The New College
FRENCH & ENGLISH
Dictionary

THIRD EDITION

The New College
FRENCH & ENGLISH
Dictionary

THIRD EDITION

ROGER J. STEINER
Emeritus Professor of Linguistics
University of Delaware

AMSCO SCHOOL PUBLICATIONS, INC.
315 Hudson Street / New York, N.Y. 10013

THE NEW COLLEGE FRENCH & ENGLISH DICTIONARY, THIRD EDITION

Cover design by Merrill Haber
Cover photograph of Annecy, Savoie, France: Getty Images
Composition by Maryland Composition Co. Inc.

When ordering this book, please specify:
either **R 778 P** or FRENCH DICTIONARY

Please visit our Website at:
www.amscopub.com

ISBN 978-1-56765-323-6
NYC Item 56765-323-5

Published by Amsco School Publications, Inc., by arrangement with the
copyright owners.

Printed in the United States of America

4 5 6 7 8 9 10   09 08 07 06

CONTENTS

PREFACE TO THE THIRD EDITION

A. *The New College French & English Dictionary* provides more grammatical help than any other French and English dictionary of its size. Features in the Third Edition show the user (1) which preposition to use after an adjective, (2) whether the adjective precedes the noun it modifies, and (3) which preposition follows a verb before a dependent infinitive. These features are added to the unusually complete grammatical material already in the previous editions, such as the different meanings an adjective has when it precedes or when it follows a noun. A dictionary-grammar cross-referenced to the body of the Dictionary provides abundant grammatical information.

With the new additions on pronunciation, this Dictionary affords more help on pronunciation of French and English words than any other bilingual dictionary of its kind.

The inclusion of over three thousand new words and meanings is another major attraction in the Third Edition—terms that reflect recent scientific developments as well as current colloquial speech.

B. Inasmuch as the basic function of a bilingual dictionary is to provide semantic equivalences, syntactical constructions are shown in both the source and target languages on both sides of the Dictionary. In performing this function, a bilingual dictionary must fulfill six purposes. For example, a French and English bilingual dictionary must provide (1) French words that an English-speaking person wishes to use in speaking and writing (by means of the English-French part), (2) English meanings of French words that an English-speaking person encounters in listening and reading (by means of the French-English part), (3) the spelling, pronunciation, and inflection of French words and the gender of French nouns that an English-speaking person needs, to use French words correctly (by means of the French-English part), (4) English words that a French-speaking person wishes to use in speaking and writing (by means of the French-English part), (5) French meanings of English words that a French-speaking person encounters in listening and reading (by means of the English-French part), and (6) the spelling, pronunciation, and inflection of English words that a French-speaking person needs, to use English words correctly (by means of the English-French part).

It may seem logical to provide the pronunciation and inflection of English words and the pronunciation and inflection of French words and the gender of French nouns where these words appear as target words inasmuch as target words, according to (1) and (4) above, are sought for the purpose of speaking and writing. Thus the users would find not only the words they seek but all the information they need about them at one and the same place. But this technique is impractical because target words are not alphabetized and could, therefore, be found only by the roundabout and uncertain way of seeking them through their translations in the other part of the dictionary. And this would be particularly inconvenient for persons using the dictionary for purposes (2) and (5) above. It is much more convenient to provide immediate alphabetized access to pronunciation and inflection where the words appear as source words. Showing the gender of nouns takes so little space that this information is provided with both source and target words.

C. Prepositional phrases and expressions containing a verb and a noun are listed under the noun, e.g.,

> **channel** [tʃænəl] *s* . . . ; **through channels** par la voie hiérarchique
> **sky** [skaɪ] *s* (*pl* **skies**) ciel *m;* **to praise to the skies** porter aux nues
> **scrutin** [skrytɛ̃] *m* . . . ; **dépouiller le scrutin** to count the votes

D. All subentries are listed alphabetically, e.g.,
avis [avi] *m* . . . ; **à mon avis** . . . ; **avis au lecteur** . . . ; **changer d'avis** . . .

E. French expressions consisting of a noun and an adjective or a noun and an adjective phrase are listed under the noun, e.g.,
scaphandre [skafɑ̃dr] *m* diving suit; spacesuit; **scaphandre autonome** aqualung
portrait [portrɛ] *m* . . . ; **portrait à mi-corps** half-length portrait

F. All solid, hyphenated, and spaced compound English words are listed as separate entries, e.g.,

mail′man′ *s* (*pl* **-men′**) facteur *m*
point′-blank′ *adj & adv* . . . à bout portant
tape′ record′er *s* magnétophone *m*

G. All words are treated in a fixed order according to the parts of speech and the functions of verbs, as follows: article, adjective, substantive, pronoun, adverb, preposition, conjunction, transitive verb, intransitive verb, impersonal verb, auxiliary verb, reflexive verb, impersonal reflexive verb, interjection.

H. Meanings with subject and usage labels come after more general meanings. Subject and usage labels (printed in roman and in parentheses) refer to the preceding entry or phrase (printed in boldface). However, when labels come immediately, i.e., without any intervening punctuation mark, after a target word, they refer to that target word and the preceding word or words separated from it only by commas, e.g.,

optometrist [ɑptɑmɪtrist] *s* opticien *m;* optométriste *mf* (Canad)

I. English adjectives are always translated by the French masculine form regardless of whether the translation of the exemplary noun modified would be masculine or feminine, e.g.,

close [klos] *adj* . . . ; (*friendship*) étroit; (*room*) renfermé

J. In order to facilitate the finding of the meaning and use sought for, changes within a vocabulary entry in part of speech and function of verb, in irregular inflection, in the gender of French nouns, and in the pronunciation of French and English words are marked with parallels: ‖, instead of the usual semicolons.

K. Since vocabulary entries are not determined on the basis of etymology, homographs are included in a single entry. When the pronunciation of a homograph changes, this is shown in the proper place after parallels.

Note, however, that plurals and words spelled with capitals are shown as run-on entries. They must be preceded by parallels only when there is a change in part of speech, in pronunciation, or in inflection.

L. Peculiarities in the pronunciation of the plural of French nouns and run-on entries are generally shown, e.g.,

guet-apens [gɛtapɑ̃] *m* (*pl* **guets-apens** [gɛtapɑ̃])
œil [œj] *m* . . . ; **entre quatre yeux** [ɑ̃trəkatzjø]

M. Periods are omitted after labels and grammatical abbreviations and at the end of vocabulary entries.

N. Proper nouns and abbreviations are listed in their alphabetical position in the main body of the Dictionary. Thus **Algérie** and **algérien** or **Suède** and **suédois** do not have to be looked up in two different parts of the book. And all subentries are listed in strictly alphabetical order.

O. The feminine form of a French adjective used as a noun (or a French feminine noun having identical spelling with the feminine form of an adjective) that falls alphabetically in a separate position from the adjective is treated in that position and is listed again as a cross reference under the adjective, e.g.,

cher chère [ʃɛr] *adj* . . . ‖ *f* see **chère** ‖ . . .
chère [ʃɛr] *f* fare, food and drink; . . .

P. In French, the adjective most often follows the noun it modifies, and those adjectives that behave differently are identified in this Dictionary. In some cases the entry for the adjective includes the explanation ''(precedes the noun it modifies),'' e.g.,

jeune [ʒœn] (precedes the noun it modifies) *adj* young . . .

In other cases the meaning of the adjective differs according to its position, and the indication ''(when standing before noun)'' is used, e.g.,

propre [prɔpr] *adj* clean, neat; . . . ‖ (when standing before noun) *adj* own . . .

Note (1) that adjectives of color (e.g., **rouge**), nationality (e.g., **français**), and religion (e.g., **catholique**) always follow the modified noun; (2) that there is a literary and stylistic practice of setting any adjective before a modified noun: **d'excellentes récoltes, d'innocents touristes, l'impossible Français, un malhonnête homme, cette étonnante variété, un immonde marchandage.** In these last examples the sense of the adjective has been subdued and the importance of the noun has been increased.

Q. The centered period is used in vocabulary entries of inflected words to mark off, according to standard orthographic principles in the two languages, the final syllable that has to be detached before the syllable showing the inflection is added, e.g.,

> **habi•tant** [abitã] **-tante** [tãt] *mf*
> **satis•fy** [sætɪs,faɪ] *v* (*pret & pp* **-fied**) *tr*

R. Where the orthographic break, according to some authorities, is not permitted, for example, between a **y** and a following vowel, the centered period is not used, e.g.,

> **croyant** [krwajã] **croyante** [krwajãt]
> **moyen** [mwajẽ] **moyenne** [mwajɛn]

S. If the two components of an English solid compound are not separated by an accent mark, a centered period is used to mark off the division between them, e.g., **la′dy•bird′.**

T. Boldface numbers preceded by the paragraph sign § refer to the section on French Irregular Verbs (§1–§76) or to the section on French Grammatical References (§77–§102).

ROGER J. STEINER

Français-Anglais
French-English

A

A, a [ɑ], *[ɑ] *m invar* first letter of the French alphabet ‖ [a] *v* **see avoir**

à [a] *prep* to, into; at; by, e.g., **à l'année** by the year; from, e.g., **arracher à** to snatch from; in, e.g., **à l'italienne** in the Italian manner; on, e.g., **à temps** on time; with, e.g., **la jeune fille aux yeux bleus** the young woman with the blue eyes

abaisse-langue [abɛslɑ̃g] *m invar* tongue depressor

abaissement [abɛsmɑ̃] *m* lowering; drop; humbling

abaisser [abɛse] *tr* to lower; humble ‖ **§96** *ref* to go down; humble oneself; to condescend

abandon [abɑ̃dɔ̃] *m* abandon; abandonment; desertion; neglect

abandonner [abɑ̃dɔne] **§96** *tr* to abandon; forsake; give up ‖ *ref* to neglect oneself, become slovenly; **s'abandonner à** to give way to

abasourdir [abazurdir] *tr* to dumfound, flabbergast; deafen

abasourdis·sant [abazurdisɑ̃] **-sante** [sɑ̃] *adj* astounding

abâtardir [abɑtardir] *tr* to debase ‖ *ref* to deteriorate, degenerate

abâtardissement [abɑtardismɑ̃] *m* debasement; deterioration, degeneration

abat·jour [abaʒur] *m invar* lampshade; eyeshade, sun visor; skylight

abats [aba] *mpl* giblets

abattage [abataʒ] *m* slaughtering (*of animals*); felling (*of trees*); demolition (*of a building*); bag, bagging (*of game*)

abattant [abatɑ̃] *m* drop leaf; toilet seat

abattement [abatmɑ̃] *m* dejection, despondency; prostration; tax deduction

abatteur [abatœr] *m* slaughterer; woodcutter; **abatteur de besogne** hard worker

abattis [abati] *m* felling (*of trees*); clearing (*of woods*); (mil) abatis; **abattis** *mpl* giblets; (slang) arms and legs

abattoir [abatwar] *m* slaughterhouse

abattre [abatr] **§7** *tr* to pull down, demolish; fell; slaughter; overthrow; discourage; shoot down, bring down (*a bird, airplane, etc.*); lay (*dust*); (cards) to lay down (*one's hand*) ‖ *ref* to abate, subside; be dejected; swoop down; pounce; crash (*said of airplane*)

abat·tu -tue [abaty] *adj* dejected, downcast

abat·vent [abavɑ̃] *m invar* chimney pot

abat·voix [abavwa] *m invar* sounding board

abbaye [abei] *f* abbey

abbé [abe] *m* abbot; abbé, father; **bonjour, monsieur l'abbé!** hello, father!

abbesse [abɛs] *f* abbess

a b c [abese] *m* (letterword) ABC's; speller

abcès [apsɛ] *m* abscess

abdiquer [abdike] *tr & intr* to abdicate

abdomen [abdɔmɛn] *m* abdomen

abécédaire [abesedɛr] *m* speller

abeille [abɛj] *f* bee; **abeille ouvrière** worker bee

abêtir [abɛtir] *tr* to make stupid ‖ *intr & ref* to become stupid

abhorrer [abɔre] *tr* to abhor

abîme [abim] *m* abyss; depth

abîmer [abime] *tr* to spoil; damage ‖ *ref* to sink; be sunk; get spoiled

ab·ject -jecte [abʒɛkt] *adj* abject

abjurer [abʒyre] *tr* to abjure

abla·tif [ablatif] **-tive** [tiv] *adj & m* ablative

aboiement [abwamɑ̃] *m* barking; yelp, cry, outcry

abois [abwa] *mpl* desperate straits; **aux abois** at bay; hard pressed

abolir [abɔlir] *tr* to abolish; annul

abomination [abɔminasjɔ̃] *f* abomination

abondamment [abɔ̃damɑ̃] *adv* abundantly

abondance [abɔ̃dɑ̃s] *f* abundance, plenty; wealth; flow (*of words*); **parler d'abondance** to ad-lib

abon·dant [abɔ̃dɑ̃] **-dante** [dɑ̃t] *adj* abundant, plentiful; wordy

abon·né -née [abɔne] *mf* subscriber; season-ticket holder; consumer (*of gas, electricity, etc.*); commuter (*on railroad*)

abonnement [abɔnmɑ̃] *m* subscription

abonner [abɔne] *tr* to take out a subscription for (*s.o.*) ‖ *ref* to subscribe, take out a subscription

abord [abɔr] *m* approach; **abords** outskirts, surroundings; **d'abord** at first; **d'un abord facile** easy to approach; **tout d'abord** first of all

abordable [abɔrdabl] *adj* approachable, accessible; reasonable (*price*)

abordage [abɔrdaʒ] *m* (naut) boarding; (naut) collision

aborder [abɔrde] *tr* to approach, accost; board; collide with, run afoul of ‖ *intr* to land, go ashore

aborigène [abɔriʒɛn] *adj & m* native, aboriginal

abor·tif [abɔrtif] **-tive** [tiv] *adj* abortive

aboucher [abuʃe] *tr* to join; bring together ‖ *ref* to have an interview

aboutir [abutir] **§96** *intr* to end; come to an end

aboutissement [abutismɑ̃] *m* outcome, result; success (*of a plan*)

aboyer [abwaje] §47 *intr* to bark; bay

abracada•brant [abrakadabrɑ̃] **-brante** [brɑ̃t] *adj* amazing, breath-taking

abra•sif [abrazif] **-sive** [ziv] *adj & m* abrasive

abrégé [abreʒe] *m* abridgment, summary; **en abrégé** in miniature; in brief, in an abbreviated form

abrégement [abreʒmɑ̃] *m* abridgment

abréger [abreʒe] §1 *tr* to abridge; shorten, curtail

abreuvage [abrœvaʒ] *m* watering

abreuver [abrœve] *tr* to water; soak; overwhelm, shower ‖ *ref* to drink

abreuvoir [abrœvwar] *m* drinking trough, watering trough, horsepond

abréviation [abrevjɑsjɔ̃] *f* abbreviation; abridgment, curtailment

abri [abri] *m* shelter, refuge, cover; air-raid shelter; carport; **abri fiscal** tax shelter; **à l'abri de** protected from

abribus [abribys] *m* bus shelter

abricot [abriko] *m* apricot

abricotier [abrikɔtje] *m* apricot tree

abri•promenade [abriprɔmnad] *m* hurricane deck, shelter deck

abriter [abrite] *tr* to shelter, protect, shield, screen ‖ *ref* to take shelter

abroger [abrɔʒe] §38 *tr* to abrogate, repeal

a•brupt -brupte [abrypt] *adj* abrupt, steep; rough, crude; blunt

abru•ti -tie [abryti] *adj* stunned, dazed, stupefied; idiotic ‖ *mf* idiot; sot

abrutir [abrytir] *tr* to brutalize; besot, deaden; overwhelm, exhaust

abrutis•sant [abrytisɑ̃] **-sante** [sɑ̃t] *adj* stupefying; deadening

absence [apsɑ̃s] *f* absence

ab•sent [apsɑ̃] **-sente** [sɑ̃t] *adj* absent; absent-minded ‖ *mf* absentee

absenter [apsɑ̃te] §97 *ref* to absent oneself, be absent, stay away

abside [apsid] *f* apse

absinthe [apsɛ̃t] *f* absinthe, wormwood; absinthe (*liqueur*)

abso•lu -lue [apsɔly] *adj* absolute

absolument [apsɔlymɑ̃] *adv* absolutely

absor•bant [apsɔrbɑ̃] **-bante** [bɑ̃t] *adj* absorbent; absorbing ‖ *m* absorbent

absorber [apsɔrbe] *tr* to absorb, soak up; eat up; drink ‖ *ref* to become absorbed, be deeply interested

absoudre [apsudr] §60, §97 (*pp* **absous, absoute**; no *pret* or *imperf subj*) *tr* to absolve; to forgive; to acquit

abstenir [apstənir] §72, §97, §99 *ref* to abstain, refrain

absti•nent [apstinɑ̃] **-nente** [nɑ̃t] *adj* abstinent; abstemious ‖ *mf* moderate eater or drinker

abstraction [apstraksjɔ̃] *f* abstraction; **faire abstraction de** to leave out, disregard

abstraire [apstrɛr] §68 (no *pret* or *imperf subj*) *tr* to abstract ‖ *ref* to become engrossed

abs•trait [apstrɛ] **-traite** [trɛt] *adj* abstract

abs-trus [apstry] **-truse** [tryz] *adj* abstruse

absurde [apsyrd] *adj* absurd

absurdité [apsyrdite] *f* absurdity

abus [aby] *m* abuse; **abus de l'information privilégiée** insider trading; **abus d'enfant** child abuse; **abus sexuel** sexual abuse

abuser [abyze] *tr* to deceive ‖ *intr* to exaggerate; **abuser de** to take advantage of, impose upon; indulge unwisely in ‖ §96 *ref* to be mistaken

abu•sif [abyzif] **-sive** [ziv] *adj* abusive, wrong; excessive

acacia [akasja] *m* locust tree; **faux acacia** black locust tree

académicien [akademisjɛ̃] *m* academician

académie [akademi] *f* academy; (fa) nude; **académie militaire** military academy

académique [akademik] *adj* academic

acagnarder [akanarde] *tr* to make lazy ‖ *ref* to grow lazy; lounge

acajou [akaʒu] *m* mahogany; mahogany tree; **acajou à pommes** (bot) cashew

acariâtre [akarjɑtr] *adj* grumpy

acca•blant [akablɑ̃] **-blante** [blɑ̃t] *adj* overwhelming

accabler [akɑble] *tr* to overwhelm; weigh down

accalmie [akalmi] *f* lull, standstill

accaparer [akapare] *tr* to corner (*the market*); monopolize

accéder [aksede] §10 *intr* to accede; acquiesce; have access

accéléra•teur [akseleratœr] **-trice** [tris] *adj* accelerating ‖ *m* accelerator

accéléré [akselere] *m* fast action; **en accéléré, à l'accéléré** (mov) speeded-up, high-speed

accélérer [akselere] §10 *tr, intr, & ref* to accelerate

accent [aksɑ̃] *m* accent; tone; stress, emphasis; **accent aigu** acute accent; **accent circonflexe** circumflex accent; **accent de hauteur** pitch accent; **accent d'insistance** emphasis; **accent d'intensité** stress accent; **accent grave** grave accent; **accent orthographique** written accent; **accent tonique** tonic accent; **mettre l'accent sur** to stress, emphasize

accentuer [aksɑ̃tɥe] *tr* to accent ‖ *ref* to become more marked

acceptable [aksɛptabl] *adj* acceptable

acceptation [aksɛptasjɔ̃] *f* acceptance

accepter [aksɛpte] §97 *tr* to accept ‖ *intr*—**accepter de** to agree to

acception [aksɛpsjɔ̃] *f* sense, meaning, preference, partiality

accès [aksɛ] *m* access, admission; outburst; (pathol) attack, bout; **accès aléatoire, accès direct** (comp) random access; **accès auprès de** admittance to; **accès aux quals** (public sign) to the docks

accessible [aksɛsibl] *adj* accessible; susceptible

accession [aksɛsjɔ̃] *f* accession

accessit [aksesit] *m* honorable mention

accessoire [aksɛswar] *adj* accessory ‖ *m* accessory; moonlighting job; (theat) prop; **accessoires** (theat) properties

accident [aksidɑ̃] *m* accident; unevenness (*of ground*); (mus) accidental; **accident de circulation** traffic accident; **accident ferroviaire** train crash

acciden·té -tée [aksidɑ̃te] *adj* rough, uneven; bumpy (*road*); eventful (*life*); (coll) wrecked (*car*) ‖ *mf* (coll) casualty, victim

acciden·tel -telle [aksidɑ̃tɛl] *adj* accidental

accidenter [aksidɑ̃te] *tr* to make uneven; vary; injure

accise [aksiz] *f* excise tax

acclamer [aklame] *tr* to acclaim

acclimater [aklimate] *tr* to acclimate ‖ *ref* to become acclimated

accolade [akɔlad] *f* embrace; accolade; (mus, typ) brace

accoler [akɔle] *tr* to hug; join side by side; couple (*names*); (typ) to brace

accommo·dant [akɔmɔdɑ̃] **-dante** [dɑ̃t] *adj* accommodating, obliging

accommodation [akɔmɔdɑsjɔ̃] *f* accommodation

accommodement [akɔmɔdmɑ̃] *m* settlement, compromise; arrangement

accommoder [akɔmɔde] *tr* to accommodate; conciliate; arrange (*furniture*); prepare (*food*) ‖ *ref* **s'accommoder à** to adapt oneself to; **s'accommoder de** to put up with

accompagna·teur [akɔ̃paɲatœr] **-trice** [tris] *mf* accompanist

accompagnement [akɔ̃paɲmɑ̃] *m* accompaniment

accompagner [akɔ̃paɲe] *tr* to accompany

accom·pli -plie [akɔ̃pli] *adj* completed; polished; accomplished

accomplir [akɔ̃plir] *tr* to accomplish; complete; fulfill (*a promise*) ‖ *ref* to come to pass

accomplissement [akɔ̃plismɑ̃] *m* accomplishment, performance

accord [akɔr] *m* accord, agreement, consent; harmony; settlement, bargain; (mus) chord; (mus) tuning; **accord global** package deal; **d'accord** in accord; **d'accord!** O.K.!, agreed!; check!, sure thing!; **d'un commun accord** by common consent

accordage [akɔrdaʒ] *m* tuning

accordéon [akɔrdeɔ̃] *m* accordion; **en accordéon** squashed; accordion-pleated

accorder [akɔrde] §97, §98 *tr* to grant; reconcile; (mus, rad) to tune ‖ *intr*—**accorder à qn de** to allow s.o. to ‖ §96 *ref* to harmonize; tally; agree

ac·cort [akɔr] **ac·corte** [akɔrt] *adj* sprightly, engaging (*e.g., young lady*)

accostage [akɔstaʒ] *m* (naut) coming alongside; (rok) docking

accoster [akɔste] *tr* to approach ‖ *intr* to dock, berth

accotement [akɔtmɑ̃] *m* shoulder (*of a road*); **accotement non-stabilisé** soft shoulder

accoter [akɔte] *tr* to shore up ‖ *ref* to lean

accotoir [akɔtwar] *m* arm rest, chair arm

accouchement [akuʃmɑ̃] *m* childbirth

accoucher [akuʃe] *tr* to deliver ‖ *intr* (*aux:* ETRE) to be confined, be delivered ‖ *intr* (*aux:* AVOIR)—**accoucher de** to give birth to

accou·cheur [akuʃœr] **-cheuse** [ʃøz] *mf* obstetrician

accouder [akude] *ref* to lean on one's elbows

accoudoir [akudwar] *m* armrest

accouple [akupl] *f* leash

accouplement [akupləmɑ̃] *m* coupling; (aerosp) linkage; **accouplement consanguin** inbreeding

accoupler [akuple] *tr* to couple; yoke; bring together for breeding; link; (elec) to hook up ‖ *ref* to mate

accourir [akurir] §14, §95 *intr* (*aux:* AVOIR or ETRE) to run up; **accourir à** *or* **vers** to rush up to

accoutrement [akutrəmɑ̃] *m* togs, get-up

accoutrer [akutre] *tr* to rig out ‖ *ref* to dress ridiculously

accoutu·mé -mée [akutyme] §92 *adj* accustomed; **à l'accoutumée** as usual ‖ *mf* regular customer; frequent visitor

accoutumer [akutyme] §96, §100 *tr* to accustom ‖ *ref*—**s'accoutumer à** to get used to

accouvage [akuvaʒ] *m* artificial incubation

accouver [akuve] *tr* to set (*a hen*) ‖ *intr* to set (*said of a hen*) ‖ *ref* to begin to set

accréditer [akredite] *tr* to accredit; win a hearing for; **accrédité auprès de** accredited to ‖ *ref* to gain credence or favor

accréditeur [akreditœr] *m* bondsman

accroc [akro] *m* tear (*in a dress*); (fig) snag, hitch; **accroc à** blot on; breach of; **sans accroc** without a hitch

accrochage [akroʃaʒ] *m* hanging; hooking; clinch (*in boxing*); collision; (mil) encounter; (rad) receiving; (coll) squabble

accroche [akroʃ] *m* hanger

accrocher [akroʃe] *tr* to hang, hang up; hook; catch; (mil) to come to grips with; (rad) to pick up; (coll) to buttonhole ‖ *ref* (coll) to come to blows; cling; catch; get caught

accroire [akrwar] (used only in *inf* after **faire**) *tr*—**faire accroire à qn** to make s.o. believe ‖ *ref*—**s'en faire accroire** to get a swelled head

accroissement [akrwasmɑ̃] *m* growth; accumulation (*of capital*); increment

accroître [akrwatr] §17 (*pp* accru; *pres ind* accrois; *pret* accrus, etc.) *tr & ref* to increase

accroupir [akrupir] *ref* to squat, crouch

accu [aky] *m* storage battery

accueil [akœj] *m* reception, welcome

accueil·lant [akœjɑ̃] **-lante** [jɑ̃t] *adj* hospitable, gracious, welcoming, friendly

accueillir [akœjir] §18 *tr* to welcome; honor (*a bill*)

aculer [akyle] *tr* to corner

accumulateur [akymylatœr] *m* storage battery

accumuler [akymyle] *tr, intr,* & *ref* to accumulate

accusa•teur [akyzatœr] **-trice** [tris] *adj* incriminating ‖ *mf* accuser

accusatif [akyzatif] *m* accusative

accusation [akyzɑsjɔ̃] *f* accusation; charge

accu•sé -sée [akyze] *adj* marked; prominent (*features*) ‖ *mf* defendant ‖ *m* acknowledgment (*of receipt*)

accuser [akyze] §97, §99 *tr* to accuse; acknowledge (*receipt*)

acerbe [asɛrb] *adj* sour; sharp; caustic (*remark*)

acé•ré -rée [asere] *adj* keen (*edge*); sharp (*tongue*)

acétate [asetat] *m* acetate

acétique [asetik] *adj* acetic

acétone [asetɔn] *f* acetone

achalandage [aʃalɑ̃daʒ] *m* customers

achalander [aʃalɑ̃de] *tr* to attract customers to ‖ *ref* to get customers

achar•né -née [aʃarne] *adj* fierce; relentless (*pursuit*); inveterate (*gambler*); bitter (*enemy*); **acharné à** bent on, set on

acharnement [aʃarnəmɑ̃] *m* fierceness, fury; stubbornness; eagerness

acharner [aʃarne] *tr* to set, sic (*dogs*); bait (*a trap*) ‖ §96 *ref* to fight bitterly; **s'acharner à** to work away at; be bent on, persist in; **s'acharner contre** to attack fiercely; **s'acharner sur** to light into; swoop down upon; bear down on; be dead set against

achat [aʃa] *m* purchase; **achat à terme** installment buying; **achat comptant** cash purchase; **achat d'impulsion** impulse buying; **aller aux achats** to go shopping

ache [aʃ] *f* wild celery

acheminement [aʃminmɑ̃] *m* forwarding; progress

acheminer [aʃmine] *tr* to direct ‖ *ref* to proceed

acheter [aʃte] §2 *tr* to buy; **acheter à** to buy from; buy for; **acheter de** to buy from; **acheter pour** to buy for

achèvement [aʃɛvmɑ̃] *m* completion

achever [aʃve] §2, §97 *tr* to complete; finish off, kill ‖ *intr* to end; be just finishing ‖ *ref* to come to an end

Achille [aʃil] *m* Achilles

achoppement [aʃɔpmɑ̃] *m* obstacle; impact

achopper [aʃɔpe] *intr* & *ref* to stumble

achromatique [akrɔmatik] *adj* achromatic

acide [asid] *adj* & *m* acid; **acide désoxyribonucléique** [dezɔksiribɔnykleik] (ADN *or* A.D.N.) *s* deoxyribonucleic acid (DNA); **acide phénique** carbolic acid

acidité [asidite] *f* acidity

acidu•lé -lée [asidyle] *adj* acid; fruit-flavored

aciduler [asidyle] *tr* to acidulate

acier [asje] *m* steel; (fig) sword; **acier inoxydable** stainless steel

aciérie [asjeri] *f* steelworks, steel mill

acmé [akme] *f* acme; (pathol) crisis

acné [akne] *f* acne

acolyte [akɔlit] *m* acolyte; accomplice

acompte [akɔ̃t] *m* installment; deposit, down payment; **acompte provisionnel** payment on estimated income tax

Açores [asɔr] *fpl* Azores

à•côté [akote] *m* (*pl* **-côtés**) sidelight; path (*beside road*); kickback, perquisite

à•coup [aku] *m* (*pl* **-coups**) jerk; **par à-coups** by fits and starts

acoustique [akustik] *adj* acoustic, acoustical ‖ *f* acoustics

acquéreur [akerœr] *m* buyer

acquérir [akerir] §3 *tr* to acquire, get

acquiescement [akjɛsmɑ̃] *m* acquiescence

acquiescer [akjɛse] §51 *intr* to acquiesce

ac•quis [aki] **-quise** [kiz] *adj* established ‖ *m* know-how

acquisition [akizisjɔ̃] *f* acquisition

acquit [aki] *m* receipt; **pour acquit** paid in full

acquit-à-caution [akitakosjɔ̃] *m* (*pl* **acquits-à-caution**) permit to transport in bond

acquittement [akitmɑ̃] *m* acquittal

acquitter [akite] *tr* to acquit; receipt (*a bill*); pay, discharge ‖ *ref* to pay one's debts; **s'acquitter de** to fulfill, perform

acre [akr] *f* acre

âcre [ɑkr] *adj* acrid

acrylique [akrilik] *adj* acrylic

acrimo•nieux [akrimɔnjø] **-nieuse** [njøz] *adj* acrimonious

acrobate [akrɔbat] *mf* acrobat

acrobatie [akrɔbasi] *f* acrobatics

acropole [akrɔpɔl] *f* acropolis

acrostiche [akrɔstiʃ] *m* acrostic

acte [akt] *m* action; bill; act; certificate, deed; **acte de présence** personal appearance; **acte de vente** bill of sale; **actes** minutes; **faire acte** to make a declaration; **prendre acte** to take minutes

acteur [aktœr] *m* actor

ac•tif [aktif] **-tive** [tiv] *adj* active; live (*microphone*); full (*citizen*) ‖ *m* credit side (*of an account*); assets; (gram) active voice; **actifs corporels** tangible assets; **actifs incorporels** intangible assets

action [aksjɔ̃] *f* action; share (*of stock*); **action de grâces** thanksgiving; **action ordinaire** share of common stock; **action privilégiée** share of preferred stock; **action replay** (telv) replay (*of a play in a game*)

actionnaire [aksjɔnɛr] *mf* stockholder; investor

actionner [aksjɔne] *tr* to actuate; drive; sue

activer [aktive] *tr* to activate; hasten ‖ *ref* to hasten

activité [aktivite] *f* activity; active service; **en pleine activité** in full swing

actrice [aktris] *f* actress

actuaire [aktɥɛr] *mf* actuary

actualisation [aktɥalizɑsjɔ̃] *f* modernization

actualiser [aktɥalize] *tr* to modernize, bring up to date

actualité [aktɥalite] *f* present condition; **actualités** current events; newsreel; **d'actualité** newsworthy

ac·tuel -tuelle [aktɥɛl] *adj* present, present-day, current, existing

actuellement [aktɥɛlmɑ̃] *adv* now, at the present time

acuité [akɥite] *f* acuity

adage [adaʒ] *m* adage

Adam [adɑ̃] *m* Adam

adapta·teur [adaptatœr] **-trice** [tris] *mf* adapter ‖ *m* (mov) adapter

adaptation [adaptasjɔ̃] *f* adaptation

adapter [adapte] *tr & ref* to adapt

addenda [adɛ̃da] *m invar* addendum

addi·tif [aditif] **-tive** [tiv] *adj & m* additive

addition [adisjɔ̃] *f* addition; check (*for a restaurant meal*)

additionner [adisjɔne] *tr* to add up; add; dilute, mix

additionneuse [adisjɔnøz] *f* adding machine

adénoïde [adenɔid] *adj* adenoid

adent [adɑ̃] *m* dovetail

adepte [adɛpt] *mf* adept

adé·quat [adekwa] **-quate** [kwat] *adj* adequate

adhérence [aderɑ̃s] *f* adherence; traction; (pathol) adhesion

adhé·rent [aderɑ̃] **-rente** [rɑ̃t] *adj & mf* adherent

adhérer [adere] §10 *intr* to adhere; stick; **adhérer à la route** to hold the road

adhé·sif [adezif] **-sive** [ziv] *adj & m* adhesive

adhésion [adezjɔ̃] *f* adhesion

adieu [adjø] *m* (*pl* **adieux**) farewell ‖ *interj* adieu!, bon voyage!; good riddance!; **sans adieu!** see you later!

adja·cent [adʒasɑ̃] **-cente** [sɑ̃t] *adj* adjacent

adjec·tif [adʒɛktif] **-tive** [tiv] *adj & m* adjective

adjoindre [adʒwɛ̃dr] §35 *tr & ref* to join

ad·joint [adʒwɛ̃] **-jointe** [ʒwɛ̃t] *adj & mf* assistant, stand-by

adjudant [adʒydɑ̃] *m* warrant officer; sergeant major; (pej) martinet

adjudication [adʒydikɑsjɔ̃] *f* auction; awarding (*of a contract*)

adjuger [adʒyʒe] §38 *tr* to adjudge, award; knock down (*at auction*)

admettre [admɛtr] §42, §96 *tr* to admit

administra·teur [administratœr] **-trice** [tris] *mf* administrator, director

administration [administrɑsjʒ] *f* administration; **administration des ponts et chaussées** highway department

administrer [administre] *tr* to administer

admira·teur [admiratœr] **-trice** [tris] *mf* admirer

admira·tif [admiratif] **-tive** [tiv] *adj* admiring; amazed

admiration [admirɑsjɔ̃] *f* admiration; wonder

admirer [admire] §97, §99 *tr* to admire; wonder at

admissible [admisibl] *adj* admissible; eligible

admission [admisjɔ̃] *f* admission; (aut) intake

admonester [admɔnɛste] *tr* to admonish

ADN *or* **A.D.N.** [edeɛn] *m* (letterword) (**acide désoxyribonucléique**) DNA (deoxyribonucleic acid)

adolescence [adɔlesɑs] *f* adolescence

adoles·cent [adɔlesɑ̃] **-cente** [sɑ̃t] *adj & mf* adolescent

adonner [adɔne] §96 *ref* to devote oneself; **s'adonner à** to give oneself up to

adopter [adɔpte] *f* to adopt

adop·tif [adɔptif] **-tive** [tiv] *adj* adopted; adoptive

adoption [adɔpsjɔ̃] *f* adoption; **adoption plénière** adoption (*equivalent to American adoption*); **adoption simple** adoption (*with visits by the genetic parents*)

adorable [adɔrabl] *adj* adorable

adora·teur [adɔratœr] **-trice** [tris] *mf* adorer; worshiper

adoration [adɔrɑsjɔ̃] *f* adoration

adorer [adɔre] *tr* to adore, worship

adosser [adɔse] *tr*—**adosser q.ch. à** to turn the back of s.th. against ‖ *ref*—**s'adosser à** to lean back against

adouber [adube] *tr* to dub

adoucir [adusir] *tr* to soften ‖ *ref* to soften; grow milder

adrénaline [adrenalin] *f* adrenalin

adressage [adrɛsaʒ] *m* mailing

adresse [adrɛs] *f* address; skill, dexterity; neatness; expertness, expertise; **adresse électronique** (comp) E-mail address; **adresse particulière** home address

adresser [adrɛse] *tr* to address ‖ *ref* to apply

Adriatique [adriatik] *adj & f* Adriatic

a·droit [adrwa] **-droite** [drwat] *adj* adroit, clever; neat

aduler [adyle] *tr* to adulate

adulte [adylt] *adj & mf* adult

adultère [adyltɛr] *adj* adulterous ‖ *m* adultery; adulterer ‖ *f* adulteress

adultérer [adyltere] §10 *tr* to adulterate; falsify (*a text*)

adulté·rin [adylterɛ̃] **-rine** [rin] *adj* born in adultery

advenir [advənir] §72 (used only in *inf*; *pp*; 3d *pers sg & pl*) *intr* (aux: ÊTRE) to come to pass; **advienne que pourra** come what may

adventice [advɑ̃tis] *adj* adventitious

adverbe [advɛrb] *m* adverb

adversaire [advɛrsɛr] *mf* adversary; **adversaire dans un match de boxe** sparring partner

adverse [advɛrs] *adj* adverse; opposite (*side*)

adversité [advɛrsite] *f* adversity

aération [aerɑsjɔ̃] *f* ventilation

aérer [aere] §10 *tr* to ventilate; to air

aé·rien [aerjɛ̃] **-rienne** [rjɛn] *adj* aerial ‖ *m* elevated railway

aéro [aero] *m* airplane

aérobic [aerɔbik] *m* aerobics

aérodynamique [aerodinamik] *adj* aerodynamic; streamlined ‖ *f* aerodynamics

aérogare [aerɔgar] *f* air terminal

aéroglisseur [aerɔglisœr] *m* hydrofoil

aérogramme [aerɔgram] *m* air letter

aérolite *or* **aérolithe** [aerɔlit] *m* meteorite, aerolite

aéronef [aerɔnɛf] *m* aircraft
aérophare [aerɔfar] *m* air beacon
aéroport [aerɔpɔr] *m* airport
aéropor‧té -tée [aerɔpɔrte] *adj* airborne
aéropos‧tal -tale [aerɔpɔstal] *adj* (*pl* **-taux** [to]) air-mail
aérosol [aerɔsɔl] *m* aerosol
aérospa‧tial -tiale [aerɔspasjal] *adj* (*pl* **-tiaux** [sjo]) aerospace
A.F. *abbr* (**allocations familiales**) family (social-security) allotments
affable [afabl] *adj* affable
affadir [afadir] *tr & ref* to stale
affaiblir [afɛblir] *tr & ref* to weaken
affaire [afɛr] *f* affair; job; business; trouble; (law) case; (coll) belongings; **affaire à saisir** bargain; **affaire d'or** (fig) gold mine; **affaire en instance** unfinished business; **affaires** business; **bonne affaire** bargain; **cela fait mon affaire** that is just what I want
affai‧ré-rée [afɛre] *adj* busy, bustling
affairiste [afɛrist] *m* slicker, operator
affaissement [afɛsmɑ̃] *m* sagging; cave-in, collapse
affaisser [afɛse] *tr* to weigh down; depress ‖ *ref* to sag; cave in, collapse
affaler [afale] *tr* to haul down ‖ *ref* to drop, sink, flop
affa‧mé -mée [afame] *adj* famished, starved
affamer [afame] *tr* to starve
affectable [afɛktabl] *adj* impressionable; mortgageable
affectation [afɛktasjɔ̃] *f* affectation; assignment; allotment
affec‧té -tée [afɛkte] *adj* affected; §92 assigned
affecter [afɛkte] §97 *tr* to affect; assign; assume (*various shapes or manners*) ‖ *ref* to grieve
affec‧tif [afɛktif] **-tive** [tiv] *adj* affective, emotional
affection [afɛksjɔ̃] *f* affection; mental state; disease, affection
affection‧né -née [afɛksjɔne] *adj* loving, fond, devoted
affectionner [afɛksjɔne] *tr* to be fond of ‖ *ref* to become attached
affectueusement [afɛktɥøzmɑ̃] *adv* affectionately
affec‧tueux [afɛktɥø] **-tueuse** [tɥøz] *adj* affectionate
affé‧rent [aferɑ̃] **-rente** [rɑ̃t] *adj* due, accruing
affermer [afɛrme] *tr* to lease, rent
affermir [afɛrmir] *tr* to strengthen, harden ‖ *ref* to become stronger, sounder
affichage [afiʃaʒ] *m* billposting
affiche [afiʃ] *f* poster, bill; (theat) playbill
afficher [afiʃe] *tr* to post, post up; display; (theat) to bill; (comp) to display (*on a screen*) ‖ *ref* to seek the limelight; **s'afficher avec** to hang around with
afficheur [afiʃœr] *m* billposter
affi‧lé -lée [afile] *adj* sharpened; sharp (*tongue*) ‖ *adv*—**d'affilée** in a row

affiler [afile] *tr* to sharpen, whet; hone, strop; set (*a saw*)
affiliation [afiljɑsjɔ̃] *f* affiliation; franchising
affi‧lié -liée [afilje] *adj & mf* affiliate; **affilié** franchise
affilier [afilje] *tr & ref* to affiliate
affiloir [afilwar] *m* sharpener; whetstone; hone, strop
affiner [afine] *tr* to improve; refine; sift ‖ *ref* to improve; mature, ripen
affinité [afinite] *f* affinity; in-law relationship
affirma‧tif [afirmatif] **-tive** [tiv] *adj & f* affirmative
affirmer [afirme] *tr* §95 to affirm ‖ *ref* to assert oneself; **s'affirmer comme** to take one's place as
affixe [afiks] *m* affix
affleurer [aflœre] *tr* to level; come up to the level of ‖ *intr* to come to the surface
affliction [afliksjɔ̃] *f* affliction
affli‧gé -gée [afliʒe] *adj* sorrowful
affli‧geant [afliʒɑ̃] **-geante** [ʒɑ̃t] *adj* sorrowful (*news*)
affliger [afliʒe] §38 *tr* to afflict, distress ‖ §97 *ref*—**s'affliger de** to be distressed about
affluence [aflyɑ̃s] *f* crowd
af‧fluent [aflyɑ̃] **-fluente** [flyɑ̃t] *adj & m* tributary
affluer [aflye] *intr* to flow; throng, crowd, flock
afflux [afly] *m* afflux, flow; rush
affo‧lé -lée [afɔle] *adj* panic-stricken
affolement [afɔlmɑ̃] *m* distraction, panic; infatuation; unsteadiness (*of a compass*)
affoler [afɔle] *tr* to distract, panic; infatuate; disturb (*a compass*) ‖ *ref* to be distracted; stampede; become infatuated; spin (*as a compass*)
affran‧chi -chie [afrɑ̃ʃi] *adj* emancipated; postpaid ‖ *mf* freethinker
affranchir [afrɑ̃ʃir] *tr* to emancipate, free; pay the postage for
affranchissement [afrɑ̃ʃismɑ̃] *m* emancipation; payment of postage; cancellation (*of mail*); **affranchissement insuffisant** postage due
affres [afr] *fpl* pangs
affrètement [afrɛtmɑ̃] *m* chartering (*of a boat*)
affréter [afrete] §10 *tr* to charter (*a boat*)
af‧freux [afrø] **-freuse** [frøz] *adj* frightful
affront [afrɔ̃] *m* affront
affronter [afrɔ̃te] *tr* to confront; face
affubler [afyble] *tr & ref* to dress in a bizarre fashion
affût [afy] *m* hunting blind; mount (*for cannon*); **être à l'affût de** to lie in wait for
affûter [afyte] *tr* to sharpen
af‧ghan [afgɑ̃] **-ghane** [gan] *adj & m* afghan ‖ (*cap*) *mf* Afghan
Afghanistan [afganistɑ̃] *m* Afghanistan
afin [afɛ̃] *adv*—**afin de** in order to; **afin que** + *subj* in order that, so that
afri‧cain [afrikɛ̃] **-caine** [kɛn] *adj* African ‖ (*cap*) *mf* African
Afrique [afrik] *f* Africa: **l'Afrique** Africa

afro-américain [afroamerikɛ̃] **-caine** [kɛn] *adj* Afro-American, African-American ‖ (*cap*) *mf* Afro-American, African-American

agacement [agasmɑ̃] *m* irritation, annoyance

agacer [agase] §51 *tr* to irritate, annoy; tease; set on edge

agape [agap] *f* agape; **agapes** banquet

âge [aʒ] *m* age; **âge scolaire** school age; **d'un certain âge** middle-aged; **quel âge avez-vous?** how old are you?

â•gé -gée [aʒe] *adj* old, aged; old, e.g., **âgé de seize ans** sixteen years old

agence [aʒɑ̃s] *f* agency, office, service, bureau; **agence de location** rental service; real-estate office; **agence de recouvrement** collection agency; **agence de tourisme** travel agency; **agence de voyages** travel bureau, travel agency; **agence immobilière** real-estate office

agencement [aʒɑ̃smɑ̃] *m* arrangement; furnishing (*of a house*); construction (*of a sentence*); **agencements** fixtures

agencer [aʒɑ̃se] §51 *tr* to arrange

agenda [aʒɛ̃da] *m* engagement book

agenouiller [aʒnuje] *ref* to kneel

agent [aʒɑ̃] *m* agent; policeman; **agent comptable** accountant; **agent de change** stockbroker; **agent de dépannage** (rad & telv) repairman; **agent de fret** cargo agent; **agent de la circulation** traffic cop; **agent de location** real-estate agent, realtor; **agent touristique** travel agent; **pardon, monsieur l'agent** excuse me, officer

agglomeration [aglɔmerasjɔ̃] *f* agglomeration; metropolitan area; built-up area

agglomé•ré -rée [aglɔmere] *adj* compressed ‖ *m* briquette; adobe; composition board

agglomérer [aglɔmere] §10 *tr & ref* to agglomerate

aggraver [agrave] *tr* to aggravate ‖ *ref* to become more serious

agile [aʒil] *adj* agile, nimble

agilité [aʒilite] *f* agility

agio•teur [aʒjɔtœr] **-teuse** [tøz] *mf* speculator

agir [aʒir] *intr* to act; take action ‖ *ref*—**il s'agit de** it is a question of

agis•sant [aʒisɑ̃] **-sante** [sɑ̃t] *adj* active

agissements [aʒismɑ̃] *mpl* machinations

agita•teur [aʒitatœr] **-trice** [tris] *mf* agitator (*person*) ‖ *m* stirrer; swizzle stick

agi•té -tée [aʒite] *adj* restless; rough (*sea*)

agiter [aʒite] *tr* to agitate; stir; wave; discuss ‖ *ref* to move about

a•gneau [aɲo] *m* (*pl* **-gneaux**) lamb

agnostique [agnɔstik] *adj & mf* agnostic

agonie [agɔni] *f* agony, death throes

agrafe [agraf] *f* clasp, pin; paper clip; staple (*for papers*); belt buckle; snap, hook; (med) clamp

agrafer [agrafe] *tr* to clasp, pin; buckle; snap; hook; fasten, clip; staple; (med) to clamp

agrafeuse [agraføz] *f* stapler

agraire [agrɛr] *adj* agrarian

agrandir [agrɑ̃dir] *tr* to enlarge ‖ *ref* to grow, become larger

agrandissement [agrɑ̃dismɑ̃] *m* enlargement

agréable [agreabl] *adj* agreeable, pleasant; neighborly

agréé agréée [agree] *adj* approved ‖ *m* attorney

agréer [agree] *tr* to accept, approve; **veuillez agréer l'expression de mes sentiments distingués** (complimentary close) sincerely yours ‖ *intr*—**agréer à** to agree with, please

agrégat [agrega] *m* aggregate

agrégation [agregasjɔ̃] *f* aggregation; admittance (*as a member of an organization*); competitive teacher's examination

agré•gé -gée [agreʒe] *adj* aggregate ‖ *mf* one who has passed his *agrégation*

agréger [agreʒe] §1 *tr* to attach, add ‖ *ref*—**s'a-gréger (a)** to join

agrément [agremɑ̃] *m* approval; pleasantness; pleasure, pastime; **agréments** adornments

agrès [agrɛ] *mpl* rigging; gym equipment

agresseur [agresœr] *adj & m* aggressor

agres•sif [agresif] **-sive** [siv] *adj* aggressive

agression [agresjɔ̃] *f* aggression; (law) assault

agreste [agrɛst] *adj* rustic, rural

agricole [agrikɔl] *adj* agricultural

agriculture [agrikyltyr] *f* agriculture

agronomie [agrɔnɔmi] *f* agronomy

agrumes [agrym] *mpl* citrus fruit

aguerrir [agerir] §96 *tr* to season, inure ‖ *ref* to become seasoned, inured

aguets [agɛ] *mpl* watch, lookout; **être aux aguets** to be on the lookout

agui•chant [agiʃɑ̃] **-chante** [ʃɑ̃t] *adj* alluring ‖ *adj fem* sexy

ah [a] *interj* ah!; **ah ça!** now then!

ahu•ri -rie [ayri] *adj* dumfounded

ahurir [ayrir] *tr* to dumfound

ahurissement [ayrismɑ̃] *m* stupefaction

ai [e] *v* see **avoir**

aide [ɛd] *mf* aid, assistant, helper ‖ *f* aid, assistance, help; **aide à la navigation** instrument landing system; **aide sociale** welfare department

aider [ede] §96, §100 *tr* to aid, help; **aider à** + *inf* to help to + *inf* ‖ *intr* to help ‖ *ref*—**s'aider de** to use

aide-soignante [ɛdswaɲɑ̃t] *f* (*pl* **aides-soignante**) nurse's aid

aie [e] *v* (**aies, ait, aient**) see **avoir**

aïe [aj] *interj* ouch!

aïeul aïeule [ajœl] *mf* grandparent ‖ *m* grandparent ‖ *m* (*pl* **aieux** [ajø]) ancestor ‖ *f* grandmother

aigle [ɛgl] *mf* eagle; **aigle de mer** eagle ray; **aigle pêcheur, grand aigle de mer** osprey, fish hawk; **grand aigle** spread eagle

aiglefin [ɛgləfɛ̃] *m* haddock

ai•glon [ɛglɔ̃] **-glonne** [glɔn] *mf* eaglet

aigre [ɛgr] *adj* sour, tart, bitter; harsh (*voice*)

aigre-doux [ɛgrədu] **-douce** [dus] *adj* bittersweet, sweet-and-sour

aigrefin [ɛgrəfɛ̃] *m* crook

aigre·let [ɛgrəlɛ] **-lette** [lɛt] adj tart

aigrir [egrir] tr to turn (s.th.) sour ‖ intr & ref to turn sour

ai·gu -guë [egy] adj sharp; acute; shrill, high-pitched ‖ m (mus) treble

aigue-marine [ɛgmarin] f (pl **aigues-marines**) aquamarine

aiguille [egɥij] f needle; peak; spire (of steeple); hand (of clock); (rr) switch; **chercher une aiguille dans une botte de foin** to look for a needle in a haystack

aiguiller [agɥije] tr to switch, shunt ‖ ref to be switched, shunted

aiguilleur [egɥijœr] m (rr) tower man; (aer) air-traffic controller

aiguillon [egɥijɔ̃] m goad; sting

aiguillonner [egɥijɔne] tr to goad on, spur on, excite

aiguiser [egɥize] tr to sharpen; whet (appetite)

ail [aj] m (pl **ails** or **aulx** [o]) garlic

aile [ɛl] f wing; flank (of army); fender (of auto); brim (of hat); blade (of propeller); vane, arm (of windmill); **aile en flèche** (aer) swept-back wing

aileron [ɛlrɔ̃] m aileron

aille [aj] v (**ailles, aillent**) see **avoir**

ailleurs [ajœr] adv elsewhere; **d'ailleurs** moreover, besides; from somewhere else; **par ailleurs** furthermore

aimable [ɛmabl] adj kind, likeable; **voulez-vous être assez aimable de** will you be good enough to

aimant [ɛmɑ̃] m magnet

aimanter [ɛmɑ̃te] tr to magnetize

aimer [eme], [ɛme] §95 tr to love; like; like to; **aimer à** to like to; **aimer bien** to like, be fond of; like to; **aimer mieux** to prefer; prefer to

aîne [ɛn] f groin

aî·né -née [ɛne] adj & mf elder, eldest, oldest; senior

aînesse [ɛnɛs] f seniority

ainsi [ɛ̃si] adv thus; **ainsi de suite** and so forth; **ainsi nommé** so-called; **ainsi que** as well as; **ainsi soit-il** amen

air [ɛr] m air; look, appearance; **air de famille** family resemblance; **avoir l'air de** to seem to; **en l'air** empty, idle (threats, talk)

airain [ɛrɛ̃] m brass; bronze

aire [ɛr] f area; threshing floor; eyrie; **aire d'attente** (aer) holding bay; **aire d'atterrissage** landing strip; **aire de lancement** launching pad; **aire de stationnement** parking area

airelle [ɛrɛl] f—**airelle coussinette** cranberry; **airelle myrtille, airelle noire** huckleberry, blueberry

air-sol [ɛrsol] adj invar air-to-ground

aisance [ɛzɑ̃s] f ease, comfort

aise [ɛz] adj—**bien aise** glad, content ‖ f ease; **aises** comforts; **à son aise** well-to-do

ai·sé -sée [eze] adj easy; natural; well-to-do

aisément [ezemɑ̃] adv easily

aisselle [ɛsɛl] f armpit

ajonc [aʒɔ̃] m furze

ajou·ré -rée [aʒure] adj openwork, perforated

ajourer [aʒure] tr to cut openings in

ajournement [aʒurnəmɑ̃] m adjournment, postponement; subpoenaing; rejection (of a candidate)

ajourner [aʒurne] tr to postpone; to subpoena; to reject (a candidate in an examination)

ajouter [aʒute] tr & intr to add ‖ ref to be added

ajus·té -tée [aʒyste] adj tight-fitting

ajuster [aʒyste] tr to adjust; arrange; fit; aim at

ajusteur [aʒystœr] m fitter

alacrité [alakrite] f gaiety, vivacity

alaise or **alèze** [alez] f mattress cover

alambic [alɑ̃bik] m still

alambi·qué -quée [alɑ̃bike] adj fine-spun, far-fetched

alanguir [alɑ̃gir] tr to weaken ‖ ref to languish

alar·mant -mante [alarmɑ̃] [mɑ̃t] adj alarming

alarme [alarm] f alarm

alarmer [alarme] tr to alarm ‖ ref to be alarmed

Alaska [alaska] m Alaska

alba·nais -naise [albanɛ] [nɛz] adj Albanian ‖ m Albanian (language) ‖ (cap) mf Albanian (person)

albâtre [albɑtr] m alabaster

albatros [albatros] m albatross

albi·geois -geoise [albiʒwa] [ʒwaz] adj Albigensian ‖ (cap) mf Albigensian

albinos [albinos] adj & m albino

album [albɔm] m album; scrapbook

albumen [albymɛn] m albumen

alcali [alkali] m alkali

alca·lin -line [alkalɛ̃] [lin] adj alkaline

alchimie [alʃimi] f alchemy

alcool [alkɔl] m alcohol; **alcool à friction** rubbing alcohol; **alcool dénaturé** denatured alcohol

alcoolique [alkɔɔlik], [alkɔlik] adj & mf alcoholic; **Alcooliques Anonymes** Alcoholics Anonymous

alcoolisme [alkɔlism] m alcoholism; **alcoolisme au volant** drunken driving

alcotest [alkɔtɛst] m breath analyzer

alcôve [alkov] f alcove; cubicle; **d'alcôve** amatory, gallant

ale [ɛl] f ale

aléa [alea] m risk

aléatoire [aleatwar] adj risky; aleatory

ALENA [alena] m (acronym) (**accord de libre-échange nord-américain**) NAFTA (North American Free Trade Agreement)

alêne [alɛn] f awl

alentour [alɑ̃tur] adv round about ‖ **alentours** mpl neighborhood

Aléoutiennes [aleusjɛn] fpl Aleutian (Islands)

alerte [alɛrt] adj & f alert; **alerte aérienne** air-raid alarm

alerter [alɛrte] tr to alert

alésage [alezaʒ] m bore (of cylinder)

aléser [aleze] §10 tr to ream; bore

ale·zan -zane [alzɑ̃] [zan] adj chestnut (colored)

algarade [algarad] f altercation

algèbre [alʒɛbr] *f* algebra
Alger [alʒe] *m* Algiers
Algérie [alʒeri] *f* Algeria
algé•rien [alʒerjɛ̃] **-rienne** [rjɛn] *adj* Algerian ‖ (*cap*) *mf* Algerian
algé•rois [alʒerwa] **-roise** [rwaz] *adj* of Algiers; Algerian ‖ (*cap*) *mf* native of Algiers; Algerian
algues [alg] *fpl* algae
alias [aljɑs] *adv* alias
alibi [alibi] *m* (law) alibi
alié•né -née [aljene] *adj* alienated; insane ‖ *mf* insane person
aliéner [aljene] **§10** *tr* to transfer, alienate ‖ *ref* to alienate (*s.o.*); to lose (*e.g., s.o.'s sympathy*)
alignement [aliɲmɑ̃] *m* alignment
aligner [aliɲe] *tr* to align; **aligner ses phrases** to choose one's words with care ‖ *ref* to line up
aliment [alimɑ̃] *m* aliment, food; **aliments** (law) necessities; **aliments pour bébés (premier âge)** baby foods
alimentaire [alimɑ̃tɛr] *adj* alimentary; subsistence, e.g., **pension alimentaire** subsistence allowance
alimentation [alimɑ̃tasjɔ̃] *f* nourishment; supplying; feeding (*a fire, a machine*)
alimenter [alimɑ̃te] *tr* to nourish; supply; feed (*a fire, a machine*)
alinéa [alinea] *m* indentation (*of the first line of a paragraph*); paragraph
aliter [alite] *tr* to keep in bed ‖ *ref* to be confined to bed
alizés [alize] *mpl* trade winds
Allah [ala] *m* Allah
allaitement [alɛtmɑ̃] *m* feeding, nursing; **allaitement au biberon** bottle feeding; **allaitement maternel** breast feeding
allaiter [alɛte] *tr* to nurse
al•lant [alɑ̃] **-lante** [lɑ̃t] *adj* active ‖ *m*—**allants et venants** passersby; **beaucoup d'allant** (coll) a lot of pep
allé•chant [ale/ɑ̃] **-chante** [/ɑ̃t] *adj* enticing, tempting
allécher [ale/e] **§10** *tr* to allure
allée [ale] *f* walk, path; going; city street, boulevard; aisle (*of theater*)
allégeance [aleʒɑ̃s] *f* allegiance; lightening (*of care*); handicapping (*of a race*)
alléger [aleʒe] **§1** *tr* to lighten; alleviate, mitigate, relieve
allégorie [allegɔri] *f* allegory
allègre [allɛgr] *adj* lively, cheerful
alléguer [allege] **§10** *tr* to allege as an excuse; cite (*an authority*)
Allemagne [almaɲ] *f* Germany; **l'Allemagne** Germany
alle•mand [almɑ̃] **-mande** [mɑ̃d] *adj* German ‖ *m* German (*language*) ‖ (*cap*) *mf* German (*person*)
aller [ale] *m* going; go; **aller (et) retour** round trip; round-trip ticket; **au pis aller** at the worst

‖ **§4, §95** *intr* (*aux:* ÉTRE) to go; work, function; **aller** + *inf* to be going to + *inf*, e.g., **je vais au magasin acheter des souliers** I am going to the store to buy some shoes; **aller à** to suit, fit, become, e.g., **la robe lui va bien** the dress beomes her; **allez!, allons!, allons donc!** well!, come on!, all right!; **allez-y doucement!** take it easy!; **ça va?, comment allez-vous?** how are you? ‖ *ref*—**s'en aller** to go away ‖ *aux*—**aller** + *inf* to be going to + *inf* (to express futurity), e.g., **il va se marier** he is going to get married
allergie [alerʒi] *f* allergy
allergique [alerʒik] *adj* allergic
aller-retour [alerətur] *m*—**faire l'aller-retour** to go and come back
alliage [aljaʒ] *m* alloy
alliance [aljɑ̃s] *f* alliance; marriage; wedding ring; **ancienne alliance** Old Covenant; **nouvelle alliance** New Covenant
al•lié-liée [alje] *adj* allied (*by treaty*); united (*in marriage*) ‖ *mf* ally; kin, in-law
allier [alje] *tr* to ally; to alloy ‖ *ref* to become allied, to ally oneself
alligator [alligatɔr] *m* alligator
allô [alo] *interj* hello!
allocation [allɔkasjɔ̃] *f* allocation, allotment; **allocation de chômage** unemployment insurance; **allocations familiales** family (social-security) allotments
allocution [allɔkysjɔ̃] *f* short speech
allonger [alɔ̃ʒe] **§38** *tr, intr, & ref* to lengthen
allouer [alwe] *tr* to allow, allocate
allumage [alymaʒ] *m* lighting; switching on (*of a light*); kindling (*of a fire*); ignition; firing
allume-feu [alymfø] *m invar* kindling
allumer [alyme] *tr* to ignite; light (*a cigarette*); light up (*a room*); put on, switch on (*a light; a radio; a heater*); provoke (*anger*) ‖ *ref* to go on (*said of a light*); light up (*said of eyes*); catch fire
allumette [alymɛt] *f* match; **allumette de sûreté** safety match
allumette-gaz [alymɛtgaz] *m* pilot light
allumeur [alymœr] *m* ignition system; **allumeur de réverbères** lamplighter
allumeuse [alymøz] *f* (coll) vamp
allure [alyr] *f* speed, pace; gait, bearing, aspect; **à l'allure de l'escargot** at a snail's pace; **à toute allure** at top speed
allusion [allyzjɔ̃] *f* allusion
almanach [almana] *m* almanac; yearbook
aloès [alɔɛs] *m* aloes
aloi [alwa] *m* legal alloy; quality; **de bon aloi** genuine
alors [alɔr] *adv* then; **alors même que** even though; **alors que** whereas
alose [aloz] *f* shad
alouette [alwɛt] *f* lark, skylark; **alouette sans tête** rolled veal
alourdir [alurdir] *tr* to weigh down, make heavy ‖ *ref* to become heavy
aloyau [alwajo] *m* (*pl* **aloyaux**) sirloin

Alpes [alp] *fpl*—**les Alpes** the Alps
alphabet [alfabɛ] *m* alphabet; **alphabet phonétique international (API)** international phonetic alphabet (IPA)
alpinisme [alpinism] *m* mountain climbing
alpiniste [alpinist] *mf* mountain climber
alpiste [alpist] *m* birdseed
al-Qaïda [alkaida] *m* al Qaeda
alsa•cien [alzasjɛ] **-cienne** [sjɛn] *adj* Alsatian ‖ *m* Alsatian (*dialect*) ‖ (*cap*) *mf* Alsatian (*person*)
alté•rant [alterɑ̃] **-rante** [rɑ̃t] *adj* thirst-provoking
altération [alterɑsjɔ̃] *f* alteration, falsification; deterioration; heavy thirst; (*mus*) accidental
altérer [altere] §10 *tr* to alter, falsify; ruin (*one's health*); weaken, impair; make thirsty ‖ *ref* to undergo a change for the worse; become thirsty
alternance [altɛrnɑ̃s] *f* alternation; (agr) rotation
alterna•tif [altɛrnatif] **-tive** [tiv] *adj* alternative; alternating; alternate ‖ *f* alternative, dilemma; alternation
alterne [altɛrn] *adj* alternate (*angles*)
alterner [altɛrne] *tr* to rotate (*crops*) ‖ *intr* to alternate
al•tier [altje] **-tière** [tjɛr] *adj* haughty
altitude [altityd] *f* altitude
alto [alto] *m* alto; viola
altruiste [altrɥist] *adj & mf* altruist
aluminium [alyminjɔm] *m* aluminum
alun [alœ̃] *m* alum
alunir [alynir] *intr* to land on the moon
alunissage [alynisaʒ] *m* landing on the moon
alvéole [alveɔl] *m & f* alveolus; cavity; cell (*of honeycomb*); socket (*of tooth*)
amadou [amadu] *m* punk, tinder
amadouer [amadwe] *tr* to wheedle
amaigrir [amɛgrir] *tr* to emaciate; make thin ‖ *ref* to grow thin
amalgame [amalgam] *m* amalgam
amalgamer [amalgame] *tr & ref* to amalgamate
aman [amɑ̃] *m*—**demander l'aman** to give in
amande [amɑ̃d] *f* almond; kernel; **amande de Malaga** Jordan almond
amandier [amɑ̃dje] *m* almond tree
a•mant [amɑ̃] **-mante** [-mɑ̃t] *mf* lover
amareyeur [amarɛjœr] *m* oysterman
amariner [amarine] *tr* to season (*a crew*); impress (*a ship*)
amarre [amar] *f* hawser
amarrer [amare] *tr & ref* to moor
amas [ama] *m* mass; heap; cluster (*of stars*); **amas de neige** snowdrift
amasser [amase] *tr* to amass; gather ‖ *intr* to hoard ‖ *ref* to pile up, crowd
amateur [amatœr] *adj* amateur ‖ *m* amateur; (coll) prospective buyer
amatir [amatir] *tr* to mat, dull (*metal or glass*)
amazone [amazon] *f* amazon; horsewoman; riding habit; **monter en amazone** to ride side-saddle ‖ (*cap*) *f* Amazon

ambages [ɑ̃baʒ] *fpl* circumlocutions; **sans ambages** without beating around the bush
ambassade [ɑ̃basad] *f* embassy
ambassadeur [ɑ̃basadœr] *m* ambassador
ambassadrice [ɑ̃basadris] *f* ambassadress; wife of an ambassador; emissary
ambiance [ɑ̃bjɑ̃s] *f* environment, milieu; atmosphere, tone
ambidextre [ɑ̃bidɛkstrə] *adj* ambidextrous ‖ *mf* ambidextrous person
ambi•gu -guë [ɑ̃bigy] *adj* ambiguous ‖ *m* ambiguousness; buffet lunch; odd mixture
ambiguïté [ɑ̃bigɥite] *f* ambiguity
ambi•tieux [ɑ̃bisjø] **-tieuse** [sjøz] *adj* ambitious
ambition [ɑ̃bisjɔ̃] *f* ambition
amble [ɑ̃bl] *m* amble; pacing
ambler [ɑ̃ble] *intr* (equit) to amble; pace
ambre [ɑ̃br] *m*—**ambre gris** ambergris; **ambre** (**jaune** or **succin**) amber
ambulance [ɑ̃bylɑ̃s] *f* ambulance
ambulan•cier [ɑ̃bylɑ̃sje] **-cière** [sjɛr] *mf* ambulance driver or attendant
ambu•lant [ɑ̃bylɑ̃] **-lante** [lɑ̃t] *adj* ambulant ‖ *m* railway mail clerk
ambulatoire [ɑ̃bylatwar] *adj* ambulatory; itinerant
âme [ɑm] *f* soul; spirit, heart, mind; core (*of cable*); bore (*of cannon*); web (*or rail*); sound post (*of violin*); **âme damnée** evil genius; **âme soeur** soulmate; **rendre l'âme** to give up the ghost
améliorer [ameljɔre] *tr & ref* to ameliorate, improve
amen [amɛn] *m invar* Amen
aménagement [amenaʒmɑ̃] *m* arrangement, equipping; preparation, development (*of land*); adjustment (*of taxes*); **aménagements** furnishings
aménager [amenaʒe] §38 *tr* to arrange, equip; remodel; parcel out; grade (*a roadbed*); feed (*a machine*); harness (*a waterfall*)
aménageur [amenaʒœr] *m* (land) developer
amende [amɑ̃d] *f* fine; forfeit (*in a game*); **faire amende honorable** (coll) to apologize
amendement [amɑ̃dmɑ̃] *m* amendment; fertilizer
amender [amɑ̃de] *tr* to amend; manure ‖ *ref* to mend one's ways, amend
amène [amɛn] *adj* pleasant
amener [amne] §2, §96 *tr* to bring; lead; bring on; furnish (*proof*); (naut) to lower; **amener pavillon** to surrender ‖ *ref* (coll) to arrive; **amenez-vous!** (slang) get a move on!
aménité [amenite] *f* amenity; **aménités** (ironical) cutting remarks
amenuiser [amənɥize] *tr* to whittle ‖ *ref* to be whittled down
a•mer -mère [amɛr] *adj* bitter ‖ *m* bitters; seamark; gall (*of animal*)
améri•cain [amerikɛ̃] **-caine** [kɛn] *adj* American ‖ *m* American English ‖ *f* phaeton; bicycle relay ‖ (*cap*) *mf* American (*person*)

américanisme [amerikanism] *m* Americanism; American studies

amérin·dien [amerɛ̃djɛ̃] **-dienne** [djɛn] *adj* Amerindian ‖ (*cap*) *mf* Amerindian

Amérique [amerik] *f* America; **l'Amérique** America; **l'Amérique du Nord** North America

amerrir [amɛrir] *intr* to land on water, alight on water

amerrissage [amɛrisaʒ] *m* landing (on water); (rok) splashdown; **amerrissage forcé** ditching; **faire un amerrisage forcé** to ditch

amertume [amɛrtym] *f* bitterness

améthyste [ametist] *f* amethyst

ameublement [amœbləmã] *m* furnishings; furniture, suite

ameublir [amœblir] *tr* (agr) to soften, mellow (*soil*)

ameuter [amøte] *tr* to rouse (*the pack*) ‖ *ref* to riot

a·mi -mie [ami] *adj* friendly ‖ *mf* friend; **ami(e) intime, ami(e) de cœur** bosom friend ‖ *m* lover; **bon ami** sweetheart, sweetie, boyfriend; **faux ami** (ling) false friend, deceptive cognate ‖ *f* mistress; **petite-amie, bonne amie** sweetheart, sweetie, girlfriend

amiable [amjabl] *adj* amicable; **à l'amiable** privately, out of court

amiante [amjɑ̃t] *m* asbestos

amibe [amib] *f* amoeba, ameba

ami·bien [amibjɛ̃] **-bienne** [bjɛn] *adj* amoebic

ami·cal -cale [amikal] *adj* (*pl* **-caux** [ko]) amicable ‖ *f* professional club

amidon [amidɔ̃] *m* starch

amidonner [amidɔne] *tr* to starch

amincir [amɛ̃sir] *tr* to make more slender, attenuate ‖ *ref* to grow thinner

ami·ral [amiral] *m* (*pl* **-raux** [ro]) admiral

amirale [amiral] *f* admiral's wife

amirauté [amirote] *f* admiralty

amitié [amitje] *f* friendship; **amitiés** (complimentary close) cordially yours; **faites mes amitiés à** give my regards to; **faites-moi l'amitié de** do me the favor of

ammo·niac -niaque [amɔnjak] *adj* ammoniacal ‖ *m* ammonia (*gas*) ‖ *f* ammonia (*gas dissolved in water*)

amnésie [amnezi] *f* amnesia

amniocentèse [amnjɔsɛ̃tɛz] *f* amniocentesis

amnios [amnjɔs] *m* amnion

amnistie [amnisti] *f* amnesty

amnistier [amnistje] *tr* to amnesty

amoindrir [amwɛ̃drir] *tr* to lessen ‖ *ref* to diminish

amollir [amɔlir] *tr* & *ref* to soften

amollissement [amɔlismã] *m* softening

amonceler [amɔ̃sle] **§34** *tr* to pile up, gather ‖ *ref* to pile up, gather; drift (*said of snow*)

amont [amɔ̃] *m* upper waters; **en amont** upstream; **en amont de** above

amorçage [amɔrsaʒ] *m* baiting; priming

amorce [amɔrs] *f* bait, lure; fuse, percussion cap; beginning; leader (*of strip of film*); (mov) preview

amorcer [amɔrse] **§51** *tr* to bait; prime; entice; begin

amorphe [amɔrf] *adj* amorphous; passive, apathetic (*student; spirit*)

amortir [amɔrtir] *tr* to absorb (*shock*); subdue (*color; pain; passions*); damp (*waves*); amortize

amortissement [amɔrtismã] *m* absorption (*of shock, sound, etc.*); amortization

amortisseur [amɔrtisœr] *m* shock absorber

amour [amur] *m* love; love affair; **amour courtois** courtly love; **premières amours** puppy love ‖ (*cap*) *m* Cupid

amou·reux -reuse [amurø] [røz] *adj* amorous; loving; fond, devoted; **amoureux de** in love with ‖ *m* lover ‖ *f* sweetheart

amour-propre [amurprɔpr] *m* (*pl* **amours-propres**) self-esteem; vanity

amovible [amɔvibl] *adj* removable; detachable; (jur) revocable

ampère [ɑ̃pɛr] *m* ampere; **ampère-heure** ampere-hour

ampèremètre [ɑ̃pɛrmɛtr] *m* ammeter

amphibie [ɑ̃fibi] *adj* amphibious, amphibian ‖ *m* amphibian

amphibien [ɑ̃fibjɛ̃] *m* amphibian

amphithéâtre [ɑ̃fiteɑtr] *m* amphitheater; auditorium (*with raised seats*)

amphitryon [ɑ̃fitrijɔ̃] *m* host at dinner ‖ (*cap*) *m* Amphitryon

ample [ɑ̃pl] *adj* ample; long (*speech*); liberal (*reward*); full (*skirt; voice*)

amplifica·teur -trice [tris] *adj* amplifying ‖ *mf* exaggerator ‖ *m* amplifier; (phot) enlarger

amplifier [ɑ̃plifje] *tr* to amplify, enlarge

amplitude [ɑ̃plityd] *f* amplitude; **amplitude de bande** (comp) bandwidth

ampoule [ɑ̃pul] *f* ampule; (elec) bulb; (pathol) blister, water blister

ampu·té -tée [ɑ̃pyte] *mf* amputee

amputer [ɑ̃pyte] *tr* to amputate; cut (*an article, speech*)

amuïr [amɥir] *ref* to become silent

amuïssement [amɥismã] *m* (phonet) silencing

amulette [amylɛt] *f* amulet

amure [amyr] *f* tack (*of sail*)

amu·sant -sante [amyzã] [zɑ̃t] *adj* amusing, fun

amuse-bouche [amyzbuʃ] *m* (*pl* **amuse-bouche** [s]) (*pl* **-bouche** *or* **bouches**) (coll) appetizer, snack

amuse-gueule [amyzgœl] *m* (*pl* **-gueule** *or* **-gueules**) (coll) appetizer, snack

amusement [amyzmã] *m* amusement

amuser [amyze] *tr* to amuse; to mislead ‖ **§96** *ref* to have a good time; to sow one's wild oats; **s'amuser à** to pass the time by; **s'amuser de** to play with; to make fun of

amygdale [amigdal] *f* tonsil

an [ɑ̃] *m* year; **de six ans** six-year-old; **l'an de grâce** the year of Our Lord; **le nouvel an, le jour de l'an** New Year's Day

anacarde [anakard] *m* cashew nut

anachronisme [anakrɔnism] *m* anachronism

analogie [analɔʒi] *f* analogy

analogue [analɔg] *adj* analogous; similar

analphabète [analfabɛt] *adj & mf* illiterate

analphabétisme [analfabetism] *m* illiteracy

analyse [analiz] *f* analysis; **analyse des renseignements** data processing

analyser [analize] *tr* to analyze

analyseur [analizœr] *m* analyzer, tester; **analyseur de lexique** (comp) scanner; **analyseur d'haleine** breath tester

analyste [analist] *mf* analyst

analytique [analitik] *adj* analytic(al)

ananas [anana] *m* pineapple

anarchie [anarʃi] *f* anarchy

anarchiste [anarʃist] *mf* anarchist

anathème [anatɛm] *m* anathema

anatife [anatif] *m* barnacle

anatomie [anatɔmi] *f* anatomy

anatomique [anatɔmik] *adj* anatomic(al)

ances•tral -trale [ãsɛstral] *adj* (*pl* **-traux** [tro]) ancestral

ancêtre [ãsɛtr] *m* ancestor

anche [ãʃ] *f* (mus) reed

anchois [ãʃwa] *m* anchovy

an•cien [ãsjɛ̃] **-cienne** [sjɛn] *adj* ancient, old, long-standing; antiquated; antique ǁ (when standing before noun) *adj* former, previous, old; retired (*businessman*); ancient (*Greece, Rome*) ǁ *mf* senior (*in rank*); oldster; **les Anciens** the Ancients

anciennement [ãsjɛnmã] *adv* formerly

ancienneté [ãsjɛnte] *f* antiquity; seniority (*in rank*)

ancre [ãkr] *f* anchor; **ancres levées** anchors aweigh

ancrer [ãkre] *tr & intr* to anchor ǁ *ref* to become established

andain [ãdɛ̃] *m* swath; row of shocks

andouille [ãduj] *f* (coll) fool, sap

andouiller [ãduje] *m* antler

âne [ɑn] *m* ass, donkey

anéantir [aneãtir] *tr* to annihilate; prostrate ǁ *ref* to disappear; humble oneself (*before God*)

anéantissement [aneãtismã] *m* annihilation; prostration

anecdote [anɛgdɔt] *f* anecdote

anémie [anemi] *f* anemia

anesse [anɛs] *f* she-ass

anesthésie [anɛstezi] *f* anesthesia

anesthésier [anɛstezje] *tr* to anesthetize

anesthésique [anɛstezik] *adj abbr m* anesthetic

anesthésiste [anɛstezist] *mf* anesthetist

anévrisme [anevrism] *m* aneurysm

anfractuosité [ãfraktɥozite] *f* rough outline (*of coast*); ruggedness, cragginess

ange [ãʒ] *m* angel; **ange gardien, ange tutélaire** guardian angel; **être aux anges** to walk on air; **mon ange** my darling, my sweetheart, sweetie

angélique [ãʒelik] *adj* angelic(al)

angélus [ãʒelys] *m* Angelus

angine [ãʒin] *f* tonsillitis, quinsy; **angine de poitrine** angina pectoris

an•glais [ãglɛ] **-glaise** [glɛz] *adj* English; **à l'anglaise** in the English manner; **filer à l'anglaise** to take French leave ǁ *m* English (*language*) ǁ (*cap*) *m* Englishman; **les Anglais** the English ǁ *f* Englishwoman

angle [ãgl] *m* angle, corner

Angleterre [ãglətɛr] *f* England; **l'Angleterre** England

anglophone [ãglofɔn] *adj* English-speaking ǁ *mf* English speaker

anglo-sa•xon [ãglosaksɔ̃] **-xonne** [sɔn] *adj & m* Anglo-Saxon ǁ (*cap*) *mf* Anglo-Saxon

angois•sant [ãgwasã] **-sante** [sãt] *adj* agonizing

angoisse [ãgwas] *f* anguish

anguille [ãgij] *f* eel; **anguille de mer** conger eel

angulaire [ãgylɛr] *adj* angular

angu•leux [ãgylø] **-leuse** [løz] *adj* angular, sharp

anhydre [anidrə] *adj* anhydrous

anicroche [anikrɔʃ] *f* (coll) hitch, snag

aniline [anilin] *f* aniline

ani•mal -male [animal] (*pl* **-maux** [mol]) *adj* animal ǁ *m* animal, brute, beast; (coll) blockhead

anima•teur [animatœr] **-trice** [tris] *adj* animating ǁ *mf* animator, moving spirit; master of ceremonies; DJ; **animateur de théâtre** theatrical producer

animation [animasjɔ̃] *f* animation

animer [anime] *tr* to animate; encourage ǁ §96 *ref* to become alive, liven up

animosité [animozite] *f* animosity

anion [anjɔ̃] *m* anion

anis [ani] *m* anise

annales [anal] *fpl* annals

an•neau [ano] *m* (*pl* **-neaux**) ring

année [ane] *f* year; **année bissextile** leap year; **année de lumière** light-year; **bonne année** Happy New Year

année-lumière [anelymjɛr] *f* (*pl* **années-lumière**) light-year

annexe [anɛks] *adj* annexed ǁ *f* annex

annexer [anɛkse] *tr* to annex

annexion [anɛksjɔ̃] *f* annexation

annihiler [aniile] *tr* to annihilate

anniversaire [anivɛrsɛr] *adj & m* anniversary; **anniversaire de naissance** birthday

annonce [anɔ̃s] *f* announcement; advertisement; (cards) bid; **petites annonces** classified ads

annoncer [anɔ̃se] §51 *tr* to announce; advertise; (cards) to bid, declare; **annoncer la couleur** (fig) to lay one's cards on the table ǁ *ref* to augur; promise to be

annonceur [anɔ̃sœr] *m* advertiser

annoncia•teur [anɔ̃sjatœr] **-trice** [tris] *adj* betokening, foreboding ǁ *m* harbinger

annoter [anɔte] *tr* to annotate

annuaire [anɥɛr] *m* annual, yearbook, directory; catalog, bulletin (*e.g., of a school*); **annuaire de la haute société** social register, blue book; **annuaire du téléphone** telephone directory, phone book

an·nuel -nuelle [anɥɛl] *adj* annual
annuité [anɥite] *f* annuity
annuler [anyle] *tr* to cancel; invalidate (*a contract*); annul (*a marriage*)
ano·din [anɔdɛ̃] **-dine** [din] *adj & m* anodyne
ano·mal -male [anɔmal] *adj* anomalous
anomalie [anɔmali] *f* anomaly
ânon [ɑnɔ̃] *m* foal of an ass
ânonner [anɔne] *tr* to recite in a stumbling manner
anonymat [anɔnimal] *m* anonymity
anonyme [anɔnim] *adj* anonymous; incorporated; (fig) colorless, drab ‖ *mf* unidentified person
anorak [anɔrak] *m* anorak; ski jacket, parka
anor·mal -male [anɔrmal] (*pl* **-maux** [mo]) *adj* abnormal ‖ *mf* abnormal person
anse [ɑ̃s] *f* handle; cove; loop; **faire danser l'anse du panier** to pad the bill
antagonisme [ɑ̃tagɔnism] *m* antagonism
antan [ɑ̃tɑ̃] *m* yesteryear
Antarctique [ɑ̃tarktik] *adj & m* Antarctic ‖ *f* Antarctic (*region*); **l'Antarctique** Antarctica
antécé·dent [ɑ̃tesedɑ̃] **-dente** [dɑ̃t] *adj & m* antecedent; **antécédents** track record; **antécédents médicaux** (med) case history
antenne [ɑ̃tɛn] *f* antenna (*feeler; aerial*); outpost; (naut) lateen yard; **antenne parabolique** dish antenna; **porter à l'antenne** to put on the air
antépénultième [ɑ̃tepenyltjɛm] *adj* antepenultimate ‖ *f* antepenult
anté·rieur -rieure [ɑ̃terjœr] *adj* anterior; former; previous, preceding; earlier; front
antériorité [ɑ̃terjɔrite] *f* priority
anthologie [ɑ̃tɔlɔʒi] *f* anthology
anthracite [ɑ̃trasit] *m* anthracite
anthrax [ɑ̃traks] *m* anthrax; **anthrax cutané** cutaneous anthrax
anthropoïde [ɑ̃trɔpɔid] *adj & m* anthropoid
anthropologie [ɑ̃trɔpɔlɔʒi] *f* anthropology
anthropophage [ɑ̃trɔpɔfaʒ] *adj & mf* cannibal
antiaé·rien [ɑ̃tiɑerjɛ̃] **-rienne** [rjɛn] *adj* antiaircraft
antialcoolique [ɑ̃tialkɔɔlik] *adj* antialcoholic ‖ *mf* teetotaler; temperance worker
antiaméri·cain [ɑ̃ntiamerikɛ̃] **-caine** [kɛn] *adj* anti-American, un-American
antibalistique [ɑ̃tibalɪstɪk] *adj* antiballistic
antibiotique [ɑ̃tibjɔtik] *adj & m* antibiotic
antiblocage [ɑ̃tiblɔkaʒ] *m* antilock
antichambre [ɑ̃tiʃɑ̃br] *f* antechamber, anteroom
antichar [ɑ̃tiʃar] *adj* antitank
anticipation [ɑ̃tisipasjɔ̃] *f* anticipation; **anticipations** prophecies (*of science fiction*); **d'anticipation** science fiction (*stories, films, etc.*); **par anticipation** in advance
antici·pé -pée [ɑ̃tisipe] *adj* anticipated, advanced, ahead of time; premature (*e.g., death*)
anticiper [ɑ̃tisipe] *tr* to anticipate; advance ‖ *intr* to act ahead of time; **anticiper sur** to

encroach on; pay ahead of time; spend ahead of time
anticléri·cal -cale [ɑ̃tiklerikal] *adj* (*pl* **-caux** [ko]) anticlerical
anticonception·nel -nelle [ɑ̃tikɔ̃sɛpsjɔnɛl] *adj* contraceptive
anticorps [ɑ̃tikɔr] *m* antibody
antidater [ɑ̃tidate] *tr* to antedate
antidéra·pant [ɑ̃tiderapɑ̃] **-pante** [pɑ̃t] *adj* nonskid ‖ *m* nonskid tire
antidéto·nant [ɑ̃tidetɔnɑ̃] **-nante** [nɑ̃t] *adj & m* antiknock
antidote [ɑ̃tidɔt] *m* antidote
antienne [ɑ̃tjɛn] *f* antiphon, anthem; **chanter toujours la même antienne** to harp on the same subject
antigel [ɑ̃tiʒɛl] *m* antifreeze
antigi·vrant [ɑ̃tiʒivrɑ̃] **-vrante** [vrɑ̃t] *adj* deicing, defrosting ‖ *m* deicer
antigivre [ɑ̃tiʒivr] *m* deicer, defroster
Antilles [ɑ̃tij] *fpl* West Indies, Antilles
antilope [ɑ̃tilɔp] *f* antelope
antimite [ɑ̃timit] *adj* mothproof ‖ *m* moth killer
antimoine [ɑ̃timwan] *m* antimony
antiparasite [ɑ̃tiparazit] *adj* (rad) static-eliminating ‖ *m* (rad) static eliminator; insecticide
antipathie [ɑ̃tipati] *f* antipathy
antiquaire [ɑ̃tiker] *m* antique dealer
antique [ɑ̃tik] *adj* antique, classic; old-fashioned ‖ *m* antique
antiquité [ɑ̃tikite] *f* antiquity; **antiquités** antiques
antisèche [ɑ̃tisɛʃ] *m & f* (slang) crib (*for cheating during exams*)
antisémite [ɑ̃tisemit] *adj* anti-Semitic ‖ *mf* anti-Semite
antisémitique [ɑ̃tisemitik] *adj* anti-Semitic
antiseptique [ɑ̃tisɛptik] *adj & m* antiseptic
antiso·cial -ciale [ɑ̃tisɔsjal] *adj* (*pl* **-ciaux** [sjo]) antisocial
antispor·tif [ɑ̃tispɔrtif] **-tive** [tiv] *adj* unsportsmanlike
antithèse [ɑ̃titɛz] *f* antithesis
antitoxine [ɑ̃titɔksin] *f* antitoxin
antitranspirant [ɑ̃titrɑ̃spirɑ̃] *m* antiperspirant
antitrust [ɑ̃titrœst] *adj invar* antitrust
antivol [ɑ̃tivɔl] *adj inv* anti-theft ‖ *m* **—antivol de bicyclette** bicycle lock; **antivol de moto** car alarm system
Antoine [ɑ̃twan] *m* Anthony
antonyme [ɑ̃tɔnim] *m* antonym
antre [ɑ̃tr] *m* den, lair; cave
anxiété [ɑ̃ksjete] *f* anxiety
anxieux [ɑ̃ksjø] **anxieuse** [ɑ̃ksjøz] *adj* anxious, worried
aorte [aɔrt] *f* aorta
août [u], [ut] *m* August
A.P. *abbr* (**assistance publique**) welfare department
apache [apaʃ] *m* apache, hoodlum
apaisement [apɛzmɑ̃] *m* appeasement
apaiser [apɛze] *tr* to appease ‖ *ref* to quiet down
apanage [apanaʒ] *m* attribute

aparté [aparte] *m* stage whisper, aside; **en aparté** privately

apartheit [apartɛd] *m* apartheid

apathie [apati] *f* apathy

apathique [apatik] *adj* apathetic

apatride [apatrid] *adj* stateless ‖ *mf* stateless person

apercevoir [apɛrsəvwar] §59, §95 *tr* to perceive ‖ §97 *ref* to notice; realize; **s'apercevoir de** to notice, realize, be aware of

aperçu [apɛrsy] *m* glimpse; view, look; outline

apéri•tif [aperitif] **-tive** [tiv] *adj* appetizing ‖ *m* apéritif

aperture [apɛrtyr] *f* (phonet) aperture

apesanteur [apəzãtœr] *f* weightlessness

à-peu-près [apøprɛ] *m invar* approximation, rough estimate

apeu-ré -rée [apœre] *adj* frightened

aphone [afɔn] *adj* voiceless, aphonic

aphorisme [afɔrism] *m* aphorism

aphrodisiaque [afrɔdizjak] *adj & m* aphrodisiac

aphte [aft] *m* mouth canker, cold sore

API [epiaj] *m* (letterword) (**alphabet phonétique international**) IPA (International Phonetic Alphabet)

apiculteur [apikyltœr] *m* beekeeper

apiculture [apikyltyr] *f* beekeeping

apitoiement [apitwamã] *m* compassion

api•toyant [apitwajã] **-toyante** [twajãt] *adj* piteous, pitiful

apitoyer [apitwaje] §47 *tr* to move (*s.o.*) to pity ‖ *ref*—**s'apitoyer sur** to feel compassion for

ap. J.-C. *abbr* (**après Jésus-Christ**) A.D.

aplanir [aplanir] *tr* to even off; iron out (*difficulties*)

aplatir [aplatir] *tr* to flatten ‖ *ref* to go flat; grovel

aplomb [aplɔ̃] *m* aplomb; hang (*of gown*); (coll) cheek, rudeness; **aplombs** stand (*of horse*); **d'aplomb** plumb; steadily

apocalyptique [apɔkaliptik] *adj* apocalyptic

apocryphe [apɔkrif] *adj* apocryphal ‖ **Apocryphes** *mpl* Apocrypha

apogée [apɔʒe] *m* apogee

Apollon [apɔllɔ̃] *m* Apollo

apologie [apɔlɔʒi] *f* apology

apophonie [apɔfɔni] *f* ablaut

apoplectique [apɔplɛktik] *adj & mf* apoplectic

apoplexie [apɔplɛksi] *f* apoplexy

apostille [apɔstij] *f* endorsement

apostiller [apɔstije] *tr* to endorse

apostolat [apɔstɔla] *m* apostleship

apostrophe [apɔstrɔf] *f* apostrophe; sharp reprimand

apostropher [apɔstrɔfe] *tr* to apostrophize; reprimand sharply

apothicaire [apɔtikɛr] *m* apothecary

apôtre [apotr] *m* apostle; **faire le bon apôtre** to play the hypocrite

apparaître [aparɛtr] §12 *intr* (*aux:* AVOIR or ÉTRE) to appear, come into view; become evident

apparat [apara] *m* pomp, ostentation

apparaux [aparo] *mpl* rigging

appareil [aparɛj] *m* apparatus, machine, appliance; apparel; radio set, hi-fi set; airplane; pomp, show, display; camera; telephone; (archit) bond; **à l'appareil!** speaking!; **appareil à sous** slot machine; **appareil auditif** hearing aid; **appareil photo à disque** disk camera; **appareil photo** camera; **appareil plâtré** plaster cast; **appareil supplémentaire** (telp) extension telephone

appareillage [aparɛjaʒ] *m* equipment; (naut) getting under way

appareiller [aparɛje] *tr* to prepare; bond (*stones*); pair, match; (naut) to rig ‖ *intr* to set sail

apparemment [aparamã] *adv* apparently

apparence [aparãs] *f* appearance

appa•rent [aparã] **-rente** [rãt] *adj* apparent

apparenter [aparãte] *tr* to relate by marriage ‖ *ref* to become related

apparier [aparje] *tr* to pair off, match

apparition [aparisjɔ̃] *f* apparition; appearance

apparoir [aparwar] (used only in: *inf*; 3d *sg pres ind* **appert**) *impers*—**il appert de** it follows from; **il appert que** it is evident that

appartement [apartəmã] *m* apartment

appartenance [apartənãs] *f* membership, belonging, adherence

appartenir [apartənir] §72 *intr*—**appartenir à** to belong to; pertain to ‖ *impers*—**il appartient à qn de** it behooves s.o. to ‖ *ref* to be one's own master

appas [apɑ] *mpl* charms; bosom

appât [apɑ] *m* bait

appâter [apɑte] *tr* to lure; fatten up (*fowl*)

appauvrir [apovrir] *tr* to impoverish ‖ *ref* to become impoverished

ap•peau [apo] *m* (*pl* **-peaux**) decoy; bird call

appel [apɛl] *m* call; appeal; summons; roll call; ring (*on telephone*); (mil) draft; **appel interurbain** long-distance call; **appel nominal** roll call; **faire l'appel** to call the roll

appe•lant [aplã] **-lante** [lãt] *adj* appellant ‖ *mf* appellant ‖ *m* decoy

appelé [aple] *m* draftee; **appelé volontaire** volunteer

appeler [aple] §34 *tr* to call; name; summon; subpoena; require; call up, draft ‖ §96 *intr* to call; appeal (*in court*); **en appeler à** to appeal to ‖ *ref* to be named, e.g., **elle s'appelle Marie** she is named Mary, her name is Mary

appelette [aplɛt] *f* (comp) applet

appendice [apɛ̃dis] *m* appendix

appendicectomie [apɛ̃disɛktɔmi] *f* appendectomy

appendicite [apɛ̃disit] *f* appendicitis

appentis [apɑ̃ti] *m* lean-to

appesantir [apzɑ̃tir] *tr* to weigh down; slow down (*e.g., bodily activity*); make (*a burden*) heavier ‖ *ref* to be weighed down; **s'appesantir sur** to dwell on, expatiate on

appéstis•sant [apetisɑ̃] **-sante** [sɑ̃t] *adj* appetizing, tempting appétit [apeti] *m* appetite

applaudir [aplodir] *tr* to applaud; **applaudir qn de** to commend, applaud s.o. for ‖ *intr* to applaud; **applaudir à** to approve, commend, applaud ‖ §97 *ref*—**s'applaudir de** to congratulate oneself on, pat oneself on the back for

applaudissement [aplodismɑ̃] *m* round of applause; **applaudissements** applause

applet [aplɛ] *m* (comp) (Canad) applet

applicable [aplikabl] *adj* applicable

application [aplikɑsjɔ̃] *f* application

applique [aplik] *f* appliqué; sconce

appli•qué -quée [aplike] *adj* industrious, studious; applied (*science*)

appliquer [aplike] *tr* to apply ‖ §96 *ref* to apply; apply oneself

appliquette [aplikɛt] *f* (comp) applet

appoint [apwɛ̃] *m* addition; balance; aid, help; **faire l'appoint** to have the right change

appointements [apwɛ̃tmɑ̃] *mpl* salary

appointer [apwɛ̃te] *tr* to point, sharpen; pay a salary to

appontage [apɔ̃taʒ] *m* deck-landing

appontement [apɔ̃tmɑ̃] *m* jetty (*landing pier*); wharf

apponter [apɔ̃te] *intr* to deck-land

apport [apɔr] *m* contribution

apporter [apɔrte] *tr* to bring; supply, provide, give; take, use, exercise (*care*)

apposer [apoze] *tr* to affix; insert (*a clause in a contract*)

appréciable [apresjabl] *adj* appreciable

appréciation [apresjɑsjɔ̃] *f* appreciation, appraisal

apprécier [apresje] *tr* to appreciate

appréhender [apreɑde] §97 *tr* to apprehend; be apprehensive about

appréhension [apreɑ̃sjɔ̃] *f* apprehension

apprendre [aprɑ̃dr] §56, §96, §101 *tr* to learn; **apprendre à vivre à qn** to teach s.o. manners; **apprendre q.ch. à qn** to inform s.o. of s.th.; teach s.o. s.th. ‖ *intr* to learn

appren•ti -tie [aprɑ̃ti] *mf* apprentice; beginner, learner

apprentissage [aprɑ̃tisaʒ] *m* apprenticeship

apprêt [aprɛ] *m* preparation, finishing touches; **sans apprêt** unaffectedly

apprêter [aprɛte] §96 *tr* & *ref* to prepare

apprivoi•sé -sée [aprivwaze] *adj* tame, domesticated

apprivoiser [aprivwaze] *tr* to tame; contain (*sorrow*) ‖ *ref* to become tame; become sociable

approba•teur [aprɔbatœr] -trice [tris] *adj* approving ‖ *m* (slang) yes man

approbation [aprɔbɑsjɔ̃] *f* approbation, approval, consent

appro•chant [aprɔʃɑ] -chante [ʃɑ̃t] *adj* similar ‖ **approchant** *adv* thereabouts

approche [aprɔʃ] *f* approach

approcher [aprɔʃe] *tr* to approach; draw up (*e.g., a chair*) ‖ *intr* to approach; **approcher de** to approach, approximate ‖ *ref* to approach,

come near; **s'approcher de** to approach, come near to, go up to

approfon•di -die [aprɔfɔ̃di] *adj* thorough, deep

approfondir [aprɔfɔ̃dir] *tr* to deepen; go deep into, get to the bottom of

appropriation [aprɔprijɑsjɔ̃] *f* appropriation; adaptation

appro•prié -priée [aprɔprije] *adj* appropriate

approprier [aprɔprije] *tr* to fit, adapt ‖ *ref* to appropriate, preempt

approuver [apruve] *tr* to approve, approve of

approvisionnement [aprɔvizjɔnmɑ̃] *m* provisioning, stocking; **approvisionnements** supplies

approvisionner [aprɔvizjɔne] *tr* to provision, stock ‖ *ref* to lay in supplies

approxima•tif [aprɔksimatif] -tive [tiv] *adj* approximate

appui [apɥi] *m* support; endorsement

appui-bras [apɥibra] *m* (*pl* **appuis-bras**) armrest

appui-livres [apɥilivr] *m* (*pl* **appuis-livres**) bookend

appui-main [apɥimɛ̃] *m* (*pl* **appuis-main**) maulstick

appui-tête [apɥitɛt] *m* (*pl* **appuis-tête**) headrest

appuyer [apɥije] §27 *tr* to support; prop; rest, lean; endorse (*a candidate*); **appuyer le doigt sur** to push (*a button, a lever, a switch*) with the finger ‖ *intr*—**appuyer sur** to lean on; press (*a button*); move (*a lever*); pull (*a trigger*); bear down on (*a pen or pencil*); stress (*a syllable*) ‖ *ref*—**s'appuyer sur** to lean on; be based on; rely on; (slang) to put up with

âpre [ɑpr] *adj* harsh, rough; bitter; greedy (*for gain*)

après [aprɛ] *adv* after, afterward; behind; **après que** after ‖ *prep* after; behind; **après Jésus-Christ (ap. J.-C.)** after Christ (A.D.); **d'après** after, from; by, according to

après-demain [aprɛdəmɛ̃] *adv* & *m* the day after tomorrow

après-guerre [aprɛgɛr] *m* & *f* (*pl* **-guerres**) postwar period

après-midi [aprɛmidi] *m* & *f invar* afternoon

âpreté [aprəte] *f* harshness; bitterness

à-propos [aprɔpo] *m* opportuneness, aptness

apte [apt] *adj* apt; **apte à** suitable for

aptitude [aptityd] *f* aptitude; proficiency, qualification

apurement [apyrmɑ̃] *m* audit, check

apurer [apyre] *tr* to audit, check

apyre [apir] *adj* fireproof

aquafortiste [akwafɔrtist] *mf* etcher

aquaplane [akwaplan] *m* aquaplane

aquarelle [akwarɛl] *f* watercolor

aquarium [akwarjɔm] *m* aquarium

aquatique [akwatik] *adj* aquatic

aqueduc [akdyk] *m* aqueduct

aquilin [akilɛ̃] *adj masc* aquiline

aquilon [akilɔ̃] *m* north wind

ara [ara] *m* (orn) macaw

arabe [arab] *adj* Arabian, Arab ‖ *m* Arabic; Arab (*horse*) ‖ (*cap*) *mf* Arabian, Arab

Arabie [arabi] *f* Arabia; **Arabie Saoudite** [sudit] Saudi Arabia

arachide [araʃid] *f* peanut

araignée [areɲe] *f* spider; grapnel; **araignée de mer** spider crab; **avoir une araignée dans le plafond** (coll) to have bats in the belfry

aratoire [aratwar] *adj* agricultural

arbalète [arbalɛt] *f* crossbow

arbitrage [arbitraʒ] *m* arbitration

arbitraire [arbitrɛr] *adj* arbitrary ‖ *m* arbitrariness, despotism

arbitre [arbitr] *m* arbiter; arbitrator; umpire, judge; **libre arbitre** free will

arbitrer [arbitre] *tr* & *intr* to arbitrate; umpire

arborer [arbɔre] *tr* to hoist (*a flag*); show off (*new clothes*)

arbouse [arbuz] *f* arbutus berry

arbousier [arbuzje] *m* arbutus

arbre [arbr] *m* tree; (mach) arbor, shaft; **arbre de Noël** Christmas tree; **arbre généalogique** family tree; **arbre vert** evergreen, conifer

arbris•seau [arbriso] *m* (*pl* **-seaux**) bushy tree

arbuste [arbyst] *m* shrub

arc [ark] *m* bow; arch; (elec, geom) arc

arcade [arkad] *f* arcade, archway

arcanes [arkan] *mpl* mysteries, secrets

arcanson [arkɑ̃sɔ̃] *m* rosin

arc-boutant [arkbutɑ̃] *m* (*pl* **arcs-boutants**) flying buttress

arc-en-ciel [arkɑ̃sjɛl] *m* (*pl* **arcs-en-ciel** [arkɑ̃sjɛl]) rainbow

archaïque [arkaik] *adj* archaic

archaïsme [arkaism] *m* archaism

archange [arkɑ̃ʒ] *m* archangel

arche [arʃ] *f* arch (*of bridge*); Ark

archéologie [arkeɔlɔʒi] *f* archaeology

archéologue [arkeɔlɔg] *mf* archaeologist

archer [arʃe] *m* archer, bowman

archet [arʃe] *m* bow

archétype [arketip] *m* archetype

archevêque [arʃəvɛk] *m* archbishop

archiduc [arʃidyk] *m* archduke

archipel [arʃipɛl] *m* archipelago

archiprêtre [arʃiprɛtr] *m* archpriest

architecte [arʃitɛkt] *m* architect

architecture [arʃitɛktyr] *f* architecture; **architecture ouverte** (comp) open architecture

archives [arʃiv] *fpl* archives

arçon [arsɔ̃] *m* saddletree

Arctique [arktik] *adj* & *m* Arctic ‖ *f* Arctic (*region*)

ardemment [ardamɑ̃] *adv* ardently

ar•dent [ardɑ̃] **-dente** [dɑ̃t] *adj* ardent; burning; bright-red (*hair*)

ardeur [ardœr] *f* ardor; intense heat

ardoise [ardwaz] *f* slate

ardoi•sier [ardwazje] **-sière** [zjɛr] *adj* slate ‖ *m* slate-quarry worker ‖ *f* slate quarry

ar•du -due [ardy] *adj* steep; arduous

arène [arɛn] *f* arena; sand; (fig) arena; **arènes** arena, coliseum, amphitheater

arête [arɛt] *f* fishbone; beard (*of wheat*); angle, ridge

argent [arʒɑ̃] *m* silver; money; **argent comptant** cash, cash down; **argent vif** cash flow

argenter [arʒɑ̃te] *tr* to silver ‖ *ref* to turn silvery (*i.e., gray*)

argenterie [arʒɑ̃tri] *f* silver plate, silverware

argentier [arʒɑ̃tje] *m* silverware cabinet; (hist) Treasurer

argen•tin [arʒɑ̃tɛ̃] **-tine** [tin] *adj* silvery (*voice*); Argentinian ‖ (*cap*) *mf* Argentinian (*person*) ‖ **l'Argentine** *f* Argentina

argile [arʒil] *f* clay

argot [argo] *m* slang; jargon, cant

argotique [argɔtik] *adj* slangy

arguer [argɥe] (many authorities write: **j'arguë, tu arguës,** etc.) *tr* to argue, imply; **arguer de faux** to doubt the authenticity of (*a document*) ‖ *intr* to draw a conclusion; **arguer de** to use as a pretext

argument [argymɑ̃] *m* argument

argumentation [argymɑ̃tasjɔ̃] *f* argument

argumenter [argymɑ̃te] *intr* to argue

argus [argys] *m* look-out, spy; **argus de la presse** clipping service; **argus de l'automobile** price list, blue book (*e.g., for used cars*)

aria [arja] *m* (coll) fuss, bother ‖ *f* aria

aride [arid] *adj* arid; (*subject, speaker, etc.*) dry

aridité [aridite] *f* aridity; (fig) dryness, dullness

aristocrate [aristɔkrat] *adj* aristocratic ‖ *mf* aristocrat

aristocratie [aristɔkrasi] *f* aristocracy

Aristote [aristɔt] *m* Aristotle

arithméti•cien [aritmetisjɛ̃] **-cienne** [sjɛn] *mf* arithmetician

arithmétique [aritmetik] *f* arithmetic

arlequin [arləkɛ̃] *m* goulash; wrench ‖ (*cap*) *m* Harlequin

armateur [armatœr] *m* ship outfitter; shipowner

armature [armatyr] *f* framework; keeper (*of a horseshoe magnet*); (mus) key signature

arme [arm] *f* arm; weapon; **arme blanche** cold steel; steel blade; **armes portatives** small arms; **faire ses premières armes** to make one's début

armée [arme] *f* army

armement [arməmɑ̃] *m* armament; fire power; (naut) outfitting

armé•nien [armenjɛ̃] **-nienne** [njɛn] *adj* Armenian ‖ *m* Armenian (*language*) ‖ (*cap*) *mf* Armenian (*person*)

armer [arme] *tr* to arm; cock (*a gun*); reinforce (*concrete*); **armer chevalier** to knight ‖ *ref* to arm oneself, arm

armistice [armistis] *m* armistice

armoire [armwar] *f* wardrobe, closet; **armoire à pharmacie** medicine cabinet; **armoire frigorifique** freezer

armoiries [armwari] *fpl* arms, coat of arms

armoise [armwaz] *f* sagebrush

armorier [armɔrje] *tr* to emblazon
armure [armyr] *f* armor; (tex) weave
arnaquer [arnake] *tr* (slang) to rip off, bamboozle
aromatique [arɔmatik] *adj* aromatic
arôme [arom] *m* aroma
aronde [arɔ̃d] *f* swallow
arpège [arpɛʒ] *m* arpeggio
arpent [arpɑ̃] *m* acre
arpentage [arpɑ̃taʒ] *m* surveying
arpenter [arpɑ̃te] *tr* to survey; (coll) to pace (*the floor*)
arpenteur [arpɑ̃tœr] *m* surveyor
ar•qué -quée [arke] *adj* arched, bowed; cambered (*beam*); hooked (*nose*)
arquer [arke] *tr* to arch, bow ‖ *ref* to arch, be bowed
arraché [araʃe] *m* (weight lifting) snatch
arrache-clou [araʃklu] *m* (*pl* **-clous**) claw hammer
arrache-pied [araʃpje] *adv*—**d'arrache-pied** at a stretch, without stopping
arracher [araʃe] *tr* to dig up, uproot, tear out, pull out; snatch; wheedle (*money; a confession*); **arracher q.ch. à qn** to take away, snatch, or pry s.th. from s.o.; **arracher q.ch. de q.ch.** to pull s.th. off, from, or out of s.th.; strip s.th. of s.th.; **arracher qn à** to deliver s.o. from (*evil; temptation; death*); **arracher qn de** to make s.o. get out of (*e.g., bed*) ‖ *ref* to tear oneself away
arra•cheur [araʃœr] **-cheuse** [ʃøz] *mf* puller ‖ *f* (mach) picker
arraisonnement [arɛzɔnmɑ̃] *m* port inspection
arraisonner [arɛzɔne] *tr* to inspect (*a ship*)
arrangement [arɑ̃ʒmɑ̃] *m* arrangement
arranger [arɑ̃ʒe] §38 *tr* to arrange; settle (*a difficulty*); fix (*repair; punish*) ‖ *ref* to be arranged; get ready; agree
arrérages [areraʒ] *mpl* arrears
arrestation [arɛstasjɔ̃] *f* arrest
arrêt [arɛ] *m* stop; stopping; arrest; decree; **arrêt complet** standstill; **arrêt de tabulateur** tabulator setting; **arrêt d'urgence** emergency shutdown; **arrêt facultatif** whistle stop; **arrêt par épuisement** burnout; **arrêt sur image** (electron) stop action; **mettre aux arrets** to keep in, confine to quarters
arrê•té -tée [arɛte] *adj* stopped, standing; decided, fixed ‖ *m* decree; authorization; (com) closing out (*of an account*); **arrêté de police** police ordinance; **prendre un arrêté** to pass a decree
arrêter [arɛte] §97, §99 *tr* to stop; arrest; fix (*one's gaze*); settle, decide upon; hire, engage; point (*game, as hunting dog does*) ‖ *intr* to stop; point (*said of hunting dog*) ‖ *ref* to stop; **s'arrêter à** to decide on; **s'arrêter de** + *inf* to stop + *ger*
arrhes [ar] *fpl* deposit, down payment; earnest money, guarantee
arrière [arjɛr] *adj invar* back, rear; tail (*wind*) ‖ *m* back, rear; stern; **à l'arrière** in back;

astern; **en arrière** backward; **en arrière de** behind ‖ *adv* back
arrié•ré -rée [arjere] *adj* backward; delinquent (*in payment*); back (*pay, taxes, etc.*); old-fashioned ‖ *mf* backward child ‖ *m* arrears; back pay; back payment; backlog
arrière-boutique [arjɛrbutik] *f* (*pl* **-boutiques**) back room (*of a shop*)
arrière-cour [arjɛrkur] *f* (*pl* **-cours**) backyard
arrière-garde [arjɛrgard] *f* (*pl* **-gardes**) rear guard
arrière-goût [arjɛrgu] *m* (*pl* **-goûts**) after-taste
arrière-grand-mère [arjɛrgrɑ̃mɛr] *f* (*pl* **-grands-mères**) great-grandmother
arrière-grand-père [arjɛrgrɑ̃pɛr] *m* (*pl* **-grands-pères**) great-grandfather
arrière-pays [arjɛrpei] *m invar* back country
arrière-pensée [arjɛrpɑ̃se] *f* (*pi* **-pensées**) mental reservation, ulterior motive
arrière-plan [arjɛrplɑ̃] *m* (*pl* **-plans**) background
arriérer [arjere] §10 *tr* to delay ‖ *ref* to fall behind (*in payment*)
arrière-train [arjɛrtrɛ̃] *m* (*pl* **-trains**) rear (*of a vehicle*); hindquarters
arrimage [arimaʒ] *m* stowage; docking, linkup (*of space vehicle*)
arrimer [arime] *tr* to stow; (aer) to dock
arrimeur [arimœr] *m* stevedore
arrivage [arivaʒ] *m* arrival (*of goods or ships*)
arrivée [arive] *f* arrival; intake; (sports) finish, goal; **arrivée en douceur** (rok) soft landing
arriver [arive] §96 *intr* (*aux:* ÉTRE) to arrive; succeed; happen; **arriver à** to attain, reach; **en arriver à** + *inf* to be reduced to + *ger*
arriviste [arivist] *mf* upstart, parvenu
arrogance [arɔgɑ̃s] *f* arrogance
arro•gant [arɔgɑ̃] **-gante** [gɑ̃t] *adj* arrogant
arroger [arɔʒe] §38 *ref* to arrogate to oneself
arrondir [arɔ̃dir] *tr* to round, round off, round out ‖ *ref* to become round
arrondissement [arɔ̃dismɑ̃] *m* district
arrosage [arozaʒ] *m* sprinkling; irrigation; (mil) heavy bombing
arroser [aroze] *tr* to sprinkle, water; irrigate; flow through (*e.g., a city*); wash down (*a meal*); (coll) to bribe; (coll) to drink to (*a success*)
arro•seur [arozœr] **-sense** [zøz] *mf* sprinkler (*person*) ‖ *f* street sprinkler
arrosoir [arozwar] *m* sprinkling can
arse•nal [arsanal] *m* (*pl* **-naux** [no]) shipyard, navy yard; (fig) storehouse; (archaic) arsenal, armory
arsenic [arsanik] *m* arsenic
art [ar] *m* art; **Art déco** Art deco *ou* deco; **arts d'agréments** music, drawing, dancing, etc.; **art de parler** speaking; **arts ménagers** home economics; **le huitième art** television; **les arts du spectacle** the performing arts; **le septième art** the cinema
artère [artɛr] *f* artery
arté•riel -rielle [arterjɛl] *adj* arterial

artériosclé·reux [arterjosklerø] **-reuse** [røz] *adj & mf* arteriosclerotic

arté·sien [artezjɛ̃] **-sienne** [zjɛn] *adj* of Artois; artesian (*well*)

arthrite [artrit] *f* arthritis

arthritique [artritik] *adj* arthritic

artichaut [arti ʃo] *m* artichoke

article [artikl] *m* article; entry (*in a dictionary*); **à l'article de la mort** on the point of death; **article de fond** leader; editorial; **article de montre, article de démonstration** floor sample; **article de tête** front-page story; **articles divers** sundries; **articles durables** durable goods

articuler [artikyle] *tr & ref* to articulate

artifice [artifis] *m* artifice; craftsmanship

artifi·ciel -cielle [artifisjɛl] *adj* artificial

artificier [artifisje] *m* fireworks maker; soldier in charge of ammunition supply

artifi·cieux [artifisjø] **-cieuse** [sjøz] *adj* artful, cunning

artillerie [artijəri] *f* artillery

artilleur [artijœr] *m* artilleryman

arti·san [artizɑ̃] **-sane** [zan] *mf* artisan, artificer ‖ *m* craftsman

artiste [artist] *adj* artistic; artist, of art, e.g., **le monde artiste** the world of art ‖ *mf* artist; actor; **artiste invité** guest artist

artistique [artistik] *adj* artistic

ar·yen [arjɛ̃] **-yenne** [jɛn] *adj* Aryan ‖ (*cap*) *mf* Aryan (*person*)

as [as] *m* ace; **as du volant** speed king ‖ [a] *v* see **avoir**

A.S. *abbr* (**assurances sociales**) social security

a/s *abbr* (**aux bons soins de**) c/o

asbeste [asbɛst] *m* asbestos

ascendance [asɑ̃dɑ̃s] *f* lineal ancestry; rising (*of air; of star*)

ascenseur [asɑ̃sœr] *m* elevator; **renvoyer l'ascenseur** to do a favòr in return

ascension [asɑ̃sjɔ̃] *f* ascension; **Ascension** *f* Ascension Day

ascèse [asɛz] *f* asceticism

ascète [asɛt] *mf* ascetic

ascétique [asetik] *adj* ascetic

ascétisme [asetism] *m* asceticism

aseptique [asɛptik] *adj* aseptic

asiatique [azjatik] *adj* Asian, Asiatic ‖ **Asiatique** *mf* Asian, Asiatic

Asie [azi] *f* Asia; **Asie Mineure** Asia Minor; **l'Asie** Asia; **l'Asie Mineure** Asia Minor

asile [azil] *m* asylum, shelter, home

aspect [aspɛ], [aspɛk] *m* aspect

asperge [aspɛrʒ] *f* asparagus; **des asperges** asparagus (*stalks and tips used as food*)

asperger [aspɛrʒe] *§38 tr* to sprinkle

aspérité [asperite] *f* roughness; harshness; gruffness

aspersion [aspɛrsjɔ̃] *f* sprinkling

asphalte [asfalt] *m* asphalt

asphyxier [asfiksje] *tr* to asphyxiate ‖ *ref* to be asphyxiated

aspic [aspik] *m* asp

aspi·rant [aspirɑ̃] **-rante** [rɑ̃t] *adj* aspirant, aspiring; suction (*pump*) ‖ *mf* candidate (*for a degree*) ‖ *m* midshipman

aspirateur [aspiratœr] *m* vacuum cleaner; **aspirateur de buée** kitchen fan

aspi·ré -rée [aspire] *adj & m* (phonet) aspirate

aspirer [aspire] *tr* to inhale; suck in ‖ *§96 intr*—**aspirer à** to aspire to

aspirine [aspirin] *f* aspirin; **aspirine tamponnée** buffered aspirine

assagir [asaʒir] *tr* to make wiser ‖ *ref* to become wiser

assail·lant [asajɑ̃] **-lante** [jɑ̃t] *adj* attacking ‖ *mf* assailant

assaillir [asajir] *§69 tr* to assail, assault

assainir [asɛnir] *tr* to purify, clean up; drain (*a swamp*)

assainissement [asɛnismɑ̃] *m* purification; draining

assaisonnement [asɛzɔnmɑ̃] *m* seasoning

assaisonner [asɛzɔne] *tr* to season, flavor

assas·sin [asasɛ̃] **-sine** [sin] *adj* murderous ‖ *m* assassin

assassinat [asasina] *m* assassination; **assassinat du caractère** character assassination

assassiner [asasine] *tr* to assassinate; (coll) to bore to death

assaut [aso] *m* assault, attack; match, bout

assèchement [asɛʃmɑ̃] *m* drainage, drying; dryness

assécher [aseʃe] *§10 tr* to drain, dry up

assemblage [asɑ̃blaʒ] *m* assemblage; assembling (*e.g., of printed pages*); (woodworking) joint, joining

assemblée [asɑ̃ble] *f* assembly, meeting

assembler [asɑ̃ble] *tr* to assemble ‖ *ref* to assemble, convene, meet

assembleur [asɑ̃blœr] *m* (comp) assembly language

assener [asne] *§2 tr* to land (*a blow*)

assentiment [asɑ̃timɑ̃] *m* assent, consent

asseoir [aswar] *§5 tr* to seat, sit, place; base (*an opinion*) ‖ *ref* to sit down

assermen·té -tée [asɛrmɑ̃te] *adj* sworn in, under oath

assertion [asɛrsjɔ̃] *f* assertion

asser·vi -vie [asɛrvi] *adj* subservient

asservir [asɛrvir] *tr* to enslave; to subdue (*e.g., passions*) ‖ *ref* to submit (*to convention; to tyranny*)

asservissement [asɛrvismɑ̃] *m* enslavement; subservience

assesseur [asɛsœr] *adj & m* assistant; associate (*judge*)

asseyez [aseje] *v* (**assieds** [asje]) see **asseoir**

assez [ase] *adv* enough; fairly, rather; **assez de** enough; **en voilà assez!** that's enough!, cut it out!, ‖ *interj* enough!, stop!

assi·du -due [asidy] *adj* assiduous; **assidu à** attentive to

assidûment [asidymɑ̃] *adv* assiduously

assié·geant [asjeʒɑ̃] **-geante** [ʒɑ̃t] *adj* besieging ‖ *mf* besieger

assiéger [asjeʒe] §1 *tr* to besiege

assiette [asjɛt] *f* plate, dish; plateful; seat (*of a rider on horseback*); position, condition; **assiette anglaise, assiette de viandes froides** cold cuts; **assiette au beurre** (fig) gravy train; **assiette creuse** soup plate; **assiette fiscale** tax basis, tax base; **je ne suis pas dans mon assiette** I'm in low spirits

assignation [asiɲasjɔ̃] *f* assignation; subpoena, summons

assi•gné -gnée [asiɲe] *mf* appointee; **assigné à résidence** permanent appointee; **assigné intérim** temporary appointee

assigner [asiɲe] §96 *tr* to assign, allot; fix (*a date*); subpoena, summon

assimilable [asimilabl] *adj* assimilable; comparable

assimilation [asimilɑsjɔ̃] *f* assimilation

assimiler [asimile] *tr* to assimilate; compare; identify with ‖ *ref* to assimilate

as•sis [asi] **-sise** [siz] *adj* seated, sitting; firmly established ‖ *f* foundation; stratum; **assises** assizes ‖ *v* see **asseoir**

assistance [asistɑ̃s] *f* assistance; audience, persons present; presence; **assistance judiciaire** public defender; **assistance publique** welfare department; **assistance sociale** social service

assis•tant [asistɑ̃] **-tante** [tɑ̃t] *adj* assistant ‖ *mf* assistant; bystander, spectator; **assistance sociale** public health nurse; social worker

assister [asiste] *tr* to assist, help ‖ *intr*—**assister à** to attend, be present at

association [asɔsjɑsjɔ̃] *f* association; (sports) soccer; **association des spectateurs** theater club; **association sans but lucratif** nonprofit organization

asso•cié -ciée [asɔsje] *adj* & *mf* associate

associer [asɔsje] *tr* to associate ‖ *ref* to go into partnership

assoif•fé -fée [aswafe] *adj* thirsty

assolement [asɔlmɑ̃] *m* rotation (*of crops*)

assombrir [asɔ̃brir] *tr* & *ref* to darken

assom•mant [asɔmɑ̃] **-mante** [mɑ̃t] *adj* (coll) boring, fatiguing

assommer [asɔme] *tr* to kill with a heavy blow; beat up; stun; (coll) to heckle; (coll) to bore

assommoir [asɔmwar] *m* bludgeon; (coll) gin mill, dive, clip joint

Assomption [asɔ̃psjɔ̃] *f* Assumption

assonance [asɔnɑ̃s] *f* assonance

assor•ti -tie [asɔrti] *adj* assorted (*e.g., cakes*); well-matched (*couple*); stocked, supplied (*store*); to match, e.g., **une cravate assortie** a necktie to match

assortiment [asɔrtimɑ̃] *m* assortment; matching (*of colors*); set (*of dishes*); platter (*of cold cuts*)

assortir [asɔrtir] *tr* to assort, match; stock ‖ *ref* to match; harmonize; **s'assortir de** to be accompanied with

assoupir [asupir] *tr* to make drowsy, lull; deaden (*pain*) ‖ *ref* to doze off; lessen (*with time*)

assoupissement [asupismɑ̃] *m* drowsiness; lethargy

assouplir [asuplir] *tr* to make supple, flexible; break in (*a horse*) ‖ *ref* to become supple, manageable

assouplissement [asuplismɑ̃] *m* suppleness, flexibility; limbering up; relaxation (*of a rule*)

assourdir [asurdir] *tr* to deafen; tone down, muffle

assouvir [asuvir] *tr* to assuage, appease, satiate; satisfy (*e.g., a thirst for vengeance*)

assouvissement [asuvismɑ̃] *m* assuagement, appeasement, satisfying

assujet•ti -tie [asyʒɛti] *adj* fastened; subject, liable ‖ *mf* taxpayer; contributor (*e.g., to social security*)

assujettir [asyʒɛtir] *tr* to subjugate; subject; fasten, secure ‖ §96 *ref* to submit

assujettis•sant [asyʒɛtisɑ̃] **-sante** [sɑ̃t] *adj* demanding

assujettissement [asyʒɛtismɑ̃] *m* subjugation, subduing; submission (*to a stronger force*); fastening, securing

assumer [asyme] *tr* to assume, take upon oneself

assurance [asyrɑ̃s] *f* assurance; insurance; **assurances sociales** social security; **assurance incendie** fire insurance; **assurance invalidité** disability insurance; **assurance maladie-sécurité** health insurance; **assurance multirisque** comprehensive insurance

assurance-maladie [asyrɑ̃smaladi] *f* (*pl* **assurances-maladie**) health insurance

assurance-vie [asyrɑ̃svi] *f* (*pl* **assurances-vie**) life insurance

assu•ré -rée [asyre] *adj* assured, satisfied; insured ‖ *mf* insured, policy holder

assurément [asyremɑ̃] *adv* assuredly

assurer [asyre] §95 *tr* to assure; secure; insure ‖ *ref* to be assured; make sure; be insured

astate [astat] *m* astatine

aster [astɛr] *m* (bot) aster

astérie [asteri] *f* starfish

astérisque [asterisk] *m* asterisk

asthénie [asteni] *f* debility

asthme [asm] *m* asthma

asticot [astiko] *m* maggot

astiquer [astike] *tr* to polish

as•tral -trale [astral] *adj* (*pl* **-traux** [tro]) astral

astre [astrə] *m* star, heavenly body; leading light; **astre de la nuit** moon; **astre du jour** sun

astreindre [astɛ̃dr] §50 *tr* to force, compel, subject ‖ §96 *ref* to force oneself; be subjected

astrologie [astrɔlɔʒi] *f* astrology

astrologue [astrɔlɔg] *m* astrologer

astronaute [astrɔnot] *mf* astronaut

astronautique [astrɔnotik] *f* astronautics

astronef [astrɔnɛf] *m* spaceship

astronome [astrɔnɔm] *mf* astronomer

astronomie [astrɔnɔmi] *f* astronomy

astronomique [astrɔnɔmik] *adj* astronomical

astrophysique [astrɔfizik] *f* astrophysics

astuce [astys] *f* slyness, guile; tricks (*of a trade*)

astu•cieux [astysjø] **-cieuse** [sjøz] *adj* astute, crafty

atelier [atəlje] *m* studio; workshop; **atelier de carrosserie** (aut) body shop

atermoiement [atɛrmwamã] *m* procrastination; extension of a loan

athée [ate] *adj* atheistic ‖ *mf* atheist

athéisme [ateism] *m* atheism

Athènes [atɛn] *f* Athens

athlète [atlɛt] *mf* athlete; jock (coll)

athlétique [atletik] *adj* athletic

athlétisme [atletism] *m* athletics

Atlantique [atlãtik] *adj & m* Atlantic

atlas [atlɑs] *m* atlas ‖ (*cap*) *m* Atlas

atmosphère [atmɔsfɛr] *f* atmosphere

atome [atom] *m* atom

atomique [atɔmik] *adj* atomic

atomi•sé -sée [atɔmize] *adj* afflicted with radiation sickness

atomiser [atɔmize] *tr* to atomize

atomiseur [atomizœr] *m* spray; atomizer

atone [atɔn] *adj* dull, expressionless; drab (*life*); (phonet) unaccented

atours [atur] *mpl* finery

atout [atu] *m* trump; **sans atout** no-trump

atrabilaire [atrabilɛr] *adj & mf* hypochondriac

âtre [ɑtr] *m* hearth

atroce [atrɔs] *adj* atrocious

atrocité [atrɔsite] *f* atrocity

atrophie [atrɔfi] *f* atrophy

atrophier [atrɔfje] *tr & ref* to atrophy

atta•chant [ata∫ã] **-chante** [∫ã] *adj* appealing, attractive

attache [ata∫] *f* attachment, tie; paper clip; (anat) joint; **attache parisienne** paper clip

atta•ché -chée [ata∫e] *adj* attached ‖ *mf* attaché; **attaché(e) de presse** press agent

attachement [ata∫mã] *m* attachment

attacher [ata∫e] *tr* to attach; tie up ‖ *intr* (culin) to stick ‖ §96 *ref* to be fastened, tied; **s'attacher à** to stick to; become devoted to

attaque [atak] *f* attack; (pathol) stroke; **attaque brusque** or **attaque brusquée** surprise attack; **attaque de nerfs** case of nerves

attaquer [atake] *tr & intr* to attack ‖ *ref-* —**s'attaquer à** to attack

attar•dé -dée [atarde] *adj* retarded; behind the times; belated, delayed ‖ *mf* mentally retarded person; lover of the past

attarder [atarde] *tr* to delay, retard ‖ *ref* to be delayed; stay, remain

atteindre [atɛ̃dr] §50 *tr* to attain; reach ‖ *intr*—**atteindre à** to attain; reach; attain to

at•teint [atɛ̃] **-teinte** [tɛ̃t] *adj* stricken ‖ *f* reaching; injury; **hors d'atteinte** out of reach; **porter atteinte à** to endanger; **premières atteintes** first signs (*of illness*)

attelage [atlaʒ] *m* harnessing; coupling

atteler [atle] §34 *tr* to harness; hitch; couple (*cars on a railroad*) ‖ *ref*—**s'atteler à** (coll) to buckle down to

attelle [atɛl] *m* splint; **attelles** hames

atte•nant [atənã] **-nante** [nãt] *adj* adjoining

attendre [atãdr] §97 *tr* to wait for, await; expect ‖ *intr* to wait ‖ §96 *ref*—**s'attendre à** to expect; rely on; **s'attendre à** + *inf* to expect to + *inf*; **s'attendre à ce que** + *subj* to expect (*s.o.*) to + *inf*, e.g., **il s'attend à ce que je lui raconte toute l'affaire** he expects me to tell him the whole story; **s'y attendre** to expect it or them

attendrir [atãdrir] *tr* to tenderize; soften ‖ *ref* to become tender; be deeply touched or moved

attendrissement [atãdrismã] *m* softening; compassion

atten•du -due [atãdy] *adj* expected ‖ **attendus** *mpl* (law) grounds ‖ *adv*—**attendu que** whereas, inasmuch as ‖ **attendu** *prep* in view of

attentat [atãta] *m* attempt, assault; outrage (*to decency*); offense (*against the state*); **attentat suicidant au plastic** suicide bombing

attente [atãt] *f* wait; expectation; **en attente!** stand by!

attenter [atãte] *intr*—**attenter à** to attempt (*e.g., s.o.'s life*); **attenter à ses jours** to attempt suicide

atten•tif [atãtif] **-tive** [tiv] *adj* attentive

attention [atãsjɔ̃] *f* attention; **attentions** attention, care, consideration ‖ *interj* attention!, be careful!

attention•nè-née [atãsjɔne] *adj* considerate

atténuation [atenɥasjɔ̃] *f* attenuation

atténuer [atenɥe] *tr* to subdue, soften (*color; pain; passions*); attenuate (*words; bacteria*); extenuate (*a fault*) ‖ *ref* to soften; lessen

atterrer [atɛre] *tr* to dismay

atterrir [atɛrir] *intr* (*aux:* AVOIR or ÉTRE) to land

atterrissage [atɛrisaʒ] *m* landing; **atterrissage dur** hard landing; **atterrissage forcé** forced landing; **atterrissage sans visibilité** blind landing; **atterrissage sur le ventre** pancake landing

attestation [atɛstasjɔ̃] *f* attestation; **attestation d'études** transcript

attester [atɛste] *tr* to attest, attest to; **attester qn de q.ch.** to call s.o. to witness to s.th.

attiédir [atjedir] *tr & ref* to cool off; warm up

attifer [atife] *tr & ref* to spruce up

attirail [atiraj] *m* gear, tackle, outfit; (coll) paraphernalia

attirance [atirãs] *f* attraction, lure, attractiveness

atti•rant [atirã] **-rante** [rãt] *adj* appealing, attractive

attirer [atire] *tr* to attract ‖ *ref* to be attracted; attract each other; call forth (*criticism*)

attiser [atize] *tr* to stir, stir up, poke

atti•tré -trée [atitre] *adj* regular (*dealer*); **attitré de la cour** appointed by the court

attitude [atityd] *f* attitude

attrac•tif [atraktif] **-tive** [tiv] *adj* attractive (*force*)

attraction [atraksjɔ̃] *f* attraction; **les attractions** vaudeville

attrait [atrɛ] *m* attraction, attractiveness, appeal; **attraits** charms

attrape [atrap] *f* trap; (coll) trick, joke

attrape-mouche [atrapmuʃ] *m* (*pl* **-mouche** or **-mouches**) flypaper; Venus's-flytrap

attrape-nigaud [atrapnigo] *m* (*pl* **-nigauds**) booby trap

attraper [atrape] *tr* to catch; snare, trap; trick ‖ *ref* to trick each other; hang on

at•trayant [atrɛjɑ̃] **-trayante** [trɛjɑ̃t] *adj* attractive

attribuer [atribɥe] *tr* to ascribe, attribute; assign (*a share*) ‖ *ref* to claim, assume

attribut [atriby] *m* attribute; predicate

attribu•tif [atribytif] **-tive** [tiv] *adj* (gram) predicative

attribution [atribysjɔ̃] *f* attribution, assignment, assignation

attris•té -tée [atriste] *adj* sorrowful

attrister [atriste] *tr* to sadden ‖ §97 *ref* to become sad

attrition [atrisjɔ̃] *f* attrition

attroupement [atrupmɑ̃] *m* mob

attrouper [atrupe] *tr* to bring together in a mob ‖ *ref* to flock together in a mob

au [o] §77 to the

aubaine [obɛn] *f* windfall, godsend, bonanza

aube [ob] *f* dawn; (mach) paddle, blade, vane

aubépine [obepin] *f* hawthorn

auberge [obɛrʒ] *f* inn; **auberge de la jeunesse** youth hostel

aubergine [obɛrʒin] *f* eggplant; (Parisian slang) meter maid

aubergiste [obɛrʒist] *mf* innkeeper

auburn [obœrn] *adj invar* auburn

au•cun [okœ̃] **-cune** [kyn] *adj*—**aucun . . . ne** or **ne . . . aucun** §90 no, none, not any ‖ *pron indef*—**aucun ne** §90B no one, nobody; **d'aucuns** some, some people

aucunement [okynmɑ̃] §90 *adv*—**ne . . . aucunement** not at all, by no means

audace [odas] *f* audacity

auda•cieux [odasjø] **-cieuse** [sjøz] *adj* audacious

au-deçà [odəsa] *adv* (obs) on this side; **au-deçà de** (obs) on this side of

au-dedans [odədɑ̃] *adv* inside; **au-dedans de** inside, inside of

au-dehors [odəɔr] *adv* outside; **au-dehors de** outside, outside of

au-delà [odəla] *m*—**l'au-delà** the beyond ‖ *adv* beyond; **au-delà de** beyond

au-dessous [odəsu] *adv* below; **au-dessous de** under

au-dessus [odəsy] *adv* above; **au-dessus de** above

au-devant [odəvɑ̃] *adv*—**aller au devant de** to go to meet; anticipate (*s.o.'s wishes*); court (*defeat*)

audience [odjɑ̃s] *f* audience

audio [odjo] *adj invar* & *m* audio

audio-fréquence [odjofrekɑ̃s] *f* audio frequency

audiomètre [odjɔmɛtr] *m* audiometer

audio-vi•suel -suelle [odjovizɥɛl] *adj* audiovisual ‖ *m* audiovisual aids

audi•teur [oditœr] **-trice** [tris] *mf* listener; auditor (*in class*); **auditeur libre** auditor (*in class*)

audi•tif [oditif] **-tive** [tiv] *adj* auditory

audition [odisjɔ̃] *f* audition; public hearing; musical recital

auditionner [odisjɔne] *tr* & *intr* to audition

auditoire [oditwar] *m* audience; courtroom

auditorium [oditɔrjɔm] *m* auditorium; concert hall; projection room

auge [oʒ] *f* trough

augmentation [ɔgmɑ̃tasjɔ̃] *f* augmentation; raise (*in salary*)

augmenter [ɔgmɑ̃te] *tr* to augment; increase or supplement (*income*); raise (*prices*); raise the salary of (*an employee*) ‖ *intr* to augment, increase; **augmenter de** to increase by (*a stated amount*)

augure [ɔgyr] *m* augur; augury

augurer [ɔgyre] *tr* & *intr* to augur

auguste [ɔgyst] *adj* august

aujourd'hui [oʒurdɥi], [oʒordɥi] *m* & *adv* today; **d'aujourd'hui en huit** a week from today; **d'aujourd'hui en quinze** two weeks from today

aumône [omon] *f* alms; **faire l'aumône** to give alms; **faire l'aumône de** (fig) to hand out

aumônier [omonje] *m* chaplain

aune [on] *m* alder ‖ *f* ell

auparavant [oparavɑ̃] *adv* before, previously

auprès [oprɛ] *adv* close by, in the neighborhood; **auprès de** near, close to; at the side of; to, at the side of; to (*a king, a government*); with; compared with

auquel [okɛl] (*pl* **auxquels**) §78

aurai [ɔre] *v* (**auras, aura, aurons, etc.**) see **avoir**

auréole [ɔreɔl] *f* aureole, halo

auréomycine [ɔreomisin] *f* aureomycin

auriculaire [ɔrikylɛr] *adj* firsthand (*witness*); auricular (*confession*) ‖ *m* little finger

auricule [ɔrikyl] *f* auricle

aurifier [ɔrifje] *tr* to fill (*a tooth*) with gold

aurore [ɔrɔr] *f* aurora, dawn

ausculter [ɔskylte] *tr* to auscultate

auspice [ospis] *m* omen; **sous les auspices de** under the auspices of

aussi [osi] *adv* also, too; therefore, and so; so; **aussi. . . que** as. . . as

aussitôt [osito] *adv* right away, immediately; **aussitôt dit, aussitôt fait** no sooner said than done; **aussitôt que** as soon as

austère [ostɛr] *adj* austere

austérité [ɔsterite] *f* austerity

Australie [ɔstrali] *f* Australia; **l'Australie** Australia

austra•lien [ɔstraljɛ̃] **-lienne** [ljɛn] *adj* Australian ‖ (*cap*) *mf* Australian

autant [otɑ̃] *adv* as much, as many; as far, as long; **autant** + *inf*, e.g., **autant dire que** it's as if, that's like saying; e.g. **autant vous dire**

que... I might as well tell you that...; **autant de** so many; **autant que** as much as, as far as; **d'autant** by so much; **d'autant plus** all the more; **d'autant plus** (or **moins**)... **que... plus** (or **moins**) all the more (or less)... as (or in proportion as)... more (or less); **d'autant que** inasmuch as

autel [ɔtɛl], [otɛl] m altar

auteur [otœr] adj—**une femme auteur** an authoress ‖ m author

authentifier [ɔtɑ̃tifje] tr to authenticate

authentique [otɑ̃tik] adj authentic; genuine (antique); notarized

authentiquer [otɑ̃tike] tr to notarize

autistique [ɔtistik] adj autistic

auto [ɔto], [oto] f auto

auto-allumage [ɔtoalymaʒ] m preignition

autobiographie [ɔtobjɔgrafɪ] f autobiography

auto-buffet [ɔtobyfɛ] m drive-in; curb service

autobus [ɔtobys] m bus, city bus

autocar [ɔtokar] m interurban bus

autochenille [ɔtoʃənij] f caterpillar (tractor)

autochtone [ɔtɔktɔn] adj & mf native

autoclave [ɔtoklav] m pressure cooker; autoclave, sterilizer

autocollant [ɔtokɔlɑ̃] m bumpersticker

autocopie [ɔtokɔpi] f duplicating, multicopying; duplicated copy

autocopier [ɔtokɔpje] tr to run off, duplicate, ditto

auto-couchette [ɔtokuʃɛt] f—**en auto-couchette** piggyback

autocrate [ɔtokrat] mf autocrat

autocratique [ɔtokratik] adj autocratic

autocritique [ɔtokritik] f self-criticism

autocuiseur [ɔtokɥizœr] m pressure cooker

autodétermination [ɔtodetɛrminasjɔ̃] f self-determination

autodidacte [ɔtodidakt] adj self-taught ‖ mf self-taught person

autodrome [ɔtodrom] m race track; test strip

auto-école [ɔtoekɔl] f (pl **-écoles**) driving school

autogare [ɔtogar] f bus station

autographe [ɔtograf] adj & m autograph

autographie [ɔtografi] f multicopying

autographier [ɔtografje] tr to duplicate

autogreffe [ɔtogrɛf] f skin grafting

auto-grue [ɔtogry] f (pl **-grues**) tow truck

autoguidage [ɔtogidaʒ] m automatic piloting

auto-intoxication [ɔtoɛ̃tɔksikasjɔ̃] f autointoxication

automate [ɔtomat] m automaton

automation [ɔtomasjɔ̃] f automation

automatique [ɔtomatik] adj automatic ‖ m dial telephone

automatisation [ɔtomatizasjɔ̃] f automation

automatiser [ɔtomatize] tr to automate

automitrailleuse [ɔtomitrajøz] f armored car mounting machine guns

autom·nal -nale [ɔtomnal] adj (pl **-naux** [no]) autumnal

automne [ɔtɔn], [otɔn] m fall, autumn; **à l'automne, en automne** in the fall

automobile [ɔtomɔbil], [otomɔbil] adj automotive ‖ f automobile

automobilisme [ɔtomɔbilism] m driving, motoring

automobiliste [ɔtomɔbilist] mf motorist

automo·teur [ɔtomɔtœr] **-trice** [tris] adj self-propelling, automatic ‖ m self-propelled river barge ‖ f rail car

autonome [ɔtonɔm] adj autonomous, independent; (comp) off line

autonomie [ɔtonɔmi] f autonomy; cruising radius, range (of ship, plane, or tank)

autoplastie [ɔtoplasti] f plastic surgery

autoportrait [ɔtopɔrtrɛ] m self-portrait

auto-propul·sé -sée [ɔtoprɔpylse] adj self-propelled

autopsie [ɔtopsi] f autopsy

autopsier [ɔtopsje] tr to perform an autopsy on

autorail [ɔtoraj] m rail car

autorisation [ɔtorizasjɔ̃] f authorization

autoriser [ɔtorize] §96, §100 tr to authorize ‖ ref—**s'autoriser de** to take as authority, to base one's opinion on

autoritaire [ɔtoritɛr] adj authoritarian, bossy

autorité [ɔtorite] f authority

autoroute [ɔtorut] f superhighway, highway; **autoroute à péage** turnpike; **autoroute de l'information, autoroute électronique** (comp) information highway

autosable [ɔtosabl] f dune buggy

auto-stop [ɔtostɔp] m hitchhiking; **faire de l'auto-stop** to hitchhike

auto-stop·peur [ɔtostɔpœr] **-peuse** [pøz] mf (pl **-peurs -peuses**) hitchhiker

autostrade [ɔtostrad] f superhighway

autour [otur] m goshawk ‖ adv around; **autour de** around; about

autre [otr] adj indef other; **autre chose** (coll) something else; **nous autres** we, e.g., **nous autres Américains** we Americans; **vous autres** you ‖ pron indef other; **d'autres** others; **j'en ai vu bien d'autres** I have seen worse than that; **l'un l'autre, les uns les autres** each other, one another; **l'un et l'autre** both; **l'un ou l'autre** either; **ni l'un ni l'autre** neither; **quelqu'un d'autre** someone else; **un autre** another

autrefois [otrəfwa] adv formerly, of old; **d'autrefois** of yore

autrement [otrəmɑ̃] adv otherwise

Autriche [otriʃ] f Austria; **l'Autriche** Austria

autri·chien [otriʃjɛ̃] **-chienne** [ʃjɛn] adj Austrian ‖ (cap) mf Austrian

autruche [otryʃ] f ostrich

autrui [otrɥi] pron indef others

auvent [ovɑ̃] m canopy (over door); flap (of tent)

aux [o] §77 to the

auxiliaire [oksiljɛr] adj auxiliary, standby; ancillary ‖ m (gram) auxiliary ‖ f noncombatant unit

aux•quels -quelles [okɛl] §78

avachir [avaʃir] *tr* to make limp, flabby ‖ *ref* to become limp, flabby

aval [aval] *m* lower waters; **en aval** downstream; **en aval de** below ‖ *m* (*pl* **avals**) endorsement

avalanche [avalɑ̃ʃ] *f* avalanche

avaler [avale] *tr* to swallow ‖ *intr* to go downstream

ava•leur [avalœr] **-leuse** [løz] *mf* swallower; **avaleur de sabres** sword swallower

avaliser [avalize] *tr* to endorse

avance [avɑ̃s] *f* advance; **en avance** fast (*clock*); **avance image par image** (electron) frame advance; **grosse avance** head start

avan•cé -cée [avɑ̃se] *adj* advanced; overripe; tainted (*meat*)

avancement [avɑ̃smɑ̃] *m* advancement

avancer [avɑ̃se] §51 *tr, intr,* & *ref* to advance

avanie [avani] *f* snub, insult; **essuyer une avanie** to swallow an affront

avant [avɑ̃] *adj invar* front ‖ *m* front; (aer) nose; (naut) bow; **d'avant** previous; **en avant** forward; **en avant de** in front of, ahead of ‖ *adv* before; **avant de** (with *inf*) before; **avant que** + *subj* before; **bien** (or **très**) **avant dans** late into; far into; deep into; **plus avant** farther on ‖ *prep* before; **avant Jésus-Christ (av. J. -C.)** before Christ (B.C.)

avantage [avɑ̃taʒ] *m* advantage; perk; (tennis) add; **avantages en nature** payment in kind; **avantages sociaux** fringe benefits

avanta•geux [avɑ̃taʒø] **-geuse** [ʒøz] *adj* advantageous; bargain (*price*); becoming (*e.g., hairdo*); conceited (*manner*)

avant-bras [avɑ̃bra] *m invar* forearm

avant-cour [avɑ̃kur] *f* (*pl* **-cours**) front yard

avant-coureur [avɑ̃kurœr] (*pl* **-coureurs**) *adj masc* presaging (*signs*) ‖ *m* forerunner, precursor, harbinger

avant-goût [avɑ̃gu] *m* (*pl* **-goûts**) foretaste

avant-guerre [avɑ̃gɛr] *m* & *f* (*pl* **-guerres**) prewar period

avant-hier [avɑ̃tjɛr], [avɑ̃jɛr] *adv* & *m* the day before yesterday

avant-port [avɑ̃pɔr] *m* (*pl* **-ports**) outer harbor

avant-poste [avɑ̃pɔst] *m* (*pl* **-postes**) outpost; **avant-postes** front lines

avant-première [avɑ̃prəmjɛr] *f* (*pl* **-premières**) review (*of a play*); premiere (*for the drama critics*); preview

avant-projet [avɑ̃prɔʒɛ] *m* (*pl* **-projets**) rough draft; draft (*of a law*)

avant-propos [avɑ̃propo] *m invar* foreword

avant-scène [avɑ̃sɛn] *f* (*pl* **-scènes**) forestage, proscenium

avant-toit [avɑ̃twa] *m* (*pl* **-toits**) eave

avant-train [avɑ̃trɛ̃] *m* (*pl* **-trains**) front end, front assembly (*of vehicle*)

avant-veille [avɑ̃vɛj] *f* (*pl* **-veilles**) two days before

avare [avar] *adj* avaricious, miserly; saving, economical ‖ *mf* miser

avarice [avaris] *f* avarice

avari•cieux [avarisjø] **-cieuse** [sjøz] *adj* avaricious

avarie [avari] *f* damage; breakdown; spoilage; (naut) average

avarier [avarje] *tr* to damage; spoil ‖ *ref* to spoil

avatar [avatar] *m* avatar; **avatars** vicissitudes

avec [avɛk] *adv* (coll) with it; (coll) along, with me, etc. ‖ *prep* with

aveline [avlin] *f* filbert

ave•nant [avnɑ̃] **-nante** [nɑ̃t] *adj* gracious, charming; **à l'avenant** in keeping, to match; **à l'avenant de** in accord with ‖ *m* (ins) endorsement; codicil, rider

avènement [avɛnmɑ̃] *m* Advent; accession (*to the throne*)

avenir [avnir] *m* future; **à l'avenir** in the future

Avent [avɑ̃] *m* Advent

aventure [avɑ̃tyr] *f* adventure; **à l'aventure** at random; aimlessly; **d'aventure** by chance; **la bonne aventure** fortunetelling; **par aventure** by chance

aventurer [avɑ̃tyre] *tr* to venture ‖ *ref* to take a chance; **s'aventurer à** to venture to

aventu•reux [avɑ̃tyrø] **-reuse** [røz] *adj* adventurous

aventurier [avɑ̃tyrje] *m* adventurer

aventurière [avɑ̃tyrjɛr] *f* adventuress; (pej) gold digger

avenue [avny] *f* avenue

avé•ré -rée [avere] *adj* established, authenticated

avérer [avere] §10 *tr* to aver ‖ *ref* to prove to be (*e.g., difficult*)

avers [avɛr] *m* heads (*of coin*), face (*of medal*)

averse [avɛrs] *f* shower; **averse météorique** meteor shower

aversion [avɛrsjɔ̃] *f* aversion

avertir [avɛrtir] §97, §99 *tr* to warn; **avertir qn de** + *inf* to warn s.o. to + *inf*

avertissement [avɛrtismɑ̃] *m* warning; notification; foreword

avertisseur [avɛrtisœr] *adj masc* warning ‖ *m* alarm; (aut) horn; (theat) callboy; **avertisseur d'incendie** fire alarm

a•veu [avø] *m* (*pl* **-veux**) avowal, confession; consent; **sans aveu** unscrupulous

aveu•glant [avœglɑ̃] **-glante** [glɑ̃t] *adj* blinding

aveugle [avœgl] *adj* blind ‖ *mf* blind person; **en aveugle** without thinking

aveuglement [avœgləmɑ̃] *m* (fig) blindness

aveuglément [avœglemɑ̃] *adv* blindly

aveugler [avœgle] *tr* to blind; dazzle; stop up, plug; board up (*a window*) ‖ *ref*—**s'aveugler sur** to shut one's eyes to

aveuglette [avœglɛt] *adv*—**à l'aveuglette** blindly

aveulir [avølir] *tr* to enervate, deaden ‖ *ref* to become limp, enervated

aveulissement [avølismɑ̃] *m* enervation

aviateur [avjatœr] *m* aviator

aviation [avjasjɔ̃] *f* aviation

aviatrice [avjatris] *f* aviatrix

avide [avid] *adj* avid, eager; greedy; voracious; **avide de** avid for

avidité [avidite] *f* avidity, eagerness; greed; voracity

avilir [avilir] *tr* to debase, dishonor; (com) to lower the price of ‖ §96 *ref* to debase oneself; (com) to deteriorate

avilis•sant [avilisɑ̃] **-sante** [sɑ̃t] *adj* debasing

avilissement [avilismɑ̃] *m* debasement; (com) depreciation

avi•né -née [avine] *adj* drunk

aviner [avine] *tr* to soak (*a new barrel*) with wine ‖ *ref* (coll) to booze

avion [avjɔ̃] *m* airplane; **avion affété, avion nolisé, avion de transport à la demande** charter (air)plane; **avion à réaction** jet; **avion-avion** air-to-air; **avion de chasse** fighter plane; **avion de transport militaire** troop carrier; **avion fugitif** spy plane; **avion long-courrier** long-range plane; **en avion** by plane; **par avion** air mail

avion-cargo [avjɔ̃kargo] *m* (*pl* **avions-cargos**) cargo liner, freighter

avion-géant [avjɔ̃ʒeɑ̃] *m* jumbo jet

avion-taxi [avjɔ̃taksi] *m* (*pl* **avions-taxis**) taxi-plane

aviron [avirɔ̃] *m* oar; **aviron de couple** scull

avis [avi] *m* opinion; advice; notice, warning; decision; **à mon avis** in my opinion; **avis au lecteur** note to the reader; **changer d'avis** to change one's mind; **envoyer avec avis de réception** to send by certified mail

avi•sé -sée [avize] *adj* prudent, shrewd; **bien avisé** well-advised

aviser [avize] §99 *tr* to glimpse, descry; advise, inform, warn ‖ *intr* to decide; **aviser à** to think of, look into; deal with ‖ §97 *ref*—**s'aviser de** to contrive, think up; be on the look-out for; **s'aviser de** + *inf* to take it into one's head to + *inf*

aviso [avizo] *m* dispatch boat, sloop

avivage [avivaʒ] *m* brightening; polishing

aviver [avive] *tr* to revive, stir up (*fire; passions*); brighten (*colors*); (med & fig) to open (*a wound*)

av. J.-C. *abbr* (**avant Jésus-Christ**) B.C.

avo•cat [avɔka] **-cate** [kat] *mf* lawyer; advocate; barrister (Brit); **avocat commis d'office** defense lawyer; **avocat du diable** devil's advocate ‖ *m* avocado

avoine [avwan] *f* oats

avoir [avwar] *m* wealth; credit side (*of ledger*) ‖ §6 *tr* to have; get; **avoir ... ans to** be ... years old, e.g., **mon fils a dix ans** my son is ten years old; **avoir beau** + *inf* §95 no matter how (much) (s.o.) + *v* (*expressing futility*), e.g., **j'ai beau travailler** no matter how much I work; **avoir froid** to be cold; **avoir raison** to be right ‖ *intr*—**avoir à** to have to; **en avoir à** or **contre** to be angry with ‖ *impers*—**il y a** there is, there are, e.g., **il n'y a pas d'espoir** there is no hope ‖ *aux* to have, e.g., **j'ai couru trop vite** I have run too fast

avoisiner [avwazine] *tr* to neighbor, be near

avortement [avɔrtəmɑ̃] *m* abortion; miscarriage

avorter [avɔrte] *intr* to abort; miscarry

avorton [avɔrtɔ̃] *m* runt; (biol) stunt

avoué [avwe] *m* lawyer (*doing notarial work*); solicitor (Brit)

avouer [avwe] §95 *tr* to avow, admit; claim, acknowledge authorship of ‖ *ref* to be admitted; **s'avouer vaincu** to admit defeat

avril [avril] *m* April

axe [aks] *m* axis

axénique [aksenik] *adj* germ-free

axer [akse] *tr* to set on an axis; orient

axiomatique [aksjɔmatik] *adj* axiomatic

axiome [aksjom] *m* axiom

axonge [aksɔ̃ʒ] *f* lard

ayant droit [ejɑ̃drwa] *m* (*pl* **ayants droit**) claimant; beneficiary

ayez [eje] *v* (**ayons**) see **avoir**

azalée [azale] *f* azalea

azimut or **azimuth** [azimyt] *m* azimuth

azote [azɔt] *m* nitrogen

azo•té -tée [azɔte] *adj* nitrogenous

Aztèques [aztɛk] *mpl* Aztecs

azur [azyr] *adj* & *m* azure

azyme [azim] *adj* unleavened ‖ *m* unleavened bread

B

B, b [be] *m invar* second letter of the French alphabet

baba [baba] *adj* (coll) flabbergasted, wide-eyed ‖ *m* baba

babeurre [babœr] *m* buttermilk

babil [babil], [babi] *m* babble, chatter; **babil enfantin** baby talk

babillage [babijaʒ] *m* babbling

babil•lard [babijar] **-larde** [jard] *adj* babbling ‖ *mf* babbler ‖ *f* (slang) letter

babiller [babije] *intr* to babble, chatter

babine [babin] *f* chop (*mouth*); **s'essuyer les babines, se lécher les babines** to lick one's chops

babiole [babjɔl] *f* (coll) bauble, gewgaw

bâbord [babɔr] *m* (naut) port, portside; **à bâbord** port; **bâbord armures** port sail

babouche [babuʃ] *f* babouche, slipper

babouin [babwɛ̃] *m* baboon; pimple on the lips; brat

baby-foot [babifut] *m invar* (*football de table*) table soccer, fuzball

bac [bak] *m* ferryboat; tub, vat; box, bin; tray (*for ice cubes*); drawer (*of refrigerator*); case (*of battery*); (slang) baccalaureate

baccalauréat [bakalɔrea] *m* baccalaureate, bachelor's degree

bacchanale [bakanal] *f* bacchanal

bâche [bɑʃ] *f* tarpaulin; hot-water tank

bache•lier [baʃəlje] **-lière** [ljɛr] *mf* bachelor (*holder of degree*) ‖ *m* (hist) bachelor (*young knight*)

bâcher [bɑʃe] *tr* to cover with a tarpaulin

bachique [baʃik] *adj* bacchanalian, bacchic; drinking (*song*)

bachot [baʃo] *m* dinghy, punt; (coll) baccalaureate

bachotage [baʃɔtaʒ] *m* (coll) cramming (*for an exam*)

bachoter [baʃɔte] *intr* (coll) to cram

bacille [basil] *m* bacillus

bâclage [baklaʒ] *m* blocking up (*of harbor*); (slang) botching (*of work*)

bâcle [bakl] *f* bolt (*of door*)

bâc•lé -lée [bakle] *adj* botched, slipshod

bâcler [bakle] *tr* to bolt (*a door*); close up (*a harbor*); (coll) to botch, to hurry through carelessly

bâ•cleur [baklœr] **-cleuse** [kløz] *mf* (coll) botcher

bacon [bakɔ̃] *m* bacon

bactéricide [bakterisid] *adj* bactericidal ‖ *m* bactericide

bactérie [bakteri] *f* bacterium; **bactéries** bacteria

bactériologie [bakterjɔlɔʒi] *f* bacteriology

ba•daud [bado] **-daude** [dod] *mf* rubber-neck, gawk, idler

badauder [badode] *intr* to stand and stare

badigeon [badiʒɔ̃] *m* whitewash

badigeonner [badiʒɔne] *tr* to whitewash; (med) to paint (*e.g., the throat*)

ba•din [badɛ̃] **-dine** [din] *adj* sprightly, playful, teasing ‖ *mf* tease ‖ *m* (aer) air-speed indicator ‖ *f* cane, switch

badinage [badinaʒ] *m* banter; **badinage amoureux** necking

badiner [badine] *intr* to joke, tease; trifle, be flippant

badinerie [badinri] *f* teasing; childishness

badminton [badmintɔn] *m* badminton

baffe [baf] *f* (coll) slap, blow, cuff

bafouer [bafwe] *tr* to heckle, humiliate

bafouiller [bafuje] *intr* (coll) to stammer, mumble, babble

bâfrer [bafre] *tr & intr* (slang) to guzzle

bagage [bagaʒ] *m* baggage; **bagages** baggage, luggage; **bagages à main** hand baggage; **ba-gages non accompagnés** baggage sent on ahead; **menus bagages** hand luggage; **plier bagage** to pack one's bags; (coll) to scram; (coll) to kick the bucket

bagarre [bagar] *f* brawl, row, riot; **chercher la bagarre** (coll) to be looking for a fight

bagarrer [bagare] *intr & ref* to riot; (coll) to brawl, scrap, scuffle

bagar•reur [bagarœr] **-reuse** [røz] *mf* (coll) rioter, brawler

bagatelle [bagatɛl] *f* trifle, bagatelle; frivolity; **s'occuper de bagatelles** to putter around ‖ *interj* nonsense!

bagnard [baɲar] *m* convict

bagne [baɲ] *m* penitentiary, penal colony; (nav) prison ship; (slang) sweatshop

bagnole [baɲɔl] *f* (slang) jalopy

bagou [bagu] *m* (coll) gift of gab

bague [bag] *f* ring; cigar band; (mach) collar, sleeve; **bague de fiançailles** engagement ring

baguenauder [bagnode] *intr* to waste time, fool around ‖ *ref* (coll) to wander about

baguer [bage] *tr* to band (*a tree*); baste (*cloth*)

baguette [bagɛt] *f* stick, switch, rod; baton; long thin loaf of bread; chopstick; **baguette de fée** fairy wand; **baguettes de tambour** drumsticks; **mener qn à la baguette** (coll) to lead s.o. by the nose; **passer par les baguettes** to run the gauntlet

baguier [bagje] *m* jewel box

bahut [bay] *m* trunk, chest; cupboard; (slang) high school

bai baie [bɛ] *adj* bay (*horse*) ‖ *m* bay; berry; bayberry; bay window

baignade [bɛɲad] *m* bathing, swimming; swimming hole, bathing spot

baigner [bɛɲe] *tr* to bathe; wash (*the coast*) ‖ *intr* to be immersed, soak ‖ *ref* to bathe; go bathing

bai•gneur [bɛɲœr] **-gneuse** [ɲøz] *mf* bather; vacationist at a spa or seaside resort; bathhouse attendant ‖ *m* doll

baignoire [bɛɲwar] *m* bathtub; (theat) orchestra box

bail [baj] *m* (*pl* **baux** [bo]) lease; **passer un bail** to sign a lease; **prendre à bail** to lease

bâillement [bɑjmɑ̃] *m* yawn

bailler [baje] *tr*—**vous me la baillez belle** (coll) you're pulling my leg

bâiller [bɑje] *intr* to yawn; be ajar, be half open

bail•leur [bajœr] **-leresse** [jərɛs] *mf* lessor; **bailleur de fonds** lender

bailli [baji] *m* bailiff

bailliage [bajaʒ] *m* bailiwick

bâillon [bɑjɔ̃] *m* gag, muzzle

bâillonner [bɑjɔne] *tr* to gag; (fig) to muzzle

bain [bɛ̃] *m* bath; **bain de soleil** sun bath; **bain de vapeur** steam bath; **bain moussant, bain de mousse** bubble bath; **bains** watering place, spa; bathing establishment; **être dans le bain** (coll) to be in hot water

bain•marie [bɛ̃mari] *m* (*pl* **bains-marie**) double boiler, bain-marie

baïonnette [bajɔnɛt] *f* bayonet

baiser [beze], [bɛze] *m* kiss ‖ *tr* (very vulgar) to have sex with; (archaic) to kiss

baisoter [bɛzɔte] *tr* (coll) to keep on kissing ‖ *ref* (coll) to bill and coo

baisse [bɛs] *f* fall; **jouer à la baisse** (com) to bear the market

baissement [bɛsmɑ̃] *m* lowering

baisser [bɛse] *m* lowering; **baisser du rideau** curtain fall ‖ *tr* to lower; take in (*sail*); dim (*headlights*) ‖ *intr* to fall, drop, sink ‖ *ref* to bend, stoop

baissier [bɛsje] *m* bear (*on the stock exchange*)

bajoue [baʒu] *f* jowl

bal [bal] *m* (*pl* **bals**) ball, dance; **bal masqué** masquerade ball; **bal travesti** fancy-dress ball

balade [balad] *f* stroll; **balade en auto** joy ride

balader [balade] *ref* to go for a stroll; **se balader en auto** to go joy-riding

bala·deur [baladœr] **-deuse** [døz] *adj* strolling ‖ *mf* stroller ‖ *m* gear; Walkman (trademark) ‖ *f* cart (*of street vendor*); drop-cord light

baladin [baladɛ̃] *m* mountebank, showman; oaf

balafre [balɑfr] *f* gash, scar

balafrer [balafre] *tr* to gash, scar

balai [balɛ] *m* broom; **balai à laver** mop; **balai de sorcière** witches'-broom; **balai électrique** vacuum cleaner; **balai mécanique** carpet sweeper; **donner un coup de balai à** to make a clean sweep of (*s.th.*); to kick (*s.o.*) out

balai-éponge [balɛepɔ̃ʒ] *m* (*pl* **balais-éponges**) mop

balance [balɑ̃s] *f* balance; scales; **faire la balance de** (bk) to balance; **la Balance** (astr, astrol) Libra

balancement [balɑ̃smɑ̃] *m* swaying, teetering; (fig) indecision, wavering; (fig) harmony (*of phrase*)

balancer [balɑ̃se] §51, §96 *tr* to balance; move (*arms or legs*) in order to balance; balance (*an account*); weigh (*the pros and cons*); swing, rock; (coll) to fire (*s.o.*); **elle est bien balancée** she is stacked (*well built*) ‖ *intr* to swing, rock; hesitate, waver ‖ *ref* to swing, seesaw; sway, rock; ride (*at anchor*)

balancier [balɑ̃sje] *m* pendulum; balance wheel; pole (*of tightrope walker*)

balançoire [balɑ̃swar] *f* swing; seesaw, teeter-totter; (slang) nonsense

balayage [balɛjaʒ] *m* sweeping; (telv) scanning

balayer [balɛje], [baleje] §49 *tr* to sweep, sweep up; sweep out; scour (*the sea*); (telv) to scan

balayeur [balɛjœr] **balayeuse** [balɛjøz] *mf* sweeper, scavenger ‖ *f* street-cleaning truck

balayures [balɛjyr] *fpl* sweepings

balbutiement [balbysimɑ̃] *m* stammering, mumbling; initial effort

balbutier [balbysje] *tr* to stammer out ‖ *intr* to stammer, mumble

balbuzard [balbyzar] *m* osprey, bald buzzard, sea eagle

balcon [balkɔ̃] *m* balcony; (theat) dress circle

baldaquin [baldakɛ̃] *m* canopy, tester

Baléares [balear] *fpl* Balearic Islands

baleine [balɛn] *f* right whale, whalebone whale; whalebone; rib (*of umbrella*); stay (*of a corset*)

baleinier [balɛnje] *m* whaling vessel

baleinière [balɛnjɛr] *f* whaleboat; lifeboat

balisage [balizaʒ] *m* (aer) ground lights; (naut) buoys

balise [baliz] *f* buoy, marker; ground light, beacon; landing signal

baliser [balize] *tr* to furnish with markers, buoys, landing lights, beacons, or radio signals

balistique [balistik] *adj* ballistic ‖ *f* ballistics

baliverne [balivɛrn] *f* nonsense, humbug

balkanique [balkanik] *adj* Balkan

ballade [balad] *f* ballade

bal·lant [balɑ̃] **-lante** [lɑ̃t] *adj* waving, swinging, dangling ‖ *m* oscillation, shaking

balle [bal] *f* ball; bullet; hull, chaff; bale; **balle de caoutchouc** rubber bullet; **balle de set, balle de match** (tennis) match point; **balle traçante** tracer bullet; **prendre** or **saisir la balle au bond** to seize time by the forelock

ballerine [balrin] *f* ballerina

ballet [balɛ] *m* ballet

ballon [balɔ̃] *m* balloon; ball; football, soccer ball; round-bottom flask; rounded mountain-top; **ballon d'essai** trial balloon

ballonner [balɔne] *tr, intr, & ref* to balloon

ballot [balo] *m* pack; bundle; (slang) blockhead, chump

ballottage [balɔtaʒ] *m* tossing, shaking; second ballot

ballotter [balɔte] *tr & intr* to toss about

ball-trap [baltrap] *m* trapshooting

balnéaire [balneɛr] *adj* seaside

ba·lourd [balur] **-lourde** [lurd] *adj* awkward, lumpish ‖ *mf* blockhead, bumpkin ‖ *m* wobble

balte [balt] *adj* Baltic ‖ (cap) *mf* Balt

Baltique [baltik] *f* Baltic (*sea*)

balustrade [balystrad] *f* balustrade, banisters

balustre [balystr] *m* baluster, banister

bal·zan [balzɑ̃] **-zane** [zan] *adj* white-footed (*horse*) ‖ *f* white spot (*on horse's foot*)

bam·bin [bɑ̃bɛ̃] **-bine** [bin] *mf* (coll) babe

bambo·chard [bɑ̃bɔʃar] **-charde** [ʃard] *adj* (coll) carousing ‖ *mf* (coll) carouser

bamboche [bɑ̃bɔʃ] *f* (slang) jag, bender

bambocher [bɑ̃bɔʃe] *intr* (coll) to carouse, go on a spree

bambo·cheur [bɑ̃bɔʃœr] **-cheuse** [ʃøz] *adj* (coll) carousing ‖ *mf* (coll) carouser

bambou [bɑ̃bu] *m* bamboo

ban [bɑ̃] *m* ban; cadenced applause; **ban de mariage** banns; **convoquer le ban et l'arrière-ban** to invite everyone and his brother; **mettre au ban** to banish, ban

ba·nal -nale [banal] *adj* (*pl* **-nals -nales**) banal, trite, commonplace ‖ *adj* (*pl* **-naux** [no] **-nales**) (archaic) common, public, in common

banaliser [banalize] *tr* to vulgarize, make commonplace

banalité [banalite] *f* banality; triteness

banane [banan] *f* banana

bananier [bananje] *m* banana tree

banc [bɑ̃] *m* bench; shoal; school (*of fish*); pew (*reserved for church officials*); (hist) privy council; **banc de neige** snowbank; **banc de sable** sandbank; **être sur les bancs** to go to high school

bancaire [bɑ̃kɛr] *adj* banking, of banks

ban•cal -cale [bɑ̃kal] *adj* (*pl* **-cals -cales**) bow-legged, bandy-legged

bandage [bɑ̃daʒ] *m* bandage; bandaging; truss; tire (*of metal or rubber*)

bande [bɑ̃d] *f* band; movie film; recording tape; cushion (*in billiards*); wrapper (*of a newspaper*); strip (*of stamps*); **bande de coiffeuse** vanity strip; **bande de fréquences** waveband; **bande dessinée** comic strip; **bande génératrice, bande mère** master tape; **bande magnétique** recording tape, magnetic tape; **bande magnétique (vidéo)** videotape; **bande sonore** or **parlante** sound track; **bande souche** master tape; **bande vidéo** videotape; **donner de la bande** to heel, to list; **faire bande à part** to keep to oneself

bande-annonce [bɑ̃danɔ̃s] *f* (**bandes-annonces**) film clip

ban-deau [bɑ̃do] *m* (*pl* **-deaux**) blindfold; headband, sweatband; bending (*of a bow*); **bandeau royal** diadem; **bandeaux** hair parted in the middle

bander [bɑ̃de] *tr* to band, put a band on; bandage; blindfold; bend (*a bow*); put a tire on; draw taut; (vulg) to have or get a hard-on ‖ *ref* to band together; put up resistance; **elle est bandante** (vulg) she is a sexpot

banderole [bɑ̃derɔl] *f* pennant, streamer; strap (*of gun*)

bandière [bɑ̃djɛr] *f* battle, e.g., **front de bandière** battle front

bandit [bɑ̃di] *m* bandit

bandoulière [bɑ̃duljɛr] *f* shoulder strap, sling; **en bandoulière** slung over the shoulder

banlieue [bɑ̃ljø] *f* suburbs; **de banlieue** suburban

banlieu•sard [bɑ̃ljøzar] **-sarde** [zard] *mf* suburbanite (*especially of a Parisian suburb*)

banne [ban] *f* awning (*of store*)

ban•ni -nie [bani] *adj* banished, exiled ‖ *mf* exile

bannière [banjɛr] *f* banner, flag

bannir [banir] *tr* to banish

bannissement [banismɑ̃] *m* banishment

banque [bɑ̃k] *f* bank; **banque de données** (comp) data bank; **banque des yeux** eye bank; **banque du sang** blood bank; **faire sauter la banque** to break the bank

banqueroute [bɑ̃krut] *f* bankruptcy (*with blame for negligence or fraud*)

banquerou•tier [bɑ̃krutje] **-tière** [tjɛr] *adj & mf* bankrupt (*with culpability*)

banquet [bɑ̃kɛ] *m* banquet

banqueter [bɑ̃kte] §34 *intr* to banquet

banquette [bɑ̃kɛt] *f* seat (*in a train, bus, automobile*); bank (*of earth or sand*); bunker (*in a golf course*); **banquette arrière** back seat;

banquette de tir (mil) emplacement for shooting; **jouer devant les banquettes** to play to an empty house

ban•quier [bɑ̃kje] **-quière** [kjɛr] *mf* banker

banquise [bɑ̃kiz] *f* pack ice

banquiste [bɑ̃kist] *m* charlatan, quack

baptême [batɛm] *m* baptism; christening; **baptême de la ligne, baptême des tropiques** or **du tropique** polliwog initiation

baptiser [batize] *tr* to baptize; christen; (slang) to dilute (*wine*) with water

baptis•mal -male [batismal] *adj* (*pl* **-maux** [mo]) baptismal

baptistaire [batistɛr] *adj* baptismal (*certificate*)

baptiste [batist] *mf* Baptist

baptistère [batistɛr] *m* baptistery

baquet [bakɛ] *m* wooden tub, bucket; (aut) bucket seat

bar [bar] *m* bar; (ichth) bass, perch; **bar payant** cash bar

baragouin [baragwɛ̃] *m* (slang) gibberish

baragouiner [baragwine] *tr* (coll) to murder (*a language*); (coll) to stumble through (*a speech*) ‖ *intr* (coll) to jabber

baraque [barak] *f* booth, stall; shanty, hovel

baraterie [baratri] *f* barratry

baratin [baratɛ̃] *m* (coll) sweet talk, hot air, sales talk

baratiner [baratine] (coll) *tr & intr* to sweet talk

baratte [barat] *f* churn

baratter [barate] *tr* to churn

Barbade [barbad] *f* Barbados; **la Barbade** Barbados

barbare [barbar] *adj* barbarous, barbaric, savage ‖ *mf* barbarian

barbaresque [barbarɛsk] *adj* of Barbary

barbarie [barbari] *f* barbarity, barbarism ‖ (*cap*) *f* Barbary

barbarisme [barbarism] *m* barbarism (*in speech or writing*)

barbe [barb] *f* beard; bristle; whiskers (*of an animal*); barbel; **barbe à papa** cotton candy; **barbes vane** (*of a feather*); deckle edge; **faire q.ch. à la barbe de qn** to do s.th. right under the nose of s.o.; **rire dans sa barbe** to laugh up one's sleeve; **se faire la barbe** to shave ‖ *interj* **c'est la barbe!** what a bore!; **la barbe!** shut up!

bar•beau [barbo] *m* (*pl* **-beaux**) cornflower; (ichth) barbel; (slang) pimp

barbe•lé -lée [barbəle] *adj* barbed ‖ **barbelés** *mpl* barbed wire

bar•bet [barbɛ] **-bette** [bɛt] *mf* water spaniel

barbiche [barbiʃ] *f* goatee

barbier [barbje] *m* barber

barbillon [barbijɔ̃] *m* barb

barbiturique [barbityrik] *m* barbiturate

barbon [barbɔ̃] *m* (pej) old fogy

barboter [barbɔte] *intr* to paddle (*like ducks*); wallow (*like pigs*); bubble (*like carbonated water*); (coll) to splutter; (slang) to steal

barbo•teur [barbɔtœr] **-teuse** [tøz] *mf* (slang) muddler ‖ *m* duck; wash bottle ‖ *f* rompers

barbotine [barbɔtin] *f* watery paste; slushy cement mix; (culin) slush drink

barbouiller [barbuje] *tr* to smear, blur; daub; (coll) to scribble; **barbouiller le cœur à** to nauseate

barbouil·leur [barbujœr] **-leuse** [jøz] *mf* dauber; messy person; scribbler

barbouze [barbuz] *f* (slang) beard; (slang) secret agent; (slang) bodyguard

bar·bu -bue [barby] *adj* bearded

bard [bar] *m* handbarrow

bardage [bardaʒ] *m* siding (*of house*)

bardane [bardan] *f* burdock

barde [bard] *m* bard ‖ *f* blanket of bacon

bar·deau [bardo] *m* (*pl* **-deaux**) shingle; lath

barder [barde] *tr* to carry with a handbarrow; armor (*a horse*); blanket (*a roast*); **barder de** to cover with ‖ *intr* to rage

bardot [bardo] *m* hinny

barème [barɛm] *m* schedule (*of rates, taxes, etc.*)

baréter [barete] §10 *intr* to trumpet (*like an elephant*)

barge [barʒ] *f* barge; haystack; godwit, black-tailed godwit

barguigner [barginje] *intr* to shilly-shally, have trouble deciding

bargui·gneur [barginœr] **-gneuse** [nøz] *mf* shilly-shallyer, procrastinator

baricaut [bariko] *m* small cask, keg

baril [baril], [bari] *m* small barrel, cask, keg

barillet [barije] *m* small barrel; revolver cylinder; spring case

bariolage [barjɔlaʒ] *m* (coll) motley, mixture of colors

bario·lé -lée [barjɔle] *adj* speckled, multicolored, variegated

barioler [barjɔle] *tr* to variegate

bariolure [barjɔlyr] *f* clashing colors, motley

bar·man [barman] *m* (*pl* **-men** [mɛn] or **-mans**) bartender

baromètre [barɔmɛtr] *m* barometer; **baromètre anénoïde** aneroid barometer

barométrique [barɔmetrik] *adj* barometric

baron [barɔ̃] *m* baron

baronne [barɔn] *f* baroness

baroque [barɔk] *adj & m* baroque

baroud [barud] *m* rumble (*gang war*); (mil) **baroud d'honneur** gallant last stand

barque [bark] *f* boat

barrage [baraʒ] *m* dam; barrage, cordon (*of police*); tollgate; barricade, roadblock, checkpoint; (sports) playoff

barre [bar], [bar] *f* bar; crossbar (*of a t*); tiller, helm; bore (*tidal flood*); **barre d'aimant** bar magnet; **barre de contrôle** (nucl) control rod; **barre de dopage** (nucl) booster rod; **barre de justice** rod to hold shackles; **barre de menu** (comp) menu bar; **barre des témoins** witness stand; **barre d'outils** (comp) tool bar; **barre du gouvernail** helm; **barres** (typ) parallels; **jouer aux barres** to play prisoner's base

bar·reau [baro] *m* (*pl* **-reaux**) bar, cross-bar, rail; rung (*of ladder or chair*); (law) bar

barrer [bare] *tr* to cross out, strike out, cancel; cross (*a t; a check in a British bank*); bar (*the door; the way*); block off (*a street*); dam (*a stream*); steer (*a boat*)

barrette [barɛt], [barɛt] *f* biretta; bar; slide; pin; name tag

barreur [barœr] *m* helmsman

barricade [barikad] *f* barricade

barricader [barikade] *tr* to barricade

barrière [barjɛr] *f* barrier; gate (*of a town; of a grade crossing*); tollgate; neighborhood shopping district

barrique [barik] *f* cask; hogshead, large barrel

barrir [barir] *intr* to trumpet (*like an elephant*)

barrot [baro] *m* beam (*of a ship*)

baryton [baritʒ] *m* baritone; alto (*saxhorn*)

baryum [barjɔm] *m* barium

bas [ba] **basse** [bas] *adj* low; base, vile; cloudy (*weather*) ‖ (when standing before noun) *adj* low; base, vile; early (*age*) ‖ *m* stocking; lower part, bottom; **à bas. . .!** down with . . .!; **bas de casse** (typ) lower case; **bas de laine** nest egg, savings; **en bas** at the bottom; downstairs ‖ *f* see **basse** ‖ **bas** *adv* softly; down, low

ba·sal -sale [bazal] *adj* (*pl* **-saux** [zo]) basic; basal (*metabolism*)

basalte [bazalt] *m* basalt

basa·né -née [bazane] *adj* tanned, sunburned

basaner [bazane] *tr* to tan, sunburn

bas-bleu [bablø] *m* (*pl* **-bleus**) bluestocking

bas-côté [bakote] *m* (*pl* **-côtés**) aisle (*of a church*); footpath (*beside a road*)

bascule [baskyl] *f* scale; rocker; seesaw

basculement [baskylmɑ̃] *m* rocking, seesawing, tipping; dimming

basculer [baskyle] *tr* to tip over ‖ *intr* to tip over; seesaw, rock, swing; **faire basculer** to dim (*the headlights*)

bas-dessus [badəsy] *m* mezzo-soprano

base [baz] *f* base; basis; **à la base** at heart, to the core; **base de données** (comp) data base; **base fiscale** tax base, tax basis; **de base** basic

base-ball [bɛzbol] *m* baseball

baser [baze] *tr* to base; ground, found (*an opinion*) ‖ *ref* to be based

bas-fond [bafɔ̃] *m* (*pl* **-fonds**) lowland; shallows; **bas-fonds** dregs, underworld; slums

basilic [bazilik] *m* basil

basilique [bazilik] *f* basilica

basin [bazɛ̃] *m* dimity

basique [bazik] *adj* basic, alkaline

basket [baskɛt] *m* basketball

basketteur [baskɛtœr] *m* basketball player

basoche [bazɔʃ] *f* law, legal profession

basque [bask] *adj* Basque ‖ *m* Basque (*language*) ‖ *f* coattail ‖ (*cap*) *mf* Basque (*person*)

basse [bas] *f* shoal; tuba; (mus) bass; **basse chiffrée** (mus) figured bass

basse-contre [baskɔ̃tr] *f* (*pl* **basses-contre**) basso profundo

basse-cour [bɑskur] f (pl **basses-cours**) barnyard, farmyard; barnyard animals; poultry yard

bassesse [bɑsɛs] f baseness; base act

bassin [basɛ̃] m basin; dock; artificial lake; collection plate; pelvis; **bassin à flot** tidal basin; **bassin de lit** bedpan; **bassin de radoub** dry dock; **bassin hygiénique** bedpan

bassine [basin] f dishpan

bassinoire [basinwar] f bedwarmer

basson [basɔ̃] m bassoon

baste [bast] m ace of clubs; saddle basket || interj enough!

bastille [bastij] f small fortress

bastion [bastjɔ̃] m bastion

bastonnade [bastɔnad] f beating

bas-ventre [bavɑ̃tr] m abdomen, lower part of the belly

bât [bɑ] m packsaddle

bataclan [bataklɑ̃] m—**tout le bataclan** (slang) the whole caboodle

bataille [batɑj], [bataj] f battle, fight

batailler [batɑje], [bataje] intr to battle, fight

batail•leur [batajœr] **-leuse** [jøz] adj belligerent || mf fighter

bataillon [batajɔ̃] m battalion

bâ•tard [batar] **-tarde** [tard] adj & mf mongrel; bastard || m one-pound loaf of short-length type of bread || f cursive handwriting

bâtar•deau [batardo] m (pl **-deaux**) cofferdam, caisson

ba•teau [bato] m (pl **-teaux**) boat; **bateau automobile** motorboat, motor launch; **bateau à vapeur** steamboat; **bateau à voiles** sailboat; **bateau de guerre** warship; **bateau de pêche** fishing boat; **bateau de sauvetage** lifeboat; **monter un bateau à qn** (slang) to pull s.o.'s leg; **par (le) bateau** by boat

bateau-citerne [batositɛrn] m (pl **bateaux-citernes**) tanker

bateau-feu [batofø] m (pl **bateaux-feux**) lightship

bateau-maison [batomezɔ̃] m (pl **bateaux-maisons**) houseboat

bateau-mouche [batomuʃ] m (pl **bateaux-mouches**) excursion boat

bateau-pompe [batopɔ̃p] m (pl **bateaux-pompes**) fireboat

batelage [batlaʒ] m lighterage; juggling; tumbling

batelée [batle] f boatload

bateler [batle] §34 tr to lighter || intr to juggle; tumble

bateleur [batlœr] **-leuse** [løz] mf juggler; tumbler

bate•lier [batlje] **-lière** [ljɛr] mf skipper || m boatman; ferryman

batellerie [batɛlri] f lighterage

bâter [bate] tr to packsaddle

bath [bat] adj (slang) A-one, swell

bâ•ti -tie [bati] adj built; **bien bâti** well-built (person) || m frame; basting (thread); basted garment

batifoler [batifɔle] intr (coll) to frolic

bâtiment [batimɑ̃] m building; ship

bâtir [batir] tr to build; baste, tack || ref to be built

bâtisse [batis] f masonry, construction; building, edifice; ramshackle house

bâtis•seur [batisœr] **-seuse** [søz] mf builder

bâton [batɔ̃] m stick; baton; staff, cane; rung (of a chair); stroke (of a pen); stick (of gum); **à bâtons rompus** by fits and starts; impromptu; (archit) with zigzag molding; **bâton de reprise** (mus) repeat bar; **bâton de rouge à lèvres** lipstick; **bâton de vieillesse** helper or nurse for the aged; **mettre des bâtons dans les roues** to throw a monkey wrench into the works

bâtonner [batɔne] tr to cudgel; cross out

bâtonnet [batɔnɛ] m rod (in the retina); chopstick; **bâtonnet de poisson** fish stick

battage [bataʒ] m beating; threshing; churning; (slang) ballyhoo

bat•tant [batɑ̃] **-tante** [tɑ̃t] adj beating; pelting, driving; swinging (door) || m flap; clapper (of bell); **à deux battants** double (door)

batte [bat] f mallet, beater; dasher, plunger; bench for beating clothes; wooden sword (for slapstick comedy); (sports) bat; **batte de l'or** goldbeating

battement [batmɑ̃] m beating, beat; throbbing, pulsing; clapping (of hands); dance step; wait (e.g., between trains)

batterie [batri] f (elec, mil, mus) battery; train service (in one direction); ruse, scheming; **batterie de cuisine** kitchen utensils

batteur [batœr] m beater; thresher; (sports) batter; **batteur de grève** beachcomber; **batteur de pieux** pile driver; **batteur électrique** electric mixer

batteuse [batøz] f threshing machine

battoir [batwar] m bat, beetle (for washing clothes); tennis racket

battre [batr] §7 tr to beat; clap (one's hands); flap, flutter; wink; bang; pound (the sidewalk); search; shuffle (the cards); **battre la mesure** to beat time; **battre monnaie** to mint money || intr to beat || ref to fight

bau [bo] m (pl **baux**) beam (of a ship)

baud [bo] m (comp) baud

baudet [bodɛ] m ass, donkey; stallion ass; sawhorse; (slang) jackass, idiot

baudrier [bodrije] m shoulder belt

bauge [boʒ] f lair, den; clay and straw mortar; (coll) pigsty

baume [bom] m balsam; (consolation) balm

ba•vard [bavar] **-varde** [vard] adj talkative, loquacious; tattletale || mf chatterer; tattletale; gossip

bavardage [bavardaʒ] m chattering; gossiping

bavarder [bavarde] intr to chatter; gossip

bava•rois [bavarwa] **-roise** [rwaz] adj Bavarian || (cap) mf Bavarian (person)

bave [bav] f dribble, froth, spittle; (fig) slander

baver [bave] intr to dribble, drool; run (like a pen); **baver sur** to besmirch

bavette [bavɛt] *f* bib

ba•veux [bavø] **-veuse** [vøz] *adj* drooling; tendentious, wordy; undercooked

Bavière [bavjɛr] *f* Bavaria; **la Bavière** Bavaria

bavocher [bavɔʃe] *intr* to smear

bavochure [bavɔʃyr] *f* smear

bavure [bavyr] *f* bur (*of metal*); smear

bayer [baje] **§49** *intr*—**bayer aux corneilles** to gawk, stargaze

bazar [bazar] *m* bazaar; five-and-ten; **tout le bazar** (slang) the whole shebang

béant [beɑ̃] **béante** [beɑ̃t] *adj* gaping, wideopen

béat [bea] **béate** [beat] *adj* smug, complacent, sanctimonious

béatifier [beatifje] *tr* to beatify

béatitude [beatityd] *f* beatitude

beau [bo] (or **bel** [bɛl] before vowel or mute **h**) **belle** [bɛl] (*pl* **beaux belles**) *adj* beautiful; handsome; **bel et bien** truly, for sure; **de plus belle** more than ever; **il fait beau** it is nice out, we are having fair weather; **tout beau!** steady!, easy does it! ‖ (when standing before noun) *adj* beautiful; handsome; fine, good; considerable, large, long; fair (*weather*); oddnumbered or recto (*page*) ‖ *mf* fair one; **faire le beau, faire la belle** to strut, swagger; sit up and beg (*said of a dog*); **la belle** the deciding match; **la Belle au bois dormant** Sleeping Beauty ‖ **beau** *adv*—**j'ai beau faire**...no matter what I do..., it's no use for me...‖ **belle** *adv*—**la bailler belle** (slang) to tell a whopper; **l'échapper belle** to have a narrow escape

beaucoup [boku] **§91** *adv* much, many; **beaucoup de** much, many; **de beaucoup** by far

beau-fils [bofis] *m* (*pl* **beaux-fils**) son-in-law; stepson

beau-frère [bofrɛr] *m* (*pl* **beaux-frères**) brother-in-law

beau-père [bopɛr] *m* (*pl* **beaux-pères**) father-in-law; stepfather

beau-petit-fils [bopətifis] *m* (*pl* **beaux-petits-fils**) son of a stepson or of a stepdaughter

beaupré [bopre] *m* bowsprit

beauté [bote] *f* beauty; **beauté du diable** (coll) bloom of youth; **se faire une beauté** (coll) to doll up

beaux-arts [bozar] *mpl* fine arts

beaux-parents [boparɑ̃] *mpl* in-laws

bébé [bebe] *m* baby; **bébé éprouvette** test-tube baby

bec [bɛk] *m* beak; nozzle, jet, burner; point (*of a pen*); (mus) mouthpiece; (slang) beak, face, mouth; **avoir bon bec** to be gossipy; **claquer du bec** (coll) to be hungry; **clore, clouer le bec à qn** (coll) to shut s.o. up; **tomber sur un bec** (coll) to encounter an unforeseen obstacle

bécane [bekan] *f* (coll) bike, bicycle

bécarre [bekar] *m* (mus) natural

bécasse [bekas] *f* woodcock; (slang) stupid woman

bécas•seau [bekaso] *m* (*pl* **bécas-seaux**) sandpiper

bec-de-cane [bɛkdəkan] *m* (*pl* **becs-de-cane**) door handle; flat-nosed pliers

bec-de-corbeau [bɛkdəkɔrbo] *m* (*pl* **becs-de-corbeau**) wire cutters

bec-de-corbin [bɛkdəkɔrbɛ̃] *m* (*pl* **becs-de-corbin**) crowbar

bec-de-lièvre [bɛkdəljɛvr] *m* (*pl* **becs-de-lièvre**) harelip

bêche [bɛʃ] *f* spade

bêcher [bɛʃe] *tr* to dig; (slang) to run (*s.th.*) down, to give (*s.o.*) a dig

bê•cheur [bɛʃœr] **-cheuse** [ʃøz] *mf* (coll) detractor, critic; (slang) stuffed shirt

bêchoir [bɛʃwar] *m* hoe

bécotage [bekɔtaʒ] *m* smooching, necking

bécoter [bekɔte] *tr* to give (*s.o.*) a peck or little kiss on the cheek ‖ *intr* to smooch, neck

becqueter [bɛkte] **§34** *tr* to peck at; (coll) to eat ‖ *ref* to bill and coo

bedaine [bədɛn] *f* paunch, beer belly

bédane [bedan] *m* cold chisel

be•deau [bədo] *m* (*pl* **-deaux**) beadle

bé-douin [bedwɛ̃] **-douine** [dwin] *adj* Bedouin ‖ (*cap*) *mf* Bedouin (*person*)

bée [be] *adj*—**bouche bée** mouth agape, flabbergasted ‖ *f* penstock

beep [bip] *m* beep; **émettre un beep** to beep

beffroi [befrwa] *m* belfry

bégaiement [begɛmɑ̃] *m* stammering, stuttering

bégayer [begɛje] **§49** *tr* & *intr* to stammer, stutter

bègue [bɛg] *adj* stammering, stuttering ‖ *mf* stammerer

bégueter [begte] **§2** *intr* to bleat

bégueule [begœl] *adj* (coll) prudish ‖ *f* (coll) prudish woman

béguin [begɛ̃] *m* hood, cap; sweetheart; (coll) infatuation

béguine [begin] *f* Beguine; sanctimonious woman

beige [bɛʒ] *adj* & *m* beige

beignet [bɛɲɛ] *m* fritter

béjaune [beʒon] *m* nestling; greenhorn, novice, ninny

bel [bɛl] *adj* see **beau**

bêlement [bɛlmɑ̃] *m* bleat, bleating

bêler [bɛle] *intr* to bleat

belette [bəlɛt] *f* weasel

belge [bɛlʒ] *adj* Belgian ‖ (*cap*) *mf* Belgian (*person*)

Belgique [bɛlʒik] *f* Belgium; **la Belgique** Belgium

bélier [belje] *m* ram; battering ram; **le Bélier** (astr, astrol) Aries

bélière [beljɛr] *f* sheepbell

bélinogramme [belinɔgram] *m* Wirephoto (*trademark*)

bélinographe [belinɔgraf] *m* Wirephoto transmitter

bélître [belitr] *m* scoundrel

belladone [bɛladɔn] *f* belladonna

bellâtre [bɛlɑtr] *adj* foppish ‖ *m* fop

belle [bɛl] *adj* see **beau**

belle-dame [bɛldam] *f* belladonna

belle-de-jour [bɛldəʒur] *f* (*pl* **belles-de-jour**) morning glory

belle-de-nuit [bɛldənɥi] *f* (*pl* **belles-de-nuit**) marvel-of-Peru

belle-d'un-jour [bɛldœ̃ʒur] *f* (*pl* **belles-d'un-jour**) day lily

belle-famille [bɛlfamij] *f* (*pl* **belles-familles**) in-laws

belle-fille [bɛlfij] *f* (*pl* **belles-filles**) daughter-in-law; stepdaughter

belle-mère [bɛlmɛr] *f* (*pl* **belles-mères**) mother-in-law; stepmother

belle-petite-fille [bɛlpətitfij] *f* (*pl* **belles-petites-filles**) daughter of a stepson or of a stepdaughter

belles-lettres [bɛllɛtr] *fpl* belles-lettres, literature

belle-sœur [bɛlsœr] *f* (*pl* **belles-sœurs**) sister-in-law

belliciste [bɛlisist] *mf* warmonger

belligé•rant [bɛliʒerɑ̃] **-rante** [rɑ̃t] *adj & m* belligerent

belli-queux [bɛlikø] **-queuse** [køz] *adj* bellicose, warlike

bel•lot [bɛlo] **-lote** [lɔt] *adj* pretty, cute; dapper

bémol [bemɔl] *adj invar & m* (mus) flat

bémoliser [bemɔlize] *tr* to flat (*a note*); provide (*a key signature*) with flats

ben [bɛ̃] *interj* (slang) well!

bénédicité [benedisite] *m* grace (*before a meal*)

bénédic•tin [benediktɛ̃] **-tine** [tin] *adj & m* Benedictine ‖ (*cap*) *f* Benedictine (liqueur)

bénédiction [benediksjɔ̃] manna from heaven

bénéfice [benefis] *m* profit; benefit; benefice; parsonage, rectory; **à bénéfice** benefit (*performance*); **bénéfice extra** perk; **sous bénéfice d'inventaire** with grave reservations

bénéficiaire [benefisjɛr] *adj* profit, e.g., **marge bénéficiaire** profit margin ‖ *mf* beneficiary

bénéficier [benefisje] *intr* to profit, benefit

benêt [bənɛ] *adj masc* simple-minded ‖ *m* simpleton, numskull

bénévolement [benevɔlmɑ̃] *adv* voluntarily, free of charge, for nothing

bé-nin [benɛ̃] **-nigne** [niɲ] *adj* benign; mild, slight; benignant, accommodating

béni-oui-oui [beniwiwi] *mpl* yes men

bénir [benir] *tr* to bless, to consecrate

bé•nit [beni] **-nite** [nit] *adj* consecrated (*bread*); holy (*water*)

bénitier [benitje] *m* font (*for holy water*)

benja•min [bɛ̃ʒamɛ̃] **-mine** [min] *mf* baby (*the youngest child*) ‖ (*cap*) *m* Benjamin

benne [bɛn] *f* bucket, bin, hopper; dumper; cage (*in mine*); **benne preneuse** (mach) scoop, jaws (*of crane*)

be•noît [bənwa] **-noîte** [nwat] *adj* indulgent; sanctimonious ‖ (*cap*) *m* Benedict

benzène [bɛ̃zɛn] *m* (chem) benzene

benzine [bɛ̃zin] *f* benzine

béquille [bekij] *f* crutch

béquiller [bekije] *intr* to walk with a crutch or crutches

bercail [bɛrkaj] *m* fold, bosom (*of church or family*)

ber•ceau [bɛrso] *m* (*pl* **-ceaux**) cradle, crib; bower; **berceau de verdure** or **de chèvre-feuille** arbor

bercelonnette [bɛrsəlɔnɛt] *f* bassinet

bercer [bɛrse] §51 *tr* to cradle, rock; beguile; assuage (*grief, pain*) ‖ *ref* to rock, swing; delude oneself (*with vain hopes*)

ber•ceur [bɛrsœr] **-ceuse** [søz] *adj* rocking, cradling ‖ *f* rocking chair; cradle song, lullaby

béret [bere] *m* beret

berge [bɛrʒ] *f* bank, steep bank

berger [bɛrʒe] *m* shepherd; shepherd dog

bergère [bɛrʒɛr] *f* shepherdess; wing chair

bergerie [bɛrʒəri] *f* sheepfold; pastoral poem

berkélium [bɛrkeljɔm] *m* berkelium

berle [bɛrl] *f* water parsnip

Berlin [bɛrlɛ̃] *m* Berlin

berline [bɛrlin] *f* sedan (*automobile*); berlin (*carriage*)

berlingot [bɛrlɛ̃go] *m* caramel candy; milk carton

berli•nois [bɛrlinwa] **-noise** [nwaz] *adj* Berlin ‖ *mf* Berliner (*person*)

berlue [bɛrly] *f*—**avoir la berlue** (coll) to be blind to what is going on

berme [bɛrm] *f* berm

Bermudes [bɛrmyd] *fpl*—**les Bermudes** Bermuda

bernacle [bɛrnakl] *f* (orn) anatid; (zool) barnacle

berne [bɛrn] *f* hazing; **en berne** at half-mast

berner [bɛrne] *tr* to toss in a blanket; ridicule; fool

bernique [bɛrnik] *interj* (coll) shucks!, heck!, what a shame!

berthe [bɛrt] *f* corsage; cape

béryllium [beriljɔm] *m* beryllium

besace [bəzas] *f* beggar's bag; mendicancy

besicles [bəzikl] *fpl* (archaic) spectacles; **prenez donc vos besicles!** (coll) put your specs on!

besogne [bəzɔɲ] *f* work, task; **abattre de la besogne** to accomplish a great deal of work; **aller vite en besogne** to work too hastily

besogner [bəzɔɲe] *intr* to drudge, slave

beso•gneux [bəzɔɲø] **-gneuse** [ɲøz] *adj* needy ‖ *mf* needy person

besoin [bəzwɛ̃] *m* need, urge; necessity; poverty, distress; **au besoin** if necessary; **avoir besoin de** to need; **faire ses besoins** to go to the toilet; **si besoin est** if need be

bes•son [besɔ̃] **-sonne** [sɔn] *mf* (dial) twin

bestiaire [bɛstjɛr] *m* bestiary

bes•tial -tiale [bɛstjal] (*pl* **-tiaux** [tjo]) *adj* bestial ‖ *mpl* see **bestiaux**

bestialité [bɛstjalite] *f* bestiality

bestiaux [bɛstjo] *mpl* livestock, cattle and horses

bestiole [bɛstjɔl] *f* bug, vermin

bê·ta [bɛtɑ] **-tasse** [tɑs] *adj* (coll) silly ‖ *mf* (coll) sap, dolt

betacam [betakam] *m* camcorder

bétail [betaj] *m invar* grazing animals (*on a farm*); **gros bétail** cattle and horses; **menu bétail, petit bétail** sheep, goats, pigs, etc.

bête [bɛt] *adj* stupid, foolish ‖ *f* animal; beast; **bête à bon Dieu** (ent) ladybird; **bête de charge, bête de somme** pack animal; **bonne bête** harmless fool

Bethléem [bɛtleɛm] *m* Bethlehem

bêtifier [bɛtifje], [betifje] *tr* to make stupid ‖ *intr* to play the fool, talk foolishly

bêtise [bɛtiz], [betiz] *f* foolishness, stupidity, nonsense; trifle; **faire des bêtises** to blunder, do stupid things; throw money around

béton [betɔ̃] *m* concrete; **béton armé** reinforced concrete; **béton précontraint** prestressed concrete

bétonner [betɔne] *tr* to make of concrete

bétonnière [betɔnjɛr] *f* cement mixer

bette [bɛt] *f* Swiss chard; **bette à carde** Swiss chard

betterave [bɛtrav] *f* beet; **betterave sucrière** sugar beet

beuglement [bøɡləmɑ̃] *m* bellow, bellowing, lowing

beugler [bøɡle], [bœɡle] *tr* (slang) to bawl out (*a song*) ‖ *intr* to bellow (*like a bull*); low (*like cattle*)

beurre [bœr] *m* butter; (slang) dough; **faire son beurre** (coll) to feather one's nest

beurrée [bœre] *f* slice of bread and butter

beurrer [bœre] *tr* to butter

beur·rier [bœrje] **-rière** [jɛr] *adj* butter ‖ *m* butter dish

beuverie [bœvri] *f* drinking party

bévue [bevy] *f* blunder, slip, boner

biais [bjɛ] **biaise** [bjɛz] *adj* bias, oblique, slanting; skew (*arch*) ‖ *m* bias, slant; skew (*of an arch*); **de biais, en biais** aslant, askew

biaiser [bjɛze] *intr* to slant; (fig) to be evasive

bibelot [biblo] *m* curio, trinket, knickknack; gewgaw

bibeloter [biblɔte] *intr* to buy or collect curios

bibe·ron [bibrɔ̃] **-ronne** [rɔn] *adj* addicted to the bottle ‖ *mf* heavy drinker ‖ *m* nursing bottle

bibi [bibi] *m* (hum) me, yours truly

Bible [bibl] *f* Bible

bibliobus [bibliɔbys] *m* bookmobile

bibliographe [bibliɔɡraf] *m* bibliographer

bibliographie [bibliɔɡrafi] *f* bibliography

bibliomane [bibliɔman] *mf* book collector

bibliothécaire [bibliɔtekɛr] *mf* librarian

bibliothéconomie [bibljɔtekɔnɔmi] *f* library science

bibliothèque [bibliɔtɛk] *f* library; bookstand; **bibliothèque vivante** walking encyclopedia

biblique [biblik] *adj* Biblical

biceps [bisɛps] *m* biceps

biche [biʃ] *f* hind; doe; **ma biche** (coll) my darling

bicher [biʃe] *intr*—**ça biche!** (slang) fine!

bichlamar [biʃlamar] *m* pidgin

bichof [biʃɔf] *m* spiced wine

bi·chon [biʃɔ̃] **-chonne** [ʃɔn] *mf* lap dog

bichonner [biʃɔne] *tr* to curl (*one's hair*); doll up ‖ *ref* to doll up

bicoque [bikɔk] *f* shack, ramshackle house

bicorne [bikɔrn] *adj* two-cornered ‖ *m* cocked hat

bicot [biko] *m* (coll) kid (*goat*); (offensive) North African, Arab

bicyclette [bisiklɛt] *f* bicycle; **aller à bicyclette** to bicycle; **bicyclette d'entraînement** exercise bicycle; **faire de la bicyclette** to go bicycling

bident [bidɑ̃] *m* two-pronged fork

bidet [bidɛ] *m* bidet (*bathroom fixture providing means for spot-bathing and rinsing after use of the toilet*); nag (*horse*)

bidon [bidɔ̃] *m* drum (*for liquids*); canteen, water bottle

bidonville [bidɔ̃vil] *m* shantytown

bidule [bidyl] *m* (slang) gadget

bief [bjɛf] *m* millrace; reach, level (*of a stream or canal*)

bielle [bjɛl] *f* connecting rod, tie rod

bien [bjɛ̃] *m* good; welfare; estate, fortune; **biens** property, possessions; **bien à vous** Sincerely yours; **biens consomptibles** consumer goods; **biens d'équipement, biens de production** capital goods; **biens immeubles** real estate; **biens meubles** personal property ‖ *adv* §91 well; rightly, properly, quite; indeed, certainly; fine, e.g., **je vais bien** I'm fine; **bien de** + *art* much, e.g., **bien de l'eau** much water; many, e.g., **bien des gens** many people; **bien entendu** of course; **bien que** + *subj* although; **eh bien!** so!; **si bien que** so that; **tant bien que mal** so-so, as well as possible ‖ *interj* good!; all right!; that's enough!

bien-ai·mé -mée [bjɛ̃neme] *adj* & *mf* beloved, darling, sweetie

bien·dire [bjɛ̃dir] *m* gracious speech, eloquent delivery; **être sur son bien-dire** to be on one's best behavior

bien-di·sant [bjɛ̃dizɑ̃] **-sante** [zɑ̃t] *adj* smooth-spoken, smooth-tongued

bien-être [bjɛ̃nɛtr] *m* well-being, welfare

bienfaisance [bjɛ̃fəzɑ̃s] *f* charity, beneficence

bienfai·sant [bjɛ̃fəzɑ̃] **-sante** [zɑ̃t] *adj* charitable, beneficent

bienfait [bjɛ̃fɛ] *m* good turn, good deed, favor; **bienfaits** benefits

bienfai·teur [bjɛ̃fɛtœr] **-trice** [tris] *mf* benefactor ‖ *f* benefactress

bien-fondé [bjɛ̃fɔ̃de] *m* cogency

bien-fonds [bjɛ̃fɔ̃] *m* (*pl* **biens-fonds**) real estate

bienheu·reux [bjɛ̃nœrø] **-reuse** [røz] *adj* & *mf* blessed

bien·nal -nale [bjɛnnal] *adj* (*pl* **-naux** [no]) biennial ‖ *f* biennial exposition

bienséance [bjɛ̃seɑ̃s] *f* propriety

bien·séant [bjɛ̃seã] **-séante** [seãt] *adj* fitting, proper, appropriate

bientôt [bjɛ̃to] *adv* soon; **à bientôt!** so long!

bienveillance [bjɛ̃vɛjɑ̃s] *f* benevolence, kindness

bienveil·lant [bjɛ̃vɛjɑ̃] **-lante** [jãt] *adj* benevolent, kindly, kind

bienvenir [bjɛ̃vnir] *intr*—**se faire bienvenir** to make oneself welcome

bienve·nu **-nue** [bjɛ̃vny] *adj* welcome ‖ *m*—**soyez le bienvenu!** welcome! ‖ *f* welcome; **souhaiter la bienvenue à** to welcome

bière [bjɛr] *f* beer; coffin; **bière à la pression** draft beer

biffer [bife] *tr* to cross out, cancel, erase; (slang) to cut (*class*)

biffin [bifɛ̃] *m* (slang) ragman; (slang) doughboy, G.I. Joe

bifo·cal **-cale** [bifɔkal] *adj* (*pl* **-caux** [ko]) bifocal

bifteck [biftɛk] *m* beefsteak

bifurquer [bifyrke] *tr* to bifurcate, divide into two branches ‖ *intr & ref* to bifurcate, fork; branch off

bigame [bigam] *adj* bigamous ‖ *mf* bigamist

bigamie [bigami] *f* bigamy

bigar·rée [bigare] *adj* mottled, variegated; motley (*crowd*)

bigar·reau [bigaro] *m* (*pl* **-reaux**) white-heart cherry

bigarrer [bigare] *tr* to mottle, variegate, streak

bigarrure [bigaryr] *f* variegation, medley, mixture

bigle [bigl] *adj* cross-eyed

bigler [bigle] *intr* to squint; be cross-eyed

bigorne [bigɔrn] *f* two-horn anvil

bigorner [bigɔrne] *tr* to form on the anvil; (slang) to smash

bi·got [bigo] **-gote** [gɔt] *adj* sanctimonious ‖ *mf* religious bigot

bigoterie [bigɔtri] *f* religious bigotry

bigoudi [bigudi] *m* hair curler, roller

bihebdomadaire [biɛbdɔmadɛr] *adj* semi-weekly

bi·jou [biʒu] *m* (*pl* **-joux**) jewel

bijouterie [biʒutri] *f* jewelry; jewelry shop; jewelry business

bijou·tier [biʒutje] **-tière** [tjɛr] *mf* jeweler

bilan [bilɑ̃] *m* balance sheet; balance; petition of bankruptcy; **bilan de santé** (med) checkup; **faire le bilan** to tabulate the results

bilboquet [bilbɔkɛ] *m* job printing

bile [bil] *f* bile; **se faire de la bile** (coll) to worry, fret

bi·lieux [biljø] **-lieuse** [ljøz] *adj* bilious; irascible, grouchy

bilingue [bilɛ̃g] *adj* bilingual

billard [bijar] *m* billiards; billiard table; billiard room

bille [bij] *f* ball; ball bearing; billiard ball; marble; log; **à bille** ballpoint (*pen*)

billet [bijɛ] *m* note; ticket; bill (*currency*); **billet à ordre** promissory note; **billet d'abonne-**

ment season ticket; **billet d'aller et retour** round-trip ticket; **billet de banque** bank note; **billet de correspondance** transfer; **billet de faire-part** announcement, notification (*of birth, wedding, death*); **billet de logement** billet; **billet doux** love letter; **billet simple** one-way ticket

billette [bijɛt] *f* billet

billetterie [bijɛtri] *f* ticketing (*at events*)

billevesée [bijvəze], [bilvəze] *f* nonsense

billion [biljɔ̃] *m* trillion (U.S.A.); billion (Brit); (obs) billion, milliard

billot [bijo] *m* block, chopping block; executioner's block

biloquer [bilɔke] *tr* to plow deeply

bimen·suel **-suelle** [bimɑ̃sɥɛl] *adj* semi-monthly

bimes·triel **-trielle** [bimɛstriɛl] *adj* bimonthly (*every two months*)

bimoteur [bimɔtœr] *adj* twin-motor ‖ *m* twin-motor plane

binaire [binɛr] *adj* binary

biner [bine] *tr* to hoe; cultivate, work over (*the soil*) ‖ *intr* to say two masses the same day

binette [binɛt] *f* hoe; (hist) wig; (slang) phiz

bineur [binœr] *m* or **bineuse** [binøz] *f* cultivator (*implement*)

binocle [binɔkl] *m* pince-nez

binoculaire [binɔkylɛr] *adj & f* binocular

binôme [binom] *adj & m* binomial

binon [binɔ̃] *m* (comp) bit

bioastronomie [bjo•astronɔmi] *f* bioastronomy

biochemie [bjoʃimi] *f* biochemistry

biochimique [bjoʃimik] *adj* biochemical

biodégradable [bjodegradablə] *adj* biodegradable

[bjoetik] *f* bioethics

biographe [bjɔgraf] *mf* biographer

biographie [bjɔgrafi] *f* biography

biographique [bjɔgrafik] *adj* biographical

biologie [bjɔlɔʒi] *f* biology

biologique [bjɔlɔʒik] *adj* biological; organic (*food, agriculture*)

biologiste [bjɔlɔʒist] *mf* biologist

biomécanique [bjomekanik] *f* biomechanics

biomédical [bjomedikal] *adj* biomedical

biométrie [bjometri] *f* biometrics

bionique [bjɔnik] *adj* bionic ‖ *f* bionics

biophysique [bjofizik] *f* biophysics

biopsie [bjɔpsi] *f* biopsy

bioscopie [bjɔskɔpi] *f* bioscopy

biosphère [bjosfɛr] *f* biosphere

biotechnique [bjotɛknik] *f* biotechnology

biotechnologie [bjotɛknɔlɔʒi] *f* biotechnology

bioterrorisme [bjotɛrɔrism] *m* bioterrorism

bioxyde [bjɔksid] *m* dioxide

bip [bip] *m* bleep, beep, blip

bipar·ti **-tie** [biparti] *adj* bipartite

bipartisme [bipartism] *m* bipartisanship

bipartite [bipartit] *adj* bipartite; bipartisan

bip-bip [bipbip] *m* bleep, beep, blip

biped [bipɛd] *adj & mf* biped ‖ *m* pair of legs of a horse

biper [bipe] *tr* (med) to bleep, to beep

biplan [biplɑ̃] *m* biplane

bique [bik] *f* nanny goat

bir·man [birmɑ̃] **-mane** [man] *adj* Burmese ‖ (*cap*) *mf* Burmese (*person*)

Birmanie [birmani] *f* Burma; **la Birmanie** Burma (Myanmar)

bis [bi] **bise** [biz] *adj* gray-brown ‖ [bis] *m*—**un bis** an encore ‖ *f* see **bise** ‖ **bis** [bis] *adv* twice; (mus) repeat; **sept bis** seven A, seven and a half ‖ **bis** [bis] *interj* encore!

bisaïeul bisaïeule [bizajœl] *mf* great-grandparent ‖ *m* great-grandfather ‖ *f* great-grandmother

bisan·nuel -nuelle [bizanɥɛl] *adj* biennial

bisbille [bisbij] *f* (coll) squabble

biscaïen [biskajɛ̃] **biscaïenne** [biskajɛn] *adj* Biscayan ‖ (*cap*) *mf* Biscayan (*person*)

biscor·nu -nue [biskɔrny] *adj* misshapen, distorted

biscotin [biskɔtɛ̃] *m* hardtack

biscotte [biskɔt] *f* zwieback

biscuit [biskɥi] *m* hardtack; cracker; cookie; unglazed porcelain; **biscuit soda** soda cracker

bise [biz] *f* north wind; (fig) winter; (slang) kiss

bi·seau [bizo] *m* (*pl* **-seaux**) bevel, chamfer; **en biseau** beveled, chamfered

biseauter [bizote] *tr* to bevel, chamfer; to mark (*cards*)

biser [bize] *tr* to redye ‖ *intr* to blacken

bi·son [bizɔ̃] **-sonne** [zɔn] *mf* bison, buffalo

bisque [bisk] *f* bisque

bisquer [biske] *intr* (coll) to be resentful

bissac [bisak] *m* bag, sack

bisser [bise] *tr* to encore; repeat

bissextile [bisɛkstil] *adj* bissextile, leap, e.g., **année bissextile** leap year

bis·sexué -sexuée [bisɛksɥe] *adj* bisexual

bis·sexuel -sexuelle [bisɛksɥɛl] *adj* bisexual

bistouri [bisturi] *m* scalpel

bistournage [bisturnaʒ] *m* castration

bistre [bistr] *adj invar* soot-brown ‖ *m* bister, soot-brown

bis·tré -trée [bistre] *adj* swarthy

bistrot [bistro] *or* **bistro** [bistro] *m* bistro, tavern, café

bisulfate [bisylfat] *m* bisulfate

bisulfite [bisylfit] *m* bisulfite

bitte [bit] *f* (vulg) penis

bitter [bitɛr] *m* bitters

bitume [bitym] *m* bitumen

bitumer [bityme] *tr* to asphalt

bitumi·neux [bityminø] **-neuse** [nøz] *adj* bituminous

bivouac [bivwak] *m* bivouac

bivouaquer [bivwake] *intr* to bivouac

bizarre [bizar] *adj* bizarre, strange, queer

bizutage [bizytaʒ] *m* (slang) initiation, hazing

bizuth [bizyt] *m* (slang) freshman

blackbouler [blakbule] *tr* to blackball; (coll) to flunk

bla·fard [blafar] **-farde** [fard] *adj* pallid, pale, wan; lambent (*flame*)

blague [blag] *f* tobacco pouch; (coll) yarn, tall story, blarney; **blague à part** (coll) all joking aside; **faire une blague** (coll) to play a trick; **sale blague** (coll) dirty trick; **sans blague!** (coll) no kidding!

blaguer [blage] *tr* (coll) to kid; **blaguer qn** (coll) to pull s.o.'s leg ‖ *intr* (coll) to kid, tell tall stories

bla·gueur [blagœr] **-gueuse** [gøz] *adj* (coll) kidding, tongue-in-cheek ‖ *mf* (coll) kidder, joker

blai·reau [blɛro] *m* (*pl* **-reaux**) badger; shaving brush

blâmable [blɑmabl] *adj* blameworthy

blâme [blɑm] *m* blame; **s'attirer un blâme** to receive a reprimand

blâmer [blɑme] §97, §99 *tr* to blame; disapprove of

blanc [blɑ̃] **blanche** [blɑ̃ʃ] *adj* white; blank; clean; sleepless (*night*); expressionless (*voice*); unconsummated (*marriage*); **blanc comme un linge** white as a sheet ‖ *m* white; blank; white meat; white man; white goods; chalk; bull's-eye; **à blanc** with blank cartridges; blank, unrecorded (*tape*); **blanc cassé** off-white; **blanc de baleine** spermaceti; **blanc de chaux** whitewash; **en blanc** blank; **en blanc et noir** in black and white ‖ *f* white woman

blanc-bec [blɑ̃bɛk] *m* (*pl* **blancs-becs**) (coll) greenhorn, callow youth

blanchâtre [blɑ̃ʃatr] *adj* whitish

blancheur [blɑ̃ʃœr] *f* whiteness

blanchir [blɑ̃ʃir] *tr* to whiten; wash or bleach; whitewash; blanch (*almonds*) ‖ *intr* to blanch, whiten; grow old

blanchissage [blɑ̃ʃisaʒ] *m* laundering; sugar refining

blanchisserie [blɑ̃ʃisri] *f* laundry

blanchis·seur [blɑ̃ʃisœr] **-seuse** [søz] *mf* launderer ‖ *m* laundryman ‖ *f* laundress, washerwoman

blanc-manger [blɑ̃maʒe] *m* (*pl* **blancs-manger**) blancmange

blanc-seing [blɑ̃sɛ̃] *m* (*pl* **blancs-seings**) carte blanche

bla·sé -sée [blaze] *adj* blasé, jaded

blaser [blaze] *tr* to cloy, blunt

blason [blazɔ̃] *m* (heral) blazon

blasonner [blazɔne] *tr* (heral) to blazon

blasphéma·teur [blasfematœr] **-teuse** [tøz] *adj* blasphemous, blaspheming ‖ *mf* blasphemer

blasphématoire [blasfematwar] *adj* blasphemous

blasphème [blasfɛm] *m* blasphemy

blasphémer [blasfeme] §10 *tr & intr* to blaspheme

blatte [blat] *f* cockroach

blé [ble] *m* wheat; (slang) dough; **blé à moudre** grist; **blé de Turquie** corn; **blé froment** wheat; **blé noir** buckwheat; **manger son blé en herbe** to spend one's money before one has it

bled [blɛd] *m* (coll) backwoods, hinterland

blême [blɛm] *adj* pale; livid, sallow, wan; ghastly

blêmir [blemir] *intr* to turn pale or livid, blanch; grow dim

blennorragie [blɛnɔraʒi] *f* gonorrhea

blèse [blɛz] *adj* lisping ‖ *mf* lisper

blèsement [blɛzmɑ̃] *m* lisping

bléser [bleze] §10 *intr* to lisp

bles•sé -sée [blɛse] *adj* wounded ‖ *mf* injured person; victim; casualty

blesser [blɛse], [blese] *tr* to wound; injure; be disagreeable to

blessure [blɛsyr] *f* wound; injury

blet blette [blɛt] *adj* overripe ‖ *f* chard

blettir [blɛtir] *intr* to overripen

bleu bleue [blø] (*pl* **bleus bleues**) *adj* blue; fairy (*stories*); violent (*anger*); rare (*meat*) ‖ *m* blue; bluing; bruise; sauce for cooking fish; telegram or pneumatic letter; (coll) raw recruit, greenhorn; **bleu barbeau** light blue; **bleu marine** navy blue; **bleus** coveralls, dungarees; (mil) fatigues; **passer au bleu** to avoid, elude (*a question*); **petit bleu** bad wine

bleuâtre [bløɑtr] *adj* bluish

bleuet [bløɛ] *m* bachelor's-button

bleuir [bløir] *tr & intr* to turn blue

bleu•té -tée [bløte] *adj* bluish

blindage [blɛ̃daʒ] *m* armor plate; armor plating; (elec) shield

blin•dé -dée [blɛ̃de] *adj* armored; armor-plated; (elec) shielded ‖ *m* (mil) tank

blinder [blɛ̃de] *tr* to armor-plate; (elec) to shield

bloc [blɔk] *m* block; blocking; tablet, pad (*of paper*); (*de bureau*) desk pad; (elec, mach) unit; brick (*of ice cream*); **à bloc** tight; **bloc de touches** (comp) keypad; **en bloc** all together, in a lump; **envoyer** or **mettre au bloc** (slang) to throw (*s.o.*) in the jug; **serrer le frein à bloc** to jam on the brakes

blocage [blɔkaʒ] *m* blockage, blocking; lumping together; rubble; freezing (*of prices; of wages*); application (*of brakes*)

blocaille [blɔkɑj] *f* rubble

bloc-diagramme [blɔkdjagram] *m* (*pl* **blocs-diagrammes**) cross section

bloc-moteur [blɔkmɔtœr] *m* (aut) motor and transmission system

bloc-notes [blɔknɔt] *m* (*pl* **blocs-notes**) scratch pad, note pad, desk pad

blocus [blɔkys] *m* blockade

blond [blɔ̃] **blonde** [blɔ̃d] *adj* blond ‖ *m* blond ‖ *f* see **blonde**

blondasse [blɔ̃das] *adj* washed-out blond

blonde [blɔ̃d] *f* blonde; blond lace; **blonde platinée** platinum blonde

blon•din [blɔ̃dɛ̃] **-dine** [din] *adj* fair-haired ‖ *mf* blond ‖ *m* cableway; hopper for concrete; (obs) fop

blondir [blɔ̃dir] *tr* to bleach ‖ *intr* to turn yellow, become blond

bloquer [blɔke] *tr* to blockade; block up; fill with rubble; jam on (*the brakes*); stop (*a car*) by jamming on the brakes; pocket (*a billiard*

ball); run on (*two paragraphs*); tighten (*a nut or bolt*) as much as possible; freeze (*wages*)

blottir [blɔtir] *ref* to cower; curl up

blouse [bluz] *f* smock; billiard pocket

blouser [bluze] *tr* to deceive, take in ‖ *intr* to pucker around the waist ‖ *ref* to be mistaken

blouson [bluzɔ̃] *m* jacket; windbreaker

blouson-noir [bluzɔ̃war] *m* (*pl* **blousons-noirs**) juvenile delinquent; hood

blue-jean [bludʒin] *m* blue jeans

bluet [blyɛ] *m* bachelor's-button; (Canad) blueberry

bluette [blyɛt] *f* piece of light fiction; spark, flash

bluffer [blyfe] *tr & intr* to bluff

bluf•feur [blyfœr] **-feuse** [føz] *mf* bluffer

blutage [blytaʒ] *m* bolting, sifting; boltings, siftings

bluter [blyte] *tr* to bolt, sift

blutoir [blytwar] *m* bolter, sifter

B.N. *abbr* (**Bibliothèque Nationale**) National Library

boa [bɔa] *m* boa

bobard [bɔbar] *m* (coll) fish story, tall tale

bobèche [bɔbɛʃ] *f* bobeche (*disk to catch drippings of candle*)

bobine [bɔbin] *f* bobbin; spool, reel; (elec) coil; **bobine d'allumage** (aut) ignition coil

bobiner [bɔbine] *tr* to spool, wind

bobo [bɔbo] *m* (*language used with children*) sore; cut; **avoir bobo** to have a pain

bocage [bɔkaʒ] *m* grove

boca•ger [bɔkaʒe] **-gère** [ʒɛr] *adj* wooded

bo•cal [bɔkal] *m* (*pl* **-caux** [ko]) jar, bottle; globe; fishbowl

boche [bɔʃ] *adj & mf* (slang & pej) German

bock [bɔk] *m* beer glass (*half pint*); glass of beer; enema; douche

boëte [bwɛt] *f* fish bait

bœuf [bœf] *m* (*pl* **bœufs** [bø]) beef; head of beef; steer; ox; **bœuf en conserve** corned beef; **bœuf haché** ground beef

boggie [bɔʒi] *m* (rr) truck

Bohême [bɔɛm] *f* Bohemia; **la Bohême** Bohemia

bohème [bɔɛm] *adj & mf* Bohemian (*artist*) ‖ *f*—**la bohème** Bohemia (*of the artistic world*)

bohé•mien [bɔɛmjɛ̃] **-mienne** [mjɛn] *adj* Bohemian; gypsy ‖ (*cap*) *mf* Bohemian; gypsy

boire [bwar] *m* drink; drinking; **le boire et le manger** food and drink ‖ §8 *tr* to drink; swallow (*an affront*) ‖ *intr* to drink; **boire à la santé de** to drink to the health of; **boire à** (**même**) to drink out of (*a bottle*); **boire comme un trou** to drink like a fish; **boire dans** to drink out of (*a glass*)

bois [bwɑ] [bwa] *m* wood; woods; horns, antlers; **bois de chauffage** firewood; **bois de lit** bedstead; **bois de placage** plywood; **bois flotté** driftwood; **bois fondu** plastic wood; **les bois** (mus) the woodwinds; **toucher du bois** to knock on wood

boisage [bwazaʒ] *m* timbering

boi•sé -sée [bwaze] *adj* wooded; paneled

boiser [bwaze] *tr* to panel, wainscot; timber (*a mine*); reforest

boiserie [bwazri] *f* woodwork, paneling, wainscoting

bois•seau [bwaso] *m* (*pl* **-seaux**) bushel

boisson [bwasɔ̃] *f* drink, beverage; **boissons hygiéniques** light wines, beer, and soft drinks

boîte [bwat] *f* box; can; canister; (slang) joint, dump; **boîte aux lettres** mailbox; **boîte chaude** (rr) hotbox; **boîte de nuit** night club; **boîte d'essieu** (mach) journal box; **boîte de vitesses** transmission-gear box; **boîte postale** post-office box; **en boîte** boxed; canned; **ferme ta boîte!** (slang) shut up!, **mettre en boîte** to box; can; (slang) to make fun of

boiter [bwate] *intr* to limp

boiterie [bwatəri] *f* limp

boi•teux [bwatø] **-teuse** [tøz] *adj* lame, limping; unsteady, wobbly (*chair*) ‖ *mf* lame person

boî•tier [bwatje] **-tière** [tjɛr] *mf* boxmaker; mail collector (*from mailboxes*) ‖ *m* box, case; kit; medicine kit; (mach) housing; **boîtier de montre** watchcase

boitte [bwat] *f* fish bait

bol [bɔl] *m* bowl, basin; cud; bolus, pellet

bolchevique [bɔlʃəvik] *adj* Bolshevik ‖ (*cap*) *mf* Bolshevik

bolcheviste [bɔlʃəvist] *adj* Bolshevik ‖ (*cap*) *mf* Bolshevik

bolduc [bɔldyk] *m* colored ribbon

bolée [bɔle] *f* bowlful

bolide [bɔlid] *m* meteorite, fireball; racing car

bombance [bɔ̃bɑ̃s] *f* (coll) feast; **faire bombance** (coll) to have a blowout

bombardement [bɔ̃bardəmɑ̃] *m* bombing; bombardment; **bombardement en tapis** carpet bombing, saturation bombing; **bombardement par ricochet** skip bombing

bombarder [bɔ̃barde] *tr* to bomb; bombard; (coll) to appoint at the last minute

bombardier [bɔ̃bardje] *m* bomber; bombardier

bombe [bɔ̃b] *f* bomb; **bombe à hydrogène** hydrogen bomb; **bombe atomique** atomic bomb; **bombe de plastique** plastic bomb; **bombe glacée** molded ice cream; **bombe intelligente** smart bomb; **bombe volante** buzz bomb; **faire la bombe** (fig) to paint the town red

bom•bé -bée [bɔ̃be] *adj* convex, bulging

bomber [bɔ̃be] *tr* to bend, arch; stick out (*one's chest*); **bomber le torse** (fig) to stick one's nose up ‖ *intr & ref* to bulge

bon [bɔ̃] **bonne** [bɔn] §91, §92 *adj* good; (slang) cool; **à quoi bon?** what's the use?; **sentir bon** to smell good; **tenir bon** to hold fast ‖ (when standing before noun) *adj* §91 good; fast (*color*) ‖ *m* coupon; **bon cadeau** gift certificate; **bon d'alimentation** food stamp; **bon de change** voucher; **bon de commande** order blank; **bon de travail** work order; **pour (tout)**

de bon for good, really ‖ *f* see **bonne** ‖ **bon** *interj* good!; what!

bonace [bɔnas] *f* calm (*of the sea*)

bonasse [bɔnas] *adj* simple, naïve

bon-bec [bɔ̃bɛk] *m* (*pl* **bons-becs**) fast talker

bonbon [bɔ̃bɔ̃] *m* bonbon, piece of candy

bonbonne [bɔ̃bɔn] *f* demijohn

bonbonnière [bɔ̃bɔnjɛr] *f* candy dish; candy box

bond [bɔ̃] *m* bound, bounce; leap, jump; **faire faux bond** to miss an appointment; **faux bond** misstep

bonde [bɔ̃d] *f* plug; bunghole; sluice gate

bon•dé -dée [bɔ̃de] *adj* crammed

bondir [bɔ̃dir] *intr* to bound, bounce; leap, jump; **faire bondir** to make (*s.o.*) hit the ceiling

bondissement [bɔ̃dismɑ̃] *m* bouncing, leaping

bondon [bɔ̃dɔ̃] *m* bung

bonheur [bɔnœr] *m* happiness; good luck; **au petit bonheur** by chance, at random; **par bonheur** luckily

bonheur-du-jour [bɔnœrdyʒur] *m* (*pl* **bonheurs-du-jour**) escritoire

bonhomie [bɔnɔmi] *f* good nature; credulity

bonhomme [bɔnɔm] *adj* good-natured, simple-minded ‖ *m* (*pl* **bonshommes** [bɔ̃zɔm]) fellow, guy; old fellow; **bonhomme de neige** snowman; **Bonhomme Hiver** Jack Frost; **faux bonhomme** humbug; **petit bonhomme** little man (*child*)

boni [bɔni] *m* bonus; discount coupon; surplus (*over estimated expenses*)

bonification [bɔnifikasjɔ̃] *f* improvement; discount; bonus; advantage

bonifier [bɔnifje] *tr* to improve; give a discount to

boniment [bɔnimɑ̃] *m* sales talk, smooth talk

bonimenteur [bɔnimɑ̃tœr] *m* huckster, charlatan

bonjour [bɔ̃ʒur] *m* good day, good morning, good afternoon, hello

bonne [bɔn] *f* maid; **bonne à tout faire** maid of all work ‖ *adj* see **bon**

bonne-maman [bɔnmamɑ̃] *f* (*pl* **bonnes-mamans**) grandma

bonnement [bɔnmɑ̃] *adv* honestly, plainly

bonnet [bɔnɛ] *m* bonnet; stocking cap; cup (*of a brassiere*); (mil) undress hat; **bonnet d'âne** dunce cap; **bonnet de nuit** nightcap; **gros bonnet** (coll) VIP

bonneterie [bɔnɛtri] *f* hosiery; knitwear

bon-papa [bɔ̃papa] *m* (*pl* **bons-papas**) grandpa

bonsoir [bɔ̃swar] *m* good evening; (coll) good night

bonté [bɔ̃te] *f* goodness; kindness

bookmaker [bukmɛkœr] bookmaker, bookie (coll)

boomer [bumɛr] *m* (electron) boomer

booster [bustœr] *m* (rok) booster

borborygme [bɔrbɔrigm] *m* rumbling (*in the stomach*)

bord [bɔr] *m* edge, border; rim, brim; side (*of*

a ship); ship, e.g., **les porteurs du bord** the ship's porters; e.g., **les hommes du bord** the ship's company; **à bord** on board; **à pleins bords** overflowing; without hindrance; **à ras bords** full to the brim; **bord de mer** beachfront, seaside; **être du (même) bord de** to be of the same mind as; **faux bord** list (*of ship*); **jeter par-dessus bord** to throw overboard

bordage [bɔrdaʒ] *m* edging (*of dress*); planking (*of ship*)

bordé [bɔrde] *m* border, edging

bordeaux [bɔrdo] *adj invar* maroon, burgundy ‖ *m* **Bordeaux** (wine); **bordeaux rouge** claret

bordée [bɔrde] *f* broadside, volley; (naut) tack; **bordée de bâbord** port watch; **bordée de tribord** starboard watch; **courir une bordée** to go skylarking on shore leave; **tirer une bordée** to jump ship

bordel [bɔrdɛl] *m* (vulgar) brothel

borde·lais [bɔrdəlɛ] **-laise** [lɛz] *adj* of Bordeaux ‖ *f* Bordeaux cask ‖ (*cap*) *mf* native or inhabitant of Bordeaux

border [bɔrde] *tr* to border; hem; sail along (*the coast*); **border un lit** to make a bed

borde·reau [bɔrdəro] *m* (*pl* **-reaux**) itemized account, memorandum

bordure [bɔrdyr] *f* border

bore [bɔr] *m* boron

boréal -éale [bɔreal] *adj* (*pl* **boréaux** [bɔreo] or **boréals**) boreal; northern

borgne [bɔrɲ] *adj* one-eyed; blind in one eye; disreputable (*bar, house, etc.*) ‖ *mf* one-eyed person

borne [bɔrn] *f* landmark; boundary stone; milestone; (elec) binding post, terminal; (slang) kilometer; **bornes** bounds, limits

bor·né -née [bɔrne] *adj* limited, narrow; dull (*mind*)

borner [bɔrne] *tr* to mark out the boundary of; set limits to ‖ §96 *ref* to restrain oneself

bosquet [bɔskɛ] *m* grove

bosse [bɔs] *f* hump; bump; (coll) flair

bosseler [bɔsle] §34 *tr* to emboss; to dent

bossoir [bɔswar] *m* davit; bow (*of ship*)

bos·su -sue [bɔsy] *adj* hunchbacked ‖ *mf* hunchback; **rire comme un bossu** to split one's sides laughing

botanique [bɔtanik] *adj* botanical ‖ *f* botany

botte [bɔt] *f* boot; bunch (*e.g., of radishes*); sword thrust; **lécher les bottes à qn** (coll) to lick s.o.'s boots

botteler [bɔtle] §34 *tr* to tie in bunches

botter [bɔte] *tr* to boot, boot out; **cela me botte** that suits me ‖ *ref* to put on one's boots

botteur [bɔtœr] *m* (sports) kicker

bottier [bɔtje] *m* custom shoemaker

Bottin [bɔtɛ̃] *m* business directory

bottine [bɔtin] *f* high button shoe

boubouler [bubule] *intr* to hoot like an owl

bouc [buk] *m* billy goat; goatee; **bouc émissaire** scapegoat

boucan [bukɑ̃] *m* smokehouse; (coll) uproar

boucaner [bukane] *tr* to smoke (*meat*)

boucanier [bukanje] *m* buccaneer

boucharde [buʃard] *f* bushhammer

bouche [buʃ] *f* mouth; muzzle (*of gun*); door (*of oven*); entrance (*to subway*); **bouche à bouche** mouth-to-mouth, e.g., **méthode insufflatoire bouche à bouche** mouth-to-mouth resuscitation; **bouche close!** mum's the word!; **bouche d'égout** catch basin; **bouche d'incendie** fire hydrant; **bouches** mouth (*of river*); **faire la petite bouche à, faire la fine bouche devant** to turn up one's nose at

bouchée [buʃe] *f* mouthful; patty; chocolate cream (*candy*)

boucher [buʃe] *m* butcher ‖ *tr* to stop up, plug; wall up; cut off (*the view*); bung (*a barrel*); cork (*a bottle*); **bouché à l'émeri** (coll) completely dumb ‖ *ref* to be stopped up

boucherie [buʃri] *f* butcher shop; **boucherie chevaline** horsemeat butcher shop

bouche-trou [buʃtru] *m* (*pl* **-trous**) stopgap

bouchon [buʃɔ̃] *m* cork, stopper; bob (*on a fishline*); **bouchon de circulation** traffic jam; **bouchon de vapeur** vapor lock

bouclage [buklaʒ] *m* closing of circuit; (mil) encirclement

boucle [bukl] *f* buckle; earring; curl; (aer) loop; **boucler la boucle** to loop the loop

boucler [bukle] *tr* to buckle; curl (*the hair*); lock up (*prisoners*); put a nose ring on (*a bull*); **boucler son budget** (coll) to make ends meet; **la boucler** (slang) to shut up, button one's lip ‖ *intr* to curl

bouclier [buklije] *m* shield; **bouclier antithermique** heat shield; **bouclier thermique** thermal cone

bouddhisme [budism] *m* Buddhism

bouddhiste [budist] *adj* (coll) *mf* Buddhist

bouder [bude] *tr* to be distant toward ‖ *intr* to pout, sulk

bou·deur [budœr] **-deuse** [døz] *adj* pouting ‖ *mf* sullen person

boudin [budɛ̃] *m* blood sausage; **à boudin** spiral

boudiner [budine] *tr* to twist

boue [bu] *f* mud

bouée [bwe] *f* buoy; **bouée de sauvetage** life preserver

boueur [bwœr] *m* garbage collector; scavenger

boueux [bwø] **boueuse** [bwøz] *adj* muddy; grimy; (typ) smeary

bouf·fant [bufɑ̃] **-fante** [fɑ̃t] *adj* puffed (*sleeves*); baggy (*trousers*)

bouffe [buf] *adj* comic (*opera*) ‖ *f* (slang) grub; **mauvaise bouffe** junk food

bouffée [bufe] *f* puff, gust

bouffer [bufe] *tr* (slang) to gobble up ‖ *intr* to puff out

bouf·fi -fie [bufi] *adj* puffed up or out

bouffir [bufir] *tr* & *intr* to puff up

bouffissure [bufisyr] *f* swelling

bouf·fon [bufɔ̃] **-fonne** [fɔn] *adj* & *m* buffoon, comic

bouffonnerie [bufɔnri] *f* buffoonery

bouge [buʒ] *m* bulge; hovel, dive

bougeoir [buʒwar] *m* flat candlestick

bougeotte [buʒɔt] *f* (coll) wanderlust

bouger [buʒe] §38 *tr*—**ne bougez rien!** (coll) don't move a thing! ‖ *intr* to budge, stir; **(ne) bouge pas!** don't move!

bougie [buʒi] *f* candle; candlepower; spark plug; **bougies de gâteaux d'anniversaire** birthday candles

bou·gon [bugɔ̃] **-gonne** [gɔn] *adj* grumbling ‖ *mf* grumbler

bougran [bugrɑ̃] *m* buckram

bou·gre [bugr] **-gresse** [grɛs] *mf* (slang) customer; **bougre d'âne** (slang) perfect ass ‖ *m* (slang) guy; **bon bougre** (slang) swell guy ‖ *f* (slang) wench

bougrement [bugrəmɑ̃] *adv* (slang) awfully, darned

bouillabaisse [bujabɛs] *f* bouillabaisse, fish stew, chowder

bouil·lant [bujɑ̃] **-lante** [jɑ̃t] *adj* boiling; fiery, impetuous

bouilleur [bujœr] *m* distiller (*of brandy*); boiler tube; small nuclear reactor

bouilli [buji] *m* beef stew

bouillir [bujir] §9 *tr & intr* to boil; **faire bouillir la marmite** (coll) to bring home the bacon

bouilloire [bujwar] *f* kettle

bouillon [bujɔ̃] *m* **broth,** bouillon; bubble; bubbling; cheap restaurant; **à gros bouillons** gushing; **boire un bouillon** (coll) to gulp water; (coll) to suffer business losses; **bouillon de culture** (bact) broth; **bouillon d'onze heures** poisoned drink; **bouillons** unsold copies, remainders

bouillonnement [bujɔnmɑ̃] *m* boiling; effervescence

bouillonner [bujɔne] *tr* to put puffs in (*a dress*) ‖ *intr* to boil up; have copies left over

bouillotte [bujɔt] *f* hot-water bottle

boulan·ger [bulɑʒe] **-gère** [ʒɛr] *mf* baker ‖ §38 *intr* to bake bread

boulangerie [bulɑʒri] *f* bakery

boule [bul] *f* ball; (slang) nut, head; **boule d'eau chaude** hot-water bottle; **boule de neige** snowball; **boule noire** blackball; **boules** bowling; **en boule** (fig) tied in a knot, on edge; **perdre la boule** (slang) to go off one's rocker; **se mettre en boule** (coll) to get mad

bou·leau [bulo] *m* (*pl* **-leaux**) birch

boule-de-neige [buldənɛʒ] *f* (*pl* **boules-de-neige**) guelder-rose; meadow mushroom

bouledogue [buldɔg] *m* bulldog

bouler [bule] *tr* to pad (*a bull's horn*) ‖ *intr* to roll like a ball; **envoyer bouler** (slang) to send (*s.o.*) packing

boulet [bulɛ] *m* cannonball; (coll) cross to bear

boulette [bulɛt] *f* ball, pellet

boulevard [bulvar] *m* boulevard; **boulevard périphérique** belt road

boulevar·dier [bulvardje] **-dière** [djɛr] *adj* fashionable ‖ *m* boulevardier, man about town

bouleversement [bulvɛrsmɑ̃] *m* upset

bouleverser [bulvɛrse] *tr* to upset; overthrow

boulier [bulje] *m* abacus (*for scoring billiards*)

bouline [bulin] *f* (naut) bowline

boulingrin [bulɛ̃grɛ̃] *m* bowling green

bouliste [bulist] *mf* bowler

boulodrome [bulɔdrɔm] *m* bowling alley

boulon [bulɔ̃] *m* bolt; **boulon à œil** eyebolt

boulonner [bulɔne] *tr* to bolt ‖ *intr* (slang) to work

bou·lot [bulo] **-lotte** [lɔt] *adj* (coll) dumpy, squat ‖ *m* (slang) cylindrical loaf of bread; (slang) work

boulotter [bulɔte] *tr* (slang) to eat

boum [bum] *f* (coll) party, jam (*session*); dance ‖ *interj* boom!

bouquet [bukɛ] *m* bouquet; clump (*of trees*); prawn; jack rabbit; **c'est le bouquet** (coll) it's tops; (coll) that's the last straw

bouquetière [buktjɛr] *f* flower girl

bouquin [bukɛ̃] *m* (coll) book; (coll) old book

bouquiner [bukine] *intr* to shop around for old books; (coll) to read

bouquinerie [bukinri] *f* secondhand books; secondhand bookstore

bouqui·neur [bukinœr] **-neuse** [nøz] *mf* collector of old books; browser in bookstores

bouquiniste [bukinist] *mf* secondhand book-dealer

bourbe [burb] *f* mire

bour·beux [burbø] **-beuse** [bøz] *adj* miry, muddy

bourbier [burbje] *m* quagmire

bourbillon [burbijɔ̃] *m* core (*of boil*)

bourde [burd] *f* (coll) boner

bourdon [burdɔ̃] *m* bumblebee; big bell; (mus) bourdon; **avoir le bourdon** (slang) to have the blues; **faux bourdon** drone

bourdonnement [burdɔnmɑ̃] *m* buzzing

bourdonner [burdɔne] *tr* (coll) to hum (*a tune*) ‖ *intr* to buzz

bourg [bur] *m* market town

bourgade [burgad] *f* small town

bour·geois [burʒwa] **-geoise** [ʒwaz] *adj* bourgeois, middle-class ‖ *mf* commoner, middle-class person; Philistine; **gros bourgeois** solid citizen ‖ *m* businessman; **en bourgeois** in civies ‖ *f* (slang) old woman (*wife*)

bourgeoisie [burʒwazi] *f* middle class; **haute bourgeoisie** upper middle class; **petite bourgeoisie** lower middle class

bourgeon [burʒɔ̃] *m* bud; pimple

bourgeon·nant [burʒɔnɑ̃] **-nante** [nɑ̃t] *adj* burgeoning, budding, growing

bourgeonnement [burʒɔnmɑ̃] *m* budding

bourgeonner [burʒɔne] *intr* to bud; break out in pimples

bourgeron [burʒərɔ̃] *m* jumper, overalls; sweat shirt

bourgogne [burgɔɲ] *m* Burgundy (wine) ‖ (*cap*) *f* Burgundy (*province*); **la Bourgogne** Burgundy

bourgui·gnon [burgiɲ̃] **-gnonne** [ɲɔn] *adj* Burgundian ‖ *m* Burgundian (*dialect*) ‖ (*cap*) *mf* Burgundian

bourlinguer [burlɛ̃ge] *intr* to labor (*in high seas*); (coll) to travel, venture forth

bourrade [burad] *f* sharp blow; poke

bourrage [buraʒ] *m* cramming; **bourrage de crâne** (coll) ballyhoo

bourre [bur] *f* stuffing, animal hair

bour•reau [buro] *m* (*pl* **-reaux**) executioner; torturer; **bourreau des cœurs** lady-killer; **bourreau de travail** workaholic

bourrée [bure] *f* fagot of twigs

bourreler [burle] §34 *tr* to torment

bourrelet [burlɛ] *m* weather stripping; roll (*of fat*); contour pillow

bourrer [bure] *tr* to stuff, cram; **bourrer de coups** to pummel, slug ‖ *ref* to stuff

bourriche [buriʃ] *f* hamper

bourrique [burik] *f* female donkey; (coll) ass

bour•ru -rue [bury] *adj* rough; grumpy; unfermented (*wine*)

bourse [burs] *f* purse; scholarship, fellowship; stock exchange, bourse; **bourse de commerce** commodity exchange; **bourse du travail** labor union hall; **bourses** scrotum

bourse-à-pasteur [bursapastœr] *f* (*pl* **bourses-à-pasteur** [bursapastœr]) (bot) shepherd's-purse

boursicaut or **boursicot** [bursiko] *m* little purse; nest egg

boursicoter [bursikɔte] *intr* to dabble in the stock market

bour•sier -sière [bursje] [sjɛr] *adj* scholarship (*student*); stock-market (*operation*) ‖ *mf* scholar (*holder of scholarship*); speculator

boursoufler [bursufle] *tr* to puff up

bousculer [buskyle] *tr* to jostle

bouse [buz] *f*—**bouse de vache** cow dung

bouseux [buzø] *m* (slang) peasant

bousillage [buzijaʒ] *m* cob (*mixture of clay and straw*); (coll) botched job

bousiller [buzije] *tr* (coll) to bungle; (slang) to smash up ‖ *intr* to build with cob

boussole [busɔl] *f* compass; **perdre la boussole** (coll) to go off one's rocker

boustifaille [bustifɑj] *f* (slang) feasting; (slang) good food

bout [bu] *m* end; piece, scrap, bit; head (*of a match; of a table*); **à bout** exhausted; **à bout de bras** at arm's length; **à bout portant** point-blank; **à tout bout de champ** at every turn, repeatedly; **au bout du compte** after all; **bout de fil** (telp) (coll) ring, call; **bout de l'an** watch night; **bout d'essai** screen test; **bout d'homme** wisp of a man; **bout filtre** filter tip; **de bout en bout** from start to finish; **haut bout** head (*of a table; of a lake*); **montrer le bout de l'oreille** to show one's true colors; **rire du bout des dents** to force a laugh; **sur le bout du doigt** at one's fingertips; **venir à bout de** to succeed in, to triumph over

boutade [butad] *f* sally, quip; whim

bout-dehors [budɔɔr] *m* (*pl* **bouts-dehors**) (naut) boom

boute-en-train [butãtrɛ̃] *m invar* life of the party, live wire

boute•feu [butfø] *m* (*pl* **-feux**) firebrand

bouteille [butɛj] *f* bottle; **bouteille isolante** vacuum bottle

bouteiller [butɛje] *m* (hist) cupbearer

bouterolle [butrɔl] *f* ward (*of lock*); rivet snap

boute-selle [butsɛl] *m* boots and saddles (*trumpet call*)

bouteur [butœr] *m* bulldozer

boutique [butik] *f* shop; stock, goods; workshop; set of tools; **boutique cadeaux, boutique de souvenirs** gift shop; **boutique de modiste** millinery shop; **boutique franche** duty-free shop; **quelle boutique!** (coll) what a hellhole!, what an awful place!

boutiquier [butikje] *m* shopkeeper

bouton [butɔ̃] *m* button; pimple; doorknob; bud; **bouton d'ascenseur** elevator button; **bouton de porte** doorbell button; **bouton de puissance** volume control; **bouton de rester en ligne** hold button

bouton-d'argent [butɔ̃darʒɑ̃] *m* (*pl* **boutons-d'argent**) sneezewort

bouton-d'or [butɔ̃dɔr] *m* (*pl* **boutons-d'or**) buttercup

boutonner [butɔne] *tr* to button ‖ *intr* to bud

bouton•neux -neuse [butɔnø] [nøz] *adj* pimply

boutonnière [butɔnjɛr] *f* buttonhole

bouton-pression [butɔ̃prɛsjɔ̃] *m* (*pl* **boutons-pression**) snap (fastener)

bouture [butyr] *f* cutting (*from a plant*)

bouturer [butyre] *tr* to propagate (*plants*) by cuttings ‖ *intr* to shoot suckers

bouverie [buvri] *f* cowshed

bou•vier -vière [buvje] [vjɛr] *mf* cowherd

bouvillon [buvijɔ̃] *m* steer, young bullock

bouvreuil [buvrœj] *m* bullfinch; **bouvreuil cramoisi** scarlet grosbeak

bovins [bɔvɛ̃] *mpl* cattle

box [bɔks] *m* (*pl* **-boxes**) stall; cubicle;

boxe [bɔks] *f* boxing; **la boxe anglaise** boxing (*with fists only*); **la boxe française** kickboxing (savate)

boxer [bɔksœr] *m* boxer (*dog*) ‖ [bɔkse] *tr* & *intr* to box

boxer-short [bɔksœrʃɔrt] *m* boxer shorts

boxeur [bɔksœr] *m* (sports) boxer; **boxeur avec qui on s'entraîne** sparring partner

boxon [bɔksɔ̃] *m* whorehouse

boy [bɔj] *m* houseboy; chorus boy

boyau [bwajo] *m* (*pl* **boyaux**) intestine, gut; inner tube; (mil) communication trench

boycottage [bɔjkɔtaʒ] *m* boycott

boycotter [bɔjkɔte] *tr* to boycott

boy-scout [bɔjskut] *m* (*pl* **-scouts**) boy scout

b. p. f. *abbr* (**bon pour francs**) value in francs

bracelet [braslɛ] *m* bracelet; wristband; **bracelet de caoutchouc** rubber band; **bracelet à breloques** charm bracelet; **bracelet de cheville** anklet

bracelet-montre [braslɛmɔ̃tr] *m* (*pl* **bracelets-montres**) wrist watch

braconnage [brakɔnaʒ] *m* poaching

braconner [brakɔne] *intr* to poach

bracon•nier [brakɔnje] **-nière** [njɛr] *mf* poacher

brader [brade] *tr* to sell off

braderie [bradəri] *f* clearance sale; garage sale, yard sale

braguette [bragɛt] *f* fly (*of trousers*)

brahmane [braman] *m* Brahman

brai [brɛ] *m* resin, pitch

braille [brɑj] *m* braille

brailler [brɑje] *tr & intr* to bawl

brail•leur [brɑjœr] **-leuse** [jøz] *adj* loudmouthed ‖ *mf* loudmouth

braiment [brɛmã] *m* bray

braire [brɛr] §68 (usually used in: *inf; ger; pp;* 3d *sg & pl*) *intr* to bray

braise [brɛz] *f* embers, coals

braiser [brɛze] *tr* to braise

braisière [brɛzjɛr] *f* braising pan

bramer [brame] *intr* to bell

bran [brã] *m* bran; (slang) dung; **bran de scie** sawdust

brancard [brãkar] *m* stretcher; shaft (*of carriage*)

brancardier [brãkardje] *m* stretcher-bearer

branche [brãʃ] *f* branch; blade (*of a scissors*); leg (*of a compass*); temple (*side-piece of a pair of glasses*)

brancher [brãʃe] *tr* to branch, fork; hook up, connect; (elec) to plug in ‖ *intr* to perch

brande [brãd] f heather; heath

brandir [brãdir] *tr* to brandish

brandon [brãdɔ̃] *m* torch; firebrand; **brandon de discorde** mischief-maker

bran•lant [brãlã] **-lante** [lãt] *adj* shaky, tottering, unsteady

branle [brãl] *m* oscillation; impetus; **mener le branle** to lead the dance; **mettre en branle** to set in motion

branle-bas [brãlɑbɑ] *m invar* call to battle stations; bustle, commotion

branler [brãle] *tr* to shake (*the head*) ‖ *intr* to shake; oscillate; be loose (*said of tooth*); **branler dans le manche** to be about to fall

braque [brak] *adj* (coll) featherbrained ‖ *mf* (coll) featherbrain ‖ *m* pointer (*dog*)

braquer [brake] *tr* to aim, point; fix (*the eyes*); turn (*a steering wheel*); **braquer contre** to turn (*e.g., an audience*) against ‖ *intr* to steer

bras [bra] *m* arm; handle; shaft; **à bras raccourcis** violently; **bras de mer** sound (*passage of water*); **bras de pick-up** pickup arm, tone arm; **bras dessus bras dessous** arm in arm; **en bras de chemise** in shirt sleeves; **être resté sur les bras de** to be left on the hands of; **manquer de bras** to be short-handed

braser [braze] *tr* to braze

brasero [brazero] *m* brazier

brasier [brazje] *m* glowing coals; blaze

bras-le-corps [bralkɔr] *m*—**à bras-le-corps** around the waist

brassage [brasaʒ] *m* brewing

brasse [brɑs], [bras] *f* fathom; breast stroke

brassée [brase] *f* armful; stroke (*in swimming*)

brasser [brase] *tr* to brew

brasserie [brasri] *f* brewery; restaurant, lunchroom

bras•seur [brasœr] **-seuse** [søz] *mf* brewer; swimmer doing the breast stroke; **brasseur d'affaires** person with many irons in the fire

brassière [brasjɛr] *f* sleeved shirt (*for an infant*); shoulder strap; **brassière de sauvetage** life preserver

bravache [bravaʃ] *adj & m* braggart

bravade [bravad] *f* bravado

brave [brav] *adj* brave ‖ (when standing before noun) *adj* worthy, honest ‖ *m* brave man

braver [brave] *tr* to brave

bravoure [bravur] *f* bravery, gallantry

break [brɛk] *m* station wagon; (coll) (*moment de repos*) break

brebis [brəbi] *f* ewe; sheep, lamb; **brebis galeuse** black sheep

brèche [brɛʃ] *f* breach (*in a wall*); gap (*between mountains*); nick (*e.g., on china*); (fig) dent (*in a fortune*); **battre en brèche** to batter; (fig) to disparage; **mourir sur la brèche** to go down fighting

bredouille [brəduj]—**rentrer** or **revenir bredouille** to return empty-handed

bredouiller [brəduje] *tr* to stammer out (*an excuse*) ‖ *intr* to mumble

bref [brɛf] **brève** [brɛv] *adj* brief, short; curt ‖ *m* papal brief ‖ *f* short syllable; **brèves et longues** dots and dashes ‖ **bref** *adv* briefly, in short

brelan [brəlã] *m* (cards) three of a kind

breloque [brəlɔk] *f* trinket, charm; **battre la breloque** to sound the all clear; keep irregular time; (coll) to have a screw loose somewhere

brème [brɛm] *f* (ichth) bream

Brésil [brezil] *m*—**le Brésil** Brazil

brési•lien [breziljẽ] **-lienne** [ljɛn] *adj* Brazilian ‖ (*cap*) *mf* Brazilian

Bretagne [brətaɲ] *f* Brittany; **la Bretagne** Brittany

bretelle [brətɛl] *f* strap, sling; access route; ramp; **bretelle de liaison** (aer) exit taxi-way; **bretelles** suspenders

bre•ton [brətɔ̃] **-tonne** [tɔn] *adj* Breton ‖ *m* Breton (*language*) ‖ (*cap*) *mf* Breton (*person*)

bretteur [brɛtœr] *m* swashbuckler

bretzel [brɛtzɛl] *m* pretzel

breuvage [brœvaʒ] *m* beverage, drink

brevet [brəvɛ] *m* diploma; license; (mil) commission; **brevet d'invention** patent

breve•té -tée [brəvte] *adj* commissioned; patented; **non breveté** noncommissioned ‖ *m* commissioned officer

breveter [brəvte] §34 *tr* to patent

bréviaire [brevjɛr] *m* (eccl) breviary

bribe [brib] *f* hunk of bread; **bribes** scraps, leavings, fragments

bric [brik] *m*—**de bric et de broc** with odds and ends; somehow

bric-à-brac [brikabrak] *m invar* secondhand merchandise; junk shop

brick [brik] *m* brig (*kind of ship*)

bricolage [brikɔlaʒ] *m* do-it-yourself

bricole [brikɔl] *f* trifle

bricoler [brikɔle] *intr* to do odd jobs; putter around

brico·leur [brikɔlœr] **-leuse** [løz] *mf* jack-of-all-trades || *m* handyman

bride [brid] *f* bridle; strap; clamp; **à toute bride** or **à bride abattue** full speed ahead

bridge [bridʒ] *m* (cards, dentistry) bridge; **bridge aux enchères** auction bridge: **bridge contrat** contract bridge

bridger [bridʒe] *intr* to play bridge

brid·geur [bridʒœr] **-geuse** [ʒøz] *mf* bridge player

briefing [brifiŋ] *m* briefing

brièvement [brijɛvmã] *adv* briefly

brièveté [brijɛvte] *f* brevity

brigade [brigad] *f* brigade

brigadier [brigadje] *m* corporal; police sergeant; noncom

brigand [brigã] *m* brigand

brigantin [brigãtɛ̃] *m* brigantine

brigue [brig] *f* intrigue, lobbying

briguer [brige] *tr* to influence underhandedly; lobby for (*s.th.*); court (*favor, votes*)

brigueur [brigœr] *m* schemer

bril·lant [brijã] **-lante** [jãt] *adj* brilliant, bright || *m* brilliancy, luster; fingernail polish

briller [brije] *intr* to shine; sparkle; **faire briller** to show (*s.o.*) off

brimade [brimad] *f* hazing; putdown

brimborion [brɛ̃bɔrjɔ̃] *m* mere trifle

brimer [brime] *tr* to haze

brin [brɛ̃] *m* blade; sprig, shoot; staple (*of hemp, linen*); strand (*of rope*); belt (*of pulley*); (coll) (little) bit, e.g., **un brin d'air** a (little) bit of air; **ne...brin §90** (archaic) not a bit, not a single; **un beau brin de fille** (coll) a fine figure of a girl

brinde [brɛ̃d] *f* (archaic) toast

brindille [brɛ̃dij] *f* twig, sprig

brioche [brijɔʃ] *f* brioche, breakfast roll

brique [brik] *f* brick

briquer [brike] *tr* (coll) to polish up, scour

briquet [brikɛ] *m* lighter

briquetage [briktaʒ] *m* brickwork

briqueter [brikte] §34 *tr* to brick (up)

briqueterie [brikɔtri] *f* brickyard

briqueteur [briktœr] *m* bricklayer

brisant [brizã] *m* breakers; **brisants** surf

brise [briz] *f* breeze

bri·sé -sée [brize] *adj* broken; folding (*door*) || *fpl* see **brisées**

brise-bise [brizbiz] *m invar* weather stripping; café curtain

brisées [brize] *fpl* track, footsteps

brise-glace [brizglas] *m invar* (naut) icebreaker

brise-jet [brizʒɛ] *m invar* (anti) splash attachment (*for water faucet*), spray filter

brise-lames [brizlam] *m invar* breakwater

brisement [brizmã] *m* breaking

briser [brize] *tr, intr, & ref* to break

brise-tout [briztu] *m invar* (coll) butterfingers, clumsy person

bri·seur [brizœr] **-seuse** [zøz] *mf* breaker (*person*); **briseur de grève** strikebreaker

brise-vent [brizvã] *m invar* windbreak

brisque [brisk] *f* service stripe

bristol [bristɔl] *m* Bristol board, pasteboard; visiting card

brisure [brizyr] *f* break; joint

britannique [britanik] *adj* British || (*cap*) *mf* Briton

broc [bro] *m* pitcher, jug

brocanter [brɔkãte] *tr* to buy, sell, or trade (*secondhand articles*) || *intr* to deal in secondhand articles

brocan·teur [brɔkãtœr] **-teuse** [tøz] *mf* secondhand dealer

brocard [brɔkar] *m* lampoon, brickbat; (zool) brocket; **lancer des brocards** to make sarcastic remarks, gibe

brocart [brɔkar] *m* brocade

broche [brɔʃ] *f* brooch; pin; (culin) spit, skewer

bro·ché -chée [brɔʃe] *adj* paperback, paperbound

brocher [brɔʃe] *tr* to brocade; sew (*book bindings*); (coll) to hurry through

brochet [brɔʃɛ] *m* (ichth) pike

brochette [brɔʃɛt] *f* skewer; skewerful; string (*of decorations*)

bro·cheur [brɔʃœr] **-cheuse** [ʃøz] *mf* bookbinder || *f* stapler

brochure [brɔʃyr] *f* brochure, pamphlet

brocoli [brɔkɔli] *m* broccoli

brodequin [brɔdkɛ̃] *m* buskin

broder [brɔde] *tr & intr* to embroider

broderie [brɔdri] *f* embroidery

brome [brom] *m* (chem) bromine

bromure [brɔmyr] *m* bromide

bronche [brɔ̃ʃ] *f* bronchial tube

broncher [brɔ̃ʃe] *intr* to stumble; flinch; grumble

bronchique [brɔ̃ʃik] *adj* bronchial

bronchite [brɔ̃ʃit] *f* bronchitis

bronze [brɔ̃z] *m* bronze

bron·zé -zée [brɔ̃ze] *adj* bronze; suntanned

bronzer [brɔ̃ze] *tr & ref* to bronze; suntan

brook [bruk] *m* (turf) water jump

broquette [brɔkɛt] *f* brad, tack

brossage [brɔsaʒ] *m* brushing

brosse [brɔs] *f* brush; **brosse à cheveux** hairbrush; **brosse à dents** toothbrush; **brosse à habits** clothesbrush; **brosse de chiendent** scrubbing brush; **brosses** shrubs, bushes

brosser [brɔse] *tr* to brush; paint the broad outlines of (*a picture*); (fig) to sketch; (slang) to beat, conquer || *ref* to brush one's clothes; (coll) to skimp, to scrimp

brouet [bruɛ] *m* gruel, broth

brouette [bruɛt] *f* wheelbarrow

brouetter [bruɛte] *tr* to carry in a wheelbarrow

brouhaha [bruaa] *m* (coll) babel, hubbub

brouillage [brujaʒ] *m* (rad) jamming, jam

brouillamini [brujamini] *m* (coll) mess

brouillard [brujar] *adj masc* blotting (*paper*) ‖ *m* fog, mist; (com) daybook

brouillasse [brujas] *f* (coll) to drizzle

brouillasser [brujase] *intr* (coll) to drizzle

brouille [bruj] *f* discord, misunderstanding

brouiller [bruje] *tr* to mix up; jam (*a broadcast*); scramble (*eggs*); **brouiller mes (ses,** etc.) **pistes** to cover my (his, etc.) tracks ‖ *ref* to quarrel; to cloud over

brouil•lon [brujʒ] **-lonne** [jɔn] *adj* crackpot; blundering; at loose ends ‖ *mf* crackpot ‖ *m* scratch pad; draft; outline, rough copy

broussailles [brusaj] *fpl* underbrush, brushwood; **en broussailles** disheveled

broussail•leux [brusajø] **-leuse** [jøz] *adj* bushy

broussard [brusar] *m* (coll) bushman, colonist

brousse [brus] *f* veldt, bush

broutage [brutaʒ] *m* grazing (*of animal*); ratatat (*of a machine*)

brouter [brute] *intr* to browse, graze; jerk, grab (*said of clutch, cutting tool, brake*)

broutille [brutij] *f* twig; trifle, bauble

broyage [brwajaʒ] *m* grinding, crushing

broyer [brwaje] §47 *tr* to grind, crush; **broyer du noir** (coll) to be down in the dumps

broyeur [brwajœr] **broyeuse** [brwajøz] *adj* grinding, crushing ‖ *mf* grinder, crusher; **broyeur d'ordures** garbage disposal ‖ *f* (mach) grinder

bru [bry] *f* daughter-in-law

bruant [bryɑ̃] *m* (orn) bunting; **bruant jaune** yellowhammer

brucelles [brysɛl] *fpl* tweezers

brugnon [brynɔ̃] *m* nectarine

bruine [bruin] *f* drizzle

bruiner [bruine] *intr* to drizzle

bruire [bruir] (usually used in: *inf;* 3d *sg pres ind* **bruit;** 3d *sg & pl imperf ind* **bruyait** or **bruissait, bruyaient** or **bruissaient**) *intr* to rustle; to hum, buzz; to splash

bruissement [bruismɑ̃] *m* rustling

bruit [brui] *m* noise; stir, fuss; **bruit de fond** background noise; **le bruit court que** it is rumored that

bruitage [bruitaʒ] *m* sound effects

brû•lant [brylɑ̃] **-lante** [lɑ̃t] *adj* burning; ardent; ticklish (*question*)

brû•lé -lée [bryle] *adj* burned ‖ *m* smell of burning; burned taste ‖ *f* (slang) beating

brûle-gueule [brylgœl] *m invar* (slang) short pipe (*for smoking*)

brûle-parfum [brylparfœ̃] *m invar* incense burner

brûle-pourpoint [brylpurpwɛ̃] **—à brûle-pourpoint** point-blank

brûler [bryle] §97 *tr* to burn; burn out (*a fuse*); go through (*a red light*); pass (*another car*); roast (*coffee*); distill (*liquor*); **brûler la cervelle à qn** to blow s.o.'s brains out ‖ *intr* to burn, burn up; **je brûle de vous voir** I long to see you ‖ *ref* to burn up, be burned

brû•leur [brylœr] **-leuse** [løz] *mf* arsonist; distiller ‖ *m* (mach) burner; **brûleur à café** coffee roaster

brûloir [brylwar] *m* roaster

brûlure [brylyr] *f* burn

brume [brym] *f* fog, mist

brumer [bryme] *intr* to be foggy

bru•meux [brymø] **-meuse** [møz] *adj* foggy, misty

brun [brœ̃] **brune** [bryn] *adj* brown, dark brown (*hair*); brown (*eyes; beer*); dusky, swarthy (*skin*); tanned, brown (*complexion*); dark (*tobacco*) ‖ *m* brown, dark brown; dark-haired man ‖ *f* see **brune**

brunâtre [brynɑtr] *adj* brownish

brune [bryn] *f* brunette; twilight; ale, stout

bru•net [brynɛ] **-nette** [nɛt] *adj* black-haired ‖ *m* dark-haired man, brunet ‖ *f* brunette

bru•ni -nie [bryni] *adj* burnished, polished ‖ *m* burnishment, polish

brunir [brynir] *tr* to brown; burnish, polish ‖ *intr* to turn brown

brunissoir [bryniswar] *m* (mach) buffer

brusque [brysk] *adj* brusque; sudden; surprise (*attack*); quick (*movements; decision*)

brusquement [bryskəmɑ̃] *adv* brusquely; abruptly, bluntly; suddenly, quickly

brusquer [bryske] *tr* to hurry, rush through; be blunt with

brusquerie [bryskri] *f* brusqueness; suddenness

brut [bryt] **brute** [bryt] *adj* crude, unpolished, unrefined, uncivilized; uncut (*diamond*); raw (*material*); dry (*champagne*); brown (*sugar*); gross (*weight*) ‖ *f* see **brute** ‖ **brut** *adv*—**peser brut** to have a gross weight of

bru•tal -tale [brytal] (*pl* **-taux** [to]) *adj* brutal, rough; outspoken; coarse, beastly ‖ *mf* brute, bully

brutaliser [brytalize] *tr* to bully; mistreat

brutalité [brytalite] *f* brutality; **brutalité policière** police brutality

brute [bryt] *f* brute

Bruxelles [brysɛl] *f* Brussels

bruxel•lois [brysɛlwa] **-loise** [lwaz] *adj* of Brussels ‖ (*cap*) *mf* native or inhabitant of Brussels

bruyamment [bruijamɑ̃] *adv* noisily

bruyant [bruijɑ̃] **bruyante** [bruijɑ̃t] *adj* noisy

bruyère [bruijɛr] *f* heather; heath

bu bue [by] *v* see **boire**

buanderie [buɑ̃dəri] *f* laundry room

buan•dier [buɑ̃dje] **-dière** [djɛr] *mf* laundry worker ‖ *f* laundress

bubonique [bybɔnik] *adj* bubonic

bûche [byʃ] *f* log; (slang) dunce; **bûche de Noël** yule log; cake decorated as a yule log; **ramasser une bûche** (slang) to take a tumble

bûcher [byʃe] *m* woodshed; pyre; stake (*e.g., for burning witches*) ‖ *tr* to roughhew; (slang) to bone up on ‖ *intr* (slang) to keep on working; slave away ‖ *ref* (slang) to fight

bûche•ron [byʃrɔ̃] **-ronne** [rɔn] *mf* woodcutter ‖ *m* lumberjack

bûchette [byʃɛt] *f* stick of wood

bû•cheur [byʃœr] **-cheuse** [ʃøz] *mf* (coll) eager beaver

budget [bydʒɛ] *m* budget; **boucler son budget** (coll) to make ends meet

budgétaire [bydʒetɛr] *adj* budgetary

buée [bɥe] *f* steam, mist

buffet [byfɛ] *m* buffet; snack bar; station restaurant; **buffet de salades** salad bar; **danser devant le buffet** to miss a meal

buffle [byfl] **bufflonne** [byflɔn] *mf* water buffalo; Cape buffalo

bugle [bygl] *m* (mus) saxhorn; bugle ‖ *f* (bot) bugle

building [bildiŋ] *m* large office building, skyscraper

buire [bɥir] *f* ewer

buis [bɥi] *m* boxwood

buisson [bɥisɔ̃] *m* bush

buisson•neux [bɥisɔnø] **-neuse** [nøz] *adj* bushy

buisson•nier [bɥisɔnje] **-nière** [njɛr] *adj*—**faire l'école buissonnière** (coll) to play hooky

bulbe [bylb] *m* bulb

bul•beux [bylbø] **-beuse** [bøz] *adj* bulbous

bulgare [bylgar] *adj* Bulgarian ‖ *m* Bulgarian (*language*) ‖ (*cap*) *mf* Bulgarian (*person*)

Bulgarie [bylgari] *f* Bulgaria; **la Bulgarie** Bulgaria

bulle [byl] *m* wrapping paper ‖ *f* bubble; blister; (eccl) bull

bulletin [byltɛ̃] *m* bulletin; ballot; **bulletin d'adhésion** membership blank; **bulletin de bagages** baggage check; **bulletin de commande** order blank; **bulletin de naissance** birth certificate; **bulletin scolaire** report card

bul•leux [bylø] **-leuse** [løz] *adj* blistery

burca [byrka] *m* (*voile qui couvre une femme des pieds à la tête*) burqa (*body veil that covers a woman from head to toe*)

bure [byr] *m* mine shaft ‖ *f* drugget, sackcloth

bu•reau [byro] *m* (*pl* **-reaux**) desk; office; **bureau à cylindre** roll-top desk; **bureau ambulant** post-office car; **bureau d'aide sociale** welfare department; **bureau de dactylos** typing pool; **bureau de l'état civil** bureau of vital statistics; **bureau de location** box office; **bureau de placement** employment agency; **bureau de poste** post office; **bureau des objets trouvés** lost-and-found department; **bureau de tabac** tobacco shop; **bureau directoire** cabinet, committee; **deuxième bureau** intelligence division

bureaucrate [byrokrat] *mf* bureaucrat

bureaucratie [byrokrasi] *f* bureaucracy

bureaucratique [byrokratik] *adj* bureaucratic

burette [byrɛt] *f* cruet; oilcan

burin [byrɛ̃] *m* engraving; burin (*tool*)

burlesque [byrlɛsk] *adj & m* burlesque

bus [bys] *m* city bus; (comp) bus; **bus d'adresse** (comp) address bus **bus de contrôle** (comp) control bus; **bus de données** (comp) data bus

busard [byzar] *m* harrier, marsh hawk

busc [bysk] *m* whalebone

buse [byz] *f* buzzard

business [biznɛs] *m* (slang) work; (slang) complicated business

bus•qué -quée [byske] *adj* arched

buste [byst] *m* bust

but [by], [byt] *m* mark, goal, target; aim, end, purpose; point (*scored in game*); **aller droit au but** to come straight to the point; **de but en blanc** point-blank

bu•té -tée [byte] *adj* obstinate, headstrong ‖ *f* abutment

buter [byte] *tr* to prop up; (slang) to bump off, kill ‖ *intr*—**buter contre** to bump into, stumble on ‖ *ref*—**se buter à** to butt up against; (fig) to be dead set on

buteur [bytœr] *m* scorer

butin [bytɛ̃] *m* booty; profits, savings

butiner [bytine] *tr* to pillage; gather honey from ‖ *intr* to pillage; gather honey (*said of bees*); **butiner dans** to browse among (*books*)

butoir [bytwar] *m* buffer, stop, catch

bu•tor [bytɔr] **-torde** [tɔrd] *mf* (slang) lout, good-for-nothing

butte [byt] *f* butte, knoll; **butte de tir** butt, mound (*for target practice*); **être en butte à** to be exposed to

butter [byte] *tr* to hill (*plants*)

buttoir [bytwar] *m* (agr) hiller

buty•reux [bytirø] **-reuse** [røz] *adj* buttery

buvable [byvabl] *adj* drinkable; (pharm) to be taken by mouth

buvard [byvar] *adj* blotting (*paper*) ‖ *m* blotter

buvette [byvɛt] *f* bar, fountain

buvette-buffet [byvɛtbyfɛ] *f* (coll) snack bar

bu•veur [byvœr] **-veuse** [vøz] *mf* drinker; **buveur d'eau** abstainer; vacationist at a spa

byzan•tin [bizɑ̃tɛ̃] **-tine** [tin] *adj* Byzantine

C

C, c [se] *m invar* third letter of the French alphabet

C / *abbr* (**compte**) account

ça [sa] *pron indef* (coll) that; **ah ça non!** no indeed!; **avec ça!** tell me another!; **ça y est** that's that; that's it, that's right; **comment ça!** how so?; **et avec ça?** what else?; **où ça,** where?

çà [sa] *adv*—**ah çà!** now then! **çà et là** here and there

cabale [kabal] *f* cabal, intrigue

cabaler [kabale] *intr* to cabal, intrigue

caban [kabɑ̃] *m* (naut) peacoat
cabane [kaban] *f* cabin, hut
cabanon [kabanɔ̃] *m* hut, padded cell
cabaret [kabarɛ] *m* tavern; cabaret, night club; liquor closet
cabas [kabɑ] *m* basket; shopping bag
cabestan [kabɛstɑ̃] *m* capstan
cabillaud [kabijo] *m* haddock; (coll) fresh cod
cabine [kabin] *f* cabin (*of ship or airplane*); bathhouse; car (*of elevator*); cab (*of locomotive or truck*); **cabine de cinéma** projection booth; **cabine de péage** tollbooth; **cabine téléphonique** telephone booth, phone booth
cabinet [kabinɛ] *m* cabinet (*small room; room for displaying collections; political committee; antique chest of drawers*); toilet, rest room; storeroom closet; clientele, practice; office (*of a professional person*); study (*of a scholar*); staff (*of a cabinet officer*); **cabinet d'aisance** rest room; **cabinet de débarras** storeroom closet; **cabinet de dentiste** dentist's office; **cabinet de stratèges** think tank; **cabinet de toilette** powder room, toilet; **cabinet fantôme** shadow cabinet; **cabinets (d'aisances)** rest rooms
câble [kɑbl] *m* cable; cable television, cable; **câble coaxial** coaxial cable; **câble de démarrage** jumper cable; **câble numérique** digital cable television
câbler [kɑble] *tr & intr* to cable
câblier [kɑblije] *m* cable ship
câblodistribution [kɑblɔdistribysjɔ̃] *f* cable television
câblogramme [kɑblɔgram] *m* cablegram
cabo•chard [kabɔ•ʃar] **-charde** [ʃard] *adj* obstinate, pigheaded
caboche [kabɔʃ] *f* hobnail; (coll) noodle (*head*)
cabochon [kabɔʃɔ̃] *m* uncut gem; stud, upholstery nail
cabot [kabo] *m* (ichth) miller's-thumb, bullhead; (coll) ham (actor)
cabotage [kabɔtaʒ] *m* coastal navigation, coasting trade
cabo•tin [kabɔtɛ̃] **-tine** [tin] *mf* barnstormer; (coll) ham (actor); **cabotin de la politique** (coll) corny politician, political orator given to histrionics
cabotinage [kabɔtinaʒ] *m* barnstorming; (coll) ham acting
cabotiner [kabɔtine] *intr* to barnstorm; (coll) to play to the grandstand
cabrer [kabre] *tr* to make (*a horse*) rear; nose up (*a plane*) ‖ *ref* to rear; kick over the traces; (aer) to nose up
cabri [kabri] *m* (zool) kid
cabriole [kabrijɔl] *f* caper
cabrioler [kabrijɔle] *intr* to caper
caca [kaka] *m*—**caca d'oie** greenish-yellow; **faire caca** (*children's language*) to go potty
cacahouète or **cacahuète** [kakawɛt] *f* peanut
cacao [kakao] *m* cocoa; cocoa bean
cacaotier [kakaɔtje] *m* (bot) cacao
cacaoyer [kakaɔje] *m* (bot) cacao

cacarder [kakarde] *intr* to cackle
cacatoès [kakatɔɛs] or **cacatois** [kakatwa] *m* cockatoo
cachalot [kaʃalo] *m* sperm whale
cache [kaʃ] *m* masking tape ‖ *f* hiding place
cache-cache [kaʃkaʃ] *m invar* hide-and-seek
cache-col [kaʃkɔl] *m invar* scarf
cachemire [kaʃmir] *m* cashmere
cache-nez [kaʃne] *m invar* muffler
cache-poussière [kaʃpusjɛr] *m invar* duster (*overgarment*)
cacher [kaʃe] *tr* to hide; **cacher q.ch. à qn** to hide s.th. from s.o. ‖ *ref* to hide; **se cacher à** to hide from; **se cacher de q.ch.** to make a secret of s.th.
cache-radiateur [kaʃradjatœr] *m invar* radiator cover
cache-sexe [kaʃsɛks] *m invar* G-string; minimum (male) swimwear
cachet [kaʃɛ] *m* seal; postmark; fee; price of a lesson; meal ticket; (pharm, phila) cachet; (fig) seal; stylishness; **payer au cachet** to pay a set fee
cacheter [kaʃte] §34 *tr* to seal, seal up; seal with wax
cachette [kaʃɛt] *f* hiding place; **en cachette** secretly
cachot [kaʃo] *m* dungeon; prison
cacophonie [kakɔfɔni] *f* cacophony
cactier [kaktje] or **cactus** [kaktys] *m* cactus
c.-à-d. *abbr* (**c'est-à-dire**) that is
cadastre [kadastr] *m* land-survey register
cadavre [kadavr] *m* corpse, cadaver; (slang) dead soldier (*bottle*)
ca•deau [kado] *m* (*pl* **-deaux**) gift
cadenas [kadna] *m* padlock
cadenasser [kadnase] *tr* to padlock
cadence [kadɑ̃s] *f* cadence, rhythm, time; output (*of worker, of factory; etc.*); **cadence de tir** rate of firing
cadencer [kadɑ̃se] §51 *tr* to cadence ‖ *intr* to call out cadence
ca•det [kadɛ] **-dette** [dɛt] *adj* younger ‖ *mf* youngest; junior; (sports) player fifteen to eighteen years old; **le cadet de mes soucis** (coll) the least of my worries ‖ *m* caddy; (mil) cadet; younger brother; younger son ‖ *f* younger sister; younger daughter
cadmium [kadmjɔm] *m* cadmium
cadrage [kadraʒ] *m* (mov, telv) framing; (phot) centering
cadran [kadrɑ̃] *m* dial; **cadran d'appel** telephone dial; **cadran solaire** sundial; **faire le tour du cadran** to sleep around the clock
cadre [kadr] *m* frame; framework; setting; outline, framework (*of a literary work*); limits, scope (*of activities or duties*); (mil) cadre; (naut) cot; **cadres** officials; (mil) regulars; **cadres sociaux** memorable dates or events
cadrer [kadre] *tr* to frame (*film*) ‖ *intr* to conform, tally
cadreur [kadrœr] *m* (mov) cameraman
ca•duc -duque [kadyk] *adj* decrepit, frail; out-

lived (*custom*); deciduous (*leaves*); lapsed (*insurance policy*); (law) null and void

caducée [kadyse] *m* caduceus

C.A.F. *abbr* (**coût, assurance, fret**) C.I.F. (*cost, insurance, and freight*)

ca•fard [kafar] **-farde** [fard] *adj* sanctimonious ‖ *mf* hypocrite; (coll) squealer ‖ *m* (coll) cockroach; (coll) blues

café [kafe] *adj invar* tan ‖ *m* coffee; café; coffeehouse; **café au lait** coffee with hot milk; **café chantant** music hall (*with tables*); **café complet** coffee, hot milk, rolls, butter, and jam; **café crème** white coffee; **café décaféiné** decaffeinated coffee; **café en poudre** instant coffee; **café express** espresso coffee; **café filtre** drip coffee; **café instantané** instant coffee; **café liégeois** coffee ice cream topped with whipped cream; **café lyophilisé** freeze-dried coffee; **café nature, café noir** black coffee; **café vert** unroasted coffee; **café soluble** powdered coffee

café-concert [kafekɔ̃sɛr] *m* (*pl* **cafés-concerts**) music hall (*with tables*), cabaret

caféier [kafeje] *m* coffee plant

caféière [kafejɛr] *f* coffee plantation

caféine [kafein] *f* caffeine

café-restaurant [kaferɛstɔrɑ̃] *m* (*pl* **cafés-restaurants**) café, bistro

cafétéria [kafeterja] *f* cafeteria

cafe•tier [kaftje] **-tière** [tjɛr] *mf* café owner ‖ *f* coffeepot

cafouiller [kafuje] *intr* (slang) to miss (*said of engine*); (slang) to flounder around

cage [kaʒ] *f* cage; **cage d'un ascenseur** elevator shaft; **cage d'un escalier** stairwell; **cage thoracique** thoracic cavity; **en cage** (coll) in the clink, in the pen

cageot [kaʒo] *m* crate

ca•gnard [kaɲar] **-gnarde** [ɲard] *adj* indolent, lazy ‖ *m* (coll) sunny spot

ca•gneux [kaɲø] **-gneuse** [ɲøz] *adj* knock-kneed; pigeon-toed

cagnotte [kaɲɔt] *f* kitty, pool

ca•got [kago] **-gotte** [gɔt] *adj* hypocritical ‖ *mf* hypocrite

cagoule [kagul] *f* cowl; hood (*with eyeholes*)

cahier [kaje] *m* notebook; **cahier à feuilles mobiles** loose-leaf notebook; **cahier d'écolier** (*à couverture bleue pour écrire des examens*) blue book; **cahier des charges** (com) specifications; **cahier (d'imprimerie)** (bb) signature, gathering

cahin-caha [kaɛ̃kaa] *adv* (coll) so-so

cahot [kao] *m* jolt, bump

cahoter [kaɔte] *tr & intr* to jolt

caho•teux [kaɔtø] **-teuse** [tøz] *adj* bumpy (*road*)

cahute [kayt] *f* hut, shack

caille [kaj] *f* quail

cail•lé -lée [kaje] *adj* curdled ‖ *m* curd

caillebotis [kajbɔti] *m* boardwalk; (mil) duckboard; (naut) grating

caillebotte [kajbɔt] *f* curds

caillebotter [kajbɔte] *tr & intr* to curdle

cailler [kaje] *tr & ref* to clot, curdle, curd

caillot [kajo] *m* clot; blood clot

cail•lou [kaju] *m* (*pl* **-loux**) pebble; (coll) bald head; **caillou du Rhin** rhinestone

caillou•teux [kajutø] **-teuse** [tøz] *adj* stony (*road*); pebbly (*beach*)

cailloutis [kajuti] *m* crushed stone, gravel

Caïn [kaɛ̃] *m* Cain

Caire [kɛr] *m*—**Le Caire** Cairo

caisse [kɛs] *f* chest, box; case (*for packing; of a clock or piano*); chestful, boxful; till, cash register, coffer, safe; cashier, cashier's window; desk (*in a hotel*); **caisse à eau** water tank; **caisse claire** snare drum; **caisse d'épargne** savings bank; **caisse des écoles** scholarship fund; **caisse de sortie** checkout counter; **grosse caisse** bass drum; bass drummer; **petite caisse** petty cash

caisson [kɛsɔ̃] *m* caisson; crate, box

cajoler [kaʒɔle] *tr* to cajole, wheedle

cajolerie [kaʒɔlri] *f* cajolery

cajou [kaʒu] *m* cashew nut

cake [kɛk] *m* fruit cake

cal [kal] *m* (*pl* **cals**) callus, callosity; **cal vicieux** badly knitted bone

calage [kalaʒ] *m* wedging, chocking; stalling (*of motor*)

calamité [kalamite] *f* calamity

calami•teux [kalamitø] **-teuse** [tøz] *adj* calamitous

calandre [kalɑ̃dr] *f* mangle (*for clothes*); calender (*for paper*); grill (*for car radiator*); (ent) weevil; (orn) lark

calandrer [kalɑ̃dre] *tr* to calender

calcaire [kalkɛr] *adj* calcareous; chalky; hard (*water*) ‖ *m* limestone

calcifier [kalsifje] *tr & ref* to calcify

calciner [kalsine] *tr & ref* to burn to a cinder

calcium [kalsjɔm] *m* calcium

calcul [kalkyl] *m* calculation; (math, pathol) calculus; **calcul au pifomètre** (coll) guestimate; **calcul biliaire** gallstone; **calcul mental** mental arithmetic; **calcul rénal** kidney stone

calculable [kalkylablə] *adj* computable

calcula•teur [kalkylatœr] **-trice** [tris] *adj* calculating ‖ *mf* calculator (*person*) ‖ *m* (mach) calculator ‖ *f* adding machine; **calculatrice de poche** pocket calculator

calculer [kalkyle] *tr & intr* to calculate

calculette [kalkylɛt] *f* pocket calculator

cale [kal] *f* wedge, chock; hold (*of ship*); **cale de construction** stocks; **cale sèche** dry dock

ca•lé -lée [kale] *adj* stalled; (coll) well-informed; (slang) involved, difficult; **calé en** (coll) strong in, up on

calebasse [kalbas] *f* calabash

calèche [kalɛʃ] *f* open carriage

caleçon [kalsɔ̃] *m* drawers, shorts; **caleçon de bain** swimming trunks

calembour [kalɑ̃bur] *m* pun

calendes [kalɑ̃d] *fpl* calends; **aux calendes grecques** (coll) when pigs fly

calendrier [kalɑ̃drije] *m* calendar; **calendrier musulman** Muslim calendar

calepin [kalpɛ̃] *m* notebook

caler [kale] *tr* to wedge, chock; jam; stall; lower (*sail*); (naut) to draw ‖ *intr* to stall (*said of motor*); (coll) to give in ‖ *ref* to stall; get nicely settled

calfater [kalfate] *tr* to caulk

calfeutrer [kalføtre] *tr* to stop up ‖ *ref* to shut oneself up

calibre [kalibr] *m* caliber; template

calibrer [kalibre] *tr* to calibrate

calice [kalis] *m* chalice; (bot) calyx

calicot [kaliko] *m* calico; sign, banner; (slang) sales clerk

califat•**kalifa**] *m* caliphate

calife [kalif] *m* caliph

Californie [kalifɔrni] *f* California; **la basse Californie** Lower California; **la Californie** California

califourchon [kalifurʃɔ̃]—**à califourchon** astride, astraddle; **s'asseoir à califourchon** to straddle

câ•lin [kɑlɛ̃] **-line** [lin] *adj* coaxing; caressing

câliner [kaline] *tr* to coax; caress

cal•leux [kalø] **-leuse** [løz] *adj* callous, calloused

callisthénie [kalisteni] *f* calisthenics

cal•mant [kalmɑ̃] **-mante** [mɑ̃t] *adj* calming ‖ *m* sedative

calmar [kalmar] *m* squid

calme [kalm] *adj* & *m* calm

calmement [kalməmɑ̃] *adv* calmly

calmer [kalme] *tr* to calm ‖ *ref* to become calm, calm down

calmir [kalmir] *intr* to abate

calomnie [kalɔmni] *f* calumny, slander

calomnier [kalɔmnje] *tr* to calumniate

caloporteur [kalɔpɔrtœr] *m* coolant

calorie [kalɔri] *f* calory

calorifère [kalɔrifɛr] *adj* heating, heat-conducting ‖ *m* heater; **calorifère à air chaud** hot-air heater; **calorifère à eau chaude** hot-water heater

calorifuge [kalɔrifyʒ] *adj* insulating ‖ *m* insulator

calorifuger [kalɔrifyʒe] §38 *tr* to insulate

caloriporteur [kalɔripɔrtœr] *m* coolant

calorique [kalɔrik] *adj* caloric

calot [kalo] *m* policeman's hat, kepi

calotte [kalɔt] *f* skullcap; dome; (coll) box on the ear; (coll) clergy; **calotte des cieux** vault of heaven; **calotte glaciaire polaire** polar ice-cap; **flanquer une calotte à** (coll) to box on the ear

calotter [kalɔte] *tr* (coll) to box on the ear, cuff; (slang) to snitch

calque [kalk] *m* tracing; decal; calque (*word-for-word correspondence between two languages*); slavish imitation; spitting image

calquer [kalke] *tr* to trace; imitate slavishly

calumet [kalymɛ] *m* calumet; **calumet de paix** peace pipe

calvados [kalvados] *m* applejack

calvaire [kalvɛr] *m* calvary

calviniste [kalvinist] *adj* & *mf* Calvinist

calvitie [kalvisi] *f* baldness

camarade [kamarad] *mf* comrade; **camarade de chambre** roommate; **camarade de travail** fellow worker; **camarade d'étude** schoolmate

camaraderie [kamaradri] *f* comradeship; camaraderie, fellowship

ca•mard [kamar] **-marde** [mard] *adj* snub-nosed

cambouis [kɑ̃bwi] *m* axle grease

cambrer [kɑ̃bre] *tr* to curve, arch

cambrioler [kɑ̃brijɔle] *tr* to break into, burglarize

cambrio•leur [kɑ̃brijɔlœr] **-leuse** [løz] *mf* burglar

cambrure [kɑ̃bryr] *f* curve, arch

cambuse [kɑ̃byz] *f* (naut) storeroom between decks

came [kam] *f* cam

ca•mé **-mée** [kame] *mf* drug user

camée [kame] *m* cameo

caméléon [kameleɔ̃] *m* chameleon

camélia [kamelja] *m* camellia

camelot [kamlo] *m* cheap woolen cloth; huckster; newsboy

camelote [kamlɔt] *f* shoddy merchandise, rubbish, junk; **camelote alimentaire** junk food

caméra [kamera] *f* (mov, telv) camera

caméscope [kameskɔp] *m* camcorder, video camera

camion [kamjɔ̃] *m* truck; paint bucket; **camion à remorque** trailer (truck); **camion à semi-remorque** semitrailer; **camion citerne** fuel truck; **camion de déménagement** moving van; **camion d'enregistrement** (mov) sound truck; **camion de remorquage** tow truck; **camion pour le transport d'automobiles** car-carrier

camion-benne [kamjɔ̃bɛn] *m* (*pl* **camions-bennes**) dump truck

camion-citerne [kamjɔ̃sitɛrn] *m* (*pl* **camions-citernes**) tank truck

camion-grue [kamjɔ̃gry] *m* (*pl* **camions-grues**) tow truck

camionnage [kamjɔnaʒ] *m* trucking

camionner [kamjɔne] *tr* to truck

camionnette [kamjɔnɛt] *f* van; **camionnette de police** police wagon; **camionnette sanitaire** mobile health unit

camionneur [kamjɔnœr] *m* trucker; truck-driver, teamster

camisole [kamizɔl] *f* camisole; **camisole de force** strait jacket

camomille [kamɔmij] *f* camomile

camouflage [kamuflaʒ] *m* camouflage

camoufler [kamufle] *tr* to camouflage

camp [kɑ̃] *m* camp; **camp de base** base camp; **camp de concentration** concentration camp; **camp de vacances** resort; **changer de camp** to change sides

campa·gnard [kɑ̃paɲar] **-gnarde** [ɲard] *adj* & *mf* rustic

campagne [kɑ̃paɲ] *f* campaign; country

cam·pé -pée [kɑ̃pe] *adj* encamped; **bien campé** well-built (*man*); clearly presented (*story*); firmly fixed

campement [kɑ̃pmɑ̃] *m* encampment; camping

camper [kɑ̃pe] *tr* to camp; (coll) to clap (*e.g.*, *one's hat on one's head*); **camper là qn** (coll) to run out on s.o. ‖ *intr* & *ref* to camp

cam·peur [kɑ̃pœr] **-peuse** [pøz] *mf* camper

camphre [kɑ̃fr] *m* camphor

camping [kɑ̃piɲ] *m* campground; trailer; camping; **camping sauvage** wilderness camping

campos [kɑ̃po] *m* (coll) vacation, day off

campus [kɑ̃pys] *m* campus

ca·mus [kamy] **-muse** [myz] *adj* snub-nosed, pug-nosed, flat-nosed

Canada [kanada] *m*—**le Canada** Canada

cana·dien [kanadjɛ̃] **-dienne** [djɛn] *adj* Canadian ‖ *f* sheepskin jacket; station wagon ‖ (*cap*) *mf* Canadian

canaille [kanɑj] *adj* vulgar, coarse ‖ *f* rabble, riffraff; scoundrel

ca·nal [kanal] *m* (*pl* **-naux** [no]) canal; tube; pipe; ditch, drain; (rad, telv) channel; **canal de Panama** Panama Canal; **canal de Suez** [sɥɛz] Suez Canal; **par le canal de** through the good offices of

canapé [kanape] *m* sofa, davenport; (culin) canapé; **canapé à deux places** settee

canapé-lit [kanapeli] *m* (*pl* **canapés-lits**) sofa bed, day bed

canard [kanar] *m* duck; sugar soaked in coffee, brandy, etc.; (mus) false note; (coll) hoax, canard; (coll) rag, paper; **canard mâle** drake; **canard publicitaire** publicity stunt; **canard sauvage** wild duck

canarder [kanarde] *tr* to snipe at ‖ *intr* to snipe

canari [kanari] *m* canary

cancan [kɑ̃kɑ̃] *m* cancan (*dance*); (coll) gossip

cancaner [kɑ̃kane] *intr* to quack; (coll) to gossip

canca·nier [kɑ̃kanje] **-nière** [njɛr] *adj* (coll) catty ‖ *mf* (coll) gossip

cancer [kɑ̃sɛr] *m* cancer; **le Cancer** (astr, astrol) Cancer

cancé·reux [kɑ̃serø] **-reuse** [røz] *adj* cancerous

cancérigène [kɑ̃seriʒɛn] or **cancérogène** [kɑ̃seroʒɛn] *adj* carcinogenic ‖ *m* carcinogen

cancre [kɑ̃kr] *m* (coll) dunce, lazy student; (coll) tightwad; (zool) crab

candélabre [kɑ̃delabr] *m* candelabrum; espaliered fruit tree; cactus; lamppost

candeur [kɑ̃dœr] *f* naïveté; guilelessness

candi [kɑ̃di] *adj* candied (*fruit*) ‖ *m* rock candy

candi·dat [kɑ̃dida] **-date** [dat] *mf* candidate; nominee

candidature [k̃didatyr] *f* candidacy

candide [kɑ̃did] *adj* naïve; ingenuous

candir [kɑ̃dir] *intr*—**faire candir** to candy, crystallize (*sugar*) ‖ *ref* to candy, crystallize

cane [kan] *f* duck, female duck

caner [kane] *intr* (slang) to chicken out

caneton [kantɔ̃] *m* duckling

canette [kanɛt] *f* female duckling; beer bottle; **canette de bière** can of beer

canevas [kanva] *m* canvas (*cloth*); outline (*of novel, story, etc.*); embroidery netting; triangulation (*in artillery, in cartography*)

canezou [kanzu] *m* sleeveless lace blouse

caniche [kaniʃ] *m* poodle

canicule [kanikyl] *f* dog days

canif [kanif] *m* penknife, pocketknife

ca·nin [kanɛ̃] **-nine** [nin] *adj* canine ‖ *f* canine (*tooth*)

canitie [kanisi] *f* grayness (*of hair*)

cani·veau [kanivo] *m* (*pl* **-veaux**) gutter; (elec) conduit

cannaie [kanɛ] *f* sugar plantation

canne [kan] *f* cane; reed; cane, walking stick; **canne à pêche** fishing rod; **canne à sucre** sugar cane

canneberge [kanbɛrʒ] *f* cranberry

canneler [kanle] §34 *tr* to groove; corrugate; flute (*a column*)

cannelle [kanɛl] *f* cinnamon; spout

cannelure [kanlyr] *f* groove, channel; corrugation; fluting (*of column*)

canner [kane] *tr* to cane (*a chair*)

cannibale [kanibal] *adj* & *mf* cannibal

canoë [kanɔe] *m* canoe

canoéiste [kanɔeist] *mf* canoeist

canon [kanɔ̃] *m* canon; cannon; gun barrel; tube; nozzle, spout; **canon à électrons** electron gun

cañon [kaɲɔ̃] *m* canyon

cano·nial -niale [kanɔnjal] *adj* (*pl* **-niaux** [njo]) canonical

canonique [kanɔnik] *adj* canonical

canoniser [kanɔnize] *tr* to canonize

cannonade [kanɔnad] *f* cannonade

canonner [kanɔne] *tr* to cannonade

canonnier [kanɔnje] *m* cannoneer

canonnière [kanɔnjɛr] *f* gunboat; popgun

canot [kano] *m* rowboat, launch; **canot automobile** speedboat, motorboat; **canot de sauvetage** lifeboat

canotage [kanɔtaʒ] *m* boating

canoter [kanɔte] *intr* to go boating

canotier [kanɔtje] *m* rower; skimmer

cant [kɑ̃] *m* cant

cantaloup [kɑ̃talu] *m* cantaloupe

cantate [kɑ̃tat] *f* cantata

cantatrice [kɑ̃tatris] *f* singer

cantilever [kɑ̃tilevœr] *adj* & *m* cantilever

cantine [kɑ̃tin] *f* canteen (*restaurant*); **cantine d'officier** officer's kit

cantique [kɑ̃tik] *m* canticle, ode; **cantique de Noël** (eccl) Christmas carol; **Cantique des Cantiques** (Bib) Song of Songs

canton [kɑ̃tɔ̃] *m* canton, district; **Cantons de l'Est** Eastern Townships (*in Canada*)

cantonade [kɑ̃tɔnad] *f* (theat) wings; **à la cantonade** (theat) offstage; **crier à la cantonade** to yell out (*s.th.*); **parler à la cantonade** to seem to be talking to oneself; (theat) to speak toward the wings

cantonnement [kɑ̃tɔnmɑ̃] *m* billeting

cantonner [kɑ̃tɔne] *tr* to billet

cantonnier [kɑ̃tɔnje] *m* road laborer; (rr) section hand

canular [kanylar] *m* (coll) practical joke, hoax, canard

canule [kanyl] *f* nozzle (*of syringe or injection needle*)

canuler [kanyle] *tr* (slang) to bother

caoutchouc [kautʃu] *m* rubber; **caoutchouc mousse** foam rubber; **caoutchoucs** rubbers, overshoes

caoutchouter [kautʃute] *tr* to rubberize

caoutchou·teux [kautʃutø] **-teuse** [tøz] *adj* rubbery

cap [kap] *m* cape, headland; bow, head (*of ship*); **Cap de Bonne Espérance** Cape of Good Hope; **mettre le cap sur** (coll) to set a course for

capable [kapabl] §93 *adj* capable

capacité [kapasite] *f* capacity; ability; **capacité d'autofinancement** (bk) cash flow

cape [kap] *f* cape; hood; derby; outer leaf, wrapper (*of cigar*); **à la cape** (naut) hove to; **de cape et d'épée** cloak-and-dagger (*novel, movie, etc.*); **rire sous cape** to laugh up one's sleeve; **vendre sous cape** (coll) to sell under the counter

C.A.P.E.S. [kapɛs] *m* (acronym) (**certificat d'aptitude au professorat de l'enseignement du second degré**) secondary-school teachers certificate

capillaire [kapillɛr] *adj* capillary ‖ *m* (bot) maidenhair (*fern*)

capitaine [kapitɛn] *m* captain; **capitaine des pompiers** fire chief

capi·tal -tale [kapital] (*pl* **-taux** [to] **-tales**) *adj* capital, principal, essential; capital (*city; punishment; crime; letter*); death (*sentence*); deadly (*sins*) ‖ *m* capital, assets; principal (*main sum*); **avec de minces capitaux** on a shoestring; **capital circulant, capital d'exploitation** working capital; **capital fixe** fixed assets; **capitaux** capital; **capitaux fébriles** (slang) hot money ‖ *f* capital (*city; letter*)

capitalisation [kapitalizasjɔ̃] *f* capitalization; hoarding (*of money*)

capitaliser [kapitalize] *tr* to capitalize (*an income*); compound (*interest*) ‖ *intr* to hoard

capitalisme [kapitalism] *m* capitalism

capitaliste [kapitalist] *adj* capitalist ‖ *mf* capitalist; investor

capital-risque [kapitalrisk] *msg* venture capital

capi·teux [kapitø] **-teuse** [tøz] *adj* heady (*wine, champagne, etc.*); intoxicating, alluring (*beauty; woman*)

Capitole [kapitɔl] *m* Capitol

capitonner [kapitɔne] *tr* to upholster

capituler [kapityle] *intr* to capitulate; parley

ca·pon [kapɔ̃] **-ponne** [pɔn] *adj* cowardly ‖ *mf* coward; sneak; tattletale

capo·ral [kapɔral] *m* (*pl* **-raux** [ro]) corporal;

shag, caporal (*tobacco*); **Caporal a dit . . .** Simon says . . .

caporalisme [kapɔralism] *m* militarism; dictatorial government

capot [kapo] *adj invar* speechless, confused; (cards) trickless ‖ *m* cover; hood (*of automobile*); (naut) hatch

capotage [kapɔtaʒ] *m* overturning

capote [kapɔt] *f* coat with a hood; hood (*of baby carriage*); **capote anglaise** condom, prophylactic; **capote rebattable** (aut) folding top

capoter [kapɔte] *intr* to capsize; overturn, upset

câpre [kɑpr] *f* (bot) caper

caprice [kapris] *m* caprice, whim

capri·cieux [kaprisjø] **-cieuse** [sjøz] *adj* capricious, whimsical

Capricorne [kaprikɔrn] *m*—**le Capricorne** (astr, astrol) Capricorn

capsule [kapsyl] *f* capsule; bottle cap; percussion cap; (bot) capsule, pod; (rok) capsule; **capsule du temps** time capsule; **capsule spatiale** space capsule; **capsules surrénales** adrenal glands

capsuler [kapsyle] *tr* to cap

captage [kaptaʒ] *m* picking up, receiving, capturing; **captage de données** (comp) data capture

capter [kapte] *tr* to win over; harness (*a river*); tap (*electric current; a water supply*); (rad, telv) to receive, pick up

capteur [kaptœr] *m* (rok) sensor

cap·tieux [kapsjø] **-tieuse** [sjøz] *adj* captious, insidious; specious

cap·tif [kaptif] **-tive** [tiv] *adj* & *mf* captive

captiver [kaptive] *tr* to captivate

captivité [kaptivite] *f* captivity

capture [kaptyr] *f* capture

capturer [kaptyre] *tr* to capture

capuce [kapys] *m* (eccl) pointed hood

capuchon [kapyʃɔ̃] *m* hood (*of coat*); cap (*of pen*); (aut) valve cap; (eccl) cowl

capucine [kapysin] *f* nasturtium

caque [kak] *f* keg, barrel

caquet [kakɛ] *m* cackle

caqueter [kakte] §34 *intr* to cackle; gossip

car [kar] *m* bus, sightseeing bus, interurban; **car de police** patrol wagon; **car sonore** loudspeaker truck ‖ *conj* for, because

carabe [karab] *m* ground beetle

carabine [karabin] *f* carbine

carabi·né -née [karabine] *adj* (coll) violent (*wind, cold, criticism*)

caraco [karako] *m* loose blouse

caractère [karaktɛr] *m* character; **caractères gras** (typ) boldface; **caractères penchés** (typ) italics

caractériser [karakterize] *tr* to characterize

caractéristique [karakteristik] *adj* & *f* characteristic

carafe [karaf] *f* carafe; **carafe à eau** water bottle; **rester en carafe** (slang) to be left out in the cold

carafon [karafɔ̃] *m* small carafe

caraïbe [karaib] *adj* Caribbean, Carib ‖ *(cap)* *mf* Carib *(person)*

carambolage [karɑ̃bɔlaʒ] *m* jostling; (coll) bumping *(e.g., of autos)*

caramboler [karɑ̃bɔle] *tr* (coll) to strike, bump into ‖ *intr* (billiards) to carom

caramel [karamɛl] *m* caramel

carapace [karapas] *f* turtle shell, carapace

carapater [karapate] *ref* (slang) to beat it

carat [kara] *m* carat

caravane [karavan] *f* caravan; house trailer; group *(of tourists)*

caravaning [karavaniŋ] *m* trailer camping

caravansérail [karavɑ̃seraj] *m* caravansary; (fig) world crossroads

caravelle [karavɛl] *f* caravel

carbonade [karbɔnad] *f* see **carbonnade**

carbone [karbɔn] *m* carbon

carbonique [karbɔnik] *adj* carbonic

carboniser [karbɔnize] *tr* to carbonize, char

carbonnade [karbɔnad] *f* charcoal-grilled steak (ham, etc.); beef and onion stew *(in northern France)*; **à la carbonnade** charcoal-grilled

carburant [karbyrɑ̃] *m* motor fuel

carburateur [karbyratœr] *m* carburetor

carbure [karbyr] *m* carbide

carburéacteur [karbyreaktœr] *m* jet fuel

carcan [karkɑ̃] *m* pillory

carcasse [karkas] *f* skeleton; framework; (coll) carcass

cardan [kardɑ̃] *m* (mach) universal joint

carde [kard] *f* card; leaf rib; teasel head

carder [karde] *tr* to card

cardiaque [kardjak] *adj* & *mf* cardiac

cardi•nal -nale [kardinal] *adj* & *m (pl* **-naux** [no]*)* cardinal

cardiogramme [kardjɔgram] *m* cardiogram

carême [karɛm] *m* Lent; **de carême** Lenten; **faire carême** to fast during Lent

carême-prenant [karɛmprɔnɑ̃] *m (pl* **carêmes-prenants***)* Shrovetide

carence [karɑ̃s] *f* lack, deficiency; failure

carène [karɛn] *f* hull

caréner [karene] §10 *tr* to streamline; (naut) to careen

caren•tiel-tielle [karɑ̃sjɛl] *adj* deficiency *(disease)*

cares•sant [karɛsɑ̃] **-sante** [sɑ̃t] *adj* caressing; lovable; nice to pet; soothing *(e.g., voice)*

caresse [karɛs] *f* caress; endearment

caresser [karɛse] *tr* to caress; pet; nourish *(a hope)*

cargaison [kargɛzɔ̃] *f* cargo

cargo [kargo] *m* freighter; **cargo mixte** freighter carrying passengers

cari [kari] *m* curry

cariatide [karjatid] *f* caryatid

caricature [karikatyr] *f* caricature; cartoon

caricaturer [karikatyre] *tr* to caricature

caricaturiste [karikatyrist] *mf* caricaturist; cartoonist

carie [kari] *f* caries; **carie sèche** dry rot

carillon [karijɔ̃] *m* carillon

carillonner [karijɔne] *tr* & *intr* to carillon, chime

carlingue [karlɛ̃g] *f* (aer) cockpit

carmin [karmɛ̃] *adj* & *m* carmine

carnage [karnaʒ] *m* carnage

carnas•sier [karnasje] **-sière** [sjɛr] *adj* carnivorous ‖ *m* carnivore ‖ *f* game bag

carnation [karnɑsjɔ̃] *f* flesh tint

carna•val [karnaval] *m (pl* **-vals***)* carnival; parade dummy

car•né -née [karne] *adj* "flesh"-colored; meat *(diet)*

carnet [karnɛ] *m* notebook, address book; memo pad; book *(of tickets, checks, stamps, etc.)*; **carnet à feuilles mobiles** loose-leaf notebook

carnier [karnje] *m* hunting bag

carotte [karɔt] *f* carrot; (min) core sample; **les carottes sont cuites** the die is cast; **tirer une carotte à** (coll) to cheat

carotter [karɔte] *tr* (coll) to cheat; chisel

carpe [karp] *m* (anat) wrist bones ‖ *f* carp; **être muet comme une carpe** to be still as a mouse

carpette [karpɛt] *f* rug, mat; **être une vraie carpette** to let s.o. walk all over one

carquois [karkwa] *m* quiver

carre [kar] *f* thickness *(of board)*; crown *(of hat)*; edge *(of ice skate)*; square toe *(of shoe)*; **d'une bonne carre** broad-shouldered *(man)*

car•ré -rée [kare] *adj* square; forthright ‖ *m* square; landing *(of staircase)*; patch *(in garden)*; (cards) four of a kind; (naut) wardroom ‖ *f* (slang) room, pad

car•reau [karo] *m (pl* **-reaux***)* tile, flagstone; windowpane; stall *(in market)*; pithead *(of mine)*; goose *(of tailor)*; quarrel *(square-headed arrow)*; (cards) diamond; (cards) diamonds; **à carreaux** checked *(design)*; **rester sur le carreaux** (coll) to be left out of the running; **se garder à carreau** (coll) to be on one's guard

carrefour [karfur] *m* crossroads; square *(in a city)*

carrelage [karlaʒ] *m* tiling

carreler [karle] §34 *tr* to tile

carrément [karemɑ̃] *adv* squarely; frankly

carrer [kare] *tr* to square ‖ *ref* (coll) to plunk oneself down; (coll) to strut

carrier [karje] *m* quarryman

carrière [karjɛr] *f* career; course *(e.g., of the sun)*; quarry; **donner carrière à** to give free rein to

carriole [karjɔl] *f* light cart, trap; (coll) jalopy

carrossable [karɔsabl] *adj* passable

carrosse [karɔs] *m* carriage, coach

carrosserie [karɔsri] *f* (aut) body

carrossier [karɔsje] *m* coachmaker

carrousel [karuzɛl] *m* carrousel; parade ground; tiltyard

carrure [karyr] *f* width *(of shoulders, garment, etc.)*; build; **d'une belle carrure** broad-shouldered *(man)*

cartable [kartabl] *m* briefcase

cartayer [karteje] §49 *intr* to avoid the ruts

carte [kart] *f* card; map, chart; bill (*to pay*); bill of fare, menu; **carte avec courbes de niveau** contour map; **carte bancaire** debit card; **carte d'abonnement** commutation ticket; season ticket; **carte de bits** (comp) bitmap; **carte de crédit** credit card; **carte d'embarquement** boarding pass; **carte de lecteur** *or* **bibliothèque** library card; **carte de Noël** Christmas card; **carte d'entrée** pass, ticket of admission; **carte de priorité** courtesy card; **carte des vins** wine list; **carte de téléphone** phone card; **carte d'identité** identification card; **carte grise** automobile registration; **carte infographique** computer map; **carte intelligente** (com) smart card; **carte mère** (comp) image map; **carte perforée** punch card; **carte postale** post card; **carte routière** road map; **cartes truquées** marked cards, stacked deck; **carte verte** (govt) green card; **faire une carte de France** (slang) to have a wet dream; **manger à la carte** to eat a la carte; **tirer les cartes à qn** to tell s.o.'s fortunes with cards

cartel [kartɛl] *m* cartel; wall clock; challenge (*to a duel*)

carte-lettre [kartəlɛtr] *f* (*pl* **cartes-lettres**) gummed letter-envelope

carter [kartɛr] *m* housing; bicycle chain guard; (aut) crankcase

carte-retrait [kartərətrɛ] *f* (*pl* **cartes-retrait**) bank card

cartilage [kartilaʒ] *m* cartilage, gristle

cartographe [kartɔgraf] *m* cartographer

cartomancie [kartɔmɑ̃si] *f* fortune-telling with cards

carton [kartɔ̃] *m* pasteboard, cardboard; cardboard box, carton; carton (*of cigarettes*); cartoon (*preliminary sketch*); (typ) cancel; **carton à chapeau** hatbox; **carton à dessin** portfolio for drawings and plans; **carton ondulé** corrugated cardboard

carton-pâte [kartɔ̃pat] *m* papier-mâché

cartouche [kartuʃ] *m* (archit) cartouche, tablet; inset (*in a picture*) ‖ *f* cartridge; carton (*of cigarettes*); canister (*of gas mask*); refill (*of pen*); **cartouche à blanc** blank cartridge

cartouchière [kartuʃjɛr] *f* cartridge belt, cartridge case

carvi [karvi] *m* caraway

cas [kɑ] *m* case; **cas d'espèce** individual case; **cas limite** borderline case; **cas urgent** emergency; **en aucun cas** under no circumstances; **en cas de** in the event of, in a time of; **en cas d'imprévu** in case of emergency; **en cas que, au cas que, au cas où, dans le cas où** in the event that; **faire cas de** to esteem, to make much of; **le cas échéant** should the occasion arise, if necessary; **ne jamais faire aucun cas de** to never pay any attention to; **selon le cas** as the case may be

casa•nier [kazanje] -nière [njɛr] *adj* home-loving ‖ *mf* homebody

casaque [kazak] *f* jockey coat; blouse; **tourner casaque** to be a turncoat

cascade [kaskad] *f* cascade; jerk; spree; **faire une cascade** (mov) to do a stunt; **prendre à la cascade** to ad-lib

cascader [kaskade] *intr* to cascade; (slang) to lead a wild life

casca•deur [kaskadœr] -deuse [døz] *mf* (mov) double ‖ *m* stunt man ‖ *f* stunt girl

case [kɑz] *f* compartment; pigeonhole; square (*e.g., of checkerboard or ledger*); box (*to be filled out on a form*); hut, cabin; **case postale** post-office box; **cochez la case correspondante** check the appropriate box; **se retrouver à la case départ** (slang) to find oneself back on square one

caséine [kazein] *f* casein

caser [kaze] *tr* to put away (*e.g., in a drawer*); arrange (*e.g., a counter display in a store*); (coll) to place, find a job for ‖ *ref* (coll) to get settled

caserne [kazɛrn] *f* barracks; **caserne de pompiers** firehouse; **de caserne** off-color (*jokes*); regimented

caserner [kazɛrne] *tr & intr* to barrack

ca•sher -shère [kaʃɛr] *adj* kosher

cash-flow [kaʃflo] *m* cash flow

casier [kasje] *m* rack (*for papers, magazines, letters, bottles*); cabinet; locker; **casier à homards** lobster pot; **casier à tiroirs** music cabinet; **casier judiciaire** police record

casino [kazino] *m* casino

casque [kask] *m* helmet; earphones, headset; comb (*of rooster*); **casque à méche** nightcap; **casque à pointe** spiked helmet; **casque blindé** crash helmet; **les Casques bleus** the U.N. peace-keeping force

casquer [kaske] *intr* to fall into a trap; (slang) to shell out

casquette [kaskɛt] *f* cap

cas•sant [kasɑ̃] -sante [sɑ̃t] *adj* brittle; abrupt, curt

casse [kɑs] *m* (slang) burglarizing ‖ *f* breakage ‖ [kas], [kɑs] *f* ladle, scoop; crucible; (bot) cassia; (pharm) senna; (typ) case; (coll) scrap heap, junk

cas•sé -sée [kɑse] *adj* broken-down; shaky, weak (*voice*)

casse-cou [kɑsku] *m invar* (coll) daredevil; (coll) stunt man; (coll) danger spot ‖ *interj* look out!

casse-croûte [kɑskrut] *m invar* snack

casse-gueule [kɑsgœl] *adj invar* (slang) risky ‖ *m invar* (coll) risky business

casse-langue [kɑslɑg] *m invar* tongue twister

casse-noisettes [kɑsnwazɛt] *m invar* nutcracker

casse-noix [kɑsnwa], [kɑsnwa] *m invar* nutcracker

casse-pieds [kɑspje] *m invar* (coll) pain in the neck

casser [kɑse] *tr* to break; crack, shatter; (law) to break (*a will*); (mil) to break, bust; (coll) to split (*one's eardrums*); **casser sa pipe** (coll) to kick the bucket ‖ *ref* to break; (coll) to rack (*one's brains*); **se casser le nez** (coll) to fail

casserole [kɑsrɔl] *f* saucepan; (slang) jalopy; **casserole à double fond** double boiler; **passer à la casserole** (slang) to screw; bump off, kill

casse-tête [kɑstɛt] *m invar* truncheon; din; brain teaser, puzzler; **casse-tête chinois** jigsaw puzzle

cassette [kɑsɛt], [kɑsɛt] *f* strongbox, coffer; casket (*for jewels*); (phot, electron) cassette; **cassette magnétique** cassette

cassis [kɑsi], [kɑsis] *m* black currant; cassis (*liqueur*); gutter

cassolette [kɑsɔlɛt] *f* incense burner

cassonade [kɑsɔnad] *f* brown sugar

cassoulet [kɑsulɛ] *m* pork and beans

cassure [kɑsyr] *f* break; crease; rift

castagnettes [kɑstaɲɛt] *fpl* castanets

caste [kɑst] *f* caste; **hors caste** outcaste

castil•lan [kɑstijɑ̃] **-lane** [jan] *adj* Castilian ‖ *m* Castilian (*language*) ‖ (*cap*) *mf* Castilian (*person*)

Castille [kɑstij] *f* Castile; **la Castille** Castile

castor [kɑstɔr] *m* beaver

castrat [kɑstra] *m* castrato

castrer [kɑstre] *tr* to castrate

ca•suel -suelle [kɑzɥɛl] *adj* casual; (coll) brittle ‖ *m* perquisites

cataclysme [kataklism] *m* cataclysm

catacombes [katakɔ̃b] *fpl* catacombs

catafalque [katafalk] *m* catafalque

cataire [katɛr] *f* catnip

Catalogne [katalɔɲ] *f* Catalonia; **la Catalogne** Catalonia

catalogue [katalɔg] *m* catalogue

cataloguer [katalɔge] *tr* to catalogue

catalyseur [katalizœr] *m* catalyst

cataplasme [kataplasm] *m* poultice

catapulte [katapylt] *f* catapult

catapulter [katapylte] *tr* to catapult

cataracte [katarakt] *f* cataract

catarrhe [katar] *m* catarrh; bad cold

catastrophe [katastrɔf] *f* catastrophe

catch [katʃ] *m* wrestling, freestyle wrestling

catcheur [katʃœr] *m* wrestler

catéchiser [kateʃize] *tr* to catechize; reason with

catéchisme [kateʃism] *m* catechism

catégorie [kategɔri] *f* category

catégorique [kategɔrik] *adj* categorical

catgut [katgyt] *m* (surg) catgut

cathartique [katartik] *adj* cathartic

cathédrale [katedral] *f* cathedral

cathéter [katetɛr] *m* (med) catheter

cathode [katɔd] *f* cathode

catholicisme [katɔlisism] *m* Catholicism

catholicité [katɔlisite] *f* catholicity; Catholicism; Catholics

catholique [katɔlik] *adj* catholic; Catholic; orthodox; **pas très catholique** (coll) questionable ‖ *mf* Catholic

cati [kati] *m* glaze, gloss

catimini [katimini]—**en catimini** (coll) on the sly

catir [katir] *tr* to glaze

cauca•sien [kɔkɑzjɛ̃] **-sienne** [zjɛn] *adj* Caucasian ‖ (*cap*) *mf* Caucasian

caucasique [kɔkɑzik] *adj* Caucasian

cauchemar [koʃmar] *m* nightmare

cause [koz] *f* cause; (law) case; **à cause de** because of, on account of, for the sake of; **cause de décès** cause of death; **et pour cause** with good reason; **hors de cause** irrelevant, beside the point; **mettre q.ch. en cause** to question s.th.; **mettre qn en cause** to implicate s.o.

causer [koze] *tr* to cause ‖ *intr* to chat

causerie [kozri] *f* chat; informal lecture

causette [kozɛt] *f*—**faire la causette** (coll) to chat

cau•seur [kozœr] **-seuse** [zøz] *adj* talkative, chatty ‖ *mf* speaker, conversationalist ‖ *f* love seat

caustique [kostik] *adj* caustic

caute•leux [kotlø] **-leuse** [løz] *adj* crafty, wily; cunning (*mind*)

cautériser [koterize] *tr* to cauterize

caution [kosjɔ̃] *f* security, collateral; guarantor, bondsman; **mettre en liberté sous caution** to let out on bail; **se porter caution pour qn** to put up bail for s.o.; **sujet à caution** unreliable; **verser une caution** to make a deposit

cautionnement [kosjɔnmɑ̃] *m* surety bond, guaranty; bail; deposit

cautionner [kosjɔne] *tr* to bail out; guarantee

cavalcade [kavalkad] *f* cavalcade

cavalerie [kavalri] *f* cavalry

cava•lier [kavalje] **-lière** [ljɛr] *adj* cavalier; bridle (*path*) ‖ *mf* horseback rider; dance partner ‖ *m* cavalier, horseman; escort; (chess) knight; **faire cavalier seul** to go it alone ‖ *f* horsewoman

cave [kav] *adj* hollow (*cheeks*) ‖ *f* cellar; liquor cabinet; liquor store; night club; bank (*in game of chance*); stake (*in gambling*); **cave à vin** wine cellar

ca•veau [kavo] *m* (*pl* **-veaux**) small cellar; vault, crypt; rathskeller

caver [kave] *tr* to hollow out ‖ *intr* to ante ‖ *ref* to become hollow (*said of eyes*); wager

caverne [kavɛrn] *f* cave, cavern; (pathol) cavity (*e.g., in lung*)

caver•neux [kavɛrnø] **-neuse** [nøz] *adj* cavernous; hollow (*voice*)

caviar [kavjar] *m* caviar; **caviar rouge** salmon roe; **passer au caviar** to blue-pencil, censor

caviarder [kavjarde] *tr* to censor

cavité [kavite] *f* cavity, hollow

caw•cher -chère [kaʃɛr] *adj* kosher

Cayes [kaj] *fpl*—**Cayes de la Floride** Florida Keys

C.C.P. *abbr* (**Compte chèques postaux**) postal banking account

CD [sede] *m* (letterword) (**Compact Disc, disque compact**) CD (Compact Disk)

CD-ROM *or* **CD-Rom** [sederɔm] *m* (letter-word) CD-ROM

ce [sə] (or **cet** [sɛt] before vowel or mute **h**) **cette** [sɛt] *adj dem* (*pl* **ces** [se]) **§82A** ‖ **ce** *pron* **§82B, §85A4**

C.E.A. *abbr* (**Commissariat à l'Énergie atomique**) Atomic Energy Commission

céans [seɑ̃] *adv* herein

ceci [sesi] *pron dem indef* this, this thing, this matter

cécité [sesite] *f* blindness

céder [sede] **§10** *tr* to cede, transfer; yield, give up; **ne le céder à personne** to be second to none ‖ *intr* to yield, succumb, give way

cédérom [sederɔm] *m* CD-ROM

cédille [sedij] *f* cedilla

cédrat [sedra] *m* citron

cèdre [sɛdr] *m* cedar

cédule [sedyl] *f* rate, schedule; (law) notification

C.E.E. *abbr* (**Communauté économique européenne**) European Economic Community

cégétiste [seʒetist] *mf* unionist

ceindre [sɛ̃dr] **§50** *tr* to buckle on; gird; encircle; wreathe (*one's head*); **ceindre la couronne** to assume the crown ‖ *ref*—**se ceindre de** to gird on

ceinture [sɛ̃tyr] *f* belt; waist, waistline; sash, waistband; girdle; **ceinture de chasteté** chastity belt; **ceinture de sauvetage** life belt; **ceinture de sécurité** safety belt; **ceinture herniaire** truss; **se mettre la ceinture** or **se serrer la ceinture** to tighten one's belt

ceinturer [sɛ̃tyre] *tr* to girdle, belt; encircle, belt; (wrestling) to grip around the waist

cela [səla] *pron dem indef* that, that thing; that matter; **à cela près** with that one exception; **et avec cela?** what else?

célébrant [selebrɑ̃] *m* (eccl) celebrant

célébration [selebrasjɔ̃] *f* celebration

célèbre [selɛbr] *adj* famous

célébrer [selebre] **§10** *tr* to celebrate

célébrité [selebrite] *f* celebrity

celer [səle] **§2** *tr* to hide, conceal

céleri [selri], [sɛlri] *m* celery

céleste [selɛst] *adj* celestial

célibat [seliba] *m* celibacy

célibataire [selibatɛr] *adj* single ‖ *mf* celibate ‖ *m* bachelor ‖ *f* spinster

celle [sɛl] **§83**

celle-ci [sɛlsi] **§84**

celle-là [sɛlla] **§84**

cellier [selje] *m* wine cellar; fruit cellar

cellophane [selɔfan] *f* cellophane

cellulaire [selylɛr] *adj* cellular

cellule [selyl], [sɛlyl] *f* cell **cellule électrogène** *or* **solaire** fuel cell; **cellule germe** germ cell; **cellule photoélectrique** photoelectric cell; **cellule souche, cellule mère** stem cell

celluloïd [selylɔid] *m* celluloid

celte [sɛlt] *adj* Celtic ‖ (*cap*) *mf* Celt

celtique [sɛltik] *adj & m* Celtic

celui [səlɥi] **celle** [sɛl] (*pl* **ceux** [sø] **celles**) **§83**

celui-ci [səlɥisi] **celle-ci** [sɛlsi] (*pl* **ceux-ci** [søsi] **celles-ci**) **§84**

celui-là [səlɥila] **celle-là** [sɛlla] (*pl* **ceux-là** [søla] **celles-là**) **§84**

cémentation [semɑ̃tasjɔ̃] *f* casehardening

cendre [sɑ̃dr] *f* cinder; **cendres** ashes

cendrée [sɑ̃dre] *f* shot; buckshot; (sports) cinder track

cendrer [sɑ̃dre] *tr* to cinder

cendrier [sɑ̃drije] *m* ashtray

Cendrillon [sɑ̃drijɔ̃] *f*—**la Cendrillon** Cinderella

cène [sɛn] *f* (eccl) Holy Communion ‖ (*cap*) *f* (eccl) Last Supper

cens [sɑ̃s] *m* census; poll tax

cen·sé -sée [sɑ̃se] **§95** *adj* supposed to, e.g., **je ne suis pas censé le savoir I** am not supposed to know it; reputed to be, e.g., **il est censé juge infaillible** he is reputed to be an infallible judge

censément [sɑ̃semɑ̃] *adv* supposedly, apparently, allegedly

censeur [sɑ̃sœr] *m* censor; census taker; critic; auditor; proctor

censure [sɑ̃syr] *f* censure; censorship; (psychoanal) censor

censurer [sɑ̃syre] **§97** *tr* to censure; censor

cent [sɑ̃] **§94** *adj & pron* (*pl* **cents** in multiples when standing before modified noun, e.g., **trois cents œufs** three hundred eggs) one hundred, a hundred, hundred; **cent pour cent** one hundred percent; **cent un** [sɑ̃œ̃] one hundred and one, a hundred and one, hundred and one; **l'an deux cent quatre** the year two thousand four; **page deux cent** page two hundred ‖ *m* hundred, one hundred ‖ [sɛnt] *m* cent

centaine [sɑ̃tɛn] *f* hundred; **par centaines** by the hundreds; **une centaine de** about a hundred

centaure [sɑ̃tɔr] *m* centaur

centenaire [sɑ̃tnɛr] *adj* centenary ‖ *mf* centenarian ‖ *m* centennial

centen·nal -nale [sɑ̃tɛnnal] *adj* (*pl* **-naux** [no]) centennial

centième [sɑ̃tjɛm] **§94** *adj, pron* (*masc, fem*), & *m* hundredth ‖ *f* hundredth performance

centigrade [sɑ̃tigrad] *adj & m* centigrade

centime [sɑ̃tim] *m* centime

centimètre [sɑ̃timɛtr] *m* centimeter; tape measure

centrage [sɑ̃traʒ] *m* centering

cen·tral -trale [sɑ̃tral] *adj* (*pl* **-traux** [tro]) central; main (*office*) ‖ *m* (telp) central ‖ *f* powerhouse; labor union; **centrale atomique** or **nucléaire** atomic generator

centralisation [sɑ̃tralizasjɔ̃] *f* centralization

centraliser [sɑ̃tralize] *tr & ref* to centralize

centre [sɑ̃tr] *m* center; **centre commercial** shopping district; **centre commercial de quartier** convenience store; **centre de dépression** storm center; **centre de (la) ville** center city; **centre de triage** (rr) switchyard;

centre d'études college; **centre de villégia-ture** resort; **centre social des étudiants** student center, student union; **centre spatial** space center

centrer [sãtre] *tr* to center

centrifuge [sãtrifyʒ] *adj* centrifugal

centuple [sãtypl] *adj & m* hundredfold; **au centuple** hundredfold

cep [sɛp] *m* vine stock

cépage [sepaʒ] *m* (bot) vine

cèpe [sɛp] *f* cepe mushroom

cependant [səpãdã] *adv* meanwhile; however, but, still; **cependant que** while, whereas; **et cependant** and yet

céramique [seramik] *adj* ceramic ‖ *f* (art of) ceramics; ceramic piece; **céramiques** ceramics (*objects*)

cerbère [sɛrbɛr] *m* (coll) watchdog ‖ (*cap*) *m* Cerberus

cer•ceau [sɛrso] *m* (*pl* **-ceaux**) hoop; **cerceaux** pinfeathers

cercle [sɛrkl] *m* circle; circle, club, society; clubhouse; hoop; **en cercle** in the cask

cercler [sɛrkle] *tr* to ring, encircle; to hoop

cercueil [sɛrkœj] *m* coffin

céréale [sereal] *adj & f* cereal

céré•bral -brale [serebral] *adj* (*pl* **-braux** [bro]) cerebral

cérémo•nial -niale [seremɔnjal] *adj & m* ceremonial

cérémonie [seremɔni] *f* ceremony; **faire des cérémonies** to stand on ceremony

cérémo•niel -nielle [seremɔnjɛl] *adj* ceremonial

cérémo•nieux [seremɔnjø] **-nieuse** [njøz] *adj* ceremonious, formal, stiff

cerf [sɛr] *m* deer, red deer; stag, buck

cerf-volant [sɛrvɔlã] *m* (*pl* **cerfs-volants**) kite

cerisaie [sərize] *f* cherry orchard

cerise [səriz] *f* cherry

cerisier [sərizje] *m* cherry tree

cerne [sɛrn] *m* annual ring (*of tree*); ring (*around moon, black eye, wound*)

cer•neau [sɛrno] *m* (*pl* **-neaux**) unripe nutmeat

cerner [sɛrne] *tr* to ring, encircle; hem in, besiege; shell (*nuts*)

cer•tain [sɛrtɛ̃] **-taine** [tɛn] §93 *adj* certain, sure ‖ (when standing before noun) *adj* certain, some; **certain auteur** a certain author; **depuis un certain temps** for some time; **d'un certain âge** middle-aged ‖ **certains** *pron indef pl* certain people

certainement [sɛrtɛnmã] *adv* certainly, surely

certes [sɛrt] *adv* indeed, certainly

certificat [sɛrtifika] *m* certificate; recommendation, attestation; **certificat d'actions** share *ou* stock certificate; **certificat d'aptitude au professorat de l'enseignement du second degré (C.A.P.E.S.)** secondary-school teachers certificate; **certificat d'aptitude pédagogique (C.A.P.)** teachers license; **certificat d'urbanisation** zoning permit

certifier [sɛrtifje] *tr* to certify

certitude [sɛrtityd] *f* certainty

cérumen [serymɛn] *m* earwax

céruse [seryz] *f* white lead

cer•veau [sɛrvo] *m* (*pl* **-veaux**) brain; mind; **cerveau brûlé** (coll) hothead; **laver le cerveau à** (coll) to brainwash

cerveauté [sɛrvote] *f* brain trust

cervelas [sɛrvəla] *m* salami

cervelet [sɛrvəlɛ] *m* cerebellum

cervelle [sɛrvɛl] *f* brains; **brûler la cervelle à qn** (coll) to shoot s.o.'s brains out; **sans cervelle** brainless

ces [se] §82A

césa•rien [sezarjɛ̃] **-rienne** [rjɛn] *adj* Caesarean ‖ *f* Caesarean section

cesse [sɛs] *f* cessation, ceasing; **sans cesse** unceasingly, incessantly

cesser [sɛse] §97 *tr* to stop, cease, leave off (*e.g., work*) ‖ *intr* to cease, stop; **cesser de + *inf*** to stop, cease, quit + *ger*

cessez-le-feu [sɛselføˈ] *m invar* cease-fire

cession [sɛsjɔ̃] *f* ceding, surrender; (law) transfer

c'est-à-dire [sɛtadir] *conj* that is, namely

césure [sezyr] *f* caesura

cet [sɛt] §82A

cette [sɛt] §82A

ceux [sø] §83

ceux-ci [søsi] §84

ceux-là [sølã] §84

Ceylan [sɛlã] *m* Ceylon (Sri Lanka)

C.G.T. [seʒete] *f* (letterword) (**confédération générale du travail**) national labor union ‖ *abbr* (**Cie Générale transatlantique**) French Line

cha•cal [ʃakal] *m* (*pl* **-cals**) jackal

cha•cun [ʃakœ̃] **-cune** [kyn] *pron indef* each, each one, every one; everybody, everyone; **chacun pour soi** every man for himself; **chacun son goût** every man to his own taste; **tout chacun** (coll) every Tom, Dick, and Harry

chadburn [tʃadbœrn] *m* (naut) public-address system

chadouf [ʃaduf] *m* well sweep

cha•grin [ʃagrɛ̃] **-grine** [grin] *adj* sad, downcast ‖ *m* grief, sorrow

chagriner [ʃagrine] *tr* to grieve, distress; make into shagreen leather ‖ *intr* to grieve, worry ‖ §97 *ref* to grieve

chah [ʃa] *m* shah

chahut [ʃay] *m* (coll) horseplay, row

chahuter [ʃayte] *tr* (coll) to upset; (coll) to boo, heckle ‖ *intr* (coll) to create a disturbance

chai [ʃɛ] *m* wine cellar

chaîne [ʃɛn] *f* chain; warp (*of fabric*); necklace; (archit) pier; (archit) tie; (naut) cable; (rad, telv) network; (telv) channel; **chaîne antidérapante** skid chain; **chaîne de fabrication, chaîne de montage** assembly line; **chaîne volontaire** franchise, franchising; **faire la chaîne** to form a bucket brigade; **travailler à la chaîne** to work on the assembly line

chaînon [ʃɛnɔ̃] *m* link; **chaînon manquant** (gen) missing link

chair [ʃɛr] f flesh; pulp (*of fruits*); meat (*of animals*); **avoir la chair de poule** to have goose pimples; **chair à canon** cannon fodder; **chair de sa chair** one's flesh and blood; **chairs** (painting, sculpture) nude parts; **en chair et en os** in the flesh; **ni chair ni poisson** neither fish nor fowl

chaire [ʃɛr] f pulpit; lectern; chair (*held by university professor*)

chaise [ʃɛz] f chair; bowline knot; (mach) bracket; **chaise à bascule** rocking chair; **chaise à fond de paille** rush-bottomed chair; **chaise à porteurs** sedan chair; **chaise berceuse** rocking chair; **chaise brisée** folding chair; **chaise cannée** cane chair; **chaise d'enfant** high chair; **chaise électrique** electric chair; **chaise percée** commode, toilet; **chaise pivotante** swivel chair; **chaise pliante** folding chair; **chaise roulante** wheelchair; **faire de la chaise longue** to relax in a deck chair; put one's feet up

cha‧land [ʃalɑ̃] **-lande** [lɑ̃d] mf customer ‖ m barge; **chaland de débarquement** (mil) landing craft

châle [ʃal] m shawl

chalet [ʃalɛ] m chalet, cottage, summer home; **chalet de nécessité** public rest room

chaleur [ʃalœr] f heat; warmth; **les grandes chaleurs de l'été** the hot weather of summer

chaleu‧reux [ʃalœrø] **-reuse** [røz] adj warm, heated

châlit [ʃali] m bedstead

chaloupe [ʃalup] f launch

chalu‧meau [ʃalymo] m (pl **-meaux**) reed; blowtorch; (mus) pipe; **chalumeau oxhydrique, chalumeau oxyacétylénique** acetylene torch

chalut [ʃaly] m trawl

chalutier [ʃalytje] m trawler

chamade [ʃamad] f—**battre la chamade** to beat wildly (*said of the heart*)

chamailler [ʃamaje] ref to squabble

chamarrer [ʃamare] tr to decorate, ornament; bedizen, bedeck; (slang) to cover (*s.o.*) with ridicule

chambarder [ʃɑ̃barde] tr (slang) to upset, turn upside down

chambellan [ʃɑ̃bɛllɑ̃] m chamberlain

chambouler [ʃɑ̃bule] tr (slang) to upset, turn topsy-turvy

chambranle [ʃɑ̃brɑ̃l] m frame (*of a door or window*); mantelpiece

chambre [ʃɑ̃br] f chamber; room; **chambre à air** inner tube; **chambre à coucher** bedroom; **chambre d'ami** guest room; **chambre de compensation** clearing house; **chambre d'hôtel** hotel room; **chambre noire** darkroom; **chambre sourde** soundproof(ed) room

chambrée [ʃɑ̃bre] f dormitory, barracks; bunkmates

chambrer [ʃɑ̃bre] tr to keep under lock and key; keep (*wine*) at room temperature

cha‧meau [ʃamo] **-melle** [mɛl] mf (pl **-meaux** camel ‖ m (slang) bitch (*person*)

chamois [ʃamwa] adj & m chamois

champ [ʃɑ̃] m field; **aux champs** salute (*played on trumpet or drum*); **champ clos** lists, dueling field; **champ de courses** race track; **champ de foire** fairground; **champ de repos** cemetery; **champ de tir** firing range; **champ libre** clear field; **champs Élysées** Elysian Fields; **Champs Elysées** Champs Elysées (*street*); **en champ clos** behind closed doors

champagne [ʃɑ̃paɲ] m champagne; **champagne brut** extra dry champagne; **champagne d'origine** vintage champagne ‖ (cap) f Champagne; **la Champagne** Champagne

champe‧nois [ʃɑ̃pənwa] **-noise** [nwaz] adj Champagne ‖ m Champagne dialect ‖ (cap) mf inhabitant of Champagne

champêtre [ʃɑ̃pɛtr] adj rustic, rural

champignon [ʃɑ̃piɲɔ̃] m mushroom; fungus; (slang) accelerator pedal; **champignon de couche** cultivated mushroom; **champignon vénéneux** toadstool

champignonner [ʃɑ̃piɲɔne] intr to mushroom

cham‧pion [ʃɑ̃pjɔ̃] **-pionne** [pjɔn] mf champion; best seller ‖ f championess

championnat [ʃɑ̃pjɔna] m championship

champlever [ʃɑ̃lve] §2 tr to chase out, gouge out

chan‧çard [ʃɑ̃sar] **-çarde** [sard] adj (slang) in luck ‖ mf (slang) lucky person

chance [ʃɑ̃s] f luck; good luck; **avoir de la chance** to be lucky; **bonne chance!** good luck! **chance du premier coup** beginner's luck; **chance moyenne** off chance; **chances** chances, risks, probability, possibility

chance‧lant [ʃɑ̃slɑ̃] **-lante** [lɑ̃t] adj shaky, unsteady, tottering; delicate (*health, constitution*)

chanceler [ʃɑ̃sle] §34 intr to stagger, totter, teeter; waver

chancelier [ʃɑ̃səlje] m chancellor

chancellerie [ʃɑ̃sɛlri] f chancellery

chan‧ceux [ʃɑ̃sø] **-ceuse** [søz] adj lucky; risky

chanci [ʃɑ̃si] m manure pile for mushroom growing

chancir [ʃɑ̃sir] intr to grow moldy

chancre [ʃɑ̃kr] m chancre; ulcer, canker

chandail [ʃɑ̃daj] m sweater; **chandail à col roulé** turtleneck sweater

chandeleur [ʃɑ̃dlœr] f—**la chandeleur** Candlemas

chandelier [ʃɑ̃dəlje] m candlestick; chandler

chandelle [ʃɑ̃dɛl] f tallow candle; prop, stay (*used in construction*); **chandelle de glace** icicle; **en chandelle** vertically; **voir trente-six chandelles** to see stars (*on account of a blow*)

chanfrein [ʃɑ̃frɛ̃] m forehead (*of a horse*); chamfer, beveled edge

chanfreiner [ʃɑ̃frɛne] tr to chamfer, bevel

change [ʃɑ̃ʒ] m exchange; rate of exchange; **de change** in reserve, extra; **donner le change à** to throw off the trail; **prendre le change** to let one self be duped; **rendre le change à qn** to give s.o. a taste of his own medicine

changeable [ʃãʒabl] *adj* changeable

chan·geant [ʃãʒã] **-geante** [ʒãt] *adj* changeable, changing, fickle; iridescent

changement [ʃãʒmã] *m* change; shift, shifting; **changement de propriétaire** under new ownership; **changement de vitesse** gearshift

changer [ʃãʒe] §38 *tr* to change; **changer contre** to exchange for ‖ *intr* to change; **changer d'avis** to change one's mind; **changer de place** to change one's seat; **changer de ton** (coll) to change one's tune; **changer de visage** to blush; change color ‖ *ref* to change, change clothes

chanoine [ʃanwan] *m* (eccl) canon

chanson [ʃãsɔ̃] *f* song; **chanson bachique** drinking song; **chanson de geste** medieval epic; **chanson de Noël** Christmas carol; **chanson du terroir** folk song; **chanson sentimentale** torch song

chansonner [ʃãsɔne] *tr* to lampoon in a satirical song

chansonneur [ʃãsɔnœr] *m* lampooner (*who writes satirical songs*)

chanson·nier [ʃãsɔnje] **-nière** [njɛr] *mf* songwriter ‖ *m* chansonnier; song book

chant [ʃã] *m* singing; song, chant; canto; crowing (*of rooster*); side (*e.g., of a brick*); **chant du cygne** swan song; **chant de Noël** Christmas carol; **chants** poetry; **de chant** on end, edgewise

chantage [ʃãtaʒ] *m* blackmail

chan·tant [ʃãtã] **-tante** [tãt] *adj* singable, melodious; singsong (*accent*); musical (*evening*)

chan·teau [ʃãto] *m* (*pl* **-teaux**) chunk (*of bread*); remnant

chantepleure [ʃãplœr] *f* wine funnel; tap (*of cask*); sprinkler; weep hole

chanter [ʃãte] *tr* to sing ‖ *intr* to sing; crow (*as a rooster*); to pay blackmail; **chanter faux** to sing out of tune; **chanter juste** to sing in tune; **faire chanter** to blackmail

chanterelle [ʃãtrɛl] *f* first string (*of violin*); decoy bird; mushroom; **appuyer sur la chanterelle** (coll) to rub it in

chan·teur [ʃãtœr] **-teuse** [tøz] *adj* singing; song (*bird*) ‖ *mf* singer; **chanteur de charme** crooner; **chanteur de rythme** jazz singer

chantier [ʃãtje] *m* shipyard; stocks, slip; workshop, yard; gantry, stand (*for barrels*); (public sign) men at work; **chantier de construction** building site; **chantier de démolition** junkyard, scrap heap; **mettre en** or **sur le chantier** to start work on

chantilly [ʃãtiji] *m* whipped cream

chantonner [ʃãtɔne] *tr & intr* to hum

chantoung [ʃãtuŋ] *m* shantung

chantourner [ʃãturne] *tr* to jigsaw

chantre [ʃãtr] *m* cantor, chanter; precentor; songster; bard, poet

chanvre [ʃãvr] *m* hemp; **en chanvre** hempen; flaxen (*color*)

chan·vrier [ʃãvrije] **-vrière** [vrijɛr] *adj* hemp (*industry*) ‖ *mf* dealer in hemp; hemp dresser

chaos [kao] *m* chaos; (fig) chaos, three-ring circus; **dans le chaos** in a state of chaos

chaotique [kaɔtik] *adj* chaotic

chaparder [ʃaparde] *tr* (coll) to pilfer, filch; gyp

chape [ʃap] *f* cover, covering; tread (*of tire*); coping (*of bridge*); frame, shell (*of pulley block*); (eccl) cope; **à chape usée** treadless

cha·peau [ʃapo] *m* (*pl* **-peaux**) hat; head (*of mushroom*); lead (*of magazine or newspaper article*); cap (*of fountain pen; of valve*); cowl (*of chimney*); **chapeau à cornes** cocked hat; **chapeau bas** hat in hand; **chapeau bas!** hats off!; **chapeau chinois** Chinese bells; **chapeau de cotillon** little hat for New Year's Eve; **chapeau de paille** straw hat; **chapeau de roue** hubcap; **chapeau haut de forme** top hat; **chapeau melon** derby; **chapeau mou** fedora

chapeau-cloche [ʃapoklɔʃ] *m* (*pl* **chapeaux-cloches** cloche (hat)

chapeauter [ʃapote] *tr* (coll) to put a hat on (*e.g., a child*)

chapelain [ʃaplɛ̃] *m* chaplain (*of a private chapel*)

chapeler [ʃaple] §34 *tr* to scrape the crust off of (*bread*)

chapelet [ʃaplɛ] *m* chaplet, rosary; string (*of onions; of islands; of insults*); chain (*of events; of mountains*); series (*e.g., of attacks*); (mil) stick (*of bombs*); **chapelet hydraulique** bucket conveyor; **défiler son chapelet** (coll) to speak one's mind; **dire son chapelet** to tell one's beads; **en chapelet** (elec) in series

chape·lier [ʃapəlje] **-lière** [ljɛr] *mf* hatter ‖ *f* Saratoga trunk

chapelle [ʃapɛl] *f* chapel; clique, coterie; **chapelle ardente** mortuary chamber lighted by candles; hearse

chapellerie [ʃapɛlri] *f* hatmaking; millinery; hat shop; millinery shop

chapelure [ʃaplyr] *f* bread crumbs

chaperon [ʃaprɔ̃] *m* chaperon; hood; cape with a hood; coping (*of wall*); **le Petit Chaperon rouge** Little Red Ridinghood

chaperonner [ʃaprɔne] *tr* to chaperon

chapi·teau [ʃapito] *m* (*pl* **-teaux**) capital (*of column*); circus tent

chapitre [ʃapitr] *m* chapter; **commencer un nouveau chapitre** to turn over a new leaf

chapitrer [ʃapitre] *tr* to reprimand, admonish, lecture; divide into chapters

chapon [ʃapɔ̃] *m* capon; (culin) crust rubbed with garlic

chaque [ʃak] *adj indef* each, every ‖ *pron indef* (coll) each, each one

char [ʃar] *m* chariot; float (*in parade*); (mil) tank; **char d'assaut** or **char de combat** (mil) tank; **char funèbre** hearse

charabia [ʃarabja] *m* gibberish, mumbo jumbo

charançon [ʃarɑ̃sɔ̃] *m* weevil

charbon [ʃarbɔ̃] *m* coal; soft coal; charcoal; carbon (*of an electric cell or arc*); cinder (*in the eye*); **charbon ardent** live coal; **charbon de bois** charcoal; **charbon de terre** coal; **être sur les charbons ardents** to be on pins and needles

charbonnage [ʃarbɔnaʒ] *m* coal mining; coal mine

charbonner [ʃarbɔne] *tr* to char; draw (*a picture*) with charcoal ‖ *intr* & *ref* to char, carbonize

charbon·neux [ʃarbɔnø] **-neuse** [nøz] *adj* sooty; anthrax-carrying

charbon·nier [ʃarbɔnje] **-nière** [njɛr] *adj* coal (*e.g., industry*) ‖ *mf* coal dealer ‖ *m* charcoal burner; coaler ‖ *f* coal scuttle; charcoal kiln; (orn) coal titmouse

charcuter [ʃarkyte] *tr* to butcher, mangle

charcuterie [ʃarkytri] *f* delicatessen; pork butcher shop

charcu·tier [ʃarkytje] **-tière** [tjɛr] *mf* pork butcher; (coll) sawbones

chardon [ʃardɔ̃] *m* thistle

chardonneret [ʃardɔnrɛ] *m* (orn) goldfinch

charge [ʃarʒ] *f* charge; load, burden; caricature; public office; **à charge de** on condition of, with the proviso of; **à charge de revanche** on condition of getting the same thing in return; **charges de famille** dependents; **charge utile** payload; **être à charge à** to be dependent upon; **être à la charge de** to be supported by; **faire la charge de** to do a takeoff of

char·gé -gée [ʃarʒe] §93 *adj* loaded; full; overcast (*sky*); registered (*letter*) ‖ *m* assistant, deputy, envoy; **chargé de cours** assistant professor

chargement [ʃarʒəmɑ̃] *m* charging; loading; cargo

charger [ʃarʒe] §38, §97, §99 *tr* to charge; drive, take (*s.o. in one's car*); (comp) to boot (up), load ‖ *intr* (mil) to charge; (naut) to load ‖ *ref* to be loaded; **se charger de** to take charge of; take up (*a question*)

chargeur [ʃarʒœr] *m* loader; stoker; shipper; clip (*of gun*); (elec) charger

chariot [ʃarjo] *m* wagon, cart; typewriter carriage; **chariot d'enfant** walker; **chariot élévateur** fork-lift truck; **Grand Chariot, Chariot de David** Big Dipper; **Petit Chariot** Little Dipper

charismatique [sarismatik] *adj* charismatic

charitable [ʃaritabl] *adj* charitable

charité [ʃarite] *f* charity; **faire la charité** to give alms; **faites la charité de, ayez la charité de** have the goodness to; **par charité** for charity's sake

charlatan [ʃarlatɑ̃] *m* charlatan

charlemagne [ʃarləmaɲ] *m* (cards) king of hearts; **faire charlemagne** to quit while winning

char·mant [ʃarmɑ̃] **-mante** [mɑ̃t] *adj* charming

charme [ʃarm] *m* charm; (*Carpinus betulus*) hornbeam; **se porter comme un charme** to be fit as a fiddle

charmer [ʃarme] *tr* to charm

char·meur [ʃarmœr] **-meuse** [møz] *adj* charming ‖ *mf* charmer

charmille [ʃarmij] *f* bower, arbor

char·nel -nelle [ʃarnɛl] *adj* carnal

charnière [ʃarnjɛr] *f* hinge

char·nu -nue [ʃarny] *adj* fleshy; plump; pulpy

charogne [ʃarɔɲ] *f* carrion

charpentage [ʃarpɑ̃taʒ] *m* carpentry

charpente [ʃarpɑ̃t] *f* framework; scaffolding; frame, build (*of body*)

charpenter [ʃarpɑ̃te] *tr* to square (*timber*); outline, map out, plan (*a novel, speech, etc.*); **être solidement charpenté** to be well built or well constructed ‖ *intr* to carpenter

charpenterie [ʃarpɑ̃tri] *f* carpentry; structure (*of building*)

charpentier [ʃarpɑ̃tje] *m* carpenter

charpie [ʃarpi] *f* lint; **en charpie** in shreds

charrée [ʃare] *f* lye

charre·tier [ʃartje] **-tière** [tjɛr] *mf* teamster; **jurer comme un charretier** to swear like a trooper

charrette [ʃarɛt] *f* cart

charriage [ʃarjaʒ] *m* cartage; drifting (*of ice*); (slang) exaggeration

charrier [ʃarje] *tr* to cart, transport; carry away (*sand, as the river does*); (slang) to poke fun at ‖ *intr* to be full of ice (*said of river*); (slang) to exaggerate

charroi [ʃarwɑ], [ʃarwa] *m* cartage

charron [ʃarɔ̃], [ʃarɔ̃] *m* wheelwright, cartwright

charroyer [ʃarwaje] §47 *tr* to cart

charrue [ʃary] *f* plow; **mettre la charrue devant les bœufs** to put the cart before the horse

charte [ʃart] *f* charter; title deed; fundamental principle

chas [ʃɑ] *m* eye (*of needle*)

chasse [ʃas] *f* hunt, hunting; hunting song; chase; bag (*game caught*); **aller à la chasse** to go hunting; **chasse à courre** riding to the hounds; **chasse aux appartements** house hunting; **chasse aux fauves** big-game hunting; **chasse aux sorcières** witch hunt; **chasse aux trésor** treasure hunt; **chasse d'eau** flush; **chasse gardée** game preserve; **chasse réservée** (public sign) no shooting; **tirer la chasse** to pull the toilet chain

châsse [ʃɑs] *f* reliquary; frame (*e.g., for eyeglasses*) ‖ **châsses** *mpl* (slang) blinkers, eyes

chasse-ballon [ʃasbalɔ̃] *m invar* dodge ball

chasse-bestiaux [ʃasbɛstjo] *m invar* cowcatcher

chasse-clou [ʃasklu] *m* (*pl* **-clous**) punch, nail set; countersink

chassé-croisé [ʃasekrwaze] *m* (*pl* **chassés-croisées**) futile efforts; Double-Crostic (trademark)

chasselas [ʃasla] *m* white table grape

chasse-mouches [ʃasmuʃ] *m invar* fly swatter; fly net

chasse-neige [ʃasnɛʒ] *m invar* snowplow; snowblower

chasse-pierres [ʃaspjɛr] *m invar* (rr) cowcatcher

chasser [ʃase] *tr* to hunt; chase; chase away, put to flight; drive (*e.g., a herd of cattle*); (coll) to fire (*e.g., a servant*) ‖ *intr* to hunt; skid; come, e.g., **le vent chasse du nord** the wind is coming from the north; **chasser de race** (coll) to be a chip off the old block

chasseresse [ʃasrɛs] *f* huntress

chas•seur [ʃasœr] **-seuse** [søz] *mf* hunter; bellhop ‖ *m* chasseur; fighter pilot; **chasseur à réaction** jet fighter; **chasseur d'assaut** fighter plane; **chasseur d'autographes** autograph hunter; **chasseur de chars** antitank tank; **chasseur de sous-marins** submarine chaser; **chasseur d'images** camera bug

chasseur-bombardier [ʃasœrbɔ̃bardje] *m* fighter-bomber

chassie [ʃasi] *f* gum (*on eyelids*)

chas•sieux [ʃasjø] **-seuse** [søz] *adj* gummy (*eyelids*)

châssis [ʃasi] *m* chassis; window frame; chase (*for printing*); **châssis à demeure** or **dormant** sealed window frame; **châssis couche** (hort) hotbed; **châssis mobile** movable sash

châssis-presse [ʃasiprɛs] *m* (*pl* **-presses**) printing frame

chaste [ʃast] *adj* chaste

chasteté [ʃastəte] *f* chastity

chat [ʃa] **chatte** [ʃat] *mf* cat ‖ *m* tomcat; **à bon chat bon rat** tit for tat; **acheter chat en poche** (coll) to buy a pig in a poke; **appeler un chat un chat** (coll) to call a spade a spade; **chat à neuf queues** cato'-nine-tails; **chat dans la gorge** (coll) frog in the throat; **chat de gouttière** alley cat; **chat de goutfourré** (coll) judge; **chat sauvage** wildcat; **d'autres chats à fouetter** (coll) other fish to fry; **il ne faut pas réveiller le chat qui dort** let sleeping dogs lie; **le Chat botté** Puss in Boots; **mon petit chat!** darling!; **pas un chat** (coll) not a soul ‖ *f* see **chatte** ‖

chat [tʃat] *m* (comp) chat room

châtaigne [ʃatɛɲ] *f* chestnut

châtaignier [ʃatɛɲe] *m* chestnut tree

chataire [ʃatɛr] *f* catnip

châ•teau [ʃato] *m* (*pl* **-teaux**) chateau; palace; estate, manor; **château d'eau** water tower; **château de cartes** house of cards; **château fort** castle, fort, citadel; **château en Espagne** castles in the air; **mener une vie de château** to live like a prince

châteaubriand or **châteaubriant** [ʃatobriɑ̃] *m* filet mignon, fillet, tenderloin

châte•lain [ʃatlɛ̃] **-laine** [lɛn] *mf* proprietor of a country estate ‖ *f* wife of the lord of the manor; bracelet

châtelet [ʃatlɛ] *m* small chateau

chat-huant [ʃayɑ̃] *m* (*pl* **chats-huants** [ʃayɑ̃]) screech owl

châtier [ʃatje] *tr* to chasten, chastise; correct; purify (*style*)

chatière [ʃatjɛr] *f* ventilation hole; cathole

châtiment [ʃatimɑ̃] *m* punishment; **châtiment corporel** corporal punishment

chatoiement [ʃatwamɑ̃] *m* glisten, sparkle; sheen, shimmer; play of colors

chaton [ʃatɔ̃] *m* kitten; setting (*of ring*); (bot) catkin

chatonner [ʃatɔne] *tr* to set (*a gem*) ‖ *intr* to have kittens

chatouillement [ʃatujmɑ̃] *m* tickle; tickling sensation

chatouiller [ʃatuje] *tr* to tickle; (fig) to excite, arouse ‖ *intr* to tickle

chatouil•leux [ʃatujø] **-leuse** [jøz] *adj* ticklish; touchy

chatoyer [ʃatwaje] §47 *intr* to glisten, sparkle; shimmer

chat-pard [ʃapar] *m* (*pl* **chats-pards**) ocelot

châtrer [ʃatre] *tr* to castrate

chatte [ʃat] *adj fem* kittenish ‖ *f* cat, female cat

chatterie [ʃatri] *f* cajoling; sweets

chatterton [ʃatɛrtɔn] *m* friction tape

chaud [ʃo] **chaude** [ʃod] *adj* hot, warm; lastminute (*news flash*); **il fait chaud** it is warm (weather); **pleurer à chaudes larmes** to cry one's eyes out ‖ *m* heat, warmth; **à chaud** emergency (*operation*); (med) in the acute stage; **avoir chaud** to be warm, be hot (*said of person*); **il a eu chaud** (coll) he had a narrow escape ‖ *adv*—**coûter chaud** (coll) to cost a pretty penny; **servir chaud** to serve (*s.th.*) piping hot

chaude-pisse [ʃodpis] *f* (vulg) clap, gonorrhea

chaudière [ʃodjɛr] *f* boiler

chaudron [ʃodrɔ̃] *m* cauldron

chaudron•nier [ʃodrɔnje] **-nière** [njɛr] *mf* coppersmith; boilermaker

chauffage [ʃofaʒ] *m* heating; stoking; (coll) coaching

chauffard [ʃofar] *m* road hog, Sunday driver

chauffe [ʃof] *f* stoking; furnace

chauffe-assiettes [ʃofasjɛt] *m invar* hot plate

chauffe-bain [ʃofbɛ̃] *m* (*pl* **-bains**) bathroom water heater

chauffe-eau [ʃofo] *m invar* water heater

chauffe-lit [ʃofli] *m* (*pl* **-lits**) bed warmer

chauffe-pieds [ʃofpje] *m invar* foot warmer

chauffe-plats [ʃofpla] *m invar* chafing dish

chauffer [ʃofe] *tr* to heat; warm up; limber up; (coll) to coach; (slang) to snitch, filch ‖ *intr* to heat up; get up steam; overheat; **ça va chauffer!** (coll) watch the fur fly! ‖ *ref* to warm oneself; heat up

chaufferette [ʃofrɛt] *f* foot warmer; space heater; car heater

chauffeur [ʃofœr] *m* driver; chauffeur; (rr) stoker, fireman

chauffeuse [ʃoføz] *f* fireside chair

chaume [ʃom] *m* stubble; thatch

chaumière [ʃomjɛr] *f* thatched cottage

chaussée [ʃose] *f* pavement, road; causeway

chausse-pied [ʃospje] m (pl **-pieds**) shoehorn

chausser [ʃose] tr to put on (*shoes, skis, glasses, tires, etc.*); shoe; fit ‖ intr to fit (*said of shoe*); **chausser de** to wear (*a certain size shoe*) ‖ ref to put one's shoes on

chausses [ʃos] fpl hose (*in medieval dress*); **aux chausses de** on the heels of; **c'est elle qui porte les chausses** (coll) she wears the pants

chausse-trape [ʃostrap] f (pl **-trapes**) trap; booby trap

chaussette [ʃosɛt] f sock

chausseur [ʃosœr] m shoe salesman

chausson [ʃosɔ̃] m pump, slipper, savate; **chausson aux pommes** apple turnover

chaussure [ʃosyr] f footwear, shoes; shoe; **chaussure de gym** gym shoe; **trouver chaussure à son pied** to find what one needs

chauve [ʃov] adj bald

chauve-souris [ʃovsuri] f (pl **chauves-souris**) (zool) bat

chau•vin [ʃovɛ̃] **-vine** [vin] adj chauvinistic ‖ mf chauvinist

chauvir [ʃovir] intr—**chauvir de l'oreille, chauvir des oreilles** to prick up the ears (*said of horse, mule, donkey*)

chaux [ʃo] f lime

chavirement [ʃavirmɑ̃] m capsizing, overturning

chavirer [ʃavire] tr & intr to tip over, capsize

cheeseburger [tʃizbœrgœr] or [tʃizburgœr] m cheeseburger

chef [ʃɛf] m head, chief, leader; boss; scoutmaster; **au premier chef** essentially; **chef de bande** ringleader, gang leader; **chef de cuisine** chef; **chef de file** leader, standard-bearer; **chef de gare** station-master; **chef de l'exécutif** chief executive; **chef de musique** bandmaster; **chef de rayon** floorwalker; **chef de tribu** chieftain; **chef d'orchestre** conductor; bandleader; **chef d'une section** (educ) chairman, chair, chairwoman; **de son propre chef** by one's own authority, on one's own ‖ f—**chef d'une section** (coll) chairwoman

chef-d'œuvre [ʃɛdœvr] m (pl **chefs-d'œuvre**) masterpiece

chef-lieu [ʃɛfljø] m (pl **chefs-lieux**) county seat, capital city

cheftaine [ʃɛftɛn] f Girl Scout unit leader

cheik [ʃɛk] m sheik

chelem [ʃlɛm] m slam (*at bridge*); **être chelem** (cards) to be shut out

chemin [ʃmɛ̃] m way; road; **chemin battu** beaten path; **chemin de la Croix** (eccl) Way of the Cross; **chemin de fer** railroad; **chemin de roulement** (aer) taxiway; **chemin des écoliers** (coll) long way around; **chemin de table** table runner; **chemin de traverse** side road; shortcut; **chemin de velours** primrose path; **n'y pas aller par quatre chemins** (coll) to come straight to the point

chemi•neau [ʃmino] m (pl **-neaux**) hobo, tramp; deadbeat

cheminée [ʃmine] f chimney, stack, smoke-stack; fireplace; (naut) funnel

cheminer [ʃmine] intr to trudge, tramp; make headway

cheminot [ʃmino] m railroader

chemise [ʃmiz] f shirt; dust jacket (*of book*); folder, file; jacket, shell, metal casing; **chemise classeur** folder; **chemise de femme** chemise; **chemise de mailles** coat of mail; **chemise de nuit** nightgown; **chemise polo** polo shirt

chemiser [ʃmize] tr (mach) to case, jacket

chemiserie [ʃmizri] f haberdashery

chemisette [ʃmizɛt] f short-sleeved shirt

chemi•sier [ʃmizje] **-sière** [zjɛr] mf haberdasher ‖ m shirtwaist

che•nal [ʃnal] m (pl **-naux** [no]) channel; mill-race

chenapan [ʃnapɑ̃] m rogue, scoundrel

chêne [ʃɛn] m oak

ché•neau [ʃeno] m (pl **-neaux**) rain spout

chêne-liège [ʃɛnljɛʒ] m (pl **chênes-lièges**) cork oak

chenet [ʃnɛ] m andiron

chènevis [ʃɛnvi] m hempseed, birdseed

chenil [ʃni] m kennel

chenille [ʃnij] f caterpillar; chenille; caterpillar tread

chenil•lé -lée [ʃnije] adj with a caterpillar tread

che•nu -nue [ʃny] adj hoary

cheptel [ʃɛptɛl], [ʃɛtɛl] m livestock; **cheptel mort** implements and buildings

chèque [ʃɛk] m check; **chèque certifié** certified check; **chèque de la caisse** cashier's check; **chèque de voyage** traveler's check; **chèque en blanc** blank check; **chèque en bois** bad check; **chèque prescrit** invalidated (*old*) check; **chèque sans provision** bad check

chéquier [ʃekje] m checkbook

cher chère [ʃɛr] adj expensive, dear ‖ (when standing before noun) adj dear, beloved ‖ f see **chère** ‖ **cher** adv dear(ly); **coûter cher** to cost a great deal

chercher [ʃɛrʃe] §96 tr to look for, search for, seek, hunt; try to get; **aller chercher** to go and get; **envoyer chercher** to send for ‖ intr to search; **chercher à** to try to, endeavor to ‖ intr to look for each other; feel one's way

cher•cheur [ʃɛrʃœr] **-cheuse** [ʃøz] adj inquiring (*mind*); homing (*device*) ‖ mf seeker; researcher, scholar, investigator; prospector (*for gold, uranium, etc.*); **chercheur sur le terrain** field worker

chère [ʃɛr] f fare, food and drink; **faire bonne chère** to live high

chèrement [ʃɛrmɑ̃] adv fondly, lovingly; dearly (*bought or won*)

ché•ri -rie [ʃeri] adj & mf darling; sweetheart; **mon chéri, ma chérie** sweetie

chérir [ʃerir] tr to cherish

cherry [ʃeri] m cherry cordial

cherté [ʃɛrte] f high price; **cherté de la vie** high cost of living

chérubin [ʃerybɛ̃] *m* cherub

ché•tif [ʃetif] **-tive** [tiv] *adj* puny, sickly; poor, wretched

che•val [ʃəval] *m* (*pl* **-vaux** [vol]) horse; metric or French horsepower (*735 watts*); **à cheval** on horseback; **à cheval sur** astride; insistent upon; **cheval à bascule** rocking horse; **cheval de bât** pack horse; **cheval de bataille** charger, warhorse; (fig) main issue (*in a political campaign*); **cheval de bois** or **cheval d'arçons** horse (*for vaulting*); **cheval de course** race horse; **cheval de race** thoroughbred; **cheval de retour** (coll) jailbird; **cheval de selle** saddle horse; **cheval de trait** draft horse; **cheval de Troie** Trojan horse; **cheval entier** stallion; **cheval vapeur** horsepower; **monter sur ses grands chevaux** (fig) to get up on one's high horse

chevalement [ʃəvalmɑ̃] *m* support, shoring; (min) headframe

chevaler [ʃvale] *tr* to shore up

chevaleresque [ʃvalrɛsk] *adj* knightly, chivalrous

chevalerie [ʃvalri] *f* chivalry

chevalet [ʃvalɛ] *m* easel; sawhorse; stand, frame; bridge (*of violin*)

chevalier [ʃvalje] *m* knight; (orn) sandpiper; **chevalier d'industrie** manipulator, swindler; **chevalier errant** knight-errant; **Chevaliers du taste-vin** wine-tasting club

chevalière [ʃvaljɛr] *f* signet ring

cheva•lin [ʃvalɛ̃] **-line** [lin] *adj* equine

cheval-vapeur [ʃvalvapœr] *m* (*pl* **chevaux-vapeur**) metric or French horsepower (*735 watts*)

chevauchée [ʃəvoʃe] *f* ride

chevaucher [ʃəvoʃe] *tr* to straddle ‖ *intr* to ride horseback; overlap

cheve•lu -lue [ʃəvly] *adj* hairy; long-haired

chevelure [ʃəvlyr] *f* hair, head of hair; tail (*of a comet*)

chevet [ʃəvɛ] *m* headboard; bolster; **de chevet** bedside (*lamp, table, book*)

che•veu [ʃəvø] *m* (*pl* **-veux**) hair; **avoir mal aux cheveux** (coll) to have a hangover; **cheveux** hair (*of the head*); hairs; **cheveux en brosse** crew cut; **couper les cheveux en quatre** (coll) to split hairs; **en cheveux** hatless; **faire dresser les cheveux** (coll) to make one's hair stand on end; **ne tenir qu'à un cheveu** (coll) to hang by a thread; **saisir l'occasion aux cheveux** (coll) to take time by the forelock; **se faire des cheveux** (coll) to worry oneself gray; **tiré par les cheveux** (coll) farfetched

chevillard [ʃəvijar] *m* wholesale cattle dealer or jobber

cheville [ʃəvij] *f* ankle; peg; pin; bolt; padding (*of verse*); **cheville ouvrière** (mach) kingbolt; (fig) mainspring (*of an enterprise*); **être en cheville avec** (coll) to be in cahoots with; **ne pas arriver à la cheville de qn** (coll) not to hold a candle to s.o.

chèvre [ʃɛvr] *f* goat; nanny goat

che•vreau [ʃəvro] *m* (*pl* **-vreaux**) kid

chèvrefeuille [ʃɛvrəfœj] *m* honeysuckle

chevrette [ʃəvrɛt] *f* kid; doe (*roe deer*); shrimp; tripod

chevreuil [ʃəvrœj] *m* roe deer; roebuck

chevron [ʃəvrɔ̃] *m* rafter; chevron, hash mark; **en chevron** in a herringbone pattern

chevron•né -née [ʃəvrɔne] *adj* wearing chevrons; experienced, oldest

chevronner [ʃəvrɔne] *tr* to put rafters on; give chevrons to

chevroter [ʃəvrɔte] *intr* to bleat; sing or speak in a quavering voice

chewing-gum [ʃwiŋgɔm], [tʃuwiŋgɔm] *m* chewing gum

chez [ʃe] *prep* at the house, home, office, etc., of, e.g., **chez mes amis** at my friends' house; e.g., **chez le boulanger** at the baker's; in the country of, among, e.g., **chez les Français** among the French; in the time of, e.g., **chez les anciens Grecs** in the time of the ancient Greeks; in the work of, e.g., **chez Homère** in Homer's works; with, e.g., **c'est chez lui une habitude** it's a habit with him

chez-soi [ʃeswa] *m invar* home

chialer [ʃjale] *intr* (slang) to cry

chiasse [ʃjas] *f* flyspecks; (metallurgy) dross; (coll) loose bowels

chic [ʃik] *adj invar* stylish, chic; **un chic type** (coll) a good egg ‖ *m* style; skill, knack; (coll) smartness, elegance; (slang) ovation; **bon chic, bon genre (B.C.B.G.)** preppie; **de chic** from memory ‖ *interj* (coll) fine!, grand!

chicane [ʃikan] *f* chicanery; shady lawsuit; baffle, baffle plate; **chercher chicane à** to engage in a petty quarrel with; **en chicane** staggered, zigzag; curved (*tube*)

chicaner [ʃikane] *tr* to pick a fight with; **chicaner q.ch. à qn** to quibble over s.th. with s.o. ‖ *intr* to quibble

chicanerie [ʃikanri] *f* chicanery

chiche [ʃiʃ] *adj* stringy; small, dwarf ‖ *interj* (coll) I dare you!

chichi [ʃiʃi] *m* fuss; **sans chichis** informally

chicon [ʃikɔ̃] *m* (coll) romaine

chicorée [ʃikɔre] *f* chicory; **chicorée frisée** endive

chicot [ʃiko] *m* stump (*of tree*); (coll) stump, stub (*of tooth*)

chien [ʃjɛ̃] **chienne** [ʃjɛn] *mf* dog ‖ *m* hammer (*of gun*); glamour; **à la chien** (coll) with bangs; **chien couchant** setter; (slang) apple polisher; **chien d'arrêt** pointer; **chien d'aveugle** Seeing Eye dog; **chien de** or **chienne de** (coll) dickens of a; **chien de garde** watchdog; **chien de traîneau** sled dog; **chien de mer** (ichth) seadog; **chien du jardinier** (coll) dog in the manger; **chien savant** performing dog; **chien** (coll) miserable (*weather, life, etc.*); **en chien de fusil** (coll) curled up (*e.g., to sleep*); **entre chien et loup** (coll) at dusk; **les chiens écrasés** (slang) the accident page (*of newspaper*); **petit chien** pup; **se regarder en chiens de faïence** (coll) to glare at one another ‖ *f* see **chienne**

chiendent [ʃjɛ̃dɑ̃] *m* couch grass; (coll) trouble

chienlit [ʃjɑ̃li] *mf* (vulg) person who soils his bed ‖ *m* carnival mask; masquerade, fantastic costume ‖ *f* (vulg) crap (*rowdyness, havoc*), e.g., **réforme, oui! chienlit, non!** reform, yes! crap, no!

chien-loup [ʃjɛ̃lu] *m* (*pl* **chiens-loups**) wolf-hound

chienne [ʃjɛn] *f* bitch

chienner [ʃjɛne] *intr* to whelp

chiennerie [ʃjɛnri] *f* stinginess, meanness

chier [ʃje] *tr* & *intr* (vulg) to crap, defecate; **tu me fais chier!** (vulg) you're a pain in the ass!

chiffe [ʃif] *f* rag; (coll) weakling

chiffon [ʃifɔ̃] *m* rag; scrap of paper; **chiffons** (coll) fashions

chiffonnade [ʃifɔnad] *f* salad greens

chiffonner [ʃifɔne] *tr* to rumple, crumple; make (*a dress*); (coll) to ruffle (*tempers*), bother ‖ *intr* to pick rags; make dresses

chiffon·nier [ʃifɔnje] **-nière** [njɛr] *mf* scavenger, ragpicker ‖ *m* chiffonier

chiffrage [ʃifraʒ] *m* coding, encoding; numbering, marking

chiffre [ʃifr] *m* figure, number; cipher, code; sum total; combination (*of lock*); monogram; **chiffre d'affaires** turnover; **chiffres romains** roman numerals

chiffrer [ʃifre] *tr* to number; monogram; figure the cost of; cipher, code; **chiffrer des messages** to encode ‖ *intr* to calculate; mount up; cipher, code ‖ *ref*—**se chiffrer par** to amount to

chignole [ʃiɲɔl] *f* breast drill, hand drill; (coll) jalopy

chignon [ʃiɲɔ̃] *m* chignon, bun, knot

chiite [ʃi·it] *adj* & *mf* Shiite

Chili [ʃili] *m*—**le Chili** Chile

chimère [ʃimɛr] *f* chimera; **se forger des chimères** to indulge in wishful thinking

chimie [ʃimi] *f* chemistry

chimiothérapie [ʃimjɔterapi] *f* chemotherapy

chimique [ʃimik] *adj* chemical

chimiste [ʃimist] *mf* chemist

chimpanzé [ʃɛ̃pɑ̃ze] *m* chimpanzee

Chine [ʃin] *f* China; **la Chine** China; **les deux Chine** the two Chinas

chi·né -née [ʃine] *adj* mottled, figured

chiner [ʃine] *tr* to mottle (*cloth*); (coll) to make fun of

chi·nois -noise [ʃinwa] [nwaz] *adj* Chinese ‖ *m* Chinese (*language*) ‖ (*cap*) *mf* Chinese (*person*)

chinoiserie [ʃinwazri] *f* Chinese curio; **chinoiseries administratives** (coll) red tape

chiot [ʃjo] *m* puppy

chiourme [ʃjurm] *f* chain gang

chip [ʃip] *m* (electron) chip

chiper [ʃipe] *tr* (slang) to swipe; gyp

chipie [ʃipi] *f* (coll) shrew

chipoter [ʃipɔte] *intr* to haggle; nibble, pick at one's food

chips [ʃips] *mpl* potato chips; French fries (Brit)

chique [ʃik] *f* chew, quid (*of tobacco*); (ent) chigger

chiqué [ʃike] *m* (slang) sham, bluff

chiquenaude [ʃiknod] *f* fillip, flick

chiquer [ʃike] *tr* to chew (*tobacco*) ‖ *intr* to chew tobacco

chiromancie [kirɔmɑ̃si] *f* palmistry

chiroman·cien [kirɔmɑ̃sjɛ̃] **-cienne** [sjɛn] *mf* palm reader

chiropracteur [kirɔpraktœr] *m* chiropractor

chiropraxie [kirɔpraksi] *f* chiropractic

chirurgi·cal -cale [ʃiryrʒikal] *adj* (*pl* **-caux** [ko]) surgical

chirurgie [ʃiryrʒi] *f* surgery; **chirurgie esthétique** cosmetic surgery; **chirurgie plastique** plastic surgery

chirur·gien [ʃiryrʒjɛ̃] **-gienne** [ʒjɛn] *mf* surgeon

chirurgien-dentiste [ʃiryrʒjɛ̃dɑ̃tist] *m* (*pl* **chirurgiens-dentistes**) dental surgeon

chiure [ʃiyr] *f* flyspeck

chlamydiose [klamidjoz] *f* chlamydia

chlore [klɔr] *m* chlorine

chlo·ré -rée [klɔre] *adj* chlorinated

chlorhydrique [klɔridrik] *adj* hydrochloric

chloroforme [klɔrɔfɔrm] *m* chloroform

chloroformer [klɔrɔfɔrme] *tr* to chloroform

chlorophylle [klɔrɔfil] *f* chlorophyll

chlorure [klɔryr] *m* chloride; **chlorure de soude** sodium chloride

choc [ʃɔk] *m* shock; clash; bump; clink (*of glasses*)

chocolat [ʃɔkɔla] *adj invar* & *m* chocolate

chocolaterie [ʃɔkɔlatri] *f* chocolate factory

chœur [kœr] *m* choir, chorus; choir loft

choir [ʃwar] (usually used only in *inf* and *pp* **chu;** sometimes used in *pres ind* **chois,** etc.; *pret* **chus,** etc; *fut* **choirai,** etc.) *intr* (*aux:* ÉTRE *or* AVOIR) to fall; **se laisser choir** to drop, flop

choi·si -sie [ʃwazi] *adj* choice, select; chosen; selected (*works*)

choisir [ʃwazir] §97 *tr* & *intr* to choose

choix [ʃwa] *m* choice; **au choix** at one's discretion; **de choix** choice

choléra [kɔlera] *m* cholera

cholérique [kɔlerik] *mf* cholera victim

cholestérol [kɔlɛsterɔl] *m* cholesterol

chômage [ʃomaʒ] *m* unemployment; **en chômage** unemployed

chô·mé -mée [ʃome] *adj* closed for business, off, e.g., **jour chômé** day off

chômer [ʃome] *tr* to take (*a day*) off; observe (*a holiday*) ‖ *intr* to take off (*from work*); be unemployed

chô·meur [ʃomœr] **-meuse** [møz] *mf* unemployed worker

chope [ʃɔp] *f* stein, beer mug

choper [ʃɔpe] *tr* (coll) to catch

chopine [ʃɔpin] *f* half-liter measure; (slang) bottle

chopper [ʃɔpe] *intr* to stumble; blunder

choquer [ʃɔke] *tr* to shock; bump; clink (*glasses*); (elec) to shock ‖ *ref* to collide; take offense

cho•ral -rale [kɔral] *adj* (*pl* **-raux** [ro]) choral ‖ *m* (*pl* **-rals**) chorale ‖ *f* choral society, glee club

chorégraphie [kɔregrafi] *f* choreography

choriste [kɔrist] *mf* chorister

chorus [kɔrys] *m*—**faire chorus** to repeat in unison; chime in; approve unanimously

chose [ʃoz] *adj invar* (coll) odd; **être tout chose** (coll) to feel funny ‖ *m* thingamajig; **Monsieur Chose** (coll) Mr. what's-his-name ‖ *f* thing; **chose saillante** standout ‖ *pron indef masc*—**autre chose** something else; **quelque chose** something

chou [ʃu] **choute** [ʃut] *mf*—**ma choute, mon chou** (coll) sweetheart ‖ *m* (*pl* **choux**) cabbage; **chou à la crème** cream puff; **chou de Bruxelles** Brussels sprouts; **de chou** (coll) of little value; **faire chou blanc** (coll) to draw a blank; **finir dans le chou** (coll) to come in last

choucas [ʃukɑ] *m* jackdaw

choucroute [ʃukrut] *f* sauerkraut; **choucroute garnie** sauerkraut with ham or sausage

chouette [ʃwɛt] *adj* (coll) swell; **chouette alors!** (coll) oh boy! ‖ *f* owl; (coll) radio; **chouette épervière** hawk owl

chou-fleur [ʃuflœr] *m* (*pl* **choux-fleurs**) cauliflower

chou-rave [ʃurav] *m* (*pl* **choux-raves**) kohlrabi

chow-chow [ʃuʃu] *m* (*pl* **-chows**) chow (*dog*)

choyer [ʃwaje] §47 *tr* to pamper, coddle; cherish (*a hope*); entertain (*an idea*)

chrestomatie [krɛstɔmati]. [krɛstɔmasi] *f* chrestomathy

chré•tien [kretjɛ̃] **-tienne** [tjɛn] *adj* & *mf* Christian

chrétiennement [kretjɛnmɑ̃] *adv* in the faith

chrétienté [kretjɛ̃te] *f* Christendom

christ [krist] *m* crucifix ‖ (*cap*) *m* Christ; **le Christ** Christ

christianiser [kristjanize] *tr* to Christianize

christianisme [kristjanism] *m* Christianity

chromatique [krɔmatik] *adj* chromatic

chrome [krom] *m* chrome, chromium

chromer [krome] *tr* to chrome

chromocodé [krɔmokɔde] *adj* (chem) color-coded

chromosome [krɔmozom] *m* chromosome

chronique [krɔnik] *adj* chronic ‖ *f* chronicle; column (*in newspaper*); **chronique financière** financial page; **chronique mondaine** society news; **chronique théâtrale** theater page

chroniqueur [krɔnikœr] *m* chronicler; columnist; **chroniqueur dramatique** drama critic

chrono [krɔno] *m*—**faire du 60 chrono** (coll) to do 60 by the clock

chronologie [krɔnɔlɔʒi] *f* chronology

chronologique [krɔnɔlɔʒik] *adj* chronological

chronomètre [krɔnɔmɛtr] *m* chronometer; stopwatch

chronométrer [krɔnɔmetre] §10 *tr* to clock, time

chronométreur [krɔnɔmetrœr] *m* timekeeper

chrysalide [krizalid] *f* chrysalis

chrysanthème [krizɑ̃tɛm] *m* chrysanthemum

chuchotement [ʃyʃɔtmɑ̃] *m* whisper, whispering

chuchoter [ʃyʃɔte] *tr* & *intr* to whisper

chuinter [ʃɥɛ̃te] *intr* to hoot (*said of owl*); make a swishing sound, hiss (*said of escaping gas*); pronounce [ʃ] instead of [s] and [ʒ] instead of [z]

chut [ʃyt] *interj* sh!

chute [ʃyt] *f* fall; downfall; drop (*in prices, voltage, etc.*); **chute d'eau** waterfall; **chute libre** (phys) free fall

chuter [ʃyte] *tr* to hush; hiss (*an actor*) ‖ *intr* (coll) to fall; (cards) to be down

Chypre [ʃipr] *f* Cyprus

ci [si] *pron indef*—**comme ci comme ça** so-so ‖ *adv*—**entre ci et là** between now and then

-ci [si] §82, §84

ci-après [siaprɛ] *adv* hereafter, below, further on

ci-bas [siba] *adv* below

cible [sibl] *f* target; (*pour le jeu de fléchettes*) dartboard

ciboule [sibul] *f* chive, scallion

ciboulette [sibulɛt] *f* chive, chives

cicatrice [sikatris] *f* scar

cicatriser [sikatrize] *tr* to heal; scar ‖ *ref* to heal

Cicéron [siserɔ̃] *m* Cicero

cicérone [siseron] *m* guide

ci-contre [sikɔ̃tr] *adv* opposite, on the opposite page; in the margin

ci-dessous [sidəsu] *adv* further on, below, hereunder

ci-dessus [sidəsy] *adv* above

ci-devant [sidəvɑ̃] *mf invar* (hist) aristocrat; (coll) back number ‖ *adv* previously, formerly

cidre [sidr] *m* cider

Cie *abbr* (**Compagnie**) Co.

ciel [sjɛl] *m* (*pl* **cieux** [sjø]) sky, heavens (*firmament*); heaven (*state of great happiness*) ‖ *m* (*pl* **ciels**) heaven (*abode of the blessed*); sky (*upper atmosphere, especially with reference to meteorological conditions; representation of sky in a painting*); canopy (*of a bed*) ‖ *m* (*pl* **cieux** or **ciels**) clime, sky

cierge [sjɛrʒ] *m* wax candle; cactus; **droit comme un cierge** straight as a ramrod; **en cierge** straight up

cigale [sigal] *f* cicada, grasshopper

cigare [sigar] *m* cigar

cigarette [sigarɛt] *f* cigarette

ci•gît [siʒi] see **gésir**

cigogne [sigɔɲ] *f* stork

ciguë [sigy] *f* hemlock (*herb and poison*)

ci-in•clus [siɛ̃kly] **-cluse** [klyz] *adj* enclosed ‖ **ci-inclus** *adv* enclosed

ci-joint [sijwɛ̃] **-jointe** [jwɛ̃t] *adj* enclosed ‖ **ci-joint** *adv* enclosed

cil [sil] *m* eyelash; **cils** eyelash (*fringe of hair*)

cilice [silis] *m* hair shirt

ciller [sije] *tr & intr* to blink

cime [sim] *f* summit, top

ciment [simɑ̃] *m* cement; **ciment armé** reinforced concrete

cimentation [simɑ̃tasjɔ̃] *f* cementing

cimenter [simɑ̃te] *tr* to cement

cimeterre [simtɛr] *m* scimitar

cimetière [simtjɛr] *m* cemetery

cinéaste [sineast] *mf* film producer; movie director; scenarist; movie technician

cinégraphiste [sinegrafist] *mf* scenarist

cinéma [sinema] *m* movies; moving-picture theater; cinema; **cinéma auto** drive-in movie; **cinéma d'essai** preview theater; **cinéma muet** silent movie

cinémathèque [sinematɛk] *f* film library

cinématographique [sinematografik] *adj* motion-picture, film

ciné-park [sinepark] *m* (*pl* **ciné-parks**) drive-in (movie) theater

cinéphile [sinefil] *mf* movie fan

cinéprojecteur [sineprɔʒɛktœr] *m* motion-picture projector

ciné-roman [sinerɔmɑ̃] *m* (*pl* **-romans**) novelization (*of a film*)

cinétique [sinetik] *adj* kinetic ‖ *f* kinetics

cin•glant -glante [sɛ̃glɑ̃] **-glante** [glɑ̃t] *adj* scathing

cin•glé -glée [sɛ̃gle] *adj* (slang) screwy ‖ *mf* (slang) screwball

cingler [sɛ̃gle] *tr* to whip; cut to the quick ‖ *intr* to go full sail

cinq [sɛ̃(k)] §94 *adj & pron* five; the Fifth, e.g., **Jean cinq** John the Fifth; **cinq heures** five o'clock ‖ *m* five; fifth (*in dates*); **il était moins cinq** (coll) it was a close shave

cinquantaine [sɛ̃kɑ̃tɛn] *f* about fifty; age of fifty, fifty mark, fifties

cinquante [sɛ̃kɑ̃t] §94 *adj, pron, & m* fifty; **cinquante et un** fifty-one; **cinquante et unième** fifty-first

cinquantième [sɛ̃kɑ̃tjɛm] §94 *adj, pron* (*masc, fem*) *& m* fiftieth

cinquième [sɛ̃kjɛm] §94 *adj, pron* (*masc, fem*) *& m* fifth

cintre [sɛ̃tr] *m* arch; coat hanger; bend; **plein cintre** semicircular arch

cin•tré -trée [sɛ̃tre] *adj* (slang) crazy

cintrer [sɛ̃tre] *tr* to arch, bend

cirage [siraʒ] *m* waxing; shoe polish; **cirage automatique des chaussures** shoeshining in an automatic machine; **dans le cirage** (coll) in the dark

circoncire [sirkɔ̃sir] §66 (*pp* **circoncis**) *tr* to circumcise

circoncision [sirkɔ̃sizjɔ̃] *f* circumcision

circonférence [sirkɔ̃ferɑ̃s] *f* circumference

circonflexe [sirkɔ̃flɛks] *adj & m* circumflex

circonscription [sirkɔ̃skripsjɔ̃] *f* circumscription; ward, district

circonscrire [sirkɔ̃skrir] §25 *tr* to circumscribe

circons•pect [sirkɔ̃spɛ], [sirkɔ̃spɛk(t)] **-pecte** [pɛkt] *adj* circumspect

circonstance [sirkɔ̃stɑ̃s] *f* circumstance; **circonstances et dépendances** appurtenances; **de circonstance** proper for the occasion, topical; emergency (*measure*); guest, e.g., **orateur de circonstance** guest speaker

circonstan•cié -ciée [sirkɔ̃stɑ̃sje] *adj* circumstantial, in detail

circonstan•ciel -cielle [sirkɔ̃stɑ̃sjɛl] *adj* (gram) adverbial

circonvenir [sirkɔ̃vnir] §72 *tr* to circumvent

circonvoi•sin [sirkɔ̃vwazɛ̃] **-sine** [zin] *adj* nearby, neighboring

circuit [sirkɥi] *m* circuit; circumference; detour; tour; **circuit d'attente** (aer) holding point; **circuit imprimé** printed circuit

circulaire [sirkylɛr] *adj & f* circular

circulation [sirkylɑsjɔ̃] *f* circulation; traffic; **circulation interdite** (public sign) no thoroughfare

circuler [sirkyle] *intr* to circulate; go, move; **circulez au pas!** walk!

cire [sir] *f* wax; **cire à cacheter** sealing wax; **cire molle** (fig) wax in one's hands

ci•ré -rée [sire] *adj* waxed ‖ *m* waterproof garment; raincoat

cirer [sire] *tr* to wax; polish

ci•reur [sirœr] **-reuse** [røz] *mf* waxer, polisher (*person*); shoeblack, bootblack ‖ *f* floor waxer (*machine*)

ci•reux [sirø] **-reuse** [røz] *adj* waxy

ciron [sirɔ̃] *m* mite

cirque [sirk] *m* circus; amphitheater

cirrhose [siroz] *f* cirrhosis

cisaille [sizɑj] *f* metal clippings, scissel; **cisailles** clippers, shears; pruning shears; wire cutter

cisaillement [sizajmɑ̃] *m* cutting, clipping, pruning; shearing off; **cisaillement du vent** wind shear

cisailler [sizaje] *tr* to shear

ci•seau [sizo] *m* (*pl* **-seaux**) chisel; **ciseau à froid** cold chisel; **ciseaux** scissors; **ciseaux à ongles** nail scissors; **ciseaux à raisin** pruning shears; **ciseaux à tondre** sheep shears

ciseler [sizle] §2 *tr* to chisel; chase; cut, shear; prune

ciseleur [sizlœr] *m* chaser, tooler

citadelle [sitadɛl] *f* citadel

cita•din [sitadɛ̃] **-dine** [din] *adj* urban ‖ *mf* city dweller

citation [sitɑsjɔ̃] *f* citation, quotation; citation, summons

cité [site] *f* housing development; (hist) fortified city, citadel; **cité ouvrière** low-cost housing development; **cité sainte** Holy City; **cité universitaire** university dormitory complex; **la Cité** the City (*district within ancient boundaries*)

cité-dortoir [sitedɔrtwar] *f* bedroom community

cité-jardin [sitezardɛ̃] *f* (*pl* **cités-jardins**) landscaped housing development with parks

citer [site] *tr* to cite, quote; summon, subpoena

citerne [sitɛrn] *f* cistern; tank; **citerne flottante** tanker

cithare [sitar] *f* cither, zither

citoyen [sitwajɛ̃] **citoyenne** [sitwajɛn] *mf* citizen; (coll) individual, person; **citoyens** citizenry

citoyenneté [sitwajɛnte] *f* citizenship; citizenry

citrique [sitrik] *adj* citric

citron [sitrɔ̃] *adj & m* lemon

citronnade [sitrɔnad] *f* lemonade

citron•né -née [sitrɔne] *adj* lemon-flavored

citronnelle [sitrɔnɛl] *f* citronella

citronner [sitrɔne] *tr* to flavor with lemon

citronnier [sitrɔnje] *m* lemon tree

citrouille [sitruj] *f* pumpkin, gourd

cive [siv] *f* chive, scallion

civet [sivɛ] *m* stew

civette [sivɛt] *f* civet; civet cat; chive, chives

civière [sivjɛr] *f* stretcher, litter

ci•vil -vile [sivil] *adj* civil; civilian; secular ‖ *m* civilian; layman; **en civil** plainclothes (*person*); in civies

civilisation [sivilizasjɔ̃] *f* civilization

civiliser [sivilize] *tr* to civilize ‖ *ref* to become civilized

civilité [sivilite] *f* civility; **civilités** kind regards; amenities

civique [sivik] *adj* civic; civil (*rights*); national (*guard*)

civisme [sivism] *m* good citizenship

clabauder [klabode] *intr* to clamor

claie [klɛ] *f* wickerwork; trellis

clair claire [klɛr] *adj* clear, bright; evident, plain; light, pale ‖ *m* light, brightness; **clair de lune** moonlight; **clairs** highlights ‖ *f* oyster bed

clairance [klɛrɑ̃s] *f* (aer) clearance

clai•ret [klɛrɛ] **-rette** [rɛt] *adj* light-red; thin, high-pitched (*voice*) ‖ *m* light, red wine ‖ *f* light sparkling wine

claire-voie [klɛrvwa] *f* (*pl* **claires-voies**) latticework, slats; clerestory; **à claire-voie** with open spaces

clairière [klɛrjɛr] *f* clearing, glade

clairon [klɛrɔ̃] *m* bugle; bugler

claironner [klɛrɔne] *tr* to announce ‖ *intr* to sound the bugle

clairse•mé -mée [klɛrsəme] *adj* scattered, sparse; thin, thinned out

clairvoyance [klɛrvwajɑ̃s] *f* clear-sightedness, clairvoyance

clairvoyant [klɛrvwajɑ̃] **clairvoyante** [klɛrvwajɑ̃t] *adj* clear-sighted, clairvoyant

clamer [klame] *tr & intr* to cry out

clameur [klamœr] *f* clamor, outcry

clamp [klɑ̃] *m* (med) clamp

clampin [klɑ̃pɛ̃] *m* (mil) straggler

clan [klɑ̃] *m* clan, clique

clandes•tin [klɑ̃dɛstɛ̃] **-tine** [tin] *adj* clandestine

clapet [klapɛ] *m* valve; **ferme ton clapet!** (slang) shut your trap

clapier [klapje] *m* rabbit hutch

clapoter [klapɔte] *intr* to splash; be choppy

claque [klak] *m* opera hat ‖ *f* slap, smack; claque, paid applauders

cla•qué -quée [klake] *adj* dog-tired; sprained

claquement [klakmɑ̃] *m* clapping; slam (*of a door*); chattering (*of teeth*)

claquemurer [klakmyre] *tr* to shut in ‖ *ref* to shut oneself up at home

claquer [klake] *tr* to slap; clap; smack (*the lips*); slam (*the door*); crack (*the whip*); click (*the heels*); snap (*the fingers*); (coll) to tire out; (coll) to waste ‖ *intr* to clap, slap, slam; crack; (slang) to fail; (slang) to die ‖ *ref* to sprain; (slang) to work oneself to death

claquettes [klakɛt] *fpl* tap-dancing

claqueur [klakœr] *m* applauder, member of a claque

clarifier [klarifje] *tr* to clarify ‖ *ref* to become clear

clarine [klarin] *f* cowbell

clarinette [klarinɛt] *f* clarinet

clarté [klarte] *f* clarity; brightness; **clarté du soleil** sunshine

classe [klɑs] *f* class; classroom; **classe de rattrapage** refresher course (*for backward children*); **classe de travaux pratiques** lab class

clas•sé -sée [klɑse] *adj* pigeonholed, tabled; standard (*literary work*); listed; **non classé** (sports) also-ran

classer [klɑse] *tr* to class; sort out, file; pigeonhole, table ‖ *ref* to come in, rank, finish; **se classer premier** (sports) to come in first

classeur [klɑsœr] *m* file (*for letters, documents*); filing cabinet

classicisme [klasisism] *m* classicism

classification [klasifikasjɔ̃] *f* classification

classifier [klasifje] *tr* to classify; sort out

classique [klasik] *adj* classic, classical; standard (*author, work*) ‖ *mf* classicist ‖ *m* classic; standard work

claudication [klodikasjɔ̃] *f* limping

clause [kloz] *f* clause, stipulation, provision; **clause additionnelle** rider; **clause ambiguë** joker clause; **clause des droits acquis** grandfather clause; **clause de style** unwritten provision; **clause d'indexation** escalator clause

claustration [klostrasjɔ̃] *f* confinement; cloistering

clavecin [klavsɛ̃] *m* harpsichord

claveciniste [klavsinist] *mf* harpsichordist

clavette [klavɛt] *f* pin, cotter pin; key

clavicorde [klavikɔrd] *m* clavichord

clavicule [klavikyl] *f* collarbone

clavier [klavje] *m* keyboard; key ring; range (*e.g., of the voice*); **clavier universel** standard keyboard

claviste [klavist] *mf* keyboard operator; (comp) keyboarder; (printing) linotypist

clayère [klɛjɛr] *f* oyster bed

clé [kle] *f* see **clef**

clebs [klɛps] *m* (coll) mutt

clef [kle] *adj invar* key ‖ *f* key; wrench; (mus) valve; (mus) clef; (wrestling) lock; **clef anglaise** monkey wrench; **clef à tube** socket wrench; **clef crocodile** alligator wrench; **clef d'allumage** ignition key; **clef de fa** bass clef; **clef des champs** vacation; **clef de sol** treble clef; **clef de voûte** keystone; **clef d'ut** tenor clef; **fausse clef** skeleton key; **sous clef** under lock and key

clématite [klematit] *f* clematis

clémence [klemɑ̃s] *f* clemency

clé•ment [klemɑ̃] **-mente** [mɑ̃t] *adj* mild, clement

clenche [klɑ̃ʃ] *f* latch

cleptomane [klɛptɔman] *mf* kleptomaniac

clerc [klɛr] *m* cleric, clergyman; scholar; clerk

clergé [klɛrʒe] *m* clergy

clergie [klɛrʒi] *f* learning, scholarship; clergy

cléri•cal -cale [klerikal] *adj & mf* (*pl* **-caux** [ko]) clerical

clic [klik] *m* (comp) (*avec le bouton de la souris*) click; **double clic** double click; **faire un clic** (comp) to click ‖ *interj* click!

cliché [kliʃe] *m* cliché; (phot) negative; (typ) plate, stereotype; **prendre un cliché** (phot) to make an exposure

clicher [kliʃe] *tr* (typ) to stereotype

client [klijɑ̃] **cliente** [kljɑ̃t] *mf* client; patient; customer; guest (*of a hotel*)

clientèle [klijɑ̃tɛl] *f* clientele; adherents; customers

clignement [kliɲmɑ̃] *m* blinking

cligner [kliɲe] *tr* to squint (*one's eyes*) ‖ *intr* to squint, blink; **cligner de l'œil à** to wink at

cligno•tant [kliɲɔtɑ̃] **-tante** [tɑ̃t] *adj* blinking ‖ *m* (aut) directional signal; (aut) flasher

clignotement [kliɲɔtmɑ̃] *m* blinking; twinkling; flickering

clignoter [kliɲɔte] *intr* to blink; twinkle; flicker

clignoteur [kliɲɔtœr] *m* (aut) directional signal

climat [klima] [klima] *m* climate

climatisation [klimatizasjɔ̃] *f* air conditioning

climati•sé -sée [klimatize] *adj* air-conditioned

climatiseur [klimatizœr] *m* airconditioner

clin [klɛ̃] *m*—**à clin** (carpentry) overlapping, covering; **clin d'œil** wink; **en un clin d'œil** in the twinkling of an eye

clinicien [klinisjɛ̃] *adj masc* clinical ‖ *m* clinician

clinique [klinik] *adj* clinical ‖ *f* clinic; private hospital

clinquant [klɛ̃kɑ̃] *m* foil, tinsel; flashiness; tawdriness

clip [klip] *m* clip, brooch

clique [klik] *f* drum and bugle corps; (coll) gang; **cliques** wooden shoes

cliquet [klikɛ] *m* (mach) pawl, catch

cliqueter [klikte] §34 *intr* to click, clink, clank, jangle

cliquetis [klikti] *m* click, clink, clank, jangle

cliquette [klikɛt] *f* castanets; (fishing) sinker

clisse [klis] *f* draining rack, wicker bottleholder

clitoris [klitɔris] *m* clitoris

clivage [klivaʒ] *m* cleavage

cliver [klive] *tr* to cleave; cut

cloaque [klɔak] *m* cesspool

clo•chard [klɔʃar] **-charde** [ʃard] *mf* beggar, tramp

cloche [klɔʃ] *adj* bell (*skirt*) ‖ *f* bell; bell; glass; blister (*on skin*); **cloche de plongeur** diving bell; **cloche de sauvetage** escape hatch (*on submarine*); **déménager à la cloche de bois** (coll) to skip out without paying; **la cloche** (slang) beggars

clochement [klɔʃmɑ̃] *m* limp, limping

cloche-pied [klɔʃpje]—**à cloche-pied** on one foot, hopping

clocher [klɔʃe] *m* steeple; belfry; parish, home town; **de clocher** local (*politics*) ‖ *intr* to limp; **quelque chose cloche** something jars, is not right

clocheton [klɔʃtɔ̃] *m* little steeple

clochette [klɔʃɛt] *f* little bell; (bot) bellflower

cloison [klwazɔ̃] *f* partition; division, barrier (*e.g., between classes*); (anat, bot) septum, dividing membrane; (naut) bulkhead; **cloison étanche** (naut) watertight compartment

cloisonner [klwazɔne] *tr* to partition

cloître [klwatr] *m* cloister

cloîtrer [klwatre] *tr* to cloister; confine

clonage [klɔnaʒ] *m* cloning; **faire du clonage** to clone

clone [klɔn] *m* clone

clopin-clopant [klɔpɛ̃klɔpɑ̃l] *adv* (coll) so-so; **aller clopin-clopant** (coll) to go hobbling along

clopiner [klɔpine] *intr* to hobble

cloque [klɔk] *f* blister

cloquer [klɔke] *tr & intr* to blister

clore [klɔr] §24 *tr & intr* to close

clos [klo] **close** [kloz] *adj* closed ‖ *m* enclosure; **clos de vigne** vineyard

clôture [klotyr] *f* fence; wall; cloistered life; closing of an account

clôturer [klotyre] *tr* to enclose, wall in; close out (*an account*); conclude (*a discussion*)

clou [klu] *m* nail; (coll) boil; (coll) jalopy; (coll) feature attraction; (slang) pawnshop; **clou de girofle** clove; **clous** pedestrian crossing; **des clous!** (slang) nothing at all!

clouer [klue] *tr* to nail; immobilize, rivet; **clouer le bec à qn** (coll) to shut s.o.'s mouth

clouter [klute] *tr* to stud; trim or border with studs, e.g., **passage clouté** pedestrian crossing (bordered with studs)

clown [klun] *m* clown; **faire le clown** to clown (around)

clownerie [klunri] *f* high jinks, clowning

club [klyb] *m* (literary) society; (political) association ‖ [klœb] *m* club (*for social and athletic purposes, etc.*); clubhouse; (golf) club; armchair

club-house [klybbaus] *m* clubhouse

clubiste [klybist] *mf* (coll) club member; (coll) joiner

clubman [klœbman] *m* club member

coaccu•sé -sée [kɔakyze] *mf* codefendant

coaguler [koagyle] *tr & ref* to coagulate

coaliser [koalize] *tr* to form into a coalition ‖ *ref* to form a coalition

coalition [koalisjɔ̃] *f* coalition

coassement [kɔasmɑ̃] *m* croak, croaking

coasser [kɔase] *intr* to croak

coasso•cié -ciée [kɔasɔsje] *mf* copartner

coauteur [kɔotœr] *m* coauthor

coa•xial -xiale [kɔaksjal] *adj* coaxial ‖ *m* coaxial cable

cobalt [kɔbalt] *m* cobalt

cobaye [kɔbaj] *m* guinea pig

Coca [kɔka] *m* (trademark) (coll) Coke

Coca-Cola [kɔkakɔla] *m* (trademark) Coca-Cola

cocaïne [kɔkain] *f* cocaine

cocarde [kɔkard] *f* cockade; rosette of ribbons; **avoir sa cocarde** (coll) to be tipsy; **prendre la cocarde** (coll) to enlist

cocar•dier -dière [kɔkardje] **-dière** [djɛr] *mf* jingoist, chauvinist

cocasse [kɔkas] *adj* (coll) funny, ridiculous

coccinelle [kɔksinɛl] *f* ladybug

coche [kɔʃ] *m* coach, stagecoach; two-door sedan; barge; **manquer le coche** *or* **rater le coche** (fig) to miss the bus ‖ *f* notch, score; (zool) sow

cocher [kɔʃe] *m* coachman, driver ‖ *tr* to notch, score; check off

cochère [kɔʃɛr] *adj* carriage (*entrance*)

co•chon [kɔʃɔ̃] **-chonne** [ʃɔn] *mf* (coll) skunk, slob ‖ *m* pig, hog; **chochon de lait** suckling pig; **cochon de mer** porpoise; **cochon de phallocrate** (slang) male chauvinist pig; **cochon d'Inde** guinea pig

cochonnerie [kɔʃɔnri] *f* (slang) dirty trick; (slang) filthy speech, smut

cocker [kɔkɛr] *m* cocker spaniel

cockney [kɔknɛj] *adj & mf* cockney ‖ *m* (*language*) cockney

cockpit [kɔkpit] *m* (aer) cockpit

cocktail [kɔktɛ] *m* cocktail; cocktail party

coco [kɔko], [koko] *m* coconut; licorice water; **mon coco** (coll) my darling; **un joli coco** (coll) a stinker ‖ *f* (slang) cocaine

cocon [kɔkɔ̃] *m* cocoon

co-conducteur [kɔkɔ̃dyktœr] *m* co-driver

cocorico [kɔkɔriko] *m* cockcrow ‖ *interj* cock-a-doodle-doo!

cocotier [kɔkɔtje] *m* coconut tree

cocotte [kɔkɔt] *f* saucepan; cocotte, floozy; **ma cocotte** (coll) my little chick, my baby doll

co•cu -cue [kɔky] *adj & m* cuckold

cocufier [kɔkyfje] *tr* (slang) to cuckold

codage [kɔdaʒ] *m* coding, encoding

code [kɔd] *m*; **code à barres** bar code; **code binaire** binary code; **code de construction** building code; **code de la route** traffic regulations; **code de la zone, code territorial** (telp) area code; **code génétique** genetic code; **code pénal** criminal code; **codes** (slang) dimmers; **Code Universel de Produit** (*le code à barres plus une numérotation*) Universal Product Code (UPC); **se mettre en code** to dim one's headlights

coder [kɔde] *tr* to code, encode

codeur [kɔdœr] *m* (comp) encoder

codex [kɔdɛks] *m* pharmacopoeia

codicille [kɔdisil] *m* codicil

codifier [kɔdifje] *tr* to codify; **codifiez vos adresses postales!** use the zip code!

coéducation [kɔedykasjɔ̃] *f* coeducation

coefficient [kɔefisjɑ̃] *m* coefficient; **coefficient de sécurité** (aer) safety factor

coéqui•pier [kɔekipje] **-pière** [pjɛr] *mf* teammate; running mate (*of a political candidate*)

coercition [kɔɛrsisjɔ̃] *f* coercion

cœur [kœr] *m* heart; core; courage, spirit; bosom, breast; depth (*of winter*); center (*of the city*); (cards) heart; (cards) hearts; **à cœur joie** to one's heart's content; **avoir du cœur** to be kind-hearted; **avoir du cœur au ventre** (coll) to have guts; **avoir le cœur sur la main** (coll) to be open-handed; **avoir le cœur sur les lèvres** to wear one's heart on one's sleeve; **cœur de bronze** heart of stone; **de bon cœur** willingly, heartily; **de mauvais cœur** reluctantly; **en avoir le cœur net** to get to the bottom of it; **épancher son cœur à** to open one's heart to; **fendre le cœur à** to break the heart of; **le cœur gros** with a heavy heart; **mal au cœur, mal de cœur** stomach ache; nausea; **par cœur** by heart; **prendre à cœur** to take to heart; **se ronger le cœur** to eat one's heart out; **soulever le cœur** to turn the stomach

coexistence [kɔegzistɑ̃s] *f* coexistence

coexister [kɔegziste] *intr* to coexist

coffre [kɔfr] *m* chest; coffer, bin; safe-deposit box; trunk (*of car*); buoy (*for mooring*); cofferdam

coffre-fort [kɔfrəfɔr] *m* (*pl* **coffres-forts**) safe, strongbox, vault

coffret [kɔfrɛ] *m* gift box

cognac [kɔɲak] *m* cognac

cognat [kɔɲa] *m* blood kin

cognée [kɔɲe] *f* ax, hatchet

cogner [kɔɲe] *tr, intr, & ref* to knock, bump

cohabiter [kɔabite] *intr* to cohabit

cohé•rent [kɔerɑ̃] **-rente** [rɑ̃t] *adj* coherent

cohériter [kɔerite] *intr* to inherit jointly

cohéri•tier [kɔeritje] **-tière** [tjɛr] *mf* coheir

cohésion [kɔesjɔ̃] *f* cohesion

cohorte [kɔɔrt] *f* cohort

cohue [kɔy] *f* crowd, throng, mob

coi [kwa] **coite** [kwat] *adj* quiet; **demeurer coi, se tenir coi** to keep still

coiffe [kwaf] *f* cap; headdress; caul

coif•fé -fée [kwafe] *adj*—**coiffé de** wearing (*a hat*); (fig) crazy about (*a person*); **être coiffé** to be wearing a hairdo; **être né coiffé** (fig) to be lucky

coiffer [kwafe] *tr* to put a hat or cap on (*s.o.*);

dress or do the hair of; to have overall responsibility for; (mil) to reach (*an objective*) ‖ *intr*—**coiffer de** to wear (*a certain size hat*) ‖ *ref* to do one's hair; **se coiffer de** (coll) to set one's cap for

coif·feur [kwafœr] **-feuse** [føz] *mf* hairdresser; barber; **coiffeur pour dames** coiffeur ‖ *f* dresser, dressing table, vanity

coiffure [kwafyr] *f* coiffure; headdress; **coiffure en brosse** crew cut

coin [kwɛ̃] *m* corner; angle; nook; wedge, coin; stamp, die (*for coining money*); (typ) quoin; **coin de détente, coin de retraite** den; **le petit coin** (coll) the powder room

coinçage [kwɛ̃saʒ] *m* wedging

coincer [kwɛ̃se] §51 *tr* to wedge, jam; (coll) to pinch, arrest ‖ *ref* to jam

coïncidence [koɛ̃sidɑ̃s] *f* coincidence

coïncider [koɛ̃side] *intr* to coincide

coin-coin [kwɛ̃kwɛ̃] *m invar* quack (*of duck*); toot (*of horn*)

coing [kwɛ̃] *m* quince

coït [kɔit] *m* coition, coitus

coke [kɔk] *m* coke (*coal*)

cokéfier [kɔkefje] *tr & ref* to coke

col [kɔl] *m* neck (*of bottle; of womb*); collar (*of dress*); mountain pass; (coll) head (*on beer*); **col blanc** white-collar worker; **col de fourrure** neckpiece; **col roulé** turtleneck; **faux col** detachable collar

colback [kɔlbak] *m* busby

colère [kɔlɛr] *f* anger; **en colère** angry; **se mettre en colère** to become angry

colé·reux [kɔlerø] **-reuse** [røz] *adj* irascible, choleric

colérique [kɔlerik] *adj* choleric

colibri [kɔlibri] *m* hummingbird

colifichet [kɔlifiʃɛ] *m* knicknack, trinket

colimaçon [kɔlimasɔ̃] *m* snail; **en colimaçon** spiral

colin [kɔlɛ̃] *m* hake

colin-maillard [kɔlɛ̃majar] *m* blindman's buff

colique [kɔlik] *f* colic

colis [kɔli] *m* piece of baggage, package, parcel; **colis postal** parcel post

colisée [kɔlize] *m* coliseum; **Colisée** (*à Rome*) Colosseum

colis·tier [kɔlistje] **-tière** [tjɛr] *mf* (pol) running mate

collabora·teur [kɔlabɔratœr] **-trice** [tris] *mf* collaborator; contributor

collaborationniste [kɔlabɔrasjɔnist] *mf* collaborationist

collaborer [kɔlabɔre] *intr* to collaborate; **collaborer à** to contribute to

collage [kɔlaʒ] *m* pasting, mounting; collage; sizing; clarifying (*of wine*); (coll) common-law marriage

col·lant [kɔlɑ̃] **-lante** [lɑ̃t] *adj* sticky; tight, close-fitting ‖ *m* tights; panty hose

collapsus [kɔlapsys] *m* (pathol) collapse

collaté·ral -rale [kɔlateral] (*pl* **-raux** [ro]) *adj* collateral; parallel; intermediate (*points of the compass*) ‖ *mf* collateral (relative) ‖ *m* side aisle of a church

collation [kɔllasjɔ̃] *f* conferring (*of titles, degrees, etc.*); collation (*of texts*) ‖ [kɔlɑsjɔ̃] *f* snack

collationner [kɔllasjɔne] *tr* to collate, to compare; **faire collationner un télégramme** to request a copy of a telegram ‖ *intr* to have a snack

colle [kɔl] *f* paste, glue; (coll) brain teaser, stickler; (slang) detention; (slang) oral exam; (slang) flunking; **colle forte** glue; **poser une colle** (slang) to ask a hard one

collecte [kɔlɛkt] *f* collection (*for charitable cause*); (eccl) collect

collecteur [kɔlɛktœr] *adj* main, e.g., **égout collecteur** main sewer ‖ *m* collector; commutator (*of motor or dynamo*); (aut) manifold; **collecteur d'ondes** aerial

collec·tif [kɔlɛktif] **-tive** [tiv] *adj* collective

collection [kɔlɛksjɔ̃] *f* collection

collectionner [kɔlɛksjɔne] *tr* to collect

collection·neur [kɔlɛksjɔnœr] **-neuse** [nøz] *mf* collector

collège [kɔlɛʒ] *m* high school; preparatory school; college (*of cardinals, electors, etc.*); **collège universitaire** junior college

collé·gial -giale [kɔleʒjal] (*pl* **-giaux** [ʒjo]) *adj* collegiate ‖ *f* collegiate church

collé·gien [kɔleʒjɛ̃] **-gienne** [ʒjɛn] *adj* high-school ‖ *m* schoolboy ‖ *f* schoolgirl; coed

collègue [kɔlɛg] *mf* colleague

coller [kɔle] *tr* to paste, stick, glue; clarify (*wine*); mat (*e.g., with blood*); (coll) to floor, stump; (coll) to punish (*a pupil*); (coll) to flunk; (coll) to sock (*e.g., on the jaw*) ‖ *intr* to cling, fit tightly (*said of dress*); (coll) to stick close; **ça colle!** (slang) O.K.!; **coller à** to jibe with (*be in accord with*) ‖ *ref* (slang) to have a common-law marriage; **se coller contre** to stand close to; cling to

collet [kɔlɛ] *m* collar; neck (*of person; of tooth*); neck, scrag (*e.g., of mutton*); cape; snare; stalk and roots; lasso, noose; **collet monté** (coll) stuffed shirt

colleter [kɔlte] §34 *tr* to collar; ‖ *ref* to fight, scuffle

colley [kɔlɛ] *m* collie

collier [kɔlje] *m* necklace; collar; dog collar; horse collar; **à collier** ring-necked; **collier de chien** dog collar; **reprendre le collier** (coll) to get back into harness

colliger [kɔlliʒe] §38 *tr* to make a collection of

colline [kɔlin] *f* hill

collision [kɔllizjɔ̃] *f* collision; **collision manquée** near collision, near miss

colloï·dal -dale [kɔllɔidal] *adj* (*pl* **-daux** [do]) colloid, colloidal

colloïde [kɔllɔid] *m* colloid

colloque [kɔllɔk] *m* colloquy, symposium

colloquer [kɔllɔke] *tr* to classify (*creditors' claims*); **colloquer q.ch. à qn** (coll) to palm off s.th. on s.o.

collusion [kɔllyzjɔ̃] *f* collusion
collyre [kɔllir] *m* (med) eyewash
Cologne [kɔlɔɲ] *f* Cologne
Colomb [kɔlɔ̃] *m* Columbus
colombe [kɔlɔ̃b] *f* dove
Colombie [kɔlɔ̃bi] *f* Columbia; **la Colombie** Colombia
colombier [kɔlɔ̃bje] *m* dovecote; large-size paper
colom•bin [kɔlɔ̃bɛ̃] **-bine** [bin] *adj* columbine ‖ *m* stock dove; lead ore ‖ *f* bird droppings; (bot) columbine
colon [kɔlɔ̃] *m* colonist; tenant farmer; summer camper
côlon [kolɔ̃] *m* (anat) colon
colonel [kɔlɔnɛl] *m* colonel
colonelle [kɔlɔnɛl] *f* colonel's wife; (theat) performance for the press
colonie [kɔlɔni] *f* colony; **colonie de déportation** penal settlement; **colonie de vacances** summer camp
coloniser [kɔlɔnize] *tr* to colonize
colonnade [kɔlɔnad] *f* colonnade
colonne [kɔlɔn] *f* column; pillar; **cinquième colonne** fifth column; **colonne de direction** (aut) steering column; **colonne vertébrale** spinal column
colophane [kɔlɔfan] *f* rosin
colophon [kɔlɔfɔ̃] *m* colophon
colo•rant [kɔlɔrɑ̃] **-rante** [rɑ̃t] *adj* coloring ‖ *m* dye, stain
colorer [kɔlɔre] *tr & ref* to color
colorier [kɔlɔrje] *tr* to paint, color
coloris [kɔlɔri] *m* hue; brilliance
colos•sal -sale [kɔlɔsal] *adj* (*pl* **-saux** [so]) colossal
colosse [kɔlɔs] *m* colossus
colporter [kɔlpɔrte] *tr* to peddle
colporteur [kɔlpɔrtœr] *m* peddler
coltiner [kɔltine] *tr* to lug on one's back or on one's head
coma [kɔma] *m* (pathol) coma
coma•teux [kɔmatø] **-teuse** [tøz] *adj* comatose ‖ *mf* person in a coma
combat [kɔ̃ba] *m* combat; **combat asymétrique** asymmetrical warfare; **combat tournoyant** (aer) dogfight; **combat rapproché** (mil) close combat; **hors de combat** disabled
comba•tif [kɔ̃batif] **-tive** [tiv] *adj* combative
combat•tant [kɔ̃batɑ̃] **-tante** [tɑ̃t] *adj & mf* combatant; **anciens combattants** veterans
combattre [kɔ̃batr] §7 *tr & intr* to combat
combien [kɔ̃bjɛ̃] *adv* how much, how many; how far; how long; how, e.g., **combien il était brave!** how brave he was! ‖ *m invar*—**du combien chaussez-vous?** what size shoes do you wear?; **du combien coiffez-vous?** what size hat do you wear?; **le combien?** which one (*in a series*)?; **le combien êtes-vous?** (coll) what rank do you have?; **le combien sommes-nous?** (coll) what day of the month is it?; **tous les combien?** how often?
combinaison [kɔ̃binɛzɔ̃] *f* combination; jump

suit; coveralls; slip, undergarment; **combinaison de danse** leotard; **combinaison de plongée** wetsuit
combi•né -née [kɔ̃bine] *adj* combined ‖ *m* French telephone, handset; radio phonograph
combiner [kɔ̃bine] *tr* to combine; arrange, group; concoct (*a scheme*) ‖ *ref* (chem) to combine
comble [kɔ̃bl] *adj* full, packed ‖ *m* summit; roof, coping; **au comble de** at the height of; **c'est le comble!, c'est un comble!** (coll) that's the limit!, that takes the cake!; **sous les combles** in the attic
combler [kɔ̃ble] *tr* to heap up; fill to the brim; overwhelm; **combler d'honneurs** to shower honors upon
combustible [kɔ̃bystibl] *adj & m* combustible, fuel
combustion [kɔ̃bystjɔ̃] *f* combustion
comédie [kɔmedi] *f* comedy; play; sham; **comédie de situation** (*sitcom*) situation comedy
comé•dien [kɔmedjɛ̃] **-dienne** [djɛn] *mf* comedian; actor; hypocrite; **comédien ambulant** strolling player ‖ *f* comedienne; actress
comédon [kɔmedɔ̃] *m* blackhead
comestible [kɔmɛstibl] *adj* edible ‖ **comestibles** *mpl* foodstuffs
comète [kɔmɛt] *f* comet
comics [kɔmiks] *mpl* (*bandes dessinées*) comics
comique [kɔmik] *adj* comic ‖ *m* comedian, comic; humorist, writer of comedies; comic aspect of the situation
comité [kɔmite] *m* committee; **comité de conseillers** think tank
commandant [kɔmɑ̃dɑ̃] *m* commandant, commander; major
commande [kɔmɑ̃d] *f* order (*for goods or services*); control, command; **à la commande** (paid) down; **commande à distance** remote control; **commande postale** mail order; **commandes de vol** flight controls; **de commande** operating; **double commande** dual controls; **(fait) sur commande** (made) to order
commandement [kɔmɑ̃dəmɑ̃] *m* command, order; (mil) command; **les dix commandements** the Ten Commandments
commander [kɔmɑ̃de] §97, §98 *tr* to order (*goods or services*); command, order ‖ *intr* (mil) to command; **commander à** to control, have command over; **commander à qn de** + *inf* to order s.o. to + *inf* ‖ *ref* to control oneself
commanditaire [kɔmɑ̃ditɛr] *adj* sponsoring ‖ *mf* (com) sponsor, backer
commandite [kɔmɑ̃dit] *f* joint-stock company
commanditer [kɔmɑ̃dite] *tr* to back, to finance; (rad, telv) to sponsor
comme [kɔm] *adv* as; how; **comme ci comme ça** so-so ‖ *prep* as, like ‖ *conj* as; since
commémoratifs [kɔmemɔratif] *mpl* (phila) commemoratives
commémorer [kɔmmemɔre] *tr* to commemorate

commen•çant [kɔmɑ̃sɑ̃] **-çante** [sɑ̃t] *mf* beginner

commencement [kɔmɑ̃smɑ̃] *m* beginning

commencer [kɔmɑ̃se] §51, §96, §97 *tr & intr* to begin; **commencer à** to begin to

comment [kɔmɑ̃] *m invar* how; wherefore || *adv* how; why; **mais comment donc!** by all means!; **n'importe comment** any way || *interj* what!; indeed!

commentaire [kɔmɑ̃tɛr] *m* commentary; unfriendly comment

commenta•teur [kɔmɑ̃tatœr] **-trice** [tris] *mf* commentator

commenter [kɔmɑ̃te] *tr* to comment on; make a commentary on; criticize

commérage [kɔmeraʒ] *m* (coll) gossip

commer•çant [kɔmɛrsɑ̃] **-çante** [sɑ̃t] *adj* commercial, business || *mf* merchant, dealer

commerce [kɔmɛrs] *m* commerce, trade; business, store; merchants

commercer [kɔmɛrse] §51 *intr* to trade

commer•cial -ciale [kɔmɛrsjal] *adj* (*pl* **-ciaux** [sjo] **-ciales**) commercial || *f* station wagon

commercialisation [kɔmɛrsjalizɑsjɔ̃] *f* marketing

commercialiser [kɔmɛsjalize] *tr* to commercialize

commère [kɔmɛr] *f* (coll) busybody, gossip

commettre [kɔmɛtr] §42 *tr* to commit; compromise || *ref* to compromise oneself

commis [kɔmi] *m* clerk; **commis voyageur** traveling salesman

commisération [kɔmizerɑsjɔ̃] *f* commiseration

commissaire [kɔmisɛr] *m* commissioner; commissary

commissaire-priseur [kɔmisɛrprizœr] *m* (*pl* **commissaires-priseurs**) appraiser; auctioneer

commissariat [kɔmisarja] *m* commissariat; **commissariat de police** police station

commission [kɔmisjɔ̃] *f* commission; errand; committee; (com) service charge; **commission d'éthique** ethics committee

commissionnaire [kɔmisjɔnɛr] *m* agent, broker; messenger

commissionner [kɔmisjɔne] *tr* to commission

commissure [kɔmisyr] *f* corner (*of lips*)

commode [kɔmɔd] *adj* convenient; comfortable; easygoing || *f* chest of drawers, bureau

commodité [kɔmɔdite] *f* comfort, accommodation; **à votre commodité** at your convenience; **commodités** comfort station; utilities

commotion [kɔmɔsjɔ̃] *f* commotion; concussion; shock

commotionner [kɔmɔsjɔne] *tr* to shake up, injure, shock

commuer [kɔmɥe] *tr* (law) to commute

com•mun [kɔmœ̃] **com•mune** [kɔmyn] *adj* common || *m* common run || *f* see **commune**

commu•nal -nale [kɔmynal] (*pl* **-naux** [no]) *adj* communal, common || *mpl* common property, commons

communautaire [kɔmynotɛr] *adj* communal

communauté [kɔmynote] *f* community; joint estate (*of husband and wife*); **Communauté économique européenne** (CEE) European Economic Community; **communauté familiale** extended family

commune [kɔmyn] *f* commune; **communes** Commons

commu•niant [kɔmynjɑ̃] **-niante** [njɑ̃t] *mf* communicant

communicable [kɔmynikabl] *adj* communicable

communi•cant [kɔmynikɑ̃] **-cante** [kɑ̃t] *adj* communicating

communica•teur [kɔmynikatœr] **-trice** [tris] *adj* connecting (*wire*) || *m* broadcaster

communica•tif [kɔmynikatif] **-tive** [tiv] *adj* communicative; infectious (*laughter*)

communication [kɔmynikɑsjɔ̃] *f* communication; telephone call; (telp) connection; **communication avec avis d'appel** (telp) messenger call; **communication avec préavis** person-to-person call; **communication payable à l'arrivée, communication P.C.V.** collect call; **communication urbaine** local call; **en communication** in touch; **fausse communication** (telp) wrong number; **vous avez la communication!** (telp) go ahead!

communier [kɔmynje] *intr* to take communion; have a common bond of sympathy, be in accord

communion [kɔmynjɔ̃] *f* communion

communiqué [kɔmynike] *m* communiqué

communiquer [kɔmynike] *tr & intr* to communicate

communi•sant [kɔmynizɑ̃] **-sante** [zɑ̃t] *adj* fellow-traveling || *mf* fellow traveler

communisme [kɔmynism] *m* communism

communiste [kɔmynist] *adj & mf* communist

commutateur [kɔmytatœr] *m* (elec) changeover switch, two-way switch

commutation [kɔmytɑsjɔ̃] *f* commutation

commutatrice [kɔmytatris] *f* (elec) rotary converter

com•pact -pacte [kɔ̃pakt] *adj* compact || *m* compact disk (CD); **Compact Disc** Compact Disk

compagne [kɔ̃paɲ] *f* companion; helpmate

compagnie [kɔ̃paɲi] *f* company; **compagnie aérienne de transport régulier** scheduled airline; **de compagnie, en compagnie** together; **fausser compagnie à** to give (*s.o.*) the slip; **tenir compagnie à** to keep (*s.o.*) company

compagnon [kɔ̃paɲɔ̃] *m* companion; helpmate; journeyman; **compagnon d'armes** comrade in arms; **compagnon de jeu** playmate; **compagnon de route** fellow traveler; **compagnon d'infortune** fellow sufferer; **joyeux compagnon** good fellow

comparaison [kɔ̃parɛzɔ̃] *f* comparison; **en comparaison de** compared to; **par comparaison** in comparison; **sans comparaison** beyond comparison

comparaître [kɔ̃parɛtr] §12 *intr* (law) to appear (in court)

compara•tif [kɔ̃paratif] **-tive** [tiv] *adj & m* comparative

compa•ré -rée [kɔ̃pare] *adj* comparative

comparer [kɔ̃pare] *tr* to compare

comparoir [kɔ̃parwar] (used only in; *inf; ger* **comparant**) *intr* (law) to appear in court

comparse [kɔ̃pars] *mf* (theat) walk-on; (fig) nobody, unimportant person

compartiment [kɔ̃partimɑ̃] *m* compartment

comparution [kɔ̃parysjɔ̃] *f* appearance in court

compas [kɔ̃pa] *m* compasses (*for drawing circles*); calipers; (naut) compass; **avoir le compas dans l'œil** to have a sharp eye

compas•sé -sée [kɔ̃pase] *adj* stiff, studied

compasser [kɔ̃pase] *tr* to measure out, lay off; **compasser ses discours** to speak like a book

compassion [kɔ̃pasjɔ̃] *f* compassion

compatibilité [kɔ̃patibilite] *f* compatibility

compatible [kɔ̃patibl] *adj* compatible; **compatible avec** consistent with, compatible with

compatir [kɔ̃patir] *intr*—**compatir à** to take pity on, feel for; be indulgent toward; share in (*s.o.'s bereavement*); **ne pouvoir compatir** to be unable to agree

compatis•sant [kɔ̃patisɑ̃] **-sante** [sɑ̃t] *adj* compassionate, sympathetic, indulgent

compatriote [kɔ̃patriɔt] *mf* compatriot

compensa•teur [kɔ̃pɑ̃satœr] **-trice** [tris] *adj* compensating, equalizing

compensation [kɔ̃pɑ̃sasjɔ̃] *f* compensation

compenser [kɔ̃pɑ̃se] *tr* to compensate; compensate for; to clear (*a check*) ‖ *ref* to balance each other

compérage [kɔperaʒ] *m* complicity

compère [kɔ̃pɛr] *m* accomplice; comrade; stooge (*for a clown*)

compétence [kɔ̃petɑ̃s] *f* competence, expertise, proficiency, qualification; (law) jurisdiction

compé•tent [kɔ̃petɑ̃] **-tente** [tɑ̃t] *adj* competent, proficient, qualified; (law) having jurisdiction, expert

compéter [kɔ̃pete] §10 *intr*—**compéter à** to belong to by right; be within the competency of (*a court*)

compéti•teur [kɔ̃petitœr] **-trice** [tris] *mf* rival, competitor

compétition [kɔ̃petisjɔ̃] *f* competition; **compétition acharnée** cutthroat competition

compila•teur [kɔ̃pilatœr] **-trice** [tris] *mf* compiler; (pej) plagiarist ‖ *m* (comp) compiler

compilation [kɔ̃pilasjɔ̃] *f* compilation

compiler [kɔ̃pile] *tr* to compile; (pej) plagiarize

complainte [kɔ̃plɛ̃t] *f* sad ballad; (law) complaint

complaire [kɔ̃plɛr] §52 *intr* to please, gratify; **complaire à** to please, gratify, e.g., **les fils complaisent au père** the sons (try to) please the father ‖ §96 *ref* (*pp* **complu** *invar*)—**se complaire à** to take pleasure in

complaisance [kɔ̃plɛzɑ̃s] *f* compliance; courtesy; complacency; **auriez-vous la complai**-

sance de... ? would you be so kind as to ...?; **de complaisance** out of kindness

complai•sant [kɔ̃plɛzɑ̃] **-sante** [zɑt] *adj* complaisant, obliging; complacent

complément [kɔ̃plemɑ̃] *m* complement; (gram) object; **complément d'attribution** (gram) indirect object

com•plet [kɔ̃plɛ] **-plète** [plɛt] *adj* complete, full; **c'est complet!** that's the last straw! ‖ *m* suit (*of clothes*); **au complet** full (*house*); **au grand complet** at full strength

complètement [kɔ̃plɛtmɑ̃] *adv* completely; right through from cover to cover

compléter [kɔ̃plete] §10 *tr* to complete ‖ *ref* to be completed; complement one another

complet-veston [kɔ̃plɛvɛstɔ̃] *m* (*pl* **complets-veston**) man's suit

complexe [kɔ̃plɛks] *adj & m* complex; **complexe de culpabilité** guilt complex; **complexe touristique** tourist resort

complexé complexée [kɔ̃plɛkse] *adj* (coll) timid, withdrawn ‖ *mf* person with complexes

complexion [kɔ̃plɛksjɔ̃] *f* constitution, disposition

complication [kɔ̃plikasjɔ̃] *f* complication

complice [kɔ̃plis] *adj* accessory, abetting ‖ *mf* accomplice; **complice d'adultère** correspondent

complicité [kɔ̃plisite] *f* complicity

compliment [kɔ̃plimɑ̃] *m* compliment

complimenter [kɔ̃plimɑ̃te] *tr* to compliment; congratulate

complimen•teur [kɔ̃plimɑ̃tœr] **-teuse** [tøz] *adj* complimentary ‖ *mf* flatterer, yes man

compli•qué -quée [kɔ̃plike] *adj* complicated

compliquer [kɔ̃plike] *tr* to complicate ‖ *ref* to become complicated; have complications

complot [kɔ̃plo] *m* plot, conspiracy

comploter [kɔ̃plɔte] *tr & intr* to plot, conspire

comploteur [kɔ̃plɔtœr] *m* conspirator

comportement [kɔ̃pɔrtəmɑ̃] *m* behavior

comporter [kɔ̃pɔrte] *tr* to permit; include ‖ *ref* to behave

compo•sant [kɔ̃pozɑ̃] **-sante** [zɑ̃t] *adj* constituent ‖ *m* (chem) component ‖ *f* (mech) component

compo•sé -sée [kɔ̃poze] *adj & m* compound

composer [kɔ̃poze] *tr* to compose; compound; dial (*a telephone number*) ‖ *intr* to take an exam; come to terms ‖ *ref*—**se composer de** to be composed of

composeur [kɔ̃pozœr] *m* (telp)—**composeur de numéros** automatic dialing

composi•teur [kɔ̃pozitœr] **-trice** [tris] *mf* composer; compositor; **amiable compositeur** (law) arbitrator

composition [kɔ̃pozisjɔ̃] *f* composition; compound; dialing (*of telephone number*); term paper; **composition programmée** (printing) computer composition, page set-up; **de bonne composition** easygoing, reasonable; **entrer en composition** to reach an agreement

composteur [kɔ̃pɔstœr] *m* composing stick; dating and numbering machine, dating stamp

compote [kɔ̃pɔt] *f* compote; **compote de pommes** applesauce

compotier [kɔ̃pɔtje] *m* compote (*dish*)

compréhensible [kɔ̃preɑ̃sibl] *adj* comprehensible

compréhen•sif [kɔ̃preɑ̃sif] **-sive** [siv] *adj* understanding; comprehensive

compréhension [kɔ̃preɑ̃sjɔ̃] *f* comprehension, understanding

comprendre [kɔ̃prɑ̃dr] §56 *tr* to understand; comprehend, include, comprise ‖ *intr* to understand ‖ *ref* to be understood; be included

compresse [kɔ̃prɛs] *f* (med) compress

compresseur [kɔ̃prɛsœr] *m* compressor; **compresseur pneumatique** air pump

compression [kɔ̃prɛsjɔ̃] *f* compression; repression; reduction

compri•mé -mée [kɔ̃prime] *adj* compressed ‖ *m* (pharm) tablet, lozenge

comprimer [kɔ̃prime] *tr* to compress; repress

com•pris [kɔ̃pri] **-prise** [priz] *adj* understood; included, including, e.g., **la ferme comprise** or **y compris la ferme** the farm included, including the farm

compromet•tant [kɔ̃prɔmɛtɑ̃] **-tante** [tɑ̃t] *adj* compromising, incriminating

compromettre [kɔ̃prɔmɛtr] §42 *tr* to compromise ‖ *intr* to submit to arbitration ‖ *ref* to compromise oneself

compromis [kɔ̃prɔmi] *m* compromise

comptabiliser [kɔ̃tabilize] *tr* (com) to enter into the books

comptabilité [kɔ̃tabilite] *f* bookkeeping, accounting; accounting department, accounts; **comptabilité en partie double** double-entry bookkeeping; **comptabilité simple** single-entry bookkeeping; **tenir la comptabilité** to keep the books

comptable [kɔ̃tabl] *adj* accountable, responsible; accounting (*machine*) ‖ *mf* bookkeeper; **comptable agréé** or **expert comptable** certified public accountant; **comptable contrôleur** auditor

comp•tant [kɔ̃tɑ̃] **-tante** [tɑ̃t] *adj* spot (*cash*); down, e.g., **argent comptant** cash down ‖ *m*—**au comptant** cash, for cash ‖ **comptant** *adv* cash (down), e.g., **payer comptant** to pay cash

compte [kɔ̃t] *m* account; accounting; (sports) count; **à bon compte** cheap; **à ce compte** in that case; **à compte** on account; **au bout du compte** or **en fin de compte** when all is said and done; **compte à rebours** countdown; **compte courant** current account; charge account; **compte de couverture** margin account; **compte de dépôt** checking account; **compte de profits et pertes** profit and loss statement; **compte en banque** bank account; **compte rendu** report, review; **compte rendu de fin de mission** debriefing; **compte rond** round numbers; **donner son compte à** to give the final paycheck to, to discharge; **être en compte à demi** to go fifty-fifty; **faire un compte rendu à** to debrief; **loin de compte** wide of the mark; **rendre compte de** to review; **se rendre compte de** to realize, to be aware of; **tenir compte de** to bear in mind

compte-fils [kɔ̃tfil] *m invar* cloth prover

compte-gouttes [kɔ̃tgut] *m invar* dropper; **au compte-gouttes** in driblets

compte-minutes [kɔ̃tminyt] *m invar* timer

compter [kɔ̃te] §95 *tr* to count; number, have; **compter + inf** to count on + *ger*; **sans compter** not to mention ‖ *intr* to count; **à compter de** starting from; **compter avec** to reckon with; **compter sur** to count on

compte-tours [kɔ̃tətur] *m invar* tachometer, r.p.m. counter

comp•teur [kɔ̃tœr] **-teuse** [tøz] *mf* counter, checker (*person*) ‖ *m* meter; counter; speedometer; **compteur de gaz** gas meter; **compteur de Geiger** Geiger counter; **compteur de stationnement** parking meter; **relever le compteur** to read the meter

compteur-indicateur [kɔ̃tœrɛ̃dikatœr] *m* (*pl* **compteurs-indicateurs**) speedometer

comptine [kɔ̃tin] *f* counting-out rhyme

comptoir [kɔ̃twar] *m* counter; branch bank; bank; **comptoir postal** mail-order house

compulser [kɔ̃pylse] *tr* to go through, examine (*books, papers, etc.*)

computer [kɔ̃pyte] *tr* to compute

comte [kɔ̃t] *m* count

comté [kɔ̃te] *m* county

comtesse [kɔ̃tɛs] *f* countess

con [kɔ̃] *m* (vulg) vagina; (vulg) stupid and contemptible person

concasser [kɔ̃kase] *tr* to crush, pound

concasseur [kɔ̃kasœr] *adj masc* crushing ‖ *m* (mach) crusher

concave [kɔ̃kav] *adj* concave

concéder [kɔ̃sede] §10 *tr & intr* to concede

concentration [kɔ̃sɑ̃trɑsjɔ̃] *f* concentration

concentrationnaire [kɔ̃sɑ̃trɑsjɔnɛr] *adj* concentration-camp, in concentration camps

concen•tré -trée [kɔ̃sɑ̃tre] *adj* concentrated; condensed (*milk*); reserved (*person*)

concentrer [kɔ̃sɑ̃tre] *tr* to concentrate; repress, hold back

concentrique [kɔ̃sɑ̃trik] *adj* concentric

concept [kɔ̃sɛpt] *m* concept

conception [kɔ̃sɛpsjɔ̃] *f* conception; **l'Immaculée Conception** (rel) the Immaculate Conception

concerner [kɔ̃sɛrne] *tr* to concern; **en ce qui concerne** concerning

concert [kɔ̃sɛr] *m* concert; **de concert** together, in concert

concer•tant [kɔ̃sɛrtɑ̃] **-tante** [tɑ̃t] *adj* performing together ‖ *mf* (mus) performer

concerter [kɔ̃sɛrte] *tr & ref* to concert, plan

concertiste [kɔ̃sɛrtist] *mf* concert performer

concession [kɔ̃sɛsjɔ̃] *f* concession

concessionnaire [kɔ̃sɛsjɔnɛr] *mf* grantee,

licensee; dealer (*in automobiles*); agent (*for insurance*)

concetti [kɔtʃeti] *mpl* conceits

concevable [kɔ̃səvabl] *adj* conceivable

concevoir [kɔ̃səvwar] **§59** *tr* to conceive; compose (*a letter, telegram*)

concierge [kɔ̃sjɛrʒ] *mf* concierge, building superintendent

concile [kɔ̃sil] *m* (eccl) council

concilia•teur [kɔ̃siljatœr] **-trice** [tris] *adj* conciliating ‖ *mf* conciliator

conciliatoire [kɔ̃siljatwar] *adj* conciliatory

concilier [kɔ̃silje] *tr* to reconcile (*two parties, two ideas, etc.*); win (*e.g., favor*) ‖ *ref* to win, gain (*friendship, esteem*)

con•cis [kɔ̃si] **-cise** [siz] *adj* concise

concitoyen [kɔ̃sitwajɛ̃] **concitoyenne** [kɔ̃sitwajɛn] *mf* fellow citizen

concluant [kɔklyɑ̃] **concluante** [kɔklyɑ̃t] *adj* conclusive

conclure [kɔklyr] **§11** *tr* to conclude ‖ *intr* to conclude; **conclure à** to decide on, decide in favor of

conclusion [kɔklyzjɔ̃] *f* conclusion

concombre [kɔkɔbr] *m* cucumber

concomi•tant [kɔkɔmitɑ̃] **-tante** [tɑ̃t] *adj* concomitant

concordance [kɔkɔrdɑ̃s] *f* agreement; concordance (*of Bible*)

concor•dant [kɔkɔrdɑ̃] **-dante** [dɑ̃t] *adj* in agreement; supporting (*evidence*)

concorde [kɔkɔrd] *f* concord

concorder [kɔkɔrde] *intr* to agree

concourir [kɔkurir] **§14, §96** *intr* to compete; cooperate; converge, concur

concours [kɔkur] *m* crowd; cooperation; contest, competition, meet; competitive examination; **concours de beauté** beauty contest; **concours de créanciers** meeting of creditors; **concours hippique** horse show; **hors concours** not competing; in a class by itself

con•cret [kɔkrɛ] **-crète** [krɛt] *adj & m* concrete

concrétiser [kɔkretize] *tr* to put in concrete form

con•çu -çue [kɔsy] *v* see **concevoir**

concubine [kɔkybin] *f* concubine

concurrence [kɔkyrɑ̃s] *f* competition; competitors; **jusqu'à concurrence de** to the amount of; **libre concurrence** free enterprise

concurrencer [kɔkyrɑ̃se] **§51** *tr* to rival, compete with

concur•rent [kɔkyrɑ̃] **-rente** [rɑ̃t] *adj* competitive ‖ *mf* competitor; contestant

concurren•tiel -tielle [kɔkyrɑ̃sjɛl] *adj* competitive

concussion [kɔkysjɔ̃] *f* extortion; embezzlement

condamnable [kɔdɑnabl] *adj* blameworthy

condamnation [kɔdɑnɑsjɔ̃] *f* condemnation; conviction, sentence

condam•né -née [kɔdɑne] *mf* convict

condamner [kɔdɑne] **§96, §100** *tr* to condemn; give up (*an incurable patient*); forbid the use

of; board up (*a window*); batten down (*the hatches*)

condensateur [kɔdɑ̃satœr] *m* (elec) condenser

condenser [kɔdɑ̃se] *tr & ref* to condense

condenseur [kɔdɑ̃sœr] *m* condenser

condescendance [kɔdesɑ̃dɑ̃s] *f* condescension

condescen•dant [kɔdesɑ̃dɑ̃] **-dante** [dɑ̃t] *adj* condescending, patronizing

condescendre [kɔdesɑ̃dr] **§96** *intr* to condescend; to yield, comply

condiment [kɔdimɑ̃] *m* condiment

condisciple [kɔdisipl] *mf* classmate

condition [kɔdisjɔ̃] *f* condition; **à condition, sous condition** conditionally; on approval; **à condition de, à condition que** on condition that; **dans de bonnes conditions** in good condition; **sans conditions** unconditional

condition•nel -nelle [kɔdisjɔnɛl] *adj & m* conditional

conditionnement [kɔdisjɔnmɑ̃] *m* packaging; conditioning

conditionner [kɔdisjɔne] *tr* to condition; (com) to package

condoléances [kɔdɔleɑ̃s] *fpl* condolence

condom [kɔdɔm] *m* condom, prophylactic

conduc•teur [kɔdyktœr] **-trice** [tris] *adj* conducting; driving; (elec) power (*line*); (elec) lead (*wire*) ‖ *adj masc* (elec, phys) (in predicate after **être**, it may be translated by a noun) conductor, e.g., **les métaux sont bons conducteurs de l'électricité** metals are good conductors of electricity ‖ *mf* guide; leader; driver; **conducteur qui prend la fuite** hit-and-run driver ‖ *m* motorman; foreman; pressman; (elec, phys) conductor; **conducteur du char** charioteer

conduire [kɔdɥir] **§19, §95, §96** *tr* to conduct; to lead; drive; see (*s.o. to the door*) ‖ *intr* to drive ‖ *ref* to conduct oneself

conduit [kɔdɥi] *m* conduit; **conduit d'aération** ventilation shaft; **conduit auditif** auditory canal; **conduits lacrymaux** tear ducts

conduite [kɔdɥit] *f* conduct, behavior; management, command; driving (*of a car; of cattle*); pipeline; duct, flue; **avoir de la conduite** to be well behaved; **conduite d'eau** water main; **conduite intérieure** closed car; **conduite pendant la nuit** night driving; **faire la conduite a** to escort; **faire une conduite de Grenoble à qn** (coll) to kick s.o. out

cône [kon] *m* cone

confection [kɔfɛksjɔ̃] *f* manufacture; construction (*e.g., of a machine*); ready-made clothes; **de confection** ready-made (*suit, dress, etc.*)

confectionner [kɔfɛksjɔne] *tr* to manufacture; prepare (*a dish*)

confection•neur [kɔfɛksjɔnœr] **-neuse** [nøz] *mf* manufacturer (*esp. of ready-made clothes*)

confédération [kɔfederɑsjɔ̃] *f* confederation, confederacy; **Confédération suisse** Federal Republic of Switzerland confédérer [kɔ̃federe] §10 *tr* & *ref* to confederate

conférence [kɔ̃ferɑ̃s] *f* conference; lecture, speech; **conférence au sommet** summit conference; **conférence de presse** press conference

conféren•cier [kɔ̃ferɑ̃sje] -cière [sjɛr] *mf* lecturer, speaker

conférer [kɔ̃fere] §10 *tr* to confer, award; administer (*a sacrament*); collate, compare || *intr* to confer

confesse [kɔ̃fɛs] *f*—**à confesse** to confession; **de confesse** from confession

confesser [kɔ̃fese] §95 *tr* to confess; (coll) to pump (*s.o.*) || *ref* to confess

confesseur [kɔ̃fɛsœr] *m* confessor

confession [kɔ̃fɛsjɔ̃] *f* confession; (eccl) denomination

confessionnal [kɔ̃fɛsjɔnal] *m* confessional

confession•nel -nelle [kɔ̃fɛsjɔnɛl] *adj* denominational

confiance [kɔ̃fjɑ̃s] *f* confidence; **confiance en soi** self-confidence; **de confiance** reliable; confidently; **en confiance** with confidence

con•fiant [kɔ̃fjɑ̃] -fiante [fjɑ̃t] *adj* confident; confiding, trusting

confidence [kɔ̃fidɑ̃s] *f* confidence, secret

confi•dent [kɔ̃fidɑ̃] -dente [dɑ̃t] *mf* confident

confiden•tiel -tielle [kɔ̃fidɑ̃sjɛl] *adj* confidential

confier [kɔ̃fje] *tr* to entrust; confide, disclose; commit (*to memory*); consign; **confier à** to put (*seed*) in (*the ground*) || *ref*—**se confier à** to confide in, to trust; **se confier en** to put one's trust in

confinement [kɔ̃finmɑ̃] *m* imprisonment; (nucl) containment (*in a reactor*)

confiner [kɔ̃fine] *tr* to confine || *intr*—**confiner à** to border on, verge on || *ref* to confine oneself; **se confiner dans** to confine oneself to

confins [kɔ̃fɛ̃] *mpl* confines

confire [kɔ̃fir] §66 (*pp* **confit**) *tr* to preserve; pickle; candy; can (*goose, chicken, etc.*); dip (*skins*) || *ref* to become immersed (*in work, prayer, etc.*)

confirmer [kɔ̃firme] *tr* to confirm

confiscation [kɔ̃fiskasjɔ̃] *f* confiscation

confiserie [kɔ̃fizri] *f* confectionery

confi•seur [kɔ̃fizœr] -seuse [zøz] *mf* confectioner, candymaker

confisquer [kɔ̃fiske] *tr* to confiscate

con•fit [kɔ̃fi] -fite [fit] *adj* preserved; pickled; candied; steeped (*e.g., in piety*); incrusted (*in bigotry*) || *m* canned chicken, goose, etc.

confiture [kɔ̃fityr] *f* preserves, jam

confitu•rier [kɔ̃fityrje] -rière [rjɛr] *mf* manufacturer of jams || *m* jelly glass, jam jar

conflagration [kɔ̃flagrasjɔ̃] *f* conflagration, turmoil

conflit [kɔ̃fli] *m* conflict

confluer [kɔ̃flye] *intr* to meet, come together (*said of two rivers*)

confondre [kɔ̃fɔ̃dr] *tr* to confuse, mix up,

mingle; confound || *ref* to become bewildered, mixed up; **se confondre en excuses** to fall all over oneself apologizing

conforme [kɔ̃fɔrm] *adj* corresponding; certified, e.g., **pour copie conforme** certified copy; **conforme à** conformable to, consistent with; **conforme à l'échantillon** identical with sample; **conforme aux normes** according to specifications; **conforme aux règles** in order

confor•mé -mée [kɔ̃fɔrme] *adj* shaped, built; **bien conformé** well-built; **mal conformé** misshapen

conformément [kɔ̃fɔrmemɑ̃] *adv*—**conformément à** in compliance with

conformer [kɔ̃fɔrme] *tr* & *ref* to conform

conformiste [kɔ̃fɔrmist] *mf* conformist

conformité [kɔ̃fɔrmite] *f* conformity, conformance

confort [kɔ̃fɔr] *m* comfort; convenience

confortable [kɔ̃fɔrtabl] *adj* comfortable || *m* comfort; easy chair

confrère [kɔ̃frɛr] *m* confrere, colleague

confrérie [kɔ̃freri] *f* brotherhood

confronter [kɔ̃frɔ̃te] *tr* to confront; compare, collate

con•fus [kɔ̃fy] -fuse [fyz] *adj* confused; vague, blurred; embarrassed

confusion [kɔ̃fyzjɔ̃] *f* confusion; embarrassment

congé [kɔ̃ʒe] *m* leave; vacation; dismissal; **congé de maternité** maternity leave; **congé libérable** military discharge; **congé payé** vacation with pay; **donner congé à** to lay off; **donner son congé à** to give notice to; **prendre congé de** to take leave of

congédiement [kɔ̃ʒedimɑ̃] *m* dismissal, discharge; paying off (*of crew*)

congédier [kɔ̃ʒedje] *tr* to dismiss

congélateur [kɔ̃ʒelatœr] *m* freezer (*for frozen foods*)

congélation [kɔ̃ʒelasjɔ̃] *f* freezing

congeler [kɔ̃ʒəle] §2 *tr* & *ref* to freeze; congeal; **congeler à basse température** to deep-freeze

congénère [kɔ̃ʒenɛr] *adj* cognate (*words*); (biol) of the same species || *mf* fellow creature; **lui et ses congénères** he and his like

congéni•tal -tale [kɔ̃ʒenital] *adj* (*pl* -taux [to]) congenital

congère [kɔ̃ʒer] *f* snowdrift

congestion [kɔ̃ʒɛstjɔ̃] *f* congestion; **congestion cérébrale** stroke; **congestion pulmonaire** pneumonia

congestionner [kɔ̃ʒɛstjɔne] *tr* & *ref* to congest

conglomération [kɔ̃glɔmerasjɔ̃] *f* conglomeration

conglomérer [kɔ̃glɔmere] §10 *tr* & *ref* to conglomerate

congratulation [kɔ̃gratylasjɔ̃] *f* congratulation

congratuler [kɔ̃gratyle] *tr* to congratulate

congre [kɔ̃gr] *m* conger eel

congrégation [kɔ̃gregasjɔ̃] *f* (eccl) congregation

congrès [kɔ̃grɛ] *m* congress, convention, meeting, conference

congressiste [kɔ̃grɛsist] *mf* delegate ‖ *m* congressman ‖ *f* congresswoman

con•gru -grue [kɔ̃gry] *adj* precise, suitable; scanty; (math) congruent

conifère [kɔnifɛr] *adj* coniferous ‖ *m* conifer, evergreen

conique [kɔnik] *adj* conical ‖ *f* conic section

conjecture [kɔ̃ʒɛktyr] *f* conjecture

conjecturer [kɔ̃ʒɛktyre] *tr & intr* to conjecture, surmise

conjoindre [kɔ̃ʒwɛ̃dr] **§35** *tr* to join in marriage

con•joint [kɔ̃ʒwɛ̃] **-jointe** [ʒwɛ̃t] *adj* united, joint ‖ *mf* spouse, consort

conjoncteur [kɔ̃ʒɔ̃ktœr] *m* automatic switch

conjonction [kɔ̃ʒɔ̃ksjɔ̃] *f* conjunction

conjoncture [kɔ̃ʒɔ̃ktyr] *f* juncture, situation; **de haute conjoncture** boom

conjugaison [kɔ̃ʒygɛzɔ̃] *f* conjugation

conju•gal -gale [kɔ̃ʒygal] *adj* (*pl* **-gaux** [go]) conjugal, connubial

conjuguer [kɔ̃ʒyge] *tr* to combine (*e.g., forces*); conjugate

conjuration [kɔ̃ʒyrɑsjɔ̃] *f* conjuration; conspiracy; **conjurations** entreaties

conju•ré -rée [kɔ̃ʒyre] *mf* conspirator

conjurer [kɔ̃ʒyre] **§97** *tr* to conjure; conjure away; conjure up; conspire for, plot; **conjurer qn de** + *inf* to entreat s.o. to + *inf* ‖ *intr* to hatch a plot ‖ *ref* to plot together, conspire

connaissance [kɔnɛsɑ̃s] *f* knowledge; acquaintance; consciousness; attention; **connaissance des temps** nautical almanac; **connaissances** knowledge; **en connaissance de** with full knowledge of; **faire connaissance avec** to become acquainted with; **faire la connaissance de** to meet; **parler en connaissance de cause** to know what one is talking about; **perdre connaissance** to lose consciousness; **sans connaissance** unconscious

connaissement [kɔnɛsmɑ̃] *m* bill of lading

connais•seur [kɔnɛsœr] **-seuse** [søz] *mf* connoisseur; expert

connaître [kɔnɛtr] **§12** *tr* to know; be acquainted with ‖ *intr*—**connaître de** (law) to have jurisdiction over ‖ *ref* to be acquainted (with); become acquainted; **se connaître à** or **en** to know a lot about; **s'y connaître** to know what one is talking about; **s'y connaître en** to know a lot about

connecter [kɔnɛkte] *tr* to connect ‖ *ref* (comp) to interface

connerie [kɔnri] *f* stupidity; (vulg) bullshit; **faire une connerie** to foul up

connétable [kɔnetabl] *m* constable

connexe [kɔnɛks] *adj* connected

connexion [kɔnɛksjɔ̃] *f* connection

connexité [kɔnɛksite] *f* connection

con•nu -nue [kɔny] *adj* well-known ‖ *m*—**le connu** the known ‖ *v* see **connaître**

conque [kɔ̃k] *f* conch

conqué•rant -rante [kɔ̃kerɑ̃ -rɑ̃t] *adj* (coll) swaggering ‖ *mf* conqueror

conquérir [kɔ̃kerir] **§3** *tr* to conquer

conquête [kɔ̃kɛt] *f* conquest

consa•cré -crée [kɔ̃sakre] *adj* accepted, time-honored, stock

consacrer [kɔ̃sakre] **§96** *tr* to consecrate; devote, dedicate (*time, energy, effort*); give, spare (*e.g., time*); to sanction, confirm ‖ *ref*—**se consacrer à** to devote or dedicate oneself to

consan•guin [kɔ̃sɑ̃gɛ̃] **-guine** [gin] *adj* consanguineous; on the father's side ‖ *mf* blood relation

consciemment [kɔ̃sjamɑ̃] *adv* consciously

conscience [kɔ̃sjɑ̃s] *f* conscience; conscientiousness; consciousness; **avoir la conscience large** to be broad-minded; **en conscience** conscientiously

conscien•cieux [kɔ̃sjɑ̃sjø] **-cieuse** [sjøz] *adj* conscientious

cons•cient [kɔ̃sjɑ̃] **-ciente** [sjɑt] **§93** *adj* conscious, aware, knowing

conscription [kɔ̃skripsjɔ̃] *f* draft, conscription

conscrit [kɔ̃skri] *m* draftee, conscript

consécration [kɔ̃sekrɑsjɔ̃] *f* consecration; confirmation

consécu•tif [kɔ̃sekytif] **-tive** [tiv] *adj* consecutive; dependent (*clause*); **consécutif à** resulting from

conseil [kɔ̃sɛj] *m* advice, counsel; counselor; council, board, committee; **conseil d'administration** board of directors; **conseil de guerre** court-martial; staff meeting of top brass; **conseil de prud'hommes** arbitration board; **conseil de révision** draft board; **conseils** advice; **un conseil** a piece of advice

conseil•ler [kɔ̃seje] **-lère** [jɛr] *mf* councilor; counselor, adviser ‖ *f* councilor's wife; counselor's wife ‖ **conseiller §97, §98** *tr* to advise, counsel (*s.o. or s.th.*); **conseiller q.ch. à qn** to recommend s.th. to s.o. ‖ *intr* to advise, counsel; **conseiller à qn de** + *inf* to advise s.o. to + *inf*

conseil•leur [kɔ̃sɛjɛr] **-leuse** [jøz] *mf* adviser; know-it-all

consensus [kɔ̃sɛ̃sys] *m* consensus

consentement [kɔ̃sɑ̃tmɑ̃] *m* consent; **consentement tacite** gentleman's agreement (*tacit agreement*)

consentir [kɔ̃sɑ̃tir] **§41, §96** *tr* to grant, allow; accept, recognize; **consentir (à ce) que** + *subj* to permit (*s.o.*) to + *inf* ‖ *intr* to consent; **consentir à** to consent to, agree to, approve of

conséquemment [kɔ̃sekamɑ̃] *adv* consequently; consistently; **conséquemment à** as a result of

conséquence [kɔ̃sekɑ̃s] *f* consequence; consistency; **en conséquence** accordingly

consé•quent [kɔ̃sekɑ̃] **-quente** [kɑt] *adj* consequent; consistent; important ‖ *m* (logic, math) consequent; **par conséquent** consequently

conserva•teur [kɔ̃sɛrvatœr] **-trice** [tris] *adj* conservative ‖ *mf* conservative; curator, keeper; warden, ranger; registrar

conservation [kɔ̃sɛrvɑsjɔ̃] *f* conservation, preservation; curatorship; curator's office
conservatisme [kɔ̃sɛrvatism] *m* conservatism
conservatoire [kɔ̃sɛrvatwar] *m* conservatory (*of music*); museum, academy
conserve [kɔ̃sɛrv] *f* canned food, preserves; escort, convoy; **conserves** dark glasses; **conserves au vinaigre** pickles; **mettre en conserve** to can; **voler de conserve avec** to fly alongside of
conserver [kɔ̃sɛrve] *tr* to conserve; preserve; keep (*one's health; one's equanimity; a secret*); escort, convoy (*a ship*) || *ref* to stay in good shape; take care of oneself
conserverie [kɔ̃sɛrvəri] *f* canning factory; canning
considérable [kɔ̃siderabl] *adj* considerable; important; large, great
considérant [kɔ̃siderɑ̃] *m* motive, grounds; **considérant que** whereas
considération [kɔ̃siderɑsjɔ̃] *f* consideration
considé•ré -rée [kɔ̃sidere] respected
considérer [kɔ̃sidere] §10 *tr* to consider, examine; esteem, consider
consignataire [kɔ̃siɲatɛr] *m* consignee, trustee
consignation [kɔ̃siɲɑsjɔ̃] *f* consignment; **en consignation** on consignment
consigne [kɔ̃siɲ] *f* password; baggage room, checkroom; checking fee; confinement to barracks, detention; bottle deposit; (mil) orders, instructions; **consigne ordinaire** baggage check; **en consigne à la douane** held up in customs; **être de consigne** to be on duty; **manquer à la consigne** to disobey orders
consigner [kɔ̃siɲe] *tr* to consign; check (*baggage*); put down in writing, enter in the record; confine to barracks, keep (*a student*) in; put out of bounds (*e.g., for military personnel*); close (*a port*); **consigner sa** (or **la**) **porte** to be at home to no one
consistance [kɔ̃sistɑ̃s] *f* solidity, consistency; stability (*of character*); credit, reality, standing; **en consistance de** consisting of
consis•tant -tante [kɔ̃sistɑ̃] [tɑ̃t] *adj* consistent; stable (*character*); solid, substantial; well-founded (*information*); **consistant en** consisting of
consister [kɔ̃siste] §96 *intr*—**consister à** + *inf* to consist in + *ger;* **consister dans** or **en** to consist in; consist of
consistoire [kɔ̃sistwar] *m* consistory
consola•teur [kɔ̃sɔlatœr] **-trice** [tris] *adj* consoling || *mf* comforter
consolation [kɔ̃sɔlɑsjɔ̃] *f* consolation
console [kɔ̃sɔl] *f* console; console table; bracket; (comp) console; **console graphique, console de visualisation** (comp) desktop
consoler [kɔ̃sɔle] §97, §99 *tr* to console
consolider [kɔ̃sɔlide] *tr* to consolidate; fund (*a debt*)
consomma•teur [kɔ̃sɔmatœr] **-trice** [tris] *mf* consumer; customer (*in a restaurant or bar*)
consommation [kɔ̃sɔmɑsjɔ̃] *f* consummation

(*e.g., of a marriage*); perpetration (*e.g., of a crime*); consumption, use; drink (*e.g., in a café*)
consom•mé -mée [kɔ̃sɔme] *adj* consummate; skilled (*e.g., technician*); consumed, used up || *m* consommé
consommer [kɔ̃sɔme] *tr* to consummate, complete; perpetrate (*e.g., a crime*); consume
consomp•tif [kɔ̃sɔ̃ptif] **-tive** [tiv] *adj* wasting away
consomption [kɔ̃sɔ̃psjɔ̃] *f* wasting away, decline
conso•nant [kɔ̃sɔnɑ̃] **-nante** [nɑt] *adj* consonant, harmonious
consonne [kɔ̃sɔn] *f* consonant
consorts [kɔ̃sɔr] *mpl* partners, associates; (pej) confederates
conspira•teur [kɔ̃spiratœr] **-trice** [tris] *mf* conspirator
conspiration [kɔ̃spirɑsjɔ̃] *f* conspiracy
conspirer [kɔ̃spire] §96 *tr & intr* to conspire
conspuer [kɔ̃spɥe] *tr* to boo, hiss
constamment [kɔ̃stamɑ̃] *adv* constantly
constance [kɔ̃stɑ̃s] *f* constancy
cons•tant [kɔ̃stɑ̃] **-tante** [tɑ̃t] *adj* constant; true; established, evident || *f* constant
constat [kɔ̃sta] *m* affidavit
constatation [kɔ̃statɑsjɔ̃] *f* authentication; declaration, claim
constater [kɔ̃state] *tr* to certify; find out; prove, establish
constellation [kɔ̃stɛllɑsjɔ̃] *f* constellation
consteller [kɔ̃stɛlle] *tr* to spangle
consterner [kɔ̃stɛrne] *tr* to dismay
constipation [kɔ̃stipɑsjɔ̃] *f* constipation
constiper [kɔ̃stipe] *tr* to constipate
consti•tuant [kɔ̃stitɥɑ̃] **-tuante** [tɥɑ̃t] *adj & m* constituent
constituer [kɔ̃stitɥe] *tr* to constitue; settle (*a dowry*); form (*a cabinet; a corporation*); empanel (*a jury*); appoint (*a lawyer*) || *ref* to be formed; **se constituer prisonnier** to give oneself up
constitu•tif [kɔ̃stitytif] **-tive** [tiv] *adj* constituent
constitution [kɔ̃stitysjɔ̃] *f* constitution; settlement (*of a dowry*); **constitution en société** incorporation
construc•teur [kɔ̃stryktœr] **-trice** [tris] *adj* constructive, building || *mf* constructor, builder
construc•tif [kɔ̃stryktif] **-tive** [tiv] *adj* constructive
construction [kɔ̃stryksjɔ̃] *f* construction; **construction mécanique** mechanical engineering
construire [kɔ̃strɥir] §19 *tr* to construct, build; draw (*e.g., a triangle*); (gram) to construe
consul [kɔ̃syl] *m* consul
consulaire [kɔ̃sylɛr] *adj* consular
consulat [kɔ̃syla] *m* consulate
consul•tant [kɔ̃syltɑ̃] **-tante** [tɑ̃t] *adj* consulting || *mf* consultant
consulta•tif [kɔ̃syltatif] **-tive** [tiv] *adj* advisory
consultation [kɔ̃syltɑsjɔ̃] *f* consultation;

consultation externe outpatient clinic; **consultation populaire** poll, referendum
consulte [kɔ̃sylt] *f* (eccl, law) consultation
consulter [kɔ̃sylte] *tr* to consult ‖ *intr* to consult, give consultations ‖ *ref* to deliberate
consumer [kɔ̃syme] *tr* to consume, use up, destroy ‖ **§96** *ref* to burn out; waste away; fail
contact [kɔ̃takt] *m* contact; **mettre en contact** to put in touch, to connect; **prendre contact** to make contact
contacter [kɔ̃takte] *tr* (coll) to contact
conta•gieux [kɔ̃taʒiø] **-gieuse** [ʒjøz] *adj* contagious
contagion [kɔ̃taʒjɔ̃] *f* contagion
contamination [kɔ̃taminɑsjɔ̃] *f* contamination
contaminer [kɔ̃tamine] *tr* to contaminate
conte [kɔ̃t] *m* tale, story; (pej) tall tale, snow job; **conte à dormir debout** cock-and-bull story, baloney; **conte de fées** fairy tale
contemplation [kɔ̃tɑ̃plɑsjɔ̃] *f* contemplation
contempler [kɔ̃tɑ̃ple] *tr* to contemplate
contempo•rain [kɔ̃tɑ̃pɔrɛ̃] **-raine** [rɛn] *adj & m* contemporary, coeval *m*
contemp•teur [kɔ̃tɑ̃ptœr] **-trice** [tris] *mf* scoffer
contenance [kɔ̃tnɑ̃s] *f* capacity; area; countenance; **faire bonne contenance** to put up a bold front
conte•nant [kɔ̃tnɑ̃] **-nante** [nɑ̃t] *adj* containing ‖ *m* container
conteneur [kɔ̃tnœr] *m* container
conteneuriser [kɔ̃tnœrize] *tr* to containerize
contenir [kɔ̃tnir] **§72** *tr* to contain; restrain ‖ *ref* to contain oneself, hold oneself back
con•tent [kɔ̃tɑ̃] **-tente** [tɑ̃t] **§93** *adj* content; happy, glad, pleased; **content de** satisfied with ‖ *m* fill, e.g., **avoir son content** to have one's fill
contentement [kɔ̃tɑ̃tmɑ̃] *m* contentment
contenter [kɔ̃tɑ̃te] *tr* to content, satisfy ‖ **§97, §99** *ref* to satisfy one's desires; **se contenter de** to be content or satisfied with
conten•tieux [kɔ̃tɑ̃sjø] **-tieuse** [sjøz] *adj* contentious ‖ *m* contention, litigation; claims department
contention [kɔ̃tɑ̃sjɔ̃] *f* application, intentness
conte•nu -nue [kɔ̃tny] *adj* contained, restrained, stifled ‖ *m* contents
conter [kɔ̃te] *tr* to relate, tell; **en conter à** (coll) to take (*s.o.*) in; **en conter (de belles)** (coll) to tell tall tales ‖ *intr* to narrate, tell a story
contestation [kɔ̃tɛstɑsjɔ̃] *f* argument, dispute; **sans contestation** without opposition
conteste [kɔ̃tɛst] *f*—**sans conteste** incontestably, unquestionably
contester [kɔ̃tɛste] *tr & intr* to contest
con•teur [kɔ̃tœr] **-teuse** [tøz] *mf* story teller, narrator
contexte [kɔ̃tɛkst] *m* context
contexture [kɔ̃tɛkstyr] *f* texture; structure, makeup
conti•gu -guë [kɔ̃tigy] *adj* contiguous; **contigue à** adjoining
continence [kɔ̃tinɑ̃s] *f* continence

conti•nent [kɔ̃tinɑ̃] **-nente** [nɑ̃t] *adj & m* continent
continen•tal -tale [kɔ̃tinɑ̃tal] *adj* (*pl* **-taux** [to]) continental
contingence [kɔ̃tɛ̃ʒɑ̃s] *f* contingency
contin•gent [kɔ̃tɛ̃ʒɑ̃] **-gente** [ʒɑ̃t] *adj* contingent ‖ *m* contingent; quota
conti•nu -nue [kɔ̃tiny] *adj* continuous; nonstop; direct (*current*) ‖ *m* continuum
continuation [kɔ̃tinɥɑsjɔ̃] *f* continuation
conti•nuel -nuelle [kɔ̃tinɥɛl] *adj* continual
continuer [kɔ̃tinɥe] **§96, §97** *tr* to continue; carry on (with), go on with ‖ *intr & ref* to go on, continue
continuité [kɔ̃tinɥite] *f* continuity
continûment [kɔ̃tinymɑ̃] *adv* continuously
conton•dant [kɔ̃tɔ̃dɑ̃] **-dante** [dɑ̃t] *adj* blunt
contorsion [kɔ̃tɔrsjɔ̃] *f* contortion
contour [kɔ̃tur] *m* contour
contourner [kɔ̃turne] *tr* to contour; go around, skirt; get around (*the law*); twist, distort
contrac•tant [kɔ̃traktɑ̃] **-tante** [tɑ̃t] *adj* contracting (*parties*) ‖ *mf* contracting party
contracter [kɔ̃trakte] *tr* to contract; float (*a loan*) ‖ *ref* to contract; be contracted
contraction [kɔ̃traksjɔ̃] *f* contraction
contractuelle [kɔ̃traktɥɛl] *f* meter maid
contradiction [kɔ̃tradiksjɔ̃] *f* contradiction
contradictoire [kɔ̃tradiktwar] *adj* contradictory
contraindre [kɔ̃trɛ̃dr] **§15, §97** *tr* to compel, force, constrain; restrain; curb ‖ *ref* to restrain oneself
con•traint [kɔ̃trɛ̃] **-trainte** [trɛ̃t] **§93** *adj* constrained, forced; stiff (*person*) ‖ *f* constraint; restraint; exigencies (*e.g., of the rhyme*)
contraire [kɔ̃trɛr] *adj* contrary; opposite (*e.g., direction*); injurious (*e.g., to health*) ‖ *m* contrary, opposite; antonym; **au contraire** on the contrary
contrairement [kɔ̃trɛrmɑ̃] *adv* contrary
contrarier [kɔ̃trarje] *tr* to thwart; vex, annoy; contrast (*e.g., colors*)
contrariété [kɔ̃trarjete] vexation, annoyance; clashing (*e.g., of colors*)
contraste [kɔ̃trast] *m* contrast
contraster [kɔ̃traste] *tr & intr* to contrast
contrat [kɔ̃tra] *m* contract, agreement; (game) highest bid (*specifying the exact number of tricks to be scored*; **remplir son contrat** (bridge) to make one's contract
contravention [kɔ̃travɑ̃sjɔ̃] *f* infraction; **dresser une contravention** to write out a (traffic) ticket; **recevoir une contravention** to get a ticket
contre [kɔ̃tr] *m* opposite, con; (cards) double; **par contre** on the contrary ‖ *adv* against; nearby; **contre à contre** alongside ‖ *prep* against; contrary to; to, e.g., **dix contre un** ten to one; for, e.g., **échanger contre** to exchange for; e.g., **remède contre la toux** remedy for a cough; (sports) versus; **contre remboursement** (com) collect on delivery

contre-allée [kɔ̃trale] *f* (*pl* **-allées**) parallel walk

contre-amiral [kɔ̃tramiral] *m* (*pl* **-amiraux** [amiro]) rear admiral

contre-appel [kɔ̃trapɛl] *m* (*pl* **-appels**) second roll call; double-check

contre-attaque [kɔ̃tratak] *f* (*pl* **-attaques**) counterattack

contre-attaquer [kɔ̃tratake] *tr* to counterattack

contrebalancer [kɔ̃trəbalɑ̃se] **§51** *tr* to counterbalance

contrebande [kɔ̃trəbɑ̃d] *f* contraband; smuggling; **faire la contrebande** to smuggle

contreban•dier [kɔ̃trəbɑ̃dje] **-dière** [djɛr] *adj* smuggled, contraband ‖ *mf* smuggler

contrebas [kɔ̃trəbɑ]—**en contrebas** downward

contrebasse [kɔ̃trəbas] *f* contrabass

contre-biais [kɔ̃trəbjɛ]—**à contre-biais** the wrong way, against the grain

contre-boutant [kɔ̃trəbutɑ̃] *m* (*pl* **-boutants**) shore

contrecarrer [kɔ̃trəkare] *tr* to stymie, thwart

contre-chant [kɔ̃trəʃɑ̃] *m* (*pl* **-chants**) counter melody

contrecœur [kɔ̃trəkœr] *m* smoke shelf; **à contrecœur** unwillingly

contrecoup [kɔ̃trəku] *m* rebound, recoil, backlash; repercussion

contre-courant [kɔ̃trəkurɑ̃] *m* (*pl* **courants**) countercurrent; **à contre-courant** upstream; behind the times

contredire [kɔ̃trədir] **§40** *tr* to contradict ‖ *ref* to contradict oneself

contrée [kɔ̃tre] *f* region, countryside

contre-écrou [kɔ̃trekru] *m* (*pl* **-écrous**) lock nut

contre-espion [kɔ̃trɛspjɔ̃] *m* (*pl* **-espions**) counterspy

contre-espionnage [kɔ̃trɛspjɔnaʒ] *m* (*pl* **-espionnages**) counterespionage

contrefaçon [kɔ̃trəfasɔ̃] *f* infringement (*of patent or copyright*); forgery; counterfeit; plagiarism

contrefacteur [kɔ̃trəfaktœr] *m* forger; counterfeiter; plagiarist

contrefaction [kɔ̃trəfaksjɔ̃] *f* forgery; counterfeiting

contrefaire [kɔ̃trəfɛr] **§29** *tr* to forge; counterfeit; imitate, mimic; disguise

contre•fait [kɔ̃trəfɛ] **-faite** [fɛt] *adj* counterfeit; deformed

contre-fenêtre [kɔ̃trəfnɛtr] *f* (*pl* **-fenêtres**) inner sash; storm window

contre-feu [kɔ̃trəfø] *m* (*pl* **-feux**) backfire (*in fire fighting*)

contreficher [kɔ̃trəfiʃe] *ref* (slang) to not give a rap

contre-fil [kɔ̃trəfil] *m* (*pl* **-fils**) opposite direction, wrong way; **à contre-fil** upstream; against the grain

contre-filet [kɔ̃trəfilɛ] *m* short loin (*club and porterhouse steaks*)

contrefort [kɔ̃trəfɔr] *m* buttress, abutment; foothills

contre-haut [kɔ̃tro]—**en contre-haut** on a higher level; from top to bottom

contre-interrogatoire [kɔ̃trɛ̃tɛrɔgatwar] *m* cross-examination

contre-interroger [kɔ̃trɛ̃tɛrɔʒe] **§38** *tr* to cross-examine

contre-jour [kɔ̃trəʒur] *m invar* backlighting; **à contre-jour** against the light

contremaî•tre [kɔ̃trəmɛtr] **-tresse** [trɛs] *mf* overseer ‖ *m* foreman; (naut) (hist) boatswain's mate; (nav) petty officer ‖ forewoman

contremander [kɔ̃trəmɑ̃de] *tr* to countermand; call off

contremarche [kɔ̃trəmarʃ] *f* countermarch; riser (*of stair step*)

contremarque [kɔ̃trəmark] *f* countersign; passout check

contremarquer [kɔ̃trəmarke] *tr* to countersign

contre-mesure [kɔ̃trəmzyr] *f* (*pl* **-mesures**) countermeasure

contre-offensive [kɔ̃trɔfɑ̃siv] *f* (*pl* **-offensives**) counteroffensive

contrepartie [kɔ̃trəparti] *f* counterpart; (bk) duplicate entry; **en contrepartie** as against this

contre-pas [kɔ̃trəpa] *m invar* half step (*taken in order to get in step*)

contre-pente [kɔ̃trəpɑ̃t] *f* (*pl* **-pentes**) reverse slope

contre-performance [kɔ̃trəpɛrfɔrmɑ̃s] *f* (*pl* **-performances**) unexpected defeat

contrepèterie [kɔ̃trəpɛtri] *f* spoonerism

contre-pied [kɔ̃trəpje] *m* (*pl* **-pieds**) backtrack; opposite opinion; **à contre-pied** off balance

contre-plaqué [kɔ̃trəplake] *m* (*pl* **-plaqués**) plywood

contre-plaquer [kɔ̃trəplake] *tr* to laminate

contrepoids [kɔ̃trəpwa] *m invar* counterweight, counterbalance

contre-poil [kɔ̃trəpwal] *m* wrong way (*e.g., of fur*); **à contre-poil** the wrong way; at the wrong end

contrepoint [kɔ̃trəpwɛ̃] *m* counterpoint

contre-pointe [kɔ̃trəpwɛ̃t] *f* (*pl* **-pointes**) false edge (*of sword*); tailstock (*of lathe*)

contre-pointer [kɔ̃trəpwɛ̃te] *tr* to quilt

contrepoison [kɔ̃trəpwazɔ̃] *m* antidote

contrer [kɔ̃tre] *tr & intr* (cards) to double; (coll) to counter

contreseing [kɔ̃trəsɛ̃] *m* countersignature

contresens [kɔ̃trəsɑ̃s] *m invar* misinterpretation; mistranslation; wrong way; **à contresens** in the wrong sense; in the wrong direction

contresigner [kɔ̃trəsiɲe] *tr* to countersign

contretemps [kɔ̃trətɑ̃] *m*—**à contre-temps** at the wrong moment; syncopated

contre-torpilleur [kɔ̃trətɔrpijœr] *m* (*pl* **-torpilleurs**) (nav) torpedo-boat destroyer

contreve•nant [kɔ̃trəvnɑ̃] **-nante** [nɑ̃t] *mf* lawbreaker, delinquent

contrevenir [kɔ̃trəvnir] **§72** *intr*—**contrevenir à** to contravene, break (*a law*)

contrevent [kɔ̃trəvɑ̃] *m* shutter, window shutter

contre-voie [kɔ̃trəvwa] *f* (*pl* **-voies**) parallel route; **à contre-voie** in reverse (*of the usual direction*); on the side opposite the platform

contribuable [kɔ̃tribɥabl] *adj* taxpaying ‖ *mf* taxpayer

contribuer [kɔ̃tribɥe] §96 *intr* to contribute

contribution [kɔ̃tribysjɔ̃] *f* contribution; tax

contrister [kɔ̃triste] *tr* to sadden

con•trit [kɔ̃tri] **-trite** [trit] *adj* contrite

contrôlable [kɔ̃trolabl] *adj* verifiable

contrôle [kɔ̃trol] *m* inspection, verification, check; supervision, observation; auditing; inspection booth, ticket window; (mil) muster roll; **contrôle des naissances** birth control; **contrôle de soi** self-control; **contrôle par sondage** spot check

contrôler [kɔ̃trole] *tr* to inspect, verify, check; supervise, put under observation; audit; criticize ‖ *ref* to control oneself

contrô•leur [kɔ̃trolœr] **-leuse** [løz] *mf* inspector, checker; supervisor, observer; auditor, comptroller; conductor, ticket collector; **contrôleur de la navigation aérienne, contrôleur aérien** air-traffic controller ‖ *m* gauge; **contrôleur des rayons béta** beta tester; **contrôleur de vitesse** speedometer; **contrôleur de vol** flight indicator

controversable [kɔ̃trɔversabl] *adj* controversial

controverse [kɔ̃trɔvers] *f* controversy

controverser [kɔ̃trɔverse] *tr* to controvert

contumace [kɔ̃tymas] *f* contempt of court

con•tus [kɔ̃ty] **-tuse** [tyz] *adj* bruised

contusion [kɔ̃tyzjɔ̃] *f* contusion, bruise

contusionner [kɔ̃tyzjɔne] *tr* to bruise

convain•cant [kɔ̃vɛ̃kɑ̃] **-cante** [kɑ̃t] *adj* convincing

convaincre [kɔ̃vɛ̃kr] §70, §97, §99 *tr* to convince; to convict ‖ *ref* to be satisfied

convain•cu -cue [kɔ̃vɛ̃ky] *adj* convinced, dyed-in-the-wool; convicted

convalescence [kɔ̃valesɑ̃s] *f* convalescence

convales•cent [kɔ̃valesɑ̃] **-cente** [sɑ̃t] *adj & mf* convalescent

convenable [kɔ̃vnabl] *adj* suitable, proper; opportune (*moment*)

convenance [kɔ̃vnɑ̃s] *f* suitability, propriety; conformity; **convenances** conventions

convenir [kɔ̃vnir] §72, §97 *intr* to agree; **convenir à** to fit, suit, e.g., **ce travail lui convient** this work suits him; **convenir de** to admit, admit to, admit the truth of; agree on ‖ *ref* (*pp* **convenu** *invar*) to agree with one another ‖ *impers*—**il convient** it is fitting, it is appropriate

convention [kɔ̃vɑ̃sjɔ̃] *f* convention

convention•nel -nelle [kɔ̃vɑ̃sjɔnɛl] *adj* conventional

conve•nu -nue [kɔ̃vny] *adj* settled; stipulated (*price*); appointed (*time, place*); trite, stereotyped (*language*)

converger [kɔ̃verʒe] §38 *intr* to converge

conversation [kɔ̃versasjɔ̃] *f* conversation

conversation•nel -nelle [kɔ̃versasjɔnɛl] *adj* (comp) interactive

converser [kɔ̃verse] *intr* to converse

conversion [kɔ̃versjɔ̃] *f* conversion; turning

conver•ti -tie [kɔ̃verti] *adj* converted ‖ *mf* convert

convertible [kɔ̃vertibl] *adj* convertible

convertir [kɔ̃vertir] *tr* to convert ‖ *ref* to convert, be converted; change one's mind

convertissable [kɔ̃vertisabl] *adj* convertible

convertisseur [kɔ̃vertisœr] *m* converter; (elec) converter

convexe [kɔ̃veks] *adj* convex

conviction [kɔ̃viksjɔ̃] *f* conviction

convier [kɔ̃vje] §96 *tr* to invite

convive [kɔ̃viv] *mf* dinner guest; table companion

convocation [kɔ̃vɔkasjɔ̃] *f* convocation; summoning

convoi [kɔ̃vwa] *m* convoy; funeral procession

convoiter [kɔ̃vwate] *tr* to covet

convoi•teur [kɔ̃vwatœr] **-teuse** [tøz] *adj* covetous ‖ *mf* covetous person

convoitise [kɔ̃vwatiz] *f* covetousness, cupidity

covoquer [kɔ̃vɔke] *tr* to convoke; summon

convoyer [kɔ̃vwaje] §47 *tr* to convoy

convoyeur [kɔ̃vwajœr] *adj* convoying ‖ *m* (mach) conveyor; (nav) escort

convulser [kɔ̃vylse] *tr* to convulse

convulsion [kɔ̃vylsjɔ̃] *f* convulsion

convulsionner [kɔ̃vylsjɔne] *tr* to convulse

coopéra•tif [kɔɔperatif] **-tive** [tiv] *adj* cooperative ‖ *f*—**coopérative vinicole** cooperative winery

coopération [kɔɔperasjɔ̃] *f* cooperation

coopérer [kɔɔpere] *intr* to cooperate; **coopérer à** to cooperate in

coordination [kɔɔrdinasjɔ̃] *f* coordination

coordon•né -née [kɔɔrdɔne] *adj & f* coordinate; **coordonnées** address and telephone number

coordonner [kɔɔrdɔne] *tr* to coordinate

co•pain [kɔpɛ̃] **-pine** [pin] *mf* (coll) pal, chum

co•peau [kɔpo] *m* (*pl* **-peaux**) chip, shaving

copie [kɔpi] *f* copy; exercise, composition (*at school*); **copie au net** fair copy; **copie supplémentaire, copie de réserve** backup copy; **pour copie conforme** true copy

copier [kɔpje] *tr & intr* to copy; **copier et coller** (comp) copy and paste

co•pieux [kɔpjø] **-pieuse** [pjøz] *adj* copious

copilote [kɔpilɔt] *m* copilot

copinisme [kɔpinism] *m* cronyism

copiste [kɔpist] *mf* copyist; copier

coposséder [kɔpɔsede] §10 *tr* to own jointly

copropriété [kɔprɔprijete] *f* joint ownership

copula•tif [kɔpylatif] **-tive** [tiv] *adj* (gram) coordinating

copulation [kɔpylasjɔ̃] *f* copulation

copule [kɔpyl] *f* (gram) copula

coq [kɔk] *adj* bantam ‖ *m* cock, rooster; (naut) cook

coq-à-l'âne [kɔkalɑn] *m invar* cock-and-bull story

coquart [kɔkar] *m* black eye, shiner

coque [kɔk] *f* shell; cocoon; hull; **à la coque** soft-boiled; **coque de noix** coconut

coquelicot [kɔkliko] *m* poppy

coqueluche [kɔkly ʃ] *f* whooping cough; (coll) rage, vogue

coquemar [kɔkmar] *m* teakettle

coquerie [kɔkri] *f* (naut) galley

coqueriquer [kɔkrike] *intr* to crow

co•quet [kɔkɛ] **-quette** [kɛt] *adj* coquettish; stylish; considerable (*sum*)

coqueter [kɔkte] §34 *intr* to flirt

coquetier [kɔkɛtje] *m* eggcup; egg man

coquetterie [kɔkɛtri] *f* coquetry

coquillage [kɔkijaʒ] *m* shellfish; shell

coquille [kɔkij] *f* shell; typographical error (*of transposed letters*); pat (*of butter*); **coquille de noix** nutshell; **coquille Saint-Jacques** scallop

co•quin [kɔkɛ̃] **-quine** [kin] *adj* deceitful; mischievous ‖ *mf* scoundrel; rascal

cor [kɔr] *m* horn; corn (*on foot*); prong (*of antler*); horn player; **à cor et à cri** with hue and cry; **cor anglais** English horn; **cor de chasse** hunting horn; **cor d'harmonie** French horn

co•rail [kɔraj] *m* (*pl* **-raux** [ro]) coral

Coran [kɔrɑ̃] *m* Koran

coranique [kɔranik] *adj* Koranic

cor•beau [kɔrbo] *m* (*pl* **-beaux**) crow, raven

corbeille [kɔrbɛj] *f* basket; flower bed; (theat) dress circle; **corbeille à papier** wastebasket; **corbeille de marriage** wedding present

corbillard [kɔrbijar] *m* hearse

corbillon [kɔrbijɔ̃] *m* small basket; word game

cordage [kɔrdaʒ] *m* cordage, rope; (naut) rigging

corde [kɔrd] *f* rope, cord; tightrope; thread (*of a carpet or cloth*); inside track; (geom) chord; (mus) string; **corde à** or **de boyau** catgut (*for, e.g., violin*); **corde à linge** wash line; **corde à nœuds** knotted rope; **corde à piano** piano wire; **cordes vocales** vocal cords; **en double corde** on two strings; **être sur la corde raide** to be out on a limb; **les cordes** (mus) the strings; **toucher la corde sensible** to touch a sympathetic cord; **usé jusqu'à la corde** threadbare

cor•dé -dée [kɔrde] *adj* heart-shaped ‖ *f* cord (*of wood*); roped party (*of mountain climbers*)

cor•deau [kɔrdo] *m* (*pl* **-deaux**) tracing line; tracing thread; mine fuse; **tiré au cordeau** in a straight line

cordelier [kɔrdəlje] *m* Franciscan friar

corder [kɔrde] *tr* to twist; string (*a tennis racket*)

cor•dial -diale [kɔrdjal] *adj & m* (*pl* **-diaux** [djo]) cordial

cordialement [kɔrdjalmɑ̃] *adv* cordially; **cordialement à vous** Sincerely yours

cordialité [kɔrdjalite] *f* cordiality

cordier [kɔrdje] *m* ropemaker; tailpiece (*of violin*)

cordon [kɔrdɔ̃] *m* cordon; cord; latchstring; **cor-**don de sonnette bellpull; **cordon de soulier** shoestring; **cordon vert** (ecol) green belt

cordon-bleu [kɔrdɔ̃blø] *m* (*pl* **cordons-bleus**) cordon bleu

cordonnerie [kɔrdɔnri] *f* shoemaking; shoe repairing; shoe store; shoemaker's

cordon•nier [kɔrdɔnje] **-nière** [njɛr] *mf* shoemaker

Corée [kɔre] *f* Korea; **la Corée** Korea

coréen [kɔreɛ̃] **coréenne** [kɔreɛn] *adj* Korean ‖ *m* Korean (*language*) ‖ (*cap*) *mf* Korean (*person*)

coriace [kɔrjas] *adj* tough, leathery; (coll) stubborn

coricide [kɔrisid] *m* corn remover

cormoran [kɔrmɔrɑ̃] *m* cormorant

cornac [kɔrnak] *m* mahout

cor•nard [kɔrnar] **-narde** [nard] *adj* horned; (slang) cuckold; wheezing (*of horse*) ‖ *m* (slang) cuckold

corne [kɔrn] *f* horn; dog-ear (*of page*); hoof; shoehorn; **corne d'abondance** horn of plenty; **faire les cornes à** (coll) to make a face at

cor•né -née [kɔrne] *adj* horny ‖ *f* cornea

corneille [kɔrnɛj] *f* crow, rook; **corneille d'église** jackdaw

cornemuse [kɔrnəmyz] *f* bagpipe

cornemuseur [kɔrnəmyzœr] *m* bagpiper

corner [kɔrne] *tr* to dog-ear; give (*s.o.*) the horn; (coll) to trumpet (*news*) about ‖ *intr* to blow the horn, honk; ring (*said of ears*); (mus) to blow a horn; **cornez!** sound your horn!

cornet [kɔrnɛ] *m* cornet; horn; dice-box; cornetist; mouthpiece (*of microphone*); receiver (*of telephone*); **cornet acoustique** ear trumpet; **cornet à pistons** cornet; **cornet de glace** ice-cream cone

cornette [kɔrnɛt] *m* (mil) cornet ‖ *f* (*headdress*) cornet

cornettiste [kɔrnɛtist] *mf* cornetist

corniche [kɔrni ʃ] *f* cornice

cornichon [kɔrni ʃɔ̃] *m* pickle, gherkin; (*fool*) (coll) dope, drip

cor•nier [kɔrnje] **-nière** [njɛr] *adj* corner ‖ *f* valley (*joining roofs*); angle iron

corniste [kɔrnist] *mf* horn player

Cornouailles [kɔrnwaj] *f* Cornwall

cornouiller [kɔrnuje] *m* dogwood

cor•nu -nue [kɔrny] *adj* horned; preposterous (*ideas*) ‖ *f* (chem) retort

corollaire [kɔrɔllɛr] *m* corollary

coronaire [kɔrɔnɛr] *adj* coronary

coroner [kɔrɔnœr] *m* coroner

corporation [kɔrpɔrasjɔ̃] *f* association, guild

corpo•rel -relle [kɔrpɔrɛl] *adj* corporal, bodily

corps [kɔr] *m* body; corps; **à corps perdu** without thinking; **à mon (ton,** etc.) **corps défendant** in self-defense; reluctantly; **corps à corps** hand-to-hand; in a clinch; **corps céleste** heavenly body; **corps composé** (chem) compound; **corps d'armée** army corps; **corps de**

garde guardhouse, guardroom; **corps de logis** main part of the building; **corps diplomatique** diplomatic corps; **corps du délit** corpus delicti; **corps enseignant** faculty; **corps noir** (phys) black body; **corps simple** (chem) simple substance; **prendre corps** to take shape; **saisir au corps** (law) to arrest

corps-à-corps [kɔrakɔr] *m* hand-to-hand combat; (boxing) infighting

corpulence [kɔrpylɑ̃s] *f* corpulence

corpuscule [kɔrpyskyl] *m* (phys) corpuscle

corral [kɔral] *m* corral

cor•rect -recte [kɔrɛkt] *adj* correct

correc•teur [kɔrɛktœr] **-trice** [tris] *mf* corrector; proofreader; **correcteur des copies** *or* **épreuves** copy reader

correc•tif [kɔrɛktif] **-tive** [tiv] *adj & m* corrective

correction [kɔrɛksjɔ̃] *f* correction; correctness; proofreading; punishment; **correction de copies** (educ) marking; **correction en course** (aer) mid-course correction

corrélation [kɔrelasjɔ̃] *f* correlation

correspondance [kɔrɛspɔ̃dɑ̃s] *f* correspondence; transfer, connection

correspon•dant [kɔrɛspɔ̃dɑ̃] **-dante** [dɑ̃t] *adj* corresponding, correspondent ‖ *mf* correspondent; party (*person who gets a telephone call*)

correspondre [kɔrɛspɔ̃dr] *intr* to correspond; **correspondre à** to correspond to, correlate with; **correspondre avec** to correspond with (*a letter writer*); connect with (*e.g., a train*)

corridor [kɔridɔr] *m* corridor

corrigé [kɔriʒe] *m* fair copy

corriger [kɔriʒe] §38 *tr* to correct; proofread ‖ *ref* to reform

corroborer [kɔrɔbɔre] *tr* to corroborate

corroder [kɔrɔde] *tr & ref* to corrode; erode

corrompre [kɔrɔ̃pr] (3d *sg pres ind* **corrompt**) *tr* to corrupt; rot; bribe; seduce; spoil

corro•sif [kɔrɔzif] **-sive** [ziv] *adj & m* corrosive

corrosion [kɔrɔsjɔ̃] *f* corrosion; erosion

corroyer [kɔrwaje] §47 *tr* to weld; to plane (*wood*); to prepare (*leather*)

corruption [kɔrrypsjɔ̃] *f* corruption; bribery; seduction

corsage [kɔrsaʒ] *m* blouse; bodice, corsage, waist; (archaic) bust

corsaire [kɔrsɛr] *m* corsair; pedal pusher; **corsaire de finance** ruthless businessman, robber baron

corse [kɔrs] *adj* Corsican ‖ *m* Corsican (*language*) ‖ (*cap*) *f* Corsica; **la Corse** Corsica ‖ (*cap*) *mf* Corsican (*person*)

cor•sé -sée [kɔrse] *adj* full-bodied, heavy; spicy, racy

corser [kɔrse] *tr* to spike, give body to (*wine*); spice up (*a story*) ‖ *ref* to become serious; **ça se corse** the plot thickens

corset [kɔrsɛ] *m* corset

cortège [kɔrtɛʒ] *m* cortege; parade; **cortège funèbre** funeral procession

cortisone [kɔrtizɔn] *f* cortisone

corvée [kɔrve] *f* chore; forced labor; work party

coryphée [kɔrife] *m* coryphée; (fig) leader

cosaque [kɔzak] *adj* Cossack ‖ (*cap*) *mf* Cossack

cosmétique [kɔsmetik] *adj* cosmetic ‖ *m* cosmetic; hair set, hair spray ‖ *f* beauty culture

cosmique [kɔsmik] *adj* cosmic

cosmonaute [kɔsmɔnot] *mf* cosmonaut

cosmopolite [kɔsmɔpɔlit] *adj & mf* cosmopolitan

cosmos [kɔsmos], [kɔsmɔs] *m* cosmos; outer space

cosse [kɔs] *f* pod; **avoir la cosse** (slang) to be lazy

cos•su -sue [kɔsy] *adj* rich; well-to-do

cos•taud [kɔsto] **-taude** [tod] *adj* (slang) husky, strapping ‖ *m* (slang) muscleman

costume [kɔstym] *m* costume; suit; **costume sur mesure** custom-made or tailor-made suit; **costume tailleur** lady's tailor-made suit

costumer [kɔstyme] *tr & ref* to dress up (*for a fancy-dress ball*); **se costumer en** to come dressed as a

costu•mier [kɔstymje] **-mière** [mjɛr] *mf* costumer

cote [kɔt] *f* assessment, quota; identification mark, letter, or number; call number (*of book*); altitude (*above sea level*); bench mark; book value (*of, e.g., used cars*); racing odds; public-opinion poll; (telv) rating; **avoir la cote** (coll) to be highly thought of; **cote d'alerte** danger point; **cote d'amour** moral qualifications; **cote de la Bourse** stock-market quotations; **cote mal taillée** rough compromise

côte [kɔt] *f* rib; chop; coast; slope; **à côtes** ribbed, corded; **aller** *or* **se mettre à la côte, faire côte** to run aground; **avoir les côtes en long** (coll) to feel lazy; **côte à côte** side by side; **côte d'Azur** French Riviera; **côtes découvertes, plates côtes** spareribs; **en côte** uphill; **être à la côte** to be broke; **faire côte** to run aground

co•té -tée [kɔte] *adj* listed (*on the stock market*); (fig) esteemed

côté [kote] *m* side; **à côté** in the next room; near; **à côté!** a miss!; **à côté de** beside; **à côtés** fringe benefits; **à trois côtés** three-sided; **côté cour** (theat) stage right; **côté jardin** (theat) stage left; **d'à côté** next-door; **de côté** sideways; sidelong; aside; **de mon côté** for my part; **donner, passer,** *or* **toucher à côté** to miss the mark; **du côté de** in the direction of, toward; on the side of; **d'un côté . . . de l'autre côté** *or* **d'un autre côté** on the one hand . . . on the other hand; **répondre à côté** to miss the point

co•teau [kɔto] *m* (*pl* **-teaux**) knoll; slope

Côte-de-l'Or [kotdəlɔr] *f* Gold Coast

côte•lé -lée [kotle] *adj* ribbed, corded

côtelette [kotlɛt] *f* cutlet, chop; **côtelettes découvertes** spareribs

coter [kɔte] *tr* to assess; mark; number; esteem;

(com) to quote, give a quotation on; (geog) to mark the elevations on

coterie [kɔtri] *f* coterie, clique

cothurne [kɔtyrn] *m* buskin

cô‧tier [kotje] **-tière** [tjɛr] *adj* coastal

cotir [kɔtir] *tr* to bruise (*fruit*)

cotisation [kɔtizɑsjɔ̃] *f* dues; assessment

cotiser [kɔtize] *tr* to assess (*each member of a group*) ‖ *intr* to pay one's dues ‖ *ref* to club together

coton [kɔtɔ̃] *m* cotton; **c'est coton** (slang) it's difficult; **coton de verre** glass wool; **coton hydrophile** absorbent cotton; cotton batting; **élever dans le coton** to coddle; **filer un mauvais coton** (coll) to be in a bad way

cotonnade [kɔtɔnad] *f* cotton cloth

cotonner [kɔtɔne] *tr* to pad or stuff with cotton ‖ *ref* to become fluffy; become spongy or mealy

cotonnerie [kɔtɔnri] *f* cotton field; cotton mill

coton‧neux [kɔtɔnø] **-neuse** [nøz] *adj* cottony; spongy, mealy

coton‧nier [kɔtɔnje] **-nière** [njɛr] *adj* cotton ‖ *mf* cotton picker ‖ *m* cotton plant

côtoyer [kotwaje] **§47** *tr* to skirt (*the edge*); hug (*the shore*); border on (*the truth, the ridiculous, etc.*)

cotre [kɔtr] *m* (naut) cutter

cotte [kɔt] *f* petticoat; peasant skirt; overalls; **cotte de mailles** coat of mail

cou [ku] *m* neck; **sauter au cou de** to throw one's arms around

couard [kwar] **couarde** [kward] *adj mf* coward

couardise [kwardiz] *f* cowardice

couchage [kuʃaʒ] *m* bedding; bed for the night

cou‧chant [kuʃɑ̃] **-chante** [ʃɑ̃t] *adj* setting ‖ *m* west; decline, old age

couche [kuʃ] *f* layer, stratum; coat (*of paint*); diaper; (hort) hotbed; **couche de fond** primer, prime coat; **couche d'ozone** ozone layer; **couches** strata; childbirth, e.g., **une femme en couches** a woman in childbirth; **fausse couche** miscarriage

coucher [kuʃe] *m* setting (*of sun*); going to bed; **coucher du soleil** sunset; **le coucher et la nourriture** room and board ‖ *tr* to put to bed; put down, lay down; bend down, flatten; mention (*in one's will*); **coucher en joue** to aim at; **coucher par écrit** to set down in writing ‖ *intr* to spend the night; **coucher avec** to sleep with (*have sex with*); (naut) to heel over ‖ *ref* to go to bed, lie down; set (*said of sun*); bend; **allez vous coucher!** (coll) go to blazes! **une Marie-couche-toi-là** a promiscuous woman

couchette [kuʃɛt] *f* berth; crib

couci-couça [kusikusa] or **couci-couci** [kusikusi] *adv* so-so

coucou [kuku] *m* cuckoo; cuckoo clock; (coll) marsh marigold

coude [kud] *m* elbow; angle, bend, turn; **coude à coude** shoulder to shoulder; **jouer des coudes à travers** to elbow one's way through (*a crowd*)

coudée [kude] *f* cubit; **avoir ses coudées franches** to have a free hand; to have elbowroom

cou-de-pied [kudpje] *m* (*pl* **cous-de-pied**) instep

couder [kude] *tr* to bend like an elbow

coudoiement [kudwamɑ̃] *m* elbowing

coudoyer [kudwaje] **§47** *tr* to elbow, to jostle; to rub shoulders with

coudraie [kudrɛ] *f* hazel grove

coudre [kudr] **§13** *tr* & *intr* to sew

coudrier [kudrije] *m* hazel tree

couenne [kwan] *f* pigskin; rind, crackling; mole, birthmark

couette [kwɛt] *f* feather bed; (little) tail; (mach) bearing; **couette de lapin** scut; **couettes** (naut) ship

cougouar or **couguar** [kugwar] *m* cougar

couiner [kwine] *intr* to send Morse code; (coll) to squeak (*said of animal*)

coulage [kulaʒ] *m* flow; leakage; casting (*of metal*); pouring (*of concrete*); (naut) scuttling; (coll) wasting

cou‧lant [kulɑ̃] **-lante** [lɑ̃t] *adj* flowing, running; permissive; accommodating (*person*) ‖ *m* sliding ring; (bot) runner

coule [kul] *f* cowl; **être à la coule** (slang) to know the ropes

cou‧lé -lée [kule] *adj* cast; sunken; (coll) sunk ‖ *m* (mus) slur ‖ *f* casting; run (*of wild beasts*); **coulée volcanique** outflow of lava

couler [kule] *tr* to pour; cast (*e.g., a statue*); scuttle; pass (*e.g., many happy hours*); (mus) to slur ‖ *intr* to flow; run; leak; sink; slip (away) ‖ *ref* to slip, slide; (coll) to be done for, be sunk; **se la couler douce** (coll) to take it easy

couleur [kulœr] *f* color; policy (*of newspaper*); (cards) suit; **de couleur** colored; **les trois couleurs** the tricolor; **sous couleur de** with the pretext of, with a show of

couleuvre [kulœvr] *f* snake; **avaler des couleuvres** (coll) to swallow insults; (coll) to be gullible; **couleuvre à collier** grass snake

coulis [kuli] *m*—**coulis de tomates** tomato sauce

coulisse [kulis] *f* groove; slide (*of trombone*); (com) curb exchange; (pol) lobby; **à coulisse** sliding; **coulisses** (theat) wings; (theat) backstage; **dans les coulisses** behind the scenes, out of sight; **travailler dans les coulisses** to pull strings

coulis‧seau [kuliso] *m* (*pl* **-seaux**) slide, runner

couloir [kulwar] *m* corridor; hallway; lobby; **couloir aérien** air lane; **couloir de la mort** death row

couloire [kulwar] *f* strainer

coup [ku] *m* blow; stroke; coup; blast (*of whistle*); jolt; move (*in a chess game*); **à coup de** with the aid of; **à coup sûr** certainly; **après coup** when it is too late; **à tout coup** each time; **beau coup de batte** (baseball) clout; **boire à petits coups** to sip; **coup de bélier** water hammer (*in pipe*); **coup de chance**

lucky hit; **coup de coude** nudge; **coup de dés** throw of the dice; risky business; **coup de fer** pressing, ironing; **coup de feu, coup de fusil** shot, gunshot; **coup de fil** telephone call; **coup de fion** (slang) finishing touch; **coup de foudre** thunderbolt; love at first sight; bolt from the blue; **coup de fouet** whiplash; stimulus; **coup de froid** cold snap; **coup de grâce** last straw; deathblow; **coup de Jarnac** [ʒarnak] stab in the back; **coup de lapin** (aut) whiplash; **coup de patte** expert stroke (*e.g., of the brush*); (coll) dig, insult; **coup de pied** kick; **coup d'épingle** pinprick; **coup de poing** punch; **coup de pouce** final touch; help, little push; **coup de sang** (pathol) stroke; **coup de semonce** warning shot; **coup de sifflet** whistle, toot; **coup de soleil** sunburn; (coll) sunstroke; **coup d'état** coup d'etat; **coup de téléphone** telephone call; **coup de tête** butt; sudden impulse; **coup de théâtre** dramatic turn of events; **coup de tonnerre** thunderclap; **coup d'œil** glance, look; **coup manqué, coup raté** miss; **coup monté** put-up job, frame-up; **coups et blessures** assault and battery; **coup sur coup** one right after the other; **donner un coup de main (à)** to lend a helping hand (to); **encore un coup** once again; **en venir aux coups** to come to blows; **être dans le coup** (coll) to be in on it; **faire coup double** to kill two birds with one stone; **faire les quatre coups** (coll) to live it up, to dissipate; **faire un coup de main** to go on a raid; **manquer son coup** to miss one's chance; **se faire donner un coup de piston** (coll) to pull wires, to use influence; **sous le coup de** under the (immediate) influence of; **sur le coup** on the spot, outright; **tout à coup** suddenly; **tout d'un coup** at one shot, at once

coupable [kupabl] §93 *adj* guilty ‖ *mf* culprit

cou•pant [kupɑ̃] **-pante** [pɑ̃t] *adj* cutting, sharp ‖ *m* (cutting) edge

coup-de-poing [kudpwɛ̃] *m* (*pl* **coups-de-poing**) brass knuckles

coupe [kup] *f* champagne glass; loving cup, trophy; cup competition; cutting; cross section; wood acreage to be cut; cut (*of cloth; of clothes; of playing cards*); division (*of verse*); **coupe claire** cutover forest; **coupe de cheveux** haircut; **coupe sombre** harvested forest; **être sous la coupe de qn** (coll) to be under s.o.'s thumb; **il y a loin de la coupe aux lèvres** there is many a slip between the cup and the lip; **mettre en coupe réglée** (coll) to fleece

cou•pé -pée [kupe] *adj* cut, cut off; interrupted (*sleep*); diluted (*wine*) ‖ *m* coupé ‖ *f* gangway

coupe-circuit [kupsirkɥi] *m invar* (elec) fuse

coupe-coupe [kupkup] *m invar* machete

coupe-feu [kupfø] *m invar* firebreak

coupe-fil [kupfil] *m invar* wire cutter

coupe-file [kupfil] *m invar* police pass (*for emergency vehicles*)

coupe-gorge [kupgɔrʒ] *m invar* death trap, dangerous territory

coupe-herbe [kupɛrb] *m* lawn trimmer (*nylon cord*)

coupe-jarret [kupʒarɛ] *m* (*pl* **-jarrets**) cutthroat

coupe-ongles [kupɔ̃gl] *m invar* nail clippers

coupe-papier [kuppapje] *m invar* paper knife, letter opener

couper [kupe] *tr* to cut; cut off; cut out; break off, interrupt; cut, water down; turn off; trump; castrate, geld; **ça te la coupe!** (coll) top that!; **couper en fin de ligne** to divide (*a word*) at the end of a line; **couper la file** (aut) to leave one's lane; **couper la parole à** to interrupt; **couper menu** to mince ‖ *intr* to cut; **couper court à** to cut (*s.o. or s.th.*) short ‖ *ref* to cut oneself; intersect; (coll) to contradict oneself; (coll) to give oneself away

couperet [kuprɛ] *m* cleaver; guillotine blade

couperose [kuproz] *f* (pathol) acne

cou•peur [kupœr] **-peuse** [pøz] *mf* cutter; **coupeur de bourses** (coll) purse snatcher; **coupeur d'oreilles** (coll) hatchet man, hired thug

couplage [kuplaʒ] *m* (mach) coupling

couple [kupl] *m* couple (*e.g., of friends, cronies, thieves, etc.; man and wife*); pair (*e.g., of pigeons*); (mech) couple, torque; **couple thermo-électrique** thermoelectric couple; **maître couple** (naut) midship frame ‖ *f* yoke (*of oxen*); couple; leash

coupler [kuple] *tr* to couple; pair

coupleur [kuplœr] *m* (mach) coupler

coupole [kupɔl] *f* cupola

coupon [kupɔ̃] *m* coupon; remnant (*of cloth*); theater ticket; **coupon date libre** open ticket

coupon-réponse [kupɔ̃repɔ̃s] *m*—**coupon-réponse international** international (postal) reply coupon; **coupon-réponse postal** return-reply post card or letter

coupure [kupyr] *f* cut, incision, slit; cut, deletion; newspaper clipping; small note; interruption, break; drain (*e.g., through a marsh*); denomination

cour [kur] *f* court; courtyard; courtship; **bien en cour** in favor; **cour anglaise** courtyard or court (*of apartment building*); **cour d'appel** appellate court; **cour d'assises** criminal court; **cour de cassation** supreme court of appeals; **cour d'école** school playground; **faire la cour à** to court; **la Cour suprême** (U.S.A.) the Supreme Court; **mal en cour** out of favor

courage [kuraʒ] *m* courage; **reprendre courage** to take heart; **travailler avec courage** to work hard ‖ *interj* buck up!, cheer up!

coura•geux [kuraʒø] **-geuse** [ʒøz] *adj* courageous; hard-working

courailler [kuraje] *intr* to gallivant

couramment [kuramɑ̃] *adv* currently; fluently, easily

cou•rant [kurɑ̃] **-rante** [rɑ̃t] *adj* current; running (*water*); present-day (*language, customs, etc.*) ‖ *m* current; flow; shift (*of opinion,* *population, etc.*); **courant alternatif** alternating current; **courant continu** direct current; **courant d'air** draft; **Courant du Golfe** Gulf Stream; **dans le courant du mois (de la semaine, etc.)** in the course of the month (of the week, etc.); **être au courant de** to be informed about

courant-jet [kurɑ̃ʒɛ] *m* (meteo) jet stream

courba•tu -tue [kurbaty] *adj* stiff in the joints, aching all over

courbature [kurbatyr] *f* stiffness, aching

courbaturer [kurbatyre] *tr* to make stiff; exhaust (*the body*)

courbe [kurb] *adj* curved ‖ *f* curve; **courbe de niveau** contour line

cour•bé -bée [kurbe] *adj* curved, bent, crooked

courber [kurbe] *tr* to bend, curve ‖ *intr & ref* to bend, curve; give in

courbure [kurbyr] *f* curve, curvature; **double courbure** S-curve

courette [kurɛt] *f* small courtyard

cou•reur -reuse [kurœr] [røz] *mf* runner; **coureur cycliste** bicycle racer; **coureur de cotillons** (coll) wolf; **coureur de dot** fortune hunter; **coureur de filles** Casanova, Don Juan; **coureur de girls** stage-door Johnny; **coureur de spectacles** play-goer; **coureur de vitesse** sprinter

courge [kurʒ] *f* gourd, squash

courir [kurir] §14, §95 *tr* to run; run after; roam; frequent ‖ *intr* to run; **le bruit court que** rumor has it that; **par le temps qui court** at the present time

courlis [kurli] *m* curlew

couronne [kurɔn] *f* crown; wreath; coronet; rim (*of atomic structures*)

couronnement [kurɔnmɑ̃] *m* crowning; coronation; capstone

couronner [kurɔne] *tr* to crown; top, cap; reward ‖ *ref* to be crowned; be covered (*with flowers*)

courrier [kurje] *m* courier; mail; **courrier du cœur** advice to the lovelorn; **courrier électronique** (comp) E-mail; **courrier mondain** gossip column; **courrier théâtral** theater section

courriériste [kurjerist] *mf* columnist

courroie [kurwa] *f* strap; belt

courroucer [kuruse] §51 *tr* (lit) to anger

courroux [kuru] *m* (lit) wrath, anger

cours [kur] *m* course; current (*of river*); tree-lined walk; rate (*of exchange*); market quotation; style, vogue; **au cours de** in the course of; **avoir cours** to be in circulation; to be legal tender; to have classes; **cours d'eau** stream, river; **cours d'été** *or* **cours de vacances** summer school; **cours du soir** night school; **cours en clôture** closing price; **de cours** in length (*said of a river*); **de long cours** long-range; **suivre un cours** to take a course (*in school*) ‖ *v* see **courir**

course [kurs] *f* running; race; errand; trip; ride (*e.g., in a taxi*); course, path; privateering;

stroke (*of a piston*); **course à pied** foot race; **course attelée** harness race; **course au trot** trotting race; **course aux armements** arms race; **course de bolides** stock-car race; **course de chevaux** horse race; **course de côte** hill climb; **course de taureaux** bullfight; **course de vitesse** sprint; **course d'obstacles** steeplechase; **course spatiale** space race; **courses sur route** road racing; **de course** at a run; racing (*car; track; crowd*); (mil) on the double; **en pleine course** in full swing; **faire des courses** to go shopping

cour•sier -sière [sjɛr] *mf* messenger ‖ *m* errand boy; steed

coursive [kursiv] *f* (naut) alleyway, gangway (*connecting staterooms*)

court [kur] **courte** [kurt] *adj* short; brief; concise; choppy (*sea*); thick (*sauce, gravy*); close (*victory*); **à court** short; **de court** by surprise; **prendre le plus court** to take a shortcut; **tenir de court** to hold on a short leash ‖ (when standing before noun) *adj* short, brief (*interval, time, life*) ‖ *m* court (*for tennis*) ‖ **court** *adv* short; **demeurer court** to forget what one wanted to say; **tourner court** to turn sharp; to stop short, to change the subject; **tout court** simply, merely; plain ‖ **court** *v* see **courir**

courtage [kurtaʒ] *m* brokerage; broker's commission

cour•taud -taude [tod] *adj* stocky, short and stocky

court-circuit [kursirkɥi] *m* (*pl* **courts-circuits**) short circuit

court-circuiter [kursirkɥite] *tr* to short-circuit

court-courrier [kurkurje] *s* (*pl* **courts-courriers**) short-range plane

courtepoint [kurtəpwɛ̃] *f* counterpane

cour•tier -tière [tjɛr] *mf* broker; agent; **courtier électoral** canvasser

courtisan [kurtizɑ̃] *m* courtier

courtisane [kurtizan] *f* courtesan

courtiser [kurtize] *tr* to court

cour•tois -toise [twaz] *adj* courteous; courtly

courtoisie [kurtwazi] *f* courtesy

court-vê•tu -tue [kurvety] *adj* short-skirted

cou•ru -rue [kury] *adj* sought after, popular; **c'est couru** (coll) it's a sure thing ‖ *v* see **courir**

couscous [kuskus] *m* couscous

cou•seur -seuse [zøz] *mf* sewer ‖ *f* seamstress; (mach) stitcher

cou•sin -sine [zin] *mf* cousin; **cousin germain** first cousin; **cousin** *or* **cousine issu(e) d'un(e) cousin(e) germain(e)** first cousin once removed; **cousin** *or* **cousine issu(e) d'un(e) cousin(e) germaine(e) du père** *or* **de la mère** second cousin ‖ *m* mosquito

cousinage [kuzinaʒ] *m* cousinship; (coll) relatives

coussin [kusɛ̃] *m* cushion; **coussin gonflable** (aut) air bag

coussinet [kusinɛ] *m* little cushion; (mach) bearing

cou·su -sue [kusy] *v* see **coudre**

coût [ku] *m* cost; **coût de la vie** cost of living

cou·teau [kuto] *m* (*pl* **-teaux**) knife; **couteau à cran d'arrêt** clasp knife with safety catch; switchblade knife; **couteau à découper** carving knife; **couteau à resort** switchblade knife; **couteau pliant, couteau de poche** jackknife

coutelas [kutlɑ] *m* cutlass; butcher knife

coutellerie [kutɛlri] *f* cutlery

coûter [kute] §96 *tr* to cost; **coûte que coûte** cost what it may; **il m'en coûte de** + *inf* it's hard for me to + *inf*

coû·teux -teuse [kutø] [tøz] *adj* costly, expensive

coutil [kuti] *m* duck (*cloth*); mattress ticking

coutume [kutym] *f* custom; habit; common law; **de coutume** ordinarily

coutu·mier [kutymje] **-mière** [mjɛr] *adj* customary; common (*law*); accustomed ‖ *m* book of common law

couture [kutyr] *f* needlework; sewing; seam; suture; scar; **battre qn à plate couture** (coll) to beat s.o. hollow; **examiner sur toutes les coutures** to examine inside and out or from every angle; **haute couture** fashion designing, haute couture; **sans couture** seamless

couturer [kutyre] *tr* to scar

coutu·rier [kutyrje] **-rière** [rjɛr] *mf* dressmaker ‖ *m* dress designer ‖ *f* seamstress

couvaison [kuvɛzɔ̃] *f* incubation period

couvée [kuve] *f* brood

couvent [kuvɑ̃] *m* convent; monastery; convent school

couver [kuve] *tr* to brood, hatch ‖ *intr* to brood; smolder

couvercle [kuvɛrkl] *m* cover, lid; **couvercle à pas de vis** screwtop

cou·vert [kuvɛr] **-verte** [vɛrt] *adj* covered; dressed, clothed; cloudy (*weather*); wooded (*countryside*) ‖ *m* cover; setting (*of table*); service (*fork and spoon*); cover charge; room, lodging; authority (*given by a superior*); **à couvert** sheltered; **mettre le couvert** to set the table; **sous le couvert de** under cover of; **sous les couverts** under cover (*of trees*) ‖ *f* glaze

couverture [kuvɛrtyr] *f* cover; coverage; covering; wrapper; blanket, bedspread

couveuse [kuvøz] *f* brood hen; incubator

couvre-chef [kuvrəʃɛf] *m* (*pl* **-chefs**) (coll) headgear

couvre-feu [kuvrəfø] *m* (*pl* **-feux**) curfew

couvre-lit [kuvrəli] *m* (*pl* **-lits**) bedspread

couvre-livre [kuvrəlivr] *m* (*pl* **-livres**) dust jacket

couvre-oreille [kuvrɔrɛj] *m* (*pl* **-oreilles**) earmuff

couvre-pieds [kuvrəpje] *m invar* bedspread; quilt

couvre-plat [kuvrəpla] *m* (*pl* **-plats**) dish cover

couvre-théière [kuvrətejɛr] *m* (*pl* **-théières**) tea cozy

couvreur [kuvrœr] *m* roofer

couvrir [kuvrir] §65 *tr* to cover ‖ *ref* to cover; cover oneself; get cloudy; put one's hat on

co-voiturage [kɔvwatyraʒ] *m* car pool

cow-boy [kaubɔj], [kobɔj] *m* (*pl* **-boys**) cowboy

C.P. *abbr* (**case postale**) post-office box

C.R. [seɛr] *adv* (letterword) (**contre remboursement**) C.O.D.; **envoyez-le-moi C.R.** send it to me C.O.D.

crabe [krab] *m* crab; caterpillar (tractor)

crachat [kraʃa] *m* sputum, spit

cra·ché -chée [kraʃe] *adj* (coll) spitting (*image*)

cracher [kraʃe] *tr & intr* to spit

crachin [kraʃɛ̃] *m* light drizzle

crachoir [kraʃwar] *m* spittoon; **tenir le crachoir** (slang) to have the floor, speak

crachoter [kraʃɔte] *intr* to keep on spitting; sputter

crack [krak] *m* favorite (*the horse favored to win*); (*drug*) crack; (coll) champion, ace; (coll) crackerjack

cracking [krakin] *m* cracking (*of oil*)

craie [krɛ] *f* chalk; piece of chalk; **craie de tailleur** tailor's chalk

craignez [krɛɲe] *v* (**craignons**) see **craindre**

crailler [kraje] *intr* to caw

craindre [krɛ̃dr] §15, §97 *tr* to fear, be afraid of, dread; respect ‖ *intr* to be afraid

crainte [krɛ̃t] *f* fear, dread; **dans la crainte que** or **de crainte que** for fear that

crain·tif [krɛ̃tif] **-tive** [tiv] *adj* fearful; timid

cramoi·si -sie [kramwazi] *adj & m* crimson

crampe [krɑ̃p] *f* cramp (*in a muscle*)

crampon [krɑ̃pɔ̃] *m* clamp; cleat (*on a shoe*); (coll) pest, bore

cramponner [krɑ̃pɔne] *tr* to clamp together; (coll) to pester ‖ *ref* to hold fast, hang on, cling

cran [krɑ̃] *m* notch; cog, catch, tooth; **avoir du cran** (coll) to be game (*for anything*); **baisser un cran** to come down a peg; **être à cran** (coll) to be exasperated, cross

crâne [krɑn] *adj* bold, daring ‖ *m* skull, cranium; **bourrer le crâne à qn** (coll) to hand s.o. a line

crâner [krane] *intr* (coll) to swagger

cra·neur [krɑnœr] **-neuse** [nøz] *adj* (coll) *mf* (coll) braggart

crapaud [krapo] *m* toad; baby grand; flaw (*in diamond*); low armchair; (coll) brat; **avaler un crapaud** (coll) to put up with a lot

crapule [krapyl] *f* underworld, scum; bum; punk; **vivre dans la crapule** to live in debauchery

crapu·leux -leuse [krapylø] [løz] *adj* debauched, lewd, filthy

craquage [krakaʒ] *m* cracking (*of petroleum*)

craquement [krakmɑ̃] *m* crack, crackle

craquer [krake] *intr* to crack; burst; (coll) to crash, fail

craqueter [krakte] §34 *intr* to crackle

crash [kraʃ] *m* crash landing

crasher [kraʃe] *intr* (aer) to crash

crasse [kras] *adj* gross; crass (*ignorance*) ‖ *f* filth, squalor; avarice; dross; **faire une crasse à qn** (slang) to play a dirty trick on s.o.

cras·seux [krasø] **-seuse** [søz] *adj* filthy, squalid; (coll) stingy

crassier [krasje] *m* slag heap

cratère [kratɛr] *m* crater; ewer

cravache [kravaʃ] *f* riding whip, horsewhip

cravacher [kravaʃe] *tr* to horsewhip

cravate [kravat] *f* necktie, cravat; scarf; sling (*for unloading goods*); **cravate de chanvre** (coll) noose; **cravate de drapeau** pennant; **derrière la cravate!** down the hatch!

cravater [kravate] *tr* to tie a necktie on (*s.o.*) ‖ *intr* (slang) to tell a fish story

crawl [krol] *m* crawl (*in swimming*)

crayeux [krɛjø] **crayeuse** [krɛjøz] *adj* chalky

crayon [krɛjɔ̃] *m* pencil; **crayon à bille** ball-point pen; **crayon de pastel** wax crayon; **crayon de rouge à lèvres** lipstick

crayon-feutre [krɛjɔ̃føtr] *m* (*pl* **crayons-feutres**) magic-marker pen

crayonnages [krɛjɔnaʒ] *mpl* doodles, doodling

crayonner [krɛjɔne] *tr* to crayon, pencil, sketch

créance [kreɑ̃s] *f* belief, credence; **créances gelées** frozen assets; **créances véreuses** bad debts

créan·cier [kreɑ̃sje] **-cière** [sjɛr] *mf* creditor; **créancier hypothécaire** mortgage holder, mortgagee

créa·teur [kreatœr] **-trice** [tris] *adj* creative ‖ *mf* creator; originator

création [kreasjɔ̃] *f* creation

créature [kreatyr] *f* creature

crécelle [kresɛl] *f* rattle; chatterbox; **de crécelle** rasping

crèche [krɛʃ] *f* manger; crèche; day nursery, day-care center

crédence [kredɑ̃s] *f* buffet, sideboard, credenza

crédibilité [kredibilite] *f* credibility

crédit [kredi] *m* credit; (govt) appropriation; **crédit au consommateur** consumer credit; **crédit croisé** swap

crédit-bail [kredibaj] *m* (*pl* **credits-bails**) leasing

créditer [kredite] *tr* (com) to credit

crédi·teur [kreditœr] **-trice** [tris] *adj* credit (*side, account*) ‖ *mf* creditor

credo [kredo] *m invar* credo, creed

crédule [kredyl] *adj* credulous

créer [kree] *tr* to create

crémaillère [kremajɛr] *f* pothook; rack; rack rail; **crémaillère et pignon** rack and pinion; **pendre la crémaillère** to have a house-warming

crémation [kremasjɔ̃] *f* cremation

crématoire [krematwar] *adj & m* crematory

crème [krɛm] *f* cream; **crème à raser** shaving cream; **crème chantilly** whipped cream; **crème de démaquillage** cleansing cream;

crème fouettée whipped cream; **crème fraîche** sour cream; **crème glacée** ice cream

crémer [kreme] §10 *intr* to cream

crémerie [krɛmri] *f* dairy; milkhouse (*on a farm*); dairy luncheonette

cré·meux [kremø] **-meuse** [møz] *adj* creamy

crémier [kremje] *m* dairyman

crémière [kremjɛr] *f* dairymaid; cream pitcher

crémone [kremɔn] *f* casement bolt

cré·neau [kreno] *m* (*pl* **-neaux**) crenel; loophole; marked lane (*on a highway*); extra passing lane; space between two cars; **créneau temporel** time slot; **créneaux** battlements

créneler [krɛnle] §34 *tr* to crenelate; tooth (*a wheel*); mill (*a coin*)

créole [kreɔl] *adj* Creole ‖ *m* Creole (*language*) ‖ (*cap*) *mf* Creole (*person*)

crêpe [krɛp] *m* crepel; mourning band ‖ *f* pancake

crépi [krepi] *m* roughcast

crépir [krepir] *tr* to roughcast

crépitation [krepitasjɔ̃] *f* crackle

crépitement [krepitmɑ̃] *m* crackling

crépiter [krepite] *intr* to crackle

cré·pu -pue [krepy] *adj* crimped, frizzly, crinkled

crépuscule [krepyskyl] *m* twilight

cresson [krɛsɔ̃] *m* cress; **cresson de fontaine** watercress

crête [krɛt] *f* crest; **crête de coq** cockscomb

Crète [krɛt] *f* Crete; **la Crète** Crete

crête-de-coq [krɛtdəkɔk] *f* (*pl* **crêtes-de-coq**) (bot) cockscomb

cré·tin [kretɛ̃] **-tine** [tin] *mf* cretin; (coll) jackass, fathead

cré·tois [kretwa] **-toise** [twaz] *adj* Cretan ‖ (*cap*) *mf* Cretan

creuser [krøze] *tr* to dig, excavate; hollow out; furrow; go into thoroughly ‖ *ref*—**se creuser la tête** (coll) to rack one's brains

creuset [krøzɛ] *m* crucible

creux [krø] **creuse** [krøz] *adj* hollow; concave; sunken, deep-set; empty (*stomach*); deep (*voice*); off-peak (*hours*); **songer creux** to dream idle dreams; **sonner creux** to sound hollow ‖ *m* hollow (*of hand*); hole (*in ground*); pit (*of stomach*); trough (*of wave*); **creux de l'aisselle** armpit; **creux des reins** small of the back

crevaison [krəvɛzɔ̃] *f* blowout

crevasse [krəvas] *f* crevice; crack (*in skin*); rift (*in clouds*); flaw (*in metal*)

crevasser [krəvase] *tr* to chap ‖ *intr & ref* to crack, chap

crève-cœur [krɛvkœr] *m invar* heartbreak, keen disappointment

crever [krəve] §2 *tr* to burst; work to death (*e.g., a horse*) ‖ *intr* to burst; split; burst, go flat (*said of a tire*); (slang) to die, kick the bucket ‖ *ref* to work oneself to death

crevette [krəvɛt] *f* shrimp; **crevette grise**

shrimp; **crevette rose, crevette bouquet** prawn

C.-R.F. *abbr* (**Croix-Rouge française**) French Red Cross

cri [kri] *m* cry; shout; whine, squeal; **dernier cri** last word, latest thing; **dernier cri de la technique** state of the art

criailler [kriɑje] *intr* to honk (*said of goose*); (coll) to whine, complain, grouse; **criailler après, criailler contre** (coll) to nag at

criaillerie [kriɑjri] *f* (coll) shouting; (coll) whining, complaining; (coll) nagging

criant [krijɑ̃] **criante** [krijɑ̃t] *adj* crying (*shame*); obvious (*truth*); flagrant (*injustice*)

criard [krijar] **criarde** [krijard] *adj* complaining; shrill (*voice*); loud (*color*); pressing (*debts*) ‖ *mf* complainer ‖ *f* scold, shrew

crible [kribl] *m* sieve; **crible à gravier** gravel screen; **crible à mineral** jig; **passer au crible** to sift or screen

cri•blé -blée [krible] *adj* riddled (*with, e.g., debts*); pitted (*by, e.g., smallpox*)

cribler [krible] *tr* to sift, screen; riddle; **cribler de ridicule** to cover with ridicule

cric [krik] *m* (aut) jack ‖ *interj* crack!, snap!

cricket [krikɛt] *m* (sports) cricket

cricri [krikri] *m* (ent) cricket

crier [krije] §97, §98 *tr* to cry; cry out; shout; cry for (*revenge*); **crier misère** to complain of being poor; cry poverty (*said of clothing, furniture, etc.*) ‖ *intr* to cry; cry out; shout; creak, squeak; squeal; **crier à** to cry out against (*scandal, injustice, etc.*); cry for (*help*); **crier après** to yell at, bawl out; **crier contre** to cry out against; to rail at

crieur [krijœr] **crieuse** [krijøz] *mf* crier; hawker, peddler; **crieur public** town crier

crime [krim] *m* crime; felony; **crime de guerre** war crime: **crimes des employés de bureau** white-collar crimes

crimi•nel -nelle [kriminɛl] *adj & mf* criminal

criminologie [kriminɔlɔʒi] *s* criminology

criminologiste [kriminɔlɔʒist] *mf* criminologist

criminologue [kriminɔlɔg] *mf* criminologist

crin [krɛ̃] *m* horsehair (*on mane and tail*); **à tous crins** out-and-out, hard-core (*e.g., revolutionist*)

crinière [krinjɛr] *f* mane

crique [krik] *f* cove

criquet [krikɛ] *m* locust; weak wine; (coll) shrimp (*person*)

crise [kriz] *f* crisis; **crise d'appendicite** appendicitis attack; **crise de foi** shaken faith; **crise de main-d'œuvre** labor-shortage; **crise de nerfs** fit of hysterics; **crise du foie** liver upset; **crise du logement** housing shortage; **crise économique** (com) depression; **crise énergétique** energy crisis

cris•pant [krispɑ̃] **-pante** [pɑ̃t] *adj* irritating, annoying

crispation [krispɑsjɔ̃] *f* contraction, shriveling up; (coll) fidgeting

cris•pé -pée [krispe] *adj* nervous, strained, tense

crisper [krispe] *tr* to contract, clench; (coll) to make fidgety ‖ *ref* to contract, curl up

crisser [krise] *tr* to grind or grit (*one's teeth*) ‖ *intr* to grate, crunch

cris•tal [kristal] *m* (*pl* **-taux** [to]) crystal; **cristal de roche** rock crystal; **cristal taillé** cut glass; **cristaux** glassware; **cristaux de soude** washing soda

cristal•lin [kristalɛ̃] **-line** [lin] *adj* crystalline ‖ *m* crystalline lens (*of the eye*)

cristalliser [kristalize] *tr, intr, & ref* to crystallize

critère [kritɛr] *m* criterion

critérium [kriterjɔm] *m* championship game

critiquable [kritikabl] *adj* open to criticism, questionable

critique [kritik] *adj* critical ‖ *mf* critic ‖ *f* criticism; critics; critique; **critiques** censure

critiquer [kritike] *tr* to criticize, find fault with ‖ *intr* to find fault

critiqueur [kritikœr] *m* critic, fault-finder

croassement [krɔasmɑ̃] *m* croak, caw, croaking (*of raven*)

croasser [krɔase] *intr* to croak, caw

croate [krɔat] *adj* Croation ‖ *m* Croat, Croatian (*language*) ‖ (*cap*) *mf* Croatian (*person*)

croc [kro] *m* hook; fang (*of dog*); tusk (*of walrus*)

croc-en-jambe [krɔkɑ̃jɑ̃b] *m* (*pl* **crocs-en-jambes** [krɔkɑ̃jɑ̃b])—**faire un croc-en-jambe à qn** to trip s.o. up

croche [krɔʃ] *f* (mus) quaver

crochet [krɔʃɛ] *m* hook; fang (*of snake*); crochet work; crochet needle; picklock; **crochet radiophonique** talent show; **crochets** (typ) brackets; **faire un crochet** to swerve; **vivre aux crochets de** to live on or at the expense of

crocheter [krɔʃte] §2 *tr* to pick (*a lock*)

crocheteur [krɔʃtœr] *m* picklock; porter

cro•chu -chue [krɔʃy] *adj* hooked (*e.g., nose*); crooked; **avoir les mains crochues** to be light-fingered

crocodile [krɔkɔdil] *m* crocodile

crocus [krɔkys] *m* crocus

croire [krwar] §16, §95 *tr* to believe; **croire + inf** to think that + *ind*; **croire qn + adj** to believe s.o. to be + *adj*; **croire que non** to think not; **croire que oui** to think so; **je crois bien** or **je le crois bien** I should say so ‖ *intr* to believe; **croire à** to believe in; **croire en Dieu** to believe in God; **j'y crois** I believe in it ‖ *ref* to believe oneself to be

croisade [krwazad] *f* crusade

croi•sé -sée [krwaze] *adj* crossed; twilled (*cloth*); double-breasted (*suit*); alternate (*rhymes*) ‖ *m* Crusader ‖ *f* crossing, crossroads

croisement [krwazmɑ̃] *m* crossing; intersection; meeting, passing (*of two vehicles*); cross-breeding; **croisement en trèfle** cloverleaf, cloverleaf intersection

croiser [krwaze] *tr* to cross; fold over; meet,

pass ‖ *intr* to fold over, lap; cruise ‖ *ref* to cross, intersect; go on a crusade

croiseur [krwazœr] *m* cruiser; **croiseur de bataille** battle cruiser

croisière [krwazjɛr] *f* cruise; **en croisière** cruising

croissance [krwasɑ̃s] *f* growth

crois·sant [krwasɑ̃] **-sante** [sɑ̃t] *adj* growing, increasing, rising ‖ *m* crescent; crescent roll; billhook

croître [krwɑtr] §17 *intr* to grow; to increase, to rise

croix [krwa] *f* cross; (typ) dagger; **croix de bois, croix de fer, si je mens je vais en enfer** cross my heart and hope to die; **croix gammée** swastika; **en croix** crossed, crosswise

Croix-du-Sud [krwadysyd] *f* Southern Cross

Croix-Rouge [krwaruʒ] *f* Red Cross

cro·quant [krɔkɑ̃] **-quante** [kɑ̃t] *adj* crisp, crunchy ‖ *m* wretch

croque-mitaine [krɔkmitɛn] *m* (*pl* **-mitaines**) bugaboo, bogeyman

croque-monsieur [krɔkməsjø] *m invar* grilled ham-and-cheese sandwich

croque-mort [krɔkmɔr] *m* (*pl* **-morts**) (coll) funeral attendant

croquer [krɔke] *tr* to munch; sketch; dissipate (*a fortune*) ‖ *intr* to crunch

croquet [krɔkɛ] *m* croquet; almond cookie

croquis [krɔki] *m* sketch; draft, outline; **croquis coté** diagram, sketch, rough sketch;

cross [krɔs] *or* **cross-country** [krɔskœntri] *m* cross-country race

crosse [krɔs] *f* crosier; butt (*of gun*); hockey stick; lacrosse stick; golf club; **chercher des crosses à** (slang) to pick a fight with; **mettre la crosse en l'air** to show the white flag, to surrender

crotale [krɔtal] *m* rattlesnake

crotte [krɔt] *f* dung; mud; **crotte de chocolat** chocolate cream (candy)

crotter [krɔte] *tr* to dirty ‖ *ref* to get dirty; commit a nuisance (*said of dog*)

crottin [krɔtɛ̃] *m* horse manure

crou·lant [krulɑ̃] **-lante** [lɑ̃t] *adj* crumbling ‖ *m* (slang) old fogy

crouler [krule] *intr* to collapse

croup [krup] *m* (pathol) croup

croupe [krup] *f* croup, rump; ridge, brow; **en croupe** behind the rider

croupetons [kruptɔ̃]—**à croupetons** squatting

crou·pi -pie [krupi] *adj* stagnant

croupier [krupje] *m* croupier; financial partner

croupière [krupjɛr] *f* crupper; **tailler des croupieres à** (coll) to make it hard for

croupion [krupjɔ̃] *m* rump

croupir [krupir] *intr* to stagnate; wallow (*in vice, filth*); remain (*e.g., in ignorance*)

croustil·lant [krustijɑ̃] **-lante** [jɑ̃t] *adj* crisp, crunchy; spicy (*story*)

croustille [krustij] *f* piece of crust; snack; **croustilles** potato chips

croustiller [krustije] *intr* to munch, nibble

croustil·leux [krustijø] **-leuse** [jøz] *adj* spicy (*story*)

croûte [krut] *f* crust; pastry shell (*of meat pie*); scab (*of wound*); (coll) daub, worthless painting; **casser la croûte** (coll) to have a snack

croû·teux [krutø] **-teuse** [tøz] *adj* scabby

croûton [krutɔ̃] *m* crouton; heel (*of bread*); **vieux croûton** (coll) old dodo

croyable [krwɑjabl], [krwajabl] *adj* believable

croyance [krwajɑ̃s] *f* belief

croyant [krwjɑ̃] **croyante** [krwjɑ̃t] *adj* believing ‖ *mf* believer

C.R.S. [seɛrɛs] *fpl* (letterword) (**Compagnies républicaines de sécurité**) state troopers

cru crue [kry] *adj* raw, uncooked; indigestible; crude (*language; art*); glaring, harsh (*light*); hard (*water*); plain (*terms*); **à cru** directly; bareback ‖ *m* region (*in which s.th. is grown*); vineyard; vintage; **de son cru** of his own intention; **du cru** local, at the vineyard ‖ *f* see **crue**

crue ‖ *v* see **croire**

crû crue [kry] *v* see **croître**

cruauté [kryote] *f* cruelty; **cruauté mentale** mental cruelty

cruche [kryʃ] *f* pitcher, jug

cruchon [kryʃɔ̃] *m* small pitcher or jug

cru·cial -ciale [krysjal] *adj* (*pl* **-ciaux** [sjo]) crucial; cross-shaped

crucifiement [krysifimɑ̃] *m* crucifixion

crucifier [krysifje] *tr* to crucify

crucifix [krysifi] *m* crucifix

crucifixion [krysifiksjɔ̃] *f* crucifixion

crudité [krydite] *f* crudity; indigestibility; rawness (*of food*); harshness (*of light*); hardness (*of water*); **crudités** raw fruits and vegetables; off-color remarks

crue [kry] *f* overflow (*of river*); growth

cruel cruelle [kryɛl] *adj* cruel

cruellement [kryɛlmɑ̃] *adv* cruelly; sorely

crû·ment [krymɑ̃] *adv* crudely; roughly

crustacé [krystase] *m* crustacean

crypte [kript] *f* crypt

crypter [kripte] *tr* to encrypt

cryptographie [kriptɔgrafi] *f* cryptography

C^te^C^t^ *abbr* (**compte courant**) current account

cubage [kybaʒ] *m* volume

cu·bain [kybɛ̃] **-baine** [bɛn] *adj* Cuban ‖ (*cap*) *mf* Cuban

cube [kyb] *adj* cubic ‖ *m* cube

cuber [kybe] *tr* to cube

cubique [kybik] *adj* cubic

cueillaison [kœjɛzɔ̃] *f* picking, gathering; harvest time

cueil·leur [kœjœr] **-leuse** [jøz] *mf* picker; fruit picker

cueillir [kœjir] §18 *tr* to pick; pluck; gather; win (*laurels*); steal (*a kiss*); (coll) to nab (*a thief*); (coll) to pick up (*a friend*)

cuiller *or* **cuillère** [kɥijɛr] *f* spoon; ladle (*for molten metal*); scoop (*of a dredger*); **cuiller à bouche** tablespoon; **cuiller à café** teaspoon; **cuiller à pot** ladle; **cuiller à soupe** soup-spoon; **cuiller et fourchette** fork and spoon

cuillerée [kɥijre] f spoonful

cuilleron [kɥijrɔ̃] m bowl (of spoon)

cuir [kɥir] m leather; hide; **cuir chevelu** scalp; **cuir synthétique** synthetic leather; **cuir verni** patent leather; **cuir vert** rawhide; **faire des cuirs** to make mistakes in liaison

cuirasse [kɥiras] f cuirass, breastplate; armor

cuiras·sé -sée [kɥirase] adj armored ‖ m battleship

cuirasser [kɥirase] tr to armor ‖ ref to steel oneself

cuire [kɥir] §19 tr to cook; ripen; **c'est du tout cuit** (coll) it's in the bag ‖ intr to cook; to sting, smart; **faire cuire** to cook; **il vous en cuira** you'll suffer for it

cui·sant [kɥizɑ̃] **-sante** [zɑ̃t] adj stinging, smarting

cuisez [kɥize] v (**cuisons**) see **cuire**

cuisine [kɥizin] f kitchen; cooking; cuisine; (coll) skulduggery; **cuisine roulante** chuck wagon, field kitchen; **faire la cuisine** to cook

cuisiner [kɥizine] tr to cook; (coll) to grill (a suspect); (coll) to fix (an election) ‖ intr to cook

cuisinette [kɥizinɛt] f kitchenette

cuisi·nier [kɥizinje] **-nière** [njɛr] mf cook ‖ f kitchen stove, cookstove

cuissardes [kɥisard] fpl hip boots

cuisse [kɥis] f thigh; (culin) drumstick; **cuisses de grenouille** frogs' legs; **il se croit sorti de la cuisse de Jupiter** (coll) he thinks he is the Lord God Almighty

cuis·seau [kɥiso] m (pl **-seaux**) leg of veal

cuisson [kɥisɔ̃] f baking, cooking; (fig) burning sensation, smarting; **en cuisson** on the stove, on the grill, in the oven

cuissot [kɥiso] m leg (of game)

cuistre [kɥistr] m pedant, prig

cuit [kɥi] **cuite** [kɥit] adj cooked; **nous sommes cuits** (coll) our goose is cooked ‖ f firing (in a kiln); **prendre une cuite** (slang) to get soused ‖ v see **cuire**

cuivre [kɥivr] m copper; **cuivre jaune** brass; **les cuivres** (mus) the brasses

cui·vré -vrée [kɥivre] adj copper-colored, bronzed; brassy, metallic (sound or voice)

cuivrer [kɥivre] tr to copper; bronze, tan; make (a sound or one's voice) brassy or metallic ‖ ref to become copper-colored

cui·vreux [kɥivrø] **-vreuse** [vrøz] adj (chem) cuprous

cul [ky] m bottom (of bottle, bag); (slang) ass, hind end, rump; **bouche en cul de poule** (slang) pursed lips; **faire cul sec** (slang) to chug-a-lug

culasse [kylas] f breechblock; (mach) cylinder head

cul-blanc [kyblɑ̃] m (pl **culs-blancs**) wheatear, whitetail

culbute [kylbyt] f somersault; tumble, bad fall; (coll) failure; (coll) fall (of a cabinet); **faire la culbute** to sell at double the purchase price

culbuter [kylbyte] tr to overthrow; overwhelm (the enemy) ‖ intr to tumble, fall backwards; somersault

culbuteur [kylbytœr] m (mach) rocker arm

cul-de-basse-fosse [kydbɑsfos] m (pl **culs-de-basse-fosse**) dungeon

cul-de-jatte [kydəʒat] mf (pl **culs-de-jatte**) legless person

cul-de-sac [kydəsak] m (pl **culs-de-sac**) dead end; (public sign) no outlet

culée [kyle] f abutment

culer [kyle] intr to back water

culinaire [kylinɛr] adj culinary

culmi·nant [kylminɑ̃] **-nante** [nɑ̃t] adj culminating; highest (point)

culmination [kylminɑsjɔ̃] f (astr) culmination

culminer [kylmine] intr to rise high, tower; (astr) to culminate

culot [kylo] m base, bottom; (coll) baby of the family; **avoir du culot** (slang) to have a lot of nerve

culotte [kylɔt] f breeches, pants; forked pipe; panties (feminine undergarment); (culin) rump; **culotte de golf** plus fours; **culotte de peau** (slang) old soldier; **culotte de sport** shorts; **porter la culotte** (coll) to wear the pants; **prendre une culotte** (slang) to lose one's shirt; (slang) to have a jag on

culot·té -tée [kylɔte] adj (coll) nervy, fresh

culotter [kylɔte] tr to cure (a pipe) ‖ ref to put one's pants on

culte [kylt] m worship; cult; divine service, ritual; religion, creed; **avoir un culte pour** to worship, adore (e.g., one's parents); **culte de la personalité** personality cult

cul-terreux [kytɛrø] m (pl **culs-terreux**) (coll) clodhopper, hayseed

cultivable [kyltivabl] adj arable, tillable

cultiva·teur [kyltivatœr] **-trice** [tris] adj farming ‖ mf farmer; grower ‖ m (mach) cultivator

cultiver [kyltive] tr to cultivate; culture

cultu·ral -rale [kyltyral] adj (pl **-raux** [ro]) agricultural

culture [kyltyr] f culture; cultivation; **culture hydroponique** tank farming; **culture sèche** dry farming

cultu·rel -relle [kyltyrɛl] adj cultural

culturisme [kyltyrism] m body-building exercises

cumula·tif [kymylatif] **-tive** [tiv] adj cumulative

cumuler [kymyle] intr to moonlight

cunéiforme [kyneifɔrm] adj cuneiform

cunnilingue [kynilɛ̃g] f cunnilingus

cunnilingus [kynilɛ̃gys] m or **cunnilinctus** [kynilɛ̃ktys] m cunnilingus

cupide [kypid] adj greedy

cupidité [kypidite] f cupidity

Cupidon [kypidɔ̃] m Cupid

curage [kyraʒ] m cleansing, cleaning out; unstopping (of a drain)

curatelle [kyratɛl] f guardianship, trusteeship

cura·teur [kyratœr] **-trice** [tris] mf guardian, trustee

cura•tif [kyratif] **-tive** [tiv] *adj* curative

cure [kyr] *f* treatment, cure; vicarage, rectory; parish; sun porch; **n'avoir cure de rien, n'en avoir cure** not to care

curé [kyre] *m* parish priest

cure-dent [kyrdɑ̃] *m* (*pl* **-dents**) toothpick

curée [kyre] *f* quarry (*given to the hounds*); scramble, mad race (*for gold, power, recognition, etc.*)

cure-oreille [kyrɔrɛj] *m* (*pl* **-oreilles**) earpick

cure-pipe [kyrpip] *m* (*pl* **-pipes**) pipe cleaner

curer [kyre] *tr* to clean out; dredge ‖ *ref* to pick (*one's nails, one's teeth, etc.*)

cu•rieux [kyrjø] **-rieuse** [rjøz] §93 *adj* curious, strange, queer

curiosité [kyrjozite] *f* curiosity; curio; connoisseurs, e.g., **le langage de la curiosité** the jargon of connoisseurs; **curiosités** sights; **visiter les curiosités** to go sightseeing

curseur [kyrsœr] *m* slide, runner; (comp) cursor

cur•sif [kyrsif] **-sive** [siv] *adj* cursory; cursive (*handwriting*) ‖ *f* cursive

cuta•né -née [kytane] *adj* cutaneous

cuticule [kytikyl] *f* cuticle

cuti-réaction [kytireaksjɔ̃] *f* skin test

cuve [kyv] *f* vat, tub, tank

cu•veau [kyvo] *m* (*pl* **-veaux**) small vat or tank

cuver [kyve] *tr* to leave to ferment; **cuver son vin** (coll) to sleep it off ‖ *intr* to ferment in a wine vat

cuvette [kyvɛt] *f* basin, pan; bulb (*of a thermometer*); (chem, phot) tray

cuvier [kyvje] *m* washtub

C.V. [seve] *m* (letterword) (**cheval-vapeur**) hp, horsepower

cyanamide [sjanamid] *f* cyanamide

cyanose [sjanoz] *f* cyanosis

cyanure [sjanyr] *m* cyanide

cybermonde [sibɛrmɔ̃d] *m* cyberspace

cyberespace [sibɛrəspas] *m* cyberspace

cybernétique [sibɛrnetik] *adj* cybernetic ‖ *f* cybernetics

cyclable [siklabl] *adj* reserved for bicycles

cycle [sikl] *m* cycle

cyclique [siklik] *adj* cyclic(al)

cycliste [siklist] *mf* cyclist

cyclomoteur [siklɔmɔtœr] *m* motorbike, moped

cyclone [siklon] *m* cyclone

cyclope [siklɔp] *m* cyclops

cyclotron [siklɔtrɔ̃] *m* cyclotron

cygne [siɲ] *m* swan

cylindrage [silɛ̃draʒ] *m* rolling (*of roads, gardens, etc.*); calendering, mangling

cylindre [silɛ̃dr] *m* cylinder; roller (*e.g., of rolling mill*); steam roller

cylindrée [silɛ̃dre] *f* piston displacement

cylindrer [silɛ̃dre] *tr* to roll (*a road, garden, etc.*); calender, mangle

cylindrique [silɛ̃drik] *adj* cylindrical

cymbale [sɛ̃bal] *f* cymbal

cynique [sinik] *adj* & *m* cynic

cynisme [sinism] *m* cynicism

cyprès [siprɛ] *m* cypress

cyrillique [sirilik] *adj* Cyrillic

cytologie [sitɔlɔʒi] *f* cytology

cytoplasme [sitɔplasm] *m* cytoplasm

czar [ksar] *m* czar

czarine [ksarin] *f* czarina

D

D, d [de] *m invar* fourth letter of the French alphabet

d' = de before vowel or mute **h**

d'abord [dabɔr] see **abord**

dactylo [daktilo] *mf* (coll) typist

dactylographe [daktilɔgraf] *mf* typist

dactylographie [daktilɔgrafi] *f* typewriting; **dactylographie au toucher** touch typewriting, touch typing

dactylographier [daktilɔgrafje] *tr* to type

dactyloscopie [daktilɔskɔpi] *f* fingerprinting

dada [dada] *m* hobby-horse; hobby, fad, pet subject; **enfourcher son dada** to ride one's hobby

dague [dag] *f* dagger; first antler; tusk

dahlia [dalja] *m* dahlia

daigner [deɲe] §95 *intr*—**daigner** + *inf* to deign to, condescend to + *inf*; **daignez** please

d'ailleurs [dajœr] see **ailleurs**

daim [dɛ̃] *m* fallow deer; suede

daine [dɛn] *f* doe

dais [dɛ] *m* canopy

dalle [dal] *f* flagstone, slab, paving block; **se rincer la dalle** (slang) to wet one's whistle

daller [dale] *tr* to pave with flagstones

dalto•nien [daltɔnjɛ̃] **-nienne** [njɛn] *adj* color-blind ‖ *mf* color-blind person

dam [dɑ̃] *m*—**au dam de** to the detriment of

damas [damɑ] *m* damask ‖ (*cap*) [damɑs] *f* Damascus

damasquiner [damaskine] *tr* to damascene

damas•sé -sée [damase] *adj* & *m* damask

dame [dam] *f* dame; lady; tamp, tamper; rowlock; (cards, chess) queen; (checkers) king; **aller à dame** (checkers) to crown a man king; (chess) to queen a pawn; **dame d'honneur** lady-in-waiting; **dame pipi** (slang) female toilet attendant; **dames** (public sign) ladies; **Première Dame** First Lady (*President's wife*) ‖ *interj* for heaven's sake!

damer [dame] *tr* to tamp (*the earth*); (checkers)

to crown (*a checker*); (chess) to queen (*a pawn*); **damer le pion à qn** to outwit s.o.

damier [damje] *m* checkerboard

damnation [dɑnɑsjɔ̃] *f* damnation

dam•né -née [dɑne] *adj & mf* damned

damner [dɑne] *tr* to damn

damoi•seau [damwazo] **-selle** [zɛl] *mf* (*pl* **-seaux**) (archaic) young member of the nobility ‖ *m* lady's man ‖ *f* (archaic) damsel

dancing [dɑsiŋ] *m* dance hall

dandiner [dɑ̃dine] *tr* to dandle ‖ *ref* to waddle along

dandy [dɑ̃di] *m* dandy, fop

Danemark [danmark] *m*—**le Danemark** Denmark

danger [dɑ̃ʒe] *m* danger

dange•reux [dɑ̃ʒrø] **-reuse** [røz] *adj* dangerous

da•nois [danwa] **-noise** [nwaz] *adj* Danish ‖ *m* Danish (*language* ‖ (*cap*) *mf* Dane

dans [dɑ̃] *prep* in; into; in (*at the end of*), e.g., **dans deux jours** in two days; **boire dans un verre** to drink out of a glass; **dans la suite** later

danse [dɑ̃s] *f* dance; **danse de Saint Guy** St. Vitus's dance; **danse guerrière** war dance

danser [dɑ̃se] *tr & intr* to dance; **faire danser** to mistreat

dan•seur [dɑ̃sœr] **-seuse** [søz] *mf* dancer; **danseur de corde** tightrope walker; **danseuse orientale** *f* belly dancer; **en danseuse** in a standing position (*taken by cyclist*)

Danube [danyb] *m* Danube

d'après [daprɛ] see **après**

dard [dar] *m* dart; sting; snake's tongue; harpoon

darder [darde] *tr* to dart, hurl

dare-dare [dardar] *adv* (coll) on the double

darse [dars] *f* wet dock

date [dat] *f* date; **date d'échéance** expiration date; **date limite** cutoff date; **de fraîche date** recent; **de longue date** of long standing; **en date de** from; **faire date** to mark an epoch; **prendre date** to make an appointment

dater [date] *tr & intr* to date; **à dater de** dating from

datif [datif] *m* dative

datte [dat] *f* date

dattier [datje] *m* date palm

daube [dob] *f* braised meat; **en daube** braised

dauber [dobe] *tr* to braise; heckle; slander; (coll) to pummel ‖ *intr* **dauber sur qn** to heckle s.o., slander s.o.

dau•beur [dobœr] **-beuse** [bøz] *mf* heckler

dauphin [dofɛ̃] *m* dolphin; dauphin

dauphine [dofin] *f* dauphiness

dauphinelle [dofinɛl] *f* delphinium

davantage [davɑ̃taʒ] **§90** *adv* more; any more; any longer; **ne ... davantage** no more; **pas davantage** no longer

de [də] **§77, §78, §79** *prep* of, from; with, e.g., **frapper d'une épée** to strike with a sword; (to indicate the agent with the passive voice) by, e.g., **ils sont aimés de tous** they are loved

by all; (to indicate the point of departure) from, e.g., **de Paris à Madrid** from Paris to Madrid; (to indicate the point of arrival) for, e.g., **le train de Paris** the train for Paris; (with a following infinitive after certain verbs) to, e.g., **il essaie d'écrire la lettre** he is trying to write the letter; (with a following infinitive after an adjective used with the impersonal expression **il est**) to, e.g., **il est facile de chanter cette chanson** it is easy to sing that song; (after **changer, se souvenir, avoir besoin,** etc.), e.g., **changer de vêtements** to change clothes; (after a comparative and before a numeral) than, e.g., **plus de quarante** more than forty; (to express the indefinite plural or partitive idea), e.g., **de l'eau** water, some water; (to form prepositional phrases with some adverbs), e.g., **auprès de vous** near you; (with the historical infinitive), e.g., **et chacun de pleurer** and everyone cried

dé [de] *m* die (*singular of dice*); thimble; domino; golf tee; **dés** dice

dealer [dilœr] *m* (slang) drug dealer

déambulateur [deɑ̃bylatœr] *m* walker (*used by an infirm person*)

déambuler [deɑ̃byle] *intr* to stroll

débâcle [debakl] *f* debacle; breakup (*of ice*)

débâcler [debakle] *intr* to break up (*said of ice in a river*)

déballage [debalaʒ] *m* unpacking; cut-rate merchandise (*sold by street vendor*)

déballer [debale] *tr* to unpack (*merchandise*); display (*merchandise*)

débandade [debɑ̃dad] *f* rout, stampede; **à la débandade** in confusion, helter-skelter

débander [debɑ̃de] *tr* to rout, stampede; slacken (*s.th. under tension*); unwind; **débander les yeux à qn** to take the blindfold from s.o.'s eyes ‖ *intr* to flee, stampede

débaptiser [debatize] *tr* to change the name of, rename

débarbouiller [debarbuje] *tr* to wash the face of

débarcadère [debarkadɛr] *m* wharf, dock, landing platform

débarder [debarde] *tr* to unload

débardeur [debardœr] *m* stevedore, longshoreman; (clothing) tank top

débar•qué -quée [debarke] *adj* disembarking ‖ *mf* new arrival ‖ *m* disembarkment; **au débarqué** on arrival

débarquement [debarkmɑ̃] *m* disembarkation

débarquer [debarke] *m*—**au débarquer de qn** at the moment of s.o.'s arrival ‖ *tr* to unload, lower (*a lifeboat, seaplane, etc.*); (coll) to sack (*s.o.*) ‖ *intr* to disembark, get off

débarras [debara] *m* catchall

débarrasser [debarase] *tr* to disencumber, disentangle; clear (*the table*); rid ‖ *ref*—**se débarrasser de** to get rid of

débarrasseur [debarasœr] *m* busboy

débarrer [debare] *tr* to unbar

débat [deba] *m* debate; dispute; **débats** discussion (*in a meeting*); proceedings (*in a court*)

débâter [debate] *tr* to unsaddle

débattre [debatr] §7 *tr* to debate, argue, discuss; haggle over (*a price*); question (*items in an account*) ‖ *ref* to struggle; be debated

débauche [deboʃ] *f* debauch, debauchery; riot (*e.g., of colors*); overeating; striking, quitting work

débaucher [deboʃe] *tr* to debauch; induce (*a worker*) to strike; lay off (*workers*); steal (*a worker*) from another employer ‖ *ref* to become debauched

débile [debil] *adj* weak ‖ *mf* mental defective

débilité [debilite] *f* debility

débiliter [debilite] *tr* to debilitate

débiner [debine] *tr* (slang) to run (*s.o.*) down ‖ *ref* (slang) to fly the coop

débit [debi] *m* debit; retail sale; shop; cutting up (*of wood*); output; way of speaking

débiter [debite] *tr* to debit; cut up in pieces; retail; produce; speak (*one's part*); repeat thoughtlessly

débi·teur [debitœr] **-trice** [tris] *adj* debit (*account, balance*); delivery (*spool*) ‖ *mf* debtor; **débiteur hypothécaire** mortgagor ‖ **-teur** [tœr] **-teuse** [tøz] *mf* gossip, talebearer; salesclerk

déblai [deblɛ] *m* excavation; **déblais** rubble, fill

déblaiement [deblɛmã] *m* clearing away

déblatérer [deblatere] §10 *tr* to bluster or fling (*threats, abuse*) ‖ *intr*—**déblatérer contre** to rail at

déblayer [debleje] §49 *tr* to clear, clear away

débloquer [deblɔke] *tr* to unblock; unfreeze (*funds, credits, etc.*)

déboguer [debɔge] *tr* (comp) to debug

déboire [debwar] *m* unpleasant aftertaste; disappointment

déboisement [debwazmã] *m* deforestation

déboîter [debwate] *tr* to disconnect (*pipe*); dislocate (*a shoulder*) ‖ *intr* to move into another lane (*said of automobile*); (naut) to haul (*out of line*)

débonder [debõde] *tr* to unbung

débonnaire [debɔnɛr] *adj* good-natured, easygoing; (Bib) meek

débor·dant [debɔrdã] **-dante** [dãt] *adj* overflowing

débor·dé -dée [debɔrde] *adj* overwhelmed

débordement [debɔrdmã] *m* overflowing; outburst; overlap; **débordements** excesses

déborder [debɔrde] *tr* to extend beyond, jut out over; trim the border from; overwhelm; untuck (*a bed*); (mil) to outflank ‖ *intr* to overflow; (naut) to shove off

débotté [debɔte] *m*—**au débotté** immediately upon arrival, at once

débouché [debuʃe] *m* outlet; opening (*for trade; of an attack*); outlet (*market for goods; discount house*)

déboucher [debuʃe] *tr* to free from obstruction; uncork ‖ *intr*—**déboucher dans** to empty into

(*said of river*); **déboucher sur** to open onto, to emerge into

débouchoir [debuʃwar] *m* plunger

déboucler [debukle] *tr* to unbuckle; take the curls out of

débouler [debule] *tr* to fly down (*e.g., a stairway*) ‖ *intr* to run suddenly out of cover (*said of rabbits*); dash; **débouler dans** to roll down (*a stairway*)

déboulonner [debulɔne] *tr* to unbolt; (coll) to ruin, have fired; (coll) to debunk

débourber [deburbe] *tr* to clear of mud, clean

débourrer [debure] *tr* to unhair (*a hide*); remove the stuffing from (*a chair*); knock (*a pipe*) clean

débours [debur] *m* disbursement; **rentrer dans ses débours** to recover one's investment

déboursement [debursmã] *m* disbursing

débourser [deburse] *tr* to disburse

débousso·lé -lée [debusɔle] *adj* adrift, without direction, lost

debout [dəbu] *adv* upright, on end; standing; up (*out of bed*)

déboutonner [debutɔne] *tr* to unbutton; **à ventre déboutonné** immoderately ‖ *ref* (coll) to get something off one's chest

débrail·lé -lée [debraje] *adj* untidy, mussed up, unkempt; loose (*morals*); vulgar (*speech*) ‖ *m* untidiness

débrancher [debrãʃe] *tr* to switch (*railroad cars*) to a siding; (elec) to disconnect

débrayage [debrɛjaʒ] *m* (aut) clutch release; (coll) walkout

débrayer [debrɛje] §49 *tr* to disengage, throw out (*the clutch*) ‖ *intr* to throw out the clutch; (coll) to walk out (*said of strikers*)

débri·dé -dée [debride] *adj* unbridled

débris [debri] *mpl* debris; remains

débrouil·lard [debrujar] **-larde** [jard] *adj* (coll) resourceful ‖ *mf* (coll) smart customer

débrouiller [debruje] *tr* to disentangle, unravel; clear up (*a mystery*); make out (*e.g., a signature*); (coll) to teach (*s.o.*) to be resourceful ‖ *ref* to clear (*said of sky*); (coll) to manage to get along, take care of oneself; (coll) to extricate oneself (*from a difficult situation*)

débucher [debyʃe] *tr* to flush out (*game*) ‖ *intr* to run out of cover (*said of game*)

débusquer [debyske] *tr* to flush out (*game; the enemy*)

début [deby] *m* debut; beginning, commencement; opening play

débu·tant [debytã] **-tante** [tãt] *adj* beginning ‖ *mf* beginner; newcomer (*e.g., to stage or screen*) ‖ *f* debutante

débuter [debyte] *intr* to make one's debut, begin; start up a business; make the opening play

deçà [dəsa] *adv*—**deçà delà** here and there; **en deçà de** on this side of

décacheter [dekaʃte] §34 *tr* to unseal

décade [dekad] *f* period of ten days; (hist, lit) decade

décadence [dekadɑ̃s] *f* decadence

déca•dent [dekadɑ̃] **-dente** [dɑ̃t] *adj & mf* decadent

décaféi•né -née [dekafeine] *adj* decaffeinated, caffeine-free

décagénaires [dekaʒenɛr] *mfpl* teenagers

décaisser [dekɛse] *tr* to uncrate; disburse, pay out

décalage [dekalaʒ] *m* unkeying; shift; slippage; (aer) stagger

décalcomanie [dekalkɔmani] *f* decal

décaler [dekale] *tr* to unkey; shift

décalquage [dekalkaʒ] or **décalque** [dekalk] *m* decal

décalquer [dekalke] *tr* to transfer (*a decal*) onto paper, canvas, metal, etc.; **décalquer sur** to transfer (*a decal*) onto (*e.g., paper*)

décamper [dekɑ̃pe] *intr* to decamp

décanat [dekana] *m* deanship

décanter [dekɑ̃te] *tr* to decant

décapant [dekapɑ̃] *m* scouring agent

décaper [dekape] *tr* to scour, scale

décapant [dekapɑ̃] *m* paint remover, stripper

décapiter [dekapite] *tr* to behead, decapitate; top (*a tree*)

décapotable [dekapɔtabl] *adj & f* (aut) convertible

décapsuleur [dekapsylœr] *m* bottle opener

déca•ti -tie [dekati] *adj* haggard, worn-out, faded

décatir [dekatir] *tr* to steam (*cloth*)

décaver [dekave] *tr* (coll) to fleece

décéder [desede] §10 *intr* (*aux;* ÉTRE) to die (*said of human being*)

décèlement [desɛlmɑ̃ *m* disclosure

déceler [desle] §2 *tr* to uncover, detect; to betray (*confusion*)

décélération [deselerasjɔ̃] *f* deceleration

décembre [desɑ̃br] *m* December

décemment [desamɑ̃] *adv* decently

décennie [desɛni] *f* decade

dé•cent [desɑ̃] **-cente** [sɑ̃t] *adj* decent

décentraliser [desɑ̃tralize] *tr* to decentralize

déception [desɛpsjɔ̃] *f* disappointment

décernement [desɛrnəmɑ̃] *m* awarding

décerner [desɛrne] *tr* to award (*a prize*); confer (*an honor*); issue (*a writ*)

décès [desɛ] *m* decease, demise

déce•vant [desvɑ̃] **-vante** [vɑ̃t] *adj* disappointing; deceptive

décevoir [desvwar] §59 *tr* to disappoint; deceive

déchaînement [deʃɛnmɑ̃] *m* unchaining, unleashing; outburst, wave

déchaîner [deʃɛne] *tr* to unchain, let loose ‖ *ref* to fly into a rage; break out (*said of storm*)

déchanter [deʃɑ̃te] *intr* (coll) to sing a different tune

décharge [deʃarʒ] *f* discharge; drain; rubbish heap; storeroom, shed; **à décharge** (law) for the defense; **à sa décharge** in his or her defense

déchargement [deʃarʒəmɑ̃] *m* unloading

décharger [deʃarʒe] §38 *tr* to discharge; unload; unburden; exculpate (*a defendant*); (comp) to download ‖ *ref* to vent one's anger; go off (*said of gun*); run down (*said of battery*); **se décharger de q.ch. sur qn** to shift the responsibility for s.th. on s.o.

déchargeur [deʃarʒœr] *m* porter (*e.g., in a market*); dock hand

déchar•né -née [deʃarne] *adj* emaciated, skinny, bony

décharner [deʃarne] *tr* to strip the flesh from; emaciate ‖ *ref* to waste away

déchaus•sé -sée [deʃose] *adj* barefoot

déchausser [deʃose] *tr* to take the shoes off of (*s.o.*); expose the roots of (*a tree, a tooth*) ‖ *ref* to take off one's shoes; shrink (*said of gums*)

déchéance [deʃeɑ̃s] *f* downfall; lapse, forfeiture (*of a right*); expiration, term (*of a note or loan*)

déchet [deʃɛ] *m* loss, decrease; **déchet de route** loss in transit; **déchets** waste products; **déchets hasardeux** hazardous waste

décheveler [deʃəvle] §34 *tr* to dishevel, muss (*s.o.'s hair*)

déchiffonner [deʃifɔne] *tr* to iron (*wrinkled material*)

déchiffrable [deʃifrabl] *adj* legible; decipherable

déchiffrement [deʃifrəmɑ̃] *m* deciphering, decoding; sight-reading

déchiffrer [deʃifre] *tr* to decipher; sight-read (*music*)

déchif•freur [deʃifrœr] **-freuse** [frøz] *mf* decipherer, decoder; sight-reader

déchique•té -tée [deʃikte] *adj* jagged, torn

déchiqueter [deʃikte] §34 *tr* to cut into strips; shred; slash

déchi•rant [deʃirɑ̃] **-rante** [rɑ̃t] *adj* heart-rending

déchi•ré -rée [deʃire] *adj* torn; sorry

déchirer [deʃire] *tr* to tear, tear up; split (*a country; one's eardrums*); pick (*s.o.'s character*) to pieces ‖ *ref* to skin (*e.g., one's knee*)

déchirure [deʃirur] *f* tear, rent; sprain

déchoir [deʃwar] (usually used only in: *inf; pp* **déchu;** sometimes used in: *pres ind* **déchois,** etc.; *fut* **déchoirai,** etc.; *cond* **déchoirais,** etc.) *intr* (*aux:* AVOIR or ÉTRE) to fall (*from high estate*); decline, fail

dé•chu -chue [deʃy] *adj* fallen; deprived (*of rights*); expired (*insurance policy*)

décibel [desibɛl] *m* decibel

décider [deside] §97, §100 *tr* to decide, decide on; **décider qn à** + *inf* to persuade s.o. to + *inf* ‖ *intr* to decide; **décider de** to decide, determine the outcome of, e.g., **le coup a décidé de la partie** the trick decided the (outcome of the) game; **décider de** + *inf* to decide to *inf* ‖ §96, §97 *ref* to decide, make up one's mind; resolve; **se décider à** + *inf* to decide to + *inf*

déci•mal -male [desimal] *adj* (*pl* **-maux** [mo]) decimal ‖ *f* decimal

décimer [desime] *tr* to decimate
déci•sif [desizif] **-sive** [ziv] *adj* decisive
décision [desizjɔ̃] *f* decision; decisiveness
déclama•teur [deklamatœr] **-trice** [tris] *adj* bombastic ‖ *mf* declaimer
déclamatoire [deklamatwar] *adj* declamatory
déclamer [deklame] *tr* to declaim ‖ *intr* to rant; **déclamer contre** to inveigh against
déclara•tif [deklaratif] **-tive** [tiv] *adj* declarative
déclaration [deklarasjɔ̃] *f* declaration; **déclaration de revenus** income-tax return; **déclaration douanière** customs declaration
déclarer [deklare] **§95** *tr & intr* to declare ‖ *ref* to declare oneself; arise, break out, occur
déclassement [deklɑsmɑ̃] *m* disarrangement; drop in social status; transfer to another class (*on ship, train, etc.*); dismantling; demoting
déclasser [deklɑse] *tr* to disarrange; dismantle; demote
déclenchement [deklɑ̃ʃmɑ̃] *m* releasing; launching (*of an attack*)
déclencher [deklɑ̃ʃe] *tr* to unlatch, disengage; release (*the shutter*); open (*fire*); launch (*an attack*)
déclencheur [deklɑ̃ʃœr] *m* (mach, phot) release
déclic [deklik] *m* pawl, catch; hair trigger; (*bruit*) click; (phot) shutter mechanism
déclin [deklɛ̃] *m* decline
déclinaison [deklinɛzɔ̃] *f* (astr) declination; (gram) declension
décliner [dekline] *tr & intr* to decline
déclive [dekliv] *adj* sloping ‖ *f* slope
déclivité [deklivite] *f* declivity
dé•clos [deklo] **-close** [kloz] *adj* in bloom
déco [deko] *m* Deco, Art Deco, art deco
décocher [dekɔʃe] *tr* to let fly; flash (*a smile*)
décodage [dekɔdaʒ] *m* decoding
décoder [dekɔde] *tr* to decode
déco•deur [dekɔdœr] **-deuse** [døz] *mf* decoder ‖ *m* (comp, mil, telv) decoder
décoiffer [dekwafe] *tr* to loosen or muss the hair of; uncap (*a bottle*) ‖ *ref* to muss one's hair; take one's hair down
décoincer [dekwɛ̃se] **§51** *tr* to unwedge, loosen (*a jammed part*)
décolérer [dekɔlere] **§10** *intr* to calm down
décollage [dekɔlaʒ] *m* unsticking, ungluing; takeoff (*of airplane*)
décoller [dekɔle] *tr* to unstick, detach ‖ *intr* (aer) to take off
décolletage [dekɔltaʒ] *m* low-cut neck; screw cutting; topping
décolle•té -tée [dekɔlte] *adj* décolleté ‖ *m* low-cut neckline; bare neck and shoulders
décolleter [dekɔlte] **§34** *tr* to cut the neck of (*a dress*) low; bare the neck and shoulders of ‖ *ref* to wear a low-necked dress
décoloration [dekɔlɔrasjɔ̃] *f* discoloration
décolorer [dekɔlɔre] *tr & ref* to bleach; fade
décombres [dekɔ̃br] *mpl* debris, ruins
décommander [dekɔmɑ̃de] *tr* to cancel an order for; call off (*a dinner*); cancel the invitation to (*a guest*) ‖ *ref* to cancel a meeting

décompléter [dekɔ̃plete] **§10** *tr* to break up (*a set*)
décomposer [dekɔ̃poze] *tr & ref* to decompose
décomposition [dekɔ̃pozisjɔ̃] *f* decomposition
décompresser [dekɔ̃prɛse] *intr* to relax
décompression [dekɔ̃prɛsjɔ̃] *f* decompression
décomprimer [dekɔ̃prime] *tr* to decompress
décompte [dekɔ̃t] *m* itemized statement; discount (*to be deducted from total*); disappointment
décompter [dekɔ̃te] *tr* to deduct (*a sum from an account*) ‖ *intr* to strike the wrong hour
déconcerter [dekɔ̃sɛrte] *tr* to disconcert
décon•fit [dekɔ̃fi] **-fite** [fit] *adj* discomfited, baffled, confused
déconfiture [dekɔ̃fityr] *f* discomfiture; downfall, rout; business failure
décongeler [dekɔ̃ʒle] **§2** *tr* to thaw; defrost
décongestion [dekɔ̃ʒɛstjɔ̃] *f* decongestion
décongestionner [dekɔ̃ʒɛstjɔne] *tr* to relieve congestion in
déconseiller [dekɔ̃sɛje] *tr* to dissuade; **déconseiller q.ch. à qn** to advise s.o. against s.th. ‖ *intr*—**déconseiller à qn de** + *inf* to advise s.o. against + *ger*
déconsidération [dekɔ̃siderasjɔ̃] *f* disrepute
déconsidérer [dekɔ̃sidere] **§10** *tr* to bring into disrepute, discredit
déconsigner [dekɔ̃siɲe] *tr* to take (*one's baggage*) out of the checkroom; free (*soldiers*) from detention
décontenancer [dekɔ̃tnɑ̃se] **§51** *tr* to discountenance, abash ‖ *ref* to lose one's self-assurance
décontrac•té -tée [dekɔ̃trakte] *adj* relaxed, at ease; indifferent
décontracter [dekɔ̃trakte] *tr* to loosen up (*one's muscles*) ‖ *intr* to stretch one's muscles; relax
déconvenue [dekɔ̃vny] *f* disappointment, mortification
décor [dekɔr] *m* décor, decoration; (theat) setting; **décor découpé** cutout; **décors** (theat) set, stage setting
décora•teur [dekɔratœr] **-trice** [tris] *mf* interior decorator; stage designer
décora•tif [dekɔratif] **-tive** [tiv] *adj* decorative, ornamental
décoration [dekɔrasjɔ̃] *f* decoration
décorum [dekɔrɔm] *m invar* decorum
découcher [dekuʃe] *intr* to sleep away from home
découdre [dekudr] **§13** *tr* to unstitch, rip up; gore ‖ *intr*—**en découdre** to cross swords ‖ *ref* to come unsewn, rip at the seam
découler [dekule] *intr* to trickle; proceed, arise, be derived
découpage [dekupaʒ] *m* shooting script; **découpage des circonscriptions electorales** gerrymandering
découper [dekupe] *tr* to carve (*e.g., a turkey*); cut out (*a design*); indent (*the coast*) ‖ *ref*—**se découper sur** to stand out against (*the horizon*)

décou·plé -plée [dekuple] *adj* well-built, brawny

découpler [dekuple] *tr* to unleash

découpure [dekupyr] *f* cutting out; ornamental cutout; indentation (*in coast*)

découragement [dekuraʒmɑ̃] *m* discouragement

décourager [dekuraʒe] §38, §97, §99 *tr* to discourage ‖ *ref* to become discouraged

décours [dekur] *m* wane

décou·su -sue [dekuzy] *adj* unsewn; disjointed, unsystematic; incoherent (*words*); desultory (*remarks*) ‖ *v* see **découdre**

décou·vert [dekuvɛr] **-verte** [vɛrt] *adj* uncovered, open, exposed ‖ *m* deficit; overdraft ‖ *f* uncovering; discovery

décou·vreur [dekuvrœr] **-vreuse** [vrøz] *mf* discoverer

découvrir [dekuvrir] §65 *tr* to discover; discern (*in the distance*); pick out (*with a searchlight*); uncover ‖ *intr* to become visible (*said of rocks at low tide*) ‖ *ref* to take off one's hat; lower one's guard; clear up (*said of the sky*); say what one is thinking; come to light, be revealed

décrasser [dekrase] *tr* to clean; polish up; get the dirt out of

décré·pit [dekrepi] **-pite** [pit] *adj* decrepit

décret [dekrɛ] *m* decree; order

décrier [dekrije] *tr* to decry, disparage, run down

décrire [dekrir] §25 *tr* to describe

décrochage [dekrɔʃaʒ] *m* (aer) stall

décrocher [dekrɔʃe] *tr* to unhook, take down; (coll) to wangle; **décrocher la timbale** (coll) to hit the jackpot ‖ *intr* to withdraw, retire; (telp) to pick up the receiver ‖ *ref* to come unhooked

décrochez-moi-ça [dekrɔʃemwasa] *m invar* (coll) secondhand clothing store; (coll) hand-me-down

décroît [dekrwa] *m* last quarter (*of moon*)

décroître [dekrwatr] §17 (*pp* **décru;** *pres ind* **décrois,** etc.; *pret* **décrus,** etc.) *intr* to decrease; shorten (*said of days*); to fall (*said of river*)

décrotter [dekrɔte] *tr* to remove mud from; (coll) teach how to behave

décrotteur [dekrɔtœr] *m* shoeshine boy

décrottoir [dekrɔtwar] *m* doormat; scraper (*for shoes*)

décrue [dekry] *f* fall, drop, subsiding

décrypter [dekripte] *tr* to decipher

déculottage [dekylɔtaʒ] *m* undressing

déculotter [dekylɔte] *tr* to take the pants off of ‖ *ref* to take off one's pants

décuple [dekypl] *adj & m* tenfold

décupler [dekyple] *tr & intr* to increase tenfold

dédaigner [dedɛɲe] §97 *tr* to disdain; reject (*e.g., an offer*); **dédaigner de** + *inf* not to condescend to + *inf*

dédai·gneux [dedɛɲø] **-gneuse** [ɲøz] *adj* disdainful

dédain [dedɛ̃] *m* disdain

dédale [dedal] *s* maze, labyrinth

dedans [dədɑ̃] *m* inside; **en dedans** inside ‖ *adv* inside, within; **mettre dedans** (coll) to take in, to fool

dédicace [dedikas] *f* dedication

dédicacer [dedikase] §51 *tr* to dedicate, autograph

dédicatoire [dedikatwar] *adj* dedicatory

dédier [dedje] *tr* to dedicate; offer (*e.g., a collection to a museum*)

dédire [dedir] §40 *tr*—**dédire qn** to disavow s.o.'s words or actions ‖ *ref* to make a retraction, back down; **se dédire de** to go back on, fail to keep

dédit [dedi] *m* penalty (*for breaking a contract*); breach of contract

dédommagement [dedɔmaʒmɑ̃] *m* compensation, damages, indemnity

dédommager [dedɔmaʒe] §38 *tr* to compensate for a loss, indemnify

dédouaner [dedwane] *tr* to clear through customs; rehabilitate (*a politician, statesman, etc.*)

dédoublement [dedubləmɑ̃] *m* splitting; subdivision; unfolding

dédoubler [deduble] *tr* to divide or split in two; remove the lining from; unfold; put on another section of (*a train*)

déduction [dedyksjɔ̃] *f* deduction; **déduction pour remplacement** deduction allowance (*on taxes*)

déduire [dedɥir] §19 *tr* to deduce; infer; (com) to deduct

déesse [deɛs] *f* goddess

défaillance [defajɑ̃s] *f* failure, failing; faint; lapse (*of memory*); nonappearance (*of witness*); **défaillance cardiaque** heart failure; **sans défaillance** unflinching

défail·lant [defajɑ̃] **-lante** [jɑ̃t] *adj* failing, faltering

défaillir [defajir] §69 *intr* to fail; falter, weaken, flag; faint

défaire [defɛr] §29 *tr* to undo; untie, unwrap, unpack; rearrange; let down (*one's hair*); rid; defeat, rout; wear (*s.o.*) down, tire (*s.o.*) out ‖ *ref* to come undone; **se défaire de** to get rid of

dé·fait [defɛ] **-faite** [fɛt] *adj* undone, untied; loose; disheveled; drawn (*countenance*) ‖ *f* defeat; disposal, turnover; (fig) loophole

défaitisme [defɛtism] *m* defeatism

défaitiste [defɛtist] *mf* defeatist

défalcation [defalkasjɔ̃] *f* deduction

défalquer [defalke] *tr* to deduct

défaufiler [defofile] *tr* to untack

défausser [defose] *tr* to straighten ‖ *ref*—**se défausser (de)** to discard

défaut [defo] *m* defect, fault; lack (*of knowledge, memory, etc.*); flaw; chink (*in armor*); **à défaut de** in default of, lacking; **faire défaut à** to abandon, fail (*e.g., one's* *friends*); (law) to default; **mettre en défaut** to foil

défaveur [defavær] *f* disfavor

défavorable [defavɔrabl] *adj* unfavorable

défavoriser [defavɔrize] *tr* to handicap, put at a disadvantage

défécation [defekasjɔ̃] *f* defecation

défec•tif [defɛktif] **-tive** [tiv] *adj* (gram) defective

défection [defɛksjɔ̃] *f* defection; **faire défection** to defect

défec•tueux [defɛktɥø] **-tueuse** [tɥøz] *adj* defective, faulty

défectuosité [defɛktɥozite] *f* imperfection

défen•deur [defɑ̃dœr] **-deresse** [drɛs] *mf* defendant

défendre [defɑ̃dr] §97, §98 *tr* to defend; protect (*e.g., against the cold*); **à son corps défendant** in self-defense; against one's will; **défendre q.ch. à qn** to forbid s.o. s.th. ‖ *intr*—**défendre à qn de** + *inf* to forbid s.o. to + *inf* ‖ *ref* to defend oneself; (coll) to hold one's own; **se défendre de** to deny (*e.g., having said s.th.*); refrain from, to keep from

défen•du -due [defɑ̃dy] *adj* forbidden

défense [defɑ̃s] *f* defense; tusk; defense lawyer; **défense passive** civil defense (*against air raids*); (public signs): **défense d'afficher** post no bills; **défense de dépasser** no passing; **défense de déposer des ordures** no dumping, no littering; **défense de doubler** no passing; **défense de faire des ordures** commit no nuisance; **défense de fumer** no smoking; **défense d'entrer** private, keep out, no admittance, no entry

défenseur [defɑ̃sœr] *m* defender; lawyer for the defense; stand-by

défen•sif [defɑ̃sif] **-sive** [siv] *adj & f* defensive

déféquer [defeke] *intr* to defecate

déférence [deferɑ̃s] *f* deference

défé•rent [deferɑ̃] **-rente** [rɑ̃t] *adj* deferential

déférer [defere] §10 *tr* to confer, award; refer (*a case to a court*); **déférer en justice** to haul into court ‖ *intr* to comply; **déférer à** to defer to, comply with

déferler [defɛrle] *tr* to unfurl; set (*the sails of a ship*) ‖ *intr* to spread out (*said of a crowd*); break (*said of waves*)

défeuiller [defœje] *tr* to defoliate ‖ *ref* to lose its leaves

défi [defi] *m* challenge, dare; **défi à l'autorité** defiance of authority; **porter un défi à** to defy; **relever un défi** to take a dare

défiance [defjɑ̃s] *f* distrust

défi•ant [defjɑ̃] **-fiante** [fjɑ̃t] *adj* distrustful

déficeler [defisle] §34 *tr* to untie

déficience [defisjɑ̃s] *f* deficiency

défi•cient [defisjɑ̃] **-ciente** [sjɑ̃t] *adj* deficient

déficit [defisit] *m* deficit

déficitaire [defisitɛr] *adj* deficit; meager (*crop*); lean (*year*)

défier [defje] §97, §99 *tr* to challenge; defy (*death, time, etc.*); **défier qn de** to dare s.o. to ‖ *ref*—**se défier de** to mistrust

défiger [defiʒe] §38 *tr* to liquefy

défiguration [defigyrasjɔ̃] *f* disfigurement; defacement

défigurer [defigyre] *tr* to disfigure; deface; distort

défilé [defile] *m* defile (*in mountains*); parade, procession, line of march; **défilé de modes** fashion parade

défilement [defilmɑ̃] *m* (mil) defilade, cover

défiler [defile] *tr* to unstring; (mil) to put under cover ‖ *intr* to march by, parade, defile ‖ *ref* to come unstrung; take cover; (coll) to goldbrick

défi•ni -nie [defini] *adj* definite; defined

définir [definir] *tr* to define ‖ *ref* to be defined

définissable [definisabl] *adj* definable

défini•tif [definitif] **-tive** [tiv] *adj* definitive; standard (*edition*); **en définitive** in short, all things considered

définition [definisjɔ̃] *f* definition; **définition de fonction** job description

définitivement [definitivmɑ̃] *adv* definitively, for good, permanently

déflation [deflasjɔ̃] *f* deflation (*of currency*); sudden drop (*in wind*)

déflecteur [deflɛktœr] *m* vent window (*of an automobile*)

défleurir [deflœrir] *tr* to deflower, strip of flowers ‖ *intr & ref* to lose its flowers

déflexion [deflɛksjɔ̃] *f* deflection

défloraison [deflɔrɛzɔ̃] *f* dropping of petals

déflorer [deflɔre] *tr* to deflower

défon•cé -cée [defɔ̃se] *adj* battered, smashed, crumpled; bumpy

défoncer [defɔ̃se] §51 *tr* to batter in; stave in (*a cask*); remove the seat of (*a chair*); break up (*ground; a road*) ‖ *ref* to be broken up (*said of road*)

déformation [defɔrmasjɔ̃] *f* deformation, distortion; **déformation dans l'espace-temps** time warp; **déformation professionelle** professional idiosyncracy, vocational bias

défor•mé -mée [defɔrme] *adj* out of shape; rough (*road*)

déformer [defɔrme] *tr* to deform, distort ‖ *ref* to become deformed

défoulement [defulmɑ̃] *m* (psychoanal) insight, recall; (coll) relief

défraî•chi -chie [defrɛʃi] *adj* dingy, faded

défraîchir [defrɛʃir] *tr* to make stale, fade

défrayer [defreje] §49 *tr* to defray the expenses of (*s.o.*); **défrayer la conversation** to be the subject of the conversation

défricher [defriʃe] *tr* to reclaim; clear up (*a puzzler*)

défricheur [defriʃœr] *m* pioneer, explorer

défriser [defrize] *tr & ref* to uncurl

défroncer [defrɔ̃se] §51 *tr* to remove the wrinkles from

défroque [defrɔk] *f* piece of discarded clothing

défroquer [defrɔke] *tr* to unfrock ‖ *ref* to give up the frock

dé•funt [defœ̃] **-funte** [fœ̃t] *adj* & *mf* deceased

déga•gé -gée [degaʒe] *adj* breezy, jaunty, nonchalant; free, detached

dégagement [degaʒmɑ̃] *m* disengagement; clearing, relieving of congestion; liberation (*e.g., of heat*); exit; retraction (*of promise*); redemption, taking out of hock

dégager [degaʒe] §38 *tr* to disengage; free, clear, release; draw, extract (*the moral or essential points*); give off, liberate; take back (*one's word*); redeem, take out of hock

dégaine [degɛn] *f* (coll) awkward bearing; ridiculous posture

dégainer [degɛne] *tr* to unsheathe ‖ *intr* to take up a sword

dégar•ni -nie [degarni] *adj* empty, depleted, stripped

dégarnir [degarnir] *tr* to clear (*a table*); withdraw soldiers from (*a sector*); prune ‖ *ref* to thin out

dégât [dega] *m* damage, havoc

dégauchir [degoʃir] *tr* to smooth out the rough edges of (*stone, wood; an inexperienced person*)

dégel [deʒɛl] *m* thaw

dégeler [deʒle] §2 *tr* to thaw, defrost; loosen up, relax ‖ *intr* to thaw out; **il dégèle** it is thawing

dégéné•ré -rée [deʒenere] *adj* & *mf* degenerate

dégénérer [deʒenere] §10 *intr* to degenerate

dégénérescence [deʒeneresɑ̃s] *f* degeneration

dégingan•dé -dée [deʒɛ̃gɑ̃de] *adj* gangling, ungainly

dégivrage [deʒivraʒ] *m* defrosting

dégivrer [deʒivre] *tr* to defrost, deice

dégivreur [deʒivrœr] *m* defroster, deicer

déglacer [deglase] §51 *tr* to deice; remove the glaze from (*paper*)

dégommer [degɔme] *tr* to ungum; (coll) to fire (*s.o.*)

dégon•flé -flée [degɔ̃fle] *adj* flat (*tire*)

dégonflement [degɔ̃fləmɑ̃] *m* deflation

dégonfler [degɔ̃fle] *tr* to deflate ‖ *ref* to go flat; go down, subside (*said of swelling*); (slang) to lose one's nerve

dégorger [degɔrʒe] §38 *tr* to disgorge; unstop, open (*a pipe*); scour (*e.g., wool*) ‖ *intr* to discharge, overflow

dégour•di -die [degurdi] *adj* limbered up, lively, sharp, adroit ‖ *mf* smart aleck

dégourdir [degurdir] *tr* to remove stiffness or numbness from (*e.g., legs*); stretch (*one's limbs*); take the chill off; teach (*s.o.*); polish (*s.o.*) ‖ *ref* to limber up

dégoût [degu] *m* distaste, dislike

dégoû•tant [degutɑ̃] **-tante** [tɑ̃t] *adj* disgusting, distasteful

dégoû•té -tée [degute] §93 *adj* fastidious, hard to please ‖ *mf* finicky person

dégoûter [degute] §97, §99 to disgust; **dégoûter**

qn de to make s.o. dislike ‖ *ref* to become fed up

dégoutter [degute] *intr* to drip, trickle

dégradation [degradasjɔ̃] *f* degradation; defacement; shading off, graduation; worsening (*of a situation*); (mil) demotion; **dégradation civique** loss of civil rights

dégrader [degrade] *tr* to degrade, bring down; deface; shade off, graduate; (mil) to demote, break ‖ *ref* to debase oneself; become dilapidated

dégrafer [degrafe] *tr* to unhook, unclasp

dégraissage [degrɛsaʒ] *m* dry cleaning

dégraisser [degrɛse] *tr* to remove grease from; dry-clean

dégrais•seur [degrɛsœr] **-seuse** [søz] *mf* dry cleaner, cleaner and dyer

degré [dəgre] *m* degree; step (*of stairs*); **monter d'un degré** to take a step up (*on the ladder of success*)

dégrèvement [degrɛvmɑ̃] *m* tax relief

dégringolade [degrɛ̃gɔlad] *f* (coll) tumble; (coll) comedown, collapse, downfall

dégringoler [degrɛ̃gɔle] *tr* to bring down (*a government*) ‖ *intr* (coll) to tumble, tumble down

dégriser [degrize] *tr* & *ref* to sober up

dégrossir [degrosir] *tr* to rough-hew; make the preliminary sketches of; refine, polish (*a hick*)

déguenil•lé -lée [degənije] *adj* ragged, in tatters ‖ *mf* ragamuffin

déguerpir [degɛrpir] *intr* (coll) to clear out, beat it; **fair déguerpir** to evict

déguisement [degizmɑ̃] *m* disguise

déguiser [degize] *tr* to disguise

dégusta•teur [degystatœr] **-trice** [tris] *mf* wine-taster

dégustation [degystasjɔ̃] *f* tasting, art of tasting; consumption (*of beverages*)

déguster [degyste] *tr* to taste discriminatingly; sip, drink; consume

déhancher [deɑ̃ʃe] *tr* to dislocate the hip of ‖ *intr* to swing one's hips

déharnacher [dearnaʃe] *tr* to unsaddle, unharness ‖ *ref* (coll) to throw off one's heavy clothing

dehors [dəɔr] *m* outside; **dehors** *mpl* outward appearance; **du dehors** from without, foreign, external; **en dehors** outside; **en dehors de** outside of; beyond ‖ *adv* outside, out; out-of-doors

déification [deifikɑsjɔ̃] *f* deification

déifier [deifje] *tr* to deify

déiste [deist] *dj* & *mf* deist

déité [deite] *f* deity

déjà [deʒa] *adv* already; yet; before

déjanter [deʒɑ̃te] *tr* to take (*a tire*) off the rim ‖ *ref* to come off

déjection [deʒɛksjɔ̃] *f* excretion; volcanic debris

déjeter [deʒte] §34 *tr* & *ref* to warp, spring

déjeuner [deʒœne] *m* lunch; breakfast; breakfast set; **déjeuner d'affaires, déjeuner de travail** business lunch; **déjeuner d'affaires** (*ren-*

contre stratégique avec des personnes haut placées) power lunch; **petit déjeuner** breakfast ‖ *intr* to have lunch; have breakfast

déjouer [deʒwe] *tr* to foil, thwart

déjucher [deʒyʃe] *tr* to unroost ‖ *intr* to come off the roost (*said of fowl*)

déjuger [deʒyʒe] §38 *ref* to change one's mind

delà [dəla] *adv*—**au delà de** beyond; **par delà** beyond

délabrement [delabrəmɑ̃] *m* decay, dilapidation; impairment (*of health*)

délabrer [delabre] *tr* to ruin, wreck ‖ *ref* to become dilapidated

délacer [delase] §51 *tr* to unlace

délai [delɛ] *m* term, duration, period (*of time*); postponement, extension; time limit; **à bref délai** at short notice; **dans le plus bref délai** in the shortest possible time; **dans un délai de** within; **dans un délai record** in record time; **dernier délai** deadline; **sans délai** without delay

délais·sé -sée [delɛse] *adj* forsaken, forlorn, neglected

délaissement [delɛsmɑ̃] *m* abandonment

délaisser [delɛse] *tr* to abandon, desert; relinquish (*a right*)

délassement [delasmɑ̃] *m* relaxation

délasser [delase] *tr* to rest, refresh, relax ‖ *ref* to rest up

déla·teur -trice [delatœr] [tris] *mf* informer

délation [delasjɔ̃] *f* paid informing

déla·vé -vée [delave] *adj* washed-out, weak

délayer [delɛje] §49 *tr* to add water to, dilute; **délayer un discours** to stretch out a speech

deleatur [deleatyr] *m* dele

délébile [delebil] *adj* erasable

délectable [delɛktabl] *adj* delectable

délectation [delɛktasjɔ̃] *f* pleasure

délecter [delɛkte] *ref*—**se délecter à** to find pleasure in

délégation [delegasjɔ̃] *f* delegation

délé·gué -guée [delege] *adj* delegated ‖ *mf* delegate, spokesman

déléguer [delege] §10 *tr* to delegate

délester [delɛste] *tr* to unballast; unburden, relieve

délétère [deletɛr] *adj* deleterious

délibération [deliberasjɔ̃] *f* deliberation

délibé·ré -rée [delibere] *adj* deliberate, firm, decided

délibérer [delibere] §10, §97 *tr* & *intr* to deliberate

déli·cat [delika] **-cate** [kat] *adj* delicate; fine, sensitive (*ear, mind, taste*); touchy; tactful; scrupulous, honest

délicatesse [delikatɛs] *f* delicacy; refinement, fineness; fastidiousness; fragility, weakness

délice [delis] *m* great pleasure ‖ **délices** *f pl* delights, pleasures

déli·cieux [delisjø] **-cieuse** [sjøz] *adj* delicious, delightful, charming

dé·lié -liée [delje] *adj* slender (*figure*); nimble

(*mind*); fine (*handwriting*); glib (*tongue*) ‖ *m* upstroke, thin stroke

délier [delje] *tr* to untie, loosen, release ‖ *ref* to come loose

délinéament [delineamɑ̃] *m* delineation

délinéer [delinee] *tr* to delineate

délinquance [delɛ̃kɑ̃s] *f* delinquency; **délinquance juvénile** juvenile delinquency

délin·quant [delɛ̃kɑ̃] **-quante** [kɑ̃t] *adj* & *mf* delinquent; **délinquant primaire** first offender

déli·rant [delirɑ̃] **-rante** [rɑ̃t] *adj* delirious, raving

délire [delir] *m* delirium; **en délire** delirious, in a frenzy

délirer [delire] *intr* to be delirious, rave

délit [deli] *m* offense, wrong, crime; **en flagrant délit** in the act

délivrance [delivrɑ̃s] *f* deliverance; delivery; rescue

délivre [delivr] *m* afterbirth, placenta

délivrer [delivre] *tr* to deliver; rescue

déloger [deloʒe] §38 *tr* to dislodge; (coll) to oust, evict ‖ *intr* to move out (*of a house*)

déloyal déloyale [delwajal] *adj* (*pl* **déloyaux** [delwajo]) disloyal; unfair, dishonest

déloyauté [delwajote] *f* disloyalty; disloyal act; dishonesty

delta [dɛlta] *m* delta

deltaplane [dɛltaplan] *m* hang glider

déluge [delyʒ] *m* deluge, flood

délu·ré -rée [delyre] *adj* smart, clever; smart-alecky, forward

délurer [delyre] *tr* & *ref* to wise up

délustrer [delystre] *tr* to take the gloss off of

démagnétiser [demaɲetize] *tr* to demagnetize

démagogie [demagoʒi] *f* demagogy

démagogique [demagoʒik] *adj* demagogic

démagogue [demagog] *adj* demagogic ‖ *mf* demagogue

démaigrir [demɛgrir] *tr* to thin down

démailler [demaje] *tr* to unshackle (*a chain*); unravel (*e.g., a knitted sweater*); make a run in (*a stocking*) ‖ *ref* to run (*said of stocking*)

démailloter [demajote] *tr* to take the diaper off of

demain [dəmɛ̃] *adv* & *m* tomorrow; **à demain** until tomorrow; so long; **de demain en huit** a week from tomorrow; **de demain en quinze** two weeks from tomorrow; **demain matin** tomorrow morning

démancher [demɑ̃ʃe] *tr* to remove the handle of; (coll) to dislocate

demande [dəmɑ̃d] *f* request; application (*for a position*); inquiry; demand (*by buyers for goods*)

demander [dəmɑ̃de] §96, §97, §98 *tr* to ask (*a favor; one's way*); ask for (*a package; a porter*); require, need (*attention*); **demander q.ch. à qn** to ask s.o. for s.th. ‖ *intr*—**demander à** or **de** + *inf;* to ask permission to + *inf;* to insist upon + *ger;* **demander après** to ask about, ask for (*s.o.*); **demander à qn**

de + *inf* to ask s.o. to + *inf*; **je ne demande pas mieux** I wish I could ‖ *ref* to be needed; wonder

deman·deur [dəmãdœr] **-deuse** [døz] *mf* asker; buyer ‖ **-deur** [dœr] **-deresse** [drɛs] *mf* plaintiff

démangeaison [demãʒezɔ̃] *f* itch

démanger [demãʒe] **§38** *tr* & *intr* to itch ‖ *intr*—**démanger à** to itch, e.g., **l'épaule lui démange** his shoulder itches, **la langue lui démange** he is itching to speak

démanteler [demãtle] **§2** *tr* to dismantle (*a fort or town*); uncover (*a spy ring*)

démaquillage [demakijaʒ] *m* removal of paint or make-up

démaquillant [demakijã] *m* cleansing cream, make-up remover

démaquiller [demakije] *tr* & *ref* to take the paint or make-up off

démarcation [demarkɑsjɔ̃] *f* demarcation

démarchage [demarʃaʒ] *m* door-to-door selling, house-to-house selling

démarche [demarʃ] *f* gait, step, bearing; method; step, move, action

démarier [demarje] *tr* to thin out (*plants*)

démarque [demark] *f* (com) markdown

démarquer [demarke] *tr* to remove the identification marks from; plagiarize; mark down

démarrage [demaraʒ] *m* start; **démarrage au moyen de câbles** jump start

démarrer [demare] *tr* to unmoor; to start; (comp) to boot, to boot up; (fam) to kick off, begin ‖ *intr* to cast off (*said of ship*); start (*said of train or car*); kick off (*said of event or project*); spurt (*said of racing contestant; said of economy*); **démarrer au moyen de câbles** jump-start; **démarrer trop tôt** to jump the gun; **faire démarrer** to start (*a car*); **ne démarrez pas!** don't stir!

démarreur [demarœr] *m* starter (*of car*)

démasquer [demaske] *tr* & *ref* to unmask

démâter [demɑte] *tr* to dismast ‖ *intr* to lose her masts (*said of ship*)

démêlé [demɛle] *m* quarrel, dispute; **avoir des démêlés avec** to be at odds with, run afoul of

démêler [demɛle] *tr* to disentangle, unravel; bring to light, uncover (*a plot*); make out, discern

démembrement [demãbrəmã] *m* dismemberment

déménagement [demenaʒmã] *m* moving

déménager [demenaʒe] **§38** *tr* to move (*household effects*) to another residence; move the furniture from (*a house*) ‖ *intr* to move, change one's residence; (coll) to become childish; **tu déménages!** (coll) you're out of your mind!

déménageur [demenaʒœr] *m* mover

démence [demãs] *f* madness, insanity; **en démence** demented

démener [demne] **§2** *ref* to struggle, be agitated; take great pains

dé·ment [demã] **-mente** [mãt] *adj* & *mf* lunatic

démenti [demãti] *m* contradiction, denial; proof to the contrary; (coll) shame (*on account of a failure*)

démentir [demãtir] **§41** *tr* to contradict, deny; give the lie to, belie ‖ *intr* to go back on one's word; be inconsistent

démerdard [demɛrdar] *m* (slang) shark, sharp customer; **petit démerdard** streetwise kid

démériter [demerite] *intr* to lose esteem, become unworthy

démesure [deməzyr] *f* lack of moderation, excess

démesu·ré -rée [deməzyre] *adj* measureless, immense; immoderate, excessive

démettre [demɛtr] **§42** *tr* to dismiss (*from a job or position*); dislocate (*an arm*) ‖ *ref* to resign, retire

démeubler [demœble] *tr* to remove the furniture from

demeurant [dəmœrã]—**au demeurant** all things considered, after all

demeure [dəmœr] *f* home, abode, dwelling; **à demeure** permanently; **dernière demeure** final resting place; **en demeure** in arrears; **mettre qn en demeure de** to oblige s.o. to; **sans plus longue demeure** without further delay

demeurer [dəmœre] **§96** *intr* to live, dwell ‖ *intr* (*aux:* ETRE) to stay, remain; **en demeurer to** leave off; **en demeurer là** to stop, rest there; leave it at that

demi [dəmi] *m* half; (sports) center; (sports) half-back; **à demi** half; **et demi** and a half, e.g., **un centimètre et demi** a centimeter and a half; (after **midi** or **minuit**) half past, e.g., **midi et demi** half past twelve

demi-bas [dəmibɑ] *m* half hose

demi-botte [dəmibɔt] *f* (*pl* **-bottes**) half boot

demi-cercle [dəmisɛrkl] *m* (*pl* **-cercles**) semicircle

demi-clef [dəmikle] *f* (*pl* **-clefs**) half hitch; **demi-clef à capeler** clove hitch; **deux demi-clefs** two half hitches

demi-congé [dəmikɔ̃ʒe] *m* (*pl* **-congés**) half-holiday

demi-deuil [dəmidœj] *m* (*pl* **-deuils**) half mourning

demi-dieu [dəmidjø] *m* (*pl* **-dieux**) demigod

demi-douzaine [dəmiduzɛn] *f* (*pl* **-douzaines**) half-dozen

demie [dəmi] *f* half hour; **et demie** half past, e.g., **deux heures et demie** half past two

demi-finale [dəmifinal] *f* (*pl* **-finales**) semifinal

demi-frère [dəmifrɛr] *m* (*pl* **-frères**) half brother; stepbrother

demi-heure [dəmiœr] *f* (*pl* **-heures**) half-hour; **toutes les demi-heures à la demi-heure juste** every half-hour on the half-hour

demi-interligne [dəmiɛ̃tɛrliɲ] *m*—**demi-interligne de base** half-line space (*on typewriter*)

demi-jour [dəmiʒur] *m invar* twilight, halflight

demi-journée [dəmiʒurne] *f* (*pl* **-journées**) half-day; **à demi-journée** half-time

démilitariser [demilitarize] *tr* to demilitarize

demi-longueur [dəmilɔ̃gœr] *f* half-length

demi-lune [dəmilyn] *f* (*pl* **-lunes**) half-moon

demi-mondaine [dəmimɔ̃dɛn] *f* (*pl* **-mondaines**) demimondaine

demi-monde [dəmimɔ̃d] *m* demimonde

demi-mot [dəmimo] *m* (*pl* **-mots**) understatement, euphemism; **comprendre à demi-mot** to get the drift of; to take the hint

déminer [demine] *tr* to clear of mines

demi-pause [dəmipoz] *f* (*pl* **-pauses**) (mus) half rest

demi-pension [dəmipɑ̃sjɔ̃] *f* (*pl* **-pensions**) breakfast and one meal

demi-place [dəmiplas] *f* (*pl* **-places**) half fare; half-price seat

demi-reliure [dəmirəljyr] *f* (*pl* **-reliures**) quarter binding; **demi-reliure à petits coins** half binding

demi-saison [dəmisɛzɔ̃] *f* in-between season; **de demi-saison** spring-and-fall (*coat*)

demi-sang [dəmisɑ̃] *m invar* half-bred horse

demi-sœur [dəmisœr] *f* (*pl* **-sœurs**) half sister; stepsister

demi-solde [dəmisɔld] *m invar* pensioned officer || *f* (*pl* **-soldes**) army pension, half pay

demi-soupir [dəmisupir] *m* (*pl* **-soupirs**) (mus) eighth rest

démission [demisjɔ̃] *f* resignation

démissionnaire [demisjɔnɛr] *adj* outgoing || *mf* former incumbent

démissionner [demisjɔne] *tr* (coll) to fire || *intr* to resign

demi-tasse [dəmitɑs] *f* (*pl* **-tasses**) half-cup; small cup, demitasse

demi-teinte [dəmitɛ̃t] *f* (*pl* **-teintes**) halftone

demi-ton [dəmitɔ̃] *m* (*pl* **-tons**) (mus) half tone

demi-tour [dəmitur] *m* (*pl* **-tours**) about-face; half turn; **demi-tour, (à) droite!** about face!, to the rear!; **donner un demi-tour** to make a half turn; **faire demi-tour** to do an about-face; to turn back

demi-volte [dəmivɔlt] *f* U-turn

démobiliser [demɔbilize] *tr* to demobilize

démocrate [demɔcrat] *mf* democrat

démocratie [demɔkrasi] *f* democracy

démocratique [demɔkratik] *adj* democratic

démo·dé -dée [demɔde] *adj* old-fashioned, out-of-date, outmoded

démoder [demɔde] *ref* to be outmoded

demoiselle [dəmwazɛl] *f* single woman, young woman, young lady, miss; dragonfly; (slang) girl; **demoiselle de magasin** saleswoman, female salesperson; **demoiselle d'honneur** maid of honor, bridesmaid; lady-in-waiting

démolir [demɔlir] *tr* to demolish; overturn (*a cabinet or government*)

démolition [demɔlisjɔ̃] *f* demolition; **démolitions** scrap, rubble

démon [demɔ̃] *m* demon

démoniaque [demɔnjak] *adj* demonic, demoniac(al) || *mf* demoniac

démonstra·teur [demɔ̃stratœr] **-trice** [tris] *mf* demonstrator

démonstra·tif [demɔ̃stratif] **-tive** [tiv] *adj & m* demonstrative

démontable [demɔ̃tabl] *adj* collapsible, detachable; knockdown

démonte-pneu [demɔ̃tpnø] *m* (*pl* **-pneus**) tire iron

démonter [demɔ̃te] *tr* to dismount; dismantle || *ref* to come apart; go to pieces (*while taking an exam*)

démontrable [demɔ̃trabl] *adj* demonstrable

démontrer [demɔ̃tre] *tr* to demonstrate

démoraliser [demɔralize] *tr* to demoralize

démouler [demule] *tr* to remove from a mold

démoustication [demustikasjɔ̃] *f* mosquito control

dému·ni -nie [demyni] *adj* out of money; **démuni de** out of; devoid of

démunir [demynir] *tr* to strip, deprive; deplete (*a garrison*) || *ref* to deprive oneself

démystifier [demistifje] *tr* to debunk

dénationaliser [denasjɔnalize] *tr* to denationalize

dénaturaliser [denatyralize] *tr* to denaturalize

dénatu·ré -rée [denatyre] *adj* denatured; unnatural, perverse

dénaturer [denatyre] *tr* to denature; pervert; distort

dénébulation [denebylasjɔ̃] *f* defogging

dénégation [denegasjɔ̃] *f* denial

déneigement [denɛʒmɑ̃] *m* snow removal

déni [deni] *m* refusal; (law) denial

dénicher [deniʃe] *tr* to dislodge; take out of the nest; make (*s.o.*) move; search out || *intr* to leave the nest

déni·cheur [deniʃœr] **-cheuse** [ʃøz] *mf* hunter (*of rare books, antiques, etc.*); **dénicheur de vedettes** talent scout

denier [dənje] *m* (fig) penny, farthing; **denier à Dieu** gratuity; **deniers** money, funds; **de ses deniers** with his own money

dénier [denje] *tr* to deny, refuse

dénigrer [denigre] *tr* to disparage

déniveler [denivle] §34 *tr* to make uneven, change the level of

dénivellation [denivɛllasjɔ̃] *f* or **dénivellement** [denivɛlmɑ̃] *m* unevenness; depression, settling

dénombrement [denɔ̃brəmɑ̃] *m* census, enumeration

dénombrer [denɔ̃bre] *tr* to take a census of, enumerate

dénomination [denɔminasjɔ̃] *f* denomination, appellation, designation

dénommer [denɔme] *tr* to denominate, name

dénoncer [denɔ̃se] §51 *tr* to renounce; indicate, reveal || *ref* to give oneself up

dénonciation [denɔ̃sjasjɔ̃] *f* denunciation; declaration

dénoter [denɔte] *tr* to denote

dénouement [denumɑ̃] *m* outcome, denouement; untying

dénouer [denwe] *tr* to untie; unravel

dénoyer [denwaje] **§47** *tr* to pump out

denrée [dɑ̄re] *f* commodity; **denrées** provisions, products

dense [dɑ̄s] *adj* dense

densité [dɑ̄site] *f* density

dent [dɑ̄] *f* tooth; cog; scallop (*of an edge*); **dent d'éléphant** tusk; **dents de lait** baby teeth; **dents de sagesse** wisdom teeth; **sur les dents** on one's toes

dentaire [dɑ̄tɛr] *adj* dental

den·tal -tale [dɑ̄tal] *adj & f* (*pl* **-taux** [to] **-tales**) dental

dent-de-chien [dɑ̄dəʃjɛ̃] *f* (*pl* **dents-de-chien**) dogtooth violet

dent-de-lion [dɑ̄dəljɔ̃] *f* (*pl* **dents-de-lion**) dandelion

denteler [dɑ̄tle] **§34** *tr* to notch, indent; perforate (*stamps*)

dentelle [dɑ̄tɛl] *f* lace; lacework

dentelure [dɑ̄tlyr] *f* notching; serration; scalloping; (phila) perforation

denter [dɑ̄te] *tr* to furnish with cogs or teeth

dentier [dɑ̄tje] *m* false teeth, denture

dentifrice [dɑ̄tifris] *m* dentifrice

dentiste [dɑ̄tist] *mf* dentist

denture [dɑ̄tyr] *f* denture; **denture artificielle** false teeth

dénuder [denyde] *tr* to strip, denude

dé·nué -nuée [denɥe] **§93** *adj* stripped; **denué de** devoid of, lacking in; **dénue de tout fondement** completely unfounded

dénuement [denymɑ̄] *m* destitution

dénuer [denɥe] *tr* to deprive, strip

déodorant [deɔdɔrɑ̄] *m* deodorant

déodoriser [deɔdɔrize] *tr* to deodorize

déontologie [deɔ̃tɔlɔʒi] *f* study of ethics; **déontologie médicale** (med) code of medical ethics

dépannage [depanaʒ] *m* emergency service, repairs

dépanner [depane] *tr* to give emergency service to; (coll) to get (*s.o.*) out of a scrape

dépan·neur [depanœr] **-neuse** [nøz] *adj* repairing ‖ *m* serviceman, repairman ‖ *f* tow truck, wrecker

dépaqueter [depakte] **§34** *tr* to unpack, unwrap

dépareil·lé -lée [deparɛje] *adj* incomplete, broken (*set*); odd (*sock*)

dépareiller [deparɛje] *tr* to break (*a set*)

déparer [depare] *tr* to mar, spoil the beauty of; strip of ornaments

déparier [deparje] *tr* to break, split up the pair of

départ [depar] *m* departure; beginning; division; sorting out; **départ usine** F.O.B.; **faux départ** false start

département [departəmɑ̄] *m* department, section; (govt) department

départir [departir] **§64** (or sometimes like **finir**) *tr* to divide up, distribute ‖ *ref*—**se départir de** to give up; depart from

dépassement [depasmɑ̄] *m* passing

dépasser [depase] *tr* to pass, overtake; go beyond; overshoot (*the mark*); exceed; extend beyond; be longer than; (coll) to surprise ‖ *intr* to pass; stick out, overlap, show

dépayser [depɛize] *tr* to take out of one's familiar surroundings; bewilder ‖ *ref* to leave one's country

dépecer [depəse] **§20** *tr* to carve, cut up

dépêche [depɛʃ] *f* dispatch; telegram

dépêcher [depɛʃe] *tr* to dispatch ‖ **§97** *ref* to hurry

dépeigner [depɛɲe] *tr* to tousle, muss up (*the hair*)

dépeindre [depɛ̃dr] **§50** *tr* to depict

dépendance [depɑ̄dɑ̄s] *f* dependence; **dépendances** outbuildings, annex; dependencies, possessions

dépen·dant [depɑ̄dɑ̄] **-dante** [dɑ̄t] *adj* dependent

dépendre [depɑ̄dr] *tr* to take down ‖ *intr* to depend; **dépendre de** to depend on; belong to; **il dépend de vous ce** it is for you to

dépens [depɑ̄] *mpl* expenses, costs; **aux dépens de** at the expense of

dépense [depɑ̄s] *f* expense; pantry; dispensary (*of hospital*); flow (*of water*); consumption (*of fuel*)

dépenser [depɑ̄se] **§96** *tr* to spend, expend ‖ *ref* to exert oneself, spend one's energy

dépen·sier [depɑ̄sje] **-sière** [sjɛr] *adj & mf* spendthrift

déperdition [depɛrdisjɔ̃] *f* loss; **déperdition de chaleur due au vent** wind-chill factor

dépérir [deperir] *intr* to waste away, decline

dépêtrer [depɛtre] *tr* to get (*s.o.*) out of a jam

dépeupler [depœple] *tr* to depopulate; unstock (*a pond*)

dépha·sé -sée [defaze] *adj* out of phase; out of step, out of touch

dépiauter [depjote] *tr* to skin

dépiécer [depjese] **§58** *tr* to dismember

dépiler [depile] *tr* to remove the hair from

dépistage [depistaʒ] *m* tracking down; (med) screening

dépister [depiste] *tr* to track down

dépit [depi] *m* spite, resentment; **en dépit de** in spite of

dépiter [depite] *tr* to spite, vex ‖ *ref* to take offense

dépla·cé -cée [deplase] *adj* displaced (*person*); misplaced, out of place

déplacement [deplasmɑ̄] *m* displacement; movement; travel; transfer (*of an official*); shift (*in votes*); change (*in schedule*); (naut) displacement

déplacer [deplase] **§51** *tr* to displace; move; **déplacer la question** to stray from the subject ‖ *ref* to move

déplaire [deplɛr] **§52** *intr* to displease, e.g., **la réplique déplaît à la jeune fille** the reply displeases the young woman; to dislike, e.g., **le lait lui déplaît** he dislikes milk; **ne vous en déplaise** if you have no objection, by your leave || *ref* (*pp* **déplu** *invar*) to be displeased, e.g., **ils se sont déplu** they were displeased; **se déplaire à** not to like it in, e.g., **je me déplais à la campagne** I don't like it in the country

déplai•sant [deplɛzɑ̃] **-sante** [zɑ̃t] *adj* unpleasant, disagreeable

déplaisir [deplezir] *m* displeasure

déplanter [deplɑ̃te] *tr* to dig up for transplanting

déplantoir [deplɑ̃twar] *m* garden trowel

dépliant [deplijɑ̃] *m* folder, brochure

déplier [deplie] *tr & ref* to unfold

déplisser [deplise] *tr* to unpleat

déploiement [deplwamɑ̃] *m* unfolding, unfurling; display, array; (mil) deployment

déplorable [deplɔrabl] *adj* deplorable

déplorer [deplɔre] *tr* to deplore; grieve over

déployer [deplwaje] §47 *tr* to unfold, unfurl; display; (mil) to deploy || *ref* (mil) to deploy

dé•plu -plue [deply] *v* see **déplaire**

déplumer [deplyme] *tr* to pluck (*a chicken*) || *ref* (coll) to lose one's hair

dépoitrail•le -lée [depwatraje] *adj* with breast indecently exposed

dépolariser [depɔlarize] *tr* to depolarize

dépo•li -lie [depɔli] *adj* ground (*glass*)

dépolir [depɔlir] *tr* to remove the polish from; frost (*glass*)

déport [depɔr] *m* disqualifying of oneself; (com) commission; **sans déport** without delay

déportation [depɔrtasjɔ̃] *f* deportation; internment in a concentration camp

dépor•té -tée [depɔrte] *mf* deported criminal, convict; prisoner in a concentration camp

déportement [depɔrtəmɑ̃] *m* swerve; **déportements** misconduct, immoral conduct, bad habits

déporter [depɔrte] *tr* to deport; send to a concentration camp; make (*an automobile*) swerve; deflect (*an airplane*) from its course || *intr* to swerve

dépo•sant [depozɑ̃] **-sante** [zɑ̃t] *adj* testifying; depositing || *mf* deponent, witness, depositor

dépose [depoz] *f* removal

déposer [depoze] §95 *tr* to deposit; depose; drop, leave off; register (*a trademark*); lodge (*a complaint*); file (*a petition*) || *intr & ref* to depose; settle, form a deposit

dépositaire [depozitɛr] *mf* trustee, holder; dealer

déposséder [deposede] §10 *tr* to dispossess

dépôt [depo] *m* deposit; depository, depot; warehouse; delivery, handing in; **dépôt d'autobus** carbarn; **dépôt de locomotives** roundhouse; **dépôt de mendicité** poorhouse; **dépôt d'épargne** savings account; **dépôt des bagages** baggage room; **dépôt d'essence** filling station; **dépôt de vivres** commissary; **dépôt d'ordures** dump

dépotoir [depɔtwar] *m* landfill, dump; garbage can; storeroom

dépouille [depuj] *f* castoff skin; hide (*taken from*

animal); **dépouille mortelle** mortal remains; **dépouilles** spoils (*of war*)

dépouillement [depujmɑ̃] *m* gathering, selection, sifting; despoilment; counting (*of votes*); **dépouillement volontaire** relinquishing

dépouiller [depuje] *tr* to skin; strip, slough off; gather, select, sift; count (*votes*) || *ref* to shed one's skin (*said of insects and reptiles*); strip oneself, divest oneself, to slough

dépour•vu -vue [depurvy] *adj* destitute; **au dépourvu** unaware; **dépourvu de** devoid of, lacking in

dépoussiérer [depusjere] §10 *tr* to vacuum

dépravation [depravasjɔ̃] *f* depravity

dépraver [deprave] *tr* to deprave

déprécation [deprekasjɔ̃] *f* supplication

dépréciation [depresjasjɔ̃] *f* depreciation

déprécier [depresje] *tr & ref* to depreciate

déprédation [depredasjɔ̃] *f* depredation; embezzlement, misappropriation

déprendre [deprɑ̃dr] §56 *ref* to detach oneself; come loose; melt

dépres•sif [depresif] **-sive** [siv] *adj* depressive

dépression [depresjɔ̃] *f* depression

déprimer [deprime] *tr* to depress, lower || *ref* to be depressed

dépriser [deprize] *tr* to undervalue

déprogrammer [deprograme] *tr* to deprogram

depuis [dəpɥi] *adv* since; **depuis que** since || *prep* since, for, e.g., **je suis à Paris depuis trois jours** I have been in Paris for three days; **depuis ... jusqu'à** from ... to

dépurer [depyre] *tr* to purify

députation [depytasjɔ̃] *f* deputation

député [depyte] *m* deputy

députer [depyte] *tr* to deputize

der [dɛr] *f*—**la der des der** (*la dernière guerre des dernières guerres*) (coll) the war to end all wars

déraci•né -née [derasine] *adj* uprooted || *mf* uprooted person, wanderer

déraciner [derasine] *tr* to uproot, root out; eradicate

déraillement [derajmɑ̃] *m* derailment

dérailler [deraje] *intr* to jump the track; (coll) to get off the track

déraison [derezɔ̃] *f* unreasonableness, irrationality

déraisonnable [derezɔnabl] *adj* unreasonable

déraisonner [derezɔne] *intr* to talk nonsense

dérangement [derɑ̃ʒmɑ̃] *m* derangement; breakdown; disturbance, bother; **en dérangement** out of order

déranger [derɑ̃ʒe] §38 *tr* to derange, put out of order; disturb, trouble || *ref* to move, change jobs; become disordered, upset; **ne vous dérangez pas!** don't get up!; don't bother!

dérapage [derapaʒ] *m* skidding

déraper [derape] *intr* to skid, sideslip; weigh anchor

dératé [derate] *m*—**courir comme un dératé** to run like a jack rabbit

dératiser [deratize] *tr* to derat

derby [dɛrbi] *m* derby (*race*)

derechef [dərəʃɛf] *adv* (lit) once again

déré•glé -glée [deregle] *adj* out of order, irregular (*pulse*); disorderly, excessive

dérégler [deregle] §10 *tr* to put out of order, upset ‖ *ref* to get out of order; run wild

déridage [deridaʒ] *m* face-lift

dérider [deride] *tr* to smooth, unwrinkle; cheer up ‖ *ref* to cheer up

dérision [derizjɔ̃] *f* derision

dérisoire [derizwar] *adj* derisive

dériva•tif [derivatif] **-tive** [tiv] *adj* derivative ‖ *m* diversion, distraction

dérivation [derivɑsjɔ̃] *f* derivation; drift; bypass; diversion (*of river, stream, etc.*); **en dérivation** shunted (*circuit*)

dérive [deriv] *f* drift; (aer) fin; (naut) centerboard; **à la dérive** adrift

déri•vé -vée [derive] *adj* drifting; shunted (*current*) ‖ *m* derivative

dériver [derive] *tr* to derive; divert (*e.g., a river*); unrivet ‖ *intr* to derive; be derived; result; drift

dermatologie [dɛrmatɔlɔʒi] *f* dermatology

der•nier [dɛrnje] **-nière** [njɛr] §92 *adj* last; latest; latter; final; last (*just elapsed*), e.g., **la semaine dernière** last week ‖ (when standing before noun) *adj* last (*in a series*), e.g., **la dernière semaine de la guerre** the last week of the war

dernièrement [dɛrnjɛrmɑ̃] *adv* lately

dernier-né [dɛrnjene] **dernière-née** [dɛrnjɛrne] *mf* (*pl* **-nés -nées**) last-born child

dérobade [derɔbad] *f* side-stepping; cop-out; (equit) refusal

déro•bé -bée [derɔbe] *adj* secret; **à la dérobée** stealthily, on the sly

dérober [derɔbe] *tr* to steal; hide; **dérober à** to steal from; rescue from (*e.g., death*) ‖ *ref* to steal away, disappear; hide; shy away; balk; shirk; give way (*said of knees or one's footing*); **se dérober à** to slip away from, escape from

dérogation [derɔgɑsjɔ̃] *f*—**dérogation à** departure from (*custom*); waiving of (*principle*); deviation from (*instructions*); release, exemption from; **par dérogation à** notwithstanding

déroger [derɔʒe] §38 *intr*—**déroger à** to depart from (*custom*); waive (*a principle*); derogate from (*dignity; one's rank*)

dérouiller [deruje] *tr* to remove the rust from; polish (*s.o.*); (coll) to limber up; (coll) to brush up on ‖ *ref* to lose its rust; brush up; limber up

dérouler [derule] *tr & ref* to unroll, unfold

dérou•tant [derutɑ̃] **-tante** [tɑ̃t] *adj* baffling, misleading

déroute [derut] *f* rout, downfall

dérouter [derute] *tr* to steer off the course; reroute; disconcert, baffle ‖ *ref* to go astray; become confused

derrick [derik] *m* oil derrick, drilling rig

derrière [dɛrjɛr] *m* rear, backside ‖ *adv & prep* behind

derviche [dɛrviʃ] *m* dervish

des [de] §77

dès [dɛ] *prep* by (*a certain time*); from (*a certain place*); as early as, as far back as; from, beginning with; **dès lors** from that time, ever since; **dès lors que** since, inasmuch as; **dès que** as soon as

désabonner [dezabɔne] *tr* to cancel the subscription of ‖ *ref* to cancel one's subscription

désabu•sé -sée [dezabyze] *adj* disillusioned

désabuser [dezabyze] *tr* to disabuse, disillusion ‖ *ref* to have one's eyes opened

désaccord [dezakɔr] *m* disagreement, discord

désaccorder [dezakɔrde] *tr* to put (*an instrument*) out of tune ‖ *ref* to get out of tune

désaccoupler [dezakuple] *tr* to unpair; uncouple

désaccoutumer [dezakutyme] §97 *tr* to break (*s.o.*) of a habit ‖ *ref* to break oneself of a habit

désaffecter [dezafɛkte] *tr* to turn from its intended use

désagréable [dezagreabl] *adj* disagreeable; unpleasant

désagréger [dezagreʒe] §1 *tr* to break up, dissolve, disintegrate

désagrément [dezagremɑ̃] *m* unpleasantness, annoyance

désaimanter [dezɛmɑ̃te] *tr* to demagnetize

désalté•rant [dezalterɑ̃] **-rante** [rɑ̃t] *adj* thirst-quenching, refreshing

désaltérer [dezaltere] §10 *tr* to quench the thirst of; refresh with a drink ‖ *ref* to quench one's thirst

désamorcer [dezamɔrse] §51 *tr* to deactivate, disconnect the fuse of; unprime

désappointement [dezapwɛ̃tmɑ̃] *m* disappointment

désappointer [dezapwɛ̃te] *tr* to disappoint; break the point of, blunt

désapprendre [dezaprɑ̃dr] §56, §96, §97 *tr* to unlearn, forget

désapproba•teur [dezaprɔbatœr] **-trice** [tris] *adj* disapproving ‖ *mf* critic

désapprouver [dezapruve] *tr* to disapprove of, disapprove

désarçonner [dezarsɔne] *tr* to unhorse, buck off; (coll) to dumfound

désarmement [dezarməmɑ̃] *m* disarmament; disarming; dismantling (*of ship*)

désarmer [dezarme] *tr* to disarm; deactivate; dismantle; appease ‖ *intr* to disarm; slacken, let up (*said of hostility*)

désarroi [dezarwa] *m* disorder, disarray, confusion

désarticulation [dezartikylɑsjɔ̃] *f* dislocation

désassembler [dezasɑ̃ble] *tr* to disassemble

désastre [dezastr] *m* disaster

désas•treux [dezastrø] **-treuse** [trøz] *adj* disastrous

désavantage [dezavɑ̃taʒ] *m* disadvantage

désavantager [dezavɑ̃taʒe] §38 *tr* to put at a disadvantage, to handicap

désavanta•geux [dezavɑ̃taʒø] **-geuse** [ʒøz] *adj* disadvantageous

désa•veu [dezavø] *m* (*pl* **-veux**) disavowal, denial, repudiation

désavouer [dezavwe] *tr* to disavow, deny, repudiate, disown

désaxé désaxée [dezakse] *adj* unbalanced, out of joint

desceller [desɛle] *tr* to unseal

descendance [desɑ̃dɑ̃s] *f* descent

descendeur [desɑ̃dœr] *m* ski jumper

descendre [desɑ̃dr], [dɛsɑ̃dr] §95, §96 *tr* to descend, go down (*a hill, street, stairway*); take down, to lower (*a picture*); (coll) to bring down (*an airplane; luggage*); (coll) to drop off, let off at the door ‖ *intr* (*aux:* ETRE) to descend; go down, go downstairs; stay, stop (*at a hotel*); **descendre** + *inf* to go down to + *inf*; stop off to + *inf*; **descendre court** to undershoot (*said of airplane*); **descendre de** to come down from (*a mountain, ladder, tree*); be descended from

descente [desɑ̃t] *f* descent; invasion, raid; stay (*at a hotel*); stop (*en route*); **descente à terre** (nav) shore leave; **descente de lit** bedside rug

descriptible [dɛskriptibl] *adj* describable

descrip•tif [dɛskriptif] **-tive** [tiv] *adj* descriptive

description [dɛskripsjɔ̃] *f* description

déségrégation [desegregasjɔ̃] *f* desegregation

désembrouillage [dezɑ̃brujaʒ] *m* (electron) descrambling

désempa•ré -rée [dezɑ̃pare] *adj* disconcerted; disabled (*ship*)

désemparer [dezɑ̃pare] *tr* to disable (*a ship*) ‖ *intr*—**sans désemparer** continuously, without intermission

désemplir [dezɑ̃plir] *intr*—**ne pas désemplir** to be always full

désenchaîner [dezɑ̃ʃɛne] *tr* to unchain

désenchantement [dezɑ̃ʃɑ̃tmɑ̃] *m* disenchantment

désenchanter [dezɑ̃ʃɑ̃te] *tr* to disenchant

désencombrer [dezɑ̃kɔ̃bre] *tr* to disencumber, clear, free

désengager [dezɑ̃gaʒe] §34 *tr* to release from a promise

désengorger [dezɑ̃gɔrʒe] §38 *tr* to unstop

désengrener [dezɑ̃grəne] §2 *tr* to disengage, throw out of gear

désenivrer [dezɑ̃nivre] *tr & intr* to sober up

désenlacer [dezɑ̃lase] §51 *tr* to unbind

désennuyer [dezɑ̃nɥije] §27 *tr* to divert, cheer up ‖ *ref* to find relief from boredom

désensabler [dezɑ̃sable] *tr* to free (*a ship*) from the sand; dredge the sand from (*a canal*)

désensibiliser [desɑ̃sibilize] *tr* to desensitize

désensorceler [dezɑ̃sɔrsəle] §34 *tr* to remove the spell from

désentortiller [dezɑ̃tɔrtije] *tr* to straighten out

désenvelopper [dezɑ̃vlɔpe] *tr* to unwrap

déséquilibre [dezekilibr] *m* mental instability

déséquili•bré -brée [dezekilibre] *adj* mentally unbalanced ‖ *mf* unbalanced person

déséquilibrer [dezekilibre] *tr* to unbalance

dé•sert [dezɛr] **-serte** [zɛrt] *adj & m* desert

déserter [dezɛrte] *tr & intr* to desert

déserteur [dezɛrtœr] *m* deserter

désertion [dezɛrsjɔ̃] *f* desertion

désespérance [dezɛsperɑ̃s] *f* despair

désespé•ré -rée [dezɛspere] *adj* desperate, hopeless ‖ *mf* desperate person

désespérer [dezɛspere] §10, §97 *tr* to be the despair of ‖ *ref* to lose hope

désespoir [dezɛspwar] *m* despair; **en désespoir de cause** as a last resort

déshabillage [dezabijaʒ] *m* striptease

déshabillé [dezabije] *m* morning wrap

déshabiller [dezabije] *tr & ref* to undress; **déshabiller saint Pierre pour habiller saint Paul** to rob Peter to pay Paul; **faire déshabiller et fouiller** to stripsearch

déshabituer [dezabitɥe] §97 *tr* to break (*s.o.*) of a habit

déshéri•té -tée [dezerite] *adj* underprivileged; **les déshérités** the underprivileged

déshériter [dezerite] *tr* to disinherit; disadvantage

déshonnête [dezɔnɛt] *adj* improper, immodest

déshonnêteté [dezɔnɛtəte] *f* impropriety, immodesty, indecency

déshonneur [dezɔnœr] *m* dishonor

déshono•rant [dezɔnɔrɑ̃] **-rante** [rɑ̃t] *adj* dishonorable, discreditable

déshonorer [dezɔnɔre] *tr* to dishonor

déshydratation [dezidratasjɔ̃] *f* dehydration

déshydrater [dezidrate] *tr* to dehydrate

désignation [deziɲasjɔ̃] *f* designation; appointment, nomination

dési•gné -gnée [desiɲe] *mf* nominee

désigner [desiɲe] *tr* to designate; indicate, point out; appoint, nominate; signify, mean; set (*the hour of an appointment*) ‖ *ref*—**se désigner à l'attention de** to bring oneself to the attention of

désillusion [dezillyzjɔ̃] *f* disillusion; disappointment

désillusionner [dezillyzjɔne] *tr* to disillusion; disappoint

désinence [dezinɑ̃s] *f* (gram) ending

désinfecter [dezɛ̃fɛkte] *tr* to disinfect

désinformation [dezɛ̃fɔrmasjɔ̃] *f* disinformation

désintégration [dezɛ̃tegrasjɔ̃] *f* disintegration

désintégrer [dezɛ̃tegre] §10 *tr & ref* to disintegrate

désintéres•sé -sée [dezɛ̃terɛse] *adj* disinterested, impartial; unselfish

désintéressement [dezɛ̃terɛsmɑ̃] *m* disinterestedness, impartiality; payment, satisfaction (*of a debt*); buyout; paying off (*of a creditor*), payoff; **désintéressement avec le financement en dehors du actif** leveraged buyout

désintéresser [dezɛ̃terɛse] *tr* to pay off; buy out ‖ *ref*—**se désintéresser de** to lose interest in

désintoxication [dezɛ̃tɔksikɑsjɔ̃] *f* detoxification

désintoxiquer [dezɛ̃tɔksike] *tr* to detoxify

désinvolte [dezɛ̃vɔlt] *adj* free and easy, casual; offhanded, impertinent

désinvolture [dezɛ̃vɔltyr] *f* free and easy manner, offhandedness; impertinence

désir [dezir] *m* desire

désirable [dezirabl] *adj* desirable

désirer [dezire] §95, §96 *tr* to desire, wish

dési•reux [dezirø] **-reuse** [røz] *adj* desirous

désister [deziste] *ref* to desist; withdraw from a runoff election, **se désister de** to waive (*a claim*); drop (*a lawsuit*)

désobéir [dezɔbeir] *intr* to disobey; **désobéir à** to disobey, e.g., **le fils désobéira à son père** the son will disobey his father; **être désobéi** to be disobeyed

désobli•geant [dezɔbliʒɑ̃] **-geante** [ʒɑ̃t] *adj* disagreeable, ungracious

désobliger [dezɔbliʒe] §38 *tr* to offend, displease, disoblige

désodori•sant [dezɔdɔrizɑ̃] **-sante** [zɑ̃t] *adj & m* deodorant

désodoriser [dezɔdɔrize] *tr* to deodorize

désœu•vré -vrée [dezœvre] *adj* idle, unoccupied, out of work; **les désœuvrés** the unemployed

désœuvrement [dezœvrəmɑ̃] *m* idleness, unemployment

déso•lant [dezɔlɑ̃] **-lante** [lɑ̃t] *adj* distressing, sad

désolation [dezɔlɑsjɔ̃] *f* desolation; grief, distress

déso•lé -lée [dezɔle] *adj* desolate; distressed

désoler [dezɔle] *tr* to desolate, destroy; distress ‖ *ref* to be distressed

désopi•lant [dezɔpilɑ̃] **-lante** [lɑ̃t] *adj* hilarious, sidesplitting

désordon•né -née [dezɔrdɔne] *adj* disordered, untidy; disorderly

désordonner [dezɔrdɔne] *tr* to upset, confuse

désordre [dezɔrdr] *m* disorder, confusion, moral laxity

désorganisa•teur [dezɔrganizatœr] **-trice** [tris] *adj* disorganizing ‖ *mf* troublemaker

désorganisation [dezɔrganizɑsjɔ̃] *f* disorganization

désorganiser [dezɔrganize] *tr* to disorganize

désorien•té -tée [dezɔrjɑ̃te] *adj* disoriented, bewildered

désorienter [dezɔrjɑ̃te] *tr* to disorient; mislead; disconcert ‖ *ref* to become confused; lose one's bearings

désormais [dezɔrme] *adv* henceforth

désosser [dezɔse] *tr* to bone

désoxyder [dezɔkside] *tr* deoxidize

despote [dɛspɔt] *m* despot

despotique [dɛspɔtik] *adj* despotic

despotisme [dɛspɔtism] *m* despotism

des•quels -quelles [dekɛl] §78

dessaisir [desɛzir] *tr* to dispossess; let go, release ‖ *ref*—**se dessaisir de** to relinquish

dessalement [desalmɑ̃] *m* desalinization

dessaler [desale] *tr* to desalt, desalinate ‖ *ref* (coll) to wise up

dessécher [deseʃe] §10 *tr* to dry up, wither; drain (*a pond*); dehydrate (*the body*); sear (*the heart*) ‖ *ref* to dry up; waste away

dessein [desɛ̃] *m* design, plan, intent; **à dessein** on purpose

desseller [desɛle] *tr* to unsaddle

desserrer [desɛre] *tr* to loosen; **ne pas desserrer les dents** to keep mum

dessert [desɛr] *m* dessert, last course

desserte [desɛrt] *f* buffet, sideboard; branch (*of railroad or bus line*); ministry (*of a substituting clergyman*)

dessertir [desɛrtir] *tr* to remove (*a gem*) from its setting

desservant [desɛrvɑ̃] *m* parish priest

desserveur [desɛrvœr] *m* busboy

desservir [desɛrvir] §63 *tr* to clear (*the table*); be of disservice to, harm; (aer, aut, rr) to stop at (*a town or station*); (aer, aut, eccl, rr) to serve (*a locality*); (elec) to supply (*a region*)

dessiller [desije] *tr*—**dessiller les yeux à qn** or **de qn** to open s.o.'s eyes, undeceive s.o.

dessin [desɛ̃] *m* drawing, sketch, design; profile (*of face*); **dessins animés** (mov) animated cartoons

dessina•teur [desinatœr] **-trice** [tris] *mf* designer; cartoonist

dessiner [desine] *tr* to draw, sketch, design; delineate, outline ‖ *ref* to stand out, be outlined

dessoûler or **dessouler** [desule] *tr & intr* to sober up

dessous [dəsu] *m* underpart; reverse side, wrong side; coaster (*underneath a glass*); seamy side, machinations behind the scenes; **au dessous de** below; **avoir le dessous** to get the short end of the deal; **du dessous** below; **en dessous** underneath; **les dessous** lingerie, undergarments ‖ *adv & prep* under, underneath, below

dessous-de-bouteille [dəsudəbutɛj] *m invar* coaster

dessous-de-bras [dəsudəbra] *m invar* underarm pad

dessous-de-carafe [dəsudəkaraf] *m invar* coaster

dessous-de-plat [dəsudəpla] *m invar* hot pad

dessous-de-table [dəsudətabl] *m invar* under-the-counter money

dessus [dəsy] *m* upper part; back (*of the hand*); right side (*of material*); (mus) treble part; **au dessus de** beyond, above; **avoir le dessus** to have the upper hand; **le dessus du panier** the cream of the crop ‖ *adv* above ‖ *prep* on, above, over

dessus-de-cheminée [dəsydəʃmine] *m invar* mantelpiece

dessus-de-lit [dəsydəli] *m invar* bedspread

dessus-de-porte [dəsydəpɔrt] *m invar* overdoor

dessus-de-table [dəsydətabl] *m invar* table cover

destin [dɛstɛ̃] *m* destiny, fate

destinataire [dɛstinatɛr] *mf* addressee; payee; **destinataire inconnu** or **absent** (formula stamped on envelope) not at this address

destination [dɛstinɑsjɔ̃] *f* destination; **à destination de** to, bound for

destinée [dɛstine] *f* destiny

destiner [dɛstine] §96, §100 *tr* to destine; set aside, reserve; **destiner q.ch. à qn** to mean or intend s.th. for s.o.

destituer [dɛstitɥe] *tr* to remove from office

destitution [dɛstitysjɔ̃] *f* dismissal, removal from office

destrier [dɛstrije] *m* (hist) steed, charger

destroyer [dɛstrɔjœr] *m* (nav) destroyer

destruc•teur [dɛstryktœr] **-trice** [tris] *adj* destroying, destructive ‖ *mf* destroyer

destruc•tif [dɛstryktif] **-tive** [tiv] *adj* destructive

destruction [dɛstryksjɔ̃] *f* destruction

dé•suet [dezɥɛ] **-suète** [zɥɛt] *adj* obsolete, antiquated, out-of-date

désuétude [dezɥetyd] *f* desuetude, disuse

désu•ni -nie [dezyni] *adj* at odds, divided against itself; uncoordinated

désunion [dezynjɔ̃] *f* dissension

désunir [dezynir] *tr* to disunite, divide; estrange

détachant [detaʃɑ̃] *m* stain remover, cleaning fluid

déta•ché -chée [detaʃe] *adj* detached; clean; spare (*parts*); acting, temporary (*official*); staccato (*note*)

détachement [detaʃmɑ̃] *m* detachment; (mil) detail

détacher [detaʃe] *tr* to detach; let loose; clean; make (*s.th.*) stand out in relief ‖ *ref* to come loose; break loose; stand out in relief; **se détacher net** to break off

détacheur [detaʃœr] *m* spot remover

détail [detaj] *m* detail; retail; item (*of an account*); **au détail** at retail; **en détail** detailed

détail•lant [detajɑ̃] **-lante** [jɑ̃t] *adj* retail ‖ *mf* retailer

détailler [detaje] *tr* to detail; cut up into pieces; retail; itemize (*an account*)

détartrer [detartre] *tr* to remove the scale from (*a boiler*); remove the tartar from (*teeth*)

détaxation [detaksɑsjɔ̃] *f* lowering or removal of taxes

détaxer [detakse] *tr* to lower or remove the tax from

détecter [detɛkte] *tr* to detect

détecteur [detɛktœr] *m* detector; **détecteur de fumée** smoke detector; **détecteur de mines** mine detector

détection [detɛksjɔ̃] *f* detection

détective [detɛktiv] *m* detective, private detective; box camera

déteindre [detɛ̃dr] §50 *tr* to fade, bleach ‖ *intr* to fade, run

dételer [detle] §34 *tr* to unharness ‖ *intr* to let up; settle down

détendre [detɑ̃dr] *tr* to relax; stretch out (*one's legs*); lower (*the gas*) ‖ *ref* to relax, enjoy oneself

déten•du -due [detɑ̃dy] *adj* relaxed; slack ‖ *v* see **détendre**

détenir [detnir] §72 *tr* to detain (*in prison*); hold, withhold; own

détente [detɑ̃t] *f* trigger; relaxation, easing (*of tension*); relaxation of tension (*in international affairs*); spring, thrust, expansion

déten•teur [detɑ̃tœr] **-trice** [tris] *mf* holder (*of stock; of a record*); keeper (*of a secret*)

détention [detɑ̃sjɔ̃] *f* detention, custody; possession; **détention préventive** pretrial imprisonment, custody

déte•nu -nue [detny] *adj* detained, imprisoned; **détenu dans le temps** stuck in a time warp ‖ *mf* prisoner

déter•gent [detɛrʒɑ̃] **-gente** [ʒɑ̃t] *adj & m* detergent

déterger [detɛrʒe] §38 *tr* to clean

détérioration [deterjɔrɑsjɔ̃] *f* deterioration

détériorer [deterjɔre] *tr* to damage ‖ *intr* to deteriorate

détermination [detɛrminɑsjɔ̃] *f* determination

déterminer [detɛrmine] §97, §100 *tr* to determine ‖ §96 *ref* to decide

déter•ré -rée [detɛre] *adj* disinterred ‖ *mf* (fig) corpse, ghost

déterrer [detɛre] *tr* to dig up; exhume

déter•sif [detɛrsif] **-sive** [siv] *adj & m* detergent

détester [detɛste] §95, §97 *tr* to detest, hate

déto•nant -nante [detɔnɑ̃] [nɑ̃t] *adj & m* explosive

détoner [detɔne] *intr* to detonate, explode

détonner [detɔne] *intr* to sing or play off key; clash (*said of colors*)

détordre [detɔrdr] *tr* untwist

détortiller [detɔrtije] *tr* to untangle

détour [detur] *m* turn, curve, bend; round-about way, detour; **sans détour** frankly, honestly

détour•né -née [deturne] *adj* off the beaten track, isolated; indirect, roundabout; twisted (*meaning*)

détournement [deturnəmɑ̃] *m* diversion, rerouting; embezzlement; hijacking (*of an airplane*); **détournement de mineur** child abuse

détourner [deturne] §97, §99 *tr* to divert; deter; embezzle; lead astray; distort, twist

détrac•teur [detraktœr] **-trice** [tris] *adj* disparaging ‖ *mf* detractor

détra•qué -quée [detrake] *adj* out of order; broken (*in health*); unhinged, deranged ‖ *mf* nervous wreck

détraquer [detrake] *tr* to put out of commission; (coll) to upset, unhinge ‖ *ref* to break down

détrempe [detrɑ̃p] *f* distemper (*painting*); annealing (*of steel*)

détremper [detrɑ̃pe] *tr* to soak; dilute; anneal (*steel*)

détresse [detrɛs] *f* distress

détriment [detrimɑ̃] *m* detriment

détritus [detritys] *m* debris, rubbish, refuse

détroit [detrwa] *m* strait, sound

détromper [detrɔ̃pe] *tr* to undeceive, enlighten

détrôner [detrone] *tr* to dethrone

détrousser [detruse] *tr* to let down (*e.g., one's sleeves*); hold up (*s.o.*) in the street ‖ *ref* to let down a garment

détrousseur [detrusœr] *m* highwayman

détruire [detrɥir] §19 *tr* to destroy; put an end to ‖ *ref* (coll) to commit suicide

dette [dɛt] *f* debt, indebtedness; **dette active** asset; **dette passive** liability

deuil [dœj] *m* mourning; grief, sorrow; bereavement; funeral procession; **deuil de veuve** widow's weeds; **faire son deuil de** (coll) to say good-bye to

deux [dø] §94 *adj & pron* two; the Second, e.g., **Charles deux** Charles the Second; **deux heures** two o'clock ‖ *m* two; second (*in dates*)

deuxième [døzjɛm] §94 *adj & m* second

deux-pièces [døpjɛs] *m invar* two-piece suit

deux-points [døpwɛ̃] *m invar* colon

deux-ponts [døpɔ̃] *m invar* (aer, naut) double-decker

dévaler [devale] *tr* to descend (*a slope*) ‖ *intr* to descend quickly

dévaloriser [devalɔrize] *tr* to reduce the value of, devalue, devaluate; depreciate, underrate ‖ *ref* to depreciate, fall in value

dévaluation [devalɥasjɔ̃] *f* devaluation

dévaluer [devalɥe] *tr* to devaluate

devancer [dəvɑ̃se] *tr* to get ahead; arrive ahead of; anticipate

devan·cier [dəvɑ̃sje] **-cière** [sjɛr] *mf* precursor, predecessor; **nos devanciers** those who have come before us, our forefathers

devant [dəvɑ̃] *m* front; **par devant** in front; **prendre les devants** to make the first move; to get ahead; to take precautions ‖ *adv* before, in front ‖ *prep* before, in front of

devanture [dəvɑ̃tyr] *f* show window; display; storefront

dévasta·teur [devastatœr] **-trice** [tris] *adj* devastating

dévastation [devastasjɔ̃] *f* devastation

dévaster [devaste] *tr* to devastate

déveine [devɛn] *f* bad luck

développé [devlɔpe] *m* press (*in weight lifting*)

développement [devlɔpmɑ̃] *m* development; unwrapping (*of package*); expansion; **développement urbain** urban development

développer [devlɔpe] *tr* to develop; unwrap (*a package*); reveal, show (*e.g., a card*); spread out, open out; expand (*an algebraic expression*) ‖ *ref* to develop

devenir [dəvnir] §72 *intr* (*aux:* ÊTRE) to become; **qu'est devenu Robert?** what has become of Robert?

dévergondage [devɛrgɔ̃daʒ] *m* profligacy

dévergon·dé -dée [devɛrgɔ̃de] *adj & mf* profligate

dévergonder [devɛrgɔ̃de] *ref* to become dissolute

dévernir [devɛrnir] *tr* to remove the varnish from

déverrouiller [devɛruje] *tr* to unbolt

dé·vers [devɛr] **-verse** [vɛrs] *adj* warped; out of alignment ‖ *m* inclination, slope; banking

déverser [devɛrse] *tr* to pour out; slope, bank ‖ *intr* to pour out; lean, become lopsided ‖ *ref* to empty, flow (*said of river*)

dévêtir [devɛtir] §73 *tr & ref* to undress

déviation [devjɑsjɔ̃] *f* deviation; detour; **déviation magnétique** magnetic deviation

dévider [devide] *tr* to unwind, reel off

dévier [devje] *tr* deflect, by-pass ‖ *intr* to deviate, swerve

de·vin [dəvɛ̃] **-vineresse** [vinrɛs] *mf* fortune-teller

deviner [dəvine] *tr* to guess

devinette [dəvinɛt] *f* riddle

dévirer [devire] *tr* to turn back; bend back; feather (*an oar*)

devis [dəvi] *m* estimate

dévisager [devizaʒe] §38 *tr* to stare at, stare down

devise [dəviz] *f* motto, slogan; heraldic device; name of a ship; currency; **devise forte** strong currency

deviser [dəvize] *intr* to chat

dévisser [devise] *tr* to unscrew

dévitaliser [devitalize] *tr* to kill the nerve of (*a tooth*)

dévoiler [devwale] *tr* to unveil; straighten (*e.g., a bent wheel*) ‖ *ref* to unveil; come to light

devoir [dəvwar] *m* duty; exercise, homework; **devoirs** respects; homework ‖ §21 *tr* §95 to owe ‖ *aux* used to express 1) necessity, e.g., **il doit s'en aller** he must go away; **il devra s'en aller** he will have to go away; **il a dû s'en aller** he had to go away; 2) obligation, e.g., **il devrait s'en aller** he ought to go away, he should go away; **il aurait dû s'en aller** he ought to have gone away, he should have gone away; 3) conjecture, e.g., **il doit être malade** he must be ill; **il a dû être malade** he must have been ill; 4) what is expected or scheduled, e.g., **que dois-je faire maintenant?** what am I to do now? **le train devait arriver à six heures** the train was to arrive at six o'clock

dévo·lu -lue [devɔly] *adj*—**dévolu à** devolving upon, vested in ‖ *m*—**jeter son dévolu sur** to fix one's choice upon

dévora·teur [devɔratœr] **-trice** [tris] *adj* devouring

dévorer [devɔre] *tr* to devour, eat up

dévo·reur [devɔrœr] **-reuse** [røz] *mf* devourer; (fig) glutton

dé·vot [devo] **-vote** [vɔt] *adj* devout, pious ‖ *mf* devout, pious person; devotee; **faux dévot** hypocrite

dévotion [devosjɔ̃] *f* devotion, devoutness; **à votre dévotion** at your service, at your disposal; **être à la dévotion de qn** to be at s.o.'s beck and call

dé·voué -vouée [devwe] *adj* devoted; **dévoué à vos ordres** (complimentary close) at your service; **votre dévoué** (complimentary close) yours truly

dévouement [devumã] *m* devotion

dévouer [devwe] *tr* §96 to sacrifice ‖ *ref*—**se dévouer à** to devote or dedicate oneself to

dévoyé dévoyée [devwaje] *adj* delinquent (*young person*) ‖ *mf* delinquent

dévoyer [devwaje] §47 *tr* to lead astray

dextérité [dɛksterite] *f* dexterity

dextrose [dɛkstroz] *m* dextrose

diabète [djabɛt] *m* diabetes

diabétique [djabetik] *adj & mf* diabetic

diable [djɑbl] *m* devil; hand truck, dolly; (coll) fellow; **à la diable** haphazardly; **au diable vauvert** miles from anywhere, far away; **c'est là le diable** (coll) there's the rub; **diable à ressort** jack-in-the-box; **du diable** extreme; **en diable** extremely; **faire le diable à quatre** (coll) to raise Cain; **tirer le diable par la queue** (coll) to be hard up

diablerie [djɑbləri] *f* deviltry

diabolique [djabɔlik] *adj* diabolic(al)

diaconesse [djakɔnɛs] *f* deaconess

diacre [djakr] *m* deacon

diacritique [djakritik] *adj* diacritical

diadème [djadɛm] *m* diadem; (*woman's head-dress*) tiara, coronet

diagnose [djagnoz] *f* diagnostics, diagnosis

diagnostic [djagnɔstik] *m* diagnosis

diagnostiquer [djagnɔstike] *tr* to diagnose

diago•nal -nale [djagɔnal] *adj & f* (*pl* **-naux** [no] **-nales**) diagonal

diagonalement [djagɔnalmã] *adv* diagonally, cater-cornered

diagramme [djagram] *m* diagram

dialecte [djalɛkt] *m* dialect

dialogue [djalɔg] *m* dialogue; **de dialogue** (comp) conversational; **dialogue de sourds** irreconcilable argument

dialoguer [djalɔge] *tr* to dialogue, adapt (*a novel for the screen*) ‖ *intr* to carry on a dialogue

diamant [djamã] *m* diamond

diamantaire [djamãtɛr] *adj* diamond-bright ‖ *m* dealer in diamonds

diamé•tral -trale [djametral] *adj* (*pl* **-traux** [tro]) diametric(al)

diamètre [djamɛtr] *m* diameter

diane [djan] *f* reveille

diantre [djãtr] *interj* the dickens!

diapason [djapazɔ̃] *m* range (*of voice or instrument*); pitch, standard pitch; tuning fork; **être au diapason de** (fig) to be on the same wavelength as

diaphane [djafan] *adj* diaphanous

diaphragme [djafragm] *m* diaphragm

diapo [djapo] *f* (coll) slide

diapositive [diapozitiv] *f* (phot) transparency, slide

diaprer [djapre] *tr* to variegate

diarrhée [djare] *f* diarrhea

diastole [djastɔl] *f* diastole

diathermie [djatɛrmi] *f* diathermy

diatribe [djatrib] *f* diatribe

dichotomie [dikɔtɔmi] *f* dichotomy; split fee (*between physicians*)

dictaphone [diktafɔn] *m* dictaphone

dictateur [diktatœr] *m* dictator

dictature [diktatyr] *f* dictatorship

dictée [dikte] *f* dictation; **écrire sous la dictée de** to take dictation from

dicter [dikte] *tr & intr* to dictate

diction [diksjɔ̃] *f* diction

dictionnaire [diksjɔnɛr] *m* dictionary; **dictionnaire vivant** (coll) walking encyclopedia

dicton [diktɔ̃] *m* saying, proverb

didacticiel [didaktisjɛl] *m* (comp) instructional software

didactique [didaktik] *adj* didactic(al)

dièdre [diɛdr] *adj & m* dihedral

diérèse [djerɛz] *f* diaeresis

dièse [djɛz] *adj & m* (mus) sharp

diesel [dizɛl] *m* diesel motor

diesel-électrique [dizɛlelɛktrik] *adj & m* (*pl* **diesels-électriques**) diesel-electric

diéser [djeze] §10 *tr* (mus) to sharp

diète [djɛt] *f* diet

diététi•cien [djetetisjɛ̃] **-cienne** [sjɛn] *mf* dietitian

diététique [djetetik] *adj* dietetic ‖ *f* dietetics

dieu [djø] *m* (*pl* **dieux**) god ‖ (*cap*) *m* God; **Dieu merci!** thank heavens!; **mon Dieu!** good gracious!

diffamation [difamasjɔ̃] *f* defamation

diffamer [difame] *tr* to defame

diffé•ré -rée [difere] *adj* deferred; delayed (*action*) ‖ *m* (rad, telv) prerecording; **en différé** (rad, telv) prerecorded

différemment [diferamã] *adv* differently

différence [diferãs] *f* difference; **à la différence de** unlike, contrary to

différencier [diferãsje] *tr & ref* to differentiate

différend [diferã] *m* dispute, disagreement, difference; **partager le différend** to split the difference

diffé•rent [diferã] **-rente** [rãt] *adj* different; **différent de** different from ‖ (when standing before noun) *adj* different, various

différen•tiel -tielle [diferãsjɛl] *adj* differential ‖ *m* (mach) differential ‖ *f* (math) differential

différer [difere] §10, §96, §97 *tr* to defer, put off ‖ *intr* to differ; disagree

difficile [difisil] §92 *adj* difficult, hard; hard to please, crotchety; **faire le difficile** to be hard to please

difficulté [difikylte] *f* difficulty

difforme [difɔrm] *adj* deformed

difformité [difɔrmite] *f* deformity

dif•fus [dify] **-fuse** [fyz] *adj* diffuse; verbose, windy

diffuser [difyze] *tr* to broadcast ‖ *ref* to diffuse

diffuseur [difyzœr] *m* spreader (*of news*); loudspeaker; nozzle

digérer [diʒere] §10 *tr & intr* to digest ‖ *ref* to be digested

digeste [diʒɛst] *adj* (coll) easy to digest ‖ *m* (law) digest

digestible [diʒɛstibl] *adj* digestible
diges·tif [diʒɛstif] **-tive** [tiv] *adj* digestive
digestion [diʒɛstjɔ̃] *f* digestion
digi·tal -tale [diʒital] *adj* (*pl* **-taux** [to]) digital ‖ *f* digitalis, foxglove
digitaline [diʒitalin] *f* (pharm) digitalis
digne [diɲ] §93 *adj* worthy; dignified; haughty, uppish; **digne d'éloges** praiseworthy, laudable
dignitaire [diɲitɛr] *mf* dignitary
dignité [diɲite] *f* dignity
digression [digrɛsjɔ̃] *f* digression
digue [dig] *f* dike; breakwater; (fig) barrier
dilacérer [dilasere] §10 *tr* to lacerate
dilapider [dilapide] *tr* to squander; embezzle
dilater [dilate] *tr & ref* to dilate
dilatoire [dilatwar] *adj* dilatory
dilemme [dilɛm] *m* dilemma
dilettante [diletɑ̃t] *mf* dilettante
diligemment [diliʒamɑ̃] *adv* diligently
diligence [diliʒɑ̃s] *f* diligence; **à la diligence de** at the request of
dili·gent [diliʒɑ̃] **-gente** [ʒɑ̃t] *adj* diligent
diluer [dilɥe] *tr* to dilute
dilution [dilysjɔ̃] *f* dilution
dimanche [dimɑ̃ʃ] *m* Sunday; **du dimanche** (coll) Sunday (*driver*); (coll) amateur (*painter*); **le dimanche des Rameaux** Palm Sunday
dîme [dim] *f* tithe
dimension [dimɑ̃sjɔ̃] *f* dimension
diminuer [diminɥe] *tr* to reduce, cut down, decrease ‖ *intr* to diminish, decrease
diminu·tif [diminytif] **-tive** [tiv] *adj & m* diminutive
diminution [diminysjɔ̃] *f* reduction; diminishing
dinde [dɛ̃d] *f* turkey hen; (culin) turkey; (coll) silly girl
dindon [dɛ̃dɔ̃] *m* turkey; tom turkey; (coll) dupe
dindonner [dɛ̃dɔne] *tr* to dupe, take in
dîner [dine] *m* dinner; **dîner de garçons** stag dinner; **dîner prié** formal dinner ‖ *intr* to dine
dînette [dinɛt] *f* family meal; children's playtime meal
dî·neur [dinœr] **-neuse** [nøz], *mf* diner, dinner guest
dingue [dɛ̃g] *adj* (slang) crazy, nuts, nutty, goffy ‖ *mf* nutty person, goof
dinosaure [dinozɔr] *m* dinosaur
diocèse [djɔsɛz] *m* diocese
diode [djɔd] *f* diode
dionée [djɔne] *f* Venus's-flytrap
diphtérie [difteri] *f* diphtheria
diphtongue [diftɔ̃g] *f* diphthong
diplomate [diplɔmat] *adj* diplomatic ‖ *mf* diplomat
diplomatie [diplɔmasi] *f* diplomacy
diplomatique [diplɔmatik] *adj* diplomatic
diplôme [diplom] *m* diploma
diplô·mé -mée [diplome] *adj* qualified ‖ *mf* holder of a diploma; alumnus, alumna
dire [dir] §95, §97, §98 *m* statement; **au dire de** according to ‖ §22 *tr* to say, tell, relate; **à l'heure dite** at the appointed time; **à qui le dites-vous?** (coll) you're telling me!; **autrement dit** in other words; **dire que ...** to think that; **dites-lui bien des choses de ma part** say hello for me; **tu l'as dit!** (coll) you said it! ‖ *intr* to say; **à vrai dire** to tell the truth; **cela va sans dire** it goes without saying; **c'est beaucoup dire** (coll) that's going rather far; **c'est pas peu dire** (slang) that's saying a lot; **comme on dit** as the saying goes; **dites donc!** hey!, say!; **il n'y a pas à dire** make no mistake about it ‖ *ref* to be said; to say to oneself or to each other; to claim to be, to call oneself
di·rect -recte [dirɛkt] *adj* direct ‖ *m* (boxing) solid punch; **en direct** (rad, telv) live
direct·teur [dirɛktœr] **-trice** [tris] *adj* directing, guiding; principal; driving (*rod, wheel*) ‖ *mf* director; **directeur commercial** sales manager; **directeur de jeu** referee; **directeur des services municipaux** city manager ‖ *f* directress
direction [dirɛksjɔ̃] *f* direction; administration, management, board; head office; (aut) steering
direction·nel -nelle [dirɛksjɔnɛl] *adj* directional
directive [dirɛktiv] *f* directive, order
directorat [dirɛktɔra] *m* directorship
dirigeable [diriʒabl] *adj & m* dirigible
diri·geant [diriʒɑ̃] **-geante** [ʒɑ̃t] *adj* governing, ruling ‖ *mf* ruler, leader, head, executive
diriger [diriʒe] §38 *tr* to direct, control, manage; steer ‖ *ref* to go; **se diriger vers** to head for
dirigisme [diriʒism] *m* government economic planning and control
dis [di] *v* (**disant, disons**) see **dire**
discernable [disɛrnabl] *adj* discernible
discernement [disɛrnəmɑ̃] *m* discernment, perception
discerner [disɛrne] *tr* to discern
disciple [displ] *m* disciple
disciplinaire [disiplinɛr] *adj* disciplinary ‖ *m* military policeman
discipline [disiplin] *f* discipline; scourge
discipliner [disipline] *tr* to discipline
disc-jockey [diskʒɔkɛ] *mf* (*pl* **disc-jockeys**) disk jockey
disconti·nu -nue [diskɔ̃tiny] *adj* discontinuous
discontinuer [diskɔ̃tine] §97 *tr* to discontinue
disconvenir [diskɔ̃vnir] §72, §97 *tr* to deny ‖ *intr*—**disconvenir à** to not suit, displease ‖ *intr* (*aux:* ETRE)—**ne pas disconvenir de** to admit, not deny
discophile [diskɔfil] *mf* record collector
discord [diskɔr] *adj masc* out of tune ‖ *m* instrument out of tune
discordance [diskɔrdɑ̃s] *f* discordance
discor·dant [diskɔrdɑ̃] **-dante** [dɑ̃t] *adj* discordant
discorde [diskɔrd] *f* discord
discorder [diskɔrde] *intr* to be discordant, jar

discothèque [diskɔtɛk] *f* record cabinet; record library; discotheque

discourir [diskurir] §14 *intr* to discourse

discours [diskur] *m* discourse; speech

discour·tois [diskurtwa] **-toise** [twaz] *adj* discourteous

discourtoisie [diskurtwazi] *f* discourtesy

discrédit [diskredi] *m* discredit

discréditer [diskredite] *tr* to discredit

dis·cret [diskrɛ] **-crète** [krɛt] *adj* discreet; discrete

discrétion [diskresjɔ̃] *f* discretion; **à discrétion** as much as one wants

discrimination [diskriminɑsjɔ̃] *f* discrimination

discriminatoire [diskriminatwar] *adj* discriminatory

discriminer [diskrimine] *tr* to discriminate

disculper [diskylpe] §97 *tr* to clear, exonerate ‖ *ref* to clear oneself

discur·sif [diskyrsif] **-sive** [siv] *adj* discursive

discussion [diskysjɔ̃] *f* discussion

discuter [diskyte] *tr & intr* to discuss; question, debate

di·sert [dizɛr] **-serte** [zɛrt] *adj* eloquent, fluent

disertement [dizɛrtəmɑ̃] *adv* eloquently, fluently

disette [dizɛt] *f* shortage, scarcity; famine

di·seur [dizœr] **-seuse** [zøz] *mf* talker, speaker; monologuist; **diseuse de bonne aventure** fortuneteller

disgrâce [disgrɑs] *f* disfavor; misfortune; surliness, gruffness

disgra·cié -ciée [disgrasje] *adj* out of favor; ill-favored, homely; unfortunate

disgracier [disgrasje] *tr* to deprive of favor

disgra·cieux [disgrasjø] **-cieuse** [sjøz] *adj* awkward; homely, ugly; disagreeable

disjoindre [disʒwɛ̃dr] §35 *tr* to sever, separate

disjoncteur [disʒɔ̃ktœr] *m* circuit breaker

dislocation [dislɔkɑsjɔ̃] *f* dislocation; separation; dismemberment

disloquer [dislɔke] *tr* to dislocate; disperse; dismember ‖ *ref* to break up, disperse

disparaître [disparɛtr] §12 *intr* to disappear

disparate [disparat] *adj* incongruous ‖ *f* incongruity; clash (*of colors*)

disparité [disparite] *f* disparity

disparition [disparisjɔ̃] *f* disappearance

dispa·ru -rue [dispary] *adj* disappeared; missing (*in battle*) ‖ *mf* missing person; **le disparu** the deceased ‖ *v* see **disparaître**

dispen·dieux [dispɑ̃djø] **-dieuse** [djøz] *adj* expensive

dispensaire [dispɑ̃sɛr] *m* dispensary, outpatient clinic

dispensa·teur [dispɑ̃satœr] **-trice** [tris] *mf* dispenser

dispense [dispɑ̃s] *f* dispensation, exemption

dispenser [dispɑ̃se] §97, §99 *tr* to dispense; **dispensé du timbrage** (label on envelope) mailing permit

disperser [dispɛrse] *tr & ref* to disperse

dispersion [dispɛrsjɔ̃] *f* dispersion, dissipation

disponibilité [disponibilite] *f* availability; **disponibilités** liquid assets; **en disponibilité** in the reserves

disponible [disponibl] *adj* available; vacant (*seat*); (govt, mil) subject to call

dis·pos [dispo] **-pose** [poz] *adj* alert, fit, in good condition

dispo·sé -sée [dispoze] §92 *adj* disposed; arranged; **disposé d'avance** predisposed; **peu disposé** reluctant

disposer [dispoze] §96, §100 *tr* to dispose ‖ *intr* to dispose; **disposer de** to dispose of, have at one's disposal; have at hand; make use of; **disposer pour** to provide for (*e.g., the future*); **vous pouvez disposer** you may leave ‖ *ref*—**se disposer à** to be disposed to; plan on

dispositif [dispozitif] *m* apparatus, device; (mil) disposition; **dispositif d'accès** (comp) access mechanism

disposition [dispozisjɔ̃] *f* disposition; disposal; **dispositions** arrangements; aptitude; provisions (*of a legal document*)

disproportion·né -née [disprɔpɔrsjɔne] *adj* disproportionate, incompatible

dispute [dispyt] *f* dispute

disputer [dispyte] *tr* to dispute; (coll) to bawl out ‖ *ref* to dispute

disquaire [diskɛr] *m* record dealer

disqualification [diskalifikɑsjɔ̃] *f* disqualification

disqualifier [diskalifje] *tr & ref* to disqualify

disque [disk] *m* disk; record, disk; (sports) discus; **changer de disque** (coll) to change the subject; **disque compact** (CD) compact disk; **disque de longue durée** long-playing record; **disque dur** (comp) hard drive, hard disk; **disque souple** (comp) diskette; **disque volant** Frisbee (trademark)

disquette [diskɛt] *f* (comp) diskette, floppy disk

dissection [disɛksjɔ̃] *f* dissection

dissemblable [disɑ̃blabl] *adj* dissimilar

dissemblance [disɑ̃blɑ̃s] *f* dissimilarity

disséminer [disemine] *tr* to disseminate

dissension [disɑ̃sjɔ̃] *f* dissension

dissentiment [disɑ̃timɑ̃] *m* dissent

disséquer [diseke] §10 *tr* to dissect

dissertation [disɛrtɑsjɔ̃] *f* dissertation; (*in school*) essay, term paper

dissidence [disidɑ̃s] *f* dissent

dissi·dent [disidɑ̃] **-dente** [dɑ̃t] *adj* dissenting ‖ *mf* dissenter, dissident

dissimiler [disimile] *tr* (phonet) to dissimilate

dissimulation [disimylɑsjɔ̃] *f* dissemblance

dissimuler [disimyle] *tr & intr* to dissemble; **dissimuler q.ch. à qn** to conceal s.th. from s.o. ‖ *ref* to hide, skulk

dissipation [disipɑsjɔ̃] *f* dissipation

dissi·pé -pée [disipe] *adj* dissipated; pleasure-seeking; unruly (*schoolboy*)

dissiper [disipe] *tr & ref* to dissipate

dissocier [disɔsje] *tr & ref* to dissociate

disso•lu -lue [disɔly] *adj* dissolute ‖ *mf* profligate

dissolution [disɔlysjɔ̃] *f* dissolution; dissoluteness; rubber cement

dissol•vant [disɔlvɑ̃] **-vante** [vɑ̃t] *adj & m* solvent

dissonance [disɔnɑ̃s] *f* dissonance

dissoudre [disudr] **§60** (*pp* **dissous, dissoute**; no *pret* or *imperf subj*) *tr & ref* to dissolve

dissuader [disɥade] **§97, §99** *tr* to dissuade, deter

distance [distɑ̃s] *f* distance; **à distance** at a distance

distancer [distɑ̃se] **§51** *tr* to outdistance, distance (*a race horse*)

dis•tant [distɑ̃] **-tante** [tɑ̃t] *adj* distant

distendre [distɑ̃dr] *tr & ref* to distend; strain (*a muscle*)

distillation [distiasjɔ̃] *f* distillation

distiller [distile] *tr* to distill

distillerie [distilri] *f* distillery; distilling industry

dis•tinct [distɛ̃], [distɛ̃kt] **-tincte** [tɛ̃kt] *adj* distinct

distinc•tif [distɛ̃ktif] **-tive** [tiv] *adj* distinctive

distinction [distɛ̃ksjɔ̃] *f* distinction

distin•gué -guée [distɛ̃ge] *adj* distinguished; famous; sincere, e.g., **veuillez accepter nos sentiments distingués** (complimentary close) please accept our sincere regards

distinguer [distɛ̃ge] *tr* to distinguish ‖ *ref* to be distinguished; distinguish oneself

distordre [distɔrdr] *tr* to twist, sprain

dis•tors [distɔr] **-torse** [tɔrs] *adj* twisted

distorsion [distɔrsjɔ̃] *f* sprain; convulsive twist; (electron, opt) distorsion

distraction [distraksjɔ̃] *f* distraction; heedlessness, lapse; embezzlement; appropriation (*of a sum of money*)

distraire [distrɛr] **§68** *tr* to distract, amuse; separate, set aside (*e.g., part of one's savings*) ‖ *ref* to amuse oneself

dis•trait [distrɛ] **-traite** [trɛt] *adj* absentminded

distribuer [distribɥe] *tr* to distribute; arrange the furnishings of (*an apartment*)

distribu•teur [distribytœr] **-trice** [tris] *mf* distributor (*person*) ‖ *m* (mach) distributor; **distributeur automatique** vending machine; **distributeur de musique** jukebox

distribution [distribysjɔ̃] *f* distribution; mail delivery; supply system (*of gas, water, or electricity*); valve gear (*of steam engine*); timing gears (*of internal-combustion engine*); (theat) cast

district [distrik], [distrikt] *m* district

dit [di] **dite** [dit] *adj* agreed upon, stated ‖ *m* saying ‖ *v* see **dire**

dites [dit] *v* see **dire**

dito [dito] *adv* ditto

diurétique [djyretik] *adj & m* diuretic

diva [diva] *f* diva

divaguer [divage] *intr* to ramble

divan [divɑ̃] *m* divan, sofa

diverger [divɛrʒe] **§38** *intr* to diverge

di•vers [divɛr] **-verse** [vɛrs] *adj* changing, varied; miscellaneous (*expenses; remarks;* **faits divers** news items; **un fait divers** an incident ‖ **di•vers -verses** (when standing before or after noun) *adj pl* diverse, different, varied; various, several, e.g., **diverses personnes** several persons, **en diverses occasions** on various occasions

diversifier [divɛrsifje] *tr & ref* to diversify

diversion [divɛrsjɔ̃] *f* diversion

diversité [divɛrsite] *f* diversity

divertir [divɛrtir] **§96** *tr* to divert, amuse ‖ *ref* to be diverted, amused

divertis•sant [divɛrtisɑ̃] **-sante** [sɑ̃t] *adj* entertaining, diverting, amusing

divertissement [divɛrtismɑ̃] *m* diversion, relaxation; entertainment; amusement; (mus) divertissement

dividende [dividɑ̃d] *m* dividend

di•vin [divɛ̃] **-vine** [vin] *adj* divine

divination [divinasjɔ̃] *f* divination

divinité [divinite] *f* divinity

diviser [divize] *tr & ref* to divide

diviseur [divizœr] *m* (math) divisor; (fig) troublemaker

divisible [divizibl] *adj* divisible

division [divizjɔ̃] *f* division

divisionnaire [divizjɔnɛr] *adj* divisional ‖ *m* division head

divorce [divɔrs] *m* divorce

divor•cé -cée [divɔrse] *mf* divorced person ‖ *f* divorcee

divorcer [divɔrse] **§51** *tr* to divorce (*a married couple*) ‖ *intr* to divorce, get a divorce; **divorcer avec** to withdraw from (*the world*); **divorcer d'avec** to get a divorce from, be divorced from, divorce (*husband or wife*); withdraw from (*the world*)

divulguer [divylge] *tr* to divulge

dix [di(s)] **§94** *adj & pron* ten; the Tenth, e.g., **Jean dix** John the Tenth; **dix heures** ten o'clock ‖ *m* ten; tenth (*in dates*)

dix-huit [dizɥi], [dizɥit] **§94** *adj & pron* eighteen; the Eighteenth, e.g., **Jean dix-huit** John the Eighteenth ‖ *m* eighteen; eighteenth (*in dates*)

dix-huitième [dizɥitjɛm] **§94** *adj & m* eighteenth

dixième [dizjɛm] **§94** *adj, pron* (*masc, fem*), & *m* tenth

dix-neuf [diznœf] **§94** *adj & pron* nineteen; the Nineteenth, e.g., **Jean dix-neuf** John the Nineteenth ‖ *m* nineteen; nineteenth (*in dates*)

dix-neuvième [diznœvjɛm] **§94** *adj & m* nineteenth

dix-sept [dissɛt] **§94** *adj & pron* seventeen; the Seventeenth, e.g., **Jean dix-sept** John the Seventeenth ‖ *m* seventeen; seventeenth (*in dates*)

dix-septième [dissɛtjɛm] **§94** *adj & m* seventeenth

DJ [didʒe] *or* [didʒi] *mf invar* (letterword) (**disc-jockey**) DJ (disk jockey)

djinn [dʒin] *m* jinn

d° *abbr* (**dito**) do. (ditto)

docile [dɔsil] *adj* docile

dock [dɔk] *m* dock; warehouse; **dock flottant** floating dry dock

docker [dɔkɛr] *m* dock worker

docte [dɔkt] *adj* learned, scholarly ‖ *mf* scholar ‖ *m* learned man

doc•teur [dɔktœr] **-toresse** [tɔrɛs] *mf* doctor; **le docteur Marie Dupont** Dr. Mary Dupont

docto•ral -rale [dɔktɔral] *adj* (*pl* **-raux** [ro]) doctoral

doctorat [dɔktɔra] *m* doctorate

doctrine [dɔktrin] *f* doctrine

document [dɔkymɑ̃] *m* document

documentaire [dɔkymɑ̃tɛr] *adj & m* documentary

documentation [dɔkymɑ̃tasjɔ̃sjɔ̃] *f* documentation; literature (*about a region, business, etc.*)

documenter [dɔkymɑ̃te] *tr* to document ‖ *ref* to gather documentary evidence

dodeliner [dɔdline] *tr & intr* to sway, rock

dodo [dodo] *m* (orn) dodo; **aller au dodo** (*baby talk*) to go to bed; **faire dodo** to sleep

do•du -due [dɔdy] *adj* (coll) plump

dogmatique [dɔgmatik] *adj* dogmatic ‖ *mf* dogmatic person ‖ *f* dogmatics

dogmatiser [dɔgmatize] *intr* to dogmatize

dogme [dɔgm] *m* dogma

dogue [dɔg] *m* bulldog

doigt [dwa] *m* finger; **à deux doigts de** a hairbreadth away from; **doigt annulaire** ring finger; **doigt de Dieu** hand of God; **doigt du pied** toe; **mettre le doigt dessus** to hit the nail on the head; **mon petit doigt m'a dit** (coll) a little bird told me; **montrer du doigt** to single out (*for ridicule*); to point at; **petit doigt** little finger; **se mettre le doigt dans l'œil** (coll) to fool oneself; **se mordre les doigts** to be sorry; **un doigt de vin** very little wine

doigté [dwate] *m* touch; adroitness, skillfulness; fingering

doigter [dwate] *m* fingering ‖ *tr & intr* to finger

doigtier [dwatje] *m* fingerstall

dois [dwa] *v* (**doit**) see **devoir**

doit [dwa] *m* debit

doléances [dɔleɑ̃s] *fpl* grievances; (pathol) symptoms

do•lent -lente [dɔlɑ̃] [lɑ̃t] *adj* doleful

dollar [dɔlar] *m* dollar

domaine [dɔmɛn] *m* domain

dôme [dom] *m* dome; cathedral

domestication [dɔmɛstikasjɔ̃] *f* domestication

domesticité [dɔmɛstisite] *f* domesticity; staff of servants

domestique [dɔmɛstik] *adj & mf* domestic

domestiquer [dɔmɛstike] *tr* to domesticate

domicile [dɔmisil] *m* residence

domicilier [dɔmisilje] *tr* to domicile ‖ *ref* to take up residence

dominance [dɔminɑ̃s] *f* (genetics) dominance

domi•nant [dɔminɑ̃] **-nante** [nɑ̃t] *adj* dominant ‖ *f* dominating trait; (mus) dominant

domina•teur [dɔminatœr] **-trice** [tris] *adj* domineering, overbearing ‖ *mf* ruler, conqueror

domination [dɔminasjɔ̃] *f* domination

dominer [dɔmine] *tr & intr* to dominate ‖ *ref* to control oneself

domini•cal -cale [dɔminikal] *adj* (*pl* **-caux** [ko]) Sunday; dominical

domino [dɔmino] *m* domino

dommage [dɔmaʒ] *m* loss; injury; **c'est dommage!** that's too bad!; **dommages accessoires et fortuits** collateral damage; **dommages et intérêts** (law) damages; **quel dommage!** what a pity!

dommageable [dɔmaʒabl] *adj* injurious

dommages-intérêts [dɔmaʒɛtɛrɛ] *mpl* (law) damages

dompter [dɔ̃te] *tr* to tame; train (*animals*); subdue

domp•teur [dɔ̃tœr] **-teuse** [tøz] *mf* tamer, trainer; conquerer

don [dɔ̃] *m* gift; don (*Spanish title*)

donataire [dɔnatɛr] *mf* legatee

dona•teur [dɔnatœr] **-trice** [tris] *mf* (law) donor, legator

donation [dɔnasjɔ̃] *f* donation, gift, grant

donc [dɔ̃k], [dɔ̃] *adv* therefore, then; thus; now, of course; (often used for emphasis), e.g., **entrez donc!** do come in!

donjon [dɔ̃ʒɔ̃] *m* keep, donjon; (nav) turret

don•nant [dɔnɑ̃] **-nante** [nɑ̃t] *adj* generous, open-handed; **donnant donnant** tit for tat; cash down; **peu donnant** closefisted

donne [dɔn] *f* (cards) deal; doña (*Spanish title*); **fausse donne** misdeal

don•né -née [dɔne] *adj* given; **étant donné que** whereas, since ‖ *f* datum; **données** data, facts

donner [dɔne] §96 *tr* to give; (cards) to deal ‖ *intr* to give; **donner sur** to open onto, look out on; **donner sur les doigts** to rap one's knuckles

don•neur [dɔnœr] **-neuse** [nøz] *mf* donor; **donneur universel** type-O blood donor ‖ *m* (cards) dealer

dont [dɔ̃] §79

donzelle [dɔ̃zɛl] *f* woman of easy virtue

doper [dɔpe] *tr* to dope

doping [dɔpiŋ] *m* dope, pep pill

dorade [dɔrad] *f* gilthead

dorénavant [dɔrenavɑ̃] *adv* henceforth

dorer [dɔre] *tr* to gild; (fig) to sugar-coat

d'ores [dɔr] see **ores**

dorlotement [dɔrlɔtmɑ̃] *m* coddling

dorloter [dɔrlɔte] *tr* to coddle

dor•mant [dɔrmɑ̃] **-mante** [mɑ̃t] *adj* stagnant, immovable ‖ *m* doorframe

dor•meur [dɔrmœr] **-meuse** [møz] *adj* sleeping ‖ *mf* sleeper ‖ *f* earring

dormir [dɔrmir] §23 *intr* to sleep; lie dormant; **à dormir debout** boring, dull; **dormir de-**

bout to sleep standing up; **dormir sur les deux oreilles** to feel secure

dors [dɔr] *v* (**dort**) see **dormir**

dortoir [dɔrtwar] *m* dormitory

dorure [dɔryr] *f* gilding; gilt; icing

dos [do] *m* back; bridge (*of nose*); **dans le dos de** behind the back of; **dos d'âne** (aut) speed bump; **en dos d'âne** saddle-backed, hog-backed; **se mettre qn à dos** to make an enemy of s.o.; **voir au dos** see other side

dosage [dozaʒ] *m* dosage

dose [doz] *f* dose; proportion, amount, share; (fig) tinge, suspicion; (slang) fix (*shot of a drug*)

doser [doze] *tr* to dose out, measure out, proportion

dossier [dosje] *m* chair back, back rest; dossier; case history; **dossier médical** medical records

dot [dɔt] *f* dowry

dotation [dɔtasjɔ̃] *f* endowment

doter [dɔte] *tr* to endow; dower; give a dowry to

douaire [dwɛr] *m* dower

douairière [dwɛrjɛr] *f* dowager

douane [dwan] *f* customs, duty; customhouse

doua·nier [dwanje] **-nière** [njɛr] *adj* customs ‖ *m* customs officer

doublage [dublaʒ] *m* doubling; metal plating of a ship; lining (*act of lining*); dubbing (*on tape or film*)

double [dubl] *adj & adv* double; **à double face** two-faced; **double page centrale** centerfold; **se garer en double fil** to double-park ‖ *m* double; duplicate, copy; **au double** twice; **double au carbone** carbon copy; **en double** in duplicate

doublement [dubləmɑ̃] *m* doubling ‖ *adv* doubly

doubler [duble] *tr* to double; parallel, run alongside; pass (*s.o., s.th. going in the same direction*); line (*a coat*); dub (*a film*); copy, dub (*a sound tape*); replace (*an actor*); gain one lap on (*another contestant*); (coll) to cheat ‖ *intr* to double; pass (*on highway*)

doublure [dublyr] *f* lining; (theat) understudy, replacement

douce-amère [dusamɛr] *f* (*pl* **douces-amères**) (bot) bittersweet

douceâtre [dusɑtr] *adj* sweetish; mawkish

doucement [dusmɑ̃] *adv* softly; slowly ‖ *interj* easy now!, just a minute!

douce·reux [dusrø] **-reuse** [røz] *adj* unpleasantly sweet, cloying; mealy-mouthed

douceur [dusœr] *f* sweetness; softness, gentleness; **douceurs** sweets

douche [duʃ] *f* shower bath; douche; (coll) dressing down; (coll) shock, disappointment

doucher [duʃe] *tr* to give a shower bath to; (coll) reprimand; (coll) to disappoint ‖ *ref* to take a shower bath

doucir [dusir] *tr* to polish, rub

doué douée [dwe] *adj* gifted, endowed

douer [dwe] *tr* to endow; **douer de** to endow or gift (*s.o.*) with

douille [duj] *f* cartridge case; sconce (*of candlestick*); bushing; (elec) socket

douil·let [dujɛ] **-lette** [jɛt] *adj* soft, delicate; oversensitive ‖ *f* child's padded coat

douleur [dulœr] *f* pain; sorrow; soreness

doulou·reux [dulurø] **-reuse** [røz] *adj* painful; sad; sore

doute [dut] *m* doubt; **sans doute** no doubt, surely

douter [dute] §97 *tr* to doubt, e.g., **je doute qu'il vienne** I doubt that he will come ‖ *intr* to doubt; **à n'en pas douter** beyond a doubt; **douter de** to doubt; distrust ‖ *ref*—**se douter de** to suspect; **se douter que** to suspect that

dou·teur [dutœr] **-teuse** [tøz] *adj* doubting ‖ *mf* doubter

dou·teux [dutø] **-teuse** [tøz] *adj* doubtful; dubious

Douvres [duvr] Dover

doux [du] **douce** [dus] *adj* sweet; soft; pleasing; suave; quiet; new (*wine*); fresh (*water*); gentle (*slope*); mild (*weather, climate*); **en douce** on the sly, on the q.t. ‖ **doux** *interj*—**tout doux!** easy there!

douzain [duzɛ̃] *m* twelve-line verse

douzaine [duzɛn] *f* dozen; **à la douzaine** by the dozen; **une douzaine de** a dozen

douze [duz] §94 *adj & pron* twelve; the Twelfth, e.g., **Jean douze** John the Twelfth ‖ *m* twelve; twelfth (*in dates*)

douzième [duzjɛm] §94 *adj, pron* (*masc, fem*), & *m* twelfth

doyen [dwajɛ̃] **doyenne** [dwajɛn] *mf* dean; **doyen d'âge** oldest member

doyenneté [dwajɛnte] *f* seniority

Dʳ *abbr* (**Docteur**) Dr.

drachme [drakm] *m* drachma; dram

dragage [dragaʒ] *m* dredging

dragée [draʒe] *f* sugar-coated almond; (pharm) pill; (coll) bitter pill; **tenir la dragée haute à qn** to make s.o. pay through the nose; be high-handed with s.o.

drageon [draʒɔ̃] *m* (bot) sucker

dragon [dragɔ̃] *m* dragon; dragoon; shrew; **dragon de vertu** prude

dragonne [dragɔn] *f* tassel, sword knot

drague [drag] *f* dredge; minesweeping apparatus

draguer [drage] *tr* to dredge, drag; sweep for mines ‖ *intr* to be on the make

dragueur [dragœr] *adj* minesweeping ‖ *m* dredger; **dragueur de mines** minesweeper

drain [drɛ̃] *m* drainpipe; (med) drain

drainage [drenaʒ] *m* drainage

drainer [drene] [drene] *tr* to drain

draisine [drezin] *f* (rr) handcar

dramatique [dramatik] *adj* dramatic

dramatiser [dramatize] *tr* to dramatize

dramaturge [dramatyrʒ] *mf* playwright

dramaturgie [dramatyrʒi] *f* dramatics

drame [dram] *m* drama; tragic event

drap [dra] *m* cloth; sheet; **drap à quatre points** fitted sheet; **être dans de beaux draps** to be in a pretty pickle

dra·peau [drapo] *m* (*pl* **-peaux**) flag; **au drapeau!** colors (*bugle call*)!; **drapeau parlementaire** flag of truce; **être sous les drapeaux** to be a serviceman

draper [drape] *tr* to drape ‖ *ref* to drape oneself

draperie [drapəri] *f* drapery; drygoods business; textile industry

dra·pier [drapje] **-pière** [pjɛr] *mf* draper; textile manufacturer

drastique [drastik] *adj* (med) drastic

drêche [drɛʃ] *f* draff, residue of malt

drège [drɛʒ] *f* dragnet

drelin [drəlɛ̃] *m* ting-a-ling

drépanocytose [drepanɔsitoz] *f* sickle-cell anemia

dressage [drɛsaʒ] *m* training (*of animals*); erection

dresser [drɛse] §96, §100 *tr* to raise, hold erect; train; put up, erect; set (*the table; a trap*); draw up, draft; plane, smooth; **dresser l'oreille** to prick up one's ears ‖ *ref* to stand up straight, sit up straight; **se dresser contre** to be dead set against

dressoir [drɛswar] *m* sideboard, buffet, dish closet

dribble [dribl] *m* (sports) dribble

dribbler [drible] *tr* & *intr* (sports) to dribble

drille [drij] *m*—**joyeux drille** gay blade ‖ *f* jeweler's drill brace; **drilles** rags (*for paper-making*)

drisse [dris] *f* halyard, rope

drogue [drɔg] *f* drug; chemical; nostrum, concoction; narcotic; (coll) trash, rubbish; **drogues miracles** miracle drugs

dro·gué -guée [drɔge] *adj* drugged; high ‖ *mf* drug addict; **drogué du travail** workaholic

droguer [drɔge] *tr* to drug or dope (*with too much medicine*) ‖ *intr* (coll) to cool one's heels ‖ *ref* to drug or dope oneself

droguerie [drɔgri] *f* drysaltery (Brit)

droguiste [drɔgist] *mf* drysalter (Brit)

droit [drwɑ], [drwa] **droite** [drwat], [drwat] *adj* right; honest, sincere; fair, just ‖ *m* law; right, justice; tax; right angle; **à bon droit** with reason; **de (plein) droit** rightfully, by rights, incontestably; **droit-à-la-vie** right-to-life; **droit coutumier** common law; **droit d'asile** right of asylum; **droit de cité** key to the city; acceptability; **droit d'entrée** admittance; **droits** duties, customs; rights; **droits civils** rights to manage property; **droits civiques** civil rights; **droits politiques** civil rights; **droits d'auteur** royalty; **droits de douane** customs duties; **droits de reproduction réservés** copyrighted; **tous droits réservés** all rights reserved, copyrighted ‖ *f* right, right-hand side; right hand; straight line; **à droite** to or on the right ‖ **droit** *adv*—**droit au but** straight to the point; **tout droit** straight ahead

droit-fil [drwafil] *m* direct tradition

droi·tier [drwatje], [drwatje] **-tière** [tjɛr] *adj* right-handed ‖ *mf* right-handed person; rightist

droiture [drwatyr], [drwatyr] *f* integrity

drolatique [drɔlatik] *adj* droll, comic

drôle [drol] *adj* droll, funny, strange, queer; **drôle de** funny, e.g., **une drôle d'idée** a funny idea; **drôle de guerre** phony war; **drôle d'homme, de corps, de pistolet,** or **de pierrot** (coll) queer duck ‖ *mf* (coll) queer duck, strange person; **drôle d'oiseau, drôle de numéro** kook

drôlerie [drolri] *f* drollery

drôlesse [drolɛs] *f* wench, hussy

dromadaire [drɔmadɛr] *m* dromedary

dronte [drɔ̃t] *m* (orn) dodo

droppage [drɔpaʒ] *m* airdrop

drosser [drɔse] *tr* to drive, carry (*as the wind drives a ship ashore*)

dru drue [dry] *adj* thick, dense; fine (*rain*) ‖ **dru** *adv* thickly, heavily

druide [drɥid] *m* druid

du [dy] §77

dû due [dy] *adj* & *m* due ‖ *v* see **devoir**

duc [dyk] *m* duke; horned owl

ducat [dyka] *m* ducat

duché [dyʃe] *m* duchy, dukedom

duchesse [dyʃɛs] *f* duchess

duègne [dɥɛɲ] *f* duenna

duel [dɥɛl] *m* duel; dual number; **duel oratoire** verbal battle

duelliste [ddɥelist] *m* duelist

dulcifier [dylsifje] *tr* to sweeten

dum-dum [dumdum] *adj invar*—**balle dum-dum** dumdum bullet

dûment [dymɑ̃] *adv* duly

dune [dyn] *f* dune

dunette [dynɛt] *f* (naut) poop

Dunkerque [dœ̃kɛrk] *f* Dunkirk

duo [dɥo] *m* duet; duo; **duo d'injures** exchange of words, insults

duodénum [dɥɔdenɔm] *m* duodenum

dupe [dyp] *f* dupe

duper [dype] *tr* to dupe

duperie [dypri] *f* deception, trickery

duplex [dyplɛks] *adj* two-way ‖ *m* duplex apartment

duplicata [dyplikata] *m* duplicate

duplicateur [dyplikatœr] *m* duplicating machine

duplication [dyplikasjɔ̃] *f* duplication

duplicité [dyplisite] *f* duplicity

duquel [dykɛl] §78

dur dure [dyr] *adj* hard; tough; difficult; **coucher sur la dure** to sleep on the bare ground or floor; **dur à la détente** tight-fisted; **dur d'oreille** hard of hearing; **élever un enfant à la dure** to give a child a strict upbringing ‖ *mf* (coll) tough customer ‖ *m* hard material, concrete ‖ **dur** *adv* hard, e.g., **travailler dur** to work hard

durable [dyrabl] *adj* durable

durant [dyrɑ̃] *prep* during; (sometimes stands after noun), e.g., **sa vie durant** during his life

durcir [dyrsir] *tr, intr & ref* to harden

durcissement [dyrsismɑ̃] *m* hardening

durée [dyre] *f* duration; wear

durer [dyre] *intr* to last, endure

dureté [dyrte] *f* hardness; cruelty

durillon [dyrijɔ̃] *m* callus, corn

duvet [dyvɛ] *m* down, fuzz; nap (*of cloth*)

duve•té -tée [dyvte] *adj* downy

duve•teux [dyvtø] **-teuse** [tøz] *adj* fuzzy

DVD [devede] *m invar* (letterword) (**disque numérique à usages variés**) DVD (digital versatile disk)

dynamique [dinamik] *adj* dynamic ‖ *f* dynamics

dynamiser [dinamize] *tr* (slang) to psych out

dynamite [dinamit] *f* dynamite

dynamiter [dinamite] *tr* to dynamite

dynamo [dinamo] *f* dynamo

dynaste [dinast] *m* dynast

dynastie [dinasti] *f* dynasty

dysenterie [disɑ̃tri] *f* dysentery

dysfonctionnement [disfɔ̃ksjɔnmɑ̃] *m* dysfunction

dyspepsie [dispɛpsi] *f* dyspepsia

E

E, e [ə], ***[ə] *m invar* fifth letter of the French alphabet

E.A.O. [eao] *m* (letterword) (**enseignement assisté par ordinateur**) CAI (*computer-assisted instruction*)

eau [o] *f* (*pl* **eaux**) water; wake (*of ship*); **à l'eau de rose** maudlin; **de la plus belle eau** of the first water; **eau calcaire** hard water; **eau de cale** bilge water; **eau de Javel** bleach; **eau dentifrice** mouthwash; **eau de Seltz** club soda; **eau dormante** still water; **eau douce** soft water; fresh water; **eau dure** hard water; **eau lourde** heavy water; **eau oxygénée** hydrogen peroxide; **eau vive** running water; **eaux** waters; waterworks; **eaux d'égouts** sewage; **eaux juvéniles** mineral waters; **eaux thermales** hot springs; **eaux usées, eaux résiduelles** polluted water; **eaux vives** swift current; **être en eau** to sweat; **faire de l'eau** to take in water; **faire eau** to leak; **grandes eaux** fountains; **nager entre deux eaux** to float under the surface; to play both sides of the street; **pêcher en eau trouble** to fish in troubled waters; **porter de l'eau à la rivière** or **à la mer** to carry coals to Newcastle; **tomber à l'eau** to fizzle out

eau-de-vie [odvi] *f* (*pl* **eaux-de-vie**) brandy; spirits

eau-forte [ofɔrt] *f* (*pl* **eaux-fortes**) aqua fortis; etching

éba•hi -hie [ebai] *adj* dumfounded

ébattre [ebatr] §7 *ref* to frolic, gambol, frisk about

ébauche [eboʃ] *f* rough sketch or draft; suspicion (*of a smile*)

ébaucher [eboʃe] *tr* to sketch, make a rough draft of

ébène [ebɛn] *f* ebony

ébénier [ebenje] *m* ebony (*tree*)

ébéniste [ebenist] *m* cabinetmaker

ébénisterie [ebenistri] *f* cabinetmaking

éberluer [ebɛrlɥe] *tr* to astonish

éblouir [ebluir] *tr* to dazzle, blind

éblouissement [ebluismɑ̃] *m* dazzle; glare; (pathol) dizziness

éboueur [ebwœr] *m* street cleaner, trash man; garbage collector

ébouillanter [ebujɑ̃te] *tr* to scald

éboulement [ebulmɑ̃] *m* cave-in, landslide

ébouler [ebule] *tr & ref* to cave in

ébourif•fant [eburifɑ̃] **-fante** [fɑ̃t] *adj* (coll) astounding

ébouriffer [eburife] *tr* to ruffle; (coll) to astound

ébouter [ebute] *tr* to cut off the end of

ébranchage [ebrɑ̃ʃaʒ] *m* pruning

ébrancher [ebrɑ̃ʃe] *tr* to prune

ébranlement [ebrɑ̃lmɑ̃] *m* shaking; shock

ébranler [ebrɑ̃le] *tr* to shake, jar ‖ *ref* to start out; be shaken

ébrécher [ebreʃe] §10 *tr* to nick, chip; make a dent in (*e.g., a fortune*) ‖ *ref* to be nicked, chipped; break off (*a tooth*)

ébriété [ebrijete] *f* inebriation

ébrouer [ebrue] *ref* to snort (*said of horse*); splash about; shake the water off oneself

ébruiter [ebrɥite] *tr* to noise about, blab ‖ *ref* to get around (*said of news*); leak out (*said of secret*)

ébullition [ebylisjɔ̃] *f* boiling; ebullience, ferment

ébur•né -née [ebyrne] *adj* ivory

écaille [ekɑj] *f* scale (*of fish, snake*); shell; tortoise shell

écail•ler [ekɑje] **-lère** [jɛr] *mf* oyster opener ‖ *m* oysterman ‖ *f* oysterwoman ‖ **écailler** *tr & ref* to scale

écale [ekal] *f* shell, husk, hull

écaler [ekale] *tr* to shell, husk, hull

écarlate [ekarlat] *adj & f* scarlet

écarquiller [ekarkije] *tr* (coll) to open wide, spread apart

écart [ekar] *m* swerve, side step; digression, flight (*of imagination*); difference, gap, spread; error, (*in range*); lapse (*in good conduct*); (cards) discard; **à l'écart** aside; aloof; **à l'écart de** far from; **faire le grand**

écart to do the splits; **faire un écart** to shy (*said of horse*) swerve (*said of car*); step aside (*said of person*)

écar·té -tée [ekarte] *adj* lonely, secluded; wide-apart

écartèlement [ekartɛlmɑ̃] *m* quartering

écarteler [ekartəle] §2 *tr* to quarter

écartement [ekartəmɑ̃] *m* removal, separation; spreading; space between; spark gap; gauge (*of rails*)

écarter [ekarte] *tr* to put aside; keep away; ward off; draw aside; spread; (cards) to discard ‖ *ref* to turn away; stray

ecchymose [ɛkimoz] *f* black-and-blue mark

ecclésiastique [eklezastik] *adj & m* ecclesiastic

écerve·lé -lée [esɛrvəle] *adj* scatterbrained ‖ *mf* scatterbrain

échafaud [eʃafo] *m* scaffold

échafaudage [eʃafodaʒ] *m* scaffolding

échafauder [eʃafode] *tr* to pile up; lay the ground work for ‖ *intr* to erect a scaffolding

échalasser [eʃalase] *tr* to stake

échalote [eʃalɔt] *f* shallot

échancrer [eʃɑ̃kre] *tr* to make a V-shaped cut in (*the neck of a dress*); cut (*a dress*) low in the neck; indent; to hollow out

échange [eʃɑ̃ʒ] *m* exchange

échanger [eʃɑ̃ʒe] §38 *tr* to exchange; **échanger pour** or **contre** to exchange (*s.th.*) for

échangeur [eʃɑ̃ʒœr] *m* interchange; **échangeur en trèfle** (aut) cloverleaf

échanson [eʃɑ̃sɔ̃] *m* cupbearer

échantillon [eʃɑ̃tijɔ̃] *m* sample; **comparer à l'échantillon** to spot-check

échantillonnage [eʃɑ̃tijɔnaʒ] *m* sampling; spot check

échantillonner [eʃɑ̃tijɔne] *tr* to cut samples of; spot-check; select (*a sampling to be polled*)

échappatoire [eʃapatwar] *f* loophole, way out

échap·pé -pée [eʃape] *mf* escapee ‖ *f* escape; short period; glimpse; (sports) spurt; **à l'échappée** stealthily

échappement [eʃapmɑ̃] *m* escape; leak; exhaust; escapement (*of watch*); **échappement libre** cutout

échapper [eʃape] *tr*—**l'échapper belle** to have a narrow escape ‖ *intr* to escape; **échapper à** to escape from; **échapper de** to slip out of ‖ *ref* to escape

écharde [eʃard] *f* splinter, sliver

écharpe [eʃarp] *f* scarf; sash; sling; **en écharpe** diagonally, crosswise; in a sling; across the shoulder

écharper [eʃarpe] *tr* to slash, cut up

échasse [eʃas] *f* stilt

échauder [eʃode] *tr* to scald; white-wash; gouge (*a customer*)

échauffement [eʃofmɑ̃] *m* heating; over-excitement

échauffer [eʃofe] *tr* to heat; warm; **échauffer les oreilles à qn** to get s.o.'s dander up ‖ *ref* to heat up; become excited

échauffourée [eʃofure] *f* skirmish; rash under-taking

éche [ɛʃ] *f* bait

échéance [eʃeɑ̃s] *f* due date, expiration; **à courte échéance** before long; **à longue échéance** in the long run

échec [eʃɛk] *m* check; chess piece, chessman; failure; **échec et mat** checkmate; **échecs** [eʃɛ] chess; chess set; **être échec** to be in check; **jouer aux échecs** to play chess; **voué à l'échec** doomed to failure

échelle [eʃɛl] *f* ladder; scale; **échelle coulisse** extension ladder; **échelle de sauvetage** fire escape; **échelle d'incendie** fire ladder; **échelle mobile** sliding scale; **échelle pliante** stepladder; **monter à l'échelle** (coll) to bite, be fooled

échelon [eʃlɔ̃] *m* echelon; rung (*of ladder*)

échelonner [eʃlɔne] *tr* to spread out, space out ‖ *ref* (aer) to stack

écheniller [eʃnije] *tr* to remove caterpillars from; exterminate (*pests*); eradicate (*corruption*)

éche·veau [eʃvo] *m* (*pl* **-veaux**) skein

écheve·lé -lée [eʃəvle] *adj* disheveled; wild (*dance, race*)

écheveler [eʃəvle] §34 *tr* to dishevel

échevin [eʃvɛ̃] *m* (hist) alderman

échine [eʃin] *f* spine, backbone; **avoir l'échine souple** (coll) to be a yes man

échiner [eʃine] *tr* to break the back of; beat, kill ‖ *ref* to tire oneself out

échiquier [eʃikje] *m* chessboard; exchequer

écho [eko] *m* echo; piece of gossip; **échos** gossip column; **faire écho** to echo

échoir [eʃwar] (usually used only in: *inf; ger* **échéant;** *pp* **échu;** 3d *sg: pres ind* **échoit;** *pret* **échut;** *fut* **échoira;** *cond* **échoirait**) *intr* (*aux:* AVOIR *or* ETRE) to fall, devolve; fall due

échoppe [eʃɔp] *f* burin; (com) stand, booth; workshop

échopper [eʃɔpe] *tr* to scoop out

échotier [ekɔrje] *m* gossip columnist, society editor

échouer [eʃwe] *tr* to ground, beach; **faire échouer** (coll) to spoil, queer ‖ *intr* to sink; run aground; fail ‖ *ref* to run aground

é·chu -chue [eʃy] *adj* due, payable

écimer [esime] *tr* to top

éclaboussement [eklabusmɑ̃] *m* splash

éclabousser [eklabuse] *tr* to splash

éclair [eklɛr] *adj* lightning (*e.g., speed*); flash (*bulb*) ‖ *m* flash (*of light, of lightning, of the eyes, of wit*); (culin) éclair; **éclairs** lightning; **éclairs de chaleur** heat lightning; **éclairs en nappe** sheet lightning; **il fait des éclairs** it is lightening; **passer comme un éclair** to flash by

éclairage [eklɛraʒ] *m* lighting; **sous cet éclairage** (fig) in this light

éclairagiste [eklɛraʒist] *mf* lighting engineer

éclaircle [eklɛrsi] *f* break, clearing; spell of good weather; glade

éclaircir [eklɛrsir] *tr* to lighten; clear up, solve; make thin ‖ *ref* to clear up; thin out

éclaircissement [eklɛrsismɑ̃] *m* explanation, clearing up

éclairement [eklɛrmɑ̃] *m* illumination

éclairer [eklɛre] *tr* to light; enlighten; **éclairer sa lanterne** (fig) to ring a bell for s.o. ‖ *intr* to light up, glitter; **il éclaire** it is lightening ‖ *ref* to be lighted

éclai·reur [eklɛrœr] **-reuse** [røz] *mf* scout ‖ *m* boy scout ‖ *f* girl scout

éclat [ekla] *m* splinter; ray (*of sunshine*); peal (*of thunder*); burst (*of laughter*); brightness, splendor

éclatement [eklatmɑ̃] *m* explosion; blowout (*of tire*); (fig) split

éclater [eklate] *intr* to splinter; sparkle, glitter; burst; break out; blow up, explode

éclateur [eklatœr] *m* spark gap (*of induction coil*)

éclectique [eklɛktik] *adj* eclectic

éclipse [eklips] *f* eclipse; **à éclipses** flashing, blinking

éclipser [eklipse] *tr* to eclipse ‖ *ref* to be eclipsed; (coll) to vanish; (coll) to sneak off

éclisse [eklis] *f* splinter; (med) splint; (rr) fishplate

éclisser [eklise] *tr* to splint

éclo·pé -pée [eklɔpe] *adj* lame ‖ *mf* cripple

éclore [eklɔr] §24 *intr* (*aux*: ÊTRE) to hatch; blossom out

éclosion [eklozjɔ̃] *f* hatching; blooming

écluse [eklyz] *f* lock (*of canal, river, etc.*); floodgate

écluser [eklyze] *tr* to close (*a canal*) by a lock; pass (*a boat*) through a lock

écœurer [ekœre] *tr* to sicken; dishearten

école [ekɔl] *f* school; **école à tir** artillery practice; **école d'application** model school; **école d'arts et métiers** trade school; **école dominicale, école du dimanche** Sunday School; **école libre** private school; **école maternelle** nursery school; **école mixte** co-educational school; **école privée** *or* **libre** private school; **être à bonne école** to be in good hands; **faire école** to set a fashion; to form a school (*to set up a doctrine, gain adherents*); **faire l'école buissonnière** (coll) to play hooky

éco·lier [ekɔlje] **-lière** [ljɛr] *adj* schoolboy ‖ *mf* pupil, scholar; novice ‖ *m* schoolboy ‖ *f* schoolgirl

écologie [ekɔlɔʒi] *f* ecology

écologique [ekɔlɔʒik] *adj* ecological

écologiste [ekɔlɔʒist] *mf* ecologist

éconduire [ekɔ̃dɥir] §19 *tr* to show out

économat [ekɔnɔma] *m* comptroller's office; commissary, company or co-op store; **économats** chain stores

économe [ekɔnɔm] *adj* economical ‖ *mf* treasurer; housekeeper ‖ *m* bursar

économie [ekɔnɔmi] *f* economy; **économie de l'offre** supply-side economics; **économie de marché** free enterprise; **économie domesti-**que home economics; **économie politique** economics; **économies** savings

économique [ekɔnɔmik] *adj* economic; economical ‖ *f* economics

économiser [ekɔnɔmize] *tr & intr* to economize, save

écope [ekɔp] *f* scoop (*for bailing*)

écoper [ekɔpe] *tr* to bail out ‖ *intr* (coll) to get a bawling out

écorce [ekɔrs] *f* bark (*of tree*); peel, peeling, rind; crust (*of earth*); **écorce de citron, écorce d'orange** lemon peel, orange peel

écorcer [ekɔrse] §51 *tr* to peel, strip off; to skin

écorcher [ekɔrʃe] *tr* to peel; chafe; fleece; overcharge; grate on (*the ears*); burn (*the throat*); murder (*a language*) ‖ *ref* to skin (*e.g., one's arm*)

écor·cheur [ekɔrʃœr] **-cheuse** [ʃøz] *mf* skinner; fleecer, swindler

écorchure [ekɔrʃyr] *f* scratch, abrasion

écorner [ekɔrne] *tr* to poll, break the horns of; dog-ear; to make a hole in (*e.g., a fortune*)

écornifler [ekɔrnifle] *tr* to cadge; **écornifler un dîner à qn** to bum a dinner off s.o.

écorni·fleur [ekɔrniflœr] **-fleuse** [fløz] *mf* sponger, moocher

écos·sais [ekɔse] **-saise** [sɛz] *adj* Scotch, Scottish ‖ *m* Scotch, Scottish (*language*); Scotch plaid ‖ (*cap*) *mf* Scot; **les Ecossais** the Scotch ‖ *m* Scotchman

Écosse [ekɔs] *f* Scotland; **l'Écosse** Scotland

écosser [ekɔse] *tr* to shell, hull, husk

écosystème [ekɔsistɛm] *m* ecosystem

écot [eko] *m* share; tree stump; **payer son écot** to pay one's share

écoulement [ekulmɑ̃] *m* flow; (com) sale, turnover; (pathol) discharge; **écoulement d'eau** drainage

écouler [ekule] *tr* to sell, dispose of ‖ *ref* to run (*said, e.g., of water*); flow; drain; leak; elapse, go by

écourter [ekurte] *tr* to shorten (*a dress, coat, etc.*); crop (*the tail, ears, etc.*); cut short, curtail

écoute [ekut] *f* listening post; monitoring; (naut) sheet; **écoute des appels** (electron) call screening; **écoutes** wild boar's ears; **être aux écoutes** to eavesdrop, keep one's ears to the ground; **se mettre à l'écoute** to listen to the radio

écouter [ekute] §95 *tr* to listen to; **écouter parler** to listen to (*s.o.*) speaking ‖ *intr* to listen; **écouter aux portes** to eavesdrop ‖ *ref* to coddle oneself; **s'écouter parler** to be pleased with the sound of one's own voice

écou·teur [ekutœr] **-teuse** [tøz] *mf* listener; **écouteur aux portes** eavesdropper ‖ *m* telephone receiver; earphone

écoutille [ekutij] *f* hatchway

écouvillon [ekuvijɔ̃] *m* swab, mop

écrabouiller [ekrabuje] *tr* (coll) to squash

écran [ekrɑ̃] *m* screen; (comp) monitor screen; (photo) filter; **écran de cheminée** fire screen;

écran de protection aérienne air umbrella; **écran de visualisation** (comp) desktop; **écran en fil de fer** window screen; **écran plat** (telv) flat screen; **le petit écran** television screen; **porter à l'écran** to put on the screen

écra·sant [ekrazɑ̃] **-sante** [zɑ̃t] *adj* crushing

écraser [ekraze] *tr* to crush; overwhelm; run over ‖ *ref* to be crushed; crash

écrémer [ekreme] §10 *tr* to skim; (fig) to skim the cream off

écrémeuse [ekremøz] *f* cream separator

écrevisse [ekrəvis] *f* crayfish

écrier [ekrije] *ref* to cry out, exclaim

écrin [ekrɛ̃] *m* jewel case

écrire [ekrir] §25, §97, §98 *tr* to write; spell ‖ *intr* to write ‖ *ref* to write to each other; be written; be spelled

é·crit [ekri] **-crite** [krit] *adj* written; **c'était écrit** it was fate ‖ *m* writing, written word; written examination; **écrits** writings, works; **par écrit** in writing

écri·teau [ekrito] *m* (*pl* **-teaux**) sign, placard

écritoire [ekritwar] *f* desk set

écriture [ekrityr] *f* handwriting; writing (*style of writing*); **écriture aérienne** skywriting; **écriture de chat** scrawl; **écritures** accounts; **Écritures** Scriptures; **écritures publiques** government documents

écrivailleur [ekrivajœr] *m* (coll) scribbler, hack writer

écrivain [ekrivɛ̃] *adj*—**femme écrivain** woman writer ‖ *m* writer; **écrivain public** public letter writer

écrivasser [ekrivase] *intr* (coll) to scribble

écrou [ekru] *m* nut (*with internal thread*); register (*on police blotter*); **écrou à oreille** thumb nut

écrouer [ekrue] *tr* to jail, book

écrouler [ekrule] *ref* to collapse; crumble; flop (*in a chair*)

é·cru -crue [ekry] *adj* raw; unbleached

écu [eky] *m* shield; crown (*money*); **écus** money

écrubier [ekrybje] *m* (naut) hawsehole

écueil [ekœj] *m* reef, sandbank; stumbling block

écuelle [ekɥɛl] *f* bowl

éculer [ekyle] *tr* to wear down at the heel

écu·mant [ekymɑ̃] **-mante** [mɑ̃t] *adj* foaming; fuming (*with rage*)

écume [ekym] *f* foam; froth; lather; dross; scum (*on liquids; on metal; of society*); **écume de mer** meerschaum

écumer [ekyme] *tr* to skim, scum; pick up (*e.g., gossip*); scour (*the seas*) ‖ *intr* to foam; scum; fume (*with anger*)

écu·meur [ekymœr] **-meuse** [møz] *mf* drifter; **écumeur de marmite** hanger-on; **écumeur de mer** pirate

écu·meux [ekymø] **-meuse** [møz] *adj* foamy, frothy

écumoire [ekymwar] *f* skimmer

écurage [ekyraʒ] *m* scouring; cleaning out

écurer [ekyre] *tr* to scour; clean out

écureuil [ekyrœj] *m* squirrel

écurie [ekyri] *f* stable (*for horses, mules, etc.*); string of horses

écusson [ekysɔ̃] *m* escutcheon; bud (*for grafting*); (mil) identification tag

écuyer [ekɥije] **écuyère** [ekɥijɛr] *mf* horseback rider ‖ *m* horseman; squire; riding master ‖ *f* horsewoman

eczéma [ɛkzema], [ɛgzema] *m* eczema

edelweiss [edəlvajs], [edɛlvɛs] *m* edelweiss

éden [edɛn] *m* Eden ‖ (*cap*) *m* Garden of Eden

éden·té -tée [edɑ̃te] *adj* toothless

E.D.F. *abbr* (**Électricité de France**) French national electric company

édicter [edikte] *tr* to decree, promulgate

édicule [edikyl] *m* kiosk; street urinal

édi·fiant [edifjɑ̃] **-fiante** [fjɑ̃t] *adj* edifying

édification [edifikasjɔ̃] *f* edification; construction, building

édifice [edifis] *m* edifice, building

édifier [edifje] *tr* to edify; inform, enlighten; construct, build; found

édit [edi] *m* edict

éditer [edite] *tr* to publish; edit (*a manuscript*)

édi·teur [editœr] **-trice** [tris] *mf* publisher; editor (*of a manuscript*)

édition [edisjɔ̃] *f* edition; publishing; **édition à tirage limité** limited edition; **édition électronique** desktop publishing

edito·rial -riale [editɔrjal] *adj & m* (*pl* **-riaux** [rjo]) editorial

édredon [edrədɔ̃] *m* eiderdown

éduca·teur [edykatœr] **-trice** [tris] *adj* educational ‖ *mf* educator

éduca·tif [edykatif] **-tive** [tiv] *adj* educational

éducation [edykasjɔ̃] *f* education, bringing-up; nurture; **éducation physique et sportive** physical education; **éducation sexuelle** sex education; **éducation spéciale, éducation pour des étudiants handicapés** special education

édulco·rant [edylkɔrɑ̃] **-rante** [rɑ̃t] *adj* sweetening ‖ *m* sweetener

éduquer [edyke] *tr* to bring up (*children*); educate, train

éfaufiler [efofile] *tr* to unravel

effacement [efasmɑ̃] *m* effacement, erasing; self-effacement

effacer [efase] §51 *tr* to efface; erase ‖ *ref* to efface oneself; stand aside

effarement [efarmɑ̃] *m* fright, scare

effaroucher [efaruʃe] *tr* to frighten, scare off

effec·tif [efɛktif] **-tive** [tiv] *adj* actual, real ‖ *m* personnel, manpower; strength (*of military unit*); complement (*of ship*); size (*of class*)

effectivement [efɛktivmɑ̃] *adv* actually, really, sure enough, indeed

effectuer [efɛktɥe] *tr* to make, effect, perform, execute ‖ *ref* to be made; take place, go off

effémi·né -née [efemine] *adj* effeminate

efféminer [efemine] *tr* to make a sissy of; unman ‖ *ref* to become effeminate

effervescence [efɛrvesɑ̃s] *f* effervescence; excitement, ferment

efferves•cent [efɛrvesɑ̃] **-cente** [sɑ̃t] *adj* effervescent

effet [efɛ] *m* effect; (billiards) english; **à cet effet** for that purpose; **en effet** indeed, actually, sure enough; **effet de commerce** bill of exchange; **effet de serre** greenhouse effect; **effets publics** government bonds; **faire de l'effet** to be striking; **faire l'effet de** to give the impression of

effeuillage [efœjaʒ] *m* thinning of leaves; striptease

effeuillaison [efœjɛzɔ̃] *f* fall of leaves

effeuiller [efœje] *tr* to thin out the leaves of, pluck off the petals of ‖ *ref* to shed its leaves

effeuilleuse [efœjøz] *f* (coll) stripteaser

efficace [efikas] *adj* effective

efficacement [efikasmɑ̃] *adv* effectively

efficacité [efikasite] *f* efficacy, efficiency

efficience [efisjɑ̃s] *f* efficiency

effi•cient [efisjɑ̃] **-ciente** [sjɑ̃t] *adj* efficient

effigie [efiʒi] *f* effigy

effiler [efile] *tr* to unravel; taper

effilocher [efilɔʃe] *tr* to unravel

efflan•qué -quée [eflɑ̃ke] *adj* skinny

effleurer [eflœre] *tr* to graze; touch on

effluve [eflyv] *m* effluvium, emanation

effondrement [efɔ̃drəmɑ̃] *m* collapse; (pathol) breakdown

effondrer [efɔ̃dre] *tr* to break open; break (*ground*) ‖ *ref* to collapse, cave in; sink

efforcer [efɔrse] **§51, §96, §97** *ref*—**s'efforcer à** or **de** to try hard to, strive to

effort [efɔr] *m* effort; (med) hernia, rupture; **effort de rupture** breaking stress; **effort de tension** torque; **faire effort sur soi-même** to get a hold of oneself

effraction [efraksjɔ̃] *f* housebreaking, break-in, breaking and entering

effraie [efrɛ] *f* screech owl

effranger [efrɑ̃ʒe] **§38** *tr & ref* to fray

ef•frayant [efrɛjɑ̃] **-frayante** [frɛjɑ̃t] *adj* frightful, dreadful

effrayer [efrɛje] **§49** *tr* to frighten ‖ **§97** *ref* to be frightened

effré•né -née [efrene] *adj* unbridled

effritement [efritmɑ̃] *m* crumbling

effriter [efrite] *tr & ref* to crumble

effroi [efrwa] *m* fright

effron•té -tée [efrɔ̃te] *adj* impudent; shameless; (slang) saucy, sassy

effronterie [efrɔ̃tri] *f* effrontery

effroyable [efrwajabl] *adj* frightful

effusion [efyzjɔ̃] *f* effusion; shedding (*of blood*); (fig) gushing

égailler [egɑje] *ref* to scatter

é•gal -gale [egal] (*pl* **-gaux** [go]) *adj* equal; level; (coll) indifferent; **ça m'est égal** (coll) it's all the same to me, it's all right ‖ *mf* equal; **à l'égal de** as much as, no less than

également [egalmɑ̃] *adv* equally, likewise, also

égaler [egale] *tr* to equal, match

égaliser [egalize] *tr* to equalize; equate

égalitaire [egalitɛr] *adj & mf* equalitarian

égalité [egalite] *f* equality; evenness; **égalité des chances** equality of opportunity; **être à égalité** to be tied, neck and neck

égard [egar] *m* respect; **à l'égard de** with regard to; **à tous (les) égards** in all respects; **eu égard à** in consideration of

éga•ré -rée [egare] *adj* stray, lost

égarement [egarmɑ̃] *m* wandering (*of mind, senses, etc.*); frenzy (*of sorrow, anger, etc.*)

égarer [egare] *tr* to mislead; misplace; bewilder ‖ *ref* to get lost, stray; be on the wrong track

égayer [egeje] **§49, §96** *tr & ref* to cheer up; brighten

égide [eʒid] *f* aegis

églefin [egləfɛ̃] *m* haddock

église [egliz] *f* church

églogue [eglɔg] *f* eclogue

égoïne [egɔin] *f* handsaw

égoïsme [egɔism] *m* egoism

égoïste [egɔist] *adj* selfish ‖ *mf* egoist

égorgement [egɔrʒəmɑ̃] *m* slaughter

égorger [egɔrʒe] **§38** *tr* to cut the throat of; (coll) to overcharge

égosiller [egozije] *ref* to shout oneself hoarse

égotisme [egɔtism] *m* egotism

égotiste [egɔtist] *adj* egotistical ‖ *mf* egotist

égout [egu] *m* drainage; sewer; sink, cesspool (*e.g., of iniquity*)

égoutier [egutje] *m* sewer worker

égoutter [egute] *tr* to drain; let drip ‖ *ref* to drip

égouttoir [egutwar] *m* drainboard

égrapper [egrape] *tr* to pick off from the cluster

égratigner [egratiɲe] *tr* to scratch; take a dig at, to tease

égratignure [egratiɲyr] *f* scratch; gibe, dig

égrener [egrəne] **§2** *tr* to shell (*e.g., peas*); gin (*cotton*); pick off (*grapes*); unstring (*pearls*); tell (*beads*) ‖ *ref* to drop one by one; be strung out

égril•lard [egrijar] **-larde** [jard] *adj* spicy, lewd ‖ *mf* shameless, unblushing person

égrugeoir [egryʒwar] *m* mortar (*for pounding or grinding*)

égruger [egryʒe] **§38** *tr* to pound (*in a mortar*)

égueuler [egœle] *tr* to break the neck of (*e.g., a bottle*)

Égypte [eʒipt] *f* Egypt; **l'Égypte** Egypt

égyp•tien [eʒipsjɛ̃] **-tienne** [sjɛn] *adj* Egyptian ‖ (*cap*) *mf* Egyptian

eh [e] *interj* well!; **en bien!** well, well!; very well!

éhon•té -tée [eɔ̃te] *adj* shameless

eider [ɛjdɛr] *m* eider duck

éjaculation [eʒakylɑsjɔ̃] *f* ejaculation; (eccl) short, fervent prayer

éjaculer [eʒakyle] *tr & intr* to ejaculate

éjecter [eʒɛkte] *tr* to eject; (coll) to oust

éjection [eʒɛksjɔ̃] *f* ejection

élabo•ré -rée [elabɔre] *adj* elaborated; prepared, elaborate

élaborer [elabɔre] *tr* to elaborate; work out, develop

élaguer [elage] *tr* to prune

élan [elɑ̃] *m* dash; impulse, outburst; spirit, glow; (zool) elk, moose; **avec élan** with enthusiasm

élan•cé -cée [elɑ̃se] *adj* slender, slim

élancement [elɑ̃smɑ̃] *m* throbbing, twinge; yearning (*e.g., for God*)

élancer [elɑ̃se] **§51** *intr* to throb, twinge ‖ *ref* to rush, spring, dash; spurt out

élargir [elarʒir] *tr* to widen; broaden; release (*a prisoner*) ‖ *ref* to widen; become more lax

élasticité [elastisite] *f* elasticity

élastique [elastik] *adj* elastic ‖ *m* elastic; rubber band

élec•teur [elɛktœr] **-trice** [tris] *adj* voting ‖ *mf* voter, constituent; (hist) elector; **électeurs** electorate

élec•tif [elɛktif] **-tive** [tiv] *adj* elective

élection [elɛksjɔ̃] *f* election; choice; **élection blanche** election without a valid result

électorat [elɛktɔra] *m* right to vote; (hist) electorate

électri•cien [elɛktrisjɛ̃] **-cienne** [sjɛn] *adj* electrical (*worker*) ‖ *mf* electrician

électricité [elɛktrisite] *f* electricity

électrifier [elɛktrifje] *tr* to electrify

électrique [elɛktrik] *adj* electric(al)

électriser [elɛktrize] *tr* to electrify

électro [elɛktro] *m* electromagnet

électro-aimant [elɛktrɔɛmɑ̃] *m* (*pl* **-aimants**) electromagnet

électrocardiogramme [elɛktrokardjɔgram] *m* electrocardiogram

électrochoc [elɛktrɔʃɔk] *m* (med) electric shock treatment

électro-culinaire [elɛktrɔkyⅼinɛr] *adj* electric kitchen (*appliances*)

électrocuter [elɛktrɔkyte] *tr* to electrocute

électrode [elɛktrɔd] *f* electrode

électrodomestique [elɛktrɔdɔmɛstik] *adj* & *m* electric appliance

électrolyse [elɛktrɔliz] *f* electrolysis

électrolyte [elɛktrɔlit] *m* electrolyte

électromagnétique [elɛktrɔmaɲetik] *adj* electromagnetic

électroména•ger [elɛktrɔmenaʒe] **-gère** [ʒɛr] *adj* household-electric

électromo•teur [elɛktrɔmɔtœr] **-trice** [tris] *adj* electromotive ‖ *m* electric motor

électron [elɛktrɔ̃] *m* electron

électronique [elɛktrɔnik] *adj* electronic ‖ *f* electronics

électron-volt [elɛktrɔ̃vɔlt] *m* (*pl* **électrons-volts**) electron-volt

électrophone [elɛktrɔfɔn] *m* electric phonograph

électrostatique [elɛktrɔstatik] *adj* electrostatic ‖ *f* electrostatics

électrotype [elɛktrɔtip] *m* electrotype

électrotyper [elɛktrɔtipe] *tr* to electrotype

élégamment [elegamɑ̃] *adv* elegantly

élégance [elegɑ̃s] *f* elegance

élé•gant [elegɑ̃] **-gante** [gɑ̃t] *adj* elegant

élégiaque [eleʒjak] *adj* elegiac ‖ *mf* elegist

élégie [eleʒi] *f* elegy

élément [elemɑ̃] *m* element; (*of an electric battery*) cell, element; (elec, mach) unit; **élément standard** standard part

élémentaire [elemɑ̃tɛr] *adj* elementary

éléphant [elefɑ̃] *m* elephant

éléphantesque [elefɑ̃tɛsk] *adj* (coll) gigantic, elephantine

élevage [elvaʒ], [ɛlvaʒ] *m* rearing, raising, breeding; **élevage des bovins** cattle raising

éléva•teur [elevatœr] **-trice** [tris] *adj* lifting ‖ *m* elevator; hoist

élévation [elevɑsjɔ̃] *f* elevation; promotion; increase; (rok) lift-off

élève [elɛv] *mf* pupil, student; **ancien élève** alumnus; **élève externe** day student; **élève interne** boarding student ‖ *f* breeder (*animal*); (hort) seedling

éle•vé -vée [elve] *adj* high, elevated; lofty, noble; **bien élevé** well-bred; **mal élevé** ill-bred

élever [elve] **§2** *tr* to raise; raise, bring up, nurture; erect ‖ *ref* to rise; arise; be built, stand

éle•veur [elvœr] **-veuse** [vøz] *mf* breeder, rancher

elfe [ɛlf] *m* elf

élider [elide] *tr* to elide

éligible [eliʒibl] *adj* eligible

élimer [elime] *tr* & *ref* to wear threadbare

éliminatoire [eliminatwar] *adj* (sports) preliminary ‖ *f* (sports) preliminaries

éliminer [elimine] *tr* to eliminate

élire [elir] **§36** *tr* to elect

élision [elizjɔ̃] *f* elision

élite [elit] *f* elite

elle [ɛl] *pron disj* **§85** her ‖ *pron conj* **§87** she

elle-même [ɛlmɛm] **§86** herself, itself

elles [ɛl] *pron disj* **§85** them ‖ *pron conj* **§87** they

ellipse [elips] *f* (gram) ellipsis; (math) ellipse

elliptique [eliptik] *adj* elliptic(al)

élocution [elɔkysjɔ̃] *f* elocution; choice and arrangement of words

éloge [elɔʒ] *m* eulogy; praise

élo•gieux [elɔʒjø] **-gieuse** [ʒjøz] *adj* full of praise

éloi•gné -gnée [elwaɲe] *adj* distant

éloignement [elwaɲəmɑ̃] *m* remoteness; aversion; postponement

éloigner [elwaɲe] *tr* to move away; remove; drive away; postpone ‖ *ref* to move away; digress, deviate; become estranged

élongation [elɔ̃gɑsjɔ̃] *f* stretching

élonger [elɔ̃ʒe] **§38** *tr* to lay (*e.g., a cable*); **élonger la terre** to skirt the coast

éloquence [elɔkɑ̃s] *f* eloquence

élo•quent [elɔkɑ̃] **-quente** [kɑ̃t] *adj* eloquent

é•lu -lue [ely] *adj* elected ‖ *mf* chosen one; **les élus** the elect ‖ *v* see **élire**

élucider [elyside] *tr* to elucidate

éluder [elyde] *tr* to elude, avoid

éma•cié -ciée [emasje] *adj* emaciated

émacier [emasje] *ref* to become emaciated

é•mail [emaj] *m* (*pl* **-maux** [mo]) enamel ‖ *m* (*pl* **-mails**) nail polish; car or bicycle paint

e-mail [imɛl] *m* (*pl* **e-mails**) (comp) E-mail

émaillage [emajaʒ] *m* enameling

émailler [emaje] *tr* to enamel; sprinkle (*e.g., with quotations, metaphors, etc.*); dot (*e.g., the fields, as flowers do*)

émanation [emanɑsjɔ̃] *f* emanation; manifestation (*e.g., of authority*)

émanciper [emɑ̃sipe] *tr* to emancipate ‖ *ref* to be emancipated; (coll) to get out of hand

émaner [emane] *intr* to emanate

émarger [emarʒe] §38 *tr* to trim (*e.g., a book*); initial (*a document*) ‖ *intr* to get paid; **émarger à** to be paid from

émasculer [emaskyle] *tr* to emasculate

embâcle [ɑ̃bɑkl] *m* pack ice, ice floe

emballage [ɑ̃balaʒ] *m* packing, wrapping; **emballage consigné** returnable bottle; **emballage perdu** nonreturnable bottle

emballer [ɑ̃bale] *tr* to wrap up, pack; race (*a motor*); (coll) to thrill; (coll) to bawl out; **emballer sous vide** to vacuum-pack ‖ *ref* to bolt, run away; (mach) to race; (coll) to get worked up

embal·leur [ɑ̃balœr] **-leuse** [løz] *mf* packer

embarbouiller [ɑ̃barbuje] *tr* to besmear; (coll) to muddle, confuse ‖ *ref* (coll) to get tangled up

embarcadère [ɑ̃barkadɛr] *m* wharf; (rr) platform

embarcation [ɑ̃barkɑsjɔ̃] *f* small boat

embardée [ɑ̃barde] *f* lurch; (aut) swerve; (aer, naut) yaw

embarder [ɑ̃barde] *intr* (aut) to swerve; (aer, naut) to yaw

embargo [ɑ̃bargo] *m* embargo

embarquement [ɑ̃barkəmɑ̃] *m* embarkation; shipping; loading

embarquer [ɑ̃barke] *tr* to embark; ship (*a sea*); load (*in car, plane, etc.*); (coll) to put in the clink ‖ *ref* to embark; board; get into a car

embarras [ɑ̃bara] *m* embarrassment; trouble, inconvenience; encumbrance, obstruction; perplexity; financial difficulties; **embarras de voitures** traffic jam; **embarras du choix** too much to choose from; **faire des embarras** (coll) to put on airs

embarras·sé -sée [ɑ̃barase] *adj* embarrassed; awkward, ill-at-ease; confused, muddled; upset (*stomach*)

embarrasser [ɑ̃barase] *tr* to embarrass; hamper, obstruct; stump, perplex ‖ *ref*—**s'embarrasser de** to take an interest in; bother with

embaucher [ɑ̃boʃe] *tr* to hire, sign on; (coll) to entice (*soldiers*) to desert ‖ *intr* to hire; **on n'embauche pas** (*public sign*) no help wanted

embauchoir [ɑ̃boʃwar] *m* shoetree

embaumement [ɑ̃bomǝmɑ̃] *m* embalming; perfuming

embaumer [ɑ̃bome] *tr* to embalm; perfume ‖ *intr* to smell good

embaumeur [ɑ̃bomœr] *m* embalmer

embellir [ɑ̃bɛlir] *tr* to embellish ‖ *intr* to clear up (*said of weather*); improve in looks ‖ *ref* to grow more beautiful

embellissement [ɑ̃bɛlismɑ̃] *m* embellishment

embêtement [ɑ̃bɛtmɑ̃] *m* (coll) annoyance

embêter [ɑ̃bɛte], [ɑ̃bete] *tr* (coll) to annoy

emblave [ɑ̃blav] *f* grainfield

emblaver [ɑ̃blave] *tr* to sow

emblée [ɑ̃ble]—**d'emblée** then and there, right off; without difficulty

emblématique [ɑ̃blematik] *adj* emblematic(al)

emblème [ɑ̃blɛm] *m* emblem

embobeliner [ɑ̃bɔbline] *tr* (coll) to bamboozle

embobiner [ɑ̃bɔbine] *tr* to wind up (*e.g., on a reel*); (coll) to bamboozle

emboîter [ɑ̃bwate] *tr* to encase; nest (*boxes, boats, etc.*); (mach) to interlock, joint; **emboîter le pas** to fall into step

embolie [ɑ̃bɔli] *f* (pathol) embolism

embonpoint [ɑ̃bɔ̃pwɛ̃] *m* portliness; **prendre de l'embonpoint** to put on flesh

embouche [ɑ̃buʃ] *f* pasture

embou·ché -chée [ɑ̃buʃe] *adj*—**mal embouché** foul-mouthed

emboucher [ɑ̃buʃe] *tr* to blow, sound

embouchoir [ɑ̃buʃwar] *m* mouthpiece

embouchure [ɑ̃buʃyr] *f* mouth (*of a river*); mouthpiece

embourber [ɑ̃burbe] *tr* to stick in the mud; vilify, implicate

embout [ɑ̃bu] *m* tip, ferrule; rubber tip (*for chair*)

embouteillage [ɑ̃butɛjaʒ] *m* bottling; bottleneck, traffic jam

emboutir [ɑ̃butir] *tr* to stamp, emboss; smash (*e.g., a fender*) ‖ *ref* to bump

embranchement [ɑ̃brɑ̃/mɑ̃] *m* branching (off); branch; branch line; junction (*of roads, track, etc.*); **embranchement particulier** private siding

embrasement [ɑ̃brazmɑ̃] *m* conflagration; illumination, glow

embraser [ɑ̃braze] *tr* to set aflame or aglow ‖ *ref* to flame up; glow

embrassade [ɑ̃brasad] *f* embrace; kissing

embrasse [ɑ̃bras] *f* curtain tieback

embrassement [ɑ̃brasmɑ̃] *m* embrace

embrasser [ɑ̃brase] *tr* to embrace; kiss; join; undertake; take in (*at a glance*); take (*the opportunity*) ‖ *ref* to embrace; neck

embras·seur [ɑ̃brasœr] **-seuse** [søz] *mf* smoocher

embrasure [ɑ̃brazyr] *f* embrasure, loop-hole; opening (*for door or window*)

embrayage [ɑ̃brɛjaʒ] *m* coupling engagement; (aut) clutch

embrayer [ɑ̃brɛje], [ɑ̃breje] §49 *tr* to engage, connect; throw into gear ‖ *intr* to throw the clutch in

embrocher [ɑ̃brɔ/e] *tr* to put on a spit

embrouillage [ɑ̃brujaz] *m* (electron) scrambling

embrouiller [ɑ̃bruje] *tr* to embroil ‖ *ref* to become embroiled

embroussail·lé -lée [ãbrusaje] *adj* bushy; tangled; complicated, complex

embru·mé -mée [ãbryme] *adj* foggy, misty

embruns [ãbrœ̃] *mpl* spray

embryologie [ãbrijɔlɔʒi] *f* embryology

embryon [ãbrijɔ̃] *m* embryo

embryonnaire [ãbrijɔnɛr] *adj* embryonic

em·bu -bue [ãby] *adj* lifeless, dull ‖ *m* dull tone (*of a painting*)

embûche [ãbyʃ] *f* snare, trap

embuer [ãbɥe] *tr* to cloud with steam; **embué de larmes** dimmed with tears

embuscade [ãbyskad] *f* ambush

embus·qué -quée [ãbyske] *adj* in ambush; **se tenir embusqué** to lie in ambush ‖ *m* (mil) goldbricker, shirker

embusquer [ãbyske] *tr* to ambush, trap ‖ *ref* to lie in ambush; (mil) to get a safe assignment

émé·ché -chée [emeʃe] *adj* (coll) tipsy, high

émender [emãde] *tr* to amend (*a sentence, decree, etc.*)

émeraude [ɛmrod] *f* emerald

émergence [emɛrʒãs] *f* emergence

émerger [emɛrʒe] §38 *intr* to emerge

émeri [ɛmri] *m* emery

émerillon [ɛmrijɔ̃] *m* swivel; (orn) merlin

émerillon·né -née [ɛmrijɔne] *adj* lively, gay

émérite [emerit] *adj* experienced; distinguished, eminent; (*titre*) emeritus; (coll) confirmed (*smoker*); **professeur émérite** emeritus professor, professor emeritus

émersion [emɛrsjɔ̃] *f* emersion

émerveillement [emɛrvɛjmã] *m* wonderment

émerveiller [emɛrvɛje] *tr* to astonish, amaze

émétique [emetik] *adj* & *m* emetic

émet·teur [emetœr] **-trice** [tris] *adj* issuing; transmitting ‖ *mf* maker (*of check, draft*); issuer ‖ *m* broadcasting station; (rad) transmitter

émetteur-récepteur [emɛtœrresɛptœr] *m* (*pl* **émetteurs-récepteurs**) (rad) walkie-talkie

émettre [emɛtr] §42 *tr* to emit; express (*an opinion*); issue (*stamps, bank notes, etc.*); transmit (*a radio signal*) ‖ *intr* to transmit, broadcast

é·meu [emø] *m* (*pl* **-neus**) (zool) emu

émeute [emøt] *f* riot

émeutier [emøtje] *m* rioter

émietter [emjɛte] *tr* to crumble; break up (*an estate*)

émi·grant [emigrã] **-grante** [grãt] *adj* & *mf* emigrant; migrant

émi·gré -grée [emigre] *adj* emigrating ‖ *mf* emigrant; émigré

émigrer [emigre] *intr* to emigrate; migrate

émincer [emɛ̃se] §51 *tr* to cut in thin slices

éminemment [eminamã] *adv* eminently

éminence [eminãs] *f* eminence

émi·nent [eminã] **-nente** [nãt] *adj* eminent

émissaire [emisɛr] *m* emissary; outlet (*of lake, basin, etc.*)

émission [emisjɔ̃] *f* emission; utterance; issue

(*of stamps, bank notes, etc.*) (rad) transmission, broadcast

emmagasiner [ãmagazine] *tr* to put in storage; store up; stockpile

emmailloter [ãmajɔte] *tr* to swathe; bandage

emmancher [ãmãʃe] *tr* to put a handle on ‖ *ref* (coll) to begin; **s'emmancher bien** (coll) to get off to a good start; **s'emmancher mal** (coll) to get off to a bad start

emmêler [ãmɛle], [ãmele] *tr* to tangle up; mix up

emménagement [ãmenaʒmã] *m* moving in; installation

emménager [ãmenaʒe] §38 *tr* & *intr* to move in

emmener [ãmne] §2 *tr* to take or lead away; take out (*e.g., to dinner*); take (*on a visit*)

emmenthal [ãmɛtal], [emɛ̃tal] *m* Swiss cheese

emmer·dant [ãmɛrdã] **-dante** [dãt] *adj* (slang) damned annoying, damned boring

emmerder [ãmɛrde] *tr* (slang) to annoy, bore, bug ‖ *ref* (slang) to be pissed off; (slang) to be bored stiff

emmiel·lé -lée [ãmjɛle], [ãmjele] *adj* honeyed (*e.g., words*)

emmitoufler [ãmitufle] *tr* & *ref* to bundle up (*in warm clothing*)

emmurer [ãmyre] *tr* to wall in, immure

émoi [emwa] *m* agitation, alarm

émolument [emɔlymã] *m* share; **émoluments** emolument, fee, salary

émonder [emɔ̃de] *tr* to prune, trim

émo·tif [emɔtif] **-tive** [tiv] *adj* emotional ‖ *mf* emotional person

émotion [emɔsjɔ̃] *f* emotion; commotion

émotionnable [emɔsjɔnabl] *adj* emotional

émotion·nant [emɔsjɔnã] **-nante** [nãt] *adj* stirring, moving

émotionner [emɔsjɔne] *tr* to move deeply, thrill, affect ‖ *ref* to get excited, flustered

émoucher [emuʃe] *tr* to chase flies away from

émouchet [emuʃɛ] *m* sparrow hawk

émouchoir [emuʃwar] *m* whisk, fly swatter

émoudre [emudr] §43 *tr* to grind, sharpen

émoulage [emulaʒ] *m* grinding, sharpening

émou·lu -lue [emuly] *adj*—**frais émoulu de** (fig) fresh from, just back from

émous·sé -sée [emuse] *adj* blunt

émousser [emuse] *tr* to dull, blunt

émoustiller [emustije] *tr* (coll) to exhilarate, rouse; tantalize

émou·vant [emuvã] **-vante** [vãt] *adj* moving, touching, stirring

émouvoir [emuvwar] §45 (*pp* **ému**) *tr* to move; excite ‖ *ref* to be moved; be excited

empailler [ãpaje] *tr* to stuff (*animals*); cane (*a chair*)

empail·leur [ãpajœr] **-leuse** [jøz] *mf* taxidermist; caner

empaler [ãpale] *tr* to impale

empan [ãpã] *m* span (*of hand*)

empanacher [ãpanaʃe] *tr* to plume

empaquetage [ãpaktaʒ] *m* packaging; package

empaqueter [ɑ̃pakte] §34 *tr* to package

emparer [ɑ̃pare] *ref*—**s'emparer de** to seize, take hold of

empâter [ɑ̃pɑte] *tr* to make sticky; fatten up (*chickens, turkeys, etc.*); coat (*the tongue*); (typ) to overlink ‖ *ref* to put on weight; become coated (*said of tongue*); become husky (*said of voice*)

empathie [ɛ̃pati] *f* empathy

empattement [ɑ̃patmɑ̃] *m* foundation, footing; (aut) wheelbase

empaumer [ɑ̃pome] *tr* to catch in the hand; hit with a racket; palm (*a card*); (coll) to hoodwink

empêchement [ɑ̃pɛʃmɑ̃] *m* impediment, bar; hindrance, obstacle

empêcher [ɑ̃pɛʃe] §97, §99 *tr* to hinder; **empêcher qn de** + *inf* to prevent or keep s.o. from + *ger*; **n'empêche que** all the same, e.g., **n'empêche qu'il est très poli** he's very polite all the same ‖ §97 *ref*—**ne pouvoir s'empêcher de** + *inf* not to be able to help + *ger*, e.g., **je n'ai pu m'empêcher de rire** I could not help laughing

empê•cheur [ɑ̃pɛʃœr] **-cheuse** [ʃøz] *mf*—**empêcheur de danser en rond** (coll) wet blanket

empeigne [ɑ̃pɛɲ] *f* upper (*of shoe*)

empennage [ɑ̃penaʒ] *m* feathers (*of arrow*); fins, vanes; (aer) empennage

empereur [ɑ̃prœr] *m* emperor

emperler [ɑ̃pɛrle] *tr* to ornament with pearls; cover with drops; **la sueur emperlait son front** his forehead was covered with beads of perspiration

empe•sé -sée [ɑ̃pəze] *adj* starched, stiff, wooden (*style*)

empeser [ɑ̃pəze] §2 *tr* to starch

empes•té -tée [ɑ̃pɛste] *adj* pestilential; stinking; reeking; depraved

empester [ɑ̃pɛste] *tr* to stink; corrupt ‖ *intr* to stink

empêtrer [ɑ̃pɛtre] *tr* to hamper; involve; entangle ‖ *ref* to become involved, entangled

emphase [ɑ̃faz] *f* overemphasis; bombast, pretentiousness

emphatique [ɑ̃fatik] *adj* overemphasized; bombastic, pretentious

emphysème [ɑ̃fizɛm] *m* emphysema

empiècement [ɑ̃pjɛsmɑ̃] *m* yoke (*of shirt, blouse, etc.*)

empierrer [ɑ̃pjɛre] *tr* to pave with stones; (rr) to ballast

empiètement [ɑ̃pjɛtmɑ̃] *m* encroachment, incursion

empiéter [ɑ̃pjete] §10 *intr* to encroach

empiffrer [ɑ̃pifre] *tr* (coll) to stuff, fatten ‖ *ref* (coll) to stuff oneself, guzzle

empiler [ɑ̃pile] *tr* to pile up, stack; (slang) to dupe ‖ *ref* to pile up; **se faire empiler** (slang) to be had

empire [ɑ̃pir] *m* empire; control, supremacy; **Empire romain** Roman Empire

empirer [ɑ̃pire] *tr* to make worse, aggravate ‖ *intr* (*aux:* AVOIR *or* ETRE) to grow worse

empirique [ɑ̃pirik] *adj* empiric(al) ‖ *m* empiricist; charlatan, quack

emplacement [ɑ̃plasmɑ̃] *m* emplacement; location, site

emplâtre [ɑ̃plɑtr] *m* patch (*on tire*); (med) plaster; (coll) boob

emplette [ɑ̃plɛt] *f* purchase; **aller faire des emplettes** to go shopping

emplir [ɑ̃plir] *tr & ref* to fill up

emploi [ɑ̃plwa] *m* employment, job; employment, use; (theat) type (*of role*); **double emploi** useless duplication; **emploi du temps** schedule

em•ployé -ployée [ɑ̃plwaje] *mf* employee; clerk

employer [ɑ̃plwaje] §47, §100 *tr* to employ; to use ‖ §96 *ref* to be employed; **s'employer à** to try to, do one's best to

em•ployeur [ɑ̃plwajœr] **-ployeuse** [plwajøz] *mf* employer

empocher [ɑ̃pɔʃe] *tr* (coll) to pocket

empoi•gnant [ɑ̃pwaɲɑ̃] **-gnante** [ɲɑ̃t] *adj* exciting, arresting, thrilling

empoigner [ɑ̃pwaɲe] *tr* to grasp; collar (*a crook*); grip, move (*an audience*)

empois [ɑ̃pwa] *m* starch

empoisonnement [ɑ̃pwazɔnmɑ̃] *m* poisoning; **avoir des empoisonnements** (coll) to be annoyed

empoisonner [ɑ̃pwazɔne] *tr* to poison; infect (*the air*); corrupt; (coll) to bother ‖ *intr* to reek ‖ *ref* to be poisoned

empoison•neur [ɑ̃pwazɔnœr] **-neuse** [nøz] *adj* poisoning ‖ *mf* poisoner; corrupter

empoissonner [ɑ̃pwasɔne] *tr* to stock with fish

empor•té -tée [ɑ̃pɔrte] *adj* quick-tempered, impetuous

emportement [ɑ̃pɔrtəmɑ̃] *m* anger, temper

emporte-pièce [ɑ̃pɔrtəpjɛs] *m* (*pl* **-pièces**) punch; **à l'emporte-pièce** trenchant, cutting, biting (*style, words, etc.*)

emporter [ɑ̃pɔrte] *tr* to take away; carry off; remove; **à emporter** to take out, to go (*e.g., said of food to take out of the restaurant*); **l'emporter sur** to have the upper hand over ‖ *ref* to be carried away; lose one's temper; run away

emporte-restes [ɑ̃pɔrtrɛst] *m invar* (coll) doggy bag

empo•té -tée [ɑ̃pɔte] *adj* (coll) clumsy ‖ *mf* (coll) butterfingers

empoter [ɑ̃pɔte] *tr* to pot (*a plant*)

empourprer [ɑ̃purpre] *tr* to set aglow ‖ *ref* to turn crimson; flush

empoussiérer [ɑ̃pusjere] §10 *tr* to cover with dust

empreindre [ɑ̃prɛ̃dr] §50 *tr* to imprint, stamp

empreinte [ɑ̃prɛ̃t] *f* imprint, stamp; **empreinte des roues** wheel tracks; **empreinte digitale** fingerprint; **empreinte du pied** or **empreinte de pas** footprint; **empreinte génétique** genetic fingerprint

empres•sé -sée [ɑ̃prɛse] *adj* eager

empressement [ɑ̃prɛsmɑ̃] *m* haste, alacrity; eagerness, readiness

empresser [ɑ̃prɛse] **§96, §97** *ref* to hasten; **s'empresser à** to be anxious to; **s'empresser auprès de** to be attentive to, make a fuss over; press around; **s'empresser de** to hasten to

emprise [ɑ̃priz] *f* expropriation; control, ascendancy

emprisonment [ɑ̃prizɔnmɑ̃] *m* imprisonment

emprisonner [ɑ̃prizɔne] *tr* to imprison

emprunt [ɑ̃prœ̃] *m* loan; loan word; **d'emprunt** feigned, assumed

emprun•té -tée [ɑ̃prœ̃te] *adj* timid, self-conscious, awkward; feigned, sham

emprunter [ɑ̃prœ̃te] *tr* to borrow; take (*a road, a route*); take on (*false appearances*); **emprunter q.ch. à** to borrow s.th. from; get s.th. from

empuantir [ɑ̃pɥɑ̃tir] *tr* to stink up

empyème [ɑ̃pjɛm] *m* empyema

empyrée [ɑ̃pire] *m* empyrean

é•mu -mue [emy] *adj* moved, touched; tender (*memory*); **ému de** alarmed by ‖ *v see* **émouvoir**

émulation [emylɑsjɔ̃] *f* emulation, rivalry

émule [emyl] *mf* emulator, rival

émulsion [emylsjɔ̃] *f* emulsion

émulsionner [emylsjɔne] *tr* to emulsify

en [ɑ̃] *pron indef & adv* **§87** ‖ *prep* in; into; to, e.g., **aller en France** to go to France; e.g., **de mal en pis** from bad to worse; at, e.g., **en mer** at sea; e.g., **en guerre** at war; on, e.g., **en congé** on leave; by, e.g., **en chemin de fer** by rail; of, made of, e.g., **en bois** (made) of wood; as, e.g., **il est mort en soldat** he died (as) a soldier

enamourer [ɑ̃namure] *ref* to become enamored, fall in love

énarque [enark] *mf* (fig) bureaucrat

encabaner [ɑ̃kabane] *ref* (Canad) to hole up, dig in (*e.g., for the winter*)

encablure [ɑ̃kablyr] *f* cable's length (*unit of measure*)

encadrement [ɑ̃kɑdrəmɑ̃] *m* framing; frame: framework; window frame; doorframe; border, edge; staffing; officering (*furnishing with officers*)

encadrer [ɑ̃kɑdre] *tr* to frame; staff (*an organization*); officer (*troops*); incorporate (*recruits*) into a unit; train, supervise

encadreur [ɑ̃kɑdrœr] *m* framer (*person*)

encager [ɑ̃kaʒe] **§38** *tr* to cage

encaisse [ɑ̃kɛs] *f* cash on hand, cash balance; **encaisse métallique** bullion

encais•sé -sée [ɑ̃kɛse] *adj* deeply embanked, sunken

encaissement [ɑ̃kɛsmɑ̃] *m* cashing (*e.g., of check*); boxing, crating; embankment

encaisser [ɑ̃kɛse], [ɑ̃kese] *tr* to cash; box, crate; receive (*a blow*); embank (*a river*); (coll) to put up with; **encaisser des coups, encaisser des critiques** (coll) to take it on the chin, to stand up to criticism ‖ *ref* to be steeply embanked

encaisseur [ɑ̃kɛsœr] *m* collector; payee; cashier

encan [ɑ̃kɑ̃] *m* auction

encanailler [ɑ̃kanɑje] *tr* to debase ‖ *ref* to acquire bad habits; keep low company

encapuchonner [ɑ̃kapyʃɔne] *tr* to hood

encaquer [ɑ̃kake] *tr* to barrel; pack (*sardines*); (coll) to pack in like sardines

encart [ɑ̃kar] *m* inset, insert

encarter [ɑ̃karte] *tr* to card (*buttons, pins, etc.*); (bb) to tip in

en-cas [ɑ̃ka] *m invar* snack; reserve, emergency supply

encasernement [ɑ̃kazɛrnəmɑ̃] *m*—**encasernement de conscience** thought control, regimentation

encaserner [ɑ̃kazɛrne] *tr* to quarter, barrack (*troops*)

encastrement [ɑ̃kastrəmɑ̃] *m* groove; fitting

encas•tré -trée [ɑ̃kastre] *adj* built-in

encastrer [ɑ̃kastre] *tr & ref* to fit

encaustique [ɑ̃kɔstik] *f* furniture polish; floor wax; encaustic painting

encaustiquer [ɑ̃kɔstike] *tr* to wax

encaver [ɑ̃kave] *tr* to cellar (*wine*)

enceindre [ɑ̃sɛ̃dr] **§50** *tr* to enclose, encircle

enceinte [ɑ̃sɛ̃t] *adj fem* pregnant ‖ *f* enclosure; walls, ramparts; precinct, compass; (boxing) ring

encens [ɑ̃sɑ̃] *m* incense; flattery

encenser [ɑ̃sɑ̃se] *tr* to incense, perfume with incense; flatter

encensoir [ɑ̃sɑ̃swar] *m* censer

encéphalite [ɑ̃sefalit] *f* encephalitis

encéphalopathie [ɑ̃sefalɔpati] *f* brain disease; **encéphalopathie spongiforme** mad cow disease

encercler [ɑ̃sɛrkle] *tr* to encircle

enchaînement [ɑ̃ʃɛnmɑ̃] *m* chaining up; chain, sequence

enchaîner [ɑ̃ʃɛne], [ɑ̃ʃene], *tr* to chain; to connect ‖ *intr* to go on speaking ‖ *ref* to be connected

enchan•té -tée [ɑ̃ʃɑ̃te] **§93** *adj* delighted, pleased

enchantement [ɑ̃ʃɑ̃tmɑ̃] *m* enchantment

enchanter [ɑ̃ʃɑ̃te] *tr* to enchant

enchan•teur [ɑ̃ʃɑ̃tœr] **-teresse** [trɛs] *adj* enchanting, bewitching ‖ *m* enchanter, magician ‖ *f* enchantress

enchâsser [ɑ̃ʃɑse] *tr* to enshrine; insert; set, chase (*a gem*)

enchère [ɑ̃ʃɛr] *f* bid, bidding; **folle enchère** bid that cannot be made good; folly

enchérir [ɑ̃ʃerir] *tr* to bid on; raise the price of ‖ *intr* to bid; rise in price; **enchérir sur** to improve on; outbid

enchérisseur [ɑ̃ʃerisœr] *m* bidder; **dernier enchérisseur** highest bidder

enchevêtrement [ɑ̃ʃvɛtrəmɑ̃] *m* entanglement; network; jumble

enchevêtrer [ɑ̃ʃvɛtre] *tr* to tangle up; halter (*a*

horse) ‖ *ref* to become complicated or confused

enchifre•né -née [ãʃifrəne] *adj* stuffed-up (*with a cold*)

enclave [ãklav] *f* enclave

enclaver [ãklave] *tr* to enclose; dovetail

enclencher [ãklãʃe] *tr* & *ref* to interlock

en•clin [ãklɛ̃] **-cline** [klin] *adj* inclined, prone

encliquetage [ãkliktaʒ] *m* ratchet

encliqueter [ãklikte] §34 *tr* to cog, mesh

enclitique [ãklitik] *adj* & *m* & *f* enclitic

enclore [ãklɔr] §24 (has also 1st & 2d *pl pres ind* **enclosons, enclosez**) *tr* to close in, wall in

enclos [ãklo] *m* enclosure, close

enclume [ãklym] *f* anvil; **se trouver entre l'enclume et le marteau** (coll) to be between the devil and the deep blue sea

encoche [ãkɔʃ] *f* notch, nick; slot; thumb index

encocher [ãkɔʃe] *tr* to notch, nick; slot

encodage [ãkɔdaʒ] *m* encoding

encoder [ãkɔde] *tr* to encode

encodeur [ãkɔdœr] *m* (comp) encoder

encoignure [ãkɔɲyr] *f* corner; corner piece; corner cabinet

encollage [ãkɔlaʒ] *m* gluing; sizing

encoller [ãkɔle] *tr* to glue; size

encolure [ãkɔlyr] *f* collar size; neck line; neck and withers (*of horse*); **gagner par une encolure** to win by a neck

encombre [ãkɔ̃br] *m*—**sans encombre** without a hitch, without hindrance

encombrement [ãkɔ̃brəmã] *m* encumbrance, congestion

encombrer [ãkɔ̃bre] *tr* to encumber; crowd, congest; block up, jam; litter; load down ‖ *ref*—**s'encombrer de** (coll) to be saddled with

encontre [ãkɔ̃tr]—**à l'encontre de** counter to, against; contrary to

encore [ãkɔr] *adv* still, e.g., **il est encore ici** he is still here; yet, e.g., **encore mieux** better yet; e.g., **pas encore** not yet; only, e.g., **si encore vous m'en aviez parlé!** if only you had told me!; even, e.g., **il est encore plus intelligent que vous** he is even more intelligent than you; **encore que** although; **encore une fois** once more, once again; **en voulez-vous encore?** do you want some more? ‖ *interj* again!, oh no, not again! (*expressing impatience or astonishment*)

encorner [ãkɔrne] *tr* to gore, toss

encouragement [ãkuraʒmã] *m* encouragement

encourager [ãkuraʒe] §38, §96, §100 *tr* to encourage

encourir [ãkurir] §14 *tr* to incur

encrasser [ãkrase] *tr* to soil, dirty; soot (*a chimney*); foul (*a gun*) ‖ *ref* to get dirty; stop up, clog; soot up

encre [ãkr] *f* ink; **encre de Chine** India ink; **encre de couleur** colored ink; **encre sympathique** invisible ink

encrer [ãkre] *tr* to ink

encreur [ãkrœr] *adj* inking (*ribbon, roller*) ‖ *m* ink roller

encrier [ãkrije] *m* inkwell

encroûter [ãkrute] *tr* to encrust; plaster (*walls*) ‖ *ref* to become encrusted; get rusty; become hidebound, prejudiced

encyclique [ãsiklik] *adj* & *f* encyclical

encyclopédie [ãsiklɔpedi] *f* encyclopedia

encyclopédique [ãsiklɔpedik] *adj* encyclopedic

endauber [ãdobe] *tr* to braise

endémie [ãdemi] *f* endemic

endémique [ãdemik] *adj* endemic

endenter [ãdãte] *tr* to tooth, cog; mesh (*gears*); **bien endenté** (coll) with plenty of teeth; (coll) with a hearty appetite

endetter [ãdɛte] *tr* & *ref* to run into debt

endêver [ãdɛve] *intr*—**faire endêver** to bedevil, drive wild

endia•blé -blée [ãdjable] *adj* devilish, reckless; full of pep

endiguement [ãdigmã] *m* damming up; embankment

endiguer [ãdige] *tr* to dam up

endimancher [ãdimãʃe] *tr* & *ref* to put on Sunday clothes, dress up

endive [ãdiv] *f* endive

endocrine [ãdɔkrin] *adj* endocrine

endoctriner [ãdɔktrine] *tr* to indoctrinate; win over

endolo•ri -rie [ãdɔlɔri] *adj* painful, sore

endommagement [ãdɔmaʒmã] *m* damage

endommager [ãdɔmaʒe] §38 *tr* to damage ‖ *ref* to suffer damage

endor•mi -mie [ãdɔrmi] *adj* asleep, sleeping; sluggish, apathetic; dormant; numb (*arm or leg*)

endormir [ãdɔrmir] §23 *tr* to put to sleep; lull, put off guard ‖ *ref* to go to sleep; slack off; let down one's guard

endos [ãdo] *m* endorsement

endosse [ãdos] *f* responsibility

endossement [ãdosmã] *m* endorsement

endosser [ãdose] *tr* to endorse; take on the responsibility of

endosseur [ãdosœr] *m* endorser

endroit [ãdrwa], [ãdrwɑ] *m* place, spot; right side (*of cloth*); **à l'endroit** right side out; **à l'endroit de** with regard to; **le petit endroit** (coll) the toilet; **mettre à l'endroit** to put on right side out

enduire [ãdɥir] §19 *tr* to coat, smear

enduit [ãdɥi] *m* coat, coating

endurance [ãdyrãs] *f* endurance

endu•rant -rante [ãdyrã] [rãt] *adj* untiring; meek, patient

endur•ci -cie [ãdyrsi] *adj* hardened; tough, calloused; inveterate

endurcir [ãdyrsir] *tr* to harden; inure, toughen ‖ *ref* to harden; **s'endurcir à** to become accustomed to, become inured to

endurcissement [ãdyrsismã] *m* hardening

endurer [ãdyre] *tr* to endure

énergétique [enɛrʒetik] *adj* energy, energy-giving, energizing ‖ *f* energetics

énergie [enɛrʒi] *f* energy; **énergie nucléaire** nuclear energy, nuclear power

énergique [enɛrʒik] *adj* energetic

énergumène [enɛrgymɛn] *mf* ranter, wild person, nut

éner·vant [enɛrvɑ̃] **-vante** [vɑ̃t] *adj* annoying, nerve-racking, irritating, enervating

énervement [enɛrvmɑ̃] *m* annoyance, nervousness, irritation, edginess

énerver [enɛrve] *tr* to enervate; unnerve, set (*s.o.'s*) nerves on edge ‖ *ref* to get nervous; be exasperated; to get excited, worked up

enfance [ɑ̃fɑ̃s] *f* childhood; infancy; dotage, second childhood; **c'est l'enfance de l'art** (coll) it's child's play; **enfance délinquante** juvenile delinquents; **première enfance** infancy

enfant [ɑ̃fɑ̃] *adj invar* childish, childlike; **bon enfant** good-natured ‖ *mf* child; **enfant de chœur** altar boy; **enfant de la balle** child who follows in his father's footsteps; **enfant en bas âge** infant; **enfant en placement** foster child; **enfant terrible** (fig) stormy petrel, troublemaker; **enfant trouvé** foundling; **mon enfant!** my boy!; **petit enfant** infant

enfantement [ɑ̃fɑ̃tmɑ̃] *m* childbirth

enfanter [ɑ̃fɑ̃te] *tr* to give birth to

enfantillage [ɑ̃fɑ̃tijaʒ] *m* childishness

enfan·tin [ɑ̃fɑ̃tɛ̃] **-tine** [tin] *adj* childish, infantile

enfari·né -née [ɑ̃farine] *adj* smeared with flour

enfer [ɑ̃fɛr] *m* hell; erotica (*restricted section of a library*)

enfermer [ɑ̃fɛrme] *tr* to enclose; shut up, lock up ‖ *ref* to shut oneself in; closet oneself

enferrer [ɑ̃fɛre] *tr* to pierce, run through ‖ *ref* to run oneself through with a sword; bite (*said of fish*); (fig) to be caught in one's own trap

enfiévrer [ɑ̃fjevre] §10 *tr* to inflame, make feverish

enfilade [ɑ̃filad] *f* row, string, series; (mil) enfilade; **en enfilade** connecting, e.g., **chambres en enfilade** connecting rooms

enfile-aiguille [ɑ̃filɛɥij] *m invar* threader, needle threader

enfiler [ɑ̃file] *tr* to pierce; thread (*a needle*); string (*beads*); start down (*a street*); (coll) to put on (*clothes*)

enfin [ɑ̃fɛ̃] *adv* finally, at last; in short; after all, anyway

enflam·mé -mée [ɑ̃flɑme], [ɑ̃flame] *adj* flaming; bright red; inflamed

enflammer [ɑ̃flɑme], [ɑ̃flame] *tr* to inflame ‖ *ref* to be inflamed; flare up

enfler [ɑfle] *tr* to swell; puff up or out; exaggerate ‖ *intr & ref* to swell, puff up

enflure [ɑ̃flyr] *f* swelling; (fig) exaggeration

enfon·cé -cée [ɑ̃fɔ̃se] *adj* sunken, deep; deepset; broken (*ribs*); (coll) taken, had (*bested*)

enfoncement [ɑ̃fɔ̃smɑ̃] *m* driving in; breaking open; hollow, recess

enfoncer [ɑ̃fɔ̃se] §51 *tr* to drive in; push in, break open; (coll) to get the better of ‖ *intr* to sink to the bottom ‖ *ref* to sink, plunge; give way; disappear; penetrate (*said of root, bullet, etc.*)

enforcir [ɑ̃fɔrsir] *tr* to reinforce ‖ *intr & ref* to become stronger; grow

enfouir [ɑ̃fwir] *tr* to bury; hide ‖ *ref* to burrow; bury oneself (*e.g., in an out-of-the-way locality*)

enfourcher [ɑ̃furʃe] *tr* to stick a pitchfork into; mount, straddle

enfourchure [ɑ̃furʃyr] *f* crotch

enfourner [ɑ̃furne] *tr* to put in the oven; (coll) to gobble down

enfreindre [ɑ̃frɛ̃dr] §50 *tr* to violate, break (*e.g., a law*)

enfuir [ɑ̃fɥir] §31 *ref* to run away; escape; elope

enfu·mé -mée [ɑ̃fyme] *adj* blackened; smoky (*color*)

enfumer [ɑ̃fyme] *tr* to smoke up, blacken; smoke out

enfutailler [ɑ̃fytaje] *tr* to cask, barrel

enga·gé -gée [ɑ̃gaʒe] *adj* committed; hocked ‖ *m* (mil) enlisted man

enga·geant -geante [ʒɑ̃t] *adj* winsome, charming, engaging

engagement [ɑ̃gaʒmɑ̃] *m* engagement; hocking; obligation; promise; (mil) enlistment; (mil) engagement

engager [ɑ̃gaʒe] §38, §96, §97, §100 *tr* to engage; hock; enlist, urge, involve; open, begin (*negotiations, the conversation, etc.*) ‖ *ref* to commit oneself; promise, pledge; enter a contest; become engaged to be married; (mil) to enlist; **s'engager dans** to begin (*battle; a conversation*); plunge into; fit into

engainer [ɑ̃gɛne] *tr* to sheathe, envelop

engazonner [ɑ̃gazɔne] *tr* to sod

engeance [ɑ̃ʒɑs] *f* (pej) breed, brood

engelure [ɑ̃ʒlyr] *f* chilblain

engendrer [ɑ̃ʒɑ̃dre] *tr* to engender

engin [ɑ̃ʒɛ̃] *m* device; **engin balistique** balistic missile; **engin guidé, engin spécial** guided missile; **engin non-identifié** unidentified flying object; **engins de pêche** fishing tackle

englober [ɑ̃glɔbe] *tr* to put together, unite; embrace, comprise

engloutir [ɑ̃glutir] *tr* to gobble down; swallow up, engulf

engluer [ɑ̃glye] *tr* to lime (*a trap*); catch; take in, hoodwink ‖ *ref* to be caught; fall into a trap, be taken in

engommer [ɑ̃gɔme] *tr* to gum

engon·cé -cée [ɑ̃gɔ̃se] *adj* awkward, stiff (*air*)

engoncer [ɑ̃gɔ̃se] §51 *tr* to bundle up; cramp

engorgement [ɑ̃gɔrʒəmɑ̃] *m* obstruction, blocking

engorger [ɑ̃gɔrʒe] §38 *tr* to obstruct, block

engouement [ɑ̃gumɑ̃] *m* infatuation; fad; (pathol) obstruction

engouer [ɑ̃gwe] *tr* to obstruct ‖ *ref* **—s'engouer de** (coll) to be infatuated with, be wild about

engouffrer [ãgufre] *tr* to engulf; gobble up; eat up (*e.g., a fortune*) ‖ *ref* to be swallowed up; dash; surge

engour·di -die [ãgurdi] *adj* numb

engourdir [ãgurdir] *tr* to numb; dull ‖ *ref* to grow numb

engourdissement [ãgurdismã] *m* numbness; dullness, torpidity

engrais [ãgrɛ] *m* fertilizer; manure; fodder; **mettre à l'engrais** to fatten

engraisser [ãgrɛse], [ãgrese] *tr* to fatten; fertilize; enrich ‖ *intr* (*aux:* AVOIR *or* ETRE) to fatten up, get fat ‖ *ref* to become fat; become rich

engranger [ãgrãʒe] §38 *tr* to garner; get in, put in the barn

engraver [ãgrave] *tr, intr, & ref* to silt up; (naut) to run aground

engrenage [ãgrənaʒ] *m* gear; gearing; (coll) mesh, toils; **engrenage à vis sans fin** worm gear; **engrenages de distribution** timing gears

engrener [ãgrəne] §2 *tr* to feed (*a hopper, a thresher; a fowl*); put into gear, mesh ‖ *intr & ref* (mach) to mesh, engage

engrenure [ãgrənyr] *f* engaging (*of toothed wheels*)

engrosser [ãgrose] *tr* (slang) to knock up, make pregnant

engrumeler [ãgrymle] §34 *tr & ref* to clot, curdle

engueulade [ãgœlad] *f* (coll) violent argument; bawling out, tongue lashing

engueuler [ãgœle] *tr* (coll) to bawl out, to give (*s.o.*) hell ‖ *ref* to argue violently

enguirlander [ãgirlãde] *tr* to garland; adorn; (coll) to bawl out

enhardir [ãardir], §96, §97 *tr* to embolden ‖ *ref* —s'enhardir à to be so bold as to, umpteenth

énième [ɛnjɛm] *adj* nth, umpteenth

énigmatique [enigmatik] *adj* enigmatic(al), puzzling

énigme [enigm] *f* enigma, riddle, puzzle

eni·vrant [ãnivrã] **-vrante** [vrãt] *adj* intoxicating, exhilarating

enivrement [ãnivrəmã] *m* intoxication

enivrer [ãnivre] *tr* to intoxicate; elate ‖ *ref* to get drunk

enjambée [ãʒãbe] *f* stride

enjambement [ãʒãbmã] *m* enjambment

enjamber [ãʒãbe] *tr* to stride over, span ‖ *intr* to stride along; run on (*said of line of poetry*); **enjamber sur** to project over; encroach on

en·jeu [ãʒø] *m* (*pl* **-jeux**) stake, bet

enjoindre [ãʒwɛ̃dr] §35, §97 *tr* to enjoin

enjôler [ãʒole] *tr* (coll) to cajole

enjô·leur [ãʒolœr] **-leuse** [løz] *adj* cajoling ‖ *mf* cajoler, wheedler

enjoliver [ãʒolive] *tr* to embellish

enjoli·veur [ãʒolivœr] **-veuse** [vøz] *mf* embellisher ‖ *m* hubcap

en·joué -jouée [ãʒwe] *adj* sprightly

enjouement [ãʒumã] *m* playfulness

enlacement [ãlasmã] *m* embrace, hug; lacing, interweaving

enlacer [ãlase] §51 *tr & ref* to enlace, entwine; embrace

enlaidir [ãledir], [ãledir] *tr* to disfigure ‖ *intr* to grow ugly ‖ *ref* to disfigure oneself

enlèvement [ãlɛvmã] *m* removal; kidnapping, abduction; **enlèvement de bébé** infant kidnaping; **enlèvement d'enfant** *or* **de mineur** child snatching

enlever [ãlve] §2 *tr* to take away, take off, remove; carry off; lift, lift up; send up; (*a balloon*); (fig) to carry away (*an audience*); **enlever le couvert** to clear the table; **enlever q.ch. à** to take s.th. from, remove s.th. from ‖ *ref* to come off, wear off; rise; boil over; (fig) to flare up

enliasser [ãljase] *tr* to tie up in bundles

enliser [ãlize] *tr* to get (*s.th.*) stuck in the mud ‖ *ref* to get stuck

enluminer [ãlymine] *tr* to illuminate; make colorful

enluminure [ãlyminyr] *f* illuminated drawing; (painting) illumination

enneiger [ãnɛʒe], [ãneʒe] §38 *tr* to cover with snow

enne·mi -mie [ɛnmi] *adj* hostile, inimical; enemy, e.g., **en pays ennemi** in enemy country ‖ *mf* enemy

ennoblir [ãnoblir] *tr* to ennoble

ennui [ãnɥi] *m* ennui, boredom; nuisance, bother; worry, trouble; **sans ennuis** trouble-free

ennuyer [ãnɥije] §27, §96, §97 *tr* to bore; bother ‖ *ref* to be bored

en·nuyeux [ãnɥijø] **-nuyeuse** [nɥijøz] *adj* boring, tedious; annoying, bothersome; sad, troublesome

énon·cé -cée [enɔ̃se] *m* statement; wording (*of a document*); terms (*of a theorem*)

énoncer [enɔ̃se] §51 *tr* to state, enunciate; utter

enorgueillir [ãnɔrgœjir] *tr* to make proud or boastful ‖ §97 *ref*—s'enorgueillir de to pride oneself on, boast of, glory in

énorme [enɔrm] *adj* enormous; (coll) shocking; (coll) outrageous

énormément [enɔrmemã] *adv* enormously, tremendously; (coll) awfully; **énormément de** lots of

énormité [enɔrmite] *f* enormity; (coll) nonsense; (coll) blunder

enquérir [ãkerir] §3 *ref*—s'enquérir de to ask or inquire about

enquête [ãkɛt] *f* investigation, inquiry; inquest; **enquête par sondage** public-opinion poll

enquêter [ãkɛte] *intr* to conduct an investigation

enraciner [ãrasine] *tr* to root; instill ‖ *ref* to take root

enra·gé -gée [ãraʒe] *adj* enraged, hotheaded; mad (*dog*); rabid (*communist*); out-and-out (*socialist*); inveterate (*gambler*); enthusiastic (*sportsman*) ‖ *mf* enthusiast, fan; fanatic, fiend

enrager [ɑ̃raʒe] §38, §97 *intr* to be mad; **faire enrager** to enrage

enrayer [ɑ̃rɛje], [ɑ̃reje] §49 *tr* to put spokes to; jam, lock; stem, halt ‖ *ref* to jam

enrayure [ɑ̃rɛjyr] *f* (mach) skid, shoe

enrégimenter [ɑ̃reʒimɑ̃te] *tr* to regiment

enregistrement [ɑ̃rəʒistrəmɑ̃] *m* recording; registration; transcription; checking (*of baggage*); **enregistrement numérique** digital recording; **enregistrement sur bande** *or* **sur ruban** tape recording; videocassette recording

enregistrer [ɑ̃rəʒistre] *tr* to record; register; transcribe; check (*baggage*); **enregistrer en vidéo** (mov, telv) to videotape

enregis•treur [ɑ̃rəʒistrœr] **-treuse** [trøz] *adj* recording ‖ *mf* recorder ‖ *m* recording machine; **enregistreur d'accident** crash recorder, black box; **enregistreur de vol** flight recorder

enrhumer [ɑ̃ryme] *tr* to give a cold to ‖ *ref* to catch cold

enrichir [ɑ̃riʃir] *tr* to enrich ‖ *ref* to become rich

enrichissement [ɑ̃riʃismɑ̃] *m* enrichment

enrober [ɑ̃rɔbe] *tr* to coat; wrap

enrôlement [ɑ̃rolmɑ̃] *m* enrollment; enlistment

enrôler [ɑ̃role] *tr & ref* to enroll, enlist

enrouement [ɑ̃rumɑ̃] *m* hoarseness, huskiness

enrouer [ɑ̃rwe] *tr* to make hoarse ‖ *ref* to become hoarse

enrouiller [ɑ̃ruje] *tr & ref* to rust

enroulement [ɑ̃rulmɑ̃] *m* coil; (archit) volute; (elec) winding

enrouler [ɑ̃rule] *tr & ref* to wind, coil; roll up

ensabler [ɑ̃sable] *tr & ref* to run aground on the sand

ensacher [ɑ̃saʃe] *tr* to bag

ensanglanter [ɑ̃sɑ̃glɑ̃te] *tr* to stain with blood; steep in blood

ensei•gnant [ɑ̃sɛɲɑ̃] **-gnante** [ɲɑ̃t] *adj* teaching ‖ *mf* teacher

enseigne [ɑ̃sɛɲ] *m* (nav) ensign ‖ *f* flag, ensign; sign (*on tavern, store*)

enseignement [ɑ̃sɛɲəmɑ̃] *m* teaching, instruction, education; **enseignement confessionnel** parochial school education; **enseignement libre** or **privé** private-school education; **enseignement mixte** coeducation; **enseignement par correspondance** correspondence courses; **enseignement programmé** computer programed courses; **enseignement public** public education; **enseignement secondaire** secondary education; **enseignement séquentiel** programed learning; **enseignment supérieur** higher education

enseigner [ɑ̃sɛɲe] §96, §101 *tr* to teach; show; **enseigner q.ch. à qn** to teach s.o. s.th. ‖ *intr* to teach; **enseigner à qn à** + *inf* to teach s.o. to + *inf*

ensemble [ɑ̃sɑ̃bl] *m* ensemble; **avec ensemble** in harmony, with one mind; **dans son ensemble** as a whole; **d'ensemble** general, comprehensive, overall; **ensemble immobilier** housing development; **grand ensemble** housing project ‖ *adv* together

ensemencement [ɑ̃smɑ̃smɑ̃] *m* sowing

ensemencer [ɑ̃smɑ̃se] §51 *tr* to seed, sow; culture (*microorganisms*)

enserrer [ɑ̃sɛre] *tr* to enclose; squeeze, clasp

ensevelir [ɑ̃səvlir] *tr* to bury; shroud

ensevelissement [ɑ̃səvlismɑ̃] *m* burial; shrouding

ensilage [ɑ̃silaʒ] *m* storing in a pit or silo

ensiler [ɑ̃sile] *tr* to ensilage

ensoleiller [ɑ̃sɔlɛje] *tr* to make sunny, brighten

ensommeil•lé -lée [ɑ̃sɔmeje] *adj* drowsy

ensorceler [ɑ̃sɔrsəle] §34 *tr* to bewitch, enchant

ensorce•leur [ɑ̃sɔrsəlœr] **-leuse** [løz] *adj* bewitching, enchanting ‖ *m* sorcerer, wizard; charmer ‖ *f* witch; enchantress

ensorcellement [ɑ̃sɔrsɛlmɑ̃] *m* sorcery, enchantment; spell, charm

ensuite [ɑ̃sɥit] *adv* then, next; afterwards, after; **ensuite?** what then?, what next?; anything else?

ensuivre [ɑ̃sɥivr] §67 (used only in 3rd *sg & pl*) *ref* to ensue; **il s'ensuit que . . .** it follows that . . .

entacher [ɑ̃taʃe] *tr* to blemish; **entaché de nullité** null and void

entaille [ɑ̃taj] *f* notch, nick; gash

entailler [ɑ̃taje] *tr* to notch, nick; gash

entame [ɑ̃tam] *f* top slice, first slice, end slice

entamer [ɑ̃tame] *tr* to cut the first slice of; begin; engage in, start (*a conversation*); make a break in (*the skin; a battle line*); cast a slur upon; open (*a bottle; negotiations; a card suit*); (coll) to make a dent in (*e.g., one's savings*)

entartrer [ɑ̃tartre] *tr & ref* to scale, fur

entassement [ɑ̃tasmɑ̃] *m* piling up

entasser [ɑ̃tase] *tr & ref* to pile up, accumulate; crowd

ente [ɑ̃t] *f* paintbrush handle; (hort) graft, scion

entendement [ɑ̃tɑ̃dmɑ̃] *m* understanding; consciousness

entendre [ɑ̃tɑ̃dr] §95 *tr* to hear; understand; mean; **entendre chanter** to hear (*s.o.*) singing, to hear (*s.o.*) sing; hear (*s.th.*) sung; **entendre dire que** to hear that; **entendre parler de** to hear of or about; **entendre raison** to listen to reason; **il entend que je le fasse** he expects me to do it, he insists that I do it ‖ *intr* to hear ‖ §96 *ref* to understand one another; get along; **s'entendre à** to be skilled in, know

enten•du -due [ɑ̃tɑ̃dy] *adj* agreed; **bien entendu** of course; **c'est entendu!** all right!

enténébrer [ɑ̃tenebre] §10 *tr* to plunge into darkness

entente [ɑ̃tɑ̃t] *f* understanding; agreement, pact; **à double entente** with a double meaning, e.g., **expression à double entente** expression with a double meaning, double entendre; **entente industrielle** (com) combine

enter [ɑ̃te] *tr* to graft; splice (*pieces of wood*)

entérinement [ãterinmã] *m* ratification

entériner [ãterine] *tr* to ratify

enterrement [ãtɛrmã] *m* burial, interment; funeral procession; funeral; funeral expenses; pigeonholing

enterrer [ãtɛre] *tr* to bury, inter; pigeonhole, sidetrack; (coll) to attend the funeral services of; **enterrer sa vie de garçon** (coll) to give a farewell stag party ‖ *ref* to bury oneself; (mil) to dig oneself in

en-tête [ãtɛt] *m* (*pl* **-têtes**) headline; chapter heading; letterhead

enté•té -tée [ãtɛte] *adj* obstinate, stubborn

entêtement [ãtɛtmã] *m* obstinacy, stubbornness

entêter [ãtɛte] *tr* to give a headache to; make giddy ‖ *intr* to go to one's head ‖ *ref* to persist

enthousiasme [ãtuzjasm] *m* enthusiasm

enthousiasmer [ãtuzjasme] *tr & ref* to enthuse

enthousiaste [ãtuzjast] *adj* enthusiastic ‖ *mf* enthusiast, fan, buff

entichement [ãti∫mã] *m* infatuation

enticher [ãti∫e] *tr* to infatuate ‖ *ref* to become infatuated

en•tier [ãtje] **-tière** [tjɛr] *adj* entire, whole, full, obstinate ‖ *m* whole, entirety; **en entier** in full

entièrement [ãtjɛrmã] *adv* entirely

entité [ãtite] *f* entity, being

entoiler [ãtwale] *tr* to put a backing on, mount

entomologie [ãtɔmɔlɔʒi] *f* entomology

entonner [ãtɔne] *tr* to barrel; intone, start off (*a song*); sing (*s.o.'s praises*) ‖ *ref* to rush up and down (*said of wind*)

entonnoir [ãtɔnwar] *m* funnel; shell hole

entorse [ãtɔrs] *f* sprain; infringement (*of a rule*); stretching (*of the truth*)

entortiller [ãtɔrtije] *tr & ref* to twist

entour [ãtur] *m*—**à l'entour** in the vicinity; **à l'entour de** around; **entours** surroundings

entourage [ãturaʒ] *m* setting; surroundings; entourage; (mach) casing

entourer [ãture] *tr* to surround ‖ *ref*—**s'entourer de** to surround oneself with

entourloupette [ãturlupɛt] *f* (coll) double cross; **faire une entourloupette à** (coll) to double-cross

entournure [ãturnyr] *f* armhole; **gêné dans les entournures** ill at ease

entraccuser [ãtrakyze] *ref* to accuse one another

entracte [ãtrakt] *m* intermission

entraide [ãtrɛd] *f* mutual assistance

entrailles [ãtraj] *fpl* entrails; tenderness, pity; bowels (*of the earth*); **sans entrailles** (fig) heartless

entr'aimer [ãtrɛme], [ãtreme] *ref* to love each other

entrain [ãtrɛ̃] *m* spirit, gusto, pep

entraînement [ãtrɛnmã] *m* training; enthusiasm

entraîner [ãtrɛne] §96, §100 *tr* to carry along or away, entrain; involve, entail; pull (*railroad cars*); work (*a pump*); train (*an athlete*) ‖ *ref* (sports) to train

entraîneur [ãtrɛnœr] *m* trainer, coach

entraîneuse [ãtrɛnøz] *f* B-girl

entr'apercevoir [ãtrapɛrsəvwar] §59 *tr* to catch a glimpse of

entrave [ãtrav] *f* shackle; hindrance; (fig) drag

entra•vé -vée [ãtrave] *adj* impeded, hampered; checked (*vowel*)

entraver [ãtrave] *tr* to shackle; hinder, impede

entre [ãtr] *prep* between; among; in or into, e.g., **entre les mains de** in or into the hands of; **d'entre** among; from among, out of; of, e.g., **l'un d'entre eux** one of them; **entre deux eaux** under the surface of the water

entrebâillement [ãtrəbajmã] *m* chink, slit, crack

entrebâiller [ãtrəbaje] *tr* to leave ajar

entrechat [ãtrə∫a] *m* caper; entrechat

entrechoquer [ãtrə∫ɔke] *tr* to bump together ‖ *ref* to clash

entrecôte [ãtrəkot] *f* sirloin steak, loin of beef; top chuck roast

entrecouper [ãtrəkupe] *tr* to interrupt; intersect ‖ *ref* to intersect

entrecroiser [ãtrəkrwaze] *tr & ref* to interlace; intersect

entre-deux [ãtrədø] *m invar* space between; interval; partition; (sports) jump ball

entre-deux-guerres [ãtrədøgɛr] *m & f invar* period between the wars (*the First and Second World War*)

entrée [ãtre] *f* entrance, entry; admission, admittance; beginning; headword, entry word (*of a dictionary*); customs duty; (culin) first course; (culin) course before the main course; **avoir ses entrées à, chez,** or **dans** to have the entree into; **d'entrée** at the start, right off; **entrée de serrure** keyhole; **entrée d'un chapeau** hat size; **entrée en matière** introduction; **entrée en scène** (theat) entrance; **entrée interdite** (public sign) keep out, no admittance, no entry; **entrée libre** or **gratuite** free admission; **entrée principale** main entrance

entrefaites [ãtrəfɛt] *fpl*—**sur ces entre-faites** meanwhile

entrefer [ãtrəfɛr] *m* (elec) air gap

entrefermer [ãtrəfɛrme] *tr* to close part way

entrefilet [ãtrəfilɛ] *m* short feature, special item

entregent [ãtrəʒã] *m* tact, diplomacy, savoir-faire; **avoir de l'entregent** to be a good mixer

entrejambe [ãtrəʒãb] *m* crotch

entrelacer [ãtrəlase] §51 *tr & ref* to interlace, entwine, intertwine

entrelarder [ãtrəlarde] *tr* to lard; interlard

entre-ligne [ãtrəliɲ] *m* (*pl* **-lignes**) space (*between the lines*); insertion (*written between the lines*); **à l'entre-ligne** double-spaced

entremêler [ãtrəmɛle] *tr* to mix, mingle; intersperse

entremets [ãtrəmɛ] *m* side dish; dessert

entremet•teur [ãtrəmɛtœr] **-teuse** [tøz] *mf* go-between ‖ *m* (pej) pimp

entremettre [ãtrəmɛtr] §42 *ref* to intervene, intercede

entremise [ãtrəmiz] *f* intervention; **par l'entre-mise de** through the medium of
entre-nuire [ãtrənɥir] §19 (*pp* **-nui** *invar*) to hurt each other
entrepont [ãtrəpõ] *m* (naut) between-decks
entreposer [ãtrəpoze] *tr* to place in a warehouse, store; bond
entrepôt [ãtrəpo] *m* warehouse; **en entrepôt** in bond; **entrepôt des douanes** bonded warehouse
entrepre•nant [ãtrəprənã] **-nante** [nãt] *adj* enterprising; bold, audacious; gallant
entreprendre [ãtrəprãdr] §56, §97 *tr* to undertake; contract for; enter upon; (coll) to try to win over ‖ *intr*—**entreprendre sur** to encroach upon
entrepre•neur [ãtrəprənœr] **-neuse** [nøz] *mf* contractor; **entrepreneur de camionnage** trucker; **entrepreneur de pompes funèbres** undertaker
entreprise [ãtrəpriz] *f* undertaking; business, firm; contract; **libre entreprise** free enterpise
entrer [ãtre] *tr* to introduce, bring in ‖ *intr* (*aux:* ÉTRE) to enter; go in, come in; **entrer à, dans,** or **en** to enter; enter into; begin; **entrer pour** to enter into, be an ingredient of
entre-rail [ãtrəraj] *m* (rr) gauge
entre-regarder [ãtrərəgarde] *ref* to exchange glances
entresol [ãtrəsɔl] *m* mezzanine
entre-temps [ãtrətã] *m invar* interval; **dans l'entre-temps** in the meantime ‖ *adv* meanwhile
entreteneur [ãtrətnœr] *m* keeper of a mistress
entretenir [ãtrətnir] §72 *tr* to maintain, keep up; carry on (*a conversation*); keep (*a mistress*); entertain, harbor ‖ *ref* to converse, talk
entrete•nu -nue [ãtrətny] *adj* kept (*woman*); continuous, undamped (*waves*)
entretien [ãtrətjẽ] *m* maintenance, upkeep; support (*of family, army, etc.*); interview; **entretien courant** servicing
entretoise [ãtrətwaz] *f* strut, brace, crosspiece
entre-tuer [ãtrətɥe] *ref* to kill each other, fight to the death
entre-voie [ãtrəvwa] *f* (rr) gauge
entrevoir [ãtrəvwar] §75 *tr* to glimpse; foresee
entre•vu -vue [ãtrəvy] *adj* half-seen; vaguely foreseen ‖ *f* interview
entrouvrir [ãtruvrir] §65 *tr & ref* to open part way
enture [ãtyr] *f* splice (*of pieces of wood*)
énumérer [enymere] §10 *tr* to enumerate
envahir [ãvair] *tr* to invade
envahissement [ãvaismã] *m* invasion
envaser [ãvaze] *tr* to fill with mud; stick in the mud
enveloppe [ãvlɔp] *f* envelope; **enveloppe à fenêtre** window envelope
envelopper [ãvlɔpe] *tr* to envelop; wrap up
envenimer [ãvnime] *tr* to inflame, make sore; (fig) to envenom, embitter

envergure [ãvɛrgyr] *f* span; wingspread; spread of sail; span, scope
enverrai [ãvere] *v* (**enverras, enverra, enverrons,** etc.) see **envoyer**
envers [ãvɛr] *m* wrong side, reverse, back; **à l'envers** inside out; upside down; back to front; topsy-turvy; **mettre à l'envers** to put on backwards ‖ *prep* toward; with regard to; **envers et contre tous** in spite of everyone else
envi [ãvi]—**à l'envi** vying with each other; **à l'envi de** vying with
enviable [ãvjabl] *adj* enviable
envie [ãvi] *f* desire, longing; envy; birthmark; hangnail; **avoir envie de** to feel like, to have a notion to
envier [ãvje] *tr* to envy; desire; **envier q.ch. à qn** to begrudge s.o. s.th.
en•vieux [ãvjø] **-vieuse** [vjøz] *adj* envious ‖ *mf* envious person
environ [ãvirõ] *m* outlying section; **aux environs de** in the vicinity of; around, about; **environs** surroundings ‖ *adv* about, approximately
environnement [ãvirɔnmã] *m* environment
environner [ãvirɔne] *tr* to surround
envisager [ãvizaʒe] §38 *tr* to envisage ‖ *intr*—**envisager de** + *inf* to plan to + *inf,* to expect to + *inf*
envoi [ãvwa] *m* consignment; remittance; envoy (*of ballad*)
envol [ãvɔl] *m* flight; (aer) takeoff
envolée [ãvɔle] *f* flight; (aer) takeoff
envoler [ãvɔle] *ref* to fly (*said of time*); (aer) to take off
envoûtement [ãvutmã] *m* spell, voodoo
envoûter [ãvute] *tr* to cast a spell on
envoyé envoyée [ãvwaje] *mf* envoy; messenger; **envoyé spécial** special correspondent (*of newspaper*)
envoyer [ãvwaje] §26, §95 *tr* to send; send out; throw (*e.g., a stone*); give (*a kick*); **envoyer promener** to send (*s.o.*) about his business; **envoyer qn** + *inf* to send s.o. to + *inf;* **envoyer qn chercher q.ch.** or **qn** to send s.o. for s.th. or s.o. ‖ *intr*—**envoyer chercher** to send for (*s.o.* or *s.th.*) ‖ *ref* (coll) to gulp down
enzyme [ãzim] *m & f* enzyme
épa•gneul -gneule [epaɲœl] *mf* spaniel
épais [epɛ] **épaisse** [epɛs] *adj* thick ‖ **épais** *adv* thickly
épaisseur [epɛsœr] *f* thickness
épaissir [epesir] *tr, intr, & ref* to thicken
épanchement [epãʃmã] *m* outpouring, effusion; (pathol) discharge
épancher [epãʃe] *tr* to pour out; unburden (*e.g., one's feelings*) ‖ *ref* to pourout; **s'épancher auprès de** to unbosom oneself to; **s'épancher de q.ch.** to get s.th. off one's chest
épandre [epãdr] *tr & ref* to spread; scatter
épanouir [epanwir] *tr* to make (*flowers*) bloom; light up (*the face*) ‖ *ref* to bloom; beam (*said of face*)

épanouissement [epanwismɑ̃] *m* blossoming; brightening up (*of a face*)

épar•gnant [eparɲɑ̃] **-gnante** [ɲɑ̃t] *adj* thrifty ‖ *mf* depositor

épargne [eparɲ] *f* saving, thrift; **épargnes** savings

épargner [eparɲe] §97 *tr* to save; spare; husband

éparpillement [eparpijmɑ̃] *m* scattering

éparpiller [eparpije] *tr* to scatter; dissinate (*e.g., one's efforts*)

épars [epar] **éparse** [epars] *adj* scattered, sparse; in disorder

épa•tant [epatɑ̃] **-tante** [tɑ̃t] *adj* (coll) wonderful, terrific

épate [epat] *f*—**faire de l'épate** (slang) to make a big show, to splurge

épa•té -tée [epate] *adj* flattened; (slang) flabbergasted

épater [epate] *tr* (coll) to shock, amaze

épaulard [epolar] *m* killer whale

épaule [epol] *f* shoulder; **donner un coup d'épaule à qn** (coll) to give s.o. a hand; **par-dessus l'épaule** (fig) contemptuously

épaulé-jeté [epoleʒte] *m* clean and jerk (*in weight lifting*)

épaulement [epolmɑ̃] *m* breastworks

épauler [epole] *tr* to back, support ‖ *intr* to take aim

épaulette [epolɛt] *f* epaulet

épave [epav] *f* wreck; derelict, stray; **épaves** wreckage

épée [epe] *f* sword

épéiste [epeist] *m* swordsman

épeler [eple] §34 *tr* to spell, spell out; read letter by letter

épellation [epɛllaasjɔ̃] *f* spelling

éper•du -due [epɛrdy] *adj* bewildered; desperate (*resistance*); mad (*with pain*); wild (*with joy*)

éperdument [epɛrdymɑ̃] *adv* desperately, madly, wildly

éperlan [epɛrlɑ̃] *m* smelt

éperon [eprɔ̃] *m* spur

éperonner [eprɔne] *tr* to spur

épervier [epɛrvje] *m* sparrow hawk; fish net; (pol & fig) hawk

éphémère [efemɛr] *adj* ephemeral ‖ *m* mayfly

épi [epi] *m* ear, cob, spike; cowlick; **épi de maïs** corncob

épice [epis] *f* spice

épicéa [episeɑ] *m* Norway spruce

épicer [epise] §51 *tr* to spice

épicerie [episri] *f* grocery store; canned goods; **épicerie de dépannage** convenience store

épi•cier [episje] **-cière** [sjɛr] *mf* grocer

épicu•rien [epikyrjɛ̃] **-rienne** [rjɛn] *adj & mf* epicurean

épidémie [epidemi] *f* epidemic

épidémiologie [epidemjɔlɔʒi] *f* epidemiology

épidémique [epidemik] *adj* epidemic; contagious (*e.g., laughter*)

épiderme [epidɛrm] *m* epidermis

épier [epje] *tr* to spy upon; be on the lookout for ‖ *intr* to ear, head

épieu [epjø] *m* (*pl* **épieux**) pike

épiglotte [epiglɔt] *f* epiglottis

épigone [epigɔn] *m* imitator, follower

épigramme [epigram] *f* epigram

épigraphe [epigraf] *f* epigraph

épilepsie [epilɛpsi] *f* epilepsy

épileptique [epilɛptik] *adj & mf* epileptic

épiler [epile] *tr* to pluck (*one's eyebrows*); remove hair from

épilogue [epilɔg] *m* epilogue

épiloguer [epilɔge] *intr* to split hairs; **épiloguer sur** to carp at

épinard [epinar] *m* spinach; **des épinards** spinach (*leaves used as food*)

épine [epin] *f* thorn; **épine dorsale** backbone; **épine noire** blackthorn; **être sur les épines** to be on pins and needles

épinette [epinɛt] *f* spinet; hencoop

épi•neux [epinø] **-neuse** [nøz] *adj* thorny; ticklish (*question*)

épingle [epɛ̃gl] *f* pin; **épingle à chapeau** hatpin; **épingle à cheveux** hairpin; **épingle à linge** clothespin; **épingle anglaise** safety pin; **épingle dans une meule de foin** needle in a haystack; **épingle de cravate** stickpin; **épingle de nourrice, épingle de sûreté** safety pin; **monter en épingle** (coll) to make much of; **tiré à quatre épingles** (coll) spic-and-span; (coll) all dolled up; **tirer son épingle du jeu** (coll) to get out by the skin of one's teeth

épingler [epɛ̃gle] *tr* to pin; (coll) to pin down (*s.o.*)

épinière [epinjɛr] *adj fem* spinal (*cord*)

Epiphanie [epifani] *f* Epiphany, Twelfth-night

épique [epik] *adj* epic

épisco•pal -pale [episkɔpal] (*pl* **-paux** [po]) *adj* episcopal; Episcopalian ‖ *mf* Episcopalian

épiscope [episkɔp] *m* (mil) periscope of a tank

épisode [epizɔd] *m* episode

épisodique [epizɔdik] *adj* episodic

épisser [epise] *tr* to splice

épissure [episyr] *f* splice; **épissure génétique** gene splicing

épistémologie [epistemɔlɔʒi] *f* epistemology; theory of knowledge

épitaphe [epitaf] *f* epitaph

épithète [epitɛt] *f* epithet

épitoge [epitɔʒ] *f* shoulder band (*worn by French lawyers and holders of French degrees*)

épitomé [epitɔme] *m* epitome

épître [epitr] *f* epistle

éplo•ré -rée [eplɔre] *adj* in tears

épluchage [eplyʃaʒ] *m* peeling; examination

éplucher [eplyʃe] *tr* to peel, pare; clean, pick; (fig) to find fault with, pick holes in

éplu•cheur [eplyʃœr] **-cheuse** [ʃøz] *mf* (coll) faultfinder ‖ *m* potato peeler, orange peeler, peeling knife ‖ *f*—**éplucheuse électrique** electric peeler épluchure [eply∫yr] f peelings; épluchure de maïs cornhusks

épointer [epwɛ̃te] tr to dull the point of

éponge [epɔ̃ʒ] f sponge

éponger [epɔ̃ʒe] §38 tr to sponge off, mop up

épopée [epɔpe] f epic

époque [epɔk] f epoch; time; period; à l'époque de at the time of; d'époque a real antique; faire époque to be epoch-making

épouiller [epuje] tr to delouse

époumoner [epumɔne] ref to shout oneself out of breath

épousailles [epuzɑj] fpl wedding

épouser [epuze] tr to marry; espouse; épouser la forme de to take the exact shape of

époussetage [epustaʒ] m dusting

épousseter [epuste] §34 tr to dust

époussette [epusɛt] f duster

épouvantable [epuvɑ̃tabl] adj frightful, terrible

épouvantail [epuvɑ̃taj] m scarecrow

épouvante [epuvɑ̃t] f fright, terror

épouvanter [epuvɑ̃te] tr to frighten, terrify

époux [epu] épouse [epuz] mf spouse || m husband; les époux husband and wife || f wife

éprendre [eprɑ̃dr] §56 ref—s'éprendre de to fall in love with; hold fast to (liberty, justice, etc.)

épreuve [eprœv] f proof, test, trial; ordeal; examination; (phot, typ) proof; corriger les épreuves (de) to proofread; épreuve de mise en pages, épreuve de pages page proof; épreuve en placard, épreuve sous le galet galley proof; épreuves (mov) rushes

épris [epri] éprise [epriz] adj infatuated; épris de in love with

éprouver [epruve] tr to prove, test, try; experience, feel; put to the test

éprouvette [epruvɛt] f test tube; specimen; (med) probe

epsomite [epsɔmit] f Epsom salts

épucer [epyse] §51 tr to clean of fleas, delouse

épui•sé -sée [epɥize] adj exhausted, tired out; sold out

épuisement [epɥizmɑ̃] m exhaustion; diminution, draining off

épuiser [epɥize] tr to exhaust, use up; wear out; tire out || ref to run out; wear out

épuration [epyrasjɔ̃] f purification; refining (e.g., of petroleum); (pol) purge

épure [epyr] f working drawing

épurement [epyrmɑ̃] m expurgation

épurer [epyre] tr to purify; expurgate; weed out, purge

équanimité [ekwanimite] f equanimity

équarrir [ekarir] tr to cut up, quarter (an animal); square off

équateur [ekwatœr] m equator; l'Equateur Ecuador

équation [ekwasjɔ̃] f equation

équato•rial -riale [ekwatɔrjal] adj (pl -riaux [rjo]) equatorial

équerrage [ekɛraʒ] m bevel; beveling

équerre [ekɛr] f square (L- or T-shaped instrument); d'équerre square, true; mettre d'équerre to square, to true

équerrer [ekɛre] tr to bevel

équestre [ekɛstr] adj equestrian

équilaté•ral -rale [ekɥilateral] adj (pl -raux [ro]) equilateral

équilibre [ekilibr] m equilibrium, balance; equipoise

equili•bré -brée [ekilibre] adj balanced, well-balanced

équilibrer [ekilibre] tr & ref to balance

équilibriste [ekilibrist] mf balancer, rope-dancer

équinoxe [ekinɔks] m equinox

équipage [ekipaʒ] m crew; retinue, suite; attire

équipe [ekip] f team; crew; gang, work party; (naut) train of boats; équipe de jour day shift; équipe de nuit night shift; équipe de secours rescue squad; équipe suicide (football) suicide squad

équipée [ekipe] f escapade, lark; crazy project

équipement [ekipmɑ̃] m equipment; équipement de survie survival kit

équiper [ekipe] tr to equip

équi•pier [ekipje] -pière [pjɛr] mf teammate; crew member

équitable [ekitabl] adj equitable

équitation [ekitasjɔ̃] f horseback riding

équité [ekite] f equity

équiva•lent [ekivalɑ̃] -lente [lɑ̃t] adj & m equivalent

équivaloir [ekivalwar] §71 intr—équivaloir à to be equivalent to; be tantamount to

équivoque [ekivɔk] adj equivocal; questionable (e.g., reputation) || f double entendre; uncertainty; sans équivoque without equivocation

équivoquer [ekivɔke] intr to equivocate, quibble; pun

érable [erabl] m maple; érable à sucre sugar maple

érafler [erafle] tr to graze, scratch

éraflure [eraflyr] f graze, scratch

érail•lé -lée [eraje] adj bloodshot (eyes); hoarse (voice); frayed (rope)

érailler [eraje] tr to fray

ère [ɛr] f era

érection [erɛksjɔ̃] f erection

érein•té -tée [erɛ̃te] adj all in, worn out, tired out

éreinter [erɛ̃te] tr to exhaust, tire out; (coll) to criticize unmercifully, run down (an author, play, etc.) || ref to wear oneself out; drudge

erg [ɛrg] m erg

ergol [ɛrgɔl] m (rok) propellant

ergot [ɛrgo] m spur (of rooster); monter or se dresser sur ses ergots (fig) to get up on a high horse

ergotage [ɛrgotaʒ] m (coll) quibbling

ergoter [ɛrgote] tr (coll) to quibble

ériger [eriʒe] §38 tr to erect || ref—s'ériger en to set oneself up as

ermitage [ɛrmitaʒ] m hermitage

ermite [ɛrmit] m hermit

éroder [erɔde] *tr* to erode

érosion [erozjɔ̃] *f* erosion

érotique [erɔtik] *adj* erotic

érotisme [erɔtism] *m* eroticism

érotothèque [erɔtɔtɛk] *f* adult book shop

er•rant [ɛrɑ̃] **-rante** [rɑ̃t] *adj* wandering, stray; errant

erratique [ɛratik] *adj* intermittent, irregular, erratic

erre [ɛr] *f* (naut) headway; **erres** track (*e.g., of deer*)

errements [ɛrmɑ̃] *mpl* ways, methods; (pej) erring ways, bad habits

errer [ɛre] *intr* to wander; err; play (*said of smile*)

erreur [ɛrœr] *f* error, mistake; **erreur de frappe** typing error

erro•né -née [ɛrɔne] *adj* erroneous

éructation [eryktɑsjɔ̃] *f* belch

éructer [erykte] *tr* (fig) to belch forth ‖ *intr* to belch

éru•dit [erydi] **-dite** [dit] *adj* erudite, learned ‖ *mf* scholar, erudite

érudition [erydisjɔ̃] *f* erudition

éruption [erypsjɔ̃] *f* eruption; blowout (*of an oil well*)

es [e] *v* see **être**

ès [ɛs] *prep* §77

esbroufe [ɛsbruf] *f* showing off; shoving

esc. *abbr* (**escompte**) discount

esca•beau [ɛskabo] *m* (*pl* **-beaux**) stool; stepladder

escadre [ɛskadr] *f* squadron; fleet

escadron [ɛskadrɔ̃] *m* (mil) squadron

escalade [ɛskalad] *f* scaling, climbing; escalation (*of a war*)

escalader [ɛskalade] *tr* to scale, climb; clamber over or up

escalator [ɛskalatɔr] *m* escalator

escale [ɛskal] *f* port of call, stop; **faire escale** to make a stop; **sans escale** nonstop

escalier [ɛskalje] *m* stairway; **escalier à vis** circular stairway; **escalier de sauvetage** fire escape; **escalier en colimaçon** spiral staircase; **escalier mécanique, escalier roulant** escalator

escalope [ɛskalɔp] *f* thin slice, escalope, scallop; **escalope de veau** veal cutlet

escamotable [ɛskamɔtabl] *adj* retractable (*e.g., landing gear*); concealable (*piece of furniture*)

escamotage [ɛskamɔtaʒ] *m* sleight of hand; side-stepping, avoiding; theft

escamoter [ɛskamɔte] *tr* to palm (*a card*); pick (*a wallet*); dodge (*a question*); slur (*a word*); hush up (*a scandal*); (aer) to retract (*landing gear*)

escamo•teur [ɛskamɔtœr] **-teuse** [tøz] *mf* prestidigitator; pickpocket

escapade [ɛskapad] *f* escapade, escape

escarbille [ɛskarbij] *f* cinder, clinker

escarbot [ɛskarbo] *m* beetle

escarboucle [ɛskarbukl] *f* (mineral) carbuncle

escargot [ɛskargo] *m* snail

escarmouche [ɛskarmuʃ] *f* skirmish; dust-up (coll); **escarmouche de frontière** border clash

escarmoucher [ɛskarmuʃe] *intr* to skirmish

escarpe [ɛskarp] *m* ruffian, bandit ‖ *f* escarpment (*of a fort*)

escar•pé -pée [ɛskarpe] *adj* steep

escarpement [ɛskarpəmɑ̃] *m* escarpment

escarpin [ɛskarpɛ̃] *m* pump, dancing shoe

escarpolette [ɛskarpɔlɛt] *f* swing

escarre [ɛskar] *f* scab

escarrifier [ɛskarifje] *tr* to form a scab on

esche [ɛʃ] *f* bait

Eschyle [ɛsʃil] [eʃil] *m* Aeschylus

escient [ɛsjɑ̃]—**à bon escient** knowingly, wittingly; **à mon (ton,** etc.) **escient** to my (your, etc.) certain knowledge

esclaffer [ɛsklafe] *ref* to burst out laughing

esclandre [ɛsklɑ̃dr] *m* scandal

esclavage [ɛsklavaʒ] *m* slavery

esclavagiste [ɛsklavaʒist] *adj* pro-slavery ‖ *mf* advocate of slavery

esclave [ɛsklav] *adv* & *mf* slave

escompte [ɛskɔ̃t] *m* discount, rebate; **escompte au comptant** cash discount; **escompte de caisse** cash discount; **escompte en dehors** bank discount; **prendre à l'escompte** to discount

escompter [ɛskɔ̃te] *tr* to discount (*a premature note*); anticipate

escompteur [ɛskɔ̃tœr] *adj* discounting (*banker*) ‖ *m* discount broker

escopette [ɛskɔpɛt] *f* blunderbuss

escorte [ɛskɔrt] *f* escort

escorter [ɛskɔrte] *tr* to escort

escouade [ɛskwad] *f* infantry section; gang (*of laborers*)

escrime [ɛskrim] *f* fencing

escrimer [ɛskrime] *intr* & *ref* to fence; **s'escrimer à** to work with might and main at; **s'escrimer contre** to fence with

escri•meur [ɛskrimœr] **-meuse** [møz] *mf* fencer

escroc [ɛskro] *m* crook, swindler

escroquer [ɛskrɔke] *tr* to swindle

escroquerie [ɛskrɔkri] *f* swindling, cheating; racket, swindle

ésotérique [ezɔterik] *adj* esoteric

espace [ɛspas] *m* space; room; **espace cosmique** outer space; **espace lointain** deep space ‖ *f* (typ) space

espacement [ɛspasmɑ̃] *m* spacing

espace-temps [ɛspastɑ̃] *m* (*pl* **espaces-temps**) space-time

espacer [ɛspase] §51 *tr* to space

espadon [ɛspadɔ̃] *m* swordfish

espadrille [ɛspadrij] *f* tennis shoe; beach sandal; esparto sandal

Espagne [ɛspaɲ] *f* Spain; **l'Espagne** Spain

espa•gnol -gnole [ɛspaɲɔl] *adj* Spanish ‖ *m* Spanish (*language*) ‖ (*cap*) *mf* Spaniard (*person*); **les Espagnols** the Spanish

espagnol-anglais [ɛspaɲɔlɑ̃gle] *m invar* Spanglish

espagnolette [ɛspaɲɔlɛt] *f* espagnolette (*door fastener for French casement window*)

espalier [ɛspalje] *m* espalier

espèce [ɛspɛs] *f* species; sort, kind; **en espèces** in specie; **en l'espèce** in the matter; **espèces sonnantes** hard cash; **sale espèce** cad, bounder ‖ *mf*—**espèce de** (coll) damn, e.g., **cet espèce d'idiot** that damn fool

espérance [ɛsperɑ̃s] *f* hope; **espérance de vie** life expectancy; **espérances** expectations; prospects

espéranto [ɛsperɑ̃to] *m* Esperanto

espérer [ɛspere] §10, §95 *tr* to hope, hope for; (coll) to wait for; **espérer** + *inf* to hope to + *inf* ‖ *intr* to trust; (coll) to wait

esperluète [ɛspɛrlɥɛt] *f* ampersand

espiègle [ɛspjɛgl] *adj* mischievous ‖ *mf* rogue

espièglerie [ɛspjɛgləri] *f* mischievousness; prank

es•pion [ɛspjɔ̃] **-pionne** [pjɔn] *mf* spy ‖ *m* concealed microphone; busybody (*mirror*)

espionnage [ɛspjɔnaʒ] *m* espionage

espionner [ɛspjɔne] *tr* to spy on

espoir [ɛspwar] *m* hope; promise

esprit [ɛspri] *m* spirit; mind; intelligence; wit; spirits (*of wine*); **à l'esprit clair** clearheaded; **avoir l'esprit de l'escalier** to think of what to say too late; **bel esprit** man of letters; **esprit d'équipe** teamwork; **esprit de système** love of order; (pej) pigheadedness; **esprit fort** freethinker; **rendre l'esprit** to give up the ghost

esquif [ɛskif] *m* skiff

esqui•mau [ɛskimo] **-maude** [mod] (*pl* **-maux**) *adj* Eskimo ‖ *m* husky, Eskimo dog; Eskimo (*language*) ‖ (*cap*) *mf* Eskimo (*person*)

esquinter [ɛskɛ̃te] *tr* (coll) to tire out; (coll) to wear out; (coll) to run down, knock, criticize

esquisse [ɛskis] *f* sketch; outline, draft; beginning (*e.g., of a smile*)

esquisser [ɛskise] *tr* to sketch; outline, draft; begin

esquiver [ɛskive] *tr* to dodge, side-step; **esquiver de la tête** to duck ‖ *ref* to sneak away

essai [ese] *m* essay; trial, test; tryout; **à l'essai** on trial; **essai de résistance contre les collisions** crash test; **essai d'un rôle** (theat) tryout; **essais** first attempts (*of artist, writer, etc.*); **essai sur le terrain** field test; **faire l'essai de** to try out

essaim [esɛ] *m* swarm

essaimer [eseme] *intr* to swarm

essarter [esarte] *tr* to clear (*brush*)

essarts [esar] *mpl* clearings

essayage [esɛjaʒ] *m* fitting, trying on

essayer [esɛje], [eseje] §49, §96, §97 *tr* to try on, try out; assay (*ore*) ‖ *intr* to try; **essayer de** to try to ‖ §96 *ref*—**s'essayer à** to try one's skill at

essayeur [esɛjœr] **essayeuse** [esɛjøz] *mf* assayer

essayiste [esɛjist] *mf* essayist

esse [ɛs] *f* S-hook; sound hole (*of violin*)

essence [esɑ̃s] *f* essence; gasoline; kind, species; **par essence** by definition

essen•tiel -tielle [esɑ̃sjɛl] *adj & m* essential

essentiellement [esɑ̃sjɛlmɑ̃] *adv* essentially

esseu•lé -lée [esœle] *adj* abandoned

es•sieu [esjø] *m* (*pl* **-sieux**) axle, axletree

essor [esɔr] *m* flight; development; boom (*in business*); **donner libre essor à** to give vent to; give full scope to; **prendre son essor** to take wing

essorer [esɔre] *tr* to spin-dry; wring; centrifuge

essoreuse [esɔrøz] *f* spin-drier; wringer; centrifuge

essouf•flé -flée [esufle] *adj* breathless, out of breath

essuie-glace [esɥiglas] *m* (*pl* **-glaces**) windshield wiper

essuie-mains [esɥimɛ̃] *m invar* towel; **essuie-mains en papier** paper toweling

essuie-plume [esɥiplym] *m* (*pl* **-plumes**) pen-wiper

essuyer [esɥije] §27 *tr* to wipe; wipe off; wipe away; suffer, endure; undergo; weather (*a storm*); **essuyer les plâtres** (coll) to be the first to occupy a house

est [ɛst] *adj invar* east, eastern ‖ *m* east; **de l'est** eastern; **faire l'est** to steer eastward; **vers l'est** eastward ‖ [e], [ɛ] *v* see **être**

estacade [ɛstakad] *f* breakwater; pier; boom (*barrier of floating logs*); railway trestle

estafette [ɛstafɛt] *f* messenger

estaminet [ɛstaminɛ] *m* bar, café

estampe [ɛstɑ̃p] *f* print, engraving; (*tool*) stamp

estamper [ɛstɑ̃pe] *tr* to stamp (*with a design*); engrave; overcharge, fleece

estampille [ɛstɑ̃pij] *f* identification mark; trademark; hallmark

est-ce que [ɛskə] see **être**

ester [ɛstɛr] *m* ester ‖ [ɛste] *intr*—**ester en justice** to go to law, to sue

esthète [ɛstɛt] *mf* aesthete

esthéti•cien [ɛstetisjɛ̃] **-cienne** [sjɛn] *mf* aesthetician ‖ *f* beautician

esthétique [ɛstetik] *adj* aesthetic; plastic (*surgery*); ‖ *f* aesthetics

estimable [ɛstimabl] *adj* estimable

estimateur [ɛstimatœr] *m* estimator, appraiser

estimation [ɛstimasjɔ̃] *f* estimation, appraisal

estime [ɛstim] *f* esteem; **à l'estime** by guesswork; (naut) by dead reckoning

estimer [ɛstime] §95 *tr* to esteem; estimate, assess; **estimer** + *inf* to think that + *inf.* e.g., **j'estime avoir fait mon devoir** I think that I did my duty

esti•val -vale [ɛstival] *adj* (*pl* **-vaux** [vol]) summer

esti•vant [ɛstivɑ̃] **-vante** [vɑ̃t] *mf* summer vacationist, summer resident

estiver [ɛstive] *intr* to summer

estocade [ɛstɔkad] *f* thrust (*in fencing*); unexpected attack

estomac [ɛstɔma] *m* stomach

estomaquer [ɛstɔmake] *tr* (coll) to astound ‖ *ref* (coll) to be angered

estomper [ɛstɔ̃pe] *tr* to shade off, rub away (*a drawing*); blur ‖ *ref* to be blurred

estrade [ɛstrad] *f* platform

estragon [ɛstragɔ̃] *m* tarragon

estro•pié -piée [ɛstrɔpje] *adj* crippled ‖ *mf* cripple

estuaire [ɛstɥɛr] *m* estuary

estudian•tin [ɛstydjɑ̃tɛ̃] **-tine** [tin] *adj* student

esturgeon [ɛstyrʒɔ̃] *m* sturgeon

et [e] *conj* and; **et . . . et** both . . . and

Établ. *abbr* (**Établissement**) company, establishment

étable [etabl] *f* stable, cowshed

établer [etable] *tr* to stable

établi [etabli] *m* workbench

établir [etablir] *tr* to establish ‖ *ref* to settle down; set up headquarters

établissement [etablismɑ̃] *m* establishment; business; factory; **établissement d'enseigne-ment, établissement scolaire** school; **éta-blissements** company, firm, e.g., **les Établis-sements Martin** Martin & Co.

étage [etaʒ] *m* floor, story; tier, level; rank, social level; (rok) stage; **de bas étage** lower-class; **dernier étage** top floor; **premier étage** first floor above ground floor, second floor

étager [etaʒe] **§38** *tr* to arrange in tiers; stagger; perform in stages

étagère [etaʒɛr] *f* rack, shelf

étai [etɛ] *m* prop, stay

étain [etɛ̃] *m* tin; pewter

étais [ete] *v* (**était, étions**) see **être**

étal [etal] *m* (*pl* **étals** or **étaux** [eto]) stall, stand; butcher's block

étalage [etalaʒ] *m* display

étalager [etalaʒe] **§38** *tr* to display

étalagiste [etalaʒist] *mf* window dresser, display artist; demonstrator

étaler [etale] *tr* to display; spread out ‖ *ref* (coll) to sprawl

étalon [etalɔ̃] *m* stallion; monetary standard

étalonner [etalɔne] *tr* to verify, control; standardize; graduate, calibrate

étalon-or [etalɔ̃ɔr] *m* gold standard

étambot [etɑ̃bo] *m* (naut) sternpost

étamer [etame] *tr* to tin-plate; silver (*a mirror*)

étamine [etamin] *f* stamen; sieve; cheese-cloth

étampe [etɑ̃p] *f* stamp, die, punch

étamper [etɑ̃pe] *tr* to stamp, punch

étanche [etɑ̃ʃ] *adj* watertight, airtight

étancher [etɑ̃ʃe] *tr* to check, stanch the flow of; quench (*one's thirst*); make watertight or airtight

étang [etɑ̃] *m* pond

étape [etap] *f* stage; stop, halt; day's march; (sports) lap; **brûler les étapes** to go straight through

état [eta] *m* state; statement, record; trade, occupation; government; (hist) estate; **en tout état de cause** at all costs; in any case; **état civil** marital status, birth and death record; **état de**

la technique, **état présent** state of the art; **état providence** welfare state; **état tampon** buffer state; **être dans tous ses états** to stew; **être en état de** to be in a position to; **faire état de** to take into account; expect to; **hors d'état** out of order, unfit; **tenir en état** to keep in shape, repair

étatisation [etatizɑsjɔ̃] *f* nationalization

étatiser [etatize] *tr* to nationalize

étatisme [etatism] *m* statism

état-major [etamaʒɔr] *m* (*pl* **états-majors**) headquarters, staff

état-providence [etaprɔvidɑ̃s] *m* welfare state

États-Unis [etazyni] *mpl* United States; **les États-Unis d'Amérique** the United States of America; **les États-Unis de Brésil** the United States of Brazil

étau [eto] *m* (*pl* **étaux**) vise

étayer [eteje] **§49** *tr* to prop, stay

etc. [ɛtsetera] *abbr* (**et caetera, et cetera**) etc.

et Cⁱᵉ *abbr* (**et Compagnie**) & Co.

été [ete] *m* summer; **en été** in (the) summer ‖ *v* see **être**

éteignoir [etɛɲwar] *m* candle snuffer; (coll) kill-joy, wet blanket

éteindre [etɛ̃dr] **§50** *tr* to extinguish, put out; turn off; wipe out; appease (*e.g., one's thirst*); dull (*a color*) ‖ *intr* to put out the light ‖ *ref* to go out; (fig) to die, pass away

éteint [etɛ̃] **éteinte** [etɛ̃t] *adj* extinguished; exinct; dull, dim

étendard [etɑ̃dar] *m* flag, banner

étendoir [etɑ̃dwar] *m* clothesline; drying rack

étendre [etɑ̃dr] *tr* to extend, spread out ‖ *ref* to stretch out; spread

éten•du -due [etɑ̃dy] *adj* outspread; extensive; vast; diluted, adulterated ‖ *f* stretch; range, scope

éter•nel -nelle [etɛrnɛl] *adj* eternal

éterniser [etɛrnize] *tr* to perpetuate (*a name*); drag out ‖ *ref* (coll) to drag on; **s'éterniser chez qn** (coll) to overstay an invitation

éternité [etɛrnite] *f* eternity

éternuement [etɛrnymɑ̃] *m* sneeze; sneezing

éternuer [etɛrnɥe] *intr* to sneeze

êtes [ɛt] *v* see **être**

étêter [etɛte] *tr* to top (*a tree*); take the head off (*a fish, nail, etc.*)

éteule [etœl] *f* stubble

éther [etɛr] *m* ether

éthé•ré -rée [etere] *adj* ethereal

Éthiopie [etjɔpi] *f* Ethiopia; **l'Éthiopie** Ethiopia

éthio•pien [etjɔpjɛ̃] **-pienne** [pjɛn] *adj* Ethiopian ‖ *m* Ethiopian (*language*) ‖ (*cap*) *mf* Ethiopian (*person*)

éthique [etik] *adj* ethical ‖ *f* ethics

ethnique [ɛtnik] *adj* ethnic(al)

ethnographie [ɛtnɔgrafi] *f* ethnography

ethnologie [ɛtnɔlɔʒi] *f* ethnology

éthyle [etil] *m* ethyl

éthylène [etilɛn] *m* ethylene

étiage [etjaʒ] *m* low-water mark

étince•lant [etɛ̃slɑ̃] **-lante** [lɑ̃t] *adj* sparkling, glittering

étinceler [etɛ̃sle] §34 *intr* to sparkle, glitter

étincelle [etɛ̃sɛl] *f* spark; (fig) flash

étiolement [etjɔlmɑ̃] *m* wilting

étioler [etjɔle] *tr & ref* to wilt

étique [etik] *adj* lean, emaciated

étiquetage [etiktaʒ] *m* labeling

étiqueter [etikte] §34 *tr* to label

étiquette [etikɛt] *f* etiquette; label; **étiquette gommée** sticker

étirer [etire] *tr* to stretch, lengthen, elongate || *ref* (coll) to stretch one's limbs

étoffe [etɔf] *f* stuff; material, fabric; quality, worth

étoffer [etɔfe] *tr* to fill out; enrich; stuff (*furniture*)

étoile [etwal] *f* star; traffic circle; **à la belle étoile** out of doors; **étoile de mer** starfish; **étoile filante** shooting or falling star; **étoile polaire** polestar

étoi•lé -lée [etwale] *adj* star-spangled, starry

étole [etɔl] *f* stole

éton•nant -nante [etɔnɑ̃] [nɑ̃t] *adj* astonishing

étonnement [etɔnmɑ̃] *m* surprise, astonishment; fissure, crack

étonner [etɔne] *tr* to surprise, astonish; shake or crack (*masonry*) || §97 *ref* to be surprised

étouf•fant -fante [etufɑ̃] [fɑ̃t] *adj* suffocating; sweltering

étouffée [etufe] *f* braising; **cuire à l'étouffée** to braise

étouffer [etufe] *tr, intr, & ref* to suffocate; stifle; choke

étoupe [etup] *f* oakum, tow

étourderie [eturdri] *f* thoughtlessness

étour•di -die [eturdi] *adj* scatterbrained || *mf* scatterbrain

étourdir [eturdir] *tr* to stun, daze; numb; deafen (*with loud noise*) || *ref* to try to forget, get in a daze

étourdissement [eturdismɑ̃] *m* dizziness; numbing

étour•neau [eturno] *m* (*pl* **-neaux**) starling

étrange [etrɑ̃ʒ] *adj* strange

étran•ger [etrɑ̃ʒe] **-gère** [ʒɛr] *adj* foreign; irrelevant; unknown, strange; **être étranger à** to be unacquainted with || *mf* foreigner; stranger; **à l'étranger** abroad, in a foreign country

étrangeté [etrɑ̃ʒte] *f* strangeness

étrangler [etrɑ̃gle] *tr & intr* to strangle || *ref* to choke; narrow (*said of passageway, valley, etc.*)

étran•gleur [etrɑ̃glœr] **-gleuse** [gløz] *mf* strangler

étrave [etrav] *f* (naut) stempost; **de l'étrave à l'etambot** from stem to stern

être [ɛtr] *m* being || §28, §95 *intr* to be; to go to + *inf* (usually in the past tense), e.g., **elle a été chanter à Paris** she went to sing in Paris, **où as-tu été passer les vacances?** Where did you go for your vacation?; **en être pour sa peine** to have nothing for one's trou-

ble; **est-ce que** (not translated in questions), e.g., **est-ce qu'ils sont riches?** are they rich?; **être à** + *pron disj* to be + *pron poss,* e.g., **le livre est à moi** the book is mine; **n'est-ce pas** see **ne; s'il en fut** it surely was, to be sure; **s'il en fut jamais** if ever there was one || *aux* (used with some intransitive verbs and all reflexive verbs) to have, e.g., **elles sont arrivées** they have arrived; (used to form the passive voice) to be, e.g., **il est aimé de tout le monde** he is loved by everybody

étrécir [etresir] *tr & ref* to shrink

étreindre [etrɛ̃dr] §50 *tr* to embrace; grip, seize

étreinte [etrɛ̃t] *f* embrace; hold, grasp

étrenne [etrɛn] *f* first sale of the day; **avoir l'étrenne de** to have the first use of; **étrennes** New-Year gifts

étrenner [etrɛne] *tr* to put on for the first time; be the first to wear || *intr* (coll) to be the first to catch it

étrier [etrije] *m* stirrup

étrille [etrij] *f* currycomb

étriller [etrije] *tr* to curry; (coll) to thrash, tan the hide of; (coll) to overcharge, fleece

étriper [etripe] *tr* to gut, disembowel

étri•qué -quée [etrike] *adj* skimpy, tight; narrow, cramped

étriquer [etrike] *tr* to make too tight; shorten (*e.g., a speech*)

étroit [etrwa] **étroite** [etrwat] *adj* narrow; strict; tight; close; **à l'étroit** confined, cramped

étroitesse [etrwatɛs] *f* narrowness; **étroitesse d'esprit, étroitesse de vues** narrow-mindedness, tunnel vision

Éts. *abbr* **Établissements**

étude [etyd] *f* study; law office; law practice; spadework, planning; **à l'étude** under consideration; **étude de faisabilité** feasibility study; **étude des ovnis** UFOlogy; **étude sur dossier** case work; **hautes études** advanced studies; **mettre à l'étude** to study; **terminer ses études** to finish one's courses

étu•diant -diante [etydjɑ̃] [djɑ̃t] *mf* student; **ancien étudiant** alumnus; **ancienne étudiante** alumna

étu•dié -diée [etydje] *adj* studied; set (*speech*); artificial, affected

étudier [etydje] *tr* to study; practice, rehearse; learn by heart; design || *intr* to study || §96 *ref* to be overly introspective; **s'étudier à** to take pains to, make a point of

étui [etɥi] *m* case, box

étuve [etyv] *f* steam bath or room; drying room; steam sterilizer; incubator (*for breeding cultures*)

étuver [etyve] *tr* to stew; steam; dry

étymologie [etimɔlɔʒi] *f* etymology

étymon [etimɔ̃cb] *m* etymon

eucalyptus [økaliptys] *m* eucalyptus

Eucharistie [økaristi] *f* Eucharist

eugénique [øʒenik] *f* eugenics

eugénisme [øʒenism] *m* eugenics

eunuque [ønyk] *m* eunuch

euphémique [øfemik] *adj* euphemistic
euphémisme [øfemism] *m* euphemism
euphonie [øfɔni] *f* euphony
euphonique [øfɔnik] *adj* euphonic
euphorie [øfɔri] *f* euphoria
euro [øro] *m* euro
eurodollar [ørɔdɔlar] *m* Eurodollar
Europe [ørɔp] *f* Europe; **l'Europe** Europe
européen [ørɔpeɛ̃] **européenne** [ørɔpeɛn] *adj* European ‖ (*cap*) *mf* European
eus [y] *v* (**eut, eûmes,** etc.) see **avoir**
eux [ø] §85
eux-mêmes [ømɛm] §86
evacuation [evakɥɑsjɔ̃] *f* evacuation; emptying, draining; **evacuation du ventre** bowel movement
évacuer [evakɥe] *tr & ref* to evacuate
éva·dé -dée [evade] *mf* escapee
évader [evade] *ref* to escape, evade
évaluer [evalɥe] *tr* to evaluate, appraise; estimate
évanes·cent [evanesɑ̃] **-cente** [sɑ̃t] *adj* evanescent
évangélique [evɑ̃ʒelik] *adj* evangelic(al)
évangéliste [evɑ̃ʒelist] *m* evangelist
évangile [evɑ̃ʒil] *m* gospel
évanouir [evanwir] *ref* to faint; lose consciousness; vanish; (rad) to fade
évanouissement [evanwismɑ̃] *m* fainting; disappearance; (rad, telv) fading
évapo·ré -rée [evapɔre] *adj* flighty, fickle, giddy
évaporer [evapɔre] *tr & ref* to evaporate
évaser [evɑze] *tr & ref* to widen
éva·sif [evazif] **-sive** [ziv] *adj* evasive
évasion [evɑzjɔ̃] *f* evasion; escape; **d'évasion** escapist (*literature*)
Ève [ev] *f* Eve; **je ne le connais ni d'Ève ni d'Adam** (coll) I don't know him from Adam
évêché [eveʃe] *m* bishopric
éveil [evɛj] *m* awakening; alarm, warning
éveil·lé -lée [eveje] *adj* alert, lively; sharp, intelligent
éveiller [eveje] *tr & ref* to wake up
événement [evenəmɑ̃], [evɛnmɑ̃] *m* event; outcome, development; **faire événement** to cause quite a stir
évent [evɑ̃] *m* vent; staleness
éventail [evɑ̃taj] *m* fan; range, spread; screen
éventaire [evɑ̃tɛr] *m* tray (*carried by flower girl, cigarette girl, etc.*); sidewalk display
éven·té -tée [evɑ̃te] *adj* stale, flat
éventer [evɑ̃te] *tr* to fan; ventilate; get wind of (*a secret*); **éventer la mèche** (coll) to let the cat out of the bag ‖ *ref* to fan oneself; fade away (*said of odor*); go stale or flat
éventrer [evɑ̃tre] *tr* to disembowel; smash open
éventualité [evɑ̃tɥalite] *f* eventuality, contingency; possibility
éven·tuel -tuelle [evɑ̃tɥɛl] *adj* possible; contingent; forthcoming ‖ *m* possibility; possibilities (*e.g., of a job*)

éventuellement [evɑ̃tɥɛlmɑ̃] *adv* possibly; if need be
évêque [evɛk] *m* bishop
évertuer [evɛrtɥe] §96 *ref*—**s'évertuer à** or **pour** + *inf* to strive to + inf
éviction [eviksjɔ̃] *f* eviction, removal; **éviction scolaire** quarantine
évidement [evidmɑ̃] *m* hollowing out
évidemment [evidamɑ̃] *adv* evidently
évidence [evidɑ̃s] *f* evidence, obviousness; conspicuousness; **de toute évidence** by all appearances; **se mettre en évidence** to come to the fore
évi·dent [evidɑ̃] **-dente** [dɑ̃t] *adj* evident
évider [evide] *tr* to hollow out
évier [evje] *m* sink
évincer [evɛ̃se] §51 *tr* to evict, oust; discriminate against
éviter [evite] §97 *tr* to avoid, escape
évoca·teur [evɔkatœr] **-trice** [tris] *adj* evocative, suggestive
évocation [evɔkɑsjɔ̃] *f* evocation
évoluer [evɔlɥe] *intr* to evolve; change one's mind
évolution [evɔlysjɔ̃] *f* evolution; **évolution du cas social** case history; **évolution de la maladie** (med) case history
évoquer [evɔke] *tr* to evoke; recall, call to mind
ex [ɛks] *mf* (coll) ex (*ex-husband, ex-wife; person with whom romantic relations have been cut off*)
ex- [ɛks] *adj* (*ancien*) ex-, e.g., **l'ex-ministre** the ex-premier
exact [ɛgza], [ɛgzakt] **exacte** [ɛgzakt] *adj* exact; punctual, on time
exactement [ɛgzaktəmɑ̃] *adv* exactly; on time
exactitude [ɛgzaktityd] *f* exactness; punctuality
exagération [ɛgzaʒerɑsjɔ̃] *f* exaggeration
exagérer [ɛgzaʒere] §10 *tr* to exaggerate; overdo
exal·té -tée [ɛgzalte] *adj* impassioned; high-strung, wrought-up ‖ *mf* hothead, fanatic
exalter [ɛgzalte] *tr* to exalt; excite (*e.g., the imagination*) ‖ *ref* to get excited
examen [ɛgzamɛ̃] *m* examination; **à l'examen** under consideration; on approval; **examen cytologique des seins** Pap smear, Pap test; **examen de fin d'études** or **examen de fin de classe** final examination; **examen de la vision** eye test; **examen de routine** routine examination; **examen médical** medical examination; **examen probatoire** placement exam; **libre examen** free inquiry; **se présenter à, passer,** or **subir un examen** to take an examination
examina·teur [ɛgzaminatœr] **-trice** [tris] *mf* examiner
examiner [ɛgzamine] *tr* to examine
exaspération [ɛgzasperɑsjɔ̃] *f* exasperation; crisis, aggravation
exaspérer [ɛgzaspere] §10 *tr* to exasperate; make worse

exaucer [ɛgzose] §51 *tr* to answer the prayer of; fulfill (*a wish*)

excava•teur [ɛskavatœr] -trice [tris] *m* & *f* excavator, steam shovel

excaver [ɛkskave] *tr* to excavate

excé•dant [ɛksedɑ̃] -dante [dɑ̃t] *adj* excess; tiresome

excédent [ɛksedɑ̃] *m* excess, surplus

excédentaire [ɛksedɑ̃tɛr] *adj* excess

excéder [ɛksede] §10 *tr* to exceed; tire out; overtax

excellence [ɛksɛlɑ̃s] *f* excellence; **Votre Excellence** Your Excellency

exceller [ɛksɛle] §96 *intr* to excel

excentricité [ɛksɑ̃trisite] *f* eccentricity

excentrique [ɛksɑ̃trik] *adj* eccentric; remote, outlying ‖ *mf* eccentric ‖ *m* (mach) eccentric

excep•té -tée [ɛksɛpte] *adj* excepted ‖ **excepté** *adv*—**excepté que** except that ‖ **excepté** *prep* except, except for

exception [ɛksɛpsjɔ̃] *f* exception; **à l'exception de** with the exception of

exception•nel -nelle [ɛksɛpsjɔnɛl] *adj* exceptional

exceptionnellement [ɛksɛpsjɔnɛlmɑ̃] *adv* exceptionally; as an exception

excès [ɛksɛ] *m* excess; **excès de pose** (phot) overexposure; **excès de vitesse** speeding

exces•sif [ɛksɛsif] -sive [siv] *adj* excessive

exciper [ɛksipe] *intr*—**exciper de** (law) to offer a plea of, allege

excitable [ɛksitabl] *adj* excitable

exci•tant [ɛksitɑ̃] -tante [tɑ̃t] *adj* stimulating ‖ *m* stimulant

exciter [ɛksite] §96, §100 *tr* to excite, stimulate; stir, incite; provoke (*e.g., laughter*) ‖ §96 *ref* to get excited; become (sexually) aroused

exclamation [ɛksklamɑsjɔ̃] *f* exclamation

exclamer [ɛksklame] *ref* to exclaim

exclure [ɛksklyr] §11 *tr* to exclude

exclu•sif [ɛksklyzif] -sive [ziv] *adj* exclusive

exclusion [ɛksklyzjɔ̃] *f* exclusion; **à l'exclusion de** exclusive of, excluding

exclusivité [ɛksklyzivite] *f* exclusiveness; exclusive rights; newsbeat; (journ) scoop; **en exclusivité** (public sign in front of a theater) exclusive showing

excommunication [ɛkskɔmynikɑsjɔ̃] *f* excommunication

excommunier [ɛkskɔmynje] *tr* to excommunicate

excorier [ɛkskɔrje] *tr* to scratch, skin

excrément [ɛkskremɑ̃] *m* excrement

excroissance [ɛkskrwasɑ̃s] *f* growth, tumor

excursion [ɛkskyrsjɔ̃] *f* excursion; tour, trip; outing

excursionner [ɛkskyrsjɔne] *intr* to go on an excursion

excusable [ɛkskyzabl] *adj* excusable

excuse [ɛkskyz] *f* excuse; **des excuses** apologies

excuser [ɛkskyze] §97, §99 *tr* to excuse ‖ *ref* to excuse oneself, apologize; **je m'excuse!** (coll) excuse me!

exécrer [ɛgzekre] §10 *tr* to execrate

exécu•tant [ɛgzekytɑ̃] -tante [tɑ̃t] *mf* performer

exécuter [ɛgzekyte] *tr* to execute; perform; make (*copies*) ‖ *ref* to comply

exécuteur [ɛgzekytœr] *m*—**exécuteur testamentaire** executor; **exécuteur des hautes œuvres** hangman

exécu•tif [ɛgzekytif] -tive [tiv] *adj* & *m* executive

exécution [ɛgzekysjɔ̃] *f* execution; performance; fulfillment; **mettre à exécution** to carry out

exécutrice [ɛgzekytris] *f* executrix

exemplaire [ɛgzɑ̃plɛr] *adj* exemplary ‖ *m* exemplar, model; sample, specimen; copy (*e.g., of book*); **en double exemplaire** with carbon copy; **exemplaire dédicacé** autographed copy; **exemplaires de passe** extra copies

exemple [ɛgzɑ̃pl] *m* example; **à l'exemple de** after the example of; **par exemple** for example; **par exemple!** the idea!, well I never!; **prêcher d'exemple** to practice what one preaches; **sans exemple** unprecedented

exempt [ɛgzɑ̃] **exempte** [ɛgzɑ̃t] *adj* exempt ‖ *m* (hist) police officer

exempter [ɛgzɑ̃te] §97, §99 *tr* to exempt

exemption [ɛgzɑ̃psjɔ̃] *f* exemption; **exemption d'impôts** tax exemption

exer•cé -cée [ɛgzɛrse] *adj* practiced, experienced

exercer [ɛgzɛrse] §51 *tr* to exercise; exert; practice (*e.g., medicine*) ‖ §96 *ref* to exercise; practice, drill

exercice [ɛgzɛrsis] *m* exercise; drill; practice; **exercice budgétaire** fiscal year; **exercices isométriques** isometrics

exergue [ɛgzɛrg] *m* inscription; place on a medal for an inscription, **mettre en exergue** to inscribe (*e.g., a proverb*)

exhalaison [ɛgzalɛzɔ̃] *f* exhalation (*of gas, vapors, etc.*)

exhalation [ɛgzalɑsjɔ̃] *f* exhalation (*of air from lungs*)

exhaler [ɛgzale] *tr*, *intr*, & *ref* to exhale

exhaure [ɛgzɔr] *f* pumping out (*of a mine*); drain pumps

exhaussement [ɛgzosmɑ̃] *m* raising; rise

exhausser [ɛgzose] *tr* to raise, increase the height of ‖ *ref* to rise

exhaus•tif [ɛgzostif] -tive [tiv] *adj* exhaustive

exhiber [ɛgzibe] *tr* to exhibit; show (*a ticket, passport, etc.*) ‖ *ref* to make an exhibition of oneself

exhibition [ɛgzibisjɔ̃] *f* exhibition

exhibitionniste [ɛgzibisjɔniste] *mf* exhibitionist; flasher

exhorter [ɛgzɔrte] §96, §100 *tr* to exhort

exhumer [ɛgzyme] *tr* to exhume

exi•geant [ɛgziʒɑ̃] -geante [ʒɑ̃t] *adj* exigent, exacting; unreasonable

exigence [ɛgziʒɑ̃s] *f* demand, claim; requirement; unreasonableness; **exigences** exigencies

exiger [ɛgziʒe] §38 *tr* to demand, require, exact

exigible [ɛgziʒibl] *adj* required; due, on demand

exi•gu -guë [ɛgzigy] *adj* tiny; insufficient

exiguïté [ɛgzigɥite] *f* smallness; insufficiency

exil [ɛgzil] *m* exile

exi•lé -lée [ɛgzile] *adj & mf* exile

exiler [ɛgzile] *tr* to exile

exis•tant [ɛgzistɑ̃] **-tante** [tɑ̃t] *adj* existing, in existence

existence [ɛgzistɑ̃s] *f* existence

existentialisme [ɛgzistɑ̃sjalism] *m* existentialism

exister [ɛgziste] *intr* to exist

ex-ministre [ɛksministrə] *m* (pol) ex-premier

exobiologie [ɛgzɔbjɔlɔʒi] *f* exobiology

exode [ɛgzɔd] *m* exodus; flight (*of capital; of emigrants, refugees, etc.*)

exonération [ɛgzɔnerasjɔ̃] *f* exemption, exoneration

exonérer [ɛgzɔnere] §10 *tr* to exempt, exonerate || *ref* to pay up a debt

exorbi•tant [ɛgzɔrbitɑ̃] **-tante** [tɑ̃t] *adj* exorbitant

exorciser [ɛgzɔrsize] *tr* to exorcise

exorde [ɛgzɔrd] *m* introduction

exotique [ɛgzɔtik] *adj* exotic

expan•sif [ɛkspɑ̃sif] **-sive** [siv] *adj* expansive

expansion [ɛkspɑ̃sjɔ̃] *f* expansion; expansiveness; spread (*of a belief*)

expa•trié -triée [ɛkspatrije] *adj & mf* expatriate

expatrier [ɛkspatrije] *tr* to expatriate

expectorer [ɛkspɛktɔre] *tr & intr* to expectorate

expé•dient [ɛkspedjɑ̃] **-diente** [djɑ̃t] *adj* expedient || *m* expedient; (coll) makeshift; **expédient provisoire** emergency measure; **vivre d'expédients** to live by one's wits

expédier [ɛkspedje] *tr* to expedite; ship; make a certified copy of; (coll) to dash off, do hurriedly

expédi•teur [ɛkspeditœr] **-trice** [tris] *adj* forwarding (*station, agency, etc.*) || *mf* sender, shipper

expédi•tif [ɛkspeditif] **-tive** [tiv] *adj* expeditious

expédition [ɛkspedisjɔ̃] *f* expedition; shipping; shipment; certified copy

expéditionnaire [ɛkspedisjɔnɛr] *adj* expeditionary || *mf* sender; clerk

expérience [ɛksperjɑ̃s] *f* experience; experiment; qualifications

expérimen•tal -tale [ɛksperimɑ̃tal] *adj* (*pl* **-taux** [to]) experimental; tentative

expérimen•té -tée [ɛksperimɑ̃te] *adj* experienced

expérimenter [ɛksperimɑ̃te] *tr* to try out, test || *intr* to conduct experiments

ex•pert [ɛkspɛr] **-perte** [pɛrt] *adj* expert || *m* expert; connoisseur; appraiser; **expert en médecine légale** forensic expert

expert-comptable [ɛkspɛrkɔ̃tabl] *m* (*pl* **experts-comptables**) certified public accountant

expertise [ɛkspɛrtiz] *f* expert appraisal; **expertise médico-légale** forensic evidence

expertiser [ɛkspɛrtise] *tr* to appraise

expier [ɛkspje] *tr* to expiate, atone for

expiration [ɛkspirasjɔ̃] *f* expiration

expirer [ɛkspire] *tr & intr* to expire; exhale

explicable [ɛksplikabl] *adj* explicable, explainable

explica•tif [ɛksplikatif] **-tive** [tiv] *adj* explanatory

explication [ɛksplikasjɔ̃] *f* explanation; interpretation (*of a text*); **avoir une explication avec qn** to have it out with s.o.

explicite [ɛksplisit] *adj* explicit

expliciter [ɛksplisite] *tr* to make explicit

expliquer [ɛksplike] §98 *tr* to explain; give an interpretation of || *ref* to explain oneself; understand

exploit [ɛksplwa] *m* exploit; **exploit d'ajournement** subpoena; **signifier un exploit** to serve a summons

exploi•tant [ɛksplwatɑ̃] **-tante** [tɑ̃t] *adj* operating, working || *mf* operator (*of enterprise*); developer; cultivator; (mov) exhibitor

exploitation [ɛksplwatasjɔ̃] *f* exploitation; management, development, cultivation; land under cultivation; **exploitation des esclaves** slave labor

exploiter [ɛksplwate] *tr* to exploit; manage, develop, cultivate || *intr* to serve summonses

explora•teur [ɛksplɔratœr] **-trice** [tris] *mf* explorer

exploration [ɛksplɔrasjɔ̃] *f* exploration; **exploration visuelle** (electron) picture search

explorer [ɛksplɔre] *tr* to explore; (astr, comp, mil, telv) to scan

exploser [ɛksplɔze] *intr* to explode

explosible [ɛksplɔzibl] *adj* explosive

explo•sif [ɛksplɔzif] **-sive** [ziv] *adj & m* explosive; **explosif plastique** plastic explosive

explosion [ɛksplɔzjɔ̃] *f* explosion; **à explosion** internal-combustion (*engine*)

exporta•teur [ɛkspɔrtatœr] **-trice** [tris] *adj* exporting || *mf* exporter

exportation [ɛkspɔrtasjɔ̃] *f* export; exportation

exporter [ɛkspɔrte] *tr & intr* to export

expo•sant [ɛkspozɑ̃] **-sante** [zɑ̃t] *mf* exhibitor; petitioner || *m* (math) exponent

exposé [ɛkspoze] *m* exposition, account, statement; report (*given by a student in class*)

exposer [ɛkspoze] §96 *tr* to expose; explain, expound; exhibit, display

exposition [ɛkspozisjɔ̃] *f* exposition; exposure (*to one of the points of the compass*); introduction (*of a book*); lying in state; **exposition canine** dog show; **exposition d'horticulture** flower show; **exposition hippique** horse show; **exposition interprofessionelle** trade show

ex•près [ɛksprɛ] **-presse** [prɛs] *adj* express || **exprès** *adj invar* special-delivery (*letter, package, etc.*) || *m* express; **par exprès** by special delivery || **exprès** *adv* expressly, on purpose

express [ɛksprɛs] *adj & m* express (*train*)

expressément [ɛkspresemɑ̃] *adv* expressly

expres•sif [ɛksprɛsif] **-sive** [siv] *adj* expressive
expression [ɛksprɛsjɔ̃] *f* expression; **d'expression anglaise** *or* **espagnole** *or* **française** English-speaking, Spanish-speaking, French-speaking
exprimer [ɛksprime] *tr* to express; squeeze out
exproprier [ɛksprɔprije] *tr* to expropriate
expul•sé -sée [ɛkspylse] *adj* deported ‖ *mf* deportee
expulser [ɛkspylse] *tr* to expel; evict; throw out
expulsion [ɛkspylsjɔ̃] *f* expulsion
expurger [ɛkspyrʒe] §38 *tr* to expurgate
ex•quis [ɛkski] **-quise** [kiz] *adj* exquisite; sharp (*pain*)
exsangue [ɛksɑ̃g] *adj* bloodless, anemic
exsuder [ɛksyde] *tr* & *intr* to exude
extase [ɛkstɑz] *f* ecstasy
exta•sié -siée [ɛkstɑzje] *adj* enraptured, ecstatic, in ecstasy
extasier [ɛkstɑzje] *ref* to be enraptured
extatique [ɛkstatik] *adj* & *mf* ecstatic
extempora•né -née [ɛkstɑ̃pɔrane] *adj* (law) unpremeditated; (pharm) ready for use
exten•sif [ɛkstɑ̃sif] **-sive** [siv] *adj* wide (*meaning*); (mech) tensile
extension [ɛkstɑ̃sjɔ̃] *f* extension
exténuer [ɛkstenɥe] *tr* to exhaust, tire out ‖ *ref* to tire oneself out
exté•rieur -rieure [ɛksterjœr] *adj* exterior; external; outer, outside; foreign (*policy*) ‖ *m* exterior; outside; (mov) location shot; **à l'extérieur** outside; abroad; **en extérieur** (mov) on location
extérieurement [ɛksterjœrmɑ̃] *adv* externally; superficially; on the outside
extérioriser [ɛksterjɔrize] *tr* to reveal, show ‖ *ref* to open one's heart
exterminer [ɛkstɛrmine] *tr* to exterminate
externat [ɛkstɛrna] *m* day school
externe [ɛkstɛrn] *adj* external ‖ *m* day student; outpatient; (med) nonresident intern
extinc•teur [ɛkstɛ̃ktœr] **-trice** [tris] *adj* extinguishing ‖ *m* fire extinguisher; **extincteur à mousse** foam extinguisher
extinction [ɛkstɛ̃ksjɔ̃] *f* extinction; extinguishing; loss (*of voice*); **extinction d'un traité** termination of a treaty; **l'extinction des feux** (mil) lights out, taps
extirper [ɛkstirpe] *tr* to extirpate
extorquer [ɛkstɔrke] *tr* to extort

extor•queur [ɛkstɔrkœr] **-queuse** [køz] *mf* extortionist
extorsion [ɛkstɔrsjɔ̃] *f* extortion
extra [ɛkstra] *adj invar* (coll) extraspecial, extra ‖ *m invar* extra
extracteur [ɛkstraktœr] *n* extractor; **extracteur de fumée** smoke evacuator
extraction [ɛkstraksjɔ̃] *f* extraction; descent, e.g., **d'extraction allemande** of German descent
extrader [ɛkstrade] *tr* to extradite
extradition [ɛkstradisjɔ̃] *f* extradition
extra•fin [ɛkstrafɛ̃] **-fine** [fin] *adj* high-quality
extraire [ɛkstrɛr] §68 *tr* to extract; excerpt; get out ‖ *ref* to extricate oneself
extrait [ɛkstrɛ] *m* extract; excerpt; abstract; certified copy; **extrait de baptême** baptismal certificate; **extrait de bœuf** beef extract; **extrait de naissance** birth certificate; **extraits** selections (*e.g., in an anthology*)
extra-muros [ɛkstramyros] *adj invar* extramural; suburban ‖ *adv* outside the town
extraordinaire [ɛkstraɔrdinɛr], [ɛkstrɔrdinɛr] *adj* extraordinary
extrapoler [ɛkstrapɔle] *tr* to extrapolate
extra-sensoriel -sensorielle [ɛkstrasɑ̃sɔrjɛl] *adj* extrasensory
extravagance [ɛkstravagɑ̃s] *f* extravagance; excess; absurdity, wildness
extrava•gant [ɛkstravagɑ̃] **-gante** [gɑ̃t] *adj* excessive, extravagant; absurd, wild, eccentric ‖ *mf* eccentric, screwball
extraver•ti -tie [ɛkstravɛrti] *adj* & *mf* extrovert
extrême [ɛkstrɛm] *adj* & *m* extreme
extrêmement [ɛkstrɛmmɑ̃] *adv* extremely
extrême-onction [ɛkstrɛmɔ̃ksjɔ̃] *f* extreme unction
Extrême-Orient [ɛkstrɛmɔrjɑ̃] *m* Far East
extrémiste [ɛkstremist] *adj* & *mf* extremist
extrémité [ɛkstremite] *f* extremity; **en venir à des extrémités** to resort to violence; **être à toute extrémité** to be at death's door
extrinsèque [ɛkstrɛ̃sɛk] *adj* extrinsic
exubé•rant [ɛgzyberɑ̃] **-rante** [rɑ̃t] *adj* exuberant
exulter [ɛgzylte] *intr* to exult
exutoire [ɛgzytwar] *m* outlet; means of escape; (med) exutory
ex-voto [ɛksvoto] *m invar* votive inscription or tablet

F

F, f [ɛf], *[ɛf] m invar* sixth letter of the French alphabet
F (*abbr*) (**franc**) franc
fable [fɑbl] *f* fable; laughingstock
fabri•cant [fabrikɑ̃] **-cante** [kɑ̃t] *mf* manufacturer

fabrica•teur [fabrikatœr] **-trice** [tris] *mf* fabricator (*e.g., of lies*); forger; counterfeiter
fabrication [fabrikasjɔ̃] *f* manufacture; forging; counterfeiting
fabrique [fabrik] *f* factory; factory workers; mill hands; (obs) church trustees; (obs)

church revenue; **fabrique de papier** paper mill

fabriquer [fabrike] *tr* to manufacture; fabricate; forge; counterfeit; **fabriquer en série** to mass-produce

fabu‧leux [fɑbylø] **-leuse** [løz] *adj* fabulous

façade [fasad] *f* façade; frontage; **en façade sur** facing, overlooking

face [fas] *f* face; side (*of a diamond; of a phonograph record*); surface; heads (*of coin*); **de face** full-faced (*portrait*); **en face (de)** opposite, facing; **faire face à** to face; face up to; meet (*an obligation*); **perdre la face** to lose face; **sauver la face** to save face

face-à-main [fasamɛ̃] *m* (*pl* **faces-à-main**) lorgnette

facétie [fasesi] *f* off-color joke; practical joke

facé‧tieux [fasesjø] **-tieuse** [sjøz] *adj* droll, funny ‖ *mf* wag

facette [fasɛt] *f* facet

fâ‧ché -chée [fɑ/e] *adj* angry; sorry; **fâché avec** at odds with; **fâché contre** angry with (*a person*); **fâché de** angry at (*a thing*); sorry for

fâcher [fɑ/e] *tr* to anger ‖ *ref* to get angry; be sorry

fâ‧cheux [fɑ/ø] **-cheuse** [/øz] *adj* annoying, tiresome; unfortunate ‖ *mf* nuisance, bore

fa‧cial -ciale [fasjal] *adj* (*pl* **-ciaux** [sjo]) facial; face (*value*)

facile [fasil] §92 *adj* easy; easygoing; facile, glib

facilité [fasilite] *f* facility; opportunity (*e.g., to meet s.o.*); **facilités de paiement** installments; easy terms

faciliter [fasilite] *tr* to facilitate

façon [fasɔ̃] *f* fashion; fashioning; way, manner; fit (*of clothes*); **à façon** job (*work; workman*); **à la façon de** like; **de façon à** so as to; **de façon que** or **de telle façon que** so that, e.g., **parlez de telle façon qu'on vous comprenne** speak so that you can be understood; **de toute façon** in any event; **façons** manners; **faire des façons** to stand on ceremony; **sans façon** informal

faconde [fakɔ̃d] *f* glibness, gift of gab

façonnage [fasonaʒ] *m* shaping; fashioning; manufacturing; (comp) processing

façonner [fasone] *tr* to fashion, shape; work (*the land*); accustom

façon‧nier [fasonje] **-nière** [njɛr] *adj* jobbing; fussy ‖ *mf* pieceworker; stuffed shirt

fac-sim [faksim] *m* (comp) hard copy

fac-similé [faksimile] *m* (*pl* **-similés**) facsimile

factage [faktaʒ] *m* delivery service; home delivery

facteur [faktœr] *m* factor; mail carrier, mailman; expressman; auctioneer (*at a market*); maker (*of musical instruments*); **facteur Rhésus** Rhesus factor

factice [faktis] *adj* imitation, artificial

fac‧tieux [faksjø] **-tieuse** [sjøz] *adj* factious, seditious ‖ *mf* troublemaker, agitator

faction [faksjɔ̃] *f* faction; **être de faction** to be on sentry duty

factionnaire [faksjonɛr] *m* sentry

factorerie [faktorəri] *f* trading post

factotum [faktotɔm] *m* factotum; meddler; jack-of-all-trades

factrice [faktris] *f* woman letter carrier

factum [faktɔm] *m* political pamphlet; (law) brief

facturation [faktyrasjɔ̃] *f* billing, invoicing

facture [faktyr] *f* invoice; bill; workmanship; **établir une facture** to make out an invoice; **suivant facture** as per invoice

facturer [faktyre] *tr* to bill

factu‧rier [faktyrje] **-rière** [rjɛr] *mf* billing clerk ‖ *m* invoice book

faculta‧tif [fakyltatif] **-tive** [tiv] *adj* optional

faculté [fakylte] *f* faculty; school, college (*of law, medicine, etc.*); **la Faculté** medical men

fadaise [fadɛz] *f* piece of nonsense; **fadaises** drivel

fade [fad] *adj* tasteless, flat; insipid, namby-pamby

fader [fade] *tr* (coll) to beat; (coll) to share the swag with; **il est fadé** (coll) he's done for

fadeur [fadœr] *f* insipidity; pointlessness; **fadeurs** platitudes

fagot [fago] *m* fagot (*bundle of sticks*); **fagot d'épines** ill-tempered person; **sentir le fagot** to smell of heresy

fagoter [fagote] *tr* to tie up in bundles; fagot; (coll) to dress like a scarecrow

faible [fɛbl] *adj* feeble, weak; low (*figure; moan*); poor (*harvest*); slight (*difference*) ‖ *mf* weakling ‖ *m* weakness; foible, weak spot; **faible d'esprit** feeble-minded person

faiblesse [fɛblɛs] *f* feebleness, weakness, frailty

faiblir [feblir] *intr* to weaken; diminish

faïence [fajɑ̃s] *f* earthenware, pottery

faille [faj] *f* (geol) fault; (tex) faille; (fig) defect; (fig) rift ‖ *v* see **falloir**

fail‧li -lie [faji] *adj & mf* bankrupt

faillible [fajibl] *adj* fallible

faillir [fajir] §95 *intr* to fail, go bankrupt ‖ (used only in: *inf; ger* **faillant;** *pp &* compound tenses; *pret; fut; cond*) *intr* to fail; give way; **faillir à** to fail, let (*s.o.*) down; fail in (*a duty*); fail to keep (*a promise*); **faillir à** + *inf* to fail to + *inf;* **sans faillir** without fail ‖ (used only in *pret* and *past indef*) *intr*—nearly, almost, e.g., **il a failli être écrasé** he was nearly run over

faillite [fajit] *f* bankruptcy; **faire faillite** to go bankrupt

faim [fɛ̃] *f* hunger; **avoir faim** to be hungry; **avoir une faim de loup** to be hungry as a bear; **manger à sa faim** to eat one's fill

fainéant [fɛneɑ̃] **fainéante** [fɛneɑ̃t] *adj* lazy ‖ *mf* loafer, do-nothing

fainéanter [fɛneɑ̃te] *intr* (coll) to loaf

faire [fɛr] *m* making, doing ‖ §29, §95 *tr* to make; do; give (*an order; a lecture; alms, a* *gift; thanks*); take (*a walk; a step*); pack (*a trunk*); clean (*the room, the shoes, etc.*); follow (*a trade*); keep (*silence*); perform (*a play; a miracle*); play the part of; charge for, e.g., **combien faites-vous ces souliers?** how much do you charge for these shoes?; to say, e.g., **oui, fit-il** yes, said he; (coll) to estimate the cost of; for expressions like **il fait chaud** it is warm, see the noun; **cela ne fait rien** it doesn't matter; **faire** + *inf* to have + *inf*, e.g., **je le ferai aller** I shall have him go; **faire** + *inf* to make + *inf*, e.g., **je le ferai parler** I will make him talk; **faire** + *inf* to have + *pp*, e.g., **je vais faire faire un complet** I am going to have a suit made; **il n'en fait pas d'autres** that's just like him; **ne faire que** + *inf* to keep on + *ger*, e.g., **il ne fait que crier** he keeps on yelling ‖ *intr* to go, e.g., **la cravate fait bien avec la chemise** the tie goes well with the shirt; to act; **comment faire?** what shall I do?; **faire dans** to make a mess in; **ne faire que de** + *inf* to have just + *pp*, e.g., **il ne fait que d'arriver** he has just arrived ‖ *ref* to become (*a doctor, lawyer, etc.*); grow (*e.g., old*); improve; happen; pretend to be; **se faire à** to get accustomed to, adjust to; **s'en faire** to worry, e.g., **ne vous en faites pas!** don't worry!

faire-part [fɛrpar] *m invar* announcement (*of birth, marriage, death*)

faire-valoir [fɛrvalwar] *m invar* turning to account; **faire-valoir direct** farming by the owner

faisable [fəzabl] *adj* feasible

fai·san [fəzɑ̃] **-sane** [zan] *or* **-sande** [zɑ̃d] *mf* pheasant

faisander [fəzɑ̃de] *tr* to jerk (*game*) ‖ *intr* to become gamy, get high

fais·ceau [fɛso] *m* (*pl* **-ceaux**) bundle, cluster; beam (*of light*); pencil (*of rays*); **faisceaux** fasces; **faisceaux de preuves** cumulative evidence; **former les faisceaux** to stack or pile arms

fai·seur [fəzœr] **-seuse** [zøz] *mf*—**bon faiseur** first-rate workman; **faiseur de marriages** matchmaker; **faiseur de vers** versifier, poetaster ‖ *m* bluffer; schemer

fait [fɛ] **faite** [fɛt] *adj* well-built, shapely; full-grown; made-up (*with cosmetics*); **fait à la main** hand-made; **tout fait** ready-made ‖ *m* deed, act; fact; **dire son fait à qn** (coll) to give s.o. a piece of one's mind; **prendre fait et cause pour** to take up the cudgels for; **si fait** yes, indeed; **sur le fait** redhanded, in the act; **tout à fait** entirely ‖ [fɛt] *m*—**au fait** to the point; after all; **de fait** de facto; **du fait que** owing to the fact that; **en fait** as a matter of fact

faîtage [fɛtaʒ] *m* ridgepole; roofs; roofing

fait-divers [fɛdivɛr] *m* (*pl* **faits-divers**) news item

faîte [fɛt] *m* peak; top (*of tree*); ridge (*of roof*); coping

faîtière [fɛtjɛr] *adj fem* ridge ‖ *f* ridge tile; skylight

fait-tout [fɛtu] *m invar* stewpan, casserole

faix [fɛ] *m* load, burden; (archit) settling; (physiol) fetus and placenta

falaise [falɛz] *f* cliff, bluff

falla·cieux [falasjø] **-cieuse** [sjøz] *adj* fallacious

fallait [falɛ] *v see* **falloir**

falloir [falwar] §30, §95 *impers* to be necessary; **c'est plus qu'il n'en faut** that's more than enough; **comme il faut** proper; properly; the right kind of, e.g., **un chapeau comme il faut** the right kind of hat; **il fallait le dire!** why didn't you say so!; **il faut** + *inf* it is necessary to + *inf*, one must + *inf*; **il faut qu'il** + *subj* it is necessary that he + *subj*, it is necessary for him to + *inf*; he must + *inf* (expressing conjecture), e.g., **il n'est pas venu, il faut qu'il soit malade** he did not come, he must be sick; **il faut qu'il** + *subj* + **pas** he must not + *inf*, e.g., **il faut qu'il ne vienne pas** he must not come; **il faut une connaissance des affaires à ce travail** the work requires business experience; **il faut une heure** it takes an hour; **il leur a fallu trois jours** it took them three days; **il leur faut** + *inf* they have to + *inf*, they must + *inf*; **il leur faut du repos** they need rest; **il leur faut sept dollars** they need seven dollars; **il ne faut pas** + *inf* one must or should not + *inf*, e.g., **il ne faut pas se fier à ce garçon** one must not trust that boy; **il ne faut pas qu'il** + *subj* he must not + *inf*; **que leur faut-il?** what do they need?, what do they require?; **qu'il ne fallait pas** wrong, e.g., **la police a arrêté l'homme qu'il ne fallait pas** the police arrested the wrong man ‖ *ref*—**il s'en faut de beaucoup** not by a long shot, far from it, not by any means; **il s'en faut de dix dollars** there is a shortage of ten dollars; **peu m'en est fallu que . . .** it very nearly happened that . . .; **peu s'en faut** very nearly; **tant s'en faut que** far from, e.g., **tant s'en faut qu'il soit artiste** he is far from being an artist

fallut [faly] *v see* **falloir**

fa·lot [falo] **-lotte** [lɔt] *adj* wan, colorless; quaint, droll ‖ *m* lantern

falsification [falsifikɑsjɔ̃] *f* falsification; adulteration; debasement (*of coin*)

falsifier [falsifje] *tr* to falsify; adulterate; debase (*coin*)

fa·mé -mée [fame] *adj*—**mal famé** disreputable

famélique [famelik] *adj* famished

fa·meux [famø] **-meuse** [møz] *adj* famous ‖ (when standing before noun) *adj* (coll) notorious; well-known

fami·lial -liale [familjal] *adj* (*pl* **-liaux** [ljo]) family, domestic ‖ *f* station wagon

familiariser [familjarize] *tr* to familiarize ‖ *ref* to become familiar

familiarité [familjarite] *f* familiarity

fami·lier [familje] **-lière** [ljɛr] *adj* familiar, intimate; household (*gods*); pet (*animal*) ‖ *mf* familiar, intimate; pet animal

famille [famij] *f* family; **en famille** in the family circle, at home; (Canad) pregnant; **famille de placement** foster family; **famille étendue** extended family; **famille monoparentale** single parent family

famine [famin] *f* famine

fa·nal [fanal] *m* (*pl* **-naux** [no]) lantern; (naut) running light

fanatique [fanatik] *adj* fanatic(al) ‖ *mf* fanatic; enthusiast, fan; **fanatique de la gymnastique** fitness buff (coll)

fanatisme [fanatism] *m* fanaticism

faner [fane] *tr* & *ref* to fade

fanfare [fɑ̃far] *f* fanfare; brass band

fanfa·ron [fɑ̃farɔ̃] **-ronne** [rɔn] *adj* bragging ‖ *mf* braggart

fanfaronner [fɑ̃farɔne] *intr* to brag

fange [fɑ̃ʒ] *f* mire, mud; (fig) mire, gutter

fan·geux [fɑ̃ʒø] **-geuse** [ʒøz] *adj* muddy; (fig) dirty, soiled

fanion [fanjɔ̃] *m* pennant, flag

fanon [fanɔ̃] *m* dewlap (*of ox*); whalebone; fetlock; wattle

fantaisie [fɑ̃tezi] *f* imagination; fantasy; fancy, whim; **de fantaisie** fanciful; fancy, e.g., **pain de fantaisie** fancy bread

fantaisiste [fɑ̃tezist] *adj* fantastic, whimsical ‖ *mf* whimsical person; singing comedian

fantasque [fɑ̃task] *adj* fantastic; whimsical, temperamental

fantassin [fɑ̃tasɛ̃] *m* foot soldier

fantastique [fɑ̃tastik] *adj* fantastic

fantoche [fɑ̃tɔʃ] *m* puppet

fantôme [fɑ̃tom] *adj* shadow (*government*) ‖ *m* phantom, ghost

fanum [fanɔm] *m* hallowed ground

faon [fɑ̃] *m* fawn

faonner [fane] *intr* to bring forth young (*said especially of deer*)

faquin [fakɛ̃] *m* rascal

farami·neux [faraminø] **-neuse** [nøz] *adj* (coll) staggering, fantastic, astronomical

fa·raud [faro] **-raude** [rod] *adj* (coll) swanky ‖ *mf* (coll) fop, bumpkin; **faire le faraud** (coll) to show off

farce [fars] *f* farce; trick, joke; (culin) stuffing

far·ceur [farsœr] **-ceuse** [søz] *mf* practical joker; phony

farcir [farsir] *tr* to stuff

fard [far] *m* make-up; **fard à paupières** eye shadow; **parler sans fard** to speak plainly, to tell the unvarnished truth; **piquer un fard** (coll) to blush

far·deau [fardo] *m* (*pl* **-deaux**) load, burden; weight (*of years*)

farder [farde] *tr* to make up (*an actor*); disguise (*the truth*) ‖ *ref* to weigh heavily; (archit) to sink; (theat) to make up

fardier [fardje] *m* dray, cart

farfe·lu -lue [farfəly] *adj* (coll) harebrained, cockeyed, bizarre

farfouiller [farfuje] *tr* (coll) to rummage about in ‖ *intr* (coll) to rummage about; **farfouiller dans** (coll) to rummage about in

farine [farin] *f* flour, meal; **farine de froment** whole-wheat flour; **farine de riz** ground rice; **farine lactée** malted milk

fariner [farine] *tr* (culin) to flour

fari·neux [farinø] **-neuse** [nøz] *adj* white with flour; mealy; starchy

farouche [faruʃ] *adj* wild, savage; unsociable; shy; stubborn (*resistance*); fierce (*look*)

fart [fart] *m* ski wax

fascicule [fasikyl] *m* fascicle; **fascicule de mobilisation** marching orders

fascina·teur [fasinatœr] **-trice** [tris] *adj* fascinating ‖ *mf* spellbinder

fasciner [fasine] *tr* to fascinate; spellbind

fascisme [faʃism] *m* fascism

fasciste [faʃist] *adj* & *mf* fascist

fasse [fas] *v* (**fasses, fassions,** etc.) see **faire**

faste [fast] *adj* auspicious; feast (*day*) ‖ *m* pomp; **fastes** annals

fast food [fɛstfud] *m* fast food(s)

fasti·dieux [fastidjø] **-dieuse** [djøz] *adj* tedious, wearisome

fas·tueux [fastɥø] **-tueuse** [tɥøz] *adj* pompous, ostentatious

fat [fat] *adj masc* conceited, foppish ‖ *m* fop

fa·tal -tale [fatal] *adj* (*pl* **-tals**) fatal; fateful; inevitable

fatalement [fatalmɑ̃] *adv* inevitably

fatalisme [fatalism] *m* fatalism

fataliste [fatalist] *adj* fatalistic ‖ *mf* fatalist

fatalité [fatalite] *f* fatality; fatalism; fate; curse; misfortune

fatidique [fatidik] *adj* fateful; prophetic

fati·gant [fatigɑ̃] **-gante** [gɑ̃t] *adj* fatiguing; tiresome (*person*)

fatigue [fatig] *f* fatigue

fati·gué -guée [fatige] §93 *adj* fatigued; worn-out (*clothing*); well-thumbed (*book*)

fatiguer [fatige] *tr* to fatigue; wear out; weary ‖ *intr* to strain, labor; pull (*said of engine*); bear a heavy strain (*said of beam*) ‖ §96, §97 *ref* to get tired

fatras [fatra] *m* jumble, hodgepodge

fatuité [fatɥite] *f* conceit; foppishness

fatwa [fatwa] *m* (*décret religieux et légal fait par un clerc musulman*) fatwa (*religious and legal decree issued by a Muslim cleric*)

faubert [fobɛr] *m* (naut) swab

faubourg [fobur] *m* suburb; outskirts; quarter, district (*especially of Paris*)

faubou·rien [foburjɛ̃] **-rienne** [rjɛn] *adj* working-class, vulgar ‖ *mf* resident of the outskirts of a city; local inhabitant

fau·ché -chée [foʃe] *adj* (coll) broke (*without money*)

faucher [foʃe] *tr* to mow, reap; (coll) to swipe

fau·cheur [foʃœr] **-cheuse** [ʃøz] *mf* reaper ‖ *m* (ent) daddy-longlegs ‖ *f* (mach) reaper, mower

faucheux [foʃø] *m* (ent) daddy-longlegs

faucille [fosij] *f* sickle

faucon [fokɔ̃] *m* falcon; (pol) hawk

fauconnier [fokɔnje] *m* falconer

faudra [fodra] *v* see **falloir**

faufil [fofil] *m* basting thread

faufiler [fofile] *tr* to baste ‖ *ref* to thread one's way, worm one's way

faune [fon] *m* faun ‖ *f* fauna

faunesse [fonɛs] *f* female faun

faussaire [fosɛr] *mf* forger

fausser [fose] *tr* to falsify, distort; bend; twist; warp (*the judgment*); force (*a lock*); strain (*the voice*); **fausser compagnie à qn** (coll) to give s.o. the slip ‖ *intr* to sing or play out of tune ‖ *ref* to bend, buckle; crack (*said of voice*)

fausset [fosɛ] *m* falsetto; plug (*for wine barrel*)

fausseté [foste] *f* falsity; double-dealing

faut [fo] *v* see **falloir**

faute [fot] *f* fault; mistake; blame; lack, need, want; (sports) foul; (sports) error; **faute** to be lacking; **faute de** for want of; **faute de copiste** clerical error; **faute de frappe** typing error; **faute d'entretien familial** nonsupport; **faute de prononciation** mispronunciation; **faute d'impression** misprint; **sans faute** without fail

fauter [fote] *intr* (coll) to go wrong (*said of a woman*)

fauteuil [fotœj] *m* armchair, easy chair; seat (*of member of an academy*); chair (*of presiding officer; presiding officer himself*); **fauteuil à bascule** or **à balançoire** rocking chair; **fauteuil à oreilles** wing chair; **fauteuil de dentiste** dentist's chair; **fauteuil d'orchestre** orchestra seat; **fauteuil pliant** folding chair; **fauteuil roulant pour malade** wheelchair; **siéger au fauteuil présidentiel** to preside

fau·teur [fotœr] **-trice** [tris] *mf* instigator, agitator

fau·tif [fotif] **-tive** [tiv] *adj* faulty

fautivement [fotivmɑ̃] *adv* by mistake, in error

fauve [fov] *adj* fawn (*color*); musky (*odor*); wild (*beast*) ‖ *m* fawn color; wild beast; **fauves** big game

fauvette [fovɛt] *f* warbler

faux [fo] **fausse** [fos] (usually stands before noun) *adj* false; counterfeit; off key; wrong, e.g., **fausse date** wrong date; e.g., **fausse note** wrong note ‖ *m* imitation; forgery; **à faux** wrongly ‖ **faux** *f* scythe ‖ **faux** *adv* out of tune, off key; **chanter faux** to sing off key

faux-bourdon [foburdɔ̃] *m* (*pl* **-bourdons**) *m* (ent) drone

faux-col [fokɔl] *m* (*pl* **-cols**) collars, detachable collar; **faux-col d'ecclésiastique** dog collar (*clerical collar*)

faux-filet [fofilɛ] *m* (*pl* **-filets**) sirloin

faux-fuyant [fofɥijɑ̃] *m* (*pl* **-fuyants**) subterfuge, pretext

faux-jour [foʒur] *m* (*pl* **-jours**) half-light

faux-monnayeur [fomɔnɛjœr] *m* (*pl* **-monnayeurs**) counterfeiter

faux-pas [fopɑ] *m invar* faux pas, slip, blunder

faux-semblant [fosɑ̃blɑ̃] *m* (*pl* **-semblants**) false pretense

faveur [favœr] *f* favor; **à la faveur de** under cover of; **en faveur de** in favor of; on behalf of

favorable [favɔrabl] *adj* favorable

favoritisme [favɔritism] *m* favoritism

favo·ri [favɔri] **-rite** [rit] *adj & mf* favorite ‖ **favoris** *mpl* sideburns ‖ *f* mistress

favoriser [favɔrize] *tr* to favor; encourage, promote

fax [faks] *m* (electron) fax

F^co or **fco** *abbr* (**franco**) postpaid

fébrile [febril] *adj* feverish

fèces [fɛs] *fpl* feces

fé·cond [fekɔ̃] **-conde** [kɔ̃d] *adj* fecund, fertile

féconder [fekɔ̃de] *tr* to impregnate; to pollinate

fécondité [fekɔ̃dite] *f* fecundity, fertility

fécule [fekyl] *f* starch; **fécule de maïs** cornstarch

fécu·lent [fekylɑ̃] **-lente** [lɑ̃t] *adj* starchy ‖ *m* starchy food

fédé·ral **-rale** [federal] *adj & m* (*pl* **-raux** [ro]) federal

fédéra·tif [federatif] **-tive** [tiv] *adj* federated, federative

fédération [federasjɔ̃] *f* federation

fédérer [federe] §10 *tr & ref* to federate

fée [fe] *f* fairy; **de fée** fairy; meticulous (*work*); **vieille fée** old bag

feed-back [fidbak] *m invar* feedback

féerie [feri] *f* fairyland; fantasy

féerique [ferik] *adj* fairy, magic(al)

feindre [fɛ̃dr] §50, §97 *tr* to feign ‖ *intr* to feign; limp (*said of horse*)

feinte [fɛ̃t] *f* feint

feinter [fɛ̃te] *tr* (coll) to trick ‖ *intr* to feint

feldspath [fɛldspat], [fɛlspat] *m* feldspar

fê·lé **-lée** [fele] *adj* (coll) cracked, crazy

fêler [fele] *tr* to crack

félicitations [felisitasjɔ̃] *fpl* congratulations

féliciter [felisite] *tr* to congratulate; **féliciter qn de** + *inf* to congratulate s.o. for + *ger;* **féliciter qn de** or **pour** to congratulate s.o. for ‖ §97 *ref*—**se féliciter de** to congratulate oneself on, be pleased with oneself because of

fellation [fɛlasjɔ̃] *f* fellatio *ou* fellation

fé·lon [felɔ̃] **-lonne** [lɔn] *adj* disloyal, treasonable

félonie [feloni] *f* disloyalty, treason

fêlure [felyr] *f* crack, chink

femelle [fəmɛl] *adj & f* female

fémi·nin [feminɛ̃] **-nine** [nin] *adj & m* feminine

féminisme [feminism] *m* feminism

femme [fam] *f* woman; wife; bride; **bonne femme** (coll) simple, good-natured woman; **femme agent** (*pl* **femmes agents**) policewoman; **femme auteur** (*pl* **femmes auteurs**), authoress; **femme de chambre** chambermaid; **femme de charge** housekeeper; **femme de journée** cleaning woman; **femme de ménage** cleaning woman; **femme d'intérieur** homebody; **femme docteur** woman doctor (*e.g., with Ph.D. degree*); **femme juge**

woman judge; **femme médecin** woman doctor (*physician*); **femme pasteur** woman preacher; **femme porteuse** surrogate mother; **femme torero** woman bullfighter

fendiller [fɑ̃dije] *tr & ref* to crack

fendoir [fɑ̃dwar] *m* cleaver, chopper

fendre [fɑ̃dr] *tr* to crack; split (*e.g., wood*); cleave (*e.g., the air*); break (*one's heart*); elbow one's way through (*a crowd*) ‖ *ref* to crack; (*escr*) to lunge

fenêtre [fənɛtr] *f* window; **double fenêtre** storm window; **fenêtre à battants** casement window, French window; **fenêtre à guillotine** sash window; **fenêtre dépliante** (comp) pop-up window; **fenêtre en saillie** bay window

fenil [fənil], [fəni] *m* hayloft

fenouil [fənuj] *m* fennel; **fenouil bâtard** dill

fente [fɑ̃t] *f* crack, split, fissure; notch; slot (*e.g., in a coin telephone*); (escr) lunge

féo·dal -dale [feɔdal] *adj* (*pl* **-daux** [do]) feudal

féodalisme [feɔdalism] *m* feudalism

fer [fɛr] *m* iron; head (*of tool*); point (*of weapon*); **croiser le fer avec** to cross swords with; **fer à cheval** horseshoe; **fer à friser** curling iron; **fer à marquer** or **flétrir** branding iron; **fer à repasser** iron, flatiron; **fer à souder** soldering iron; **fer de fonte** cast iron; **fer forgé** wrought iron; **fers** irons, chains, fetters; **marquer au fer** to brand; **remuer le fer dans la plaie** (coll) to rub it in

ferai [fəre], [fre] *v* see **faire**

ferblanterie [fɛrblɑ̃tri] *f* tinware; tinwork, sheet-metal work; tinsmith's shop

ferblantier [fɛrblɑ̃tje] *m* tinsmith

fé·rié -riée [ferje] *adj* feast (*day*)

férir [ferir] *tr*—**sans coup férir** without striking a blow

ferler [fɛrle] *tr* (naut) to furl

fermage [fɛrmaʒ] *m* tenant farming; rent

ferme [fɛrm] *adj* firm ‖ *f* farm, tenant farm; farmhouse ‖ *adv* firmly, fast; without parole

fer·mé -mée [fɛrme] *adj* exclusive, restricted; inscrutable (*countenance*)

ferment [fɛrmɑ̃] *m* ferment

fermenter [fɛrmɑ̃te] *intr* to ferment

fermer [fɛrme] *tr* to close, shut; turn off; **fermer à clef** to lock; **fermer au verrou** to bolt; **la ferme!** (slang) shut up!, shut your trap! ‖ *intr & ref* to close, shut

fermeté [fɛrməte] *f* firmness

fermeture [fɛrmətyr] *f* closing; fastening; **fermeture éclair, fermeture à glissière** zipper

fer·mier -mière [fɛrmje] *adj* farming ‖ *m* farmer; tenant farmer; lessee ‖ *f* farmer's wife

fermoir [fɛrmwar] *m* snap, clasp

féroce [ferɔs] *adj* ferocious

férocité [ferɔsite] *f* ferocity

ferraille [fɛraj] *f* scrap iron; (coll) small change; **mettre à la ferraille** to junk

ferrailleur [fɛrajœr] *m* dealer in scrap iron; sword rattler

fer·ré -rée [fɛre] *adj* ironclad; hobnailed (*shoe*);

paved (*road*); iron-tipped; **ferré sur** well versed in

ferrer [fɛre] *tr* to shoe (*a horse*)

ferret [fɛre] *m* tag (*of shoelace*); (geol) hard core

ferronnerie [fɛrɔnri] *f* ironwork; hardware

ferron·nier [fɛrɔnje] **-nière** [njɛr] *mf* ironworker; hardware dealer

ferrotypie [fɛrɔtipi] *f* tintype

ferroviaire [fɛrɔvjɛr] *adj* railway

ferrure [fɛryr] *f* horseshoeing; **ferrures** hardware; metal trim

ferry-boat [fɛribot] *m* (*pl* **-boats**) train ferry

fertile [fɛrtil] *adj* fertile

fertilisation [fɛrtilizasjɔ̃] *f* fertilization; **fertilisation croisée** cross-fertilization

fertiliser [fɛrtilize] *tr* to fertilize

fertilité [fɛrtilite] *f* fertility

fé·ru -rue [fery] *adj*—**féru de** wrapped up in (*an idea, an interest*)

fer·vent [fɛrvɑ̃] **-vente** [vɑ̃t] *adj* fervent ‖ *mf* devotee

ferveur [fɛrvœr] *f* fervor

fesse [fɛs] *f* buttock

fessée [fɛse] *f* spanking

fesse-mathieu [fɛsmatjø] *m* (*pl* **-mathieux**) usurer; skinflint

fesser [fɛse] *tr* to spank

fes·su -sue [fɛsy] *adj* broad-bottomed

festin [fɛstɛ̃] *m* feast, banquet

festi·val [fɛstival] *m* (*pl* **-vals**) music festival

festivité [fɛstivite] *f* festivity

feston [fɛstɔ̃] *m* festoon

festonner [fɛstɔne] *tr* to festoon; scallop

festoyer [fɛstwaye] §47 *tr* to fete, regale ‖ *intr* to feast

fê·tard [fɛtar] **-tarde** [tard] *mf* merrymaker; boisterous drinker

fête [fɛt] *f* festival; feast day, holiday; name day; party, festivity; **être à la fête** (coll) to be very pleased or gratified; **faire fête à** to receive with open arms; **faire la fête** (coll) to carouse; **fête foraine** carnival; **fête légale** legal holiday; **Fête nationale** Bastille Day, national holiday; **la Fête des mères** Mother's Day; **la Fête des morts** All Souls' Day; **la Fête des pères** Father's Day; **la Fête des Rois** Twelfthnight, the Three Wise Men's Day; **se faire une fête de** to look forward with pleasure to; **souhaiter une bonne fête à qn** to wish s.o. many happy returns

Fête-Dieu [fɛtdjø] *f* (*pl* **Fêtes-Dieu**)—**la Fête-Dieu** Corpus Christi

fêter [fɛte] *tr* to fete; celebrate (*a special event*)

fétiche [fetiʃ] *m* fetish

fétide [fetid] *adj* fetid

fétu [fety] *m* straw; trifle

feu [fø] *adj* (*pl* **feus**) (standing before noun) late, deceased, e.g., **la feue reine** the late queen ‖ **feu** *adj invar* (standing before article and noun) late, deceased, e.g., **feu la reine** the late queen ‖ *m* (*pl* **feux**) fire; flame; traffic light; burner (*of stove*); **à petit feu** by inches;

dans un feu roulant de questions in a crossfire of questions; **du feu** a light (*to ignite a cigar, etc.*); **être sous les feux de la rampe** to be in the limelight; **faire du feux** to light a fire; **faire long feu** to hang fire; to fail; (arti) to miss; **feux croisés** crossfire; **feu d'artifice** fireworks; **feu de joie** bonfire; **feu de paille** (fig) flash in the pan; **feu follet** will-o'-the-wisp; **feux de position, feux de stationnement** parking lights; **feux masqués** (mil) blackout; **mettre le feu à** to set on fire; **prendre feu** to catch fire ‖ **feu** *interj* fire! (*command to fire*); **au feu!** fire! (*warning*)

feuillage [fœjaʒ] *m* foliage; **feuillages** fallen branches

feuille [fœj] *f* leaf; sheet; form (*to be filled out*); **feuille de chou** (coll) rag (*newspaper of little value*); **feuille de présence** time sheet; **feuille d'étain** tin foil; **feuille de température** temperature chart; **feuille d'imposition, feuille d'impôt** income-tax form

feuil·lé -lée [fœje] *adj* leafy, foliaged ‖ *f* bower; **feuillées** (mil) camp latrine

feuiller [fœje] *intr* to leaf

feuille·té -tée [fœjte] *adj* foliated; in flaky layers

feuilleter [fœjte] §34 *tr* to leaf through; foliate; (culin) to roll into thin layers

feuilleton [fœjtɔ̃] *m* newspaper serial (*printed at bottom of page*); (rad, telv) serial

feuil·lu -lue [fœjy] *adj* leafy ‖ *m* foliage

feuillure [fœjyr] *f* groove

feuler [føle] *intr* to growl (*said of cat*)

feutre [føtr] *m* felt

feu·tré -trée [føtre] *adj* velvetlike; muffled (*steps*)

feutrer [føtre] *tr* to felt

fève [fɛv] *f* bean; **fève des Rois** bean or figurine baked in the Twelfth-night cake; **fèves au lard** pork and beans

février [fevrie] *m* February

fi [fi] *interj* fie!; **faire fi de** to scorn

fiabilité [fjabilite] *f* reliability

fiable [fjabl] *adj* reliable

fiacre [fjakr] *m* horse-drawn cab

fiançailles [fjɑ̃saj] *fpl* engagement, betrothal

fian·cé -cée [fjɑ̃se] *mf* betrothed ‖ *m* fiancé ‖ *f* fiancée

fiancer [fjɑ̃se] §51 *tr* to betroth ‖ *ref* to become engaged

fiasco [fjasko] *m* (coll) fiasco, failure; **faire fiasco** to flop, fail

fibre [fibr] *f* fiber; (fig) feeling, sensibility; **avoir la fibre sensible** to be easily moved; **fibre de verre** fiberglass

fi·breux [fibrø] **-breuse** [brøz] *adj* fibrous

fibrose [fibroz] *f* (pathol) fibrosis; **fibrose cystique** cystic fibrosis

ficeler [fisle] §34 *tr* to tie up

ficelle [fisɛl] *adj* (coll) knowing ‖ *f* string; **connaître les ficelles** (fig) to know the ropes; **tenir** or **tirer les ficelles** (fig) to pull strings; **vieille ficelle** (coll) old hand

fiche [fiʃ] *f* peg; slip, form, blank; filing card, index card; membership card; (cards) chip, counter; (elec) plug; **fiche de consolation** booby prize; **fiche femelle** (elec) jack; **fiche perforée** punch card; **fiche scolaire** report card

ficher [fiʃe] *tr* to drive in (*a stake*); to take down (*information on a form*); to fasten, fix, stick ‖ **ficher** or **fiche** *v* (*p fichu*) *tr* (vulg) (dated) to have sex with; **ficher qn à la porte** (coll) to kick s.o. out; **ficher une gifle à qn** (coll) to box s.o. on the ear; **fichez-le dans ta poche!** (vulg) shove it in your pocket!; **fichez-moi la paix!** (coll) lay off!; **fichez-moi le camp!** (coll) beat it!; **je m'en fiche!** (vulg) I don't give a damn!; **qu'est-ce que tu fiches ici?** (coll) what are you doing here? ‖ *ref*—**se ficher de** or **se fiche de** (coll) to make fun of

fichier [fiʃje] *m* card catalogue; cabinet, file (*for cards or papers*); (comp) file

fichtre [fiʃtr] *interj* (coll) gosh!

fi·chu -chue [fiʃy] *adj* (coll) wretched, ugly, lousy, rotten; (coll) done for, kaput; **fichu de** capable of ‖ *m* scarf, shawl

fic·tif [fiktif] **-tive** [tiv] *adj* fictitious

fiction [fiksjɔ̃] *f* fiction

fidéicommis [fideikɔmi] *m* (law) trust

fidèle [fidɛl] *adj* faithful; regular ‖ *mf* supporter; **les fidèles** (eccl) the congregation, the faithful

fidèlement [fidɛlmɑ̃] *adv* faithfully; regularly

fidélité [fidelite] *f* fidelity, faithfulness; **haute fidélité** high fidelity

fief·fé -fé [fjefe] *adj* (coll) downright, real, regular (*liar, coward, etc.*)

fiel [fjɛl] *m* bile; gall

fiel·leux [fjelø] **-leuse** [løz] *adj* galling

fiente [fjɑ̃t] *f* droppings

fier fière [fjɛr] §93 *adj* proud; haughty ‖ **fier** [fje] *tr* (archaic) to entrust ‖ *ref*—**se fier à** or **en** to trust, to have confidence in, to rely upon; **se fier à qn de** to entrust s.o. with; **s'y fier** to trust it

fier-à-bras [fjɛrabra] *m* (*pl* **fier-à-bras** or **fiers-à-bras** [fjɛrabra]) braggart

fierté [fjɛrte] *f* pride

fièvre [fjɛvr] *f* fever; **fièvre aphteuse** foot-and-mouth disease; **fièvre jaune** yellow fever

fifre [fifr] *m* fife; fife player

fi·gé -gée [fiʒe] *adj* curdled; fixed, set; frozen (*smile*); **figé sur place** rooted to the spot

figement [fiʒmɑ̃] *m* clotting, coagulation

figer [fiʒe] §38 *tr* to curdle; stop dead ‖ *ref* to curdle; set, freeze (*said, e.g., of smile*)

fignoler [fiɲɔle] *tr* to work carefully at ‖ *intr* to be finicky

figue [fig] *f* fig; **faire la figue à** (coll) to snap one's fingers at; **figue de Barbarie** prickly pear

figuier [figje] *m* fig tree

figu·rant [figyrɑ̃] **-rante** [rɑ̃t] *mf* (theat) supernumerary, extra

figura·tif [figyratif] **-tive** [tiv] *adj* figurative, emblematic

figure   147   **finesse**

figure [figyr] *f* figure; face (*of a person*); face card; chess piece (other than a pawn); **faire figure** to cut a figure; **figure de proue** (naut) figurehead; **prendre figure** to take shape

figu•ré -rée [figyre] *adj* figurative; figured ‖ *m* figurative sense

figurer [figyre] *tr* to figure ‖ *intr* to figure, take part; (theat) to walk on ‖ *§95 ref* to imagine, believe

fil [fil] *m* thread; wire; edge (*e.g., of knife*); grain (*of wood*); **au fil de l'eau** with the stream; **droit fil** with the grain; **elle lui a donné du fil à retordre** (fig) she gave him more than he bargained for; **fil à plomb** plumb line; **fil de fer barbelé** barbed wire; **fil de lin** yarn; **fil d'or** spun gold; **fils de la vierge** gossamer; **passer au fil de l'épée** to put to the sword; **plein de fils** stringy; **sans fil** wireless

filage [filaʒ] *m* spinning; (telv) ghost image

filament [filamɑ̃] *m* filament

filamen•teux [filamɑ̃tø] **-teuse** [tøz] *adj* stringy

filan•dreux [filɑ̃drø] **-dreuse** [drøz] *adj* stringy (*meat*); long, drawn-out

fi•lant [filɑ̃] **-lante** [lɑ̃t] *adj* ropy (*liquid*); shooting (*star*)

filasse [filas] *f* tow, oakum

filature [filatyr] *f* manufacture of thread; spinning mill; shadowing (*of a suspect*)

fil-de-fériste [fildəferist] *mf* tightwire walker

file [fil] *f* file, row, lane; **à la file** one after another, in a row; **file d'attente** waiting line; (aer) stack; **marcher en file indienne** to walk Indian file

filer [file] *tr* to spin; pay out (*rope, cable*); prolong; shadow (*a suspect*) ‖ *intr* to ooze; smoke (*said of lamp*); (coll) to go fast; **filer à l'anglaise** (coll) to take French leave; **filer doux** (coll) to back down, to give in; **filez!** (coll) get out!

filet [file] *m* net; trickle (*of water*); streak (*of light*); thread (*of screw or nut*); (culin) fillet; (typ) rule; **faux filet** sirloin; **filet à bagage** baggage rack; **filet à cheveux** hair net; **filet à provisions** string bag, mesh bag

fileter [filte] *§2 tr* to thread (*a screw*); draw (*wire*)

fi•leur [filœr] **-leuse** [løz] *mf* spinner

fi•lial -liale [filjal] *adj* (*pl* **-liaux** [ljo]) filial ‖ *f* (com) branch, subsidiary

filiation [filjɑsjɔ̃] *f* filiation

filière [filjɛr] *f* (mach) die; (mach) drawplate; **filière administrative** official channels; **passer par la filière** (coll) to go through channels; (coll) to work one's way up

filigrane [filigran] *m* filigree; watermark (*in paper*)

filigraner [filigrane] *tr* to filigree

filin [filɛ̃] *m* (naut) rope

fille [fij] *f* daughter; unmarried young woman or girl; servant; (pej) tart; **fille de joie, des rues,** or **de vie, fille publique** prostitute; **fille de salle** nurse's aid; **fille d'honneur** bridesmaid; **fille en placement** foster daughter;

jeune fille (unmarried) young woman; **petite fille** girl (under thirteen years of age); **vieille fille** old maid

fillette [fijɛt] *f* young girl, little lass

fil•leul -leule [fijœl] *mf* godchild ‖ *m* godson ‖ *f* goddaughter

film [film] *m* film; movie, film; (fig) train (*of events*); **film sonore** sound film; **film vidéo** (mov, telv) video film

filmage [filmaʒ] *m* filming

filmer [filme] *tr* to film

filmique [filmik] *adj* film

filon [filɔ̃] *m* vein, lode; (coll) soft job; (coll) bonanza, strike; **filon guide** leader vein

filoselle [filɔzɛl] *f* floss silk

filou [filu] *m* sneak thief; cheat, sharper

filouter [filute] *tr* (coll) to swindle, cheat; **filouter q.ch. à qn** (coll) to do s.o. out of s.th. ‖ *intr* to cheat at cards

fils [fis] *m* son; (when following proper name) junior; **fils à papa** (coll) rich man's son, playboy; **fils de ses œuvres** (fig) self-made man; **fils en placement** foster son

filtrage [filtraʒ] *m* filtering; screening; surveillance (*by the police*)

fil•trant [filtrɑ̃] **-trante** [trɑ̃t] *adj* filterable; filter, e.g., **papier filtrant** filter paper

filtre [filtrə] *m* filter

filtrer [filtre] *tr & intr* to filter; (*café*) to perk

fin [fɛ̃] **fine** [fin] *adj* fine; thin; exquisite; keen, discriminating ‖ (when standing before noun) *adj* clever, sly, smart; secret, hidden; **au fin fond de** deep in the interior of; **le fin mot de l'histoire** the truth of the story ‖ *m* fine linen; smart person; **le fin du fin** the finest of the fine ‖ **fin** *f* end; **à la fin** at last; **à seule fin de** for the sole purpose of; **à toutes fins utiles** for your information; **c'est la fin des haricots** (slang) that takes the cake; **en fin de compte** in the end; to get to the point; **fin de semaine** weekend; **fins de série** (com) remnant, leftover article; **fin d'interdiction de dépasser** (*public sign*) end of no passing; **mettre fin à** to put an end to; **mot de la fin** clincher; **sans fin** endless ‖ **fin** *adv* absolutely; finely (*ground*); small, e.g., **écrire fin** to write small

fi•nal -nale [final] (*pl* **-nals** or **-naux** [no]) *adj* final ‖ *m* finale ‖ *f* last syllable or letter; (mus) keynote; (sports) finals

finalement [finalmɑ̃] *adv* finally

finaliste [finalist] *mf* finalist

finance [finɑ̃s] *f* finance

financement [finɑ̃smɑ̃] *m* financing

financer [finɑ̃se] *§51 tr* to finance

finan•cier [finɑ̃sje] **-cière** [sjɛr] *adj* financial; spicy (*sauce for vol-au-vent*) ‖ *m* financier

finasser [finase] *intr* (coll) to use finesse, finagle

finasserie [finasri] *f* shrewdness

fi•naud [fino] **-naude** [nod] *adj* wily, sly ‖ *mf* sly fox; smart aleck

finesse [finɛs] *f* finesse; fineness; **savoir les finesses** to know the fine points or niceties

fi•ni -nie [fini] *adj* finished; finite; ruined (*in health, financially, etc.*) arrant (*rogue*) ‖ *m* finish; finite

finir [finir] §97 *tr & intr* to finish; **en finir avec** to have done with; **finir de** + *inf* to finish + *ger;* **finir par** + *inf* to finish by + *inf*

finissage [finisaʒ] *m* finishing touch, final step

finition [finisjɔ̃] *f* finish; **finitions** finishing touches

finlan•dais [fɛ̃lɑ̃dɛ] **-daise** [dɛz] *adj* Finnish ‖ *m* Finnish (*language*) ‖ (*cap*) *mf* Finn

Finlande [fɛ̃lɑ̃d] *f* Finland; **la Finlande** Finland

fin•noise [finwa] **-noise** [nwaz] *adj* Finnish ‖ *m* Finnish (*language*); Finnic (*branch of Uralic*) ‖ (*cap*) *mf* Finn

fiole [fjɔl] *f* phial

fioriture [fjɔrityr] *f* flourish, curlicue

firmament [firmamɑ̃] *m* firmament

firme [firm] *f* firm, house, company

fis [fi] *v* (**fit, fîmes,** etc.) see **faire**

fisc [fisk] *m* bureau of internal revenue, tax-collection agency

fis•cal -cale [fiskal] *adj* (*pl* **-caux** [ko]) fiscal; revenue, taxation

fiscaliser [fiskalize] *tr* to subject to tax

fiscalité [fiskalite] *f* tax collections; fiscal policy

fissile [fisil] *adj* fissionable

fission [fisjɔ̃] *f* fission; **fission nucléaire** nuclear fission

fissure [fisyr] *f* fissure, crack

fissurer [fisyre] *tr & ref* to fissure

fiston [fistɔ̃] *m* (slang) sonny

fixa•teur [fiksatœr] **-trice** [tris] *adj* fixing, fixative ‖ *m* fixer; hair cream; (phot) fixing bath

fixation [fiksɑsjɔ̃] *f* fixation; fixing; **fixations** bindings (*on ski equipment*)

fixe [fiks] *adj* fixed; permanent (*ink*); glassy (*stare*); regular (*time*); set (*price*); standing (*rule*) ‖ *m* fixed income ‖ *interj* (mil) eyes front!

fixe-chaussette [fiksəʃosɛt] *m* (*pl* **-chaussettes**) garter (*for men's socks*)

fixement [fiksəmɑ̃] *adv* fixedly

fixer [fikse] *tr* to fix; appoint; (coll) to stare at; **fixer son choix sur** to fix on; **pour fixer les idées** for the sake of argument ‖ *ref* to be fastened; establish residence; make up one's mind

flacon [flakɔ̃] *m* small bottle; flask

flagada [flagada] *adj* (slang) pooped

flageller [flaʒɛlle] *tr* to flagellate

flageoler [flaʒɔle] *intr* to quiver

flageolet [flaʒɔlɛ] *m* flageolet; kidney bean

flagorner [flagɔrne]*tr* to flatter

fla•grant [flagrɑ̃] **-grante** [grɑ̃t] *adj* flagrant, glaring, obvious

flair [flɛr] *m* scent, sense of smell; (*discernment*) flair, keen nose

flairer [flɛre] *tr* to smell, sniff; scent, smell out

fla•mand [flamɑ̃] **-mande** [mɑ̃d] *adj* Flemish ‖ *m* Flemish (*language*) ‖ (*cap*) *mf* Fleming (*person*)

flamant [flamɑ̃] *m* flamingo

flam•bant [flɑ̃bɑ̃] **-bante** [bɑ̃t] *adj* flaming; **flambant neuf** (coll) brand-new

flam•beau [flɑ̃bo] *m* (*pl* **-beaux**) torch; candlestick; large wax candle; (fig) light

flambée [flɑ̃be] *f* blaze; flare-up

flamber [flɑ̃be] *tr* to singe; sterilize; (culin) to flambé; **être flambé** (coll) to be all washed up, ruined ‖ *intr* to flame; burn

flamberge [flɑ̃bɛrʒ] *f* (archaic) sword, blade; **mettre flamberge au vent** to unsheathe the sword

flambeur [flɑ̃bœr] *m* high roller; big gambler

flamboiement [flɑ̃bwamɑ̃] *m* glow, flare

flamboyant [flɑ̃bwajɑ̃] **flamboyante** [flɑ̃bwajɑ̃t] *adj* flaming, blazing; (archit) flamboyant

flamboyer [flɑ̃bwaje] §47 *intr* to flame

flamme [flɑm], [flam] *f* flame; pennant

flammèche [flamɛʃ] *f* ember, large spark

flan [flɑ̃] *m* custard; blank (*coin, medal, record*); **à la flan** (slang) happy-go-lucky; botched (*job*); **c'est du flan** (slang) it's ridiculous

flanc [flɑ̃] *m* flank; side (*of ship, mountain, etc.*); **battre du flanc** to pant; **être sur le flanc** (coll) to be laid up; **flancs** (archaic) womb; bosom; **prêter le flanc à** to lay oneself open to; **se battre les flancs** to go to a lot of trouble for nothing; **tirer au flanc** (coll) to gold-brick, to malinger

flancher [flɑ̃ʃe] *intr* (coll) to give in; (coll) to weaken, give way

flanchet [flɑ̃ʃɛ] *m* flank (*of beef*)

Flandre [flɑ̃dr] *f* Flanders; **la Flandre** Flanders

flanelle [flanɛl] *f* flannel

flâner [flɑne] *intr* to stroll, saunter; loaf

flânerie [flɑnri] *f* strolling; loafing

flâ•neur [flɑnœr] **-neuse** [nøz] *mf* stroller; loafer (*shoe*)

flanquer [flɑ̃ke] *tr* to flank; (coll) to throw, fling; **flanquer à la porte** (coll) to kick out; **flanquer un coup à** (coll) to take a swing at

fla•pi-pie [flapi] *adj* (coll) tired out, fagged out

flaque [flak] *f* puddle, pool

flash [flaʃ] *m* (*pl* **flashes**) news flash; flash pictures; (phot) flash attachment; (phot) flash bulb

flasque [flask] *adj* flabby ‖ *m* metal trim ‖ *f* flask; powder horn

flatter [flate] *tr* to flatter; stroke; delight; cater to; delude ‖ *intr* to flatter ‖ §97 *ref*—**se flatter de** to flatter oneself on

flatterie [flatri] *f* flattery

flat•teur [flatœr] **-teuse** [tøz] *adj* flattering ‖ *mf* flatterer

flatulence [flatylɑ̃s] *f* (pathol) flatulence

flatuosité [flatyozite] *f* (pathol) flatulence

fléau [fleo] *m* (*pl* **fléaux**) flail; beam (*of balance*); (fig) scourge, plague

flèche [flɛʃ] *f* arrow; spire (*of church*); boom (*of crane*); flitch (*of bacon*); **en flèche** like an arrow; in tandem; **faire flèche de tout bois**

to leave no stone unturned; **flèche d'eau** (bot) arrowhead

fléchette [fle∫ɛt] *f* dart (*used in game*); **jouer aux fléchettes** to play darts

fléchir [fle∫ir] *tr* to bend; move (*e.g., to pity*) ‖ *intr* to bend, give way; weaken, flag; go down, sag (*said of prices*)

flegmatique [flɛgmatik] *adj* phlegmatic, stolid

flegme [flɛgm] *m* phlegm

flem•mard [flɛmar] **-marde** [mard] *adj* idle, lazy ‖ *mf* idler, loafer

flemme [flɛm] *f* (slang) sluggishness; **tirer sa flemme** (slang) to not lift a finger

flet [flɛ] *m* flounder

flétan [fletɑ̃] *m* halibut

flétrir [fletrir] *tr & ref* to fade, wither; weaken

flétrissure [fletrisyr] *f* fading, withering; branding (*of criminals*); blot, stigma

fleur [flœr] *f* flower; blossom; **à fleur de** level with, even with; on the surface of; **à fleur de peau** skin-deep; **à fleur de tête** bulging (*eyes*); **elle est fleur bleue** (slang) she is a prude; **en fleur** in bloom; **en fleurs** in bloom (*said of group of different varieties*); **fleur de farine** fine white flour; **fleur de l'âge** prime of life; **fleur de lis** [flœrdəlis] fleur-de-lis; **fleur des pois** (coll) pick of the lot; **fleurs** mold (*on wine, cider, etc.*)

fleurer [flœre] *intr* to give off an odor; **fleurer bon** to smell good

fleuret [flœrɛ] *m* fencing foil

fleurette [flœrɛt] *f* little flower; **conter fleurette** to flirt

fleu•ri -rie [flœri] *adj* in bloom; flowery; florid (*complexion; style*)

fleurir [flœrir] *tr* to decorate with flowers ‖ *intr* to flower, bloom ‖ *intr* (*ger* **florissant**; *imperf* **florissais**, etc.) to flourish

fleuriste [flœrist] *mf* florist; floral gardener; maker or seller of artificial flowers

fleuron [flœrɔ̃] *m* floret; (archit) finial; **fleuron à sa couronne** feather in his cap

fleuve [flœv] *m* river (*flowing directly to the sea*); (fig) river (*of tears, blood, etc.*)

flexible [flɛksibl] *adj* flexible; (fig) pliant

flexion [flɛksjɔ̃] *f* bending, flexion; (gram) inflection

flibuster [flibyste] *tr* to rob, snitch ‖ *intr* to filibuster

flibustier [flibystje] *m* filibuster (*pirate*)

flic [flik] *m* (coll) cop, copper; cops

flicaille [flikaj] *f* (slang) (pej) fuzz, cops

flic flac [flikflak] *interj* splash!

flingot [flɛ̃go] *m* (slang) rod, gat

flingue [flɛ̃g] *m* (slang) rod, gat

flipper [flipɛr] *m* pinball machine ‖ [flipe] *intr* (slang) to be high; (slang) to feel low

flirt [flœrt] *m* flirt; flirtation

flirter [flœrte] *intr* to flirt

flir•teur [flœrtœr] **-teuse** [tøz] *adj* flirtatious ‖ *mf* flirt

flocon [flɔkɔ̃] *m* flake; snowflake; tuft (*e.g., of*

wool); **flocons d'avoine** oatmeal; **flocons de maïs** cornflakes; **flocons de neige** snowflakes

floconner [flɔkɔne] *intr* to form flakes; become fleecy

flocon•neux [flɔkɔnø] **-neuse** [nøz] *adj* flaky; fleecy

flopée [flɔpe] *f*—(slang) **une flopée de** loads of, lots of

floraison [flɔrɛzɔ̃] *f* flowering, blooming

flo•ral -rale [flɔral] *adj* (*pl* **-raux** [ro]) floral

floralies [flɔrali] *fpl* flower show

flore [flɔr] *f* flora

floren•tin [flɔrɑ̃tɛ̃] **-tine** [tin] *adj* Florentine; **à la florentine** with spinach ‖ (*cap*) *mf* Florentine (*native or inhabitant of Florence*)

Floride [flɔrid] *f* Florida; **la Floride** Florida

florilège [flɔrilɛʒ] *m* anthology

floris•sant -sante [flɔrisɑ̃] [sɑ̃t] *adj* flourishing

floss [flɔs] *m* (coll) dental floss

flot [flo] *m* wave; tide; flood, multitude; **à flot** afloat; **à flots** in torrents, abundantly; **flots** waters (*of a lake, the sea, etc.*); **flots de** lots of

flottabilité [flɔtabilite] *f* buoyancy

flottable [flɔtabl] *adj* buoyant; navigable (*for rafts*)

flottage [flɔtaʒ] *m* log driving

flottaison [flɔtɛzɔ̃] *f* water line

flot•tant [flɔtɑ̃] **-tante** [tɑ̃t] *adj* floating; vacillating, undecided

flotte [flɔt] *f* fleet buoy; float (*on fishline*); (slang) water, rain; **flotte en réserve** (nav) mothball fleet

flottement [flɔtmɑ̃] *m* floating; hesitation, vacillation; undulation

flotter [flɔte] *intr* to float; waver, hesitate; fly (*said of flag*); **il flotte** (slang) it is raining

flotteur [flɔtœr] *m* log driver; float (*of fishline, carburetor, etc.*); pontoon, float (*of seaplane*)

flottille [flɔtij] *f* flotilla; **flottille de pêche** fishing fleet

flou floue [flu] *adj* blurred, hazy; fluffy (*hair*); loose-fitting (*dress*); light and soft (*tones, lines in a painting*) ‖ *m* blur, fuzziness; dressmaking

flouer [flue] *tr* to dupe, swindle; **se faire flouer** to be had

fluctuation [flyktɥasjɔ̃] *f* fluctuation

fluctuer [flyktɥe] *intr* to fluctuate

fluet [flyɛ] **fluette** [flyɛt] *adj* thin, slender

fluide [flɥid] *adj & m* fluid

fluidifier [flɥidifje] *tr* to liquefy

fluor [flyɔr] *m* fluorine

fluores•cent [flyɔresɑ̃] **-cente** [sɑ̃t] *adj* fluorescent

fluoridation [flyɔridɑsjɔ̃] *f* fluoridation

fluorider [flyɔride] *tr & intr* to fluoridate

fluorure [flyɔryr] *m* fluoride

flûte [flyt] *f* flute; long thin loaf of French bread; tall champagne glass; **flûte à bec** recorder; **flûte de Pan** Pan's pipes; **flûtes** (slang) legs; **grande flûte** concert flute; **jouer** or **se tirer**

des flûtes (slang) to run for it; **petite flûte** piccolo ‖ *interj* shucks! rats!

flûtiste [flytist] *mf* flutist

flux [fly] *m* flow; flood tide; (cards) flush; (chem, elec, med, metallurgy) flux; **flux de caisse** cash flow; **flux de données** (comp) data flow; **flux de sang** flush, blush; dysentery; **flux de textes** (comp) text flow; **flux de ventre** diarrhea; **flux et reflux** ebb and flow

fluxion [flyksjɔ̃] *f* inflammation

foc [fɔk] *m* (naut) jib

fo•cal -cale [fɔkal] *adj* (*pl* **-caux** [ko]) focal

fœtus [fetys] *m* fetus

foi [fwa] *f* faith; word (*of a gentleman*); **ajouter foi à** to give credence to; **bonne foi** good faith, sincerity; **de bonne foi** sincere; sincerely; **de mauvaise foi** dishonest; dishonestly; **en foi de quoi** in witness whereof; **faire foi de** to be evidence of; **ma foi!** upon my word!; **manquer de foi à** to break faith with; **mauvaise foi** bad faith, insincerity; **sur la foi de** on the strength of

foie [fwa] *m* liver; **avoir les foies** (slang) to be scared stiff; **foie gras** goose liver

foin [fwɛ̃] *m* hay; **avoir du foin dans ses bottes** (coll) to be well heeled; **faire du foin** (slang) to kick up a fuss

foire [fwar] *f* fair; market; (coll) chaos, mess; **faire la foire** to raise hell; **foire d'empoigne** free-for-all

foirer [fware] *intr* (slang) to flop, fail; (slang) to hang fire; (slang) to be stripped (*said of screw, nut, etc.*)

fois [fwa] *f* time, e.g., **visiter trois fois par semaine** to visit three times a week; times, e.g., **deux fois deux font quatre** two times two is four; **à la fois** at the same time, together; **des fois** sometimes; **deux fois** twice; twofold; **encore une fois** once more, again; **il y avait une fois** once upon a time there was; **maintes et maintes fois** time and time again; **une fois** one time, once; **une fois pour toutes** or **une bonne fois** once and for all

foison [fwazɔ̃] *f*—**à foison** in abundance

foison•nant [fwazɔnɑ̃] **-nante** [nɑ̃t] *adj* abundant, plentiful

foisonner [fwazɔne] *intr* to abound

fol *adj* see **fou**

folâtre [fɔlɑtr] *adj* frisky, playful

folâtrer [fɔlɑtre] *intr* to frolic, romp

folie [fɔli] *f* madness, insanity; folly, piece of folly; country lodge, hideaway (*for romantic trysts*); **à la folie** madly, passionately; **faire une folie** to do something crazy; **folie de la persécution** persecution complex

folio [fɔljo] *m* folio

folioter [fɔljɔte] *tr* to folio

folle [fɔl] *f* crazy woman ‖ *adj* see **fou**

follement [fɔlmɑ̃] *adv* madly

fol•let [fɔlɛ] **-lette** [lɛt] *adj* merry, playful; elfish

follicule [fɔlikyl] *m* follicle

fomenta•teur [fɔmɑ̃tatœr] **-trice** [tris] *mf* agitator, troublemaker

fomenter [fɔmɑ̃te] *tr* to foment

fon•cé -cée [fɔ̃se] *adj* dark; deep

foncer [fɔ̃se] §51 *tr* to darken; dig (*a well*); fit a bottom to (*a cask*) ‖ *intr* to charge, rush

fon•cier [fɔ̃sje] **-cière** [sjɛr] *adj* landed (*property*); property (*tax*); fundamental, natural ‖ *m* real-estate tax

foncièrement [fɔ̃sjɛrmɑ̃] *adv* fundamentally, naturally

fonction [fɔ̃ksjɔ̃] *f* function; duty; **faire fonction de** to function as; **fonction publique** government work; **mauvaise fonction** malfunction

fonctionnaire [fɔ̃ksjɔnɛr] *mf* civil servant; officeholder

fonctionnarisme [fɔ̃ksjɔnarism] *m* bureaucracy

fonction•nel -nelle [fɔ̃ksjɔnɛl] *adj* functional

fonctionnement [fɔ̃ksjɔnmɑ̃] *m* working, functioning, operation; **bon fonctionnement** good working order

fonctionner [fɔ̃ksjɔne] *intr* to function, work; **mal fonctionner** to malfunction

fond [fɔ̃] *m* bottom; back, far end; background; foundation; dregs; core, inner meaning, main issue; **à fond** thoroughly; **à fond de train** at full speed; **au fond, dans le fond,** or **par le fond** actually, really, basically; **de fond** fundamental, main; **de fond en comble** from top to bottom; **faire fond sur** to rely on; **fond de tarte** bottom pie crust; **fonds de placement fermé** investment trust fund; **fond sonore** background noise; **râcler les fonds du tiroir** to scrape the bottom of the barrel; **sans fond** bottomless; **y aller au fond** to go the whole way ‖ see **fonds**

fondamen•tal -tale [fɔ̃damɑ̃tal] *adj* (*pl* **-taux** [to]) fundamental, fundamentalistic ‖ *f* (mus) fundamental ‖ *mpl* fundamentals

fondamentalisme [fɔ̃damɑ̃talism] *m* (rel) fundamentalism; **fondamentalisme islamique** Islamic fundamentalism

fondamentaliste [fɔ̃damɑ̃talist] *mf* (rel) fundamentalist

fon•dant [fɔ̃dɑ̃] **-dante** [dɑ̃t] *adj* melting; juicy, luscious ‖ *m* fondant (*candy*); (metallurgy) flux

fonda•teur [fɔ̃datœr] **-trice** [tris] *mf* founder

fondation [fɔ̃dɑsjɔ̃] *f* foundation; founding; endowment

fon•dé -dée [fɔ̃de] §92 *adj* founded; justified; authorized; **bien fondé** well-founded ‖ *m*—**fondé de pouvoir** proxy, authorized agent

fondement [fɔ̃dmɑ̃] *m* foundation, basis; (coll) behind; **sans fondement** unfounded

fonder [fɔ̃de] *tr* to found

fonderie [fɔ̃dri] *f* foundry; smelting

fondeur [fɔ̃dœr] *m* founder, smelter

fondre [fɔ̃dr] *tr* to melt, dissolve; smelt; cast (*metal*); blend (*colors*); merge (*companies*) ‖ *intr* to melt; (coll) to lose weight; **fondre en larmes** to burst into tears; **fondre sur** to pounce on

fondrière [fɔ̃drijɛr] *f* quagmire; mudhole, rut, pothole

fonds [fɔ̃] *m* land (*of an estate*); business, good will; fund; **bon fonds** good nature; **fonds** *mpl* capital; **fonds commun à placement dirigé au développement** growth fund; **fonds de commerce** business house; **fonds de prévoyance** reserve fund; **fonds en fidéicommis** trust fund; **fonds d'État** *mpl* government bonds; **fonds servant à des pots-de-vin** slush fund

fon•du -due [fɔ̃dy] *adj* melted; molten ‖ *m* blending (*of colors*); (mov, telv) dissolve, fade-out ‖ *f* fondue ‖ *v* see **fondre**

fongicide [fɔ̃ʒisid] *adj* fungicidal ‖ *m* fungicide

font [fɔ̃] *v* see **faire**

fontaine [fɔ̃tɛn] *f* fountain; spring; well; cistern; **fontaine de Jouvence** Fountain of Youth; **fontaines vivantes** dancing waters

fonte [fɔ̃t] *f* melting; casting; cast iron; holster; (typ) font; **venir de fonte avec** to be cast in one piece with

fonts [fɔ̃] *mpl*—**fonts baptismaux** baptismal font

football [futbol] *m* soccer; **football américain** football

footballeur [futbolœr] *m* soccer player

footing [futiŋ] *m* walking

for [fɔr] *m*—**dans son for intérieur** in his heart of hearts; **for intérieur** conscience

forage [fɔraʒ] *m* drilling; **forage d'exploration, forage sauvage** wildcat drilling

fo•rain [fɔrɛ̃] **-raine** [rɛn] *adj* traveling, itinerant ‖ **forains** *mpl* carnival people

forban [fɔrbã] *m* pirate

forçage [fɔrsaʒ] *m* (agr) forcing

forçat [fɔrsa] *m* convict; (hist) galley slave; (fig) drudge

force [fɔrs] *f* force; strength; **à force de** by dint of, as a result of; **à toute force** at all costs; **de première force** foremost (*musician, artist, scientist, etc.*) **de toutes ses forces** with all one's might; **force de frappe** striking force; **force m'est de ...** (lit) I am obliged to ...; **force majeure** (law) act of God; **forces** sheep shears; **force vive** (phys) kinetic energy; **la force de l'âge** the prime of life ‖ *adj invar* (archaic) many

forcément [fɔrsemã] *adv* inevitably, necessarily

force•né -née [fɔrsəne] *adj* frenzied, frantic ‖ *m* madman ‖ *f* crazy woman

forceps [fɔrsɛps] *m* (obstet) forceps

forcer [fɔrse] §51, §96, §97, §100 *tr* to force; do violence to; bring to bay; increase (*the dose*); strain (*a muscle*); mark up (*a receipt*); **forcer la main à qn** to force s.o.'s hand; **forcer la note** (coll) to overdo it; **forcer le respect de qn** to compel respect from s.o.; **forcer qn à** or **de** + *inf* to force s.o. to + *inf* ‖ *ref* to overdo; do violence to one's feelings

forclore [fɔrklɔr] (used only in *inf* and *pp* **forclos**) *tr* to foreclose

forclusion [fɔrklyzjɔ̃] *f* foreclosure

forer [fɔre] *tr* to drill, bore

fores•tier [fɔrɛstje] **-tière** [tjɛr] *adj* forest ‖ *m* forester

foret [fɔrɛ] *m* drill

forêt [fɔrɛ] *f* forest; **forêt vierge équatoriale** or **forêt amazonienne** rain forest

fo•reur [fɔrœr] **-reuse** [røz] *adj* drilling ‖ *mf* driller ‖ *f* drill, machine drill

forfaire [fɔrfɛr] §29 (used only in *inf;* 1st, 2d, & 3d *sg pres ind;* compound tenses) *intr*—**forfaire à** to forfeit (*one's honor*); fail in (*a duty*)

forfait [fɔrfɛ] *m* heinous crime; contract; package deal; (turf) forfeit; **à forfait** for a lump sum

forfaitaire [fɔrfɛtɛr] *adj* contractual

forfaiture [fɔrfɛtyr] *f* malfeasance

forfanterie [fɔrfãtri] *f* bragging

forge [fɔrʒ] *f* forge; steel mill

forger [fɔrʒe] §38 *tr* to forge

forgeron [fɔrʒərɔ̃] *m* blacksmith

forgeur [fɔrʒœr] *m* forger, smith; coiner (*e.g., of new expressions*); fabricator (*of false stories*)

formaldéhyde [fɔrmaldeid] *m* formaldehyde

formaliser [fɔrmalize] *ref* to take offense

formaliste [fɔrmalist] *adj* formalistic, conventional ‖ *mf* formalist

formalité [fɔrmalite] *f* formality, convention

format [fɔrmal] *m* size, format

formation [fɔrmasjɔ̃] *f* formation; education, training; qualifications

forme [fɔrm] *f* form; **en forme** fit, in shape; **en forme, en bonne forme,** or **en bonne et due forme** in order, in due form; **pour la forme** for appearances

for•mel -melle [fɔrmɛl] *adj* explicit; strict; formal, superficial

formellement [fɔrmɛlmã] *adv* absolutely, strictly

former [fɔrme] *tr & ref* to form; educate

formidable [fɔrmidabl] *adj* formidable; (coll) tremendous, terrific

formulaire [fɔrmylɛr] *m* formulary; form (*with spaces for answers*); **formulaire de commande** order form

formule [fɔmyl] *f* formula; form, blank; format; **formule de politesse** complimentary close

formuler [fɔrmyle] *tr* to formulate; draw up

forniquer [fɔrnike] *intr* to fornicate

fort [fɔr] **forte** [fɔrt] *adj* strong; fortified (*city*); **c'est fort!** it's hard to believe! ‖ (when standing before noun) *adj* high (*fever*); large (*sum*); hard (*task*) ‖ *m* fort; strong man; forte; height (*of summer*) ‖ **fort** *adv* exceedingly; loud; hard

fort-en-thème [fɔratɛm] *adj* (slang) grind (*student*)

forteresse [fɔrtərɛs] *f* fortress, fort

forti•fiant [fɔrtifjã] **-fiante** [fjãt] *adj & m* tonic

fortification [fɔrtifikasjɔ̃] *f* fortification

fortifier [fɔrtifje] *tr* to fortify; confirm (*one's opinions*)

fortin [fɔrtɛ̃] *m* small fort

for·tuit [fɔrtɥi] **-tuite** [tɥit] *adj* fortuitous, accidental

fortune [fɔrtyn] *f* fortune; **faire fortune** to make a fortune

fortu·né -née [fɔrtyne] *adj* fortunate; rich

fosse [fos] *f* pit; grave; **fosse aux lions** lions' den; **fosse commune** pauper's grave; **fosse d'aisances** cesspool; **fosse septique** septic tank

fossé [fose] *m* ditch, trench; moat; **fossé des générations** generation gap; **sauter le fossé** to take the plunge

fossette [fosɛt] *f* dimple

fossile [fosil] *adj* & *m* fossil ‖ *mf* fossil (*person*)

fossoyeur [foswajœr] *m* gravedigger

fosterage [fɔsteraʒ] *m* foster parenting

fou [fu] or **fol** [fɔl] **folle** [fɔl] (*pl* **fous folles**) *adj* mad, insane; foolish; extravagant; unsteady; loose (*pulley*); (coll) tremendous (*success*); **être fou à lier** to be raving mad; **être fou de** to be wild about; to be wild with (*joy, pain, etc.*) ‖ **fou** *m* madman; fool; jester; (cards) joker; (chess) bishop ‖ *f* see **folle**

foucade [fukad] *f* whim, impulse

foudre [fudr] *m* thunderbolt (*of Zeus*); large cask; **foudre de guerre** great captain; **foudre d'éloquence** powerful orator ‖ *f* lightning; **foudres** displeasure (*e.g., of a prince*); **foudres de l'Église** excommunication

foudroyant [fudrwajɑ̃] **foudroyante** [fudrwajɑ̃t] *adj* lightning-like; crushing, overwhelming

foudroyer [fudrwaje] §47 *tr* to strike with lightning; strike suddenly; dumfound; **foudroyer d'un regard** to cast a withering glance at ‖ *intr* to hurl thunderbolts

fouet [fwɛ] *m* whip; (culin) beater

fouetter [fwɛte] *tr* & *intr* to whip

fougère [fuʒɛr] *f* fern

fougue [fug] *f* spirit, ardor

fou·gueux [fugø] **-gueuse** [gøz] *adj* spirited, fiery, impetuous

fouille [fuj] *f* excavation; search

fouiller [fuje] *tr* to excavate; search, comb, inspect

fouillis [fuji] *m* jumble, disorder

fouine [fwin] *f* beech marten; pitchfork; harpoon

fouiner [fwine] *intr* (coll) to pry, meddle

fouir [fwir] *tr* to dig, burrow

foulard [fular] *m* scarf, neckerchief

foule [ful] *f* crowd, mob; **en foule** in great numbers

fouler [fule] *tr* to tread on, press; sprain ‖ *ref* to sprain; (slang) to put oneself out, to tire oneself out

foulque [fulk] *f* (zool) coot

foulure [fulyr] *f* sprain

four [fur] *m* oven; kiln, furnace; (coll) flop, turkey; **faire cuire au four** to bake; to roast; **faire four** (coll) to flop; **four à briques** brick-kiln; **four à chaux** limekiln; **four auto-nettoyant** self-cleaning oven; **petit four** teacake

fourbe [furb] *adj* deceiving, cheating ‖ *mf* deceiver, cheat

fourberie [furbəri] *f* deceit, cheating

fourbir [furbir] *tr* to furbish, polish

fourbissage [furbisaʒ] *m* furnishing, polishing

four·bu -bue [furby] *adj* broken-down (*horse*); (coll) dead tired, all in

fourche [furʃ] *f* fork; pitchfork; **fourche avant** front fork (*of bicycle*); **fourches patibulaires** (hist) gallows

fourcher [furʃe] *tr* & *intr* to fork; **la langue lui a fourché** (coll) he made a slip of the tongue

fourchette [furʃɛt] *f* fork; wishbone; **posséder une bonne fourchette** to have a hearty appetite

four·chu -chue [furʃy] *adj* forked; cloven

fourgon [furgɔ̃] *m* truck; poker; (rr) baggage car; (rr) boxcar; **fourgon bancaire** armored car; **fourgon de queue** caboose; **fourgon funèbre** hearse

fourmi [furmi] *f* ant; (slang) pusher (*of drugs*); **avoir des fourmis** (coll) to have ants in one's pants; **fourmi blanche** white ant, termite

fourmilier [furmilje] *m* anteater

fourmilière [furmiljɛr] *f* ant hill

fourmiller [furmije] *intr* to swarm; tingle (*said, e.g., of foot*); **fourmiller de** to teem with

fournaise [furnɛz] *f* furnace; (fig) oven

four·neau [furno] *m* (*pl* **-neaux**) furnace; cooking stove; **haut fourneau** blast furnace

fournée [furne] *f* batch

four·ni -nie [furni] *adj* bushy, thick; **bien fourni** well-stocked

fourniment [furnimɑ̃] *m* (mil) kit

fournir [furnir] *tr* to furnish, supply; provide; play (*a card of the same suit that has been led*); **fournir q.ch. à qn** to supply or provide s.o. with s.th. ‖ *intr* to supply (*s.o.'s needs*), e.g., **ses parents fournissent à ses besoins** his parents supply his needs; defray (*expenses*); (cards) to follow suit, e.g., **fournir à trèfle** to follow suit in clubs ‖ *ref* to grow thick; be a customer

fournissement [furnismɑ̃] *m* contribution, holdings (*of each shareholder*); statement of holdings

fournisseur [furnisœr] *m* supplier, dealer

fourniture [furnityr] *f* furnishing, supplying; (culin) seasoning; **fournitures** supplies

fourrage [furaʒ] *m* fodder

fourrager [furaʒe] §38 *tr* to forage; rummage, rummage through ‖ *intr* to rummage (about), forage

fourragère [furaʒɛr] *f* lanyard; tailboard

four·ré -rée [fure] *adj* lined with fur; furred (*tongue*); stuffed (*dates*); filled (*candies*); sham, hollow (*peace*) ‖ *m* thicket

four·reau [furo] *m* (*pl* **-reaux**) sheath; scabbard; tight skirt; **coucher dans son fourreau** (coll) to sleep in one's clothes

fourrer [fure] *tr* to line with fur; (coll) to cram, stuff; (coll) to shut up (*in prison*); (coll) to stick, poke ‖ *ref* (coll) to turn, go; (coll) to curl up (*in bed*); **se fourrer dans** (coll) to stick one's nose in

fourre-tout [furtu] *m invar* catchall; duffel bag; tote bag

fourreur [furœr] *m* furrier

fourrier [furje] *m* quartermaster

fourrière [furjɛr] *f* pound (*for automobiles; for stray dogs*)

fourrure [furyr] *f* fur

fourvoyer [furvwaje] §47 *tr* to lead astray

foutre [futr] §7 (*pres* **je, tu fous; il fout**) *tr* (vulg) (dated) to have sex with; **fous-le dans ta poche!** shove it in your pocket!; **fous-moi la paix!** lay off!; **fous-moi le camp!** get the hell out!; **je t'en fous!** the hell with you!; **qu'est-ce qu'il fout?** what in hell is he doing? ‖ *ref* (vulg) (dated) to be had; **je m'en fous!** to hell with it!; **se foutre de** not to give a damn about; to make fun of

foutu [futy] *adj* (slang) damned; lousy, rotten; done for, kaput; **foutu de** capable of

fox [fɔks] *m* fox terrier

fox-terrier [fɔkstɛrje] *m* fox terrier

fox-trot [fɔkstrɔt] *m invar* fox trot

foyer [fwaje] *m* foyer, lobby; hearth, fireside; firebox; focus; home; greenroom; center (*of learning; of infection*); **à double foyer** bifocal; **foyer des étudiants** student center; **foyer du soldat** service club; **foyers** native land

frac [frak] *m* cutaway coat

fracas [fraka] *m* crash; roar (*of waves*); peal (*of thunder*)

fracasser [frakase] *tr & ref* to break; shatter, break to pieces

fraction [fraksjɔ̃] *f* fraction; breaking (*e.g., of bread*); **fraction de seconde** split-second

fractionnaire [fraksjɔnɛr] *adj* fractional

fractionnement [fraksjɔnmɑ̃] *m* cracking (*of petroleum*)

fractionner [fraksjɔne] *tr* to divide into fractions

fracture [fraktyr] *f* fracture; breaking open

fracturer [fraktyre] *tr* to fracture; break open

fragile [fraʒil] *adj* fragile

fragment [fragmɑ̃] *m* fragment

fragmenter [fragmɑ̃te] *tr* to fragment

frai [frɛ] *m* spawning; spawn, roe

fraîche [frɛʃ] *f* cool of the day

fraîchement [frɛʃmɑ̃] *adv* in the open air; recently; (coll) cordially

fraîcheur [frɛʃœr] *f* coolness; freshness; newness

fraîchir [frɑʃir] *intr* to become cooler; freshen (*said of wind*)

frais [frɛ] **fraîche** [frɛʃ] *adj* cool; fresh; wet (*paint*); ready (*cash*); **frais et dispos, frais comme une rose** fresh as a daisy; **il fait frais** it is cool out ‖ (when standing before noun) *adj* recent (*date*); latest (*news*) ‖ *m* cool place; fresh air; **aux frais de** at the expense of; **de frais** just, freshly; **faire les frais de la conversation** (coll) to take the lead in the conversation; be the subject of the conversa-

tion; **frais** *mpl* expenses; **frais généraux** overhead expenses; **se mettre en frais** (coll) to go to a great deal of expense or trouble ‖ *f* see **fraîche** ‖ **frais** *adv*—**boire frais** to have a cool drink ‖ **frais fraîche** *adv* (agrees with following *pp*) just, freshly, e.g., **garçon frais arrivé de l'école** boy just arrived from school; e.g., **roses fraîches cueillies** freshly gathered roses

fraise [frɛz] *f* strawberry; wattle (*of turkey*); (mach) countersink

fraiser [frɛze] *tr* (mach) to countersink

fraisier [frɛzje] *m* strawberry plant

framboise [frɑ̃bwaz] *f* raspberry

framboisier [frɑ̃bwazje] *m* raspberry bush

franc [frɑ̃] **franche** [frɑ̃ʃ] *adj* free; frank, sincere; complete ‖ (when standing before noun) *adj* arrant (*knave*); downright (*fool*) ‖ **franc franque** [frɑ̃k] *adj* Frankish ‖ *m* franc (*unit of currency*) ‖ (*cap*) *m* Frank (*medieval German*) ‖ **franc** *adv* frankly

fran•çais [frɑ̃sɛ] **-çaise** [sɛz] *adj* French ‖ *m* French (*language*); **en bon français** in correct French ‖ (*cap*) *m* Frenchman; **les Français** the French ‖ *f* Frenchwoman

franc-alleu [frɑ̃kalø] *m* (*pl* **francs-alleux** [frɑ̃kalø]) (hist) freehold

France [frɑ̃s] *f* France; **la France** France

franchement [frɑ̃ʃmɑ̃] *adv* frankly, sincerely; without hesitation

franchir [frɑ̃ʃir] *tr* to cross, go over or through; jump over; overcome (*an obstacle*)

franchise [frɑ̃ʃiz] *f* exemption; frankness; freedom; **franchise postale** frank

francique [frɑ̃sik] *m* Frankish

franciser [frɑ̃size] *tr* to make French

franc-maçon [frɑ̃masɔ̃] *m* (*pl* **francs-maçons**) Freemason

franc-maçonnerie [frɑ̃masɔnri] *f* Freemasonry

franco [frɑ̃ko] *adv* free, without shipping costs; **franco de bord** free on board; **franco de port** postpaid

franco-cana•dien [frɑ̃kokanadjɛ̃] **-dienne** [djɛn] *adj* French-Canadian ‖ **Franco-Cana•dien -dienne** *mf* French Canadian

francophone [frɑ̃kɔfɔn] *adj* French-speaking ‖ *mf* French speaker

franc-parler [frɑ̃parle] *m*—**avoir son franc-parler** to be free-spoken

franc-tireur [frɑ̃tirœr] *m* (*pl* **francs-tireurs**) freelance; sniper

frange [frɑ̃ʒ] *f* fringe; **à frange** fringed; **frange des dingues** lunatic fringe

franger [frɑ̃ʒe] §38 *tr* to fringe

franglais [frɑ̃glɛ] *m* Franglais

franquette [frɑ̃kɛt] *f*—**à la bonne franquette** (coll) simply, without fuss

frap•pant [frapɑ̃] **-pante** [pɑ̃t] *adj* striking, surprising

frappe [frap] *f* minting, striking; stamp (*on coins, medals, etc.*); touch (*in typing*); space (*in typing*), e.g., **une ligne de 65 frappes** a 65-space line

frap·pé -pée [frape] *adj* struck; iced; (slang) crazy ‖ *m* (mus) downbeat

frapper [frape] *tr* to strike, hit, knock; mint (coin); stamp (*cloth*); ice (*e.g., champagne*) ‖ *intr* to strike, hit, knock ‖ *ref* (coll) to become panic-stricken

frasque [frask] *f* escapade

frater·nel -nelle [fratɛrnɛl] *adj* fraternal, brotherly

fraterniser [fratɛrnize] *intr* to fraternize

fraternité [fratɛrnite] *f* fraternity, brotherhood

fraude [frod] *f* fraud; smuggling; **en fraude** fraudulently; **faire la fraude** to smuggle; **fraude fiscale** tax evasion

fraudu·leux [frodylø] **-leuse** [løz] *adj* fraudulent

frayer [frɛje], [freje] §49 *tr* to mark out (*a path*) ‖ *intr* to spawn; **frayer avec** to associate with

frayeur [frɛjœr] *f* fright, scare

fredaine [frədɛn] *f* (coll) escapade, prank, spree

fredon [frədɔ̃] *m* (cards) three of a kind

fredonnement [frədɔnmɑ̃] *m* hum, humming

fredonner [frədɔne] *tr & intr* to hum

frégate [fregat] *f* frigate

frein [frɛ̃] *m* bit (*of bridle*); brake (*of car*); **frein à disque** disk brake; **frein à main** hand brake; **frein à pied** foot brake; **frein à tambour** drum brake; **mettre le frein** to put the brake on; **mettre un frein à** to curb, check; **ronger son frein** to champ at the bit

freiner [frɛne] *tr & intr* to brake

frelater [frəlate] *tr* to adulterate

frêle [frɛl] *adj* frail

frelon [frəlɔ̃] *m* hornet

frémir [fremir] §97 *intr* to shudder

frémissement [fremismɑ̃] *m* shudder

frêne [frɛn] *m* ash tree

frénésie [frenezi] *f* frenzy

frénétique [frenetik] *adj* frenzied

fréquemment [frekamɑ̃] *adv* frequently

fréquence [frekɑ̃s] *f* frequency; **basse fréquence** low frequency; **fréquence du pouls** pulse rate; **haute fréquence** high frequency

fré·quent [frekɑ̃] **-quente** [kɑ̃t] *adj* frequent, rapid (*pulse*)

fréquenter [frekɑ̃te] *tr* to frequent; associate with; (coll) to go steady with (*a boy or girl*)

frère [frɛr] *m* brother; **frère consanguin** half brother (*by the father*); **frère convers** (eccl) lay brother; **frère de lait, frère de placement** foster brother; **frére de sang** blood brother; **frère germain** whole brother; **frère jumeau** twin brother; **frères siamois** Siamese twins; **frère utérin** half brother (*by the mother*)

fresque [frɛsk] *f* fresco

fret [frɛ] *m* freight; chartering; cargo

fréter [frete] §10 *tr* to charter (*a ship*); rent (*a car*)

fréteur [fretœr] *m* shipowner

frétiller [fretije] *intr* to wriggle; quiver; **frétiller de** to wag (*its tail*)

fretin [frətɛ̃] *m*—**le menu fretin** small fry

frette [frɛt] *f* hoop, iron ring

freudisme [frødism] *m* Freudianism

freux [frø] *m* rook, crow

friand [frijɑ̃] **friande** [frijɑ̃d] *adj* tasty; fond (*of food, praise, etc.*) ‖ *m* sausage roll

friandise [frijɑ̃diz] *f* candy, sweet; delicacy, tidbit

fric [frik] *m* (slang) jack, money

fricasser [frikase] *tr* to fricassee; squander

fric-frac [frikfrak] *m* (coll) break-in

friche [friʃ] *f* fallow land; **en friche** fallow

friction [friksjɔ̃] *f* friction; massage

frictionner [friksjɔne] *tr* to rub, massage

Frigidaire [friʒidɛr] *m* (trademark) refrigerator

frigide [friʒid] *adj* frigid

frigidité [friʒidite] *f* frigidity

frigorifier [frigɔrifje] *tr* to refrigerate

frigorifique [frigɔrifik] *adj* refrigerating ‖ *m* cold-storage plant

fri·leux [frilø] **-leuse** [løz] *adj* chilly, shivery

frimas [frima] *m* icy mist, rime

frime [frim] *f* (coll) sham, fake, hoax

frimer [frime] *intr* (coll) to show off, to attract attention

frimousse [frimus] *f* (coll) little face, cute face

fringale [frɛ̃gal] *f* (coll) mad hunger

frin·gant [frɛ̃gɑ̃] **-gante** [gɑ̃t] *adj* dashing, spirited

fringuer [frɛ̃ge] *tr* (slang) to dress ‖ *intr* (obs) to frisk about

fringues [frɛ̃g] *fpl* (slang) duds

fri·pé -pée [fripe] *adj* rumpled, mussed; worn, tired (*face*)

friper [fripe] *tr* to wrinkle, rumple

friperie [fripri] *f* secondhand clothes; secondhand furniture

fri·pier [fripje] **-pière** [pjɛr] *mf* old-clothes dealer; junk dealer

fri·pon [fripɔ̃] **-ponne** [pɔn] *adj* roguish ‖ *mf* rogue, rascal

friponnerie [fripɔnri] *f* rascality, cheating

fripouille [fripuj] *f* (slang) scoundrel

frire [frir] §22 (used in *inf; pp;* 1st, 2d, 3d *sg pres ind; sg imperv;* rarely used in *fut; cond*) *tr* to fry; deep-fry; **être frit** (coll) to be done for ‖ *intr* to fry

frise [friz] *f* frieze

friselis [frizli] *m* soft rustling; gentle lapping (*of water*)

friser [frize] *tr* to curl; border on; graze ‖ *intr* to curl

frisoir [frizwar] *m* curling iron

fri·son [frizɔ̃] **-sonne** [zɔn] *adj* Frisian ‖ *m* wave, curl; Frisian (*language*) ‖ (*cap*) *mf* Frisian

fris·quet [friskɛ] **-quette** [kɛt] *adj* (coll) chilly

frisson [frisɔ̃] *m* shiver; shudder; thrill; **frissons** shivering

frissoner [frisɔne] *intr* to shiver

frisure [frizyr] *f* curling; curls

frit [fri] **frite** [frit] *v* see **frire**

frites [frit] *fpl* French fries

frittage [fritaʒ] *m* (metallurgy) sintering

friture [frityr] *f* frying; deep fat; fried fish; (rad, telv) static

frivole [frivɔl] *adj* frivolous, trifling

froc [frɔk] *m* (eccl) frock

froid [frwɑ] **froide** [frwɑd] *adj* cold; chilly (*manner*) ‖ *m* cold; coolness (*between persons*); **avoir froid** to be cold; **il fait froid** it is cold; **jeter un froid sur** (fig) to put a damper on

froideur [frwɑdœr] *f* coldness; coolness

froissement [frwɑsmɑ̃] *m* bruising; rumpling; crumpling; clash (*of interests*); ruffling (*of feelings*)

froisser [frwɑse] *tr* to bruise; rumple, crumple ‖ *ref* to take offense

frôlement [frolmɑ̃] *m* grazing; rustle

frôler [frole] *tr* to graze, brush against; (coll) to have a narrow escape from

fromage [frɔmaʒ] *m* cheese; (coll) soft job; **fromage à tartiner** cheese spread; **fromage blanc** cream cheese; **fromage de tête** headcheese; **fromage fondu** processed cheese

froma•ger [frɔmaʒe] **-gère** [ʒɛr] *adj* cheese (*industry*) ‖ *m* cheesemaker; (bot) silkcotton tree

fromagerie [frɔmaʒri] *f* cheese factory; cheese store

froment [frɔmɑ̃] *m* wheat

fronce [frɔ̃s] *f* crease, fold; **à fronces** shirred

froncement [frɔ̃smɑ̃] *m* puckering; **froncement de sourcils** frown

froncer [frɔ̃se] §51 *tr* to pucker; **froncer les sourcils** to frown, wrinkle one's brow

frondaison [frɔ̃dɛzɔ̃] *f* foliation; foliage

fronde [frɔ̃d] *f* slingshot

fronder [frɔ̃de] *tr* to scoff at

fron•deur [frɔ̃dœr] **-deuse** [døz] *adj* bantering, irreverent ‖ *mf* scoffer

front [frɔ̃] *m* forehead; impudence; brow (*of hill*); (geog, mil, pol) front; **de front** abreast; frontal; at the same time; **faire front à** to face up to; **front de mer** beachfront; **un front froid** (meteo) a cold front

fronta•lier [frɔ̃talje] **-lière** [ljɛr] *adj* frontier ‖ *m* frontiersman ‖ *f* frontier woman

frontière [frɔ̃tjɛr] *adj* & *f* frontier, border; **passer la frontière** to cross the border

frontispice [frɔ̃tispis] *m* frontispiece; title page

frottement [frɔtmɑ̃] *m* rubbing, friction

frotter [frɔte] *tr* to rub; polish; strike (*a match*); **frotter les oreilles à qn** (coll) to box s.o.'s ears ‖ *ref*—**se frotter à** (coll) to attack, challenge; (coll) to rub shoulders with

frottis [frɔti] *m* smear; **frottis sanguin Papanicolau** Pap smear, Pap test

froufrou [frufru] *m* rustle, swish

frousse [frus] *f* (slang) jitters

fructifier [fryktifje] *intr* to bear fruit

fruc•tueux [fryktɥø] **-tueuse** [tɥøz] *adj* fruitful, profitable

fru•gal -gale [frygal] *adj* (*pl* **-gaux** [go]) temperate; frugal (*meal*)

fruit [frɥi] *m* fruit; **des fruits** fruit; **fruits civils** income (*from rent, interest, etc.*); **fruits de mer** seafood; **fruit sec** (fig) flop, failure

fruiterie [frɥitri] *f* fruit store

frui•tier [frɥitje] **-tière** [tjɛr] *adj* fruit; fruit-bearing ‖ *mf* fruit vendor

fruste [fryst] *adj* worn; rough, uncouth

frustrer [frystre] *tr* frustrate, disappoint; cheat, defraud

f.s. *abbr* (**faux sens**) mistranslation

fuel [fjul] *m* fuel oil, heating oil

fuel-oil [fjulɔl] *m* fuel oil

fugace [fygas] *adj* fleeting, evanescent

fugi•tif [fyʒitif] **-tive** [tiv] *adj* & *mf* fugitive

fugue [fyg] *f* sudden disappearance; (mus) fugue

fuir [fɥir] §31 *tr* to flee, run away from ‖ *intr* to flee; leak; recede (*said of forehead*)

fuite [fɥit] *f* flight; leak

fulgu•rant [fylgyrɑ̃] **-rante** [rɑ̃t] *adj* flashing; vivid; stabbing (*pain*)

fulguration [fylgyrasjɔ̃] *f* sheet lightning

fulgurer [fylgyre] *intr* to flash

fuligi•neux [fyliʒinø] **-neuse** [nøz] *adj* sooty

fumage [fymaʒ] *m* smoking (*of meat*); manuring (*of fields*)

fume-cigare [fymsigar] *m invar* cigar holder

fume-cigarette [fymsigarɛt] *m invar* cigarette holder

fumée [fyme] *f* smoke; steam; **fumées** fumes; **fumée exhalée par les fumeurs** secondhand smoke

fumer [fyme] *tr* & *intr* to smoke; fume; manure

fumerie [fymri] *f* opium den; smoking room

fumet [fymɛ] *m* aroma; bouquet (*of wine*)

fu•meur [fymœr] **-meuse** [møz] *mf* smoker; **fumeur à la file** chain smoker

fu•meux [fymø] **-meuse** [møz] *adj* smoky; foggy, hazy (*ideas*)

fumier [fymje] *m* manure; dunghill; (slang) skunk, scoundrel

fumiger [fymiʒe] §38 *tr* to fumigate

fumillard [fymijar] *m* smog

fumiste [fymist] *m* heater man; (coll) practical joker

fumisterie [fymistri] *f* heater work; heater shop; (coll) hooey

fumoir [fymwar] *m* smoking room; smokehouse

funambule [fynɑ̃byl] *mf* tightrope walker

funèbre [fynɛbr] *adj* funereal; funeral (*march, procession, service*)

funérailles [fynerɑj] *fpl* funeral

funéraire [fynerɛr] *adj* funeral

funeste [fynɛst] *adj* baleful, fatal

funiculaire [fynikylɛr] *adj* & *m* funicular

fur [fyr] *m*—**au fur et à mesure** progressively, gradually; **au fur et à mesure de** in proportion to; **au fur et à mesure que** as, in proportion as

furet [fyrɛ] *m* ferret; snoop; ring-in-the-circle (*parlor game*)

fureter [fyrte] §2 *intr* to ferret

fureur [fyrœr] *f* fury; **à la fureur** passionately; **faire fureur** to be the rage

furi•bond [fyribɔ̃] **-bonde** [bɔ̃d] *adj* furious; withering (*look*) ‖ *mf* irascible individual

furie [fyri] *f* fury; termagant

fu•rieux [fyrjø] **-rieuse** [rjøz] *adj* furious; angry (*wind*)

furoncle [fyrɔ̃kl] *m* boil

fur•tif [fyrtif] **-tive** [tiv] *adj* furtive, stealthy

fus [fy] *v* (**fut, fûmes,** etc.) see **être**

fusain [fyzɛ̃] *m* charcoal; charcoal drawing; spindle tree

fu•seau [fyzo] *m* (*pl* **-seaux**) spindle; **à fuseau** tapering; **fuseau horaire** time zone (*between two meridians*)

fusée [fyze] *f* rocket; spindleful; spindle (*of axle*); (coll) ripple, burst (*of laughter*); **fusée à retard** delayed-action fuse; **fusée à vent comprimé** air rifle; **fusée d'artifice** or **fusée volante** skyrocket; **fusée éclairante, fusée de signalisation** flare; **fusée engin** rocket engine; **fusée fusante** time fuse; **fusée percutante** percussion fuse

fuselage [fyzlaʒ] *m* fuselage

fuse•lé -lée [fyzle] *adj* spindle-shaped; tapering, slender (*fingers*); streamlined

fuseler [fyzle] §34 *tr* to taper; streamline

fuser [fyze] *intr* to melt; run (*said of colors*); fizz, spurt; stream in or out (*said of light*)

fusible [fyzibl] *adj* fusible ‖ *m* fuse

fusil [fyzi] *m* gun, rifle; whetstone rifleman; **fusil à canon scié** sawed-off shotgun; **fusil à deux coups** double-barreled gun; **fusil de** chasse shot gun; **fusil mitrailleur** light machine gun; **un bon fusil** a good shot (*person*)

fusillade [fyzijad] *f* fusillade

fusiller [fyzije] *tr* to shoot, execute by a firing squad

fusion [fyzjɔ̃] *f* fusion; **fusion nucléaire** nuclear fusion

fusionner [fyzjɔne] *tr & intr* to blend, fuse; (com) to merge

fustiger [fystiʒe] §38 *tr* to thrash, flog; castigate

fût [fy] *m* cask, keg; barrel (*of drum*); stock (*of gun*); trunk (*of tree*); shaft (*of column*); stem (*of candelabrum*)

futaie [fytɛ] *f* stand of timber; **de haute futaie** full-grown

futaille [fytɑj] *f* cask, barrel

futaine [fytɛn] *f* fustian

fu•té -tée [fyte] *adj* (coll) cunning, shrewd ‖ *f* mastic, filler

futile [fytil] *adj* futile

futilité [fytilite] *f* futility; **futilités** trifles

fu•tur -ture [fytyr] *adj* future ‖ *m* future; husband-to-be ‖ *f* future wife

futuriste [fytyrist] *adj* futuristic

fuyant [fɥijɑ̃] **fuyante** [fɥijɑ̃t] *adj* fleeting; receding (*forehead*)

fuyard [fɥijar] **fuyarde** [fɥijard] *adj & mf* runaway

G

G, g [ʒe] *m invar* seventh letter of the French alphabet

gabardine [gabardin] *f* gabardine

gabare [gabar] *f* barge

gabarit [gabari] *m* template; (rr) maximum structure; (coll) size

gabelle [gabɛl] *f* (hist) salt tax

gâche [gɑʃ] *f* catch (*at a door*); trowel; wooden spatula

gâcher [gɑʃe] *tr* to mix (*cement*); spoil, bungle, squander

gâchette [gɑʃɛt] *f* trigger; pawl, spring catch

gâ•cheur [gɑʃœr] **-cheuse** [ʃøz] *adj* bungling ‖ *f* bungler

gâchis [gɑʃi] *m* wet cement; mud, slush; (coll) mess, muddle

gaélique [gaelik] *adj & m* Gaelic

gaffe [gaf] *f* gaff; (coll) social blunder, faux pas

gaffer [gafe] *tr* to hook with a gaff ‖ *intr* (coll) to make a blunder

gaga [gaga] *adj* (coll) doddering ‖ *mf* (coll) dotard

gage [gaʒ] *m* pledge, pawn; forfeit (*in a game*); **gages** wage, wages; **prêter sur gages** to pawn

gager [gaʒe] §38, §97 *tr* to wager, bet; pay wages to

ga•geur [gaʒœr] **-geuse** [ʒøz] *mf* bettor

gageure [gaʒyr] *f* wager, bet

gagiste [gaʒist] *mf* pledger; wage earner; (theat) extra

ga•gnant [gaɲɑ̃] **-gnante** [ɲɑ̃t] *adj* winning ‖ *mf* winner

gagne-pain [gaɲpɛ̃] *m invar* breadwinner; livelihood, bread and butter

gagne-petit [gaɲpəti] *m invar* cheapjack, low-salaried worker

gagner [gaɲe] §96 *tr* to gain; win; earn; reach; save (*time*) ‖ *intr* to improve; gain; spread ‖ *ref* to be catching (*said of disease*)

ga•gneur [gaɲœr] **-gneuse** [ɲøz] *mf* winner; earner

gai gaie [ge] *adj* cheerful, merry, happy; (*couleur*) bright, lively, brilliant; (*homosexuel*) gay; (coll) tipsy; **avoir le vin gai** to be in drunken high spirits; **une soirée gaie** a lively, good-spirited party ‖ *m* gay ‖ *f* (rare) gay, lesbian

gaiement [gemɑ̃] *adv* gaily, cheerfully, merrily, happily

gaieté [gete] *f* gaiety; **de gaieté de cœur** of one's own free will

gail•lard [gajar] **-larde** [jard] *adj* healthy,

hearty; merry; ribald, spicy ‖ *m* sturdy fellow; tricky fellow; **gaillard d'arrière** quarterdeck; **gaillard d'avant** forecastle ‖ *f* bold young lady; husky young woman

gaillardise [gajardiz] *f* cheerfulness; **gaillardises** spicy stories

gaîment [gemɑ̃] *adv* see **gaiement**

gain [gɛ̃] *m* gain; earnings; winning (*e.g., of bet*); **avoir gain de cause** to win one's case

gaine [gɛn] *f* sheath; case, covering; girdle (*corset*); **gaine d'aération** ventilation shaft

gainer [gene] *tr* to sheath, encase

gaîté [gete] *f* gaiety

gala [gala] *m* gala; state dinner

galamment [galamɑ̃] *adv* gallantly

ga•lant [galɑ̃] **-lante** [lɑ̃t] *adj* gallant; amorous; kept (*woman*) ‖ *m* gallant; **vert gallant** gay old blade

galanterie [galɑ̃tri] *f* gallantry; libertinism

galaxie [galaksi] *f* galaxy

galbe [galb] *m* curve, sweep, graceful outline

gale [gal] *f* mange; (coll) backbiter, cad

galée [gale] *f* (typ) galley

galéjade [galeʒad] *f* joke, far-fetched story

galère [galɛr] *f* galley; drudgery; mason's hand truck

galerie [galri] *f* gallery; cornice, rim; baggage rack; **galerie de tableaux** (*shop*) art gallery; **galerie marchande** shopping center; shopping mall

galérien [galerjɛ̃] *m* galley slave

galet [galɛ] *m* pebble; (mach) roller

galetas [galta] *m* hovel

galette [galɛt] *f* cake; buckwheat pancake; hardtack; (slang) dough, money, **galette des Rois** twelfth-cake (*eaten at Epiphany*)

ga•leux [galø] **-leuse** [løz] *adj* mangy

galimatias [galimatja] *m* nonsense, gibberish

galion [galjɔ̃] *m* galleon

Galles [gal]—**le pays de Galles** Wales; **prince de Galles** Prince of Wales

gal•lois [galwa] **gal•loise** [galwaz] *adj* Welsh ‖ *m* Welsh (*language*) ‖ (*cap*) *m* Welshman; **les Gallois** the Welsh ‖ (*cap*) *f* Welshwoman

gallon [galɔ̃] *m* gallon (*imperial or American*)

galoche [galɔʃ] *f* clog (*shoe*); **de** or **en galoche** pointed (*chin*)

galon [galɔ̃] *m* galloon, braid; (mil) stripe, chevron; **prendre du galon** to move up

galonner [galɔne] *tr* to trim with braid

galop [galo] *m* gallop; **petit galop** canter

galoper [galɔpe] *tr & intr* to gallop

galopin [galɔpɛ̃] *m* (coll) urchin

galvaniser [galvanize] *tr* to galvanize

galvanoplastie [galvãnɔplasti] *f* electroplating

galvauder [galvode] *tr* (coll) to botch; (coll) to waste (*e.g., one's talent*); (coll) to sully (*a name*) ‖ *intr* (slang) to walk the streets ‖ *ref* (slang) to go bad

gambade [gãbad] *f* gambol

gambader [gãbade] *intr* to gambol

gambit [gãbi] *m* gambit

gamelle [gamɛl] *f* mess kit

ga•min [gamɛ̃] **-mine** [min] *mf* street urchin; youngster

gaminerie [gaminri] *f* mischievousness

gamme [gam] *f* gamut, range; set (*of tools*); (mus) scale, gamut; **gamme de fréquence** (comp) frequency range; **gamme de gris** (comp) gray scale; **gamme de l'entrée** (comp) entry level; **haut de gamme** top-of-the-line; **haute gamme** (comp) high-level

Gand [gɑ] *m* Ghent

ganglion [gãglijɔ̃] *m* ganglion

gangrène [gãgrɛn] *f* gangrene

gangrener [gãgrəne] §2 *tr & ref* to gangrene

ganse [gãs] *f* braid, piping

gant [gɑ̃] *m* glove; **gant à laver** glove washcloth; **gants chirurgicaux** surgical gloves; **jeter le gant** to throw down the gauntlet; **prendre des gants pour** to put on kid gloves to; **relever le gant** to take up the gauntlet; **se donner des gants** to take all the credit

gantelet [gãtlɛ] *m* protective glove

ganter [gãte] *tr* to put gloves on (*s.o.*); fit, become (*s.o.; said of gloves*); **cela me gante** (coll) that suits me ‖ *intr*—**ganter de** to wear, take (*a certain size of glove*) ‖ *ref* to put on one's gloves

garage [garaʒ] *m* garage; turnout, passing place; service station, repair shop; used-car lot; **garage d'autobus** bus depot; **garage d'avions** hangar

garagiste [garaʒist] *m* garageman, mechanic; car dealer

ga•rant [garã] **-rante** [rãt] *adj* guaranteeing ‖ *mf* guarantor, warrantor; **se porter garant de** to guarantee ‖ *m* guarantee, warranty

garantie [garãti] *f* guarantee, warranty; earnest money

garantir [garãtir] *tr* to guarantee; vouch for; shelter, protect

garce [gars] *f* (coll) wench; (coll) bitch

garçon [garsɔ̃] *m* boy; young man; bachelor; apprentice; waiter; **être bon garçon** to be nice; **garçon de café** café waiter; **garçon de courses** errand boy; **garçon de recette** bank messenger; **garçon de salle** orderly; **garçon d'honneur** best man; **garçon manqué** tomboy; **petit garçon** boy (*two to thirteen years of age*); **vieux garçon** old bachelor

garçonne [garsɔn] *f* bachelor woman, female bachelor

garçonnet [garsɔnɛ] *m* little boy

garçon•nier [garsɔnje] **-nière** [njɛr] *adj* bachelor; tomboyish ‖ *f* bachelor apartment; tomboy

garde [gard] *m* guard, guardsman; keeper, custodian; **garde champêtre** constable; **garde de nuit** night watchman; **garde forestier** ranger ‖ *f* guard; custody; nurse; flyleaf; **de garde** on duty; **garde à vous!** (mil) attention!; **garde civique** national guard; **monter la garde** to go on guard duty; **prendre garde à** to look out for, to take notice of; **prendre garde de** to take care not to; to be careful to; **prendre garde que** to notice that; **prendre**

garde que ... ne + *subj* to be careful lest, to be careful that ... not; **sur ses gardes** on one's guard

garde-à-vous [gardavu] *m invar* attention (*military position*)

garde-à-vue [gardavy] *f* custody, imprisonment

garde-barrière [gardəbarjɛr] *mf* (*pl* **gardes-barrière** or **gardes-barrières**) crossing guard

garde-bébé [gardəbebe] *mf* (*pl* **-bébés**) baby-sitter

garde-boue [gardəbu] *m invar* mudguard

garde-chasse [gardəʃas] *m* (*pl* **gardes-chasse** or **gardes-chasses**) gamekeeper

garde-corps [gardəkɔr] *m invar* guardrail; (naut) life line

garde-côte [gardəkot] *m* (*pl* **-côtes**) coastguard cutter ‖ *m* (*pl* **gardes-côtes**) (obs) coastguardsman; (obs) coast guard

garde-feu [gardəfø] *m invar* fire screen

garde-fou [gardəfu] *m* (*pl* **-fous**) guardrail

garde-frein [gardəfrɛ̃] *m* (*pl* **gardes-frein** or **gardes-freins**) brakeman

garde-magasin [gardəmagazɛ̃] *m* (*pl* **gardes-magasin** or **gardes-magasins**) warehouseman

garde-malade [gardəmalad] *mf* (*pl* **gardes-malades**) nurse

garde-manger [gardəmɑ̃ʒe] *m invar* icebox; larder

garde-meuble [gardəmœbl] *m* (*pl* **-meuble** or **meubles**) furniture warehouse

garde-nappe [gardənap] *m* (*pl* **-nappe** or **nappes**) table mat, place mat

garde-pêche [gardəpɛʃ] *m* (*pl* **gardes-pêche**) fish warden ‖ *m invar* fishery service boat

garder [garde] §97 *tr* to guard; keep; **garder à vue** to hold in custody; **garder jusqu'à l'arrivée** (formula on envelope) hold for arrival; **garder la chambre** to stay in one's room; **garder la ligne** to keep one's figure ‖ *ref* to keep (*to stay free of deterioration*); **se garder de** to protect oneself from; watch out for; take care not to

garde-rats [gardəra] *m invar* rat guard

garderie [gardəri] *f* nursery, day care; forest reserve

garde-robe [gardərɔb] *f* (*pl* **-robes**) wardrobe

gar·deur [gardœr] **-deuse** [døz] *mf* keeper, herder

garde-voie [gardəvwa] *m* (*pl* **gardes-voie** or **gardes-voies**) trackwalker

garde-vue [gardəvy] *m invar* eyeshade, visor

gar·dien [gardjɛ̃] **-dienne** [djɛn] *adj* guardian (*angel*) ‖ *mf* guard, guardian; keeper; caretaker; attendant (*at a garage*); **gardien de but** goalkeeper; **gardien de la paix** policeman

gardiennage [gardjɛnaʒ] *m* baby-sitting; **gardiennage électronique** security system

gare [gar], [gar] *f* station; **gare aérienne** airport; **gare de fret** cargo terminal; **gare de triage** switchyard; **gare maritime** port, dock; **gare routière** or **gare d'autobus** bus station ‖ [gar] *interj* look out!; **sans crier gare** without warning

garer [gare] *tr* to park; put in the garage; (naut) to dock; (rr) to shunt; (coll) to secure (*e.g., a fortune*) ‖ *ref* to get out of the way; park, park one's car; **se garer de** to look out for

gargariser [gargarize] *ref* to gargle

gargarisme [gargarism] *m* gargle

gargote [gargɔt] *f* (coll) hash house, beanery

gargouille [garguj] *f* gargoyle

gargouillement [gargujmɑ̃] *m* gurgling; rumbling (*in stomach*)

gargouiller [garguje] *intr* to gurgle

garnement [garnəmɑ̃] *m* scamp, bad boy

gar·ni -nie [garni] *adj* furnished (*room*) ‖ *m* furnished room; furnished house

garnir [garnir] *tr* to garnish, adorn; furnish; strengthen; line (*a brake*) ‖ *ref* to fill up (*said of crowded room, theater seats, etc.*)

garnison [garnizɔ̃] *f* garrison

garniture [garnityr] *f* garniture, decoration; fittings; accessories; complete set; (culin) garnish; **garniture de feu** fire irons; **garniture de lit** bedding

garrot [garo] *m* garrote (*instrument of torture*); (med) tourniquet; (zool) withers

garrotte [garɔt] *f* garrotte (*torture*)

garrotter [garɔte] *tr* to garrote; pinion

gars [ga] *m* (coll) lad; **c'est un gars!** (coll) he's a brave young man!

Gascogne [gaskɔɲ] *f* Gascony; **la Gascogne** Gascony

gasconnade [gaskɔnad] *f* gasconade; insincere invitation

gas-oil or **gasoil** [gazwal] *m* diesel oil, diesel fuel

Gaspésie [gaspezi] *f* Gaspé Peninsula

gaspiller [gaspije] *tr* to waste, squander

gastrique [gastrik] *adj* gastric

gastronomie [gastrɔnɔmi] *f* gastronomy

gâ·teau [gato] *adj invar* (coll) fond (*papa*); (coll) fairy (*godmother*) ‖ *m* (*pl* **-teaux**) cake; (coll) booty, loot; **gâteau de miel** honeycomb; **gâteau des Rois** twelfth-cake; **gâteau roulé** jelly roll

gâte-métier [gatmetje] *m invar* undercutter

gâte-papier [gatpapje] *m invar* hack writer

gâter [gate] *tr* & *ref* to spoil

gâte-sauce [gātsos] *m invar* poor cook; kitchen boy

gâ·teux [gatø] **-teuse** [tøz] *adj* (coll) senile ‖ *mf* (coll) dotard

gâtisme [gatism] *m* senility

gauche [goʃ] *adj* left; left-hand; crooked; awkward ‖ *f* left hand; left side; (pol) left wing; **à gauche** to the left; **à gauche, gauche!** (mil) left, face!

gauchement [goʃmɑ̃] *adv* clumsily, awkwardly

gau·cher [goʃe] **-chère** [ʃɛr] *adj* left-handed ‖ *mf* left-hander

gauchir [goʃir] *tr* & *intr* to warp

gauchiste [goʃist] *adj* & *mf* leftist

gaudriole [godrijɔl] *f* broad joke

gaufre [gofr] *f* waffle; **gaufre de miel** honeycomb

gaufrer [gofre] *tr* to emboss, figure; flute; corrugate

gaufrette [gofrɛt] *f* wafer

gaufrier [gofrije] *m* waffle iron

gaule [gol] *f* pole; **la Gaule** Gaul

gauler [gole] *tr* to bring down (*e.g., fruit*) with a pole

gau•lois [golwa] **-loise** [lwaz] *adj* Gaulish, Gallic; broad (*humor*) ‖ *m* Gaulish (*language*) ‖ (*cap*) *mf* Gaul ‖ (*cap*) *f* gauloise (*cigarette*)

gauloiserie [golwazri] *f* racy joking

gaulthèrie [goteri] *f* (bot) wintergreen

gausser [gose] *ref*—**se gausser de** (coll) to poke fun at

gaver [gave] *tr & ref* to cram

gavroche [gavrɔʃ] *mf* street urchin

gaz [gɑz] *m* gas; gaslight; gas company; **gaz d'échappement** exhaust; **gaz d'éclairage** illuminating gas; **gaz de combat** poison gas; **gaz en cylindre** bottled gas; **gaz hilarant** laughing gas; **gaz lacrimogène** tear gas; **mettre les gaz** (aut) to step on the gas

gaze [gɑz] *f* gauze; cheesecloth

ga•zé -zée [gɑze] *adj* gassed ‖ *mf* gas casualty

gazéifier [gɑzeifje] *tr* to gasify; carbonate, charge

gazelle [gazɛl] *f* gazelle

gazer [gɑze] *tr* to gas; cover with gauze; tone down ‖ *intr* (coll) to go full steam ahead; **ça gaze?** (coll) how goes it?

ga•zeux [gɑzø] **-zeuse** [zøz] *adj* gaseous; carbonated

ga•zier [gɑzje] **-zière** [zjɛr] *adj* gas ‖ *m* gasman; gas fitter

gazoduc [gɑzɔdyk] *m* gas pipeline

gazogène [gɑzɔʒɛn] *m* gas producer

gazoline [gɑzɔlin] *f* petroleum ether

gazomètre [gɑzɔmɛtr] *m* gasholder, gas tank

gazon [gɑzɔ̃] *m* lawn; turf, sod

gazonner [gɑzɔne] *tr* to sod

gazouiller [gazuje] *intr* to chirp, twitter; warble; babble

gazouillis [gazuji] *m* chirping; warbling; babbling

geai [ʒɛ] *m* jay

géant [ʒeɑ̃] **géante** [ʒeɑ̃t] *adj* gigantic ‖ *m* giant ‖ *f* giantess

Gédéon [ʒedeɔ̃] *m* (Bib) Gideon

Géhenne [ʒeɛn] *f* Gehenna

gei•gnard [ʒɛɲar] **-gnard** [ɲar] *adj* (coll) whining ‖ *mf* (coll) whiner

geignement [ʒɛɲmɑ̃] *m* whinning, whimper

geindre [ʒɛ̃dr] §50 *intr* to whine, whimper; (coll) to complain

gel [ʒɛl] *m* frost, freezing; (chem) gel

gélatine [ʒelatin] *f* gelatin

gelée [ʒɔle] *f* frost; (culin) jelly; **gelée blanche** hoarfrost

geler [ʒɔle] §2 *tr, intr, & ref* to freeze; to congeal

gelure [ʒɔlyr] *f* frostbite

Gémeaux [ʒemo] *mpl*—**les Gémeaux** (astr, astrol) Gemini

gémi•né -née [ʒemine] *adj* twin; coeducational (*school*)

gémir [ʒemir] §97 *intr* to groan, moan

gémissement [ʒemismɑ̃] *m* groaning, moaning

gemme [ʒɛm] *f* gem; bud; pine resin

gemmer [ʒɛmme] *tr* to tap for resin ‖ *intr* to bud

gê•nant [ʒɛnɑ̃] **-nante** [nɑ̃t] *adj* troublesome, embarrassing

gencive [ʒɑ̃siv] *f* (anat) gum

gendarme [ʒɑ̃darm] *m* policeman; military policeman; rock pinnacle; flaw (*of gem*); (coll) virago; (slang) red herring

gendarmerie [ʒɑ̃darmri] *f* police headquarters

gendre [ʒɑ̃dr] *m* son-in-law

gêne [ʒɛn] *f* discomfort, embarrassment; **être dans la gêne** to be hard up; **être sans gêne** (coll) to be rude, casual

gène [ʒɛn] *m* (biol) gene

généalogie [ʒenealɔʒi] *f* genealogy

gêner [ʒɛne] §97 *tr* to embarrass; inconvenience; hinder; embarrass financially; pinch (*the feet*) ‖ *ref* to put oneself out, be inconvenienced; **ne vous gênez pas!** don't be disturbed; make yourself at home!

géné•ral -rale [ʒeneral] *adj & m* (*pl* **-raux** [ro]) general; **en général** in general; **général de brigade** brigadier general; **général de corps d'armée** lieutenant general; **général de division** major general ‖ *f* general's wife; (theat) opening night; **battre la générale** (mil) to sound the alarm

généralat [ʒenerala] *m* generalship

généralement [ʒeneralmɑ̃] *adv* generally

généraliser [ʒeneralize] *tr & intr* to generalize

généralissime [ʒeneralisim] *m* generalissimo

généraliste [ʒeneralist] *m* (med) general practitioner, family doctor

généralité [ʒeneralite] *f* generality; **la généralité de** the general run of

généra•teur [ʒeneratœr] **-trice** [tris] *adj* generating ‖ *m* boiler ‖ *f* generator

génération [ʒenerasjɔ̃] *f* generation; **les générations montantes** the generations to come

générer [ʒenere] §10 *tr* to generate

géné•reux [ʒenerø] **-reuse** [røz] *adj* generous; full (*bosom*); rich, full (*wine*)

générique [ʒenerik] *adj* generic ‖ *m* (mov) credit line

générosité [ʒenerozite] *f* generosity; **générosités** acts of generosity

Gênes [ʒɛn] *f* Genoa

genèse [ʒənɛz] *f* genesis

genet [ʒɔnɛ] *m* jennet (horse)

genêt [ʒɔnɛ] *m* (bot) broom; **genêt pineux** furze

généti•cien [genetisjɛ̃] **-cienne** [sjɛn] *mf* geneticist

génétique [ʒenetik] *adj* genetic ‖ *f* genetics

gê•neur [ʒɛnœr] **-neuse** [nøz] *mf* intruder, spoilsport

Genève [ʒɛnɛv] *f* Geneva

gene•vois [ʒɔnɛvwa], [ʒɛnvwa] **-voise** [vwaz] *adj* Genevan ‖ (*cap*) *mf* Genevan (*person*)

genévrier [ʒənevrije] *m* juniper

ge·nial -niale [ʒenjal] *adj* (*pl* **-niaux** [njo]) brilliant, ingenious; geniuslike, of genius

génie [ʒeni] *m* genius; bent, inclination; genie; engineer corps; **génie civil** civil engineering; **génie industriel** industrial engineering; **génie logiciel** software engineering; **génie maritime** naval construction

genièvre [ʒenjɛvr] *m* juniper; juniper berry; gin

génisse [ʒenis] *f* heifer

géni·tal -tale [ʒenital] *adj* (*pl* **-taux** [to]) genital

géni·teur [ʒenitœr] **-trice** [tris] *adj* engendering ‖ *m* sire ‖ *f* genetrix

géni·tif [ʒenitif] **-tive** [tiv] *adj* & *m* genitive

génocide [ʒenɔsid] *m* genocide

gé·nois [ʒenwa] **-noise** [nwaz] *adj* Genoese ‖ (*cap*) *mf* Genoese

génome [ʒenom] *m* genome

ge·nou [ʒənu] *m* (*pl* **-noux**) knee; (mach) joint

genouillère [ʒənujɛr] *f* kneecap; kneepad

genre [ʒɑ̃r] *m* genre; genus; kind, sort; manner, way; fashion, taste; (gram) gender; **dans votre genre** like you; **de genre** (fa) genre; **faire du genre** (coll) to put on airs; **genre humain** humankind

gens [ʒɑ̃] (an immediately preceding adjective that varies in its feminine form is put in that form, and so are **certain, quel, tel,** and **tout** that precede that preceding adjective, but the noun remains masculine for pronouns that stand for it, for past participles that agree with it, and for adjectives in all other positions, e.g., **toutes ces vieilles gens sont intéressants** all these old people are interesting) ‖ *mpl* people; nations, e.g., **droit des gens** law of nations; men, e.g., **gens de lettres** men of letters; **gens d'affaires** businesspeople, businessmen; **gens d'Eglise** clergy; **gens de la presse** news persons, newsmen; **gens de mer** seamen; **gens de robe** bar; **jeunes gens** young people (*men and women*); young men

gent [ʒɑ̃] *f* (obs) nation, race

gentiane [ʒɑ̃sjan] *f* gentian

gen·til [ʒɑ̃ti] **-tille** [tij] *adj* nice, kind; cool (slang) ‖ (*cap*) *m* (hist) pagan, gentile

gentilhomme [ʒɑ̃tijɔm] *m* (*pl* **gentils-hommes** [ʒɑ̃tizɔm]) nobleman

gentillesse [ʒɑ̃tijɛs] *f* niceness, kindness; **gentillesses** nice things, kind words

gentil·let [ʒɑ̃tijɛ] **-lette** [jɛt] *adj* rather nice

gentiment [ʒɑ̃timɑ̃] *adv* nicely; gracefully

gentleman [ʒɛntləman] *m* (*pl* **gentlemen** [ʒɛntləmɛn]) (nineteenth-century) gentleman

gentleman's agreement [dʒɛntləmansagrimɛnt] *m* gentleman's agreement (*type of international agreement*)

genuflexion [ʒɛnyflɛksjɔ̃] *f* genuflection

géographie [ʒeɔgrafi] *f* geography

geôle [ʒol] *f* jail

geô·lier [ʒolje] **-lière** [ljɛr] *mf* jailer

géologie [ʒeɔlɔʒi] *f* geology

géologique [ʒeɔlɔʒik] *adj* geologic(al)

géologue [ʒeɔlɔg] *mf* geologist

géomé·tral -trale [ʒeɔmetral] *adj* (*pl* **-traux** [tro]) flat (*projection*)

géométrie [ʒeɔmetri] *f* geometry

géométrique [ʒeɔmetrik] *adj* geometric(al)

géophysique [ʒeɔfizik] *f* geophysics

géopolitique [ʒeɔpɔlitik] *f* geopolitics

Georges [ʒɔrʒ] *m* George

gérance [ʒerɑ̃s] *f* management; board of directors

géranium [ʒeranjɔm] *m* geranium

gé·rant [ʒerɑ̃] **-rante** [rɑ̃t] *mf* manager; **gérant d'une publication** managing editor

gerbe [ʒɛrb] *f* sheaf; spray (*of flowers; of water; of bullets*); shower (*of sparks*)

gerbée [ʒɛrbe] *f* straw

gerber [ʒɛrbe] *tr* to sheave; stack

gerce [ʒɛrs] *f* crack, split; clothes moth

gercer [ʒɛrse] §51 *tr, intr,* & *ref* to crack, chap

gerçure [ʒɛrsyr] *f* crack, chap

gérer [ʒere] §10 *tr* to manage, run

gériatrie [ʒerjatri] *f* geriatrics

ger·main [ʒɛrmɛ̃] **-maine** [mɛn] *adj* german, first (*cousin*)

germanophone [ʒɛrmanɔfɔn] *adj* German-speaking ‖ *mf* German speaker

germe [ʒɛrm] *m* germ

germer [ʒɛrme] *intr* to germinate

germicide [ʒɛrmisid] *adj* germicidal ‖ *m* germicide

germi·nal -nale [ʒɛrminal] *adj* germ

gérondif [ʒerɔ̃dif] *m* gerund

gérontologie [ʒerɔ̃tɔlɔʒi] *f* gerontology

gésier [ʒesje] *m* gizzard

gésir [ʒezir] (used only in *inf:* **ger gisant;** 3d *sg pres ind* **git;** 1st, 2d 3d *pl pres ind* **gisons, gisez, gisent;** *imperf ind* **gisais, gisait, gisions, gisiez, gisaient**) *intr* to lie; **ci-gît** here lies (*buried*)

gesse [ʒɛs] *f* vetch; **gesse odorante** sweet pea

gestation [ʒɛstasjɔ̃] *f* gestation

geste [ʒɛst] *m* gesture ‖ *f* medieval epic poem

gesticuler [ʒɛstikyle] *intr* to gesticulate

gestion [ʒɛstjɔ̃] *f* management, administration; **gestion d'extension** (comp) extension manager

gestionnaire [ʒɛstjɔnɛr] *adj* managing ‖ *mf* manager, administrator

gestualité [ʒɛstɥalite] *f* body language

ges·tuel -tuelle [ʒɛstɥɛl] *adj* gestural ‖ *f* body language

geyser [ʒɛzɛr], [ʒɛjzɛr] *m* geyser

ghetto [geto], [gɛtto] *m* ghetto

gib·beux [ʒibø] **-beuse** [bøz] *adj* humped, hunchbacked

gibecière [ʒibsjɛr] *f* game bag; sack (*for papers, books, etc.*)

gibelotte [ʒiblɔt] *f* rabbit stew

gibet [ʒibɛ] *m* gibbet, gallows

gibier [ʒibje] *m* game; **gibier à plume** feathered game; **gibier de potence** gallows bird

giboulée [ʒibule] *f* shower; hailstorm

giboyeux [ʒibwajø] **giboyeuse** [ʒibwajøz] *adj* full of game

gibus [ʒibys] *m* opera hat
giclée [ʒikle] *f* spurt
gicler [ʒikle] *intr* to spurt
gicleur [ʒiklœr] *m* atomizer; (aut) spray nozzle
(*of carburetor*)
gifle [ʒifl] *f* slap in the face
gifler [ʒifle] *tr* to slap in the face
gigantesque [ʒigãtɛsk] *adj* gigantic
gigogne [ʒigɔɲ] *adj*—**table gigogne** nest of tables ‖ (*cap*) *f*—**la mère Gigogne** the old
woman who lived in a shoe
gigolo [ʒigɔlo] *m* (coll) gigolo
gigot [ʒigo] *m* leg of lamb, leg of mutton; **à**
gigot leg-of-mutton (*sleeve*)
gigue [ʒig] *f* jig; haunch (*of venison*); (coll) leg;
(slang) long-legged gawky girl
gilet [ʒilɛ] *m* vest; **gilet de sauvetage** life jacket;
gilet pare-balles bulletproof vest; **pleurer**
dans le gilet de qn (coll) to cry on s.o.'s
shoulder
gimmick [gimik] *m* gadget
gingembre [ʒɛ̃ʒãbr] *m* ginger
girafe [ʒiraf] *f* giraffe
giration [ʒirasjɔ̃] *f* gyration
girl [gœrl] *f* chorus girl
girofle [ʒirɔfl] *m* clove
giroflée [ʒirɔfle] *f* gillyflower
giron [ʒirɔ̃] *m* lap; bosom (*of the Church*)
girouette [ʒirwɛt] *f* weather vane
gisement [ʒizmã] *m* deposit; lode, seam; (naut)
bearing; **gisement de pétrole** oil field
gi•tan [ʒitã] **-tane** [tan] *adj & mf* gypsy
gîte [ʒit] *m* lodging; lair, cover; deposit (*of ore*);
gîte à la noix round steak ‖ *f* (naut) list; **don-**
ner de la gîte to heel
gîter [ʒite] *intr* to lodge; lie, couch; perch; (naut)
to list, heel ‖ *ref* to find shelter
givre [ʒivr] *m* rime, hoarfrost
givrer [ʒivre] *tr* to frost
glabre [glabr] *adj* beardless
glaçage [glasaʒ] *m* icing (*on cake*)
glace [glas] *f* ice; ice cream; mirror; plate glass;
car window; glaze, icing; flaw (*of gem*); **être**
de glace (fig) to be hard as stone; **glace au**
sirop sundae; **glace panachée** Neapolitan ice
cream; **rompre la glace** (fig) to break the ice
gla•cé -cée [glase] *adj* frozen; iced, chilled; icy,
frosty; glazed, glossy
glacer [glase] §51 *tr* to freeze; chill; glaze; ice
(*a cake*); **à vous glacer le sang** spine-chilling
glacerie [glasri] *f* glass factory
glaciaire [glasjɛr] *adj* glacial
gla•cial -ciale [glasjal] *adj* (*pl* **-cials**) glacial,
freezing
glacier [glasje] *m* glacier; ice-cream man
glacière [glasjɛr] *f* icehouse; icebox; freezer
glacis [glasi] *m* slope; ramp; (mil) glacis; (painting) glaze; (pol) buffer states
glaçon [glasɔ̃] *m* icicle; ice cube; ice floe; (fig)
cold fish, iceberg
glaçure [glasyr] *f* (ceramics) glaze
gladiateur [gladjatœr] *m* gladiator
glaïeul [glajœl] *m* gladiola

glaire [glɛr] *f* white of egg; mucus
glaise [glɛz] *f* clay, loam
glaisière [glɛzjɛr] *f* clay pit
glaive [glɛv] *m* (lit) sword
glamour [glamur] *adj & m* glamour
gland [glã] *m* acorn; tassel
glande [glãd] *f* gland
glane [glan] *f* gleaning; cluster
glaner [glane] *tr* to glean
glanure [glanyr] *f* gleaning
glapir [glapir] *intr* to yelp, yap
glas [gla] *m* knell, tolling
glasnost [glasnɔst] *m* glasnost
glaucome [glokɔm] *m* glaucoma
glauque [glok] *adj & m* blue-green
glèbe [glɛb] *f* clod (*sod*); soil (*land*)
glène [glɛn] *f* (anat) socket; (naut) coil of rope
glissade [glisad] *f* slip; sliding; (dancing) glide;
glissade de terre landslide; **glissade sur**
l'aile (aer) sideslip; **glissade sur la queue**
(aer) tail dive
glis•sant [glisã] **-sante** [sãt] *adj* slippery
glissement [glismã] *m* sliding; gliding; **glisse-**
ment de terrain landslide
glisser [glise] *tr* to slip; drop (*a word into s.o.'s*
ear) ‖ *intr* to slip; slide; skid; glide ‖ *ref* to
slip
glissière [glisjɛr] *f* slide, groove; **à glissière**
sliding; zippered; **glissière de sécurité** guard
rail
glissoire [gliswar] *f* slide (*on ice or snow*)
glo•bal -bale [glɔbal] *adj* (*pl* **-baux** [bo]) global;
lump (*sum*)
globe [glɔb] *m* globe; **globe de feu** fireball;
globe de l'œil eyeball
globule [glɔbyl] *m* globule; (physiol) corpuscle;
globule blanc white blood cell, white blood
corpuscle; **globule rouge** red blood cell, red
blood corpuscle
gloire [glwar] *f* glory; pride; halo; **pour la gloire**
for fun, for nothing; **se faire gloire de** to glory
in
gloriette [glɔrjɛt] *f* arbor, summerhouse
glo•rieux [glɔrjø] **-rieuse** [rjøz] *adj* glorious;
blessed; vain
glorifier [glɔrifje] *tr* to glorify ‖ §97 *ref*—**se**
glorifier de to glory in
gloriole [glɔrjɔl] *f* vainglory
glose [gloz] *f* gloss; (coll) gossip
gloser [gloze] *intr* (coll) to gossip
glossaire [glɔsɛr] *m* glossary
glotte [glɔt] *f* glottis
glouglou [gluglu] *m* gurgle, glug; gobble-
gobble; coo (*of dove*)
glouglouter [gluglute] *intr* to gurgle; gobble
(*said of turkey*)
glousser [gluse] *intr* to cluck; chuckle
glou•ton [glutɔ̃] **-tonne** [tɔn] *adj* gluttonous ‖
mf glutton ‖ *m* (zool) glutton, wolverine
gloutonnerie [glutɔnri] *f* gluttony
glu [gly] *f* birdlime; (coll) trap
gluant [glyã] **gluante** [glyãt] *adj* sticky,
gummy; (fig) tenacious

glucose [glykoz] *m* glucose

glycérine [gliserin] *f* glycerine

gnognote [ɲɔɲɔt] *f* (coll) junk

gnome [gnom] *m* gnome

gnomon [gnɔmɔ̃] *m* sundial

gnon [ɲɔ̃] *m* (slang) blow, punch

go [go]—**tout de go** (coll) straight off, at once

goal [gol] *m* goalkeeper

gobelet [gɔblɛ] *m* cup, tumbler, mug; **gobelets utilisés** (public sign) used paper drinking cups

gobe-mouches [gɔbmuʃ] *m invar* (zool) fly-catcher; (fig) sucker, gull

gober [gɔbe] *tr* to gulp down, gobble; suck (*an egg*); (coll) to swallow, be a sucker for

goberger [gɔbɛrʒe] **§38** *ref* (coll) to guzzle; (coll) to live in comfort

gobeter [gɔbte] **§34** *tr* to plaster, fill in the cracks of

go•beur [gɔbœr] **-beuse** [bøz] *mf* (coll) sucker, gullible person

godet [gɔdɛ] *m* cup; basin; bucket (*of water wheel*); (bot) calyx; **à godets** flared

godille [gɔdij] *f* scull, oar; **à la godille** without rhyme or reason, erratically

godiller [gɔdije] *intr* to scull

godillot [gɔdijo] *m* (slang) clodhopper (*shoe*)

goéland [gɔelɑ̃] *m* seal gull

goélette [gɔelɛt] *f* (naut) schooner

goémon [gɔemɔ̃] *m* seaweed

gogo [gɔgo] *m* (coll) sucker, gull; **à gogo** (coll) galore

gogue•nard [gɔgnar] **-narde** [nard] *adj* jeering, mocking

goguenarder [gɔgnarde] *intr* to jeer

goguette [gɔgɛt] *f*—**en goguette** (coll) tipsy

goinfre [gwɛ̃fr] *m* glutton, guzzler

goitre [gwatr] *m* goiter

golf [gɔlf] *m* golf; golf course, golf links; **golf miniature** miniature golf

golfe [gɔlf] *m* gulf; **Golfe du Mexique** Gulf of Mexico; **Golfe Persique** Persian Gulf

golfeur [gɔlfœr] *m* golfer

gomme [gɔm] *f* gum; eraser; **gomme à claquer** bubble gum; **gomme à mâcher** chewing gum; **gomme d'épinette** spruce gum; **gomme de sapin** balsam; **gomme élastique** India rubber; **mettre la gomme** (slang) to speed it up

gomme-laque [gɔmlak] *f* (*pl* **gommes-laques**) shellac

gommelaquer [gɔmlake] *tr* to shellac

gommer [gɔme] *tr* to gum; erase ‖ *intr* to stick, gum up

gond [gɔ̃] *m* hinge; **sortir de ses gonds** (coll) to fly off the handle

gondole [gɔ̃dɔl] *f* gondola

gondoler [gɔ̃dɔle] *intr* & *ref* to buckle up

gondolier [gɔ̃dɔlje] *m* gondolier

gonfalon [gɔ̃falɔ̃] *m* pennant

gonflement [gɔ̃flǝmɑ̃] *m* swelling

gonfler [gɔ̃fle] *tr* to swell, inflate ‖ *intr* to swell up, puff up ‖ *ref* to become inflated; (coll) to swell up with pride

gonfleur [gɔ̃flœr] *m* tire pump

gong [gɔ̃g] *m* gong

gonococcie [gɔnokɔksi] *f* gonorrhea

goret [gɔrɛ] *m* piglet; (coll) slob

gorge [gɔrʒ] *f* throat; bust, breasts (*of woman*); gorge; **à pleine gorge** or **à gorge déployée** at the top of one's voice; **avoir la gorge serrée** to have a lump in one's throat; **faire des gorges chaudes de** (coll) to scoff at; to gloat over; **rendre gorge** to make restitution

gorger [gɔrʒe] **§38** *tr* & *ref* to gorge, stuff

gorille [gɔrij] *m* gorilla; (slang) strong-arm man, bodyguard; (slang) bouncer (*in a night club*)

gosier [gozje] *m* throat, gullet; **à plein gosier** loudly, lustily; **gosier serré** with one's heart in one's mouth; **s'humecter** or **se rincer le gosier** (slang) to wet one's whistle

gosse [gɔs] *mf* (coll) kid, youngster

gothique [gɔtik] *adj* Gothic ‖ *m* Gothic (*language*); Gothic art ‖ *f* black letter, Old English

gouailler [gwaje] *tr* to jeer at ‖ *intr* to jeer

gouape [gwap] *f* (slang) hoodlum, blackguard

gouaper [gwape] *intr* (slang) to lead a disreputable life

goudron [gudrɔ̃] *m* tar; **goudron de houille** coal tar

goudronner [gudrɔne] *tr* to tar

gouffre [gufr] *m* gulf, abyss; whirlpool

gouge [guʒ] *f* gouge; harlot

gouger [guʒe] **§38** *tr* to gouge

gouine [gwin] *f* (vulg) (*lesbienne*) queer (pej)

goujat [guʒa] *m* boor, cad

goujon [guʒɔ̃] *m* gudgeon, pin; pintle (*of hinge*); dowel; (ichth) gudgeon; **taquiner le goujon** to go fishing

goulasch [gulaʃ] *m* & *f* goulash

goule [gul] *f* ghoul

goulet [gulɛ] *m* narrows, sound; **goulet d'étranglement** bottleneck

goulot [gulo] *m* neck (*of bottle*); **boire au goulot** to drink right out of the bottle

gou•lu -lue [guly] *adj* gluttonous

goupil [gupi] *m* (obs) fox

goupille [gupij] *f* pin; **goupille fendue** cotter pin

goupiller [gupije] *tr* to cotter; (slang) to contrive, wangle

goupillon [gupijɔ̃] *m* bottle brush; sprinkler (*for holy water*); **goupillon nettoie-pipes** pipe cleaner

gourd [gur] **gourde** [gurd] *adj* numb (*with cold*) ‖ *adj fem* (coll) dumb ‖ *f* gourd; canteen, metal flask; (coll) dumbbell

gourdin [gurdɛ̃] *m* cudgel

gourgandine [gurgɑ̃din] *f* (hist) low-necked bodice; (coll) trollop

gourer [gure] *intr* (coll) to make a booboo

gour•mand [gurmɑ̃] **-mande** [mɑ̃d] *adj* & *mf* gourmand, gourmet

gourmander [gurmɑ̃de] *tr* to bawl out

gourmandise [gurmɑ̃diz] *f* gluttony; love of good food; **gourmandises** delicacies

gourme [gurm] *f* impetigo; **jeter sa gourme** (coll) to sow one's wild oats

gour•mé -mée [gurme] *adj* stiff, stuckup

gourmet [gurmɛ] *m* gourmet

gourmette [gurmɛt] *f* curb (*of harness*); curb watch chain

gousse [gus] *f* pod; clove (*of garlic*)

gousset [guse] *m* vest pocket; fob, watch pocket (*in trousers*)

goût [gu] *m* taste; flavor; sense of taste; **au goût du jour** up to date

goûter [gute] *m* afternoon snack ‖ *tr* to taste; sample; relish, enjoy ‖ *intr* to have a bite to eat; **goûter à** to sample, try; **goûter de** (coll) to try out (*e.g., a trade*)

goutte [gut] *f* drop, drip; (pathol) gout; **boire la goutte** (coll) to take a nip of brandy; **la goutte d'eau qui a fait déborder le vase** the straw that broke the camel's back; **ne ... goutte** §90 (used only with **comprendre, connaître, entendre,** and **voir**) (archaic & hum) not at all, e.g., **je n'y vois goutte** I don't see at all; **tomber goutte à goutte** to drip

goutte-à-goutte [gutagut] *m invar* (med) dropping bottle (*for intravenous drip*); (med) I.V. stand

gouttelette [gutlɛt] *f* droplet

goutter [gute] *intr* to drip

gouttière [gutjɛr] *f* eavestrough, gutter; (med) splint

gouvernail [guvɛrnaj] *m* rudder, helm; **gouvernail de profondeur** (aer) elevator

gouver·nant [guvɛrnɑ̃] **-nante** [nɑ̃t] *adj* governing ‖ *governants mpl* powers that be, rulers ‖ *f* governess; housekeeper

gouverne [guvɛrn] *f* guidance; **gouvernes** (aer) controls; **pour votre gouverne** for your guidance

gouvernement [guvɛrnəmɑ̃] *m* government; **gouvernement fantoche** puppet government

gouvernemen·tal -tale [guvɛrnəmɑ̃tal] *adj* (*pl* **-taux** [to]) governmental

gouverner [guvɛrne] *tr* to govern, control; steer; manage with care ‖ *intr* to govern; (naut) to answer to the helm

gouverneur [guvɛrnœr] *m* governor; tutor; director (*e.g., of a bank*)

goyave [gɔjav] *f* guava

goyavier [gɔjavje] *m* guava tree

Graal [gral] *m* Grail

grabat [graba] *m* pallet, straw bed

grâce [grɑs] *f* grace; **de bonne grâce** willingly; **de grâce** for mercy's sake; **de mauvaise grâce** unwillingly; **faire grâce à** to pardon; to spare; **faites-moi la grâce de** be kind enough to; **grâce!** mercy!; **grâce à** thanks to

gracier [grasje] *tr* to reprieve

gra·cieux [grasjø] **-cieuse** [sjøz] *adj* gracious; graceful

gracile [grasil] *adj* slender, slim

gradation [gradɑsjɔ̃] *f* gradation

grade [grad] *m* grade; rank; degree (*in school*); **en prendre pour son grade** (coll) to get called down

gra·dé -dée [grade] *adj* noncommissioned ‖ *mf* noncommissioned officer

gradient [gradjɑ̃] *m* gradient

gradin [gradɛ̃] *m* tier

graduation [graduɑsjɔ̃] *f* graduation

gra·dué -duée [gradɥe] *adj* graduated (*scale*); graded (*lessons*) ‖ *mf* graduate

gra·duel -duelle [gradɥɛl] *adj* & *m* gradual

graduer [gradɥe] *tr* to graduate

grailler [graje] *intr* to speak hoarsely; sound the horn to recall the dogs

grain [grɛ̃] *m* grain; particle, speck; bean; squall; **grain de beauté** beauty spot, mole; **grain de raisin** grape; **grains** grain, cereals; **veiller au grain** (fig) to be on one's guard

graine [grɛn] *f* seed; **graine d'anis** aniseed; **mauvaise graine** (coll) incorrigible youth; **monter en graine** to run to seed; to soon be on the shelf (*said of young girl*); (coll) to grow; **prendre de la graine de** (coll) to follow the example of

graissage [grɛsaʒ] *m* (aut) lubrication

graisse [grɛs] *f* grease; fat; mother (*of wine*)

graisser [grɛse], [grese] *tr* to grease; lubricate; get grease stains on; **graisser la patte à qn** (coll) to grease s.o.'s palm

grais·seux [grɛsø] **-seuse** [søz] *adj* greasy

grammaire [gramɛr] *f* grammar

grammai·rien [gramɛrjɛ̃] **-rienne** [rjɛn] *mf* grammarian

grammati·cal -cale [gramatikal] *adj* (*pl* **-caux** [ko]) grammatical

gramme [gram] *m* gram

grand [grɑ̃] **grande** [grɑ̃d] *adj* tall, e.g., **un homme grand** a tall man ‖ (when standing before noun) *adj* large; great; important; tall; high (*priest; mass; society; explosive*), vain, empty (*words*); broad (*daylight*); grand (*dignitary; officer; lady*); main (*road*); long (*arms or legs*); greater, e.g., **le Grand Londres** Greater London; (fig) big (*heart*) ‖ *m* adult, grownup; grandee, noble; **en grand** life-size; on a grand scale; enlarged (*copy*); wide (*open*); **grands et petits** young and old ‖ **grand** *adv*—**voir grand** to see big, to envisage great projects

grand-angle [grɑ̃tɑ̃gl] *or* **grand-angulaire** [grɑ̃tɑ̃gylɛr] *m* (*pl* **grands-angles, grands-angulaires**) (phot) wide-angle lens

grand-chose [grɑ̃ʃoz] *mf invar*—**pas grand-chose** (coll) nobody, person of no importance ‖ *adv*—**pas grand-chose** not much

grand-duc [grɑ̃dyk] *m* (*pl* **grands-ducs**) grand duke

grand-duché [grɑ̃dyʃe] *m* (*pl* **grands-duchés**) grand duchy

Grande-Bretagne [grɑ̃dbrətaɲ] *f* Great Britain; **la Grande-Bretagne** Great Britain

grande-duchesse [grɑ̃dədyʃɛs] *f* (*pl* **grandes-duchesses**) grand duchess

grande·let [grɑ̃dlɛ] **-lette** [lɛt] *adj* tall for his or her age

grandement [grɑ̃dmɑ̃] *adv* highly; handsomely; **se tromper grandement** to be very mistaken

grand-erre [grɑ̃tɛr] *adv* at full speed

gran•det [grɑ̃dɛ] **-dette** [dɛt] *adj* rather big; rather tall

grandeur [grɑ̃dœr] *f* size; height; greatness; (astr) magnitude

grandiose [grɑ̃djoz] *adj* grandiose

grandir [grɑ̃dir] *tr* to enlarge; increase ‖ *intr* to grow; grow up

grandissement [grɑ̃dismɑ̃] *m* magnification, enlargement; growth

grand-livre [grɑ̃livr] *m* (*pl* **grands-livres**) ledger

grand-maman [grɑ̃mamɑ̃] *f* (*pl* **-mamans**) grandma, mom-mom

grand-mère [grɑ̃mɛr] *f* (*pl* **-mères** or **grands-mères**) grandmother; (coll) old lady

grand-messe [grɑ̃mɛs] *f* (*pl* **-messes**) high mass

grand-oncle [grɑ̃tɔ̃kl] *m* (*pl* **grands-oncles**) granduncle

Grand-Orient [grɑ̃tɔrjɑ̃] *m* grand lodge

grand-papa [grɑ̃papa] *m* (*pl* **grands-papas**) grandpa, pop-pop

grand-peine [grɑ̃pɛn]—**à grand-peine** with great difficulty

grand-père [grɑ̃pɛr] *m* (*pl* **grands-pères**) grandfather

grand-route [grɑ̃rut] *f* (*pl* **-routes**) highway

grand-rue [grɑ̃ry] *f* (*pl* **-rues**) main street

Grands Lacs [grɑ̃lak] *mpl* Great Lakes

grands-parents [grɑ̃parɑ̃] *mpl* grandparents

grand-tante [grɑ̃tɑ̃t] *f* (*pl* **-tantes**) grandaunt

grange [grɑ̃ʒ] *f* barn

granit [grani], [granit] *m* granite

granite [granit] *m* granite

granulaire [granylɛr] *adj* granular

granule [granyl] *m* granule

granu•lé -lée [granyle] *adj* granulated ‖ *m* little pill; medicine in granulated form

granuler [granyle] *tr & ref* to granulate

graphie [grafi] *f* spelling

graphique [grafik] *adj* graphic(al) ‖ *m* graph

graphite [grafit] *m* graphite

grappe [grap] *f* bunch, cluster; string (*of onions*); **une grappe humaine** a bunch of people

grappillage [grapijaʒ] *m* gleaning; (coll) graft

grappiller [grapije] *tr & intr* (*in vineyard*) to glean; (coll) to pilfer

grappillon [grapijɔ̃] *m* little bunch

grappin [grapɛ̃] *m* grapnel; **jeter** or **mettre le grappin sur qn** (coll) to get one's hooks into s.o.

gras [grɑ] **grasse** [grɑs] *adj* fat; greasy; rich (*soil*); carnival (*days*); smutty (*stories*); (typ) bold-faced ‖ *m* fatty part; calf (*of leg*); foggy weather; **au gras** with meat sauce; **faire gras** to eat meat ‖ **gras** *adv*—**parler gras** to speak with uvular r; to tell smutty stories

gras-double [grɑdubl] *m* (*pl* **-doubles**) tripe

grassement [grɑsmɑ̃] *adv* comfortably; generously, handsomely

grasseyer [grɑseje] §32 *tr* to make (*one's r's*) uvular ‖ *intr* to speak with uvular r

grassouil•let [grɑsujɛ] **-lette** [jɛt] *adj* (coll) plump, chubby

gratification [gratifikɑsjɔ̃] *f* tip, gratuity

gratifier [gratifje] *tr* to favor, reward; **gratifier qn de q.ch.** to bestow s.th. upon s.o.

gratin [gratɛ̃] *m* cooking au gratin; dish of food prepared au gratin; friction surface (*of a matchbox*); (culin) crust; (coll) upper crust; **au gratin** au gratin (*breaded and/or with grated cheese*)

gratiner [gratine] *tr* to cook au gratin ‖ *intr* to brown, crisp

gratis [gratis] *adv* gratis

gratitude [gratityd] *f* gratitude

gratte [grat] *f* scraper; (coll) graft

gratte-ciel [gratsjɛl] *m invar* skyscraper

gratte-cul [gratky] *m invar* (bot) hip

gratte-dos [gratdo] *m invar* back scratcher

gratte-papier [gratpapje] *m invar* (coll) pencil pusher, office drudge

gratte-pieds [gratpje] *m invar* shoe scraper

gratter [grate] *tr* to scratch; scratch out; scrape up, scrape together; itch; (coll) to pocket ‖ *intr* to knock gently ‖ *ref* to scratch

grattoir [gratwar] *m* scraper; knife eraser

gra•tuit [gratɥi] **-tuite** [tɥit] *adj* free of charge; gratuitous; unfounded

gratuité [gratɥite] *f* gratuity

grave [grav], [grɑv] *adj* grave; low (*frequency*); (mus) bass; (mus) flat

grave•leux -leuse [gravlø] [løz] *adj* gravelly, gritty; smutty, licentious

gravelle [gravɛl] *f* (pathol) gravel

graver [grave] *tr* to engrave; cut (*a phonograph record*)

graveur [gravœr] *m* engraver; etcher

gravier [gravje] *m* gravel

gravillons [gravijɔ̃] *mpl* gravel (*on roadway*)

gravir [gravir] *tr* to climb, climb up

gravitation [gravitɑsjɔ̃] *f* gravitation

gravité [gravite] *f* gravity

graviter [gravite] *intr* to gravitate

gravure [gravyr] *f* engraving; etching; cutting (*of phonograph record*)

gré [gre] *m* will; **à son gré** to one's liking; **bon gré mal gré** willy-nilly; **de bon gré** willingly; **de gré à gré** by mutual consent; **de gré ou de force** willy-nilly; **savoir (bon) gré de** to be grateful for; **savoir mauvais gré de** to be displeased with

grec grecque [grɛk] *adj* Greek; classic (*profile*) ‖ *m* Greek (*language*) ‖ *f* Greek fret ‖ (*cap*) *mf* Greek

Grèce [grɛs] *f* Greece; **la Grèce** Greece

gre•din [grədɛ̃] **-dine** [din] *mf* scoundrel

gréement [gremɑ̃] *m* (naut) rigging

green [grin] *s* (golf) green, putting green

gréer [gree] *tr* (naut) to rig

greffe [grɛf] *m* (jur) office of the court clerk ‖ *f* grafting; (hort, med) graft; **greffe du cœur** heart transplant; **greffe du rein** kidney transplant

greffer [grɛfe] *tr* to graft; add ‖ *ref* to be added

greffier [grɛfje] *m* clerk of court, recorder; court reporter

greffon [grɛfɔ̃] *m* (hort) graft; (surg) transplant

grégaire [gregɛr] *adj* gregarious

grège [grɛʒ] *adj* raw (*silk*) ‖ *f* raw silk

grégo•rien [gregɔrjɛ̃] **-rienne** [rjɛn] *adj* Gregorian

grêle [grɛl] *adj* slender, slim; thin, high-pitched ‖ *f* hail; (fig) shower

grê•lé -lée [grɛle] *adj* pockmarked

grêler [grɛle] *tr* to damage by hail; pockmark ‖ *intr* (fig) to rain down thick; **il grêle** it is hailing

grêlon [grɛlɔ̃] *m* hailstone

grelot [grəlo] *m* sleigh bell

grelottement [grələtmɑ̃] *m* shivering, trembling; jingle, jingling

grelotter [grələte] *intr* to shiver, tremble; jingle

grenade [grənad] *f* grenade; (bot) pomegranate; **grenade à main** hand grenade; **grenade éclairante** flare; **grenade lacrymogène** tear bomb; **grenade sous-marine** depth charge

grenadier [grənadje] *m* pomegranate tree; (mil) grenadier

grenadine [grənadin] *f* grenadine

grenaille [grənaj] *f* shot; **grenaille de plomb** buckshot

grenailler [grənaje] *tr* to granulate

grenat [grəna] *adj invar & m* garnet

grenier [grənje] *m* attic, loft; granary

grenouille [grənuj] *f* frog; **grenouille mugissante** or **taureau** bullfrog; **manger la grenouille** (coll) to make off with the money, to abscond

grenouillère [grənujɛr] *f* marsh

gre•nu -nue [grəny] *adj* full of grain; grainy (*leather*); granular (*marble*) ‖ *m* graininess; granularity

grès [grɛ] *m* gritstone, sandstone; stoneware; terra cotta (*for drainpipes*)

grésil [grezil] *m* sleet

grésillement [grezijmɑ̃] *m* sizzling; chirping (*of cricket*)

grésiller [grezije] *tr* to scorch, shrivel up ‖ *intr* to sizzle, sputter; **il grésille** it is sleeting

grève [grɛv] *f* beach; strike; (*armor*) greave; **faire (la) grève** to strike; **faire la grève de la faim** to go on a hunger strike; **grève avec occupation de l'usine, grève avec occupation des locaux** sitdown strike; **grève de solidarité** sympathy strike; **grève du zèle** work-to-rule strike, job action (*rigid application of rules*); **grève générale** general strike; **grève improvisée, grève inattendue, grève surprise** walkout; **grève perlée** slowdown strike; **grève sauvage, grève spontanée** wildcat strike; **grève sur le tas** sitdown strike; **grève tournante** strike in one industry at a time or for several hours at a time; **se mettre en grève** to go on strike

grever [grəve] §2 *tr* to burden; assess (*property*); **grever de** to burden with

gréviste [grevist] *mf* striker

gribouillage [gribujaʒ] *m* (coll) scribble, scrawl; (coll) daub (*in painting*)

gribouiller [gribuje] *tr* (coll) to scribble off (*a note*) ‖ *intr* (coll) to scribble, scrawl; (coll) to daub

grief [grijɛf] *m* grievance, complaint; **faire grief de q.ch. à qn** to complain to s.o. about s.th.

grièvement [grijɛvmɑ̃] *adv* seriously, badly

griffe [grif] *f* claw, talon; signature stamp; (bot) tendril; (mach) hook, grip; **faire ses griffes** to sharpen its claws (*said of cat*); **griffe à papiers** paper clip; **porter la griffe de** to carry the stamp of; **tomber sous la griffe de** (coll) to fall into the clutches of

griffer [grife] *tr* to claw, scratch

griffon [grifɔ̃] *m* griffin

griffonner [grifɔne] *tr* to scrawl; (coll) to scribble off (*a letter*)

grignoter [griɲɔte] *tr* to nibble on or at; wear down (*e.g., the enemy*) ‖ *intr* (coll) to make a little profit, get a cut

gril [gril] *m* gridiron, grid, grill; (theat) upper flies; **être sur le gril** (coll) to be on tenterhooks

grillade [grijad] *f* grilled meat; broiling

grillage [grijaʒ] *m* grating, latticework, trellis; broiling; roasting; toasting; burning out (*of a light bulb*); (tex) singeing

grille [grij] *f* grille; grate, grating; bars; railing; gate; squares (*of crossword puzzle*); grid (*of storage battery and vacuum tube*); **grille d'entrée** iron gate; **grille des salaires** salary schedule

grille-pain [grijpɛ̃] *m invar* toaster

grille-pain-four [grijpɛ̃fur] *m* toaster oven

griller [grije] *tr* to grill, broil; put a grill on; roast (*coffee*); toast (*bread*); burn out (*a fuse, lamp, electric iron, etc.*); singe, scorch; nip (*a bud, as the frost does*) ‖ *intr* to grill; toast; burn out; **griller de** to long to

grilloir [grijwar] *m* roaster; (culin) broiler

grillon [grijɔ̃] *m* cricket

grimace [grimas] *f* grimace; **faire des grimaces** to make faces; smirk, simper; be full of wrinkles

grimacer [grimase] §51 *intr* to grimace; make wrong creases

grime [grim] *m* dotard, old fogey

grimer [grime] *tr* to make up (*an actor*) ‖ *ref* to make up

grimper [grɛ̃pe] *tr* to climb ‖ *intr* to climb; **grimper à** or **sur** to climb up on

grimpe•reau [grɛ̃pro] *m* (*pl* **-reaux**) (orn) tree creeper

grim•peur [grɛ̃pœr] **-peuse** [pøz] *adj* climbing ‖ *m* climber

grincement [grɛ̃smɑ̃] *m* grating

grincer [grɛ̃se] §51 *tr* to gnash, grit (*the teeth*) ‖ *intr* to grate, grind, creak; scratch (*said of pen*)

grin•cheux [grɛ̃ʃø] **-cheuse** [ʃøz] *adj* grumpy ‖ *mf* grumbler, sorehead

gringa•let [grɛ̃gale] **-lette** [lɛt] *adj* weak, puny ‖ *m* (coll) weakling, shrimp

griot [grijo] **griotte** [grijɔt] *mf* witch doctor ‖ *m* seconds (*in milling grain*) ‖ *f* sour cherry

grippe [grip] *f* gripper; **grippe asiatique** Asian flu; **prendre en grippe** to take a dislike to

grippeminaud [gripmino] *m* (coll) smoothly, hypocrite

gripper [gripe] *tr* to snatch; (slang) to steal ‖ *intr* (mach) to jam ‖ *ref* to get stuck

grippe-sou [gripsu] *m* (*pl* **-sou** or **-sous**) (coll) tightwad, skinflint

gris [gri] **grise** [griz] *adj* gray; cloudy; brown (*paper*); (coll) tipsy, high

grisailler [grizaje] *tr* to paint gray ‖ *intr* to turn gray

grisâtre grizɑtr] *adj* grayish

griser [grize] *tr* to paint gray; (coll) to intoxicate; **les succès l'ont grisé** (coll) success has gone to his head ‖ *ref* to get tipsy; **se griser de** (coll) to revel in

griserie [grizri] *f* intoxication

grisette [grizɛt] *f* gay working girl

gris-gris [grigri] *m* lucky charm

grisonner [grizɔne] *intr* to turn gray

grisotte [grizɔt] *f* clock (*in stocking*)

grisou [grizu] *m* firedamp

grive [griv] *f* thrush; **grive mauvis** song thrush; **grive migratoire** (*Turdus migratorius*) robin

grive•lé -lée [grivle] *adj* speckled

grivèlerie [grivɛlri] *f* sneaking out without paying the check

gri•vois [grivwa] **-voise** [vwaz] *adj* spicy, off-color

grizzly [grizli] *m* grizzly bear

Groënland [grɔɛnlɑ̃d] *m*—**le Groënland** Greenland

grog [grɔg] *m* grog

gro•gnard [grɔɲar] **-gnarde** [ɲard] *adj* grumbling ‖ *mf* grumbler

grogner [grɔɲe] *intr* to grunt, growl; grumble, grouch

gro•gnon [grɔɲɔ̃] **-gnonne** [ɲɔn] *adj* grouchy, grumbling ‖ *mf* grouch, grumbler

grognonner [grɔɲɔne] *intr* to grunt; be a complainer, whine

groin [grwɛ̃] *m* snout; (coll) ugly mug

grommeler [grɔmle] §34 *tr & intr* to mutter, grumble; growl

grondement [grɔ̃dmɑ̃] *m* growl; rumble

gronder [grɔ̃de] §97 *tr* to scold ‖ *intr* to scold; growl; grumble

gron•deur [grɔ̃dœr] **-deuse** [døz] *adj* scolding, grumbling ‖ *mf* grumbler

groom [grum] *m* bellhop, pageboy

gros [gro] **grosse** [gros] *adj* big (*with child*); heavy (*heart*) ‖ (when standing before noun) *adj* big, large, bulky; coarse; plain (*common sense*); main (*walls*); high (*stakes*); rich (*merchant*); booming (*voice*); bad (*weather*); heavy, rough (*sea*); swear (words) ‖ *m* bulk, main part; **en gros** wholesale; roughly, without going into detail; **faire le gros et le détail**

to deal in wholesale and retail ‖ *f* see **grosse** ‖ **gros** *adv* much, a great deal; (fig) probably

gros-bec [grobɛk] *m* (*pl* **-becs**) grosbeak

groseille [grozɛj] *f* currant; **groseille à maque-reau** gooseberry

groseillier [grozɛje] *m* currant bush

Gros-Jean [groʒɑ̃] *m*—**être Gros-Jean comme devant** to be in the same fix again

gros-porteur [groprtœr] *m* (*pl* **-porteurs**) (aer) jumbo jet

grosse [gros] *f* fat woman; (com) gross; (law) engrossed copy

grosserie [grosri] *f* silver dishes

grossesse [grosɛs] *f* pregnancy

grosseur [grosœr] *f* size; swelling, tumor

gros•sier [grosje] **-sière** [sjɛr] *adj* coarse; crude, rude; vulgar, ribald; glaring (*error*)

grossièrement [grosjɛrmɑ̃] *adv* grossly

grossièreté [grosjɛrte] *f* coarseness, grossness, vulgarity

grossir [grosir] *tr* to enlarge; increase ‖ *intr* to grow larger; put on weight

grossis•sant [grosisɑ̃] **-sante** [sɑ̃t] *adj* swelling, magnifying (*glasses*)

grossiste [grosist] *m* wholesaler, jobber

grotesque [grotɛsk] *adj* grotesque ‖ *mf* grotesque person ‖ *m* grotesque ‖ *f* grotesque (*ornament*)

grotte [grot] *f* grotto

grouillement [grujmɑ̃] *m* swarming; rumbling

grouiller [gruje] *intr* to swarm; **grouiller de** to teem with ‖ *ref* (slang) to get a move on

grouillot [grujo] *m* (coll) gofer, errand boy

groupe [grup] *m* group; (mach & mil) unit; **groupe de pression** lobby; **groupe d'experts** think tank; **groupe franc** (mil) commando; **groupe sanguin** blood type; **groupe témoin** control group

groupement [grupmɑ̃] *m* grouping; organization

grouper [grupe] *tr & ref* to group

gruau [gryo] *m* (*pl* **gruaux**) groats; (culin) gruel; (orn) small crane

grue [gry] *f* crane; (orn) crane; (coll) tart

gruger [gryʒe] §38 *tr* to sponge on, exploit; crunch

grume [grym] *f* bark; **en grume** rough (*timber*)

gru•meau [grymo] *m* (*pl* **-meaux**) gob; curd

grumeler [grymle] §34 *intr* to curdle, clot

gruyère [gryjɛr] *m* Gruyère cheese

guatémaltèque [gwatemaltɛk] *adj* Guatemalan ‖ (*cap*) *mf* Guatemalan

gué [ge] *m* ford, crossing; **sonder le gué** (coll) to see how the land lies ‖ *interj* hurrah!

guéable [geabl] *adj* fordable

guéer [gee] *tr* to ford; water (*a horse*)

guelte [gɛlt] *f* commission, percentage

guenille [gənij] *f* ragged garment; **en guenilles** in tatters

guenon [gənɔ̃] *f* female monkey; long-tailed monkey; (coll) hag, old bag

guépard [gepar] *m* cheetah

guêpe [gɛp] *f* wasp

guère [gɛr] §90 *adv* hardly ever; **ne ... guère** hardly, scarcely; hardly ever; not very; **ne ... guère de** hardly any; **ne ... guère que** hardly any but; hardly anyone but; **ne ... plus guère** hardly ever any more; not much longer

guères [gɛr] *adv* (poetic) var of **guère**

guéret [gerɛ] *m* fallow land

guéridon [geridɔ̃] *m* pedestal table

guérilla [gerija] *f* guerrilla warfare

guérillero [gerijero] *m* guerrilla

guérir [gerir] *tr* to cure ‖ *intr* to get well; get better; heal ‖ *ref* to cure oneself; recover

guérison [gerizɔ̃] *f* cure, healing; recovery

guérissable [gerisabl] *adj* curable

guéris•seur [gerisœr] **-seuse** [søz] *mf* healer; quack

guérite [gerit] *f* sentry box; (rr) signal box; **guérite téléphonique** call box

guerre [gɛr] *f* war; **de guerre lasse** for the sake of peace and quiet; **être de bonne guerre** to be fair, to be cricket; **guerre à outrance** all-out war; **guerre chimique** chemical warfare; **guerre commercial** trade war; **guerre des nerfs** war of nerves; **Guerre de Troie** Trojan War; **guerre d'usure** war of attrition; **guerre éclair** blitzkrieg; **guerre froide** cold war; **guerre presse-bouton** push-button war; **guerre sacrée** sacred war, jihad; **guerre sainte** holy war; **la guerre du Golfe** the Gulf War

guer•rier [gɛrje] **-rière** [rjɛr] *adj* warlike, martial ‖ *m* warrior ‖ *f* amazon

guerroyant [gɛrwajɑ̃] **guerroyante** [gɛrwajɑ̃t] *adj* warlike, bellicose

guerroyer [gɛrwaje] §47 *intr* to make war

guer•royeur [gɛrwajœr] **-royeuse** [wajøz] *adj* fighting (*spirit*) ‖ *mf* fighter

guet [gɛ] *m* watch, lookout

guet-apens [gɛtapɑ̃] *m* (*pl* **guets-apens** [gɛtapɑ̃]) ambush, trap

guêtre [gɛtr] *f* gaiter, legging

guêtrer [gɛtre] *tr & ref* to put gaiters on

guetter [gɛte] *tr* to watch; watch for; (coll) to lie in wait for

guetteur [gɛtœr] *m* lookout, sentinel

gueu•lard [gœlar] **-larde** [lard] *adj* (slang) loud-mouthed; (slang) fond of good eating ‖ *mf* gourmet; (slang) loud-mouth ‖ *m* mouth (*of blast furnace; of cannon*); (naut) megaphone

gueule [gœl] *f* mouth (*of animal; of furnace, cannon, etc.*); (slang) mouth, mug (*of person*); **avoir de la gueule** (coll) to have a certain air; **avoir la gueule de bois** (coll) to have a hangover; **fine gueule** (coll) gourmet; **gueule cassée** (coll) disabled veteran; **gueule noire** (coll) miner; **ta gueule!** (slang) shut up!

gueule-de-loup [gœldəlu] *f* (*pl* **gueules-de-loup**) (bot) snapdragon

gueuler [gœle] *tr & intr* (slang) to bellow

gueuleton [gœltɔ̃] *m* (slang) big feed

gueux [gø] **gueuse** [gøz] *adj* beggarly, wretched ‖ *mf* beggar; scamp ‖ *f* pig iron; pig (*mold*); woolen jacket; (coll) whore; **courir la gueuse** (coll) to go whoring

gugusse [gygys] *m* clown

gui [gi] *m* mistletoe; (naut) boom

guichet [giʃe] *m* window (*in post office, bank, box office, etc.*); counter (*e.g., in bank*); wicket; **guichet libre-service** automated teller machine

guidage [gidaʒ] *m* (rok) guidance

guide [gid] *m* guide; guidebook ‖ *f* rein; **mener la vie à grandes guides** to live extravagantly ‖ **Guide** Girl Scout

guide-âne [gidɑn] *m* (*pl* **-âne** or **-ânes**) manual, guide

guider [gide] *tr* to guide

guidon [gidɔ̃] *m* handlebars; sight, bead (*of gun*); (naut) pennant

guigne [giɲ] *f* heart cherry; (coll) jinx

guigner [giɲe] *tr* to steal a glance at; (coll) to covet ‖ *intr* to peep

guignol [giɲɔl] *m* puppet theater; (pej) clown, buffoon, bumpkin; **Grand Guignol** Parisian puppet theater (*1897–1962*); (aer) king post

guignolet [giɲɔlɛ] *m* cherry brandy

guillaume [gijom] *m* rabbet plane; **Guillaume** William

guilledou [gijdu] *m*—**courir le guilledou** (coll) to make the rounds

guillemet [gijmɛ] *m* quotation mark; **entre guillements** in quotation marks, in quotes; **fermer les guillemets** to close quotes; **fermez les guillemets** unquote, end of quote; **ouvrez les guillemets** quote; **ouvrir les guillemets** to quote

guillemeter [gijməte] §34 *tr* to put in quotes

guiller [gije] *intr* to ferment

guille•ret [gijrɛ] **-rette** [rɛt] *adj* chipper, lively, cheerful

guillotine [gijɔtin] *f* guillotine; **à guillotine** sliding; sash (*window*)

guillotiner [gijɔtine] *tr* to guillotine

guimauve [gimov] *f* (bot) marshmallow

guimbarde [gɛ̃bard] *f* (mus) jew's-harp; (coll) jalopy

guimpe [gɛ̃p] *f* wimple

guin•dé -dée [gɛ̃de] *adj* affected, stiff

guin•deau [gɛ̃do] *m* (*pl* **-deaux**) windlass

guinder [gɛ̃de] *tr* to hoist ‖ *ref* to put on airs

guinée [gine] *f* guinea (*coin*); **Guinée** Guinea (*the region*); **la Guinée** Guinea (*the region*)

guingan [gɛ̃gɑ̃] *m* gingham

guingois [gɛ̃gwa] *m*—**de guingois** askew; lopsidedly

guinguette [gɛ̃gɛt] *f* roadside inn, roadside park

guipage [gipaʒ] *m* wrapping, lapping

guiper [gipe] *tr* to wind; cover (*a wire*)

guipure [gipyr] *f* pillow lace

guirlande [girlɑ̃d] *f* garland, wreath

guirlander [girlɑ̃de] *tr* to garland

guise [giz] *f* manner; **à sa guise** as one pleases; **en guise de** by way of

guitare [gitar] *f* guitar
guitariste [gitarist] *mf* guitarist
guppy [gypi] *m* guppy
gustation [gystɑsjɔ̃] *f* tasting; drinking
guttu•ral -rale [gytyral] (*pl* **-raux** [ro] **-rales**)
　adj & *f* guttural
Guyane [gɥijan] *f* Guyana; **la Guyane** Guyana
gym [ʒim] *f* (coll) gymnastics
gymnase [ʒimnɑz] *m* gymnasium; fitness center
gymnaste [ʒimnast] *mf* gymnast

gymnastique [ʒimnastik] *adj* gymnastic ‖ *f*
　gymnastics; physical fitness
gymnote [ʒimnɔt] *m* electric eel
gynécologie [ʒinekɔlɔʒi] *f* gynecology
gynécologue [ʒinekɔlɔg] *mf* gynecologist
gypse [ʒips] *m* gypsum
gyrocompas [ʒirɔkɔ̃pa] *m* gyrocompass
gyrophare [ʒirɔfar] *m* (aut) emergency light,
　dome light (*flashing, revolving*)
gyroscope [ʒirɔskɔp] *m* gyroscope

H

H, h [aʃ], *[aʃ] *m invar* eighth letter of the
　French alphabet
habile [abil] *adj* skillful; clever
habileté [abilte] *f* skill; cleverness
habiliter [abilite] *tr* to qualify, entitle
habillage [abijaʒ] *m* preparation; dressing;
　cover, outside surface; assembly; packaging
　and presentation; labeling and sealing; (mach)
　casing
habillement [abijmɑ̃] *m* clothing; clothes
habiller [abije] *tr* to dress; clothe; put together
　‖ *intr* to be becoming, e.g., **robe qui habille
　bien** becoming dress ‖ *ref* to dress; get
　dressed; **s'habiller chez** to buy one's clothes
　at or from
habit [abi] *m* dress suit; habit, frock; **habit de
　cérémonie** or **soirée, habit à queue de pie,
　habit à queue de morue** tails; **habits** clothes
habitacle [abitakl] *m* (aer) cockpit; (naut) binna-
　cle; (poetic) dwelling
habi•tant [abitɑ̃] **-tante** [tɑ̃t] *mf* inhabitant
habitat [abita] *m* habitat; living conditions,
　housing
habitation [abitɑsjɔ̃] *f* habitation; dwelling; res-
　idence; **habitation à bon marché** or **à loyer
　modéré** low-rent apartment
habi•té -tée [abite] *adj* inhabited; (rok) manned
habiter [abite] *tr* to live in, inhabit ‖ *intr* to live,
　reside
habitude [abityd] *f* habit, custom; **comme d'ha-
　bitude** as usual; **d'habitude** usually
habi•tuel -tuelle [abitɥɛl] *adj* habitual
habituer [abitɥe] §96, §100 *tr* to accustom
　ref—**s'habituer à** to get used to
hâbler *[able] *intr* to brag, to boast
hâblerie *[ablǝri] *f* bragging
hâ•bleur *[ablœr] **-bleuse** [bløz] *adj* boastful ‖
　mf braggart, boaster
hache *[aʃ] *f* ax, hatchet
ha•ché -chée *[aʃe] *adj* ground, chopped;
　hachured; choppy (*sea*); jerky (*style*); dotted
　(*line*)
hacher *[aʃe] *tr* to hack; grind, chop up; **hacher
　menu** to mince
hache•reau *[aʃro] *m* (*pl* **-reaux**) hatchet

hachette *[aʃɛt] *f* hatchet
hachis *[aʃi] *m* hash, forcemeat; chopped vege-
　tables
hachisch *[aʃiʃ] *m* hashish
hachoir *[aʃwar] *m* cleaver; chopping board
hachure *[aʃyr] *f* shading
hachurer *[aʃyre] *tr* to shade, hatch
haddock *[adɔk] *m* finnan haddie
ha•gard *[agar] **-garde** [gard] *adj* haggard
haie *[ɛ] *f* hedge; hurdle; line, row
haïe *[aj] *interj* giddap!
haillon *[ɑjɔ̃] *m* old piece of clothing; **en hail-
　lons** in rags and tatters
haillon•neux *[ɑjɔnø] **-neuse** [nøz] *adj* ragged,
　tattered
haine *[ɛ] *f* hate
hai•neux *[ɛnø] **-neuse** [nøz] *adj* full of hate,
　spiteful, malevolent
haïr *[air] §33, §96, §97 *tr* to hate, detest ‖
　intr—**haïr de** to hate to
haire *[ɛr] *f* hair shirt
haïssable *[aisabl] *adj* hateful
Haïti [aiti] *f* Haiti
haï•tien [aisjɛ̃] **-tienne** [sjɛn] *adj* Haitian ‖ (*cap*)
　mf Haitian
halcyon [alsjɔ̃] *m* (orn) kingfisher
hâle *[ɑl] *m* suntan
haleine [alɛn] *f* breath; **avoir l'haleine courte**
　to be short-winded; (fig) to have little inspira-
　tion; **de longue haleine** hard, arduous (*work*);
　en haleine in good form; **hors d'haleine** out
　of breath; **perdre haleine** to get out of breath;
　reprendre haleine to catch one's breath;
　tenir en haleine to hold (*an audience*) breath-
　less
halenée [alne] *f* whiff; strong breath
haler *[ale] *tr* to haul, tow
hâler *[ale] *tr* to tan
hale•tant *[altɑ̃] **-tante** [tɑ̃t] *adj* breathless,
　panting
haleter [alte] §2 *intr* to pant, puff
hall *[ol] *m* lobby; hall, auditorium
halle *[al] *f* market, marketplace; exchange
hallebarde *[albard] *f* halberd; **il pleut des hal-
　lebardes** (coll) it's raining cats and dogs

hallebardier [albardje] *m* halberdier
hallier *[alje] *m* thicket
halluci•nant [allysinã] **-nante** [nãt] *adj* staggering, incredible
hallucination [allysinasjɔ̃] *f* hallucination
halo *[alo] *m* halo
halogène [aloʒɛn] *m* halogen
halte *[alt] *f* halt; stop; (rr) flag stop, way station; **faire faire halte à** to halt ‖ *interj* halt!
halte-là * [altla] *interj* (mil) halt!
haltère [altɛr] *m* dumbbell, barbell
haltérophile [alterɔfil] *m* weight lifter
haltérophilie [alterɔfili] *f* weight lifting
hamac *[amak] *m* hammock
hamburger [ãburgœr], [ãbyrʒe] *m* hamburger
ha•meau *[amo] *m* (*pl* **-meaux**) hamlet
hameçon [amsɔ̃] *m* hook, fishhook; (fig) bait
hammam *[ammam] *m* Turkish bath
hampe *[ãp] *f* staff, pole; shaft; downstroke; (culin) flank
hamster *[amstɛr] *m* hamster
han *[ã], [hã] *m* grunt
hanap *[anap] *m* hanap, goblet
hanche *[ã∫] *f* hip; haunch
hancher *[ã∫e] *intr* to lean on one leg ‖ *ref* (mil) to stand at ease
handball *[ãbol] *m* handball
handicap *[ãdikap] *m* handicap; **handicap physique** physical handicap
handicaper *[ãdikape] *tr* to handicap
hangar *[ãgar] *m* hangar; shed
hanneton *[antɔ̃] *m* June bug, chafer
hanter *[ãte] *tr* to haunt
hantise *[ãtiz] *f* obsession
happe *[ap] *f* crucible tongs; (carp) cramp, staple
happer *[ape] *tr* to snap up; (coll) to nab ‖ *intr* to stick
haquenée *[akne] *f* palfrey
haquet *[akɛ] *m* dray; **haquet à main** pushcart
harangue *[arãg] *f* harangue
haranguer *[arãge] *tr* & *intr* to harangue
haras *[arɑ] *m* stud farm
harasser *[arase] *tr* to tire out
harcèlement *[arsɛlmã] *m* harassment; **harcèlement sexuel** sexual harassment
harceler *[arsəle] §2 or §34 *tr* to harass, harry; pester; dun
harde *[ard] *f* herd; leash; set (*of dogs*); **hardes** old clothes
har•di -die *[ardi] *adj* bold, daring; audacious, brazen ‖ **hardi** *interj* up and at them!
hardiesse *[ardjɛs] *f* boldness
hardiment *[ardimã] *adv* boldly; audaciously, brazenly
harem *[arɛm] *m* harem
hareng *[arã] *m* herring; **hareng fumé** kipper; **hareng saur** red herring; **sec comme un hareng** (coll) long and thin; **serrés comme des harengs** (coll) packed like sardines
harengère *[arãʒɛr] *f* fishwife; (coll) shrew
harenguet *[arãgɛ] *m* sprat
hargne *[arɲ] *f* bad temper

har•gneux *[arɲø] **-gneuse** [ɲøz] *adj* bad-tempered, peevish, surly
haricot *[ariko] *m* bean; **haricot beurre** lima bean, butter bean; **haricot de Lima** lima bean; **haricot de mouton** haricot (*stew*); **haricot de Soissons** kidney bean; **haricot vert** string bean, green bean
harmonica [armɔnika] *m* mouth organ
harmonie [armɔni] *f* harmony; (mus) band
harmo•nieux [armɔnjø] **-nieuse** [njøz] *adj* harmonious
harmonique [armɔnik] *adj* harmonic
harmoniser [armɔnize] *tr* & *ref* to harmonize
harnachement *[arna∫mã] *m* harness; harnessing
harnacher *[arna∫e] *tr* to harness; rig out
harnais *[arnɛ] *m* harness
haro *[aro] *m*—**crier haro sur** (coll) to make a hue and cry against
harpagon [arpagɔ̃] *m* scrooge
harpe *[arp] *f* harp
harpie *[arpi] *f* harpy
harpiste *[arpist] *mf* harpist
harpon *[arpɔ̃] *m* harpoon
harponner *[arpɔne] *tr* to harpoon; (coll) to nab (*e.g., a thief*)
hart *[ar] *f* noose
hasard *[azar] *m* hazard, chance; **à tout hasard** just in case, come what may; **au hasard** at random; **par hasard** by chance
hasar•dé -dée *[azarde] *adj* hazardous
hasarder *[asarde] §96, §97 *tr* to risk, hazard, gamble ‖ §96 *ref* to venture, risk
hasar•deux *[azardø] **-deuse** [døz] *adj* risky, uncertain; hazardous
has been *[azbin] *mf invar* has-been
hase *[az] *f* doe hare
hâte *[ɑt] *f* haste; **à la hâte** hastily; **avoir hâte de** to be eager to; **en hâte, en toute hâte** posthaste
hâter *[ɑte] §97 *tr* & *ref* to hasten
hâ•tif *[ɑtif] **-tive** [tiv] *adj* premature; (hort) early
hauban *[obã] *m* (naut) shroud; (naut) guy
haubert *[obɛr] *m* coat of mail
hausse *[os] *f* rise, increase; block, wedge, prop; (mil) elevation, range; **jouer à hausse** to bull the market
haussement *[osmã] *m* shrug
hausser *[ose] *tr* to raise, lift; shrug (*one's shoulders*) ‖ *intr* to rise
haussier *[osje] *m* bull (*on the stock exchange*)
haussière *[osjɛr] *f* (naut) hawser
haut *[o] **haute** *[ot] *adj* high; loud; high and mighty ‖ (when standing before noun) *adj* high; loud; upper, higher; extra (*pay*); early (*antiquity, Middle Ages, etc.*) ‖ *m* top; height; **de haut en bas** from top to bottom; **en haut** up; upstairs; **haut de casse** (typ) upper case; **haut des côtes** sparerib; **le prendre de haut** to get on one's high horse; **traiter de haut en bas** to high-hat ‖ *f* see **haute** ‖ **haut** *adv* high; up high; loudly; **haut les bras!** start

working!; **haut les cœurs!** lift up your hearts!; **haut les mains!** hands up!

hau·tain *[otɛ̃] **-taine** [tɛn] *adj* haughty

hautbois *[obwa] *m* oboe

haut-de-chausses *[odə ʃos] *m* (*pl* **hauts-de-chausses**) trunk hose, breeches

haut-de-forme *[odəfɔrm] *m* (*pl* **hauts-de-forme**) top hat

haute *[ot] *f* high society

haute-fidélité *[otfidelite] *f* high fidelity, hi-fi

hautement *[otmɑ̃] *adv* loudly; openly, clearly; high (*qualified*); proudly

hauteur *[otœr] *f* height; hill, upland; altitude; nobility; haughtiness; (phys) pitch (*of sound*); **à la hauteur de** equal to, up to; (naut) off

haut-fond *[ofɛ̃] *m* (*pl* **hauts-fonds**) shoal, shallows

haut-le-cœur *[oləkœr] *m invar* nausea

haut-le-corps *[oləkɔr] *m invar* jump, sudden start

haut-parleur *[oparlœr] *m* (*pl* **haut-parleurs**) loudspeaker

hautu·rier *[otyrje] **-rière** [rjɛr] *adj* deep-sea

havage *[avaʒ] *m* (min) cutting

havane *[avan] *adj invar* tan, brown ‖ *m* Havana cigar ‖ (*cap*) *f*—**La Havane** Havana

hâve *[av] *adj* haggard, peaked

havir *[avir] *tr* (culin) to sear

havre *[avr] *m* haven, harbor

havresac *[avrəsak] *m* haversack, knapsack; tool bag

hawaïen or **hawaiien** [awajɛ̃], [avajɛ̃] **hawaïenne** or **hawaiienne** [awajɛn], [avajɛn] *adj* Hawaiian ‖ (*cap*) *mf* Hawaiian

Hawaii [awai], [awaji] **l'île Hawaii** Hawaii; **les îles Hawaii** the Hawaiian Islands

Haye *[ɛ] *f*—**La Haye** The Hague

hayon *[ajɔ̃] *m* (aut) hatchback

H.B.M. [a ʃbeɛm] *f* (letterword) (**habitation à bon marché**) low-rent apartment

he *[e], [hə] *interj* hey!

heaume *[om] *m* helmet

hebdomadaire [ɛbdɔmadɛr] *adj & m* weekly

héberger [ebɛrʒe] §38 *tr* to lodge

hébé·té -tée [ebete] *adj* dazed

hébéter [ebete] §10 *tr* to daze, stupefy

hébraïque [ebraik] *adj* Hebrew

hébraï·sant [ebraizɑ̃] **-sante** [zɑ̃t] *mf* Hebraist

hébraïser [ebraize] *tr & intr* to Hebraize

hé·breu [ebrø] (*pl* **-breux**) *adj masc* Hebrew ‖ *m* Hebrew (*language*); **c'est de l'hébreu pour moi** it's Greek to me ‖ (*cap*) *m* Hebrew (*man*)

hécatombe [ekatɔ̃b] *f* hecatomb

hégire [eʒir] *f* Hegira

hein *[ɛ̃] *interj* (coll) eh!, what!

hélas [elas] *interj* alas!

Hélène [elɛn] *f* Helen

héler *[ele] §10 *tr* to hail, call

hélice [elis] *f* (aer) propeller; (math) helix, spiral; (naut) screw

hélicoptère [elikɔptɛr] *m* helicopter

héliport [elipɔr] *m* heliport

hélistation [elistasjɔ̃] *f* helicopter landing

hélium [eljɔm] *m* helium

hélix [eliks] *m* helix

hellène [ɛlɛn] *adj* Hellenic ‖ (*cap*) *mf* Hellene

helvétique [ɛlvetik] *adj* Swiss

hématie [emati] *f* red blood corpuscle

hémisphere [emisfɛr] *m* hemisphere

hémistiche [emisti ʃ] *m* hemistich

hémoglobine [emoglɔbin] *f* hemoglobin

hémophile [emɔfil] *adj* hemophilic ‖ *mf* hemophiliac

hémophilie [emɔfili] *f* hemophilia

hémorragie [emɔraʒi] *f* hemorrhage

hémorroïdes [emɔrɔid] *fpl* hemorrhoids

hémostatique [emɔstatik] *adj* hemostatic ‖ *m* hemostatic, hemostat

henné *[ɛnne] *m* henna

hennir *[enir] *intr* to neigh, whinny

hennissement *[enismɑ̃] *m* neigh, whinny

Henri [ɑ̃ri], *[ɑ̃ri] *m* Henry

hépatite [epatit] *f* hepatitis

héraldique [eraldik] *adj* heraldic

héraut *[ero] *m* herald

herbe [ɛrb] *f* grass; lawn; herb; **couper l'herbe sous le pied de qn** (coll) to pull the rug from under s.o. 's feet; **en herbe** unripe; budding; **fines herbes** herbs for seasoning; **herbe à la puce** (*Canad*) poison ivy; **herbe aux chats** catnip; **herbes médicinales** or **officinales** (pharm) herbs; **herbes potagères** potherbs; **mauvaise herbe** weed

her·beux [ɛrbø] **-beuse** [bøz] *adj* grassy

herbicide [ɛrbisid] *adj* herbicidal ‖ *m* weed killer

herboriste [ɛrbɔrist] *mf* herbalist

herboristerie [ɛrbɔristri] *f* herb shop

her·bu -bue [ɛrby] *adj* grassy

her·culéen [ɛrkyleɛ̃] **-culéenne** [kyleɛn] *adj* herculean

hère *[ɛr] *m* wretch

héréditaire [ereditɛr] *adj* hereditary

hérédité [eredite] *f* heredity

hérésie [erezi] *f* heresy

hérétique [eretik] *adj & mf* heretic

héris·sé -sée *[erise] *adj* bristly; shaggy; prickly; surly

hérisser *[erise] *tr & intr* to bristle

hérisson *[erisɔ̃] *m* hedgehog

héritage [eritaʒ] *m* heritage; inheritance

hériter [erite] *tr* to inherit ‖ *intr* to inherit; **hériter de** to become the heir of; inherit, come into

héri·tier [eritje] **-tière** [tjɛr] *mf* heir ‖ *f* heiress

hermétique [ɛrmetik] *adj* hermetic(al), airtight; (fig) obscure

hermine [ɛrmin] *f* ermine

herminette [ɛrminɛt] *f* adze

hernie *[ɛrni] *f* hernia; **hernie discale** slipped disc

her·nieux [ɛrnjø] **-nieuse** [njøz] *adj* ruptured

héroïne [erɔin] *f* heroine; (*drug*) heroin

héroïque [erɔik] *adj* heroic

héroïsme [erɔism] *m* heroism

héron *[erɔ̃] *m* heron

héros *[ero] *m* hero
herpès [ɛrpɛs] *m* herpes
herse *[ɛrs] *f* harrow; portcullis; **les herses** (theat) stage lights
herser *[ɛrse] *tr* to harrow
hési•tant [ezitã] **-tante** [tãt] *adj* hesitant
hésitation [ezitɑsjɔ̃] *f* hesitation
hésiter [ezite] §96 *intr* to hesitate
hétéroclite [eterɔklit] *adj* unusual, odd
hétérodoxe [eterɔdɔks] *adj* heterodox
hétérodyne [eterɔdin] *adj* heterodyne
hétérogène [eterɔʒɛn] *adj* heterogeneous
hêtre *[ɛtr] *m* beech, beech tree
heur [œr] *m* pleasure; **heur et malheur** joys and sorrows
heure [œr] *f* hour; time (*of day*); o'clock; **à la bonne heure!** fine!; **à l'heure** on time; by the hour, per hour; **à l'heure juste, à l'heure sonnante** on the hour; **à tout à l'heure!** see you later!; **à toute heure** at any time; **de bonne heure** early; **heure de fermeture** closing time; **heure d'été** daylight-saving time; **heure H** zero hour; **heure légale** twelve-month daylight time (standard time); **heure militaire** sharp, e.g., **huit heures, heure militaire** eight sharp; **heures creuses** off-peak hours; **heures d'affluence** rush hours; **heures de consultation** office hours; **heures de pointe** rush hours; **heures d'ouverture** business hours; **heure semestrielle** semester hour; **heures perdues** spare time; **heures supplémentaires** overtime; **l'heure du déjeuner** lunch hour; **tout à l'heure** in a little while; a little while ago
heu•reux [œrø], [ørø] **-reuse** [røz] §93 *adj* happy, pleased; lucky, fortunate
heurt *[œr] *m* knock, bump; clash; bruise; **heurt sans des dégats importants** fenderbender; **sans heurt** without a hitch
heur•té -tée *[œrte] *adj* clashing (*colors*); abrupt (*style*)
heurter *[œrte] *tr* to knock against, bump into; antagonize ‖ *intr*—**heurter contre** to bump into ‖ *ref* to clash, collide; **se heurter à** to come up against
heurtoir *[œrtwar] *m* door knocker; (rr) buffer
hexagone [ɛgzagɔn] *m* hexagon; **l'Hexagone (national)** (fig) France
hi *[i] *m* *invar*—**hi hi hi!** ho ho ho!; **pousser des hi et des ha** to sputter in amazement
hiatus [jatys], *[jatys] *m* hiatus
hiberner [ibɛrne] *intr* to hibernate
hibiscus [ibiskys] *m* hibiscus
hi•bou *[ibu] *m* (*pl* **-boux**) owl
hic *[ik] *m*—**violà le hic!** (coll) there's the rub!
hi•deux [idø] **-deuse** [døz] *adj* hideous
hie *[i] *f* pile driver
hièble [jɛbl] *f* (bot) elder
hié•mal -male [jemal] *adj* (*pl* **-maux** [mo]) winter
hier [jɛr] *adv & m* yesterday; **hier soir** last evening, last night
hiérarchie *[jerarʃi] *f* hierarchy

hiéroglyphe [jerɔglif] *m* hieroglyphic
hiéroglyphique [jerɔglifik] *adj* hieroglyphic
hi-fi *[ifi] *f* *invar* (coll) (*haute fidélité*) hi-fi (*high fidelity*)
high-tech *[ajtɛk] *adj invar* high-tech ‖ *m invar* high technology
hi-han *[iã] *interj* heehaw
hila•rant [ilarã] **-rante** [rãt] *adj* hilarious; laughing (*gas*)
hilare [ilar] *adj* hilarious
hin•dou -doue [ɛ̃du] *adj* Hindu ‖ (*cap*) *mf* Hindu
hippique [ipik] *adj* horse (*race, show*)
hippisme [ipism] *m* horse racing
hippodrome [ipɔdrom] *m* hippodrome, race track
hippopotame [ipɔpɔtam] *m* hippopotamus
hirondelle [irɔ̃dɛl] *f* (orn) swallow; (coll) bicycle cop
hispanique [ispanik] *adj* Hispanic
hispani•sant [ispanizã] **-sante** [zãt] *mf* Hispanist
hispanophone [ispanɔfɔn] *adj* Spanish-speaking ‖ *mf* Spanish speaker
hisser *[ise] *tr* to hoist, to raise
histoire [istwar] *f* history; story; **faire des histoires à** (coll) to make trouble for; **histoire à dormir debout** (coll) tall tale; **histoire de rire** (coll) just for fun; **histoire de s'informer** (coll) out of curiosity; **pas d'histoires** (coll) no fuss
histologie [istolɔʒi] *f* histology
histo•rien [istɔrjɛ̃] **-rienne** [rjɛn] *mf* historian
historier [istɔrje] *tr* to illustrate, adorn
historique [istɔrik] *adj* historic(al) ‖ *m* historical account
histrion [istrijɔ̃] *m* ham actor
hiver [ivɛr] *m* winter
hiveriser [ivɛrize] *tr* (aut) to winterize
hiver•nal -nale [ivɛrnal] *adj* (*pl* **-naux** [no]) winter
hiverner [ivɛrne] *intr* to winter
H.L.M. [aʃɛlɛm] *m* (letterword) (**habitation à loyer modéré**) low-rent apartment
ho *[o], [ho] *interj* hey there!; what!
hobe•reau *[ɔbro] *m* (*pl* **-reaux**) (orn) hobby; (coll) squire
hoche *[ɔʃ] *f* nick on a blade
hochement *[ɔʃmã] *m* shake, toss
hochepot *[ɔʃpo] *m* (culin) hotchpotch
hochequeue *[ɔʃkø] *m* (orn) wagtail
hocher *[ɔʃe] *tr* to shake; nod
hochet *[ɔʃɛ] *m* rattle (*toy*); bauble
hockey *[ɔkɛ] *m* hockey; **hockey sur glace** ice hockey
hockeyeur [ɔkɛjœr] *m* hockey player
hoirie [wari] *f* legacy
holà *[ɔla], [hɔla] *m* *invar*—**mettre le holà à** (coll) to put a stop to ‖ *interj* hey!; stop!
holding *[ɔldiŋ] *m* holding company
hold-up *[ɔldœp] *m* *invar* holdup
hollan•dais *[ɔlãdɛ] **-daise** [dɛz] *adj* Dutch ‖ *m* Dutch (*language*) ‖ (*cap*) *mf* Hollander (*person*)

hollande *[ɔlãd] *m* Edam cheese || *f* Holland (*linen*) || (*cap*) *f* Holland; **la Hollande** Holland

Hollywood *[ɔliwud] *m* (*centre de l'industrie cinématographique*) Hollywood

Hollywoo·dien *[ɔliwudjẽ] **-dienne** [djɛn] *adj* Hollywood

holocauste [ɔlɔkost] *m* holocaust

homard *[ɔmar] *m* lobster

home *[om] *m* home

homélie [ɔmeli] *f* homily

homéopathie [ɔmeɔpati] *f* homeopathy

home-trainer [omtrɛnœr] *m* exercise bicycle

homicide [ɔmisid] *adj* homicidal || *mf* homicide (*person*) || *m* homicide, murder; **homicide involontaire, homicide par imprudence** manslaughter

hommage [ɔmaʒ] *m* homage; **hommage de l'auteur** (formula in presenting complimentary copies) with the compliments of the author; **hommages** respects, compliments

hommasse [ɔmas] *adj* mannish (*woman*)

homme [ɔm] *m* man; **brave homme** fine man, honest man; **être homme à** to be the man to, to be capable of; **homme à tout faire** jack-of-all-trades; handyman; **homme d'affaires** businessman; **homme d'armes** man-at-arms; **homme de droite** rightist; **homme de gauche** leftist; **homme d'église** churchman; **homme de guerre** or **d'épée** military man; **homme de la rue** man in the street, first comer; **homme de l'espace** spaceman; **homme de lettres** man of letters; **homme de paille** figurehead, stooge, front man; **homme de peine** workingman; **homme des bois** orangutan; **homme d'Etat** statesman; **homme de troupe** (*pl* **hommes des troupes**) (mil) enlisted man, private; **homme d'expédition** go-getter; **homme d'intérieur** homebody; **homme du monde** man of the world; **homme galant** ladies' man; **homme orchestra** one-man band; **hommes de bien** men of good will; **honnête homme** upright man; man of culture, gentleman; **jeune homme** young man; teen-age boy; **le vieil homme** (Bib) the old Adam; **un homme à la mer!** man overboard!

homme-grenouille [ɔmgrənuj] *m* (*pl* **hommes-grenouilles**) frogman

homme-sandwich [ɔmsãdwitʃ], [ɔmsãdwiʃ] *m* (*pl* **hommes-sandwichs**) sandwich man

homogène [ɔmɔʒɛn] *adj* homogeneous

homogénéiser [ɔmɔʒeneize] *tr* to homogenize

homologation [ɔmɔlɔgasjõ] *f* validation

homologue [ɔmɔlɔg] *adj* homologous || *mf* (fig) opposite number

homologuer [ɔmɔlɔge] *tr* to confirm, endorse; probate (*e.g., a will*)

homonyme [ɔmɔnim] *adj* homonymous || *m* homonym; namesake

homosexualité [ɔmɔsɛksɥalite] *f* homosexuality

homo·sexuel -sexuelle [ɔmɔsɛksɥɛl] *adj & mf* homosexual

hongre *[ɔ̃gr] *adj* gelded || *m* gelding

hongrer *[ɔ̃gre] *tr* to geld

Hongrie *[ɔ̃gri] *f* Hungary; **la Hongrie** Hungary

hon·grois *[ɔ̃grwa] **-groise** [grwaz] *adj* Hungarian || *m* Hungarian (*language*) || (*cap*) *mf* Hungarian (*person*)

honnête [ɔnɛt] *adj* honest, honorable

honnêteté [ɔnɛtəte] *f* honesty, uprightness

honneur [ɔnœr] *m* honor; **faire honneur à sa parole** to keep one's word

honnir *[ɔnir] *tr* to shame

honorabilité [ɔnɔrabilite] *f* respectability

honorable [ɔrɔrabl] *adj* honorable

honoraire [ɔnɔrɛr] *adj* honorary, emeritus || **honoraires** *mpl* honorarium, fee

honorer [ɔnɔre] *tr* to honor || *ref*—**s'honorer de** to pride oneself on

honorifique [ɔnɔrifik] *adj* honorific

honte *[ɔ̃t] *f* shame; **avoir honte** to be ashamed; **faire honte à qn** to make s.o. ashamed; **faire honte à ses parents** to be a disgrace to one's parents; **fausse honte** bashfulness; **sans honte** unashamedly

hon·teux *[ɔ̃tø], **-teuse** [tøz] *adj* ashamed; shameful; sheepish, shamefaced, bashful; venereal (*diseases*)

hop *[ɔp] *interj* go!, off with you!

hôpi·tal *[ɔpital] *m* (*pl* **-taux** [to]) hospital; charity hospital

hoquet *[ɔkɛ] *m* hiccough

hoqueter *[ɔkte] **§34** *intr* to hiccough

horaire [ɔrɛr] *adj* hourly, by hour || *m* timetable; schedule; **horaire flottant** flex(i)time

horde *[ɔrd] *f* horde

horion *[ɔrjɔ̃] *m* punch, clout

horizon [ɔrizɔ̃] *m* horizon

horizon·tal -tale [ɔrizɔ̃tal] (*pl* **-taux** [to] **-tales**) *adj & f* horizontal

horloge [ɔrlɔʒ] *f* clock; **horloge à eau, horloge d'eau** water clock; **horloge à sable, horloge de sable** hourglass; **horloge atomique, horloge moléculaire** atomic clock; **horloge comtoise, horloge normande, horloge parquet** grandfather's clock; **horloge numérique** digital clock; **horloge solaire** sundial

horlo·ger [ɔrlɔʒe] **-gère** [ʒɛr] *adj* clockmaking, watchmaking || *mf* clockmaker, watchmaker

horlogerie [ɔrlɔʒri] *f* clockmaking, watchmaking; **d'horlogerie** clockwork

hormis *[ɔrmi] *prep* (lit) except for

hormone [ɔrmɔn] *f* hormone

horoda·té -tée [ɔrɔdate] *adj* stamped with the hour and date

horoscope [ɔrɔskɔp] *m* horoscope; **tirer l'horoscope de qn** to cast s.o.'s horoscope

horreur [ɔrœr] *f* horror; **avoir horreur de** to have a horror of; **commettre des horreurs** to commit atrocities; **dire des horreurs** to say obscene things; **dire des horreurs de** to say shocking things about

horrible [ɔribl] *adj* horrible

horrifier [ɔrifje] *tr* to horrify

horripi•lant [ɔrripilɑ̃] **-lante** [lɑ̃t] (coll) *adj* hair-raising

horripilation [ɔrripilɑsjɔ̃] *f* gooseflesh; (coll) exasperation

horripiler [ɔrripile] *tr* to give gooseflesh to; (coll) to exasperate

hors *[ɔr] *prep* out, beyond, outside; except, except for, save; **hors de** out of, outside of; **hors de soi** beside oneself, frantic; **hors d'ici!** get out!; **hors tout** overall

hors-bord *[ɔrbɔr] *m invar* outboard (*motor or motorboat*)

hors-caste *[ɔrkast] *mf invar* outcaste

hors-concours *[ɔrkɔ̃kur] *adj invar* excluded from competition ‖ *m invar* contestant excluded from competition

hors-d'œuvre *[ɔrdœvr] *m invar* hors d'œuvre; **le déjeuner commence par des hors-d'œuvre** the dinner begins with the hors d'œuvres

hors-jeu *[ɔrjø] *m invar* offside position

hors-la-loi *[ɔrlalwa] *m invar* outlaw

hors-ligne *[ɔrliɲ] *adj invar* (coll) exceptional ‖ *m invar* roadside

hors-texte *[ɔrtɛks] *m invar* (bb) insert

hortensia [ɔrtɑ̃sja] *m* hydrangea

horticole [ɔrtikɔl] *adj* horticultural

horticulture [ɔrtikyltyr] *f* horticulture

hospice [ɔspis] *m* hospice; home (*for the old, infirm, orphaned, etc.*)

hospita•lier [ɔspitalje] **-lière** [ljɛr] *adj* hospitable; hospital ‖ *mf* hospital employee

hospitaliser [ɔspitalize] *tr* to hospitalize

hospitalité [ɔspitalite] *f* hospitality

hostie [ɔsti] *f* (eccl) Host

hostile [ɔstil] *adj* hostile

hostilité [ɔstilite] *f* hostility

hôte [ot] *mf* guest ‖ *m* host

hôtel [otɛl], [ɔtɛl] *m* hotel; mansion; **hôtel des Monnaies** mint; **hôtel des Postes** main post office; **hôtel des ventes** auction house; **hôtel de ville** city hall; **hôtel meublé** rooming house, residential hotel; **hôtel particulier** mansion

hôtel-Dieu [otɛldjø], [ɔtɛldjø] *m* (*pl* **hôtels-Dieu**) city hospital

hôte•lier [otəlje], [ɔtəlje] **-lière** [ljɛr] *adj* hotel (*business*) ‖ *mf* hotel manager

hôtellerie [otɛlri], [ɔtɛlri] *f* hotel business; fine restaurant; hostelry, hostel

hôtesse [otɛs] *f* hostess; **hôtesse de l'air** air hostess, stewardess

hotte *[ɔt] *f* basket (*carried on back*); hod (*of mason*); hood (*of chimney*); **hotte aspirante** exhaust hood

hou *[u] *interj* oh no!

houache *[waʃ] *f* wake (*of ship*)

houblon *[ublɔ̃] *m* hop (*vine*); hops (*dried flowers*)

houe *[u] *f* hoe

houer *[we] *tr* to hoe

houille *[uj] *f* coal; **houille blanche** water power; **houille bleue** tide power; **houille d'or** energy from the sun; **houille grasse** or **col-**

lante soft coal; **houille incolore** wind power; **houille maigre** or **éclatante** hard coal; **houille rouge** energy from the heat of the earth

houil•ler *[uje] **houil•lère** *[ujɛr] *adj* coal-bearing, carboniferous; coal (*industry*) ‖ *f* coal mine

houilleur *[ujœr] *m* coal miner

houle *[ul] *f* swell

houlette *[ulɛt] *f* crook (*of shepherd*); (hort) trowel

hou•leux *[ulø] **-leuse** [løz] *adj* swelling (*sea*); (fig) stormy, turbulent

houp *[up], [hup] *interj* go to it!

houppe *[up] *f* tuft; crest; tassel; **houppe à poudre** powder puff

houppelande *[uplɑ̃d] *f* greatcoat

houppette *[upɛt] *f* tuft; powder puff

hourra *[ura], [hura] *m*—**pousser trois hourras** to give three cheers ‖ *interj* hurrah!, yippie!

hourvari *[urvari] *m* call to the hounds; (coll) uproar

houspiller *[uspije] *tr* to jostle, knock around; to rake over the coals, to tell off

housse *[us] *f* slipcover; cover (*e.g., for typewriter*); garment bag; housing, horsecloth; (aut) seat cover; **housse de protection** dust cover

housser *[use] *tr* to dust (*with feather duster*)

houssine *[usin] *f* rug beater; switch

houssoir *[uswar] *m* feather duster; whisk broom

houx *[u] *m* holly

hoyau *[wajo] *m* (*pl* **hoyaux**) mattock; pickax

hublot *[yblo] *m* porthole

huche *[yʃ] *f* hutch; bin

hucher *[yʃe] *tr* to call, shout to

hue *[y] *interj* gee!; gee up! **tirer à hue et à dia** (fig) to pull in opposite directions

huée *[ɥe] *f* hoot, boo

huer *[ɥe] *tr & intr* to hoot, boo

hugue•not *[ygno] **-note** [nɔt] *ad* Huguenot ‖ *f* pipkin ‖ (*cap*) *mf* Huguenot (*person*)

huile *[ɥil] *f* oil; big shot; **ça baigne dans l'huile** (coll) everything is going smoothly; **d'huile** calm, e.g., **mer d'huile** calm sea; **huile de coude** elbow grease; **huile de foie de morue** cod-liver oil; **huile de freins** brake fluid; **huile de ricin** castor oil; **huile lourde** diesel fuel; **huile solaire** suntan oil; **les huiles** (coll) the VIP's; **sentir l'huile** (fig) to smell of midnight oil; **verser de l'huile sur le feu** (fig) to add fuel to the fire

huiler [ɥile] *tr* to oil; grease

hui•leux [ɥilø] **-leuse** [løz] *adj* oily; greasy

huilier [ɥilje] *m* oil-and-vinegar cruet

huis [ɥi] *m* (archaic) door; **à huis clos** behind closed doors; (law) in camera; **à huis ouvert** spectators admitted ‖ *[ɥi] *m*—**demander le huis clos** to request a closed-door session

huisserie [ɥisri] *f* doorframe

huissier [ɥisje] *m* doorman; usher (*before a per-*

son of rank); **huissier audiencier** bailiff; **huissier exploitant** process server

huit *[ɥi(t)] §94 *adj & pron* eight; the Eighth, e.g., **Jean huit** John the Eighth; **huit heures** eight o'clock ‖ *m* eight; eighth (*in dates*); **faire des huit** to cut figures of eight (*in figure skating*)

huitain *[ɥitɛ̃] *m* eight-line verse

huitaine *[ɥitɛn] *f* (grouping of) eight; week; **à huitaine** the same day next week; **une huitaine de** about eight

huitième *[ɥitjɛm] §94 *adj, pron* (*masc, fem*), *& m* eighth

huître [ɥitr] *f* oyster

huit-reflets *[ɥirəflɛ] *m invar* top hat

huî-trier [ɥitrije] **-trière** [trijɛr] *adj* oyster (*industry*) ‖ *m* (orn) oystercatcher ‖ *f* oyster bed

hulotte *[ylɔt] *f* hoot owl

hululer *[ylyle] *intr* to hoot

hum *[œm], [hœm] *interj* hum!

hu•main [ymɛ̃] **-maine** [mɛn] *adj* human; humane

humaniste [ymanist] *adj & m* humanist

humanitaire [ymanitɛr] *adj & mf* humanitarian

humanité [ymanite] *f* humanity; **humanités** (**classiques**) humanities (*Greek & Latin classics*); **humanités modernes** humanities, belles-letters; **humanités scientifiques** liberal studies (*concerned with the observation and classification of facts*)

humble [œ̃bl] *adj* humble

humecter [ymɛkte] *tr* to moisten ‖ *ref* to become damp; **s'humecter le gosier** (slang) to wet one's whistle

humer *[yme] *tr* to suck, suck up; sip; inhale, breathe in

humérus [ymerys] *m* humerus

humeur [ymœr] *f* humor, body fluid; humor, mood, spirits; **avec humeur** testily; **avoir de l'humeur** to be in a bad mood; **être de bonne humeur** to be in a good humor

humide [ymid] *adj* humid, damp; wet

humidifier [ymidifje] *tr* to humidify

humidité [ymidite] *f* humidity

humi•liant [ymiljɑ̃] **-liante** [ljɑ̃t] *adj* humiliating

humiliation [ymiljɑsjɔ̃] *f* humiliation

humilier [ymilje] *tr* to humiliate, humble ‖ *ref* to humble oneself

humilité [ymilite] *f* humility

humoriste [ymɔrist] *adj* humorous (*writer*) ‖ *mf* humorist

humoristique [ymɔristik] *adj* humorous

humour [ymur] *m* humor; **humour noir** macabre humor, sick humor

humus [ymys] *m* humus

hune *[yn] *f* (naut) top; **hune de vigie** (naut) crow's-nest

huppe *[yp] *f* tuft, crest (*of bird*); (orn) hoopoe

hup•pé -pée *[ype] *adj* tufted, crested; (coll) smart, stylish

hure *[yr] *f* head (*of boar, salmon, etc.*); (culin) headcheese

hurlement *[yrlmɑ̃] *m* howl, roar; howling, roaring (*e.g., of wind*)

hurler *[yrle] *tr* to cry out, yell ‖ *intr* to howl, roar

hur•leur *[yrlœr] **-leuse** [løz] *adj* howling ‖ *mf* howler ‖ *m* (zool) howler

hurluberlu [yrlybɛrly] *m* (coll) scatterbrain

hu•ron *[yrɔ̃] **-ronne** [rɔn] *adj* (coll) boorish, uncouth ‖ *mf* (coll) boor

hurricane *[urikan], *[œrikɛn] *m* hurricane

hutte *[yt] *f* hut, cabin

hyacinthe [jasɛ̃t] *f* hyacinth (*stone*)

hya•lin [jalɛ̃] **-line** [lin] *adj* glassy

hybride [ibrid] *adj & m* hybrid

hydrate [idrat] *m* hydrate

hydrater [idrate] *tr & ref* to hydrate

hydraulique [idrolik] *adj* hydraulic ‖ *f* hydraulics

hydravion [idravjɔ̃] *m* hydroplane

hydre [idr] *f* hydra

hydrocarbure [idrɔkarbyr] *m* hydrocarbon

hydro-électrique [idrɔelɛktrik] *adj* hydroelectric

hydrofoil [idrɔfɔjl] *m* hydrofoil

hydrofuge [idrɔfyʒ] *adj* waterproof

hydrofuger [idrɔfyʒe] §38 *tr* to waterproof

hydrogène [idrɔʒɛn] *m* hydrogen

hydroglisseur [idrɔglisœr] *m* speedboat

hydromètre [idrɔmɛtr] *m* hydrometer ‖ *f* (ent) water spider

hydrophile [idrɔfil] *adj* absorbent ‖ *m*—**hydrophile brun** (ent) water devil

hydrophobie [idrɔfɔbi] *f* hydrophobia

hydropisie [idrɔpizi] *f* dropsy

hydroptère [idrɔptɛr] *m* hydrofoil

hydroscope [idrɔskɔp] *m* drowser

hydroxyde [idrɔksid] *m* hydroxide

hyène [jɛn] *f* hyena

hygiène [iʒjɛn] *f* hygiene; **hygiène mentale** mental hygiene

hygiénique [iʒjenik] *adj* hygienic

hymen [imɛn] *m* (anat) hymen

hymnaire [imnɛr] *m* hymnal

hymne [imnə], [im] *m* hymn, ode, anthem; **hymne national** national anthem ‖ *f* (eccl) hymn, canticle

hyperacidité [iperasidite] *f* hyperacidity

hyperac•tif [iperaktif] **-tive** [tiv] *adj* hyperactive, hyper ‖ *mf* hyperactive

hyperbole [ipɛrbɔl] *f* (math) hyperbola; (rhet) hyperbole

hyperconnexion [ipɛrkɔnɛksjɔ̃] *f* (comp) hyperlink

hypersensible [ipɛrsɑ̃sibl] *adj* hypersensitive, supersensitive

hypersensi•tif [ipɛrsɑ̃sitif] **-tive** [tiv] *adj* hypersensitive, supersensitive

hyper•sexué -sexuée [ipɛrsɛksɥe] *adj* oversexed

hypertension [ipɛrtɑ̃sjɔ̃] *f* high blood pressure, hypertension

hypertexte [ipɛrtɛkst] *m* (comp) hypertext

hyperventilation [ipɛrvɑ̃tilasjɔ̃] *f* hyperventilation

hypnose [ipnoz] *f* hypnosis

hypnotique [ipnɔtik] *adj* & *m* hypnotic

hypnotiser [ipnɔtize] *tr* to hypnotize ‖ *ref*—**s'hypnotiser sur** (fig) to be hypnotized by

hypnoti•seur [ipnɔtizœr] **-seuse** [zøz] *mf* hypnotist

hypnotisme [ipnɔtism] *m* hypnotism

hypocondriaque [ipɔkɔ̃drijak] *adj* & *mf* hypochondriac

hypocrisie [ipɔkrizi] *f* hypocrisy

hypocrite [ipɔkrit] *adj* hypocritical ‖ *mf* hypocrite

hypodermique [ipɔdɛrmik] *adj* hypodermic

hyposulfite [ipɔsylfit] *m* hyposulfite

hypotension [ipɔtɑ̃sjɔ̃] *f* low blood pressure

hypoténuse [ipɔtenyz] *f* hypotenuse

hypothèque [ipɔtɛk] *f* mortgage; **prendre une hypothèque sur** to put a mortgage on; **purger une hypothèque** to pay off a mortgage

hypothéquer [ipɔteke] **§10** *tr* to mortgage

hypothèse [ipɔtɛz] *f* hypothesis

hypothétique [ipɔtetik] *adj* hypothetic(al)

hystérie [isteri] *f* hysteria

hystérique [isterik] *adj* hysteric(al)

I

I, i [i], *[i] *m invar* ninth letter of the French alphabet

IA [i'a] *f* (letterword) **(intelligence artificielle)** AI (artificial intelligence)

ïambique [jɑ̃bik] *adj* iambic

ibé•rien [iberjɛ̃] **-rienne** [rjɛn] *adj* Iberian ‖ (*cap*) *mf* Iberian

ibérique [iberik] *adj* Iberian

iceberg [isbɛrg] *m* iceberg

ichtyologie [iktjɔlɔʒi] *f* ichthyology

ici [isi] *adv* here; this is, e.g., **ici Paris** (rad, telv) this is Paris; e.g., **ici Robert** (telp) this is Robert; **d'ici** hereabouts; from today; **d'ici demain** before tomorrow; **d'ici là** between now and then, in the meantime; **d'ici peu** before long; **jusqu'ici** up to now, hitherto; **par ici** this way, through here

ici-bas [isibɑ] *adv* here below, on earth

icône [ikon] *f* icon

iconoclaste [ikɔnɔklast] *adj* iconoclastic ‖ *mf* iconoclast

iconographie [ikɔnɔgrafi] *f* iconography; pictures, pictorial material

iconoscope [ikɔnɔskɔp] *m* iconoscope

ictère [iktɛr] *m* jaundice

ictérique [ikterik] *adj* jaundiced

idéal idéale [ideal] *adj* & *m* (*pl* **idéaux** [ideo] or **idéals**) ideal

idéaliser [idealize] *tr* idealize

idéaliste [idealist] *adj* & *mf* idealist

idée [ide] *f* idea; mind, head; opinion, esteem; (coll) shade, touch; **changer d'idée** to change one's mind

idem [idɛm] *adv* idem, the same, ditto

identification [idɑ̃tifikasjɔ̃] *f* identification

identifier [idɑ̃tifje] *tr* to identify

identique [idɑ̃tik] *adj* identic(al)

identité [idɑ̃tite] *f* identity

idéologie [ideɔlɔʒi] *f* ideology; (pej) utopianism

idéologique [ideɔlɔʒik] *adj* ideologic(al); conceptual

ides [id] *fpl* ides

idiolecte [idjɔlɛkt] *m* idiolect (*individual linguistic style of a person*)

idiomatique [idjɔmatik] *adj* idiomatic

idiome [idjom] *m* idiom, language (*the linguistic communication used in a country or community*)

idiosyncrasie [idjɔsɛ̃krazi] *f* idiosyncrasy

i•diot [idjo] **-diote** [djɔt] *adj* idiotic ‖ *mf* idiot

idiotie [idjɔsi] *f* idiocy

idiotisme [idjɔtism] *m* idiom, idiomatic expression (*expression that is contrary to the usual patterns of the language*)

idolâtrer [idɔlatre] *tr* to idolize

idolâtrie [idɔlatri] *f* idolatry

idole [idɔl] *f* idol

idylle [idil] *f* idyll; romance, love affair

idyllique [idilik] *adj* idyllic

if [if] *m* yew

IGAME [igam] *m* (acronym) **(Inspecteur Général de l'Administration en Mission Extraordinaire)** head prefect

igname [iɲam], [ignam] *f* yam

ignare [iɲar] *adj* ignorant

ig•né -née [igne] *adj* igneous

ignifuge [ignifyʒ] *adj* fireproof ‖ *m* fireproofing

ignifuger [ignifyʒe] **§38** *tr* to fireproof

ignition [ignisjɔ̃] *f* ignition; red heat (*of metal*)

ignoble [iɲɔbl] *adj* ignoble; disgusting

ignomi•nieux [iɲɔminjø] **-nieuse** [njøz] *adj* ignominious

ignorance [iɲɔrɑ̃s] *f* ignorance

igno•rant [iɲɔrɑ̃] **-rante** [rɑ̃t] *adj* ignorant ‖ *mf* ignoramus

ignorer [iɲɔre] *tr* not to know, be ignorant of; be unacquainted with

iguane [igwan] *m* (zool) iguana

il [il] **§87, §92** *pron* he, it

île [il] *f* island, isle; **les îles Britanniques** the British Isles; **les îles Normandes** the Channel Islands

illé·gal -gale [illegal] *adj* (*pl* **-gaux** [go]) illegal

illégitime [illeʒitim] *adj* illegitimate; unjustified

illet·tré -trée [illɛtre] *adj & mf* illiterate

illicite [illisit] *adj* illicit; foul (*blow*)

illimi·té -tée [illimite] *adj* unlimited

illisible [illizibl] *adj* illegible; unreadable (*book*)

illogique [illɔʒik] *adj* illogical

illumination [illyminasjɔ̃] *f* illumination

illumi·né -née [illymine] *adj & mf* fanatic, visionary

illuminer [illymine] *tr* to illuminate

illusion [illyzjɔ̃] *f* illusion; **illusion de la vue** optical illusion; **se faire des illusions** to indulge in wishful thinking

illusionner [illyzjɔne] *tr* to delude ‖ *ref* to delude oneself

illusionniste [illyzjɔnist] *mf* magician

illusoire [illyzwar] *adj* illusory, illusive

illustra·teur [illystratœr] *m* illustrator

illustration [illystrasjɔ̃] *f* illustration; glorification; glory; celebrity

illustre [illystr] *adj* illustrious, renowned

illus·tré -trée [illystre] *adj* illustrated ‖ *m* illustrated magazine

illustrer [illystre] *tr* to illustrate ‖ *ref* to distinguish oneself

îlot [ilo] *m* small island, isle; block (*of houses*)

ils [il] §87 *pron* they

image [imaʒ] *f* image; picture; **images** imagery; **image de marque** name brand; **images** imagery; **images d'archives** file film; **une image vaut mieux que dix mille mots** a picture is worth a thousand words

imager [imaʒe] §38 *tr* to embellish with metaphors, to color

imagerie [imaʒri] *f*—**imagerie d'Epinal** cardboard cutouts

imaginaire [imaʒinɛr] *adj* imaginary

imagination [imaʒinasjɔ̃] *f* imagination

imaginer [imaʒine] §97 *tr* to imagine; invent ‖ *intr* to imagine; **imaginer de** + *inf* to have the idea of + *ger* ‖ §95 *ref* to imagine oneself; **imaginez-vous!** imagine!

imbattable [ɛ̃batabl] *adj* unbeatable

imbat·tu -tue [ɛ̃baty] *adj* unbeaten

imbécile [ɛ̃besil] *adj & mf* imbecile

imbécillité [ɛ̃besilite] *f* imbecility

imberbe [ɛ̃bɛrb] *adj* beardless

imbi·bé -bée [ɛ̃bibe] *adj* (coll) drunk, tipsy; **imbibé de** soaked with; steeped in

imbiber [ɛ̃bibe] *tr & ref* to soak; **s'imbiber de** to soak up; be imbued with; (coll) to imbibe (*liquor*)

imbrication [ɛ̃brikasjɔ̃] *f* overlapping

imbriquer [ɛ̃brike] *tr* to overlap; interweave; fit (*s.th.*) into ‖ *ref* to overlap; be linked; be interwoven; **ça s'imbrique l'un dans l'autre** they fit into each other; they are linked

imbrisable [ɛ̃brizabl] *adj* unbreakable

imbrûlable [ɛ̃brylabl] *adj* fireproof

im·bu -bue [ɛ̃by] *adj*—**imbu de** imbued with, steeped in

imbuvable [ɛ̃byvabl] *adj* undrinkable; unbearable, insufferable, awful

imita·teur [imitatœr] **-trice** [tris] *mf* imitator

imitation [imitasjɔ̃] *f* imitation

imiter [imite] *tr* to imitate

immacu·lé -lée [immakyle] *adj* immaculate

immangeable [ɛ̃mɑ̃ʒabl] *adj* inedible

immanquable [ɛ̃mɑ̃kabl] *adj* infallible; inevitable

immaté·riel -rielle [immaterjɛl] *adj* immaterial

immatriculation [immatrikylasjɔ̃] *f* registration; enrollment; **immatriculation de livraison** dealer's plate

immatriculer [immatrikyle] *tr* to register

immature [immatyr] *adj* unmatured

immé·diat [immedja] **-diate** [djat] *adj* immediate

immédiatement [immedjatmɑ̃] *adv* immediately

immémo·rial -riale [immemɔrjal] *adj* (*pl* **-riaux** [rjo]) immemorial

immense [immɑ̃s] *adj* immense

immensurable [immɑ̃syrabl] *adj* immeasurable, immensurable

immerger [immɛrʒe] §38 *tr* to immerse, dip; throw overboard; lay (*a cable*)

imméri·té -tée [immerite] *adj* undeserved

immersion [immɛrsjɔ̃] *f* immersion

immettable [ɛ̃mɛtabl] *adj* unwearable

immeuble [immœbl] *adj* real, e.g., **biens immeubles** real estate ‖ *m* building, apartment building; **immeuble à beaucoup d'étages** high-rise; **immeuble à copropriété** condominium

immi·grant [immigrɑ̃] **-grante** [grɑ̃t] *adj & mf* immigrant

immigration [immigrasjɔ̃] *f* immigration

immi·gré -grée [immigre] *adj & mf* immigrant

immigrer [immigre] *intr* to immigrate

immi·nent [imminɑ̃] **-nente** [nɑ̃t] *adj* imminent, impending

immiscer [immise] §51 *ref*—**s'immiscer dans** to interfere with, meddle with

immixtion [immiksjɔ̃] *f* interference; **immixtions** intrusions upon privacy (*e.g.*, *wiretapping*)

immobile [immɔbil] *adj* motionless; immobile (*resolute*); dead (*typewriter key*)

immobi·lier -lière [immɔbilje] [ljer] *adj* real-estate, property; real, e.g., **biens immobiliers** real estate

immobiliser [immɔbilize] *tr* to immobilize; tie up ‖ *ref* to come to a stop

immodé·ré -rée [immɔdere] *adj* immoderate

immonde [immɔ̃d] *adj* foul, filthy; (eccl) unclean

immondices [immɔ̃dis] *fpl* garbage, refuse

immo·ral -rale [immɔral] *adj* (*pl* **-raux** [ro]) immoral

immortaliser [immɔrtalize] *tr* to immortalize

immor·tel -telle [immɔrtɛl] *adj & mf* immortal ‖ *f* (bot) everlasting

immoti·vé -vée [immɔtive] *adj* groundless

immuable [immчabl] *adj* changeless

immuniser [immynize] *tr* to immunize

immunité [immynite] *f* immunity

immunodéficience [ımynɔdefisjɑ̃s] *f* immunodeficiency

immunologie [imynɔlɔʒi] *f* immunology

impact [ɛ̃pakt] *m* impact; **impact résistant** unbreakable (*e.g., glasses*)

im·pair -paire [ɛ̃pɛr] *adj* odd, uneven ‖ *m* (coll) blunder

impardonnable [ɛ̃pardɔnabl] *adj* unpardonable

impar·fait [ɛ̃parfɛ] **-faite** [fɛt] *adj & m* imperfect

imparité [ɛ̃parite] *f* inequality, disparity

impar·tial -tiale [ɛ̃parsjal] *adj* (*pl* **-tiaux** [sjo]) impartial

impartir [ɛ̃partir] *tr* to grant

impasse [ɛ̃pɑs] *f* blind alley, dead-end street; impasse, deadlock, standoff; (cards) finesse; **faire l'impasse à** (cards) to finesse

impassible [ɛ̃pasibl] *adj* impassible; impassive (*look, face, etc.*)

impatiemment [ɛ̃pasjamɑ̃] *adv* impatiently

impatience [ɛ̃pasjɑ̃s] *f* impatience; **impatiences** (coll) attack of nerves

impa·tient -tiente [ɛ̃pasjɑ̃] *adj* impatient

impatienter [ɛ̃pasjɑ̃te] *tr* to make impatient ‖ §97 *ref* to lose patience

impatroniser [ɛ̃patrɔnize] *ref* to take charge; take hold

impavide [ɛ̃pavid] *adj* fearless

impayable [ɛ̃pɛjabl] *adj* (coll) priceless, very funny

im·payé -payée [ɛ̃peje] *adj* unpaid

impec [ɛ̃pɛk] *adj* (coll) impeccable

impeccable [ɛ̃pɛkabl] *adj* impeccable

impénétrable [ɛ̃penetrabl] *adj* impenetrable

impéni·tent [ɛ̃penitɑ̃] **-tente** [tɑ̃t] *adj* impenitent, obdurate, inveterate

impensable [ɛ̃pɑ̃sabl] *adj* unthinkable

imper [ɛ̃pɛr] *m* (coll) raincoat

impéra·tif [ɛ̃peratif] **-tive** [tiv] *adj & m* imperative

impératrice [ɛ̃peratris] *f* empress

imperceptible [ɛ̃pɛrsɛptibl] *adj* imperceptible; negligible

imperdable [ɛ̃pɛrdabl] *adj* unlosable

imperfection [ɛ̃pɛrfɛksjɔ̃] *f* imperfection, defect

impé·rial -riale [ɛ̃perjal] *adj* (*pl* **-riaux** [rjo]) imperial ‖ *f* goatee; upper deck (*of bus, coach, etc.*)

impérialiste [ɛ̃perjalist] *adj & mf* imperialist

impé·rieux [ɛ̃perjø] **-rieuse** [rjøz] *adj* imperious, haughty; imperative, urgent

impérissable [ɛ̃perisabl] *adj* imperishable

impéritie [ɛ̃perisi] *f* incompetence

imperméabiliser [ɛ̃pɛrmeabilize] *tr* to waterproof

imperméable [ɛ̃pɛrmeabl] *adj* waterproof; impervious ‖ *m* raincoat

imperson·nel -nelle [ɛ̃pɛrsɔnɛl] *adj* impersonal; commonplace; ordinary

imperti·nent [ɛ̃pɛrtinɑ̃] **-nente** [nɑ̃t] *adj* impertinent ‖ *mf* impertinent person

impesanteur [ɛ̃pɛsɑ̃tœr] *f* weightlessness

impé·trant [ɛ̃petrɑ̃] **-trante** [trɑ̃t] *mf* holder (*of a title or degree*)

impé·tueux [ɛ̃petцø] **-tueuse** [tцøz] *adj* impetuous

impie [ɛ̃pi] *adj* impious, ungodly; blasphemous ‖ *mf* unbeliever; blasphemer

impiété [ɛ̃pjete] *f* impiety; disrespect

impitoyable [ɛ̃pitwajabl] *adj* unmerciful

implacable [ɛ̃plakabl] *adj* implacable

implanter [ɛ̃plɑ̃te] *tr* to implant; introduce ‖ *ref* to take root; **s'implanter chez** (coll) to thrust oneself upon

implication [ɛ̃plikɑsjɔ̃] *f* implication

implicite [ɛ̃plisit] *adj* implicit

impliquer [ɛ̃plike] *tr* to implicate; imply

implorer [ɛ̃plɔre] *tr* to implore

imployable [ɛ̃plwajabl] *adj* pitiless; inflexible

impo·li -lie [ɛ̃pɔli] *adj* impolite

impolitique [ɛ̃pɔlitik] *adj* ill-advised

impondérable [ɛ̃pɔ̃derabl] *adj & m* imponderable

impopulaire [ɛ̃pɔpylɛr] *adj* unpopular

impopularité [ɛ̃pɔpylarite] *f* unpopularity

importance [ɛ̃pɔrtɑ̃s] *f* importance; size; **d'importance** large, of consequence; thoroughly, very hard

impor·tant [ɛ̃pɔrtɑ̃] **-tante** [tɑ̃t] *adj* important; large, considerable ‖ *m* main thing; **faire l'important** (coll) to act big

importa·teur [ɛ̃pɔrtatœr] **-trice** [tris] *adj* importing ‖ *mf* importer

importation [ɛ̃pɔrtɑsjɔ̃] *f* importation

importer [ɛ̃pɔrte] *tr* to import ‖ *intr* to matter; be important; **n'importe** no matter, never mind; **n'importe comment** any way; **n'importe où** anywhere; **n'importe quand** anytime; **n'importe quel . . .** any . . . ; **n'importe qui** anybody; **n'importe quoi** anything; **peu m'importe** it doesn't matter to me; **qu'importe?** what does it matter?

impor·tun [ɛ̃pɔrtœ̃] **-tune** [tyn] *adj* bothersome ‖ *mf* pest, nuisance

importuner [ɛ̃pɔrtyne] *tr* to importune

imposable [ɛ̃pozabl] *adj* taxable

impo·sant [ɛ̃pozɑ̃] **-sante** [zɑ̃t] *adj* imposing

impo·sé -sée [ɛ̃poze] *adj* taxed; fixed (*price*) ‖ *mf* taxpayer

imposer [ɛ̃poze] §97, §98 *tr* to impose; levy a tax on ‖ *intr*—**en imposer à** to make an impression on; impose on ‖ *ref* to assert oneself; be indispensable; **ça s'impose** that's obvious, that's self-evident; **s'imposer à** to force itself upon; **s'imposer chez** to foist oneself upon

imposition [ɛ̃pozisjɔ̃] *f* imposition; taxation; laying on, levying; **niveau d'imposition** tax bracket

impossibilité [ɛ̃pɔsibilite] *f* impossibility; **être dans l'impossibilité de** to be unable to

impossible [ɛ̃pɔsibl] *adj* impossible

imposte [ɛ̃pɔst] *f* transom; (archit) impost
imposteur [ɛ̃pɔstœr] *m* impostor
imposture [ɛ̃pɔstyr] *f* imposture
impôt [ɛ̃po] *m* tax; **impôt du sang** (lit) military duty; **impôt foncier** property tax; **impôt retenu à la source** withholding tax; **impôt sur le revenu** income tax; **impôt sur les plus-values (en capital)** capital gains tax
impotence [ɛ̃pɔtɑ̃s] *f* lameness, infirmity
impo·tent [ɛ̃pɔtɑ̃] **-tente** [tɑ̃t] *adj* crippled; bed-ridden ‖ *mf* cripple
impraticable [ɛ̃pratikabl] *adj* impracticable; impassable (*e.g.*, road)
impré·cis [ɛ̃presi] **-cise** [siz] *adj* vague, hazy
imprégner [ɛ̃preɲe] §10 *tr* to impregnate
imprenable [ɛ̃prənabl] *adj* impregnable
impréparation [ɛ̃preparasjɔ̃] *f* unpreparedness
imprésario [ɛ̃presarjo] *m* impresario
impression [ɛ̃prɛsjɔ̃] *f* impression; printing; (phot) print; **impression subordonnée** (comp) background printing
impression·nant [ɛ̃prɛsjɔnɑ̃] **-nante** [nɑ̃t] *adj* impressive
impressionner [ɛ̃prɛsjɔne] *tr* to impress, affect; (phot) to expose
impressionnisme [ɛ̃prɛsjɔnism] *m* (painting) impressionism
imprévisible [ɛ̃previzibl] *adj* unforeseeable
imprévision [ɛ̃previzjɔ̃] *f* lack of foresight
im·prévoyant [ɛ̃prevwajɑ̃] **-prévoyante** [prevwajɑ̃t] *adj* improvident, short-sighted
impré·vu [ɛ̃prevy] *adj* & *m* unforeseen, unexpected; **sauf imprévu** unless something unforeseen happens
imprimante [ɛ̃primɑ̃t] *f* (comp) printer; **imprimante à jet d'encre** ink-jet printer; **imprimante à laser** laser printer; **imprimante matricielle** dot-matrix printer
impri·mé -mée [ɛ̃prime] *adj* printed ‖ *m* print, calico; printed work, book; printing (*as opposed to script*); **imprimés** printed matter
imprimer [ɛ̃prime] *tr* to print; imprint; impress; impart (*e.g.*, movement)
imprimerie [ɛ̃primri] *f* printing; printing office, print shop
imprimeur [ɛ̃primœr] *m* printer
imprimeur-éditeur [ɛ̃primœreditœr] *m* (*pl* **imprimeurs-éditeurs**) printer and publisher
imprimeur-libraire [ɛ̃primœrlibrɛr] *m* (*pl* **imprimeurs-libraires**) printer and publisher
imprimeuse [ɛ̃primøz] *f* printing press
improbable [ɛ̃prɔbabl] *adj* improbable
improba·tif [ɛ̃prɔbatif] **-tive** [tiv] *adj* disapproving
improbité [ɛ̃prɔbite] *f* dishonesty
improduc·tif [ɛ̃prɔdyktif] **-tive** [tiv] *adj* unproductive
impromp·tu -tue [ɛ̃prɔ̃pty] *adj* impromptu ‖ *m* impromptu play; (mus) impromptu ‖ **impromptu** *adv* impromptu
impropre [ɛ̃prɔpr] *adj* improper (*not right*); **impropre à** unfit for
impropriété [ɛ̃prɔprijete] *f* incorrectness

improviser [ɛ̃prɔvize] *tr* & *intr* to improvise
improviste [ɛ̃prɔvist]—**à l'improviste** unexpectedly, impromptu; **prendre à l'improviste** to catch napping
impru·dent [ɛ̃prydɑ̃] **-dente** [dɑ̃t] *adj* imprudent
impubère [ɛ̃pybɛr] *adj* under the age of puberty
impubliable [ɛ̃pybljabl] *adj* unpublishable, not fit to print
impu·dent [ɛ̃pydɑ̃] **-dente** [dɑ̃t] *adj* impudent
impudeur [ɛ̃pydœr] *f* immodesty
impudicité [ɛ̃pydisite] *f* indecency
impudique [ɛ̃pydik] *adj* immodest
impuissance [ɛ̃pɥisɑ̃s] *f* powerlessness, helplessness; ineffectiveness; (pathol) impotence: **être dans l'impuissance de faire q.ch.** to be incapable of doing s.th.
impuis·sant [ɛ̃pɥisɑ̃] **-sante** [sɑ̃t] *adj* impotent, powerless, helpless; (pathol) impotent
impul·sif [ɛ̃pylsif] **-sive** [siv] *adj* impulsive ‖ *mf* impulsive person
impulsion [ɛ̃pylsjɔ̃] *f* impulse; **donner l'impulsion à** to give an impetus to; **sous l'impulsion du moment** on the spur of the moment
impunément [ɛ̃pynemɑ̃] *adv* with impunity
impu·ni -nie [ɛ̃pyni] *adj* unpunished
impunité [ɛ̃pynite] *f* impunity
im·pur -pure [ɛ̃pyr] *adj* impure
impureté [ɛ̃pyrte] *f* impurity; unchastity
imputation [ɛ̃pytasjɔ̃] *f* imputation; (com) charge; (com) deduction
imputer [ɛ̃pyte] §97, §98 *tr* to impute, ascribe; (com) **imputer q.ch. à** to charge s.th. to
inabordable [inabɔrdabl] *adj* unapproachable, inaccessible; prohibitive (*price*)
inaccessible [inaksesibl] *adj* inaccessible
inaccoutu·mé -mée [inakutyme] *adj* unusual; **inaccoutumé à** unaccustomed to, unused to
inache·vé -vée [inaʃve] *adj* unfinished, uncompleted
inac·tif [inaktif] **-tive** [tiv] *adj* inactive
inaction [inaksjɔ̃] *f* inaction
inactivité [inaktivite] *f* inactivity
inadaptation [inadaptasjɔ̃] *f* maladjustment
inadap·té -tée [inadapte] *adj* maladjusted ‖ *mf* misfit
inadvertance [inadvɛrtɑ̃s] *f*—**par inadvertance** inadvertently
inalté·ré -rée [inaltere] *adj* unspoiled
inamovible [inamɔvibl] *adj* fixed, unmovable; not removable
inani·mé -mée [inanime] *adj* inanimate
inappréciable [inapresjabl] *adj* inappreciable, imperceptible; invaluable
inapprivoisable [inaprivwazabl] *adj* untamable
inapte [inapt] *adj* inept; **inapte à** unfit for, unsuitable for ‖ *mf* dropout, washout; **les inaptes** the unfit; the unemployable
inaptitude [inaptityd] *f* unfitness
inarticu·lé -lée [inartikyle] *adj* inarticulate
inassou·vi -vie [inasuvi] *adj* unsatisfied
inattaquable [inatakabl] *adj* unquestionable;

inattendu unassailable; **inattaquable par** unaffected by, resistant to

inatten•du -due [inatɑ̃dy] *adj* unexpected

inatten•tif [inatɑ̃tif] **-tive** [tiv] *adj* inattentive; careless

inattention [inatɑ̃sjɔ̃] *f* inattentiveness, carelessness

inaudible [inodibl] *adj* inaudible

inaugu•ral -rale [inogyral] *adj* (*pl* **-raux** [ro]) inaugural

inauguration [inogyrɑsjɔ̃] *f* inauguration

inaugurer [inogyre] *tr* to inaugurate; unveil (*a statue*)

inauthentique [inotɑ̃tik] *adj* unauthentic

inavouable [inavuabl] *adj* shameful

ina•voué -vouée [inavwe] *adj* unacknowledged

inca [ɛ̃ka] *adj invar* Inca ‖ (*cap*) *m* Inca

incandes•cent [ɛ̃kɑ̃desɑ̃] **-cente** [sɑ̃t] *adj* incandescent; wild, stirred up (*crowd*)

incapable [ɛ̃kapabl] §93 *adj* incapable; (law) incompetent ‖ *mf* (law) incompetent person

incapacité [ɛ̃kapasite] *f* incapacity; disability

incarcérer [ɛ̃karsere] §10 *tr* to incarcerate

incar•nat [ɛ̃karna] **-nate** [nat] *adj* "flesh" -colored; rosy ‖ *m* "flesh" color

incarnation [ɛ̃karnɑsjɔ̃] *f* incarnation

incar•né -née [ɛ̃karne] *adj* incarnate; ingrowing (*nail*)

incarner [ɛ̃karne] *tr* to incarnate, embody ‖ *ref* to become incarnate; (pathol) to become ingrown; **s'incarner dans** to become the embodiment of

incartade [ɛ̃kartad] *f* indiscretion; prank

incassable [ɛ̃kɑsabl] *adj* unbreakable

incendiaire [ɛ̃sɑ̃djɛr] *adj* & *mf* incendiary

incendie [ɛ̃sɑ̃di] *m* fire, conflagration; **incendie volontaire** arson

incen•dié -diée [ɛ̃sɑ̃dje] *adj* burnt down ‖ *mf* fire victim

incendier [ɛ̃sɑ̃dje] *tr* to set on fire; burn down; (fig) to fire, inflame; (slang) to give a tongue-lashing to

incer•tain [ɛ̃sɛrtɛ̃] **-taine** [tɛn] *adj* uncertain; indistinct; unsettled (*weather*)

incertitude [ɛ̃sɛrtityd] *f* incertitude, uncertainty; **dans l'incertitude** in doubt

incessamment [ɛ̃sɛsamɑ̃] *adv* incessantly; without delay, at any moment

inces•sant -sante [ɛ̃sɛsɑ̃] **-sante** [sɑ̃t] *adj* incessant

inceste [ɛ̃sɛst] *m* incest

inces•tueux -tueuse [ɛ̃sɛstɥø] **-tueuse** [tɥøz] *adj* incestuous

inchan•gé -gée [ɛ̃ʃɑ̃ʒe] *adj* unchanged

incidemment [ɛ̃sidamɑ̃] *adv* incidentally

incidence [ɛ̃sidɑ̃s] *f* incidence

inci•dent -dente [ɛ̃sidɑ̃] **-dente** [dɑ̃t] *adj* & *m* incident

incinérer [ɛ̃sinere] §10 *tr* to incinerate; cremate

incirconcis [ɛ̃sirkɔ̃si] *adj masc* uncircumcised

inciser [ɛ̃size] *tr* to make an incision in; tap (*a tree*); (med) to lance

inci•sif -sive [ɛ̃sizif] **-sive** [ziv] *adj* incisive ‖ *f* incisor

incision [ɛ̃sizjɔ̃] *f* incision

incitation [ɛ̃sitɑsjɔ̃] *f* incitement

inciter [ɛ̃site] §96, §100 *tr* to incite

inci•vil -vile [ɛ̃sivil] *adj* uncivil

incivili•sé -sée [ɛ̃sivilize] *adj* uncivilized

inclassable [ɛ̃klɑsabl] *adj* unclassifiable

inclé•ment [ɛ̃klemɑ̃] **-mente** [mɑ̃t] *adj* inclement

inclinaison [ɛ̃klinɛzɔ̃] *f* inclination; slope

inclination [ɛ̃klinɑsjɔ̃] *f* inclination; bow; love, affection

incliner [ɛ̃kline] §96 *tr* & *ref* to incline; bend; bow; obey

inclure [ɛ̃klyr] §11 (*pp* **inclus**) *tr* to include; enclose

in•clus -cluse [ɛ̃kly] **-cluse** [klyz] *adj* including, e.g., **jusqu'à la page dix incluse** up to and including page ten; inclusive, e.g., **de mercredi à samedi inclus** from Wednesday to Saturday inclusive

inclu•sif -sive [ɛ̃klyzif] **-sive** [ziv] *adj* inclusive

inclusivement [ɛ̃klyzivmɑ̃] *adv* inclusively, inclusive

incognito [ɛ̃kɔɲito] *m* & *adv* incognito

incohé•rent [ɛ̃kɔerɑ̃] **-rente** [rɑ̃t] *adj* incoherent; inconsistent, illogical

incollable [ɛ̃kɔlabl] *adj* (coll) knowing all the answers, not to be stumped

incolore [ɛ̃kɔlɔr] *adj* colorless

incomber [ɛ̃kɔ̃be] *intr*—**incomber à** to devolve on, fall upon; **il incombe à qn de** it behooves s.o. to

incombustible [ɛ̃kɔ̃bystibl] *adj* incombustible; fireproof

incommode [ɛ̃kɔmɔd] *adj* inconvenient; unwieldy

incommoder [ɛ̃kɔmɔdite] *tr* to inconvenience

incommodité [ɛ̃kɔmɔdite] *f* inconvenience

incomparable [ɛ̃kɔ̃parabl] *adj* incomparable

incompatible [ɛ̃kɔ̃patibl] *adj* incompatible; conflicting

incompétence [ɛ̃kɔ̃petɑ̃s] *f* incompetence; lack of jurisdiction

incompé•tent [ɛ̃kɔ̃petɑ̃] **-tente** [tɑ̃t] *adj* incompetent; lacking jurisdiction

incom•plet [ɛ̃kɔ̃plɛ] **-plète** [plɛt] *adj* incomplete

incompréhensible [ɛ̃kɔ̃preɑsibl] *adj* incomprehensible

incom•pris -prise [kɔ̃pri] **-prise** [priz] *adj* misunderstood

inconcevable [ɛ̃kɔ̃svabl] *adj* inconceivable

inconciliable [ɛ̃kɔ̃siljabl] *adj* irreconcilable

incondition•nel -nelle [ɛ̃kɔ̃disjɔnɛl] *adj* unconditional

inconduite [ɛ̃kɔ̃dɥit] *f* misconduct

inconfort [ɛ̃kɔ̃fɔr] *m* discomfort

incon•gru -grue [ɛ̃kɔ̃gry] *adj* incongruous

incon•nu -nue [ɛ̃kɔny] *adj* unknown; **inconnu à cette adresse** address unknown ‖ *mf* unknown (*person*) ‖ *m* unknown (*what is not known*); (cadavre) John Doe (*unidentified dead body*) ‖ *f* (math) unknown; (cadavre) Jane Doe (*unidentified dead body*)

inconsciemment [ɛ̃kɔ̃sjamɑ̃] *adv* subconsciously; unconsciously

inconscience [ɛ̃kɔ̃sjɑ̃s] f unconsciousness; unawareness

incons•cient [ɛ̃kɔ̃sjɑ̃] **-ciente** [sjɑ̃t] adj unconscious, unaware, oblivious; thoughtless; subconscious ‖ mf dazed person ‖ m unconscious

inconséquence [ɛ̃kɔ̃sekɑ̃s] f inconsistency; thoughtlessness, inconsiderateness

inconsé•quent [ɛ̃kɔ̃sekɑ̃] **-quente** [kɑ̃t] adj inconsistent; thoughtless, inconsiderate

inconsidé•ré -rée [ɛ̃kɔ̃sidere] adj inconsiderate

inconsistance [ɛ̃kɔ̃sistɑ̃s] f inconsistency; flimsiness, instability

inconsis•tant [ɛ̃kɔ̃sistɑ̃] **-tante** [tɑ̃t] adj inconsistent; flimsy, unstable

inconsolable [ɛ̃kɔ̃sɔlabl] adj inconsolable

incons•tant [ɛ̃kɔ̃stɑ̃] **-tante** [tɑ̃t] adj inconstant

inconstitution•nel -nelle [ɛ̃kɔ̃stitysjɔnɛl] adj unconstitutional

incontestable [ɛ̃kɔ̃tɛstabl] adj incontestable, unquestionable, indisputable

inconti•nent [ɛ̃kɔ̃tinɑ̃] **-nente** [nɑ̃t] adj incontinent ‖ **incontinent** adv at once, forthwith

incontrôlable [ɛ̃kɔ̃trolabl] adj unverifiable

incontrô•lé -lée [ɛ̃kɔ̃trole] adj unverified; unchecked, uncontrollable

inconvenance [ɛ̃kɔ̃vnɑ̃s] f impropriety

inconve•nant [ɛ̃kɔ̃vnɑ̃] **-nante** [nɑ̃t] adj improper, indecent

inconvénient [ɛ̃kɔ̃venjɑ̃] m inconvenience, disadvantage; **voir un inconvénient à** to have an objection to

incorporation [ɛ̃kɔrpɔrɑsjɔ̃] f incorporation; (mil) induction

incorpo•ré -rée [ɛ̃kɔrpɔre] adj built-in

incorpo•rel -relle [ɛ̃kɔrpɔrɛl] adj incorporeal; intangible (property)

incorporer [ɛ̃kɔrpɔre] tr to incorporate; (mil) to induct ‖ ref to incorporate

incor•rect -recte [ɛ̃kɔrɛkt] adj incorrect; unfair; improper; discourteous; indecent

incorrectement [ɛ̃kɔrɛktəmɑ̃] adv incorrectly; improperly; discourteously; in an underhand way

incorrection [ɛ̃kɔrɛksjɔ̃] f impropriety; incorrectness; impolite behavior; dishonesty

incrédule [ɛ̃kredyl] adj incredulous; unbelieving ‖ mf unbeliever, freethinker

incrédulité [ɛ̃kredylite] f incredulity; disbelief

incrément [ɛ̃kremɑ̃] m (comp) increment

incrémenter [ɛ̃kremɑ̃te] tr (comp) to increment

increvable [ɛ̃krəvabl] adj punctureproof; (slang) untiring

incriminer [ɛ̃krimine] tr to incriminate

incrochetable [ɛ̃krɔʃtabl] adj burglarproof (lock)

incroyable [ɛ̃krwajabl] adj unbelievable

in•croyant [ɛ̃krwajɑ̃] **-croyante** [krwajɑ̃t] adj unbelieving ‖ mf unbeliever

incrustation [ɛ̃krystɑsjɔ̃] f incrustation; inlay; (sewing) insert

incruster [ɛ̃kryste] tr to incrust; inlay ‖ ref to take root, become ingrained

incubateur [ɛ̃kybatœr] m incubator

incuber [ɛ̃kybe] tr to incubate

inculpation [ɛ̃kylpɑsjɔ̃] f indictment; **sous l'inculpation de** on a charge of

incul•pé -pée [ɛ̃kylpe] adj indicted; **inculpé de** charged with, accused of ‖ mf accused, defendant

inculper [ɛ̃kylpe] tr to indict, charge

inculquer [ɛ̃kylke] tr to inculcate

inculte [ɛ̃kylt] adj uncultivated; uncouth

incunables [ɛ̃kynabl] mpl incunabula

incurable [ɛ̃kyrabl] adj & mf incurable

incurie [ɛ̃kyri] f carelessness

incursion [ɛ̃kyrsjɔ̃] f incursion, foray

Inde [ɛ̃d] f India; **Indes Occidentales** West Indies; **l'Inde** India

indébrouillable [ɛ̃debrujabl] adj inextricable, hopelessly involved

indécence [ɛ̃desɑ̃s] f indecency

indé•cent [ɛ̃desɑ̃] **-cente** [sɑ̃t] adj indecent

indéchiffrable [ɛ̃deʃifrabl] adj undecipherable; incomprehensible; illegible

indé•cis [ɛ̃desi] **-cise** [siz] adj indecisive; uncertain, undecided; blurred

indéclinable [ɛ̃deklinabl] adj indeclinable

indécrottable [ɛ̃dekrɔtabl] adj (coll) incorrigible, hopeless

indéfectible [ɛ̃defɛktibl] adj everlasting; unfailing

indéfendable [ɛ̃defɑ̃dabl] adj indefensible

indéfi•ni -nie [ɛ̃defini] adj indefinite

indéfinissable [ɛ̃definisabl] adj indefinable

indéfrisable [ɛ̃defrizabl] adj permanent (wave) ‖ f permanent wave

indélébile [ɛ̃delebil] adj indelible

indéli•cat [ɛ̃delika] **-cate** [kat] adj indelicate; dishonest

indémaillable [ɛ̃demajabl] adj runproof

indemne [ɛ̃dɛmn] adj undamaged, unharmed

indemnisation [ɛ̃dɛmnizɑsjɔ̃] f indemnification, compensation

indemniser [ɛ̃dɛmnize] tr to compensate

indemnité [ɛ̃dɛmnite] f indemnity; allowance, grant; compensation; **indemnité journalière** workmen's compensation; **indemnité parlementaire** salary of members (of parliamentary body); **indemnités** fringe benefits

indéniable [ɛ̃denjabl] adj undeniable

indépendamment [ɛ̃depɑ̃damɑ̃] adv independently; **indépendamment de** apart from; regardless of

indépendance [ɛ̃depɑ̃dɑ̃s] f independence

indépen•dant [ɛ̃depɑ̃dɑ̃] **-dante** [dɑ̃t] adj & mf independent

indéréglable [ɛ̃dereglabl] adj foolproof

indescriptible [ɛ̃dɛskriptibl] adj indescribable

indésirable [ɛ̃dezirabl] adj undesirable

indestructible [ɛ̃dɛstryktibl] adj indestructible

indétermi•né -née [ɛ̃detɛrmine] adj indeterminate

indétraquable [ɛ̃detrakabl] adj foolproof

index [ɛ̃dɛks] m index; forefinger; index number; **Index** (eccl) Index; **index de matières** subject index

indexa·teur [ɛ̃dɛksasjɔ̃] *f*—**indexation des traitements sur le coût de la vie** consumer price index, CPI

indica·teur [ɛ̃dikatœr] **-trice** [tris] *adj* indicating ‖ *mf* informer ‖ *m* gauge; indicator, pointer; timetable; indicator, pointer; road sign; guidebook; street guide

indica·tif [ɛ̃dikatif] **-tive** [tiv] *adj* indicative, suggestive | *m* (gram) indicative; (rad) station identification; **indicatif d'appel** (rad, telg) call letters or number; **indicatif postal** zip code

indication [ɛ̃dikɑsjɔ̃] *f* indication; **fausse indication** wrong piece of information; **indications** directions; **sauf indication contraire** unless otherwise directed; **sur l'indication de** at the suggestion of

indice [ɛ̃dis] *m* indication, sign; clue; **indice de pose** exposure index; **indice de refroidissement** chill factor; **indice des prix** price index; **indice des prix de consommation** consumer price index; **indice d'octane** octane number; **indice du coût de la vie** cost-of-living index

indicible [ɛ̃disibl] *adj* inexpressible

in·dien [ɛ̃djɛ̃] **-dienne** [djɛn] *adj* Indian ‖ *f* calico, chintz ‖ (*cap*) *mf* Indian

indifféremment [ɛ̃diferamɑ̃] *adv* indiscriminately

indiffé·rent [ɛ̃diferɑ̃] **-rente** [rɑ̃t] *adj* indifferent; unimportant; **cela m'est indifférent** it's all the same to me

indigence [ɛ̃diʒɑ̃s] *f* indigence, poverty

indigène [ɛ̃diʒɛn] *adj* indigenous, native ‖ *mf* native

indi·gent [ɛ̃diʒɑ̃] **-gente** [ʒɑ̃t] *adj* indigent ‖ *mf* pauper; **les indigents** the poor

indigeste [ɛ̃diʒɛst] *adj* indigestible; heavy, stodgy; undigested, mixed up

indigestion [ɛ̃diʒɛstjɔ̃] *f* indigestion

indignation [ɛ̃diɲɑsjɔ̃] *f* indignation

indigne [ɛ̃diɲ] *adj* unworthy; shameful

indi·gné -gnée [ɛ̃diɲe] *adj* indignant

indigner [ɛ̃diɲe] *tr* to outrage ‖ §97 *ref* to be indignant

indignité [ɛ̃diɲite] *f* unworthiness; indignity, outrage

indigo [ɛ̃digo] *adj invar & m* indigo

indi·qué -quée [ɛ̃dike] *adj* advisable, appropriate; **être tout indiqué pour** to be just the thing for; be just the man for

indiquer [ɛ̃dike] *tr* to indicate; name; **indiquer du doigt** to point to, point out

indi·rect -recte [ɛ̃dirɛkt] *adj* indirect

indisciplinable [ɛ̃disiplinabl] *adj* unruly

indiscipline [ɛ̃disiplin] *f* lack of discipline, disobedience

indiscipli·né -née [ɛ̃disipline] *adj* undisciplined

indis·cret [ɛ̃diskrɛ] **-crète** [krɛt] *adj* indiscreet

indiscrétion [ɛ̃diskresjɔ̃] *f* indiscretion; **sans indiscrétion ...** if I may ask ...

indiscutable [ɛ̃diskytabl] *adj* unquestionable

indiscu·té -tée [ɛ̃diskyte] *adj* unquestioned

indispensable [ɛ̃dispɑ̃sabl] *adj & m* indispensable, essential

indisponible [ɛ̃dispɔnibl] *adj* unavailable; out of commission (*said of car, machine, etc.*)

indispo·sé -sée [ɛ̃dispoze] *adj* indisposed (*slightly ill*); ill-disposed

indisposer [ɛ̃dispoze] *tr* to indispose

indissoluble [ɛ̃disɔlybl] *adj* indissoluble

indis·tinct [ɛ̃distɛ̃], [ɛ̃distɛ̃kt] **-tincte** [tɛ̃kt] *adj* indistinct

indistinctement [ɛ̃distɛ̃ktəmɑ̃] *adv* indistinctly; indiscriminately

individu [ɛ̃dividy] *m* individual; (coll) fellow, guy

individualiser [ɛ̃dividɥalize] *tr* to individualize

individualité [ɛ̃dividɥalite] *f* individuality

indivi·duel -duelle [ɛ̃dividɥɛl] *adj* individual; separate

indi·vis [ɛ̃divi] **-vise** [viz] *adj* joint; **par indivis** jointly

indivisible [ɛ̃divizibl] *adj* indivisible

Indochine [ɛ̃dɔʃin] *f* Indochina; **l'Indochine** Indochina

Indochi·nois [ɛ̃dɔʃinwa] **-noise** [nwaz] *adj & mf* Indo-Chinese

indocile [ɛ̃dɔsil] *adj* rebellious, unruly

indo-européen [ɛ̃dɔørɔpeɛ̃] **-européenne** [ørɔpeɛn] *adj* Indo-European ‖ *m* Indo-European (*language*) ‖ (*cap*) *mf* Indo-European

indolemment [ɛ̃dɔlamɑ̃] *adv* indolently

indo·lent [ɛ̃dɔlɑ̃] **-lente** [lɑ̃t] *adj* indolent; apathetic; painless (*e.g., tumor*) ‖ *mf* idler

indolore [ɛ̃dɔlɔr] *adj* painless

indomptable [ɛ̃dɔ̃tabl] *adj* indomitable

indomp·té -tée [ɛ̃dɔ̃te] *adj* untamed

Indonésie [ɛ̃dɔnezi] *f* Indonesia; **l'Indonésie** Indonesia

indoné·sien [ɛ̃dɔnezjɛ̃] **-sienne** [zjɛn] *adj* Indonesian ‖ *m* Indonesian (*language*) ‖ (*cap*) *mf* Indonesian (*person*)

in-douze [ɛ̃duz] *adj invar & m invar* duodecimo

in·du -due [ɛ̃dy] *adj* unseemly (*e.g., hour*); undue (*haste*); unwarranted (*remark*) ‖ *m* something not due

indubitable [ɛ̃dybitabl] *adj* indubitable; **c'est indubitable** there's no doubt about it

inducteur [ɛ̃dyktœr] *m* (elec) field

induction [ɛ̃dyksjɔ̃] *f* (elec, logic) induction

induire [ɛ̃dɥir] §19, §96 *tr* to induce; **induire en** to lead into (*temptation, error, etc.*)

in·duit -duite [ɛ̃dɥi] **-duite** [dɥit] *adj* induced ‖ *m* (elec) armature

indulgence [ɛ̃dylʒɑ̃s] *f* indulgence

indul·gent [ɛ̃dylʒɑ̃] **-gente** [ʒɑ̃t] *adj* indulgent

indûment [ɛ̃dymɑ̃] *adv* unduly

indurer [ɛ̃dyre] *tr & ref* to harden

industrialiser [ɛ̃dystrijalize] *tr* to industrialize ‖ *ref* to become industrialized

industrie [ɛ̃dystri] *f* industry; trickery; (obs) occupation, trade; **industrie du bâtiment** building industry, construction; **industrie en pleine expansion** growth industry; **l'industrie du spectacle** show business

industrie-clef [ɛ̃dystrikle] *f* (*pl* **industries-clefs**) key industry

indus•triel -trielle [ɛ̃dystrijɛl] *adj* industrial ‖ *m* industrialist

indus•trieux [ɛ̃dystrijø] **-trieuse** [trijøz] *adj* industrious; skilled

inébranlable [inebrɑ̃labl] *adj* unshakable

inéchangeable [ineʃɑ̃ʒabl] *adj* unexchangeable

iné•dit [inedi] **-dite** [dit] *adj* unpublished; new, novel

inéducable [inedykabl] *adj* unteachable

ineffable [inɛfabl] *adj* ineffable

ineffaçable [inɛfasabl] *adj* indelible

inefficace [inɛfikas] *adj* ineffective, inefficient

inefficacité [inefikasite] *f* ineffectiveness, inefficiency

iné•gal -gale [inegal] *adj* (*pl* **-gaux** [go]) unequal; uneven

inégalité [inegalite] *f* inequality; unevenness

inélégamment [inelegamɑ̃] *adv* inelegantly

inéligible [ineliʒibl] *adj* ineligible

inéluctable [inelyktabl] *adj* unavoidable

inem•ployé -ployée [inɑ̃plwaje] *adj* unused

inénarrable [inenarabl] *adj* beyond words, too funny for words

inepte [inɛpt] *adj* inept, inane

ineptie [inɛpsi] *f* ineptitude, inanity; inane remark

inépuisable [inepɥizabl] *adj* inexhaustible

inerme [inɛrm] *adj* thornless

inertie [inɛrsi] *f* inertia

inescomptable [inɛskɔ̃tabl] *adj* not subject to discount

inespé•ré -rée [inɛspere] *adj* unhoped-for, unexpected

inestimable [inɛstimabl] *adj* inestimable, invaluable, priceless

inévitable [inevitabl] *adj* inevitable

inexact inexacte [inɛgzakt] *adj* inexact, inaccurate; unpunctual

inexactitude [inɛgzaktityd] *f* inexactness, inaccuracy; unpunctuality

inexau•cé -cée [inɛgzose] *adj* unfulfilled, unanswered

inexcitable [inɛksitabl] *adj* unexcitable

inexcusable [inɛkskyzabl] *adj* inexcusable

inexécutable [inɛgzekytabl] *adj* impracticable

inexécution [inɛgzekysjɔ̃] *f* nonfulfillment

inexer•cé -cée [inɛgzɛrse] *adj* untried; untrained

inexhaustible [inɛgzostibl] *adj* inexhaustible

inexigible [inɛgziʒibl] *adj* uncollectable

inexis•tant [inɛksistɑ̃] **-tante** [tɑ̃t] *adj* nonexistent

inexorable [inɛgzɔrabl] *adj* inexorable

inexpérience [inɛksperjɑ̃s] *f* inexperience

inexpérimen•té -tée [inɛksperimɑ̃te] *adj* inexperienced; untried; unskilled

inex•pié -piée [inɛkspje] *adj* unexpiated

inexplicable [inɛksplikabl] *adj* inexplicable, unexplainable

inexpli•qué -quée [inɛksplike] *adj* unexplained

inexploi•té -tée [inɛksplwate] *adj* untapped

inexplo•ré -rée [inɛksplɔre] *adj* unexplored

inexpres•sif [inɛksprɛsif] **-sive** [siv] *adj* expressionless

inexprimable [inɛksprimabl] *adj* inexpressible

inexpri•mé -mée [inɛksprime] *adj* unexpressed

inexpugnable [inɛkspygnabl] *adj* impregnable

inextinguible [inɛkstɛ̃gibl], [inɛkstɛ̃gɥibl] *adj* inextinguishable; uncontrollable; unquenchable

infaillible [ɛ̃fajibl] *adj* infallible

infaisable [ɛ̃fəzabl] *adj* unfeasible

infa•mant [ɛ̃famɑ̃] **-mante** [mɑ̃t] *adj* opprobrious

infâme [ɛ̃fam] *adj* infamous; squalid

infamie [ɛ̃fami] *f* infamy; **dire des infamies à** to hurl insults at; **noter d'infamie** to brand as infamous

infant [ɛ̃fɑ̃] *m* infante

infante [ɛ̃fɑ̃t] *f* infanta

infanterie [ɛ̃fɑ̃tri] *f* infantry; **infanterie de l'air, infanterie aéroportée** parachute troops; **infanterie de marine** overseas troops; **infanterie portée, infanterie motorisée** motorized troops

infantile [ɛ̃fɑ̃til] *adj* infantile

infarctus [ɛ̃farktys] *m* (pathol) infarct, infarction; **infarctus du myocarde** coronary thrombosis

infatigable [ɛ̃fatigabl] *adj* indefatigable

infatuation [ɛ̃fatɥasjɔ̃] *f* conceit, false pride

infa•tué -tuée [ɛ̃fatɥe] *adj* infatuated with oneself, conceited

infé•cond [ɛ̃fekɔ̃] **-conde** [kɔ̃d] *adj* sterile, barren

in•fect -fecte [ɛ̃fɛkt] *adj* stinking; foul, vile

infecter [ɛ̃fɛkte] *tr* to infect; pollute; stink up

infec•tieux [ɛ̃fɛksjø] **-tieuse** [sjøz] *adj* infectious

infection [ɛ̃fɛksjɔ̃] *f* infection; stench

inférer [ɛ̃fere] §10 *tr* to infer, conclude

infé•rieur -rieure [ɛ̃ferjœr] *adj* lower; inferior; **inférieur à** below; less than ‖ *mf* subordinate, inferior

infériorité [ɛ̃ferjɔrite] *f* inferiority

infer•nal -nale [ɛ̃fɛrnal] *adj* (*pl* **-naux** [no]) infernal

infester [ɛ̃fɛste] *tr* to infest

infidèle [ɛ̃fidɛl] *adj* infidel; unfaithful ‖ *mf* infidel ‖ *m* unfaithful husband ‖ *f* unfaithful wife

infidélité [ɛ̃fidelite] *f* infidelity; inaccuracy, unfaithfulness

infiltration [ɛ̃filtrɑsjɔ̃] *f* infiltration

infiltrer [ɛ̃filtre] *ref* to infiltrate; seep, percolate; **s'infiltrer à travers** or **dans** to infiltrate

infime [ɛ̃fim] *adj* very small, infinitesimal; very low; trifling, negligible

infi•ni -nie [ɛ̃fini] *adj* infinite ‖ *m* infinite; (math) infinity; **à l'infini** infinitely

infiniment [ɛ̃finimɑ̃] *adv* infinitely; (coll) greatly, deeply, terribly

infinité [ɛ̃finite] *f* infinity

infini•tif [ɛ̃finitif] **-tive** [tiv] *adj* & *m* infinitive

infirme [ɛ̃firm] *adj* infirm, crippled, disabled ‖ *mf* invalid, cripple

infirmer [ɛ̃firme] *tr* (law) to invalidate

infirmerie [ɛ̃firməri] *f* infirmary; (nav) sick bay
infir·mier [ɛ̃firmje] **-mière** [mjɛr] *mf* nurse; **infirmière bénévole** volunteer nurse; **infirmière diplômée** registered nurse ‖ *m* male nurse; orderly, attendant
infirmière-major [ɛ̃firmjɛrmaʒɔr] *f* head nurse
infirmité [ɛ̃firmite] *f* infirmity
infixe [ɛ̃fiks] *m* infix
inflammable [ɛ̃flamabl] *adj* inflammable
inflammation [ɛ̃flamɑsjɔ̃] *f* inflammation
inflammatoire [ɛ̃flamatwar] *adj* inflammatory
inflation [ɛ̃flɑsjɔ̃] *f* inflation
inflationniste [ɛ̃flɑsjɔnist] *adj* inflationary
infléchir [ɛ̃fleʃir] *tr* to inflect, bend ‖ *ref* to bend, curve
inflexible [ɛ̃flɛksibl] *adj* inflexible
inflexion [ɛ̃flɛksjɔ̃] *f* inflection; change; bend, curve; metaphony
infliger [ɛ̃fliʒe] §38 *tr* to inflict; **infliger q.ch. à** to inflict s.th. on
influence [ɛ̃flyɑ̃s] *f* influence
influencer [ɛ̃flyɑ̃se] §51 *tr* to influence
in·fluent [ɛ̃flyɑ̃] **-fluente** [flyɑɑt] *adj* influential
influenza [ɛ̃flyɑ̃za] *f* influenza
influer [ɛ̃flye] *intr*—**influer sur** to influence
infographie [infografi] *f* (comp) graphing and imaging, mapmaking
in-folio [ɛ̃fɔljo] *adj & m* (*pl* **-folio** or **-folios**) folio
informa·teur [ɛ̃fɔrmatœr] **-trice** [tris] *mf* informant; informer
informati·cien [ɛ̃fɔmatisjɛ̃] **-cienne** [sjɛn] *mf* informant; computer specialist
information [ɛ̃fɔrmɑsjɔ̃] *f* information; piece of information; (law) investigation; **aller aux informations** to make inquiries: **information génétique** genetic characteristics; **informations** news; information; **information de presse** press reports
informatique [ɛ̃fɔrmatik] *adj* informational; computer ‖ *f* computer science, information science; data processing; information storage; **faire de l'informatique** to operate a computer
informatisation [ɛ̃fɔrmatizɑsjɔ̃] *f* computerization
informatiser [ɛ̃fɔrmatize] *tr* to computerize
informe [ɛ̃fɔrm] *adj* formless, shapeless
informer [ɛ̃fɔrme] *tr* to inform, advise ‖ *intr* —**informer contre** to inform on ‖ *ref* to inquire, keep oneself informed
inforoute [ɛ̃fɔrut] *f* (comp) information highway
infortune [ɛ̃fɔrtyn] *f* misfortune
infortu·né -née [ɛ̃fɔrtyne] *adj* unfortunate
infraction [ɛ̃frɑksjɔ̃] *f* infraction
infranchissable [ɛ̃frɑ̃ʃisabl] *adj* insuperable; impassable (*e.g., mountain*)
infrarouge [ɛ̃fraruʒ] *adj & m* infrared
infrason [ɛ̃frasɔ̃] *m* infrasonic vibration
infrastructure [ɛ̃frastryktyr] *f* infrastructure; (rr) roadbed

infroissable [ɛ̃frwasabl] *adj* creaseless, wrinkleproof
infruc·tueux [ɛ̃fryktɥø] **-tueuse** [tɥøz] *adj* unfruitful, fruitless
in·fus [ɛ̃fy] **-fuse** [fyz] *adj* inborn, innate, intuitive
infuser [ɛ̃fyze] *tr* to infuse; brew; **infuser un sang nouveau à** to put new blood or life into ‖ *intr* to steep
infusion [ɛ̃fyzjɔ̃] *f* steeping; brew
ingambe [ɛ̃gɑ̃b] *adj* spry, nimble, alert
ingénier [ɛ̃ʒenje] §96 *ref* to strive hard
ingénierie [ɛ̃ʒeniri] or **ingéniérie** [ɛ̃ʒenjeri] *f* engineering
ingénieur [ɛ̃ʒenjœr] *m* engineer; **ingénieur chimique** chemical engineer; **ingénieur des ponts et chaussées** civil engineer; **ingénieur système** (comp) computer engineer
ingé·nieux [ɛ̃ʒenjø] **-nieuse** [njøz] *adj* ingenious
ingéniosité [ɛ̃ʒenjozite] *f* ingenuity
ingé·nu -nue [ɛ̃ʒeny] *adj* ingenuous, artless ‖ *mf* naïve person ‖ *f* ingénue
ingénuité [ɛ̃ʒenɥite] *f* ingenuousness
ingérer [ɛ̃ʒere] §10 *tr* to ingest ‖ §97 *ref* to meddle
ingouvernable [ɛ̃guvɛrnabl] *adj* unruly, unmanageable
in·grat [ɛ̃gra] **-grate** [grat] *adj* ungrateful; disagreeable; thankless (*task*); unprofitable (*work*); barren (*soil*); awkward (*age*) ‖ *mf* ingrate
ingratitude [ɛ̃gratityd] *f* ingratitude
ingrédient [ɛ̃gredjɑ̃] *m* ingredient
inguérissable [ɛ̃gerisabl] *adj & mf* incurable
ingurgiter [ɛ̃gyrʒite] *tr* to swallow; gulp down
inhabile [inabil] *adj* unfitted, unqualified; incompetent; clumsy; incapable, inefficient
inhabileté [inabilte] *f* unfitness, inability; incompetence; clumsiness; lack of skill; (law) incompetency, legal incapacity
inhabitable [inabitabl] *adj* uninhabitable
inhabi·té -tée [inabite] *adj* uninhabited
inhabi·tuel -tuelle [inabitɥel] *adj* unusual
inhaler [inale] *tr & intr* to inhale, breathe in
inhé·rent [inerɑ̃] **-rente** [rɑ̃t] *adj* inherent
inhiber [inibe] *tr* to inhibit
inhibition [inibisjɔ̃] *f* inhibition
inhospita·lier [inɔspitalje] **-lière** [ljɛr] *adj* inhospitable
inhu·main [inymɛ̃] **-maine** [mɛn] *adj* inhuman
inhumanité [inymanite] *f* inhumanity
inhumation [inymɑsjɔ̃] *f* burial
inhumer [inyme] *tr* to bury, inter
inimitable [inimitabl] *adj* inimitable
inimitié [inimitje] *f* enmity
ininflammable [inɛ̃flamabl] *adj* nonflammable, non-inflammable
inintelli·gent [inɛ̃tɛliʒɑ̃] **-gente** [ʒɑ̃t] *adj* unintelligent
inintéres·sant [inɛ̃terɛsɑ̃] **-sante** [sɑ̃t] *adj* uninteresting
ininterrom·pu -pue [inɛ̃terɔ̃py] *adj* uninterrupted

inique [inik] *adj* iniquitous, unjust, unfair

iniquité [inikite] *f* iniquity; unjustness, unfairness

ini·tial -tiale [inisjal] (*pl* **-tiaux** [sjo] **-tiales**) *adj* & *f* initial

initia·teur [inisjatœr] **-trice** [tris] *adj* initiating || *mf* initiator

initiation [inisjɑsjɔ̃] *f* initiation

initiative [inisjativ] *f* initiative

initier [inisje] *tr* to initiate; introduce || *ref* to become initiated

injecter [ɛ̃ʒɛkte] *tr* to inject; impregnate || *ref* to become bloodshot

injec·teur [ɛ̃ʒɛktœr] **-trice** [tris] *adj* injecting || *m* injector; nozzle (*in motor*)

injection [ɛ̃ʒɛksjɔ̃] *f* injection; impregnation; redness (*of eyes*); (geog) intrusion; **injection de rappel** booster shot; **injection dans l'économie** pump-priming; **injection intraveineuse** intravenous injection (IV)

injonction [ɛ̃ʒɔ̃ksjɔ̃] *f* injunction, order

injouable [ɛ̃ʒwabl] *adj* unplayable

injure [ɛ̃ʒyr] *f* insult; wrong; **l'injure des ans** the ravages of time

injurier [ɛ̃ʒyrje] *tr* to insult, abuse

inju·rieux [ɛ̃ʒyrijø] **-rieuse** [rjøz] *adj* insulting, abusive; harmful, offensive

injuste [ɛ̃ʒyst] *adj* unjust

injustice [ɛ̃ʒystis] *f* injustice

injusti·fié -fiée [ɛ̃ʒystifje] *adj* unjustified

inlassable [ɛ̃lɑsabl] *adj* untiring

in·né -née [inne] *adj* innate, inborn

innocemment [inɔsamɑ̃] *adv* innocently

innocence [inɔsɑ̃s] *f* innocence

inno·cent [inɔsɑ̃] **-cente** [sɑ̃t] *adj* & *mf* innocent

innocenter [inɔsɑ̃te] *tr* to exonerate

innocuité [inɔkɥite] *f* innocuousness

innombrable [inɔ̃brabl] *adj* innumerable

innova·teur [inɔvatœr] **-trice** [tris] *adj* innovating || *mf* innovator

innovation [inɔvɑsjɔ̃] *f* innovation

innover [inɔve] *tr* & *intr* to innovate

innocu·pé -pée [inɔkype] *adj* unoccupied; unemployed, idle || *mf* idler

in-octavo [inɔktavo] *adj* & *m* (*pl* **-octavo** or **-octavos**) octavo

inoculation [inɔkylɑsjɔ̃] *f* inoculation

inoculer [inɔkyle] *tr* to inoculate

inodore [inɔdɔr] *adj* odorless

inoffen·sif [inɔfɑ̃sif] **-sive** [siv] *adj* inoffensive

inondation [inɔ̃dɑsjɔ̃] *f* flood

inonder [inɔ̃de] *tr* to flood

inopi·né -née [inɔpine] *adj* unexpected

inoppor·tun [inɔpɔrtœ̃] **-tune** [tyn] *adj* untimely, inconvenient

inopportunité [inɔpɔrtynite] *f* untimeliness

inorganique [inɔrganik] *adj* inorganic

inorgani·sé -sée [inɔrganize] *adj* unorganized (*workers*), nonunion

inoubliable [inublijabl] *adj* unforgettable

inouï inouïe [inwi] *adj* unheard-of

inoxydable [inɔksidabl] *adj* inoxidizable, stainless, rustproof

inqualifiable [ɛ̃kalifjabl] *adj* unspeakable

in·quiet [ɛ̃kjɛ] **-quiète** [kjɛt] *adj* anxious, worried, uneasy; restless

inquié·tant [ɛ̃kjetɑ̃] **-tante** [tɑ̃t] *adj* disquieting, worrisome

inquiéter [ɛ̃kjete] §10 *tr* & *intr* to worry

inquiétude [ɛ̃kjetyd] *f* uneasiness, worry

inquisi·teur [ɛ̃kizitœr] **-trice** [tris] *adj* inquisitorial; searching (*e.g., look*) || *m* inquisitor; investigator

inquisition [ɛ̃kizisjɔ̃] *f* inquisition; investigation

inracontable [ɛ̃rakɔ̃tabl] *adj* untellable

insaisissable [ɛ̃sezisabl] *adj* hard to catch; elusive

insalubre [ɛ̃salybr] *adj* unhealthy

insane [ɛ̃san] *adj* insane, crazy

insanité [ɛ̃sanite] *f* insanity; piece of folly

insatiable [ɛ̃sasjabl] *adj* insatiable

insatisfaction [ɛ̃satisfaksjɔ̃] *f* dissatisfaction

inscription [ɛ̃skripsjɔ̃] *f* inscription; registration, enrollment; **inscription de** or **en faux** (law) plea of forgery; **prendre ses inscriptions** to register at a university

inscrire [ɛ̃skrir] §25 *tr* to inscribe; register; record || *ref* to register, enroll; **s'inscrire à** to join; **s'inscrire en faux contre** to deny; **s'inscrire pour** to sign up for

ins·crit [ɛ̃skri] **-crite** [krit] *adj* inscribed; registered, enrolled || *mf* registered student; (sports) entry; **inscrit maritime** naval recruit

insecte [ɛ̃sɛkt] *m* insect, bug

insecticide [ɛ̃sɛktisid] *adj* insecticidal || *m* insecticide

insen·sé -sée [ɛ̃sɑ̃se] *adj* senseless, insane, crazy || *m* madman || *f* madwoman

insensible [ɛ̃sɑ̃sibl] *adj* insensitive; imperceptible

inséparable [ɛ̃separabl] *adj* inseparable || *m* lovebird

insérer [ɛ̃sere] §10 *tr* to insert

insertion [ɛ̃sɛrsjɔ̃] *f* insertion

insi·dieux [ɛ̃sidjø] **-dieuse** [djøz] *adj* insidious

insigne [ɛ̃siɲ] *adj* signal, noteworthy; notorious || *m* badge, mark; **insigne d'identité** name tag; **insignes** insignia

insigni·fiant [ɛ̃siɲifjɑ̃] **-fiante** [fjɑ̃t] *adj* insignificant

insincère [ɛ̃sɛ̃sɛr] *adj* insincere

insinuation [ɛ̃sinɥɑsjɔ̃] *f* insinuation

insinuer [ɛ̃sinɥe] *tr* to insinuate; hint, hint at; work in, introduce || *ref*—**s'insinuer dans** to worm one's way into

insipide [ɛ̃sipid] *adj* insipid, tasteless; insipid, dull

insister [ɛ̃siste] *intr* to insist; (coll) to continue, persevere; **insister pour** to insist on; **insister sur** to stress, emphasize

insociable [ɛ̃sɔsjabl] *adj* unsociable

insolateur [ɛ̃sɔlatœr] *m* solar heater

insolation [ɛ̃sɔlɑsjɔ̃] *f* exposure to the sun; sunstroke

insolence [ɛ̃sɔlɑ̃s] *f* insolence

inso•lent [ɛ̃sɔlɑ̃] **-lente** [lɑ̃t] *adj* insolent; extraordinary, unexpected

insolite [ɛ̃sɔlit] *adj* bizarre

insoluble [ɛ̃sɔlybl] *adj* insoluble

insolvabilité [ɛ̃sɔlvabilité] *f* insolvency

insolvable [ɛ̃sɔlvabl] *adj* insolvent

insomnie [ɛ̃sɔmni] *f* insomnia

insondable [ɛ̃sɔ̃dabl] *adj* unfathomable

insonore [ɛ̃sɔnɔr] *adj* soundproof; noiseless

insonorisation [ɛ̃sɔnɔrisasjɔ̃] *f* soundproofing

insonoriser [ɛ̃sɔnɔrize] *tr* to soundproof

insouciance [ɛ̃susjɑ̃s] *f* carefreeness; indifference, carelessness

insou•ciant [ɛ̃susjɑ̃] **-ciante** [sjɑ̃t] *adj* carefree, unconcerned

insou•cieux [ɛ̃susjø] **-cieuse** [sjøz] *adj* carefree, unmindful

insou•mis [ɛ̃sumis] **-mise** [miz] *adj* unruly; unsubjugated ‖ *mf* rebel ‖ *m* (mil) A.W.O.L.

insoumission [ɛ̃sumisjɔ̃] *f* insubordination, rebellion; (mil) absence without leave

insoupçonnable [ɛ̃supsɔnabl] *adj* above suspicion

insoupçon•né -née [ɛ̃supsɔne] *adj* unsuspected

insoutenable [ɛ̃sutnabl] *adj* untenable; unbearable

inspecter [ɛ̃spɛkte] *tr* to inspect

inspec•teur [ɛ̃spɛktœr] **-trice** [tris] *mf* inspector

inspection [ɛ̃spɛksjɔ̃] *f* inspection; inspectorship

inspiration [ɛ̃spirasjɔ̃] *f* inspiration

inspirer [ɛ̃spire] §97, §98 *tr* to inspire; breathe in; **inspirer à qn de** to inspire s.o. to; **inspirer q.ch. à qn** to inspire s.o. with s.th. ‖ *ref*—**s'inspirer de** to be inspired by

instable [ɛ̃stabl] *adj* unstable

installa•teur [ɛ̃stalatœr] **-trice** [tris] *mf* installer ‖ *m* heater man; fitter, plumber; (comp) installer

installation [ɛ̃stalasjɔ̃] *f* installation; equipment, outfit; appointments, fittings; **installation d'évacuation des vidanges** sewage disposal plant

installer [ɛ̃stale] *tr* to install; equip, furnish; **être bien installé** to be comfortably settled ‖ *ref* to settle down, set up shop; **s'installer chez** to foist oneself on

instamment [ɛ̃stamɑ̃] *adv* urgently, earnestly

instance [ɛ̃stɑ̃s] *f* insistence; **avec instance** earnestly; **en instance** pending; **en instance de** on the point of; **en seconde instance** on appeal; **instances** entreaties; **introduire une instance** to start proceedings

ins•tant [ɛ̃stɑ̃] **-tante** [tɑ̃t] *adj* urgent, pressing ‖ *m* instant, moment, **à chaque instant, à tout instant** continually; **à l'instant** at once, right away; just now; at the moment; **par instants** from time to time

instanta•né -née [ɛ̃stɑ̃tane] *adj* instantaneous ‖ *m* snapshot

instantanément [ɛ̃stɑ̃tanemɑ̃] *adv* instantaneously; instantly

instar [ɛ̃star]—**à l'instar de** in the manner of

instauration [ɛ̃stɔrasjɔ̃] *f* establishment

instaurer [ɛ̃stɔre] *tr* to establish

instigation [ɛ̃stigasjɔ̃] *f* instigation

instiller [ɛ̃stile] *tr* to instill

instinct [ɛ̃stɛ̃] *m* instinct; **d'instinct, par instinct** by instinct

instinc•tif [ɛ̃stɛ̃ktif] **-tive** [tiv] *adj* instinctive

instituer [ɛ̃stitɥe] *tr* to found; institute (*e.g., proceedings*)

institut [ɛ̃stity] *m* institute; **institut de beauté** beauty parlor; **institut de coupe** tonsorial parlor; **institut dentaire** dental school

institu•teur [ɛ̃stitytœr] **-trice** [tris] *mf* schoolteacher; founder

institution [ɛ̃stitysjɔ̃] *f* institution

instructeur [ɛ̃stryktœr] *m* instructor

instruc•tif [ɛ̃stryktif] **-tive** [tiv] *adj* instructive

instruction [ɛ̃stryksjɔ̃] *f* instruction; directive; education; (comp) statement; **instruction judiciaire** (law) preliminary investigation; **instruction phonique** phonics; **instructions** directions (*for use*); **instructions permanentes** standing orders

instruire [ɛ̃strɥir] §19, §96 *tr* to instruct; (law) to conduct the investigation of; **instruire qn de** to inform s.o. of ‖ *ref* to improve one's mind

instrument [ɛ̃strymɑ̃] *m* instrument; **instrument à anche** reed instrument; **instrument à cordes** stringed instrument; **instrument à vent** wind instrument; **instrument en bois** woodwind; **instrument en cuivre** brass

instrumen•tal -tale [ɛ̃strymɑ̃tal] *adj* (*pl* -**taux** [to]) instrumental

instrumenter [ɛ̃strymɑ̃te] *tr* to instrument

instrumentiste [ɛ̃strymɑ̃tist] *mf* instrumentalist

insu [ɛ̃sy] *m*—**à l'insu de** unknown to; **à mon insu** unknown to me

insubmersible [ɛ̃sybmɛrsibl] *adj* unsinkable

insubordon•né -née [ɛ̃sybɔrdɔne] *adj* insubordinate

insuccès [ɛ̃syksɛ] *m* failure

insuffisamment [ɛ̃syfizamɑ̃] *adv* insufficiently

insuffi•sant [ɛ̃syfizɑ̃] **-sante** [zɑ̃t] *adj* insufficient

insulaire [ɛ̃sylɛr] *adj* insular ‖ *mf* islander

insuline [ɛ̃sylin] *f* insulin

insulte [ɛ̃sylt] *f* insult

insulter [ɛ̃sylte] *tr* to insult ‖ *intr*—**insulter à** to offend, outrage

insupportable [ɛ̃sypɔrtabl] *adj* unbearable

insur•gé -gée [ɛ̃syrʒe] *adj* & *mf* insurgent

insurger [ɛ̃syrʒe] §38 *ref* to revolt, rebel

insurmontable [ɛ̃syrmɔ̃tabl] *adj* insurmountable

insurrection [ɛ̃syrɛksjɔ̃] *f* insurrection

in•tact -tacte [ɛ̃takt] *adj* intact, untouched

intangible [ɛ̃tɑ̃ʒibl] *adj* intangible

intarissable [ɛ̃tarisabl] *adj* inexhaustible

inté•gral -grale [ɛ̃tegral] *adj* (*pl* -**graux** [gro]) integral; complete (*e.g., edition*); full (*e.g., payment*) ‖ *f* complete works; (math) integral

inté•grant [ɛ̃tegrɑ̃] **-grante** [grɑ̃t] *adj* integral

intégration [ɛ̃tegrɑsjɔ̃] f integration
intègre [ɛ̃tɛgr] adj honest, upright
intégrer [ɛ̃tegre] §10 tr to integrate ‖ ref to form an integral part; (slang) to be accepted (at an exclusive school)
intégrité [ɛ̃tegrite] f integrity
intellect [ɛ̃telɛkt] m intellect
intellec•tuel -tuelle [ɛ̃telɛktɥɛl] adj & mf intellectual
intelligemment [ɛ̃teliʒamɑ̃] adv intelligently
intelligence [ɛ̃teliʒɑ̃s] f intelligence; intellect (person); en bonne intelligence avec on good terms with; être d'intelligence to be in collusion; intelligence artificielle artificial intelligence
intelli•gent [ɛ̃teliʒɑ̃] -gente [ʒɑ̃t] adj intelligent
intelligentsia [ɛ̃teliʒɛ̃sja] f intelligentsia
intelligible [ɛ̃teliʒibl] adj intelligible
intempé•rant [ɛ̃tɑ̃perɑ̃] -rante [rɑ̃t] adj intemperate
intempéries [ɛ̃tɑ̃peri] fpl bad weather
intempes•tif [ɛ̃tɑ̃pɛstif] -tive [tiv] adj untimely
intenable [ɛ̃tnabl] adj untenable
intendance [ɛ̃tɑ̃dɑ̃s] f stewardship; controllership, office of bursar; Intendance (mil) Quartermaster Corps
inten•dant [ɛ̃tɑ̃dɑ̃] -dante [dɑ̃t] mf steward, superintendent; controller, bursar; intendant militaire quartermaster
intense [ɛ̃tɑ̃s] adj intense
inten•sif [ɛ̃tɑ̃sif] -sive [siv] adj intensive
intensifier [ɛ̃tɑ̃sifje] tr & ref to intensify
intensité [ɛ̃tɑ̃site] f intensity
intenter [ɛ̃tɑ̃te] tr to start (a suit); bring (an action)
intention [ɛ̃tɑ̃sjɔ̃] f intention, intent; à l'intention de for (the sake of)
intention•né -née [ɛ̃tɑ̃sjɔne] adj motivated; bien intentionné well-meaning; mal intentionné ill-disposed
intention•nel -nelle [ɛ̃tɑ̃sjɔnɛl] adj intentional
inter [ɛ̃tɛr] m (coll) long distance
interac•tif [ɛ̃tɛraktif] -tive [tiv] adj (comp) interactive
interaction [ɛ̃tɛraksjɔ̃] f interaction, interplay
intercaler [ɛ̃tɛrkale] tr to intercalate; insert, sandwich
intercéder [ɛ̃tɛrsede] §10 intr to intercede
intercepter [ɛ̃tɛrsɛpte] tr to intercept
intercepteur [ɛ̃tɛrsɛptœr] m interceptor
interchangeable [ɛ̃tɛrʃɑ̃ʒabl] adj interchangeable
interclasse [ɛ̃tɛrklɑs] m (educ) break between classes
intercontinen•tal -tale [ɛ̃tɛrkɔ̃tinɑ̃tal] (pl -taux [to]) adj intercontinental
intercourse [ɛ̃tɛrkurs] f (naut) free entry
interdépen•dant [ɛ̃tɛrdepɑ̃dɑ̃] -dante [dɑ̃t] adj interdependent
interdiction [ɛ̃tɛrdiksjɔ̃] f interdiction; suspension; interdiction de séjour forbidden entry
interdire [ɛ̃tɛrdir] §40, §97, §98 tr to prohibit,

forbid; confound, abash; interdict; suspend; interdire q.ch. à qn to forbid s.o. s.th.
interdisciplinaire [ɛ̃tɛrdisipliner] adj interdisciplinary
inter•dit [ɛ̃tɛrdi] -dite [dit] adj prohibited, forbidden; dumfounded, abashed; deprived of rights; (mil) off limits ‖ m interdict
intéres•sant [ɛ̃terɛsɑ̃] -sante [sɑ̃t] adj interesting; attractive (offer)
intéres•sé -sée [ɛ̃terese] adj interested; self-seeking ‖ mf interested party
intéresser [ɛ̃terese] tr to interest; involve ‖ §96 ref—s'intéresser à or dans to be interested in
intérêt [ɛ̃terɛ] m interest; intérêts composés compound interest
interface [ɛ̃tɛrfas] f (comp) interface
interférence [ɛ̃tɛrferɑ̃s] f interference
interférer [ɛ̃tɛrfere] §10 intr (phys) to interfere ‖ ref to interfere with each other
inté•rieur -rieure [ɛ̃terjœr] adj interior; inner, inside ‖ m interior; inside; house, home; à l'intérieur (de) inside
intérieurement [ɛ̃terjœrmɑ̃] adv inwardly, internally; to oneself
intérim [ɛ̃terim] m invar interim; dans l'intérim in the meantime; par intérim acting, pro tem, interim
intérimaire [ɛ̃terimer] adj temporary, acting
interjection [ɛ̃tɛrʒɛksjɔ̃] f interjection
interligne [ɛ̃tɛrliɲ] m space between the lines; writing in the space between the lines; à double interligne double-spaced; à simple interligne single-spaced ‖ f lead
interligner [ɛ̃tɛrliɲe] tr to interline; (typ) to lead out
interlocu•teur [ɛ̃tɛrlɔkytœr] -trice [tris] mf interlocutor; intermediary; party (with whom one is conversing)
interlope [ɛ̃tɛrlɔp] adj illegal, shady ‖ m (naut) smuggling vessel
interloquer [ɛ̃tɛrlɔke] tr to disconcert
interlude [ɛ̃tɛrlyd] m interlude
intermède [ɛ̃tɛrmɛd] m (theat & fig) interlude
intermédiaire [ɛ̃tɛrmedjer] adj intermediate, intermediary ‖ mf intermediary ‖ m (com) middleman; par l'intermédiaire de by means of, by the medium of
interminable [ɛ̃tɛrminabl] adj interminable
intermit•tent [ɛ̃tɛrmitɑ̃] -tente [tɑ̃t] adj intermittent
internat [ɛ̃tɛrna] m boarding school; boarding-school life; (med) internship
internatio•nal -nale [ɛ̃tɛrnasjɔnal] adj (pl -naux [no]) international
internaute [ɛ̃tɛrnot] mf (comp) Internet user
internautique [ɛ̃tɛrnotik] adj (comp) Internet
interne [ɛ̃tɛrn] adj inner; (math) interior ‖ mf boarder (at a school); (med) intern
inter•né -née [ɛ̃tɛrne] mf internee
internement [ɛ̃tɛrnəmɑ̃] m internment; confinement (of a mental patient)
interner [ɛ̃tɛrne] tr to intern

Internet *or* **internet** [ɛ̃tɛrnɛt] *m* (comp) Internet; **à Internet** *or* **à l'Internet** online; **se connecter à Internet** to go online; **surfer sur Internet** to surf the Internet
interpeller [ɛ̃tɛrpele] *tr* to question, interrogate; yell at; heckle
interphone [ɛ̃tɛrfɔn] *m* intercom
interplanétaire [ɛ̃tɛrplanetɛr] *adj* interplanetary
interpoler [ɛ̃tɛrpɔle] *tr* to interpolate
interposer [ɛ̃tɛrpoze] *tr* to interpose
interprétation [ɛ̃tɛrpretɑsjɔ̃] *f* interpretation
interprète [ɛ̃tɛrprɛt] *mf* interpreter; spokesperson; intermediary, go-between, agent, helper; (theat) performer; **les interprètes** (theat) the cast
interpréter [ɛ̃tɛrprete] §10 *tr* to interpret; **mal interpréter** to misinterpret
interra·cial -ciale [ɛ̃tɛrrasjal] *adj* interracial
interrogation [ɛ̃tɛrɔgɑsjɔ̃] *f* interrogation
interroger [ɛ̃tɛrɔʒe] §38 *tr* to interrogate, question
interrompre [ɛ̃tɛrɔ̃pr] (3d *sg pres ind* **interrompt** [ɛ̃tɛrɔ̃]) *tr* to interrupt; heckle ‖ §97 *ref* to break off, be interrupted
interrup·teur [ɛ̃tɛryptœr] **-trice** [tris] *adj* interrupting; circuit-breaking ‖ *m* switch; contact breaker, circuit breaker; **interrupteur à couteau** knife switch; **interrupteur à culbuteur** *or* **à bascule** toggle switch; **interrupteur d'escalier** two-way switch; **interrupteur encastré** flush switch; **interrupteur olive** pear switch
interruption [ɛ̃tɛrypsjɔ̃] *f* interruption
intersection [ɛ̃tɛrsɛksjɔ̃] *f* intersection
intersigne [ɛ̃tɛrsiɲ] *m* omen, portent
interstellaire [ɛ̃tɛrstelɛr] *adj* interstellar
interstice [ɛ̃tɛrstis] *m* interstice
interur·bain [ɛ̃tɛryrbɛ̃] **-baine** [bɛn] *adj* interurban, intercity; (telp) long-distance ‖ *m* (telp) long distance
intervalle [ɛ̃tɛrval] *m* interval
intervenir [ɛ̃tɛrvnir] §72 (*aux:* ÉTRE) *intr* to intervene; take place, happen; (med) to operate; **faire intervenir** to call in
intervention [ɛ̃tɛrvɑ̃sjɔ̃] *f* intervention; (med) operation; **intervention de changement de sexe** sex change operation
intervertir [ɛ̃tɛrvɛrtir] *tr* to invert, transpose
interview [ɛ̃tɛrvju] *f* (jour) interview
interviewer [ɛ̃tɛrvjuvœr] *m* interviewer ‖ [ɛ̃tɛrvjuve] *tr* to interview
intervox [ɛ̃tɛrvɔks] *m* intercom
intestat [ɛ̃tɛsta] *adj* & *mf invar* intestate
intes·tin [ɛ̃tɛstɛ̃] **-tine** [tin] *adj* intestine, internal ‖ *m* intestine; **gros intestin** large intestine; **intestin grêle** small intestine
intimation [ɛ̃timɑsjɔ̃] *f* (law) summons
intime [ɛ̃tim] *adj* & *mf* intimate
inti·mé -mée [ɛ̃time] *mf* (law) defendant
intimer [ɛ̃time] *tr* to notify; give (*an order*)
intimider [ɛ̃timide] *tr* to intimidate

intimité [ɛ̃timite] *f* intimacy; privacy; depths (*of one's being*)
intituler [ɛ̃tityle] *tr* to entitle
intolérable [ɛ̃tɔlerabl] *adj* intolerable
intolé·rant [ɛ̃tɔlerɑ̃] **-rante** [rɑ̃t] *adj* intolerant
intonation [ɛ̃tɔnɑsjɔ̃] *f* intonation
intouchable [ɛ̃tuʃabl] *adj* & *mf* untouchable
intoxication [ɛ̃tɔksikasjɔ̃] *f* poisoning; **intoxication alimentaire** food poisoning
intoxiquer [ɛ̃tɔksike] *tr* to poison
intraduisible [ɛ̃tradɥizibl] *adj* untranslatable
intraitable [ɛ̃trɛtabl] *adj* intractable
Intranet *or* **intranet** [ɛ̃tranɛt] *m* (comp) Intranet
intransi·geant [ɛ̃trɑ̃ziʒɑ̃] **-geante** [ʒɑ̃t] *adj* intransigent ‖ *mf* diehard, standpatter
intransi·tif [ɛ̃trɑ̃zitif] **-tive** [tiv] *adj* intransitive
intrant [ɛ̃trɑ̃] *m* input
intravei·neux [ɛ̃travɛnø] **-neuse** [nøz] *adj* intravenous
intrépide [ɛ̃trepid] *adj* intrepid; persistent
intri·gant [ɛ̃trigɑ̃] **-gante** [gɑ̃t] *adj* intriguing ‖ *mf* plotter, schemer
intrigue [ɛ̃trig] *f* intrigue, plot; love affair; **intrigues de couloir** lobbying
intriguer [ɛ̃trige] *tr* & *intr* to intrigue
intrinsèque [ɛ̃trɛ̃sɛk] *adj* intrinsic
introduction [ɛ̃trɔdyksjɔ̃] *f* introduction; admission
introduire [ɛ̃trɔdɥir] §19 *tr* to introduce, bring in; show in; interject (*e.g., a remark*); insert (*a coin*) ‖ *ref* to be introduced; **s'introduire dans** to slip in
intronisation [ɛ̃trɔnizasjɔ̃] *f* investiture, inauguration
introniser [ɛ̃trɔnize] *tr* to enthrone
introspec·tif [ɛ̃trɔspɛktif] **-tive** [tiv] *adj* introspective
introuvable [ɛ̃truvabl] *adj* unfindable
introver·ti -tie [ɛ̃trɔvɛrti] *adj* & *mf* introvert
in·trus [ɛ̃try] **-truse** [tryz] *adj* intruding ‖ *mf* intruder
intrusion [ɛ̃tryzjɔ̃] *f* intrusion
intuition [ɛ̃tɥisjɔ̃] *f* intuition
inusable [inyzabl] *adj* durable, wearproof
inusi·té -tée [inyzite] *adj* obsolete
inutile [inytil] *adj* useless, unnecessary
inutilement [inytilmɑ̃] *adv* in vain, uselessly; unnecessarily
inutilité [inytilite] *f* uselessness
invain·cu -cue [ɛ̃vɛ̃ky] *adj* unconquered
invalide [ɛ̃valid] *adj* invalid ‖ *mf* invalid, cripple; **invalide de guerre** disabled veteran
invalider [ɛ̃valide] *tr* to invalidate
invalidité [ɛ̃validite] *f* invalidity; disability
invariable [ɛ̃variabl] *adj* invariable
invasion [ɛ̃vɑzjɔ̃] *f* invasion
invective [ɛ̃vɛktiv] *f* invective
invectiver [ɛ̃vɛktive] *tr* to rail at ‖ *intr* to inveigh
invendable [ɛ̃vɑ̃dabl] *adj* unsalable
inven·du -due [ɛ̃vɑ̃dy] *adj* unsold ‖ *m*—**les invendus** the unsold copies; the unsold articles
inventaire [ɛ̃vɑ̃tɛr] *m* inventory

inventer [ɛ̃vɑ̃te] *tr* to invent
inven‧teur [ɛ̃vɑ̃tœr] **-trice** [tris] *mf* inventor; (law) finder
inven‧tif [ɛ̃vɑ̃tif] **-tive** [tiv] *adj* inventive
invention [ɛ̃vɑ̃sjɔ̃] *f* invention
inventorier [ɛ̃vɑ̃tɔrje] *tr* to inventory
inversable [ɛ̃vɛrsabl] *adj* untippable, uncapsizable
inverse [ɛ̃vɛrs] *adj* opposite, inverse ‖ *m* opposite, reverse, converse; (math) inverse (*function*), reciprocal (*function*); **faire l'inverse de** to do the opposite of
inverser [ɛ̃vɛrse] *tr* to invert, reverse ‖ *intr* (elec) to reverse
inverseur [ɛ̃vɛrsœr] *m* reversing device; **inverseur des phares** (aut) dimmer
inversion [ɛ̃vɛrsjɔ̃] *f* inversion
inverté‧bré -brée [ɛ̃vɛrtebre] *adj & m* invertebrate
inver‧ti -tie [ɛ̃vɛrti] *mf* invert
invertir [ɛ̃vɛrtir] *tr* to invert, reverse
investiga‧teur [ɛ̃vɛstigatœr] **-trice** [tris] *adj* investigative; searching ‖ *mf* investigator
investigation [ɛ̃vɛstigasjɔ̃] *f* investigation
investir [ɛ̃vɛstir] *tr* to invest; vest; **investir qn de sa confiance** to place one's confidence in s.o.
investissement [ɛ̃vɛstismɑ̃] *m* investment; **investissement astucieux** smart money
investis‧seur [ɛ̃vɛstisœr] **-seuse** [søz] *mf* investor; **investisseurs bien informés** smart money, insiders
investiture [ɛ̃vɛstityr] *f* investiture; nomination (*as a candidate for election*); primary election
invété‧ré -rée [ɛ̃vetere] *adj* inveterate
invétérer [ɛ̃vetere] *ref* to become inveterate
invincible [ɛ̃vɛ̃sibl] *adj* invincible
invisible [ɛ̃vizibl] *adj* invisible; (coll) hiding, keeping out of sight
invitation [ɛ̃vitasjɔ̃] *f* invitation
invite [ɛ̃vit] *f* invitation, inducement; **répondre à l'invite de qn** (cards) to return s.o.'s lead; (fig) to respond to s.o.'s advances
invi‧té -tée [ɛ̃vite] §92 *adj* invited ‖ *mf* guest
inviter [ɛ̃vite] §96, §100 *tr* to invite
involontaire [ɛ̃vɔlɔ̃tɛr] *adj* involuntary
invoquer [ɛ̃vɔke] *tr* to invoke
invraisemblable [ɛ̃vrɛsɑ̃blabl] *adj* improbable, unlikely, hard to believe; (coll) strange, weird
invraisemblance [ɛ̃vrɛsɑ̃blɑ̃s] *f* improbability, unlikelihood; (coll) queerness
invulnérable [ɛ̃vylnerabl] *adj* invulnerable
iode [jɔd] *m* iodine
iodure [jɔdyr] *m* iodide
ion [jɔ̃] *m* ion
ioniser [jɔnize] *tr* to ionize
iota [jɔta] *m* iota
irai [ire] *v* see **aller**
Irak [irak] *m*—**l'Irak** Iraq
ira‧kien [irakjɛ̃] **-kienne** [kjɛn] *adj* Iraqi ‖ (*cap*) *mf* Iraqi
Iran [irɑ̃] *m*—**l'Iran** Iran
ira‧nien [iranjɛ̃] **-nienne** [njɛn] *adj* Iranian ‖ *m*

Iranian (*language*) ‖ (*cap*) *mf* Iranian (*person*)
iras [ira] *v* (**ira, irez**) see **aller**
iris [iris] *m* iris
irlan‧dais [irlɑ̃dɛ] **-daise** [dɛz] *adj* Irish ‖ *m* Irish (*language*) ‖ (*cap*) *m* Irishman; **les Irlandais** the Irish ‖ (*cap*) *f* Irishwoman
Irlande [irlɑ̃d] *f* Ireland; **l'Irlande** Ireland
ironie [irɔni] *f* irony
ironique [irɔnik] *adj* ironic(al)
ironiser [irɔnize] *tr* to say ironically ‖ *intr* to speak ironically, jeer
irons [irɔ̃] *v* (**iront**) see **aller**
irradier [iradje] *tr & ref* to irradiate
irraison‧né -née [irɛzɔne] *adj* unreasoning
irration‧nel -nelle [irasjɔnɛl] *adj* irrational
irréalisable [irealizabl] *adj* impractical, unattainable
irréalité [irealite] *f* unreality
irrecevable [irəsvabl] *adj* inadmissable (*evidence*); unacceptable (*demand*)
irrécouvrable [irekuvrabl] *adj* uncollectible
irrécupérable [irekyperabl] *adj* irretrievable
irrécusable [irekyzabl] *adj* unimpeachable, incontestable, indisputable
ir‧réel -réelle [ireɛl] *adj* unreal
irréflé‧chi -chie [irefleʃi] *adj* rash, thoughtless
irréfutable [irefytabl] *adj* irrefutable
irrégu‧lier [iregylje] **-lière** [ljɛr] *adj & m* irregular
irréli‧gieux [irelizjø] **-gieuse** [zjøz] *adj* irreligious
irrémédiable [iremedjabl] *adj* irremediable
irremplaçable [irɑ̃plasabl] *adj* irreplaceable
irréparable [ireparabl] *adj* irreparable; irretrievable (*loss, mistake, etc.*)
irrépressible [irepresibl] *adj* irrepressible
irréprochable [ireprɔʃabl] *adj* irreproachable
irrésistible [irezistibl] *adj* irresistible
irréso‧lu -lue [irezɔly] *adj* irresolute
irrespect [irɛspɛ] *m* disrespect
irrespec‧tueux [irɛspɛktɥø] **-tueuse** [tɥøz] *adj* disrespectful
irrespirable [irɛspirabl] *adj* unbreathable
irresponsable [irɛspɔ̃sabl] *adj* irresponsible
irrétrécissable [iretresisabl] *adj* preshrunk, unshrinkable
irrévéren‧cieux [ireverɑ̃sjø] **-cieuse** [sjøz] *adj* irreverent
irréversible [ireversibl] *adj* irreversible
irrévocable [irevɔkabl] *adj* irrevocable
irrigation [irigasjɔ̃] *f* irrigation
irriguer [irige] *tr* to irrigate
irri‧tant [iritɑ̃] **-tante** [tɑ̃t] *adj* irritating ‖ *m* irritant
irritation [iritasjɔ̃] *f* irritation
irriter [irite] *tr* to irritate ‖ *ref* to become irritated
irruption [irypsjɔ̃] *f* irruption; invasion; **faire irruption** to burst in
isabelle [izabɛl] *m* dun or light-bay horse ‖ (*cap*) *f* Isabel
Isaïe [izai] *m* Isaiah
Islam [islam] *m*—**l'Islam** Islam

islamique [islamik] *adj* Islamic

islan•dais [islɑ̃dɛ] **-daise** [dɛz] *adj* Icelandic ‖ *m* Icelandic (*language*) ‖ (*cap*) *mf* Icelander

Islande [islɑ̃d] *f* Iceland; **l'Islande** Iceland

isocèle [izɔsɛl] *adj* isosceles

iso•lant [izɔlɑ̃] **-lante** [lɑ̃t] *adj* insulating ‖ *m* insulator

isolation [izɔlɑsjɔ̃] *f* insulation; **isolation phonique** soundproofing

isolationniste [izɔlɑsjɔnist] *adj & mf* isolationist

iso•lé -lée [izɔle] *adj* isolated; independent; insulated

isolement [izɔlmɑ̃] *m* isolation; insulation

isolément [izɔlemɑ̃] *adv* separately, independently

isoler [izɔle] *tr* to isolate; insulate ‖ *ref* to cut oneself off

isoloir [izɔlwar] *m* polling booth

isométrique [izɔmetrik] *adj* isometric

isotope [izɔtɔp] *m* isotope

Israël [israɛl] *m* Israel; **à Israël** (*to give*) to Israel; **d'Israël** of Israel, e.g., **l'état d'Israël** the state of Israel; **en Israël** in Israel; (*to go*) to Israel

israé•lien [israeljɛ̃] **-lienne** [ljɛn] *adj* Israeli ‖ (*cap*) *mf* Israeli

israélite [israelit], [izraelit] *adj* Israelite ‖ (*cap*) *mf* Israelite

is•su -sue [isy] *adj*—**issu de** descended from, born of ‖ *f* exit, way out; outlet; outcome, issue; **à l'issue de** on the way out from; at the end of; **issues** sharps, middlings (*in milling flour*); offal (*in butchering*); **sans issue** without exit; without any way out

isthme [ism] *m* isthmus

Italie [itali] *f* Italy; **l'Italie** Italy

ita•lien [italjɛ̃] **-lienne** [ljɛn] *adj* Italian ‖ *m* Italian (*language*) ‖ (*cap*) *mf* Italian (*person*)

italique [italik] *adj* Italic; (typ) italic ‖ *m* (typ) italics

item [itɛm] *m* question (*in a test*) ‖ *adv* ditto

itinéraire [itinerɛr] *adj & m* itinerary

itiné•rant [itinerɑ̃] **-rante** [rɑ̃t] *adj & mf* itinerant

itou [itu] *adv* (slang) also, likewise

I.V.G. [iveʒe] *f* (letterword) (**interruption volontaire de grossesse**) abortion

ivoire [ivwar] *m* ivory

ivraie [ivrɛ] *f* darnel, cockle; (Bib) tares

ivre [ivr] *adj* drunk, intoxicated

ivresse [ivrɛs] *f* drunkenness; ecstasy, rapture

ivrogne [ivrɔɲ] *adj* hard-drinking ‖ *m* drunkard

ivrognerie [ivrɔɲri] *f* drunkenness

ivrognesse [ivrɔɲɛs] *f* drinking woman

J

J, j [ʒi] *m invar* tenth letter of the French alphabet

jabot [ʒabo] *m* jabot; crop (*of bird*)

jabotage [ʒabɔtaʒ] *m* jabbering

jaboter [ʒabɔte] *tr & intr* to jabber

jacasse [ʒakas] *f* magpie; chatterbox

jacasser [ʒakase] *intr* to chatter, jabber

jacasserie [ʒakasri] *f* chatter, jabber

jachère [ʒaʃɛr] *f* fallow ground

jacinthe [ʒasɛ̃t] *f* hyacinth; **jacinthe des bois** bluebell

jacquard [ʒakar] *m* loom; weave; **jacquard à losanges** argyl

Jacques [ʒak] *m* James, Jacob; **Jacques Bonhomme** the typical Frenchman

Jacquot [ʒako] *m* (*sobriquet*) Jimmy, Jim

jactance [ʒaktɑ̃s] *f* bragging

jade [ʒad] *m* jade

jadis [ʒadis] *adv* formerly of yore

jaguar [ʒagwar] *m* jaguar

jaillir [ʒajir] *intr* to gush, burst forth

jaillis•sant [ʒajisɑ̃] **-sante** [sɑ̃t] *adj* gushing

jaillissement [ʒajismɑ̃] *m* gush

jais [ʒɛ] *m* jet

jalon [ʒalɔ̃] *m* stake; landmark; surveying staff

jalonner [ʒalɔne] *tr* to stake out; mark (*a way, a channel*)

jalousie [ʒaluzi] *f* jealousy; awning; Venetian blind

ja•loux [ʒalu] **-louse** [luz] *adj* jealous

Jamaï•cain [dʒamaikɛ̃] **-caine** [kɛn] *adj & mf* Jamaican

Jamaï•quain [dʒamaikɛ̃] **-quaine** [kɛn] *adj & mf* Jamaican

jamais [ʒamɛ] *adv* ever; never; **à jamais** forever; **jamais de la vie!** not on your life! **jamais plus** never again; **ne ... jamais §90** never; **pour jamais** forever

jambe [ʒɑ̃b] *f* leg; **à toutes jambes** as fast as possible; **prendre ses jambes à son cou** to take to one's heels

jambière [ʒɑ̃bjɛr] *f* leg warmer

jambon [ʒɑ̃bɔ̃] *m* ham; **jambon d'York** boiled ham

jambon•neau [ʒɑ̃bɔno] *m* (*pl* **-neaux**) ham knuckle

jamboree [ʒɑ̃bɔre], [dʒambɔri] *m* jamboree

jante [ʒɑ̃t] *f* felloe; rim (*of auto wheel*)

janvier [ʒɑ̃vje] *m* January

Japon [ʒapɔ̃] *m*—**le Japon** Japan

japo•nais [ʒapɔnɛ] **-naise** [nɛz] *adj* Japanese ‖ *m* Japanese (*language*) ‖ (*cap*) *mf* Japanese (*person*)

japper [ʒape] *intr* to yap, yelp

jaquemart [ʒakmar] *m* jack (*figurine striking the time on a bell*)

jaquette [ʒakɛt] *f* coat, jacket; cut-away coat, morning coat; book jacket

jardin [ʒardɛ̃] *m* garden; **jardin d'acclimatation** zoo; **jardin d'enfants** kindergarten; **jardin d'hiver** greenhouse

jardiner [ʒardine] *tr* to clear out, trim ‖ *intr* to garden

jardinerie [ʒardinri] *f* (com) garden center

jardi·nier [ʒardinje] **-nière** [njɛr] *adj* garden ‖ *mf* gardener ‖ *m* flower stand; mixed vegetables; spring wagon ‖ *f* kindergartner (*teacher*); window box

jargon [ʒargɔ̃] *m* jargon; **jargon journalistique** (pej) journalese

jarre [ʒar] *f* earthenware jar

jarret [ʒarɛ] *m* hock, gambrel; shin (*of beef or veal*); back of the knee

jarretelle [ʒartɛl] *f* garter

jarretière [ʒartjɛr] *f* garter

jars [ʒar] *m* gander

jaser [ʒɑze] *intr* to babble; prattle; blab, gossip

jasmin [ʒasmɛ̃] *m* jasmine

jaspe [ʒasp] *m* jasper; (bb) marbling

jasper [ʒaspe] *tr* to marble, speckle

jatte [ʒat] *f* bowl

jauge [ʒoʒ] *f* gauge; (agr) trench; (naut) tonnage; **jauge d'huile, jauge à tige** dipstick

jauger [ʒoʒe] §38 *tr* to gauge, measure; (naut) to draw

jaunâtre [ʒonɑtr] *adj* yellowish, sallow

jaune [ʒon] *adj* yellow ‖ *mf* yellow person (*Oriental*) ‖ *m* yellow; yolk (*of egg*); scab, strikebreaker

jaunir [ʒonir] *tr* & *intr* to yellow

jaunisse [ʒonis] *f* jaundice

Javel [ʒavɛl] *f*—**eau de Javel** bleach

javelle [ʒavɛl] *f* swath (*of grain*); bunch (*of twigs*)

javelliser [ʒavɛlize] *tr* to chlorinate (*water*)

javelot [ʒavlo] *m* javelin

jazz [dʒaz] *m* jazz

je [ʒə] §87 I

Jean [ʒɑ̃] *m* John

Jeanne [ʒɑn] *f* Jane, Jean, Joan

jeannette [ʒanɛt] *f* gold cross (*ornament*); sleeveboard

Jeannot [ʒano] *m* (coll) Johnny, Jack

jeep [dʒip] *f* jeep

Jéhovah [ʒeɔva] *m* Jehovah

je-m'en-fichisme [ʒmɑ̃fiʃism] *m* (slang) what-the-hell attitude

je-ne-sais-quoi [ʒensekwa] *m invar* what-you-call-it

Jérôme [ʒerom] *m* Jerome

jerrycan [dʒɛrikan] *m* gasoline can

jersey [ʒɛrse] *m* jersey, sweater

Jérusalem [ʒeryzalɛm] *f* Jerusalem

jésuite [ʒezɥit] *adj* Jesuit; (pej) hypocritical ‖ (*cap*) *m* Jesuit; (pej) hypocrite

Jésus [ʒezy] *m* Jesus

Jésus-Christ [ʒezykri] *m* Jesus Christ

jet [ʒɛ] *m* throw, cast; jet; spurt, gush; flash (*of light*); **du premier jet** at the first try; **jet à la mer** jettison; **jet d'eau** fountain; **jet d'encre** (comp) ink jet; **jet dentaire** water pick; **jet de pierre** stone's throw

jetable [ʒɛtabl] *adj* disposable

jetée [ʒəte] *f* breakwater, jetty

jeter [ʒəte] §34 *tr* to throw; throw away; throw down; hurl, fling; toss; cast (*a glance*); shed (*the skin*); pour forth; utter; to drop (*anchor*); lay (*the foundations*) ‖ *intr* to sprout ‖ *ref* to throw oneself; rush; empty (*said of a river*)

jeton [ʒətɔ̃] *m* token, counter; slug

jeu [ʒø] *m* (*pl* **jeux**) play; game, sport; gambling; pack, deck (*of cards*); set (*of chess pieces; of tools*); playing, acting; execution, performance; **en jeu** in gear; at stake; **franc jeu** fair play; **gros jeu** high stakes; **hors jeu** out of play; offside; **jeu d'arcade** video arcade; **jeu d'eau** dancing waters; **jeu de chaises musicales** musical chairs; **jeu de dames** checkers; **jeu de devinettes** guessing game; **jeu de fléchettes** darts; **jeu de hasard** game of chance; **jeu de massacre** hit-the-baby (*game at fair*); **jeu de mots** pun, play on words; **jeu d'enfant** child's play; **jeu de patience** jigsaw puzzle; **jeu de puce** tiddly-winks; **jeu de société** parlor game; **jeu d'orgue** organ stop; **jeu vidéo** video game; **jouer un jeu d'enfer** to play for high stakes; **vieux jeu** old hat

jeudi [ʒødi] *m* Thursday; **jeudi saint** Maundy Thursday

jeun [ʒœ̃]—**à jeun** fasting; on an empty stomach

jeune [ʒœn] (precedes the noun it modifies) *adj* young; youthful; junior, younger ‖ *m* young man; **jeunes délinquants** juvenile delinquents; **les jeunes** young people; the young (*of an animal*)

jeûne [ʒøn] *m* fast, fasting

jeûner [ʒøne] *intr* to fast; abstain; eat sparingly

jeunesse [ʒœnɛs] *f* youth; youthfulness; boyhood, girlhood; **jeunesse dorée** young people of wealth and fashion

jeu·net [ʒœnɛ] **-nette** [nɛt] *adj* youngish

jeû·neur [ʒønœr] **-neuse** [nøz] *mf* faster

jex [ʒɛks] *m* steel wool

joaillerie [ʒɔɑjri] *f* jewelry; jewelry business; jewelry shop

joail·lier [ʒɔɑje] **-lière** [jɛr] *mf* jeweler

jobard [ʒɔbar] *m* (coll) dupe

jobarderie [ʒɔbardri] *f* gullibility

jockey [ʒɔkɛ] *m* jockey

jodler [ʒɔdle] *tr* & *intr* to yodel

jog·geur [ʒɔgœr] **-geuse** [gøz] *mf* jogger

jogging [dʒɔgiŋ] *m* jogging; sweat suit, track-suit

joie [ʒwa] *f* joy; **joies** pleasures

joindre [ʒwɛ̃dr] §35 *tr* to join; add; adjoin; catch up with; **joindre les deux bouts** to make both ends meet ‖ *intr* to join ‖ *ref* to join, unite; be adjacent, come together

joint [ʒwɛ̃] **jointe** [ʒwɛ̃t] *adj* joined; joint (*effort*); **joint à** added to ‖ *m* joint; **joint de car-**

dan (mach) universal joint; **joint de culasse** (aut) gasket (*of cylinder head*); **joint de dilatation thermique** expansion joint; **trouver le joint** (coll) to hit on the solution ‖ *v* see **joindre**

jointoiement [ʒwɛ̃twamɑ̃] *m* (archit) pointing

jointure [ʒwɛ̃tyr] *f* knuckle; joint

joker [ʒɔkɛr] *m* joker; wild card

jo•li -lie [ʒɔli], [ʒɔli] (precedes the noun it modifies) *adj* pretty; tidy (*income*)

joliment [ʒɔlimɑ̃] *adv* nicely; (coll) extremely, awfully

Jonas [ʒɔnɑs], [ʒɔnɑ] *m* Jonah

jonc [ʒɔ̃] *m* rush; **jonc d'Inde** rattan

jonchée [ʒɔ̃ʃe] *f* litter (*things strewn about*); cottage cheese

joncher [ʒɔ̃ʃe] *tr* to strew; litter

jonction [ʒɔ̃ksjɔ̃] *f* junction

jongler [ʒɔ̃gle] *intr* to juggle

jonglerie [ʒɔ̃gləri] *f* jugglery

jongleur [ʒɔ̃glœr] *m* juggler; jongleur

jonque [ʒɔ̃k] *f* (naut) junk

jonquille [ʒɔ̃kij] *adj invar* pale-yellow ‖ *m* pale yellow ‖ *f* jonquil

Jordanie [ʒɔrdani] *f* Jordan; **la Jordanie** Jordan

Jorda•nien [dʒɔrdanjɛ̃] **–nienne** [njɛn] *adj & mf* Jordanian

joue [ʒu] *f* cheek; **se caler les joues** (slang) to stuff oneself

jouer [ʒwe] §96 *tr* to play; gamble away; feign; act (*a part*) ‖ *intr* to play; gamble; feign; **faire jouer** to spring (*a lock*); **jouer à** to play (*a game*); **jouer à la baisse** to bear the market; **jouer à la hausse** to bull the market; **jouer de** to play (*a musical instrument*) ‖ *ref* to frolic; **se jouer de** to make fun of; be independent of; make light of

jouet [ʒwɛ] *m* toy, plaything

joueur [ʒwœr] **joueuse** [ʒwøz] *mf* player (*of games; of musical instruments*); gambler; **beau joueur** good sport; **joueur à la baisse** bear; **joueur à la hausse** bull; **joueur d'échecs** chess player; **joueur de football** football player; **mauvais joueur** poor sport

jouf•flu -flue [ʒufly] *adj* chubby

joug [ʒu] *m* yoke

jouir [ʒwir] §97 *intr* to enjoy oneself, enjoy life; come (*have an orgasm*); **jouir de** to enjoy

jouissance [ʒwisɑ̃s] *f* enjoyment; use, possession

jouis•seur [ʒwisœr] **-seuse** [søz] *adj* pleasure-loving ‖ *mf* pleasure lover

jou•jou [ʒuʒu] *m* (pl **-joux**) toy, plaything

jour [ʒur] *m* day; daylight; light, window, opening; **à jour** openwork; up to date; **de nos jours** nowadays; **du jour au lendemain** overnight, suddenly; **grand jour** broad daylight; **huit jours** a week; **il fait jour** it is getting light; **jour chômé** day off; **jour de ma fête** my birthday; **jour férié** legal holiday; **Jour du Travail** Labor Day; **jour ouvrable** workday; **le jour de l'An** New Year's day; **le jour J** D-Day; **quinze jours** two weeks; **sous un**

faux jour in a false light; **vivre au jour le jour** to live from hand to mouth

Jourdain [ʒurdɛ̃] *m* Jordan (*river*)

jour•nal [ʒurnal] *m* (pl **-naux** [no]) newspaper; journal; diary; (naut) logbook, journal; **journal parlé** newscast; **journal télévisé** telecast

journa•lier [ʒurnalje] **-lière** [ljɛr] *adj* daily ‖ *m* day laborer

journalisme [ʒurnalism] *m* journalism

journaliste [ʒurnalist] *mf* journalist

journalistique [dʒurnalistik] *adj* journalistic

journée [ʒurne] *f* day; day's journey; day's pay; day's work; **journée d'accueil** open house; **toute la journée** all day long

journellement [ʒurnɛlmɑ̃] *adv* daily

joute [ʒut] *f* joust

jouter [ʒute] *intr* to joust

jo•vial -viale [ʒɔvjal] *adj* (pl **-vials** or **-viaux** [vjo] **-viales**) jovial, jocose

joyau [ʒwajo] *m* (pl **joyaux**) jewel; **joyaux de la couronne** crown jewels

joyeux [ʒwajø] **joyeuse** [ʒwajøz] *adj* joyful, cheerful; jocose

jubi•lant -lante [ʒybilɑ̃] **-lante** [lɑ̃t] *adj* jubilant

jubilé [ʒybile] *m* jubilee; golden-wedding anniversary

jucher [ʒyʃe] *tr & intr* to perch ‖ *ref* to go to roost

judaïque [ʒydaik] *adj* Jewish

judaïsme [ʒydaism] *m* Judaism

judas [ʒyda] *m* peephole ‖ (*cap*) *m* Judas

judicature [ʒydikatyr] *f* judiciary

judiciaire [ʒydisjɛr] *adj* legal, judicial

judi•cieux [ʒydisjø] **-cieuse** [sjøz] *adj* judicious, judicial

juge [ʒyʒ] *m* judge; umpire; **juge arbitre** umpire; **juge assesseur** associate judge

jugement [ʒyʒmɑ̃] *m* judgment

juger [ʒyʒe] §38, §95 *tr & intr* to judge; **juger bon de** to consider it a good thing to; **jugez de ma surprise!** imagine my surprise!; **si j'en juge par mon expérience** judging by my experience

jugulaire [ʒygylɛr] *adj* jugular ‖ *f* chin strap

juif [ʒɥif] **juive** [ʒɥiv] *adj* Jewish ‖ (*cap*) *mf* Jew

juillet [ʒɥijɛ] *m* July

juin [ʒɥɛ̃] *m* June

Jules [ʒyl] *m* Julius; (coll) Mack; (slang) pimp; (slang) chamber pot

ju•lien [ʒyljɛ̃] **-lienne** [ljɛn] *adj* Julian ‖ *f* (*soup*) julienne; (bot) rocket

ju•meau [ʒymo] **-melle** [mɛl] (pl **-meaux -melles**) *adj & mf* twin ‖ *m* twin brother ‖ *f* twin sister; see **jumelles**

jumelage [ʒymlaʒ] *m* twinning

jume•lé -lée [ʒymle] *adj* double; twin (*cities*); semidetached (*house*); bilingual (*text*)

jumeler [ʒymle] §34 *tr* to couple, join; pair

jumelles [ʒymɛl] *fpl* opera glasses; field glasses; **jumelles de manchettes** cuff links

jument [ʒymɑ̃] *f* mare

jungle [ʒɔ̃gl] *f* jungle

jupe [ʒyp] *f* skirt; **jupe portefeuille** wrap-around skirt

jupe-culotte [ʒypkylɔt] *f* split skirt

jupon [ʒypɔ̃] *m* petticoat

ju•ré [ʒyre] **-rée** [re] *adj* sworn ‖ *mf* juror; member of an examining board; **premier juré** foreman; **première jurée** *f* forewoman

jurer [ʒyre] §95, §97, §98 *tr* to swear ‖ *intr* to swear; clash

juridiction [ʒyridiksjɔ̃] *f* jurisdiction

juridique [ʒyridik] *adj* legal, judicial

juriste [ʒyrist] *m* writer on legal matters

juron [ʒyrɔ̃] *m* oath

jury [ʒyri] *m* jury; examining board

jus [ʒy] *m* juice; gravy; (slang) drink (*body of water*)

jusqu'au-boutiste [ʒyskobutist] *mf* (coll) bitter-ender, diehard

jusque [ʒysk(ə)] *adv* even; **jusqu'à** as far as, down to, up to; until; even; **jusqu'à ce que** until; **jusqu'après** until after; **jusqu'à quand** how long ‖ *prep* as far as; until; **jusques et y compris** [ʒyskəzeikɔ̃pri] up to and including; **jusqu'ici** this far; until now; **jusqu'où** how far

jusque-là [ʒyskəla] *adv* that far, until then

jusquiame [ʒysykjam] *f* henbane

juste [ʒyst] *adj* just, righteous; accurate; just enough; sharp, e.g., **à six heures justes** at six o'clock sharp; (mus) in tune, on key; (slang) cool ‖ *adv* justly; correctly, exactly

justement [ʒystəmɑ̃] *adv* just; justly; exactly; as it happens

juste-milieu [ʒystəmiljø] *m* happy medium, golden mean

juterie [ʒytri] *f* juice bar

justesse [ʒystɛs] *f* justness; precision, accuracy; **de justesse** barely

justice [ʒystis] *f* justice; **faire justice de** to mete out just punishment to; to make short work of

justiciable [ʒystisjabl] *adj*—**justiciable de** accountable to; subject to

justifier [ʒystifje] *tr* to justify ‖ *intr*—**justifier de** to account for, prove ‖ *ref* to clear oneself

jute [ʒyt] *m* jute

ju•teux [ʒytø] **-teuse** [tøz] *adj* juicy

juvénile [ʒyvenil] *adj* juvenile, youthful

juxtaposer [ʒykstapoze] *tr* to juxtapose

K

K, k [kɑ] *m invar* eleventh letter of the French alphabet

kakatoès [kakatɔɛs] *m* cockatoo

kaki [kaki] *adj invar* & *m* khaki

kaléidoscope [kaleidɔskɔp] *m* kaleidoscope

kamikaze [kamikaze] *m* kamikaze

kangourou [kɑ̃guru] *m* kangaroo

karaté [karate] *m* karate

kascher or **kasher** [ka/ɛr] *adj* kosher; **c'est kascher** it's kosher

kayak [kajak] *m* kayak; **faire du kayak** to go canoeing

keepsake [kipsɛk] *m* giftbook, keepsake

képi [kepi] *m* kepi

kermesse [kɛrmɛs] *f* charity bazaar

kérosène [kerozɛn] *m* kerosene; **kérosène aviation** jet fuel; rocket fuel

ketchup [kɛt/œp] *m* ketchup

khan [kɑ̃] *m* khan

kidnapper [kidnape] *tr* to kidnap

kidnap•peur [kidnapœr] **-peuse** [pøz] *mf* kidnaper

kif [kif] *m* (coll) pot, marijuana

kif-kif [kifkif] *adj invar* (coll) all the same; **c'est kif-kif** (coll) it's fifty-fifty

kilo [kilo] *m* kilo, kilogram

kilocycle [kilɔsikl] *m* kilocycle

kilogramme [kilɔgram] *m* kilogram

kilomètre [kilɔmɛtr] *m* kilometer, kilo

kilowatt [kilɔwat] *m* kilowatt

kilowatt-heure [kilɔwatœr] *m* (*pl* **kilowatts-heures**) kilowatt-hour

kilt [kilt] *m* kilt

kimono [kimɔno] *m* kimono

kinescope [kinɛskɔp] *m* kinescope

kiosque [kjɔsk] *m* newsstand; bandstand; summerhouse

kipper [kipœr], [kipɛr] *m* kipper

kitsch *or* **kitch** [kit/] *adj invar* & *m invar* kitsch

kiwi [kiwi] *m* kiwi

klaxon [klaksɔn] *m* (aut) horn

klaxonner [klaksɔne] *intr* to sound the horn

kleptomane [klɛptɔman] *adj* & *mf* kleptomaniac

km/h *abbr* (**kilomètres-heure, kilomètres à l'heure**) kilometers per hour

knock-out [nɔkaut], [nɔkut] *adj invar* (boxing) knocked out, groggy ‖ *m* (boxing) knockout

k.o. [kao] *adj* (letterword) (**knock-out**) k.o., knocked out; **mettre k.o.** to knock out ‖ *m* k.o., knockout

Koweït [kɔwe•it] *m* Kuwait

kowe•ï•tien [kɔwe•isjɛ̃] **-tienne** [sjɛn] *adj* Kuwaiti ‖ (*cap*) *mf* Kuwaiti

krach [krak] *m* crash (*e.g., on the stock market*)

kraft [kraft] *m* strong wrapping paper

krak [krak] *m* medieval castle

Kremlin [krɛmlɛ̃] *m*—**le Kremlin** the Kremlin

kyrielle [kirjɛl] *f* rigmarole, string

kyste [kist] *m* cyst

L

L, l [ɛl], *[ɛl] *m invar* twelfth letter of the French alphabet

l' = **le** or **la** before a vowel or mute *h* ‖ often untranslated, e.g., **plus que je ne l'ai fait** more than I did; never translated when used for euphony, e.g., **comme l'on** as one, **que l'on** that one, **si l'on** if one

la [la] *art* §77 the ‖ *m* (mus) la ‖ *pron* §87 her; it

là [la] *adv* there; here, e.g., **je suis là** I am here; in, e.g., **est-il là?** is he in?; **il n'était pas là** he was out; **là, là!** there, there! (*it's not as bad as that!*)

-là [la] § 82, §84

là-bas [labɑ] *adv* yonder, over there

label [labɛl] *m* union label

labeur [labœr] *m* labor, toil

la•bial -biale [labjal] (*pl* **-biaux** [bjo] **-biales**) *adj & f* labial

laboran•tin [labɔrɑ̃tɛ̃] **-tine** [tin] *mf* laboratory assistant

laboratoire [labɔratwar] *m* laboratory; **laboratoire d'analyses** pathology laboratory; **laboratoire de langues** language laboratory; **laboratoire de prothèse dentaire** dental laboratory; **laboratoire du ciel**; Skylab; **laboratoire médico-légal** forensic laboratory; **laboratoire nucléaire** nuclear research laboratory

labo•rieux [labɔrjø] **-rieuse** [rjøz] *adj* laborious; arduous; industrious; working (*classes*); **c'est laborieux!** (coll) it's endless!

labour [labur] *m* tilling, plowing

labourable [laburabl] *adj* arable, tillable

labourer [labure] *tr* to till, plow; furrow (*the brow*); scratch

laboureur [laburœr] *m* farm hand, plowman

Labrador [labradɔr] *m*—**le Labrador** Labrador

labyrinthe [labirɛ̃t] *m* labyrinth, maze

lac [lak] *m* lake; **Grands Lacs** Great Lakes; **tombé dans le lac** (coll) all washed up, left with nothing, kaput

lacer [lɑse] §51 *tr* to lace; tie (*one's shoes*)

lacération [laserɑsjɔ̃] *f* tearing

lacérer [lasere] §10 *tr* to lacerate; tear up

lacet [lasɛ] *m* lace; snare, noose; bowstring (*for strangling*); hairpin curve; **en lacet** winding (*road*); **lacet de soulier** shoelace

lâche [lɑʃ] *adj* slack, loose; lax, careless; cowardly ‖ *mf* coward

lâcher [lɑʃe] *tr* to loosen; let go, release; turn loose; blurt out (*a word*); fire (*a shot*); (coll) to drop (*one's friends*); **lâcher pied** to give ground; **lâcher prise** to let go

lâcheté [lɑʃte] *f* cowardice

lâ•cheur [lɑʃœr] **-cheuse** [ʃøz] *mf* fickle friend, turncoat

lacis [lɑsi] *m* network (*of threads, nerves*)

laconique [lakɔnik] *adj* laconic

lacrymogène [lakrimɔʒɛn] *adj* tear (*gas*)

lacs [lɑ] *m* noose, snare; **lacs d'amour** love knot

la•té -tée [lakte] *adj* milky, milk (*diet*)

lacune [lakyn] *f* lacuna, gap, blank

lad [lad] *m* stableboy

là-dedans [ladədɑ̃] §85A *adv* in it, within, in that, in there

là-dessous [ladəsu] §85A *adv* under it, under that, under there

là-dessus [ladəsy] §85A *adv* on it, on that; thereupon

ladre [lɑdr] *adj* stingy, niggardly ‖ *mf* miser

ladrerie [lɑdrəri] *f* miserliness

lagon [lagɔ̃] *m* lagoon

lagune [lagyn] *f* lagoon

lai laie [lɛ] *adj* lay ‖ *m* lay (*poem*) ‖ *f* see **laie**

laïc laïque [laik] *adj* lay, secular ‖ *mf* layman ‖ *f* laywoman

laiche [lɛʃ] *f* (bot) sedge, reed grass

laïcisation [laisizasjɔ̃] *f* secularization

laïciser [laisize] *tr* to secularize

laid [lɛ] **laide** [lɛd] *adj* ugly; plain, homely; mean, low-down

laide•ron [lɛdrɔ̃] **-ronne** [rɔn] *adj* homely, ugly ‖ **laideron** *m* or *f* ugly wench

laideur [lɛdœr] *f* ugliness; meanness

laie [lɛ] *f* (zool) wild sow

lainage [lɛnaʒ] *m* woolens

laine [lɛn] *f* wool; **laine d'acier** steel wool; **manger** or **tondre la laine sur le dos à** (fig) to fleece

lainer [lɛne] *tr* to teasel, nap

lai•neux [lɛnø] **-neuse** [nøz] *adj* wooly; downy

lai•nier [lɛnje] **-nière** [njɛr] *adj* wool (*industry*) ‖ *mf* dealer in wool; worker in wool

laïque [laik] *adj* lay, secular ‖ *mf* layman ‖ *f* laywoman

laisse [lɛs] *f* leash; foreshore

laissé-pour-compte laissée-pour-compte [lesepurkɔ̃t] *adj* returned (*merchandise*) ‖ *m* (*pl* **laissés-pour-compte**)   reject;   leftover merchandise

laisser [lɛse], [lese] §95, §96, §97 *tr* to leave, quit; let, allow; let go (*at a low price*); let have, e.g., **il me l'a laissé pour trois dollars** he let me have it for three dollars; **laisser +** *inf* **+ qn** to let s.o. + *inf*, e.g., **il a laissé Marie aller au théâtre** he let Mary go to the theater; e.g., **il me l'a laissé peindre** or **il m'a laissé le peindre** he let me paint it ‖ *intr*—**ne pas laisser de** to not fail to, to not stop ‖ *ref* to let oneself, e.g., **se laisser aller** to let oneself go; **se laisser aller à** to give way to

laisser-aller [leseale] *m* abandon, easygoingness; slovenliness, negligence

laisser-passer [lesepɑse] *m invar* permit, pass

lait [lɛ] *m* milk; **lait condensé** condensed milk; **lait de chaux** whitewash; **lait de poule** eggnog; **lait écrémé** skim milk; **lait entier** whole milk; **se mettre au lait** to go on a milk diet

laitage [lɛtaʒ] *m* dairy products

laitance [lɛtɑ̃s] f milt

laiterie [lɛtri] f dairy, creamery; dairy farming

lai•tier [letje] -tière [tjɛr] adj dairy; milch (cow) ‖ m milkman; (metallurgy) slag, dross ‖ f dairymaid; milch cow

laiton [lɛtɔ̃] m brass; brass wire

laitonner [lɛtɔne] tr to plate with brass

laitue [lety] f lettuce; laitue romaine romaine

laïus [lajys] m (coll) speech, impromptu remarks; (coll) hot air

laïus•seur [lajysœr] -seuse [søz] mf (coll) windbag

laize [lɛz] f width (of cloth)

lamanage [lamanaʒ] m harborage

lamaneur [lamanœr] m harbor pilot

lam•beau [lɑ̃bo] m (pl -beaux) scrap, bit; rag; en lambeaux in tatters, in shreds

lam•bin [lɑ̃bɛ̃] -bine [bin] adj (coll) slow ‖ mf (coll) slowpoke

lambiner [lɑ̃bine] intr (coll) to dawdle

lambris [lɑ̃bri] m paneling, wainscoting; plaster (of ceiling); lambris dorés (fig) palatial home

lambrisser [lɑ̃brise] tr to panel, wainscot; plaster

lame [lam] f blade; slat (of blinds); runner (of skate); wave; lamina, thin plate, sword; (fig) swordsman; lame de fond ground swell

la•mé -mée [lame] adj gold-trimmed, silver-trimmed, spangled ‖ m—de lamé, e.g., une robe de lamé a spangled dress

lamelle [lamɛl] f lamella, thin strip; slide (of microscope)

lamentable [lamɑ̃tabl] adj lamentable

lamentation [lamɑ̃tasjɔ̃] f lamentation, lament

lamenter [lamɑ̃te] intr & ref to lament

laminer [lamine] tr to laminate; roll (a metal)

laminoir [laminwar] m rolling mill; calender

lampadaire [lɑ̃padɛr] m lamppost; floor lamp

lampe [lɑ̃p] f lamp; (electron) tube; lampe à pétrole kerosene lamp; lampe à rayons ultraviolets sun lamp; lampe à souder blowtorch; lampe au néon neon light; lampe de chevet bedlamp; lampe de poche flashlight; lampe survoltée photo-flood bulb; s'en mettre plein la lampe (slang) to stuff one's face

lampée [lɑ̃pe] f (coll) gulp, swig

lamper [lɑ̃pe] tr (coll) to gulp down, guzzle

lampe-tempête [lɑ̃ptɑ̃pɛt] f (pl lampes-tempête) hurricane lamp

lampion [lɑ̃pjɔ̃] m Chinese lantern; les lampions rhythmical call or rhythmical stamping of feet to denote impatience

lampiste [lɑ̃pist] m lightman; (coll) scapegoat; (coll) underling

lamproie [lɑ̃prwa] f lamprey

lampyre [lɑ̃pir] m glowworm

lance [lɑ̃s] f lance; nozzle (of hose); rompre une lance avec to cross swords with

lan•cé -cée [lɑ̃se] adj flying (start); in the swim

lance-bombes [lɑ̃sbɔ̃b] m invar trench mortar; (aer) bomb release

lancée [lɑ̃se] f impetus

lance-flammes [lɑ̃sflam] m invar flamethrower

lance-fusées [lɑ̃sfyze] m invar rocket launcher

lancement [lɑ̃smɑ̃] m launching, throwing; launching (of ship; of new product on the market); (aer) airdrop; (aer) release; (baseball) pitching

lance-mines [lɑ̃smin] m invar minelayer

lance-pierres [lɑ̃spjɛr] m invar slingshot

lancer [lɑ̃se] m (baseball) pitch; (sports) throw: lancer franc (basketball) free throw ‖ §51 tr to throw, fling, cast; launch (e.g., a ship, a new product); issue (e.g., an appeal); (baseball) to pitch ‖ ref to rush, dash; se lancer dans to launch out into, take up

lance-roquettes [lɑ̃srɔkɛt] m invar (arti) bazooka

lance-torpilles [lɑ̃stɔrpij] m invar torpedo tube

lancette [lɑ̃sɛt] f (surg) lancet

lan•ceur [lɑ̃sœr] -ceuse [søz] mf promoter; (baseball) pitcher; (sports) hurler, thrower; lanceur de disque discus thrower; lanceurs de réserve (baseball) bull pen ‖ m (rok) booster; launcher

lanci•nant [lɑ̃sinɑ̃] -nante [nɑ̃t] adj shooting, throbbing (pain); gnawing (regret)

lanciner [lɑ̃sine] tr to torment ‖ intr to shoot; throb

lan•dau [lɑ̃do] m (pl -daus) landau; baby carriage

lande [lɑ̃d] f moor, heath

landier [lɑ̃dje] m kitchen firedog with pothangers

langage [lɑ̃gaʒ] m language, speech; idiom (individual linguistic style of a person or of a group); langage d'assemblage (comp) assembly language; langage de bas niveau (comp) low-level language; langage de programmation, langage machine computer language; langage gestuel, langage par signes sign language

lange [lɑ̃ʒ] m diaper

langer [lɑ̃ʒe] §38 tr to swaddle, diaper

langou•reux [lɑ̃gurø] -reuse [røz] adj languorous

langouste [lɑ̃gust] f spiny lobster, crayfish

langous•tier [lɑ̃gustje] -tière [tjɛr] m & f lobster net ‖ m lobster boat

langoustine [lɑ̃gustin] f prawn

langue [lɑ̃g] f tongue; language, speech; avoir la langue bien pendue (coll) to have the gift of gab; donner sa langue au chat (coll) to give up; langue cible target language; langue d'arrivée target language; langue de départ source language; langue de terre tongue (neck or narrow strip) of land; langue source source language; langues romanes Romance languages; langue verte racy underworld slang; langues vivantes modern languages; langue verte slang; mauvaise langue backbiter, gossip; prendre langue avec to open up a conversation with; tirer la langue à to stick out one's tongue at

langue-de-chat [lãgdəʃa] *f* (*pl* **langues-de-chat**) (*culin*) ladyfinger

languette [lãgɛt] *f* tongue (*e.g., of shoe*); pointer (*of scale*); flap, strip

langueur [lãgœr] *f* languor

languir [lãgir] *intr* to languish; to pine away

languis•sant [lãgisã] **-sante** [sãt] *adj* languid; languishing; long-drawn-out, tiresome

lanière [lanjɛr] *f* strap, strip, thong

lanoline [lanɔlin] *f* lanolin

lanterne [lãtɛrn] *f* lantern; (aut) parking light; (obs) street lamp; **conter des lanternes** (coll) to talk nonsense; **lanterne d'agrandissement** (phot) enlarger; **lanterne de projection, lanterne à projections** slide projector, filmstrip projector; **lanterne rouge** (slang) tail end, last to arrive; **lanterne sourde** dark lantern; **lanterne vénitienne** Japanese lantern; **oublier d'éclairer** or **d'allumer sa lanterne** (coll) to leave out the most important point

lanterner [lãtɛrne] *tr* (coll) to string along, put off ‖ *intr* to loaf around, dawdle; **faire lanterner qn** to keep s.o. waiting

lapider [lapide] *tr* to stone; vilify

la•pin [lapɛ̃] **-pine** [pin] *mf* rabbit; **lapin de garenne** wild rabbit; **lapin russe** albino rabbit; **poser un lapin à qn** (coll) to stand s.o. up

la•pon [lapɔ̃] **-pone** [pɔn] *adj* Lappish ‖ *m* Lapp, Lappish (*language*) ‖ (*cap*) *mf* Lapp, Laplander (*person*)

Laponie [lapɔni] *f* Lapland; **la Laponie** Lapland

lapsus [lapsys] *m* slip (*of tongue, pen, etc.*)

laquais [lakɛ] *m* lackey, footman

laque [lak] *m & f* lacquer ‖ *m* lacquer ware ‖ *f* lac; shellac; hair spray

laquelle [lakɛl] §78

laquer [kake] *tr* to shellac; lacquer

larcin [larsɛ̃] *m* petty larceny; plagiarism

lard [lar] *m* bacon, side pork; (coll) fat (*of a person*); (slang) fat slob; **se faire du lard** (coll) to get fat

larder [larde] *tr* to lard; pierce, riddle

large [larʒ] *adj* wide, broad; generous; ample; loose-fitting ‖ (when standing before noun) *adj* wide, broad; generous; ample; large, e.g., **pour une large part** to a large extent ‖ *m* width, breadth; open sea; room, e.g. **donner du large à qn** to give s.o. room; **au large** within sight of shore; **au large de** off, e.g. **au large du Havre** off Le Havre; **de large** wide, e.g., **trois mètres de large** three meters wide; **je suis au large dans cet habit** this suit is roomy for me; **passer au large de** to give a wide berth to; **prendre le large** (coll) to shove off ‖ *adv* boldly; **calculer large** to figure roughly; **habiller large** to dress in loose-fitting clothes; **il n'en mène pas large** (fig) he gets rattled in a tight spot; **voir large** (fig) to think big

largement [larʒəmã] *adv* widely; abundantly; fully; plenty, e.g., **vous avez largement le temps** you have plenty of time

largesse [larʒɛs] *f* largess

largeur [larʒœr] *f* width, breadth; (naut) beam; **dans les grandes largeurs** (coll) in a big way; **grande largeur** double-width (*cloth*); **largeur de bande** (comp) bandwidth; **largeur d'esprit** broadmindedness

larguer [large] *tr* to let go, release

larme [larm] *f* tear; (coll) drop; **fondre en larmes** to burst into tears; **pleurer à chaudes larmes** to shed bitter tears

lar•moyant [larmwajã] **-moyante** [mwajãt] [mwajɑt] *adj* tearful; watery (*eyes*)

larmoyer [larmwaje] §47 *intr* to water (*said of eyes*); snivel, blubber

lar•ron [larɔ̃] **lar•ronnesse** [larɔnɛs] *mf* thief; **s'entendre comme larrons en foire** to be as thick as thieves

larve [larv] *f* larva

laryn•gé -gée [larɛ̃ʒe] *adj* laryngeal

laryn•gien [larɛ̃ʒjɛ̃] **-gienne** [ʒjɛn] *adj* laryngeal

laryngite [larɛ̃ʒit] *f* laryngitis

laryngoscope [larɛ̃gɔskɔp] *m* laryngoscope

larynx [larɛ̃ks] *m* larynx

las [la] **lasse** [las] *adj* weary ‖ **las** [las], [la] *interj* alas!

lascar [laskar] *m* character, rogue

las•cif [lasif] **las•cive** [lasiv] *adj* lascivious

lasciveté [lasivte] *f* lasciviousness

laser [lazɛr] *m* laser

las•sant [lasã] **-sante** [sãt] *adj* tiring, tedious

lasser [lase] §96, §97 *tr* to tire, weary; wear out (*s.o.'s patience*) ‖ *ref*—**sans se lasser** unceasingly; **se lasser de** + *inf* to tire of + *ger*; to tire oneself out + *ger*

lassitude [lasityd] *f* lassitude, weariness

lasso [laso] *m* lasso

latence [latãs] *f* latency

la•tent [latã] **-tente** [tãt] *adj* latent

laté•ral -rale [lateral] *adj* (*pl* **-raux**) lateral

la•tin [latɛ̃] **-tine** [tin] *adj* Latin ‖ *m* Latin (*language*); **latin vulgaire** Vulgar Latin ‖ (*cap*) *mf* Latin (*person*)

latino-améri•cain [latinɔamerikɛ̃] **-caine** [kɛn] (*pl* **-américains**) *adj* Latin-American ‖ (*cap*) *mf* Latin American

latitude [latityd] *f* latitude

latrines [latrin] *fpl* latrine

latte [lat] *f* lath; broadsword; **latte de plancher** floorboard

latter [late] *tr* to lath

lattis [lati] *m* lathing, laths

laudanum [lodanɔm] *m* laudanum

lauda•tif [lodatif] **-tive** [tiv] *adj* laudatory

lau•réat -réate [lɔrea] *adj* laureate ‖ *mf* winner, laureate

laurier [lɔrje] *m* laurel, sweet bay; **laurier rose** rosebay; **s'endormir sur ses lauriers** to rest on one's laurels

lavable [lavabl] *adj* washable

lavabo [lavabo] *m* washbowl; washroom; **lavabos** toilet, lavatory

lavage [lavaʒ] *m* washing; **lavage de cerveau** (coll) brainwashing; **lavage des titres** wash sale; **lavage de tête** (coll) dressing down, scolding

lavallière [lavaljɛr] *f* loosely tied bow

lavande [lavɑ̃d] *f* lavender

lavandière [lavɑ̃djɛr] *f* washerwoman

lavasse [lavas] *f* (coll) dishwater

lave [lav] *f* lava

lave-glace [lavglas] *m* (*pl* **-glaces**) (aut) windshield washer

lavement [lavmɑ̃] *m* enema

laver [lave] *tr* to wash; **laver la tête à qn** (coll) to haul s.o. over the coals; **laver le cerveau à** (coll) to brainwash ‖ *intr* to wash ‖ *ref* to wash oneself, wash; **elle s'en est lavé les mains** (fig) she washed her hands of it

laverie [lavri] *f* (min) washery; **laverie automatique, laverie libre-service** self-service laundry

lavette [lavɛt] *f* dishcloth

la•veur [lavœr] **-veuse** [vøz] *mf* washer; **laveur de vaisselle** dishwasher (*person*); **laveur de vitres** window washer (*person*) ‖ *f* washerwoman; washing machine

lavoir [lavwar] *m* place for washing clothes

lavure [lavyr] *f* dishwater; (coll) swill, hogwash

laxa•tif [laksatif] **-tive** [tiv] *adj & m* laxative

layer [leje] §49 *tr* to blaze a trail through; blaze (*trees to mark a trail*)

layette [lɛjɛt] *f* layette; packing case

lazzi [lazi] *mpl* jeers

le [lə] *art* §77 the ‖ *pron* §87 him; it

leader [lidœr] *m* leader

lèche [lɛʃ] *f* (coll) thin slice (*e.g., of bread*); **faire de la lèche à qn** (slang) to lick s.o.'s boots

lèche-carreaux [lɛʃkaro] *m invar* (slang) window-shopping

lèchefrite [lɛʃfrit] *f* dripping pan

lècher [leʃe] §10 *tr* to lick; over-polish (*one's style*)

lé•cheur [leʃœr] **-cheuse** [ʃøz] *mf* (coll) bootlicker, flatterer

lèche-vitrines [lɛʃvitrin] *m invar* window-shopping; **faire du lèche-vitrines** to go window-shopping

leçon [ləsɔ̃] *f* lesson; reading (*of manuscript*); **faire la leçon à** to lecture, sermonize; prime on what to say

lec•teur [lɛktœr] **-trice** [tris] *mf* reader; lecturer (*of university rank*) ‖ *m* playback; **lecteur CD** CD player; **lecteur de cassettes** cassette player; **lecteur de disque compact** compact disk player

lecture [lɛktyr] *f* reading; playback; **lecture optique** optical scanner; **lecture sur les lèvres** lip reading

ledit [lədi] **ladite** [ladit] *adj* (*pl* **lesdits** [ledi] **lesdites** [ledit]) the aforesaid

lé•gal **-gale** [legal] *adj* (*pl* **-gaux** [go]) legal; statutory

légalisation [legalizasjɔ̃] *f* legalization

légaliser [legalize] *tr* to legalize

légalité [legalite] *f* legality

légat [legal] *m* papal legate

légataire [legatɛr] *mf* legatee; **légataire universel** residual heir

légation [legɑsjɔ̃] *f* legation

légendaire [leʒɑ̃dɛr] *adj* legendary

légende [leʒɑ̃d] *f* legend; caption

lé•ger [leʒe] **-gère** [ʒɛr] §92 *adj* light; slight (*accent, difference, pain, mistake, etc.*); faint (*sound, tint, etc.*); delicate (*odor, perfume, etc.*); mild, weak (*drink*); scanty (*dress*); graceful (*figure*); empty (*stomach*); agile, active; frivolous, carefree; **à la légère** lightly; without due consideration

légèrement [leʒɛrmɑ̃] *adv* lightly; slightly; flippantly, thoughtlessly

légèreté [leʒɛrte] *f* lightness; gracefulness; frivolity; fickleness

leggings [legiŋs] *mpl & fpl* leggings

leghorn [legɔrn] *f* leghorn (*chicken*)

légiférer [leʒifere] §10 *intr* to legislate

légion [leʒjɔ̃] *f* legion

législa•teur [leʒislatœr] **-trice** [tris] *mf* legislator

législa•tif [leʒislatif] **-tive** [tiv] *adj* legislative

législation [leʒislɑsjɔ̃] *f* legislation

législature [leʒislatyr] *f* legislative session; legislature

légiste [leʒist] *m* jurist

légitime [leʒitim] *adj* legitimate ‖ *f* (slang) lawful spouse; **ma légitime** (slang) my better half

légitimer [leʒitime] *tr* to legitimate; justify

légitimité [leʒitimite] *f* legitimacy

legs [lɛ], [lɛg] *m* legacy

léguer [lege] §10 *tr* to bequeath

légume [legym] *m* vegetable; legume (*pod*) ‖ *f*—**grosse légume** (slang) bigwig, big wheel

légu•mier [legymje] **-mière** [mjɛr] *adj* vegetable (*garden, farming, etc.*) ‖ *m* vegetable dish

lemme [lɛm] *m* lemma

lendemain [lɑ̃dmɛ̃] *m* next day; results, outcome, e.g., **avoir d'heureux lendemains** to have happy results or a happy outcome; **au lendemain de** the day after; **le lendemain matin** the next morning; **sans lendemain** short-lived

lénifier [lenifje] *tr* (med) to soothe

lent [lɑ̃] **lente** [lɑ̃t] §92 *adj* slow ‖ *f* nit

lentement [lɑ̃tmɑ̃] *adv* slowly; deliberately

lenteur [lɑ̃tœr] *f* slowness, sluggishness; **lenteurs** delays, dilatoriness

lentille [lɑ̃tij] *f* lens; (bot) lentil; **lentilles** freckles; **lentilles cornéennes** contact lenses

léopard [leɔpar] *m* leopard

lèpre [lɛpr] *f* leprosy

lé•preux [leprø] **-preuse** [prøz] *adj* leprous ‖ *mf* leper

lequel [ləkɛl] §78

les [le] *art* §77 the ‖ *pron* §87 them ‖ *prep* near (*in place names*)

lesbianisme [lɛsbjanism] *m* lesbianisme

les•bien [lɛsbjɛ̃] **-bienne** [bjɛn] *adj & f* lesbian

lèse-majesté [lɛzmaʒɛste] *f*—**crime de lèse-majesté** lese majesty, high treason

léser [leze] §10 *tr* to injure

lésine [lezin] *f* stinginess

lésiner [lezine] *intr* to haggle, be stingy

lésion [lezjɔ̃] *f* lesion; wrong, damage; **lésion traumatique** whiplash injury

les•quels -quelles [lekɛl] §78

lessivage [lesivaʒ] *m* washing; **lessivage de crâne** (coll) brainwashing

lessive [lesiv] *f* washing (*of clothes*); wash; washing soda, lye; **faire la lessive** to do the wash

lessiver [lesive] *tr* to wash; scrub (*with a cleaning agent*); (slang) to clean out (*e.g., another poker player*); **être lessivé** (slang) to be exhausted

lessiveuse [lesivøz] *f* washing machine

lest [lɛst] *m* ballast

leste [lɛst] *adj* nimble, quick; suggestive, broad; flippant

lestement [lɛstəmã] *adv* nimbly, deftly

lester [lɛste] *tr* to ballast; (coll) to fill (*one's stomach, pockets, etc.*) ‖ *ref* (coll) to stuff oneself

léthargie [letarʒi] *f* lethargy

léthargique [letarʒik] *adj* lethargic ‖ *mf* lethargic person

lettrage [lɛtraʒ] *m* lettering

lettre [lɛtr] *f* letter; **à la lettre, au pied de la lettre** to the letter; **avant la lettre** before complete development; **en toutes lettres** in full; in so many words; **lettre anonyme venimeuse** poison-pen letter; **lettre de change** bill of exchange; **lettre de faire-part** announcement; **lettre de voiture** bill of lading; **lettre d'imprimerie** printed letter; **lettre majuscule** capital letter; **lettre par avion** airmail letter; **lettre recommandée** registered letter; **lettres** letters (*literature*); **lettres numérales** roman numerals; **mettre une lettre à la poste** to mail a letter

let•tré -trée [lɛtre] *adj* lettered, literate ‖ *mf* learned person

lettre-morte [lɛtrəmɔrt] *f* letter returned to sender

lettrine [letrin] *f* catchword; initial letter

leu [lø] *m*—**à la queue leu leu** in single file

leucémie [løsemi] *f* leukemia

leucorrhée [løkɔre] *f* leucorrhea

leur [lœr] *adj poss* §88 their ‖ *pron poss* §89 theirs *pron pers* §87 them; to them

leurre [lœr] *m* lure; delusion

leurrer [lœre] *tr* to lure; trick, delude ‖ *ref* to be deceived

levain [ləvɛ̃] *m* leaven

levant [ləvã] *adj masc* rising (*sun*) ‖ *m* east ‖ (*cap*) *m* Levant

levan•tin -tine [ləvãtɛ̃] -[tin] *adj* Levantine ‖ (*cap*) *mf* Levantine

le•vé -vée [ləve] *adj* rising (*sun*); raised (*e.g., hand*); up, e.g., **le soleil est levé** the sun is up ‖ *m* (mus) upbeat; (surv) survey ‖ *f* levee, embankment; collection (*of mail*); levying (*of troops, taxes, etc.*); raising (*of siege*); lifting (*of embargo*); striking (*of camp*); breaking (*of seals*); upstroke (*of piston*); **faire une levée** (cards) to take a trick; **levée de boucliers** public protest, outcry; **levée d'écrou** discharge (*from prison*); **levée de séance** adjournment; **levée du corps** removal of the body; funeral service (*in front of the coffin*); **levées manquantes** (cards) undertricks

lever [ləve] *m* rising; (surv) survey; **lever du rideau** rise of the curtain; curtain raiser; **lever du soleil** sunrise ‖ §2 *tr* to lift; raise; collect, pick up (*the mail*); levy (*troops, taxes, etc.*); strike (*camp*); adjourn (*a meeting*); weigh (*anchor*); relieve (*a guard*); remit (*a punishment*); flush (*e.g., a partridge*); effect (*a survey*); break (*the seals*) ‖ *intr* to come up (*said of plants*); rise (*said of dough*) ‖ *ref* to get up; stand up; rise; heave (*said of sea*); clear up (*said of weather*)

léviathan [levjatã] *m* leviathan

levier [ləvje] *m* lever, crowbar; **être aux leviers de commande** (aer) to be at the controls; (fig) to be in control; **levier de changement de vitesse** gearshift lever; **levier d'interligne et de retour du chariot** return lever (*of a typewriter*)

lévitation [levitasjɔ̃] *f* levitation

levraut [ləvro] *m* young hare, leveret

lèvre [lɛvr] *f* lip; rim; **du bout des lèvres** halfheartedly, guardedly; **embrasser sur les lèvres** to kiss; **serrer les lèvres** to purse one's lips

lèvrier [levrije] *m* greyhound

levure [ləvyr] *f* yeast, **levure anglaise** or **chimique** baking powder; **levure de bière** brewer's yeast

lexi•cal -cale [lɛksikal] *adj* (*pl* **-caux** [ko]) lexical

lexicographe [lɛksikɔgraf] *mf* lexicographer

lexicographie [lɛksikɔgrafi] *f* lexicography

lexicographique [lɛksikɔgrafik] *adj* lexicographic(al)

lexicologie [lɛksikɔlɔʒi] *f* lexicology

lexique [lɛksik] *m* lexicon, vocabulary; abridged dictionary

lez [le] *prep* near (*in place names*)

lézard [lezar] *m* lizard; **faire le lézard** (coll) to sun oneself, loaf

lézarde [lezard] *f* crack, split, crevice; gimp (*of furniture*); braid; (mil) gold braid

lézarder [lezarde] *tr & ref* to crack, split ‖ *intr* (coll) to bask in the sun

liaison [ljɛzɔ̃] *f* liaison; (comp) linkage; (rad, telv) linkup

liant [ljã] **liante** [ljã] *adj* flexible, supple; sociable, affable ‖ *m* flexibility; sociability; binder, binding material; **avoir du liant** to be a good mixer

liard [ljar] *m* (fig) farthing

liasse [ljas] *f* packet, bundle (*e.g., of letters*); wad (*of bank notes*)

Liban [libã] *m*—**le Liban** Lebanon

liba·nais [libanɛ] **-naise** [nɛz] *adj* Lebanese ‖ (*cap*) *mf* Lebanese

libation [libasjɔ̃] *f* libation

libelle [libɛl] *m* lampoon

libellé [libɛlle] *m* wording

libeller [libele], [libɛlle] *tr* to word; draw up (*e.g., a contract*); make out (*a check*)

libellule [libɛlyl] *f* dragonfly

libé·ral -rale [liberal] *adj & mf* (*pl* **-raux** [ro]) liberal

libéralisme [liberalism] *m* liberalism

libéralité [liberalite] *f* liberality

libéra·teur [liberatœr] **-trice** [tris] *adj* liberating ‖ *mf* liberator

libération [liberasjɔ̃] *f* liberation; freeing; **libération conditionnelle** release on parole; **libération sous caution** release on bail

libérer [libere] §10 *tr* to liberate ‖ *ref* to free oneself; pay up

liberté [libɛrte] *f* liberty, freedom; **liberté d'association** or **liberté de réunion** right of assembly; **liberté de langage** freedom of speech; **liberté de la presse** freedom of the press; **liberté de la propriété** right to own private property; **liberté du commerce et de l'industrie** free enterprise; **liberté du culte** freedom of worship

liber·tin [libɛrtɛ̃] **-tine** [tin] *adj* libertine; (archaic) freethinking ‖ *mf* libertine; (archaic) freethinker

libidi·neux [libidinø] **-neuse** [nøz] *adj* libidinous

libido [libido] *f* libido

libraire [librɛr] *mf* bookseller; publisher

libraire-éditeur [librɛreditœr] *m* (*pl* **libraires-éditeurs**) publisher and bookseller

librairie [librɛri] *f* bookstore; book trade; publishing house; **librarie d'occasion** second-hand bookstore

libre [libr] §93 *adj* free; vacant; available; (*public sign*) not in use, empty; for hire; **je suis libre de mon temps** my time is my own; **libre arbitre** free will; **libre de** free to, at liberty to

libre-échange [librəʃɑ̃ʒ] *m* free trade

libre-échangiste [librəʃɑ̃ʒist] *m* (*pl* **-échangistes**) free trader

libre-pen·seur [librəpɑ̃sœr] **-seuse** [søz] *mf* (*pl* **libres-penseurs**) freethinker

libre-service [librəsɛrvis] *m* (*pl* **libres-services**) self-service; self-service store

lice [lis] *f* enclosure or fence (*of race track, fairground, tiltyard, etc.*); (zool) hound bitch; **de basse lice** (tex) low-warp; **de haute lice** (tex) high-warp; **entrer en lice** to enter the lists

licence [lisɑ̃s] *f* license; **licence ès lettres** advanced liberal-arts degree, master of arts; **prendre des licences avec** to take liberties with

licen·cié -ciée [lisɑ̃sje] *mf* holder of a master's degree

licenciement [lisɑ̃simɑ̃] *m* discharge, layoff

licencier [lisɑ̃sje] *tr* to discharge, lay off

licen·cieux [lisɑ̃sjø] **-cieuse** [sjøz] *adj* licentious

lichen [likɛn] *m* lichen

licher [liʃe] *tr* (slang) to gulp down

licite [lisit] *adj* lawful, licit

licorne [likɔrn] *f* unicorn

licou [liku] *m* halter

lie [li] *f* dregs, lees; (fig) dregs, scum

lie-de-vin [lidvɛ̃] *adj invar* maroon

liège [ljɛʒ] *m* cork

lien [ljɛ̃] *m* tie, bond, link, linkup, linkage

lier [lje] *tr* to tie, bind, link ‖ *ref* to bind together; make friends; **lier conversation avec** to fall into conversation with; **se lier d'amitié avec** to become friends with

lierre [ljɛr] *m* ivy

liesse [ljɛs] *f*—**en liesse** in festive mood, gay

lieu [ljø] *m* (*pl* **lieux**) place; **au lieu de** instead of, in lieu of; **avoir lieu** to take place; **avoir lieu de** to have reason to; **donner lieu à** to give rise to; **en aucun lieu** nowhere; **en dernier lieu** finally; **en haut lieu** high up, in responsible circles; **en premier lieu** first of all; **en quelque lieu que** wherever; **en tous lieux** everywhere; **il y a lieu à** there is room for; **lieu commun** commonplace; platitude; **lieu de jugement** or **procès** (law) venue; **lieu de villégiature** resort; **lieu géométrique** locus; **lieux** premises; **lieux d'aisances** restrooms; **lieux payants** comfort station, public lavatory; **sur les lieux** on the spot; on the premises; **tenir lieu** to take place; **tenir lieu de** to take the place of

lieu-dit [ljødi] *m* (*pl* **lieux-dits**)—**le lieu-dit . . .** the place called . . .

lieue [ljø] *f* league (*unit of distance*)

lieur [ljœr] **lieuse** [ljøz] *mf* binder ‖ *f* (mach) binder

lieutenant [ljøtnɑ̃] *m* lieutenant; (merchant marine) mate; **lieutenant de port** harbor master; **lieutenant de vaisseau** (nav) lieutenant commander

lieutenant-colonel [ljøtnɑ̃kɔlɔnɛl] *m* (*pl* **lieutenants-colonels**) lieutenant colonel

lièvre [ljɛvr] *m* hare; **c'est là que gît le lièvre** there's the rub; **lever un lièvre** (fig) to raise an embarrassing question; **prendre le lièvre au gîte** (fig) to catch s.o. napping

ligament [ligamɑ̃] *m* ligament

ligature [ligatyr] *f* ligature

ligaturer [ligatyre] *tr* to tie up

lignage [liɲaʒ] *m* lineage

ligne [liɲ] *f* line; figure, waistline; (*of an automobile*) lines; **aller à la ligne** to begin a new paragraph; **avoir de la ligne** to have a good figure; **en ligne** (comp) on line; **en première ligne** of the first importance; on the firing line; **entrer en ligne de compte** to be under consideration; **garder sa ligne** to keep one's figure; **grande ligne** (rr) main line; **grandes lignes** broad outline; **hors ligne** unrivaled, outstanding; **la ligne est occupée** the line is busy, I hear the busy signal; **ligne à postes groupés**

(telp) party line; **ligne brisée** dotted line; **ligne de but** goal line; **ligne de changement de date** international date line; **ligne de faille** fault line; **ligne de flottaison** water line; **ligne de mire, ligne de visée** (arti) line of sight; **ligne de partage des eaux, ligne de faîte** watershed; **ligne des arbres** timber line; **ligne d'horizon** skyline; **ligne droite** straight line; **ligne partagée** (telp) party line; **ligne pointillée** or **hachée** dotted line

ligne-bloc [liɲblɔk] (*pl* **lignes-blocs**) *m* linotype slug

lignée [liɲe] *f* lineage, offspring

li•gneux -gneuse [liɲø] [ɲøz] *adj* woody

lignifier [liɲifje] *tr & ref* to turn into wood

ligot [ligo] *m* firewood (*in tied bundle*)

ligoter [ligɔte] *tr* to tie up, bind

ligue [lig] *f* league

liguer [lige] *tr & ref* to league

lilas [lila] *adj invar & m* lilac

li•lial -liale [liljal] *adj* (*pl* **-liaux** [ljo]) lily-white, lily-like

lillipu•tien [lilipysjɛ̃] **-tienne** [sjɛn] *adj & mf* Lilliputian

limace [limas] *f* (zool) slug; (coll) slowpoke; (slang) shirt

limaçon [limasɔ̃] *m* snail; **en limaçon** spiral

limaille [limɑj] *f* filings

limbe [lɛ̃b] *m* (astr, bot) limb; **limbes** limbo

lime [lim] *f* file; (*Citrus limetta*) sweet lime; **dernier coup de lime** finishing touches; **enlever à la lime** to file off; **lime à ongles** nail file; **lime émeri** emery board

limer [lime] *tr* to file; fray; (fig) to polish

limette [limɛt] *f* (*Citrus limetta*) sweet lime

limier [limje] *m* bloodhound; (coll) sleuth

liminaire [liminɛr] *adj* preliminary

limitation [limitasjɔ̃] *f* limitation

limite [limit] *f* limit; maximum, e.g., **vitesse limite** maximum speed; **dernière limite** deadline; **limite des neiges permanentes** snow line, snow limit; **limite de temps** time limit

limiter [limite] *tr* to limit ‖ *ref* to be limited; limit oneself

limitrophe [limitrɔf] *adj* frontier; **limitrophe de** adjacent to

limogeage [limɔʒaʒ] *m* (coll) removal from office

limoger [limɔʒe] §38 *tr* (coll) to remove from office, relieve of a command

limon [limɔ̃] *m* silt; clay; mud; shaft (*of wagon*)

limonade [limɔnad] *f* lemon soda

limona•dier [limɔnadje] **-dière** [djɛr] *mf* soft-drink manufacturer; café manager

limo•neux -neuse [limɔnø] [nøz] *adj* silty; muddy

limousine [limuzin] *f* heavy cloak; (aut) limousine

limpide [lɛ̃pid] *adj* limpid

lin [lɛ̃] *m* flax; linen

linceul [lɛ̃sœl] *m* shroud; cover (*of snow*)

linéaire [lineɛr] *adj* linear

linéament [lineamɑ̃] *m* lineament

linge [lɛ̃ʒ] *m* linen (*sheets, tablecloths, un-*

derclothes, etc.); piece of linen; **il faut laver son linge sale en famille** one must wash one's dirty linen in private; **laver le linge** to do the wash; **linge de corps** underclothes

lingère [lɛ̃ʒɛr] *f* linen maid; linen closet

lingerie [lɛ̃ʒri] *f* linen (*sheets, tablecloths, underclothes, etc.*); linen closet; utility room (*for washing and hanging clothes*); **lingerie de dame** lingerie; **lingerie d'homme** men's underwear

lingot [lɛ̃go] *m* ingot

lin•gual -guale [lɛ̃gwal] (*pl* **-guaux** [gwo] **-guales**) *adj & f* lingual

linguiste [lɛ̃gɥist] *mf* linguist

linguistique [lɛ̃gɥistik] *adj* linguistic ‖ *f* linguistics

linkage [lɛ̃kaʒ] *m* (gen) linkage

liniment [linimɑ̃] *m* liniment

linoléum [linɔleɔm] *m* linoleum

linon [linɔ̃] *m* lawn (*sheer linen*)

linotte [linɔt] *f* (orn) linnet

linotype [linɔtip] *f* linotype

linotypiste [linɔtipist] *mf* linotype operator

lin•teau [lɛ̃to] *m* (*pl* **-teaux**) lintel

lion [ljɔ̃] **lionne** [ljɔn] *mf* lion ‖ *m*—**le Lion** (astr, astrol) Leo ‖ *f* lioness

lion•ceau [ljɔso] *m* (*pl* **-ceaux**) lion cub

lippe [lip] *f* thick lower lip, blubber lip

lip•pu -pue [lipy] *adj* thick-lipped

liquéfier [likefje] *tr* to liquefy

liqueur [likœr] *f* liqueur; liquid; (chem, pharm) liquor

liquidation [likidasjɔ̃] *f* liquidation; settlement; clearance sale

liquide [likid] *adj & m* liquid ‖ *f* liquid (*consonant*)

liquider [likide] *tr* to liquidate; settle (*a score*); wind up (*a piece of business*); (coll) to get rid of; put an end to

liquidité [likidite] *f* liquidity

liquo•reux [likɔrø] **-reuse** [røz] *adj* sweet, syrupy

lire [lir] §36 *tr & intr* to read; **lire à haute voix** to read aloud; **lire à vue** to sight-read; **lire sur les lèvres** to lip-read ‖ *ref* to read; show, e.g., **la surprise se lit sur votre visage** your face shows surprise

lis [lis] *m* lily; **lis blanc** lily; **lis jaune** day lily

Lisbonne [lizbɔn] *f* Lisbon

liseré [lizre] or **liséré** [lizere] *m* braid, border, strip

li•seur [lizœr] **-seuse** [zøz] *mf* reader ‖ *f* bookmark; reading lamp; book jacket; bed jacket

lisibilité [lizibilite] *f* legibility

lisible [lizibl] *adj* legible; readable

lisière [lisjɛr] *f* edge, border; list, selvage; **tenir en lisières** to keep in leading strings

lissage [lisaʒ] *m* face-lift

lisse [lis] *adj* smooth, polished, sleek ‖ *f* (naut) handrail

lissé [lise] *m* smoothness

lisser [lise] *tr* to smooth, polish, sleek; glaze

(*paper*) ‖ *ref* to become smooth; **se lisser les plumes** to preen its feathers

lisseuse [lisøz] *f* ice resurfacer

listage [lista ʒ] *m* (comp) listing

liste [list] *f* list; (comp) listing; **liste des invités** guest list; **liste de vérification** check list; **liste rouge** (telp) list of telephone subscribers with unlisted numbers

lister [liste] *tr* (comp) to list

lit [li] *m* bed; layer; stratum; **dans le lit de la marée** in the tideway; **dans le lit du vent** in the wind's eye; **du premier lit** by or of the first marriage; **lit de mort** deathbed; **lit d'époque** period bed; **lit de repos** day bed; **lit de sangle, lit de camp** folding cot, camp bed; **lit en portefeuille** apple-pie bed; **lit escamotable, lit à rabattement** Murphy bed (trademark); **lit pliant** foldaway bed; **lits jumeaux** twin beds; **lits superposés** bunk beds

litanie [litani] *f* litany; tale of woe

lit-cage [lika ʒ] *m* (*pl* **lits-cages**) foldaway bed

lit-canapé [likanape] *m* (*pl* **lits-canapés**) sofa bed

litée [lite] *f* litter (*of animals*)

literie [litri] *f* bedding, bedclothes

lithine [litin] *f* lithia

lithium [litjɔm] *m* lithium

lithographe [litɔgraf] *mf* lithographer

lithographie [litɔgrafi] *f* lithography; lithograph

lithographier [litɔgrafje] *tr* to lithograph

litière [litjɛr] *f* litter (*bedding for animals*); **faire litière de** to trample

litige [liti ʒ] *m* litigation

liti·gieux [liti ʒjø] **-gieuse** [ʒjøz] *adj* litigious

litre [litr] *m* liter

littéraire [literɛr] *adj* literary ‖ *mf* teacher of literature; belletrist

litté·ral -rale [literal] *adj* (*pl* **-raux** [ro]) literal; literary, written

littérature [literatyr] *f* literature

litto·ral -rale [litɔral] (*pl* **-raux** [ro]) *adj* littoral, coastal ‖ *m* coast, coastline

liturgie [lityr ʒi] *f* liturgy

liturgique [lityr ʒik] *adj* liturgic(al)

livid [livid] *adj* livid

living [liviŋ] *m* living room; all-purpose room in a studio apartment

Livourne [livurn] *f* Leghorn

livrable [livrabl] *adj* ready for delivery

livraison [livrɛzɔ̃] *f* delivery; installment; **livraison contre remboursement** cash on delivery

livre [livr] *m* book; **à livre ouvert** at sight; **faire un livre** to write a book; (racing) to make book; **feuilleter un livre** to glance through a book; **grand livre** (bk) ledger; **livre broché, livre de poche** paperback; **livre de bandes dessinées** comic book; **livre de bord** (aer, naut) logbook; **livre de chevet** bedside book; **livre de classe** textbook; **livre de cuisine, livre de recettes** cookbook; **livre d'or** blue book; testimonial volume; guest book; **livre jaune** white book; **petit livre** (bk) journal,

day book; **porter au grand livre** (bk) to post ‖ *f* pound (*weight; currency*)

livrée [livre] *f* livery; appearances; coat (*of horse, deer, etc.*)

livrer [livre] *tr* to deliver; surrender; betray ‖ *ref*—**se livrer à** to surrender oneself to; give way to, indulge in

livresque [livrɛsk] *adj* bookish

livret [livrɛ] *m* booklet; (mus) libretto; **livret de caisse d'épargne** bankbook; **livret de famille** marriage certificate; **livret d'instruction** instruction manual; **livret militaire** military record; **livret scolaire** transcript (*of grades*)

li·vreur [livrœr] **-vreuse** [vrøz] *mf* deliverer (*of parcels, packages, etc.*) ‖ *m* delivery-man ‖ *f* woman who makes deliveries; delivery truck

lobby [lɔbi] (*pl* **lobbies**) *m* lobby; **lobby environnementaliste** environmental-protection lobby; **lobby des marchands de revolvers** gun lobby

lobe [lɔb] *m* lobe; **lobe de l'oreille** ear lobe

lo·cal -cale [lɔkal] (*pl* **-caux** [ko]) *adj* local ‖ *m* place, premises, quarters; headquarters; **locaux** (sports) home team; **locaux commerciaux** office space

localiser [lɔkalize] *tr* to locate; localize

localité [lɔkalite] *f* locality

locataire [lɔkatɛr] *mf* tenant, renter

location [lɔkasjɔ̃] *f* rental; reservation

loch [lɔk] *m* (naut) log (*to determine speed*)

lock-out [lɔkaut] *m invar* lockout

locomotive [lɔkɔmɔtiv] *f* locomotive; (fig) mover; (fig) price leader

locuste [lɔkyst] *f* (ent) locust

locu·teur [lɔkytœr] **-trice** [tris] *mf* speaker

locution [lɔkysjɔ̃] *f* locution; phrase

lof [lɔf] *m* windward side; **aller** or **venir au lof** to sail into the wind

logarithme [lɔgaritm] *m* logarithm

loge [lɔ ʒ] *f* lodge; circus cage; concierge's room; chamber, cell; (theat) dressing room; (theat) box

logeabilité [lɔ ʒabilite] *f* spaciousness

logeable [lɔ ʒabl] *adj* livable, inhabitable

logement [lɔ ʒmɑ̃] *m* lodging, lodgings

loger [lɔ ʒe] §38 *tr, intr, & ref* to lodge

lo·geur [lɔ ʒœr] **-geuse** [ʒøz] *mf* proprietor of a boardinghouse ‖ *m* landlord ‖ *f* landlady

logiciel [lɔ ʒisjel] *m* (comp) software

logi·cien [lɔ ʒisjɛ̃] **-cienne** [sjɛn] *mf* logician

logique [lɔ ʒik] *adj* logical ‖ *f* logic

logis [lɔ ʒi] *m* abode

logistique [lɔ ʒistik] *adj* logistic(al) ‖ *f* logistics

logo [lɔgo] *m* logo

loi [lwa] *f* law; **faire des lois** to legislate; **faire la loi** to lay down the law; **loi concernant la prescription** statute of limitations; **loi exceptionnelle** emergency legislation; **loi sélective du plus fort, loi du mieux adapté** survival of the fittest

loin [lwɛ̃] *adv* far; far away, far off; **au loin** in the distance; **d'aussi loin que, du plus loin que** as soon as; as far back as; **de loin** from afar; far from; far be it from (*e.g., me*); **de loin en loin** now and then; **il y a loin de** it is a far cry from; **loin des yeux, loin du cœur** out of sight, out of mind

loin•tain [lwɛ̃tɛ̃] **-taine** [tɛn] *adj* faraway, distant, remote; early (*e.g., memories*) ‖ *m* distance, background; **le lointain** (theat) upstage

loir [lwar] *m* dormouse; **dormir comme un loir** to sleep like a log

loisible [lwazibl] *adj*—**il m'est** (**lui est,** etc.) **loisible de** I am (he is, etc.) free to or entitled to, it is open for me (him, etc.)

loisir [lwazir] *m* leisure, spare time; **à loisir** at one's convenience; **loisirs** diversions

lolo [lolo] *m* (coll) milk (*in baby talk*)

lombes [lɔ̃b] *mpl* loins

londo•nien [lɔ̃dɔnjɛ̃] **-nienne** [njɛn] *adj* London ‖ (*cap*) *mf* Londoner

Londres [lɔ̃dr] *m* London

londrès [lɔ̃drɛs] *m* Havana cigar

long [lɔ̃] **longue** [lɔ̃g] *adj* long; lengthy (*speech*); long (*syllable, vowel*); thin, weak (*sauce, gravy*); slow (*to understand, to decide*) ‖ (when standing before noun) *adj* long; **de longue main** of long standing ‖ *m* length; extent; **au long** at length; **de long** lengthwise; **de long en large** up and down, back and forth; **le long de** along; **tout au long** without forgetting anything ‖ *f* see **longue** ‖ **long** *adv* much; **en dire long** to talk a long time; to speak volumes; **en savoir long sur** to know a great deal about; **en savoir plus long** to know more about it

longanimité [lɔ̃ganimite] *f* long-suffering

long-courrier [lɔ̃kurje] (*pl* **-courriers**) *adj* long-range ‖ *m* airliner; liner, ocean liner

longe [lɔ̃ʒ] *f* tether, leash; (culin) loin

longer [lɔ̃ʒe] **§38** *tr* to walk along, go beside; extend along, skirt

longeron [lɔ̃ʒrɔ̃] *m* crossbeam, girder

longévité [lɔ̃ʒevite] *f* longevity

longitude [lɔ̃ʒityd] *f* longitude

longtemps [lɔ̃tɑ̃] *m* a long time; **avant longtemps** before long; **depuis longtemps** for a long time since; **ne . . . plus longtemps** no . . . longer ‖ *adv* long; for a long time

longue [lɔ̃g] *f* long syllable; long vowel; long suit (*in cards*); **à la longue** in the long run

longuement [lɔ̃gmɑ̃] *adv* at length, a long time

lon•guet [lɔ̃gɛ] **-guette** [gɛt] *adj* (coll) longish, rather long

longueur [lɔ̃gœr] *f* length; lengthiness; **à longueur de journée** all day long; **de longueur, dans la longueur** lengthwise; **d'une longueur** by a length, by a head; **longueur d'onde** wavelength; **longueurs** slowness, delays; tedious passages (*e.g., of a book*); **traîner en longueur** to drag on

longue-vue [lɔ̃gvy] *f* (*pl* **longues-vues**) telescope, spyglass

looping [lupiŋ] *m* loop-the-loop

lopin [lɔpɛ̃] *m* patch of ground, plot

loquace [lɔkwas], [lɔkas] *adj* loquacious

loque [lɔk] *f* rag; **être comme une loque** to feel like a dishrag; **être en loques** to be in tatters

loquet [lɔkɛ] *m* latch

loque•teux [lɔktø] **-teuse** [tøz] *adj* in tatters ‖ *mf* tatterdemalion

lorgner [lɔrɲe] *tr* to cast a sidelong glance at; ogle; have one's eyes on (*a job, an inheritance, etc.*)

lorgnette [lɔrɲet] *f* opera glasses

lorgnon [lɔrɲɔ̃] *m* pince-nez; lorgnette

loriot [lɔrjo] *m* golden oriole

lorry [lɔri] *m* lorry, small flatcar

lors [lɔr] *adv*—**lors de** at the time of; **lors même que** even if

lorsque [lɔrsk] *conj* when

losange [lɔzɑ̃ʒ] *m* (geom) lozenge; **en losange** diamond-shaped; oval-shaped

lot [lo] *m* lot; prize (*e.g., in lottery*); **gagner le gros lot** to hit the jackpot

loterie [lɔtri] *f* lottery

lo•ti -tie [lɔti] *adj* built-up (*area*); **bien loti** well off; **mal loti** badly off

lotion [losjɔ̃] *f* lotion; **lotion après-rasage** aftershave (lotion), shaving lotion; **lotion capillaire** hair tonic

lotionner [losjɔne] *tr* to bathe (*a wound*)

lotir [lɔtir] *tr* to parcel out; to subdivide (*for development*); **lotir qn de q.ch.** to allot s.th. to s.o.

lotissement [lɔtismɑ̃] *m* allotment, apportionment; building lot; (building) development, subdivision

louable [lwabl] *adj* praiseworthy; for hire

louage [lwaʒ] *m* hire

louange [lwɑ̃ʒ] *f* praise; **à la louange de** in praise of

louanger [lwɑ̃ʒe] **§38** *tr* to praise, extol

louan•geur [lwɑ̃ʒœr] **-geuse** [ʒøz] *adj* laudatory, flattering

loubard [lubar] *m* hood (*gangster*); punk

louche [luʃ] *adj* ambiguous; suspicious, queer, shady; cross-eyed; cloudy (*e.g., wine*) ‖ *f* ladle; basting spoon

loucher [luʃe] *intr* to be cross-eyed, squint; **faire loucher qn de jalousie** (coll) to turn s.o. green with envy; **loucher sur** (coll) to cast longing eyes at

louchet [luʃɛ] *m* spade (*for digging*)

louer [lwe] **§97** *tr* to rent, hire; to reserve (*a seat*); praise ‖ *ref* to be rented; hire oneself out; **se louer de** to be satisfied with

loueur [lwœr] **loueuse** [lwøz] *mf* operator of a rental service; flatterer

loufoque [lufɔk] *adj* (slang) cracked ‖ *m* (slang) crackpot

lougre [lugr] *m* (naut) lugger

Louisiane [lwizjan] *f* Louisiana; **la Louisiane** Louisiana

lou•lou [lulu] **-loute** [lut] *mf* (coll) darling, pet ‖ *m*—**loulou de Poméranie** Pomeranian, spitz

loup [lu] *m* wolf; mask (*around the eyes*); flaw; **avoir vu le loup** to have lost one's innocence; **crier au loup** to cry wolf; **loup de mer** (ichth) wolf eel; (coll) old salt; **mon petit loup** (coll) my pet ‖ see **louve**

loup-cervier [lusɛrvje] *m* (*pl* **loups-cerviers**) lynx

loupe [lup] *f* magnifying glass; gnarl (*on tree*); (pathol) wen

lou•pé -pée [lupe] *adj* bungled; defective ‖ *m* defect

louper [lupe] *tr* (coll) to goof up, muff; (coll) to miss (*e.g., one's train*) ‖ *intr* (coll) to fail, goof

loup-garou [lugaru] *m* (*pl* **loups-garous**) werewolf

lou•piot -piotte [pjɔt] *mf* (coll) kid, child; **loupiots** (coll) small fry

lourd [lur] **lourde** [lurd] §92 *adj* heavy; hefty; clumsy; sultry (*weather*); off-color (*joke*); dull (*mind*); (agr) hard to cultivate ‖ (when standing before noun) *adj* heavy; grave; clumsy (*e.g., compliments*); off-color (*joke*) ‖ **lourd** *adv* heavy, heavily

lour•daud -daude [dod] *adj* clumsy, loutish, dull ‖ *mf* lout, oaf

lourdement [lurdəmɑ̃] *adv* heavily; clumsily; **avancer** or **rouler lourdement** to lumber along

lourdeur [lurdœr] *f* heaviness; clumsiness; sultriness; dullness

loustic [lustik] *m* wag, clown; (coll) screwball, character

loutre [lutr] *f* otter

louve [luv] *f* she-wolf

louve•teau [luvto] *m* (*pl* **-teaux**) wolf cub; cub scout

louvoyer [luvwaje] §47 *intr* to be evasive; (naut) to tack

lovelace [lɔvlas] *m* seducer, Don Juan

lover [lɔve] *tr* & *ref* to coil

loyal loyale [lwajal] *adj* (*pl* **loyaux** [lwajo]) loyal; honest; fair, just

loyaliste [lwajalist] *mf* loyalist

loyauté [lwajote] *f* loyalty; honesty; fairness

loyer [lwaje] *m* rent

lu lue [ly] *v* see **lire**

lubie [lybi] *f* whim; fad

lubricité [lybrisite] *f* lubricity, lewdness

lubri•fiant [lybrifjɑ̃] **-fiante** [fjɑ̃t] *adj* & *m* lubricant

lubrifier [lybrifje] *tr* to lubricate

lubrique [lybrik] *adj* lecherous, lustful, lewd

lucarne [lykarn] *f* dormer window; skylight

lucide [lysid] *adj* lucid

luciole [lysjɔl] *f* firefly

lucra•tif [lykratif] **-tive** [tiv] *adj* lucrative; **sans but lucratif** nonprofit

lucre [lykr] *m* lucre

ludiciel [lydisjɛl] *m* games software

luette [lɥet] *f* uvula

lueur [lɥœr] *f* glimmer, gleam; flash, blink

luge [lyʒ] *f* sled

lugubre [lygybr] *adj* gloomy

lui [lɥi] *pron disj* §85 him ‖ *pron conj* §87 him; her; it; to him; to her; to it

lui-même [lɥimɛm] §86 himself; itself

luire [lɥir] §37 *intr* to shine; to gleam, glow, glisten; to dawn

lui•sant [lɥizɑ̃] **-sante** [zɑ̃t] *adj* shining

lulu [lyly] *m* (orn) tree pipit

lumbago [lɔ̃bago] *m* lumbago

lumière [lymjɛr] *f* light; aperture; (*person*) luminary; **avoir des lumières de** to have knowledge of; **lumière du coffre** (aut) trunk light; **lumière ultraviolette** ultraviolet light

lumignon [lymiɲɔ̃] *m* feeble light

luminaire [lyminɛr] *m* luminary

lumines•cent [lyminɛsɑ̃] **-cente** [sɑ̃t] *adj* luminescent

lumi•neux [lyminø] **-neuse** [nøz] *adj* luminous; light (*e.g., spot*); bright (*idea*)

lunaire [lynɛr] *adj* lunar ‖ *f* (bot) honesty

lunatique [lynatik] *adj* whimsical, eccentric ‖ *mf* whimsical person, eccentric

lunch [lœntʃ], [lœ̃ʃ] *m* buffet lunch

lundi [lœ̃di] *m* Monday

lune [lyn] *f* moon; **être dans la lune** to be daydreaming; **lune de miel** honeymoon; **lune des moissons** harvest moon; **vieilles lunes** good old days, bygone days

lu•né -née [lyne] *adj* moon-shaped; **bien luné** in a good mood; **mal luné** in a bad mood

lune•tier [lyntje] **-tière** [tjɛr] *mf* optician

lunette [lynɛt] *f* telescope, spyglass; toilet seat; hole (*in toilet seat*); wishbone (*of turkey, chicken*); (archit) lunette; (aut) rear window; **lunettes** eyeglasses, spectacles; goggles; **lunettes auditives** eyeglass hearing aid; **lunettes de lecture, lunettes pour lire** reading glasses; **lunettes de soleil** sunglasses; **lunettes noires** dark glasses; **lunettes prescrites** prescription glasses; **lunettes (protectrices) de ski** skiing goggles

lurette [lyrɛt] *f*—**il y a belle lurette** (coll) ages ago

luron [lyrɔ̃] *m* (coll) playboy

luronne [lyrɔn] *f* (coll) hussy

lustre [lystr] *m* luster; five-year period; chandelier

lus•tré -trée [lystre] *adj* glossy, shiny

lustrine [lystrin] *f* cotton satin

lut [lyt] *m* (chem) lute

luth [lyt] *m* (mus) lute

lutherie [lytri] *f* violin making

luthé•rien [lyterjɛ̃] **-rienne** [rjɛn] *adj* Lutheran ‖ (*cap*) *mf* Lutheran

luthier [lytje] *m* violin maker

lu•tin [lytɛ̃] **-tine** [tin] *adj* impish ‖ *m* imp, urchin, scamp; sprite, brownie

lutiner [lytine] *tr* to tease

lutrin [lytrɛ̃] *m* lectern

lutte [lyt] *f* struggle, fight; wrestling; **de bonne lutte** aboveboard; **de haute lutte** by force; in open competition; hard-won; **lutte à la corde**

de traction tug of war; **lutte libre** catch-as-catch-can, freestyle wrestling
lutter [lyte] *intr* to fight, struggle; wrestle
lut•teur [lytœr] **-teuse** [tøz] *mf* wrestler; (fig) fighter
luxation [lyksɑsjɔ̃] *f* dislocation
luxe [lyks] *m* luxury; **avec un trés grand luxe** luxury (*e.g., apartment*)
Luxembourg [lyksãbur] *m*—**le Luxembourg** Luxembourg
luxer [lykse] *tr* to dislocate
lu•xueux [lyksɥø] **-xueuse** [ksɥøz] *adj* luxurious
luxure [lyksyr] *f* lechery, lust
luxu•riant [lyksyrjɑ̃] **-riante** [rjɑ̃t] *adj* luxuriant
luxu•rieux [lyksyrjø] **-rieuse** [rjøz] *adj* lecherous, lustful
luzerne [lyzɛrn] *f* alfalfa
lycée [lise] *m* high school (with academic courses); lyceum

ly•céen [liseɛ̃] **-céenne** [seɛn] *mf* secondary-school student
lymphatique [lɛ̃fatik] *adj* lymphatic
lymphe [lɛ̃f] *f* lymph
lynchage [lɛ̃ʃaʒ] *m* lynching
lyncher [lɛ̃ʃe] *tr* to lynch
lynx [lɛ̃ks] *m* lynx
Lyon [ljɔ̃] *m* Lyons
lyon•nais [lionɛ] **-naise** [nɛz] *adj* Lyonese; **à la lyonnaise** lyonnaise
lyophilisation [ljɔfilizasjɔ̃] *f* freeze drying
lyophiliser [ljɔfilize] *tr* to freeze-dry
lyre [lir] *f* lyre
lyrique [lirik] *adj* lyric(al) ‖ *m* lyric poet ‖ *f* lyric poetry
lyrisme [lirism] *m* lyricism
lys [lis] *m* lily; **lys blanc** lily; **lys jaune** day lily
lysimaque [lizimak] *f* loosestrife

M

M, m [ɛm], *[ɛm] *m invar* thirteenth letter of the French alphabet
M. *abbr* (**Monsieur**) Mr.
m' = me before vowel or mute **h**
ma [ma] §88 my
ma•boul -boule [mabul] *adj* (slang) nuts, balmy ‖ *mf* (slang) nut
macabre [makɑbr] *adj* macabre
macadam [makadam] *m* macadam
macadamiser [makadamize] *tr* to macadamize
macaron [makarɔ̃] *m* macaroon; (coll) bumper sticker
macchabée [makabe] *m* (slang) stiff (*corpse*)
macédoine [masedwan] *f* macédoine, medley; **macédoine de fruits** fruit salad; **macédoine de légumes** mixed vegetables
macérer [masere] §10 *tr* to macerate; mortify (*the flesh*); soak, steep ‖ *intr* to soak, steep
mâchefer [mɑʃɛr] *m* clinker
mâcher [mɑʃe] *tr* to chew; **mâcher la besogne à qn** to do all one's work for one; **ne pas mâcher ses mots** to not mince words
machiavélique [makjavelik] *adj* Machiavellian
machin [maʃɛ̃] *m* (coll) what-do-you-call-it; (coll) what's-his-name, so-and-so
machi•nal -nale [maʃinal] *adj* (*pl* **-naux** [no]) mechanical
machination [maʃinɑsjɔ̃] *f* machination
machine [maʃin] *f* machine; engine; **faire machine arrière** to go into reverse; **machine à calculer** adding machine; **machine à coudre** sewing machine; **machine à écrire** typewriter; **machine à écrire portative** portable typewriter; **machine à laver** washing machine; **machine à laver la vaisselle** dishwasher; **machine à sous** slot machine;

machine à vapeur steam engine; **machine de télégestion bancaire** automated teller machine; **machines** machinery
machine-outil [maʃinuti] *f* (*pl* **machines-outils**) machine tool
machinerie [maʃinri] *f* machinery; engine room
machiniste [maʃinist] *m* (theat) stagehand
machisme [matʃism] *or* [maʃism] *m* male chauvinism
machiste [matʃist] *or* [maʃist] *adj & m* (male) chauvinist
mâchoire [mɑʃwar] *f* jaw; jawbone; lower jaw
mâchonner [mɑʃɔne] *tr* to chew, munch; mumble (*e.g., the end of a sentence*)
mâchurer [mɑʃyre] *tr* to crush; smudge
maçon [masɔ̃] *m* mason
maçonner [masɔne] *tr* to mason, wall up
maçonnerie [masɔnri] *f* masonry
macule [makyl] *f* spot, blotch; inkblot; birthmark
maculer [makyle] *tr* to soil, spot; (typ) to smear
madame [madam] *f* (*pl* **mesdames** [medam]) madam; Mrs.; (not translated), e.g., **madame votre femme** your wife
Madeleine [madlɛn] *f* Madeleine, Magdalen; sponge cake; **pleurer comme une Madeleine** to weep bitterly
mademoiselle [madmwazɛl] *f* (*pl* **mesdemoiselles** [medmwazɛl]) Miss; eldest daughter; (not translated), e.g., **mademoiselle votre fille** your daughter
Madone [madɔn] *f* Madonna
ma•dré -drée [madre] *adj* sly, cagey ‖ *mf* sly one
madrier [madrije] *m* beam
mafia *or* **maffia** [mafja] *f* Mafia, Maffia; **la Maf(f)ia** the Mafia

maf•flu -flue [mafly] *adj* heavy-jowled

magasin [magazɛ̃] *m* store; warehouse; magazine (*of gun or camera; for munitions or powder*); **avoir en magasin** to have in stock; **grands magasins** department store; **magasin à libre service** self-service store; **magasin à prix unique** variety store; **magasin à succursales multiples** chain store; **magasin d'antiquités** antique shop; **magasin de modes** dress shop; **magasin de rabais** discount store; **magasin diététique** health-food store; **magasin entrepôt** outlet, discount house; **magasin qui vend de tout** general store

magasinage [magazinaʒ] *m* storage, warehousing; storage charges; (Canad) shopping

magasinier [magazinje] *m* warehouseman

magazine [magazin] *m* magazine; (mov, telv) hour, program, e.g., **magazine féminin** woman's hour

mages [maʒ] *mpl* Magi

magi•cien [maʒisjɛ̃] **-cienne** [sjɛn] *mf* magician

magie [maʒi] *f* magic

magique [maʒik] *adj* magic

magis•tral -trale [maʒistral] *adj* (*pl* **-traux** [tro]) masterful, masterly; magisterial; (pharm) magistral

magistrat [maʒistra] *m* magistrate

magnanime [maɲanim] *adj* magnanimous

magnat [magna] *m* magnate

magnésium [maɲezjɔm] *m* magnesium

magnétique [maɲetik] *adj* magnetic; hypnotic

magnétiser [maɲetize] *tr* to magnetize; hypnotize; spellbind

magnétisme [maɲetism] *m* magnetism

magnéto [maɲeto] *f* magneto

magnétophone [maɲetɔfɔn] *m* tape recorder; **magnétophone à fil d'acier** wire recorder

magnétoscope [maɲetɔskɔp] *m* video recorder, videotape recorder; video recording; videotape recording; **magnétoscope à cassettes** cassette recorder; videocassette recorder

magnétoscoper [maɲetɔskɔpe] *tr* to tape, to video, to videotape

magnifier [maɲifje] *tr* to extol, glorify

magnifique [maɲifik] *adj* magnificent; lavishly generous

magnitude [magnityd] *f* (astr) magnitude

magot [mago] *m* Barbary ape; figurine; (coll) hoard, pile (*of money*)

Mahomet [maɔmɛ] *m* Muhammad

mahomé•tan [maɔmetɑ̃] **-tane** [tan] *adj & m* Mohammedan

mai [mɛ] *m* May; Maypole

maie [mɛ] *f* bread bin; kneading trough

maigre [mɛgr] *adj* lean; thin; meager; meatless (*day*); **faire maigre** to abstain from meat

maigreur [mɛgrœr] *f* leanness; meagerness

maigri•chon [megriʃɔ̃] **-chonne** [ʃɔn] *adj* (coll) skinny

maigrir [megrir] *tr* to slim; make (*s.o.*) look thinner ‖ *intr* to lose weight

mail [maj] *m* mall

maille [mɑj] *f* link; stitch; mesh, loop; **avoir**

maille à partir avec qn to have a bone to pick with s.o.; **mailles** mail

maillet [majɛ] *m* mallet

maillon [mɑjɔ̃] *m* link (*of a chain*); **maillon qui manque à la chaîne** missing link

maillot [majo] *m* swimming suit; jersey; **maillot de bain** swimming suit; **maillot de corps** undershirt; **maillot de danseur** tights, leotard; **maillot de gym** leotard; **maillot tank** tank top; **maillot des acrobates** tights; **maillot de sport** sweat shirt

main [mɛ] *f* hand; quire; **à la main** by hand; **à main levée** by show of hands; in one stroke; **avoir la haute main sur** to control; **avoir la main, être la main** (cards) to be the dealer; **battre des mains** to applaud; **de la main à la main** privately; **de longue main** carefully; for a long time; **de main à main** from one person to another; **de première main** firsthand; **donner les mains à q.ch.** to be in favor of s.th.; **en venir aux mains** to come to blows; **faire main basse sur** to grab, to steal; **haut les mains!** hands up!; **main dans la main** hand in hand; **passer la main dans le dos à qn** to soft-soap s.o.; **serrer la main à** to shake hands with; **sous main** secretly; **tout main** handmade

main-d'œuvre [mɛ̃dœvr] *f* (*pl* **mains-d'œuvre**) labor; laborers, manpower

maint [mɛ̃] **mainte** [mɛ̃t] *adj* many a; **à maintes reprises** time and again

maintenant [mɛ̃tənɑ̃] *adv* now

maintenir [mɛ̃tnir] §72 *intr* to maintain; hold up ‖ *ref* to keep on; keep up

maintien [mɛ̃tjɛ̃] *m* maintenance; bearing

maire [mɛr] *m* mayor

mairesse [mɛrɛs] *f* (coll) mayor's wife

mairie [meri] *f* town hall, city hall

mais [mɛ] *m* but ‖ *adv* why, well; **mais non** certainly not ‖ *conj* but

maïs [mais] *m* corn, maize; **maïs en épi** corn on the cob; **maïs explosé** popcorn

maison [mɛzɔ̃] *f* house; home; household, family; house, firm, business; **à la maison** at home, home; **fait à la maison** homemade; **la Maison Blanche** the White House; **maison centrale** state or federal prison; **maison close, borgne, publique, mal famée, de débauche, de passe, de rendez-vous, de tolérance** house of ill fame; **maison d'accouchement** lying-in hospital; **maison d'antiquités, de meubles d'époque, or d'originaux** antique shop; **maison de commerce** firm; **maison de confiance** (com) trustworthy firm; **maison de correction** reform school; **maison de couture** dressmaking establishment; **maison de fous** madhouse; **maison de jeux** gambling house; **maison de plaisance or de campagne** cottage, summer home; **maison de rapport** apartment house; **maison de repos** rest home; **maison de retraite** old-people's home; **maison de santé** nursing home; **maison jumelée** semi-detached house; **maison mère** head office; parent company; **maison mortuaire** home of the deceased; **maison religieuse** convent

maisonnée [mɛzɔne] *f* household

maisonnette [mezɔnɛt] *f* little house, cottage

maî•tre [mɛtr] **-tresse** [trɛs] *adj* expert, capable; basic, key; main (*beam, girder*); utter (*fool*); arrant (*knave*); high (*card*) ‖ *m* master; Mr. (*when addressing a lawyer*); (naut) mate; (naut) petty officer; **être passé maître en** to be a past master of or in; **maître chanteur** blackmailer; **maître d'armes** fencing master; **maître de chapelle** choirmaster; **maître d'école** schoolmaster; **maître de conférences** associate professor; **maître de forges** ironmaster; **maître de maison** man of the house, householder; **maître d'équipage** boatswain; **maître d'études** monitor, supervisor; **maître d'hôtel** headwaiter; butler; **maître d'œuvre** foreman; **maître Jacques** jack-of-all-trades; **maître mécanicien** chief engineer; **maître mineur** mine foreman; **maître queue** chef; **passer maître** to know one's trade ‖ *f* see **maîtresse**

maître-autel [mɛtrotɛl] *m* (*pl* **maîtres-autels**) high altar

maîtresse [mɛtrɛs] *f* mistress; **maîtresse d'école** schoolmistress; **maîtresse de maison** lady of the house

maîtrise [metriz] *f* mastery, command; master's degree; **maîtrise de soi** self-control

maîtriser [metrize] *tr* to master, control; subdue

maj. *abbr* (**majuscule**) cap.

majesté [maʒɛste] *f* majesty

majes•tueux [maʒɛstɥø] **-tueuse** [tɥøz] *adj* majestic

ma•jeur -jeure [maʒœr] *adj* & *m* major

major [maʒɔr] *m* regimental quartermaster; army doctor; **être le major de sa promotion** to be at the head of one's class

majordome [maʒɔrdɔm] *m* major-domo

majorer [maʒɔre] *tr* to increase the price of; overprice; raise (*the price*)

majoritaire [maʒɔritɛr] *adj* majority

majorité [maʒɔrite] *f* majority; time of being of full legal age

Majorque [maʒɔrk] *f* Majorca

major•quin [maʒɔrkɛ̃] **-quine** [kin] *adj* Majorcan ‖ (*cap*) *mf* Majorcan

majuscule [maʒyskyl] *adj* capital (*letter*) ‖ *f* capital letter

mal [mal] *adj*—**de mal** bad, e.g., **dire q.ch. de mal** to say s.th. bad; **pas mal** not bad, quite good-looking ‖ *m* (*pl* **maux** [mo]) evil; trouble; hurt; pain; wrong; **avoir du mal à** + *inf* to have a hard time + *ger,* to have difficulty in + *ger;* **avoir mal à la tête** to have a headache; **avoir mal au cœur** to be nauseated; **avoir mal aux dents** to have a toothache; **avoir mal de gorge** to have a sore throat; **dire du mal de qn** to speak ill of s.o.; **faire mal à, faire du mal à** to hurt, to harm; **le Mal** Evil; **mal aux reins** backache; **mal blanc** whitlow;

mal de l'air airsickness; **mal d'altitude, mal des montagnes** altitude sickness; **mal de la route** carsickness; **mal de mer** seasickness; **mal des rayons** radiation sickness; **mal du pays** homesickness; **mal du siècle** Weltschmerz, romantic melancholy; **se donner du mal** to take pains ‖ *adv* §91 badly, bad; **de mal en pis** from bad to worse; **être mal avec qn** to be on bad terms with s.o.; **pas mal** not bad; **pas mal de** a lot of, quite a few

malade [malad] *adj* sick, ill ‖ *mf* patient, sick person

maladie [maladi] *f* disease, sickness; distemper; **elle va en faire une maladie** (coll) she'll be terribly upset over it; **maladie d'altitude** flying sickness; **maladie d'Alzheimer** Alzheimer's disease; **maladie de carence** *or* **par carence** deficiency disease; **maladie de cœur** heart trouble; **maladie de la vache folle** mad cow disease; **maladie des caissons** bends, decompression sickness; **maladie diplomatique** malingering; **maladie du sommeil** sleeping sickness; **maladie sexuellement transmissible** (MST) sexually transmitted disease STD; **revenir de maladie** to convalesce

mala•dif [maladif] **-dive** [div] *adj* sickly; morbid

maladresse [maladrɛs] *f* awkwardness; blunder

mala•droit [maladrwa] **-droite** [drwat] *adj* clumsy, awkward

ma•lais [malɛ] **-laise** [lɛz] *adj* Malay (*language*) ‖ *m* see **malaise** *m* ‖ (*cap*) *mf* Malay (*person*)

malaise [malɛz] *m* malaise, discomfort

malai•sé -sée [maleze] *adj* difficult

malap•pris [malapri] **-prise** [priz] *adj* uncouth, ill-bred ‖ *mf* ill-bred person

malard [malar] *m* (orn) mallard

malaria [malarja] *f* malaria

malavi•sé -sée [malavize] *adj* ill-advised, indiscreet

malaxer [malakse] *tr* to knead; churn (*butter*); massage

malaxeur [malaksœr] *m* churn; (mach) mixer

malchance [malʃɑ̃s] *f* bad luck; **par malchance** unluckily; **une malchance** a piece of bad luck

malchan•ceux [malʃɑ̃sø] **-ceuse** [søz] *adj* unlucky

malcommode [malkɔmɔd] *adj* inconvenient; unsuitable, impracticable

maldonne [maldɔn] *f* misdeal

mâle [mɑl] *adj* male; energetic, virile ‖ *m* male

malédiction [malediksjɔ̃] *f* curse

maléfice [malefis] *m* evil spell

maléfique [malefik] *adj* baleful

malencon•treux [malɑ̃kɔ̃trø] **-treuse** [trøz] *adj* untimely, unfortunate

malentendu [malɑ̃tɑ̃dy] *m* misunderstanding

malfaçon [malfasɔ̃] *f* defect

malfai•sant [malfəzɑ̃] **-sante** [zɑ̃t] *adj* mischievous, harmful

malfaiteur [malfɛtœr] *m* malefactor

malfa·mé -mée [malfame] *adj* ill-famed

malgra·cieux [malgrasjø] **-cieuse** [sjøz] *adj* ungracious

malgré [malgre] *prep* in spite of; **malgré que** in spite of the fact that, although

malhabile [malabil] *adj* inexperienced, clumsy

malheur [malœr] *m* misfortune; unhappiness; bad luck; **faire un malheur** to commit an act of violence; (theat) to be a howling success; **jouer de malheur** to be unlucky

malheureusement [malœrøzmɑ̃] *adv* unfortunately

malheu·reux [malœrø] **-reuse** [røz] *adj* unfortunate; unhappy; unlucky; paltry ‖ *m* poor man, wretch; **les malheureux** the unfortunate ‖ *f* poor woman, wretch

malhonnête [malɔnɛt] *adj* dishonest; (slang) rude, uncivil

malhonnêteté [malɔnɛtte] *f* dishonesty

malice [malis] *f* mischievousness; malice; trick

mali·cieux [malisjø] **-cieuse** [sjøz] *adj* malicious, mischievous

malignité [maliɲite] *f* malignancy

ma·lin [malɛ̃] **-ligne** [liɲ] *adj* cunning, sly, smart; mischievous; malignant; (med) malignant; **ce n'est pas malin** (coll) it's easy ‖ *mf* sly one; **Le Malin** the Evil One

malingre [malɛ̃gr] *adj* weakly, puny

malintention·né-née [malɛ̃tɑ̃sjɔne] *adj* evil-minded, ill-disposed

mal-jugé [malʒyʒe] *m* miscarriage (*of justice*)

malle [mal] *f* trunk; mailboat; **faire ses malles** to pack

malléable [maleabl] *adj* malleable; compliant; pliable

mallette [malɛt] *f* valise; case

malmener [malmǝne] **§2** *tr* to rough up

malodo·rant [malɔdɔrɑ̃] **-rante** [rɑ̃t] *adj* malodorous; bad (*breath*)

malo·tru -true [malɔtry] *adj* coarse, uncouth ‖ *mf* ill-bred person, oaf

malpropre [malprɔpr] *adj* dirty; improper; crude, clumsy (*workmanship*)

mal·sain [malsɛ̃] **-saine** [sɛn] *adj* unhealthy

mal·séant [malseɑ̃] **-séante** [seɑ̃t] *adj* improper

malson·nant [malsɔnɑ̃] **-nante** [nɑ̃t] *adj* offensive, objectionable

malt [malt] *m* malt

maltraiter [maltrete] *tr* to mistreat

malveil·lant [malvɛjɑ̃] **-lante** [jɑ̃t] *adj* malevolent

malve·nu -nue [malvǝny] *adj* ill-advised, out of place; poorly developed

malversation [malvɛrsɑsjɔ̃] *f* embezzlement

maman [mamɑ̃] *f*, mama, ma, mom, mamma

mamelle [mamɛl] *f* breast; udder

mamelon [mamlɔ̃] *m* nipple, teat; knoll

mamie [mami] *f* (coll) my dear

mammectomie [mamɛktɔmi] *f* mastectomy

mammifère [mamifɛr] *adj* mammalian ‖ *m* mammal

mammographie [mamɔgrafi] *f* mammogram, mammograph

mammouth [mamut] *m* mammoth

mamours [mamur] *mpl* (coll) caresses

mam'selle or **mam'zelle** [mamzɛl] *f* (coll) Miss

manant [manɑ̃] *m* hick, yokel

manche [mɑ̃ʃ] *m* handle; stick, stock; neck (*of violin*); (culin) knuckle; **branler au manche** or **dans le manche** to be shaky; **manche à balai** broomstick; (aer) joystick; **manche à gigot** holder (*for carving*) ‖ *f* sleeve; hose; channel; game, heat, round; shaft, chute; (baseball) inning; (bridge) game; (tennis) set; **en manches de chemise** in shirt sleeves; **la Manche** the English Channel; **manche à air** windsock; **manche à manche** neck and neck, even up; **manches à gigot** leg-of-mutton sleeves

manchette [mɑ̃ʃɛt] *f* cuff; (journ) headline

manchon [mɑ̃ʃɔ̃] *m* muff; mantle (*of gaslight*); (mach) casing, sleeve

man·chot [mɑ̃ʃo] **-chote** [ʃɔt] *adj* one-armed; one-handed; (coll) clumsy ‖ *mf* one-armed person; one-handed person ‖ *m* (orn) penguin

mandarine [mɑ̃darin] *f* mandarin orange

mandat [mɑ̃da] *m* mandate; term of office; money order; power of attorney; proxy; **mandat d'arrêt** warrant; **mandat de perquisition** search warrant

mandataire [mɑ̃datɛr] *mf* representative; proxy; defender

mandat-carte [mɑ̃dakart] *m* (*pl* **mandats-carte**) postal-card money order

mandat-poste [mɑ̃dapɔst] *m* (*pl* **mandats-poste**) postal money order

Mandchourie [mɑ̃tʃuri] *f* Manchuria; **la Mandchourie** Manchuria

mander [mɑ̃de] **§97** *tr* to summon

mandoline [mɑ̃dɔlin] *f* mandolin

mandragore [mɑ̃dragɔr] *f* mandrake

mandrin [mɑ̃drɛ̃] *m* (mach) punch; (mach) chuck

manécanterie [manekɑ̃tri] *f* choir school

manège [manɛʒ] *m* horsemanship; riding school; trick, little game; **manège de chevaux de bois** merry-go-round

mânes [mɑn] *mpl* shades, spirits (*of ancestors*)

maneton [mantɔ̃] *m* crank handle; pin (*of crankshaft*)

manette [manɛt] *f* lever, switch

manganèse [mɑ̃ganɛz] *m* manganese

mangeable [mɑ̃ʒabl] *adj* edible; barely fit to eat

mangeaille [mɑ̃ʒaj] *f* swill; (coll) grub, chow

mangeotter [mɑ̃ʒɔte] *tr* to pick at (*one's food*)

manger [mɑ̃ʒe] *m* food, e.g., **le boire et le manger** food and drink; (slang) meal ‖ **§38** *tr* to eat; eat up; mumble (*one's words*); **manger du bout des lèvres** to nibble at ‖ *intr* to eat; **manger à la fortune du pot** to take potluck

mangerie [mɑ̃ʒri] *f* (coll) big meal

mange-tout [mɑ̃ʒtu] *m invar* sugar pea

man·geur [mɑ̃ʒœr] **-geuse** [ʒøz] *mf* eater; wastrel, spendthrift; **mangeur d'hommes** man-eater

mangouste [mɑ̃gust] *f* mongoose

maniable [manjabl] *adj* maneuverable, easy to handle, supple

maniaco-dépres•sif [manjakɔdeprɛsif] **-sive** [siv] *adj* manic-depressive

maniaque [manjak] *adj & mf* maniac

manie [mani] *f* mania; **manie de la persécution** persecution complex

maniement [manimɑ̃] *m* handling

manier [manje] *tr* to handle ‖ *ref* (coll) to get a move on

manière [manjɛr] *f* manner; **à la manière de** in the manner of; **de manière à** so as to; **de manière que** so that; **de toute manière** in any case; **d'une manière ou d'une autre** one way or another; **en aucune manière** by no means; **faire des manières** to pretend to be indifferent, to want to be coaxed; **manière de voir** point of view; **manières** manners

manié•ré -rée [manjere] *adj* mannered, affected

maniérisme [manjerism] *m* mannerism

ma•nieur [manjœr] **-nieuse** [njøz] *mf* handler; **grand manieur d'argent** tycoon

manifes•tant [manifɛstɑ̃] **-tante** [tɑ̃t] *mf* demonstrator

manifestation [manifɛstasjɔ̃] *f* demonstration, manifestation

manifeste [manifɛst] *adj* manifest ‖ *m* manifesto; (naut) manifest

manifester [manifɛste] *tr* to manifest ‖ *intr* to demonstrate ‖ *ref* to reveal oneself

manigance [manigɑ̃s] *f* trick, intrigue

manipuler [manipyle] *tr* to manipulate; handle (*e.g., packages*); arrange (*equipment*) for an experiment

manitou [manitu] *m* manitou; (coll) bigwig

manivelle [manivɛl] *f* crank

manne [man] *f* manna

mannequin [mankɛ̃] *m* model; mannequin, dummy; scarecrow

manœuvre [manœvr] *m* hand, laborer ‖ *f* maneuver; (naut) handling, maneuvering; (rr) shifting; **fausse manœuvre** wrong move; **manœuvres** rigging

manœuvrer [manœvre] *tr & intr* to maneuver; (rr) to shift

manoir [manwar] *m* manor, manor house

man•quant [mɑ̃kɑ̃] **-quante** [kɑ̃t] *adj* missing ‖ *mf* absentee ‖ *m* missing article; **manquants** shortages

manque [mɑ̃k] *m* lack; shortage; insufficiency; **manque à gagner** lost opportunity; **manque de parole** breach of faith; **par manque de** for lack of ‖ *f*—**à la manque** (coll) rotten, poor, dud

man•qué -quée [mɑ̃ke] *adj* missed, unsuccessful; broken (*engagement*); (with abilities which were not professionally developed), e.g., **le docteur est un cuisinier manqué** the doctor could have been a cook by profession

manquement [mɑ̃kmɑ̃] *m* breach, lapse

manquer [mɑ̃ke] §96, §97 *tr* to miss; flunk ‖ *intr* to misfire; be missing, e.g., **il en manque trois** three are missing; be missed, e.g., **vous lui manquez beaucoup** you are very much missed by him, he misses you very much; be short, e.g., **il lui manque cinq francs** he is five francs short; **manquer à** to break (*one's word*); disobey (*an order*); fail to observe (*a rule*); fail, e.g., **le cœur lui a manqué** his heart failed him; **manquer de** to lack, be short of, to run out of; **manquer de** + *inf* to nearly + *inf*, e.g., **il a manqué de se noyer** he nearly drowned; **sans manquer** without fail ‖ *ref* to miss each other; to fail

mansarde [mɑ̃sard] *f* mansard roof; mansard

manse [mɑ̃s] *m & f* (hist) small manor

mante [mɑ̃t] *f* mantle; **mante religieuse** (ent) praying mantis

man•teau [mɑ̃to] *m* (*pl* **-teaux** [to]) overcoat; mantle, cloak; mantelpiece; **sous le manteau** sub rosa

mantille [mɑ̃tij] *f* mantilla

manucure [manykyr] *mf* manicurist

ma•nuel -nuelle [manɥɛl] *adj* manual ‖ *mf* laborer, blue-collar worker ‖ *m* manual, handbook

manufacture [manyfaktyr] *f* factory, plant

manufacturer [manyfaktyre] *tr* to manufacture

manus•crit [manyskri] **-crite** [krit] *adj & m* manuscript

manutention [manytɑ̃sjɔ̃] *f* handling (*of goods*); stopping for unloading

manutentionner [manytɑ̃sjɔne] *tr* to handle (*merchandise*)

mappemonde [mapmɔ̃d] *f* world map; **mappemonde céleste** map of the heavens

maque•reau [makro] **-relle** [rɛl] (*pl* **-reaux -relles**) *mf* (slang) procurer ‖ *m* mackerel; (slang) pimp ‖ *f* (slang) madam (*of a brothel*)

maquette [makɛt] *f* maquette, model; dummy (*of book*); rough sketch

maquignon [makiɲɔ̃] *m* horse trader; wholesale cattle dealer; (coll) go-between

maquignonnage [makiɲɔnaʒ] *m* horse trading

maquignonner [makiɲɔne] *intr* to horse-trade

maquillage [makijaʒ] *m* make-up; fakery

maquiller [makije] *tr* to make up; fake, distort ‖ *ref* to make up

maquil•leur [makijœr] **-leuse** [jøz] *mf* make-up artist ‖ *m* make-up man

maquis [maki] *m* bush; maquis; **prendre le maquis** to go underground

maraî•cher [mareʃe] **-chère** [ʃɛr] *adj* truck-farming ‖ *mf* truck farmer

marais [marɛ] *m* marsh; truck farm; **marais salant** saltern

marasme [marasm] *m* depression; doldrums, standstill

marathon [maratɔ̃] *m* marathon

marâtre [maratr] *f* stepmother; cruel mother

maraude [marod] *f* marauding; **en maraude** cruising (*taxi*)

marauder [marode] *intr* to maraud; cruise (*said of taxi*)

marau•deur [marodœr] **-deuse** [døz] *adj* marauding ‖ *mf* marauder

marbre [marbr] *m* marble; (typ) stone

marbrer [marbre] *tr* to marble; mottle, vein; bruise, blotch

marc [mar] *m* mark (*old coin*); marc, pulp; **marc de café** coffee grounds; **marc de thé** tea leaves ‖ [mark] (*cap*) *m* Mark

marcassin [markasɛ̃] *m* young wild boar

mar·chand [marʃɑ̃] **-chande** [ʃɑ̃d] *adj* marketable; sale (*value*); trading (*center*); wholesale (*price*); merchant (*marine*) ‖ *mf* merchant; **marchand ambulant** peddler, street vendor, pitchman; **marchand clandestin** fence (*seller of stolen goods*); **marchand de canons** munitions maker; **marchand de couleurs** paint dealer, dealer in household articles; **marchand de ferraille** junk dealer; **marchand de journaux** newsdealer; **marchand des quatre-saisons** fruit vendor; **marchand en gros** wholesaler; **marchand forain** hawker ‖ *f*—**marchande d'amour** or **de plaisir** prostitute

marchandage [marʃɑ̃daʒ] *m* bargaining; haggling; deal, underhanded arrangement

marchander [marʃɑ̃de] *tr* to bargain over; haggle over; be stingy with (*e.g., one's compliments*) ‖ *intr* to haggle

marchan·deur [marʃɑ̃dœr] **-deuse** [døz] *mf* bargainer; haggler

marchandisage [marʃɑ̃dizaʒ] *m* merchandising

marchandise [marʃɑ̃diz] *f* merchandise; **marchandises** goods

mar·chant [marʃɑ̃] **-chante** [ʃɑ̃t] *adj* marching; militant (*wing of political party*); (mil) wheeling (*flank*)

marche [marʃ] *f* march; step (*of stairway*); walking; movement; progress, course; (aut) gear; **à dix minutes de marche** ten minutes' walk from here; **attention à la marche!** watch your step!; **en marche** in motion, running, operating; **faire marche arrière** to back up; to reverse; **fermer la marche** to bring up the rear; **marche funèbre** funeral march; **ouvrir la marche** to lead off the procession

marché [marʃe] *m* market; shopping; deal, bargain; **à bon marché** cheap; cheaply; **à meilleur marché** cheaper; more cheaply; **bon marché** cheapness; cheap; cheaply; **faire bon marché de** to set little store by; **faire son marché** to do the marketing; **lancer, mettre,** or **vendre sur le marché** to market; **marché à option** futures market; **marché aux puces** flea market; **marché de matières premières** commodities market; **marché noir** black market; **par-dessus le marché** into the bargain

marchepied [marʃəpje] *m* footstool; little stepladder; running board; footboard; (fig) stepping stone

marcher [marʃe] *intr* to walk; run; operate; march; **ça marche** it works; **ça marche?** O.K.?; **ça marche!** that's cool! (slang); **faire marcher qn** to pull someone's leg; **marcher à grands pas** to stride; **marcher au pas** to walk in step; **marcher dans l'espace** to take a space walk; **marcher sur** to tread on, walk on; **marchez au pas** (*public sign*) drive slowly

mar·cheur [marʃœr] **-cheuse** [ʃøz] *mf* walker

mardi [mardi] *m* Tuesday; **mardi gras** Shrove Tuesday; Mardi gras

mare [mar] *f* pool, pond

marécage [marekaʒ] *m* marsh, swamp

maréca·geux [marekaʒø] **-geuse** [ʒøz] *adj* marshy, swampy

maré·chal [mareʃal] *m* (*pl* **-chaux** [ʃo]) marshal; blacksmith; **maréchal des logis** artillery or cavalry sergeant

maréchale [mareʃal] *f* marshal's wife

maréchal-ferrant [mareʃalfɛrɑ̃] *m* (*pl* **maréchaux-ferrants**) blacksmith, farrier

marée [mare] *f* tide; fresh seafood; **marée descendante** ebb tide; **marée montante** flood tide

marelle [marɛl] *f* hopscotch

marémo·teur [maremɔtœr] **-trice** [tris] *adj* tide-driven

margarine [margarin] *f* margarine

marge [marʒ] *f* margin; border, edge; lee-way, room; **en marge de** on the fringe of; a footnote to; **marge bénéficiaire** margin of profit; **marge brute d'autofinancement (MBA)** cash flow; **marge de sécurité** margin of safety

margelle [marʒɛl] *f* curb, edge (*of well, fountain, etc.*)

margeur [marʒœr] *m* margin stop

margi·nal **-nale** [marʒinal] *adj* (*pl* **-naux** [no]) marginal

margot [margo] *f* (coll) magpie; (coll) chatterbox; **Margot** (coll) Maggie

margotin [margɔtɛ̃] *m* kindling

margouillis [marguji] *m* (coll) rotten stinking mess

margou·lin [margulɛ̃] **-line** [lin] *mf* sharpster, shyster

marguerite [margərit] *f* daisy (comp) daisy wheel; **Marguerite** Margaret

marguillier [margije] *m* churchwarden

mari [mari] *m* husband

mariable [marjabl] *adj* marriageable

mariage [marjaʒ] *m* marriage; wedding; blend, combination; **mariage blanc** unconsummated marriage

Marianne [marjan] *f* Marian; Marianne (*symbol of the French Republic*)

ma·rié **-riée** [marje] *adj* married ‖ *m* bridegroom; **jeunes mariés** newlyweds; **les mariés** the bride and groom ‖ *f* bride

marier [marje] *tr* to marry, join in wedlock; marry off; blend, harmonize ‖ *ref* to get married; **se marier avec** to marry

marie-salope [marisalɔp] *f* (*pl* **maries-salopes**) dredger; (slang) slut

ma·rieur [marjœr] **-rieuse** [rjøz] *mf* (coll) matchmaker

marihuana [mariɥana] *or* **marijuana** [mariʒɥana] *f* marijuana

ma·rin [marɛ̃] **-rine** [rin] *adj* marine; sea-going; sea, e.g., **brise marine** sea breeze ‖ *m* sailor, seaman; **sailor suit** ‖ *f* navy; seascape; **marine marchande** merchant marine

mariner [marine] *tr & intr* to marinate

mari·nier [marinje] **-nière** [njɛr] *adj* naval; petty (*officer*); **à la marinière** cooked in gravy with onions ‖ *m* waterman ‖ *f* blouse; (swimming) sidestroke

marionnette [marjɔnɛt] *f* marionette; (fig) puppet

mari·tal -tale [marital] *adj* (*pl* **-taux** [to]) of the husband

maritime [maritim] *adj* maritime

maritorne [maritɔrn] *f* slut

marivaudage [marivodaʒ] *m* playful flirting; sophisticated conversation

marjolaine [marʒɔlɛn] *f* marjoram

marketing [marketiŋ] *m* marketing

marlou [marlu] *m* (slang) pimp

marmaille [marmaj] *f* (coll) brats

marmelade [marməlad] *f* marmalade; (coll) mess

marmite [marmit] *f* pot, pan; (geol) pothole; (mil) shell, heavy shell; **marmite autoclave, marmite sous pression** pressure cooker; **marmite norvégienne** double boiler

marmiton [marmitɔ̃] *m* cook's helper

marmonner [marmɔne] *tr & intr* to mumble

marmot [marmo] *m* (coll) lad; (coll) grotesque figurine (*on knocker*); **croquer le marmot** (coll) to cool one's heels; **marmots** (coll) urchins, kids

marmotte [marmɔt] *f* woodchuck; **dormir comme une marmotte** to sleep like a log; **marmotte d'Amérique** groundhog; **marmotte de commis voyageur** traveling salesman's sample case

marmouset [marmuzɛ] *m* grotesque figurine; little man

marner [marne] *tr* to marl ‖ *intr* (naut) to flow, rise; (coll) to drudge

Maroc [marɔk] *m*—**le Maroc** Morocco

maro·cain [marɔkɛ̃] **-caine** [kɛn] *adj* Moroccan ‖ (*cap*) *mf* Moroccan

maronner [marɔne] *intr* (coll) to grumble

maroquin [marɔkɛ̃] *m* morocco leather

maroquinerie [marɔkinri] *f* leather goods

marotte [marɔt] *f* fad; whim; dummy head (*of milliner*); jester's staff

marquage [markaʒ] *m* marking; (*on an animal*) branding; (*on a tree*) blazing

mar·quant [markɑ̃] **-quante** [kɑ̃t] *adj* remarkable; outstanding; purple (*passages*)

marque [mark] *f* mark; brand, make; hallmark; token, sign; **à vos marques!** on your mark(s)!; **de marque** distinguished; **marque déposée** trademark

marquer [marke] *tr* to mark; brand; score; indicate, show ‖ *intr* to make a mark, leave an impression

marqueterie [markətri], [markɛtri] *f* marquetry, inlay

mar·queur [markœr] **-queuse** [køz] *mf* marker ‖ *m* scorekeeper; scorer ‖ *f* (mach) stenciler

marquis [marki] *m* marquis

marquise [markiz] *f* marchioness, marquise; marquee, awning; (rr) roof (*over platform*)

marraine [marɛn] *f* godmother, sponsor; christener; **marraine de guerre** war mother

mar·rant [marɑ̃] **-rante** [rɑ̃t] *adj* (slang) side-splitting; (slang) funny, queer

marre [mar] *adv*—**en avoir marre** (coll) to be fed up

marrer [mare] *ref* (slang) to have a good laugh

mar·ron [marɔ̃] **-ronne** [rɔn] *adj* quack (*doctor*); shyster (*lawyer*) ‖ **marron** *adj invar* brown ‖ *m* chestnut; **marron d'Inde** horse chestnut

marronnier [marɔnje] *m* chestnut tree; **marronnier d'Inde** horse-chestnut tree

mars [mars] *m* March; **Mars** Mars

Marseille [marsɛj] *f* Marseilles

marsouin [marswɛ̃] *m* porpoise

marte [mart] *f* (zool) marten

mar·teau [marto] (*pl* **-teaux**) *adj* (coll) cracked; balmy ‖ *m* hammer; (ichth) hammerhead; **marteau de porte** knocker

marteau-pilon [martopilɔ̃] *m* (*pl* **marteaux-pilons**) drop hammer

marteau-piqueur [martopikœr] *m* (*pl* **marteaux-piqueurs**) pneumatic drill

marteler [martəle] §2 *tr* to hammer; hammer at; hammer out

Marthe [mart] *f* Martha

mar·tial -tiale [marsjal] *adj* (*pl* **-tiaux** [sjo]) martial

mar·tien [marsjɛ̃] **-tienne** [sjɛn] *adj & mf* Martian

martinet [martinɛ] *m* triphammer; scourge, cat-o'-nine-tails; (orn) martin, swift

martin-pêcheur [martɛ̃pɛʃœr] *m* (*pl* **martins-pêcheurs**) (orn) kingfisher

martre [martr] *f* (zool) marten

mar·tyr -tyre [martir] *adj & mf* martyr ‖ **martyre** *m* martyrdom

martyriser [martirize] *tr* to martyr

marxiste [marksist] *adj & mf* Marxist

maryland [marilɑ̃] *m* choice tobacco ‖ (*cap*) *m*—**le Maryland** Maryland

mas [ma], [mas] *m* farmhouse or farm (*in Provence*)

mascarade [maskarad] *f* masquerade

mascaret [maskarɛ] *m* bore

mascaron [maskarɔ̃] *m* mask, mascaron

mascotte [maskɔt] *f* mascot

mascu·lin [maskylɛ̃] **-line** [lin] *adj & m* masculine

maso [mazo] *adj* (coll) masochistic ‖ *mf* masochist

masochiste [mazɔʃist] *adj* masochistic ‖ *mf* masochist

masque [mask] *m* mask; **masque à gaz** gas mask; **masque de beauté** face pack; **masque mortuaire** death mask

masquer [maske] *tr & ref* to mask

massacre [masakr] *m* massacre; botched job

massacrer [masakre] *tr* to massacre; to botch

massage [masaʒ] *m* massage

masse [mas] *f* mass; sledgehammer; mace; pool, common fund; (elec) ground (*e.g., of an automobile*); **masse d'air froid** cold front; **mettre à la masse** (elec) to ground; **une masse de** (coll) a lot of

massepain [maspɛ̃] *m* marzipan

masser [mase] *tr* to mass; massage || *ref* to mass; massage oneself

massette [masɛt] *f* sledge hammer (*of stonemason*); (bot) bulrush

mas·seur -seuse [masœr] [søz] *mf* masseur || *m* massager (*instrument*)

massicot [masiko] *m* paper cutter

mas·sif -sive [masif] [siv] *adj* massive; heavy-set; solid (*e.g., gold*) || *m* massif, high plateau; clump (*of flowers, trees, etc.*)

massue [masy] *f* club, bludgeon

mastectomie [mastɛktɔmi] *f* mastectomy

mastic [mastik] *m* putty

mastiquer [mastike] *tr* to masticate; putty

mastoc [mastɔk] *adj invar* heavy, massive

masturbation [mastyrbasjɔ̃] *f* masturbation

masturber [mastyrbe] *tr & ref* to masturbate

m'as-tu-vu -vue [matyvy] (*pl* **-vu -vue**) *adj* (coll) stuck-up || *mf* (coll) show-off; smart aleck; (coll) bragging actor

masure [mazyr] *f* hovel, shack, shanty

mat mate [mat] *adj* dull, flat || **mat** *adj invar* checkmated || *m* checkmate || **mat** *adv* dull

mât [ma] *m* mast; pole

mataf [mataf] *m* (slang) gob (*sailor*)

matamore [matamɔr] *m* braggart

match [matʃ] *m* (*pl* **matchs** *or* **matches**) match, contest, game; **match de baseball** ball game; **match de bienfaisance** benefit game *ou* match; **match de boxe** boxing match

matelas [matla] *m* mattress; (coll) roll (*of bills*); **matelas à eau** water bed

matelasser [matlase] *tr* to pad, cushion

matelot [matlo] *m* sailor, seaman

matelote [matlɔt] *f* fish stew in wine

mater [mate] *tr* to dull; checkmate; subdue

matérialiser [materjalize] *ref* to materialize

matérialiste [materjalist] *adj* materialistic || *mf* materialist

maté·riau [materjo] *m* (*pl* **-riaux**) material

maté·riel -rielle [materjɛl] *adj* material; materialistic || *m* material; equipment; (comp) hardware; (mil) material; **matériel roulant** (rr) rolling stock || *f* (slang) living

maternage [maternaʒ] *m* nursing; mothering

mater·nel -nelle [maternɛl] *adj* maternal || *f* nursery school

maternité [maternite] *f* maternity; maternity hospital

math *or* **maths** [mat] *fpl* (coll) math

mathémati·cien -cienne [matematisjɛ̃] [sjɛn] *mf* mathematician

mathématique [matematik] *adj* mathematical || **mathématiques** *fpl* mathematics

matière [matjɛr] *f* matter; subject matter; material; **matière première** raw material

matin [matɛ̃] *m* morning; early part of the morning; **au petit matin** in the wee hours of the morning; **de bon matin, de grand matin** very early; **du matin** in the morning, A.M., e.g., **onze heures du matin** eleven o'clock in the morning, eleven A.M. || *adv* early

mâ·tin [matɛ̃] **-tine** [tin] *mf* (coll) sly one || *m* (zool) mastiff || **mâtin** *adv* indeed!, well I'll be!

mati·nal -nale [matinal] *adj* (*pl* **-naux** [no]) morning; early-rising

mâti·né -née [matine] *adj* crossbred; **mâtiné de** mixed with, crossbred with

matinée [matine] *f* morning; matinée; **faire la grasse matinée** to sleep late

mâtiner [matine] *tr* to crossbreed

matines [matin] *fpl* matins

matité [matite] *f* dullness

ma·tois -toise [matwa] [twaz] *adj* sly, cunning || *mf* sly dog

matou [matu] *m* tomcat

matraque [matrak] *f* bludgeon; club, billy

matraquer [matrake] *tr* to club, bludgeon

matriarcat [matrijarka] *m* matriarchy

matrice [matris] *f* matrix; **matrice active** (comp) active matrix; **matrice de points** dot matrix

matricide [matrisid] *mf* matricide (*person*) || *m* matricide (*action*)

matricule [matrikyl] *adj* serial (*number*) || *m* serial number || *f* roll, register

matrimo·nial -niale [matrimɔnjal] *adj* (*pl* **-niaux** [njo]) matrimonial, marital

matrone [matrɔn] *f* matron; matriarch; old hag; midwife; abortionist

mâture [matyr] *f* masts (*of ship*)

maudire [modir] §39 *tr* to curse, damn

mau·dit [modi] **-dite** [dit] *adj* cursed

maugréer [mogree] *intr* to grumble, gripe

maure [mɔr] *adj* Moorish || (*cap*) *m* Moor

mauresque [mɔrɛsk] *adj* Moorish || (*cap*) *f* Moorish woman

mausolée [mozɔle] *m* mausoleum

maussade [mosad] *adj* sullen, gloomy

mau·vais [mɔvɛ], [movɛ] **-vaise** [vɛz] (precedes the noun it modifies) §91, §92 *adj* bad; evil; wrong; **il fait mauvais** the weather is bad; **sentir mauvais** to smell bad || *mf* wicked person; **le Mauvais** the Evil One || *m* evil

mauve [mov] *adj* mauve || *f* (bot) mallow

mauviette [movjɛt] *f* (orn) lark; (coll) milquetoast

mauvis [movi] *m* (orn) redwing

maxillaire [maksilɛr] *m* jawbone

maxime [maksim] *f* maxim

maximum [maksimɔm] *adj & m* maximum

mayonnaise [majɔnɛz] *f* mayonnaise

mazette [mazɛt] *f* duffer || *interj* gosh!

mazout [mazut] *m* fuel oil

mazouter [mazute] *intr* to fuel up

M^e *abbr* (**Maître**) Mr.

me [mə] §87 me, to me

méandre [meãdr] *m* meander

mec [mɛk] *m* (slang) guy; (slang) tough egg

mécanicien [mekanisjẽ] *m* mechanic; machinist; engineer (*of locomotive*); **mécanicien dentiste** dental technician

mécanicienne [mekanisjɛn] *f* sewing-machine operator

mécanique [mekanik] *adj* mechanical ‖ *f* mechanism; mechanics

mécaniser [mekanize] *tr* to mechanize

mécanisme [mekanism] *m* mechanism

mécano [mekano] *m* (coll) mechanic

mécène [mesɛn] *m* patron, Maecenas

méchamment [meʃamã] *adv* maliciously, nastily; (coll) fantastically

méchanceté [meʃãste] *f* malice, wickedness; nastiness

mé•chant [meʃã] **-chante** [ʃãt] *adj* malicious, wicked; nasty; naughty (*child*) ‖ *mf* mean person; **faire le méchant** to threaten; (coll) to strike back; **les méchants** the wicked; **méchant!** naughty boy!

mèche [mɛʃ] *f* wick; fuse; lock (*of hair*); bit (*of drill*); **être de mèche avec** (coll) to be in cahoots with; **éventer** or **découvrir la mèche** to discover the plot; **il n'y a pas mèche** (coll) it's no go, nothing doing; **vendre la mèche** (coll) to let the cat out of the bag

mécompte [mekɔ̃t] *m* miscalculation; disappointment

méconnaissable [mekɔnɛsabl] *adj* unrecognizable

méconnaître [mekɔnɛtr] §12 *tr* to ignore; underestimate

mécon•nu -nue (mekɔny] *adj* underestimated, misunderstood

mécon•tent [mekɔ̃tã] **-tente** [tãt] *adj* dissatisfied, displeased ‖ *mf* grumbler

mécontentement [mekɔ̃tãtmã] *m* dissatisfaction, displeasure

mécontenter [mekɔ̃tãte] *tr* to displease

Mecque [mɛk] *f*—**La Mecque** Mecca

mécréant [mekreã] **mécréante** [mekreãt] *adj* unbelieving ‖ *mf* unbeliever

médaille [medaj] *f* medal

médaillon [medajɔ̃] *m* medallion; locket; thin round slice (*e.g., of meat*); pat (*of butter*)

médecin [medsẽ] *m* doctor; **femme médecin** woman doctor

médecine [medsin], [mɛtsin] *f* medicine (*science and art*); **médecine légale, médecine médico-légale** forensic medicine

média [medja] *m* mass media

mé•dian [medjã] **-diane** [djan] *adj* & *f* median

média•teur [medjatœr] **-trice** [tris] *mf* mediator, arbitrator

médiation [medjɑsjɔ̃] *f* mediation

médi•cal -cale [medikal] *adj* (*pl* **-caux** [ko]) medical

médicament [medikamã] *m* (pharm) medicine; **médicament miracle** wonder drug

médicamenter [medikamãte] *tr* to dose

médicamen•teux [medikamãtø] **-teuse** [tøz] *adj* medicinal

médici•nal -nale [medisinal] *adj* (*pl* **-naux** [no]) medicinal

médico-légal [medikɔlegal] *adj* (*pl* **médico-légaux**) forensic

médié•val -vale [medjeval] *adj* (*pl* **-vaux** [vo]) medieval

médiéviste [medjevist] *mf* medievalist

médiocre [medjɔkr] *adj* mediocre, poor, inferior, second-rate

médiocrité [medjɔkrite] *f* mediocrity

médire [medir] §40 *intr* to backbite; **médire de** to run down, to disparage

médisance [medizãs] *f* disparagement, backbiting

médi•sant [medizã] **-sante** [zãt] *adj* disparaging, backbiting ‖ *mf* slanderer

méditation [meditɑsjɔ̃] *f* meditation

méditer [medite] §97 *tr* & *intr* to meditate

méditerra•né -née [mediterane] *adj* Mediterranean; inland ‖ (*cap*) *f* Mediterranean (Sea)

méditerranéen [mediteranẽ] **méditerra•néenne** [mediteraneɛn] *adj* Mediterranean

médium [medjɔm] *m* medium (*in spiritualism*); range (*of voice*)

médiumnique [medjɔmnik] *adj* psychic

médius [medjys] *m* middle finger

méduse [medyz] *f* jellyfish, medusa ‖ (*cap*) *f* Medusa

méduser [medyze] *tr* to petrify (*with terror*)

meeting [mitiŋ] *m* rally, meet, meeting; **meeting d'aviation** air show (*flying display*)

méfait [mefɛ] *m* misdeed; **méfaits** ravages

méfiance [mefjãs] *f* mistrust

mé•fiant [mefjã] **-fiante** [fjãt] *adj* mistrustful

méfier [mefje] *ref* to beware; **se méfier de** to guard against, to mistrust

mégacycle [megasik] *m* megacycle

mégaphone [megafɔn] *m* megaphone

mégarde [megard] *f*—**par mégarde** inadvertently

mégère [meʒɛr] *f* shrew

mégohm [megɔm] *m* megohm

mégot [mego] *m* butt (*of cigarette or cigar*)

meil•leur -leure [mɛjœr] (precedes the noun it modifies) §91 *adj comp* & *super* better; best; **meilleur marché** cheaper

mél [mel] *m* (comp) E-mail

mélancolie [melãkɔli] *f* melancholy, melancholia

mélancolique [melãkɔlik] *adj* melancholy

mélange [melãʒ] *m* mixing, blending; mixture, blend; **mélanges** homage volume, Festschrift

mélanger [melãʒe] §38 *tr* to mix, blend

mélan•geur [melãʒœr] **-geuse** [ʒøz] *m* & *f* mixer

mélasse [melas] *f* molasses; **dans la mélasse** (coll) in the soup

mê•lé -lée [mele] *adj* mixed ‖ *f* melee

mêler [mele] §97 *tr* to mix; tangle; shuffle (*the cards*) ‖ *ref* to mix; **se mêler à** to mingle with; join in; **se mêler de** to meddle with, interfere with

mélèze [melɛz] *m* (bot) larch

méli-mélo [melimelo] *m* mishmash

mélodie [melɔdi] *f* melody

mélo•dieux [melɔdjø] **-dieuse** [djøz] *adj* melodious

mélodique [melɔdik] *adj* melodic

mélodramatique [melɔdramatik] *adj* melodramatic

mélomane [melɔman] *adj* music-loving ‖ *mf* music lover

melon [məlɔ̃] *m* melon; derby; **melon d'eau** watermelon

mélopée [melɔpe] *f* singsong, chant

membrane [mɑ̃bran] *f* membrane; **membrane vibrante** (elec) diaphragm

membre [mɑ̃br] *m* member; limb, member; **membre actif** active member; **membre bienfaiteur** sustaining member; **membre de phrase** clause; **membre donateur** contributing member; **membre perpétuel** life member

membrure [mɑ̃bryr] *f* frame, limbs

même [mɛm] *adj indef* very, e.g., **le jour même** on that very day ‖ (when standing before noun) *adj indef* same, e.g., **en même temps** at the same time ‖ *pron indef* same, same one; **à même de** + *inf* up to + *ger*, in a position to + *inf;* **à même le (la,** etc.) straight out of the (*e.g., bottle*); flush with the (*e.g., pavement*); next to one's (*e.g., skin*); on the bare (*ground, sand, etc.*) **cela revient au même** that amounts to the same thing; **de même** likewise; **de même que** in the same way as; **tout de même** nevertheless ‖ *adv* even; **même quand** even when; **même si** even if

-même [mɛm] §86

mémé [meme] *f* (*children's language*) granny, grandma, mom-mom, grandmom

mémento [memɛ̃to] *m* memento; memo book

mémère [memɛr] *f* (coll) granny; (coll) blowsy dame

mémoire [memwar] *m* memorandum; statement, account; term paper; treatise; petition; **mémoires** memoirs ‖ *f* memory; (comp) data storage; **de mémoire** from memory; **de mémoire d'homme** within memory; **mémoire morte** (comp) read-only memory, ROM; **mémoire vive** (comp) random-access memory, RAM; **pour mémoire** for the record

mémorandum [memɔrɑ̃dɔm] *m* memorandum; **mémorandum de combat** battle orders

mémo•rial [memɔrjal] *m* (*pl* **-riaux** [rjo]) memorial; (dipl) memorandum; memoirs

mena•çant [mənasɑ̃] **-çante** [sɑ̃t] *adj* menacing

menace [mənas] *f* menace, threat

menacer [mənase] §51, §97, §99 *tr & intr* to menace, threaten

ménage [menaʒ] *m* household; family; married couple; furniture; **de ménage** homemade; **faire bon ménage** to get along well; **faire des ménages** to do housework (*for hire*); **faire le ménage** to do the housework; **se mettre en**

ménage to set up housekeeping; (coll) to live together (*without being married*)

ménagement [menaʒmɑ̃] *m* discretion; consideration

ména•ger [menaʒe] **-gère** [ʒɛr] *adj* household; **ménager de** thrifty with ‖ *f* housewife, homemaker; silverware; silverware case ‖ **ménager** §38 *tr* to be careful with, spare (*money, one's strength*); husband (*one's resources, one's strength*); be considerate of, handle with kid gloves; arrange, bring about; install, provide; make (*e.g., a hole*); **ménager un espace pour** leave a space for ‖ *intr* to save ‖ *ref* to take good care of oneself

ménagerie [menaʒri] *f* menagerie

men•diant [mɑ̃djɑ̃] **-diante** [djɑ̃t] *adj & mf* beggar; **des mendiants** dessert (*of dried fruits and nuts*)

mendier [mɑ̃dje] *tr & intr* to beg

menées [məne] *fpl* intrigues, schemes

mener [məne] §2, §95 *tr* to lead; take; manage; draw (*e.g., a line*) ‖ *intr* to lead

ménestrel [menɛstrɛl] *m* wandering minstrel

ménétrier [menetrije] *m* fiddler

me•neur [mənœr] **-neuse** [nøz] *mf* leader; ringleader; **meneur de jeu** master of ceremonies; narrator; moving spirit

menotte [mənɔt] *f* tiny hand; **menottes** handcuffs; **mettre** or **passer les menottes à** to handcuff

mens [mɑ̃] *v* (**ment**) see **mentir**

mensonge [mɑ̃sɔ̃ʒ] *m* lie; **pieux mensonge** white lie

mensonger [mɑ̃sɔ̃ʒe] **-gère** [ʒɛr] *adj* lying, false; illusory, deceptive

men•struel -struelle [mɑ̃stryɛl] *adj* menstrual

menstrues [mɑ̃stry] *fpl* menses

mensualité [mɑ̃sɥalite] *f* monthly installment; monthly salary

men•suel -suelle [mɑ̃sɥɛl] *adj* monthly

men•tal -tale [mɑ̃tal] *adj* (*pl* **-taux** [to]) mental

mentalité [mɑ̃talite] *f* mentality

men•teur [mɑ̃tœr] **-teuse** [tøz] *adj* lying ‖ *mf* liar

menthe [mɑ̃t] *f* mint; **menthe poivrée** peppermint; **menthe verte** spearmint

mention [mɑ̃sjɔ̃] *f* mention; **avec mention** with honors; **biffer les mentions inutiles** to cross out the questions which do not apply; **être reçu sans mention** to receive just a passing grade

mentionner [mɑ̃sjɔne] *tr* to mention

mentir [mɑ̃tir] §41 *intr* to lie

menton [mɑ̃tɔ̃] *m* chin

mentonnière [mɑ̃tɔnjɛr] *f* chin rest; chin strap

me•nu -nue [məny] *adj* small, little; tiny, fine ‖ *m* menu; minute detail; **menu dépliant** (comp) pull-down menu

menuet [mənɥɛ] *m* minuet

menuiserie [mənɥizri] *f* carpentry; woodwork

menuisier [mənɥizje] *m* carpenter

méprendre [meprɑ̃dr] §56 *ref* to be mistaken; **à s'y méprendre** enough to take one for the other; **il n'y a pas à s'y méprendre** there's no mistake about it

mépris [mepri] *m* contempt, scorn ·

méprisable [meprizabl] *adj* contemptible, despicable

mépri•sant [meprizɑ̃] **-sante** [zɑ̃t] *adj* contemptuous, scornful

méprise [mepriz] *f* mistake

mépriser [meprize] *tr* to despise, scorn

mer [mɛr] *f* sea; **basse mer** low tide; **de haute mer** seagoing; **haute mer, pleine mer** high seas; high tide; **Mer des Antilles, Mer des Caraïbes, Mer Caraïbe** Caribbean Sea; **mer des Indes** Indian Ocean; **Mer Rouge** Red Sea; **sur mer** afloat

mercanti [mɛrkɑ̃ti] *m* profiteer

mercantile [mɛrkɑ̃til] *adj* profiteering, mercenary

mercenaire [mɛrsənɛr] *adj & mf* mercenary

mercerie [mɛrsəri] *f* notions

merci [mɛrsi] *m* thanks, thank you; **merci de** + *inf* thank you for + *ger;* **merci de** or **pour** thank you for ‖ *f*—**à la merci de** at the mercy of; **Dieu merci!** thank heavens! ‖ *interj* thanks!, thank you!; no thanks!, no thank you!

mercredi [mɛrkrədi] *m* Wednesday; **mercredi des Cendres** Ash Wednesday

mercure [mɛrkyr] *m* mercury

mercuriale [mɛrkyrjal] *f* reprimand; market quotations; mercury (*weed*)

merde [mɛrd] *f* excrement; **merde alors!** (coll) well I'll be!

mère [mɛr] *f* mother; **la mère Gigogne** the old woman who lived in a shoe; **mère adoptive** (*selon l'adoption plénière*) adoptive mother; **mère de placement** foster mother

méri•dien [meridjɛ̃] **-dienne** [djɛn] *adj & m* meridian ‖ *f* meridian line; couch, sofa; siesta

méridio•nal -nale [meridjɔnal] (*pl* **-naux** [no]) *adj* meridional, southern ‖ (*cap*) *mf* inhabitant of the Midi

meringue [mərɛ̃g] *f* meringue

merise [məriz] *f* wild cherry

merisier [mərizje] *m* wild cherry (tree)

méri•tant [meritɑ̃] **-tante** [tɑ̃t] *adj* deserving, worthy

mérite [merit] *m* merit

mériter [merite] §97 *tr* to merit, deserve; win, earn ‖ *intr*—**mériter bien de** to deserve the gratitude of

méritoire [meritwar] *adj* deserving, meritorious

merlan [mɛrlɑ̃] *m* (ichth) whiting

merle [mɛrl] *m* (orn) blackbird; **merle blanc** (fig) rara avis; **vilain merle** (fig) dirty dog

merlin [mɛrlɛ̃] *m* ax; poleax; (naut) marline

merluche [mɛrly ʃ] *f* (ichth) hake, cod

merveille [mɛrvɛj] *f* marvel, wonder; **à merveille** marvelously, wonderfully

merveil•leux [mɛrvɛjø] **-leuse** [jøz] *adj* marvelous, wonderful

mes [me] §88 my

mésalliance [mezaljɑ̃s] *f* misalliance, mismatch

mésallier [mezalje] *tr* to misally ‖ *ref* to marry beneath one's station

mésange [mezɑ̃ʒ] *f* (orn) chickadee, titmouse

mésaventure [mezavɑ̃tyr] *f* misadventure

mesdames *fpl* see **madame**

mesdemoiselles *fpl* see **mademoiselle**

mésentente [mezɑ̃tɑ̃t] *f* misunderstanding

mésestimer [mezɛstime] *tr* to underestimate

mésintelligence [mezɛ̃teliʒɑ̃s] *f* misunderstanding, discord

mes•quin [mɛskɛ̃] **-quine** [kin] *adj* mean; stingy; petty

mess [mɛs] *m* officer's mess

message [mesaʒ] *m* message; **messages commerciaux non solicités envoyés par e-mail** (comp) spam (slang)

messa•ger [mesaʒe] **-gère** [ʒɛr] *mf* messenger

messagerie [mesaʒri] *f* express; **messagerie électronique** (comp) E-mail; **messageries express** express company; **messageries aériennes** air freight

messe [mɛs] *f* (eccl) Mass; **dire** or **faire des messes basses** (coll) to speak in an undertone; **messe basse, petite messe** Low Mass; **première messe, messe du début** early Mass

Messie [mesi] *m* Messiah

messieurs *mpl* see **monsieur**

messieurs-dames [mɛsjødam] *interj* ladies and gentlemen!

mesure [məzyr] *f* measure; measurement; (mus, poetic) measure; **à mesure** successively, one by one; **à mesure que** as; according as, proportionately as; **battre la mesure** to keep time; **dans la mesure de** insofar as; **dans une certaine mesure** to a certain extent; **être en mesure de** to be in a position to; **faire sur mesure** to make (*clothing*) to order; (fig) to tailormake; **mesure de circonstance** emergency measure; **mesure en ruban** tape measure; **prendre des mesures de** to take measures to; **prendre la mesure de** to size up; **prendre les mesures de** to measure

mesurer [məzyre] *tr* to measure; measure off or out ‖ *ref* to measure; **se mesurer avec** to measure swords with

métairie [metɛri] *f* farm (*of a sharecropper*)

mé•tal [metal] *m* (*pl* **-taux** [to]) metal

métallique [metalik] *adj* metallic

métalloïde [metalɔid] *m* nonmetal

métallurgie [metalyrʒi] *f* metallurgy

métamorphose [metamɔrfoz] *f* metamorphosis

métaphore [metafɔr] *f* metaphor

métaphorique [metafɔrik] *adj* metaphorical

métathèse [metatɛz] *f* metathesis

métayage [metejaʒ] *m* sharecropping, tenant farming

mé•tayer [meteje] **-tayère** [tejɛr] *mf* sharecropper

méteil [metɛj] *m* wheat and rye

météo [meteo] *adj invar* meteorological ‖ *m* weatherman ‖ *f* meteorology; weather bureau; weather report

météore [meteɔr] *m* meteor; (fig) meteor

météorite [meteɔrit] *m & f* meteorite

météorologie [meteɔrɔlɔʒi] *f* meteorology; weather bureau; weather report

météorologiste [meteɔlɔdʒist] *mf* weather forecaster

métérologue [meterɔlɔg] *mf* weather forecaster

métèque [metɛk] *m* (pej) foreigner

méthane [metan] *m* methane

méthode [metɔd] *f* method; **méthode insufflatoire bouche à bouche** mouth-to-mouth resuscitation

méthodique [metɔdik] *adj* methodic(al)

méthodiste [metɔdist] *adj & mf* Methodist

méticu·leux [metikylø] **-leuse** [løz] *adj* meticulous

métier [metje] *m* trade, craft; loom; **faites votre métier!** mind your own business!; **métiers du bâtiment** building trades; **sur le métier** on the stocks

mé·tis -tisse [metis] *adj & mf* half-breed

métisser [metise] *tr* to crossbreed

métrage [metraʒ] *m* length in meters; length (*of remnant, film, etc.*); (mov) length of film in meters (*in English: footage, i.e., length of film in feet*); **court métrage** (mov) short subject, short; **long métrage** (mov) full-length movie, feature

mètre [mɛtr] *m* meter; **mètre à ruban** tape measure; **mètre pliant** folding rule

métrer [metre] §10 *tr* to measure out by the meter

métrique [metrik] *adj* metric(al) ‖ *f* metrics

métro [metro] *m* subway

métronome [metrɔnɔm] *m* metronome

métropole [metrɔpɔl] *f* metropolis; mother country

métropoli·tain [metrɔpɔlitɛ̃] **-taine** [tɛn] *adj* metropolitan ‖ *m* subway; (eccl) metropolitan

mets [mɛ] *m* dish, food

mettable [mɛtabl] *adj* wearable

met·teur [mɛtœr] **-teuse** [tøz] *mf*—**metteur au point** mechanic; **metteur en œuvre** setter; (fig) promoter; **metteur en ondes** (rad) director, producer; **metteur en pages** (typ) make-up man; **metteur en scène** (mov, theat) director, producer

mettre [mɛtr] §42, §95, §96 *tr* to put, lay, place; put on (*clothes*); set (*the table*); take (*time*); **mettre à feu** (rok) to fire; **mettre au point** to carry out, complete; tune up, adjust; (opt) to focus; (rad) to tune; **mettre au rancart** to pigeonhole; **mettre en accusation** to indict; **mettre en marche** to start; **mettre en œuvre** to put into action; **mettre en scène** (theat) to direct; (theat & fig) to stage; **mettre en valeur** to develop, improve; set off, enhance; **mettre en vigueur** to enforce; **mettre feu à** to set fire to; **mettre que** (coll) to suppose that ‖ *intr*—**mettre bas** (zool) to litter ‖ §96 *ref* to sit or stand; go; **se mettre à** to begin to; **se mettre à table** to sit down to eat; (slang) to confess; **se mettre en colère** to get angry; **se**

mettre en route to set out; **se mettre mal avec** to quarrel with

meuble [mœbl] *adj* uncemented; loose (*ground*); personal (*property*) ‖ *m* piece of furniture; **meubles** furniture; **meubles d'occasion** secondhand furniture

meubler [mœble] *tr* to furnish

meuglement [møgləmɑ̃] *m* lowing (*of cow*)

meugler [møgle] *intr* to low

meuh! meuh! [mœmœ] *interj* moo! moo!

meule [møl] *f* millstone; grindstone; stack (*e.g., of hay*)

meuler [møle] *tr* to grind

meu·nier [mønje] **-nière** [njɛr] *adj* milling (*e.g., industry*) ‖ *m* miller ‖ *f* miller's wife; **à la meunière** sautéed in butter

meurs [mœr] *v* (**meurt**) see **mourir**

meurt-de-faim [mœrdəfɛ̃] *mf invar* starveling; **de meurt-de-faim** starvation (*wages*)

meurtre [mœrtr] *m* manslaughter; (fig) shame, crime; **meurtre commis avec préméditation** murder

meur·trier [mœrtrije] **-trière** [trijɛr] *adj* murderous; deadly ‖ *m* murderer ‖ *f* murderess; gun slit, loophole

meurtrir [mœrtrir] *tr* to bruise

meurtrissure [mœrtrisyr] *f* bruise

meute [møt] *f* pack, band

mévente [mevɑ̃t] *f* slump (*in sales*)

mexi·cain [mɛksikɛ̃] **-caine** [kɛn] *adj* Mexican ‖ (*cap*) *mf* Mexican

Mexico [mɛksiko] Mexico City

Mexique [mɛksik] *m*—**le Mexique** Mexico

mezzanine [mɛdzanin] *m & f* (theat) mezzanine ‖ *f* mezzanine; mezzanine window

miam! miam! [mjɑ̃mjɑ̃] *interj* purr! purr!

miaou [mjau] *m* meow

miaulement [mjolmɑ̃] *m* meow; caterwauling; catcall

miauler [mjole] *intr* to meow

mi-bas [miba] *m invar* half hose

mica [mika] *m* mica

miche [miʃ] *f* round loaf of bread

mi-chemin [miʃmɛ̃] *m*—**à mi-chemin** halfway

micheton [miʃtɔ̃] *m* (slang) john (*prostitute's customer*)

mi-clos [miklo] **-close** [kloz] *adj* (*pl* **-clos -closes**) half-shut

micmac [mikmak] *m* (coll) underhand dealing

mi-corps [mikɔr]—**à mi-corps** to the waist

mi-côte [mikot]—**à mi-côte** halfway up the hill

micro [mikro] *m* home computer, desktop computer, personal computer, microcomputer

microbe [mikrɔb] *m* microbe

microbicide [mikrɔbisid] *adj & m* germicide

microbiologie [mikrɔbjɔlɔʒi] *f* microbiology

microbiologiste [mikrɔbjɔlɔʒist] *mf* microbiologist

microchip [mikrɔtʃip] *m* microchip

microchirurgie [mikroʃiryrʒi] *f* microsurgery

microeconomie [mikrɔekɔnɔmi] *f* microeconomics

microédition [mikrɔedisjɔ̃] *f* desktop publishing

microfilm [mikrɔfilm] *m* microfilm

microfilmer [mikrɔfilme] *tr* to microfilm

micro-onde [mikrɔɔ̃d] *f* (*pl* **-ondes**) microwave

micro-ondes [mikrɔɔ̃d] *m* (culin) microwave (oven)

micro-ordinateur [mikrɔɔrdinatœr] *m* (*pl* **-ordinateurs**) home computer, desktop computer, personal computer, microcomputer, minicomputer

microphone [mikrɔfɔn] *m* microphone

micro-plastron [mikrɔplastrɔ̃] *m* chest microphone

microprocesseur [mikrɔprɔsɛsœr] *m* (comp, electron) word processor

microscope [mikrɔskɔp] *m* microscope; **microscope électronique** electron microscope

microscopique [mikrɔskɔpik] *adj* microscopic

microsillon [mikrɔsijɔ̃] *adj & m* microgroove

midi [midi] *m* noon; south; twelve, e.g., **midi dix** ten minutes after twelve; **chercher midi à quatorze heures** (fig) to look for difficulties where there are none; **Midi** south of France

midinette [midinɛt] *f* dressmaker's assistant; working girl

mie [mi] *f* soft part, crumb; female friend; **ne ... mie** §90 (archaic) not a crumb, not, e.g., **je n'en veux mie** I don't want any

miel [mjɛl] *m* honey

miel‧leux [mjɛlø] **-leuse** [løz] *adj* honeyed, unctuous

mien [mjɛ̃] **mienne** [mjɛn] §89 mine

miette [mjɛt] *f* crumb

mieux [mjø] §91 *adv comp & super* better; **aimer mieux** to prefer; **à qui mieux mieux** trying to outdo each other; **de mieux en mieux** better and better; **être mieux, aller mieux** to feel better; **tant mieux** so much the better; **valoir mieux** to be better

mieux-être [mjøzɛtr] *m* improved well-being

mièvre [mjɛvr] *adj* dainty, affected

mi-figue [mifig] *f*—**mi-figue mi-raisin** half one way half the other; half in jest half in earnest

mi‧gnard [miɲar] **-gnarde** [ɲard] *adj* affected, mincing

mi‧gnon [miɲɔ̃] **-gnonne** [ɲɔn] *adj* cute, darling ‖ *mf* darling

mignon‧net [miɲɔnɛ] **-nette** [nɛt] *adj* dainty ‖ *f* fine lace; pepper; (bot) pink

mignoter [miɲɔte] *tr* (coll) to pet (*a child*)

migraine [migrɛn] *f* migraine; headache

migratoire [migratwar] *adj* migratory

mi-jambe [miʒɑ̃b] *f*—**à mi-jambe** up to one's knee

mijoter [miʒɔte] *tr* to simmer; (coll) to cook up, brew ‖ *intr* to simmer

mijoteuse [miʒɔtøz] *f* crockpot

mil [mil] *adj* one thousand, e.g., **mil neuf cent quatorze** nineteen fourteen (*year*) ‖ *m* Indian club; millet

milan [milɑ̃] *m* (orn) kite

milice [milis] *f* militia

mi‧lieu [miljø] *m* (*pl* **-lieux**) middle; milieu; **milieu de table** centerpiece

militaire [militɛr] *adj* military ‖ *m* soldier; **le militaire** the military

mili‧tant [militɑ̃] **-tante** [tɑ̃t] *adj & mf* militant

militariser [militarize] *tr* to militarize

militarisme [militarism] *m* militarism

militer [milite] *intr* to militate

milk-shake [milkʃɛk] *m* milk shake

mille [mil] *adj & pron* thousand ‖ *m* thousand; mile; **mettre dans le mille** to hit the bull's-eye; **mille marin** international nautical mile

mille-feuille [milfœj] *f* (*pl* **-feuilles**) (bot) yarrow ‖ *m* (culin) napoleon

millénaire [milenɛr] *adj* millennial ‖ *m* millennium

mille-pattes [milpat] *m invar* centipede

millésime [milezim] *m* date, vintage; year of issue

millet [mijɛ] *m* millet; birdseed

milliard [miljar] *m* billion

milliardaire [miljardɛr] *mf* billionaire

millième [miljɛm] *adj, pron* (*masc, fem*) thousandth ‖ *m* thousandth; mill (*thousandth part of a dollar*)

millier [milje] *m* thousand; about a thousand; **par milliers** by the thousands; **un millier de** a thousand

milligramme [miligram] *m* milligram

millimètre [milimɛtr] *m* millimeter

million [miljɔ̃] *m* million; **un million de** a million

millionième [miljɔnjɛm] *adj, pron* (*masc, fem*), & *m* millionth

millionnaire [miljɔnɛr] *adj & m* millionaire

mime [mim] *mf* mime; mimic

mimer [mime] *tr & intr* to mime; mimic

mimique [mimik] *adj* sign (*language*) ‖ *f* mimicry

mi-moyen [mimwajɛ̃] *m* (*pl* **-moyens**) welterweight

minable [minabl] *adj* wretched, shabby; (coll) pitiful (*performance, existence, etc.*) ‖ *mf* unfortunate

minaret [minarɛ] *m* minaret

minauder [minode] *intr* to simper, smirk

minau‧dier [minodje] **-dière** [djɛr] *adj* mincing

mince [mɛ̃s] *adj* thin, slim, slight; **mince!** or **mince alors!** golly!

mine [min] *f* mine; lead (*of pencil*); look, face; looks; (fig) mine (*of information*); **avoir bonne mine** to look well; **avoir la mine d'être** to look to be; **avoir mauvaise mine** to look badly; **faire bonne mine à** to be nice to; **faire des mines** to simper; **faire la mine à** to pout at; **faire mauvaise mine à** to be unpleasant to; **faire mine de** to make as if to

miner [mine] *tr* to mine; undermine; wear away

minerai [minrɛ] *m* ore

miné‧ral -rale [mineral] (*pl* **-raux** [ro]) *adj & m* mineral

minéralogie [mineralɔʒi] *f* mineralogy

mi·net [minɛ] **-nette** [nɛt] *mf* (coll) kitty, pussy; (coll) darling

mi·neur -neure [minœr] *adj* minor (*secondary in importance*); minor (*underaged*); (mus) minor (*key*) ‖ *mf* minor (*less than legal age*) ‖ *m* miner; (mus) minor mode

miniature [minjatyr] *f* miniature

miniaturisation [minjatyrizɑsjɔ̃] *f* miniaturization

miniaturiser [minjatyrize] *tr* to miniaturize

minigolf [minigolf] *m* miniature golf

minijupe [miniʒyp] *f* miniskirt

mini·mal -male [minimal] *adj* (*pl* **-maux** [mo]) minimum (*temperature*)

minimarge [minimarʒ] *f* discount house

minime [minim] *adj* tiny; derisory (*salary*)

minimiser [minimize] *tr* to minimize

minimum [minimɔm] *adj & m* minimum; **minimum vital** minimum wage

ministère [ministɛr] *m* ministry; **ministère des affaires étrangères** ministry of foreign affairs (department of state)

ministé·riel -rielle [ministerjel] *adj* ministerial

ministre [ministr] *m* minister; **ministre des affaires étrangères** minister of foreign affairs (secretary of state); **premier ministre** premier, prime minister

minium [minjɔm] *m* red lead

minois [minwa] *m* (coll) pretty little face

minoritaire [minɔritɛr] *adj* minority

minorité [minɔrite] *f* minority; time of being under legal age

Minorque [minɔrk] *f* Minorca

minoterie [minɔtri] *f* flour mill; flour industry

minotier [minɔtje] *m* miller

minuit [minɥi] *m* midnight; twelve, e.g. **minuit et demi** twelve-thirty

minuscule [minyskyl] *adj* tiny; small (*letter*) ‖ *f* small letter

minus habens [minysabɛ̃s] *mf invar* (coll) moron, idiot

minutage [minytaʒ] *m* timing

minute [minyt] *f* minute; moment, instant; **à la minute** that very moment ‖ *interj* (coll) just a minute!

minuter [minyte] *tr* to itemize; time

minuterie [minytri] *f* delayed-action switch; (mach) timing mechanism

minuteur [minytœr] *m* timer

minutie [minysi] *f* minute detail; great care; **minuties** minutiae

minu·tieux [minysjø] **-tieuse** [sjøz] *adj* meticulous, thorough

mioche [mjɔʃ] *mf* (coll) brat

mi-pente [mipɑ̃t]—**à mi-pente** halfway up or halfway down

mirabilis [mirabilis] *m* (bot) marvel-of-Peru

miracle [mirakl] *m* miracle; wonder, marvel; miracle play; **crier au miracle** to go into ecstasies

miracu·leux [mirakylø] **-leuse** [løz] *adj* miraculous; wonderful, marvelous

mirador [miradɔr] *m* watchtower

mirage [miraʒ] *m* mirage

mire [mir] *f* sight (*of gun*); surveyor's pole; (telv) test pattern

mire-œufs [mirø] *m invar* candler

mirer [mire] *tr* to candle (*eggs*) ‖ *ref* to look at oneself; be reflected

mirifique [mirifik] *adj* (coll) marvelous

mirobo·lant [mirɔbɔlɑ̃] **-lante** [lɑ̃t] *adj* (coll) astounding

miroir [mirwar] *m* mirror; **miroir à alouettes** decoy

miroiter [mirwate] *intr* to sparkle, gleam; **faire miroiter q.ch. à qn** to lure s.o. with s.th.

miroton [mirɔtɔ̃] *m* Irish stew

mis [mi] **mise** [miz] *v* see **mettre**

misaine [mizɛn] *f* foresail

misanthrope [mizɑ̃trɔp] *mf* misanthrope

miscellanées [miselane], [misɛllane] *fpl* miscellany

mise [miz] *f* placing, putting; dress, attire; (cards) stake, ante; **de mise** acceptable, proper; **mise à feu** firing (*e.g., of missile*); **mise à l'eau** launching; **mise à prix** opening bid; **mise au point** carrying out, completion; tuning up, adjustment; (opt) focusing; (rad) tuning; **mise au rancart** pigeonholing; **mise bas** delivery (*of litter*); **mise de fonds** investment, funding; **mise en accusation** indictment; **mise(s) en chantier** construction start(s); **mise en code** coding; **mise en demeure** (law) injunction; **mise en marche** starting; **mise en œuvre** putting into action; **mise en placement** fosterage (*of children*); **mise en plis** set; **mise en scène** (theat) direction; (theat & fig) staging; **mise en valeur** development, improvement; **mise en vigueur** enforcement; **mise sur ordinateur** computerization

mise-en-garde [mizɑ̃gard] *f* (electron) hold

miser [mize] *tr & intr* to ante; stake, bet; bid (*e.g., at auction*)

misérable [mizerabl] *adj* miserable ‖ *mf* wretch

misère [mizɛr] *f* misery, wretchedness; poverty; worry; (coll) trifle; **crier misère** to make a poor mouth; to look forsaken; **faire des misères à** to pester; **misères** woes, misfortunes

misé·reux [mizerø] **-reuse** [røz] *adj* destitute, wretched ‖ *mf* pauper

miséricorde [mizerikɔrd] *f* mercy

miséricor·dieux [mizerikɔrdjø] **-dieuse** [djøz] *adj* merciful

missel [misɛl] *m* missal

missile [misil] *m* guided missile; **missile croisière** cruise missile

mission [misjɔ̃] *f* mission

missionnaire [misjɔnɛr] *adj & m* missionary

missive [misiv] *adj & f* missive

mitaine [mitɛn] *f* mitt

mite [mit] *f* (ent) mite; (ent) clothes moth

mi·té -tée [mite] *adj* moth-eaten; (coll) shabby

mi-temps [mitɑ̃] *f invar* (sports) half time; **à mi-temps** half time

miter [mite] *ref* to become moth-eaten

mi·teux [mitø] **-teuse** [tøz] *adj* shabby ‖ *mf* (coll) shabby-looking person

miti·gé -gée [mitiʒe] *adj* mitigated, reserved, qualified

mitiger [mitiʒe] §38 *tr* to mitigate

mitonner [mitɔne] *tr* to simmer; pamper; (coll) to contrive, devise ‖ *intr* to simmer

mitoyen [mitwajɛ̃] **mitoyenne** [mitwajɛn] *adj* midway, intermediate, dividing; jointly owned, common

mitraille [mitrɑj] *f* scrap iron; grapeshot; artillery fire

mitrailler [mitrɑje] *tr* to machine-gun; pepper (*with gunfire, flash bulbs, etc.*)

mitraillette [mitrɑjɛt] *f* submachine gun, Tommy gun

mitrail·leur [mitrɑjœr] **-leuse** [jøz] *adj* repeating, automatic (*firearm*) ‖ *m* machine gunner ‖ *f* machine gun

mitre [mitr] *f* miter; chimney pot

mitron [mitrɔ̃] *m* baker's boy

mi-voix [mivwa]—**à mi-voix** in a low voice, under one's breath

mixer or **mixeur** [miksœr] *m* electric food mixer

mixte [mikst] *adj* mixed; coeducational; composite; joint (*e.g., commission*); (rr) freight-and-passenger

mixtion [mikstjɔ̃] *f* mixing; mixture

mixture [mikstyr] *f* mixture

M.L.F. [ɛmɛlɛf] *m* (letterword) (**mouvement de libération de la femme**) women's liberation movement

Mlle *abbr* (**Mademoiselle**) Miss

MM. *abbr* (**Messieurs**) Messrs.

Mme *abbr* (**Madame**) Mrs.; Mme.

mobile [mɔbil] *adj* mobile ‖ *m* motive; (fa) mobile

mobil-home [mɔbilom] *m* mobile home

mobi·lier [mɔbilje] **-lière** [ljɛr] *adj* personal ‖ *m* furniture

mobilisable [mɔbilizabl] *adj* (mil) subject to call

mobilisation [mɔbilizasjɔ̃] *f* mobilization

mobiliser [mɔbilize] *tr & intr* to mobilize

mobilité [mɔbilite] *f* mobility; **mobilité sociale ascendante** upward mobility

mobylette [mɔbilɛt] *f* (trademark) moped

moche [mɔʃ] *adj* (coll) ugly; (coll) lousy

modalité [mɔdalite] *f* modality, manner, method; **modalités** terms

mode [mɔd] *m* kind, method, mode; (gram) mood; (mus) mode; **mode d'emploi** directions for use; **mode dialogué** (comp) conversational mode; **mode subordonné** (comp) background mode ‖ *f* fashion; **à la mode** in style, fashionable; **à la mode de** in the manner of; **modes** fashions; millinery

modèle [mɔdɛl] *adj & m* model; sample, e.g., **villa modèle** sample home

modelé [mɔdle] *m* (fa) modeling

modeler [mɔdle] §2 *tr* to model; shape, mold ‖ *ref*—**se modeler sur** to take as a model

modélisation [mɔdelisasjɔ̃] *f* (comp, econ) modeling

modélisme [mɔdelism] *m* modeling (*making models*)

modéliste [mɔdelist] *mf* model-airplane designer, etc.; dress designer

modem [mɔdɛm] *m* (comp) (*modulateur démodulateur*) modem (*modulator demodulator*)

modéra·teur [mɔderatœr] **-trice** [tris] *adj* moderating ‖ *mf* moderator; regulator; moderator (*for slowing down neutrons*); **modérateur de son** volume control

modé·ré -rée [mɔdere] *adj* moderate

modérer [mɔdere] §10 *tr & ref* to moderate

moderne [mɔdɛrn] *adj* modern

moderniser [mɔdɛrnize] *tr* to modernize

modeste [mɔdɛst] *adj* modest

modestie [mɔdɛsti] *f* modesty

modicité [mɔdisite] *f* paucity (*of resources*); lowness (*of price*)

modifica·teur [mɔdifikatœr] **-trice** [tris] *adj* modifying ‖ *m* modifier

modifier [mɔdifje] *tr* to modify

modique [mɔdik] *adj* moderate, reasonable

modiste [mɔdist] *f* milliner

modulation [mɔdylasjɔ̃] *f* modulation; **modulation d'amplitude** amplitude modulation; **modulation de fréquence** frequency modulation

module [mɔdyl] *m* module; **module lunaire** (rok) lunar module

moduler [mɔdyle] *tr & intr* to modulate

moelle [mwal] *f* marrow; (bot) pith; **moelle épinière** spinal cord; **moelle osseuse** bone marrow

moel·leux [mwalø] **-leuse** [løz] *adj* soft; mellow; flowing (*brush stroke*)

moellon [mwalɔ̃] *m* building stone; ashlar

mœurs [mœr], [mœrs] *fpl* customs, habits; morals; **mœurs spéciales** (coll) homosexual lifestyle

mohair [mɔɛr] *m* mohair

moi [mwa] §85, §87 me

moignon [mwaɲɔ̃] *m* stump

moi-même [mwamɛm] §86 myself

moindre [mwɛ̃dr] (precedes the noun it modifies) §91 *adj comp & super* less; lesser; least, slightest

moine [mwan] *m* monk

moi·neau [mwano] *m* (*pl* **-neaux**) sparrow

moins [mwɛ̃] *m* less; minus; **au moins** or **du moins** at least; **(le) moins** (the) least; **moins de** fewer ‖ *adv comp & super* §91 less; fewer; **à moins de** + *inf* without + *ger*, unless + *ind*; **à moins que** unless; **de moins en moins** less and less; **en moins de rien** in no time at all; **moins de** (followed by numeral) less than; **moins que** less than; **rien moins que** anything but ‖ *prep* minus; to, e.g., **dix heures moins le quart** a quarter to ten

moire [mwar] *f* moire; **moire de soie** watered silk

moi·ré -rée [mware] *adj* watered (*silk*) ‖ *m* wavy sheen

mois [mwa] *m* month

Moïse [mɔiz] *m* Moses

moi·si -sie [mwazi] *adj* moldy ‖ *m* mold; **sentir le moisi** to have a musty smell

moisir [mwazir] *tr* to mold ‖ *intr* to become moldy, mold; (fig) to vegetate ‖ *ref* to mold

moisissure [mwazisyr] *f* mold

moisson [mwasɔ̃] *f* harvest

moissonner [mwasɔne] *tr* to harvest, reap

moisson·neur [mwasɔnœr] **-neuse** [nøz] *mf* reaper ‖ *f* (mach) reaper

moite [mwat] *adj* moist, damp; clammy

moiteur [mwatœr] *f* moistness, dampness; **moiteur froide** clamminess

moitié [mwatje] *f* half; (coll) better half (*wife*); **à moitié, la moitié** half; **à moitié chemin** halfway; **à moitié prix** at half price; **de moitié** by half ‖ *adv* half

moka [mɔka] *m* mocha coffee; mocha cake

mol *adj* see **mou**

molaire [mɔlɛr] *adj* & *f* molar

môle [mol] *m* mole, breakwater ‖ *f* (ichth) sunfish

molécule [mɔlekyl] *f* molecule

moleskine [mɔlɛskin] *f* (*fabric*) moleskin; imitation leather

molester [mɔlɛste] *tr* to molest

moleter [mɔlte] §34 *tr* to knurl, mill

mollas·son [mɔlasɔ̃] **-sonne** [sɔn] *mf* (coll) softy

molle *adj* see **mou**

mollement [mɔlmɑ̃] *adv* flabbily; listlessly

mollesse [mɔlɛs] *f* flabbiness; apathy; permissiveness; softness (*of contour*); mildness (*of climate*)

mol·let [mɔlɛ] **-lette** [lɛt] *adj* soft, downy; soft-boiled (*egg*) ‖ *m* (anat) calf

molletière [mɔltjɛr] *f* puttee, legging

molleton [mɔltɔ̃] *m* flannel

mollir [mɔlir] *intr* to weaken

mollusque [mɔlysk] *m* mollusk

molosse [mɔlɔs] *m* watchdog

molybdène [mɔlibdɛn] *m* molybdenum

môme [mom] *adj* (slang) little ‖ *mf* (coll) kid ‖ *f* (slang) babe

moment [mɔmɑ̃] *m* moment; **à aucun moment** at no time; **à ce moment-là, en ce moment-là** then, at that time; **à tout moment, à tous moments** continually; **au moment où** just when; **c'est le moment** now is the time; **d'un moment à l'autre** at any moment; **en ce moment** now; at this moment; **moments de loisir** spare time; **par moments** now and then; **sur le moment** at the very moment; **un petit moment** a little while

momenta·né -née [mɔmɑ̃tane] *adj* momentary

momerie [mɔmri] *f* mummery

momie [mɔmi] *f* mummy

mon [mɔ̃] §88 my

M^{on} *abbr* (**Maison**) (com) House

mona·cal -cale [mɔnakal] *adj* (*pl* **-caux** [ko]) monastic, monkish

monachisme [mɔnaʃism], [mɔnakism] *m* monasticism

monarchique [mɔnarʃik] *adj* monarchic

monarque [mɔnark] *m* monarch

monastère [mɔnastɛr] *m* monastery

monastique [mɔnastik] *adj* monastic

mon·ceau [mɔ̃so] *m* (*pl* **-ceaux**) heap, pile

mon·dain [mɔ̃dɛ̃] **-daine** [dɛn] *adj* worldly; social (*life, functions, etc.*); sophisticated ‖ *mf* worldly-minded person; socialite

mondanité [mɔ̃danite] *f* worldliness; **mondanités** social events; (journ) social news

monde [mɔ̃d] *m* world; people; **avoir du monde chez soi** to have company; **il y a du monde, il y a un monde fou** there is a big crowd; **le beau monde, le grand monde** high society, fashionable society; **mettre au monde** to give birth to; **tout le monde** everybody, everyone

monder [mɔ̃de] *tr* to hull; blanch; stone

mon·dial -diale [mɔ̃djal] *adj* (*pl* **-diaux** [djo]) world; worldwide

monétaire [mɔnetɛr] *adj* monetary

mon·gol -gole [mɔ̃gɔl] *adj* Mongol ‖ *m* Mongol (*language*) ‖ (*cap*) *mf* Mongol (*person*)

moni·teur [mɔnitœr] **-trice** [tris] *mf* coach, trainer, instructor; monitor (*at school*); (comp, telv) monitor, visual display unit, video display unit; (comp) desktop

monnaie [mɔnɛ] *f* change, small change; money (*legal tender of a country*); **fausse monnaie** counterfeit money; **la Monnaie** the Mint; **monnaie forte** hard currency; **payer en monnaie de singe** to give lip service to

monnayer [mɔneje] §49 *tr* to mint, coin; convert into cash; cash in on

monnayeur [mɔnɛjœr] *m*—**faux monnayeur** counterfeiter

monocle [mɔnɔkl] *m* monocle

monogamie [mɔnɔgami] *f* monogamy

monogramme [mɔnɔgram] *m* monogram

monographie [mɔnɔgrafi] *f* monograph

monokini [mɔnɔkini] *m* topless swimsuit

monolithique [mɔnɔlitik] *adj* monolithic

monolingue [mɔnɔlɛ̃g] *adj* monolingual

monologue [mɔnɔlɔg] *m* monologue

monologuer [mɔnɔlɔge] *tr* to soliloquize

monologuiste [mɔnɔlɔgist] *mf*—**monologuiste comique** stand-up comedian

monomanie [mɔnɔmani] *f* monomania

monôme [mɔnom] *m* single file (*of students*); (math) monomial

monoplan [mɔnɔplɑ̃] *m* monoplane

monopole [mɔnɔpɔl] *m* monopoly

monopoliser [mɔnɔpɔlize] *tr* to monopolize

monorail [mɔnɔraj] *m* monorail

monosyllabe [mɔnɔsilab] *m* monosyllable

monothéiste [mɔnɔteist] *adj* & *mf* monotheist

monotone [mɔnɔtɔn] *adj* monotonous

monotonie [mɔnɔtɔni] *f* monotony

monotype [mɔnɔtip] *adj* monotypic ‖ *m* monotype ‖ *f* Monotype (*machine to set type*)

monseigneur [mɔ̃sɛɲœr] *m* (*pl* **messeigneurs** [mesɛɲœr] monseigneur

monsieur [məsjø] *m* (*pl* **messieurs** [mesjø]) gentleman; sir; mister; Mr.; (often untranslated) e.g., **oui, monsieur!** yes, of course!, yes, I will!, etc. (*instead of "yes, Sir!"*)

monstre [mɔ̃str] *adj* huge, monster ‖ *m* monster; freak; **monstres sacrés** (fig) sacred cows, idols

mons•trueux [mɔ̃stryø] **-trueuse** [tryøz] *adj* monstrous

mont [mɔ̃] *m* mount; mountain; **par monts et par vaux** over hill and dale; **passer les monts** to cross the Alps

montage [mɔ̃taʒ] *m* hoisting; setting up (*of a machine*); (elec) hookup; (mov) cutting, editing

monta•gnard [mɔ̃taɲar] **-gnarde** [ɲard] *adj* mountain ‖ *mf* mountaineer

montagne [mɔ̃taɲ] *f* mountain; **montagnes russes** roller coaster

monta•gneux [mɔ̃taɲø] **-gneuse** [ɲøz] *adj* mountainous

mon•tant [mɔ̃tɑ̃] **-tante** [tɑ̃t] *adj* rising, ascending; uphill; vertical; high-necked (*dress*) ‖ *m* upright, riser; gatepost; total (*sum*); allure; (culin) tang; **montants** goal posts; (slang) pair of trousers

mont-de-piété [mɔ̃dpjete] *m* (*pl* **monts-de-piété**) pawnshop

mon•té -tée [mɔ̃te] *adj* mounted; organized; equipped, well-provided; worked-up, angry ‖ *f* climb; slope

monte-charge [mɔ̃tʃarʒ] *m invar* freight elevator

monte-plats [mɔ̃tpla] *m invar* dumbwaiter

monter [mɔ̃te] §95, §96 *tr* to go up, climb; mount; set up; carry up, take up, bring up ‖ *intr* (*aux:* ÉTRE) to go up, come up; come upstairs; rise; come in (*said of tide*); **monter** + *inf* to go up to + *inf;* **monter à** or **en** to go up, climb, ascend, mount; **monter sur** to mount (*the throne*); go on (*the stage*) ‖ *ref*—**se monter à** to amount to; **se monter en** to lay in a supply of; **se monter la tête** to get excited

montre [mɔ̃tr] *f* show, display; watch; **en montre** in the window, on display; **faire montre de** to show off, parade; **montre à affichage numérique** digital watch; **montre à remontoir** stem-winder; **montre à répétition** repeater

montre-bracelet [mɔ̃trəbraslɛ] *f* (*pl* **montres-bracelets**) wristwatch

montrer [mɔ̃tre] §96 *tr* to show; **montrer du doigt** to point out or at ‖ *ref* to appear; show oneself to be (*e.g., patient*)

mon•treur [mɔ̃trœr] **-treuse** [trøz] *mf* showman, exhibitor

mon•tueux [mɔ̃tɥø] **-tueuse** [tɥøz] *adj* rolling, hilly

monture [mɔ̃tyr] *f* mounting; assembling; mount (*e.g., horse*)

monument [mɔnymɑ̃] *m* monument; **monument aux morts** memorial monument

moquer [mɔke] §97 *tr & ref* to mock; **se moquer de** to make fun of, laugh at

moquerie [mɔkri] *f* mockery

moquette [mɔkɛt] *f* pile carpet; wall-to-wall carpeting

mo•ral -rale [mɔral] (*pl* **-raux** [ro]) *adj* moral ‖ *m* morale ‖ *f* ethics; moral (*of a fable*); **faire la morale à qn** to lecture s.o.

moralité [mɔralite] *f* morality; moral (*e.g., of a fable*)

morasse [mɔras] *f* final proof (*of newspaper*)

moratoire [mɔratwar] *m* moratorium

moratorium [mɔratɔrjɔm] *m* moratorium

morbide [mɔrbid] *adj* morbid

morbleu [mɔrblø] *interj* (obs) zounds!

mor•ceau [mɔrso] *m* (*pl* **-ceaux**) piece, bit; morsel; **bas morceaux** (culin) cheap cuts; **en morceaux** in cubes (*of sugar*); **morceaux choisis** selected passages

morceler [mɔrsəle] §34 *tr* to parcel out

morcellement [mɔrsɛlmɑ̃] *m* parceling out, division

mordancer [mɔrdɑ̃se] §51 *tr* to size

mor•dant -dante [dɑ̃t] *adj* mordant, caustic ‖ *m* mordant; cutting edge; fighting spirit; (mus) mordent

mordicus [mɔrdikys] *adv* (coll) stoutly, tenaciously

mordiller [mɔrdije] *tr & intr* to nibble; nip

mordo•ré -rée [mɔrdɔre] *adj* golden-brown, bronze-colored

mordre [mɔrdr] *tr* to bite ‖ *intr* to bite; **mordre à** to bite on; take to, find easy; **mordre dans** to bite into; **mordre sur** to encroach upon ‖ *ref* to bite; **s'en mordre la langue** to feel like biting off one's tongue because of it

mor•du -due [mɔrdy] *adj* bitten; smitten ‖ *mf* (coll) fan (*person*)

morelle [mɔrɛl] *f* nightshade

morfondre [mɔrfɔ̃dr] *tr* to chill to the bone ‖ *ref* to be bored waiting

morgue [mɔrg] *f* morgue; haughtiness

mori•caud [mɔriko] **-caude** [kod] *adj* (coll) dark-skinned, dusky

morigéner [mɔriʒene] §10 *tr* to scold

morillon [mɔrijɔ̃] *m* rough emerald; duck; **morillon à dos blanc** canvasback

mor•mon [mɔrmɔ̃] **-mone** [mɔn] *adj & mf* Mormon

morne [mɔrn] *adj* dismal, gloomy ‖ *m* hillock, knoll

mornifle [mɔrnifl] *f* (coll) slap

morose [mɔroz] *adj* morose

morphine [mɔrfin] *f* morphine

morphologie [mɔrfɔlɔʒi] *f* morphology

morpion [mɔrpjɔ̃] *m* tick-tack-toe; (*youngster*) (slang) squirt; (*Phthirus pubis*) (slang) crab louse

mors [mɔr] *m* bit; jaw (*of vise*)

morse [mɔrs] *m* Morse code; walrus

morsure [mɔrsyr] *f* bite

mort [mɔr] **morte** [mɔrt] *adj* dead; spent (*bullet*); (aut) neutral; motionless, e.g., **au point**

mort at a standstill ‖ *mf* dead person, corpse ‖ *m* (bridge) dummy; **faire le mort** to play dead ‖ **mort** *f* death; **attraper la mort** to catch one's death of cold; **mort à la naissance** still-birth; **mort subite** sudden death; **mort subite** *or* **inexpliquée du nourrisson** crib death, cot death, sudden death ‖ *v* see **mourir**

mortadelle [mɔrtadɛl] *f* bologna

mortaise [mɔrtɛl] *f* mortise

mortaiser [mɔrteze] *tr* to mortise

mortalité [mɔrtalite] *f* mortality

mort-aux-rats [mɔrtora], [mɔrora] *f invar* rat poison

mort-bois [mɔrbwa] *m* deadwood

morte-eau [mɔrto] *f* (*pl* **mortes-eaux** [mɔrtəzo]) low tide

mor•tel -telle [mɔrtɛl] *adj & mf* mortal

morte-saison [mɔrtəsɛzɔ̃] *f* (*pl* **mortes-saisons**) off-season

mortier [mɔrtje] *m* mortar; round judicial cap

mortifier [mɔrtifje] *tr* to mortify; tenderize (*meat*)

mort-né -née [mɔrne] (*pl* **-nés**) *adj* stillborn ‖ *mf* stillborn child

mortuaire [mɔrtɥɛr] *adj* mortuary; funeral (*e.g., service*); death (*notice*)

morue [mɔry] *f* cod

morve [mɔrv] *f* snot

mor•veux -veuse [vøz] *adj* snotty ‖ *mf* (coll) young snot, brat, whippersnapper

mosaïque [mɔzaik] *adj* mosaic; Mosaic ‖ *f* mosaic

Moscou [mɔsku] *m* Moscow

mosquée [mɔske] *f* mosque

mot [mo] *m* word; answer (*to riddle*); **à mots couverts** guardedly; **au bas mot** at least; **avoir toujours le mot pour rire** to be always cracking jokes; **bon mot** witticism; **grand mot** buzz word; **gros mots** foul words; **le mot à mot** the word-for-word translation; **mot à double sens** double entendre; **mot d'entrée** headword, entry word (*of a dictionary*); **mot de passe** password; **mot d'ordre** slogan; **mot pour mot** word for word; **mot résonant, prétentieux et emphatique** buzz word; **mots croisés** crossword puzzle; **mot impudique de quatre lettres** four-letter word; **ne ... mot** §90 (lit) not a word, nothing; **placer un mot** to put in a word; **prendre qn au mot** to take s.o. at his word; **sans mot dire** without a word

motard [mɔtar] *m* (coll) motorcyclist; (coll) motorcycle cop

mot-clé [mokle] *m* (*pl* **mots-clés**) key word

motel [mɔtɛl] *m* motel

mo•teur [mɔtœr] **-trice** [tris] *adj* driving (*wheel*); drive (*shaft*); motive (*power*); power (*brake*); motor (*nerve*) ‖ *m* motor, engine; prime mover; instigator; **moteur à deux temps** two-cycle engine; **moteur à explosion** internal-combustion engine; **moteur à injection** fuel-injection engine; **moteur à quatre temps** four-cycle engine; **moteur à réaction** jet engine; **moteur hors bord** outboard motor

moteur-fusée *m* (*pl* **moteurs-fusées**) rocket engine

motif [mɔtif] *m* motive; (fa, mus) motif

motion [mosjɔ̃] *f* (parl) motion

motiver [mɔtive] *tr* to state the reason for, account for, explain, justify; motivate; warrant; **motiver une décision sur** to base a decision on

moto [mɔto] *f* motorcycle

motoculteur [mɔtɔkyltœr] *m* rototiller

motoneige [mɔtɔnɛʒ] *f* snowmobile

motoriser [mɔtɔrize] *tr* to motorize

mot-outil [mouti] *m* (*pl* **mots-outils**) link word

mot-piège [mopjɛʒ] *m* (*pl* **mots-pièges**) tricky word

mots-croisés [mokrwaze] *mpl* crossword puzzle

mot-souche [mosuʃ] *m* (*pl* **mots-souches**) headword, entry word; (typ) catchword

motte [mɔt] *f* clod, lump; slab (*of butter*); **motte de gazon** turf, divot

motus [mɔtys] *interj* mum's the word!

mou [mu] (or **mol** [mɔl] before vowel or mute h) **molle** [mɔl] (*pl* **mous molles**) *adj* soft; limp, flabby, slack; spineless, listless ‖ *m* slack; lights, lungs; (coll) softy; **bourrer le mou à qn** to hand s.o. a line

mou•chard [muʃar] **-charde** [ʃard] *mf* (coll) stool pigeon, squealer

moucharder [muʃarde] *tr* (coll) to spy on; (coll) to squeal on ‖ *intr* (coll) to squeal

mouche [muʃ] *f* fly; beauty spot; **faire d'une mouche un éléphant** to make a mountain out of a molehill; **faire la mouche** to fly into a rage; **faire mouche** to hit the bull's-eye; **fine mouche** sly, cagey person; **mouche à miel** honeybee; **mouche d'Espagne** (pharm) Spanish fly; **mouche du coche** busybody

moucher [muʃe] *tr* to blow (*one's nose*); to snuff, trim; (coll) to scold ‖ *ref* to blow one's nose

moucherolle [muʃrɔl] *f* (orn) flycatcher

moucheron [muʃrɔ̃] *m* gnat; snuff (*of candle*)

moucheter [muʃte] §34 *tr* to speckle

mouchoir [muʃwar] *m* handkerchief; **mouchoirs à jeter** disposable tissues; **mouchoirs en papier** paper handkerchiefs

moudre [mudr] §43 *tr* to grind

moue [mu] *f* wry face; **faire la moue** to pout

mouette [mwɛt] *f* gull, sea gull; **mouette rieuse** black-headed gull

mouffette [mufɛt] *f* skunk

moufle [mufl] *m & f* pulley block ‖ *f* mitten

mouillage [mujaʒ] *m* anchorage; wetting; watering, diluting

mouil•lé -lée [muje] *adj* wet; at anchor; palatalized; liquid (*l*)

mouiller [muje] *tr* to wet; water, dilute; palatalize; drop (*anchor*) ‖ *intr* to drop anchor ‖ *ref* to get wet; water; (coll) to become involved

moulage [mulaʒ] *m* molding, casting; mold, cast; grinding, milling

moule [mul] *m* mold, form; **moule à gaufre**

waffle iron ‖ *f* mussel; (slang) fleabrain; (slang) jellyfish

mouler [mule] *tr* to mold; outline, e.g., **corsage qui moule le buste** blouse that outlines the bosom

moulin [mulɛ̃] *m* mill; **moulin à café** coffee grinder; **moulin à paroles** (coll) windbag; **moulin à vent** windmill

moulinet [mulinɛ] *m* winch; reel (*of casting rod*); turnstile; pinwheel (*child's toy*); **faire le moulinet avec** to twirl

moult [mult] *adv* (obs) much, many

mou•lu -lue [muly] *adj* ground; (coll) done in ‖ *v* see **moudre**

moulure [mulyr] *f* molding

mou•rant [murɑ̃] **-rante** [rɑ̃t] *adj* dying ‖ *mf* dying person

mourir [murir] §44, §97 *intr* (*aux:* ÉTRE) to die ‖ *ref* to be dying

mouron [murɔ̃] *m* (bot) starwort, stitchwort; (bot) pimpernel

mousquetaire [muskətɛr] *m* musketeer

mousse [mus] *adj* dull ‖ *m* cabin boy ‖ *f* moss; froth, foam; lather, suds; whipped cream; (culin) mousse; **mousse à raser** shaving foam

mousseline [muslin] *f* muslin; **mousseline de soie** chiffon

mousser [muse] *intr* to froth, foam; lather; **faire mousser** (coll) to crack up, build up; (slang) to enrage

mous•seux [musø] **-seuse** [søz] *adj* mossy; frothy, foamy; sudsy; sparkling (*wine*)

mousson [musɔ̃] *f* monsoon

moustache [mustaʃ] *f* mustache; **moustaches** whiskers (*of, e.g., cat*); **moustaches en croc** handle-bar mustache

moustiquaire [mustikɛr] *f* mosquito net

moustique [mustik] *m* mosquito

moût [mu] *m* must; wort

moutard [mutar] *m* (slang) kid

moutarde [mutard] *f* mustard

moutier [mutje] *m* (obs) monastery

mouton [mutɔ̃] *m* sheep; mutton; (slang) stool pigeon; **doux comme un mouton** gentle as a lamb; **moutons** whitecaps; **moutons de Panurge** (fig) chameleons, yes men; **revenons à nos moutons** let's get back to our subject

mouton•né -née [mutone] *adj* fleecy; frothy (*sea*); mackerel (*sky*)

moutonner [mutone] *tr* to curl ‖ *intr* to break into whitecaps

mouton•neux [mutonø] **-neuse** [nøz] *adj* frothy; fleecy (*e.g., cloud*)

mouture [mutyr] *f* grinding; mixture of wheat, rye, and barley; (fig) reworking

mouvement [muvmɑ̃] *m* movement; motion; **mouvement d'horlogerie** clockwork; **mouvement d'humeur** fit of bad temper; **mouvement ondulatoire** wave motion; **mouvements oculaires rapides** rapid eye movements (REM)

mouvemen•té -tée [muvmɑ̃te] *adj* lively; eventful; hilly, broken (*terrain*)

mouvementer [muvmɑ̃te] *tr* to enliven

mouvoir [muvwar] §45 *tr* to move; set in motion, drive ‖ *ref* to move, stir

moyen [mwajɛ̃] **moyenne** [mwajɛn] *adj* average; ordinary; middle, intermediate; medium ‖ *m* way, manner; **au moyen de** by means of; **moyens** means ‖ *f* average; mean; passing mark; **en moyenne** on an average

moyen-âge [mwajɛnɑʒ] *m* Middle Ages

moyenâ•geux [mwajɛnɑʒø] **-geuse** [ʒøz] *adj* medieval; outdated

moyen-courrier [mwajɛ̃kurje] *m* (*pl* **moyens-courriers**) medium-range plane

moyennant [mwajɛnɑ̃] *prep* in exchange for ‖ *conj* provided that

Moyen-Orient [mwajɛnɔrjɑ̃] *m* Middle East

moyeu [mwajø] *m* (*pl* **moyeux**) hub

MST [ɛmɛste] *f* (letterword) (**maladie sexuelle-ment transmissible**) STD (*sexually transmitted disease*)

mû mue [my] *adj* (*pl* **mus mues** [my]) *adj* driven, propelled ‖ *f* see **mue** ‖ *v* see **mouvoir**

mucosité [mykozite] *f* mucus

mucus [mykys] *m* mucus

mue [my] *f* molt, shedding

muer [mɥe] *intr* to molt; shed, slough; (*said of voice*) to break, change

muet [mɥɛ] **muette** [mɥɛt] *adj* mute; silent; nonspeaking (*rôle*); blank; dead (*key*) ‖ *mf* mute ‖ *m* silent movie

muezzin [mɥedzin] *m* muezzin

mufle [myfl] *m* muzzle, snout; (coll) cad, skunk

mugir [myʒir] *intr* to bellow

mugissement [myʒismɑ̃] *m* bellow

muguet [mygɛ] *m* lily of the valley

Muhammad [myamad] *m* Muhammad

mulâ•tre [mylɑtr] **-tresse** [trɛs] *mf* mulatto

mule [myl] *f* mule

mulet [mylɛ] *m* mule; (ichth) mullet

mule•tier [myltje] **-tière** [tjɛr] *adj* mule (*e.g., trail*) ‖ *mf* muleteer

mulette [mylɛt] *f* freshwater clam

mulot [mylo] *m* field mouse

multilaté•ral -rale [myltilateral] *adj* (*pl* **-raux** [ro]) multilateral

multinatio•nal -nale [myltinasjɔnal] *adj* multinational ‖ *f* multinational corporation, multinational

multiple [myltipl] *adj* & *m* multiple; **plus petit commun multiple (P.P.C.M.)** least common denominator (L.C.D.)

multiplet [myltiplɛ] *m* (comp) byte

multiplex *or* **multiplexe** [myltiplɛks] *adj* & *m* (mov) multiplex

multiplicité [myltiplisite] *f* multiplicity

multi•plié -pliée [myltiplje] *adj* multiplied; **multiplié par** times

multiplier [myltiplije] *tr* & *ref* to multiply

multiprocesseur [myltiprɔsɛsœr] *m* (comp) multiprocessor

multiprogram•mé -mée [myltiprɔgrame] *adj* (comp) multitasked

multiprogrammation [myltiprɔgramasjɔ̃] *f* (comp) multitasking

multisalle [myltisal] *adj* having several projection rooms (of a multiplex)

multitâche [myltitɑʃ] *adj* (comp) multitasked

multitraitement [myltitrɛtmɑ̃] *m* (comp) multiprocessing

multitude [myltityd] *f* multitude

munici•pal -pale [mynisipal] *adj* (*pl* **-paux** [po]) municipal

municipalité [mynisipalite] *f* municipality; city officials; city hall

munifi•cent [mynifisɑ̃] **-cente** [sɑ̃t] *adj* munificent

munir [mynir] *tr* to provide, equip ‖ *ref*—**se munir de** to provide oneself with

munitions [mynisjɔ̃] *fpl* munitions; **munitions de combat** live ammunition

mu•queux [mykø] **-queuse** [køz] *adj* mucous ‖ *f* mucous membrane

mur [myr] *m* wall; **mettre au pied du mur** to corner; **mur de soutènement** retaining wall; **mur sonique, mur du son** sound barrier

mûr mûre [myr] *adj* ripe, mature ‖ *f* see **mûre**

muraille [myrɑj] *f* wall, rampart

mu•ral -rale [myral] *adj* (*pl* **-raux** [ro]) mural

mûre [myr] *f* mulberry; blackberry

murer [myre] *tr* to wall up or in ‖ *ref* to shut oneself up

mûrier [myrje] *m* mulberry tree

mûrir [myrir] *tr & intr* to ripen, mature

murmure [myrmyr] *m* murmur

murmurer [myrmyre] *tr & intr* to murmur

musaraigne [myzarɛɲ] *f* (zool) shrew

musarder [myzarde] *intr* to dawdle

musc [mysk] *m* musk

muscade [myskad] *f* nutmeg; **passez muscade!** presto!

muscardin [myskardɛ̃] *m* dormouse

muscat [myska] *m* muscatel

muscle [myskl] *m* muscle

mus•clé -clée [myskle] *adj* muscular; (coll) powerful (*e.g., drama*); (slang) difficult

musculaire [myskylɛr] *adj* muscular

musculation [myskylasjɔ̃] *f* body building exercises

muscu•leux [myskylø] **-leuse** [løz] *adj* muscular

muse [myz] *f* muse; **les Muses** the Muses

mu•seau [myzo] *m* (*pl* **-seaux**) snout; (coll) mug, face

musée [myze] *m* museum; **musée d'art** art gallery

museler [myzle] §**34** *tr* to muzzle

muselière [myzəljɛr] *f* muzzle

muser [myze] *intr* to dawdle

musette [myzɛt] *f* feed bag; kit bag; haversack; (mus) musette

muséum [myzeɔm] *m* museum of natural history

musi•cal -cale [myzikal] *adj* (*pl* **-caux** [ko]) musical

musical-hall [myzikol] *m* (*pl* **-halls**) vaudeville; vaudeville house; music hall (Brit)

musi•cien [myzisjɛ̃] **-cienne** [sjɛn] *mf* musician

musicologie [myzikɔlɔʒi] *f* musicology

musique [myzik] *f* music; band; **musique de fond** background music; **musique rustique** country music; **toujours la même musique** (coll) the same old song

mus•qué -quée [myske] *adj* musk-scented

musul•man [myzylmɑ̃] **-mane** [man] *adj & mf* Muslim

mutation [mytɑsjɔ̃] *f* mutation; transfer; (biol) mutation, sport

muter [myte] *tr* to transfer

muti•lé -lée [mytile] *mf* disabled veteran

mutiler [mytile] *tr* to mutilate; deface; disable; garble (*e.g., the truth*)

mu•tin [mytɛ̃] **-tine** [tin] *adj* roguish ‖ *mf* mutineer

muti•né -née [mytine] *adj* mutinous ‖ *mf* mutineer

mutiner [mytine] *ref* to mutiny

mutualité [mytɥalite] *f* mutual insurance

mu•tuel -tuelle [mytɥel] *adj* mutual ‖ *f* mutual benefit association

myope [mjɔp] *adj* near-sighted ‖ *mf* near-sighted person

myriade [mirjad] *f* myriad

myrrhe [mir] *f* myrrh

myrte [mirt] *m* myrtle

myrtille [mirtij] *f* blueberry

mystère [mistɛr] *m* mystery

mysté•rieux [misterjø] **-rieuse** [rjøz] *adj* mysterious

mysticisme [mistisism] *m* mysticism

mystification [mistifikɑsjɔ̃] *f* mystification; hoax, ripoff

mystifier [mistifje] *tr* to mystify; hoax

mystique [mistik] *adj & mf* mystic

mythe [mit] *m* myth

mythique [mitik] *adj* mythical

mythologie [mitɔlɔʒi] *f* mythology

mythologique [mitɔlɔʒik] *adj* mythological

N, n [ɛn], *[ɛn] *m invar* fourteenth letter of the French alphabet

n' = **ne** before vowel or mute **h**

na•bot [nabo] **-bote** [bɔt] *adj* dwarfish ‖ *mf* dwarf, midget

nacelle [nasɛl] *f* (aer) nacelle; (naut) wherry, skiff; (fig) boat

nacre [nakr] *f* mother-of-pearl

na•cré -crée [nacre] *adj* pearly

nage [naʒ] *f* swimming; rowing, paddling; **être (tout) en nage** to be wet with sweat; **nage à la pagaie** paddling; **nage de côté** sidestroke; **nage en couple** sculling; **nage en grenouille** breaststroke; **nage libre** freestyle swimming

nagée [naʒe] *f* swimming stroke

nageoire [naʒwar] *f* fin; flipper (*of seal*); float (*for swimmers*)

nager [naʒe] §38 *intr* to swim; float; row; **nager à culer** (naut) to back water; **nager debout** to tread water; to row standing up; **nager entre deux eaux** to swim under water; (fig) to carry water on both shoulders

na•geur [naʒœr] **-geuse** [ʒøz] *adj* swimming; floating ‖ *mf* swimmer; rower

naguère or **naguères** [nagɛr] *adv* lately, just now

naïf [naif] **naïve** [naiv] *adj* naïve ‖ *mf* simple-minded person; easy mark, patsy

nain [nɛ̃] **naine** [nɛn] *adj* & *mf* dwarf

naissain [nɛsɛ̃] *m* seed oysters

naissance [nɛsɑ̃s] *f* birth; lineage; descent; beginning; (archit) springing line; **de basse naissance** lowborn; **de haute naissance** highborn; **de naissance** by birth; **donner naissance à** to give birth to; to give rise to; **naissance de la gorge** bosom, throat; **naissance des cheveux** hairline; **naissance du jour** daybreak; **prendre naissance** to arise, originate

nais•sant [nɛsɑ̃] **-sante** [sɑ̃t] *adj* nascent, rising, budding, burgeoning

naître [nɛtr] §46 *intr* (*aux:*ETRE) to be born; bud; arise, originate; dawn; **faire naître** to give birth to; give rise to

naïveté [naivte] *f* naïveté; artlessness

nana [nana] *f* (slang) chick (*girl*)

nanan [nanɑ̃], [nɑ̃nɑ̃] *m* (coll) goody; **du nanan** (coll) nice

nanotechnologie [nanɔtɛknɔlɔʒi] *f* nanotechnology

nantir [nɑ̃tir] *tr* to give security or a pledge to; **nantir de** to provide with ‖ *intr* to stock up; feather one's nest ‖ *ref*—**se nantir de** to provide oneself with

nantissement [nɑ̃tismɑ̃] *m* security

napée [nape] *f* wood nymph

napel [napɛl] *m* monkshood, wolfsbane

naphte [naft] *m* naphtha

napoléo•nien [napɔleɔnjɛ̃] **-nienne** [njɛn] *adj* Napoleonic

nappage [napaʒ] *m* table linen

nappe [nap] *f* tablecloth; sheet (*of water, flame*);

net (*for fishing; for bird catching*); **mettre la nappe** to set the table; **nappe d'autel** altar cloth; **ôter la nappe** to clear the table

napperon [naprɔ̃] *m* tablecloth cover; **petit napperon** doily

narcisse [narsis] *m* narcissus; **narcisse des bois** daffodil; **Narcisse** Narcissus

narcotique [narkɔtik] *adj* & *m* narcotic

narcotiser [narkɔtize] *tr* to dope

nargue [narg] *f* scorn, contempt; **faire nargue de** to defy; **nargue de . . .!** fie on . . .!

narguer [narge] *tr* to flout, snap one's fingers at

narguilé [nargile] *m* hookah

narine [narin] *f* nostril

nar•quois [narkwa] **-quoise** [kwaz] *adj* sly, cunning; sneering

narra•teur [naratœr] **-trice** [tris] *mf* narrator, storyteller

narra•tif [naratif] **-tive** [tiv] *adj* narrative

narration [narɑsjɔ̃] *f* narration; narrative

narrer [nare] *tr* to narrate, relate

na•sal -sale [nazal] *adj* (*pl* **-saux** [zo]) nasal ‖ *f* nasal (*vowel*)

nasaliser [nazalize] *tr* & *intr* to nasalize

nasarde [nazard] *f* fillip on one's nose (*in contempt*); snub, insult

na•seau [nazo] *m* (*pl* **-seaux**) nostril (*of horse, etc.*); **naseaux** (coll) snout

nasil•lard [nazijar] **-larde** [jard] *adj* nasal

nasiller [nazije] *intr* to talk through one's nose; squawk, quack

nasse [nas] *f* fish trap; (sports) basket

na•tal -tale [natal] *adj* (*pl* **-tals**) natal, of birth, native

nataliste [natalist] *mf* right-to-lifer

natalité [natalite] *f* birth rate; **natalité dirigée** birth control

natation [natɑsjɔ̃] *f* swimming

na•tif [natif] **-tive** [tiv] *adj* & *mf* native

nation [nɑsjɔ̃] *f* nation; **Nations Unies** United Nations

natio•nal -nale [nɑsjɔnal] *adj* & *mf* (*pl* **-naux** [no] **-nales**) national

nationaliser [nɑsjɔnalize] *tr* to nationalize

nationalité [nɑsjɔnalite] *f* nationality; **double nationalité** dual citizenship

nativité [nativite] *f* nativity; nativity scene; **Nativité** Nativity

natte [nat] *f* mat, matting; braid

natter [nate] *tr* to weave; braid

naturalisation [natyralizɑsjɔ̃] *f* naturalization

naturaliser [natyralize] *tr* to naturalize

naturalisme [natyralism] *m* naturalism

naturaliste [natyralist] *adj* & *mf* naturalist

nature [natyr] *adj* & *invar* raw; black (*coffee*) ‖ *f* nature; **en nature** in kind; **nature morte** (painting) still life

natu•rel -relle [natyrɛl] *adj* natural; native ‖ *m* naturalness; native, citizen; disposition, nature

naturellement [natyrɛlmɑ̃] *adv* naturally; of course

naufrage [nofraʒ] *m* shipwreck

naufra•gé -gée [nofraʒe] *adj* shipwrecked || *mf* shipwrecked person; **naufragés de l'espace** persons lost in space

nauséa•bond [nozeabɔ̃] **-bonde** [bɔ̃d] *adj* nauseating

nausée [noze] *f* nausea

nau•séeux [nozeø] **-séeuse** [zeøz] *adj* nauseous

nautique [notik] *adj* nautical

nautisme [notism] *m* yachting

nauto•nier [notɔnje] **-nière** [njɛr] *mf* pilot

na•val -vale [naval] *adj* (*pl* **-vals**) naval; nautical, maritime

navel [navɛl] *f* navel orange

navet [navɛ] *m* turnip

navette [navɛt] *f* shuttle; shuttle train; **faire la navette** to shuttle, to ply back and forth; **navette aérienne** air shuttle; **navette spatiale** space shuttle

navigable [navigabl] *adj* navigable (*river*); seaworthy (*ship*)

naviga•teur [navigatœr] **-trice** [tris] *adj* seafaring || *m* navigator

navigation [navigasjɔ̃] *f* navigation; sailing; **navigation de plaisance** (sports) sailing; **navigation spatiale** astronavigation

naviguer [navige] *intr* to navigate, sail; **naviguer sur** to navigate, sail (*the sea*)

navire [navir] *m* ship; **navire de débarquement** landing craft; **navire marchand** merchantman

navire-citerne [navirsitɛrn] *m* (*pl* **navires-citernes**) tanker

navire-école [navirekɔl] *m* (*pl* **navires-écoles**) training ship

navire-jumeau [navirʒymo] *m* (*pl* **navires-jumeaux**) sister ship

na•vrant [navrɑ̃] **-vrante** [vrɑ̃t] *adj* distressing, heartrending

na•vré -vrée [navre] *adj* sorry, grieved

navrer [navre] *tr* to distress, grieve

nazaréen [nazareɛ̃] **nazaréenne** [nazareɛn] *adj* Nazarene || (*cap*) *mf* Nazarene

na•zi -zie [nazi] *adj & mf* Nazi

N.-D. *abbr* (**Notre-Dame**) Our Lady

ne [nə] §87, §90; **n'est-ce pas?** isn't that so? La traduction précédente est généralement remplacée par diverses locutions. Si l'énoncé est négatif, la question qui équivaut à **n'est-ce pas?** sera affirmative, par ex., **Vous ne travaillez pas. N'est-ce pas?** You are not working. Are you? Si l'énoncé est affirmatif, la question sera négative, par ex., **Vous travaillez. N'est-ce pas?** You are working. Are you not? ou Aren't you? Si l'énoncé contient un auxiliaire, la question contiendra cet auxiliaire moins l'infinitif ou moins le participe passé, par ex., **Il arrivera demain. N'est-ce pas?** He will arrive tomorrow. Won't he?; par ex., **Paul est déjà arrivé. N'est-ce pas?** Paul has already arrived. Hasn't he? Si l'énoncé

ne contient ni auxiliaire ni forme de la copule "to be," la question contiendra l'auxiliaire "do" ou "did" moins l'infinitif, par ex., **Marie parle anglais. N'est-ce pas?** Mary speaks English. Doesn't she?

né née [ne] *adj* born; by birth; **bien né** highborn; **né libre** freeborn; **né pour** cut out for

néanmoins [neɑ̃mwɛ̃] *adv* nevertheless

néant [neɑ̃] *m* nothing, nothingness; worthlessness; obscurity; none (*as a response on the appropriate blank of an official form*)

nébu•leux [nebylø] **-leuse** [løz] *adj* nebulous; gloomy (*facial expression*); worried (*brow*) || *f* nebula

nécessaire [nesesɛr] *adj* necessary, needful; **nécessaire à** required for || *m* necessities; kit, dressing case

nécessairement [nesesɛrmɑ̃] *adv* necessarily

nécessité [nesesite] *f* necessity; need; **nécessité préalable** prerequisite

nécessiter [nesesite] §96 *tr* to necessitate

nécessi•teux [nesesitø] **-teuse** [tøz] *adj* needy || *mf* needy person; **les nécessiteux** the needy

nécrologie [nekrɔlɔʒi] *f* necrology, obituary

nectar [nɛktar] *m* nectar

néerlan•dais [neɛrlɑ̃dɛ] **-daise** [dɛz] *adj* Dutch || *m* Dutch (*language*) || (*cap*) *mf* Netherlander

nef [nɛf] *f* nave; (archaic) ship; **nef latérale** aisle

néfaste [nefast] *adj* ill-starred, unlucky

nèfle [nɛfl] *f* medlar

néflier [neflije] *m* medlar tree

néga•teur [negatœr] **-trice** [tris] *adj* negative

néga•tif [negatif] **-tive** [tiv] *adj* negative || *m* (phot) negative || *f* negative (*side of a question*)

négation [negasjɔ̃] *f* negation; (gram) negative

négli•gé -gée [negliʒe] *adj* careless; unadorned, unstudied || *m* carelessness; negligee, dressing gown

négligeable [negliʒabl] *adj* negligible

négligence [negliʒɑ̃s] *f* negligence; (med) malpractice; **avec négligence** slovenly; **négligence criminelle** criminal negligence

négli•gent [negliʒɑ̃] **-gente** [ʒɑ̃t] *adj* negligent || *mf* careless person

négliger [negliʒe] §38, §97 *tr* to neglect || *ref* to neglect oneself

négoce [negɔs] *m* trade, commerce; (com) company

négociable [negɔsjabl] *adj* negotiable

négo•ciant [negɔsjɑ̃] **-ciante** [sjɑ̃t] *mf* wholesaler, dealer

négocia•teur [negɔsjatœr] **-trice** [tris] *mf* negotiator

négociation [negɔsjasjɑ̃] *f* negotiation

négocier [negɔsje] *tr* to negotiate || *intr* to negotiate; deal

nègre [nɛgr] *adj* (*qui appartient aux Noirs*) Black; African Black || **nè•gre** [nɛgr] **-gresse** [grɛs] *mf* (usually offensive) Black; **les nègres d'une plantation** (hist) the Negro slaves of a plantation; **travailler comme un nègre**

to work like a dog ‖ *m* (coll) ghost writer; **petit nègre** pidgin, Creole
négrerie [negrəri] *f* slave quarters
négrier [negrije] *adj masc* slave ‖ *m* slave driver; slave ship; slave trader
neige [nɛʒ] *f* snow
neiger [neʒe] §38 *intr* to snow
Némésis [nemezis] *f* Nemesis
nenni [nani], [neni], [nɛni] *adv* (archaic) no, not
nénuphar [nenyfar] *m* water lily
néologisme [neɔlɔʒism] *m* neologism
néon [neɔ̃] *m* neon
néophyte [neɔfit] *mf* neophyte, convert; beginner
neptunium [nɛptynjɔm] *m* neptunium
nerf [nɛr] *m* nerve; tendon, sinew; (archit, bb) rib; (fig) backbone, sinew; **avoir du nerf** to have nerves of steel; **avoir les nerfs à fleur de peau** to be on edge; **nerf de bœuf** scourge; **porter sur les nerfs à qn** to get on s.o.'s nerves
Néron [nerɔ̃] *m* Nero
ner•veux [nɛrvø] **-veuse** [vøz] *adj* nervous; nerve; jittery; sinewy, muscular; forceful (*style*)
nervosité [nɛrvozite] *f* nervousness; irritability; agitation
nervure [nɛrvyr] *f* rib; vein, nervure
net nette [nɛt] *adj* clean; clear, sharp, distinct; net; **net d'impôt** tax-exempt ‖ *m*—**mettre au net** to make a fair copy of ‖ **net** *adv* flatly, point-blank, outright
netteté [nɛtte] *f* neatness; clearness, sharpness
nettoiement [nɛtwamɑ̃] *m* cleaning
nettoyage [nɛtwajaʒ] *m* cleaning; **nettoyage à sec** dry cleaning
nettoyant [nɛtwajɑ̃] *m* cleaning product
nettoyer [nɛtwaje] §47 *tr* to clean; wash up or out; **nettoyer à sec** to dry-clean ‖ *ref* to wash up, clean oneself
net•toyeur [nɛtwajœr] **-toyeuse** [twajøz] *mf* cleaner
neuf [nœf] **neuve** [nœv] §94 *adj* new; **flambant neuf, tout neuf** brand-new ‖ **neuf** *adj & pron* nine; the Ninth, e.g., **Jean neuf** John the Ninth; **neuf heures** nine o'clock ‖ *m* nine; ninth (*in dates*)
neutraliser [nøtralize] *tr* to neutralize
neutralité [nøtralite] *f* neutrality
neutre [nøtr] *adj & m* neuter; neutral
neuvième [nœvjɛm] §94 *adj, pron* (*masc, fem*), *& m* ninth
névasse [nevɑs] *f* slush
ne•veu [nəvø] *m* (*pl* **-veux**) nephew; **nos neveux** our posterity
névralgie [nevralʒi] *f* neuralgia
névrose [nevroz] *f* neurosis
névro•sé -sée [nevroze] *adj & mf* neurotic
New York [nujɔrk], [nœjɔrk] *m* New York
newyor•kais [nœjɔrkɛ] **-kaise** [kɛz] *adj* New York ‖ (*cap*) *mf* New Yorker
nez [ne] *m* nose; cape, headland; **à plein nez**

entirely, really; **nez à nez** face to face; **parler du nez** to talk through one's nose
ni [ni] §90 *conj*—**ne ... ni ... ni** neither ... nor, e.g., **elle n'a ni papier ni stylo** she has neither paper nor pen; **ni ... ni** neither ... nor; **ni ... non plus** nor ... either
niable [njabl] *adj* deniable
niais [njɛ] **niaise** [njɛz] *adj* foolish, silly, simple-minded ‖ *mf* fool, simpleton
niaiserie [njɛzəri] *f* foolishness, silliness, simpleness
niche [niʃ] *f* niche; alcove; prank; **niche à chien** doghouse
nichée [niʃe] *f* brood
nicher [niʃe] *tr* to niche, lodge ‖ *intr* to nestle; nest; hide ‖ *ref* to nest
nickel [nikɛl] *adj* (slang) spic and span ‖ *m* nickel
nickeler [nikle] §34 *tr* to nickel-plate
nickelure [niklyr] *f* nickel plate
nicotine [nikɔtin] *f* nicotine
nid [ni] *m* nest; **en nid d'abeilles** honeycombed; **nid de pie** crow's-nest
nid-à-feu [nidafø] *m* (*pl* **nids-à-feu**) fire trap
nid-de-poule [nidəpul] *m* (*pl* **nids-de-poule**) pothole
nièce [njɛs] *f* niece
nième [njɛm] *adj* nth
nier [nje] §97 *tr* to deny ‖ *intr* to plead not guilty
ni•gaud [nigo] **-gaude** [god] *adj* silly ‖ *mf* nincompoop
nigauderie [nigodri] *f* silliness
nihilisme [niilism] *m* nihilism
Nil [nil] *m* Nile
nimbe [nɛ̃b] *m* halo, nimbus
nimber [nɛ̃be] *tr* to halo
nimbus [nɛ̃bys] *m* (meteo) nimbus
nipper [nipe] *tr* (coll) to tog ‖ *ref* (coll) to tog oneself out
nippes [nip] *fpl* (coll) worn-out clothes; (slang) duds
nique [nik] *f*—**faire la nique à** to turn up one's nose at
nitouche [nituʃ] *f*—**de sainte nitouche** hypocritically pious
nitrate [nitrat] *m* nitrate
nitre [nitr] *m* niter, nitrate
ni•treux [nitrø] **-treuse** [trøz] *adj* nitrous
nitrière [nitrijɛr] *f* saltpeter bed
nitrique [nitrik] *adj* nitric
nitrogène [nitrɔʒɛn] *m* nitrogen
nitroglycérine [nitrɔgliserin] *f* nitroglycerin
ni•veau [nivo] *m* (*pl* **-veaux**); **à deux niveaux** split-level; **au niveau de** on a par with; **de haut niveau** top-level, top-ranking; **niveau à bulle d'air** spirit level; **niveau à lunettes** surveyor's level; **niveau d'essence** gasoline gauge; **niveau de vie** standard of living; **niveau d'huile** oil gauge; **niveau d'imposition** tax bracket; **niveau mental** I.Q.
niveler [nivle] §34 *tr* to level; survey
nive•leur [nivlœr] **-leuse** [løz] *mf* leveler ‖ *m* harrow ‖ *f* (agr) leveler

nivellement [nivɛlmɑ̃] *m* leveling; surveying

Nᵒ, nᵒ *abbr* (**numéro**) no.

noble [nɔbl] *adj* & *mf* noble

noblesse [nɔblɛs] *f* nobility; nobleness

noce [nɔs] *f* wedding; wedding party; **faire la noce** to go on a spree; **ne pas être à la noce** to be in trouble; **noces** wedding

no•ceur [nɔsœr] **-ceuse** [søz] *adj* (coll) bacchanalian, reveling ‖ *mf* (coll) reveler, debauchee

no•cif [nɔsif] **-cive** [siv] *adj* noxious

noctambule [nɔktɑ̃byl] *mf* nighthawk; sleepwalker

nocturne [nɔktyrn] *adj* nocturnal; night; nightly ‖ *m* (mus) nocturne ‖ *f* open night (*of store*)

nodosité [nɔdozite] *f* nodule (*of root*); node, wart

Noé [nɔe] *m* Noah

noël [nɔɛl] *m* Christmas carol; (coll) Christmas present; **Noël** Christmas

nœud [nø] *m* knot; rosette; finger joint; Adam's apple; tie, alliance; crux (*of question, plot, crisis*); node; (naut) knot; **nœud de vache** granny knot; **nœud plat** square knot; **nœuds** coils (*of snake*); **nœud vital** nerve center

noir noire [nwar] *adj* black; **noir comme poix** pitch-black ‖ (*cap*) *adj* & *mf* (*person*) Black ‖ *m* black; bruise; **broyer du noir** to be blue, down in the dumps; **noir de fumée** lampblack ‖ *f* (mus) quarter note

noirâtre [nwarɑtr] *adj* blackish

noi•raud [nwaro] **-raude** [rod] *adj* swarthy

noirceur [nwarsœr] *f* blackness; black spot

noircir [nwarsir] *tr* to blacken ‖ *intr* & *ref* to burn black; turn dark

noircissure [nwarsisyr] *f* black spot, smudge

noise [nwaz] *f* squabble; **chercher noise à** to pick a quarrel with

noisetier [nwaztje] *m* hazelnut tree

noisette [nwazɛt] *adj invar* reddish-brown ‖ *f* hazelnut

noix [nwɑ], [nwa] *f* walnut; nut; **à la noix** (slang) trifling; **noix d'acajou, noix de cajou** cashew nut; **noix du Brésil** Brazil nut; **noix de coco** coconut; **noix de galle** nutgall; **noix de muscade** nutmeg; **noix de veau** round of veal

nolis [nɔli] *m* freight

noliser [nɔlize] *tr* to charter (*a ship*)

nom [nɔ̃] *m* name; noun; **de nom** by name; **nom à rallonges, nom à tiroirs** (coll) word made up of several parts; **nom commercial** trade name; **nom de baptême** baptismal name, Christian name; **nom de demoiselle** maiden name; **nom de Dieu!** God damn!, for Chrissakes!; **nom de famille** surname; **nom de guerre** fictitious name, assumed name; **nom de jeune fille** maiden name; **nom d'emprunt** assumed name; **nom de nom!** God damn!; **nom de théâtre** stage name; **nom marchand** trade name; **petit nom d'amitié** pet name; **sans nom** nameless; **sous le nom de** by the name of

nomade [nɔmad] *adj* & *mf* nomad

nombre [nɔ̃br] *m* number, quantity

nombrer [nɔ̃bre] *tr* to number

nom•breux [nɔ̃brø] **-breuse** [brøz] *adj* numerous; rhythmic, harmonious (*e.g., prose*)

nombril [nɔ̃bri] *m* navel

nomenclature [nɔmɑ̃klatyr] *f* nomenclature; vocabulary; body (*of dictionary*)

nomi•nal -nale [nɔminal] *adj* (*pl* **-naux** [no]) nominal; **appel nominal** roll call

nomina•tif [nɔminatif] **-tive** [tiv] *adj* nominative; registered (*stocks, bonds, etc.*) ‖ *m* nominative

nomination [nɔminasjɔ̃] *f* appointment

nom•mé -mée [nɔme] *adj* named; appointed; called ‖ *m*—**le nommé . . .** the man called . . .

nommément [nɔmemɑ̃] *adv* namely, particularly

nommer [nɔme] *tr* to name, call; appoint ‖ *ref* to be named, e.g., **je me nomme . . .** my name is . . .

non [nɔ̃] *m invar* no ‖ *adv* no, not; **non pas** not so; **non plus** neither, not, nor . . . either, e.g., **moi non plus** nor I either; **non point!** by no means!; **que non!** no indeed!

non-belligé•rant [nɔ̃belliʒerɑ̃] **-rante** [rɑ̃t] *adj* & *mf* nonbelligerent

nonce [nɔ̃s] *m* nuncio

nonchalamment [nɔ̃ʃalamɑ̃] *adv* nonchalantly

noncha•lant [nɔ̃ʃalɑ̃] **-lante** [lɑ̃t] *adj* nonchalant

non-combat•tant [nɔ̃kɔ̃batɑ̃] **-tante** [tɑ̃t] *adj* & *mf* noncombatant

non-conformiste [nɔ̃kɔ̃fɔrmist] *adj* & *mf* nonconformist

non-enga•gé -gée [nɔnɑ̃gaʒe] *adj* unaligned, uncommitted

non-ingérence [nɔ̃ɛ̃ʒerɑ̃s] *f* noninterference

nonnain [nɔnɛ̃] *f* (pej) nun

nonne [nɔn] *f* nun

nonobstant [nɔnɔpstɑ̃] *adv* notwithstanding; **nonobstant que** although ‖ *prep* in spite of

non-pesanteur [nɔ̃pəzɑ̃tœr] *f* weightlessness

non-rési•dent [nɔ̃rezidɑ̃] **-dente** [dɑ̃t] *adj* & *mf* nonresident

non-réussite [nɔ̃reysit] *f* failure

non-sens [nɔ̃sɑ̃s] *m* absurdity, nonsense

non-usage [nɔnyzaʒ] *m* disuse

non-violence [nɔ̃vjɔlɑ̃s] *f* nonviolence

nord [nɔr] *adj invar* north, northern ‖ *m* north; **du nord** northern; **faire le nord** to steer northward; **perdre le nord** to become disoriented, not to know one's way; **vers le nord** northward

nord-améri•cain [nɔrdamerikɛ̃] **-caine** [kɛn] *adj* North American ‖ (*cap*) *mf* North American

nord-est [nɔrɛst] *adj invar* & *m* northeast

nordique [nɔrdik] *adj* & *mf* Nordic

nord-ouest [nɔrwɛst] *adj invar* & *m* northwest

nor•mal -male [nɔrmal] *adj* (*pl* **-maux** [mo]) normal; regular, standard; perpendicular ‖ *f* normal; perpendicular; normalcy

norma•lien [nɔrmaljɛ̃] **-lienne** [ljɛn] *mf* student at a teachers college

nor•mand [nɔrmɑ̃] **-mande** [mɑ̃d] *adj* Norman ‖ *m* Norman (*dialect*) ‖ (*cap*) *mf* Norman (*person*)

Normandie [nɔrmɑ̃di] *f* Normandy; **la Normandie** Normandy

norme [nɔrm] *f* norm; specifications

nor•rois [nɔrwa] **nor•roise** [nɔrwaz] *adj* Norse ‖ *m* Norse (*language*) ‖ (*cap*) *m* Norseman

Norvège [nɔrvɛʒ] *f* Norway; **la Norvège** Norway

norvé•gien [nɔrveʒjɛ̃] **-gienne** [ʒjɛn] *adj* Norwegian ‖ *m* Norwegian (*language*) ‖ *f* round-stemmed rowboat ‖ (*cap*) *mf* Norwegian (*person*)

nos [no] **§88** our

nostalgie [nɔstalʒi] *f* nostalgia, homesickness

nostalgique [nɔstalʒik] *adj* nostalgic, homesick

nota bene [nɔtabene] *m invar* memo (*preceded by "N.B."*)

notable [nɔtabl] *adj* notable, noteworthy ‖ *m* notable

notaire [nɔtɛr] *m* notary; lawyer

notamment [nɔtamɑ̃] *adv* especially

notation [nɔtasjɔ̃] *f* notation

note [nɔt] *f* note; bill (*to be paid*); grade, mark (*in school*); footnote; **être dans la note** to be in the swing of things; **note de rappel** reminder; **prendre note de** to note down

noter [nɔte] *tr* to note; note down; notice; mark (*a student*); write down (*a tune*)

notice [nɔtis] *f* notice; instructions, directions; instruction manual; preface; **notice d'un livre** review of a book

notification [nɔtifikasjɔ̃] *f* notification, notice

notifier [nɔtifje] **§97** *tr* to report on; serve (*a summons*)

notion [nosjɔ̃] *f* notion

notoire [nɔtwar] *adj* well-known

notoriété [nɔtɔrjete] *f* fame

notre [nɔtr] **§88** our

nôtre [notr] **§89** ours; **serez-vous des nôtres?** will you join us?

noue [nu] *f* pasture land; roof gutter

noué nouée [nwe] *adj* afflicted with rickets

nouer [nwe] *tr* to knot; tie; form; cook up (*a plot*) ‖ *ref* to form knots; be tied; (*hort*) to set

noueux [nwø] **noueuse** [nwøz] *adj* knotty, gnarled

nouille [nuj] *f* noodle

nounou [nunu] *f* nanny

nour•ri -rie [nuri] *adj* heavy, sustained; rich (*style*)

nourrice [nuris] *f* wet nurse; can; (aut) reserve tank

nourricerie [nurisri] *f* baby farm; stock farm; silkworm farm

nourri•cier [nurisje] **-cière** [sjɛr] *adj* nutritive; nourishing; foster

nourrir [nurir] *tr* to nourish; suckle; to feed (*a fire*); nurse (*plants; hopes*) ‖ *intr* to be nourishing ‖ *ref* to feed; thrive

nourrisseur [nurisœr] *m* stock raiser, dairyman

nourrisson [nurisɔ̃] *m* nursling, suckling; foster child

nourriture [nurityr] *f* nourishment, food; nourishing; nursing; feeding; **nourriture du feu** firewood

nous [nu] **§85, §87** we; us; to us; **nous autres Américains** we Americans

nous-mêmes [numɛm] **§86** ourselves

nou•veau [nuvo] (or **-vel** [vɛl] before vowel or mute **h**) **-velle** [vɛl] (*pl* **-veaux -velles**) *adj* new (*recent*) ‖ (when standing before noun) *adj* new (*other, additional, different*) ‖ *m* freshman; **à nouveau** anew; **de nouveau** again; **du nouveau** something new; **le nouveau** the new; **le Nouveau Monde** the New World ‖ *f* see **nouvelle**

nouveau-né -née [nuvone] *adj* & *mf* (*pl* **nés**) newborn

nouveauté [nuvote] *f* newness, novelty

nouvelle [nuvɛl] *f* piece of news; novelette, short story; **donnez-moi de vos nouvelles** let me hear from you; **nouvelles** news ‖ *adj* see **nouveau**

Nouvelle-Angleterre [nuvɛlɑ̃glətɛr] *f* New England; **la Nouvelle-Angleterre** New England

Nouvelle-Ecosse [nuvɛlekɔs] *f* Nova Scotia; **la Nouvelle-Ecosse** Nova Scotia

Nouvelle-Orléans [nuvɛlɔrleɑ̃] *f*—**la Nouvelle-Orléans** New Orleans

Nouvelle-Zélande [nuvɛlzelɑ̃d] *f* New Zealand; **la Nouvelle-Zélande** New Zealand

nouvelliste [nuvɛlist] *mf* short-story writer

nova•teur [nɔvatœr] **-trice** [tris] *adj* innovating ‖ *mf* innovator

novembre [nɔvɑ̃br] *m* November

novice [nɔvis] *adj* inexperienced, new ‖ *mf* novice, neophyte

noviciat [nɔvisja] *m* novitiate

novocaïne [nɔvɔkain] *f* novocaine

noyade [nwajad] *f* drowning

noyau [nwajo] *m* (*pl* **noyaux**) nucleus; stone, kernel; pit (*of fruit*); core (*of electromagnet*); newel; hub; core, center (*of the city*); (fig) cell (*of conspirators*); (fig) bunch (*of card players*), **noyau d'atome** atomic nucleus

noyautage [nwajotaʒ] *m* infiltration (*e.g., of communists*)

noyer [nwaje] *m* walnut tree; **en noyer** in walnut (*wood*) ‖ **§47** *tr* & *ref* to drown

nu nue [ny] *adj* naked, nude; bare; barren; uncarpeted; unharnessed, unsaddled (*horse*); (aut) stripped ‖ *m* nude; **à nu** exposed; bareback ‖ *f* see **nue**

nuage [nɥaʒ] *m* cloud

nua•geux [nɥaʒø] **-geuse** [ʒøz] *adj* cloudy

nuance [nɥɑ̃s] *f* hue, shade, tone, nuance

Nubie [nybi] *f* Nubia

nu•bien [nybjɛ̃] **-bienne** [bjɛn] *adj* & *mf* Nubian

nucléaire [nykleɛr] *adj* nuclear

nucléole [nykleɔl] *m* nucleolus

nucléon [nykleɔ̃] *m* nucleon

nudiste [nydist] *adj* & *mf* nudist

nudité [nydite] *f* nakedness; nudity; plainness (*of style*); nude

nue [ny] *f* clouds; sky; **mettre** or **porter aux nues** to praise to the skies

nuée [nye] *f* cloud, storm cloud; flock

nuire [nɥir] §19 (*pp* nui *invar*) *intr*—**nuire à** to harm, injure, e.g., **cette accusation lui a beaucoup nui** that accusation hurt him very much

nuisible [nɥizibl] *adj* harmful

nuit [nɥi] *f* night; **à la nuit close** after dark; **bonne nuit** good night; **cette nuit** last night; **nuit blanche** sleepless night

nuitamment [nɥitamɑ̃] *adv* at night

nu-jambes [nyʒɑ̃b] *adj invar* bare-legged

nul nulle [nyl] *adj indef* no; **ne . . . nul** or **nul . . . ne** §90 no; **nul et non avenu, nulle et non avenue** [nylenɔnavny] null and void ‖ *f* dummy word or letter ‖ **nul** *pron indef*—**nul ne** §90B no one, nobody

nullement [nylmɑ̃] §90 *adv* not at all

nullité [nylite] *f* nonentity, nobody; invalidity

nûment [nymɑ̃] *adv* candidly, frankly

numéraire [nymerɛr] *m* specie; **payer en numéraire** to pay in cash

numé·ral -rale [nymeral] *adj & m* (*pl* **-raux** [ro]) numeral

numération [nymerɑsjɔ̃] *f* numeration; **numération globulaire** blood count

numérique [nymerik] *adj* numerical; digital

numériser [nymerize] *tr* digitize

numéro [nymero] *m* numeral; number; issue, number (*of a periodical*), e.g., **dernier numéro** current issue; e.g., **numéro ancien** back number; (slang) queer duck; **faire un numéro** to dial **numéro de classification** call number; **numéro de dossiers** case load; **numéro de vestiaire** check (*of checkroom*); **numéro d'ordre** serial number

numérotage [nymerɔtaʒ] *m* numbering, numeration

numérotation [nymerɔtasjɔ̃] *f* numbering, numeration; **numérotation décimale** call number

numéroter [nymerɔte] *tr* to number

numismatique [nymismatik] *adj* numismatic ‖ *f* numismatics

nu-pieds [nypje] *adj invar* barefooted

nup·tial -tiale [nypsjal] *adj* (*pl* **-tiaux** [sjo]) nuptial

nuque [nyk] *f* nape, scruff

nurse [nœrs] *f* children's nurse

nu-tête [nytɛt] *adj invar* bareheaded

nutri·tif [nytritif] **-tive** [tiv] *adj* nutritive; nutritious

nutrition [nytrisjɔ̃] *f* nutrition

nylon [nilɔ̃] *m* nylon

nymphe [nɛ̃f] *f* nymph; (Ent) nympha, chrysalis, pupa

O

O, o [o], *[o] m invar* fifteenth letter of the French alphabet

oasis [ɔazis] *f* oasis

obéir [ɔbeir] *intr* to obey; yield to; be subject to; **obéir à** to obey, e.g., **je leur obéis** I obey them, **j'obéis à la loi** I obey the law; **obéir au doigt et à l'œil** to obey blindly; **vous êtes obéi** you are obeyed

obéissance [ɔbeisɑ̃s] *f* obedience

obéis·sant [ɔbeisɑ̃] **-sante** [sɑ̃t] *adj* obedient

obélisque [ɔbelisk] *m* obelisk

obérer [ɔbere] §10 *tr* to burden with debt ‖ *ref* to run into debt

obèse [ɔbez] *adj* obese

obésité [ɔbezite] *f* obesity

objecter [ɔbʒɛkte] *tr* to object, e.g., **objecter que . . .** to object that . . .; to bring up, e.g., **objecter q.ch. à qn** to bring up s.th. against s.o.; put forward (*in opposition*), e.g., **objecter de bonnes raisons à** or **contre un argument** to put forward good reasons against an argument

objecteur [ɔbʒɛktœr] *m*—**objecteur de conscience** conscientious objector

objec·tif [ɔbʒɛktif] **-tive** [tiv] *adj* objective ‖ *m* objective; lens; (mil) target; **objectif angle plat** fish-eye lens

objection [ɔbʒɛksjɔ̃] *f* objection; **faire des objections** to object

objectivité [ɔbʒɛktivite] *f* objectivity

objet [ɔbʒɛ] *m* object; **menus objets** notions; **objet d'art** work of art; **objet de risée** laughingstock; **objets de première nécessité** articles of everyday use; **objet volant non-identifié** unidentified flying object; **remplir son objet** to attain one's end

obligation [ɔbligasjɔ̃] *f* obligation; (com) bond, debenture; **être dans l'obligation de** to be obliged to

obligatoire [ɔbligatwar] *adj* required, obligatory; (coll) inevitable

obli·gé -gée [ɔbliʒe] §93 *adj* obliged, compelled; necessary, indispensable; **bien obligé** much obliged; **c'est obligé** (coll) it has to be; **être obligé de** to be obliged to

obli·geant [ɔbliʒɑ̃] **-geante** [ʒɑ̃t] *adj* obliging

obliger [ɔbliʒe] §38, §96, §97, §100 *tr* to oblige ‖ §96 *ref*—**s'obliger à** + *inf* to undertake to + *inf*; **s'obliger pour qn** to stand surety for s.o.

oblique [ɔblik] *adj* oblique
oblitération [ɔbliterasjɔ̃] *f* obliteration; cancellation (*of postage stamp*); (pathol) occlusion
oblitérer [ɔblitere] §10 to obliterate; cancel (*a postage stamp*); obstruct (*e.g., a vein*)
o•blong [ɔblɔ̃] **-blongue** [blɔ̃g] *adj* oblong
obnubiler [ɔbnybile] *tr* to cloud, befog
obole [ɔbɔl] *f* widow's mite
obscène [ɔpsɛn] *adj* obscene
obscénité [ɔpsenite] *f* obscenity
obs•cur -cure [ɔpskyr] *adj* obscure
obscurcir [ɔpskyrsir] *tr* to obscure; dim ‖ *ref* to grow dark; grow dim
obscurité [ɔpskyrite] *f* obscurity
obséder [ɔpsede] §10 *tr* to obsess; importune, harass
obsèques [ɔpsɛk] *fpl* obsequies, funeral rites
obsé•quieux [ɔpsekjø] **-quieuse** [kjøz] *adj* obsequious
observance [ɔpsɛrvɑ̃s] *f* observance
observa•teur [ɔpsɛrvatœr] **-trice** [tris] *adj* observant ‖ *mf* observer
observation [ɔpsɛrvɑsjɔ̃] *f* observation
observatoire [ɔpsɛrvatwar] *m* observatory
observer [ɔpsɛrve] *tr* to observe ‖ *ref* to watch oneself; watch each other
obsession [ɔpsesjɔ̃] *f* obsession
obsolète [ɔpsɔlɛt] *adj* obsolete
obstacle [ɔpstakl] *m* obstacle
obstétrique [ɔpstetrik] *adj* obstetrical ‖ *f* obstetrics
obstination [ɔpstinɑsjɔ̃] *f* obstinacy
obsti•né -née [ɔpstine] *adj* obstinate
obstruction [ɔpstryksjɔ̃] *f* obstruction; (sports) blocking; **faire de l'obstruction** (pol) to filibuster; **obstruction systématique** filibustering
obstruer [ɔpstrye] *tr* to obstruct
obtempérer [ɔptɑ̃pere] §10 *intr*—**obtempérer à** to comply with, obey
obtenir [ɔptənir] §72, §97 *tr* to obtain, get
obtention [ɔptɑ̃sjɔ̃] *f* obtaining
obtura•teur [ɔptyratœr] **-trice** [tris] *adj* stopping, closing ‖ *m* (mach) stopcock; (phot) shutter; **obturateur à guillotine** drop shutter
obturation [ɔptyrɑsjɔ̃] *f* stopping up; filling (*of tooth*); **obturation des lumières** blackout
obturer [ɔptyre] *tr* to stop up; fill (*a tooth*)
ob•tus -tuse [ɔpty] **-tuse** [tyz] *adj* obtuse
obus [ɔby] *m* (mil) shell; plunger (*of tire valve*); **obus à balles** shrapnel; **obus à mitraille** shrapnel; **obus de rupture** armor-piercing shell
obvier [ɔbvje] *intr*—**obvier à** to obviate, prevent
oc [ɔk] *adv* (Old Provençal) yes
occasion [ɔkazjɔ̃], [ɔkɑzjɔ̃] *f* occasion; opportunity; bargain; **à l'occasion** on occasion; **à l'occasion de** for (*e.g., s.o.'s birthday*); **d'occasion** secondhand (*clothing*); used (*car*); **venez me voir à votre première occasion** come to see me at your first opportunity

occasion•nel -nelle [ɔkazjɔnɛl] *adj* occasional; chance (*meeting*); determining (*cause*)
occasionnellement [ɔkazjɔnɛlmɑ̃] *adv* occasionally; by chance, accidentally
occasionner [ɔkazjɔne] *tr* to occasion
occident [ɔksidɑ̃] *m* occident, west
occiden•tal -tale [ɔksidɑ̃tal] *adj* & *mf* (*pl* **-taux** [to]) occidental
occlu•sif [ɔklyzif] **-sive** [ziv] *adj* & *f* occlusive
occlusion [ɔklyzjɔ̃] *f* occlusion
occulte [ɔkylt] *adj* occult
occu•pant [ɔkypɑ̃] **-pante** [pɑ̃t] *adj* occupying ‖ *mf* occupant
occupation [ɔkypɑsjɔ̃] *f* occupation; **occupation sauvage** sit-in
occu•pé -pée [ɔkype] *adj* occupied; **occupé** (public sign) in use
occuper [ɔkype] *tr* to occupy ‖ §96, §97 *ref* to find something to do; **s'occuper de** to be occupied with, be busy with; take care of, handle
occurrence [ɔkyrɑ̃s] *f* occurrence; **en l'occurrence** under the circumstances; **être en occurrence** to occur; **selon l'occurrence** as the case may be
océan [ɔseɑ̃] *m* ocean; **océan glacial arctique** Arctic Ocean; **océan Indien** Indian Ocean
océanique [ɔseanik] *adj* oceanic
ocre [ɔkr] *f* ochre
octane [ɔktan] *m* octane
octave [ɔktav] *f* octave
octa•von [ɔktavɔ̃] **-vonne** [vɔn] *mf* octoroon
octet [ɔktɛ] *m* (comp) byte (of eight bits)
octobre [ɔktɔbr] *m* October
octroi [ɔktrwa] *m* granting (*of a favor*); tax on provisions being brought into town
octroyer [ɔktrwaje] §47 *tr* to grant, concede; bestow
oculaire [ɔkylɛr] *adj* ocular, eye ‖ *m* ocular, eyepiece
oculariste [ɔkylarist] *mf* optician (*who specializes in glass eyes*)
oculiste [ɔkylist] *mf* oculist
ode [ɔd] *f* ode
odeur [ɔdœr] *f* odor, scent; **odeur du corps** body odor
o•dieux [ɔdjø] **-dieuse** [djøz] *adj* odious ‖ *m* odium, odiousness
odo•rant [ɔdɔrɑ̃] **-rante** [rɑ̃t] *adj* fragrant
odorat [ɔdɔra] *m* (sense of) smell
Odyssée [ɔdise] *f* Odyssey
œcuménique [ekymenik] *adj* ecumenical
œdème [edɛm] *m* (pathol) edema
œdipe [edip] *m* Oedipus
œil [œj] *m* (*pl* **yeux** [jø] **les yeux** [lezjø]) eye; typeface, font; bud; **avoir l'œil (américain)** (coll) to be observant; **coûter les yeux de la tête** (coll) to cost a fortune; **donner de l'œil à** to give a better appearance to; **entre quatre yeux** [ɑ̃trəkatzjø] (coll) between you and me; **faire les gros yeux à** (coll) to glare at; **faire les yeux doux à** to make eyes at; **ne pas avoir les yeux dans la poche** (coll) to keep one's eyes peeled; (coll) to be no shrinking violet;

œil au beurre noir (coll) black eye; **œil de pie** (naut) eyelet; **œil de verre** glass eye; **œil électrique** electric eye; **pocher un œil à qn** to give s.o. a black eye; **sale œil** disapproving or dirty look; **sauter aux yeux, crever les yeux** to be obvious; **se mettre le doigt dans l'œil** (coll) to put one's foot in one's mouth; **se rincer l'œil** (slang) to get an eyeful; **taper dans l'œil à** or **de qn** (coll) to take s.o.'s fancy; **voir d'un mauvais œil** to take a dim view of

œil-de-bœuf [œjdəbœf] *m* (*pl* **œils-de-bœuf**) bull's-eye, small oval window

œil-de-chat [œjdəʃa] *m* (*pl* **œils-de-chat**) cat's-eye (*gem*)

œil-de-perdrix [œjdəpɛrdri] *m* (*pl* **œils-de-perdrix**) (pathol) soft corn

œillade [œjad] *f* glance, leer, wink; **lancer, jeter,** or **décocher une œillade à** to ogle

œillère [œjɛr] *f* eyecup; blinker; **avoir des œillères** to be biased

œillet [œjɛ] *m* eyelet; eyelet hole; carnation, clove pink; **œillet d'Inde** (*Tagetes*) marigold

œilleton [œjtɔ̃] *m* eye, bud; eyepiece; sight (*of rifle, camera, etc.*)

œillette [œjɛt] *f* opium poppy

œnologie [enɔlɔʒi] *f* science of viniculture, oenology

œsophage [ezɔfaʒ] *m* esophagus

œstres [ɛstr] *mpl* botflies, nose flies

œuf [œf] *m* (*pl* **œufs** [ø]) egg; **marcher sur des œufs** to walk on thin ice; **œuf à la coque** soft-boiled egg; **œuf à repriser** darning egg; **œuf de Colomb** ingenious, though obvious, solution to a problem; **œuf de Pâques** or **œuf rouge** Easter egg; **œuf dur** hard-boiled egg; **œuf mollet** soft-boiled egg; **œuf poché** poached egg; **œufs** spawn, roe; **œufs au lait** custard; **œufs au miroir** fried eggs; **œufs brouillés** scrambled eggs; **œuf sur le plat** fried egg; **plein comme un œuf** chock-full; **tondre un œuf** to squeeze blood out of a turnip; **tuer, écraser,** or **étouffer dans l'œuf** to nip in the bud

œuvre [œvr] *m* works (*of a painter*); **dans œuvre** inside (*measurements*); **hors d'œuvre** out of alignment; **le grand œuvre** the philosopher's stone; **le gros œuvre** (archit) the foundation, walls, and roof ‖ *f* work; piece of work; **bonnes œuvres** good works; **mettre en œuvre** to implement, to use; **mettre qn à l'œuvre** to set s.o. to work; **mettre tout en œuvre** to leave no stone unturned; **œuvres complètes** collected works; **œuvres mortes** (naut) topsides; **œuvre pie** good deed, good work; **œuvres vives** (naut) hull below water line; **se mettre à l'œuvre** to get to work

offen·sant [ɔfɑ̃sɑ̃] **-sante** [sɑ̃t] *adj* offensive

offense [ɔfɑ̃s] *f* offense; **faire offense à qn** to offend s.o.; **soit dit sans offense** with all due respect

offenser [ɔfɑ̃se] *tr* to offend ‖ *ref* to be offended

offen·sif [ɔfɑ̃sif] **-sive** [siv] *adj* & *f* offensive

of·fert [ɔfɛr] **-ferte** [fɛrt] *v* see **offrir**

office [ɔfis] *m* office; (eccl) office, service; **d'office** ex officio; **faire l'office de** to act as; **office d'ami** friendly turn; **remplir son office** (fig) to do its job ‖ *f* pantry

offi·ciel -cielle [ɔfisjɛl] *adj* & *mf* official

officier [ɔfisje] *m* officer; (naut) mate; **officier de service** (mil) officer of the day; **officier ministériel** notary public; **officier supérieur** (mil) field officer ‖ *intr* to officiate

offi·cieux [ɔfisjø] **-cieuse** [sjøz] *adj* unofficial, off-the-cuff; zealous; well-meant (*lie*); **faire l'officieux** to be officious

officine [ɔfisin] *f* pharmacy; den (*of thieves*); **officine d'intrigue** hotbed of intrigue

offrant [ɔfrɑ̃] *m*—**le plus offrant** the highest bidder

offre [ɔfr] *f* offer; **l'offre et la demande** supply and demand; **offres d'emploi** (formula in want ads) help wanted

offrir [ɔfrir] §65, §97, §98 *tr* to offer ‖ §96 *ref* to offer oneself; offer itself, occur

offset [ɔfsɛt] *m invar* offset

offusquer [ɔfyske] *tr* to obfuscate, obscure; irritate, displease ‖ *ref*—**s'offusquer de** to take offense at

ogive [ɔʒiv] *f* ogive; (rok) nose cone

ogre [ɔgr] **ogresse** [ɔgrɛs] *mf* ogre; **manger comme un ogre** (coll) to eat like a horse

ohé [ɔe] *interj* hey!; **ohé du navire!** ship ahoy!

ohm [om] *m* ohm

oie [wa] *f* goose; simpleton; **oie blanche** simple little goose (*naïve girl*); **oie sauvage** wild goose

oignon [ɔɲɔ̃] *m* onion; (hort) bulb; (pathol) bunion; (coll) turnip, pocket watch; **aux petits oignons** (coll) perfect; **ce ne sont pas mes oignons** it's no business of mine; **occupe-toi de tes oignons** (coll) mind your own business

oïl [ɔil], [ɔj] *adv* (Old French) yes

oindre [wɛ̃dr] §35 *tr* to anoint

oi·seau [wazo] *m* (*pl* **-seaux**) bird; hod (*of mason*); (coll) character; **être comme l'oiseau sur la branche** to be here today and gone tomorrow; **oiseau de paradis, oiseau des îles** bird of paradise; **oiseau des tempêtes** stormy petrel; **oiseaux domestiques, oiseaux de basse-cour** poultry

oiseau-mouche [wazomuʃ] *m* (*pl* **-mouches**) hummingbird

oiseler [wazle] §34 *tr* to train (*hawks*) ‖ *intr* to trap birds

oiselet [wazlɛ] *m* little bird

oiseleur [wazlœr] *m* fowler

oise·lier [wazəlje] **-lière** [ljɛr] *mf* bird fancier

oi·seux [wazø] **-seuse** [zøz] *adj* useless

oi·sif [wazif] **-sive** [ziv] *adj* idle ‖ *mf* idler

oisillon [wazijɔ̃] *m* fledgling

oisiveté [wazivte] *f* idleness

oison [wazɔ̃] *m* gosling; (coll) ninny

O.K. [oke] *interj* (letterword) O.K.!

oléagi·neux [ɔleaʒinø] **-neuse** [nøz] *adj* oily

oléoduc [ɔleɔdyk] *m* oil pipeline

olfac•tif [ɔlfaktif] **-tive** [tiv] *adj* olfactory
olibrius [ɔlibrijys] *m* pedant; pest; braggart (*in medieval plays*)
oligarchie [ɔligarʃi] *f* oligarchy
olivaie [ɔlivɛ] *f* olive grove
olivâtre [ɔlivɑtr] *adj* olive (*complexion*)
olive [ɔliv] *adj invar* & *f* olive
olivette [ɔlivɛt] *f* olive grove; plum tomato
olivier [ɔlivje] *m* olive tree; olive wood; **Olivier** Oliver
O.L.P. [ɔɛlpe] *f* (letterword) (**Organisation de la libération de la Palestine**) PLO
olympiade [ɔlɛ̃pjad] *f* olympiad
olym•pien [ɔlɛ̃pjɛ̃] **-pienne** [pjɛn] *adj* Olympian
olympique [ɔlɛ̃pik] *adj* Olympic
ombilic [ɔ̃bilik] *m* umbilicus
ombili•cal -cale [ɔ̃bilikal] *adj* (*pl* **-caux** [ko]) umbilical
ombrage [ɔ̃braʒ] *m* shade; **porter ombrage à** to offend; **prendre ombrage (de)** to take offense (at)
ombrager [ɔ̃braʒe] §38 *tr* to shade
ombra•geux [ɔ̃braʒø] **-geuse** [ʒøz] *adj* shy, skittish; touchy; distrustful
ombre [ɔ̃br] *f* shadow; shade; **ombres (chinoises)** shadow play, shadowgraph; **une ombre au tableau** (coll) a fly in the ointment
ombrelle [ɔ̃brɛl] *f* parasol; (aer) umbrella
ombrer [ɔ̃bre] *tr* to shade; apply eye shadow to
om•breux [ɔ̃brø] **-breuse** [brøz] *adj* shady
omelette [ɔmlɛt] *f* omelet
omettre [ɔmɛtr] §42, §97 *tr* to omit
omission [ɔmisjɔ̃] *f* omission
omnibus [ɔmnibys] *adj* omnibus; local (*train*) ‖ *m* omnibus; local (train)
omnipo•tent [ɔmnipɔtɑ̃] **-tente** [tɑ̃t] *adj* omnipotent
omnis•cient [ɔmnisjɑ̃] **-ciente** [sjɑ̃t] *adj* omniscient
omnium [ɔmnjɔm] *m* (com) holding company, general trading company; (sports) open race
omnivore [ɔmnivɔr] *adj* omnivorous
omoplate [ɔmɔplat] *f* shoulder blade
on [ɔ̃] §87 *pron indef* one, they, people; (coll) we, e.g., **y va-t-on?** are we going there?; (coll) I, e.g., **on est fatigué** I am tired; (often translated by passive forms), e.g., **on sait que** it is generally known that
once [ɔ̃s] *f* ounce
oncle [ɔ̃kl] *m* uncle; **oncle à la mode de Bretagne** first cousin once removed; **l'Oncle Sam** Uncle Sam; **l'Oncle Tom** (*bon nègre*) Uncle Tom (pej)
onction [ɔ̃ksjɔ̃] *f* unction; eloquence
onc•tueux [ɔ̃ktɥø] **-tueuse** [tɥøz] *adj* unctuous; greasy; bland
onde [ɔ̃d] *f* wave; watering (*of silk*); (poetic) water; **les petites ondes** (rad) shortwave; **mettre en ondes** to put on the air; **onde de choc** (aer) shock wave; **onde encéphalique** brain wave; **onde porteuse** (rad) carrier wave; **ondes amorties** (rad) damped waves;

ondes entretenues (rad) continuous waves; **ondes radiophoniques** airwaves; **onde sonore** sound wave
ondée [ɔ̃de] *f* shower
on-dit [ɔ̃di] *m invar* gossip, scuttlebutt
on•doyant [ɔ̃dwajɑ̃] **-doyante** [dwajɑ̃t] *adj* undulating, wavy; wavering (*person*)
ondoyer [ɔ̃dwaje] §47 *tr* to baptize in an emergency ‖ *intr* to undulate, wave
ondulation [ɔ̃dylɑsjɔ̃] *f* undulation, waving; flowing (*e.g., of drapery*); wave (*of hair*); **à ondulations** rolling (*ground*); **ondulation permanente** permanent wave
ondu•lé -lée [ɔ̃dyle] *adj* wavy; corrugated
onduler [ɔ̃dyle] *tr* to wave (*hair*) ‖ *intr* to wave, undulate
oné•reux [ɔnerø] **-reuse** [røz] *adj* onerous
ongle [ɔ̃gl] *m* nail, fingernail; **jusqu'au bout des ongles** to or at one's fingertips; **ongle des pieds** toenail
onglée [ɔ̃gle] *f* numbness in the fingertips
onglet [ɔ̃glɛ] *m* nail hole, groove (*in blade*); thimble; **à onglets** thumb-indexed; **monter sur onglet** (bb) to insert (*a page*)
onguent [ɔ̃gɑ̃] *m* ointment, salve
ont [ɔ̃] *v* see **avoir**
O.N.U. [ɔny] (acronym) or [ɔɛny] (letterword) *f* (**Organisation des Nations Unies**) UN (United Nations)
onu•sien [ɔnyzjɛ̃] **-sienne** [zjɛn] *adj* UN
onyx [ɔniks] *m* onyx
onzain *[ɔ̃zɛ̃] *m* eleven-line verse
onze *[ɔ̃z] §94 *adj* & *pron* eleven; the Eleventh, e.g., **Jean onze** John the Eleventh; **onze heures** eleven o'clock ‖ *m* eleven; eleventh (*in dates*), e.g., **le onze mai** the eleventh of May
onzième *[ɔ̃zjɛm] §94 *adj*, *pron* (*masc, fem*), & *m* eleventh
opale [ɔpal] *f* opal
opaque [ɔpak] *adj* opaque
O.P.E.P. [ɔpɛp] *f* (acronym) (**organisation des pays exportateurs de pétrole**) OPEC
opéra [ɔpera] *m* opera; opera house; **grand opéra, opéra sérieux** grand opera; **opéra bouffe** comic opera, opéra bouffe
opéra-comique [ɔperakɔmik] *m* (*pl* **opéras-comiques**) light opera
opéra•teur [ɔperatœr] **-trice** [tris] *mf* operator; **opérateur (de) console** (comp) keyboarder; **opérateur de permanence** operator on duty ‖ *m* cameraman
opération [ɔperɑsjɔ̃] *f* operation; **opérations à terme** (com) futures; **opération test** exploratory operation
opé•ré -rée [ɔpere] *mf* surgical patient
opérer [ɔpere] §10 *tr* to operate on; **opérer à chaud** to perform an emergency operation on (*s.o.*); **opérer qn de q.ch.** (med) to operate on s.o. for s.th. ‖ *intr* to operate; work ‖ *ref* to occur, take place
opérette [ɔperɛt] *f* operetta, musical comedy
opia•cé -cée [ɔpjase] *adj* opiate

opiner [ɔpine] *intr* to opine; **opiner du bonnet** (coll) to be a yes man

opiniâtre [ɔpinjɑtr] *adj* stubborn

opiniâtreté [ɔpinjɑtrəte] *f* stubbornness

opinion [ɔpinjɔ̃] *f* opinion; public opinion; **avoir bonne opinion de** to think highly of; **avoir une piètre opinion de** to take a dim view of

opium [ɔpjɔm] *m* opium

oponce [ɔpɔ̃s] *m* prickly pear

opossum [ɔpɔsɔm] *m* opossum

oppor·tun [ɔpɔrtœ̃] **-tune** [tyn] *adj* opportune, timely, expedient

opportuniste [ɔpɔrtynist] *adj* opportunistic *mf* opportunist

opportunité [ɔpɔrtynite] *f* opportuneness, timeliness; appropriateness

oppo·sant [ɔpozɑ̃] **-sante** [zɑ̃t] *adj* opposing ‖ *mf* opponent

oppo·sé -sée [ɔpoze] §92 *adj & m* opposite, contrary; **à l'opposé de** contrary to

opposer [ɔpoze] *tr* to raise (*an objection*); **opposer q.ch. à** to set up s.th. against; place s.th. opposite; contrast s.th. with ‖ *ref*—**s'opposer à** to oppose, object to

opposite [ɔpozit] *m*—**à l'opposite (de)** opposite

opposition [ɔpozisjɔ̃] *f* opposition; contrast

oppresser [ɔprɛse] *tr* to oppress; impede (*respiration*); weigh upon (*one's heart*)

oppresseur [ɔprɛsœr] *m* oppressor

oppres·sif [ɔprɛsif] **-sive** [siv] *adj* oppressive

oppression [ɔprɛsjɔ̃] *f* oppression; difficulty in breathing

opprimer [ɔprime] *tr* to oppress

opprobre [ɔprɔbr] *m* opprobrium, shame

opter [ɔpte] *intr* to opt, choose

opticien [ɔptisjɛ̃] *m* optician

optimisme [ɔptimism] *m* optimism

optimiste [ɔptimist] *adj* optimistic ‖ *mf* optimist

option [ɔpsjɔ̃] *f* option; **option d'achat** (com) call option; **option de vente** put option

optique [ɔptik] *adj* optic(al) ‖ *f* optics; perspective; **sous cette optique** from that point of view

opu·lent [ɔpylɑ̃] **-lente** [lɑ̃t] *adj* opulent

opuscule [ɔpyskyl] *m* opuscule, treatise; brochure, pamphlet

or [ɔr] *m* gold; **rouler sur l'or** to be rolling in money ‖ *adv* now; therefore

oracle [ɔrakl] *m* oracle

orage [ɔraʒ] *m* storm

ora·geux [ɔraʒø] **-geuse** [ʒøz] *adj* stormy

oraison [ɔrɛzɔ̃] *f* prayer; **oraison dominicale** Lord's Prayer; **oraison funèbre** funeral oration; **prononcer l'oraison funèbre de** (coll) to write off (*a custom, institution, etc.*)

o·ral -rale [ɔral] *adj* (*pl* **-raux** [ro]) oral

orange [ɔrɑ̃ʒ] *adj invar* orange (*color*) ‖ *m* orange (*color*) ‖ *f* orange (*fruit*)

oran·gé -gée [ɔrɑ̃ʒe] *adj & m* orange (*color*)

orangeade [ɔrɑ̃ʒad] *f* orangeade

oranger [ɔrɑ̃ʒe] *m* orange tree

orangeraie [ɔrɑ̃ʒrɛ] *f* orange grove

orangerie [ɔrɑ̃ʒri] *f* orangery; orange grove

orang-outan [ɔrɑ̃utɑ̃] *m* (*pl* **orangs-outans**) orangutan

ora·teur [ɔratœr] **-trice** [tris] *mf* orator; speaker; **orateur de circonstance** guest speaker; **orateur de fin de banquet** after-dinner speaker; **orateur invité** guest speaker

oratoire [ɔratwar] *adj* oratorical ‖ *m* (eccl) oratory

oratorio [ɔratɔrjo] *m* oratorio

orbite [ɔrbit] *f* orbit; socket (*of eye*); **placer sur son orbite, mettre en orbite** to orbit; **sur orbite** in orbit

orchestre [ɔrkɛstr] *m* orchestra; band; **orchestre de typique** rumba band

orchestrer [ɔrkɛstre] *tr* to orchestrate

orchidée [ɔrkide] *f* orchid

ordalie [ɔrdali] *f* (hist) ordeal

ordinaire [ɔrdinɛr] *adj* ordinary ‖ *m* ordinary; regular bill of fare; (mil) mess; **d'ordinaire, à l'ordinaire** ordinarily

ordi·nal -nale [ɔrdinal] *adj & m* (*pl* **-naux** [no]) ordinal

ordinateur [ɔrdinatœr] *m* (comp) computer; **fait à l'ordinateur** computerized; **mettre sur ordinateur** to computerize; **mise sur ordinateur** computerization; **ordinateur de poche** pocket computer; **ordinateur domestique** home computer; **ordinateur individuel** personal computer, desktop computer; **ordinateur personnel** personal computer, desktop computer; **ordinateur portatif** laptop computer

ordination [ɔrdinasjɔ̃] *f* ordination

ordonnance [ɔrdɔnɑ̃s] *f* ordinance; order, arrangement; (pharm) prescription

ordonna·teur [ɔrdɔnatœr] **-trice** [tris] *mf* organizer; marshal; **ordonnateur des pompes funèbres** funeral director

ordon·né -née [ɔrdɔne] *adj* orderly

ordonner [ɔrdɔne] §97, §98 *tr* to arrange, put in order; order; prescribe (*e.g., medicine*); (eccl) to ordain; **ordonner à qn de** + *inf* to order s.o. to + *inf*; **ordonner q.ch. à qn** to order s.o. to do s.th.

ordre [ɔrdr] *m* order; **avoir de l'ordre** to be neat, orderly; **à vos ordres** at your service; **dans l'ordre d'entrée en scène** (theat) in order of appearance; **de premier ordre** first-rate; **en ordre** in order; **jusqu'à nouvel ordre** until further notice; as things stand; **les ordres** (eccl) orders; **ordre du jour** (mil) order of the day; (parl) agenda; **ordre public** law and order; **payez à l'ordre de** (com) pay to the order of; **sous les ordres de** under the command of

ordure [ɔrdyr] *f* rubbish, filth; **ordures ménagères** garbage

ordu·rier [ɔrdyrje] **-rière** [rjɛr] *adj* lewd, filthy

orée [ɔre] *f* edge (*of a forest*)

oreille [ɔrɛj] *f* ear; **avoir l'oreille basse** to be humiliated; **dormir sur les deux oreilles** to sleep soundly; **dresser** or **tendre l'oreille** to prick up one's ears; **échauffer les oreilles à qn** to rile s.o. up; **faire la sourde oreille** to turn a deaf ear; **oreille externe** outer ear; **oreille interne** inner ear; **rompre les oreilles à qn** (coll) to talk s.o.'s head off; **se faire tirer l'oreille** (coll) to play hard to get

oreiller [ɔreje] *m* pillow

oreillette [ɔrɛjɛt] *f* earflap (*of cap*); (anat) auricle

oreillons [ɔrɛjɔ̃] *mpl* mumps

ores [ɔr] *adv*—**d'ores et déjà** [dɔrzedeʒa] from now on

Orfée [ɔrfe] *m* Orpheus

orfèvre [ɔrfɛvr] *m* goldsmith; silversmith; **être orfèvre en la matière** (coll) to know one's onions

orfèvrerie [ɔrfɛvrəri] *f* goldsmith's shop; goldsmith's trade; gold plate; gold or silver jewelry

orfraie [ɔrfrɛ] *f* osprey, fish hawk

organdi [ɔrgɑ̃di] *m* organdy

organe [ɔrgan] *m* organ; part (*of a machine*)

organique [ɔrganik] *adj* organic

organisa•teur [ɔrganizatœr] **-trice** [tris] *adj* organizing ‖ *mf* organizer

organisation [ɔrganizasjɔ̃] *f* organization

organiser [ɔrganize] *tr* to organize

organisme [ɔrganism] *m* organism; organization

organiste [ɔrganist] *mf* organist

orgasme [ɔrgasm] *m* orgasm

orge [ɔrʒ] *f* barley

orgelet [ɔrʒəlɛ] *m* (pathol) sty

orgie [ɔrʒi] *f* orgy

orgue [ɔrg] *m* organ; **orgue de Barbarie** hand organ; **orgue de cinéma** theater organ ‖ *f*—**les grandes orgues** the pipe organ

orgueil [ɔrgœj] *m* pride, conceit; **avoir l'orgueil de** to take pride in

orgueil•leux [ɔrgœjø] **-leuse** [jøz] *adj* proud, haughty

orient [ɔrjɑ̃] *m* orient; east; **Orient** Orient, East

orien•tal -tale [ɔrjɑ̃tal] (*pl* **-taux** [to]) *adj* oriental; eastern, east ‖ (*cap*) *mf* Oriental (*person*)

orientation [ɔrjɑ̃tasjɔ̃] *f* orientation; **orientation professionnelle** vocational guidance; **orientation sexuelle** sexual orientation

orienter [ɔrjɑ̃te] *tr* to orient; guide ‖ *ref* to take one's bearings

orien•teur [ɔrjɑ̃tœr] **-teuse** [tøz] *mf* guidance counselor

orifice [ɔrifis] *m* orifice, hole, opening

origan [ɔrigɑ̃] *m* marjoram

originaire [ɔriʒinɛr] *adj* native; original, first

origi•nal -nale [ɔriʒinal] *adj* (*pl* **-naux** [no]) original; eccentric, peculiar ‖ *m* antique (*piece of furniture*); eccentric, card (*person*); (typ) copy, original

originalité [ɔriʒinalite] *f* originality; eccentricity

origine [ɔriʒin] *f* origin

origi•nel -nelle [ɔriʒinɛl] *adj* original (*sin; meaning*); primitive, early

ori•gnal [ɔriɲal] *m* (*pl* **-gnaux** [ɲo]) moose, elk

orillon [ɔrijɔ̃] *m* ear, handle; (archit) projection

ori•peau [ɔripo] *m* (*pl* **-peaux**) tinsel; **oripeaux** cheap finery

Orléans [ɔrleɑ̃] *f* Orléans; **la Nouvelle Orléans** New Orleans

orme [ɔrm] *m* elm; **attendez-moi sous l'orme** (coll) I won't be there

ornement [ɔrnəmɑ̃] *m* ornament

ornemen•tal -tale [ɔrnəmɑ̃tal] *adj* (*pl* **-taux** [to]) ornamental

orner [ɔrne] *tr* to ornament, adorn

ornière [ɔrnjɛr] *f* rut, groove

ornithologie [ɔrnitɔlɔʒi] *f* ornithology

orphe•lin [ɔrfəlɛ̃] **-line** [lin] *adj* & *mf* orphan

orphelinat [ɔrfəlina] *m* orphanage (*asylum*)

orphéon [ɔrfeɔ̃] *m* male choir, glee club; brass band

ORSEC [ɔrsɛk] (**PLAN**) *f* (acronyme) (**Organisation des Secours**) state of emergency plan

orteil [ɔrtɛj] *m* toe; big toe; **gros orteil** big toe

O.R.T.F. [ɔɛrteɛf] *m* (letterword) (**Office de radio-télévision française**) French radio and television system

orthodoxe [ɔrtɔdɔks] *adj* orthodox

orthographe [ɔrtɔgraf] *f* spelling, orthography

orthographier [ɔrtɔgrafje] *tr* to spell

orthopédie [ɔrθɔpedi] *f* orthopedics

ortie [ɔrti] *f* nettle

orviétan [ɔrvjetɑ̃] *m* nostrum

O.S. [ɔɛs] *f* (letterword) (**ouvrière spécialisée**) specialist

os [ɔs] *m* (*pl* **os** [o]) bone; **à gros os** big-boned; **os à moelle** marrowbone; **tomber sur un os** (coll) to meet up with a problem; **trempé jusqu'aux os** soaked to the skin

osciller [ɔsile] *intr* to oscillate; waver, hesitate

o•sé -sée [oze] *adj* daring, bold; risqué, off-color

oseille [ozɛj] *f* sorrel; (slang) dough

oser [oze] §95 *tr* & *intr* to dare

osier [ozje] *m* osier; **d'osier** wicker

osmose [ɔsmoz] *f* osmosis

ossature [ɔsatyr] *f* bone structure; framework, skeleton

ossements [ɔsmɑ̃] *mpl* bones, remains

os•seux [ɔsø] **-seuse** [søz] *adj* bony

ossifier [ɔsifje] *tr* & *ref* to ossify

os•su -sue [ɔsy] *adj* bony; big-boned

ostensible [ɔstɑ̃sibl] *adj* conspicuous, ostensible; ostentatious

ostensoir [ɔstɑ̃swar] *m* monstrance

ostentatoire [ɔstɑ̃tatwar] *adj* ostentatious

ostracisme [ɔstrasism] *m* ostracism

otage [ɔtaʒ] *m* hostage

otalgie [ɔtalʒi] *f* earache

O.T.A.N. *or* **OTAN** [ɔtan], [ɔtɑ̃] *f* (acronym) (**Organisation du traité de l'Atlantique Nord**) (**l'O.T.A.N.**) NATO (North Atlantic Treaty Organization)

otarie [ɔtari] *f* sea lion

OTASE [ɔtaz] *f* (acronym) (**Organisation du**

traité de l'Asie du Sud-Est) (l'OTASE) SEATO (Southeast Asia Treaty Organization)

ôter [ote] *tr* to remove, take away; take off; tip (*one's hat*); **ôter q.ch. à qn** to remove or take away s.th. from s.o.; **ôter q.ch. de q.ch.** to take s.th. away from s.th. || *ref* to withdraw, get out of the way

otto•man [ɔtɔmã] **-mane** [man] *adj* Ottoman || *m* ottoman (*corded fabric*) || *f* ottoman (*divan*) || (*cap*) *mf* Ottoman (*person*)

ou [u] *conj* or; **ou ... ou** either ... or

où [u] *adv* where; **d'où** from where, whence; **où que** wherever; **par où** which way || *conj* where; when; **d'où** from where, whence; **par où** through which; **partout où** wherever

ouailles [wɑj] *fpl* (eccl) flock

ouais [wɛ] *interj* (coll) oh yeah!

ouate *[wat] *f* cotton batting, wadding

ouater *[wate] *tr* to pad, wad

oubli [ubli] *m* forgetfulness; omission, oversight; **tomber dans l'oubli** to fall into oblivion

oublier [ublije] §97 *tr & intr* to forget || *ref* to forget oneself; be forgotten

oubliettes [ublijɛt] *fpl* dungeon of oblivion

ou•blieux [ublijø] **-blieuse** [blijøz] *adj* forgetful, oblivious, unmindful

ouche [uʃ] *f* orchard; vegetable garden

ouest [wɛst] *adj invar* west, western || *m* west; **de l'ouest** western; **faire l'ouest** to steer westward; **ouest américain** far West; **vers l'ouest** westward

ouest-alle•mand [wɛstalmã] **-mande** [mãd] *adj* West German || (*cap*) *mf* West German

ouf *[uf] *interj* whew!

oui [wi] *m invar* yes; **les oui l'emportent** the ayes have it || *adv* yes; **je crois que oui** I think so; **oui madame** yes ma'am; **oui monsieur** yes sir; **oui mon capitaine** (**mon général,** etc.) yes sir

ouï-dire [widir] *m invar* hearsay; **simples ouï-dire** (law) hearsay evidence

ouïe [wi] *f* hearing; **être tout ouïe** [tutwi] to be all ears; **ouïs** gills; sound holes (*of violin*) || *interj* oh my!

ouïr [wir] §95 (used only in: *inf,* compound tenses with *pp* **ouï,** and 2d *pl impv* **oyez**) *tr* to hear; **oyez ...!** hear ye ...!

ouragan [uragã] *m* hurricane

ourdir [urdir] *tr* to warp (*cloth before weaving*); hatch (*e.g., a plot*)

ourler [urle] *tr* to hem; **ourler à jour** to hemstitch

ourlet [urlɛ] *m* hem; **ourlet de la jupe** hemline

ours [urs] *m* bear; (fig) lone wolf; **ours en peluche** teddy bear; **ours mal léché** unmannerly boor; **ours marin** (zool) seal; **vendre la peau de l'ours avant de l'avoir tué** to count one's chickens before they are hatched

ourse [urs] *f* she-bear; **la Grande Ourse** the Great Bear; **la Petite Ourse** the Little Bear

oursin [ursɛ̃] *m* sea urchin

ourson [ursɔ̃] *m* bear cub

ouste [ust] *interj* (coll) out!, out you go!

outarde [utard] *f* (orn) bustard

outil [uti] *m* tool, implement; **outil à moteur** power tool

outillage [utijaʒ] *m* tools; equipment

outil•lé -lée [utije] *adj* equipped with tools; tooled-up (*factory*)

outiller [utije] *tr* to equip with tools; tool up (*a factory*) || *ref* to supply oneself with equipment; tool up

outilleur [utijœr] *m* toolmaker

outrage [utraʒ] *m* outrage, affront; ravages (*of time*); contempt of court; **faire outrage à qn** to outrage s.o.; **outrage à la justice** contempt of court; **outrage aux bonnes mœurs** traffic in pornography; **outrage public à la pudeur** indecent exposure

outrager [utraʒe] §38 *tr* to outrage, affront

outra•geux [utraʒø] **-geuse** [ʒøz] *adj* outrageous, insulting

outrance [utrãs] *f* excess; exaggeration; **à outrance** to the limit

outran•cier [utrãsje] **-cière** [sjɛr] *adj* extreme, excessive, out-and-out; *mf* extremist, out-and-outer

outre [utr] *f* goatskin canteen || *adv* further; **d'outre en d'outre** right through; **en outre** besides, moreover; **passer outre à** to ignore (*e.g., an order*) || *prep* in addition to, apart from; beyond

ou•tré -trée [utre] *adj* overdone, exaggerated; exasperated

outrecui•dant [utrəkɥidã] **-dante** [dãt] *adj* self-satisfied; insolent, presumptuous

outre-Manche [utrəmãʃ] *adv* across the Channel

outremer [utrəmɛr] *m* ultramarine, lapis lazuli (*color*)

outre-mer [utrəmɛr] *adv* overseas

outre-monts [utrəmɔ̃] *adv* over the mountains (*i.e., the Alps*)

outrepasser [utrəpase] *tr* to go beyond, to exceed

outrer [utre] *tr* to overdo, exaggerate; exasperate

outre-tombe [utrətɔ̃b] *adv*—**d'outre-tombe** posthumous

ou•vert -verte [uvɛr] **-verte** [vɛrt] *adj* open; exposed; frank, candid; on (*said of meter, gas, etc.*); || *v* see **ouvrir**

ouverture [uvɛrtyr] *f* opening; hole, gap; (mus) overture; (phot) aperture; **ouverture en fondu** (mov) fade-in

ouvrable [uvrabl] *adj* working, e.g., **jour ouvrable** working day

ouvrage [uvraʒ] *m* work, handiwork; piece of work; work, treatise

ouvrager [uvraʒe] §38 *tr* to work (*e.g., iron*); turn (*wood*)

ou•vré -vrée [uvre] *adj* worked, wrought; finished (*product*)

ouvre-boîtes [uvrəbwat] *m invar* can opener

ouvre-bouteilles [uvrəbutɛj] *m invar* bottle opener
ouvreur [uvrœr] *m* opener (*in poker*)
ouvreuse [uvrøz] *f* usher
ou•vrier [uvrije] **-vrière** [vrijɛr] *adj* working, worker; worker's, workingman's ‖ *mf* worker ‖ *m* workman, laborer; workingman ‖ *f* working-woman; (ent) worker ant; (ent) worker bee
ouvrir [uvrir] §65 *tr* to open; turn on (*the light; the radio or television; the gas*); **ouvrir boutique** to set up shop ‖ *intr* to be open; open (*said of store, school, etc.; said of card player*) ‖ *ref* to open; be opened; **s'ouvrir à** to open up to, confide in
ouvroir [uvrwar] *m* workroom
ovaire [ovɛr] *m* ovary
ovale [ɔval] *adj & m* oval

ovation [ɔvɑsjɔ̃] *f* ovation
ovationner [ɔvɑsjɔne] *tr* to give an ovation to
Ovide [ɔvid] *m* Ovid
O.V.N.I. [ɔvni] *m* (acronym) (**objet volant non-identifié**) UFO
oxford [ɔksfɔr] *m* oxford cloth
oxycarbonisme [ɔksikarbɔnism] *m* carbon-monoxide poisoning
oxyde [ɔksid] *m* oxide
oxyder [ɔkside] *tr & ref* to oxidize
oxygène [ɔksiʒɛn] *m* oxygen
oxygéner [ɔksiʒene] §10 *tr* to oxygenate; bleach (*hair*) ‖ *ref*—**s'oxygéner les poumons** (coll) to fill one's lungs full of pure air
oxyton [ɔksitɔ̃] *adj & m* oxytone
ozone [ozɔn] *m* ozone
ozonosphère [ozɔnɔsfɛr] *f* ozonosphere

P

P, p [pe] *m invar* sixteenth letter of the French alphabet
pacage [pakaʒ] *m* pasture
pacifica•teur [pasifikatœr] **-trice** [tris] *mf* pacifier
pacifier [pasifje] *tr* to pacify
pacifique [pasifik] *adj* pacific ‖ **Pacifique** *adj & m* Pacific
pacifisme [pasifism] *m* pacifism
pacifiste [pasifist] *mf* pacifist
pacotille [pakɔtij] *f* junk; **de pacotille** shoddy; junky
pacte [pakt] *m* pact, covenant; **pacte de non-agression** nonaggression pact
pactiser [paktize] *intr* to compromise; traffic (*with the enemy*)
paf [paf] *adj* (slang) tipsy, tight ‖ *interj* bang!
pagaie [pagɛ] *f* paddle
pagaïe or **pagaille** [pagaj] *f* disorder; **en pagaïe** (coll) in great quantity; (coll) in a mess
paganisme [paganism] *m* paganism
pagayer [pageje] §49 *tr & intr* to paddle
page [paʒ] *m* page ‖ *f* page (*of a book*); **être à la page** to be up to date; **page de calcul** spreadsheet
paginer [paʒine] *tr* to page
pagne [paɲ] *m* loincloth
paie [pɛ] *f* pay, wages
paiement [pɛmɑ̃] *m* payment; **paiement comptant** cash payment
païen [pajɛ̃] **païenne** [pajɛn] *adj & mf* pagan
pail•lard [pajar] **-larde** [jard] *adj* ribald ‖ *mf* debauchee
paillasse [pajas] *m* buffoon ‖ *f* straw mattress; (slang) whore
paillasson [pajasɔ̃] *m* doormat
paille [paj] *f* straw; flaw; (Bib) mote; **paille de fer** iron shavings

pail•lé -lée [paje] *adj* rush-bottomed (*chair*)
pailler [paje] *m* straw stack ‖ *tr* to bottom (*a chair*) with straw; mulch
pailleter [pajte] §34 *tr* to spangle
paillette [pajɛt] *f* spangle; flake (*of mica; of soap*); grain (*of gold*); flaw (*in a diamond*); **paillette de maïs** corn flakes
pain [pɛ̃] *m* bread; loaf (*of bread, of sugar*); cake (*of soap*); pat (*of butter*); **avoir du pain sur la planche** (coll) to have a lot to do; **pain à cacheter** sealing wafer; **pain aux raisins** raisin roll; **pain bis** brown bread; **pain complet** whole-wheat bread; **pain de fantaisie** bread sold by the loaf (*instead of by weight*); **pain de mie** sandwich bread; **pain d'épice** gingerbread; **pain de viande** meat loaf; **pain grillé** toast; **pain perdu** French toast; **petit pain** roll; **se vendre comme des petits pains** (coll) to sell like hot cakes
pair paire [pɛr] *adj* even (*number*) ‖ *m* peer; equal; (com) par; **hors de pair, hors pair** unrivaled; **marcher de pair avec** to keep abreast of; **travailler au pair** (coll) to work for one's keep; **au pair** at par ‖ *f* pair; couple; brace (*of dogs, pistols, etc.*); yoke (*of oxen*)
pairesse [pɛrɛs] *f* peeress
pairie [pɛri], [peri] *f* peerage
pais [pe] *v* (**paît**) see **paître**
paisible [pezibl] *adj* peaceful
paître [pɛtr] §48 *tr & intr* to graze; **envoyer paître** (coll) to send packing
paix [pɛ] *f* peace
Pakistan [pakistɑ̃] *m*—**le Pakistan** Pakistan
pakista•nais [pakistane] **-naise** [nɛz] *adj* Pakistani ‖ (*cap*) *mf* Pakistani
pal [pal] *m* (*pl* **paux** [po] or **pals**) pale, stake
palabre [palabr] *m & f* palaver
palace [palas] *m* luxury hotel

palais [palɛ] *m* palace; palate; courthouse, law courts

palan [palɑ̃] *m* block and tackle

palanque [palɑ̃k] *f* stockade

pala•tal -tale [palatal] (*pl* **-taux** [to] **-tales**) *adj & f* palatal

pale [pal] *f* blade (*of, e.g., oar*); stake; sluice gate; (eccl) pall

pâle [pɑl] *adj* pale

palefrenier [palfrənje] *m* groom; (coll) hick, oaf

palefroi [palfrwa] *m* palfrey

paleron [palrɔ̃] *m* bottom chuck roast

palet [palɛ] *m* disk, flat stone; puck

paletot [palto] *m* topcoat

palette [palɛt] *f* palette; paddle

pâleur [pɑlœr] *f* pallor; paleness

palier [palje] *m* landing (*of stairs*); plateau (*of curve of a graph*); (mach) bearing; **en palier** on the level; **palier à billes** ball bearing; **par paliers** graduated (*e.g., tax*); in stages

pâlir [pɑlir] *tr & intr* to pale, turn pale

palis [pali] *m* picket fence

palissade [palisad] *f* palisade; fence

palissandre [palisɑ̃dr] *m* rosewood

pallier [palje] *tr* to palliate ‖ *intr*—**pallier à** to mitigate

palmarès [palmarɛs] *m* list of winners; hit parade

palme [palm] *f* (bot) palm; **palmes fins** (*for swimming*)

palmeraie [palmərɛ] *f* palm grove

palmier [palmje] *m* palm tree

palmipède [palmipɛd] *adj* webfooted ‖ *m* webfoot

palombe [palɔ̃b] *f* ringdove

palourde [palurd] *f* clam

palpable [palpabl] *adj* palpable; plain, obvious

palper [palpe] *tr* to feel; palpate; (coll) to pocket (*money*)

palpiter [palpite] *intr* to palpitate

palsambleu [palsɑ̃blø] *interj* zounds!

paltoquet [paltɔkɛ] *m* nonentity

palu•déen [palydeɛ̃] **-déenne** [deɛn] *adj* marsh (*plant*); swamp (*fever*)

paludisme [palydism] *m* malaria

pâmer [pɑme] *ref* to swoon

pâmoison [pɑmwazɔ̃] *f* swoon

pamphlet [pɑ̃flɛ] *m* lampoon

pamplemousse [pɑ̃pləmus] *m & f* grapefruit

pan [pɑ̃] *m* tail (*of shirt or coat*); section; side, face; patch (*of sky*); **Pan** Pan ‖ *interj* bang!

panacée [panase] *f* panacea

panachage [panaʃaʒ] *m* mixing; **faire du panachage** to split one's vote

panache [panaʃ] *m* plume; wreath (*of smoke*); **aimer le panache** to be fond of show; **avoir son panache** (coll) to be tipsy; **faire panache** to somersault, turn over

pana•ché -chée [panaʃe] *adj* variegated; mixed (*salad*); motley (*crowd*)

panacher [panaʃe] *tr* to variegate; plume; split (*one's vote*) ‖ *ref* to become variegated

panais [panɛ] *m* parsnip

panama [panama] *m* panama hat; **le Panama** Panama; **Panama** Panama City

panaris [panari] *m* (pathol) whitlow, felon

pancarte [pɑ̃kart] *f* placard; poster, sign

panchromatique [pɑ̃krɔmatik] *adj* panchromatic

pancréas [pɑ̃kreas] *m* pancreas

pandémonium [pɑ̃demɔnjɔm] *m* den of iniquity; pandemonium

pa•né -née [pane] *adj* breaded

panetière [pantjɛr] *f* breadbox

panier [panje] *m* basket; hoop (*of skirt*); creel (*trap*); **être dans le même panier** to be in the same boat; **panier à ouvrage** work basket; **panier à papier** wastepaper basket; **panier à provisions** shopping basket; **panier à salade** wire salad washer; (coll) paddy wagon; **panier percé** spendthrift

panier-repas [panjerəpɑ] *m* (*pl* **paniers-repas**) box lunch

panique [panik] *adj & f* panic

panne [pan] *f* breakdown, trouble; plush; fat (*of pig*); peen (*of hammer*); tip (*of soldering iron*); bank (*of clouds*); purlin (*of roof*); daub; (theat) small part; **(en) panne sèche** (*public sign*) out of gas; **être dans la panne** (coll) to be hard up; **être en panne** (coll) to be unable to continue; **être en panne de** (coll) to be deprived of; **laisser en panne** to leave in the lurch; **mettre en panne** (naut) to heave to; **panne fendue** claw (*of hammer*); **rester en panne** to come to a standstill; **tomber en panne** to have a breakdown

pan•né -née [pane] *adj* (slang) hard up

pan•neau [pano] *m* (*pl* **-neaux**) panel; snare, net; **condamner les panneaux** (naut) to batten down the hatches; **donner dans le panneau** to walk into the trap; **panneau d'affichage** billboard; **panneau de tête** headboard (*of bed*); **panneaux** paneling; **panneaux de signalisation** traffic signs; **tomber** or **donner dans le panneau** to be taken in, to fall into a trap

panoplie [panɔpli] *f* panoply

panorama [panɔrama] *m* panorama

panoramiquer [panɔramike] *intr* (mov, telv) to pan

panse [pɑ̃s] *f* belly; rumen, first stomach

pansement [pɑ̃smɑ̃] *m* (surg) dressing

panser [pɑ̃se] *tr* to dress, bandage; groom (*an animal*)

pan•su -sue [pɑ̃sy] *adj* potbellied

pantalon [pɑ̃talɔ̃] *m* trousers, pair of trousers; panties; slacks; **pantalon à pattes d'éléphant** bell-bottomed trousers; **pantalon corsaire** pedal pushers; **pantalon de coutil** ducks; blue jeans; **pantalon de golf** knickers; **pantalon de ski** ski pants

pante [pɑ̃t] *m* (slang) guy

panteler [pɑ̃tle] §34 *intr* to pant

panthéisme [pɑ̃teism] *m* pantheism

panthéon [pɑ̃teɔ̃] *m* pantheon

panthère [pɑ̃tɛr] *f* panther

pantin [pɑ̃tɛ̃] *m* puppet; jumping jack; **pantin articulé** string puppet
pantois [pɑ̃twa] *adj* flabbergasted
pantomime [pɑ̃tɔmim] *f* pantomime
pantou•flard [pɑ̃tuflar] **-flarde** [flard] *mf* (coll) homebody
pantoufle [pɑ̃tufl] *f* slipper
pantoufler [pɑ̃tufle] *intr* to leave government service
paon [pɑ̃] *m* peacock, peafowl; peacock butterfly
paonne [pan] *f* peahen
papa [papa] *m* papa; **à la papa** (coll) cautiously; **de papa** (coll) outmoded; **papa gâteau** (coll) sugar daddy
papas [papɑs] *m* pope (*in Orthodox Church*)
papauté [papote] *f* papacy
pape [pap] *m* pope
pape•lard [paplar] **-larde** [lard] *adj* hypocritical ‖ *mf* hypocrite ‖ *m* scrap of paper
paperasse [papras] *f* old paper
paperasserie [paprasri] *f* red tape
paperas•sier [paprasje] **-sière** [sjɛr] *adj* fond of red tape ‖ *mf* bureaucrat
papeterie [paptri] *f* paper mill; stationery store
pape•tier [paptje] **-tière** [tjɛr] *mf* stationer
papier [papje] *m* paper; newspaper article; document; piece of paper; **être dans les petits papiers de** (coll) to be in the good graces of; **gratter du papier** to scribble; **papier à calquer, papier végétal** tracing paper; **papier à cigarettes** cigarette paper; **papier à en-tête** letterhead (stationery); **papier à lettres** writing paper; **papier alu** aluminum foil; **papier à machine** typewriter paper; **papier à musique** staff paper; **papier bible, indien,** or **pelure** Bible paper, onionskin; **papier buvard** blotting paper; **papier carbone** carbon paper; **papier collant** Scotch tape; **papier d'emballage** wrapping paper; **papier de soie** tissue paper; **papier d'étain** tin foil; **papier de verre** sandpaper; **papier fort** cardboard; **papier hygiénique** toilet paper; **papier journal** newsprint; **papier kraft** cardboard (*for packing*); **papier mâché** papier-mâché; **papier ministre** foolscap; **papier paraffiné** wax paper; **papier peint** wallpaper; **papier rayé** lined paper; **papiers** (*public sign*) waste paper; **papier sensible** photographic paper; **papier tue-mouches** flypaper; **rayez cela de vos papiers!** (coll) don't count on it!
papier-filtre [papjefiltrə] *m* filter paper
papier-monnaie [papjemɔnɛ] *m* paper money
papier-pierre [papjepjɛr] *m* (*pl* **papiers-pierre**) papier-mâché
papille [papij], [papil] *f* papilla; **papille gustative** taste bud
papillon [papijɔ̃] *m* butterfly; flier, handbill; inset; form, application; thumbscrew, wing nut; butterfly valve; rider (*to document*); (coll) parking ticket; **papillon de nuit** moth; **papillons noirs** gloomy thoughts
papillonner [papijɔne] *intr* to flit about

papillote [papijɔt] *f* curlpaper; (culin) paper wrapper
papilloter [papijɔte] *intr* to blink; to flicker
papoter [papɔte] *intr* to chitchat
paprika [paprika] *m* paprika
papyrus [papirys] *m* papyrus
pâque [pɑk] *f* Passover; **la pâque russe** Russian Easter; **Pâque** Passover
paquebot [pakbo] *m* liner
pâquerette [pɑkrɛt] *f* white daisy
Pâques [pɑk] *m* Easter ‖ *fpl* Easter; **faire ses pâques** or **Pâques** to take Easter Communion; **Pâques fleuries** Palm Sunday
paquet [pakɛ] *m* packet, bundle; package; parcel; pack (*of cigarettes*); dressing down; **être un paquet d'os** [dɔs] to be nothing but skin and bones; **faire son paquet** (coll) to pack up; **mettre le paquet** (coll) to shoot the works; **paquet de mer** heavy sea; **petit paquet** parcel (*under a kilogram*); **petits paquets** parcel post; **un paquet de** a lot of
paquetage [pakta3] (comp) batch
par [par] *prep* by; through; out of, e.g., **par la fenêtre** out of the window; per, a, e.g., **huit dollars par jour** eight dollars per day, eight dollars a day; on, e.g., **par une belle matinée** on a beautiful morning; in, e.g., **par temps de brume** in foggy weather; **de par la loi** in the name of the law; **de par le monde** throughout the world; **par ailleurs** furthermore; **par avion** (*formula on envelope*) air mail; **par delà** beyond; **par derrière** at the back, the back way; **par devant** in front, before; **par exemple** for example; **par ici** this way; **par là** that way; **par où?** which way?
para [para] *m* (coll) paratrooper
parabole [parabɔl] *f* parable; (*curve*) parabola
parachever [paraʃve] §2 *tr* to finish off
parachutage [paraʃyta3] *m* airdrop, airdropping
parachute [paraʃyt] *m* parachute
parachuter [paraʃyte] *tr* to airdrop; (coll) to appoint in haste
parachutisme [paraʃytism] *m* parachuting; (sports) skydiving
parachutiste [paraʃytist] *mf* parachutist; (sports) skydiver ‖ *m* paratrooper
parade [parad] *f* show; parry; sudden stop (*of horse*); come-on (*in front of sideshow*); (mil) inspection, parade; **à la parade** on parade; **faire parade de** to show off, to display
parader [parade] *intr* to show off
paradis [paradi] *m* paradise; (theat) peanut gallery
parado•xal -xale [paradɔksal] *adj* (*pl* **-xaux** [kso]) paradoxical
paradoxe [paradɔks] *m* paradox
parafe [paraf] *m* flourish; initials
parafer [parafe] *tr* to initial
paraffine [parafin] *f* paraffin
paraffiner [parafine] *tr* to paraffin
parages [para3] *mpl* region, vicinity; **dans ces parages** in these parts
paragraphe [paragraf] *m* paragraph

Paraguay [paragɛ] *m*—le **Paraguay** Paraguay

para·guayen [paragɛjɛ̃] **-guayenne** [gɛjɛn] *adj* Paraguayan ‖ (*cap*) *mf* Paraguayan

paraître [parɛtr] §12, §95 *intr* to appear; seem; come out; show off; **à ce qu'il paraît** from all appearances; **faire paraître** to publish; **vient de paraître** just out

parallèle [paralɛl] *adj* parallel ‖ *m* parallel, comparison; (geog) parallel ‖ *f* (geom) parallel

paralyser [paralize] *tr* to paralyze

paralysie [paralizi] *f* paralysis

paralytique [paralitik] *adj & mf* paralytic

parangon [parɑ̃gɔ̃] *m* paragon

paranoïaque [paranɔjak] *adj & mf* paranoiac

parapet [parapɛ] *m* railing, parapet; (mil) parapet

paraphe [paraf] *m* flourish; initials

parapher [parafe] *tr* to initial

paraphrase [parafrɑz] *f* circumlocution, paraphrase; commentary

paraphraser [parafrɑze] *tr* to paraphrase

parapluie [paraplɥi] *m* umbrella; cover, front

parasite [parazit] *adj* parasitic(al) ‖ *m* parasite; **parasites** (rad) static

parasiter [parazite] *tr* to live as a parasite on or in (*a host*); (fig) to sponge on

parasol [parasɔl] *m* parasol; beach umbrella

paratonnerre [paratɔnɛr] *m* lightning rod

parâtre [parɑtr] *m* stepfather; cruel father

paravent [paravɑ̃] *m* folding screen

parbleu [parblø] *interj* rather!, by Jove!, you bet!

parc [park] *m* park; sheepfold; corral, pen; playpen; grounds, property; (mil) supply depot; (rr) rolling stock; **parc à huîtres** oyster bed; **parc automobile** motor pool; **parc d'attractions** amusement park; **parc de stationnement (payant)** parking lot

parcage [parkaʒ] *m* parking

parcelle [parsɛl] *f* particle; plot, lot (*in a subdivision*)

parce que [pars(ə)kə] *conj* because

parchemin [parʃəmɛ̃] *m* parchment; (coll) sheepskin (*diploma*)

parchemi·né -née [parʃəmine] *adj* wrinkled

parcheminer [parʃəmine] *tr* to parchmentize ‖ *ref* to shrivel up

par-ci [parsi] *adv*—**par-ci par-là** here and there

parcimo·nieux [parsimɔnjø] **-nieuse** [njøz] *adj* parsimonious

parcomètre [parkɔmɛtr] *m* parking meter

parcourir [parkurir] §14 *tr* to travel through, tour; wander about; cover (*a distance*); scour (*the country*); glance through

parcours [parkur] *m* run, trip; route, distance covered; round (*e.g., of golf*); stroke (*of piston*)

par-delà [pardəla] *adv & prep* beyond

par-derrière [pardɛrjɛr] *adv & prep* behind

par-dessous [pardəsu] *adv & prep* underneath

pardessus [pardəsy] *m* overcoat

par-dessus [pardəsy] *adv* on top, over ‖ *prep* on top of, over

par-devant [pardəvɑ̃] *adv* in front ‖ *prep* in front of, before

par-devers [pardəvɛr] *prep* in the presence of; **par-devers soi** in one's own possession

pardi [pardi] *interj* (coll) of course!

pardon [pardɔ̃] *m* pardon; Breton pilgrimage ‖ *adv* to contradict a negative statement or question) yes, e.g., **Vous ne parlez pas français, n'est-ce pas? Pardon, je le parle très bien** You don't speak French, do you? Yes, I speak it very well ‖ *interj* pardon me!; (slang) oh boy!

pardonnable [pardɔnabl] *adj* pardonable

pardonner [pardɔne] §98 *tr* to pardon, forgive, excuse, e.g., **Marie pardonne à Robert d'avoir manqué le rendez-vous** Mary forgives Robert for missing the date; **pardonnez-moi de vous avoir dérangé** excuse me for disturbing you; **pardonnez-moi, mais . . .** excuse me, but . . . ; **pardonner q.ch. à qn** to pardon s.o. s.th. ‖ *intr* (**à qn**) to pardon, forgive, e.g., **Marie pardonnera à Robert** Mary will forgive Robert; **ne pas pardonner** to be fatal (*said of illness, mistake, etc.*)

pare-balles [parbal] *adj invar* bulletproof

pare-boue [parbu] *m invar* mudguard

pare-brise [parbriz] *m invar* windshield

pare-chocs [parʃɔk] *m invar* (aut) bumper; **pare-chocs contre pare-chocs** bumper to bumper

pare-étincelles [paretɛ̃sɛl] *m invar* fire screen

pa·reil -reille [parɛj] *adj* identical, the same; such, such a ‖ *mf* equal, match; **sans pareil, sans pareille** without parallel, unequaled ‖ *m*—**c'est du pareil au même** (coll) it's six of one and half dozen of the other ‖ *f* same (thing); **rendre la pareille à qn** to pay s.o. back in his own coin

pareillement [parɛjmɑ̃] *adv* likewise

parement [parmɑ̃] *m* cuff; facing; trimming; (eccl) parament

pa·rent [parɑ̃] **-rente** [rɑ̃t] *adj* like ‖ *mf* relative; **parent de placement** foster parent; **parent par le sang** blood relation; **parents** parents; relatives; ancestors; **plus proche parent** next of kin

parenté [parɑ̃te] *f* relationship; relations

parenthèse [parɑ̃tɛz] *f* parenthesis; **entre parenthèses** in parentheses

parer [pare] *tr* to adorn; parry; prepare ‖ *intr*—**parer à** to provide for ‖ *ref* to show off

pare-soleil [parsɔlɛj] *m invar* sun visor

paresse [parɛs] *f* laziness

paresser [parese] *intr* (coll) to loaf

pares·seux [parɛsø] **-seuse** [søz] *adj* lazy ‖ *mf* lazy person, lazybones; malingerer ‖ *m* (zool) sloth

par ex. *abbr* (**par exemple**) e.g.

parfaire [parfɛr] §29 *tr* to perfect; make up (*e.g., a sum of money*)

par·fait [parfɛ] **-faite** [fɛt] *adj & m* perfect ‖ **parfait** *interj* fine!, excellent!

parfaitement [parfɛtmɑ̃] *adv* perfectly; completely; certainly, of course

parfois [parfwa] *adv* sometimes

parfum [parfœ̃] *m* perfume; aroma; bouquet (*of wines*); flavor (*of ice cream*); **au parfum** in the know

parfumer [parfyme] *tr* to perfume; flavor ‖ *ref* to use perfume

parfumerie [parfymri] *f* perfume shop; perfumery

pari [pari] *m* bet, wager; **pari gagnant** winning bet, sure thing

paria [parja] *m* pariah

parier [parje] §97 *tr & intr* to bet, wager

Paris [pari] *m* Paris

pari•sien [parizjɛ̃] **-sienne** [zjɛn] *adj* Parisian ‖ (*cap*) *mf* Parisian

parité [parite] *f* parity; likeness; evenness (*of numbers*)

parjure [parʒyr] *adj* perjured ‖ *mf* perjurer ‖ *m* perjury

parking [parkiŋ] *m* parking lot

par•lant [parlɑ̃] **-lante** [lɑ̃t] *adj* speaking; talking (*e.g., picture*); eloquent, expressive

parlement [parləmɑ̃] *m* parliament

parlementaire [parləmɑ̃tɛr] *adj* parliamentary ‖ *mf* peace envoy; member of a parliament, legislator

parlementer [parləmɑ̃te] *intr* to parley

parler [parle] *m* speech, way of speaking; dialect ‖ §97, §98 *tr & intr* to speak, talk; **tu parles Charles!** you don't say!

par•leur [parlœr] **-leuse** [løz] *mf*—**beau parleur** good talker; windbag

parloir [parlwar] *m* reception room

parlote [parlɔt] *f* (coll) talk, gossip, rumor

parmi [parmi] *prep* among

Parnasse [parnɑs] *m*—**le Parnasse** Parnassus (*poetry*); Mount Parnassus

parodie [parɔdi] *f* parody, travesty

parodier [parɔdje] *tr* to parody, travesty

paroi [parwa] *f* partition, wall; inner side; (anat) wall

paroisse [parwas] *f* parish

parois•sial -siale [parwasjal] *adj* (*pl* **-siaux** [sjo]) parochial, parish

parois•sien [parwasjɛ̃] **-sienne** [sjɛn] *mf* parishioner ‖ *m* prayer book; (coll) fellow

parole [parɔl] *f* word; speech; word, promise; **avoir la parole** to have the floor; **donner la parole à** to recognize, to give the floor to; **sur parole** on one's word

paro•lier [parɔlje] **-lière** [ljɛr] *mf* lyricist; librettist

parpaing [parpɛ̃] *m* concrete block; building block

parquer [parke] *tr* to park; pen in ‖ *intr* to be penned in ‖ *ref* to park

Parque [park] *f* (lit) destiny, death; **les Parques** (myth) the Fates

parquet [parkɛ] *m* parquet, floor; floor (*of stock exchange*); public prosecutor's office

parqueter [parkəte] §34 *tr* to parquet, floor

parrain [parɛ̃] *m* godfather; sponsor

parrainer [parɛne] *tr* to sponsor

parraineur [parɛnœr] *m* sponsor

parricide [parisid] *mf* parricide, patricide (*person*) ‖ *m* parricide, patricide (*act*)

parsemer [parsəme] §2 *tr* to sprinkle; spangle

part [par] *m* newborn child; dropping (*of young by animal in labor*) ‖ *f* part, share; **aller quelque part** (coll) to go to the toilet; **à part** aside; aside from; **à part entière** with full privileges; **autre part** elsewhere; **avoir part au gâteau** (coll) to have a slice of the pie; **d'autre part** besides; **de la part de** on the part of, from; **de part en part** through and through; **de toutes parts** on all sides; **d'une part . . . d'autre part** on the one hand . . . on the other hand; **faire la part de** to make allowance for; **faire part de** to announce; **faire part de q.ch. à qn** to inform s.o. of s.th.; **nulle part** nowhere; **nulle part ailleurs** nowhere else; **pour ma part** as for me, for my part; **prendre en bonne part** to take goodnaturedly; **prendre en mauvaise part** to take offense at; **prendre part à** to take part in; **quelque part** somewhere

partage [partaʒ] *m* division, partition; sharing; share; tie vote; **échoir en partage à qn** to fall to s.o.'s lot; **partage de temps** (comp) time sharing

partager [partaʒe] §38 *tr* to share; divide; **partager l'affiche** to co-star

partance [partɑ̃s] *f* departure; **en partance** leaving; **en partance pour** bound for

partant [partɑ̃] *m* (sports) starter; **partants** departing guests, departing travelers, etc. ‖ *adv* (lit) consequently

partenaire [partənɛr] *mf* partner; sparring partner; (mov, telv) co-star; **partenaires qui habitent sous le même toit** domestic partners

parterre [partɛr] *m* orchestra circle; flower bed

parthénogenèse [partenɔʒənɛz] *f* parthenogenesis

Parthénon [partenɔ̃] *m* Parthenon

parti [parti] *m* party; side; match, good catch; **faire un mauvais parti à** to rough up; to mistreat; **parti pris** fixed opinion; prejudice; **prendre le parti de** to decide to; **prendre le parti de qn** to take s.o.'s side; **prendre parti** to take sides; **prendre son parti** to make up one's mind; **prendre son parti de** to resign oneself to; **tirer parti de** to take advantage of

par•tial -tiale [parsjal] *adj* (*pl* **-tiaux** [sjo]) partial, biased

partici•pant [partisipɑ̃] **-pante** [pɑ̃t] *adj & mf* participant

participation [partisipasjɔ̃] *f* participation; **participation majoritaire** controlling interest

participe [partisip] *m* participle

participer [partisipe] *intr*—**participer à** to participate in; **participer de** to partake of

particulariser [partikylarize] *tr* to specify ‖ *ref* to make oneself conspicuous

particularité [partikylarite] *f* peculiarity; detail

particule [partikyl] *f* particle

particu·lier [partikylje] **-lière** [ljɛr] *adj* particular; special; private ‖ *mf* private citizen; (coll) odd person; **de particulier à particulier** (journ) personals ‖ *m* particular

particulièrement [partikyljɛrmɑ̃] *adv* particularly

partie [parti] *f* part; line, specialty; game, winning score; contest; party (*diversion*); (law) party; **avoir partie liée avec** to be in league with; **faire partie de** to belong to; **faire partie intégrante de** to be part and parcel of; **partie civile** plaintiff; **partie de chasse** hunting party; **partie de plaisir** outing, picnic; **partie nulle** tie game; **prendre à partie** to take to task

par·tiel -tielle [parsjɛl] *adj* partial

partir [partir] (used only in *inf*) *tr*—**avoir maille à partir** to have a bone to pick ‖ §64, §95, §96 *intr* (*aux:* ÊTRE) to leave; go off (*said of firearm*); begin; **à partir de** from; from . . . on, e.g., **à partir de maintenant** from now on; **faire partir** to send off; remove (*a spot*); set off (*an explosive*); fire (*a gun*); **partir +** *inf* to leave in order to + *inf*; **partir de** to come from; start with; **partir pour** or **à** to leave for

parti·san [partizɑ̃] **-sane** [zan] *adj & mf* partisan

partition [partisjɔ̃] *f* (mus) score

partout [partu] *adv* everywhere; **partout ailleurs** anywhere else; everywhere else; **partout où** wherever; everywhere

parure [paryr] *f* ornament; set; finery; necklace

parution [parysjɔ̃] *f* appearance, publication

parvenir [parvǝnir] §72, §96 *intr* (*aux:* ÊTRE)—**parvenir à** to reach; **parvenir à +** *inf* to succeed in + *ger*

parve·nu -nue [parvǝny] *adj & mf* upstart

parvis [parvi] *m* square (*in front of a church*)

pas [pɑ] *m* step; pace; footprint; footfall; pass; straits; pitch (*of screw*); **allonger le pas** to quicken one's pace; to put one's best foot forward; **à pas comptés** with measured tread; **à pas de loup, à pas feutrés** stealthily; **à pas de tortue** at a snail's pace; **à quatre pas** nearby; **au pas** at a walk; **au pas de course** double-quick; **céder le pas (à)** to stand aside (for); to keep clear (*in front of a driveway*); **de ce pas** at once; **être au pas** to be in step; **faire le premier pas** to make the first move; **faire les cent pas** to come and go; **faux pas** misstep; blunder; **marcher sur les pas de** to follow in the footsteps of; **marquer le pas** to mark time; **mauvais pas** tight squeeze, fix; **pas à pas** little by little, cautiously; **pas d'armes** passage at arms; **Pas de Calais** Straits of Dover; **pas de cheval** hoofbeat; **pas de clerc** blunder; **pas de deux** two-step; **pas de la porte** doorstep; **pas de l'oie** goosestep; **pas de porte** (com) price paid for good will; **prendre le pas sur** to get ahead of ‖ *adv*—**ne . . . pas** §90 not, e.g., **je ne sais pas** I do not

know; e.g., **ne pas signer** to not sign; (used with **non**), e.g., **non pas** no; (used without **ne**) (slang) not, e.g., **je fais pas de politique** I don't meddle in politics; **n'est-ce pas?** see **ne; pas?** (coll) not so?; **pas de** no; **pas du tout** not at all; **pas encore** not yet

pas·cal -cale [paskal] *adj* (*pl* **-caux** [ko]) Passover; Easter

passable [pɑsabl] *adj* passable, fair; mediocre, so-so

passade [pɑsad] *f* passing fancy

passage [pɑsaʒ] *m* passage; crossing; pass; **barrer le passage** to block the way; **du passage** in passing, in parentheses; **livrer passage à** to let through; **passage à niveau** grade crossing; **passage au-dessous de la voie, passage souterrain** underpass; **passage au-dessus de la voie** overpass; **passage clouté, passage zébré** pedestrian crossing, crosswalk; **passage de vitesses** gear shifting; **passage interdit** (*public sign*) do not enter; (*public sign*) no thoroughfare; **passage protégé** arterial crossing (*vehicles intersecting highway must stop*)

passa·ger [pɑsaʒe] **-gère** [ʒɛr] *adj* passing, fleeting; migratory; busy (*road*) ‖ *mf* passenger; **passenger clandestin, passager de cale** stowaway; **passager d'entrepont** steerage passenger

pas·sant [pɑsɑ̃] **-sante** [sɑ̃t] *adj* busy (*street*) ‖ *mf* passerby

passation [pɑsasjɔ̃] *f* handing over

passavant [pɑsavɑ̃] *m* permit; (naut) gangway

passe [pɑs] *m* master key ‖ *f* pass; channel; **être en bonne passe de** to be in a fair way to; **être en passe de** to be about to; **mauvaise passe** tight spot

pas·sé -sée [pɑse] *adj* past; faded; overripe; last (*week*) ‖ *m* past; past tense ‖ **passé** *prep* past, beyond, after

passe-bouillon [pɑsbujɔ̃] *m invar* soup strainer

passe-droit [pɑsdrwa] *m* (*pl* **-droits**) illegal favor; injustice

passe-lacet [pɑslasɛ] *m* (*pl* **-lacets**) bodkin

passe-lait [pɑslɛ] *m invar* milk strainer

passe-lettres [pɑslɛtr] *m* (*pl* **-lettres**) letter drop

passement [pɑsmɑ̃] *m* braid, trimming

passementer [pɑsmɑ̃te] *tr* to trim

passementerie [pɑsmɑ̃tri] *f* trimmings

passe-montagne [pɑsmɔ̃taɲ] *m* (*pl* **-montagnes**) storm hood, ski mask

passe-partout [pɑspartu] *m invar* master key; slip mount

passe-passe [pɑspɑs] *m invar* legerdemain; sleight of hand

passepoil [pɑspwal] *m* piping, braid

passeport [pɑspɔr] *m* passport

passer [pɑse] §96 *tr* to pass; ferry; get across (*e.g., a river*); spend, pass (*e.g., the evening*); take (*an exam*); slip on (*e.g., a dressing gown*); show (*a film*); make (*a telephone call*); go on (*one's way*); **passer q.ch. à qn** to hand or lend s.o. s.th.; forgive s.o. s.th. ‖ *intr* (*aux:* AVOIR *or* ETRE) to pass; pass away;

become; **en passer par là** to knuckle under; **faire passer** to get (*e.g., a message*) through; while away (*the time*); **passer à** to pass over to; **passer chez** or **passer voir** to drop in on; **passer outre à** to override; **passer par** to pass through, go through; **passer pour** to pass for or as; **passons!** let's skip it! || §97 *ref* to happen, take place; also **passer de** to do without

passe•reau [pɑsro] *m* (*pl* **-reaux**) sparrow

passerelle [pɑsrɛl] *f* footbridge; gangplank; (naut) bridge; **passerelle couverte extensible** (aer) enclosed swinging gangplank; **passerelle télescopique** telescopic corridor

passe-temps [pɑstɑ̃] *m invar* pastime, hobby

passe-thé [pɑste] *m invar* tea strainer

pas•seur [pɑsœr] **-seuse** [søz] *mf* smuggler || *m* ferryman

passible [pasibl] *adj*—**passible de** liable for, subject to

pas•sif [pasif] **-sive** [siv] *adj* passive || *m* passive; debts, liabilities

passiflore [pasiflɔr] *f* passionflower

passion [pɑsjɔ̃], [pɑsjɔ̃] *f* passion

passion•nant [pɑsjɔnɑ̃] **-nante** [nɑ̃t] *adj* thrilling, fascinating

passion•né -née [pɑsjɔne] *adj* passionate; impassioned; **passionné de** or **pour** passionately fond of || *mf* enthusiast, fan

passion•nel -nelle [pɑsjɔnɛl] *adj* of passion, of jealousy

passionner [pɑsjɔne] *tr* to excite the interest of, arouse || *ref*—**se passionner pour** or **à** to be passionately fond of

passoire [pɑswar] *f* colander; strainer; (fig) sieve

pastel [pastɛl] *m* pastel; (bot) woad

pastèque [pastɛk] *f* watermelon

pasteur [pastœr] *m* pastor, minister; shepherd

pasteuriser [pastœrize] *tr* to pasteurize

pastiche [pastiʃ] *m* pastiche; parody

pastille [pastij] *f* lozenge, drop; tire patch; polka dot; (comp) chip; **pastille pectorale** cough drop

pasto•ral -rale [[pastoral] (*pl* **-raux** [ro] **-rales**) *adj & f* pastoral

pastorat [pastora] *m* pastorate

pat [pat] *adj invar* (chess) in stalemate; **faire pat** to stalemate || *m* (chess) stalemate

patache [pataʃ] *f* police boat; (coll) rattletrap

patachon [pataʃɔ̃] *m*—**mener une vie de patachon** to lead a wild life

patapouf [patapuf] *m* (coll) roly-poly || *interj* flop!

pataquès [patakɛs] *m* faulty liaison; blooper, goof

patate [patat] *f* sweet potato; (coll) spud

patati [patati]—**et patati et patata** (coll) and so on and on

patatras [patatra] *interj* bang!, crash!

pa•taud [pato] **-taude** [tod] *adj* clumsy, loutish || *mf* lout

pataugeoire [patoʒwar] *f* wading pool

patauger [patoʒe] §38 *intr* to splash; to wade; (coll) to flounder

pâte [pɑt] *f* paste; dough, batter; **en pâte** (typ) pied; **mettre la main à la pâte** to put one's shoulder to the wheel; **pâte à papier** wood pulp; **pâte brisée, pâte feuilletée** puff paste; **pâte dentifrice** toothpaste; **pâte molle** spineless person; **pâtes (alimentaires)** pasta (*macaroni, noodles, spaghetti, etc.*); **peindre à la pâte** to paint with a full brush; **une bonne pâte d'homme** (coll) a good sort

pâté [pate] *m* blot, splotch; (typ) pi; **pâté de foie gras** minced goose livers; **pâté de maisons** block of houses; **pâté en croûte** meat or fish pie; **pâté maison** chef's-special pâté

pâtée [pate] *f* dog food, cat food; chicken feed

pate•lin [patlɛ̃] **-line** [lin] *adj* fawning, wheedling || *m* wheedler; (coll) native village

patenôtre [patnotr] *f* prayer; (archaic) mumbo jumbo

pa•tent [patɑ̃] **-tente** [tɑ̃t] *adj* patent || *f* license; tax; **patente (de santé)** (naut) bill of health

paten•té -tée [patɑ̃te] *adj* licensed || *mf* licensed dealer

patenter [patɑ̃te] *tr* to license

Pater [patɛr] *m invar* Lord's Prayer

patère [patɛr] *f* clothes hook; curtain hook

paterne [patɛrn] *adj* mawkish, mealy-mouthed

pater•nel -nelle [patɛrnɛl] *adj* paternal; fatherly || *m* (slang) pop, dad

paternité [patɛrnite] *f* paternity; fatherhood; authorship

pâ•teux [patø] **-teuse** [tøz] *adj* pasty; thick; coated (*tongue*)

pathétique [patetik] *adj* pathetic || *m* pathos

pathologie [patɔlɔʒi] *f* pathology

pathos [patos] *m* bathos

patibulaire [patibylɛr] *adj* hangdog (*look*)

patience [pasjɑ̃s] *f* patience; (cards) solitaire

pa•tient [pasjɑ̃] **-tiente** [sjɑ̃t] *adj & mf* patient

patienter [pasjɑ̃te] *intr* to be patient

patin [patɛ̃] *m* skate; runner; sill, sleeper; (*sole*) patten; (aer) skid; (rr) base, flange (*of rails*); **patin à glace** ice skate; **patin à roulettes** roller skate; **patin de frein** brake shoe; **patin en ligne** in-line skates

patinage [patinaʒ] *m* ice skating

patiner [patine] *intr* to skate; slide; skid; **patiner sur glace, faire du patin à glace** to ice skate

patinette [patinɛt] *f* scooter

pati•neur [patinœr] **-neuse** [nøz] *mf* ice skater

patinoire [patinwar] *f* skating rink

patio [patjo], [pasjo] *m* patio

pâtir [pɑtir] *intr*—**pâtir de** to suffer from

pâtisserie [pɑtisri] *f* pastry; pastry shop; pastry making

pâtis•sier [pɑtisje] **-sière** [sjɛr] *mf* pastry cook; proprietor of a pastry shop

patoche [patɔʃ] *f* (coll) hand, paw

patois [patwa] *m* patois; jargon, lingo

patouiller [patuje] *tr* (coll) to paw, maul || *intr* (coll) to splash

patraque [patrak] *adj* in bad shape ‖ *f* (coll) turnip (*old watch*)
pâtre [pɑtr] *m* herdsman
patriarche [patrijar*ʃ*] *m* patriarch
patrice [patris] *m* patrician; **Patrice** Patrick
patri•cien [patrisjɛ̃] **-cienne** [sjɛn] *adj & mf* patrician
patrie [patri] *f* native land, fatherland
patrimoine [patrimwan] *m* patrimony
patrio•tard [patrijɔtar] **-tarde** [tard] *adj* flag-waving, chauvinistic
patriote [patrijɔt] *adj* patriotic ‖ *mf* patriot
patriotique [patrijɔtik] *adj* patriotic
patriotisme [patrijɔtism] *m* patriotism
pa•tron [patrɔ̃] **-tronne** [trɔn] *mf* patron saint; proprietor; boss; sponsor ‖ *m* pattern, model, template; captain, skipper; coxswain; master, lord; medium size; **grand patron** large size; **patron à jours** stencil; **patron de thèse** thesis sponsor ‖ *f* mistress of the house; (slang) better half
patronage [patrɔnaʒ] *m* patronage, protection; sponsorship; (eccl) social center
patronat [patrɔna] *m* management
patronner [patrɔne] *tr* to patronize, protect; sponsor; stencil
patrouille [patruj] *f* patrol
patrouiller [patruje] *intr* to patrol
patte [pat] *f* paw; foot (*of bird*); leg (*of insect*); flap, tab; hook; (coll) hand, foot, or leg (*of person*); **à pattes d'éléphant** bell-bottom (*trousers*); **à quatre pattes** on all fours; **faire patte de velours** (coll) to pull in one's claws; **graisser la patte à** (coll) to grease the palm of; **patte d'épaule** shoulder strap; **pattes de mouche** (coll) scrawl
patte-d'oie [patdwa] *f* (*pl* **pattes-d'oie**) crow's-foot; crossroads; (bot) goosefoot
pattemouille [patmuj] *f* damp cloth
pâturage [pɑtyraʒ] *m* pasture; pasturage; pasture rights
pâture [pɑtyr] *f* fodder; pasture; (fig) food
paume [pom] *f* palm; (archaic) tennis
pau•mé -mée [pome] *adj* (coll) lost
paupière [popjɛr] *f* eyelid
pause [poz] *f* pause; (mus) full rest; **pause café** coffee break
pauvre [povr] *adj* poor; **pauvre de moi!** woe is me!; **pauvre d'esprit** (coll) dimwitted ‖ (when standing before noun) *adj* poor, wretched; late (*deceased*) ‖ *mf* pauper; **les pauvres** the poor
pauvreté [povrəte] *f* poverty
P.A.V. [peave] *adj* (letterword) (**payable avec préavis**) person-to-person (*telephone call*)
pavaner [pavane] *ref* to strut
pavé [pave] *m* pavement, street; paving stone; paving block; (culin) slab; **sur le pavé** pounding the streets, out of work
pavement [pavmɑ̃] *m* paving (*act*); mosaic or marble flooring
paver [pave] *tr* to pave
pavillon [pavijɔ̃] *m* pavilion; tent, canopy; lodge, one-story house; wing, pavilion; hospital ward; flag; bell (*of trumpet*); **amener son pavillon** to strike one's colors; **baisser pavillon** to knuckle under; **pavillon de chasse** hunting lodge; **pavillon des sports** field house; **pavillon noir** Jolly Roger
pavois [pavwa] *m* shield; **élever sur le pavois** to extol
pavoiser [pavwaze] *tr* to deck out with bunting, decorate
pavot [pavo] *m* poppy
payable [pɛjabl] *adj* payable
payant [pɛjɑ̃] **payante** [pɛjɑ̃t] *adj* paying
paye [pɛj] *f* pay, wages
payement [pɛjmɑ̃] *m* payment
payer [peje] §49 *tr* to pay; pay for; **payer comptant** to pay cash for; **payer de retour** to pay back; **payer q.ch. à qn** to pay s.o. for s.th.; pay for s.th. for s.o.; **payer qn de q.ch.** to pay s.o. for s.th.; **payer rubis sur l'ongle** to pay down on the nail ‖ *intr* to pay; **payer et prends** cash and carry ‖ *ref* to treat oneself to; take what is due; **pouvoir se payer** to be able to afford; **se payer de** to be satisfied with
pays [pei] *m* country; region; town; (coll) fellow countryman; **du pays** local; **le pays de** the land of; **pays de cocagne** land of milk and honey; **pays non-alignés** nonaligned nations
paysage [peizaʒ] *m* landscape, scenery; (painting) landscape; **paysage lunaire** moonscape
paysagiste [peizaʒist] *m* landscape painter
pay•san [peizɑ̃] **-sane** [zan] *adj & mf* peasant
Pays-Bas [peiba], [pɛiba], *mpl*—**les Pays-Bas** The Netherlands
payse [peiz] *f* countrywoman
PC (ordinateur personnel) PC (personal computer)
P.C. [pese] *m* (letterword) (**parti communiste**) Communist party; (**poste de commandement**) command post
P.c.c. *abbr* (**pour copie conforme**) certified copy
p.c.v. *or* **P.C.V.** [peseve] *m* (letterword) (**payable chez vous**) *or* (**à percevoir**)—**téléphoner en p.c.v.** to telephone collect
péage [peaʒ] *m* toll
peau [po] *f* (*pl* **peaux**) skin; pelt; hide; film (*on milk*); (slang) bag, whore; **entrer dans la peau d'un personnage** (theat) to get right inside a part; **faire peau neuve** to turn over a new leaf; **la peau!** (slang) nothing doing!; **peau d'âne** (coll) sheepskin; **peau de tambour** drumhead; **vendre la peau de l'ours avant de l'avoir tué** to count one's chickens before they are hatched
peau-rouge [poruʒ] *mf* (*pl* **peaux-rouges**) redskin
pêche [pɛ*ʃ*] *f* peach; fishing; **pêche à la mouche noyée** fly casting; **pêche au coup** fishing with hook, line, and pole; **pêche au lancer** casting; **pêche sous-marine** deep-sea fishing; **pêche sportive** fishing with a fly rod or casting rod
péché [pe*ʃ*e] *m* sin

pécher [pe∫e] §10 *intr* to sin

pêcher [pe∫e] *m* peach tree ‖ *tr* to fish, fish for; (coll) to get ‖ *intr* to fish; **pêcher à la mouche** to fly-fish

pêcherie [pɛ∫ri] *f* fishery

pé•cheur [pe∫œr] **-cheresse** [∫rɛs] *mf* sinner

pê•cheur [pɛ∫œr] **-cheuse** [∫øz] *mf* fisher; **pêcheur de perles** pearl diver ‖ *m* fisherman

pécore [pekɔr] *f* (coll) silly goose

pecque [pɛk] *f* (coll) silly affected woman

péculat [pekyla] *m* embezzlement

pécule [pekyl] *m* nest egg

pédagogie [pedagɔʒi] *f* pedagogy, education

pédagogue [pedagɔg] *adj* pedagogical ‖ *mf* pedagogue; teacher

pédale [pedal] *f* pedal; treadle; (slang) pederast; **de la pédale** (pej) gay, homosexual; **pédale d'embrayage** (aut) clutch pedal

pédaler [pedale] *intr* to pedal; **pédaler dans la choucroute** (slang) to be mixed up

pédalier [pedalje] *m* pedal keyboard; pedal and sprocket-wheel assembly

pédalo [pedalo] *m* water bicycle

pé•dant [pedɑ̃] **-dante** [dɑ̃t] *adj* pedantic ‖ *mf* pedant

pédanterie [pedɑ̃tri] *f* pedantry

pédantesque [pedɑ̃tɛsk] *adj* pedantic

pédé [pede] *m* (pej) queer (*homosexual*)

pédéraste [pederast] *m* pederast

pédestre [pedɛstr] *adj* on foot

pédiatrie [pedjatri] *f* pediatrics

pédicure [pedikyr] *mf* chiropodist, podiatrist

pedigree [pedigri] *m* pedigree

Pégase [pegɑz] *m* Pegasus

pègre [pɛgr] *f* underworld

peigne [pɛɲ] *m* comb; card (*for wool*); reed (*of loom*); (zool) scallop

peigner [peɲe] *tr* to comb; to card ‖ *ref* to comb one's hair

peignez [peɲe] *v* (**peignons**) see **peindre**; see **peigner**

peignoir [pɛɲwar] *m* bathrobe; dressing gown, peignoir

peindre [pɛ̃dr] §50 *tr & intr* to paint

peine [pɛn] *f* pain; trouble; difficulty; penalty; **à peine** hardly, scarcely; **en être pour sa peine** to have nothing to show for one's trouble; **faire (de la) peine à** to grieve; **faire peine à voir** to be pathetic; **peine capitale** capital punishment; **peine de cœur** heartache; **peine de mort** death penalty; **peine pécuniaire** financial distress; **purger sa peine** to serve one's sentence; **valoir la peine** to be worth while; **veuillez vous donner la peine de** please be so kind as to

peiner [pene] *tr* to pain, grieve; fatigue ‖ *intr* to labor

peint [pɛ̃] **peinte** [pɛ̃t] *v* see **peindre**

peintre [pɛ̃tr] *m* painter

peinture [pɛ̃tyr] *f* paint; painting; **attention à la peinture** (*public sign*) wet paint; **je ne peux pas le voir en peinture** (coll) I can't stand him

peinturer [pɛ̃tyre] *tr* to lay a coat of paint on; to daub

peinturlurer [pɛ̃tyrlyre] *tr* (coll) to paint in all the colors of the rainbow

péjora•tif [peʒɔratif] **-tive** [tiv] *adj & m* pejorative

pékin [pekɛ̃] *m* pekin; **en pékin** (slang) in civies; **Pékin** Peking

péki•nois [pekinwa] **-noise** [nwaz] *adj* Pekingese ‖ *m* Pekingese (*language; dog*) ‖ (*cap*) *mf* Pekingese (*inhabitant*)

pelage [pəlaʒ] *m* coat (*of animal*)

pe•lé -lée [pəle] *adj* bald; bare

pêle-mêle [pɛlmɛl] *m invar* jumble ‖ *adv* pell-mell

peler [pəle] §2 *tr, intr, & ref* to peel, peel off

pèle•rin [pɛlrɛ̃] **-rine** [rin] *mf* pilgrim ‖ *m* peregrine falcon; basking shark ‖ *f* see **pèlerine**

pèlerinage [pɛlrinaʒ] *m* pilgrimage

pèlerine [pɛlrin] *f* pelerine, cape; hooded cape

péliade [peljad] *f* adder

pélican [pelikɑ̃] *m* pelican

pellagre [pelagr] *f* pellagra

pelle [pɛl] *f* shovel; scoop; **pelle à poussière** dustpan; **pelle à vapeur** steam shovel; **pelle mécanique** power shovel; **ramasser à la pelle** to shovel, to shovel up

pelletée [pɛlte] *f* shovelful

pelleter [pɛlte] §34 *tr* to shovel

pelleterie [pɛltri] *f* fur trade; skin, pelt

pelleteuse [pɛltøz] *f* power shovel

pellicule [pelikyl] *f* film; pellicle; speck of dandruff; (biol) film; **pellicules** dandruff

pelote [plɔt] *f* ball (*of string, of snow, etc.*); **faire sa pelote** (coll) to make one's pile; **pelote basque** pelota; **pelote d'épingles** pincushion

peloter [plɔte] *tr* to wind into a ball; (fig) to flatter; (slang) to feel up, to paw ‖ *intr* to bat the ball back and forth

pelo•teur [plɔtœr] **-teuse** [tøz] *adj* flattering, ingratiating; (coll) fresh, amorous, spoony ‖ *mf* (coll) masher, spooner

peloton [plɔtɔ̃] *m* little ball (*e.g., of wool*); group (*of racers*); (mil) platoon, troop, detachment; **peloton d'exécution** firing squad

pelotonner [plɔtɔne] *tr* to wind into a ball ‖ *ref* to curl up, snuggle

pelouse [pluz] *f* lawn; (golf) green

peluche [ply∫] *f* plush; lint

pelure [plyr] *f* peel, peeling, skin; rind; (coll) coat

pénaliser [penalize] *tr* to penalize

pénalité [penalite] *f* penalty

pe•naud -naude [pəno] [nod] *adj* bashful, shy; shamefaced; crestfallen

penchant [pɑ̃∫ɑ̃] *m* penchant, bent

pen•ché -chée [pɑ̃∫e] *adj* leaning; stooping; bent over

pencher [pɑ̃∫e] §96 *tr, intr, & ref* to lean, bend, incline; **se pencher sur** to make a close study of

pendable [pɑ̃dabl] *adj* outrageous; (archaic) hangable

pendaison [pãdɛzɔ̃] *f* hanging
pen·dant [pãdã] **-dante** [dãt] *adj* hanging; pending ‖ *m* pendant; counterpart; **pendant d'oreille** eardrop; **se faire pendant** to make a pair ‖ **pendant** *adv*—**pendant que** while ‖ **pendant** *prep* during
pendeloque [pãdlɔk] *f* pendant; jewel (*of eardrop*)
pendentif [pãdãtif] *m* pendant; eardrop; lavaliere
penderie [pãdri] *f* clothes closet
pendoir [pãdwar] *m* meat hook
pendre [pãdr] *tr* to hang; hang up; **être pendu à** to hang on (*e.g., the telephone*) ‖ *intr* to hang; hang down; sag; **ça lui pend au nez** he's got it coming to him ‖ *ref* to hang oneself; **se pendre à** to hang on to
pen·du -due [pãdy] *adj* hanging; hanged ‖ *mf* hanged person
pendule [pãdyl] *m* pendulum ‖ *f* clock; **pendule à pile** battery clock
pêne [pɛn] *m* bolt; latch
pénétration [penetrasjɔ̃] *f* penetration; permeation
pénétrer [penetre] §10 *tr* to penetrate, permeate ‖ *intr* to penetrate; enter ‖ *ref* to mix; **se pénétrer de** to become imbued with
pénible [penibl] *adj* hard, painful
péniche [peniʃ] *f* barge; houseboat; **péniche de débarquement** landing craft
pénicilline [penisilin] *f* penicillin
pé·nien [penjɛ̃] **-nienne** [njɛn] penile, penis
péninsulaire [penɛ̃sylɛr] *adj* peninsular
péninsule [penɛ̃syl] *f* large peninsula
pénis [penis] *m* penis
pénitence [penitãs] *f* penitence; penalty (*in games*); punishment; **en pénitence** in disgrace; **faire pénitence** to do penance
pénitencier [penitãsje] *m* penitentiary; penal colony
péni·tent -tente [penitã] **-tente** [tãt] *adj & mf* penitent
penne [pɛn] *f* quill, feather
Pennsylvanie [pɛnsilvani] *f* Pennsylvania; **la Pennsylvanie** Pennsylvania
pénombre [penɔ̃br] *f* penumbra; half-light; **dans la pénombre** out of the limelight
pense-bête [pãsbɛt] *m* (*pl* **-bêtes**) (coll) reminder
pensée [pãse] *f* thought; thinking; (bot) pansy
penser [pãse] §95 *tr* to think; **penser de** to think of (*to have as an opinion of*); **penser + inf** to intend to + *inf* ‖ *intr* to think; **penser à** to think of (*to direct one's thoughts toward*); **y penser** to think of it, e.g., **pendant que j'y pense** while I think of it
penseur [pãsœr] *m* thinker
pen·sif [pãsif] **-sive** [siv] *adj* pensive; absentminded
pension [pãsjɔ̃] *f* pension (*annuity; room and board; boardinghouse*); **avec pension complète** with three meals; **pension alimentaire** alimony; **pension de famille** residential hotel; **pension de retraite, pension viagère** an-

nuity, retirement pension; **prendre pension** to board; **sans pension** without meals
pensionnaire [pãsjɔnɛr] *mf* boarder; guest (*in hotel*); resident student ‖ *f* naïve woman or girl
pensionnat [pãsjɔna] *m* boarding school
pension·né -née [pãsjɔne] *adj* pensioned ‖ *mf* pensioner
pensionner [pãsjɔne] *tr* to pension
pensum [pɛ̃sɔm] *m* thankless task
Pentagone, le [pɛtagɔn] *m* the Pentagon
pente [pãt] *f* slope; inclination, bent; fall (*of the river*); **en pente** sloping; **pente savonneuse** (fig) slippery slope
Pentecôte [pãtkot] *f*—**la Pentecôte** Pentecost, Whitsunday
pénultième [penyltjɛm] *adj* next to the last ‖ *f* penult
pénurie [penyri] *f* lack, shortage
pépé [pepe] *m* (*children's language*) pop-pop, grandpop, grandpa
pépée [pepe] *f* doll; (slang) doll
pépère [pepɛr] *adj* (coll) easygoing ‖ *m* grandpa; (coll) old duffer; (coll) overgrown boy
pépètes [pepɛt] *fpl* (slang) dough
pépie [pepi] *f* (vet) pip; **avoir le pépie** (coll) to be thirsty
pépiement [pepimã] *m* chirp
pépier [pepje] *intr* to chirp
pépin [pepɛ̃] *m* pip, seed; (coll) umbrella; **avoir un pépin** (coll) to strike a snag
pépinière [pepinjɛr] *f* (hort) nursery; (fig) training school; (fig) hotbed
pépiniériste [pepinjerist] *m* nurseryman
pépite [pepit] *f* nugget
péque·naud [pɛkno] **-naude** [nod] *adj & mf* (slang) peasant
péquenot [pɛkno] *m* (slang) peasant
perçage [pɛrsaʒ] *m* drilling, boring
per·çant [pɛrsã] **-çante** [sãt] *adj* piercing, penetrating
perce [pɛrs] *f* drill, bore; **en perce** on tap
percée [pɛrse] *f* opening, gap; clearing; breakthrough; discovery
perce-neige [pɛrsənɛʒ] *m invar* (bot) snowdrop
percepteur [pɛrsɛptœr] *m* tax collector
perceptible [pɛrsɛptibl] *adj* perceptible; collectable, payable
perception [pɛrsɛpsjɔ̃] *f* perception; tax collection; tax; tax department, bureau of internal revenue
percer [pɛrse] §51 *tr* to pierce; drill; tap (*a barrel*); break through ‖ *intr* to come through or out; burst (*said, e.g., of abscess*); to make a name for oneself
perceuse [pɛrsøz] *f* drill; machine drill
percevoir [pɛrsəvwar] §59 *tr* to perceive; collect
perche [pɛrʃ] *f* pole; (ichth) perch; (sports) pole vaulting; (coll) beanpole; **perche à sauter** vaulting pole; **perche à son** microphone stand; **tendre la perche à** to lend a helping hand to

percher [pɛrʃe] *tr* to perch ‖ *intr* to perch, roost
perchoir [pɛrʃwar] *m* perch
per•clus [pɛrkly] **-cluse** [klyz] *adj* crippled, paralyzed
percolateur [pɛrkɔlatœr] *m* large coffee maker
percuter [pɛrkyte] *tr* to strike; crash into; percuss ‖ *intr* to crash
percuteur [pɛrkytœr] *m* firing pin
per•dant [pɛrdɑ̃] **-dante** [dɑ̃t] *adj* losing ‖ *mf* loser
perdition [pɛrdisjɔ̃] *f* perdition; **en perdition** (naut) in distress
perdre [pɛrdrə] §96 *tr* to lose; ruin ‖ *intr* to lose; leak; deteriorate ‖ *ref* to get lost; disappear
per•dreau [pɛrdro] *m* (*pl* **-dreaux**) young partridge
perdrix [pɛrdri] *f* partridge
per•du -due [pɛrdy] *adj* lost; spare (*time*); stray (*bullet*); remote (*locality*); advance (*sentry*)
père [pɛr] *m* father; senior, e.g., **M. Martin père** Mr. Martin, senior; **père adoptif** (*selon l'adoption plénière*) adoptive father; **père de famille** head of the household; **père de placement** adoptive father; **père spirituel** father confessor
péremptoire [perɑ̃ptwar] *adj* peremptory
péréquation [perekwɑsjɔ̃] *f* equalizing
perfection [pɛrfɛksjɔ̃] *f* perfection
perfectionner [pɛrfɛksjɔne] *tr* to perfect ‖ *ref* to improve
perfide [pɛrfid] *adj* perfidious ‖ *mf* treacherous person
perfidie [pɛrfidi] *f* perfidy
perforation [pɛrfɔrɑsjɔ̃] *f* perforation; puncture
perforatrice [pɛrfɔratris] *f* pneumatic drill; perforator; keypunch (machine)
perforer [pɛrfɔre] *tr* to perforate; drill, bore; punch (*a card*)
performance [pɛrfɔrmɑ̃s] *f* (sports) performance
pergélisol [pɛrʒelisɔl] *m* permafrost
péricliter [periklite] *intr* to fail
péril [peril] *m* peril
péril•leux -leuse [perijø] [jøz] *adj* perilous
péri•mé -mée [perime] *adj* expired, elapsed; out-of-date
périmer [perime] *intr* & *ref* to lapse
période [perjɔd] *f* period; (phys) cycle; (phys) half-life
périodique [perjɔdik] *adj* periodic(al)
péripétie [peripesi] *f* vicissitude
périphérie [periferi] *f* periphery; suburbs
périphérique [periferik] *adj* peripheral; suburban
périple [peripl] *m* journey
périr [perir] *intr* to perish
périscope [periskɔp] *m* periscope
périssable [perisabl] *adj* perishable
perle [pɛrl] *f* pearl; bead
perler [pɛrle] *tr* to pearl; do to perfection ‖ *intr* to form beads
permanence [pɛrmanɑ̃s] *f* permanence; headquarters, station; **en permanence** at all hours

perma•nent [pɛrmanɑ̃] **-nente** [nɑ̃t] *adj* permanent; standing; continuous, nonstop ‖ *f* permanent
perme [pɛrm] *f* (coll) furlough
permettre [pɛrmɛtr] §42, §97, §98 *tr* to permit; **permettre q.ch. à qn** to allow s.o. s.th. ‖ *intr*—**permettez!** excuse me!; **permettre à qn de** + *inf* to permit s.o. to or let s.o. + *infr;* **vous permettez?** may I? ‖ *ref*—**se permettre de** to take the liberty of
permis [pɛrmi] *m* permit, license; **permis de chasse** hunting permit; **permis de conduire** driver's license; **permis de construire** construction permit; **permis de port d'armes** gun permit
permission [pɛrmisjɔ̃] *f* permission; (mil) furlough, leave
permissionnaire [pɛrmisjɔnɛr] *m* soldier on leave
permutation [pɛrmytɑsjɔ̃] *f* permutation; exchange of posts; transposition
permuter [pɛrmyte] *tr* to permute; exchange ‖ *intr* to change places
perni•cieux [pɛrnisjø] **-cieuse** [sjøz] *adj* pernicious
péroné [perɔne] *m* (anat) fibula
pérorer [perɔre] *intr* to hold forth
Pérou [peru] *m*—**le Pérou** Peru
peroxyde [perɔksid] *m* peroxide
perpendiculaire [pɛrpɑ̃dikylɛr] *adj* & *f* perpendicular
perpète [pɛrpɛt]—**à perpète** (slang) forever
perpétrer [pɛrpetre] §10 *tr* to perpetrate
perpé•tuel -tuelle [pɛrpetɥɛl] *adj* perpetual; life (*imprisonment*); constant, continual
perpétuer [pɛrpetɥe] *tr* to perpetuate ‖ *ref* to be perpetuated
perpétuité [pɛrpetɥite] *f* perpetuity; **à perpétuité** forever; for life
perplexe [pɛrplɛks] *adj* perplexed; **rendre perplexe** to perplex
perplexité [pɛrplɛksite] *f* perplexity
perquisition [pɛrkizisjɔ̃] *f* search
perquisitionner [pɛrkizisjɔne] *intr* to make a search
perron [pɛrɔ̃] *m* front-entrance stone steps
perroquet [pɛrɔkɛ] *m* parrot
perruche [peryʃ] *f* parakeet; hen parrot
perruque [peryk] *f* wig; **vieille perruque** (coll) old fogey
per•san [pɛrsɑ̃] **-sane** [san] *adj* Persian ‖ *m* Persian (*language*) ‖ (*cap*) *mf* Persian (*person*)
perse [pɛrs] *adj* Persian ‖ (*cap*) *mf* Persian ‖ (*cap*) *f* Persia; **la Perse** Persia
persécuter [pɛrsekyte] *tr* to persecute
persécution [pɛrsekysjɔ̃] *f* persecution
persévérer [pɛrsevere] §10, §96 *intr* to persevere
persienne [pɛrsjɛn] *f* Persian blind, slatted shutter
persil [pɛrsi] *m* parsley
persis•tant [pɛrsistɑ̃] **-tante** [tɑ̃t] *adj* persistent

persister [pɛrsiste] §96 *intr* to persist; **persister à** to persist in

personnage [pɛrsɔnaʒ] *m* personage; (theat) character

personnalité [pɛrsɔnalite] *f* personality

personne [pɛrsɔn] *f* person; self; appearance; lady, e.g., **belle personne** beautiful lady; e.g., **jolie personne** pretty lady; **grande personne** grown-up; **par personne** per person; **payer de sa personne** to not spare one's efforts; **personne remarquable** standout; **s'assurer de la personne de** to arrest; **une tierce personne** a third party ‖ *pron indef* no one, nobody; **personne ne** or **ne . . . personne** §90B no one, nobody, not anyone

person·nel -nelle [pɛrsɔnɛl] *adj* personal ‖ *m* personnel; **personnel navigant** (aer) flying personnel; **personnel de route** (rr) train crew

personnifier [pɛrsɔnifje] *tr* to personify

perspective [pɛrspɛktiv] *f* perspective; outlook; **en perspective** in view

perspicace [pɛrspikas] *adj* perspicacious

persuader [pɛrsɥade] §97, §99 *tr* to persuade; **persuader q.ch. à qn** or **persuader qn de q.ch** to persuade s.o. of s.th. ‖ §98 *intr*—**persuader à qn de** to persuade s.o. to ‖ *ref* to be convinced

persuasion [pɛrsɥazjɔ̃] *f* persuasion

perte [pɛrt] *f* loss; ruin, downfall; **à perte de vue** as far as the eye can see; **perte de réclamation** tax loss; **en pure perte** uselessly; **pertes parmi la population civile** (mil) collateral damage

perti·nent [pɛrtinɑ̃] **-nente** [nɑ̃t] *adj* pertinent

perturba·teur [pɛrtyrbatœr] **-trice** [tris] *adj* disturbing ‖ *mf* troublemaker

perturbation [pɛrtyrbasjɔ̃] *f* disruption; perturbation; **perturbation atmosphérique** atmospheric disturbance

perturber [pɛrtyrbe] *tr* to perturb; disturb

péru·vien [peryvjɛ̃] **-vienne** [vjɛn] *adj* Peruvian ‖ (*cap*) *mf* Peruvian

pervenche [pɛrvɑ̃ʃ] *f* periwinkle

per·vers [pɛrvɛr] **-verse** [vɛrs] *adj* perverted ‖ *mf* pervert

perversion [pɛrvɛrsjɔ̃] *f* perversion

perversité [pɛrvɛrsite] *f* perversity, depravity

pervertir [pɛrvɛrtir] *tr* to pervert

pesage [pəzaʒ] *m* weigh-in; paddock

pesamment [pəzamɑ̃] *adv* heavily

pe·sant [pəzɑ̃] **-sante** [zɑ̃t] *adj* heavy ‖ *m*—**valoir son pesant d'or** to be worth one's weight in gold

pesanteur [pəzɑ̃tœr] *f* heaviness; weight; (phys) gravity

pèse-bébé [pezbebe] *m* (*pl* **-bébés**) baby scale

pesée [pəze] *f* weighing; leverage

pèse-lettre [pezlɛtr] *m* (*pl* **-lettres**) letter scale

pèse-personne [pezpɛrsɔn] *m* (*pl* **personnes**) bathroom scale

peser [pəze] §2 *tr* to weigh ‖ *intr* to weigh; **peser à** to hang heavy on; **peser sur** to bear down

on; lie down on; lie heavy on; stress ‖ *ref* to weigh oneself; weigh in

peson [pəzɔ̃] *m* spring scale

pessimisme [pesimism] *m* pessimism

pessimiste [pesimist] *adj* pessimistic ‖ *mf* pessimist

peste [pɛst] *f* plague; pest, nuisance ‖ *interj* gosh!

pester [pɛste] *intr* to grouse; **pester contre** to rail at

pestifé·ré -rée [pɛstifere] *adj* plague-ridden ‖ *mf* victim of the plague

pestilence [pɛstilɑ̃s] *f* pestilence

pet [pɛ] *m* recyclable plastic; (coll) hard blow; (coll) dent; (coll) wind (*intestinal gas*); **ça ne vaut pas un pet (de lapin)** (coll) it's not worth a wooden nickel ‖ *interj* (coll) look out!

pétale [petal] *m* petal

pétanque [petɑ̃k] *f* petanque

pétarade [petarad] *f* series of explosions; backfire; (vulg) making wind

pétard [petar] *m* firecracker; blast; (slang) gat, revolver; (slang) backside; **faire du pétard** (coll) to kick up a fuss; **lancer un pétard** (coll) to drop a bombshell

pet-de-loup [pɛdlu] *m* (*pl* **pets-de-loup**) absent-minded professor

pet-de-nonne [pɛdnɔn] *m* (*pl* **pets-de-nonne**) fritter

pet-en-l'air [pɛtɑ̃lɛr] *m invar* short jacket

péter [pete] §10 *tr*—**péter du feu** (coll) to be a live wire ‖ *intr* (coll) to go bang; (vulg) to break wind, fart

pètesec [pɛtsɛk] *adj invar* (coll) bossy, despotic ‖ *m invar* (coll) martinet, bossy fellow

pétil·lant [petijɑ̃] **-lante** [jɑ̃t] *adj* crackling; sparkling

pétiller [petije] *intr* to crackle; to sparkle

pe·tiot [pətjo] **-tiote** [tjɔt] *adj* (coll) tiny, wee ‖ *mf* (coll) tot

pe·tit [pəti] **-tite** [tit] (precedes the noun it modifies) §91 *adj* small, little; short; minor, lower; **en petit** shortened; miniature; **petit à petit** little by little, bit by bit ‖ *mf* youngster; young (*of an animal*); poor little thing ‖ *m* little boy ‖ *f* little girl

petit-beurre [pətibœr] *m* (*pl* **petits-beurre**) cookie

petit-cou·sin [pətikuzɛ̃] **-sine** [zin] *mf* (*pl* **petits-cousins**) second cousin

petite-fille [pətitfij] *f* (*pl* **petites-filles**) granddaughter

petite-nièce [pətitnjɛs] *f* (*pl* **petites-nièces**) great-niece

petitesse [pətitɛs] *f* smallness

petit-fils [pətifis] *m* (*pl* **petits-fils**) grandson; grandchild

petit-gris [pətigri] *m* (*pl* **petits-gris**) miniver; snail

pétition [petisjɔ̃] *f* petition; **faire une pétition de principe** to beg the question

petit-lait [pətilɛ] *m* (*pl* **petits-laits**) whey

petit-neveu [pətinvø] *m* (*pl* **petits-neveux**) great-nephew

petits-enfants [pətizãfã] *mpl* grandchildren

petit-suisse [pətisɥis] *m* (*pl* **petits-suisses**) cream cheese

peton [pətɔ̃] *m* (coll) tiny foot

pétoncle [petɔ̃kl] *m* scallop

Pétrarque [petrark] *m* Petrarch

pétrifier [petrifje] *tr & ref* to petrify

pétrin [petrɛ̃] *m* kneading trough; (coll) mess, jam

pétrir [petrir] *tr* to knead; mold

pétrochimique [petroʃimik] *adj* petrochemical

pétrole [petrɔl] *m* petroleum; **à pétrole** kerosene (*lamp*); **pétrole brut** crude oil; **pétrole lampant** kerosene

pétro•lier [petrolje] **-lière** [ljɛr] *adj* oil ‖ *m* tanker; oil baron

P et T [peete] *fpl* (letterword) (**Postes et télécommunications**) post office, telephone, and telegraph

pétu•lant [petylã] **-lante** [lãt] *adj* lively, frisky

peu [pø] *m* bit, little; **peu de** few; not much; not many; **peu de chose** not much ‖ *adv* §91 little; not very; **à peu près** about, practically; **depuis peu** of late; **peu ou prou** more or less; **peu probable** improbable; **peu s'en faut** very nearly; **pour peu que, si peu que** however little; **quelque peu** somewhat; **sous peu** before long; **tant soit peu** ever so little

peuplade [pœplad] *f* tribe

peuple [pœpl] *adj* plebeian, common ‖ *m* people

peuplement [pœpləmã] *m* populating; planting; stocking (*e.g., with fish*)

peupler [pœple] *tr* to people; plant; stock ‖ *intr* to multiply, breed

peuplier [pøplje] *m* poplar

peur [pœr] *f* fear; **avoir peur (de)** to be afraid (of); **de peur que** lest, for fear that; **une peur bleue** (coll) an awful fright

peu•reux [pœrø] **-reuse** [røz] *adj* fearful, timid

peux [pø] (*v* **peut, peuvent**) see **pouvoir**

peut-être [pøtɛtr] *adv* perhaps; **peut-être que non** perhaps not

p. ex. *abbr* (**par exemple**) e.g.

phalange [falãʒ] *f* phalanx

phalène [falɛn] *m & f* moth

phallique [falik] *adj* phallic

phallocrate [falɔkrat] *adj & m* (male) chauvinist

phallus [falys] *m* phallus, penis

Pharaon [faraɔ̃] *m* Pharaoh

phare [far] *m* lighthouse; beacon; (aut) headlight; **phare antibrouillard** foglight; **phares code** dimmers

phari•sien [farizjɛ̃] **-sienne** [zjɛn] *adj* pharisaic ‖ *mf* pharisee

pharmaceutique [farmasøtik] *adj* pharmaceutical ‖ *f* pharmaceutics

pharmacie [farmasi] *f* drugstore, pharmacy; medicine chest; drugs

pharma•cien [farmasjɛ̃] **-cienne** [sjɛn] *mf* pharmacist

pharynx [farɛ̃ks] *m* pharynx

phase [faz] *f* phase

Phébé [febe] *f* Phoebe

Phénicie [fenisi] *f* Phoenicia; **la Phénicie** Phoenicia

phéni•cien [fenisjɛ̃] **-cienne** [sjɛn] *adj* Phoenician ‖ (*cap*) *mf* Phoenician

phénix [feniks] *m* phoenix

phénomé•nal **-nale** [fenɔmenal] *adj* (*pl* **-naux** [no]) phenomenal

phénomène [fenɔmɛn] *m* phenomenon; (coll) monster, freak

philanthrope [filãtrɔp] *mf* philanthropist

philanthropie [filãtrɔpi] *f* philanthropy

philatélie [filateli] *f* philately

philatéliste [filatelist] *mf* philatelist

philip•pin [filipɛ̃] **-pine** [pin] *adj* Philippine ‖ (*cap*) *mf* Filipino

Philippines [filipin] *fpl* Philippines

philistin [filistɛ̃] *adj masc & m* Philistine

philologie [filɔlɔʒi] *f* philology

philologue [filɔlɔg] *mf* philologist

philosophe [filozof] *adj* philosophic ‖ *mf* philosopher

philosophie [filozofi] *f* philosophy

philosophique [filozofik] *adj* philosophic(al)

philtre [filtr] *m* philter

phlébite [flebit] *f* phlebitis

phobie [fɔbi] *f* phobia

phonème [fonɛm] *m* phoneme

phonétique [fonetik] *adj* phonetic ‖ *f* phonetics

phoniatrie [fɔnjatri] *f* speech therapy

phono [fɔno] *m* (coll) phonograph

phonographe [fɔnɔgraf] *m* phonograph

phonologie [fɔnɔlɔʒi] *f* phonology

phonothèque [fɔnɔtɛk] *f* record library

phoque [fɔk] *m* seal; **phoque commun** seadog

phosphate [fɔsfat] *m* phosphate

phosphore [fɔsfɔr] *m* phosphorus

phosphores•cent [fɔsfɔresã] **-cente** [sãt] *adj* phosphorescent

photo [fɔto] *f* photo, snapshot

photocopier [fɔtɔkɔpje] *tr* to photocopy, to photostat; to Xerox (trademark)

photocopieur [fɔtɔkɔpjœr] *m* photocopier

photogénique [fɔtɔʒenik] *adj* photogenic

photographe [fɔtɔgraf] *mf* photographer

photographie [fɔtɔgrafi] *f* photography; photograph; **photographie aérienne** aerial photograph

photographier [fɔtɔgrafje] *tr* to photograph

photogravure [fɔtɔgravyr] *f* photoengraving

photostat [fɔtɔsta] *m* photostat

photothèque [fɔtɔtɛk] *f* photograph library

phrase [fraz] *f* sentence; (mus) phrase; **phrase de choc** punch line

phrénologie [frenɔlɔʒi] *f* phrenology

physi•cien [fizisjɛ̃] **-cienne** [sjɛn] *mf* physicist

physiologie [fizjɔlɔʒi] *f* physiology

physiologique [fizjɔlɔʒik] *adj* physiological

physionomie [fizjɔnɔmi] *f* physiognomy

physique [fizik] *adj* physical; material ‖ *m* physique; appearance ‖ *f* physics; **physique de la**

particule particle physics; **physique de l'état solide** solid-state physics; **physique nucléaire** nuclear physics

piaffer [pjafe] *intr* to paw the ground; fidget, fume

piailler [pjɑje] *intr* (coll) to cheep; (coll) to squeal

pianiste [pjanist] *mf* pianist

piano [pjano] *m* piano; **piano à queue** grand piano; **piano droit** upright piano ‖ *adv* (coll) quietly

pianoter [pjanɔte] *intr* to strum; to drum, to thrum; to rattle away

piastre [pjastr] *f* (Canad) dollar

piaule [pjol] *f* (slang) pad (*one's home*)

piauler [pjole] *intr* to peep; screech (*said of pulley*); (coll) to whine

pic [pik] *m* peak; (*tool*) pick; (orn) woodpecker; **à pic** sheer, steep; (coll) in the nick of time; **couler à pic** to sink like a stone

picaillons [pikajɔ̃] *mpl* (slang) dough

picaresque [pikarɛsk] *adj* picaresque

piccolo [pikɔlo] *m* piccolo

pichet [pi∫ɛ] *m* pitcher, jug

pick-up [pikœp] *m invar* pickup; record player; pickup truck

picoler [pikɔle] *intr* (slang) to get pickled

picorer [pikɔre] *tr & intr* to peck

picoter [pikɔte] *tr* to prick; peck at; sting

picotin [pikɔtɛ̃] *m* peck (*measure*)

pictu•ral -rale [piktyral] *adj* (*pl* **-raux** [ro]) pictorial

pidgin [pidʒin] *m* (ling) pidgin

pie [pi] *adj invar* piebald ‖ *f* magpie

pièce [pjɛs] *f* piece; patch; room; play; document; coin; wine barrel; **à la pièce** separately; **donner la pièce** to tip; **faire pièce à** to play a trick on; to put a check on; **inventé de toutes pièces** made up out of the whole cloth; **la pièce** apiece; **pièce à conviction** (law) exhibit; **pièce comptable** voucher; **pièce d'eau** ornamental pond; **pièce de rechange, pièce détachée** spare part; **pièce de résistance** pièce de résistance; (culin) entree; **pièce rapportée** in-law; **pièces rendues** change; **reprenez alors votre pièce au retour de monnaies** take your change from the coin return; **tout d'une pièce** in one piece; (coll) rigid; (coll) stiffly ‖ *adv* apiece

pied [pje] *m* foot; foothold; **à pied** on foot; **à pied d'œuvre** on the site, on the spot, where the work is being done; **au pied de la lettre** literally; **au pied levé** offhand; **c'est des pieds!** (slang) that's cool!, that's fresh!; **de pied en cap** from head to toe; **faire le pied de grue** (coll) to cool one's heels, to stand around waiting; **faire les pieds à** (coll) to give what's coming to; **faire un pied de nez** (coll) to thumb one's nose; **lever le pied** to abscond; **mettre à pied** to dismiss, fire; **mettre les pieds dans le plat** (coll) to put one's foot in one's mouth; **mettre pied à terre** to dismount; **mettre qn au pied du mur** to corner

s.o.; force s.o. to a showdown; **pied d'athlète** (pathol) athlete's foot; **pied équin** clubfoot; **travailler comme un pied** (coll) to botch one's work; **vous avez pied?** can you touch bottom?

pied-à-terre [pjetatɛr] *m invar* hangout, temporary base

pied-bot [pjebo] *m* (*pl* **pieds-bots**) club-footed person

pied-d'alouette [pjedalwɛt] *m* (*pl* **pieds-d'alouette**) delphinium

pied-de-poule [pjedəpul] *adj invar* hound's-tooth (*design or pattern*)

pied-droit [pjedrwa] *m* (*pl* **pieds-droits**) (archit) pier

piédes•tal -tale [pjedɛstal] *m* (*pl* **-taux** [to]) pedestal

pied-noir [pjenwar] *m* (*pl* **pieds-noirs**) Algerian of European descent

piège [pjɛʒ] *m* trap, snare; **piège de police pour contrôle de vitesse** (aut) speed trap

piéger [pjeʒe] §1 *tr* to trap, snare; booby-trap

pie-grièche [pigrijɛ∫] *f* (*pl* **pies-grièches**) shrike; shrew

pierraille [pjɛrɑj] *f* rubble

pierre [pjɛr] *f* stone; **faire d'une pierre deux coups** to kill two birds with one stone; **Pierre** Peter; **pierre à aiguiser** whetstone; **pierre à briquet** flint; **pierre à chaux, pierre à plâtre** gypsum; **pierre à feu, pierre à fusil** gunflint; **pierre angulaire** cornerstone; **pierre à rasoir** hone; **pierre calcaire** limestone; **pierre d'achoppement** stumbling block; **pierre de gué** stepping stone; **pierre de taille** ashlar; **pierre de touche** touchstone; **pierre tombale** tombstone

pierreries [pjɛri] *fpl* precious stones

pier•reux -reuse [pjɛrø] [røz] *adj* stony ‖ *f* (coll) streetwalker

pierrot [pjɛro] *m* clown; sparrow; (coll) oddball; (coll) greenhorn

piété [pjete] *f* piety; devotion

piéter [pjete] §10 *intr* to toe the line ‖ *ref* to stand firm

piétiner [pjetine] *tr* to trample on ‖ *intr* to stamp; mark time

piéton [pjetɔ̃] *m* pedestrian

piètre [pjɛtr] *adj* poor, wretched

pieu [pjø] *m* (*pl* **pieux**) post, stake; (archit) pile

pieuvre [pjœvr] *f* octopus; (coll) leech

pieux pieuse [pjø] [pjøz] *adj* pious; dutiful; white (*lie*)

pif [pif] *m* (slang) snout (*nose*) ‖ *interj* bang!

pifomètre [pifɔmɛtr] *m* (coll) intuition, instinct; **au pifomètre** at a rough guess

pige [piʒ] *f* (slang) year; **à la pige** (journ) so much a line; on a free-lance basis; **faire la pige à** (slang) to outdo

pigeon [piʒɔ̃] *m* pigeon; **pigeon voyageur** homing pigeon

pigeonner [piʒɔne] *tr* (coll) to dupe

pigeonnier [piʒɔnje] *m* dovecote

piger [piʒe] §38 *tr* (slang) to look at; (slang) to get ‖ *intr*—**tu piges?** (slang) do you get it?

pigment [pigmã] *m* pigment

pignocher [piɲɔʃe] *intr* to pick at one's food

pignon [piɲɔ̃] *m* gable; (mach) pinion; **avoir pignon sur rue** (coll) to have a home of one's own; (coll) to be well off; **pignon de chaîne** sprocket wheel

pile [pil] *f* stack, pile; pier; (elec) battery (*primary cell*); (coll) thrashing; **pile atomique** atomic pile; **pile ou face** heads or tails; **pile sèche** dry cell ‖ *adv* (coll) short; (coll) exactly; **tomber pile** (coll) to happen at the right moment

piler [pile] *tr* to grind, crush

pilier [pilje] *m* pillar; **pilier de cabaret** barfly

pillage [pijaʒ] *m* looting

pil·lard [pijar] **-larde** [jard] *adj* looting ‖ *mf* looter

piller [pije] *tr* & *intr* to loot; plagiarize

pil·leur [pijœr] **-leuse** [jøz] *mf* pillager

pilon [pilɔ̃] *m* pestle; (coll) drumstick (*of chicken*); (coll) wooden leg; **pilon à vapeur** steam hammer

pilonnage [pilɔnaʒ] *m* crushing; **pilonnage aérien** saturation bombing

pilonner [pilɔne] *tr* to crush; bomb

pilori [pilɔri] *m* pillory

pilot [pilo] *m* pile (*in piling*); rags (*for paper*)

pilotage [pilɔtaʒ] *m* piloting; **pilotage sans visibilité** blind flying; **pilotage terroriste suicide** suicide bombing

pilote [pilɔt] *mf* pilot; **pilote de ligne** airline pilot; **pilote d'émission** (telv) anchor, anchorperson; **pilote d'essai** test pilot; **pilote terroriste suicidant** suicide bomber ‖ *m* (telv) anchorman; **pilote automatique** (electron) automatic pilot

piloter [pilɔte] *tr* to pilot; guide; drive piles into ‖ *intr* to pilot; be a guide

pilotis [pilɔti] *m* piles

pilule [pilyl] *f* pill; (coll) bitter pill; **dorer la pilule** to sweeten the pill

piment [pimã] *m* allspice (*berry*); (fig) spice; **piment doux** sweet pepper; **piment rouge** red or hot pepper

pimenter [pimãte] *tr* to season with red pepper; (fig) to spice

pim·pant [pɛ̃pã] **-pante** [pãt] *adj* smart, spruce

pin [pɛ̃] *m* pine; **pin de Weymouth** (*Pinus strobus*) white pine; **pin sylvestre** (*Pinus sylvestris*) Scotch pine

pinacle [pinakl] *m* pinnacle

pince [pɛ̃s] *f* tongs; pliers; forceps; crowbar; gripper; grip; pleat; claw (*of crab*); **aller à pinces** (slang) to hoof it; **petites pinces, pince à épiler** tweezers; **pince à linge** clothespin; **pince à sucre** sugar tongs; **pince hémostatique** hemostat; **pinces** tongs; pincers, pliers; **pinces de cycliste** bicycle clips; **serrer la pince à** (slang) to shake hands with

pin·cé -cée [pɛ̃se] *adj* prim, tight-lipped; thin, pinched ‖ *f* see **pincée**

pin·ceau [pɛ̃so] *m* (*pl* **-ceaux**) paintbrush; pencil (*of light*)

pincée [pɛ̃se] *f* pinch

pincement [pɛ̃smã] *m* pinching; plucking

pince-monseigneur [pɛ̃smɔ̃sɛɲœr] *f* (*pl* **pinces-monseigneur**) jimmy

pince-nez [pɛ̃sne] *m invar* nose glasses

pincer [pɛ̃se] §51 *tr* to pinch; grip; nip off; pluck; top (*plants*); purse (*the lips*); pleat; (coll) to nab, to catch ‖ *intr* to bite (*said of cold*); **en pincer pour** (slang) to have a crush on; **pincer de** (mus) to strum on

pince-sans-rire [pɛ̃ssãrir] *adj invar* deadpan ‖ *mf invar* deadpan comic

pincette [pɛ̃sɛt] *f* tweezers; **pincettes** tweezers; fire tongs

pinçon [pɛ̃sɔ̃] *m* bruise (*from pinch*)

pinède [pinɛd] *f* pine grove

pingouin [pɛ̃gwɛ̃] *m* (*family:* Alcidae) auk

ping-pong [piŋpɔ̃g] *m* table tennis, Ping-Pong

pingre [pɛ̃gr] *adj* (coll) stingy ‖ *mf* (coll) tightwad

pinson [pɛ̃sɔ̃] *m* (orn) finch

pintade [pɛ̃tad] *f* guinea fowl

pin up [pinœp] *f invar* (coll) pinup girl

pioche [piɔʃ] *f* pickax

piocher [pjɔʃe] *tr* & *intr* to dig, pick; (coll) to cram

pio·cheur [pjɔʃœr] **-cheuse** [ʃøz] *mf* digger; (coll) grind ‖ *f* (mach) cultivator

piolet [pjɔlɛ] *m* ice ax

pion [pjɔ̃] *m* (checkers) man; (chess & fig) pawn; (slang) proctor; **damer le pion à** (coll) to get the better of

pionnier [pjɔnje] *m* pioneer, trailblazer; young student chess player

pipe [pip] *f* pipe; **casser sa pipe** (slang) to kick the bucket

pi·peau [pipo] *m* (*pl* **-peaux**) bird call; shepherd's pipe; lime twig

piper [pipe] *tr* to snare, catch; load (*the dice*); mark (*the cards*) ‖ *intr*—**ne pipe pas!** (coll) not a peep out of you!

pi·quant [pikã] **-quante** [kãt] *adj* piquant, intriguing; racy, spicy ‖ *m* sting; prickle; quill (*of porcupine*); piquancy, pungency; point (*of story*); (fig) bite

pique [pik] *m* (cards) spade; (cards) spades ‖ *f* pike; pique

pi·qué -quée [pike] *adj* stung; sour; (mus) staccato; (coll) batty; **ne pas être piqué des vers** (slang) to be first rate; **piqué de** studded with ‖ *m* quilt; **descendre en piqué** to nose-dive

pique-assiette [pikasjɛt] *mf* (*pl* **-assiettes**) (coll) sponger

pique-feu [pikfø] *m invar* poker

pique-fleurs [pikflœr] *m invar* flower holder

pique-nique [piknik] *m* (*pl* **-niques**) picnic

pique-niquer [piknike] *intr* to picnic

piquer [pike] *tr* to sting; prick; pique; stimulate; quilt; spur; give a shot to; (mus) to play staccato; (slang) to filch; (slang) to pinch, nab ‖ *intr* to turn sour; (aer) to nose-dive §97 *ref* to be piqued; spot; give oneself a shot; **se piquer de** to take pride in; **se piquer pour** to take a fancy to

piquet [pikɛ] *m* peg, stake; picket; **piquet de grève** picket line

piqueter [pikte] **§34** *tr* to stake out; spot, dot

piquette [pikɛt] *f* poor wine; (coll) crushing defeat

pi•queur [pikœr] **-queuse** [køz] *mf* stitcher ‖ *m* huntsman; outrider

piqûre [pikyr] *f* sting, bite; prick; injection, shot; stitching; puncture; **piqûre de rappel** booster shot; **piqûre de ver** moth hole

pirate [pirat] *m* pirate; (comp) hacker; **pirate de l'air** hijacker; **pirate informatique** hacker

pirater [pirate] *tr* (comp) to access by means of hacking, to hack into; (electron) to copy without permission, to pirate ‖ *intr* (comp) to hack; (electron) to pirate

piraterie [piratri] *f* piracy; (comp) hacking; **piraterie aérienne** hijacking; **piraterie informatique** hacking; **piraterie vidéo** video piracy

pire[pir] (precedes the noun it modifies) **§91** *adj comp & super* worse; worst ‖ *m* (the) worst

pirouette [pirwɛt] *f* pirouette

pirouetter [pirwete] *intr* to pirouette

pis [pi] *adj comp & super* worse; worst ‖ *m* udder; **au pis aller** at worst; **de pis en pis** worse and worse; **(le) pis** (the) worst; **qui pis est** what's worse; **tant pis** so much the worse ‖ *adv comp & super* **§91** worse; worst

pis-aller [pizale] *m invar* makeshift

piscine [pisin] *f* swimming pool

pisse [pis] *f* (slang) piss (vulg)

pisse-chaude *f invar* (coll) gonorrhea

pisse-froid *m invar* wet blanket, cold fish (coll)

pissenlit [pisɑ̃li] *m* dandelion

pisser [pise] *tr* (coll) to spout (*water*); (coll) to leak; (slang) to pass (*e.g., blood*); **pisser de la copie** (slang) to be a hack writer ‖ *intr* (slang) to piss (vulg)

pisse-vinaigre [pisvinɛgr] *m invar* (coll) skinflint; wet blanket

pissoir [piswar] *m* (coll) urinal

pissotière [pisɔtjɛr] *f* (coll) street urinal

pistache [pistaʃ] *f* pistachio

pistage [pistaʒ] *m* tracking

piste [pist] *f* track; trail; ring (*of, e.g., circus*); rink; lane (*of highway*); **à double piste** four-lane (*highway*); runway; **piste cavalière** bridle path; **piste cyclable** bicycle path; **piste d'atterrissage** landing strip; **piste de danse** dance floor; **piste d'envol** runway; **piste pour les courses de levriers** dog track; **piste pour skieurs** ski run; **piste sonore** sound track

pister [piste] *tr* to track, trail

pistolet [pistɔlɛ] *m* pistol; spray gun; (coll) card; **pistolet à bouchon** popgun; **pistolet à souder** welding gun; **pistolet d'arçon** horse pistol; **pistolet mitrailleur** submachine gun

piston [pistɔ̃] *m* piston; (coll) pull

pistonner [pistɔne] *tr* (coll) to push, back

pitance [pitɑ̃s] *f* ration; food

pi•teux [pitø] **-teuse** [tøz] *adj* pitiful, sorry, sad

pitié [pitje] *f* pity; **à faire pitié** (coll) very badly; **par pitié!** for pity's sake!; **quelle pitié!** how awful!

piton [pitɔ̃] *m* screw eye; peak; **piton adhésif** adhesive hook

pitou [pitu] *m* (Canad) dog; (Canad) tyke

pitoyable [pitwajabl] *adj* pitiful

pitre [pitr] *m* clown

pittoresque [pitɔrɛsk] *adj* picturesque

pivoine [pivwan] *f* peony

pivot [pivo] *m* pivot

pivoter [pivɔte] *intr* to pivot

P.J. [peʒi] *f* (letterword) **(police judiciaire)** (coll) police (*dealing with criminal cases*)

placage [plakaʒ] *m* veneering; plating

placard [plakar] *m* cupboard; closet; placard, poster; (typ) galley; **placards de presse** press passes

placarder [plakarde] *tr* to placard; (typ) to print in galleys

place [plas] *f* place; city square; room; seat; job, position; fare; **place de loge** box seat; **places debout** standing room; **sur place** on the spot

placement [plasmɑ̃] *m* placement; investment; **de placement** employment (*agency*); **placement d'enfants** foster care; **mettre en placement** to place in foster care; **prendre qn en placement** to take s.o. into a foster family

placer [plase] **§51** *tr* to place; invest; slip in ‖ *ref* to seat oneself; rank; get a job; take place

pla•ceur [plasœr] **-ceuse** [søz] *mf* employment agent ‖ *m* usher

placide [plasid] *adj* placid

pla•cier [plasje] **-cière** [sjɛr] *mf* agent, representative

placoplâtre [plakɔplɑtr] *m* plasterboard

plafond [plafɔ̃] *m* ceiling

plafonner [plafɔne] *intr*—**plafonner (à)** to hit the top (at)

plafonnier [plafɔnje] *m* ceiling light; (aut) dome light; courtesy light

plage [plaʒ] *f* beach; band (*of record*); (poetic) clime

plagiaire [plaʒjɛr] *mf* plagiarist

plagiat [plaʒja] *m* plagiarism

plagier [plaʒje] *tr & intr* to plagiarize

plagiste [plaʒist] *mf* beach concessionaire

plaider [plede] *tr* to argue (*a case*); plead (*e.g., ignorance*) ‖ *intr* to plead; go to law

plai•deur [plɛdœr] **-deuse** [døz] *mf* litigant

plaidoirie [plɛdwari] *f* pleading

plaidoyer [plɛdwaje] *m* appeal (*of lawyer to judge or jury*)

plaie [plɛ] *f* wound, sore; plague; **plaie en séton** flesh wound

plai•gnant [plɛɲɑ̃] **-gnante** [ɲɑt] *mf* plaintiff

plain [plɛ̃] *m* high tide

plaindre [plɛ̃dr] **§15, §97** *tr* to pity ‖ *ref* to complain

plaine [plɛn] *f* plain

plain-pied [plɛ̃pje] *m*—**de plain-pied** on the same floor; (fig) on an equal footing

plainte [plɛ̃t] *f* complaint; moan

plain•tif [plɛ̃tif] **-tive** [tiv] *adj* plaintive

plaire [plɛr] §52 *intr* to please; **plaire à** to be pleasing to, appeal to, e.g., **cette musique leur plaît** that music appeals to them; to inspire liking in, e.g., **le lait lui plaît** he likes milk, **le dîner m'a plu** I liked the dinner; to be suitable for, e.g., **ce plan lui plaît** that plan suits her; **s'il vous plaît** please ‖ §96 *ref* (*pp* **plu** *invar*) to be pleased; enjoy oneself; like one another; **se plaire à** to like it in, e.g., **je me plais à la campagne** I like it in the country

plaisance [plɛzɑ̃s] *f*—**de plaisance** pleasure (*e.g., boat*)

plai•sant [plɛzɑ̃] **-sante** [zɑ̃t] *adj* pleasant; funny ‖ *m*—**mauvais plaisant** practical joker

plaisanter [plɛzɑ̃te] *tr* to poke fun at ‖ *intr* to joke

plaisanterie [plɛzɑ̃tri] *f* joke; joking

plaisantin [plɛzɑ̃tɛ̃] *adj masc* roguish, waggish ‖ *m* wag, kidder

plaisent [plɛz] *v* (**plaisons**) see **plaire**

plaisir [plɛzir] *m* pleasure; **à plaisir** without cause; at one's pleasure; **au plaisir (de vous revoir)** good-by; **faire plaisir à** to please, give pleasure to

plaît [plɛ] *v* see **plaire**

plan [plɑ̃] **plane** [plan] *adj* even, flat; plane (*angle*) ‖ *m* plan; design; (geom) plane; **au deuxième plan** in the background; **au premier plan** in the foreground; downstage; **au troisième plan** far in the background; **gros plan** (mov) close-up; **laisser en plan** (coll) to leave stranded; (coll) to put off, delay; **lever un plan** to survey; **plan d'attaque** line of attack; **plan de paix** peace plan; **plan de travail** work schedule; **plan de vol** flight plan; **plan d'occupation des sols (P.O.S.)** zoning code; **rester en plan** (coll) to remain in suspense; **sur le plan de** from the point of view of ‖ *f* see **plane**

planche [plɑ̃ʃ] *f* board; plank; (hort) bed; (typ) plate; (slang) blackboard; **faire de la planche à voile** to go windsurfing; **faire la planche** to float on one's back; **planche à pain** breadboard; (slang) flat-chested woman; **planche à repasser** ironing board; **planche à roulettes** skateboard; **planche de bord** instrument panel; **planche de débarquement** gangplank; **planche de messages** (comp) message board; **planche de plancher** floorboard; **planche de salut** sheet anchor; last hope; **planche pourrie** (slang) dubious character

planchéier [plɑ̃ʃeje] *tr* to floor; board

plancher [plɑ̃ʃe] *m* floor; **le plancher des vaches** (coll) terra firma

planchette [plɑ̃ʃɛt] *f* small board; shelf; **planchette à papiers attachées** clipboard

plane [plan] *f* drawknife

planer [plane] *tr* to plane ‖ *intr* to hover; glide;

float; **planer sur** to overlook, sweep (*e.g., a landscape with one's eyes*); (fig) to hover over

planète [planɛt] *f* planet

planeur [planœr] *m* glider

planeuse [planøz] *f* planing machine

planification [planifikɑsjɔ̃] *f* planning; **planification des naissances** family planning

planifier [planifje] *tr* to plan

planisme [planism] *m*—**planisme familial** family planning

planning [planiŋ] *m* detailed plan; **planning familial** birth control

plan-plan [plɑ̃plɑ̃] *adv* (coll) quietly, without hurrying

planque [plɑ̃k] *f* (coll) soft job; (slang) hideout

planquer [plɑ̃ke] *tr* to hide ‖ *ref* (mil) to take cover; (slang) to hide out

plant [plɑ̃] *m* planting; bed, patch; seedling, sapling

plantation [plɑ̃tɑsjɔ̃] *f* planting; plantation; **plantation de cheveux** hairline; head of hair

plante [plɑ̃t] *f* plant; sole

plan•té -tée [plɑ̃te] *adj* set, situated

planter [plɑ̃te] *tr* to plant; set; **planter là** to give the slip to ‖ *ref* to stand

planteur [plɑ̃tœr] *m* planter

plantoir [plɑ̃twar] *m* (hort) dibble

planton [plɑ̃tɔ̃] *m* (mil) orderly

plantu•reux [plɑ̃tyrø] **-reuse** [røz] *adj* abundant; fertile; (coll) buxom

plaque [plak] *f* plate; plaque; splotch; **plaque à crêpes** pancake griddle; **plaque croûteuse** scab; **plaque dentaire** plaque; **plaque d'identité** identification tag, identity tag; **plaque d'immatriculation, plaque minéralogique** (aut) license plate; **plaque logique** (comp) logic board; **plaque tournante** (rr) turntable; (fig) hub (*of a city, airline, enterprise*)

plaquer [plake] *tr* to plate; veneer; plaster down (*one's hair*); strike (*a chord*); (football) to tackle; (coll) to jilt; **plaquer à l'électricité** to electroplate ‖ *ref* to lie flat; (aer) to pancake

plaquette [plakɛt] *f* plaque; pamphlet; (histology) platelet; **plaquette de silicium** silicon chip

plasma [plasma] *m* plasma: **plasma germinal** germ plasma

plastic [plastik] *m* plastic bomb

plastique [plastik] *adj* plastic ‖ *m* plastics ‖ *f* plastic art

plasti•queur [plastikœr] **-queuse** [køz] *mf* bomber; **plastiqueur suicidant, plastiqueuse suicidante** suicide bomber

plastron [plastrɔ̃] *m* shirt front; breastplate; hostile contingent (*in war games*)

plastronner [plastrɔne] *intr* (fig) to throw out one's chest

plat [pla] **plate** [plat] *adj* flat; even; smooth (*sea*); dead; (*calm*); corny (*joke*); **à plat** rundown; flat; **tomber plat** (coll) to fall unluckily ‖ *m* dish; platter; course (*of meal*); flat (*of* *hand*); blade (*of oar*); face (*of hammer*); **plat cuisiné** platter, short-order meal; **plat de côtes** sparerib; **plat du jour** today's special, chef's special; **plat principal, plat de résistance** entree; **plats** (bb) boards

platane [platan] *m* plane tree; **faux platane** sycamore

pla·teau [plato] *m* (*pl* **-teaux**) plateau; tray; shelf; platform; plate; pan (*of scale*); (mov, telv) set; (rr) flatcar; (theat) stage; **plateau porte-disque** turntable (*of phonograph*); **pleateau repas congelé** frozen dinner; **plateau tournant** revolving stage; lazy Susan

plate-bande [platbãd] *f* (*pl* **plates-bandes**) flower bed

plate-forme [platfɔrm] *f* (*pl* **plates-formes**) platform; drilling rig (*at sea*); (rr) flatcar

platine [platin] *m* platinum ‖ *f* plate; platen; lock (*of gun*); stage (*of microscope*); **platine de magnétophone** tape deck

plati·né -née [platine] *adj* platinum-plated; platinum

platitude [platityd] *f* platitude; flatness; obsequiousness

Platon [platɔ̃] *m* Plato

plâtre [plɑtr] *m* plaster; plaster cast; **essuyer les plâtres** to be the first occupant of a new house; **plâtre à mouler** plaster of Paris

plâtrer [plɑtre] *tr* to plaster; put in a cast; fertilize ‖ *ref* (coll) to pile on the make-up or face powder

plausible [plozibl] *adj* plausible

plé·béien [plebejɛ̃] **-béienne** [bejɛn] *adj & mf* plebeian

plein [plɛ̃] **pleine** [plɛn] *adj* full; round, plump; solid (*bar, wheel, wire, etc.*); continuous (*line*); heavy (*heart*); in foal, with calf, etc.; (coll) drunk; **plein aux as** (coll) well-heeled; **plein de** full of; covered with; preoccupied with; **plein de soi** self-centered ‖ (when standing before noun) *adj* full; high (*tide*); **en plein** + *noun* in the midst of the + *noun*, right in the + *noun*; at the height of the (*season*); in the open (*air*); out at (*sea*), on the high (*seas*); in broad (*daylight*); in the dead of (*winter*) ‖ *m* full (*of the moon*); bull's-eye; downstroke; **battre son plein** to be in full swing; **en plein** plumb, plump, squarely; **faire le plein (de)** to fill up the tank (with) ‖ **plein** *adv* full; (coll) plenty, a lot, e.g., **j'en ai plein** I've got a lot, I have plenty; **plein de monde** a lot of people; **plein d'égards** (coll) considerate; **tout plein** very much, entirely

plein-emploi [plɛ̃ɑ̃plwa] *m* full employment

pleu·rard [plœrar] **-rarde** [rard] *adj* (coll) whimpering ‖ *mf* (coll) whimperer

pleurer [plœre] *tr* to weep over; shed (*tears*); **pleurer misère** to complain of being poor ‖ *intr* to cry, weep; **pleurer à chaudes larmes** to weep bitterly; **pleurer dans le gilet de qn** (coll) to cry on s.o.'s shoulder

pleurésie [plœrezi] *f* pleurisy

pleu·reur [plœrœr] **-reuse** [røz] *adj* weeping ‖ *f* paid mourner

pleurnicher [plœrniʃe] *intr* to whimper, snivel

pleurs [plœr] *mpl* tears

pleutre [pløtr] *adj* (coll) cowardly ‖ *m* (coll) coward

pleuvasser [pløvase] *intr* (coll) to drizzle

pleuvoir [pløvwar] §53 *intr & impers* to rain; **pleuvoir à verse, à flots,** or **à seaux** to rain buckets

pli [pli] *m* fold; pleat; bend (*of arm or leg*); hollow (*of knee*); letter; envelope; undulation (*of ground*); (cards) trick; **faire des plis (dans)** to crimple; **faux pli** crease, wrinkle; **petit pli** tuck; **pli creux** box pleat; **sous ce pli** enclosed, herewith; **sous pli cacheté** in a sealed envelope; **sous pli distinct** or **séparé** under separate cover; **sous pli fermé** in a sealed envelope

pliage [plijaʒ] *m* folding

pliant [plijɑ̃] **pliante** [plijɑ̃t] *adj* folding; collapsible; pliant ‖ *m* campstool, folding chair

plier [plije] *tr* to fold; bend; force; **plier bagage** to leave ‖ *intr* to fold; bend; yield; **ne pas plier, s.v.p.** (*formula on envelope*) please do not bend ‖ §96 *ref* to fold; yield; fall back (*said of army*)

plinthe [plɛ̃t] *f* baseboard

plisser [plise] *tr* to pleat; crease; wrinkle, crimple; squint (*the eyes*) ‖ *intr* to fold ‖ *ref* to wrinkle, crimple; pucker up (*said of mouth*)

plomb [plɔ̃] *m* lead; shot; seal; plumb; sinker (*of fishline*); (elec) fuse; **à plomb** plumb, vertical; straight down, directly; **faire sauter un plomb** to burn or blow out a fuse

plombage [plɔ̃baʒ] *m* filing (*of tooth*); sealing (*e.g., at customs*)

plombagine [plɔ̃baʒin] *f* graphite

plom·bé -bée [plɔ̃be] *adj* leaden; in bond, sealed; filled (*tooth*); livid (*hue*)

plomber [plɔ̃be] *tr* to cover with lead; seal; plumb; fill (*a tooth*); make livid; roll (*the ground*)

plomberie [plɔ̃bri] *f* plumbing; plumbing-supply store; leadwork

plombeur [plɔ̃bœr] *m* (mach) roller

plombier [plɔ̃bje] *m* plumber; worker in lead

plonge [plɔ̃ʒ] *f* dishwashing

plon·geant [plɔ̃ʒɑ̃] **-geante** [ʒɑ̃t] *adj* plunging; from above

plongée [plɔ̃ʒe] *f* plunge; dive; dip, slope; **en plongée** submerged

plongeoir [plɔ̃ʒwar] *m* diving board

plongeon [plɔ̃ʒɔ̃] *m* plunge; dive; (football) tackle; **plongeon de haut vol** high dive

plonger [plɔ̃ʒe] §38 *tr* to plunge; thrust, stick ‖ *intr* to plunge; dive; (coll) to have a good view; **plonger raide** to crash-dive ‖ *ref—se* **plonger dans** to immerse oneself in; give oneself over to

plon·geur [plɔ̃ʒœr] **-geuse** [ʒøz] *adj* diving ‖ *mf* diver; dishwasher (*in restaurant*) ‖ *m* (mach) plunger; (orn) diver

plot [plo] *m* (elec) contact point

plouc [pluk] *m* (coll) peasant, hick

ployer [plwaje] §47 *tr & intr* to bend

plu [ply] *v* see **plaire;** see **pleuvoir**

pluches [plyʃ] *fpl* (mil) K.P.

pluie [plɥi] *f* rain; shower; **pluie acide** acid rain; **pluies radioactives** fallout

plumage [plymaʒ] *m* plumage

plumard [plymar] *m*—**aller au plumard** (slang) to hit the hay

plume [plym] *f* feather; pen; penpoint

plu•meau [plymo] *m* (*pl* -**meaux**) feather duster

plumer [plyme] *tr* to pluck; (coll) to fleece ‖ *intr* to feather one's oar

plumet [plymɛ] *m* plume

plu•meux [plymø] -**meuse** [møz] *adj* feathery

plumier [plymje] *m* pencil box

plupart [plypar] *f*—**la plupart** most; the most; for the most part; **la plupart de** most; the most; most of, the majority of; **la plupart d'entre nous (eux)** most of us (them); **pour la plupart** for the most part

plu•riel -**rielle** [plyrjɛl] *adj & m* plural; **au pluriel** in the plural

plus [ply] ([plyz] before vowel; [plys] in final position) *m* plus; **au plus, tout au plus** at the most, at best; at the latest; at the outside; **d'autant plus** all the more so; **de plus** more; moreover, besides; **de plus en plus** more and more; **en plus** extra; **en plus de** in addition to, besides; **le plus, la plus, les plus** (the) most; **le plus de** the most; **le plus que** as much as, as fast as; **ni . . . non plus** nor . . . either, e.g., **ni moi non plus** nor I either; **ni plus ni moins** neither more nor less; **non plus** neither, not . . . either; **plus de** more, e.g., **plus de chaleur** more heat; no more, e.g., **plus de potage** no more soup; **qui plus est** what is more, moreover ‖ *adv comp & super* §91 more; **des plus** + *adj* most + *adj*, extremely + *adj;* **(le)** plus . . . (the) most . . . , e.g., **ce que j'aime le plus** what I like (the) most; **le** (or **son,** etc.) **plus** + *adj* the (or his, etc.) most; **ne . . . plus** §90 no more, no longer; **ne . . . plus que** §90 now only, e.g., **il n'y a plus que mon oncle** there is now only my uncle; **on ne peut plus** + *adj* or *adv* extremely + *adj* or *adv;* **plus de** (followed by numeral) more than; **plus jamais** never more; **plus . . . plus** (or **moins**) the more . . . the more (or the less); **plus que** more than; **plus tôt** sooner ‖ *prep* plus

plusieurs [plyzjœr] *adj & pron indef* several

plus-que-parfait [plyskəparfɛ] *m* pluperfect

plus-value [plyvaly] *f* (*pl* -**values**) appreciation; increase; surplus; extra cost; surplus value; **plus-values (en capital)** capital gains

Plutarque [plytark] *m* Plutarch

Pluton [plytɔ̃] *m* Pluto

plutonium [plytɔnjɔm] *m* plutonium

plutôt [plyto] *adv* rather; instead; **plutôt . . . que** rather . . . than

pluvier [plyvje] *m* (orn) plover

plu•vieux [plyvjø] -**vieuse** [vjøz] *adj* rainy

P.N.B. [peɛnbe] *m* (letterword) (**produit national brut**) G.N.P. (*gross national product*)

pneu [pnø] *m* (*pl* **pneus**) tire; express letter; **pneu à flanc blanc** whitewall tire; **pneu ballon** or **confort** balloon tire; **pneu de secours** spare tire; **pneu radial** radial tire; **pneus à clous** studded tires; **pneu sans chambre à air** tubeless tire; **pneus neiges** snow tires

pneumatique [pnømatik] *adj* pneumatic ‖ *m* tire; express letter (*by Parisian tube*); **pneumatiques à carcasse radiale** radial tires

pneumonie [pnømɔni] *f* pneumonia

pneumopathie [pnømɔpati] *f*—**pneumopathie atypique** SARS; **pneumopathie infectieuse** pneumonia

pochade [pɔʃad] *f* sketch

po•chard [pɔʃar] -**charde** [ʃard] *mf* (coll) boozer, guzzler

poche [pɔʃ] *f* pocket; bag, pouch; crop (*of bird*)

po•ché -**chée** [pɔʃe] *adj* poached; black (*eye*)

pocher [pɔʃe] *tr* to poach; dash off (*a sketch*)

pochette [pɔʃɛt] *f* folder; book (*of matches*); kit; fancy handkerchief; **pochette à disque** record jacket; **pochette surprise** surprise package

pocheuse [pɔʃøz] *f* egg poacher

pochoir [pɔʃwar] *m* stencil

poêle [pwal] *m* stove; pall; canopy ‖ *f* frying pan

poêlon [pwalɔ̃] *m* saucepan

poème [pɔɛm] *m* poem; **poème symphonique** tone poem

poésie [pɔezi] *f* poetry; poem

poète [pɔɛt] *mf* poet

poétesse [pɔetɛs] *f* poetess

poétique [pɔetik] *adj* poetic(al) ‖ *f* poetics

pognon [pɔɲɔ̃] *m* (coll) dough (slang)

pogrom [pɔgrɔm] *m* pogrom

poids [pwa], [pwɑ] *m* weight; **deux poids deux mesures** double standard; **poids brut, poids total** gross weight; **poids coq** bantamweight; **poids et haltères** weightlifting; weights; **poids léger** lightweight; **poids lourd** heavy truck; (boxing) heavyweight; **poids mort** (& fig) dead weight; **poids mouche** flyweight; **poids moyen** middleweight; **poids net** net weight; **poids plume, poids mouche** featherweight; **poids welter** welterweight

poi•gnant [pwaɲɑ̃] -**gnante** [ɲɑ̃t] *adj* poignant

poignard [pwaɲar] *m* dagger

poignarder [pwaɲarde] *tr* to stab

poigne [pwaɲ] *f* grip, grasp; **à poigne** strong, energetic

poignée [pwaɲe] *f* handful; handle; grip; hilt; **poignée de main** handshake

poignet [pwaɲɛ] *m* wrist; cuff; **poignet mousquetaire** French cuff

poil [pwal] *m* hair; bristle; nap, pile; coat (*of animals*); **à long poil** shaggy; **à poil** naked; bareback; **au poil** (slang) peachy; **avoir un poil dans la main** (coll) to be lazy; **de mauvais poil** (coll) in a bad mood; **de tout poil** (coll) of every shade and hue; **poil follet** down; **reprendre du poil de la bête** (coll) to be one's own self again; **se mettre à poil** to strip to the skin

poi·lu -lue [pwaly] *adj* hairy ‖ *m* (mil) doughboy

poinçon [pwɛ̃sɔ̃] *m* punch; stamp; hallmark; **poinçon à glace** ice pick

poinçonner [pwɛ̃sɔne] *tr* to punch; stamp; prick; hallmark

poinçonneuse [pwɛ̃sɔnøz] *f* stamping machine; ticket punch

poindre [pwɛ̃dr] §35 (*used especially in inf, pres ind, fut*) *intr* to dawn; sprout

poing [pwɛ̃] *m* fist; **dormir à poings fermés** to sleep like a log

point [pwɛ̃] *m* point; stitch; period (*used also in French to mark the divisions of whole numbers*); hole (*in a strap*); mark (*on a test*); (aer, naut) position; (typ) point; **à point** at the right moment; to a turn, medium; **à point nommé** in the nick of time; **à tel point que** to such a degree that; **au dernier point** to the utmost degree; **de point en point** exactly to the letter; **de tout point, en tout point** entirely; **deux points** colon; **faire le point** to take stock, get one's bearings; **mettre au point** to focus; adjust, tune up; develop, perfect, fine-tune; **mettre les points sur les i** to dot one's i's; **point d'appui** fulcrum; base of operations; **point de bâti** (sewing) tack; **point de coupure** cutoff; **point de départ** starting point; **point de détonation d'une bombe nucléaire** ground zero; **point de mire** target; **point de repère** point of reference, guide; (surv) bench mark; (fig) landmark; **point d'estime** dead reckoning; **point de vue** viewpoint; **point d'exclamation** exclamation point; **point d'explosion** ground zero; **point d'interrogation** question mark; **point d'orgue** (mus) pause; **point du jour** break of day; **point et virgule** semicolon; **point mort** dead center; (aut) neutral; **point noir** construction (*on highway*); **points et traits** dots and dashes ‖ *adv*—**ne . . . point** §90 not; not at all

pointage [pwɛ̃taʒ] *m* checking; check mark; aiming

point-com [pwɛ̃kɔm] *s* (comp) (*.com*) dot-com

pointe [pwɛ̃t] *f* point; tip; peak; head (*of arrow*); nose (*e.g., of bullet*); toe (*of shoe*); twinge (*of pain*); dash (*of, e.g., vanilla*); suggestion, touch; witty phrase, quip; (geog) cape, point; (mil) spearhead; **à pointes** spiked (*shoes*); **de pointe** peak (*e.g., hours*); **discuter sur les pointes d'épingle** to split hairs; **en pointe** tapering; **faire des pointes** to toe-dance; **pointe d'aiguille** needlepoint; **pointe de Paris** wire nail; **pointe de vitesse** spurt; **pointe du jour** daybreak; **sur la pointe des pieds** on tiptoe

poin·teau [pwɛ̃to] *m* (*pl* **-teaux**) checker; needle

pointer [pwɛ̃tœr] *m* pointer (*dog*) ‖ [pwɛ̃te] *tr* to check off; check in; prick up (*the ears*); dot ‖ *intr* to rise, soar skywards; stand out; sprout; **pointer sur** (coll) zero in on ‖ *ref* to check in, show up

poin·teur [pwɛ̃tœr] **-teuse** [tøz] *mf* checker; scorer; timekeeper; gunner; (*dog*) pointer ‖ *m* (comp) pointer, pointing

pointillé [pwɛ̃tije] *m* perforated line

pointil·leux [pwɛ̃tijø] **-leuse** [jøz] *adj* punctilious; touchy; captious

poin·tu -tue [pwɛ̃ty] *adj* pointed; shrill; (fig) touchy

pointure [pwɛ̃tyr] *f* size

poire [pwar] *f* pear; bulb (*of camera, syringe, horn, etc.*); (slang) mug; (slang) sucker, sap; **couper la poire en deux** to split the difference; **garder une poire pour la soif** to put something aside for a rainy day; **poire à poudre** powder flask; **poire électrique** pear-shaped switch

poi·reau [pwaro] *m* (*pl* **-reaux**) (bot) leek; **faire le poireau** (slang) to cool one's heels

poirée [pware] *f* (bot) Swiss chard

poirier [pwarje] *m* pear tree

pois [pwa], [pwɑ] *m* pea; polka dot; **petits pois, pois verts** peas; **petit pois sauteur** jumping bean; **pois cassés** split peas; **pois chiche** chickpea; **pois de senteur** sweet pea

poison [pwazɔ̃] *m* poison

pois·sard [pwasar] **-sarde** [sard] *adj* vulgar ‖ *f* fishwife

poisser [pwase] *tr* to coat with wax or pitch ‖ *intr* to be sticky

pois·seux [pwasø] **-seuse** [søz] *adj* sticky

poisson [pwasɔ̃] *m* fish; **les Poissons** (astr, astrol) Pisces; **poisson d'avril** April Fool (*joke, trick*); **poisson rouge** goldfish

poisson-chat [pwasɔ̃ʃa] *m* (*pl* **poissons-chats**) catfish

poissonnerie [pwasɔnri] *f* fish market

poisson·nier [pwasɔnje] **-nière** [njɛr] *mf* dealer in fish ‖ *f* fishwife; fish kettle

poitrail [pwatraj] *m* breast

poitrinaire [pwatrinɛr] *adj & mf* (pathol) consumptive

poitrine [pwatrin] *f* chest; breast; bosom

poivre [pwavr] *m* pepper

poivrer [pwavre] *tr* to pepper

poivrier [pwavrije] *m* pepper plant; pepper shaker

poivrière [pwavrijɛr] *f* pepper shaker; pepper plantation; **en poivrière** bulblike, turreted

poivron [pwavrɔ̃] *m* pepper; sweet pepper plant

poix [pwa], [pwɑ] *f* pitch; **poix sèche** resin

poker [pɔkɛr] *m* poker; four of a kind

polaire [pɔlɛr] *adj* pole, polar

polariser [pɔlarize] *tr* to polarize

pôle [pol] *m* pole

po·li -lie [pɔli] *adj* polished; polite ‖ *m* polish, gloss

police [pɔlis] *f* police; policy; **police d'assurance** insurance policy

policer [pɔlise] §51 *tr* to civilize; (obs) to police

Polichinelle [pɔliʃinɛl] *m* Punch; **de polichinelle** open (*secret*)

poli·cier [pɔlisje] **-cière** [sjɛr] *adj* police (*inves-*

tigation, dog, etc.); detective (*e.g., story*) ‖ *m* plain-clothes man, detective

polio [pɔljo] *mf* (coll) polio victim ‖ *f* (coll) polio

polir [pɔlir] *tr* to polish

polissoir [pɔliswar] *m* polisher

polis•son [pɔlisɔ̃] **-sonne** [sɔn] smutty ‖ *mf* scamp, rascal

politesse [pɔlitɛs] *f* politeness; **politesses** civilities, compliments

politicard [pɔlitikar] *m* unscrupulous politician

politi•cien [pɔlitisjɛ̃] **-cienne** [sjɛn] *adj* shortsighted; insincere ‖ *mf* (sometimes pej) politician; **politicien marron** (pej) politico

politique [pɔlitik] *adj* political; prudent, wise ‖ *m* politician; statesman ‖ *f* politics; policy; cunning, shrewdness; **politique du place-sous** patronage

politiquement [pɔlitikmɑ̃] *adv*—**politiquement correct** politically correct

pollen [pɔlɛn] *m* pollen

pol•luant [pɔlɥɑ̃] **-luante** [lɥɑ̃t] *adj* polluting

polluer [pɔlɥe] *tr* to pollute

pollution [pɔlysjɔ̃] *f* pollution; **pollution de l'environnement** environmental pollution; **pollutions nocturnes** wet dreams

polo [pɔlo] *m* polo

poloéiste [pɔlɔeist] *mf* polo player

Pologne [pɔlɔɲ] *f* Poland; **la Pologne** Poland

polo•nais [pɔlɔnɛ] **-naise** [nɛz] *adj* Polish ‖ *m* Polish (*language*) ‖ (*cap*) *mf* Pole

polonium [pɔlɔnjɔm] *m* polonium

pol•tron [pɔltrɔ̃] **-tronne** [trɔn] *adj* cowardly ‖ *mf* coward

polycopie [pɔlikɔpi] *f* mimeographing; **tiré à la polycopie** mimeographed

polycopié [pɔlikɔpje] *m* mimeographed university lectures

polycopier [pɔlikɔpje] *tr* to mimeograph

polygame [pɔligam] *adj* polygamous ‖ *mf* polygamist

polyglotte [pɔliglɔt] *adj* polyglot ‖ *mf* polyglot, linguist

polygone [pɔligon] *m* polygon; shooting range

polynôme [pɔlinom] *m* polynomial

polype [pɔlip] *m* polyp

polythéiste [pɔliteist] *adj* polytheistic ‖ *mf* polytheist

pom [pɔ̃] *interj* bang!

pommade [pɔmad] *f* pomade; **passer de la pommade à** (coll) to soft-soap

pomme [pɔm] *f* apple; ball, knob; head (*of lettuce*); **pomme à couteau** eating apple; **pomme de discorde** bone of contention; **pomme de pin** pine cone; **pomme de terre** potato; **pommes chips** potato chips; **pommes de terre au four** baked potatoes; scalloped potatoes; **pommes de terre en robe de chambre, en robe des champs,** or **en chemise** potatoes in their jackets; **pommes de terre sautées** fried potatoes; **pommes frites** French fried potatoes; **pommes soufflées** potato puffs; **pommes vapeur** boiled potatoes; steamed potatoes

pom•meau [pɔmo] *m* (*pl* **-meaux**) pommel; butt (*of fishing pole*)

pomme•lé -lée [pɔmle] *adj* dappled; fleecy (*clouds*); mackerel (*sky*)

pommette [pɔmɛt] *f* cheekbone

pommier [pɔmje] *m* apple tree

pompe [pɔ̃p] *f* pomp; pump; **à la pompe** on draught; **aller à toute pompe** (slang) to go lickety-split; **être en dehors de ses pompes** (slang) to be absent-minded; **pompe à incendie** fire engine; **pompe aspirante** suction pump; **pompe à vélo** bicycle pump; **pompe de chaleur** heat pump; **pompes funèbres** funeral

pomper [pɔ̃pe] *tr* to pump; suck in

pompette [pɔ̃pɛt] *adj* (coll) tipsy

pom•peux [pɔ̃pø] **-peuse** [pøz] *adj* pompous; high-flown

pom•pier [pɔ̃pje] **-pière** [pjɛr] *adj* conventional; pretentious ‖ *mf* fitter ‖ *m* fireman

pompiste [pɔ̃pist] *mf* filling-station attendant

pomponner [pɔ̃pɔne] *tr & ref* to dress up

ponçage [pɔ̃saʒ] *m* sandpapering; pumicing

ponce [pɔ̃s] *f* pumice stone

pon•ceau [pɔ̃so] (*pl* **-ceaux**) *adj* poppy-red ‖ *m* rude bridge; culvert

poncer [pɔ̃se] §51 *tr* to sandpaper; pumice

ponceuse [pɔ̃søz] *f* sander

poncho [pɔ̃tʃo] *m* poncho

poncif [pɔ̃sif] *m* banality

ponctualité [pɔ̃ktɥalite] *f* punctuality

ponctuation [pɔ̃ktɥasjɔ̃] *f* punctuation

ponc•tuel -tuelle [pɔ̃ktɥɛl] *adj* punctual

ponctuer [pɔ̃ktɥe] *tr* to punctuate

pondération [pɔ̃derasjɔ̃] *f* balance; weighting

pondé•ré -rée [pɔ̃dere] *adj* moderate, well-balanced; weighted

pondérer [pɔ̃dere] §10 *tr* to balance; weight

pondeuse [pɔ̃døz] *f* layer (*hen*); (coll) prolific woman

pondre [pɔ̃dr] *tr* to lay (*an egg*); (coll) to turn out (*a book*); (slang) to bear (*a child*) ‖ *intr* to lay

poney [pɔnɛ] *m* pony

pongiste [pɔ̃ʒist] *mf* table-tennis player, Ping-Pong player

pont [pɔ̃] *m* bridge; (naut) deck; **faire le pont** (coll) to take the intervening day or days off; **pont aérien** airlift; **pont arrière** (aut) rear-axle assembly; **pont cantilever, pont à consoles** cantilever bridge; **ponts et chaussées** [pɔ̃zeʃose] highway department; **ponts restaurants** turnpike restaurants; **pont suspendu** suspension bridge

ponte [pɔ̃t] *f* egg laying; eggs

pontet [pɔ̃tɛ] *m* trigger guard

pontife [pɔ̃tif] *m* pontiff

pont-levis [pɔ̃lvi] *m* (*pl* **ponts-levis**) drawbridge

ponton [pɔ̃tɔ̃] *m* pontoon; landing stage

pont-promenade [pɔ̃prɔmnad] *m* (*pl* **ponts-promenades**) promenade deck

pool [pul] *m* pool (*combine*)

pope [pɔp] *m* Orthodox priest

popeline [pɔplin] *f* poplin

popote [pɔpɔt] *adj invar* (coll) stay-at-home ‖ *f* (mil) mess; (coll) cooking; **faire la popote** (coll) to do the cooking oneself

populace [pɔpylas] *f* populace, rabble

populaire [pɔpylɛr] *adj* popular; vulgar, common

populariser [pɔpylarize] *tr* to popularize

popularité [pɔpylarite] *f* popularity

population [pɔpylɑsjɔ̃] *f* population

popu·leux [pɔpylø] **-leuse** [løz] *adj* populous; crowded

populo [pɔpylo] *m* (coll) rabble

porc [pɔr] *m* pig, hog; pork

porcelaine [pɔrsəlɛn] *f* porcelain; china

porcelet [pɔrsəlɛ] *m* piglet

porc-épic [pɔrkepik] *m* (*pl* **porcs-épics** [pɔrkepik] porcupine

porche [pɔrʃ] *m* porch, portico

porcher [pɔrʃe] *m* swineherd

porcherie [pɔrʃəri] *f* pigpen

pore [pɔr] *m* pore

po·reux [pɔrø] **-reuse** [røz] *adj* porous

porno [pɔrno] *m & f* (coll) porn

pornographie [pɔrnɔgrafi] *f* pornography

pornographique [pɔrnɔgrafik] *adj* pornographic

porphyre [pɔrfir] *m* porphyry

port [pɔr] *m* port; carryings; wearing; bearing; shipping charges; **arriver à bon port** to arrive safe; **port d'attache** home port; **port d'escale** port of call; **port franc** duty-free; free port; **port payé** postpaid

portable [pɔrtabl] *adj* portable; wearable

portail [pɔrtaj] *m* portal, gate

por·tant [pɔrtɑ̃] **-tante** [tɑ̃t] *adj* bearing; lifting; **être bien portant** to be in good health ‖ *m* handle

porta·tif [pɔrtatif] **-tive** [tiv] *adj* portable ‖ *m* cellphone, cellular telephone

porte [pɔrt] *f* door; doorway; gate; **fausse porte** blind door; **porte à deux battants** double door; **porte à porte** door to door (*selling*); **porte à tambour** revolving door; **porte battante** swinging door; **porte cochère** covered carriage entrance

porte-à-faux [pɔrtafo] *m invar*—**en porte-à-faux** out of line; (fig) in an untenable position

porte-aiguilles [pɔrtegɥi] *m invar* needle case

porte-allumettes [pɔrtalymɛt] *m invar* matchbox

porte-assiette [pɔrtasjɛt] *m* (*pl* **-assiette** or **-assiettes**) place mat

porte-avions [pɔrtavjɔ̃] *m invar* aircraft carrier

porte-bagages [pɔrtbagaʒ] *m invar* baggage rack

porte-bannière [pɔrtbanjɛr] *mf* (*pl* **-bannière** or **-bannières**) colorbearer

porte-bonheur [pɔrtbɔnœr] *m invar* goodluck charm

porte-carte [pɔrtəkart] *m* (*pl* **-carte** or **-cartes**) card case

porte-chapeaux [pɔrtʃapo] *m invar* hatrack

porte-cigarette [pɔrtsigarɛt] *m invar* cigarette holder

porte-cigarettes [pɔrtsigarɛt] *m invar* cigarette case

porte-clés or **porte-clefs** [pɔrtəkle] *m invar* key ring

porte-disques [pɔrtdisk] *m invar* record case

porte-documents [pɔrtdɔkymɑ̃] *m invar* letter case, portfolio

porte-drapeau [pɔrtdrapo] *m* (*pl* **-drapeau** or **-drapeaux**) standard-bearer

portée [pɔrte] *f* range, reach; import, significance; litter; (mus) staff; **à la portée de** within reach of; **à portée de voix** within speaking distance, within earshot; **à portée de l'oreille** within hearing distance; **hors de la portée de** out of reach of

portefaix [pɔrtəfɛ] *m* porter; dock hand

porte-fenêtre [pɔrtfənɛtr], [pɔrtəfnɛtr] *f* (*pl* **portes-fenêtres**) French window, French door

portefeuille [pɔrtəfœj] *m* portfolio; wallet, billfold

porteman·teau [pɔrtmɑ̃to] *m* (*pl* **-teaux**) clothes tree; **en portemanteau** square (*shoulders*)

porte-mine [pɔrtəmin] *m* (*pl* **-mine** or **mines**) mechanical pencil

porte-monnaie [pɔrtmɔnɛ] *m invar* change purse

porte-parapluies [pɔrtparaplɥi] *m invar* umbrella stand

porte-parole [pɔrtparɔl] *m invar* spokesperson, spokesman, mouthpiece

porte-plume [pɔrtəplym] *m invar* penholder; **porte-plume réservoir** fountain pen

porter [pɔrte] **§96, §100** *tr* to carry; bear; wear; propose (*a toast*); **être porté à** to be inclined to; **être porté sur** to have a weakness for; **porter à l'écran** (mov) to put on the screen; **porter qn sur son testament** to put s.o. in one's will; **portez ... arme!** present ... arms! ‖ *intr* to carry; **porter sur** to bear down on, emphasize; be aimed at ‖ *ref* to be worn; proceed, go; to be, e.g., **comment vous portez-vous?** how are you?; **se porter à** to indulge in; **se porter candidat** to run as a candidate

porte-savon [pɔrtsavɔ̃] *m* (*pl* **-savon** or **-savons**) soap dish

porte-serviettes [pɔrtsɛrvjɛt] *m invar* towel rack

por·teur [pɔrtœr] **-teuse** [tøz] *mf* porter; bearer; holder; **être porteur du virus du sida** to be HIV positive; **porteur de germes** germ carrier

porte-vêtement [pɔrtəvɛtmɑ̃] *m invar* clothes hanger

porte-voix [pɔrtəvwa] *m invar* megaphone; **mettre les mains en porte-voix** to cup one's hands

por·tier [pɔrtje] **-tière** [tjɛr] *mf* concierge ‖ *m* doorman ‖ *f* door (*of car*); portiere

portillon [pɔrtijɔ̃] *m* gate; (rr) side gate (*at crossing*); **refouler du portillon** (slang) to have bad breath

portion [pɔrsjɔ̃] *f* portion; share

portique [pɔrtik] *m* portico

porto [pɔrto] *m* port wine

portori·cain [pɔrtorikɛ̃] **-caine** [kɛn] *adj* Puerto Rican ‖ (*cap*) *mf* Puerto Rican

Porto Rico [pɔrtoriko] *f* Puerto Rico

portrait [pɔrtrɛ] *m* portrait; **être tout le portrait de** to be the very image of; **portrait à mi-corps** half-length portrait; **portrait de face** full-faced portrait

portraitiste [pɔrtretist] *mf* portrait painter

portu·gais [pɔrtygɛ] **-gaise** [gɛz] *adj* Portuguese ‖ *m* Portuguese (*language*) ‖ (*cap*) *mf* Portuguese (*person*)

Portugal [pɔrtygal] *m*—**le Portugal** Portugal

P.O.S. [peoɛs] *m* (letterword) (**plan d'occupation des sols**) zoning code

pose [poz] *f* pose; laying, setting in place; (phot) exposure

po·sé -sée [poze] *adj* poised, steady; trained (*voice*)

pose-marge [pozmarʒ] *f invar* margin setter (*on a typewriter*)

posément [pozemɑ̃] *adv* calmly, steadily, carefully

posemètre [pozmɛtr] *m* (phot) light meter, exposure meter

poser [poze] *tr* to place; arrange; ask (*a question*); set up (*a principle*) ‖ *intr* to pose ‖ *ref* to pose; alight; land; **se poser en** to set oneself up as

po·seur [pozœr] **-seuse** [zøz] *mf* layer; artist's model; poseur; phony; **poseur d'affiches** billposter

posi·tif [pozitif] **-tive** [tiv] *adj & m* positive

position [pozisjɔ̃] *f* position

posologie [pɔzɔlɔʒi] *f* dosage

posséder [posede] §10 *tr* to possess, own; have a command of, know perfectly ‖ *ref* to control oneself

possession [posesjɔ̃] *f* possession

possibilité [pɔsibilite] *f* possibility

possible [pɔsibl] *adj & m* possible

postage [pɔstaʒ] *m* mailing

pos·tal -tale [pɔstal] *adj* (*pl* **-taux** [to]) postal

postalage [pɔstalaʒ] *m* selling by mail

postcombustion [pɔstkɔ̃bystjɔ̃] *f* afterburner

postdate [pɔstdat] *f* postdate

postdater [pɔstdate] *tr* to postdate

poste [pɔst] *m* post; station; set; position, job; **poste de commande** (naut) control room; **poste de contrôle** (mil) control room; **poste de contrôle de frontière** border crossing; **poste de douane** port of entry; **poste d'émetteur** broadcasting station; **poste de pilotage** cockpit; **poste de radio** radio set; **poste de repérage** tracking station; **poste de secours** first-aid station; **poste des malades** (nav) sick

bay; **poste d'essence** gas station; **poste de travail** (work) shift, job; **poste d'incendie** fire station; **poste supplémentaire** (telp) extension ‖ *f* post, mail; **mettre à la poste** to mail; **poste restante** general delivery; **postes** post office department

poster [pɔste] *tr* to post ‖ *ref* to lie in wait

postérité [pɔsterite] *f* posterity

posthume [pɔstym] *adj* posthumous

postiche [pɔstiʃ] *adj* false; detachable ‖ *m* toupee; switch, false hair

pos·tier [pɔstje] **-tière** [tjɛr] *mf* postal clerk

postscolaire [pɔstskɔlɛr] *adj* adult (*education*); extension (*courses*)

post-scriptum [pɔstskriptɔm] *m invar* postscript

postu·lant [pɔstylɑ̃] **-lante** [lɑ̃t] *mf* applicant, candidate; postulant

postuler [pɔstyle] *tr* to apply for ‖ *intr* to apply; **postuler pour** to represent (*a client*)

posture [pɔstyr] *f* posture; situation

pot [po] *m* pot; pitcher, jug; jar; can; **avoir du pot** (coll) to be lucky; **découvrir le pot aux roses** (coll) to discover the secret; **payer les pots cassés** (coll) to pay the piper; **pot à bière** beer mug; **pot à fleurs** flowerpot; **pot catalytique** (aut) catalytic converter; **pot de café** coffee mug; **pot de chambre** chamber pot; **pot d'échappement** (aut) muffler; **pot de noir** cloudy weather; **pot d'étain** pewter tankard; **tourner autour du pot** (coll) to beat about the bush

potable [pɔtabl] *adj* drinkable; (coll) acceptable, passable

potache [pɔtaʃ] *m* (coll) schoolboy

potage [pɔtaʒ] *m* soup; **potage à vermicelle** noodle soup; **potage de maïs** hominy; **pour tout potage** (lit) all told

pota·ger [pɔtaʒe] **-gère** [ʒɛr] *adj* vegetable ‖ *m* vegetable garden; dinner pail

potasse [pɔtas] *f* potash

potasser [pɔtase] *tr* (coll) to bone up on ‖ *intr* (coll) to grind away

potas·seur [pɔtasœr] **-seuse** [søz] *mf* (coll) grind

potassium [pɔtasjɔm] *m* potassium

pot-au-feu [pɔtofø] *adj invar* (coll) homeloving ‖ *m invar* beef stew

pot-de-vin [podvɛ̃] *m* (*pl* **pots-de-vin**) bribe, money under the table

po·teau [pɔto] *m* (*pl* **-teaux**) post, pole; **franchir le poteau** to reach the goal (*to succeed*); **poteau de but** goal post; **poteau indicateur** signpost

pote·lé -lée [pɔtle] *adj* chubby

potence [pɔtɑ̃s] *f* gallows; bracket

potentat [pɔtɑ̃ta] *m* potentate

poten·tiel -tielle [pɔtɑ̃sjɛl] *adj & m* potential

poterie [pɔtri] *f* pottery; metalware; **poterie mordorée** lusterware

poterne [pɔtɛrn] *f* postern

potiche [pɔtiʃ] *f* large Oriental vase; (fig) figurehead

potin [pɔtɛ̃] *m* piece of gossip; racket; **faire du potin** (coll) to raise a row; **potins** gossip

potiner [pɔtine] *intr* to gossip

potion [posjɔ̃] *f* potion

potiron [pɔtirɔ̃] *m* pumpkin; **potiron lumineux** jack-o'-lantern

pou [pu] *m* (*pl* **poux**) louse

poubelle [pubɛl] *f* garbage can

pouce [pus] *m* thumb; big toe; inch; **manger sur le pouce** (coll) to eat on the run

poudre [pudr] *f* powder; face powder; **en poudre** powdered; granulated (*sugar*); **il n'a pas inventé la poudre** (coll) he's not so smart; **jeter de la poudre aux yeux de** to deceive; **poudre à pâte** baking powder; **poudre dentifrice** tooth powder; **se mettre de la poudre** to powder one's nose

poudrer [pudre] *tr* to powder

poudrerie [pudrəri] *f* powder mill

pou•dreux [pudrø] **-dreuse** [drøz] *adj* powdery; dusty || *f* sugar shaker

poudrier [pudrije] *m* compact

poudrière [pudrijɛr] *f* powder magazine; (fig) powder keg

poudroyer [pudrwaje] §47 *intr* to raise the dust; shine through the dust

pouf [puf] *m* hassock, pouf || *interj* plop!; **faire pouf** (slang) to flop

pouffer [pufe] *intr* to burst out laughing

pouil•leux [pujø] **-leuse** [jøz] *adj* lousy; sordid || *mf* person covered with lice

pouillot [pujo] *m* (orn) warbler

poulailler [pulaje] *m* henhouse; (theat) peanut gallery

poulain [pulɛ̃] *m* colt, foal

poule [pul] *f* hen; chicken; (*in games*) pool; jackpot; (turf) sweepstakes; (coll) skirt, dame; (slang) tart, mistress; **ma poule** (coll) my pet; **poule au pot** chicken stew; **poule de luxe** (slang) high-class prostitute; call girl; **poule d'Inde** turkey hen; **poule mouillée** (coll) milksop, coward; **tuer la poule aux œufs d'or** to kill the goose that lays the golden eggs

poulet [pulɛ] *m* chicken; (coll) love letter; (slang) cop; **mon petit poulet** (coll) my pet; **poulet d'Inde** turkey cock

poulette [pulɛt] *f* pullet; (coll) gal; **ma poulette** (coll) darling

pouliche [pulif] *f* filly

poulie [puli] *f* pulley; block

pou•lot [pulo] **-lotte** [lɔt] *mf* child, kid, lovie, baby (*term of affection*); **attention aux petits poulots** (*public sign*) watch children

poulpe [pulp] *m* octopus

pouls [pu] *m* pulse; **tâter le pouls à** to feel the pulse of

poumon [pumɔ̃] *m* lung

poupe [pup] *f* (naut) stern, poop

poupée [pupe] *f* doll; dummy; sore finger; (mach) headstock

pou•pon [pupɔ̃] **-ponne** [pɔn] *mf* baby; chubby-faced youngster

pouponnière [pupɔnjɛr] *f* nursery

pour [pur] *m*—**le pour et le contre** the pros and the cons || *adv*—**pour lors** then; **pour peu que** however little; **pour que** in order that; **pour . . . que** however, e.g., **pour charmante qu'elle soit** however charming she may be || *prep* for; in order to; **pour ainsi dire** so to speak; **pour cent** percent

pourboire [purbwar] *m* tip

pour•ceau [purso] *m* (*pl* **-ceaux**) swine, hog, pig

pourcentage [pursɑ̃taʒ] *m* percentage

pourchasser [purʃase] *tr* to hound

pourlécher [purleʃe] §10 *ref* to smack one's lips

pourparlers [purparle] *mpl* talks, parley, conference

pourpoint [purpwɛ̃] *m* doublet

pourpre [purpr] *adj* purple || *m* purple (*violescent*) || *f* purple (*deep red, crimson*)

pourquoi [purkwa] *m* why; **le pourquoi et le comment** the why and the wherefore || *adv &* *conj* why; **pourquoi pas?** why not?

pour•ri -rie [puri] *adj* rotten; spoiled || *m* rotten part

pourrir [purir] *tr, intr, & ref* to rot; spoil; corrupt

pourriture [purityr] *f* rot; decay; corruption

poursuite [pursɥit] *f* pursuit; (aer) tracking; (law) action, suit; (coll) spotlight

poursui•vant [pursɥivɑ̃] **-vante** [vɑ̃t] *mf* pursuer; (law) plaintiff

poursuivre [pursɥivr] §67 *tr* to pursue, chase; proceed with; persecute; sue || *intr* to continue || *ref* to be continued

pourtant [purtɑ̃] *adv* however, nevertheless, yet

pourtour [purtur] *m* circumference

pourvoi [purvwa] *m* (law) appeal

pourvoir [purvwar] §54, §95 *tr*—**pourvoir de** to supply with, provide with; favor with || *intr*—**pourvoir à** to provide for, attend to || *ref* (law) to appeal

pour•voyeur [purvwajœr] **-voyeuse** [vwajœz] *mf* provider, supplier; caterer; **pourvoyeurs** gun crew

pourvu que [purvykə] *conj* provided that

pousse [pus] *f* shoot, sprout

pous•sé -sée [puse] *adj* elaborate; searching, exhaustive || *f* push, shove; thrust; rise; pressure; (rok) thrust

pousse-café [puskafe] *m invar* liqueur

pousser [puse] §96, §100 *tr* to push, shove, egg on, urge; utter (*a cry*); heave (*a sigh*); **pousser plus loin** to carry further || *intr* to push, shove; grow; push on || *ref* to push oneself forward

poussette [pusɛt] *f* baby carriage

poussier [pusje] *m* coal dust

poussière [pusjɛr] *f* dust; powder; **poussière d'eau** spray; **une poussière** a trifle; **une poussière de** a lot of

poussié•reux [pusjerø] **-reuse** [røz] *adj* dusty; powdery

pous•sif [pusif] **-sive** [siv] *adj* wheezy

poussin [pusɛ̃] *m* chick

poussoir [puswar] *m* push button

poutre [putr] *f* beam; joist; girder

poutrelle [putrɛl] *f* small girder

pouvoir [puvwar] *m* power; **pouvoir d'achat** purchasing power ‖ §55, §95 *tr* to be able to do; **je n'y puis rien** I can't or cannot help it, I can do nothing about it ‖ *intr* to be able; **on ne peut mieux** couldn't be better; **on ne peut plus** I (we, they, etc.) can do no more; I'm (we're, they're, etc.) all in ‖ *aux* used to express 1) ability, e.g., **elle peut prédire l'avenir** she is able to predict the future, she can predict the future; 2) permission, e.g., **vous pouvez partir** you may go; e.g., **puis-je partir?** may I go?; 3) possibility, e.g., **il peut pleuvoir** it may rain; e.g., **il a pu oublier son parapluie** he may have forgotten his umbrella; 4) optative, e.g., **puisse-t-il venir!** may he come! ‖ *impers ref*—**il se peut que** it is possible that, e.g., **il se peut qu'il vienne ce soir** it is possible that he may come this evening, he may come this evening; **il se pourrait bien que** it might well be that, e.g., **il se pourrait bien qu'il vînt ce soir** it might well be that he will come this evening, he might come this evening ‖ *ref* to be possible; **cela ne se peut pas** that is not possible

pragmatique [pragmatik] *adj* pragmatic(al)

Prague [prag] Prague

prairie [prɛri], [preri] *f* meadow; **les Prairies** the prairie

praticable [pratikabl] *adj* practicable; passable ‖ *m* practicable stage property; (mov, telv) camera platform

prati·cien [pratisjɛ̃] **-cienne** [sjɛn] *mf* practitioner

prati·quant [pratikɑ̃] **-quante** [kɑ̃t] *adj* practicing (*e.g., Catholic*); churchy ‖ *mf* churchgoer

pratique [pratik] *adj* practical ‖ *f* practice; contact, company; customer; **libre pratique** freedom of worship; (naut) freedom from quarantine

pratiquement [pratikmɑ̃] *adv* practically, in practice

pratiquer [pratike] *tr* to practice; cut, make (*e.g., a hole*); frequent; read a great deal of ‖ *intr* to practice (*said, e.g., of doctor*); practice one's religion ‖ *ref* to be practiced, done; rule, prevail (*said of prices*)

pré [pre] *m* meadow; **pré et marée** surf and turf; **sur le pré** on the field of honor (*dueling ground*)

préalable [prealabl] *adj* previous; preliminary ‖ *m* prerequisite; **au préalable** before, in advance

préambule [preɑ̃byl] *m* preamble

préau [preo] *m* (*pl* **préaux**) yard

préavis [preavi] *m* advance warning; **avec préavis** person-to-person (*telephone call*)

précaire [prekɛr] *adj* precarious

précaution [prekosjɔ̃] *f* precaution

précautionner [prekosjone] *tr* to caution ‖ *intr* to be on one's guard

précaution·neux [prekosjɔnø] **-neuse** [nøz] *adj* precautious

précédemment [presedamɑ̃] *adv* before, previously

précé·dent [presedɑ̃] **-dente** [dɑ̃t] *adj* preceding ‖ *m* precedent

précéder [presede] §10 *tr* & *intr* to precede

précepte [presɛpt] *m* precept

précep·teur [presɛptœr] **-trice** [tris] *mf* tutor

prêche [prɛʃ] *m* sermon

prêcher [preʃe] *tr* to preach; preach to ‖ *intr* to preach; **prêcher d'exemple** to practice what one preaches

prê·cheur [preʃœr] **-cheuse** [ʃøz] *adj* preaching ‖ *mf* sermonizer

pré·cieux [presjø] **-cieuse** [sjøz] *adj* precious; valuable; affected

préciosité [presjozite] *f* preciosity (*French literary style corresponding to English euphuism*)

précipice [presipis] *m* precipice

précipi·té -tée [presipite] *adj* hurried, precipitous ‖ *m* precipitate

précipiter [presipite] *tr* to hurl ‖ *ref* to hurl oneself; precipitate; hurry, rush

pré·cis [presi] **-cise** [siz] *adj* precise; sharp, e.g., **trois heures précises** three o'clock sharp ‖ *m* abstract, summary

précisément [presizemɑ̃] *adv* precisely, exactly; clearly, accurately

préciser [presize] *tr* to specify ‖ *intr* to be precise ‖ *ref* to become clear; take shape, jell

précision [presizjɔ̃] *f* precision; **précisions** data

préci·té -tée [presite] *adj* aforementioned

précoce [prekɔs] *adj* precocious; (bot) early

précon·çu -çue [prekɔ̃sy] *adj* preconceived

préconiser [prekɔnize] *tr* to advocate, recommend

précurseur [prekyrsœr] *adj masc* precursory ‖ *m* forerunner, harbinger

prédateur [predatœr] *adj masc* predatory ‖ *m* predatory animal

prédécesseur [predesesœr] *m* predecessor

prédicateur [predikatœr] *m* preacher

prédiction [prediksjɔ̃] *f* prediction

prédire [predir] §40 *tr* to predict

prédisposer [predispoze] *tr* to predispose

prédomi·nant [predɔminɑ̃] **-nante** [nɑ̃t] *adj* predominant

préémi·nent [preeminɑ̃] **-nente** [nɑ̃t] *adj* preeminent

préfabri·qué -quée [prefabrike] *adj* prefabricated

préface [prefas] *f* preface

préfacer [prefase] §51 *tr* to preface

préfecture [prefɛktyr] *f* prefecture; **préfecture de police** police headquarters

préférable [preferabl] *adj* preferable

préférence [preferɑ̃s] *f* preference

préférer [prefere] §10, §95 *tr* to prefer

préfet [prefɛ] *m* prefect; **préfet de police** police commissioner

préfixe [prefiks] *m* prefix

préfixer [prefikse] *tr* to prefix
préhistorique [preistɔrik] *adj* prehistoric
préjudice [preʒydis] *m* prejudice, detriment; **porter préjudice à** to injure, to harm; **sans préjudice de** without affecting
préjudiciable [preʒydisjabl] *adj* detrimental
préjudicier [preʒydisje] *intr*—**préjudicier à** to harm, damage
préjugé [preʒyʒe] *m* prejudice
préjuger [preʒyʒe] §38 *tr* to foresee ‖ *intr*—**préjuger de** to prejudge
prélart [prelar] *m* tarpaulin
prélasser [prelɑse] *ref* to lounge
prélat [prela] *m* prelate
prélèvement [prelɛvmɑ̃] *m* deduction; sample; levy
prélever [prelve] §2 *tr* to set aside, deduct; take (*a sample*); levy; **prélever à** to take from
préliminaire [preliminɛr] *adj & m* preliminary
prélude [prelyd] *m* prelude
préluder [prelyde] *intr* to warm up (*said of singer, musician, etc.*); **préluder à** to prelude
prématu•ré -rée [prematyre] *adj* premature
préméditer [premedite] *tr* to premeditate
prémices [premis] *fpl* first fruits; beginning
pre•mier [prəmje] **-mière** [mjɛr] §92 *adj* first; raw (*materials*); prime (*number*); the First, e.g., **Jean premier** John the First ‖ (when standing before noun) *adj* first; prime (*minister*); maiden (*voyage*); early (*infancy*) ‖ *m* first; **jeune premier** leading man; **premier de cordée** leader ‖ *f* first; first class; (theat) première; **jeune première** leading lady ‖ *pron* (*masc & fem*) first
premièrement [prəmjɛrmɑ̃] *adv* firstly, first, in the first place, to begin with
premier-né [prəmjene] **-née** [ne] (*pl* **premiers-nés**) *adj & mf* first-born
prémisse [premis] *f* premise
prémonition [premɔnisjɔ̃] *f* premonition
prémunir [premynir] *tr* to forewarn ‖ *ref*—**se prémunir contre** to protect oneself against
pre•nant [prənɑ̃] **-nante** [nɑ̃t] *adj* sticky; winning, pleasing
prendre [prɑ̃dr] §56 *tr* to take; take on; take up; catch; get (*to obtain and bring*); steal (*a kiss*); buy (*a ticket*); make (*an appointment*); **à tout prendre** all things considered; **prendre de l'âge** to be getting old; **prendre la mer** to take to sea; **prendre l'eau** to leak; **prendre le large** to take to the open sea; **prendre q.ch. à qn** to take s.th. from s.o.; charge s.o. s.th. (*i.e., a certain sum of money*); **prendre son temps** to take one's time ‖ *intr* to catch (*said of fire*); take root; form (*said of ice*); set (*said of mortar*); stick (*to a pan or dish*); catch on (*said of a style*); to turn (*right or left*); **prendre à droite** to bear to the right; **qu'est-ce qui lui prend?** what's come over him? ‖ §96 *ref* to get caught, catch (*e.g., on a nail*); congeal; clot; curdle; jam; take from each other; **pour qui se prend-il?** who does he think he is?; **s'en prendre à qn de q.ch.** to

blame s.o. for s.th.; **se prendre à** to begin to; **se prendre d'amitié** to strike up a friendship; **se prendre de vin** to get drunk; **s'y prendre** to go about it
pre•neur [prənœr] **-neuse** [nøz] *mf* taker; buyer; payee; lessee
prenne [prɛn] *v* (**prennes, prennent**) see **prendre**
prénom [prenɔ̃] *m* first name
prénommer [prenɔme] *tr* to name ‖ *ref*—**il (elle, etc.) se prénomme** his (her, etc.) first name is
préoccupation [preɔkypasjɔ̃] *f* preoccupation
préoccuper [preɔkype] *tr* to preoccupy ‖ *ref*—**se préoccuper de** to pay attention to; be concerned about
prépara•teur [preparatœr] **-trice** [tris] *mf* laboratory assistant
préparatifs [preparatif] *mpl* preparations
préparation [preparasjɔ̃] *f* preparation; notice, warning
préparatoire [preparatwar] *adj* preparatory
préparer [prepare] §96, §100 *tr, intr, & ref* to prepare
prépondé•rant [prepɔ̃derɑ̃] **-rante** [rɑ̃t] *adj* preponderant
prépo•sé -sée [prepoze] *mf* employee, clerk; mail carrier, postman; **préposé de la douane** customs officer; **préposée au vestiaire** hatcheck person, hatcheck girl
préposer [prepoze] *tr*—**préposer qn à q.ch.** to put s.o. in charge of s.th.
préposition [prepozisjɔ̃] *f* preposition
prérogative [prerɔgativ] *f* prerogative
près [prɛ] *adv* near; **à beaucoup près** by far; **à cela près** except for that; **à peu d'exceptions près** with few exceptions; **à peu près** about, practically; **à . . . près** except for; within, e.g., **je peux vous dire l'heure à cinq minutes près** I can tell you what time it is within five minutes; **au plus près** to the nearest point; **de près** close; closely; **ici près** near here; **près de** near; nearly, about; alongside, at the side of; **près de + inf** about to + *inf;* **tout près** nearby, right here ‖ *prep* near; to, at
présage [prezaʒ] *m* presage, foreboding
présager [prezaʒe] §38 *tr* to presage, forebode; anticipate
pré-salé [presale] *m* (*pl* **prés-salés**) salt-meadow sheep; salt-meadow mutton
presbyte [prɛsbit] *adj* far-sighted ‖ *mf* far-sighted person
presbytère [prɛsbitɛr] *m* presbytery
presbyté•rien [prɛsbiterjɛ̃] **-rienne** [rjɛn] *adj & mf* Presbyterian
presbytie [prɛsbisi] *f* far-sightedness
préscolaire [preskɔlɛr] *adj* preschool
prescription [preskripsjɔ̃] *f* prescription
prescrire [preskrir] §25, §97, §98 *tr* to prescribe ‖ *ref* to be prescribed
préséance [preseɑ̃s] *f* precedence
présélection [preselɛksjɔ̃] *f*—**présélection des candidats** screening of candidates

présence [prezɑ̃s] *f* presence; attendance; **en présence** face to face; under consideration

pré•sent [prezɑ̃] **-sente** [zɑ̃t] *adj* present ‖ *m* present, gift; (gram) present; **les présents** those present

présentable [prezɑ̃tabl] *adj* presentable

présenta•teur [prezɑ̃tatœr] **-trice** [tris] *mf* (rad) announcer; (telv) anchor; **présentateur de disques** disk jockey

présentateur-tronc [prezɑ̃tatœrtrɔ̃] *m* (telv) anchorman

présentation [prezɑ̃tasjɔ̃] *f* presentation; introduction; appearance; look, form (*of a new product*)

presentatrice-tronc [prezɑ̃tatristrɔ̃] *f* (telv) anchor

présentement [prezɑ̃tmɑ̃] *adv* right now

présenter [prezɑ̃te] *tr* to present; introduce; offer; pay (*one's respects*) ‖ *ref* to present oneself; present itself; **se présenter à** to be a candidate for

présérie [preseri] *f* (com) trial run, sample run

préservatif [prezɛrvatif] *m* preventive; condom, prophylactic

préserver [prezɛrve] *tr* to preserve

présidence [prezidɑ̃s] *f* presidency; chairmanship; presidential mansion

prési•dent [prezidɑ̃] **-dente** [dɑ̃t] *mf* president; chairperson; chairman; presiding judge ‖ *f* president's wife; chairwoman; **madame la présidente** madam chairman

présiden•tiel -tielle [prezidɑ̃sjɛl] *adj* presidential

présider [prezide] *tr* to preside over ‖ *intr* to preside; **présider à** to preside over

présomp•tif [prezɔ̃ptif] **-tive** [tiv] *adj* presumptive, presumed

présomption [prezɔ̃psjɔ̃] *f* presumption

présomp•tueux [prezɔ̃ptɥø] **-tueuse** [tɥøz] *adj* presumptuous

présonorisation [presɔnɔrizasjɔ̃] *f* playback

presque [prɛsk(ə)] *adv* almost, nearly; **presque jamais** hardly ever; **presque personne** scarcely anybody

presqu'île [prɛskil] *f* peninsula

pres•sant [presɑ̃] **-sante** [sɑ̃t] *adj* pressing, urgent

presse [prɛs] *f* press; hurry, rush; crowd; hand screw, clamp; **mettre sous presse** to go to press; **presse typographique** printing press

pres•sé -sée [prese] §93 *adj* pressed; pressing, urgent; squeezed

presse-bouton [prɛsbutɔ̃] *adj invar* pushbutton (*warfare*)

presse-citron [prɛssitrɔ̃] *m invar* lemon squeezer

pressentiment [presɑ̃timɑ̃] *m* presentiment, foreboding

pressentir [presɑ̃tir] §41 *tr* to have a foreboding of; sound out

presse-papiers [prɛspapje] *m invar* paperweight

presse-purée [prɛspyre] *m invar* potato masher

presser [prese], [prɛse] §97 *tr* to press; squeeze; hurry, hasten ‖ *intr* to be urgent ‖ *ref* to hurry; **se presser à** to crowd around

pressing [presiŋ] *m* dry cleaner's

pression [prɛsjɔ̃] *f* pressure; snap fastener; **à la pression** on draught; **pression artérielle** blood pressure

pressoir [prɛswar] *m* press

pressurer [presyre] *tr* to press, squeeze; bleed white, wring money out of

pressuriser [presyrize] *tr* to pressurize

prestance [prɛstɑ̃s] *f* commanding appearance, dignified bearing

prestation [prɛstasjɔ̃] *f* taking (*of oath*); tax; allotment, allowance, benefit; services; performance; **prestation à domicile** (culin) catering

preste [prɛst] *adj* nimble

prestidigita•teur [prɛstidiʒitatœr] **-trice** [tris] *mf* magician

prestidigitation [prɛstidiʒitasjɔ̃] *f* sleight of hand, legerdemain

prestige [prɛstiʒ] *m* prestige; illusion, magic

presti•gieux [prɛstiʒjø] **-gieuse** [ʒjøz] *adj* prestigious, famous; marvelous

présumer [prezyme] §95, §97 *tr* to presume; presume to be ‖ *intr* to presume; **présumer de** to presume upon

présupposer [presypoze] *tr* to presuppose

présure [prezyr] *f* rennet

prêt [prɛ] **prête** [prɛt] §92 *adj* ready; **prêt à porter** ready-to-wear, ready-made; **prêt à tout** ready for anything ‖ *m* loan

prêt-à-monter [prɛtamɔ̃te] *m* (*pl* **prets-à-monter** [prɛzamɔ̃te]) kit

prétantaine [pretɑ̃tɛn] *f*—**courir la prétantaine** (coll) to be on the loose; (coll) to have many love affairs

prêt-à-porter [prɛtaporte] *m* (*pl* **prêts-à-porter** [prɛtaporte]) ready-to-wear, ready-made clothes

prêt-bail [prɛbaj] *m invar* lend-lease

préten•dant [pretɑ̃dɑ̃] **-dante** [dɑ̃t] *mf* pretender ‖ *m* suitor

prétendre [pretɑ̃dr] §95, §96 *tr* to claim; require ‖ *intr*—**prétendre à** to aspire to; lay claim to

préten•du -due [pretɑ̃dy] *adj* so-called, alleged ‖ *m* fiancé ‖ *f* fiancée

prête-nom [prɛtnɔ̃] *m* (*pl* **-noms**) dummy, figurehead, straw man

préten•tieux [pretɑ̃sjø] **-tieuse** [sjøz] *adj* pretentious

prétention [pretɑ̃sjɔ̃] *f* pretention, pretense; claim, pretensions

prêter [prete], [prɛte] *tr* to lend; give (*e.g., help*); pay (*attention*); take (*an oath*); impart (*e.g., luster*); attribute, ascribe *to* lend; stretch; **prêter à** to lend itself to ‖ *ref*—**se prêter à** to lend itself to; be a party to; countenance; indulge in

prê•teur [pretœr] **-teuse** [tøz] *mf* lender; **prêteur sur gages** pawnbroker

prétexte [pretɛkst] *m* pretext; **sous des prétex-**

tes fallacieux under false pretenses, under false colors

prétexter [pretɛkste] *tr* to give as a pretext

prétonique [pretɔnik] *adj* pretonic

prêtre [prɛtr] *m* priest

prêtresse [prɛtrɛs] *f* priestess

prêtrise [pretriz] *f* priesthood

preuve [prœv] *f* proof, evidence; **preuve d'acidité** (chem) litmus test; **preuve déterminante** *or* **décisive** (fig) litmus test

preux [prø] *adj masc* valiant ‖ *m* doughty knight

prévaloir [prevalwar] §71 (*subj* **prévale,** etc.) *intr* to prevail ‖ *ref*—**se prévaloir de** to avail oneself of; pride oneself on

prévarication [prevarikɑsjɔ̃] *f* breach of trust

prévariquer [prevarike] *intr* to betray one's trust

prévenance [prevnɑ̃s] *f* kindness, thoughtfulness

préve•nant [prevnɑ̃] **-nante** [nɑ̃t] *adj* attentive, considerate; prepossessing

prévenir [prevnir] §72 *tr* to anticipate; avert, forestall; ward off, prevent; notify, inform; bias, prejudice

préven•tif [prevɑ̃tif] **-tive** [tiv] *adj* preventive; pretrial (*detention*)

prévention [prevɑ̃sjɔ̃] *f* bias, prejudice; predisposition; custody, imprisonment; prevention (*of accidents*); **prévention routière** traffic police; road safety

préve•nu -nue [prevny] *adj* biased, prejudiced; forewarned; accused ‖ *mf* prisoner, accused, defendant

prévision [previzjɔ̃] *f* anticipation, estimate; **prévision du temps** weather forecast; **prévisions** expectations

prévoir [prevwar] §57 *tr* to foresee, anticipate; forecast

prévoyance [prevwajɑ̃s] *f* foresight

pré•voyant [prevwajɑ̃] **-voyante** [vwajɑ̃t] *adj* far-sighted, provident

prie-dieu [pridjø] *m invar* prie-dieu ‖ *f* praying mantis

prier [prije] §96, §97, §99 *tr* to ask, beg; pray (*God*); **je vous en prie!** I beg your pardon!; by all means!; you are welcome!; please have some!; **je vous prie!** please!; **prier qn de** + *inf* to ask, beg s.o. to + *inf* ‖ *intr* to pray

prière [prijɛr] *f* prayer; **prière de ...** please ...; **prière de faire suivre** please forward; **prière de garder jusqu'à l'arrivée** please hold until arrival; **prière d'insérer** publisher's insert for reviewers

primaire [primɛr] *adj* primary; first (*offender*); (coll) narrow-minded ‖ *m* (elec) primary; (coll) primitive

primat [prima] *m* (eccl) primate

primate [primat] *m* (zool) primate

primauté [primote] *f* supremacy

prime [prim] *adj* early (*youth*); (math) prime ‖ *f* premium; bonus; free gift; (eccl) prime; **prime de transport** traveling expenses

primer [prime] *tr* to excel; take priority over; award a prize to

primerose [primroz] *f* hollyhock

primesau•tier [primsotje] **-tière** [tjɛr] *adj* impulsive, quick

primeur [primœr] *f* freshness; first fruit; early vegetable; (journ) beat, scoop; **primeurs** fruits and vegetables out of season

primevère [primvɛr] *f* primrose

primi•tif [primitif] **-tive** [tiv] *adj* primitive; original, early; primary (*colors; tense*) ‖ *mf* primitive

primo [primo] *adv* firstly

primor•dial -diale [primɔrdjal] *adj* (*pl* **-diaux** [djo]) primordial; fundamental, prime, primary

prince [prɛ̃s] *m* prince; **le Prince Charmant** Prince Charming; **prince consort** prince consort; **prince de Galles** Prince of Wales

princesse [prɛ̃sɛs] *f* princess

prin•cier [prɛ̃sje] **-cière** [sjɛr] *adj* princely

princi•pal -pale [prɛ̃sipal] *adj* & *m* (*pl* **-paux** [po]) principal, chief

principauté [prɛ̃sipote] *f* principality

principe [prɛ̃sip] *m* principle; beginning; source

printa•nier [prɛ̃tanje] **-nière** [njɛr] *adj* spring; springlike

printemps [prɛ̃tɑ̃] *m* spring; springtime; **au printemps** in the spring

priorité [prijɔrite] *f* priority; right of way; **de priorité** preferred (*stock*); main (*road*); **priorité à droite, priorité à gauche** (*public sign*) yield; **priorité piétons** pedestrian right of way

pris [pri] **prise** [priz] *adj* set, frozen; **être pris** to be busy; **pris de vin** drunk ‖ *f* capture, seizure; taking; hold; setting; tap, faucet; (med) dose; (naut) prize; **donner prise à** to lay oneself open to; **être aux prises avec** to be struggling with; **hors de prise** out of gear; **lâcher prise** to let go; **mettre en prise** (aut) to put into gear; **prise d'air** ventilator; **prise d'antenne** (rad) lead-in; **prise d'armes** military parade; **prise d'eau** water faucet; hydrant; **prise de bec** (coll) quarrel; **prise de conscience** awakening, awareness; **prise de courant** (elec) plug; (elec) tap, outlet; **prise de position** statement of opinion; **prise de sang** blood specimen; **prise de son** recording; **prise de tabac** pinch of snuff; **prise de terre** (elec) ground connection; **prise de vue(s)** (phot) shot, picture taking; **prise de vues aérienne** aerial survey; **prise de vue directe** (telv) live broadcast; **prise directe** high gear ‖ *v* see **prendre**

prisée [prize] *f* appraisal

priser [prize] *tr* to value; snuff up ‖ *intr* to take snuff

pri•seur [prizœr] **-seuse** [zøz] *mf* snuffer ‖ *m* appraiser

prisme [prism] *m* prism

prison [prizɔ̃] *f* prison

prison•nier [prizɔnje] **-nière** [njɛr] *mf* prisoner

privautés [privote] *fpl* liberties

pri•vé -vée [prive] *adj* private; tame, pet ‖ *m* private life ‖ *v* see **priver**

priver [prive] §97 *tr* to deprive ‖ *ref* to deprive oneself; **se priver de** to do without, abstain from

privilège [privilɛʒ] *m* privilege

privilé•gié -giée [privileʒje] *adj* privileged; preferred (*stock*)

prix [pri] *m* price; prize; value; **à aucun prix** not at any price; by no means; **à tout prix** at all costs; **au prix de** at the price of; at the rate of; compared with; **dans mes prix** within my means; **grand prix** championship race; **hors de prix** at a prohibitive cost; **prix courant** list price; **prix de consolation** consolation prize; **prix de départ** upset price; **prix de détail** retail price; **prix de fabrique** factory price; **prix de gros** wholesale price; **prix de lancement** introductory offer; **prix de la vie** cost of living; **prix de location** rent; **prix de revient** cost price; **prix de sang** blood money; **prix de vente** selling price; **prix fixe** table d'hôte; **prix unique** variety store

probabilité [prɔbabilite] *f* probability

probable [prɔbabl] *adj* probable, likely

probablement [prɔbabləmɑ̃] *adv* probably

pro•bant [prɔbɑ̃] **-bante** [bɑ̃t] *adj* convincing; conclusive (*evidence*)

probatoire [prɔbatwar] *adj* experimental, preliminary

probe [prɔb] *adj* honest, upright

problème [prɔblɛm] *m* problem

procédé [prɔsede] *m* process; procedure; tip (*of cue*); **procédés** proceedings; behavior

procéder [prɔsede] §10, §96 *intr* to proceed; **procéder à** to carry out, conduct, undertake, perform; **procéder de** to arise from

procédure [prɔsedyr] *f* procedure; proceedings

procès [prɔsɛ] *m* lawsuit, case; trial; **intenter un procès à** to sue; to prosecute; **procès collectif** class action (suit); **sans autre forme de procès** then and there, without appeal

proces•sif -sive [prɔsesif] [siv] *adj* litigious

procession [prɔsesjɔ̃] *f* procession

processus [prɔsesys] *m* process

procès-verbal [prɔsɛvɛrbal] *m* (*pl* **-verbaux** [vɛrbo]) report; minutes; ticket (*e.g., for speeding*)

pro•chain [prɔʃɛ̃] **-chaine** [ʃɛn] *adj* next; impending; (lit) nearest, immediate; **la prochaine semaine** the next week; **la semaine prochaine** next week ‖ *m* neighbor, fellowman ‖ *f*—**à la prochaine!** (coll) so long!

prochainement [prɔʃɛnmɑ̃] *adv* shortly ‖ *interj* so long!

proche [prɔʃ] *adj* near; nearby; close (*relative*) ‖ **proches** *mpl* close relatives ‖ *adv*—**de proche en proche** little by little

proclamer [prɔklame] *tr* to proclaim

proclitique [prɔklitik] *adj & m* proclitic

procuration [prɔkyrasjɔ̃] *f* power of attorney; **par procuration** by proxy

procurer [prɔkyre] *tr & ref* to procure, get

procureur [prɔkyrœr] *m* attorney; **procureur de la république** district attorney; **procureur général** attorney general

prodige [prɔdiʒ] *m* prodigy; wonder

prodi•gieux [prɔdiʒjø] **-gieuse** [ʒjøz] *adj* prodigious, wonderful; terrific

prodigue [prɔdig] *adj* prodigal, lavish ‖ *mf* prodigal, spendthrift

prodiguer [prɔdige] *tr* to squander, waste; lavish ‖ *ref* to not spare oneself; show off

prodrome [prɔdrom] *m* harbinger; introduction

produc•teur [prɔdyktœr] **-trice** [tris] *adj* productive ‖ *mf* producer

produc•tif [prɔdyktif] **-tive** [tiv] *adj* productive; producing

production [prɔdyksjɔ̃] *f* production

produire [prɔdɥir] §19 *tr* to produce; create; introduce ‖ *ref* to take place; be produced; show up

produit [prɔdɥi] *m* product; proceeds; offspring; **produit de luxe** luxury item; **produit national brut (P.N.B.)** gross national product (G.N.P.); **produit pharmaceutique** patent medicine, drug; **produits agricoles** agricultural produce; **produits de beauté** cosmetics; **produits laitiers** dairy products

proémi•nent [prɔeminɑ̃] **-nente** [nɑ̃t] *adj* prominent, protuberant

profane [prɔfan] *adj* profane; lay, uninformed ‖ *mf* profane; layman

profaner [prɔfane] *tr* to profane; (fig) to prostitute

proférer [prɔfere] §10 *tr* to utter

professer [prɔfese] *tr* to profess; teach ‖ *intr* to teach

professeur [prɔfesœr] *m* teacher; professor; **professeur suppléant** substitute teacher

profession [prɔfesjɔ̃] *f* profession; occupation, trade

profession•nel -nelle [prɔfesjɔnɛl] *adj & mf* professional

profil [prɔfil] *m* profile; pattern; side face; cross section; skyline (*of city*)

profi•lé -lée [prɔfile] *adj* streamlined, aerodynamic

profiler [prɔfile] *tr* to profile ‖ *ref*—**se profiler sur** to stand out against

profit [prɔfi] *m* profit; **mettre à profit** to take advantage of; **profits et pertes** profit and loss

profitable [prɔfitabl] *adj* profitable

profiter [prɔfite] *intr* to profit; to thrive, grow; **profiter à qn** to benefit s.o.; **profiter de** to profit from, take advantage of

profi•teur [prɔfitœr] **-teuse** [tøz] *mf* profiteer

pro•fond [prɔfɔ̃] **-fonde** [fɔ̃d] *adj* profound; deep; low (*bow; voice*); **peu profond** shallow ‖ *m* depths ‖ *f* (slang) pocket ‖ **profond** *adv* deep

profondément [prɔfɔ̃demɑ̃] *adv* profoundly, deeply; soundly; deep

profondeur [prɔfɔ̃dœr] *f* depth

progéniture [prɔʒenityr] *f* progeny; off-spring, child

programma•teur [prɔgramatœr] **-trice** [tris] *mf* (mov, rad, telv) programer

programmation [prɔgramɑsjɔ̃] *f* programing

programme [prɔgram] *m* program; **programme de comptabilité** (comp) spreadsheet; **programme de prévoyance** retirement program; **programme des études** curriculum; **programme intensif** crash program

programmer [prɔgrame] *tr* to program

programmerie [prɔgramri] *f* (comp) software

program•meur [prɔgramœr] **-meuse** [møz] *mf* (comp) programer

progrès [prɔgrɛ] *m* progress; **faire des progrès** to make progress

progresser [prɔgrese] *intr* to progress

progres•sif [prɔgresif] **-sive** [siv] *adj* progressive

progressiste [prɔgresist] *adj & mf* progressive

prohiber [prɔibe] *tr* to prohibit

prohibition [prɔibisjɔ̃] *f* prohibition

proie [prwa], [prwɑ] *f* prey; **de proie** predatory; **en proie à** a prey to

projecteur [prɔʒɛktœr] *m* projector; searchlight; (mov) movie projector

projectile [prɔʒɛktil] *m* projectile; **projectile téléguidé** guided missile

projection [prɔʒɛksjɔ̃] *f* projection; **projection en boucle fermée** endless strip

projectionniste [prɔdʒɛk/ɔnist] *mf* projectionist

projet [prɔʒɛ] *m* project; draft; sketch, plan; **faire des projets** to make plans; **projet de loi** bill

projeter [prɔʒte] §34, §97 *tr* to project; pour fourth (*smoke*); cast (*a shadow*); plan ‖ *intr* to plan

prolétaire [prɔletɛr] *m* proletarian

prolétariat [prɔletarja] *m* proletariat

proléta•rien [prɔletarjɛ̃] **-rienne** [rjɛn] *adj* proletarian

proliférer [prɔlifere] §10 *intr* to proliferate

prolifique [prɔlifik] *adj* prolific

prolixe [prɔliks] *adj* prolix

prologue [prɔlɔg] *m* prologue; preface

prolongateur [prɔlɔ̃gatœr] *m* extension cord

prolongation [prɔlɔ̃gɑsjɔ̃] *f* extension (*of time*); overtime period

prolonger [prɔlɔ̃ʒe] §38 *tr* to prolong; extend ‖ *ref* to be prolonged; continue, extend

promenade [prɔmnad] *f* promenade; walk; ride; drive; sail; **faire une promenade (en auto, à cheval, à motocyclette, en bateau,** etc.) to take a ride; **promenade dans l'espace** space walk

promener [prɔmne] §2 *tr* to take for a walk; take for a ride; walk (*e.g., a dog*); take along; **envoyer promener qn** (coll) to send s.o. packing; **promener . . . sur** to run (*e.g., one's hand, eyes*) over ‖ *ref* to stroll; go for a walk, ride, drive, or sail; **allez vous promener!** get out of here!; **se promener dans l'espace** to spacewalk

prome•neur [prɔmnœr] **-neuse** [nøz] *mf* walker, stroller

promenoir [prɔmnwar] *m* ambulatory, cloister; (theat) standing room

promesse [prɔmɛs] *f* promise

promettre [prɔmɛtr] §42, §98 *tr* to promise; **promettre q.ch. à qn** to promise s.th. to s.o. ‖ *intr* to look promising; **promettre à qn de** + *inf* to promise s.o. to + *inf* ‖ §97 *ref* to promise oneself; **se promettre de** to resolve to

pro•mis [prɔmi] **-mise** [miz] *adj* promised; **promis à** headed for

promiscuité [prɔmiskɥite] *f* indiscriminate mixture; lack of privacy

promontoire [prɔmɔ̃twar] *m* promontory

promo•teur [prɔmotœr] **-trice** [tris] *mf* promoter; originator; **promoteur immobilier** housing developer

promotion [prɔmosjɔ̃] *f* promotion; uplift; class (*in school*)

promouvoir [prɔmuvwar] §45 (*pp* **promu**) *tr* to promote

prompt [prɔ̃] **prompte** [prɔ̃t] *adj* prompt, ready, quick

promptitude [prɔ̃tityd] *f* promptness

promulguer [prɔmylge] *tr* to promulgate

prône [pron] *m* homily

prôner [prone] *tr* to extol

pronom [prɔnɔ̃] *m* pronoun

pronomi•nal -nale [prɔnɔminal] *adj* (*pl* **-naux** [no]) pronominal; reflexive (*verb*)

pronon•cé -cée [prɔnɔ̃se] *adj* marked; sharp (*curve*); prominent (*nose*)

prononcer [prɔnɔ̃se] §51 *tr* to pronounce; utter; deliver (*a speech*); pass (*judgment*) ‖ *intr* to decide ‖ *ref* to be pronounced; express an opinion

prononciation [prɔnɔ̃sjɑsjɔ̃] *f* pronunciation

pronostic [prɔnɔstik] *m* prognosis; **pronostics sur les matchs de football** football pool

pronostiquer [prɔnɔstike] *tr* to prognosticate

propagande [prɔpagɑ̃d] *f* propaganda; publicity, advertising

propager [prɔpaʒe] §38 *tr* to propagate; spread ‖ *ref* to be propagated; spread

propédeutique [prɔpedøtik] *f* (educ) preliminary study

propension [prɔpɑ̃sjɔ̃] *f* propensity

prophète [prɔfɛt] *m* prophet

prophétesse [prɔfetɛs] *f* prophetess

prophétie [prɔfesi] *f* prophecy

prophétiser [prɔfetize] *tr* to prophesy

prophylactique [prɔfilaktik] *adj* prophylactic

propice [prɔpis] *adj* propitious; lucky (*star*)

proportion [prɔpɔrsjɔ̃] *f* proportion; **en proportion de** in proportion to

proportion•né -née [prɔpɔrsjɔne] *adj* proportionate

proportion•nel -nelle [prɔpɔrsjɔnɛl] *adj* proportional

proportionner [prɔpɔrsjɔne] *tr* to proportion

propos [prɔpo] *m* remark; purpose; **à ce propos**

in this connection; **à propos** by the way; timely, fitting; at the right moment; **à propos de** with regard to, concerning; **à tout propos** at every turn; **changer de propos** to change the subject; **de propos délibéré** on purpose; **des propos en l'air** idle talk; **hors de propos** out of place; irrelevant

proposer [prɔpoze] **§97, §98** *tr* to propose; nominate; recommend (*s.o.*) ‖ *ref* to have in mind; apply (*for a job*); **se proposer de** to intend to

proposition [prɔpozisjɔ̃] *f* proposition; proposal; clause

propre [prɔpr] *adj* clean, neat; original (*meaning*); proper (*name*); literal (*meaning*); **propre à** fit for, suited to ‖ (when standing before noun) *adj* own ‖ *m* characteristic; **au propre** in the literal sense; **c'est du propre!** (coll) what a dirty trick! **en propre** in one's own right

proprement [prɔprəmɑ̃] *adv* neatly; cleanly; properly; exactly, literally; strictly

pro•pret [prɔprɛ] **-prette** [prɛt] *adj* (coll) clean, bright

propreté [prɔprəte] *f* cleanliness, neatness

propriétaire [prɔprijetɛr] *mf* proprietor, owner; landowner ‖ *m* landlord ‖ *f* proprietress; landlady

propriété [prɔprijete] *f* property; propriety, appropriateness

propulseur [prɔpylsœr] *m* engine, motor; outboard motor; (rok) booster

propulsion [prɔpylsjɔ̃] *f* propulsion; **propulsion à quatre roues motrices** four-wheel drive; **propulsion à réaction** jet propulsion

prorata [prɔrata] *m invar*—**au prorata de** in proportion to

proroger [prɔrɔʒe] **§38** *tr* to postpone; extend; adjourn ‖ *ref* to be adjourned

prosaïque [prozaik] *adj* prosaic

prosateur [prozatœr] *m* prose writer

proscrire [prɔskrir] **§25** *tr* to proscribe; banish, outlaw

pros•crit [prɔskri] **-crite** [krit] *adj* banished ‖ *mf* outlaw

prose [proz] *f* prose; (coll) style (*of writing*)

prosélyte [prɔzelit] *mf* proselyte

prosodie [prɔzɔdi] *f* prosody

prospecter [prɔspɛkte] *tr & intr* to prospect

prospec•teur [prɔspɛktœr] **-trice** [tris] *mf* prospector

prospecteur-placier [prɔspɛktœrplasje] *m* head hunter (*for employment*)

prospectus [prɔspɛktys] *m* prospectus; handbill

prospère [prɔspɛr] *adj* prosperous

prospérer [prɔspere] **§10** *intr* to prosper, thrive

prospérité [prɔsperite] *f* prosperity

prostate [prɔstat] *f* prostate (gland)

prosternation [prɔstɛrnasjɔ̃] *f* prostration; groveling

prosterner [prɔstɛrne] *tr* to bend over ‖ *ref* to prostrate oneself; grovel

prostituée [prɔstitɥe] *f* prostitute

prostituer [prɔstitɥe] *tr* to prostitute

prostration [prɔstrasjɔ̃] *f* prostration

pros•tré -trée [prɔstre] *adj* prostrate

protagoniste [prɔtagɔnist] *m* protagonist

prote [prɔt] *m* (typ) foreman

protection [prɔtɛksjɔ̃] *f* protection; **protection civile** civil defense; **protection de données, protection de l'information** (comp) data protection

proté•gé -gée [prɔteʒe] *adj* guarded; arterial (*crossing*); **automatiquement protégé** failsafe ‖ *m* protégé, dependent; pet

protège-cahier [prɔtɛʒkaje] *m* (*pl* **-cahiers**) notebook cover

protège-livre [prɔtɛʒlivr] *m* (*pl* **-livres**) dust jacket

protège-oreille [prɔtɛʒɔrɛj] *m* earmuff

protège-slip [prɔtɛʒslip] *m* (*pl* **-slips** [slip]) panty liner

protéger [prɔteʒe] **§1** *tr* to protect; be a patron of; (comp) save

protège-tympan [prɔtɛʒtimpɑ̃] *m invar* ear plug

protéine [prɔtein] *f* protein

protes•tant [prɔtɛstɑ̃] **-tante** [tɑ̃t] *adj & mf* Protestant; protestant

protestation [prɔtɛstasjɔ̃] *f* protest

protester [prɔtɛste] **§97** *tr & intr* to protest; **protester de** to protest

protêt [prɔtɛ] *m* (com) protest

protocole [prɔtɔkɔl] *m* protocol

proton [prɔtɔ̃] *m* proton

protoplasme [prɔtɔplasm] *m* protoplasm

prototype [prɔtɔtip] *m* prototype

protozoaire [prɔtɔzɔɛr] *m* protozoan

protubérance [prɔtyberɑ̃s] *f* protuberance

proue [pru] *f* prow, bow

prouesse [pruɛs] *f* prowess

prouver [pruve] *tr* to prove

provenance [prɔvnɑ̃s] *f* origin; **en provenance de** from

proven•çal -çale [prɔvɑ̃sal] (*pl* **-çaux** [so]) *adj* Provençal ‖ *m* Provençal (*language*) ‖ (*cap*) *mf* Provençal (*person*)

provenir [prɔvnir] **§72** *intr* (*aux:* ETRE)—**provenir de** to come from

proverbe [prɔvɛrb] *m* proverb

providence [prɔvidɑ̃s] *f* providence

providen•tiel -tielle [prɔvidɑ̃sjɛl] *adj* providential

province [prɔvɛ̃s] *adj invar* (coll) provincial ‖ *f* province; **la province** the provinces (*all of France outside of Paris*)

proviseur [prɔvizœr] *m* headmaster

provision [prɔvizjɔ̃] *f* stock, store; deposit; **aller aux provisions** to go shopping; **faire provision de** to stock up on; **provision pour amortissement** depreciation allowance; **provisions** provisions, foodstuffs; **sans provision** bad (*check*)

provisoire [prɔvizwar] *adj* provisional, temporary; emergency

provo•cant [prɔvɔkɑ̃] **-cante** [kɑ̃t] *adj* provocative

provoquer [prɔvɔke] §96 *tr* to provoke; cause, bring about; arouse

proxénète [prɔksenɛt] *mf* procurer ‖ *m* pimp

proximité [prɔksimite] *f* proximity; **à proximité de** near

prude [pryd] *adj* prudish ‖ *f* prude

prudemment [prydamɑ̃] *adv* carefully, prudently

prudence [prydɑ̃s] *f* prudence

pru•dent [prydɑ̃] **-dente** [dɑ̃t] *adj* prudent

pruderie [prydri] *f* prudery

prud'homme [prydɔm] *m* arbitrator; (obs) solid citizen

prudhommesque [prydɔmɛsk] *adj* pompous

pruine [prɥin] *f* bloom

prune [pryn] *f* plum; **des prunes!** (slang) nuts!; **pour des prunes** (coll) for nothing

pru•neau [pryno] *m* (*pl* **-neaux**) prune; (slang) bullet

prunelle [prynɛl] *f* pupil (*of eye*); sloe; sloe gin; **jouer de la prunelle** (coll) to ogle; **prunelle de ses yeux** apple of his (one's, etc.) eye

prunellier [prynelje] *m* sloe, blackthorn

prunier [prynje] *m* plum tree

prus•sien [prysjɛ̃] **-sienne** [sjɛn] *adj* Prussian ‖ (*cap*) *mf* Prussian

P.-S. [peɛs] *m* (letterword) (**post-scriptum**) P.S.

psalmodier [psalmɔdje] *tr & intr* to speak in a singsong

psaume [psom] *m* psalm

psautier [psotje] *m* psalter

pseudonyme [psødɔnim] *adj* pseudonymous ‖ *m* pseudonym; nom de plume

psitt [psit] *interj* (coll) hist!

P.S.V. [peɛsve] *m* (letterword) (**pilotage sans visibilité**) blind flying

psychanalyse [psikanaliz] *f* psychoanalysis

psychanalyser [psikanalize] *tr* to psychoanalyze

psyché [psi/e] *f* psyche; cheval glass

psychédélique [psikedelik] *adj* psychedelic

psychiatre [psikjatr] *mf* psychiatrist

psychiatrie [psikjatri] *f* psychiatry

psychique [psi/ik] *adj* psychic

psychologie [psikɔlɔʒi] *f* psychology

psychologique [psikɔlɔʒik] *adj* psychologic(al)

psychologue [psikɔlɔg] *mf* psychologist

psychopathe [psikɔpat] *mf* psychopath

psychose [psikoz] *f* psychosis

psychotique [psikɔtik] *adj & mf* psychotic

ptomaïne [ptɔmain] *f* ptomaine

P.T.T. [petete] *fpl* (letterword) (**Postes, télégraphes et téléphones**) post office, telephone, and telegraph

pu [py] *v* see **pouvoir;** see **paître**

puant [pɥɑ̃] **puante** [pɥɑ̃t] *adj* stinking, fetid

puanteur [pɥɑ̃tœr] *f* stench, stink

pub [pyb] *abbr* (**publicité**) publicity; (rad, telv) commercial

puberté [pybɛrte] *f* puberty

pu•blic **-blique** [pyblik] *adj* public; notorious ‖ *m* public; audience

publication [pyblikɑsjɔ̃] *f* publication; proclamation; **publication assistée par ordinateur** desktop publishing

publiciste [pyblisist] *mf* public-relations expert

publicitaire [pyblisitɛr] *adj* advertising ‖ *m* advertising specialist

publicité [pyblisite] *f* publicity; advertising; (rad, telv) commercial; **publicité aérienne** skywriting

publier [pyblije] *tr* to publish; publicize, proclaim

puce [pys] *f* flea; (comp) chip; **mettre la puce à l'oreille à qn** (fig) to put a bug in s.o.'s ear

pu•ceau [pyso] **-celle** [sɛl] (*pl* **-ceaux**) *adj & mf* (coll) virgin ‖ *f* maid

puceron [pysrɔ̃] *m* plant louse

pudding [pudiŋ] *m* plum pudding

puddler [pydle] *tr* to puddle

pudeur [pydœr] *f* modesty

pudi•bond [pydibɔ̃] **-bonde** [bɔ̃d] *adj* prudish

pudibonderie [pydibɔ̃dri] *f* false modesty

pudique [pydik] *adj* modest, chaste

puer [pɥe] *tr* to reek of ‖ *intr* to stink

pué•ril **-rile** [pɥeri] *adj* puerile

puérilité [pɥerilite] *f* puerility

pugilat [pyʒila] *m* fight, brawl

pugiliste [pyʒilist] *m* pugilist

pugnace [pygnas] *adj* pugnacious

puî•né **-née** [pɥine] *adj* younger ‖ *mf* younger child

puis [pɥi] *adv* then; next; **et puis** besides; **et puis aprés?** (coll) what next? ‖ *v* see **pouvoir**

puisard [pɥizar] *m* drain, cesspool; sump

puisatier [pɥizatje] *m* well digger

puiser [pɥize] *tr* to draw (*water*); **puiser à** or **dans** to draw (*s.th.*) from ‖ *intr*—**puiser à** or **dans** to draw from or on; dip or reach into

puisque [pɥisk(ə)] *conj* since, as, seeing that

puissamment [pɥisamɑ̃] *adv* powerfully; exceedingly

puissance [pɥisɑ̃s] *f* power

puis•sant [pɥisɑ̃] **-sante** [sɑ̃t] *adj* powerful

puisse [pɥis] *v* (**puisses, puissions,** etc.) see **pouvoir**

puits [pɥi] *m* well; pit; (min) shaft; (naut) locker; **puits absorbant, puits perdu** cesspool; **puits de pétrole** oil well; **puits de science** fountain of knowledge

pull-over [pulɔvœr], [pylɔvɛr] *m* (*pl* **-overs**) sweater, pullover

pulluler [pylyle] *intr* to swarm, to teem

pulmonaire [pylmɔnɛr] *adj* pulmonary ‖ *f* (bot) lungwort

pulpe [pylp] *f* pulp

pulsation [pylsɑsjɔ̃] *f* pulsation; beat; pulse

pulsion [pylsjɔ̃] *f* (psychoanal) impulse

pulvérisateur [pylverizatœr] *m* spray, atomizer

pulvérisation [pylverisɑsjɔ̃] *f* (med) spray (*for nose or throat*)

pulvériser [pylverize] *tr* to pulverize; spray

punaise [pynɛz] *f* bug; bedbug; thumbtack

punch [pɔ̃ʃ] *m* punch (*drink*) ‖ [pœnʃ] *m* (boxing) punch
punching-ball [pœnʃiŋbol] *m* punching bag
punir [pynir] §97 *tr & intr* to punish
punition [pynisjɔ̃] *f* punishment
pupille [pypil], [pypij] *mf* ward ‖ *f* pupil (*of eye*)
pupitre [pypitr] *m* desk; stand, rack; lectern; console, controls; **pupitre à musique** music stand
pur pure [pyr] *adj* pure ‖ *mf* diehard; **les purs** the pure in heart
purée [pyre] *f* purée; mashed potatoes; (coll) wretch; **être dans la purée** (coll) to be broke; **purée de pois** (culin, fig) pea soup ‖ *interj* (slang) how awful!
pureté [pyrte] *f* purity
purga•tif [pyrgatif] **-tive** [tiv] *adj & m* purgative
purgatoire [pyrgatwar] *m* purgatory
purge [pyrʒ] *f* purge
purger [pyrʒe] §38 *tr* to purge; pay off (*e.g., a mortgage*); serve (*a sentence*)
purifier [pyrifje] *tr* to purify
puri•tain [pyritɛ̃] **-taine** [tɛn] *adj & mf* puritan; Puritan
pur-sang [pyrsɑ̃] *adj & m invar* thorough-bred
pus [py] *m* pus ‖ *v* (**put, pûmes,** etc.) see **pouvoir**
pusillanime [pyzilanim] *adj* pusillanimous
pustule [pystyl] *f* pimple, pustule

putain [pytɛ̃] *adj invar* (coll) amiable, agreeable ‖ *f* (vulg) whore
puta•tif [pytatif] **-tive** [tiv] *adj* (law) putative
putois [pytwa] *m* skunk, polecat
putréfier [pytrefje] *tr & ref* to decompose, rot
putride [pytrid] *adj* putrid
putt [pœt] *m* (golf) (*coup roulé*) putt
putter [pœtœr] *s* (golf) putter ‖ [pœte] *intr* to putt
putting [pœtiŋ] *m* (golf) putting
puy [pɥi] *m* volcanic peak
puzzle [pœzl] *m* jigsaw puzzle
p.-v. [peve] *m* (letterword) (**procès-verbal**) (coll) ticket, e.g., **attraper un p.-v.** to get a ticket
pygargue [pigarg] *m* osprey, fish hawk
pygmée [pigme] *m* pygmy
pygméen [pigmeɛ̃] **pygméenne** [pigmeɛn] *adj* pygmy
pyjama [piʒama] *m* pajamas; **un pyjama** a pair of pajamas
pylône [pilon] *m* pylon; tower
pyramide [piramid] *f* pyramid
Pyrénées [pirene] *fpl* Pyrenees
pyrite [pirit] *f* pyrites
pyrotechnie [pirɔtɛkni] *f* pyrotechnics
pyrotechnique [pirɔtɛknik] *adj* pyrotechnical
python [pitɔ̃] *m* python
pythonisse [pitɔnis] *f* pythoness
pyxide [piksid] *f* pyx

Q

Q, q [ky] *m invar* seventeenth letter of the French alphabet
Q.I. [kyi] *m* (letterword) (**quotient intellectuel**) I.Q.
quadrant [kwadrɑ̃], [kadrɑ̃] *m* (math) quadrant
quadrilatère [kwadrilatɛr] *m* quadrilateral
quadrupède [kwadrypɛd] *m* quadruped
quadruple [kwadrypl] *adj & m* quadruple
quadrupler [kwadryple] *tr & intr* to quadruple
quadru•plés -plées [kwadryple] *mfpl* quadruplets
quai [ke] *m* quay, wharf; platform (*e.g., in a railroad station*); embankment, levee; **amener à quai** to berth; **le Quai d'Orsay** the French foreign office
qua•ker [kwɛkœr], [kwakɛr] **-keresse** [krɛs] *mf* Quaker
qualifiable [kalifjabl] *adj* describable
qualification [kalifikasjɔ̃] *f* (sports) qualification (*testing to allow participation in a contest et activity*)
quali•fié -fiée [kalifje] *adj* qualified; qualifying; aggravated (*crime*); (*ouvrier; athlète*) qualified, e.g., **une équipe qualifiée** a qualified team (*a team that has passed the qualifying games*)

qualifier [kalifje] *tr & intr* to qualify
qualité [kalite] *f* quality; title, capacity; **avoir qualite pour** to be authorized to; **de première qualité** first-rate, upscale; **en qualité de** in the capacity of
quand [kɑ̃] *adv* when; how soon; **n'importe quand** anytime; **quand même** though, just the same ‖ *conj* when; **quand même** even if
quant [kɑ̃] *adv*—**quant à** as for, as to, as far as; **quant à cela** for that matter
quant-à-soi [kɑ̃taswa] *m* dignity, reserve; **rester** or **se tenir sur son quant-à-soi** to keep one's distance
quantique [kwɑ̃tik] *adj* quantum
quantité [kɑ̃tite] *f* quantity
quan•tum [kwɑ̃tɔm] *m* (*pl* **-ta** [ta]) quantum
quarantaine [karɑ̃tɛn] *f* age of forty, forty mark, forties; quarantine; **une quarantaine de** about forty
quarante [karɑ̃t] §94 *adj, pron, & m* forty; **quarante et un** forty-one; **quarante et unième** forty-first
quarante-deux [karɑ̃tdø] §94 *adj, pron, & m* forty-two
quarante-deuxième [karɑ̃tdøzjɛm] §94 *adj, pron* (*masc, fem*), *& m* forty-second

quarantième [karɑ̃tjɛm] §94 *adj, pron* (*masc, fem*), & *m* fortieth

quart [kar] *m* quarter; fourth (*in fractions*); quarter of a pound; quarter of a liter; **au quart de tour** immediately; **bon quart!** (naut) all's well!; **passer un mauvais quart d'heure** to have a trying time; **petit quart** (naut) dog-watch; **prendre le quart** (naut) to come on watch; **quart de cercle** quadrant; **quart de soupir** (mus) sixteenth-note rest; **quart d'heure de Rabelais** day of reckoning; **tous les quarts d'heure au quart d'heure juste** every quarter-hour on the quarter-hour; **trois quarts** three quarters; **un petit quart d'heure** a quarter of an hour or so

quarte [kart] *adj* quartan (*fever*) ‖ *f* half-gallon; (escr) quarte; (mus) fourth

quarte•ron [kartərɔ̃] **-ronne** [rɔn] *mf* quadroon ‖ *m* handful (*e.g., of people*)

quartette [kwartɛt] *m* combo (*foursome*)

quartier [kartje] *m* quarter; neighborhood; section (*of orange*); portion; **à quartier** aloof; apart; **avoir quartier libre** (mil) to have a pass; to be off duty; **le quartier chinois** Chinatown; **les beaux quartiers** the upper-class residential district; **mettre en quartiers** to dismember; **quartier d'affaires** business district; **quartier général** (mil) headquarters; **quartier réservé** red-light district; **quartiers** quarters, barracks

quartier-maître [kartjemɛtr] *m* (*pl* **quartiers-maîtres**) quartermaster

quartz [kwarts] *m* quartz

quasar [kwazar], [kazar] *m* quasar

quasi [kazi] *m* butt (*of a loin cut*) ‖ *adv* almost

quasi-collision [kazikɔlisjɔ̃] *f* (aer) near collision, near miss

quasiment [kazimɑ̃] *adv* (coll) almost

quatorze [katɔrz] §94 *adj & pron* fourteen; the Fourteenth, e.g., **Jean quatorze** John the Fourteenth; **c'est parti comme en quatorze** (slang) it's off to a good start ‖ *m* fourteen; fourteenth (*in dates*)

quatorzième [katɔrzjɛm] §94 *adj, pron* (*mas, fem*), & *m* fourteenth

quatrain [katrɛ̃] *m* quatrain

quatre [katr] §94 *adj & pron* four; the Fourth, e.g., **Jean quatre** John the Fourth; **quatre à quatre** four at a time; **quatre heures** four o'clock ‖ *m* four; fourth (*in dates*); **se mettre en quatre pour** to fall all over oneself for; **se tenir à quatre** to keep oneself under control

quatre-épices [katrepis] *m & f invar* allspice (*plant*); **des quatre-épices** allspice (*spice*)

quatre-quarts [katrəkar] *m invar* pound cake

quatre-saisons [katrəsezɔ̃], [katsezɔ̃] *f invar* everbearing small strawberry

quatre-temps [katrətɑ̃] *mpl* Ember days

quatre-vingt-deux [katrəvɛ̃dø] *adj, pron,* & *m* eighty-two

quatre-vingt-deuxième [katrəvɛ̃døzjɛm] *adj, pron* (*masc, fem*), & *m* eighty-second

quatre-vingt-dix [katrəvɛ̃di(s)] §94 *adj, pron,* & *m* ninety

quatre-vingt-dixième [katrəvɛ̃dizjɛm] §94 *adj, pron* (*masc, fem*), & *m* ninetieth

quatre-vingtième [katrəvɛ̃tjɛm] §94 *adj, pron* (*masc, fem*), & *m* eightieth

quatre-vingt-onze [katrəvɛ̃ɔ̃z] §94 *adj, pron,* & *m* ninety-one

quatre-vingt-onzième [katrəvɛ̃ɔ̃zjɛm] §94 *adj, pron* (*masc, fem*), & *m* ninety-first

quatre-vingts [katrəvɛ̃] §94 *adj & pron* eighty; **quatre-vingt** eighty, e.g., **page quatre-vingt** page eighty ‖ *m* eighty

quatre-vingt-un [katrəvɛ̃œ̃] §94 *adj, pron,* & *m* eighty-one

quatre-vingt-unième [katrəvɛ̃ynjɛm] §94 *adj, pron* (*masc, fem*), & *m* eighty-first

quatrième [katrijɛm] §94 *adj, pron* (*masc, fem*), & *m* fourth

quatuor [kwatɥɔr] *m* (*mus*) quartet

que [kə] (or **qu'** [k] before a vowel or mute **h**) *pron rel* whom; which; that; **ce que** that which, what ‖ *pron interr* what; **qu'est-ce que . . . ?** what (as direct object) . . . ?; **qu'est-ce qui . . . ?** what (as subject) . . . ? ‖ *adv* why, e.g., **qu'avez-vous besoin de tant de livres?** why do you need so many books?; how!, e.g., **que cette femme est belle!** how beautiful that woman is!; **que de** what a lot of, e.g., **que de difficultés!** what a lot of difficulties! ‖ *conj* that; when, e.g., **un jour que je suis allé chez le dentiste** once when I went to the dentist; since, e.g., **il y a trois jours qu'il est arrivé** it is three days since he came; until, e.g., **attendez qu'il vienne** wait until he comes; than, e.g., **plus grand que moi** taller than I; as, e.g., **aussi grand que moi** as tall as I; but, e.g., **personne que vous** no one but you; whether, e.g., **qu'il parte ou qu'il reste** whether he leaves or stays; (in a conditional sentence without **si**, to introduce the conditional in a dependent clause which represents the main clause of the corresponding sentence in English), e.g., **il ferait faillite que cela ne m'étonnerait pas** if he went bankrupt it would not surprise me; (as a repetition of another conjunction), e.g., **si elle chante et que la salle soit comble** if she sings and there is a full house; e.g., **comme il avait soif et que le vin était bon** as he was thirsty and the wine was good; (in a prayer or exhortation), e.g., **que Dieu vous bénisse!** may God bless you!, God bless you!; (in a command), e.g., **qu'il parle (aille, parte,** etc.) let him speak (go, leave, etc.); **ne . . . que** §90 only, but

québé•cois [kebekwa] **-coise** [kwaz] *adj & mf* Quebecois *ou* Québécois, Quebec(k)er

quel quelle [kɛl] §80

quelconque [kɛlkɔ̃k] *adj indef* any; any, whatever; any at all; some kind of ‖ (when standing before noun) *adj indef* some, some sort of ‖ *adj* ordinary, nondescript, mediocre

quelque [kɛlkə] *adj indef* some, any; **quelque**

chose (always *masc*) something; **quelque chose de bon** something good; **quelque part** somewhere; **quelque ... qui** or **quelque ... que** whatever ... ; whichever ... ; **quelques** a few ‖ *adv* some, about; **quelque peu** somewhat; **quelque + *adj* or *adv* ... que** however **+ *adj* or *adv***

quelquefois [kɛlkəfwa] *adv* sometimes

quel·qu'un [kɛlkœ̃] **-qu'une** [kyn] §81

quémander [kemɑ̃de] *tr* to beg for ‖ *intr* to beg

qu'en-dira-t-on [kɑ̃diratɔ̃] *m invar* what other people will say, gossip

quenotte [kənɔt] *f* (coll) baby tooth

quenouille [kənuj] *f* distaff; distaff side

querelle [kərɛl] *f* quarrel; **chercher querelle à** to pick a quarrel with; **une querelle d'Allemand, une mauvaise querelle** a groundless quarrel

quereller [kərɛle] *tr* to nag, scold ‖ *ref* to quarrel

querel·leur [kərɛlœr] **-leuse** [løz] *adj* quarrelsome ‖ *mf* wrangler ‖ *f* shrew

quérir [kerir] (used only in *inf*) *tr* to go for, to fetch

question [kɛstjɔ̃] *f* question; **question discutable** moot point

questionnaire [kɛstijɔner] *m* questionnaire

questionner [kɛstjɔne] *tr* to question

question·neur [kɛstjɔnœr] **-neuse** [nøz] *adj* inquisitive ‖ *mf* inquisitive person ‖ *m* (rad, telv) quizmaster

quête [kɛt] *f* quest; **faire la quête** to take up the collection

quêter [kete] *tr* to beg or fish for (*votes, praise, etc.*); hunt for (*game*); collect (*contributions*) ‖ *intr* to take up a collection

quetsche [kwɛtʃ] *f* quetsch

queue [kø] *f* tail; queue; billiard cue; train (*of dress*); handle (*of pan*); bottom (*of class*); stem, stalk; **à la queue leu leu** in single file; **en queue** at the back; **faire la queue** to line up, to queue up; **fausse queue** miscue; **queue de cheval** (bot) horsetail; **queue de loup** (bot) purple fox-glove; **queue de poisson** (aut) fishtail; **queue de vache** cat's-tail (*cirrus*); **sans queue ni tête** without head or tail; **venir en queue** to bring up the rear

queue-d'aronde [kødarɔ̃d] *f* (*pl* **queues-d'aronde**) dovetail; **assembler à queue-d'aronde** to dovetail

queue-de-cheval [kødʃval] *f* (*pl* **queues-de-cheval**) ponytail

queue-de-morue [kødmɔry] *f* (*pl* **queues-de-morue**) tails, swallow-tailed coat; (painting) flat brush

queue-de-rat [kødəra] *f* (*pl* **queues-de-rat**) rat-tail file; taper

qui [ki] *pron rel* who, whom; which, that; **ce qui** that which, what; **n'importe qui** anyone; **qui que** anyone, no one; whoever, e.g., **qui que vous soyez** whoever you are ‖ *pron interr* who, whom; **qui est-ce que ... ?** whom ... ?; **qui est-ce qui ... ?** who ... ?

quia [kɥija]—**mettre** or **réduire qn à quia** (obs) to stump or floor s.o.

quiconque [kikɔ̃k] *pron indef* whoever, whosoever; whomever; anyone

quidam [kɥidam], [kidam] *m* individual, person

quiétude [kɥijetyd], [kjetyd] *f* peace of mind; quiet, calm

quignon [kiɲɔ̃] *m* hunk (*of bread*)

quille [kij] *f* keel; pin (*for bowling*); **quilles** ninepins

quincaillerie [kɛ̃kɑjri] *f* hardware; hardware store

quincail·lier [kɛ̃kɑje] **-lière** [jɛr] *mf* hardware dealer

quinconce [kɛ̃kɔ̃s] *m* quincunx; **en quinconce** quincuncially

quinine [kinin] *f* quinine

quinquen·nal -nale [kɥɛ̃kɥɛnal] *adj* (*pl* **-naux** [no]) five-year

quinquet [kɛ̃ke] *m*—**allume tes quinquets!** (slang) open your eyes!

quinquina [kɛ̃kina] *m* cinchona

quin·tal [kɛ̃tal] *m* (*pl* **-taux** [to]) hundredweight; one hundred kilograms

quinte [kɛ̃t] *f* whim; (cards) sequence of five; (mus) fifth; **quinte de toux** fit of coughing

quintessence [kɛ̃tesɑ̃s] *f* quintessence

quintette [kɥɛ̃tɛt], [kɛ̃tɛt] *m* (mus) quintet; (coll) five-piece combo; **quintette à cordes** string quintet

quin·teux [kɛ̃tø] **-teuse** [tøz] *adj* crotchety, fitful, restive

quintu·plés -plées [kɛ̃typle] *mfpl* quintuplets

quinzaine [kɛ̃zɛn] *f* (group of) fifteen; two weeks, fortnight; **une quinzaine de** about fifteen

quinze [kɛ̃z] §94 *adj & pron* fifteen; the Fifteenth, e.g., **Jean quinze** John the Fifteenth ‖ *m* fifteen; fifteenth (*in dates*)

quinzième [kɛ̃zjɛm] §94 *adj, pron (masc, fem), & m* fifteenth

quiproquo [kiprɔko] *m* mistaken identity, misunderstanding

quiscale [kɥiskal] *m* (orn) purple grackle

quittance [kitɑ̃s] *f* receipt

quitte [kit] *adj* free (*from obligation*); clear (*of debts*); **(en) être quitte pour** to get off with; **être quitte** to be quits; **tenir qn quitte de** to release s.o. from ‖ *m*—**jouer (à) quitte ou double** to play double or nothing ‖ *adv*—**quitte à** even if it means

quitter [kite] *tr* to leave; take off (*e.g., a coat*) ‖ *intr* to leave, go away; **ne quittez pas!** (telp) hold the line! ‖ *ref* to part, separate

quitus [kɥitys] *m* discharge, acquittance

qui-vive [kiviv] *m invar*—**sur le quivive** on the qui vive ‖ *interj* (mil) who goes there?

quoi [kwa] *pron indef* what, which; **à quoi bon?** what's the use? **de quoi** enough; **moyennant quoi** in exchange for which; **n'importe quoi** anything; **quoi que** whatever; **quoi qu'il en soit** be that as it may; **sans quoi** otherwise

quoique [kwakə] *conj* although, though

quolibet [kɔlibɛ] *m* gibe, quip

quorum [kwɔrɔm], [kɔrɔm] *m* quorum

quota [kwɔta], [kɔta] *m* quota
quote-part [kɔtpar] *f invar* quota, share
quoti‧dien [kɔtidjɛ̃] **-dienne** [djɛn] *adj* daily ‖
  m daily newspaper

quotient [kɔsjɑ̃] *m* quotient; **quotient cours-
  bénéficié** price-earnings ratio; **quotient intellectuel** intelligence quotient
quotité [kɔtite] *f* share, amount

R

R, r [ɛr], *[ɛr] *m invar* eighteenth letter of the
  French alphabet
rabâcher [rabɑ/e] *tr* to harp on ‖ *intr* to harp
  on the same thing
rabais [rabɛ] *m* reduction, discount
rabaisser [rabese] *tr* to lower; to disparage
rabat [raba] *m* flap (*vestment*)
rabat-joie [rabaʒwa] *m invar* kill-joy
rabattre [rabatr] §7 *tr* to lower; discount; turn
  down; fold up; pull down; cut back; flush
  (*game*) ‖ *intr* to turn; **en rabattre** to come
  down a peg or two; **rabattre de** to reduce (*a
  price*) ‖ *ref* to fold; drop down; turn the other
  way; **se rabattre sur** to fall back on
rabat‧tu -tue [rabaty] *adj* turndown
rabbin [rabɛ̃] *m* rabbi
rabibocher [rabibɔ/e] *tr* (coll) to patch up ‖ *ref*
  (coll) to make up
rabiot [rabjo] *m* overtime; extra bit; (mil) extra
  service; (coll) graft
rabioter [rabjɔte] *tr & intr* to graft
râ‧blé -blée [rɑble] *adj* husky
rabot [rabo] *m* plane
raboter [rabɔte] *tr* to plane
rabo‧teux [rabɔtø] **-teuse** [tøz] *adj* rough, uneven ‖ *f* (mach) planer
rabou‧gri -grie [rabugri] *adj* scrub, scrawny
rabrouer [rabrue] *tr* to snub
racaille [rakɑj] *f* riffraff
raccommodage [rakɔmɔdaʒ] *m* mending; darning; patching
raccommodement [rakɔmɔdmɑ̃] *m* (coll) rec-
  onciliation
raccommoder [rakɔmɔde] *tr* to mend; darn;
  patch; (coll) to patch up
raccompagner [rakɔ̃paɲe] *tr* to see back, see
  home
raccord [rakɔr] *m* connection; coupling; joint;
  adapter; **faire un raccord à** to touch up
raccordement [rakɔrdəmɑ̃] *m* connecting, linking, joining
raccorder [rakɔrde] *tr & ref* to connect
raccour‧ci -cie [rakursi] *adj* shortened;
  abridged; squat, dumpy; bobbed (*hair*) ‖ *m*
  abridgment; shortcut, cutoff; foreshortening;
  en raccourci in miniature; in a nutshell
raccourcir [rakursir] *tr* to shorten; abridge;
  foreshorten ‖ *intr* to grow shorter
raccourcissement [rakursismɑ̃] *m* shortening;
  abridgment; shrinking
raccroc [rakro] *m* (billiards) fluke

raccrocher [rakrɔ/e] *tr & intr* to hang up ‖
  ref—**se raccrocher à** to hang on to
race [ras] *f* race; **de race** thoroughbred
ra‧cé -cée [rase] *adj* thoroughbred
rachat [ra/a] *m* repurchase; redemption; ransom
racheter [ra/te] §2 *tr* to buy back; redeem;
  ransom
rachitique [ra/itik] *adj* rickety
rachitisme [ra/itism] *m* rickets
ra‧cial -ciale [rasjal] *adj* (*pl* **-ciaux** [sjo]) race,
  racial
racine [rasin] *f* root; **racine carrée** square root;
  racine cubique cube root
racisme [rasism] *m* racism
raciste [rasist] *adj & mf* racist
racket [rakɛt] *m* (coll) racket
racketter or **racketteur** [rakɛtœr] *m* racketeer
raclée [rakle] *f* beating
racler [rakle] *tr* to scrape
raclette [raklɛt] *f* scraper; hoe; (phot) squeegee
racloir [raklwar] *m* scraper
raclure [raklyr] *f* scrapings
racolage [rakɔlaʒ] *m* soliciting
racoler [rakɔle] *tr* (coll) to solicit; (archaic) to
  shanghai
raco‧leur [rakɔlœr] **-leuse** [løz] *mf* recruiter ‖ *f*
  (coll) hustler, streetwalker
racontar [rakɔ̃tar] *m* (coll) gossip
raconter [rakɔ̃te] *tr* to tell, narrate; describe
racon‧teur [rakɔ̃tœr] **-teuse** [tøz] *mf* storyteller
racornir [rakɔrnir] *tr & intr* to harden; shrivel
radar [radar] *m* radar
rade [rad] *f* roadstead; **en rade** (coll) abandoned
ra‧deau [rado] *m* (*pl* **-deaux**) raft
ra‧diant [radjɑ̃] **-diante** [djɑ̃t] *adj* (astr, phys)
  radiant
radiateur [radjatœr] *m* radiator
radiation [radjɑsjɔ̃] *f* radiation; striking off
radi‧cal -cale [radikal] *adj & mf* (*pl* **-caux** [ko])
  radical ‖ *m* (chem, gram, math) radical
radier [radje] *tr* to cross out, strike out or off
ra‧dieux [radjø] **-dieuse** [djøz] *adj* radiant
radin [radɛ̃] *adj masc & fem* (slang) stingy
radio [radjo] *m* radiogram; radio operator ‖ *f*
  radio; radio set; X-ray
radioac‧tif [radjɔaktif] **-tive** [tiv] *adj* radioactive
radioamateur [radjɔamatœr] *m* ham operator,
  radio ham
radio-crochet [radjɔkrɔ/e] *m* (*pl* **-crochets**) talent show

radiodiffuser [radjɔdifyze] *tr* to broadcast
radiodiffusion [radjɔdifyzjɔ̃] *f* broadcasting
radiofréquence [radjɔfrekɑ̃s] *f* radiofrequency
radiogramme [radjɔgram] *m* radiogram
radiographie [radjɔgrafi] *f* X-ray
radiographier [radjɔgrafje] *tr* to X-ray
radiographique [radjɔgrafik] *adj* X-ray
radioguidage [radjɔgidaʒ] *m* radio control; radio guidance; **radioguidage d'aérodrome** instrument-landing system
radiogui•dé **-dée** [radjɔgide] *adj* radio-controlled; guided (*missile*)
radio-journal [radjɔʒurnal] *m* (*pl* **-journaux** [ʒurno]) radio newscast
radiologie [radjɔlɔʒi] *f* radiology
radiophare [radjɔfar] *m* radio beacon
radioreportage [radjɔrəpɔrtaʒ] *m* news broadcast; sports broadcast
radio-réveil [radjɔrevɛj] *m* (*pl* **radios-réveils**) clock radio
radioscopie [radjɔskɔpi] *f* radioscopy, fluoroscopy
radio-taxi [radjɔtaksi] *m* (*pl* **-taxis**) radio taxi
radiotéléphone [radjɔtelefɔn] *m* radiophone, cellular telephone, cellphone, car telephone
radiotélévi•sé **-sée** [radjɔtelevize] *adj* broadcast over radio and television
radiothérapie [radjɔterapi] *f* X-ray treatment, radiotherapy
radis [radi] *m* radish
radium [radjɔm] *m* radium
radius [radjys] *m* (anat) radius
radotage [radɔtaʒ] *m* drivel, twaddle
radoter [radɔte] *intr* to talk nonsense, ramble
radoub [radu] *m* (naut) graving
radouber [radube] *tr* (naut) to grave
radoucir [radusir] *tr & ref* to calm down
rafale [rafal] *f* squall, gust; burst of gunfire
raffermir [rafɛrmir] *tr & ref* to harden
raffinage [rafinaʒ] *m* refining
raffinement [rafinmɑ̃] *m* refinement
raffiner [rafine] *tr* to refine ‖ *intr* to be subtle; **raffiner sur** to overdo
raffinerie [rafinri] *f* refinery
raffoler [rafɔle] *intr*—**raffoler de** to dote on, to be wild about
raffut [rafy] *m* (coll) uproar
rafistolage [rafistɔlaʒ] *m* (coll) patching up
rafistoler [rafistɔle] *tr* (coll) to patch up
rafle [rɑfl] *f* raid, mass arrest; stalk; corncob
rafler [rɑfle] *tr* (coll) to carry away, make a clean sweep of
rafraîchir [rafreʃir] *tr* to cool; refresh; freshen up; trim (*the hair*) ‖ *intr* to cool ‖ *ref* to cool off; refresh oneself
rafraîchissement [rafreʃismɑ̃] *m* refreshment; cooling off
ragaillardir [ragajardir] *tr* to cheer up
rage [raʒ] *f* rage; rabies; **à la rage** madly; **faire rage** to rage
rager [raʒe] §38 *intr* (coll) to be enraged
ra•geur **-geuse** [raʒœr] [ʒøz] *adj* bad-tempered
ragot [rago] *m* (coll) gossip

ragoût [ragu] *m* stew, ragout; (obs) spice, relish
ragoû•tant **-tante** [ragutɑ̃] [tɑ̃t] *adj* tempting, inviting; pleasing; **peu ragoûtant** not very appetizing
rai [rɛ] *m* ray; spoke
raid [rɛd] *m* raid; air raid; endurance test
raide [rɛd] *adj* stiff; tight, taut; steep; (coll) incredible ‖ *adv* suddenly
raideur [rɛdœr] *f* stiffness
raidillon [rɛdijɔ̃] *m* short steep path
raidir [rɛdir] *tr & ref* to stiffen
raie [rɛ] *f* stripe, streak; stroke; line (*of spectrum*); part (*of hair*); (ichth) ray, skate
raifort [rɛfɔr] *m* horseradish
rail [raj] *m*; **rail conducteur** third rail; **remettre sur les rails** (fig) to put back on the track; **sortir des rails** to jump the track
railler [raje] *tr* to make fun of ‖ *intr* to joke ‖ *ref*—**se railler de** to make fun of
raillerie [rajri] *f* raillery, banter
rail•leur **-leuse** [rajœr] [jøz] *adj* teasing, bantering ‖ *mf* teaser
rainette [rɛnɛt] *f* tree frog
rainure [renyr] *f* groove
raisin [rɛzɛ̃] *m* grapes; grape; **raisin d'ours** (bot) bearberry; **raisins de Corinthe** currants; **raisins de mer** cuttlefish eggs; **raisins de Smyrne** seedless raisins; **raisins secs** raisins
raisiné [rezine] *m* grape jelly; (slang) blood
raison [rɛzɔ̃] *f* reason; ratio, rate; **à raison de** at the rate of; **avoir raison** to be right; **avoir raison de** to get the better of; **donner raison à** to back, support; **en raison de** because of; **raison sociale** trade name; **se faire une raison** to resign oneself
raisonnable [rɛzɔnabl] *adj* reasonable; rational
raison•né **-née** [rɛzɔne] *adj* rational; detailed
raisonnement [rɛzɔnmɑ̃] *m* reasoning; argument
raisonner [rɛzɔne] *tr* to reason out; reason with ‖ *intr* to reason; argue ‖ *ref* to reason with oneself
raison•neur **-neuse** [rɛzɔnœr] [nøz] *adj* rational; argumentative ‖ *mf* reasoner; arguer
rajeunir [raʒœnir] *tr* to rejuvenate ‖ *intr* to grow young again ‖ *ref* to pretend to be younger than one is
rajeunissement [raʒœnismɑ̃] *m* rejuvenation
rajouter [raʒute] *tr* to add again; (coll) to add more
rajuster [raʒyste] *tr* to readjust; adjust ‖ *ref* to adjust one's clothes
râle [rɑl] *m* rale; death rattle; (orn) rail
ralen•ti **-tie** [ralɑ̃ti] *adj* slow ‖ *m* slowdown; **au ralenti** slowdown (*work*); go-slow (*policy*); slow-motion (*moving picture*); idling (*motor*); **tourner au ralenti** (aut) to idle
ralentir [ralɑ̃tir] *tr, intr, & ref* to slow down; **ralentir** (*public sign*) slow
ralentissement [ralɑ̃tismɑ̃] *m* slowdown; slowing down, slowing up; letting up, easing off
ralliement [ralimɑ̃] *m* rally
rallier [ralje] *tr & ref* to rally

rallonge [ralɔʒ] *f* extra piece; extension cord; extra (*in building a new house*); (coll) raise (*in pay*); leaf (*of table*); (coll) under-the-table payment; **à rallonges** extension (*table*)

rallonger [ralɔʒe] §38 *tr & intr* to lengthen ‖ *ref* to grow longer

rallumer [ralyme] *tr* to relight; (fig) to rekindle ‖ *intr* to put on the lights again ‖ *ref* to be rekindled

rallye [rali] *m* rally; **rallye d'aviation** air show (*flying display*)

RAM [er α εm] *f invar* (letterword) (**mémoire vive**) RAM (random-access memory)

Ramadan [ramadɑ̃] *m* (rel) Ramadan

ramage [ramaʒ] *m* floral design; warbling

ramas [ramɑ] *m* heap; pack (*e.g., of thieves*)

ramassage [ramɑsaʒ] *m* gathering; **ramassage scolaire** school-bus service

ramas•sé -sée [ramɑse] *adj* stocky; compact (*style*)

ramasse-poussière [ramaspusjεr] *m invar* dustpan

ramasser [ramɑse] *tr* to gather; gather together; pick up; (coll) to catch (*a scolding; a cold*) ‖ *ref* to gather; gather oneself together

rambarde [rɑ̃bard] *f* handrail

rame [ram] *f* prop, stick; oar, pole; ream (*of paper*); string (*e.g., of barges*); (rr) train, section; **rame de métro** subway train

ra•meau [ramo] *m* (*pl* **-meaux**) branch; sprig

ramée [rame] *f* boughs

ramener [ramne] §2 *tr* to lead back; bring back; reduce; restore

ramer [rame] *tr* to stake (*a plant*) ‖ *intr* to row

ra•meur [ramœr] **-meuse** [møz] *mf* rower

ramier [ramje] *m* wood pigeon

ramifier [ramifje] *tr & ref* to ramify, branch out

ramol•li -lie [ramɔli] *adj* sodden; (coll) half-witted ‖ *mf* (coll) half-wit

ramollir [ramɔlir] *tr & ref* to soften

ramoner [ramɔne] *tr* to sweep (*a chimney*)

ramoneur [ramɔnœr] *m* chimney sweep

ram•pant -pante [rɑ̃pɑ̃] [pɑ̃t] *adj* crawling; creeping; (hum) ground (*crew*)

rampe [rɑ̃p] *f* ramp; grade, gradient; banister; flight (*of stairs*); (aer) runway lights; (theat) footlights; **rampe de lancement** launching pad

ramper [rɑ̃pe] *intr* to crawl; grovel; (bot) to creep

ramure [ramyr] *f* branches; antlers

rancart [rɑ̃kar] *m* (slang) rendezvous; **mettre au rancart** (coll) to scrap, to shelve

rance [rɑ̃s] *adj* rancid

ranch [rɑ̃tʃ] *m* ranch

rancir [rɑ̃sir] *intr & ref* to turn rancid

rancœur [rɑ̃kœr] *f* rancor

rançon [rɑ̃sɔ̃] *f* ransom; price (*e.g., of fame*); **mettre à rançon** to hold for ransom

rançonner [rɑ̃sɔne] *tr* to ransom, to hold for ransom; extort money from; steal from; to overcharge, e.g., **cet hôtelier rançonne ses** clients that hotel manager overcharges his guests

rancune [rɑ̃kyn] *f* grudge

rancu•nier [rɑ̃kynje] **-nière** [njεr] *adj* vindictive, spiteful, rancorous

randonnée [rɑ̃dɔne] *f* long walk; long ride

rang [rɑ̃] *m* rank; **au premier rang** in the first row; ranking; **en rang d'oignons** in a line

ran•gé -gée [rɑ̃ʒe] *adj* orderly; pitched (*battle*); steady (*person*)

ranger [rɑ̃ʒe] §38 *tr* to range; rank ‖ *ref* to take one's place; get out of the way; mend one's ways; **se ranger à** to adopt, take (*e.g., a suggestion*)

ranimer [ranime] *tr & ref* to revive

raout [raut] *m* reception

rapace [rapas] *adj* rapacious ‖ *m* bird of prey

rapatriement [rapatrimɑ̃] *m* repatriation

rapatrier [rapatrije] *tr* to repatriate

râpe [rɑp] *f* rasp; grater

râ•pé -pée [rɑpe] *adj* grated; threadbare ‖ *m* (coll) grated cheese

râper [rɑpe] *tr* to rasp, grate

rapetasser [raptase] *tr* (coll) to patch up

rapetisser [raptise] *tr, intr, & ref* to shrink, shorten

râ•peux [rɑpø] **-peuse** [pøz] *adj* raspy, grating

ra•piat [rapja] **-piate** [pjat] *adj* (coll) stingy ‖ *mf* (coll) skinflint

rapide [rapid] *adj* rapid; steep ‖ *m* rapids; (rr) express; **rapides** rapids

rapidement [rapidmɑ̃] *adv* rapidly

rapidité [rapidite] *f* rapidity; steepness

rapiéçage [rapjesaʒ] *m* patching

rapiécer [rapjese] §58 *tr* to patch

rapière [rapjεr] *f* rapier

rapin [rapɛ̃] *m* dauber; (coll) art student

rapine [rapin] *f* rapine, pillage

rappel [rapεl] *m* recall; reminder; call-up; recurrence; booster (*shot*); (*public sign*) end of speed limit, resume speed; (theat) curtain call; **battre le rappel** to call to arms; **rappel au règlement** point of order; **rappel de chariot** backspacer

rappeler [raple] §34 *tr* to recall; remind; call back; call up ‖ §95, §97 *ref* to remember

rapport [rapɔr] *m* yield, return; report; connection, bearing; (math) ratio; (mil) debriefing; **avoir de bons rapports avec** to be on good terms with; **en rapport avec** in touch with; in keeping with; **par rapport à** in comparison with; **rapports** relations; sexual relations; **sous le rapport de** from the standpoint of; **sous tous les rapports** in all respects

rapporter [rapɔrte] *tr* to bring back; yield; report; relate; repeal, call off; attach; retrieve (*game*); (bk) to post ‖ *intr* to yield; (coll) to squeal ‖ *ref*—**s'en rapporter à** to leave it up to; **se rapporter à** to be related to, refer to, have to do with

rappor•teur [rapɔrtœr] **-teuse** [tøz] *mf* tattletale ‖ *m* recorder; (geom) protractor

rapprochement [raprɔ∫mɑ̃] *m* bringing together; parallel; rapprochement

rapprocher [raprɔ∫e] *tr* to bring closer; reconcile; compare ‖ *ref* to draw closer, approach; **se rapprocher de** to approximate, resemble

rapt [rapt] *m* kidnapping

raquette [rakɛt] *f* racket; snowshoe; tennis player; (bot) prickly pear

rare [rar] *adj* rare; scarce; sparse, thin (*hair*)

rarement [rarmɑ̃] *adv* rarely, seldom

rareté [rarte] *f* rarity; scarcity; rareness

R.A.S. [ɛraɛs] (letterword) (**rien à signaler**) nothing worth talking about

ras [ra] **rase** [raz] *adj* short (*hair, nap, etc.*); level; close-cropped; close-shaven; open (*country*) ‖ *m*—**à ras de, au ras de** flush with; **ras d'eau** water line; **ras du cou** crew neck; **voler au ras du sol** to skim along the ground

rasade [razad] *f* bumper, glassful

rasage [razaʒ] *m* shearing; shaving

ra•sant [razɑ̃] **-sante** [zɑ̃t] *adj* level; grazing; close to the ground; (coll) boring

rase-mottes [razmɔt] *m invar* hedgehopper; **faire du rase-mottes** or **voler en rasemottes** to hedgehop

raser [raze] *tr* to shave; raze; graze ‖ *ref* to shave

ra•seur [razœr] **-seuse** [zøz] *adj* (coll) boring ‖ *mf* (coll) bore

rasoir [razwar] *adj invar* (slang) boring ‖ *m* razor; (slang) bore; **rasoir à manche** straight razor; **razoir de sûreté** safety razor

rassasiement [rasazimɑ̃] *m* satiation

rassasier [rasazje] *tr* to satisfy; satiate ‖ *ref* to have one's fill

rassemblement [rasɑ̃bləmɑ̃] *m* assembling; crowd; muster; (*trumpet call*) assembly; **rassemblement!** (mil) fall in!

rassembler [rasɑ̃ble] *tr & ref* to gather together

rasseoir [raswar] **§5** *tr* to reseat; set in place again ‖ *ref* to sit down again

rasséréner [raserene] **§10** *tr & ref* to calm down

rassir [rasir] *intr & ref* (coll) to get stale

ras•sis [rasi] **-sise** [siz] *adj* level-headed; stale (*bread*)

rassortir [rasɔrtir] *tr* to restock ‖ *ref* to lay in a new stock

rassurer [rasyre] *tr* to reassure ‖ *ref* to be reassured

rastaquouère [rastakwɛr] *m* (coll) flashy stranger

rat [ra] *m* rat; (coll) tightward; **fait comme un rat** caught like a rat in a trap; **mon rat** (coll) my turtledove; **rat à bourse** gopher; **rat de bibliothèque** bookworm; **rat de cale** stowaway; **rat de cave** thin candle; tax collector; **rat d'égout** sewer rat; **rat des champs** field mouse; **rat d'hôtel** hotel thief; **rat d'Opéra** ballet girl; **rat musqué** muskrat

ratatiner [ratatine] *ref* to shrivel up

ratatouille [ratatuj] *f* ratatouille; (coll) stew; (coll) bad cooking; (coll) blows

rate [rat] *f* spleen; female rat

ra•té -tée [rate] *adj* miscarried; bad (*shot, landing, etc.*) ‖ *mf* failure, dropout

râ•teau [rato] *m* (*pl* **-teaux**) rake

râteler [ratle] **§34** *tr* to rake

râtelier [ratəlje] *m* rack; set of false teeth; **manger à deux râteliers** (coll) to play both sides of the street; **râtelier d'armes** gun rack

rater [rate] *tr* to miss ‖ *intr* to miss, misfire; fail

ratiboiser [ratibwaze] *tr* (coll) to take to the cleaners; **ratiboiser q.ch. à qn** (coll) to clean s.o. out of s.th.

ratière [ratjɛr] *f* rattrap

ratifier [ratifje] *tr* to ratify

ration [rasjɔ̃] *f* ration

ration•nel -nelle [rasjɔnɛl] *adj* rational

rationnement [rasjɔnmɑ̃] *m* rationing

rationner [rasjɔne] *tr* to ration

ratisser [ratise] *tr* to rake; rake in; search with a fine-tooth comb; (coll) to fleece

ratissoire [ratiswar] *f* hoe

raton [ratɔ̃] *m* little rat; **raton laveur** raccoon

rattacher [rata∫e] *tr* to tie again; link; unite ‖ *ref* to be connected

rattrapage [ratrapaʒ] *m* catch-up; (typ) catchword

rattraper [ratrape] *tr* to catch up to; recover; recapture ‖ *ref* to catch up; **se rattraper à** to catch hold of; **se rattraper de** to make good, recoup

rature [ratyr] *f* erasure

raturer [ratyre] *tr* to cross out

rauque [rok] *adj* hoarse, raucous

ravage [ravaʒ] *m* ravage

ravager [ravaʒe] **§38** *tr* to ravage

ravalement [ravalmɑ̃] *m* trimming down; resurfacing; disparagement

ravaler [ravale] *tr* to choke down; disparage; drag down; resurface; eat (*one's words*) ‖ *ref* to lower oneself

ravaudage [ravodaʒ] *m* mending; darning; (fig) patchwork

ravauder [ravode] *tr* to mend; darn

ra•vi -vie [ravi] **§93** *adj* delighted, happy, charmed

ravier [ravje] *m* hors-d'œuvre dish

ravigoter [ravigɔte] *tr* (coll) to revive

ravilir [ravilir] *tr* to debase

ravin [ravɛ̃] *m* ravine

ravine [ravin] *f* mountain torrent

raviner [ravine] *tr* to furrow

ravir [ravir] *tr* to ravish; kidnap, abduct; delight; entrance; **ravir q.ch. à qn** to snatch, take s.th. from s.o. ‖ *intr*—**à ravir** marvelously

raviser [ravize] *ref* to change one's mind

ravis•sant [ravisɑ̃] **-sante** [sɑ̃t] *adj* ravishing, entrancing

ravis•seur [ravisœr] **-seuse** [søz] *mf* kidnaper

ravitaillement [ravitajmɑ̃] *m* supplying; supplies

ravitailler [ravitaje] *tr* to supply; fill up the gas tank of (*a vehicle*) ‖ *ref* to lay in supplies; fill up (*to get gas*)

raviver [ravive] *tr* to revive; brighten up; reopen (*an old wound*) ‖ *ref* to revive; break out again

ravoir [ravwar] (used only in *inf*) *tr* to get back again

rayer [reje] §49 *tr* to cross out, strike out; rule, line; stripe, pinstripe; rifle (*a gun*)

rayon [rɛjɔ̃] *m* ray; radius; spoke; shelf; honeycomb; department (*in a store*); point (*of star*); **ce n'est pas mon rayon** (coll) that's not in my line; **rayon de la mort** death ray; **rayon de lune** moonbeam; **rayon laser** laser beam; **rayons X** X rays; **rayon visuel** line of sight

rayonnage [rɛjɔnaʒ] *m* set of shelves, shelving

rayon•nant [rɛjɔnɑ̃] **-nante** [nɑ̃t] *adj* radiant; radiating; radioactive; (rad) transmitting

rayonne [rɛjɔn] *f* rayon

rayonnement [rɛjɔnmɑ̃] *m* radiance; influence, diffusion; (phys) radiation; **rayonnement de faible (grande) énergie** low-level (high-level) radiation; **rayonnement diffusé** scattered radiation; **rayonnement ionisant** ionizing radiation; **rayonnement parasite** stray radiation; **rayonnement solaire** solar radiation

rayonner [rɛjɔne] *intr* to radiate

rayure [rejyr] *f* stripe; scratch; rifling

raz [rɑ] *m* race (*channel and current of water*); **raz de marée** tidal wave; landslide (*in an election*)

razzia [razja] *f* raid

razzier [razje] *tr* to raid

réacteur [reaktœr] *m* reactor; **réacteur nucléaire** nuclear reactor

réactif [reaktif] *m* (chem) reagent

réaction [reaksjɔ̃] *f* reaction; kick (*of rifle*); **à réaction** jet; **réaction en chaîne** chain reaction

réactionnaire [reaksjɔnɛr] *adj & mf* reactionary

réactiver [reaktive] *tr* to reactivate

réadaptation [readaptasjɔ̃] *f* rehabilitation; readjustment; **réadaptation fonctionnelle** occupational therapy

réadapter [readapte] *tr* to rehabilitate; readjust ‖ *ref* to be rehabilitated

réaffirmer [reafirme] *tr* to reaffirm

réagir [reaʒir] *intr* to react

réalimentation [realimɑ̃tasjɔ̃] *f* (electron) feedback

réalisable [realizabl] *adj* feasible; (com) saleable

réalisa•teur [realizatœr] **-trice** [tris] *adj* producing ‖ *mf* achiever; producer ‖ *m* (mov, rad, telv) director

réalisation [realizasjɔ̃] *f* accomplishment; work; (mov, rad, telv) production; (com) liquidation

réaliser [realize] *tr* to accomplish; realize; sell out; (mov) to produce ‖ *ref* to come to pass, be realized

réalisme [realism] *m* realism

réaliste [realist] *adj* realistic ‖ *mf* realist

réalité [realite] *f* reality; **en réalité** in reality, really, in actual fact

réanimer [reanime] *tr* to revive

réapparaître [reaparɛtr] §12 *intr* to reappear

réapparition [reaparisjɔ̃] *f* reappearance

réarmement [rearmǝmɑ̃] *m* rearmament

réassortir [reasɔrtir] *tr* to restock ‖ *ref* to lay in a new stock

réassurer [reasyre] *tr* to reinsure

rébarba•tif [rebarbatif] **-tive** [tiv] *adj* forbidding, repulsive

rebâtir [rǝbɑtir] *tr* to rebuild

rebattre [rǝbatr] §7 *tr* to beat; reshuffle; repeat over and over again

rebat•tu -tue [rǝbaty] *adj* hackneyed

rebelle [rǝbɛl] *adj* rebellious ‖ *mf* rebel

rebeller [rǝbele], [rǝbɛlle] *ref* to rebel

rébellion [rebeljɔ̃] *f* rebellion

rebiffer [rǝbife] *ref* to kick over the traces

reboisement [rǝbwazmɑ̃] *m* reforestation

rebond [rǝbɔ̃] *m* rebound

rebon•di -die [rǝbɔ̃di] *adj* plump, buxom; paunchy

rebondir [rǝbɔ̃dir] *intr* to bounce; (fig) to come up again

rebord [rǝbɔr] *m* edge, border; sill, ledge; hem; brim (*of hat*); rim (*of saucer*); lip (*of cup*)

reboucher [rǝbuʃe] *tr* to recork; stop up ‖ *ref* to be stopped up

rebours [rǝbur] *m*—**à rebours** backwards; against the grain; the wrong way; backhanded (*compliment*); **à** or **au rebours de** contrary to

rebouter [rǝbute] *tr* to set (*a bone*)

rebrousse-poil [rǝbruspwal]—**à rebrousse-poil** against the grain, the wrong way

rebrousser [rǝbruse] *tr* to brush up; **rebrousser chemin** to turn back; **rebrousser qn** (coll) to rub s.o. the wrong way ‖ *ref* to turn up, bend back

rebuffade [rǝbyfad] *f* rebuff; **essuyer une rebuffade** to be snubbed

rebut [rǝby] *m* castoff; waste; scum (*of society*); rebuff; **de rebut** castoff; waste; unclaimed (*letter*); **mettre au rebut** to discard

rebu•tant [rǝbytɑ̃] **-tante** [tɑ̃t] *adj* dull, tedious; repugnant

rebuter [rǝbyte] *tr* to rebuff; bore; be repulsive to

recaler [rǝkale] *tr* (coll) to flunk

récapitulation [rekapitylasjɔ̃] *f* recapitulation

recéder [rǝsede] §10 *tr* to give back; sell back; resell

recel [rǝsɛl] *m* concealment (*of stolen goods; of criminals*)

receler [rǝsle] §2 or **recéler** [rǝsele] §10 *tr* to conceal; receive (*stolen goods*); harbor (*a criminal*) ‖ *intr* to hide

rece•leur [rǝslœr] **-leuse** [løz] *mf* fence, receiver of stolen goods

récemment [resamɑ̃] *adv* recently, lately

recensement [rǝsɑ̃smɑ̃] *m* census; **recensement du contingent** draft registration

recenser [rǝsɑ̃se] *tr* to take the census of; take a count of

recenseur [rǝsɑ̃sœr] *m* census taker

ré•cent [resɑ̃] **-cente** [sɑ̃t] *adj* recent

récépissé [resepise] *m* receipt; certificate, permit

réceptacle [reseptakl] *m* receptacle

récep•teur [reseptœr] **-trice** [tris] *adj* receiving ‖ *m* receiver

récep•tif [reseptif] **-tive** [tiv] *adj* receptive

réception [resepsjɔ̃] *f* reception; receipt; approval; admission (*to a club*); registration desk (*of hotel*); landing (*of, e.g., a parachutist*); (sports) catch; **accuser réception de** to acknowledge receipt of

réceptionnaire [resepsjɔnɛr] *mf* consignee; chief receptionist

récession [resesjɔ̃] *f* recession

recette [rəsɛt] *f* receipt; collection (*of debts, taxes, etc.*); (culin) recipe; **faire recette** to be a box-office attraction; **recettes de métier** tricks of the trade; **recette des finances** internal revenue;

recevable [rəsvabl] *adj* acceptable; admissible

rece•veur [rəsvœr] **-veuse** [vøz] *mf* collector; conductor (*of bus, streetcar, etc.*); blood recipient; **receveur des postes** postmaster; **receveur universel** recipient of blood from a universal donor

recevoir [rəsvwar] §59 *tr* to receive; accommodate; admit (*to a school, club, etc.*); **être reçu** to be admitted; pass ‖ *intr* to receive

rechange [rəʃɑ̃ʒ] *m* replacement, change; **de rechange** spare (*e.g., parts*)

rechaper [rəʃape] *tr* to recap, retread

réchapper [reʃape] *intr*—**en réchapper** to get away with it; to get well; **réchapper à** or **de** to escape from

recharge [rəʃarʒ] *f* refill; recharging; reloading

recharger [rəʃarʒe] §38 *tr* to recharge; refill; reload; ballast (*a roadbed*)

réchaud [reʃo] *m* hot plate

réchauffer [reʃofe] *tr & ref* to warm up

rêche [rɛʃ] *adj* rough, harsh

recherche [rəʃɛrʃ] *f* search; quest; investigation, piece of research; refinement; **recherches** research

recher•ché -chée [rəʃɛrʃe] *adj* sought-after, in demand; elaborate; studied, affected

rechercher [rəʃɛrʃe] *tr* to seek, look for

rechigner [rəʃiɲe] *intr*—**rechigner à** to balk at

rechute [rəʃyt] *f* relapse

rechuter [rəʃyte] *intr* to relapse

récidive [residiv] *f* recurrence; second offense

récidiver [residive] *intr* to recur; relapse

récif [resif] *m* reef

récipiendaire [resipjɑ̃dɛr] *m* new member, inductee; recipient

récipient [resipjɑ̃] *m* container, receptacle, recipient

réciprocité [resiprɔsite] *f* reciprocity

réciproque [resiprɔk] *adj* reciprocal ‖ *f* converse

récit [resi] *m* recital, account

réci•tal [resital] *m* (*pl* **-tals**) recital

récitation [resitasjɔ̃] *f* recitation

réciter [resite] *tr* to recite

récla•mant [reklamɑ̃] **-mante** [mɑ̃t] *mf* claimant

réclamation [reklamɑsjɔ̃] *f* complaint; demand

réclame [reklam] *f* advertising; advertisement; (theat) cue; (typ) catchword; **faire de la réclame** to advertise, to ballyhoo; **réclame à éclipse** flashing sign; **réclame lumineuse** illuminated sign

réclamer [reklame] *tr* to claim; clamor for; demand ‖ *intr* to lodge a complaint; intercede ‖ *ref*—**se réclamer de** to appeal to; claim kinship with; **se réclamer de qn** to use s.o.'s name as a reference

reclassement [rəklɑsmɑ̃] *m* reclassification

reclasser [rəklɑse] *tr* to reclassify

re•clus [rəkly] **-cluse** [klyz] *adj & mf* recluse

recoin [rəkwɛ̃] *m* nook, cranny

récollection [rekɔlɛksjɔ̃] *f* religious meditation

recoller [rəkɔle] *tr* to paste again

récolte [rekɔlt] *f* harvest

récolter [rekɔlte] *tr* to harvest

recommander [rəkɔmɑ̃de] §97, §98 *tr* to recommend; register (*a letter*); **envoyer en recommandé** to send by certified mail ‖ *ref*—**se recommander à** to seek the protection of; **se recommander de** to ask (*s.o.*) for a reference

recommencer [rəkɔmɑ̃se] §51, §96, §97 *tr & intr* to begin again

récompense [rekɔ̃pɑ̃s] *f* recompense, reward; award

récompenser [rekɔ̃pɑ̃se] *tr* to recompense

réconcilier [rekɔ̃silje] *tr* to reconcile

reconduction [rəkɔ̃dyksjɔ̃] or **réconduction** [rekɔ̃dyksjɔ̃] *f* continuation; renewal (*of a lease*)

reconduire [rəkɔ̃dɥir] §19 *tr* to escort; (coll) to kick out, to send packing

réconfort [rekɔ̃fɔr] *m* comfort

réconfor•tant [rekɔ̃fɔrtɑ̃] **-tante** [tɑ̃t] *adj* consoling; stimulating

réconforter [rekɔ̃fɔrte] *tr* to comfort; revive ‖ *ref* to recuperate; cheer up

reconnaissance [rəkɔnɛsɑ̃s] *f* recognition; gratitude; (mil) reconnaissance; **aller en reconnaissance** to reconnoiter; **reconnaissance de** or **pour** gratitude for

reconnais•sant [rəkɔnɛsɑ̃] **-sante** [sɑ̃t] *adj* grateful; **être reconnaissant de** + *inf* to be grateful for + *ger*; **être reconnaissant de** or **pour** to be grateful for

reconnaître [rəkɔnɛtr] §12, §95 *tr* to recognize; (mil) to reconnoiter ‖ *ref* to recognize oneself; know where one is; acknowledge oneself (*e.g., guilty*); **s'y reconnaître** to know where one is

reconquérir [rəkɔ̃kerir] §3 *tr* to reconquer

reconquête [rəkɔ̃kɛt] *f* reconquest

reconsidérer [rəkɔ̃sidere] §10 *tr* to reconsider

reconstituant [rəkɔ̃stitɥɑ̃] *m* tonic

reconstituer [rəkɔ̃stitɥe] *tr* to reconstruct; restore

reconstruire [rəkɔ̃strɥir] §19 *tr* to reconstruct

record [rəkɔr] *adj invar & m* record

recordman [rəkɔrdman] *m* record holder

recoudre [rəkudr] §13 *tr* to sew up

recoupement [rəkupmã] *m* cross-check, cross-checking; **faire un recoupement** to cross-check

recouper [rəkupe] *tr* to cut again; blend (*wines*)

recourir [rəkurir] §14 *intr* to run again; **recourir à** to resort to; appeal to

recours [rəkur] *m* recourse; **avoir recours à** to resort to; call on for help; **en dernier recours** as a last resort; **recours en grâce** petition for pardon

recouvrement [rəkuvrəmã] *m* recovery

recouvrer [rəkuvre] *tr* to recover

recouvrir [rəkuvrir] §65 *tr* to cover; cover up; mask; resurface (*e.g., a road*) ‖ *ref* to overlap

récréation [rekreasjɔ̃] *f* recreation; recess (*at school*)

recréer [rəkree] *tr* to re-create

récréer [rekree] *tr & ref* to relax

récrier [rekrije] *ref* to cry out

récrire [rekrir] §25 *tr* to rewrite; write again

recroquevil•lé -lée [rəkrɔkvije] *adj* shriveled up, curled up; huddled up

recroqueviller [rəkrɔkvije] *tr & ref* to shrivel up, curl up

re•cru -crue [rəkry] *adj* exhausted

recrue [rəkry] *f* recruit

recruter [rəkryte] *tr* to recruit; **recrutons** (*public sign for job openings*) help wanted ‖ *ref* to be recruited

rectangle [rɛktãgl] *m* rectangle

rectificateur [rɛktifikatœr] *m* rectifier

rectifier [rɛktifje] *tr* to rectify; true up; grind (*a cylinder*)

rectum [rɛktɔm] *m* rectum

re•çu -çue [rəsy] *adj* received; accepted, recognized; successful ‖ *m* receipt ‖ *v* see **recevoir**

recueil [rəkœj] *m* collection; compilation

recueillement [rəkœjmã] *m* meditation

recueillir [rəkœjir] §18 *tr* to collect, gather; take in (*a needy person*); receive (*a legacy*) ‖ *ref* to collect oneself, meditate

recuire [rəkɥir] §19 *tr* to anneal, temper; cook over again ‖ *intr* (fig) to stew

recul [rəkyl] *m* backing, backward movement; kick, recoil; **être en recul** to be losing ground; **prendre du recul** to consider in perspective

reculer [rəkyle] *tr* to move back; put off (*e.g., a decision*) ‖ *intr* to move back; back out; recoil; **reculer devant** to shrink from ‖ *ref* to move back

reculons [rəkylɔ̃]—**à reculons** backwards

récupération [rekyperasjɔ̃] *f* recovery

récurer [rekypere] §10 *tr* to salvage, recover; recuperate; make up (*e.g., lost hours*); find another job for ‖ *intr* to recuperate

récurer [rekyre] *tr* to scour

récur•rent [rekyrã] **-rente** [rãt] *adj* recurrent

récusable [rekyzabl] *adj* (law) untrustworthy, unreliable

récuser [rekyze] *tr* to take exception to ‖ *ref* to refuse to give one's opinion

recyclage [rəsiklaʒ] *m* recycling; retraining, reorientation

recycler [rəsikle] *tr* to recycle; retrain, reorient

rédac•teur [redaktœr] **-trice** [tris] *mf* editor; **rédacteur en chef** editor in chief; **rédacteur gérant** managing editor; **rédacteur publicitaire** copywriter; **rédacteur sportif** sports editor

rédaction [redaksjɔ̃] *f* editorial staff; editorial office; edition; editing

reddition [redisjɔ̃] *f* surrender

redécouvrir [rədekuvrir] §65 *tr* to rediscover

rédemp•teur [redãptœr] **-trice** [tris] *adj* redemptive ‖ *mf* redeemer

rédemption [redãpsjɔ̃] *f* redemption

redevable [rədvabl] *adj* indebted

redevance [rədvãs] *f* dues, fees; rent; tax (*on radio sets*); royalty

rédiger [rediʒe] §38 *tr* to edit; draft; write up

redingote [rədɛ̃gɔt] *f* frock coat

redire [rədir] §22 *tr* to repeat; give away (*a secret*) ‖ *intr*—**trouver à redire à** to find fault with

redon•dant [redɔ̃dã] **-dante** [dãt] *adj* redundant

redoublement [rədubləmã] *m* redoubling; repeating (*of a course*)

redoutable [rədutabl] *adj* frightening

redoute [rədut] *f* redoubt

redouter [rədute] §97 *tr* to dread

redressement [rədrɛsmã] *m* straightening out; redress; (elec) rectifying

redresser [rədrese] *tr* to straighten; hold up (*e.g., the head*); redress; (elec) to rectify ‖ *ref* to straighten up

redresseur [rədrɛsœr] *m* (elec) rectifier; **redresseur de torts** knight-errant; (coll) reformer

réduction [redyksjɔ̃] *f* reduction; **réduction des effectifs** reduction in force, downsizing

réduire [redɥir] §19, §96, §100 *tr* to reduce; set (*a bone*); **réduire des effectifs** to downsize ‖ §96 *ref* to boil down; **se réduire à** to amount to; **se réduire en** to be reduced to

réduit [redɥi] *m* retreat, nook; redoubt

rééditer [reedite] *tr* to reedit

réel réelle [reɛl] *adj & m* real, actual

réélection [reelɛksjɔ̃] *f* reelection

réellement [reɛlmã] *adv* really

réémetteur [reemɛtœr] *m* (electron) relay transmitter

réescompte [reɛskɔ̃t] *m* rediscount

réexamen [reɛgzamɛ̃] *m* reexamination

réexpédier [reɛkspedje] *tr* to reship; return to sender

réexpédition [reɛkspedisjɔ̃] *f* reshipment; return

refaire [rəfɛr] §29 *tr* to redo ‖ *intr*—**à refaire** to be done over; be dealt over ‖ *ref* to recover; make good one's losses

réfection [refɛksjɔ̃] *f* repairing, rebuilding, remaking

référence [referãs] *f* reference

référendum or **referendum** [referɛ̃dɔm] *m* referendum

référer [refere] §10 *intr*—**en référer à** to appeal to ‖ *ref*—**s'en référer à** to leave it up to; **se référer à** to refer to

refermer [rəfɛrme] *tr* & *ref* to close again, to close

refiler [rəfile] *tr*—**refiler à qn** (slang) to palm off on s.o.

réflé•chi -chie [refleʃi] *adj* thoughtful; well-thought-out; (gram) reflexive ‖ *m* (gram) reflexive

réfléchir [refleʃir] *tr* & *intr* to reflect; **réfléchir à, réfléchir sur** to think about, ponder ‖ *ref* to be reflected

réflec•teur [reflɛktœr] **-trice** [tris] *adj* reflecting ‖ *m* reflector

reflet [rəflɛ] *m* reflection; glint, gleam

refléter [rəflete] §10 *tr* to reflect, mirror ‖ *ref* to be mirrored

réflexe [reflɛks] *adj* & *m* reflex

réflexion [reflɛksjɔ̃] *f* reflection; **réflexion faite** on second thought

refluer [rəflye] *intr* to ebb

reflux [rəfly] *m* ebb

refonte [rəfɔ̃t] *f* recasting

réforma•teur [reformatœr] **-trice** [tris] *mf* reformer

réformation [reformasjɔ̃] *f* reformation

réforme [reform] *f* reform; **la Réforme** the Reformation

réfor•mé -mée [reforme] *adj* (eccl) Reformed; (mil) disabled

reformer [rəforme] *tr* & *ref* to regroup

réformer [reforme] *tr* to reform; (mil) to discharge ‖ *ref* to reform

refou•lé -lée [rəfule] *adj* (coll) inhibited

refoulement [rəfulmɑ̃] *m* driving back; (psychoanal) repression

refouler [rəfule] *tr* to drive back; choke back (*a sob*); sail against (*the current*); compress, stem; (psychoanal) to repress ‖ *intr* to flow back

réfractaire [refraktɛr] *adj* refractory; rebellious ‖ *mf* insubordinate; draft dodger

réfraction [refraksjɔ̃] *f* refraction

refrain [rəfrɛ̃] *m* refrain; hum; **le même refrain** the same old tune; **refrain publicitaire** (advertising) jingle

refréner [rəfrene] §10 *tr* to curb

réfrigérateur [refriʒeratœr] *m* refrigerator

réfrigérer [refriʒere] §10 *tr* to refrigerate; (coll) to chill to the bone

refroidir [rəfrwadir] *tr* to cool; (slang) to rub out ‖ *intr* to cool ‖ *ref* to cool; catch cold

refroidissement [rəfrwadismɑ̃] *m* cooling

refuge [rəfyʒ] *m* refuge; shelter; safety zone

réfu•gié -giée [refyʒje] *mf* refugee

réfugier [refyʒje] *ref* to take refuge

refus [rəfy] *m* refusal; **refus seulement** regrets only (*to invitation*)

refuser [rəfyze] §96, §97, §98 *tr* to refuse; refuse; recognize; flunk; decline ‖ *intr* to refuse; **refuser de** or **à** to refuse to ‖ §96 *ref* to be refused; **se refuser à** to refuse to accept

réfuter [refyte] *tr* to refute

regagner [rəgaɲe] *tr* to regain

regain [rəgɛ̃] *m* second growth; (fig) aftermath; **regain de** new lease on

ré•gal [regal] *m* (*pl* **-gals**) treat

régaler [regale] *tr* to treat; level ‖ *intr* to treat

regard [rəgar] *m* look, glance; **couver du regard** to gloat over; look fondly at; look greedily at; **en regard** facing, opposite

regar•dant [rəgardɑ̃] **-dante** [dɑ̃t] *adj* (coll) penny-pinching

regarder [rəgarde] §95 *tr* to look at; face; concern ‖ *intr* to look; **regarder à** to pay attention to; watch (*one's money*); mind (*the price*); **y regarder à deux fois** to watch one's step, think twice ‖ *ref* to face each other

régate [regat] *f* regatta

régence [reʒɑ̃s] *f* regency

régénération [reʒenerasjɔ̃] *f* regeneration; (chem) feedback

régénérer [reʒenere] §10 *tr* & *ref* to regenerate

ré•gent [reʒɑ̃] **-gente** [ʒɑ̃t] *mf* regent

régenter [reʒɑ̃te] *tr* & *intr* to boss

régicide [reʒisid] *mf* regicide (*person*) ‖ *m* regicide (*act*)

régie [reʒi] *f* commission, administration; excise tax; stage management; (rad, telv) control room; **en régie** state-owned or -operated

regimber [rəʒɛ̃be] *intr* & *ref* to revolt; balk

régime [reʒim] *m* government, form of government; administration; system; diet; performance, working conditions; rate (*of speed; of flow; of charge or discharge of a storage battery*); bunch, cluster; stem (*of bananas*); (gram) complement; (gram) government; **en régime permanent** under steady working conditions

régiment [reʒimɑ̃] *m* regiment

régimentaire [reʒimɑ̃tɛr] *adj* regimental

région [reʒjɔ̃] *f* region, area

régir [reʒir] *tr* to govern

régisseur [reʒisœr] *m* manager; stage manager

registre [rəʒistr] *m* register; damper; throttle valve

réglable [reglabl] *adj* adjustable

réglage [reglaʒ] *m* setting, adjusting; lines (*on paper*); (mach, rad, telv) tuning

règle [rɛgl] *f* rule; ruler; **en règle** in order; **en règle générale** as a general rule; **règle à calcul** slide rule; **règles** menstrual period

ré•glé -glée [regle] *adj* regulated; adjusted; tuned; well-behaved, orderly; ruled (*paper*); finished, decided

règlement [rɛglamɑ̃] *m* regulation, rule; settlement; **en règlement judiciaire** in bankruptcy proceedings; **règlement complet** payment in full, payoff; **règlement intérieur** bylaws

réglementaire [reglamɑ̃tɛr] *adj* regular; regulation

réglementer [reglamɑ̃te] *tr* to regulate, control

régler [regle] §10 *tr* to regulate, put in order; set (*a watch*); settle (*an account*); rule (*paper*); (aut, rad, telv) to tune ‖ *intr* to pay

réglisse [reglis] *m* & *f* licorice

ré·gnant [reɲɑ̃] **-gnante** [ɲɑ̃t] *adj* reigning; ruling; prevailing, prevalent

règne [rɛɲ] *m* reign; (biol) kingdom

régner [reɲe] §10 *intr* to reign

regorger [rəgɔrʒe] §38 *intr* to overflow; **regorger de** to abound in

regratter [rəgrate] *tr* to scrape ‖ *intr* to pinch pennies

regret [rəgrɛ] *m* regret; **à regret** regretfully

regrettable [rəgrɛtabl] *adj* regrettable

regretter [rəgrete] *tr* to regret; long for, miss; **regretter** + *subj* to be sorry that + *ind* ‖ §97 *intr* to be sorry, regret, e.g., **je regrette d'avoir fait cela** I regret having done that

régulariser [regylarize] *tr* to regularize; adjust, regulate

régularité [regylarite] *f* regularity

régula·teur [regylatœr] **-trice** [tris] *adj* regulating ‖ *m* (mach) governor

régulation [regylɑsjɔ̃] *f* regulation

régu·lier [regylje] **-lière** [ljɛr] *adj* regular; scheduled; exact, prompt; legitimate; honest, aboveboard, on the level ‖ *m* (mil, rel) regular ‖ *f*—**ma régulière** (slang) my woman

réhabiliter [reabilite] *tr* to rehabilitate

rehausser [rəose] *tr* to heighten; enhance

Reims [rɛ̃s] *m* Rheims

rein [rɛ̃] *m* kidney

réincarnation [reɛ̃karnɑsjɔ̃] *f* reincarnation

reine [rɛn] *f* queen; **reine du carnaval, reine de la fête** carnival queen

reine-claude [rɛnklod] *f* (*pl* **-claudes** or **reines-claudes**) greengage

reine-des-prés [rɛndepre] *f* (*pl* **reines-des-prés**) meadowsweet

reine-marguerite [rɛnmargərit] *f* (*pl* **reines-marguerites**) aster

réintégrer [reɛ̃tegre] §10 *tr* to reinstate; return to

réitérer [reitere] §10 *tr* reiterate

rejaillir [rəʒajir] *intr* to spurt out; bounce; splash; **rejaillir sur** to reflect on

rejet [rəʒɛ] *m* casting up; rejection; enjambment; (bot) shoot

rejeter [rəʒte] §34 *tr* to reject; throw back; throw up; shift (*responsibility*) ‖ *ref* to fall back

rejeton [rəʒtɔ̃] *m* shoot; offshoot, offspring; (coll) child

rejeu [rəʒø] *m* (electron) playback

rejoindre [rəʒwɛ̃dr] §35 *tr* to rejoin; overtake ‖ *ref* to meet

réjouir [reʒwir] *tr* to gladden, cheer ‖ §97 *ref* to rejoice, be delighted

réjouissance [reʒwisɑ̃s] *f* rejoicing; **réjouissances** festivities

réjouis·sant [reʒwisɑ̃] **-sante** [sɑ̃t] *adj* cheery; amusing

relâche [rəlɑʃ] *m* & *f* respite, letup ‖ *f* (naut) stop; **faire relâche** (naut) to make a call; (theat) to close (*for a day or two*); **relâche** (*public sign*) no performance today

relâ·ché -chée [rəlɑʃe] *adj* lax; loose

relâchement [rəlɑʃmɑ̃] *m* relaxation; letting up

relâcher [rəlɑʃe] *tr* to loosen; relax; release ‖ *intr* (naut) to make a call ‖ *ref* to loosen; become lax

relais [rəlɛ] *m* relay; shift; **prendre le relais** (slang) to take up the slack

relance [rəlɑ̃s] *f* raise (*e.g., in poker*); outbreak

relancer [rəlɑ̃se] §51 *tr* to start up again; harass, hound; return (*the ball*); raise (*the ante*) ‖ *intr* (cards) to raise

re·laps -lapse [rəlaps] *mf* backslider

relater [rəlate] *tr* to relate

rela·tif [rəlatif] **-tive** [tiv] *adj* relative

relation [rəlɑsjɔ̃] *f* relation; **en relation avec, en relations avec** in touch with; **relations** connections

relativité [rəlativite] *f* relativity

relaxation [rəlaksɑsjɔ̃] *f* relaxation

relaxer [rəlakse] *tr* to relax; free ‖ *ref* to relax

relayer [rəleje] §49 *tr* to relay; relieve ‖ *ref* to work in relays or shifts

reléguer [rəlege] §10 *tr* to relegate

relent [rəlɑ̃] *m* musty smell

relève [rəlɛv] *f* relief; change (*of the guard*); **prendre la relève** to take over

rele·vé -vée [rəlve] *adj* lofty, elevated; turned up; graded (*curve*); spicy ‖ *m* check list; tuck (*in dress*); (culin) next course; **faire le relevé de** to survey; to check off; **relevé de compte** bank statement; **relevé de compteur** meter reading; **relevé de notes des écoles** transcript of grades

relèvement [rəlɛvmɑ̃] *m* raising; recovery, improvement; picking up (*e.g., of wounded*); (naut) bearing

relever [rəlve] §2 *tr* to raise; turn up; restore; relieve, enhance; pick out; take a reading of; season; (mil) to relieve ‖ *intr*—**relever de** to recover from; depend on ‖ *ref* to rise; recover; right itself; take turns

re·lié -liée [rəlje] *adj* (bb) hardbound, hardcover; **relié cuir** leather-bound; **relié plein chagrin** entirely bound in grained leather

relief [rəljɛf] *m* relief; **en relief** in relief; **reliefs** leavings

relier [rəlje] *tr* to bind; to link

re·lieur [rəljœr] **-lieuse** [ljøz] *mf* bookbinder

reli·gieux [rəliʒjø] **-gieuse** [ʒjøz] *adj* religious ‖ *m* monk ‖ *f* nun; cream puff

religion [rəliʒjɔ̃] *f* religion

reliquat [rəlika] *m* remainder

relique [rəlik] *f* relic

relire [rəlir] §36 *tr* to read again; read over again

reliure [rəljyr] *f* binding; bookbinding

reloger [rələʒe] §38 *tr* to find a new home for, relocate

reluire [rəlɥir] §37 *intr* to shine, gleam, sparkle

relui·sant [rəlɥizɑ̃] **-sante** [zɑ̃] *adj* shiny, gleaming; **peu reluisant** unpromising, not brilliant

reluquer [rəlyke] *tr* to have an eye on

remâcher [rəmɑʃe] *tr* (coll) to stew over

remailler [rəmaje] *tr* to mend the meshes of

remanier [rəmanje] *tr* to revise, revamp; to re-shuffle

remarier [rəmarje] *tr & ref* to remarry

remarquable [rəmarkabl] *adj* remarkable

remarque [rəmark] *f* remark; **accompagner de remarques** to annotate; **des remarques?** any comments?; **faire une remarque** to make a remark; remark, make a critical observation

remarquer [rəmarke] *tr & intr* to remark, notice; **faire remarquer** to point out ‖ *ref*—**se fair remarquer** to make oneself conspicuous

remballer [rɑ̃bale] *tr* to repack

rembarquer [rɑ̃barke] *tr, intr, & ref* to reembark

rembarrer [rɑ̃bare] *tr* to snub, rebuff

remblai [rɑ̃blɛ] *m* fill; embankment

remblayer [rɑ̃bleje] §49 *tr* to fill; bank up

rembobiner [rɑ̃bɔbine] *tr* to rewind

remboîter [rɑ̃bwate] *tr* to reset (*a bone*); recase (*a book*)

rembourrer [rɑ̃bure] *tr* to upholster; stuff; pad

rembourrure [rɑ̃buryr] *f* stuffing

remboursement [rɑ̃bursəmɑ̃] *m* reimbursement; **contre remboursement** C.O.D.; with cash, e.g., **envoi contre remboursement** cash with order; **remboursement dans le bas de l'appareil** coin return

rembourser [rɑ̃burse] *tr* to reimburse

rembrunir [rɑ̃brynir] *tr* to darken; sadden ‖ *ref* to cloud over

remède [rəmɛd] *m* remedy

remédier [rəmedje] *intr*—**remédier à** to remedy

remembrement [rəmɑ̃brəmɑ̃] *m* regrouping

remémorer [rəmemɔre] *tr*—**remémorer q.ch. à qn** to remind s.o. of s.th. ‖ *ref* to remember

remerciement [rəmɛrsimɑ̃] *m* thanking; **remerciements** thanks; **mille remerciements de** or **pour** a thousand thanks for

remercier [rəmɛrsje] §97 *tr* to thank; dismiss (*an employee*); refuse with thanks; **remercier qn de** + *inf* to thank s.o. for + *ger;* **remercier qn de** or **pour** to thank s.o. for

remettre [rəmɛtr] §42 *tr* to remit, deliver; put back; put back on; give back; put off; reset ‖ *ref* to resume; recover; pull oneself together; (*said of weather*) clear; **s'en remettre à** to leave it up to, depend on

remise [rəmiz] *f* remittance; discount; delivery; postponement; surrender, return; garage; cover (*for game*); **de remise** rented (*car*); **remise au comptant** cash discount

remiser [rəmize] *tr* to put away; park ‖ *ref* to take cover

rémission [remisjɔ̃] *f* remission

remmailler [rɑ̃maje] *tr* to darn

remmener [rɑ̃mne] §2 *tr* to take back

remodelage [rəmɔdlaʒ] *m* remodeling; plastic surgery

remon•tant [rəmɔ̃tɑ̃] **-tante** [tɑ̃t] *adj* fortifying; remontant (*rose*) ‖ *m* tonic

remonte [rəmɔ̃t] *f* ascent

remontée [rəmɔ̃te] *f* climb; surfacing; comeback

remonte-pente [rəmɔ̃tpɑ̃t] *m* (*pl* **-pentes**); ski lift

remonter [rəmɔ̃te] *tr* to remount; pull up; wind (*a clock*); pep up; (theat) to put on again ‖ *intr* (*aux:* ÊTRE) to go up again; date back ‖ *ref* to pep up

remontoir [rəmɔ̃twar] *m* knob (*of stemwinder*); key, winder

remontrance [rəmɔ̃trɑ̃s] *f* remonstrance

remontrer [rəmɔ̃tre] *tr* to show again; point out ‖ *intr*—**en remontrer à** to outdo, best

remords [rəmɔr] *m* remorse

remorque [rəmɔrk] *f* tow rope; trailer; **à la remorque** in tow

remorquer [rəmɔrke] *tr* to tow; haul

remorqueur [rəmɔrkœr] *m* tugboat

rémouleur [remulœr] *m* knife grinder, scissors grinder

remous [rəmu] *m* eddy; wash (*of boat*); agitation

rempailler [rɑ̃paje] *tr* to cane

rempart [rɑ̃par] *m* rampart

remplaçable [rɑ̃plasabl] *adj* replaceable

rempla•çant [rɑ̃plasɑ̃] **-çante** [sɑ̃t] *mf* replacement, substitute

remplacement [rɑ̃plasmɑ̃] *m* replacement

remplacer [rɑ̃plase] §51 *tr* to replace; take the place of; **remplacer par** to replace with

rem•pli -plie [rɑ̃pli] *adj* full ‖ *m* tuck

remplir [rɑ̃plir] *tr* to fill; fill up; fill out or in; fulfill ‖ *ref* to fill up

remplissage [rɑ̃plisaʒ] *m* filling up

remplumer [rɑ̃plyme] *ref* (coll) to put on flesh again; (coll) to make a comeback

remporter [rɑ̃pɔrte] *tr* to take back; carry off; win

remue-ménage [rəmymenaʒ] *m invar* stir, bustle, to-do

remue-méninges [rəmymenɛ̃ʒ] *f invar* (slang) brainstorming

remuer [rəmɥe] *tr* to move; stir; remove (*e.g., a piece of furniture*) ‖ *intr* to move ‖ *ref* to move; hustle

rémunération [remynerasjɔ̃] *f* remuneration

renâcler [rənɑkle] *intr* to snort; **renâcler à** (coll) to shrink from, bridle at

renaissance [rənɛsɑ̃s] *f* renascence, rebirth; renaissance

renais•sant [rənɛsɑ̃] **-sante** [sɑ̃t] *adj* renascent, reviving; Renaissance

renaître [rənɛtr] §46 *tr* to be reborn; revive; grow again

re•nard [rənar] **-narde** [nard] *mf* fox

renché•ri -rie [rɑ̃ʃeri] *adj* fastidious

renchérir [rɑ̃ʃerir] *tr* to make more expensive ‖ *intr* to go up in price; **renchérir sur** to improve on; **renchérir sur la perfection** to gild the lily

rencontre [rɑ̃kɔ̃tr] *f* meeting, encounter; clash; collision; **aller à la rencontre de** to go to meet; **de rencontre** chance (*e.g., acquaintance*)

rencontrer [rɑ̃kɔ̃tre] *tr* to meet, encounter ‖ *ref* to meet; collide; occur

rendement [rɑ̃dmɑ̃] *m* yield; (mech) output, efficiency

rendez-vous [rɑ̃devu] *m* appointment, date; rendezvous; **donner (un) rendez-vous à, fixer (un) rendez-vous à** to make an appointment with; **sur rendez-vous** by appointment

rendre [rɑ̃dr] *tr* to render; yield; surrender; make; translate; vomit ‖ *intr* to bring in, yield ‖ *ref* to surrender; **se rendre à** to go to; **se rendre compte de** to realize

ren·du -due [rɑ̃dy] *adj* arrived; translated; all in, exhausted ‖ *m* rendering; returned article

rêne [rɛn] *f* rein

rené·gat [rənega] **-gate** [gat] *mf* renegade

renfer·mé -mée [rɑ̃fɛrme] *adj* closemouthed, stand-offish ‖ *m* close smell; **sentir le renfermé** to smell stuffy

renfermer [rɑ̃fɛrme] *tr* to contain; include ‖ *ref*—**se renfermer dans** to withdraw into; confine oneself

renfler [rɑ̃fle] *ref* to swell up

renflouage [rɑ̃flua ʒ] *m* refloating, bailing out; **renflouage de l'économie** (govt) pump-priming

renflouer [rɑ̃flue] *tr* to keep afloat; salvage

renfoncement [rɑ̃fɔ̃smɑ̃] *m* recess; hollow; dent

renfoncer [rɑ̃fɔ̃se] §51 *tr* to recess; dent; pull down (*e.g., one's hat*) ‖ *ref* to recede; draw back

renforcement [rɑ̃fɔrsəmɑ̃] *m* reinforcement

renforcer [rɑ̃fɔrse] §51 *tr* to reinforce

renforcir [rɑ̃fɔrsir] *tr* (slang) to strengthen ‖ *intr* (slang) to grow stronger

renfort [rɑ̃fɔr] *m* reinforcement

renfro·gné -gnée [rɑ̃frɔɲe] *adj* sullen, glum

renfrogner [rɑ̃frɔɲe] *ref* to scowl

rengager [rɑ̃gaʒe] §38 *tr* to rehire ‖ *intr & ref* to reenlist

rengaine [rɑ̃gɛn] *f*—**la même rengaine** the same old story; **vieille rengaine** old refrain

rengorger [rɑ̃gɔrʒe] §38 *ref* to strut

reniement [rənimɑ̃] *m* denial

renier [rənje] *tr* to deny; repudiate

renifler [rənifle] *tr & intr* to sniff

renne [rɛn] *m* reindeer

renom [rənɔ̃] *m* renown, fame

renom·mé -mée [rənɔme] *adj* renowned, well-known ‖ *f* fame; reputation

renommer [rənɔme] *tr* to reelect; reappoint

renoncement [rənɔ̃smɑ̃] *m* renunciation

renoncer [rənɔ̃se] §51, §96 *tr* (lit) to renounce, repudiate ‖ *intr* to give up; (cards) to renege; **renoncer à** to renounce; give up, abandon, e.g., **lui renoncer** to abandon her (or him); **y renoncer** to give it up

renonciation [rənɔ̃sjɑsjɔ̃] *f* renunciation; waiver

renoncule [rənɔ̃kyl] *f* buttercup; **renoncule**

double bachelor's-button; **renoncule langue** spearwort

renouer [rənwe] *tr* to tie again; resume (*e.g., a conversation*) ‖ *intr* to renew a friendship

renou·veau [rənuvo] *m* (*pl* **-veaux**) springtime; revival

renouvelable [rənuvlabl] *adj* renewable

renouveler [rənuvle] §34 *tr & ref* to renew

renouvellement [rənuvɛlmɑ̃] *m* renewal

rénover [renɔve] *tr* to renew; renovate

renseignement [rɑ̃sɛɲmɑ̃] *m* piece of information; **de renseignements** (mil) intelligence; **renseignements** information

renseigner [rɑ̃sɛɲe] *tr* to inform ‖ *ref* to find out; **se renseigner auprès de qn** to inquire of s.o.

rentable [rɑ̃tabl] *adj* profitable

rente [rɑ̃t] *f* revenue, income; annuity; dividend, return; **rente viagère** life annuity

ren·té -tée [rɑ̃te] *adj* well-off

renter [rɑ̃te] *tr* to endow

ren·tier -tière [rɑ̃tje] [tjɛr] *mf* person of independent means

ren·tré -trée [rɑ̃tre] *adj* sunken (*eyes*); suppressed (*feelings*) ‖ *f* return; reopening (*of school*); yield, income; (comp) reentry

rentrer [rɑ̃tre] §95 *tr* to bring in or back; put in; hold back (*e.g., one's tears*); draw in (*claws*) ‖ *intr* (*aux:* ETRE) to return, reenter; go or come home; be paid or collected; **rentrer dans** to fit into; come back to; get back, recover; **rentrer en soi-même** to take stock of oneself

renverse [rɑ̃vɛrs] *f* shift, turn; **à la renverse** backwards

renversement [rɑ̃vɛrsəmɑ̃] *m* reversal, shift; upset, overturn; overthrow

renverser [rɑ̃vɛrse] *tr* to reverse; overthrow; bowl over, astonish ‖ *intr & ref* to capsize

renvoi [rɑ̃vwa] *m* dismissal; postponement; reference; return; belch, burp; (law) change of venue

renvoyer [rɑ̃vwaje] §26 *tr* to dismiss; fire (*an employee*); postpone; refer; send back

réorganiser [reɔrganize] *tr & ref* to reorganize

réouverture [reuvɛrtyr] *f* reopening

repaire [rəpɛr] *m* den

repaître [rəpɛtr] §12 *tr* to graze; **repaître de** to feast (*e.g., one's eyes*) on ‖ *ref* to eat one's fill (*said of only animals*); **se repaître de** to indulge in, to wallow in

répandre [repɑ̃dr] *tr* to spread; strew, scatter; spill; shed ‖ *ref* to spread; **se répandre en** to be profuse in

répan·du -due [repɑ̃dy] *adj* widespread; widely known

reparaître [rəparɛtr] §12 *intr* to reappear

répara·teur [reparatœr] **-trice** [tris] *adj* restorative ‖ *m* repairman; **réparateur de hautes cheminées et de clochers** steeplejack

réparation [reparɑsjɔ̃] *f* repair; reparation; restoration

réparer [repare] *tr* to repair, fix; mend, patch;

make up (*a loss*); redress (*a wrong*); restore (*one's strength*)

repartie [rəparti], [rəparti] *f* repartee

repartir [rəpartir] **§64** *tr* to retort ‖ *intr* (*aux:* ETRE) to start again; leave again; **repartir à zéro** to go back to square one

répartir [rəpartir] *tr* to distribute

répartiteur [rəpartitœr] *m* distributor; assessor; dispatcher

répartition [rəpartisjɔ̃] *f* distribution; apportionment; range (*of words*)

repas [rəpa] *m* meal, repast; **dernier repas** (rel) last supper; **repas champêtre** picnic; **repas de noce** wedding breakfast; **repas froid** cold snack; **repas principal** main meal; **repas sur le pouce** takeout meal; **repas tiré du sac** brown-bag lunch

repassage [rəpasaʒ] *m* recrossing; ironing; stropping; whetting

repasser [rəpase] *tr* to pass again; go over, review; iron; strop; whet ‖ *intr* to pass by again; drop in again

repêcher [rəpɛʃe] *tr* to fish out; give another chance to; (coll) to get (*s.o.*) out of a scrape

repentance [rəpɑ̃tɑ̃s] *f* repentance

repen•tant [rəpɑ̃tɑ̃] **-tante** [tɑ̃t] *adj* repentant

repen•ti -tie [rəpɑ̃ti] *adj* repentant

repentir [rəpɑ̃tir] *m* repentance ‖ **§41, §97** *ref* to repent; **se repentir de** to be sorry for, to repent

repérage [rəperaʒ] *m* spotting, locating; tracking; marking with a reference mark; (mov) synchronization

répercussion [repɛrkysjɔ̃] *f* repercussion; reverberation

répercuter [repɛrkyte] *tr* to reflect ‖ *ref* to reverberate; have repercussions

repère [rəpɛr] *m* mark, reference

repérer [rəpere] **§10** *tr* to locate, spot; mark with a reference mark; (mov) to synchronize

répertoire [repɛrtwar] *m* repertory; index; **répertoire à onglets** thumb index; **répertoire d'adresses** address book; **répertoire vivant** walking encyclopedia

répéter [repete] **§10** *tr* & *ref* to repeat

répéti•teur [repetitœr] **-trice** [tris] *mf* assistant teacher; coach, tutor

répétition [repetisjɔ̃] *f* repetition; private lesson, tutoring; rehearsal; **répétition des couturières** next-to-last dress rehearsal; **répétition générale** final dress rehearsal

repeupler [rəpœple] *tr* to repeople; restock

repiquer [rəpike] *tr* to plant out (*seedlings*); repave; restitch; rerecord; (phot) to retouch ‖ *intr*—**repiquer à** (slang) to come back to

répit [repi] *m* respite, letup

replacement [rəplasmɑ̃] *m* replacement; reinvestment

replacer [rəplase] **§51** *tr* to replace; find a new job for; reinvest ‖ *ref* to find a new job

replâtrage [rəplatraʒ] *m* replastering; makeshift; (fig) patchwork

re•plet [rəplɛ] **-plète** [plɛt] *adj* fat, plump

repli [rəpli] *m* crease, fold; dip, depression; (mil) falling back

replier [rəplije] *tr* to refold; turn up; close (*e.g., an umbrella*) ‖ *ref* to curl up, coil up; (mil) to fall back

réplique [replik] *f* reply, retort; replica; **donner la réplique à qn** to answer s.o.; (theat) to give s.o. his cue; (theat) to play the straight man or stooge for s.o.

répliquer [replike] *tr* & *intr* to reply

replonger [rəplɔ̃ʒe] **§38** *tr* to plunge again ‖ *intr* to dive again ‖ *ref*—**se replonger dans** to get back into

répon•dant [repɔ̃dɑ̃] **-dante** [dɑ̃t] *mf* guarantor; (eccl) server; **avoir du répondant** (coll) to have money behind one

répon•deur [repɔ̃dœr] **-deuse** [døz] *adj* (coll) back-talking ‖ *m*—**répondeur automatique, répondeur téléphonique** (telephone) answering machine

répondre [repɔ̃dr] **§98** *tr* to answer (*e.g., yes or no*); assure ‖ *intr* to answer, reply; answer back, be saucy; reecho; **répondre à** to answer (*e.g., a question, a letter*); correspond to; **répondre de** to answer for (*a person*); guarantee (*a thing*) ‖ *ref* to answer each other; correspond to each other; be in harmony

réponse [repɔ̃s] *f* answer, response; **réponse normande** evasive answer

report [rəpɔr] *m* carrying forward or over; carryover

reportage [rəpɔrtaʒ] *m* reporting

reporter [rəpɔrtɛr] *m* reporter; **reporter d'images** news cameraman ‖ [rəpɔrte] *tr* to carry back; to postpone; (math) to carry forward ‖ *intr* (com) to carry stock; **à reporter** carried forward ‖ *ref*—**se reporter à** to be carried back to (*e.g., childhood days*); refer to

reporteur [rəpɔrtœr] *m* broker

repos [rəpo] *m* rest, repose; **au repos** not running, still; **de tout repos** reliable; **en repos** at rest; **repos!** (mil) at ease!; **sans repos** restless

repo•sé -sée [rəpoze] *adj* refreshed, relaxed

reposer [rəpoze] *tr* to rest ‖ *intr* to rest; **ici repose . . .** here lies . . . ‖ *ref* to rest; **s'en reposer sur** to rely on

repous•sant [rəpusɑ̃] **-sante** [sɑ̃t] *adj* repulsive

repousser [rəpuse] *tr* to push, shove; repulse, repel; reject, refuse; postpone; emboss ‖ *intr* to grow again; be offensive; (arti) to recoil

repoussoir [rəpuswar] *m* foil; contrast; (mach) driving bolt

reprendre [rəprɑ̃dr] **§56, §97** *tr* to take back; resume; regain (*consciousness*); find fault with; take in (*e.g., a dress*); catch (*one's breath*); (theat) to put on again ‖ *intr* to start again; pick up, improve; criticize ‖ *ref* to pull oneself together; correct oneself in speaking

représailles [rəprezaj] *fpl* reprisal

représen•tant [rəprezɑ̃tɑ̃] **-tante** [tɑ̃t] *adj* & *mf* representative; **représentant de commerce** traveling salesman

représenta•tif [rəprezãtatif] **-tive** [tiv] *adj* representative

représentation [rəprezãtɑsjɔ̃] *f* representation; performance; remonstrance; **représentation de bienfaisance** benefit performance

représenter [rəprezãte] *tr* to represent; put on, perform ‖ *intr* to make a good showing

répression [represjɔ̃] *f* repression

réprimande [reprimãd] *f* reprimand

réprimander [reprimãde] §97 *tr* to reprimand

réprimer [reprime] *tr* to repress

re•pris [rəpri] **-prise** [priz] *adj* recaptured; **être repris de** to suffer from a recurrence of ‖ *m*—**repris de justice** hardened criminal, habitual offender ‖ *f* see **reprise**

reprisage [rəprizaʒ] *m* darning

reprise [rəpriz] *f* recapture; resumption; darning; pickup (*acceleration of motor*); (mov) rerun; (theat) revival; **à plusieurs reprises** several times; **faire une reprise à** to darn; **par reprises** a little at a time

repriser [rəprize] *tr* to darn; mend

réproba•teur [reprɔbatœr] **-trice** [tris] *adj* reproving

reproche [rəprɔʃ] *m* reproach

reprocher [rəprɔʃe] §98 *tr* to reproach; begrudge; (law) to take exception to (*a witness*); **reprocher q.ch. à qn** to reproach s.o. for s.th.; begrudge s.o. s.th.; remind s.o. reproachfully of s.th.

reproduction [rəprɔdyksjɔ̃] *f* reproduction; **reproduction embryonnaire asexuée** embryonic cloning

reproduire [rəprɔdɥir] §19 *tr & ref* to reproduce

reprographieur [rəprɔgrafjœr] *m* copying machine

réprou•vé -vée [repruve] *adj & mf* outcast; damned

réprouver [repruve] *tr* to disapprove

reps [rɛps] *m* baize

reptile [rɛptil] *m* reptile

re•pu -pue [rəpy] *adj* satiated

républi•cain [repyblikɛ̃] **-caine** [kɛn] *adj & mf* republican

république [repyblik] *f* republic; **République fédérale d'Allemagne** Federal Republic of Germany; **République tchèque** Czech Republic

répudier [repydje] *tr* to repudiate

répu•gnant [repyɲã] **-gnante** [ɲãt] *adj* repugnant

répugner [repyɲe] §96, §97 *intr*—**répugner à** to be repugnant to, disgust, repel, e.g., **cette odeur leur répugne** that odor disgusts them; **il me (te, lui,** etc.**) répugne de** it is distasteful for me (you, him, etc.) to; **répugner à** or **de** + *inf* to be reluctant or loath to + *inf*, balk at + *ger*

répul•sif [repylsif] **-sive** [siv] *adj* repulsive

réputation [repytɑsjɔ̃] *f* reputation

répu•té -tée [repyte] *adj* of high repute; **être réputé** to be reputed to be

requérir [rəkerir] §3 *tr* to demand; ask; require; summon

requête [rəkɛt] *f* petition, appeal

requiem [rekɥijɛm] *m* requiem

requin [rəkɛ̃] *m* shark

re•quis [rəki] **-quise** [kiz] *adj* required, requisite ‖ *mf* conscript ‖ *v* see **requérir**

réquisition [rekizisjɔ̃] *f* requisition

réquisitionner [rekizisjɔne] *tr* to requisition

réquisitoire [rekizitwar] *m* indictment

res•capé -capée [rɛskape] *adj* rescued ‖ *mf* survivor

rescinder [resɛ̃de] *tr* to rescind

rescousse [rɛskus] *f* rescue

ré•seau [rezo] *m* (*pl* **-seaux**) net; network, system; **réseau de barbelés** barbed wire entanglement; **réseau ferroviaire urbain** rapid transit

réséda [rezeda] *m* mignonette

réservation [rezɛrvɑsjɔ̃] *f* reservation; booking

réserve [rezɛrv] *f* reserve; reservation; reserve room (*in a library*); **de réserve** emergency, reserve (*rations, fund, etc.*); **réserve des imprimés** periodical room (*in a library*); **sous réserve que** on condition that; **sous toutes réserves** without committing oneself

réserver [rezɛrve] §97 *tr* to reserve; set aside ‖ *ref* to set aside for oneself; wait and see, hold off

réserviste [rezɛrvist] *m* reservist

réservoir [rezɛrvwar] *m* reservoir, tank; **réservoir de bombes** bomb bay

résidanat [rezidana] *m* (med) residency

résidence [rezidãs] *f* residence; **résidence mobile** mobile home; **résidence surveillée** house arrest; **résidence universitaire** college dormitory

rési•dent [rezidã] **-dente** [dãt] *mf* alien, foreigner; (dipl) resident

résiden•tiel -tielle [rezidãsjɔl] *adj* residential

résider [rezide] *intr* to reside

résidu [rezidy] *m* residue; refuse

resi•duel -duelle [rezidɥɛl] *adj* residual

résignation [reziɲɑsjɔ̃] *f* resignation

résigner [reziɲe] *tr* to resign ‖ §96 *ref* to be or become resigned

résilier [rezilje] *tr* to cancel

résille [rezij] *f* hair net

résine [rezin] *f* resin

résistance [rezistãs] *f* resistance

résis•tant [rezistã] **-tante** [tãt] *adj* resistant; strong; fast (*color*) ‖ *mf* (hist) Resistance fighter

résister [reziste] §96 *intr* to be fast, not run (*said of colors or dyes*); **résister à** to weather (*e.g., a storm*); resist, hold out against, withstand, e.g., **inutile de lui résister** useless to resist him; **résister à** + *inf* to resist + *ger*

réso•lu -lue [rezɔly] §92 *adj* resolute, resolved ‖ *v* see **résoudre**

résolution [rezɔlysjɔ̃] *f* resolution; canceling

résonance [rezɔnãs] *f* resonance

résonner [rezɔne] *intr* to resound; to reecho, ring, clank; twang

résorber [rezɔrbe] *tr* to absorb ‖ *ref* to become absorbed

résoudre [rezudr] §60, §96, §97 *tr* to resolve; decide; solve; persuade; cancel; **être résolu à** to be resolved to ‖ *intr*—**résoudre de** to decide to ‖ §96—*ref*—**se résoudre à** to decide to; reconcile oneself to; **se résoudre en** to turn into

résout [rezu] *v* see **résoudre**

respect [rɛspɛ] *m* respect; **présenter ses respects (à)** to pay one's respects (to); **respect de soi** or **soi-même** self-respect; **respect humain** [rɛspɛkymɛ̃] fear of what people might say; **sauf votre (mon,** etc.) **respect** with all due respect; pardon the language; **tenir en respect** to keep at a respectful distance

respectable [rɛspɛktabl] *adj* respectable

respecter [rɛspɛkte] *tr* to respect; **respecter les fleurs** (*public sign*) keep off the flowers ‖ *ref* to keep one's self-respect

respec•tif [rɛspɛktif] **-tive** [tiv] *adj* respective

respec•tueux [rɛspɛktɥø] **-tueuse** [tɥøz] *adj* respectful

respirer [rɛspire] *tr* to breathe ‖ *intr* to breathe; catch one's breath

resplendis•sant [rɛsplɑ̃disɑ̃] **-sante** [sɑ̃t] *adj* radiant, beaming, shining, aglow, resplendent

responsabilité [rɛspɔ̃sabilite] *f* responsibility

responsable [rɛspɔ̃sabl] *adj* responsible; **responsable de** responsible for; **responsable envers** accountable to; **solidairement responsable** jointly liable ‖ *mf* person responsible, person in charge

resquiller [rɛskije] *tr* (coll) to obtain by fraud ‖ *intr* (coll) to crash the gate

resquil•leur [rɛskijœr] **-leuse** [jøz] *mf* (coll) gate-crasher

ressac [rəsak] *m* surf; undertow

ressaisir [rəsezir] *tr* to recapture ‖ *ref* to regain one's self-control

ressasser [rəsase] *tr* to go over and over again

ressaut [rəso] *m* projection; sharp rise

ressemblance [rəsɑ̃blɑ̃s] *f* resemblance

ressembler [rəsɑ̃ble] *intr*—**ressembler à** to look like, resemble, e.g., **le fils lui ressemble** the son looks like him ‖ *ref* (*pp* **ressemblé** *invar*) to resemble one another; be alike, look alike

ressemeler [rəsəmle] §34 *tr* to resole

ressentiment [rəsɑ̃timɑ̃] *m* resentment

ressentir [rəsɑ̃tir] §41 *tr* to feel keenly, be hurt by (*an insult*); experience (*joy, pain, surprise*) ‖ *ref*—**se ressentir de** to feel the aftereffects of

resserre [rəsɛr] *f* shed, storeroom

resserrer [rəsere] *tr* to tighten; contract; close; lock up (*e.g., valuables*) again ‖ *ref* to tighten; contract

ressort [rəsɔr] *m* spring; springiness; motive; **du ressort de** within the jurisdiction of; **en dernier ressort** without appeal; as a last re-

sort; **ressort à boudin** coil spring; **sans ressort** slack

ressortir [rəsɔrtir] *intr*—**ressortir à** to come under the jurisdiction of; fall under the head of ‖ §64 *intr* (*aux:* ÊTRE) to go out again; stand out, be evident; **faire ressortir** to set off; **il ressort de** it follows from; **il ressort que** it follows that

ressortis•sant [rəsɔrtisɑ̃] **-sante** [sɑ̃t] *adj*—**ressortissant à** under the jursidiction of ‖ *mf* national

ressource [rəsurs] *f* resource; **de ressource** resourceful; **sans ressources** without resources

ressouvenir [rəsuvnir] §72, §97 *ref* to reminisce; **se ressouvenir de** to recall

ressusciter [resysite] *tr* to resuscitate; to resurrect ‖ *intr* (*aux:* ÊTRE) to rise from the dead; get well

res•tant [rɛstɑ̃] **-tante** [tɑ̃t] *adj* remaining ‖ *m* remainder

restaupouce [rɛstɔpus] *m* fast-food restaurant

restaurant [rɛstɔrɑ̃] *m* restaurant; café (*small restaurant*); **restaurant libre-service** self-service restaurant

restauration [rɛstɔrasjɔ̃] *f* restoration; restaurant business; **restauration rapide** fast food

restaurer [rɛstɔre] *tr* to restore ‖ *ref* (coll) to take some nourishment

reste [rɛst] *m* rest, remainder; remnant; relic; **au reste, du reste** moreover; **de reste** spare; **restes** remains; leftovers

rester [rɛste] §96 *intr* (*aux:* ÊTRE) to remain, stay; be left over; **en rester** to stop, leave off; **en rester là** to stop right there; **il me (te, leur,** etc.) **reste q.ch.** I (you, they, etc.) have s.th. left

restituer [rɛstitɥe] *tr* to restore; give back; (comp) to print out

restitution [rɛstitysjɔ̃] *f* restitution; restoration

restoroute [rɛstɔrut] *m* drive-in restaurant; service stop, rest stop (*on a superhighway*)

restreindre [rɛstrɛ̃dr] §50 *tr* to restrict; curtail ‖ *ref* to become limited; cut down expenses

res•treint [rɛstrɛ̃] **-treinte** [trɛ̃t] *adj* limited

restriction [rɛstriksjɔ̃] *f* restriction; **restriction mentale** mental reservation

résultat [rezylta] *m* result; **résultat financier** bottom line

résulter [rezylte] *intr* to result; **il en résulte que** it follows that

résumé [rezyme] *m* summary, recapitulation; **en résumé** in short, in a word

résumer [rezyme] *tr* to summarize ‖ *ref* to be summed up

résurrection [rezyrɛksjɔ̃] *f* resurrection

rétablir [retablir] *tr* to restore ‖ *ref* to recover

rétablissement [retablismɑ̃] *m* restoration; recovery

retailler [rətaje] *tr* to resharpen

retape [rətap] *f* (slang) streetwalking

retaper [rətape] *tr* (coll) to straighten up; (coll) to give a lick and a promise to ‖ *ref* (coll) to perk up

retard [rətar] *m* delay; **en retard** late; slow (*clock*); **en retard sur** behind

retardataire [rətardatɛr] *adj* tardy; retarded ‖ *mf* latecomer, straggler

retar·dé -dée [rətarde] *adj* retarded ‖ *mf* (pej) retard

retarder [rətarde] *tr* to delay; put off; set back ‖ *intr* to go slow, be behind

retenir [rətnir] §72 *tr* to hold back, keep back; detain; remember, note; reserve; retain (*a lawyer*); carry (*a number*) ‖ §97 *ref*—**se retenir à** to cling to; **se retenir de** to refrain from

retentir [rətãtir] *intr* to resound

rete·nu -nue [rətny] *adj* reserved; held back ‖ *f* withholding; reserve; **retenue à la source** withholding tax

réticence [retisãs] *f* evasiveness, concealment; hesitation; reservation, misgiving

réti·cent [retisã] **-cente** [sãt] *adj* evasive; hesitant; reserved, withdrawn

réticule [retikyl] *m* handbag

ré·tif [retif] **-tive** [tiv] *adj* restive

rétine [retin] *f* retina

reti·ré -rée [rətire] *adj* remote, out-of-the-way; retired

retirement [rətirmã] *m* contraction

retirer [rətire] *tr* to withdraw; take off; fire again ‖ *intr* to fire again ‖ *ref* to withdraw; retire

retombée [rətõbe] *f* fall; hang (*of cloth*); **retombées radioactives** fallout

retomber [rətõbe] *intr* (*aux:* ÊTRE) to fall again; fall; fall back; hang, hang down; relapse

retordre [rətɔrdrə] *tr* to twist; wring out

rétorquer [retɔrke] *tr* to retort

re·tors [rətɔr] **-torse** [tɔrs] *adj* twisted; wily; curved (*beak*) ‖ *mf* rascal

retouche [rətuʃ] *f* retouch; (phot) retouching; **retouches** alterations

retoucher [rətuʃe] *tr* to retouch; make alterations on

retour [rətur] *m* return; turn, bend; reversal (*e.g., of opinion*); **de retour** in return; **en retour d'équerre** at right angles; **être de retour** to be back; **par retour du courrier** by return mail; **retour à la masse** (elec) ground (*on chassis of auto, radio, etc.*); **retour à la terre** (elec) ground; **retour à l'envoyeur** return to sender (*on letter*); **retour d'âge** change of life; **retour de flamme** backfire; **retour de manivelle** kick (of the crank); (fig) backlash; **retour de monnaie** coin return; **retour en arrière** flashback

retourner [rəturne] §95 *tr* to send back, return; upset; turn over (*e.g., the soil*); turn inside out ‖ *intr* (*aux:* ÊTRE) to go back, return ‖ *ref* to turn around, look back; turn over; (fig) to veer, shift; **s'en retourner** to go back; **se retourner contre** to turn against

retracer [rətrase] §51 *tr* to retrace; bring to mind, recall ‖ *ref* to recall

rétracter [retrakte] *tr* & *ref* to retract

rétraction [retraksjõ] *f* contraction

retrait [rətrɛ] *m* withdrawal; shrinkage; running out (*of tide*); **en retrait** set back, recessed; (typ) indented; **retrait de permis** suspension of driver's license

retraite [rətrɛt] *f* retreat; retirement; pension; **battre en retraite** to retreat; **en retraite** retired; **prendre sa retraite** to retire; **retraite anticipée** early retirement; **toucher sa retraite** to draw one's pension

retrai·té -tée [rətrete] *adj* pensioned, retired ‖ *mf* pensioner

retranchement [rətrãʃmã] *m* retrenchment; cutting out

retrancher [rətrãʃe] *tr* to cut off or out, retrench ‖ *ref* to become entrenched

retransmettre [rətrãsmɛtr] §42 *tr* to retransmit; rebroadcast

retransmission [rətrãsmisjõ] *f* retransmission; rebroadcast

rétré·ci -cie [retresi] *adj* narrow; shrunk

rétrécir [retresir] *tr* to shrink; take in (*a garment*) ‖ *intr* & *ref* to shrink; narrow

rétrécissement [retresismã] *m* shrinkage, contraction; **rétrécissement du champ visuel** (opt) tunnel vision

retremper [rətrãpe] *tr* to soak again; retemper; give new strength to ‖ *ref* to take another dip; get new vigor

rétribuer [retribɥe] *tr* to remunerate

rétribution [retribysjõ] *f* retribution; salary, fee

rétro [retro] *adj invar* (coll) (*inspiré par les années 1920 à 1960*) retro, e.g., **la mode rétro** retro fashions; e.g., **le style rétro** retro styles ‖ *m* recoil; rearview mirror

rétroaction [retrɔaksjõ] *f* (mech) feedback

rétrocontrôle [retrɔkõtrol] *m* (physiol) feedback

rétrofusée [retrɔfyze] *f* retrorocket

rétrograder [retrɔgrade] *intr* to retrogress

rétroprojecteur [retrɔprɔʒɛktœr] *m* overhead projector

rétrospec·tif [retrɔspɛktif] **-tive** [tiv] *adj* retrospective ‖ *m* flashback

rétrospection [retrɔspɛksjõ] *f* restrospection

retrousser [rətruse] *tr* to roll up, turn up; curl up (*one's lip*) ‖ *ref* to turn up or pull up one's clothes

retrouve [rətruv] *f* (comp) retrieval

retrouver [rətruve] *tr* to find again; recover ‖ *ref* to be back again; meet again; get one's bearings

rétroviseur [retrɔvizœr] *m* rear-view mirror

rets [rɛ] *m*—**prendre dans des rets** to snare

réunification [reynifikasjõ] *f* reunification

réunion [reynjõ] *f* reunion; meeting; **réunion de service** staff meeting

réunir [reynir] *tr* to unite, join; reunite; call together, convene ‖ *ref* to meet; reunite

réus·si -sie [resyi] *adj* successful

réussir [reysir] §96 *tr* to make a success of, be good at; accomplish ‖ *intr* to succeed; **réussir à** to succeed in; pass (*an exam*)

réussite [reysit] *f* success; **faire une réussite** (cards) to play solitaire

réutilisable [reytilizabl] *adj* reusable

revaloir [rəvalwar] **§71** *tr*—**revaloir q.ch à qn** to pay s.o. back for s.th.

revaloriser [rəvalɔrize] *tr* to revalue, reassert the value of; raise (*a salary*)

revan•chard [rəvɑ̃ʃar] **-charde** [ʃard] *adj* (coll) vengeful ‖ *mf* (coll) avenger

revanche [rəvɑ̃ʃ] *f* revenge; return bout or engagement, return match; **en revanche** on the other hand; **prendre sa revanche sur** to get even with

revancher [rəvɑ̃ʃe] *ref* to get even

rêvasser [rɛvase] *intr* to daydream

rêvasserie [rɛvasri] *f* fitful dreaming; daydreaming

rêve [rɛv] *m* dream

revêche [rəvɛʃ] *adj* sullen, crabbed

réveil [revɛj] *m* awakening; recovery; alarm clock; (mil) reveille

réveille-matin [revɛjmatɛ̃] *m invar* alarm clock

réveiller [reveje] *tr & ref* to wake up

réveillon [revɛjɔ̃] *m* Christmas Eve supper; New Year's Eve party

réveillonner [revɛjɔne] *intr* to celebrate Christmas Eve *ou* New Year's Eve

révéla•teur [revelatœr] **-trice** [tris] *adj* revealing; telltale ‖ *mf* informer ‖ *m* (phot) developer

révélation [revelasjɔ̃] *f* revelation

révéler [revele] **§10** *tr* to reveal; (phot) to develop

revenant [rəvnɑ̃] *m* ghost

reven•deur [rəvɑ̃dœr] **-deuse** [døz] *mf* retailer; secondhand dealer

revendication [rəvɑ̃dikasjɔ̃] *f* claim

revendiquer [rəvɑ̃dike] *tr* to claim; insist upon; assume (*a responsibility*)

revendre [rəvɑ̃dr] *tr* to resell

revenez-y [rəvnezi] *m invar* (coll) return; **un goût de revenez-y** (coll) a taste like more

revenir [rəvnir] **§72, §95** *intr* (*aux:* ÉTRE) to return, come back; **en revenir** to have a narrow escape; **faire revenir** (culin) to brown; **n'en pas revenir** to not get over it; **revenir à** to come to, amount to; come to (*e.g., mind*); **revenir à soi** to come to; **revenir bredouille** to come back empty-handed; **revenir de** to recover from; realize (*a mistake*); **revenir de loin** to have been at death's door; **revenir sur** to go back on (*e.g., one's word*) ‖ *ref*—**s'en revenir** to come back

revente [rəvɑ̃t] *f* resale

revenu [rəvny] *m* revenue, income; **revenu imposable** taxable income; **revenu national brut** **(R.N.B.)** gross national product (G.N.P.); **revenu net** net income; **revenus salariaux** earned income

revenue [rəvny] *f* new growth (*of trees*)

rêver [rɛve] *tr* to dream ‖ *intr* to dream; **rêver à** to dream of (*think about*); **rêver de** to dream of (*in sleep*); to long to + *inf*

réverbère [revɛrbɛr] *m* streetlight

réverbérer [revɛrbere] **§10** *tr* to reflect (*light, heat, etc.*); re-echo, reverberate ‖ *ref* to be reflected

reverdir [rəvɛrdir] *tr* to make green ‖ *intr* to grow green; become young again

révérence [reverɑ̃s] *f* reverence; curtsy; **révérence parler** (coll) pardon the language; **tirer sa révérence** to bow out

révéren•cieux [reverɑ̃sjø] **-cieuse** [sjøz] *adj* obsequious

révé•rend [reverɑ̃] **-rende** [rɑ̃d] *adj & m* reverend

révérer [revere] **§10** *tr* to revere

rêverie [rɛvri] *f* reverie

revers [rəvɛr] *m* reverse; lapel; (tennis) backhand; **à revers** from behind; **revers de main** slap with the back of the hand

reverser [rəvɛrse] *tr* to pour back; pour out again

réversible [revɛrsibl] *adj* reversible

revêtement [rəvɛtmɑ̃] *m* surfacing; facing; lining; casing

revêtir [rəvɛtir] **§73** *tr* to put on; clothe, dress up; invest; surface; line; face; assume (*a form; an aspect*)

rê•veur [rɛvœr] **-veuse** [vøz] *adj* dreamy ‖ *mf* dreamer; **cela me laisse rêveur** that leaves me puzzled

revirement [rəvirmɑ̃] *m* sudden reversal; (naut) tack

réviser [revize] *tr* to revise; review; overhaul; recondition

réviseur [revizœr] *m* proofreader

révision [revizjɔ̃] *f* revision; review; overhauling; proofreading

révisionniste [revizjɔnist] *adj & mf* revisionist

revivre [rəvivr] **§74** *tr* to live again, relive ‖ *intr* to live again

révocation [revɔkasjɔ̃] *f* dismissal; revocation

revoici [rəvwasi] *prep*—**me (vous,** etc.) **revoici** (coll) here I am (you are, etc.) again

revoilà [rəvwala] *prep*—**le (la,** etc.) **voilà** (coll) there it, he (she, etc.) is again

revoir [rəvwar] *m*—**au revoir** good-by ‖ **§75** *tr* to see again; review; revise ‖ *ref* to meet again; **on se reverra** we'll see each other again, so long

révol•tant [revɔltɑ̃] **-tante** [tɑ̃t] *adj* revolting

révolte [revɔlt] *f* revolt, rebellion

révol•té -tée [revɔlte] *adj & mf* rebel

révolter [revɔlte] *tr & ref* to revolt; **se révolter devant** to be revolted by

révo•lu -lue [revɔly] *adj* completed; elapsed; bygone

révolution [revɔlysjɔ̃] *f* revolution

révolutionnaire [revɔlysjɔnɛr] *adj & mf* revolutionary

revolver [revɔlvɛr] *m* revolver

révoquer [revɔke] *tr* to revoke; countermand; dismiss; recall

re•vu -vue [rəvy] *adj* revised ‖ *f* see **revue**

revue [rəvy] *f* review; magazine, journal; (theat)

revue; **passer en revue** to review (*past events; troops*)

rez-de-chaussée [redʃose] *m invar* first floor, ground floor

R.F. *abbr* (**République Française**) French Republic

Rh. *abbr* (**facteur Rhésus**) Rh (Rhesus factor)

rhabiller [rabije] *tr* to repair; dress again; refurbish ‖ *ref* to change one's clothes; **va te rhabiller!** (pej) get out!

rhapsodie [rapsɔdi] *f* rhapsody

Rhénanie [renani] *f* Rhineland

rhéostat [reɔsta] *m* rheostat

Rhésus [resys] *adj & m* (gen) rhesus ‖ **rhésus** *m* rhesus monkey, rhesus

rhétorique [retɔrik] *adj* rhetorical ‖ *f* rhetoric

Rhin [rɛ̃] *m* Rhine

rhinocéros [rinɔserɔs] *m* rhinoceros

rhubarbe [rybarb] *f* rhubarb

rhum [rɔm] *m* rum

rhumati•sant [rymatizɑ̃] **-sante** [zɑ̃t] *adj & mf* rheumatic

rhumatis•mal -male [rymatismal] *adj* (*pl* **-maux** [mo]) rheumatic

rhumatisme [rymatism] *m* rheumatism

rhume [rym] *m* cold; **rhume des foins** hay fever

ri [ri] *v* see **rire**

riant [rjɑ̃] **riante** [rjɑ̃t] *adj* smiling; cheerful, pleasant

ribambelle [ribɑ̃bɛl] *f* (coll) long string, swarm, lot

ri•baud [ribo] **-baude** [bod] *adj* licentious ‖ *mf* camp follower; debauchee

ricanement [rikanmɑ̃] *m* snicker

ricane [rikane] *intr* to snicker

ri•chard [riʃar] **-charde** [ʃard] *mf* (coll) moneybags

riche [riʃ] *adj* rich ‖ *m* rich man; **nouveaux riches** newly rich

riche•lieu [riʃəljø] *m* (*pl* **-lieu** or **-lieus**) oxford

richesse [riʃɛs] *f* wealth; richness; **richesses** riches; **richesses naturelles** natural resources

ricin [risɛ̃] *m* castor-oil plant; castor bean

ricocher [rikɔʃe] *intr* to ricochet, rebound

ricochet [rikɔʃɛ] *m* ricochet; fun; **faire des ricochets** to play ducks and drakes; **par ricochet** indirectly

rictus [riktys] *m* rictus; grin

ride [rid] *f* wrinkle; ripple

ri•dé -dée [ride] *adj* wrinkled; corrugated

ri•deau [rido] *m* (*pl* **-deaux**) curtain; **rideau d'arbres** line of trees; **rideau de fer** iron curtain; safety blind (*of a store*); (theat) fire curtain; **rideau de feu** (mil) cover of artillery fire; **rideau de fumée** smoke, screen

ridectomie [ridɛktɔmi] *f* face-lift

ridelle [ridɛl] *f* rave, side rails (*of wagon*)

rider [ride] *tr* to wrinkle; ripple

ridicule [ridikyl] *adj* ridiculous ‖ *m* ridicule

ridiculiser [ridikylize] *tr* to ridicule

rien [rjɛ̃] *m* trifle; **comme un rien** with no trouble at all; **un rien de** just a little (bit) of; **un rien de temps** no time at all ‖ *pron indef*—**de**

rien don't mention it, you're welcome; of no importance; **il n'en est rien** such is not the case; **rien ne** or **ne ... rien §90B** nothing, not anything; **rien de moins (que)** nothing less (than); **rien que** nothing but

rieur [rjœr] **rieuse** [rjøz] *adj* laughing ‖ *mf* laugher, mocker ‖ *f* (orn) black-headed gull

riflard [riflar] *m* coarse file; jack plane; paring chisel

rigide [riʒid] *adj* rigid; stiff; strict

rigidité [riʒidite,] *f* rigidity; **rigidité cadavérique** rigor mortis

rigolade [rigɔlad] *f* (coll) good time; fun; (coll) big joke

rigole [rigɔl] *f* drain; ditch

rigoler [rigɔle] *intr* (slang) to laugh, joke

rigo•lo [rigɔlo] **-lote** [lɔt] *adj* (coll) comical; (coll) queer, funny ‖ *mf* (coll) card ‖ *m* (slang) rod, gat

rigou•reux [rigurø] **-reuse** [røz] *adj* rigorous; severe

rigueur [rigœr] *f* rigor, strictness; **à la rigueur** to the letter; as a last resort; **de rigueur** compulsory, de rigueur

rillons [rijɔ̃] *mpl* cracklings

rimail•leur [rimajœr] **-leuse** [jøz] *mf* (coll) rhymester

rime [rim] *f* rhyme; **rimes croisées** alternate rhymes; **rimes plates** couplets of alternate masculine and feminine rhymes

rimer [rime] *tr & intr* to rhyme

rimmel [rimɛl] *m* mascara

rinçage [rɛ̃saʒ] *m* rinse

rince-bouche [rɛ̃buʃ] *m invar* mouthwash

rince-bouteilles [rɛ̃•utej] *m invar* (mach) bottle-washing machine

rince-doigts [rɛ̃sdwa] *m invar* fingerbowl

rincer [rɛ̃se] **§51** *tr* to rinse; (slang) to ruin, take to the cleaners

rinçure [rɛ̃syr] *f* rinsing water

ring [riŋ] *m* ring (*for, e.g., boxing*)

ringard [rɛ̃gar] *m* poker (*for fire*)

ripaille [ripaj] *f* (coll) blowout; **faire ripaille** (coll) to carouse

ripe [rip] *f* scraper

riper [ripe] *tr* to scrape; (naut) to slip ‖ *intr* to slip; skid

riposte [ripɔst] *f* riposte, retort

riposter [ripɔste] *tr* to riposte, retort

rire [rir] *m* laugh; laughter; laughing; **fou rire** uncontrollable laughter; **gros rire** guffaw; **rire jaune** forced laugh ‖ **§61** (*pp* **ri** *invar*) *intr* to laugh, joke, smile; **pour rire** for fun, in jest; **rire dans sa barbe, rire sous cape** to laugh up one's sleeve; **rire de** to laugh at or over; **rire du bout des lèvres, rire du bout des dents** to titter; **rire jaune** to force a laugh ‖ **§97** *ref*—**se rire de** to laugh at

ris [ri] *m* (naut) reef; (obs) laughter; **ris d'agneau** or **de veau** sweetbread

risée [rize] *f* scorn; laughingstock; light squall

risible [rizibl] *adj* laughable

risque [risk] *m* risk; **à risques élevés** high-risk

ris•qué -quée [riske] *adj* risky; risqué

risquer [riske] §97 *tr* to risk; hasard (*e.g., a remark*) ‖ *intr*—**risquer de** + *inf* to risk + *ger;* have a good chance of + *ger*

risque-tout [riskətu] *mf invar* daredevil

rissoler [risɔle] *tr & intr* to brown

ristourne [risturn] *f* rebate, refund; dividend

ristourner [risturne] *tr* to refund

ritournelle [riturnɛl] *f*—**c'est toujours la même ritournelle** it's always the same old story; **ritournelle publicitaire** advertising jingle or slogan

ri•tuel -tuelle [rityɛl] *adj & m* ritual

rivage [rivaʒ] *m* shore; bank

ri•val -vale [rival] (*pl* -**vaux** [vo] -**vales**) *adj & mf* rival

rivaliser [rivalize] *intr* to compete; **rivaliser avec** to compete with, rival

rivalité [rivalite] *f* rivalry

rive [riv] *f* shore; bank; **rive droite** Right Bank; **rive gauche** Left Bank

river [rive] *tr* to rivet

rive•rain [rivrɛ̃] -**raine** [rɛn] *adj* waterfront; bordering ‖ *mf* riversider; dweller along a street or road

riveraineté [rivrɛnte] *f* riparian rights

rivet [rivɛ] *m* rivet

rivière [rivjɛr] *f* river, stream, tributary; (turf) water jump; **rivière de diamants** diamond necklace

rixe [riks] *f* brawl, dust-up (coll)

riz [ri] *m* rice; **riz au lait** rice pudding; **riz glacé** polished rice; **riz intégral** brown rice; **riz précuit** minute rice

rizière [rizjɛr] *f* rice field

robe [rɔb] *f* dress; gown; robe; wrapper (*of cigar*); skin (*of onion, sausage, etc.*); husk (*of, e.g., bean*); **robe de chambre** dressing gown; **robe de cocktail** cocktail dress; **robe de grossesse** maternity dress; **robe de mariée** wedding dress; **robe d'intérieur** housecoat; **robe du soir** evening gown; **robe tunique** smock

robe-chemisier [rɔbʃəmizje] *f* chemise (*dress*)

rober [rɔbe] *tr* to husk, skin; wrap (*a cigar*)

roberts [rɔbɛr] *mpl* (slang) breasts

robin [rɔbɛ̃] *m* (coll) judge; (pej) shyster

robinet [rɔbinɛ] *m* faucet, tap; cock; **robinet d'eau tiède** (coll) bore; **robinet mélangeur** mixing faucet

robinier [rɔbinje] *m* (bot) locust tree

robot [rɔbo] *m* robot; pilotless (*airplane*); **robot cireur** automatic shoeshiner

robotique [rɔbɔtik] *adj* robotic ‖ *f* robotics

robotiser [rɔbɔtize] *tr* to robotize

robre [rɔbr] *m* rubber (*in bridge*)

robuste [rɔbyst] *adj* robust; firm

roc [rɔk] *m* rock

rocade [rɔkad] *f* bypass (*of a road*)

rocaille [rɔkaj] *adj* rococo ‖ *f* stones; rocky ground; stonework

rocail•leux [rɔkajø] -**leuse** [jøz] *adj* rocky, stony; harsh

roche [rɔʃ] *f* rock; boulder

rocher [rɔʃe] *m* rock; crag

rochet [rɔʃɛ] *m* ratchet; bobbin

ro•cheux [rɔʃø] -**cheuse** [ʃøz] *adj* rocky

rodage [rɔdaʒ] *m* grinding; breaking in; **en rodage** being broken in, new

roder [rɔde] *tr* to grind (*a valve*); break in (*a new car*); polish up (*a new play*)

rôder [rode] *intr* to prowl

rô•deur [rodœr] -**deuse** [døz] *adj* prowling ‖ *mf* prowler

rogatons [rɔgatɔ̃] *mpl* (coll) scraps

rogne [rɔɲ] *f* (coll) anger; **mettre qn èn rogne** (coll) to make s.o. see red

rogner [rɔɲe] *tr* to pare, trim

rognon [rɔɲɔ̃] *m* kidney

rogomme [rɔgɔm] *m*—**de rogomme** (coll) husky, beery (*voice*)

rogue [rɔg] *adj* arrogant

roi [rwa], [rwɑ] *m* king; **tirer les rois** to gather to eat the Twelfth-night cake

roitelet [rwatlɛ] *m* kinglet; (orn) kinglet

rôle [rol] *m* role; roll, muster

ROM [ɛroɛm] *f invar* (letterword) (**mémoire morte**) ROM (read-only memory)

ro•main [rɔmɛ̃] -**maine** [mɛn] *adj* Roman; roman (*type*); romaine (*lettuce*) ‖ *m* (typ) roman ‖ *f* romaine (lettuce); **bon comme la romaine** (slang) done for ‖ (*cap*) *mf* Roman (*person*)

ro•man [rɔmɑ̃] -**maine** [man] *adj* Romance (*language*); (archit) Romanesque ‖ *m* novel; **roman à l'eau de rose** romance; **roman d'anticipation, roman de science fiction** science-fiction novel; **roman de série noire** thriller; **roman noir** whodunit; Gothic novel; **roman policier** detective story

romance [rɔmɑ̃s] *f* ballad

romanche [rɔmɑ̃ʃ] *m* Romansh

roman•cier [rɔmɑ̃sje] -**cière** [sjɛr] *mf* novelist; **romancier d'anticipation** science-fiction writer

ro•mand [rɔmɑ̃] -**mande** [mɑ̃d] *adj* French-speaking (*Switzerland*)

romanesque [rɔmanɛsk] *adj* romanesque, romantic, fabulous

roman-feuilleton [rɔmɑ̃fœjtɔ̃] *m* (*pl* **romans-feuilletons**) newspaper serial

roman-fleuve [rɔmɑ̃flœv] *m* (*pl* **romans-fleuves**) saga novel

romani•chel -chelle [rɔmaniʃɛl] *mf* gypsy, vagrant

romantique [rɔmɑ̃tik] *adj & mf* romantic

romantisme [rɔmɑ̃tism] *m* romanticism

romarin [rɔmarɛ̃] *m* (bot) rosemary

Rome [rɔm] *f* Rome

rompre [rɔ̃pr] (3d *sg pres ind* **rompt** [rɔ̃]) *tr* to break; burst; break in, train; break off ‖ *intr & ref* to break

rom•pu -pue [rɔ̃py] *adj*—**rompu à** accustomed to, experienced in; **rompu de** tired out from or by, exhausted with

romsteck [rɔmstɛk] *m* rump steak

ronce [rɔ̃s] *f* bramble; curly grain (*of wood*); **en ronces artificielles** barbed-wire (*fence*)

ronchonner [rɔ̃ʃɔne] *intr* (coll) to bellyache, grumble

rond [rɔ̃] **ronde** [rɔ̃d] *adj* round; rounded; plump; straightforward; (slang) tight, drunk ‖ *m* ring, circle; round slice; (coll) dough, money; **en rond** in a circle; **faire les ronds de jambes** (slang) to bow and scrape; **rond comme une queue de pelle** (slang) soused, stoned, dead drunk; **rond de fumée** smoke ring; **rond de serviette** napkin ring ‖ *f* round; beat, round; round dance; radius; round hand; (mus) whole note; **à la ronde** around; **s'amuser à la ronde, faire la ronde** to go ring-around-a-rosy ‖ **rond** *adv*—**tourner rond** to work or go smoothly

rond-de-cuir [rɔ̃dkɥir] *m* (*pl* **ronds-de-cuir**) leather seat; (pej) bureaucrat

ron•deau [rɔ̃do] *m* (*pl* **-deaux**) rondeau; field roller

ronde•let [rɔ̃dlɛ] **-lette** [lɛt] *adj* plump; tidy (*sum*)

rondelle [rɔ̃dɛl] *f* disk; slice; washer (*of faucet, bolt, etc.*)

rondement [rɔ̃dmɑ̃] *adv* briskly; **mener rondement** to make short work of; **parler rondement** to be blunt

rondeur [rɔ̃dœr] *f* roundness; plumpness; frankness

rond-point [rɔ̃pwɛ̃] *m* (*pl* **ronds-points**) intersection, crossroads; traffic circle; circus, roundabout (Brit)

ronéo [rɔneo] *f* Mimeograph machine

ronéotyper [rɔneotipe] *tr* to mimeograph

ron•flant [rɔ̃flɑ̃] **-flante** [flɑ̃t] *adj* snoring; roaring; whirring, humming; (pej) high-sounding, pretentious

ronflement [rɔ̃fləmɑ̃] *m* snore; roar; whirr, hum

ronfler [rɔ̃fle] *intr* to snore; roar; whirr, hum

ron•fleur [rɔ̃flœr] **-fleuse** [fløz] *mf* snorer ‖ *m* vibrator (*replacing bell*)

ronger [rɔ̃ʒe] §38 *tr* to gnaw, nibble; eat away; bite (*one's nails*); corrode; torment ‖ *ref* to be worn away; be eaten away; eat one's heart out, fret

ron•geur [rɔ̃ʒœr] **-geuse** [ʒøz] *adj* gnawing ‖ *m* rodent

ronron [rɔ̃rɔ̃] *m* purr; drone

ronronnement [rɔ̃rɔnmɑ̃] *m* purring

ronronner [rɔ̃rɔne] *intr* to purr

roquer [rɔke] *intr* (chess) to castle

roquet [rɔkɛ] *m* cur, yapper; (*breed of dog*) pug

roquette [rɔkɛt] *f* (*plant; missile*) rocket

rosace [rozas] *f* rose window; (archit) rosette

rosa•cé -cée [rozase] *adj* roselike ‖ *f* skin eruption

rosaire [rozɛr] *m* rosary

rosâtre [rozɑtr] *adj* dusty-pink

rosbif [rɔsbif] *m* roast beef

rose [roz] *adj & m* rose, pink (*color*) ‖ *f* rose; rose window; **dire la rose** to box the compass; **rose des vents** compass card; **rose d'Inde** (*Tagetes*) marigold

ro•sé -sée [roze] *adj* rose, rose-colored ‖ *m* rosé wine ‖ *f* see **rosée**

ro•seau [rozo] *m* (*pl* **-seaux**) reed

rosée [roze] *f* dew

roséole [rozeɔl] *f* rash; rose rash

roseraie [rozrɛ] *f* rose garden

rosette [rozɛt] *f* bowknot; rosette; red ink; red chalk

rosier [rozje] *m* rosebush; **rosier églantier** sweetbrier

rosse [rɔs] *adj* nasty, mean; strict, stern; cynical ‖ *f* (coll) beast, stinker; (coll) nag; **sale rosse** (coll) dirty bitch

rossée [rɔse] *f* (coll) thrashing

rosser [rɔse] *tr* to beat up, thrash; (coll) to beat, best

rossignol [rɔsiɲɔl] *m* skeleton key; (orn) nightingale; (coll) piece of junk, drug on the market

rot [ro] *m* (slang) burp, belch

rota•tif [rɔtatif] **-tive** [tiv] *adj* rotary ‖ *f* rotary press

rotation [rɔtɑsjɔ̃] *f* rotation; turnover (*of merchandise*)

rotatoire [rɔtatwar] *adj* rotary

roter [rɔte] *intr* (slang) to burp

rô•ti -tie [roti] *adj* roasted ‖ *m* roast ‖ *f* piece of toast; **rôtie à l'anglaise** Welsh rarebit

rotin [rɔtɛ̃] *m* rattan; **de** or **en rotin** cane (*chair*); **pas un rotin!** not a penny!

rôtir [rotir] *tr, intr, & ref* to roast; toast; scorch

rôtisserie [rotisri] *f* rotisserie shop (*where roasted fowl is sold*); grillroom (*restaurant*)

rôtissoire [rotiswar] *f* rotisserie

rotogravure [rɔtɔgravyr] *f* rotogravure

rotonde [rɔtɔ̃d] *f* rotunda; (rr) roundhouse

rotor [rɔtɔr] *m* rotor

rotule [rɔtyl] *f* kneecap

roture [rɔtyr] *f* common people

rotu•rier [rɔtyrje] **-rière** [rjɛr] *adj* plebeian, of the common people ‖ *mf* commoner

rouage [rwaʒ] *m* cog; **rouages** movement (*of a watch*)

rou•blard [rublar] **-blarde** [blard] *adj* (coll) wily ‖ *mf* (coll) schemer

roublardise [rublardiz] *f* (coll) cunning

roucoulement [rukulmɑ̃] *m* cooing; billing and cooing

roucouler [rukule] *tr & intr* to coo

roue [ru] *f* wheel; **faire la roue** to turn cartwheels; to strut; **roue de secours** spare wheel (*with tire*)

roué rouée [rwe] *adj* slick; knocked out ‖ *mf* slicker ‖ *m* rake

rouelle [rwɛl] *f* fillet (*of veal*)

rouer [rwe] *tr* to break upon the wheel; **rouer de coups** to thrash, beat up

rouerie [ruri] *f* trickery; trick

rouet [rwɛ] *m* spinning wheel

rouflaquette [ruflakɛt] *f* spit curl

rouge [ruʒ] *adj* red ‖ *m* red; rouge; blush; **porter au rouge** to heat red-hot; **rouge à lèvres** lipstick ‖ *adv* red

rou•geaud [ruʒo] **-geaude** [ʒod] *adj* ruddy ‖ *mf* ruddy-faced person

rouge-gorge [ruʒgɔrʒ] *m* (*pl* **rouges-gorges**) robin (*Erithacus rubecula*)

rougeole [ruʒɔl] *f* measles

rougeoyer [ruʒwaje] §47 *intr* to glow red; turn red

rougeur [ruʒœr] *f* redness; blush; **rougeurs** red spots

rougir [ruʒir] §97 *tr* to redden ‖ *intr* to turn red; blush

rouille [ruj] *f* rust

rouil•lé -lée [ruje] *adj* rusty; (*out of practice; blighted*) rusty

rouiller [ruje] *tr, intr, & ref* to rust

roulade [rulad] *f* trill; (mus) run

rou•lant -lante [lɑ̃t] *adj* rolling; (coll) funny

rou•leau [rulo] *m* (*pl* **-leaux**) roller; roll; spool; rolling pin; **rouleau compresseur** road roller; **rouleau du printemps** egg rolling

roulement [rulmɑ̃] *m* roll; rotation; rattle, clatter; exchange; (swing) shift; **par roulement** in rotation; **roulement à billes** ball bearing

rouler [rule] *tr* to roll; (coll) to take in, cheat ‖ *intr* to roll; roll along; **rouler sur** to roll in (*wealth*); turn on ‖ *ref* to roll; roll up; toss and turn; to twiddle (*one's thumbs*); **se les rouler** (coll) to not turn a hand

roule-ta-bille [rultabij] *m invar* (coll) rolling stone

roulette [rulɛt] *f* small wheel; castor; roulette; **aller comme sur des roulettes** to go well, to work smoothly

rou•leur [rulœr] **-leuse** [løz] *mf* drifter (*from one job to another*) ‖ *m* freight handler ‖ *f* streetwalker

roulis [ruli] *m* (naut) roll

roulotte [rulɔt] *f* trailer; gypsy wagon

rou•main [rumɛ̃] **-maine** [mɛn] *adj* Rumanian ‖ *m* Rumanian (*language*) ‖ (*cap*) *mf* Rumanian (*person*)

roupiller [rupije] *intr* to take a snooze

rou•quin [rukɛ̃] **-quine** [kin] *adj* (coll) redheaded; ‖ *mf* (coll) redhead ‖ *m* (slang) red wine; **Rouquin** Red (*nickname*)

rouspéter [ruspete] §10 *intr* (coll) to bellyache, complain, kick

rouspé•teur [ruspetœr] **-teuse** [tøz] *mf* (coll) bellyacher, complainer

roussâtre [rusɑtr] *adj* auburn

rousse [rus] *f* redhead, auburn-haired woman; (slang) cops

roussette [rusɛt] *f* (ichth) dogfish, seadog

rousseur [rusœr] *f* reddishness; freckle

roussir [rusir] *tr* to scorch; singe ‖ *intr* to become brown; **faire roussir** (culin) to brown

route [rut] *f* road, highway; route, itinerary; **bonne route!** happy motoring!; **en route!**

let's go!; **faire fausse route** to take the wrong road; (fig) to be on the wrong track; **mettre en route** to start; **route à chaussées séparées, route à quatre voies** divided highway; **route déformée** rough road; **route déviée** detour; **route express** expressway; **route secondaire** back road

rou•tier [rutje] **-tière** [tjɛr] *adj* road (*e.g., map*) ‖ *m* trucker; bicycle racer; Explorer, Rover (*boy scout*); (naut) track chart; **vieux routier** veteran, old hand

routine [rutin] *f* routine

routi•nier [rutinje] **-nière** [njɛr] *adj* routine; one-track (*mind*)

rouvieux [ruvjø] *adj masc* mangy ‖ *m* mange

rouvrir [ruvrir] §65 *tr & intr* to reopen

roux [ru] **rousse** [rus] *adj* russet, reddish; red, auburn (*hair*); browned (*butter*) ‖ *mf* redhead ‖ *m* russet, reddish brown, auburn (*color*); brown sauce ‖ *f* see **rousse**

royal royale [rwajal] *adj* (*pl* **royaux** [rwajo]) royal ‖ *f* imperial, goatee

royaliste [rwajalist] *adj & mf* royalist

royaume [rwajom] *m* kingdom

royauté [rwajote] *f* royalty

R.S.V.P. [ɛrɛsvepe] *m* (letterword) (**répondez, s'il vous plaît**) R.S.V.P.

R.T.F. [ɛrteɛf] *f* (letterword) (**radio-diffusion-télévision française**) French radio and television

ruade [ryad] *f* kick, buck

ruban [rybɑ̃] *m* ribbon; tape; **ruban adhésif** adhesive tape; **ruban adhésif transparent** transparent tape; **ruban cache** masking tape; **ruban de chapeau** hatband; **ruban de frein** brake lining; **ruban encreur** typewriter ribbon; **ruban magnétique** recording tape

rubéole [rybeɔl] *f* German measles

rubis [rybi] *m* ruby; jewel (*of watch*); **payer rubis sur l'ongle** to pay down on the nail

rubrique [rybrik] *f* rubric; caption, heading; label (*in a dictionary*)

ruche [ryʃ] *f* beehive

rude [ryd] *adj* rude, rough; rugged; hard; steep; (coll) amazing

rudement [rydmɑ̃] *adv* roughly; (coll) awfully, mighty

rudesse [rydɛs] *f* rudeness, roughness; harshness

rudiment [rydimɑ̃] *m* rudiment

rudoyer [rydwaje] §47 *tr* to bully, browbeat; abuse, treat roughly

rue [ry] *f* street; **rue à double sens** two-way street; **rue à sens unique** one-way street; **rue barrée** (*public sign*) no thoroughfare; (*public sign*) closed for repairs; **rue piétonne** pedestrian mall; **rue sans issue** (*public sign*) no outlet

ruée [rɥe] *f* rush; **ruée vers l'or** gold rush

ruelle [rɥɛl] *f* alley, lane; space between bed and wall

ruer [rɥe] *intr* to kick, buck; **ruer dans les**

brancards to kick over the traces ‖ *ref*—**se ruer sur** to rush at

rugir [ryʒir] *intr* to roar, bellow

rugissement [ryʒismɑ̃] *m* roar

rugosité [rygozite] *f* roughness; ruggedness; bumpiness; coarseness

ru·gueux [rygø] **-gueuse** [gøz] *adj* rough, rugged; coarse; gnarled (*tree*)

ruine [rɥin] *f* ruin

ruiner [rɥine] *tr* to ruin ‖ *ref* to ruin oneself; fall into ruins

ruis·seau [rɥiso] *m* (*pl* **-seaux**) stream, brook; (fig) gutter

ruisseler [rɥisle] §34 *intr* to stream; drip, trickle

ruisselet [rɥislɛ] *m* little stream

ruissellement [rɥisɛlmɑ̃] *m* streaming; (*e.g., of light*) flood

rumeur [rymœr] *f* rumor; hum (*e.g., of voices*); roar (*of the sea*); **rumeur publique** public opinion

ruminer [rymine] *tr & intr* to ruminate; ruminate on or over

ru·pin [rypɛ̃] **-pine** [pin] *adj* (slang) rich ‖ *mf* (slang) swell

rupiner [rypine] *tr & intr* (coll) to do well

rupteur [ryptœr] *m* (elec) contact breaker

rupture [ryptyr] *f* rupture; breach; break; breaking off

ru·ral -rale [ryral] (*pl* **-raux** [ro]) *adj* rural ‖ *mf* farmer; **ruraux** country people

ruse [ryz] *f* ruse

ru·sé -sée [ryze] *adj* cunning, crafty ‖ *mf* sly one

russe [rys] *adj* Russian ‖ *m* Russian (*language*) ‖ (*cap*) *mf* Russian (*person*)

Russie [rysi] *f* Russia; **la Russie** Russia

rus·taud [rysto] **-taude** [tod] *adj* rustic, clumsy ‖ *mf* bumpkin

rustine [rystin] *f* bicycle repair patch

rustique [rystik] *adj* rustic; hardy

rustre [rystr] *adj* oafish ‖ *m* bumpkin, oaf; (obs) peasant

rut [ryt] *m* (zool) rut

ruti·lant [rytilɑ̃] **-lante** [lɑ̃t] *adj* bright-red; gleaming

rutiler [rytiler] *intr* to gleam, glow

rythme [ritm] *m* rhythm; rate (*of production*)

ryth·mé -mée [ritme] *adj* rhythmic(al); cadenced

rythmer [ritme] *tr* to cadence; mark with a rhythm

rythmique [ritmik] *adj* rhythmic(al)

S

S, s [ɛs], *[ɛs] *m invar* nineteenth letter of the French alphabet

S. *abbr* (**saint**) St.

s' = **se** before vowel or mute **h**

sa [sa] §88 his, her, its

S.A. [ɛsa] *f* (letterword) (**société anonyme**) Inc.

sabbat [saba] *m* Sabbath (*Friday night to Saturday night*); witches' Sabbath; racket, uproarious gaiety; **sabbat des chats** caterwauling

sabir [sabir] *m* (ling) pidgin; (pej) jargon

sable [sabl] *m* sand; sable; **sable mouvant** quicksand

sabler [sable] *tr* to sandblast; drink in one gulp; toss off (*some champagne*)

sa·bleux [sablø] **-bleuse** [bløz] *adj* sandy ‖ *f* sandblast; sandblaster

sablier [sablije] *m* hourglass; (*for drying ink*) sandbox; dealer in sand

sablière [sablijɛr] *f* sandpit; wall plate; (rr) sandbox

sablon·neux [sablɔnø] **-neuse** [nøz] *adj* sandy

sablonnière [sablɔnjɛr] *f* sandpit

sabord [sabɔr] *m* porthole

saborder [sabɔrde] *tr* to scuttle

sabot [sabo] *m* wooden shoe; hoof; whipping top; bungled work; ferrule; caster cup; **dormir comme un sabot** to sleep like a top; **sabot de frein** brake shoe; **sabot d'enrayage** wedge, block, scotch

sabotage [sabotaʒ] *m* sabotage

saboter [sabote] *tr* to sabotage; bungle ‖ *intr* (coll) to make one's wooden shoes clatter

sabo·teur [sabotœr] **-teuse** [tøz] *mf* saboteur; bungler

sabo·tier [sabotje] **-tière** [tjɛr] *mf* maker and seller of wooden shoes ‖ *f* clog dance

sabre [sabr] *m* saber

sabrer [sabre] *tr* to saber; (coll) to botch; (coll) to cut, condense

sac [sak] *m* sack, bag; **être un sac d'os** [dos] to be nothing but skin and bones; **mettre à sac** (coll) to rifle; **sac à main** handbag; **sac à malice** bag of tricks; **sac à provisions** shopping bag; **sac congélateur** freezer bag; **sac de couchage** sleeping bag; **sac de nœuds** (slang) can of worms; **sac de voyage** traveling bag, overnight suitcase; **sac poubelle** trash bag; **vider son sac** (slang) to get something off one's chest

saccade [sakad] *f* jerk

sacca·dé -dée [sakade] *adj* jerky

saccager [sakaʒe] §38 *tr* to sack; (coll) to upset, turn topsy-turvy

saccha·rin [sakarɛ̃] **-rine** [rin] *adj* saccharine ‖ *f* saccharin

saccharose [sakaroz] *m* sucrose

sacerdoce [sasɛrdɔs] *m* priesthood

sacerdo·tal -tale [sasɛrdɔtal] *adj* (*pl* **-taux** [to]) sacerdotal, priestly

sac-filtre [sakfiltrə] *m* (*pl* **sacs-filtres**) filter bag

sache [saʃ] *v* (**saches, sachions,** etc.) see **savoir**

sachet [saʃɛ] *m* sachet; packet (*of needles, medicine,* etc.); powder charge

sacoche [sakɔʃ] *f* satchel

sacramen•tel -telle [sakramɑ̃tɛl] *adj* sacramental

sacre [sakr] *m* crowning, consecration

sa•cré -crée [sakre] *adj* sacred; (anat) sacral ‖ (when standing before noun) *adj* (coll) darned, blasted

sacrement [sakrəmɑ̃] *m* sacrament

sacrer [sakre] *tr* to crown, consecrate ‖ *intr* to curse

sacrifice [sakrifis] *m* sacrifice

sacrifier [sakrifje] *tr* to sacrifice

sacrilège [sakrilɛʒ] *adj* sacrilegious ‖ *mf* sacrilegious person ‖ *m* sacrilege

sacristain [sakristɛ̃] *m* sexton

sadique [sadik] *adj* sadistic ‖ *mf* sadist

safran [safrɑ̃] *m* saffron

sagace [sagas] *adj* sagacious, shrewd

sage [saʒ] *adj* wise; well-behaved; modest (*woman*); good (*child*); **soyez sage!** be good! ‖ *mf* sage

safe-femme [saʒfam] *f* (*pl* **sages-femmes**) midwife

sagesse [saʒɛs] *f* wisdom; good behavior

Sagittaire [saʒitɛr] *m*—**le Sagittaire** (astr, astrol) Sagittarius

sai•gnant -gnante [sɛɲɑ̃] [ɲɑ̃t] *adj* bleeding; (*wound*) fresh; (*meat*) rare

saignée [seɲe] *f* bloodletting; bend of the arm, small of the arm; (fig) drain on the purse

saignement [sɛɲmɑ̃] *m* bleeding; **saignement de nez** nosebleed

saigner [seɲe], [seɲe] *tr & intr* to bleed; **saigner à blanc, saigner aux quatre veines** to bleed white

sail•lant -lante [sajɑ̃] [jɑ̃t] *adj* prominent, salient; projecting; high (*cheekbones*)

saillie [saji] *f* projection; spurt; sally, outburst; **faire saillie** to jut out, project

saillir [sajir] (used only in *inf, ger,* & 3d *sg* & *pl*) *tr* (agr) to cover ‖ **§69** *intr* to protrude, project; spurt

sain [sɛ̃] **saine** [sɛn] *adj* healthy; **sain d'esprit** sane; **sain et sauf, saine et sauve** safe and sound

saindoux [sɛdu] *m* lard

sainement [sɛnmɑ̃] *adv* soundly

sais [se] *v* (**sait**) see **savoir**

saint [sɛ̃] **sainte** [sɛt] *adj* saintly; sacred, holy ‖ *mf* saint

Saint-Esprit [sɛtɛspri] *m* (rel) Holy Spirit

sainteté [sɛtəte] *f* holiness

Saint-Siège [sɛsjɛz] *m* Holy See

saisie [sezi] *f* seizure; foreclosure

saisie-arrêt [seziarɛ] *f* (*pl* **-arrêts**) attachment, garnishment

saisir [sezir] *tr* to seize; sear (*meat*); grasp (*to understand*); strike, startle; overcome; **saisir**

un tribunal de to lay before a court ‖ *ref*—**se saisir de** to take possession of

saisis•sant -sante [sezisɑ̃] **-sante** [sɑ̃t] *adj* gripping, arresting; startling, striking

saisissement [sezismɑ̃] *m* chill; shock

saison [sezɔ̃] *f* season

salace [salas] *adj* salacious

salade [salad] *f* salad; (fig) mess; **raconter des salades** (slang) to tell fish stories; **salade de chou** slaw, cabbage salad; **salade de fruits** fruit salad

saladier [saladje] *m* salad bowl

salaire [salɛr] *m* salary, wage; recompense, punishment; **salaires** earned income

salariat [salarja] *m* salaried workers, employees; salary (*fixed wage*)

sala•rié -riée [salarje] *adj* salaried, hired ‖ *mf* wage earner; employee

sa•laud [salo] **-laude** [lod] *adj* (coll) slovenly ‖ *mf* (slang) skunk, scoundrel

sale [sal] *adj* dirty; dull (*color*) ‖ *mf* dirty person

sa•lé -lée [sale] *adj* salty, salted; dirty (*joke*); padded (*bill*); (slang) exaggerated ‖ *m* salt pork

saler [sale] *tr* to salt

saleté [salte] *f* dirtiness; piece of dirt; (slang) dirty trick; (slang) dirt

saleuse [saløz] *f* road-salting truck

salière [saljɛr] *f* saltcellar

salir [salir] *tr & ref* to soil

salive [saliv] *f* saliva

saliver [salive] *intr* to salivate

salle [sal] *m* room; hall; auditorium; ward (*in a hospital*); (theat) audience, house; **grande salle municipale** city center; **salle à manger** dining room; **salle d'armes** fencing room; **salle d'attente** waiting room; **salle de bains** bathroom; **salle de commande** (mil) control room; **salle de concert** concert hall; **salle d'écoute** language laboratory; **salle de détente** rec room; **salle de jeux électroniques** amusement arcade; **salle d'embarquement** (aer) gate; **salle de la réserve** rare-book room; **salle de police** (mil) guardhouse; **salle de réveil, salle de réanimation** (med) recovery room; **salle de rédaction** city room; **salle des accouchées** maternity ward; **salle de séjour** living room; **salle de services du prêt** reserve-book room; **salle des fêtes** hall, auditorium; **salle des machines** engine room; **salle des pas perdus** lobby, waiting room; **salle de spectacle** movie house; **salle des urgences** emergency room; **salle des ventes** salesroom, showroom; **salle de travail** delivery room; **sallee d'exposition** showroom

salmigondis [salmigɔ̃di] *m* hodgepodge

salon [salɔ̃] *m* living room, parlor; exposition; saloon (*ship's lounge*); **salon de beauté** beauty parlor; **salon de l'aéronautique** air show; **salon de l'automobile** automobile show; **salon de thé** tearoom

salon•nard [salɔnar] **-narde** [nard] *mf* sycophant

saloperie [salɔpri] *f* (slang) trash

salopette [salɔpɛt] *f* coveralls, overalls; bib; smock

salpêtre [salpɛtr] *m* saltpeter

salsepareille [salsəparɛj] *f* sarsaparilla

saltimbanque [saltɛ̃bɑ̃k] *mf* tumbler; mountebank, charlatan

salubre [salybr] *adj* salubrious, healthful

saluer [salɥe] *tr* to salute; greet, bow to, wave to

salut [saly] *m* health; safety; salvation; salute; greeting, bow; nod; **salut!** (coll) hi!, howdy!; **salut les gars!, salut les copains!** hi, fellows!

salutaire [salytɛr] *adj* healthy, salutary, beneficial

salutation [salytɑsjɔ̃] *f* greeting; **salutations distinguées** or **sincères salutations** (complimentary close) yours truly

salve [salv] *f* salvo, salute

samari•tain [samaritɛ̃] **-taine** [tɛn] *adj* Samaritan || (*cap*) *mf* Samaritan

samedi [samdi] *m* Saturday

samouraî [samuraj] *m* samurai

sanatorium [sanatɔrjɔm] *m* sanitarium

sanctifier [sɑ̃ktifje] *tr* to sanctify

sanction [sɑ̃ksjɔ̃] *f* sanction; penalty

sanctionner [sɑ̃ksjɔne] *tr* to sanction; penalize

sanctuaire [sɑ̃ktɥɛr] *m* sanctuary

sandale [sɑ̃dal] *f* sandal; gym shoe

sandwich [sɑ̃dwitʃ], [sɑ̃dviʃ] *m* (*pl* **sandwiches, sandwichs**) sandwich

sang [sɑ̃] *m* blood; **avoir le sang chaud** (coll) to be a go-getter; **bon sang!** (coll) darn it!; **sang et tripes** blood and guts; **se faire du bon sang** to enjoy oneself; **se faire du mauvais sang** to get all stewed up

sang-froid [sɑ̃frwa] *m* self-control

san•glant [sɑ̃glɑ̃] **-glante** [glɑ̃t] *adj* bloody; cruel

sangle [sɑ̃gl] *f* cinch

sanglier [sɑ̃glije] *m* wild boar; **tirer sur un sanglier de carton** (coll) to tear down a straw man

sanglot [sɑ̃glo] *m* sob

sangloter [sɑ̃glɔte] *intr* to sob

sang-mêlé [sɑ̃mɛle] *m invar* half-breed

sangsue [sɑ̃sy] *f* bloodsucker, leech

san•guin [sɑ̃gɛ̃] **-guine** [gin] *adj* sanguine || *f* (fa) sanguine

sanitaire [sanitɛr] *adj* sanitary; hospital; e.g., **avion sanitaire** hospital plane

sans [sɑ̃] *adv*—**sans que** without; **sans quoi** or else || *prep* without; **sans cesse** ceaselessly; **sans façon** informally; **sans fil** wireless

sans-abri [sɑ̃zabri] *mf invar* homeless person

sans-cœur [sɑ̃kœr] *mf invar* heartless person

sans-filiste [sɑ̃filist] *mf* (*pl* **-filistes**) radio operator; radio amateur

sans-gêne [sɑ̃ʒɛn] *adj invar* offhanded || *mf invar* offhanded person || *m* offhandedness

sansonnet [sɑ̃sɔnɛ] *m* starling; blackbird

sans-travail [sɑ̃travaj] *mf invar* unemployed worker

san•tal [sɑ̃tal] *m* (*pl* **-taux** [to]) (bot) sandalwood

santé [sɑ̃te] *f* health; sanity; **santé publique** public-health service

saou•dien [sudjɛ̃] **-dienne** [djɛn] *adj* Saudi || (*cap*) *mf* Saudi

saoudite [sudit] *adj* Saudi

sape [sap] *f* sap (*undermining*)

saper [sape] *tr* to sap, undermine

sapeur [sapœr] *m* (mil) sapper; **fumer comme un sapeur** (coll) to smoke like a chimney

sapeur-pompier [sapœrpɔ̃pje] *m* (*pl* **sapeurs-pompiers**) fireman; **sapeurs-pompiers** fire department

saphir [safir] *m* sapphire; sapphire needle

sapin [sapɛ̃] *m* fir

sapristi [sapristi] *interj* hang it!

saquer [sake] *tr* (slang) to fire, sack

sarbacane [sarbakan] *f* blowgun

sarcasme [sarkasm] *m* sarcasm

sarcastique [sarkastik] *adj* sarcastic

sarcler [sarkle] *tr* to weed, root out

sarcloir [sarklwar] *m* hoe

Sardaigne [sardɛɲ] *f* Sardinia; **la Sardaigne** Sardinia

sarde [sard] *adj* Sardinian || *m* Sardinian (*language*) || (*cap*) *mf* Sardinian (*person*)

sardine [sardin] *f* sardine

S.A.R.L. *abbr* (**société à responsabilité limitée**) corporation

sarment [sarmɑ̃] *m* vine; vine shoot

sarra•sin [sarazɛ̃] **-sine** [zin] *adj* Saracen || *m* buckwheat || *f* portcullis || (*cap*) *mf* Saracen

sar•rau [saro] *m* (*pl* **-raus**) smock

sarriette [sarjɛt] *f* (bot) savory

sas [sɑ], [sɑs] *m* sieve; lock (*of canal, submarine, etc.*); air lock (*of caisson, spaceship, etc.*); **sas d'évacuation** (aer) escape hatch

sasser [sɑse] *tr* to sift, screen; pass through a lock

satanique [satanik] *adj* satanic; fiendish, wicked

satelliser [satelize] *tr* to make a satellite of; (rok) to put into orbit

satellite [satelit] *adj & m* satellite; **satellite de relais** relay satellite

satin [satɛ̃] *m* satin

satinette [satinɛt] *f* sateen

satire [satir] *f* satire

satirique [satirik] *adj* satiric(al)

satiriser [satirize] *tr* to satirize

satisfaction [satisfaksjɔ̃] *f* satisfaction

satisfaire [satisfɛr] §29 *tr* to satisfy || *intr*—**satisfaire à** to satisfy, fulfill, meet, e.g., **avez-vous satisfait à tous les besoins?** have you met all the needs? || *ref* to be satisfied

satisfai•sant [satisfəzɑ̃] **-sante** [zɑ̃t] *adj* satisfactory; satisfying

saturer [satyre] *tr* to saturate

Saturne [satyrn] *m* Saturn

saturnisme [satyrnism] *m* lead poisoning

sauce [sos] *f* sauce; gravy; drawing pencil; (tech) solution

saucer [sose] §51 *tr* to dip in sauce or gravy; (coll) to soak to the skin; (coll) to reprimand severely

saucière [sosjɛr] *f* gravy bowl

saucisse [sosis] *f* sausage; frankfurter

saucisson [sosisɔ̃] *m* bologna, sausage

sauf [sof] **sauve** [sov] *adj* safe ‖ **sauf** *prep* save, except; barring; subject to (*e.g., correction*)

sauf-conduit [sofkɔ̃dɥi] *m* (*pl* **-conduits**) safe-conduct

sauge [soʒ] *f* (bot) sage, salvia

saugre•nu -nue [sogrəny] *adj* absurd, silly

saule [sol] *m* willow

saumâtre [somɑtr] *adj* brackish

saumon [somɔ̃] *m* salmon; pig (*of crude metal*)

saumure [somyr] *f* brine

sauner [sone] *intr* to make salt

saupoudrer [sopudre] *tr* to sprinkle (*with powder, sugar; citations*)

saurai [sɔre] *v* (**sauras, saura, saurons,** etc.) see **savoir**

saurer [sɔre] *tr* to kipper

saut [so] *m* leap, jump; falls, waterfall; **au saut du lit** on getting out of bed; **faire le saut** to take the fatal step; **faire un saut chez** to drop in on; **par sauts et par bonds** by fits and starts; **saut à la perche** pole vault; **saut dans le temps** time warp; **saut de carpe** jackknife; **saut de l'ange** swan dive; **saut en chute libre** skydiving; **saut en hauteur** high jump; **saut en longueur** long jump; **saut périlleux** somersault

saut-de-lit [sodli] *m invar* wrap

saut-de-mouton [sodmutɔ̃] *m* (*pl* **sauts-de-mouton**) overpass

saute [sot] *f* change in direction, shift

saute-mouton [sotmutɔ̃] *m* leapfrog

sauter [sote] *tr* to leap over; skip ‖ *intr* to leap, jump; blow up; **faire sauter** to sauté; flip (*a pancake*); fire (*an employee*); **sauter à cloche-pied** to hop on one foot; **sauter à pieds joints** to do a standing jump; **sauter aux nues** to get mad

sauterelle [sotrɛl] *f* grasshopper; **sauterelle d'Amérique** katydid

sauterie [sotri] *f* (coll) hop (*dancing party*)

sau•teur [sotœr] **-teuse** [tøz] *adj* jumping ‖ *mf* jumper; **sauteur (sauteuse) en hauteur** high jumper; ‖ *m* jumper, jumping horse ‖ *f* frying pan

sautiller [sotije] *intr* to hop

sautoir [sotwar] *m* St. Andrew's cross; **en sautoir** crossways

sauvage [sovaʒ] *adj* savage; wild; shy ‖ *mf* savage

sauvagerie [sovaʒri] *f* savagery; wildness; shyness

sauvegarde [sovgard] *f* safeguard

sauvegarder [sovgarde] *tr* to safeguard

sauve-qui-peut [sovkipø] *m invar* panic, stampede, rout

sauver [sove] *tr* to save; rescue ‖ *intr*—**sauve qui peut!** every man for himself! ‖ *ref* to run

away; escape; (theat) to exit; **sauve-toi!** (coll) scram!

sauvetage [sovtaʒ] *m* salvage; lifesaving, rescue; **sauvetage financier** (com) bailout

sauveteur [sovtœr] *adj masc* lifesaving ‖ *m* lifesaver

sauveur [sovœr] *adj masc* Saviour ‖ *m* savior; **Le Sauveur** the Saviour

savamment [savamɑ̃] *adv* knowingly; skillfully

savane [savan] *f* prairie, savanna

sa•vant [savɑ̃] **-vante** [vɑ̃t] *adj* scholarly, learned ‖ *mf* scientist, scholar, savant; **savant atomiste** nuclear physicist

savate [savat] *f* old slipper; kickboxing; (coll) butterfingers; **traîner la savate** to be down at the heel

saveur [savœr] *f* savor, taste

savoir [savwar] *m* learning ‖ §62, §95 *tr & intr* to know; know how to; **à savoir** namely, to wit; **à savoir que** with the understanding that; **en savoir long** to know all about it; **pas que je sache** not that I know of

savoir-faire [savwarfɛr] *m invar* know-how

savon [savɔ̃] *m* soap; (slang) sharp reprimand, tongue lashing; **savon à barbe** shaving soap; **passer un savon à** (slang) to shout at; **savon en paillettes** soap flakes

savonnage [savonaʒ] *m* soaping

savonner [savone] *tr* to soap

savonnerie [savonri] *f* soap factory

savonnette [savonɛt] *f* toilet soap

savon•neux [savonø] **-neuse** [nøz] *adj* soapy

savourer [savure] *tr* to savor

savou•reux [savurø] **-reuse** [røz] *adj* savory, tasty

saxon [saksɔ̃] **saxonne** [saksɔn] *adj* Saxon ‖ *m* Saxon (*language*) ‖ (*cap*) *mf* Saxon (*person*)

saxophone [saksofɔn] *m* saxophone

saynète [sɛnɛt] *f* sketch, playlet

sca•bieux [skabjø] **-bieuse** [bjøz] *adj* scabby ‖ *f* scabious

sca•breux [skabrø] **-breuse** [brøz] *adj* rough (*road*); risky (*business*); scabrous (*remark*)

scalpel [skalpɛl] *m* scalpel

scalper [skalpe] *tr* to scalp

scandale [skɑ̃dal] *m* scandal; disturbance

scanda•leux [skɑ̃dalø] **-leuse** [løz] *adj* scandalous

scandaliser [skɑ̃dalize] *tr* to lead astray; scandalize ‖ *ref* to take offense

scander [skɑ̃de] *tr* to scan (*verses*)

scandinave [skɑ̃dinav] *adj* Scandinavian ‖ *m* Scandinavian (*language*) ‖ (*cap*) *mf* Scandinavian (*person*); **Scandinaves** Scandinavian countries

scanner [skanɛr] *m* scanner; **scanner numérique** digital scanner

scanographe [skanograf] *m* (med) CAT scanner

scansion [skɑ̃sjɔ̃] *f* scansion

scaphandre [skafɑ̃dr] *m* diving suit; spacesuit; **scaphandre autonome** aqualung, scuba; **scaphandre spatial** spacesuit

scaphandrier [skafɑ̃drije] *m* diver, scuba diver

scarlatine [skarlatin] *f* scarlet fever

scarole [skarɔl] *f* escarole

sceau [so] *m* (*pl* **-seaux**) seal

scélé·rat [selera] **-rate** [rat] *adj* villainous ‖ *mf* villain

scellé [sɛle] *m* seal

sceller [sɛle] *tr* to seal

scénario [senarjo] *m* scenario

scénariste [skenarist] *mf* scenarist

scène [sɛn] *f* scene; stage; theater; **en scène** on stage

scénique [senik] *adj* scenic

scepticisme [sɛptisism] *m* skepticism

sceptique [sɛptik] *adj* & *mf* skeptic

sceptre [sɛptr] *m* scepter

schah [ʃa] *m* shah

schelem [ʃlɛm] *m* slam (*at bridge*)

schéma [ʃema] *m* diagram, sketch; outline; pattern

schisme [ʃism] *m* schism

schiste [ʃist] *m* schist, shale

schizophrène [skizɔfrɛn] *adj* & *mf* schizophrenic

schlague [ʃlag] *f* flogging

schooner [skunœr], [ʃunœr] *m* schooner

sciatique [sjatik] *adj* sciatic ‖ *f* (pathol) sciatica

scie [si] *f* saw; (coll) bore, nuisance; **scie à découper, scie sauteuse** jig saw

sciemment [sjamã] *adv* knowingly

science [sjãs] *f* science; learning, knowledge; **science de l'information** computer science

science-fiction [sjãsfiksjɔ̃] *f* science fiction

scientifique [sjãtifik] *adj* scientific ‖ *mf* scientist

scier [sje] *tr* to saw; (coll) to bore ‖ *intr* (naut) to row backwards

scierie [siri] *f* sawmill

scieur [sjœr] *m* sawyer

scinder [sɛ̃de] *tr* to divide ‖ *ref* to be divided

scintil·lant [sɛ̃tijã] **-lante** [jãt] *adj* scintillating; twinkling

scintillation [sɛ̃tijãsjɔ̃] *f* twinkling, twinkle; (phys) scintillation

scintillement [sɛ̃tijmã] *m* twinkling

scintiller [sɛ̃tije] *intr* to scintillate; twinkle

scion [sjɔ̃] *m* scion; tip (*of fishing rod*)

scission [sisjɔ̃] *f* schism; (biol & phys) fission

sciure [sjyr] *f* sawdust

sclérose [skleroz] *f* sclerosis

scolaire [skɔlɛr] *adj* school

scolastique [skɔlastik] *adj* & *m* scholastic ‖ *f* scholasticism

sconse [skɔ̃s] *m* skunk fur; skunk

scories [skɔri] *fpl* slag, dross, clinker

scorpion [skɔrpjɔ̃] *m* scorpion; **le Scorpion** (astr, astrol) Scorpion

scout scoute [skut] *adj* & *m* scout

scoutisme [skutism] *m* scouting

scribe [skrib] *m* scribe

script [skript] *m* scrip; (typ) script

scripturaire [skriptyrɛr] *adj* Scriptural ‖ *m* fundamentalist

scrofule [skrɔfyl] *f* scrofula

scrotum [skrɔtɔm] *m* scrotum

scrupule [skrypyl] *m* scruple

scrupu·leux [skrypylø] **-leuse** [løz] *adj* scrupulous

scruter [skryte] *tr* to scrutinize

scrutin [skrytɛ̃] *m* ballot; balloting, voting, poll; **dépouiller le scrutin** to count the votes; **scrutin de ballottage** runoff election

scrutiner [skrytine] *intr* to ballot

sculpter [skylte] *tr* to sculpture; carve (*wood*)

sculpteur [skyltœr] *m* sculptor

sculpture [skyltyr] *f* sculpture

s.d. *abbr* (**sans date**) n.d.

S.D.E.C. [esdeəse] *m* (letterword) (**Service de Documentation Extérieure et de Contre-espionnage**) (*équivalence aux U.S.A.*) CIA (*Central Intelligence Agency*)

S.D.N. [ɛsdeɛn] *f* (letterword) (**Société des Nations**) League of Nations

se [sə] **§87** *ref pron*

séance [seãs] *f* session, sitting; seat (*in an assembly*); performance, showing; séance; **séance tenante** on the spot

séant [seã] **séante** [seãt] *adj* fitting, decent; sitting (*as a king or a court in session*) ‖ *m* buttocks, bottom; **se mettre sur son séant** to sit up (*in bed*)

seau [so] *m* (*pl* **seaux**) bucket, pail; **il pleut à seaux** it's raining cats and dogs; **seau à charbon** coal scuttle

sébile [sebil] *f* wooden bowl; (telp) coin return

sec [sɛk] **sèche** [sɛʃ] *adj* dry; sharp; rude; unguarded (*card*); total (*loss*); **en cinq sec** in a jiffy; **sec comme un hareng** (coll) long and thin; **tout sec** and nothing more ‖ *m* dryness; **à sec** dry; (coll) broke ‖ *f* *see* **sèche** ‖ **sec** *adv*—**aussi sec** (slang) on the spot; **boire sec** to drink one's liquor straight; **frapper sec** to land a hard fast punch; **parler sec** to talk tough

sécession [sesesjɔ̃] *f* secession

sèche [sɛʃ] *f* (slang) fag, cigarette

sèche-cheveux [sɛʃʃəvø] *m invar* hair drier

sèche-linge [sɛʃlɛ̃ʒ] *m invar* clothes drier

sécher [seʃe] **§10** *tr* to dry; season; cut (*a class*) ‖ *intr* to become dry

sécheresse [sɛʃrɛs] *f* dryness; drought; baldness (*of style*); curtness (fig) coldness

séchoir [seʃwar] *m* drier; drying room; hair drier; clotheshorse

séchoir-chevalet [seʃwarʃəvale] *m invar* clotheshorse

se·cond [səgɔ̃] **-conde** [gɔ̃d] *adj* & *pron* second; **en second** next in rank ‖ *m* second ‖ *f* *see* **seconde**

secondaire [səgɔ̃dɛr] *adj* & *m* secondary

seconde [səgɔ̃d] *f* second (*in time; musical interval; of angle*); second class

seconder [səgɔ̃de] *tr* to help, second

se·coué -couée [səkwe] *adj* (slang) nuts, crazy

secouer [səkwe] *tr* to shake; shake off or down ‖ *ref* to pull oneself together

secourable [səkurabl] *adj* helpful

secourir [səkurir] **§14** *tr* to help, aid

secourisme [səkurism] *m* first aid
secouriste [səkurist] *mf* first-aider; first-aid worker
secours [səkur] *m* help, aid; **au secours!** help!; **de secours** emergency; spare (*tire*); **des secours** supplies, relief
secousse [səkus] *f* shake, jolt; (elec) shock
se•cret [səkrɛ] **-crète** [krɛt] *adj* secret; secretive ‖ *m* secret; secrecy; **au secret** in solitary confinement ‖ *f* see **secrète**
secrétaire [səkretɛr] *mf* secretary; **secrétaire de rédaction** copy editor; copy reader ‖ *m* secretary (*desk*)
secrète [səkrɛt] *f* central intelligence
sécréter [sekrete] §10 *tr* to secrete
sectaire [sɛktɛr] *adj* & *mf* sectarian
secte [sɛkt] *f* sect
secteur [sɛktœr] *m* sector; (elec) house current, local supply circuit; **secteur postal** postal zone; (mil) A.P.O. number
section [sɛksjɔ̃] *f* section; cross section
sectionner [sɛksjɔne] *tr* to section; cut ‖ *ref* to break apart
séculaire [sekylɛr] *adj* secular
sécu•lier [sekylje] **-lière** [ljɛr] *adj* & *m* secular
sécurité [sekyrite] *f* security
séda•tif [sedatif] **-tive** [tiv] *adj* & *m* sedative
sédation [sedasjɔ̃] *f* sedation
sédentaire [sedɑ̃tɛr] *adj* sedentary
sédiment [sedimɑ̃] *m* sediment
sédi•tieux [sedisjø] **-tieuse** [sjøz] *adj* seditious
sédition [sedisjɔ̃] *f* sedition
séduc•teur [sedyktœr] **-trice** [tris] *adj* seducing, bewitching ‖ *mf* seducer ‖ *f* vamp
séduction [sedyksjɔ̃] *f* seduction
séduire [sedɥir] §19 *tr* to seduce; charm, bewitch; bribe
sédui•sant [sedɥizɑ̃] **-sante** [zɑ̃t] *adj* seductive, tempting
segment [sɛgmɑ̃] *m* segment; **segment de piston** piston ring
ségrégation [segregasjɔ̃] *f* segregation; **supprimer** *or* **éliminer la ségrégation raciale de** to integrate, to desegregate
ségrégationniste [segregasjɔnist] *adj* segregationist
seiche [sɛʃ] *f* cuttlefish; tidal wave; **chasser la seiche** (slang) to look for the end of the rainbow
séide [seid] *m* henchman
seigle [sɛgl] *m* rye
seigneur [sɛɲœr] *m* lord
sein [sɛ̃] *m* breast; bosom; womb; **au sein de** in the heart of
seine [sɛn] *f* dragnet
seing [sɛ̃] *m* signature; **sous seing privé** privately witnessed
seize [sɛz] §94 *adj* & *pron* sixteen; the Sixteenth, e.g., **Jean seize** John the Sixteenth ‖ *m* sixteen; sixteenth (*in dates*)
seizième [sɛzjɛm] §94 *adj, pron* (*masc, fem*), & *m* sixteenth
séjour [seʒur] *m* stay, visit

séjourner [seʒurne] *intr* to reside; stay, visit
sel [sɛl] *m* salt; **gros sel** coarse salt; (fig) dirty joke; **sel ammoniac** sal ammoniac; **sel fin, sel de table** table salt; **sel gemme** rock salt
sélec•tif [selɛktif] **-tive** [tiv] *adj* selective
sélection [selɛksjɔ̃] *f* selection
sélectionner [selɛksjɔne] *tr* to select
self [sɛlf] *f* (elec) coil, spark coil
self-service [sɛlfsɛrvis] *m* self-service
selle [sɛl] *f* saddle; seat (*of bicycle, motorcycle, etc.*); sculptor's tripod; stool, movement; (culin) saddle; **aller à la selle** to go to the toilet
seller [sɛle] *tr* to saddle
sellier [sɛlje] *m* saddler
selon [səlɔ̃] *adv*—**c'est selon** that depends; **selon que** according as ‖ *prep* according to; after (*e.g., my own heart*)
selva *var de* **selve**
selve [sɛlv] *f* rain forest
semailles [səmaj] *fpl* sowing, seeding
semaine [səmɛn] *f* week; week's wages; set of seven; **à la petite semaine** day-to-day, hand-to-mouth; short-sighted; **de semaine** on duty during the week; **la semaine des quatre jeudis** (coll) never; **semaine anglaise** five-day workweek
semai•nier [səmenje] **-nière** [njɛr] *mf* week worker ‖ *m* highboy; office calendar
sémantique [semɑ̃tik] *adj* semantic ‖ *f* semantics
sémaphore [semafɔr] *m* semaphore
semblable [sɑ̃blabl] *adj* similar, like ‖ *m* fellowman, equal
semblant [sɑ̃blɑ̃] *m* semblance, appearance; **faire semblant** to pretend
sembler [sɑ̃ble] §95 *intr* to seem; seem to
semelle [səmɛl] *f* sole; foot (*of stocking*); tread (*of tire*); bed (*of concrete*); **battre la semelle** to stamp one's feet
semence [səmɑ̃s] *f* seed; semen; brad; **semence de perles** seed pearls
semer [səme] §2 *tr* to seed, sow; scatter, strew; lay (*mines*); (slang) to outdistance; (slang) to drop (*an acquaintance*)
semestre [səmɛstr] *m* semester; six-month period
semes•triel -trielle [səmɛstrijɛl] *adj* six-month; semester
se•meur [səmœr] **-meuse** [møz] *mf* sower; spreader of gossip ‖ *f* seeder, drill
semi-chenillé [səmiʃnije] *m* half-track
semi-conduc•teur [səmikɔ̃dyktœr] **-trice** [tris] *adj* semiconductive ‖ *m* semiconductor
semifi•ni -nie [səmifini] *adj* unfinished
sémil•lant [semijɑ̃] **-lante** [jɑ̃t] *adj* sprightly, lively
séminaire [seminɛr] *m* seminary; seminar; conference
semi-remorque [səmirəmɔrk] *f* (*pl* **-remorques**) semitrailer
semis [səmi] *m* sowing; seedling; seedbed
sémite [semit] *adj* Semitic ‖ (*cap*) *mf* Semite

sémitique [semitik] *adj* Semitic

semoir [səmwar] *m* seeder, drill

semonce [səmɔ̃s] *f* reprimand; (naut) order to heave to

semoncer [səmɔ̃se] §51 *tr* to reprimand; (naut) to order to heave to

semoule [səmul] *f* (culin) semolina

sénat [sena] *m* senate

sénateur [senatœr] *m* senator

sénile [senil] *adj* senile

sens [sɑ̃s] *m* sense, meaning; opinion; direction; **à double sens** ambiguous, e.g., **mot à double sens** double entendre; **en sens inverse** in the opposite direction; **sens antihoraire** counterclockwise; **sens de l'humour** sense of humor; **sens dessus dessous** [sɑ̃dəsydəsu] upside down; **sens devant derrière** [sɑ̃dəvɑ̃derjɛr] back to front; **sens interdit** (*public sign*) no entry; **sens obligatoire** (*public sign*) right way, this way; **sens unique** (*public sign*) one way

sensation [sɑ̃sɑsjɔ̃] *f* sensation

sensation•nel -nelle [sɑ̃sɑsjɔnɛl] *adj* sensational

sen•sé -sée [sɑ̃se] *adj* sensible

sensibiliser [sɑ̃sibilize] *tr* to sensitize

sensibilité [sɑ̃sibilite] *f* sensitivity, sensitiveness; compassion, feeling

sensible [sɑ̃sibl] *adj* sensitive; considerable, appreciable; perceptible; (mus) leading (*note*)

sensiblement [sɑ̃sibləmɑ̃] *adv* approximately; appreciably, noticeably; acutely, keenly

sensi•tif -tive [sɑ̃sitif] **-tive** [tiv] *adj* sensory; sensitive, touchy

senso•riel -rielle [sɑ̃sɔrjɛl] *adj* sensory

sen•suel -suelle [sɑ̃sɥɛl] *adj* sensual

sent-bon [sɑ̃bɔ̃] *m invar* odor, perfume

sentence [sɑ̃tɑ̃s] *f* proverb; (law) sentence

senteur [sɑ̃tœr] *f* odor, perfume

sentier [sɑ̃tje] *m* path; **hors des sentiers battus** off the beaten track

sentiment [sɑ̃timɑ̃] *m* feeling; opinion; **nos meilleurs sentiments** (*formula in letter writing*) our best wishes

sentimen•tal -tale [sɑ̃timɑ̃tal] *adj* (*pl* **-taux** [to]) sentimental

sentine [sɑ̃tin] *f* bilge

sentinelle [sɑ̃tinɛl] *f* sentinel

sentir [sɑ̃tir] §41, §95 *tr* to feel; smell; smell like, smell of; taste of; have all the earmarks of; show the effects of; **ne pas pouvoir sentir qn** to be unable to stand s.o. ‖ *intr* to smell; smell bad ‖ *ref* to feel; be felt; **se sentir de** to feel the effects of

seoir [swar] §5A (3d *pl pres ind* **siéent;** used only in 3d *sg & pl* of most simple tenses) *intr*—**seoir à** to be fitting for, proper to; be suitable to, suit, become, e.g., **cette robe lui sied** that dress suits her, that dress becomes her ‖ (used only in *inf* and 2d *sg & pl* and 1st *pl impv*) *ref* (coll & poetic) to sit down, have a seat

séparation [separasjɔ̃] *f* separation

séparer [separe] *tr & ref* to separate, divide

sept [sɛt] §94 *adj & pron* seven; the Seventh, e.g., **Jean sept** John the Seventh; **sept heures** seven o'clock ‖ *m* seven; seventh (*in dates*)

septembre [sɛptɑ̃br] *m* September

septentrio•nal -nale [sɛptɑ̃trijɔnal] (*pl* **-naux** [no]) *adj* northern

septième [sɛtjɛm] §94 *adj, pron* (*masc, fem*), & *m* seventh

septique [sɛptik] *adj* septic

sépulcre [sepylkr] *m* sepulcher

sépulture [sepyltyr] *f* grave, tomb, burial place; burial

séquelle [sekɛl] *f* gang; (pathol) complications; **séquelles** aftermath

séquence [sekɑ̃s] *f* sequence; (*in poker*) straight

séquestrer [sekɛstre] *tr* to sequester

serai [səre], [sre] *v* (**seras, sera, serons,** etc.) see **être**

sérail [seraj] *m* (*pl* **sérails**) seraglio

séraphin [serafɛ̃] *m* seraph; (coll) angel

serbe [sɛrb] *adj* Serb, Serbian ‖ (*cap*) *mf* Serbe, Serbian ‖ (*l.c.*) *m* (*langue*) Serbe, Serbian

serbo-croate [sɛrbɔkrɔat] *m* (*langue*) Serbo-Croatian

se•rein -reine [sərɛ̃] **-reine** [rɛn] *adj* serene ‖ *m* night dew

sérénade [serenad] *f* serenade

sérénité [serenite] *f* serenity

serf [sɛr], [sɛrf] **serve** [sɛrv] *mf* serf

serge [sɛrʒ] *f* serge; baize

sergent [sɛrʒɑ̃] *m* sergeant

série [seri] *f* series, string, set; (elec) series; **de série** standard; stock (*car*); **en série** in (a) series; mass, e.g., **fabrication en série** mass production; **hors série** outsize (*wearing apparel*); discontinued (*as an item of manufacture*); custom-built; almost unheard of; **série noire** run of bad luck

sé•rieux -rieuse [serjø] **-rieuse** [rjøz] *adj* serious; **prendre au sérieux** to take seriously

serin [sərɛ̃] *m* canary; (coll) simpleton

seringa [sərɛ̃ga] *m* mock orange

seringue [sərɛ̃g] *f* syringe; (hort) spray gun; **seringue à graisse** grease gun; **seringue à injections** hypodermic syringe; **seringue à instillations** nasal spray

serment [sɛrmɑ̃] *m* oath; **prêter serment** to take oath

sermon [sɛrmɔ̃] *m* sermon

sermonner [sɛrmɔne] *tr* to sermonize

seroposi•tif [serɔpozitif] **-tive** [tiv] *adj* seropositive; HIV positive

serpe [sɛrp] *f* billhook

serpent [sɛrpɑ̃] *m* snake, serpent; **serpent à sonnettes** rattlesnake; **serpent caché sous les fleurs** snake in the grass

serpenter [sɛrpɑ̃te] *intr* to wind

serpen•tin -tine [sɛrpɑ̃tɛ̃] **-tine** [tin] *adj* serpentine ‖ *m* coil; worm (*of still*); paper streamer

serpillière [sɛrpijɛr] *f* floorcloth; sacking, burlap

serpolet [sɛrpɔlɛ] *m* thyme

serre [sɛr] *f* greenhouse; **serres** claws, talons

ser•ré -rée [sɛre] *adj* tight; narrow; compact; close || **serré** *adv*—**jouer serré** to play it close to the vest

serre-fils [sɛrfil] *m invar* (elec) binding post

serre-freins [sɛrfrɛ̃] *m invar* brakeman

serre-livres [sɛrlivr] *m invar* book end

serrement [sɛrmɑ̃] *m* squeezing, pressing; (min) partition (*to keep out water*); (pathol) pang; **serrement de cœur** heaviness of heart; **serrement de main** handshake

serrer [sɛre] *tr* to press; squeeze; wring; tighten; close up (*ranks*); clasp, shake, e.g., **serrer la main à** to shake hands with; grit (*one's teeth*); put on (*the brakes*) || *intr*—**serrez à droite** (*public sign*) squeeze to right || *ref* to squeeze together, be close together

serre-tête [sɛrtɛt] *m invar* headband; kerchief; crash helmet; (telp) headset

serrure [sɛryr] *f* lock; **serrure de sûreté** safety lock

serrurier [seryrje] *m* locksmith

sers [sɛr] *v* (**sert**) see **servir**

sertir [sɛrtir] *tr* to set (*a stone*)

sérum [serɔm] *m* serum

servage [sɛrvaʒ] *m* serfdom

ser•veur [sɛrvœr] **-veuse** [vøz] *mf* (tennis) server || *m* waiter; barman (comp) server; **serveur à distance** (comp) remote server; **serveur de chat** (comp) chat server || *f* waitress; barmaid; extra maid; (mach) coffee maker

serviable [sɛrvjabl] *adj* obliging

service [sɛrvis] *m* service; agency; service charge; **service après vente** warranty service; **être de service** to be on duty; **service compris** tip included; **service de déminage** bomb squad; **Service de Documentation Extérieure et Contre-espionage (S.D.E.C.)** (*equivalence aux U.S.A.*) Central Intelligence Agency (CIA); **service de garde** twenty-four-hour service; **service de livraison** delivery service; **service des abonnes absents** telephone answering service; **service des renseignements téléphoniques** information; **service des urgences** emergency room; **service sanitaire** ambulance corps

serviette [sɛrvjɛt] *f* napkin; towel; brief case; **serviette de bain** bath towel; **serviette de table** table napkin; **serviette de toilette en papier** paper towel; **serviette en papier** paper napkin; **serviette éponge** washcloth; Turkish towel; **serviette hygiénique** sanitary napkin

servile [sɛrvil] *adj* servile

servir [sɛrvir] **§63, §96** *tr* to serve; deal (*cards*) || *intr* to serve; **servir à** to be useful for, to serve as; **servir à qn de** to serve s.o. as; **servir de** to serve as, to function as || *ref* to help oneself; **se servir chez** to patronize; **se servir de** to use

serviteur [sɛrvitœr] *m* servant

servitude [sɛrvityd] *f* servitude; (law) easement

servofrein [sɛrvofrɛ̃] *m* power brake

ses [se] **§88**

sésame [sezam] *m* sesame

session [sesjɔ̃] *f* session

seuil [sœj] *m* threshold

seul seule [sœl] **§92** *adj* alone; lonely || (when standing before noun) *adj* sole, single, only || *pron indef* single one, only one; single person, only person || **seul** *adv* alone

seulement [sœlmɑ̃] *adv* only, even || *conj* but

sève [sɛv] *f* sap; vim

sévère [sever] *adj* severe; stern; strict

sévices [sevis] *mpl* cruelty, brutality

sévir [sevir] *intr* to rage

sevrage [sɔvraʒ] *m* weaning

sevrer [sɔvre] **§2** *tr* to wean

sexe [sɛks] *m* sex; **le beau sexe** the fair sex; **le sexe fort** the sterner sex

sexisme [sɛksism] *m* sexism

sexiste [sɛksist] *adj & mf* sexist

sex-shop [sɛksʃɔp] *m* (*pl* **-shops**) adult book store

sextant [sɔkstɑ̃] *m* sextant

sextuor [sɛkstɥɔr] *m* (mus) sextet

sexualité [sɛksɥalite] *f* sexuality

sexuel sexuelle [sɛksɥɛl] *adj* sexual

seyant [sɛjɑ̃] **seyante** [sɛjɑ̃t] *adj* becoming

SF *abbr* **science-fiction**

shampouiner [ʃɑ̃puine] *tr* to shampoo (*the hair*)

shampoui•neur [ʃɑ̃puinœr] **-neuse** [nøz] *mf* (*person*) shampooer || *m & f* (mach) rug shampooer

shampooing [ʃɑ̃pwɛ̃] *m* shampoo

shérif [ʃerif] *m* sheriff

shooter [ʃute] *ref* (slang) to shoot up (*intravenously*)

short [ʃɔrt] *m* shorts

si [si] *m invar* if; **des si et des cars** ifs and buts || *adv* so; as; (to contradict a negative statement or question) yes, e.g., **Vous ne le saviez pas. Si!** You didn't know. Yes, I did!; **si bien que** so that, with the result that; **si peu que** so little that; **si peu que ce soit** however little it may be; **si** + *adj* or *adv* + **que** + *subj* however + *adj* or *adv* + *ind*, e.g., **si vite qu'il s'en aille** however fast he goes away || *conj* if; whether; **si . . . ne** unless, e.g., **si je ne me trompe** unless I am mistaken; **si ce n'est** unless; **si tant est que** if it is true that

sia•mois [sjamwa] **-moise** [mwaz] *adj* Siamese || (*cap*) *mf* Siamese

sibé•rien [siberjɛ̃] **-rienne** [rjɛn] *adj* Siberian || (*cap*) *mf* Siberian

sibylle [sibil] *f* sibyl

Sicile [sisil] *f* Sicily; **la Sicile** Sicily

sici•lien [sisiljɛ̃] **-lienne** [ljɛn] *adj* Sicilian || (*cap*) *mf* Sicilian

SIDA [sida] *m* (acronym) (**syndrome d'immuno-déficience acquise**)—**le SIDA** AIDS (*acquired immune-deficiency syndrome*)

sidé•ral -rale [sideral] *adj* (*pl* **-raux** [ro]) sidereal

sidérer [sidere] **§10** *tr* (coll) to flabbergast

sidérurgie [sideryrʒi] *f* iron-and-steel industry

sidérurgique [sideryrʒik] *adj* iron-and-steel

siècle [sjɛkl] *m* century; age; (eccl) world

siège [sjeʒ] *m* seat; headquarters; (eccl) see; (mil) siege; **siège à glissière** glider; **siège arrière** back seat; **siège avant** front seat; **siège baquet** (*pl* **sièges baquets**) bucket seat; **siège billes** bean-bag chair; **siège des cabinets** toilet seat; **siège éjectable** ejection seat

siéger [sjeʒe] §1 *intr* to sit, be in session; (*said of malady*) be seated

sien [sjɛ̃] **sienne** [sjɛn] §89

sieste [sjɛst] *f* siesta; **faire le sieste** to take a siesta; (coll) to be caught napping

sifflement [sifləmɑ̃] *m* whistle; hiss; swish, whiz; wheezing

siffler [sifle] *tr* to whistle (*e.g., a tune*); to hiss, boo; whistle to ‖ *intr* to whistle; hiss; swish, whiz

sifflet [siflɛ] *m* whistle; **sifflet à gaz** protective whistle in a woman's handbag

sif•fleur [siflœr] **-fleuse** [fløz] *mf* whistler

siffloter [siflɔte] *tr & intr* to whistle (a tune)

sigle [sigl] *m* abbreviation; word formed by literation; acronym

si•gnal [siɲal] *m* (*pl* **-gnaux** [ɲo]) signal; sign; (telp) busy signal; **signal de fumée** smoke signal

signa•lé -lée [siɲale] *adj* signal, noteworthy

signalement [siɲalmɑ̃] *m* description

signaler [siɲale] *tr* to signal; point out ‖ *ref* to distinguish oneself

signalisation [siɲalizɑsjɔ̃] *f* signs

signataire [siɲatɛr] *adj & mf* signatory

signature [siɲatyr] *f* signature; signing

signe [siɲ] *m* sign; **faire signe à** to motion to, to signal; **signe de la Croix** (eccl) Sign of the Cross; **signe de ponctuation** punctuation mark; **signe de tête** nod

signer [siɲe] *tr* to sign ‖ *ref* to cross oneself

signet [siɲɛ] [sinɛ] *m* bookmark

significa•tif [siɲifikatif] **-tive** [tiv] *adj* significant

signifier [siɲifje] §97 *tr* to signify; mean

sikh [sik] *adj & mf* Sikh

silence [silɑ̃s] *m* silence

silen•cieux [silɑ̃sjø] **-cieuse** [sjøz] *adj* silent ‖ *m* silencer (*of a gun*); (aut) muffler

silex [silɛks] *m* flint

silhouette [silwɛt] *f* silhouette

silhouetter [silwete] *tr* to silhouette

silicium [silisjɔm] *m* silicon

silicone [silikon] *f* silicone

sillage [sijaʒ] *m* wake

sillet [sijɛ] *m* (mus) nut

sillon [sijɔ̃] *m* furrow; groove; **sillon sonore** sound track

sillonner [sijɔne] *tr* to furrow; groove; cross, streak

silo [silo] *m* silo

silure [silyr] *m* catfish

simagrée [simagre] *f* pretense

similaire [similɛr] *adj* similar

similigravure [similigravyr] *f* halftone

similitude [similityd] *f* similarity

similor [similɔr] *m* ormolu

simple [sɛ̃pl] *adj* simple; one-way (*ticket*); **à simple interligne** (typ) single-spaced; **passer en simple police** to go to police court; **simple particulier** private citizen; **simple soldat** private ‖ *mf* simple-minded person ‖ *m* simple (*herb*); (tennis) singles

simplement [sɛ̃pləmɑ̃] *adv* simply, plainly, naturally; simply, merely, just; with a simple mind

sim•plet [sɛ̃plɛ] **-plette** [plɛt] *adj* artless

simplicité [sɛ̃plisite] *f* simplicity; simpleness; simple-mindedness; **en toute simplicité** naturally, without affectation; **venez en toute simplicité** come as you are

simplifier [sɛ̃plifje] *tr* to simplify

simpliste [sɛ̃plist] *adj* oversimple

simulacre [simylakr] *m* sham; **simulacre de combat** sham battle

simulateur [simylatœr] *m* (comp) simulator

simuler [simyle] *tr* to simulate

simulta•né -née [simyltane] *adj* simultaneous; **en simultané** simultaneous (*translation*)

sinapisme [sinapism] *m* mustard plaster

sincère [sɛ̃sɛr] *adj* sincere

sincérité [sɛ̃serite] *f* sincerity

sinécure [sinekyr] *f* sinecure

singe [sɛ̃ʒ] *m* monkey; (slang) boss; **grimacer comme un vieux singe** to grin like a Cheshire cat

singer [sɛ̃ʒe] §38 *tr* to ape

singerie [sɛ̃ʒri] *f* monkeyshine; grimace; monkey cage

singulariser [sɛ̃gylarize] *tr* to draw attention to ‖ *ref* to stand out

singu•lier [sɛ̃gylje] **-lière** [ljɛr] *adj & m* singular

sinistre [sinistr] *adj* sinister ‖ *m* disaster

sinis•tré -trée [sinistre] *adj* damaged, ruined; homeless; shipwrecked ‖ *mf* victim

sinon [sinɔ̃] *adv* if not; perhaps even; **sinon que** except for the fact that ‖ *prep* except for, except to ‖ *conj* except, unless; or else, else, otherwise

si•nueux [sinɥø] **-nueuse** [nɥøz] *adj* sinuous, winding

sinus [sinys] *m* sinus; (trig) sine

sionisme [sjɔnism] *m* Zionism

siphon [sifɔ̃] *m* siphon; siphon bottle; trap (*double-curved pipe*)

siphonner [sifɔne] *tr* to siphon

sire [sir] *m* sire; (archaic) sir; **un triste sire** a miserable wretch

sirène [sirɛn] *f* siren; foghorn; mermaid

sirop [siro] *m* syrup; **sirop pectoral** cough syrup

siroter [sirɔte] *tr & intr* (coll) to sip

sis [si] **sise** [siz] *adj* located

sismique [sismik] *adj* seismic

sismographe [sismɔgraf] *m* seismograph

sismologie [sismɔlɔʒi] *f* seismology

sitcom [sitkɔm] *m* (telv) sitcom

site [sit] *m* site; lay of the land

sitôt [sito] *adv* immediately; **sitôt dit, sitôt fait** no sooner said than done; **sitôt que** as soon as

sittelle [sitɛl] *f* (orn) nuthatch

situation [sitɥɑsjɔ̃] *f* situation; **situation sans issue** deadlock, impasse

situer [sitɥe] *tr* to situate, locate

six [si(s)] §94 *adj & pron* six; the Sixth; **Jean six** John the Sixth; **six heures** six o'clock ‖ *m* six; sixth (*in dates*)

sixième [sizjɛm] §94 *adj, pron* (*masc, fem*), & *m* sixth

six-quatre-deux [siskatdø]—**à la six-quatre-deux** (coll) slapdash

sizain [sizɛ̃] *m* six-line verse; pack (*of cub scouts*)

sizerin [sizrɛ̃] *m* (orn) redpoll

skate [skɛt] *m* skateboard

skate′board′ [skɛtbɔrd] *m* skateboard

ski [ski] *m* ski; skiing; **faire du ski** to go skiing; **ski de fond** cross-country ski; **ski nautique** water-skiing

skier [skje] *intr* to ski

skieur [skjœr] **skieuse** [skjøz] *mf* skier

slalom [slalɔm] *m* slalom

slave [slav] *adj* Slav; Slavic ‖ *m* Slavic (*language*) ‖ (*cap*) *mf* Slav (*person*)

slip [slip] *m* supporter; swimming trunks; (women's) panties; **slip de soutien, slip coquille** supporter, jockstrap; **slip minimum** bikini

s.l.n.d. *abbr* (**sans lieu ni date**) n.p. & n.d.

slogan [slɔgɑ̃] *m* (com) slogan

slovaque [slɔvak] *adj* Slovak ‖ *m* Slovak (*language*) ‖ (*cap*) *mf* Slovak (*person*)

Slovaquie, la [slɔvaki] *f* Slovakia

SMIC *or* **S.M.I.C.** [smik] *m* (acronym) (*salaire minimum interprofessionnel de croissance*) minimum wage

smi•card [smikar] **-carde** [kard] *mf* (coll) minimum-wage earner

smoking [smɔkiŋ] *m* tuxedo; formal wear, black tie

smurf [smyrf] *m* break dancing

snack [snak] *m* snack bar

S.N.C.F. [ɛsɛnseɛf] *f* (letterword) (**Société nationale des chemins de fer français**) French railroad

snob [snɔb] *adj invar* snobbish ‖ *mf* (*pl* **snob** *or* **snobs**) snob

snober [snɔbe] *tr* to snub

snobisme [snɔbism] *m* snobbery

sobre [sɔbr] *adj* sober, moderate; simple (*ornamentation*)

sobriété [sɔbrijete] *f* sobriety; moderation (*in eating, speaking*)

sobriquet [sɔbrikɛ] *m* nickname

soc [sɔk] *m* plowshare

sociable [sɔsjabl] *adj* sociable, neighborly; social (*creature*)

so•cial -ciale [sɔsjal] *adj* (*pl* **-ciaux** [sjo]) social

sociali•sant [sɔsjalizɑ̃] **-sante** [zɑ̃t] *adj* socialistic ‖ *mf* socialist sympathizer

socialiser [sɔsjalize] *tr* to socialize

socialisme [sɔsjalism] *m* socialism

socialiste [sɔsjalist] *adj & mf* socialist

sociétaire [sɔsjetɛr] *mf* stockholder; member (*e.g., of an acting company*)

société [sɔsjete] *f* society; company; firm, partnership; **société anonyme** stock company, corporation; **société de gardiennage** security-systems company; **société de prévoyance** benefit society; **Société des Nations** League of Nations; **société d'investissement à capital variable** mutual-fund society; **société d'unigestion** holding company; **société mère** parent company; **société multinationale** multinational corporation

sociologie [sɔsjɔlɔʒi] *f* sociology

socle [sɔkl] *m* pedestal; footing, socle; **socle roulant** portable stand (*e.g., for a television set*)

socque [sɔk] *m* clog, sabot; (theat) comedy

socquette [sɔkɛt] *f* anklet

Socrate [sɔkrat] *m* Socrates

soda [sɔda] *m* soda water

sodium [sɔdjɔm] *m* sodium

sodomie [sɔdɔmi] *f* sodomy

sœur [sœr] *f* sister; **et ta sœur!** (slang) knock it off!; **ma sœur** (eccl) sister; **sœur de placement, sœur de lait** foster sister

sofa [sɔfa] *m* sofa

soi [swa] §85, §85B; **à part soi** to oneself (himself, etc.); **de soi, en soi** in itself

soi-disant [swadizɑ̃] *adj invar* so-called, self-styled ‖ *adv* supposedly

soie [swa] *f* silk; bristle

soierie [swari] *f* silk goods; silk factory

soif [swaf] *f* thirst; **avoir soif** to be thirsty

soi•gné -gnée [swaɲe] *adj* well-groomed, trim; polished (*speech*)

soigner [swaɲe] *tr* to nurse, take care of; groom; polish (*one's style*)

soigneur [swaɲœr] *m* (sports) trainer

soi•gneux [swaɲø] **-gneuse** [ɲøz] *adj* careful, meticulous

soi-même [swamɛm] §86

soin [swɛ̃] *m* care, attention; treatment; **aux bons soins de** in care of (*c/o*); **être aux petits soins auprès de** to wait on (*s.o.*) hand and foot; **premiers soins** first aid; **soins à domicile** home-care nursing; **soins des pieds** pedicure; podiatry; **soins d'urgence** first aid; **soins infirmière** nursing

soir [swar] *m* evening, night; **hier soir** last night; **le soir** in the evening, at night

soirée [sware] *f* evening; evening party; **en soirée** evening (*performance*); **soirée dansante** dance; **soirée-hébergement** pajama party

sois [swa] *v* (**soit, soient**) see **être**

soit [swa], [swat] *conj* take for instance, e.g., **soit quatre multiplié par deux** take for instance four multiplied by two; say, e.g., **bien des hommes étaient perdus, soit un million** many men were lost, say a million; **soit . . . soit** either . . . or, whether . . . or; **soit que . . .**

soit que whether . . . or ‖ [swat] *interj* so be it!, all right!

soixante [swasɑ̃t] §94 *adj, pron, & m* sixty; **soixante et onze** seventy-one; **soixante et onzième** seventy-first; **soixante et un** sixty-one; **soixante et unième** sixty-first

soixante-dix [swasɑ̃tdi(s)] §94 *adj, pron, & m* seventy

soixante-dixième [swasɑ̃tizjɛm] §94 *adj, pron* (*masc, fem*)*, & m* seventieth

soixante-douze [swasɑ̃tduz] §94 *adj, pron, & m* seventy-two

soixante-douzième [swasɑ̃tduzjɛm] §94 *adj, pron* (*masc, fem*)*, & m* seventy-second

soixantième [swasɑ̃tjɛm] §94 *adj, pron* (*masc, fem*)*, & m* sixtieth

soja [sɔʒa] *m* soybean

sol [sɔl] *m* soil; ground; floor

solaire [sɔlɛr] *adj* solar

soldat [sɔlda] *m* soldier

soldatesque [sɔldatɛsk] *adj* barrack-room (*humor; manners*) ‖ *f* rowdies

solde [sɔld] *m* balance (*of an account*); remnant; clearance sale; **en solde** reduced (*in price*) ‖ *f* (mil) pay

solder [sɔlde] *tr* to settle (*an account*); to sell out; (mil) to pay ‖ *intr* to sell out

sol•deur [sɔldœr] **-deuse** [døz] *mf* dealer in seconds and remnants

sole [sɔl] *f* sole (*fish*); field (*used for crop rotation*)

soleil [sɔlɛj] *m* sun; sunshine, sunlight; sunflower; pinwheel; **il fait** (**du**) **soleil** it is sunny

solen•nel -nelle [sɔlanɛl] *adj* solemn

solenniser [sɔlanize] *tr* to solemnize

solénoïde [sɔlenɔid] *m* solenoid

solfège [sɔlfɛʒ] *m* sol-fa

solidage [sɔlidaʒ] *f* goldenrod

solidaire [sɔlidɛr] *adj* interdependent; jointly binding; **être solidaire** to show solidarity; **se déclarer solidaire de** to declare solidarity with **solidaire de** responsible for; answerable to; integral with, in one piece with

solidariser [sɔlidarize] *ref* to join together; **se solidariser avec** to declare solidarity with

solidarité [sɔlidarite] *f* solidarity, interdependence

solide [sɔlid] *adj & m* solid

solidité [sɔlidite] *f* solidity; soundness; strength (*e.g., of a fabric*)

soliloque [sɔlilɔk] *m* soliloquy

soliste [sɔlist] *mf* soloist

solitaire [sɔlitɛr] *adj* solitary; lonely ‖ *m* solitary, anchorite; old wild boar; solitaire; tapeworm

solitude [sɔlityd] *f* solitude

solive [sɔliv] *f* joist

soli•veau [sɔlivo] *m* (*pl* **-veaux**) small joist; (coll) nobody

sollicitation [sɔlisitasjɔ̃] *f* solicitation

solliciter [sɔllisite] *tr* to solicit; apply for; incite; attract (*attention; iron*); induce; **to start** *ou* **prompt** (*an engine*) ‖ *intr* to seek favors

sollici•teur [sɔllisitœr] **-teuse** [tøz] *mf* solicitor, office seeker, petitioner, lobbyist

solo [sɔlo] *adj invar & m* solo

solstice [sɔlstis] *m* solstice

soluble [sɔlybl] *adj* soluble; solvable

solution [sɔlysjɔ̃] *f* solution

solutionner [sɔlysjɔne] *tr* to solve

solvabilité [sɔlvabilite] *f* solvency

solvable [sɔlvabl] *adj* solvent

solvant [sɔlvɑ̃] *m* solvent

sombre [sɔ̃br] *adj* somber; sullen

sombrer [sɔ̃bre] *intr* to sink; vanish (*as a fortune*)

sommaire [sɔmɛr] *adj & m* summary

sommation [sɔmasjɔ̃] *f* summons; sentry challenge; **faire les trois sommations** to read the riot act

somme [sɔm] *m* nap ‖ *f* sum; **en somme, somme toute** in short, when all is said and done

sommeil [sɔmɛj] *m* sleep; **avoir sommeil** to be sleepy

sommeiller [sɔmɛje] *intr* to doze; lie dormant

sommelier [sɔməlje] *m* wine steward

sommer [sɔme] §97 *tr* to add up; summon, issue a legal writ to

sommes [sɔm] *v* see **être**

sommet [sɔme] *m* summit, top; apex (*of a triangle*); vertex (*of an angle*); (fig) acme

sommier [sɔmje] *m* bedspring; ledger; crossbeam; (archaic) pack animal; **sommier élastique** spring mattress

sommité [sɔmite] *f* pinnacle, crest; leader, authority

somnambule [sɔmnɑ̃byl] *adj* sleepwalking ‖ *mf* sleepwalker; Walkman (trademark)

somnifère [sɔmnifɛr] *adj* sleep-inducing, soporific ‖ *m* sleeping pill

somnolence [sɔmnɔlɑ̃s] *f* drowsiness; indolence, laziness

somno•lent [sɔmnɔlɑ̃] **-lente** [lɑ̃t] *adj* somnolent, drowsy; indolent

somnoler [sɔmnɔle] *intr* to doze

somptuaire [sɔ̃ptɥɛr] *adj* luxury (*tax*)

somp•tueux [sɔ̃ptɥø] **-tueuse** [tɥøz] *adj* sumptuous

son [sɔ̃] *adj poss* §88 his, her, its ‖ *m* sound; sounding; bran; **son stéréophonique de haute fidélité** hi-fi stereo sound

sonal [sɔnal] *m* (advertising) jingle

sonate [sɔnat] *f* sonata

sondage [sɔ̃daʒ] *m* sounding, probing; **sondage de l'opinion** public-opinion poll; **sondage d'exploration** wildcat (*well*); **sondage isoloir** exit poll; **sondage(s)** sounding

sonde [sɔ̃d] *f* lead, probe; borer, drill; **sonde spatiale** space probe

sonder [sɔ̃de] *tr* to sound, probe, bore, fathom; explore, reconnoiter; poll (*e.g., public opinion*); sound out (*s.o.*)

son•deur [sɔ̃dœr] **-deuse** [døz] *mf* prober, sounder

songe [sɔ̃ʒ] *m* dream

songe-creux [sɔ̃ʒkrø] *m invar* visionary, pipe dreamer

songer [sɔ̃ʒe] §38, §96 *tr* to dream up ‖ *intr* to dream; think; intend to; **songer à** to think of; imagine, dream of; **songez-y!** think it over!

songerie [sɔ̃ʒri] *f* reverie, daydreaming

son•geur [sɔ̃ʒœr] **-geuse** [ʒøz] *adj* dreamy, pre-occupied ‖ *mf* daydreamer

sonique [sɔnik] *adj* sonic, of sound

sonnaille [sɔnɑj] *f* cowbell, sheepbell

sonnailler [sɔnɑje] *m* bellwether ‖ *intr* to ring often and without cause

son•nant [sɔnɑ̃] **-nante** [nɑ̃t] *adj* striking (*clock*); metal (*money*); at the stroke of, e.g., **à huit heures sonnantes** at the stroke of eight

son•né -née [sɔne] *adj* past, e.g., **deux heures sonnées** past two o'clock; over, e.g., **il a soixante ans sonnés** he is over sixty; (slang) cuckoo, nuts; (slang) stunned; **être sonné** (slang) to be knocked out

sonner [sɔne] *tr* to ring; ring for; sound ‖ *intr* to ring; strike; sound

sonnerie [sɔnri] *f* chimes, chiming; set of bells, carillon; fanfare; ring (*of a telephone, door-bell, etc.*); alarm or striking mechanism (*of clock*)

sonnet [sɔnɛ] *m* sonnet

sonnette [sɔnɛt] *f* doorbell; pile driver

sonneur [sɔnœr] *m* bellringer; trumpeter

sonore [sɔnɔr] *adj* sonorous; sound (*wave, track*); echoing (*hall, cathedral, etc.*); (pho-net) voiced ‖ *f* voiced consonant

sonorisation [sɔnɔrizɑsjɔ̃] *f* public-address sys-tem; (mov) sound track

sonoriser [sɔnɔrize] *tr* to record sound effects on (*a film*); equip (*an auditorium*) with loud-speakers

sonorité [sɔnɔrite] *f* sonority, resonance

sonotone [sɔnɔtɔn] *m* hearing aid

sont [sɔ̃] *v* see **être**

sophistication [sɔfistikɑsjɔ̃] *f* adulteration

sophisti•qué -quée [sɔfistike] *adj* adulterated; artificial, counterfeit; (comp) sophisticated

sophistiquer [sɔfistike] *tr* to adulterate; subtil-ize

Sophocle [sɔfɔkl] *m* Sophocles

sopraniste [sɔpranist] *m* male soprano

sopra•no [sɔprano] *mf* (*pl* **-ni** [ni] or **-nos**) so-prano ‖ *m* soprano (*voice*)

sorbet [sɔrbɛ] *m* sherbet

sorbetière [sɔrbətjɛr] *f* ice-cream freezer

sorbon•nard [sɔrbɔnar] **-narde** [nard] *mf* (coll) Sorbonne student; (coll) Sorbonne professor

sorcellerie [sɔrsɛlri] *f* sorcery

sor•cier [sɔrsje] **-cière** [sjɛr] *adj* sorcerer's; **cela n'est pas sorcier** there's no trick to that ‖ *m* sorcerer, wizard ‖ *f* sorceress, witch; **vieille sorcière** old hag

sordide [sɔrdid] *adj* sordid

sornette [sɔrnɛt] *f* nonsense

sors [sɔr] *v* (**sort**) see **sortir**

sort [sɔr] *m* fate, destiny; fortune, lot; spell, charm

sortable [sɔrtabl] *adj* suitable, acceptable; pre-sentable

sor•tant [sɔrtɑ̃] **-tante** [tɑ̃t] *adj* retiring (*congressman*); winning (*number*) ‖ *mf* per-son leaving

sorte [sɔrt] *f* sort, kind; state, condition; way, manner; **de la sorte** this way, thus; **de sorte que** so that, with the result that; **en quelque sorte** in a certain way; **en sorte que** in such a way that

sortie [sɔrti] *f* exit, way out; outing, jaunt; quit-ting time; outburst, tirade; (mil) sortie; **faire une sortie à** (slang) to bawl out; **sortie de bain** bathrobe; **sortie de bal** evening wrap; **sortie de secours** emergency exit, fire exit; **sortie de voiture(s)** driveway

sortilège [sɔrtilɛʒ] *m* spell, charm

sortir [sɔrtir] §64 *tr* to take out, bring out; pub-lish ‖ *intr* (*aux:* ETRE) to go out, come out; come forth; stand out; **au sortir de** on coming out of; **sortir de +** *inf* (coll) to have just + *pp*

S.O.S. [ɛsoɛs] *m* (letterword) S.O.S.

sosie [sozi] *m* double

sot [so] **sotte** [sɔt] (precedes the noun it modi-fies) *adj* stupid, silly ‖ *mf* fool, simpleton

sottise [sɔtiz] *f* stupidity, silliness, foolishness

sou [su] *m* sou; (fig) penny, farthing; **sans le sou** penniless; **sou à sou** or **sou par sou** a penny at a time

soubassement [subɑsmɑ̃] *m* subfoundation, infrastructure

soubresaut [subrəso] *m* sudden start, jerk; pal-pitation, jump (*of the heart*)

soubrette [subrɛt] *f* (theat) soubrette; (coll) at-tractive chambermaid

souche [suʃ] *f* stump; stock; master tape; stack (*of fireplace*); strain (*of virus*); (coll) dolt; **de pure souche** full-blooded

souci [susi] *m* care; marigold; **sans souci** care-free

soucier [susje] §97 *ref* to care, concern oneself

soucieusement [susjøzmɑ̃] *adv* uneasily, anx-iously; with concern

sou•cieux [susjø] **-cieuse** [sjøz] *adj* solicitous, concerned; uneasy, anxious

soucoupe [sukup] *f* saucer; **soucoupe volante** flying saucer; Frisbee (trademark)

soudage [sudaʒ] *m* soldering; welding

sou•dain [sudɛ̃] **-daine** [dɛn] *adj* sudden ‖ **sou-dain** *adv* suddenly

soudainement [sudɛnmɑ̃] *adv* suddenly

soudaineté [sudɛnte] *f* suddenness

souda•nais [sudanɛ] **-naise** [nɛz] *adj* Sudanic ‖ *m* Sudanic (*language*) ‖ (*cap*) *mf* Sudanese (*person*)

soude [sud] *f* (chem) soda

souder [sude] *tr* to solder; weld ‖ *ref* to knit (*as bones do*)

soudeur [sudœr] *m* welder

soudoyer [sudwaje] §47 *tr* to bribe; hire (*assas-sins*)

soudure [sudyr] *f* solder; soldering; soldered

joint; knitting (*of bones*); **faire la soudure** to bridge the gap; **soudure autogène** welding

soue [su] *f* pigsty

soufflage [sufla3] *m* blowing; glass blowing

souf•fert [sufɛr] **-ferte** [fɛrt] *v* see **souffrir**

souffle [sufl] *m* breath; breathing; **second souffle** second wind

souf•flé -flée [sufle] *adj* puffed up ‖ *m* soufflé

souffler [sufle] *tr* to blow; blow out (*a candle*); blow up (*a balloon*); prompt (*an actor*); huff (*a checker*); suggest (*an idea*); **ne pas souffler mot** not to breathe a word; **souffler à l'oreille** to whisper; **souffler q.ch. à qn** to take s.th. from s.o. ‖ *intr* to blow; pant, puff; take a breather, catch one's breath

soufflerie [sufləri] *f* bellows; wind tunnel

soufflet [suflɛ] *m* slap in the face; affront, insult; bellows; gore (*of dress*); (rr) flexible cover (*between two cars*)

souffleter [sufləte] §34 *tr* to slap in the face; affront

souf•fleur [suflœr] **-fleuse** [fløz] *mf* (theat) prompter ‖ *m* glass blower ‖ *f* (mach) blower

soufflure [suflyr] *f* blister, bubble

souffrance [sufrɑ̃s] *f* suffering; **en souffrance** unfinished (*business*); outstanding (*bill*); unclaimed (*parcel*); at a standstill, suspended

souf•frant [sufrɑ̃] **-frante** [frɑ̃t] *adj* suffering; sick, ailing

souffre-douleur [sufrədulœr] *m invar* butt (*of a joke*), laughingstock

souffre•teux [sufrətø] **-teuse** [tøz] *adj* sickly; destitute, half-starved

souffrir [sufrir] §65, §96, §97 *tr* to suffer; stand, bear, tolerate; permit ‖ *intr* to suffer ‖ *ref* to put up with each other

soufre [sufr] *m* sulfur

soufrer [sufre] *tr* to sulfurate

souhait [swɛ] *m* wish; **à souhait** to one's liking, to perfection; **à vos souhaits!** (salutation) gesundheit!; **souhaits** good wishes; **souhaits de bonne année** New Year's greetings

souhaitable [swɛtabl] *adj* desirable

souhaiter [swɛte] §95, §97 *tr* to wish; wish for; wish to; **je vous la souhaite bonne et heureuse** I wish you a happy New Year

souille [suj] *f* wallow

souiller [suje] *tr* to dirty, spot, stain, soil, sully

souillon [sujɔ̃] *f* (coll) scullery maid

souillure [sujyr] *f* spot, stain

soûl [su] **soûle** [sul] *adj* drunk; sottish ‖ *m* fill, e.g., **manger son soûl** to eat one's fill

soulagement [sulaʒmɑ̃] *m* relief; comfort

soulager [sulaʒe] §38 *tr* to relieve; comfort

soûler [sule] *tr* (slang) to cram down one's throat; (slang) to get (*s.o.*) drunk ‖ *ref* (fig) to have one's fill; (slang) to get drunk

soulèvement [sulɛvmɑ̃] *m* upheaval; uprising; surge; **soulèvement de cœur** nausea

soulever [sulve] §2 *tr* to raise, heave, lift (up); stir up ‖ *ref* to rise; raise oneself; revolt

soulier [sulje] *m* shoe; **être dans ses petits souliers** (coll) to feel awkward; **souliers à talons**

hauts high-heeled shoes; **souliers bas** low-heeled shoes; **souliers compensés** elevator shoes; **souliers de marche** walking shoes; **souliers montants** boots; **souliers richelieu** oxfords

soulignement [suliɲəmɑ̃] *m* underlining

souligner [suliɲe] *tr* to underline; emphasize

soulte [sult] *f* balance due

soumettre [sumɛtr] §42 *tr* to submit; subject; overcome, subdue ‖ *ref* to submit, surrender

sou•mis [sumi] **-mise** [miz] *adj* submissive, subservient; subject; amenable (*to a law*)

soumission [sumisjɔ̃] *f* submission, surrender; bid (*to perform a service*); guarantee

soumissionnaire [sumisjɔnɛr] *mf* bidder

soupape [supap] *f* valve; **soupape à réglage** or **à papillon** damper; **soupape de sûreté** safety valve; **soupape électrique** rectifier

soupçon [supsɔ̃] *m* suspicion; misgiving; dash, touch (*small amount*)

soupçonner [supsɔne] §97 *tr & intr* to suspect

soupçon•neux [supsɔnø] **-neuse** [nøz] *adj* suspicious

soupe [sup] *f* vegetable soup; sop (*bread*); (mil) mess; **de soupe** on K.P.; **soupe au lait** (coll) mean-tempered person; **soupe populaire** soup kitchen; **trempé comme une soupe** soaking wet

soupente [supɑ̃t] *f* attic

souper [supe] *m* supper ‖ *intr* to have supper

soupeser [supəze] §2 *tr* to heft, weigh (*e.g., a package*) in one's hand

soupière [supjɛr] *f* soup tureen

soupir [supir] *m* sigh; breath; (mus) quarter rest

soupi•rail [supiraj] *m* (*pl* **-raux** [ro]) cellar window

soupirant [supirɑ̃] *m* suitor

soupirer [supire] *intr* to sigh; **soupirer après** or **pour** to long for

souple [supl] *adj* supple; flexible, pliant; versatile, adaptable

souplesse [suplɛs] *f* suppleness, flexibility

souquer [suke] *tr* to haul taut ‖ *intr* to pull hard (*on the oars*)

source [surs] *f* source; spring, fountain; **source de pétrole** oil well; **source jaillissante** gusher

sourcier [sursje] *m* dowser

sourcil [surci] *m* eyebrow

sourciller [sursije] *intr* to knit one's brows; **sans sourciller** without batting an eye

sourcil•leux [sursijø] **-leuse** [jøz] *adj* supercilious

sourd [sur] **sourde** [surd] *adj* deaf; quiet; dull (*sound, color*); deep (*voice*); undeclared (*war*); (phonet) unvoiced; **sourd comme un pot** (coll) stone-deaf ‖ *mf* deaf person ‖ *f* unvoiced consonant

sourdement [surdəmɑ̃] *adv* secretly; heavily; dully

sourdine [surdin] *f* (mus) mute; **à la sourdine** muted; **en sourdine** on the sly

sourd-muet [surmɥɛ] **sourde-muette** [surdəmɥɛt] (*pl* **sourds-muets**) *adj* deaf and dumb, deaf-mute ‖ *mf* deaf-mute

sourdre [surdr] (used in: *inf;* 3d *sg & pl pres ind* **sourd, sourdent**) *intr* to spring, well up

souricier [surisje] *m* mouser

souricière [surisjɛr] *f* mousetrap; (fig) trap

sourire [surir] *m* smile ‖ **§61, §97** *intr* to smile; **sourire à** to smile at; smile on; look good to

souris [suri] *m* (obs) smile ‖ *f* mouse

sour-nois [surnwa] **-noise** [nwaz] *adj* sly, cunning, artful

sous [su] *prep* under; on (*a certain day; certain conditions*); **sous caoutchouc** rubber-covered; **sous clef** under lock and key; **sous la main** at hand; **sous les drapeaux** in the army; **sous main** underhandedly; **sous peu** shortly; **sous un certain angle** from a certain point of view

sous-alimentation [suzalimɑ̃tɑsjɔ̃] *f* undernourishment

sous-bois [subwa] *m* underbrush, undergrowth

sous-chef [su/ɛf] *m* (*pl* **-chefs**) assistant (*to the head person*), deputy, second-in-command

souscripteur [suskriptœr] *m* subscriber (*to a loan or charity*); signer (*of a commercial paper*)

souscription [suskripsjɔ̃] *f* signature; subscription; **souscription de soutien** sustaining membership

souscrire [suskrir] **§25** *tr & intr* to subscribe

sous-cuta-né -née [sukytane] *adj* subcutaneous

sous-dévelop-pé -pée [sudɛvlɔpe] *adj* underdeveloped

sous-diacre [sudjakr] *m* subdeacon

sous-direc-teur [sudirɛktœr] **-trice** [tris] *mf* (*pl* **-directeurs**) second-in-command

sous-entendre [suzɑ̃tɑ̃dr] *tr* to understand (*what is not expressed*); to imply

sous-entendu [suzɑ̃tɑ̃dy] *m* inference, implication, innuendo, double meaning, double entendre

sous-entente [suzɑ̃tɑ̃t] *f* mental reservation; hidden, cryptic meaning

sous-entrepreneur [suzɑ̃trəprənœr] *m* (*pl* **-entrepreneurs**) subcontractor

sous-estimer [suzɛstime] *tr* to underestimate

sous-fifre [sufifr] *m* (*pl* **-fifres**) (coll) underling

sous-garde [sugard] *f* trigger guard

sous-lieutenant [suljøtnɑ̃] *m* (*pl* **-lieutenants**) second lieutenant

sous-location [sulɔkɑsjɔ̃] *f* sublease

sous-louer [sulwe] *tr* to sublet, sublease

sous-main [sumɛ̃] *m invar* desk blotter; **en sous-main** underhandedly

sous-marin -marine [sumarɛ̃] [marin] *adj & m* (*pl* **-marins**) submarine

sous-marinier [sumarinje] *m* (*pl* **-mariniers**) submarine crewman

sous-mentonnière [sumɑ̃tɔnjər] *f* (*pl* **-mentonnières**) chin strap

sous-nappe [sunap] *f* (*pl* **-nappes**) table pad

sous-off [suzɔf] *m* (*pl* **-offs**) noncom

sous-officier [suzɔfisje] *m* (*pl* **-officiers**) noncommissioned officer

sous-ordre [suzɔrdr] *m* (*pl* **-ordres**) underling, subordinate; (biol) suborder; **en sousordre** subordinate; subordinately

sous-production [suprɔdyksjɔ̃] *f* underproduction

sous-produit [suprɔdɥi] *m* (*pl* **-produits**) by-product

sous-secrétaire [suskretɛr] *m* (*pl* **-secrétaires**) undersecretary

sous-secrétariat [suskretarja] *m* undersecretaryship

sous-seing [susɛ̃] *m invar* privately witnessed document

soussi•gné -gnée [sisiɲe] *adj & mf* undersigned

sous-sol [susɔl] *m* (*pl* **-sols**) subsoil; basement

sous-titre [sutitr] *m* (*pl* **-titres**) subtitle

sous-titrer [sutitre] *tr* to subtitle

soustraction [sustraksjɔ̃] *f* subtraction; (law) purloining

soustraire [sustrɛr] **§68** *tr* to remove; take away; subtract; deduct; **soustraire de** to subtract from; **soustraire q.ch. à qn** to take s.th. away from s.o.; steal s.th. from s.o. ‖ *ref* to withdraw; **se soustraire à** to escape from

sous-traitant [sutrɛtɑ̃] *m* (*pl* **-traitants**) subcontractor; sublessee

sous-traité [sutrɛte] *m* (*pl* **-traités**) subcontract

sous-traiter [sutrɛte] *tr & intr* to subcontract

sous-ventrière [suvɑ̃trijer] *f* (*pl* **-ventrières**) girth

sous-verre [suvɛr] *m invar* passe-partout; coaster

sous-vêtement [suvɛtmɑ̃] *m* (*pl* **-vêtements**) undergarment

soutache [suta/] *f* braid

soutacher [suta/e] *tr* to trim with braid

soutane [sutan] *f* soutane, cassock

soutanelle [sutanɛl] *f* frock coat; choir robe

soute [sut] *f* (naut) storeroom; **soute à charbon** coal bunker

soutenable [sutnabl] *adj* supportable, tenable

soutenance [sutnɑ̃s] *f* defense (*of an academic thesis*)

soutènement [sutɛnmɑ̃] *m* support

souteneur [sutnœr] *m* pimp

soutenir [sutnir] **§72, §95** *tr* to support, bear; sustain; insist; claim; defend (*a thesis*) ‖ *ref* to stand up; keep afloat

soute•nu -nue [sutny] *adj* sustained; elevated (*style*); steady (*market*); true (*colors*)

souter•rain -raine [sutɛrɛ̃] [rɛn] *adj* subterranean, underground; underhanded ‖ *m* tunnel, subway (*for pedestrians*)

soutien [sutjɛ̃] *m* support; stand-by

soutien-gorge [sutjɛ̃gɔrʒ] *m* (*pl* **soutiens-gorge**) brassiere

soutirage [sutiraʒ] *m* racking

soutirer [sutire] *tr* to rack (*wine*); **soutirer q.ch. à qn** to get s.th. out of s.o., sponge on s.o. for s.th.

souvenir [suvnir] *m* memory, remembrance;

souvenir; **en souvenir de** in remembrance of ‖ §72 *intr*—**faire souvenir qn de q.ch.** to remind s.o. of s.th. ‖ §97 *ref* to remember; **se souvenir de** to remember

souvent [suvɑ̃] *adv* often

souve•rain [suvrɛ̃] **-raine** [rɛn] *adj & mf* sovereign ‖ *m* sovereign (*coin*)

souveraineté [suvrɛnte] *f* sovereignty

soviet [sɔvjɛt] *m* soviet

soviétique [sɔvjetik] *adj* Soviet ‖ (*cap*) *mf* Soviet Russian

soya [sɔja] *m* soybean

soyeux [swajø] **soyeuse** [swajøz] *adj* silky

soyez [swaje] *v* (**soyons**) see **être**

S.P. *abbr* (**sapeurs-pompiers**) fire department

spa•cieux [sapsjø] **-cieuse** [sjøz] *adj* spacious, roomy

spadassin [spadasɛ̃] *m* hatchet man, hired thug

spaghetti [spagɛti] *mpl* spaghetti

sparadrap [sparadra] *m* adhesive tape

spartiate [sparsjat] *adj* Spartan ‖ (*cap*) *mf* Spartan

spasme [spasm] *m* spasm

spasmodique [spasmɔdik] *adj* spasmodic; (pathol) spastic

spath [spat] *m* (mineral) spar

spa•tial -tiale [spasjal] *adj* (*pl* **-tiaux** [sjo]) spatial

spatiocarte [spasjɔkart] *f* maps drawn from satellite pictures

spationef [spasjɔnɛf] *m* space vehicle

spatule [spatyl] *f* spatula; (orn) spoon-bill

spea•ker [spikœr] **-kerine** [krin] *mf* (rad, telv) announcer ‖ *m* speaker (*presiding officer*)

spé•cial -ciale [spesjal] *adj* (*pl* **-ciaux** [sjo]) special, especial, particular; specialized; peculiar, odd

spécialiser [spesjalize] *tr & ref* to specialize

spécialiste [spesjalist] *mf* specialist; expert

spécialité [spesjalite] *f* specialty, speciality; specialization; patent medicine

spécialement [spesjalmɑ̃] *adv* specially, especially, particularly

spé•cieux [spesjø] **-cieuse** [sjøz] *adj* specious

spécifier [spesifje] *tr* to specify

spécifique [spesifik] *adj & m* specific

spécimen [spesimɛn] *m* specimen; sample copy

spectacle [spɛktakl] *m* spectacle, sight; show; play; **à grand spectacle** spectacular (*production*); **spectacle solo** one-man show

specta•teur [spɛktatœr] **-trice** [tris] *mf* spectator

spectre [spɛktr] *m* ghost; spectrum; (fig) specter

spécula•teur [spekylatœr] **-trice** [tris] *mf* speculator

spéculer [spekyle] *tr* to speculate

spéléologie [speleɔlɔʒi] *f* speleology

sperme [spɛrm] *m* sperm

sphère [sfɛr] *f* sphere

sphérique [sferik] *adj* spherical

sphinx [sfɛ̃ks] *m* sphinx

spider [spider] *m* (aut) rumble seat

spi•nal -nale [spinal] *adj* (*pl* **-naux** [no]) spinal

spi•ral -rale [spiral] *adj* (*pl* **-raux** [ro]) spiral ‖ *m* hairspring (*of watch*) ‖ *f* spiral; **en spirale** spiral

spire [spir] *f* turn (*in a wire*); whorl (*of a shell*)

spirée [spire] *f* (bot) spirea

spirite [spirit] *adj & mf* spiritualist

spiri•tuel -tuelle [spirituɛl] *adj* spiritual; sacred (*music*); witty ‖ *m* ecclesiastical power

spiri•tueux [spirituø] **-tueuse** [tuøz] *adj* spirituous ‖ *m* spirituous liquor

spleen [splin] *m* boredom, melancholy

splendeur [splɑ̃dœr] *f* splendor

splendide [splɑ̃did] *adj* splendid; bright, brilliant

spolia•teur [spɔljatœr] **-trice** [tris] *adj* despoiling ‖ *mf* despoiler

spolier [spɔlje] *tr* to despoil

spon•gieux [spɔ̃ʒjø] **-gieuse** [ʒjøz] *adj* spongy

sponta•né -née [spɔ̃tane] *adj* spontaneous

sporadique [spɔradik] *adj* sporadic(al)

sport [spɔr] *adj invar* sport, sporting; sportsmanlike ‖ *m* sport

spor•tif [spɔrtif] **-tive** [tiv] *adj* sport, sporting ‖ *mf* athlete, player ‖ *m* sportsman

spot [spɔt] *m* spotlight; (radar) blip

spoutnik [sputnik] *m* sputnik

spu•meux [spymø] **-meuse** [møz] *adj* frothy, foamy

squale [skwal] *m* (ichth) dogfish

squelette [skəlɛt] *m* skeleton

squelettique [skəletik] *adj* skeletal

S.R. *abbr* (**service de renseignements**) information desk or bureau

SRAS *abbr* (**syndrome respiratoire aigu sévère**) SARS (severe acute respiratory syndrome)

stabiliser [stabilize] *tr* to stabilize

stabilité [stabilite] *f* stability

stable [stabl] *adj* stable

stade [stad] *m* stadium; (fig) stage (*of development*); **stade de baseball** ball park; **stade de football** football stadium

stage [staʒ] *m* probationary period, apprenticeship; training period

stagiaire [staʒjɛr] *adj* apprentice ‖ *mf* trainee, apprentice; student teacher

stag•nant [stagnɑ̃] **-nante** [nɑ̃t] *adj* stagnant

stalle [stal] *f* stall; parking spot; **stalle d'études (dans une bibliothèque)** carrel

stance [stɑ̃s] *f* stanza

stand [stɑ̃d] *m* stands; shooting gallery; pit (*for motor racing*)

standard [stɑ̃dar] *adj invar* standard ‖ *m* standard; switchboard

standardiser [stɑ̃dardize] *tr* to standardize

standardiste [stɑ̃dardist] *mf* switchboard operator, telephone operator

standing [stɑ̃diŋ] *m* status, standing; standard of living; **de grand standing** luxury (*apartments*)

star [star] *f* (mov, theat) star

starter [startɛr], [startœr] *m* (aut) choke; (sports) starter

station [stɑsjɔ̃] f station; resort; (rr) flag station; **station balnéaire** beach resort, seaside resort; **station d'autobus** bus stop; **station d'écoute** monitoring station; **station d'émission** broadcasting station; **station de repérage** tracking station; **station de taxis** taxi stand; **station libre-service** self-service station; **station météorologique** weather station; **station orbitale** orbital space station; **stations de la Croix** (rel) Stations of the Cross; **station spatiale** space station

stationnaire [stɑsjɔnɛr] adj stationary ‖ m gunboat

stationnement [stɑsjɔnmɑ̃] m parking; **stationnement interdit** (public sign) no parking

stationner [stɑsjɔne] intr to stop; park

station-service [stɑsjɔ̃sɛrvis] f (pl **stations-service**) service station

statique [statik] adj static

statisti•cien [statistisjɛ̃] **-cienne** [sjɛn] mf statistician

statistique [statistik] adj statistical ‖ f statistics

statuaire [statɥɛr] adj statuary ‖ mf sculptor ‖ f statuary

statue [staty] f statue

statuer [statɥe] tr to hand down (a ruling) ‖ intr to hand down a ruling

statu quo [statykwo], [statuko] m status quo

stature [statyr] f stature

statut [staty] m statute; legal status; **le statut de** the status of

statutaire [statytɛr] adj statutory

Ste abbr (**Sainte**) St. (female saint)

Sté abbr (**Société**) Inc.

sténo [steno] f stenographer; stenography

sténodactylo [stenɔdaktilo] f shorthand typist; shorthand typing

sténogramme [stenɔgram] m shorthand notes

sténographe [stenɔgraf] mf stenographer

sténographie [stenɔgrafi] f stenography

sténographier [stenɔgrafje] tr to take down in shorthand

stéréo [stereo] adj invar stereo ‖ f—**en stéréo** (electron) in stereo

stéréophonie [stereɔfɔni] f stereophonic sound system; **en stéréophonie** stereophonic (e.g., broadcast)

stéréoscopique [stereɔskɔpik] adj stereo, stereoscopic

stéréoty•pé -pée [stereɔtipe] adj stereotyped

stérile [steril] adj sterile

stériliser [sterilize] tr to sterilize

stérilité [sterilite] f sterility

sterling [stɛrliŋ] adj invar sterling

stéthoscope [stetɔskɔp] m stethoscope

stick [stik] m walking stick

stigmate [stigmat] m stigma

stigmatiser [stigmatize] tr to stigmatize

stimu•lant -lante [stimylɑ̃] [lɑ̃t] adj stimulating, exhilarating ‖ m stimulant

stimulateur [stimylatœr] m (cardiaque) pacemaker, heart pacemaker

stimuler [stimyle] tr to stimulate

stimu•lus [stimylys] m (pl **-li** [li]) (physiol) stimulus

stipendier [stipɑ̃dje] tr to hire (e.g., an assassin); bribe

stipuler [stipyle] tr to stipulate

stock [stɔk] m goods, stock; hoard; store

stockage [stɔkaʒ] m storage; **stockage de données** (comp) data storage

stocker [stɔke] tr & intr to stockpile; (comp) to store

stockiste [stɔkist] m authorized dealer (carrying parts, motors, etc.)

stoï•cien [stɔisjɛ̃] **-cienne** [sjɛn] adj & mf Stoic

stoïque [stɔik] adj stoical ‖ mf stoic

stop [stɔp] m stop; stoplight; **du stop** (coll) hitchhiking ‖ interj stop!

stoppage [stɔpaʒ] m reweaving, invisible mending

stopper [stɔpe] tr to reweave; stop ‖ intr to stop

store [stɔr] m blind; window awning; outside window shade

strabique [strabik] adj squint-eyed

strabisme [strabism] m squint

strapontin [strapɔ̃tɛ̃] m jump seat; (theat) attached folding seat

strass [stras] m paste (jewelry)

stratagème [strataʒɛm] m stratagem

strate [strat] f (geol) stratum

stratège [stratɛʒ] m strategist

stratégie [strateʒi] f strategy

stratégique [strateʒik] adj strategic(al)

stratégiste [strateʒist] m strategist

stratifier [stratifje] tr & ref to stratify

stratosphère [stratɔsfɛr] f stratosphere

streptococcie [strɛptɔkɔksi] f streptococcus infection

streptocoque [strɛptɔkɔk] m streptococcus

streptomycine [strɛptɔmisin] f (pharm) streptomycin

strict stricte [strikt] adj strict

stri•dent [stridɑ̃] **-dente** [dɑ̃t] adj strident

strie [stri] f streak; stripe

strier [strije] tr to streak; score, groove

strip-teaseur [striptizœr] m (pl **-teaseurs**) (male) stripper, stripteaser

strip-teaseuse [striptizøz] f (pl **-teaseuses**) (female) stripper, stripteaser

stroboscope [strɔbɔskɔp] m stroboscope, strobe (light)

stroboscopique [strɔbɔskɔpik] adj stroboscopic

strontium [strɔ̃sjɔm] m strontium

strophe [strɔf] f verse, stanza; strophe

structu•ral -rale [stryktyral] adj (pl **-raux** [ro]) structural

structure [stryktyr] f structure

strychnine [striknin] f strychnine

stuc [styk] m stucco; **enduire de stuc** to stucco

stu•dieux [stydjø] **-dieuse** [djøz] adj studious

studio [stydjo] m studio

stupé•fait [stypefɛ] **-faite** [fɛt] adj dumfounded, amazed

stupé•fiant [stypefjɑ̃] **-fiante** [fjɑ̃t] adj astounding ‖ m drug, narcotic

stupéfier [stypefje] tr to astound; stupefy (as with a drug)

stupeur [stypœr] *f* stupor; amazement

stupide [stypid] *adj* stupid

stupidité [stypidite] *f* stupidity

stuquer [styke] *tr* to stucco

style [stil] *m* style; stylus; **style de vie** lifestyle

styler [stile] *tr* to train

stylet [stilɛ] *m* stiletto

styliser [stilize] *tr* to stylize

stylo [stilo] *m* pen, fountain pen; **stylo à bille** ballpoint pen; **stylo à réservoir** fountain pen

stylo-bille [stilobij] *m* (*pl* **stylos-billes**) ball-point pen

stylo-feutre [stiloføtr] *m* (*pl* **stylos-feutres**) felt-tip pen

styptique [stiptik] *adj & m* styptic

suaire [sɥɛr] *m* shroud, winding sheet

suave [sɥav] *adj* sweet (*perfume, music, etc.*); bland (*food*); suave

subcons•cient [sypkɔ̃sjɑ̃] **-ciente** [sjɑ̃t] *adj & m* subconscious

subdiviser [sybdivize] *tr* to subdivide

subdivision [sybdivizjɔ̃] *f* subdivision

subir [sybir] *tr* to submit to; undergo; feel, experience; take (*an exam*); serve (*a sentence*)

su•bit [sybi] **-bite** [bit] *adj* sudden

subjec•tif [sybʒɛktif] **-tive** [tiv] *adj* subjective

subjonc•tif [sybʒɔ̃ktif] **-tive** [tiv] *adj & m* subjunctive

subjuguer [sybʒyge] *tr* to dominate; spellbind

sublime [syblim] *adj* sublime

sublimer [syblime] *tr* to sublimate

submerger [sybmɛrʒe] §38 *tr* to submerge

submersible [sybmɛrsibl] *adj & m* submersible

submersion [sybmɛrsjɔ̃] *f* submersion

subodorer [sybɔdɔre] *tr* to scent (*game*); (fig) to scent (*a plot*)

subordon•né -née [sybɔrdɔne] *adj & mf* subordinate

subordonner [sybɔrdɔne] *tr* to subordinate

suborner [sybɔrne] *tr* to bribe

subrécargue [sybrekarg] *m* supercargo

subreptice [sybrɛptis] *adj* surreptitious

subsé•quent [sypsekɑ̃] **-quente** [kɑ̃t] *adj* subsequent

subside [sypsid], [sybzid] *m* subsidy

subsidiaire [sypsidjɛr] *adj* subsidiary

subsistance [sybzistɑ̃s], [sypsistɑ̃s] *f* subsistence; (mil) rations

subsister [sybziste], [sypsiste] *intr* to subsist

substance [sypstɑ̃s] *f* substance; **en substance** briefly

substan•tiel -tielle [sypstɑ̃sjɛl] *adj* substantial

substan•tif [sypstɑ̃tif] **-tive** [tiv] *adj & m* substantive

substituer [sypstitɥe] *tr*—**substituer qn** or **q.ch. à** to substitute s.o. or s.th. for, e.g., **une biche fut substituée à Iphigénie** a hind was substituted for Iphigenia ‖ *ref*—**se substituer à** to take the place of

substitut [sypstity] *m* substitute

substitution [sypstitysjɔ̃] *f* substitution

substrat [sypstra] *m* substratum

subterfuge [sypterfyʒ] *m* subterfuge

sub•til -tile [syptil] *adj* subtle; fine (*powder, dust, etc.*); quick (*poison*); delicate (*scent*); clever (*crook*)

subtiliser [syptilize] *tr* to pick (*a purse*) ‖ *intr* to split hairs

subtilité [syptilite] *f* subtlety

subur•bain [sybyrbɛ̃] **-baine** [bɛn] *adj* suburban

subvenir [sybvənir] §72 *intr* to supply, provide, satisfy

subvention [sybvɑ̃sjɔ̃] *f* subsidy, subvention

subventionner [sybvɑ̃sjɔne] *tr* to subsidize

subver•sif [sybvɛrsif] **-sive** [siv] *adj* subversive

subvertir [sybvɛrtir] *tr* to subvert

suc [syk] *m* juice; sap; (fig) essence

succéda•né -née [syksedane] *adj & m* substitute

succéder [syksede] §10 *intr* to happen; **succéder à** to succeed, follow, e.g., **son fils lui succédera** his son will succeed him ‖ *ref* (*pp* **succédé** *invar*) to follow one another, follow one after the other

succès [syksɛ] *m* success; outcome; **avoir du succès** to be a success

succes•sif [syksɛsif] **-sive** [siv] *adj* successive

succession [syksɛsjɔ̃] *f* succession; inheritance; heirs

suc•cinct [syksɛ̃] **-cincte** [sɛ̃t] *adj* succinct; scanty; meager

succion [syksjɔ̃] *f* suction

succomber [sykɔ̃be] *intr* to succumb

succursale [sykyrsal] *f* branch

sucer [syse] §51 *tr* to suck

sucette [sysɛt] *f* pacifier; lollipop, sucker

su•ceur [sysœr] **-ceuse** [søz] *adj* sucking ‖ *m* nozzle

suçon [sysɔ̃] *m* (coll) hickie

suçoter [sysɔte] *tr* to suck away at

sucre [sykr] *m* sugar; **sucre brut** brown sugar; **sucre candi** rock candy; **sucre de canne** cane sugar; **sucre d'érable** maple sugar; **sucre en morceaux** cube sugar, lump sugar; **sucre glace** confectioners' sugar; **sucre semoule** granulated sugar

su•cré -crée [sykre] *adj* sugary; with sugar, e.g., **du café sucré** coffee with sugar ‖ *f*—**faire la sucrée** to be mealy-mouthed

sucrer [sykre] *tr* to sugar; (slang) to take away, cut out ‖ *ref* (slang) to grab the lion's share

sucrerie [sykrəri] *f* sugar refinery; **sucreries** candy

su•crier [sykrije] **-crière** [krijɛr] *adj* sugar ‖ *m* sugar bowl

sud [syd] *adj invar* south, southern ‖ *m* south; **du sud** southern; **faire le sud** to steer southward; **vers le sud** southward

sud-améri•cain [sydamerikɛ̃] **-caine** [kɛn] *adj* South American ‖ (*cap*) *mf* (*pl* **Sud-Américains**) South American

sudation [sydɑsjɔ̃] *f* sweating

sud-est [sydɛst] *adj invar & m* southeast

sudiste [sydist] *mf* Southerner (*in U.S.A.*)

sud-ouest [sydwɛst] *adj invar & m* southwest

suède [sɥɛd] *m* suede ‖ *(cap) f* Sweden; **la Suède** Sweden

sué•dois [sɥedwa] **-doise** [dwaz] *adj* Swedish ‖ *m* Swedish *(language)* ‖ *(cap) mf* Swede

suée [sɥe] *f* sweating

suer [sɥe] *tr & intr* to sweat

sueur [sɥœr] *f* sweat

suffire [syfir] §66, §96 *intr* to suffice; **il suffit de** + *inf* it suffices to + *inf;* **suffire à** to be sufficient for, be adequate to, meet, satisfy, e.g., **suffire à mes besoins** to meet my needs; **suffire à** + *inf* to suffice to + *inf;* **suffit!** enough! ‖ *ref (pp* **suffi** *invar)* to be self-sufficient

suffisamment [syfizamã] *adv* sufficiently, adequately

suffisance [syfizãs] *f* sufficiency; self-sufficiency, smugness

suffi•sant [syfizã] **-sante** [zãt] *adj* sufficient; smug, sophomoric; impudent ‖ *mf* prig

suffixe [syfiks] *m* suffix

suffo•cant [syfɔkã] **-cante** [kãt] *adj* suffocating, stifling; astonishing, stunning

suffoquer [syfɔke] *tr & intr* to suffocate, choke, stifle, smother

suffrage [syfraʒ] *m* suffrage, vote; public approval; **au suffrage universel** by popular vote; **suffrage capacitaire** suffrage contingent upon literacy tests; **suffrage censitaire** suffrage upon payment of taxes

suggérer [sygʒere] §10, §97, §98 *tr* to suggest

sugges•tif [sygʒɛstif] **-tive** [tiv] *adj* suggestive

suggestion [sygʒɛstjɔ̃] *f* suggestion

suggestionner [sygʒɛstjɔne] *tr* to influence by means of suggestion

suicide [sɥisid] *adj* suicidal ‖ *m* suicide *(act)*

suici•dé -dée [sɥiside] *adj* dead by suicide ‖ *mf* suicide *(person)*

suicider [sɥiside] *ref* to commit suicide

suie [sɥi] *f* soot

suif [sɥif] *m* tallow

suint [sɥɛ̃] *m* wool fat, wool grease

suinter [sɥɛ̃te] *intr* to seep, ooze; sweat *(said of wall)*; run *(said of wound)*

suis [sɥi] *v* see **être**; see **suivre**

suisse [sɥis] *adj* Swiss; **faire suisse** to eat or drink by oneself; to go Dutch ‖ *m* Swiss guard; uniformed usher; **petit suisse** cream cheese ‖ *(cap) f* Switzerland; **la Suisse** Switzerland ‖ **Suisse Suissesse** [sɥisɛs] *mf* Swiss *(person)*

suite [sɥit] *f* suite; consequence; continuation, sequel *(of literary work)*; sequence, series; **à la suite de** after; **de suite** in succession; in a row; **par la suite** later on; **par suite** consequently; **par suite de** because of

sui•vant [sɥivã] **-vante** [vãt] *adj* next, following, subsequent ‖ *mf* follower; next *(person)* ‖ *f* servant, confidante ‖ **suivant** *adv* —**suivant que** according as ‖ **suivant** *prep* according to

sui•veur [sɥivœr] **-veuse** [vøz] *adj* follow-up *(e.g., car)* ‖ *mf* follower

sui•vi -vie [sɥivi] *adj* connected, coherent; popular

suivre [sɥivr] §67 *tr* to follow; take *(a course in school)*; **suivre la mode** (fig) to follow suit ‖ *intr* to follow; **à suivre** to be continued ‖ *ref* to follow in succession; follow one after the other

su•jet [syʒɛ] **-jette** [ʒɛt] *adj* subject; apt, liable; inclined ‖ *mf* subject *(of a government)*; **mauvais sujet** ne'er-do-well ‖ *m* subject, topic; (gram) subject; **au sujet de** about, concerning; **sujet brûlant** hot potato (fig), hot-button issue

sujétion [syʒesjɔ̃] *f* subjection

sulfamide [sylfamid] *m* sulfa drug

sulfate [sylfat] *m* sulphate

sulfure [sylfyr] *m* sulfide

sulfurique [sylfyrik] *adj* sulfuric

sultan [syltã] *m* sultan

sumac [symak] *m* sumac; **sumac vénéneux** poison ivy

sunlight [sœnlait] *m invar* (mov, telv) projector

sunnite [synit] *adj & mf* Sunni

super [sypɛr] *m* (coll) high-test gas

superbe [sypɛrb] *adj* superb; proud ‖ *m* proud person ‖ *f* pride

supercarburant [sypɛrkarbyrã] *m* high-test gasoline

supercherie [sypɛrʃəri] *f* hoax, swindle

superdécrochage [sypɛrdekrɔʃaʒ] *m* (aer) deep stall

superfétatoire [sypɛrfetatwar] *adj* redundant

superficie [sypɛrfisi] *f* surface, area

superfi•ciel -cielle [sypɛrfisjɛl] *adj* superficial

super•flu -flue [sypɛrfly] *adj* superfluous ‖ *m* superfluity, excess

supé•rieur -rieure [syperjœr] *adj* superior; higher; upper *(e.g., story)*; advanced; **supérieur a** above; more than ‖ *mf* superior

supérieurement [syperjœrmã] *adv* superlatively, exceptionally

supériorité [syperjɔrite] *f* superiority

superla•tif [sypɛrlatif] **-tive** [tiv] *adj & m* superlative; **au superlatif** superlatively; in the superlative

supermarché [sypɛrmarʃe] *m* supermarket

superposer [sypɛrpoze] *tr* to superimpose ‖ *ref* to intervene

superproduction [sypɛrprɔdyksjɔ̃] *f* (mov) blockbuster

supersonique [sypɛrsɔnik] *adj* supersonic

supersti•tieux [sypɛrstisjø] **-tieuse** [sjøz] *adj* superstitious

superstition [sypɛrstisjɔ̃] *f* superstition

superstrat [sypɛrstra] *m* superstratum

superviser [sypɛrvize] *tr* to inspect; revise; correct; supervise

supplanter [syplãte] *tr* to supplant

suppléance [sypleãs] *f* substituting; temporary post

sup•pléant [sypleã] **-pléante** [pleãt] *adj* substituting ‖ *mf* substitute *(e.g., a teacher, judge)*

suppléer [syplee] *tr* to supply; take the place of; make up for *(what is lacking)*; fill in *(the* *gaps*); substitute for (*s.o.*); fill (*a vacancy*) ‖ *intr*—**suppléer à** to make up for (*s.th.*)

supplément [syplemɑ̃] *m* supplement; extra charge

supplémentaire [syplemɑ̃tɛr] *adj* supplementary, additional, extra; supplemental

supplé•tif [sypletif] **-tive** [tiv] *adj & m* (mil) auxiliary

sup•pliant [syplijɑ̃] **-pliante** [plijɑ̃t] *adj & mf* suppliant, supplicant

supplice [syplis] *m* torture; punishment; **être au supplice** to be in agony

supplicier [syplisje] *tr* to torture to death; torment

supplier [syplije] **§97, §99** *tr* to beseech, implore, supplicate; **je vous en supplie** I beg you; **supplier qn de** to implore s.o. to

supplique [syplik] *f* petition

support [sypɔr] *m* support, prop, pillar, bracket, strut; standard (*e.g., for a lamp*)

support-chaussette [sypɔrʃosɛt] *m* (*pl* **supports-chaussette**) garter (*for men*)

supporter [sypɔrtœr], [sypɔrtɛr] *m* fan, devotee, supporter, partisan ‖ [sypɔrte] *tr* to support, prop up; bear, endure; stand, tolerate, put up with ‖ *intr*—**supporter de** + *inf* to tolerate or stand for + *ger* ‖ *ref* to be tolerated; put up with each other

suppo•sé -sée [sypoze] *adj* supposed, admitted; spurious, assumed ‖ **supposé** *prep* supposing, admitting, granting

supposer [sypoze] **§95** *tr* to suppose; imply; **à supposer que . . .** suppose that . . .; **supposer un testament** to palm off a forged will

supposition [sypozisjɔ̃] *f* supposition; forgery, fraudulent substitution or alteration; **supposition de part** or **supposition d'enfant** false claim of maternity and maternal rights

suppositoire [sypozitwar] *m* suppository

suppôt [sypo] *m* henchman, tool, agitator, hireling; **suppôt de Bacchus** drunkard; **suppôt du diable** imp

suppression [sypresjɔ̃] *f* suppression; elimination (*of a job*); discontinuance (*of a festival*); killing (*of a person*); **suppression de part** or **suppression d'enfant** concealment of a child's birth or death

supprimer [syprime] *tr* to suppress, cancel, abolish; cut out, omit; (slang) to eliminate, liquidate ‖ *ref* to kill oneself

suppurer [sypyre] *intr* to suppurate

supputation [sypytasjɔ̃] *f* calculation, evaluation, reckoning

supputer [sypyte] *tr* to calculate (*e.g., forthcoming profits, expenses*)

suprématie [sypremasi] *f* supremacy

suprême [syprɛm] *adj* supreme; last

sur sure [syr] *adj* sour ‖ **sur** *prep* on, over; about, concerning; with (*on the person of*); out of, in, e.g., **un jour sur quatre** one day out of four, one day in four; after, e.g., **page sur page** page after page; **sur ce, sur quoi** whereupon; **sur le fait** in the act

sûr sûre [syr] **§93** *adj* sure; trustworthy; safe; certain; **à coup sûr, pour sûr** for sure, without fail; **bien sûr!** sure thing!

surabon•dant [syrabɔ̃dɑ̃] **-dante** [dɑ̃t] *adj* superabundant

surabonder [syrabɔ̃de] *intr* to superabound; **surabonder de** or **en** to be glutted with

surajouter [syraʒute] *tr* to add on

suralimentation [syralimɑ̃tɑsjɔ̃] *f* forced feeding; (aut) supercharging

suran•né -née [syrane] *adj* outmoded, out-of-date, superannuated; expired (*driver's license, passport, etc.*)

surboum [syrbum] *f* (slang) dance, hop

surcharge [syrʃarʒ] *f* surcharge; overwriting; (sports) handicap (*of weight on a horse*); (comp) overload(ing)

surcharger [syrʃarʒe] **§38** *tr* to surcharge; write a word over (*another word*); write a word over a crossed-out word on (*a document*)

surchauffe [syrʃof] *f* superheating; overheating (*of the economy*)

surchauffer [syrʃofe] *tr* to superheat (*steam; an oven*); overheat (*an oven, iron, etc.*)

surchoix [syrʃwa] *m* finest quality

surclasser [syrklase] *tr* to outclass

surcompo•sé -sée [syrkɔ̃poze] *adj* (gram) double-compound

surcompression [syrkɔ̃presjɔ̃] *f* pressurization, high compression

surcompri•mé -mée [syrkɔ̃prime] *adj* high-compression (*engine*)

surcomprimer [syrkɔ̃prime] *tr* to supercharge; pressurize

surcontrer [syrkɔ̃tre] *tr* (cards) to redouble

surcouper [syrkupe] *tr* (cards) to overtrump

surcroît [syrkrwa], [syrkrwa] *m* addition, increase; **de surcroît** or **par sucroît** in addition, extra

surdi-mutité [syrdimytite] *f* deaf-muteness

surdité [syrdite] *f* deafness

surdosage [syrdosaʒ] *m* overdose

su•reau [syro] *m* (*pl* **-reaux**) elderberry

surélévation [syrelevasjɔ̃] *f* escalation, excessive increase; extra story (*added to a building*)

surélever [syrelve] **§2** *tr* to raise, raise up; drive up; jack up

sûrement [syrmɑ̃] *adv* surely, certainly; safely; steadily, confidently

surenchère [syrɑ̃ʃɛr] *f* higher bid; **surenchère électorale** campaign promise, political outbidding

surenchérir [syrɑ̃ʃerir] *intr* to make a higher bid; **surenchérir sur qn** to outbid s.o.

surestimer [syrɛstime] *tr* to overestimate

su•ret [syrɛ] **-rette** [rɛt] *adj* tart

sûreté [syrte] *f* safety, security; sureness (*of touch; of taste*); surety; **à sûreté intégrée** failsafe; **en sûreté** out of harm's way; in custody, confined (*e.g., in prison*); **sûreté individuelle** legal protection (*e.g., against arbitrary arrest*); **Sûreté nationale** or **la Sûreté** central intelligence; **sûretés** precautions; guarantees, security (*for a loan*)

surévaluer [syrevalɥe] *tr* to overvalue

surexciter [syrɛksite] *tr* to overexcite

surexposer [syrɛkspoze] *tr* (phot) to overexpose

surexposition [syrɛkspozisjɔ̃] *f* (phot) overexposure

surface [syrfas] *f* surface; financial backing; **faire surface** to surface (*said of a submarine*)

surfaire [syrfɛr] §29 *tr* & *intr* to overprice; to overrate

surfer [syrfe] *tr* to surf

sur•fin [syrfɛ̃] **-fine** [fin] *adj* superfine

surgélation [syrʒelɑsjɔ̃] *f* deep freezing

surge•lé -lée [syrʒəle] *adj* frozen (*foods*)

surgeon [syrʒɔ̃] *m* offshoot, sucker

surgir [syrʒir] *intr* to spring up; arise, appear; arrive, reach port

surglacer [syrglase] §51 *tr* to glaze; ice (*cake*)

surhaussement [syrosmɑ̃] *m* heightening, raising; banking (*of road*)

surhausser [syrose] *tr* to heighten, raise; force up (*prices*); force up the price of (*s.th.*); bank (*a road*)

surhomme [syrɔm] *m* superman

surhu•main [syrymɛ̃] **-maine** [mɛn] *adj* superhuman

surimpression [syrɛ̃presjɔ̃] *f* superimposition; (mov) montage

surintendant [syrɛ̃tɑ̃dɑ̃] *m* superintendent, administrator

surir [syrir] *intr* to turn sour

surjeu [syrʒø] *m* playback

sur-le-champ [syrlʃɑ̃] *adv* on the spot, immediately

surlendemain [syrlɑ̃dmɛ̃] *m*—**le surlendemain** the second day after, two days later

surlier [syrlje] *tr* to whip (*a rope*)

surliure [syrljyr] *f* whipping (*of rope*)

surmédicaliser [syrmedikalize] *intr* (med) to overprescribe, overmedicate

surmenage [syrmənaʒ] *m* overworking, fatigue

surmener [syrməne] §2 *tr* & *ref* to overwork

sur•moi [syrmwa] *m* superego

surmonter [syrmɔ̃te] *tr* to surmount ‖ *intr* to come to the top (*said of oil in water*)

surmouler [syrmule] *tr* to cast from another mold

surmultiplication [syrmyltiplikɑsjɔ̃] *f* (aut) overdrive

surnager [syrnaʒe] §38 *intr* to float; survive

surnatu•rel -relle [syrnatyrɛl] *adj* & *m* supernatural

surnom [syrnɔ̃] *m* nickname, sobriquet

surnombre [syrnɔ̃br] *m* excess number; **en surnombre** supernumerary; spare; **rester en surnombre** to be odd man; **surnombre des habitants** overpopulation

surnommer [syrnɔme] *tr* to name, call, nickname

surnuméraire [syrnymerɛr] *adj* supernumerary, extra ‖ *mf* substitute, supernumerary

suroffre [syrɔfr] *f* better or higher offer

suroît [syrwa] *m* southwest wind

surpasser [syrpɑse] *tr* to surpass; astonish ‖ *ref* to outdo oneself

surpaye [syrpɛj] *f* extra pay

surpayer [syrpɛje] §49 *tr* to pay too much to; pay too much for

surpeu•plé -plée [syrpœple] *adj* overpopulated

surpeuplement [syrpœpləmɑ̃] *m* overpopulation

surplis [syrpli] *m* surplice

surplomber [syrplɔ̃be] *tr* & *intr* to overhang; to look down upon

surplus [syrply] *m* surplus; **au surplus** moreover; **surplus militaires** army surplus

surpopulation [syrpɔpylɑsjɔ̃] *f* overpopulation

surprendre [syrprɑ̃dr] §56, §96 *tr* to surprise; come upon by chance; detect; overtake, catch

surprise [syrpriz] *f* surprise

surprise-party or **surprise-partie** [syrprizparti] *f* (*pl* **surprises-parties**) private dancing party

surproduction [syrprɔdyksjɔ̃] *f* overproduction

surréalisme [syrrealism] *m* surrealism

surrégénérateur [syreʒeneratœr] **-trice** [tris] *adj* (nucl) breeder (reactor)

surréservation [syresɛrvɑsjɔ̃] *f* overbooking

sursaut [syrso] *m* sudden start; **en sursaut** with a start

sursauter [syrsote] *intr* to give a jump, start, jerk

surseoir [syrswar] §5B (*fut* **surseoirai**, etc.) *intr*—**surseoir à** (law) to defer, postpone, stay, e.g., **surseoir à une exécution** to stay an execution

sursis [syrsi] *m* suspension (*of penalty*); postponement, deferment, stay; **en sursis, avec sursis** suspended (*sentence*)

surtaxe [syrtaks] *f* surtax, surcharge; **surtaxe postale** postage due

surtaxer [syrtakse] *tr* to surtax

surtension [syrtɑ̃sjɔ̃] *f* (elec) surge

surtout [syrtu] *m* topcoat; centerpiece, epergne ‖ *adv* especially, particularly

surveillance [syrvɛjɑ̃s] *f* supervision; (*by the police*) surveillance

surveil•lant [syrvɛjɑ̃] **-lante** [jɑ̃t] *mf* supervisor, superintendent, overseer; **surveillant d'études** study-hall proctor

surveiller [syrvɛje] *tr* to inspect, put under surveillance; supervise, watch over, monitor

survenir [syrvənir] §72 *intr* (*aux:* ETRE) to arrive unexpectedly, happen suddenly, crop up

survenue [syrvəny] *f* unexpected arrival

survêt [syrvɛ] *m* (coll) tracksuit, sweat suit

survêtement [syrvɛtmɑ̃] *m* tracksuit, sweat suit

survie [syrvi] *f* survival; afterlife; (law) survivorship; **survie du plus apte** survival of the fittest

survivance [syrvivɑ̃s] *f* survival

survi•vant [syrvivɑ̃] **-vante** [vɑ̃t] *adj* surviving ‖ *mf* survivor

survivre [syrvivr] §74 *intr* to survive; **survivre**

à to survive, outlive, e.g., **elle lui survécut** she survived him ‖ *ref* (*pp* **survécu** *invar*) (fig) to outlive one's time; **se survivre dans** to live on in

survoler [syrvɔle] *tr* to fly over; skim over (*e.g., a problem*)

survol•té -tée [syrvɔlte] *adj* electrified, charged with emotion

sus [sys], [sy] *adv*—**en sus de** in addition to ‖ *interj* up and at it (them)!

susceptible [syseptibl] *adj* sensitive, touchy; **susceptible de** capable of, liable to, susceptible of

susciter [sysite] *tr* to stir up, evoke, rouse; (lit) to raise up

sus•dit [sysdi] **-dite** [dit] *adj* aforesaid

susmention•né -née [sysmãsjɔne] *adj* aforementioned

sus•pect [syspɛ], [syspɛkt] **-pecte** [pɛkt] *adj* suspect, suspicious ‖ *mf* suspect

suspecter [syspɛkte] *tr* to suspect

suspendre [syspãdr] *tr* to suspend; hang, hang up; **être suspendu aux lèvres de qn** to hang on s.o.'s every word ‖ *ref* to be hung; hang on

suspen•du -due [syspãdy] *adj* suspended; hanging

suspens [syspã] *m* suspense; **en suspens** suspended; in abeyance; outstanding; in suspense

suspension [syspãsjɔ̃] *f* suspension; **suspension hydraulique** hydraulic suspension

suspi•cieux [syspisjø] **-cieuse** [sjøz] *adj* suspicious

suspicion [syspisjɔ̃] *f* suspicion

sustenter [systãte] *tr* to sustain ‖ *ref* to sustain oneself

susurrer [sysyre] *tr & intr* to murmur, whisper

susvi•sé -sée [sysvize] *adj* above-mentioned

suture [sytyr] *f* suture

suturer [sytyre] *tr* to suture

suze•rain [syzrɛ̃] **-raine** [rɛn] *adj & mf* suzerain

svastika [svastika] *m* swastika

svelte [svɛlt] *adj* slender, lithe, willowy

S.V.P. [ɛsvepe] *m* (letterword) (**s'il vous plaît**) if you please, please

sweat [swɛt] *m* sweatshirt

sweater [switœr] *m* sweater; **sweater à col roulé** turtleneck sweater

sweat-shirt [switʃœrt] *or* [swɛtʃœrt] *m* (*pl* **sweat-shirts**) sweatshirt

sycophante [sikɔfãt] *m* informer

syllabe [silab] *f* syllable

syllogisme [silɔʒism] *m* syllogism

sylphe [silf] *m* sylph

sylvestre [silvɛstr] *adj* sylvan

symbole [sɛ̃bɔl] *m* symbol; **Symbole des apôtres** Apostles' Creed

symbolique [sɛ̃bɔlik] *adj* symbolic(al)

symboliser [sɛ̃bɔlize] *tr* to symbolize

symbolisme [sɛ̃bɔlism] *m* symbolism

symétrie [simetri] *f* symmetry

symétrique [simetrik] *adj* symmetric(al)

sympa [sɛ̃pa] *adj* (coll) likable, attractive

sympathie [sɛ̃pati] *f* fondness, liking; sympathy

sympathique [sɛ̃patik] *adj* likable, attractive; (*ink*) invisible; (anat) sympathetic

sympathi•sant [sɛ̃patizɑ̃] **-sante** [zɑ̃t] *adj* sympathetic ‖ *mf* sympathizer

sympathiser [sɛ̃patize] *intr* to get along well; **sympathiser avec** to be drawn toward; support

symphonie [sɛ̃fɔni] *f* symphony

symptôme [sɛ̃ptom] *m* symptom

synagogue [sinagɔg] *f* synagogue

synchrone [sɛ̃krɔn] *adj* synchronous

synchronisation [sɛ̃krɔnisajɔ̃] *f* synchronization, sync, synch

synchroniser [sɛ̃krɔnize] *tr* to synchronize; **être synchronisé avec** to be synchronized with, to be in sync with

syncope [sɛ̃kɔp] *f* faint, swoon, syncope; syncopation

synco•pé -pée [sɛ̃kɔpe] *adj* syncopated

syndicat [sɛ̃dika] *m* labor union; **syndicat de distribution** (journ) syndicate; **syndicat d'initiative** chamber of commerce; **syndicat patronal** employers' association

syndicats-patrons [sɛ̃dikapatrɔ̃] *adj invar* labor-management

syndi•qué -quée [sɛ̃dike] *adj* union ‖ *mf* union member

syndiquer [sɛ̃dike] *tr & ref* to unionize

syndrome [sɛ̃drom] *m* syndrome; **syndrome de choc toxique** toxic shock syndrome; **syndrome de l'usure au travail** burnout; **syndrome d'immunodéficience acquise** acquired immune-deficiency syndrome, AIDS

synonyme [sinɔnim] *adj* synonymous ‖ *m* synonym

synopsis [sinɔpsis] *m & f* (mov) synopsis

syntaxe [sɛ̃taks] *f* syntax

synthèse [sɛ̃tɛz] *f* synthesis

synthétique [sɛ̃tetik] *adj* synthetic

synthétiser [sɛ̃tetize] *tr* to synthesize

syntonisation [sɛ̃tɔnizɑsjɔ̃] *f* tuning (*of radio*)

syntoniser [sɛ̃tɔnize] *tr* to tune in

syphilis [sifilis] *f* syphilis

Syrie [siri] *f* Syria; **la Syrie** Syria

sy•rien [sirjɛ̃] **-rienne** [rjen] *adj* Syrian ‖ (*cap*) *mf* Syrian (*person*)

systématique [sistematik] *adj* systematic; routine

systématiser [sistematize] *tr* to systematize

système [sistɛm] *m* system; **courir, porter,** or **taper sur le système à qn** (slang) to get on s.o.'s nerves; **système D** (coll) resourcefulness; **système d'exploitation** (comp) operating system

systole [sistɔl] *f* systole

T

T, t [te] *m invar* twentieth letter of the French alphabet

t. *abbr* (**tome**) vol.

t' = **te** before vowel or mute **h**

ta [ta] §88 your

tabac [taba] *m* tobacco; tobacco shop; **avoir le gros tabac** (slang) to be a hit; **passer qn à tabac** (coll) to give s.o. the third degree; **tabac à chiquer** chewing tobacco; **tabac à priser** snuff

tabagie [tabaʒi] *f* smoke-filled room

tabasser [tabase] *tr* (slang) to give a licking to, shellac

tabatière [tabatjɛr] *f* snuffbox; skylight, dormer window

tabernacle [tabɛrnakl] *m* tabernacle

table [tabl] *f* table; **aimer la table** to like good food; **à table!** dinner is served!; **dresser** or **mettre la table** to set the table; **faire table rase** to make a clean sweep; **sainte table** altar rail; **se mettre à table** (slang) to tell all, to confess, to squeal; **table à abattant** drop table; **table à abattants, table à volets** drop-leaf table; **table à abattants sur pieds mobiles** gate-leg table; **table à ouvrage** worktable; **table à rallonges** extension table; **table à salade** salad bar; **table de chevet, table de nuit** bedside table; **table d'écoute** wiretap; **table de jeu** card table; **table des matières** table of contents; **table de toilette** dressing table; **table d'harmonie** (mus) sounding board; **table d'hôte** table d'hôte; chef's special; **table d'opération** operating table; **table du téléphone** telephone table; **table gigogne** nest of tables; **table interurbaine** long-distance switchboard; **table roulante** serving cart; **tenir table ouverte** to keep open house

ta•bleau [tablo] *m* (*pl* **-bleaux**) painting, picture; scoreboard; board; table, catalogue; panel (*of jurors*); **former un tableau** (law) to empanel a jury; **jouer sur les deux tableaux** (slang) to play both sides of the street; **tableau d'affichage** bulletin board; **tableau d'avancement** seniority list; **tableau de bord** dashboard; instrument panel; **tableau de distribution** switchboard; **tableau d'honneur** honor roll; **tableau noir** blackboard; **tableau vivant** tableau

tableautier [tablotje] *m* tabulator (*of typewriter*)

tabler [table] *intr*—**tabler sur** to count on; use as a base

tablette [tablɛt] *f* shelf; mantelpiece; bar (*e.g., of chocolate*); **rayez cela de vos tablettes** don't count on it; **tablettes** pocket notebook

table-valise [tabləvaliz] *f* (*pl* **tables-valises**) folding table

tablier [tablije] *m* apron; roadway (*of bridge*); hood (*of chimney*); **tablier de fer** protective shutter (*on store window*)

ta•bou -bou or **-boue** [tabu] *adj & m* taboo

tabouret [taburɛ] *m* stool; footstool

tabulaire [tabylɛr] *adj* tabular

tabulateur [tabylatœr] *m* tabulator

tac [tak] *m* click, clack; **du tac au tac** tit for tat; **tac tac tac tac!** rat-a-tat-tat!

tache [taʃ] *f* spot, stain; blemish, flaw; blot, smear; speck; **faire tache** to be out of place; **faire tache d'huile** to spread; **sans tache** spotless, unblemished; **tache de rousseur, tache de son** freckle; **tache de vin** birthmark; **tache originelle** original sin; **tache solaire** sunspot

tâche [tɑʃ] *f* task, job; **prendre à tâche de** to try to; **travailler à la tâche** to do piecework

tacher [taʃe] *tr & ref* to spot, stain

tâcher [taʃe] §96, §97 *tr*—**tâcher que** to see to it that ‖ *intr*—**tâcher de** to try to; **y tâcher** to try

tâcheron [tɑʃrɔ̃] *m* small jobber; pieceworker; hard worker; wage slave

tacheter [taʃte] §34 *tr* to spot, speckle

tacite [tasit] *adj* tacit

taciturne [tasityrn] *adj* taciturn

tacot [tako] *m* (coll) jalopy

tact [takt] *m* tact; sense of touch

tacticien [taktisjɛ̃] *m* tactician

tactique [taktik] *adj* tactical ‖ *f* tactics

taffetas [tafta] *m* taffeta; **taffetas gommé** adhesive tape

Tage [taʒ] *m* Tagus

taïaut [tajo] *interj* tallyho!

taie [tɛ] *f* (pathol) leukoma; **avoir une taie sur l'œil** (fig) to be blinded by prejudice; **taie d'oreiller** pillowcase

taillader [tajade] *tr & ref* to slash, cut

taille [tɑj] *f* cutting (*e.g., of diamond*); trimming (*e.g., of hedge*); height, stature; waist, waistline; size; cut (*of garment*); **à la taille de, de la taille de** to the measure of, suitable for; **avoir la taille fine** to have a slim waist; **de taille** big enough, strong enough; (coll) big; **être de taille à** to be up to, to be big enough to; **taille de guêpe** wasp waist; **taille en dessous** next size smaller; **taille en dessus** next size larger

tail•lé -lée [tɑje] *adj* cut; trimmed; **bien taillé** well-built; **taillé pour** cut out for

taille-crayon [tɑjkrɛjɔ̃] *m* (*pl* **-crayon** or **-crayons**) pencil sharpener

taille-douce [tɑjdus] *f* (*pl* **tailles-douces**) copperplate; intaglio

taille-haies [tɑj-ɛ] *m invar* hedge cutter

taille-pain [tɑjpɛ̃] *m invar* bread knife; bread slicer

tailler [tɑje] *tr* to cut; sharpen (*a pencil*); prune, trim (*a tree*); carve (*stone*); clip (*hair*) ‖ *intr* (cards) to deal ‖ *ref* to carve out (*a path; a career*); (coll) to beat it

tailleur [tɑjœr] *m* tailor; woman's suit; (cards) dealer; **en tailleur** squatting (*while tailoring*); **tailleur de diamants** diamond cutter; **tailleur**

de pierre stonecutter; **tailleur sur mesure** lady's tailor-made suit

taillis [taji] *m* thicket, copse

tain [tɛ̃] *m* silvering (*of mirror*)

taire [tɛr] §52 (3d *sg pres ind* **tait**) *tr* to hush up, hide; **la tairas-tu?** (slang) will you shut your trap?; **taire q.ch. à qn** to keep s.th. from s.o. ‖ *intr*—**faire taire** to silence ‖ *ref* to keep quiet, keep still; **se taire sur** to say nothing about; **tais-toi!** shut up!

Taïwan [tajwan] *f* Taiwan

talent [talɑ̃] *m* talent

talen·tueux [talɑ̃tɥø] -**tueuse** [tɥøz] *adj* talented

talkie-walkie [tɔkiwɔki] *m* (*pl* **talkies-walkies**) walkie-talkie

taloche [talɔʃ] *f* plastering trowel; (coll) clout, smack

talon [talɔ̃] *m* heel; stub

talonnage [talɔnaʒ] *m* tailgating

talonner [talɔne] *tr* to tail; tailgate; harass; dig one's spurs into ‖ *intr* to bump

talus [taly] *m* slope; embankment; **talus de neige** snowbank

tambour [tɑ̃bur] *m* drum; drummer; entry-way; spool (*of reel*); **tambour battant** (coll) roughly; (coll) quickly; **tambour cylindrique** revolving door; **tambour de basque** tambourine; **tambour de freins** brake drum; **tambour de ville** town crier

tambouriner [tɑ̃burine] *tr* to drum; broadcast far and wide ‖ *intr* to beat a tattoo; drum

tambour-major [tɑ̃burmaʒɔr] *m* (*pl* **tambours-majors**) drum major

tamis [tami] *m* sieve; **passer au tamis** to sift; **tamis à farine** flour sifter

Tamise [tamiz] *f* Thames

tamiser [tamize] *tr & intr* to sift

tampon [tɑ̃pɔ̃] *m* plug; bung; swab; rubber stamp; buffer; cancellation, postmark; (surg) tampon; **tampon abrasif** scouring sponge; **tampon buvard** hand blotter; **tampon encreur** stamp pad

tamponner [tɑ̃pɔne] *tr* to swag, dab; bump; bump into; (surg) to tampon

tan [tɑ̃] *adj invar* tan ‖ *m* tanbark

tancer [tɑ̃se] §51 *tr* to scold

tandem [tɑ̃dɛm] *m* tandem; **en tandem** tandem

tandis que [tɑ̃dikə], [tɑ̃diskə] *conj* while; whereas

tangage [tɑ̃gaʒ] *m* (naut) pitching

Tanger [tɑ̃ʒe] *m* Tangier

tangible [tɑ̃ʒibl] *adj* tangible

tanguer [tɑ̃ge] *intr* to pitch (*said of ship*)

tanière [tanjɛr] *f* den, lair

tanker [tɑ̃kɛr] *m* oil tanker

tan·nant [tanɑ̃] -**nante** [nɑ̃t] *adj* (coll) boring

tanne [tan] *f* spot (*on leather*); blackhead

tanner [tane] *tr* to tan; (coll) to pester

tannerie [tanri] *f* tannery

tanneur [tanœr] *m* tanner

tan-sad [tɑ̃sad] *m* (*pl* **-sads**) rear seat (*of motorcycle*)

tant [tɑ̃] *adv* so, so much; so long; **en tant que** as; insofar as; **si tant est que** if it is true that; **tant bien que mal** somehow or other; **tant de** so many; so much; **tant mieux** so much the better; **tant pis** so much the worse; never mind, so what!; **tant qu'à faire** while we're (you're, etc.) at it; **tant que** as well as; as long as; **tant s'en faut** far from it; **tant soit peu** ever so little; **vous m'en direz tant** (coll) you've just said a mouthful

tante [tɑ̃t] *f* aunt; (pej) queer; **ma tante** (coll) the hockshop; **tante à la mode de Bretagne** first cousin once removed

tantième [tɑ̃tjɛm] *m* percentage

tantine [tɑ̃tin] *f* (coll) auntie

tantôt [tɑ̃to] *m* (coll) afternoon ‖ *adv* in a little while; a little while ago; (coll) in the afternoon; **à tantôt** see you soon; **tantôt. . .tantôt** sometimes. . .sometimes

taon [tɑ̃] *m* horsefly

tapage [tapaʒ] *m* uproar, three-ring circus (fig)

tapa·geur [tapaʒœr] -**geuse** [ʒøz] *adj* loud

tape [tap] *f* tap, slap

ta·pé -**pée** [tape] *adj* dried (*fruit*); rotten in spots; (coll) crazy; (slang) worn (*with age or fatigue*); **bien tapé** (coll) well done; (coll) nicely served; (coll) to the point

tape-à-l'œil [tapalœj] *adj* gaudy, showy ‖ *m invar* mere show

taper [tape] *tr* to tap, slap; type; (coll) to hit (*s.o. for money*) ‖ *intr* to tap, slap; type; (coll) to go to the head (*said of wine*); **ça tape ici** (slang) it hurts here; **taper dans** (coll) to use; **taper dans le mille** (coll) to succeed; **taper dans l'œil de qn** (coll) to make a hit with s.o.; **taper de** to hit (*e.g., 100 m.p.h.*); **taper des pieds** to stamp one's feet; **taper sur** (coll) to get on (*s.o.'s nerves*); **taper sur le ventre de qn** (coll) to give s.o. a poke in the ribs; **taper sur qn** (coll) to run down s.o., give s.o. a going-over

tapette [tapɛt] *f* carpet beater; fly swatter; handball; (slang) homo, fruit (*homosexual*); **avoir une fière tapette** (coll) to be a chatterbox; **tapette tue-mouche** fly swatter

tapin [tapɛ̃] *m* (coll) drummer boy; (slang) solicitation (*by a prostitute*)

tapinois [tapinwa]—**en tapinois** stealthily

tapir [tapir] *ref* to crouch, squat; hide

tapis [tapi] *m* carpet; rug; game of chance; **mettre sur le tapis** to bring up for discussion; **tapis de bain** bath mat; **tapis de sol** ground cloth; **tapis de table** table covering; **tapis d'orient** oriental rug; **tapis mur à mur** wall-to-wall carpeting; **tapis roulant** conveyor belt; moving sidewalk

tapis-brosse [tapibrɔs] *m* (*pl* **-brosses**) doormat

tapisser [tapise] *tr* to upholster; tapestry; wallpaper

tapisserie [tapisri] *f* upholstery; tapestry; **faire tapisserie** to be a wallflower

tapis·sier [tapisje] -**sière** [sjɛr] *mf* upholsterer; tapestry maker; paperhanger

tapoter [tapɔte] *tr & intr* to tap

taquet [takɛ] *m* wedge, peg; (mach) tappet; (naut) cleat; **taquet d'arrêt** (rr) scotch, wedge

ta•quin [takɛ̃] **-quine** [kin] *adj* teasing ‖ *mf* tease

taquiner [takine] *tr* to tease

taquinerie [takinri] *f* teasing

taraud [taro] *m* (mach) tap

tarauder [tarode] *tr* (mach) to tap; (coll) to pester

taraudeuse [tarodøz] *f* tap wrench

tard [tar] *m*— **sur le tard** late in the day; late in life ‖ *adv* late; **pas plus tard que** no later than; **plus tard** later on

tarder [tarde] §96, §97 *intr* to delay; **tarder à** to be long in ‖ *impers*—**il me (te,** etc.**) tarde de** + *inf* I (you, etc.) long to + *inf* e.g., **il lui tarde de vous voir** he longs to see you

tar•dif [tardif] **-dive** [div] *adj* late; backward; tardy

tardivement [tardivmɑ̃] *adv* belatedly

tare [tar] *f* defect, blemish; taint; loss in value; tare (*weight*)

tarer [tare] *tr* to damage; taint; tare ‖ *ref* to spoil

targette [tarʒɛt] *f* latch

targuer [targe] *ref*—**se targuer de** to pride oneself on

tarière [tarjɛr] *f* auger, drill

tarif [tarif] *m* price list; rate, tariff; **plein tarif** full fare; **tarifs postaux** postal rates

tarifaire [tarifɛr] *adj* tariff

tarifer [tarife] *tr* to price; rate

tarir [tarir] *tr* to drain, exhaust, dry up ‖ *intr* to dry up, run dry; **ne pas tarir** to never run out ‖ *ref* to dry up; be exhausted

tarse [tars] *m* tarsus; instep

tartare [tartar] *adj* tartar (*sauce*); Tartar ‖ (*cap*) *mf* Tartar

tarte [tart] *adj* (coll) silly, stupid; (coll) ugly ‖ *f* pie, tart; (slang) slap; **c'est pas de la tarte** (slang) it's no easy matter; **tarte à la crème** custard pie; (slang) slapstick comedy; **tarte mousseline** chiffon pie

tartine [tartin] *f* slice of bread and butter or jam; (coll) long-winded speech; (coll) rambling article

tartiner [tartine] *tr* to spread

tartre [tartr] *m* tartar; scale

tartuferie [tartyfri] *f* hypocrisy

tas [tɑ] *m* heap, pile; **mettre en tas** to pile up; **prendre sur le tas** to catch red-handed; **tas de foin** haystack; **un tas de** (coll) a lot of

tasse [tɑs] *f* cup; **tasse à café** coffee cup; **tasse à thé** teacup; **tasse de café** cup of coffee

tas•sé -sée [tɑse] *adj* squat, dumpy; shrunk; curled up, slumped; complete; well-filled; packed tight; stiff (*drink*)

tas•seau [tɑso] *m* (*pl* **-seaux**) bracket; cleat; lug (*on casting*)

tasser [tɑse] *tr* to cram; tamp, pack down ‖ *intr* to grow thick ‖ *ref* to settle; huddle; (coll) to go back to normal

taste-vin [tastəvɛ̃] *m invar* wine taster (*cup*); sampling tube

tata [tata] *f* (slang) auntie

tâter [tɑte] *tr* to feel, touch; test, feel out; **tâter le pouls à qn** to feel s.o.'s pulse ‖ *intr*—**tâter de** to taste; experience; try 'one's hand at ‖ *ref* to stop to think, ponder

tâte-vin [tɑtvɛ̃] *m invar* wine taster (*cup*); sampling tube

tatil•lon [tatijɔ̃] **-lonne** [jɔn] *adj* fussy, hairsplitting ‖ *mf* hairsplitter

tâtonner [tɑtone] *intr* to grope

tâtons [tɑtɔ̃]—**à tâtons** gropingly

tatouage [tatwaʒ] *m* tattoo

tatouer [tatwe] *tr* to tattoo

taudis [todi] *m* hovel; **taudis** *mpl* slums

taule [tol] *f* (slang) fleabag; (slang) jug, clink; **faire de la taule** (slang) to do a stretch

taupe [top] *f* mole; moleskin

taupin [topɛ̃] *m* (mil) sapper; (coll) engineering student

taupinière [topinjɛr] *f* molehill

tau•reau [toro] *m* (*pl* **-reaux**) bull; **le Taureau** (astr, astrol) Taurus

taux [to] *m* rate; ratio; degree (*of disability*); **taux de base** prime rate; **taux de change** exchange rate; **taux d'escompte** discount rate; **taux d'intérêt** interest rate

taveler [tavle] §34 *tr* to spot ‖ *ref* to become spotted

taverne [tavɛrn] *f* inn, tavern

taxation [taksɑsjɔ̃] *f* fixing (*of prices, wages,* etc.); assessment; taxation

taxe [taks] *f* fixed price; rate; tax; **taxe à l'achat** sales tax; **taxe à la valeur ajoutée (TVA)** value-added tax (VAT); **taxe de luxe** luxury tax; **taxe de séjour** nonresident tax; **taxe directe** sales tax; **taxe perçue** postage paid; **taxe sur les cadeaux** gift tax; **taxe supplémentaire** postage due; **taxe sur les spectacles** entertainment tax; **taxe sur le tabac** cigarette tax

taxer [takse] *tr* to fix the price of; regulate the rate of; assess; tax; **taxer qn de** to tax or charge s.o. with ‖ *ref* to set an offering price; **se taxer de** to accuse oneself of

taxi [taksi] *m* taxi; (coll) cabdriving; **hep taxi!** taxi! ‖ *mf* (coll) cabdriver

taxidermie [taksidɛrmi] *f* taxidermy

taxiphone [taksifɔn] *m* pay phone

tchao *or* **ciao** [tʃao] *interj* (coll) so long!, I'll be seeing you; (Midi) hello!, hi!

tchèque [tʃɛk] *adj* Czech ‖ *m* Czech (*language*) ‖ (*cap*) *mf* Czech (*person*)

te [tə] §87 you, to you

techni•cien [tɛknisjɛ̃] **-cienne** [sjɛn] *mf* technician; engineer

technique [tɛknik] *adj* technical ‖ *f* technique; engineering; technics

technologie [tɛknɔlɔʒi] *f* technology; **de la haute technologie** high-tech; **technologie de pointe** up-to-date technology; **technologies avancées** new technologies

teck [tɛk] *m* teak

teckel [tɛkɛl] *m* dachshund

teigne [tɛɲ] _f_ moth; ringworm; (fig) pest, nuisance

teindre [tɛ̃dr] §50 _tr_ to dye; tint ‖ _ref_ to be tinted; dye or tint (_one's hair_)

teint [tɛ̃] **teinte** [tɛ̃t] _adj_ dyed; with dyed hair ‖ _m_ dye; complexion; **bon teint** fast color ‖ _f_ tint, shade; (fig) tinge

teinter [tɛ̃te] _tr_ to tint; tinge

teinture [tɛ̃tyr] _f_ dye; dyeing; tincture; (fig) smattering; **teinture d'iode** (pharm) iodine

teinturerie [tɛ̃tyrri] _f_ dry cleaner's; dyer's; dyeing

teintu·rier [tɛ̃tyrje] **-rière** [rjɛr] _mf_ dry cleaner; dyer

tel telle [tɛl] _adj_ such; like, e.g., **tel père tel fils** like father like son; **de telle sorte que** so that; **tel ou tel** such and such a; **tel que** such as, the same as, as; **tel quel** as is ‖ _mf_—**un tel** or **une telle** so-and-so ‖ _pron_ such a one, such

télé [tele] _f_ (coll) TV; (coll) TV set

télécommander [telekɔmɑ̃de] _tr_ to operate by remote control; (fig) to inspire, influence

télécommunications [telekɔmynikɑsjɔ̃] _fpl_ telecommunications

télécopie [telekɔpi] _f_ (_fax_) fax (_copy_)

télécopieur [telekɔpjœr] _m_ (_fax_) fax (_machine_)

télédistribution [teledistribysjɔ̃] _f_ cable television

téléenseignement [teleɑ̃sɛɲmɑ̃] _m_ educational television

téléfax [telefaks] _m_ (trademark) fax

téléférique [teleferik] _m_ skyride, cableway

télégramme [telegram] _m_ telegram

télégraphe [telegraf] _m_ telegraph

télégraphier [telegrafje] _tr & intr_ to telegraph

télégraphiste [telegrafist] _mf_ telegrapher

télégui·dé -dée [telegide] _adj_ remote-controlled

téléguider [telegide] _tr_ to guide (_e.g., a missile_); (coll) to influence

téléimprimeur [teleɛ̃primœr] _m_ teletype, teleprinter

télémarketing [telemarkitiŋ] _m_ telemarketing

télémercatique [telemɛrkatik] _m_ telemarketing

télémessagerie [telemesaʒri] _f_ (comp) E-mail

télémètre [telemɛtr] _m_ telemeter; range finder

télémétrie [telemetri] _f_ telemetry

téléobjectif [teleɔbʒɛktif] _m_ telephoto lens

télépathie [telepati] _f_ telepathy, mental telepathy

téléphérique [teleferik] _m_ skyride, cableway

téléphone [telefɔn] _m_ telephone; **téléphone à clavier** tone telephone, digital telephone, push-button telephone; **téléphone cellulaire** cellular telephone, cellphone; **téléphone mobile** cellular telephone, cellphone, mobile telephone; **téléphone numérique** digital telephone; **téléphone portatif** cellphone, cellular telephone; **téléphone public** public telephone; **téléphone payant** coin telephone; **téléphone rouge** (pol) hot line; **téléphone sur la liste rouge** unlisted telephone

téléphoner [telefɔne] _tr & intr_ to telephone

téléphoniste [telefɔnist] _mf_ telephone operator ‖ _m_ lineman

télescope [telɛskɔp] _m_ telescope

télescoper [telɛskɔpe] _intr & ref_ to telescope

télescopique [telɛskɔpik] _adj_ telescopic

téléscripteur [teleskriptœr] _m_ teletype, teletypewriter

télésiège [telesjɛʒ] _m_ chairlift

téléski [teleski] _m_ ski lift

télésouffleur [telesuflœr] _m_ teleprompter

téléspecta·teur [telespɛktatœr] **-trice** [tris] _mf_ (television) viewer; **téléspectateurs** television audience

télétexte [teletɛkst] _m_ teletext

télétraitement [teletrɛtmɑ̃] _m_ (comp) processing by modem

télétype [teletip] _m_ teletype

téléviser [televize] _tr_ to televise

téléviseur [televizœr] _m_ television set; **téléviseur à servo-réglage** remote-control television set

télévision [televizjɔ̃] _f_ television; (coll) television set; **télévision par câble** cable television; **télévision payante** pay television

télévi·suel -suelle [televizɥɛl] _adj_ television

tellement [tɛlmɑ̃] _adv_ so much, so; **tellement de** so much, so many; **tellement que** to such an extent that

téméraire [temerɛr] _adj_ rash, reckless, foolhardy

témérité [temerite] _f_ temerity, rashness

témoignage [temwaɲaʒ] _m_ testimony, witness; **en témoignage de quoi** in witness whereof; **rendre témoignage à** or **pour** to testify in favor of

témoigner [temwaɲe] §95 _tr_ to show; testify ‖ _intr_ to testify; **témoigner de** to give evidence of; bear witness to

témoin [temwɛ̃] _adj invar_ type, model; pilot; sample, model (_home or apartment_) ‖ _m_ witness; control (_in scientific experiment_); second (_in duel_); **prendre à témoin** to call to witness; **témoin à charge** witness for the prosecution; **témoin à décharge** witness for the defense; **témoin oculaire** eyewitness; **Témoins de Jéhovah** Jehovah's Witnesses

tempe [tɑ̃p] _f_ (anat) temple

tempérament [tɑ̃peramɑ̃] _m_ temperament; amorous nature; **à tempérament** on the installment plan

tempérance [tɑ̃perɑ̃s] _f_ temperance

tempé·rant [tɑ̃perɑ̃] **-rante** [rɑ̃t] _adj_ temperate

température [tɑ̃peratyr] _f_ temperature

tempé·ré -rée [tɑ̃pere] _adj_ temperate; tempered; restrained

tempérer [tɑ̃pere] §10 _tr_ to temper ‖ _ref_ to moderate

tempête [tɑ̃pɛt] _f_ tempest, storm; **affronter la tempête** (fig) to face the music; **tempête dans un verre d'eau** tempest in a teapot; **tempête de neige** blizzard; **tempête de poussière** dust storm; **tempête de sable** sandstorm

tempêter [tɑ̃pɛte] _intr_ to storm

tempé·tueux [tɑ̃petɥø] **-tueuse** [tɥøz] adj tempestuous

temple [tɑ̃pl] m temple; chapel, church

tempo [tɛmpo], [tĕpo] m tempo

temporaire [tɑ̃pɔrɛr] adj temporary

tempo·ral -rale [tɑ̃pɔral] adj (pl **-raux** [ro]) (anat) temporal

tempo·rel -relle [tɑ̃pɔrɛl] adj temporal

temporiser [tɑ̃pɔrize] intr to temporize, stall

temps [tɑ̃] m time; times; cycle (of internal-combustion engine); position, movement (in gymnastics, fencing, carrying of arms); weather, e.g., **quel temps fait-il?** what is the weather like?; (gram) tense; (mus) beat, measure; **à temps** in time; **au temps de** in the time of; **avoir fait son temps** to have seen better days; **dans le bon vieux temps, en le bon vieux temps** in the good old days; **dans le temps** formerly; **de temps en temps** from time to time; **en même temps** at the same time; **en temps de crise** in the time of crisis; **en temps et lieu** in due course; **en temps partagé** (comp) time-sharing; **en temps utile** in due course; **faire son temps** to do time (in prison); **gagner du temps** to save time; **le bon vieux temps** the good old days; **Le Temps** Father Time; **temps atomique** atomic era; **temps d'accès** (comp) turnaround time; **temps d'arrêt** pause, halt; **temps de chien** (slang) lousy weather; **temps mort** (sports) time-out; **temps partagé** (comp) time sharing; **temps réel** (comp) real time

tenable [tənabl] adj—**pas tenable** untenable; unbearable

tenace [tənas] adj tenacious

ténacité [tenasite] f tenacity

tenailler [tənɑje] tr to torture

tenailles [tənɑj] fpl pliers, pincers

tenan·cier [tənɑ̃sje] **-cière** [sjɛr] mf share-cropper; lessee; keeper (e.g., of a dive)

te·nant [tənɑ̃] **-nante** [nɑ̃t] adj attached (collar) ‖ mf (sports) holder (of a title) ‖ m champion, supporter; **connaître les tenants et les aboutissants** to know the ins and outs; **d'un seul tenant** in one piece

tendance [tɑ̃dɑ̃s] f tendency

tendan·cieux [tɑ̃dɑ̃sjø] **-cieuse** [sjøz] adj tendentious, slanted

ten·deur [tɑ̃dœr] **-deuse** [døz] mf paperhanger; layer (of traps) ‖ m stretcher

tendoir [tɑ̃dwar] m clothesline

tendon [tɑ̃dɔ̃] m tendon

tendre [tɑ̃dr] adj tender ‖ §96 tr to stretch; hang; bend (a bow); lay (a trap); strain (one's ear); hold out, reach out ‖ intr—**tendre à** to aim at; tend toward ‖ ref to become strained

tendresse [tɑ̃drɛs] f tenderness, love, affection; (coll) partiality; **mille tendresses** (closing of letter) fondly

tendreté [tɑ̃drəte] f tenderness

ten·du -due [tɑ̃dy] adj tense, taut; strained; stretched out; **tendu de** hung with

ténèbres [tenɛbr] fpl darkness

téné·breux [tenebrø] **-breuse** [brøz] adj dark; somber (person); shady (deal); obscure (style)

te·neur [tənœr] **-neuse** [nøz] mf holder; **teneur de livres** bookkeeper ‖ **teneur** f tenor, gist; text; grade (e.g., of ore)

ténia [tenja] m tapeworm

tenir [tənir] §72, §96 tr to hold; keep; take up (space); **être tenu à** to be obliged to; **être tenu de** to be responsible for ‖ intr to hold; **il ne tient qu'à vous** it's up to you; **tenez!** here!; **tenir à** to insist upon; care for, value; be caused by; **tenir dans** to fit in; **tenir de** to take after, resemble; **tenir debout** (fig) to hold water, ring true; **tenir q.ch. de qn** to have s.th. from s.o., learn s.th. from s.o.; **tiens!** well!, hey! ‖ ref to stay, remain; sit up; stand up; behave; contain oneself; **à quoi s'en tenir** what to believe; **s'en tenir à** to limit oneself to; abide by

tennis [tɛnis] m tennis; tennis court; **tennis de table** table tennis, Ping-Pong

ténor [tenor] adj masc tenor ‖ m tenor; star performer

tension [tɑ̃sjɔ̃] f tension; blood pressure; pressure; voltage; **avoir de la tension** to have high blood pressure; **haute tension** (elec) high tension; **tension artérielle, tension du sang** blood pressure

tentacule [tɑ̃takyl] m tentacle

tenta·teur [tɑ̃tatœr] **-trice** [tris] mf tempter

tentation [tɑ̃tasjɔ̃] f temptation

tentative [tɑ̃tativ] f attempt

tente [tɑ̃t] f tent; awning; **tente de plage** beach tent

tente-abri [tɑ̃tabri] f (pl **tentes-abris** [tɑ̃tabri]) pup tent

tenter [tɑ̃te] §97 tr to tempt; attempt ‖ intr—**tenter de** to attempt to

tenture [tɑ̃tyr] f drape; hangings; wallpaper

te·nu -nue [təny] §93 adj firm (securities, market, etc.); **bien tenu** well-kept ‖ f see **tenue** ‖ v see **tenir**

té·nu -nue [teny] adj tenuous; thin

tenue [təny] f holding; managing; upkeep, maintenance; behavior; bearing; dress, costume; uniform; session; (mus) hold; **avoir de la tenue** to have good manners; **avoir une bonne tenue** (equit) to have a good seat; **en bonne tenue physique** in good shape physically; **en tenue** in uniform; **grande tenue** (mil) full dress; **petite tenue** (mil) undress; **tenue des livres** bookkeeping; **tenue de soirée** evening clothes; **tenue de ville** street clothes

térébenthine [terebɑ̃tin] f turpentine

tergiverser [tɛrʒivɛrse] intr to duck, equivocate, vacillate

terme [tɛrm] m term; end, limit; quarterly payment; **avant terme** prematurely; **terme fatal** last day of grace

terminaison [tɛrminɛzɔ̃] f ending, termination

termi•nal -nale [tɛrminal] *adj & m* (*pl* **-naux** [no]) terminal

terminer [tɛrmine] *tr & ref* to terminate; **se terminer par** to end with ‖ *interj*—**terminé** over (*in CB language*)

terminus [tɛrminys] *m* terminal ‖ *interj* the end has come!

termite [tɛrmit] *m* termite

terne [tɛrn] *adj* dull, drab

ternir [tɛrnir] *tr & ref* to tarnish

terrain [tɛrɛ̃] *m* ground; terrain; playing field; dueling field; **ne pas être sur son terrain** to be out of one's depth; **tâter le terrain** to find out the lay of the land; **terrain à bâtir** or **à lotir** building plot; **terrain brûlant** (fig) unsafe ground; **terrain d'atterrissage** landing field; **terrain d'aviation** airfield; **terrain de courses** race track; **terrain de golf** golf course, golf links; **terrain de jeux** playground; **terrain de manœuvres** parade ground; **terrain glissant** (fig) slippery slope; **terrain vague** vacant lot; **tout terrain** all-surface (vehicle)

terrasse [tɛras] *f* terrace; sidewalk café; **terrasse en plein air** outdoor café

terrasser [tɛrase] *tr* to embank; floor, knock down

terre [tɛr] *f* earth; land; (elec) ground; **descendre à terre** to go ashore; **la Terre Sainte** the Holy Land; **mettre pied à terre** to dismount; **par terre** on the floor; on the ground; **terre cuite** terra cotta; **Terre de Feu** Tierra del Fuego; **terre ferme** terra firma; **terre franche** loam

ter•reau [tɛro] *m* (*pl* **-reaux**) compost

terre-neuve [tɛrnœv] *m invar* Newfoundland dog ‖ *f*—**Terre-Neuve** Newfoundland

terre-plein [tɛrplɛ̃] *m* (*pl* **-pleins**) median, divider (*of road*); fill, embankment; earthwork, rampart; terrace; (rr) roadbed

terrer [tɛre] *tr* to earth up (*e.g., a tree*); earth over (*seed*) ‖ *ref* to burrow; entrench oneself

terrestre [tɛrɛstr] *adj* land; terrestrial

terreur [tɛrœr] *f* terror; **la Terreur** the Reign of Terror

ter•reux -reuse [tɛrø] [røz] *adj* earthy; dirty; sallow (*complexion*)

terrible [tɛribl] *adj* terrible; terrific

ter•rien -rienne [tɛrjɛ̃] [rjɛn] *adj* landed (*gentry*) ‖ *mf* landowner; landlubber ‖ *m* earthman

terrier [tɛrje] *m* hole, burrow; (*dog*) terrier

terrifier [tɛrifje] *tr* to terrify

terrir [tɛrir] *intr* to come close to shore (*said of fish*)

territoire [tɛritwar] *m* territory

terroir [tɛrwar] *m* soil; homeland

terroriser [tɛrɔrize] *tr* to terrorize

tertiaire [tɛrsjɛr] *adj* tertiary

tertre [tɛrtr] *m* mound, knoll

tes [te] §88 your

tesson [tɛsɔ̃] *m* shard; broken glass

test [tɛst] *m* test; (zool) shell; **test de capacité intellectuelle** intelligence test; **test de la des-** cendance paternity test; **test de niveau** placement test; **test d'intelligence pratique, test de talent** aptitude test; **test nucléaire** nuclear test

testament [tɛstamɑ̃] *m* testament; will

testa•teur [tɛstatœr] **-trice** [tris] *mf* testator

tester [tɛste] *tr* to test ‖ *intr* to make one's will

testicule [tɛstikyl] *m* testicle

testostérone [tɛstɔsterɔn] *f* testosterone

tétanos [tetanos] *m* tetanus

têtard [tɛtar] *m* tadpole; (bot) pollard

tête [tɛt] *f* head; heading (*e.g., of chapter*); **à la tête de** in charge of, at the head of; **à tête reposée** at (one's) leisure; **avoir la tête près du bonnet** (coll) to be quick-tempered; **avoir une bonne tête** to have a pleasant look or expression; **de tête** in one's mind's eye, mentally; capable, e.g., **une femme de tête** a capable woman; **en avoir par-dessus la tête** (coll) to be fed up with it; **en tête** foremost, at the front, leading; **en tête à tête avec** alone with; **faire la tête à** to frown at, give a dirty look to; **faire une tête** to wear a long face; **forte tête** strong-minded person; **jeter à la tête à qn** (fig) to cast in s.o.'s face; **la tête en bas** head downwards, upside down; **la tête la première** headfirst, headlong; **laver la tête à qn** (coll) to give s.o. a dressing down; **mauvaise tête** troublemaker; **monter à la tête de qn** to go to s.o.'s head; **n'en faire qu'à sa tête** to be a law unto oneself; **par tête** per capita, per head; **piquer une tête** to take a header, dive; **saluer de la tête** to nod; **se mettre en tête de** to take it into one's head to; **se payer la tête de qn** (coll) to pull s.o.'s leg; **tenir tête à** to face up to, to stand up to; **tête baissée** headlong, heedless; **tête bêche** from top to bottom; head to foot; **tête brûlée** dare-devil; **tête chercheuse** homing head (*of missile*); **tête d'affiche** (theat) headliner; **tête de bois** blockhead; **tête de cuvée** choice wine; **tête de graveur** recording head; **tête de lecture** (elec) playback head; **tête de ligne** truck terminal; railhead; **tête de linotte** scatterbrain; **tête de pont** (mil) bridgehead, beachhead; **tête de Turc** butt, scapegoat, fall guy, patsy; **tête montée** excitable person; **tête morte et tibias** skull and crossbones; **tomber sur la tête** (coll) to be off one's rocker

tête-à-queue [tɛtakø] *m invar* about-face, slue

tétée [tete] *f* sucking; feeding time

téter [tete] §10 *tr & intr* to suck

tétine [tetin] *f* nipple; teat

téton [tetɔ̃] *m* (coll) tit

tétras [tetrɑ] *m* grouse

tette [tɛt] *f* (coll) tit

tê•tu -tue [tɛty] *adj* stubborn

teuf-teuf [tœftœf] *m* (*pl* **teuf-teuf** or **teufs-teufs**) (coll) jalopy ‖ *interj* chug! chug!

tévé [teve] *f* (acronym) (**télévision**) TV

texte [tɛkst] *m* text; (mov, telv) script; **apprendre son texte** (theat) to learn one's lines

textile [tɛkstil] *adj & m* textile

tex·tuel -tuelle [tɛkstɥɛl] *adj* textual; verbatim

texture [tɛkstyr] *f* texture

thaï [tai] *adj invar & m* Thai

thaïlan·dais [tajlɑ̃dɛ] **-daise** [dɛz] *adj* Thai ‖ (*cap*) *mf* Thai

Thaïlande [tajlɑ̃d] *f* Thailand

thaumaturge [tomatyrʒ] *m* miracle worker, magician

thé [te] *m* tea

théâ·tral -trale [teatral] *adj* (*pl* **-traux** [tro]) theatrical

théâtre [teɑtr] *m* theater; stage, boards; scene (*e.g., of the crime*)

théier [teje] **théière** [tejɛr] *adj* tea ‖ *m* tea (*shrub*) ‖ *f* see **théière**

théière [tejɛr] *f* teapot

thème [tɛm] *m* theme; translation (*into a foreign language*)

théocratie [teɔkrasi] *f* theocracy

théologie [teɔlɔʒi] *f* theology

théorème [teɔrɛm] *m* theorem

théorie [teɔri] *f* theory; procession; **faire de la théorie** to theorize; **théorie de l'information** information theory; **théorie germinale** germ theory

théorique [teɔrik] *adj* theoretical

thérapeutique [terapøtik] *adj* therapeutic ‖ *f* therapeutics

thérapie [terapi] *f* therapy; **thérapie familiale** group therapy (*of a family*); **thérapie physique** physical therapy

Thérèse [terɛz] *f* Theresa

ther·mal -male [tɛrmal] *adj* (*pl* **-maux** [mo]) thermal

thermique [tɛrmik] *adj* thermal

thermocouple [tɛrmɔkupl] *m* thermocouple

thermodynamique [tɛrmɔdinamik] *adj* thermodynamic ‖ *f* thermodynamics

thermomètre [tɛrmɔmɛtr] *m* thermometer

thermonucléaire [tɛrmɔnykleɛr] *adj* thermonuclear

Thermopyles [tɛrmɔpil] *fpl*—**les Thermopyles** Thermopylae

thermos [tɛrmɔs] *f* thermos bottle

thermosiphon [tɛrmɔsifɔ̃] *m* hot-water heater

thermostat [tɛrmɔsta] *m* thermostat

thésauriser [tezorize] *tr & intr* to hoard

thésauri·seur [tezorizœr] **-seuse** [zøz] *mf* hoarder

thèse [tɛz] *f* thesis; viewpoint, idea, position

thon [tɔ̃] *m* tuna

thorax [tɔraks] *m* thorax

thrène [trɛn] *m* threnody

thrombose [trɔ̃boz] *f* thrombosis

thuriféraire [tyriferɛr] *m* incense bearer; flatterer

thym [tɛ̃] *m* thyme

thyroïde [tirɔid] *adj & f* thyroid

tiare [tjar] *f* tiara (*papal miter*); papacy

tibia [tibja] *m* tibia; shin; **tibias croisés et tête de mort** skull and crossbones

tic [tik] *m* (pathol) tic; **tic tac** ticktock

ticket [tikɛ] *m* ticket (*of bus, subway, etc.*); check (*for article in baggage room*); ration stamp; **sans tickets** unrationed; **ticket de quai** platform ticket

tic-tac [tiktak] *m invar* tick

tiède [tjɛd] *adj* lukewarm; mild

tiédeur [tjedœr] *f* lukewarmness; mildness

tiédir [tjedir] *tr* to take the chill of ‖ *intr* to become lukewarm

tien [tjɛ̃] **tienne** [tjɛn] §89 yours

tiens [tjɛ̃] *interj* well!, hey! ‖ *v* see **tenir; un "tiens" vaux mieux que deux "tu l'auras"** a bird in the hand is worth two in the bush

tiers [tjɛr] **tierce** [tjɛrs] *adj* third; tertian (*fever*) ‖ *m* third (*in fractions*); **le tiers** a third; the third party; **le tiers et le quart** (coll) everybody and anybody; **le Tiers Monde** the Third World ‖ *f* (typ) press proof

tige [tiʒ] *f* stem; trunk; shaft; shank; piston rod; leg (*of boot*); stock (*of genealogy*)

tignasse [tiɲas] *f* shock, mop (*of hair*)

tigre [tigr] *m* tiger

ti·gré -grée [tigre] *adj* striped; speckled, spotted

tigresse [tigrɛs] *f* tigress

tillac [tijak] *m* top deck (*of old-time ships*)

tilleul [tijœl] *m* linden

tilt [tilt] *m*—**faire tilt** to give an out-of-order signal; (slang) to strike home

timbale [tɛ̃bal] *f* metal cup, mug; (culin) mold; (mus) kettledrum; **décrocher la timbale** (coll) to carry off the prize

timbalier [tɛ̃balje] *m* kettledrummer

timbrage [tɛ̃braʒ] *m* stamping; cancellation (*of mail*)

timbre [tɛ̃br] *m* bell; doorbell; buzzer; seal, stamp; postage stamp; postmark; snare (*of drum*); (phonet, phys) timbre; **timbre aéropostal** airmail stamp

tim·bré -brée [tɛ̃bre] *adj* stamped; ringing (*voice*); (coll) cracked, crazy

timbre-poste [tɛ̃brəpɔst] *m* (*pl* **timbres-poste**) postage stamp

timbrer [tɛ̃bre] *tr* to stamp; postmark

timbres-prime [tɛ̃brəprim] *mpl* trading stamps

timide [timid] *adj* timid, shy

timon [timɔ̃] *m* pole (*of carriage*); beam (*of plow*); (naut) helm

timonier [timɔnje] *m* helmsman; wheel horse

timo·ré -rée [timɔre] *adj* timorous

tin [tɛ̃] *m* chock

tinette [tinɛt] *f* firkin (*tub*); bucket (*for fecal matter*)

tintamarre [tɛ̃tamar] *m* uproar

tintement [tɛ̃tɑ̃] *m* tolling (*of bell*); tinkle (*of bell*); ringing (*in ears*)

tinter [tɛ̃te] *tr* to toll ‖ *intr* to toll; tinkle; jingle, clink; ring (*said of ears*)

tintin [tɛ̃tɛ̃] *m*—**faire tintin** (slang) to do without ‖ *interj* (slang) nothing doing!

tintouin [tɛ̃twɛ̃] *m* (coll) trouble

tique [tik] *f* (ent) tick

tiquer [tike] *intr* to twitch; (coll) to wince; **sans tiquer** (coll) without turning a hair

tir [tir] *m* shooting; firing; aim; shooting gallery; **tir à la cible** target practice; **tir à l'arc** archery; **tir au fusil** gunnery; **tir au pigeon** trapshooting

tirade [tirad] *f* (theat) long speech

tirage [tiraʒ] *m* drawing; towing; draft (*of chimney*); printing; circulation (*of newspaper*); (comp) hard copy; (coll) tension, friction; **tirage à part** offprint; **tirage au sort** lottery drawing; **tirage de luxe** deluxe edition

tiraillement [tirajmã] *m* pain, cramp; conflict, tension

tirailler [tiraje] *tr* to pull about, tug at; pester ‖ *intr* to blaze away; **tirailler sur** to snipe at ‖ *ref* to have a misunderstanding

tirailleur [tirajœr] *m* sharpshooter; sniper; (fig) free lance

tirant [tirã] *m* string; strap; **tirant d'eau** draft (*of ship*)

tire [tir] *f* (heral) row (*of vair*); (slang) car, auto; (Canad) taffy pull

ti•ré -rée [tire] *adj* drawn; printed ‖ *m* shooting preserve; payee; **tiré à part** offprint

tire-au-flanc [tiroflã] *m invar* (coll) malingerer, shirker, goof-off, loafer

tire-botte [tirbɔt] *m* (*pl* **-bottes**) bootjack

tire-bouchon [tirbuʃɔ̃] *m* (*pl* **-bouchons**) corkscrew; corkscrew curl

tire-bouchonner [tirbuʃɔne] *tr* to twist in a spiral

tire-bouton [tirbutɔ̃] *m* (*pl* **-boutons**) buttonhook

tire-clou [tirklu] *m* (*pl* **-clous**) nail puller

tire-d'aile [tirdɛl]—**à tire-d'aile** with wings outspread, swiftly

tire-fond [tirfɔ̃] *m invar* spike; screw eye

tire-larigot [tirlarigo]—**boire à tire-larigot** to drink like a fish

tire-ligne [tirliɲ] *m* (*pl* **-lignes**) ruling pen

tirelire [tirlir] *f* piggy bank; (*face*) (coll) mug; (*head*) (coll) noggin; (slang) belly

tire-l'œil [tirlœj] *m invar* eye catcher

tirer [tire] *tr* to draw; pull, tug; shoot, fire; run off, print; take out; take, get; stick out (*one's tongue*); **tirer au clair** to bring out into the open; **tirer parti de** to turn to account ‖ *intr* to pull; shoot; draw (*e.g., to a close*); draw (*said of chimney*); **tirer à, vers,** or **sur** to border on ‖ *ref* to extricate oneself; **s'en tirer** to manage; get off (*get out of a difficulty*); **se tirer d'affaire** to pull through, get along

tiret [tirɛ] *m* dash; blank (*on an exam*)

tirette [tirɛt] *f* slide (*of desk*); damper (*of chimney*)

tireur [tirœr] *m* marksman; drawer, payer (*of check*); printer; **tireur de bois flotté** log driver; **tireur d'élite** sharpshooter; **tireur d'épée** fencer; **tireur isolé** sniper

tireuse [tirøz] *f* markswoman; **tireuse de cartes** fortuneteller

tiroir [tirwar] *m* drawer; (mach) slide valve; **à tiroirs** episodic (*play, novel, etc.*)

tiroir-caisse [tirwarkɛs] *m* (*pl* **tiroirs-caisses**) cash register

tisane [tizan] *f* tea, infusion; (coll) bad champagne; (slang) slap

tison [tizɔ̃] *m* ember; (fig) firebrand

tisonner [tizɔne] *tr* to poke

tisonnier [tizɔnje] *m* poker

tissage [tisaʒ] *m* weaving

tisser [tise] *tr & intr* to weave

tisse•rand [tisrã] **-rande** [rãd] *mf* weaver

tis•seur [tisœr] **-seuse** [søz] *mf* weaver

tissu [tisy] *m* tissue; cloth; fabric, material; pack (*of lies*)

tissu-éponge [tisyepɔ̃ʒ] *m* (*pl* **tissus-éponges**) toweling, terry cloth

tissure [tisyr] *f* texture; (fig) framework

titane [titan] *m* titanium

titanesque [titanɛsk] *adj* titanic

titanique [titanik] *adj* (chem) titanic

titi [titi] *m* (slang) street urchin

Titien [tisjɛ̃] *m*—**le Titien** Titian

titre [titr] *m* title; title page; heading; headline; fineness (*of coinage*); claim, right; concentration (*of a solution*); **à juste titre** rightly so; **à titre de** in the capacity of; by virtue of; **à titre d'emprunt** as a loan; **à titre d'essai** on trial; **à titre expérimental** as an experiment; **à titre gratuit** or **gracieux** free of charge; **titre d'actions** share certificate; **titres** qualifications; **titres flamboyants** banner headlines; (com) securities

titrer [titre] *tr* to title; subtitle (*films*)

tituber [titybe] *intr* to stagger

titulaire [titylɛr] *adj* titular ‖ *mf* incumbent; holder (*of passport, license, degree, post, lock box, etc.*)

titulariser [titylarize] *tr* to confirm the appointment of

toast [tost] *m* toast; **porter un toast à** to toast

toboggan [tɔbɔgã] *m* toboggan; toboggan run; slide, chute

toc [tɔk] *adj invar* (coll) worthless; (coll) crazy ‖ *m* (mach) chuck; (coll) imitation; **en toc** (coll) worthless; **toc, toc!** knock, knock!

tofu [tɔfy] *m* tofu

tohu-bohu [tɔybɔy] *m* hubbub

toi [twa] §85, §87 you

toile [twal] *f* cloth; linen; canvas, painting; (theat) curtain; **La Toile** (comp) the Web; **La Toile mondiale** (comp) the World-Wide Web; **toile à coton** calico; **toile à laver** dishrag; **toile à matelas** ticking; **toile à voile** sailcloth; **toile cirée** oilcloth; **toile d'araignée** cobweb; **toile de fond** backdrop

toilette [twalɛt] *f* toilet; dressing table; dress, outfit (*of a woman*); **aimer la toilette** to be fond of clothing; **faire la toilette de** to lay out (*a corpse*); **la toilette** (Belgique) toilets; **toilettes** toilets

toi-même [twamɛm] §86 yourself

toise [twaz] *f* fathom; **passer à la toise** to measure the height of

toiser [twaze] *tr* to size up

toison [twazɔ̃] *f* fleece; mop (*of hair*); **Toison d'or** Golden Fleece

toit [twa] *m* roof; rooftop; home, house; **crier sur les toits** to shout from the housetops; **toit ouvrant** (aut) sunroof

toiture [twatyr] *f* roofing

tôle [tol] *f* sheet metal; tole (*decorative metalware*); **tôle de blindage** armor plate; **tôle étamée** tin plate; **tôle galvanisée** galvanized iron; **tôle noire** sheet iron; **tôle ondulée** corrugated iron

tolérable [tɔlerabl] *adj* tolerable, bearable

tolérance [tɔlerɑ̃s] *f* tolerance

tolérer [tɔlere] §10 *tr* to tolerate

tôlerie [tolri] *f* sheet metal; rolling mill

tolet [tɔlɛ] *m* oarlock

tollé [tɔle] *m* outcry, protest

tomaison [tɔmɛzɔ̃] *f* volume number

tomate [tɔmat] *f* tomato

tombe [tɔ̃b] *f* tomb; grave; tombstone

tom•beau [tɔ̃bo] *m* (*pl* -**beaux**) tomb; **à tombeau couvert** lickety-split

tombée [tɔ̃be] *f* fall (*of rain, snow, etc.*); **tombée de la nuit** nightfall

tomber [tɔ̃be] *tr* to throw (*a wrestler*); (coll) to remove (*a piece of clothing*); (slang) to seduce (*a woman*) ‖ *intr* (*aux:* ÉTRE) to fall, drop; **tomber amoureux** to fall in love; **tomber bien** to happen just in time; **tomber en panne** to have a breakdown; **tomber sur** to run into, chance upon; turn to (*said of conversation*)

tombe•reau [tɔ̃bro] *m* (*pl* -**reaux**) dump truck; dumpcart; load

tombola [tɔ̃bɔla] *m* raffle

tome [tɔm] *m* tome, volume

tomodensitomètre [tɔmɔdɑ̃sitɔmɛtr] *m* CAT scanner

tomodensitométrie [tɔmɔdɑ̃sitɔmetri] *f* CAT (*computerized axial tomography*)

ton [tɔ̃] *adj poss* §88 your ‖ *m* tone; (mus) key

to•nal -nale [tɔnal] *adj* (*pl* -**nals**) tonal

tonalité [tɔnalite] *f* tonality; (telp) dial tone; **tonalité continue** dial tone; **tonalité d'appel** ring; **tonalité insolite** warning tone; out-of-order signal; **tonalité-pulsation** (telp) tone pulse

ton•deur [tɔ̃dœr] -**deuse** [døz] *mf* shearer ‖ *f* shears; **tondeuse à cheveux** hair clippers; **tondeuse à fouet** lawn trimmer (*nylon cord*); **tondeuse à gazon** lawn mower; **tondeuse (à gazon) à moteur** power mower; **tondeuse auto-portée** riding mower; **tondeuse électrique** electric clippers; **tondeuse mécanique** cropper; power mower

tondre [tɔ̃dr] *tr* to clip; shear; mow

toni•fiant [tɔnifjɑ̃] -**fiante** [fjɑ̃t] *adj & m* tonic

tonifier [tɔnifje] *tr* to tone up

tonique [tɔnik] *adj & m* tonic

toni•truant [tɔnitryɑ̃] -**truante** [tryɑ̃t] *adj* (coll) thunderous

tonnage [tɔnaʒ] *m* tonnage

tonne [tɔn] *f* ton; tun

ton•neau [tɔno] *m* (*pl* -**neaux**) barrel; cart; roll (*of automobile, airplane, etc.*); (naut) ton; **au tonneau** on draught; **tonneau de poudre** powder keg

tonnelet [tɔnlɛ] *m* keg

tonnelier [tɔnəlje] *m* cooper

tonnelle [tɔnɛl] *f* arbor

tonner [tɔne] *intr* to thunder

tonnerre [tɔnɛr] *m* thunder

tonte [tɔ̃t] *f* clipping; shearing; mowing

tonton [tɔ̃tɔ̃] *m* (slang) uncle

top [tɔp] *m* beep

topaze [tɔpaz] *f* topaz

toper [tɔpe] *intr* to shake hands on it; **tope là!** it's a deal!

topinambour [tɔpinɑ̃bur] *m* Jerusalem artichoke

topique [tɔpik] *adj* local, regional

topographie [tɔpɔgrafi] *f* topography

toquade [tɔkad] *f* (coll) infatuation

toquante [tɔkɑ̃t] *f* (coll) ticker (*watch*)

toque [tɔk] *f* toque; cap (*of chef; of judge*)

to•qué -quée [tɔke] *adj* (coll) crazy, cracked ‖ *mf* (coll) nut

toquer [tɔke] *tr* to infatuate ‖ *intr* (coll) to rap, tap ‖ *ref*—**se toquer de** to be infatuated with

torche [tɔrʃ] *f* torch; **se mettre en torche** to fail to open (*said of parachute*); **torche électrique** flashlight

torcher [tɔrʃe] *tr* to wipe clean; rush through, botch; daub with clay and straw; (vulg) **je m'en torche!** to hell with it!

torchère [tɔrʃɛr] *f* candelabrum; floor lamp

torchis [tɔrʃi] *m* adobe

torchon [tɔrʃɔ̃] *m* dishcloth; rag; (coll) scribble; **le torchon brûle** they're squabbling

torchonner [tɔrʃɔne] *tr* (coll) to botch

tor•dant [tɔrdɑ̃] -**dante** [dɑ̃t] *adj* (coll) sidesplitting

tord-boyaux [tɔrbwajo] *m invar* (coll) rot-gut

tordeuse [tɔrdøz] *f* moth

tordoir [tɔrdwar] *m* wringer; rope-making machine

tordre [tɔrdr] *tr* to twist; wring ‖ *ref* to twist; writhe; **se tordre de rire** to split one's sides laughing

toréador [tɔreadɔr] *m* (obs) toreador

tornade [tɔrnad] *f* tornado

toron [tɔrɔ̃] *m* strand (*of rope*)

torpédo [tɔrpedo] *f* (archaic) open touring car

torpeur [tɔrpœr] *f* torpor

torpille [tɔrpij] *f* torpedo; (arti) mine

torpiller [tɔrpije] *tr* to torpedo

torpilleur [tɔrpijœr] *m* torpedo boat; torpedoman

torque [tɔrk] *f* coil of wire; twist (*of tobacco*)

torréfaction [tɔrefaksjɔ̃] *f* roasting

torréfier [tɔrefje] *tr* to roast

torrent [tɔrɑ̃] *m* torrent

torride [tɔrid] *adj* torrid

tors [tɔr] **torse** [tɔrs] *adj* twisted; crooked ‖ *m* twist ‖ see **torse** *m*

torsade [tɔrsad] *f* twisted cord; coil (*of hair*); **à torsades** fringed; cable-knit

torsader [tɔrsade] *tr* to twist

torse [tɔrs] *m* torso, trunk

torsion [tɔrsjɔ̃] *f* twisting, torsion

tort [tɔr] *m* wrong; harm; **à tort** wrongly; **à tort et à travers** at random, wildly; carelessly; inconsiderately; **à tort ou à raison** rightly or wrongly; **avoir tort** to be wrong; **donner tort à** to lay the blame on; **faire tort à** to wrong

torticolis [tɔrtikɔli] *m* stiff neck

tortillard [tɔrtijar] *adj masc* knotty ‖ *m* (coll) jerkwater train

tortiller [tɔrtije] *tr* to twist, twirl; (slang) to gulp down ‖ *intr* to wriggle; (coll) to beat about the bush ‖ *ref* to wriggle, squirm; writhe, twist

tor·tu -tue [tɔrty] *adj* crooked ‖ *f* turtle, tortoise

tor·tueux [tɔrtɥø] **-tueuse** [tɥøz] *adj* winding; devious, underhanded

torture [tɔrtyr] *f* torture

torturer [tɔrtyre] *tr* to torture

torve [tɔrv] *adj* menacing

tos·can [tɔskɑ̃] **-cane** [kan] *adj* Tuscan ‖ *m* Tuscan (*dialect*) ‖ (*cap*) *mf* Tuscan (*person*)

tôt [to] *adv* soon; early; **au plus tôt** as soon as possible; at the earliest; **le plus tôt possible** as soon as possible; **pas de si tôt** not soon; **tôt ou tard** sooner or later

to·tal -tale [tɔtal] *adj & m* (*pl* **-taux** [to]) total

totaliser [tɔtalize] *tr* to total

totalitaire [tɔtalitɛr] *adj* totalitarian

totem [tɔtɛm] *m* totem

toton [tɔtɔ̃] *m* teetotum

toubib [tubib] *m* (coll) medical officer; (coll) doctor, physician

tou·chant [tu∫ɑ̃] **-chante** [∫ɑ̃t] *adj* touching ‖ **touchant** *prep* touching, concerning

touche [tu∫] *f* touch; key (*of piano or typewriter*); stop (*of organ*); fret (*of guitar*); fingerboard (*of violin*); hit (*in fencing*); bite (*on fishline*); goad (*for cattle*); tab (*of file index*); thumb index; (elec) contact; (coll) look, appearance; **touche de blocage** shift lock; **touche de manœuvre** shift key; **touche de recul** backspacer; **touche marge libre, touche passemarge** margin release

touche-à-tout [tu∫atu] *m invar* (coll) busy-body

toucher [tu∫e] *m* touch, sense of touch ‖ *tr* to touch; concern; cash (*a check*); draw out (*money*); goad (*cattle*); (mus) to pluck (*the strings*) ‖ *intr* to touch; **toucher à** to touch (*one's food, capital, etc.*); touch on; call at (*a port*); be about to achieve (*one's aim*); **toucher de** to play (*e.g., the piano*) ‖ *ref* to touch

touer [twe] *tr* to warp, kedge

touffe [tuf] *f* tuft; clump (*of trees*)

touffeur [tufœr] *f* suffocating heat

touf·fu -fue [tufy] *adj* bushy; (fig) dense

touille [tuj] *m* dogfish, shark

touiller [tuje] *tr* (coll) to stir; (coll) to mix; (coll) to shuffle

toujours [tuʒur] *adv* always; still; anyhow; **M.**

Toujours (coll) yes man; **pour toujours** forever

toupet [tupɛ] *m* tuft (*of hair*); forelock (*of horse*); (coll) nerve, brass

toupie [tupi] *f* top; molding board; silly woman

tour [tur] *m* turn; tour; trick; lathe; **à tour de bras** with all one's might; **à tour de rôle** in turn; **en un tour de main** in a jiffy, in a flash; **faire le tour de** to tour, to visit; to walk or ride around; **faire un tour de** to take a walk or ride in; **faire un tour de cochon à** (slang) to play a dirty trick on; **fermer à double tour** to double-lock; **tour à tour** by turns; **tour de bâton** (coll) rake-off; killing; **tour de contrôle** control tower; **tour de main, tour d'adresse** sleight of hand; **tour de poitrine** chest size; **tour de reins** sudden back pain; **tour de taille** waist measurement; **tour de tête** hat size; **tours et retours** twists and turns; **tours mn.** revolutions per minute ‖ *f* tower; (chess) castle, rook; (mil) turret; **tour de contrôle** control tower; **tour de forage** oil rig, derrick; **tour de guet** lookout tower; **tours jumelles** twin towers

tourbe [turb] *f* peat; mob

tourbillon [turbijɔ̃] *m* whirl; whirlpool; whirlwind

tourbillonner [turbijɔne] *intr* to whirl, to swirl

tourelle [turɛl] *f* turret

tourillon [turijɔ̃] *m* axle; trunnion

tourisme [turism] *m* tourism; tourist industry; sightseeing; **de tourisme** tourist; **faire du tourisme** to do some sightseeing

touriste [turist] *adj & mf* tourist

tourment [turmɑ̃] *m* torment

tourmente [turmɑ̃t] *f* storm

tourmenter [turmɑ̃te] *tr* to torment ‖ *ref* to fret

tour·nant [turnɑ̃] **-nante** [nɑ̃t] *adj* turning, revolving ‖ *m* turn; turning point; water wheel

tourne-à-gauche [turnago∫] *m invar* wrench; saw set; diestock

tournebroche [turnəbrɔ∫] *m* roasting jack, turnspit

tourne-disque [turnədisk] *m* (*pl* **-disques**) record player

tournedos [turnədo] *m* filet mignon

tournée [turne] *f* round; **en tournée** (theat) on tour; **faire une tournée** to take a trip; **offrir la tournée générale** (coll) to treat everyone to a round of drinks; **tournée de distribution de journaux** newspaper route; **tournée électorale** political campaign

tournemain [turnəmɛ̃] **—en un tournemain** in a split second

tourne-pierre [turnɛpjɛr] *m* (*pl* **-pierres**) (orn) turnstone

tourner [turne] *tr* to turn; turn over; shoot (*a moving picture; a scene*); outflank; **tourner et retourner** to turn over and over ‖ *intr* to turn; (mov) to shoot a picture; (theat) to tour; **la tête me** (**lui,** etc.) **tourne** my (his, etc.) head is turning, I feel (he feels, etc.) dizzy; **silence, on tourne!** quiet on the set!; **tourner**

à or **en** to turn into; **tourner autour du pot** (coll) to beat about the bush; **tourner bien** to turn out well; **tourner court** to make a sharp turn; **tourner en rond** to go around in circles, spin; **tourner mal** to go bad ‖ *ref* to turn

tournesol [turnəsɔl] *m* litmus; sunflower

tournevis [turnəvis] *m* screwdriver

tourniquet [turnikɛ] *m* turnstile; revolving door; revolving display stand; (surg) tourniquet; **passer au tourniquet** (slang) to be court-martialed

tournoi [turnwa] *m* tournament

tournoyer [turnwaje] §47 *intr* to turn, wheel; twirl; tourney

tournure [turnyr] *f* turn, course (*of events*); wording, phrasing, turn (*of phrase*); expression; shape, figure; **prendre tournure** to take shape

tourte [turt] *adj* (slang) stupid ‖ *f* (coll) dolt; **tourte à la viande** meat pie

tour•teau [turto] *m* (*pl* **-teaux**) oil cake; crab

tourte•reau [turtəro] *m* (*pl* **-reaux**) turtledove; young lover

tourterelle [turtərɛl] *f* turtledove

tourtière [turtjɛr] *f* pie pan

toussailler [tusɑje] *intr* to keep on coughing

Toussaint [tusɛ̃] *f* All Saints' Day; **la Toussaint** All Saints' Day

tousser [tuse] *intr* to cough; clear one's throat

tousserie [tusri] *f* constant coughing

toussotement [tusɔtmɑ̃] *m* slight coughing

toussoter [tusɔte] *intr* to cough slightly

tout [tu] **toute** [tut] (*pl* **tous toutes**) *adj* any, every, all; all, all of, e.g., **tous les hommes** all men, all of the men; whole, entire, e.g., **toute la journée** the whole day; **à tout coup** every time; **à toute heure** at any time; **tous les deux** both; **tout le monde** everybody, everyone ‖ *m* (*pl* **touts**) whole, all; everything; sum; **du tout** (coll) not at all; **en tout** wholly, in all; **jouer le tout pour le tout** (slang) to shoot the works; **pas du tout** not at all; **tout de même** all the same, surely ‖ **tout toute** (*pl* **tous** [tus] **toutes**) *pron* all, everything, anything; **à tout prendre** on the whole; **tout compté** all things considered ‖ **tout** *adv* all, quite, completely; very, e.g., **un des tout premiers** one of the very foremost; **tout à côté de** right next to; **tout à coup** suddenly; **tout à fait** quite; **tout à l'heure** in a little while; a little while ago; **tout au plus** at most; **tout de même** however, all the same; **tout de suite** at once, immediately; **tout d'un coup** all at once; **tout en** while, e.g., **tout en parlant** while talking; **tout éveillé** wide awake; **tout fait** ready-made; **tout haut** aloud; **tout neuf** brand-new; **tout nu** stark-naked; **tout près** nearby; **tout . . . que** despite the fact that, e.g., **tout vieux qu'il était** despite the fact that he was old ‖ **toute toutes** *adv* (before a feminine word beginning with a consonant or an aspirate **h**) all, quite, completely, e.g., **elles sont**

toutes seules they are all (or quite or completely) alone

tout-à-l'égout [tutalegu] *m invar* sewerage

toute-épice [tutepis] *f* (*pl* **toutes-épices** [tutepis]) allspice (*berry*)

toutefois [tutfwa] *adv* however

toute-puissance [tutpɥisɑ̃s] *f* omnipotence

toutou [tutu] *m* (coll) doggie

Tout-Paris [tupari] *m invar* high society, smart set (*in Paris*)

tout-petit [tupəti] *m* (*pl* **-petits**) toddler

tout-puissant [tupɥisɑ̃] **toute-puissante** [tutpɥisɑ̃t] (*pl* **tout-puissants toutes-puissantes**) *adj* almighty ‖ **le Tout-Puissant** the Almighty

tout-venant [tuvnɑ̃] *m invar* all comers; run-of-the-mine coal; run-of-the-mill product; ordinary run of people

toux [tu] *f* cough

toxico [tɔksiko] *m* (coll) junkie; **toxico qui s'adonne au crack** crackhead

toxicomane [tɔksikɔman] *adj* addicted ‖ *mf* drug addict, junkie

toxicomanie [tɔksikɔmani] *f* drug addiction

toxique [tɔksik] *adj* toxic ‖ *m* poison

tph *abbr* (**telephone**) tel.

trac [trak] *m* (coll) stage fright; **avoir le trac** (coll) to lose one's nerve; **tout à trac** without thinking

tracas [traka] *m* worry, trouble

tracasser [trakase] *tr & ref* to worry

tracasserie [trakasri] *f* bother; **tracasseries** interference

tracassin [trakasɛ̃] *m* (coll) worry

trace [tras] *f* trace; track, trail; sketch; footprint; **marcher sur les traces de** to follow in the footsteps of

tracé [trase] *m* tracing; **faire le tracé de** to lay out; (math) to plot

tracer [trase] §51 *tr* to trace, draw

tra•ceur [trasœr] **-ceuse** [søz] *mf* tracer ‖ *m* tracer (*radioactive substance*)

trachée [traʃe] *f* trachea, windpipe

trachée-artère [traʃeartɛr] *f* (*pl* **trachées-artères**) windpipe

tract [trakt] *m* tract

tractation [traktɑsjɔ̃] *f* underhanded deal

tracteur [traktœr] *m* tractor

traction [traksjɔ̃] *f* traction; **faire des tractions** to do chin-ups; **traction avant** frontwheel drive

tradition [tradisjɔ̃] *f* tradition

tradition•nel -nelle [tradisjɔnɛl] *adj* traditional

traduc•teur [tradyktœr] **-trice** [tris] *mf* translator

traduction [tradyksjɔ̃] *f* translation

traduire [tradɥir] §19 *tr* to translate; **traduire en justice** to haul into court

trafic [trafik] *m* traffic, trade; **trafic d'influence** influence peddling; **trafic routier** highway traffic

trafi•quant [trafikɑ̃] **-quante** [kɑ̃t] *mf* racketeer; **trafiquant en stupéfiants** dope peddler

trafiquer [trafike] *tr* to traffic in ‖ *intr* to traffic; **trafiquer de** to traffic in or on
trafi•queur [trafikœr] **-queuse** [køz] *mf* racketeer
tragédie [traʒedi] *f* tragedy
tragé•dien [traʒedjɛ̃] **-dienne** [djɛn] *mf* tragedian
tragique [traʒik] *adj* tragic
trahir [trair] *tr* to betray
trahison [traizɔ̃] *f* betrayal; treason
train [trɛ̃] *m* pace, speed; manner, way; series; raft (*of logs*); (rr) train; (coll) row, racket; (slang) hind end; **aller son petit train** to go along nicely; **être en train de** + *inf* to be in the act or process of + *ger;* (translated by a progressive form of the verb), e.g., **je suis en train d'écrire** I am writing; **mettre en train** to start; **se magner le train** (slang) to get a move on; **train arrière** (aut) rear-axle assembly; (rr) rear car; **train avant** (aut) front-axle assembly; **train d'atterrissage** landing gear; **train de banlieue** suburban train; **train de marchandises** freight train; **train d'enfer** furious pace; **train de vie** way of life; standard of living; **train de voyageurs** passenger train; **train direct** express train; **train omnibus** local train; **train sanitaire** military hospital train
traî•nant [trɛnɑ̃] **-nante** [nɑ̃t] *adj* trailing; creeping; drawling; languid
traî•nard [trɛnar] **-narde** [nard] *mf* straggler
traîne [trɛn] *f* train (*of dress*); dragnet; **à la traîne** dragging; straggling; in tow
traî•neau [trɛno] *m* (*pl* **-neaux**) sleigh; sled; sledge; dragnet
traînée [trene] *f* trail, train; streak; (aer) drag; (coll) streetwalker
traîner [trene] *tr* to drag, lug; drawl; shuffle (*the feet*) ‖ *intr* to drag; straggle; lie around ‖ *ref* to crawl; creep; limp
traî•neur [trɛnœr] **-neuse** [nøz] *mf* straggler; loiterer
train-train [trɛ̃trɛ̃] *m* routine
traire [trɛr] §68 *tr* to milk
trait [trɛ] *m* arrow, dart; dash; stroke; feature (*of face*); trait, characteristic; trace (*of harness*); **avoir trait à** to refer to; **de trait** draft (*horse*); **d'un trait** in one gulp; **partir comme un trait** to be off like a shot; **tracer à grands traits** to trace in broad outlines; **trait d'esprit** witticism; **trait d'héroïsme** heroic deed; **trait d'union** hyphen; **trait pour trait** exactly ‖ *f* see **traite** ‖ **trait** [trɛ] **traite** [trɛt] *v* see **traire**
traitable [trɛtabl] *adj* tractable
traite [trɛt] *f* trade, traffic; milking; (com) draft; **tout d'une traite** at a single stretch ‖ *v* see **traire**
traité [trete] *m* treatise; treaty
traitement [trɛtmɑ̃] *m* treatment; salary; (comp) processing, turnaround; **mauvais traitements** affront, mistreatment; **traitement des données, traitement de l'information** infor-

mation processing, data processing; **traitement de texte(s)** word processing; **traitements** earned income
traiter [trete] *tr* to treat; receive; **traiter les données** (comp) to data-process; **traiter qn de** to call s.o. (*a name*) ‖ *intr* to negotiate; **traiter de** to deal with
traiteur [trɛtœr] *m* caterer; (obs) restaurateur
traî•tre [trɛtr] **-tresse** [trɛs] *adj* traitorous; treacherous; (coll) single ‖ *mf* traitor; (theat) villain ‖ *f* traitress
traîtrise [tretriz] *f* treachery
trajectoire [traʒɛktwar] *f* trajectory; **trajectoire d'attente** (aer) holding pattern
trajet [traʒɛ] *m* distance, trip, passage; (aer) flight
tralala [tralala] *m* (coll) fuss
trame [tram] *f* weft; web (*of life*); conspiracy
tramer [trame] *tr* to weave; hatch (*a plot*) ‖ *ref* to be plotted
traminot [tramino] *m* traction-company employee
tramontane [tramɔ̃tan] *f* north wind; **perdre la tramontane** to lose one's bearings
tramp [trɑ̃p] *m* tramp steamer
tramway [tramwɛ] *m* streetcar
tran•chant [trɑ̃ʃɑ̃] **-chante** [ʃɑ̃t] *adj* cutting; glaring; trenchant ‖ *m* cutting edge; knife; side (*of hand*); **à double tranchant** or **à deux tranchants** two-edged
tranche [trɑ̃ʃ] *f* slice; section; portion, installment; group (*of figures*); cross section; tax bracket; **doré sur tranches** (bb) gilt-edged; (coll) gilded (*e.g., youth*); **une tranche de vie** a slice of life
tranchée [trɑ̃ʃe] *f* trench; **tranchées** colic
trancher [trɑ̃ʃe] *tr* to cut off; slice; decide, settle ‖ *intr* to decide once and for all; stand out; **trancher avec** to contrast with; **trancher dans le vif** to cut to the quick; (fig) to take drastic measures; **trancher de** (lit) to affect the manners of
trancheuse [trɑ̃ʃøz] *f* food slicer
tranquille [trɑ̃kil] *adj* quiet, tranquil; **laissez-moi tranquille** leave me alone; **soyez tranquille** don't worry
tranquillement [trɑ̃kilmɑ̃] *adv* quietly, tranquilly
tranquilli•sant [trɑ̃kilizɑ̃] **-sante** [zɑ̃t] *adj* tranquilizing ‖ *m* tranquilizer
tranquilliser [trɑ̃kilize] *tr* to tranquilize; to reassure ‖ *ref* to calm down
tranquillité [trɑ̃kilite] *f* tranquillity
transaction [trɑ̃zaksjɔ̃] *f* transaction; compromise
transat [trɑ̃zat] *m* (coll) transatlantic liner; (coll) deck chair ‖ **la Transat** (coll) the French Line
transatlantique [trɑ̃zatlɑ̃tik] *adj* transatlantic ‖ *m* transatlantic liner; deck chair
transbordement [trɑ̃sbɔrdəmɑ̃] *m* transshipment, transfer

transborder [trɑ̃sbɔrde] *tr* to transship, transfer
transbordeur [trɑ̃sbɔrdœr] *m* transporter bridge
transcender [trɑ̃sɑ̃de] *tr* & *ref* to transcend
transcription [trɑ̃skripsjɔ̃] *f* transcription
transcrire [trɑ̃skrir] §25 *tr* to transcribe; **transcrire en clair** to decode
transe [trɑ̃s] *f* apprehension, anxiety; trance; **être dans des transes** to be quaking in one's boots
transept [trɑ̃sɛpt] *m* transept
transférer [trɑ̃sfere] §10 *tr* to transfer; convey
transfert [trɑ̃sfɛr] *m* transfer, transference
transfo [trɑ̃sfo] *m* (coll) transformer
transforma•teur [trɑ̃sfɔrmatœr] **-trice** [tris] *adj* (elec) transforming ‖ *m* (elec) transformer; **transformateur abaisseur (de tension)** step-down transformer; **transformateur de sonnerie** doorbell transformer; **transformateur élévateur (de tension)** step-up transformer
transformer [trɑ̃sfɔrme] *tr* & *ref* to transform; **transformer en une arme** to weaponize
transfuge [trɑ̃sfyʒ] *m* turncoat
transfuser [trɑ̃sfyze] *tr* to transfuse; instill
transfusion [trɑ̃sfyzjɔ̃] *f* transfusion
transgresser [trɑ̃sgrese] *tr* to transgress
transgression [trɑ̃sgrɛsjɔ̃] *f* transgression
transhumer [trɑ̃zyme] *tr* & *intr* to move from winter to summer pasture
tran•si -sie [trɑ̃zi], [trɑ̃si] *adj* chilled to the bone; numb, transfixed (*with fright*)
transiger [trɑ̃ziʒe] §38 *intr* to compromise
transistor [trɑ̃zistɔr] *m* transistor; transistor radio
transit [trɑ̃zit] *m* transit
transi•tif [trɑ̃zitif] **-tive** [tiv] *adj* transitive
transition [trɑ̃zisjɔ̃] *f* transition
transitoire [trɑ̃zitwar] *adj* transitory; transitional
translation [trɑ̃slɑsjɔ̃] *f* transfer, translation
translitérer [trɑ̃slitere] §10 *tr* to transliterate
translucide [trɑ̃slysid] *adj* translucent
transmetteur [trɑ̃smɛtœr] *adj masc* transmitting ‖ *m* (telg, telp) transmitter; **transmetteur d'ordres** (naut) engine-room telegraph
transmettre [trɑ̃smɛtr] §42 *tr* to transmit; transfer; (sports) to pass
transmission [trɑ̃smisjɔ̃] *f* transmission; broadcast; **transmission de données** (comp) data transmission; **transmission de pensée** thought transference; **transmission d'information du satellite à la tierre** downlink; **transmission en différé** recorded broadcast; **transmission en direct** live broadcast; **transmissions** (mil) signal corps
transmuer [trɑ̃smɥe] *tr* to transmute
transmuter [trɑ̃smyte] *tr* to transmute
transparaître [trɑ̃sparɛtr] §12 *intr* to show through
transparence [trɑ̃sparɑ̃s] *f* transparency; (mov) back projection
transpa•rent [trɑ̃sparɑ̃] **-rente** [rɑ̃t] *adj* transparent ‖ *m* transparent screen; transparency
transpercer [trɑ̃spɛrse] §51 *tr* to transfix

transpiration [trɑ̃spirɑsjɔ̃] *f* perspiration
transpirer [trɑ̃spire] *tr* to sweat ‖ *intr* to sweat, perspire; leak out (*said of news*)
transplanter [trɑ̃splɑ̃te] *tr* to transplant
transport [trɑ̃spɔr] *m* transport; transportation; (nav) troop carrier; **transport au cerveau** cerebral hemorrhage; **transport de troupes** (aut) troop carrier; **transport en commun** public transportation
transpor•té -tée [trɑ̃spɔrte] *adj* enraptured, carried away
transporter [trɑ̃spɔrte] *tr* to transport
transpor•teur [trɑ̃spɔrtœr] **-teuse** [tøz] *adj* transporting, hauling, carrying ‖ *m* transporter; **transporteur d'appoint** (aer) commuter airline
transposer [trɑ̃spoze] *tr* to transpose
transver•sal -sale [trɑ̃svɛrsal] *adj* (*pl* **-saux** [so]) transversal; cross (*street*)
trapèze [trapɛz] *m* trapeze; trapezoid
trappe [trap] *f* trap door; pitfall, trap; Trappist monastery; **Trappe** Trappist order
trappeur [trapœr] *m* trapper
tra•pu -pue [trapy] *adj* stocky, squat
traque [trak] *f* driving of game
traquenard [traknar] *m* trap, booby trap, pitfall
traquer [trake] *tr* to hem in, bring to bay
trauma [troma] *m* (psychol) trauma
traumatique [tromatik] *adj* traumatic
traumatisme [tromatism] *m* trauma
tra•vail [travaj] *m* (*pl* **-vaux** [vo]) work; workmanship; **en travail** in labor; **Travail** Labor; **travail à la pièce, travail à la tâche** piecework; **travail d'équipe** teamwork; **travail de Romain** herculean task; **travail du forçat** (fig) slave labor; **travail en réseau** networking; **travail sur le terrain** fieldwork; **travaux de ville** (printing) job work, job printing; **travaux forcés** hard labor; **travaux ménagers** housework ‖ *m* (*pl* **-vails**) stocks (*for horses*)
travail•lé -lée [travaje] *adj* finely wrought, elaborate; labored
travailler [travaje] §96 *tr* to work; worry ‖ *intr* to work; warp (*said of wood*); **travailler à son compte, travailler pour son compte, travailler à la pige** to freelance; **travailler d'arrache-pied** (coll) to work like a beaver
travail•leur [travajœr] **-leuse** [jøz] *adj* hard-working ‖ *mf* worker, toiler; **travailleur en construction** construction worker
travailliste [travajist] *adj* & *mf* Labourite (Brit)
travaillomane [travajɔman] *mf* (coll) workaholic
travée [trave] *f* span (*of bridge*); row of seats; (archit) bay
traveling [travliŋ] *m* (mov, telv) dolly (*for camera*)
travers [travɛr] *m* breadth; fault, failing; **à travers** across, through; **de travers** awry; **en travers de** across; **par le travers de** abreast of
traverse [travɛrs] *f* crossbeam; cross street; setback; rung (*of ladder*); (rr) tie; **de traverse**

cross (*e.g., street*); **mettre à la traverse de** to oppose

traversée [travɛrse] *f* crossing; **traversée d'une frontière** border crossing

traverser [travɛrse] *tr* to cross; cut across

traver•sier [travɛrsje] **-sière** [sjɛr] *adj* cross, crossing

traversin [travɛrsɛ̃] *m* bolster (*of bed*)

traves•ti -tie [travɛsti] *adj* disguised; costume (*ball*) ‖ *m* fancy costume, disguise; transvestite; female impersonator

travestir [travɛstir] *tr* to travesty; disguise

travestissement [travɛstismɑ̃] *m* travesty; disguise

trébucher [trebyʃe] *intr* to stumble

tréfiler [trefile] *tr* to wiredraw

trèfle [trɛfl] *m* clover; trefoil; cloverleaf (*intersection*); (cards) club; (cards) clubs

tréfonds [trefɔ̃] *m* secret depths

treillage [trɛjaʒ] *m* trellis

treillager [trɛjaʒe] **§38** *tr* to trellis

treille [trɛj] *f* grape arbor

treillis [trɛji] *m* latticework; iron grating; denim; **treillis métallique** wire netting

treilliser [trɛjise] *tr* to trellis

treize [trɛz] **§94** *adj & pron* thirteen; the Thirteenth, e.g., **Jean treize** John the Thirteenth ‖ *m* thirteen; thirteenth (*in dates*); **treize à la douzaine** baker's dozen

treizième [trɛzjɛm] **§94** *adj, pron* (*masc, fem*), & *m* thirteenth

tréma [trema] *m* dieresis

tremble [trɑ̃bl] *m* aspen (*tree*)

tremblement [trɑ̃bləmɑ̃] *m* trembling; **tremblement de terre** earthquake

trembler [trɑ̃ble] **§96, §97** *intr* to tremble

trembleur [trɑ̃blœr] *m* vibrator, buzzer; (rel) Shaker; (rel) Quaker

trembloter [trɑ̃blɔte] *intr* to quiver; quaver

trémie [tremi] *f* hopper

trémolo [tremɔlo] *m* tremolo

trémoussement [tremusmɑ̃] *m* fluttering, flutter; jiggling, jiggle

trémousser [tremuse] *ref* to flutter; jiggle; (coll) to bustle

trempage [trɑ̃paʒ] *m* soaking

trempe [trɑ̃p] *f* temper; soaking; (slang) scolding

trempée [trɑ̃pe] *f* tempering

tremper [trɑ̃pe] *tr* to temper; dilute; dunk ‖ *intr* to soak; become involved (*in, e.g., a crime*)

trempette [trɑ̃pɛt] *f*—**faire la trempette, faire une trempette** to dunk; **faire trempette** to take a dip

tremplin [trɑ̃plɛ̃] *m* springboard, diving board; trampoline; ski jump; (fig) springboard

trentaine [trɑ̃tɛn] *f* age of thirty; **une trentaine de** about thirty

trente [trɑ̃t] **§94** *adj & pron* thirty; **sur son trente et un** (coll) all spruced up; **trente et un** thirty-one; **trente et unième** thirty-first ‖ *m* thirty; thirtieth (*in dates*); **trente et un**

thirty-one; thirty-first (*in dates*); **trente et unième** thirty-first

trente-deux [trɑ̃tdø] **§94** *adj, pron, & m* thirty-two

trente-deuxième [trɑ̃tdøzjɛm] **§94** *adj, pron* (*masc, fem*), & *m* thirty-second

trente-six [trɑ̃tsi(s)] **§94** *adj, pron, & m* thirty-six; **tous les trente-six du mois** (coll) once in a blue moon

trentième [trɑ̃tjɛm] **§94** *adj, pron* (*masc, fem*), & *m* thirtieth

trépas [trepa] *m* (lit) death; **passer de vie à trépas** (lit) to pass away

trépasser [trepase] *intr* (lit) to die

trépied [trepje] *m* tripod

trépigner [trepiɲe] *intr* to stamp one's feet

très [trɛ] *adv* very; **le très honorable** the Right Honorable

trésor [trezɔr] *m* treasure; **Trésor** Treasury

trésorerie [trezɔrri] *f* treasury

tréso•rier [trezɔrje] **-rière** [rjɛr] *mf* treasurer

tressaillement [tresajmɑ̃] *m* start, quiver

tressaillir [tresajir] **§69** *intr* to give a start, quiver

tressauter [tresote] *intr* to start

tresse [trɛs] *f* tress

tresser [trɛse] *tr* to braid, plait; weave (*e.g., a basket*)

tré•teau [treto] *m* (*pl* **-teaux**) trestle; **sur les tréteaux** (theat) on the boards

treuil [trœj] *m* windlass; winch

trêve [trɛv] *f* truce; respite; **faire trève à q.ch.** to interrupt or suspend s.th.; **trève de. . .** that's enough. . .

tri [tri] *m* sorting

triage [trijaʒ] *m* sorting, selection; classification; (rr) shifting

triangle [trijɑ̃gl] *m* triangle

tribord [tribɔr] *m* starboard

tribu [triby] *f* tribe

tribu•nal [tribynal] *m* (*pl* **-naux** [no]) tribunal, court; **en plein tribunal** in open court; **tribunal de police** police court; **tribunal tutélaire de mineurs** juvenile court, family court; **tribunaux pour enfants** juvenile courts

tribune [tribyn] *f* rostrum, tribune; gallery; grandstand; **monter à la tribune** to take the floor; **tribune des journalistes** press box; **tribune d'orgue** organ loft; **tribune libre** open forum; **tribune téléphonique** phone-in show

tribut [triby] *m* tribute

tributaire [tribytɛr] *adj & m* tributary; **être tributaire de** to be dependent upon

tricher [triʃe] *tr & intr* to cheat

tricherie [triʃri] *f* cheating

tri•cheur [triʃœr] **-cheuse** [ʃøz] *mf* cheater; **tricheur professionnel** cardsharper

tricolore [trikɔlɔr] *adj & m* tricolor

tricorne [trikɔrn] *m* tricorn, three-cornered hat

tricot [triko] *m* knitting; knitted garment; **tricot de corps, tricot de peau** undershirt

tricotage [trikɔtaʒ] *m* knitting

tricoter [trikɔte] *tr & intr* to knit

trictrac [triktrak] *m* backgammon; backgammon board

trier [trije] *tr* to pick out, screen; **trier sur le volet** to hand-pick

trieur [trijœr] **trieuse** [trijøz] *mf* sorter ‖ *m & f* (mach) sorter

trigonométrie [trigɔnɔmetri] *f* trigonometry

trille [trij] *m* trill

triller [trije] *tr & intr* to trill

trillion [triljɔ̃] *m* quintillion (U.S.A.); trillion (Brit)

trilogie [trilɔʒi] *f* trilogy

trimbaler [trɛ̃bale] *tr* to cart around

trimer [trime] *intr* to slave

trimestre [trimɛstr] *m* quarter (*of a year*); quarter's salary; quarter's rent; (educ) term

tringle [trɛ̃gl] *f* rod; **tringle de rideau** curtain rod

trinité [trinite] *f* trinity

trinquer [trɛ̃ke] *intr* to clink glasses, toast; (slang) to drink; **trinquer avec** to hobnob with

trio [trijo] *m* trio

triom•phant [trijɔ̃fɑ̃] **-phante** [fɑ̃t] *adj* triumphant

triomphe [trijɔ̃f] *m* triumph; **faire triomphe à** to welcome in triumph

tripar•ti -tie [triparti] *adj* tripartite

tripartite [tripartit] *adj* tripartite

tripatouiller [tripatuje] *tr* (coll) to tamper with

tripette [tripɛt] *f*—**ça ne vaut pas tripette** it's not worth a wooden nickel

triple [tripl] *adj & m* triple

tri•plé -plée [triple] *mf* triplet

tripler [triple] *tr & intr* to triple

triplicata [triplikata] *m invar* triplicate

tripot [tripo] *m* gambling den; house of ill repute

tripoter [tripɔte] *tr* to finger, toy with ‖ *intr* to dabble, potter around; rummage

trique [trik] *f* (coll) cudgel

triste [trist] *adj* sad

tristesse [tristɛs] *f* sadness, sorrow

triturer [trityre] *tr* to pulverize, grind ‖ *ref*—**se triturer la cervelle** to rack one's brain

tri•vial -viale [trivjal] *adj* (*pl* **-viaux** [vjo]) trivial; vulgar, coarse

trivialité [trivjalite] *f* triviality; vulgarity, coarseness

tr/mn *abbr* (**tours par minute**) r.p.m.

troc [trɔk] *m* barter; swap; **troc pour troc** even up

troglodyte [trɔglɔdit] *m* cave dweller; (orn) wren

trognon [trɔɲɔ̃] *m* core; (slang) darling, pet

Troie [trwa] *f* Troy

trois [trwa] §94 *adj & pron* three; the Third, e.g., **Jean trois** John the Third; **trois heures** three o'clock ‖ *m* three; third (*in dates*)

troisième [trwazjɛm] §94 *adj, pron* (*masc, fem*), *& m* third

trolley [trɔlɛ] *m* trolley

trolleybus [trɔlɛbys] *m* trackless trolley

trombe [trɔb] *f* waterspout; **entrer en trombe** to dash in; **trombe d'eau** deluge

trombone [trɔ̃bɔn] *m* trombone; paper clip

trompe [trɔ̃p] *f* horn; trunk (*of elephant*); beak (*of insect*); **trompe d'Eustache** Eustachian tube

trompe-la-mort [trɔ̃plamɔr] *mf invar* daredevil

trompe-l'œil [trɔ̃plœj] *m invar* dummy effect; (coll) bluff, fake; **en trompe-l'œil** in perspective

tromper [trɔ̃pe] *tr* to deceive, cheat ‖ *ref* to be wrong; **se tromper de** to be mistaken about

tromperie [trɔ̃pri] *f* deceit; fraud; illusion

trompeter [trɔ̃pte] §34 *tr & intr* to trumpet

trompette [trɔ̃pɛt] *m* trumpeter ‖ *f* trumpet; **en trompette** turned up

trom•peur [trɔ̃pœr] **-peuse** [pøz] *adj* false, lying ‖ *mf* deceiver

tronc [trɔ̃] *m* trunk; (slang) head; **tronc des pauvres** poor box

tronche [trɔ̃ʃ] *f* (slang) noodle

tronçon [trɔ̃sɔ̃] *m* stump; section (*e.g., of track*)

tronçonneuse [trɔ̃sɔnøz] *f* chain saw

trône [tron] *m* throne

trôner [trone] *intr* to sit in state ‖ *ref*—**se trôner sur** to lord it over

tronquer [trɔ̃ke] *tr* to truncate, cut off; mutilate

trop [tro] *m* excess; too much; **de trop** too much; to excess; in the way, e.g., **il est de trop ici** he is in the way here; **par trop** altogether, excessively; **trop de ...** too much ...; too many ... ‖ *adv* too; too much; **trop lourd** overweight

trophée [trɔfe] *m* trophy

tropi•cal -cale [trɔpikal] *adj* (*pl* **-caux** [ko]) tropical

troposphère [trɔpɔsfɛr] *f* troposphere

trop-plein [trɔplɛ̃] *m* (*pl* **-pleins**) overflow

troquer [trɔke] *tr* to barter; **troquer contre** to swap for

trot [tro] *m* trot; **au trot** at a trot; (coll) on the double, quickly

trotte [trɔt] *f* (coll) quite a distance to walk

trotter [trɔte] *intr* to trot

trot•teur [trɔtœr] **-teuse** [tøz] *mf* (turf) trotter ‖ *f* second hand; **trotteuse centrale** sweep-second

trottin [trɔtɛ̃] *m* errand girl

trottinette [trɔtinɛt] *f* scooter

trottoir [trɔtwar] *m* sidewalk; **faire le trottoir** to walk the streets (*said of prostitute*); **trottoir roulant** moving walkway, moving sidewalk

trou [tru] *m* hole; pothole; eye (*of needle*); gap; jerkwater town; **boire comme un trou** to drink like a fish; **faire son trou** to feather one's nest; **faire un trou à la lune** to fly the coop; **trou d'air** air pocket; **trou de balle, trou du cul** (vulg) asshole; (fig) asshole; **trou de clef** keyhole (*of clock*); **trou de la serrure** keyhole; **trou de mémoire** amnesia, blackout; **trou de souris** mousehole; **trou d'homme** manhole; **trou d'obus** shell hole;

trou d'ozone ozone hole; **trou du souffleur** prompter's box; **trou individuel** (mil) foxhole; **trou noir** (astr) black hole

trouble [trubl] *adj* muddy, cloudy, turbid (*liquid*); murky (*sky*); misty (*glass*); blurred (*image; sight*); dim (*light*); vague, disquieting ‖ *m* disquiet; unrest; trouble (*illness*); **troubles dûs au décalage horaire** jet lag

trouble-fête [trubləfɛt] *mf invar* wet blanket, kill-joy

troubler [truble] *tr* to upset, trouble; make muddy; disturb; make cloudy; blur ‖ *ref* to become muddy or cloudy; lose one's composure

trouée [true] *f* gap, breach; (mil) breakthrough

trouille [truj] *f*—**avoir la trouille** (slang) to get cold feet

troupe [trup] *f* troop; band, party; (theat) troupe

trou‧peau [trupo] *m* (*pl* **-peaux**) flock; herd; **attention aux troupeaux** (*public sign*) cattle crossing

troupier [trupje] *m* (coll) soldier; **jurer comme un troupier** to swear like a trooper

trousse [trus] *f* case, kit; **avoir qn à ses trousses** to have s.o. at one's heels; **trousse de première urgence** first-aid kit

trous‧seau [truso] *m* (*pl* **-seaux**) trousseau; outfit; bunch (*of keys*)

troussequin [truskɛ̃] *m* cantle

trousser [truse] *tr* to turn up; tuck up; polish off; (culin) to truss ‖ *ref* to lift one's skirts

trouvaille [truvɑj] *f* find

trouver [truve] §96 *tr* to find ‖ §95 *ref* to be found; find oneself; to be, e.g., **où se trouve-t-il?** where is he?; **il se trouve que . . .** it happens that . . .; **se trouver mal** to feel ill

troyen [trwajɛ̃] **troyenne** [trwajɛn] *adj* Trojan ‖ (*cap*) *mf* Trojan

truand [tryɑ̃] **truande** [tryɑ̃d] *adj & m* good-for-nothing

truc [tryk] *m* gadget, device; (coll) trick, gimmick; (coll) thing; (coll) what's-his-name; (coll) condom

truchement [tryʃmɑ̃] *m* spokesman; interpreter; **par le truchement de** thanks to, through

trucu‧lent [trykylɑ̃] **-lente** [lɑ̃t] *adj* truculent

truelle [tryɛl] *f* trowel

truffe [tryf] *f* truffle

truie [trɥi] *f* sow

truisme [tryism] *m* truism

truite [trɥit] *f* trout; **truite arc-en-ciel** rainbow trout; **truite saumonée** salmon trout

tru‧meau [trymo] *m* (*pl* **-meaux**) trumeau (*mirror with painting above in same frame*)

truquage [trykaʒ] *m* faking

truquer [tryke] *tr* to fake; cook (*the accounts*); stack (*the deck*); load (*the dice*); fix (*the outcome of a fight*) ‖ *intr* to resort to fakery

trust [trœst] *m* trust, holding company

T.S.F. [teɛsɛf] *f* (letterword) (**télégraphie sans fil**) wireless; radio

t.s.v.p. *abbr* (**tournez s'il vous plaît**) over (*please turn the page*)

tu [ty] §87 you; **être à tu et à toi avec** to hobnob with

T.U. [tey] *m* (letterword) (**temps universel**) universal time, Greenwich Mean Time

tube [tyb] *m* tube; pipe; (anat) duct; (slang) hit; **tube digestif** alimentary canal

tubercule [tybɛrkyl] *m* tubercle; tuber

tuberculose [tybɛrkyloz] *f* tuberculosis

tue-mouches [tymuʃ] *m invar* flypaper

tuer [tɥe] *tr* to kill ‖ §96 *ref* to be killed; kill oneself

tuerie [tyri] *f* slaughter

tue-tête [tytɛt]—**à tue-tête** at the top of one's voice

tuile [tɥil] *f* tile; (coll) nasty blow

tuilerie [tɥilri] *f* tileworks

tulipe [tylip] *f* tulip

tumeur [tymœr] *f* tumor

tumulte [tymylt] *m* tumult, hubbub

tungstène [tœ̃kstɛn] *m* tungsten

tunique [tynik] *f* tunic; membrane; (bot) coat, envelope, skin

tunnel [tynɛl] *m* tunnel; **passer sous un tunnel** to go through a tunnel; **tunnel aérodynamique** wind tunnel

turban [tyrbɑ̃] *m* turban

turbine [tyrbin] *f* turbine

turbopropulseur [tyrbɔproɔpylsœr] *m* turboprop

turboréacteur [tyrbɔreaktœr] *m* turbojet

turbu‧lent [tyrbylɑ̃] **-lente** [lɑ̃t] *adj* turbulent

turc turque [tyrk] *adj* Turkish ‖ *m* Turkish (*language*) ‖ (*cap*) *mf* Turk (*person*)

turf [tyrf] *m*—**le turf** the turf, the track

turfiste [tyrfist] *m* turfman, racegoer

turlututu [tyrlytyty] *interj* fiddlesticks!, nonsense!

Turquie [tyrki] *f* Turkey; **la Turquie** Turkey

turquoise [tyrkwaz] *m* turquoise (*color*) ‖ *f* turquoise (*stone*)

tutelle [tytɛl] *f* guardianship, tutelage; trusteeship

tu‧teur [tytœr] **-trice** [tris] *mf* guardian ‖ *m* (hort) stake, prop

tutoyer [tytwaje] §47 *tr* to address familiarly; use familiar grammatical forms (**toi, tu,** etc.) in speaking to an intimate, an inferior, or (if a Protestant) to God (*to "thou"*) ‖ *ref* to be on a first-name basis

tuyau [tɥijo], [tyjo] *m* (*pl* **tuyaux**) pipe, tube; fluting; (coll) tip; **tuyau d'arrosage** garden hose; **tuyau d'échappement** exhaust; **tuyau d'incendie** fire hose

tuyauter [tɥijote], [tyjote] *tr* to flute; (coll) to tip off ‖ *intr* (coll) to crib

tuyauterie [tɥijotri] *f* pipe mill; piping; (aut) manifold; **tuyauterie d'admission** intake manifold; **tuyauterie d'échappement** exhaust manifold

TVA *or* **T.V.A.** *f* (letterword) (**taxe à la valeur ajoutée**) VAT (value-added tax)

tympan [tɛ̃pɑ̃] *m* eardrum; (archit, mus) tympanum

type [tip] *m* type; (coll) fellow, character

typesse [tipɛs] *f* (slang) dame, broad, gal
typhoïde [tifɔid] *adj & f* typhoid
typhon [tifɔ̃] *m* typhoon
typique [tipik] *adj* typical; South American (*music*)
typographie [tipɔgrafi] *f* typography

typographique [tipɔgrafik] *adj* typographic(al)
typon [tipɔ̃] *m* offset film
tyran [tirɑ̃] *m* tyrant; (orn) kingbird
tyrannie [tirani] *f* tyranny
tyrannique [tiranik] *adj* tyrannic(al)

U

U, u [y], *[y] *m invar* twenty-first letter of the French alphabet
Ukraine [ykrɛn] *f* Ukraine
ukrai·nien [ykrɛnjɛ̃] **-nienne** [njɛn] *adj* Ukrainian ‖ *m* Ukrainian (*language*) ‖ (*cap*) *mf* Ukrainian (*person*)
ulcère [ylsɛr] *m* ulcer, sore
ulcérer [ylsere] §10 *tr* to ulcerate; embitter ‖ *ref* to ulcerate; fester
ulté·rieur -rieure [ylterjœr] *adj* ulterior; subsequent
ultimatum [yltimatɔm] *m* ultimatum
ultime [yltim] *adj* ultimate, final
ultra [yltra] *m* (pol) extremist
ultra-court [yltrakur] **-courte** [kurt] *adj* (electron) ultrashort
ultrason [yltrasɔ̃] *m* (electron) ultrasound
ultravio·let [yltravjɔlɛ] **-lette** [lɛt] *adj & m* ultraviolet
ululer [ylyle] *intr* to hoot
un [œ̃] **une** [yn] §77 *adj & pron* one; **l'un à l'autre** to each other, to one another; **l'un et l'autre** both; **l'un l'autre** each other, one another; **ni l'un ni l'autre** neither, neither one; **un à un** one by one; **une heure** one o'clock ‖ *art indef* a ‖ *m* one ‖ *f*—**il était moins une** it was a narrow escape; **la une** the front page
unanime [ynanim] *adj* unanimous
unanimité [ynanimite] *f* unanimity
Unesco [ynɛsko] *f* (acronym) (**Organisation des Nations Unies pour l'Éducation, la Science et la Culture**)—**l'Unesco** UNESCO
u·ni -nie [yni] *adj* united; smooth, level; uneventful; plain; solid (*color*); together (*said, e.g., of the hands of a clock*) ‖ *m* plain cloth
unicorne [ynikɔrn] *m* unicorn
unième [ynjɛm] *adj* first, e.g., **vingt et unième** twenty-first
unification [ynifikɑsjɔ̃] *f* unification
unifier [ynifje] *tr* to unify ‖ *ref* to consolidate, merge; become unified
uniforme [ynifɔrm] *adj & m* uniform
uniformément [ynifɔrmemɑ̃] *adv* uniformly; regularly; steadily
uniformiser [ynifɔrmize] *tr* to make uniform
uniformité [ynifɔrmite] *f* uniformity

unijambiste [yniʒɑ̃bist] *adj* one-legged ‖ *mf* one-legged person
unilaté·ral -rale [ynilateral] *adj* (*pl* **-raux** [ro]) unilateral
union [ynjɔ̃] *f* union; **union libre** common-law marriage
Union européenne [ynjɔ̃ørɔpeɛn] *f* European Union
unique [ynik] *adj* only, single; unique; **enfant unique** only child
unir [ynir] *tr & ref* to unite
unisson [ynisɔ̃] *m* unison
unitaire [ynitɛr] *adj* unit
unité [ynite] *f* unity; unit; battleship; (coll) one million old francs; **unité centrale** (comp) disk drive; **unités de valeur** (educ) hours of credit
univers [ynivɛr] *m* universe
univer·sel -selle [ynivɛrsɛl] *adj & m* universal
universitaire [ynivɛrsitɛr] *adj* university; academic ‖ *mf* academic
université [ynivɛrsite] *f* university
Untel [œ̃tɛl] *mf* so-and-so, e.g., **Monsieur/ Madame Untel** Mr. and Mrs. So-and-so
uranium [yranjɔm] *m* uranium
Uranus [yranus] *m* Uranus
ur·bain [yrbɛ̃] **-baine** [bɛn] *adj* urban; urbane
urbaniser [yrbanize] *tr* to urbanize
urbanisme [yrbanism] *m* city planning
urbaniste [yrbanist] *adj* zoning (*ordinance*) ‖ *mf* city planner
urbanité [yrbanite] *f* urbanity
urètre [yrɛtr] *m* urethra
urgence [yrʒɑ̃s] *f* urgency; emergency; emergency case; **d'urgence** emergency (*e.g., hospital ward*); right away, without delay
ur·gent [yrʒɑ̃] **-gente** [ʒɑ̃t] *adj* urgent; emergency (*case*); (formula on letter or envelope) rush ‖ *m* urgent matter
urinaire [yrinɛr] *adj* urinary
uri·nal [yrinal] *m* (*pl* **-naux** [no]) urinal (*for use in bed*)
urine [yrin] *f* urine
uriner [yrine] *tr & intr* to urinate
urinoir [yrinwar] *m* urinal (*place*)
urne [yrn] *f* urn; ballot box; **aller aux urnes** to go to the polls
urologie [yrɔlɔʒi] *f* urology
U.R.S.S. [yɛrɛsɛs] *f* (letterword) (**Union des**

Républiques Socialistes Soviétiques) U.S.S.R.

Ursse [yrs] *f* (acronym) (**Union des Républiques Socialistes Soviétiques**) U.S.S.R.

urticaire [yrtikɛr] *f* hives

urubu [yryby] *m* turkey vulture

us [ys] *mpl*—**les us et (les) coutumes** the manners and customs

U.S. [yɛs] *adj* (letterword) (**United States**) U.S., e.g., **l'aviation U.S.** U.S. aviation

U.S.A. [yɛsa] *mpl* (letterword) (**United States of America**) U.S.A.

usage [yzaʒ] *m* usage; custom; use; **faire de l'usage** to wear well; **hors d'usage** outmoded; (gram) obsolete; **manquer d'usage** to lack good breeding; **usage du monde** good breeding, savoir-vivre

usa•gé -gée [yzaʒe] *adj* secondhand; worn-out, used

usa•ger [yzaʒe] **-gère** [ʒɛr] *mf* user

usant [yzɑ̃] **usante** [yzɑ̃t] *adj* exhausting, wearing

u•sé -sée [yze] *adj* worn-out; trite, commonplace

user [yze] *tr* to wear out; wear away; ruin (*e.g., health*) ‖ *intr*—**en user bien avec** to treat well; **user de** to use ‖ *ref* to wear out

usine [yzin] *f* factory, mill, plant; **usine à gaz** gasworks

usiner [yzine] *tr* to machine, tool

usi•nier [yzinje] **-nière** [njɛr] *adj* manufacturing; factory (*town*) ‖ *m* manufacturer

usi•té -tée [yzite] *adj* used, in use; **peu usité** out of use, rare

ustensile [ystɑ̃sil] *m* utensil, implement

u•suel -suelle [yzɥɛl] *adj* usual

usure [yzyr] *f* usury; wear and tear

usurper [yzyrpe] *tr* to usurp

uté•rin [yterɛ̃] **-rine** [rin] *adj* uterine; on the side of the mother

utérus [yterys] *m* uterus, womb

utile [ytil] §92 *adj* useful, helpful; **puis-je vous être utile?** can I be of help?

utilisable [ytilazabl] *adj* usable

utilisa•teur [ytilizatœr] **-trice** [tris] *mf* user

utilitaire [ytilitɛr] *adj* utilitarian; utility (*vehicle, goods, etc.*)

utilité [ytilite] *f* utility, usefulness, use; (theat) support; (theat) supporting rôle; **jouer les utilités** (fig) to play second fiddle; **utilités** (theat) small parts

utopique [ytɔpik] *adj* utopian

utopiste [ytɔpist] *mf* utopian

V

V, v [ve] *m invar* twenty-second letter of the French alphabet

v. *abbr* (**voir**) see; (**volume**) vol.

va [va] *v* see **aller**

vacance [vakɑ̃s] *f* vacancy, opening; **vacances** vacation

vacancier [vakɑ̃sje] *m* vacationist

va•cant [vakɑ̃] **-cante** [kɑ̃t] *adj* vacant

vacarme [vakarm] *m* din, racket

vacation [vakɑsjɔ̃] *f* investigation; **vacations** fee; recess

vaccin [vaksɛ̃] *m* vaccine

vaccination [vaksinɑsjɔ̃] *f* vaccination

vaccine [vaksin] *f* cowpox

vacciner [vaksine] *tr* to vaccinate

vache [vaʃ] *adj* embarrassing (*question*); cantankerous (*person*) ‖ *f* cow; cowhide; (*woman*) (slang) bitch; (*man*) (slang) swine, rat; (*policeman*) (slang) flatfoot, bull; **en vache** leather (*e.g., suitcase*); **manger de la vache enragée** (coll) not to have a red cent to one's name; **oh, la vache!** damn it!; **parler français comme une vache espagnole** (coll) to murder the French language; **vache à eau** canvas bucket (*for camping*); **vache à lait** milch cow; (coll) gull, sucker

vachement [vaʃmɑ̃] *adv* (slang) tremendously

va•cher [vaʃe] **-chère** [ʃɛr] *mf* cowherd

vacherie [vaʃri] *f* cowshed; dairy farm; (coll) dirty trick

vachette [vaʃɛt] *f* young calf; calf (*leather*)

vaciller [vasije] *intr* to vacillate, waver; flicker; totter

vacuité [vakɥite] *f* vacuity, emptiness

vacuum [vakɥɔm] *m* vacuum

vade-mecum [vademekɔm] *m invar* handbook, vade mecum

vadrouille [vadruj] *f* (naut) mop, swab; plunger (*plumber's*); (slang) bender, spree

vadrouiller [vadruje] *intr* (slang) to ramble around, gad about

vadrouil•leur [vadrujœr] **-leuse** [jøz] *mf* (slang) rounder

va-et-vient [vaevjɛ̃] *m invar* backward-and-forward motion; hurrying to and fro; comings and goings; ferryboat; (elec) two-way switch

vaga•bond [vagabɔ̃] **-bonde** [bɔ̃d] *adj* vagabond ‖ *mf* vagabond, tramp

vagabondage [vagabɔ̃daʒ] *m* vagrancy; **vagabondage interdit** (*public sign*) no loitering, no begging

vagabonder [vagabɔ̃de] *intr* to wander about, roam, tramp

vagin [vaʒɛ̃] *m* vagina

vagi•nal -nale [vaʒinal] (*pl* **-naux** [no]) *adj* vaginal

vagir [vaʒir] *intr* to cry, wail

vague [vag] *adj* vague; vacant (*look; lot*); waste (*land*) ‖ *m* vagueness; (fig) space, thin air; **vague à l'âme** uneasy sadness ‖ *f* wave; **la nouvelle vague** the wave of the future; **vague de fond** ground swell

vaguemestre [vagmɛstr] *m* (mil, nav) mail clerk

vaguer [vage] *intr* to wander

vaillance [vajɑ̃s] *f* valor

vail·lant [vajɑ̃] **-lante** [jɑ̃t] *adj* valiant; up to scratch

vaille [vaj] *v* (**vailles, vaillent**) see **valoir**

vain [vɛ̃] **vaine** [vɛn] *adj* vein; **en vain** in vain

vaincre [vɛ̃kr] §70 *tr* to defeat, conquer; overcome (*fear, instinct, etc.*) ‖ *intr* to conquer ‖ *ref* to control oneself

vaincs [vɛ̃] *v* (**vainc**) see **vaincre**

vain·cu **-cue** [vɛ̃ky] *adj* defeated, beaten, conquered ‖ *mf* loser ‖ *v* see **vaincre**

vainquant [vɛ̃kɑ̃] *v* (**vainquez, vainquons**) see **vaincre**

vainqueur [vɛ̃kœr] *adj masc* victorious ‖ *m* victor, winner

vairon [vɛrɔ̃] *adj masc* whitish (*eye*); **vairons** of different colors (*said of eyes*) ‖ *m* (ichth) minnow

vais [ve] *v* see **aller**

vais·seau [vɛso] *m* (*pl* **-seaux**) vessel; nave (*of church*); **vaisseau amiral** flagship; **vaisseau sanguin** blood vessel; **vaisseau spatial** spaceship

vaisseau-école [vɛsoekɔl] *m* (*pl* **vaisseaux-écoles**) (nav) training ship

vaisselier [vɛsəlje] *m* china closet

vaisselle [vɛsɛl] *f* dishes; **faire la vaisselle** to wash the dishes; **vaisselle plate** plate (*of gold or silver*)

val [val] *m* (*pl* **vaux** [vo] or **vals**) (obs) valley; **à val** going down the valley; **à val de** (obs) down from

valable [valabl] *adj* valid; worthwhile (*e.g., experience*)

valence [valɑ̃s] *f* (chem) valence

valen·tin [valɑ̃tɛ̃] **-tine** [tin] *mf* valentine (*sweetheart*)

valet [valɛ] *m* valet; holdfast, clamp; (cards) jack; **valet de chambre** valet; **valet de ferme** hired man; **valet de pied** footman

valeur [valœr] *f* value, worth, merit; valor; (*person, thing, or quality worth having*) asset; (com) security, stock; **de valeur** able; valuable; (Canad) too bad, unfortunate; **envoyer en valeur déclarée** to insure (*a package*); **mettre en valeur** to develop (*e.g., a region*); set off, enhance; **valeur d'avenir** growth stock; **valeur de tout repos, valeur de père de famille, valeur-vedette** blue chip; **valeurs négociées à terme** futures

valeu·reux [valœrø] **-reuse** [røz] *adj* valorous, brave

validation [validɑsjɔ̃] *f* validation

valide [valid] *adj* valid; fit, able-bodied

valider [valide] *tr* to validate

validité [validite] *f* validity

valise [valiz] *f* suitcase; **faire ses valises** to pack, pack one's bags; **valise diplomatique** diplomatic pouch

vallée [vale] *f* valley

vallon [valɔ̃] *m* vale, dell

valoir [valwar] §71, §95 *tr* to equal; **un service en vaut un autre** one good turn deserves another; **valoir q.ch. à qn** to get or bring s.o. s.th., e.g., **cela lui a valu une amélioration** that got him a raise; e.g., **la condamnation lui a valu cinq ans de prison** the verdict brought him five years in prison ‖ *intr* to be worth; **autant vaut y renoncer** might as well give up; **cela ne vaut rien** it's worth nothing; **faire valoir** to set off to advantage; use to advantage; develop (*one's land*); invest (*funds, capital*); put forward (*one's reasons*); **faire valoir que . . .** to argue that . . .; **vaille que vaille** somehow or other ‖ *impers*—**il vaut mieux** it would be better to, e.g., **il vaut mieux attendre** it would be better to wait; **mieux vaut tard que jamais** better late than never ‖ *ref*—**les deux se valent** one is as good as the other

valse [vals] *f* waltz

valser [valse] *tr & intr* to waltz

va·lu **-lue** [valy] *v* see **valoir**

valve [valv] *f* (aut, bot, zool) valve; (elec) vacuum tube

valvule [valvyl] *f* valve

vamp [vɑ̃p] *f* vamp

vamper [vɑ̃pe] *tr* (coll) to vamp

vampire [vɑ̃pir] *m* vampire

van [vɑ̃] *m* van (*for moving horses*)

vandale [vɑ̃dal] *adj* vandal; Vandal ‖ *m* vandal ‖ (*cap*) *mf* Vandal

vandalisme [vɑ̃dalism] *m* vandalism

vanille [vanij] *f* vanilla

vani·teux [vanitø] **-teuse** [tøz] *adj* vain, conceited

vanne [van] *f* sluice gate, floodgate; butterfly valve; (slang) gibe

van·neau [vano] *m* (*pl* **-neaux**) (orn) lapwing

vanner [vane] *tr* to winnow; tire out

vannerie [vanri] *f* basketry

vannier [vanje] *m* basket maker

van·tail [vɑ̃taj] *m* (*pl* **-taux** [to]) leaf (*of door, shutter, sluice gate, etc.*)

van·tard [vɑ̃tar] **-tarde** [tard] *adj* bragging, boastful ‖ *mf* braggart

vantardise [vɑ̃tardiz] *f* bragging, boasting

vanter [vɑ̃te] §97 *tr* to praise; boost, push (*a product on the market*) ‖ *ref* to brag, boast

va-nu-pieds [vanypje] *mf invar* (coll) tramp

vapeur [vapœr] *m* steamship ‖ *f* steam; vapor, mist; **à la vapeur** steamed (*e.g., potatoes*); under steam; (coll) at full speed; **à vapeur** steam (*e.g., engine*); **vapeur d'eau** water vapor; **vapeurs** low spirits

vaporisateur [vaporizatœr] *m* atomizer, spray

vaporiser [vaporize] *tr & ref* to vaporize; spray

vaquer [vake] *intr* to take a recess; **vaquer à** to attend to ‖ *impers*—**il vaque** there is vacant

varappe [varap] f cliff; rock climbing

varech [varɛk] m wrack, seaweed

vareuse [varøz] f (mil) blouse; (nav) peacoat

variable [varjabl] adj & f variable

va·riant [varjɑ̃] **-riante** [rjɑ̃t] adj & f variant

variation [varjɑsjɔ̃] f variation

varice [varis] f varicose veins

varicelle [varisɛl] f chicken pox

va·rié -riée [varje] adj varied

varier [varje] tr & intr to vary

variété [varjete] f varity; **variétés** selections (*from literary works*); vaudeville

variole [varjɔl] f smallpox

vari·queux [varikø] **-queuse** [køz] adj varicose

Varsovie [varsɔvi] f Warsaw

vase [vɑs] m vase; vessel; chamber pot; **en vase clos** shut up; in an airtight chamber; **vase de nuit** chamber pot ‖ f mud, slime

vas [va] v see **aller**

vaseline [vazlin] f petroleum jelly, Vaseline

va·seux [vazø] **-seuse** [zøz] adj muddy, slimy; (coll) all in, tired; (coll) fuzzy, obscure

vasistas [vazistɑs] m transom

vasouiller [vazuje] tr (coll) to make a mess of ‖ intr (coll) to go badly

vasque [vask] f basin (*of fountain*)

vas·sal -sale [vasal] (*pl* **-saux** [so] **-sales**) adj & mf vassal

vaste [vast] adj vast

vastement [vastəmɑ̃] adv (coll) very

Vatican [vatikɑ̃] m Vatican

vaticane [vatikan] adj fem Vatican

va-tout [vatu] m—**jouer son va-tout** to stake one's all, play one's last card

vaudeville [vodvil] m vaudeville (*light theatrical piece interspersed with songs*); (obs) satirical song

vaudou [vodu] adj invar & m voodoo

vaudrai [vodre] v (**vaudras, vaudra, vaudrons,** etc.) see **valoir**

vau-l'eau [volo]—**à vau-l'eau** downstream; **s'en aller à vau-l'eau** (fig) to go to pot

vau·rien [vorjɛ̃] **-rienne** [rjɛn] mf good-for-nothing

vautour [votur] m vulture

vautrer [votre] ref to wallow

vaux [vo] v (**vaut**) see **valoir**

veau [vo] m (*pl* **veaux**) calf; veal; calfskin; (coll) lazybones, dope; **pleurer comme un veau** to cry like a baby; **veau marin** seal

vé·cu -cue [veky] adj true to life ‖ v see **vivre**

vedette [vədɛt] f patrol boat; scout; lead, star; **en vedette** in the limelight; **mettre en vedette** to headline, to highlight; **vedette de l'écran** movie star; **vedette du petit écran** television star

végé·tal -tale [veʒetal] (*pl* **-taux** [to]) adj vegetable, vegetal ‖ m vegetable

végéta·rien [veʒetarjɛ̃] **-rienne** [rjɛn] adj & mf vegetarian; **végétarien qui ne mange pas les produits laitiers** vegan

végétation [veʒetɑsjɔ̃] f vegetation; **végétations (adénoïdes)** adenoids

végéter [veʒete] §10 intr to vegetate

véhémence [veemɑ̃s] f vehemence

véhé·ment [veemɑ̃] **-mente** [mɑ̃t] adj vehement

véhicule [veikyl] m vehicle

veille [vej] f watch, vigil; wakefulness; **à la veille de** on the eve of; just before; on the verge or point of; **la veille de** the eve of; the day before; **la Veille de Noël** Christmas Eve; **la Veille du jour de l'An** New Year's Eve; **veilles** sleepless nights, late nights; night work

veillée [veje] f evening; social evening; **veillée funèbre, veillée du corps** wake

veiller [veje] tr to sit up with, watch over ‖ intr to sit up, stay up; keep watch; **veiller à** to look after, see to

veil·leur [vejœr] **-leuse** [jøz] mf watcher ‖ m watchman; **veilleur de nuit** night watchman ‖ f see **veilleuse**

veilleuse [vejøz] f night light; rushlight; pilot light; **mettre en veilleuse** to turn down low; to dim (*the headlights*); to slow down (*production in a factory*)

vei·nard [venar] **-narde** [nard] adj (coll) lucky ‖ mf (coll) lucky person

veine [vɛn] f vein; luck; **veine alors!** (coll) swell!

veiner [vene] tr to vein

vei·neux [venø] **-neuse** [nøz] adj veined; venous

vélaire [velɛr] adj & f velar

vêler [vele] intr to calve

vélin [velɛ̃] m vellum

velléitaire [veleitɛr] adj & mf erratic

velléité [veleite] f stray impulse; fancy; **velléité de sourire** slight smile

vélo [velo] m bike; **faire du vélo** to go bicycle riding

vélocité [velɔsite] f velocity; speed; agility

vélomoteur [velɔmɔtœr] m motorbike

velours [vəlur] m velvet; **velours côtelé** corduroy

velou·té -tée [vəlute] adj velvety ‖ m velvetiness

velouter [vəlute] tr to make velvety

ve·lu -lue [vəly] adj hairy

vélum [velɔm] m awning

velvet [vɛlvɛt] m velveteen

venaison [vənɛzɔ̃] f venison

ve·nant [vənɑ̃] **-nante** [nɑ̃t] adj coming; thriving ‖ mf comer; **à tout venant** to all comers

vendange [vɑ̃dɑ̃ʒ] f grape harvest; vintage

vendanger [vɑ̃dɑ̃ʒe] §38 tr to pick (*the grapes*) ‖ intr to harvest grapes

ven·deur [vɑ̃dœr] **-deuse** [døz] mf seller, vendor; salesclerk; **vendeur ambulant** peddler, street vendor, pitchman; **vendeur de choc** pitchman; **vendeuse de choc** pitchwoman ‖ m salesman ‖ f saleswoman, saleslady

vendre [vɑ̃dr] tr to sell; sell out, betray; **à vendre** for sale; **vendre à découvert** to sell short; **vendre au détail** to retail; **vendre aux enchères** to auction off; **vendre en gros** to wholesale ‖ ref to sell; sell oneself, sell out

vendredi [vɑ̃drədi] *m* Friday; **vendredi saint** Good Friday

ven•du -due [vɑ̃dy] *adj* sold; corrupt ‖ *mf* traitor

véné•neux [venenø] **-neuse** [nøz] *adj* poisonous

vénérable [venerabl] *adj* venerable

vénérer [venere] §10 *tr* to venerate

véné•rien [venerjɛ̃] **-rienne** [rjɛn] *adj* venereal ‖ *mf* person with venereal disease

vengeance [vɑ̃ʒɑ̃s] *f* vengeance, revenge

venger [vɑ̃ʒe] §38 *tr* to avenge ‖ *ref* to get revenge

ven•geur [vɑ̃ʒœr] **-geuse** [ʒøz] *adj* avenging ‖ *mf* avenger

veni•meux [vənimø] **-meuse** [møz] *adj* venomous

venin [vənɛ̃] *m* venom

venir [vənir] §72, §95, §96, §97 *intr* (*aux:* ETRE) to come; **à venir** forthcoming; **faire venir** to send for; **où voulez-vous en venir?** what are you getting at?; **venez avec** (coll) come along; **venir de** to have just, e.g., **il vient de partir** he has just left ‖ *impers*—**il me** (**nous,** etc.) **vient à l'esprit que** it occurs to me (to us, etc.) that

Venise [vəniz] *f* Venice

véni•tien [venisjɛ̃] **-tienne** [sjɛn] *adj* Venetian ‖ (*cap*) *mf* Venetian

vent [vɑ̃] *m* wind; **avoir le vent en poupe** to be in luck; **avoir vent de** to get wind of; **contre vents et marées** through thick and thin; **en plein vent** in the open air; **être dans le vent** to be up to date; **il fait du vent** it is windy; **les vents** (mus) the woodwinds; **vent arrière** tailwind; **vent coulis** draft; **vent debout** headwind; **vent d'est** east wind; **vent en poupe** (naut) tailwind

vente [vɑ̃t] *f* sale; felling (*of timber*); **en vente** on sale; **en vente libre** (pharm) on sale without a prescription; **jeunes ventes** new overgrowth; **vente à l'éventaire** sidewalk sale; **vente amiable** private sale; **vente à tempérament** installment selling; **vente à terme** sale on time; **vente au détail** retailing; **vente aux enchères** auction; **vente bric-à-brac** garage sale, yard sale; **vente en gros** wholesaling; **vente par correspondance** mail-order business

ventilateur [vɑ̃tilatœr] *m* ventilator; fan; electric fan

ventilation [vɑ̃tilasjɔ̃] *f* ventilation; **ventilation artificielle** artificial respiration

ventiler [vɑ̃tile] *tr* to ventilate; to value separately; (bk) to apportion

ventouse [vɑ̃tuz] *f* sucker; suction cup; suction grip; nozzle (*of vacuum cleaner*); vent; plunger (*for clogged drain*)

ventre [vɑ̃tr] *m* belly; stomach; womb; **à plat ventre** prostrate; **à ventre déboutonné** (coll) excessively; (coll) with all one's might; **avoir q.ch. dans le ventre** (coll) to have s.th. on the ball; **bas ventre** (fig) genitals; **ventre à terre** (coll) lickety-split

ventricule [vɑ̃trikyl] *m* ventricle

ventriloque [vɑ̃trilɔk] *mf* ventriloquist

ventriloquie [vɑ̃trilɔki] *f* ventriloquism

ventripo•tent [vɑ̃tripɔtɑ̃] **-tente** [tɑ̃t] *adj* (coll) potbellied

ven•tru -true [vɑ̃try] *adj* potbellied

ve•nu -nue [vəny] *adj*—**bien venu** successful; welcome ‖ *mf*—**le premier venu** the first comer; just anyone; **les nouveaux venus** the newcomers ‖ *f* coming, advent ‖ *v* see **venir**

Vénus [venys] *f* Venus

vénusté [venyste] *f* charm, grace

vêpres [vɛpr] *fpl* vespers

ver [vɛr] *m* worm; **tirer les vers du nez à** to worm secrets out of, to pump; **ver à soie** silkworm; **ver de terre** earthworm; **ver luisant** glowworm; **ver solitaire** tapeworm

véracité [verasite] *f* veracity

véranda [verɑ̃da] *f* veranda, sunporch

ver•bal -bale [vɛrbal] *adj* (*pl* **-baux** [bo]) verbal; (gram) verb

verbaliser [vɛrbalize] *intr* to write out a report or summons; **verbaliser contre qn** to give s.o. a ticket (*e.g., for speeding*)

verbe [vɛrb] *m* verb; **avoir le verbe haut** to talk loud; **Verbe** (eccl) Word

ver•beux [vɛrbø] **-beuse** [bøz] *adj* verbose, wordy

verbiage [vɛrbjaʒ] *m* verbiage

verdâtre [vɛrdɑtr] *adj* greenish

verdeur [vɛrdœr] *f* greenness; vigor, spryness; crudeness (*of speech*)

verdict [vɛrdik], [vɛrdikt] *m* verdict; **verdict instantané** (sports) sudden death

verdir [vɛrdir] *tr & intr* to turn green

verdoyer [vɛrdwaje] §47 *intr* to become green

verdure [vɛrdyr] *f* verdure; greens

vé•reux -reuse [verø] **-reuse** [røz] *adj* wormy

verge [vɛrʒ] *f* rod; shank (*of anchor*); penis

verger [vɛrʒe] *m* orchard

verglas [vɛrgla] *m* glare ice; sleet

vergogne [vɛrgɔɲ] *f*—**sans vergogne** immodest, brazen; immodestly, brazenly

véridique [veridik] *adj* veracious

vérifica•teur [verifikatœr] **-trice** [tris] *mf* inspector, examiner; **vérificateur comptable** auditor; **vérificateur orthographique** (comp) spell checker

vérification [verifikasjɔ̃] *f* verification; auditing; ascertainment

vérifier [verifje] *tr* to verify; audit; ascertain

vérin [verɛ̃] *m* jack; (aer) control; **vérin hydraulique** hydraulic lift, hydraulic jack

véritable [veritabl] *adj* veritable; real, genuine

vérité [verite] *f* truth; **à la vérité** to tell the truth; **dire à qn ses quatre vérités** (coll) to give s.o. a piece of one's mind; **en vérité** truly, in truth

ver•meil -meille [vɛrmɛj] *adj* rosy

vermillon [vɛrmijɔ̃] *adj invar & m* vermilion

vermine [vɛrmin] *f* vermin

vermou•lu -lue [vɛrmuly] *adj* worm-eaten

vermout or **vermouth** [vɛrmut] *m* vermouth

vernaculaire [vɛrnakylɛr] *adj* vernacular

vernir [vɛrnir] *tr* to varnish; **être verni** (coll) to be lucky

vernis [vɛrni] *m* varnish; (fig) veneer

vernissage [vɛrnisaʒ] *m* varnishing; private viewing (*of pictures*)

vernisser [vɛrnise] *tr* to glaze

vérole [verɔl] *f* (slang) syphilis; **petite vérole** smallpox

verrai [vere] *v* (**verras, verra, verrons,** etc.) see **voir**

verre [vɛr] *m* glass; crystal (*of watch*); **verre à vitre** windowpane; **verre consigné** bottle with deposit; **verre de contact** contact lens; **verre de lampe** lamp chimney; **verre dépoli** frosted glass; **verre perdu** disposable bottle (*no deposit*); **verres eyeglasses**; **verres de soleil** sunglasses; **verres grossissants** magnifying glasses; **verre taillé** cut glass

verrière [vɛrjɛr] *f* stained-glass window

verrou [vɛru] *m* bolt; **être sous les verrous** to be locked up

verrouiller [vɛruje] *tr* to bolt; lock up ‖ *ref* to lock oneself in

verrue [vɛry] *f* wart

vers [vɛr] *m* verse; **les vers** verse, poetry ‖ *prep* toward; about, e.g., **vers les cinq heures** about five o'clock

Versailles [vɛrsaj] *f* Versailles

versant [vɛrsɑ̃] *m* slope, side

versatile [vɛrsatil] *adj* fickle

verse [vɛrs] *f*—**pleuvoir à verse** to pour

ver‧sé -sée [vɛrse] *adj*—**versé dans** versed in

Verseau [vɛrso] *m*—**le Verseau** (astr, astrol) Aquarius

versement [vɛrsəmɑ̃] *m* deposit; installment; **versement anticipé** payment in advance

verser [vɛrse] *tr* to pour; upset; tip over; deposit ‖ *intr* to overturn

verset [vɛrsɛ] *m* (Bib) verse

versification [vɛrsifikɑsjɔ̃] *f* versification

versifier [vɛrsifje] *tr* & *intr* to versify

version [vɛrsjɔ̃] *f* version; translation from a foreign language

verso [vɛrso] *m* verso; **au verso** on the back

vert [vɛr] **verte** [vɛrt] *adj* green; verdant; vigorous (*person*); new (*wine*); raw (*leather*); sharp (*scolding*); spicy (*story*); **ils sont trop verts!** sour grapes! ‖ *m* green; greenery; **mettre au vert** to put out to pasture; **se mettre au vert** to take a rest in the country

vert-de-gris [vɛrdəgri] *m invar* verdigris

vertèbre [vɛrtɛbr] *f* vertebra

verté‧bré -brée [vɛrtebre] *adj* & *m* vertebrate

verti‧cal -cale [vɛrtikal] (*pl* **-caux** [ko] **-cales**) *adj* vertical ‖ *m* (astr) vertical circle ‖ *f* vertical

vertige [vɛrtiʒ] *m* vertigo, dizziness

vertigo [vɛrtigo] *m* staggers (*of horse*); caprice

vertu [vɛrty] *f* virtue

ver‧tueux [vɛrtɥø] **-tueuse** [tɥøz] *adj* virtuous

verve [vɛrv] *f* verve

ver‧veux [vɛrvø] **-veuse** [vøz] *adj* lively, animated ‖ *m* fishnet

vésanie [vezani] *f* madness

vesce [vɛs] *f* vetch

vésicule [vezikyl] *f* vesicle; blister; **vésicule biliaire** gall bladder

vespasienne [vɛspazjɛn] *f* street urinal

vessie [vesi] *f* bladder; **vessie à glace** ice bag

veste [vɛst] *f* coat, suit coat; **remporter une veste** (coll) to suffer a setback; **retourner sa veste** (coll) to do an about-face; **veste croisée** double-breasted coat; **veste de pyjama** pajama top; **veste de sport** sport coat; **veste d'intérieur, veste d'appartement** lounging robe; **veste droite** single-breasted coat

vestiaire [vɛstjɛr] *m* checkroom, cloakroom; dressing room

vestibule [vɛstibyl] *m* vestibule

vestige [vɛstiʒ] *m* vestige; footprint

veston [vɛstɔ̃] *m* coat

Vésuve [vezyv] *m*—**le Vésuve** Vesuvius

vêtement [vɛtmɑ̃] *m* garment; **vêtements assortis, vêtements coordonnés** mix-and-match clothes; **vêtements de bébé** baby clothes; **vêtements de rechange** spare clothes; **vêtements de travail** working clothes

vétéran [veterɑ̃] *m* veteran

vétérinaire [veterinɛr] *adj* & *mf* veterinary

vétille [vetij] *f* trifle

vétiller [vetije] *intr* to split hairs

vêtir [vɛtir] §73 *tr* & *ref* to dress

veto [veto] *m* veto; **mettre** or **opposer son veto à** to veto

vê‧tu -tue [vɛty] *v* see **vêtir**

vétuste [vetyst] *adj* decrepit, rickety

veuf [vœf] **veuve** [vœv] *adj* widowed ‖ *m* widower ‖ *f* see **veuve**

veuille [vœj] *v* (**veuilles, veuillent**) see **vouloir**

veule [vøl] *adj* (coll) feeble, weak

veuvage [vœvaʒ] *m* widowhood; widowerhood

veuve [vœv] *adv* widow

veux [vø] *v* (**veut**) see **vouloir; en veux-tu en voilà** (slang) as many as you want

vexation [vɛksɑsjɔ̃] *f* vexation

vexer [vɛkse] *tr* to vex

via [vja] *prep* via

viaduc [vjadyk] *m* viaduct

via‧ger [vjaʒe] **-gère** [ʒɛr] *adj* life, for life ‖ *m* life annuity

viande [vjɑ̃d] *f* meat; **amène ta viande!** (slang) get over here!

vibration [vibrɑsjɔ̃] *f* vibration

vibrer [vibre] *intr* to vibrate

vicaire [vikɛr] *m* vicar

vice [vis] *m* vice; defect; **vice de conformation** physical defect; **vice de forme** (law) irregularity, flaw; **vice versa** vice versa

vice-amiral [visamiral] *m* (*pl* **-amiraux** (amiro)) vice-admiral

vice-président [visprezidɑ̃] **-présidente** [prezidɑ̃t] *mf* (*pl* **-présidents**) vice-president

vice-roi [visrwa] *m* (*pl* **-rois**) viceroy

vice-versa [visvɛrsa], [visvɛrsa] *adv* vice versa

vi‧cié -ciée [visje] *adj* foul, polluted; poor, thin (*blood*)

vicier [visje] *tr* to foul, pollute; taint, spoil

vi•cieux [visjø] **-cieuse** [sjøz] *adj* vicious; wrong (*use*); libertine; balky

vici•nal -nale [visinal] *adj* (*pl* **-naux** [no]) local, side (*road*)

vicissitude [visisityd] *f* vicissitude

vicomte [vikɔ̃t] *m* viscount

victime [viktim] *f* victim

victoire [viktwar] *f* victory

victo•rieux [viktɔrjø] **-rieuse** [rjøz] *adj* victorious

victuailles [viktɥɑj] *fpl* victuals, foods

vidange [vidɑ̃ʒ] *f* draining; night soil; drain (*of pipe, sink, etc.*)

vidanger [vidɑ̃ʒe] §38 *tr* to drain

vide [vid] *adj* empty; blank; vacant ‖ *m* emptiness, void; vacuum; **emballé sous vide** vacuum packed; **vide d'air** air space

vi•dé -dée [vide] *adj* cleaned (*fish, fowl, etc.*); played out, exhausted

vide-bouteille [vidbutɛj] *m* (*pl* **-bouteilles**) siphon

vide-cave [vidkav] *m invar* sump pump

vidéo [video] *adj invar* & *f* video

vidéocassette [videokasɛt] *f* videocassette, videotape

vidéo-clip [videoklip] *m* (*pl* **video-clips**) video clip

vidéoclub [videoklœb] *m* video club

vidéocommunication [videokɔmynikasjɔ̃] *f* video communication

vidéoconférence *var* de **visioconférence**

vidéodisque [videodisk] *m* videodisk, videodisc

vidéofréquence [videofrekɑ̃s] *f* video signal

vidéogramme [videogram] *m* video recorder, videotape recorder; video recording, videotape recording

vidéographie [videografi] *f* **vidéographie diffusée** teletext; **vidéographie interactive** videotex(t)

vidéographique [videografik] *adj* of teletex, of videotex

vidéolecteur [videolɛktœr] *m* videodisk player

vide-ordures [vidɔrdyr] *m invar* garbage shoot

vidéosurveillance [videosyrvɛjɑ̃s] *f* video surveillance

vidéotex [videotɛks] *m* videotex, videotext

vidéothèque [videotɛk] *f* video library

vidéotransmission [videotrɑ̃smisjɔ̃] *f* transmission of television programs on large screens in theaters and conference rooms

vide-poche *or* **vide-poches** [vidpɔʃ] *m invar* (aut) console

vider [vide] *tr* to empty; drain; clean (*fish, fowl, etc.*); settle (*a question*); **se faire vider de** (coll) to get thrown out of; be fired from; be expelled from

vi•deur [vidœr] **-deuse** [døz] *mf* (coll) bouncer (*in a night club*)

viduité [vidɥite] *f* widowhood

vidure [vidyr] *f* guts (*e.g., of cleaned fish*); **vidures de poubelle** garbage

vie [vi] *f* life; livelihood, living; **à vie** for life;

de ma (sa, etc.) vie in my (his, etc.) life, e.g., **je ne l'ai jamais vu de ma vie** I have never seen it in my life; **jamais de la vie!** not on your life!; **vie de bâton de chaise** disorderly life; **vie de château** life of ease

vieil [vjɛj] *adj* see **vieux**

vieillard [vjɛjar] *m* old man; **les vieillards** old people

vieille [vjɛj] *f* old woman ‖ *adj* see **vieux**

vieilleries [vjɛjri] *fpl* old things; old ideas

vieillesse [vjɛjɛs] *f* old age

vieil•li -lie [vjeji] *adj* aged; out-of-date, antiquated

vieillir [vjejir] *tr* to age; make (*s.o.*) look older ‖ *intr* to age, grow old ‖ *ref* to make oneself look older

vieil•lot [vjɛjo] **-lotte** [jɔt] *adj* (coll) oldish, quaint

vielle [vjɛl] *f* (hist) hurdy-gurdy

viendrai [vjɛ̃dre] *v* (**viendras, viendra, viendrons,** etc.) see **venir**

Vienne [vjɛn] *f* Vienna; Vienne (*city in France*)

vien•nois [vjɛnwa] **-noise** [nwaz] *adj* Viennese ‖ (*cap*) *mf* Viennese

viens [vjɛ̃] *v* (**vient**) see **venir**

vierge [vjɛrʒ] *adj* virginal; virgin; blank; unrecorded (*tape or cassette*); unexposed (*film*) ‖ *f* virgin; **la Vierge** (astr, astrol) Virgo

Vietnam [vjɛtnam] *m*—**le Vietnam** Vietnam

vietna•mien [vjɛtnamjɛ̃] **-mienne** [mjɛn] *adj* Vietnamese ‖ (*cap*) *mf* Vietnamese

vieux [vjø] (*or* **vieil** [vjɛj] before vowel or mute **h**) **vieille** [vjɛj] *adj* old (*wine*) ‖ (when standing before noun) *adj* old; old-fashioned; obsolete (*word, meaning, etc.*) ‖ *mf* old person ‖ *m* old man; **les vieux** old people; **mon vieux** (coll) my boy ‖ *f* see **vieille**

vif [vif] **vive** [viv] *adj* alive, living; lively, quick; bright, intense; hearty, heartfelt; sharp (*criticism*); keen (*pleasure*); spring (*water*) ‖ *m* quick; **couper dans le vif** to take drastic measures; **entrer dans le vif de** to get to the heart of; **peindre au vif** to paint from life; **piqué au vif** stung to the quick

vif-argent [vifarʒɑ̃] *m* quicksilver; (*person*) live wire

vigie [viʒi] *f* lookout

vigilance [viʒilɑ̃s] *f* vigilance

vigi•lant [viʒilɑ̃] **-lante** [lɑ̃t] *adj* vigilant ‖ *m* night watchman

vigile [viʒil] *m* night watchman ‖ *f* (eccl) vigil

vigne [viɲ] *f* vine; vineyard; **vigne blanche** clematis; **vigne de Judas** bittersweet; **vigne vierge** Virginia creeper

vigne•ron [viɲrɔ̃] **-ronne** [rɔn] *mf* winegrower; vintner

vignette [viɲɛt] *f* vignette; tax stamp; gummed tab

vignoble [viɲɔbl] *m* vineyard

vigou•reux [vigurø] **-reuse** [røz] *adj* vigorous

vigueur [vigœr] *f* vigor; **entrer en vigueur** to go into effect

VIH *or* **V.I.H.** [veiaʃ] *m* (letterword) (**Virus de**

l'Immunodéficience Humaine) HIV (Human Immunodeficiency Virus)

vil vile [vil] *adj* vile; cheap

vi·lain [vilɛ̃] **-laine** [lɛn] (precedes the noun it modifies) *adj* nasty; ugly; naughty ‖ *mf* nasty person

vilebrequin [vilbrəkɛ̃] *m* brace (*of brace and bit*); crankshaft

vilenie [vilni] *f* villainy; abuse

villa [villa] *f* villa; cottage, small one-story home

village [vilaʒ] *m* village

villa·geois [vilaʒwa] **-geoise** [ʒwaz] *mf* villager

ville [vil] *f* city; town; **aller en ville** to go downtown; **la Ville Lumière** the City of Light (*Paris*); **ville champignon** boom town; **ville satellite** suburban town; **villes jumelées, villes réunies** twin cities

ville-dortoir [vildɔrtwar] *f* bedroom community

villégiature [vileʒjatyr] *f* vacation

vin [vɛ̃] *m* wine; **avoir le vin gai** to be hilariously drunk; **être entre deux vins** to be tipsy; **vin d'honneur** reception (*at which toasts are offered*); **vin d'orange** sangaree; **vin mousseux** sparkling wine; **vin ordinaire** table wine

vinaigre [vinɛgr] *m* vinegar

vinaigrette [vinɛgrɛt] *f* French dressing, vinaigrette sauce

vindica·tif [vɛ̃dikatif] **-tive** [tiv] *adj* vindictive

vingt [vɛ̃] §94 *adj & pron* twenty; the Twentieth, e.g., **Jean vingt** John the Twentieth; **vingt et un** [vɛ̃teœ̃] twenty-one; Twenty-first, e.g., **Jean vingt et un** John the Twenty-first; **vingt et unième** twenty-first ‖ *m* twenty; twentieth (*in dates*); **vingt et un** twenty-one; twenty-first (*in dates*); **vingt et unième** twenty-first

vingtaine [vɛ̃tɛn] *f* score; **une vingtaine de** about twenty

vingt-deux [vɛ̃tdø] §94 *adj & pron* twenty-two; the Twenty-second, e.g., **Jean vingt-deux** John the Twenty-second ‖ *m* twenty-two; twenty-second (*in dates*) ‖ *interj* (slang) watch out!, cheese it!

vingt-deuxième [vɛ̃tdøzjɛm] §94 *adj, pron* (*masc, fem*), & *m* twenty-second

vingt-et-un [vɛ̃teœ̃] *m* (cards) twenty-one

vingtième [vɛ̃tjɛm] §94 *adj, pron* (*masc, fem*), & *m* twentieth

vinyle [vinil] *m* vinyl

viol [vjɔl] *m* rape; **viol collectif** gang rape

viola·teur [vjɔlatœr] **-trice** [tris] *mf* violator; lawbreaker; **violateur méprisant** scofflaw

violation [vjɔlɑsjɔ̃] *f* violation

violence [vjɔlɑ̃s] *f* violence

vio·lent [vjɔlɑ̃] **-lente** [lɑ̃t] *adj* violent

violenter [vjɔlɑ̃te] *tr* to do violence to

violer [vjɔle] *tr* to violate; break (*the faith*); rape, ravish

vio·let [vjɔlɛ] **-lette** [lɛt] *adj & m* violet (*color*) ‖ *f* (bot) violet

violon [vjɔlɔ̃] *m* violin; (slang) calaboose, jug;

payer les violons (coll) to pay the piper; **violon d'Ingres** hobby

violoncelle [vjɔlɔ̃sɛl] *m* violoncello

violoniste [vjɔlɔnist] *mf* violinist

vipère [vipɛr] *f* viper

virage [viraʒ] *m* turning; turn, e.g., **pas de virage à gauche** no left turn; (aer) bank; (phot) toning; **virage en épingle à cheveux** hairpin curve; **virages** (*public sign*) winding road; **virage sur place** U-turn

virago [virago] *f* mannish woman

virée [vire] *f* (coll) spin (*in a car*); (coll) round (*of bars*)

virement [virmɑ̃] *m* transfer (*of funds*); (naut) tacking

virer [vire] *tr* to transfer (*funds*); (phot) to tone ‖ *intr* to turn; (aer) to bank; **virer à** to turn (*sour, red, etc.*); **virer de bord** (naut) to tack

virevolte [virvɔlt] *f* turn; about-face

virevolter [virvɔlte] *intr* to make an about-face; go hither and thither

virginité [virʒinite] *f* virginity, maidenhood

virgule [virgyl] *f* (gram) comma; (*used in French to set off the decimal fraction from the integer*) decimal point

virilité [virilite] *f* virility

virole [virɔl] *f* ferrule

virologie [virɔlɔʒi] *f* virology

vir·tuel [virtɥɛl] **-tuelle** [virtɥɛl] *adj* potential; (mech, opt, phys) virtual

virtuose [virtɥoz] *mf* virtuoso

virtuosité [virtɥozite] *f* virtuosity

virulence [virylɑ̃s] *f* virulence

viru·lent [virylɑ̃] **-lente** [lɑ̃t] *adj* virulent

virus [virys] *m* virus; (comp) computer virus; **virus de l'immunodéficience humaine (VIH)** human immunodeficiency virus (HIV); **virus informatique** computer virus

vis [vis] *f* screw; thread (*of screw*); spiral staircase; **fermer à vis** to screw shut; **serrer la vis à** (fig) to put the screws on; **vis à ailettes** wing nut; **vis à bois** wood screw; **vis à métaux, vis à tôle** machine screw; **vis à tête plate** flat-headed screw; **vis à tête ronde** round-headed screw; **vis de blocage** setscrew ‖ [vi] *v* (**vit**) see **vivre**; see **voir**

visa [viza] *m* visa; (fig) approval

visage [vizaʒ] *m* face; **à deux visages** two-faced; **faire bon visage à** to pretend to be friendly to; **trouver visage de bois** to find the door closed; **visages pâles** palefaces; **voir qn sous son vrai visage** to see s.o. in his true colors

visagiste [vizaʒist] *mf* beautician

vis-à-vis [vizavi] *adv* vis-à-vis; **vis-à-vis de** vis-à-vis; toward; in the presence of ‖ *m* vis-à-vis; **en vis-à-vis** facing

viscère [visɛr] *m* organ; **viscères** viscera

visée [vize] *f* aim

viser [vize] §96 *tr* to aim; aim at; concern; visa ‖ *intr* to aim; **viser à** to aim at; aim to

viseur [vizœr] *m* viewfinder; sight (*of gun*); **viseur de lancement** bombsight

visibilité [vizibilite] *f* visibility; **sans visibilité** blind (*flying*)

visible [vizibl] *adj* visible; obvious; (coll) at home, free; (coll) open to the public

visière [vizjɛr] *f* visor; sight (*of gun*); **rompre en visière à** to take a stand against

visioconférence [visjɔkɔ̃ferɑ̃s] *or* **vidéoconférence** [videokɔ̃ferɑ̃s] *f* videoconference

vision [vizjɔ̃] *f* vision

visionnaire [vizjɔnɛr] *adj & mf* visionary

visionner [vizjɔne] *tr* to view, inspect

visionneuse [vizjɔnøz] *f* viewer

visite [vizit] *f* visit; inspection; **en** or **de visite** visiting; **faire** or **rendre visite à** to visit; **visite de politesse** courtesy call; **visite sur le terrain** field trip

visiter [vizite] *tr* to visit; inspect

visi•teur [vizitœr] **-teuse** [tøz] *adj* visiting (*e.g., nurse*) ‖ *mf* visitor; inspector

vison [vizɔ̃] *m* mink

vis•queux [viskø] **-queuse** [køz] *adj* viscous

visser [vise] *tr* to screw; screw on; (coll) to put the screws on

visualiser [vizɥalize] *tr* to visualize

vi•suel -suelle [vizɥɛl] *adj* visual

vi•tal -tale [vital] *adj* (*pl* **-taux** [to]) vital

vitaliser [vitalize] *tr* to vitalize

vitalité [vitalite] *f* vitality

vitamine [vitamin] *f* vitamin

vite [vit] *adj* fast, swift ‖ *adv* fast, quickly; **faites vite!** hurry up!

vitesse [vitɛs] *f* speed, velocity; rate; **à toute vitesse** at full speed; **changer de vitesse** (aut) to shift gears; **en grande vitesse** (rr) by express; **en petite vitesse** (rr) by freight; **en première (seconde,** etc.**) vitesse** (aut) in first (second, etc.) gear; **vitesse acquise** momentum

viticole [vitikɔl] *adj* wine

viticulteur [vitikyltœr] *m* winegrower

vitrage [vitraʒ] *m* glasswork; small window curtain; sash; glazing

vi•trail [vitraj] *m* (*pl* **-traux** [tro]) stained-glass window

vitre [vitr] *f* windowpane, pane; (aut) window; **casser les vitres** (coll) to kick up a fuss

vi•tré -trée [vitre] *adj* glazed; vitreous (*humor*); glassed-in

vi•treux [vitrø] **-treuse** [trøz] *adj* glassy; vitreous

vitrier [vitrije] *m* glazier

vitrine [vitrin] *f* show window, store window; showcase; glass cabinet; **lécher les vitrines** (coll) to go window-shopping

vitupérer [vitypere] §10 *tr* to vituperate, abuse ‖ *intr*—**vitupérer contre** (coll) to vituperate

vivace [vivas] *adj* hardy, vigorous; long-lived; (bot) perennial

vivacité [vivasite] *f* vivacity

vivan•dier [vivɑ̃dje] **-dière** [djɛr] *mf* sutler ‖ *f* camp follower

vi•vant [vivɑ̃] **-vante** [vɑ̃t] *adj* living, alive; lively; modern, spoken (*language*) ‖ *m*—**bon vivant** high liver, jolly companion; **du vivant de** during the lifetime of; **les vivants et les morts** the quick and the dead

vivat [viva] *m* viva ‖ *interj* viva!

vivement [vivmɑ̃] *adv* quickly, warmly; deeply; sharply, briskly

viveur [vivœr] *m* pleasure seeker, rounder

vivier [vivje] *m* fish preserve, fishpond

vivi•fiant [vivifjɑ̃] **-fiante** [fjɑ̃t] *adj* invigorating, exhilarating

vivifier [vivifje] *tr* to vivify, vitalize

vivisection [vivisɛksjɔ̃] *f* vivisection

vivoir [vivwar] *m* (Canad) living room

vivoter [vivɔte] *intr* (coll) to live from hand to mouth

vivre [vivr] *m*—**le vivre et le couvert** room and board; **le vivre et le vêtement** food and clothing; **vivres** provisions; (mil) rations, supplies ‖ §74 *tr* to live (*one's life, faith, art*); live through, experience ‖ *intr* to live; **être difficile à vivre** to be difficult to live with; **qui vive?** (mil) who is there?; **qui vivra verra** time will tell; **vive!, vivent!** viva! long live!; **vivre au jour le jour** to live from hand to mouth; **vivre de** to live on

vizir [vizir] *m* vizier

vlan [vlɑ̃] *interj* whack!, wham!

vocable [vɔkabl] *m* word

vocabulaire [vɔkabylɛr] *m* vocabulary

vo•cal -cale [vɔkal] *adj* (*pl* **-caux** [ko]) vocal

vocaliser [vɔkalize] *tr, intr, & ref* to vocalize

vocatif [vɔkatif] *m* vocative

vocation [vɔkɑsjɔ̃] *f* vocation, calling; **vocation pédagogique** teaching career

vociférer [vɔsifere] §10 *tr* to shout (*e.g., insults*) ‖ *intr* to vociferate

vœu [vø] *m* (*pl* **vœux**) vow; wish; resolution; **meilleurs vœux!** best wishes!; **tous mes vœux!** my best wishes!

vogue [vɔg] *f* vogue, fashion; **en vogue** in vogue, in fashion

voguer [vɔge] *intr* to sail; **vogue la galère!** let's chance it, here goes!

voici [vwasi] *prep* here is, here are; for, e.g., **voici quatre jours qu'elle est partie** she has been gone for four days; **voici he is**; **nous voici** here we are; **que voici** here, e.g., **mon frère que voici va vous accompagner** my brother here is going to accompany you

voie [vwa] *f* way; road; lane (*of highway*); (anat) tract; (rr) track; **en voie de** on the road to, nearing; **être en bonne voie** to be doing well; **voie d'eau** leak; **voie de desserte** frontage road; **voie de garage** driveway; **voie de raccordement** access route; **voie d'évitement** siding; **voie lactée** Milky Way; **voie maritime** seaway; **voie(s) de fait** (law) assault and battery; **voie ferrée** surface mail

voilà [vwala] *prep* there is, there are; here is, here are; that's e.g., **voilà pourquoi** that's why; ago, e.g., **voilà quatre jours qu'elle est partie** she left four days ago; **voilà, monsieur** there you are, sir

voile [vwal] *m* veil; (phot) fog (*on negative*); **voile du palais** soft palate; **voile noir** (pathol) blackout; **voile qui couvre le corps** body veil ‖ *f* sail; sailboat; **faire voile sur** to set sail for

voi•lé -lée [vwale] *adj* veiled; overcast; muffled; warped; husky (*voice*); (phot) fogged; **peu voilé** thinly veiled, broad (*e.g., hint*)

voiler [vwale] *tr* to veil; (phot) to fog ‖ *ref* to cloud over; become warped

voi•lier [vwalje] **-lière** [ljɛr] *adj* sailing ‖ *m* sailboat; sailmaker; migratory bird

voilure [vwalyr] *f* sails; warping

voir [vwar] §75, §95 *tr* to see; **faire voir** to show; **voir jouer** to see (*s.o.*) playing, to see (*s.o.*) play; to see (*s.th.*) played; **voir qn qui vient** to see s.o. coming, see s.o. come; **voir venir qn** to see s.o. coming, see s.o. come; (fig) to see through s.o. ‖ *intr* to see; **faites voir!** let's see it!, let me see it!; **j'en ai vu bien d'autres** I have seen worse than that; **n'avoir rien à voir avec, à,** or **dans** to have nothing to do with; **voir à** + *inf* to see that + *ind*, e.g., **voir à nous loger** to see that we are housed; **voir au dos** see other side, turn the page; **voyons!** see here!, come now! ‖ *ref* to see oneself; see one another; be obvious; be seen, be found

voire [vwar] *adv* nay, indeed; **voire même** or even, and even

voirie [vwari] *f* highway department; garbage collection; dump

voi•sé -sée [vwaze] *adj* voiced

voi•sin [vwazɛ̃] **-sine** [zin] *adj* neighboring; adjoining; **voisin de** near ‖ *mf* neighbor

voisinage [vwazinaʒ] *m* neighborhood; neighborliness

voisiner [vwazine] *intr* to visit one's neighbors; **voisiner avec** to be placed next to

voiture [vwatyr] *f* vehicle; carriage; (aut, rr) car; **en voiture!** all aboard!; **petite voiture** (coll) wheelchair; **voiture à bras** handcart; **voiture banalisée** unmarked police car; **voiture de location** rented car; **voiture d'enfant** baby carriage; **voiture de police** police car; **voiture de pompier** fire engine; **voiture de remise** rented car; **voiture de ronde** patrol car; **voiture de série** stock car; **voiture de tourisme** pleasure car; **voiture d'infirme** wheelchair; **voiture d'occasion** used car; **voiture école** school bus

voiture-bar [vwatyrbar] *f* (*pl* **voitures-bars**) club car

voiturette [vwatyrɛt] *f*—**voiturette de golf** golf cart

voiture-lit [vwatyrli] *f* (*pl* **voitures-lits**) sleeping car

voiturer [vwatyre] *tr* to transport, convey

voiture-restaurant [vwatyrrɛstorɑ̃] *f* (*pl* **voitures-restaurants**) dining car

voiture-salon [vwatyrsalɔ̃] *f* (*pl* **voitures-salons**) parlor car

voix [vwa], [vwɑ] *f* voice; vote; **à haute voix** aloud; in a loud voice; **à pleine voix** at the top of one's voice; **avoir voix au chapitre** (coll) to have a say in the matter; **à voix basse** in a low voice; **à voix haute** in a loud voice; **de vive voix** by word of mouth; **voix de tête, voix de fausset** falsetto

vol [vɔl] *m* theft; robbery; flight; flock; **au vol** in flight; in passing; **à vol d'oiseau** as the crow flies; **de haut vol** high-flying; big-time (*crook*); **vol à la demande** charter flight; **vol à la tire** purse snatching; **vol à l'étalage** shoplifting; **vol avec effraction** burglary; **vol à voile** gliding; **vol cosmique** space flight; **vol plané** volplane; **vol régulier** scheduled flight; **vol sans visibilité** blind flying; **vol sur aile delta, vol libre** hang gliding

volage [vɔlaʒ] *adj* fickle, changeable

volaille [vɔlɑj] *f* fowl; (slang) hens (*women*); (slang) gal

vo•lant [vɔlɑ̃] **-lante** [lɑ̃t] *adj* flying ‖ *m* steering wheel; flywheel; shuttlecock; sail (*of windmill*); flounce (*of dress*); leaf (*attached to stub*); **volant de sécurité** safety margin, reserve

vola•til -tile [vɔlatil] *adj* volatile ‖ *m* bird; fowl

volatiliser [vɔlatilize] *tr & ref* to volatilize

volcan [vɔlkɑ̃] *m* volcano

volcanique [vɔlkanik] *adj* volcanic

vole [vɔl] *f*—**faire la vole** to take all the tricks

volée [vɔle] *f* volley; flight (*of birds; of stairs*); flock; **à la volée** on the wing; at random; **à toute volée** loud and clear; **de haute volée** upper-class; **de la première volée** first-class, crack; **sonner à toute volée** to peal out

voler [vɔle] §95 *tr* to rob; steal; fly at; **ne l'avoir pas volé** to deserve all that is coming; **voler à** to steal from ‖ *intr* to rob; steal; fly

volet [vɔlɛ] *m* shutter; inside flap; endpaper; (aer) flap; **trier sur le volet** to choose with care

voleter [vɔlte] §34 *intr* to flutter

vo•leur [vɔlœr] **-leuse** [løz] *adj* thievish ‖ *mf* thief; **au voleur!** stop thief!; **voleur à la tire** pickpocket; **voleur à l'étalage** shoplifter; **voleur de bétail** rustler; **voleur de grand chemin** highwayman

volition [vɔlisjɔ̃] *f* volition

volley-ball [vɔlɛbol] *m* volleyball

vol•leyeur [vɔlɛjœr] **-leyeuse** [lɛjøz] *mf* volleyball player

volontaire [vɔlɔ̃tɛr] *adj* voluntary; headstrong; willful; determined (*chin*) ‖ *mf* volunteer

volonté [vɔlɔ̃te] *f* will; wishes; **à volonté** at will; **bonne volonté** good will; **faire ses quatre volontés** (coll) to do just as one pleases; **mauvaise volonté** ill will

volontiers [vɔlɔ̃tje] *adv* gladly, willingly

volt [vɔlt] *m* volt

voltage [vɔltaʒ] *m* voltage

volte-face [vɔltəfas] *f invar* volte-face, turnaround

voltige [vɔltiʒ] *f* acrobatics

voltiger [vɔltiʒe] §38 *intr* to flit about; flutter

voltmètre [vɔltmɛtr] *m* voltmeter

volubile [vɔlybil] *adj* voluble
volume [vɔlym] *m* volume; **faire du volume** (coll) to put on airs
volumi·neux [vɔlyminø] **-neuse** [nøz] *adj* voluminous
volupté [vɔlypte] *f* voluptuousness, ecstasy
volup·tueux [vɔlyptɥø] **-tueuse** [tɥøz] *adj* voluptuous ‖ *mf* voluptuary
vomir [vɔmir] *tr & intr* to vomit
vomissure [vɔmisyr] *f* vomit
vont [vɔ̃] *v* see **aller**
vorace [vɔras] *adj* voracious
voracité [vɔrasite] *f* voracity
vos [vo] §88 your
vo·tant [vɔtɑ̃] **-tante** [tɑ̃t] *mf* voter
vote [vɔt] *m* vote; **passer au vote** to vote on; **vote affirmatif** yea; **vote négatif** nay; **vote par correspondance** absentee ballot; **vote par procuration** proxy
voter [vɔte] *tr* to vote; vote for ‖ *intr* to vote; **voter à mains levées** to vote by show of hands; **voter par assis et levé** to give one's vote by standing or by remaining seated
vo·tif [vɔtif] **-tive** [tiv] *adj* votive
votre [vɔtr] §88 your
vôtre [votr] §89 yours
voudrai [vudre] *v* (**voudras, voudra, voudrons,** etc.) see **vouloir**
vouer [vwe] *tr* to vow, dedicate; doom, condemn; **voué à** headed for; doomed to ‖ §96 *ref*—**se vouer à** to dedicate oneself to
vouloir [vulwar] *m* will ‖ §76, §95 *tr* to want, wish; require; **je voudrais** I would like; I would like to; **veuillez** + *inf* please + *inf*; **voulez-vous vous taire?** will you be quiet?; **vouloir bien** to be glad to, be willing to; **vouloir dire** to mean ‖ *intr*—**en vouloir à** to bear a grudge against; **je veux!** (slang) and how!; **je veux bien** I'm quite willing; **si vous voulez bien** if you don't mind ‖ *ref*—**s'en vouloir** to have it in for each other
vou·lu -lue [vuly] *adj* required; deliberate ‖ *v* see **vouloir**
vous [vu] §85, §87 you, to you; **vous autres Américans** you Americans
vous-même [vumɛm] §86 yourself
voussoir [vuswar] *m* (archit) arch stone
voussoyer *or* **vousoyer** [vuswaje] *var* de **vouvoyer**
voussure [vusyr] *f* arch, arching
voûte [vut] *f* vault; **voûte céleste** canopy of heaven
voûter [vute] *tr* to vault; bend ‖ *ref* to become round-shouldered
vouvoyer [vuvwaje] §47 *tr* to address with formality; use formal grammatical forms (**vous,** etc.) in speaking to a stranger, a superior, or, often (if a Catholic), to God ‖ *ref* to use **vous** and corresponding verbal forms in speaking with one another

voy. *abbr* (**voyez**) see
voyage [vwajaʒ] *m* trip, journey, voyage; ride (*in car, train, plane, etc.*); **voyage à forfait** all-expense tour; **voyage aller et retour** round trip; **voyage d'affaires** business trip; **voyage de noces** honeymoon; **voyage organisé** package tour
voyager [vwajaʒe] §38 *intr* to travel
voya·geur [vwajaʒœr] **-geuse** [ʒøz] *mf* traveler; passenger
voyance [vwajɑ̃s] *f* clairvoyance
voyant [vwajɑ̃] **voyante** [vwajɑ̃t] *adj* loud, gaudy ‖ *mf* clairvoyant ‖ *m* signal; (aut) gauge ‖ *f* fortuneteller
voyelle [vwajɛl] *f* vowel
voyeur [vwajœr] **voyeuse** [vwajøz] *mf* voyeur ‖ *m* Peeping Tom
voyez [vwaje] *v* (**voyons**) see **voir**
voyou [vwaju] **voyoute** [vwajut] *adj* gutter (*e.g., language*) ‖ *mf* guttersnipe; brat; hoodlum
vrac [vrak]—**en vrac** unpacked, loose; in bulk; in disorder
vrai vraie [vrɛ], [vre] *adj* true, real, genuine ‖ *m* truth; **à vrai dire** to tell the truth; **pour vrai** (coll) for good
vraiment [vrɛmɑ̃] *adv* truly, really; surely, frankly
vraisemblable [vrɛsɑ̃blabl] *adj* probable, likely; true to life, realistic (*play, novel*)
vraisemblance [vrɛsɑ̃blɑ̃s] *f* probability, likelihood; realism
vrille [vrij] *f* drill; (aer) spin; (bot) tendril
vriller [vrije] *tr* to bore ‖ *intr* to go into a tailspin
vrombir [vrɔ̃bir] *intr* to throb; buzz; hum, purr (*said of motor*)
vu vue [vy] *adj* seen, regarded; **bien vu de** in favor with; **mal vu de** out of favor with ‖ *m*—**au vu de** upon presentation of; **au vu et au su de tout le monde** openly ‖ *f* view; sight; eyesight; **avoir à vue** to have in mind; **à vue** in sight; (com) on demand; **à vue de nez** at first sight; at a rough estimate; **à vue d'œil** visibly, quickly; the eye by sight; **en vue** in evidence; in sight; **en vue de** in order to; **garder à vue** to keep under observation, keep locked up; **perdre qn de vue** to lose sight of s.o.; get out of touch with s.o.; **vue à vol d'oiseau** bird's-eye view; **vues sur** designs on ‖ **vu** *prep* considering, in view of; **vu que** whereas ‖ *v* see **voir**
vulcaniser [vylkanize] *tr* to vulcanize
vulgaire [vylgɛr] *adj* common, vulgar; ordinary, everyday; vernacular ‖ *m* common herd; vernacular
vulgariser [vylgarize] *tr* to popularize; make vulgar
vulgarité [vylgarite] *f* vulgarity
vulnérable [vylnerabl] *adj* vulnerable
Vve *abbr* (**veuve**) widow

W

W, w [dubləve] *m invar* twenty-third letter of the French alphabet

wagon [vagɔ̃] *m* (rr) car, coach; (coll) big car; **un wagon** (coll) a lot; **wagon à bagages** baggage car; **wagon à bestiaux** cattle car; **wagon couvert** boxcar; **wagon de marchandises** freight car; **wagon de voyageurs** passenger car; **wagon frigorifique** or **réfrigérant** refrigerator car; **wagon plat** flat car; **wagon pour le transport d'automobiles** car-carrier

wagon-bar [vagɔ̃bar] *m* (*pl* **wagons-bars**) club car

wagon-citerne [vagɔ̃sitɛrn] *m* (*pl* **wagons-citernes**) tank car

wagon-lit [vagɔ̃li] *m* (*pl* **wagons-lits**) sleeping car

wagon-poste [vagɔ̃pɔst] *m* (*pl* **wagons-poste**) mail car

wagon-réservoir [wagɔ̃rezɛrvwar] *m* (*pl* **wagons-réservoirs**) tank car

wagon-restaurant [vagɔ̃rɛstɔrɑ̃] *m* (*pl* **wagons-restaurants**) dining car

wagon-salon [vagɔ̃salɔ̃] *m* (*pl* **wagons-salons**) parlor car

wagon-tombereau [vagɔ̃tɔ̃bro] *m* (*pl* **wagons-tombereaux**) dump truck

walkman [wɔkman] *m* Walkman (trademark)

wallace [valas] *f* drinking fountain

wal•lon [walɔ̃] **-lonne** [lɔn] *adj* Walloon ‖ *m* Walloon (*dialect*) ‖ (*cap*) *mf* Walloon

warrant [warɑ̃], [varɑ̃] *m* receipt

WASP [wasp] *adj invar* & *mf invar* (acronym) **(de race blanche, d'origine anglo-saxonne, de religion protestante)** WASP (White, Anglo-Saxon, Protestant)

water-polo [watɛrpɔlo] *m* water polo

waterproof [watɛrpruf] *adj invar* waterproof ‖ *m invar* raincoat

waters [watɛr], [vater] *mpl* toilet

watt [wat] *m* watt

watt-heure [watœr] *m* (*pl* **watts-heures**) watt-hour

wattman [watman] *m* motorman

wattmètre [watmɛtr] *m* wattmeter

W.-C. [vese] *or* [dublɔvese] *m* (letterword) **(water-closet)** toilet

Web, web [wɛb] *m* (comp) Web

week-end [wikɛnd] *m* (*pl* **-ends**) weekend

whisky [wiski] *m* whiskey; **whisky écossais** Scotch

wolfram [vɔlfram] *m* wolfram

WWW *or* **www** *abbr* (**Web, La Toile**) www. (World-Wide Web)

X

X, x [iks], *[iks] *m invar* twenty-fourth letter of the French alphabet

Xavier [gzavje] *m* Xavier

xénon [gsenɔ̃] *m* xenon

xénophobe [gsenɔfɔb] *adj* xenophobic ‖ *mf* xenophobe

xénophobie [gzenɔfɔbi] *f* xenophobia

Xérès [kerɛs], [gzerɛs] *m* Jerez; sherry

xérocopie [gzerɔkɔpi], [kserɔkɔpi] *f* Xerox (trademark), Xerox copy

xérographie [gzerɔgrafi], [kserɔgrafi] *f* xeroxing, xerography

Xerxès [gzɛrsɛs] *m* Xerxes

xylème [gzilɛm], [ksilɛm] *m* xylem

xylographie [ksilɔgrafi] *f* xylograph

xylophone [ksilɔfɔn] *m* xylophone

Y

Y, y [igrɛk], *[igrɛk] *m invar* twenty-fifth letter of the French alphabet

y [i] *pron pers* §87 to it, to them; at it, at them; in it, in them; by it, by them; of it, of them, e.g., **j'y pense** I am thinking of it or them; (untranslated with certain verbs), e.g., **je n'y vois pas** I don't see; e.g., **il s'y connaît** (coll) he's an expert, he knows what he's talking about; him, her, e.g., **je m'y fie** I trust him; **allez-y!** go ahead!, start!; **ça y est!** that's it!; **je n'y suis pour personne** I am not at home

for anybody; **je n'y suis pour rien** I have nothing to do with it; **j'y suis!** I've got it! ‖ *adv* there; here, in, e.g., **Monsieur votre père y est-il?** is your father here?, is your father in?

yacht [jɔt], [jak] *m* yacht; **yacht à glace** iceboat

yacht-club [jɔtklœb] *m* yacht club

yankee [jɑ̃ki] *adj masc* Yankee ‖ (*cap*) *mf* Yankee

yaourt [jaurt] *or* [jaur] *m* yogurt

yèble [jɛbl] *f* (bot) elder; **l'yèble** the elder

yeoman [jɔman] *m* yeoman
yeuse [jøz] *f* holm oak; **l'yeuse** the holm oak
yeux [jø] *mpl* see œil
yé-yé [jeje] (*pl* -yés) *adj & mf* jitterbug
yi•dich -diche [jidiʃ] *adj & m* Yiddish
yiddish [jidiʃ] *adj invar & m invar* Yiddish
yoga [jɔga] *m* yoga
yogi [jɔgi] *m* yogi
yogourt *or* yoghourt [jɔgur] *m* yogurt

yole [jɔl] *f* yawl
Yonne [jɔn] *f* Yonne; **l'Yonne** the Yonne
yougoslave [jugɔslav] *adj* Yugoslav ‖ (*cap*) *mf* Yugoslav
Yougoslavie [jugɔslavi] *f* Yugoslavia; **la You-goslavie** Yugoslavia
youyou [juju] *m* dinghy
ypérite [iperit] *f* mustard gas
yuppie [jupi] *mf* yuppie, yuppy

Z

Z, z [sɛd] *m invar* twenty-sixth letter of the French alphabet
za•zou -zoue [zazu] *adj* (coll) jazzy ‖ *m* (coll) zoot suiter
zèbre [zɛbr] *m* zebra; (slang) guy
zébrer [zebre] §10 *tr* to stripe; **le soleil zèbre** the sun casts streaks of light on
zébrure [zebryr] *f* stripe
zéla•teur [zelatœr] -trice [tris] *mf* zealot
zèle [zɛl] *m* zeal
zénith [zenit] *m* zenith
zéphyr [zefir] *m* zephyr
zeppelin [zɛplɛ̃] *m* zeppelin
zéro [zero] *m* zero; **les avoir à zéro** (slang) to be scared stiff
zest [zɛst] *m*—**entre le zist et le zest** (coll) betwixt and between ‖ *interj* tush!
zeste [zɛst] *m* peel (*of citrus fruit*); dividing membrane (*of nut*); **pas un zeste** (fig) not a particle of difference
Zeus [zøs] *m* Zeus
zézaiement [zezɛmɑ̃] *m* lisp
zézayer [zezeje] §49 *intr* to lisp

zibeline [ziblin] *f* sable
zieuter [zjøte] *tr* (slang) to get a load of
zigzag [zigzag] *m* zigzag; gypsy moth
zigzaguer [zigzage] *intr* to zigzag
zinc [zɛ̃g] *m* zinc; (coll) bar
zircon [zirkɔ̃] *m* zircon
zirconium [zirkɔnjɔm] *m* zirconium
zizanie [zizani] *f* wild rice; tare; **semer la ziza-nie** to sow discord
zodiaque [zɔdjak] *m* zodiac
zonage [zɔnaʒ] *m* zoning
zone [zon] *f* zone; **zone bleue** center city with limited parking; **zone chic** fashionable neighborhood; **zones urbaines en déclin** inner city, inner core
zoning [zoniŋ] *m* zoning
zoo [zoo] *m* zoo
zoologie [zɔɔlɔʒi] *f* zoology
zoologique [zɔɔlɔʒik] *adj* zoologic(al)
zoom [zum] *m* zoom; zoom lens
zouave [zwav] *m* Zouave; **faire le zouave** (coll) to play the fool
zut [zyt] *interj* heck!; hang it!
zygote [zigɔt] *m* zygote

English-French
Anglais-Français

A

A, a [e] *s* Iière lettre de l'alphabet

a *art indef* un

aback [ə'bæk] *adv* avec le vent dessus; **taken aback** déconcerté

abandon [ə'bændən] *s* abandon *m* ‖ *tr* abandonner

abase [ə'bes] *tr* abaisser, humilier

abasement [ə'besmeənt] *s* abaissement *m*

abash [ə'bæʃ] *tr* décontenancer

abashed *adj* confus, confondu

abate [ə'bet] *tr* (*to reduce*) diminuer, réduire; (*part of price*) rabattre ‖ *intr* se calmer; (*said of wind*) tomber

abbess ['æbɪs] *s* abbesse *f*

abbey ['æbi] abbaye *f*

abbot ['æbət] *s* abbé *m*

abbreviate [ə'brivɪ,et] *tr* abréger

abbreviation [ə,brivɪ'eʃən] *s* abréviation *f*

A B C's [,e,bi'siz] *spl* (letterword) a b c *m*

abdicate ['æbdɪ,ket] *tr & intr* abdiquer

abdomen ['æbdəmən], [æb'domən] *s* abdomen *m*

abduct [æb'dʌkt] *tr* enlever, ravir

abet [ə'bɛt] *v* (*pret & pp* **abetted**; *ger* **abetting**) *tr* encourager

abettor [ə'bɛtər] *s* complice *mf*

abeyance [ə'be·əns] *s* suspension *f*; **in abeyance** en suspens

ab·hor [æb'hɔr] *v* (*pret & pp* **-horred**; *ger* **-horring**) *tr* abhorrer, détester

abhorrent [æb'hɔrənt] *adj* détestable, répugnant

abide [ə'baɪd] *v* (*pret & pp* **abode** or **abided**) *tr* attendre‖ *intr* demeurer, continuer, persister; **to abide by** s'en tenir à; rester fidèle à

abili·ty [ə'bɪlɪti] *s* (*pl* **-ties**) (*power to perform*) capacité *f*, compétence *f*; (*proficiency*) aptitude *f*; (*cleverness*) habileté *f*, talent *m*

abject [æb'dʒɛkt] *adj* abject

ablative ['æblətɪv] *adj & s* ablatif *m*

ablaut ['æblaʊt] *s* apophonie *f*

ablaze [ə'blez] *adj* (*on fire*) enflammé; (*colorful*) replendissant ‖ *adv* en feu

able ['ebəl] *adj* capable, habile; **to be able to** pouvoir

a'ble-bod'ied *adj* robuste, vigoureux; (*seaman*) breveté

abloom [ə'blum] *adj & adv* en fleur

abnormal [æb'nɔrməl] *adj* anormal

abnormali·ty [,æbnɔr'mælɪti] *s* (*pl* **-ties**) anomalie *f*, irrégularité *f*; (*of body*) difformité *f*

aboard [ə'bɔrd] *adv* à bord; **all aboard!** en voi-

ture!; **to go aboard** s'embarquer ‖ *prep* à bord de

abode [ə'bod] *s* demeure *f*, résidence *f*

abolish [ə'balɪʃ] *tr* abolir

A-bomb ['e,bam] *s* bombe *f* atomique

abomination [ə,bamɪ'neʃən] *s* abomination *f*

aborigines [,æbə'rɪdʒɪ,niz] *spl* aborigènes *mpl*

abort [ə'bɔrt] *intr* avorter

abortion [ə'bɔrʃən] *s* avortement *m*, I.V.G. *f*

abound [ə'baʊnd] *intr* abonder

about [ə'baʊt] *adv* (*all round*) à la ronde, tout autour; (*almost*) presque; (*here and there*) çà et là; **to be about to** être sur le point de ‖ *prep* (*around*) autour de, aux environs de; (*approximately*) environ; vers, e.g., **about six o'clock** vers six heures; (*concerning*) au sujet de; **it is about** (*it concerns*) . . . il s'agit de . . .

about'-face' *ou* **about'-face'** *s* volte-face *f*; (mil) demi-tour *m* ‖ **about'-face'** *intr* faire volte-face

above [ə'bʌv] *adv* (*overhead*) en haut, audessus; (*earlier*) ci-dessus ‖ *prep* audessus de; (*more than*) plus que, outre; (*another point on the river*) en amont de; **above all** surtout

above'-men'tioned *adj* susmentionné

abrasive [ə'bresɪv] *adj & s* abrasif *m*

abreast [ə'brɛst] *adj & adv* de front; **three abreast** par rangs de trois; **to be abreast of** or **with** être en ligne avec; **to keep abreast of** se tenir au courant de

abridge [ə'brɪdʒ] *tr* abréger

abridgment [ə'brɪdʒmənt] *s* (*shortened version*) abrégé *m*, résumé *m*; (*shortening*) diminution *f*, réduction *f*

abroad [ə'brɔd] *adv* au loin; (*in foreign parts*) à l'étranger

abrogate ['æbrə,get] *tr* abroger

abrupt [ə'brʌpt] *adj* (*steep; impolite*) abrupt; (*hasty*) brusque, précipité

abscess ['æbsɛs] *s* abcès *m*

abscond [æb'skand] *intr* s'enfuir, déguerpir; **to abscond with** lever le pied avec

absence ['æbsəns] *s* absence *f*

absent ['æbsənt] *adj* absent ‖ [æb'sɛnt] *tr*—**to absent oneself** s'absenter

absentee [,æbsən'ti] *s* absent *m*

ab'sentee bal'lot *s* vote *m* par correspondance

ab'sent-mind'ed *adj* absent, distrait

absolute ['æbsə,lut] *adj & s* absolu *m*

absolutely [,æbsə'lutli] *adv* absolument

absolve [æb'salv] *tr* absoudre

absorb [æb`sɔrb] *tr* absorber; **to be** *ou* **become absorbed in** s'absorber dans

absorbent [æb`sɔrbənt] *adj* absorbant; (*cotton*) hydrophile ‖ *s* absorbant *m*

absorbing [æb`sɔbɪŋ] *adj* absorbant

abstain [æb`sten] *intr* s'abstenir

abstemious [æb`stimɪ•əs] *adj* abstinent, sobre

abstinent [`æbstmənt] *adj* abstinent

abstract [`æbstrækt] *adj* abstrait ‖ *s* abrégé *m*, résumé *m* ‖ *tr* résumer ‖ [æb`strækt] *tr* abstraire; (*to remove*) soustraire

abstractedly [æb`stræktɪdli] *adv* d'un œil distrait

abstruse [æb`strus] *adj* abstrus

absurd [æb`sʌrd] *adj* absurde

absurdi•ty [æb`sʌrdɪti] *s* (*pl* **-ties**) absurdité *f*

abundance [ə`bʌndəns] *s* abondance *f*

abundant [ə`bʌndənt] *adj* abondant

abuse [ə`bjus] *s* abus *m*; (*mistreatment*) maltraitement *m*; (*insulting words*) insultes *fpl* ‖ [ə`bjuz] *tr* abuser de; maltraiter; insulter

abusive [ə`bjusɪv] *adj* (*insulting*) injurieux; (*wrong*) abusif

abut [ə`bʌt] *v* (*pret* & *pp* **abutted**; *ger* **abutting**) *intr*—**to abut on** border, confiner

abutment [ə`bʌtmənt] *s* (*of wall*) contrefort *m*; (*of bridge*) culée *f*; (*of arch*) pied-droit *m*

abyss [ə`bɪs] *s* abîme *m*

A.C. [`e`si] *s* (letterword) (**alternating current**) courant *m* alternatif

academic [,ækə`dɛmɪk] *adj* (*of a college*) universitaire; (*of an academy*) académique; (*theoretical*) théorique ‖ *s* étudiant *m* or professeur *m* de l'université

academician [ə,kædə`mɪʃən] *s* académicien *m*

acade•my [ə`kædəmi] *s* (*pl* **-mies**) académie *f*; (*preparatory school*) collège *m*

accede [æk`sid] *intr* acquiescer; **to accede to** accéder à; (*the throne*) monter sur

accelerate [æk`sɛlə,ret] *tr* & *intr* accélérer

accelerator [æk`sɛlə,retər] *s* accélérateur *m*

accent [`æksɛnt] *s* accent *m* ‖ [`æksɛnt], [æk`sɛnt] *tr* accentuer

ac′cent mark′ *s* accent *m* (orthographique)

accentuate [æk`sɛntʃu,et] *tr* accentuer

accept [æk`sɛpt] *tr* accepter

acceptable [æk`sɛptəbəl] *adj* acceptable

acceptance [æk`sɛptəns] *s* acceptation *f*; (*approval*) approbation *f*

acceptation [,æksɛp`teʃən] *s* acceptation *f*; (*meaning*) acception *f*

access [`æksɛs] *s* accès *m* ‖ *tr* (comp) (*to gain access to*) accéder

accessible [æk`sɛsɪbəl] *adj* accessible

accession [æk`sɛʃən] *s* accession *f*

ac′cess mech′anism *s* (comp) dispositif *m* d'accès

accesso•ry [æk`sɛsəri] *adj* accessoire ‖ *s* (*pl* **-ries**) accessoire *m*; (*to a crime*) complice *mf*

ac′cess route′ *s* voie *f* de raccordement, bretelle *f*

accident [`æksɪdənt] *s* accident *m*; **by accident** par accident

accidental [,æksɪ`dɛntəl] *adj* accidentel ‖ *s* (mus) accident *m*

ac′cident-prone′ *adj* prédisposé aux accidents

acclaim [ə`klem] *tr* acclamer

acclimate [`æklɪ,met] *tr* acclimater

accommodate [ə`kamə,det] *tr* accommoder; (*to oblige*) rendre service à; (*to lodge*) loger

accommodating [ə`kamə,detɪŋ] *adj* accommodant, serviable

accommodation [ə,kamə`deʃən] *s* accommodation *f*; **accommodations** commoditiés *fpl*; (*in a train*) place *f*; (*in a hotel*) chambre *f*; (*room and board*) le vivre et le couvert

accompaniment [ə`kʌmpənɪmənt] *s* accompagnement *m*

accompanist [ə`kʌmpənist] *s* accompagnateur *m*

accompa•ny [ə`kʌmpəni] *v* (*pret* & *pp* **-nied**) *tr* accompagner

accomplice [ə`kamplɪs] *s* complice *mf*

accomplish [ə`kamplɪʃ] *tr* accomplir

accomplishment [ə`kamplɪʃmənt] *s* accomplissement *m*, réalisation *f*; (*thing itself*) œuvre *f* accomplie; **accomplishments** arts *mpl* d'agrément, talents *mpl*

accord [ə`kɔrd] *s* accord *m*; **in accord** d'accord; **of one's own accord** de son plein gré ‖ *tr* accorder ‖ *intr* se mettre d'accord

accordance [ə`kɔrdəns] *s* accord *m*; **in accordance with** conformément à

according [ə`kɔrdɪŋ] *adj*—**according as** selon que; **according to** selon, d'après, suivant; **according to expert advice** au dire d'experts

accordingly [ə`kɔrdɪŋli] *adv* en conséquence

accordion [ə`kɔrdɪ•ən] *s* accordéon *m*

accost [ə`kɔst] *tr* accoster

account [ə`kaunt] *s* (*calculation; bill; bank account; report*) compte *m*; (*benefit*) profit *m*, avantage *m*; (*narration*) récit *m*; (*report*) compte rendu; (*explanation*) explication *f*; **of no account** sans importance; **on account of** à cause de; **on no account** en aucune façon; **to call to account** demander des comptes à ‖ *intr*—**to account for** expliquer; (*money*) rendre compte de

accountable [ə`kauntəbəl] *adj* responsable; (*explainable*) explicable

accountant [ə`kauntənt] *s* comptable *mf*

account′ book′ *s* registre *m* de comptabilité

accounting [ə`kauntɪŋ] *s* (*profession*) comptabilité *f*

accouterments [ə`kutərmənts] *spl* équipement *m*

accredit [ə`krɛdɪt] *tr* accréditer

accretion [ə`kriʃən] *s* accroissement *m*

accrue [ə`kru] *intr* s'accroître; **to accrue from** dériver de; **to accrue to** échoir à

accumulate [ə`kjumjə,let] *tr* accumuler ‖ *intr* s'accumuler

accuracy [`ækjərəsi] *s* exactitude *f*

accurate [`ækjərɪt] *adj* exact; (*aim*) juste; (*translation*) fidèle

accursed [ə`kʌrsɪd], [ə`kʌrst] *adj* maudit

accusation [ˌækjəˈzeʃən] s accusation f
accusative [əˈkjuzətɪv] adj & s accusatif m
accuse [əˈkjuz] tr accuser
accused s accusé m, inculpé m
accustom [əˈkʌstəm] tr accoutumer; **to become accustomed** s'accoutumer
ace [es] s as m; **to have an ace up one's sleeve** avoir un atout dans la manche
acetate [ˈæsɪˌtet] s acétate m
ace′tic ac′id [əˈsitɪk] s acide m acétique
acetone [ˈæsɪˌton] s acétone f
acet′ylene torch′ [əˈsɛtɪˌlin] s chalumeau m oxyacétylénique
ache [ek] s douleur f ‖ intr faire mal; **my head aches** j'ai mal à la tête; **to be aching to** (coll) brûler de
achieve [əˈtʃiv] tr (a task) accomplir; (an aim) atteindre; (success) obtenir; (a victory) remporter
achievement [əˈtʃivmənt] s (completion) accomplissement m, réalisation f; (thing itself) œuvre f remarquable, réussite f; (heroic deed) exploit m
Achil′les′ heel′ [əˈkɪliz] s talon m d'Achille
acid [ˈæsɪd] adj & s acide m
acidi•ty [əˈsɪdɪti] s (pl -ties) acidité f
ac′id rain′ s pluie f acide
ac′id test′ s (fig) épreuve f définitive
acknowledge [ækˈnɑlɪdʒ] tr reconnaître; **to acknowledge receipt of** accuser réception de
acknowledgment [ækˈnɑlɪdʒmənt] s (recognition) reconnaissance f; (of an error) aveu m; (of a letter) accusé m de réception; (receipt) récépissé m
acme [ˈækmi] s comble m, sommet m
acne [ˈækni] s acné f
acolyte [ˈækəˌlaɪt] s enfant m de chœur; (priest) acolyte m; assistant m
acorn [ˈekɔrn] s gland m
acoustic [əˈkustɪk] adj acoustique ‖ **acoustics** s & spl acoustique f
acquaint [əˈkwent] tr informer; **to be acquainted** se connaître; **to be acquainted with** connaître
acquaintance [əˈkwentəns] s connaissance f
acquiesce [ˌækwiˈɛs] intr acquiescer
acquiescence [ˌækwiˈɛsəns] s acquiescement m; contentement m
acquire [əˈkwaɪr] tr acquérir; (friends; a reputation) s'acquérir
acquired′immune′-defi′ciency syn′drome [əˈkwaɪrd] s syndrome m d'immunodéficience acquise (le SIDA)
acquirement [əˈkwaɪrmənt] s acquisition f
acquisition [ˌækwɪˈzɪʃən] s acquisition f
acquisitive [əˈkwɪzɪtɪv] adj âpre au gain, avide
acquit [əˈkwɪt] v (pret & pp acquitted; ger acquitting) tr acquitter; **to acquit oneself** se comporter
acquittal [əˈkwɪtəl] s acquittement m
acre [ˈekər] s acre f
acrid [ˈækrɪd] adj âcre
acrimonious [ˌækrɪˈmoni•əs] adj acrimonieux

acrobat [ˈækrə, bæt] s acrobate mf
acrobatic [ˌækrəˈbætɪk] adj acrobatique ‖ **acrobatics** s (profession) acrobatie f; **acrobatics** spl (stunts) acrobatics
acronym [ˈækrənɪm] s sigle m
acropolis [əˈkrɑpəlɪs] s acropole f
across [əˈkrɔs] adv en travers, à travers; (sidewise) en largeur ‖ prep en travers de; (e.g., the street) de l'autre côté de; **across country** à travers champs; **to come across** rencontrer par hasard; **to go across** traverser
acrostic [əˈkrɔstɪk] s acrostiche m
acrylic [əˈkrɪlɪk] adj acrylique
act [ækt] s action f, acte m; (circus, rad, telv) numéro m; (govt) loi f; (law, theat) acte; (coll) allure f affectée, comédie f; **in the act** sur le fait, en flagrant délit ‖ tr jouer; **to act the fool** faire le pitre ‖ intr agir; se conduire; (theat) jouer; **to act as** servir de; **to act on** influer sur
acting [ˈæktɪŋ] adj intérimaire, par intérim ‖ s (actor's art) jeu m; (profession) théâtre m
action [ˈækʃən] s action f; (law) acte m; (mach) jeu m; (theat) intrigue f; **out of action** hors de service; **to go into action** (mil) aller au feu; **to suit the action to the word** joindre le geste à la parole; **to take action** prendre des mesures
activate [ˈæktɪˌvet] tr activer, actionner
active [ˈæktɪv] adj actif
ac′tive ma′trix s (comp) matrice f active
activi•ty [ækˈtɪvɪti] s (pl -ties) activité f
actor [ˈæktər] s acteur m
actress [ˈæktrɪs] s actrice f
actual [ˈæktʃʊ•əl] adj véritable, réel, effectif
actually [ˈæktʃʊ•əli] adv réellement, en réalité, effectivement
actuar•y [ˈæktʃʊˌɛri] s (pl -ies) actuaire m
actuate [ˈæktʃʊˌet] tr (to turn on) actionner; (to motivate) animer
acuity [əˈkju•ɪti] s acuité f
acumen [əˈkjumən] s finesse f
acupuncture [ˈækjʊpˌʌŋktʃər] s acupuncture f, acuponcture f
acute [əˈkjut] adj aigu; (fig) avisé
acute′ac′cent s accent m aigu
acutely [əˈkjutli] adv profondément
A.D. [ˈeˈdi] adj (letterword) (**Anno Domini**) ap. J.-C.
ad [æd] s (coll) annonce f
adage [ˈædɪdʒ] s adage m
Adam [ˈædəm] s Adam m; **I don't know him from Adam** (coll) je ne le connais ni d'Eve ni d'Adam
adamant [ˈædəmənt] adj inflexible
Ad′am's ap′ple s pomme f d'Adam
adapt [əˈdæpt] tr adapter
adaptation [ˌædæpˈteʃən] s adaptation f
adapter [əˈdæptər] s adaptateur m; (phot) bague f porte-objectif
add [æd] tr ajouter; **to add up** additionner ‖ intr additionner; **to add up to** s'élever à
adder [ˈædər] s (zool) vipère f

addict [ˈædɪkt] *s* (pathol) toxicomane *mf*; (sports) fanatique *mf* ‖ [əˈdɪkt] *tr* atteindre de toxicomanie; **to be addicted to** (*drugs; alcohol*) s'adonner à; (*to enjoy*) s'adonner à

addiction [əˈdɪkʃən] *s* toxicomanie *f*; **addiction to** penchant *m* pour; (pathol) dépendance *f* à

add'ing machine' *s* machine *f* à calculer, additionneuse *f*, calculatrice *f*

addition [əˈdɪʃən] *s* addition *f*; **in addition to** en plus de

additive [ˈædɪtɪv] *adj & s* additif *m*

addle [ˈædəl] *tr* brouiller

address [əˈdrɛs], [ˈædrɛs] *s* adresse *f* ‖ [əˈdrɛs] *s* discours *m*; **to deliver an address** prononcer un discours ‖ *tr* adresser; s'adresser à; (*an audience*) faire un discours à

address' book' *s* carnet *m* d'adresses

address'bus' *s* (comp) bus *m* d'adresse

addressee [ˌædrɛˈsi] *s* destinataire *mf*

adduce [əˈd(j)us] *tr* alléguer; (*proof*) fournir

adenoids [ˈædəˌnɔɪdz] *spl* végétations *fpl* adénoïdes

adept [əˈdɛpt] *adj* habile ‖ *s* adepte *mf*

adequate [ˈædɪkwɪt] *adj* suffisant, adéquat; **adequate to** à la hauteur de, proportionné à

adhere [ædˈhɪr] *intr* adhérer

adherence [ædˈhɪrəns] *s* adhérence *f*

adherent [ædˈhɪrənt] *adj & s* adhérent *m*

adhesion [ædˈhiʒən] *s* adhésion *f*; (pathol) adhérence *f*

adhesive [ædˈhisɪv] *adj & s* adhésif *m*

adhe'sive hook' *s* piton *m* adhésif

adhe'sive tape' *s* sparadrap *m*

adieu [əˈd(j)u] *s* (*pl* **adieus** or **adieux**) adieu *m* ‖ *interj* adieu!

ad infinitum [ˌædˌɪnfɪˈnaɪtəm] *adv* sans fin

adjacent [əˈdʒesənt] *adj* adjacent

adjective [ˈædʒɪktɪv] *adj & s* adjectif *m*

adjoin [əˈdʒɔɪn] *tr* avoisiner ‖ *intr* être contigus

adjoining [əˈdʒɔɪnɪŋ] *adj* contigu

adjourn [əˈdʒʌrn] *tr* (*to postpone*) remettre, reporter; (*a meeting, a session*) lever; (*sine die; for resumption at another time or place*) ajourner ‖ *intr* s'ajourner; lever la séance

adjournment [əˈdʒʌrnmənt] *s* suspension *f* de séance

adjudge [əˈdʒʌdʒ] *tr* adjuger; (*a criminal*) condamner

adjudicate [əˈdʒudɪˌket] *tr & intr* juger

adjunct [ˈædʒʌŋkt] *adj & s* adjoint *m*; **adjuncts** accessoires *mpl*

adjust [əˈdʒʌst] *tr* ajuster ‖ *intr* s'adapter

adjustable [əˈdʒʌstəbəl] *adj* réglable; (*antenna*) orientable

adjustment [əˈdʒʌstmənt] *s* (*act of adjusting*) ajustage *m*, réglage *m*; (*wages, prices*) rajustement *m*; (*arrangement*) ajustement *m*, règlement *m*; (telv) mise *f* au point

adjutant [ˈædʒətənt] *s* adjutant *m*

ad-lib [ˌædˈlɪb] *adj* improvisé ‖ *v* (*pret & pp* **-libbed**; *ger* **-libbing**) *tr & intr* improviser (en cascade)

administer [ædˈmɪnɪstər] *tr* administrer; **to ad-minister an oath** faire prêter serment ‖ *intr*—**to administer to** pourvoir à, aider, assister

administration [ædˌmɪnɪsˈtreʃən] *s* (*management*) administration *f*; (*government*) gouvernement *m*

administrator [ædˈmɪnɪsˌtretər] *s* administrateur *m*

admiral [ˈædmɪrəl] *s* amiral *m*

admiration [ˌædmɪˈreʃən] *s* admiration *f*

admire [ædˈmaɪr] *tr* admirer

admirer [ædˈmaɪrər] *s* admirateur *m*; (*suitor*) soupirant *m*

admission [ædˈmɪʃən] *s* admission *f*; (*entry*) entrée *f*, accès *m*; (*confession*) aveu *m*; **free admission** entrée gratuite *or* libre

ad·mit [ædˈmɪt] *v* (*pret & pp* **-mitted**; *ger* **-mitting**) *tr* admettre; (*e.g., a mistake*) avouer; **admit bearer** laisser passer

admittance [ædˈmɪtəns] *s* droit *m* d'entrée, admission *f*; **admittance to** accès *m* auprès de; **no admittance** accès interdit, entrée *f* interdite

admittedly [ædˈmɪtɪdli] *adv* manifestement

admonish [ædˈmɑnɪʃ] *tr* admonester

ad nauseam [ædˈnɔʃiˌæm], [ædˈnɔsɪˌæm] *adv* jusqu'au dégoût

ado [əˈdu] *s* agitation *f*; **much ado about nothing** beaucoup de bruit pour rien; **without further ado** sans plus de façons

adolescence [ˌædəˈlɛsəns] *s* adolescence *f*

adolescent [ˌædəˈlɛsənt] *adj & s* adolescent *m*

adopt [əˈdɑpt] *tr* adopter

adoption [əˈdɑpʃən] *s* adoption *f* (*adoption plénière*)

adoptive [əˈdɑptɪv] *adj* adoptif

adop'tive fath'er *s* père *m* adoptif (*selon l'adoption plénière*)

adop'tive moth'er *s* mère *f* adoptive (*selon l'adoption plénière*)

adorable [əˈdorəbəl] *adj* adorable

adoration [ˌædəˈreʃən] *s* adoration *f*

adore [əˈdor] *tr* adorer

adorn [əˈdɔrn] *tr* orner, parer

adornment [əˈdɔrnmənt] *s* parure *f*

adre'nal glands' [ædˈrinəl] *spl* (capsules) surrénales *fpl*

adrenaline [əˈdrɛnəlɪn] *s* adrénaline *f*

Adriatic [ˌedrɪˈætɪk] *adj & s* Adriatique *f*

adrift [əˈdrɪft] *adj & adv* à la dérive

adroit [əˈdrɔɪt] *adj* adroit, habile

adulate [ˈædʒəˌlet] *tr* aduler

adult [əˈdʌlt] *adj & s* adulte *mf*

adult' book' shop' *s* érotothèque *f*

adulterate [əˈdʌltəˌret] *tr* frelater

adulteration [əˌdʌltəˈreʃən] *s* frelatage *m*

adulterer [əˈdʌltərər] *s* adultère *m*

adulteress [əˈdʌltərɪs] *s* adultère *f*

adulterous [əˈdʌltərəs] *adj* adultère

adulter·y [əˈdʌltəri] *s* (*pl* **-ies**) adultère *m*

adumbrate [əˈdʌməmˌbret] *tr* ébaucher; (*to foreshadow*) présager

advance [ædˈvæns] *s* avance *f*; **advances** propositions *fpl*; propositions malhonnêtes; **in advance** d'avance; en avance ‖ *tr* avancer ‖ *intr* avancer, s'avancer; (*said of prices*) augmenter; (*said of stocks*) monter

advanced [æd'vænst] *adj* supérieur; **advanced in years** d'un age avancé

advanced' stud'ies *spl* hautes études *fpl*

advancement [æd'vænsmənt] *s* avancement *m*

advance' not'ice *s* préavis *m*

advance' pay'ment *s* versement *m* anticipé

advantage [æd'væntɪdʒ] *s* avantage *m*; **to take advantage of** profiter de

advent [ˈædvɛnt] *s* venue *f*; **Advent** (eccl) Avent *m*

adventitious [ˌædvɛn'tɪʃəs] *adj* adventice

adventure [æd'vɛntʃər] *s* aventure *f*

adventurer [æd'vɛntʃərər] *s* aventurier *m*

adventuress [æd'vɛntʃərɪs] *s* adventurière *f*

adventurous [æd'vɛntʃərəs] *adj* aventureux

adverb [ˈædvʌrb] *s* adverbe *m*

adversar•y [ˈædvər,sɛri] *s* (*pl* **-ies**) adversaire *mf*

adverse [æd'vʌrs] *adj* adverse

adversi•ty [æd'vʌrsɪti] *s* (*pl* **-ties**) adversité *f*

advertise [ˈædvər,taɪz] *tr* & *intr* annoncer

advertisement [æd'vʌrtɪzmənt] *s* annonce *f*

advertiser [ˈædvər,taɪzər] *s* annonceur *m*

advertising [ˈædvər,taɪzɪŋ] *s* réclame *f*

ad'vertising a'gency *s* agence *f* de publicité

ad'vertising spe'cialist *s* publicitaire *mf*, entrepreneur *m* de publicité

advice [æd'vaɪs] *s* conseil *m*; conseils; **a piece of advice** un conseil

advisable [æd'vaɪzəbəl] *adj* opportun, recommandable

advise [æd'vaɪz] *tr* (*to counsel*) conseiller; (*to inform*) aviser; **to advise against** déconseiller; **to advise s.o. to** + *inf* conseiller à qn de + *inf*

advisedly [æd'vaɪzɪdli] *adv* en connaissance de cause

advisement [æd'vaɪzmənt] *s* conseils *mpl*; **to take under advisement** mettre en délibération

adviser [æd'vaɪzər] *s* conseiller *m*

advisory [æd'vaɪzəri] *adj* consultatif

advocacy [ˈædvəkəsi] *s* plaidoyer *m*

advocate [ˈædvə,ket] *s* partisan *m*; (*lawyer*) avocat *m* ‖ *tr* préconiser

Aege'an Sea' [ɪ'dʒi•ən] *s* mer *f* Égée, mer de l'Archipel

aegis [ˈidʒɪs] *s* égide *f*

aerial [ˈɛri•əl] *adj* aérien ‖ *s* antenne *f*

aer' ial pho' tograph *s* photographie *f* aérienne

aer' ial sur' vey *s* prise *f* de vues aérienne

aerobics [ə'robɪks] *s* aérobic *m*

aerodynamic [ˌɛrodaɪ'næmɪk] *adj* aérodynamique ‖ **aerodynamics** *s* aérodynamique *f*

aeronautic [ˌɛro'nɔtɪk] *adj* aéronautique ‖ **aeronautics** *s* aéronautique *f*

aerosol [ˈɛrə,sol] *s* aérosol *m*

aerospace [ˈɛrə,spes] *adj* aérospatial

Aeschylus [ˈɛskɪləs] *s* Eschyle *m*

aesthete [ˈɛsθit] *s* esthète *mf*

aesthetic [ɛs'θɛtɪk] *adj* esthétique ‖ **aesthetics** *s* esthétique *f*

afar [ə'fɑr] *adv* au loin

affable [ˈæfəbəl] *adj* affable

affair [ə'fɛr] *s* affaire *f*; (*of lovers*) affaire de cœur

affect [ə'fɛkt] *tr* affecter

affectation [ˌæfɛk'te/ən] *s* affectation *f*

affected *adj* affecté, maniéré

affection [ə'fɛk/ən] *s* affection *f*

affectionate [ə'fɛk/ənɪt] *adj* affectueux

affidavit [ˌæfɪ'devɪt] *s* déclaration *f* sous serment

affiliate [ə'fɪlɪ,et] *s* (com) société *f* affiliée ‖ *tr* affilier ‖ *intr* s'affilier

affini•ty [ə'fɪnɪti] *s* (*pl* **-ties**) affinité *f*; (*connection, resemblance*) rapport *m*, ressemblance *f*; (*liking*) attrait *m*, attraction *f*

affirm [ə'fʌrm] *tr* & *intr* affirmer

affirmative [ə'fʌrmətɪv] *adj* affirmatif ‖ *s* affirmative *f*

affir'mative ac'tion *s* (pol) discrimination *f* positive (*visée à favoriser quelques groupes désavantagés*)

affix [ˈæfɪks] *s* affixe *m* ‖ [ə'fɪks] *tr* (*a signature*) apposer; (*guilt*) attribuer; (*a stamp*) coller

afflict [ə'flɪkt] *tr* affliger

affliction [ə'flɪk/ən] *s* (*sorrow*) affliction *f*; (*disorder*) infirmité *f*

affluence [ˈæflu•əns] *s* affluence *f* de biens, richesse *f*

afford [ə'fɔrd] *tr* (*to provide*) fournir; (*to be able to pay for*) se permettre, avoir de quoi payer, avoir les moyens d'acheter

affront [ə'frʌnt] *s* affront *m* ‖ *tr* insulter

afghan [ˈæfgæn] *adj* & *m* afghan *m* ‖ (*cap*) *mf* *s* Afghan *m*, Afghane *f*

Afghanistan [æf'gænɪ,stæn] *s* l'Afghanistan *m*

afire [ə'faɪr] *adj* & *adv* en feu

aflame [ə'flem] *adj* & *adv* en flammes

afloat [ə'flot] *adj* & *adv* à flot; (*rumor*) en circulation; **to keep afloat on the water** se tenir sur l'eau

afoot [ə'fut] *adj* & *adv* à pied; (*underway*) en œuvre

aforesaid [ə'for,sɛd] *adj* susdit, susmentionné, précité

afraid [ə'fred] *adj* effrayé; **to be afraid** avoir peur

afresh [ə'frɛ/] *adv* à nouveau

Africa [ˈæfrɪkə] *s* Afrique *f*; l' Afrique

African [ˈæfrɪkən] *adj* africain ‖ *s* Africain *m*

African-American [ˈæfrɪkənə'mɛrɪkən] *adj* afro-américain ‖ *mf* Afro-Américain *m*, Afro-Américaine *f*

Afro-American [ˈæfro•ə'mɛrɪkən] *adj* afro-américain ‖ *mf* Afro-Américain *m*, Afro-Américaine *f*

after [ˈæftər] *adj* suivant, postérieur ‖ *adv* après; plus tard; **soon after** bientôt après ‖ *prep* après, à la suite de; (*in the manner or style* *of*) d'après; (*not translated in expressions of time*), e.g., **eight minutes after ten** dix heures huit; **after all** *conj* après que ‖ *conj* après que

af′ter·burn′er *s* (aer) *s* postcombustion *f* (*dispositif de postcombustion*)

af′ter-din′ner *adj* d'après dîner

af′ter-din′ner speak′er *s* orateur *m* de fin de banquet

af′ter-effect′ *s* contrecoup *m*; **after-effects** (pathol) séquelles *fpl*

af′ter·glow′ *s* lueur *f* du coucher

af′ter-im′age *s* image *f* consécutive

af′ter-life′ *s* survie *f*

aftermath [`æftər,mæθ] *s* conséquences *fpl* sérieuses, suites *fpl*; (agr) regain *m*

af′ter·noon′ *s* après-midi *m* & *f*; **good afternoon!** bonjour!

af′tershave′ (lo′tion) *s* lotion *f* après-rasage

af′ter·taste′ *s* arrière-goût *m*

af′ter·thought′ *s* réflexion *f* après coup

afterward [`æftərwərd] *adv* après, ensuite

again [ə`gɛn] *adv* encore; (*besides, moreover*) de plus, d'ailleurs, en outre; (*once more*) de nouveau, encore une fois; **as much again** deux fois autant; **not again** ne . . . plus, e.g., **I won't do it again** je ne le ferai plus; **now and again** de temps en temps

against [ə`gɛnst] *prep* contre; **against the grain** à rebrousse-poil; **over against** en face de; par contraste que

age [edʒ] *s* âge *m*; (*about a hundred years*) siècle *m*; **for ages** depuis longtemps; **of age** majeur; **to come of age** atteindre sa majorité; **under age** mineur ‖ *tr* & *intr* vieillir

age′ brack′et *s* tranche *f* d'âge

aged [edʒd] *adj* (*wine, cheese, etc.*) vieilli; (*of the age of*) âgé de ‖ [`edʒɪd] *adj* âgé, vieux

age′less *adj* sans âge, toujours jeune

agen·cy [`edʒənsi] *s* (*pl* **-cies**) agence *f*; (*means*) action *f*

agenda [ə`dʒɛndə] *s* ordre *m* du jour

agent [`edʒənt] *s* agent *m*; (*means*) moyen *m*; (com) commissionnaire *m*

agglomeration [ə,glɑmə`reʃən] *s* agglomération *f*

aggrandizement [ə`grændɪzmənt] *f* agrandissement *m*

aggravate [`æɡrə,vet] *tr* aggraver; (coll) exaspérer

aggregate [`æɡrɪ,get] *adj* global ‖ *s* agrégat *m* ‖ *tr* assembler; (coll) s'élever à

aggression [ə`grɛʃən] *s* agression *f*

aggressive [ə`grɛsɪv] *adj* agressif; (*live-wire*) entreprenant

aggressor [ə`grɛsər] *s* agresseur *m*

aghast [ə`gæst] *adj* abasourdi

agile [`ædʒɪl] *adj* agile

agility [ə`dʒɪlɪti] *s* agilité *f*

agitate [`ædʒɪ,tet] *tr* agiter

agitator [`ædʒɪ,tetər] *s* agitateur *m*

aglow [ə`glo] *adj* & *adv* rougeoyant

agnostic [æg`nɑstɪk] *adj* & *s* agnostique *mf*

ago [ə`go] *adv* il y a, e.g., **two days ago** il y a deux jours

agog [ə`gɑg] *adj* & *adv* en émoi

agonizing [`æɡə,naɪzɪŋ] *adj* angoissant

ago·ny [`æɡəni] *s* (*pl* **-nies**) (*physical pain*) douleur *f* atroce; (*mental pain*) angoisse *f*; (*death struggle*) agonie *f*

agrarian [ə`grɛrɪ·ən] *adj* agraire; (law) agrarien ‖ *s* agrairien *m*

agree [ə`gri] *intr* être d'accord, s'accorder; **agreed!** d'accord!; **to agree to** consentir à

agreeable [ə`gri·əbəl] *adj* agréable, sympathique; (*consenting*) d'accord

agreement [ə`grimənt] *s* accord *m*

agriculture [`æɡrɪ,kʌlt/ər] *s* agriculture *f*

agronomy [ə`grɑnəmi] *s* agronomie *f*

aground [ə`graʊnd] *adj* (naut) échoué ‖ *adv*—**to run aground** échouer

ague [`egju] *s* fièvre *f* intermittente

ahead [ə`hɛd] *adj* & *adv* en avant; **ahead of** avant; devant; **straight ahead** tout droit; **to get ahead of** devancer

ahem [ə`hɛm] *interj* hum!

ahoy [ə`hɔɪ] *interj*—**ship ahoy!** ohé du navire!

AI [`e`aɪ] *s* (letterword) (**artificial intelligence**) IA (intelligence artificielle)

aid [ed] *s* (*assistance*) aide *f*; (*assistant*) aide *mf* ‖ *tr* aider

aide-de-camp [`eddə`kæmp] *s* (*pl* **aides-de-camp**) officier *m* d'ordonnance, aide *m* de camp

AIDS [edz] *s* (acronym) (**acquired immune-deficiency syndrome**) le SIDA (syndrome d'immuno-déficience acquise)

ail [el] *tr* affliger; **what ails you?** qu'avez-vous? ‖ *intr* être souffrant

ailment [`elmənt] *s* indisposition *f*, maladie *f*

aim [em] *s* (*purpose*) but *m*, objectif *m*; (*of gun*) pointage *m* ‖ *tr* diriger; (*a blow*) allonger; (*a telescope, cannon, etc.*) pointer, viser ‖ *intr* viser

air [ɛr] *s* air *m*; **on the air** à la radio, à la télévision, à l'antenne; **to put on airs** prendre des airs; **to put on the air** radio-diffuser; **to walk on air** ne pas toucher terre; **up in the air** confondu, sidéré; (*angry*) très monté ‖ *tr* aérer; (*a question*) ventiler; (*feelings*) donner libre cours à

air′ bag′ *s* (aut) coussin *m* gonflable

air-borne [`ɛr,born] *adj* aéroporté

air′ brake′ *s* frein *m* à air comprimé

air′-condi′tion *tr* climatiser

air′ condi′tioner *s* climatiseur *m*

air′ condi′tioning *s* climatisation *f*

air controller *var* de **air traffic controller**

air′craft′ *s* aéronef *m*, appareil *m* d'aviation

air′craft car′rier *s* porte-avions *m*

air′drop′ *s* parachutage *m* ‖ *tr* parachuter

air′field′ *s* terrain *m* d'aviation, aérodrome *m*

air′foil′ *s* voilure *f*

air′ force′ *s* forces *fpl* aériennes

air′ freight′ *s* (*parcels*) transport *m* par avion,

fret *m* par avion; (*company*) messageries *fpl* aériennes

air′ gap′ *s* (elec) entrefer *m*

air′ in′take *s* entrée *f* d'air, prise *f* d'air

air′ lane′ *s* couloir *m* aérien, couloir de navigation aérienne

air′ let′ter *s* aérogramme *m*

air′lift′ *s* pont *m* aérien

air′line′ *s* ligne *f* aérienne

air′line pi′lot *s* pilote *m* de ligne

air′lin′er *s* avion *m* de transport

air′mail′ *adj* aéropostal ‖ *s* poste *f* aérienne; by airmail par avion

air′mail let′ter *s* lettre *f* par avion

air′mail stamp′ *s* timbre *m* aéropostal

air′ mat′tress *s* matelas *m* pneumatique

air′plane′ *s* avion *m*

air′ pock′et *s* trou *m* d'air

air′ pollu′tion *s* pollution *f* de l'air

air′port′ *s* aéroport *m*

air′port police′ *s* police *f* de l'air

air′ pump′ *s* compresseur *m* pneumatique

air′ raid′ *s* attaque *f* aérienne

air′-raid drill′ *s* exercice *m* d'alerte aérienne

air′-raid shel′ter *s* abri *m*

air′-raid ward′en *s* chef *m* d'îlot

air′-raid warn′ing *s* alarme *f* aérienne

air′ ri′fle *s* fusil *m* à vent comprimé

air′ show′ *s* (*airplane display*) salon *m* de l'aéronautique; (*flying display*) meeting *m* d'aviation rallye *m* d'aviation

air′ shut′tle *s* navette *f* aérienne

air′sick′ *adj* atteint du mal de l'air

air′sick′ness *s* mal *m* de l'air

air′ sleeve′ or sock′ *s* manche *f* à air

air′term′inal *s* aérogare *f*

air′tight′ *adj* hermétique

air′-to-air′ *adj* avion-avion *inv*

air′-to-ground′ *adj* air-sol *inv*

air′ (traf′fic) control′ler *s* contrôleur *m* aérien, aiguilleur *m* (du ciel), contrôleur de la navigation aérienne

air′waves′ *spl* ondes *fpl* radiophoniques

air′way′ *s* route *f* aérienne

air·y [′εri] *adj* (*comp* -ier; *super* -iest) (*room*) bien aéré; (*casual, light*) léger; (*graceful*) gracieux; (coll) maniéré

aisle [aɪl] *s* (*through rows of seats*) passage *m* central, allée *f*; (*in a train*) couloir *m*; (*long passageway in a church*) nef *f* latérale

ajar [ə′dʒɑr] *adj* entrebâillé

akimbo [ə′kɪmbo] *adj & adv*—with arms akimbo les poings sur les hanches

akin [ə′kɪn] *adj* apparenté

alabaster [′ælə,bæstər] *s* albâtre *m*

alacrity [ə′lækrɪti] *s* vivacité *f*, empressement *m*

alarm [ə′lɑrm] *s* alarme *f*; (*of clock*) sonnerie *f* ‖ *tr* alarmer

alarm′ clock′ *s* réveille-matin *m*, réveil *m*

alarming [ə′lɑrmɪn] *adj* alarmant

alas [ə′læs] *interj* hélas!

Alaska [ə′læskə] *s* Alaska *m*

Albanian [æl′beni·ən] *adj* albanais ‖ *s* (*language*) albanais *m*; (*person*) Albanais

albatross [′ælbə,trɔs] *s* albatros *m*

albi·no [æl′baino] *adj* albinos ‖ *s* (*pl* -nos) albinos *m*

album [′ælbəm] *s* album *m*

albumen [′ælbjumən] *s* albumen *m*

alchemy [′ælkɪmi] *s* alchimie *f*

alcohol [′ælkə,hɔl] *s* alcool *m*

alcoholic [,ælkə′hɔlɪk] *adj & s* alcoolique *mf*

Alcohol′ics Anon′ymous *s* Alcooliques *mpl* Anonymes (*société d'entraide des alcooliques*)

alcove [′ælkov] *s* niche *f*; (*for a bed*) alcôve *f*

alder [′ɔldər] *s* aune *m*

alder·man [′ɔldərmən] *s* (*pl* -men) conseiller *m* municipal

ale [el] *s* ale *f*

alembic [ə′lεmbɪk] *s* alambic *m*; (fig) creuset *m*

alert [ə′lʌrt] *adj & s* alerte *f* ‖ *tr* alerter

Aleut′ian Is′lands [ə′luʃən] *spl* (îles *fpl*) Aléoutiennes

alfalfa [æl′fælfə] *s* luzerne *f*

algae [′ældʒi] *spl* algues *fpl*

algebra [′ældʒɪbrə] *s* algèbre *f*

Algeria [æl′dʒɪri·ə] *s* Algérie *f*

Algerian [æl′dʒɪri·ən] *adj* (*of Algeria*) algérien; (*of Algiers, the Barbary state*) algérois ‖ *s* Algérien *m*; Algérois *m*

Algiers [æl′dʒɪrz] *s* Alger *m*

alias [′eli·əs] *s* nom *m* d'emprunt ‖ *adv* alias, autrement dit

ali·bi [′ælɪ,baɪ] *s* (*pl* -bis) excuse *f*; (law) alibi *m*

alien [′eljən] *adj & s* étranger *m*

alienate [′eljə,net] *tr* aliéner, s'aliéner

alight [ə′laɪt] *adj* allumé ‖ *v* (*pret & pp* alighted or alit [ə′lɪt]) *intr* descendre, se poser; (aer) (*on land*) atterrir; (aer) (*on sea*) amerrir

align [ə′laɪn] *tr* aligner ‖ *intr* s'aligner

alignment [ə′laɪnmənt] *s* alignement *m*

alike [ə′laɪk] *adj* pareils, e.g., these books are alike ces livres sont pareils; to look alike se ressembler ‖ *adv* de la même façon

alimentary canal′ [,ælɪ′mεntəri] *m* tube *m* digestif

alimony [′ælɪ,moni] *s* pension *f* alimentaire après divorce

alive [ə′laɪv] *adj* vivant; vif; alive to sensible à

alka·li [′ælkə,laɪ] *s* (*pl* -lis or -lies) alcali *m*

alkaline [′ælkə,laɪn] *adj* alcalin

all [ɔl] *adj indef* tout; tout le ‖ *s* tout *m* ‖ *pron indef* tout; tous; all of tout le; first of all tout d'abord; is that all? c'est tout?; (*ironically*) ce n'est que ça?; not at all pas du tout ‖ *adv* tout; all at once tout à coup; all but presque; all in (coll) éreinté; all in all à tout prendre; all off (slang) abandonné; all right bon, ça va, très bien; all's well! (naut) bon quart!; all the better tant mieux; all told en tout; fifteen (thirty, etc.) all (tennis) égalité à quinze (trente, etc.); partout, e.g., **thirty all** trente partout; **to be all for** ne demander mieux que

Allah [`ælə], [`ɑlə] *m* Allah *m*

all-American [`ɔlə`mɛrɪkən] *adj* cent pour cent américain

all-around [`ɔlə`raʊnd] *adj* complet; général, sur toute la ligne

allay [ə`le] *tr* apaiser

all´-clear´ *s* fin *f* d'alerte

allege [ə`lɛdʒ] *tr* (*to assert*) alléguer; (*to assert without proof*) affirmer sans preuve; (law) déclarer sous serment

alleged *adj* présumé, prétendu, censé

allegedly [ə`lɛdʒɪdli] *adv* prétendument, censément

allegiance [ə`lidʒəns] *s* allégeance *f*

allegoric(al) [ælɪ`gɔrɪk(əl)] *adj* allégorique

allego·ry [`ælɪˌgori] *s* (*pl* **-ries**) allégorie *f*

allergic [ə`lʌrdʒɪk] *adj* allergique

aller·gy [`ælərdʒi] *s* (*pl* **-gies**) allergie *f*

alleviate [ə`livɪˌet] *tr* soulager, alléger

alley [`æli] *s* ruelle *f*; **that is up my alley** (slang) cela est dans mes cordes

al´ley cat´ *s* chat *m* de gouttière

alliance [ə`laɪ•əns] *s* alliance *f*

alligator [`ælɪˌgetər] *s* alligator *m*

al´ligator clip´ *s* pince *f* crocodile

al´ligator pear´ *s* poire *f* d'avocat

al´ligator wrench´ *s* clef *f* crocodile

alliteration [əˌlɪtə`reʃən] *s* allitération *f*

all´-know´ing *adj* omniscient

allocate [`æloˌket] *tr* allouer, assigner

allot [ə`lɑt] *v* (*pret & pp* **allotted**; *ger* **allotting**) *tr* répartir

allotment [ə`lɑtmənt] *s* allocation *f*

all´-out´ *adj* total

allow [ə`laʊ] *tr* (*to permit*) permettre, tolérer; (*to concede*) admettre; (*as a grant*) allouer, accorder || *intr*—**to allow for** tenir compte de

allowance [ə`laʊ•əns] *s* (*money*) allocation *f*, indemnité *f*; (com) réduction *f*, rabais *m*, concession *f*; **to make allowances for** tenir compte de

alloy [`ælɔɪ] *s* alliage *m* || [ə`lɔɪ] *tr* allier

all´-pow´erful *adj* tout-puissant

all´-pur´pose *adj* qui répond à tous les besoins; (*knife*) universel

all´ right´ *interj* bon!, très bien!, ça va!; (*agreed!*) c'est entendu!, d'accord!

all´-round´ *adj* (*athlete*) complet; (*man*) universel; total, global

All´ Saints´´ Day´ *s* la Toussaint

All´ Souls´´ Day´ *s* la fête des Morts

all´spice´ *s* (*plant*) quatre-épices *f*; (*berry*) toute-épice *f*; piment *m*

all´-time´ *adj* record

allude [ə`lud] *intr*—**to allude to** faire allusion à

allure [ə`lʊr] *tr* séduire, tenter

allurement [ə`lʊrmənt] *s* charme *m*

alluring [ə`lʊrɪn] *adj* séduisant

allusion [ə`luʒən] *s* allusion *f*

all´-weath´er *adj* de toute saison, tous temps

all´ wet´ *adj* (coll) fichu, erroné

al·ly [`ælaɪ] *s* (*pl* **-lies**) allié *m* || [ə`laɪ] *v* (*pret & pp* **-lied**) *tr* allier

almanac [`ɔlmə,næk] *s* almanach *m*

almighty [ɔl`maɪti] *adj* omnipotent, toutpuissant

almond [`ɑmənd], [`æmənd] *s* amande *f*

al´mond tree´ *s* amandier *m*

almost [`ɔlmost] *adv* presque; **I almost fell** j'ai failli tomber

alms [ɑmz] *s & spl* aumône *f*

alms´house´ *s* hospice *m*

aloe [`ælo] *s* aloès *m*

aloft [ə`lɔft] *adv* en l'air, en haut; (aer) en vol; (naut) en haut

alone [ə`lon] *adj* seul, e.g., **my arm alone suffices** mon bras seul suffit; e.g., **the metropolis alone** la seule métropole; **let alone . . .** sans compter . . .; **to leave alone** laisser tranquille || *adv* seulement

along [ə`lɔn] *adv* avec; **all along** tout le temps; **come along!** venez donc!; **to get along** s'en aller; se porter, faire des progrès || *prep* le long de; sur

along´side´ *adv* à côté || *prep* à côté de

aloof [ə`luf] *adj* isolé, peu abordable || *adv* à l'écart, à distance

aloud [ə`laʊd] *adv* à haute voix

alpenstock [`ælpən,stɑk] *s* bâton *m* ferré

alphabet [`ælfə,bɛt] *s* alphabet *m*

alpine [`ælpaɪn] *adj* alpin

Alps [ælps] *spl*—**the Alps** les Alpes *fpl*

al Quaeda [al`kedɑ] *s* al-Qaïda *m*

already [ɔl`rɛdɪ] *adv* deja

alright *var de* **all right**

Alsatian [æl`seʒən] *adj* alsacien || *s* (*dialect*) alsacien *m*; (*person*) Alsacien *m*

also [`ɔlso] *adv* aussi, également

altar [`ɔltər] *s* autel *m*

al´tar boy´ *s* enfant *m* de chœur

al´tar cloth´ *s* nappe *f* d'autel

al´tar·piece´ *s* rétable *m*

al´tar rail´ *s* grille *f* du chœur, grille de l'autel

alter [`ɔltər] *tr* (*to transform*) changer, modifier; (*to date; evidence*) falsifier, fausser; (*a text*) altérer; (*a suit of clothes*) retoucher, faire des retouches à; (*an animal*) châtrer || *intr* changer, se modifier

alteration [ˌɔltə`reʃən] *s* (*transformation*) changement *m*; (*falsification*) altération *f*; (*in a building*) modification *f*; **alterations** (*in clothing*) retouches *fpl*

alternate [`ɔltərnɪt] *adj* alternatif; (*angle*) alterne; (*rhyme*) croisé || [`ɔltər,net] *tr* faire alternance à || *intr* alterner

al´ternating cur´rent *s* courant *m* alternatif

alternative [ɔl`tʌrnətɪv] *adj* alternatif || *s* alternative *f*

although [ɔl`ðo] *conj* bien que, quoique

altitude [`æltɪ,t(j)ud] *s* altitude *f*

al´titude sick´ness *s* mal *m* d'altitude, mal des montagnes

al·to [`ælto] *s* (*pl* **-tos**) alto *m*

altogether [ˌɔltəˈgɛðər] *adv* (*wholly*) entièrement, tout à fait; (*on the whole*) somme toute, tout compte fait; (*with everything included*) en tout, tout compris
altruist [ˈæltrʊ•ɪst] *adj & s* altruiste *mf*
alum [ˈæləm] *s* alun *m*
aluminum [əˈlumɪnəm] *s* aluminium *m*
alu′minum foil′ *s* papier *m* alu
alum•na [əˈlʌmnə] *s* (*pl* **-nae** [ni]) diplômée *f*, ancienne étudiante *f*
alum•nus [əˈlʌmnəs] *s* (*pl* **-ni** [naɪ]) diplômé *m*, ancien étudiant *m*
alveo•lus [ælˈvi•ələs] *s* (*pl* **-li** [ˌlaɪ]) alvéole *m*
always [ˈɔlwɪz], [ˈɔlwez] *adv* toujours
Alz′heimer's disease′ [ˈɑltsˌhaɪmərz] *s* maladie *f* d'Alzheimer
AM [ˈeˈɛm] *s* (letterword) (**amplitude modulation**) modulation *f* d'amplitude
A.M. [ˈeˈɛm] *adv* (letterword) (**ante meridiem**) du matin, a.m.
Am. *abbr* **America, American**
amalgam [əˈmælgəm] *s* amalgame *m*
amalgamate [əˈmælgəˌmet] *tr* amalgamer ‖ *intr* s'amalgamer
amass [əˈmæs] *tr* amasser
amateur [ˈæmətʃər] *adj & s* amateur *m*
amaze [əˈmez] *tr* étonner
amazing [əˈmezɪŋ] *adj* étonnant
amazon [ˈæməˌzɑn] *s* amazone *f*; **Amazon** Amazone *f*; (*river*) fleuve *m* des Amazones
ambassador [æmˈbæsədər] *s* ambassadeur *m*
ambassadress [æmˈbæsədrɪs] *s* ambassadrice *f*, ambassadeur *m*
amber [ˈæmbər] *adj* ambré ‖ *s* ambre *m* jaune, ambre succin
ambidextrous [ˌæmbɪˈdɛkstrəs] *adj* ambidextre
ambigui•ty [ˌæmbɪˈgju•ɪti] *s* (*pl* **-ties**) ambiguïté *f*
ambiguous [æmˈbɪgju•əs] *adj* ambigu
ambition [æmˈbɪʃən] *s* ambition *f*
ambitious [æmˈbɪʃəs] *adj* ambitieux
amble [ˈæmbəl] *s* amble *m* ‖ *intr* (*to stroll*) déambuler; (equit) ambler
ambulance [ˈæmbjələns] *s* ambulance *f*
am′bulance corps′ *s* service *m* sanitaire
am′bulance driv′er *s* ambulancier *m*
ambulatory [ˈæmbjələˌtori] *adj* ambulatoire
ambush [ˈæmbʊʃ] *s* embuscade *f* ‖ *tr* embusquer
ame•ba [əˈmibə] *s* (*pl* **-bas** *ou* **-bae** [bi]) amide *f*
ameliorate [əˈmiljəˌret] *tr* améliorer ‖ *intr* s'améliorer
amen [ˈeˈmɛn], [ˈɑˈmɛn] *s* amen *m* ‖ *interj* ainsi soit-il!
amenable [əˈminəbəl] *adj* docile; **amenable to** (*a court*) justiciable de; (*a fine*) passible de; (*a law*) soumis à; (*persuasion*) disposé à; (*a superior*) responsable envers
amend [əˈmɛnd] *tr* amender ‖ *intr* s'amender
amendment [əˈmɛndmənt] *s* amendement *m*
amends [əˈmɛndz] *spl* dédommagement *m*; **to make amends to** dédommager
ameni•ty [əˈmɛnɪti] *s* (*pl* **-ties**) aménité *f*; **amenities** agréments *mpl*; civilités *fpl*
America [əˈmɛrɪkə] *s* Amérique *f*; l'Amérique
American [əˈmɛrɪkən] *adj* américain; (*of the U.S.A.*) états-unien ‖ *s* Américain *m*, Américaine *f*; (*from the U.S.A.*) États-Unien *m*, États-Unienne *f*
Amer′ican Eng′lish *s* américain *m*, anglo-américain *m* (*anglais parlé aux États-Unis*)
Amer′ican In′dian *s* amérindien *m*
Americanism [əˈmɛrɪkəˌnɪzəm] *s* (*word*) américanisme *m*; patriotisme *m* américain
Amer′ican plan′ *s* pension *f* complète
Amer′ican way of life′ *s* mode *m* de vie américain
Amerindian [ˌæməˈrɪndi•ən] *adj* amérindien ‖ *s* Amérindien *m*
amethyst [ˈæmɪθɪst] *s* améthyste *f*
amiable [ˈemɪ•əbəl] *adj* aimable
amicable [ˈæmɪkəbəl] *adj* amical
amid [əˈmɪd] *prep* au milieu de
amid′ships *adv* au milieu du navire
amidst [əˈmɪdst] *prep* au milieu de
amiss [əˈmɪs] *adj* détraqué; **not amiss** pas mal; **something amiss** quelque chose qui manque, quelque chose qui cloche ‖ *adv* de travers; **to take amiss** prendre en mauvaise part
ami•ty [ˈæmɪti] *s* (*pl* **-ties**) amitié *f*
ammeter [ˈæmˌmitər] *s* ampèremètre *m*
ammonia [əˈmonɪ•ə] *s* (*gas*) ammoniac *m*; (*gas dissolved in water*) ammoniaque *f*
ammunition [ˌæmjəˈnɪʃən] *s* munitions *fpl*
amnesia [æmˈniʒə] *s* amnésie *f*
amnes•ty [ˈæmnɪsti] *s* (*pl* **-ties**) amnistie *f* ‖ *v* (*pret & pp* **-tied**) *tr* amnistier
amniocentesis [ˌæmnɪ•osɛnˈtisɪs] *s* amniocentèse *f*
amnion [ˈæmnɪ•ɑn] *s* amnios *m*
amoeba [əˈmibə] *s* amibe *f*
among [əˈmʌŋ] *prep* entre, parmi
amorous [ˈæmərəs] *adj* amoureux
amorphous [əˈmɔrfəs] *adj* amorphe
amortize [ˈæmərˌtaɪz] *tr* amortir
amount [əˈmaʊnt] *s* montant *m*, quantité *f* ‖ *intr*—**to amount to** s'élever à
ampere [ˈæmpɪr] *s* ampère *m*
am′pere-hour′ *s* ampère-heure *m*
ampersand [ˈæmpərˌsænd] *s* esperluète *f*
amphibian [æmˈfɪbɪ•ən] *adj & s* amphibie *mf*; amphibien *m*
amphibious [æmˈfɪbɪ•əs] *adj* amphibie
amphitheater [ˈæmfɪˌθi•ətər] *s* amphithéâtre *m*
ample [ˈæmpəl] *adj* ample; (*speech*) satisfaisant; (*reward*) suffisant
amplifier [ˈæmplɪˌfaɪ•ər] *s* amplificateur *m*
ampli•fy [ˈæmplɪˌfaɪ] *v* (*pret & pp* **-fied**) *tr* amplifier
amplitude [ˈæmplɪˌt(j)ud] *s* amplitude *f*
am′plitude modula′tion *s* modulation *f* d'amplitude
ampule [ˈæmpjul] *s* ampoule *f*
amputate [ˈæmpjəˌtet] *tr* amputer
amputee [ˌæmpjəˈti] *s* amputé *m*

amuck [əˈmʌk] *adv*—**to run amuck** s'emballer

amulet [ˈæmjəlɪt] *s* amulette *f*

amuse [əˈmjuz] *tr* amuser

amusement [əˈmjuzmənt] *s* amusement *m*

amuse′ment arcade′ *s* salle *f* de jeux électroniques

amuse′ment park′ *s* parc *m* d'attractions

amusing [əˈmjuzɪŋ] *adj* amusant

an [æn], [ən] *art indef* (devant un son vocalique) un

anachronism [əˈnækrə,nɪzəm] *s* anachronisme *m*

analogous [əˈnæləgəs] *adj* analogue

analo‧gy [əˈnælədʒi] *s* (*pl* -**gies**) analogie *f*

analy‧sis [əˈnælɪsɪs] *s* (*pl* -**ses**) [,sɪz] analyse *f*

analyst [ˈænəlɪst] *s* analyste *mf*

analytic(al) [,ænəˈlɪtɪk(əl)] *adj* analytique

analyze [ˈænə,laɪz] *tr* analyser

anarchist [ˈænərkɪst] *s* anarchiste *mf*

anarchy [ˈænərki] *s* anarchie *f*

anathema [əˈnæθɪmə] *s* anathème *m*

anatomic(al) [,ænəˈtɑmɪk(əl)] *adj* anatomique

anato‧my [əˈnætəmi] *s* (*pl* -**mies**) anatomie *f*

ancestor [ˈænsɛstər] *s* ancêtre *m*

ances‧try [ˈænsɛstri] *s* (*pl* -**tries**) ancêtres *mpl*, aïeux *mpl*; (*line*) ascendance *f*

anchor [ˈæŋkər] *s* ancre *f*; (telv) présentateur-tronc *m*, présentatrice-tronc *f*, pilote *mf* d'émission; **anchors aweigh!** ancres levées!; **to cast anchor** jeter l'ancre, mouiller l'ancre; **to weigh anchor** lever l'ancre ‖ *tr & intr* ancrer

an′chor‧man′ *s* (telv) présentateur-tronc *m*, pilote *m* d'émission

an′chor‧per′son *s* présentateur-tronc *m*, présentatrice-tronc *f*, pilote *mf* d'émission

ancho‧vy [ˈænt∫ovi] *s* (*pl* -**vies**) anchois *m*

ancient [ˈen∫ənt] *adj* ancien

and [ænd] *conj* et; **and/or** et/ou; **and so forth** et ainsi de suite

andiron [ˈænd,aɪˈərn] *s* chenet *m*

anecdote [ˈænɪk,dot] *s* anecdote *f*

anemia [əˈnimɪ‧ə] *s* anémie *f*

an′eroid barom′eter [ˈænə,rɔɪd] *s* baromètre *m* anéroïde

anesthesia [,ænɪsˈθiʒə] *s* anesthésie *f*

anesthetic [,ænɪsˈθɛtɪk] *adj & s* anesthésique *m*

anesthetist [æˈnɛsθɪtɪst] *s* anesthésiste *mf*

anesthetize [æˈnɛsθɪ,taɪz] *tr* anesthésier

aneurysm [ˈænjɛ‧ə,rɪzəm] *s* anévrisme *m*

anew [əˈn(j)u] *adv* à (*or* de) nouveau

angel [ˈendʒəl] *s* ange *m* (*financial backer*) (coll) bailleur *m* de fonds

angelic(al) [ænˈdʒɛlɪk(əl)] *adj* angélique

anger [ˈæŋgər] *s* colère *f* ‖ *tr* mettre en colère, fâcher

angina pectoris [ænˈdʒaɪnəˈpɛktərɪs] *s* angine *f* de poitrine

angle [ˈæŋgəl] *s* angle *m* ‖ *tr* (journ) présenter sous un certain angle ‖ *intr* pêcher à la ligne; **to angle for** essayer d'attraper; (*a compliment*) quêter

angler [ˈæŋglər] *s* (*fisherman*) pêcheur *m* à la ligne; (*schemer*) intrigant *m*

Anglo-Saxon [,æŋgloˈsæksən] *adj & s* anglo-saxon *m* ‖ *s* Anglo-Saxon *m*, Anglo-Saxonne *f*

an‧gry [ˈæŋgri] *adj* (*comp* -**grier**; *super* -**griest**) fâché; **angry at** fâché de; **angry with** fâché contre; **to become angry** se mettre en colère

anguish [ˈæŋgwɪ∫] *s* angoisse *f*

angular [ˈæŋgjələr] *adj* angulaire; (*features*) anguleux

anhydrous [ænˈhaɪdrəs] *adj* anhydre

an′iline dyes′ [ˈænɪlɪn] *ou* [ˈænɪ,laɪn] *spl* colorants *mpl* à base d'aniline

animal [ˈænɪməl] *adj & s* animal *m*

animate [ˈænɪmɪt] *adj* animé ‖ [ˈænɪ,met] *tr* animer

an′imated cartoon′ *s* dessins *mpl* animés

animation [,ænɪˈme∫ən] *s* animation *f*

animosi‧ty [,ænɪˈmɑsɪti] *s* (*pl* -**ties**) animosité *f*

animus [ˈænɪməs] *s* animosité *f*; intention *f*

anion [ˈæn,aɪ‧ən] *s* anion *m*

anise [ˈænɪs] *s* anis *m*

aniseed [ˈænɪ,sid] *s* graine *f* d'anis

ankle [ˈæŋkəl] *s* cheville *f*

anklet [ˈæŋklɪt] *s* (*sock*) socquette *f*; (*ornamental circlet*) bracelet *m* de cheville

annals [ˈænəlz] *spl* annales *fpl*

anneal [əˈnil] *tr* recuire, détremper

annex [ˈænɛks] *s* annexe *f* ‖ [əˈnɛks] *tr* annexer, rattacher

annexation [,ænɛksˈe∫ən] *s* annexion *f*, rattachement *m*

annihilate [əˈnaɪ‧ɪ,let] *tr* annihiler

annihilation [ə,naɪ‧ɪˈle∫ən] *s* anéantissement *m*

anniversa‧ry [,ænɪˈvʌrsəri] *adj* anniversaire ‖ *s* (*pl* -**ries**) anniversaire *m*

annotate [ˈænə,tet] *tr* annoter

announce [əˈnaʊns] *tr* annoncer

announcement [əˈnaʊnsmənt] *s* annonce *f*, avis *m*

announcer [əˈnaʊnsər] *s* annonceur *m*; (rad) présentateur *m*, speaker *m*

annoy [əˈnɔɪ] *tr* ennuyer, tourmenter

annoyance [əˈnɔɪ‧əns] *s* ennui *m*, énervement *m*

annoying [əˈnɔɪ‧ɪŋ] *adj* ennuyeux

annual [ˈænju‧əl] *adj* annuel ‖ *s* annuaire *m*; plante *f* annuelle

annui‧ty [əˈn(j)u‧ɪti] *s* (*pl* -**ties**) (*annual payment*) annuité *f*; (*of a retired person*) pension *f* de retraite, pension viagère

an‧nul [əˈnʌl] *v* (*pret & pp* -**nulled**; *ger* -**nulling**) *tr* annuler; abolir

anode [ˈænod] *s* anode *f*

anodyne [ˈænə,daɪn] *adj & s* anodin *m*

anoint [əˈnɔɪnt] *tr* oindre

anomalous [əˈnɑmələs] *adj* anomal

anoma‧ly [əˈnɑməli] *s* (*pl* -**lies**) anomalie *f*

anon [əˈnɑn] *adv* tout à l'heure

anonymity [,ænəˈnɪmɪti] *s* anonymat *m*

anonymous [əˈnɑnɪməs] *adj* anonyme

another [ə'nʌðər] *adj & pron indef* un autre; (*an additional*) encore un; **many another** beaucoup d'autres

answer ['ænsər] *s* réponse *f;* (math) solution *f* ‖ *tr* (e.g., *yes or no*) répondre; (*a question, a letter*) répondre à ‖ *intr* répondre; **to answer for** répondre de

an'swer book' *s* livre *m* du maître

an'swering machine' *s* répondeur *m* automatique

an'swering ser'vice *s* (telp) service *m* des abonnés absents

ant [ænt] *s* fourmi *f;* **to have ants in one's pants** avoir des fourmis

antagonism [æn'tægə,nɪzəm] *s* antagonisme *m*

antagonize [æn'tægə,naɪz] *tr* contrarier; (*a friend*) s'aliéner

Antarctic [ænt'arktɪk] *adj & s* Antarctique *f*

Antarctica [ænt'arktɪkə] *s* l'Antarctique *f*

Antarc'tic O'cean *s* Océan *m* glacial antarctique

ante ['ænti] *s* mise *f* ‖ *tr* miser ‖ *intr* miser, caver; **ante up!** misez!

anteater ['ænt,itər] *s* fourmilier *m*

antecedent [,ænti'sidənt] *adj & s* antécédent *m*

antechamber ['ænti,t∫embər] *s* antichambre *f*

antedate ['ænti,det] *tr* antidater; (*to come before*) précéder

antelope ['ænti,lop] *s* antilope *f*

anten•na [æn'tɛnə] *s* (*pl* **-nae** [ni]) (ent) antenne *f* ‖ *s* (*pl* **-nas**) (rad) antenne *f*

antepenult [,ænti'pinʌlt] *s* antépénultième *f*

anterior [æn'tɪrɪ•ər] *adj* antérieur

anteroom ['ænti,rum] *s* antichambre *f,* vestibule *m*

anthem ['ænθəm] *s* hymne *m;* (eccl) antienne *f,* hymne *f*

ant' hill' *s* fourmilière *f*

antholo•gy [æn'θalədʒi] *s* (*pl* **-gies**) anthologie *f*

Anthony ['ænθəni] *s* Antoine *m*

anthracite ['ænθrə,saɪt] *s* anthracite *m*

anthrax ['ænθræks] *s* (*disease*) charbon *m;* (*group of boils*) anthrax *m*

anthropoid ['ænθro,pɔɪd] *adj & s* anthropoïde *m*

anthropology [,ænθrə'palədʒi] *s* anthropologie *f*

antiaircraft [,ænti'ɛr,kræft] *adj* antiaérien, contre-avions

anti'ballist'ic mis'sile ['æntibə 'lɪstɪk] *s* missile *m* antibalistique

antibiotic [,æntibaɪ'atɪk] *adj & s* antibiotique *m*

antibod•y ['ænti,badi] *s* (*pl* **-ies**) anticorps *m*

anticipate [æn'tɪsɪ,pet] *tr* anticiper; (*to expect*) s'attendre à; devancer

anticipation [æn,tɪsɪ'pe∫ən] *s* anticipation *f*

anticlimax [,ænti'klaɪmæks] *s* chute *f* dans le trivial, désillusion *f*

antics ['æntɪks] *spl* bouffonnerie *f*

antidote ['ænti,dot] *s* antidote *m*

antifreeze [,ænti'friz] *s* antigel *m*

antiglare [,ænti'glɛr] *adj* antiaveuglant

antiknock [,ænti'nak] *adj & s* antidétonant *m*

Antilles [æn'tɪliz] *spl* Antilles *fpl*

anti'lock brakes' ['ænti'lak] *spl* freins *mpl* antiblocage

an'timis'sile mis'sile [,ænti'mɪsəl] *s* missile *m* antimissile

antimony ['ænti,moni] *s* antimoine *m*

antipa•thy [æn'tɪpəθi] *s* (*pl* **-thies**) antipathie *f*

antiperspirant [,ænti'pʌrspərənt] *s* antitranspirant *m*

antiphon ['ænti,fan] *s* antienne *f*

antiquar•y ['ænti,kwɛri] *s* (*pl* **-ies**) collectionneur *m* d'antiquités; (*dealer*) antiquaire *mf*

antiquated ['ænti,kwetɪd] *adj* vieilli, démodé

antique [æn'tik] *adj* antique; ancien ‖ *s* (*piece of furniture*) original *m;* **antiques** meubles *mpl* d'époque

antique' deal'er *s* antiquaire *m*

antique' shop' *s* magasin *m* d'antiquités, maison *f* de meubles d'époque

antiqui•ty [æn'tɪkwɪti] *s* (*pl* **-ties**) antiquité *f;* (*oldness*) ancienneté *f*

anti-Semitic [,æntɪsɪ'mɪtɪk] *adj* antisémite, antisémitique

antiseptic [,æntɪ'sɛptɪk] *adj & s* antiseptique *m*

an'titank' gun' [,ænti'tæŋk] *s* canon *m* antichar

antithe•sis [æn'tɪθɪsɪs] *s* (*pl* **-ses** [,siz]) antithèse *f*

antitoxin [,ænti'taksɪn] *s* antitoxine *f*

antitrust' law' [,ænti'trʌst] *s* loi *f* antitrust *invar*

antiwar [,ænti'wɔr] *adj* antimilitariste

antler ['æntlər] *s* andouiller *m*

antonym ['æntənɪm] *s* antonyme *m*

anvil ['ænvɪl] *s* enclume *f*

anxie•ty [æŋ'zaɪ•əti] *s* (*pl* **-ties**) anxiété *f,* inquiétude *f*

anxious ['æŋk∫əs] *adj* inquiet, soucieux; **to be anxious to** avoir envie de, tenir beaucoup á

any ['ɛni] *adj indef* quelque; du, e.g., **do you have any butter?** avez-vous du beurre?; aucun, e.g., **he reads more than any other child** il lit plus qu'aucun autre enfant; **any day** n'importe quel jour; **any place** n'importe où; **any time** n'importe quand, à tout moment; **any way** n'importe comment, de toute façon ‖ *pron indef* quiconque; quelques-uns §81; **not . . . any** ne . . . aucun §90; ne . . . en . . . pas, e.g., **I will not give him any** je ne lui en donnerai pas ‖ *adv* un peu

an'y•bod'y *pron indef* quelqu'un §81; n'importe qui; **not . . . anybody** ne . . . personne

an'y•how' *adv* en tout cas

an'y•one' *pron indef* quelqu'un §81; n'importe qui; quiconque; **not . . . anyone** ne . . . personne, e.g., **I don't see anyone** je ne vois personne

an'y•thing' *pron indef* quelque chose; n'importe quoi, e.g., **say anything (at all)** dites n'importe quoi; **anything at all** quoi que se soit, si peu que ce soit; **anything but** rien moins que; **anything else?** et avec ça?, ensuite?; **not . . . anything** ne . . . rien

an′y•way′ *adv* en tout cas

an′y•where′ *adv* n'importe où; **not . . . anywhere** ne . . . nulle part

aor•ta [e′ɔrtə] *s* (*pl* **-tas** *ou* **-tae** [ti]) aorte *f*

apace [ə′pes] *adv* vite, rapidement

apache [ə′pæʃ] *s* apache *m* ‖ (*cap*) [ə′pætʃi] *s* apache *m*

apart [ə′part] *adj* séparé ‖ *adv* à part, à l'écart; **apart from** en dehors de

apartheid [ə′partet] *s* apartheid *m*

apartment [ə′partmənt] *s* appartement *m*

apart′ment house′ *s* maison *f* de rapport, immeuble *m* d'habitation

apathetic [,æpə′θεtɪk] *adj* apathique, amorphe

apa•thy [′æpəθi] *s* (*pl* **-thies**) apathie *f*

ape [ep] *s* singe *m* ‖ *tr* singer

aperture [′æpərtʃər] *s* ouverture *f*; (phonet) aperture *f*

apex [′epεks] *s* (*pl* **apexes** or **apices** [′æpɪ,siz]) sommet *m*; (astr) apex *m*

aphid [′æfɪd] *s* puceron *m*

aphorism [′æfə,rɪzəm] *s* aphorisme *m*

aphrodisiac [,æfrə′dɪzɪ,æk] *adj* & *s* aphrodisiaque *m*

apiar•y [′epɪ,εri] *s* (*pl* **-ies**) rucher *m*

apiece [ə′pis] *adv* la pièce, chacun

apish [′epɪʃ] *adj* simiesque; (fig) imitateur

aplomb [ə′plam] *s* aplomb *m*

apocalyptic(al) [ə,pakə′lɪptɪk(əl)] *adj* apocalyptique

Apocrypha [ə′pakrɪfə] *s* apocryphes *mpl*

apogee [′æpə,dʒi] *s* apogée *m*

Apollo [ə′palo] *s* Apollon *m*

apologetic [ə,palə′dʒεtɪk] *adj* prêt à s'excuser, humble, penaud

apologize [ə′palə,dʒaɪz] *intr* faire des excuses, s'excuser

apolo•gy [ə′palədʒi] *s* (*pl* **-gies**) excuse *f*; (*makeshift*) semblant, *m*, prétexte *m*; (*apologia*) apologie *f*

A.P.O. number [′e′pi′o,nʌmbər] *s* (letter-word) (**Army Post Office**) secteur *m* postal

apoplectic [,æpə′plεktɪk] *adj* & *s* apoplectique *mf*

apoplexy [′æpə,plεksi] *s* apoplexie *f*

apostle [ə′pasəl] *s* apôtre *m*

Apos′tles′ Creed′ *s* symbole *m* des apôtres

apos′tle•ship′ *s* apostolat *m*

apostrophe [ə′pastrəfi] *s* apostrophe *f*

apothecar•y [ə′paθɪ,kεri] *s* (*pl* **-ies**) apothicaire *m*

appall [ə′pɔl] *tr* épouvanter, effrayer, consterner

appalling [ə′pɔlɪŋ] *adj* épouvantable

appara•tus [,æpə′retəs] *s* (*pl* **-tus** or **tuses**) appareil *m*, dispositif *m*

appar•el [ə′pærəl] *s* (*equipment; clothes*) appareil *m*; (*clothes*) habillement *m* ‖ *v* (*pret* & *pp* **-eled** or **-elled**; *ger* **-eling** or **elling**) *tr* habiller, vêtir; parer

apparent [ə′pærənt] *adj* apparent; (*heir*) présomptif

apparition [,æpə′rɪʃən] *s* apparition *f*

appeal [ə′pil] *s* (*call*) appel *m*; (*attraction*) charme *m*, attrait *m*; (law) pourvoi *m*, appel ‖ *tr* (*a case*) faire appeler ‖ *intr* (*to request publicly*) lancer un appel; (*to beg*) faire appel; (law) pouvoir en appel; **to appeal to** (*to attract*) séduire, charmer

appealing [ə′pilɪŋ] *adj* séduisant, attrayant, sympathique

appear [ə′pɪr] *intr* (*to come into view; to be published; to seem*) paraître; (*to come into view*) apparaître

appearance [ə′pɪrəns] *s* (*look*) apparence *f*, aspect *m*; (*act of showing up*) apparition *f*; (*in print*) parution *f*; **to all appearances** selon toute vraisemblance; **to make one's appearance** faire acte de présence

appease [ə′piz] *tr* apaiser

appeasement [ə′pizmənt] *s* apaisement *m*

appeaser [ə′pizər] *s* conciliateur *m*, pacificateur *m*

appel′late court′ [ə′pεlet] *s* tribunal *m* d'appel; **highest appellate court** cour *f* de cassation

append [ə′pεnd] *tr* apposer, ajouter

appendage [ə′pεndɪdʒ] *s* dépendance *f*, accessoire *m*

appendecto•my [,æpən′dεktəmi] *s* (*pl* **-mies**) appendicectomie *f*

appendicitis [ə,pεndɪ′saɪtɪs] *s* appendicite *f*

appen•dix [ə′pεndɪks] *s* (*pl* **-dixes** or **dices** [dɪ,siz]) appendice *m*

appertain [,æpər′ten] *intr* se rapporter

appetite [′æpɪ,taɪt] *s* appétit *m*

appetizer [′æpɪ,taɪzər] *s* stimulant *m*, tonique *m*; (culin) premier plat *m*; (culin) amuse-bouche *m*, amuse-gueule *m*

appetizing [′æpɪ,taɪzɪŋ] *adj* appétissant

applaud [ə′plɔd] *tr* (*to give applause to*) applaudir; (*to approve*) applaudir à; **to applaud s.o. for** applaudir qn de ‖ *intr* applaudir

applause [ə′plɔz] *s* applaudissements *mpl*

apple [′æpəl] *s* pomme *f*; (*tree*) pommier *m*

ap′ple•jack′ *s* calvados *m*

ap′ple of the eye′ *s* prunelle *f* des yeux

ap′ple or′chard *s* pommeraie *f*, verger *m* à pommes

ap′ple pie′ *s* tarte *f* aux pommes

ap′ple pol′isher *s* (coll) chien *m* couchant, flagorneur *m*

ap′ple•sauce′ *s* compote *f* de pommes; (slang) balivernes *fpl*

applet [′æplεt] *s* (comp) appliquette *f*, appelette *f*, applet *m* (Canad)

ap′ple tree′ *s* pommier *m*

ap′ple turn′over *s* chausson *m* (aux pommes)

appliance [ə′plaɪəns] *s* (*machine or instrument*) appareil *m*; (*act of applying*) application *f*; **appliances** accessoires *mpl*

applicable [′æplɪkəbəl] *adj* applicable

applicant [′æplɪkənt] *s* candidat *m*, postulant *m*

application [,æplɪ′keʃən] *s* (*putting into effect*) application *f*; (*for a job*) demande *f*, sollicitation *f*

applica′tion blank′ *s* formule *f*

applied' arts' *spl* arts *mpl* industriels

ap•ply [ə`plaɪ] *v* (*pret & pp* **-plied**) *tr* appliquer ‖ *intr* s'appliquer; **to apply for** solliciter, postuler; **to apply to s.o.** s'adresser à qn

appoint [ə`pɔɪnt] *tr* nommer, désigner; (obs) équiper

appointed *adj* (*person*) nommé, désigné; (*time*) convenu, dit

appointment [ə`pɔɪntmənt] *s* (*engagement*) rendez-vous *m*; (*to a position*) désignation *f*, nomination *f*; **appointments** (*of a room*) aménagements *mpl*; **by appointment** sur rendez-vous

apportion [ə`pɔrʃən] *tr* répartir; (com) ventiler

appraisal [ə`prezəl] *s* appréciation *f*, estimation *f*, évaluation *f*

appraise [ə`prez] *tr* estimer, évaluer

appraiser [ə`prezər] *s* estimateur *m*, évaluateur *m*

appreciable [ə`priʃi•əbəl] *adj* appréciable, sensible

appreciate [ə`priʃi,et] *tr* (*to value, esteem*) apprécier; (*to be grateful for*) reconnaître; (*to be aware of*) être sensible à, s'apercevoir de ‖ *intr* augmenter, hausser

appreciation [ə,priʃi`eʃən] *s* (*judgment, estimation*) appréciation *f*; (*gratitude*) reconnaissance *f*; (*rise in value*) plus-value *f*

appreciative [ə`priʃi,etɪv] *adj* reconnaissant

apprehend [,æprɪ`hɛnd] *tr* (*to understand*) comprendre; (*to seize; fear*) appréhender

apprehension [,æprɪ`hɛnʃən] *s* appréhension *f*

apprehensive [,æprɪ`hɛnsɪv] *adj* craintif

apprentice [ə`prɛntɪs] *s* apprenti *m*, stagiaire *mf*

appren'tice•ship' *s* apprentissage *m*, stage *m*

apprise [ə`praɪz] *tr* prévenir, informer, mettre au courant

approach [ə`protʃ] *s* approche *f*; **to make approaches to** faire des avances à ‖ *tr* approcher, approcher de, s'approcher de ‖ *intr* approcher, s'approcher

approachable [ə`protʃəbəl] *adj* abordable, accessible

approbation [,æprə`beʃən] *s* approbation *f*

appropriate [ə`propri•ɪt] *adj* approprié ‖ [ə`propri,et] *tr* (*to take for oneself*) s'approprier; (*to assign*) affecter

appropriation [ə,propri`eʃən] *s* appropriation *f*; (*assigning*) affectation *f*; (govt) crédit *m* budgétaire

approval [ə`pruvəl] *s* approbation *f*, consentement *m*; **on approval** à l'essai, à condition

approve [ə`pruv] *tr* approuver ‖ *intr* être d'accord; **to approve of** approuver

approximate [ə`praksɪmɪt] *adj* approximatif ‖ [ə`praksɪ,met] *tr* se rapprocher de

apricot [`æprɪ,kɑt] *s* abricot *m*; (*tree*) abricotier *m*

April [`eprɪl] *s* avril *m*

A'pril fool' *s* (*joke*) poisson *m* d'avril; (*victim*) dupe *f*, dindon *m*

A'pril Fools'' Day' *s* le jour du poisson d'avril

apron [`eprən] *s* tablier *m*; (aer) aire *f* de manœuvre

apropos [,æprə`po] *adj* opportun ‖ *adv* opportunément; **apropos of** quant à, à l'égard de

apse [æps] *s* abside *f*

apt [æpt] *adj* apte; bien à propos; **apt to** enclin à, porté à

aptitude [`æptɪ,t(j)ud] *s* aptitude *f*

ap'titude test' *s* test *m* d'intelligence pratique, test de talent

aquacade [`ækwə,ked] *s* féerie *f* sur l'eau, spectacle *m* aquatique

aqualung [`ækwə,lʌŋ] *s* scaphandre *m* autonome

aquamarine [,ækwəmə`rin] *s* aiguemarine *f*

aquaplane [`ækwə,plen] *s* aquaplane *m*

aquari•um [ə`kwɛri•əm] *s* (*pl* **-ums** *ou* **-a** [ə]) aquarium *m*

Aquarius [ə`kwɛri•əs] *s* (astr, astrol) le Verseau

aquatic [ə`kwætɪk] *adj* aquatique ‖ **aquatics** *spl* sports *mpl* nautiques

aqueduct [`ækwə,dʌkt] *s* aqueduc *m*

aquiline [`ækwɪ,laɪn] *adj* aquilin

Arab [`ærəb] *adj* arabe ‖ *s* (*horse*) arabe *m*; (*person*) Arabe *mf*

Arabia [ə`rebi•ə] *s* Arabie *f*

Arabian [ə`rebi•ən] *adj* arabe ‖ *s* Arabe *mf*

Arabic [`ærəbɪk] *adj* arabique ‖ *s* (*language*) arabe *m*

Ar'abic nu'meral *s* chiffre *m* arabe

arbiter [`ɑrbɪtər] *s* arbitre *m*

arbitrary [`ɑrbɪ,trɛri] *adj* arbitraire

arbitrate [`ɑrbɪ,tret] *tr & intr* arbitrer

arbitration [,ɑrbɪ`treʃən] *s* arbitrage *m*

arbitrator [`ɑrbɪ,tretər] *s* arbitre *m*, médiateur *m*; (law) amiable compositeur *m*

arbor [`ɑrbər] *s* (*shady recess*) berceau *m*, charmille *f*; (mach) arbre *m*

arbore•tum [,ɑrbə`ritəm] *s* (*pl* **-tums** *ou* **-ta** [tə]) jardin *m* botanique d'arbres

arbutus [ɑr`bjutəs] *s* arbousier *m*

arc [ɑrk] *s* (elec, geom) arc *m*

arcade [ɑr`ked] *s* (*for shopping*) galerie *f* marchande; (*amusement arcade*) salle *f* de jeux électroniques; (architt) arcade *f*

arcane [ɑr`ken] *adj* mystérieux

arch [ɑrtʃ] *adj* insigne; espiègle ‖ *s* (*of a building, cathedral, etc.*) arc *m*; (*of bridge*) arche *f*; (*of vault*) voûte *f* ‖ *tr* (*the back*) arquer; (archit) voûter ‖ *intr* s'arquer; se voûter

archaic [ɑr`ke•ɪk] *adj* archaïque

archaism [`ɑrke,ɪzəm] *s* archaïsme *m*

archangel [`ɑrk,endʒəl] *s* archange *m*

arch'bish'op *s* archevêque *m*

arch'duke' *s* archiduc *m*

arched [ɑrtʃt] *adj* voûté, courbé, arqué

archeologist [,ɑrkɪ`ɑlədʒɪst] *s* archéologue *mf*

archeology [,ɑrkɪ`ɑlɪdʒi] *s* archéologie *f*

archer [`ɑrtʃər] *s* archer *m*

archery [`ɑrtʃəri] *s* tir *m* à l'arc

archetype [`ɑrkɪ,taɪp] *s* archétype *m*

archipela•go [,ɑrkɪ`pɛləgo] *s* (*pl* **-gos** *ou* **goes**) archipel *m*

architect [ˈɑrkɪˌtɛkt] s architecte m
architecture [ˈɑrkɪˌtɛktʃər] s architecture f
archives [ˈɑrkɑɪvz] spl archives fpl
arch'priest' s archiprêtre m
arch'way' s voûte f, arcade f
Arctic [ˈɑrktɪk] adj & s (ocean) Arctique m; (region) Arctique f
arc' weld'ing s soudure f à l'arc
ardent [ˈɑrdənt] adj ardent
ardor [ˈɑdər] s ardeur f
arduous [ˈɑrdjuˑəs] adj ardu, difficile
area [ˈɛrɪˑə] s région f, e.g., **the New York area** la région de New York; (surface measure) aire f, superficie f, e.g., **area of a triangle** aire d'un triangle; (of knowledge; field) domaine m, champ m; (geog; pol) territoire m; (mil) secteur m, zone f; **in this area** (on this subject) à ce propos
ar'ea code' s (telp) code m de la zone, code territorial
ar'ea way' s courette f en contrebas
arena [əˈrinə] s arène f
aren't contr **are not**
Argentina [ˌɑrdʒənˈtinə] s Argentine f; l'Argentine
argue [ˈɑgju] tr (a question) discuter; (a case) plaider; (a point) soutenir; (to imply) arguer; **to argue s.o. into** + ger persuader à qn de + inf || intr discuter, argumenter; plaider
argument [ˈɑrgjəmənt] s (proof; reason; theme) argument m; (debate) discussion f, dispute f
argumentative [ˌɑrgjəˈmɛntətɪv] adj disposé à argumenter, raisonneur
argyl ou **argyll** [ˈɑrgɪl] adj jacquard à losanges
aria [ˈɑrɪˑə] s aria f
arid [ˈærɪd] adj aride
aridity [əˈrɪdɪti] s aridité f
Aries [ˈɛriz] s (astr, astrol) le Bélier
arise [əˈraɪz] v (pret **arose** [əˈroz]; pp **arisen** [əˈrɪzən]) intr (to rise) se lever; (to originate) provenir, prendre naissance; (to occur) se produire; (to be raised, as objections) s'élever
aristocra·cy [ˌærɪsˈtɑkrəsi] s (pl -cies) aristocratie f
aristocrat [əˈrɪstəˌkræt] s aristocrate mf
aristocratic [əˌrɪstəˈkrætɪk] adj aristocrate
Aristotle [ˈærɪˌstɑtəl] s Aristote m
arithmetic [əˈrɪθmətɪk] s arithmétique f
arithmetician [əˌrɪθməˈtɪʃən] s arithméticien m
ark [ɑrk] s arche f
arm [ɑrm] s bras m; (mil) arme f; **arm in arm** bras dessus bras dessous; **at arm's length** à bout de bras; **under my (your, etc.) arm** sous mon (ton, etc.) aisselle; **up in arms** en rébellion ouverte || tr armer || intr s'armer
armada [ɑrˈmɑdə] s armada f, grande flotte f
armadil·lo [ˌɑrməˈdɪlo] s (pl -los) tatou m
armament [ˈɑrməmənt] s armement m
armature [ˈɑrməˌtʃər] f (elec) induit m
arm'band' s brassard m
arm'chair' s fauteuil m, chaise f à bras

Armenian [ɑrˈminɪˑən] adj arménien || s (language) arménien m; (person) Arménien
armful [ˈɑrmˌful] s brassée f
arm'hole' s emmanchure f, entournure f
armistice [ˈɑrmɪstɪs] s armistice m
armor [ˈɑrmər] s (personal) armure f; (on ships, tanks, etc.) cuirasse f, blindage m || tr cuirasser, blinder || intr se mettre l'armure
ar'mored car' s fourgon m blindé
ar'mor plate' s plaque f de blindage
ar'mor-plate' tr cuirasser, blinder
armor·y [ˈɑrməri] s (pl -ies) ateliers mpl d'armes, salle f d'armes
arm'pit' s aisselle f
arm'rest' s appui-bras m, accoudoir m
arms' race' s course f aux armements
arms' reduc'tion s contrôle m des armes
arm'wres'tle intr faire le bras de fer
ar·my [ˈɑrmi] adj militaire || s (pl -mies) armée f
ar'my corps' s corps m d'armée
ar'my sur'plus s surplus mpl militaires
aroma [əˈromə] s arôme m
aromatic [ˌærəˈmætɪk] adj aromatique
around [əˈraund] adv (nearby) autour, alentour; **all around** de tous côtés || prep autour de; (approximately) environ, à peu près; **around 2010** (coll) vers 2010
arouse [əˈrauz] tr éveiller; (from sleep) réveiller
arpeg·gio [ɑrˈpɛdʒo] s (pl -gios) arpège m
arraign [əˈren] tr accuser; (law) mettre en accusation
arrange [əˈrendʒ] tr arranger || intr s'arranger
arrangement [əˈrendʒmənt] s arrangement m
array [əˈre] s (display) étalage m; (adornment) parure f; (mil) ordre m, rang m || tr ranger, disposer; (to adorn) parer
arrearage [əˈrɪrɪdʒ] s arriéré m
arrears [əˈrɪrz] spl arriéré m; **in arrears** arriéré
arrest [əˈrɛst] s (capture) arrestation f; (halt) arrêt m || tr arrêter; fixer; (attention) retenir
arresting [əˈrɛstɪŋ] adj frappant, saisissant
arrhythmia [əˈrɪθmɪˑə] s changement du rythme du battement du coeur
arrival [əˈraɪvəl] s arrivée f; (of goods or ships) arrivage m
arrive [əˈraɪv] intr arriver
arrogance [ˈærəgəns] s arrogance f
arrogant [ˈærəgənt] adj arrogant
arrogate [ˈærəˌget] tr—**to arrogate to oneself** s'arroger
arrow [ˈæro] s flèche f
ar'row·head' s (point) tête f de flèche; (bot) sagittaire m
arsenal [ˈɑrsənəl] s (stock) arsenal m; (factory) manufacture f d'armes
arsenic [ˈɑrsɪnɪk] s arsenic m
arson [ˈɑrsən] s incendie m volontaire
arsonist [ˈɑrsənɪst] s incendiaire mf
art [ɑrt] s art m
Art' De'co ou **art de'co** s Art m déco, déco m
arterial [ɑrˈtɪrɪˑəl] adj artériel

arteriosclerotic [ɑr,tɪrɪ•oskli`rɑtɪk] *adj* artério-scléreux

arter•y [`ɑrtəri] *s* (*pl* **-ies**) artère *f*

arte'sian well' [ɑr`tiʒən] *s* puits *m* artésien

artful [`ɑrtfəl] *adj* (*skillful*) ingénieux; (*crafty*) artificieux, sournois; artificiel

art' gal'lery *s* musée d'art; (*shop*) galerie *f* de tableaux

arthritic [ɑr`θrɪtɪk] *adj* arthritique

arthritis [ɑr`θraɪtɪs] *s* arthrite *f*

artichoke [`ɑrtɪ,tʃok] *s* artichaut *m*

article [`ɑrtɪkəl] *s* article; **article of clothing** objet *m* d'habillement

articulate [ɑr`tɪkjəlɪt] *adj* articulé; (*expressing oneself clearly*) clair, expressif; (*speech*) intelligible; (*creature*) doué de la parole ‖ [ɑr`tɪkjə,let] *tr* articuler ‖ *intr* s'articuler

artifact [`ɑrtɪ,fækt] *s* objet *m* fabriqué; (biol) artefact *m*

artifice [`ɑrtɪfɪs] *s* artifice *m*

artificial [,ɑrtɪ`fɪʃəl] *adj* artificiel

artifi'cial insem'ina'tion *s* fécondation *f* artificielle

artifi'cial intel'ligence *s* intelligence *f* artificielle

artificiali•ty [,ɑrtɪ,fɪʃi`ælɪti] *s* (*pl* **-ties**) manque *m* de naturel

artifi'cial respira'tion *s* respiration *f* artificielle, ventilation *f* artificielle

artillery [ɑr`tɪləri] *s* artillerie *f*

artil'lery•man *s* (*pl* **-men**) artilleur *m*

artisan [`ɑrtɪzən] *s* artisan *m*

artist [`ɑrtɪst] *s* artiste *mf*

artistic [ɑr`tɪstɪk] *adj* artistique, artiste

artistry [`ɑrtɪstri] *s* art *m*, habileté *f*

artless [`ɑrtlɪs] *adj* (*uncontrived*) naturel; (*ingenuous*) ingénu, naïf; (*lacking art*) sans art

arts' and crafts' *spl* arts et métiers *mpl*

Aryan [`ɛrɪ•ən] *adj* aryen ‖ *s* (*person*) Aryen *m*

as [æz], [əz] *pron* tel que, e.g., **the same as** le même que ‖ *adv* aussi, e.g., **as . . . as** aussi . . . que; **as for** quant à; **as is** tel quel; **as of** (*a certain date*) en date du; **as regards** en ce qui concerne; **as soon as** aussitôt que; **as though** comme si; **as yet** jusqu'ici ‖ *prep* comme; (*in the capacity of*) en tant que, en qualité de, à titre de; (*in such a way as*) en manière de; (*such as*) tel que; (*considered as*) considéré comme; (*insofar as*) dans la mesure où; (*at the same time as and to the same degree as*) au fur et à mesure que ‖ *conj* puisque; comme; que

asbestos [æs`bɛstəs] *s* amiante *m*, asbeste *m*

ascend [ə`sɛnd] *tr* (*a ladder*) monter à; (*a mountain*) gravir; (*a river*) remonter ‖ *intr* monter, s'élever

ascendancy [ə`sɛndənsi] *s* supériorité *f*, domination *f*

ascension [ə`sɛnʃən] *s* ascension *f*

Ascen'sion Day' *s* Ascension *f*

ascent [ə`sɛnt] *s* ascension *f*

ascertain [,æsər`ten] *tr* vérifier

ascertainment [,æsər`tenmənt] *s* constatation *f*

ascetic [ə`sɛtɪk] *adj* ascétique ‖ *s* ascéte *mf*

asceticism [ə`sɛtɪ,sɪzəm] *s* ascétisme *m*, ascése *f*

ascor'bic ac'id [ə`skɔrbɪk] *s* acide *m* ascorbique

ascribe [ə`skraɪb] *tr* attribuer, imputer

aseptic [e`sɛptɪk] *adj* aseptique

ash [æʃ] *s* cendre *f*; (*tree*) frêne *m*

ashamed [ə`ʃemd] *adj* honteux; **to be ashamed** avoir honte

ash'can' *s* poubelle *f*

ashen [`æʃən] *adj* cendré

ashore [ə`ʃor] *adv* à terre; **to go ashore** débarquer

ashlar [`æʃlər] *s* pierre *f* de taille; (*small, unhewn stone*) moellon *m*

ash'tray' *s* cendrier *m*

Ash' Wednes'day *s* le mercredi des Cendres

Asia [`eʒə] *s* Asie *f*; l'Asie

A'sia Mi'nor *s* Asie *f* Mineure; l'Asie Mineure

Asian [`eʒən] *ou* **Asiatic** [,eʒɪ`ætɪk] *adj* asiatique ‖ *s* Asiatique *mf*

As'ian flu' *s* grippe *f* asiatique

aside [ə`saɪd] *s* aparté *m* ‖ *adv* de côté, à part; (*aloof, at a distance*) à l'écart; **aside from** en dehors de, à part; **to step aside** s'écarter; (fig) quitter la partie

asinine [`æsɪ,naɪn] *adj* stupide

ask [æsk] *tr* (*a favor; one's way*) demander; (*a question*) poser; **to ask s.o. about s.th.** interroger qn au sujet q.ch.; **to ask s.o. for s.th.** demander q.ch. à qn; **to ask s.o. to** + *inf* demander à qn de + *inf*, prier qn de + *inf* ‖ *intr*—**to ask about** s'enquérir de; **to ask for** (*a package; a porter*) demander; (*to inquire about*) demander après; **you asked for it** (*you're in for it*) (coll) c'est bien fait pour vous

askance [ə`skæns] *adv* de côté; **to look askance at** regarder de travers

askew [ə`skju] *adj & adv* de travers, en biais, de biais

asleep [ə`slip] *adj* endormi; **to fall asleep** s'endormir

asp [æsp] *s* aspic *m*

asparagus [ə`spærəgəs] *s* asperge *f*; (*stalks and tips used as food*) des asperges

aspect [`æspɛkt] *s* aspect *m*

aspen [`æspən] *s* tremble *m*

aspersion [ə`spʌrʒən] *s* (*sprinkling*) aspersion *f*; (*slander*) calomnie *f*

asphalt [`æsfɔlt] *s* asphalte *m*

asphyxiate [æs`fɪksɪ,et] *tr* asphyxier

aspirate [`æspɪrɪt] *adj & s* (phonet) aspiré *m* ‖ [`æspɪ,ret] *tr* aspirer

aspire [ə`spaɪr] *intr*—**to aspire to** aspirer à

aspirin [`æspɪrɪn] *s* aspirine *f*

ass [æs] *s* âne *m*; (anat & vulg) cul *m*; (*person*) (vulg) imbécile *mf*, crétin *m*, âne

assail [ə`sel] *tr* assaillir

assailant [ə`selənt] *s* assaillant *m*

assassin [ə`sæsɪn] *s* assassin *m*

assassinate [ə'sæsɪ,net] *tr* assassiner
assassination [ə,sæsɪ'neʃən] *s* assassinat *m*
assault [ə'sɔlt] *s* (*military attack*) assault *m*; (*unlawful physical attack*) agression *f*; (*rape*) viol *m*; (law) voie *f* de fait ‖ *tr* assaillir
assault' and bat'tery *s* (law) voies *fpl* de fait
assay [ə'se], [`æse] *s* essai *m*; métal *m* titré ‖ [ə'se] *t* essayer; titrer
assayer [ə'se•ər] *s* essayeur *m*
as'say val'ue *s* teneur *f*
assemblage [ə'sɛmblɪdʒ] *s* assemblage *m*
assemble [ə'sɛmbəl] *tr* assembler ‖ *intr* s'assembler, se réunir
assem•bly [ə'sɛmbli] *s* (*pl* -blies) (*meeting*) assemblée *f*, réunion *f*; (*assembling*) assemblage *m*, montage *m*
assemb'ly hall' *s* salle *f* de conférences; (educ) grand amphithéâtre *m*
assem'bly lan'guage *s* (comp) langage *m* d'assemblage, assembleur *m*
assem'bly line' *s* chaîne *f* de fabrication, chaîne de montage
assem'bly room' *s* salle *f* de réunion; (mach) atelier *m* de montage
assent [ə'sɛnt] *s* assentiment *m* ‖ *intr* assentir
assert [ə'sʌrt] *tr* affirmer; (*one's rights*) revendiquer; **to assert oneself** imposer le respect, s'imposer
assertion [ə'sʌrʃən] *s* assertion *f*
assess [ə'sɛs] *tr* (*damages, taxes, etc.*) évaluer; (*value of property*) coter; (*property for tax purposes*) grever
assessment [ə'sɛsmənt] *s* (*estimation*) évaluation *f*; (*of real estate*) calcul *m* (de la valeur imposable); (*amount of tax*) charge *f*, taxe *f*
assessor [ə'sɛsər] *s* répartiteur *m* d'impôts
asset [`æsɛt] *s* (*advantage*) avantage *m*, atout *m*; **assets** biens *mpl*, avoirs, *mpl*, actif *m*
ass'hole' *s* (anat, fig, vulg) trou *m* de cul, trou de balle
assiduous [ə'sɪdju•əs] *adj* assidu
assign [ə'saɪn] *tr* (*task, date, etc.*) assigner; (mil) affecter
assignation [,æsɪg'neʃən] *s* attribution *f*, allocation *f*, affectation *f*; (*lovers' tryst*) rendez-vous *m* illicite
assignment [ə'saɪnmənt] *s* (*allocation*) attribution *f*; (*schoolwork*) devoirs *mpl*; (law) assignation *f*, transfer *m*; (mil) affectation *f*
assimilate [ə'sɪmɪ,let] *tr* assimiler ‖ *intr* s'assimiler
assimilation [ə,sɪmɪ'leʃən] *s* assimilation *f*
assist [ə'sɪst] *tr* assister, aider, secourir ‖ *intr* être assistant
assistance [ə'sɪstəns] *s* assistance *f*, aide *f*, secours *m*
assistant [ə'sɪstənt] *adj* & *s* assistant *m*, adjoint *m*
assis'tant profes'sor *s* professeur *m* assistant, maître *m* assistant
assizes [ə'saɪzɪz] *spl* assises *fpl*
associate [ə'soʃi•ɪt] *adj* associé *s* ‖ associé *m* ‖ [ə'soʃi,et] *tr* associer ‖ *intr* s'associer

association [ə,soʃi'eʃən] *s* association *f*
assonance [`æsənəns] *s* assonance *f*
assort [ə'sɔrt] *tr* assortir ‖ *intr* s'associer
assorted *adj* assorti
assortment [ə'sɔrtmənt] *s* assortiment *m*
assuage [ə'swedʒ] *tr* assouvir; soulager, apaiser
assume [ə's(j)um] *tr* (*to suppose*) supposer; (*various forms*) affecter; (*a fact*) présumer; (*a name*) emprunter; (*duties*) assumer, se charger de
assumed *adj* (*supposed*) supposé; (*borrowed*) d'emprunt, emprunté; (*feigned*) feint
assumed' name' *s* nom *m* d'emprunt, nom de guerre
assuming [ə's(j)umɪŋ] *adj* prétentieux
assumption [ə'sʌmpʃən] *s* (*supposition*) présomption *f*, hypothèse *f*; (*of virtue*) affectation *f*; (*of power*) appropriation *f*; **Assumption** (eccl) Assomption *f*
assurance [ə'ʃurəns] *s* (*certainty; self-confidence*) assurance; (*guarantee*) promesse *f*
assure [ə'ʃur] *tr* assurer, garantir
astatine [`æstə,tin] *s* astate *m*
aster [`æstər] *s* aster *m*; (*China aster*) reine-marguerite *f*
asterisk [`æstə,rɪsk] *s* astérisque *m*
astern [ə'stʌrn] *adv* à l'arrière
asthma [`æzmə] *s* asthme *m*
astonish [ə'stanɪʃ] *tr* étonner
astonishing [ə'stanɪʃɪŋ] *adj* étonnant
astonishment [ə'stanɪʃmənt] *s* étonnement *m*
astound [ə'staund] *tr* stupéfier, ahurir, étonner
astounding [ə'staundɪŋ] *adj* étonnant, stupéfiant, abasourdissant
astraddle [ə'strædəl] *adv* à califourchon
astray [ə'stre] *adv*—**to go astray** s'égarer; **to lead astray** égarer
astride [ə'straɪd] *adv* à califourchon ‖ *prep* à califourchon sur
astrologer [ə'straladʒər] *s* astrologue *m*
astrology [ə'straladʒər] *s* astrologie *m*
astronaut [`æstrə,nɔt] *s* astronaute *mf*
astronautics [,æstrə'nɔtɪks] *s* astronautique *f*
astronavigation [,æstro,nævɪ'geʃən] *s* navigation *f* spatiale
astronomer [ə'stranəmər] *s* astronome *m*
astronomic(al) [,æstrə'namɪk(əl)] *adj* astronomique
as'tronom'ical year' *s* année *f* solaire, année tropique
astronomy [ə'stranəmi] *s* astronomie *f*
astrophysics [,æstro'fɪzɪks] *s* astrophysique *f*
astute [ə'st(j)ut] *adj* astucieux, fin
asunder [ə'sʌndər] *adj* séparé ‖ *adv* en deux
asylum [ə'saɪləm] *s* asile *m*
asymmetrical [`esɪ'mɛtrɪkəl] *adj* asymétrique
a'symme'trical war'fare *s* (*warfare between two enemies of very different size and capabilities*) (le) combat *m* asymétrique (*guerre entre deux ennemis qui possèdent des forces inégales et des moyens différents*)
at (@) [æt] *prep* (comp) at; escargot (obs)
at [æt], [ət] *prep* à, e.g., **at Paris** à Paris; chez,

e.g., **at John's** chez Jean; en, e.g., **at the same time** en même temps

atheism [ˈeθiˌɪzəm] *s* athéisme *m*

atheist [ˈeθiˌɪst] *s* athée *mf*

atheistic [ˌeθiˈɪstɪk] *adj* athée

Athens [ˈæθɪnz] *s* Athènes *f*

athlete [ˈæθlit] *s* athlète *m*, sportif *m*

ath′lete's foot′ *s* pied *m* d'athlète

athletic [æθˈlɛtɪk] *adj* athlétique ‖ **athletics** *s* athlétisme *m*

athlet′ic support′er *s* slip *m* de soutien

athwart [əˈθwɔrt] *adv* par le travers

Atlantic [ætˈlæntɪk] *adj & s* Atlantique *m*

atlas [ˈætləs] *s* atlas *m*

ATM [ˈeˈtiˈɛm] *s* (letterword) (automated teller machine) machine *f* de télégestion bancaire, guichet *m* libre service

atmosphere [ˈætməsˌfɪr] *s* atmosphère *f*

atmospheric [ˌætməsˈfɛrɪk] *adj* atmosphérique ‖ **atmospherics** *spl* parasites *mpl* atmosphériques

atom [ˈætəm] *s* atome *m*

atomic [əˈtɑmɪk] *adj* atomique

atomi′ic bomb′ *s* bombe *f* atomique

atom′ic nuc′leus *s* noyau *m* d'atome

atom′ic pile′ *s* pile *f* atomique

atom′ic struc′ture *s* édifice *m* atomique

atom′ic weight′ *s* poids *m* atomique, masse *f* atomique

atomize [ˈætəˌmaɪz] *tr* atomiser

atomizer [ˈætəˌmaɪzər] *s* atomiseur *m*, vaporisateur *m*; (e.g., of hair spray) bombe *f*

at′om smash′er *s* *mécanisme qui casse des atomes*

atone [əˈton] *intr*—**to atone for** expier

atonement [əˈtonmənt] *s* expiation *f*

atrocious [əˈtroʃəs] *adj* atroce

atroci•ty [əˈtrɑsɪti] *s* (*pl* **-ties**) atrocité *f*

atro•phy [ˈætrəfi] *s* atrophie *f* ‖ *v* (*pret & pp* **-phied**) *tr* atrophier ‖ *intr* s'atrophier

attach [əˈtætʃ] *tr* (to join; attribute) attacher; (property) saisir; (salary) mettre opposition sur; **to be attached to** s'attacher à

attaché [ataˈʃe] *s* attaché(e) *mf*

attachment [əˈtætʃmənt] *s* (fastener) attache *f*; (of the sentiments) attachement *m*; (supplementary device) accessoire *m*; (law) opposition *f*, saisie-arrêt *f*

attack [əˈtæk] *s* attaque *f* ‖ *tr* attaquer; s'attaquer à ‖ *intr* attaquer

attacker [əˈtækər] *s* assaillant *m*

attain [əˈten] *tr* atteindre

attainment [əˈtenmənt] *s* acquisition *f*, réalisation *f*; **attainments** connaissances *fpl*

attar [ˈætər] *s* essence *f*

attempt [əˈtɛmpt] *s* tentative *f*, effort *m*; (try) essai *m*; (assault) attentat *m* ‖ *tr* tenter; (s.o.'s life) attenter à

attend [əˈtɛnd] *tr* (a performance) assister à; (a sick person) soigner; (a person) servir; **to attend classes** suivre des cours ‖ *intr*—**to attend to** vaquer à, s'occuper de

attendance [əˈtɛndəns] *s* (number of people

present) assistance *f*; (being present) présence *f*; (med) soins *mpl*

attendant [əˈtɛndənt] *adj* concomitant ‖ *s* assistant *m*; (to royalty) serviteur *m*; **attendants** suite *f*

attention [əˈtɛnʃən] *s* attention *f*; (mil) garde-à-vous *m*; **attention: Mr. Doe** à l'attention de M. Dupont; **attentions** égards *mpl*; **to come to attention** (mil) se mettre au garde-à-vous; **to pay attention to** se prêter attention à, faire attention à ‖ *interj* attention!; (mil) garde à vous!

attentive [əˈtɛntɪv] *adj* attentif

attenuate [əˈtɛnjuˌet] *tr* (to make thin) amincir; (words; bacteria) atténuer

attest [əˈtɛst] *tr* attester ‖ *intr*—**to attest to** attester

Attic [ˈætɪk] *adj* attique ‖ (l.c.) *s* mansarde *f*, grenier *m*, soupente *f*

attire [əˈtaɪr] *s* vêtement *m*, parure *f* ‖ *tr* habiller, vêtir, parer

attitude [ˈætɪˌt(j)ud] *s* attitude *f*

attorney [əˈtɑrni] *s* avoué *m*, avocat *m*

attor′ney gen′eral *s* procureur *m* général, ministre *m* de la justice

attract [əˈtrækt] *tr* attirer

attraction [əˈtrækʃən] *s* attraction *f*

attractive [əˈtræktɪv] *adj* (person, manner) attirant, attrayant; (said, e.g., of a force) attractif; (price, offer; idea) intéressant

attribute [ˈætrɪˌbjut] *s* attribut *m* ‖ [əˈtrɪbjut] *tr* attribuer

attrition [əˈtrɪʃən] *s* attrition *f*, usure *f*

attune [əˈt(j)un] *tr* accorder

auburn [ˈɔbərn] *adj* auburn, brun rougeâtre

auction [ˈɔkʃən] *s* vente *f* aux enchères ‖ *tr* vendre aux enchères

auc′tion bridge′ *s* bridge *m* aux enchères

auctioneer [ˌɔkʃənˈɪr] *s* adjudicateur *m*, commissaire-priseur *m* ‖ *tr & intr* vendre aux enchères

auc′tion house′ *s* hôtel *m* des ventes

audacious [ɔˈdeʃəs] *adj* audacieux

audacity [ɔˈdæsɪti] *s* audace *f*

audience [ˈɔdi•əns] *s* (hearing; formal interview) audience *f*; (assembly of hearers or spectators) assistance *f*, salle *f*, auditoire *m*; (of a writer or performer) public *m*

audio [ˈɔdi•o] *adj* audio invar ‖ *s* audio *m*

au′dio fre′quency [ˈɔdiˌo] *s* audio-fréquence *f*

audiometer [ˌɔdiˈɑmɪtər] *s* audiomètre *m*

audiovisual [ˌɔdi•oˈvɪʒu•əl] *adj* audio-visuel

au′dio•vis′ual aids′ *spl* support *m* audio-visuel, moyens *mpl* audio-visuels

audit [ˈɔdɪt] *s* apurement *m* ‖ *tr* apurer; **to audit a class** assister à la classe en auditeur libre

audition [ɔˈdɪʃən] *s* audition *f* ‖ *tr & intr* auditionner

auditor [ˈɔdɪtər] *s* (com) comptable *m* agréé, expert comptable *m*; (educ) auditeur *m* libre

auditorium [ˌɔdiˈtori•əm] *s* auditorium *m*, salle *f*, amphithéâtre *m*

auditory [ˈɔdiˌtori] *adj* auditif

auger [ˈɔgər] *s* tarière *f*

aught [ɔt] *s* zéro *m* ‖ *pron indef*—**for aught I know** autant que je sache ‖ *adv* du tout

augment [ɔgˈmɛnt] *tr & intr* augmenter

augur [ˈɔgər] *s* augure *m* ‖ *tr & intr* augurer; **to augur well** être de bon augure

augu•ry [ˈɔgjəri] *s* (*pl* **-ries**) augure *m*

august [ɔˈgʌst] *adj* auguste ‖ **August** [ˈɔgəst] *s* août *m*

auk [ɔk] *s* guillemot *m*

aunt [ænt], [ɑnt] *s* tante *f*

aureomycin [ˌɔrɪ•oˈmaɪsɪn] *s* (pharm) auréomycine *f*

auricle [ˈɔrɪkəl] *s* auricule *f*, oreillette *f*

aurora [əˈrorə] *s* aurore *f*

auscultate [ˈɔskəl،tet] *tr* ausculter

auspices [ˈɔspɪsɪz] *spl* auspices *mpl*

auspicious [ɔsˈpɪ/əs] *adj* propice, favorable

austere [ɔsˈtɪr] *adj* austère

Australia [ɔˈstreljə] *s* Australie *f*; l'Australie

Australian [ɔˈstreljən] *adj* australien ‖ *s* (*person*) Australien *m*

Austria [ˈɔstrɪ•ə] *s* Autriche *f*; l'Autriche

Austrian [ˈɔstrɪ•ən] *adj* autrichien ‖ *s* (*person*) Autrichien *m*

authentic [ɔˈθɛntɪk] *adj* authentique

authenticate [ɔˈθɛntɪ،ket] *tr* authentifier, constater l'authenticité de

author [ˈɔθər] *s* auteur *m*

authoress [ˈɔθərɪs] *s* femme *f* auteur

authoritarian [ɔ،θɑrɪˈtɛrɪ•ən], [ɔ،θɔrɪˈtɛrɪ•ən] *adj* autoritaire ‖ *s* homme *m* autoritaire

authoritative [ɔˈθɔrɪ،tetɪv] *adj* autorisé; (*dictatorial*) autoritaire

authority [ɔˈθɔrɪti] *s* (*pl* **-ties**) autorité *f*; **on good authority** de bonne part

authorize [ˈɔθə،raɪz] *tr* autoriser

au′thor•ship′ *s* paternité *f*

autistic [ɔˈtɪstɪk] *adj* autistique

au•to [ˈɔto] *s* (*pl* **-tos**) (coll) auto *f*, voiture *f*

autobiogra•phy [ˌɔtobaɪˈagrəfi] *s* (*pl* **-phies**) autobiographie *f*

autocrat [ˈɔtə،kræt] *s* autocrate *mf*

autocratic(al) [ˌɔtəˈkrætɪk(əl)] *adj* autocratique

autograph [ˈɔtə،græf] *s* autographe *m* ‖ *tr* écrire l'autographe sur, dédicacer

au′tographed cop′y *s* exemplaire *m* dédicacé

au′tograph′ hunt′er *s* chasseur *m* d'autographes

au′to•intox′ica′tion *s* auto-intoxication *f*

automat [ˈɔtə،mæt] *s* restaurant *m* libre service

automate [ˈɔtə،met] *tr* automatiser

au′tomat′ed tell′er machine′ (**ATM**) *s* (com) machine *f* de télégestion bancaire, guichet *m* libre service

automatic [ˌɔtəˈmætɪk] *adj* automatique ‖ *s* revolver *m*

au′tomat′ic dial′ing *s* (telp) composeur *m* de numéros

au′tomat′ic laun′dry *s* laverie *f* automatique

au′tomat′ic pi′lot *s* pilote *m* automatique

automat′ic transmis′sion *s* transmission *f* automatique

automation [ˌɔtəˈme/ən] *s* automatisation *f*, automation *f*

automa•ton [ɔˈtɑmə،tɑn] *s* (*pl* **-tons** *ou* **-ta**) [tə] automate *m*

automobile [ˌɔtəmoˈbil] *s* automobile *f*

automobile′ show′ *s* salon *m* de l'automobile

automotive [ˌɔtəˈmotɪv] *adj* automobile; automoteur

autonomous [ɔˈtɑnəməs] *adj* autonome

autonomy [ɔˈtɑnəmi] *s* autonomie *f*

autop•sy [ˈɔtɑpsi] *s* (*pl* **-sies**) autopsie *f*

autumn [ˈɔtəm] *s* automne *m*

autumnal [ɔˈtʌmnəl] *adj* automnal, d'automne

auxilia•ry [ɔgˈzɪljəri] *adj* auxiliaire ‖ *s* (*pl* **-ries**) auxiliaire *mf*; **auxiliaries** (mil) troupes *fpl* auxiliaires

avail [əˈvel] *s* utilité *f* ‖ *tr* profiter à; **to avail oneself of** avoir recours à, profiter de ‖ *intr* être utile, servir

available [əˈveləbəl] *adj* disponible; (*e.g., train*) accessible; **to make available to** mettre à la disposition de

avalanche [ˈævə،lænt/] *s* avalanche *f*

avarice [ˈævərɪs] *s* avarice *f*

avaricious [ˌævəˈrɪ/əs] *adj* avaricieux

avenge [əˈvɛndʒ] *tr* venger

avenger [əˈvɛndʒər] *s* vengeur *m*

avenue [ˈævə،n(j)u] *s* avenue *f*

aver [əˈvʌr] *v* (*pret & pp* **averred**; *ger* **averring**) *tr* avérer, affirmer

average [ˈævərɪdʒ] *adj* moyen ‖ *s* moyenne *f*; **on the average** en moyenne ‖ *tr* prendre la moyenne de ‖ *intr* atteindre une moyenne

averse [əˈvʌrs] *adj*—**averse to** hostile à, opposé à, ennemi de

aversion [əˈvʌrʒən] *s* aversion *f*

avert [əˈvʌrt] *tr* (*one's eyes: a blow*) détourner, écarter; (*an accident*) éviter

aviar•y [ˈvɪ،ɛri] *s* (*pl* **-ies**) volière *f*

aviation [،evɪˈe/ən] *s* aviation *f*

aviator [ˈevɪ،etər] *s* aviateur *m*

avid [ˈævɪd] *adj* avide; **avid for** avide de

avidity [əˈvɪdɪti] *s* avidité *f*

avoca•do [ˌævoˈkado] *s* (*pl* **-dos**) avocat *m*

avocation [ˌævəˈke/ən] *s* occupation *f*, profession *f*; (*hobby*) distraction *f*

avoid [əˈvɔɪd] *tr* éviter

avoidable [əˈvɔɪdəbəl] *adj* évitable

avoidance [əˈvɔɪdəns] *s* dérobade *f*

avow [əˈvau] *tr* avouer

avowal [əˈvau•əl] *s* aveu *m*

avowedly [əˈvau•ɪdli] *adv* ouvertement, franchement

await [əˈwet] *tr* attendre

awake [əˈwek] *adj* éveillé ‖ *v* (*pret & pp* **awoke** [əˈwok] *ou* **awaked**) *tr* éveiller ‖ *intr* s'éveiller

awaken [əˈwekən] *tr* éveiller, réveiller ‖ *intr* se réveiller

awakening [əˈwekənɪŋ] *s* réveil *m*

award [əˈwɔrd] *s* (*prize*) prix *m*; (law) dommages et intérêts *mpl* ‖ *tr* (*a prize*) décerner; (*a sum of money*) allouer; (*damages*) accorder

aware [ə'wɛr] *adj* conscient; **to become aware of** se rendre compte de

awareness [ə'wɛrnɪs] *s* conscience *f*

away [ə'we] *adj* absent ‖ *adv* au loin, loin; **away from** éloigné de, loin de; **to do away with** abolir; **to get away** s'absenter; (*to escape*) échapper; **to go away** s'en aller; **to make away with** (*to steal*) dérober; **to run away** se sauver; **to send away** renvoyer; **to take away** enlever ‖ *interj* hors d'ici!; **away with!** à bas!

awe [ɔ] *s* crainte *f* révérentielle ‖ *tr* inspirer de la crainte à

awesome ['ɔsəm] *adj* impressionnant

awful ['ɔfəl] *adj* terrible; (coll) terrible, affreux

awfully ['ɔfəli] *adj* terriblement; (coll) joliment, rudement

awhile [ə'hwaɪl] *adv* quelque temps, un peu, un moment

awkward ['ɔkwərd] *adj* (*clumsy*) gauche, maladroit; (*moment*) embarrassant; (*problem, situation*) délicat

awl [ɔl] *s* alène *f*

awning ['ɔnɪŋ] *s* (*over a window*) tente *f*; (*in front of store*) banne *f*

A.W.O.L. ['ewɔl] *s* (acronym) (**absent without leave**) absence *f* illégale; **to be A.W.O.L.** être absent sans permission

awry [ə'raɪ] *adv* de travers

ax [æks] *s* hache *f*

axiom ['æksɪ•əm] *s* axiome *m*

axiomatic [,æksɪ•ə'mætɪk] *adj* axiomatique

axis ['æksɪs] *s* (*pl* **axes** ['æksiz]) axe *m*

axle ['æksəl] *s* essieu *m*

ax'le grease' *s* cambouis *m*

ax'le-tree' *s* essieu *m*

ay or **aye** [aj] *s* oui *m*; **aye, aye, sir!** oui, commandant!, bien, capitaine!; **the ayes have it** les oui l'emportent ‖ [e] *adv* toujours

azalea [ə'zeljə] *s* azalée *f*

azimuth ['æzɪməθ] *s* azimut *m*

Azores [ə'zorz] *spl* Açores *fpl*

Aztecs ['æztɛks] *spl* Aztèques *mpl*

azure ['eʒər] *adj* azuré, d'azur ‖ *s* azur *m* ‖ *tr* azurer

B

B, b [bi] *s* II*ᵉ* lettre de l'alphabet

babble ['bæbəl] *s* babil *m* ‖ *tr* (*secrets*) dire à tort et à travers ‖ *intr* babiller; (*said of birds*) jaser; (*said of brook*) murmurer

babbling ['bæblɪŋ] *adj* (*gossiper*) babillard; (*brook*) murmurant ‖ *s* babillage *m*

babe [beb] *s* bébé *m*, bambin *m*; (*naive person*) (coll) enfant *mf*; (*pretty girl*) (coll) pépée *f*, môme *f*

babel ['bebəl] *s* brouhaha *m*, vacarme *m*

baboon [bæ'bun] *s* babouin *m*

ba•by ['bebi] *s* (*pl* **-bies**) bébé *m*; (*youngest child*) cadet *m*, benjamin *m*; **baby!** (*honey!*) (coll) ma choute! ‖ *v* (*pret & pp* **-bied**) *tr* traiter en bébé, dorloter; (*e.g., a machine*) traiter avec soin

ba'by boom'ers *spl génération née pendant les vingt années qui suivent la Seconde Guerre Mondiale*

ba'by car'riage *s* voiture *f* d'enfant, poussette *f*; (*with hood*) landau *m*

ba'by foods' *spl* aliments *mpl* pour bébés premier âge, nourriture *f* pour enfants premier âge, la diététique infantile

ba'by grand' *s* piano *m* demi-queue

ba'by-sit'ter *s* gardienne *f* d'enfants, garde-bébé *mf*

ba'by-sit'ting *s* gardiennage *m* d'enfants

ba-by talk' *s* babil *m* enfantin

ba'by teeth' *spl* dents *fpl* de lait

baccalaureate [,bækə'lɔrɪ•ɪt] *s* baccalauréat *m*

bacchanal ['bækənəl] *adj* bachique ‖ *s* bacchanale *f*; (*person*) noceur *m*

bachelor ['bætʃələr] *s* (*single person*) célibataire *m*; (*graduate*) bachelier *m*

bach'elor apart'ment *s* garçonnière *f*

bach'elor girl' *s* garçonne *f*

bach'elor's degree' *s* baccalauréat *m*

bacil•lus [bə'sɪləs] *s* (*pl* **-li** [laɪ]) bacille *m*

back [bæk] *adj* postérieur ‖ *s* (*part of the body; of a living being, hand, tongue, garment, chair, page*) dos *m*; (*of house; of head or body*) derrière *m*; (*of house; of car*) arrière *m*; (*of room*) fond *m*; (*of fabric*) envers *m*; (*of seat*) dossier *m*; (*of medal; of hand*) revers *m*; (*of page*) verso *m*; (sports) arrière *m*; **at the back** en queue; **back to back** dos à dos; **with one's back to the wall** poussé au pied du mur, aux abois ‖ *adv* en arrière, à l'arrière; **as far back as** déjà en, dès, **back and forth** de long en large; **back of** derrière; **back to front** sens devant derrière; **in back** par derrière; **some weeks back** il y a quelques semaines; **to be back** être de retour; **to come back** revenir; **to go back** revenir; **to go back home** rentrer; **to go back on** (coll) abandonner; **to go back to** (*to hark back to*) remonter à; **to make one's way back** s'en retourner ‖ *tr* faire faire marche arrière à; (*e.g., a car*) faire reculer; (*to support*) appuyer, soutenir; (*to reinforce*) renforcer; (*e.g. a racehorse*) parier pour; **to back s.o. up** soutenir qn; **to back water** nager à culer ‖ *intr* reculer; faire marche arrière; **to back down** (fig) se rétracter, se retirer; **to back out of** (*e.g., an agreement*) se dédire de, se soustraire à; **to back up** reculer

back'ache' *s* mal *m* de dos

back'bite' *v* (*pret* -**bit**; *pp* -**bitten** or **bit**) *tr* médire de ‖ *intr* médire

back'bit'er *s* médisant *m*

back'bone' *s* (*spinal column*) colonne *f* vertébrale, épine *f* dorsale, échine *f*; (*of a fish*) grande arête *f*; (*of an enterprise*) colonne *f*, appui *m*; (fig) caractère *m*, cran *m*; **to have no backbone** (fig) avoir l'échine souple

back'break'ing *adj* éreintant, dur

back'door' *adj* (fig) secret, clandestin

back'door' *s* porte *f* de derrière; (fig) petite porte

back'down' *s* (coll) palinodie *f*

back'drop' *s* toile *f* de fond

backer [ˈbækər] *s* (*of team, party, etc.*) supporter *m*; (com) bailleur *m* de fonds, commanditaire *m*

back'fire' *s* retour *m* de flamme, pétarade *f*; (*for firefighting*) contre-feu *m*; (mach) contre-allumage *m* ‖ *intr* donner des retours de flamme; (fig) produire un résultat imprévu

backgammon [ˈbækˌgæmən] *s* trictrac *m*, jacquet *m*

back'ground' *s* fond *m*; (*of person*) origines *fpl*, éducation *f*; (*music, sound effects, etc.*) fond sonore

back'ground mode' *s* (comp) mode *m* subordonné

back'ground mus'ic *s* musique *f* de fond

back'ground noise' *s* bruit *m* de fond, fond *m* sonore

back'ground print'ing *s* (comp) impression *f* subordonnée

back'hand' *s* (tennis) revers *m*

back'hand'ed *adj* de revers; (*compliment*) à rebours, équivoque

backing [ˈbækɪŋ] *s* (*support*) appui *m*, soutien *m*; (*reinforcement*) renforcement *m*; (*backing up*) recul *m*

back' in'terest *m* arrérages *mpl*

back'lash' *s* contrecoup *m*

back'light'ing *s* contre-jour *m*

back'log' *s* arriéré *m*, accumulation *f*

back' num'ber *s* (*of newspaper, magazine*) vieux numéro *m*; (coll) vieux jeu *m*

back'pain *s* tour *m* de reins

back' pay' *s* salaire *m* arriéré; (mil) arriéré *m* de solde

back' pay'ment *s* arriéré *m*

back' rest' *s* dossier *s*

back' road' *s* route *f* secondaire

back' scratch'er *s* gratte-dos *m*; (slang) lèche-bottes *m*

back' seat' *s* banquette *f* arrière; **to take a back seat** (fig) aller au second plan

back'side' *s* derrière *m*, postérieur *m*

back'slide' *intr* récidiver

back'slid'er *s* récidiviste *mf*, relaps *m*

back'spac'er *s* touche *f* d'espace arrière, touche de recul

back'spin' *s* (*of ball*) coup *m* en bas, effet *m*

back'stage' *adv* dans les coulisses

back'stairs' *adj* caché, indirect

back'stairs' *spl* escalier *m* de service

back'stitch' *s* point *m* arrière

back'stop' *s* (*baseball*) attrapeur *m* ‖ *v* (*pret & pp* -**stopped**; *ger* -**stopping**) *tr* (coll) soutenir

back'stroke' *s* (*of piston*) course *f* de retour; (*swimming*) brasse *f* sur le dos

back'swept wing' *s* aile *f* en flèche

back' talk' *s* réplique *f* impertinente

back' tax'es *spl* impôts *mpl* arriérés

back'-to-back' *adj* consécutif

back'track' *intr* rebrousser chemin

back'up' *s* appui *m*, soutien *m*

back'up cop'y *s* copie *f* supplémentaire, copie de réserve

back'up light' *s* phare *m* de recul

backward [ˈbækwərd] *adj* (*in direction*) en arrière, rétrograde; (*in time*) en retard; (*in development*) arriéré, attardé ‖ *adv* en arrière; (*opposite to the normal*) à rebours; (*walking*) à reculons; (*flowing*) à contre-courant; (*stroking of the hair*) à contre-poil; **backward and forward** de long en large; **to go backward and forward** aller et venir

back'ward-and-for'ward mo'tion *s* va-et-vient *m*

backwardness [ˈbækwərdnɪs] *s* retard *m*, lenteur *f*

backwards [ˈbækwərdz] *adv* var of **backward**

back'wash' *s* remous *m*

back'wa'ter *s* (*of river*) bras *m* mort; (*e.g., of water wheel*) remous *m*; (fig) endroit *m* isolé, trou *m*

back' wheel' *s* roue *f* arrière

back'woods' *spl* forêts *fpl* de l'intérieur; (*godforsaken place*) bled *m*, brousse *f*

back'woods'man *s* (*pl* -**men**) défricheur *m* de forêts, coureur *m* des bois

back'yard' *s* derrière *m* (de la maison)

bacon [ˈbekən] *s* lard *m*, bacon *m*; (slang) butin *m*; **bacon and eggs** œufs au bacon; **to bring home the bacon** (coll) remporter la timbale

bacteria [bækˈtɪrɪə] *spl* bactéries *fpl*

bacteriology [bækˌtɪrɪˈɑlədʒɪ] *s* bactériologie *f*

bacteri·um [bækˈtɪrɪəm] *s* (*pl* -**a** [ə]) bactérie *f*

bad [bæd] *adj* mauvais §91; (*wicked*) méchant; (*serious*) grave; **from bad to worse** de mal en pis; **too bad!** c'est dommage!

bad' breath' *s* haleine *f* forte

bad' check' *s* chèque *m* en bois, chèque sans provision

bad' com'pany *s* mauvaises fréquentations *fpl*

bad' debt' *s* mauvaise créance *f*

bad' egg' *s* (slang) mauvais sujet *m*

bad' exam'ple *s* exemple *m* pernicieux

badge [bædʒ] *s* insigne *m*, plaque *f*

badger [ˈbædʒər] *s* blaireau *m* ‖ *tr* harceler, ennuyer

bad' lot' *s* voyou *mpl*, racaille *f*

badly [ˈbædlɪ] *adv* mal §91; (*seriously*) gravement; **to want badly** avoir grande envie de

bad'man *s* (*pl* -**men'**) bandit *m*

badminton [ˈbædmɪntən] *s* badminton *m*

badness [ˈbædnɪs] *s* mauvaise qualité *f;* (*of character*) méchanceté *f*

bad'-tem'pered *adj* susceptible, méchant; (*e.g., horse*) vicieux, rétif

bad' trip' *s* (slang) (*on drugs*) voyage *m* trop poussé

baffle [ˈbæfəl] *s* déflecteur *m,* chicane *f* ‖ *tr* déconcerter, confondre

baffling [ˈbæflɪŋ] *adj* déconcertant

bag [bæg] *s* sac *m;* (*suitcase*) valise *f;* (*of game*) chasse *f;* **it's in the bag** (coll) c'est du tout cuit ‖ *v* (*pret & pp* **bagged;** *ger* **bagging**) *tr* ensacher, mettre en sac; (*game*) abattre, tuer ‖ *intr* (*said of clothing*) faire poche

bagel [ˈbegəl] *s* petit pain *m* en forme d'anneau

bagful [ˈbæg,fʊl] *s* sachée *f*

baggage [ˈbægɪdʒ] *s* bagage *m,* bagages

bag'gage car' *s* (rr) fourgon *m* à bagages

bag'gage check' *s* (*receipt*) bulletin *m* de bagages; (*checking*) consigne *f* ordinaire

bag'gage rack' *s* (aer) casier *m* à bagages; (rr) porte-bagages *m invar,* filet *m*

bag'gage room' *s* bureau *m* de gare expéditeur; (*checkroom*) consigne *f*

bag'gage truck' *s* chariot *m* à bagages; (*hand truck*) diable *m*

bag•gy [ˈbægi] *adj* (*comp* **-gier;** *super* **-giest**) bouffant

bag' of tricks' *s* sac *m* à malice

bag'pipe' *s* cornemuse *f*

bail [bel] *s* caution *f;* **to be out on bail** être libre sous caution; **to put up bail** se porter caution ‖ *tr* cautionner; **to bail out** se porter caution pour; (*a boat*) écoper ‖ *intr*—**to bail out** (aer) sauter en parachute

bailiff [ˈbelɪf] *s* (*of a court*) huissier *m,* bailli *m;* (*on a farm*) régisseur *m*

bailiwick [ˈbelɪwɪk] *s* bailliage *m,* rayon *m;* (fig) domaine *m*

bail'out' *s* (com) sauvetage *m* financier

bait [bet] *s* appât *m,* amorce *f* ‖ *tr* appâter, amorcer; (*to harass*) harceler

baize [bez] *s* serge *f,* reps *m*

bake [bek] *tr* faire cuire au four; **to bake bread** boulanger, faire le pain ‖ *intr* cuire au four

baked' pota'toes *spl* pommes *fpl* de terre au four

bakelite [ˈbekə,laɪt] *s* bakélite *f*

baker [ˈbekər] *s* boulanger *m*

bak'er's doz'en *s* treize *m* à la douzaine

baker•y [ˈbekəri] *s* (*pl* **-ies**) boulangerie *f*

baking [ˈbekɪŋ] *s* cuisson *f* au four

bak'ing pow'der *s* levure *f* anglaise, poudre *f* à pâte, levure chimique

bak'ing so'da *s* bicarbonate *m* de soude

balance [ˈbæləns] *s* balance *f,* équilibre *m;* (*scales*) balance *f;* (*what is left*) reste *m;* (com) solde *m,* report *m* ‖ *tr* balancer; (*an account*) solder ‖ *intr* se balancer; se solder

balanced [ˈbælənst] *adj* équilibré

bal'ance of pay'ments *s* balance *f* des comptes

bal'ance of pow'er *s* équilibre *m* politique

bal'ance of trade' *s* balance *f* du commerce

bal'ance sheet' *s* bilan *m*

bal'ance wheel' *s* balancier *m*

balancing [ˈbælənsɪŋ] *s* (*oscillation*) balancement *m;* (*evening up*) équilibrage *m,* ajustement *m;* (com) règlement *m* des comptes

balco•ny [ˈbælkəni] *s* (*pl* **-nies**) balcon *m;* (*in a theater*) galerie *f*

bald [bɔld] *adj* chauve; (*fact, statement, etc.*) simple, net, carré

baldness [ˈbɔldnɪs] *s* calvitie *f*

bale [bɔl] *s* balle *f* ‖ *tr* emballer

baleful [ˈbelfəl] *adj* funeste, fatal; triste

balk [bɔk] *s* (*disappointment*) déception *f,* contretemps *m;* (*beam*) poutre *f;* (baseball) feinte *f* illégale ‖ *tr* frustrer ‖ *intr* regimber

Balkan [ˈbɔlkən] *adj* balkanique

balk•y [ˈbɔki] *adj* (*comp* **-ier;** *super* **-iest**) regimbé, rétif

ball [bɔl] *s* balle *f;* (*in billiards; in bearings*) bille *f;* (*spherical body*) boule *f;* (*dance*) bal *m;* (baseball) balle *f;* **balls** (vulg) couilles *fpl* **to be on the ball** (slang) être toujours là pour le coup; **to have s.th. on the ball** (slang) avoir q.ch. dans le ventre; **to play ball** jouer à la balle, jouer au ballon; (slang) coopérer; (*to be in cahoots*) (slang) être en tandem ‖ *tr*—**to ball up** (slang) bousiller, embrouiller

ballad [ˈbæləd] *s* (*song*) romance *f,* complainte *f;* (*poem*) ballade *f*

ball' and chain' *s* boulet *m;* (slang) femme *f,* épouse *f*

ball'-and-sock'et joint' *s* joint *m* à rotule

ballast [ˈbæləst] *s* (aer, naut) lest *m;* (rr) ballast *m* ‖ *tr* lester; ballaster

ball'bear'ing *s* bille *f,* roulement *m* à billes

ball' cock' *s* robinet *m* à flotteur

ballerina [ˌbæləˈrinə] *s* ballerine *f*

ballet [ˈbæle] *s* ballet *m*

ball' game' *s* match *m* de base-ball

ballistic [bəˈlɪstɪk] *adj* balistique ‖ **ballistics** *s* balistique *f*

ballis'tic mis'sile *s* engin *m* balistique

balloon [bəˈlun] *s* ballon *m* ‖ *tr* ballonner ‖ *intr* ballonner, se ballonner

ballot [ˈbælət] *s* (*balloting*) scrutin *m;* (*individual ballot*) bulletin *m* (de vote) ‖ *intr* scrutiner, voter

bal'lot box' *s* urne *f;* **to stuff the ballot boxes** bourrer les urnes

balloting [ˈbælətɪn] *s* scrutin *m*

ball' park' *s* stade *m* de base-ball

ball'-point pen' *s* stylo *m* à bille, crayon *m* à bille

ball' room' *s* salon *m* de bal, salle *f* de danse

ballyhoo [ˈbælɪ,hu] *s* publicité *f* tapageuse ‖ *tr* faire de la réclame pour

balm [bɑm] *s* baume *m* ‖ *tr* parfumer

balm•y [ˈbɑmi] *adj* (*comp* **-ier;** *super* **-iest**) embaumé; (slang) toqué

baloney [bəˈloni] *s* (culin) mortadelle *f;* (slang) fadaises *fpl*

balsam [ˈbɔlsəm] *s* baume *m*
bal'sam fir' *s* sapin *m* baumier
bal'sam pop'lar *s* peuplier *m* baurnier
Balt [bɔlt] *s* Balte *mf*
Baltic [ˈbɔltɪk] *adj* Baltique
Bal'timore o'riole [ˈbɔltɪˌmor] *s* loriot *m* de Baltimore
baluster [ˈbæləstər] *s* balustre *m*
balustrade [ˌbæləsˈtred] *s* balustrade *f*, rampe *f*
bamboo [bæmˈbu] *s* bambou *m*
bamboozle [bæmˈbuzəl] *tr* (slang) mystifier
ban [bæn] *s* ban *m*, interdiction *f*; **bans** bans *mpl* ‖ *v* (*pret & pp* **banned**; *ger* **banning**) *tr* mettre au ban
banal [ˈbænəl], [bəˈnæl] *adj* banal
banali·ty [bəˈnælɪti] *s* (*pl* **-ties**) banalité *f*
banana [bəˈnænə] *s* banane *f*
banan'a tree' *s* bananier *m*
band [bænd] *s* (*strap, connection*) bande *f*, lien *m*; (*group*) bande, troupe *f*; (*brass band*) musique *f*, fanfare *f*; (*dance band*) orchestre *m*; (*strip of color*) raie *f*; **to beat the band** (slang) sans pareille; (*hastily*) vivement ‖ *tr* entourer de bandes; (*a bird*) marquer de bandes ‖ *intr*—**to band together** se grouper
bandage [ˈbændɪdʒ] *s* (*dressing*) pansement *m*; (*holding the dressing in place*) bandage *m* ‖ *tr* panser; bander
band'box' *s* carton *m* de modiste
bandit [ˈbændɪt] *s* bandit *m*
band'mas'ter *s* chef *m* de musique
band'saw' *s* scie *f* à ruban
band'stand' *s* kiosque *m*
band'wag'on *s* char *m* de la victoire; **to jump on the bandwagon** suivre la majorité victorieuse
band'width' *s* (comp) largeur *f* de bande; (electron) amplitude *f* de bande
ban·dy [ˈbændi] *adj* tortu ‖ *v* (*pret & pp* **-died**) *tr* renvoyer, échanger; **to bandy words** se renvoyer des paroles ‖ *intr* se disputer
ban'dy-leg'ged *adj* bancal
bane [ben] *s* poison *m*; ruine *f*
baneful [ˈbenfəl] *adj* funeste, nuisible
bang [bæŋ] *s* coup *m*; (*of a door*) claquement *m*; (*of fireworks; of a gun*) détonation *f*; **bangs** frange *f*; **to go off with a bang** détoner; (slang) réussir ‖ *tr* frapper; (*a door*) faire claquer; **to bang down** (*e.g., a lid*) abattre violemment; **to bang up** (slang) rosser, cogner ‖ *intr* claquer avec fracas; **to bang against** cogner; **to bang on** frapper à ‖ *interj* pan!; pom!
bang'-up' *adj* (slang) de premier ordre, à la hauteur
banish [ˈbænɪʃ] *tr* bannir, exiler
banishment [ˈbænɪʃmənt] *s* bannissement *m*
banister [ˈbænɪstər] *s* balustre *m*; **banisters** balustrade *f*, rampe *f*
bank [bæŋk] *s* (*for money, blood, data, etc.*) banque *f*; (*of river*) rive *f*, bord *m*; (*shoal*) banc *m*; (*slope*) talus *m*, terrasse *f*; (*in a gambling game*) cave *f*; (aer) virage *m* incliné; **to**

break the bank faire sauter la banque ‖ *tr* terrasser; (*money*) déposer; (*an airplane*) incliner ‖ *intr* (aer) virer, virer sur l'aile, s'incliner; **to bank on** compter sur
bank' account' *s* compte *m* en banque
bank'book' *s* carnet *m* de banque
bank' card' *s* carte-retrait *f*
banked *adj* incliné
banker [ˈbæŋkər] *s* banquier *m*
banking [ˈbæŋkɪŋ] *adj* bancaire
bank' note' *s* billet *m* de banque
bank'roll' *s* paquet *m* de billets, liasse *f* de billets
bankrupt [ˈbæŋkrʌpt] *adj & s* failli *m*; (*with guilt*) banqueroutier *m*; **to go bankrupt** faire banqueroute ‖ *tr* mettre en faillite
bankrupt·cy [ˈbæŋkrʌptsi] *s* (*pl* **-cies**) faillite *f*, banqueroute *f*; (fig) ruine *f*
bank' vault' *s* chambre *f* forte
banner [ˈbænər] *s* bannière *f*
ban'ner cry' *s* cri *m* de guerre
ban'ner head' lines *spl* titres *mpl* flamboyants
ban'ner year' *s* année *f* record
banquet [ˈbæŋkwɪt] *s* banquet *m* ‖ *intr* banqueter
bantam [ˈbæntəm] *adj* nain ‖ *s* poulet *m* nain, poulet *m* de bantam
ban'tam·weight' *s* poids *m* bantam; (boxing) poids bantam, poids coq
banter [ˈbæntər] *s* badinage *m* ‖ *tr & intr* badiner
bantering [ˈbæntərɪŋ] *adj* railleur, goguenard
baptism [ˈbæptɪzəm] *s* baptême *m*
baptismal [bæpˈtɪzməl] *adj* baptismal
baptis'mal certif'icate *s* extrait *m* de baptême
baptis'mal font' *s* fonts *mpl* baptismaux
Baptist [ˈbæptɪst] *s* baptiste *mf*
baptister·y [ˈbæptɪstəri] *s* (*pl* **-ies**) baptistère *m*
baptize [ˈbæptaɪz] *tr* baptiser
bar [bar] *s* barre *f*, barreau *m*; (*obstacle*) barrière *f*, empêchement *m*; (*barroom; counter*) bar *m*; (*profession of law*) barreau; (*of public opinion*) tribunal *m*; (*of chocolate*) tablette *f*, plaquette *f*; (*mus*) mesure *f*; (phys) bar; **behind bars** sous les barreaux ‖ *prep*—**bar none** sans exception ‖ *v* (*pret & pp* **barred**; *ger* **barring**) *tr* barrer
barb [barb] *s* (*of a fishhook, arrow, feather*) barbillon *m*; (*arrowhead*) dent *f* d'une flèche; (*in metalwork*) barbe *f* ‖ *tr* garnir de barbillons
Barbados [barˈbedoz] *s* la Barbade
barbarian [barˈbɛrɪən] *adj & s* barbare *mf*
barbaric [barˈbærɪk] *adj* barbare
barbarism [ˈbarbəˌrɪzəm] *s* barbarie *f*; (*in speech or writing*) barbarisme *m*
barbari·ty [barˈbærɪti] *s* (*pl* **-ties**) barbarie *f*
barbarous [ˈbarbərəs] *adj* barbare
barbecue [ˈbarbɪˌkju] *s* grillade *f* en plein air ‖ *tr* griller à la sauce piquante et au charbon de bois
bar'becue pit' *s* rôtisserie *f* en plein air
barbed *adj* barbelé, pointu
barbed' wire' *s* fil *m* de fer barbelé

barbed′-wire entan′glement *s* réseau *m* de barbelés

bar′bell′ *s* haltère *m*

barber [ˈbɑrbər] *s* coiffeur *m; (who shaves)* barbier *m*

bar′ber pole′ *s* enseigne *f* de barbier

bar′ber•shop *s* salon *m* de coiffeur

bar′ber•shop quartet′ *s* ensemble *m* harmonique de chanteurs amateurs

barbiturate [bɑrˈbɪtʃə,ret], [ˌbɑrbɪˈtjʊret] *adj & s* barbiturique *m*

bar′ code′ *s* code-barres *m*, code *m* à barres

bard [bɑrd] *s* barde *m*

bare [bɛr] *adj* nu; *(uncovered)* découvert; *(wire)* dénudé, à nu; *(necessities)* simple, strict; *(ace, king, queen)* sec ‖ *tr* mettre à nu

bare′back′ *adv* à nu

bare′faced′ *adj* éhonté, effronté

bare′foot′ *adj* nu-pieds

bare′head′ed *adj* nu-tête

bare′leg′ged *adj* nu-jambes

barely [ˈbɛrli] *adv* à peine

bareness [ˈbɛrnɪs] *s* nudité *f,* dénuement *m; (of style)* pauvreté *f*

barf [bɑrf] *intr* (slang) dégueler

bar′fly′ *s* (*pl* **-flies**) (slang) pilier *m* de cabaret

bargain [ˈbɑrgɪn] *s (deal)* marché *m,* affaire *f; (cheap purchase)* solde *m,* occasion *f;* **into the bargain** par-dessus le marché ‖ *tr***—to bargain away** vendre à perte ‖ *intr* entrer en négociations; **she gave him more than he bargained for** (fig) elle lui a donné du fil à retordre; **to bargain over** marchander; **to bargain with** traiter avec

bar′gain coun′ter *s* rayon *m* des soldes

bar′gain sale′ *s* vente *f* de soldes

barge [bɑrdʒ] *s* barge *f,* chaland *m,* péniche *f* ‖ *intr***—to barge into** entrer sans façons

baritone [ˈbærɪ,ton] *adj* de baryton ‖ *s* baryton *m*

barium [ˈbɛ,rɪ•əm] *s* baryum *m*

bark [bɑrk] *s (of tree)* écorce *f; (of dog)* aboiement *m; (boat)* trois-mâts *m;* **his bark is worse than his bite** il fait plus de bruit que de mal ‖ *tr***—to bark out** dire d'un ton sec ‖ *intr* aboyer; **to bark up the wrong tree** suivre une mauvaise piste

bar′keep′er *s* barman *m*

barker [ˈbɑrkər] (coll) *s* bonimenteur *m,* barnum *m*

barley [ˈbɑrli] *s* orge *f*

bar′ mag′net *s* barre *f* d'aimant

bar′maid′ *s* fille *f* comptoir, demoiselle *f* de comptoir, serveuse *f*

barn [bɑrn] *s (for grain)* grange *f; (for horses)* écurie *f; (for livestock)* étable *f*

barnacle [ˈbɑrnəkəl] *s (on a ship)* anatife *m,* patelle *f; (goose)* bernacle *f*

barn′ owl′ *s (Tyto alba)* effraie *f*

barn′storm′ *intr* aller en tournée

barn′yard′ *s* basse-cour *f*

barometer [bəˈrɑmɪtər] *s* baromètre *m*

barometric [ˌbærəˈmɛtrɪk] *adj* barométrique

baron [ˈbærən] *s* baron *m; (of steel, coal, lumber)* (coll) magnat *m*

baroness [ˈbærənɪs] *s* baronne *f*

baroque [bəˈrok] *adj & s* baroque *m*

barracks [ˈbærəks] *spl* caserne *f*

barrage [bəˈrɑʒ] *s* barrage *m*

barred *adj* barré; *(excluded)* exclu

barrel [ˈbærəl] *s* tonneau *m,* fût *m;* **large barrel** barrique *f;* **small barrel** baril *m,* baricaut *m,* barillet *m*

bar′rel or′gan *s* orgue *m* de Barbarie

barren [ˈbærən] *adj* stérile; *(bare)* nu; *(of style)* aride, sec

barricade [ˌbærɪˈked] *s* barricade *f* ‖ *tr* barricader

barrier [ˈbærɪ•ər] *s* barrière *f*

bar′rier reef′ *s* récif-barrière *m*

barring [ˈbɑrɪŋ] *prep* sauf

barrister [ˈbærɪstər] *s* (Brit) avocat *m*

bar′room′ *s* cabaret *m,* bar *m,* bistrot *m*

bar′tend′er *s* barman *m*

barter [ˈbɑrtər] *s* échange *m,* troc *m* ‖ *tr* échanger

ba′sal metab′olism [ˈbesəl] *s* métabolisme *m* basal

basalt [bəˈsɔlt], [ˈbæsɔlt] *s* basalte *m*

base [bes] *adj* bas, vil ‖ *s (main ingredient; starting point; lowest part)* base *f; (fundamental, principal)* fondement *m,* ligne *f* d'appui, principe *m; (pedestal)* socle *m; (baseball)* but *m* ‖ *tr* baser; fonder

base′ball′ *s* base-ball *m; (ball)* balle *f*

base′board′ *s* plinthe *f*

base′less *adj* sans fondement

basement [ˈbesmənt] *s* sous-sol *m,* cave *f*

base′ment win′dow *s* soupirail *m*

bash [bæʃ] *tr* cogner, assommer

bashful [ˈbæʃfəl] *adj* timide

basic [ˈbesɪk] *adj* fondamental, de base, essentiel; *(alkaline)* basique

basil [ˈbæzəl] *s* basilic *m*

basilica [bəˈsɪlkə] *s* basilique *f*

basin [ˈbesɪn] *s (bowl; pond; dock)* bassin *m; (washbasin)* cuvette *f; (bowl)* bol *m*

ba•sis [ˈbesɪs] *s (pl* **-ses** [siz]) base *f,* fondement *m;* **on the basis of** sur la base de, par suite de

bask [bæsk] *intr* se chauffer

basket [ˈbæskɪt] *s* panier *m; (with a handle)* corbeille *f; (carried on the back)* hotte *f*

bas′ket•ball′ *s* basket-ball *m,* basket *m*

bas′ket•ball play′er *s* basketteur *m*

bas′ket case′ *s* (coll) cas *m* perdu

bas′ket lunch′ *s* panier-repas *m*

bas′ket•mak′er *s* vannier *m*

bas′ket•work′ *s* vannerie *f*

Basque [bæsk] *adj* basque ‖ *s (language)* basque *m; (person)* Basque *mf*

bass [bes] *adj* grave, bas ‖ *s* (mus) basse *f* ‖ [bæs] *s* (ichth) bar *m*

bass′ clef′ *s* clef *f* de fa

bass′ drum′ [bes] *s* grosse caisse *f*

bassinet [ˌbæsɪˈnɛt] *s* bercelonnette *f*

bassoon [bə`sun] s bassoon m
bass viol [`bes`vaɪ•əl] s basse f de viole
basswood [`bæs,wʊd] s tilleul m
bastard [`bæstərd] adj bâtard ‖ s bâtard m; (vulg) salaud m, saligaud m
baste [best] tr (to thrash) rosser; (to scold) éreinter; (culin) arroser; (sewing) faufiler, baguer, bâtir
bastion [`bæst∫ən] s bastion m
bat [bæt] s (cudgel) bâton m; (for cricket) bat m; (sports) batte f; (zool) chauve-souris f; (blow) (coll) coup m; **right off the bat** sur-le-champ; **to be at bat** tenir la batte; **to go to bat for** (coll) intervenir au profit de; **to have bats in the belfry** (coll) avoir une araignée dans le plafond ‖ v (pret & pp **batted;** ger **batting**) tr battre
batch [bæt∫] s (of papers) liasse f; (comp) paquetage m; (coll) fournée f, lot m
batch' proc'essing (comp) traitement m par lots
bated [`betɪd] adj—**with bated breath** en baissant la voix, dans un souffle
bath [bæθ] s bain m; (bathroom) salle f de bains; **to take a bath** prendre un bain, se baigner
bathe [beð] tr baigner ‖ intr se baigner
bather [`beðər] s baigneur m
bath'house' s établissement m de bains; (at the seashore) cabine f
bath'ing suit' s costume m de bain
bath'ing trunks' s slip m de bain
bath' mat' s tapis m de bain
bath'robe' s peignoir m
bath'room' s salle f de bains
bath'room fix'tures spl appareils mpl sanitaires
bath'room scale' s pèse-personne m
bath' tow'el s serviette f de bain
bath'tub' s baignoire f
baton [bæ`tan] s (scepter) bâton m; (mus) baguette f, bâton de chef d'orchestre; (sports) bâton de relais, témoin m
battalion [bə`tæljən] s bataillon m
batten [`bætən] tr—**to batten down the hatches** condamner les panneaux
batter [`bætər] s (culin) pâte f; (sports) batteur m ‖ tr battre
bat'tering ram' s bélier m
batter•y [`bætəri] s (pl -ies) (elec, mil, mus) batterie f; (primary cell) pile f; (secondary cell or cells) accumulateur m, accu m
bat'ting or'der s (baseball) formation f des frappeurs
battle [`bætəl] s bataille f; **to do battle** livrer combat ‖ tr & intr combattre
bat'tle-ax' s hache f d'armes; (shrew) (slang) harpie f, mégère f
bat'tle cruis'er s croiseur m de bataille
bat'tle cry' s cri m de guerre
bat'tledore' and shut'tle cock' [`bætəldɔr] spl raquette f et volant m
bat'tle-field' s champ m de bataille
bat'tle-front' s front m de bataille

bat'tle line' s ligne f de feu
battlement [`bætəlmənt] s créneau m; **battlements** parapet m, rempart m
bat'tle roy'al s mêlée f générale
bat'tle•ship' s cuirassé m, navire m de guerre
bat•ty [`bæti] adj (comp **-tier;** super **-tiest**) (slang) dingo, maboul, braque
bauble [`bɔbəl] s babiole f, bagatelle f; (of jester) marotte f
baud [bɔd] s (comp) baud m
baud' rate' s (comp) rapidité moyenne du signal transmis
Bavaria [bə`vɛrɪ•ə] s la Bavière
Bavarian [bə`vɛrɪ•ən] adj bavarois ‖ s Bavarois m
bawd•y [`bɔdi] adj (comp **-ier;** super **-iest**) obscène, impudique
bawl [bɔl] tr—**to bawl out** (slang) faire une sortie à, engueuler ‖ intr gueuler; (to cry) sangloter
bawl'ing out' s (slang) engueulade f
bay [be] adj & s baie f; **at bay** aux abois ‖ intr aboyer, hurler
bay'ber'ry s (pl -ries) baie f
bay'berry tree' s laurier m
bayonet [`be•ənɪt] s baïonnette f ‖ tr percer d'un coup de baïonnette
bayou [`baɪ•u] s anse f
bay' rum' s eau f de toilette au laurier
bay' win'dow s fenêtre f en saillie; (slang) bedaine f, gros ventre m
bazaar [bə`zɑr] s bazar m; (social event) kermesse f
B.C. [`bi si] adv (letterword) (**before Christ**) av. J.-C.
be [bi] v (pres **am** [æm], **is** [ɪz], **are** [ɑr]; pret **was** [wɑz] or [wʌz], **were** [wʌr]; pp **been** [bɪn]) intr être; avoir, e.g., **to be five years old** avoir cinq ans; e.g., **to be ten feet long** avoir dix pieds de long; e.g., **what is the matter with you?** qu'avez-vous?; **here is** or **here are** voici; **how are you?** comment allez-vous?, ça va?, comment vous portez-vous?; **how much is that?** combien coûte cela?, c'est combien ça?; **so be it** ainsi soit-il; **there is** or **there are** il y a; (in directing the attention) voilà; for expressions like **it is warm** il fait chaud or **I am cold** j'ai froid, see the noun ‖ aux (to form the passive voice) être, e.g., **he is loved by everybody** il est aimé de tout le monde; (progressive not expressed in French), e.g., **he is eating** il mange; **to be to** + inf devoir + inf, e.g., **I am to give a speech** je dois prononcer un discours
beach [bit∫] s plage f, bord m de la mer; grève f, rivage m ‖ tr & intr échouer
beach' ball' s ballon m de plage
beach' bug'gy s buggy m
beach'comb'er s batteur m de grève
beach'front' s front m de mer, bord m de mer
beach'head' s (mil) tête f de pont
beach' resort' s station f balnéaire

beach′ robe′ s sortie f de bain, peignoir m de bain

beach′ shoe′ s claquette f

beach′ tent′ s tente f de plage

beach′ umbrel′la s parasol m de plage

beach′wear′ s tenue f de plage

beacon [′bikən] s signal m, phare m ‖ tr éclairer ‖ intr briller

bead [bid] s (girder) perle f, grain m; (of a gun) guidon m; **beads** collier m; (of sweat) gouttes fpl; (eccl) chapelet m; **to draw a bead on** viser; **to tell one's beads** égrener son chapelet

beagle [′bigəl] s beagle m, briquet m

beak [bik] s bec m; (nose) (slang) pif m; grand nez m crochu

beaker [′bikər] s coupe f, vase m à bec, verre m à expérience

beam [bim] s (girder) poutre f; (plank) madrier m; (of roof) solive f; (of ship) bau m, barrot m; (of light; of hope) rayon m; (rad) faisceau m; **on the beam** (slang) sur la bonne piste; **to be off the beam** (slang) faire fausse route ‖ tr (light, waves, etc.) émettre; **to beam a broadcast** faire une émission ‖ intr rayonner

bean [bin] s haricot m; (broad bean) fève f; (slang) caboche f; **to spill the beans** (coll) vendre la mèche

bean′-bag chair′ s siège billes m

bean′ pole′ s perche f à fèves; (person) (slang) asperge f

bean′stalk′ s tige f de fève, tige de haricot

bear [bɛr] s ours m; (in the stock market) baissier m ‖ v (pret **bore** [bor]; pp **borne** [born]) tr porter; (a child) enfanter; (interest on money) rapporter; (to put up with) souffrir, supporter; **to bear the market** jouer à la baisse ‖ intr porter; **to bear down** appuyer; **to bear up against** résister à; **to bear upon** avoir du rapport à; **to bring to bear** mettre en jeu

bearable [′bɛrəbəl] adj supportable

bear′ cub′ s ourson m

beard [bɪrd] s barbe f ‖ tr braver, narguer

bearded adj barbu

beardless [′bɪrdlɪs] adj imberbe, sans barbe

bearer [′bɛrər] s porteur m

bearing [′bɛrɪŋ] s (posture; behavior) port m, maintien m; (mach) roulement m, coussinet m; (naut) relèvement m; **to get one's bearings** se retrouver; **to have a bearing on** s'appliquer à; **to take bearings** (naut) faire le point

bear′ mar′ket s marché m à la baisse

bear′skin′ s peau f d'ours; colback m

beast [bist] s bête f, animal m; (person) brute f, animal m

beast·ly [′bistli] adj (comp **-lier**; super **-liest**) brutal, bestial; (coll) abominable, détestable

beast′ of bur′den s bête f de somme, bête de charge

beat [bit] s (of heart, pulse, drums) battement m; (of policeman) ronde f; (mus) measure f, temps m ‖ v (pret **beat**; pp **beat** or **beaten**) tr battre; (to defeat) vaincre, battre; **that beats**

me! (slang) ça me dépasse!; **to beat back** or **down** rabattre; **to beat in** enfoncer; **to beat it** (slang) filer, décamper; **to beat s.o. hollow** (coll) battre qn à plate couture; **to beat s.o. out of money** (slang) escroquer qn; **to beat time** battre la mesure; **to beat up** (slang) rosser ‖ intr battre; **to beat around the bush** (coll) tourner autour du pot

beat′en track′ ou **path′** s sentier m battu

beater [′bitər] s batteur m; (culin) fouet m

beati·fy [bɪ′ætɪ,faɪ] v (pret & pp **-fied**) tr béatifier

beating [′bitɪŋ] s (of wings, heart, pulse, drums) battement m; (thrashing) correction f, rossée f, raclée f; (defeat) défaite f, raclée; **to take a beating** se faire battre à plate couture

beatitude [bɪ′ætɪ,t(j)ud] s béatitude f

beau [bo] s (pl **beaus** or **beaux** [boz]) beau m, galant m

beautician [bju′tɪʃən] s coiffeur m, coiffeuse f, esthéticienne f

beautiful [′bjutɪfəl] adj beau

beautifully [′bjutɪfəli] adv admirablement

beauti·fy [′bjutɪ,faɪ] v (pret & pp **-fied**) tr embellir

beau·ty [′bjuti] s (pl **-ties**) beauté f

beau′ty con′test s concours m de beauté

beau′ty par′lor ou **beau′ty shop′** s salon m de beauté, institut m de beauté

beau′ty queen′ s reine f de beauté

beau′ty sleep′ s sommeil m avant minuit

beau′ty spot′ s (place) coin m délicieux; (on face) grain m de beauté

beaver [′bivər] s castor m

becalm [bɪ′kɑm] tr calmer, apaiser; (naut) abriter

because [bɪ′kɔz] conj parce que; **because of** à cause de, par suite de

beck [bɛk] s—**to be at s.o.'s beck and call** obéir à qn au doigt et à l'œil

beckon [′bɛkən] tr faire signe à, appeler ‖ intr appeler

be·come [bɪ′kʌm] v (pret **-came**; pp **-come**) tr convenir à, aller à, seoir à ‖ intr devenir; se faire, e.g., **to become a doctor** se faire médecin; e.g., **to become known** se faire connaître; **to become accustomed** s'accoutumer; **to become old** vieillir; **what has become of him?** qu'est-ce qu'il est devenu?

becoming [bɪ′kʌmɪŋ] adj convenable, seyant

bed [bɛd] s lit m; couche f; **to go to bed** se coucher; **to put to bed** coucher

bed′ and board′ s le vivre et le couvert

bed′ and break′fast s (Brit) chambre f avec petit déjeuner

bed′bug′ s punaise f (des lits)

bed′ clothes′ spl couvertures fpl et draps mpl

bedding [′bɛdɪŋ] s literie f

bedeck [bɪ′dɛk] tr parer, orner, chamarrer; **to bedeck oneself** s' attifer

bed′fast′ adj cloué au lit

bed′fel′low s camarade m de lit

bed′jack′et s liseuse f

bedlam [ˈbɛdləm] *s* pétaudière *f,* tumulte *m*
bed'lamp' *s* lampe *f* de chevet
bed'lin'en *s* literie *f,* draps *mpl* en toile de fil
bed'pan' *s* bassin *m* (de lit)
bedraggled [bɪˈdrægəld] *adj* crotté, échevelé
bedridden [ˈbɛdˌrɪdən] *adj* alité, cloué au lit
bed'rock' *s* roche *f* de fond; (geol) soubassement *m;* (fig) fondement *m,* base *f*
bed'room' *s* chambre *f* à coucher
bed'room' commun'ity *s* cité-dortoir *f,* ville-dortoir *f*
bed'room lamp' *s* lampe *f* de chevet
bed'side' *s* bord *m* du lit, chevet *m*
bed'side book' *s* livre *m* de chevet
bed'side ta'ble *s* table *f* de chevet, table de nuit
bed'sore' *s* escarre *f*
bed'spread' *s* dessus-de-lit *m invar*
bed'spring' *s* sommier *m*
bed'stead' *s* bois *m* de lit
bed'tick' *s* coutil *m*
bed'time' *s* l'heure *f* du coucher
bed'warm'er *s* chauffe-lit *m*
bed'wet'ting *s* énurésie *f*
bee [bi] *s* abeille *f;* (*get-together*) réunion *f;* (*contest*) concours *m*
beech [bitʃ] *s* hêtre *m*
beech' mar'ten *s* (zool) fouine *f*
beech' nut' *s* faîne *f*
beef [bif] *s* bœuf *m* ‖ *tr*—**to beef up** (coll) renforcer ‖ *intr* (slang) rouspéter
beef' cat'tle *s* bœufs *mpl* de boucherie
beef' ex'tract *s* extrait *m* de bœuf
beef'steak' *s* bifteck *m*
beef' stew' *s* ragoût *m* de bœuf
bee'hive' *s* ruche *f*
bee'keep'er *s* apiculteur *m*
bee'keep'ing *s* apiculture *f*
bee'line' *s*—**to make a beeline for** aller en droite ligne à
beep [bip] *s* bip *m;* (aut) coup *m* de klaxon ‖ *tr* (med) biper ‖ *intr* émettre un bip
beeper [ˈbipər] *s* bip-bip *m*
beer [bɪr] *s* bière *f*
beer' bel'ly *s* (coll) panse *f* (*du buveur de bière*)
beer' bot'tle *ou* **beer' can** *s* canette *f* (de bière)
bees'wax' *s* circe *f* d'abeille
beet *s* betterave *f*
beetle [ˈbitəl] *s* scarabée *m,* escarbot *m*
bee'tle-browed' *adj* à sourcils épais, à sourcils fournis
be·fall [bɪˈfɔl] *v* (*pret.* **-fell;** *pp* **-fallen**) *tr* arriver à ‖ *intr* arriver
befitting [bɪˈfɪtɪŋ] *adj* convenable, seyant
before [bɪˈfor] *adv* avant, auparavant ‖ *prep* avant; (*in front of*) devant; **before** + *ger* avant de + *inf* ‖ *conj* avant que
before'hand' *adv* d'avance, préalablement, auparavant
befriend [bɪˈfrɛnd] *tr* venir en aide à
befuddle [bɪˈfʌdəl] *tr* embrouiller
beg [bɛg] *v* (*pret & pp* **begged;** *ger* **begging**) *tr* mendier; (*to entreat*) supplier ‖ *intr* mendier;

(*said of dog*) faire le beau; **I beg of you** je vous en prie; **to beg for** solliciter; **to beg off** s'excuser; **to beg off from** se faire excuser de; **to go begging** (fig) rester pour compte
be·get [bɪˈgɛt] *v* (*pret* **-got;** *pp* **-gotten** or **-got;** *ger* **-getting**) *tr* engendrer
beggar [ˈbɛgər] *s* mendiant *m*
beggarly [ˈbɛgərli] *adj* chétif, misérable
be·gin [bɪˈgɪn] *v* (*pret* **-gan** [ˈgæn]; *pp* **-gun** [ˈgʌn]; *ger* **-ginning**) *tr & intr* commencer; **beginning with** à partir de; **to begin to** commencer à
beginner [bɪˈgɪnər] *s* débutant *m,* commençant *m;* (*tyro*) blanc-bec *m,* novice *m,* béjaune *m;* (mil) bleu *m*
begin'ner's luck' *s* coup *m* de chance, la chance *f* du premier coup; "coup d'essai, coup de maître"
beginning [bɪˈgɪnɪŋ] *s* commencement *m,* début *m*
begrudge [bɪˈgrʌdʒ] *tr* donner à contrecœur; **to begrudge s.o. s.th.** envier q.ch. à qn
beguile [bɪˈgaɪl] *tr* charmer, tromper
behalf [bɪˈhæf] *s*—**on behalf of** de la part de, au nom de
behave [bɪˈhev] *intr* se comporter, se conduire; (*to behave well*) se comporter bien
behavior [bɪˈhevjər] *s* comportement *m,* conduite *f;* (mach) fonctionnement *m*
behaviorism [bɪˈhevjərɪzəm] *s* behaviorisme *m*
behead [bɪˈhɛd] *tr* décapiter
beheading [bɪˈhɛdɪŋ] *s* décapitation *f*
behest [bɪˈhɛst] *s* ordre *m,* demande *f*
behind [bɪˈhaɪnd] *s* derrière *m* ‖ *adv* derrière, par derrière; **to be behind** être en retard; **to fall behind** traîner en arrière ‖ *prep* derrière; en arrière de; **behind the back of** dans le dos de; **behind time** en retard
be·hold [bɪˈhold] *v* (*pret & pp* **-held** [ˈhɛld]) *tr* contempler ‖ *interj* voyez!, voici!
behoove [bɪˈhuv] *impers*—**it behooves him to** il lui appartient de; **it does not behoove him to** mal lui sied de
being [ˈbiɪŋ] *adj*—**for the time being** pour le moment ‖ *s* être *m*
belabor [bɪˈlebər] *tr* rosser; (fig) trop insister sur
belated [bɪˈletɪd] *adj* attardé, tardif
belch [bɛltʃ] *s* éructation *f,* rot *m* (slang) ‖ *tr & intr* éructer
bel·fry [ˈbɛlfri] *s* (*pl* **-fries**) beffroi *m,* clocher *m*
Belgian [ˈbɛldʒən] *adj* belge ‖ *s* Belge *mf*
Belgium [ˈbɛldʒəm] *s* Belgique *f;* la Belgique
be·lie [bɪˈlaɪ] *v* (*pret & pp* **-lied** [ˈlaɪd]; *ger* **-lying** [ˈlaɪɪŋ]) *tr* démentir
belief [bɪˈlif] *s* croyance *f*
believable [bɪˈlivəbəl] *adj* croyable
believe [bɪˈliv] *tr & intr* croire; **to believe in** croire à or en; **to make believe** faire semblant, feindre
believer [bɪˈlivər] *s* croyant *m*
belittle [bɪˈlɪtəl] *tr* rabaisser

bell [bɛl] *s* (*hollow instrument*) cloche *f;* (*of a clock or gong*) timbre *m;* (*small bell*) sonnette *f;* clochette *f;* (*big bell*) bourdon *m;* (*on animals*) grelot *m,* clarine *f,* sonnaille *f;* (*of a trumpet*) pavillon *m;* **bells** sonnerie *f* ‖ *tr* attacher un grelot à

belladonna [ˌbɛləˈdɑnə] *s* belladone *f*

bell′-bot′tom trou′sers *spl* pantalon *m* à pattes d'éléphant

bell′boy′ *s* chasseur *m,* garçon *m* d'hôtel

bell′ glass′ *s* globe *m,* garde-poussière *m*

bell′hop′ *s* chasseur *m,* garçon *m* d'hôtel

bellicose [ˈbɛlɪˌkos] *adj* belliqueux

belligerent [bəˈlɪdʒərənt] *adj & s* belligérant *m*

bell′ jar′ *s* var of **bell glass**

bellow [ˈbɛlo] *s* mugissement *m;* **bellows** (*of camera; of fireplace*) soufflet *m;* (*of organ; of forge*) soufflerie *f* ‖ *intr* mugir, beugler

bell′pull′ *s* cordon *m* de sonnette

bell′ ring′er *s* sonneur *m;* carillonneur *m*

bell′-shaped′ *adj* en forme de cloche

bell′ tow′er *s* clocher *m,* campanile *m*

bellwether [ˈbɛlˌwɛðər] *s* sonnailler *m*

bel-ly [ˈbɛli] *s* (*pl* **-lies**) ventre *m* ‖ *v* (*pret & pp* **-lied**) *intr*—**to belly out** s'enfler

bel′ly·ache′ *s* (coll) mal *m* de ventre ‖ *intr* (slang) rouspéter

bel′ly·but′ton *s* (coll) nombril *m*

bel′ly dance′ *s* (coll) danse *f* du ventre

bel′ly danc′er *s* danseuse *f* orientale

bel′ly flop′ *s* plat ventre *m* (acrobatique)

bellyful [ˈbɛlɪˌful] *s* (slang) ventrée *f*

bel′ly-land′ *intr* (aer) aterrir sur le ventre

belong [bɪˈlɔŋ] *intr* (*to have the proper qualities*) aller bien; **to belong in** devoir être dans, e.g., **this chair belongs in that corner** cette chaise doit être dans ce coin-là; **to belong to** appartenir à; **to belong together** aller ensemble

belongings [bɪˈlɔŋɪŋz] *spl* biens *mpl,* effets *mpl*

beloved [bɪˈlʌvɪd], [bɪˈlʌvd] *adj & s* bien-aimé *m*

below [bɪˈlo] *adv* dessous, au-dessous, en bas; (*as follows, following*) ci-dessous, ci-après ‖ *prep* sous, au-dessous de; (*another point on the river*) en aval de

belt [bɛlt] *s* (*encircling band or strip*) ceinture *f;* (*tract of land, region*) zone *f;* (*blow*) coup *m;* (*of a machine*) courroie *f;* **to tighten one's belt** se serrer la ceinture ‖ *tr* ceindre; (slang) cogner

belt′ buck′le *s* boucle *f* de ceinturon

belt′ convey′or *s* tapis *m* roulant

belted *adj* à ceinture

belt′way′ *s* route *f* de ceinture, boulevard *m* périphérique

bemoan [bɪˈmon] *tr* déplorer

bemuse [bɪˈmjuz] *tr* stupéfier, hébéter

bench [bɛntʃ] *s* banc *m;* (law) siège *m;* (sports) banc *m* de joueurs

bench′ mark′ *s* repère *m*

bend [bɛnd] *s* (*curvature*) courbure *f* (*of river, tube, road*) coude *m;* (*of arm, knee*) pli *m;*

bends mal *m* des caissons ‖ *v* (*pret & pp* **bent** [bɛnt]) *tr* courber; (*the elbow; a person to one's will*) plier; (*the knee*) fléchir ‖ *intr* courber; plier; **do not bend** (label) ne pas plier; **to bend down** se courber

bender [ˈbɛndər] *s*—**to go on a bender** (slang) faire la bombe

beneath [bɪˈniθ] *adv* dessous, au-dessous, en bas ‖ *prep* sous, au-dessous de

benediction [ˌbɛnɪˈdɪkʃən] *s* bénédiction *f*

benefactor [ˈbɛnɪˌfæktər] *s* bienfaiteur *m*

beneficence [bɪˈnɛfɪsəns] *s* bienfaisance *f*

beneficent [bɪˈnɛfɪsənt] *adj* bienfaisant

beneficial [ˌbɛnɪˈfɪʃəl] *adj* profitable, avantageux; (*remedy*) salutaire

beneficiar-y [ˌbɛnɪˈfɪʃɪˌɛri] *s* (*pl* **-ies**) bénéficiaire *mf,* ayant droit *m*

benefit [ˈbɛnɪfɪt] *s* profit *m;* (theat) bénéfice *m;* **benefits** bienfaits *mpl,* avantages *mpl;* **for the benefit of** au profit de ‖ *tr* profiter à ‖ *intr* se trouver bien, gagner

ben′efit game′ *s* match *m* de bienfaisance

ben′efit match′ *s* match *m* de bienfaisance

ben′efit perfor′mance *s* représentation *f* de bienfaisance

ben′efit soci′ety *s* société *f* de prévoyance

benevolent [bɪˈnɛvələnt] *adj* bienveillant, bienfaisant, bénévole

benign [bɪˈnaɪn] *adj* bénin

bent [bɛnt] *adj* courbé, plié; (*person's back*) voûté; (*determined*) résolu; **bent over** (*shoulders*) voûté; (*figure, person*) courbé; **to be bent on** être acharné à ‖ *s* penchant *m;* **to have a bent for** avoir du goût pour

benzene [bɛnˈzin] *s* (chem) benzène *m*

benzine [bɛnˈzin] *s* benzine *f*

bequeath [bɪˈkwið] *tr* léguer

bequest [bɪˈkwɛst] *s* legs *m*

berate [bɪˈret] *tr* gronder

be·reave [bɪˈriv] *v* (*pret & pp* **-reaved** or **-reft** [ˈrɛft]) *tr* priver; (*to cause sorrow to*) affliger

bereavement [bɪˈrivmənt] *s* (*loss*) privation *f;* (*sorrow*) deuil *m,* affliction *f*

berkelium [bərˈkɪlɪˌəm] *s* berkélium *m*

Berlin [bərˈlɪn] *adj* berlinois ‖ *s* Berlin *m*

Berliner [bərˈlɪnər] *s* berlinois *m*

berm [bʌrm] *s* berme *f*

Bermuda [bərˈmjudə] *s* les Bermudes *fpl*

ber·ry [ˈbɛri] *s* (*pl* **-ries**) baie *f;* (*seed*) grain *m*

berserk [bərˈzʌrk] *adv* frénétiquement; **to go berserk** frapper à tort et à travers

berth [bʌrθ] *s* (*sleeping space*) couchette *f;* (*at a dock*) emplacement *m;* (*space to move about*) évitage *m;* (fig) poste *m,* situation *f* ‖ *tr* (*a ship*) acoster

beryllium [bəˈrɪlɪˌəm] *s* béryllium *m*

be·seech [bɪˈsitʃ] *v* (*pret & pp* **-sought** [ˈsɔt] or **-seeched**) *tr* supplier

be·set [bɪˈsɛt] *v* (*pret & pp* **-set;** *ger* **-setting**) *tr* assiéger, assaillir

beside [bɪˈsaɪd] *prep* à côté de, auprès de; **to be beside oneself** être hors de soi; **to be beside oneself with** (*e.g., joy*) être transporté de

besides [bɪ'saɪdz] *adv* (*in addition*) en outre, de plus; (*otherwise*) d'ailleurs ‖ *prep* en sus de, en plus de, outre

besiege [bɪ'sidʒ] *tr* assiéger

besmear [bɪ'smɪr] *tr* barbouiller

besmirch [bɪ'smʌrtʃ] *tr* souiller

best [bɛst] *adj super* (le) meilleur §91 ‖ *s* (le) meilleur *m;* **at best** au mieux; **to do one's best** faire de son mieux; **to get the best of it** avoir le dessus; **to make the best of** s'accommoder de ‖ *adv super* (le) mieux §91 ‖ *tr* l'emporter sur

best' girl' *s* (coll) petite amie *f,* atitrée *f*

bestial ['bɪstjəl] *adj* bestial, brutal

best' man' *s* garçon *m* d'honneur

bestow [bɪ'sto] *tr* accorder, conférer

bestowal bɪ'sto•əl] *s* don *m,* dispensation *f*

best'sel'ler *s* livre *m* à succès, succès *m* de librairie, champion *m*

bet [bɛt] *s* pari *m,* gageure *f;* **make your bets!** faites vos jeux! ‖ *v* (*pret & pp* **bet** or **betted;** *ger* **betting**) *tr & intr* parier; **you bet!** (slang) je vous crois!, tu parles!

be•take [bɪ'tek] *v* (*pret* **-took;** *pp* **-taken**) *tr*—**to betake oneself** se rendre

be'ta test'er ['beta] *s* contrôleur *m* des rayons béta

Bethlehem ['bɛθlɪ,hɛm] *s* Bethléem

betray [bɪ'tre] *tr* trahir

betrayal [bɪ'tre•əl] *s* trahison *f*

betrayer [bɪ'tre•ər] *s* traître *m*

betrothal [bɪ'troðəl] *s* fiançailles *fpl*

better ['bɛtər] *adj comp* meilleur §91; **better than** meilleur que ‖ *adv comp* mieux §91; **better than** mieux que; (followed by numeral) plus de; **it is better to** il vaut mieux de; **so much the better** tant mieux; **to be better to** (*in better health*) aller mieux; **to be better to** valoir mieux; **to get better** s'améliorer; **to get the better of** l'emporter sur; **to think better** se raviser ‖ *tr* améliorer ‖ *intr* s'améliorer

bet'ter half' *s* (coll) chère moitié *f*

bet'ting odds' *spl* cote *f* (des paris)

bettor ['bɛtər] *s* parieur *m,* gageur *m*

between [bɪ'twin] *adv* au milieu, dans l'intervalle ‖ *prep* entre; **between friends** dans l'intimité

between'-decks' *s* (naut) entrepont *m*

bev•el ['bɛvəl] *adj* biseauté, taillé en biseau ‖ *s* (*instrument*) équerre *f;* (*sloping part*) biseau *m* ‖ *v* (*pret & pp* **-eled** *ou* **-elled;** *ger* **-eling** *ou* **-elling**) *tr* biseauter, chanfreiner, équerrer

beverage ['bɛvərɪdʒ] *s* boisson *f*

bev•y ['bɛvi] *s* (*pl* **-ies**) bande *f*

bewail [bɪ'wel] *tr* lamenter, pleurer

beware [bɪ'wɛr] *tr* se bien garder de ‖ *intr* pendre garde; **to beware of** prendre garde à ‖ *interj* gare!, prenez garde!

bewilder [bɪ'wɪldər] *tr* confondre, ahurir

bewilderment [bɪ'wɪldərmənt] *s* confusion *f,* ahurissement *m*

bewitch [bɪ'wɪtʃ] *tr* ensorceler

bewitching [bɪ'wɪtʃɪŋ] *adj* enchanteur

beyond [bɪ'jand] *s*—**the beyond** l'au-delà *m* ‖ *adv* au-delà ‖ *prep* au-delà de; **beyond a doubt** hors de doute; **it's beyond me** (coll) je n'y comprends rien; **to go beyond** dépasser

biannual [baɪ'ænju•əl] *adj* semi-annuel

bias ['baɪ•əs] *adj* biais ‖ *s* biais *m;* (fig) prévention *f,* préjugé *m* ‖ *tr* prédisposer, prévenir, rendre partial

bib [bɪb] *s* bavette *f*

Bible ['baɪbəl] *s* Bible *f*

Biblical ['bɪblɪkəl] *adj* biblique

bibliographer [,bɪblɪ'agrəfər] *s* bibliographe *m*

bibliogra•phy [,bɪblɪ'agrəfi] *s* (*pl* **-phies**) bibliographie *f*

biceps ['baɪsɛps] *s* biceps *m*

bicker ['bɪkər] *intr* se quereller, se chamailler

bickering ['bɪkərɪŋ] *s* bisbille *f*

bicuspid [baɪ'kʌspɪd] *s* prémolaire *f*

bicycle ['baɪsɪkəl] *s* bicyclette *f,* vélo *m* ‖ *intr* faire de la bicyclette, aller à bicyclette

bi'cycle lock' *s* antivol *m* de bicyclette

bi'cycle path' *s* piste *f* cyclable

bi'cycle pump' *s* pompe *f* à vélo

bi'cycle repair' patch' *s* rustine *f*

bicyclist ['baɪsɪklɪst] *s* cycliste *mf*

bid [bɪd] *s* (*offer*) enchère *f,* offre *f,* mise *f;* (*e.g., to build a school*) soumission *f;* (cards) demande *f* ‖ *v* (*pret* **bade** [bæd] or **bid;** *ger* **bidden** ['bɪdən]) *tr* inviter; (*to order*) commander; (cards) demander; **to bid ten thousand on** mettre une enchère de dix mille sur ‖ *intr*—**to bid on** mettre une enchère sur

bidder ['bɪdər] *s* enchérisseur *m,* offrant *m;* (*person who submits an estimate*) soumissionnaire *mf*

bidding ['bɪdɪŋ] *s* enchères *fpl;* **at s.o.'s bidding** aux ordres de qn

bide [baɪd] *tr*—**to bide one's time** attendre l'heure *or* le bon moment

bidet [bi'de] *s* (*bathroom fixture providing means for spot-bathing and rinsing after use of the toilet*) bidet *m*

biennial [baɪ'ɛnɪ•əl] *adj* biennal

bier [bɪr] *s* (*frame or stand*) catafalque *m;* (*coffin*) cercueil *m*

biff [bɪf] *s* (slang) gnon *m,* beigne *f* ‖ *tr* (slang) gifter, cogner

bifocal [baɪ'fokəl] *adj* bifocal ‖ **bifocals** *spl* lunettes *fpl* bifocales

big [bɪg] *adj* (*comp* **bigger;** *super* **biggest**) gros, grand; (*man*) de grande taille ‖ *adv*—**to grow big** grossir, grandir; **to talk big** (slang) se vanter

bigamist ['bɪgəmɪst] *s* bigame *mf*

bigamous ['bɪgəməs] *adj* bigame

bigamy ['bɪgəmi] *s* bigamie *f*

big'-bel'lied *adj* au gros ventre

big'boned' *adj* ossu, à gros os

big' broth'er *s* grand frère *m*

big' busi'ness *s* (pej) les grosses affaires *fpl*

Big' Dip'per *s* Grand Chariot *m*

big' game' *s* fauves *mpl,* gros gibier *m*

big'-heart'ed *adj* généreux, cordial

big′mouth′ *s* (slang) gueulard *m*
bigot [ˈbɪgət] *s* bigot *m*
bigoted [ˈbɪgətɪd] *adj* bigot
bigot•ry [ˈbɪgətri] *s* (*pl* **-ries**) bigoterie *f*
big′ shot′ *s* (slang) grand manitou *m*, gros bonnet *m*, grand caïd *m*, grosse légume *f*
big′ sis′ter *s* grande sœur *f*
big′ splash′ *s* (slang) sensation *f* à tout casser
big′ stiff′ *s* (slang) personnage *m* guindé
big′ talk′ *s* (slang) vantardise *f*
big′ toe′ *s* orteil *m*, gros orteil
big′ top′ *s* (*circus tent*) chapiteau *m*
big′ wheel′ *s* (slang) gros bonnet *m*, grand manitou *m*, grosse légume *f*
big′wig′ *s* (coll) gros bonnet *m*, grand manitou *m*, grosse légume *f*
bike [baɪk] *s* (coll) bécane *f*, vélo *m*
bikini [bɪˈkini] *s* slip *m* minimum
bile [baɪl] *s* bile *f*
bilge [bɪldʒ] *s* sentine *f*, cale *f*
bilge′ wa′ter *s* eau *f* de cale
bilingual [baɪˈlɪŋgwəl] *adj* bilingue
bilious [ˈbɪljəs] *adj* bilieux
bilk [bɪlk] *s* tromperie *f*, escroquerie *f* ∥ *tr* tromper, escroquer
bill [bɪl] *s* (*invoice*) facture *f*, mémoire *m;* (*in a hotel*) note *f;* (*in a restaurant*) addition *f;* (*currency*) billet *m;* (*of a bird*) bec *m;* (*posted*) affiche *f*, placard *m*, écriteau *m;* (*in a legislature*) projet *m* de loi; **post no bills** (public sign) défense d'afficher; **to head the bill** (theat) avoir la vedette ∥ *tr* facturer
bill′board′ *s* tableau *m* d'affichage, panneau *m* d'affichage
billet [ˈbɪlɪt] *s* (*order*) billet *m* de logement; (*of metal or wood*) billette *f* ∥ *tr* loger, cantonner
bill′fold′ *s* portefeuille *m*
bil′liard ball′ *s* bille *f*
billiards [ˈbɪljərdz] *s* & *spl* billard *m*
bil′liard ta′ble *s* billard *m*
billion [ˈbɪljən] *s* (U.S.A.) milliard *m;* (Brit) billion *m*
billionaire [ˌbɪljənˈɛr] *s* milliardaire *mf*
bill′ of exchange′ *s* lettre *f* de change, traite *f*
bill′ of fare′ *s* carte *f* du jour
bill′ of health′ *s* patente *f* de santé
bill′ of lad′ing *s* connaissement *m*
bill′ of rights′ *s* déclaration *f* des droits de l'homme
bill′ of sale′ *s* acte *m* de vente
billow [ˈbɪlo] *s* flot *m*, grosse vague *f* ∥ *intr* ondoyer
billowy [ˈbɪloˑi] *adj* onduleux, ondoyant
bill′post′er *s* colleur *m* d'affiches, afficheur *m*
bil•ly [ˈbɪli] *s* (*pl* **-lies**) bâton *m*
bil′ly goat′ *s* (coll) bouc *m*
bimonthly [baɪˈmʌnθli] *adj* bimestriel
bin [bɪn] *s* huche *f*, coffre *m*
binary [ˈbaɪnəri] *adj* & *s* binaire *f*
bi′nary code′ *s* code *m* binaire
binaural [barˈnɔrəl] *adj* stéréophonique; à deux oreilles
bind [baɪnd] *v* (*pret* & *pp* **bound** [baʊnd] *tr* (*to*

fasten) lier, attacher; (*a book*) relier; (*s.o. to an agreement*) obliger; **to bind with** (*to encircle*) entourer de ∥ *intr* (*to be obligatory*) être obligatoire; (*to cohere*) adhérer
binder [ˈbaɪndər] *s* (*person*) lieur *m;* (*of books*) relieur *m;* (*agreement*) conventions *fpl;* (mach) lieuse *f*
binder•y [ˈbaɪndəri] *s* (*pl* **-ies**) atelier *m* de reliure
binding [ˈbaɪndɪŋ] *adj* obligatoire; (med) astringent; **binding on all concerned** solidaire ∥ *s* reliure *f*
bind′ing post′ *s* (elec) borne *f*
binge [bɪndʒ] *s* (coll) noce *f*, bombe *f*
bingo [ˈbɪŋgo] *s* loto *m*
binocular [bɪˈnɑkjələr] *adj* & *s* binoculaire *m;* **binoculars** jumelles *fpl*
binomial [baɪˈnomɪˑəl] *adj* & *s* binôme *m*
bioastronomy [ˌbaɪˑoˑəˈstrɑnəmi] *s* bioastronomie *f*
biochemical [ˌbaɪˑoˈkɛmɪkəl] *adj* biochimique
biochemistry [ˌbaɪˑoˈkɛmɪstri] *s* biochimie *f*
biodegradable [ˈbaɪˑodɪˈgredəbəl] *adj* biodégradable
bioethics [ˌbaɪˑoˈɛθɪks] *s* bioéthique *f*
biographer [baɪˈɑgrəfər] *s* biographe *mf*
biographic(al) [ˌbaɪˑəˈgræfɪk(əl)] *adj* biographique
biogra•phy [baɪˈɑgrəfi] *s* (*pl* **-phies**) biographie *f*
biological [ˈbaɪˑəˈlɑdʒɪkel] *adj* biologique
bi′ological clock′ *s* horloge *f* biologique, horloge interne
bi′ological fath′er *s* père *m* biologique
bi′ological moth′er *s* mère *f* biologique
bi′ological war′fare *s* guerre *f* biologique
bi′ological weap′on *s* arme *f* biologique
biologist [baɪˈɑlədʒɪst] *s* biologiste *mf*
biology [baɪˈɑlədʒi] *s* biologie *f*
biomechanics [ˌbaɪˑoməˈkænɪks] *s* biomécanique *f*
biomedical [baɪˑoˈmɛdɪkəl] *adj* biomédical
biometrics [ˈbaɪˑoˈmɛtrɪks] *s* biométrie *f*
bionic [ˌbaɪˈɑnɪk] *adj* bionique ∥ **bionics** *s* bionique *f*
biophysics [ˌbaɪˑəˈfɪzɪks] *s* biophysique *f*
biop•sy [ˈbaɪˑɑpsi] *s* (*pl* **-sies**) biopsie *f*
bioscopy [baɪˈɑskəpi] *s* bioscopie *f*
biosphere [ˈbaɪˑosfɪr] *s* biosphère *f*
biotechnology [ˈbaɪˑotekˈnɑlədʒi] *s* biotechnologie *f*, biotechnique *f*
bioterrorism [baɪˑoˈtɛrerɪzəm] *s* bioterrorisme *m*
bipartisan [baɪˈpɑrtɪzən] *adj* bipartite
bipartite [baɪˈpɑrtaɪt] *adj* biparti
biped [ˈbaɪpɛd] *adj* & *s* bipède *m*
biplane [ˈbaɪˌplen] *s* biplan *m*
birch [bʌrtʃ] *s* bouleau *m;* (*for whipping*) verges *fpl* ∥ *tr* battre à coups de verges
birch′ rod *s* verges *fpl*
bird [bʌrd] *s* oiseau *m;* (slang) type *m*, individu *m;* **a bird in the hand is worth two in the bush** un "tiens" vaut mieux que deux "tu

l'auras''; **to give s.o. the bird** (slang) envoyer qn promener; **to kill two birds with one stone** faire d'une pierre deux coups

bird′ bath′ s bain m pour oiseaux

bird′ cage′ s cage f d'oiseau

bird′ call′ s appeau m, pipeau m

bird′ dog′ s chien m pour la plume

bird′ fan′cier s oiselier

birdie [ˈbʌrdi] s oiselet m, oisillon m

bird′lime′ s glu f

bird′ of pas′sage s oiseau m de passage

bird′ of prey′ s oiseau m de proie

bird′seed′ s alpiste m, chènevis m

bird's′-eye′ s (*pattern*) œil-de-perdrix m

bird's′-eye view′ s vue f à vol d'oiseau, tour m d'horizon, vue d'ensemble

biretta [bɪˈrɛtə] s barette f

birth [bʌrθ] s naissance f; **by birth** de naissance; **to give birth to** donner naissance à

birth′ certif′icate s acte m de naissance, extrait m de naissance, bulletin m de naissance

birth′ control′ s contrôle m des naissances, natalité f dirigée

birth′day′ s anniversaire m; **happy birthday!** heureux anniversaire!

birth′day cake′ s gâteau m d'anniversaire

birth′day can′dles spl bougies fpl de gâteaux d'anniversaire

birth′day pres′ent s cadeau m d'anniversaire

birth′mark′ s tache f, envie f

birth′place′ s lieu m de naissance

birth′ rate′ s natalité f, taux m de natalité

birth′right′ s droit m de naissance

biscuit [ˈbɪskɪt] s petit pain m, crêpe f au beurre, gâteau m feuilleté

bisect [baɪˈsɛkt] tr couper en deux, diviser en deux

bisexual [baɪˈsɛkʃʊ•əl] adj bissexuel

bishop [ˈbɪʃəp] s évêque m; (chess) fou m

bishopric [ˈbɪʃəprɪk] f évêché m

bison [ˈbaɪzən] s bison m

bistro [ˈbɪstro] s bistrot m, bistro m, café; café-restaurant m; boîte f de nuit

bisulfate [baɪˈsʌlfet] s bisulfate m

bisulfite [baɪˈsʌlfaɪt] s bisulfite m

bit [bɪt] s (*morsel*) morceau m, bout m, brin m; (*of a bridle*) mors m; (*of a drill*) mèche f; (comp) binon m, bit m; **bit by bit** petit à petit

bitch [bɪtʃ] s (*dog*) chienne f; (*fox*) renarde f; (*wolf*) louve f, (vulg) vache f, salope f, ordure f

bite [baɪt] s (*of food*) bouchée f; (*by an animal*) morsure f; (*by an insect*) piqûre f; (*by a fish on a hook*) touche f || v (*pret* **bit** [bɪt]; *pp* **bit** or **bitten** [ˈbɪtən]) tr mordre; (*said of an insect or snake*) piquer; **to bite off** mordre d'un coup de dent; **to feel like biting off one's tongue because of it** s'en mordre la langue

biting [ˈbaɪtɪŋ] adj mordant; (*cold*) piquant; (*wind*) coupant

bit′map′ s (comp) carte f de bits

bit′ play′er s figurant m

bitter [ˈbɪtər] adj amer; (*cold*) âpre noir, (*flight*) acharné; (*style*) mordant || **bitters** spl bitter m

bit′ter end′ s—**to the bitter end** jusqu'au bout

bit′ter-end′er s (coll) intransigeant m, jusqu'au-boutiste mf

bitterness [ˈbɪtərnɪs] s amertume f; (*of winter*) âpreté f; (fig) aigreur f

bit′ter-sweet′ adj aigre-doux || s douceamère f

bitumen [bɪˈt(j)umən] s bitume m

bivou•ac [ˈbɪvʊ,æk] s bivouac m, cantonnement m || v (*pret & pp* **-acked;** *ger* **-acking**) intr bivouaquer

biweekly [baɪˈwikli] adj bimensuel || adv bimensuellement

biyearly [baɪˈjɪrli] adj semestriel || adv semestriellement

bizarre [bɪˈzɑr] adj bizarre

blab [blæb] v (*pret & pp* **blabbed;** *ger* **blabbing**) tr ébruiter || intr jaser

blabber [ˈblæbər] intr jaser

blab′ber•mouth′ s (slang) jaseur m

black [blæk] adj & s noir m; **black is beautiful** nous sommes fiers d'être Noirs || (*cap*) adj & s (*person*) Noir m, Noire f || tr noircir; **to black out** faire le black-out dans

black′-and-blue′ adj couvert de bleus

black′-and-white′ adj en blanc et noir

black′ball′ tr blackbouler

black′ber′ry s (*pl* **-ries**) mûre f, mûre de ronce

black′bird′ s (*Turdus merula*) merle m

black′board′ s tableau m noir

black′board eras′er s éponge f, chiffon m

black′ bod′y s (phys) corps m noir

black′ box′ s (aer) enregistreur m d'accident

black′ cur′rant s cassis m

black′ damp′ s mofette f

blacken [ˈblækən] tr noircir

black′ eye′ s œil m poché; (*shiner*) coquart m; **to give s.o. a black eye** pocher l'œil à qn; (fig) ruiner la réputation de qn

black′-eyed Su′san [ˈsuzən] s marguerite f américaine

blackguard [ˈblægɑrd] s vaurien m, salaud m

black′head′ s comédon m, tanne f, point m noir

black′-headed gull′ s mouette f rieuse

black′ hole′ s (astr) trou m noir

blacking [ˈblækɪŋ] s cirage m noir

blackish [ˈblækɪʃ] adj noirâtre

black′jack′ s assommoir m; (cards) vingt-et-un m || tr assommer

black′ lead′ [lɛd] s mine f de plomb

black′ let′ter s caractère m gothique

black′ list′ s liste f noire

black′-list′ tr mettre à l'index, mettre en quarantaine

black′ lo′cust s (bot) faux acacia m

black′ mag′ic s magie f noire

black′mail′ s chantage m || tr faire chanter || intr faire du chantage

blackmailer [ˈblæk,melər] s maître m chanteur

black′ mark′ s (*of censure*) tache f

black′ mar′ket s marché m noir

black′ marketeer′ [ˌmɑrkɪˈtir] *s* trafiquant *m* du marché noir

black′ out′ *s* (*accidental*) panne *f* d'électricité; (*planned for protection*) feux *mpl* masqués, black-out *m;* (*of aviator*) cécité *f* temporaire; (*amnesia*) trou *m* de mémoire, voile *m* noir; (theat) obscurcissement *m* de la scène

black′ pep′per *s* poivre *m* noir

black′ sheep′ *s* (fig) brebis *f* galeuse

black′ smith′ *s* forgeron *m*, maréchal-ferrant *m*

black′ tie′ (*indication to wear formal clothes*) smoking *m*, en smoking

black′top *s* (*surface of road*) asphalte *m* ‖ *tr* asphalter

bladder [ˈblædər] *s* vessie *f*

bladderwort [ˈblædər,wʌrt] *s* utriculaire *f*

blade [bled] *s* (*of knife, tool, weapon, razor*) lame *f;* (*of scissors*) branche *f;* (*of grass*) brin *m;* (*of propeller*) aile *f*, pale *f;* (*of oar; of tongue*) plat *m;* (*of guillotine*) couperet *m;* (*of windshield wiper*) caoutchouc *m;* (*young man*) gaillard *m;* (mach) ailette *f*, palette *f*, aube *f*

blah [blɑ] *s* (slang) sornettes *fpl*, fadaises *fpl*, bêtises *fpl* ‖ *interj* patati-patata!

blah-blah [ˈblɑˈblɑ] *s* baratin *m*

blamable [ˈblemɔbəl] *adj* blâmable, coupable

blame [blem] *s* (*censure*) blâme *m*, reproches *mpl;* (*responsibility*) faute *f* ‖ *tr* blâmer; reprocher; s'en prendre à

blameless [ˈblemlɪs] *adj* sans reproche

blame′ wor′thy *adj* blâmable

blanch [blæntʃ] *tr & intr* blanchir

bland [blænd] *adj* doux, suave; (*with dissimulation*) narquois

blandish [ˈblændɪʃ] *tr* flatter, cajoler

blandishment [ˈblændɪʃmənt] *s* flatterie

blank [blæŋk] *adj* blanc; (*check; form*) en blanc; (*mind*) confondu, déconcerté; (*page*) vierge; (*cassette, tape*) vierge, à blanc ‖ *s* (*void*) blanc *m;* (*gap*) trou *m*, vide *m*, lacune *f;* (*metal mold*) flan *m;* (*form to be filled out*) fiche *f*, formule *f*, feuille *f;* (*space to be filled in*) tiret *m* ‖ *tr*—**to blank out** effacer ‖ *intr*—**to blank out** (coll) s'évanouir

blank′ check′ *s* chèque *m* en blanc; (fig) chèque en blanc

blanket [ˈblæŋkɪt] *adj* général ‖ *s* couverture *f* ‖ *tr* envelopper

blank′ tape′ *s* bande magnétique à blanc

blank′ verse′ *s* vers *mpl* blancs

blare [blɛr] *s* bruit *m* strident; (*of trumpet*) sonnerie *f* ‖ *tr* faire retentir; (*like a trumpet*) sonner ‖ *intr* retentir

blarney [ˈblɑrni] *s* (coll) flagornerie *f* ‖ *tr* (coll) flagorner

blaspheme [blæsˈfim] *tr & intr* blasphémer

blasphemous [ˈblæsfɪməs] *adj* blasphématoire, blasphémateur

blasphe•my [ˈblæsfɪmi] *s* (*pl* **-mies**) blasphème *m*

blast [blæst] *s* (*gust*) rafale *f*, souffle *m;* (*of bomb*) explosion *f;* (*of dynamite*) charge *f;* (*of whistle*) coup *m;* (*of trumpet*) sonnerie *f;* **at full blast** à toute allure ‖ *tr* (*to blow up*) faire sauter; (*hopes*) ruiner; (*a plant*) flétrir ‖ *intr* (*said of plant*) se faner; **to blast off** (*said of rocket*) se mettre à feu

blast′ fur′nace *s* haut fourneau *m*

blasting [ˈblæstɪŋ] *s* abattage *m* à la poudre; (*of hopes*) anéantissement *m;* (coll) abattage *m*, verte semonce *f*

blast′ing cap′ *s* capsule *f* fulminante

blast′ off′ *s* mise *f* à feu, lancement *m*

blatant [ˈbletənt] *adj* criard; (*injustice*) criant

blaze [blez] *s* (*fire*) flamme *f*, flambée *f;* (*e.g., blazing house*) incendie *m;* **to run like blazes** (slang) courir furieusement ‖ *tr*—**to blaze the trail** frayer la piste ‖ *intr* flamboyer, s'embraser

blazing [ˈblezɪŋ] *adj* (*building, etc.*) embrasé, en feu; (*sun*) flamboyant ‖ *s* (*on a tree*) marquage *m*

blazon [ˈblezən] *s* (heral) blason *m* ‖ *tr* célébrer; exalter; (heral) blasonner

bleach [blitʃ] *s* (*for washing clothes*) décolorant *m*, eau *f* de Javel; (*for hair*) eau oxygénée *f* ‖ *tr* blanchir, décolorer

bleachers [ˈblitʃərz] *spl* gradins *mpl*, tribune *f*

bleak [blik] *adj* froid, morne, nu

blear-eyed [ˈblɪrˈaɪd] *adj* (*teary*) chassieux, larmoyant; (*dull*) d'un esprit épais

blear•y [ˈblɪri] *adj* (*comp* **-ier;** *super* **-iest**) (*eyes*) chassieux; (*prospect*) voilé, incertain

bleat [blit] *s* bêlement *m* ‖ *intr* bêler, bégueter

bleed [blid] *v* (*pret & pp* **bled** [blɛd]) *tr & intr* saigner; **to bleed white** saigner à blanc

bleeding [ˈblidɪŋ] *adj* saignant ‖ *s* saignement *m;* (*bloodletting*) saignée *f*

bleep [blip] *s* top *m;* (med) bip *m* ‖ *tr* (med) biper ‖ *intr* émettre des signaux

blemish [ˈblɛmɪʃ] *s* défaut *m*, tache *f* ‖ *tr* défigurer; (*a reputation*) tacher

blench [blɛntʃ] *intr* (*to turn pale*) pâlir; (*to draw back*) broncher

blend [blɛnd] *s* mélange *m* ‖ *v* (*pret & pp* **blended** or **blent** [blɛnt]) *tr* mêler, mélanger; fondre, marier ‖ *intr* se fondre, se marier

bless [blɛs] *tr* bénir

blessed [ˈblɛsɪd] *adj* (*holy*) béni, saint; (*happy*) bienheureux

blessing [ˈblɛsɪŋ] *s* bénédiction *f;* (*at meals*) bénédicité *m*

blight [blaɪt] *s* (*of cereals, plants*) rouille *f*, nielle *f;* (*of peaches*) cloque *f;* (*of potatoes; of vines*) brunissure *f;* (fig) flétrissure *f* ‖ *tr* rouiller, nieller; (*hopes, aspirations*) flétrir, frustrer

blimp [blɪmp] *s* vedette *f* (aérienne)

blind [blaɪnd] *adj* aveugle; **blind by birth** aveugle-né; **blind in one eye** borgne; **blind person** aveugle *m* ‖ *s* store *m;* (*for hunting*) guet-apens *m;* (fig) feinte *f;* (cards) talon *m* ‖ *tr* aveugler; (*by dazzling*) éblouir

blind′ al′ley *s* cul-de-sac *m*, impasse *f*

blind′ date′ *s* rendez-vous *m* arrangé; (*person*)

inconnu *m*, inconnue *f* (*avec qui on a rendez-vous*)

blinder [`blaɪndər] *s* œillère *f*

blind´ flight´ *s* vol *m* à l'aveuglette

blind´ fly´ing *s* (aer) pilotage *m* sans visibilité

blind´fold´ *adj* les yeux bandés ‖ *s* bandeau *m* ‖ *tr* bander les yeux de

blind´ land´ing *s* (aer) atterrissage *m* sans visibilité

blindly [`blaɪndli] *adv* aveuglément

blind´ man´ *s* aveugle *m*

blind´ man's bluff´ *s* colin-maillard *m*

blindness [`blaɪndnɪs] *s* cécité *f*; (fig) aveuglement *m*

blind´ spot´ *s* côté *m* faible

blink [blɪŋk] *s* clignotement *m* ‖ *tr* faire clignoter ‖ *intr* clignoter

blinker [`blɪŋkər] *s* (*signal*) feu *m* clignotant; (*for horses*) œillère *f*; (*for signals*) projecteur *m* clignotant

blink´er light´ *s* feu *m* à éclipses

blinking [`blɪŋkɪŋ] *s* clignement *m*

blip [blɪp] *s* spot *m*, bip *m*

bliss [blɪs] *s* félicité *f*, béatitude *f*

blissful [`blɪsfəl] *adj* bienheureux

blister [`blɪstər] *s* ampoule *f*, bulle *f* ‖ *tr* couvrir d'ampoules; (*paint*) boursoufler ‖ *intr* se couvrir d'ampoules; se boursoufler

blithe [blaɪθ] *adj* gai, joyeux

blitzkrieg [`blɪts,krig] *s* guerre *f* éclair

blizzard [`blɪzərd] *s* tempête *f* de neige

bloat [blot] *tr* boursoufler, enfler ‖ *intr* se boursoufler, enfler

blob [blɑb] *s* motte *f*; (*of color*) tache *f*; (*of ink*) pâté *m*

block [blɑk] *s* (*stone*) bloc *m*; (*toy*) cube *m*; (*of shares*) tranche *f*; (*of houses*) pâté *m*, îlot *m* ‖ *tr* (*a project*) contrecarrer; (*a wall*) condamner, murer; **to block up** boucher, bloquer

blockade [blɑ`ked] *s* blocus *m*; **to run the blockade** forcer le blocus ‖ *tr* bloquer

block´ and tac´kle *s* palan *m*

block´bust´er *s* (coll) bombe *f* de gros calibre; (mov) superproduction *f*

block´head´ *s* sot *m*, niais *m*

blond [blɑnd] *adj & s* blond *m*

blonde [blɑnd] *adj & s* blonde *f*

blood [blʌd] *s* sang *m*; **in cold blood** de sang-froid; **to put new blood into** infuser un sang nouveau à

blood´ and guts´ *spl* sang *m* et tripes

blood´bank´ *s* banque *f* du sang

blood´ broth´er *s* frère *m* de sang

blood´ count´ *s* numération *f* globulaire

blood´ curd´ling *adj* horripilant

blood´ don´or *s* donneur *m* de sang

blood´hound´ *s* limier *m*

bloodless [`blʌdlɪs] *adj* (*without blood*) exsangue; (*revolution*) sans effusion de sang

bloodletting [`blʌd,lɛtɪŋ] *s* saignée *f*; (fig) effusion *f* de sang

blood´ mon´ey *s* prix *m* du sang

blood´ plas´ma *s* plasma *m* sanguin

blood´ poi´soning *s* septicémie *f*, empoisonnement *m* du sang

blood´ pres´sure *s* tension *f* artérielle

blood´ rela´tion *s* parent *m* or parente *f* par le sang

blood´ sam´ple *s* échantillon *m* de sang

blood´shed´ *s* effusion *f* de sang

blood´shot´ *adj* injecté, éraillé

blood´ spec´imen *s* prise *f* de sang

blood´stained´ *adj* taché de sang

blood´stream´ *s* circulation *f* du sang

blood´suck´er *s* sangsue *f*

blood´ test´ *s* examen *m* du sang, analyse *f* de sang

blood´thirst´y *adj* sanguinaire

blood´ transfu´sion *s* transfusion *f* de sang, transfusion sanguine

blood´ type´ *s* groupe *m* de sang

blood´ ves´sel *s* vaisseau *m* sanguin

blood•y [`blʌdi] *adj* (*comp* **-ier;** *super* **-iest**) sanglant

bloom [blum] *s* fleur *f*; (*of a fruit*) velouté *m*, duvet *m*; **in bloom** en fleur; **in full bloom** en pleine floraison ‖ *intr* fleurir

bloomers [`blumərz] *spl* culotte *f* de femme

blooper [`blupər] *s* (coll) gaffe *f*, bévue *f*; (rad) poste *m* brouilleur

blossom [`blɑsəm] *s* fleur *f*; **in blossom** en fleur ‖ *intr* fleurir; **to blossom out** s'épanouir

blot [blɑt] *s* (& fig) tache *f*, pâté *m* ‖ *v* (*pret & pp* **blotted;** *ger* **blotting**) *tr* tacher, barbouiller; (*ink*) sécher; **to blot out** rayer ‖ *intr* (*said of ink*) boire

blotch [blɑtʃ] *s* tache *f* ‖ *tr* couvrir de taches; (*the skin*) marbrer

blotch•y [`blɑtʃi] *adj* (*comp* **-ier;** *super* **-iest**) brouillé, tacheté

blotter [`blɑtər] *s* buvard *m*

blot´ting pa´per *s* papier *m* buvard

blouse [blaʊs] *s* (*women's wear*) corsage *m*; (*children's*) chemise *f*; (mil) vareuse *f*

blow [blo] *s* coup *m*; **to come to blows** en venir aux coups ‖ *v* (*pret* **blew** [blu]; *pp* **blown**) *tr* souffler; **to blow one's nose** se moucher; **to blow out** (*a candle*) éteindre; **to blow up** faire sauter; (*a photograph*) agrandir; (*a balloon*) gonfler ‖ *intr* souffler; (slang) décamper en vitesse; **to blow out** (*said of a tire*) éclater; **to blow over** passer; **to blow up** éclater; (slang) se mettre en colère

blower [`blo•ər] *s* soufflerie *f*; (mach) ventilateur *m*

blow´fly´ *s* (*pl* **-flies**) mouche *f* à viande

blow´gun´ *s* sarbacane *f*

blow´hard´ *s* (slang) hâbleur *m*

blow´hole´ *s* (*of tunnel*) ventilateur *m*; (*of whale*) évent *m*

blowing [`blo•ɪŋ] *s* soufflage *m*; (*of the wind*) soufflement *m*

blow´out´ *s* (*of a tire*) éclatement *m*; (*of an oil well*) éruption *f*; (*orgy*) (slang) gueuleton *m*

blow´pipe´ *s* chalumeau *m*

blow´torch´ *s* lampe *f* à souder

blubber [ˈblʌbər] *s* graisse *f* de baleine ‖ *tr* bredouiller ‖ *intr* pleurer comme un veau

bludgeon [ˈblʌdʒən] *s* matraque *f* ‖ *tr* assommer

blue [blu] *adj* bleu; **to be blue** (coll) broyer du noir, avoir le cafard ‖ *s* bleu *m;* **from out of the blue** du ciel, à l'improviste; **the blues** le cafard, l'humeur *f* noire ‖ *tr* bleuir

blue′bell′ *s* jacinthe *f* des bois

blue′ber′ry *s* (*pl* **-ries**) myrtille *f*

blue′bird′ *s* oiseau *m* bleu

blue′-black′ *adj* noir tirant sur le bleu

blue′blood′ *s* sang *m* royal, sang noble

blue′ book′ *s* (*social register*) annuaire *m* de la haute société; (*price list*) argus *m;* (aut) (*price list of used cars*) argus de l'automobile; (educ) cahier *m* d'écolier à couverture bleue (*pour écrire des examens*)

blue′bot′tle *s* bluet *m,* barbeau *m*

blue′cheese′ *s* roquefort *m* américain

blue′ chip′ *s* valeur-vedette *f,* valeur *f* de tout repos, valeur de père de famille

blue′-gray′ *adj* gris bleuté, gris-bleu

blue′jay′ *s* geai *m* bleu

blue′ jeans′ *spl* blue-jean *m*

blue′ moon′ *s*—**once in a blue moon** tous les trente-six du mois

blue′nose′ *s* puritain *m,* collet *m* monté

blue′-pen′cil *v* (*pret & pp* **-ciled** or **-cilled;** *ger* **-ciling** or **-cilling**) *tr* (*to make corrections*) corriger au crayon bleu; (*to censure*) couper, censurer

blue′print′ *s* dessin *m* négatif, photocalque *m;* (fig) plan *m,* schéma *m* ‖ *tr* planifier

blue′ rib′bon *adj* select, distingué, d'élite ‖ *s* premier prix *m*

blue′stock′ing *s* (coll) bas-bleu *m*

bluff [blʌf] *adj* (*steep*) abrupt; (*cliff*) accore, escarpé; (*person*) brusque ‖ *s* (*cliff*) falaise *f,* cap *m* à pic; (*deception*) bluff *m;* **to call s.o.'s bluff** relever un défi ‖ *tr & intr* bluffer

bluffer [ˈblʌfər] *s* bluffeur *m*

bluish [ˈbluˑɪʃ] *adj* bleuté, bleuâtre

blunder [ˈblʌndər] *s* bévue *f,* gaffe *f* ‖ *intr* faire une bévue, gaffer; **to blunder into** se heurter contre; **to blunder upon** découvrir par hasard; tomber sur

blunt [blʌnt] *adj* (*blade*) émoussé; (*point*) épointé; (*person*) brusque ‖ *tr* émousser; épointer

bluntly [ˈblʌntli] *adv* (*rudely*) brusquement, sans façons; (*frankly*) carrément, sans ménagements

blur [blʌr] *s* barbouillage *m* ‖ *v* (*pret & pp* **blurred;** *ger* **blurring**) *tr* embrouiller, voiler

blurb [blʌrb] *s* (*ad*) baratin *m* publicitaire; (*on book cover*) publicité *f* au protègelivre

blurt [blʌrt] *tr*—**to blurt out** laisser échapper, lâcher

blush [blʌʃ] *s* rougeur *f;* **at first blush** au premier abord ‖ *intr* rougir

bluster [ˈblʌstər] *s* rodomontade *f,* fanfaronnade *f* ‖ *intr* (*of wind*) souffler en rafales; (*of person*) faire du fracas

blustery [ˈblʌstəri] *adj* (*wind*) orageux; (*person*) bravache, fanfaron

boar [bor] *s* (*male swine*) verrat *m;* (*wild hog*) sanglier *m*

board [bord] *s* (*piece of wood*) planche *f;* (*e.g., of directors*) conseil *m,* commission *f;* (*meals*) le couvert; **above board** cartes sur table; **on board** à bord ‖ *tr* (*a ship*) monter à bord de; (*paying guests*) nourrir ‖ *intr* monter à bord; (*said of paying guest*) prendre pension

board′ and room′ *s* pension *f* et chambre *f*

boarder [ˈbordər] *s* pensionnaire *mf;* (*student*) interne *mf*

board′ing card′ *ou* **board′ing pass′** *s* carte *f* d'embarquement

board′ing•house′ *s* pension *f* (de famille)

board′ of direc′tors *s* conseil *m* d'administration, gérance *f*

board′ of trade′ *s* association *f* des industriels et commerçants

board′ of trustees′ *s* comité *m* administrateur (*e.g., of a university*)

board′walk′ *s* promenade *f* planchéiée au bord de la mer; (*over mud*) caillebotis *m*

boast [bost] *s* vanterie *f* ‖ *intr* se vanter

boastful [ˈbostfəl] *adj* vantard

boasting [ˈbostɪŋ] *s* jactance *f*

boat [bot] *s* bateau *m;* (*small boat*) embarcation *f;* **to miss the boat** (coll) manquer le coche, rater le coche

boat′ hook′ *s* gaffe *f*

boat′house′ *s* hangar *m* à bateaux or à canots

boating [ˈbotɪŋ] *s* canotage *m;* **to go boating** faire du canotage

boat′load′ *s* batelée *f*

boat′man *s* (*pl* **-men**) batelier *m*

boat′ race′ *s* régate *f*

boatswain [ˈbosən], [ˈbot‚swen] *s* maître *m* d'équipage

bob [bab] *s* (*hair style*) coiffure *f* courte ‖ *v* (*pret & pp* **bobbed;** *ger* **bobbing**) *intr* s'agiter, danser

bobbin [ˈbabɪn] *s* bobine *f*

bob′by pin′ *s* épingle *f* à cheveux

bob′by•socks′ *spl* (coll) socquettes *fpl,* chaussettes *fpl* basses

bobbysoxer [ˈbabɪ‚saksər] *s* (coll) zazou *m,* jeune lycéenne *f*

bob′sled′ *s* bobsleigh *m*

bob′tail′ *adj* à queue écartée ‖ *tr* couper court

bock′ beer′ *s* bock *m,* bière allemande

bode [bod] *tr & intr* présager

bodily [ˈbadɪli] *adj* corporel, physique ‖ *adv* corporellement, en corps

bod•y [ˈbadi] *s* (*pl* **-ies**) corps *m;* (*dead body*) cadavre *m;* (*solidity*) consistance *f;* (*flavor of wine*) sève *f,* générosité *f;* (aer) fuselage *m;* (aut) carrosserie *f;* **to come in a body** venir en corps

bod′y build′ing *s* exercices *mpl* de culturisme, exercises de musculation

bod′y•guard′ *s* garde *m* du corps; (*group*) garde *f* du corps

bod′y lan′guage s gestuelle f, gestualité f
bod′y o′dor s mauvaise odeur f du corps
bod′y shop′ s (aut) atelier m de carrosserie
bod′y veil′ s voile m qui couvre le corps
bog [bɑg] s marécage m, fondrière f ‖ v (pret & pp **bogged;** ger **bogging**) intr—**to bog down** s'enliser
bogey•man [ˈbogiˌmæn] s (pl **-men**) croquemitaine m
bogus [ˈbogəs] adj faux, simulé
Bohemia [boˈhimɪ•ə] s (country) Bohême f, la Bohême; (of artistic world) la bohème
Bohemian [boˈhimɪ•ən] adj (of Bohemia) bohémien; (unconventional, arty) bohème, de bohème ‖ s (person living in the country of Bohemia) Bohémien m; (artist) bohème mf
boil [bɔɪl] s (boiling) ébullition f; (on the skin) furoncle m, clou m ‖ tr faire bouillir ‖ intr bouillir
boiled′ din′ner s pot-au-feu m
boiled′ ham′ s jambon m d'York
boiled′ pota′toes spl pommes fpl bouillies, pommes vapeur
boiler [ˈbɔɪlər] s chaudière f
boi′ler-mak′er s chaudronnier m
boiling [ˈbɔɪlɪŋ] adj bouillonnant ‖ s ébullition f, bouillonnement m
boil′ing point′ s point m d'ébullition
boisterous [ˈbɔɪstərəs] adj bruyant
bold [bold] adj hardi, osé, intrépide; (forward) effronté, impudent; (cliff) abrupt
bold′face′ s (typ) caractères mpl gras
bold′-faced′ adj (forward) effronté
boldness [ˈboldnɪs] s hardiesse f; effronterie f
boll′ wee′vil [bol] s anthonome m du cotonnier, charançon m du coton
bologna [bəˈlonə], [bəˈlonjə] s mortadelle f, gros saucisson m
bolster [ˈbolstər] s traversin m ‖ tr soutenir
bolt [bolt] s (of door or window) verrou m; (of lock) pêne m; (with a thread at one end) boulon m; (of cloth) rouleau m ‖ tr verrouiller; (food) gober; (e.g., a political party) lácher ‖ intr décamper
bomb [bɑm] s bombe f ‖ tr bombarder
bombard [bɑmˈbɑrd] tr bombarder
bombardier [ˌbɑmbərˈdɪr] s bombardier m
bombardment [bɑmˈbɑrdmənt] s bombardement m
bombast [ˈbɑmbæst] s boursouflure f
bombastic [bɑmˈbæstɪk] adj boursouflé
bomb′ bay′ s (aer) soute f à bombes
bomb′ cra′ter s entonnoir m, trou m d'obus
bomber [ˈbɑmər] s avion m de bombardement, bombardier m
bombing [ˈbɑmɪŋ] s bombardement m
bomb′proof′ adj à l'épreuve des bombes
bomb′shell′ s obus m; **to fall like a bombshell** tomber comme une bombe
bomb′ shel′ter s abri m à l'épreuve des bombes
bomb′sight′ s viseur m de lancement
bomb′ squad′ s service m de déminage
bona fide [ˈbonəˌfaɪdə] adj & adv de bonne foi

bonanza [boˈnænzə] s aubaine f, filon m
bonbon [ˈbɑnˌbɑn] s bonbon m
bond [bɑnd] s (link) lien m; (com) obligation f; **in bond** en entrepôt ‖ tr (com) entreposer, mettre en entrepôt
bondage [ˈbɑndɪdʒ] s esclavage m
bond′ed ware′house s entrepôt m des douanes
bond′hold′er s obligataire mf
bone [bon] s os m; (of a fish) arête f; **to have a bone to pick** avoir maille à partir ‖ tr (meat or fish) désosser ‖ intr—**to bone up on** (a subject) (slang) potasser, piocher
bone′head′ s (slang) ignorant m
boneless [ˈbonlɪs] adj sans os; sans arêtes
bone′ mar′row s moelle f (osseuse)
bone′ of conten′tion s pomme f de discorde
boner [ˈbonər] s (coll) bourde f
bonfire [ˈbɑnˌfaɪr] s feu m de joie; (for burning trash) feu de jardin
bonnet [ˈbɑnɪt] s bonnet m; chapeau m à brides; (fig) chapeau
bonus [ˈbonəs] s boni m, prime f
bon•y [ˈboni] adj (comp **-ier;** super **-iest**) osseux; (thin) décharné
boo [bu] s huée f, sifflement m; **not to say boo** ne pas souffler mot ‖ tr & intr huer, siffler ‖ interj hou!, peuh!
boob [bub] s (coll) emplâtre m
booboo [ˈbuˌbu] s (coll) connerie f; **to make a booboo** se gourer, faire une connerie
boo•by [ˈbubi] s (pl **-bies**) (coll) nigaud m
boo′by hatch′ s (slang) asile m d'aliénés; (prison) (slang) violon m
boo′by prize′ s fiche f de consolation
boo′by trap′ s engin m piégé; (fig) attrapenigaud m, traquenard m
boo′by-trap′ v (pret & pp **-trapped;** ger **-trapping**) tr piéger
booing [ˈbuɪŋ] s hués fpl
book [bʊk] s livre m; (of tickets) carnet m; (libretto) livret m; **by the book** d'après le texte, selon les rèles; **to make book** (sports) inscrire les paris ‖ tr (a seat or room) retenir, réserver
book′bind′er s relieur m
book′bind′er•y s (pl **-ies**) atelier m de reliure
book′bind′ing s reliure f
book′case′ s bibliothèque f, étagère f
book′ end′ s serre-livres m, appui-livres m
bookie [ˈbʊki] s (coll) bookmaker m
booking [ˈbʊkɪŋ] s réservation f; (theat) location f
bookish [ˈbʊkɪʃ] adj livresque; (person) studieux
book′keep′er s comptable mf, teneur m de livres
book′keep′ing s comptabilité f
book′ learn′ing s science f livresque
booklet [ˈbʊklɪt] s livret m; (notebook) cahier m; (pamphlet) brochure f
book′lov′er s bibliophile mf
book′mak′er s bookmaker m
book′mark′ s signet m
bookmobile [ˈbʊkmoˌbil] s bibliobus m

book′plate′ s ex-libris m
book′rack′ s étagère f
book′ review′ s compte m rendu
book′sel′ler s libraire mf
book′shelf′ s (pl **-shelves**) rayon m, étagère f
books′ in print′ s livres mpl disponibles
book′stand′ s étalage m de livres; (in a station) bibliothèque f
book′store′ s librairie f
book′ val′ue s (com) valeur f comptable
book′worm′ s ciron m; (fig) rat m de bibliothèque
boom [bum] s retentissement m, grondement m; (rapid rise or growth) vague f de prospérité, boom m; (naut) bout-dehors m ‖ intr retentir; (com) prospérer ‖ interj boum!
boomer [′bumər] s (electron) boomer m
boomerang [′bumə‚ræŋ] s boomerang m
boomers [′bumərz] abbr **baby boomers**
boom′ town′ s ville f champignon
boon [bun] s bienfait m, avantage m; (archaic) don m, faveur f
boor [bʊr] s rustre m, goujat m
boost [bust] s relèvement m; (help) aide f ‖ tr soulever par derrière; (prices) hausser; (to praise) faire la réclame pour
booster [′bustər] s (enthusiastic backer) réclamiste mf; (go-getter) homme m d'expédition, lanceur m d'affaires; (aut) suramplificateur m; (elec) survolteur m; (rok) booster m, propulseur m
boost′er rock′et s fusée f de lancement
boost′er rod′ s (nucl) barre f de dopage
boost′er shot′ s piqûre f de rappel, injection f de rappel
boot [but] s botte f, bottine f; **to boot** en sus; **to lick s.o.'s boots** (coll) lécher les bottes à qn ‖ tr botter; (comp) démarrer; **to boot out** flanquer à la porte; **to boot (up)** (comp) charger
boot′black′ s cireur m de bottes
booth [buθ] s (at fair) baraque f; (e.g., for telephoning) cabine f
boot′leg′ adj (slang) clandestin, de contrebande ‖ v (pret & pp **-legged;** ger **-legging**) tr (slang) faire la contrebande de ‖ intr (slang) faire la contrebande
bootlegger [′but‚lɛgər] s (slang) contrebandier m; (slang) contrebandier m d'alcool, bootlegger m
boot′leg′ging s contrebande f
boot′lick′ tr (coll) lécher les bottes à
boo•ty [′buti] s (pl **-ties**) butin m
booze [buz] s (coll) boisson f alcoolique ‖ intr (coll) s'adonner à la boisson
border [′bɔrdər] s (edge) bord m, bordure f; (of field and forest; of a piece of cloth) lisière f; (of a road) marge f; (of a country) frontière f; (edging) galon m, bordé m; **to cross the border** passer la frontière ‖ tr border; (a handkerchief) liserer ‖ intr—**to border on** confiner à, toucher à; (a color) tirer sur
bor′der clash′ s escarmouche f de frontière
bor′der cross′ing s poste m de contrôle de fron-

tière, poste frontière; (passage from on side to the other) traversée f d'une frontière
bor′der-line′ adj indéterminé ‖ s ligne f de démarcation
bor′der-line case′ s cas m limite
bore [bor] s (hole) trou m; (of gun) calibre m; (of cannon) âme f; (of cylinder) alésage m; (nuisance) ennui m; (person) raseur m; **what a bore!** c'est la barbe!, ô rasoir! ‖ tr percer; (a cylinder) aléser; (to annoy) ennuyer
boreal [′bɔrɪ•əl] adj boréal
boredom [′bordəm] s ennui m
boring [′borɪŋ] adj ennuyeux, rasant, rasoir ‖ s perçage m, percement m
born [bɔrn] adj né; **to be born** naître
borrow [′baro], [′bɔro] tr emprunter; **to borrow from** emprunter à
borrower [′baro•ər], [′bɔro•ər] s emprunteur m
bor′rower's card′ s bulletin m de prêt
borrowing [′bɔro•ɪŋ] s emprunt m
borzoi [′bɔrzɔɪ] s lévrier m russe
bosom [′buzəm] s sein m, poitrine f; (of the Church) giron m
bo′som friend′ s ami m intime, ami de coeur, amie f intime, amie de coeur
boss [bɔs] s patron m, chef m; (foreman) contremaître m ‖ tr mener, régenter
boss•y [′bɔsi] adj (comp **-ier;** super **-iest**) autoritaire, tyrannique
botanical [bə′tænɪkəl] adj botanique
botanist [′batənɪst] s botaniste mf
botany [′batəni] s botanique f
botch [batʃ] tr—**to botch up** bousiller, saloper
both [boθ] adj deux, e.g., **with both hands** à deux mains; les deux, e.g., **both books** les deux livres ‖ pron les deux, tous les deux ‖ conj à la fois; **both . . . and** aussi bien . . . que, e.g., **both in England and France** aussi bien en Angleterre qu'en France
bother [′baðər] s ennui m ‖ tr ennuyer, déranger ‖ intr se déranger
bothersome [′baðərsəm] adj importun
bottle [′batəl] s bouteille f ‖ tr mettre en bouteille, embouteiller
bot′tle cap′ s capsule f
bot′tle depos′it s consigne f
bot′tled gas′ s gaz m en cylindre
bot′tle•neck′ s goulot m; (fig) embouteillage m, goulot m d'étranglement
bot′tle o′pener s ouvre-bouteilles m, décapsuleur m
bottler [′batlər] s metteur m en bouteilles
bottling [′batlɪŋ] s mise f en bouteilles
bottom [′batəm] s fond m; **at the bottom of** au fond de; (the page) en bas de; **to reach the bottom of the barrel** (coll) être à fond de cale
bot′tom dol′lar s dernier sou m
bottomless [′batəmlɪs] adj sans fond
bot′tom line′ s (com) résultat m financier; (fig) conclusion f; point m essentiel
bough [baʊ] s rameau m
boulder [′boldər] s bloc m, rocher m

boulevard [ˈbʊləˌvard] *s* boulevard *m*
bounce [baʊns] *s* (*elasticity*) bond *m;* (*of a ball*) rebond *m* ‖ *tr* faire rebondir; (slang) flanquer à la porte ‖ *intr* rebondir
bouncer [ˈbaʊnsər] *s* (*in night club*) (coll) videur *m,* gorille *m*
bouncing [ˈbaʊnsɪŋ] *adj* (*appearing in good health*) rebondi, dodu, potelé
bound [baʊnd] *adj* (*tied*) lié; (*obliged*) obligé, tenu; **bound for** en partance pour ‖ *s* bond *m,* saut *m;* **bounds** bornes *fpl,* limites *fpl;* **out of bounds** hors jeu; (*prohibited*) défendu ‖ *tr* borner, limiter ‖ *intr* bondir
bounda•ry [ˈbaʊndəri] *s* (*pl* **-ries**) borne *f,* limite *f*
boun'dary stone' *s* borne *f*
boundless [ˈbaʊndlɪs] *adj* sans bornes
bountiful [ˈbaʊntɪfʊl] *adj* abondant; (*generous person*) généreux, libéral
boun•ty [ˈbaʊnti] *s* (*pl* **-ties**) largesse *f,* (*award*) prime *f*
bouquet [buˈke] *s* bouquet *m*
bout [baʊt] *s* (*time*) période *f,* (*of fever*) accès *m,* attaque *f;* (sports) combat *m,* rencontre *f*
bow [baʊ] *s* (*greeting*) inclination *f,* révérence *f;* (*of ship*) avant *m,* proue *f* ‖ *tr* incliner, courber ‖ *intr* s'incliner, se courber; **to bow down** se prosterner; **to bow out** se retirer; **to bow to** saluer ‖ [bo] *s* (*weapon*) arc *m;* (*bowknot*) nŒud *m;* (*of violin*) archet *m* ‖ *intr* (mus) tirer l'archet
bowdlerize [ˈbaʊdləˌraɪz] *tr* expurger
bowel [ˈbaʊ•əl] *s* intestin *m,* boyau *m;* **bowels** entrailles *fpl*
bow'el move'ment *s* évacuation *f* du ventre
bower [ˈbaʊ•ər] *s* berceau *m,* tonnelle *f*
bow'ie knife' [ˈbo•ɪ] *s* couteau-poignard *m*
bowknot [ˈbo,nɑt] *s* nŒud *m* en forme de rose, rosette *f*
bowl [bol] *s* (*container*) bol *m,* jatte *f;* (*of pipe*) fourneau *m;* (*of spoon*) cuilleron *m;* **bowls** (sports) boules *fpl* ‖ *tr* rouler, lancer; **to bowl over** (*to overturn*) (coll) renverser; (slang) déconcerter ‖ *intr*—**to bowl along** rouler rapidement
bowlegged [ˈbo,lɛgd], [ˈbo,lɛgɪd] *adj* aux jambes arquées
bowler [ˈbolər] *s* (*hat*) chapeau *m* melon; (*in cricket*) lanceur *m;* (*in bowling*) joueur *m* de boules
bowling [ˈbolɪŋ] *s* bowling *m;* (*lawn bowling*) jeu *m* de boules; (*skittles*) jeu de quilles
bowl'ing al'ley *s* boulodrome *m,* bowling *m*
bowl'ing green' *s* boulingrin *m*
bowl'ing pin' *s* quille *f*
bowsprit [ˈbaʊsprɪt] *s* beaupré *m*
bow' tie' [bo] *s* nŒud *m* papillon
bowwow [ˈbaʊˌwaʊ] *interj* oua, oua!
box [baks] *s* boîte *f;* (*in a questionnaire*) case *f;* (law) barre *f;* (theat) loge *f,* baignoire *f;* **box on the ear** claque *f* ‖ *tr* emboîter; (*to hit*) boxer; **to box the compass** réciter la rose des vents ‖ *intr* (sports) boxer

box'car' *s* (rr) wagon *m* couvert
boxer [ˈbaksər] *s* (*person*) boxeur *m;* (*dog*) boxer *m*
boxers [ˈbaksərz] *ou* **box'er shorts'** boxer-short *m*
boxing [ˈbaksɪŋ] *s* emboîtage *m;* (sports) boxe *f;* (*worldwide championship matches*) la boxe anglaise
box'ing match' *s* match *m* de boxe
box' of'fice *s* bureau *m* de location
box'-office flop' *s* (slang) four *m*
box'-office hit' *s* pièce *f* à succès
box' pleat' *s* pli *m* creux
box' seat' *s* (theat) place *f* de loge
box'wood' *s* buis *m*
boy [bɔɪ] *s* garçon *m;* (*little boy*) garçon-net *m*
boycott [ˈbɔɪkat] *s* boycottage *m* ‖ *tr* boycotter
boy'friend' *s* (*sweetheart*) bon ami *m;* (*bosom friend*) ami *m* intime *m,* camarade *m;* (*friend*) ami *m*
boyhood [ˈbɔɪhʊd] *s* enfance *f,* jeunesse *f,* adolescence *f*
boyish [ˈbɔɪ•ɪʃ] *adj* de garçon
boy' scout' *s* boy-scout *m*
bra [bra] (coll) soutien-gorge *m*
brace [bres] *s* (*support*) attache *f,* lien *m;* (*of game birds*) couple *f;* (*of pistols*) paire *f;* (*to impart a rotary movement to a bit*) vilebrequin *m;* (aer, aut) entretoise *f;* (dentistry) appareil *m;* (med) appareil orthopédique; (mus, typ) accolade *f* ‖ *tr* ancrer, entretoiser; (*to tone up*) fortifier, remonter ‖ *intr*—**to brace up** prendre courage
brace' and bit' *s* vilebrequin *m*
bracelet [ˈbreslɪt] *s* bracelet *m*
bracer [ˈbresər] *s* tonique *m*
bracing [ˈbresɪŋ] *adj* tonique, fortifiant
bracket [ˈbrækɪt] *s* (*angled support*) support *m,* console *f;* (*grouping*) group *m,* classe *f,* tranche *f;* (*level*) niveau *m;* (mach) chaise *f;* (typ) crochet *m* ‖ *tr* grouper; (typ) mettre entre crochets
brackish [ˈbrækɪʃ] *adj* saumâtre
brad [bred] *s* semence *f,* clou *m* (sans tête)
brag [bræg] *s* (*pret & pp* **bragged;** *ger* **bragging**) *intr* se vanter, se targuer
braggadoci•o [ˌbrægəˈdoʃiˌo] *s* (*pl* **-os**) fanfaronnade *f;* (*person*) fanfaron *m*
braggart [ˈbrægərt] *s* vantard *m*
bragging [ˈbrægɪŋ] *s* vanterie *f*
Brah•man [ˈbramən] *s* (*pl* **-mans**) brahmane *m*
braid [bred] *s* tresse *f,* passement *m;* (mil) galon *m;* **to trim with braid** soutacher ‖ *tr* passementer; (*the hair*) tresser
braille [brel] *s* braille *m*
brain [bren] *s* cerveau *m;* **brains** cervelle *f,* (fig) intelligence *f,* cerveau; **to rack one's brains** se creuser la cervelle ‖ *tr* casser la tête à
brain' child' *s* idée *f* de génie
brain'-dead *adj* sans des ondes encéphaliques
brain' drain' *s* évasion *f* de(s) cerveaux, fuite *f* de(s) cerveaux
brainless [ˈbrenlɪs] *adj* sans cervelle

brain′storm′ s accès m de folie; (coll) confusion f mentale; (coll) trouvaille f, bonne idée f, idée géniale

brain′storm′ing s remue-méninges m

brain′ trust′ s cerveauté f, projéticiens mpl

brain′wash′ tr faire un lavage de cerveau à

brain′wash′ing s lavage m de cerveau

brain′wave′ s onde f encéphalique; (coll) idée f géniale, inspiration f

brain′work′ s travail m intellectuel

brain•y [′breni] adj (comp -ier; super -iest) (coll) intelligent à l'esprit vif

braise [brez] tr braiser, endauber

brais′ing pan′ s braisière f

brake [brek] s frein m; **to put on the brakes** serrer les freins ‖ tr & intr freiner

brake′ drum′ s tambour m de frein

brake′ light′ s (aut) feu m de freinage

brake′ lin′ing s garniture f de frein

brake′man s (pl -men) serre-freins m

brake′ ped′al s pédale f de frein

brake′ shoe′ s sabot m de frein

bramble [′bræmbəl] s ronce f

bran [bræn] s son m, bran m

branch [brænt∫] s branche f; (of tree) rameau m, branche; (of a business) succursale, filiale ‖ intr—**to branch off** s'embrancher, se bifurquer; **to branch out** se ramifier

branch′ line′ s embranchement m

branch′ of′fice s succursale f

branch′ road′ s embranchement m

brand [brænd] s (trademark) marque f; (torch) brandon m; (coal) tison m; (on a criminal) fiétrissure f; (on cattle) marque ‖ tr marquer au fer rouge, flétrir

branding [′brændɪŋ] m marquage m

brand′ing i′ron s fer m à flétrir

brandish [′brændɪ∫] tr brandir

brand′-new′ adj tout neuf, flambant neuf

bran•dy [′brændi] s (pl -dies) eau-de-vie f

brash [bræ∫] adj impertinent

brass [bræs] s (metal) laiton m; (mil) (coll) officiers mpl supérieurs, galonnard m; (slang) toupet m, culot m; **big brass** (slang) grosses légumes fpl; **the brasses** (mus) les cuivres

brass′ band′ s fanfare f, musique f

brassiere [brə′zɪr] s soutien-gorge m

brass′ knuck′les spl coup-de-poing m

brass′ tack′ s semence f (de tapissier); **to get down to brass tacks** (coll) en venir aux faits

brat [bræt] s (coll) garnin m, gosse mf

brava•do [brə′vado] s (pl -does or -dos) bravade f

brave [brev] adj brave ‖ s guerrier m peau-rouge ‖ tr braver

bravery [′brevəri] s bravoure f

bra•vo [′bravo] (pl -vos) bravo m ‖ interj bravo!

brawl [brɔl] s bagarre f, querelle f ‖ intr se bagarrer, se quereller

brawler [′brɔlər] s bagarreur m

brawn [brɔn] s (strength) muscle m; (muscles) muscles bien développés; (culin) fromage m de cochon

brawn•y [′brɔni] adj (comp -ier; super -iest) bien découplé, musclé

bray [bre] s braiment m ‖ intr braire

braze [brez] tr braser

brazen [′brezən] adj effronté, hardi ‖ tr—**to brazen through** mener à bonne fin avec une effronterie audacieuse

Brazil [brə′zɪl] s le Brésil

Brazilian [brə′zɪljən] adj brésilien ‖ s (person) Brésilien m

Brazil′ nut′ s noix f du Brésil

breach [brit∫] s (in a wall) brèche f; (violation) infraction f ‖ tr ouvrir une brèche dans

breach′ of con′tract s rupture f de contrat

breach′ of prom′ise s rupture f de fiançailles

breach′ of the peace′ s attentat m contre l'ordre public

breach′ of trust′ s abus m de confiance

bread [brɛd] s pain m ‖ tr paner, gratiner

bread′ and but′ter s (fig) gagne-pain m

bread′bas′ket s corbeille f a pain

bread′board′ s planche f à pain

bread′ crumbs′ spl chapelure f

breaded adj (culin) au gratin

bread′ed veal′ cut′let s escalope f panée de veau

bread′fruit′ s fruit m à pain; (tree) arbre m à pain, jacquier m

bread′ knife′ s couteau m à pain

bread′ line′ s queue de gens qui attendent pour toucher les bons de pain

breadth [brɛdθ] s largeur f

bread′win′ner s soutien m de famille

break [brek] s (fracture) rupture f; (of an object) brisure f, cassure f; (in time or space) trou m, pause f; (slang) chance f ‖ v (pret **broke** [brok]; pp **broken**) tr rompre, briser, casser; (a law) violer; (the heart) fendre; (one's word) manquer à; (a will; a soldier by reducing his rank) casser; **to break bread** rompre le pain; **to break down** (for analysis) analyser; **to break in** (a door) enfoncer; (a new car) roder ‖ intr rompre, briser, se briser; (said of clouds) se dissiper; (said of waves) déferler; **to break down** avoir une panne; **to break off** se détacher net: **to break off from work** prendre un break

breakable [′brekəbəl] adj fragile

breakage [′brekɪdʒ] s casse f

break′ danc′ing s smurf m

break′down′ s (stoppage) arrêt m; (disaster) débâcle f; (of health) effondrement m, dépression f; (of negotiations) rupture f; (for analysis) analyse f, ventilation f; (mach) panne f

breaker [′brekər] s brisant m

breakfast [′brɛkfəst] s petit déjeuner m ‖ intr prendre le petit déjeuner

break′fast food′ s céréales fpl (pour le petit déjeuner)

break′-in s effraction f

break′ing and en′tering s effraction f

break′ing point′ s point m limite zéro

break′neck′ *adj* vertigineux; **at breakneck speed** à tombeau ouvert

break′ of day′ *s* point *m* du jour

break′through′ *s* (mil) percée *f*; (fig) découverte *f* sensationnelle

break′up′ *s* (*splitting up*) dissolution *f*; (*of ice*) débâcle *f*; (*of friendship*) rupture *f*

break′wa′ter *s* digue *f*, brise-lames *m*

breast [brɛst] *f* sein *m*; (*of cooked chicken*) blanc *m*; **to make a clean breast of it** se déboutonner

breast′bone′ *s* sternum *m*; (*of fowl*) bréchet *m*

breast′-feed′ing *s* allaitement *m* maternel

breast′ opera′tion *s* remodelage *m*

breast′plate′ *s* (*of high priest*) pectoral *m*; (*of armor*) plastron *m*

breast′stroke′ *s* brasse *f*

breast′work′ *s* (mil) parapet *m*

breath [brɛθ] *s* haleine *f*, souffle *m*; **last breath** dernier soupir *m*; **out of breath** hors d'haleine

breathalyzer [ˈbrɛθə,laɪzər] *s* alcotest *m*, prise *f* d'haleine

breathe [brið] *tr & intr* respirer, souffler; **not to breathe a word** ne pas souffler mot

breathing [ˈbriðɪŋ] *s* souffle *m*

breath′ing space′ *s* répit *m*

breathless [ˈbrɛθlɪs] *adj* haletant, hors d'haleine; (*silence*) ému; (*lifeless*) inanimé

breath′tak′ing *adj* émouvant, sensationnel

breech [britʃ] *s* culasse *f*

breech′es bu′oy *s* (naut) bouée-culotte *f*

breed [brid] *s* race *f* ‖ *v* (*pret & pp* **bred** [brɛd]) *tr* engendrer; (*e.g., cattle*) élever ‖ *intr* se reproduire

breeder [ˈbridər] *s* éleveur *m*

breed′er reac′tor *s* (nucl) réacteur *m* surrégénérateur

breeding [ˈbridɪŋ] *s* (*of animals*) élevage *m*; **good breeding** savoir-vivre *m*

breeze [briz] *s* brise *f*

breez•y [ˈbrizi] *adj* (*comp* **-ier**; *super* **-iest**) aéré; (coll) désinvolte, dégagé

brethren [ˈbrɛðrɪn] *spl* frères *mpl*

Breton [ˈbrɛtən] *adj* breton ‖ *s* (*language*) breton *m*; (*person*) Breton *m*

breviar•y [ˈbrɛvɪ,ɛri] *s* (*pl* **-ies**) (eccl) bréviaire *m*

brevi•ty [ˈbrɛviti] *s* (*pl* **-ties**) brièveté *f*

brew [bru] *s* breuvage *m*, infusion *f* ‖ *tr* infuser; (*beer*) brasser ‖ *intr* s'infuser

brewer [ˈbruˑər] *s* brasseur *f*

brew′er's yeast′ *s* levure *f* de bière

brewer•y [ˈbruˑəri] *s* (*pl* **-ies**) brasserie *f*

brewing [ˈbruˑɪŋ] *s* brassage *m*

bribe [braɪb] *s* pot-de-vin *m* ‖ *tr* corrompre, suborner, soudoyer, arroser (coll)

briber•y [ˈbraɪbəri] *f* (*pl* **-ies**) corruption *f*, subornation *f*

brick [brɪk] *s* brique *f*; (*of ice cream*) bloc *m* ‖ *tr* briqueter

brick′bat′ *s* brocard *m*; **to hurl brickbats** lancer des brocards

brickkiln [ˈbrɪk,kɪln] *s* four *m* à briques

brick′lay′er *s* briqueteur *m*

brick′work′ *s* briquetage *m*

brick′yard′ *s* briqueterie *f*

bridal [ˈbraɪdəl] *adj* nuptial

bride [braɪd] *s* (nouvelle) mariée *f*

bride′groom′ *s* (nouveau) marié *m*

brides′maid′ *s* demoiselle *f* d'honneur

bride′-to-be′ *s* future femme *f*

bridge [brɪdʒ] *s* pont *m*; (cards, dentistry) bridge *m*; (naut) passerelle *f*; **to burn one's bridges** couper les ponts ‖ *tr* construire un pont sur; **to bridge a gap** combler une lacune

bridge′head′ *s* (mil) tête *f* de pont

bridle [ˈbraɪdəl] *s* bride *f*; (fig) frein *m* ‖ *tr* brider; (fig) freiner ‖ *intr* se raidir

bri′dle path′ *s* piste *f* cavalière

brief [brif] *adj* bref ‖ *s* résumé *m*; (law) dossier *m*; **briefs** slip *m*; **to hold a brief for** plaider pour ‖ *tr* mettre au courant

brief′ case′ *s* serviette *f*

briefing [ˈbrifɪŋ] *s* briefing *m*, renseignements *mpl* tactiques

briefly [ˈbrifli] *adv* bref, brièvement, en substance

brier [ˈbraɪˑər] *s* ronce *f*

brig [brɪg] *s* prison *f* navale; (*ship*) brick *m*

brigade [brɪˈged] *s* brigade *f*

brigadier [,brɪgəˈdɪr] *s* général *m* de brigade

brigand [ˈbrɪgənd] *s* brigand *m*

brigantine [ˈbrɪgən,tin] *s* brigantin *m*

bright [braɪt] *adj* brillant; (*day*) clair; (*color*) vif; (*person*) (fig) brillant

brighten [ˈbraɪtən] *tr* faire briller; égayer, réjouir ‖ *intr* s'éclaircir

bright′ ide′a *s* (coll) idée *f* lumineuse

brightness [ˈbraɪtnɪs] *s* éclat *m*, clarté *f*; (*of mind*) vivacité *f*

brilliance [ˈbrɪljəns] or **brilliancy** [ˈbrɪljənsi] *s* brillant *m*, éclat *m*

brilliant [ˈbrɪljənt] *adj & s* brillant *m*

brim [brɪm] *s* bord *m* ‖ *v* (*pret & pp* **brimmed**; *ger* **brimming**) *intr*—**to brim over (with)** déborder (de)

brimful [ˈbrɪm,fʊl] *adj* à ras bords

brim′stone′ *s* soufre *m*

brine [braɪn] *s* saumure *f*

bring [brɪŋ] *v* (*pret & pp* **brought** [brɔt]) *tr* apporter; (*a person*) amener, conduire; **to bring back** rapporter; (*a person*) ramener; **to bring down** (*baggage*) descendre; (*with a gun*) abattre; **to bring in** entrer, introduire; **to bring out** faire ressortir; (*e.g., a book*) publier; **to bring together** réunir; **to bring to pass** causer, opérer; **to bring up** éduquer, élever; (*baggage*) monter

bring′ing-up′ *s* éducation *f*

brink [brɪŋk] *s* bord *m*

brisk [brɪsk] *adj* vif, actif, animé

brisket [ˈbrɪskɪt] *s* (culin) poitrine *f*

bristle [ˈbrɪsəl] *s* soie *f*; (*of brush*) poil *m* ‖ *tr* hérisser ‖ *intr* se hérisser

bristling [ˈbrɪslɪŋ] *adj* hérissé

Bris′tol board′ [ˈbrɪstəl] *s* bristol *m*
Britain [ˈbrɪtən] *s* Grande-Bretagne *f;* la Grande-Bretagne
British [ˈbrɪtɪʃ] *adj* britannique ‖ **the British** les Britanniques
Britisher [ˈbrɪtɪʃər] *s* Britannique *mf*
Brit′ish Isles′ *spl* îles *fpl* Britanniques
Briton [ˈbrɪtən] *s* Britannique *mf*
Brittany [ˈbrɪtəni] *s* Bretagne *f;* la Bretagne
brittle [ˈbrɪtəl] *adj* fragile, cassant
broach [brotʃ] *s* (*spit*) broche *f; (for tapping casks*) mèche *f* à percer, perçoir *m*, foret *m* ‖ *tr* (*e.g., a keg of beer*) mettre en perce; (*a subject*) entamer
broad [brɔd] *adj* (*wide*) large; (*immense*) vaste; (*mind, views*) libéral, tolérant; (*accent*) fort, prononcé; (*use, sense*) répandu, général; (*daylight*) plein; (*joke, story*) grossier, salé
broad′-backed′ *adj* d'une belle carrure
broad′brimmed′ *adj* à larges bords
broad′cast′ *adj* diffusé; (rad) radiodiffusé ‖ *s* (rad) radiodiffusion *f*, émission *f* ‖ *v* (*pret & pp* **-cast**) *tr* diffuser, répandre; (rad) radiodiffuser ‖ *intr* (rad) émettre
broad′cast′er *s* communicateur *m*
broad′casting sta′tion *s* station *f* d'émission
broad′cloth′ *s* popeline *f*
broaden [ˈbrɔdən] *tr* élargir ‖ *intr* s'élargir
broad′-gauge′ *adj* à voie large
broad′ jump′ *s* saut *m* en longueur
broad′-mind′ed *adj* évolué, à l'esprit large
broad′side′ *s* bordée *f;* (typ) placard *m*
brocade [broˈked] *s* brocart *m* ‖ *tr* brocher
broccoli [ˈbrakəli] *s* brocoli *m*
brochure [broˈʃʊr] *s* brochure *f*
brogue [brog] *s* accent *m* irlandais; (*shoe*) soulier *m* grossier
broil [brɔil] *s* grillade *f;* (*quarrel*) rixe *f* ‖ *tr & intr* griller
broiler [ˈbrɔilər] *s* gril *m*
broke [brok] *adj* (slang) fauché
broken [ˈbrokən] *adj* brisé, cassé; (*promise; ranks; beam*) rompu
bro′ken-down′ *adj* délabré; en panne
bro′ken-heart′ed *adj* au cœur brisé
broker [ˈbrokər] *s* courtier *m*
brokerage [ˈbrokərɪdʒ] *s* courtage *m*
bro′kerage fee′ *s* (frais *mpl* de) courtage *m*
bromide [ˈbromaɪd] *s* bromure *m;* (coll) platitude *f*
bromine [ˈbromin] *s* brome *m*
bronchial [ˈbrɑŋkɪ•əl] *adj* bronchique
bron′chial tube′ *s* bronche *f*
bronchitis [brɑŋˈkaɪtɪs] *s* bronchite *f*
bron•co [ˈbrɑŋko] *s* (*pl* **-cos**) cheval *m* sauvage
bronze [brɑnz] *adj* bronzé ‖ *s* bronze *m* ‖ *tr* bronzer ‖ *intr* se bronzer
brooch [brotʃ], [brutʃ] *s* broche *f*
brood [brud] *s* couvée *f;* (*of children*) nichée *f* ‖ *intr* couver; (*to sulk*) broyer du noir; **to brood over** songer sombrement à
brood′ hen′ *s* couveuse *f*
brood′mare′ *s* poulinière *f*

brook [brʊk] *s* ruisseau *m* ‖ *tr*—**to brook** no ne pas tolérer
brooklet [ˈbrʊklɪt] *s* ruisseau *m*
broom [brum] *s* balai *m;* (bot) genêt *m*
broom′stick′ *s* manche *m* à balai
broth [brɔθ] *s* bouillon *m*, consommé *m*
brothel [ˈbréðəl] *s* bordel *m*
brother [ˈbrʌðər] *s* frère *m*
broth′er•hood′ *s* fraternité *f*
broth′er-in-law′ *s* (*pl* **brothers-in-law**) beau-frère *m*
brotherly [ˈbrʌðərli] *adj* fraternel ‖ *adv* fraternellement
brow [braʊ] *s* (*forehead*) front *m; (eyebrow*) sourcil *m;* **to knit one's brow** froncer le sourcil
brow′beat′ *v* (*pret* **-beat;** *pp* **-beaten**) *tr* rabrouer, brusquer
brown [braʊn] *adj* marron *m; (eyes*) brun; (*hair*) brun, châtain; (*shoes*) marron; (*ale*) brune; (*bread*) bis; (*sugar*) brun; (*butter*) roux, noir; (*bear*) brun; (*tanned*) bronzé, bruni; (*dark-complexioned*) brun de peau; **brown wrapping paper** papier *m* d'emballage ‖ *s* marron *m*, brun *m* ‖ *tr* (*skin*) bronzer, brunir; (culin) faire dorer, rissoler ‖ *intr* (*sauce; leaves*) roussir; (*skin*) brunir; (culin) dorer, rissoler
brown′ bag′ lunch *s* repas *m* tiré du sac
brown′ fields′ *spl* terrain *m* contaminé par des déchets hasardeux
brownie [ˈbrauni] *s* (*sprite*) lutin *m; (cake*) gâteau *m* au chocolat et aux noix; **Brownie** (*girl scout under ten years of age*) Guide *f*
brownish [ˈbraʊnɪʃ] *adj* brunâtre
brown′ out′ *s* (*shortage of power*) panne *f* partielle; (mil) camouflage *m* partiel des lumières
brown′ rice′ *s* riz *m* intégral *or* complet
brown′ stone′ *s* (*brownstone front*) bâtiment *m* de grès brun; (mineral) grès *m* brun
brown′ stud′y *s*—**in a brown study** absorbé dans des méditations
brown′ sug′ar *s* cassonade *f*, sucre *m* brut
browse [braʊz] *intr* (*said of animals*) brouter; (*said of booklovers*) butiner; (*said of customers for secondhand books*) bouquiner
browzer [ˈbraʊzər] *s* (comp) navigateur *m*, fureteur *m*, butineur *m* (*Québec*)
bruise [bruz] *s* (*on body or fruit*) meurtrissure *f;* (*on body*) contusion *f* ‖ *tr* meurtrir, contusionner
bruiser [ˈbruzər] *s* (coll) costaud *m*
bruit [brut] *tr* ébruiter; **to bruit about** répandre
brunette [bruˈnɛt] *adj & s* brune *f*, brunette *f*
brunt [brʌnt] *s* choc *m*, assaut *m;* **to bear the brunt of** (fig) faire tous les frais de
brush [brʌʃ] *s* brosse *f*, (*countryside*) brousse *f;* (elec) balai *m* ‖ *tr* brosser; **to brush aside** écarter ‖ *intr*—**to brush against** frôler; **to brush up on** repasser, rafraîchir
brush′-off′ *s* (slang) affront *m;* **to give a brush-off to** (slang) expédier avec rudesse
brush′wood′ *fpl* broussailles *fpl*, brindilles *fpl*
brusque [brʌsk] *adj* brusque
Brussels [ˈbrʌsəlz] *s* Bruxelles *f*

Brus'sels sprouts' *mpl* chou *m* de Bruxelles
brutal [`brutəl] *adj* brutal
brutali·ty [bru`tælɪti] *s* (*pl* **-ties**) brutalité *f*
brute [brut] *adj* brutal ‖ *s* bête *f*, animal *m*; (*person*) brute *f*, animal *m*
brutish [`brutɪʃ] *adj* grossier, brut; brutal
bubble [`bʌbəl] *s* bulle *f* ‖ *intr* bouillonner; (*said of drink*) pétiller; **to bubble over** déborder
bub'ble bath' *s* bain *m* moussant, bain de mousse
bub'ble gum' *s* gomme *f* à claquer
bub·bly [`bʌbli] *adj* (*comp* **-blier;** *super* **-bliest**) bouillonnant, gazeux
bubon'ic plague' [bju`bɑnɪk] *s* peste *f* bubonique
buccaneer [,bʌkə`nɪr] *s* boucanier *m*
buck [bʌk] *s* (*red deer*) cerf *m*; (*fallow deer*) daim *m*; (*roebuck*) chevreuil *m*; (*slang*) dollar *m*; the male of many animals such as: (*goat*) bouc *m*; (*rabbit*) lapin *m*; (*hare*) lièvre *m*; **to pass the buck** (coll) renvoyer la balle ‖ *tr*—**to buck off** (*a rider*) désarçonner; **to buck up** (coll) remonter le courage de ‖ *intr*—**to buck up** (coll) reprendre courage
bucket [`bʌkɪt] *s* seau *m*; **to kick the bucket** (slang) casser sa pipe, claquer, crever
buck'et seat' *s* siège *m* baquet
buckle [`bʌkəl] *s* boucle *f* ‖ *tr* boucler ‖ *intr* arquer, gauchir; **to buckle down** s'appliquer
buck' pri'vate *s* simple soldat *m*
buckram [`bʌkrəm] *s* bougran *m*
buck'saw' *s* scie *f* à bûches
buck'shot' *s* gros plomb *m*
buck'tooth' *s* (*pl* **-teeth**) dent *f* saillante
buck'wheat' *s* sarrasin *m*
buck'wheat cake' *s* crêpe *f* de sarrasin
bud [bʌd] *s* bouton *m*, bourgeon *m* ‖ *v* (*pret & pp* **budded;** *ger* **budding**) *intr* boutonner, bourgeonner
Buddhism [`budɪzəm] *s* bouddhisme *m*
Buddhist [`budɪst] *adj & s* bouddhiste *mf*
budding [`bʌdɪŋ] *adj* en bouton; (*beginning*) en germe, naissant
bud·dy [`bʌdi] *s* (*pl* **-dies**) (coll) copain *m*
budge [bʌdʒ] *tr* faire bouger ‖ *intr* bouger
budget [`bʌdʒɪt] *s* budget *m* ‖ *tr* comptabiliser, inscrire au budget
budgetary [`bʌdʒɪ,terij] *adj* budgétaire
buff [bʌf] *adj* (*color*) chamois ‖ *s* (coll) fanatique *mf*, enthousiaste *mf* ‖ *tr* polir, émeuler
buffa·lo [`bʌfə,lo] *s* (*pl* **-loes** *ou* **-los**) bison *m*; (*water buffalo; Cape buffalo*) buffle *m*
buffer [`bʌfər] *s* (mach) brunissoir *m*; (rr) (*on cars*) tampon *m*; (rr) (*at end of track*) butoir *m*
buf'fered as'pirin [`bʌfərd] *s* aspirine *f* tamponnée
buff'er state' *s* état *m* tampon
buf'fer zone' *s* zone *f* tampon
buffet [bu`fe] *s* buffet *m* ‖ [`bʌfɪt] *tr* frapper (violemment)
buffet' lunch' [bu`fe] *s* lunch *m*
buffet' sup'per *s* buffet *m*

buffoon [bə`fun] *s* bouffon *m*
buffooner·y [bə`funəri] *s* (*pl* **-ies**) bouffonnerie *f*
bug [bʌg] *s* insecte *m*; (germ) microbe *m*; (*in a mechanical device*) vice *m*, défaut *m*; (*hidden microphone*) micro *m*; (comp) bogue *f*; (coll) idée *f* fixe, lutin *m*; (Brit) punaise *f*; **he's a bug for . . .** (coll) il est fou de . . . ‖ *v* (*pret & pp* **bugged;** *ger* **bugging**) *tr* (slang) installer une table d'écoute dans; installer un microphone dans; (*to annoy*) (slang) embêter, emmerder
bug'bear' *s* (*scare*) épouvantail *m*, croquemitaine *m*; (*pet peeve*) bête *f* noire
bug'-eyed' *adj* (slang) aux yeux saillants
bug·gy [`bʌgi] *adj* (*comp* **-gier;** *super* **-giest**) infesté d'insectes; infesté; (slang) fou ‖ *s* (*pl* **-gies**) buggy *m* à quatre roues; (*two-wheeled*) buggy, boguet *m*
bug'house' *s* (slang) cabanon *m*
bugle [`bjugəl] *s* (bot) bugle *f*; (mus) clairon *m* ‖ *tr & intr* claironner
bu'gle call' *s* sonnerie *f* de clairon
bugler [`bjuglər] *s* clairon *m*
build [bɪld] *s* (*of human body*) taille *f*, charpente *f*, carrure *f* ‖ *v* (*pret & pp* **built** [bɪlt]) *tr* bâtir, construire
builder [`bɪldər] *s* constructeur *m*; (*of bridges, roads, etc.*) entrepreneur *m*
building [`bɪldɪŋ] *s* immeuble *m*, bâtiment *m*, édifice *m*; (*erection*) construction *f*
build'ing and loan' associa'tion *s* société *f* de prêt à la construction
build'ing code' *s* code *m* de construction
build'ing lot' *s* terrain *m* à bâtir
build'ing per'mit *s* permis *m* de construire
build'ing site' *s* chantier *m* de construction; lotissement *m* à bâtir
build'ing trades' *spl* métiers *mpl* du bâtiment
build'-up *s* (*of excitement*) montée *f*; (*of pressure*) intensification *f*; (*of gas*) accumulation *f*; (fig) présentation *f* publicitaire, battage *m*
built'-in' *adj* incorporé, encastré
built'-up' *adj* aggloméré; (*heel*) renforcé; (*land*) bâti, loti
bulb [bʌlb] *s* bulbe *m*; (*of vaporizer*) poire *f*; (bot) oignon *m*; (elec) ampoule *f*
bulbous [`bʌlbəs] *adj* bulbeux
Bulgaria [bʌl`gerɪ·ə] *s* Bulgarie *f*; la Bulgarie
Bulgarian [bʌl`gerɪ·ən] *adj* bulgare ‖ *s* (*language*) bulgare *m*; (*person*) Bulgare *mf*
bulge [bʌldʒ] *s* bosse *f*, bombement *m*; (mil) saillant *m* ‖ *tr* bourrer, gonfler ‖ *intr* faire une bosse, bomber
bulk [bʌlk] *s* masse *f*, volume *m*; **in bulk** en bloc; (com) en vrac ‖ *tr* entasser (en vrac) ‖ *intr* tenir de la place; **to bulk large** devenir important
bulk'head' *s* (naut) cloison *f*
bulk·y [`bʌlki] *adj* (*comp* **-ier;** *super* **-iest**) volumineux
bull [bʊl] *s* taureau *m*; (*on the stock exchange*) haussier *m*, spéculateur *m* à la hausse; (eccl)

bulle *f;* (*policeman*) (slang) flic *m,* vache *f;* (*exaggeration*) (slang) blague *f,* boniment *m,* chiqué *m;* **like a bull in a china shop** comme un éléphant dans un magasin de porcelaine; **to take the bull by the horns** (fig) prendre le taureau par les cornes ‖ *tr*—**to bull the market** jouer à la hausse

bull′dog′ *s* bouledogue *m*

bull′doze′ *tr* passer au bulldozer; (coll) intimider

bulldozer [′bʊl‚dozər] *s* chasse-terre *m,* bouteur *m,* bouldozeur *m*

bullet [′bʊlɪt] *s* balle *f*

bulletin [′bʊlətɪn] *s* bulletin *m;* (*e.g., of a university*) annuaire *m*

bul′letin board′ *s* tableau *m* d'affichage

bul′let·proof′ *adj* à l'épreuve des balles ‖ *tr* blinder

bul′let·proof vest′ *s* gilet *m* pare-balles

bull′fight′ *s* course *f* de taureaux

bull′fight′er *s* torero *m*

bull′fight′ing *s* tauromachie *f*

bull′finch′ *s* bouvreuil *m*

bull′frog′ *s* grenouille *f* d'Amérique

bull′head′ *s* (ichth) chabot *m,* cabot *m;* (*miller's-thumb*) meunier *m,* cabot

bull′head′ed *adj* entêté

bullion [′bʊljən] *s* (*of gold*) or *m;* (*of silver*) argent *m;* encaisse *f* métallique, lingots *mpl* d'or, lingots d'argent; (*on uniform*) cordonnet *m* d'or, cordonnet d'argent

bull′ mar′ket *s* marché *m* à la hausse

bullock [′bʊlək] *s* bœuf *m*

bull′ pen′ *s* toril *m;* (*jail*) poste *m* de détention préventive; (baseball) zone *f* des exercises d'échauffement, enclos *m* des releveurs; (*pitchers*) lanceurs *mpl* de réserve

bull′ring′ *s* arène *f,* arène pour les courses de taureaux

bull′s′-eye′ *s* mouche *f;* **to hit the bull's-eye** faire mouche

bull′s′-eye win′dow *s* œil-de-bœuf *m*

bul·ly [′bʊli] *adj* (coll) épatant ‖ *s* (*pl* **-lies**) brute *f,* brutal *m;* (*at school*) brimeur *m,* tyranneau *m* ‖ *v* (*pret & pp* **-lied**) *tr* brutaliser, malmener; (*at school*) brimer, tyranniser

bulrush [′bʊl‚rʌʃ] *s* jonc *m* des marais

bulwark [′bʊlwərk] *s* rempart *m;* (naut) pavois *m* ‖ *tr* garnir de remparts; (fig) protéger

bum [bʌm] *adj* (slang) moche, de camelote ‖ *s* (slang) clochard *m* ‖ *v* (*pret & pp* **bummed;** *ger* **bumming**) *tr & intr* (slang) écornifler

bumble [′bʌmbəl] *tr* bâcler ‖ *intr* (*to stumble*) trébucher; (*in speaking*) bafouiller; (*said of bee*) bourdonner

bum′ble·bee′ *s* bourdon *m*

bump [bʌmp] *s* (*blow*) choc *m;* (*protuberance*) bosse *f;* (*of car on rough road*) cahot *m* ‖ *tr* cogner, tamponner, heurter; **to bump off** (*to kill*) (slang) buter ‖ *intr* se cogner; **to bump along** (*said of car*) cahoter; **to bump into** buter contre, choquer

bumper [′bʌmpər] *adj* exceptionnel ‖ *s* (aut)

pare-chocs *m;* (rr) tampon *m;* **bumper to bumper** pare-chocs contre pare-chocs

bump′er car′ *s* (*at a carnival*) auto *f* tamponneuse

bump′er stick′er *s* autocollant *m,* macaron *m*

bumpkin [′bʌmpkɪn] *s* péquenot *m,* rustre *m*

bumptious [′bʌmpʃəs] *adj* outrecuidant

bump·y [′bʌmpi] *adj* (*comp* **-ier;** *super* **-iest**) bosselé; (*road*) cahoteux

bun [bʌn] *s* brioche *f,* petit pain *m;* (*hair*) chignon *m*

bunch [bʌnʃ] *s* (*of vegetables*) botte *f;* (*of bananas*) régime *m;* (*of flowers*) bouquet *m;* (*of grapes*) grappe *f;* (*of keys*) trousseau *m;* (*of people*) groupe *m,* bande *f;* (*of ribbons*) flot *m;* (*of feathers, hair*) touffe *f;* (*of twigs*) paquet *m;* (*on body*) bosse *f* ‖ *tr* grouper ‖ *intr* se serrer

buncombe [′bʌŋkəm] *s* (coll) balivernes *fpl,* sornettes *fpl*

bundle [′bʌndəl] *s* paquet *m;* (*of banknotes, papers, etc.*) liasse *f* ‖ *tr* empaqueter, mattre en paquet; **to bundle up** (*in warm clothing*) emmitoufler ‖ *intr*—**to bundle up** s'emmitoufler

bung [bʌŋ] *s* bonde *f* ‖ *tr* mettre une bonde à

bungalow [′bʌŋgə‚lo] *s* bungalow *m*

bung′hole′ *s* bonde *f*

bungle [′bʌŋgəl] *s* gâchis *m,* bousillage *m* ‖ *tr* saboter, bousiller ‖ *intr* saboter

bungler [′bʌŋglər] *s* gâcheur *m,* bousilleur *m*

bungling [′bʌŋglɪŋ] *adj* gauche, maladroit ‖ *s* maladresse *f*

bunion [′bʌnjən] *s* oignon *m* (au pied)

bunk [bʌŋk] *s* (*bed*) couchette *f;* (slang) balivernes *fpl,* sornettes *fpl* ‖ *intr* (coll) se coucher

bunk′ bed′ *s* lit *m* superposé; (naut) cadre *m*

bunker [′bʌŋkər] *s* (golf) banquette *f;* (naut) soute *f;* (mil) blockhaus *m,* bunker *m*

bun·ny [′bʌni] *s* (*pl* **-nies**) petit lapin *m*

bunting [′bʌntɪŋ] *s* (*flags*) drapeaux *mpl;* (*cloth*) étamine *f;* (orn) bruant *m*

buoy [bɔɪ], [′bu·i] *s* bouée *f* ‖ *tr*—**to buoy up** faire flotter; (fig) soutenir

buoyancy [′bɔɪ·ənsi] *s* flottabilité *f*

buoyant [′bɔɪ·ənt] *adj* flottant; (*cheerful*) plein d'allant, plein de ressort

bur [bʌr] *s* (*of chestnut*) bogue *f;* (*ragged metal edge*) bavure *f,* barbe *f*

burble [′bʌrbəl] *s* murmure *m* ‖ *intr* murmurer

burden [′bʌrdən] *s* fardeau *m,* charge *f;* (mus) refrain *m* ‖ *tr* charger

bur′den of proof′ *s* fardeau *m* de la preuve

burdensome [′bʌrdənsəm] *adj* onéreux

burdock [′bʌrdɑk] *s* bardane *f*

bureau [′bjʊro] *s* (*piece of furniture*) commode *f,* chiffonier *m;* (*office*) bureau *m*

bureaucra·cy [bjʊ′rɑkrəsi] *s* (*pl* **-cies**) bureaucratie *f,* énarchie *f*

bureaucrat [′bjʊtʃrə‚kræt] *s* bureaucrate *mf,* rond-de-cuir *m,* énarque *mf*

bureaucratic [‚bjʊrə′krætɪk] *adj* bureaucratique

bur′eau of vi′tal statis′tics *s* bureau *m* de l'état civil

burgeoning [ˈbɅrdʒənɪŋ] *adj* bougeonnant, naissant

burger [ˈbɅrgər] *s* hamburger *m*

burglar [ˈbɅrglər] *s* cambrioleur *m*

bur′glar alarm′ *s* signalisateur *m* anti-vol, sonnette *f* d'alarme

burglarize [ˈbɅrglə‚raɪz] *tr* cambrioler

bur′glar‧proof′ *adj* incrochetable

burglar‧y [ˈbɅrgləri] *s* (*pl* -ies) cambriolage *m*

Burgundian [bərˈgɅndɪ•ən] *adj* bourguignon ‖ *s* (*dialect*) bourguignon *m;* (*person*) Bourguignon *m*

Burgundy [ˈbɅrgəndi] *s* Bourgogne *f;* la Bourgogne ‖ **burgun‧dy** *s* (-dies) (*wine*) bourgogne *m*

burial [ˈbɛrɔ•əl] *s* enterrement *m,* inhumation *f*

bur′ial ground′ *s* cimetière *m*

burlap [ˈbɅrlæp] *s* toile *f* d'emballage, serpillière *f*

burlesque [bərˈlɛsk] *adj & s* burlesque *m* ‖ *tr* parodier

burlesque′ show′ *s* striptease *m*

bur‧ly [ˈbɅrli] *adj* (*comp* -lier; *super* -liest) solide, costaud

Burma [ˈbɅrmə] *s* Birmanie *f;* la Birmanie

Bur‧mese [bərˈmiz] *adj* birman ‖ *s* (*pl* -mese) (*language*) birman *m;* (*person*) Birman *m*

burn [bɅrn] *s* brûlure *f* ‖ *v* (*pret & pp* burned or burnt [bɅrnt]) *tr & intr* brûler; **to burn out** (*elec*) griller

burner [ˈbɅrnər] *s* (*on which to cook*) brûleur *m;* (*using gas*) bec *m;* (*of a stove*) feu *m*

burning [ˈbɅrnɪŋ] *adj* brûlant; (*in flames*) en feu ‖ *s* brûlure *f;* (*fire*) incendie *m*

burnish [ˈbɅrnɪʃ] *tr* brunir, polir

burn′-out *s* arrêt *m* par épuisement; (*emotional breakdown*) syndrome *m* de l'usure au travail

burp [bɅrp] *s* rot *m,* renvoi *m* ‖ *tr* (*a baby*) faire faire son renvoi à ‖ *intr* roter, faire un renvoi

burqa [ˈbɅrkɑ] *s* (*body veil that covers a woman from head to toe*) burca *m* (*voile qui couvre une femme des pieds à la tête*)

burrow [ˈbɅro] *s* terrier *m* ‖ *tr* creuser ‖ *intr* se terrer

bursar [ˈbɅrsər] *s* économe *m*

burst [bɅrst] *s* éclat *m,* explosion *f* ‖ *v* (*pret & pp* burst [bɅrst]) *tr* faire éclater; (*a balloon*) crever; (*a boiler; one's buttons*) faire sauter ‖ *intr* éclater, exploser; (*said of tire*) crever; **to burst into tears** fondre en larmes; **to burst out laughing** éclater de rire

bur‧y [ˈbɛri] *v* (*pret & pp* -ied) *tr* enterrer, ensevelir; (*e.g., pirate treasure*) enfouir

bus [bɅs] *s* (*pl* busses or buses) (*city*) autobus *m,* bus *m;* (*interurban or sightseeing*) car *m,* autocar *m;* (*comp*) bus *m;* **to miss the bus** (fig) manquer le coche, rater le coche ‖ *v* (*pret & pp* bused or bussed; *ger* busing or bussing) *tr* transporter en autobus

bus′boy′ *s* aide-serveur *m,* desserveur *m,* débarasseur *m*

bush [buʃ] *s* (*shrub*) buisson *m;* (*small shrub*) arbuste *m;* (*in Africa and Australia*) brousse *f;* **to beat around the bush** tourner autour du pot, tortiller

bushed [buʃt] *adj* (coll) éreinté

bushel [ˈbuʃəl] *s* boisseau *m*

bushing [ˈbuʃɪŋ] *s* manchon *m,* douille *f,* bague *f,* coussinet *m*

bush‧y [ˈbuʃi] *adj* (*comp* -ier; *super* -iest) (*countryside*) buissonneux; (*hair*) touffu; (*eyebrows*) broussailleux

business [ˈbɪznɪs] *adj* commercial ‖ *s* affaires *fpl,* les affaires; (*subject*) sujet *m;* (*store*) commerce *m;* (*company*) établissement *m;* (theat) jeux *mpl* de scène; **it's none of your business** cela ne vous regarde pas; **mind your own business!** occupez-vous de vos affaires!, faites votre métier!; **to mean business** (coll) ne pas plaisanter; **to send about one's business** envoyer paître

busi′ness dis′trict *s* quartier *m* commerçant

busi′ness hours′ *s* heures *fpl* d'ouverture

busi′ness house′ *s* maison *f* de commerce

busi′ness-like′ *adj* pratique; (*manner, transaction*) sérieux

busi′ness lunch′ *s* déjeuner *m* d'affaires, déjeuner de travail

busi′ness‧man′ *s* (*pl* -men′) homme *m* d'affaires; **big businessman** grand industriel *m,* chef *m* d'industrie

busi′ness man′ager *s* directeur *m* commercial

busi′ness reply′ card′ *s* carte *f* postale avec réponse payée

busi′ness suit′ *s* complet *m* veston

busi′ness trip′ *s* voyage *m* d'affaires

busi′ness‧wom′an *s* (*pl* -wom′en) femme *f* d'affaires

busing [ˈbɅsɪŋ] *s* (educ) busing *m,* ramassage *m* scolaire; (pol) *le transport d'étudiants en autobus loin de leur domicile afin de favoriser l'intégration raciale*

bus′ shel′ter *s* abribus *m*

buskin [ˈbɅskɪn] *s* brodequin *m*

bus′ sta′tion *s* gare *f* routière

bus′ stop′ *s* arrêt *m* d'autobus

bust [bɅst] *s* (*statue*) buste *m;* (*of woman*) gorge *f,* buste; (slang) faillite *f* ‖ *tr* (mil) limoger; (slang) casser ‖ *intr* (slang) échouer

busting [ˈbɅstɪŋ] *s* (mil) cassation *f*

bustle [ˈbɅsəl] *s* remue-ménage *m,* affairement *m,* branle-bas *m* ‖ *intr* se remuer, s'affairer

bustling [ˈbɅslɪŋ] *adj* affairé

bus‧y [ˈbɪzi] *adj* (*comp* -ier; *super* -iest) occupé ‖ *v* (*pret & pp* -ied) *tr*—**to busy oneself with** s'occuper de

bus′y‧bod′y *s* (*pl* -ies) officieux *m*

bus′y sig′nal *s* (telp) signal *m* d'occupation, tonalité *f* occupé; **there's a busy signal** la ligne est occupée

but [bɅt] *adv* seulement; ne . . . que, e.g., **to have nothing but trouble** n'avoir que des ennuis; **but for** sans; **but for that** à part cela

‖ *prep* sauf, excepté; **all but** presque ‖ *conj* mais

butcher ['butʃər] *s* boucher *m* ‖ *tr* (*an animal for meat*) abattre, dépecer; (*to massacre; to bungle*) massacrer

butch′er knife′ *s* couperet *m*, coutelas *m* (de boucher)

butch′er shop′ *s* boucherie *f*

butler ['bʌtlər] *s* maître *m* d'hôtel, intendant *m*

butt [bʌt] *s* (*end*) bout *m*; (*cask*) futaille *f*; (*of a gun*) crosse *f*; (*of a cigarette*) mégot *m*; (*of a joke*) souffre-douleur *m*; (*blow*) coup *m* de tête, coup de corne; (slang) postérieur *m*, derrière *m* ‖ *tr* (*like a goat*) donner un coup de corne à ‖ *intr*—**to butt up against** buter contre; **to butt in** (coll) intervenir sans façon

butte [bjut] *s* butte *f*, tertre *m*, puy *m*

butt′ end′ *s* gros bout *m*

butter ['bʌtər] *s* beurre *m* ‖ *tr* beurrer; **to butter up** (coll) passer de la pommade à, pateliner

but′ter•cup′ *s* renoncule *f*, bouton-d'or *m*

but′ter dish′ *s* beurrier *m*, beurrière *f*

but′ter•fat′ *s* crème *f*

but′ter•fin′gered *adj* maladroit

but′ter•fin′gers *s* brise-tout *mf*

but′ter•fly′ *s* (*pl* **-flies**) papillon *m*

but′ter knife′ *s* couteau *m* à beurre

but′ter•milk′ *s* babeurre *m*

but′ter•scotch′ *s* caramel *m* au beurre

buttocks ['bʌtəks] *spl* fesses *fpl*

button ['bʌtən] *s* bouton *m* ‖ *tr* boutonner

but′ton cell′ *s* (*battery*) pile-bouton *f*

but′ton•hole′ *s* boutonnière *f* ‖ *tr* (coll) retenir (*qn*) par le pan de sa veste

but′ton•hook′ *s* tire-bouton *m*

buttress ['bʌtrɪs] *s* contrefort *m* ‖ *tr* arcbouter; (fig) étayer

buxom ['bʌksəm] *adj* plantureuse

buy [baɪ] *s*—**a good buy** (coll) une bonne affaire ‖ *v* (*pret & pp* **bought** [bɔt]) *tr* acheter; (*a ticket*) prendre; **to buy a drink for** payer un verre à; **to buy back** racheter; **to buy from** acheter à or de; **to buy out** (*a partner*) désin-

téresser; **to buy s.o. off** se débarrasser de qn, racheter qn; **to buy up** accaparer

buyer ['baɪ•ər] *s* acheteur *m*

buy′out′ *s* (com) désintéressement *m*

buzz [bʌz] *s* bourdonnement *m;* **to give s.o. a buzz** (*on the telephone*) (coll) passer un coup de fil à ‖ *tr* (aer) survoler à basse altitude ‖ *intr* bourdonner

buzzard ['bʌzərd] *s* buse *f*

buzz′ bomb′ *s* bombe *f* volante

buzzer ['bʌzər] *s* vibreur *m* sonore, trembleur *m*

buzz′ saw′ *s* scie *f* circulaire

buzz′ word′ *s* grand mot *m*, mot résonnant, prétentieux et emphatique

by [baɪ] *adv* près, auprès; (*aside*) de côté; **by and by** tout à l'heure, sous peu; **by and large** généralement parlant ‖ *prep* par; (*near*) près de; **by a head** (*taller*) d'une tête; **by day** pendant la journée; **by far** de beaucoup; **by Monday** d'ici à lundi; **by 2004** déjà en 2004, en 2004 au plus tard; **by profession** de profession; **by the way** à propos; **to be followed (loved, etc.) by** être suivi (aimé, etc.) de

by-and-by ['baɪ•ən'baɪ] *s* proche avenir *m;* **in the sweet by-and-by** à la Saint-Glinglin

bye-bye ['baɪ'baɪ] *interj* au revoir!, salut!

by′ gone′ *adj* d'autrefois, passé

by′law′ *s* ordonnance *f*, règlement *m*

by′-line′ *s* signature *f* de journaliste

by′-pass′ *s* (*road*) bretelle *f* de contournement, rocade *f;* (elec, med) dérivation *f* ‖ *tr* éviter, contourner; (mach) amener or placer en dérivation

by′-play′ *s* (theat) jeu *m* en aparté

by′-prod′uct *s* sous-produit *m*

by′-road′ *s* chemin *m* détourné

bystander ['baɪ,stændər] *s* spectateur *m*, assistant *m*

byte [baɪt] *s* (comp) multiplet *m;* (*of eight bits*) octet *m*

by′way′ *s* chemin *m* écarté, voie *f* indirecte

by′word′ *s* dicton *m*, proverbe *m;* objet *m* de dérision

Byzantine ['bɪzən,tin] *adj & s* byzantin *m*

C

C, c [si] *s* **III**[e] lettre de l'alphabet

cab [kæb] *s* taxi *m;* (*of locomotive or truck*) cabine *f;* (*hansom*) fiacre *m*, cab *m*

cabaret ['kæbə're] *s* boîte *f* de nuit, cabaret *m*

cabbage ['kæbɪdʒ] *s* chou *m*

cab′driv′er *s* chauffeur *m* de taxi

cabin ['kæbin] *s* (*hut*) case *f*, cabane *f;* (*of ship or airplane*) cabine *f*

cab′in boy′ *s* (naut) mousse *m*

cabinet ['kæbinit] *s* (*small room; room for displaying art; political committee*) cabinet

m; (*piece of furniture*) meuble *m* à tiroirs, cabinet; (*wall cupboard*) placard *m*, armoire *f* fixe

cab′inet-mak′er *s* ébéniste *m*, menuisier *m*

cab′inet mem′ber *s* ministre *m*

cable ['kebəl] *s* câble *m* ‖ *tr & intr* câbler

ca′ble car′ *s* funiculaire *m*, téléférique *m*, tramway *m* funiculaire

ca′ble-gram′ *s* câblogramme *m*

ca′ble-knit′ *adj* à torsades, torsadé

ca′ble ship′ *s* câblier *m*

ca'ble's length' s encablure f
ca'ble net'work s réseau m câblé
ca'ble tel'evision s câble m, câbledistribution f, télédistribution f, télévision f par câble
ca'ble T'V' var de **cable television**
caboose [kə'bus] s (naut) coquerie f; (rr) fourgon m de queue, wagon m du personnel
cab'stand' s station f de taxi
cache [kæʃ] s cachette f, cache f ‖ tr mettre dans une cachette, cacher
cachet [kæ'ʃe] s cachet m
cackle [ˈkækəl] s caquet m ‖ intr caqueter; (said of goose) cacarder
cacopho•ny [kə'kɑfəni] s (pl **-nies**) cacophonie f
cac•tus [ˈkæktəs] s (pl **-tuses** or **-ti** [taɪ]) cactus m
cad [kæd] s malotru m
cadaver [kə'dævər] s cadavre m
cad•dy [ˈkædi] s (pl **-dies**) boîte f à thé; (person) cadet m, caddie m
cadence [ˈkedəns] s cadence f
cadet [kə'dɛt] s cadet m
cadmium [ˈkædmɪ•əm] s cadmium m
Caesar'ean opera'tion [sɪ'zɛrɪ•ən] s césarienne f
café [kæ'fe] s restaurant m, café-restaurant m; café m, bistrot m; cabaret m, boîte de nuit
ca'fé soci'ety s gens mpl chic des cabarets à la mode
cafeteria [ˌkæfə'tɪrɪ•ə] s cafétéria f, restaurant m de libre-service
caffeine [kæ'fin], [ˈkæfɪ•ɪn] s caféine f
cage [kedʒ] s cage f ‖ tr mettre en cage
ca•gey [ˈkedʒi] adj (comp **-gier;** super **-giest**) prudent, peu communicatif; (secretive) dissimulé; (coll) rusé, fin
cahoots [kə'huts] s—**in cahoots** (slang) de mèche
CAI [ˈsi•e'aɪ] s (letterword) (**computer-assisted instruction**) E.A.O. (enseignement assisté par ordinateur)
Cain [ken] s Caïn m; **to raise Cain** (coll) faire le diable à quatre
Cairo [ˈkaɪro] s Le Caire
caisson [ˈkesən] s caisson m
cais'son disease' s maladie f des caissons
cajole [kə'dʒol] tr cajoler, enjôler
cajoler•y [kə'dʒoləri] s (pl **-ies**) cajolerie f, enjôlement m
cake [kek] s (dessert; shaped like a cake) gâteau m; (one-layer cake) galette f; (pastry) pâtisserie f; (of soap, wax) pain m; (of ice) bloc m; (crust) croûte f; **to sell like hot cakes** (coll) se vendre comme des petits pains; **to take the cake** (coll) être la fin des haricots ‖ tr couvrir d'une croûte ‖ intr s'agglutiner, faire croûte
calabash [ˈkælə,bæʃ] s calebasse f; (tree) calebassier m
calaboose [ˈkælə,bus] s (coll) violon m, tôle f
calamitous [kə'læmɪtəs] adj calamiteux
calami•ty [kə'læmɪti] s (pl **-ties**) calamité f
calci•fy [ˈkælsɪ,faɪ] v (pret & pp **-fied**) tr calcifier ‖ intr se calcifer

calcium [ˈkælsɪ•əm] s calcium m
calculate [ˈkælkjə,let] tr & intr calculer
calculating [ˈkælkjə,letɪŋ] adj calculateur
calculation [ˌkælkjə'leʃən] s calcul m
calcu•lus [ˈkælkjələs] s (pl **-luses** or **-li** [ˌlaɪ]) (math, pathol) calcul m
caldron [ˈkɔldrən] s (culin) chaudron m; (mach) chaudière f
calendar [ˈkæləndər] s calendrier m
cal'endar year' s année f civile
calender [ˈkæləndər] s calandre f ‖ tr calandrer, cylindrer
calf [kæf] s (pl **calves** [kævz]) veau m; (of leg) mollet m
calf'skin' s veau m, peau f de veau
calf's' liv'er s foie m de veau
caliber [ˈkælɪbər] s calibre m, ‖ graduer, jauger
calibrate [ˈkælɪ,bret] tr calibrer
cali•co [ˈkælɪ,ko] s (pl **-coes** or **-cos**) calicot m, indienne f
California [ˌkælɪ'fɔrnɪ•ə] s Californie f; la Californie
calipers [ˈkælɪpərz] spl compas m à calibrer
caliph [ˈkelɪf], [ˈkælɪf] s calife m
caliphate [ˈkælɪfet] s califat m
calisthenic [ˌkælɪs'θɛnɪk] adj callisthénique ‖ **calisthenics** spl callisthénie f
calk [kɔk] s crampon m à glace ‖ tr calfater
call [kɔl] s (signal; summons; naming) appel m; (cry) cri m; (visit) visite f; (at a port) escale f; (telp) appel téléphonique; **to have no call to** n'avoir aucune raison de ‖ tr appeler; (e.g., the doctor) faire venir; (a meeting) convoquer; **to call aside** prendre à part; **to call back** rappeler; **to call down** (from upstairs) faire descendre; (the wrath of the gods) invoquer; (to scold) (coll) gronder; **to call off** (a dog) rappeler; (coll) annuler, décommander; **to call the roll** faire l'appel; **to call to mind** rappeler; **to call to order** rappeler à l'ordre; **to call up** (coll) passer un coup de fil à; (mil) mobiliser ‖ intr appeler, crier; (to visit) faire une visite; (naut) faire escale; **to call upon** faire appel à; **to call upon s.o. to speak** inviter qn à prendre la parole
call' bell' s sonnette f
call' box' s guérite f téléphonique
call' boy' s (in a hotel) chasseur m; (theat) avertisseur m
caller [ˈkɔlər] s visiteur m
call' girl' s call-girl f
calling [ˈkɔlɪŋ] s (occupation) métier m, vocation f; (of a meeting) convocation f
call'ing card' s carte f de visite
call' let'ter s (telg, rad) indicatif m d'appel
call' mon'ey s prêts mpl au jour le jour
call' num'ber s numéro m de classification, numérotage m, numérotation f décimale
call' op'tion s (com) option f d'achat
callous [ˈkæləs] adj (foot, hand, etc.) calleux; (unfeeling) endurci, insensible
callow [ˈkælo] adj inexpérimenté, novice
cal'low youth' s blanc-bec m

call′ screen′ing *s* (electron) écoute *f* des appels

callus [ˈkæləs] *s* (*on skin*) cal *m*, durillon *m*, callosité *f;* (bot) cal *m*

calm [kɑm] *adj & s* calme *m* ‖ *tr* calmer; **to calm down** pacifier ‖ *intr*—**to calm down** se calmer; (*said of wind or sea*) calmir

calorie [ˈkæləri] *s* calorie *f*

calum•ny [ˈkæləmni] *s* (*pl* **-nies**) calomnie *f*

calva•ry [ˈkælvəri] *s* (*pl* **-ries**) calvaire *m;* **Calvary** le Calvaire

calve [kæv], [kɑv] *intr* vêler

cam [kæm] *s* came *f*

cambric [ˈkembrɪk] *s* batiste *f*

camcorder [ˈkæm,kɔrdər] *s* caméscope *m* (*caméra vidéo portative à magnétoscope intégré*)

camel [ˈkæməl] *s* chameau *m*

camellia [kəˈmiljə] *s* camélia *m*

came•o [ˈkæmi,o] *s* (*pl* **-os**) camée *m*

camera [ˈkæmərə] *s* appareil *m*, appareil photo

cam′era bug′ *s* chasseur *m* d'images

cam′era crew′ *s* cadreurs *mpl*

cam′era•man′ *s* (*pl* **-men′**) photographe *m;* (mov) cadreur *m*, cameraman *m*

camomile [ˈkæmə,maɪl] *s* camomille *f*

camouflage [ˈkæmə,flɑʒ] *s* camouflage *m* ‖ *tr* camoufler

camp [kæmp] *s* camp *m* ‖ *intr* camper; **to go camping** faire du camping

campaign [kæmˈpen] *s* campagne *f* ‖ *intr* faire campagne

campaigner [kæmˈpenər] *s* propagandiste *mf;* vétéran *m*

camp′ bed′ *s* lit *m* de camp, lit de sangle

camp′ chair′ *s* chaise *f* pliante

camper [ˈkæmpər] *s* campeur *m;* (aut) camping-car *m*

camp′fire′ *s* feu *m* de camp

camp′ground′ *s* camping *m*

camphor [ˈkæmfər] *s* camphre *m*

camping [ˈkæmpɪŋ] *s* camping *m*

camp′stool′ *s* pliant *m*

campus [ˈkæmpəs] *s* campus *m*, terrain *m* universitaire

cam′shaft′ *s* arbre *m* à cames

can [kæn] *s* (*of food, beer, film, garbage, etc.*) boîte *f;* (*e.g., for gasoline*) bidon *m* ‖ *v* (*pret & pp* **canned;** *ger* **canning**) *tr* mettre en boîte, conserver; (*to dismiss*) (slang) dégommer ‖ *v* (*pret & cond* **could** [kʊd]) *aux*—**Albert can't do it** Albert ne peut (pas) le faire; **can he swim?** sait-il nager?

Canada [ˈkænədə] *s* le Canada

Canadian [kəˈnedɪ•ən] *adj* canadien ‖ *s* (*person*) Canadien *m*

canal [kəˈnæl] *s* canal *m*

canard [kəˈnɑrd] *s* fausse nouvelle *f*, canard *m* (coll)

canar•y [kəˈnɛri] *s* (*pl* **-ies**) canari *m*, serin *m*

can•cel [ˈkænsəl] *v* (*pret & pp* **-celed** or **-celled;** *ger* **-celing** or **-celling**) *tr* annuler; (*a word*) biffer, rayer; (*a contract*) résilier; (*a postage stamp*) oblitérer; **to cancel an invitation** dé-

commander les invités; **to cancel each other out** s'annuler, se détruire

cancellation [,kænsəˈleʃən] *s* annulation *f;* (*of postage stamp*) oblitération *f;* (*of contract*) résiliation *f*

cancella′tion to or′der *s* (phila) oblitération *f* de complaisance

cancer [ˈkænsər] *s* cancer *m;* **Cancer** (astr, astrol) le Cancer

cancerous [ˈkænsərəs] *adj* cancéreux

candela•brum [,kændəˈlebrəm] *s* (*pl* **-bra** [brə] or **-brums**) candélabre *m*

candid [ˈkændɪd] *adj* franc

candida•cy [ˈkændɪdəsi] *s* (*pl* **-cies**) candidature *f*

candidate [ˈkændɪ,det] *s* candidat *m*

can′did cam′era *s* caméra *f* invisible

candied *adj* candi

can′died fruit′ *s* fruit *m* candi

candle [ˈkændəl] *s* bougie *f;* (*of tallow*) chandelle *f;* (eccl) cierge *m*

can′dle•hold′er *s* bougeoir *m*

can′dle•light′ *s* lumière *f* de bougie

can′dle•pow′er *s* (phys) bougie *f*

can′dle•stick′ *s* chandelier *m*, bougeoir *m*

can′dle ta′ble *s* guéridon *m*

candor [ˈkændər] *s* franchise *f*, loyauté *f*

can•dy [ˈkændi] *s* (*pl* **-dies**) confiserie *f*, bonbons *mpl;* **candies** douceurs *fpl;* **piece of candy** bonbon ‖ *v* (*pret & pp* **-died**) *tr* glacer, faire candir ‖ *intr* se candir

can′dy box′ *s* boîte *f* à bonbons

can′dy corn′ *s* grains *mpl* de maïs soufflés et sucrés

can′dy dish′ *s* bonbonnière

can′dy machine′ *s* distributeur *m* de friandises

can′dy store′ *s* confiserie *f*

cane [ken] *s* canne *f;* (bot) canne ‖ *tr* canner, rempailler

cane′ chair′ *s* chaise *f* cannée

cane′ sug′ar *s* sucre *m* de canne

canine [ˈkenaɪn] *adj* canin ‖ *s* (*tooth*) canine *f*

canister [ˈkænɪstər] *s* boîte *f* métallique; (mil) boîte à mitraille

canker [ˈkæŋkər] *s* chancre *m;* (*in fruit; in society*) ver *m* rongeur ‖ *tr* ronger; (*society*) corrompre

canned [kænd] *adj* (*food*) en boîte, en conserve; (*drunk*) (slang) rétamé, rond; (*fired*) (slang) flanqué à la porte, vidé

canned′ goods′ *spl* conserves *fpl*, aliments *mpl* conservés

canned′ mu′sic *s* (coll) musique *f* enregistrée, musique en conserve

canner•y [ˈkænəri] *s* (*pl* **-ies**) conserverie *f*

cannibal [ˈkænɪbəl] *adj & s* cannibale *mf*

canning [ˈkænɪŋ] *s* conservation *f*

can′ning fac′tory *s* conserverie *f*

cannon [ˈkænən] *s* canon *m*

cannonade [,kænəˈned] *s* canonnade *f* ‖ *tr* canonner

can′non•ball′ *s* boulet *m* (de canon)

can′non fod′der *s* chair *f* à canon

can•ny [ˈkæni] *adj* (*comp* **-nier;** *super* **-niest**) prudent, circonspect; rusé, malin

canoe [kəˈnu] *s* canoë *m*

canoeist [kəˈnu•ɪst] *s* canoéiste *mf*

canon [ˈkænən] *s* canon *m*

canonical [kəˈnɑnɪkəl] *adj* canonique, canonial ‖ **canonicals** *spl* vêtements *mpl* sacerdotaux

canonize [ˈkænəˌnaɪz] *tr* canoniser

can' o'pener *s* ouvre-boîtes *m*

canopy [ˈkænəpi] *s* (*pl* **-pies**) dais *m;* (*over an entrance*) marquise *f*

can't *contr* **can not** *ou* **cannot**

cant [kænt] *s* (*insincere conventional expression*) l'affectation *f* de pruderie, des phrases *fpl* toute faites; (*argot*) jargon *m* ‖ *tr* (*to tip*) incliner ‖ *intr* (*to tip*) s'incliner; (*to be hypocritical*) papelarder

cantaloupe [ˈkæntəˌlop] *s* cantaloup *m*

cantankerous [kænˈtæŋkərəs] *adj* revêche, acariâtre

cantata [kənˈtɑtə] *s* cantate *f*

canteen [kænˈtin] *s* (*shop*) cantine *f;* (*water flask*) bidon *m;* (*service club*) foyer *m* du soldat, du marin, etc.

canter [ˈkæntər] *s* petit galop *m* ‖ *intr* aller au petit galop

canticle [ˈkæntɪkəl] *s* cantique *m,* hymne *f*

cantilever [ˈkæntɪˌlivər] *adj & s* cantilever *m*

can'tilever bridge' *s* pont *m* cantilever, pont à consoles

canton [kænˈtɑn] *s* canton *m*

cantor [ˈkæntər] *s* (*in a synagogue*) chantre *m* principal

canvas [ˈkænvəs] *s* (*cloth*) canevas *m;* (*picture*) toile *f*

canvass [ˈkænvəs] *s* (*scrutiny*) enquête *f;* (*campaign*) tournée *f* électorale ‖ *tr* (*a voter*) solliciter la voix de; (*a district*) faire une tournée électorale dans; (*com*) prospecter ‖ *intr* (*com*) faire la place; **to canvass for** (*a candidate*) faire une campagne électorale en faveur de

canyon [ˈkænjən] *s* cañon *m*

cap [kæp] *s* (*with visor*) casquette *f;* (*without brim*) bonnet *m;* (*to wear with academic gown*) toque *f,* mortier *m;* (*of bottle*) capsule *f;* (*of cartridge*) amorce *f,* capsule; (*of fountain pen*) capuchon *m,* chapeau *m;* (*of valve; to cover photographic lens*) chapeau *m;* **to set one's cap for** chercher à captiver ‖ *v* (*pret & pp* **capped;** *ger* **capping**) *tr* coiffer; (*a bottle*) capsuler; (*a cartridge*) amorcer; (*a success*) couronner; (*to outdo*) (coll) surpasser

cap. *abbr* (**capital letter**) maj.

capabili•ty [ˌkepəˈbɪlɪti] *s* (*pl* **-ties**) aptitude *f,* capacité *f*

capable [ˈkepəbəl] *adj* capable

capacious [kəˈpeʃəs] *adj* spacieux, vaste, ample

capaci•ty [kəˈpæsɪti] *s* (*pl* **-ties**) capacité *f;* **filled to capacity** comble; **in the capacity of** en tant que, en qualité de, à titre de

cap' and gown' *s* costume *m* académique, toge *f* et mortier *m;* **in cap and gown** en toque et en toge

cape [kep] *s* (*clothing*) cape *f,* pèlerine *f;* (geog) cap *m,* promontoire *m*

Cape' of Good Hope' *s* Cap *m* de Bonne Espérance

caper [ˈkepər] *s* cabriole *f,* gambade *f;* (bot) câpre *f* ‖ *tr* cabrioler, gambader

Cape'town' *s* Le Cap

capital [ˈkæpɪtəl] *adj* capital; excellent ‖ *s* (*city*) capitale *f;* (archit) chapiteau *m;* (com) capital *m;* (typ) majuscule *f,* capitale; **small capital** petite capitale

cap'ital and la'bor *spl* le capital et le travail

cap'ital gains' *spl* plus-values *fpl* (en capital)

cap'ital gains' tax' *s* impôt *m* sur les plus-values (en capital)

cap'ital goods' *spl* biens *mpl* d'équipement, biens de production

capitalism [ˈkæpɪtəˌlɪzəm] *s* capitalisme *m*

capitalist [ˈkæpɪtəlɪst] *adj & s* capitaliste *mf*

capitalize [ˈkæpɪtəˌlaɪz] *tr & intr* capitaliser; (typ) écrire avec une majuscule; **to capitalize on** miser sur, tourner à son profit, tirer parti de

cap'ital let'ter *s* majuscule *f*

cap'ital pun'ishment *s* peine *f* capitale

capitol [ˈkæpɪtəl] *s* capitole *m*

capitulate [kəˈpɪtʃəˌlet] *intr* capituler

capon [ˈkepɑn] *s* chapon *m*

caprice [kəˈpris] *s* caprice *m*

capricious [kəˈprɪʃəs] *adj* capricieux

Capricorn [ˈkæprɪˌkɔrn] *s* (astr, astrol) le Capricorne

capsize [ˈkæpsaɪz] *tr* faire chavirer ‖ *intr* chavirer, capoter

capstan [ˈkæpstən] *s* cabestan *m*

cap' stone' *s* (archit) couronnement *m;* (fig) couronnement, point *m* culminant

capsule [ˈkæpsəl] *s* capsule *f;* (bot, rok) capsule

captain [ˈkæptən] *s* (*head*) chef *m,* capitaine *m;* (mil) capitaine; (naut) commandant *m;* (sports) chef d'équipe ‖ *tr* commander, diriger

captain•cy [ˈkæptənsi] *s* (*pl* **-cies**) direction *f,* commandement *m;* grade *m* de capitaine

caption [ˈkæpʃən] *s* légende *f;* (mov) soustitre *m* ‖ *tr* intituler, donner un sous-titre à

captious [ˈkæpʃəs] *adj* pointilleux, chicaneux; (*insidious*) captieux

captivate [ˈkæptɪˌvet] *tr* captiver

captive [ˈkæptɪv] *adj & s* captif *m*

captivi•ty [kæpˈtɪvɪti] *s* (*pl* **-ties**) captivité *f*

captor [ˈkæptər] *s* ravisseur *m;* (naut) auteur *m* d'une prise

capture [ˈkæptʃər] *s* capture *f,* prise *f* ‖ *tr* capturer

car [kɑr] *s* (*automobile*) auto *f,* voiture *f;* (*of elevator*) cabine *f;* (rr) wagon *m,* voiture; (*for mail, baggage, etc.*) (rr) fourgon *m*

carafe [kəˈræf] *s* carafe *f*

caramel [ˈkærəməl] *s* caramel *m*

carat [ˈkærət] *s* carat *m*

caravan [ˈkærəˌvæn] *s* caravane *f*

caravansa•ry [ˌkærəˈvænsəri] *s* (*pl* **-ries**) caravansérail *m*

caraway [ˈkærəˌwe] s carvi m
car'away seed' s graine f de carvi
car'barn' s dépôt m de tramways
carbide [ˈkɑrbaɪd] s carbure f
carbine [ˈkɑrbaɪn] s carabine f
carbol'ic ac'id [kɑrˈbɑlɪk] s acide m phénique
car' bomb' s voiture f piégée
carbon [ˈkɑrbən] s (chemical element) carbone m; (part of arc light or battery) charbon m; (in auto cylinder) calamine f; papier m carbone
car'bonated wa'ter [ˈkɑrbəˌnetɪd] s eau f gazeuse, soda m
car'bon cop'y s double m au carbone; (fig) calque m; (person) (fig) sosie m
car'bon diox'ide s gaz m carbonique
car'bon monox'ide s oxyde m de carbone
car'bon monox'ide poi'soning s oxycarbonisme m
car'bon pa'per s papier m carbone
carbuncle [ˈkɑrbʌŋkəl] s furoncle m
carburetor [ˈkɑrbəˌretər] s carburateur m
car'-car'rier s camion m pour le transport d'automobiles; (rr) wagon m pour le transport d'automobiles
carcass [ˈkɑrkəs] s (dead body) cadavre m; (without offal) carcasse f
carcinogenic [ˌkɑrsənoˈʒɛnɪk] adj cancérigène, cancérogène
carcinoma [ˌkɑrsɪˈnomə] s carcinome m
card [kɑrd] s carte f; (for filing) fiche f; (for carding) carde f; (coll) original m, numéro m, type m; **to have a card up one's sleeve** avoir un atout dans sa manche; **to put one's cards on the table** jouer cartes sur table ‖ tr carder, peigner
card'board' s carton m, papier m fort
card' case' s porte-cartes m
card' cat'alogue s fichier m
cardiac [ˈkɑrdɪˌæk] adj cardiaque ‖ s (patient) (coll) cardiaque mf
cardinal [ˈkɑrdɪnəl] adj & s cardinal m
card' in'dex s fichier m
cardiogram [ˈkɑrdɪˌoˌgræm] s cardiogramme m
card' par'ty s soirée f bridge, soirée poker, soirée whist (etc.)
card'sharp' s tricheur m
card' ta'ble s table f de jeu
card' trick' s tour m de cartes
care [kɛr] s (attention) soin m; (anxiety) souci m; (responsibility) charge f; (upkeep) entretien m; **in care of** aux bons soins de, à l'attention de; **take care!** faites attention!; **to take care not to** se garder de; **to take care of** se charger de; (a sick person) soigner; **to take care to** avoir soin de ‖ intr—**I don't care** ça m'est égal; **to care about** se soucier de, se préoccuper de; **to care for** (s.o.) avoir de la sympathie pour; (s.th.) trouver plaisir à; (a sick person) soigner; **to care to** désirer, vouloir
careen [kəˈrin] tr faire coucher sur le côté ‖ intr donner de la bande, s'incliner

career [kəˈrɪr] s carrière f
care'free' adj sans souci, insouciant
careful [ˈkɛrfəl] adj soigneux, attentif; **be careful!** soyez prudent!
careless [ˈkɛrlɪs] adj (neglectful) négligent; (nonchalant) insouciant
carelessness [ˈkɛrlɪsnɪs] s négligence f
caress [kəˈrɛs] s caresse f ‖ tr caresser, câliner
caret [ˈkærət] s guidon m de renvoi
care'tak'er s concierge mf, gardien m
care'taker gov'ernment s gouvernement m intérimaire
care'worn' adj rongé par les soucis
car'fare' s prix m du trajet, place f; **to pay carfare** payer le parcours
car•go [ˈkɑrgo] s (pl -goes or -gos) cargaison f
car'go ter'minal s gare f de fret
car' heat'er s chauffage m de voiture
car' hop' s serveur m (qui apporte à manger aux automobilistes dans leur voiture)
Car'ibbe'an Sea [ˌkærɪˈbiˈən], [kəˈrɪbiˈən] s Mer f des Caraïbes, Mer des Antilles, Mer Caraïbe
caricature [ˈkærɪkətˌʃər] s caricature f ‖ tr caricaturer
caricaturist [ˈkærɪkətˌʃərɪst] s caricaturiste mf
caries [ˈkɛriz] s carie f
carillon [ˈkærɪˌlɑn] s carillon m ‖ tr & intr carillonner
car'load' s voiturée f
carnage [ˈkɑrnɪdʒ] s carnage m
carnal [ˈkɑrnəl] adj charnel; sexuel
car'nal sin' s péché m de la chair
carnation [kɑrˈneˌʃən] s œillet m
carnival [ˈkɑrnɪvəl] s carnaval m; fête f
car'nival queen' s reine f du carnaval, reine de la fête
car•ol [ˈkærəl] s chanson f, cantique m; (Christmas carol) noël m ‖ v (pret & pp -oled or -olled; ger -oling or -olling) tr & intr chanter
carom [ˈkærəm] s carambolage m ‖ intr caramboler
carouse [kəˈrauz] intr faire la bombe
carp [kɑrp] s carpe f ‖ intr se plaindre
carpenter [ˈkɑrpəntər] s charpentier m; (joiner) menuisier m
carpentry [ˈkɑrpəntri] s charpenterie f
carpet [ˈkɑrpɪt] s tapis m ‖ tr recouvrir d'un tapis
car'pet bomb'ing s bombardement m en tapis (bombardement à saturation)
car'pet sweep'er s balai m mécanique
car' pool' s co-voiturage m
car'port' s abri m pour auto, abri d'auto
car'-rent'al serv'ice s entreprise f de location de voitures
carrel [ˈkærəl] s stalle f d'études (dans une bibliothèque)
carriage [ˈkærɪdʒ] s (horse-drawn) voiture f, équipage m; (used to transport royalty) carrosse m; (bearing) port m, maintien m; (cost of transport) frais mpl de port; (of typewriter; of rocket) chariot m; (of gun) affût m

carrier [ˈkærɪ•ər] s (*person*) porteur *m;* (*e.g., a teamster*) camionneur *m,* voiturier *m;* (*vehicle*) transporteur *m*

car′rier pig′eon s pigeon *m* voyageur

car′rier wave′ s onde *f* porteuse

carrion [ˈkærɪ•ən] s charogne *f*

carrot [ˈkærət] s carotte *f*

carrousel [ˌkærəˈzɛl] s (*merry-go-round*) manège *m* de chevaux de bois; (hist) carrousel *m*

car•ry [ˈkæri] v (*pret & pp* **-ried**) tr porter; (*in adding numbers*) retenir; **to be carried** (parl) être voté, être adopté; **to be carried away** (*e.g., with enthusiasm*) être entraîné, s'importer; **to carry away** or **off** emporter, enlever; **to carry back** rapporter; **to carry down** descendre; **to carry forward** avancer; (bk) reporter; **to carry on** continuer; (*e.g., a conversation*) soutenir; **to carry oneself straight** se tenir droit; **to carry out** (*a plan*) exécuter; **to carry over** (bk) reporter; **to carry through** mener à bonne fin; **to carry up** monter; **to carry with one** (*e.g., an audience*) entraîner ‖ intr (*said of voice or sound*) porter; **to carry on** continuer; (*in a ridiculous manner*) (coll) faire des espiègleries; (*angrily*) (coll) s'emporter

car′ sick′ness s mal *m* de la route

cart [kɑrt] s charrette *f;* (*in a supermarket*) poussette *f;* **to put the cart before the horse** mettre la charrue devant les bœufs ‖ tr charrier; (*to truck*) camionner

cartel [kɑrˈtɛl] s cartel *m*

car′ tel′ephone s radiotéléphone *m,* téléphone *m* cellulaire, téléphone mobile

cartilage [ˈkɑrtɪlɪdʒ] s cartilage *m*

cartographer [kɑrˈtɑgrəfər] s cartographe *m*

carton [ˈkɑrtən] s carton *m,* boîte *f*

cartoon [kɑrˈtun] s dessin *m* humoristique; caricature *f;* (*comic strip*) bande *f* dessinée; (fa) carton *m;* (mov) dessin animé ‖ tr caricaturer, ridiculiser

cartoonist [kɑrˈtunɪst] s caricaturiste *mf*

cartridge [ˈkɑrtrɪdʒ] s cartouche *f;* capsule *f* enregistreuse de pick-up

car′tridge belt′ s cartouchière *f*

car′tridge case′ s cartouchière *f*

cart′wheel′ s roue *f;* **to turn cartwheels** faire la roue

carve [kɑrv] tr & intr sculpter; (culin) découper

carver [ˈkɑrvər] s sculpteur *m;* (culin) découpeur *m*

carv′ing knife′ s couteau *m* à découper

car′wash′ s (*place of business*) lave-auto *m,* tunnel *m* de lavage; (*car washing*) lavage *m* de voitures

car′ wax′ s crème *f* pour auto

caryatid [ˌkærɪˈætɪd] s cariatide *f*

cascade [kæsˈked] s cascade *f* ‖ intr cascader

case [kes] s (*instance, example*) cas *m;* (*for packing; of clock or piano*) caisse *f;* (*for cigarettes, eyeglasses, cartridges*) étui *m;* (*for jewels, silver, etc.*) écrin *m;* (*for watch*) boîtier *m;* (*for pillow*) taie *f;* (*for surgical instruments*) trousse *f;* (*for sausage*) peau *f;* (*showcase*) vitrine *f;* (*covering*) enveloppe *f,* couverture *f;* (*law*) cause *f;* (typ) casse *f;* **as the case may be** selon le cas; **in any case** en tout cas; **in case** au cas où; **in case of emergency** en cas d'imprévu; **in no case** en aucun cas; **just in case** à tout hasard; **to win one's case** avoir gain de cause ‖ tr (*to put into a case*) encaisser; (*to package*) envelopper; (*to observe*) (slang) observer, épier

case′ hard′en tr aciérer, cémenter; (fig) endurcir

case′ his′tory s évolution *f* du cas social; (med) antécédents *mpl* médicaux, évolution de la maladie

casein [ˈkesi•ɪn] s caséine *f*

casement [ˈkesmənt] s croisée *f*

case′ load′ s numéro *m* de dossiers

case′ work′ s étude *f* sur dossier

case′ work′er s assistant *m* social, assistante *f* sociale

cash [kæʃ] s espèces *fpl;* **cash down** argent comptant; **cash offer** offre *f* réelle; **cash on delivery** livraison contre remboursement; **cash on hand** fonds *mpl* en caisse; **in cash** en numéraire; **to pay cash down** payer comptant, payer cash ‖ tr toucher, encaisser ‖ intr—**to cash in on** (coll) tirer parti de

cash′ and car′ry s achat *m* au comptant et à emporter, paye et prends

cash′ bal′ance s solde *m* de caisse

cash′ bar′ s bar *m* payant

cash′ dis′count s escompte *m* au comptant, remise *f* au comptant

cash′ down′ *m* argent *m* comptant

cash′ flow′ s argent *m* vif, flux *m* de caisse, cash-flow *m;* (bk) capacité *f* d'autofinancement

cashew [ˈkæʃu] s noix *f* d'acajou, anacarde *m,* cajou *m;* (*tree*) anacardier *m*

cash′ew nut′ s noix *f* d'acajou, cajou *m*

cashier [kæˈʃɪr] s caissier *m*

cash′ier′s′ check′ s chèque de la caisse

cashmere [ˈkæʃmɪr] s cachemire *m*

cash′ pay′ment s paiement *m* comptant

cash′ pur′chase s achat *m* comptant

cash′ reg′ister s caisse *f* enregistreuse

casino [kəˈsino] s casino *m*

casing [ˈkesɪŋ] s enveloppe *f,* chemise *f,* coffrage *m;* (*of door or window*) chambranle *m*

cask [kæsk] s tonneau *m,* fût *m*

casket [ˈkæskɪt] s (*for jewels*) écrin *m,* cassette *f;* (*for interment*) cercueil *m*

casserole [ˈkæsə,rol] s terrine *f*

cassette [kəˈsɛt] s cassette *f*

cassette′ deck′ s platine *f* à cassettes

cassette′ play′er s lecteur *m* de cassettes

cassette′ record′er s magnétophone *m* à cassettes

cassock [ˈkæsək] s soutane *f*

cast [kæst] s (*mold*) moule *m;* (*of metal*) fonte

f; (*of fish line*) lancer *m;* (*throw*) jet *m;* (*for broken limb*) plâtre *m;* (*squint*) léger strabisme *m;* (theat) distribution *f* ‖ *v* (*pret & pp* **cast**) *tr* fondre, jeter en moule; (*to throw*) lancer; (*a glance*) jeter; (*a play*) distribuer les rôles de; **to be cast in one piece with** venir de fonte avec; **to cast aside** mettre de côté; **to cast lots** tirer au sort; **to cast off** rejeter; **to cast out** mettre à la porte; (*a spell*) exorciser ‖ *intr* (fishing) lancer la canne; **to cast about for** chercher; **to cast off** (naut) larguer les amarres

castanets [ˌkæstəˈnɛts] *spl* castagnettes *fpl*

cast′ away′ *adj & s* naufragé *m*

caste [kæst] *s* caste *f*

caster [ˈkæstər] *s* (*wheel*) roulette *f;* (*cruet stand*) huilier *m;* (*shaker*) saupoudreuse *f*

castigate [ˈkæstɪˌget] *tr* châtier, corriger

Castile [kæsˈtil] *s* Castille *f;* la Castille

Castilian [kæsˈtɪljən] *adj* castillan ‖ *s* (*language*) castillan *m;* (*person*) Castillan *m*

casting [ˈkæstɪŋ] *s* (*act or process*) fonte *f;* (*thing cast*) pièce *f* fondue; (*act*) lancement *m;* (fishing) pêche *f* au lancer; (theat) distribution *f*

cast′ing rod′ *s* canne *f* à lancer

cast′ i′ron *s* fonte *f*

cast′-i′ron *adj* en fonte

cast′-iron stom′ach *s* estomac *m* d'autruche

castle [ˈkæsəl] *s* (*palace*) château *m;* (*fortified castle*) château fort; (*chess*) tour *f* ‖ *tr & intr* (chess) roquer

cast′ off′ *adj & s* rejeté *m*

cas′tor oil′ [ˈkæstər] *s* huile *f* de ricin

castrate [ˈkæstret] *tr* castrer

casual [ˈkæʒuˑəl] *adj* casuel; (*indifferent*) insouciant, désinvolte

casually [ˈkæʒuˑəli] *adv* nonchalamment, avec désinvolture; (*by chance*) fortuitement

casual•ty [ˈkæʒuˑəlti] *s* (*pl* **-ties**) accident *m;* (*person*) accidenté *m;* **casualties** (mil) pertes *fpl,* les morts et blessées *fpl*

cas′ualty list′ *s* état *m* des pertes

cat [kæt] *s* (*tomcat*) chat *m;* (*female cat*) chatte *f;* (naut) capon *m;* (*shrew*) (coll) cancanière *f,* chipie *f;* **a cat may look at a queen** un chien regarde un évêque; **to let the cat out of the bag** (coll) vendre *or* éventer la mèche; **to rain cats and dogs** (coll) pleuvoir à seaux

CAT [kæt] *s* (acronym) (**computerized axial tomography**) scanographie *f,* tomodensitométrie *f*

cataclysm [ˈkætəˌklɪzəm] *s* cataclysme *m*

catacombs [ˈkætəˌkomz] *spl* catacombes *fpl*

catalogue [ˈkætəˌləg] *s* catalogue *m;* (*of university*) annuaire *m* ‖ *tr* cataloguer, classer

Catalonia [ˌkætəˈloniˑə] *s* Catalogne *f;* la Catalogne

catalyst [ˈkætəlɪst] *s* catalyseur *m*

catalyt′ic convert′er [ˌkætəˈlɪtɪk] *s* (aut) pot *m* catalytique

catapult [ˈkætəˌpʌlt] *s* catapulte *f* ‖ *tr* catapulter

cataract [ˈkætəˌrækt] *s* cataracte *f*

catarrh [kəˈtɑr] *s* catarrhe *m*

catastrophe [kəˈtæstrəfi] *s* catastrophe *f*

cat′ call′ *s* huée *f;* (theat) coup *m* de sifflet ‖ *tr & intr* (theat) siffler

catch [kætʃ] *s* (*catching and thing caught*) prise *f,* capture *f;* (*on door*) loquet *m;* (*on buckle*) ardillon *m;* (*caught by fisherman*) pêche *f;* (mach) cliquet *m,* chien *m;* **good catch!** (sports) bien rattrapé! **there's a catch to it** (coll) c'est une attrape ‖ *v* (*pret & pp* **caught** [kɔt]) *tr* attraper; (*a train; a fish; fire*) prendre; (*a word or sound*) saisir; (*e.g., one's coat*) accrocher; **caught like a rat in a trap** fait comme un rat; **to catch hold of** saisir, s'accrocher à; **to catch s.o. in the act** prendre qn sur le fait; **to catch up** (*in a mistake*) surprendre ‖ *intr* prendre; (*said of fire*) s'allumer, s'enflammer, se prendre; **to catch on** (*a nail, thorn, etc.*) s'accrocher à; (*to understand*) (coll) comprendre; (*to become popular*) (coll) devenir célèbre, devenir populaire; **to catch up** se rattraper; **to catch up with** rattraper

catch′all′ *s* débarras *m,* fourre-tout *m*

catch′ ba′sin *s* bouche *f* d'égout

catcher [ˈkætʃər] *s* attrapeur *m* (*joueur qui doit attraper la balle*)

catching [ˈkætʃɪŋ] *adj* contagieux; (*e.g., smile*) communicatif

catch′ ques′tion *s* (coll) colle *f*

catch′word′ *s* mot *m* de ralliement, slogan *m;* (*cliché*) rengaine *f,* scie *f;* (*at the bottom of page*) réclame *f;* (theat) réplique *f;* (typ) mot-souche *m*

catch•y [ˈkætʃi] *adj* (*comp* **-ier;** *super* **-iest**) (*tune*) facile à retenir, entraînant; (*question*) insidieux, à traquenard

catechism [ˈkætɪˌkɪzəm] *s* catéchisme *m*

categorical [ˌkætɪˈgɔrɪkəl] *adj* catégorique

catego•ry [ˈkætɪˌgori] *s* (*pl* **-ries**) catégorie *f*

cater [ˈketər] *tr* (*e.g., a wedding*) fournir le buffet de ‖ *intr* être fournisseur; **to cater to** pourvoir à; (*to favor*) entourer de prévenances

cat′er-cor′nered [ˈkætər,kɔrnərd] *adj* diagonal ‖ *adv* diagonalement

caterer [ˈketərər] *s* fournisseur *m,* traiteur *m*

catering [ˈketərɪŋ] *s* (culin) prestation *f* à domicile

caterpillar [ˈkætərˌpɪlər] *s* chenille *f*

cat′erpillar trac′tor *s* autochenille *f*

cat′fish′ *s* poisson-chat *m*

cat′gut′ *s* boyau *m* de chat; (*string*) corde *f* à boyau, boyau *m;* (surg) catgut *m*

cathartic [kəˈθɑrtɪk] *adj* cathartique ‖ *s* purgatif *m*

cathedral [kəˈθidrəl] *s* cathédrale *f*

catheter [ˈkæθɪtər] *s* (med) cathéter *m*

catheterization [ˌkæθɪtərɪˈzeʃən] *s* (surg) cathétérisme *m*

cathode [ˈkæθod] *s* cathode *f*

catholic [ˈkæθəlɪk] *adj* (*universal*) catholique; tolérant, large, e.g., **he has a catholic mind**

il a l'esprit large, il est fort tolérant ‖ (*cap*) *adj & s* catholique *mf*

Catholicism [kə'θɑlɪ'sɪzəm] *s* catholicisme *m*

catholicity [,kæθə'lɪsɪti] *s* catholicité *f;* universalité *f;* (*tolerance*) largeur *f* d'esprit, tolérance *f*

catkin ['kætkɪn] *s* (bot) chaton *m*

cat'nap' *s* petit somme *m*

cat'nip *s* herbe-aux-chats *f*, cataire *f*

cat-o'-nine-tails [,kætə'naɪn,telz] *s* chat *m* à neuf queues

CAT' scan' *s* (med) image *m* donnée par le scanographe

CAT' scan'ner *s* (med) scanographe *m*, scanner *m*, tomodensitomètre *m*

catsup ['kætsəp] *s* = **ketchup**

cattle ['kætəl] *s* bœufs *mpl;* (*including horses*) gros bétail *m*, bestiaux *mpl*

cat'tle car' *s* fourgon *m* à bestiaux

cat'tle cross'ing *s* passage *m* de troupeaux

cat'tle•man *s* (*pl* **-men**) éleveur *m* de bétail

cat'tle rais'ing *s* élevage *m* des bovins

cat'tle ranch' *s* ranch *m*

cat'tle thief' *s* voleur *m* de bétail

cat•ty ['kæti] *adj* (*comp* **-tier;** *super* **-tiest**) (coll) cancanier, méchant

cat'ty-cor'ner *adj* (coll) diagonal ‖ *adv* (coll) diagonalement

cat'walk' *s* passerelle *f*

Caucasian [kɔ'keʃən] *adj* caucasien ‖ *s* Caucasien *m*

caucus ['kɔkəs] *s* comité *m* électoral ‖ *intr* se grouper en comité électoral

cauliflower ['kɔlɪ,flaʊ•ər] *s* chou-fleur *m*

caulk [kɔk] *tr* calfater

cause [kɔz] *s* cause *f;* **to have cause to** avoir lieu de ‖ *tr* causer; **to cause to** + *inf* faire + *inf,* e.g., **he caused him to stumble** il l'a fait trébucher

cause'way' *s* chaussée *f*

caustic ['kɔstɪk] *adj* caustique

cauterize ['kɔtə,raɪz] *tr* cautériser

caution ['kɔʃən] *s* prudence *f*, précaution *f;* (*warning*) avertissement *m* ‖ *tr* mettre en garde, avertir

cautious ['kɔʃəs] *adj* prudent, circonspect

cavalcade [,kævəl'ked] *s* cavalcade *f*

cavalier [,kævə'lɪr] *adj & s* cavalier *m*

caval•ry [,kævəlri] *s* (*pl* **-ries**) cavalerie *f*

cav'alry•man or **cav'alry•man** *s* (*pl* **-men'** or **-men**) cavalier *m*

cave [kev] *s* caverne *f* ‖ *intr*—**to cave in** s'effondrer

cave'-in' *s* effondrement *m*

cave' man' *s* homme *m* des cavernes; (coll) rustre *m*, ours *m*

cavern ['kævərn] *s* caverne *f*

caviar ['kævɪ,ɑr] *s* caviar *m*

cav•il ['kævɪl] *v* (*pret & pp* **-iled** or **-illed;** *ger* **-iling** or **illing**) *intr* ergoter, chicaner

cavi•ty ['kævɪti] *s* (*pl* **-ties**) cavité *f*

cavort [kə'vɔrt] *intr* gambader, caracoler

caw [kɔ] *s* croassement *m* ‖ *intr* croasser, crialler

C.B. ['si'bi] *s* (letterword) (**citizen band**) bande *f* publique

C.B. ra'dio *s* appareil *m* de radio émetteur-récepteur multicanaux

CD ['si'di] *s* (letterword) (**Compact Disk**) CD *m* (Compact Disc, disque compact)

C'D' play'er *s* lecteur *m* CD

CD-ROM ['si'di'rom] *s* CD-ROM or CD-Rom *m invar,* cédérom *m*

cease [sis] *s* cessation *f;* **without cease** sans cesse ‖ *tr & intr* cesser; **to cease fire** cesser le feu

cease'-fire' *s* cessez-le-feu *m*

ceaseless ['sislɪs] *adj* incessant, continuel

cedar ['sidər] *s* cèdre *m*

cede [sid] *tr & intr* céder

cedilla [sɪ'dɪlə] *s* cédille *f*

ceiling ['silɪŋ] *s* plafond *m;* **to hit the ceiling** (coll) sortir de ses gonds

ceil'ing lamp' *s* plafonnier *m*

ceil'ing price' *s* prix *m* maximum

celebrant ['sɛlɪbrənt] *s* (eccl) célébrant *m*

celebrate ['sɛlɪ,bret] *tr* célébrer

celebrated *adj* célèbre

celebration [,sɛlɪ'breʃən] *s* célébration *f*, fête *f*

celebri•ty [sɪ'lɛbrɪti] *s* (*pl* **-ties**) célébrité *f;* (*e.g., movie star*) vedette *f*

celery ['sɛləri] *m* céleri *m*

celestial [sɪ'lɛstʃəl] *adj* céleste

celiba•cy ['sɛlɪbəsi] *s* (*pl* **-cies**) célibat *m*

celibate ['sɛlɪ,bet] *adj & s* célibataire *mf*

cell [sɛl] *s* cellule *f;* (*of electric battery*) élément *m*

cellar ['sɛlər] *s* (*basement; wine cellar*) cave *f;* (*often partly above ground*) sous-sol *m*

cellist or **'cellist** ['tʃɛlɪst] *s* violoncelliste *mf*

cel•lo or **'cel•lo** ['tʃɛlo] *s* (*pl* **-los**) violoncelle *m*

cellophane ['sɛlə,fen] *s* cellophane *f*

cell'phone' *s* téléphone *m* mobile, radiotéléphone *m*, téléphone cellulaire, (téléphone) portatif

cellular ['sɛljulər] *adj* cellulaire

cel'lular tel'ephone *s* téléphone *m* cellulaire

celluloid ['sɛljə,lɔɪd] *s* celluloïd *m*

Celt [sɛlt], [kɛlt] *s* Celte *mf*

Celtic ['sɛltɪk], ['kɛltɪk] *adj* celte, celtique ‖ *s* celtique *m*

cement [sɪ'mɛnt] *s* ciment *m* ‖ *tr* cimenter

cement' mix'er *s* bétonnière *f*

cemeter•y ['sɛmɪ,tɛri] *s* (*pl* **-ies**) cimetière *m*

censer ['sɛnsər] *s* encensoir *m*

censor ['sɛnsər] *s* censeur *m* ‖ *tr* censurer

cen'sor•ship' *s* censure *f*

censure ['sɛn•ʃər] *s* blâme *m* ‖ *tr* blâmer

census ['sɛnsəs] *s* recensement *m*, dénombrement *m;* (*in Roman Empire*) cens *m*

cen'sus tak'er *s* recenseur *m;* (*in ancient Rome*) censeur *m*

cent [sɛnt] *s* cent *m;* **not to have a red cent to one's name** n'avoir pas un sou vaillant

centaur ['sɛntɔr] *s* centaure *m*

centenarian [,sɛntɪ'nɛrɪ•ən] *s* centenaire *mf*

centennial [sɛnˈtɛnɪˌəl] *adj* centennial ‖ *s* centenaire *m*

center [ˈsɛntər] *adj* central ‖ *s* centre *m;* (*middle*) milieu *m* ‖ *tr* centrer ‖ *intr*—**to center on** concentrer sur

cen′ter cit′y *s* centre *m* de (la) ville

cen′ter·fold′ *s* double page *f* centrale

centering [ˈsɛntərɪŋ] *s* centrage *m;* (phot) cadrage *m*

cen′ter·piece′ *s* milieu *m* de table, surtout *m*

centrigrade [ˈsɛntɪˌgred] *adj* & *s* centrigrade *m*

centimeter [ˈsɛntɪˌmitər] *s* centimètre *m*

centipede [ˈsɛntɪˌpid] *s* mille-pattes *m,* myriapodes *mpl*

central [ˈsɛntrəl] *adj* & *s* central *m*

Cen′tral Amer′ica *s* l'Amérique *f* centrale

Cen′tral Intel′ligence A′gency (CIA) *s* (*equivalent French agency*) Service *m* de Documentation Extérieure et contre-espionnage (S.D.E.C)

centralize [ˈsɛntrəˌlaɪz] *tr* centraliser ‖ *intr* se centraliser

centrifugal [sɛnˈtrɪfjʊgəl] *adj* centrifuge

centrifuge [ˈsɛntrɪˌfjudʒ] *s* essoreuse *f* ‖ *tr* essorer

centu·ry [ˈsɛntʃəri] *s* (*pl* **-ries**) siècle *m*

cen′tury-old′ *adj* séculaire

ceramic [sɪˈræmɪk] *adj* céramique ‖ **ceramics** *s* (art) céramique *f;* spl (*objects*) céramiques

cereal [ˈsɪrɪˌəl] *adj* céréalier ‖ *s* (*grain*) céréale *f;* (*oatmeal*) flocons *mpl* d'avoine; (*cornflakes*) flocons de maïs; (*cooked cereal*) bouillie *f,* gruau *m*

cerebral [ˈsɛrɪbrəl] *adj* cérébral

ceremonial [ˌsɛrɪˈmonɪˌəl] *adj* cérémonial; (*e.g., tribal rites*) cérémoniel ‖ cérémonial *m*

ceremonious [ˌsɛrɪˈmonɪˌəs] *adj* cérémonieux

ceremo·ny [ˈsɛrɪˌmoni] *s* (*pl* **-nies**) cérémonie *f;* **to stand on ceremony** faire des cérémonies

certain [ˈsʌrtən] *adj* certain; **a certain** certain; **certain people** certains; **for certain** pour sûr, à coup sûr; **to make certain of** s'assurer de

certainly ˈsʌrtənli] *adv* certainement

certain·ty [ˈsʌrtənti] *s* (*pl* **-ties**) certitude *f*

certificate [sərˈtɪfɪkɪt] *s* certificat *m,* acte *m;* (*of birth, of marriage, etc.*) bulletin *m,* acte *m,* extrait *m;* (*proof*) attestation *f;* (educ) diplôme *m*

cer′tified check′ *s* chèque *m* certifié

cer′tified cop′y *s* extrait *m;* (formula used on documents) pour copie conforme

cer′tified pub′lic account′ant *s* expert comptable *m,* compatable *m* agréé

certi·fy [ˈsʌrtɪˌfaɪ] *v* (*pret* & *pp* **-fied**) *tr* certifier; **to send by certified mail** envoyer en recommandé, envoyer avec avis de réception

cervix [ˈsʌrvɪks] *s* (*pl* **cervices** [sərˈvaɪsiz]) nuque *f*

cessation [sɛˈseʃən] *s* cessation *f,* cesse *f*

cesspool [ˈsɛsˌpul] *s* fosse *f* d'aisance, cloaque *m*

Ceylon [sɪˈlɑn] *s* Ceylan *m*

Ceylo·nese [ˌsiləˈniz] *adj* cingalais ‖ *s* (*pl* **-nese**) Cingalais *m*

cf *abbr* confer, compare

chafe [tʃef] *tr* écorcher, irriter ‖ *intr* s'écorcher, s'irriter

chaff [tʃæf] *s* balle *f;* (*banter*) raillerie *f* ‖ *tr* railler, persifler

chaf′ing dish′ *s* réchaud *m* de table, chauffe-plats *m*

chagrin [ʃəˈgrɪn] *s* mortification *f,* humiliation *f* ‖ *tr* mortifier, humilier

chain [tʃen] *s* chaîne *f* ‖ *tr* enchaîner

chain′ gang′ *s* forçats *mpl* à la chaîne

chain′ reac′tion *s* (phys) réaction *f* en chaîne

chain′ saw′ *s* tronçonneuse *f*

chain′ smok′er *s* fumeur *m* à la file

chain′ stitch′ *s* point *m* de chaînette

chain′ store′ *s* magasin *m* à succursales multiples, économat *m*

chair [tʃɛr] *s* (*seat*) chaise *f;* (*held by university professor*) chaire *f;* (*of presiding officer; presiding officer himself*) fauteuil *m;* (*of a committee, department, etc.*) chef *m;* (educ) chef *m* d'une section; **to take a chair** prendre un siège, s'asseoir; **to take the chair** occuper le fauteuil, présider une assemblée ‖ *tr* présider

chair′ lift′ *s* télésiège *m*

chair′man *s* (*pl* **-men**) président *m;* (educ) chef *m* d'une section

chair′man·ship′ *s* présidence *f*

chair′wom′an *s* (*pl* **-wom′en**) présidente *f;* (educ) chef *f* (coll) d'une section

chalice [ˈtʃælɪs] *s* calice *m*

chalk [tʃɔk] *s* craie *f;* **a piece of chalk** une craie, un morceau de craie ‖ *tr* marquer avec de la craie, écrire à la craie

chalk·y [ˈtʃɔki] *adj* (*comp* **-ier;** *super* **-iest**) crayeux

challenge [ˈtʃælɪndʒ] *s* (*call, summons*) défi *m;* (*objection*) contestation *f;* (mil) quivive *m;* (sports) challenge *m* ‖ *tr* défier; (*to question*) mettre en question, contester; (mil) crier qui-vive à

chamber [ˈtʃembər] *s* chambre *f*

chamberlain [ˈtʃembərlɪn] *s* chambellan *m*

cham′ber·maid′ *s* femme *f* de chambre

cham′ber mu′sic *s* musique *f* de chambre

Cham′ber of Com′merce *s* syndicat *m* d'initiative

cham′ber pot′ *s* vase *m* de nuit, pot *m* de chambre, vase *m*

chameleon [kəˈmilɪˌən] *s* caméléon *m*

chamfer [ˈtʃæmfər] *s* chanfrein *m* ‖ *tr* chanfreiner

chamois [ˈʃæmi] *s* (*pl* **-ois**) chamois *m*

champ [tʃæmp] *s* mâchonnement *m* ‖ *tr* mâcher bruyamment; **to champ at the bit** ronger son frein

champagne [ʃæmˈpen] *s* champagne *m* ‖ (*cap*) *adj* champenois ‖ (*cap*) *s* Champagne *f;* la Champagne

champion [ˈtʃæmpɪˌən] *s* champion *m* ‖ *tr* se faire le champion de, défendre

cham'pion•ship' s championnat m

chance [t∫æns] adj fortuit, de rencontre ‖ s (luck) hasard m; (good luck) chance f, coup m de chance; (possibility)) chance, possibilité f, e.g., **one chance in four** une chance sur quatre; (opportunity) occasion f, chance; **by chance** par hasard, fortuitement; **chances** chances fpl, sort m; **to take a chance** encourir un risque; acheter un billet de loterie; **to take chances** jouer gros jeu ‖ tr hasarder, risquer ‖ intr—**to chance to** venir à, avoir l'occasion de; **to chance upon** rencontrer par hasard

chance' acquaint'ance s connaissance f de rencontre

chancel ['t∫ænsəl] s chœur m, sanctuaire m

chanceller•y ['t∫ænsələri] s (pl -ies) chancellerie f

chancellor ['t∫ænsələr] s chancelier m, ministre m

chancre ['∫æŋkər] s chancre m

chandelier [,∫ændə'lɪr] s lustre m

change [t∫end3] s changement m; (coins) pièces fpl rendues, monnaie f; **change in the wind** saute f de vent; **change of address** changement de domicile; **change of clothes** vêtements mpl de rechange; **for a change** comme distraction; pour changer ‖ tr changer; changer de, e.g., **to change religions** changer de culte; **to change sides** tourner casaque ‖ intr changer; (said of voice at puberty) muer; **to change over** (e.g., from one system to another) passer

changeable ['t∫end3əbəl] adj changeable; (weather) variable; (character) changeant, mobile

changeless ['t∫end3lɪs] adj immuable

change' of life' s retour m d'âge

change' of voice' s mue f

change' o'ver s changement m, renversement m, relève f

change' purse' s porte-monnaie m

change' return' s remboursement m dans le bas de l'appareil, retour m de monnaies

chan•nel ['t∫ænəl] s (body of water joining two others) canal m; (bed of river) chenal m; (means of communication) voie f, canal; (passage) conduit m; (groove) cannelure f; (strait) bras m de mer; (for trade) débouché m; (rad) canal; (rad, telv) chaîne f; (telv) canal (Canad); **through channels** par la voie hiérarchique, par la filière ‖ v (pret & pp -neled ou -nelled; ger -neling ou -nelling) tr creuser, canneler

Chan•nel Is'lands spl îles fpl Anglo-Normandes

chant [t∫ænt] s (song; singing) chant m; (monotonous chant) mélopée f; (chanted by demonstrators) chant scandé; (mus) psalmodie f, plain-chant m ‖ tr & intr psalmodier

chanter ['t∫æntər] s chantre m

chantey ['∫ænti] s chanson f de bord

chaos ['ke•as] s chaos m

chaotic [ke'atɪk] adj chaotique

chap [t∫æp] s (fissure, crack) crevasse f, gerçure f; (coll) type m, individu m; **poor chap** (coll) pauvre vieux m; pauvre garçon m ‖ v (pret & pp chapped; ger chapping) tr crevasser, gercer ‖ intr se crevasser, se gercer

chapel ['t∫æpəl] s chapelle f; (in a house) oratoire m; (Protestant chapel) temple m

chaperon ['∫æpə,ron] s chaperon m, duègne f ‖ tr chaperonner

chaplain ['t∫æplɪn] s aumônier m

chaplet ['t∫æplɪt] s chapelet m

chapter ['t∫æptər] s chapitre m; (of an association) bureau m régional

char [t∫ar] v (pret & pp charred; ger charring) tr & intr charbonner; **to become charred** se charbonner, se carboniser

character ['kærɪktər] s caractère m; (theat) personnage m; (typ) signe m; (coll) type m, sujet m, numéro m, phénomène m

char'acter ac'tor s acteur m de genre

char'acter assas'sination s assassinat m du caractère

characteristic [,kærɪktə'rɪstɪk] adj & s caractéristique f

characterize ['kærɪktə,raɪz] tr caractériser, typer

char'acter ref'erence s certificat m de moralité, certificat de bonne vie et mœurs

char'coal' s charbon m de bois

char'coal burn'er s charbonnier m

char'coal pen'cil s charbon m, crayon m de fusain

charge [t∫ard3] s (responsibility) charge f; (cost) prix m; (person cared for) personne f à charge; (thing cared for) chose f à charge; (accusing) accusation f; (against a defendant) chef m d'accusation; (made to a jury) résumé m; (mil) charge; **on a charge of** sous l'inculpation de; **to reverse the charges** téléphoner en p.c.v.; **to take charge of** se charger de; **without charge** gratis ‖ tr charger; **to charge s.o. sth. for sth.** prendre or demander q.ch. à qn pour q.ch.; **to charge to s.o.'s account** mettre sur le compte de qn ‖ intr (mil) charger; **to charge down on** foncer sur

charge' account' s compte m courant

charger ['t∫ard3ər] s cheval m de bataille; (elec) chargeur m

chariot ['t∫ærɪ•ət] s char m

charioteer [,t∫ærɪ•ə'tɪr] s conducteur m de char

charisma [kə'rɪzmə] s charme m, don m de plaire; (theol) charisme m

charismatic [kærɪz'mætɪk] adj charismatique

charitable ['t∫ærɪtəbəl] adj charitable

chari•ty ['t∫ærɪti] s (pl -ties) (kindness) charité f; (action) acte m de charité; (alms) bienfaisance f, aumônes fpl, charité; (institution) société f or œuvre f de bienfaisance; **for charity's sake** par charité

charlatan ['∫arlətən] s charlatan m

charm [t∫arm] s charme m; (e.g., on a bracelet) breloque f, porte-bonheur m ‖ tr charmer

charm' brac'elet s bracelet m à breloques

charming [ˈtʃɑrmɪŋ] *adj* charmeur, charmant
charnel [ˈtʃɑrnəl] *adj* de charnier ‖ *s* charnier *m*, ossuaire *m*
chart [tʃɑrt] *s* (*map*) carte *f;* (*graph*) dessin *m* graphique; (*diagram*) diagramme *m;* (*table*) tableau *m* ‖ *tr* inscrire sur un dessin graphique; (*naut*) porter sur une carte, dresser la carte de
charter [ˈtʃɑrtər] *s* (*document*) charte *f;* (*authorization*) statuts *mpl;* (*of a bank*) privilège; (*chartering of a boat, bus, plane, etc.*) affrètement *m* ‖ *tr* accorder une charte à; (*a ship*) affréter, noliser; (*a bus*) louer
char′ter flight′ *s* vol *m* en charter, vol *m* à la demande
char′ter mem′ber *s* membre *m* fondateur
char′ter plane′ *s* charter *m*, avion *m* affété, avion nolisé
char′wom′an *s* (*pl* **-wom′en**) nettoyeuse *f*
chase [tʃes] *s* chasse *f*, poursuite *f;* (*for printing*) châssis *m* ‖ *tr* chasser; (*a gem*) enchâsser; (*gold*) ciseler; (*metal*) repousser; **to chase away** chasser ‖ *intr*—**to chase after** pourchasser, poursuivre
chaser [ˈtʃesər] *s* chasseur *m;* (*of women*) (coll) coureur *m;* (*taken after an alcoholic drink*) (coll) rince-gueule *m*
chasm [ˈkæzəm] *s* abîme *m*
chas•sis [ˈtʃæsi] *s* (*pl* **-sis** [siz]) châssis *m*
chaste [tʃest] *adj* chaste
chasten [ˈtʃesən] *tr* châtier
chastise [tʃæsˈtaɪz] *tr* châtier, corriger
chastisement [tʃæsˈtaɪzmənt] *s* châtiment *m*
chastity [ˈtʃæstɪtɪ] *s* chasteté *f*
chat [tʃæt] *s* causerie *f*, causette *f* ‖ *v* (*pret & pp* **chatted;** *ger* **chatting**) *intr* causer, bavarder
château [ʃæto] *s* château *m*, manoir *m*, castel *m*
chat′ room′ *s* (comp) chat *m*
chat′ serv′er *s* (comp) serveur *m* de chat
chattel [ˈtʃætəl] *s* bien *m* meuble, objet *m* mobiliaire
chatter [ˈtʃætər] *s* bavardage *m*, caquetage *m* ‖ *intr* bavarder, caqueter; (*said of teeth*) claquer
chat′ter•box′ *s* bavard *m*, babillard *m*
chauffeur [ˈʃofər] *s* chauffeur *m*
chauvinist [ˈʃovɪnɪst] *adj & mf* (pol) chauvin *m*, chauvine *f* ‖ *adj & m* (*sexist*) machiste *m*, phallocrate *m*
chauvinistic [ˌʃovɪˈnɪstɪk] *adj* chauvin
cheap [tʃip] *adj* bon marché; (coll) honteux; **to get off cheap** (coll) en être quitte à bon compte
cheapen [ˈtʃipən] *tr* baisser le prix de; diminuer la valeur de
cheap′skate′ *s* (slang) rat *m*
cheat [tʃit] *s* tricheur *m*, fraudeur *m* ‖ *tr* tricher, frauder ‖ *intr* (*e.g., at cards*) tricher; (*e.g., in an examination*) frauder
cheating [ˈtʃitɪŋ] *s* tricherie *f*, fraude *f*
check [tʃɛk] *s* (*stopping*) arrêt *m;* (*brake*) frein *m;* (*supervision*) contrôle *m*, vérification *f;* (*in a restaurant*) addition *f;* (*drawn on a bank*) chèque *m;* (*e.g., of a chessboard*) carreau *m;*

(*of the king in chess*) échec *m;* (*for baggage*) bulletin *m;* (*pass-out check*) contremarque *f;* (*chip, counter*) jeton *m;* **in check** en échec ‖ *tr* arrêter, freiner; contrôler, vérifier; (*baggage*) faire enregistrer; (*e.g., one's coat*) mettre au vestiaire; (*the king in chess*) faire échec à; **to check off** pointer, cocher ‖ *intr* s'arrêter; **to check in** (*at a hotel*) s'inscrire sur le registre; **to check out** (*of a hotel*) régler sa note; **to check up on** contrôler, examiner
check′book′ *s* carnet *m* de chèques, chéquier *m*
checked *adj* (*checkered*) à carreaux; (*syllable*) entravé
checker [ˈtʃɛkər] *s* (*inspector*) contrôleur *m;* (*piece used in game*) pion *m;* (*square of checkerboard*) carreau *m;* **checkers** jeu *m* de dames ‖ *tr* (*to divide in squares*) quadriller; (*to scatter here and there*) diaprer
check′er•board′ *s* damier *m*
checkered *adj* (*divided into squares*) quadrillé, à carreaux; (*varied*) varié, accidenté; (*career, life*) plein de vicissitudes, mouvementé
check′girl′ *s* préposée *f* au vestiaire
check′ing account′ *s* compte *m* en banque
check′ list′ *s* liste *f* de contrôle, liste de vérification
check′ mark′ *s* trait *m* de repère, repère *m*, coche *f*
check′mate′ *s* échec et mat *m;* (fig) échec *m* ‖ *tr* faire échec et mat à, mater ‖ *intr* faire échec et mat, mater ‖ *interj* échec et mat!
check′-out count′er *s* caisse *f* de sortie; (*in supermarket*) caisse de supermarché
check′point′ *s* contrôle *m* de police
check′room′ *s* (*cloakroom*) vestiaire *m;* (*baggage room*) consigne *f*
check′up′ *s* vérification *f*, examen *m* complet; (med) bilan *m* de santé
cheek [tʃik] *s* joue *f;* (coll) aplomb *m*, toupet *m*
cheek′bone′ *s* pommette *f*
cheep [tʃip] *intr* piauler
cheer [tʃir] *s* bonne humeur *f*, gaieté *f;* encouragement *m*, e.g., **word of cheer** parole *f* d'encouragement; **cheers** acclamations *fpl*, bravos *mpl*, vivats *mpl;* **three cheers for . . .!** vive . . .!; **to give three cheers** pousser trois hourras ‖ *tr* (*to cheer up*) encourager, égayer; (*to applaud*) acclamer, applaudir ‖ *intr* pousser des vivats, applaudir; **cheer up!** courage!
cheerful [ˈtʃirfəl] *adj* de bonne humeur, gai; (*place*) d'aspect agréable
cheerfully [ˈtʃirfəli] *adv* gaiement; (*willingly*) de bon cœur
cheer′lead′er *s* chef *m* de claque
cheerless [ˈtʃirlɪs] *adj* morne, triste
cheese [tʃiz] *s* fromage *m*
cheese′bur′ger *s* cheeseburger *m* (*hamburger auquel on ajoute du fromage*)
cheese′cake′ *s* (slang) les pin up *fpl*
cheese′ cake′ *s* soufflé *m* au fromage, tarte *f* au fromage
cheese′cloth′ *s* gaze *f*
cheese′ spread′ *s* fromage *m* à tartiner

chees•y [ˈtʃizi] adj (comp **-ier;** super **-iest**) caséeux; (slang) miteux

cheetah [ˈtʃitə] s guépard m

chef [ʃɛf] s chef m de cuisine, maître queux m

chemical [ˈkɛmɪkəl] adj chimique ‖ s produit m chimique

chem′ical en′gineer′ s ingénieur m chimiste

chem′ical war′fare s guerre f chimique

chemise [ʃəˈmiz] s chemise f de femme; (dress) robe-chemisier f

chemist [ˈkɛmɪst] s chimiste mf

chemistry [ˈkɛmɪstri] s chimie f

chemotherapy [ˌkimoˈθɛrəpi] s chimiothérapie f

cherish [ˈtʃɛriʃ] tr chérir; (an idea) nourrir; (a hope) caresser

cher•ry [ˈtʃɛri] s (pl **-ries**) cerise f; (tree) cerisier m

cher′ry or′chard s cerisaie f

cher′ry tree′ s cerisier m

cher•ub [ˈtʃɛrəb] s (pl **-ubim** [əbɪm]) chérubin m ‖ s (pl **-ubs**) (fig) chérubin m

chess [tʃɛs] s échecs mpl; **to play chess** jouer aux échecs

chess′board′ s échiquier m

chess′ piece′ s pièce f du jeu d'échecs; (other than pawn) figure f

chess′ play′er s joueur m d'échecs

chess′ set′ s échecs mpl

chest [tʃɛst] s caisse f; (of drawers) commode f; (anat) poitrine f; **to get s.th. off one's chest** (coll) se déboutonner, dire ce qu'on a sur le cœur

chest′ mic′rophone s micro-plastron m

chestnut [ˈtʃɛsnət] adj (color) châtain ‖ s (color) châtain m; (nut) châtaigne f, marron m; (tree) châtaignier m

chest′ of drawers′ s commode f, chiffonnier m

cheval′ glass′ [ʃəˈvæl] s psyché f

chevron [ˈʃɛvrən] s chevron m

chew [tʃu] tr mâcher; (tobacco) chiquer

chewing [ˈtʃuɪŋ] s mastication f

chew′ing gum′ s gomme f à mâcher, chewing-gum m

chic [ʃik] adj & s chic m

chicaner•y [ʃɪˈkɛnəri] s (pl **-ies**) truc m, ruse f, artifice m

chick [tʃik] s poussin m; (girl) (slang) tendron m, nana f

chickadee [ˈtʃikəˌdi] s (Parus atricapillus) mésange f boréale

chicken [ˈtʃikən] s poulet m; **to be chicken** (slang) avoir la frousse ‖ intr—**to chicken out** (slang) caner

chick′en coop′ s poulailler m

chick′en-heart′ed adj froussard, poltron

chick′en pox′ s varicelle f

chick′en stew′ s poule-au-pot m

chick′en wire′ s treillis m métallique

chick′ pea′ s pois m chiche

chico•ry [ˈtʃikəri] s (pl **-ries**) chicorée f

chide [tʃaɪd] v (pret **chided** or **chid** [tʃid]; pp

chided, chid, or **chidden** [ˈtʃidən]) tr & intr gronder

chief [tʃif] adj principal, en chef ‖ s chef m; (boss) (coll) patron m

chief′ exec′utive s chef m de l'exécutif

chief′ jus′tice s président m de la Cour suprême

chiefly [ˈtʃifli] adv principalement

chief′ of police′ s préfet m de police

chief′ of staff′ s chef m d'état-major

chief′ of state′ s chef m d'État

chieftain [ˈtʃiftən] s chef m

chiffon [ʃɪˈfɑn] s mousseline f de soie

chiffonier [ˌʃifəˈnɪr] s chiffonnier m

chilblain [ˈtʃilˌblen] s engelure f

child [tʃaɪld] s (pl **children** [ˈtʃildrən]) enfant mf; **with child** enceinte

child′ abuse′ s abus m d'enfant, détournement m de mineur

child′ molest′ing [moˈlɛstɪŋ] s détournement m de mineur

child′birth′ s accouchement m

child′hood′ s enfance f

childish [ˈtʃaɪldɪʃ] adj enfantin, puéril

child′ la′bor s travail m des enfants

child′like′ adj enfantin, d'enfant

child′s′ play′ s jeu m d'enfant; **it's child's play** c'est l'enfance de l'art

child′ snatch′ing s (coll) enlèvement m d'enfant or de mineur

child′ wel′fare s protection f de l'enfance

Chile [ˈtʃili] s le Chili

chil′i pep′per [ˈtʃili] s piment m

chill [tʃil] adj & s froid m; **sudden chill** saisissement m, coup m de froid; **to take the chill off** faire tiédir ‖ tr refroidir; (a person) transir, faire frissonner; (wine) frapper

chill′ fac′tor s indice m de refroidissement

chill•y [ˈtʃili] adj (comp **-ier;** super **-iest**) froid; (sensitive to cold) frileux; **it is chilly** il fait frisquet, il fait frais

chime [tʃaɪm] s coup m de son; **chimes** (at doorway) sonnerie f; (in bell tower) carillon m ‖ tr & intr carillonner; **to chime in** faire chorus

chimera [kaɪˈmɪrə] s chimère f

chiming [ˈtʃaɪmɪŋ] s carillonnement m, sonnerie f

chimney [ˈtʃimni] s cheminée f; (of lamp) verre m

chim′ney pot′ s abat-vent m, mitre f

chim′ney sweep′ s ramoneur m

chimpanzee [tʃimˈpænzi] s chimpanzé m

chin [tʃin] s menton m; **to take it on the chin** (coll) encaisser des coups, encaisser des critiques

china [ˈtʃaɪnə] s porcelaine f de Chine; **China** Chine f; la Chine

chi′na clos′et s vitrine f

Chi•na•town [ˈtʃaɪnəˌtaʊn] s quartier chinois

chi′na•ware′ s porcelaine f

Chi•nese [tʃaɪˈniz] adj chinois ‖ s (language) chinois m ‖ s (pl **-nese**) Chinois m (person)

Chi′nese lan′tern s lanterne f vénitienne, lampion m

Chi′nese puz′zle *s* casse-tête *m invar* chinois

chink [tʃɪŋk] *s* fente *f,* crevasse *f;* **chink in one's armor** (coll) défaut *m* de la cuirasse

chin′ strap′ *s* sous-mentonnière *f,* jugulaire *f*

chip [tʃɪp] *s* fragment *m; (of wood)* copeau *m,* éclat *m; (in gambling)* jeton *m;* (electron) microplaquette *f,* pastille *f,* chip *m;* **chips** (*potato chips*) pommes *fpl* chips; (Brit) (*french fries*) frites *fpl;* **to be a chip off the old block** (coll) chasser de race, être un rejeton de la vieille souche ‖ *v (pret & pp* **chipped;** *ger* **chipping)** *tr* enlever un copeau à ‖ *intr* s'écailler; **to chip in** contribuer

chipmunk [ˈtʃɪp,mʌŋk] *s* tamias *m* rayé

chipper [ˈtʃɪpər] *adj* (coll) en forme, guilleret

chiropodist [kaɪˈrɑpədɪst] *s* pédicure *mf*

chiropractic [ˈkaɪrə,præktɪk] *s* la chiropraxie

chiropractor [ˈkaɪrə,præktər] *s* chiropracteur *m*

chirp [tʃʌrp] *s* gazouillis *m,* pépiement *m* ‖ *intr* gazouiller, pépier

chis•el [ˈtʃɪzəl] *s* ciseau *m* ‖ *v (pret & pp* **-eled** or **-elled;** *ger* **-eling** or **-elling)** *tr* ciseler; (*a person*) (slang) escroquer, carotter; **to chisel s.o. out of s.th.** (slang) escroquer q.ch. à qn

chiseler [ˈtʃɪzələr] *s* ciseleur *m;* (slang) escroc *m*

chit [tʃɪt] *s* note *f,* ticket *m;* (coll) gamin *m*

chit′-chat′ *s* bavardage *m*

chivalrous [ˈʃɪvəlrəs] *adj* honorable, courtois; (lit) chevaleresque

chivalry [ˈʃɪvəlri] *s (of Middle Ages)* chevalerie *f;* (*politeness*) courtoisie *f,* galanterie *f*

chive [tʃaɪv] *s* ciboulette *f,* civette *f*

chloride [ˈkloraɪd] *s* chlorure *m*

chlorinate [ˈklorɪ,net] *tr* (*water*) verduniser

chlorination [,klorɪˈneʃən] *s* verdunisation *f*

chlorine [ˈklorin] *s* chlore *m*

chloroform [ˈklorə,form] *s* chloroforme *m* ‖ *tr* chloroformer

chlorophyll [ˈklorəfɪl] *s* chlorophylle *f*

chock [tʃɑk] *s* cale *f;* (naut) poulie *f* ‖ *tr* caler

chock′-full′ *adj* bondé, comble, bourré

chocolate [ˈtʃɔkəlɪt] *adj & s* chocolat *m*

choc′olate bar′ *s* tablette *f* de chocolat

choice [tʃɔɪs] *adj* de choix, choisi ‖ *m* choix *m;* **by choice** par goût, volontairement

choir [kwaɪr] *s* chœur *m*

choir′boy′ *s* enfant *m* de chœur

choir′ loft′ *s* chœur *m*

choir′mas′ter *s* chef *m* de chœur; (eccl) maître *m* de chapelle

choir′ robe′ *s* soutanelle *f*

choke [tʃok] *s* (aut) starter *m* ‖ *tr* étouffer; (*to obstruct*) obstruer, boucher; **to choke back, down,** or **off** étouffer; **to choke up** obstruer, engorger ‖ *intr* étouffer; **to choke up** (*e.g., with tears*) étouffer

choke′ coil′ *s* (elec) bobine *f* de réactance

choker [ˈtʃokər] *s* (*scarf*) foulard *m;* (*necklace*) collier *m* court

choking [ˈtʃokɪŋ] *s* étouffement *m*

cholera [ˈkɑlərə] *s* choléra *m*

choleric [ˈkɑlərɪk] *adj* coléreux

cholesterol [kəˈlɛstə,rol] *s* cholestérol *m*

choose [tʃuz] *v (pret* **chose** [tʃoz]; *pp* **chosen** [ˈtʃozən]) *tr & intr* choisir

choos•y [ˈtʃuzi] *adj (comp* **-ier;** *super* **-iest)** (coll) difficile à plaire, chipoteur

chop [tʃɑp] *s (blow)* coup *m* de hache; (culin) côtelette *f;* **to lick one's chops** (coll) se lécher or s'essuyer les babines ‖ *v (pret & pp* **chopped;** *ger* **chopping)** *tr* hacher, couper; **to chop down** abattre; **to chop off** trancher, couper; **to chop up** couper en morceaux, hacher ‖ *intr (said of waves)* clapoter

chopper [ˈtʃɑpər] *s (of butcher)* couperet *m;* (coll) hélicoptère *m;* **choppers** (slang) les dents *fpl*

chop′ping block′ *s* billot *m,* hachoir *m*

chop•py [ˈtʃɑpi] *adj (comp* **-pier;** *ger* **-piest)** agité; (*waves*) clapoteux

chop′stick′ *s* baguette *f,* bâtonnet *m*

choral [ˈkorəl] *adj* choral

chorale [koˈral] *s* choral *m*

cho′ral soci′ety *s* chorale *f*

chord [kɔrd] *s* accord *m;* (geom) corde *f*

chore [tʃor] *s* devoir *m;* (*burdensome chore*) corvée *f,* besogne *f*

choreography [,kɔriˈɑgrəfi] *s* chorégraphie *f*

chorister [ˈkɔrɪstər] *s* choriste *mf*

chortle [ˈtʃɔrtəl] *intr* glousser

chorus [ˈkorəs] *s* (*group*) chœur *m,* chorale *f;* (*of song*) refrain *m;* (*of protest*) concert *m* ‖ *tr* répéter en chœur, faire chorus

cho′rus boy′ *s* boy *m*

cho′rus girl′ *s* girl *f*

cho′sen few′ [ˈtʃozən] *s* élite *f*

chow [tʃaʊ] *s (dog)* chow-chow *m;* (mil) boustifaille *f,* mangeaille *f*

chow′-chow′ *s* (culin) macédoine *f* assaisonnée

chowder [ˈtʃaʊdər] *s* soupe *f* au poisson

Christ [kraɪst] *s* Christ *m;* le Christ

christen [ˈkrɪsən] *tr* baptiser

Christendom [ˈkrɪsəndəm] *s* chrétienté *f*

christening [ˈkrɪsənɪŋ] *s* baptême *m*

Christian [ˈkrɪstʃən] *adj & s* chrétien *m*

Christianity [,krɪstʃiˈænɪti] *s* christianisme *m*

Christianize [ˈkrɪstʃəˈnaɪz] *tr* christianiser

Christ′ian name′ *s* nom *m* de baptême

Christmas [ˈkrɪsməs] *adj* de Noël ‖ *s* Noël *m;* **Merry Christmas!** Joyeux Noël!

Christ′mas card′ *s* carte *f* de Noël

Christ′mas car′ol *s* chanson *f* de Noël, chant *m* de Noël; (eccl) cantique *m* de Noël

Christ′mas Day′ *s* le jour de Noël

Christ′mas Eve′ *s* la veille de Noël

Christ′mas gift′ *s* cadeau *m* de Noël

Christ′mas tree′ *s* arbre *m* de Noël

Christ′mas tree lights′ *spl* guirlandes *fpl*

chromatic [kroˈmætɪk] *adj* chromatique

chrome [krom] *adj* chromé ‖ *s* acier *m* chromé; (*color*) jaune *m;* (chem) chrome *m* ‖ *tr* chromer

chromium [ˈkromɪ•əm] *s* chrome *m*

chromosome [ˈkromə,som] *s* chromosome *m*

chronic [ˈkrɑnɪk] *adj* chronique

chronicle [ˈkrɑnɪkəl] s chronique f ‖ tr faire la chronique de

chronicler [ˈkrɑnɪklər] s chroniqueur m

chronologic(al) [ˌkrɑnəˈlɑdʒɪk(əl)] adj chronologique

chronolo‧gy [krəˈnɑlədʒi] s (pl -gies) chronologie f

chronometer [krəˈnɑmɪtər] s chronomètre m

chrysanthemum [krɪˈsænθɪməm] s chrysanthème m

chub‧by [ˈtʃʌbi] adj (comp **-bier**; super **-biest**) joufflu, potelé, dodu

chuck [tʃʌk] s (tap, blow, etc.) petite tape f; (under the chin) caresse f sous le menton; (of lathe) mandrin m; (bottom chuck and chuck rib) paleron m; (top chuck roast and chuck rib) entrecôte f ‖ tr tapoter; **to chuck away** jeter

chuckle [ˈtʃʌkəl] s gloussement m, petit rire m ‖ intr glousser, rire tout bas

chum [tʃʌm] s (coll) copain m ‖ v (pret & pp **chummed**; ger **chumming**) intr—**to chum around with** (coll) fraterniser avec

chum‧my [ˈtʃʌmi] adj (comp **-mier**; super **-miest**) intime, familier

chump [tʃʌmp] s (slang) ballot m, lourdaud m

chunk [tʃʌŋk] s gros morceau m; (e.g., of wood) bloc m

church [tʃʌrtʃ] s église f

church′go′er s pratiquant m

church′man s (pl **-men**) (clergyman) ecclésiastique m; (layman) membre m d'une église, fidèle mf, paroissien m

church′ mem′ber s fidèle mf

church′ ser′vice s office m, culte m

church′yard′ s cimetière m

churlish [ˈtʃʌrlɪʃ] adj rustre, grossier; (out of sorts) grincheux

churn [tʃʌrn] s baratte f ‖ tr (cream) baratter; (e.g., water) agiter; **to churn butter** battre le beurre ‖ intr bouillonner

chute [ʃut] s (inclined channel or trough) glissière f; (of river) rapide m, chute f d'eau; (aer) parachute m

CIA [ˈsiˈaɪˈe] s (letterword) (**Central Intelligence Agency**) (equivalent French agency) S.D.E.C. (service de documentation extérieure et de contre-espionnage)

ciao [tʃau] interj tchao! or ciao!

cicada [sɪˈkɑdə] s cigale f

Cicero [ˈsɪsəˌro] s Cicéron m

cider [ˈsaɪdər] s cidre m

cigar [sɪˈgɑr] s cigare m

cigarette [ˌsɪgəˈrɛt] s cigarette f

cigarette′ butt′ s mégot m

cigarette′ case′ s étui m à cigarettes

cigarette′ fiend′ s fumeur m enragé

cigarette′ hold′er s fume-cigarette m

cigarette′ light′er s briquet m

cigarette′ pa′per s papier m à cigarettes

cigarette′ tax′ s taxe f sur le tabac

cigar′ hold′er s fume-cigare m

cigar′ store′ s bureau m de tabac

cinch [sɪntʃ] s (of saddle) sangle f; **it's a cinch** (coll) c'est couru d'avance ‖ tr sangler; (to make sure of) (slang) assurer

cinder [ˈsɪndər] s cendre f ‖ tr cendrer

Cinderella [ˌsɪndəˈrɛlə] s la Cendrillon f

cin′der track′ s piste f cendrée

cinema [ˈsɪnəmə] s cinéma m

cinnamon [ˈsɪnəmən] s cannelle f

cipher [ˈsaɪfər] s zéro m; (code) chiffre m; **in cipher** en chiffres ‖ tr & intr chiffrer

circle [ˈsʌrkəl] s cercle m; (coterie) milieu m, monde m; **to have circles around the eyes** avoir les yeux cernés ‖ tr ceindre, entourer; (to travel around) faire le tour de

circuit [ˈsʌrkɪt] s circuit m; (of judge) tournée f

cir′cuit break′er s (switch) interrupteur m; (protection against excessive current) disjoncteur m

cir′cuit court′ s cour f d'assises

circuitous [sərˈkjuˈɪtəs] adj détourné, indirect

circuit‧ry [ˈsʌrkətri] s (pl **-ries**) système m de circuits

circular [ˈsʌrkjələr] adj & s circulaire f

circulate [ˈsʌrkjəˌlet] tr faire circuler ‖ intr circuler

circulation [ˌsʌrkjəˈleʃən] s circulation f; (of newspaper) tirage m

circumcise [ˈsʌrkəmˌsaɪz] tr circoncire

circumcision [ˌsʌrkəmˈsɪʒən] s circoncision f

circumference [sərˈkʌmfərəns] s circonférence f

circumflex [ˈsʌrkəmˌflɛks] adj & s circonflexe m

circumlocution [ˌsʌrkəmloˈkjuʃən] s circonlocution f

circumscribe [ˌsʌrkəmˈskraɪb] tr circonscrire

circumspect [ˈsʌrkəmˌspɛkt] adv circonspect

circumstance [ˈsʌrkəmˌstæns] s circonstance f; (pomp) cérémonie f; **in easy circumstances** aisé; **under no circumstance** sous aucun prétexte; **under the circumstances** dans ces conditions

circumstantial [ˌsʌrkəmˈstænʃəl] adj (derived from circumstances) circonstanciel; (detailed) circonstancié

cir′cumstan′tial ev′idence s preuves fpl indirectes

circumvent [ˌsʌrkəmˈvɛnt] tr circonvenir

circus [ˈsʌrkəs] s cirque m; (Brit) rond-point m

cirrhosis [sɪˈrosɪs] s cirrhose f

cistern [ˈsɪstərn] s citerne f

citadel [ˈsɪtədəl] s citadelle f

citation [saɪˈteʃən] s citation f; (award) présentation f, mention f

cite [saɪt] tr citer

cither [ˈsɪθər] s cithare f

citified [ˈsɪtɪˌfaɪd] adj urbain

citizen [ˈsɪtɪzən] s citoyen m

citizen‧ry [ˈsɪtɪzənri] s (pl **-ries**) citoyens mpl

cit′izen‧ship′ s citoyenneté f

citric [ˈsɪtrɪk] adj citrique

citron [ˈsɪtrən] s cédrat m; (tree) cédratier m

citronella [ˌsɪtrə'nɛlə] *s* citronnelle *f*

cit′rus fruit′ ['sɪtrəs] *s* agrumes *mpl*

cit•y ['sɪti] *s* (*pl* **-ies**) ville *f;* **the City** (*district within ancient boundaries*) la Cité

cit′y cen′ter *s* centre *m,* coeur *m* ou noyau *m* de la ville; (*public building*) grande salle *f* municipale; (*concert hall*) salle municipale de concert

cit′y coun′cil *s* conseil *m* municipal

cit′y hall′ *s* hôtel *m* de ville

cit′y man′ager *s* directeur *m* des services municipaux

cit′y plan′ner *s* urbaniste *mf*

cit′y plan′ning *s* urbanisme *m*

cit′y room′ *s* (journ) salle *f* de rédaction

civ′et cat′ ['sɪvɪt] *s* civette *f*

civic ['sɪvɪk] *adj* civique; **civics** instruction *f* civique

civies ['sɪviz] *spl* (coll) vêtements *mpl* civils; **in civies** en civil, en bourgeois

civil ['sɪvɪl] *adj* civil; (*courteous*) poli

civ′il defense′ *s* protection *f* civile

civ′il engineer′ing *s* génie *m* civil

civilian [sɪ'vɪljən] *adj* & *s* civil *m*

civil′ian life′ *s* vie *f* civile

civili•ty [sɪ'vɪlɪti] *s* (*pl* **-ties**) civilité *f*

civilization [ˌsɪvɪlɪ'zeʃən] *s* civilisation *f*

civilize ['sɪvɪˌlaɪz] *tr* civiliser

civ′il rights′ *spl* droits *mpl* civiques, droits politiques

civ′il ser′vant *s* fonctionnaire *mf*

civ′il serv′ice *s* fonction *f* publique

civ′il war′ *s* guerre *f* civile; **Civil War** (*of the United States*) Guerre de Sécession

clack [klæk] *s* claquement *m* ‖ *intr* claquer

clad [klæd] *adj* vêtu, habillé

claim [klem] *s* (*request*) demande *f;* (*to a right*) revendication *f;* (*assertion*) affirmation *f;* (*right*) droit *m,* titre *m;* (*insurance claim*) déclaration de sinistre, demande d'indemnité; (*in prospecting*) concession *f* ‖ *tr* (*a right*) réclamer, revendiquer; (*to require*) exiger, demander; **to claim that ...** prétendre que ...; **to claim to** prétendre

claimant ['klemənt] *s* prétendant *m,* ayant droit *m*

clairvoyance [klɛr'vɔɪ•əns] *s* voyance *f,* seconde vue *f;* (*keen insight*) clairvoyance *f*

clairvoyant [klɛr'vɔɪ•ənt] *adj* clairvoyant ‖ *s* voyante *f;* voyant *m*

clam [klæm] *s* palourde *f* ‖ *v* (*pret* & *pp* **clammed;** *ger* **clamming**) *intr*—**to clam up** (slang) se taire

clam′bake′ *s* pique-nique *m* aux palourdes

clamber ['klæmbər] *intr* grimper; **to clamber over** or **up** escalader

clam•my ['klæmi] *adj* (*comp* **-mier;** *super* **-miest**) moite; (*clinging*) collant

clamor ['klæmər] *s* clameur *f* ‖ *intr* vociférer; **to clamor for** réclamer

clamorous ['klæmərəs] *adj* bruyant

clamp [klæmp] *s* crampon *m,* agrafe *f;* (med) clamp *m* ‖ *tr* fixer, attacher; **to clamp to-gether** cramponner ‖ *intr*—**to clamp down on** (coll) visser

clan [klæn] *s* clan *m*

clandestine [klæn'dɛstɪn] *adj* clandestin

clang [klæŋ] *s* bruit *m* métallique, choc *m* retentissant, cliquetis *m* ‖ *tr* faire résonner ‖ *intr* résonner

clank [klæŋk] *s* bruit *m* sec, bruit métallique, cliquetis *m* ‖ *tr* faire résonner ‖ *intr* résonner

clannish ['klænɪʃ] *adj* partisan

clap [klæp] *s* (*sound*) bruit *m* sec, claquement *m;* (*action*) tape *f;* (*with the hands*) battement *m* ‖ *v* (*pret* & *pp* **clapped;** *ger* **clapping**) *tr* battre; (*into jail*) (coll) fourrer; **to clap the hands** claquer or battre les mains ‖ *intr* applaudir, claquer

clapper ['klæpər] *s* (*person*) applaudisseur *m;* (*of bell*) battant *m*

clapping [klæpɪŋ] *s* (*applause*) applaudissements *mpl*

claque [klæk] *s* (*paid clappers*) claque *f;* (*crush hat*) claque *m*

claret ['klærɪt] *s* bordeaux *m*

clari•fy ['klærɪˌfaɪ] *v* (*pret* & *pp* **-fied**) *tr* clarifier

clarinet [ˌklærɪ'nɛt] *s* clarinette *f*

clarity ['klærɪti] *s* clarté *f*

clash [klæʃ] *s* (*sound*) bruit *m* métallique; (*conflict*) dispute *f,* heurt *m,* choc *m;* (*between people; with police*) accrochage *m;* (*of colors*) disparate *f* ‖ *intr* se heurter, s'entre-choquer; (*said of colors*) former une disparate

clasp [klæsp] *s* (*on brooch, necklace, purse*) agrafe *f,* fermoir *m;* (*embrace*) étreinte *f* ‖ *tr* agrafer; (*to embrace*) étreindre

clasp′ knife′ *s* couteau *m* pliant

class [klæs] *s* classe *f* ‖ *tr* classer

class′ ac′tion suit′ *s* (law) procès *m* collectif

classic ['klæsɪk] *adj* & *s* classique *m*

classical ['klæsɪkəl] *adj* classique

classicism ['klæsɪˌsɪzəm] *s* classicisme *m*

classicist ['klæsɪsɪst] *s* classique *mf*

classification [ˌklæsɪfɪ'keʃən] *s* classification *f,* classement *m*

classified *adj* classifié, classé; (*documents*) secret, confidentiel

clas′sified advertise′ments *spl* petites annonces *fpl*

classi•fy ['klæsɪˌfaɪ] *v* (*pret* & *pp* **-fied**) *tr* classifier

class′mate *s* camarade *mf* de classe

class′room′ *s* salle *f* de classe, classe *f*

class•y ['klæsi] *adj* (*comp* **-ier;** *super* **-iest**) (slang) chic

clatter ['klætər] *s* fracas *m* ‖ *intr* faire un fracas

clause [klɔz] *s* clause *f,* article *m;* (gram) proposition *f*

clavichord ['klævɪˌkɔrd] *s* clavicorde *m*

clavicle ['klævɪkəl] *s* clavicule *f*

claw [klɔ] *s* (*of animal*) griffe *f;* (*of crab*) pince *f;* (*of hammer*) panne *f* fendue ‖ *tr* griffer, déchirer

clay [kle] *s* argile *f,* glaise *f*

clay′ pig′eon s pigeon m d'argile, pigeon de tir

clay′ pipe′ s pipe f en terre

clay′ pit′ s argilière f, glaisière f

clean [klin] adj propre; (precise) net ‖ adv net; tout à fait ‖ tr nettoyer; (fish) vider; (streets) balayer; **to clean out** curer; (a person) (slang) mettre à sec, décaver; **to clean up** nettoyer ‖ intr faire le nettoyage

clean′ and jerk′ s (weightlifting) épaulé-jeté m

clean′ bill′ of health′ s état m parfait de santé

clean′-cut′ adj bien délimité, net; (e.g., athlete) bien découplé

cleaner [`klinər] s (person) nettoyeur m, dégraisseur m; (cleaning agent) nettoyant m; **to be taken to the cleaners** (slang) se faire rincer

cleaning [`klinɪŋ] s nettoyage m

clean′ing flu′id s détachant m

clean′ing wom′an s femme f de ménage

cleanliness [`klɛnlɪnɪs] s propreté f, netteté f

cleanse [klɛnz] tr nettoyer, écurer; (e.g., a wound) assainir; (e.g., one's thoughts) purifier

cleanser [`klɛnzər] s produit m de nettoyage; (soap) détersif m

clean′-shav′en adj rasé de frais

cleans′ing cream′ s crème f de démaquillage

clean′up′ s nettoiement m

clear [klɪr] adj clair; (sharp) net; (free) dégagé, libre; (unmortgaged) franc d'hypothèque; **to become clear** s'éclaircir; **to keep clear of** éviter ‖ tr (to brighten) éclaircir; (e.g., a fence) franchir; (obstacles) dégager; (land) défricher; (goods in customs) dédouaner; (an account) solder; (a check) compenser; **to clear away** écarter, enlever; **to clear oneself** se disculper; **to clear out** (e.g., a garden) jardiner; **to clear the table** desservir, enlever le couvert, ôter la nappe; **to clear up** éclaircir ‖ intr (said of weather) s'éclaircir; **my check has cleared** on a compensé mon chèque; **to clear out** (coll) filer, se sauver

clearance [`klɪrəns] s (permission) permis m, laissez-passer m, autorisation f; (between two objects) espace m libre; (aer) clairance f; (com) compensation f; (mach) espace m mort, jeu m

clear′ance sale′ s vente f de soldes

clear′-cut′ adj net, tranché; (case) absolu

clear′-head′ed adj lucide, perspicace

clearing [`klɪrɪŋ] s (in clouds) éclaircie f; (in forest) clairière f, trouée f

clear′ing house′ s (com) comptoir m de règlement, chambre f de compensation

clearness [`klɪrnɪs] s clarté f, netteté f

clear′-sight′ed adj perspicace, clairvoyant

cleat [klit] s taquet m

cleavage [`klivɪdʒ] s clivage m

cleave [kliv] v (pret & pp **cleft** [klɛft] or **cleaved**) tr fendre ‖ intr se fendre; **to cleave to** s'attacher à, adhérer à

cleaver [`klivər] s couperet m, hachoir m

clef [klɛf] s (mus) clef f

cleft [klɛft] adj fendu ‖ s fente f, crevasse f

cleft′ pal′ate s palais m fendu, fissure f palatine

clematis [`klɛmətɪs] s clématite f

clemen•cy [`klɛmənsi] s (pl -cies) clémence f

clement [`klɛmənt] adj clément

clench [klɛntʃ] tr serrer, crisper

cler•gy [`klʌrdʒi] s (pl -gies) (members) clergé m; (profession) clergie f

cler′gy•man s (pl -men) ecclésiastique m, clerc m

cleric [`klɛrɪk] s clerc m, ecclésiastique m

clerical [`klɛrɪkəl] adj clerical; de bureau ‖ s—**clericals** habit m ecclésiastique

cler′ical er′ror s faute f de copiste, faute de sténographe

cler′ical work′ s travail m de bureau

clerk [klʌrk] s (clerical worker) employé m de bureau, commis m; (in lawyer's office) clerc m; (in store) vendeur m; (in bank) comptable mf; (of court) greffier m; (eccl) clerc

clever [`klɛvər] adj habile, adroit

cliché [kli`ʃe] s cliché m, expression f consacrée

click [klɪk] s cliquetis m, clic m; (of heels) bruit m sec; (of tongue) claquement m; (of a machine) déclic m; (comp) clic ‖ intr cliqueter, faire un déclic; (to succeed) (coll) réussir; (to get along well) (coll) s'entendre à merveille; (comp) (with the mouse) faire un clic

client [`klaɪ•ənt] s client m

clientele [ˌklaɪ•ən`tɛl] s clientèle f

cliff [klɪf] s falaise f, talus m raide

climate [`klaɪmɪt] s climat m

climax [`klaɪmæks] s point m culminant, comble m

climb [klaɪm] s montée f, ascension f ‖ tr & intr monter, gravir; grimper; **to climb down** descendre

climber [`klaɪmər] s grimpeur m; (bot) plante f grimpante; (social climber) parvenu m, arriviste mf

climbing [`klaɪmɪŋ] s montée f, escalade f

clinch [klɪntʃ] s (act) rivetage m; (fastener) crampon m, rivet m; (boxing) corps-à-corps m ‖ tr (a nail) river; (a bargain) boucler ‖ intr se prendre corps à corps

clincher [`klɪntʃər] s (coll) argument m sans réplique

cling [klɪŋ] v (pret & pp **clung** [klʌŋ]) intr s'accrocher, se cramponner; **to cling to** (a person) se serrer contre; (a belief) adhérer à

cling′stone peach′ s alberge f

clinic [`klɪnɪk] s clinique f

clinical [`klɪnɪkəl] adj clinique

clinician [klɪ`nɪʃən] s clinicien m

clink [klɪŋk] s cliquetis m; (e.g., of glasses) tintement m, choc m; (jail) (slang) taule f, bloc m ‖ tr (glasses, in a toast) choquer; **to clink glasses with** trinquer avec ‖ intr tinter, cliqueter

clinker [`klɪŋkər] s mâchefer m, scories fpl

clip [klɪp] s (for papers) attache f; (brooch) agrafe f, clip m; (of gun) chargeur m; (blow) (coll) taloche *f; (fast pace)* (coll) pas *m* rapide ‖ *v (pret & pp* **clipped;** *ger* **clipping**) *tr (to fasten)* attacher; *(hair)* rafraîchir; *(sheep)* tondre; *(one's words)* avaler

clip′board′ *s* planchette *f* à papiers attachés

clipper [′klɪpər] *s* (aer) clipper *m;* (naut) voilier *m* de course; **clippers** tondeuse *f*

clipping [′klɪpɪŋ] *s* tondage *m; (of sheep)* tonte *f; (of one's hair)* taille *f; (of newspaper)* coupure *f* (de presse); **clippings** *(cuttings, shavings, etc.)* rognures *fpl,* chutes *fpl*

clip′ping ser′vice *s* argus *m*

clique [klik] *s* coterie *f,* clan *m,* chapelle *f*

clitoris [′klɪtərɪs] *s* clitoris *m*

cloak [klok] *s* manteau *m* ‖ *tr* masquer

cloak′-and-dag′ger *adj (e.g., story)* de cape et d'épée

cloak′room′ *s* vestiaire *m;* (rr) consigne *f*

clock [klɑk] *s (larger type of clock)* horloge *f; (smaller type of clock)* pendule *f; (e.g., in a tower)* horloge; **to turn back the clock** retarder l'horloge; (fig) revenir en arrière ‖ *tr* chronométrer

clock′mak′er *s* horloger *m*

clock′ rad′io *s* radio-réveil *m*

clock′tow′er *s* tour *f* de l'horloge

clock′wise′ *adj & adv* dans le sens des aiguilles d'une montre

clock′work′ *s* mouvement *m* d'horlogerie; **like clockwork** (coll) comme une horloge

clod [klɑd] *s* motte *f; (person)* rustre *mf*

clod′hop′per *s* cul-terreux *m; (shoe)* godillot *m*

clog [klɑg] *s (shoe)* galoche *f,* socque *m; (hindrance)* entrave *f* ‖ *v (pret & pp* **clogged;** *ger* **clogging**) *tr (e.g., a pipe)* boucher; *(e.g., traffic)* entraver ‖ *intr* se boucher

cloister [′klɔɪstər] *s* cloître *m* ‖ *tr* cloîtrer

clone [klon] *s* clone *m;* (comp) clone *m* ‖ *tr* faire du clonage à ‖ *intr* faire du clonage

cloning [′klonɪŋ] *s* clonage *m*

close [klos] *adj* proche, tout près; *(game; weave; formation, order)* serré; *(friend)* intime; *(friendship)* étroit; *(room)* renfermé, étouffant; *(translation)* fidèle; **close to** près de ‖ *adv* près, de près ‖ [kloz] *s (enclosure)* clos *m; (end)* fin *f; (closing)* fermeture *f* ‖ *tr* fermer; *(to end)* conclure, terminer; *(an account)* régler, clôturer; *(ranks)* serrer, resserrer; *(a meeting)* lever; **close quotes** fermez les guillemets; **to close in** enfermer; **to close out** (com) liquider, solder ‖ *intr* se fermer; finir, se terminer; *(on certain days)* (theat) faire relâche; **to close in on** *(the enemy)* aborder

close′ call′ [klos] *s*—**to have a close call** (coll) l'échapper belle

close-cropped [′klos′krɑpt] *adj* coupé ras

closed [klozd] *adj* fermé; *(road)* barré; *(e.g., pipe)* obturé, bouché; *(ranks)* serré; (public sign in front of theater) relâche; **with closed eyes** les yeux clos

closed′ car′ *s* conduite *f* intérieure

closed′-cir′cuit tel′evision *s* télévision *f* en circuit fermé

closed′ sea′son *s* fermeture *f* de la chasse, fermeture de la pêche

closed′ shop′ *s* atelier *m* qui n'admet que des travailleurs syndiqués

closed′ shop′ pol′icy *s* exclusion *f* des travailleurs non syndiqués

closefisted [′klos′fɪstəd] *adj* ladre, avare

close-fitting [′klos′fɪtɪŋ] *adj* collant, ajusté, qui moule le corps

close-grained [′klos′grend] *adj* serré

close-knit [′klos′nɪt] *adj* très uni

closely [′klosli] *adv (near)* de près, étroitement; *(exactly)* exactement

close-mouthed [′klos′mauðd] *adj* peu communicatif, économe de mots

closeness [′klosnɪs] *s (nearness)* proximité *f; (accuracy)* exactitude *f; (stinginess)* avarice *f; (of weather)* lourdeur *f; (of air)* manque *m* d'air

close′out′ *s* fin *f* de série

close′ shave′ [klos] *s*—**to have a close shave** se faire raser de près; (coll) échapper à un cheveu près

closet [′klɑzɪt] *s* placard *m*

clos′et dra′ma *s* spectacle *m* dans un fauteuil

close-up [′klos,ʌp] *s* premier plan *m,* gros plan, plan serré, plan rapproché

closing [′klozɪŋ] *adj* dernier, final ‖ *s* fermeture *f; (of account; of meeting)* clôture *f*

clos′ing-out′ sale′ *s* soldes *mpl* des fins de séries

clos′ing price′ *s* dernier cours *m; (on the stock exchange)* cours *m* en clôture

clos′ing time′ *s* heure *f* de fermeture ‖ *interj* on ferme!

clot [klɑt] *s* caillot *m* ‖ *v (pret & pp* **clotted;** *ger* **clotting**) *tr* cailler ‖ *intr* se cailler

cloth [klɔθ] *s* étoffe *f; (fabric)* tissu *m; (of wool)* drap *m; (of cotton or linen)* toile *f,* **cloths** *(for cleaning)* chiffons *mpl,* torchons *mpl,* linge *m;* **the cloth** le clergé

clothe [kloð] *v (pret & pp* **clothed** or **clad** [klæd]) *tr* habiller, vêtir; *(e.g., with authority)* revêtir, investir

clothes [kloz] *spl* vêtements *mpl,* habits *mpl; (underclothes, shirts, etc.; wash)* linge *m;* **in plain clothes** en civil; **to put on one's clothes** s'habiller; **to take off one's clothes** se déshabiller

clothes′bas′ket *s* panier *m* à linge

clothes′brush′ *s* brosse *f* à habits

clothes′ clos′et *s* garde-robe *f,* penderie *f,* placard *m*

clothes′ dri′er *ou* **clothes′ dry′er** *s* sèche-linge *m invar*

clothes′ hang′er *s* cintre *m*

clothes′horse′ *s* séchoir-chevalet *m*

clothes′line′ *s* corde *f* à linge, étendoir *m*

clothes′ moth′ *s* gerce *f*

clothes′pin′ *s* pince *f* à linge

clothes′ rack′ *s* patère *f*

clothes' tree' s portemanteau m
clothier [ˈkloðjər] s confectionneur m, marchand m de confections
clothing [ˈkloðɪŋ] s vêtements mpl
cloud [klaʊd] s nuage m; (heavy cloud; multitude) nuée f; **in the clouds** dans les nues ‖ tr couvrir de nuages; (phot) voiler ‖ intr (phot) se voiler; **to cloud over** ou **up** se couvrir de nuages
cloud'burst' s averse f, rafale f de pluie
cloud-capped [ˈklaʊd͵kæpt] adj couronné de nuages
cloud' cham'ber s (phys) chambre f d'ionisation
cloudless [ˈklaʊdlɪs] adj sans nuages
cloud·y [ˈklaʊdi] adj (comp -ier; super -iest) nuageux; (phot) voilé
clout [klaʊt] s (coll) coup m de poing; (cuff) gifle f; (pull, political power) influence f, pouvoir m, autorité f; (baseball) beau coup m de batte ‖ tr (coll) donner un coup de poing à; (to cuff) gifler
clove [klov] s (spice) clou m de girofle, girofle m; (of garlic) gousse f; (bot) giroflier m
clove' hitch' s demi-clef f à capeler
clo'ven hoof' [ˈklovən] s pied m fourchu; **to show the cloven hoof** (coll) montrer le bout de l'oreille
clover [ˈklovər] s trèfle m; **to be in clover** (coll) être sur le velours
clo'ver·leaf' s (pl -leaves) (leaf) feuille f de trèfle; (intersection) croisement m en trèfle, échangeur m en trèfle
clown [klaʊn] s clown m, pitre m, bouffon m ‖ intr faire le pitre
clownish [ˈklaʊnɪʃ] adj bouffon; (clumsy) empoté, rustre
cloy [klɔɪ] tr rassasier
club [klʌb] s (weapon) massue f, gourdin m, assommoir m; (group) cercle m, amicale f, club m; (cards) trèfle m; (golf) crosse f, club m ‖ v (pret & pp clubbed; ger clubbing) tr (to strike) assommer; (to pool) mettre en commun ‖ intr—**to club together** s'associer; se cotiser
club' car' s voiture-salon f
club'foot' s (pl -feet) pied m équin, pied bot
club'foot'ed adj—**to be clubfooted** avoir le pied bot, être pied-bot
club'house' s club m, club-house m
club'man s (pl -men) clubman m
club' mem'ber s membre m d'un club
club'room' s salle f de réunion
club' so'da s eau f de Seltz
club' steak' s aloyau m de bœuf
club'wom'an s (pl -wom'en) cercleuse f
cluck [klʌk] s gloussement m ‖ intr glousser
clue [klu] s indice m, indication f; **to find the clue** trouver la clef; **to give s.o. a clue** mettre qn sur la piste; **to have the clue** tenir le bout du fil
clump [klʌmp] s (of earth) bloc m, masse f; (of trees) bouquet m; (of shrubs or flowers)

massif m; (gait) pas m lourd ‖ intr—**to clump along** marcher lourdement
clum·sy [ˈklʌmzi] adj (comp -sier; super -siest) (worker) maladroit, gauche; (work) bâclé, grossier
cluster [ˈklʌstər] s (of people) groupe m, rassemblement m; (of trees) bouquet m; (of grapes, fruit, blossoms, flowers) grappe f; (of pears) glane f; (of bananas) régime m; (of diamonds) épi m, nœud m; (of stars) amas m ‖ tr grouper ‖ intr—**to cluster around** se rassembler; **to cluster together** se conglomérer
clutch [klʌtʃ] s (grasp, grip) griffe f, serre f; (aut) embrayage m; (aut) pédale f d'embrayage; **to fall into the clutches of** tomber sous la patte de; **to let in the clutch** embrayer; **to throw out the clutch** débrayer ‖ tr saisir, empoigner ‖ intr—**to clutch at** se raccrocher à
clutter [ˈklʌtər] s encombrement m ‖ tr—**to clutter up** encombrer
Co. abbr (**Company**) Cⁱᵉ
c/o abbr (**in care of**) a/s (aux soins de)
coach [kotʃ] s (drawn by horses) coche m, carrosse f; (bus) autocar m, car m; (two-door sedan) coche m; (baseball) instructeur m; (rr) voiture f; (sports) entraîneur m, moniteur m ‖ tr donner des leçons particulières à; entraîner; (for an exam) préparer à un examen, chauffer; (an actor) faire répéter
coach'-and-four' s carrosse f à quatre chevaux
coach' box' s siège m du cocher
coach' house' s remise f
coaching [ˈkotʃɪŋ] s leçons fpl particulières, chauffage m, répétitions fpl; (sport) entraînement m
coach'man s (pl -men) cocher m
coagulate [koˈægjə͵let] tr coaguler ‖ intr se coaguler
coal [kol] adj charbonnier, houiller ‖ s houille f, charbon m; **coals** (embers) tisons mpl, charbons ardents; **to carry coals to Newcastle** porter de l'eau à la rivière
coal' bin' s coffre m à charbon
coal' bunk'er s soute f à charbon
coal' car' s wagon-tombereau m
coal' deal'er s charbonnier m
coalesce [͵koəˈlɛs] intr s'unir, se combiner, fusionner
coal' field' s bassin m houiller
coalition [͵koəˈlɪʃən] s coalition f; **to form a coalition** se coaliser
coal' mine' s houillère f
coal' oil' s pétrole m lampant
coal' scut'tle s seau m à charbon
coal' tar' s goudron m de houille
coal'yard' s charbonnerie f
coarse [kors] adj (in manners) grossier; (composed of large particles) gros; (hair, skin) rude
coarse'-grained' adj à gros grain; (wood) à gros fil

coarseness [ˈkorsnɪs] s (*in manners*) grossièreté *f;* (*of hair, skin*) rudesse *f*

coast [kost] s côte *f;* **the coast is clear** la route est libre ‖ *intr* caboter; (*said of automobile*) aller au débrayé; (*said of bicycle*) aller en roue libre; **to coast along** continuer sur sa lancée

coastal [ˈkostəl] *adj* côtier

coaster [ˈkostər] s (*under a glass*) dessous-de-verre *m,* sous-verre *m;* (*naut*) caboteur *m*

coast′er brake′ s frein *m* à contrepédalage

coast′ guard′ s service *m* de guet le long des côtes

coast′-guard cut′ter s garde-côte *m*

coast′guards′man s (*pl* **-men**) soldat *m* chargé de la garde des côtes

coasting [ˈkostɪŋ] s (*e.g., on a cycle*) descente *f* en roue libre

coast′ing trade′ s cabotage *m*

coast′line′ s littoral *m*

coast′wise′ *adj* côtier ‖ *adv* le long de la côte

coat [kot] s (*jacket*) veste *f;* (*suitcoat*) veston *m;* (*topcoat*) manteau *m;* (*of an animal*) robe *f,* pelage *m,* livrée *f;* (*of paint*) couche *f* ‖ *tr* enduire; (*with chocolate*) enrober; (*a pill*) dragéifier

coat′ hang′er s cintre *m,* portemanteau *m*

coating [ˈkotɪŋ] s enduit *m,* couche *f*

coat′ of arms′ s écu *m* armorial; (*bearings*) blason *m,* armoiries *fpl*

coat′ of mail′ s cotte *f* de mailles

coat′rack′ s portemanteau *m*

coat′room′ s vestiaire *m*

coat′tail′ s basque *f*

coauthor [koˈɔθər] s coauteur *m*

coax [koks] *tr* cajoler, amadouer, câliner

coax′ial ca′ble [koˈæksɪəl] s câble *m* coaxial, coaxial *m*

cob [kab] s (*of corn*) épi *m* de maïs; (*horse*) cob *m;* (*swan*) cygne *m* mâle

cobalt [ˈkobɔlt] s cobalt *m*

cobbler [ˈkablər] s (*shoemaker*) cordonnier *m;* (*cake*) tourte *f* aux fruits; (*drink*) boisson *f* glacée

cobblestone [ˈkabəlˌston] s pavé *m*

cob′web′ s toile *f* d'araignée

coca [ˈkokə] s (*bot*) coca *m*

Coca-Cola [ˈkokəˌkolə] s (*trademark*) Coca-Cola *m*

cocaine [koˈken] s cocaïne *f*

cock [kak] s (*rooster*) coq *m;* (*faucet*) robinet *m;* (*of gun*) chien *m* ‖ *tr* (*one's ears*) dresser, redresser; (*one's hat*) mettre sur l'oreille, retrousser; (*a rifle*) armer

cockade [kaˈked] s cocarde *f*

cock-a-doodle-doo [ˈkakəˌdudəlˈdu] *interj* cocorico!

cock′-and-bull′ sto′ry s coq-à-l'âne *m*

cock′crow′ s cocorico *m*

cocked′ hat′ s chapeau *m* à cornes; **to knock into a cocked hat** (*slang*) démolir, aplatir

cock′er span′iel [ˈkakər] s cocker *m*

cock′eyed′ *adj* (*coll*) de travers, de biais; (*slang*) insensé

cock′fight′ s combat *m* de coqs

cockle [ˈkakəl] s (*bot*) nielle *f;* (*zool*) bucarde *f,* clovisse *f*

cockney [ˈkakni] *adj & s* cockney *mf;* (*dialect*) cockney *m*

cock′pit′ s (*aer*) cockpit *m,* carlingue *f,* poste *m* de pilotage, habitacle *m*

cock′roach′ s blatte *f,* cafard *m*

cockscomb [ˈkaksˌkom] s crête *f* de coq; (*bot*) crête-de-coq *f*

cock′sure′ *adj* (*coll*) sûr et certain

cock′tail′ s cocktail *m*

cock′tail dress′ s robe *f* de cocktail

cock′tail par′ty s cocktail *m*

cock′tail shak′er s shaker *m*

cock′tail snack′ s amuse-gueule *m*

cock•y [ˈkaki] *adj* (*comp* **-ier;** *super* **-iest**) (*coll*) effronté, suffisant

cocoa [ˈkoko] s cacao *m*

co′coa bean′ s cacao *m*

coconut [ˈkokəˌnʌt] s noix *f* de coco, coco *m*

co′conut palm′ s cocotier *m*

cocoon [kəˈkun] s cocon *m*

cod [kad] s (*ichth*) morue *f*

C.O.D. [ˈsiˈoˈdi] s (*letterword*) (**Collect on Delivery**) C.R., contre remboursement, *e.g.,* **send it to me C.O.D.** envoyez-le-moi C.R.

coddle [ˈkadəl] *tr* dorloter, gâter

code [kod] s code *m;* (*secret code*) chiffre *m* ‖ *tr* chiffrer

code′ word′ s mot *m* convenu

codex [ˈkodɛks] s (*pl* **codices** [ˈkadɪˌsiz]) manuscrit *m* ancien

cod′fish′ s morue *f*

codger [ˈkadʒər] s—**old codger** (*coll*) vieux bonhomme *m*

codicil [ˈkadɪsɪl] s (*of will*) codicille *m;* (*of contract, treaty, etc.*) avenant *m*

codi•fy [ˈkadɪˌfai] *v* (*pret & pp* **-fied**) *tr* codifier

coding [ˈkodɪŋ] s mise *f* en code, chiffrage *m;* (*comp*) codage *m*

cod′-liver oil′ s huile *f* de foie de morue

co-driver [ˈkoˈdraivər] s co-conducteur *m*

coed [ˈkoˌɛd] s collégienne *f,* étudiante *f* universitaire

coeducation [ˌkoˌɛdʒəˈkeʃən] s coéducation *f,* enseignement *m* mixte

co′educa′tional school′ [ˌkoˌɛdʒəˈkeʃənəl] s école *f* mixte

coefficient [ˌkoˈfɪʃənt] s coefficient *m*

coerce [koˈʌrs] *tr* contraindre, forcer

coercion [koˈʌrʃən] s coercition *f*

coeval [koˈivəl] *adj & s* contemporain *m*

coexist [ˌkoˈɪɡˈzɪst] *intr* coexister

coexistence [ˌkoˈɪɡˈzɪstəns] s coexistence *f*

coffee [ˈkɔfi] s café *m;* **black coffee** café noir, café nature; **ground coffee** café moulu; **roasted coffee** café brûlé, café torréfié

cof′fee and rolls′ s café *m* complet

cof′fee bean′ s grain *m* de café

cof′fee break′ s pause-café *f,* pause café

cof′fee•cake′ s gimblette *f* (qui se prend avec le café)

cof′fee cup′ s tasse f à café
cof′fee grind′er s moulin m à café
cof′fee grounds′ spl marc m de café
cof′fee mak′er s percolateur m
cof′fee mill′ s moulin m à café
cof′fee mug′ s pot m de café
cof′fee planta′tion s caféière f
cof′fee•pot′ s cafetière f; (for pouring) verseuse f
cof′fee roast′er s brûloir m
cof′fee shop′ s (of hotel) hôtel-restaurant m; (in station) buffet m
cof′fee ta′ble s (petite) table f basse
cof′fee tree′ s caféier m
coffer [ˈkɔfər] s coffre m, caisse f; (archit) caisson m; **coffers** trésor m, fonds mpl
cof′fer•dam′ s coffre m, bâtardeau m
coffin [ˈkɔfɪn] s cercueil m, bière f
cog [kɑg] s dent f; (cogwheel) roue f dentée; **to slip a cog** (coll) avoir des absences
cogency [ˈkɔdʒənsi] s force f (de persuasion)
cogent [ˈkɔdʒənt] adj puissant, convaincant
cogitate [ˈkɑdʒɪˌtet] tr & intr méditer
cognac [ˈkonjæk] s cognac m
cognate [ˈkɑgnet] adj congénère, apparenté ‖ s congénère mf; (word) mot m apparenté
cognizance [ˈkɑgnɪzəns] s connaissance f
cognizant [ˈkɑgnɪzənt] adj informé
cog′wheel′ s roue f dentée
cohabit [koˈhæbɪt] intr cohabiter
coheir [koˈer] s cohéritier
cohere [koˈhɪr] intr s'agglomérer, adhérer; (said of reasoning or style) se suivre logiquement, correspondre
coherent [koˈhɪrənt] adj cohérent
cohesion [koˈhiʒən] s cohésion f
coiffeur [kwaˈfʌr] s coiffeur m pour dames
coiffure [kwaˈfjur] s coiffure f ‖ tr coiffer
coil [kɔɪl] s (something wound in a spiral) rouleau m; (single turn of spiral) tour m; (of a still) serpentin m; (of hair) boucle f; (elec) bobine f; **coils** (of snake) nœuds mpl ‖ tr enrouler; (naut) lover, gléner ‖ intr s'enrouler; (said of snake or stream) serpenter
coil′ spring′ s ressort m en spirale, ressort à boudin
coin [kɔɪn] s monnaie f; (single coin) pièce f de monnaie; (wedge) coin m; **in coin** en espèces, en numéraire; **to pay back s.o. in his own coin** rendre à qn la monnaie de sa pièce; **to toss a coin** jouer à pile ou face ‖ tr (a new word; a story or lie) forger, inventer; **to coin money** frapper de la monnaie, (coll) faire des affaires d'or, s'enrichir à vue d'œil
coinage [ˈkɔɪnɪdʒ] s monnayage m; (fig) invention f
coincide [ˌkoɪnˈsaɪd] intr coïncider
coincidence [koˈɪnsɪdəns] s coïncidence f
coin′ lock′er s consigne f automatique
coin′-op′erated adj automatique
coin′-op′erated laun′dry s laverie f automatique, laverie libre-service

coin′ return′ s retour m de monnaie; (receptacle) sébile f
coin′ tel′ephone s téléphone m payant
coition [koˈɪʃən] or **coitus** [ˈkoˌɪtəs] s coït m
coke [kok] s coke m ‖ tr cokéfier ‖ intr se cokéfier
Coke [kok] s (trademark) (coll) Coca m (trademark) (Coca-Cola)
colander [ˈkʌləndər] s passoire f
cold [kold] adj froid; **it is cold** (said of weather) il fait froid; **to be cold** (said of person) avoir froid ‖ s froid m; (indisposition) rhume m; **to be left out in the cold** (slang) rester en carafe; **to catch a cold** attraper un rhume, s'enrhumer
cold′ blood′ s—**in cold blood** de sang-froid
cold′-blood′ed adj insensible; (sensitive to cold) frileux; (zool) à sang froid
cold′ chis′el s ciseau m à froid
cold′ com′fort s maigre consolation f
cold′ cream′ s cold-cream m
cold′ cuts′ spl viandes fpl froides, assiette f anglaise
cold′ feet′ [fit] spl—**to have cold feet** (coll) avoir froid aux yeux
cold′ front′ s front m froid
cold′-heart′ed adj au cœur dur, insensible
coldness [ˈkoldnɪs] s froideur f; (in the air) froidure f
cold′ should′er s—**to give s.o. the cold shoulder** (coll) battre froid à qn
cold′ snap′ s coup m de froid
cold′ stor′age s entrepôt m frigorifique; **in cold storage** en glacière
cold′-stor′age adj frigorifique
cold′ war′ s guerre f froide
cold′ wave′ s vague f de froid
coleslaw [ˈkolˌslɔ] s salade f de chou
colic [ˈkɑlɪk] s colique f
coliseum [ˌkɑlɪˈsiˌəm] s colisée m
colitis [koˈlaɪtɪs] s colite f
collaborate [kəˈlæbəˌret] intr collaborer
collaborationist [kəˌlæbəˈreʃənɪst] s collaborationniste mf
collaborator [kəˈlæbəˌretər] s collaborateur m
collapse [kəˈlæps] s écroulement m, effondrement m; (of prices, of government) chute f; (of prices; of a beam) fléchissement m; (pathol) collapsus m ‖ intr s'écrouler, s'effondrer; (said of government) tomber; (said of structure or prices) s'effondrer; (said of balloon) se dégonfler
collapsible [kəˈlæpsɪbəl] adj démontable, rabattable, pliant
collar [ˈkɑlər] s (of dress, shirt) collet m, col m; (worn by dog; on pigeon) collier m; (mach) collier ‖ tr colleter; (coll) empoigner
col′lar•band′ s pied m de col (d'une chemise)
col′lar•bone′ s clavicule f
collate [kəˈlet] tr collationner, conférer
collateral [kəˈlætərəl] adj (fact) correspondant, concomitant; (parallel) parallèle; (subordinate) accessoire; (kin) collatéral ‖ s (kin) collatéral m; (com) nantissement m

collat′eral dam′age *s* dommages *mpl* accessoires et fortuits; (mil) pertes *fpl* parmi la population civile

collation [kə′leʃən] *s* collation *f*

colleague [′kalig] *s* collègue *mf*

collect [′kalɛkt] *s* (eccl) collecte *f* ‖ [kə′lɛkt] *tr* rassembler; (*taxes*) percevoir, lever; (*stamps, antiques*) collectionner; (*eggs; classroom papers; tickets*) ramasser; (*mail*) faire la levée de; (*debts*) recouvrer; (*gifts, money*) collecter; (*one's thoughts; anecdotes*) recueillir; **to collect oneself** se reprendre, se remettre ‖ *intr* (*for the poor*) quêter; (*to gather together*) se rassembler, se réunir; (*to pile up*) s'amasser ‖ *adv* en p.c.v., e.g., **to telephone collect** téléphoner en p.c.v.

collect′ call′ *s* (telp) communication *f* P.C.V.

collected *adj* recueilli, maître de soi

collection [kə′lɛkʃən] *s* collection *f;* (*of taxes*) perception *f,* levée *f,* recouvrement *m;* (*of mail*) levée *f;* (*of verses*) recueil *m*

collec′tion a′gency *s* agence *f* de recouvrement

collec′tion plate′ *s* plateau *m* de quête

collective [kə′lɛktɪv] *adj* collectif

collector [kə′lɛktər] *s* (*of stamps, antiques*) collectionneur *m;* (*of taxes*) percepteur *m,* receveur *m,* collecteur *m;* (*of tickets*) contrôleur *m*

college [′kalɪdʒ] *s* (*of cardinals, electors, etc.*) collège *m;* (*school in a university*) faculté *f;* (U.S.A.) école *f* des arts et sciences; **Paul is going to college** (coll) Paul s'inscrit à l'université

col′lege dor′mitory *s* résidence *f* universitaire, cité *f* universitaire

collegian [kə′lidʒɪ•ən] *s* étudiant *m*

collegiate [kə′lidʒɪ•ɪt] *adj* collégial, de l'université, universitaire

collide [kə′laɪd] *intr* se heurter, se tamponner; **to collide with** se heurter à or contre, heurter contre

collie [′kali] *s* colley *m*

collier [′kaljər] *s* houilleur *m;* (*ship*) charbonnier *m*

collier•y [′kaljəri] *s* (*pl* **-ies**) houillère *f*

collision [kə′lɪʒən] *s* collision *f*

collocate [′kalo‚ket] *tr* disposer en rapport; (*creditors*) colloquer

colloid [′kalɔɪd] *adj* colloïdal ‖ *s* colloïde *m*

colloquial [kə′lokwɪ•əl] *adj* familier

colloquialism [kə′lokwɪ•ə‚lızəm] *s* expression *f* familière

collo•quy [′kaləkwi] *s* (*pl* **-quies**) colloque *m*

collusion [kə′luʒən] *s* collusion *f;* **to be in collusion with** être d'intelligence avec

cologne [kə′lon] *s* eau *f* de Cologne

Colombia [kə′lʌmbɪ•ə] *s* Colombie *f;* la Colombie

colon [′kolən] *s* (anat) côlon *m;* (gram) deux points *mpl*

colonel [′kʌrnəl] *s* colonel *m*

colonial [kə′lonɪ•əl] *adj & s* colonial *m*

colonist [′kalənɪst] *s* colon *m*

colonize [′kalə‚naɪz] *tr & intr* coloniser

colonnade [‚kalə′ned] *s* colonnade *f*

colo•ny [′kaləni] *s* (*pl* **-nies**) colonie *f*

colophon [′kalə‚fan] *s* colophon *m*

color [′kʌlər] *s* couleur *f;* **the colors** les couleurs, le drapeau; **to call to the colors** appeler sous les drapeaux; **to give** or **lend color to** colorer; (fig) rendre vraisemblable; **to show one's true colors** se révéler sous son vrai jour; **under color of** sous couleur de; **with flying colors** enseignes déployées ‖ *tr* colorer; (*e.g., a drawing*) colorier; (*to exaggerate*) donner de l'éclat à, imager; (*to dye*) teindre ‖ *intr* se colorer; (*to blush*) rougir

col′or•bear′er *s* porte-drapeau *m*

col′or•blind′ *adj* daltonien, aveugle des couleurs

col′or-cod′ed *adj* (chem) chromocodé

colored *adj* coloré; (*ink*) de couleur; (*person: usually offensive*) de couleur; (*drawing*) colorié

colorful [′kʌlərfəl] *adj* (*striking*) coloré; (*unusual*) pittoresque

col′or guard′ *s* garde *f* d'honneur du drapeau

coloring [′kʌlərɪŋ] *adj* colorant ‖ *s* colorant *m;* (*of painting, complexion, style*) coloris *m*

colorless [′kʌlərlɪs] *adj* incolore

col′or photog′raphy *s* photographie *f* en couleurs

col′or salute′ *s* (mil) salut *m* au drapeau, salut aux couleurs

col′or ser′geant *s* sergent-chef *m,* sergent-major *m*

col′or tel′evision *s* télévision *f* en couleurs

colossal [kə′lasəl] *adj* colossal

Colosseum [‚kalə′si•əm] *s* Colisée *m*

colossus [kə′lasəs] *s* colosse *m*

colt [kolt] *s* poulain *m*

Columbus [kə′lʌmbəs] *s* Colomb *m*

column [′kaləm] *s* colonne *f;* (journ) rubrique *f,* chronique *f,* courrier *m;* (mil) colonne *f*

columnar [kə′lʌmnər] *adj* en colonne

columnist [′kaləmɪst] *s* chroniqueur *m,* courriériste *mf*

coma [′komə] *s* (pathol) coma *m*

comb [kom] *s* (*for hair*) peigne *m;* (*currycomb*) étrille *f;* (*of rooster; of wave*) crête *f;* (*filled with honey*) rayon *m* ‖ *tr* peigner; explorer minutieusement, fouiller; **to comb out** démêler ‖ *intr* (*said of waves*) déferler

com•bat [′kambæt] *s* combat *m* ‖ [′kambæt] [kəm′bæt] *v* (*pret & pp* **-bated** *ou* **-batted;** *ger* **-bating** *ou* **-batting**) *tr & intr* combattre

combatant [′kambətənt] *adj & s* combattant *m*

com′bat du′ty *s* service *m* de combat, service au front

combination [‚kambɪ′neʃən] *s* combinaison *f*

combine [′kambaɪn] *s* (com) trust *m,* combinaison *f* financière, entente *f* industrielle; (agr) moissonneuse-batteuse *f* ‖ [kəm′baɪn] *tr* combiner ‖ *intr* se liguer, fusionner; (chem) se combiner

combin′ing form′ *s* élément *m* de composition

combo [′kambo] *s* (*of four musicians*) quartette

combustible [kəm'bʌstɪbəl] *adj & s* combustible *m*

combustion [kəm'bʌstʃən] *s* combustion *f*

come [kʌm] *v* (*pret* **came** [kem]; *pp* **come**) *intr* venir; **come in!** entrez!; **to come after** succéder à, suivre; (*to come to get*) venir chercher; **to come apart** se séparer, se défaire; **to come around** (*to snap back*) se rétablir; (*to give in*) céder; **to come at** (*to attack*) se jeter sur; **to come back** revenir; (coll) revenir en vogue; **to come before** précéder; (*e.g., a legislature*) se mettre devant; **to come between** s'interposer entre; **to come by** (*to get*) obtenir; (*to pass*) passer; **to come down** descendre; **to come downstairs** descendre (en bas); **to come down with** tomber malade avec; **to come for** venir chercher; **to come from** provenir de, dériver de; (*said of wind*) chasser de; **to come in** entrer; entrer dans; (*said of tide*) monter; (*said of style*) entrer en vogue; **to come in for** avoir part à; (*e.g., an inheritance*) succéder à; (*e.g., sympathy*) s'attirer; **to come off** se détacher; (*to take place*) avoir lieu; en sortir, e.g., **to come off victorious** en sortir vainqueur; **to come out** sortir; (*said of sun, stars; said of book*) paraître; (*said of buds*) éclore; (*said of news*) se divulguer; (*said of debutante*) débuter; **to come out for** se prononcer pour; **to come over** se laisser persuader; arriver, e.g., **what's come over him?** qu'est-ce qui lui est arrivé?; **to come through** (*e.g., fields*) passer par, passer à travers; (*e.g., a wall*) pénétrer; (*an illness*) surmonter; se tirer indemne; **to come to** revenir à soi; **to come together** s'assembler, se réunir; **to come true** se réaliser; **to come up** monter; (*to occur*) se présenter; **to come upstairs** monter (en haut); **to come up to** monter jusqu'à, venir à; **to come up with** proposer

come'-and-go' *s* va-et-vient *m*

come'back' *s* (*of style*) (coll) retour *m* en vogue; (*of statesman*) (coll) retour *m* au pouvoir; (slang) réplique *f*, riposte *f*; **to stage a comeback** (coll) se réhabiliter, faire une belle remontée

comedian [kə'midɪ•ən] *s* (*comic*) comique *m*; (*on the legitimate stage*) comédien *m*; (*author*) auteur *m* comique

comedienne [kə,midɪ'ɛn] *s* comédienne *f*

come'down' *s* humiliation *f*, déchéance *f*

come•dy ['kɑmədi] *s* (*pl* **-dies**) comédie *f*

come•ly ['kʌmli] *adj* (*comp* **-lier**; *super* **-liest**) (*attractive*) avenant, gracieux; (*decorous*) convenable, bienséant

come'-on' *s* (slang) leurre *m*, attrape *f*

comet ['kɑmɪt] *s* comète *f*

comfort ['kʌmfərt] *s* (*well-being*) confort *m*; (*sympathy*) consolation *f*; (*person*) consolateur *m*; **comforts** commodités *fpl*, agréments *mpl* ‖ *tr* consoler, réconforter

comfortable ['kʌmfərtəbəl] *adj* confortable; (*in a state of comfort*) bien; (*well-off*) à l'aise

comforter ['kʌmfərtər] *s* (*person*) consolateur *m*; (*bedcover*) couvre-pieds *m* piqué; (*of wool*) cache-nez *m*; (*for baby*) tétine *f*, sucette *f*

comforting ['kʌmfərtɪŋ] *adj* consolateur, réconfortant

com'fort sta'tion *s* châlet *m* de nécessité, lieux *mpl* d'aisances, toilette *f*

comic ['kɑmɪk] *adj & s* comique *m*; **comics** (*cartoons*) dessins *mpl* humoristiques, bandes *fpl* dessinées, comics *mpl*

com'ic op'era *s* opéra *m* bouffe

com'ic book' *s* livre *m* de bandes dessinées

com'ic strip' *s* bande *f* humoristique, bande dessinée

coming ['kʌmɪŋ] *adj* qui vient; (*future*) d'avenir, de demain ‖ *s* arrivée *f*, venue *f*; **comings and goings** allées et venues

com'ing out' *s* (*of stocks, bonds, etc.*) émission *f*; (*of a book*) parution *f*; (*of a young lady*) début *m*

comma ['kɑmə] *s* virgule *f*; (*in French a period or sometimes a small space is used to mark the divisions of whole numbers*) point *m*

command [kə'mænd] *s* (*leadership*) gouvernement *m*; (*order, direction*) commandement *m*, ordre *m*; (*e.g., of a foreign language*) maîtrise *f*; (mil) commandement *m*; **to be at s.o.'s command** être aux ordres de qn; **to have a command of** (*a language*) posséder; **to have at one's command** avoir à sa disposition ‖ *tr* commander, ordonner; (*respect*) inspirer; (*to look out over*) dominer; (*a language*) connaître ‖ *intr* (mil) commander, donner les ordres

commandant [,kɑmən'dænt] *s* commandant *m*

commandeer [,kɑmən'dɪr] *tr* réquisitionner

commander [kə'mændər] *s* commandant *m*

comman'der in chief' *s* commandant *m* en chef

commanding [kə'mændɪŋ] *adj* imposant; (*in charge*) d'autorité

commemorate [kə'mɛməret] *tr* commémorer, célébrer

commence [kə'mɛns] *tr & intr* commencer

commencement [kə'mɛnsmənt] *s* commencement *m*; (educ) jour *m* de la distribution des prix, jour de la collation des grades

commence'ment ex'ercise *s* cérémonie *f* de remise des diplômes

commend [kə'mɛnd] *tr* (*to praise*) louer; (*to entrust*) confier, recommander

commendable [kə'mɛndəbəl] *adj* louable

commendation [,kɑmən'deʃən] *s* louange *f*, éloge *m*; (mil) citation *f*

comment ['kɑmənt] *s* remarque *f*, observation *f*, commentaire *m* ‖ *intr* faire des observations; **to comment on** commenter

commentar•y ['kɑmən,tɛri] *s* (*pl* **-ies**) commentaire *m*

commentator ['kɑmən,tetər] *s* commentateur *m*

commerce ['kɑmərs] *s* commerce *m*, négoce *m*

commercial [kə'mʌrʃəl] *adj* commercial, commerçant ‖ *s* annonce *f* publicitaire; (rad, telv) publicité *f*, pub *f*, spot *m*, écran *m* de publicité

commercialize [kə`mʌrʃə,laɪz] *tr* commercialiser

commiserate [kə`mɪzə,ret] *intr*—**to commiserate with** compatir aux malheurs de

commiseration [kə,mɪzə`reʃən] *s* commisération *f*

commissar [,kamɪ`sar] *s* commissaire *m*

commissar•y [`kamɪ,sɛri] *s* (*pl* **-ies**) (*person*) commissaire *m*; (*canteen*) cantine *f*

commission [kə`mɪʃən] *s* commission *f*; (*board, council*) conseil *m*; (com) guelte *f*; (mil) brevet *m*; **out of commission** hors de service; (naut) désarmé ‖ *tr* commissionner; (mil) promouvoir

commis´sioned of´ficer *s* breveté *m*

commissioner [kə`mɪʃənər] *s* commissaire *m*

com•mit [kə`mɪt] *v* (*pret* & *pp* **-mitted**; *ger* **-mitting**) *tr* (*an error, crime, etc.*) commettre; (*one's soul, one's money, etc.*) confier; (*one's word*) engager; (*to a mental hospital*) interner; **to commit to memory** apprendre par cœur; **to commit to prison** envoyer en prison; **to commit to writing** coucher par écrit

commitment [kə`mɪtmənt] *s* (*act of committing*) perpétration *f*; (*to a mental institution*) internement *m*; (*to prison*) emprisonnement *m*; (*to a cause*) engagement *m*

committal [kə`mɪtəl] *s* (*of a crime*) perpétration *f*; (*of a task*) délégation *f*; **committal to prison** mise *f* en prison

commit´tal ser´vice *s* (eccl) prières *fpl* au bord de la tombe

committee [kə`mɪti] *s* comité *m*, commission *f*

commode [kə`mod] *s* (*toilet*) chaise *f* percée; (*dressing table*) grande table *f* de nuit

commodious [kə`modɪ•əs] *adj* spacieux, confortable

commod´ities mar´ket *s* marché *m* de matières premières

commodi•ty [kə`madɪti] *s* (*pl* **-ties**) denrée *f*, marchandise *f*

commod´ity exchange´ *s* bourse *f* de commerce

common [`kamən] *adj* commun ‖ *s* terrain *m* communal; **commons** communaux *mpl*; (*of school*) réfectoire *m*; **the Commons** (Brit) les communes *fpl*

com´mon car´rier *s* entreprise *f* de transports en commun

commoner [`kamənər] *s* homme *m* du peuple, roturier *m*; (Brit) membre *m* de la Chambre des communes

com´mon law´ *s* droit *m* coutumier, coutume *f*

com´mon-law mar´riage *s* union *f* libre, collage *m*

Com´mon Mar´ket *s* Marché *m* Commun

com´mon noun´ *s* nom *m* commun

com´mon•place´ *adj* banal ‖ *s* banalité *f*

com´mon sense´ *s* sens *m* commun

com´mon-sense´ *adj* sensé

com´mon stock´ *s* action *f* ordinaire, actions ordinaires

commonweal [`kamən,wil] *s* bien *m* public

com´mon•wealth´ *s* état *m*, république *f*

commotion [kə`moʃən] *s* commotion *f*

commune [kə`mjun] *intr* s'entretenir; (eccl) communier

communicant [kə`mjunɪkənt] *s* informateur *m*; (eccl) communiant *m*

communicate [kə`mjunɪ,ket] *tr* & *intr* communiquer

communicating [kə`mjunɪ,ketɪŋ] *adj* communicant

communication [kə,mjunɪ`keʃən] *s* communication *f*

communica´tions sat´ellite *s* satellite *m* de transmission

communicative [kə`mjunɪ,ketɪv] *adj* communicatif

communion [kə`mjunjən] *s* communion *f*; **to take communion** communier

communism [`kamjə,nɪzəm] *s* communisme *m*

communist [`kamjənɪst] *adj* & *s* communiste *mf*

communi•ty [kə`mjunɪti] *s* (*pl* **-ties**) (*locality*) voisinage *m*; (*group of people living together*) communauté *f*

commu´nity chest´ *s* caisse *f* de secours

commutation [,kamjə`teʃən] *s* commutation *f*

commuta´tion tick´et *s* carte *f* d'abonnement

commutator [`kamjə,tetər] *s* (elec) collecteur *m*

commute [kə`mjut] *tr* échanger; (*e.g., a prison term*) commuer ‖ *intr* s'abonner au chemin de fer; voyager avec carte d'abonnement

commuter [kə`mjutər] *s* abonné *m* au chemin de fer

commut´er air´line *s* transporteur *m* d'appoint

compact [kəm`pækt] *adj* compact ‖ [`kampækt] *s* (*agreement*) pacte *m*; (*for cosmetics*) poudrier *m*, boîte *f* à poudre

com´pact disk´ *s* disque *m* compact, compact disc *m*, compact *m*

com´pact disk´ play´er *s* lecteur *m* de disque compact

companion [kəm`pænjən] *s* compagnon *m*; (*female companion*) compagne *f*

companionable [kəm`pænjənəbəl] *adj* sociable

compan´ion•ship´ *s* camaraderie *f*

compan´ion•way´ *s* escalier *m* des cabines

compa•ny [`kʌmpəni] *s* (*pl* **-nies**) compagnie *f*; (com) société *f*, compagnie; (naut) équipage *m*; (theat) troupe *f*; **to have company** avoir du monde; **to keep bad company** fréquenter la mauvaise compagnie; **to keep company** sortir ensemble; **to keep s.o. company** tenir compagnie à qn; **to part company** se séparer

comparative [kəm`pærətɪv] *adj* comparatif; (*anatomy, literature, etc.*) comparé ‖ *s* comparatif *m*

compare [kəm`pɛr] *s*—**beyond compare** incomparablement, sans égal ‖ *tr* comparer; **compared to** en comparaison de; **to be compared to** se comparer à

comparison [kəm`pærɪsən] *s* comparaison *f*

compartment [kəm`partmənt] *s* compartiment *m*

compass [ˈkʌmpəs] s (*for showing direction*) boussole f; (*range, reach*) portée f; (*for drawing circles*) compas m; **to box the compass** réciter la rose des vents ‖ tr—**to compass about** entourer

com′pass card′ s rose f des vents

compassion [kəmˈpæʃən] s compassion f

compassionate [kəmˈpæʃənɪt] adj compatissant

compatibility [kəmˌpætɪˈbɪlɪti] s compatibilité f, convenance f

compatible [kəmˈpætəbəl] adj compatible; **compatible with** compatible avec

com•pel [kəmˈpɛl] v (*pret & pp* **-pelled;** *ger* **-pelling**) tr contraindre, obliger; (*respect, silence*) imposer

compelling [kəmˈpɛlɪŋ] adj irrésistible; (*motive*) impérieux

compendious [kəmˈpɛndɪ•əs] adj abrégé, succinct

compensate [ˈkʌmpənˌset] tr compenser; **to compensate s.o. for** dédommager qn de ‖ intr—**to compensate for** compenser

compensation [ˌkʌmpənˈseʃən] s compensation f

compete [kəmˈpit] intr concourir

competence [ˈkʌmpɪtəns] or **competency** [ˈkʌmpɪtənsi] s compétence f

competent [ˈkʌmpɪtənt] adj compétent

competition [ˌkʌmpɪˈtɪʃən] s concurrence f, compétition f; (*contest*) concours m; (sports) compétition, épreuve f

competitive [kəmˈpɛtɪtɪv] adj compétitif

compet′itive exam′ination s concours m

competitiveness [kəmˈpɛtɪtɪvnɪs] s compétitivité f

competitor [kəmˈpɛtɪtər] s concurrent m

compilation [ˌkʌmpɪˈleʃən] s compilation f

compile [kəmˈpaɪl] tr compiler

compiler [kəmˈpaɪlər] s compilateur m, rédacteur m; (comp) compilateur

complacency [kəmˈplesənsi] s complaisance f; (*self-satisfaction*) suffisance f

complacent [kəmˈplesənt] adj complaisant; content de soi, suffisant

complain [kəmˈplen] intr se plaindre

complainant [kəmˈplenənt] s plaignant m

complaint [kəmˈplent] s plainte f; (*grievance*) grief m; (*illness*) maladie f, mal m, symptômes mpl, doléances fpl

complaisant [kəmˈplezənt] adj complaisant

complement [ˈkʌmplɪmənt] s complément m; (mil) effectif m ‖ [ˈkʌmplɪmɛnt] tr compléter

complete [kəmˈplit] adj complet ‖ tr compléter

completion [kəmˈpliʃən] s achèvement m

complex [kəmˈplɛks] adj complexe ‖ [ˈkʌmplɛks] s complexe m

complexion [kəmˈplɛkʃən] s (*texture of skin, especially of face*) teint m; (*general aspect*) caractère m; (*constitution*) complexion f

compliance [kəmˈplaɪ•əns] s complaisance f; soumission f, conformité f; **in compliance with** conformément à

complicate [ˈkʌmplɪˌket] tr compliquer

complicated adj compliqué

complication [ˌkʌmplɪˈkeʃən] s complication f

complici•ty [kəmˈplɪsɪti] s (pl **-ties**) complicité f

compliment [ˈkʌmplɪmənt] s compliment m; **compliments** (*kind regards*) civilités fpl; **to pay a compliment to** faire un compliment à; **with the compliments of the author** hommage de l'auteur ‖ tr complimenter

com′plimen′tary cop′y [ˌkʌmplɪˈmɛntəri] s exemplaire m en hommage; **to give a complimentary copy of a book** faire hommage d'un livre

com′plimen′tary tick′et s billet m de faveur

com•ply [kəmˈplaɪ] v (*pret & pp* **-plied**) intr—**to comply with** se conformer à, acquiescer à

component [kəmˈponənt] adj composant ‖ s (chem) composant m; (mech, math) composante f

comportment [kəmˈpɔrtmənt] s comportement m

compose [kəmˈpoz] tr composer; **to be composed of** se composer de; **to compose oneself** se calmer

composed adj paisible, tranquille

composer [kəmˈpozər] s compositeur m

compos′ing stick′ s composteur m

composite [kəmˈpazɪt] adj & s composé m

composition [ˌkʌmpəˈzɪʃən] s composition f

compositor [kəmˈpazɪtər] s compositeur m

compost [ˈkʌmpost] s compost m

composure [kəmˈpoʒər] s calme m, sangfroid m

compote [ˈkʌmpot] s (*stewed fruits*) compote f; (*dish*) compotier m

compound [ˈkʌmpaʊnd] adj composé ‖ s (*mixture*) composé m; (gram) mot m composé; (math) complexe m; (mil) enceinte f ‖ [kəmˈpaʊnd] tr composer, combiner; (*interest*) capitaliser

comprehend [ˌkʌmprɪˈhɛnd] tr comprendre

comprehensible [ˌkʌmprɪˈhɛnsɪbəl] adj compréhensible

comprehension [ˌkʌmprɪˈhɛnʃən] s compréhension f

comprehensive [ˌkʌmprɪˈhɛnsɪv] adj compréhensif, étendu; (*study, view, measure*) d'ensemble

comprehen′sive insur′ance s assurance f multirisque

compress [ˈkʌmprɛs] s (med) compresse f ‖ [kəmˈprɛs] tr comprimer

compression [kəmˈprɛʃən] s compression f

comprise [kəmˈpraɪz] tr comprendre, renfermer

compromise [ˈkʌmprəˌmaɪz] s compromis m; (*with one's conscience*) transaction f; **rough compromise** cote f mal taillée ‖ tr (*e.g., one's honor*) compromettre ‖ intr (*to make concessions*) transiger

comptroller [kənˈtrolər] s vérificateur m, contrôleur m

compulsive [kəmˈpʌlsɪv] *adj* obligatoire; (psychol) compulsif

compulsory [kəmˈpʌlsəri] *adj* obligatoire, forcé

computable [kəmˈpjutəbəl] *adj* calculable

computation [ˌkɑmpjuˈteʃən] *s* calcul *m*

compute [kəmˈpjut] *tr* computer, calculer, supputer || *intr* calculer

computer [kəmˈpjutər] *adj* informatique || *s* ordinateur *m*; **to operate a computer** faire de l'informatique

comput′er chip′ *s* chip *m* (*microplaquette en silicon*)

comput′er composi′tion *s* (typ) composition *f* programmée

comput′er dat′ing *s* rendez-vous arrangés par l'ordinateur

comput′er en′gineer′ *s* ingénieur *m* système

computerization [kəmˌpjutəraɪˈzeʃən] *s* informatisation *f*, mise *f* sur ordinateur

computerize [kəmˈpjutəraɪz] *tr* informatiser, mettre sur ordinateur

computerized *adj* fait à l'ordinateur

comput′er lan′guage *s* langage *m* de programmation, langage machine

comput′er map′ *s* carte *f* infographique

comput′er pro′gramer *s* programmeur *m*

comput′er pro′graming *s* programmation *f*

comput′er sci′ence *s* informatique *f*, science *f* de l'information

comput′er spe′cialist *s* informaticien *m*, informaticienne *f*

comput′er vir′us *s* virus *m* informatique

comrade [ˈkɑmræd] *s* camarade *mf*

com′rade in arms′ *s* compagnon *m* d'armes

com′rade•ship′ *s* camaraderie *f*

con [kɑn] *s* contre *m* || *v* (*pret & pp* **conned;** *ger* **conning**) *tr* étudier; (naut) gouverner; (slang) escroquer

concave [kɑnˈkev] *adj* concave

conceal [kənˈsil] *tr* dissimuler

concealment [kənˈsilmənt] *s* (*hiding*) dissimulation *f*; (*place*) cachette *f*

concede [kənˈsid] *tr & intr* concéder

conceit [kənˈsit] *s* (*vanity*) vanité *f*; (*witty expression*) saillie *f*, mot *m*; **conceits** concetti *mpl*

conceited *adj* vaniteux, vain

conceivable [kənˈsivəbəl] *adj* concevable

conceive [kənˈsiv] *tr & intr* concevoir

concentrate [ˈkɑnsənˌtret] *tr* concentrer || *intr* se concentrer

concentra′tion camp′ [ˌkɑnsənˈtreʃən] *s* camp *m* de concentration

concentric [kənˈsɛntrɪk] *adj* concentrique

concept [ˈkɑnsɛpt] *s* concept *m*

conception [kənˈsɛpʃən] *s* conception *f*

concern [kənˈsʌrn] *s* (*business establishment*) maison *f*, compagnie *f*; (*worry*) inquiétude *f*; (*relation, reference*) intérêt *m*; (*matter*) affaire *f* || *tr* concerner; **as concerns** quant à; **my book concerns . . .** mon livre traite de . . ., il s'agit dans mon livre de . . .; **persons**

concerned intéressés *mpl*; **to be concerned** être inquiet; **to be concerned about** se préoccuper de; **to concern oneself with** s'intéresser à; **to whom it may concern** à qui de droit

concerning [kənˈsʌrnɪŋ] *prep* concernant, en ce qui concerne, touchant

concert [ˈkɑnsərt] *s* concert *m*; **in concert** de concert || [kənˈsʌrt] *tr* concerter || *intr* se concerter

con′cert hall′ *s* salle *f* de concert

con′cert•mas′ter *s* premier violon *m* soliste

concer•to [kənˈtʃɛrto] *s* (*pl* **-tos** or **-ti** [ti]) concerto *m*

concession [kənˈsɛʃən] *s* concession *f*

conciliate [kənˈsɪliˌet] *tr* concilier

conciliatory [kənˈsɪliˈəˌtori] *adj* conciliatoire

concise [kənˈsaɪs] *adj* concis

conclude [kənˈklud] *tr & intr* conclure

conclusion [kənˈkluʒən] *s* conclusion *f*

conclusive [kənˈklusɪv] *adj* concluant

concoct [kənˈkɑkt] *tr* confectionner; (*a story*) inventer; (*a plan*) machiner

concoction [kɑnˈkɑkʃən] *s* confection *f*; (*mixture*) mélange *m*; (pej) drogue *f*

concomitant [kənˈkɑmɪtənt] *adj* concomitant || *s* accompagnement *m*

concord [ˈkɑŋkɔrd] *s* concorde *f*; (gram) concordance *f*; (mus) accord *m*

concordance [kɑnˈkɔrdəns] *s* concordance *f*

concourse [ˈkɑŋkors] *s* (*of people*) concours *m*, foule *f*; (*road*) boulevard *m*; (*of railroad station*) hall *m*, salle *f* des pas perdus

concrete [ˈkɑnkrit] *adj* concret; de béton || *s* concret *m*; (*for construction*) béton *m* || *tr* (*a sidewalk*) bétonner

con′crete block′ *s* parpaing *m*

con′crete mix′er *s* bétonnière *f*

concubine [ˈkɑŋkjəˌbaɪn] *s* concubine *f*

con•cur [kənˈkʌr] *v* (*pret & pp* **-curred;** *ger* **-curring**) *intr* (*said of events*) concourir; (*said of persons*) s'accorder

concurrence [kənˈkʌrəns] *s* concours *m*

concurrent [kənˈkʌrənt] *adj* concourant

concussion [kənˈkʌʃən] *s* secousse *f*, ébranlement *m*; (pathol) commotion *f*

condemn [kənˈdɛm] *tr* condamner

condemnation [ˌkɑndɛmˈneʃən] *s* condamnation *f*

condense [kənˈdɛns] *tr* condenser || *intr* se condenser

condensed′ milk′ *s* lait *m* condensé

condenser [kənˈdɛnsər] *s* condenseur *m*; (elec) condensateur *m*

condescend [ˌkɑndɪˈsɛnd] *intr* condescendre

condescending [ˌkɑndɪˈsɛndɪŋ] *adj* condescendant

condescension [ˌkɑndɪˈsɛnʃən] *s* condescendance *f*

condiment [ˈkɑndɪmənt] *s* condiment *m*

condition [kənˈdɪʃən] *s* condition *f*; **on condition that** à condition que || *tr* conditionner

conditional [kənˈdɪʃənəl] *adj & s* conditionnel *m*

condi′tioned re′flex *s* réflexe *m* conditionné

conditioning [kən'dɪʃənɪŋ] *s* conditionnement *m*

condo ['kɑndo] *s* (coll) immeuble *m* à copropriété

condole [kən'dol] *intr*—**to condole with** offrir ses condoléances à

condolence [kən'doləns] *s* condoléances *fpl*

condom ['kɑndəm] *s* préservatif *m*, capote *f* anglaise

condominium [,kɑndə'mɪni•əm] *s* immeuble *m* à copropriété

condone [kən'don] *tr* pardonner, tolérer

conducive [kən'd(j)usɪv] *adj* favorable

conduct ['kɑndʌkt] *s* conduite *f*, comportement *m* ‖ [kən'dʌkt] *tr* conduire

conductor [kən'dʌktər] *s* (*on bus or streetcar*) receveur *m;* (mus) chef *m* d'orchestre; (rr) chef de train; (elec, phys) conducteur *m;* (elec, phys) (in predicate after **to be,** it may be translated by an adjective) conducteur *m,* e.g., **metals are good conductors of electricity** les métaux sont bons conducteurs de l'électricité

conduit ['kɑndɪt], ['kɑndu•ɪt] *s* (*pipe*) conduit *m,* tuyau *m;* (elec) caniveau *m,* tube *m*

cone [kon] *s* cône *m;* (*for popcorn, ice cream*) cornet *m,* plaisir *m*

confection [kən'fɛkʃən] *s* confiserie *f*

confectioner [kən'fɛkʃənər] *s* confiseur *m*

confec′tioners′ sug′ar *s* sucre *m* glace

confectioner•y [kən'fɛkʃə,nɛri] *s* (*pl* **-ies**) confiserie *f*

confedera•cy [kən'fədərəsi] *s* (*pl* **-cies**) confédération *f;* (*for unlawful purposes*) conspiration *f,* entente *f*

confederate [kən'fɛdərɪt] *adj* confédéré ‖ complice *mf;* **Confederate** (hist) Confédéré *m* ‖ [kən'fɛdə,ret] *tr* confédérer ‖ *intr* se confédérer

con•fer [kən'fʌr] *v* (*pret & pp* **-ferred;** *ger* **-ferring**) *tr & intr* conférer

conference ['kɑnfərəns] *s* conférence *f;* (*interview*) entretien *m;* (sports) groupement *m* (d'équipes); **to be in conference** être en conférence

con′ference room′ *s* salle *f* de conférences

con′ference ta′ble *s* table *f* de conférence

conferment [kən'fʌrmənt] *s* (*of degrees*) collation *f*

confess [kən'fɛs] *tr* confesser ‖ *intr* se confesser

confession [kən'fɛʃən] *s* confession *f*

confessional [kən'fɛʃənəl] *s* confessional *m*

confessor [kən'fɛsər] *s* confesseur *m*

confidant [,kɑnfɪ'dænt] *s* confident *m*

confide [kən'faɪd] *tr* confier ‖ *intr*—**to confide in** se confier à

confidence ['kɑnfɪdəns] *s* confiance *f;* (*secret*) confidence *f;* **in strict confidence** sous toute réserve; **to have confidence in** se confier à

confident ['kɑnfɪdənt] *adj* confiant ‖ *s* confident *m*

confidential [,kɑnfɪ'dɛnʃəl] *adj* confidentiel

confiden′tial sec′retary *s* secrétaire *m* particulier, secrétaire *f* particulière

confine ['kɑnfaɪn] *s* (obs) confinement *m;* **the confines** les confins *mpl* ‖ [kən'faɪn] *tr* confiner, enfermer; (*to keep within limits*) limiter; **to be confined** (*said of woman*) accoucher; **to be confined to bed** être alité

confinement [kən'faɪnmənt] *s* limitation *f;* (*in prison*) emprisonnement *m;* (*in childbirth*) accouchement *m*

confirm [kən'fʌrm] *tr* confirmer

confirmed *adj* (*reassured*) confirmé; (*bachelor*) endurci; (*drunkard*) fieffé; (*drinker*) invétéré; (*smoker*) émérite

confiscate ['kɑnfɪs,ket] *tr* confisquer

conflagration [,kɑnflə'greʃən] *s* conflagration *f,* incendie *m*

conflict ['kɑnflɪkt] *s* conflit *m* ‖ [kən'flɪkt] *intr* être en contradiction, se heurter

conflicting [kən'flɪktɪŋ] *adj* contradictoire; (*events, class hours, etc.*) incompatible

con′flict of in′terest *s* conflit *m* d'intérêts, conflit des intérêts

conform [kən'fɔrm] *tr* conformer ‖ *intr* se conformer, s'accommoder

conformist [kən'fɔrmɪst] *s* conformiste *mf*

conformi•ty [kən'fɔrmɪti] *s* (*pl* **-ties**) conformité *f;* **in conformity with** conformément à

confound [kɑn'faʊnd] *tr* confondre ‖ ['kɑn'faʊnd] *tr* maudire; **confound it!** diable!

confounded *adj* confus; (*damned*) sacré

confrere ['kɑnfrɛr] *s* confrère *m*

confront [kən'frʌnt] *tr* (*to face boldly*) affronter, faire face à; (*witnesses; documents*) confronter; **to be confronted by** se trouver en face de

confuse [kən'fjuz] *tr* confondre

confused *adj* confus, embarrassé

confusing [kən'fjuzɪŋ] *adj* déroutant, embrouillant

confusion [kən'fjuʒən] *s* confusion *f*

confute [kən'fjut] *tr* réfuter

congeal [kən'dʒil] *tr* congeler ‖ *intr* se congeler

congenial [kən'dʒinjəl] *adj* sympathique, agréable; compatible; **congenial to** *ou* **with** apparenté à, conformer au tempérament de

congenital [kən'dʒɛnɪtəl] *adj* congénital

con′ger eel′ ['kɑŋgər] *s* congre *m,* anguille *f* de mer

congest [kən'dʒɛst] *tr* congestionner ‖ *intr* se congestionner

congestion [kən'dʒɛstʃən] *s* congestion *f*

conglomeration [kən,glɑmə're ʃən] *s* conglomération *f*

congratulate [kən'græt∫ə,let] *tr* féliciter, congratuler; **to congratulate s.o. for** féliciter qn de *or* pour; **to congratulate s.o. for** + *ger* féliciter qn de + *inf*

congratulations [kən,græt∫ə'le∫ənz] *spl* félicitations *fpl*

congregate ['kɑŋgrɪ,get] *tr* rassembler ‖ *intr* se rassembler

congregation [,kɑŋgrɪ'ge∫ən] *s* (*grouping*) rassemblement *m;* (*parishioners*) fidèles *mfpl;* (*Protestant parishioners; committee of Roman Catholic prelates*) congrégation *f*

congress [ˈkɑŋgrɪs] *s* congrès *m*

congressional [kənˈgrɛʃənəl] *adj* parlementaire

con′gress•man *s* (*pl* **-men**) congressiste *m,* parlementaire *m*

con′gress•wom′an *s* (*pl* **-wom′en**) congressiste *f,* parlementaire *f*

congruent [ˈkɑŋgruˑənt] *adj* (math) congru

conical [ˈkɑnɪkəl] *adj* conique

conifer [ˈkɑnəfər] *s* conifère *m,* arbre *m* vert

conjecture [kənˈdʒɛktʃər] *s* conjecture *f* ‖ *tr & intr* conjecturer

conjugal [ˈkɑndʒəgəl] *adj* conjugal

conjugate [ˈkɑndʒə͵get] *tr* conjuguer

conjugation [͵kɑndʒəˈgeʃən] *s* conjugaison *f*

conjunction [kənˈdʒʌŋkʃən] *s* conjonction *f*

conjuration [͵kɑndʒəreˈʃən] *s* conjuration *f*

conjure [kənˈdʒʊr] *tr* (*to appeal to solemnly*) conjurer ‖ [ˈkɑndʒər], [ˈkʌndʒər] *tr* (*to exorcise, drive away*) conjurer; **to conjure up** évoquer ‖ *intr* faire de la sorcellerie

conk [kɑnk] *vi*—**to conk out** (coll) (*person*) crever; (*engine, machine*) tomber *or* rester en panne, caler

con′ man′ *s* escroc *m*

connect [kəˈnɛkt] *tr* (*to join*) relier, joindre; (*e.g., two parties on the telephone*) mettre en communication; (*a pipe, an electrical device*) brancher, connecter ‖ *intr* se lier, se joindre; **to connect with** (*said of train*) correspondre avec

connected *adj* (*related*) connexe; (*logical*) suivi

connecting [kəˈnɛktɪŋ] *adj* de liaison; (*wire*) de connexion; (*pipe*) de raccord; (*street*) communiquant

connect′ing flight′ *s* vol *m* en transit

connect′ing rod′ *s* bielle *f*

connection [kəˈnɛkʃən] *s* connexion *f,* liaison *f;* (*between two causes*) connexité *f;* (*in families*) parenté *f,* parent *m;* (*by telephone*) communication *f;* (*of trains*) correspondance *f;* (elec) connexion; **connections** (*in the business world*) clientèle *f,* relations *fpl;* (*in families*) alliés *mpl;* consanguins *mpl;* **in connection with** à propos de

con′ning tow′er [ˈkɑnɪŋ] *s* (*e.g., on battleship*) poste *m or* tourelle *f* de commandement; (*on sub*) kiosque *m*

conniption [kəˈnɪpʃən] *s* (*coll*) rogne *f*

connive [kəˈnaɪv] *intr* être de connivence, être complice

connote [kəˈnot] *tr* (*to signify*) signifier, vouloir dire; (*to imply*) suggérer, sousentendre

connubial [kəˈn(j)ubiˑəl] *adj* conjugal

conquer [ˈkɑŋkər] *tr* conquérir

conqueror [ˈkɑŋkərər] *s* conquérant

conquest [ˈkɑŋkwɛst] *s* conquête *f*

conscience [ˈkɑnʃəns] *s* conscience *f;* **in all conscience** en conscience; **to have on one's conscience** avoir sur la conscience

conscientious [͵kɑnʃiˈɛnʃəs] *adj* consciencieux

conscien′tious objec′tor [əbˈdʒɛktər] *s* objecteur *m* de conscience

conscious [ˈkɑnʃəs] *adj* conscient; **to be conscious** (*not unconscious*) avoir connaissance; **to be conscious of** avoir conscience de

consciousness [ˈkɑnʃəsnɪs] *s* (*not sleep or coma*) connaissance *f;* (*awareness*) conscience *f*

conscript [ˈkɑnskrɪpt] *s* (mil) conscrit *m;* (nav) inscrit *m* maritime ‖ [kənˈskrɪpt] *tr* (mil) enrôler; (nav) inscrire

conscription [kənˈskrɪpʃən] *s* conscription *f*

consecrate [ˈkɑnsɪ͵kret] *tr* consacrer; (*e.g., bread*) bénir; (*a king or bishop*) sacrer

consecration [͵kɑnsɪˈkreʃən] *s* consécration *f;* (*to a task*) dévouement *m;* (*of a king or bishop*) sacre *m*

consecutive [kənˈsɛkjətɪv] *adj* de suite, consécutif

consensus [kənˈsɛnsəs] *s* consensus *m*

consent [kənˈsɛnt] *s* consentement *m;* **by common consent** d'un commun accord ‖ *intr* consentir

consequence [ˈkɑnsɪ͵kwɛns] *s* conséquence *f*

consequential [͵kɑnsɪˈkwɛnʃəl] *adj* conséquent, logique

consequently [ˈkɑnsɪ͵kwɛntli] *adv* conséquemment, par conséquent

conservation [͵kɑnsərˈveʃən] *s* conservation *f*

conservatism [kənˈsʌrvə͵tɪzəm] *s* conservatisme *m*

conservative [kənˈsʌrvətɪv] *adj & s* conservateur *m;* **at a conservative estimate** au bas mot, au moins

conservato•ry [kənˈsʌrvə͵tori] *s* (*pl* **-ries**) (*of music*) conservatoire *m;* (*greenhouse*) serre *f*

conserve [kənˈsʌrv] *tr* conserver

consider [kənˈsɪdər] *tr* considérer

considerable [kənˈsɪdərəbəl] *adj* considérable

considerate [kənˈsɪdərɪt] *adj* prévenant, plein d'égards

consideration [kən͵sɪdəˈreʃən] *s* (*thoughtfulness; careful thought; fact*) considération *f;* (*remuneration*) rétribution *f;* (*favor*) indulgence *f;* **to take into consideration** tenir compte de; **under consideration** à l'étude, en ligne de compte, en présence

considering [kənˈsɪdərɪŋ] *prep* eu égard à; **considering that** vu que

consign [kənˈsaɪn] *tr* consigner

consignee [͵kɑnsaɪˈni] *s* consignataire *m*

consignment [kənˈsaɪnmənt] *s* consignation *f,* livraison *f*

consist [kənˈsɪst] *intr*—**to consist in** consister dans *or* en; **to consist in** + *ger* consister à + *inf;* **to consist of** consister dans *or* en

consisten•cy [kənˈsɪstənsi] *s* (*pl* **-cies**) (*logical connection*) conséquence *f;* (*firmness, amount of firmness*) consistance *f*

consistent [kənˈsɪstənt] *adj* (*agreeing with itself or oneself*) conséquent; (*holding firmly to-*

gether) consistant; **consistent with** compatible avec

consisto•ry [kənˈsɪstəri] *s* (*pl* **-ries**) consistoire *m*

consolation [ˌkɑnsəˈleʃən] *s* consolation *f*

con′sola′tion prize′ *s* prix *m* de consolation

console [ˈkɑnsol] *s* console *f;* (aut) (*small storage cabinet between bucket seats*) vide-poche(s) *m;* (comp) console *f* ‖ [kənˈsol] *tr* consoler

con′sole ta′ble *s* console *f*

consolidate [kənˈsɑlɪˌdet] *tr* consolider

consonant [ˈkɑnsənənt] *adj* (*in sound*) consonant; **consonant with** d'accord avec ‖ *s* consonne *f*

consort [ˈkɑnsɔrt] *s* (*husband*) conjoint *m;* (*wife*) conjointe *f;* prince *m* consort; (*convoy*) conserve *f* ‖ [kənˈsɔrt] *tr* unir ‖ *intr* s'associer; (*to harmonize*) s'accorder; **to consort with** s'associer à or avec

conspicuous [kənˈspɪkjuˌəs] *adj* (*difference*) apparent, frappant; (*attracting special attention*) voyant; **to make oneself conspicuous** se faire remarquer

conspira•cy [kənˈspɪrəsi] *s* (*pl* **-cies**) conspiration *f,* conjuration *f*

conspirator [kənˈspɪrətər] *s* conspirateur *m,* conjuré *m*

conspire [kənˈspaɪr] *intr* conspirer

constancy [ˈkɑnstænsi] *s* constance *f*

constant [ˈkɑnstənt] *adj* constant ‖ *s* constante *f*

constantly [ˈkɑnstəntli] *adv* constamment

constellation [ˌkɑnstəˈleʃən] *s* constellation *f*

constipate [ˈkɑnstɪˌpet] *tr* constiper

constipation [ˌkɑnstɪˈpeʃən] *s* constipation *f*

constituen•cy [kənˈstɪtʃuˌənsi] *s* (*pl* **-cies**) (*persons*) électeurs *mpl,* commettants *mpl;* (*place*) circonscription *f* électorale

constituent [kənˈstɪtʃuˌənt] *adj* constituant, constitutif ‖ *s* élément *m,* constituant *m;* (*voter, client*) électeur *m,* commettant *m*

constitute [ˈkɑnstɪˌt(j)ut] *tr* constituer

constitution [ˌkɑnstɪ t(j)uʃən] *s* constitution *f*

constrain [kənˈstren] *tr* contraindre

constraint [kənˈstrent] *s* contrainte *f;* (*restraint*) retenue *f;* (*uneasiness*) gêne *f*

constrict [kənˈstrɪkt] *tr* resserrer

construct [kənˈstrʌkt] *tr* construire

construction [kənˈstrʌkʃən] *s* construction *f;* interprétation *f*

construc′tion per′mit *s* permis *m* de construire

construc′tion start′ *s* mise *f* en chantier

construc′tion work′er *s* travailleur *m* en construction

constructive [kənˈstrʌktɪv] *adj* constructif, constructeur

construe [kənˈstru] *tr* expliquer, interpréter; (gram) construire

consul [ˈkɑnsəl] *s* consul *m*

consular [ˈkɑns(j)ələr] *adj* consulaire

consulate [ˈkɑns(j)əlɪt] *s* consulat *m*

consult [kənˈsʌlt] *tr* consulter ‖ *intr* consulter; se consulter

consultant [kənˈsʌltənt] *s* conseiller *m,* consultant *m*

consultation [ˌkɑnsəlˈteʃən] *s* consultation *f;* (eccl, law) consulte *f*

consume [kənˈs(j)um] *tr* (*to make use of, use up*) consommer; (*to use up entirely; to destroy*) consumer, épuiser

consumer [kənˈs(j)umər] *s* consommateur *m;* (*of gas, electricity, etc.*) abonné *m*

consum′er cred′it *s* crédit *m* au consommateur

consum′er goods′ *spl* denrées *fpl* de consommation

consum′er price′ in′dex *s* indice *m* des prix de consommation

consummate [kənˈsʌmɪt] *adj* consommé ‖ [ˈkɑnsəˌmet] *tr* consommer

consumption [kənˈsʌmpʃən] *s* consommation *f;* (pathol) tuberculose *f* pulmonaire

contact [ˈkɑntækt] *s* contact *m;* **to put in contact** mettre en contact ‖ *tr* (coll) prendre contact avec, contacter ‖ *intr* prendre contact

con′tact break′er *s* (elec) interrupteur *m*

con′tact lens′ *s* verre *m* de contact, lentille *f* de contact, lentille cornéenne

contagion [kənˈtedʒən] *s* contagion *f*

contagious [kənˈtedʒəs] *adj* contagieux

contain [kənˈten] *tr* contenir; (*one's sorrow*) apprivoiser

container [kənˈtenər] *s* boîte *f,* contenant *m,* récipient *m;* (*to ship goods*) conteneur *m*

containment [kənˈtenmənt] *s* refoulement *m,* retenue *f;* (*in a nuclear reactor*) confinement *m*

contaminate [kənˈtæmɪˌnet] *tr* contaminer

contamination [kənˌtæmɪˈneʃən] *s* contamination *f*

contemplate [ˈkɑntəmˌplet] *tr & intr* contempler; (*e.g., a trip*) projeter; **to contemplate** + *ger* penser + *inf*

contemplation [ˌkɑntəmˈpleʃən] *s* contemplation *f*

contemporaneous [kənˌtempəˈreniˌəs] *adj* contemporain

contemporar•y [kənˈtempəˌreri] *adj* contemporain ‖ *s* (*pl* **-ies**) contemporain *m*

contempt [kənˈtempt] *s* mépris *m,* nargue *f;* (law) contumace *f;* **to hold in contempt** mépriser

contemptible [kənˈtemptɪbəl] *adj* méprisable

contempt′ of court′ *s* outrage *m* à la justice

contemptuous [kənˈtemptʃuˌəs] *adj* méprisant

contend [kənˈtend] *tr* prétendre ‖ *intr* combattre; **to contend with** lutter contre

contender [kənˈtendər] *s* concurrent *m,* compétiteur *m*

content [kənˈtent] *adj & s* content *m* ‖ [ˈkɑntent] *s* contenu *m;* **contents** contenu; (*of table of contents*) matières *fpl* ‖ [kənˈtent] *tr* contenter

contented [kənˈtentɪd] *adj* content, satisfait

contention [kənˈtenʃən] *s* (*strife*) dispute *f,* différend *m;* (*point argued for*) point *m* discuté, argument *m;* (law) contentieux *m*

contentious [kən'tɛnʃəs] *adj* contentieux

contentment [kən'tɛntmənt] *s* contentement *m*

contest ['kantɛst] *s* (*struggle, fight*) lutte *f,* dispute *f;* (*competition*) concours *m,* compétition *f* ‖ [kən'tɛst] *tr & intr* contester

contestant [kən'tɛstənt] *s* concurrent *m*

context ['kantɛkst] *s* contexte *m*

contiguous [kən'tɪgjuˑəs] *adj* contigu

continence ['kantɪnəns] *s* continence *f*

continent ['kantɪnənt] *adj & s* continent *m*

continental [,kantɪ'nɛntəl] *adj* continental

contingen·cy [kən'tɪndʒənsi] *s* (*pl* **-cies**) contingence *f,* éventualité *f*

contingent [kən'tɪndʒənt] *adj & s* contingent *m*

continual [kən'tɪnjuˑəl] *adj* continuel

continuation [kən,tɪnjuˑ'eʃən] *s* continuation *f;* (*e.g., of a story*) suite *f*

continue [kən'tɪnju] *tr & intr* continuer; **continued on page two (three, etc.)** suite page deux (trois, etc.); **to be continued** à suivre

continui·ty [,kantɪ'n(j)uˑɪti] *s* (*pl* **-ties**) continuité *f;* (mov, rad, telv) découpage *m,* scénario *m*

continuous [kən'tɪnjuˑəs] *adj* continu

contin'uous show'ing *s* (mov) spectacle *m* permanent

contin'uous waves' *spl* ondes *fpl* entretenues

contortion [kən'tɔrʃən] *s* contorsion *f*

contour ['kantʊr] *s* contour *m* ‖ *tr* contourner

con'tour line' *s* courbe *f* de niveau

con'tour map' *s* carte *f* avec courbes de niveau

contraband ['kantrə,bænd] *adj* contrebandier ‖ *s* contrebande *f*

contrabass ['kantrə,bes] *s* contrebasse *f*

contraceptive [,kantrə'sɛptɪv] *adj & s* contraceptif *m*

contract ['kantrækt] *s* contrat *m* ‖ *tr* contracter ‖ *intr* se contracter

con'tract bridge' *s* bridge *m* contrat

contraction [kən'trækʃən] *s* contraction *f*

contractor [kən'træktər], [kantræktər] *s* entrepreneur *m* du bâtiment

contradict [,kantrə'dɪkt] *tr* contredire

contradiction [,kantrə'dɪkʃən] *s* contradiction *f*

contradictory [,kantrə'dɪktəri] *adj* contradictoire

contral·to [kən'trælto] *s* (*pl* **-tos**) contralto *m*

contraption [kən'træpʃən] *s* (coll) machin *m,* truc *m*

contra·ry ['kantrɛri] *adj* contraire ‖ *adv* contrairement ‖ [kən'trɛri] *adj* (coll) obstiné, têtu ‖ ['kantrɛri] *s* (*pl* **-ries**) contraire *m;* **on the contrary** au contraire, par contre

contrast ['kantræst] *s* contraste *m* ‖ [kən'træst] *tr & intr* contraster

contravene [,kantrə'vin] *tr* contredire; (*a law*) contrevenir

contribute [kən'trɪbjut] *tr* (*e.g., a sum of money*) contribuer pour ‖ *intr* contribuer; (*to a newspaper, conference, etc.*) collaborer

contribution [,kantrɪ'bjuʃən] *s* contribution *f,* apport *m;* (*e.g., for charity*) souscription *f;* (*to a newspaper, conference, etc.*) collaboration *f*

contributor [kən'trɪbjutər] *s* (*donor*) donneur *m;* (*e.g., to a charitable cause*) souscripteur *m;* (*to a newspaper, conference, etc.*) collaborateur *m*

contrite [kən'traɪt] *adj* contrit

contrition [kən'trɪʃən] *s* contrition *f*

contrivance [kən'traɪvəns] *s* invention *f,* expédient *m;* (*gadget*) dispositif *m*

contrive [kən'traɪv] *tr* inventer ‖ *intr* s'arranger; **to contrive to** trouver moyen de

con·trol [kən'trol] *s* (*authority*) direction *f,* autorité *f;* (*mastery*) maîtrise *f;* (*surveillance*) contrôle *m;* **controls** commandes *fpl* ‖ *v* (*pret & pp* **-trolled**) *ger* **-trolling**) *tr* diriger; maîtriser; (*to give surveillance to*) contrôler; (*to handle the controls of*) commander; **to control oneself** se contrôler

control' bus' *s* (comp) bus *m* de contrôle

control' group' *s* groupe *m* témoin

controller [kən'trolər] *s* contrôleur *m,* appareil *m* de contrôle; (elec) controller *m*

controll'ing in'terest [kən'trolɪŋ] *s* participation *f* majoritaire

control' pan'el *s* (aer) planche *f* de bord, tableau *m* de bord

control' rod' *s* (nucl) barre *f* de contrôle

control' room' *s* (mil) salle *f* de commande, poste *m* de contrôle; (naut) poste *m* de commande; (rad, telv) régie *f*

control' stick' *s* (aer) manche *m* à balai

control' tow'er *s* poste-vigie *m,* tourelle *f* de commandement, tour *f* de contrôle

controversial [,kantrə'vʌrʃəl] *adj* controversable

controver·sy ['kantrə,vʌrsi] *s* (*pl* **-sies**) controverse *f;* dispute *f,* querelle *f*

controvert ['kantrə,vʌrt] *tr* controverser; contredire

contumacious [,kant(j)u'meʃəs] *adj* rebelle, récalcitrant

contume·ly ['kant(j)umɪli] *s* (*pl* **-lies**) injure *f,* outrage *m,* mépris *m*

contusion [kən't(j)uʒən] *s* contusion *f*

conundrum [kə'nʌndrəm] *s* devinette *f,* énigme *f*

convalesce [,kanvə'lɛs] *intr* guérir, se remettre, se rétablir

convalescence [,kanvə'lɛsəns] *s* convalescence *f*

convalescent [,kanvə'lɛsənt] *adj & s* convalescent *m*

convales'cent home' *s* maison *f* de repos

convene [kən'vin] *tr* assembler, convoquer ‖ *intr* s'assembler

convenience [kən'vinjəns] *s* commodité *f,* confort *m;* **at your convenience** quand cela vous conviendra; **at your earliest convenience** (com) dans les meilleurs délais; **for my own convenience** pour mon utilité personnelle

conven'ience store' *s* centre *m* commercial de quartier, épicerie *f* de dépannage

convent [ˈkɑnvɛnt] *s* couvent *m* (de religieuses)

convention [kənˈvɛnʃən] *s* (*meeting*) assemblée *f*, congrès *m;* (*agreement*) convention *f;* (*accepted usage*) convention sociale; **conventions** convenances *fpl*, bienséances *fpl*

conventional [kənˈvɛnʃənəl] *adj* conventionnel; (*in conduct*) respectueux des convenances; (*everyday*) usuel; (*model, type*) traditionnel

converge [kənˈvʌrdʒ] *intr* converger

conversant [kənˈvʌrsənt] *adj* familier, versé

conversation [ˌkɑnvərˈseʃən] *s* conversation *f*

conversational [ˌkɑnvərˈseʃənəl] *adj* de conversation; (comp) de dialogue

conversa'tional mode' *s* (comp) mode *m* dialogué

converse [ˈkɑnvʌrs] *adj & s* contraire *m*, inverse *m*, réciproque *f* ‖ [kənˈvʌrs] *intr* converser

conversion [kənˈvʌrʒən] *s* conversion *f*

convert [ˈkɑnvʌrt] *s* converti *m* ‖ [kənˈvʌrt] *tr* convertir ‖ *intr* se convertir

converter [kənˈvʌrtər] *s* convertisseur *m*

convertible [kənˈvʌrtɪbəl] *adj* (*person*) convertissable; (*thing; security*) convertible; (*sofa*) transformable; (aut) décapotable ‖ *s* (aut) décapotable *f*

convex [kɑnˈvɛks] *adj* convexe, bombé

convey [kənˈve] *tr* (*goods, passengers*) transporter; (*e.g., a message*) communiquer; (*e.g., property*) transmettre; (law) céder

conveyance [kənˈveˑəns] *s* (*of goods, passengers*) transport *m;* (*vehicle*) moyen *m* de transport, voiture *f;* (*of message*) communication *f;* (*transfer*) transmission *f;* (law) transfert *m*, cession *f*

conveyor [kənˈveˑər] *s* transporteur *m*, convoyeur *m*

convey'or belt' *s* tapis *m* roulant

convict [ˈkɑnvɪkt] *s* condamné *m*, détenu *m* ‖ [kənˈvɪkt] *tr* condamner, convaincre

conviction [kənˈvɪkʃən] *s* (*sentencing*) condamnation *f;* (*certainty*) conviction *f*

convince [kənˈvɪns] *tr* convaincre

convincing [kənˈvɪnsɪŋ] *adj* convaincant

convivial [kənˈvɪviˑəl] *adj* jovial, plein d'entrain

convocation [ˌkɑnvəˈkeʃən] *s* (*calling together*) convocation *f;* (*meeting*) assemblée *f*

convoke [kənˈvok] *tr* convoquer

convolution [ˌkɑnvəˈluʃən] *s* (*of brain*) circonvolution *f*

convoy [ˈkɑnvɔɪ] *s* convoi *m*, conserve *f*, e.g., **to sail in convoy** naviguer de conserve ‖ *tr* convoyer

convulse [kənˈvʌls] *tr* convulsionner, convulser; **to be convulsed with laughter** se tordre de rire

coo [ku] *intr* roucouler

cooing [ˈkuˑɪŋ] *s* roucoulement *m*

cook [kʊk] *s* cuisinier *m*, chef *m;* (*female cook*) cuisinière *f* ‖ *tr* cuisiner, faire cuire; **to cook** up (*a plot*) machiner, tramer ‖ *intr* faire la cuisine, cuisiner; (*said of food*) cuire

cook' book' *s* livre *m* de cuisine

cooker [ˈkʊkər] *s* réchaud *m*, cuisinière *f*

cookery [ˈkʊkəri] *s* cuisine *f*

cookie [ˈkʊki] *s* biscuit *m*, gâteau *m* sec, petit-beurre *m*

cooking [ˈkʊkɪŋ] *s* cuisine *f;* (*e.g., of meat*) cuisson *f*

cook'ing uten'sils *spl* batterie *f* de cuisine

cook'stove' *s* cuisinière *f*

cook•y [ˈkʊki] *s* (*pl* -**ies**) biscuit *m*, gâteau *m* sec, petit-beurre *m*

cool [kul] *adj* frais; (*e.g., to an idea*) indifférent; (*calm*) calme; (*unfriendly*) froid; (slang) bon, gentil, juste; **it is cool out** il fait frais; **that's cool!** ça marche!; **to keep cool** tenir au frais; se tenir tranquille ‖ *s* fraîcheur *f;* **keep your cool!** t'énerve pas! ‖ *tr* rafraîchir, refroidir; **to cool one's heels** (coll) se morfondre ‖ *intr* se refroidir, se rafraîchir; **to cool down** se calmer; **to cool off** se refroidir

coolant [ˈkulənt] *s* caloporteur *m*, caloriporteur *m*

cooler [ˈkulər] *s* frigorifique *m;* (*prison*) (slang) violon *m*, tôle *f*

cool'-head'ed *adj* imperturbable, de sangfroid

coolness [ˈkulnɪs] *s* fraîcheur *f;* (*of disposition*) sang-froid *m*, calme *m;* (*standoffishness*) froideur *f*

coon [kun] *s* raton *m* laveur

coop [kup] *s* poulailler *m;* **to fly the coop** (slang) débiner, décamper ‖ *tr* enfermer dans un poulailler; **to coop up** claquemurer

co-op [ˈkoˌɑp] *s* entreprise *f* coopérative

cooper [ˈkupər] *s* tonnelier *m*

cooperate [koˈɑpəˌret] *intr* coopérer; (*to be helpful*) faire preuve de bonne volonté

cooperation [koˌɑpəˈreʃən] *s* coopération *f*

cooperative [koˈɑpəˌretɪv] *adj* coopératif ‖ *s* coopérative *f*

coordinate [koˈɔrdɪnɪt] *adj* coordonné ‖ *s* coordonnée *f* ‖ [koˈɔrdɪˌnet] *tr* coordonner

coordination [koˌɔrdəˈneʃən] *s* coordination *f*

coot [kut] *s* foulque *f;* **old coot** (coll) vieille baderne *f*

cootie [ˈkuti] *s* (slang) pou *m*

cop [kɑp] *s* (coll) agent *m* ‖ *v* (*pret & pp* **copped; ger copping**) *tr* (slang) dérober

copartner [koˈpɑrtnər] *s* coassocié *m*, coparticipant *m;* (*in crime*) complice *mf*

co-payment [ˈkoˌpemənt] *ou* **co-'pay'** *s* (ins) portion de l'assurance médicale payée par l'assuré

cope [kop] *intr*—**to cope with** faire face à, tenir tête à

cope'stone' *s* couronnement *m*

copier [ˈkɑpiˑər] *s* (*person who copies*) copiste *mf*, imitateur *m;* (*apparatus*) appareil *m* à copier; (*making photocopies*) machine *f* à photocopier, reprographieur *m*

copilot [ˈkoˌpaɪlət] *s* copilote *m*

coping [ˈkopɪŋ] *s* faîte *m*, comble *m; (of bridge)* chape *f*

copious [ˈkopɪ•əs] *adj* copieux

cop'-out' *s* démission *f*, dérobade *f*

copper [ˈkɑpər] *adj* de cuivre, en cuivre; *(color)* cuivré ‖ *s* cuivre *m; (coin)* petite monnaie *f;* (slang) flic *m*

cop'per•smith' *s* chaudronnier *m*

coppery [ˈkɑpəri] *adj* cuivreux

coppice [ˈkɑpɪs] *s* taillis *m*

copulate [ˈkɑpjə,let] *intr* s'accoupler

copulation [,kɑpjəˈleʃən] *s* copulation *f*, accouplement *m*

cop•y [ˈkɑpi] *s (pl* **-ies**) copie *f; (of a book)* exemplaire *m; (of a magazine)* numéro *m; (for printer)* original *m;* **to make copies** exécuter des doubles ‖ *v (pret & pp* **-ied**) *tr & intr* copier

cop'y•book' *s* cashier *m*

cop'y•cat' *s* (coll) imitateur *m*, singe *m*

cop'y-and-paste' *s* (comp) copier et coller

cop'y ed'itor *s* secrétaire *mf* de rédaction

cop'ying machine' [ˈkɑpɪ•ɪŋ] *s* machine *f* à photocopier, reprographieur *m*

cop'y read'er *s* correcteur *m* des copies, correcteur des épreuves; *(of news to be published)* secrétaire *mf* de rédaction

cop'y•right' *s* propriété *f* artistique *or* littéraire, droit *m* de l'artiste *or* de l'auteur, copyright *m;* (formula on printed matter) dépôt *m* légal ‖ *tr* réserver les droits de publication de

cop'y•right'ed *adj* (formula used on printed material) droits de reproduction réservés

cop'y•writ'er *s* rédacteur *m* d'annonces publicitaires

co•quet [koˈkɛt] *v (pret & pp* **-quetted;** *ger* **-quetting**) *intr* coqueter

coquet•ry [ˈkokətri] *s (pl* **-ries**) coquetterie *f*

coquette [koˈkɛt] *s* coquette *f* ‖ *intr* coqueter

coquettish [koˈkɛtɪʃ] *adj* coquet

coral [ˈkɔrəl] *adj* de corail, en corail ‖ *s* corail *m*

cor'al reef' *s* récif *m* de corail

cord [kɔrd] *s* corde *f; (string)* ficelle *f; (attached to a bell)* cordon *m;* (elec) fil *m* ‖ *tr* corder

cordage [ˈkɔrdɪdʒ] *s* cordage *m*

cordial [ˈkɔrdʒəl] *adj & s* cordial *m*

cordiali•ty [kɔrˈdʒælɪti] *s (pl* **-ties**) cordialité *f*

corduroy [ˈkɔrdə,rɔɪ] *s* velours *m* côtelé; **corduroys** pantalon en velours côtelé

core [kor] *s (of fruit)* trognon *m*, cœur *m; (of magnet, cable, earth, atom)* noyau *m;* (nucl) cœur *m;* **rotten to the core** pourri à la base ‖ *tr* vider

corespondent [,korɪsˈpɑndənt] *s* complice *mf* d'adultère

cork [kɔrk] *s* liège *m; (of bottle)* bouchon *m;* **to take the cork out of** déboucher ‖ *tr* boucher

corking [ˈkɔrkɪŋ] *adj* (coll) épatant

cork' oak' *s* chêne-liège *m*

cork'screw' *s* tire-bouchon *m*

cork'-tipped' *adj* à bout de liège

cormorant [ˈkɔrmərənt] *s* cormoran *m*

corn [kɔrn] *s (in U.S.A.)* maïs *m; (in England)* blé *m; (in Scotland)* avoine *f; (single seed)* grain *m; (on foot)* cor *m,* durillon *m; (whiskey)* (coll) eau-de-vie *f* de grain; (slang) platitude *f,* banalité *f*

corn' bread' *s* pain *m* de maïs

corn' cob' *s* épi *m* de maïs; *(without the grain)* rafle *f*

corn'cob pipe' *s* pipe *f* en rafle de maïs

corn' crib' *s* dépôt *m* de maïs

cornea [ˈkɔrnɪ•ə] *s* cornée *f*

corned' beef' *s* bœuf *m* salé

corner [ˈkɔrnər] *adj* cornier ‖ *s* coin *m*, angle *m; (of room)* encoignure *f; (of lips)* commissure *f; (on the market)* prise *f* de contrôle; **around the corner** au tournant; **in a corner** (fig) au pied du mur, à l'accul; **to cut a corner close** prendre un virage à la corde; **to cut corners** *(in spending)* rogner les dépenses; *(in work)* bâcler un travail ‖ *tr* coincer, acculer; *(the market)* accaparer

cor'ner cup'board *s* encoignure *f*

cor'ner room' *s* pièce *f* d'angle

cor'ner•stone' *s* pierre *f* angulaire

cornet [kɔrˈnɛt] *s* cornet *m; (headdress)* cornette *f;* (mil) cornette *m;* (mus) cornet à pistons

corn' exchange' *s* bourse *f* des céréales

corn'field' *s (in U.S.A.)* champ *m* de maïs; *(in England)* champ de blé; *(in Scotland)* champ d'avoine

corn'flakes' *spl* paillettes *fpl* de maïs

corn' flour' *s* farine *f* de maïs

corn'flow'er *s* bluet *m*, barbeau *m*

corn' frit'ter *s* crêpes *fpl* de maïs

corn'husk' *s* enveloppe *f* de l'épi de maïs

cornice [ˈkɔrnɪs] *s* corniche *f*

corn' meal' *s* farine *f* de maïs

corn' on the cob' *s* maïs *m* en épi

corn' pad' *s* bourrelet *m* coricide

corn' pone' *s* pain *m* de maïs

corn' pop'per *s* appareil *m* pour faire éclater le maïs

corn' remov'er *s* coricide *m*

corn' silk' *s* barbe *f* de maïs

corn'stalk' *s* tige *f* de maïs

corn'starch' *s* fécule *f* de maïs

cornucopia [,kɔrnəˈkopɪ•ə] *s* corne *f* d'abondance

Cornwall [ˈkɔrn,wɔl] *s* la Cornouailles

corn•y [ˈkɔrni] *adj (comp* **-ier;** *super* **-iest**) (slang) banal, trivial, fade

corollar•y [ˈkɔrə,lɛri] *s (pl* **-ies**) corollaire *m*

coronary [ˈkɔrə,nɛri] *adj* coronaire

cor'onary thrombo'sis *s* (pathol) infarctus *m* du myocarde

coronation [,kɔrəˈneʃən] *s* couronnement *m*, sacre *m*

cor'oner's in'quest [ˈkɔrənərz] *s* enquête *f* judiciaire par-devant jury (en cas de mort violente ou suspecte)

coronet [ˈkɔrə,nɛt] *s (worn by lady)* diadème

m; (*worn by members of nobility*) couronne f; (*worn by earl or baron*) tortil m

corporal [ˈkɔrpərəl] adj corporel ‖ s (mil) caporal m

cor′poral pun′ishment s châtiment m corporel

corporate [ˈkɔrpərɪt] adj incorporé

corporation [ˌkɔrpəˈreʃən] s société f anonyme, compagnie f anonyme

corporeal [kɔrˈporɪ•əl] adj corporel, matériel

corps [kor] s (pl **corps** [korz]) corps m; (mil) corps d'armée

corpse [kɔrps] s cadavre m

corps′man s (pl **-men**) (mil) infirmier m

corpulent [ˈkɔrpjələnt] adj corpulent

corpuscle [ˈkɔrpəsəl] s (phys) corpuscule m; (physiol) globule m

corpus delicti [ˈkɔrpəsdɪˈlɪktaɪ] s (law) corps m du délit

cor•ral [kəˈræl] s corral m, enclos m ‖ v (*pret & pp* **-ralled;** *ger* **-ralling**) tr enfermer dans un corral; (fig) saisir

correct [kəˈrɛkt] adj correct ‖ tr corriger

correction [kəˈrɛkʃən] s correction f

corrective [kəˈrɛktɪv] adj & s correctif m

correc′tive lens′es spl verres mpl correcteurs

correctness [kəˈrɛktnɪs] s correction f

correlate [ˈkɔrə,let] tr mettre en corrélation ‖ intr correspondre; **to correlate with** correspondre à

correlation [ˌkɔrɪˈleʃən] s corrélation f

correspond [ˌkɔrɪˈspɑnd] intr correspondre

correspondence [ˌkɔrɪˈspɑndəns] s correspondance f

correspond′ence course′ s cours m de l'enseignement par correspondance

correspondent [ˌkɔrɪˈspɑndənt] adj & s correspondant m

corresponding [ˌkɔrɪˈspɑndɪŋ] adj correspondant

corridor [ˈkɔrɪdər] s corridor m, couloir m

corroborate [kəˈrɑbə,ret] tr corroborer

corrode [kəˈrod] tr corroder ‖ intr se corroder

corrosion [kəˈroʒən] s corrosion f

corrosive [kəˈrosɪv] adj & s corrosif m

corrugated [ˈkɔrə,getɪd] adj ondulé

corrupt [kəˈrʌpt] adj corrompu ‖ tr corrompre

corruption [kəˈrʌpʃən] s corruption f

corsage [kɔrˈsɑʒ] s bouquet m porté or fleur f portée à l'épaule ou à la ceinture; (*waist*) corsage m

corsair [ˈkɔr,sɛr] s corsaire m

corset [ˈkɔrsɪt] s corset m

Corsica [ˈkɔrsɪkə] s Corse f; la Corse

Corsican [ˈkɔrsɪkən] adj corse ‖ s (*dialect*) corse m; (*person*) Corse mf

cortege [kɔrˈteʒ] s cortège m

cor•tex [ˈkɔr,tɛks] s (pl **-tices** [tɪ,siz]) cortex m

cortisone [ˈkɔrtɪ,son] s cortisone f

coruscate [ˈkɔrəs,ket] intr scintiller

cosmetic [kazˈmɛtɪk] adj & s cosmétique m

cosmet′ic sur′gery s chirurgie f esthétique

cosmic [ˈkazmɪk] adj cosmique

cosmonaut [ˈkazmə,nɔt] s cosmonaute mf

cosmopolitan [ˌkazməˈpɑlɪtən] adj & s cosmopolite mf

cosmos [ˈkazməs] s cosmos m

Cossack [ˈka,sæk] adj cosaque ‖ s Cosaque mf

cost [kɔst] s coût m; (*price*) prix m; **at all costs** à tout prix, coûte que coûte; **at cost** au prix coûtant; **costs** frais mpl; (law) dépens mpl ‖ v (*pret & pp* **cost**) intr coûter

cost′ account′ing s comptabilité f industrielle

co′-star′ s (mov, theat) partenaire mf ‖ intr partager l'affiche; (public sign) **co-starring X** avec X

costliness [ˈkɔstlɪnɪs] s cherté f, haut prix m

cost•ly [ˈkɔstli] adj (*comp* **-lier;** *super* **-liest**) coûteux, cher

cost′ of liv′ing s coût m de la vie

cost′-of-liv′ing in′dex s indice m du coût de la vie

cost′ price′ s prix m coûtant; (*net price*) prix de revient

costume [ˈkast(j)um] s costume m

cos′tume ball′ s bal m costumé

cos′tume jew′elry s bijoux mpl en toc

costumer [kasˈt(j)umər] s costumier m

cot [kat] s lit m de sangle

cot′ death′ s mort f subite du nourrisson, mort inexpliquée du nourrisson

coterie [ˈkotəri] s coterie f

cottage [ˈkatɪdʒ] s chalet m, cabanon m, villa f; (*with a thatched roof*) chaumière f

cot′tage cheese′ s lait m caillé, caillé m, jonchée f

cot′ter pin′ [ˈkatər] s goupille f fendue, clavette f

cotton [ˈkatən] adj cotonnier, de coton ‖ s coton m ‖ intr—**to cotton up to** (coll) éprouver de la sympathie pour

cot′ton bat′ting s coton m or ouate f hydrophile

cot′ton can′dy s barbe f à papa

cot′ton field′ s cotonnerie f

cot′ton gin′ s égreneuse f

cot′ton mill′ s filature f de coton, cotonnerie f

cot′ton pick′er s cotonnier m

cot′ton pick′ing s récolte f du coton

cot′ton•seed′ s graine f de coton

cot′tonseed oil′ s huile f de coton

cot′ton waste′ s déchets mpl or bourre f de coton

cot′ton•wood′ s peuplier m de Virginie

cottony [ˈkatəni] adj cotonneux

couch [kautʃ] s (*without back*) divan m; (*with back*) sofa m, canapé m ‖ tr (*a demand, a letter*) rédiger ‖ intr (*to lie in wait*) se tapir

couch′ pota′to s (slang) téléspectateur m indolent

cougar [ˈkugər] s couguar m, cougouar m

cough [kɔf], [kɑf] s toux f ‖ tr—**to cough up** cracher en toussant; (slang) (*money*) cracher ‖ intr tousser

cough′ drop′ s pastille f pectorale, pastille pour la toux

cough′ syr′up s sirop m pectoral, sirop contre la toux

could [kʊd] *aux*—**he could not come** il ne pouvait pas venir; **he couldn't do it** il n'a (pas) pu le faire; **he couldn't do it if he wanted to** il ne pourrait (pas) le faire s'il le voulait, il ne saurait (pas) le faire s'il le voulait

couldn't *contr* **could not**

council [ˈkaʊnsəl] *s* conseil *m*; (eccl) concile *m*

coun′cil·man *s* (*pl* **-men**) conseiller *m* municipal

councilor [ˈkaʊnsələr] *s* conseiller *m*

coun·sel [ˈkaʊnsəl] *s* conseil *m*, avis *m*; (*lawyer*) avocat *m* ‖ *v* (*pret & pp* **-seled** or **-selled;** *ger* **-seling** *ou* **-selling**) *tr & intr* conseiller; **to counsel s.o. to** + *inf* conseiller à qn de + *inf*

counselor [ˈkaʊnsələr] *s* conseiller *m*, conseil *m*; (*lawyer*) avocat *m*

count [kaʊnt] *s* (*counting*) compte *m*; (*nobleman*) comte *m* ‖ *tr* compter; **to count the votes** dépouiller le scrutin ‖ *intr* compter; **count off!** (mil) comptez-vous!; **to count for** valoir; **to count on** (*to have confidence in*) compter sur (*s.o. or s.th.*); **to count on** + *ger* compter + *inf*

countable [ˈkaʊntəbəl] *adj* comptable

count′down′ *s* compte *m* à rebours

countenance [ˈkaʊntɪnəns] *s* mine *f*, contenance *f*; **to give countenance to** appuyer; **to keep one's countenance** garder son sérieux; **to lose countenance** perdre contenance ‖ *tr* soutenir, approuver

counter [ˈkaʊntər] *adj* contraire ‖ *s* (*counting agent or machine*) compteur *m*; (*piece of wood or metal for keeping score*) jeton *m*; (*board in shop over which business is transacted*) comptoir *m*; (*in a bar or café*) zinc *m*; **over the counter** (com) hors bourse, hors cote; **under the counter** en dessous de table, sous le comptoir, sous cape ‖ *adv* contrairement; en sens inverse; **to run counter to** aller à l'encontre de ‖ *tr* contrarier, contrecarrer; (*a move, e.g., in chess*) contrer; (*an opinion*) prendre le contre-pied de ‖ *intr* parer le coup, parer un coup; **to counter with** riposter par

coun′ter·act′ *tr* contrebalancer

coun′ter·attack′ *s* contre-attaque *f* ‖ **coun′ter··attack′** *tr* contre-attaquer

coun′ter·bal′ance *s* contrepoids *m* ‖ **coun′ter··bal′ance** *tr* contrebalancer

coun′ter·clock′wise′ *adj & adv* en sens inverse des aiguilles d'une montre, en sens antihoraire

coun′ter·cul′ture *s* contre-culture *f*

coun′ter·cur′rent *s* contre-courant *m*

coun′ter·es′pionage *s* contre-espionnage *m*

counterfeit [ˈkaʊntərfɪt] *adj* contrefait; (*beauty*) sophistiqué ‖ *s* contrefaction *f*, contrefaçon *f*; (*money*) fausse monnaie *f* ‖ *tr* contrefaire; (*e.g., an illness*) feindre

counterfeiter [ˈkaʊntərˌfɪtər] *s* contre-facteur *m*; (*of money*) faux-monnayeur *m*

coun′terfeit mon′ey *s* fausse monnaie *f*, faux billets *mpl*

coun′ter·ir′ritant *adj & s* révulsif *m*

countermand [ˈkaʊntərˌmænd] *s* contreordre *m* ‖ *tr* contremander

coun′ter·march′ *s* contremarche *f* ‖ *intr* faire une contremarche

coun′ter·meas′ure *s* contre-mesure *f*

coun′ter·offen′sive *s* contre-offensive *f*

coun′ter·pane′ *s* courtepoint *f*

coun′ter·part *s* contrepartie *f*, homologue *m*

coun′ter·point′ *s* (mus) contrepoint *m*

coun′ter·poise′ *s* contrepoids *m* ‖ *tr* faire équilibre à

coun′ter·rev′olu′tionar·y *adj* contrerévolutionnaire ‖ *s* (*pl* **-ies**) contrerévolutionnaire *mf*

coun′ter·sign′ *s* contremarque *f*; (*signature*) contreseing *m*; (mil) mot *m* d'ordre ‖ *tr* contresigner

coun′ter·sig′nature *s* contreseing *m*

coun′ter·sink′ *s* fraise *f*, chasse-clou *m* ‖ *v* (*pret & pp* **-sunk**) *tr* fraiser

coun′ter·spy′ *s* (*pl* **-spies**) contre-espion *m*

coun′ter·stroke′ *s* contrecoup *m*

coun′ter·weight′ *s* contrepoids *m*

countess [ˈkaʊntɪs] *s* comtesse *f*

countless [ˈkaʊntɪs] *adj* innombrable

countrified [ˈkʌntrɪˌfaɪd] *adj* provincial, compagnard

coun·try [ˈkʌntri] *s* (*pl* **-tries**) (*territory of a nation*) pays *m*; (*land of one's birth*) patrie *f*; (*region*) contrée *f*; (*not the city*) campagne *f*

coun′try club′ *s* club *m* privé situé hors des agglomérations

coun′try estate′ *s* domaine *m*

coun′try·folk′ *s* campagnards *mpl*

coun′try gen′tleman *s* châtelain *m*, propriétaire *m* d'un château

coun′try house′ *s* maison *f* de campagne

coun′try·man *s* (*pl* **-men**) (*of the same country*) compatriote *mf*; (*rural*) compagnard *m*

coun′try mu′sic *s* musique *f* rustique

coun′try·side′ *s* paysage *m*, campagne *f*

coun′try town′ *s* petite ville *f* de province

coun′try·wide′ *adj* national

coun′try·wom′an *s* (*pl* **-wom′en**) (*of the same country*) compatriote *f*; (*rural*) campagnarde *f*

coun·ty [ˈkaʊnti] *s* (*pl* **-ties**) comté *m*

coun′ty seat′ *s* chef-lieu *m* de comté

coup [ku] *s* coup *m*

coup d'etat [ˌkuˌdeˈtɑ] *s* (pol) coup *m* d'état

coupé [kupe] *s* coupé *m*

couple [ˈkʌpəl] *s* (*man and wife; male and female; friends*) couple *m*, paire *f*; (*of eggs, cakes, etc.*) couple *f*; (elec, mech) couple *m*; **a couple of** deux; quelques ‖ *tr* coupler, accoupler; (mach) embrayer ‖ *intr* s'accoupler

coupler [ˈkʌplər] *s* (mach) coupleur *m*

coupling [ˈkʌplɪŋ] *s* accouplement *m*; (mach) couplage *m*

coupon [ˈk(j)upɑn] *s* coupon *m*, bon *m*

courage [ˈkʌrɪdʒ] *s* courage *m*

courageous [kəˈreɪdʒəs] *adj* courageux

courier ['kurɪ•ər] *s* courrier *m;* (*on horseback*) estafette *f*

course [kors] *s* (*duration, process; course in school*) cours *m;* (*of a meal*) service *m*, plat *m;* (*of a stream*) parcours *m*, cours *m;* (*direction*) route *f*, chemin *m;* **course before the main course** (culin) entrée *f;* **first course** (culin) premier plat, entrée en matière; **in due course** en temps voulu; **in the course of** au cours de; **in the course of time** avec le temps; **main course** (culin) plat principal, pièce *f* de résistance; **of course!** naturellement!, bien entendu!; **to give a course** faire un cours; **to set a course for** (naut) mettre le cap sur; **to take a course** suivre un cours ‖ *tr & intr* courir

court [kort] *s* cour *f;* (*of law*) tribunal *m*, cour; (sports) terrain *m*, court *m;* **out of court** à l'amiable ‖ *tr* courtiser, faire la cour à; (*favor, votes*) briguer, solliciter; (*danger*) aller au-devant de

courteous ['kʌrtɪ•əs] *adj* poli, courtois

courtesan ['kortɪzən] *s* courtisane *f*

courte•sy ['kʌrtisi] *s* (*pl* **-sies**) politesse *f*, courtoisie *f;* **through the courtesy of** avec la gracieuse permission de

cour'tesy call' *s* visite *f* de politesse

cour'tesy card' *s* (com) carte *f* de priorité

cour'tesy light' *s* (aut) plafonnier *m*

court'house' *s* palais *m* de justice

courtier ['kortɪ•ər] *s* courtisan *m*

court' jest'er *s* bouffon *m* du roi

court•ly ['kortli] *adj* (*comp* **-lier;** *super* **-liest**) courtois, élegant

court'ly love' *s* amour *m* courtois

court' -mar'tial *s* (*pl* **courts-martial**) conseil *m* de guerre ‖ *v* (*pret & pp* **-tialed** or **-tialled;** *ger* **-tialing** or **-tialling**) *tr* traduire en conseil de guerre; **to be court-martialed** passer en conseil de guerre

court' plas'ter *s* taffetas *m* gommé, sparadrap *m*

court'room' *s* salle *f* du tribunal

court'ship' *s* cour *f*

court'yard' *s* cour *f*

couscous ['kuskus] *s* (culin) couscous *m*

cousin ['kʌzɪn] *s* cousin *m*

cove [kov] *s* anse *f*, crique *f*

covenant ['kʌvənənt] *s* contrat *m*, accord *m*, pacte *m;* (Bib) alliance *f*

cover ['kʌvər] *s* (*blanket; military protection; book cover*) couverture *f;* (*lid*) couvercle *m;* (*for furniture*) housse *f;* (*of wild game*) remise *f*, gîte *m;* (com) couverture *f*, provision *f*, marge *f;* (mach) chape *f;* (phila) enveloppe *f;* **from cover to cover** de la première page à la dernière; **to take cover** se mettre à l'abri; **under cover** (*e.g., of trees*) sous les couverts; (*safe from harm*) à couvert; **under cover of** sous le couvert de, dissimulé dans; **under separate cover** sous pli distinct ‖ *tr* couvrir; (*a certain distance*) parcourir; (*a newspaper story*) faire le reportage de; (*one's tracks*) brouiller; (*with, e.g., chocolate*) enrober; **to**

cover up recouvrir ‖ *intr* se couvrir; (*to brood*) couver

coverage ['kʌvərɪdʒ] *s* (*amount or space covered*) portée *f;* (*of news*) reportage *m;* (*insurance*) assurance *f*, couverture *f* d'assurance

co'ver•alls' *spl* salopette *f*, bleus *mpl*

cov'er charge' *s* couvert *m*

cov'ered wag'on *s* chariot *m* couvert

cov'er girl' *s* cover-girl *f*, pin up *f*

covering ['kʌvərɪŋ] *s* couverture *f*, recouvrement *m*

covert ['kʌvərt] *adj* couvert, caché

cov'er•up' *s* subterfuge *m;* (*reply*) réponse *f* évasive

covet ['kʌvɪt] *tr* convoiter

covetous ['kʌvɪtəs] *adj* cupide, avide

covetousness ['kʌvɪtəsnɪs] *s* convoitise *f*, cupidité *f*

covey ['kʌvi] *s* couvée *f;* (*in flight*) volée *f*

cow [kau] *s* vache *f;* (*of seal, elephant*) femelle *f* ‖ *tr* (coll) intimider

coward ['kau•ərd] *s* lâche *mf*

cowardice ['kau•ərdɪs] *s* lâcheté *f*

cowardly ['kau•ərdli] *adj* lâche ‖ *adv* lâchement, peureusement

cow'bell' *s* grelot *m*, clarine *f*

cow'boy' *s* cow-boy *m*

cow'catch'er *s* (rr) chasse-bestiaux *m*

cower ['kau•ər] *intr* se tapir

cow'herd' *s* vacher *m*, bouvier *m*

cow'hide' *s* vache *f*, peau *f* de vache; fouet *m* ‖ *tr* fouetter

cowl [kaul] *s* (*religious dress*) capuchon *m*, cagoule *f;* (*of chimney*) chapeau *m;* (aer, aut) capot *m*

cow'lick' *s* mèche *f* rebelle

cow'pox' *s* (pathol) vaccine *f*

coxcomb ['kaks,kom] *s* (*conceited person*) petit-maître *m*, fat *m;* (bot) crête-de-coq *f*

coxswain ['kaksən], ['kaks,swen] *s* (naut) patron *m* de chaloupe; (rowing) barreur *m*

coy [kɔɪ] *adj* réservé, modeste

co•zy ['kozi] *adj* (*comp* **-zier;** *super* **-ziest**) douillet, intime ‖ *s* (*pl* **-zies**) couvrethéière *m*

C.P.A. ['si'pi'e] *s* (letterword) (**certified public accountant**) expert-comptable *m*, comptable *m* agréé

CPI ['si'pi'aɪ] *s* (letterword) (**consumer price index**) indexation *f* des traitements sur le coût de la vie

crab [kræb] *s* crabe *m;* (*grouch*) grincheux *m* ‖ *v* (*pret & pp* **crabbed;** *ger* **crabbing**) *intr* (coll) se plaindre

crab' ap'ple *s* pomme *f* sauvage

crabbed ['kræbɪd] *adj* acariâtre; (*handwriting*) de chat; (*author*) hermétique; (*style*) entortillé

crab•by ['kræbi] *adj* (*comp* **-bier;** *super* **-biest**) (coll) revêche, grognon

crack [kræk] *adj* (*troops*) d'élite; (coll) expert, de premier ordre ‖ *s* (*noise*) bruit *m* sec, craquement *m;* (*of whip*) claquement *m;* (*fissure*) fente *f;* (*e.g., in a dish*) fêlure *f;* (*e.g.,* *in a wall*) lézarde *f*; (*in skin*) gerçure *f*; (*joke*) bon mot *m*; (*drug*) crack *m*; **crack of dawn** pointe *f* du jour ‖ *tr* (*one's fingers; petroleum*) faire craquer; (*a whip*) claquer; (*to split*) fendre; (*e.g., a dish*) fêler; (*e.g., a wall*) lézarder; (*the skin*) gercer; (*nuts*) casser; **to crack a joke** (slang) faire or lâcher une plaisanterie; **to crack up** (*to praise*) (coll) vanter, prôner; (*to crash*) (coll) écraser ‖ *intr* (*to make a noise*) craquer; (*said of whip*) claquer; (*to be split*) se fendre; (*said of dish*) se fêler; (*said of wall*) se lézarder; (*said of skin*) se gercer; **to crack up** (*to crash*) (coll) s'écraser; (*to break down*) (coll) craquer, s'effondrer

crack′-brained′ *adj* timbré; **to be crack-brained** avoir le cerveau fêlé

crack′down′ *s* (coll) répression *f*

cracked *adj* (*split*) fendu, fêlé; (*foolish*) (coll) timbré, toqué, cinglé

cracker [ˋkrækər] *s* biscuit *m* sec

crack′er-bar′rel *adj* (coll) en chambre, au petit pied

crack′er•jack′ *adj* (slang) expérimenté, remarquable ‖ *s* (slang) crack *m*

crack′head′ *s* (slang) toxico *m* qui s'adonne au crack

cracking [ˋkrækɪŋ] *s* (*of petroleum*) cracking *m*

crackle [ˋkrækəl] *s* crépitation *f* ‖ *intr* crépiter, pétiller

crack′le•ware′ *s* porcelaine *f* craquelée

crackling [ˋkræklɪŋ] *s* crépitement *m*, pétillement *m*; (culin) couenne *f* rissolée; **cracklings** cretons *mpl*

crack′pot′ *adj & s* (slang) original *m*, excentrique *mf*

crack′ shot′ *s* (coll) fin tireur *m*

crack′-up′ *s* (*collision*) (coll) écrasement *m*; (*breakdown*) (coll) effondrement *m*

cradle [ˋkredəl] *s* berceau *m* ‖ *tr* bercer

cra′dle-song′ *s* berceuse *f*

craft [kræft] *s* (*profession*) métier *m*; (*trickery*) artifice *m*; (naut) embarcation *f*, barque *f*

craftiness [ˋkræftɪnɪs] *s* ruse *f*, astuce *f*

crafts′man *s* (*pl* **-men**) artisan *m*

crafts′man•ship′ *s* habileté *f* technique; exécution *f*

craft•y [ˋkræfti] *adj* (*comp* **-ier**; *super* **-iest**) rusé

crag [kræg] *s* rocher *m* escarpé

cram [kræm] *v* (*pret & pp* **crammed**; *ger* **cramming**) *tr* (*with food*) bourrer, gaver; (*with people*) bonder; (*for an exam*) (coll) chauffer ‖ *intr* se bourrer, se gaver; (*for an exam*) (coll) potasser

cramp [kræmp] *s* (*metal bar; clamp*) crampon *m*; (*in a muscle*) crampe *f*; (carpentry) serre-joint *m* ‖ *tr* cramponner, agrafer; presser, serrer; (*one's movements, style, or manner of living*) gêner

cranber•ry [ˋkræn‚bɛri] *s* (*pl* **-ries**) (*Vaccinium oxycoccus or V. uliginosum*) canneberge *f*, airelle *f* coussinette

crane [kren] *s* (mach, orn) grue *f* ‖ *tr* (*one's neck*) allonger, tendre ‖ *intr* allonger le cou

crani•um [ˋkrenɪ•əm] *s* (*pl* **-a** [ə]) crâne *m*

crank [kræŋk] *s* (*which turns*) manivelle *f*; (*person*) (coll) excentrique *mf* ‖ *tr* (*a motor*) faire partir à la manivelle

crank′case′ *s* carter *m*

crank′shaft′ *s* vilebrequin *m*

crank•y [ˋkræŋki] *adj* (*comp* **-ier**; *super* **-iest**) (*person*) revêche, grincheux; (*not working well*) détraqué; (*queer*) excentrique

cran•ny [ˋkræni] *s* (*pl* **-nies**) fente *f*, crevasse *f*; (*corner*) coin *m*

crape [krep] *s* crêpe *m*

crape′hang′er *s* (slang) rabat-joie *m*

craps [kræps] *s* (slang) jeu *m* de dés; **to shoot craps** (slang) jouer aux dés

crash [kræʃ] *s* (*noise*) fracas *m*, écroulement *m*; (*of thunder*) coup *m*; (*e.g., of airplane*) écrasement *m*; (*e.g., on stock market*) krach *m* ‖ *tr* briser, fracasser; (*e.g., an airplane*) écraser ‖ *intr* retentir; (*said of airplane*) s'écraser; (*to fail*) craquer; **to crash into** emboutir, tamponner; **to crash through** enfoncer

crash′ dive′ *s* brusque plongée *f*

crash′ hel′met *s* casque *m*

crash′-land′ing *s* crash *m*, atterrissage *m* violent

crash′ pro′gram *s* programme *m* intensif

crash′ record′er *s* (aer) enregistreur *m* d'accident

crash′ test *s* (aut) essai *m* de résistance contre les collisions

crass [kræs] *adj* grossier; (*ignorance*) crasse

crate [kret] *s* caisse *f* à claire-voie, cageot *m*, caisson *m* ‖ *tr* emballer dans une caisse à claire-voie

crater [ˋkretər] *s* cratère *m*

cravat [krəˋvæt] *s* cravate *f*

crave [krev] *tr* (*drink, tobacco, etc.*) avoir un besoin maladif de; (*affection*) avoir grand besoin de; (*attention*) solliciter; **to crave s.o.'s pardon** implorer le pardon de qn ‖ *intr*—**to crave for** désirer ardemment; implorer

craven [ˋkrevən] *adj & s* poltron *m*

craving [ˋkrevɪŋ] *s* désir *m* ardent, désir obsédant

craw [krɔ] *s* jabot *m*

crawl [krɔl] *s* (*snail's pace*) allure *f* très ralentie; (swimming) crawl *m* ‖ *intr* ramper; (*to go slowly*) avancer au pas; **to be crawling with** fourmiller de, grouiller de; **to crawl along** se traîner; **to crawl on one's hands and knees** aller à quatre pattes; **to crawl over** escalader; **to crawl up** grimper

crayon [ˋkre•ən] *s* crayon *m* de pastel, pastel *m* ‖ *tr* crayonner

craze [krez] *s* manie *f*, toquade *f* ‖ *tr* rendre fou

cra•zy [ˋkrezi] *adj* (*comp* **-zier**; *super* **-ziest**) fou; (*rickety*) délabré; (coll) dingue, fou; **to be crazy about** (coll) être fou de, être toqué de; **to drive crazy** rendre fou, affoler; **to go crazy** perdre la boule

cra′zy bone′ *s* nerf *m* du coude

cra′zy quilt′ *s* courtepointe *f* multicolore

creak [krik] *s* cri *m*, grincement *m* ‖ *intr* crier, grincer

creak•y [ˈkriki] *adj* (*comp* **-ier;** *super* **-iest**) criard

cream [krim] *s* crème *f;* **creams** (*with chocolate coating*) chocolats *mpl* fourrés ‖ *tr* écrémer; (*butter and sugar together*) mélanger ‖ *intr* crémer

cream′ cheese′ *s* fromage *m* à la crème, fromage blanc, petit suisse *m*

creamer•y [ˈkriməri] *s* (*pl* **-ies**) laiterie *f;* compagnie *f* laitière

cream′ of tar′tar *s* crème *f* de tartre

cream′ pitch′er *s* crémière *f*

cream′ puff′ *s* chou *m* à la crème

cream′ sep′arator [ˈsɛpəˌretər] *s* écrémeuse *f*

cream•y [ˈkrimi] *adj* (*comp* **-ier;** *super* **-iest**) crémeux

crease [kris] *s* pli *m*, faux pli *m* ‖ *tr & intr* plisser

create [kriˈet] *tr* créer

creation [kriˈeʃən] *s* création *f*

creative [kriˈetɪv] *adj* créateur, inventif

creator [kriˈetər] *s* créateur *m*

creature [ˈkritʃər] *s* créature *f*

credence [ˈkridəns] *s* créance *f*, croyance *f*, foi *f*

credentials [krɪˈdɛnʃəlz] *spl* papiers *mpl*, pièces *fpl* justificatives, lettres *fpl* de créance

credibility [ˌkrɛdɪˈbɪlɪti] *s* crédibilité *f*

credible [ˈkrɛdɪbəl] *adj* croyable, digne de foi

credit [ˈkrɛdɪt] *s* crédit *m;* **on credit** à crédit; **to be a credit to** faire honneur à; **to take credit for** s'attribuer le mérite de ‖ *tr* croire, ajouter foi à; (*com*) créditer, porter au crédit

creditable [ˈkrɛdɪtəbəl] *adj* estimable, honorable

cred′it card′ *s* carte *f* de crédit

creditor [ˈkrɛdɪtər] *s* créditeur *m*, créancier *m*

cre•do [ˈkrido] *s* (*pl* **-dos**) credo *m*

credulous [ˈkrɛdʒələs] *adj* crédule

creed [krid] *s* credo *m;* (*denomination*) foi *f*

creek [krik] *s* ruisseau *m*

creep [krip] *v* (*pret & pp* **crept** [krɛpt]) *intr* (*to crawl*) ramper; (*stealthily*) se glisser; (*slowly*) se traîner, se couler; (*to climb*) grimper; (*with a sensation of insects*) fourmiller; **to creep up on s.o.** s'approcher de qn à pas lents

creeper [ˈkripər] *s* plante *f* rampante

creeping [ˈkripɪŋ] *adj* (*lagging*) lent, traînant; (*plant*) rampant ‖ *s* rampement *m*

creep•y [ˈkripi] *adj* (*comp* **-ier;** *super* **-iest**) (*coll*) mystérieux, terrifiant; **to feel creepy** fourmiller

cremate [ˈkrimet] *tr* incinérer

cremation [krɪˈmeʃən] *s* crémation *f*, incinération *f*

cremato•ry [ˈkriməˌtori] *adj* crématoire ‖ *s* (*pl* **-ries**) crématoire *m*, four *m* crématoire

Creole [ˈkriˌol] *adj* créole ‖ *s* (*language*) créole *m;* (*person*) Créole *mf*

crepe [krep] *s* (*paper*) crêpe *m;* (*pancake*) crêpe *f*

crepe′ pa′per *s* papier *m* crêpe

crescent [ˈkrɛsənt] *s* croissant *m*

cress [krɛs] *s* cresson *m*

crest [krɛst] *s* crête *f*

crested [ˈkrɛstɪd] *adj* à crête; (*with feathers*) huppé

crest′fall′en *adj* abattu, découragé

Cretan [ˈkritən] *adj* crétois ‖ *s* Crétois *m*

Crete [krit] *s* Crète *f;* la Crète

cretin [ˈkritən] *s* crétin *m*

crevice [ˈkrɛvɪs] *s* crevasse *f*, fente *f*

crew [kru] *s* (*rowing; group working together*) équipe *f;* (*of a ship*) équipage *m;* (*group, especially of armed men*) bande *f*, troupe *f*

crew′ cut′ *s* cheveux *mpl* en brosse

crew′ mem′ber *s* équipier *m*

crib [krɪb] *s* berceau *m;* (*manger*) crèche *f*, mangeoire *f;* (*for grain*) coffre *m;* (*student's pony*) antisèche *m & f* ‖ *v* (*pret & pp* **cribbed;** *ger* **cribbing**) *tr & intr* (*coll*) copier à la dérobée

crib′ death′ *s* mort *m* subite du nourrisson, mort inexpliquée du nourrisson

cricket [ˈkrɪkɪt] *s* (*ent*) grillon *m;* (*sports*) cricket *m;* (*coll*) franc jeu *m*, jeu loyal; **to be cricket** être de bonne guerre

crier [ˈkraɪ•ər] *s* crieur *m*

crime [kraɪm] *s* crime *m;* (*misdemeanor*) délit *m*

criminal [ˈkrɪmɪnəl] *adj & s* criminel *m*

crim′inal code′ *s* code *m* pénal

crim′inal court′ *s* cour *f* d'assises

crim′inal law′ *s* loi *f* pénale

crim′inal neg′ligence *s* négligence *f* criminelle

criminologist [ˌkrɪməˈnɑlədʒɪst] *s* criminologiste *mf or* criminologue *mf*

criminology [ˌkrɪməˈnɑlədʒi] *f* criminologie *f*

crimp [krɪmp] *s* (*in cloth*) pli *m;* (*in hair*) frisure *f;* (*recruiter*) racoleur *m;* **to put a crimp in** (*coll*) mettre obstacle à ‖ *tr* (*cloth*) plisser; (*hair*) friser, crêper; (*metal*) onduler

crimple [ˈkrɪmpəl] *tr* faire des plis dans, plisser ‖ *intr* faire des plis, se plisser

crimson [ˈkrɪmzən] *adj & s* cramoisi *m*

cringe [krɪndʒ] *intr* s'humilier, s'abaisser

cringing [ˈkrɪndʒɪŋ] *adj* craintif, servile ‖ *s* crainte *f*, servilité *f*

crinkle [ˈkrɪŋkəl] *s* pli *m*, ride *f* ‖ *tr* froisser, plisser ‖ *intr* se froisser

cripple [ˈkrɪpəl] *s* estropié *m*, boiteux *m;* (*disabled*) infirme, invalide ‖ *tr* estropier; (*a machine*) disloquer; (*business or industry*) paralyser; (*a ship*) désemparer

cri•sis [ˈkraɪsɪs] *s* (*pl* **-ses** [siz]) crise *f*

crisp [krɪsp] *adj* (*crackers, bread, etc.*) croustillant; (*tone*) tranchant, brusque; (*air*) vif, frais

crisscross [ˈkrɪsˌkrɔs] *adj* entrecroisé, treillissé ‖ *s* entrecroisement *m;* (*e.g., of wires*) enchevêtrement *m* ‖ *adv* en forme de croix ‖ *tr* entrecroiser ‖ *intr* se entrecroiser

criteri•on [kraɪˈtɪri•ən] *s* (*pl* **-a** [ə] *or* **-ons**) critère *m*

critic [ˈkrɪtɪk] *s* (*of books, music, films, etc.*)

critique *mf;* (*fault-finder*) critiqueur *m,* désapprobateur *m*

critical [ˈkrɪtɪkəl] *adj* critique

critically [ˈkrɪtɪkəli] *adv* en critique; **critically ill** gravement malade

criticism [ˈkrɪtɪˌsɪzəm] *s* critique *f*

criticize [ˈkrɪtɪˌsaɪz] *tr & intr* critiquer

critique [krɪˈtik] *s* critique *f*

croak [krok] *s* (*of raven*) croassement *m;* (*of frog*) coassement *m* ‖ *intr* (*said of raven*) croasser; (*said of frog*) coasser; (*to die*) (slang) mourir

Croat [ˈkro•æt] *s* (*language*) croate *m;* (*person*) Croate *mf*

Croatian [kroˈeʃən] *adj* croate ‖ *s* (*language*) *m;* (*person*) Croate *mf*

cro•chet [kroˈʃe] *s* crochet *m* ‖ *v* (*pret & pp* **-cheted** [ˈʃed]; *ger* **-cheting** [ˈʃe•ɪŋ]) *tr & intr* tricoter au crochet

crochet′ nee′dle *s* crochet *m*

crock [krɑk] *s* pot *m* de terre

crock′pot *s* mijoteuse *f*

crockery [ˈkrɑkəri] *s* faïence *f,* poterie *f*

croc′odile tears′ *spl* larmes *fpl* de crocodile

crocodile [ˈkrɑkəˌdaɪl] *s* crocodile *m*

crocus [ˈkrokəs] *s* crocus *m*

crone [kron] *s* vieille ratatinée *f,* vieille bique *f*

cro•ny [ˈkroni] *s* (*pl* **-nies**) copain *m*

cronyism [ˈkroni•ɪzəm] *s* copinisme *m*

crook [krʊk] *s* (*hook*) croc *m;* (*of shepherd*) houlette *f;* (*of bishop*) crosse *f;* (*in road*) courbure *f;* (*person*) (coll) escroc *m* ‖ *tr* courber ‖ *intr* se courber

crooked [ˈkrʊkɪd] *adj* (*stick*) courbé, crochu; (*path; conduct*) tortueux; (*tree; nose; legs*) tortu; (*person*) (coll) malhonnête, fourbe

croon [krun] *intr* chanter des chansons sentimentales

crooner [ˈkrunər] *s* chanteur *m* de charme

crop [krɑp] *s* (*produce*) produit *m* agricole; (*amount produced*) récolte *f;* (*head of hair*) cheveux *mpl* ras; (*of bird*) jabot *m;* (*whip*) fouet *m;* (*of whip*) manche *m;* (*of appointments, promotions, heroes, discoveries*) moisson *f* ‖ *v* (*pret & pp* **cropped;** *ger* **cropping**) *tr* tondre; (*head of hair*) couper, tailler; (*ears of animal*) essoriller ‖ *intr*—**to crop up** (coll) surgir, s'élever brusquement

crop′ dust′ing *s* pulvérisation *f* des cultures

croquet [kroˈke] *s* croquet *m*

crosier [ˈkroʒər] *s* crosse *f*

cross [krɔs] *adj* (*diagonal*) transversal, oblique; (*breed*) croisé; (*ill-humored*) maussade ‖ *s* croix *f;* (*of breeds; of roads*) croisement *m* ‖ *tr* (*e.g., one's arms or legs*) croiser; (*the sea; a street*) traverser; (*breeds*) croiser, métisser; (*the threshold*) franchir; (*said of one road with respect to another*) couper; (*the letter t*) barrer; (*e.g., s.o.'s plans*) (coll) contre-carrer; **to cross oneself** (eccl) se signer; **to cross out** biffer, rayer ‖ *intr* se croiser, passer; **to cross over** passer de l'autre côté

cross′bones′ *spl* tibias *mpl* croisés

cross′bow′ *s* arbalète *f*

cross′ breed′ *v* (*pret & pp* **-bred**) *tr* croiser, métisser

cross′-check′ *s* recoupement *m* ‖ *tr* faire un recoupement de

cross′-coun′try *adj* à travers champs

cross′-coun′try bike′ *m* vélo *m* de cross-country

cross′-coun′try race′ *m* cross-country *m,* cross *m*

cross′-country ski′ing *s* ski *m* de fonds

cross′cur′rent *s* contre-courant *m;* tendance *f* contraire

cross′-examina′tion *s* contre-interrogatoire *m*

cross′-exam′ine *tr* contre-interroger, contre-examiner

cross′-eyed′ *adj* louche

cross-fertilization [ˈkrɔs ˌfʌrtələˈzeʃən] *s* fertilisation *f* croisée

cross′fire′ *s* (mil) feux *mpl* croisés; **in a crossfire of questions** dans un feu roulant de questions

crossing [ˈkrɔsɪŋ], [ˈkrɑsɪŋ] *s* (*road junction*) croisement *m;* (*of ocean*) traversée *f;* (*of river, mountain, etc.*) passage *m;* (rr) passage *m* à niveau; (*for pedestrians*) passage *m* clouté

cross′ing gate′ *s* barrière *f* d'un passage à niveau

cross′patch′ *s* (coll) grincheux *m,* grognon *m*

cross′piece′ *s* entretoise *f*

cross′-pur′poses *spl* malentendu *m,* désaccord *m*

cross′ ref′erence *s* renvoi *m*

cross′road′ *s* voie *f* transversale, chemin *m* de traverse; **crossroads** carrefour *m,* croisement *m*

cross′ sec′tion *s* (*cut*) coupe *f* transversale; (*e.g., of building*) section *f;* (*of opinion*) sondage *m,* groupe *m* représentatif, échantillon *m*

cross′-sec′tion *tr* coupe transversalement

cross′ street′ *s* rue *f* de traverse, rue transversale

cross′walk′ *s* passage *m* clouté

cross′wise′ *adv* en croix, en sautoir

cross′word puz′zle *s* mots *mpl* croisés

crotch [krɑtʃ] *s* (*forked piece*) fourche *f;* (*between legs*) entrejambe *f,* enfourchure *f*

crotchet [ˈkrɑtʃɪt] *s* (mus) noire *f;* (coll) lubie *f*

crotchety [ˈkrɑtʃɪti] *adj* capricieux, fantasque

crouch [kraʊtʃ] *s* accroupissement *m* ‖ *intr* s'accroupir, se blottir

croup [krup] *s* (*of horse*) croupe *f;* (pathol) croup *m*

croupier [ˈkrupɪ•ər] *s* croupier *m*

crouton [ˈkrutɑn] *s* croûton *m*

crow [kro] *s* corbeau *m;* (*rook*) corneille *f,* freux *m;* **as the crow flies** à vol d'oiseau; **to eat crow** (coll) avaler des couleuvres ‖ *intr* (*said of cock*) chanter; (*said of babies*) gazouiller; **to crow over** chanter victoire sur, triompher bruyamment de

crow′bar′ s levier m; (*for forcing doors*) pince-monseigneur f

crowd [kraʊd] s foule f; (*clique, set*) bande f; monde m; **a crowd** (*of people*) du monde, beaucoup de monde ‖ tr serrer, entasser; (*to push*) pousser; (*a debtor*) presser; **to crowd out** ne pas laisser de place à ‖ intr affluer, s'amasser; **to crowd around** se presser autour de; **to crowd in** s'attrouper

crowded adj encombré, bondé

crow′foot′ s renoncule f, bouton m d'or

crowing [ˈkroʊ•ɪŋ] s chant m de coq, coco-rico m; (*of babies*) gazouillement m

crown [kraʊn] s couronne f; (*of hat*) calotte f ‖ tr couronner, sacrer; (checkers) damer; **to crown s.o.** (slang) flanquer un coup sur la tête à qn

crowning [ˈkraʊnɪŋ] s couronnement m

crown′ jew′els spl joyaux mpl de la couronne

crown′ prince′ s prince m héritier

crown′ prin′cess s princesse f héritière

crow's′-foot′ s (pl **-feet**) patte-d'oie f

crow's′-nest′ s (naut) nid m de pie, tonneau m de vigie

crucial [ˈkruʃəl] adj crucial

crucible [ˈkrusɪbəl] s creuset m

crucifix [ˈkrusɪfɪks] s crucifix m, christ m

crucifixion [ˌkrusɪˈfɪkʃən] s crucifixion f

cruci•fy [ˈkrusɪˌfaɪ] v (pret & pp **-fied**) tr crucifier

crude [krud] adj (*raw, unrefined*) cru, brut; (*lacking culture*) fruste, grossier; (*unfinished*) informe, grossier, mal développé; (*oil*) brut

crudi•ty [ˈkrudɪti] s (pl **-ties**) crudité f; (*of person*) grossièreté f

cruel [ˈkru•əl] adj cruel

cruel•ty [ˈkru•əlti] s (pl **-ties**) cruauté f

cruet [ˈkru•ɪt] s burette f

cru′et stand′ s huilier m

cruise [kruz] s croisière f ‖ intr croiser

cruise′ mis′sile s missile m croisière

cruiser [ˈkruzər] s croiseur m

cruising [ˈkruzɪŋ] adj en croisière; (*taxi*) en maraude

cruis′ing range′ s autonomie f

cruis′ing speed′ s vitesse f de route

cruller [ˈkrʌlər] s beignet m

crumb [krʌm] s miette f; (*soft part of bread*) mie f ‖ tr (*cutlets, etc.*) paner

crumble [ˈkrʌmbəl] tr émietter, réduire en miettes; (*e.g., stone*) effriter ‖ intr s'émietter; s'effriter; (*to fall to pieces*) s'écrouler

crum•my [ˈkrʌmi] adj (*comp* **-mier**; *super* **-miest**) (slang) sale, minable

crumple [ˈkrʌmpəl] tr friper, froisser; (*a fender*) mettre en accordéon ‖ intr se friper, se froisser

crunch [krʌnʃ] tr croquer, broyer ‖ intr (*said of snow*) craquer

crupper [ˈkrʌpər] s croupière f

crusade [kruˈsed] s croisade f ‖ intr se croiser, prendre part à une croisade

crush [krʌʃ] s (*crushing*) écrasement m; (*of people*) presse f, foule f; **to have a crush on** (slang) avoir un béguin pour ‖ tr écraser; (*e.g., stone*) broyer, concasser; (*to oppress, grieve*) accabler, aplatir

crush′ hat′ s claque m, gibus m

crust [krʌst] s croûte f

crustacean [krʌsˈteʃən] s crustacé m

crust•y [ˈkrʌsti] adj (*comp* **-ier**; *super* **-iest**) croustillant; (*said of person*) bourru, hargneux

crutch [krʌtʃ] s béquille f

crux [krʌks] s nœud m

cry [kraɪ] s (pl **cries**) (*loud shout*) cri m; (*of wolf*) hurlement m; (*of bull*) mugissement m; **to cry one's eyes out** pleurer à chaudes larmes; **to have a good cry** donner libre cours aux larmes ‖ v (*pret & pp* **cried**) tr crier; **to cry out** crier ‖ intr crier; (*to weep*) pleurer; **to cry for** crier à; **to cry for joy** pleurer de joie; **to cry out** pousser des cris, s'écrier; **to cry out against** crier à

cry′ba′by s (pl **-bies**) pleurard m

crying [ˈkraɪ•ɪŋ] adj pleurant; (*need*) pressant; **for crying out loud!** (coll) il ne manquait plus que ça!; **a crying shame** une honte ‖ s larmes fpl, pleurs mpl

crypt [krɪpt] s crypte f

cryptic(al) [ˈkrɪptɪk(əl)] adj secret, occulte; (*silence*) énigmatique

cryptography [krɪpˈtɑgrəfi] s cryptographie f

crystal [ˈkrɪstəl] s cristal m

crys′tal ball′ s boule f de cristal

crystalline [ˈkrɪstəlɪn] adj cristallin

crystallize [ˈkrɪstəˌlaɪz] tr cristalliser; (*sugar*) candir ‖ intr cristalliser; (*said of sugar*) se candir; (*said of one's thoughts*) (fig) se cristalliser

cub [kʌb] s (*of animal*) petit m; (*of bear*) ourson m; (*of fox*) renardeau m; (*of lion*) lionceau m; (*of wolf*) louveteau m

Cuban [ˈkjubən] adj cubain ‖ s Cubain m

cubbyhole [ˈkʌbɪˌhol] s (*room*) retraite f; (*in wall*) placard m; (*in furniture*) case f

cube [kjub] adj & s cube m; **in cubes** (*said of sugar*) en morceaux ‖ tr cuber

cube′ root′ s racine f cubique

cube′ sug′ar s sucre m en morceaux

cubic [ˈkjubɪk] adj cubique, cube

cubicle [ˈkjubɪkəl] s box m, alcôve f

cu′bic me′ter s mètre m cube

cub′ report′er s reporter m débutant

cub′ scout′ s louveteau m

cuckold [ˈkʌkəld] adj & s cocu m, cornard m ‖ tr cocufier

cuckoo [ˈkʊkʊ] adj (slang) niais, benêt ‖ s coucou m

cuck′oo clock′ s coucou m

cucumber [ˈkjukʌmbər] s concombre m

cud [kʌd] s bol m alimentaire; **to chew the cud** ruminer

cuddle [ˈkʌdəl] tr serrer doucement dans les

bras ‖ *intr* (*said of lovers*) s'étreindre; **to cuddle up** se pelotonner

cudg•el [ˈkʌdʒəl] *s* gourdin *m*, trique *f*; **to take up the cudgels for** prendre fait et cause pour ‖ *v* (*pret & pp* **-eled** or **-elled**; *ger* **-eling** or **-elling**) *tr* bâtonner, rosser

cue [kju] *s* (*notice*) signal *m*; (*hint*) mot *m*; (*rod used in billiards; persons in line*) queue *f*; (mus) indication *f* de rentrée; (theat) réclame *f*; **to give s.o. the cue** faire la leçon à qn, donner le mot à qn; **to take one's cue from** se conformer à

cuff [kʌf] *s* (*of shirt*) poignet *m*, manchette *f*; (*of coat or trousers*) parement *m*; (*blow*) taloche *f*, manchette *f* ‖ *tr* talocher, flanquer une taloche à

cuff′ link′ *s* bouton *m* de manchette

cuirass [kwɪˈræs] *s* cuirasse *f*

cuisine [kwɪˈzin] *s* cuisine *f*

culinary [ˈkjulɪˌnɛri] *adj* culinaire

cull [kʌl] *tr* (*to select*) choisir; (*to gather, pluck*) cueillir; **to cull from** recueillir dans

culm [kʌlm] *s* chaume *m*; (*coal dust*) charbonnaille *f*

culminate [ˈkʌlmɪˌnet] *intr* (astr) culminer; **to culminate in** finir par, se terminer en

culmination [ˌkʌlmɪˈneʃən] *s* point *m* culminant; (astr) culmination *f*

culottes [k(j)uˈlɑts] *spl* pantalon *m* de plage

culpable [ˈkʌlpəbəl] *adj* coupable

culprit [ˈkʌlprɪt] *s* (*guilty one*) coupable *mf*; (*accused*) accusé *m*, prévenu *m*

cult [kʌlt] *s* culte *m*

cultivate [ˈkʌltɪˌvet] *tr* cultiver

cultivation [ˌkʌltɪˈveʃən] *s* culture *f*

cultivator [ˈkʌltɪˌvetər] *s* (*person*) cultivateur *m*, exploitant *m* agricole; (mach) cultivateur *m*, scarificateur *m*

cultural [ˈkʌltʃərəl] *adj* culturel

culture [ˈkʌltʃər] *s* culture *f* ‖ *tr* cultiver

cultured *adj* (*learned*) cultivé, lettré

cul′tured pearl′ *s* perle *f* de culture

culvert [ˈkʌlvərt] *s* ponceau *m*, cassis *m*

cumbersome [ˈkʌmbərsəm] *adj* incommode, encombrant; (*clumsy*) lourd, difficile à manier

cummerbund [ˈkʌmərˌbʌnd] *s* ceinture *f* d'étoffe

cumulative [ˈkjumjəˌletɪv] *adj* croissant, cumulatif

cunnilingus [ˌkʌnɪˈlɪŋɡəs] *ou* **cunnilinctus** [ˌkʌnɪˈlɪŋktəs] *s* cunnilingus *m*, cunnilinctus, cunnilingue *f*

cunning [ˈkʌnɪŋ] *adj* (*sly*) astucieux, rusé; (*clever*) habile, fin; (*attractive*) gentil ‖ *s* (*slyness*) astuce *f*, ruse *f*; (*cleverness*) habileté *f*, finesse *f*

cup [kʌp] *s* (*for coffee or tea; cupful*) tasse *f*; (*of metal*) gobelet *m*, timbale *f*; (bot, eccl) calice *m*; (mach) godet *m* graisseur; (sports) coupe *f* ‖ *v* (*pret & pp* **cupped**; *ger* **cupping**) *tr* (surg) ventouser

cupboard [ˈkʌbərd] *s* armoire *f*; (*in wall*) placard *m*

Cupid [ˈkjupɪd] *s* Cupidon *m*

cupidity [kjuˈpɪdɪti] *s* cupidité *f*

cupola [ˈkjupələ] *s* coupole *f*

cur [kʌr] *s* (*mongrel dog*) chien *m* métis, roquet *m*; (*despicable person*) mufle *m*

curate [ˈkjurɪt] *s* vicaire *m*

curative [ˈkjurətɪv] *adj* curatif

curator [kjuˈretər] *s* conservateur *m*

curb [kʌrb] *s* (*edge of road*) bordure *f* de pavés, bord *m* de trottoir; (*of well*) margelle *f*; (*of bit*) gourmette *f*; (*market*) coulisse *f*; (*check, restraint*) frein *m* ‖ *tr* (*a horse*) gourmer; (*passions, anger, desires*) réprimer, refréner; **curb your dog** (public sign) faites faire votre chien dans le ruisseau

curb′ serv′ice *s* restoroute *m*

curb′stone′ *s* garde-pavé *m*; **curbstones** bordure *f* de pavés

curd [kʌrd] *s* caillé *m*; **curds** caillebotte *f* ‖ *tr* cailler, caillebotter ‖ *intr* se cailler, se caillebotter

curdle [ˈkʌrdəl] *tr* (*milk*) cailler; (*the blood*) figer ‖ *intr* se cailler; se figer

curds′ and whey′ *spl* lait *m* caillé sucré

cure [kjur] *s* (*recovery*) guérison *f*; (*treatment*) cure *f*; (*remedy*) remède *m* ‖ *tr* guérir; (*meat; leather*) saler; (*a pipe*) culotter

cure′-all′ *s* panacée *f*

curfew [ˈkʌrfju] *s* couvre-feu *m*

curi•o [ˈkjurɪˌo] *s* (*pl* **-os**) bibelot *m*

curiosi•ty [ˌkjurɪˈɑsɪti] *s* (*pl* **-ties**) curiosité *f*

curious [ˈkjurɪˌəs] *adj* curieux

curl [kʌrl] *s* (*of hair*) boucle *f*, frisure *f*; (*spiral-shaped*) volute *f*; (*of smoke*) spirale *f* ‖ *tr* boucler, friser; (*to coil, to roll up*) enrouler, tire-bouchonner; **to curl one's lip** faire la moue ‖ *intr* boucler, friser; (*said of smoke*) s'élever en spirales; (*said of waves*) onduler, déferler; **to curl up** (*said of leaves, paper, etc.*) se recroqueviller; (*in bed*) se rouler en boule

curlew [ˈkʌrl(j)u] *s* courlis *m*

curlicue [ˈkʌrlɪˌkju] *s* paraphe *m*

curl′ing i′ron *s* fer *m* à friser

curl′pa′per *s* papillote *f*

curl•y [ˈkʌrli] *adj* (*comp* **-ier;** *super* **-iest**) bouclé, frisé

curmudgeon [kərˈmʌdʒən] *s* (*crosspatch*) bourru *m*, sale bougre *m*; (*miser*) ladre *mf*

currant [ˈkʌrənt] *s* groseille *f*

curren•cy [ˈkʌrənsi] *s* (*pl* **-cies**) circulation *f*; (*legal tender*) monnaie *f*, devises *fpl*; **to give currency to** donner cours à

current [ˈkʌrənt] *adj* (*opinion, price, word, etc.*) courant; (*month*) en cours; (*accepted*) admis, reçu; (*present-day*) actuel ‖ *s* courant *m*; (*stream*) courant, cours *m*

cur′rent account′ *s* compte *m* courant

cur′rent events′ *spl* actualités *fpl*

cur′rent fail′ure *s* panne *f* de secteur

cur′rent is′sue *s* dernier numéro *m*

curricu‧lum [kə`rɪkjələm] *s* (*pl* **-lums** or **-la** [lə]) programme *m* scolaire, plan *m* d'études

cur‧ry [`kʌri] *s* (*pl* **-ries**) cari *m* ‖ *v* (*pret & pp* **-ried**) *tr* (*a horse*) étriller; (culin) apprêter au cari; **to curry favor with** faire la cour à

cur'ry‧comb' *s* étrille *f* ‖ *tr* étriller

cur'ry pow'der *s* cari *m*

curse [kʌrs] *s* (*imprecation*) malédiction *f;* (*swearword*) juron *m;* (*bane*) fléau *m,* malheur *m* ‖ *tr* maudire ‖ *intr* jurer, sacrer

cursed [`kʌrsɪd], [kʌrst] *adj* maudit, exécrable, sacré

cursive [`kʌrsɪv] *adj* cursif ‖ *s* cursive *f*

cursor [`kʌrsər] *s* (comp) curseur *m*

cursory [`kʌrsəri] *adj* superficiel, précipité

curt [kʌrt] *adj* brusque, court

curtail [kər`tel] *tr* (*to reduce*) raccourcir, diminuer; (*expenses*) restreindre; (*rights*) enlever

curtailment [kʌr`telmənt] *s* (*reduction*) diminution *f;* (*of rights*) privation *f*

curtain [`kʌrtən] *s* rideau *m* ‖ *tr* garnir de rideaux; (*to hide*) cacher sous des rideaux; **to curtain off** séparer par un rideau

cur'tain call' *s* rappel *m* (sur scène)

cur'tain rais'er *s* (*play*) lever *m* de rideau

cur'tain ring' *s* anneau *m* de rideau

cur'tain rod' *s* tringle *f* de rideau

curt‧sy [`kʌrtsi] *s* (*pl* **-sies**) révérence *f* ‖ *v* (*pret & pp* **-sied**) *intr* faire la révérence

curvature [`kʌrvətʃər] *s* courbure *f;* (*of spine*) déviation *f*

curve [kʌrv] *s* courbe *f;* (*of road*) virage *m;* (*curvature*) courbure *f;* (baseball) courbe *f* ‖ *tr* courber ‖ *intr* se courber

curved *adj* courbe, courbé

cushion [`kʊʃən] *s* coussin *m* ‖ *tr* (*a chair*) rembourrer; (*a shock*) amortir

cuspidor [`kʌspɪˌdɔr] *s* crachoir *m*

cuss [kʌs] *s* (*person*) (coll) vaurien *m,* chenapan *m* ‖ *tr* (coll) maudire ‖ *intr* (coll) jurer, sacrer

cuss'word' *s* (coll) juron *m*

custard [`ʌstərd] *s* flan *m,* œufs *mpl* au lait, crème *f* caramel

custodian [kəs`todɪ‧ən] *s* gardien *m;* concierge *mf*

custo‧dy [`kʌstədi] *s* (*pl* **-dies**) (*care*) garde *f;* (*imprisonment*) emprisonnement *m;* **in custody** en sûreté; **to take into custody** mettre en état d'arrestation

custom [`kʌstəm] *s* coutume *f;* (*customers*) clientèle *f;* **customs** douane *f;* (*duties*) droits *mpl* de douane

customary [`kʌstəˌmɛri] *adj* coutumier, ordinaire, habituel

custom-built [`kʌstəm`bɪlt] *adj* hors série, fait sur commande

customer [`kʌstəmər] *s* (*buyer*) client *m,* chaland *m;* (coll) individu *m,* type *m;* **customers** clientèle *f,* achalandage *m*

cus'tom‧house' *s* douanier ‖ *s* douane *f*

custom‧made [`kʌstəm`med] *adj* fait sur commande; (*clothes*) sur mesure

cus'toms clear'ance *s* expédition *f* douanière

cus'toms dec'lara'tion *s* déclaration *f* douanière

cus'toms du'ties *spl* droits *mpl* de douane

cus'toms of'ficer *s* douanier *m*

cus'toms un'ion *s* union *f* douanière

cus'tom tai'lor *s* tailleur *m* à façon

cut [kʌt] *adj* coupé; **cut out** taillé, e.g., **he is not cut out for that** il n'est pas taillé pour cela; e.g., **your work is cut out for you** voilà votre besogne taillée ‖ *s* (*of a garment; of cards; haircut; act of cutting*) coupe *f;* (*piece cut off*) tranche *f,* morceau *m;* (*slash*) coupure *f;* (*with knife, whip, etc.*) coup *m;* (*in prices, wages, etc.*) réduction *f,* (typ) gravure *f,* planche *f;* (*absence from school*) (coll) séchage *m;* (*in winnings, earnings, etc.*) (slang) part *f;* **the cheap cuts** les bas morceaux *mpl* ‖ *v* (*pret & pp* **cut;** *ger* **cutting**) *tr* couper; (*meat, bread*) trancher; (*prices*) réduire, baisser; (e.g., *a hole*) pratiquer; (*glass, diamonds*) tailler; (*fingernails*) rogner; (*an article, play, speech*) sabrer, faire des coupures à; (*a phonograph record*) enregistrer; (*a class*) (coll) sécher; **to cut down** faucher, abattre; (*expenses*) réduire; **to cut off, out,** or **up** découper, couper; **to cut short** couper court à ‖ *intr* couper; trancher; **to cut in** (*a conversation*) s'immiscer dans; (coll) enlever la danseuse d'un autre; **to cut off** (*debate*) clore; **to cut up** (slang) faire le pitre

cut'-and-dried' *adj* décidé d'avance, tout fait; monotone, rasoir

cutaneous [kju`tenɪ‧əs] *adj* cutané

cutan'eous an'thrax *s* (pathol) anthrax *m* cutané

cut'away' *s* frac *m*

cut'back' *s* réduction *f;* (mov) retour *m* en arrière

cute [kjut] *adj* (coll) mignon; (*shrewd*) (coll) rusé

cut' flowers' *spl* fleurs *fpl* coupées

cut' glass' *s* cristal *m* taillé

cuticle [`kjutɪkəl] *s* cuticule *f*

cutlass [`kʌtləs] *s* coutelas *m*

cutlery [`kʌtləri] *s* coutellerie *f*

cutlet [`kʌtlɪt] *s* (*slice of meat*) côtelette *f;* (*without bone*) escalope *f;* (*croquette of minced chicken, etc.*) croquette *f*

cut'off' *s* point *m* de coupure; (*road*) raccourci *m;* (*of river*) bras *m* mort; (*of cylinder*) obturateur *m*

cut'off' date' *s* date *f* limite

cut'out' *s* (aut) échappement *m* libre; (elec) coupe-circuit *m;* (mov) décor *m* découpé

cut'-rate' *adj* à prix réduit

cutter [`kʌtər] *s* (naut) cotre *m*

cut'throat' *s* coup-jarret *m*

cut'throat' com'peti'tion *s* compétition *f* acharnée

cutting [`kʌtɪŋ] *adj* tranchant; (*tone, remark*) mordant, cinglant ‖ *s* (*action*) coupe *f;* (*from a newspaper*) coupure *f;* (e.g., *of prices*) réduction *f;* (hort) bouture *f;* (mov) découpage *m*

cut′ting edge′ *s* point *m* extrême; (*vanguard*) avant-garde *f* (du progrès)

cuttlefish [ˈkʌtəl,fɪʃ] *s* seiche *f*

cut′wa′ter *s* (naut) étrave *f;* (*of bridge*) bec *m*

cyanamide [saɪˈænə,maɪd] *s* cyanamide *f*

cyanide [ˈsaɪ•ə,naɪd] *s* cyanure *m*

cyanosis [,saɪ•əˈnosɪs] *s* cyanose *f*

cybernetic [,saɪbərˈnɛtɪk] *adj* cybernétique ‖ **cybernetics** [,saɪbərˈnɛtɪks] *s* cybernétique *f*

cyberspace [ˈsaɪbərˈspes] *s* cybermonde *m or* cyberespace *m*

cycle [ˈsaɪkəl] *s* cycle *m;* (*of internal-combustion engine*) temps *m;* (phys) période *f* ‖ *intr* faire de la bicyclette

cyclic(al) [ˈsɪklɪk(əl)] *adj* cyclique

cyclist [ˈsaɪklɪst] *s* cycliste *mf*

cyclone [ˈsaɪklon] *s* cyclone *m*

cyclops [ˈsaɪklɑps] *s* cyclope *m*

cyclotron [ˈsaɪklo,trɑn] *s* cyclotron *m*

cylinder [ˈsɪlɪndər] *s* cylindre *m;* (*of revolver*) barillet *m*

cyl′inder block′ *s* cylindre *m*

cyl′inder bore′ *s* alésage *m*

cyl′inder head′ *s* culasse *f*

cylindric(al) [sɪˈlɪndrɪk(əl)] *adj* cylindrique

cymbal [ˈsɪmbəl] *s* cymbale *f*

cynic [ˈsɪnɪk] *adj & s* cynique *m*

cynical [ˈsɪnɪkəl] *adj* cynique

cynicism [ˈsɪnɪ,sɪzəm] *s* cynisme *m*

cynosure [ˈsaɪnə,ʃʊr] *s* guide *m*, exemple *m*, norme *f;* (*center of attention*) clou *m;* (astr) cynosure *f*

cypress [ˈsaɪprəs] *s* cyprès *m*

Cyprus [ˈsaɪprəs] *s* Chypre *f*

Cyrillic [sɪˈrɪlɪk] *adj* cyrillique

cyst [sɪst] *s* kyste *m;* (*on the skin*) vésicule *f*

cystic fibrosis [ˈsɪstɪkfaɪˈbrosəs] *s* (pathol) fibrose *f* cystique

cytology [saɪˈtɑlədʒi] *s* cytologie *f*

czar [zɑr] *s* tsar *m*, czar *m*

czarina [zɑˈrinə] *s* tsarine *f*, czarine *f*

Czech [tʃɛk] *adj* tchèque ‖ *s* (*language*) tchèque *m;* (*person*) Tchèque *mf*

Czech′ Repub′lic *s* République *f* tchèque

D

D, d [di] *s* IVe lettre de l'alphabet

dab [dæb] *s* touche *f;* (*of ink*) tache *f;* (*of butter*) petit morceau *m* ‖ *v* (*pret & pp* **dabbed;** *ger* **dabbing**) *tr* essuyer légèrement; (*to pat*) tapoter

dabble [ˈdæbəl] *tr* humecter ‖ *intr* barboter; **to dabble in** se mêler de; **to dabble in the stock market** boursicoter

dachshund [ˈdɑks,hund] *s* teckel *m*

dad [dæd] *s* (coll) papa *m*

dad•dy [ˈdædi] *s* (*pl* **-dies**) papa *m*

dad′dy-long′legs′ *s* (*pl* **-legs**) faucheux *m*

daffodil [ˈdæfədɪl] *s* jonquille *f* des prés, narcisse *m* des bois

daff•y [ˈdæfi] *adj* (*comp* **-ier;** *super* **-iest**) (coll) timbré, toqué

dagger [ˈdægər] *s* poignard *m*, dague *f;* (typ) croix *f*, obel *m;* **to look daggers at** foudroyer du regard

dahlia [ˈdæljə] *s* dahlia *m*

dai•ly [ˈdeli] *adj* quotidien, journalier ‖ *s* (*pl* **-lies**) quotidien *m* ‖ *adv* journellement

dain•ty [ˈdenti] *adj* (*comp* **-tier;** *super* **-tiest**) délicat ‖ *s* (*pl* **-ties**) friandise *f*

dair•y [ˈdɛri] *adj* laitier ‖ *s* (*pl* **-ies**) laiterie *f;* (*shop*) crémerie *f;* (*farm*) vacherie *f*

dair′y farm′ *s* vacherie *f*

dair′y•man *s* (*pl* **-men**) laitier *m*

dair′y prod′ucts *spl* produits *mpl* laitiers

dais [ˈde•ɪs] *s* estrade *f*

dai•sy [ˈdezi] *s* (*pl* **-sies**) marguerite *f*

dai′sy wheel′ *s* (comp) marguerite *f*

dai′sy wheel′ print′er *s* (comp) imprimante *f* de marguerite

dal•ly [ˈdæli] *v* (*pret & pp* **-lied**) *intr* (*to tease*) badiner; (*to delay*) s'attarder

dam [dæm] *s* (*obstruction*) barrage *m;* (*female quadruped*) mère *f* ‖ *v* (*pret & pp* **dammed;** *ger* **damming**) *tr* contenir, endiguer

damage [ˈdæmɪdʒ] *s* dommage *m*, dégâts *mpl;* (*to engine, ship, etc.*) avaries *fpl;* (*to one's reputation*) tort *m;* **damages** (law) dommages-intérêts *mpl* ‖ *tr* endommager; (*merchandise; a machine*) avarier; (*a reputation*) faire du tort à

damaging [ˈdæmɪdʒɪŋ] *adj* dommageable, préjudiciable

damascene [ˈdæmə,sin], [,dæməˈsin] *adj* damasquiné ‖ *s* damasquinage *m* ‖ *tr* damasquiner

Damascus [dəˈmæskəs] *s* Damas *f*

dame [dem] *s* dame *f;* (coll) jupon *m*, typesse *f*, gonzesse *f*

damn [dæm] *s* juron *m*, gros mot *m;* **I don't give a damn** (slang) je m'en fiche; **that's not worth a damn** (slang) ça ne vaut pas un pet de lapin, ça ne vaut pas chipette ‖ *tr* condamner; (*to criticize harshly*) éreinter; (*to curse*) maudire; **damn him!** qu'il aille au diable!; **damn it!** merde!, nom de Dieu!, oh, la vache!; **I'll be damned if . . .** que le diable m'emporte si . . . ; **to damn with faint praise** assommer avec des fleurs; **well, I'll be damned!** ça c'est trop fort! ‖ *intr* maudire

damnation [dæm'neʃən] s damnation f
damned [dæmd] adj damné m ‖ s—**the damned** les damnés ‖ [dæm] adv (slang) diablement, bigrement
damp [dæmp] adj humide, moite ‖ s humidité f; (firedamp) grisou m ‖ tr (to dampen) humecter, mouiller; (a furnace) étouffer; (sound; electromagnetic waves) amortir
dampen ['dæmpən] tr (to moisten) humecter; (enthusiasm) refroidir; (to muffle) amortir
damper ['dæmpər] s (of chimney) registre m; (of stovepipe) soupape f de réglage; (of piano) étouffoir m; **to put a damper on** (fig) jeter un froid sur
damsel ['dæmzəl] s demoiselle f
dance [dæns] s danse f; bal m, soirée f dansante ‖ tr & intr danser
dance' band' s orchestre m de danse
dance' floor' s piste f de danse
dance' hall' s dancing m, salle f de danse
dance' pro'gram s carnet m de bal
dancer ['dænsər] s danseur m
danc'ing part'ner s danseur m
danc'ing wa'ters spl fontaines fpl vivantes
dandelion ['dændɪˌlaɪ•ən] s pissenlit m
dandruff ['dændrəf] s pellicules fpl
dan•dy ['dændi] adj (comp -dier; super -diest) (coll) chic, chouette ‖ s (pl -dies) dandy m, élégant m
Dane [den] s Danois m
danger ['dendʒər] s danger m
dangerous ['dendʒərəs] adj dangereux
dangle ['dæŋgəl] tr faire pendiller ‖ intr pendiller
Danish ['denɪʃ] adj & s danois m
dank [dæŋk] adj humide, moite
Danube ['dænjub] s Danube m
dapper ['dæpər] adj fringant, élégant
dappled ['dæpəld] adj (mottled) tacheté; (sky) pommelé; (horse) moucheté, miroité
dare [dɛr] s défi m; **to take a dare** relever un défi ‖ tr défier; oser; **to dare s.o. to** + inf défier qn de + inf ‖ intr oser; **to dare** + inf oser + inf
dare'dev'il s risque-tout mf
daring ['dɛrɪŋ] adj audacieux, hardi ‖ s audace f, hardiesse f
dark [dark] adj sombre, obscur; (color) foncé; (complexion) basané, brun; **it is dark** il fait noir, il fait nuit ‖ s obscurité f, ténèbres fpl
Dark' Ag'es spl âge m des ténèbres
dark' brown' adj brun, brun foncé, chocolat
dark' choc'olate s chocolat m à croquer
dark'-complex'ioned adj brun, basané, brun de peau
darken ['darkən] tr assombrir; (the complexion) brunir; (a color) foncer ‖ intr s'assombrir; (said of forehead) se rembrunir
dark' glass'es spl lunettes fpl noires, verres mpl fumés
dark' horse' s (pol) candidat m obscur; (sports) outsider m
darkly ['darkli] adv obscurément; (mysterious-

ly) ténébreusement; (threateningly) d'un air menaçant
dark' meat' s viande f brune; (of game) viandre noire
darkness ['darknɪs] s obscurité f
dark' room' s (phot) chambre f noire
darling ['darlɪŋ] adj & s chéri m, bien-aimé m; **my darling** mon chou
darn [darn] s reprise f, raccommodage m ‖ tr repriser, raccommoder ‖ interj zut!
darn'ing egg' s œuf m à repriser
darn'ing nee'dle s aiguille f à repriser
dart [dart] s dard m; (small missile used in a game) fléchette f ‖ intr se précipiter, aller comme une flèche
dart'board' s cible f (de jeu de fléchettes)
darts [darts] s jeu m de fléchettes; **to play darts** jouer aux fléchettes
dash [dæʃ] s (sudden rush) mouvement m brusque; (small amount) soupçon m, petit brin m; (of color) pointe f, touche f; (splash) choc m, floc m; (spirit) élan m, fougue f; (in printing, writing) tiret m; (in telegraphy) trait m, longue f; (sports) sprint m ‖ tr (quickly) précipiter; (violently) heurter; (hopes) abattre; **to dash off** écrire d'un trait, esquisser; **to dash to pieces** fracasser ‖ intr se précipiter; **to dash against** se heurter contre; **to dash by** filer à grand train; **to dash in** entrer en trombe; **to dash off** or **out** s'élancer, s'élancer dehors
dash'board' s tableau m de bord
dashing ['dæʃɪŋ] adj impétueux, fougueux; (elegant) fringant
dastard ['dæstərd] adj & s lâche mf
data ['detə], ['dætə] spl données fpl, information f; (comp) données
da'ta bank' s banque f de données
da'ta base' s base f de données
da'ta bus' s (comp) bus m de données
da'ta cap'ture s (comp) captage m de données
da'ta flow' s (comp) flux m de données
da'ta-proc'ess intr (comp) traiter les données
da'ta proc'essing s analyse f des renseignements, étude f des données; (comp) traitement m de l'information or les données
da'ta protec'tion s (comp) protection f de données, protection de l'information
da'ta stor'age s (comp) stockage m de données, mémoire f
da'ta trans'mis'sion s (comp) transmission f de données
date [det] s (time) date f; (on books, on coins) millésime m; (palm) dattier m; (fruit) datte f; (of note, of loan) terme m, échéance f; (appointment) rendez-vous m; **out of date** suranné, périmé; **to date** ce jour; **up to date** à la page, au courant ‖ tr dater; (e.g., a work of art) assigner une date à; (coll) fixer un rendez-vous avec ‖ intr (to be outmoded) dater; **to date from** dater de, remonter à
date' line' s ligne f de changement de date
date' palm' s dattier m
dative ['detɪv] s datif m

daub [dɔb] *s* barbouillage *m* ‖ *tr* barbouiller
daughter [ˈdɔtər] *s* fille *f*
daugh′ter-in-law′ *s* (*pl* **daughters-in-law**) belle-fille *f*, bru *f*
daunt [dɔnt] *tr* intimider, abattre
dauntless [ˈdɔntlɪs] *adj* intrépide
dauphin [ˈdɔfɪn] *s* dauphin *m*
davenport [ˈdævən‚pɔrt] *s* canapé-lit *m*
Davey [ˈdevi] **Jones** [dʒonz] **locker** *s* port *m* des navires perdus
daw [dɔ] *s* choucas *m*
dawdle [ˈdɔdəl] *intr* flâner, muser
dawn [dɔn] *s* aube *f*, aurore *f* ‖ *intr* poindre; **to dawn on** venir à l'esprit à
day [de] *adj* (*work*) diurne; (*worker*) de journée ‖ *s* jour *m;* (*of travel, work, worry*) journée *f;* (*of the month*) quantième *m;* **a day** (*per day*) par jour; **by the day** à la journée; **day by day** au jour le jour, jour par jour; **every day** tous les jours, chaque jour; **every other day** tous les deux jours; **from day to day** de jour en jour; **good old days** bon vieux temps; **in less than a day** du jour au lendemain; **in these days** de nos jours; **in those days** à ce moment-là, à cette époque; **one fine day** un beau jour; **the day after** le lendemain; le lendemain de; **the day after tomorrow** après-demain; l'après-demain *m;* **the day before** la veille; la veille de; **the day before yesterday** avant-hier; l'avant-hier *m;* **the other day** l'autre jour, récemment; **to have had its day** avoir fait son temps
day′ bed′ *s* canapé-lit *m*, petit lit *m* de repos
day′break′ *s* pointe *f* du jour, lever *m* du jour; **at daybreak** au jour levant
day′ care′ *s* service *m* de garderie d'enfants
day′-care cen′ter *s* garderie *f* d'enfants, crèche *f*
day′ coach′ *s* (rr) voiture *f*
day′dream′ *s* rêvasserie *f*, rêverie *f* ‖ *intr* rêvasser, rêver creux
day′dream′er *s* songe-creux *m*, songeur *m*
day′dream′ing *s* rêvasserie *f*
day′ la′borer *s* journalier *m*
day′light′ *s* jour *m;* **in broad daylight** en plein jour; **to see daylight** (coll) comprendre; (coll) voir la fin d'une tâche difficile
day′light-sav′ing time′ *s* heure *f* d'été
day′ lil′y *s* lis *m* jaune, belle-d'un-jour *f*
day′ nurs′ery *s* garderie *f* d'enfants, crèche *f*
day′ off′ *s* jour *m* de congé, jour chômé
day′ of reck′oning *s* jour *m* de règlement; (*last judgment*) jour d'expiation
day′ shift′ *s* équipe *f* de jour
day′ stu′dent *s* externe *mf*
day′time′ *s* jour *m*, journée *f*
daze [dez] *s* étourdissement *m;* **in a daze** hébété ‖ *tr* étourdir
dazzle [ˈdæzəl] *s* éblouissement *m* ‖ *tr* éblouir
dazzling [ˈdæzlɪŋ] *adj* éblouissant
D.C. [ˈdiˈsi] *s* (letterword) (**District of Columbia**) le district de Columbia; (**direct current**) le courant continu

D′-day′ *s* le jour J
deacon [ˈdikən] *s* diacre *m*
deaconess [ˈdikənɪs] *s* diaconesse *f*
dead [dɛd] *adj* mort; (*tired*) épuisé; (*color*) terne; (*business*) stagnant; (*sleep*) profond; (*calm*) plat; (*loss*) sec; (*typewriter key*) immobile; **on a dead level** à franc niveau ‖ *s*—**in the dead of night** au milieu de la nuit; **the dead** les morts; **the dead of winter** le cœur de l'hiver ‖ *adv* absolument; **to stop dead** s'arrêter net
dead′beat′ *s* (slang) écornifleur *m*
dead′ bolt′ *s* pêne *m* dormant
dead′ calm′ *s* calme *m* plat
dead′ cen′ter *s* point *m* mort
dead′-drunk′ *adj* ivre mort
deaden [ˈdɛdən] *tr* amortir; (*sound*) assourdir
dead′ end′ *s* cul-de-sac *m*, impasse *f*
dead′latch′ *s* pêne *m* dormant
dead′-let′ter of′fice *s* bureau *m* des rebuts
dead′line′ *s* dernier délai *m*, date *f* limite, terme *m* de rigueur
dead′lock′ *s* serrure *f* à pêne dormant; (fig) impasse *f* ‖ *tr* faire aboutir à une impasse
dead·ly [ˈdɛdli] *adj* (*comp* **-lier;** *super* **-liest**) mortel; (*sin*) capital
dead′ pan′ *s* (slang) visage *m* sans expression
dead′ reck′oning *s* estime *f;* (*position*) point *m* d'estime
dead′ ring′er *s* (coll) portrait *m* vivant
dead′ sol′dier *s* (*bottle*) (slang) cadavre *m*
dead′ weight′ *s* poids *m* mort
dead′wood′ *s* bois *m* mort; (fig) objet *m* or individu *m* inutile
deaf [dɛf] *adj* sourd; **to turn a deaf ear** faire la sourde oreille
deaf′-and-dumb′ *adj* sourd-muet
deafen [ˈdɛfən] *tr* assourdir
deafening [ˈdɛfənɪŋ] *adj* assourdissant
deaf′-mute′ *adj* & *s* sourd-muet *m*
deafness [ˈdɛfnɪs] *s* surdité *f*
deal [dil] *s* (*bargain*) affaire *f;* (cards) main *f*, donne *f;* **a good deal (of)** or **a great deal (of)** beaucoup (de); **to think a great deal of s.o.** estimer qn ‖ *v* (*pret* & *pp* **dealt** [dɛlt]) *tr* (*a blow*) donner, porter; (cards) donner, distribuer; **to deal out** (*e.g., gifts*) distribuer, répartir; (*alms*) dispenser; (*justice*) rendre ‖ *intr* négocier; (cards) faire la donne; **to deal in** faire le commerce de; **to deal with** (*a person*) traiter avec; (*a subject*) traiter de
dealer [ˈdilər] *s* marchand *m*, négociant *m*, négociant *m*, revendeur *m;* (*of cards*) donneur *m;* (*middleman, e.g., in selling automobiles*) concessionnaire *m*, stockiste *m;* (*in drugs*) fourmi *f* (slang)
deal′er's plate′ *s* (aut) immatriculation *f* de livraison
dean [din] *s* doyen *m;* (educ) chef *m* de branche
dean′ship *s* doyenné *m*, décanat *m*
dear [dɪr] *adj* cher; **dear me!** mon Dieu!; **Dear Sir** (*salutation in a letter*) Monsieur ‖ *s* chéri *m*, chérie *f*

dearie ['dɪri] *s* (coll) chérie *f*, chéri *m*

dearth [dʌrθ] *s* disette *f*, pénurie *f*

death [dɛθ] *s* mort *f*; **at death's door** à deux doigts de la mort; **to bore to death** raser; **to put to death** mettre à mort; **to starve to death** mourir de faim; faire mourir de faim

death' bed' *s* lit *m* de mort

death' blow' *s* coup *m* mortel

death' certif'icate *s* constatation *f* de décès, extrait *m* mortuaire

death' house' *s* quartier *m* de la mort

death' knell' *s* glas *m* funèbre

deathless ['dɛθlɪs] *adj* immortel

deathly ['dɛθli] *adj* mortel ‖ *adv* mortellement, comme la mort

death' mask' *s* masque *m* mortuaire

death' pen'alty *s* peine *f* capitale, peine de mort

death' rate' *s* mortalité *f*, taux *m* de mortalité

death' rat'tle *s* râle *m* de la mort

death' ray' *s* rayon *m* de la mort

death' row' *s* couloir *m* de la mort

death' war'rant *s* ordre *m* d'exécution

death'watch' *s* veillée *f* funèbre

deb [dɛb] *s* (slang) débutante *f*

de-bar [dɪ'bɑr] *v* (*pret & pp* **-barred;** *ger* **-barring**) *tr* exclure; empêcher

debark [dɪ'bɑrk] *tr & intr* débarquer

debarkation [,dɪbɑr'keʃən] *s* débarquement *m*

debase [dɪ'bes] *tr* avilir, abaisser; (*e.g., money*) altérer

debatable [dɪ'betəbəl] *adj* discutable

debate [dɪ'bet] *s* débat *m*; **under debate** en discussion ‖ *tr & intr* discuter

debauch [dɪ'bɔtʃ] *s* débauche *f* ‖ *tr* débaucher, corrompre

debauchee [,dɛbɔ'ʃi] *s* débauché *m*

debaucher-y [dɪ'bɔtʃəri] *s* (*pl* **-ies**) débauche *f*

debenture [dɪ'bɛntʃər] *s* (*bond*) obligation *f*; (*voucher*) reçu *m*

debilitate [dɪ'bɪlɪ,tet] *tr* débiliter

debili-ty [dɪ'bɪlɪti] *s* (*pl* **-ties**) débilité *f*

debit ['dɛbɪt] *s* débit *m*; (*entry on debit side*) article *m* au débit ‖ *tr* débiter, porter au débit

deb'it bal'ance *s* solde *m* débiteur

deb'it card' *s* carte *f* bancaire

debonair [,dɛbə'nɛr] *adj* gai, jovial; élégant, charmant

debrief [,di'brif] *tr* faire faire un compte rendu à; (mil) faire faire un rapport à

debriefing [di'brifɪŋ] *s* compte rendu *m* de fin de mission; rapport *m*

debris [də'bri] *s* débris *mpl*, détritus *m*; (*from ruined buildings*) décombres *mpl*

debt [dɛt] *s* dette *f*; **to run into debt** s'endetter

debtor ['dɛtər] *s* débiteur *m*

debug [di'bʌg] *tr* (*an activity*) enlever les défauts de; (*a room*) enlever des micros de; (comp) déboguer

debut [de'bju] *s* début *m* ‖ *intr* débuter

debutante ['dɛbjə,tænt] *s* débutante *f*

decade ['dɛked] *s* décennie *f*; (hist, lit) décade *f*

decadence [dɪ'kedəns] *s* décadence *f*

decadent [dɪ'kedənt] *adj & s* décadent *m*

decaffeinated [di'kæfənetɪd] *adj* décaféiné

decal ['dikæl] *s* décalcomanie *f*

decamp [dɪ'kæmp] *intr* décamper

decanter [dɪ'kæntər] *s* carafe *f*

decapitate [dɪ'kæpɪ,tet] *tr* décapiter

decay [dɪ'ke] *s* (*rotting*) pourriture *f*; (*decline*) décadence *f*; (*falling to pieces*) délabrement *m*; (*of teeth*) carie *f* ‖ *tr* pourrir; (*teeth*) carier ‖ *intr* pourrir, se gâter; (*said of teeth*) se carier; tomber en décadence *or* ruine; délabrer

decease [dɪ'sis] *s* décès *m* ‖ *intr* décéder

deceit [dɪ'sit] *s* tromperie *f*

deceitful [dɪ'sitfəl] *adj* trompeur

deceive [dɪ'siv] *tr & intr* tromper

decelerate [di'sɛlə,ret] *tr & intr* ralentir

December [dɪ'sɛmbər] *s* décembre *m*

decen-cy ['disənsi] *s* (*pl* **-cies**) décence *f*; **decencies** convenances *fpl*

decent ['disənt] *adj* décent

decently ['disəntli] *adv* décemment

decentralize [di'sɛntrə,laɪz] *tr* décentraliser

deception [dɪ'sɛpʃən] *s* tromperie *f*

deceptive [dɪ'sɛptɪv] *adj* trompeur

decep'tive cog'nate *s* faux ami *m*

decibel ['dɛsəbɛl] *s* décibel *m*

decide [dɪ'saɪd] *tr* décider; (*the outcome*) décider de ‖ *intr* décider, se décider; **to decide to** + *inf* décider de + *inf*, se décider à + *inf*; **to decide upon a day** fixer un jour

deciduous [dɪ'sɪdʒʊ‧əs] *adj* caduc

decimal ['dɛsɪməl] *adj* décimal ‖ *s* décimale *f*

dec'imal point' *s* (*in French the comma is used to separate the decimal fraction from the integer*) virgule *f*

decimate ['dɛsɪ,met] *tr* décimer

decipher [dɪ'saɪfər] *tr* déchiffrer

decision [dɪ'sɪʒən] *s* décision *f*

decisive [dɪ'saɪsɪv] *adj* décisif

deck [dɛk] *s* (*of cards*) jeu *m*, paquet *m*; (*of ship*) pont *m*; **between decks** (naut) dans l'entrepont ‖ *tr*—**to deck out** parer, orner

deck' chair' *s* transatlantique *m*, transat *m*, chaise *f* longue de bord

deck' hand' *s* matelot *m* de pont

deck'-land' *intr* apponter

deck'-land'ing *s* appontage *m*

deck'le edge' ['dɛkəl] *s* barbes *fpl*, bords *mpl* baveux

declaim [dɪ'klem] *tr & intr* déclamer

declaration [,dɛklə're ʃən] *s* déclaration *f*

declarative [dɪ'klærətɪv] *adj* déclaratif

declare [dɪ'klɛr] *tr & intr* déclarer

declension [dɪ'klɛnʃən] *s* (gram) déclinaison *f*

declination [,dɛklɪ'neʃən] *s* (astr, geog) déclinaison *f*

decline [dɪ'klaɪn] *s* déclin *m*, décadence *f*; (*in prices*) baisse *f* ‖ *tr & intr* décliner

declivi-ty [dɪ'klɪvɪti] *s* (*pl* **-ties**) déclivité *f*, pente *f*

Deco *ou* **deco** ['dɛko] *s* Art *m* déco, déco *m*

decode [dɪ'kod] *tr* décoder, déchiffrer

decoder [dɪ'kodər] *s* (*person*) decodeur *m*, déchiffreur *m;* (comp, mil, telv) décodeur *m*

decoding [dɪ'kodɪŋ] *s* décodage *m*

decompose [‚dikəm'poz] *tr* décomposer ‖ *intr* se décomposer

decomposition [‚dikɑmpə'zɪʃən] *s* décomposition *f*

decompression [‚dikəm'prɛʃən] *s* décompression *f*

de'compres'sion sick'ness *s* maladie *f* caissons

decongestion [‚dikən'dʒɛstʃən] *s* décongestion *f*

decontamination [‚dikən‚tæmɪ'neʃən] *s* décontamination *f*

decontrol [‚dikən'trol] *tr* lever les contrôles gouvernementaux de

decorate ['dɛkə‚ret] *tr* décorer

decoration [‚dɛkə'reʃən] *s* décoration *f*

decorator ['dɛkə‚retər] *s* décorateur *m*

decorous ['dɛkərəs], [dɪ'korəs] *adj* convenable, correct, bienséant

decorum [dɪ'korəm] *s* décorum *m*

decoy ['dikɔɪ] *s* leurre *m*, appât *m;* (*bird*) appeau *m* ‖ *tr* [dɪ'kɔɪ] *tr* leurrer

decrease ['dikris] *s* diminution *f* ‖ [dɪ'kris] *tr* & *intr* diminuer

decree [dɪ'kri] *s* décret *m*, arrêté *m;* (*of divorce*) ordonnance *f* ‖ *tr* décréter, arrêter, ordonner

decrepit [dɪ'krɛpɪt] *adj* décrépit

de•cry [dɪ'kraɪ] *v* (*pret* & *pp* **-cried**) *tr* décrier, dénigrer

dedicate ['dɛdɪ‚ket] *tr* dédier

dedication [‚dɛdɪ'keʃən] *s* consécration *f;* (*e.g., in a book*) dédicace *f*

dedicatory ['dɛdɪkə‚tori] *adj* dédicatoire

deduce [dɪ'd(j)us] *tr* déduire, inférer

deduct [dɪ'dʌkt] *tr* déduire

deduction [dɪ'dʌkʃən] *s* déduction *f*

deed [did] *s* action *f*, acte *m;* (law) acte, titre *m*, contrat *m;* **deed of valor** haut fait *m;* **good deed** bonne action; **in deed** dans le fait ‖ *tr* transférer par un acte

deem [dim] *tr* estimer, juger, croire ‖ *intr* penser

deep [dip] *adj* profond; (*sound*) grave; (*color*) foncé; de profondeur, e.g., **to be twenty feet deep** avoir vingt pieds de profondeur; **deep in debt** criblé de dettes; **deep in thought** plongé dans la méditation ‖ *adv* profondément; **deep into the night** très avant dans la nuit

deepen ['dipən] *tr* approfondir ‖ *intr* s'approfondir

deep'-freeze' *v* (*pret* **-froze;** *pp* **-frozen** or *pret* & *pp* **-freezed**) *tr* surgeler

deep' freez'er *s* congélateur *m*

deep' freez'ing *s* surgélation *f*

deep'-fry' *v* (*pret* & *pp* **-fried**) *tr* faire frire (en friteuse)

deep' fry'er *s* friteuse *f*

deep'-laid' *adj* habilement ourdi

deep' mourn'ing *s* grand deuil *m*

deep'-root'ed *adj* profondément enraciné, indéracinable

deep'-sea fish'ing *s* grande pêche *f* au large, pêche maritime

deep' space' *s* espace *m* lointain

deep' stall' *s* (aer) superdécrochage *m*

deer [dɪr] *s* (*red deer*) cerf *m;* (*fallow deer*) daim *m;* (*roe deer*) chevreuil *m*

deer'skin' *s* peau *f* de daim

deface [dɪ'fes] *tr* défigurer

de facto [di'fækto] *adv* de fait, de facto

defamation [‚dɛfə'meʃən] *s* diffamation *f*, injures *fpl*

defame [dɪ'fem] *tr* diffamer

default [dɪ‚fɔlt] *s* manque *m*, défaut *m;* (*on an obligation*) carence *f;* **by default** par défaut; (sports) par forfait; **in default of** à défaut de ‖ *tr* (*a debt*) manquer de s'acquitter de ‖ *intr* ne pas tenir ses engagements; (sports) perdre par forfait

defeat [dɪ'fit] *s* défaite *f;* **unexpected defeat** contre-performance *f* ‖ *tr* vaincre, battre, défaire

defeatism [dɪ'fitɪzəm] *s* défaitisme *m*

defeatist [dɪ'fitɪst] *adj* & *s* défaitiste *mf*

defecate ['dɛfɪ‚ket] *intr* déféquer

defect ['difɛkt] *s* défaut *m*, imperfection *f*, vice *m* ‖ [dɪ'fɛkt] *intr* faire défection, déserter

defection [dɪ'fɛkʃən] *s* défection *f*

defective [dɪ'fɛktɪv] *adj* défectueux, vicieux; (gram) défectif

defend [dɪ'fɛnd] *tr* défendre

defendant [dɪ'fɛndənt] *s* (law) défendeur *m*, intimé *m*

defender [dɪ'fɛndər] *s* défenseur *m*

defense [dɪ'fɛns] *s* défense *f;* **in his** *ou* **her defense** à sa décharge

defense' law'yer *s* défense *f*, avocat *m* qui représente la défense, avocat commis d'office

defenseless [dɪ'fɛnslɪs] *adj* sans défense

defensive [dɪ'fɛnsɪv] *adj* défensif ‖ *s* défensive *f*

de•fer [dɪ'fʌr] *v* (*pret* & *pp* **-ferred;** *ger* **-ferring**) *tr* (*to postpone*) différer; (mil) mettre en sursis ‖ *intr*—**to defer to** (*to yield to*) déférer à

deference ['dɛfərəns] *s* déférence *f*

deferential [‚dɛfə'rɛnʃəl] *adj* déférent

deferment [dɪ'fʌrmənt] *s* (*postponement*) ajournement *m*, remise *f;* (*extension of time*) délai *m;* (mil) sursis *m* d'appel, sursis d'incorporation

defiance [dɪ'faɪəns] *s* défi *m*, provocation *f*, nargue *f;* **in defiance of** au mépris de, en dépit de

defiant [dɪ'faɪ•ənt] *adj* provocant, hostile, de défi

deficien•cy [dɪ'fɪʃənsi] *s* (*pl* **-cies**) déficience *f*, insuffisance *f;* (*of vitamins or minerals*) carence *f;* (com) déficit *m*

deficient [dɪ'fɪʃənt] *adj* déficient, insuffisant

deficit ['dɛfɪsɪt] *adj* déficitaire ‖ *s* déficit *m*

defile [dɪ'faɪl], ['difaɪl] *s* défilé *m* ‖ [dɪ'faɪl] *tr* souiller ‖ *intr* défiler

defilement [dɪ'faɪlmənt] *s* souillure *f*

define [dɪˈfaɪn] *tr* définir

definite [ˈdɛfɪnɪt] *adj* défini; (*opinions, viewpoints*) décidé

definitely [ˈdɛfɪnɪtli] *adv* décidément, nettement

definition [ˌdɛfɪˈnɪʃən] *s* définition *f*

definitive [dɪˈfɪnɪtɪv] *adj* définitif

deflate [dɪˈflet] *tr* dégonfler; (*currency*) amener la déflation de ‖ *intr* se dégonfler

deflation [dɪˈfleʃən] *s* dégonflement *m*; (*of prices*) déflation *f*

deflect [dɪˈflɛkt] *tr & intr* dévier

deflower [diˈflauˑər] *tr* déflorer; (*to strip of flowers*) défleurir

defogging [dɪˈfɔgɪŋ] *s* dénébulation *f*

deforest [diˈfɔrɪst] *tr* déboiser

deform [dɪˈfɔrm] *tr* déformer

deformed *adj* contrefait, difforme

deformi•ty [dɪˈfɔrmɪti] *s* (*pl* **-ties**) difformité *f*

defraud [dɪˈfrɔd] *tr* frauder

defray [dɪˈfre] *tr* payer, supporter

defrost [diˈfrɔst] *tr* décongeler, dégivrer

defroster [diˈfrɔstər] *s* déglaceur *m*, dégivreur *m*

defrosting [diˈfrɔstɪŋ] *s* dégèlement *m*, dégivrage *m*

deft [dɛft] *adj* adroit, habile; (*hand*) exercé, preste

defunct [dɪˈfʌŋkt] *adj* défunt; (*practice, style, etc.*) tombé en désuétude

de•fy [dɪˈfaɪ] *v* (*pret & pp* **-fied**) *tr* défier, braver, porter un défi à

degeneracy [dɪˈdʒɛnərəsi] *s* dégénérescence *f*

degenerate [dɪˈdʒɛnərɪt] *adj & s* dégénéré *m* ‖ [dɪˈdʒɛnəˌret] *intr* dégénérer

degrade [dɪˈgred] *tr* dégrader

degrading [dɪˈgredɪŋ] *adj* dégradant

degree [dɪˈgri] *s* degré *m*; (*from a university*) grade *m*; (*of humidity*) titre *m*; **to take a degree** obtenir ses diplômes, obtenir ses titres universitaires

dehumidi•fy [ˌdihjuˈmɪdɪˌfaɪ] *v* (*pret & pp* **-fied**) *tr* déshumidifier

dehydrate [diˈhaɪdret] *tr* déshydrater; (*the body*) dessécher

deice [diˈaɪs] *tr* déglacer, dégivrer

deicer [diˈaɪsər] *s* dégivreur *m*, antigivrant *m*

dei•fy [ˈdiˑɪˌfaɪ] *v* (*pret & pp* **-fied**) *tr* déifier

deign [den] *intr*—**to deign to** daigner

dei•ty [ˈdiˑɪti] *s* (*pl* **-ties**) divinité *f*; (mythol) déité *f*; **the Deity** Dieu *m*

dejected [dɪˈdʒɛktɪd] *adj* abattu, découragé

dejection [dɪˈdʒɛk/ən] *s* abattement *m*

delay [dɪˈle] *s* retard *m*; (*postponement*) sursis *m*, remise *f*; **without delay** sans délai; **without further delay** sans plus tarder ‖ *tr* retarder; (*to put off*) remettre, différer ‖ *intr* tarder, s'attarder

delayed′-ac′tion *adj* à action différée

delayed′-ac′tion switch′ *s* minuterie *f* d'escalier

delayed′ record′ing *s* différé *m*

delayed′-time′ switch′ *s* coupe-circuit *m* à action différée

dele [ˈdili] *s* (typ) deleatur *m*

delectable [dɪˈlɛktəbəl] *adj* délectable

delegate [ˈdɛlɪˌget] *s* délégué *m*; (*at a convention*) congressiste *mf*, délégué ‖ *tr* déléguer

delegation [ˌdɛlɪˈgeʃən] *s* délégation *f*

delete [dɪˈlit] *tr* supprimer

deletion [dɪˈliʃən] *s* suppression *f*; (*the deleted part*) passage *m* supprimé

deliberate [dɪˈlɪbərɪt] *adj* (*premeditated*) délibéré, réfléchi; (*cautious*) circonspect; (*slow*) lent ‖ [dɪˈlɪbəˌret] *tr & intr* délibérer

deliberately [dɪˈlɪbərɪtli] *adv* (*on purpose*) exprès, de propos délibéré; (*without hurrying*) posément, sans hâte

deliberation [dɪˌlɪbəˈreʃən] *s* délibération *f*; (*slowness*) lenteur *f*

delica•cy [ˈdɛlɪkəsi] *s* (*pl* **-cies**) délicatesse *f*; (*choice food*) friandise *f*, gourmandise *f*

delicate [ˈdɛlɪkɪt] *adj* délicat

delicatessen [ˌdɛlɪkəˈtɛsən] *s* charcuterie *f*

delicious [dɪˈlɪʃəs] *adj* délicieux

delight [dɪˈlaɪt] *s* délice *m*, délices *fpl*, plaisir *m* ‖ *tr* enchanter, ravir ‖ *intr*—**to delight in** se délecter à

delighted *adj* enchanté, ravi, content

delightful [dɪˈlaɪtfəl] *adj* délicieux, ravissant, enchanteur

delineate [dɪˈlɪnɪˌet] *tr* esquisser

delinquen•cy [dɪˈlɪŋkwənsi] *s* (*pl* **-cies**) délit *m*, faute *f*; (*e.g., of juveniles*) délinquance *f*

delinquent [dɪˈlɪŋkwənt] *adj* négligent, coupable; (*in payment*) arriéré; (*in guilt*) délinquant ‖ *s* délinquant *m*; créancier *m* en retard

delirious [dɪˈlɪrɪˑəs] *adj* délirant

deliri•um [dɪˈlɪrɪˑəm] *s* (*pl* **-ums** or **-a** [ə]) délire *m*

deliver [dɪˈlɪvər] *tr* délivrer; (*e.g., laundry*) livrer; (*mail*) distribuer; (*a blow*) asséner; (*an opinion*) exprimer; (*a speech*) prononcer; (*energy*) débiter, fournir; **to be delivered of a child** accoucher d'un enfant

deliver•y [dɪˈlɪvəri] *s* (*pl* **-ies**) *s* remise *f*; (*e.g., of a package*) livraison *f*; (*of mail*) distribution *f*; (*of a speech; of electricity*) débit *m*; (*of a woman in childbirth*) accouchement *m*, délivrance *f*; **free delivery** livraison franco

deliv′ery•man′ *s* (*pl* **-men**) livreur *m*

deliv′ery room′ *s* salle *f* d'accouchement, salle de travail

deliv′ery ser′vice *s* service *m* de livraison

deliv′ery truck′ *s* fourgon *m* à livraison

dell [dɛl] *s* vallon *m*

delouse [diˈlaus] *tr* épouiller

delphinium [dɛlˈfɪnɪˑəm] *s* dauphinelle *f*, pied-d'alouette *m*

delta [ˈdɛltə] *s* delta *m*

delude [dɪˈlud] *tr* duper, tromper

deluge [ˈdɛljudʒ] *s* déluge *m* ‖ *tr* inonder

delusion [dɪˈluʒən] *s* illusion *f*, tromperie *f*; **delusions** (psychopathol) hallucinations *fpl*; **delusions of grandeur** folie *f* des grandeurs

delusive [dɪˈlusɪv] or **delusory** [dɪˈlusəri] *adj* trompeur

de luxe [dɪˈlʌks] *adj & adv* de luxe

delve [dɛlv] *intr*—**to delve into** fouiller dans, approfondir

demagnetize [diˈmægnɪˌtaɪz] *tr* démagnétiser, désaimanter

demagogue [ˈdɛməˌgɑg] *s* démagogue *mf*

demand [dɪˈmænd] *s* exigence *f*; (*of the buying public*) demande *f*; **demands** exigences; **in great demand** très recherché; **on demand** sur demande ‖ *tr* exiger

demanding [dɪˈmændɪŋ] *adj* exigeant

demarcate [ˈdimɑrˌket] *tr* délimiter

demean [dɪˈmin] *tr* dégrader; **to demean one-self** se conduire

demeanor [dɪˈminər] *s* conduite *f*, tenue *f*

demented [dɪˈmɛntɪd] *adj* aliéné, fou

demerit [diˈmɛrɪt] *s* démérite *m*

demigod [ˈdɛmɪˌgɑd] *s* demi-dieu *m*

demijohn [ˈdɛmɪˌdʒɑn] *s* dame-jeanne *f*

demilitarize [diˈmɪlɪtəˌraɪz] *tr* démilitariser

demise [dɪˈmaɪz] *s* décès *m*

demitasse [ˈdɛmɪˌtæs] *s* petite tasse *f* à café; (*contents*) café *m* noir

demobilize [diˈmobɪˌlaɪz] *tr* démobiliser

democra•cy [dɪˈmɑkrəsi] *s* (*pl* **-cies**) démocratie *f*

democrat [ˈdɛməˌkræt] *s* démocrate *mf*

democratic [ˌdɛməˈkrætɪk] *adj* démocratique

demolish [dɪˈmɑlɪʃ] *tr* démolir

demolition [ˌdɛməˈlɪʃən] *s* démolition *f*

demon [ˈdimən] *s* démon *m*

demoniac [dɪˈmoniˌæk] *adj & s* démoniaque *mf*

demonic [dɪˈmɑnɪk] *adj* démoniaque

demonize [ˈdiməˌnaɪz] *tr* attribuer un caractère démoniaque à

demonstrate [ˈdɛmənˌstret] *tr* démontrer ‖ *intr* (*to show feelings in public gatherings*) manifester

demonstration [ˌdɛmənˈstreʃən] *s* démonstration *f*; (*public show of feeling*) manifestation *f*

demonstrative [dɪˈmɑnstrətɪv] *adj* démonstratif

demonstrator [ˈdɛmənˌstretər] *s* (*salesman*) démonstrateur *m*; (*agitator*) manifestant *m*

demoralize [dɪˈmɔrəˌlaɪz] *tr* démoraliser

demote [dɪˈmot] *tr* rétrograder

demotion [dɪˈmoʃən] *s* rétrogradation *f*

de•mur [dɪˈmʌr] *v* (*pret & pp* **-murred;** *ger* **-murring**) *intr* faire des objections

demure [dɪˈmjʊr] *adj* modeste, posé

demurrage [dɪˈmʌrɪdʒ] *s* (naut) surestarie *f*

den [dɛn] *s* (*of animals; of thieves*) repaire *m*, retraite *f*, officine *f*; (*of wild beasts*) antre *m*; (*of lions*) tanière *f*; (*room in a house*) cabinet *m* de travail, fumoir *m*, coin *m* de détente, coin de retraite; (Cub Scouts) sizaine *f*

denaturalize [diˈnætʃərəˌlaɪz] *tr* dénaturaliser

denial [dɪˈnaɪ•əl] *s* (*contradiction*) dénégation *f*, démenti *m*; (*refusal*) refus *m*, déni *m*

denim [ˈdɛnɪm] *s* coutil *m*

denizen [ˈdɛnɪzən] *s* habitant *m*

Denmark [ˈdɛnmɑrk] *s* le Danemark

denomination [dɪˌnɑmɪˈneʃən] *s* dénomination *f*; (*of coin or stamp*) valeur *f*; (eccl) secte *f*, confession *f*, communion *f*

denote [dɪˈnot] *tr* dénoter

denounce [dɪˈnaʊns] *tr* dénoncer

dense [dɛns] *adj* dense; (*stupid*) bête

densi•ty [ˈdɛnsɪti] *s* (*pl* **-ties**) densité *f*

dent [dɛnt] *s* (*depression*) marque *f* de coup, creux *m*; (*in a knife; in a fortune*) brèche *f*; **to make a dent in** faire une brèche à ‖ *tr* ébrécher

dental [ˈdɛntəl] *adj* dentaire; (phonet) dental ‖ *s* dentale *f*

den′tal brac′es *spl* appareil *m* dentaire

den′tal floss′ *s* fil *m* dentaire, soie *f* dentaire

den′tal lab′oratory *s* laboratoire *m* de prothèse dentaire

den′tal sur′geon *s* chirurgien-dentiste *m*

den′tal techni′cian *s* mécanicien *m* dentiste

dentifrice [ˈdɛntɪfrɪs] *s* dentifrice *m*

dentist [ˈdɛntɪst] *s* dentiste *mf*

dentistry [ˈdɛntɪstri] *s* odontologie *f*

den′tist′s chair′ *s* fauteuil *m* de dentiste

den′tist′s of′fice *s* cabinet *m* de dentiste

denture [ˈdɛntʃər] *s* (*set of teeth*) denture *f*; (*set of artificial teeth*) dentier *m*, râtelier *m*, prothèse *f* dentaire

denunciation [dɪˌnʌnsiˈeʃən] *s* dénonciation *f*

de•ny [dɪˈnaɪ] *v* (*pret & pp* **-nied**) *tr* nier, démentir; **to deny oneself** se refuser, se priver

deodorant [diˈodərənt] *adj & s* désodorisant *m*

deodorize [diˈodəˌraɪz] *tr* désodoriser

deoxidize [diˈɑksɪˌdaɪz] *tr* désoxyder

deoxyribonucleic acid (DNA) [diˈɑksɪˈrɪbəˈnukle•ɪk] *s* acide *m* désoxyribonucléique (ADN or A.D.N.)

depart [dɪˈpɑrt] *intr* partir; **to depart from** se départir de

departed *adj* (*dead*) mort, défunt

department [dɪˈpɑrtmənt] *s* département *m*; (*of hospital*) service *m*; (*of agency*) bureau *m*; (*of store*) rayon *m*, comptoir *m*; (*of university*) section *f*

Depart′ment of State′ *s* ministère *m* des affaires étrangères

depart′ment store′ *s* grands magasins *mpl*, galerie *f*

departure [dɪˈpɑrtʃər] *s* départ *m*

depend [dɪˈpɛnd] *intr* dépendre; **to depend on** or **upon** dépendre de

dependable [dɪˈpɛndəbəl] *adj* sûr; (*person*) digne de confiance

dependence [dɪˈpɛndəns] *s* dépendance *f*; **dependence on** dépendance de; (*trust in*) confiance en

dependen•cy [dɪˈpɛndənsi] *s* (*pl* **-cies**) dépendance *f*; (*country, territory*) possession *f*, colonie *f*

dependent [dɪˈpɛndənt] *adj* dépendant; **dependent on** dépendant de; (*s.o. for family support*) à la charge de ‖ *s* charge *f* de famille

depend′ent clause′ s proposition f subordonnée

depict [dɪ'pɪkt] tr dépeindre, décrire

depiction [dɪ'pɪkʃən] s peinture f

deplete [dɪ'plit] tr épuiser

depletion [dɪ'pliʃən] s épuisement m

deple′tion allow′ance s déduction f pour remplacement

deplorable [dɪ'plorəbəl] adj déplorable

deplore [dɪ'plor] tr déplorer

deploy [dɪ'plɔɪ] tr (mil) déployer ‖ intr (mil) se déployer

deployment [dɪ'plɔɪmənt] s (mil) déploiement m

depolarize [di'polə,raɪz] tr dépolariser

depopulate [di'pɑpjə,let] tr & intr dépeupler

deport [dɪ'port] tr déporter; **to deport oneself** se comporter

deportation [,dipor'teʃən] s déportation f

deportee [,dipor'ti] s déporté m

deportment [dɪ'portmənt] s comportement m, tenue f, manières fpl

depose [dɪ'poz] tr & intr déposer

deposit [dɪ'pɑzɪt] s dépôt m; (as pledge) cautionnement m, arrhes fpl, gage m; **no deposit** (bottle) perdu; **to pay a deposit** verser une provision, un acompte, or une caution; **with deposit** (on a bottle) consigné ‖ tr déposer; laisser comme provision

depos′it account′ s compte m courant

depositor [dɪ'pɑzɪtər] s déposant m

deposito‧ry [dɪ'pɑzɪ,tori] s (pl -ries) dépôt m; (person) dépositaire mf

depot ['dipo] s dépôt m; (rr) gare f

depraved [dɪ'prevd] adj dépravé

depravi‧ty [dɪ'præviti] s (pl -ties) dépravation f

deprecate ['dɛprɪ,ket] tr désapprouver

depreciate [dɪ'priʃi,et] tr déprécier ‖ intr se déprécier

depreciation [dɪ,priʃi'eʃən] s dépréciation f

deprecia′tion allow′ance s provision f pour amortissement

depredation [,dɛprɪ'deʃən] s déprédation f

depress [dɪ'prɛs] tr déprimer; (prices) abaisser

depressing [dɪ'prɛsɪŋ] adj attristant

depression [dɪ'prɛʃən] s dépression f

deprive [dɪ'praɪv] tr priver

deprogram [dɪ'progræm] tr déprogrammer

depth [dɛpθ] s profondeur f; (in sound) gravité f; **depths** abîme m; **in the depth of winter** en plein hiver; **to go beyond one's depth** perdre pied; sortir de sa compétence

depth′ bomb′ s bombe f sous-marine

depth′ charge′ s grenade f sous-marine

deputation [,dɛpjə'teʃən] s députation f

deputize ['dɛpjə,taɪz] tr députer

depu‧ty ['dɛpjəti] s (pl -ties) député m

derail [dɪ'rel] tr faire dérailler ‖ intr dérailler

derailment [dɪ'relmənt] s déraillement m

derange [dɪ'rendʒ] tr déranger

derangement [dɪ'rendʒmənt] s dérangement m; (of mind) aliénation f

der‧by ['dɑrbi] s (pl -bies) (race) derby m; (hat) chapeau m melon

deregulate [dɪ'rɛgjə,let] tr déréglementer

derelict ['dɛrɪlɪkt] adj abandonné, délaissé; (in one's duty) négligent ‖ s épave f

dereliction [,dɛrɪ'lɪkʃən] s abandon m, renoncement m

deride [dɪ'raɪd] tr tourner en dérision, ridiculiser

derision [dɪ'rɪʒən] s dérision f

derisive [dɪ'raɪsɪv] adj dérisoire

derisory [də'raɪzəri] adj dérisoire

derivation [,dɛrɪ've ʃən] s dérivation f

derivative [dɪ'rɪvətɪv] adj & s dérivé m

derive [dɪ'raɪv] tr & intr dériver

dermatitis [,dɛrmə'taɪtɪs] s dermatite f, dermite f

dermatology [,dɑrmə'talədʒi] s dermatologie f

derogatory [dɪ'rɑgə,tori] adj péjoratif

derrick ['dɛrɪk] s (crane) grue f; (for extracting oil) derrick m, tour f (de forage)

dervish ['dɑrvɪʃ] s derviche m

desalinization [di,selɪni'zeʃən] s dessalement m

desalt [di'sɔlt] tr dessaler

descend [dɪ'sɛnd] tr descendre ‖ intr descendre; (said of rain) tomber; **to be descended from** descendre de; **to be directly descended from** (e.g., an idea) être dans le droit-fil de; **to descend on** s'abattre sur

descendant [dɪ'sɛndənt] adj & s descendant m

descendent [dɪ'sɛndənt] adj descendant

descent [dɪ'sɛnt] s descente f; (drop in temperature) chute f; (lineage) descendance f, naissance f; **of German descent** d'extraction allemande

descrambling [di'skræmblɪŋ] s (electron) désembrouillage m

describe [dɪ'skraɪb] tr décrire

description [dɪ'skrɪpʃən] s description f

descriptive [dɪ'skrɪptɪv] adj descriptif

de‧scry [dɪ'skraɪ] v (pret & pp -scried) tr découvrir, apercevoir

desecrate ['dɛsɪ,kret] tr profaner

desegregate [di'sɛgrɪ,get] intr supprimer la ségrégation raciale

desegregation [di,sɛgrɪ'geʃən] s déségrégation f

desensitize [di'sɛnsɪ,taɪz] tr désensibiliser

desert ['dɛzərt] adj & s désert m ‖ [dɪ'zʌrt] s mérite m; **to get one's just deserts** recevoir son salaire, recevoir sa juste punition ‖ tr & intr déserter

deserted adj (person) abandonné; (place) désert, nu

deserter [dɪ'zʌrtər] s déserteur m

desertion [dɪ'zʌrʃən] s désertion f

deserve [dɪ'zʌrv] tr & intr mériter

deservedly [dɪ'zʌrvɪdli] adv à juste titre, dignement

deserving [dɪ'zʌrvɪŋ] adj méritoire, digne

design [dɪ'zaɪn] s (combination of details; art of designing; work of art) dessin m; (plan, scheme) dessein m, projet m, plan m; (model, *outline*) modèle *m,* type *m,* grandes lignes *fpl;* **to have designs on** avoir des desseins sur ‖ *tr* inventer, projeter; (*e.g., a dress*) dessiner; (*a secret plan*) combiner; **designed for** destiné à

designate [ˈdɛzɪgˌnet] *tr* désigner

designer [dɪˈzaɪnər] *s* dessinateur *m;* (com) concepteur-projeteur *m;* (mov, theat) décorateur *m*

designing [dɪˈzaɪnɪŋ] *adj* artificieux, intrigant ‖ *s* dessin *m*

desirable [dɪˈzaɪrəbəl] *adj* désirable

desire [dɪˈzaɪr] *s* désir *m* ‖ *tr* désirer

desirous [dɪˈzaɪrəs] *adj* désireux

desist [dɪˈzɪst] *intr* cesser

desk [dɛsk] *s* (*in office*) bureau *m;* (*in schoolroom*) pupitre *m;* (*of cashier*) caisse *f*

desk′ blot′ter *s* sous-main *m*

desk′ clerk′ *s* réceptionnaire *mf,* réceptionniste *mf*

desk′ pad′ *s* bloc *m* (de bureau), bloc-notes *m*

desk′ set′ *s* écritoire *f*

desk′top *s* (comp) moniteur *m,* écran *m* or console *f* de visualisation, console *f* graphique (*les icônes et les listes d'outils sur l'écran du moniteur*)

desk′top comput′er *s* (comp) micro-ordinateur *m,* ordinateur *m* individuel *or* personnel

desk′top pub′lishing *s* publication *f* assistée par ordinateur (PAO), édition *f* électronique, microédition *f*

desolate [ˈdɛsəlɪt] *adj* désert; (*sad*) désolé; (*alone*) abandonné ‖ [ˈdɛsəˌlet] *tr* désoler

desolation [ˌdɛsəˈleʃən] *s* désolation *f*

despair [dɪˈspɛr] *s* désespoir *m,* désespérance *f* ‖ *intr* désespérer

despairing [dɪˈspɛrɪŋ] *adj* désespéré

despera•do [ˌdɛspəˈrado] *s* (*pl* **-does** or **-dos**) hors-la-loi *m*

desperate [ˈdɛspərɪt] *adj* capable de tout, poussé à bout; (*bitter, excessive*) acharné, à outrance; (*hopeless*) désespéré; (*remedy*) héroïque

desperation [ˌdɛspəˈreʃən] *s* (*despair*) désespoir *m;* (*recklessness*) témérité *f*

despicable [ˈdɛspɪkəbəl] *adj* méprisable, mesquin

despise [dɪˈspaɪz] *tr* mépriser, dédaigner

despite [dɪˈspaɪt] *prep* en dépit de, malgré

despoil [dɪˈspɔɪl] *tr* dépouiller

desponden•cy [dɪˈspandənsi] *s* (*pl* **-cies**) abattement *m,* accablement *m*

despondent [dɪˈspandənt] *adj* abattu, accablé, déprimé

despot [ˈdɛspat] *s* despote *m,* tyran *m*

despotic [dɛsˈpatɪk] *adj* despotique

despotism [ˈdɛspəˌtɪzəm] *s* despotisme *m*

dessert [dɪˈzʌrt] *s* dessert *m*

dessert′ spoon′ *s* cuiller *f* à dessert

destination [ˌdɛstɪˈneʃən] *s* destination *f*

destine [ˈdɛstɪn] *tr* destiner

desti•ny [ˈdɛstɪni] *s* (*pl* **-nies**) destin *m,* destinée *f*

destitute [ˈdɛstɪˌt(j)ut] *adj* (*poverty-stricken*) indigent; (*lacking*) dépourvu, dénué

destitution [ˌdɛstɪˈt(j)uʃən] *s* dénuement *m,* indigence *f*

destroy [dɪˈstrɔɪ] *tr* détruire

destroyer [dɪˈstrɔɪ•ər] *s* destructeur *m;* (nav) destroyer *m*

destruction [dɪˈstrʌkʃən] *s* destruction *f*

destructive [dɪˈstrʌktɪv] *adj* destructeur, destructif

desultory [ˈdɛsəlˌtori] *adj* décousu, sans suite; (*conversation*) à bâtons rompus

detach [dɪˈtætʃ] *tr* détacher

detachable [dɪˈtætʃəbəl] *adj* détachable, démontable; (*collar*) faux

detached *adj* détaché

detachment [dɪˈtætʃmənt] *s* détachement *m*

detail [dɪˈtel], [ˈditel] *s* détail *m;* (mil) extrait *m* de l'ordre du jour; (mil) détachement *m* ‖ [dɪˈtel] *tr* détailler

detailed′ state′ment *s* bordereau *m*

detain [dɪˈten] *tr* retenir, retarder; (*in prison*) détenir

detect [dɪˈtɛkt] *tr* déceler, détecter

detection [dɪˈtɛkʃən] *s* détection *f*

detective [dɪˈtɛktɪv] *adj* (*device*) détecteur; (*film, novel*) policier ‖ *s* détective *m,* agent *m* de la sûreté

detec′tive sto′ry *s* roman *m* policier

detector [dɪˈtɛktər] *s* détecteur *m*

detention [dɪˈtɛnʃən] *s* détention *f*

de•ter [dɪˈtʌr] *v* (*pret & pp* **-terred;** *ger* **-terring**) *tr* dissuader, détourner

detergent [dɪˈtʌrdʒənt] *adj & s* détersif *m,* détergent *m*

deteriorate [dɪˈtɪri•əˌret] *tr* détériorer ‖ *intr* se détériorer

determination [di,tʌrmɪˈneʃən] *s* détermination *f*

determine [dɪˈtʌrmɪn] *tr* déterminer

determined *adj* déterminé, résolu

deterrent [dɪˈtʌrənt] *adj & s* préventif *m*

detest [dɪˈtɛst] *tr* détester

dethrone [dɪˈθron] *tr* détrôner

detonate [ˈdɛtəˌnet] *tr* faire détoner, faire éclater ‖ *intr* détoner

detour [ˈditʊr] *s* déviation *f;* (*indirect manner*) détour *m* ‖ *tr & intr* dévier

detoxification [di,taksəfəˈkeʃən] *s* désintoxication *f*

detoxi•fy [diˈtaksəˌfaɪ] *v* (*pret & pp* **-fied**) *tr* désintoxiquer

detract [dɪˈtrækt] *tr* diminuer ‖ *intr*—**to detract from** amoindrir

detractor [dɪˈtræktər] *s* détracteur *m*

detriment [ˈdɛtrɪmənt] *s* détriment *m*

detrimental [ˌdɛtrɪˈmɛntəl] *adj* préjudiciable, nuisible

deuce [d(j)us] *s* deux *m;* (*score*) égalité *f;* **what the deuce!** (coll) diantre!, que diable!

devaluate [diˈvæljʊˌet] *tr* dévaluer

devaluation [di,væljʊˈeʃən] *s* dévaluation *f*

devastate [ˈdɛvəsˌtet] *tr* dévaster

devastating [ˈdɛvəsˌtetɪŋ] *adj* dévastateur; (coll) écrasant, accablant

devastation [ˌdɛvəsˈteʃən] *s* dévastation *f*

develop [dɪˈvɛləp] *tr* développer; (*a mine*) exploiter; (*to perfect*) mettre au point, réaliser, étudier; (*e.g., a fever*) contracter, être atteint de; (phot) révéler, développer ‖ *intr* se développer; (*to become evident*) se produire, se manifester

developer [dɪˈvɛləpər] *s* entrepreneur *m*, aménager *m*; (*of houses*) promoteur *m* de construction, lotisseur *m*; (*builder*) maître *m* d'œuvre; (phot) révélateur *m*

development [dɪˈvɛləpmənt] *s* dévelopement *m*; (*event*) événement *m* récent; (*of housing*) aménagement *m*, lotissement *m*, grand ensemble *m*

deviate [ˈdivɪˌet] *s* perverti *m* ‖ *tr* faire dévier ‖ *intr* dévier

deviation [ˌdivɪˈeʃən] *s* déviation *f*

device [dɪˈvaɪs] *s* appareil *m*, dispositif *m*; (*trick*) stratagème *m*, ruse *f*; emblème *m*, devise *f*; **to leave s.o. to his own devices** abandonner qn à ses propres moyens

dev•il [ˈdɛvəl] *s* diable *m*; **speak of the devil!** (coll) je vois un loup!; **to be between the devil and the deep blue sea** (coll) se trouver entre l'enclume et le marteau; **to raise the devil** (slang) faire le diable à quatre ‖ *v* (*pret & pp* **-iled** *or* **-illed;** *ger* **-iling** *or* **-illing**) *tr* épicer fortement; (coll) tourmenter

devilish [ˈdɛvəlɪʃ] *adj* diabolique; (*roguish*) coquin

dev′il-may-care′ *adj* insouciant, étourdi

devilment [ˈdɛvəlmənt] *s* (*mischief*) diablerie *f*; (*evil*) méchanceté *f*

devil•try [ˈdɛvəltri] *s* (*pl* **-tries**) méchanceté *f*, cruauté *f*; (*mischief*) espièglerie *f*

devious [ˈdivɪəs] *adj* (*straying*) détourné, dévié; (*roundabout; shifty*) tortueux

devise [dɪˈvaɪz] *tr* combiner, inventer; (law) léguer

devoid [dɪˈvɔɪd] *adj* dépourvu, vide, dénué

devolve [dɪˈvɑlv] *intr*—**to devolve on, to,** or **upon** échoir à

devote [dɪˈvot] *tr* consacrer

devoted *adj* dévoué; **devoted to** voué à, dévoué à, attaché à

devotee [ˌdɛvəˈti] *s* dévot *m*, adepte *mf*; (sports) fervent *m*, fanatique *mf*

devotion [dɪˈvoʃən] *s* dévotion *f*; (*to study, work, etc.*) dévouement *m*; **devotions** dévotions, prières *fpl*

devour [dɪˈvaʊr] *tr* dévorer

devout [dɪˈvaʊt] *adj* dévot, pieux

dew [d(j)u] *s* rosée *f*

dew′drop′ *s* goutte *f* de rosée

dew′lap′ *s* fanon *m*, double menton *m*

dew′ point′ *s* point *m* de rosée

dew•y [ˈd(j)u•i] *adj* (*comp* **-ier;** *super* **-iest**) couvert de rosée

dexterity [dɛksˈtɛrɪti] *s* dextérité *f*, adresse *f*

diabetes [ˌdaɪ•əˈbitiz] *s* diabète *m*

diabetic [ˌdaɪ•əˈbɛtɪk] *adj & s* diabétique *mf*

diabolic(al) [ˌdaɪ•əˈbɑlɪk(əl)] *adj* diabolique

diacritical [ˌdaɪ•əˈkrɪtɪkəl] *adj* diacritique

diadem [ˈdaɪ•əˌdɛm] *s* diadème *m*

diaeresis = dieresis

diagnose [ˌdaɪ•əgˈnos] *tr* diagnostiquer

diagnosis [ˌdaɪ•əgˈnosɪs] *s* (*pl* **-ses** [siz]) diagnostic *m*

diagonal [daɪˈægənəl] *adj* diagonal ‖ *s* diagonale *f*

dia•gram [ˈdaɪ•əˌgræm] *s* diagramme *m*, croquis *m* coté ‖ *v* (*pret & pp* **-gramed** *or* **-grammed;** *ger* **-graming** *or* **-gramming**) *tr* représenter schématiquement

di•al [ˈdaɪ•əl] *s* cadran *m* ‖ *v* (*pret & pp* **-aled** *or* **-alled;** *ger* **-aling** *or* **-alling**) *tr* (*a telephone number*) composer ‖ *intr* faire un numéro

dialect [ˈdaɪ•əˌlɛkt] *s* dialecte *m*

dialing [ˈdaɪ•əlɪŋ] *s* (telp) composition *f* du numéro

dialogue [ˈdaɪ•əˌlɔg] *s* dialogue *m*; **to carry on a dialogue** dialoguer

di′al tel′ephone *s* téléphone *m* automatique, automatique *m*

di′al tone′ *s* (telp) tonalité *f*

diameter [daɪˈæmɪtər] *s* diamètre *m*

diametric(al) [ˌdaɪ•əˈmɛtrɪk(əl)] *adj* diamètral

diamond [ˈdaɪmənd] *s* (*gem*) diamant *m*; (*figure of a rhombus*) losange *m*; (baseball) petit champ *m*; (cards) carreau *m*

diaper [ˈdaɪ•əpər] *s* lange *m*, couche *f* ‖ *tr* (*to variegate*) diaprer

diaphanous [daɪˈæfənəs] *adj* diaphane

diaphragm [ˈdaɪ•əˌfræm] *s* diaphragme *m*

diarrhea [ˌdaɪ•əˈri•ə] *s* diarrhée *f*

dia•ry [ˈdaɪ•əri] *s* (*pl* **-ries**) journal *m*

diastole [daɪˈæstəli] *s* diastole *f*

diathermy [ˈdaɪ•əˌθʌrmi] *s* diathermie *f*

diatribe [ˈdaɪ•əˌtraɪb] *s* diatribe *f*

dice [daɪs] *spl* dés *mpl*; **no dice!** (slang) pas moyen!; **to load the dice** piper les dés ‖ *tr* couper en cubes

dice′box′ *s* cornet *m* à dés

dichoto•my [daɪˈkatəmi] *s* (*pl* **-mies**) dichotomie *f*

Dictaphone [ˈdɪktəˌfon] *s* (trademark) dictaphone *m*

dictate [ˈdɪktet] *s* précepte *m*, règle *f* ‖ *tr & intr* dicter

dictation [dɪkˈteʃən] *s* dictée *f*; **to take dictation from** écrire sous la dictée de

dictator [dɪkˈtetər] *s* dictateur *m*

dic′tator•ship′ *s* dictature *f*

diction [ˈdɪkʃən] *s* diction *f*

dictionar•y [ˈdɪkʃənˌɛri] *s* (*pl* **-ies**) dictionnaire *m*

dic•tum [ˈdɪktəm] *s* (*pl* **-ta** [tə]) dicton *m*; (law) opinion *f*, arrêt *m*

didactic(al) [dɪˈdæktɪk(əl)] *adj* didactique

didn't *contr* **did not**

die [daɪ] *s* (*pl* **dice** [daɪs]) dé *m*; **the die is cast** le dé en est jeté ‖ *s* (*pl* **dies**) (*for stamping coins, medals, etc.*) coin *m*; (*for cutting* *threads*) filière *f;* (*key pattern*) jeu *m* ‖ *v* (*pret & pp* died; *ger* dying) *intr* mourir; **to be dying to** se mourir; **to be dying to** (coll) mourir d'envie de; **to die away** s'éteindre; **to die laughing** (coll) mourir de rire

die′hard′ *adj* intransigeant ‖ *s* intransigeant *m,* jusqu'au-boutiste *mf*

diere•sis [daɪˈɛrɪsɪs] *s* (*pl* **-ses** [ˌsiz]) (*separation*) diérèse *f;* (*mark*) tréma *m*

dies′el-elec′tric *adj & s* diesel-électrique *m*

die′sel en′gine [ˈdizəl] *s* diesel *m,* moteur *m* diesel

dies′el fu′el *s* gas-oil *m,* gasoil *m*

die′sel oil′ *s* gas-oil *m,* gasoil *m*

die′stock′ *s* porte-filière *m*

diet [ˈdaɪ•ət] *s* (*food and drink*) nourriture *f;* (*congress; abstention from food*) diète *f;* (*special menu*) régime *m* ‖ *intr* être or se mettre au régime, suivre un régime

dietetic [ˌdaɪ•əˈtɛtɪk] *adj* diététique ‖ **dietetics** *s* diététique *f*

dietician [ˌdaɪ•əˈtɪʃən] *s* diététicien *m*

differ [ˈdɪfər] *intr* différer; **to differ with** être en désaccord avec

difference [ˈdɪfərəns] *s* différence *f;* (*controversy*) différend *m;* **to make no difference** ne rien faire; **to split the difference** partager le différend

different [ˈdɪfərənt] *adj* différent

differential [ˌdɪfəˈrɛnʃəl] *adj* différentiel ‖ *s* (mach) différentiel *m;* (math) différentielle *f*

differentiate [ˌdɪfəˈrɛnʃɪˌet] *tr* différencier ‖ *intr* se différencier

difficult [ˈdɪfɪˌkʌlt] *adj* difficile

difficul•ty [ˈdɪfɪˌkʌlti] *s* (*pl* **-ties**) difficulté *f*

diffident [ˈdɪfɪdənt] *adj* défiant, timide

diffuse [dɪˈfjus] *adj* diffus ‖ [dɪˈfjuz] *tr* diffuser ‖ *intr* se diffuser

dig [dɪg] *s*—**to give s.o. a dig** (coll) lancer un trait à qn ‖ *v* (*pret & pp* dug [dʌg]; *ger* digging) *tr* bêcher, creuser; **to dig up** déterrer ‖ *intr* bêcher

digest [ˈdaɪdʒɛst] *s* abrégé *m,* résumé *m;* (*publication*) digest *m,* sélection *f;* (law) digeste *m* ‖ [dɪˈdʒɛst] *tr & intr* digérer

digestible [dɪˈdʒɛstɪbəl] *adj* digestible

digestion [dɪˈdʒɛstʃən] *s* digestion *f*

digestive [dɪˈdʒɛstɪv] *adj* digestif

diges′tive tract′ *s* appareil *m* digestif

digit [ˈdɪdʒɪt] *s* (*numeral*) chiffre *m;* (*finger*) doigt *m;* (*toe*) doigt du pied

digital [ˈdɪdʒɪtəl] *adj* (*numerical*) numérique; (anat) digital

dig′ital clock′ *s* horloge *f* numérique

dig′ital comput′er *s* calculateur *m* numérique

digitalis [ˌdɪgɪˈtælɪs] *s* (bot) digitale *f;* (pharm) digitaline *f*

dig′ital record′ing *s* enregistrement *m* numérique

dig′ital scan′ner *s* scanner *m* numérique

dig′ital tel′ephone *s* téléphone *m* numérique

dig′ital watch′ *s* montre *f* à affichage numérique

digitize [ˈdɪdʒətaɪz] *tr* numériser

dignified *adj* distingué; (*air*) digne

digni•fy [ˈdɪgnɪˌfaɪ] *v* (*pret & pp* **-fied**) *tr* glorifier, honorer

dignitar•y [ˈdɪgnɪˌtɛri] *s* (*pl* **-ies**) dignitaire *mf*

digni•ty [ˈdɪgnɪti] *s* (*pl* **-ties**) dignité *f;* **to stand on one's dignity** rester sur son quant-à-soi, le prendre de haut

digress [dɪˈgrɛs] *intr* faire une digression

digression [dɪˈgrɛʃən] *s* digression *f*

dihedral [daɪˈhidrəl] *adj & s* dièdre *m*

dike [daɪk] *s* digue *f*

dilapidated [dɪˈlæpɪˌdetɪd] *adj* délabré, déglingué

dilate [daɪˈlet] *tr* dilater ‖ *intr* se dilater

dilatory [ˈdɪləˌtori] *adj* lent, tardif; (*strategy, answer*) dilatoire

dilemma [dɪˈlɛmə] *s* dilemme *m*

dilettan•te [ˌdɪləˈtænti] *adj* dilettante ‖ *s* (*pl* **-tes** or **-ti** [ti]) dilettante *mf*

diligence [ˈdɪlɪdʒəns] *s* diligence *f*

diligent [ˈdɪlɪdʒənt] *adj* diligent

dill [dɪl] *s* fenouil *m* bâtard, aneth *m*

dillydal•ly [ˈdɪlɪˌdæli] *v* (*pret & pp* **-lied**) *intr* traînasser

dilute [dɪˈlut] *adj* dilué ‖ *tr* diluer, délayer

dilution [dɪˈluʃən] *s* dilution *f*

dim [dɪm] *adj* faible, indistinct; (*forebodings*) obscur; (*memory*) effacé; (*color*) terne; (*idea of what is going on*) obtus, confus; **to take a dim view of** envisager sans enthousiasme ‖ *v* (*pret & pp* dimmed; *ger* dimming) *tr* affaiblir, obscurcir; (*beauty*) ternir; (*the headlights*) baisser, mettre en code ‖ *intr* s'affaiblir, s'obscurcir; (*said of color, beauty, etc.*) se ternir

dime [daɪm] *s* monnaie *f* de dix cents américains

dimension [dɪˈmɛnʃən] *s* dimension *f*

diminish [dɪˈmɪnɪʃ] *tr & intr* diminuer

diminutive [dɪˈmɪnjətɪv] *adj & s* diminutif *m*

dimi•ty [ˈdɪmɪti] *s* (*pl* **-ties**) basin *m,* brillanté *m*

dimly [ˈdɪmli] *adv* indistinctement

dimmers [ˈdɪmərz] *spl* (aut) feux *mpl* code, feux de croisement; **to put on the dimmers** se mettre en code

dimple [ˈdɪmpəl] *s* fossette *f*

dim′wit′ *s* (slang) sot *m,* niais *m*

din [dɪn] *s* tapage *m,* fracas *m,* casse-tête *m;* ‖ *v* (*pret & pp* dinned; *ger* dinning) *tr* assourdir; répéter sans cesse ‖ *intr* sonner bruyamment

dine [daɪn] *tr* fêter par un dîner ‖ *intr* dîner; **to dine out** dîner en ville

diner [ˈdaɪnər] *s* (*eater*) dîneur *m;* (*short-order restaurant*) plats-cuisinés *m;* (rr) wagon-restaurant *m*

dinette [daɪˈnɛt] *s* coin-repas *m*

ding-dong [ˈdɪŋˌdɔŋ] *s* tintement *m,* digue-din-don *m*

din•ghy [ˈdɪŋgi] *s* (*pl* **-ghies**) canot *m,* youyou *m*

din•gy [ˈdɪndʒi] *adj* (*comp* **-gier;** *super* **-giest**) défraîchi, terne

din'ing car' *s* wagon-restaurant *m*
din'ing hall' *s* salle *f* à manger; (*of university*) réfectoire *m*
din'ing room' *s* salle *f* à manger
din'ing-room suite' *s* salle *f* à manger
dinner ['dɪnər] *s* dîner *m*
din'ner coat' *s* smoking *m*
din'ner dance' *s* dîner *m* suivi de bal
din'ner guest' *s* convive *mf*, invité *m*
din'ner jack'et *s* smoking *m*
din'ner pail' *s* potager *m*
din'ner set' *s* service *m* de table
din'ner time' *s* heure *f* du dîner
dinosaur ['daɪnə,sɔr] *s* dinosaure *m*
dint [dɪnt] *s*—**by dint of** à force de
diocese ['daɪ•ə,sɪs] *s* diocèse *m*
diode ['daɪ•od] *s* diode *f*
dioxide [daɪ'aksaɪd] *s* bioxyde *m*
dip [dɪp] *s* (*immersion*) plongeon *m*; (*swim*) baignade *f*; (*slope*) pente *f*; (*of magnetic needle*) inclinaison *f* ‖ *v* (*pret & pp* **dipped;** *ger* **dipping**) *tr* plonger; (*a flag*) marquer ‖ *intr* plonger; (*said of magnetic needle*) incliner; (*said of scale*) pencher; **to dip into** (*a book*) feuilleter; (*one's capital*) prendre dans
diphtheria [dɪf'θɪrɪ•ə] *s* diphtérie *f*
diphthong ['dɪfθɔŋ] *s* diphtongue *f*
diphthongize ['dɪfθɔŋ,gaɪz] *tr* diphtonguer ‖ *intr* se diphtonguer
diploma [dɪ'plomə] *s* diplôme *m*
diploma•cy [dɪ'ploməsi] *s* (*pl* **-cies**) diplomatie *f*
diplomat ['dɪplə,mæt] *s* diplomate *mf*
diplomatic [,dɪplə'mætɪk] *adj* diplomatique, diplomate
dip'lomat'ic corps' *s* corps *m* diplomatique
dip'lomat'ic pouch' *s* valise *f* diplomatique
dipper ['dɪpər] *s* louche *f*, cuiller *f* à pot
dip'stick' *s* jauge *f* d'huile, jauge à tige
dire [daɪr] *adj* affreux, terrible
direct [dɪ'rɛkt] *adj* direct; franc, sincère ‖ *tr* diriger; (*to order*) ordonner; (*a letter, question, etc.*) adresser; (*to point out*) indiquer; (*theat*) mettre en scène
direct' cur'rent *s* courant *m* continu
direct' di'aling *s* (telp) automatique *m* interurbain
direct' hit' *s* coup *m* or tir *m* direct
direction [dɪ'rɛk/ən] *s* direction *f*; (*e.g., of a street*) sens *m*; (*theat*) mise *f* en scène; **directions** (*orders*) instructions *fpl*; (*for use*) mode *m* d'emploi, instructions
directional [dɪ'rɛk/ənəl] *adj* directionnel
direc'tional sig'nal *s* clignotant *m*
directive [dɪ'rɛktɪv] *s* ordre *m*, avis *m*, directive *f*
direct' ob'ject *s* (gram) complément *m* direct
director [dɪ'rɛktər] *s* directeur *m*, administrateur *m*, chef *m*; (*of a board*) membre *m* du conseil, votant *m*; (theat) metteur *m* en scène
direc'tor•ship' *s* direction *f*, directorat *m*
directo•ry [dɪ'rɛktəri] *s* (*pl* **-ries**) (*board of directors*) conseil *m* d'administration; (*e.g., of* telephone) annuaire *m*; (*e.g., of genealogy*) almanach *m*; (eccl) directoire *m*
dirge [dʌrdʒ] *s* hymne *f* or chant *m* funèbre
dirigible ['dɪrɪdʒɪbəl] *adj & s* dirigeable *m*
dirt [dʌrt] *s* saleté *f*, ordure *f*; (*on clothes, skin, etc.*) crasse *f*; (*mire*) crotte *f*, boue *f*; (*earth*) terre *f*; **to get the dirt out of** décrasser
dirt'-cheap' *adj* vendu à vil prix
dirt' road' *s* chemin *m* de terre
dirt•y ['dʌrti] *adj* (*comp* **-ier;** *super* **-iest**) sale, malpropre; (*clothes, skin, etc.*) crasseux; (*muddy*) crotté, boueux; (*mean*) méchant, vilain
dir'ty lin'en *s* linge *m* sale; **don't wash your dirty linen in public** il faut laver son linge sale en famille
dir'ty trick' *s* (slang) sale tour *m*; **to play a dirty trick on** (slang) faire un tour de cochon à
disabili•ty [,dɪsə'bɪlɪti] *s* (*pl* **-ties**) incapacité *f*, invalidité *f*
disabil'ity insur'ance *s* assurance *f* invalidité
disabil'ity pen'sion *s* pension *f* d'invalidité
disable [dɪs'ebəl] *tr* rendre incapable, mettre hors de combat; (*to hurt the limbs of*) estropier, mutiler
disabled *adj* (*serviceman*) invalide; (*ship*) désemparé
disa'bled vet'eran *s* invalide *m*, réformé *m*
disabuse [,dɪsə'bjuz] *tr* désabuser
disadvantage [,dɪsəd'væntɪdʒ] *s* désavantage *m* ‖ *tr* désavantager
disadvantaged *adj* défavorisé, désavantagé
disadvantageous [dɪs,ædvən'tedʒəs] *adj* désavantageux
disagree [,dɪsə'gri] *intr* différer; **to disagree with** (*to cause discomfort to*) ne pas convenir à; (*to dissent from*) donner tort à
disagreeable [,dɪsə'gri•əbəl] *adj* désagréable; (*mood, weather, etc.*) maussade
disagreement [,dɪsə'grimənt] *s* désaccord *m*, différend *m*
disallow [,dɪsə'laʊ] *tr* désapprouver, rejeter
disappear [,dɪsə'pɪr] *intr* disparaître; (phonet) s'amuïr
disappearance [,dɪsə'pɪrəns] *s* disparition *f*; (phonet) amuïssement *m*
disappoint [,dɪsə'pɔɪnt] *tr* décevoir, désappointer
disappointed *adj* déçu
disappointment [,dɪsə'pɔɪntmənt] *s* déception *f*, désappointement *m*
disapproval [,dɪsə'pruvəl] *s* désapprobation *f*
disapprove [,dɪsə'pruv] *tr & intr* désapprouver
disarm [dɪs'arm] *tr & intr* désarmer
disarmament [dɪs'arməmənt] *s* désarmement *m*
disarming [dɪs'armɪŋ] *adj* désarmant
disarray [,dɪsə're] *s* désarroi *m*, désordre *m*; **in disarray** (*said of apparel*) à demi vêtu ‖ *tr* mettre en désarroi
disassemble [,dɪsə'sɛmbəl] *tr* démonter, désassembler

disassociate [ˌdɪsəˈsoʃɪˌet] *tr* dissocier
disaster [dɪˈzæstər] *s* désastre *m*
disas′ter ar′ea *s* région *f* sinistrée
disastrous [dɪˈzæstrəs] *adj* désastreux
disavow [ˌdɪsəˈvaʊ] *tr* désavouer
disavowal [ˌdɪsəˈvaʊ•əl] *s* désaveu *m*
disband [dɪsˈbænd] *tr* licencier, congédier ‖ *intr* se débander, se disperser
dis•bar [dɪsˈbar] *v* (*pret & pp* **-barred;** *ger* **-barring**) *tr* (law) rayer du barreau
disbelief [ˌdɪsbɪˈlif] *s* incroyance *f*
disbelieve [ˌdɪsbɪˈliv] *tr & intr* ne pas croire
disburse [dɪsˈbʌrs] *tr* débourser
disbursement [dɪsˈbʌrsmənt] *s* déboursement *m;* **disbursements** débours *mpl*
disc [dɪsk] *s* disque *m*
discard [dɪsˈkard] *s* rebut *m;* (cards) écart *m;* **discards** marchandises *fpl* de rebut ‖ *tr* mettre de côté, jeter; (cards) écarter ‖ *intr* (cards) se défausser
discern [dɪˈsʌrn] *tr* discerner, percevoir
discernible [dɪˈsʌrnɪbəl] *adj* discernable
discerning [dɪˈsʌrnɪŋ] *adj* judicieux, pénétrant, éclairé
discernment [dɪˈsʌrnmənt] *s* discernement *m*
discharge [dɪsˈtʃardʒ] (*of a gun; of a battery*) décharge *f;* (*of a prisoner*) élargissement *m;* (*from a job*) congé *m,* renvoi *m;* (*from the armed forces*) libération *f;* (*from the armed forces for unfitness*) réforme *f;* (*from a wound*) suppuration *f* ‖ *tr* décharger; (*a prisoner*) élargir; (*an employee*) congédier, renvoyer, licencier; (*a soldier*) libérer, réformer ‖ *intr* se décharger; (pathol) suppurer
disciple [dɪˈsaɪpəl] *s* disciple *m*
disciplinarian [ˌdɪsɪplɪˈnɛrɪ•ən] *s* partisan *m* d'une forte discipline; personne *f* qui impose une forte discipline
disciplinary [ˈdɪsɪplɪˌnɛri] *adj* disciplinaire
discipline [ˈdɪsɪplɪn] *s* discipline *f* ‖ *tr* discipliner
disclaim [dɪsˈklem] *tr* désavouer, renier
disclaimer [dɪsˈklemər] *s* désaveu *m*
disclose [dɪsˈkloz] *tr* découvrir, révéler
disclosure [dɪsˈkloʒər] *s* découverte *f,* révélation *f*
disco [ˈdɪsko] *s* discothèque *f*
discolor [dɪsˈkʌlər] *tr* décolorer ‖ *intr* se décolorer
discoloration [dɪsˌkʌləˈreʃən] *s* décoloration *f*
discomfit [dɪsˈkʌmfɪt] *tr* décontenancer, bafouer
discomfiture [dɪsˈkʌmfɪtʃər] *s* déconfiture *f,* déconvenue *f*
discomfort [dɪsˈkʌmfərt] *s* (*uneasiness, mild pain*) malaise *f;* (*inconvenience*) gêne *f* ‖ *tr* gêner
disconcert [ˌdɪskənˈsʌrt] *tr* déconcerter
disconnect [ˌdɪskəˈnɛkt] *tr* (*to separate*) désunir, séparer; (*a mechanism*) débrayer; (*a plug*) débrancher; (*current*) couper
disconsolate [dɪsˈkansəlɪt] *adj* désolé, inconsolable

discontent [ˌdɪskənˈtɛnt] *adj* mécontent ‖ *s* mécontentement *m* ‖ *tr* mécontenter
discontented *adj* mécontent
discontinue [ˌdɪskənˈtɪnju] *tr* discontinuer
discontinuous [ˌdɪskənˈtɪnju•əs] *adj* discontinu
discord [ˈdɪskɔrd] *s* discorde *f,* désaccord *m;* (mus) discordance *f*
discordance [dɪsˈkɔrdəns] *s* discordance *f*
discotheque [ˈdɪskoˌtɛk] *s* discothéque *f*
discount [ˈdɪskaʊnt] *s* escompte *m,* remise *f,* rabais *m* ‖ [dɪsˈkaʊnt] *tr* escompter, rabattre
dis′count house′ *s* magasin *m* de rebais, minimarge *f*
dis′count rate′ *s* taux *m* d'escompte
dis′count store′ *s* magasin *m* de rebais, minimarge *f*
discourage [dɪsˈkʌrɪdʒ] *tr* décourager
discouragement [dɪsˈkʌrɪdʒmənt] *s* découragement *m*
discourse [ˈdɪskors] *s* discours *m* ‖ [dɪsˈkors] *intr* discourir
discourteous [dɪsˈkʌrtɪ•əs] *adj* impoli, discourtois
discourte•sy [dɪsˈkʌrtəsi] *s* (*pl* **-sies**) impolitesse *f,* discourtoisie *f*
discover [dɪsˈkʌvər] *tr* découvrir
discoverer [dɪsˈkʌvərər] *s* découvreur *m*
discover•y [dɪsˈkʌvəri] *s* (*pl* **-ies**) découverte *f*
discredit [dɪsˈkrɛdɪt] *s* discrédit *m* ‖ *tr* discréditer
discreditable [dɪsˈkrɛdɪtəbəl] *adj* déshonorant, peu honorable
discreet [dɪsˈkrit] *adj* discret
discrepan•cy [dɪsˈkrɛpənsi] *s* (*pl* **-cies**) désaccord *m,* différence *f*
discretion [dɪsˈkrɛʃən] *s* discrétion *f*
discriminate [dɪsˈkrɪmɪˌnet] *tr & intr* discriminer; **to discriminate against** défavoriser
discrimination [dɪsˌkrɪmɪˈneʃən] *s* discrimination *f*
discriminatory [dɪsˈkrɪmɪnəˌtori] *adj* discriminatoire
discus [ˈdɪskəs] *s* (sports) disque, *m,* palet *m*
discuss [dɪsˈkʌs] *tr & intr* discuter
discussion [dɪsˈkʌʃən] *s* discussion *f*
dis′cus throw′er *s* lanceur *m* de disque
disdain [dɪsˈden] *s* dédain *m* ‖ *tr* dédaigner
disdainful [dɪsˈdenfəl] *adj* dédaigneux
disease [dɪˈziz] *s* maladie *f*
diseased *adj* malade
disembark [ˌdɪsɛmˈbark] *tr & intr* débarquer
disembarkation [dɪsˌɛmbarˈkeʃən] *s* débarquement *m*
disembow•el [ˌdɪsɛmˈbaʊ•əl] *v* (*pret & pp* **-eled** or **-elled;** *ger* **-eling** or **-elling**) *tr* éventrer
disenchant [ˌdɪsɛnˈtʃænt] *tr* désenchanter
disenchantment [ˌdɪsɛnˈtʃæntmənt] *s* désenchantement *m*
disengage [ˌdɪsɛnˈgedʒ] *tr* dégager; (*toothed wheels*) désengrener; (*a motor*) débrayer ‖ *intr* se dégager
disengagement [ˌdɪsɛnˈgedʒmənt] *s* dégagement *m,* détachement *m*

disentangle [ˌdɪsɛn'tæŋgəl] *tr* démêler, débrouiller

disentanglement [ˌdɪsɛn'tæŋgəlmənt] *s* démêlage *m*, débrouillement *m*

disestablish [ˌdɪsɛs'tæblɪʃ] *tr* (*the Church*) séparer de l'État

disfavor [dɪs'fevər] *s* défaveur *f* ‖ *tr* défavoriser

disfigure [dɪs'fɪgjər] *tr* défigurer, enlaidir

disfigurement [dɪs'fɪgjərmənt] *s* défiguration *f*

disfranchise [dɪs'fræntʃaɪz] *tr* priver de ses droits civiques

disgorge [dɪs'gɔrdʒ] *tr & intr* dégorger

disgrace [dɪs'gres] *s* déshonneur *m* ‖ *tr* déshonorer; (*to deprive of favor*) disgracier; **to disgrace oneself** se déshonorer

disgraceful [dɪs'gresfəl] *adj* déshonorant, honteux

disgruntled [dɪs'grʌntəld] *adj* contrarié, de mauvaise humeur

disguise [dɪs'gaɪz] *s* déguisement *m* ‖ *tr* déguiser

disgust [dɪs'gʌst] *s* dégoût *m* ‖ *tr* dégoûter

disgusting [dɪs'gʌstɪŋ] *adj* dégoûtant

dish [dɪʃ] *s* plat *m*; (*food*) mets *m*, plat; **to wash the dishes** faire la vaisselle ‖ *tr*—**to dish up** servir

dish' anten'na *s* antenne *f* parabolique

dish' clos'et *s* étagère *f* à vaisselle

dish'cloth' *s* lavette *f*

dishearten [dɪs'hartən] *tr* décourager

dishev•el [dɪ'ʃɛvəl] *v* (*pret & pp* **-eled** or **-elled**; *ger* **-eling** or **-elling**) *tr* écheveler

dishonest [dɪs'anɪst] *adj* malhonnête, déloyal

dishones•ty [dɪs'anɪsti] *s* (*pl* **-ties**) malhonnêteté *f*, déloyauté *f*, improbité *f*

dishonor [dɪs'anər] *s* déshonneur *m* ‖ *tr* déshonorer

dishonorable [dɪs'anərəbəl] *adj* déshonorant

dish'pan' *s* bassine *f*

dish' rack' *s* égouttoir *m*

dish'rag' *s* lavette *f*

dish'tow'el *s* torchon *m*

dish'wash'er *s* machine *f* à laver la vaisselle, lave-vaisselle *f*; (*person*) plongeur *m*

dish'wa'ter *s* eau *f* de vaisselle

disillusion [ˌdɪsɪ'luʒən] *s* désillusion *f* ‖ *tr* désillusionner

disillusionment [ˌdɪsɪ'luʒənmənt] *s* désillusionnement *m*

disinclination [dɪs,ɪnklɪ'neʃən] *s* répugnance *f*, aversion *f*

disinclined [ˌdɪsɪn'klaɪnd] *adj* indisposé

disinfect [ˌdɪsɪn'fɛkt] *tr* désinfecter

disinfectant [ˌdɪsɪn'fɛktənt] *adj & s* désinfectant *m*

disinformation [dɪs,ɪnfər'meʃən] *s* désinformation *f*

disingenuous [ˌdɪsɪn'dʒɛnju•əs] *adj* insincère, sans franchise

disinherit [ˌdɪsɪn'hɛrɪt] *tr* déshériter

disintegrate [dɪs'ɪntɪˌgret] *tr* désagréger; (nucl) désintégrer ‖ *intr* se désagréger; (nucl) se désintégrer

disintegration [dɪs,ɪntɪ'greʃən] *s* désagrégation *f*; (nucl) désintégration *f*

disin•ter [ˌdɪsɪn'tʌr] *v* (*pret & pp* **-terred;** *ger* **-terring**) *tr* déterrer

disinterested [dɪs'ɪntəˌrɛstɪd] *adj* désintéressé

disjointed [dɪs'dʒɔɪntɪd] *adj* désarticulé; (*e.g., style*) décousu

disjunctive [dɪs'dʒʌŋktɪv] *adj* disjonctif; (*pronoun*) tonique

disk [dɪsk] *s* disque *m*

disk' brake' *s* frein *m* à disque

disk' cam'era *s* appareil *m* photo à disque

disk' drive' *s* (comp) unité *f* centrale

diskette [dɪs'kɛt] *s* (comp) disquette *f*, disque *m* souple

disk' jock'ey *s* présentateur *m* de disques, animateur *m*, disc-jockey *mf*

dislike [dɪs'laɪk] *s* aversion *f*; **to take a dislike for** prendre en aversion ‖ *tr* ne pas aimer

dislocate ['dɪslo,ket] *tr* disloquer; (*a joint*) luxer

dislodge [dɪs'lɑdʒ] *tr* déplacer; (*e.g., the enemy*) déloger

disloyal [dɪs'lɔɪ•əlti] *adj* déloyal

disloyal•ty [dɪs'lɔɪ•əlti] *s* (*pl* **-ties**) déloyauté *f*

dismal ['dɪzməl] *adj* sombre, triste

dismantle [dɪs'mæntəl] *tr* démanteler; (*a machine*) démonter; (*a ship*) désarmer

dismay [dɪs'me] *s* consternation *f* ‖ *tr* consterner

dismember [dɪs'mɛmbər] *tr* démembrer

dismiss [dɪs'mɪs] *tr* (*a thought, suggestion, or subject*) écarter; (*an employee*) congédier, renvoyer, licencier; (*an official, an officer*) destituer, casser; terminer; (*an appeal*) (law) rejeter; (*a class in school*) laisser partir, congédier; **class dismissed!** partez!

dismissal [dɪs'mɪsəl] *s* congédiement *m*, renvoi *m*, destitution *f*; (*of an idea*) abandon *m*; (*of an appeal*) (law) rejet *m*

dismount [dɪs'maunt] *tr* démonter ‖ *intr* descendre

disobedience [ˌdɪsə'bidɪ•əns] *s* désobéissance *f*

disobedient [ˌdɪsə'bidɪ•ənt] *adj* désobéissant

disobey [ˌdɪsə'be] *tr* désobéir à; **to be disobeyed** être désobéi ‖ *intr* désobéir

disorder [dɪs'ɔrdər] *s* désordre *m* ‖ *tr* désordonner

disorderly [dɪs'ɔrdərli] *adj* désordonné, déréglé; (*crowd*) turbulent, effervescent

disor'derly con'duct *s* conduite *f* désordonnée

disorganize [dɪs'ɔrgə,naɪz] *tr* désorganiser

disoriented [dɪs'ɔrɪ,ɛntɪd] *adj* désorienté; **to become disoriented** perdre le nord

disown [dɪs'on] *tr* désavouer, renier

disparage [dɪ'spærɪdʒ] *tr* dénigrer, déprécier

disparagement [dɪ'spærɪdʒmənt] *s* dénigrement *m*, dépréciation *f*

disparate ['dɪspərɪt] *adj* disparate

dispari•ty [dɪ'spærɪti] *s* (*pl* **-ties**) disparité *f*

dispassionate [dɪs'pæʃənɪt] *adj* calme; impartial

dispatch [dɪ'spætʃ] *s* envoi *m*, expédition *f*; (govt, journ, mil) dépêche *f*; (*promptness*) promptitude *f* ‖ *tr* dépêcher, expédier, envoyer; (coll & fig) expédier

dis•pel [dɪ'spɛl] *v* (*pret & pp* **-pelled;** *ger* **-pelling**) *tr* dissiper, disperser

dispensa•ry [dɪ'spɛnsəri] *s* (*pl* **-ries**) dispensaire *m*

dispensation *s* [,dɪspɛn'seʃən] (*dispensing*) dispensation *f*; (*exemption*) dispense *f*

dispense [dɪ'spɛns] *tr* dispenser, distribuer ‖ *intr*—**to dispense with** se passer de; se défaire de

dispenser [dɪ'spɛnsər] *s* dispensateur *m*; (*automatic*) distributeur *m*

disperse [dɪ'spʌrs] *tr* disperser ‖ *intr* se disperser

dispersion [dɪ'spʌrʒən] *s* dispersion *f*

dispirit [dɪ'spɪrɪt] *tr* décourager

displace [dɪs'ples] *tr* déplacer; (*to take the place of*) remplacer

displaced' per'son *s* personne *f* déplacée

displacement [dɪs'plesmənt] *s* déplacement *m*; (*substitution*) remplacement *m*

display [dɪ'sple] *s* exposition *f*, étalage *m*; (*of emotion*) manifestation *f*; (comp) visuel ‖ *tr* exposer, étaler; (*anger, courage, etc.*) manifester; (*ignorance*) révéler; (comp) afficher, visualiser

display' cab'inet *s* vitrine *f*

display' win'dow *s* vitrine *f*, devanture *f*

displease [dɪs'pliz] *tr* déplaire à

displeasing [dɪs'plizɪŋ] *adj* déplaisant

displeasure [dɪs'plɛʒər] *s* déplaisir *m*, mécontentement *m*

disposable [dɪ'spozəbəl] *adj* (*available*) disponible; (*made to be disposed of*) jetable, à jeter; (*container*) perdu, e.g., **disposable bottle** verre perdu

disposal [dɪ'spozəl] *s* disposition *f*; (*of a question*) résolution *f*; (*of trash, garbage, etc.*) destruction *f*

dispos'able tis'sues *spl* mouchoirs *mpl* à jeter

dispose [dɪ'spoz] *tr* disposer ‖ *intr* disposer; **to dispose of** disposer de; (*to get rid of*) se défaire de; (*a question*) résoudre, trancher

disposed *adj*—**to be disposed to** se disposer à, être porté à

disposition [,dɪspə'zɪʃən] *s* disposition *f*; (*mental outlook*) naturel *m*; (mil) dispositif *m*

dispossess [,dɪspə'zɛs] *tr* déposséder; expulser

disproof [dɪs'pruf] *s* réfutation *f*

disproportionate [,dɪsprə'porʃənɪt] *adj* disproportionné

disprove [dɪs'pruv] *tr* réfuter

dispute [dɪ'spjut] *s* dispute *f*; **beyond dispute** incontestable ‖ *tr* disputer ‖ *intr* se disputer

disquali•fy [dɪs'kwɑlɪ,faɪ] *v* (*pret & pp* **-fied**) *tr* disqualifier

disquiet [dɪs'kwaɪ•ət] *s* inquiétude *f* ‖ *tr* inquiéter

disquisition [,dɪskwɪ'zɪʃən] *s* essai *m*, traité *m* considérable

disregard [,dɪsrɪ'gɑrd] *s* indifférence *f*; **disre-**

gard for manque *m* d'égards envers ‖ *tr* ne pas faire cas de, passer sous silence

disrepair [,dɪsrɪ'pɛr] *s* délabrement *m*

disreputable [dɪs'rɛpjətəbəl] *adj* déshonorant, suspect; (*shabby*) débraillé, râpé

disrepute [,dɪsrɪ'pjut] *s* discrédit *m*

disrespect [,dɪsrɪ'spɛkt] *s* irrévérence *f*; manque *m* de respect, irrespect *m*

disrespectful [,dɪsrɪ'spɛktfəl] *adj* irrévérencieux, irrespectueux; **to be disrespectful to** manquer de respect à

disrobe [dɪs'rob] *tr* déshabiller ‖ *intr* se déshabiller

disrupt [dɪs'rʌpt] *tr* rompre; (*to throw into disorder*) bouleverser

disruption [dɪs'rʌpʃən] *s* bouleversement *m*, perturbation *f*, interruption *f*

dissatisfaction [,dɪssætɪs'fæʃən] *s* mécontentement *m*

dissatisfied *adj* mécontent

dissatis•fy [dɪs'sætɪs,faɪ] *v* (*pret & pp* **-fied**) *tr* mécontenter

dissect [dɪ'sɛkt] *tr* disséquer

dissection [dɪ'sɛkʃən] *s* dissection *f*

dissemble [dɪ'sɛmbəl] *tr & intr* dissimuler

disseminate [dɪ'sɛmɪ,net] *tr* disséminer

dissension [dɪ'sɛnʃən] *s* dissension *f*

dissent [dɪ'sɛnt] *s* dissentiment *m*; (*nonconformity*) dissidence *f* ‖ *intr* différer

dissenter [dɪ'sɛntər] *s* dissident *m*

dissertation [,dɪsər'teʃən] *s* dissertation *f*; (*for a degree*) thèse *f*; (*speech*) discours *m*

disservice [dɪ'sʌrvɪs] *s* mauvais service *m*, tort *m*

dissidence ['dɪsɪdəns] *s* dissidence *f*

dissident ['dɪsɪdənt] *adj & s* dissident *m*

dissimilar [dɪ'sɪmɪlər] *adj* dissemblable

dissimilate [dɪ'sɪmɪ,let] *tr* (phonet) dissimiler

dissimulate [dɪ'sɪmjə,let] *tr & intr* dissimuler

dissipate ['dɪsɪ,pet] *tr* dissiper; (*energy, heat, etc.*) disperser ‖ *intr* se dissiper

dissipated *adj* dissipé; débauché

dissipation [,dɪsɪ'peʃən] *s* dissipation *f*; (*of energy, heat, etc.*) dispersion *f*

dissociate [dɪ'soʃɪ,et] *tr* dissocier ‖ *intr* se dissocier

dissolute ['dɪsə,lut] *adj* dissolu

dissolution [,dɪsə'luʃən] *s* dissolution *f*

dissolve [dɪ'zɑlv] *tr* dissoudre ‖ *intr* se dissoudre

dissonance ['dɪsənəns] *s* dissonance *f*

dissuade [dɪ'swed] *tr* dissuader

distaff ['dɪstæf] *s* quenouille *f*

dis'taff side' *s* côté *m* maternel

distance ['dɪstəns] *s* distance *f*; **at a distance** à distance; **in the distance** au loin, dans le lointain ‖ *tr* distancer

distant ['dɪstənt] *adj* distant; (*uncle, cousin, etc.*) éloigné

distaste [dɪs'test] *s* dégoût *m*, aversion *f*

distasteful [dɪs'testfəl] *adj* dégoûtant, répugnant

distemper [dɪs'tɛmpər] *s* (*of dog*) roupie *f*; (painting) détrempe *f* ‖ *tr* peindre en détrempe

distend [dɪ'stɛnd] *tr* distendre ‖ *intr* se distendre

distension [dɪ'stɛn/ən] *s* distension *f*

distill [dɪ'stɪl] *tr* distiller

distillation [ˌdɪstɪ'le/ən] *s* distillation *f*

distiller•y [dɪs'tɪləri] *s* (*pl* **-ies**) distillerie *f*

distinct [dɪs'tɪŋkt] *adj* distinct; (*unusual*) insigne

distinction [dɪs'tɪŋk/ən] *s* distinction *f*

distinctive [dɪs'tɪŋktɪv] *adj* distinctif

distinguish [dɪs'tɪŋgwɪ/] *tr* distinguer; **to distinguish oneself** se distinguer, se faire remarquer

distinguished *adj* distingué

distort [dɪs'tɔrt] *tr* déformer

distortion [dɪs'tɔr/ən] *s* déformation *f;* (*of meaning*) sens *m* forcé; (phot, rad) distorsion *f*

distract [dɪ'strækt] *tr* (*to amuse*) distraire; (*to bewilder*) bouleverser

distracted *adj* bouleversé, éperdu

distraction [dɪ'stræk/ən] *s* (*amusement*) distraction *f;* (*madness*) folie *f*

distraught [dɪ'strɔt] *adj* bouleversé

distress [dɪ'strɛs] *s* détresse *f* ‖ *tr* affliger

distress′ call′ *s* signal *m* de détresse

distressing [dɪ'strɛsɪŋ] *adj* affligeant, pénible

distribute [dɪ'strɪbjʊt] *tr* distribuer

distribution [ˌdɪstrə'bju/ən] *s* distribution *f*

distributor [dɪ'strɪbjətər] *s* distributeur *m;* (*for a product*) concessionnaire *mf*

district ['dɪstrɪkt] *s* contrée *f*, région *f;* (*of a city*) quartier *m;* (*administrative division*) district *m*, circonscription *f* ‖ *tr* diviser en districts

dis′trict attor′ney *s* procureur *m* de la République, procureur général

distrust [dɪs'trʌst] *s* défiance *f*, méfiance *f* ‖ *tr* se défier de, se méfier de

distrustful [dɪs'trʌstfəl] *adj* défiant

disturb [dɪs'tɜrb] *tr* déranger, troubler; (*the peace*) perturber

disturbance [dɪs'tɜrbəns] *s* dérangement *m*, trouble *m;* (*riot*) bagarre *f*, émeute *f;* (*in the atmosphere or magnetic field*) perturbation *f*

disuse [dɪs'jus] *s* désuétude *f*

ditch [dɪt/] *s* fossé *m;* **to the last ditch** jusqu'à la dernière extrémité ‖ *tr* fossoyer; (slang) se défaire de ‖ *intr* (aer) faire un amerrissage forcé

ditch′ reed′ *s* (bot) laîche *f*

dither ['dɪðər] *s* agitation *f;* **to be in a dither** (coll) s'agiter sans but

dit•to ['dɪto] *s* (*pl* **-tos**) le même; (*on a duplicating machine*) copie *f*, duplicata *m* ‖ *adv* dito, de même, idem ‖ *tr* copier, reproduire

dit•ty ['dɪti] *s* (*pl* **-ties**) chansonnette *f;* **old ditty** (coll) vieux refrain *m*

diuretic [ˌdaɪə'rɛtɪk] *adj* & *s* diurétique *m*

diva ['divə] *s* diva *f*

divan ['daɪvæn], [dɪ'væn] *s* divan *m*

dive [daɪv] *s* (*of a swimmer*) plongeon *m;* (*of a submarine*) plongée *f;* (aer) piqué *m;* (coll) gargote *f*, cabaret *m* borgne ‖ *v* (*pret* & *pp* **dived** or **dove** [dov]) *intr* plonger; (*said of submarine*) plonger effectuer une plongée;

(aer) piquer; **to dive for** (*e.g., pearls*) pêcher; **to dive into** (coll) piquer une tête dans

dive′-bomb′ *tr* & *intr* bombarder en piqué

dive′ bomb′er *s* bombardier *m* à piqué

dive′ bomb′ing *s* bombardement *m* en piqué, piqué *m*

diver ['daɪvər] *s* plongeur *m;* (*person who works under water*) scaphandrier *m;* (orn) plongeon *m*

diverge [dɪ'vɜrdʒ] *intr* diverger

divers ['daɪvərz] or **diverse** [dɪ'vʌrs] *adj* divers

diversi•fy [dɪ'vʌrsɪˌfaɪ] *v* (*pret* & *pp* **-fied**) *tr* diversifier ‖ *intr* se diversifier

diversion [dɪ'vʌrʒən] *s* (*relaxation*) distraction *f*, dérivatif *m*, diversion *f;* (*of traffic*) déviation *f;* (*rerouting*) dérivation *f*, détournement *m;* (mil) diversion

diversi•ty [dɪ'vʌrsiti] *s* (*pl* **-ties**) diversité *f*

divert [dɪ'vʌrt] *tr* détourner; (*to entertain*) distraire, divertir

diverting [dɪ'vʌrtɪŋ] *adj* divertissant

divest [dɪ'vɛst] *tr* dépouiller; **to divest oneself of** se défaire de; (*property, holdings*) se déposséder de

divestment [dɪ'vɛstmənt] *s* dépossession *f*

divide [dɪ'vaɪd] *s* (geog) ligne *f* de partage ‖ *tr* diviser ‖ *intr* se diviser

divid′ed high′way *s* route *f* à chaussées séparées, route à quatre voies

dividend ['dɪvɪˌdɛnd] *s* dividende *m*

dividers [dɪ'vaɪdərz] *spl* compas *m* de mesure

dividing [dɪ'vaɪdɪŋ] *s* division *f;* **dividing up** répartition *f*, partage *m*

divination [ˌdɪvɪ'ne/ən] *s* divination *f*

divine [dɪ'vaɪn] *adj* divin ‖ *s* ecclésiastique *mf* ‖ *tr* deviner

diviner [dɪ'vaɪnər] *s* devin *m*

diving [daɪvɪŋ] *s* plongeon *m*

div′ing bell′ *s* cloche *f* à plongeur

div′ing board′ *s* plongeoir *m*, tremplin *m*

div′ing suit′ *s* scaphandre *m*

divin′ing rod′ [dɪ'vaɪnɪŋ] *s* baguette *f* divinatoire

divini•ty [dɪ'vɪnɪti] *s* (*pl* **-ties**) divinité *f;* (*subject of study*) théologie *f;* **the Divinity** Dieu *m*

divisible [dɪ'vɪzɪbəl] *adj* divisible

division [dɪ'vɪʒən] *s* division *f*

divisor [dɪ'vaɪzər] *s* diviseur *m*

divorce [dɪ'vors] *s* divorce *m;* **to get a divorce** divorcer; **to get a divorce from** (*husband or wife*) divorcer; d'avec ‖ *tr* (*the married couple*) divorcer; (*husband or wife*) divorcer d'avec ‖ *intr* divorcer

divorcee [dɪvor'si] *s* divorcée *f*

divot ['dɪvɪt] *s* (golf) motte *f* de gazon

divulge [dɪ'vʌldʒ] *tr* divulguer

dizziness ['dɪzɪnɪs] *s* vertige *m*

diz•zy ['dɪzi] *adj* (*comp* **-zier;** *super* **-ziest**) vertigineux; (coll) étourdi, farfelu; **to feel dizzy** avoir le vertige; **to make dizzy** étourdir

DJ ['di'dʒe] *s* (letterword) (**disk jockey**) DJ (disc-jockey)

DNA [ˈdiˈɛnˈe] s (letterword) (**deoxyribonucleic acid**) ADN m or A.D.N. m (acide désoxyribonucléique)

do [du] v (3d pers **does** [dʌz]; pret **did** [dɪd]; pp **done** [dʌn]; ger **doing** [ˈdu•ɪŋ]) tr faire; (homage; justice; a good turn) rendre; **to do over** refaire; **to do up** emballer, envelopper ‖ intr faire; **how do you do?** enchanté de faire votre connaissance; **that will do** c'est bien; en voilà assez; **that will never do** cela n'ira jamais; **to do away with** supprimer; **to do without** se passer de; **will I do?** suis-je bien comme ça?; **will it do?** ça va-t-il comme ça? ‖ aux used in English but not specifically expressed in French: 1) in questions, e.g., **do you speak French?** parlez-vous français?; 2) in negative sentences, e.g., **I do not speak French** je ne parle pas français; 3) as a substitute for another verb in an elliptical question, e.g., **I saw him. Did you?** je l'ai vu. L'avez-vous vu?; 4) for emphasis, e.g., **I do believe what you told me** je crois bien ce que vous m'avez dit; 5) in inversions after certain adverbs, e.g., **hardly did we finish when . . .** à peine avions-nous fini que . . . ; 6) in an imperative entreaty, e.g., **do come in!** entrez donc!

do. abbr (**ditto**) dᵒ

docile [ˈdɑsɪ] adj docile

dock [dɑk] s embarcadère m, quai m; (area including piers and waterways) bassin m, dock m; (bot) oseille f, patience f; (law) banc m des prévenus ‖ tr faire entrer au bassin; (an animal) couper la queue à; (s.o.'s salary) retrancher ‖ intr (naut) s'amarrer au quai

docket [ˈdɑkɪt] s (law) rôle m; **on the docket** pendant, non jugé; **to put on the docket** (coll) prendre en main

dock′ hand′ s docker m

docking [ˈdɑkɪŋ] s (rok) arrimage m, accostage m

dock′ work′er s docker m

dock′yard′ s chantier m

doctor [ˈdɑktər] s docteur m; (woman) femme f docteur; (med) docteur, médecin m; (med) doctoresse f; **Doctor Curie** (professor, Ph.D., etc.) Monsieur Curie; Madame Curie ‖ tr soigner; (e.g., a chipped vase) réparer; (e.g., the facts) falsifier ‖ intr pratiquer la médecine; (coll) être en traitement; (coll) prendre des médicaments

doctorate [ˈdɑktərɪt] s doctorat m

Doc′tor of Laws′ s docteur m en droit

doctrine [ˈdɑktrɪn] s doctrine f

document [ˈdɑkjəmənt] s document m ‖ [ˈdɑkjə,mɛnt] tr documenter

documenta•ry [,dɑkjəˈmɛntəri] adj documentaire ‖ s (pl -ries) documentaire m

documentation [,dɑkjəmɛnˈte/ən] s documentation f

doddering [ˈdɑdərɪŋ] adj tremblotant, gâteux

dodge [dɑdʒ] s écart m, esquive f; (coll) ruse f, truc m ‖ tr esquiver; (a question) éluder ‖ intr s'esquiver

dodge′ ball′ s chasse-ballon m invar

do•do [ˈdodo] s (pl -dos or -does) (orn) dronte m, dodo m; (coll) vieux fossile m, innocent m

doe [do] s (of fallow deer) daine f; (hind) biche f; (roe doe) chevrette f; (of hare) hase f; (of rabbit) lapine f

doe′skin′ s peau f de daim

doesn't contr **does not**

doff [dɑf] tr ôter

dog [dɔg] s chien m; **let sleeping dogs lie** il ne faut pas réveiller le chat qui dort; **to go to the dogs** (coll) se débaucher; (said of business) (coll) aller à vau-l'eau; **to put on the dog** (coll) faire de l'épate ‖ v (pret & pp **dogged**; ger **dogging**) tr poursuivre

dog′catch′er s employé m de la fourière

dog′ col′lar s collier m de chien; (clerical collar) faux-col m d'ecclésiastique

dog′ days′ spl canicule f

doge [dodʒ] s doge m

dog′face′ s (slang) troufion m

dog′fight′ s (aer) combat m aérien tournoyant et violent; (coll) bagarre f

dog′fish′ s (ichth) roussette f

dogged [ˈdɔgɪd] adj tenace, obstiné

doggerel [ˈdɔgərəl] s vers mpl de mirliton

dog•gy [ˈdɔgi] adj (comp -gier; super -giest) canin, de chien ‖ s (pl -gies) toutou m

dog′gy bag′ s emporte-restes m

dog′house′ s niche f à chien; **in the dog-house** (slang) en disgrâce

dog′ in the man′ger s chien m du jardinier

dog′ Lat′in s latin m de cuisine

dogma [ˈdɔgmə] s dogme m

dogmatic [dɔgˈmætɪk] adj dogmatique ‖ **dogmatics** s dogmatique f

dog′ pound′ s fourrière f

dog′ rac′ing s courses fpl de lévriers

dog′ rose′ s rose f des haies

dog's′-ear′ s corner f ‖ tr corner

dog′ show′ s exposition f canine

dog′ sled′ or **dog′ sledge′** s traîneau m à chiens

dog's′ life′ s vie f de chien

Dog′ Star′ s Canicule f

dog′ tag′ s (mil) plaque f d'identité

dog′-tired′ adj éreinté, fourbu

dog′tooth′ s (pl -teeth) dent f de chien, canine f; (archit, bot, mach) dent-de-chien f

dog′tooth vi′olet s dent-de-chien f

dog′ track′ s piste f pour les courses de levriers

dog′trot′ s petit-trot m

dog′watch′ s (naut) petit quart m

dog′wood′ s cornouiller m

doi•ly [ˈdɔɪli] s (pl -lies) napperon m; (underplate) garde-nappe m

doings [ˈdu•ɪŋz] spl actions fpl, œuvres fpl, faits et gestes mpl

do-it-yourself [,du•ɪtfərˈsɛlf] adj de bricolage ‖ s bricolage m

doldrums [ˈdoldrəmz] spl marasme m; (naut) zone f des calmes

dole [dol] s aumône f; indemnité f de chômage

‖ *tr*—**to dole out** distribuer parcimonieuse-ment

doleful [ˈdolfəl] *adj* dolent

doll [dɑl] *s* poupée *f* ‖ *tr*—**to be dolled up** (coll) être tiré à quatre épingles ‖ *intr*—**to doll up** (coll) se parer, s'endimancher

dollar [ˈdɑlər] *s* dollar *m*

dol·ly [ˈdɑli] *s* (*pl* **-lies**) (*low movable frame*) chariot *m;* (*hand truck*) diable *m;* (*child's doll*) poupée *f;* (mov, telv) travelling *m*

dolphin [ˈdɑlfɪn] *s* dauphin *m*

dolt [dolt] *s* nigaud *m*, lourdaud *m*

doltish [ˈdoltɪʃ] *adj* nigaud, lourdaud

domain [doˈmen] *s* domaine *m;* (*private estate*) terres *fpl*, propriété *f*

dome [dom] *s* dôme *m*, coupole *f*

dome′ light′ *s* (aut) plafonnier *m;* (aut) (*flashing, revolving outside light*) gyrophare *m*

domestic [dəˈmɛstɪk] *adj & s* domestique *mf*

domesticate [dəˈmɛstɪˌket] *tr* domestiquer

domesticity [ˌdomɛsˈtɪsɪti] *s* caractère *m* casa-nier; vie *f* familiale

domes′tic part′ners *spl* partenaires *mfpl* qui habitent sous le même toit

domicile [ˈdɑmɪsɪl] *s* domicile *m* ‖ *tr* domicilier

dominance [ˈdɑmɪnəns] *s* prédominance *f;* (ge-netics) dominance *f*

dominant [ˈdɑmɪnənt] *adj* prédominant, domi-nant ‖ *s* (mus) dominante *f*

dominate [ˈdɑmɪˌnet] *tr & intr* dominer

dominating [ˈdɑmɪˌnetɪŋ] *adj* dominateur

domination [ˌdɑmɪˈneʃən] *s* domination *f*

domineer [ˌdɑmɪˈnɪr] *intr* se montrer tyranique

domineering [ˌdɑmɪˈnɪrɪŋ] *adj* tyrannique, au-toritaire

dominion [dəˈmɪnjən] *s* domination *f;* (*of Brit-ish Commonwealth*) dominion *m*

domi·no [ˈdɑmɪˌno] *s* (*pl* **-noes** or **-nos**) domino *m;* **dominoes** *sg* (*game*) les dominos

don [dɑn] *s* (*tutor*) précepteur *m* ‖ *v* (*pret & pp* **donned;** *ger* **donning**) *tr* mettre, enfiler

donate [ˈdonet] *tr* faire un don de

donation [doˈneʃən] *s* don *m*, cadeau *m*

done [dʌn] *adj* fait; **are you done?** en avez-vous fini?; **it is done** (*it is finished*) c'en est fait; **to be done** (*e.g., beefsteak*) être cuit; **to have done with** en finir avec; **well done!** très bien!, bravo!, à la bonne heure!

done′ for′ *adj* (*tired out*) (coll) fourbu; (*ruined*) (coll) abattu; (*out of the running*) (coll) hors de combat; (*dead*) (coll) estourbi

donkey [ˈdɑŋki] *s* âne *m*, baudet *m*

donor [ˈdonər] *s* donneur *m;* (law) donateur *m*

don't *abbr* do not

doodle [ˈdudəl] *s* (*doodling*) crayonnages *mpl* ‖ *tr & intr* griffonner

doom [dum] *s* condamnation *f;* destin *m* funeste ‖ *tr* condamner

dooms′day′ *s* jugement *m* dernier

door [dor] *s* porte *f;* (*of a carriage or automo-bile*) portière *f;* (*one part of a double door*) battant *m;* **behind closed doors** à huis clos;

to see to the door conduire à la porte; **to show s.o. the door** éconduire qn, mettre qn à la porte

door′bell′ *s* timbre *m*, sonnette *f*

door′bell but′ton *s* bouton *m* de porte

door′bell transform′er *s* transformateur *m* de sonnerie

door′bell wire′ *s* fil *m* sonnerie

door′ check′ *s* arrêt *m* de porte

door′frame′ *s* chambranle *m*, huisserie *f*, dor-mant *m*

door′head′ *s* linteau *m*

door′jamb′ *s* jambage *m*

door′knob′ *s* bouton *m* de porte

door′knock′er *s* heurtoir *m*, marteau *m* de porte

door′ latch′ *s* loquet *m*

door′man *s* (*pl* **-men**) portier *m*

door′mat′ *s* essuie-pieds *m*, paillasson *m*

door′nail′ *s* clou *m* de porte; **dead as a doornail** (coll) bien mort

door′post′ *s* montant *m* de porte

door′ scrap′er [ˈskrepər] *s* décrottoir *m*, gratte-pieds *m*

door′sill′ *s* seuil *m*, traverse *f*

door′step′ *s* seuil *m*, pas *m*

door′stop′ *s* entrebâilleur *m*, butoir *m*

door′-to-door′ *adj* porte-à-porte

door′-to-door′ sell′ing *s* démarchage *m*

door′way′ *s* porte *f*, portail *m*

dope [dop] *s* (*varnish*) enduit *m;* (slang) narcoti-que *m*, stupéfiant *m;* (*information*) (slang) renseignements *mpl;* (*fool*) (slang) cornichon *m* ‖ *tr* enduire; (slang) doper, stupéfier; **to dope out** (slang) deviner, déchiffrer

dope′ fiend′ *s* (slang) toxicomane *mf*

dope′ ped′dler *s* trafiquant *m* de stupéfiants

dormant [ˈdɔrmənt] *adj* endormi, assoupi; la-tent; **to lie dormant** dormir

dor′mer win′dow [ˈdɔrmər] *s* lucarne *f*

dormito·ry [ˈdɔrmɪˌtori] *s* (*pl* **-ries**) (*room*) dor-toir *m;* (*building*) pavillon *m* des étudiants, maison *f* de résidence, foyer *m* d'étudiants

dor′mitory com′plex *s* cité *f* universitaire

dor·mouse [ˈdɔrˌmaus] *s* (*pl* **-mice**) loir *m*

dosage [ˈdosɪdʒ] *s* (*administration*) dosage *m;* (*amount*) dose *f;* (*information on medicine bottle*) posologie *f*

dose [dos] *s* dose *f* ‖ *tr* donner en doses; donner un médicament à

dossier [ˈdɑsɪˌe] *s* dossier *m*

dot [dɑt] *s* point *m;* **on the dot** (coll) à l'heure tapante; pile, e.g., **at noon on the dot** à midi pile ‖ *v* (*pret & pp* **dotted;** *ger* **dotting**) *tr* (*to make with dots*) pointiller; **to dot one's i's** mettre les points sur les i

dotage [ˈdotɪdʒ] *s* radotage *m*

dotard [ˈdotərd] *s* gâteux *m*, gaga *m*

dot-com [ˈdɑtˈkɑm] *s* (comp) (*.com*) point-com ‖ *adv* par internet

dote [dot] *intr* radoter; **to dote on** raffoler de

doting [ˈdotɪŋ] *adj* radoteur; (*loving to excess*) qui aime follement

dot′ ma′trix [ˈmetrɪks] *s* matrice *f* de points

dot'-ma'trix print'er *s* imprimante *f* matricielle

dots' and dash'es *spl* (telg) points et traits *mpl*

dot'ted line' *s* ligne *f* pointillée, ligne hachée, pointillé *m;* **to sign on the dotted line** signer en bonne et due forme

double [ˈdʌbəl] *adj & adv* double, en deux, deux fois ‖ *s* double *m;* (cards) contre *m;* (*stunt man*) (mov) cascadeur *m;* **doubles** (tennis) double; **on the double!** (coll) dare-dare!, au trot!; **to play double or nothing** jouer à quitte ou double ‖ *tr* doubler; (cards) contrer; **to double up** plier en deux ‖ *intr* doubler; (cards) contrer; **to double back** faire un crochet; **to double up** se plier, se tordre

dou'ble-act'ing *adj* à double effet

dou'ble-bar'reled *adj* (*gun*) à deux coups

dou'ble bass' [bes] *s* contrebasse *f*

dou'ble bed' *s* grand lit *m,* lit à deux places

dou'ble boil'er *s* casserole *f* à double fond; bain-marie *m*

dou'ble-breast'ed *adj* croisé

dou'ble chin' *s* double menton *m*

dou'ble click' *s* (comp) double clic *m*

dou'ble cross' *s* (slang) entourloupette *f,* double jeu *m*

dou'ble-cross' *tr* (coll) doubler, rouler, faire une entourloupette à

dou'ble-cross'er *s* (slang) personne *f* double, faux jeton *m*

Dou'ble-Cros'tic [ˈkrɔstɪk] *s* (trademark) chassé-croisé *m*

dou'ble date' *s* partie *f* carrée, sortie *f* à quatre

dou'ble-deal'er *s* personne *f* double, homme *m* à deux visages

dou'ble-deal'ing *adj* hypocrite ‖ *s* duplicité *f*

dou'ble-deck'er *s* (*bed*) lits *mpl* superposés, lit gigognes, lit à deux étages; (*bus*) autobus *m* à deux étages; (*sandwich*) double sandwich *m;* (aer, naut) deuxponts *m*

dou'ble-edged' *adj* à deux tranchants, à double tranchant

double entendre [ˈdubələnˈtandrə] *s* expression *f* à double entente, mot *m* à double sens

dou'ble-en'try book'keep'ing *s* comptabilité *f* en partie double

dou'ble-faced' *adj* à double face

dou'ble fea'ture *s* (mov) deux grands films *mpl,* double programme *m*

dou'ble-joint'ed *adj* désarticulé

dou'ble-lock' *tr* fermer à double tour

dou'ble-park' *tr* faire stationner en double file ‖ *intr* stationner en double file, se garer en double file

dou'ble-quick' *adj & adv* au pas de course, en vitesse

dou'ble room' *s* chambre *f* à deux lits

dou'ble-spaced' *adj* à l'interligne double, à double interligne

dou'ble stand'ard *s* code *m* de morale à deux aspects; **to have a double standard** avoir deux poids et deux mesures

doublet [ˈdʌblɪt] *s* (*close-fitting jacket*) pourpoint *m;* (*counterfeit stone; each of two words having the same origin*) doublet *m*

dou'ble-talk' *s* (coll) non-sens *m;* (coll) paroles *fpl* creuses *or* ambiguës, mots *mpl* couverts

dou'ble time' *s* (*for work*) salaire *m* double; (mil) pas *m* redoublé

doubleton [ˈdʌbəltən] *s* deux cartes *fpl* d'une couleur

dou'ble track' *s* double piste *f*

doubling [ˈdʌblɪŋ] *s* doublement *m*

doubly [ˈdʌbli] *adv* doublement

doubt [daut] *s* doute *m;* **beyond a doubt** à n'en pas douter; **no doubt** sans doute ‖ *tr* douter de; **to doubt that** douter que; **to doubt whether** douter si ‖ *intr* douter

doubter [ˈdautər] *s* douteur *m*

doubtful [ˈdautfəl] *adj* douteux; indécis, hésitant

doubtless [ˈdautlɪs] *adv* sans doute

douche [duʃ] *s* douche *f;* (*instrument*) seringue *f* à lavement ‖ *tr* doucher ‖ *intr* se doucher

dough [do] *s* pâte *f;* (slang) fric *m,* pognon *m,* blé *m,* beurre *m;* **big dough** (slang) grosse galette *f*

dough'boy' *s* (coll) troufion *m,* biffin *m;* (*in the First World War*) poilu *m*

dough'nut' *s* beignet *m*

dough•ty [ˈdauti] *adj* (*comp* **-tier;** *super* **-tiest**) vaillant, preux

dough•y [ˈdo•i] *adj* (*comp* **-ier;** *super* **-iest**) pâteux

dour [daur], [dur] *adj* (*severe*) austère; (*obstinate*) buté; (*gloomy*) mélancolique

douse [daus] *tr* tremper, arroser; (slang) éteindre

dove [dʌv] *s* colombe *f*

dovecote [ˈdʌv‚kot] *s* pigeonnier *m,* colombier *m*

Dover [ˈdovər] *s* Douvres

dove'tail' *s* queue-d'aronde *f,* adent *m* ‖ *tr* assembler à queue-d'aronde, adenter; (fig) raccorder, opérer le raccord entre ‖ *intr* se raccorder

dove'tailed' *adj* à queue-d'aronde

dowager [ˈdau•ədʒər] *s* douairière *f*

dow•dy [ˈdaudi] *adj* (*comp* **-dier;** *super* **-diest**) gauche, fagoté, mal habillé

dow•el [ˈdau•əl] *s* goujon *m* ‖ *v* (*pret & pp* **-eled** *or* **-elled;** *ger* **-eling** *or* **-elling**) *tr* goujonner

dower [ˈdau•ər] *s* (*widow's portion*) douaire *m;* (*marriage portion*) dot *f;* (*natural gift*) don *m* ‖ *tr* assigner un douaire à; doter

down [daun] *adj* bas; (*train*) descendant; (*storage battery*) épuisé; (*tire*) à plat; (*sun*) couché; (*wind, sea, etc.*) calmé; (*blinds; prices*) baissé; (*stocks*) en moins-value; (*sad*) abattu, triste ‖ *s* (*on a bird*) duvet *m;* (*sand hill*) dune *f* ‖ *adv* en bas, au bas, vers les bas; à terre; (*south*) au sud; **down!** (*in elevator*) on descend!, pour la descente!; **down from** du haut de; **down there** là-bas; **down to** jusqu'à; **down under** aux antipodes; **down with . . . !** à bas . . .!; for expressions like **to go down**

descendre or **to pay down** payer comptant, see the verb ‖ *prep* en bas de; (*along*) le long de; (*a stream*) en descendant ‖ *tr* descendre, abattre; (*to swallow*) (coll) avaler

down'-and-out' *adj* décavé

down'beat' *s* (mus) temps *m* fort, frappé *m*, premier accent *m*

down'cast' *adj* abattu, baissé

down'fall' *s* chute *f*, ruine *f*

down'grade' *adj* (coll) descendant ‖ *s* descente *f;* **to be on the downgrade** déchoir ‖ *adv* en déclin ‖ *tr* déclasser

down'heart'ed *adj* abattu, découragé

down'hill' *adj* descendant ‖ *adv*—**to go downhill** aller en descendant; (fig) décliner

down'link' *s* (aerosp) transmission *f* d'information du satellite à la tierre

down'load *tr* (comp) décharger ‖ *intr* (comp) accéder à une image jointe à une message électronique

down' pay'ment *s* acompte *m*

down'pour' *s* déluge *m*, averse *f*

down'right' *adj* absolu, véritable ‖ *adv* tout à fait, absolument

down'-size' *tr* réduire des effectifs

down'siz'ing *s* réduction *f* des effectifs

down'stairs' *s* rez-de-chaussée *m* ‖ *adv* en bas; **to go downstairs** descendre

down'stream' *adv* en aval

down'stroke' *s* (*of piston*) course *f* descendante; (*in writing*) jambage *m*

down'-to-earth' *adj* terre-à-terre

down'town' *adj* du centre ‖ *s* centre *m* ‖ *adv* en ville

down'trend' *s* tendance *f* à la baisse

downtrodden [ˈdaʊnˌtrɑdən] *adj* opprimé

downward [ˈdaʊnwərd] *adj* descendant ‖ *adv* en bas, en descendant

downwards [ˈdaʊnwərdz] *adv* en bas, en descendant

down'wash' *s* (aer) air *m* déplacé

down•y [ˈdaʊni] *adj* (*comp* **-ier;** *super* **-iest**) duveteux; (*velvety*) velouté; (*soft*) mou, moelleux

dow•ry [ˈdaʊri] *s* (*pl* **-ries**) dot *f*

dowser [ˈdaʊzər] *s* sourcier *m*, hydroscope *m*

doze [doz] *s* petit somme *m* ‖ *intr* sommeiller; **to doze off** s'assoupir

dozen [ˈdʌzən] *s* douzaine *f;* **a dozen** . . . une douzaine de . . . ; **by the dozen** à la douzaine

D.P. *abbr* (**displaced person**) personne *f* déplacée

Dr. *abbr* (**Doctor**) Dʳ

drab [dræb] *adj* (*comp* **drabber;** *super* **drabbest**) gris ‖ *s* gris *m*

drach•ma [ˈdrækmə] *s* (*pl* **-mas** or **-mae** [mi]) drachme *f*

draft [dræft] *s* (*air current*) courant *m* d'air; (*pulling; current of air in chimney*) tirage *m;* (*sketch, outline*) ébauche *f;* (*of a letter, novel, etc.*) brouillon *m*, premier jet *m;* (*of a bill in Congress*) projet *m;* (*of a law*) avant-projet *m;* (*drink*) trait *m*, gorgée *f;* (com) mandat *m*,

traite *f;* (mil) conscription *f;* (naut) tirant *m* d'eau; **drafts** (*game*) dames *fpl;* **on draft** à la pression; **to be exempted from the draft** être exempté du service militaire ‖ *tr* (*a document*) rédiger, faire le brouillon de; (*a bill in Congress*) dresser; (*a recruit*) appeler sous les drapeaux; **to be drafted** être appelé sous les drapeaux

draft' beer' *s* bière *f* pression

draft' board' *s* conseil *m* de révision; commission *f* locale des conscriptions

draft' call' *s* appel *m* sous les drapeaux

draft' dodg'er [ˈdɑdʒər] *s* embusqué *m*, réfractaire *mf*

draftee [ˌdræfˈti] *s* appelé *m* (sous les drapeaux), conscrit *m*

draft' horse' *s* cheval *m* de trait

drafting [ˈdræftɪŋ] *s* dessin *m* industriel

draft'ing room' *s* bureau *m* d'études

drafts'man *s* (*pl* **-men**) dessinateur *m;* (*man who draws up documents*) rédacteur *m*

draft•y [ˈdræfti] *adj* (*comp* **-ier;** *super* **-iest**) plein de courants d'air

drag [dræg] *s* (*net*) drège *f;* (*sledge or sled*) traîneau *m;* (*stone drag*) fardier *m;* (*brake*) enrayure *f;* (*impediment*) entrave *f;* (aer) traînée *f* ‖ *v* (*pret & pp* **dragged;** *ger* **dragging**) *tr* traîner; (*one's feet*) traînasser; (*a net*) draguer; (*a field*) herser; **to drag down** entraîner; **to drag in** introduire de force; **to drag on** traîner en longueur; **to drag out** faire sortir de force ‖ *intr* traîner à terre; se traîner

drag' net' *s* traîneau *m*, chalut *m*

dragon [ˈdrægən] *s* dragon *m*

drag'on•fly' *s* (*pl* **-flies**) demoiselle *f*, libellule *f*

dragoon [drəˈgun] *s* dragon *m* ‖ *tr* tyranniser, forcer, contraindre

drain [dren] *s* (*sewer*) égout *m;* (*pipe*) tuyau *m* d'égout; (*ditch*) tranchée *f* d'écoulement; (*source of continual expense*) saignée *f;* (med) drain *m* ‖ *tr* (*wet ground*) drainer; (*a glass or cup*) vider entièrement; (*a crankcase*) vidanger; (*s.o. of strength*) épuiser; (med) drainer ‖ *intr* s'égoutter, s'écouler

drainage [ˈdrenɪdʒ] *s* drainage *m*

drain'board' *s* égouttoir *m*

drain' cock' *s* purgeur *m*

drain'pipe' *s* tuyau *m* d'écoulement, drain *m*

drain' plug' *s* bouchon *m* de vidange

drake [drek] *s* canard *m* mâle

dram [dræm] *s* (*weight*) drachme *m;* (*drink*) petit verre *f*, goutte *f*

drama [ˈdrɑmə], [ˈdræmə] *s* drame *m*

dra'ma crit'ic *s* chroniqueur *m* dramatique

dra'ma review' *s* avant-première *f*

dramatic [drəˈmætɪk] *adj* dramatique ‖ **dramatics** *s* dramaturgie *f*, art *m* dramatique

dramatist [ˈdræmətɪst] *s* auteur *m* dramatique, dramaturge *mf*

dramatize [ˈdræməˌtaɪz] *tr* dramatiser

drape [drep] *s* (*curtain*) rideau *m;* (*hang of a*

curtain, skirt, etc.) drapement *m* || *tr* draper, tendre; se draper dans

draper•y [`drepəri] *s* (*pl* **-ies**) draperie *f;* **draperies** rideaux *mpl*, tentures *fpl*

drastic [`dræstɪk] *adj* énergique, radical; (*laxative*) drastique

draught [dræft] *s* (*of fish*) coup *m* de filet; (*drink*) trait *m*, gorgée *f;* (naut) tirant *m* d'eau; **draughts** (*game*) dames *fpl; on draught* à la pression

draught' beer' *s* bière *f* pression

draught' board' *s* damier *m*

draw [drɔ] *s* (*taking, drawing, pulling; in a fireplace*) tirage *m;* (*in a game or other contest*) partie *f* nulle, match *m* nul || *v* (*pret* **drew** [dru]; *pp* **drawn** [drɔn]) *tr* tirer; (*a crowd*) attirer; (*a design*) dessiner; (*a card*) tirer; (*trumps*) faire tomber; (*a bow*) bander, tendre; (*water*) puiser; **to draw a conclusion** tirer une conséquence; **to draw aside** prendre à l'écart; **to draw blood** faire saigner; **to draw interest** porter intérêt; **to draw lots** tirer au sort; **to draw off** (*e.g., a liquid*) soutirer; **to draw out** (*a person*) faire parler; (*an activity*) prolonger, traîner; **to draw up** (*a list*) dresser; (*a plan*) rédiger; (naut) jauger || *intr* tirer; dessiner; faire partie nulle, faire match nul; **to draw away** s'éloigner; **to draw back** reculer, se retirer; **to draw near** approcher; s'approcher de

draw' back' *s* désavantage *m*, inconvénient *m*

draw' bridge' *s* pont-levis *m*

drawee [ˌdrɔ`i] *s* tiré *m*, accepteur *m*

drawer [`drɔ•ər] *s* dessinateur *m;* (com) tireur *m* || [drɔr] *s* tiroir *m;* **drawers** caleçon *m*

drawing [`drɔ•ɪŋ] *s* (*sketch*) dessin *m;* (*in a lottery*) tirage *m;* **drawing off** tirage *m*

draw'ing board' *s* planche *f* à dessin

draw'ing card' *s* attrait *m*, attraction *f*

draw'ing room' *s* salon *m*

draw'knife' *s* (*pl* **-knives**) plane *f*

drawl [drɔl] *s* voix *f* traînante || *tr* dire d'une voix traînante || *intr* traîner la voix en parlant

drawn' but'ter [drɔn] *s* beurre *m* fondu; sauce *f* blanche

drawn' work' *s* broderie *f* à fils tirés

dray [dre] *s* haquet *m*, charrette *f;* (*sledge*) fardier *m*, schlitte *f*

drayage [`dre•ɪdʒ] *s* charriage *m*, charroi *m;* frais *mpl* de transport

dray' horse' *s* cheval *m* de trait

dray'man *s* (*pl* **-men**) haquetier *m*

dread [drɛd] *adj* redoutable, terrible || *s* terreur *f*, crainte *f* || *tr & intr* redouter, craindre

dreadful [`drɛdfəl] *adj* épouvantable

dream [drim] *s* rêve *m*, songe *m;* (*fancy, illusion*) rêverie *f*, songerie *f* || *v* (*pret & pp* **dreamed** or **dreamt** [drɛmt]) *tr*—**to dream up** rêver || *intr* rêver, songer; **to dream of** (*future plans*) rêver à; (*s.o.*) rêver de

dreamer [`drimər] *s* rêveur *m*

dream'land' *s* pays *m* des songes

dream' world' *s* monde *m* des rêves

dream•y [`drimi] *adj* (*comp* **-ier;** *super* **-iest**) rêveur; (slang) épatant

drear•y [`drɪri] *adj* (*comp* **-ier;** *super* **-iest**) triste, morne; monotone

dredge [drɛdʒ] *s* drague *f* || *tr* draguer

dredger [`drɛdʒər] *s* dragueur *m;* (mach) drague *f*

dredging [`drɛdʒɪŋ] *s* dragage *m*

dregs [drɛgz] *spl* lie *f*

drench [drɛntʃ] *tr* tremper, inonder

dress [drɛs] *s* habillement *m*, costume *m;* (*woman's attire*) toilette *f*, mise *f;* (*woman's dress*) robe *f* || *tr* habiller, vêtir; (*to apply a dressing to*) panser; (culin) garnir; **to dress down** (coll) passer un savon à, chapitrer; **to dress up** parer; (*ranks*) (mil) aligner; **to get dressed** s'habiller || *intr* s'habiller, se vêtir; (mil) s'aligner; **to be dressing** être à sa toilette; **to dress up** se parer

dress' ball' *s* bal *m* paré

dress' cir'cle *s* corbeille *f*, premier balcon *m*

dress' coat' *s* frac *m*

dresser [`drɛsər] *s* coiffeuse *f;* commode *f* à miroir; (*sideboard*) dressoir *m;* **to be a good dresser** être recherché dans sa mise

dress' form' *s* mannequin *m*

dress' goods' *spl* étoffes *fpl* pour costumes

dressing [`drɛsɪŋ] *s* (*providing with clothes*) habillement *m;* (*for food*) assaisonnement *m*, sauce *f;* (*stuffing for fowl*) farce *f;* (*fertilizer*) engrais *m;* (*for a wound*) pansement *m*

dress'ing down' *s* (coll) savon *m*, verte réprimande *f*, algarade *f*

dress'ing gown' *s* peignoir *m*, robe *f* de chambre

dress'ing room' *s* cabinet *m* de toilette, vestiaire *m;* (theat) loge *f*

dress'ing sta'tion *s* poste *m* de secours

dress'ing ta'ble *s* coiffeuse *f*, toilette *f*

dress'mak'er *s* couturière *f*

dress'mak'ing *s* couture *f*

dress'making estab'lishment *s* maison *f* de couture

dress' rehear'sal *s* répétition *f* en costume; **final dress rehearsal** répétition générale

dress' shield' *s* dessous-de-bras *m*

dress' shirt' *s* chemise *f* à plastron

dress' shop' *s* magasin *m* de modes

dress' suit' *s* habit *m* de cérémonie, tenue *f* de soirée

dress' tie' *s* cravate *f* de smoking, cravate-plastron *f*

dress' u'niform *s* (mil) grande tenue *f*

dress•y [`drɛsi] *adj* (*comp* **-ier;** *super* **-iest**) (coll) élégant, chic

dribble [`drɪbəl] *s* dégouttement *m;* (*of child*) bave *f;* (sports) dribble *m* || *tr* (sports) dribbler || *intr* dégoutter; (*said of child*) baver; (sports) dribbler

driblet [`drɪblɪt] *s* chiquet *m;* **in driblets** au compte-gouttes

dried' ap'ple [draɪd] *s* pomme *f* tapée

dried' beef' *s* viande *f* boucanée

dried′ fig′ s figue f sèche

dried′ fruit′ s fruit m sec

dried′ pear′ s poire f tapée

drier [′draɪ•ər] s (for clothes) séchoir m, sécheuse f; (for paint) siccatif m; (mach) sécheur m

drift [drɪft] s mouvement m, force f, poussée f; (of sand, snow) amoncellement m; (of meaning) sens m, direction f; (aer & naut) dérive f, dérivation f ‖ intr aller à la dérive; (said of snow) s'amonceler; (aer, naut) dériver; (fig) se laisser aller, flotter

drift′ ice′ s glaces fpl flottantes

drift′ wood′ s bois m flotté

drill [drɪl] s (for metal, wood) foret m, mèche f; (machine) perforatrice f, perceuse f; (fabric) coutil m, treillis m; (furrow) sillon m; (agricultural implement) semoir m; (in school; on the drill ground) exercice m ‖ tr instruire; (e.g., students) former, entraîner; (mach) forer; (mil) faire faire l'exercice à; **to drill s.th. into s.o.** seriner q.ch. à qn ‖ intr faire l'exercice; forer

driller [′drɪlər] s foreur m

drill′ field′ or **drill′ ground′** s terrain m d'exercice

drilling [′drɪlɪŋ] s (of metal; of an oil well) forage m; (dentistry) fraisage m

drill′ing rig′ s derrick m; (at sea) plate-forme f

drill′mas′ter s moniteur m; (mil) instructeur m

drill′ press′ s foreuse f à colonnes

drink [drɪŋk] s boisson f, breuvage m; boire m, e.g., **food and drink** le boire et le manger ‖ v (pret **drank** [dræŋk]; pp **drunk** [drʌŋk]) tr boire; (e.g., with a meal) prendre; **to drink down** boire d'un trait ‖ intr boire; **to drink out of** (a glass) boire dans; (a bottle) boire à; **to drink to the health of** boire à la santé de

drinkable [′drɪŋkəbəl] adj buvable, potable

drinker [′drɪŋkər] s buveur m

drink′ing cup′ s tasse f à boire, gobelet m

drink′ing foun′tain s fontaine f à boire, borne-fontaine f

drink′ing song′ s chanson f à boire

drink′ing trough′ s abreuvoir m

drink′ing wa′ter s eau f potable

drip [drɪp] s (drop) goutte f; (dripping) égout m, dégouttement m; (person) (slang) cornichon m ‖ v (pret & pp **dripped**; ger **dripping**) intr dégoutter, goutter

drip′ cof′fee s café-filtre m

drip′ cof′fee mak′er s cafetière f à filtre

drip′-dry′ adj à séchage rapide; (label on shirt) repassage inutile

dripolator [′drɪpə‚letər] s filtre m à café

drip′ pan′ s égouttoir m

dripping [′drɪpɪŋ] s ruissellement m; **drippings** graisse f de rôti

drive [draɪv] s (in an automobile) promenade f; (road) chaussée f; (vigor) énergie f, initiative f; (fund-raising) campagne f; (push for-

ward) propulsion f; (aut) (point of power application to roadway) traction f; (golf) crossée f; (mach) transmission f; **to go for a drive** faire une promenade en auto ‖ v (pret **drove** [drov]; pp **driven** [′drɪvən]) tr (an automobile, locomotive, etc.; an animal; a person in an automobile) conduire; (a nail) enfoncer; (a bargain) conclure; (the ball in a game) renvoyer, chasser; (to push, force) pousser, forcer; (to overwork) surmener; **to drive away** chasser; **to drive back** repousser; (e.g., in a car) reconduire; **to drive crazy** rendre fou; **to drive in** enfoncer; **to drive out** chasser; **to drive to despair** conduire au désespoir ‖ intr conduire; **drive slowly** (public sign) marcher au pas; **to drive away** partir, démarrer; **to drive back** rentrer en auto; **to drive on** continuer sa route; **to drive out** sortir

drive′-in′ s (motion-picture theater) cinéma m auto, ciné-park m; (restaurant) restoroute m

driv•el [′drɪvəl] s (slobber) bave f; (nonsense) bêtises fpl ‖ v (pret **-eled** or **-elled**; ger **-eling** or **-elling**) intr baver; (to talk nonsense) radoter

driver [′draɪvər] s chauffeur m, conducteur m; (of a carriage) cocher m; (of a locomotive) mécanicien m; (of pack animals) toucheur m

driv′er's li′cense s permis m de conduire

drive′ shaft′ s arbre m d'entraînement

drive′way′ s voie f de garage, sortie f de voiture

drive′ wheel′ s roue f motrice, roue de transmission

driv′ing school′ s auto-école f

drizzle [′drɪzəl] s pluie f fine, bruine f ‖ intr bruiner, brouillasser

droll [drol] adj drôle, drolatique

dromedar•y [′drɑmə‚dɛri] s (pl **-ies**) dromadaire m

drone [dron] s (humming) bourdonnement m; (of plane or engine) vrombissement m, ronron m; (do-nothing) fainéant m; (aer) avion m téléguidé, avion sans pilote; (ent) faux bourdon m ‖ intr bourdonner, ronronner

drool [drul] intr baver

droop [drup] s inclinaison f ‖ intr se baisser; (to lose one's pep) s'alanguir; (bot) languir

drooping [′drupɪŋ] adj languissant

drop [drɑp] s (e.g., of water) goutte f; (fall) chute f; (slope) précipice m; (depth of drop) hauteur f de chute; (in price; in temperature) baisse f; (lozenge) pastille f; (of supplies from an airplane) droppage m; **a drop in the bucket** une goutte d'eau dans la mer ‖ v (pret & pp **dropped**; ger **dropping**) tr laisser tomber; (a curtain; the eyes, voice) baisser; (from an airplane) lâcher; (e.g., a name from a list) omettre, supprimer; (a remark) glisser; (a conversation; relations; negotiations) cesser; (anchor) jeter, mouiller; (an idea, a habit, etc.) renoncer à; **to drop off** déposer ‖ intr tomber; se laisser tomber; baisser; cesser; **to drop in** entrer en passant; **to drop in on** faire un saut chez; **to drop off** se détacher; s'endormir; **to drop out of** (*to quit*) renoncer à, abandonner

drop′ cur′tain *s* rideau *m* d'entracte

drop′-cord light′ *s* baladeuse *f*

drop′ ham′mer *s* marteau-pilon *m*

drop′ kick′ *s* coup *m* tombé

drop′ leaf′ *s* abattant *m*

drop′-leaf′ ta′ble *s* table *f* à abattants, table à volets

drop′let *s* gouttelette *f*

drop′light′ *s* lampe *f* suspendue

drop′out′ *s* raté *m;* **to become a dropout** abandonner les études

dropper [′drɑpər] *s* compte-gouttes *m*

drop′ shut′ter *s* (phot) obturateur *m* à guillotine

dropsy [′drɑpsi] *s* anasarque *f;* hydropisie *f* (obs)

drop′ ta′ble *s* table *f* à abattant

dross [drɔs] *s* scories *mpl,* écume *f*

drought [draʊt] *s* sécheresse *f*

drove [drov] *s* (*of animals*) troupeau *m;* (*multitude*) foule *f,* flots *mpl;* **in droves** par bandes

drover [′drovər] *s* bouvier *m*

drown [draʊn] *tr* noyer; **to drown out** couvrir ‖ *intr* se noyer

drowse [draʊz] *intr* somnoler, s'assoupir

drow•sy [′draʊzi] *adj* (*comp* **-sier;** *super* **-siest**) somnolent

drub [drʌb] *v* (*pret & pp* **drubbed;** *ger* **drubbing**) *tr* flanquer une raclée à, rosser

drudge [drʌdʒ] *s* homme *m* de peine, piocheur *m;* **harmless drudge** (*e.g., who compiles dictionaries*) gratte-papier *m* inoffensif

drudger•y [′drʌdʒəri] *s* (*pl* **-ies**) corvée *f,* travail *m* pénible

drug [drʌg] *s* (*medicine*) produit *m* pharmaceutique, drogue *f;* (*narcotic*) stupéfiant *m,* drogue; **drug on the market** rossignol *m* ‖ *v* (*pret & pp* **drugged;** *ger* **drugging**) *tr* (*a person*) donner un stupéfiant à, stupéfier; (*food or drink*) ajouter un stupéfiant à

drug′ ad′dict *s* toxicomane *mf,* drogué *m,* intoxiqué *m,* camé *m*

drug′ addic′tion *s* toxicomanie *f*

druggist [′drʌgɪst] *s* pharmacien *m*

drug′ hab′it *s* toxicomanie *f,* vice *m* des stupéfiants

drug′ push′er *s* revendeur *m* (de drogues); (slang) dealer *m,* vendeur *m* de mort, fourmi *f*

drug′store′ *s* pharmacie-bazar *f,* pharmacie *f*

drug′ traf′fic *s* trafic *m* des stupéfiants

druid [′dru•ɪd] *s* druide *m*

drum [drʌm] *s* (*cylinder; instrument of percussion*) tambour *m;* (*container for oil, gasoline, etc.*) bidon *m;* **to play the drum** battre du tambour ‖ *v* (*pret & pp* **drummed;** *ger* **drumming**) *tr* (*e.g., a march*) tambouriner; rassembler au son du tambour; **to drum into** fourrer dans; **to drum up customers** racoler des

clients ‖ *intr* jouer du tambour; (*with the fingers*) tambouriner; (*on the piano*) pianoter

drum′ and bu′gle corps′ *s* clairons et tambours *mpl,* clique *f*

drum′beat′ *s* coup *m* de tambour

drum′ brake′ *s* frein *m* à tambour

drum′fire′ *s* (mil) tir *m* nourri, feu *m* roulant

drum′head′ *s* peau *f* de tambour; (naut) noix *f*

drum′ ma′jor *s* tambour-major *m*

drummer [′drʌmər] *s* tambour *m;* (*salesman*) (coll) commis *m* voyageur

drum′stick′ *s* baguette *f* de tambour; (*of chicken*) (coll) cuisse *f,* pilon *m*

drunk [drʌŋk] *adj* ivre, soûl; **to get drunk** s'enivrer; **to get s.o. drunk** enivrer qn ‖ *s* (*person*) (coll) ivrogne *m;* (*state*) ivresse *f;* **to go on a drunk** (coll) se soûler

drunkard [′drʌŋkərd] *s* ivrogne *m*

drunken [′drʌŋkən] *adj* enivré

drunk′en driv′er *s* chauffeur *m* en état d'ivresse

drunk′en driv′ing *s* conduite *f* en état d'ivresse, ivresse *f* au volant, alcoolisme *m* au volant

drunkenness [′drʌŋkənnɪs] *s* ivresse *f*

dry [drai] *adj* (*comp* **drier;** *super* **driest**) sec; (*thirsty*) assoiffé; (*boring*) aride ‖ *s* (*pl* **drys**) (*prohibitionist*) antialcoolique *mf* ‖ *v* (*pret & pp* **dried**) *tr* sécher; (*the dishes*) essuyer ‖ *intr* sécher; **to dry up** se dessécher; (slang) se taire

dry′ bat′tery *s* pile *f* sèche; (*number of dry cells*) batterie *f* de piles

dry′ cell′ *s* pile *f* sèche

dry′-clean′ *tr* nettoyer à sec

dry′ clean′er *s* nettoyeur *m* à sec, teinturier *m*

dry′ clean′er's *s* teinturerie *f*

dry′ clean′ing *s* nettoyage *m* à sec

dry′ dock′ *s* cale *f* sèche, bassin *m* de radoub

dry′-eyed′ *adj* d'un œil sec

dry′ farm′ing *s* culture *f* sèche

dry′ goods′ *spl* tissus *mpl,* étoffes *fpl*

dry′ ice′ *s* glace *f* sèche

dry′ing room′ *s* séchoir *m*

dry′ land′ *s* terre *f* ferme

dry′ meas′ure *s* mesure *f* à grains

dryness [′drainɪs] *s* sécheresse *f;* (*e.g., of a speaker*) aridité *f*

dry′ nurse′ *s* nourrice *f* sèche

dry′ rot′ *s* carie *f* sèche

dry′ run′ *s* exercice *m* simulé, répétition *f,* examen *m* blanc

dry′ sea′son *s* saison *f* sèche

dry′ wash′ *s* blanchissage *m* sans repassage

dual [′d(j)u•əl] *adj* double ‖ *s* duel *m*

du′al cit′izen•ship′ *s* double nationalité

du′al controls′ *spl* double commande *f*

dub [dʌb] *s* (slang) balourd *m* ‖ *v* (*pret & pp* **dubbed;** *ger* **dubbing**) *tr* (*to nickname*) donner un sobriquet à; (*to knight*) donner l'accolade à, adouber; (*a tape recording or movie film*) doubler

dubbing [′dʌbɪŋ] *s* (mov) doublage *m*

dubious [′d(j)ubi•əs] *adj* (*undecided*) hésitant; (*questionable*) douteux

ducat [ˈdʌkət] *s* ducat *m*

duchess [ˈdʌtʃis] *s* duchesse *f*

duch•y [ˈdʌtʃi] *s* (*pl* **-ies**) duché *m*

duck [dʌk] *s* canard *m;* (*female*) cane *f;* (*motion*) esquive *f;* **ducks** (*trousers*) pantalon *m* de coutil ‖ *tr* (*the head*) baisser ‖ *intr* se baisser; **to duck out** (coll) s'esquiver

ducking [ˈdʌkɪŋ] *s* plongeon *m*, bain *m* forcé

duckling [ˈdʌklɪŋ] *s* caneton *m;* (*female*) canette *f*

ducks' and drakes' *s*—to play at ducks and drakes faire des ricochets sur l'eau; (fig) jeter son argent par les fenêtres

duck'-toed' *adj* qui marche en canard

duct [dʌkt] *s* conduit *m*, canal *m*

duct'less glands' [ˈdʌktlɪs] *spl* glandes *fpl* closes

duct' tape' *s* bande *f* adhésive pour fermer hermétiquement les joints de conduits

duct'work' *s* tuyauterie *f*, canalisation *f*

dud [dʌd] *s* (slang) obus *m* qui a raté, fusée *f* mouillée; (slang) raté *m*, navet *m;* **duds** (*clothes*) (coll) frusques *fpl*, nippes *fpl*

dude [d(j)ud] *s* poseur *m*, gommeux *m*

dude' ranch' *s* ranch *m* d'opérette

due [d(j)u] *adj* dû; (*note*) échéant; (*bill*) exigible; (*train, bus, person*) attendu; **due to** par suite de; **in due (and proper) form** en bonne forme, en règle, en bonne et due forme; **to fall due** venir à l'échéance; **when is the train due?** à quelle heure doit arriver le train? ‖ *s* dû *m;* **dues** cotisation *f;* **to pay one's dues** cotiser ‖ *adv* droit vers, e.g., **due north** droit vers le nord

due' date' *s* échéance *f*

duel [ˈd(j)uəl] *s* duel *m;* **to fight a duel** se battre en duel ‖ *v* (*pret & pp* **dueled** or **duelled;** *ger* **dueling** or **duelling**) *intr* se battre en duel

duelist or **duellist** [ˈd(j)uəlɪst] *s* duelliste *m*

duenna [d(j)uˈɛnə] *s* duègne *f*

dues'-pay'ing *adj* cotisant

duet [d(j)uˈɛt] *s* duo *m*

duke [d(j)uk] *s* duc *m*

dukedom [ˈd(j)ukdəm] *s* duché *m*

dull [dʌl] *adj* (*not sharp*) émoussé; (*color*) terne; (*sound; pain*) sourd; (*stupid*) lourd; (*business*) lent; (*boring*) ennuyeux; (*flat*) fade, insipide; **to become dull** s'émousser; (*said of senses*) s'engourdir ‖ *tr* (*a knife*) émousser; (*color*) ternir; (*sound; pain*) amortir; (*spirits*) hébéter, engourdir ‖ *intr* s'émousser; se ternir; s'amortir; s'engourdir

dullard [ˈdʌlərd] *s* lourdaud *m*, hébété *m*

dullness [ˈdʌlnɪs] *s* (*of knife*) émoussement *m;* (*e.g., of wits*) lenteur *f*

duly [ˈd(j)uli] *adv* dûment, justement

dumb [dʌm] *adj* (*lacking the power to speak*) muet; (coll) gourde, imbécile; **completely dumb** (coll) bouché à l'émeri; **to play dumb** (coll) feindre l'innocence

dumb'bell' *s* (sports) haltère *m;* (slang) gourde *f*, imbécile *mf*

dumb' crea'ture *s* animal *m*, brute *f*

dum'dum bul'let [ˈdʌmdʌm] *s* balle *f* dum-dum

dumb'wait'er *s* monte-plats *m;* (*serving table*) table *f* roulante

dumfound [ˈdʌm,faʊnd] *tr* abasourdir, ébahir

dum•my [ˈdʌmi] *adj* faux, factice ‖ *s* (*pl* **-mies**) (*dress form*) mannequin; (*in card games*) mort *m;* (*figurehead, straw man*) prête-nom *m*, homme *m* de paille; (*skeleton copy of a book or magazine*) maquette *f;* (*object put in place of the real thing*) simulacre *m;* (slang) bêta *m*, ballot *m*

dump [dʌmp] *s* (*pile of rubbish*) amas *m*, tas *m;* (*place*) dépotoir *m;* (mil) dépôt *m;* (slang) taudis *m;* **to be down in the dumps** (coll) avoir le cafard ‖ *tr* décharger, déverser; (*on rubbish pile*) jeter au rebut; (com) vendre en faisant du dumping

dumping [ˈdʌmpɪŋ] *s* (com) dumping *m*

dumpling [ˈdʌmplɪŋ] *s* dumpling *m*, boulette *f*

dump' truck' *s* tombereau *m*

dump•y [ˈdʌmpi] *adj* (*comp* **-ier;** *super* **-iest**) (*short and fat*) courtaud, trapu, tassé; (*shabby*) râpé, minable

dun [dʌn] *adj* isabelle ‖ *s* créancier *m* importun; (*demand for payment*) demande *f* pressante ‖ *v* (*pret & pp* **dunned;** *ger* **dunning**) *tr* (*for payment*) importuner, poursuivre

dunce [dʌns] *s* âne *m*, cancre *m*

dunce' cap' *s* bonnet *m* d'âne

dune [d(j)un] *s* dune *f*

dune' bug'gy *s* autosable *m*

dung [dʌŋ] *s* fumier *m*

dungarees [ˌdʌŋgəˈriz] *spl* pantalon *m* de treillis, treillis *m*, bleu *m*

dungeon [ˈdʌndʒən] *s* cachot *m*, culde-basse-fosse *m;* (*keep of castle*) donjon *m*

dung'hill' *s* tas *m* de fumier

dunk [dʌŋk] *tr & intr* tremper

du•o [ˈd(j)uo] *s* (*pl* **-os**) duo *m*

duode•num [ˌd(j)uəˈdinəm] *s* (*pl* **-na** [nə]) duodénum *m*

dupe [d(j)up] *s* dupe *f*, dindon *m* de la farce ‖ *tr* duper, flouer, faire marcher

duplex [ˈd(j)uplɛks] *adj* double, duplex ‖ *s* (*apartment*) appartement *m* sur deux étages, duplex *m;* (*house*) maison *f* double

du'plex house' *s* maison *f* double

duplicate [ˈd(j)uplɪkɪt] *adj* double ‖ *s* duplicata *m*, polycopie *f;* **in duplicate** en double, en duplicata ‖ [ˈd(j)upli,ket] *tr* faire le double de, reproduire; (*on a machine*) polycopier, ronéocopier

du'plicating machine' *s* duplicateur *m*

duplici•ty [d(j)uˈplɪsɪti] *s* (*pl* **-ties**) duplicité *f*

durable [ˈd(j)ʊrəbəl] *adj* durable

dur'able goods' *spl* articles *mpl* durables

duration [d(j)uˈreʃən] *s* durée *f*

duress [d(j)uˈrɛs] *s* contrainte *f;* emprisonnement *m*

during [ˈd(j)ʊrɪŋ] *prep* pendant

dusk [dʌsk] *s* crépuscule *m;* **at dusk** entre chien et loup

dust [dʌst] *s* poussière *f* ‖ *tr* (*to free of dust*) épousseter; (*to sprinkle with dust*) saupoudrer; **to dust off** épousseter

dust′ bowl′ *s* région *f* dénudée

dust′ cloth′ *s* chiffon *m* à épousseter

dust′ cloud′ *s* nuage *m* de poussière

dust′ cov′er *s* housse *f* de protection

duster [ˈdʌstər] *s* (*made of feathers*) plumeau *m*; (*made of cloth*) chiffon *m*; (*overgarment*) cache-poussière *m*

dust′ jack′et *s* protège-livre *m*, couvre-livre *m*, liseuse *f*

dust′pan′ *s* pelle *f* à poussière, ramasse-poussière *m invar*

dust′ rag′ *s* chiffon *m* à épousseter

dust′ storm′ *s* tempête *f* de poussière

dust′up *s* (coll) rixe *f*, escarmouche *f*

dust•y [ˈdʌsti] *adj* (*comp* **-ier;** *super* **-iest**) poussiéreux; (*color*) cendré

Dutch [dʌtʃ] *adj* hollandais, néerlandais; (slang) allemand ‖ *s* (*language*) hollandais *m*, néerlandais *m*; (slang) allemand *m*; **in Dutch** (slang) en disgrâce; **the Dutch** les Hollandais *mpl*, les Néerlandais *mpl*; (slang) les Allemands *mpl*; **we will go Dutch** (coll) chacun paiera son écot

Dutch′man *s* (*pl* **-men**) Hollandais *m*, Néerlandais *m*; (slang) Allemand *m*

Dutch′ treat′ *s* —**to have a Dutch treat** (coll) faire suisse, payer son écot

dutiable [ˈd(j)uti•əbəl] *adj* soumis aux droits de douane

dutiful [ˈd(j)utɪfəl] *adj* respectueux, soumis, plein d'égards

du•ty [ˈd(j)uti] *s* (*pl* **-ties**) devoir *m;* **duties** fonctions *fpl;* (*taxes, customs*) droits *mpl;* **to be off duty** ne pas être de service, avoir quartier libre; **to be on duty** être de service, être de garde; **to have the duty to** avoir pour devoir de

du′ty-free′ *adj* exempt de droits

du′ty-free shop′ *s* boutique *f* franche

DVD [ˈdiˈviˈdi] *s* (letterword) (**digital versatile disk**) DVD *m invar* (disque numérique à usages variés)

dwarf [dwɔrf] *adj & s* nain *m* ‖ *tr & intr* rapetisser

dwell [dwɛl] *v* (*pret & pp* **dwelled** or **dwelt** [dwɛlt]) *intr* demeurer; **to dwell on** appuyer sur

dwelling [ˈdwɛlɪŋ] *s* demeure *f*, habitation *f*

dwell′ing house′ *s* maison *f* d'habitation

dwindle [ˈdwɪndəl] *intr* diminuer; **to dwindle away** s'affaiblir

dye [daɪ] *s* teinture *f* ‖ *v* (*pret & pp* **dyed;** *ger* **dyeing**) *tr* teindre

dyed′-in-the-wool′ *adj* intransigeant

dyeing [ˈdaɪɪŋ] *s* teinture *f*

dyer [ˈdaɪər] *s* teinturier *m*

dying [ˈdaɪɪŋ] *adj* mourant, moribond

dynamic [daɪˈnæmɪk], [dɪˈnæmɪk] *adj* dynamique ‖ **dynamics** *s* dynamique *f*

dynamite [ˈdaɪnəˌmaɪt] *s* dynamite *f* ‖ *tr* dynamiter

dyna•mo [ˈdaɪnəˌmo] *s* (*pl* **-mos**) dynamo *f*

dynas•ty [ˈdaɪnəsti] *s* (*pl* **-ties**) dynastie *f*

dysentery [ˈdɪsənˌtɛri] *s* dysenterie *f*

dysfunction [dɪsˈfʌŋʃən] *s* dysfonctionnement *m*

dyspepsia [dɪsˈpɛpsi•ə] *s* dyspepsie *f*

E

E, e [i] *s* V⁰ lettre de l'alphabet

each [itʃ] *adj indef* chaque ‖ *pron indef* chacun; **each other** nous, se; l'un l'autre; **to each other** l'un à l'autre ‖ *adv* chacun; (*apiece*) pièce, la pièce

eager [ˈigər] *adj* ardent, empressé; **eager for** avide de; **to be eager to** brûler de, désirer ardemment

ea′ger bea′ver *s* bûcheur *m*, mouche *f* du coche

eagerness [ˈigərnɪs] *s* ardeur *f*, empressement *m*

eagle [ˈigəl] *s* aigle *m*

ea′gle-eyed′ *adj* à l'œil d'aigle

ea′gle ray′ *s* (ichth) aigle *m* de mer

eaglet [ˈiglɪt] *s* aiglon *m*

ear [ɪr] *s* oreille *f;* (*of corn or wheat*) épi *m;* **to box s.o.'s ears** frotter les oreilles à qn; **to prick up one's ears** dresser l'oreille; **to turn a deaf ear** faire la sourde oreille ‖ *intr* (*said of grain*) épier

ear′ache′ *s* douleur *m* d'oreille

ear′drop′ *s* pendant *m* d'oreille

ear′drum′ *s* tympan *m*

ear′flap′ *s* lobe *m* de l'oreille; (*on a cap*) protège-oreilles *m*

earl [ʌrl] *s* comte *m*

earldom [ˈʌrldəm] *s* comté *m*

ear•ly [ˈʌrli] (*comp* **-lier;** *super* **-liest**) *adj* primitif; (*first in a series*) premier; (*occurring in the near future*) prochain; (*in the morning*) matinal; (*ahead of time*) en avance; **at an early age** dès l'enfance ‖ *adv* de bonne heure, tôt; anciennement; **as early as** dès; **earlier** plus tôt, de meilleure heure

ear′ly bird′ *s* matinal *m*

ear′ly mass′ *s* première messe *f*

ear′ly-morn′ing *adj* matinal

ear′ly retire′ment *s* retraite *f* anticipée

ear′ly ris′er *s* matinal *m*

ear′ly-ris′ing *adj* matineux, matinal

ear′ly warn′ing sys′tem *s* dispositif *m* de première alerte

ear′mark′ *s* marque *f*, cachet *m* ‖ *tr (animals)* marquer à l'oreille; *(e.g., money)* spécialiser; **to earmark for** affecter à, assigner à

ear′muff′ *s* couvre-oreille *m*, protège-oreille *m*

earn [ʌrn] *tr* gagner; *(to get one's due)* mériter; *(interest)* rapporter

earned′ in′come *s* revenus *mpl* salariaux, traitements *mpl*, salaires *mpl*

earnest [′ʌrnɪst] *adj* sérieux; **in earnest** sérieusement ‖ *s* gage *m*; (com) arrhes *fpl*

earn′est mon′ey *s* arrhes *fpl*, garantie *f*

earn′ing pow′er *s (person)* capacité *f* de gain; *(stock)* rentabilité *f*

earnings [′ʌrnɪŋz] *spl (wages)* gages *mpl*; *(profits)* profit *m*, bénéfices *mpl*

ear′phone′ *s* écouteur *m*; **earphones** casque *m*, écouteurs

ear′plug′ *s* protège-tympan *m invar*

ear′ring′ *s* boucle *f* d'oreille

ear′shot′ *s*—**within earshot** à portée de voix

ear′split′ting *adj* assourdissant

ear′wax′ *s* cérumen *m*

earth [ʌrθ] *s* terre *f*; **to come down to earth** retomber des nues; **where on earth ...?** où diable ...?

earthen [′ʌrθən] *adj* de terre, en terre

ear′then•ware′ *s* faïence *f*

earthly [′ʌrθli] *adj* terrestre

earth′man′ *s (pl* **men)** terrien *m*

earth′quake′ *s* tremblement *m* de terre

earth′work′ *s* terrassement *m*

earth′worm′ *s* lombric *m*, ver *m* de terre

earth•y [′ʌrθi] *adj (comp* **-ier;** *super* **-iest)** terreux; *(worldly)* mondain; *(unrefined)* grossier, terre à terre

ear′trum′pet *s* cornet *m* acoustique

ease [iz] *s* aise *f*; *(readiness, naturalness)* désinvolture *f*; *(comfort, well-being)* bien-être *m*, tranquillité *f*; **at ease** tranquille; (mil) au repos; **to take one's ease** prendre ses aises; **with ease** facilement ‖ *tr* faciliter; *(a burden)* alléger; *(e.g., one's mind)* calmer, apaiser; *(to let up on)* ralentir ‖ *intr* se calmer, s'apaiser

easel [′izəl] *s* chevalet *m*

easement [′izmənt] *s* (law) servitude *f*

easily [′izɪli] *adv* facilement, aisément; *(certainly)* sans doute

easiness [′izɪnɪs] *s* facilité *f*; *(of manner)* désinvolture *f*, insouciance *f*

east [ist] *adj & s* est *m* ‖ *adv* à l'est, vers l'est

Easter [′istər] *s* Pâques *m*; **Happy Easter!** Joyeuses Pâques!

East′er egg′ *s* œuf *m* de Pâques

East′er Mon′day *s* lundi *m* de Pâques

eastern [′istərn] *adj* oriental, de l'est

East′ern Stan′dard Time′ *s* l'heure *f* de l'Est

East′ern Town′ships *spl (in Canada)* Cantons *mpl* de l'Est

eastward [′istwərd] *adv* vers l'est

east′ wind′ *s* vent *m* d'est

eas•y [′izi] *adj (comp* **-ier;** *super* **-iest)** facile; *(easygoing)* aisé, désinvolte; **it's not easy to** + *inf* ce n'est pas commode à + *inf* ‖ *adv* (coll) facilement; (coll) lentement; **to take it easy** (coll) en prendre à son aise

eas′y chair′ *s* fauteuil *m*, bergère *f*

eas′y•go′ing *adj* insouciant, nonchalant, commode à vivre

eas′y mark′ *s* jobard *m*

eas′y pay′ments *spl* facilités *fpl* de paiement

eat [it] *v (pret* **ate** [et]; *pp* **eaten** [′itən]) *tr* manger; **to eat away** ronger ‖ *intr* manger

eatable [′itəbəl] *adj* comestible

eat′ing ap′ple *s* pomme *f* à couteau

eaves [ivz] *spl* avant-toits *mpl*

eaves′drop′ *v (pret & pp* **-dropped;** *ger* **-dropping)** *intr* écouter à la porte

ebb [ɛb] *s* reflux *m*, baisse *f* ‖ *intr* refluer, baisser; **to ebb and flow** monter et baisser, fluer et refluer

ebb′ and flow′ *s* flux et reflux *m*

ebb′ tide′ *s* marée *f* descendante, jusant *m*

ebon•y [′ɛbəni] *s (pl* **-ies)** ébène *f*; *(tree)* ébénier *m*

ebullient [ɪ′bʌljənt] *adj* bouillonnant; (fig) enthousiaste, exubérant

eccentric [ɛk′sɛntrɪk] *adj* excentrique ‖ *s (odd person)* excentrique *mf*; *(device)* excentrique *m*

eccentrici•ty [ˌɛksɛn′trɪsɪti] *s (pl* **-ties)** excentricité *f*

ecclesiastic [ɪˌklizɪ′æstɪk] *adj & s* ecclésiastique *m*

echelon [′ɛʃəˌlɑn] *s* échelon *m* ‖ *tr* (mil) échelonner

ech•o [′ɛko] *s (pl* **-oes)** écho *m* ‖ *tr* répéter ‖ *intr* faire écho

eclectic [ɛk′lɛktɪk] *adj & s* éclectique *mf*

eclipse [ɪ′klɪps] *s* éclipse *f* ‖ *tr* éclipser

eclogue [′ɛklɔg] *s* églogue *f*

ecological [ˌɛkə′lɑdʒɪkəl] *adj* écologique

ecologist [ɪ′kɑlədʒɪst] *s* écologiste *mf*

ecology [ɪ′kɑlədʒi] *s* écologie *f*

economic [ˌikə′nɑmɪk] *adj* économique ‖ **economics** *s* économique *f*

economical [ˌikə′nɑmɪkəl] *adj* économe

economize [ɪ′kɑnəˌmaɪz] *tr & intr* économiser

econo•my [ɪ′kɑnəmi] *s (pl* **-mies)** économie *f*

ecosystem [′ɛkoˌsɪstəm] *s* écosystème *m*

ecsta•sy [′ɛkstəsi] *s (pl* **-sies)** extase *f*

ecstatic [ɛk′stætɪk] *adj & s* extatique *mf*

Ecuador [′ɛkwəˌdɔr] *s* l'Équateur *m*

ecumenic(al) [ˌɛkjə′mɛnɪk(əl)] *adj* œcuménique

eczema [′ɛksɪmə] *s* eczéma *m*

edema [ɪ′dimə] *s* (pathol) œdème *m*

ed•dy [′ɛdi] *s (pl* **-dies)** tourbillon *m* ‖ *v (pret & pp* **-died)** *intr* tourbillonner

edelweiss [′edəlˌvaɪs] *s* edelweiss *m*, fleur *f* de neige

Eden [′idən] *s* (fig) éden *m*

edge [ɛdʒ] *s* bord *m*; *(of a knife, sword, etc.)* fil *m*, tranchant *m*; *(of a field, forest, etc.; of a strip of cloth)* lisière *f*; (slang) avantage *m*;

on edge de chant; (*nervous*) énervé, crispé; **to be on edge** avoir les nerfs à fleur de peau; **to have the edge on** (coll) enfoncer; **to set the teeth on edge** agacer les dents ‖ *tr* border; (*to sharpen*) affiler, aiguiser ‖ *intr* s'avancer de biais; **to edge away** s'écarter peu à peu; **to edge in** se glisser parmi ou dans

edge′ways′ *adv* de côté, de biais

edging [ˈɛdʒɪŋ] *s* bordure *f*

edg•y [ˈɛdʒi] *adj* (*comp* **-ier;** *super* **-iest**) (*nervous*) crispé, irritable

edible [ˈɛdɪbəl] *adj* comestible

edict [ˈidɪkt] *s* édit *m*

edification [ˌɛdɪfɪˈkeʃən] *s* édification *f*

edifice [ˈɛdɪfɪs] *s* édifice *m*

edi•fy [ˈɛdɪˌfaɪ] *v* (*pret & pp* **-fied**) *tr* édifier

edifying [ˈɛdɪˌfaɪ•ɪŋ] *adj* édifiant

edit [ˈɛdɪt] *tr* préparer la publication de; (*e.g., a newspaper*) diriger, rédiger; (*a text*) éditer

edition [ɪˈdɪʃən] *s* édition *f*

editor [ˈɛdɪtər] *s* (*of newspaper or magazine*) rédacteur *m*; (*of manuscript*) éditeur *m*; (*of feature or column*) chroniqueur *m*, courriériste *mf*

editorial [ˌɛdɪˈtori•əl] *adj & s* éditorial *m*

edito′rial of′fice *s* rédaction *f*

edito′rial pol′icy *s* ligne *f* politique

edito′rial staff′ *s* rédaction *f*

ed′itor in chief′ *s* rédacteur *m* en chef

educate [ˈɛdʒʊˌket] *tr* instruire, éduquer

educated *adj* cultivé, instruit

education [ˌɛdʒʊˈkeʃən] *s* éducation *f*, instruction *f*

educational [ˌɛdʒʊˈkeʃənəl] *adj* éducatif, éducateur

educa′tional tel′evision *s* télé-enseignement *m*, télévision *f* éducative, télévision scolaire

educator [ˈɛdʒʊˌketər] *s* éducateur *m*

eel [il] *s* anguille *f*

ee•rie *ou* **ee•ry** [ˈɪri] *adj* (*comp* **-rier;** *super* **-riest**) mystérieux, spectral

efface [ɪˈfes] *tr* effacer

effect [ɪˈfɛkt] *s* effet *m*; **in effect** en fait, effectivement; **to be in effect** être en vigueur; **to feel the effects of** se ressentir de; **to go into effect, to take effect** prendre effet; (*said of law*) entrer en vigueur ‖ *tr* effectuer, mettre à exécution

effective [ɪˈfɛktɪv] *adj* efficace; (*actually in effect*) en vigueur; (*striking*) impressionnant; **to become effective** produire son effet; (*to go into effect*) entrer en vigueur

effectual [ɪˈfɛktʃʊ•əl] *adj* efficace

effectuate [ɪˈfɛktʃʊˌet] *tr* effectuer

effeminacy [ɪˈfɛmɪnəsi] *s* effémination *f*

effeminate [ɪˈfɛmɪnɪt] *adj* efféminé; **to become effeminate** s'efféminer

effervesce [ˌɛfərˈvɛs] *intr* être en effervescence

effervescent [ˌɛfərˈvɛsənt] *adj* effervescent

effete [ɪˈfit] *adj* stérile, épuisé

efficacious [ˌɛfɪˈkeʃəs] *adj* efficace

efficacy [ˈɛfɪkəsi] *s* efficacité *f*

efficien•cy [ɪˈfɪʃənsi] *s* (*pl* **-cies**) efficacité *f*; (*of business*) efficience *f*; (*of machine*) rendement *m*; (*of person*) compétence *f*

effi′ciency ex′pert *s* ingénieur *m* en organisation

efficient [ɪˈfɪʃənt] *adj* efficace; (*of machine*) efficient, de bon rendement; (*of person*) efficient, compétent

effi•gy [ˈɛfɪdʒi] *s* (*pl* **-gies**) effigie *f*

effort [ˈɛfərt] *s* effort *m*

effronter•y [ɪˈfrʌntəri] *s* (*pl* **-ies**) effronterie *f*

effusion [ɪˈfjuʒən] *s* effusion *f*

effusive [ɪˈfjusɪv] *adj* démonstratif; **to be effusive in** se répandre en

e.g. *abbr* (Lat: *exempli gratia* for example) par ex., ex.

egg [ɛg] *s* œuf *m*; **eggs and bacon** œufs *mpl* au bacon; **good (bad) egg** (*person*) (slang) brave (sale) type; **to put all one's eggs in one basket** mettre tous ses œufs dans le même panier ‖ *tr*—**to egg on** (coll) pousser, inciter

egg′beat′er *s* fouet *m*, batteur *m* à œufs

egg′cup′ *s* coquetier *m*

egg′head′ *s* (slang) intellectuel *m*

eggnog [ˈɛgˌnɑg] *s* lait *m* de poule

egg′plant′ *s* aubergine *f*

egg′ poach′er *s* pocheuse *f*

egg′ roll′ing *s* rouleau *m* du printemps

egg′shell′ *s* coquille *f* d'œuf

egg′ white′ *s* blanc *m* d'œuf

egoism [ˈigoˌɪzəm] *s* égoïsme *m*

egoist [ˈigo•ɪst] *s* égoïste *mf*

egotism [ˈigoˌtɪzəm] *s* égotisme *m*

egotist [ˈigotɪst] *s* égotiste *mf*

egregious [ɪˈgridʒəs] *adj* insigne, notoire

egress [ˈigrɛs] *s* sortie *f*, issue *f*

egret [ˈgrɛt] *s* aigrette *f*

Egypt [ˈidʒɪpt] *s* Égypte *f*; l'Égypte

Egyptian [ɪˈdʒɪpʃən] *adj* égyptien ‖ *s* Egyptien *m*

ei′der down′ [ˈaɪdər] *s* édredon *m*

ei′der duck′ *s* eider *m*

eight [et] *adj & pron* huit ‖ *s* huit *m*; (*group of eight*) huitaine *f*; **about eight** une huitaine de; **eight o'clock** huit heures

eight′ball′ *s*—**behind the eightball** (coll) dans le pétrin

eighteen [ˈetˈtin] *adj, pron, & s* dix-huit *m*

eighteenth [ˈetˈtinθ] *adj & pron* dix-huitième (*masc, fem*); **the Eighteenth** dix-huit, e.g., **John the Eighteenth** Jean dix-huit ‖ *s* dix-huitième *m*; **the eighteenth** (*in dates*) le dix-huit

eighth [etθ] *adj & pron* huitième (*masc, fem*); **the Eighth** huit, e.g., **John the Eighth** Jean huit ‖ *s* huitième *m*; **the eighth** (*in dates*) le huit

eightieth [ˈeti•θ] *adj & pron* quatre-vingtième (*masc, fem*) ‖ *s* quatre-vingtième *m*

eigh•ty [ˈeti] *adj & pron* quatre-vingts ‖ *s* (*pl* **-ties**) quatre-vingts *m*

eight′y-first′ *adj & pron* quatre-vingt-unième (*masc, fem*) ‖ *s* quatre-vingt-unième *m*

eight′y-one′ *adj, pron, & s* quatre-vingt-un *m*

either ['iðər], ['aɪðər] adj & pron indef l'un ou l'autre; l'un et l'autre; **on either side** de chaque côté ‖ adv—**not either** non plus ‖ conj—**either ... or** ou ... ou, soit ... soit, ou bien ... ou bien

ejaculate [ɪ'dʒækjə,let] tr & intr crier; (physiol) éjaculer

eject [ɪ'dʒɛkt] tr éjecter; (to evict) expulser, chasser

ejection [ɪ'dʒɛkʃən] s éjection f; (eviction) expulsion f

ejec'tion seat' s (aer) siège m éjectable

eke [ik] tr—**to eke out** gagner avec difficulté

elaborate [ɪ'læbərɪt] adj élaboré, soigné; (ornate) orné, travaillé; (involved) compliqué, recherché ‖ [ɪ'læbə,ret] tr élaborer ‖ intr—**to elaborate on** or **upon** donner des détails sur

elapse [ɪ'læps] intr s'écouler

elastic [ɪ'læstɪk] adj & s élastique m

elasticity [,ɪlæs'tɪsɪti] s élasticité f

elated [ɪ'letɪd] adj transporté, exalté

elation [ɪ'leʃən] s transport m, exultation f

elbow ['ɛlbo] s coude m; **at one's elbow** à portée de la main; **to rub elbows with** coudoyer ‖ tr coudoyer; **to elbow one's way** se frayer un chemin à coups de coude ‖ intr jouer des coudes

el'bow grease' s (coll) huile f de coude

el'bow rest' s accotoir m, bras m de fauteuil

el'bow•room' s espace m; **to have elbowroom** avoir les coudées franches

elder ['ɛldər] adj aîné, plus âgé ‖ s aîné m; (senior) doyen m; (bot) sureau m; (eccl) ancien m

el'der•ber'ry s (pl -ries) sureau m; (berry) baie f de sureau

elderly ['ɛldərli] adj vieux, âgé

eld'er states'man s vétéran m de la politique

eldest ['ɛldɪst] adj (l')aîné, (le) plus âgé

elect [ɪ'lɛkt] adj élu ‖ s—**the elect** les élus mpl ‖ tr élire

election [ɪ'lɛkʃən] s élection f

electioneer [ɪ,lɛk'ʒə'nɪr] intr faire la campagne électorale, solliciter des voix

elective [ɪ'lɛktɪv] adj électif; (optional) facultatif ‖ s matière f à option

elec'toral col'lege [ɪ'lɛktərəl] s collège m électoral

electorate [ɪ'lɛktərɪt] s corps m électoral, électeurs mpl, votants mpl

electric(al) [ɪ'lɛktrɪk(əl)] adj électrique

elec'tric appli'ance s électrodomestique m

elec'trical engineer' s ingénieur m électricien

elec'trical engineer'ing s technique f électrique

elec'tric blan'ket s couverture f chauffante

elec'tric chair' s chaise f électrique

elec'tric clothes' dri'er s séchoir m électrique

elec'tric eel' s gymnote m

elec'tric eye' s cellule f photo-électrique

elec'tric fan' s ventilateur m électrique

elec'tric heat'er s radiateur m électrique

electrician [,ɛlɛk'trɪʃən] s électricien m

electricity [,ɛlɛk'trɪsɪti] s électricité f

elec'tric light' s lampe f électrique

elec'tric me'ter s compteur m de courant

elec'tric mix'er s batteur m électrique

elec'tric per'colator s cafetière f électrique

elec'tric range' s cuisinière f électrique

elec'tric shav'er s rasoir m électrique

elec'tric shock' treat'ment s (med) électrochoc m

elec'tric tim'er s prise f de courant programmatrice

electri•fy [ɪ'lɛktrɪ,faɪ] v (pret & pp -fied) tr (to provide with electric power) électrifier; (to communicate electricity to; to thrill) électriser

elec•tro [ɪ'lɛktro] s (pl -tros) électrotype m

electrocardiogram [ɪ,lɛktro'kardɪ•əgræm] s électrocardiogramme m

electrocute [ɪ'lɛktrə,kjut] tr électrocuter

electrode [ɪ'lɛktrod] s électrode f

electrolysis [,ɛlɛk'tralɪsɪs] s électrolyse f

electrolyte [ɪ'lɛktrə,laɪt] s électrolyte m

elec'tro•mag'net s électro-aimant m

elec'tro•magnet'ic adj électromagnétique

electron [ɪ'lɛktran] s électron m

elec'tron gun' s canon m à électrons

electronic [,ɛlɛk'tranɪk] adj électronique ‖ electronics s électronique f

electron'ic pub'lishing s édition f électronique, micro-édition

elec'tron mi'croscope s microscope m électronique

electroplate [ɪ'lɛktrə,plet] tr galvaniser

electroshock [ɪ'lɛktrə,ʃak] s électrochoc m

electrostatic [ɪ,lɛktrə'stætɪk] s électrostatique ‖ electrostatics s électrostatique f

elec'tro•type' s électrotype m ‖ tr électrotyper

elegance ['ɛlɪgəns] s élégance f

elegant ['ɛlɪgənt] adj élégant

elegiac [,ɛlɪ'dʒaɪ•æk] adj élégiaque

ele•gy ['ɛlɪdʒi] s (pl -gies) élégie f

element ['ɛlɪmənt] s élément m

elementary [,ɛlɪ'mɛntəri] adj élémentaire

elephant ['ɛlɪfənt] s éléphant m

elevate ['ɛlɪ,vet] tr élever

elevated adj élevé; (style) soutenu; (train, railway, etc) aérien

el'evated rail'way s métro m aérien

elevation [,ɛlɪ've/ən] s élévation f

elevator ['ɛlɪ,vetər] s ascenseur m; (for freight) monte-charge m; (for hoisting grain) élévateur m; (warehouse for storing grain) silo m à céréales; (aer) gouvernail m d'altitude, gouvernail de profondeur

el'eva'tor but'ton s bouton m d'ascenseur

el'evator shoes' spl souliers mpl compensés

eleven [ɪ'lɛvən] adj & pron onze ‖ s onze m; **eleven o'clock** onze heures

eleventh [ɪ'lɛvənθ] adj & pron onzième (masc, fem); **the Eleventh** onze, e.g., **John the Eleventh** Jean onze ‖ s onzième m; **the eleventh** (in dates) le onze

elev'enth hour' s dernier moment m

elf [ɛlf] s (pl elves [ɛlvz]) elfe m

elicit [ɪˈlɪsɪt] tr (e.g., a smile) provoquer, faire sortir; (e.g., help) obtenir

elide [ɪˈlaɪd] tr élider

eligible [ˈɛlɪdʒɪbəl] adj éligible; (e.g., bachelor) sortable

eliminate [ɪˈlɪmɪˌnet] tr éliminer

elision [ɪˈlɪʒən] s élision f

elite [eˈlit] s élite f

elk [ɛlk] s élan m

ellipse [ɪˈlɪps] s (geom) ellipse f

ellip·sis [ɪˈlɪpsɪs] s (pl -ses [siz]) ellipse f; (punctuation) points mpl de suspension

elliptic(al) [ɪˈlɪptɪk(əl)] adj elliptique

elm [ɛlm] s orme m

elongate [ɪˈlɔŋget] tr allonger, prolonger

elope [ɪˈlop] intr s'enfuir avec un amant

elopement [ɪˈlopmənt] s enlèvement m consenti

eloquence [ˈɛləkwəns] s éloquence f

eloquent [ˈɛləkwənt] adj éloquent

else [ɛls] adj—nobody else personne d'autre; nothing else rien d'autre; somebody else quelqu'un d'autre, un autre; something else autre chose; what else quoi encore; who else qui encore; who's else de qui d'autre ‖ adv d'une autre façon, autrement; how(ever) else de toute autre façon; nowhere else nulle part ailleurs; or else sinon, ou bien, sans quoi; somewhere else ailleurs, autre part; when else quand encore; where else où encore

else·where· adv ailleurs, autre part

elucidate [ɪˈlusɪˌdet] tr élucider

elude [ɪˈlud] tr éluder, se soustraire à; (a pursuer) échapper à

elusive [ɪˈlusɪv] adj évasif, fuyant; (baffling) insaisissable, déconcertant

emaciated [ɪˈmeʃiˌetɪd] adj émacié; to become emaciated s'émacier

E-mail ou e-mail [ˈiˈmel] s (comp) messagerie f électronique, courrier m électronique, e-mail m, mél m, courriel m (Canad)

E'-mail address' s adresse f électronique

emanate [ˈɛməˌnet] intr émaner

emancipate [ɪˈmænsɪˌpet] tr émanciper

embalm [ɛmˈbam] tr embaumer

embalming [ɛmˈbamɪŋ] s embaumement m

embankment [ɛmˈbæŋkmənt] s (of river) digue f; (of road) remblai m

embar·go [ɛmˈbargo] s (pl -goes) embargo m ‖ tr mettre un embargo sur

embark [ɛmˈbark] intr s'embarquer

embarkation [ˌɛmbarˈkeʃən] s embarquement m

embarrass [ɛmˈbærəs] tr faire honte à; (to make difficult) embarrasser

embarrassing [ɛmˈbærəsɪŋ] adj embarrassant, gênant

embarrassment [ɛmˈbærəsmənt] s honte f, confusion f, gêne f; (difficulty) embarras m

embas·sy [ˈɛmbəsi] s (pl -sies) ambassade f

em·bed [ɛmˈbɛd] v (pret & pp -bedded; ger -bedding) tr encastrer

embellish [ɛmˈbɛlɪʃ] tr embellir

embellishment [ɛmˈbɛlɪʃmənt] s embellissement m

ember [ˈɛmbər] s tison m; embers braise f

Em'ber days' spl quatre-temps mpl

embezzle [ɛmˈbɛzəl] tr détourner, s'approprier ‖ intr commettre des détournements

embezzler [ɛmˈbɛzlər] s détourneur m de fonds

embitter [ɛmˈbɪtər] tr aigrir

emblazon [ɛmˈblezən] tr embellir; exalter, célébrer

emblem [ˈɛmbləm] s emblème m

emblematic(al) [ˌɛmbləˈmætɪk(əl)] adj emblématique

embodiment [ɛmˈbadɪmənt] s personnification f, incarnation f

embod·y [ɛmˈbadi] v (pret & pp -ied) tr personnifier, incarner; (to include) incorporer

embolden [ɛmˈboldən] tr enhardir

embolism [ˈɛmbəˌlɪzəm] s embolie f

emboss [ɛmˈbɔs] tr (to raise in relief) graver en relief; (metal) bosseler; (e.g., leather) gaufrer, repousser

embouchure [ˌɑmbuˈʃur] s embouchure f; (mus) position f des lèvres

embrace [ɛmˈbres] s étreinte f, embrassement m ‖ tr étreindre, embrasser ‖ intr s'étreindre, s'embrasser

embroider [ɛmˈbrɔɪdər] tr broder

embroider·y [ɛmˈbrɔɪdəri] s (pl -ies) broderie f

embroil [ɛmˈbrɔɪl] tr (to throw into confusion) embrouiller; (to involve in contention) brouiller

embroilment [ɛmˈbrɔɪlmənt] s embrouillage m, brouillamini m, imbroglio m

embry·o [ˈɛmbrɪˌo] s (pl -os) embryon m

embryology [ˌɛmbrɪˈalədʒi] s embryologie f

embryonic [ˌɛmbrɪˈanɪk] adj embryonnaire

em'bryon'ic clon'ing s reproduction f embryonnaire asexuée

em'bryon'ic stem' cell' re'search s investigations fpl des cellules souches qui proviennent des embryons

emend [ɪˈmɛnd] tr corriger

emendation [ˌimɛnˈdeʃən] s correction f

emerald [ˈɛmərəld] s émeraude f

emerge [ɪˈmʌrdʒ] intr émerger

emergence [ɪˈmʌrdʒəns] s émergence f

emergen·cy [ɪˈmʌrdʒənsi] adj urgent, d'urgence; (exit) de secours ‖ s (pl -cies) cas m urgent

emer'gency brake' s frein m de secours

emer'gency ex'it s sortie f de secours

emer'gency land'ing s atterrissage m forcé

emer'gency opera'tion s (med) opération f à chaud

emer'gency ra'tions spls vivres mpl de réserve

emer'gency room' s salle f des urgences, service m des urgences

emer'gency shut'down s arrêt m d'urgence

emeritus [ɪˈmɛrɪtəs] adj émérite

emer'itus profes'sor s professeur m émérite

emersion [ɪˈmʌrʒən] s émersion f

emery [ˈɛməri] s émeri m
em′ery cloth′ s toile f d'émeri
em′ery wheel′ s meule f en émeri
emetic [ɪˈmɛtɪk] adj & s émétique m
emigrant [ˈɛmɪgrənt] adj & s émigrant m
emigrate [ˈɛmɪˌgret] intr émigrer
eminence [ˈɛmɪnəns] s éminence f
eminent [ˈɛmɪnənt] adj éminent; **most eminent** (eccl) éminentissime
emissar•y [ˈɛmɪˌsɛri] s (pl **-ies**) émissaire m
emit [ɪˈmɪt] v (pret & pp **emitted**; ger **emitting**) tr émettre; (a gas, an odor, etc.) exhaler
emolument [ɪˈmɑljəmənt] s émoluments mpl
emotion [ɪˈmoʃən] s émotion f
emotional [ɪˈmoʃənəl] adj émotif, émotionnable
empathy [ˈɛmpəθi] s empathie f
emperor [ˈɛmpərər] s empereur m
empha•sis [ˈɛmfəsɪs] s (pl **-ses** [ˌsiz]) (on an idea, event, project, etc.) importance f accordée, mise f en relief, insistance f; (on a word or phrase) accent m d'insistance, accentuation f; **to place emphasis on** insister vivement sur, souligner; (a word or syllable) mettre l'accent sur; **with emphasis on** en insistant particulièrement sur
emphasize [ˈɛmfəˌsaɪz] tr appuyer sur, insister sur, mettre en relief, faire ressortir, souligner; (a word or syllable) mettre l'accent sur
emphatic [ɛmˈfætɪk] adj accentué, énergique; (denial) catégorique
emphysema [ˌɛmfɪˈsimə] s emphysème m
empire [ˈɛmpaɪr] s empire m
empiric(al) [ɛmˈpɪrɪk(əl)] adj empirique
empiricist [ɛmˈpɪrɪsɪst] s empirique m
emplacement [ɛmˈplesmənt] s emplacement m
employ [ɛmˈplɔɪ] s service m ‖ tr employer
employee [ˌɛmplɔɪˈi] s employé m
employer [ɛmˈplɔɪ•ər] s employeur m, patron m, chef m
employment [ɛmˈplɔɪmənt] s emploi m
employ′ment a′gency s bureau m de placement
empower [ɛmˈpaʊ•ər] tr autoriser
empress [ˈɛmprɪs] s impératrice f
emptiness [ˈɛmptɪnɪs] s vide m
emp•ty [ˈɛmpti] adj (comp **-tier**; super **-tiest**) vide; (hollow) creux, vain; (coll) affamé ‖ v (pret & pp **-tied**) tr vider ‖ intr se vider; (said of river) se jeter; (said of auditorium) se dégarnir
emp′ty-hand′ed adj & adv les mains vides
emp′ty-head′ed adj écervelé
empye•ma [ˌɛmpɪˈimə] s (pl **-mata** [mətə]) empyème m
empyrean [ˌɛmpɪˈri•ən] s empyrée m
emu [ˈimju] s (zool) émeu m
emulate [ˈɛmjə•let] tr chercher à égaler, imiter ‖ intr rivaliser
emulator [ˈɛmjə•letər] s émule mf
emulsi•fy [ɪˈmʌlsɪˌfaɪ] v (pret & pp **-fied**) tr émulsionner
emulsion [ɪˈmʌlʃən] s émulsion f

enable [ɛnˈebəl] tr—**to enable to** rendre capable de, mettre à même de
enact [ɛnˈækt] tr (to decree) décréter, arrêter; (theat) représenter
enactment [ɛnˈæktmənt] s (establishing) établissement m; (govt) promulgation f; (law) décret m, arrête m; (theat) représentation f
enam•el [ɪˈnæməl] s émail m ‖ v (pret & pp **-eled** or **-elled**; ger **-eling** or **-elling**) tr émailler
enameling [ɪˈnæməlɪŋ] s émaillage m
enam′el•ware′ s ustensiles mpl en fer émaillé
enamor [ɛnˈæmər] tr rendre amoureux; **to become enamored with** s'énamourer de
encamp [ɛnˈkæmp] tr & intr camper
encampment [ɛnˈkæmpmənt] s campement m
encase [ɛnˈkes] tr mettre en caisse; enfermer, envelopper
encephalitis [ɛnˌsɛfəˈlaɪtɪs] s encéphalite f
enchain [ɛnˈtʃen] tr enchaîner
enchant [ɛnˈtʃænt] tr enchanter
enchanting [ɛnˈtʃæntɪŋ] adj charmant, ravissant; (casting a spell) enchanteur
enchantment [ɛnˈtʃæntmənt] s enchantement m
enchantress [ɛnˈtʃæntrɪs] s enchanteresse f
encircle [ɛnˈsʌrkəl] tr encercler, cerner; (a word) entourer d'un cercle
enclitic [ɛnˈklɪtɪk] adj & s enclitique m
enclose [ɛnˈkloz] tr enclore, entourer; (in a letter) inclure, joindre
enclosed adj (surrounded) entouré; (fenced in) clôturé; (covered) couvert; (with a letter) ci-joint, ci-inclus
enclosure [ɛnˈkloʒər] s clôture f, enceinte f, enclos m; (e.g., in a letter) pièce f jointe, pièce annexée
encode [ɛnˈkod] tr chiffrer, coder, encoder; (to translate into a foreign language) traduire (dans une langue qu'on étudie) ‖ intr chiffrer des messages
encoder [ɛnˈkodər] s (comp) codeur m, encodeur m
encoding [ɛnˈkodɪŋ] s codage m, encodage m; (translation into a foreign language) thème m
encomi•um [ɛnˈkomɪ•əm] s (pl **-ums** or **-a** [ə]) panégyrique m, éloge m
encompass [ɛnˈkʌmpəs] tr entourer, renfermer
encore [ˈankor] s rappel m, bis m ‖ tr bisser ‖ interj bis!
encounter [ɛnˈkaʊntər] s rencontre f ‖ tr rencontrer ‖ intr se rencontrer, combattre
encourage [ɛnˈkʌrɪdʒ] tr encourager
encouragement [ɛnˈkʌrɪdʒmənt] s encouragement m
encroach [ɛnˈkrotʃ] intr—**to encroach on** or **upon** empiéter sur; abuser de
encrypt [ɛnˈkrɪpt] tr crypter
encumber [ɛnˈkʌmbər] tr encombrer, embarrasser; (with debts) grever
encumbrance [ɛnˈkʌmbrəns] s encombrement m, embarras m; (law) charge f
encyclical [ɛnˈsɪklɪkəl] adj & s encyclique f

encyclopedia [ɛn,saɪklə'pidɪ•ə] *s* encyclopédie *f*

encyclopedic [ɛn,saɪklə'pidɪk] *adj* encyclopédique

end [ɛnd] *s* (*in time*) fin *f;* (*in space; small piece*) bout *m;* (*end of set period of time*) terme *m;* **at loose ends** en pagaille; **at the end, in the end** à la fin; **to be at the end of one's rope** être au bout de son rouleau; **to bring to an end** mettre fin à; **to come to an end** prendre fin; **to make both ends meet** joindre les deux bouts; **to stand on end** (*said of hair*) se dresser; **to this end** à cet effet ‖ *tr* achever, terminer ‖ *intr* s'achever, se terminer; **to end up by** finir par; **to end with** (or **in**) se terminer par

endanger [ɛn'dendʒər] *tr* mettre en danger

endear [ɛn'dɪr] *tr* faire aimer; **to endear oneself to** se faire aimer de

endeavor [ɛn'dɛvər] *s* effort *m*, tentative *f* ‖ *intr*—**to endeavor to** s'efforcer de, tâcher de

endemic [ɛn'dɛmɪk] *adj* endémique

ending ['ɛndɪŋ] *s* fin *f*, terminaison *f;* (*gram*) désinence *f*

endive ['ɛndaɪv] *s* (*blanched type*) endive *f;* (*Cichorium endivia*) chicorée *f* frisée

endless ['ɛndlɪs] *adj* sans fin

end'most' *adj* extrême

endocrine ['ɛndokrɪn] *adj* endocrine

endorse [ɛn'dɔrs] *tr* endosser; (*a candidate*) appuyer; (*a plan*) souscrire à

endorsement [ɛn'dɔrsmənt] *s* endos *m*, endossement *m;* (*approval*) appui *m*, approbation *f*

endorser [ɛn'dɔrsər] *s* endosseur *m*

endow [ɛn'daʊ] *tr* doter, fonder

endowment [ɛn'daʊmənt] *s* dotation *f*, fondation *f;* (*talent*) don *m*

endow'ment fund' *s* caisse *f* de dotation

end' pa'per *s* pages *fpl* de garde

endurance [ɛn'd(j)ʊrəns] *s* endurance *f*

endur'ance test' *s* épreuve *f* d'endurance

endure [ɛn'd(j)ʊr] *tr* endurer ‖ *intr* durer

enduring [ɛn'd(j)ʊrɪŋ] *adj* durable

enema ['ɛnəmə] *s* lavement *m*

ene•my ['ɛnəmi] *adj* ennemi ‖ *s* (*pl* **-mies**) ennemi *m*

en'emy al'ien *s* étranger *m* ennemi

energetic [,ɛnər'dʒɛtɪk] *adj* énergique

energizing ['ɛnər,dʒaɪzɪŋ] *adj* énergétique

ener•gy ['ɛnərdʒi] *s* (*pl* **-gies**) énergie *f*

en'ergy bal'ance *s* (nucl) bilan *m* énergétique

en'ergy cri'sis *s* crise *f* énergétique

enervate ['ɛnər,vet] *tr* énerver

enfeeble [ɛn'fibəl] *tr* affaiblir

enfold [ɛn'fold] *tr* envelopper, enrouler; (*to embrace*) embrasser

enforce [ɛn'fors] *tr* (*a law*) faire exécuter, mettre en vigueur; (*one's rights, one's point of view*) faire valoir, appuyer; (*e.g., obedience*) imposer

enforcement [ɛn'forsmənt] *s* contrainte *f;* (*of a law*) exécution *f*, mise *f* en vigueur

enfranchise [ɛn'fræntʃaɪz] *tr* affranchir; donner le droit de vote à

engage [ɛn'gedʒ] *tr* engager; (*to hire*) engager, embaucher; (*to reserve*) retenir, réserver, louer; (*s.o.'s attention*) fixer, attirer; (*the clutch*) embrayer; (*toothed wheels*) engrener; **to be engaged in** s'occuper de; **to be engaged to be married** être fiancé; **to engage s.o. in conversation** entamer une conversation avec qn ‖ *intr* s'engager; (mach) engrener; **to engage in** s'embarquer dans, entrer en or dans

engaged *adj* (*to be married*) fiancé; (*busy*) occupé, pris; (mach) en prise; (mil) aux prises, aux mains

engagement [ɛn'gedʒmənt] *s* engagement *m;* (*betrothal*) fiançailles *fpl;* (*appointment*) rendez-vous *m;* (mach) embrayage *m*, engrenage *m;* (mil) engagement, combat *m*

engage'ment ring' *s* bague *f* or anneau *m* de fiançailles

engaging [ɛn'gedʒɪŋ] *adj* engageant, attirant

engender [ɛn'dʒɛndər] *tr* engendrer

engine ['ɛndʒɪn] *s* machine *f;* (*of automobile*) moteur *m*

engineer [,ɛndʒə'nɪr] *s* ingénieur *m;* (*engine driver*) mécanicien *m* ‖ *tr* diriger *or* construire en qualité d'ingénieur; (coll) manigancer, machiner

engineer' corps' *s* génie *m*

engineering [,ɛndʒə'nɪrɪŋ] *s* ingénierie *f*

en'gine house' *s* dépôt *m* de pompes à incendie

en'gine•man' *s* (*pl* **-men**) mécanicien *m*

en'gine room' *s* chambre *f* des machines

en'gine-room tel'egraph *s* (naut) transmetteur *m* d'ordres

en'gine trou'ble *s* panne *f* de moteur

England ['ɪŋglənd] *s* Angleterre *f;* l'Angleterre

English ['ɪŋglɪʃ] *adj* anglais ‖ *s* (*language*) anglais *m;* (billiards) effet *m;* **the English** les Anglais

Eng'lish Chan'nel *s* Manche *f*

Eng'lish dai'sy *s* marguerite *f* des champs

Eng'lish horn' *s* cor *m* anglais

Eng'lish•man *s* (*pl* **-men**) Anglais *m*

Eng'lish-speak'ing *adj* anglophone, d'expression anglaise; (*country*) de langue anglaise

Eng'lish•wom'an *s* (*pl* **-wom'en**) Anglaise *f*

engraft [ɛn'græft] *tr* greffer; (fig) implanter

engrave [ɛn'grev] *tr* graver

engraver [ɛn'grevər] *s* graveur *m*

engraving [ɛn'grevɪŋ] *s* gravure *f*

engross [ɛn'gros] *tr* absorber, occuper; (*a document*) grossoyer

engrossing [ɛn'grosɪŋ] *adj* absorbant

engulf [ɛn'gʌlf] *tr* engouffrer, engloutir

enhance [ɛn'hæns] *tr* rehausser, relever, améliorer, mettre en valeur

enhanced [ɛn'hænst] *adj* rehaussé, amélioré

enhancement [ɛn'hænsmənt] *s* rehaussement *m*, amélioration *f;* (*splendor*) éclat *m*

enigma [ɪ'nɪgmə] *s* énigme *f*

enigmatic(al) [,ɪnɪg'mætɪk(əl)] *adj* énigmatique

enjoin [ɛn'dʒɔɪn] *tr* enjoindre; (*to forbid*) interdire

enjoy [ɛn'dʒɔɪ] *tr* jouir de; **to enjoy** + *ger* prendre plaisir à + *inf;* **to enjoy oneself** s'amuser, se divertir

enjoyable [ɛn'dʒɔɪ•əbəl] *adj* agréable, plaisant; (*show, party, etc.*) divertissant

enjoyment [ɛn'dʒɔɪmənt] *s* (*pleasure*) plaisir *m;* (*pleasurable use*) jouissance *f*

enkindle [ɛn'kɪndəl] *tr* allumer

enlarge [ɛn'lɑrdʒ] *tr* agrandir, élargir; (phot) agrandir ‖ *intr* s'agrandir, s'élargir; **to enlarge on** or **upon** discourir longuement sur, amplifier

enlargement [ɛn'lɑrdʒmənt] *s* agrandissement *m*

enlighten [ɛn'laɪtən] *tr* éclairer

enlightenment [ɛn'laɪtənmənt] *s* éclaircissements *mpl;* **the Enlightenment** le siècle des lumières

enlist [ɛn'lɪst] *tr* enrôler ‖ *intr* s'enrôler, s'engager

enlist′ed man′ *s* homme *m* de troupe

enlistment [ɛn'lɪstmənt] *s* enrôlement *m*, engagement *m*

enliven [ɛn'laɪvən] *tr* animer, égayer

enmesh [ɛn'mɛʃ] *tr* prendre dans les rets; (*e.g., in an evil design*) empêtrer; (mach) engrener

enmi•ty [`ɛnmɪti] *s* (*pl* **-ties**) inimitié *f*

ennoble [ɛn'nobəl] *tr* ennoblir; (*to confer a title of nobility upon*) anoblir

ennui [`ɑnwi] *s* ennui *m*

enormous [ɪ'nɔrməs] *adj* énorme

enormously [ɪ'nɔrməsli] *adv* énormément

enough [ɪ'nʌf] *adj*, *s*, & *adv* assez; **more than enough** plus qu'il n'en faut; **that's enough!** en voilà assez!; **to be intelligent enough** être assez intelligent; **to have enough to live on** avoir de quoi vivre ‖ *interj* assez!, ça suffit!

enounce [ɪ'naʊns] *tr* énoncer

enrage [ɛn'redʒ] *tr* faire enrager, rendre furieux; **to be enraged** enrager

enrapture [ɛn'ræptʃər] *tr* ravir, transporter

enrich [ɛn'rɪtʃ] *tr* enrichir

enrichment [ɛn'rɪtʃmənt] *s* enrichissement *m*

enroll [ɛn'rol] *tr* enrôler; (*a student*) inscrire; (*to wrap up*) enrouler ‖ *intr* s'enrôler; (*said of student*) prendre ses inscriptions, se faire inscrire

enrollment [ɛn'rolmənt] *s* enrôlement *m;* (*of a student*) inscription *f;* (*wrapping up*) enroulement *m*

ensconce [ɛn'skɑns] *tr* cacher; **to ensconce oneself** s'installer

ensemble [ɑn'sɑmbəl] *s* ensemble *m*

ensign [`ɛnsaɪn] *s* enseigne *f* ‖ [`ɛnsən] *s* (nav) enseigne *m* de deuxième classe

ensilage [`ɛnsɪlɪdʒ] *s* fourrage *m* d'un silo américain ‖ *tr* ensiler

enslave [ɛn'slev] *tr* asservir, réduire en esclavage

enslavement [ɛn'slevmənt] *s* asservissement *m*

ensnare [ɛn'snɛr] *tr* prendre au piège, attraper

ensue [ɛn's(j)u] *intr* s'ensuivre, résulter

ensuing [ɛn's(j)u•ɪŋ] *adj* suivant

ensure [ɛn'ʃʊr] *tr* assurer, garantir

entail [ɛn'tel] *tr* occasionner, entraîner

entangle [ɛn'tæŋgəl] *tr* embrouiller

entanglement [ɛn'tæŋgəlmənt] *s* embrouillement *m*, embarras *m*

enter [`ɛntər] *tr* (*a room, a house, etc.*) entrer dans; (*a school, the army, etc.*) entrer à; (*e.g., a period of convalescence*) entrer en; (*a highway, a public square, etc.*) déboucher sur; (*e.g., a club*) devenir membre de; (*a request*) enregistrer, consigner par écrit; (*a student, a contestant, etc.*) admettre, faire inscrire; (*in the customhouse*) déclarer; (*to make a record of*) inscrire, porter; **to enter one's name for** se faire inscrire à or pour ‖ *intr* entrer; (theat) entrer en scène; **to enter into** entrer à, dans, or en; (*to be an ingredient of*) entrer pour; **to enter on** or **upon** entreprendre, débuter dans

enterprise [`ɛntər,praɪz] *s* (*undertaking*) entreprise *f;* (*spirit, push*) esprit *m* d'entreprise, allant *m*, entrain *m*

enterprising [`ɛntər,praɪzɪŋ] *adj* entreprenant

entertain [,ɛntər'ten] *tr* (*to distract*) amuser, divertir; (*to show hospitality to*) recevoir; (*at a meal*) régaler; (*a hope*) entretenir, nourrir; (*an idea*) concevoir ‖ *intr* recevoir

entertainer [,ɛntər'tenər] *s* (*host*) hôte *m*, amphitryon *m* amuseur *m;* (*comedian*) comique *mf*

entertaining [,ɛntər'tenɪŋ] *adj* amusant, divertissant

entertainment [,ɛntər'tenmənt] *s* (*distraction*) amusement *m*, divertissement *m;* (*show*) spectacle *m;* (*as a guest*) accueil *m*, hospitalité *f*

en′tertain′ment tax′ *s* taxe *f* sur les spectacles

enthrall [ɛn'θrɔl] *tr* (*to charm*) captiver, charmer; (*to enslave*) asservir, rendre esclave

enthrone [ɛn'θron] *tr* introniser

enthuse [ɛn'θ(j)uz] *tr* (coll) enthousiasmer ‖ *intr* (coll) s'enthousiasmer

enthusiasm [ɛn'θ(j)uzɪ,æzəm] *s* enthousiasme *m*

enthusiast [ɛn'θ(j)uzɪ,æst] *s* enthousiaste *mf;* (*camera fiend, sports fan, etc.*) fanatique *mf*, enragé *m*

enthusiastic [ɛn,θ(j)uzɪ'æstɪk] *adj* enthousiaste; (*for sports, music, a hobby*) fanatique, enragé

entice [ɛn'taɪs] *tr* attirer, séduire; (*to evil*) tenter, chercher à séduire

enticement [ɛn'taɪsmənt] *s* attrait *m*, appât *m;* tentation *f*, séduction *f*

entire [ɛn'taɪr] *adj* entier

entirely [ɛn'taɪrli] *adv* entièrement, en entier; (*absolutely*) tout à fait, absolument

entire•ty [ɛn'taɪrti] *s* (*pl* **-ties**) totalité *f*, entier *m;* **in its entirety** dans sa totalité

entitle [ɛn'taɪtəl] *tr* (*to name*) intituler; (*to qualify*) donner le droit à; **to be entitled to** avoir droit à

enti•ty [ˈɛntɪti] *s* (*pl* **-ties**) entité *f*

entomb [ɛnˈtum] *tr* ensevelir

entombment [ɛnˈtummənt] *s* ensevelissement *m*

entomology [ˌɛntəˈmɑlədʒi] *s* entomologie *f*

entourage [ˌɑntuˈrɑʒ] *s* entourage *m*

entrails [ˈɛntrelz] *spl* entrailles *fpl*

entrain [ɛnˈtren] *tr* faire prendre le train, embarquer; (*to carry along*) entraîner ‖ *intr* embarquer, s'embarquer

entrance [ˈɛntrəns] *s* entrée *f;* (theat) entrée en scène; **entrance to . . .** (public sign) accès à . . . ‖ [ɛnˈtræns], [ɛnˈtrɑns] *tr* enchanter, ensorceler; **to be entranced** s'extasier

en′trance examina′tion *s* examen *m* d'entrée

en′trance fee′ *s* prix *m* d'entrée, droit *m* d'entrée

entrancing [ɛnˈtrænsɪŋ] *adj* enchanteur, ensorceleur

entrant [ˈɛntrənt] *s* inscrit *m;* (*in a competition*) concurrent *m*, participant *m*

en•trap [ɛnˈtræp] *v* (*pret & pp* **-trapped;** *ger* **-trapping**) *tr* attraper

entreat [ɛnˈtrit] *tr* supplier, prier, conjurer

entreat•y [ɛnˈtriti] *s* (*pl* **-ies**) supplication *f,* prière *f*

entree [ˈantre] *s* (*entrance; course preceding the roast*) entrée *f;* (*main dish*) plat *m* de résistance

entrench [ɛnˈtrɛntʃ] *tr* retrancher; **to be entrenched** se retrancher ‖ *intr*—**to entrench on** *ou* **upon** empiéter sur

entrust [ɛnˈtrʌst] *tr*—**to entrust s.o. with s.th., to entrust s.th. to s.o.** confier q.ch. à qn

en•try [ˈɛntri] *s* (*pl* **-tries**) entrée *f;* (*in a dictionary*) article *m*, entrée; (*on a register*) inscription *f;* (*in a competition*) concurrent *m*, participant *m;* (*thing entered for judging in a competition*) objet *m* exposé

en′try blank′ *s* feuille *f* d'inscription

en′try lev′el *s* (comp) gamme *f* de l'entrée

en′try vi′sa *s* visa *m* d'entrée

en′try word′ *s* (*of a dictionary*) mot *m* d'entrée, mot-souche *m*, entrée *f,* adresse *f*

entwine [ɛnˈtwaɪn] *tr* entrelacer, enlacer ‖ *intr* s'entrelacer, s'enlacer

enumerate [ɪˈn(j)umə,ret] *tr* énumérer

enunciate [ɪˈnʌnsɪ,et] *tr* énoncer, déclarer; (*to articulate*) articuler, prononcer

envelop [ɛnˈvɛləp] *tr* envelopper

envelope [ˈɛnvə,lop], [ˈɑnvə,lop] *s* enveloppe *f;* **in an envelope** sous enveloppe, sous pli

envenom [ɛnˈvɛnəm] *tr* envenimer, empoisonner

enviable [ˈɛnvɪ•əbəl] *adj* enviable, digne d'envie

envious [ˈɛnvɪ•əs] *adj* envieux

environment [ɛnˈvaɪrənmənt] *s* environnement *m*, milieu *m*

environmental [ɛn,vaɪrənˈməntəl] *adj* écologique, du milieu

envir′onmen′tal pollu′tion *s* pollution *f* de l'environnement

environs [ɛnˈvaɪrənz] *spl* environs *mpl*

envisage [ɛnˈvɪzɪdʒ] *tr* envisager

envoi [ˈɛnvɔɪ] *s* envoi *m*

envoy [ˈɛnvɔɪ] *s* envoyé *m*, émissaire *m;* (*of poem*) envoi *m*

en•vy [ˈɛnvi] *s* (*pl* **-vies**) envie *f* ‖ *v* (*pret & pp* **-vied**) *tr* envier

enzyme [ˈɛnzaɪm] *s* enzyme *m & f*

epaulet [ˈɛpə,lɛt] *s* épaulette *f*

epergne [ɪˈpʌrn], [eˈpɛrn] *s* surtout *m*

ephemeral [ɪˈfɛmərəl] *adj* éphémère

epic [ˈɛpɪk] *adj* épique ‖ *s* épopée *f*

epicure [ˈɛpɪ,kjʊr] *s* gourmet *m*, gastronome *m*

epicurean [ˌɛpɪkjuˈri•ən] *adj & s* épicurien

epidemic [ˌɛpɪˈdɛmɪk] *adj* épidémique ‖ *s* épidémie *f*

epidemiology [ˌɛpɪ,dimɪˈɑlədʒi] *s* épidémiologie *f*

epidermis [ˌɛpɪˈdʌrmɪs] *s* épiderme *m*

epiglottis [ˌɛpɪˈglɑtɪs] *s* épiglotte *f*

epigram [ˈɛpɪ,græm] *s* épigramme *f*

epilepsy [ˈɛpɪ,lɛpsi] *s* épilepsie *f*

epileptic [ˌɛpɪˈlɛptɪk] *adj & s* épileptique *mf*

epilogue [ˈɛpɪ,lɔg] *s* épilogue *m*

episcopal [ɪˈpɪskəpəl] *adj* épiscopal

Episcopalian [ɪ,pɪskəˈpeli•ən] *adj* épiscopal ‖ *s* épiscopal *m*

episode [ˈɛpɪ,sod] *s* épisode *m*

episodic [ˌɛpɪˈsɑdɪk] *adj* épisodique

epistle [ɪˈpɪsəl] *s* épître *f*

epitaph [ˈɛpɪ,tæf] *s* épitaphe *f*

epithet [ˈɛpɪ,θɛt] *s* épithète *f*

epitome [ɪˈpɪtəmi] *s* (*abridgment*) épitomé *m;* (*representative of a class*) modèle *m*, personnification *f*

epitomize [ɪˈpɪtə,maɪz] *tr* abréger; personnifier

epoch [ˈipak] *s* époque *f*

epochal [ˈɛpəkəl] *adj* mémorable

ep′och-mak′ing *adj* qui fait époque

epoxy [ɪˈpɑksi] *s* résine *f* époxyde

Ep′som salts′ [ˈɛpsəm] *spl* epsomite *f*, sels *mpl* d'Epsom

equable [ˈɛkwəbəl], [ˈikwəbəl] *adj* uniforme, égal; tranquille

equal [ˈikwəl] *adj* égal; **to be equal to** égaler, valoir; (*e.g., the occasion*) être à la hauteur de; **to be equal to** + *ger* être de force à + *inf*, être à même de + *inf;* **to get equal with** (coll) se venger de ‖ *s* égal *m*, pareil *m* ‖ *v* (*pret & pp* **equaled** *ou* **equalled;** *ger* **equaling** *ou* **equalling**) *tr* égaler

equali•ty [ɪˈkwɑlɪti] *s* (*pl* **-ties**) égalité *f*

equalize [ˈikwə,laɪz] *tr* égaliser

equally [ˈikwəli] *adv* également

e′qual opportu′nity *s* chances *fpl* égales

equanimity [ˌikwəˈnɪmɪti] *s* équanimité *f,* égalité *f* d'âme

equate [ɪˈkwet] *tr* égaliser, mettre en équation

equation [ɪˈkweʒən] *s* équation *f*

equator [ɪˈkwetər] *s* équateur *m*

equatorial [ˌikwəˈtori•əl] *adj* équatorial

equestrian [ɪˈkwɛstrɪ•ən] *adj* équestre ‖ *s* cavalier *m*, écuyer *m*

equilateral [‚ikwɪg'lætərəl] *adj* équilatéral

equilibrium [‚ikwɪ'lɪbriˑəm] *s* équilibre *m*

equinoctial [‚ikwɪ'nakʃəl] *adj* équinoxial

equinox ['ikwɪ‚naks] *s* équinoxe *m*

equip [ɪ'kwɪp] *v* (*pret* & *pp* **equipped;** *ger* **equipping**) *tr* équiper, outiller; **to equip with** munir de

equipment [ɪ'kwɪpmənt] *s* équipement *m*, matériel *m*, appareillage *m*

equipoise ['ikwɪ‚pɔɪz], ['ɛkwɪ‚pɔɪz] *s* équilibre *m* ‖ *tr* équilibrer

equitable ['ɛkwɪtəbəl] *adj* équitable

equi‧ty ['ɛkwɪti] *s* (*pl* **-ties**) équité *f;* (com) part *f* résiduaire

equivalent [ɪ'kwɪvələnt] *adj* & *s* équivalent *m*

equivocal [ɪ'kwɪvəkəl] *adj* équivoque

equivocate [ɪ'kwɪvə‚ket] *intr* équivoquer

equivocation [ɪ‚kwɪvə'keʃən] *s* tergiversation *f,* équivoque *f*

ER *abbr* **emergency room**

era ['ɪrə] *s* ère *f,* époque *f*

eradicate [ɪ'rædɪ‚ket] *tr* déraciner, extirper

erase [ɪ'res] *tr* effacer, biffer

eraser [ɪ'resər] *s* gomme *f* à effacer; brosse *f*

erasure [ɪ're‚ʃər] *s* effacement *m,* rature *f*

ere [ɛr] *prep* (poetic) avant ‖ *conj* (poetic) avant que

erect [ɪ'rɛkt] *adj* droit, debout ‖ *tr* (*to set in an upright position*) dresser, élever; (*a building*) ériger, édifier; (*a machine*) monter

erection [ɪ'rɛkʃən] *s* érection *f*

erg [ʌrg] *s* erg *m*

ermine ['ʌrmɪn] *s* hermine *f*

erode [ɪ'rod] *tr* éroder

erosion [ɪ'roʒən] *s* érosion *f*

erotic [ɪ'ratɪk] *adj* érotique

err [ʌr] *intr* se tromper, faire erreur, errer; (*to do wrong*) s'égarer, pécher

errand ['ɛrənd] *s* commission *f,* course *f;* **to go on** or **to run an errand** faire une course

er‧rand boy‧ *s* coursier *m,* garçon *m* de courses

erratic [ɪ'rætɪk] *adj* variable; capricieux, excentrique

erroneous [ɪ'roniˑəs] *adj* erroné

error ['ɛrər] *s* erreur *f*

erudite ['ɛr(j)ʊ‚daɪt] *adj* érudit

erudition [‚ɛr(j)ʊ'dɪʃən] *s* érudition *f*

erupt [ɪ'rʌpt] *intr* faire éruption

eruption [ɪ'rʌpʃən] *s* éruption *f*

escalate ['ɛskə‚let] *tr* escalader

escalation [‚ɛskə'leʃən] *s* escalade *f*

escalator ['ɛskə‚letər] *s* escalator *m,* escalier *m* mécanique ou roulant

es‧calator clause‧ *s* clause *f* d'indexation

escallop [ɛs'kæləp] *s* (*seafood*) coquille *f* Saint-Jacques, peigne *m,* pétoncle *m;* (culin) coquille au gratin ‖ *tr* (culin) gratiner et cuire au four et à la crème; (culin) servir en coquille

escapade [‚ɛskə'ped] *s* fredaine *f,* frasque *f;* (*getting away*) escapade *f*

escape [ɛs'kep] *s* (*getaway*) évasion *f,* fuite *f;* (*from responsibilities, duties, etc.*) évasion, escapade *f;* (*of gas, liquid, etc.*) échappement *m,* fuite; (*of a clock*) échappement; **to have a narrow escape** l'échapper belle; **to make one's escape** se sauver, s'échapper ‖ *tr* échapper à, éviter ‖ *intr* échapper, s'échapper, s'évader; **to escape from** échapper à

escape‧ clause‧ *s* échappatoire *f*

escapee [‚ɛskə'pi] *s* évadé *m,* échappé *m*

escape‧ hatch‧ *s* (aer) sas *m* d'évacuation

escape‧ lit'erature *s* littérature *f* d'évasion

escapement [ɛs'kepmənt] *s* issue *f,* débouché *m;* (mach) échappement *m*

escape‧ wheel‧ *s* roue *f* de rencontre

escarole ['ɛskə‚rol] *s* scarole *f*

escarpment [ɛs'karpmənt] *s* escarpement *m*

eschew [ɛs't ʃu] *tr* éviter, s'abstenir de

escort [ɛs'kɔrt] *s* escorte *f;* (*gentleman escort*) cavalier *m* ‖ ['ɛs'kɔrt] *tr* escorter

escutcheon [ɛs'kʌtʃən] *s* écusson *m*

Eski‧mo ['ɛskɪ‚mo] *adj* eskimo, esquimau ‖ *s* (*pl* **-mos** or **-mo**) (*language; dog*) esquimau *m;* (*person*) Eskimo *m,* Esquimau *m*

Es'kimo wom'an *s* Esquimaude *f,* femme *f* esquimau

esopha‧gus [i'safəgəs] *s* (*pl* **-gi** [‚dʒaɪ]) œsophage *m*

esoteric [‚ɛso'tɛrɪk] *adj* ésotérique

espalier [ɛs'pæljər] *s* espalier *m*

especial [ɛs'pɛʃəl] *adj* spécial

especially [ɛs'pɛʃəli] *adv* surtout, particulièrement

Esperanto [‚ɛspə'ranto] *s* espéranto *m*

espionage [‚ɛspiˑə'naʒ] *s* espionnage *m*

espousal [ɛs'pauzəl] *s* épousailles *f;* **espousal of** (*a cause*) adoption de, adhésion à

espouse [ɛs'pauz] *tr* épouser; (*to advocate, adopt*) adopter, embrasser

Esq. *abbr* (**Esquire**) —**John Smith, Esq.** Monsieur Jean Smith (*qui est avocat*)

esquire ['ɛskwaɪr] *s* (hist) écuyer *m*

essay ['ɛse] *s* essai *m* ‖ *tr* essayer

essayist ['ɛseˑɪst] *s* essayiste *mf*

essence ['ɛsəns] *s* essence *f*

essential [ɛ'sɛnʃəl] *adj* & *s* essentiel *m*

essentially [ə'sɛnʃəli] *adv* essentiellement, avant tout, au premier chef

establish [ɛs'tæblɪʃ] *tr* établir

establishment [ɛs'tæblɪʃmənt] *s* établissement *m;* **the Establishment** (pol) les pouvoirs *mpl* établis, les milieux *mpl* dirigeants

estate [ɛs'tet] *s* (*landed property*) domaine *m,* propriété *f,* terres *fpl;* (*a person's possessions*) biens *mpl,* possessions *fpl;* (*left by a decedent*) héritage *m,* succession *f;* (*social status*) rang *m,* condition *f;* (hist) état *m*

esteem [ɛs'tim] *s* estime *f* ‖ *tr* estimer

esthete ['ɛsθit] *s* esthète *mf*

esthetic [ɛs'θɛtɪk] *adj* esthétique ‖ **esthetics** *s* esthétique *f*

estimable ['ɛstɪməbəl] *adj* estimable

estimate ['ɛstɪ‚met] *s* évaluation *f,* appréciation *f;* (*appraisal*) estimation *f* ‖ *tr* (*to judge, deem*) apprécier, estimer; (*the cost*) estimer, évaluer

estimation [,ɛstɪ'meʃən] *s* (*opinion*) jugement *m;* (*esteem*) estime *f;* (*appraisal*) estimation *f;* **in my estimation** à mon avis

estrangement [ɛs'trendʒmənt] *s* éloignement *m;* (*a becoming unfriendly*) désaffection *f*

estuar·y ['ɛstʃʊˌɛri] *s* (*pl* **-ies**) estuaire *m*

etc. *abbr* (Lat **et cetera** and so on) et c., et ainsi de suite

etch [ɛtʃ] *tr & intr* graver à l'eau-forte

etcher ['ɛtʃər] *s* aquafortiste *m*

etching ['ɛtʃɪŋ] *s* eau-forte *f*

eternal [ɪ'tʌrnəl] *adj* éternel

eterni·ty [ɪ'tʌrnɪti] *s* (*pl* **-ties**) éternité *f*

ether ['iθər] *s* éther *m*

ethereal [ɪ'θɪrɪ·əl] *adj* éthéré

ethical ['ɛθɪkəl] *adj* éthique

ethics ['ɛθɪks] *s* (*branch of philosophy*) étique *f,* morale *f;* spl (*one's conduct, one's moral principles*) morale

eth'ics commit'tee *s* commission *f* d'éthique

Ethiopia [,iθɪ'opɪ·ə] *s* Éthiopie *f;* l'Éthiopie

Ethiopian [,iθɪ'opɪ·ən] *adj* éthiopien ‖ *s* (*language*) éthiopien *m;* (*person*) Éthiopien *m*

ethnic(al) ['ɛθnɪk(əl)] *adj* ethnique

ethnography [ɛθ'nɑgrəfi] *s* ethnographie *f*

ethnology [ɛθ'nɑlədʒi] *s* ethnologie *f*

ethyl ['ɛθɪl] *s* éthyle *m*

ethylene ['ɛθɪˌlin] *s* éthylène *m*

etiquette ['ɛtɪˌkɛt] *s* étiquette *f*

etymolo·gy [,ɛtɪ'mɑlədʒi] *s* (*pl* **-gies**) étymologie *f*

ety·mon ['ɛtɪˌmɑn] *s* (*pl* **-mons** or **-ma** [mə]) étymon *m*

eucalyp·tus [ˌjukə'lɪptəs] *s* (*pl* **-tuses** or **-ti** [taɪ]) eucalyptus *m*

Eucharist ['jukərɪst] *s* Eucharistie *f*

euchre ['jukər] *s* euchre *m* ‖ *tr* (coll) l'emporter sur

eugenics [ju'dʒɛnɪks] *s* eugénisme *m or* eugénique *f*

eulogize ['julə,dʒaɪz] *tr* faire l'éloge de

eulo·gy ['julədʒi] *s* (*pl* **-gies**) éloge *m*

eunuch ['junək] *s* eunuque *m*

euphemism ['jufɪˌmɪzəm] *s* euphémisme *m*

euphemistic [,jufɪ'mɪstɪk] *adj* euphémique

euphonic [ju'fɑnɪk] *adj* euphonique

eupho·ny ['jufəni] *s* (*pl* **-nies**) euphonie *f*

euphoria [ju'forɪ·ə] *s* euphorie *f*

euphuism ['jufjuˌɪzəm] *s* euphuisme *m;* préciosité *f*

euro ['juro] *s* (*principal currency of the European Union*) euro *m*

Eurodollar ['juro'dɑlər] *s* eurodollar *m*

Europe ['jurəp] *s* Europe *f;* l'Europe

European [,jurə'pi·ən] *adj* européen ‖ *s* Européen *m*

Europe'an Econom'ic Commun'ity *s* Communauté *f* économique européenne (CEE)

Europe'an Un'ion *s* Union *f* européenne

euthanasia [,juθə'neʒə] *s* euthanasie *f*

evacuate [ɪ'vækjuˌet] *tr* évacuer ‖ *intr* s'évacuer

evade [ɪ'ved] *tr* échapper à, éviter, esquiver ‖ *intr* s'évader

evaluate [ɪ'væljuˌet] *tr* évaluer

Evangel [ɪ'vændʒəl] *s* évangile *m*

evangelic(al) [,ɛvən'dʒɛlɪk(əl)] *adj* évangélique

evangelist [ɪ'vændʒəlɪst] *s* évangéliste *m*

evaporate [ɪ'væpəˌret] *tr* évaporer ‖ *intr* s'évaporer

evasion [ɪ'veʒən] *s* évasion *f;* subterfuge *m,* détour *m*

evasive [ɪ'vesɪv] *adj* évasif

eve [iv] *s* veille *f;* (poetic) soir *m;* **on the eve of** à la veille de; **Eve** Éve *f*

even ['ivən] *adj* (*smooth*) uni; (*number*) pair; (*equal, uniform*) égal; (*temperament*) calme, rassis, égal; **even with** à fleur de; **to be even** être quitte; (cards, sports) être manche à manche *or* point à point; **to get even with** (coll) rendre la pareille à ‖ *adv* même; **even + comp** encore **+ comp,** e.g., **even better** encore mieux; **even so** quand même ‖ *tr* aplanir, égaliser

evening ['ivnɪŋ] *adj* du soir ‖ *s* soir *m;* **all evening** toute la soirée; **every evening** tous les soirs; **in the evening** le soir; **the evening before** la veille au soir

eve'ning clothes' *s* tenue *f* de soirée; (*for women*) toilette *f* de soirée; (*for men*) habit *m* de soirée

eve'ning damp' *s* serein *m*

eve'ning gown' *s* robe *f* du soir

eve'ning prim'rose *s* onagraire *f*

eve'ning star' *s* étoile *f* du soir, étoile du berger

eve'ning wrap' *s* sortie *f* de bal

e'ven·song' *s* (eccl) vêpres *fpl*

event [ɪ'vɛnt] *s* événement *m;* **at all events** or **in any event** en tout cas; **in the event that** dans le cas où

eventful [ɪ'vɛntfəl] *adj* mouvementé; mémorable

eventual [ɪ'vɛntʃʊ·əl] *adj* final

eventuali·ty [ɪˌvɛntʃʊ'ælɪti] *s* (*pl* **-ties**) éventualité *f*

eventually [ɪ'vɛntʃʊ·əli] *adv* finalement, à la longue, en fin de compte

eventuate [ɪ'vɛntʃʊˌet] *intr*—**to eventuate in** se terminer par, aboutir à

ever ['ɛvər] *adv* (*at all times*) toujours; (*at any time*) jamais; **ever since** dès lors, depuis; **for ever and ever** à tout jamais; **hardly ever** presque jamais

ev'er·glade' *s* région *f* marécageuse

ev'er·green' *adj* toujours vert ‖ *s* arbre *m* vert, conifère *m;* **evergreens** plantes *fpl* vertes, verdure *f* décorative

ev'er·last'ing *adj* éternel; (*continual*) sempiternel, perpétuel

ev'er·more' *adv* toujours; **for evermore** à jamais

every ['ɛvri] *adj* tous les; (*each*) chaque, tout; (coll) tout, e.g., **every bit as good as** tout aussi bon que; **every man for himself** sauve qui peut; **every now and then** de temps en temps; **every once in a while** de temps à autre; **every other day** tous les deux jours; **every other one** un sur deux; **every which way** (coll) de tous côtés; (coll) en désordre

ev′ery•bod′y *pron indef* tout le monde

ev′ery•day′ *adj* de tous les jours

ev′ery•man′ *s* Monsieur Tout-le-monde

ev′ery man′ Jack′ of them′ *ou* ev′ery moth′-er's son′ *s* tous tant qu'ils sont, tous sans exception

ev′ery•one′ or ev′ery one′ *pron indef* chacun, tous, tout le monde

ev′ery•thing′ *pron indef* tout

ev′ery•where′ *adv* partout, de toutes parts; partout où; **everywhere else** partout ailleurs

evict [ɪ′vɪkt] *tr* évincer, expulser

eviction [ɪ′vɪkʃən] *s* éviction *f*

evidence [′ɛvɪdəns] *s* évidence *f;* (*proof*) preuve *f,* témoignage *m* ‖ *tr* manifester, démontrer

evident [′ɛvɪdənt] *adj* évident

evidently [′ɛvɪdəntli] *adv* évidemment

evil [′ivəl] *adj* mauvais, méchant ‖ *s* mal *m,* méchanceté *f*

evildoer [′ivəl,duəͻr] *s* malfaisant *m,* méchant *m*

e′vil-do′ing *s* malfaisance *f*

e′vil eye′ *s* mauvais œil *m*

e′vil-mind′ed *adj* malintentionné, malin

E′vil One′ *s* Esprit *m* malin

evince [ɪ′vɪns] *tr* montrer, manifester

evocative [ɪ′vɑkətɪv] *adj* évocateur

evoke [ɪ′vok] *tr* évoquer

evolution [,ɛvə′luʃən] *s* évolution *f*

evolve [ɪ′vɑlv] *tr* développer, élaborer ‖ *intr* évoluer

ewe [ju] *s* brebis *f*

ewer [′juəͻr] *s* aiguière *f*

ex [ɛks] *s* (*pl* **exes** [′ɛksɪz]) la lettre X; (coll) ex *mf* (*ex-époux ou ex-épouse; personne avec qui on a eu des relations amoureuses, maintenant terminées*)

ex- [ɛks] *adj* (*former*), ex-, e.g., **the ex-premier** le ex-ministre

exact [ɛg′zækt] *adj* exact ‖ *tr* exiger

exacting [ɛg′zæktɪŋ] *adj* exigeant

exactly [ɛg′zæktli] *adv* exactement; (*sharp, on the dot*) précisément, justement

exactness [ɛg′zæktnɪs] *s* exactitude *f*

exaggerate [ɛg′zædʒə,ret] *tr* exagérer

exalt [ɛg′zɔlt] *tr* exalter

exam [ɛg′zæm] *s* (coll) examen *m*

examination [ɛg,zæmɪ′neʃən] *s* examen *m;* **to take an examination** se présenter à, passer, *or* subir un examen

examine [ɛg′zæmɪn] *tr* examiner

examiner [ɛg′zæmɪnər] *s* inspecteur *m,* vérificateur *m;* (*in a school*) examinateur *m*

example [ɛg′zæmpəl] *s* exemple *m;* **for example** par exemple

exasperate [ɛg′zæspə,ret] *tr* exaspérer

exasperation [ɛg,zæspə′reʃən] *s* exaspération *f*

excavate [′ɛkskə,vet] *tr* excaver

exceed [ɛk′sid] *tr* excéder

exceedingly [ɛk′sidɪŋli] *adv* extrêmement

ex•cel [ɛk′sɛl] *v* (*pret & pp* -**celled;** *ger* -**celling**) *tr* surpasser ‖ *intr* exceller; **to excel in** exceller dans; **to excel in** + *ger* exceller à + *inf*

excellence [′ɛksələns] *s* excellence *f*

excellen•cy [′ɛksələnsi] *s* (*pl* -**cies**) excellence *f;* **Your Excellency** Votre Excellence

excelsior [ɛk′sɛlsɪəͻr] *s* copeaux *mpl* d'emballage

except [ɛk′sɛpt] *adv*—**except for** excepté; **except that** excepté que ‖ *prep* excepté, sauf ‖ *tr* excepter

exception [ɛk′sɛpʃən] *s* exception *f;* **to take exception to** trouver à redire à; **with the exception of** à l'exception de

exceptional [ɛk′sɛpʃənəl] *adj* exceptionnel

excerpt [′ɛksʌrpt] *s* extrait *m,* citation *f* ‖ [ɛk′sʌrpt] *tr* extraire

excess [′ɛksɛs] *adj* excédentaire ‖ [ɛk′sɛs] *s* (*amount or degree*) excédent *m,* excès *m;* (*excessive amount; immoderate indulgence*) excès *m;* **in excess of** en plus de

ex′cess bag′gage *s* excédent *m* de bagages

ex′cess fare′ *s* supplément *m*

excessive [ɛk′sɛsɪv] *adj* excessif

ex′cess-prof′its tax′ *s* contribution *f* sur les bénéfices extraordinaires

ex′cess weight′ *s* excédent *m* de poids

exchange [ɛks′tʃendʒ] *s* échange *m;* (*barter*) troc *m;* (com) bourse *f;* (telp) central *m;* **in exchange for** en contrepartie de ‖ *tr* échanger; (*to barter*) troquer; **to exchange compliments** échanger des politesses; **to exchange for** échanger contre, échanger pour

exchange′ rate′ *s* taux *m* de change

exchequer [′ɛkstʃɛkər] *s* trésor *m* public; ministère *m* des finances; (hist) échiquier *m*

excise [′ɛksaɪz] *s* contributions *fpl* indirectes ‖ *tr* effacer, rayer; (surg) exciser

excitable [ɛk′saɪtəbəl] *adj* excitable

excite [ɛk′saɪt] *tr* exciter

excited *adj* agité, surexcité; **don't get excited!** ne vous énervez pas!; **to get excited** s'emballer; **to get excited about** se passionner de or pour

excitement [ɛk′saɪtmənt] *m* agitation *f,* excitation *f*

exciting [ɛk′saɪtɪŋ] *adj* émotionnant, entraînant, passionnant

exclaim [ɛks′klem] *tr* s'écrier, e.g., **"All is lost!" he exclaimed** "Tout est perdu!" s'écria-t-il ‖ *intr* s'exclamer, se récrier

exclamation [,ɛksklə′meʃən] *s* exclamation *f*

exclama′tion mark′ *s* point *m* d'exclamation

exclude [ɛks′klud] *tr* exclure

excluding [ɛks′kludɪŋ] *prep* á l'exclusion de, sans compter

exclusion [ɛks′kluʒən] *s* exclusion *f*

exclusive [ɛks′klusɪv] *adj* exclusif; (*expensive; fashionable*) (coll) choisi, select; **exclusive of** á l'exclusion de

exclu′sive rights′ *spl* exclusivité *f*

exclu′sive show′ing *s* (public sign in front of a theater) en exclusivité

excommunicate [ˌɛkskəˈmjunɪˌket] *tr* excommunier

excommunication [ˌɛkskəˌmjunɪˈkeʃən] *s* excommunication *f*

excoriate [ɛksˈkorɪˌet] *tr* (fig) vitupérer

excrement [ˈɛkskrəmənt] *s* excrément *m*

excruciating [ɛksˈkruʃɪˌetɪŋ] *adj* affreux, atroce

exculpate [ˈɛkskʌlˌpet] *tr* disculper

excursion [ɛksˈkʌrʒən] *s* excursion *f*

excusable [ɛksˈkjuzəbəl] *adj* excusable

excuse [ɛksˈkjus] *s* excuse *f* ‖ [ɛksˈkjuz] *tr* excuser; **excuse me!** pardon!, je m'excuse!, **to excuse oneself** s'excuser

execrate [ˈɛksɪˌkret] *tr* exécrer; (*to curse*) maudire

execute [ˈɛksɪˌkjut] *tr* exécuter

execution [ˌɛksɪˈkjuʃən] *s* exécution *f*

executioner [ˌɛksɪˈkjuʃənər] *s* bourreau *m*

executive [ɛgˈzɛkjətɪv] *adj* (*powers*) exécutif; (*position*) administratif ‖ *s* exécutif *m*; (*of school, business, etc.*) directeur *m*, administrateur *m*

Exec′utive Man′sion *s* (U.S.A.) demeure *f* du Président

executor [ɛgˈzɛkjətər] *s* exécuteur *m* testamentaire

executrix [ɛgˈzɛkjətrɪks] *s* exécutrice *f* testamentaire

exemplary [ˈɛgzəmˌplɛri] *adj* exemplaire

exempli•fy [ɛgˈzɛmplɪˌfaɪ] *v* (*pret & pp* **-fied**) *tr* démontrer par des exemples; (*to be a model of*) servir d'exemple à

exempt [ɛgˈzɛmpt] *adj* exempt ‖ *tr* exempter

exemption [ɛgˈzɛmpʃən] *s* exemption *f*; **exemptions** (*from taxes*) déductions *fpl*

exercise [ˈɛksərˌsaɪz] *s* exercice *m*; **exercises** cérémonies *fpl* ‖ *tr* exercer ‖ *intr* s'exercer, s'entraîner

ex′ercise bi′cycle *s* bicyclette *f* d'entraînement, home-trainer *m*

exert [ɛgˈzʌrt] *tr* exercer; **to exert oneself** faire des efforts

exertion [ɛgˈzʌrʃən] *s* effort *m*; (*e.g., of power*) exercice *m*

exhalation [ˌɛksˈhəˈleʃən] *s* (*of air*) expiration *f*; (*of gas, vapors, etc.*) exhalaison *f*

exhale [ɛksˈhel] *tr* (*air from lungs*) expirer; (*gas, vapor*) exhaler ‖ *intr* expirer; s'exhaler

exhaust [ɛgˈzɔst] *s* (*system*) échappement *m*; (*fumes*) gaz *mpl* d'échappement ‖ *tr* épuiser; faire le vide dans

exhaust′ fan′ *s* ventilateur *m* aspirant

exhaust′ hood′ *s* hotte *f* aspirante

exhaustion [ɛgˈzɔstʃən] *s* épuisement *m*

exhaustive [ɛgˈzɔstɪv] *adj* exhaustif

exhaust′ man′ifold *s* tuyauterie *f* or collecteur *m* d'échappement

exhaust′ pipe′ *s* tuyau *m* d'échappement

exhaust′ valve′ *s* soupape *f* d'échappement

exhibit [ɛgˈzɪbɪt] *s* exhibition *f*; (*of art*) exposition *f*; (law) document *m* á l'appui, pièce *f* à conviction ‖ *tr* exhiber; (*e.g., pictures*) exposer ‖ *intr* faire une exposition

exhibition [ˌɛksɪˈbɪʃən] *s* exhibition *f*

ex′hibi′tion game′ *s* (sports) match *m* amical

exhibitionist [ˌɛksɪˈbɪʃənɪst] *s* exhibionniste *mf*

exhibitor [ɛgˈzɪbɪtər] *s* exposant *m*

exhilarate [ɛgˈzɪləˌret] *tr* égayer, animer

exhilarating [ɛgˈzɪləˌretɪŋ] *adj* stimulant, vivifiant, enivrant

exhort [ɛgˈzɔrt] *tr* exhorter

exhume [ɛksˈhjum] *tr* exhumer

exigen•cy [ˈɛksɪdʒənsi] *s* (*pl* **-cies**) exigence *f*

exigent [ˈɛksɪdʒənt] *adj* exigeant

exile [ˈɛgzaɪl] *s* exil *m*; (*person*) exilé *m* ‖ *tr* exiler

exist [ɛgˈzɪst] *intr* exister

existence [ɛgˈzɪstəns] *s* existence *f*

existing [ɛgˈzɪstɪŋ] *adj* existant, actuel

exit [ˈɛksɪt] *s* sortie *f* ‖ *intr* sortir

ex′it poll′ *s* (pol) sondage *m* post-isoloir

ex′it tax′i•way *s* (aer) bretelle *f* de liaison

exobiology [ˌɛksobaɪˈɑlədʒi] *s* exobiologie *f*

exodus [ˈɛksədəs] *s* exode *m*

exonerate [ɛgˈzanəˌret] *tr* (*to free from blame*) disculper; (*to free from an obligation*) exonérer, dispenser

exorbitant [ɛgˈzɔrbɪtənt] *adj* exorbitant

exorcize [ˈɛksɔrˌsaɪz] *tr* exorciser

exotic [ɛgˈzatɪk] *adj* exotique

expand [ɛksˈpænd] *tr* (*a gas, metal, etc.*) dilater; (*to enlarge, develop*) élargir, développer; (*to unfold, stretch out*) déplier, déployer; (*the chest*) gonfler; (math) développer ‖ *intr* se dilater; s'élargir, se développer; s'étendre, se déployer; se gonfler

expandable [ɛksˈpændəbəl] *adj* (comp) agrandissant

expanse [ɛksˈpæns] *s* étendue *f*

expansion [ɛksˈpænʃən] *s* expansion *f*

expan′sion joint′ *s* joint *m* de dilatation thermique

expansive [ɛksˈpænsɪv] *adj* expansif; (*broad*) large, étendu

expatiate [ɛksˈpeʃɪˌet] *intr* discourir, s'étendre

expatriate [ɛksˈpetrɪ•ɪt] *adj & s* expatrié *m* ‖ [ɛksˈpetrɪˌet] *tr* expatrier

expect [ɛksˈpɛkt] *tr* (*to await the coming of*) attendre; (*to look for as likely*) s'attendre à; **to expect it** s'y attendre; **to expect s.o. to** + *inf* s'attendre à ce que qn + *subj;* **to expect to** + *inf* s'attendre à + *inf*

expectan•cy [ɛksˈpɛktənsi] *s* (*pl* **-cies**) attente *f*, expectative *f*

expect′ant moth′er [ɛksˈpɛktənt] *s* future mère *f*

expectation [ˌɛkspɛkˈteʃən] *s* expectative *f*, espérance *f*

expectorate [ɛksˈpɛktəˌret] *tr & intr* expectorer

expedien•cy [ɛksˈpidɪ•ənsi] *s* (*pl* **-cies**) convenance *f*, opportunité *f*; opportunisme *m*, débrouillage *m*

expedient [ɛksˈpidɪ•ənt] *adj* expédient; (*looking out for oneself*) débrouillard ‖ *s* expédient *m*

expedite [ˈɛkspɪˌdaɪt] *tr* expédier

expedition [ˌɛkspɪˈdɪʃən] *s* expédition *f*; célérité *f*, promptitude *f*

expeditionary [ˌɛkspɪˈdɪʃənˌɛri] *adj* expéditionnaire

expeditious [ˌɛkspɪˈdɪʃəs] *adj* expéditif

ex·pel [ɛksˈpɛl] *v* (*pret & pp* **-pelled;** *ger* **-pelling**) *tr* expulser; (*from school*) renvoyer

expend [ɛksˈpɛnd] *tr* (*to pay out*) dépenser; (*to use up*) consommer

expendable [ɛksˈpɛndəbəl] *adj* non récupérable; (*soldier*) sacrifiable

expenditure [ɛksˈpɛndɪtʃər] *s* dépense *f*; consommation *f*

expense [ɛksˈpɛns] *s* dépense *f*; **at the expense of** aux dépens de; **expenses** frais *mpl*; (*for which a person will be reimbursed*) indemnité *f*; **to meet expenses** faire face aux dépenses

expense′ account′ *s* état *m* de frais, note *f* de frais

expensive [ɛksˈpɛnsɪv] *adj* cher, couteux; (*tastes*) dispendieux

experience [ɛksˈpɪri·əns] *s* expérience *f* ‖ *tr* éprouver

experienced *adj* expérimenté

experiment [ɛksˈpɛrɪmənt] *s* expérience *f* ‖ *intr* faire des expériences, expérimenter

experimental [ɪkˌspɛrəˈmɛntəl] *adj* expérimental, probatoire

expert [ˈɛkspərt] *adj & s* expert *m*

expertise [ˌɛkspərˈtiz] *s* maîtrise *f*, compétence *f*, adresse *f*

expiate [ˈɛkspɪˌet] *tr* expier

expiration [ˌɛkspəˈreʃən] *s* expiration *f*

ex′pira′tion date′ *s* date *f* d'échéance; (*pharm*) date de la perte de la force d'un médicament

expire [ɛksˈpaɪr] *tr & intr* expirer

expired *adj* (*lease; passport*) expiré; (*note; permit*) périmé; (*e.g., driver′s license*) suranné; (*insurance policy*) déchu

explain [ɛksˈplen] *tr* expliquer; **to explain oneself** s'expliquer ‖ *intr* expliquer

explainable [ɛksˈplenəbəl] *adj* explicable

explanation [ˌɛkspləˈneʃən] *s* explication *f*

explanatory [ɛksˈplænəˌtori] *adj* explicatif

explicit [ɛksˈplɪsɪt] *adj* explicite

explode [ɛksˈplod] *tr* faire sauter; (*a theory, opinion, etc.*) discréditer ‖ *intr* exploser, éclater, sauter

exploit [ˈɛksplɔɪt] *s* exploit *m* ‖ [ɛksˈplɔɪt] *tr* exploiter

exploitation [ˌɛksplɔɪˈteʃən] *s* exploitation *f*

exploration [ˌɛkspləˈreʃən] *s* exploration *f*

explore [ɛksˈplor] *tr* explorer

explorer [ɛksˈplorər] *s* explorateur *m*; (*boy scout*) routier *m*

explosion [ɛksˈploʒən] *s* explosion *f*

explosive [ɛksˈplosɪv] *adj* explosif; (*mixture*) explosible ‖ *s* explosif *m*

exponent [ɛksˈponənt] *s* interprète *mf*; (math) exposant *m*

export [ˈɛksport] *s* exportation *f* ‖ *tr & intr* exporter

exportation [ˌɛksporˈteʃən] *s* exportation *f*

exporter [ˈɛksportər] *s* exportateur *m*

expose [ɛksˈpoz] *tr* exposer; (*to unmask*) démasquer, dévoiler; (phot) impressionner

exposé [ˌɛkspoˈze] *s* dévoilement *m*, révélation *f*, mise *f* en lumière

exposition [ˌɛkspəˈzɪʃən] *s* exposition *f*

expostulate [ɛksˈpɑstʃəˌlet] *intr* faire des remontrances; **to expostulate with** faire des remontrances à

exposure [ɛksˈpoʒər] *s* exposition *f*; (*unmasking*) dévoilement *m*; (phot) exposition *f*, prise *f* de vue(s); (phot) durée *f* d'exposition, indice *m* de pose

expound [ɛksˈpaʊnd] *tr* exposer

ex-premier [ɛksˈprimˈir] *s* (pol) ex-ministre *m*

express [ɛksˈprɛs] *adj* exprès, formel; (*train; gun*) express ‖ *s* (*merchandise*) messagerie *f*; (*train*) express *m*, rapide *m*, train *m* direct; **by express** (rr) en grande vitesse ‖ *adv* (rr) en grande vitesse ‖ *tr* exprimer; (*merchandise*) envoyer en grande vitesse; (*through the express company*) expédier par les messageries; **to express oneself** s'exprimer

express′ com′pany *s* messageries *fpl*

express′ high′way *s* autoroute *f*

expression [ɛksˈprɛʃən] *s* expression *f*

expressive [ɛksˈprɛsɪv] *adj* expressif

expressly [ɛksˈprɛsli] *adv* exprès

express′man *s* (*pl* **-men**) entrepreneur *m* de messageries; facteur *m*, agent *m* d'un service de messageries

express′ train′ *s* train m express

express′ way′ *s* autoroute, route *f* express

expropriate [ɛksˈpropriˌet] *tr* exproprier

expulsion [ɛksˈpʌlʃən] *s* expulsion *f*; (*from schools*) renvoi *m*

expunge [ɛksˈpʌndʒ] *tr* effacer, supprimer, rayer

expurgate [ˈɛkspərˌget] *tr* expurger

exquisite [ˈɛkskwɪzɪt] *adj* exquis

ex-service·man [ˌɛksˈsʌrvɪsˌmæn] *s* (*pl* **-men′**) ancien combattant *m*

extant [ˈɛkstənt], [ɛksˈtænt] *adj* existant, subsistant

extemporaneous [ɛksˌtɛmpəˈreni·əs] *adj* improvisé, impromptu

extemporaneously [ɛksˌtɛmpəˈreni·əsli] *adv* à l'impromptu, d'abondance

extempore [ɛksˈtɛmpəri] *adj* improvisé ‖ *adv* d'abondance, à l'impromptu

extemporize [ɛksˈtɛmpəˌraɪz] *tr & intr* improviser

extend [ɛksˈtɛnd] *tr* (*to stretch out*) étendre; (*a period of time; a street; a line*) prolonger; (*a treaty; a session; a right; a due date*) proroger; (*a helping hand*) tendre ‖ *intr* s'étendre

extended *adj* étendu, prolongé

extend′ed fam′ily *s* communauté *f* familiale, famille *f* étendue

extension [ɛksˈtɛnʃən] *s* extension *f*; prolongation *f*; (*board for a table*) rallonge *f*; (*to build-*

ing) annexe *f;* (comp) extension *f;* (telp) poste *m*

exten'sion cord' *s* cordon *m* prolongateur, prolongateur *m,* rallonge *f*

exten'sion lad'der *s* échelle *f* à coulisse

exten'sion man'ager *s* (comp) gestion *f* d'extension

exten'sion ta'ble *s* table *f* à rallonges

exten'sion tel'ephone *s* appareil *m* supplémentaire

extensive [ɛksˈtɛnsɪv] *adj* vaste, étendu

extent [ɛksˈtɛnt] *s* étendue *f;* **to a certain extent** dans une certaine mesure; **to a great extent** en grande partie, considérablement; **to the full extent** dans toute la mesure

extenuate [ɛksˈtɛnjuˌet] *tr* atténuer; minimiser

exterior [ɛksˈtɪrɪˌər] *adj & s* extérieur *m*

exterminate [ɛksˈtʌrmɪˌnet] *tr* exterminer

external [ɛksˈtʌrnəl] *adj* extérieur; (pharm, med) externe ‖ **externals** *spl* dehors *mpl,* apparences *fpl;* (*superficialities*) choses *fpl* secondaires

extinct [ɛksˈtɪŋkt] *adj* (*volcano*) éteint; disparu; tombé en désuétude

extinction [ɛksˈtɪŋkʃən] *s* extinction *f*

extinguish [ɛksˈtɪŋgwɪʃ] *tr* éteindre

extinguisher [ɛksˈtɪŋgwɪʃər] *s* (*for candles*) éteignoir *m;* (*for fires*) extincteur *m*

extirpate [ˈɛkstərˌpet] *tr* extirper

ex•tol [ɛksˈtol] *v* (*pret & pp* **-tolled;** *ger* **-tolling**) *tr* exalter, vanter

extort [ɛksˈtɔrt] *tr* extorquer

extortion [ɛksˈtɔrʃən] *s* extorsion *f*

extortionist [ɛksˈtɔrʃənɪst] *s* extorqueur *m*

extra [ˈɛkstrə] *adj* supplémentaire; (*of high quality*) extra, extra-fin; (*spare*) de rechange ‖ *s* extra *m;* (*of a newspaper*) édition *f* spéciale; (*in building a new house*) rallonge *f;* (mov, theat) figurant *m* ‖ *adv* en plus, en sus; (*not on the bill*) non compris

ex'tra board' *s* (*for extension table*) rallonge *f*

ex'tra charge' *s* supplément *m*

extract [ˈɛkstrækt] *s* extrait *m* ‖ [ɛksˈtrækt] *tr* extraire

extraction [ɛksˈtrækʃən] *s* extraction *f*

extracurricular [ˌɛkstrəkəˈrɪkjələr] *adj* extrascolaire

extradite [ˈɛkstrəˌdaɪt] *tr* extrader

extradition [ˌɛkstrəˈdɪʃən] *s* extradition *f*

ex'tra-dry' *adj* (*champagne*) très sec

ex'tra fare' *s* supplément *m* de billet

ex'tra•galac'tic *adj* extragalactique

ex'tra•mu'ral *adj* à l'extérieur de la ville; à l'extérieur de l'université

extraneous [ɛksˈtrenɪˌəs] *adj* étranger

extraordinary [ɛksˈtrɔrdɪˌnɛri] *adj* extraordinaire

extrapolate [ɛksˈtræpəˌlet] *tr & intr* extrapoler

ex'tra•sen'sory *adj* extrasensoriel

ex'tra-spe'cial *adj* extra

ex'tra•terres'trial *adj* extraterrestre

extravagance [ɛksˈtrævəgəns] *s* (*lavishness*) prodigalité *f,* gaspillage *m;* (*folly*) extravagance *f*

extravagant [ɛksˈtrævəgənt] *adj* (*person*) dépensier, prodigue; (*price*) exorbitant; (*e.g., praise*) outré; (*e.g., claims*) exagéré, extravagant

extreme [ɛksˈtrim] *adj & s* extrême *m;* **in the extreme, to extremes** à l'extrême

extremely [ɛksˈtrimli] *adv* extrêmement

extreme' unc'tion *s* extrême-onction *f*

extremist [ɛksˈtrimɪst] *adj & s* extrémiste *mf,* ultra *mf*

extremi•ty [ɛksˈtrɛmɪti] *s* (*pl* **-ties**) extrémité *f;* **extremities** extrémités

extricate [ˈɛkstrɪˌket] *tr* dégager; (*a gas*) libérer; **to extricate oneself from** se tirer de, se dépêtrer de

extrinsic [ɛksˈtrɪnsɪk] *adj* extrinsèque

extrovert [ˈɛkstrəˌvʌrt] *adj & s* extraverti *m*

extrude [ɛksˈtrud] *intr* faire saillie, dépasser

exuberant [ɛgˈz(j)ubərənt] *adj* exubérant

exude [ɛgˈzud] *tr & intr* exsuder

exult [ɛgˈzʌlt] *intr* exulter

exultant [ɛgˈzʌltənt] *adj* triomphant

eye [aɪ] *s* œil *m;* (*of needle*) chas *m,* trou *m;* (*of hook and eye*) porte *f;* **eyes** *pl* yeux *mpl;* **to catch s.o.'s eye** tirer l'œil à qn; **to lay eyes on** jeter les yeux sur; **to make eyes at** (coll) faire les yeux doux à; **to see eye to eye with s.o.** voir les choses du même œil que qn; **with an eye to** en vue de; **without batting an eye** (coll) sans sourciller ‖ *v* (*pret & pp* **eyed;** *ger* **eying** *or* **eyeing**) *tr* toiser, reluquer

eye'ball' *s* globe *m* oculaire

eye' bank' *s* banque *f* des yeux

eye'bolt' *s* boulon *m* à œil

eye'brow' *s* sourcil *m*

eye'cup' *s* œillère *f*

eye' drops' *spl* collyre *m*

eye,' ear,' nose,' and throat' (*public sign*) yeux, nez, gorge, oreilles

eyeful [ˈaɪful] *s* vue *f,* coup *m* d'œil; **to get an eyeful** (coll) s'en mettre plein la vue, se rincer l'œil

eye'glass' *s* (*of optical instrument*) oculaire *m;* (*eyecup*) œillère *f;* **eyeglasses** lunettes *fpl*

eye'lash' *s* cil *m;* (*fringe of hair*) cils

eyelet [ˈaɪlɪt] *s* œillet *m;* (*of sail*) œil *m* de pie

eye'lid' *s* paupière *f*

eye' of the morn'ing *s* astre *m* du jour

eye' o'pener [ˈopənər] *s* révélation *f;* (coll) goutte *f* de bonne heure

eye'piece' *s* oculaire *m*

eye' shade' *s* visière *f,* abat-jour *m*

eye' shad'ow' *s* fard *m* à paupières

eye'shot' *s* portée *f* de la vue

eye'sight' *s* vue *f;* (*eyeshot*) portée *f* de la vue

eye' sock'et *s* orbite *f* de l'œil

eye'sore' *s* objet *m* déplaisant

eye′strain′ s fatigue f des yeux; **to suffer from eyestrain** avoir les yeux fatigués

eye′ test′ s examen m de la vision

eye′-test chart′ s tableau m de lecture pour la vision

eye′tooth′ s (pl **-teeth**) dent f œillère or canine; **to cut one's eyeteeth** (coll) ne pas être un blanc-bec; **to give one's eyeteeth for** (coll) donner la prunelle de ses yeux pour

eye′wash′ s collyre m; (slang) de l'eau bénite de cour, de la poudre aux yeux

eye′wit′ness s témoin m oculaire

ey•rie or **ey•ry** [ˈɛri] s (pl **-ries**) aire f (de l'aigle); (fig) nid m d'aigle

F

F, f [ɛf] s VIᵉ lettre de l'alphabet

fable [ˈfebəl] s fable f

fabric [ˈfæbrɪk] s tissu m, étoffe f

fabricate [ˈfæbrɪ͵ket] tr fabriquer

fabrication [͵fæbrɪˈkeʃən] s fabrication f; (lie) mensonge m

fabulous [ˈfæbjələs] adj fabuleux

façade [fəˈɑd] s façade f

face [fes] s visage m, figure f; (side) face f; (of the earth) surface f; (appearance, expression) mine f, physionomie f; **about face!** (mil) demi-tour! **to keep a straight face** montrer un front sérieux; **to lose face** perdre la face; **to make a face** faire une grimace; **to set one's face against** faire front à ‖ tr faire face à; (a wall) revêtir; (a garment) mettre un revers à ‖ intr—**to face about** faire demi-tour; **to face up to** faire face à, affronter

face′ card′ s figure f

face′-lift′ or **face′-lift′ing** s ridectomie f, déridage m, lissage m

face′ pack′ s masque m de beauté

face′ pow′der s poudre f de riz

facet [ˈfæsɪt] s facette f

facetious [fəˈsiʃəs] adj plaisant

face′ tow′el s serviette f de toilette

face′ val′ue s valeur f faciale, valeur nominale

facial [ˈfeʃəl] adj facial ‖ s massage m esthétique

fa′cial tis′sue s serviette f à démaquiller

facilitate [fəˈsɪlɪ͵tet] tr faciliter

facili•ty [fəˈsɪlɪti] s (pl **-ties**) facilité f; **facilities** installations fpl

facing [ˈfesɪŋ] s revêtement m; (of garment) revers m

facsimile [fækˈsɪmɪli] s fac-similé m

fact [fækt] s fait m; **in fact** en fait, de fait; **the fact is that** c'est que

faction [ˈfækʃən] s faction f; (strife) discorde f

factor [ˈfæktər] s facteur m ‖ tr résoudre or décomposer en facteurs

facto•ry [ˈfæktəri] s (pl **-ries**) usine f, fabrique f

fac′tory price′ s prix m de facture, prix usine

factual [ˈfæktʃʊ•əl] adj vrai, réel

facul•ty [ˈfækəlti] s (pl **-ties**) faculté f; (teaching staff) corps m enseignant

fad [fæd] s mode f, marotte f, lubie f; **latest fad** dernier cri m

fade [fed] tr déteindre, décolorer ‖ intr déteindre, se décolorer; (to lose vigor, freshness) se faner; **to fade in** apparaître graduellement; **to fade out** disparaître graduellement

fade′-in′ s (mov) ouverture f en fondu

fade′-out′ s (mov) fondu m

fag [fæg] s (slang) cibiche f ‖ v (pret & pp **fagged**; ger **fagging**) tr—**to fag out** éreinter

fagot [ˈfægət] s fagot m; (for filling up trenches) fascine f ‖ tr fagoter

fail [fel] s—**without fail** sans faute ‖ tr manquer à; (a student) refuser; (an examination) échouer à or dans ‖ intr manquer, faire défaut; (to not succeed) échouer, rater; (said of motor) tomber en panne; (to weaken) baisser, faiblir; **to fail completely** faire chou blanc; **to fail in** faillir à; **to fail to** manquer de, faillir à; **to fail to do** or **to keep** faillir à

failing [ˈfelɪŋ] adj défaillant ‖ s défaut m ‖ prep à défaut de

fail′-safe′ adj automatiquement protégé, à sûreté intégrée

failure [ˈfeljər] s insuccès m, échec m; (lack) manque m, défaut m; (person) raté m; (com) faillite f

faint [fent] adj faible; **to feel faint** se sentir mal ‖ s évanouissement m ‖ intr s'évanouir

faint′-heart′ed adj timide, peureux

fair [fɛr] adj juste, équitable; (honest) loyal, honnête; (average) moyen, passable; (clear) clair; (beautiful) beau; (pleasing) agréable, plaisant; (of hair) blond; (complexion) blanc; **to be fair** (to be just) être de bonne guerre ‖ s foire f, fête f; (bazaar) kermesse f ‖ adv impartialement; **to bid fair to** avoir des chances de; **to play fair** jouer franc jeu

fair′ cop′y s copie f au net

fair′ground′ s champ m de foire

fairly [ˈfɛrli] adv impartialement, loyalement; assez

fair′-mind′ed adj impartial

fairness [ˈfɛrnɪs] s impartialité f, justice f; (of complexion) clarté f

fair′ play′ s franc jeu m

fair′ sex′ s beau sexe m

fair′way′ s (golf) parcours m normal; (naut) chenal m

fair′-weath′er adj (e.g., friend) des beaux jours

fair•y [ˈfɛri] *adj* féerique ‖ *s* (*pl* **-ies**) fée *f;* (*homosexual*) (pej) tapette *f*, tante *f*,

fair′y god′mother *s* marraine *f* fée; (coll) marraine gâteau

fair′y•land′ *s* royaume *m* des fées

fair′y tale′ *s* conte *m* de fées

faith [feθ] *s* foi *f;* **to break faith with** manquer de foi à; **to keep faith with** tenir ses engagements envers; **to pin one's faith on** mettre tout son espoir en

faithful [ˈfeθfəl] *adj* fidèle ‖ *s*—**the faithful** les fidèles *mpl*

faithless [ˈfeθlɪs] *adj* infidèle

fake [fek] *adj* (coll) faux ‖ *s* faux *m*, article *m* truqué ‖ *tr* truquer

faker [ˈfekər] *s* truqueur *m*

falcon [ˈfɔkən], [ˈfɔlkən] *s* faucon *m*

falconer [ˈfɔkənər] *s* fauconnier *m*

fall [fɔl] *adj* automnal ‖ *s* chute *f;* (*of prices*) baisse *f;* (*season*) automne *m & f;* (*of fall d'eau* ‖ *v* (*pret* **fell** [fɛl]; *pp* **fallen** [ˈfɔlən]) *intr* tomber; (*said of prices*) baisser; **fall in!** (mil) rassemblement!; **fall out!** (mil) rompez les rangs!; **to fall down** (*said of person*) tomber par terre; (*said of building*) s'écrouler; **to fall for** (coll) se laisser prendre à; (*to fall in love with*) (coll) tomber amoureux de; **to fall in** s'effondrer; (mil) former des rangs; **to fall into the trap** donner dans le piège; **to fall off** tomber de; (*to decline*) baisser, diminuer; **to fall out** (*to disagree*) se brouiller; **to fall over oneself to** (coll) se mettre en quatre pour

fallacious [fəˈleʃəs] *adj* fallacieux

falla•cy [ˈfæləsi] *s* (*pl* **-cies**) erreur *f*, fausseté *f*

fall′ guy′ *s* (slang) tête *f* de Turc

fallible [ˈfælɪbəl] *adj* faillible

fall′ing star′ *s* étoile *f* filante

fall′ out′ *s* pluies *fpl* radioactives, retombées *fpl* radioactives

fall′out shel′ter *s* abri *m* antiatomique

fallow [ˈfælo] *adj* en friche, en jachère ‖ *s* friche *f*, jachère *f* ‖ *tr* laisser en friche *or* en jachère

false [fɔls] *adj* faux; artificiel, simulé; (*hair*) postiche; **under false colors** sous des prétextes fallacieux ‖ *adv* faussement; **to play false** tromper

false′ alarm′ *s* fausse alerte *f*

false′ bot′tom *s* double fond *m*

false′ cog′nate *s* faux ami *m*

false′ eye′lashes *spl* cils *mpl* postiches

false′ face′ *s* masque *m*

false′ friend′ *s* (*deceptive cognate*) faux ami *m*

false′-heart′ed *adj* perfide, traître

false′hood *s* mensonge *m*

false′ pretens′es *spl* faux-semblants *mpl*

false′ return′ *s* fausse déclaration *f* d'impôts

false′ step′ *s* faux-pas *m*

false′ teeth′ [ˈtiθ] *spl* fausses dents *fpl*

falset•to [fɔlˈsɛto] *s* (*pl* **-tos**) fausset *m*, voix *f* de tête; (*person*) fausset *m*

falsi•fy [ˈfɔlsɪˌfaɪ] *v* (*pret & pp* **-fied**) *tr* falsifier, fausser

falsi•ty [ˈfɔlsɪti] *s* (*pl* **-ties**) fausseté *f*

falter [ˈfɔltər] *s* vacillation *f*, hésitation *f;* (*of speech*) balbutiement *m* ‖ *intr* vaciller, hésiter; balbutier

fame [fem] *s* renom *m*, renommée *f*

famed *adj* renommé, célèbre

familiar [fəˈmɪljər] *adj & s* familier *m;* **to become familiar with** se familiariser avec

familiari•ty [fəˌmɪliˈærɪti] *s* (*pl* **-ties**) familiarité *f*

familiarize [fəˈmɪljəˌraɪz] *tr* familiariser

fami•ly [ˈfæmɪli] *adj* familial; **in a** *or* **the family way** (coll) dans une position intéressante; (coll) en famille (Canad) ‖ *s* (*pl* **-lies**) famille *f*

fam′ily court′ *s* tribunal *m* tutélaire de mineurs

fam′ily man′ *s* (*pl* **men′**) père *m* de famille; (*stay-at-home*) homme *m* casanier, pantouflard *m*

fam′ily name′ *s* nom *m* de famille

fam′ily physi′cian *s* médecin *m* de famille

fam′ily plan′ning *s* planisme *m* familial

fam′ily tree′ *s* arbre *m* généalogique

famine [ˈfæmɪn] *s* famine *f*

famish [ˈfæmɪʃ] *tr* affamer, priver de vivres ‖ *intr* souffrir de la faim

famished *adj* affamé, famélique; **to be famished** (coll) mourir de faim

famous [ˈfeməs] *adj* renommé, célèbre

fan [fæn] *s* éventail *m;* (mach) ventilateur *m;* (coll) fanatique *mf*, enragé *m* ‖ *v* (*pret & pp* **fanned**; *ger* **fanning**) *tr* éventer; (*to winnow*) vanner; (*e.g., passions*) exciter ‖ *intr*—**to fan out** se déployer en éventail

fanatic [fəˈnætɪk] *adj & s* fanatique *mf*

fanatical [fəˈnætɪkəl] *adj* fanatique

fanaticism [fəˈnætɪˌsɪzəm] *s* fanatisme *m*

fan′ belt′ *s* (aut) courroie *f* de ventilateur

fancied *adj* imaginaire, supposé

fanciful [ˈfænsɪfəl] *adj* fantaisiste, capricieux

fan•cy [ˈfænsi] *adj* (*comp* **-cier;** *super* **-ciest**) ornemental; (*goods, clothes, bread*) de fantaisie; (*high-quality*) fin, extra, de luxe ‖ *s* (*pl* **-cies**) fantaisie *f*, caprice *m;* **to take a fancy to** prendre du goût pour; (*a loved one*) prendre en affection ‖ *v* (*pret & pp* **-cied**) *tr* s'imaginer, se figurer; **to fancy oneself** s'imaginer; **to fancy that** imaginer que

fan′cy dress′ *s* costume *m* de fantaisie, travesti *m*

fan′cy dress′ ball′ *s* bal *m* costumé, bal travesti

fan′cy foods′ *spl* comestibles *mpl* de fantaisie

fan′cy-free′ *adj* libre, gai, sans amour

fan′cy jew′elry *s* bijouterie *f* de fantaisie

fan′cy skat′ing *s* patinage *m* de fantaisie

fan′cy•work′ *s* broderie *f*, ouvrage *m* d'agrément

fanfare [ˈfænfɛr] *s* fanfare *f*

fang [fæŋ] *s* croc *m;* (*of snake*) crochet *m*

fantastic(al) [fænˈtæstɪk(əl)] *adj* fantastique

fanta•sy [ˈfæntəsi] *s* (*pl* **-sies**) fantaisie *f*

far [fɑr] *adj* lointain; **on the far side of** à l'autre côté de ‖ *adv* loin; **as far as** autant que; (*up* *to*) jusqu'à; **as far as I am concerned** quant à moi; **as far as I know** pour autant que je sache; **by far** de beaucoup; **far and wide** partout; **far away** au loin; **far from** loin de; **far from it** tant s'en faut; **far into the night** fort avant dans la nuit; **far into the woods** avant dans le bois; **far off** au loin; **how far?** jusqu'où?; **how far is it from . . .?** combien y a-t-il de . . .?; **in so far as** dans la mesure où; **so far** or **thus far** jusqu'ici; **to go far to** contribuer pour beaucoup à

far′away′ *adj* éloigné, distant

farce [fɑrs] *s* farce *f*

farcical [ˈfɑrsɪkəl] *adj* grotesque, ridicule

fare [fɛr] *s* prix *m*, tarif *m*; (*cost of taxi*) course *f*; (*passenger in taxi*) client *m*; (*passenger in bus*) voyageur *m*; (*culin*) chère *f*, ordinaire *m*; **fares, please!** vos places, s'il vous plaît! ‖ *intr* se porter; **how did you fare?** comment ça s'est-il passé?

Far′ East′ *s* Extrême-Orient *m*

fare′well′ *s* adieu *m*; **to bid s.o. farewell** dire adieu à qn

far′-fetched′ *adj* tiré par les cheveux

far-flung [ˈfɑrˈflʌŋ] *adj* étendu, vaste, d'une grande envergure

farm [fɑrm] *s* ferme *f*; (*sharecropper's farm*) métairie *f* ‖ *tr* cultiver, exploiter; **to farm out** donner à ferme; (*work*) donner en exploitation à l'extérieur ‖ *intr* faire de la culture

farmer [ˈfɑrmər] *s* fermier *m*

farm′ hand′ *s* valet *m* de ferme

farm′house′ *s* ferme *f*, maison *f* de ferme

farming [ˈfɑrmɪŋ] *s* agriculture *f*, exploitation *f* agricole

farm′yard′ *s* cour *f* de ferme

Far′ North′ *s* Grand Nord *m*

far′-off′ *adj* lointain, éloigné

far′-reach′ing *adj* à longue portée

far′sight′ed *adj* prévoyant; (physiol) presbyte

farther [ˈfɑrðər] *adj* plus éloigné ‖ *adv* plus loin

farthest [ˈfɑrðɪst] *adj* (le) plus éloigné ‖ *adv* le plus loin; au plus

farthing [ˈfɑrðɪŋ] *s* liard *m*

Far′ West′ *s* ouest *m* américain, far ouest

fascinate [ˈfæsɪˌnet] *tr* fasciner

fascinating [ˈfæsɪˌnetɪŋ] *adj* fascinateur, fascinant

fascism [ˈfæʃɪzəm] *s* fascisme *m*

fascist [ˈfæʃist] *adj & s* fasciste *mf*

fashion [ˈfæʃən] *s* mode *f*, vogue *f*; (*manner*) façon *f*, manière *f*; **after a fashion** tant bien que mal; **in fashion** à la mode, en vogue; **out of fashion** démodé ‖ *tr* façonner

fashionable [ˈfæʃənəbəl] *adj* à la mode, élégant, chic

fash′ion design′ing *s* haute couture *f*

fash′ion parade′ *s* défilé *m* de modes

fash′ion plate′ *s* gravure *f* de mode; (*person*) (coll) élégant *m*

fash′ion show′ *s* présentation *f* de collection, présentation de modèles

fast [fæst], [fɑst] *adj* rapide; (*fixed*) solide, fixe;

(*clock*) en avance; (*friend*) fidèle; (*color*) grand, bon, e.g., **fast color** grand teint, bon teint; (*person*) (slang) dévergondé; **to make fast** fixer, fermer ‖ *s* jeûne *m*; **to break one's fast** rompre le jeûne ‖ *adv* vite, rapidement; (*firmly*) solidement, ferme; (*asleep*) profondément; **to hold fast** tenir bon; **to live fast** (coll) faire la noce, mener la vie à grandes guides; **to stand fast against** tenir tête à ‖ *intr* jeûner

fast′ day′ *s* jour *m* de jeûne, jour maigre

fasten [ˈfæsən] *tr* attacher, fixer; (*e.g., a belt*) ajuster ‖ *intr* s'attacher, se fixer

fastener [ˈfæsənər] *s* attache *f*, agrafe *f*

fast′ food′ *s* or **fast foods** *spl* fast food *m*; (*type of business*) restauration *f* rapide

fast′-food res′taurant *s* restaupouce *m*

fastidious [fæsˈtɪdiˑəs] *adj* délicat, dégoûté, difficile

fasting [ˈfæstɪŋ] *s* jeûne *m*

fat [fæt] *adj* (*comp* **fatter;** *super* **fattest**) (*plump; greasy*) gras; (*large*) gros; (*soil*) riche; (*spark*) nourri; **to get fat** engraisser ‖ *s* graisse *f*; (*of meat*) gras *m*

fatal [ˈfetəl] *adj* fatal

fatalism [ˈfetəˌlɪzəm] *s* fatalisme *m*

fatalist [ˈfetəlɪst] *s* fataliste *mf*

fatali·ty [fəˈtælɪti] *s* (*pl* **-ties**) fatalité *f*; (*in accidents, war, etc.*) mort *f*, accident *m* mortel

fate [fet] *s* sort *m*, destin *m*; **the Fates** les Parques *fpl*

fated *adj* destiné, voué

fateful [ˈfetfəl] *adj* fatal; (*prophetic*) fatidique

fat′head′ *s* (coll) crétin *m*, sot *m*

father [ˈfɑðər] *s* père *m*; **Father** (*salutation given a priest*) Monsieur l'abbé ‖ *tr* servir de père à; (*to beget*) engendrer; (*an idea, project*) inventer

fa′ther·hood′ *s* paternité *f*

fa′ther-in-law′ *s* (*pl* **fathers-in-law**) beau-père *m*

fa′ther·land′ *s* patrie *f*

fatherless [ˈfɑðərlɪs] *adj* sans père, orphelin de père

fatherly [ˈfɑðərli] *adj* paternel

Fa′ther's Day′ *s* la Fête des pères

Fa′ther Time′ *s* le Temps

fathom [ˈfæðəm] *s* brasse *f* ‖ *tr* sonder

fathomless [ˈfæðəmlɪs] *adj* insondable

fatigue [fəˈtig] *s* fatigue *f*; **fatigues** (mil) bleus *mpl*

fatigue′ clothes′ *spl* tenue *f* de corvée

fatigue′ du′ty *s* (mil) corvée *f*

fatten [ˈfætən] *tr & intr* engraisser

fat·ty [ˈfæti] *adj* (*comp* **-tier;** *super* **-tiest**) gras, graisseux; (*tissue*) adipeux; (*chubby*) (coll) potelé, dodu ‖ *s* (*pl* **-ties**) (coll) bon gros *m*

fatuous [ˈfætʃuˑəs] *adj* sot, idiot

fatwa [ˈfætwɑ] *s* (*religious and legal decree issued by a Muslim cleric*) fatwa *m* (*décret religieux et légal fait par un clerc musulman*)

faucet [ˈfɔsɪt] *s* robinet *m*

fault [fɔlt] s faute f; (geol) faille f; **to a fault** à l'excès; **to find fault with** trouver à redire à

fault′find′er s critiqueur m, éplucheur m

fault′find′ing adj chicaneur ‖ s chicanerie f, critique f

faultless [ˈfɔltlɪs] adj sans défaut

fault•y [ˈfɔlti] adj (comp **-ier;** super **-iest**) fautif, défectueux

faun [fɔn] s faune m

fauna [ˈfɔnə] s faune f

favor [ˈfevər] s faveur f; do me the favor to faites-moi le plaisir de; **to be in favor of** être partisan de; **to be in favor with** jouir de la faveur de; **to decide in s.o.'s favor** donner gain de cause à qn; **to do a favor in return** renvoyer l'ascenseur ‖ tr favoriser; (to look like) (coll) tenir de; (e.g., a sore leg) (coll) ménager

favorable [ˈfevərəbəl] adj favorable

favorite [ˈfevərɪt] adj & s favori m

favoritism [ˈfevərɪˌtɪzəm] s favoritisme m

fawn [fɔn] adj (color) fauve ‖ s faon m ‖ intr—**to fawn upon** (said of dog) faire des caresses à; (said of person) faire le chien couchant auprès de

fax [fæks] s fax m; (machine) télécopieur m; (facsimile copy) télécopie f

faze [fez] tr (coll) affecter, troubler

FBI [ˌɛfˌbiˈaɪ] s (letterword) (**Federal Bureau of Investigation**) Sûreté f nationale, Sûreté (the French equivalent)

fear [fɪr] s crainte f, peur f ‖ tr craindre, avoir peur de ‖ intr craindre, avoir peur

fearful [ˈfɪrfəl] adj (frightened) peureux, effrayé; (frightful) effrayant; (coll) énorme, effrayant

fearless [ˈfɪrlɪs] adj sans peur

feasible [ˈfizɪbəl] adj faisable

feast [fist] s festin m, régal m ‖ tr régaler ‖ intr faire bonne chère; **to feast on** se régaler de

feast′ day′ s fête f, jour m de fête

feat [fit] s exploit m, haut fait m

feather [ˈfɛðər] s plume f; **feather in one's cap** (coll) fleuron m à sa couronne; **in fine feather** (coll) plein d'entrain ‖ tr emplumer; (an oar) ramener à plat; **to feather one's nest** (coll) faire son beurre

feath′er bed′ s lit m de plumes, couette f

feath′er•bed′ding s emploi m de plus d'ouvriers qu'il n'en faut

feath′er•brained′ adj braque, étourdi

feath′er dust′er s plumeau m

feath′er•edge′ s (of board) biseau m; (of tool) morfil m

feath′er•weight′ s (boxing) poids m plume, poids mouche

feathery [ˈfɛðəri] adj plumeux

feature [ˈfitʃər] s trait m, caractéristique f; (mov) long métrage m, grand film m ‖ tr caractériser; offrir comme attraction principale

fea′ture writ′er s rédacteur m

February [ˈfɛbruˌɛri] s février m

feces [ˈfisiz] spl fèces fpl

feckless [ˈfɛklɪs] adj veule, faible

federal [ˈfɛdərəl] adj & s fédéral m

Fed′eral Repub′lic of Ger′many s République f fédérale d'Allemagne

Fed′eral Repub′lic of Swit′zerland s Confédération f suisse

federate [ˈfɛdəˌret] adj fédéré ‖ tr fédérer ‖ intr se fédérer

federation [ˌfɛdəˈreʃən] s fédération f

fedora [fɪˈdorə] s chapeau m mou

fed′ up′ [fɛd] adj—**to be fed up** (coll) en avoir marre; **to be fed up with** (coll) avoir plein le dos de

fee [fi] s honoraires mpl, cachet m; **for a nominal fee** pour une somme symbolique

feeble [ˈfibəl] adj faible

fee′ble•mind′ed adj imbécile; obtus, à l'esprit lourd

feed [fid] s nourriture f, pâture f; (mach) alimentation f; (slang) grand repas m ‖ v (pret & pp **fed** [fɛd]) tr nourrir, donner à manger à; (a machine) alimenter ‖ intr manger; **to feed upon** se nourrir de

feed′back′ s (chem) régénération f; (electron) réalimentation f; (mech) rétroaction f, feedback m invar; (physiol) rétrocontrôle m, feedback m invar; (fig) réactions fpl observées; (fig) remarques fpl données en confidence

feed′ bag′ s musette-mangeoire f; **to put on the feed bag** (slang) casser la croûte

feeder [ˈfidər] s alimenteur m; (elec) canal m d'amenée

feed′ pump′ s pompe f d'alimentation

feed′ trough′ s mangeoire f, auge f

feed′ wire′ s (elec) fil m d'amenée

feel [fil] s sensation f ‖ v (pret & pp **felt** [fɛlt]) tr sentir, éprouver; (the pulse) tâter; (to examine) palper; **to feel one's way** avancer à tâtons ‖ intr (sick, tired, etc.) se sentir; **I feel as if . . .** il me semble que . . .; **not to feel well** être mal en point; **to feel for** tâtonner, chercher à tâtons; (to sympathize with) (coll) être plein de pitié pour; **to feel like** avoir envie de

feeler [ˈfilər] s (ent) antenne f; **to put out a feeler** (coll) tâter le terrain

feeling [ˈfilɪŋ] s (with senses) toucher m, tact m; (with hands) tâtage m; (impression, emotion) sentiment m; **feelings** sensibilité f

feign [fen] tr & intr feindre

feint [fent] s feinte f ‖ intr feinter

feldspar [ˈfɛldˌspar] s feldspath m

felicitate [fəˈlɪsɪˌtet] tr féliciter

felicitous [fəˈlɪsɪtəs] adj heureux, à propos

fell [fɛl] adj cruel, féroce ‖ tr abattre

fellate [ˈfɛˌlet] tr pratiquer la fellation sur

fellatio [fəˈleʃiˌo] ou **fellation** [fəˈleʃən] s fellation f

felloe [ˈfɛlo] s jante f

fellow [ˈfɛlo] s (of a society) membre m; (holder of a fellowship) boursier m; (friend, neighbor, etc.) homme m, compagnon m; (coll) type m, bonhomme *m*, gars *m*; **poor fellow!** (coll) pauvre garçon!

fel′low cit′izen *s* concitoyen *m*

fel′low coun′tryman *s* compatriote *mf*

fel′low crea′ture *s* semblable *mf*

fel′low-man′ *s* (*pl* **-men′**) semblable *m*, prochain *m*

fel′low mem′ber *s* confrère *m*

fel′low·ship′ *s* camaraderie *f*; (*scholarship*) bourse *f*; (*organization*) association *f*

fel′low stu′dent *s* condisciple *m*

fel′low trav′eler *s* compagnon *m* de voyage; (pol) compagnon de route

felon [′fɛlən] *s* criminel *m*; (pathol) panaris *m*

felo·ny [′fɛləni] *s* (*pl* **-nies**) crime *m*

felt [fɛlt] *s* feutre *m* ‖ *tr* feutrer

felt′-tip pen′ *s* stylo-feutre *m*

female [′fimel] *adj* (*sex*) féminin; (*animal, plant, piece of a device*) femelle ‖ *s* (*person*) femme *f*; (*plant, animal*) femelle *f*

feminine [′fɛmɪnɪn] *adj & s* féminin *m*

feminism [′fɛmɪ͵nɪzəm] *s* féminisme *m*

fen [fɛn] *s* marécage *m*

fence [fɛns] *s* barrière *f*, clôture *f*; palissade *f*; (*for stolen goods*) receleur *m*, marchand *m* clandestin; (baseball) clôture *f*; **on the fence** (coll) indécis, en balance ‖ *tr* clôturer ‖ *intr* faire de l'escrime

fencing [′fɛnsɪŋ] *s* (*enclosure*) clôture *f*; (sports) escrime *f*

fenc′ing acad′emy *s* salle *f* d'armes

fenc′ing mas′ter *s* maître *m* d'armes

fenc′ing match′ *s* assaut *m* d'armes

fend [fɛnd] *tr*—**to fend off** parer ‖ *intr*—**to fend for oneself** (coll) se débrouiller, se tirer d'affaire

fender [′fɛndər] *s* (*mudguard*) aile *f*, gardeboue *m*; (*of locomotive*) chasse-pierres *m*; (*of fireplace*) garde-feu *m*

fen′ der·bend′ er *s* (coll) (aut) heurt *m* sans des dégâts importants

fennel [′fɛnəl] *s* fenouil *m*

ferment [′fʌrmɛnt] *s* ferment *m* ‖ [fər′mɛnt] *tr* faire fermenter; (*wine*) cuver ‖ *intr* fermenter

fern [fʌrn] *s* fougère *f*

ferocious [fə′roʃəs] *adj* féroce

feroci·ty [fə′rɑsɪti] *s* (*pl* **-ties**) férocité *f*

ferret [′fɛrɪt] *s* furet *m* ‖ *tr*—**to ferret out** dénicher ‖ *intr* fureter

Fer′ris wheel′ [′fɛrɪs] *s* grande roue *f*

fer·ry [′fɛri] *s* (*pl* **-ries**) bac *m*; (*to transport trains*) ferry-boat *m* ‖ *v* (*pret & pp* **-ried**) *tr & intr* passer en bac

fer′ry·boat′ *s* bac *m*; (*to transport trains*) ferry-boat *m*

fer′ry·man *s* (*pl* **-men**) passeur *m*

fertile [′fʌrtɪl] *adj* fertile, fécond

fertilize [′fʌrtɪ͵laɪz] *tr* fertiliser; (*to impregnate*) féconder

fertilizer [′fʌrtɪ͵laɪzər] *s* engrais *m*, amendement *m*; (bot) fécondateur *m*

fervent [′fʌrvənt] *adj* fervent

fervid [′fʌrvɪd] *adj* fervent

fervor [′fʌrvər] *s* ferveur *f*

fester [′fɛstər] *s* ulcère *m* ‖ *tr* ulcérer ‖ *intr* s'ulcérer

festival [′fɛstɪvəl] *adj* de fête ‖ *s* fête *f*; (mov, mus) festival *m*

festive [′fɛstɪv] *adj* de fête, gai

festivi·ty [fɛs′tɪvɪti] *s* (*pl* **-ties**) festivité *f*

festoon [fɛs′tun] *s* feston *m* ‖ *tr* festonner

fetch [fɛtʃ] *tr* aller chercher; (*a certain price*) se vendre à

fetching [′fɛtʃɪŋ] *adj* (coll) séduisant

fete [fɛt] *s* fête *f* ‖ *tr* fêter

fetid [′fɛtɪd] *adj* fétide, puant

fetish [′fɛtɪʃ] *s* fétiche *m*

fetlock [′fɛtlɑk] *s* boulet *m*; (*tuft of hair*) fanon *m*

fetter [′fɛtər] *s* lien *m*; **fetters** fers *mpl*, chaînes *fpl* ‖ *tr* enchaîner, entraver

fettle [′fɛtəl] *s* condition *f*, état *m*; **in fine fettle** en pleine forme

fetus [′fitəs] *s* fœtus *m*

feud [fjud] *s* querelle *f*, vendetta *f* ‖ *intr* se quereller, être à couteaux tirés

feudal [′fjudəl] *adj* féodal

feudalism [′fjudə͵lɪzəm] *s* féodalisme *m*

fever [′fivər] *s* fièvre *f*

fe′ver blis′ter *s* bouton *m* de fièvre

feverish [′fivərɪʃ] *adj* fiévreux

few [fju] *adj* peu de; **a few** ... quelques ...; **quite a few** pas mal de; **the few** ... les rares ... ‖ *pron indef* peu; **a few** quelques-uns §81; **quite a few** beaucoup

ff. *abbr* et seq., et suivantes; **see p. 21 ff.** voir à partir de la page 21

fiancé [͵fi·ɑn′se] *s* fiancé *m*

fiancée [͵fi·ɑn′se] *s* fiancée *f*

fias·co [fɪ′æsko] *s* (*pl* **-cos** or **-coes**) fiasco *m*, échec *m*

fiat [′faɪæt] *s* ordonnance *f*, autorisation *f*

fib [fɪb] *s* (coll) petit mensonge *m*, blague *f* ‖ *v* (*pret & pp* **fibbed;** *ger* **fibbing**) *intr* (coll) blaguer

fiber [′faɪbər] *s* fibre *f*

fi′ber·glass′ *s* fibre *f* de verre

fibrous [′faɪbrəs] *adj* fibreux

fickle [′fɪkəl] *adj* inconstant, volage

fiction [′fɪkʃən] *s* fiction *f*; (*branch of literature*) ouvrages *mpl* d'imagination, romans *mpl*

fictional [′fɪkʃənəl] *adj* romanesque, d'imagination

fictionalize [′fɪkʃənə͵laɪz] *tr* romancer

fictitious [fɪk′tɪʃəs] *adj* fictif

fiddle [′fɪdəl] *s* violon *m* ‖ *tr*—**to fiddle away** (coll) gaspiller ‖ *intr* jouer du violon; **to fiddle around** or **with** (coll) tripoter

fiddler [′fɪdlər] *s* (coll) violoneux *m*

fid′dle·stick′ *s* (coll) archet *m*; **fiddlesticks!** (coll) quelle blague!

fiddling [′fɪdlɪŋ] *adj* (coll) musard

fideli·ty [fɪ′dɛlɪti] *s* (*pl* **-ties**) fidélité *f*

fidget [′fɪdʒɪt] *intr* se trémousser; **to fidget with** tripoter

fidgety [ˈfɪdʒɪti] *adj* nerveux

fiduciar•y [fɪˈd(j)uʃɪˌɛri] *adj* fiduciaire ‖ *s* (*pl* -ies) fiduciaire *m*

fie [faɪ] *interj* fi!; **fie on . . .!** nargue de . . .!

field [fild] *s* (*piece of land*) champ *m*; (*area, activity*) domaine *m*, aire *f*; (aer, sports) terrain *m*; (elec) champ; (*of motor or dynamo*) (elec) inducteur *m*; (mil) aire *f*, théâtre *m*

field′ day′ *s* (*cleanup*) (mil) manœuvres *fpl* de garnison; (sports) manifestation *f* sportive

fielder [ˈfildər] *s* (baseball) chasseur *m*, homme *m* de champ

field′ glass′es *spl* jumelles *fpl*

field′ hock′ey *s* hockey *m* sur gazon

field′ hos′pital *s* ambulance *f*, formation *f* sanitaire

field′ house′ *s* (sports) complexe *m* sportif, pavillon *m* des sports

field′ mag′net *s* aimant *m* inducteur

field′ mar′shal *s* maréchal *m*

field′ mouse′ *s* mulot *m*

field′ piece′ *s* pièce *f* de campagne

field′ test′ *s* essai *m* sur le terrain

field′ trip′ *s* visite *f* sur le terrain

field′ work′ *s* travail *m* sur le terrain

field′ -work′er *s* chercheur *m* sur le terrain

fiend [find] *s* démon *m*; (*mischiefmaker*) (coll) espiègle *mf*; (*enthusiast*) (coll) mordu *m*; (*addict*) (coll) toxicomane *mf*

fiendish [ˈfindɪʃ] *adj* diabolique

fierce [fɪrs] *adj* féroce, farouche; (*wind*) furieux; (coll) très mauvais

fierceness [ˈfɪrsnɪs] *s* férocité *f*

fier•y [ˈfaɪri] *adj* (*comp* -ier; *super* -iest) (*coals, sun*) ardent; (*heat, sand*) brûlant; (*speech*) fougueux, enflammé; (*horse, person, etc.*) fougueux, ardent

fife [faɪf] *s* fifre *m*

fifteen [ˈfɪfˈtin] *adj, pron, & s* quinze *m*; **about fifteen** une quinzaine de

fifteenth [ˈfɪfˈtinθ] *adj & pron* quinzième (*masc, fem*); **the Fifteenth** quinze, e.g., **John the Fifteenth** Jean quinze ‖ *s* quinzième *m*; **the fifteenth** (*in dates*) le quinze

fifth [fɪfθ] *adj & pron* cinquième (*masc, fem*); **the Fifth** cinq, e.g., **John the Fifth** Jean cinq ‖ *s* cinquième; (mus) quinte *f*; **the fifth** (*in dates*) le cinq

fifth′ col′umn *s* cinquième colonne *f*

fiftieth [ˈfɪftɪ•ɪθ] *adj & pron* cinquantième (*masc, fem*) ‖ *s* cinquantième *m*

fif•ty [ˈfɪfti] *adj & pron* cinquante ‖ *s* (*pl* -ties) cinquante *m*; **about fifty** une cinquantaine *f*; **fifties** (*years of the decade*) années *fpl* cinquante

fif′ty-fif′ty *adv*—**to go fifty-fifty** (coll) être de moitié, être en compte à demi; kif, kif *m* (coll)

fig [fɪg] *s* figue *f*; (*tree*) figuier *m*; **a fig for . . .!** (coll) nargue de . . . !

fight [faɪt] *s* combat *m*, bataille *f*; (*spirit*) cœur *m*; **to pick a fight with** chercher querelle à ‖ *v* (*pret & pp* **fought** [fɔt]) *tr* combattre, se battre contre; **to fight off** repousser ‖ *intr* combattre, se battre; **to fight shy of** se défier de

fighter [ˈfaɪtər] *s* combattant *m*; (*game person*) batailleur *m*; (aer) chasseur *m*, avion *m* de chasse

fight′er pi′lot *s* chasseur *m*

fig′ leaf′ *s* feuille *f* de figuier; (*on statues*) feuille de vigne

figment [ˈfɪgmənt] *s* fiction *f*, invention *f*

figurative [ˈfɪgjərətɪv] *adj* figuratif; (*meaning*) figuré

figure [ˈfɪgjər] *s* (*diagram, drawing, image; important person; in skating, dancing*) figure *f*; (*silhouette*) forme *f*; (*bodily form*) taille *f*; (math) chiffre *m*; **to be good at figures** être bon en calcul; **to have a good figure** avoir de la ligne; **to keep one's figure** garder sa ligne ‖ *tr* figurer; (*to embellish*) orner de motifs; (*to imagine*) se figurer, s'imaginer; **to figure out** calculer; (coll) déchiffrer ‖ *intr* figurer; **to figure on** compter sur

fig′ured bass′ [bes] *s* (mus) basse *f* chiffrée

fig′ured silk′ *s* soie *f* à dessin

fig′ure-head′ *s* prête-nom *m*, homme *m* de paille; (naut) figure *f* de proue

fig′ure of speech′ *s* figure *f* de rhétorique; (fig) façon *f* de parler

fig′ure skat′ing *s* patinage *m* de fantaisie

filament [ˈfɪləmənt] *s* filament *m*

filbert [ˈfɪlbərt] *s* noisette *f*, aveline *f*; (*tree*) noisetier *m*, avelinier *m*

filch [fɪltʃ] *tr* chaparder, chiper

file [faɪl] *s* (*tool*) lime *f*; (*for papers*) classeur *m*; (*for cards*) fichier *m*; (*personal record*) dossier *m*; (*line*) file *f*; (comp) fichier *m*; **in single file** en file indienne, à la queue leu leu; **to form single file** dédoubler les rangs ‖ *tr* limer; classer, ranger; (*a petition*) déposer; **to file down** enlever à la lime ‖ *intr*—**to file off** défiler; **to file out** sortir un à un

file′ case′ *s* fichier *m*

file′ clerk′ *s* employé *m*, commis *m*

file′ film′ *s* images *fpl* d'archives

file′ num′ber *s* (*e.g., used in answering a letter*) référence *f*

filial [ˈfɪlɪ•əl] *adj* filial

filiation [ˌfɪlɪˈeʃən] *s* filiation *f*

filibuster [ˈfɪlɪˌbʌstər] *s* (*use of delaying tactics*) obstruction *f*; (*legislator*) obstructionniste *mf*; (*pirate*) flibustier *m* ‖ *tr* (*legislation*) obstruer ‖ *intr* faire de l'obstruction

filigree [ˈfɪlɪˌgri] *adj* filigrané ‖ *s* filigrane *m* ‖ *tr* filigranter

filing [ˈfaɪlɪŋ] *s* (*of documents*) classement *m*; (*with a tool*) limage *m*; **filings** limaille *f*, grains *mpl* de limaille

fil′ing cab′inet *s* classeur *m*

fil′ing card′ *s* fiche *f*

Filipi•no [ˌfɪlɪˈpino] *adj* philippin ‖ *s* (*pl* -nos) Philippin *m*

fill [fɪl] *s* (*earth, stones, etc.*) remblai *m*; **I've had my fill!** j'en ai assez!; **to eat one's fill** manger à sa faim, manger tout son content;

to have one's fill of avoir tout son soul de ‖ *tr* remplir; (*a prescription*) exécuter; (*a tooth*) plomber; (*a cylinder with gas*) charger; (*a hollow or gap*) combler; (*a job*) occuper; **to fill in** remblayer, combler; **to fill out** (*a questionnaire*) remplir ‖ *intr* se remplir; **to fill out** se gonfler; (*said of sail*) s'enfler; **to fill up** se combler; (*to fill the tank full*) faire le plein

filler [ˈfɪlər] *s* remplissage *m*; (*of cigar*) tripe *f*; (*sizing*) apprêt *m*, mastic *m*; (*in notebook*) papier *m*; (journ) pesée *f*

fillet [ˈfɪlɪt] *s* bande *f*; (*for hair*) bandeau *m*; (archit) moulure *f* ‖ [ˈfɪle], [ˈfɪlɪt] *s* (culin) filet *m* ‖ *tr* couper en filets

filling [ˈfɪlɪŋ] *adj* (*food*) rassasiant ‖ *s* (*of job*) occupation *f*; (*of tooth*) plombage *m*; (*e.g., of turkey*) farce *f*; (*of cigar*) tripe *f*

fill′ing sta′tion *s* poste *m* d'essence

fill′ing-station attend′ant *s* pompiste *mf*

fillip [ˈfɪlɪp] *s* tonique *m*, stimulant *m*; (*with finger*) chiquenaude *f* ‖ *tr* donner une chiquenaude à

fil•ly [ˈfɪli] *s* (*pl* **-lies**) pouliche *f*; (coll) fillette *f*

film [fɪlm] *s* film *m*; (*in a roll*) pellicule *f*, film ‖ *tr* filmer

film′ clip′ *s* bande-annonce *f*

filming [ˈfɪlmɪŋ] *s* filmage *m*

film′ li′brary *s* cinémathèque *f*

film′ mak′er *s* cinéaste *mf*

film′ star′ *s* vedette *f* du cinéma

film′strip′ *s* film *m* fixe

film•y [ˈfɪlmi] *adj* (*comp* **-ier;** *super* **-iest**) diaphane, voilé

filter [ˈfɪltər] *s* filtre *m* ‖ *tr & intr* filtrer

fil′ter bag′ *s* sac-filtre *m*

filtering [ˈfɪltərɪŋ] *s* filtrage *m*; (*of water*) filtration *f*

fil′ter pa′per *s* papier-filtre *m*

fil′ter tip′ *adj* à bout-filtre ‖ *s* bout-filtre *m*, bout-filtrant *m*

filth [fɪlθ] *s* saleté *f*, ordure *f*; (fig) obscénité *f*

filth•y [ˈfɪlθi] *adj* (*comp* **-ier;** *super* **-iest**) sale, immonde

filth′y lu′cre [ˈlukər] *s* (coll) lucre *m*

fin [fɪn] *s* nageoire *f*; **fins** (*for swimming*) palmes *fpl*

final [ˈfaɪnəl] *adj* final; (*last in a series*) ultime, définitif ‖ *s* examen *m* final; (sports) finale *f*

finale [fɪˈnɑli] *s* (mus) final *m*

finalist [ˈfaɪnəlɪst] *s* finaliste *mf*

finally [ˈfaɪnəli] *adv* finalement, enfin

fi′nal touch′ *s* coup *m* de pouce

finance [ˈfaɪnæns] *s* finance *f* ‖ *tr* financer

fi′nance com′pany *s* entreprise *f* de prêt, caisse *f* de prévoyance

financial [faɪˈnænʃəl] *adj* financier; (*interest; distress*) pécuniaire

financier [ˌfaɪnənˈsɪr] *s* financier *m*

financing [ˈfaɪnænsɪŋ] *s* financement *m*

finch [fɪntʃ] *s* pinson *m*

find [faɪnd] *s* trouvaille *f* ‖ *v* (*pret & pp* **found** [faʊnd]) *tr* trouver; **to find out** apprendre ‖

intr (law) déclarer; **to find out (about)** se renseigner (sur), se mettre au courant (de); **find out!** à vous de trouver!

finder [ˈfaɪndər] *s* (*of camera*) viseur *m*; (*of optical instrument*) chercheur *m*

finding [ˈfaɪndɪŋ] *s* découverte *f*; (law) décision *f*; **findings** conclusions *fpl*

fine [faɪn] *adj* fin; (*weather*) beau; (*person, manners, etc.*) distingué, excellent; **that's fine!** bien!, parfait! ‖ *s* amende *f* ‖ *tr* mettre à l'amende

fine′ arts′ *spl* beaux-arts *mpl*

fineness [ˈfaɪnnɪs] *s* finesse *f*; (*of metal*) titre *m*

fine′ print′ *s* petits caractères *mpl*; (*of a contract*) petites lignes *fpl* (illisibles)

finer•y [ˈfaɪnəri] *s* (*pl* **-ies**) parure *f*

finespun [ˈfaɪnˌspʌn] *adj* ténu; (fig) subtil

finesse [fɪˈnɛs] *s* finesse *f*; (*in bridge*) impasse *f*; **to use finesse** finasser ‖ *tr* faire l'impasse à

fine′-toothed comb′ *s* peigne *m* aux dents fines, peigne fin

fine′-tune′ *tr* mettre au point

finger [ˈfɪŋgər] *s* doigt *m*; (slang) mouchard *m*, indicateur *m*; **let's keep our fingers crossed** touchons du bois; **not to lift a finger** (fig) ne pas remuer le petit doigt; **to burn one's fingers** (fig) se faire échauder; **to put one's finger on the spot** (fig) mettre le doigt dessus; **to slip between the fingers** glisser entre les doigts; **to snap one's fingers at** (fig) faire la figue à, narguer; **to twist around one's little finger** (coll) mener par le bout du nez, faire tourner comme un toton ‖ *tr* toucher du doigt, manier; (mus) doigter; (slang) espionner; (slang) identifier

fin′ger board *s* (*of guitar*) touche *f*; (*of piano*) clavier *m*

fin′ger bowl′ *s* rince-doigts *m*

fin′ger dexter′ity *s* (mus) doigté *m*

fin′ger food′ *s* mets *m* mangé en se servant des doigts

fingering [ˈfɪŋgərɪŋ] *s* maniement *m*; (mus) doigté *m*

fin′ger•nail′ *s* ongle *m*

fin′gernail pol′ish *s* brillant *m*

fin′ger•print′ *s* empreinte *f* digitale ‖ *tr* prendre les empreintes digitales de

fin′ger•tip′ *s* bout *m* du doigt; **to have at one's fingertips** tenir sur le bout du doigt

finicky [ˈfɪnɪki] *adj* méticuleux

finish [ˈfɪnɪʃ] *s* (*perfection*) achevé *m*, fini *m*; (*elegance*) finesse *f*; (*conclusion*) fin *f*; (*gloss, coating, etc.*) fini *m* ‖ *tr & intr* finir; **to finish** + *ger* finir de + *inf*; **to finish by** + *ger* finir par + *inf*

fin′ishing touch′ *s* dernière main *f*

finite [ˈfaɪnaɪt] *adj & s* fini *m*

Finland [ˈfɪnlənd] *s* Finlande *f*; la Finlande

Finlander [ˈfɪnləndər] *s* Finlandais *m*

Finn [fɪn] *s* (*member of a Finnish-speaking group of people*) Finnois *m*; (*native or inhabitant of Finland*) Finlandais *m*

Finnish [ˈfɪnɪʃ] *adj & s* finnois *m*

fir [fʌr] *s* sapin *m*

fire [faɪr] *s* feu *m;* (*destructive burning*) incendie *m;* **to catch fire** prendre feu; **to set on fire** mettre le feu à ‖ *tr* mettre le feu à; (*e.g., passions*) enflammer; (*a weapon*) tirer; (*a rocket*) lancer; (*an employee*) (coll) renvoyer ‖ *interj* (*warning*) au feu!; (*command to fire*) feu!

fire′ alarm′ *s* avertisseur *m* d'incendie; (*box*) poste *m* avertisseur d'incendie

fire′arm′ *s* arme *f* à feu

fire′ball′ *s* globe *m* de feu; (mil) grenade *f* incendiaire

fire′bird′ *s* loriot *m* d'Amérique

fire′boat′ *s* bateau-pompe *m*

fire′box′ *s* boîte *f* à feu; (rr) foyer *m*

fire′brand′ *s* tison *m;* (coll) brandon *m* de discorde

fire′break′ *s* tranchée *f* garde-feu, pare-feu *m*

fire′brick′ *s* brique *f* réfractaire

fire′ brigade′ *s* corps *m* de sapeurs-pompiers

fire′bug′ *s* (coll) incendiaire *mf*

fire′ chief′ *s* capitaine *m* des pompiers

fire′ com′pany *s* corps *m* de sapeurs-pompiers; (*insurance company*) compagnie *f* d'assurance contre l'incendie

fire′crack′er *s* pétard *m*

fire′damp′ *s* grisou *m*

fire′ depart′ment *s* service *m* des incendies, sapeurs-pompiers *mpl*

fire′ dog′ *s* chenet *m*, landier *m*

fire′ drill′ *s* exercices *mpl* de sauvetage en cas d'incendie

fire′ en′gine *s* pompe *f* à incendie

fire′ escape′ *s* échelle *f* de sauvetage, escalier *m* de secours

fire′ ex′it *s* sortie *f* de secours

fire′ extin′guisher *s* extincteur *m*

fire′fly′ *s* (*pl* -**flies**) luciole *f*

fire′guard′ *s* (*before hearth*) pare-étincelles *m;* (*in forest*) pare-feu *m*

fire′ hose′ *s* manche *f* d'incendie

fire′house′ *s* caserne *f* de pompiers, poste *m* de pompiers

fire′ hy′drant *s* bouche *f* d'incendie

fire′ insur′ance *s* assurance *f* contre l'incendie

fire′ i′rons *spl* garniture *f* de foyer

fire′ lad′der *s* échelle *f* d'incendie

fire′less cook′er [ˈfaɪrlɪs] *s* marmite *f* norvégienne

fire′man *s* (*pl* -**men**) (*man who stokes fires*) chauffeur *m;* (*man who extinguishes fires*) sapeur-pompier *m*, pompier *m*

fire′place′ *s* cheminée *f*, foyer *m*

fire′plug′ *s* bouche *f* d'incendie

fire′ pow′er *s* puissance *f* de feu

fire′proof′ *adj* ignifuge; (*dish*) apyre ‖ *tr* ignifuger

fire′ sale′ *s* vente *f* après incendie

fire′ screen′ *s* écran *m* de cheminée, gardefeu *m*

fire′ ship′ *s* brûlot *m*

fire′ shov′el *s* pelle *f* à feu

fire′side′ *s* coin *m* du feu

fire′side chat′ *s* (pol) causerie *f* télévisée au coin du feu

fire′trap′ *s* nid-à-feu *m*

fire′ wall′ *s* coupe-feu *m*

fire′ward′en *s* garde *m* forestier, vigie *f*

fire′wa′ter *s* (slang) gnole *f*, whisky *m*

fire′wood′ *s* bois *m* de chauffage

fire′works′ *spl* feu *m* d'artifice

firing [ˈfaɪrɪŋ] (*of furnace*) chauffe *f;* (*of bricks, ceramics, etc.*) cuite *f;* (*of gun*) tir *m*, feu *m;* (*by a group of soldiers*) fusillade *f;* (*of an internal-combustion engine*) allumage *m;* (*of an employee*) (coll) renvoi *m*

fir′ing line′ *s* ligne *f* de feu, chaîne *f* de combat

fir′ing or′der *s* rythme *m* d'allumage

fir′ing pin′ *s* percuteur *m*, aiguille *f*

fir′ing squad′ *s* peloton *m* d'exécution; (*for ceremonies*) piquet *m* d'honneurs funèbres

firm [fʌrm] *adj & adv* ferme; **to stand firm** tenir bon ‖ *s* maison *f* de commerce, firme *f*

firmament [ˈfʌrməmənt] *s* firmament *m*

firm′ name′ *s* nom *m* commercial

firmness [ˈfʌrmnɪs] *s* fermeté *f*

firm′ware′ *s* (comp) programmerie *f* particulière

first [fʌrst] *adj, pron, & s* premier *m;* **a first** (*a record*) une première; **at first** au commencement, au début; **first come first served** les premiers vont devant; **from the first** depuis le premier jour; **John the First** Jean premier ‖ *adv* premièrement, d'abord; **first and last** en tout et pour tout; **first of all, first off** tout d'abord, de prime abord, premièrement

first′ aid′ *s* premiers soins *mpl*, premiers secours *mpl*

first′-aid′ kit′ *s* boîte *f* à pansements, trousse *f* de première urgence

first′-aid′ sta′tion *s* poste *m* de secours

first′-born′ *adj & s* premier-né *m*

first′-class′ *adj* de première classe, de premier ordre ‖ *adv* en première classe

first′ cous′in *s* cousin *m* germain; **first cousin once removed** cousin germain d'un père ou d'une mère, oncle ou tante à la mode de Bretagne

first′ draft′ *s* brouillon *m*, premier jet *m*

first′ fin′ger *s* index *m*

first′ floor′ *s* rez-de-chaussée *m;* (*first floor above the ground floor*) (Brit) premier étage *m*

first′ fruits′ *spl* prémices *fpl*

first′hand′ *adj & adv* de première main

first′ lieuten′ant *s* lieutenant *m* en premier

First′ La′dy *s* (*President's wife*) Première Dame *f*

firstly [ˈfʌrstli] *adv* en premier lieu, d'abord

first′ mate′ *s* (naut) second *m*

first′ name′ *s* prénom *m*, petit nom *m*

first′ night′ *s* (theat) première *f*

first-nighter [ˌfʌrstˈnaɪtər] *s* (theat) habitué *m* des premières

first′ offend′er s délinquant m primaire

first′ of′ficer s (naut) officier m en second

first′ prize′ s (in a lottery) gros lot m; **to win first prize** remporter le prix

first′ quar′ter s (of the moon) premier quartier m

first′-rate′ adj de premier ordre, de première qualité; (coll) excellent ‖ adv (coll) très bien, à merveille

first′-run mov′ie s film m en exclusivité

first′ try′ s coup m d'essai

fiscal [ˈfɪskəl] adj fiscal

fis′cal year′ s exercice m budgétaire

fish [fɪʃ] s poisson m; **cold fish** (coll) pisse-froid m; **to be like a fish out of water** être comme un poisson sur la paille; **to be neither fish nor fowl** être ni chair ni poisson; **to drink like a fish** boire comme un trou; **to have other fish to fry** avoir d'autres chiens à fouetter ‖ tr pêcher; (rr) éclisser; **to fish out** or **up** repêcher ‖ intr pêcher; **to fish for compliments** quêter des compliments; **to go fishing** aller à la pêche; **to take fishing** emmener à la pêche

fish′ and chips′ s (culin) poisson m et chips f

fish′bone′ s arête f

fish′bowl′ s bocal m

fisher [ˈfɪʃər] s pêcheur m; (zool) martre f

fish′er·man s (pl -men) pêcheur m

fisher·y [ˈfɪʃəri] s (pl -ies) (activity; business) pêche f; (grounds) pêcherie f

fish′-eye lens′ s objectif m angle plat

fish′ hawk′ s aigle m pêcheur

fish′hook′ s hameçon m

fishing [ˈfɪʃɪŋ] adj pêcheur, de pêche ‖ s pêche f

fish′ing ground′ s pêcherie f

fish′ing reel′ s moulinet m

fish′ing rod′ s canne f à pêche

fish′ing tack′le s attirail m de pêche

fish′line′ s ligne f de pêche

fish′ mar′ket s poissonnerie f

fish′net stock′ings spl bas mpl en résille

fish′plate′ s (rr) éclisse f

fish′pool′ s vivier m

fish′ spear′ s foëne f, fouëne f

fish′ stick′ s (culin) bâtonnet m de poisson

fish′ sto′ry s hâblerie f, blague f

fish′tail′ s queue f de poisson; (aer) embardée f ‖ intr (aer) embarder

fish′wife′ s (pl -wives′) poissonnière f; (foul-mouthed woman) poissarde f

fish′worm′ s asticot m

fish·y [ˈfɪʃi] adj (comp -ier; super -iest) (eyes) (coll) vitreux; (coll) véreux, louche, pas franc du collier

fission [ˈfɪʃən] s (biol) scission f; (nucl) fission f

fissionable [ˈfɪʃənəbəl] adj fissible, fissile

fissure [ˈfɪʃər] s fissure f, fente f ‖ tr fissurer ‖ intr se fissurer

fist [fɪst] s poing m; (typ) petite main f; **to shake one's fist at** menacer du poing

fist′fight′ s combat m à coup de poings

fistful [ˈfɪstful] s poignée f

fisticuffs [ˈfɪstɪˌkʌfs] spl empoignade f or rixe f à coups de poing; (sports) boxe f

fit [fɪt] adj (comp **fitter**; super **fittest**) bon, convenable; capable, digne; (in good health) en forme, sain; **fit to be tied** en colère; **fit to drink** buvable; **fit to eat** mangeable; **to feel fit** être frais et dispos ‖ s ajustement m; (of clothes) coupe f, façon f; (of fever, rage, coughing) accès m; **by fits and starts** par accès; **fit of coughing** quinte f de toux ‖ v (pret & pp **fitted**; ger **fitting**) tr ajuster; (s.th. in s.th.) emboîter; **to fit for** (e.g., a task) préparer à; **to fit out** or **up** aménager; **to fit out with** garnir de ‖ intr s'emboîter; **to fit in** tenir dans; **to fit in with** s'accorder avec, convenir à

fitful [ˈfɪtfəl] adj intermittent

fitness [ˈfɪtnɪs] s convenance f; (for a task) aptitude f; (good shape) bonne forme f

fit′ness buff′ s (coll) fanatique mf de la gymnastique

fit′ness cen′ter s gymnase m, établissement m pour pratiquer des exercices physiques

fit′ted sheet′ s drap m à quatre pointes

fitter [ˈfɪtər] s ajusteur m; (of machinery) monteur m; (of clothing) essayeur m

fitting [ˈfɪtɪŋ] adj convenable, approprié, à propos ‖ s ajustage m; (of a garment) essayage m; **fittings** aménagements mpl; (of metal) ferrures fpl

five [faɪv] adj & pron cinq ‖ s cinq m; **five o'clock** cinq heures

five′-year plan′ s plan m quinquennal

fix [fɪks] s (aer, naut) position f; (coll) mauvais pas m; (injection) (slang) piqûre f, piquouse f, dose f; **to be in a fix** (coll) être dans le pétrin; **to give oneself a fix** (slang) se shooter, se piquer ‖ tr réparer; (e.g., a date; a photographic image; prices; one's eyes) fixer; (slang) donner son compte à

fixed′ as′sets spl capital m fixe

fixedly [ˈfɪksɪdli] adv fixement

fixed′-price′ con′tract s marché m à forfait

fixing [ˈfɪksɪŋ] s fixation f; (phot) fixage m; **fixings** (slang) collation f, des mets mpl

fix′ing bath′ s bain m de fixage, fixateur m

fixture [ˈfɪkstʃər] s accessoire m, garniture f; **fixtures** meubles mpl à demeure

fizz [fɪz] s pétillement m ‖ intr pétiller

fizzle [ˈfɪzəl] s (coll) avortement m ‖ intr (coll) avorter; **to fizzle out** (coll) tomber à l'eau, échouer

flabbergasted [ˈflæbərˌgæstɪd] adj (coll) éberlué, épaté

flab·by [ˈflæbi] adj (comp -bier; super -biest) mou, flasque; **to become flabby** s'avachir

flag [flæg] s drapeau m ‖ v (pret & pp **flagged**; ger **flagging**) tr—**to flag s.o.** transmettre des signaux à qn en agitant un fanion ‖ intr faiblir, se relâcher

flag′ cap′tain s (nav) capitaine m de pavillon

flagger [ˈflægər] s employé routier ou employée routière qui régle la circulation par moyen d'un drapeau

flag'man s (pl -men) (rr) garde-voie m

flag' of truce' s drapeau m parlementaire

flag'pole' s hampe f de drapeau; (naut) mât m de pavillon; (surv) jalon m

flagrant [ˈflegrənt] adj scandaleux; (e.g., injustice) flagrant

flag'ship' s (nav) vaisseau m amiral

flag'staff' s hampe f de drapeau

flag'stone' s dalle f

flag' stop' s (rr) halte f, arrêt m facultatif

flag'-wav'ing adj cocardier ‖ s patriotisme m de façade

flail [flel] s fléau m ‖ tr (agr) battre au fléau; (fig) éreinter

flair [flɛr] s flair m; aptitude f

flak [flæk] s tir m contre-avions

flake [flek] s (of snow; of cereal) flocon m; (of soap; of mica) paillette f; (of paint) écaille f ‖ intr tomber en flocons; **to flake off** s'écailler

flak•y [ˈfleki] adj (comp -ier; super -iest) floconneux, lamelleux

flamboyant [flæmˈbɔɪənt] adj fleuri, orné, coloré; (archit) flamboyant

flame [flem] s flamme f; (coll) amant m, amante f ‖ tr flamber ‖ intr flamber, flamboyer

flamethrower [ˈflem,θroʊ•ər] s lance-flammes m

flaming [ˈflemɪŋ] adj flambant

flamin•go [fləˈmɪŋgo] s (pl -gos or -goes) flamant m

flammable [ˈflæməbəl] adj inflammable

Flanders [ˈflændərz] s Flandre f; la Flandre

flange [flændʒ] s rebord m, saillie f; (of wheel) jante f; (of rail) patin m

flank [flæŋk] s flanc m ‖ tr flanquer

flannel [ˈflænəl] s flanelle f

flap [flæp] s (part that can be folded under) rabat m; (fold in clothing) pan m; (of a cap) couvre-nuque m; (of a pocket; of an envelope) patte f; (of wings) coup m, battement m; (of a table) battant m; (of a sail, flag, etc.) claquement m; (slap) tape f; (aer) volet m ‖ v (pret & pp **flapped;** ger **flapping**) tr (wings, arms, etc.) battre; (to slap) taper ‖ intr battre; (said of sail, flag, etc.) claquer; (said of curtain) voltiger; (to hang down) pendre

flap'jack' s (coll) crêpe f

flare [flɛr] s (of light or fire) éclat m vif; (e.g., of skirt; of pipe or funnel) évasement m; (for signaling) fusée f éclairante ‖ tr évaser ‖ intr flamboyer; (to spread outward) s'évaser; **to flare up** s'enflammer; (to reappear) se produire de nouveau; (to become angry) s'emporter

flare'-up' s flambée f soudaine; (of illness) recrudescence f; (of anger) accès m de colère

flash [flæʃ] s (of lightning) éclair m; (of flame, jewels) éclat m; (of hope) lueur f, rayon m; (of wit) trait m; (of genius) éclair; (brief moment) instant m; (phot) flash m; (ostentation) (coll) tape-à-l'œil m; (last-minute news) (coll) nou-

velle f éclair; **flash in the pan** (coll) feu m de paille; **in a flash** en un clin d'œil ‖ tr projeter; (a gem) faire étinceler; (to show off) faire parade de; (a message) répandre, transmettre ‖ intr jeter des éclairs; (said of gem, eyes, etc.) étinceler; **to flash by** passer comme un éclair

flash'back' s (mov) retour m en arrière, rappel m, rétrospectif m

flash'bulb' s ampoule f flash, flash m

flasher [ˈflæʃər] s (flashing) clignotant m; (obscene) exhibitionniste m

flash' flood' s crue f subite

flashing [ˈflæʃɪŋ] adj éclatant; (light) à éclats; (signal) clignotant ‖ s bande f de solin

flash'light' s lampe f torche, lampe de poche; (phot) lampe éclair

flash'light bat'tery s pile f torche

flash•y [ˈflæʃi] adj (comp -ier; super -iest) (coll) tapageur, criard

flask [flæsk] s flacon m, gourde f; (in lab) ballon m, flacon

flat [flæt] adj (comp **flatter;** super **flattest**) (level) plat, uni; (nose) aplati; (refusal) net; (beer) éventé; (tire) dégonflé; (dull, tasteless) fade, terne; (mus) bémol ‖ s appartement m; (flat tire) crevaison f; (of sword) plat m; (mus) bémol m; (theat) châssis m ‖ adv (outright) (coll) nettement, carrément; **to fall flat** tomber à plat; (fig) manquer son effet; **to sing flat** chanter faux

flat'boat' s plate f

flat-broke [ˈflætˈbrok] adj (coll) complètement fauché, à la côte

flat'car' s plate-forme f

flat'foot' s (police) (slang) flic m, vache f

flat'-foot'ed adj aux pieds plats; (coll) franc, brutal

flat'i'ron s fer m à repasser

flatly [ˈflætli] adv net, platement

flat'-nosed' adj camard, camus

flat' screen' s (telv) écran m plat

flatten [ˈflætən] tr aplatir, aplanir; (metallurgy) laminer ‖ intr s'aplatir, s'aplanir; **to flatten out** (aer) se redresser

flatter [ˈflætər] tr & intr flatter

flatterer [ˈflætərər] s flatteur m

flattering [ˈflætərɪŋ] adj flatteur

flatter•y [ˈflætəri] s (pl -ies) flatterie f

flat' tire' s pneu m dégonflé, à plat, or crevé, crevaison f

flat'top' s (nav) porte-avions m

flatulence [ˈflætʃələns] s boursouflure f; (pathol) flatulence f

flat'ware' s couverts mpl; (plates) assiettes fpl

flaunt [flɔnt] tr faire étalage de

flautist [ˈflɔtɪst] s flûtiste mf

flavor [ˈflevər] s saveur f, goût m; (of ice cream) parfum m ‖ tr assaisonner, parfumer

flavoring [ˈflevərɪŋ] s assaisonnement m; (lemon, rum, etc.) parfum m

flaw [flɔ] s (defect) défaut m, tache f, vice m; (crack) fêlure f; (in metal) paille f; (in diamond) crapaud m

flawless [ˈflɔlɪs] *adj* sans défaut, sans tache

flax [flæks] *s* lin *m*

flaxen [ˈflæksən] *adj* de lin, blond

flax'seed' *s* graine *f* de lin

flay [fle] *tr* écorcher; (*to criticize*) rosser, fustiger

flea [fli] *s* puce *f*

flea' and tick' col'lar *s* collier *m* antiparasitaire

flea'bite' *s* piqûre *f* de puce; (*trifle*) vétille *f*

flea' mar'ket *s* marché *m* aux puces

fleck [flɛk] *s* tache *f*; (*particle*) particule *f* ‖ *tr* tacheter

fledgling [ˈflɛdʒlɪŋ] *adj* (*lawyer, teacher*) en herbe, débutant ‖ *s* oisillon *m*; (*novice*) débutant *m*, béjaune *m*

flee [fli] *v* (*pret & pp* **fled** [flɛd]) *tr & intr* fuir

fleece [flis] *s* toison *f* ‖ *tr* tondre; (*to strip of money*) (coll) écorcher, plumer

fleec•y [ˈflisi] *adj* (*comp* **-ier;** *super* **-iest**) laineux; (*snow, wool*) floconneux; (*hair*) moutonneux; (*clouds*) moutonné

fleet [flit] *adj* rapide ‖ *s* flotte *f*

fleet'-foot'ed *adj* au pied léger

fleeting [ˈflitɪŋ] *adj* passager, fugitif

Fleming [ˈflɛmɪŋ] *s* Flamand *m*

Flemish [ˈflɛmɪʃ] *adj & s* flamand *m*

flesh [flɛʃ] *s* chair *f*; **in the flesh** en chair et en os; **to lose flesh** perdre de l'embonpoint; **to put on flesh** prendre de l'embonpoint, s'empâter

flesh' and blood' *s* nature *f* humaine; (*relatives*) famille *f*, parenté *f*

flesh'-col'ored *adj* couleur *f* de chair, carné, incarnat

flesh'pot' *s* (*pot for cooking meat*) pot-au-feu *m*; **fleshpots** (*high living*) luxe *m*, grande chère *f*; (*evil places*) maisons *fpl* de débauche, mauvais lieux *mpl*

flesh' wound' [wʊnd] *s* blessure *f* en séton, blessure superficielle

flesh•y [ˈflɛʃi] *adj* (*comp* **-ier;** *super* **-iest**) charnu

flex [flɛks] *tr & intr* fléchir

flexible [ˈflɛksɪbəl] *adj* flexible

flex(i)time [ˈflɛks(ə)ˌtaɪm] *s* horaire *m* flottant

flick [flɪk] *s* (*with finger*) chiquenaude *f*; (*with whip*) petit coup *m*; **flicks** (coll) ciné *m* ‖ *tr* faire une chiquenaude à; (*a whip*) faire claquer

flicker [ˈflɪkər] *s* petite lueur *f* vacillante; (*of eyelids*) battement *m*; (*of emotion*) frisson *m* ‖ *intr* trembloter, vaciller; (*said of eyelids*) ciller

flier [ˈflaɪər] *s* aviateur *m*; (coll) spéculation *f* au hasard; (rr) rapide *m*; (*handbill*) (coll) prospectus *m*

flight [flaɪt] *s* fuite *f*; (*of airplane*) vol *m*; (*of birds*) volée *f*; (*of stairs*) volée; (*of fancy*) élan *m*; **to put to flight** mettre en fuite; **to take flight** prendre la fuite

flight' attend'ant *s* (aer) membre *m* du personnel qui sert les passagers

flight' controls' *spl* commandes *fpl* de vol

flight' deck' *s* (nav) pont *m* d'envol

flight' plan' *s* plan *m* de vol

flight' record'er *s* enregistreur *m* de vol

flight•y [ˈflaɪti] *adj* (*comp* **-ier;** *super* **-iest**) volage, léger; braque, écervelé

flim•flam [ˈflɪmˌflæm] *s* (coll) baliverne *f*; (*fraud*) (coll) escroquerie *f* ‖ *v* (*pret & pp* **-flammed;** *ger* **-flamming**) *tr* (coll) escroquer

flim•sy [ˈflɪmzi] *adj* (*comp* **-sier;** *super* **-siest**) léger; (*e.g., cloth*) fragile; (*e.g., excuse*) frivole

flinch [flɪntʃ] *intr* reculer, fléchir; **without flinching** sans broncher, sans hésiter

fling [flɪŋ] *s* jet *m*; **to go on a fling** faire la noce; **to have a fling at** tenter; **to have one's fling** jeter sa gourme ‖ *v* (*pret & pp* **flung** [flʌŋ]) *tr* lancer; (*on the floor, out the window; in jail*) jeter; **to fling open** ouvrir brusquement

flint [flɪnt] *s* silex *m*; (*of lighter*) pierre *f*

flint'lock' *s* fusil *m* à pierre

flint•y [ˈflɪnti] *adj* (*comp* **-ier;** *super* **-iest**) siliceux; (*heart*) de pierre, insensible

flip [flɪp] *adj* (*comp* **flipper;** *super* **flippest**) (coll) mutin, moqueur ‖ *s* (*flick*) chiquenaude *f*; (*somersault*) culbute *f*; (aer) petit tour *m* de vol ‖ *v* (*pret & pp* **flipped;** *ger* **flipping**) *tr* donner une chiquenaude à; (*a page*) tourner rapidement; **to flip a coin** jouer à pile ou face; **to flip over** (*a phonograph record*) retourner

flippancy [ˈflɪpənsi] *s* désinvolture *f*

flippant [ˈflɪpənt] *adj* désinvolte

flipper [ˈflɪpər] *s* nageoire *f*

flip' side' *s* autre face *f* (d'un disque)

flirt [flʌrt] *s* flirteur *m*, flirt *m* ‖ *intr* flirter; (*said only of a man*) conter fleurette

flit [flɪt] *v* (*pret & pp* **flitted;** *ger* **flitting**) *intr* voleter; **to flit away** passer rapidement; **to flit here and there** voltiger

float [flot] *s* (*raft*) radeau *m*; (*on fish line; in carburetor; on seaplane*) flotteur *m*; (*on fish line or net*) flotte *f*; (*of mason*) aplanissoire *f*; (*in parade*) char *m* de cavalcade, char de Carnaval ‖ *tr* faire flotter; (*a loan*) émettre, contracter ‖ *intr* flotter, nager; (*on one's back*) faire la planche

floater [ˈflotər] *s* (*tramp*) vagabond *m*; (*illegal voter*) faux électeur *m*

floating [ˈflotɪŋ] *adj* flottant; (*free*) libre ‖ *s* flottement *m*; (*of loan*) émission *f*

float'ing is'land *s* (culin) œufs *mpl* à la neige

flock [flɑk] *s* (*of birds*) volée *f*; (*of sheep*) troupeau *m*; (*of people*) foule *f*, bande *f*; (*of nonsense*) tas *m*; (*of faithful*) ouailles *fpl* ‖ *intr* s'assembler; **to flock in** entrer en foule; **to flock together** s'attrouper

floe [flo] *s* banquise *f*; (*floating piece of ice*) glaçon *m* flottant

flog [flɑg] *v* (*pret & pp* **flogged;** *ger* **flogging**) *tr* fouetter, flageller

flogging [ˈflɑgɪŋ] *s* fouet *m*

flood [flʌd] *s* inondation *f*; (*caused by heavy rain*) déluge *m*; (*sudden rise of river*) crue *f*; (*of tide*) flot *m*; (*of words, tears, light*) flots *mpl,* déluge ‖ *tr* inonder; (*to overwhelm*) submerger, inonder; (*a carburetor*) noyer ‖ *intr* (*said of river*) déborder; (aut) se noyer

flood′gate′ *s* (*of a dam*) vanne *f;* (*of a canal*) porte *f* d'écluse

flood′light′ *s* phare *m* d'éclairage, projecteur *m* de lumière ‖ *tr* illuminer par projecteurs

flood′tide′ *s* marée *f* montante, flux *m*

floor [flor] *s* (*inside bottom surface of room*) plancher *m,* parquet *m;* (*story of building*) étage *m;* (*of swimming pool, the sea, etc.*) fond *m;* (*of assembly hall*) enceinte *f,* parquet; (*of the court*) prétoire *m,* parquet; (naut) varangue *f;* **to ask for the floor** réclamer la parole; **to give s.o. the floor** donner la parole à qn; **to have the floor** avoir la parole; **to take the floor** prendre la parole ‖ *tr* parqueter; (*an opponent*) terrasser; (*to disconcert*) (coll) désarconner

floor′board′ *s* planche *f* de plancher, latte *f* de plancher

flooring [`florɪŋ] *s* planchéiage *m,* parquetage *m*

floor′ lamp′ *s* lampe *f* à pied, lampadaire *m*

floor′ mop′ *s* brosse *f* à parquet

floor′ sam′ple *s* article *m* de démonstration, article de montre

floor′ show′ *s* spectacle *m* de cabaret

floor′ tim′ber *s* (naut) varangue *f*

floor′walk′er *s* chef *m* de rayon

floor′ wax′ *s* cire *f* à parquet, encaustique *f*

flop [flɑp] *s* (coll) insuccès *m,* échec *m;* (*literary work or painting*) (coll) navet *m;* (*play*) (coll) four *m;* **to take a flop** (coll) faire patapouf ‖ *v* (*pret & pp* **flopped;** *ger* **flopping**) *intr* tomber lourdement; (*to fail*) (coll) échouer, rater

floppy [`flɑpi] *adj* lâche, flottant

flop′py disk′ *s* (comp) (obs) disquette *f,* disque *m* souple

flora [`florə] *s* flore *f*

floral [`florəl] *adj* floral

florescence [flo`resəns] *s* floraison *f*

florid [`florɪd] *adj* fleuri, flamboyant; (*complexion*) rubicond

Florida [`florɪdə] *s* Floride *f;* la Floride

Flor′ida Keys′ *spl* Cayes *fpl* de la Floride

floss [flɔs] *s* bourre *f;* (*of corn*) barbe *f*

floss′ silk′ *s* bourre *f* de soie, filoselle *f*

floss•y [`flɔsi] *adj* (*comp* **-ier;** *super* **-iest**) soyeux; (slang) pimpant, tapageur

flotsam [`flɑtsəm] *s* épave *f*

flot′sam and jet′sam *s* choses *fpl* de flot et de mer, épaves *fpl*

flounce [flaʊns] *s* volant *m* ‖ *tr* garnir de volants ‖ *intr* s'élancer avec emportement

flounder [`flaʊndər] *s* flet *m;* (*plaice*) carrelet *m,* plie *f* ‖ *intr* patauger

flour [flaʊr] *s* farine *f* ‖ *tr* fariner

flourish [`flʌrɪʃ] *s* fioriture *f;* (*on a signature*) paraphe *m;* (*of trumpets*) fanfare *m;* (*brandishing*) brandissement *m* ‖ *tr* brandir; (*to wave*) agiter ‖ *intr* fleurir, prospérer

flourishing [`flʌrɪʃɪŋ] *adj* florissant

flour′ mill′ *s* moulin *m,* minoterie *f*

floury [`flaʊri] *adj* farineux

flout [flaʊt] *tr* se moquer de, narguer ‖ *intr* se moquer

flow [flo] *s* (*running*) écoulement *m;* (*of tide, blood, words*) flot *m,* flux *m;* (*of blood to the head*) afflux *m;* (*current*) courant *m* ‖ *intr* écouler; (*said of tide*) monter; (*said of blood in the body*) circuler; (fig) couler; **to flow into** déboucher dans, se verser dans; **to flow over** déborder

flow′chart′ *s* organigramme *m,* ordinogramme *m*

flower [`flaʊ•ər] *s* fleur *f* ‖ *tr & intr* fleurir

flow′er bed′ *s* plate-bande *f,* parterre *m;* (*round flower bed*) corbeille *f*

flow′er gar′den *s* jardin *m* de fleurs, jardin d'agrément

flow′er girl′ *s* bouquetière *f;* (*at a wedding*) fille *f* d'honneur

flow′er•pot′ *s* pot *m* à fleurs

flow′er shop′ *s* boutique *f* de fleuriste

flow′er show′ *s* exposition *f* horticole, floralies *fpl*

flow′er stand′ *s* jardinière *f*

flowery [`flaʊ•əri] *adj* fleuri

flu [flu] *s* (coll) grippe *f*

fluctuate [`flʌktʃʊ,et] *intr* fluctuer

flue [flu] *s* tuyau *m*

fluency [`flu•ənsi] *s* facilité *f*

fluent [`flu•ənt] *adj* disert, facile; (*flowing*) coulant

fluently [`flu•əntli] *adv* couramment

fluff [flʌf] *s* (*velvety cloth*) peluche *f;* (*tuft of fur, dust, etc.*) duvet *m;* (*boner made by actor*) (coll) loup *m* ‖ *tr* lainer, rendre pelucheux; (*one's entrance*) (coll) louper; (*one's lines*) (coll) bouler ‖ *intr* pelucher

fluff•y [`flʌfi] *adj* (*comp* **-ier;** *super* **-iest**) duveteux; (*hair*) flou

fluid [`flu•ɪd] *adj & s* fluide *m*

fluke [fluk] *s* (*of anchor*) patte *f;* (billiards) raccroc *m,* coup *m* de veine

flume [flum] *s* canalisation *f,* ravin *m*

flunk [flʌŋk] *tr* (*a student*) (coll) recaler, coller; (*an exam*) rater ‖ *intr* être recalé, se faire coller

flunk•y [`flʌŋki] *s* (*pl* **-ies**) laquais *m*

fluorescent [,flu•ə`resənt] *adj* fluorescent

fluoridate [`florɪ,det] *tr & intr* fluorider

fluoridation [,florɪ`deʃən] *s* fluoridation *f*

fluoride [`flu•ə,raɪd] *s* fluorure *m*

fluorine [`flu•ə,rin] *s* fluor *m*

fluoroscopy [,flu•ə`rɑskəpi] *s* radioscopie *f*

fluorspar [`flu•ər,spɑr] *s* spath *m* fluor

flur•ry [`flʌri] *s* (*pl* **-ries**) agitation *f;* (*of wind, snow, etc.*) rafale *f* ‖ *v* (*pret & pp* **-ried**) *tr* agiter

flush [flʌʃ] *adj* (*level*) à ras; (*well-provided*) bien pourvu; (*healthy*) vigoureux; **flush with** au ras de, au niveau de ‖ *s* (*of light*) éclat *m;* (*in the cheeks*) rougeur *f;* (*of joy*) transport *m;* (*of toilet*) chasse *f* d'eau; (*in poker*) flush *m;* **in the first flush of** dans l'ivresse or le premier éclat de ‖ *adv* à ras, de niveau; (*directly*) droit ‖ *tr* (*a bird*) lever; **to flush a toilet** tirer la chasse d'eau; **to flush out** (*e.g., a drain*) laver à grande eau ‖ *intr* (*to blush*) rougir

flush′ switch′ *s* interrupteur *m* encastré

flush′ tank′ *s* réservoir *m* de chasse

flush′ toi′let *s* water-closet *m* à chasse d'eau

fluster [ˈflʌstər] *s* agitation *f;* **in a fluster** en émoi ‖ *tr* agiter

flute [flut] *s* flûte *f* ‖ *tr* (*a column*) canneler; (*a dress*) tuyauter

flutist [ˈflutɪst] *s* flûtiste *mf*

flutter [ˈflʌtər] *s* battement *m;* **all of a flutter** (coll) tout agité ‖ *intr* voleter; (*said of pulse*) battre fébrilement; (*said of heart*) palpiter

flux [flʌks] *s* flux *m;* (*for fusing metals*) acide *m* à souder; **to be in flux** être dans un état indécis

fly [flaɪ] *s* (*pl* **-flies**) mouche *f;* (*for fishing*) mouche artificielle; (*of trousers*) braguette *f;* (*of tent*) auvent *m;* **flies** (theat) cintres *mpl;* **fly in the ointment** (fig) ombre *f* au tableau; **on the fly** au vol ‖ *v* (*pret* **flew** [flu]; *pp* **flown** [flon]) *tr* (*a kite*) faire voler; (*an airplane*) piloter; (*freight or passengers*) transporter en avion; (*e.g., the Atlantic*) survoler; (*to flee from*) fuir ‖ *intr* voler; (*to flee*) fuir; (*said of flag*) flotter; **to fly blind** voler à l'aveuglette; **to fly by** voler; **to fly in the face of** porter un défi à; **to fly off** s'envoler; **to fly off the handle** (coll) sortir de ses gonds; **to fly open** s'ouvrir brusquement; **to fly over** survoler

fly′blow′ *s* œufs *mpl* de mouche

fly′-by-night′ *adj* mal financé, indigne de confiance ‖ *s* financier *m* qui lève le pied

fly′ cast′ing *s* pêche *f* à la mouche noyée

fly′catch′er *s* attrape-mouches *m;* (bot) dionée *f,* attrape-mouches; (orn) gobemouches *m*

fly′-fish′ *intr* pêcher à la mouche

flying [ˈflaɪ•ɪŋ] *adj* volant; rapide; court, passager ‖ *s* aviation *f;* vol *m*

fly′ing but′tress *s* arc-boutant *m*

fly′ing col′ors —with flying colors drapeau *m* déployé; brillamment

fly′ing field′ *s* champ *m* d'aviation

fly′ing•fish′ *s* poisson *m* volant

fly′ing sau′cer *s* soucoupe *f* volante

fly′ing sick′ness *s* maladie *f* d'altitude

fly′ing start′ *s* départ *m* lancé

fly′ing time′ *s* heures *fpl* de vol

fly′leaf′ *s* (*pl* **-leaves**) feuille *f* de garde, garde *f*

fly′ net′ *s* (*for a bed*) moustiquaire *f;* (*for a horse*) chasse-mouches *m*

fly′pa′per *s* papier *m* tue-mouches

fly′rod′ *s* canne *f* à mouche

fly′speck′ *s* chiure *f,* chiasse *f*

fly′ swat′ter [ˌswɑtər] *s* chasse-mouches *m,* émouchoir *m,* tapette *f* tue-mouche

fly′trap′ *s* attrape-mouches *m*

fly′weight′ *s* (boxing) poids *m* mouche

fly′wheel′ *s* volant *m*

FM [ˈɛfˈɛm] *s* (letterword) (**frequency modulation**) modulation *f* de fréquence

foal [fol] *s* poulain *m* ‖ *intr* mettre bas

foam [fom] *s* écume *f;* (*on beer*) mousse *f* ‖ *intr* écumer, mousser

foam′ extin′guisher *s* extincteur à mousse

foam′ rub′ber *s* caoutchouc *m* mousse

foam•y [ˈfomi] *adj* (*comp* **-ier;** *super* **-iest**) écumeux, mousseux

fob [fɑb] *s* (*pocket*) gousset *m;* (*ornament*) breloque *f* ‖ *v* (*pret & pp* **fobbed;** *ger* **fobbing**) *tr***—to fob off s.th. on s.o.** refiler q.ch. à qn

f.o.b. or **F.O.B.** [ˌɛfˌoˈbi] *adv* (letterword) (**free on board**) franco de bord, départ usine

focal [ˈfokəl] *adj* focal

fo•cus [ˈfokəs] *s* (*pl* **-cuses** or **-ci** [saɪ]) foyer *m;* **in focus** au point; **out of focus** non réglé, hors du point focal ‖ *v* (*pret & pp* **-cused** or **-cussed;** *ger* **-cusing** or **-cussing**) *tr* mettre au point, faire converger; (*a beam of electrons*) focaliser; (*e.g., attention*) concentrer ‖ *intr* converger; **to focus on** se concentrer sur

fodder [ˈfɑdər] *s* fourrage *m*

foe [fo] *s* ennemi *m,* adversaire *mf*

fog [fɔg] *s* brouillard *m;* (naut) brume *f;* (phot) voile *m* ‖ *v* (*pret & pp* **fogged;** *ger* **fogging**) *tr* embrumer; (phot) voiler ‖ *intr* s'embrumer; (phot) se voiler

fog′ bank′ *s* banc *m* de brume

fog′ bell′ *s* cloche *f* de brume

fog′bound′ *adj* arrêté par le brouillard, pris dans le brouillard

fog•gy [ˈfɔgi] *adj* (*comp* **-gier;** *super* **-giest**) brumeux; (phot) voilé; (fig) confus, flou; **it is foggy** il fait du brouillard

fog′ horn′ *s* sirène *f,* corne *f,* or trompe *f* de brume

fog′ light′ *s* phare *m* antibrouillard

fogy [ˈfogi] *s* (slang) croulant *m*

foible [ˈfɔɪbəl] *s* faible *m,* marotte *f*

foil [fɔɪl] *s* (*thin sheet of metal*) feuille *f,* lame *f;* (*of mirror*) tain *m;* (*sword*) fleuret *m;* (*person whose personality sets off another's*) repoussoir *m* ‖ *tr* déjouer, frustrer

foil′-wrapped′ *adj* ceint de papier d'argent

foist [fɔɪst] *tr***—to foist oneself upon** s'imposer chez; **to foist s.th. on s.o.** imposer q.ch. à qn

fold [fold] *s* (*crease*) pli *m,* repli *m;* (*for sheep*) parc *m,* bergerie *f;* (*of fat*) bourrelet *m;* (*of the faithful*) bercail *m* ‖ *tr* plier, replier; (*one's arms*) se croiser; **to fold in** (culin) incorporer; **to fold up** replier ‖ *intr* se replier; **to fold up** (theat) faire four; (coll) s'effondrer

folder [ˈfoldər] *s* (*covers for holding papers*) chemise *f,* chemise classeur; (*pamphlet*) dépliant *m;* (*person folding newspapers*) plieur *m*

folderol [ˈfɑldəˌrɑl] *s* sottise *f;* (*piece of foolishness*) bagatelle *f*

folding [ˈfoldɪŋ] *adj* pliant, repliant, rabattable

fold′ing cam′era *s* appareil *m* pliant

fold′ing chair′ *s* chaise *f* pliante, chaise brisée

fold′ing cot′ *s* lit *m* pliant or escamotable

fold′ing door′ *s* porte *f* à deux battants

fold′ing rule′ *s* mètre *m* pliant

fold′ing screen′ *s* paravent *m*

fold′ing seat′ *s* strapontin *m*

foliage [′folɪ·ɪdʒ] *s* feuillage *m*, feuillu *m*

foli·o [′folɪˌo] *adj* in-folio ‖ *s* (*pl* **-os**) (*sheet*) folio *m;* (*book*) in-folio ‖ *tr* folioter, paginer

folk [fok] *adj* populaire, traditionnel, du peuple ‖ *s* (*pl* **folk** or **folks**) peuple *m*, race *f;* **folks** (coll) gens *mpl*, personnes *fpl;* **my folks** (coll) les miens *mpl*, ma famille

folk′ dance′ *s* danse *f* folklorique

folk′lore′ *s* folklore *m*

folk′ mu′sic *s* musique *f* populaire

folk′ song′ *s* chanson *f* du terroir

folk·sy [′foksi] *adj* (*comp* **-sier;** *super* **-siest**) (coll) sociable, liant; (*like common people*) (coll) du terroir

folk′ways′ *spl* coutumes *fpl* traditionnelles

follicle [′falɪkəl] *s* follicule *m*

follow [′falo] *tr* suivre; (*to come after*) succéder; (*to understand*) comprendre; (*a profession*) embrasser; **to follow up** poursuivre; (*e.g., a success*) exploiter ‖ *intr* suivre; (*one after the other*) se suivre; **as follows** comme suit; **it follows that** il s'ensuit que

follower [′falo·ər] *s* suivant *m;* partisan *m*, disciple *m*, épigone *m*

following [′falo·ɪŋ] *adj* suivant ‖ *s* (*of a prince*) suite *f;* (*followers*) partisans *mpl*, disciples *mpl*

fol′low the lead′er *s* jeu *m* de la queue leu leu

fol′low-up′ *adj* de continuation, complémentaire; (*car*) suiveur ‖ *s* soins *mpl* post-hospitaliers

fol·ly [′fali] *s* (*pl* **-lies**) sottise *f;* (*madness*) folie *f;* **follies** spectacle *m* de music-hall, folies *fpl*

foment [fo′mɛnt] *tr* fomenter

fond [fand] *adj* affectueux, tendre; **to become fond of** s'attacher à

fondle [′fandəl] *tr* caresser

fondness [′fandnɪs] *s* affection *f*, tendresse *f;* (*appetite*) goût *m*, penchant *m*

font [fant] *s* source *f;* (*for holy water*) bénitier *m;* (*for baptism*) fonts *mpl;* (typ) fonte *f*

food [fud] *adj* alimentaire ‖ *s* nourriture *f*, aliments *mpl;* **food for thought** matière *f* à réflexion; **good food** bonne cuisine *f*

food′ and cloth′ing *s* le vivre et le vêtement

food′ and drink′ *s* le boire et le manger

food′ poi′soning *s* intoxication *f* alimentaire

food′ proc′essor *s* robot *m* multifonctions

food′ slic′er *s* trancheuse *f*

food′ stamp′ *s* bon *m* d'alimentation

food′stuffs′ *spl* denrées *fpl* alimentaires, vivres *mpl*

fool [ful] *s* sot *m;* (*jester*) fou *m;* (*person imposed on*) innocent *m*, niais *m;* **to make a fool of** se moquer de; **to play the fool** faire le pitre ‖ *tr* mystifier, abuser; **to fool away** gaspiller sottement ‖ *intr* faire la bête; **to fool around** (coll) gâcher son temps; **to fool with** (coll) tripoter

fooler·y [′fuləri] *s* (*pl* **-ies**) sottise *f*, ânerie *f*

fool′har′dy *adj* (*comp* **-dier;** *super* **-diest**) téméraire

fooling [′fulɪŋ] *s* tromperie *f;* **no fooling!** sans blague!

foolish [′fulɪʃ] *adj* sot, niais; ridicule, absurde

fool′proof′ *adj* à toute épreuve; infaillible

fools′cap′ *s* papier *m* ministre

fools′ er′rand *s*—**to go on a fool's errand** y aller pour des prunes

foot [fʊt] *s* (*pl* **feet** [fit]) pied *m;* (*of cat, dog, bird*) patte *f;* **on foot** à pied; **to drag one's feet** aller à pas de tortue; **to have one foot in the grave** avoir un pied dans la tombe; **to put one's best foot forward** (coll) partir du bon pied; **to put one's foot down** faire acte d'autorité; **to put one's foot in one's mouth** (coll) mettre les pieds dans le plat; **to stand on one's own feet** voler de ses propres ailes; **to tread under foot** fouler aux pieds ‖ *tr* (*the bill*) payer; **to foot it** aller à pied

footage [′fʊtɪdʒ] *s* (mov, telv) (*in French* métrage *m, i.e., length of film in meters*) longueur *f* d'un film en pieds

foot′-and-mouth′ disease′ *s* (vet) fièvre *f* aphteuse

foot′ball′ *s* football *m* américain; (*ball*) ballon *m*

foot′ball play′er *s* joueur *m* de football

foot′ball pool′ *s* pronostics *mpl* (sur les matchs de football)

foot′ball sta′dium *s* stade *m* de football

foot′board′ *s* marchepied *m*

foot′ brake′ *s* frein *m* à pédale

foot′bridge′ *s* passerelle *f*

foot′fall′ *s* pas *m* léger, bruit *m* de pas

foot′hills′ *spl* contreforts *mpl*, collines *fpl* basses

foot′hold′ *s*—**to gain a foothold** prendre pied

footing [′fʊtɪŋ] *s* équilibre *m;* (archit) empattement *m*, base *f*, socle *m;* **to be on a friendly footing** être en bons termes; **to be on an equal footing** être sur un pied d'égalité; **to lose one's footing** perdre pied

foot′lights′ *spl* (theat) rampe *f*

foot′lock′er *s* (mil) cantine *f*

foot′loose′ *adj* libre, sans entraves

foot′man *s* (*pl* **-men**) valet *m* de pied

foot′mark′ *s* empreinte *f* de pied

foot′note′ *s* note *f* au bas de la page

foot′pad′ *s* voleur *m* de grand chemin

foot′path′ *s* sentier *m* pour piétons

foot′print′ *s* empreinte *f* de pas, trace *f*

foot′ race′ *s* course *f* à pied

foot′rest′ *s* cale-pied *m*, repose-pied *m*

foot′ sol′dier *s* fantassin *m*

foot′sore′ *adj* aux pieds endoloris, éclopé

foot′step′ *s* pas *m;* **to follow in s.o.'s footsteps** suivre les traces de qn

foot′stone′ *s* pierre *f* tumulaire (au pied d'une tombe); (archit) première pierre

foot′stool′ s tabouret m

foot′warm′er s chauffe-pieds m

foot′wear′ s chaussures fpl

foot′work′ s jeu m de jambes

foot′worn′ adj usé; (person) aux pieds endoloris

fop [fɑp] s petit-maître m, bellâtre m

for [fɔr], [fər] prep pour; de, e.g., **to thank s.o. for** remercier qn de; e.g., **time for dinner** l'heure du dîner; e.g., **to cry for joy** pleurer de joie; e.g., **request for money** demande d'argent; à, e.g., **for sale** à vendre; e.g., **to sell for a high price** vendre à un prix élevé; e.g., **it is for you to decide** c'est à vous de décider; par, e.g., **famous for** célèbre par; e.g., **for example** par exemple; e.g., **for pity's sake** par pitié; contre, e.g., **a remedy for** un remède contre; **as for** quant à; **for** + ger pour + perf inf, e.g., **he was punished for stealing** il fut puni pour avoir volé; **for all that** malgré tout cela; **for short** en abrégé; **he has been in Paris for a week** il est à Paris depuis une semaine, il y a une semaine qu'il est à Paris; **he was in Paris for a week** il était à Paris pendant une semaine; **to be for** (to be in favor of) être en faveur de, être partisan de or pour; **to use s.th. for s.th.** employer q.ch. comme q.ch.; e.g., **to use coal for fuel** employer le charbon comme combustible ‖ conj car, parce que

forage [′fɔrɪdʒ] s fourrage m ‖ tr & intr fourrager

foray [′fɔre] s incursion f ‖ tr saccager, fourrager ‖ intr faire une incursion

for·bear [fɔr′bɛr] s (pret -bore; pp -borne) tr s'abstenir de ‖ intr se montrer patient

forbearance [fɔr′bɛrəns] s abstention f; patience f

for·bid [fɔr′bɪd] v (pret -bade or -bad [′bæd]; pp -bidden; ger -bidding) tr défendre, interdire; **God forbid!** qu'à Dieu ne plaise!; **to forbid s.o. s.th.** défendre q.ch. à qn; **to forbid s.o. to** défendre à qn de

forbidden [fɔr′bɪdən] adj défendu

forbidding [fɔr′bɪdɪŋ] adj rebutant, rébarbatif, sinistre

force [fɔrs] s force f; (of a word) signification f, valeur f; **in force** en vigueur; **in full force** en force; **the allied forces** les puissances alliées ‖ tr forcer; **to force back** repousser; (air; water) refouler; **to force in** (e.g., a door) enfoncer; **to force one's way into** (e.g., a house) pénétrer de force dans; **to force s.o.'s hand** forcer la main à qn; **to force s.o. to** + inf forcer qn à or de + inf; **to force s.th. into s.th.** faire entrer q.ch. dans q.ch.; **to force up** (e.g., prices) faire monter

forced′ draft′ s tirage m forcé

forced′ land′ing s atterrissage m forcé

forced′ march′ s marche f forcée

force′-feed′ tr (pret & pp -fed) gaver, suralimenter

force′-feed′ing s suralimentation f

forceful [′fɔrsfəl] adj énergique

for·ceps [′fɔrsɛps] s (pl -ceps or -cipes [sɪ‚piz]) (dent, surg) pince f; (obstet) forceps m

force′ pump′ s pompe f foulante

forcible [′fɔrsɪbəl] adj énergique, vigoureux; (convincing) convaincant; (imposed) forcé

ford [fɔrd] s gué m ‖ tr franchir à gué

fore [fɔr] adj antérieur; (naut) de l'avant ‖ s (naut) avant m; **to the fore** en vue, en vedette ‖ adv à l'avant ‖ interj (golf) gare devant!

fore′ and aft′ adv de l'avant à l'arrière

fore′arm′ s avant-bras m ‖ **fore·arm′** tr prémunir; (to warn) avertir

fore′bear′ s ancêtre m

foreboding [fɔr′bodɪŋ] s (sign) présage m; (feeling) pressentiment m

fore′cast′ s prévision f ‖ v (pret & pp -cast or -casted) tr pronostiquer

forecastle [′foksəl], [′fɔr‚kæsəl] s gaillard m d'avant

fore·close′ tr exclure; (law) forclore; **to foreclose the mortgage** saisir l'immeuble hypothéqué

foreclosure [fɔr′kloʒər] s saisie f, forclusion f

fore·doom′ tr condamner par avance

fore′ edge′ s (bb) tranche f

fore′fa′ther s aïeul m, ancêtre m

fore′fin′ger s index m

fore′foot′ s (pl -feet) patte f de devant

fore′front′ s premier rang m; **in the forefront** en première ligne

fore·go′ v (pret -went; pp -gone) tr (to give up) renoncer à

foregoing [fɔr′go‚ɪŋ] adj précédent, antérieur; (facts, text, etc., already cited) déjà cité, cidessus

fore′gone′ adj inévitable; (anticipated) décidé d'avance, prévu

fore′ground′ s premier plan m

fore′hand′ed adj prévoyant; (thrifty) ménager

forehead [′fɔrɪd] s front m

foreign [′fɔrɪn] adj étranger

for′eign affairs′ spl affaires fpl étrangères

foreigner [′fɔrɪnər] s étranger m

for′eign exchange′ s change m étranger; (currency) devises fpl

for′eign min′ister s ministre m des affaires étrangères

for′eign of′fice s ministère m des affaires étrangères

for′eign serv′ice s (dipl) service m diplomatique; (mil) service m à l'étranger

for′eign trade′ s commerce m extérieur

fore′leg′ s jambe f de devant

fore′lock′ s mèche f sur le front; (of horse) toupet m; **to take time by the forelock** saisir l'occasion par les cheveux

fore′man s (pl -men) chef m d'équipe; (in machine shop, factory) contremaître m; (of jury) premier juré m

foremast [′fɔrməst], [′fɔr‚mæst] s mât m de misaine

fore′most′ adj premier, principal ‖ adv au premier rang

fore'noon' s matinée f
forensic [fəˈrɛn(t)sɪk] adj médico-légal
foren'sic ev'idence s expertise f médico-légale
foren'sic ex'pert s expert m en médecine légale
foren'sic lab'oratory s laboratoire m médico-légal
foren'sic med'icine s médecine f légale, médecine médico-légale
fore'part' s avant m, devant m, partie f avant
fore'paw' s patte f de devant
fore'quar'ter s quartier m de devant
fore'run'ner s précurseur m, avant-coureur m; (sign) signe m avant-coureur
foresail [ˈforsəl], [ˈforˌsel] s misaine f, voile f de misaine
fore•see' v (pret -saw; pp -seen) tr prévoir
foreseeable [forˈsi•əbəl] adj prévisible
fore•shad'ow tr présager, préfigurer
fore•short'en tr dessiner en raccourci
fore•short'ening s raccourci m
fore'sight' s prévision f, prévoyance f
fore'sight'ed adj prévoyant
fore'skin' s prépuce m
forest [ˈforɪst] adj forestier ‖ s forêt f
fore'stage' s (theat) avant-scène f
fore•stall' tr anticiper, devancer
for'est rang'er s garde m forestier
forestry [ˈforɪstri] s sylviculture f
fore'taste' s avant-goût m
fore•tell' v (pret & pp -told) tr prédire
fore'thought' s prévoyance f; (law) préméditation f
for•ev'er adv pour toujours, à jamais
fore•warn' tr avertir, prévenir
fore'wom'an s (of jury) première jurée f
fore'word' s avant-propos m, avis m au lecteur
forfeit [ˈforfɪt] adj perdu ‖ s (pledge) dédit m, gage m; (fine) amende f; **to play at forfeits** jouer aux gages ‖ tr être déchu de, être privé de
forfeiture [ˈforfɪtʃər] s perte f; (fine) amende f, confiscation f
forge [fordʒ] s forge f ‖ tr forger; (e.g., documents) contrefaire, falsifier
forger [ˈfordʒər] s forgeur m; (e.g., of documents) faussaire mf
for•get [fərˈgɛt] v (pret -got; pp -got or -gotten; ger -getting) tr & intr oublier; **forget it!** n'y pensez plus!; **to forget to** + inf oublier de + inf
forgetful [fərˈgɛtfəl] adj oublieux
forget'-me-not' s myosotis m, ne-m'oubliez-pas m
forgivable [fərˈgɪvəbəl] adj pardonnable
for•give [fərˈgɪv] v (pret -gave; pp -given) tr & intr pardonner
forgiveness [fərˈgɪvnɪs] s pardon m
forgiving [fərˈgɪvɪŋ] adj indulgent, miséricordieux
for•go [fərˈgo] v (pret -went; pp -gone) tr renoncer à, s'abstenir de

fork [fork] s fourche f; (of road, tree, stem) fourche f, bifurcation f; (at table) fourchette f ‖ tr & intr fourcher, bifurquer
forked adj fourchu
forked' light'ning s éclairs mpl en zigzag
fork'lift truck' s chariot m élévateur
forlorn [fərˈlorn] adj (destitute) abandonné; (hopeless) désespéré; (wretched) misérable
forlorn' hope' s tentative f désespérée
form [form] s forme f; (paper to be filled out) formule f, fiche f, feuille f; (construction to give shape to cement) coffrage m ‖ tr former ‖ intr se former
formal [ˈforməl] adj cérémonieux, officiel; (formalistic) formaliste; (superficial) formel, de pure forme
for'mal attire' s tenue f de cérémonie
for'mal call' s visite f de politesse
formaldehyde [forˈmældəˌhaɪd] s formaldéhyde
for'mal din'ner s dîner m de cérémonie, dîner prié
formali•ty [forˈmælɪti] s (pl -ties) formalité f; (stiffness) raideur f; (polite conventions) cérémonie f, étiquette f
for'mal par'ty s soirée f de gala
for'mal speech' s discours m d'apparat
format [ˈformæt] s format m
formation [forˈmeʃən] s formation f
former [ˈformər] adj antérieur, précédent; (long past) ancien; (first of two things mentioned) premier ‖ pron—**the former** celui-là §84; le premier
formerly [ˈformərli] adv autrefois, anciennement, jadis
form'fit'ting adj ajusté, moulant
formidable [ˈformɪdəbəl] adj formidable
formless [ˈformlɪs] adj informe
form' let'ter s lettre f circulaire
formu•la [ˈformjələ] s (pl -las or -lae [ˌli]) formule f
formulate [ˈformjəˌlet] tr formuler
fornicate [ˈfornɪˌket] intr forniquer
for•sake [forˈsek] v (pret -sook [ˈsʊk]; pp -saken [ˈsekən]) tr abandonner, délaisser
fort [fort] s fort m, forteresse f; **hold the fort!** (coll) je vous confie la maison!
forte [fort] s fort m
forth [forθ] adv en avant; **and so forth** et ainsi de suite; **from this day forth** à partir de ce jour; **to go forth** sortir, se mettre en route
forth'com'ing adj à venir, à paraître, prochain
forth'right' adj net, direct ‖ adv droit, carrément; (immediately) tout de suite
forth'with' adv sur-le-champ
fortieth [ˈfortɪ•ɪθ] adj & pron quarantième (masc, fem) ‖ s quarantième m
fortification [ˌfortɪfɪˈkeʃən] s fortification f
forti•fy [ˈfortɪˌfaɪ] v (pret & pp -fied) tr fortifier; (wine) viner
fortitude [ˈfortɪˌt(j)ud] s force f d'âme
fortnight [ˈfortˌnaɪt] s quinze jours mpl, quinzaine f

fortress [ˈfɔrtrɪs] s forteresse f
fortuitous [fɔrˈt(j)uˌɪtəs] adj (accidental) fortuit; (lucky) fortuné
fortunate [ˈfɔrtʃənɪt] adj heureux
fortune [ˈfɔrtʃən] s fortune f; **to cost a fortune** coûter les yeux de la tête; **to make a fortune** faire fortune; **to tell s.o. his fortune** dire la bonne aventure à qn
for′tune hunt′er s coureur m de dots
for′tune•tel′ler s diseuse f de bonne aventure
for•ty [ˈfɔrti] adj & pron quarante ‖ s (pl -ties) quarante m; **about forty** une quarantaine
fo•rum [ˈforəm] s (pl -rums or -ra [rə]) forum m; (e.g., of public opinion) tribunal m; **open forum** tribune f libre
forward [ˈfɔrwərd] adj de devant; (precocious) avancé, précoce; (bold) audacieux, effronté ‖ s (sports) avant m ‖ adv en avant; **to bring forward** (bk) reporter; **to come forward** s'avancer; **to look forward to** compter sur, se faire une fête de ‖ tr envoyer, expédier; (a letter) faire suivre; (a project) avancer, favoriser; **please forward** prière de faire suivre
for′warding address′ s adresse f d'expédition, adresse d'envoi
fossil [ˈfɑsɪl] adj & s fossile m
foster [ˈfɔstər] adj de lait, nourricier ‖ tr encourager, entretenir
fosterage [ˈfɔstərɪdʒ] s (of children) mise f en placement
fos′ter broth′er s frère m de placement, frère du lait
fos′ter care′ s placement m d'enfants; **to place in foster care** mettre en placement
fos′ter child′ s enfant mf en placement
fos′ter daugh′ter s fille f en placement
fos′ter fam′ily s famille f de placement; **to take s.o. into a foster family** prendre qn en placement
fos′ter fath′er s père m de placement
fos′ter moth′er s mère f de placement
fos′ter par′ent s parent m de placement
fos′ter sis′ter s sœur f de placement; sœur de lait
fos′ter son′ s fils m en placement
foul [faʊl] adj immonde; (air) vicié; (wind) contraire; (weather) gros, sale; (breath) fétide; (language) ordurier; (water) bourbeux; (ball) hors jeu ‖ s (baseball) faute f; (boxing) coup m bas ‖ adv déloyalement ‖ tr (sports) commettre une faute contre; **to foul up** polluer; (a relationship) ficher en l'aire ‖ intr (said of anchor, propeller, rope, etc.) s'engager; **to foul up** faire une connerie
foul-mouthed [ˈfaʊlˈmaʊðd] adj mal embouché
foul′ play′ s malveillance f; (sports) jeu m déloyal
found [faʊnd] tr fonder, établir; (metal) fondre
foundation [faʊnˈdeʃən] s (basis; masonry support) fondement m; (act of endowing) dotation f; (endowment) fondation f
founder [ˈfaʊndər] s fondateur m; (in foundry)

fondeur m ‖ intr (said of horse) boiter bas; (said of building) s'effondrer; (naut) sombrer
foundling [ˈfaʊndlɪŋ] s enfant m trouvé
found′ling hos′pital s hospice m des enfants trouvés
found•ry [ˈfaʊndri] s (pl -ries) fonderie f
found′ry•man s (pl -men) fondeur m
fount [faʊnt] s source f
fountain [ˈfaʊntən] s fontaine f
foun′tain•head′ s source f, origine f
Foun′tain of Youth′ s fontaine f de Jouvence
foun′tain pen′ s stylo m (à réservoir)
four [for] adj & pron quatre ‖ s quatre m; **four o'clock** quatre heures; **on all fours** à quatre pattes
four′-cy′cle adj (mach) à quatre temps
four′-cyl′inder adj (mach) à quatre cylindres
four′-flush′ intr (coll) bluffer, faire le fanfaron
fourflusher [ˈforˌflʌʃər] s (coll) bluffeur m
four′-foot′ed adj quadrupède
four′ hun′dred adj & pron quatre cents ‖ s quatre cents m; **the Four Hundred** la haute société; le Tout Paris
four′-in-hand′ s (tie) cravate-plastron f; (team) attelage m à quatre
four′-lane′ adj à quatre voies
four′-leaf clo′ver s trèfle m à quatre feuilles
four′-let′ter word′ s mot m impudique de quatre lettres
four′-motor plane′ s quadrimoteur m
four′-o'clock′ s (Mirabilis jalapa) belle-de-nuit f
four′ of a kind′ s (cards) un carré
four′-post′er s lit m à colonnes
four′score′ adj quatre-vingts
foursome [ˈforsəm] s partie f double
fourteen [ˈforˈtin] adj, pron, & s quatorze m
fourteenth [ˈforˈtinθ] adj & pron quatorzième (masc, fem); **the Fourteenth** quatorze, e.g., **John the Fourteenth** Jean quatorze ‖ s quatorze m; **the fourteenth** (in dates) le quatorze
fourth [forθ] adj & pron quatrième (masc, fem); **the Fourth** quatre, e.g., **John the Fourth** Jean quatre ‖ s quatrième m; (in fractions) quart m; **the fourth** (in dates) le quatre
fourth′ estate′ s quatrième pouvoir m
four′-wheel′ drive′ s propulsion f à quatre roues motrices
fowl [faʊl] s volaille f
fox [fɑks] s renard m ‖ tr (coll) mystifier
fox′glove′ s digitale f
fox′hole′ s renardière f; (mil) gourbi m, abri m de tranchée
fox′hound′ s fox-hound m
fox′ hunt′ s chasse f au renard
fox′ ter′rier s fox-terrier m
fox′ trot′ s (of animal) petit trot m; (dance) fox-trot m
fox•y [ˈfɑksi] adj (comp -ier; super -iest) rusé, madré
foyer [ˈfɔɪˌər] s (lobby) foyer m; (entrance hall) vestibule m
fracas [ˈfrekəs] s bagarre f, rixe f

fraction [`fræk∫ən] s fraction f
fractional [`fræk∫ənəl] adj fractionnaire
frac′tional cur′rency s monnaie f division-naire
fracture [`frækt∫ər] s fracture f; **to set a fracture** réduire une fracture ‖ tr fracturer
fragile [`frædʒɪl] adj fragile
fragment [`frægmənt] s fragment m ‖ tr fragmenter
fragrance [`fregrəns] s parfum m
fragrant [`fregrənt] adj parfumé
frail [frel] adj frêle; (e.g., virtue) fragile, faible ‖ s (basket) couffe f
frail·ty [`frelti] s (pl -ties) fragilité f; (weakness) faiblesse f
frame [frem] s (of picture, mirror) cadre m; (of glasses) monture f; (of window, car) châssis m; (of window, motor) bâti m; (support, stand) armature f; (structure) charpente f; (for embroidering) métier m; (of comic strip) cadre, dessin m; (mov, telv) image f ‖ tr former, charpenter; (a picture) encadrer; (film) cadrer; (an answer) formuler; (slang) monter une accusation contre
frame′ advance′ s (electron) avance f image par image
frame′ house′ s maison f en bois
frame′ of mind′ s disposition f d'esprit
frame′-up′ s (slang) coup m monté
frame′work′ s charpente f, squelette m
framing [`fremɪŋ] s (mov, phot) cadrage m
France [fræns] s France f; la France
franchise [`frænt∫aɪz] s concession f, privilège m; (com) chaîne f volontaire; (pol) droit m de vote
franglais [`frɑnˌgle] or [`frɑ̃ˌgle] s Franglais m
frank [fræŋk] adj franc ‖ s franchise f postale; **Frank** (medieval German person) Franc m; (masculine name) François m ‖ tr affranchir
frankfurter [`fræŋkfərtər] s saucisse f de Francfort
frankincense [`fræŋkɪnˌsɛns] s oliban m
Frankish [`fræŋkɪ∫] adj franc ‖ s francique m
frankness [`fræŋknɪs] s franchise f
frantic [`fræntɪk] adj frénétique
fraternal [frə`tʌrnəl] adj fraternel
fraterni·ty [frə`tʌrnɪti] s (pl -ties) fraternité f; (association) confrérie f; (at a university) club m d'étudiants, amicale f estudiantine
fraternize [`frætərˌnaɪz] intr fraterniser
fraud [frɔd] s fraude f; (person) imposteur m, fourbe mf
fraudulent [`frɔdjələnt] adj frauduleux, en fraude
fraught [frɔt] adj—**fraught with** chargé de
fray [fre] s bagarre f ‖ tr érailler ‖ intr s'érailler
freak [frik] s (sudden fancy) caprice m; (anomaly) curiosité f; (person, animal) monstre m
freakish [`frikɪ∫] adj capricieux; bizarre; (grotesque) monstrueux
freckle [`frekəl] s tache f de rousseur, éphélide f

freckly [`frekli] adj couvert de taches de rousseur
free [fri] adj (comp **freer** [`friˑər]; super **freest** [`friˑɪst]) libre; (without charge) gratuit; (without extra charge) franc, exempt; (e.g., end of a rope) dégagé; (with money, advice, etc.) libéral, généreux; (manner, speech, etc.) franc, ouvert; **to set free** libérer, affranchir ‖ adv franco, gratis, gratuitement; (naut) largue, e.g., **running free** courant largue ‖ v (pret & pp **freed** [frid]; ger **freeing** [`friˑɪŋ]) tr libérer; (a prisoner) affranchir, élargir; (to disengage) dégager; (from an obligation) exempter
free′ admis′sion s entrée f libre, entrée gratuite
free′ and eas′y adj désinvolte, dégagé
freebooter [`friˌbutər] s flibustier m, maraudeur m
free′born′ adj né libre
free′ competi′tion s libre concurrence f
freedom [`fridəm] s liberté f
free′dom of speech′ s liberté f de la parole
free′dom of the press′ s liberté f de la presse
free′dom of the seas′ s liberté f des mers
free′dom of thought′ s liberté f de la pensée
free′dom of wor′ship s liberté f du culte, libre pratique f
free′ en′terprise′ s libre entreprise f
free′ fall′ s (phys) chute f libre
free′-for-all′ s foire f d'empoigne, mêlée f
free′ hand′ s carte f blanche
free′-hand draw′ing s dessin m à main levée
free′hand′ed adj libéral, généreux
free′hold′ s (law) propriété f foncière perpétuelle; (hist) franc-alleu m
free′ lance′ s franc-tireur m
free′-lance′ intr travailler à la pige, travailler à (or pour) son compte
free′man s (pl -men) homme m libre; (citizen) citoyen m
Free′ma′son s franc-maçon m
Free′ma′sonry s franc-maçonnerie f
free′ of charge′ adj & adv gratis, exempt de frais, gratuit, bénévolement
free′ on board′ adv franco de bord, départ usine
free′ port′ s port m franc
free′ ser′vice s service m assuré après la vente
free′ speech′ s liberté f de la parole
free′-spo′ken adj franc; **to be free-spoken** avoir son franc-parler
free′stone′ adj (bot) à noyau non-adhérent ‖ s (mas) pierre f de taille
free′style′ swim′ming s nage f libre
free′style′ wrest′ling s lutte f libre, catch m
free′think′er s libre penseur m
free′ thought′ s libre pensée f
free′ throw′ s (sports) lancer m franc
free′ tick′et s billet m de faveur
free′ trade′ s libre-échange m
free′way′ s autoroute f
free′will′ adj volontaire, de plein gré

free' will' *s* libre arbitre *m;* **of one's own free will** de son propre gré

freeze [friz] *s* congélation *f* ‖ *v* (*pret* **froze** [froz]; *pp* **frozen**) *tr* geler, congeler; (*e.g., wages*) geler, bloquer; (*foods*) surgeler ‖ *intr* geler; **it is freezing** il gèle

freeze'-dry' *v* (*pret & pp* **-dried**) *tr* lyophiliser

freeze' dry'ing *s* lyophilisation *f*

freezer [´frizər] *s* (*for making ice cream*) sorbetière *f;* (*for foods*) congélateur *m*

freez'er bag' *s* sac *m* congélateur

freezing [´frizɪŋ] *adj* glacial ‖ *s* congélation *f*

freight [fret] *s* fret *m,* chargement *m;* (*cost*) fret, prix *m* du transport; **by freight** (rr) en petite vitesse ‖ *tr* transporter; (*a ship, truck, etc.*) charger

freight' car' *s* wagon *m* de marchandises, wagon à caisse

freighter [´fretər] *s* cargo *m*

freight' plat'form *s* quai *m* de déchargement

freight' sta'tion *s* gare *f* de marchandises

freight' train' *s* train *m* de marchandises

freight' yard' *s* (rr) cour *f* de marchandises

French [frɛntʃ] *adj* français ‖ *s* (*language*) français *m;* **the French** les Français

French' Cana'dian *s* Franco-Canadien *m*

French'-Cana'dian *adj* franco-canadien

French' chalk' *s* craie *f* de tailleur, stéatite *f*

French' cuff' *s* poignet *m* mousequetaire

French' door' *s* porte-fenêtre *f*

French' dress'ing *s* vinaigrette *f*

French' fries' *spl* frites *fpl*

French' horn' *s* (mus) cor *m* d'harmonie

French' horse'power *s* (*735 watts*) cheval-vapeur *m,* cheval *m*

French' leave' *s*—**to take French leave** filer à l'anglaise

French' man *s* (*pl* **-men**) Français *m*

French' roll' *s* petit pain *m*

French'-speak'ing *adj* francophone; d'expression française; (*country*) de langue française

French' tel'ephone *s* combiné *m*

French' toast' *s* pain *m* perdu

French' win'dow *s* porte-fenêtre *f*

French' wom'an *s* (*pl* **-wom'en**) Française *f*

frenzied [´frɛnzid] *adj* frénétique

fren•zy [´frɛnzi] *s* (*pl* **-zies**) frénésie *f*

frequen•cy [´frikwənsi] *s* (*pl* **-cies**) fréquence *f*

fre'quency modula'tion *s* modulation *f* de fréquence

fre'quency range' *s* (comp) gamme *f* de fréquence

frequent [´frikwənt] *adj* fréquent ‖ [frɪ´kwɛnt] *tr* fréquenter

frequently [´frikwəntli] *adv* fréquemment

fres•co [´frɛsko] *s* (*pl* **-coes** or **-cos**) fresque *f* ‖ *tr* peindre à fresque

fresh [frɛʃ] *adj* frais; (*water*) doux; (*e.g., idea*) nouveau; (*wound*) saignant; (*cheeky*) (coll) osé, impertinent; **fresh paint!** (*public sign*) attention, peinture fraîche! ‖ *adv* nouvellement; **fresh in** (coll) récemment arrivé; **fresh out** (coll) récemment épuisé

freshen [´frɛʃən] *tr* rafraîchir ‖ *intr* se rafraîchir; (*said of wind*) fraîchir

freshet [´frɛʃɪt] *s* crue *f*

fresh'man *s* (*pl* **-men**) étudiant *m* de première année, bizut *m*

freshness [´frɛʃnɪs] *s* fraîcheur *f;* (*sauciness*) impudence *f,* impertinence *f*

fresh'-wa'ter *adj* d'eau douce

fret [frɛt] *s* (*interlaced design*) frette *f;* (*uneasiness*) inquiétude *f;* (mus) touchette *f* ‖ *v* (*pret & pp* **fretted;** *ger* **fretting**) *tr* ajourer ‖ *intr* s'inquiéter, geindre

fretful [´frɛtfəl] *adj* irritable, boudeur

fret'work' *s* ajour *m,* ornementation *f* ajourée

Freudianism [´frɔɪdɪ•ə,nɪzəm] *s* freudisme *m*

friar [´fraɪ•ər] *s* moine *m*

fricassee [,frɪkə´si] *s* fricassé *f*

friction [´frɪkʃən] *s* friction *f*

fric'tion tape' *s* chatterton *m,* ruban *m* isolant

Friday [´fraɪdi] *s* vendredi *m*

fried [fraɪd] *adj* frit

fried' egg' *s* œuf *m* sur le plat

friend [frɛnd] *s* ami *m;* **to make friends with** se lier d'amitié avec

friend•ly [´frɛndli] *adj* (*comp* **-lier;** *super* **-liest**) amical, sympathique

friend'ly fire' *s* (mil) feux *m* d'ami

friendship [´frɛndʃɪp] *s* amitié *f*

frieze [friz] *s* (archit) frise *f*

frigate [´frɪgɪt] *s* frégate *f*

fright [fraɪt] *s* frayeur *f,* effroi *m;* (*grotesque or ridiculous person*) (coll) épouvantail *m;* **to take fright at** s'effrayer de

frighten [´fraɪtən] *tr* effrayer; **to frighten away** effaroucher, faire fuir

frightful [´fraɪtfəl] *adj* effroyable; (coll) affreux; (*huge*) (coll) énorme

frigid [´frɪdʒɪd] *adj* frigide; (*zone*) glacial

frigidity [frɪ´dʒɪdɪti] *s* frigidité *f*

frill [frɪl] *s* (*on shirt front*) jabot *m;* (*frippery*) falbala *m*

fringe [frɪndʒ] *s* frange *f;* (*border*) bordure *f;* (opt) frange; **on the fringe of** en marge de ‖ *tr* franger

fringe' ben'efits *spl* supplément *m* de solde, bénéfices *mpl* marginaux, avantages *mpl* sociaux, indemnités *fpl,* à côtés *mpl*

fripper•y [´frɪpəri] *s* (*pl* **-ies**) (*flashiness*) clinquant *m;* (*inferior goods*) camelote *f*

Frisbee [´frɪzbi] *s* (trademark) disque *m* volant, soucoupe *f* volante

frisk [frɪsk] *tr* (slang) fouiller, palper ‖ *intr*—**to frisk about** gambader, folâtrer

frisk•y [´frɪski] *adj* (*comp* **-ier;** *super* **-iest**) vif, folâtre; (*horse*) fringant

fritter [´frɪtər] *s* beignet *m* ‖ *tr*—**to fritter away** gaspiller

frivolous [´frɪvələs] *adj* frivole

frizzle [´frɪzəl] *s* frisure *f* ‖ *tr* frisotter; (culin) faire frire ‖ *intr* frisotter; (culin) grésiller

friz•zly [´frɪzli] *adj* (*comp* **-zlier;** *super* **-zliest**) crépu, crépelu

fro [fro] *adv*—**to and fro** de long en large; **to go to and fro** aller et venir

frock [frak] *s* robe *f;* (*overalls, smock*) blouse *f;* (eccl) froc *m*

frock′ coat′ *s* redingote *f*

frog [frɑg], [frɔg] *s* grenouille *f;* (*in throat*) chat *m*

frog′man′ *s* (*pl* **-men′**) homme-grenouille *m*

frogs′′ legs′ *spl* cuisses *fpl* de grenouille

frol•ic [′frɑlɪk] *s* gaieté *f,* ébats *mpl* ‖ *v* (*pret & pp* **-icked;** *ger* **-icking**) *intr* s'ébattre, folâtrer

frolicsome [′frɑlɪksəm] *adj* folâtre

from [frʌm], [frɑm], [frəm] *prep* de; de la part de, e.g., **greetings from your friend** compliments de la part de votre ami; contre, e.g., **a shelter from the rain** un abri contre la pluie; **from a certain angle** sous un certain angle; **from . . . to** depuis . . . jusqu'à; **from what I hear** d'après ce que j'apprends; **the flight from** le vol en provenance de; **to drink from** (*a glass*) boire dans; (*a bottle*) boire à; **to learn from a book** apprendre dans un livre; **to steal from** voler à

front [frʌnt] *adj* antérieur, de devant ‖ *s* front *m;* (*first place*) premier rang *m;* (aut) avant *m;* (geog, mil, pol) front *m;* (*figurehead*) (coll) prête-nom *m;* **in front** par devant; **in front of** en face de, devant; **to put up a bold front** (coll) faire bonne contenance ‖ *tr* (*to face*) donner sur; (*to confront*) affronter ‖ *intr*—**to front on** donner sur

frontage [′frʌntɪdʒ] *s* façade *f;* (*along a street, lake, etc.*) largeur *f*

front′age road′ *s* voie *f* de desserte

front′ door′ *s* porte *f* d'entrée

front′ drive′ *s* (aut) traction *f* avant

frontier [frʌn′tɪr] *adj* frontalier ‖ *s* frontière *f;* (hist) front *m* de colonisation, front pionnier

frontiers′man *s* (*pl* **-men**) frontalier *m,* broussard *m*

frontispiece [′frʌntɪsˌpis] *s* frontispice *m;* (archit) façade *f* principale

front′ lines′ *spl* avant-postes *mpl*

front′ man′ *s* homme *m* de paille

front′ mat′ter *s* (*of book*) feuilles *fpl* liminaires

front′ of′fice *s* direction *f*

front′ page′ *s*—**the front page** la première page, la une

front′ porch′ *s* porche *m*

front′ room′ *s* chambre *f* sur la rue

front′ row′ *s* premier rang *m*

front′ seat′ *s* siège *m* avant; (aut) banquette *f* avant

front′ steps′ *spl* perron *m*

front′ view′ *s* vue *f* de face

front′-wheel drive′ *s* traction *f* avant

front′yard′ *s* devant *m* de la maison

frost [frɔst] *s* (*freezing*) gelée *f;* (*frozen dew*) givre *m* ‖ *tr* (*to freeze*) geler; (*to cover with frost*) givrer; (culin) glacer

frost′bite′ *s* engelure *f*

frost′ed glass′ *s* verre *m* dépoli

frosting [′frɔstɪŋ] *s* (*on glass*) dépolissage *m;* (culin) fondant *m*

frost•y [′frɔsti] *adj* (*comp* **-ier;** *super* **-iest**) couvert de givre; (*reception, welcome*) glacé, glacial

froth [frɔθ] *s* écume *f;* (*on soap, beer, chocolate*) mousse *f;* (*frivolity*) futilité *f* ‖ *intr* mousser; (*at the mouth*) écumer

froth•y [′frɔθi] *adj* (*comp* **-ier;** *super* **-iest**) écumeux; (*soap, beer, chocolate*) mousseux; (*frivolous*) creux, futile

froward [′frowərd] *adj* obstiné, revêche

frown [fraʊn] *s* froncement *m* de sourcils ‖ *intr* froncer les sourcils; **to frown at** or **on** être contraire à, désapprouver

frows•y or **frowz•y** [′fraʊzi] *adj* (*comp* **-ier;** *super* **-iest**) malpropre, négligé, peu soigné; (*smelling bad*) malodorant

fro′zen as′sets [′frozən] *spl* fonds *mpl* gelés

fro′zen din′ner *s* plateau *m* repas congelé

fro′zen foods′ *spl* aliments *mpl* surgelés

frugal [′frugəl] *adj* sobre, modéré; (*meal*) frugal

fruit [frut] *adj* fruitier ‖ *s* fruit *m;* les fruits, e.g., **I like fruit** j'aime les fruits; (*homosexual*) (pej) tapette *f,* pédé *m*

fruit′ cake′ *s* cake *m*

fruit′ cup′ *s* coupe *f* de fruits

fruit′ fly′ *s* mouche *f* du vinaigre

fruitful [′frutfəl] *adj* fructueux, fécond

fruition [fru′ɪʃən] *s* réalisation *f;* **to come to fruition** fructifier

fruit′ juice′ *s* jus *m* de fruits

fruitless [′frutlɪs] *adj* stérile, vain

fruit′ sal′ad *s* macédoine *f* de fruits, salade *f* de fruits

fruit′ stand′ *s* étalage *m* de fruits

fruit′ store′ *s* fruiterie *f*

frumpish [′frʌmpɪʃ] *adj* fagoté, négligé

frustrate [′frʌstret] *tr* frustrer

fry [fraɪ] *s* (*pl* **-fries**) (culin) friture *f;* (ichth) fretin *m* ‖ *v* (*pret & pp* **fried**) *tr* faire frire; (*to sauté*) faire sauter ‖ *intr* frire

fry′ing pan′ *s* poêle *f* à frire; **to jump from the frying pan into the fire** sauter de la poêle dans le feu

fudge [fʌdʒ] *s* fondant *m* de chocolat; (*humbug*) blague *f*

fuel [′fjuˑəl] *s* combustible *m;* (aut) carburant *m;* (fig) aliment *m* ‖ *v* (*pret & pp* **fueled** or **fuelled;** *ger* **fueling** or **fuelling**) *tr* pourvoir en combustible

fuel′ cell′ *s* cellule *f* électrogène, cellule solaire

fu′el gauge′ *s* jauge *f* de combustible

fuel′-injec′tion en′gine *s* moteur *m* à injecteur

fu′el line′ *s* conduite *f* de combustible

fu′el oil′ *s* mazout *m,* fuel-oil *m,* fuel *m*

fu′el tank′ *s* réservoir *m* de carburant; (aut) réservoir à essence

fu′el truck′ *s* camion *m* citerne

fugitive [′fjudʒɪtɪv] *adj & s* fugitif *m*

ful•crum [′fʌlkrəm] *s* (*pl* **-crums** or **-cra** [krə]) point *m* d'appui

fulfill [fʊlˈfɪl] *tr* accomplir; (*an obligation*) s'acquitter de, remplir

fulfillment [fʊlˈfɪlmənt] *s* accomplissement *m*

full [fʊl] *adj* plein; (*dress, garment*) ample, bouffant; (*schedule*) chargé; (*lips*) gros, fort; (*brother, sister*) germain; (*having no more room*) complet; **full to overflowing** plein à déborder ‖ *s* plein *m;* **in full** intégralement, entièrement; (*to spell in full*) en toutes lettres; **to the full** complètement ‖ *adv* complètement; **full in the face** en pleine figure; **full many a** bien des; **full well** parfaitement ‖ *tr* (*cloth*) fouler

full′ blast′ *adv* (coll) en pleine activité

full′-blood′ed *adj* robuste; (*thoroughbred*) pur sang, de pure souche

full-blown [ˈfʊlˈblon] *adj* achevé, développé; en pleine fleur

full′-bod′ied *adj* (*e.g., wine*) corsé

full′ dress′ *s* grande tenue *f*

full′-dress coat′ *s* frac *m*

full′-faced′ *adj* (*portrait*) de face

full′-fig′ured *adj* un peu gras, bien en chair

full-fledged [ˈfʊlˈflɛdʒd] *adj* véritable, rien moins que

full-grown [ˈfʊlˈgron] *adj* (*plant*) mûr; (*tree*) de haute futaie; (*person*) adulte

full′ house′ *s* (poker) main *f* pleine; (theat) salle *f* comble

full′-length′ *adj* (*portrait*) en pied

full′-length mir′ror *s* psyché *f*

full′-length mov′ie *s* long métrage *m*

full′ load′ *s* plein chargement *m*

full′ meas′ure *s* mesure *f* comble

full′ moon′ *s* pleine lune *f*

full′ name′ *s* nom *m* et prénoms *mpl*

full′ pow′ers *spl* pleins pouvoirs *mpl*

full′ rest′ *s* (mus) pause *f*

full′ sail′ *adv* toutes voiles dehors

full′ ses′sion *s* assemblée *f* plénière

full′-sized′ *adj* de grandeur nature

full′ speed′ *s* toute vitesse *f*

full′ stop′ *s* (gram) point *m* final; **to come to a full stop** s'arrêter net

full′ swing′ *s*—**in full swing** en pleine activité, en train

full′ tilt′ *adv* à toute vitesse

full′ time′ *adv* à pleines journées

full′-time′ *adj* à temps plein

full′ view′ *s*—**in full view** à la vue de tous

full′ weight′ *s* poids *m* juste

fully [ˈfʊli] *adv* entièrement, pleinement

fulsome [ˈfʊlsəm] *adj* écœurant, bas, servile

fumble [ˈfʌmbəl] *tr* manier maladroitement; (*the ball*) ne pas attraper, laisser tomber ‖ *intr* tâtonner

fume [fjum] *s* (*bad humor*) rage *f;* **fumes** fumées *fpl*, vapeurs *fpl* ‖ *tr & intr* fumer

fumigate [ˈfjumɪ͵get] *tr* fumiger

fun [fʌn] *adj* (coll) amusant ‖ *s* amusement *m*, gaieté *f;* (*badinage*) plaisanterie *f;* **in fun** pour rire; **to have fun** s'amuser; **to make fun of** se moquer de

function [ˈfʌŋkʃən] *s* fonction *f;* (*meeting*) cérémonie *f* ‖ *intr* fonctionner; **to function as** faire fonction de

functional [ˈfʌŋkʃənəl] *adj* fonctionnel

functionar·y [ˈfʌŋkʃə͵nɛri] *s* (*pl* **-ies**) fonctionnaire *mf*

fund [fʌnd] *s* fonds *m;* **funds** fonds *mpl* ‖ *tr* (*a debt*) consolider

fundamental [͵fʌndəˈmɛntəl] *adj* fondamental ‖ **fundamentals** *spl* fondamentaux *mpl*

fundamentalism [͵fʌndəˈmɛntəlɪsəm] *s* (rel) fondamentalisme *m*

fundamentalist [͵fʌndəˈmɛntəlɪst] *s* (rel) fondamentaliste *mf;* (*scientist*) chercheur *m* qui s'adonne à la recherche fondamentale

fundamentalistic [͵fʌndə͵mɛntəˈlɪstɪk] *adj* fondamental

funding [ˈfʌndɪŋ] *s* mise *f* de fonds

funeral [ˈfjunərəl] *adj* (*march, procession, ceremony*) funèbre; (*expenses*) funéraire ‖ *s* funérailles *fpl*

fu′neral direc′tor *s* entrepreneur *m* de pompes funèbres

fu′neral home′ *ou* **par′lor** *s* chapelle *f* mortuaire; salon *m* mortuaire (Canad); (*business*) entreprise *f* de pompes funèbres

fu′neral proces′sion *s* convoi *m* funèbre, enterrement *m*, deuil *m*

fu′neral serv′ice *s* office *m* des morts

funereal [fjuˈnɪri·əl] *adj* funèbre

fungicide [ˈfʌndʒɪ͵saɪd] *s* fongicide *m*

fungus [ˈfʌŋgəs] *s* (*pl* **funguses** or **fungi** [ˈfʌndʒaɪ]) (bot) champignon *m;* (pathol) fongus *m*

funicular [fjuˈnɪkjələr] *adj & s* funiculaire *m*

funk [fʌŋk] *s* (coll) frousse *f*, funk *m*

funky [ˈfʌŋki] *adj* (coll) funky, peureux; (slang) fruste, rustre; (slang) menant le train ‖ *s* funky *m*

fun·nel [ˈfʌnəl] *s* (*for pouring through*) entonnoir *m;* (*smokestack*) cheminée *f;* (*tube for ventilation*) tuyau *m* ‖ *v* (*pret & pp* **-neled** or **-nelled;** *ger* **-neling** or **-nelling**) *tr* verser avec un entonnoir; (*to channel*) concentrer

funnies [ˈfʌniz] *spl* pages *fpl* comiques

fun·ny [ˈfʌni] *adj* (*comp* **-nier;** *super* **-niest**) comique; amusant, drôle; (coll) bizarre, curieux; **to strike s.o. as funny** paraître drôle à qn

fun′ny pa′per *s* pages *fpl* comiques

fur [fʌr] *s* fourrure *f;* (*on tongue*) empâtement *m;* **furs** pelleteries *fpl*

furbish [ˈfʌrbɪʃ] *tr* fourbir; **to furbish up** remettre à neuf

furious [ˈfjʊri·əs] *adj* furieux

furl [fʌrl] *tr* (naut) ferler

fur′-lined′ *adj* doublé de fourrure

furlough [ˈfʌrlo] *s* permission *f;* **on furlough** en permission ‖ *tr* donner une permission à

furnace [ˈfʌrnɪs] *s* (*to heat a house*) calorifère *m;* (*to produce steam*) chaudière *f;* (*e.g., to smelt ores*) fourneau *m;* (rr) foyer *m;* (fig) fournaise *f*

furnish [`fʌrnɪʃ] *tr* fournir; (*a house*) meubler
fur′nished apart′ment *s* garni *m*, appartement *m* meublé
furnishings [`fʌrnɪʃiŋz] *spl* (*of a house*) ameublement *m;* (*things to wear*) articles *mpl* d'habillement
furniture [`fʌrnɪtʃər] *s* meubles *mpl;* **a piece of furniture** un meuble; **a suite of furniture** un mobilier
fur′niture deal′er *s* marchand *m* de meubles
fur′niture pol′ish *s* encaustique *f*
fur′niture store′ *s* maison *f* d'ameublement
fur′niture ware′house *s* garde-meuble *m*
furor [`fjurɔr] *s* fureur *f*
furrier [`fʌrɪ•ər] *s* fourreur *m*, pelletier *m*
furrow [`fʌro] *s* sillon *m* ‖ *tr* sillonner
fur•ry [`fʌri] *adj* (*comp* **-rier;** *super* **-riest**) fourré, à fourrure
further [`fʌrðər] *adj* additional, supplémentaire ‖ *adv* plus loin; (*besides*) en outre, de plus ‖ *tr* avancer, favoriser
furtherance [`fʌrðərəns] *s* avancement *m*
fur′ther-more′ *adv* de plus, d'ailleurs
furthest [`fʌrðɪst] *adj* (le) plus éloigné ‖ *adv* le plus loin
furtive [`fʌrtɪv] *adj* furtif
fu•ry [`fjuri] *s* (*pl* **-ries**) furie *f*
furze [fʌrz] *s* genêt *m* épineux, ajonc *m* d'Europe
fuse [fjuz] *s* (*tube or wick filled with explosive material*) étoupille *f*, mèche *f;* (*device for exploding a bomb or projectile*) fusée *f;* (elec) fusible *m*, plomb *m* de sûreté, plomb fusible;
to burn or **blow out a fuse** faire sauter un plomb ‖ *tr* fondre; étoupiller ‖ *intr* se fondre
fuse′ box′ *s* boîte *f* à fusibles
fuselage [`fjuzəlɪdʒ] *s* fuselage *m*
fusible [`fjuzɪbəl] *adj* fusible
fusillade [ˌfjuzɪ`led] *s* fusillade *f*
fusion [`fjuʒən] *s* fusion *f*
fuss [fʌs] *s* (*excitement*) tapage *m*, agitation *f;* (*attention*) façons *fpl*, chichi *m;* (*dispute*) bagarre *f;* **to kick up a fuss** (coll) faire un tas d'histoires; **to make a fuss over** faire grand cas de ‖ *intr* faire des embarras, simagrées, or chichis; **to fuss over** être aux petits soins auprès de
fuss•y [`fʌsi] *adj* (*comp* **-ier;** *super* **-iest**) tracassier, tatillon; (*in dress*) pomponné
fustian [`fʌstʃən] *s* (*cloth*) futaine *f;* (*bombast*) grandiloquence *f*
futile [`fjutɪl] *adj* futile
futility [fju`tɪlɪti] *s* futilité *f*
future [`fjutʃər] *adj* futur, d'avenir ‖ *s* avenir *m;* (gram) futur *m;* **futures** (com) valeurs *fpl* négociées à terme, opérations *fpl* à terme; **in the future** à l'avenir; **in the near future** à brève échéance
fu′tures mar′ket *s* marché *m* à option
futuristic [ˌfjutʃə`rɪstɪk] *adj* futuriste
fuzball [`fuzbɔl] *s* (*table game played with figurines moved on mobile rods*) baby-foot *m*
fuzz [fʌz] *s* (*on a peach*) duvet *m;* (*on a blanket*) peluche *f;* (*in pockets and corners*) bourre *f;* (pej) (*police*) flicaille *f*
fuzz•y [`fʌzi] *adj* (*comp* **-ier;** *super* **-iest**) pelucheux; (*hair*) crêpelu; (*indistinct*) flou

G

G, g [dʒi] *s* VIIe lettre de l'alphabet
gab [gæb] *s* (coll) bavardage *m*, langue *f* ‖ *v* (*pret & pp* **gabbed;** *ger* **gabbing**) *intr* (coll) bavarder
gabardine [`gæbərˌdin] *s* gabardine *f*
gabble [`gæbəl] *s* jacasserie *f* ‖ *intr* jacasser
gable [`gebəl] *s* (*of roof*) pignon *m;* (*over a door or window*) gable *m*
ga′ble end′ *s* pignon *m*
ga′ble roof′ *s* comble *m* sur pignon, toit *m* à deux pentes
gad [gæd] *v* (*pret & pp* **gadded;** *ger* **gadding**) *intr*—**to gad about** courir la prétantaine, vadrouiller
gad′about′ *s* vadrouilleur *m*
gad′fly′ *s* (*pl* **-flies**) taon *m*
gadget [`gædʒɪt] *s* dispositif *m;* (*unnamed article*) machin *m*, truc *m*, gimmick *m*
Gaelic [`gelɪk] *adj* & *s* gaélique *m*
gaff [gæf] *s* gaffe *f;* **to stand the gaff** (slang) ne pas broncher
gaffer [`gæfər] *s* (coll) vieux bonhomme *m*
gag [gæg] *s* bâillon *m;* (*interpolation by an actor*) gag *m;* (*joke*) blague *f* ‖ *v* (*pret & pp* **gagged;** *ger* **gagging**) *tr* bâillonner ‖ *intr* avoir des haut-le-cœur
gage [gedʒ] *s* (*pledge*) gage *m;* (*challenge*) défi *m*
gaie•ty [`ge•ɪti] *s* (*pl* **-ties**) gaieté *f*
gaily [`geli] *adv* gaiement
gain [gen] *s* gain *m;* (*increase*) accroissement *m* ‖ *tr* gagner; (*to reach*) atteindre, gagner ‖ *intr* gagner du terrain; (*said of invalid*) s'améliorer; (*said of watch*) avancer; **to gain on** prendre de l'avance sur
gainful [`genfəl] *adj* profitable
gain′say′ *v* (*pret & pp* **-said** [ˌsed], [ˌsɛd]) *tr* (*to deny*) nier; (*to contradict*) contredire; **not to gainsay** ne pas disconvenir de
gait [get] *s* démarche *f*, allure *f*
gaiter [`getər] *s* guêtre *f*
gala [`gælə] *adj* de gala ‖ *s* gala *m*
galax•y [`gæləksi] *s* (*pl* **-ies**) galaxie *f*
gale [gel] *s* gros vent *m;* **gales of laughter** éclats *mpl* de rire; **to weather a gale** étaler un coup de vent

gall [gɔl] s bile f, fiel m; (*something bitter*) (fig) fiel m, amertume f; (*audacity*) (coll) toupet m ‖ tr écorcher par le frottement; (fig) irriter

gallant [ˈgælənt] adj (*spirited, daring*) vaillant, brave; (*stately, grand*) fier, noble; (*showy, gay*) élégant, superbe, de fête ‖ adj galant ‖ s galant m; vaillant m ‖ [gəˈlænt] intr faire le galant

gallant‧ry [ˈgæləntri] s (*pl* -ries) galanterie f; (*bravery*) vaillance f

gall' blad'der s vésicule f biliaire

gall' duct' s conduit m biliaire

galleon [ˈgæli•ən] s (naut) galion m

galler‧y [ˈgæləri] s (*pl* -ies) galerie f; (*cheapest seats in theater*) poulailler m; **to play to the gallery** poser pour la galerie

galley [ˈgæli] s (*ship*) galère f; (*ship's kitchen*) coquerie f; (typ) galée f; placard m

gal'ley proof' s épreuve f en placard, épreuve sous le galet

gal'ley slave' s galérien m (archaic); (fig & hum) forçat m (archaic)

Gallic [ˈgælɪk] adj gaulois

Gal'lic wit' s esprit m gaulois

galling [ˈgɔlɪŋ] adj irritant, blessant

gallivant [ˈgælɪˌvænt] intr courailler

gall' nut' s noix f de galle

gallon [ˈgælən] s gallon m américain

galloon [gəˈlun] s galon m

gallop [ˈgæləp] s galop m ‖ tr faire galoper ‖ intr galoper

gal‧lows [ˈgæloz] s (*pl* -lows or -lowses) gibet m, potence f

gal'lows bird' s (coll) gibier m de potence

gall'stone' s calcul m biliaire

galore [gəˈlor] adv à foison, à gogo

galoshes [gəˈlɑˌʃiz] spl caoutchoucs mpl

galvanize [ˈgælvəˌnaɪz] tr galvaniser

gal'vanized i'ron s tôle f galvanisée

gambit [ˈgæmbɪt] s gambit m

gamble [ˈgæmbəl] s risque m, affaire f de chance ‖ tr jouer; **to gamble away** perdre au jeu ‖ intr jouer; jouer à la Bourse; (fig) prendre des risques

gambler [ˈgæmblər] s joueur m

gambling [ˈgæmblɪŋ] s jeu m

gam'bling den' s tripot m

gam'bling house' s maison f de jeu

gam'bling ta'ble s table f de jeu

gam‧bol [ˈgæmbəl] s gambade f ‖ v (*pret & pp* -boled or -bolled; ger -boling or -bolling) intr gambader

gambrel [ˈgæmbrəl] s (*hock*) jarret m; (in *butcher shop*) jambier m

gam'brel roof' s toit m en croupe

game [gem] adj (*plucky*) crâne, résolu; (*leg*) boiteux ‖ s jeu m; (*contest*) match m; (*score necessary to win*) partie f; (*animal or bird*) gibier m; **to make game of** tourner en dérision

game' bag' s carnassière f, gibecière f

game' bird' s oiseau m que l'on chasse

game'cock' s coq m de combat

game'keep'er s garde-chasse m

game' of chance' s jeu m de hasard

game' preserve' s chasse f gardée

game' war'den s garde-chasse m

gam'ing [ˈgemɪŋ] s jeu m

gamut [ˈgæmət] s gamme f

gam‧y [ˈgemi] adj (*comp* -ier; *super* -iest) (*having flavor of uncooked game*) faisandé; (*plucky*) crâne

gander [ˈgændər] s jars m

gang [gæŋ] adj multiple ‖ s (*of workmen*) équipe f, brigade f; (*of thugs*) bande f; (*of wrongdoers*) séquelle f, clique f ‖ intr—**to gang up** se concerter; **to gang up on** se liguer contre

gangling [ˈgæŋglɪŋ] adj dégingandé

gangli‧on [ˈgæŋgli•ən] s (*pl* -ons or -a [ə]) ganglion m

gang'plank' s passerelle f, planche f de débarquement

gang' rape' s viol m collectif

gangrene [ˈgæŋgrin] s gangrène f ‖ tr gangrener ‖ intr se gangrener

gangster [ˈgæŋstər] s bandit m, gangster m

gang'way' s (*passageway*) passage m, coursive f; (*gangplank*) planche f de débarquement; (in *ship's side*) coupée f ‖ interj rangez-vous!, dégagez!

gan‧try [ˈgæntri] s (*pl* -tries) (*for barrels*) chantier m; (*for crane*) portique m; (rr) pont m à signaux

gan'try crane' s grue f à portique

gap [gæp] s (*blank*) lacune f; (*in wall*) brèche f; (*between mountains*) col m, gorge f; (*between two points of view*) abîme m, gouffre m

gape [gep] s (*gap*) ouverture f, brèche f; (*yawn*) bâillement m; (*look of astonishment*) badauderie f ‖ intr (*to yawn*) bâiller; (*to look with astonishment*) badauder; **to gape at** regarder bouche bée

garage [gəˈrɑʒ] s garage m

garage' sale' s braderie f, vente f bric-à-brac

garb [gɑrb] s costume m ‖ tr vêtir

garbage [ˈgɑrbɪdʒ] s ordures fpl

gar'bage can' s poubelle f, dépotoir m (d'ordures)

gar'bage collec'tion s voirie f

gar'bage collec'tor s boueur m

gar'bage dispos'al s broyeur m d'ordures

gar'bage truck' s benne f à ordures

garble [ˈgɑrbəl] tr mutiler, tronquer

garden [ˈgɑrdən] s jardin m; (*of vegetables*) potager m; (*of flowers*) parterre m ‖ intr jardiner

gard'en cen'ter s (com) jardinerie f

gar'den cit'y s cité-jardin f

gardener [ˈgɑrdnər] s jardinier m

gardening [ˈgɑrdnɪŋ] s jardinage m

gar'den par'ty s garden-party f

gargle [ˈgɑrgəl] s gargarisme m ‖ intr se gargariser

gargoyle [ˈgɑrgɔɪl] s gargouille f

garish [ˈgærɪʃ] adj cru, rutilant, criard

garland [ˈgɑrlənd] s guirlande f ‖ tr guirlander

garlic [ˈgɑrlɪk] s ail m

garment [ˈgɑrmənt] *s* vêtement *m*

gar'ment bag' *s* housse *f* à vêtements

garner [ˈgɑrnər] *tr* (*to gather, collect*) amasser; (*cereals*) engranger

garnet [ˈgɑrnɪt] *adj* & *s* grenat *m*

garnish [ˈgɑrnɪʃ] *s* garniture *f* ‖ *tr* garnir; (*law*) effectuer une saisie-arrêt sur

garret [ˈgærɪt] *s* grenier *m;* (*dormer room*) mansarde *f*

garrison [ˈgærɪsən] *s* garnison *f* ‖ *tr* (*troops*) mettre en garnison; (*a city*) mettre des troupes en garnison dans

garrote [gəˈrɑt], [gəˈrot] *s* (*method of execution*) garrotte *f;* (*iron collar used for such an execution*) garrot *m* ‖ *tr* garrotter

garrulous [ˈgær(j)ələs] *adj* bavard

garter [ˈgɑrtər] *s* jarretelle *f*, jarretière *f;* (*for men's socks*) support-chaussette *m*, fixe-chaussette *m*

garth [gɑrθ] *s* cour *f* intérieure d'un cloître

gas [gæs] *s* gaz *m;* (coll) essence *f;* (*empty talk*) (coll) bavardage *m;* **out of gas** en panne sèche; **to step on the gas** (coll) appuyer sur le champignon ‖ *v* (*pret & pp* **gassed;** *ger* **gassing**) *tr* gazer, asphyxier ‖ *intr* dégager des gaz; (mil) gazer; (*to talk nonsense*) (coll) bavarder

gas'bag' *s* enveloppe *f* à gaz; (coll) blagueur *m*, baratineur *m*

gas' burn'er *s* bec *m* de gaz

gas' cham'ber *s* chambre *f* à gaz

Gascony [ˈgæskəni] *s* Gascogne *f;* la Gascogne

gas' en'gine *s* moteur *m* à gaz

gaseous [ˈgæsɪ•əs] *adj* gazeux

gas' gen'erator *s* gazogène *m*

gash [gæʃ] *s* entaille *f;* (*on face*) balafre *f* ‖ *tr* entailler; balafrer

gas' heat' *s* chauffage *m* au gaz

gas' heat'er *s* (*for hot water*) chauffe-eau *m* à gaz; (*for house heat*) calorifère *m* à gaz

gas'hold'er *s* gazomètre *m*

gasi•fy [ˈgæsɪˌfaɪ] *v* (*pret & pp* -**fied**) *tr* gazéifier ‖ *intr* se gazéifier

gas' jet' *s* bec *m* de gaz

gasket [ˈgæskɪt] *s* joint *m*

gas'light' *s* éclairage *m* au gaz

gas' main' *s* conduite *f* de gaz

gas' mask' *s* masque *m* à gaz

gas' me'ter *s* compteur *m* à gaz

gasoline [ˈgæsəˌlin] *s* essence *f*

gas'oline can' *s* bidon *m* d'essence

gas'oline gauge' *s* voyant *m* d'essence

gas'oline pump' *s* pompe *f* à essence

gas'oline tax' *s* taxe *f* sur l'essence

gasp [gæsp] *s* halètement *m;* (*of surprise; of death*) hoquet *m* ‖ *tr*—**to gasp out** (*a word*) dire dans un souffle ‖ *intr* haleter

gas' pipe' *s* conduite *f* de gaz

gas' produc'er *s* gazogène *m*

gas' range' *s* fourneau *m* à gaz, cuisinière *f* à gaz

gassed *adj* (*in warfare*) gasé

gas' sta'tion *s* poste *m* d'essence

gas' stove' *s* cuisinière *f* à gaz, réchaud *m* à gaz

gas' tank' *s* gazomère *m;* (aut) réservoir *m* d'essence

gastric [ˈgæstrɪk] *adj* gastrique

gastronomy [gæsˈtrɑnəmi] *s* gastronomie *f*

gas' works' *spl* usine *f* à gaz

gat [gæt] *s* (*gun*) (slang) flingue *f*

gate [get] *s* porte *f;* (*in fence or wall*) grille *f;* (*main gate*) portail *f;* (*of sluice*) vanne *f;* (*number paying admission; amount paid*) entrée *f;* (*waiting area*) (aer) salle *f* d'embarquement; (rr) barrière *f;* **to crash the gate** resquiller

gate-crasher [ˈgetˌkræʃər] *s* (coll) resquilleur *m*

gate'keep'er *s* portier *m;* (rr) garde-barrière *mf*

gate'-leg ta'ble *s* table *f* à abattants sur pieds mobiles

gate'post' *s* montant *m*

gate'way' *s* passage *m*, entrée *f;* (*main entrance*) portail *m*

gather [ˈgæðər] *tr* amasser, rassembler; (*the harvest*) rentrer; (*fruits, flowers, etc.*) cueillir, ramasser; (*one's thoughts*) recueillir; (bb) rassembler; (sewing) froncer; (*to deduce*) (fig) conclure; **to gather dust** s'encrasser; **to gather oneself together** se ramasser ‖ *intr* se réunir, s'assembler; (*said of clouds*) s'amonceler

gathering [ˈgæðərɪŋ] *s* réunion *m*, rassemblement *m;* (*of harvest*) récolte *f;* (*of fruits, flowers, etc.*) cueillette *f;* (bb) assemblage *m*, cahier *m* (d'imprimerie); (sewing) froncis *m*

gaud•y [ˈgɔdi] *adj* (*comp* -**ier;** *super* -**iest**) criard, voyant

gauge [gedʒ] *s* jauge *f*, calibre *m;* (*of liquid in a container*) niveau *m;* (*of gasoline, oil, etc.*) indicateur *m;* (*of carpenter*) trusquin *m;* (rr) écartement *m* ‖ *tr* jauger, calibrer; (*a person; s.o.'s capacities; a distance*) juger de, jauger

gauge' glass' *s* indicateur *m* de niveau

Gaul [gɔl] *s* Gaule *f;* la Gaule

Gaulish [ˈgɔlɪʃ] *adj* & *s* gaulois *m*

gaunt [gɔnt] *adj* décharné, étique, efflanqué

gauntlet [ˈgɔntlɪt] *s* gantelet *m;* **to run the gauntlet** passer par les baguettes; **to take up the gauntlet** relever le gant; **to throw down the gauntlet** jeter le gant

gauze [gɔz] *s* gaze *f*

gavel [ˈgævəl] *s* marteau *m*

gawk [gɔk] *s* (coll) godiche *mf* ‖ *intr* (coll) bayer aux corneilles; **to gawk at** (coll) regarder bouche bée

gawk•y [ˈgɔki] *adj* (*comp* -**ier;** *super* -**iest**) godiche

gay [ge] *adj* (*homosexual*) gay, gai; (obs) joyeux, riant, heureux; enjoué; éclatant ‖ *s* gay *m*, gai *m;* (rare) gaie *f*

gay' blade' *s* (coll) joyeux drille *m*

gaze [gez] *s* regard *m* fixe ‖ *intr* regarder fixement

gazelle [gəˈzɛl] *s* gazelle *f*

gazette [gəˈzɛt] *s* gazette *f;* journal *m* officiel

gazetteer [,gæzə`tır] *s* dictionnaire *m* géographique

gear [gɪr] *s* (*paraphernalia*) attirail *m*, appareil *m;* (*of transmission, steering, etc.*) mécanisme *m;* (*adjustment of automobile transmission*) marche *f,* vitesse *f;* (*two or more toothed wheels meshed together*) engrenage *m;* **out of gear** débrayé; **to throw into gear** embrayer; **to throw out of gear** débrayer; (fig) disloquer ‖ *tr & intr* engrener

gear′box′ *s* (aut) boîte *f* de vitesses

gear′shift′ *s* changement *m* de vitesse

gear′shift lev′er *s* levier *m* de changement de vitesse

gear′wheel′ roue *f* d'engrenage

gee [dʒi] *interj* sapristi!; (*to the right*) hue!; **gee up!** hue!

Gehenna [gɪ`hɛnə] *s* Géhenne *f*

Gei′ger count′er [`gaɪgər] *s* cómpteur *m* de Geiger

gel [dʒɛl] *s* (chem) gel *m*

gelatine [`dʒɛlətɪn] *s* gélatine *f*

geld [gɛld] *v* (*pret & pp* **gelded** or **gelt** [gɛlt]) *tr* châtrer

gelding [`gɛldɪŋ] *s* hongre *m*

gem [dʒɛm] *s* gemme *f;* (fig) bijou *m*

Gemini [`dʒɛmə,naɪ] *s* (astr, astrol) les Gémeaux *mpl*

gender [`dʒɛndər] *s* (gram) genre *m;* (coll) sexe *m*

gene [dʒin] *s* (biol) gène *m*

genealo·gy [,dʒɛnɪ`ælədʒi] *s* (*pl* **-gies**) généalogie *f*

general [`dʒɛnərəl] *adj & s* général *m;* **in general** en général

gen′eral deliv′ery *s* poste *f* restante

generalissi·mo [,dʒɛnərə`lɪsɪmo] *s* (*pl* **-mos**) généralissime *m*

generali·ty [,dʒɛnə`ræliti] *s* (*pl* **-ties**) généralité *f*

generalize [`dʒɛnərə,laɪz] *tr & intr* généraliser

generally [`dʒɛnərəli] *adj* généralement

gen′eral practi′tioner *s* (med) généraliste *m*

gen′eral pur′pose *adj* universel

gen′eral·ship′ *s* tactique *f;* (office) généralat *m*

gen′eral staff′ *s* état-major *m*

gen′eral store′ *s* magasin *m* qui vend de tout

gen′eral strike′ *s* grève *f* générale

generate [`dʒɛnə,ret] *tr* générer; (*to beget*) engendrer; (geom) engendrer

gen′erating sta′tion *s* usine *f* génératrice, centrale *f*

generation [,dʒɛnə`re∫ən] *s* génération *f*

genera′tion gap′ *s* fossé *m* des générations

generator [`dʒɛnə,retər] *s* (chem) gazogène *m;* (elec) génératrice *f*

generic [dʒɪ`nɛrɪk] *adj* générique

generosi·ty [,dʒɛnə`rasɪti] *s* (*pl* **-ties**) générosité *f*

generous [`dʒɛnərəs] *adj* (*action, quantity*) généreux; (*supply; harvest*) abondant; (*size*) ample

gene·sis [`dʒɛnɪsɪs] *s* (*pl* **-ses** [,siz]) genèse *f;* **Genesis** (Bib) La Genèse

gene′ splic′ing *s* épissure *f* génétique

genetic [dʒɪ`nɛtɪk] *adj* génétique ‖ **genetics** *s* génétique *f*

genet′ic code′ *s* code *m* génétique

genet′ic en′gineer′ing *s* sélection *f* eugénique

genet′ic fin′ger·print′ *s* empreinte *f* génétique

geneticist [dʒə`nɛtəsɪst] *s* généticien *m*

Geneva [dʒɪ`nivə] *s* Genève *f*

genial [`dʒinɪəl] *adj* affable

genie [`dʒini] *s* génie *m*

genital [`dʒɛnɪtəl] *adj* génital ‖ **genitals** *spl* organes *mpl* génitaux

genitive [`dʒɛnɪtɪv] *s* génitif *m*

genius [`dʒinjəs] *s* (*pl* **geniuses**) génie *m* ‖ *s* (*pl* **genii** [`dʒinɪ,aɪ]) génie *m*

Genoa [`dʒɛno•ə] *s* Gênes *f*

genocide [`dʒɛnə,saɪd] *s* génocide *m*

genome [`dʒinom] *s* (gen) génome *m*

genteel [dʒɛn`til] *adj* distingué, de bon ton, élégant

gentian [`dʒɛn∫ən] *s* gentiane *f*

gentile [`dʒɛntaɪl] *s* non-juif *m*, chrétien *m;* (hist) gentil *m*

gentili·ty [dʒɛn`tɪlɪti] *s* (*pl* **-ties**) (*birth*) naissance *f* distinguée; (*breeding*) politesse *f*

gentle [`dʒɛntəl] *adj* doux; (*in birth*) noble, bien né; (*e.g., tap on the shoulder*) léger

gen′tle·folk′ *s* gens *mpl* de bonne naissance

gen′tle·man *s* (*pl* **-men**) monsieur *m;* (*polite person*) homme *m* bien élevé; (*man of independent means*) rentier *m;* (hist) gentilhomme *m*

gentlemanly [`dʒɛntəlmənli] *adj* bien élevé, de bon ton

gen′tleman's agree′ment *s* engagement *m* sur parole, contrat *m* verbal; (*type of international agreement*) gentleman's agreement *m;* (*tactic used in the discrimination of minorities*) consentement *m* tacite

gen′tle sex′ *s* sexe *m* faible

gentry [`dʒɛntri] *s* gens *mpl* de bonne naissance; (Brit) petite noblesse *f*

genuflection [`dʒɛnjəflɛ∫ən] *s* génuflexion *f*

genuine [`dʒɛnjʊ•ɪn] *adj* véritable, authentique; (*person*) sincère, franc

genus [`dʒinəs] *s* (*pl* **genera** [`dʒɛnərə] or **genuses**) genre *m*

geogra·phy [dʒɪ`agrəfi] *s* (*pl* **-phies**) géographie *f*

geologic(al) [,dʒiə`ladʒɪk(əl)] *adj* géologique

geologist [dʒɪ`alədʒɪst] *s* géologue *mf*

geolo·gy [dʒɪ`alədʒi] *s* (*pl* **-gies**) géologie *f*

geometric(al) [,dʒiə`mɛtrɪk(əl)] *adj* géométrique

geome·try [dʒɪ`amɪtri] *s* (*pl* **-tries**) géométrie *f*

geophysics [,dʒiə`fɪzɪks] *s* géophysique *f*

geopolitics [,dʒiə`palɪtɪks] *s* géopolitique *f*

George [dʒɔrdʒ] *s* Georges *m*

geranium [dʒɪ`reni•əm] *s* géranium *m*

geriatrics [,dʒɛrɪ`ætrɪks] *s* gériatrie *f*

germ [dʒʌrm] *adj* germinal ‖ *s* germe *m*

German [ˈdʒʌrmən] adj allemand ‖ s (*language*) allemand m; (*person*) Allemand m
germane [dʒɛrˈmen] adj à propos, pertinent; **germane to** se rapportant à
Ger′man mea′sles s rubéole f
Ger′man sil′ver s maillechort m, argentan m
Ger′man speak′er s germanophone mf
Ger′man-speak′ing adj germanophone
Germa•ny [ˈdʒʌrməni] s (*pl* **-nies**) Allemagne f; l'Allemagne
germ′ car′rier s porteur m de germes
germ′ cell′ s cellule f germe
germ′-free′ adj axénique
germicidal [ˌdʒʌrmɪˈsaɪdəl] adj germicide
germicide [ˈdʒʌrmɪˌsaɪd] s germicide m
germinate [ˈdʒʌrmɪˌnet] intr germer
germ′ plas′ma s plasma m germinal
germ′ the′ory s théorie f germinale
germ′ war′fare s guerre f bactériologique
gerontology [ˌdʒɛrənˈtɑlədʒi] s gérontologie f
gerrymander [ˈgɛrɪˌmændər] ou **gerrymandering** [ˈgɛrɪˌmændərɪŋ] s découpage m des circonscriptions électorales
gerund [ˈdʒɛrənd] s gérondif m
gestation [dʒɛsˈteʃən] s gestation f
gesticulate [dʒɛsˈtɪkjəˌlet] intr gesticuler
gestural [ˈdʒɛstʃərəl] adj gestuel
ges′tural lan′guage ou **ges′ture lan′guage** var de **sign′ lan′guage**
gesture [ˈdʒɛstʃər] s geste m ‖ intr faire des gestes; **to gesture to** faire signe à
get [gɛt] v (*pret* **got** [gɑt]; *pp* **got** or **gotten** [ˈgɑtən]; *ger* **getting**) tr obtenir, procurer; (*to receive*) avoir, recevoir; (*to catch*) attraper; (*to seek*) chercher, aller chercher; (*to reach*) atteindre; (*to find*) trouver, rencontrer; (*to obtain and bring*) prendre; (*e.g., dinner*) faire; (rad) avoir, prendre, accrocher; (*to understand*) (coll) comprendre; **to get across** faire accepter; faire comprendre; **to get a kick out of** (coll) prendre plaisir à; **to get back** ravoir, se faire rendre; **to get down** descendre; (*to swallow*) avaler; **to get in** rentrer; **to get out the trump** purger les atouts; **to get s.o. to** + *inf* persuader à qn de + *inf;* **to get s.th. done** faire faire q.ch. ‖ intr (*to become*) devenir, se faire; (*to arrive*) arriver, parvenir; **get up!** (*said to an animal*) hue!; **to get about** (*said of news*) se répandre; (*said of convalescent*) être de nouveau sur pied; (*to move about*) circuler; **to get across** traverser; **to get along** circuler; (*to succeed*) se tirer d'affaire; **to get along with** faire bon ménage avec; **to get along without** se passer de; **to get angry** se fâcher; **to get away** s'évader; **to get away with** s'en aller avec; (coll) s'en tirer avec; **to get back** reculer; (*to return*) rentrer; **to get back at** (coll) rendre la pareille à, se venger sur; **to get by** passer; (*to manage, to shift*) (coll) s'en tirer sans peine; **to get dark** faire nuit; **to get down** descendre; **to get going** se mettre en marche; **to get in** or **into** entrer dans; **to get**

off (*to go free*) s'en tirer; **to get off (of)** (*a bus, a horse, etc.*) descendre de; (*a chair, the floor*) se lever de; **to get off with** en être quitte pour; **to get on** monter sur; (*a car*) monter dans; continuer; (*to succeed*) faire des progrès; **to get out** sortir; **to get rid of** se défaire de; **to get to** arriver à; (*to have an opportunity to*) avoir l'occasion de; **to get up** se lever; **to not get over it** (coll) ne pas en revenir
get′ away s démarrage m; (*flight*) fuite f
get′-togeth′er s réunion f
get′ up′ s (*style*) (coll) présentation f; (*outfit*) (coll) affublement m
gewgaw [ˈgjugɔ] s bibelot m, babiole f
geyser [ˈgaɪzər] s geyser m
ghastly [ˈgæstli] adj (*comp* **-lier;** *super* **-liest**) livide, blême; horrible, affreux
Ghent [gɛnt] s Gand m
gherkin [ˈgʌrkɪn] s cornichon m
ghet•to [ˈgɛto] s (*pl* **-tos**) ghetto m
ghost [gost] s revenant m, spectre m; (*shade, semblance*) ombre f; **not the ghost of a chance** pas la moindre chance; **to give up the ghost** rendre l'âme, rendre l'esprit
ghost′ im′age s filage m
ghostly [ˈgostli] adj (*comp* **-lier;** *super* **-liest**) spectral, fantomatique
ghost′ sto′ry s histoire f de revenants
ghost′ town′ s ville f morte
ghost′ writ′er s rédacteur m anonyme
ghoul [gul] s goule f; (*body snatcher*) déterreur m de cadavres
ghoulish [ˈgulɪʃ] adj vampirique
G.H.Q. abbr **General Headquarters**
GI [ˈdʒiˈaɪ] (letterword) (**General Issue**) adj fourni par l'armée ‖ s (*pl* **GI's**) soldat m américain, simple soldat
giant [ˈdʒaɪənt] adj & s géant m
giantess [ˈdʒaɪənˌtɪs] s géante f
gibberish [ˈdʒɪbərɪʃ] s baragouin m
gibbet [ˈdʒɪbɪt] s gibet m, potence f
gibe [dʒaɪb] s raillerie f, moquerie f ‖ tr & intr railler; **to gibe at** se moquer de, railler
giblets [ˈdʒɪblɪts] spl abattis m, abats mpl
gid•dy [ˈgɪdi] adj (*comp* **-dier;** *super* **-diest**) étourdi; (*height*) vertigineux; (*foolish*) léger, frivole
Gideon [ˈgɪdiˌən] s (Bib) Gédéon m
gift [gɪft] s cadeau m; (*natural ability*) don m, talent m ‖ tr douer
gift′ certif′icate s bon m cadeau
gifted adj doué
gift′ horse′—never look a gift horse in the mouth à cheval donné on ne regarde pas à la bride
gift′ of gab′ s (coll) bagou m, faconde f
gift′ shop′ s boutique f de souvenirs, magasin m de nouveautés
gift′ tax′ s taxe f sur les cadeaux
gift′-wrap v (*pret & pp* **-wrapped;** *ger* **-wrapping**) tr faire un paquet cadeau de
gigantic [dʒaɪˈgæntɪk] adj gigantesque

giggle [ˈgɪgəl] s petit rire m ‖ intr pousser des petits rires, glousser

gigo•lo [ˈdʒɪgəˌlo] s (pl -los) gigolo m

GI Joe [ˌdʒiˌaɪˈdʒo] s le troufion

gild [gɪld] v (pret & pp **gilded** or **gilt** [gɪlt]) tr dorer

gilding [ˈgɪldɪŋ] s dorure f

gill [gɪl] s (of cock) fanon m; **gills** (of fish) ouïes fpl, branchies fpl

gilt [gɪlt] adj & s doré m

gilt′-edged′ adj (e.g., book) doré sur tranche; (securities) de premier ordre, de tout repos

gimcrack [ˈgɪmˌkræk] adj de pacotille, de camelote ‖ s babiole f

gimlet [ˈgɪmlɪt] s vrille f, perçoir m

gimmick [ˈgɪmɪk] s (coll) truc m, machin m; (trick) tour m

gimp [gɪmp] s boiterie f ‖ intr boiter

gin [dʒɪn] s (alcoholic liquor) gin m, genièvre m; (for cotton, corn, etc.) égreneuse f; (snare) trébuchet m ‖ v (pret & pp **ginned;** ger **ginning**) tr égrener

ginger [ˈdʒɪndʒər] s gingembre m; (fig) entrain m, allant m

gin′ger ale′ s boisson f gazeuse au gingembre

gin′ger•bread′ s pain m d'épice; ornement m de mauvais goût

gingerly [ˈdʒɪndʒərli] adj précautionneux ‖ adv tout doux, avec précaution

gin′ger•snap′ s gâteau m sec au gingembre

gingham [ˈgɪŋəm] s guingan m

giraffe [dʒɪˈræf] s girafe f

gird [gʌrd] v (pret & pp **girt** [gʌrt] or **girded**) tr ceindre; **to gird on** se ceindre de; **to gird oneself for** se préparer à

girder [ˈgʌrdər] s poutre f

girdle [ˈgʌrdəl] s ceinture f; (corset) gaine f ‖ tr ceindre, entourer

girl [gʌrl] s jeune fille f; (little girl) petite fille f; (servant) bonne f

girl′ friend′ s (sweetheart) petite amie f, bonne amie f; (bosom friend) amie intime f, camarade f; (friend) amie f

girl′ hood′ s enfance f, jeunesse f d'une femme

girlish [ˈgʌrlɪʃ] adj de jeune fille, de petite fille

girl′ scout′ s éclaireuse f, guide f

girls′′ school′ s école f de filles

girth [gʌrθ] s (band) sangle f; (measure around) circonférence f; (of person) tour m de taille

gist [dʒɪst] s fond m, essence f

give [gɪv] s élasticité f ‖ v (pret **gave** [gev]; pp **given** [ˈgɪvən]) tr donner; (a speech, a lecture, a class; a smile) faire; **to give away** donner, distribuer; révéler; **to give back** rendre, remettre; **to give forth** or **off** émettre; **to give oneself up** se rendre; **to give up** renoncer à, abandonner ‖ intr donner; **to give in** se rendre; **to give out** manquer; (to become exhausted) s'épuiser; **to give way** faire place, reculer

give′-and-take′ s compromis m; échange m de propos plaisants

give′ away′ s (coll) révélation f involontaire;

(coll) trahison f; **to play giveaway** jouer à qui perd gagne

given [ˈgɪvən] adj donné; **given that** vu que, étant donné que

giv′en name′ s prénom m

giver [ˈgɪvər] s donneur m, donateur m

gizzard [ˈgɪzərd] s gésier m

glacial [ˈgleʃəl] adj glacial; (chem) en cristaux; (geol) glaciaire

glacier [ˈgleʃər] s glacier m

glad [glæd] adj (comp **gladder;** super **gladdest**) content, heureux; **to be glad to** être content or heureux de

gladden [ˈglædən] tr réjouir

glade [gled] s clairière f, éclaircie f, percée f

glad′ hand′ s (coll) accueil m chaleureux

gladiator [ˈglædiˌetər] s gladiateur m

gladiola [ˌglædɪˈolə] s glaïeul m

gladly [ˈglædli] adv volontiers, avec plaisir

gladness [ˈglædnɪs] s joie f, plaisir m

glad′ rags′ spl (slang) frusques fpl des grands jours

glamorous [ˈglæmərəs] adj ravissant, éclatant, glamour

glamour [ˈglæmər] s charme m, éclat m, glamour m

glam′our girl′ s ensorceleuse f

glance [glæns] s coup m d'œil; **at a glance** d'un seul coup d'œil; **at first glance** à première vue ‖ intr jeter un regard; **to glance at** jeter un coup d'œil sur; **to glance off** ricocher, dévier; **to glance through a book** feuilleter un livre; **to glance up** lever les yeux

gland [glænd] s glande f

glanders [ˈglændərz] spl (vet) morve f

glare [glɛr] s (light) lumière f éblouissante; (look) regard m irrité ‖ intr éblouir, briller; **to glare at** lancer un regard méchant à, foudroyer du regard

glare′ ice′ s verglas m

glaring [ˈglɛrɪŋ] adj (shining) éblouissant; (mistake, fact) évident, qui saute aux yeux; (blunder, abuse) grossier, scandaleux

glasnost [ˈglɑsˌnɑst] s transparence f, glasnost m

glass [glæs] s verre m; (mirror) glace f; **glasses** lunettes fpl

glass′ blow′er [ˈbloˌər] s verrier-souffleur m

glass′ case′ s vitrine f

glass′ ceil′ing s la barrière non reconnue qui empêche les femmes de continuer à avancer

glass′ cut′ter s (tool) diamant m; (workman) vitrier m

glass′ door′ s porte f vitrée

glassful [ˈglæsful] s verre m

glass′ house′ s serre f; (fig) maison f de verre

glass′ ware′ s verrerie f

glass′ wool′ s laine f de verre

glass′ works′ s verrerie f, glacerie f

glass•y [ˈglæsi] adj (comp **-ier;** super **-iest**) vitreux; (smooth) lisse

glaucoma [glɔˈkomə] s glaucome m

glaze [glez] s (ceramics) vernis m; (culin) glace

f; (tex) lustre m ‖ tr (*to cover with a glossy coating*) glacer; (*to fit with glass*) vitrer

glazier [ˈgleʒər] s vitrier m

gleam [glim] s rayon m; (*of hope*) lueur f ‖ intr rayonner, reluire

glean [glin] tr glaner

glee [gli] s allégresse f, joie f

glee′ club′ s orphéon m, société f chorale

glen [glɛn] s vallon m, ravin m

glib [glɪb] adj (*comp* **glibber;** *super* **glibbest**) facile; (*tongue*) délié

glide [glaɪd] s glissement m; vol m plané; (*mus*) port m de voix; (*phonet*) son m transitoire ‖ intr glisser, se glisser; (aer) planer

glider [ˈglaɪdər] s (*porch seat*) siège m à glissière; (aer) planeur m

gliding [ˈglaɪdɪŋ] s vol m à voile

glimmer [ˈglɪmər] s faible lueur f ‖ intr jeter une faible lueur

glimmering [ˈglɪmərɪŋ] adj faible, vacillant ‖ s faible lueur f, miroitement m; soupçon m, indice m

glimpse [glɪmps] s aperçu m; **to catch a glimpse of** entrevoir, aviser ‖ tr entrevoir

glint [glɪnt] s reflet m, éclair m ‖ intr jeter un reflet, étinceler

glisten [ˈglɪsən] s scintillement m ‖ intr scintiller

glitter [ˈglɪtər] s éclat m, étincellement m ‖ intr étinceler

glitz [glɪts] s (coll) clinquant m, faux brillant m

glitzy [ˈglɪtsi] adj (coll) brillant, séduisant, éblouissant

gloaming [ˈglomɪŋ] s crépuscule m, jour m crépusculaire

gloat [glot] intr éprouver un malin plaisir; **to gloat over** faire des gorges chaudes de; (*e.g., one's victim*) couver du regard

global [ˈglobəl] adj sphérique; mondial

globe [glob] s globe m

globe′-trot′ter s globe-trotter m

globule [ˈglabjʊl] s globule m

gloom [glum] s obscurité f, ténèbres fpl; tristesse f

gloom·y [ˈglumi] adj (*comp* **-ier;** *super* **-iest**) sombre, lugubre; (*ideas*) noir

glori·fy [ˈglorɪˌfaɪ] v (*pret & pp* **-fied**) tr glorifier

glorious [ˈglorɪ·əs] adj glorieux

glo·ry [ˈglori] s (*pl* **-ries**) gloire f; **to be in one's glory** être aux anges; **to go to glory** (slang) aller à la ruine ‖ v (*pret & pp* **-ried**) intr—**to glory in** se glorifier de

gloss [glɔs] s lustre m; (*on cloth*) cati m; (*on floor*) brillant m; (*note, commentary*) glose f; **to take off the gloss from** décatir ‖ tr lustrer; **to gloss over** maquiller, farder

glossa·ry [ˈglasəri] s (*pl* **-ries**) glossaire m

gloss·y [ˈglasi] adj (*comp* **-ier;** *super* **-iest**) lustré, brillant

glot′tal stop′ [ˈglatəl] s coup m de glotte

glottis [ˈglatɪs] s glotte f

glove [glʌv] s gant m ‖ tr ganter

glove′ compart′ment s boîte f à gants

glove′ wash′cloth s gant m à laver

glow [glo] s rougeoiement m ‖ intr rougeoyer

glower [ˈglau·ər] s grise mine f ‖ intr avoir l'air renfrogné

glowing [ˈglo·ɪʒ] adj rougeoyant, incandescent; (*healthy*) rayonnant; (*cheeks*) vermeil; (*reports*) enthousiaste, élogieux

glow′worm′ s ver m luisant

glucose [ˈglukos] s glucose m

glue [glu] s colle f ‖ tr coller

glue′pot′ s pot m à colle

gluey [ˈglu·i] adj (*comp* **gluier;** *super* **gluiest**) gluant

glug [glʌg] s glouglou m

glum [glʌm] adj (*comp* **glummer;** *super* **glummest**) maussade, renfrogné

glut [glʌt] s (*excess*) surabondance f, excès m; (*on the market*) engorgement m, surplus m ‖ v (*pret & pp* **glutted;** *ger* **glutting**) tr (*with food*) rassasier; (*the market*) inonder, engorger

glutton [ˈglʌtən] s glouton m

gluttonous [ˈglʌtənəs] adj glouton

glutton·y [ˈglʌtəni] s (*pl* **-ies**) gloutonnerie f

glycerine [ˈglɪsərɪn] s glycérine f

G.M.T. abbr (**Greenwich mean time** *temps moyen de Greenwich*) T.U., temps m universel

gnarl [narl] s (bot) nœud m ‖ tr tordre ‖ intr grogner

gnarled adj noueux

gnash [næʃ] tr—**to gnash the teeth** grincer des dents ou les dents

gnat [næt] s moucheron m, moustique m

gnaw [nɔ] tr ronger

gnome [nom] s gnome m

G.N.P. [ˈdʒiˈɛnˈpi] s (letterword) (**gross national product**) R.N.P. (revenue national brut), P.N.B. (produit national brut)

go [go] s (*pl* **goes**) aller m; **a lot of go** (slang) beaucoup d'allant; **it's no go** (coll) ça ne marche pas, pas mèche; **to have a go at** (coll) essayer; **to make a go of** (coll) réussir à ‖ v (*pret* **went** [wɛnt]; *pp* **gone** [gɔn], [gɑn]) tr—**to go it alone** le faire tout seul, faire cavalier seul ‖ intr aller; (*to work, operate*) marcher; y aller, e.g., **did you go?** y êtes-vous allé?; devenir, e.g., **to go crazy** devenir fou; faire, e.g., **to go quack-quack** faire couincouin; **going, going, gone!** une fois, deux fois, adjugé!; **go to it!** allez-y!; **to be going to** or **to go to** + *inf* aller + *inf*, e.g., **I am going to the store to buy some shoes** je vais au magasin acheter des souliers; (to express futurity from the point of view of the present or past) aller + *inf*, e.g., **he is going to get married** il va se marier; e.g., **he was going to get married** il allait se marier tout seul; **to go** (*to take out*) (coll) à emporter; **to go against** contrarier; **to go ahead of** dépasser; **to go away** s'en aller; **to go back** retourner; (*to return home*) rentrer; (*to back up*) reculer; (*to date back*) remonter; **to go by** passer; (*a rule, model, etc.*)

agir selon; **to go down** descendre; (*said of sun*) se coucher; (*said of ship*) sombrer; (cards) chuter; **to go fishing** aller à la pêche; **to go for** or **to go get** aller chercher; **to go in** entrer; entrer dans; (*to fit into*) tenir dans; **to go in for** se consacrer à; **to go in with** s'associer à or avec, se joindre à; **to go off** (*said of bomb, gun, etc.*) partir; **to go on** + *ger* continuer à + *inf;* **to go out** sortir; (*said of light, fire, etc.*) s'éteindre; **to go over** (*to examine*) parcourir, repasser; **to go through** (*e.g., a door*) passer par; (*e.g., a city*) traverser; (*a fortune*) dissiper, dilapider; **to go together** (*said, e.g., of colors*) s'assortir; (*said of lovers*) être très liés; **to go under** succomber; (*said, e.g., of submarine*) plonger; (*a false name*) être connu sous; **to go up** monter; **to go with** accompagner; (*a color, dress, etc.*) s'assortir avec; **to go without** se passer de; **to let go of** lâcher

goad [god] *s* aiguillon *m* ‖ *tr* aiguillonner

go′-ahead′ *adj* (coll) entreprenant ‖ *s* (coll) signal *m* d'aller en avant

goal [gol] *s* but *m*

goal′keep′er *s* goal *m*, gardien *m* de but

goal′line′ *s* ligne *f* de but

goal′ post′ *s* montant *m*, poteau *m* de but

goat [got] *s* chèvre *f;* (*male goat*) bouc *m;* (coll) dindon *m;* **to get the goat of** (slang) exaspérer, irriter

goatee [goˈti] *s* barbiche *f*

goat′herd′ *s* chevrier *m*

goat′skin′ *s* peau *f* de chèvre

goat′suck′er *s* (orn) engoulevent *m*

gob [gɑb] *s* (*lump*) (coll) grumeau *m;* (*sailor*) (slang) mataf *m*

gobble [ˈgɑbəl] *s* glouglou *m* ‖ *tr* engloutir, bâfrer ‖ *intr* bâfrer; (*said of turkey*) glouglouter

gobbledegook [ˈgɑbəldɪˌguk] *s* (coll) palabre *m* & *f*, charabia *m*

go′-between′ *s* intermédiaire *mf;* (*in shady love affairs*) entremetteur *m*

goblet [ˈgɑblɪt] *s* verre *m* à pied

goblin [ˈgɑblɪn] *s* lutin *m*

go′-by′ *s* (coll) affront *m;* **to give s.o. the go-by** (coll) brûler la politesse à qn

go′cart′ *s* chariot *m;* (*baby carriage*) poussette *f;* (*handcart*) charrette *f* à bras

god [gɑd] *s* dieu *m;* **God damn!** (pej) nom *m* de Dieu!, nom de nom!; **God forbid** qu'à Dieu ne plaise; **God grant** plût à Dieu; **my God!** bon Dieu!; **God willing** s'il plaît à Dieu

god′child′ *s* (*pl* **-chil′dren**) filleul *m*

god′damn′it *interj* nom d'une pipe!, nom d'un chien!, nom d'un petit bonhomme!, cré nom de Dieu!

god′daugh′ter *s* filleule *f*

goddess [ˈgɑdɪs] *s* déesse *f*

god′fa′ther *s* parrain *m*

God′-fear′ing *adj* dévot, pieux

God′forsak′en *adj* abandonné de Dieu; (coll) perdu, misérable

god′head′ *s* divinité *f;* **Godhead** Dieu *m*

godless [ˈgɑdlɪs] *adj* athée, impie

god•ly [ˈgɑdli] *adj* (*comp* **-lier;** *super* **-liest**) dévot, pieux

god′moth′er *s* marraine *f*

God′s′ a′cre *s* le champ de repos

god′send′ *s* aubaine *f*

god′son′ *s* filleul *m*

God′speed′ *s* bonne chance *f*, bon voyage *m*

go-getter [ˈgoˌgɛtər] *s* (coll) homme *m* d'expédition, lanceur *m* d'affaires

goggle [ˈgɑgəl] *intr* (*to open the eyes wide*) écarquiller les yeux, rouler de gros yeux ronds

gog′gle-eyed′ *adj* aux yeux saillants

goggles [ˈgɑgəlz] *spl* lunettes *fpl* protectrices

going [ˈgo•ɪŋ] *adj* en marche; **going on two o'clock** presque deux heures ‖ *s* départ *m;* **good going!** bien joué!

go′ing concern′ *s* maison *f* en pleine activité

go′ings on′ *spl* (coll) chahut *m*, tapage *m;* (coll) événements *mpl*

goiter [ˈgɔɪtər] *s* goitre *m*

gold [gold] *adj* d'or, en or ‖ *s* or *m*

gold′beat′er *s* batteur *m* d'or

gold′ beater's skin′ *s* baudruche *f*

gold′crest′ *s* roitelet *m* à tête dorée

gold′ dig′ger *s* (*woman*) (pej) aventurière *f*

golden [ˈgoldən] *adj* d'or; (*gilt*) doré; (*hair*) d'or, d'un blond doré; (*opportunity*) favorable, magnifique

gold′en age′ *s* âge *m* d'or

gold′en calf′ *s* veau *m* d'or

Gold′en Fleece′ *s* Toison *f* d'or

gold′en mean′ *s* juste-milieu *m*

gold′en plov′er *s* pluvier *m* doré

gold′en-rod′ *s* solidage *f*, gerbe *f* d'or

gold′en rule′ *s* règle *f* de la charité chrétienne

gold′en wed′ding *s* noces *fpl* d'or, jubilé *m*

gold′-filled′ *adj* (*tooth*) aurifié

gold′finch′ *s* chardonneret *m*

gold′fish′ *s* poisson *m* rouge

goldilocks [ˈgoldɪˌlɑks] *s* jeune fille *f* aux cheveux d'or

gold′ leaf′ *s* feuille *f* d'or

gold′ mine′ *s* mine *f* d'or; **to strike a gold mine** (fig) dénicher le bon filon, faire des affaires d'or

gold′ plate′ *s* vaisselle *f* d'or

gold′-plate′ *tr* plaquer d'or

gold′ rush′ *s* ruée *f* vers l'or

gold′smith′ *s* orfèvre *m*

gold′ stan′dard *s* étalon-or *m*

golf [gɑlf] *s* golf *m* ‖ *intr* jouer au golf

golf′ ball′ *s* balle *f* de golf

golf′ cart′ *s* voiturette *f* de golf

golf′ club′ *s* crosse *f* de golf, club *m;* (*association*) club *m* de golf

golf′ course′ *s* golf *m*, terrain *m* de golf

golfer [ˈgɑlfər] *s* joueur *m* de golf, golfeur *m*

golf′ links′ *spl* golf *m*, terrain *m* de golf

gondola [ˈgɑndələ] *s* gondole *f*

gondolier [ˌgɑndəˈlɪr] *s* gondolier *m*

gone [gɑn] *adj* parti, disparu; (*used up*) épuisé; (*ruined*) ruiné, fichu; (*dead*) mort; **far gone**

avancé; **gone on** (*in love with*) (coll) entiché de, épris de

gong [gɔŋ] *s* gong *m*

gonorrhea [ˌgɑnəˈri·ə] *s* blennorragie *f*, gonococcie *f*

goo [gu] *s* (slang) matière *f* collante

good [gʊd] *adj* (*comp* **better**; *super* **best**) bon §91; (*child*) sage; (*meals*) soigné; **good for you!** bien joué!; **to be good at** être fort en, être expert à; **to make good** prospérer; (*a loss*) compenser; (*a promise*) tenir; **will you be good enough to** voulez-vous être assez aimable de ‖ *s* bien *m*; **for good** pour de bon, définitivement; **goods** biens *mpl*; (com) marchandises *fpl*; **to catch with the goods** (slang) prendre la main dans le sac; **to the good** de gagné, e.g., **all** or **so much to the good** autant de gagné ‖ *interj* bon!, bien!, à la bonne heure!; **very good!** parfait!

good′ after·noon′ *s* bonjour *m*

good′-by′ or **good′-bye′** *s* adieu *m* ‖ *interj* au revoir!; (*before a long journey*) adieu!

good′ cit′izenship *s* civisme *m*

good′ day′ *s* bonjour *m*

good′ deed′ *s* bonne action *f*

good′ egg′ *s* (slang) chic type *m*

good′ eve′ning *s* bonsoir *m*

good′ faith′ *s* la bonne volonté

good′ fel′low *s* brave garçon *m*, brave type *m*

good′ fel′lowship *s* camaraderie *f*

good′-for-noth′ing *adj* inutile *m* ‖ *s* bon *m* à rien

Good′ Fri′day *s* le Vendredi saint

good′ grac′es *spl* bonnes grâces *fpl*

good′-heart′ed *adj* au cœur généreux

good′-hu′mored *adj* de bonne humeur

good′-look′ing *adj* beau, joli

good′ looks′ *spl* belle mine *f*

good′ luck′ *s* bonne chance *f*

good·ly [ˈgʊdli] *adj* (*comp* **-lier**; *super* **-liest**) considérable, important; (*quality*) bon; (*appearance*) beau

good′ morn′ing *s* bonjour *m*

good′-na′tured *adj* aimable, accommodant

goodness [ˈgʊdnɪs] *s* bonté *f*; **for goodness′ sake!** pour l'amour de Dieu!; **goodness knows** Dieu seul sait ‖ *interj* mon Dieu!

good′ night′ *s* bonne nuit *f*

good′ sense′ *s* bon sens *m*

good′-sized′ *adj* de grandeur moyenne, assez grand

good′ speed′ *s* succès *m*, bonne chance *f*

good′-tem′pered *adj* de caractère facile, d'humeur égale

good′ time′ *s* bon temps *m*; **to have a good time** prendre du bon temps, bien s'amuser; **to make good time** arriver en peu de temps

good′ turn′ *s* bienfait *m*, service *m*

good′ will′ *s* bonne volonté *f*; (com) achalandage *m*

good′ works′ *spl* bonnes œuvres *fpl*

good·y [ˈgʊdi] *adj* (coll) d'une piété affectée ‖

s (*pl* **-ies**) (coll) petit saint *m*; **goodies** friandises *fpl* ‖ *interj* chouette!; chic!

gooey [ˈgu·i] *adj* (*comp* **gooier**; *super* **gooiest**) (slang) gluant; (*sentimental*) (slang) à l'eau de rose

goof [guf] *s* (slang) toqué *m* ‖ *intr*—**to goof off** (slang) tirer au flanc

goof·y [ˈgufi] *adj* (*comp* **-ier**; *super* **-iest**) (slang) toqué, maboul

goon [gun] *s* (*roughneck*) (coll) dur *m*; (coll) terroriste *m* professionnel; (slang) niais *m*

goose [gus] *s* (*pl* **geese** [gis]) oie *f*; **to kill the goose that lays the golden eggs** tuer la poule aux œufs d'or ‖ *s* (*pl* **gooses**) (*of tailor*) carreau *m*

goose′ber′ry *s* (*pl* **-ries**) groseille *f* verte

goose′ egg′ *s* œuf *m* d'oie; (slang) zéro *m*

goose′ flesh′ *s* chair *f* de poule

goose′neck′ *s* col *m* de cygne

goose′ pim′ples *spl* chair *f* de poule

goose′ step′ *s* (mil) pas *m* de l'oie

goose′-step′ *v* (*pret* & *pp* **-stepped**; *ger* **-stepping**) *intr* marcher au pas de l'oie

gopher [ˈgofər] *s* citelle *m*

gore [gor] *s* (*blood*) sang *m* caillé; (sewing) soufflet *m* ‖ *tr* percer d'un coup de corne; (sewing) tailler en pointe

gorge [gɔrdʒ] *s* gorge *f* ‖ *tr* gorger ‖ *intr* se gorger

gorgeous [ˈgɔrdʒəs] *adj* magnifique

gorilla [gəˈrɪlə] *s* gorille *m*

gorse [gɔrs] *s* (bot) genêt *m* épineux

gor·y [ˈgori] *adj* (*comp* **-ier**; *super* **-iest**) ensanglanté, sanglant

gosh [gɑʃ] *interj* (coll) sapristi!, mon Dieu!

goshawk [ˈgɑsˌhɔk] *s* autour *m*

gospel [ˈgɑspəl] *s* évangile *m*; **Gospel** Évangile

gos′pel truth′ *s* parole *f* d'Évangile

gossamer [ˈgɑsəmər] *adj* ténu ‖ *s* toile *f* d'araignée, fils *mpl* de la Vierge; (*gauze*) gaze *f*

gossip [ˈgɑsɪp] *s* commérage *m*, cancan *m*; (*person*) commère *f*; **piece of gossip** potin *m*, racontar *m* ‖ *intr* cancaner

gos′sip col′umnist *s* échotier *m*

Gothic [ˈgɑθɪk] *adj* & *s* gothique *m*

gouge [gaʊdʒ] *s* gouge *f* ‖ *tr* gouger; (*to swindle*) empiler

goulash [ˈgulɑʃ] *s* goulasch *m* & *f*

gourd [gʊrd] *s* gourde *f*

gourmand [ˈgʊrmənd] *s* gourmand *m*; (*glutton*) glouton *m*

gourmet [ˈgʊrme] *s* gourmet *m*

gout [gaʊt] *s* goutte *f*

govern [ˈgʌvərn] *tr* gouverner; (gram) régir ‖ *intr* gouverner

governess [ˈgʌvərnɪs] *s* institutrice *f*, gouvernante *f*

government [ˈgʌvərnmənt] *s* gouvernement *m*

governmental [ˌgʌvərnˈmentəl] *adj* gouvernemental

governor [ˈgʌvərnər] *s* gouverneur *m*; (mach) régulateur *m*

gown [gaʊn] *s* robe *f*

grab [græb] *s* prise *f*; (coll) vol *m*, coup *m* ‖ *v* (*pret & pp* **grabbed;** *ger* **grabbing**) *tr* empoigner, saisir ‖ *intr*—**to grab at** s'a-gripper à

grab′ bag′ *s* sac *m* à surprises

grace [gres] *s* grâce *f;* (*prayer at table before meals*) bénédicité *m;* (*prayer at table after meals*) grâces; (*extension of time*) délai *m* de grâce; **in someone's good graces** en odeur de sainteté auprès de qn, dans les petits papiers de qn ‖ *tr* orner; honorer

graceful [′gresfəl] *adj* gracieux

grace′ note′ *s* note *f* d'agrément, appogiature *f*

gracious [′greʃəs] *adj* gracieux; (*compassionate*) miséricordieux

grackle [′grækəl] *s* (*myna*) mainate *m;* (*purple grackle*) quiscale *m*

gradation [gre′deʃən] *s* gradation *f*

grade [gred] *s* (*rank*) grade *m;* (*of oil*) grade; qualité *f;* (*school class*) classe *f*, année *f;* (*mark in school*) note *f;* **to make the grade** réussir ‖ *tr* classer; (*a school paper*) noter; (*land*) niveler

grade′ cross′ing *s* (rr) passage *m* à niveau

grade′ school′ *s* école *f* primaire

gradient [′gredɪ•ənt] *adj* montant ‖ *s* pente *f;* (phys) gradient *m*

gradual [′grædʒʊ•əl] *adj & s* graduel *m*

gradually [′grædʒʊ•əli] *adv* graduellement, peu à peu, par paliers

graduate [′grædʒʊ•ɪt] *s* diplômé *m* ‖ [′grædʒʊ•et] *tr* conférer un diplôme à, décerner des diplômes à; (*to mark with degrees*) graduer ‖ *intr* recevoir son diplôme

grad′uate school′ *s* faculté *f* des hautes études

grad′uate stu′dent *s* étudiant *m* avancé, étudiant de maîtrise, de doctorat

grad′uate work′ *s* études *fpl* avancées

grad′uat′ing class′ *s* classe *f* sortante

graduation [ˌgrædʒʊ′eʃən] *s* collation *f* des grades; (*e.g., marking on beaker*) graduation *f*

graft [græft] *s* (hort, surg) greffe *f;* (*stealing*) (coll) gratte *f*, grattage *m*, magouille *f* ‖ *tr & intr* (hort, surg) greffer; (coll) gratter

grafter [′græftər] *s* (hort) greffeur *m;* (coll) homme *m* véreux, concussionnaire *mf*

gra′ham bread′ [′gre•əm] *s* pain *m* entier

gra′ham flour′ *s* farine *f* entière

grain [gren] *s* (*small seed; tiny particle of sand, etc.; small unit of weight; small amount*) grain *m;* (*cereal seeds*) grains *mpl*, céréales *fpl;* (*in stone*) fil *m;* (*in wood*) fibres *fpl;* **against the grain** à rebours, à contre-fil, à rebrousse-poil ‖ *tr* grener; (*wood, etc.*) veiner

grain′ el′evator *s* dépôt *m* et élévateur *m* à grains

grain′field′ *s* champ *m* de blé

graining [′grenɪŋ] *s* grenage *m;* (*of painting*) veinage *m*

gram [græm] *s* gramme *m*

grammar [′græmər] *s* grammaire *f*

grammarian [grə′mɛrɪ•ən] *s* grammairien *m*

gram′mar school′ *s* école *f* primaire

grammatical [grə′mætɪkəl] *adj* grammatical

grana•ry [′grænəri] *s* (*pl* **-ries**) grenier *m*

grand [grænd] *adj* magnifique; (*person*) grand; (coll) formidable

grand′aunt′ *s* grand-tante *f*

grand′child′ *s* (*pl* **-chil′dren**) petit-fils *m;* petite-fille *f;* **grandchildren** petits-enfants *mpl*

grand′daugh′ter *s* petite-fille *f*

grand′ duch′ess *s* grande-duchesse *f*

grand′ duch′y *s* grand-duché *m*

grand′ duke′ *s* grand-duc *m*

grandee [græn′di] *s* grand *m* d'Espagne

grand′fa′ther *s* grand-père *m*

grand′father clause′ *s* clause *f* des droits aquis

grand′father's clock′ *s* pendule *f* à gaine, horloge *f* comtoise, horloge normande

grandiose [′grændɪˌos] *adj* grandiose; pompeux

grand′ ju′ry *s* jury *m* d'accusation

grand′ lar′ceny *s* grand larcin *m*

grand′ lodge′ *s* grand orient *m*

grandma [′grændˌmɑ], [′græmə] *s* (coll) grand-maman *f*

grand′mom′ *s* grand-maman *f*, mémé *f*

grand′moth′er *s* grand-mère *f*

grand′neph′ew *s* petit-neveu *m*

grand′niece′ *s* petite-nièce *f*

grand′ op′era *s* grand opéra *m*

grandpa [′grændˌpɑ], [′græmpə] *s* (coll) grandpapa *m;* (*gramps*) pépé *m*

grand′par′ent *s* grand-père *m;* grand-mère *f;* **grandparents** grands-parents *mpl*

grand′ pian′o *s* piano *m* à queue

grand′ pop′ *s* grand-papa *m*, pépé *m*

grand′ slam′ *s* grand chelem *m*

grand′ son′ *s* petit-fils *m*

grand′ stand′ *s* tribune *f*, gradins *mpl*

grand′ to′tal *s* total *m* global

grand′ un′cle *s* grand-oncle *m*

grand′ vizier′ *s* grand vizir *m*

grange [grendʒ] *s* ferme *f;* syndicat *m* d'agriculteurs

granite [′grænɪt] *s* granite *m*, granit *m*

gran•ny [′græni] *s* (*pl* **-nies**) (coll) grandmère *f*, mémé *f*

gran′ny knot′ *s* nœud *m* de vache

grant [grænt] *s* (*of land*) concession *f;* (*subsidy*) subvention *f;* (*scholarship*) bourse *f* ‖ *tr* concéder, accorder; (*a wish*) exaucer; (*e.g., a charter*) octroyer; (*a degree*) décerner; **to take for granted** escompter, tenir pour évident; traiter avec indifférence

grantee [græn′ti] *s* donataire *mf*

grantor [græn′tɔr] *s* donateur *m*

granular [′grænjələr] *adj* granulaire

granulate [′grænjəˌlet] *tr* granuler ‖ *intr* se granuler

gran′ulated sug′ar *s* sucre *m* cristallisé

granule [′grænjʊl] *s* granule *m*, granulé *m*

grape [grep] *s* (*fruit*) raisin *m;* (*vine*) vigne *f;* (*single grape*) grain *m* de raisin

grape′ ar′bor *s* treille *f*

grape′fruit′ *s* (*fruit*) pamplemousse *m & f;* (*tree*) pamplemoussier *m*

grape′ juice′ *s* jus *m* de raisin

grape′shot′ *s* mitraille *f*

grape′ vine′ s vigne f; (*chain of gossip*) source f de canards; téléphone m arabe, téléphone chinois

graph [græf] s graphique m; (gram) graphie f

graphic(al) [′græfɪk(əl)] adj graphique; (fig) vivant, net

graphite [′græfaɪt] s graphite m

graph′ pa′per s papier m quadrillé

grapnel [′græpnəl] s grappin m

grapple [′græpəl] s (*tool*) grappin m; (*fight*) corps à corps m ‖ tr (*with a grappling iron*) saisir au grappin; (*a person*) empoigner à bras le corps ‖ intr (*to fight*) lutter corps à corps; **to grapple with** en venir aux prises avec, s'attaquer à

grap′pling i′ron s grappin m

grasp [græsp] s prise f; **to have a good grasp of** avoir une profonde connaissance de; **within one's grasp** à sa portée ‖ tr saisir ‖ intr—**to grasp at** tâcher de saisir; saisir avidement

grasping [′græspɪŋ] adj avide, rapace

grass [græs] s herbe f; (*pasture*) herbage m; (*lawn*) gazon m; **keep off the grass** (*public sign*) ne marchez pas sur le gazon; **to go to grass** (fig) s'étaler par terre

grass′hop′per s sauterelle f

grass′-roots′ adj populaire, du peuple

grass′ seed′ s graine f fourragère; (*for lawns*) graine f pour gazon

grass′ snake′ s (*Tropidonotus natrix*) couleuvre f à collier

grass′ wid′ow s demi-veuve f

grass•y [′græsi] adj (*comp* **-ier;** *super* **-iest**) herbeux

grate [gret] s grille f, grillage m ‖ tr (*to put a grate on*) griller; (*e.g., cheese*) râper; **to grate the teeth** grincer des dents ‖ intr grincer; **to grate on** écorcher

grateful [′gretfəl] adj reconnaissant; **to be grateful for** être reconnaissant de or pour

grater [′gretər] s râpe f

grati•fy [′grætɪ,faɪ] v (*pret & pp* **-fied**) tr faire plaisir à, satisfaire

gratifying [′grætɪ,faɪ•ɪŋ] adj agréable, satisfaisant

grating [′gretɪŋ] adj grinçant ‖ s grillage m, grille f

gratis [′grætɪs] adj gratuit, gracieux ‖ adv gratis, gratuitement

gratitude [′grætɪ,t(j)ud] s gratitude f, reconnaissance f; **gratitude for** reconnaissance de or pour

gratuitous [grə′t(j)u•ɪtəs] adj gratuit

gratui•ty [grə′t(j)u•ɪti] s (*pl* **-ties**) gratification f, pourboire m

grave [grev] adj grave ‖ s fosse f, tombe f

grave′ ac′cent s accent m grave

gravedigger [′grev,dɪgər] s fossoyeur m

gravel [′grævəl] s (*on roadway*) gravier m, gravillons mpl; (geol) gravier; (pathol) gravelle f

grav′en im′age [′grevən] s image f taillée

grave′stone′ s pierre f tombale

grave′yard′ s cimetière m

gravitate [′grævɪ,tet] intr graviter

gravitation [,grævɪ′teʃən] s gravitation f

gravi•ty [′grævɪti] s (*pl* **-ties**) gravité f; (phys) pesanteur f, gravité

gra•vy [′grevi] s (*pl* **-vies**) (*juice from cooking meat*) jus m; (*sauce made with this juice*) sauce f; (slang) profit m facile, profit supplémentaire

gra′vy boat′ s saucière f

gra′vy train′ s (slang) assiette f au beurre

gray [gre] adj gris; (*gray-haired*) gris, chenu; **to turn gray** grisonner ‖ s gris m ‖ intr grisonner

gray′beard′ s barbon m, ancien m

gray′-haired′ adj gris, chenu

gray′hound′ s lévrier m; (*female*) levrette f

grayish [′gre•ɪʃ] adj grisâtre

gray′ mat′ter s substance f grise

gray′ scale′ s (comp) gamme f de gris

graze [grez] tr (*to touch lightly*) frôler, effleurer; (*to scratch lightly in passing*) érafler; (*to pasture*) faire paître ‖ intr paître

grease [gris] s graisse f ‖ [griz] tr graisser

grease′ cup′ [gris] s godet m graisseur

grease′ gun′ [gris] s graisseur m, seringue f à graisse

grease′ paint′ [gris] s fard m, grimage m

greas•y [′grisi] adj (*comp* **-ier;** *super* **-iest**) graisseux, gras

great [gret] adj grand; (coll) excellent, formidable; **a great deal, a great many** beaucoup

great′-aunt′ s grand-tante f

Great′ Bear′ s Grande Ourse f

Great′ Brit′ain s Grande Bretagne f; la Grande Bretagne

great′coat′ s capote f

Great′ Dane′ s danois m

Great′er New′ York′ s le Grand New York

great′-grand′ child′ s (*pl* **-chil′dren**) arrière-petit-fils m; arrière-petite-fille f; **great-grandchildren** arrière-petits-enfants mpl

great′-grand′daugh′ter s arrière-petite-fille f

great′-grand′fa′ther s arrière-grand-père m, bisaïeul m

great′-grand′moth′er s arrière-grand-mère f, bisaïeule f

great′-grand′par′ents spl arrière-grands-parents mpl

great′-grand′son s arrière-petit-fils m

Great′ Lakes′ spl Grands Lacs mpl

greatly [′gretli] adv grandement, fort, beaucoup

great′-neph′ew s petit-neveu m

greatness [′gretnɪs] s grandeur f

great′-niece′ s petite-nièce f

great′-un′cle s grand-oncle m

Grecian [′griʃən] adj grec ‖ s (*person*) Grec m

Greece [gris] s Grèce f; la Grèce

greed [grid] s avidité f

greed•y [′gridi] adj (*comp* **-ier;** *super* **-iest**) avide

Greek [grik] adj grec ‖ s (*language*) grec m; (*unintelligible language*) (coll) hébreu m, e.g., **it's Greek to me** (coll) c'est de l'hébreu pour moi; (*person*) Grec *m*

Greek' fire' *s* feu *m* grégeois

green [grin] *adj* vert; inexpérimenté, novice ‖ *s* vert *m;* (*lawn*) gazon *m;* (*golf*) green *m,* pelouse *f* d'arrivée; **greens** légumes *mpl* verts

green'back' *s* (U.S.A.) billet *m* de banque

green' bean' *s* haricot *m* vert

green' belt' *s* (ecol) cordon *m* vert

green' card' *s* (govt) carte *f* verte

greener•y [ˈgrinəri] *s* (*pl* **-ies**) verdure *f*

green'-eyed' *adj* aux yeux verts; (*envious*) jaloux

green'gage' *s* (bot) reine-claude *f*

green'gro'cer•y *s* (*pl* **-ies**) fruiterie *f*

green'horn' *s* blanc-bec *m,* bleu *m*

green'house' *s* serre *f*

green'house effect' *s* effect *m* de serre

greenish [ˈgrinɪʃ] *adj* verdâtre

Greenland [ˈgrinlənd] *s* le Groënland

green' light' *s* feu *m* vert, voie *f* libre

greenness [ˈgrinnɪs] *s* verdure *f;* (*unripeness*) verdeur *f;* inexpérience *f,* naïveté *f*

green' pep'per *s* poivron *m* vert

green'room' *s* (theat) foyer *m*

greensward [ˈgrin‚swɔrd] *s* pelouse *f*

green' thumb' *s*—**to have a green thumb** avoir la main verte

greet [grit] *tr* saluer; (*to welcome*) accueillir

greeting [ˈgritɪŋ] *s* salutation *f;* (*welcome*) accueil *m;* **greetings** (*on greeting card*) vœux *mpl* ‖ **greetings** *interj* salut!

greet'ing card' *s* carte *f* de vœux

gregarious [grɪˈgɛri•əs] *adj* grégaire

Gregorian [grɪˈgori•ən] *adj* grégorien

grenade [grɪˈned] *s* grenade *f*

grey [gre] *adj, s,* & *intr* var of **gray**

grey'hound' *s* var of **grayhound**

grid [grid] *s* (*of storage battery and vacuum tube*) grille *f;* (*on map*) quadrillage *m;* (culin) gril *m*

griddle [ˈgrɪdəl] *s* plaque *f* chauffante

grid'dle•cake' *s* var de **pancake**

grid'i'ron *s* gril *m;* (sports) terrain *m* de football

grid' leak' *s* résistance *f* de fuite de la grille

grid' line' *s* ligne *f* de quadrillage

grief [grif] *s* chagrin *m,* affliction *f;* **to come to grief** finir mal

grief'-strick'en *adj* affligé, navré

grievance [ˈgrivəns] *s* grief *m*

grieve [griv] *tr* chagriner, affliger ‖ *intr* se chagriner, s'affliger

grievous [ˈgrivəs] *adj* grave, douloureux

griffin [ˈgrɪfɪn] *s* griffon *m*

grill [grɪl] *s* gril *m;* (*grating*) grille *f* ‖ *tr* griller; (*an accused person*) (coll) cuisiner

grille [grɪl] *s* grille *f;* (aut) calandre *f*

grilled' beef'steak' *s* châteaubriand *m*

grill'room' *s* grill-room *m*

grim [grɪm] *adj* (*comp* **grimmer;** *super* **grimmest**) (*fierce*) menaçant; (*repellent*) macabre; (*unyielding*) implacable; (*stern-looking*) lugubre

grimace [ˈgrɪməs] *s* grimace *f* ‖ *intr* grimacer

grime [graɪm] *s* crasse *f,* saleté *f*

grim•y [ˈgraɪmi] *adj* (*comp* **-ier;** *super* **-iest**) crasseux, sale

grin [grɪn] *s* (*smile*) large sourire *m* ‖ *v* (*pret* & *pp* **grinned;** *ger* **grinning**) *intr* avoir un large sourire, rire à belles dents; (*in pain*) grimacer

grind [graɪnd] *s* (*of coffee*) moulure *f;* (*job*) (coll) boulot *m,* collier *m;* (*student*) (coll) bûcheur *m,* fort-en-thème *m;* **daily grind** (coll) train-train *m* quotidien ‖ *v* (*pret* & *pp* **ground** [graʊnd]) *tr* (*coffee, flour*) moudre; (*food*) broyer; (*meat*) hacher; (*a knife*) aiguiser; (*the teeth*) grincer; (*valves*) roder ‖ *intr* grincer; **to grind away at** (coll) bûcher

grinder [ˈgraɪndər] *s* (*for coffee, pepper, etc.*) moulin *m,* broyeur *m;* (*for meat*) hachoir *m;* (*for tools*) repasseur *m;* (*back tooth*) molaire *f*

grind'stone' *s* meule *f,* pierre *f* à aiguiser

grip [grɪp] *s* (*hold*) prise *f;* (*with hand*) poigne *f;* (*handle*) poignée *f;* (*handbag*) sac *m* de voyage; (*understanding*) compréhension *f;* **to come to grips** en venir aux prises; **to lose one's grip** lâcher prise ‖ *v* (*pret* & *pp* **gripped;** *ger* **gripping**) *tr* serrer, saisir fortement; (*e.g., a theater audience*) empoigner

gripe [graɪp] *s* (coll) rouspétance *f* ‖ *intr* (coll) rouspéter, ronchonner

grippe [grɪp] *s* grippe *f*

gripping [ˈgrɪpɪŋ] *adj* passionnant

gris•ly [ˈgrɪzli] *adj* (*comp* **-lier;** *super* **-liest**) horrible, macabre

grist [grɪst] *s* blé *m* à moudre

gristle [ˈgrɪsəl] *s* cartilage *m*

gris•tly [ˈgrɪsli] *adj* (*comp* **-tlier;** *super* **-tliest**) cartilagineux

grist'mill' *s* moulin *m* à blé

grit [grɪt] *s* (*sand*) grès *m,* sable *m;* (*courage*) cran *m;* **grits** gruau *m* ‖ *v* (*pret* & *pp* **gritted;** *ger* **gritting**) *tr* (*one's teeth*) grincer

grit•ty [ˈgrɪti] *adj* (*comp* **-tier;** *super* **-tiest**) sablonneux; (fig) plein de cran

griz•zly [ˈgrɪzli] *adj* (*comp* **-zlier;** *super* **-zliest**) grisonnant ‖ *s* (*pl* **-zlies**) ours *m* gris

griz'zly bear' *s* ours *m* gris

groan [gron] *s* gémissement *m* ‖ *intr* gémir

grocer [ˈgrosər] *s* épicier *m*

grocer•y [ˈgrosəri] *s* (*pl* **-ies**) épicerie *f;* **groceries** denrées *fpl*

gro'cery store' *s* épicerie *f*

grog [grɑg] *s* grog *m*

grog•gy [ˈgrɑgi] *adj* (*comp* **-gier;** *super* **-giest**) (coll) vacillant; (*shaky, e.g., from a blow*) (coll) étourdi; (*drunk*) (coll) gris, ivre

groin [grɔɪn] *s* (anat) aine *f;* (archit) arête *f*

groom [grum] *s* (*bridegroom*) marié *m;* (*stable-boy*) palefrenier *m* ‖ *tr* soigner, astiquer; (*horses*) panser; (*a politician, a starlet, etc.*) dresser, préparer

grooms'man *s* (*pl* **-men**) garçon *m* d'honneur

groove [gruv] *s* (*for sliding door, etc.*) rainure *f;* (*of pulley*) gorge *f;* (*of phonograph record*) sillon *m;* (*mark left by wheel*) ornière *f;* (*of window, door, etc.*) feuillure *f;* **in the groove** (coll) comme sur des roulettes; **to get into a groove** (coll) devenir routinier ‖ *tr* rainer, canneler

grope [grop] *intr* tâtonner; **to grope for** chercher à tâtons

gropingly [ˈgropɪŋli] *adv* à tâtons

grosbeak [ˈgrosˌbik] *s* gros-bec *m*

gross [gros] *adj* (*flagrant*) flagrant, choquant; (*error*) gros, lourd; (*fat, burly*) gras, épais; (*crass, vulgar*) grossier; (*weight; receipts*) brut; (*displacement*) global ‖ *s invar* recette *f* brute; (*twelve dozen*) grosse *f* ‖ *tr* produire en recette brute, produire brut, e.g., **the business grossed a million dollars** l'entreprise a produit un million de dollars, brut

gross′ na′tional prod′uct (G.N.P.) *s* revenu *m* national brut (R.N.B.), produit *m* national brut (P.N.B.)

gross′ weight′ *s* poids *m* brut, poids total

grotesque [groˈtɛsk] *adj* grotesque ‖ *s* grotesque *m;* (*ornament*) grotesque *f*

grot•to [ˈgrɑto] *s* (*pl* **-toes** or **-tos**) grotte *f*

grouch [graʊtʃ] *s* (coll) humeur *f* grognon; (*person*) (coll) grognon *m* ‖ *intr* (coll) grogner

grouch•y [ˈgraʊtʃi] *adj* (*comp* **-ier;** *super* **-iest**) (coll) grognon, maussade

ground [graʊnd] *s* terre *f;* (*piece of land*) terrain *m;* (*basis, foundation*) fondement *m*, base *f;* (*reason*) motif *m*, cause *f;* (elec) terre *f;* (*body of automobile corresponding to ground*) (elec) masse *f;* **ground for complaint** grief *m;* **grounds** parc *m*, terrain; fondement, cause; (*of coffee*) marc *m;* **on the ground of** pour raison de, sous prétexte de; **to be losing ground** être en recul; **to break ground** donner le premier coup de pioche; **to have grounds for** avoir matière à; **to stand one's ground** tenir bon or ferme; **to yield ground** lâcher pied ‖ *tr* fonder, baser; (elec) mettre à terre; **grounded** (aer) interdit de vol, gardé au sol; **to ground s.o. in s.th.** enseigner à fond q.ch. à qn

ground′ beef′ *s* bœuf *m* haché

ground′ connec′tion *s* prise *f* de terre

ground′ crew′ *s* équipe *f* au sol, personnel *m* rampant

ground′ floor′ *s* rez-de-chaussée *m*

ground′ glass′ *s* verre *m* dépoli

ground′ hog′ *s* marmotte *f* d'Amérique

grounding [ˈgraʊndɪŋ] *s* (aer) interdiction *f* de vol; (elec) mise *f* à la masse

ground′ installa′tions *spl* (aer) infrastructure *f*

ground′ lead′ [lid] *s* (elec) conduite *f* à terre

groundless [ˈgraʊndlɪs] *adj* sans fondement

ground′ meat′ *s* viande *f* hachée

ground′ plan′ *s* plan *m* de base; (archit) plan horizontal

ground′ speed′ *s* (aer) vitesse *f* par rapport au sol

ground′ swell′ *s* lame *f* de fond

ground′ troops′ *spl* (mil) effectifs *mpl* terrestres

ground′ wire′ *s* (elec) fil *m* de terre, fil de masse

ground′ work′ *s* fondement *m*, fond *m*

ground′ ze′ro *m* point *m* d'explosion; (mil) point de détonation d'une bombe nucléaire

group [grup] *s* groupe *m* ‖ *tr* grouper ‖ *intr* se grouper

group′ ther′apy *s* (*of a family*) thérapie *f* familiale

grouse [graʊs] *s* coq *m* de bruyère, tétras *m* ‖ *intr* (slang) grogner

grove [grov] *s* bocage *m*, bosquet *m*

grov•el [ˈgrʌvəl] *v* (*pret & pp* **-eled** or **-elled;** *ger* **-eling** or **-elling**) *intr* se vautrer; (*before s.o.*) ramper

grow [gro] *v* (*pret* **grew** [gru]; *pp* **grown** [gron]) *tr* cultiver, faire pousser; (*a beard*) laisser pousser ‖ *intr* croître; (*said of plants*) pousser; (*said of seeds*) germer; (*to become*) devenir; **to grow angry** se mettre en colère; **to grow old** vieillir; **to grow out of** se développer de; (*e.g., a suit of clothes*) devenir trop grand pour; **to grow up** grandir, profiter

grower [ˈgro•ər] *s* cultivateur *m*

growl [graʊl] *s* grondement *m*, grognement *m* ‖ *tr & intr* gronder, grogner

grown′-up′ *adj* adulte ‖ *s* (*pl* **grown-ups**) adulte *mf;* **grown-ups** grandes personnes *fpl*

growth [groθ] *s* croissance *f*, développement *m;* (*increase*) accroissement *m;* (*of trees, grass, etc.*) pousse *f;* (pathol) excroissance *f*, grosseur *f*

growth′ fund′ *s* fonds *m* commun à placement dirigé au développement

growth′ in′dustrie *s* industrie *f* en pleine expansion

growth′ stock′ *s* valeur *f* d'avenir

grub [grʌb] *s* asticot *m;* (*person*) homme *m* de peine; (*food*) (coll) boustifaille *f* ‖ *v* (*pret & pp* **grubbed;** *ger* **grubbing**) *tr* défricher ‖ *intr* fouiller

grub•by [ˈgrʌbi] *adj* (*comp* **-bier;** *super* **-biest**) sale, malpropre

grudge [grʌdʒ] *s* rancune *f;* **to have a grudge against** garder rancune à ‖ *tr* donner à contre-cœur

grudgingly [ˈgrʌdʒɪŋli] *adv* à contre-cœur

gruel [ˈgru•əl] *s* gruau *m*, bouillie *f*

grueling [ˈgru•əlɪŋ] *adj* éreintant

gruesome [ˈgrusəm] *adj* macabre

gruff [grʌf] *adj* bourru, brusque; (*voice*) rauque, gros

grumble [ˈgrʌmbəl] *s* grognement *m* ‖ *intr* grogner, grommeler

grump•y [ˈgrʌmpi] *adj* (*comp* **-ier;** *super* **-iest**) maussade, grognon

grunt [grʌnt] *s* grognement *m* ‖ *intr* grogner

G′-string′ *s* (*loincloth*) pagne *m;* (*worn by women entertainers*) cache-sexe *m;* (mus) corde *f* de sol

guarantee [ˌgærənˈti] *s* garantie *f;* (*guarantor*)

garant *m*, répondant *m; (security)* caution *f* ‖ *tr* garantir

guarantor [ˈgærənˌtɔr] *s* garant *m*

guaran‧ty [ˈgærənti] *s (pl* **-ties)** garantie *f* ‖ *v (pret & pp* **-tied)** *tr* garantir

guard [gɑrd] *s* garde *f; (person)* garde *m;* **on guard** en garde; *(on duty)* de garde; (mil) en faction, de faction; **on one's guard** sur ses gardes; **to mount guard** monter la garde; **under guard** gardé à vue ‖ *tr* garder ‖ *intr* être de faction; **to guard against** se garder de

guard′ du′ty *s* service *m* de garde

guarded *adj (remark)* prudent

guard′house′ *s* guérite *f*, corps-de-garde *m;* (mil) salle *f* de police, prison *f* militaire

guardian [ˈgɑrdɪ‧ən] *adj* gardien ‖ *s* gardien *m; (of a ward)* tuteur *m*

guard′ian an′gel *s* ange *m* gardien, ange tuté- laire

guard′ian‧ship′ *s* garde *f;* (law) tutelle *f*

guard′rail′ *s* garde-fou *m*, parapet *m*, glissière *f* de sécurité

guard′room′ *s* corps-de-garde *m*, salle *f* de po- lice; *(prison)* bloc *m*, tôle *f*

guards′man *s (pl* **-men)** garde *m*

Guatemalan [ˌgwɑtɪˈmɑlən] *adj* guatémaltèque ‖ *s* Guatémaltèque *mf*

guava [ˈgwɑvə] *s* goyave *f; (tree)* goyavier *m*

guerrilla [gəˈrɪlə] *s* guérillero *m;* **guerrillas** *(band)* guérilla *f*

guerril′la war′fare *s* guérilla *f*

guess [gɛs] *s* conjecture *f* ‖ *tr & intr* conjecturer; *(a secret, riddle, etc.)* deviner; (coll) suppo- ser, penser; **I guess so** je crois que oui; **to guess right** bien deviner

guess′ing game′ *s* jeu *m* de devinettes

guess′work′ *s* supposition *f;* **by guesswork** au jugé

guest [gɛst] *s* invité *m*, hôte *mf; (in a hotel)* client *m*, hôte

guest′ ar′tiste *s* artiste *mf* invité(e)

guest′ book′ *s* livre *m* d'or

guestimate [ˈgɛstəmət] *s* (coll) calcul *m* au pifo- mètre

guest′ list′ *s* liste *f* des invités

guest′ room′ *s* chambre *f* d'ami

guest′ speak′er *s* orateur *m* de circonstance, orateur invité

guffaw [gəˈfɔ] *s* gros rire *m* ‖ *tr* dire avec un gros rire ‖ *intr* rire bruyamment

guidance [ˈgaɪdəns] *s (advice)* conseils *mpl; (guiding)* conduite *f; (in choosing a career)* orientation *f; (of rocket)* guidage *m;* **for your guidance** pour votre gouverne

guid′ance coun′selor *s* orienteur *m*

guide [gaɪd] *s* guide *m* ‖ *tr* guider

guide′book′ *s* guide *m*

guid′ed mis′sile *s* engin *m* téléguidé

guide′ dog′ *s* chien *m* d'aveugle

guid′ed tour′ *s* visite *f* commentée, visite guidée

guide′ line′ *s* (fig) norme *f*, règle *f;* **guide lines** *(for writing straight lines)* transparent *m*, guide-âne *m*

guide′post′ *s* poteau *m* indicateur

guide′ word′ *s* lettrine *f*

guild [gɪld] *s* association *f*, corporation *f;* (eccl) confrérie *f;* (hist) guilde *f*

guild′hall′ *s* hôtel *m* de ville

guile [gaɪl] *s* astuce *f*, artifice *m*

guileful [ˈgaɪlfəl] *adj* astucieux, artificieux

guileless [ˈgaɪllɪs] *adj* candide, innocent

guillotine [ˈgɪləˌtin] *s* guillotine *f* ‖ *tr* guillotiner

guilt [gɪlt] *s* culpabilité *f*

guiltless [ˈgɪltlɪs] *adj* innocent

guilt‧y [ˈgɪlti] *adj (comp* **-ier;** *super* **-iest)** cou- pable; **found guilty** reconnu coupable

guinea [ˈgɪni] *s* guinée *f;* **Guinea** Guinée; la Guinée

guin′ea fowl′ or **hen′** *s* poule *f* de Guinée, pin- tade *f*

guin′ea pig′ *s* cobaye *m*

guise [gaɪz] *s* apparences *fpl*, déguisement *m;* **under the guise of** sous un semblant de, sous le masque de

guitar [gɪˈtɑr] *s* guitare *f*

guitarist [gɪˈtɑrɪst] *s* guitariste *mf*

gulch [gʌltʃ] *s* ravin *m*

gulf [gʌlf] *s* golfe *m;* (fig) gouffre *m*

Gulf′ of Mex′ico *s* Golfe *m* du Mexique

Gulf′ Stream′ *s* Courant *m* du Golfe

Gulf′ War′ *s* guerre *f* du Golfe

gull [gʌl] *s* mouette *f*, goéland *m;* (coll) gogo *m*, jobard *m* ‖ *tr* escroquer, duper

gullet [ˈgʌlɪt] *s* gosier *m*

gullible [ˈgʌlɪbəl] *adj* crédule, naïf

gul‧ly [ˈgʌli] *s (pl* **-lies)** ravin *m; (channel)* ri- gole *f*

gulp [gʌlp] *s* gorgée *f*, lampée *f;* **at one gulp** d'un trait ‖ *tr*—**to gulp down** avaler à grandes bouchées, lamper; *(e.g., tears)* ravaler, refou- ler ‖ *intr* avoir la gorge serrée

gum [gʌm] *s* gomme *f; (on eyelids)* chassie *f;* (anat) gencive *f* ‖ *v (pret & pp* **gummed;** *ger* **gumming)** *tr* gommer; **to gum up** encrasser; (coll) bousiller

gum′ ar′abic *s* gomme *f* arabique

gum′boil′ *s* phlegmon *m*, fluxion *f*

gum′ boot′ *s* botte *f* de caoutchouc

gum′drop′ *s* boule *f* de gomme, pâte *f* de fruits

gum‧my [ˈgʌmi] *adj (comp* **-mier;** *super* **-miest)** gommeux; *(eyelids)* chassieux

gumption [ˈgʌmpʃən] *s* (coll) initiative *f*, cran *m*

gum′shoe′ *s* caoutchouc *m;* (coll) détective *m* ‖ *intr* rôder en tapinois, marcher furtivement

gun [gʌn] *s* fusil *m; (for spraying)* pistolet *m;* **to stick to one's guns** (coll) ne pas en dé- mordre ‖ *v (pret & pp* **gunned;** *ger* **gunning)** *tr*—**to gun down** tuer d'un coup de fusil; **to gun the engine** (slang) appuyer sur le cham- pignon ‖ *intr*—**to gun for** *(game)* chasser; *(an enemy)* pourchasser

gun′ bar′rel *s* canon *m*

gun′boat′ *s* cannonière *f*

gun′ car′riage _s_ affût _m_ de canon
gun′cot′ton _s_ fulmicoton _m_
gun′ crew′ _s_ peloton _m_ de pièce, servants _mpl_ de canon
gun′fire′ _s_ canonnade _f,_ coups _mpl_ de feu
gun′ laws′ _spl_ réglementation _f_ du port d'armes
gun′ lob′by _s_ lobby _m_ des marchands de revolvers
gun′man _s_ (_pl_ **-men**) _s_ bandit _m_
gun′met′al _s_ métal _m_ bleui
gunner [ˈgʌnər] _s_ canonnier _m,_ artilleur _m;_ (aer) mitrailleur _m_
gunnery [ˈgʌnəri] _s_ tir _m,_ canonnage _m_
gunnysack [ˈgʌni,sæk] _s_ sac _m_ de serpillière
gun′ per′mit _s_ permis _m_ de port d'armes
gun′point′ _s_—**at gunpoint** à main armée
gun′pow′der _s_ poudre _f_ à canon
gun′run′ning _s_ contrebande _f_ d'armes
gun′shot′ _s_ coup _m_ de feu, coup de fusil
gun′shot wound′ _s_ blessure _f_ par balle
gun′smith′ _s_ armurier _m_
gun′stock′ _s_ fût _m_
gunwale [ˈgʌnəl] _s_ (naut) plat-bord _m_
gup•py [ˈgʌpi] _s_ (_pl_ **-pies**) guppy _m_
gurgle [ˈgʌrgəl] _s_ glouglou _m,_ gargouillement _m_ ‖ _intr_ glouglouter, gargouiller
gush [gʌʃ] _s_ jaillissement _m_ ‖ _intr_ jaillir; **to gush over** (coll) s'attendrir sur
gusher [ˈgʌʃər] _s_ puits _m_ jaillissant
gushing [ˈgʌʃɪŋ] _adj_ (_water_) jaillissant; (_person_) trop exubérant
gush•y [ˈgʌʃi] _adj_ (_comp_ **-ier;** _super_ **-iest**) (coll) démonstratif, expansif
gusset [ˈgʌsɪt] _s_ (_in garment_) soufflet _m;_ (mach) gousset _m_
gust [gʌst] _s_ bouffée _f,_ coup _m_
gusto [ˈgʌsto] _s_ goût _m,_ entrain _m_
gust•y [ˈgʌsti] _adj_ (_comp_ **-ier;** _super_ **iest**) venteux; (_wind_) à rafales
gut [gʌt] _s_ boyau _m;_ **guts** (coll) cran _m;_ **he has**

a lot of guts (pej) il est vachement gonflé ‖ _v_ (_pret & pp_ **gutted;** _ger_ **gutting**) _tr_ raser à l'intérieur; (_to take out the guts of_) vider
gutter [ˈgʌtər] _s_ (_on side of road_) caniveau _m;_ (_in street_) ruisseau _m;_ (_of roof_) gouttière _f;_ (_ditch formed by rain water_) rigole _f_
gut′ter•snipe′ _s_ (coll) voyou _m_
guttural [ˈgʌtərəl] _adj_ guttural ‖ _s_ gutturale _f_
guy [gaɪ] _s_ (_supporting cable_) câble _m_ tenseur; (naut) hauban _m;_ (coll) type _m,_ gars _m_ ‖ _tr_ haubaner; (to coll) se moquer de
Guyana [gaɪˈænə] _s_ Guyane _f;_ la Guyane
guy′ rope′ _s_ corde _f_ de tente
guy′ wire′ _s_ câble _m_ tenseur, (naut) hauban _m_
guzzle [ˈgʌzəl] _tr & intr_ boire avidement
guzzler [ˈgʌzlər] _s_ soiffard _m_
gym [dʒɪm] _s_ (coll) gymnase _m_
gymnasi•um [dʒɪmˈneziˑəm] _s_ (_pl_ **-ums** or **-a** [ə]) gymnase _m_
gymnast [ˈdʒɪmnæst] _s_ gymnaste _mf_
gymnastic [dʒɪmˈnæstɪk] _adj_ gymnastique ‖ **gymnastics** _spl_ gymnastique _f,_ gym _f_ (coll)
gym′shoe′ _s_ chaussure _f_ de gym
gynecologist [ˌgaɪnəˈkɑlədʒɪst] _ou_ [ˌdʒaɪnə-ˈkɑlədʒɪst] _s_ gynécologue _mf_
gynecology [ˌgaɪnəˈkɑlədʒi] _s_ gynécologie _f_
gyp [dʒɪp] _s_ (slang) escroquerie _f;_ (_person_) (slang) aigrefin _m_ ‖ _v_ (_pret & pp_ **gypped;** _ger_ **gypping**) _tr_ (slang) tirer une carotte à, refaire, gruger, chiper, chaparder
gypsum [ˈdʒɪpsəm] _s_ gypse _m_
gyp•sy [ˈdʒɪpsi] _adj_ bohémien ‖ _s_ (_pl_ **-sies**) bohémien _m;_ **Gypsy** (_language_) tsigane _m,_ romanichel _m;_ (_person_) gitan _m,_ tsigane _mf,_ romanichel _m_
gyp′sy moth′ _s_ zigzag _m_
gyrate [ˈdʒaɪret] _intr_ tournoyer
gyrocompass [ˈdʒaɪro,kʌmpəs] _s_ gyrocompas _m_
gyroscope [ˈdʒaɪrə,skop] _s_ gyroscope _m_

H

H, h [etʃ] _s_ VIIIᵉ lettre de l'alphabet
haberdasher [ˈhæbər,dæʃər] _s_ chemisier _m_
haberdasher•y [ˈhæbər,dæʃəri] _s_ (_pl_ **-ies**) chemiserie _f,_ confection _f_ pour hommes
habit [ˈhæbɪt] _s_ habitude _f;_ (_dress_) habit _m,_ costume _m;_ **to get into the habit of** s'habituer à
habitat [ˈhæbɪ,tæt] _s_ habitat _m_
habitual [həˈbɪtʃuˑəl] _adj_ habituel
habituate [həˈbɪtʃu,et] _tr_ habituer
hack [hæk] _s_ (_notch_) entaille _f;_ (_cough_) toux _f_ sèche; (_hackney_) voiture _f_ de louage; (_old nag_) rosse _f;_ (_writer_) écrivassier _m_ ‖ _tr_ (to chop) hacher; (_to access a computer system_)

pirater ‖ _intr_ (comp) se livrer à la piraterie; **to hack into** (comp) pirater
hacker [ˈhækər] _s_ (comp) pirate _m_ informatique; (obs) opérateur _m or_ opératrice _f_ ordinateur; (obs) spécialiste _mf_ dans l'informatique
hacking [ˈhækɪŋ] _s_ (comp) piraterie _f_ informatique
hackney [ˈhækni] _s_ voiture _f_ de louage
hackneyed [ˈhæknid] _adj_ banal, battu
hack′saw′ _s_ scie _f_ à métaux
haddock [ˈhædək] _s_ églefin _m_
hadn′t contr **had not**
hag [hæg] _s_ (_ugly woman_) guenon _f;_ (_witch_) sorcière _f;_ **old hag** vieille fée _f_

haggard [ˈhægərd] *adj* décharné, hâve; (*wild-looking*) hagard, farouche

haggle [ˈhægəl] *intr* marchander; **to haggle over** marchander

Hague [heg] *s*—**The Hague** La Haye

hail [hel] *s* (*frozen rain*) grêle *f;* **within hail** à portée de la voix ‖ *tr* saluer; (*a ship, taxi, etc.*) héler ‖ *intr* grêler; **to hail from** venir de ‖ *interj* salut!

Hail′ Mar′y *s* Ave Maria *m*

hail′stone′ *s* grêlon *m*

hail′storm′ *s* tempête *f* de grêle

hair [hɛr] *s* poil *m;* (*of person*) cheveu *m;* (*head of human hair*) cheveux *mpl;* **against the hair** à rebrousse-poil, à contrepoil; **hairs** cheveux; **to a hair** à un cheveu près; **to get in s.o.'s hair** (slang) porter sur les nerfs à qn; **to let one's hair down** (slang) en prendre à son aise; **to make s.o.'s hair stand on end** faire dresser les cheveux à qn; **to not turn a hair** ne pas tiquer; **to split hairs** fendre or couper les cheveux en quatre

hair′breadth′ *s* épaisseur *f* d'un cheveu; **to escape by a hairbreadth** l'échapper belle

hair′brush′ *s* brosse *f* à cheveux

hair′cloth′ *s* thibaude *f;* (*for furniture*) tissu-crin *m*

hair′cream′ *s* fixateur *m*

hair′curl′er [ˌkʌrlər] *s* frisoir *m;* (*pin*) bigoudi *m*

hair′cut′ *s* coupe *f* de cheveux; **to get a haircut** se faire couper les cheveux

hair′do′ *s* (*pl* **-dos**) coiffure *f*

hair′dress′er *s* coiffeur *m,* coiffeuse *f*

hair′dress′ing *s* cosmétique *m*

hair′ dri′er *ou* **hair′ dry′er** *s* sèche-cheveux *m,* séchoir *m*

hair′ dye′ *s* teinture *f* des cheveux

hair′line′ *s* (*on face of type*) délié *m;* (*along the upper forehead*) naissance *f* des cheveux, plantation *f* des cheveux

hair′net′ *s* résille *f*

hair′pin′ *s* épingle *f* à cheveux

hair′pin turn′ *s* lacet *m*

hair′-rais′ing *adj* (coll) horripilant

hair′ rib′bon *s* ruban *m* à cheveux

hair′ set′ *s* mise *f* en plis

hair′ shirt′ *s* haire *f,* cilice *m*

hair′split′ting *adj* vétilleux, trop subtil ‖ *s* ergotage *m*

hair′ spray′ *s* (*for setting hair*) laque *f,* fixatif *m*

hair′spring′ *s* spiral *m*

hair′ style′ *s* coiffure *f*

hair′ ton′ic *s* lotion *f* capillaire

hair′ trig′ger *s* détente *f* douce

hair•y [ˈhɛri] *adj* (*comp* **-ier;** *super* **-iest**) poilu, velu; (*on head*) chevelu

Haiti [ˈheti] *s* Haïti *f;* **the Republic of Haiti** la république d'Haïti

Haitian [ˈheʃən] *adj* haïtien ‖ *s* Haïtien *m*

halberd [ˈhælbərd] *s* hallebarde *f*

hal′cyon days′ [ˈhælsɪ•ən] *spl* jours *mpl* alcyoniens, jours sereins

hale [hel] *adj* vigoureux, sain; **hale and hearty** frais et gaillard ‖ *tr* haler

half [hæf] *adj* demi ‖ *s* (*pl* **halves** [hævz]) moitié *f,* la moitié; (*of the hour*) demi *m;* **by half** de moitié, à demi; **half an hour** une demi-heure; **in half** en deux; **to go halves** être de moitié ‖ *adv* moitié, à moitié; **half. . .half** moitié. . . moitié; **half past** et demie, e.g., **half past three** trois heures et demie

half′-and-half′ *adj & adv* moitié l'un moitié l'autre, en parties égales ‖ *s* (*for coffee*) mélange *m* de lait et de crème; (*beer*) mélange de bière et de porter

half′back′ *s* (football) demi-arrière *m,* demi *m*

half′-baked′ *adj* à moitié cuit; (*person*) inexpérimenté; (*plan*) prématuré, incomplet

half′ bind′ing *s* (bb) demi-reliure *f* à petits coins

half′-blood′ *s* métis *m;* demi-frère *m*

half′ boot′ *s* demi-botte *f*

half′-bound′ *adj* (bb) en demi-reliure à coins

half′-breed′ *s* métis *m,* sang-mêlé *m;* (*e.g., horse*) demi-sang *m*

half′ broth′er *s* demi-frère *m;* (*by the father*) frère consanguin; (*by the mother*) frère utérin

half′-cocked′ *adv* (coll) avec trop de hâte

half′-day′ *s* demi-journée *f*

half′-doz′en *s* demi-douzaine *f*

half′ fare′ *s* demi-tarif *m,* demi-place *f*

half′-full′ *adj* à moitié plein

half′-heart′ed *adj* sans entrain, hésitant

half′-hol′iday *s* demi-congé *m*

half′ hose′ *s* chaussettes *fpl*

half′-hour′ *s* demi-heure *f;* **every half-hour on the half-hour** toutes les demi-heures à la demi-heure juste; **on the half-hour** à la demie

half′ leath′er *s* (bb) demi-reliure *f* à petits coins

half′-length′ *s* demi-longueur *f*

half′-length por′trait *s* portrait *m* en buste

half′-life′ *s* (phys) période *f*

half′-light′ *s* demi-jour *m*

half′-line space′ *s* (*on typewriter*) demi-interligne *m* de base

half′-mast′ *s*—**at half-mast** en berne, à mi-mât

half′-moon′ *s* demi-lune *f*

half′ mourn′ing *s* demi-deuil *m*

half′ note′ *s* (mus) blanche *f*

half′ pay′ *s* demi-solde *f*

halfpen•ny [ˈhepəni], [ˈhepni] *s* (*pl* **-nies**) demi-penny *m;* (fig) sou *m*

half′ pint′ *s* demi-pinte *f;* (*little runt*) (slang) petit culot *m*

half′-seas o′ver *adj*—**to be half-seas over** avoir du vent dans les voiles

half′ shell′ *s* (*either half of a bivalve*) écaille *f;* **on the half shell** dans sa coquille

half′ sis′ter *s* demi-sœur *f;* (*by the father*) sœur consanguine; (*by the mother*) sœur utérine

half′ sole′ *s* demi-semelle *f*

half′-staff′ *s*—**at half-staff** à mi-mât

half′-tim′bered _adj_ à demi-boisage
half′ time′ _s_ (sports) mi-temps _m_
half′-time′ _adj_ à demi-journée
half′ ti′tle _s_ faux titre _m_, avant-titre _m_
half′tone′ _s_ (painting, phot) demi-teinte _f_; (typ) similigravure _f_
half′ tone′ _s_ (mus) demi-ton _m_
half′-track′ _s_ semi-chenillé _m_
half′-truth′ _s_ demi-vérité _f_
half′turn′ _s_ demi-tour _m_; (_of wheel_) demi-révolution _f_
half′way′ _adj_ & _adv_ à mi-chemin; **halfway through** à moitié de; **halfway up** à micôte; **to meet s.o. halfway** couper la poire en deux avec qn
half′-wit′ted _adj_ à moitié idiot
halibut [ˈhælɪbət] _s_ flétan _m_
halitosis [ˌhælɪˈtosɪs] _s_ mauvaise haleine _f_
hall [hɔl] _s_ (_passageway_) corridor _m_, couloir _m_; (_entranceway_) entrée _f_, vestibule _m_; (_large meeting room_) salle _f_, hall _m_, salle des fêtes; (_assembly room of a university_) amphithéâtre _m_; (_building of a university_) bâtiment _m_
halleluiah or **hallelujah** [ˌhælɪˈlujə] _s_ alléluia _m_ ‖ _interj_ alléluia!
hall′mark′ _s_ estampille _f_, poinçon _m_; (fig) cachet _m_, marque _f_
hal·lo [həˈlo] _s_ (_pl_ **-los**) holà _m_ ‖ _intr_ huer ‖ _interj_ holà!, ohé!; (hunting) taïaut!
hallow [ˈhælo] _tr_ sanctifier
hallowed _adj_ sanctifié, saint
Halloween or **Hallowe'en** [ˌhæloˈin] _s_ la veille de la Toussaint
hallucinate [həˈlusɪnet] _intr_ avoir des hallucinations
hallucination [həˌlusɪˈneʃən] _s_ hallucination _f_
hallucinogenic [həˌlusənoˈdʒɛnɪk] _adj_ hallucinogène
hall′way′ _s_ corridor _m_, couloir _m_
ha·lo [ˈhelo] _s_ (_pl_ **-los** or **-loes**) (meteo) auréole _f_, halo _m_; (_around a head_) auréole
halogen [ˈhælədʒən] _s_ halogène _m_
halt [hɔlt] _adj_ boiteux, estropié ‖ _s_ halte _f_, arrêt _m_; **to come to a halt** faire halte ‖ _tr_ faire faire halte à ‖ _intr_ faire halte ‖ _interj_ halte!; (mil) halte-là!
halter [ˈhɔltər] _s_ licou _m_; (_noose_) corde _f_
halting [ˈhɔltɪŋ] _adj_ boiteux; hésitant
halve [hæv] _tr_ diviser or partager en deux; réduire de moitié
halyard [ˈhæljərd] _s_ (naut) drisse _f_
ham [hæm] _s_ (_part of leg behind knee_) jarret _m_; (_thigh and buttock_) fesse _f_; (culin) cuisse _f_; (_cured_) (culin) jambon _m_; (rad) radio amateur _m_; (theat) cabotin _m_; **hams** fesses
hamburger [ˈhæm͵bʌrgər] _s_ sandwich _m_ à la hambourgeoise, hamburger _m_; (_Hamburg steak_) biftek _m_ haché
hamlet [ˈhæmlɪt] _s_ hameau _m_
hammer [ˈhæmər] _s_ marteau _m_; (_of gun_) chien _m_, percuteur _m_ ‖ _tr_ marteler; **to hammer out** étendre au marteau; (_to resolve_) résoudre ‖

intr—**to hammer away at** (_e.g._, _a job_) travailler d'arrache-pied à
hammock [ˈhæmək] _s_ hamac _m_
ham′ op′era′tor _s_ (_radio ham_) radioamateur _m_
hamper [ˈhæmpər] _s_ manne _f_ ‖ _tr_ embarrasser, gêner, empêcher
hamster [ˈhæmstər] _s_ hamster _m_
ham′string′ _v_ (_pret_ & _pp_ **-strung**) _tr_ couper le jarret à; (fig) couper les moyens à
hand [hænd] _s_ main, à la main, manuel ‖ _s_ main _f_; (_workman_) manœuvre _m_, ouvrier _m_; (_way of writing_) écriture _f_; (_clapping of hands_) applaudissements _mpl_; (_of clock or watch_) aiguille _f_; (_a round of play_) coup _m_, partie _f_, main; (_of God_) doigt _m_; (_measure_) palme _m_; (cards) jeu _m_; **at hand** sous la main; (_said of approaching event_) proche, prochain; **by hand** à la main; **hand in hand** main dans la main; **hands off!** n'y touchez pas!; **hands up!** haut les mains!; **hand to hand** corps à corps; **on every hand** de toutes parts, de tous côtés; **on the one hand . . . on the other hand** d'une part . . . d'autre part; **to live from hand to mouth** vivre au jour le jour; **to rule with a firm hand** avoir de la poigne; **to shake hands with** serrer la main à; **to wait on hand and foot** être aux petits soins pour; **to win hands down** gagner dans un fauteuil; **under the hand and seal of** signé et scellé de ‖ _tr_ donner, présenter; (_e.g._, _food at table_) passer; **to hand down** (_e.g._, _property_) léguer; (_a verdict_) prononcer; **to hand in** remettre; **to hand on** transmettre; **to hand out** distribuer; **to hand over** céder, livrer
hand′bag′ _s_ sac _m_ à main
hand′ bag′gage _s_ menus bagages _mpl_, bagages à main
hand′ball′ _s_ pelote _f_; (_game_) handball _m_
hand′bill′ _s_ prospectus _m_
hand′book′ _s_ manuel _m_
hand′ brake′ _s_ frein _m_ à main
hand′car′ _s_ (rr) draisine _f_
hand′cart′ _s_ voiture _f_ à bras
hand′clasp′ _s_ poignée _f_ de main
hand′ control′ _s_ commande _f_ à la main
hand′cuff′ _s_ menotte _f_ ‖ _tr_ mettre les menottes à
handful [ˈhænd͵ful] _s_ poignée _f_
hand′ glass′ _s_ miroir _m_ à main; (_magnifying glass_) loupe _f_ à main
hand′ grenade′ _s_ grenade _f_ à main
handi·cap [ˈhændɪ͵kæp] _s_ handicap _m_ ‖ _v_ (_pret_ & _pp_ **-capped;** _ger_ **-capping**) _tr_ handicaper
handicraft [ˈhændɪ͵kræft] _s_ habileté _f_ manuelle; métier _m_; **handicrafts** produits _mpl_ d'artisanat
handiwork [ˈhændɪ͵wʌrk] _s_ ouvrage _m_, travail _m_ manuel; (fig) œuvre _f_
handkerchief [ˈhæŋkərt͵ʃif] _s_ mouchoir _m_
handle [ˈhændəl] _s_ (_of basket, crock, pitcher_) anse _f_; (_of shovel, broom, knife_) manche _m_;

(*of umbrella, sword, door*) poignée *f;* (*of frying pan*) queue *f;* (*of pump*) brimbale *f;* (*of handcart*) brancard *m;* (*of wheelbarrow*) bras *m;* (*opportunity, pretext*) prétexte *m;* (mach) manivelle *f,* manette *f;* **to fly off the handle** (coll) sortir de ses gonds ‖ *tr* manier; (*with one's hands*) palper, tâter; **handle with care** (*shipping label*) fragile; **to handle roughly** malmener ‖ *intr*—**to handle well** (mach) avoir de bonnes réactions

han·dle·bars' *spl* guidon *m*

handler [ˈhændlər] *s* (sports) entraîneur *m*

handling [ˈhændlɪŋ] *s* (*e.g., of tool*) maniement *m;* (*e.g., of person*) traitement *m;* (*of merchandise*) manutention *f*

hand'made' *adj* fait à la main

hand'maid' or **hand'maid'en** *s* servante *f;* (fig) auxiliaire *mf*

hand'-me-down' *s* (coll) décrochez-moi-ça *m*

hand' or'gan *s* orgue *m* de Barbarie

hand'out' *s* (*notes*) (coll) documentation *f;* (slang) aumône *f*

hand'-picked' *adj* trié sur le volet

hand'rail' *s* main *f* courante, rampe *f*

hand'saw' *s* égoïne *f,* scie *f* à main

hand'set' *s* combiné *m*

hand'shake' *s* poignée *f* de main

handsome [ˈhænsəm] *adj* beau; (*e.g., fortune*) considérable

hand'spring' *s*—**to do a handspring** prendre appui sur les mains pour faire la culbute

hand'-to-hand' *adj* corps-à-corps

hand'-to-mouth' *adj*—**to lead a hand-to-mouth existence** vivre au jour le jour

hand' truck' *s* bard *m,* diable *m*

hand'work' *s* travail *m* à la main

hand'writ'ing *s* écriture *f*

handwritten [ˈhænd,rɪtən] *adj* manuscrit, autographe

hand·y [ˈhændi] *adj* (*comp* **-ier;** *super* **-iest**) (*easy to handle*) maniable; (*within easy reach*) accessible, sous la main; (*skillful*) adroit, habile; **to come in handy** être très à propos

hand'y·man *s* (*pl* **-men'**) homme *m* à tout faire, bricoleur *m*

hang [hæŋ] *s* (*of dress, curtain, etc.*) retombée *f,* drapé *m;* (*skill; insight*) adresse *f,* sens *m;* **I don't give a hang!** (coll) je m'en moque pas mal!; **to get the hang** (coll) saisir le truc, attraper le chic ‖ *v* (*pret & pp* **hung** [hʌŋ]) *tr* pendre; (*laundry*) étendre; (*wallpaper*) coller; (*one's head*) baisser; **hang it all!** zut alors!; **to hang up** suspendre, accrocher; (telp) raccrocher ‖ *intr* pendre, être accroché; **to hang around** flâner, rôder; **to hang on** se cramponner à, s'accrocher à; (*to depend on*) dépendre de; (*to stay put*) tenir bon; **to hang out** pendre dehors; (slang) percher, loger; **to hang over** (*to threaten*) peser sur, menacer; **to hang together** rester unis; **to hand up** (telp) raccrocher ‖ *v* (*pret & pp* **hung** or **han-**

ged) *tr* (*to execute by hanging*) pendre ‖ *intr* se pendre

hangar [ˈhæŋər], [ˈhæŋgɑr] *s* hangar *m*

hang' dog' *adj* (*look*) patibulaire

hanger [ˈhæŋər] *s* crochet *m;* (*coathanger*) cintre *m,* portemanteau *m*

hang'er-on' *s* (*pl* **hangers-on**) parasite *m,* pique-assiette *m*

hang' glid'er *s* deltaplane *m*

hang' glid'ing *s* vol *m* à libre, vol sur aile delta

hanging [ˈhæŋɪŋ] *adj* pendant, suspendu ‖ *s* pendaison *f;* **hangings** tentures *fpl*

hang'man *s* (*pl* **-men**) bourreau *m*

hang'nail' *s* envie *f*

hang'out' *s* (coll) repaire *m*

hang'o'ver *s* (coll) gueule *f* de bois

hank [hæŋk] *s* écheveau *m*

hanker [ˈhæŋkər] *intr*—**to hanker after** or **for** désirer vivement, être affamé de

Hannibal [ˈhænɪbəl] *s* Annibal *m*

haphazard [ˌhæpˈhæzərd] *adj* fortuit, imprévu; au petit bonheur ‖ *adv* à l'aventure, au hasard

hapless [ˈhæplɪs] *adj* malheureux, malchanceux

happen [ˈhæpən] *intr* arriver, se passer; (*to be the case by chance*) survenir; **happen what may** advienne que pourra; **how does it happen that . . . ?** comment se fait-il que . . . ?, d'où vient-il que . . . ?; **to happen at the right moment** tomber pile; **to happen on** tomber sur; **to happen to** + *inf* se trouver + *inf,* venir à + *inf*

happening [ˈhæpənɪŋ] *s* événement *m*

happily [ˈhæpɪli] *adv* heureusement

happiness [ˈhæpɪnɪs] *s* bonheur *m*

hap·py [ˈhæpi] *adj* (*comp* **-pier;** *super* **-piest**) heureux; (*pleased*) content; (*hour*) propice; **to be happy to** être heureux ou content de

hap'py-go-luck'y *adj* sans souci, insouciant ‖ *adv* (archaic) à l'aventure

hap'py me'dium *s* juste-milieu *m*

Hap'py New' Year' *interj* bonne année!

harangue [həˈræŋ] *s* harangue *f* ‖ *tr & intr* haranguer

harass [həˈræs] *tr* harceler; tourmenter

harbinger [ˈhɑrbɪndʒər] *s* avant-coureur *m,* précurseur *m*

harbor [ˈhɑrbər] *s* port *m* ‖ *tr* héberger, donner asile à; (*a criminal, stolen goods, etc.*) receler; (*suspicions; a hope*) entretenir, nourrir; (*a grudge*) garder

har'bor mas'ter *s* capitaine *m* de port

hard [hɑrd] *adj* dur; (*difficult*) difficile; (*water*) cru, calcaire; (*work*) assidu, dur; **to be hard on** (*to treat severely*) être dur ou sévère envers; (*to wear out fast*) user ‖ *adv* dur, fort; (*firmly*) ferme; **hard upon** de près, tout contre; **to rain hard** pleuvoir fort; **to try hard** bien essayer

hard'-and-fast' *adj* strict, inflexible, établi

hard-bitten [ˈhɑrdˈbɪtən] *adj* tenace, dur à cuire

hard'-boiled' *adj* (*egg*) dur; (coll) dur, inflexible

hard'bound edi'tion *s* édition *f* reliée

hard′ can′dy *s* bonbons *mpl;* **piece of hard candy** bonbon *m*

hard′ cash′ *s* espèces *fpl* sonnantes

hard′ ci′der *s* cidre *m*

hard′ coal′ *s* houille *f* éclatante, anthracite *m*

hard′ cop′y *s* (comp) fac-sim *m,* tirage *m*

hard′ core′ *s* (*of supporters, opponents, resistance*) noyau *m,* cercle *m,* centre *m*

hard′-core′ *adj* (*support, opposition*) inconditionnel

hard′-core′ pornog′raphy *s* pornographie *f* (dite) dure

hard′ cov′er *adj* (*hardbound*) relié ‖ *s* livre *m* relié

hard′ disk′ *s* (comp) disque *m* dur

hard′ drink′ *s* boissons *fpl* alcooliques, liqueurs *fpl* fortes

hard′ drink′er *s* grand buveur *m*

hard′ drive′ *s* (comp) disque *m* dur

hard′-earned′ *adj* péniblement gagné

harden [′hɑrdən] *tr* durcir, endurcir ‖ *intr* se durcir, s'endurcir

hardening [′hɑrdənɪŋ] *s* durcissement *m;* (fig) endurcissement *m*

hard′ fact′ *s* fait *m* brutal; **hard facts** réalités *fpl*

hard-fought [′hɑrd′fɔt] *adj* acharné, chaudement disputé

hard′-head′ed *adj* positif, à la tête froide

hard′-heart′ed *adj* dur, sans compassion

hardihood [′hɑrdɪˌhʊd] *s* endurance *f;* courage *m;* audace *f*

hardiness [′hɑrdɪnɪs] *s* vigueur *f*

hard′ la′bor *s* travaux *mpl* forcés

hard′ land′ing *s* atterrissage *m* dur

hard′ luck′ *s* guigne *f,* malchance *f*

hardly [′hɑrdli] *adv* guère, à peine, ne . . . guère, e.g., **he hardly thinks of anything else** à peine pense-t-il à autre chose, il ne pense guère à autre chose; **hardly ever** presque jamais

hardness [′hɑrdnɪs] *s* dureté *f*

hard′ of hear′ing *adj* dur d'oreille; **the hard of hearing** les malentendants

hard′-pressed′ *adj* aux abois, gêné

hard′ rub′ber *s* caoutchouc *m* durci, ébonite *f*

hard′ sell′ *s* (coll) vente *f* à l'arraché

hard′-shell′ *adj* (*clam*) à carapace dure; (coll) opiniâtre

hard′ship′ *s* peine *f;* **hardships** privations *fpl;* fatigues *fpl*

hard′ tack′ *s* biscuit *m,* biscotin *m*

hard′ times′ *spl* difficultés *fpl,* temps *mpl* difficiles

hard′ to please′ *adj* difficile à contenter, exigeant

hard′ up′ *adj* (coll) à court d'argent; **to be hard up for** (coll) être à court de

hard′ ware′ *s* quincaillerie *f;* (*trimmings*) ferrure *f;* (comp) matériel *m*

hard′ware′man *s* (*pl* **-men**) quincaillier *m*

hard′ware store′ *s* quincaillerie *f*

hard-won [′hɑrd,wʌn] *adj* chèrement disputé, conquis de haute lutte

hard′wood′ *s* bois *m* dur; arbre *m* de bois dur

hard′wood floor′ *s* parquet *m*

har•dy [′hɑrdi] *adj* (*comp* **-dier;** *super* **-diest**) vigoureux, robuste; (*rash*) hardi; (hort) résistant

hare [hɛr] *s* lièvre *m*

hare′brained′ *adj* écervelé, farfelu

hare′lip′ *s* bec-de-lièvre *m*

harem [′hɛrəm] *s* harem *m*

hark [hɑrk] *intr* écouter; **to hark back to** en revenir à ‖ *interj* écoutez!

harken [′hɑrkən] *intr*—**to harken to** écouter

harlequin [′hɑrləkwɪn] *s* arlequin *m*

harlot [′hɑrlət] *s* prostituée *f,* fille *f* publique

harm [hɑrm] *s* mal *m,* dommage *m* ‖ *tr* nuire à, faire du mal à

harmful [′hɑrmfəl] *adj* nuisible

harmless [′hɑrmlɪs] *adj* inoffensif

harmonic [hɑr′mɑnɪk] *adj* harmonique

harmonica [hɑr′mɑnɪkə] *s* harmonica *m*

harmonious [hɑr′monɪˈəs] *adj* harmonieux

harmonize [′hɑrməˌnaɪz] *tr* harmoniser ‖ *intr* s'harmoniser

harmo•ny [′hɑrməni] *s* (*pl* **-nies**) harmonie *f*

harness [′hɑrnɪs] *s* harnais *m,* harnachement *m;* **to die in the harness** (coll) mourir sous le harnais, mourir debout; **to get back in the harness** (coll) reprendre le collier ‖ *tr* harnacher; (*e.g., a river*) aménager, capter

har′ness mak′er *s* bourrelier *m,* harnacheur *m*

har′ness race′ *s* course *f* attelée

harp [hɑrp] *s* harpe *f* ‖ *intr*—**to harp on** rabâcher

harpist [′hɑrpɪst] *s* harpiste *mf*

harpoon [hɑr′pun] *s* harpon *m* ‖ *tr* harponner

harpsichord [′hɑrpsɪˌkɔrd] *s* clavecin *m*

har•py [′hɑrpi] *s* (*pl* **-pies**) harpie *f*

harrow [′hæro] *s* (agr) herse *f* ‖ *tr* tourmenter; (agr) herser

harrowing [′hæroˈɪŋ] *adj* horripilant

har•ry [′hæri] *v* (*pret & pp* **-ried**) *tr* harceler; (*to devastate*) ravager

harsh [hɑrʃ] *adj* (*life, treatment, etc.*) sévère, dur; (*to the touch*) rude; (*to the taste*) âpre; (*to the ear*) discordant

harshness [′hɑrʃnɪs] *s* dureté *f,* rudesse *f;* âpreté *f*

hart [hɑrt] *s* cerf *m*

harum-scarum [′hɛrəmˈskɛrəm] *adj & s* écervelé ‖ *adv* en casse-cou

harvest [′hɑrvɪst] *s* récolte *f;* (*of grain*) moisson *f* ‖ *tr* récolter, moissonner ‖ *intr* faire la récolte or moisson

harvester [′hɑrvɪstər] *s* moissonneur *m;* (mach) moissonneuse *f*

har′vest home′ *s* fin *f* de la moisson; fête *f* de la moisson

har′vest moon′ *s* lune *f* des moissons

has-been [′hæz,bɪn] *s* (coll) vieille croûte *f,* has been *mf invar*

hash [hæʃ] *s* hachis *m* ‖ *tr* hacher

hash′house′ *s* (slang) gargote *f*

hashish [ˈhæʃiʃ] *s* hachisch *m*

hasn′t *contr* has not

hasp [hæsp], [hɑsp] *s* moraillon *m*

hassle [ˈhæsəl] *s* (coll) querelle *f*, accrochage *m*

hassock [ˈhæsək] *s* pouf *m*

haste [hest] *s* hâte *f;* in haste à la hâte; to make haste se hâter

hasten [ˈhesən] *tr* hâter ‖ *intr* se hâter

hast•y [ˈhesti] *adj* (*comp* -ier; *super* -iest) hâtif, précipité (*rash*) inconsidéré, emporté

hat [hæt] *s* chapeau *m;* hat in hand chapeau bas; hats off to . . .! chapeau bas devant . . .!; to keep under one′s hat (coll) garder strictement pour soi; to talk through one′s hat (coll) parler à tort et à travers; to throw one′s hat in the ring (coll) descendre dans l′arène

hat′band′ *s* ruban *m* de chapeau

hat′ block′ *s* forme *f* à chapeaux

hat′box′ *s* carton *m* à chapeaux

hatch [hætʃ] *s* (*brood*) éclosion *f;* (*trap door*) trappe *f;* (*lower half of door*) demiporte *f;* (*opening in ship′s deck*) écoutille *f;* (*hood over hatchway*) capot *m;* (*lid for opening in ship′s deck*) panneau *m* de descente; down the hatch! (*bottoms up!*) derrière la cravate! ‖ *tr* (*eggs*) couver, faire éclore; (*a plot*) ourdir, manigancer; (*to hachure*) hachurer ‖ *intr* éclore; (*said of chicks*) sortir de la coquille

hatch′back′ *s* (aut) hayon *m*

hat′check girl′ *s* préposée *f* au vestiaire

hatchet [ˈhætʃit] *s* hachette *f;* to bury the hatchet faire la paix

hatch′way′ *s* écoutille *f*

hate [het] *s* haine *f* ‖ *tr* haïr, détester; to hate to haïr de

hateful [ˈhetfəl] *adj* haïssable

hat′pin′ *s* épingle *f* à chapeau

hat′rack′ *s* porte-chapeaux *m*

hatred [ˈhetrɪd] *s* haine *f*

hat′shop′ *s* chapellerie *f*

hatter [ˈhætər] *s* chapelier *m*

haughtiness [ˈhɔtɪnɪs] *s* hauteur *f*

haugh•ty [ˈhɔti] *adj* (*comp* -tier; *super* -tiest) hautain, altier

haul [hɔl] *s* (*pull, tug*) effort *m;* (*amount caught*) coup *m* de filet, prise *f;* (*distance covered*) parcours *m*, distance *f* de transport ‖ *tr* (*to tug*) tirer; (com) transporter

haulage [ˈhɔlɪdʒ] *s* transport *m;* (*cost*) frais *m* de transport

haunch [hɔntʃ] *s* (*hip*) hanche *f;* (*hind quarter of an animal*) quartier *m;* (*leg of animal used for food*) cuissot *m*

haunt [hɔnt], [hɑnt] *s* lieu *m* fréquenté, rendezvous *m;* (*e.g., of criminals*) repaire *m* ‖ *tr* (*to obsess*) hanter; (*to frequent*) fréquenter

haunt′ed house′ *s* maison *f* hantée par les fantômes

Havana [həˈvænə] *s* La Havane

have [hæv] *s*—the haves and the have-nots les riches et les pauvres ‖ *v* (3d *pers* has [hæz]; *pret & pp* had [hæd]) *tr* avoir; to have + *inf*

faire + *inf*, e.g., I shall have him go je le ferai aller; to have + *pp* faire + *inf*, e.g., I am going to have a suit made je vais faire faire un complet; to have it in for someone garder un chien de sa chienne; to have nothing to do with n′avoir rien à voir avec; to have on (*clothing*) porter; to have s.th. to + *inf* avoir q.ch. à + *inf*, e.g., I have a lot of work to do j′ai beaucoup de travail à faire ‖ *intr*—to have to avoir à; devoir; falloir, e.g., I have to go il me faut aller; falloir que, e.g., I have to read him the letter il faut que je lui lise la lettre ‖ *aux* (to form compound past tenses) avoir, e.g., I have run too fast j′ai couru trop vite; (to form compound past tenses with some intransitive verbs and all reflexive verbs) être, e.g., they have arrived elles sont arrivées; to have just + *pp* venir de + *inf*, e.g., they have just returned ils viennent de rentrer; e.g., they had just returned ils venaient de rentrer; to have been had (coll) avoir été trompé

have′lock *s* couvre-nuque *m*

haven [ˈhevən] *s* havre *m*, asile *m*

haven′t *contr* have not

haversack [ˈhævər,sæk] *s* havresac *m*

havoc [ˈhævək] *s* ravage *m;* to play havoc with causer des dégâts à

haw [hɔ] *s* (bot) cenelle *f* ‖ *tr & intr* tourner à gauche ‖ *interj* dia!, à gauche!

Hawaiian [həˈwaɪjən] *adj* hawaïen ‖ *s* Hawaïen *m*

Hawai′ian Is′lands *spl* îles *fpl* Hawaii

haw′-haw′ *s* rire *m* bête ‖ *intr* rire bêtement ‖ *interj* heu!

hawk [hɔk] *s* faucon *m;* (*mortarboard*) taloche *f;* (pol & fig) faucon *m;* (*sharper*) (coll) vautour *m* ‖ *tr* colporter; to hawk up expectorer ‖ *intr* chasser au faucon; (*to hawk up phlegm*) graillonner

hawker [ˈhɔkər] *s* colporteur *m*

hawk′ owl′ *s* chouette *f* épervière

hawks′bill tur′tle *s* caret *m*, caouane *f*

hawse [hɔz] *s* (*hole*) écubier *m;* (*prow*) nez *m;* (*distance*) évitage *m*

hawse′hole′ *s* écubier *m*

hawser [ˈhɔzər] *s* haussière *f*

haw′thorn′ *s* aubépine *f*

hay [he] *s* foin *m;* to hit the hay (slang) aller au plumard; to make hay faire les foins

hay′ fe′ver *s* rhume *m* des foins

hay′field′ *s* pré *m* à foin

hay′fork′ *s* fourche *f* à foin

hay′loft′ *s* fenil *m*, grenier *m* à foin

hay′mak′er *s* (boxing) coup *m* de poing en assommoir

haymow [ˈhe,maʊ] *s* fenil *m;* approvisionnement *m* de foin

hay′rack′ *s* râtelier *m*

hay′ride′ *s* promenade *f* en charrette de foin

hay′seed′ *s* graine *f* de foin; (coll) culterreux *m*

hay′stack′ *s* meule *f* de foin

hay′wire′ *adj* (slang) en pagaille; to go hay-

wire (slang) perdre la boussole ‖ *s* fil *m* de fer à lier le foin

hazard [ˈhæzərd] *s* risque *m*, danger *m*; (golf) obstacle *m*; **at all hazards** à tout hasard ‖ *tr* hasarder, risquer

hazardous [ˈhæzərdəs] *adj* hasardeux; (*risky*) hasardé

haz′ardous waste′ *s* les déchets *mpl* hasardeux

haze [hez] *s* brume *f*; (fig) obscurité *f* ‖ *tr* brimer

hazel [ˈhezəl] *adj* couleur de noisette, brun clair ‖ *s* (*tree*) noisetier *m*, avelinier *m*

ha′zel‧nut′ *s* noisette *f*, aveline *f*

hazing [ˈhezɪŋ] *s* brimade *f*; (*of university freshmen*) bizutage *m*

ha‧zy [ˈhezi] *adj* (*comp* **-zier**; *super* **-ziest**) brumeux; (*notion*) nébuleux, vague

H′-bomb′ *s* bombe *f* H

he [hi] *pron pers* il §87; lui §85; ce §82B; **he who** celui qui §83

head [hɛd] *s* tête *f*; (*of bed*) chevet *m*; (*of boil*) tête; (*on glass of beer*) mousse *f*; (*of drum*) peau *f*; (*of cane*) pomme *f*; (*of coin*) face *f*; (*of barrel, cylinder, etc.*) fond *m*; (*of cylinder of automobile engine*) culasse *f*; (*of celery*) pied *m*; (*of ship*) avant *m*; (*of spear, ax, etc.*) fer *m*; (*of arrow*) pointe *f*; (*of business, department, etc.*) chef *m*, directeur *m*; (*of school*) directeur, principal *m*; (*of stream*) source *f*; (*of lake; of the table*) bout *m*, haut bout; (*of a match*) bout; (*caption*) titre *m*; (*decisive point*) point *m* culminant, crise *f*; **at the head of** à la tête de; **from head to foot** des pieds à la tête; **head downwards** la tête en bas; **head of a pin** tête d'épingle; **head of cattle** bœuf *m*; **head over heels in love (with)** éperdument amoureux (de); **heads or tails** pile ou face; **over one's head** (*beyond reach*) hors de la portée de qn; (*going to a higher authority*) sans tenir compte de qn; **to be out of one's head** (coll) être timbré ou fou; **to go to one's head** monter à la tête de qn; **to keep one's head** garder son sang-froid; **to keep one's head above water** se tenir à flot; **to not make head or tail of it** n'y comprendre rien; **to put heads together** prendre conseil; **to take it into one's head to** avoir l'idée de, se mettre en tête de; **to win by a head** gagner d'une tête ‖ *tr* (*to direct*) diriger; (*a procession*) conduire, mener; (*an organization; a class in school*) être en tête de; (*a list*) venir en tête de; **to head off** détourner ‖ *intr* (*said of grain*) épier; **to head for** or **toward** se diriger vers

head′ache′ *s* mal *m* de tête

head′band′ *s* bandeau *m*

head′board′ *s* panneau *m* de tête

head′cheese′ *s* fromage *m* de tête

head′ cold′ *s* rhume *m* de cerveau

head′dress′ *s* coiffure *f*

head′first′ *adv* la tête la première; (*impetuously*) précipitamment

head′frame′ *s* (min) chevalement *m*

head′gear′ *s* garniture *f* de tête, couvre-chef *m*; (*for protection*) casque *m*

head′hunt′er *s* chasseur *m* de têtes; (*for employment*) prospecteur-placier *m*

heading [ˈhɛdɪŋ] *s* titre *m*; (*of letter*) en-tête *m*; (*of chapter*) tête *f*

headland [ˈhɛdlənd] *s* promontoire *m*

headless [ˈhɛdlɪs] *adj* sans tête; (*leaderless*) sans chef

head′light′ *s* (aut) phare *m*; (naut) fanal *m*; (rr) feu *m* d'avant

head′line′ *s* (*of newspaper*) manchette *f*; (*of article*) titre *m*; **to make the headlines** apparaître aux premières pages des journaux ‖ *tr* mettre en vedette

head′lin′er *s* (slang) tête *f* d'affiche

head′long′ *adj* précipité ‖ *adv* précipitamment

head′man′ *s* (*pl* **-men′**) chef *m*

head′mas′ter *s* principal *m*, directeur *m*

head′most′ *adj* de tête, premier

head′ of′fice *s* bureau *m* central; (*director's office*) direction *f*; (*of a corporation*) siège *m* social

head′ of hair′ *s* chevelure *f*

head′-on′ *adj & adv* de front, face à face

head′phones′ *spl* écouteurs *mpl*, casque *m*

head′piece′ *s* (*any covering for head*) casque *m*; (*headset*) écouteur *m*; (*brains, judgment*) tête *f*, caboche *f*; (typ) vignette *f*, en-tête *m*

head′quar′ters *s* bureau *m* central, siège *m* principal; (*police station*) commissariat *m* de police; (mil) quartier *m* général; (*staff headquarters*) (mil) état-major *m*

head′rest′ *s* appui-tête *m*

head′set′ *s* casque *m*, écouteurs *mpl*

heads′man *s* (*pl* **-men**) bourreau *m*

head′ start′ *s* grosse avance *f*; (govt) programme *m* préscolaire pour des enfants défavorisés

head′stone′ *s* pierre *f* tumulaire (à la tête d'une tombe); (*cornerstone*) pierre angulaire

head′strong′ *adj* têtu, entêté

head′wait′er *s* maître *m* d'hôtel

head′wa′ters *spl* cours *m* supérieur d'une rivière

head′way′ *s* progrès *m*, marche *f* avant; (*between buses*) intervalle *m*; (naut) erre *f*; **to make headway** progresser, aller de l'avant

head′wear′ *s* garniture *f* de tête

headwind [ˈhɛd,wɪnd] *s* vent *m* contraire, vent debout

head′word′ *s* (*of a dictionary*) mot *m* d'entrée, mot-souche *m*, entrée *f*, adresse *f*

head′work′ *s* travail *m* mental, travail de tête

head‧y [ˈhɛdi] *adj* (*comp* **-ier**; *super* **-iest**) (*wine*) capiteux; (*conduct*) emporté; (*news*) excitant; (*perfume*) entêtant

heal [hil] *tr* guérir; (*a wound*) cicatriser ‖ *intr* guérir

healer [ˈhilər] *s* guérisseur *m*

healing [ˈhilɪŋ] *s* guérison *f*

health [hɛlθ] *s* santé *f*; **to be in good health** se porter bien, être en bonne santé; **to be in poor**

health se porter mal, être en mauvaise santé; **to drink to the health of** boire à la santé de; **to enjoy radiant health** avoir une santé florissante; **to your health!** à votre santé!

health´-food store´ s magasin m diététique

healthful [ˈhɛlθfəl] adj sain; (air, climate, etc.) salubre; (recreation, work, etc.) salutaire

health´ insur´ance s assurance f maladie-securité, assurance-maladie f

health•y [ˈhɛlθi] adj (comp -ier; super -iest) sain; (air, climate, etc.) salubre; (person) bien portant; (appetite) robuste

heap [hip] s tas m, amas m ‖ tr entasser, amasser; **to heap** (honors, praise, etc.) **on s.o.** combler qn de; **to heap** (insults) **on s.o.** accabler qn de

hear [hɪr] v (pret & pp **heard** [hʌrd]) tr entendre, ouïr; **to hear it said** l'entendre dire; **to hear s.o. sing, to hear s.o. singing** entendre chanter qn, entendre qn qui chante; **to hear s.th. sung** entendre chanter q.ch. ‖ intr entendre; **hear! hear!** très bien!, bravo!; **hear ye!** oyez!; **to hear about** entendre parler de; **to hear from** avoir des nouvelles de; **to hear of** entendre parler de; **to hear tell of** (coll) entendre parler de; **to hear that** entendre dire que

hearer [ˈhɪrər] s auditeur m; **hearers** auditoire m

hearing [ˈhɪrɪŋ] s (sense) l'ouïe f; (act; opportunity to be heard) audition f; (law) audience f; **in the hearing of** en la présence de, devant; **within hearing** à portée de la voix

hear´ing aid´ s sonotone m, microvibrateur m, appareil m de correction auditive, appareil auditif; aide f auditive; (fitted as part of eyeglasses) lunettes fpl auditives

hear´say´ s ouï-dire m

hear´say ev´idence s simples ouï-dire mpl

hearse [hʌrs] s corbillard m, char m funèbre

heart [hɑrt] s cœur m; (cards) cœur m; **after one's heart** selon son cœur; **at heart** au fond; **by heart** par cœur; **heart and soul** corps et âme; **lift up your hearts!** haut les cœurs!; **to break the heart of** fendre le cœur à; **to die of a broken heart** mourir de chagrin; **to eat one's heart out** se ronger le cœur; **to eat to one's heart's content** manger tout son soûl; **to get to the heart of the matter** entrer dans le vif de la question; **to have one's heart in one's work** avoir le cœur à l'ouvrage; **to have one's heart in the right place** avoir le cœur bien placé; **to lose heart** perdre courage; **to open one's heart to** épancher son cœur à; **to take heart** prendre courage; **to take to heart** prendre à cœur; **to wear one's heart on one's sleeve** avoir le cœur sur les lèvres; **with a heavy heart** le cœur gros; **with all one's heart** de tout son cœur; **with one's heart in one's mouth** le gosier serré

heart´ache´ s peine f de cœur

heart´ attack´ s crise f cardiaque

heart´beat´ s battement m du cœur

heart´break´ s crève-cœur m

heartbroken [ˈhɑrtˌbrokən] adj navré, chagriné

heart´burn´ s pyrosis m

heart´ cher´ry s guigne f

heart´ disease´ s maladie f de cœur

hearten [ˈhɑrtən] tr encourager

heart´ fail´ure s arrêt m du cœur

heartfelt [ˈhɑrtˌfɛlt] adj sincère, cordial, bien senti

hearth [hɑrθ] s foyer m, âtre m

hearth´stone´ s pierre f de cheminée

heartily [ˈhɑrtɪli] adv de bon cœur, sincèrement

heartless [ˈhɑrtlɪs] adj sans cœur

heart´ of stone´ s (fig) cœur m de bronze

heart´ pace´ma´ker s (med) stimulateur m (cardiaque)

heart´-rend´ing adj désolant, navrant

heart´sick´ adj désolé, chagrin

heart´strings´ spl fibres fpl, replis mpl du cœur

heart´-to-heart´ adj franc, ouvert; sérieux ‖ adv à cœur ouvert

heart´ trans´plant s greffe f du cœur, transplantation f cardiaque

heart´ trou´ble s maladie f de cœur

heart´wood´ s bois m de cœur

heart•y [ˈhɑrti] adj (comp -ier; super -iest) cordial, sincère; (meal) copieux; (laugh) sonore; (eater) gros

heat [hit] s chaleur f; (heating) chauffage m; (rut of animals) rut m; (in horse racing) éliminatoire f; **in heat** en rut ‖ tr échauffer; (e.g., a house) chauffer ‖ intr s'échauffer; **to heat up** chauffer

heated adj chauffé; (fig) chaud, échauffé

heater [ˈhitər] s (for food) réchaud m; (for heating house) calorifère m

heath [hiθ] s bruyère f

hea•then [ˈhiðən] adj païen ‖ s (pl **-then** or **-thens**) païen m

heathendom [ˈhiðəndəm] s paganisme m

heather [ˈhɛðər] s bruyère f

heating [ˈhitɪŋ] adj échauffant ‖ s chauffage m

heat´ing oil´ s fuel m

heat´ light´ning s éclairs mpl de chaleur

heat´ pump´ s pompe f de chaleur

heat´ shield´ s (rok) bouclier m contre la chaleur, bouclier antithermique

heat´stroke´ s insolation f, coup m de chaleur

heat´ wave´ s vague f de chaleur; (phys) onde f calorifique

heave [hiv] s soulèvement m; **heaves** (vet) pousse f ‖ v (pret & pp **heaved** or **hove** [hov]) tr soulever; (to throw) lancer; (a sigh) pousser; (the anchor) lever ‖ intr se soulever; faire des efforts pour vomir; (said of bosom) palpiter

heaven [ˈhɛvən] s ciel m; **for heaven's sake** pour l'amour de Dieu; **Heaven** le ciel; **heavens** cieux mpl, ciel

heavenly [ˈhɛvənli] adj céleste

heav´enly bod´y s corps m céleste

heav•y [ˈhɛvi] adj (comp -ier; super -iest) lourd, pesant; (heart; crop; eater; baggage; rain, *sea, weather*) gros; (*meal*) copieux; (*sleep*) profond; (*work*) pénible; (*book, reading, etc.*) indigeste; (*parts*) (theat) tragique, sombre ‖ *adv* lourd, lourdement; **to hang heavy on** peser sur

heav′y drink′er *s* fort buveur *m*

heav′y·du′ty *adj* extra-fort, à grand rendement

heav′y-heart′ed *adj* au cœur lourd

heav′y·set′ *adj* de forte carrure, costaud

heav′y wa′ter *s* eau *f* lourde

heav′y·weight′ *s* (boxing) poids *m* lourd

Hebraist [ˋhibre•ɪst] *s* hébraïsant *m*

Hebrew [ˋhibru] *adj* hébreu, hébraïque ‖ *s* (*language*) hébreu *m*, langue *f* hébraïque; (*man*) Hébreu *m*, Juif *m*; (*woman*) Juive *f*

hecatomb [ˋhɛkə‚tom] *s* hécatombe *f*

heckle [ˋhɛkəl] *tr* interrompre bruyamment, chahuter; (*on account of trifles*) asticoter, harceler

heckler [ˋhɛklər] *s* interrupteur *m* impertinent, interpellateur *m*

hectic [ˋhɛktɪk] *adj* fou, bouleversant

he'd *contr* he had; he would

hedge [hɛdʒ] *s* haie *f* ‖ *tr* entourer d'une haie; **to hedge in** entourer de tous côtés ‖ *intr* chercher des échappatoires, hésiter; (com) faire la contrepartie

hedge′ cut′ter *s* taille-haies *m invar*

hedge′hog′ *s* hérisson *m*; (*porcupine*) porc-épic *m*

hedge′hop′ *v* (*pret & pp* -hopped; *ger* -hopping) *intr* (aer) voler en rasemottes

hedge′hop′per *s* rase-mottes *m invar*

hedgerow [ˋhɛdʒ‚ro] *s* bordure *f* de haies, haie *f* vive

heed [hid] *s* attention *f*, soin *m*; **to take heed** prendre garde ‖ *tr* faire attention à, prendre garde à ‖ *intr* faire attention, prendre garde

heedful [ˋhidfəl] *adj* attentif

heedless [ˋhidlɪs] *adj* inattentif

heehaw [ˋhi‚hɔ] *s* hi-han *m* ‖ *intr* pousser des hi-hans

heel [hil] *s* talon *m*; (slang) goujat *m*; **to be down at the heel** traîner la savate; **to cool one's heels** (coll) croquer le marmot, faire le pied de grue, faire le poireau

heft•y [ˋhɛfti] *adj* (*comp* -ier; *super* -iest) costaud; (*heavy*) pesant

heg., hej., ou h. *s* (*honorific applied to someone who has made a pilgrimage to Mecca*) *hadj or *hadji *mf invar*

hegira [hɪˋdʒaɪrə] *s* fuite *f* précipitée, hégire *f*; **Hegira** (rel) *hadj *or* *hadjdj [adʒ] *m invar*

heifer [ˋhɛfər] *s* génisse *f*

height [haɪt] *s* hauteur *f*; (*e.g., of folly*) comble *m*

heighten [ˋhaɪtən] *tr* rehausser; (*to increase the amount of*) augmenter; (*to set off, bring out*) relever ‖ *intr* se rehausser; augmenter

heinous [ˋhenəs] *adj* odieux, atroce

heir [ɛr] *s* héritier *m*; **to become the heir of** hériter de

heir′ appar′ent *s* (*pl* **heirs apparent**) héritier *m* présomptif

heiress [ˋɛrɪs] *s* héritière *f*

heir′loom′ *s* meuble *m*, bijou *m*, or souvenir *m* de famille

Helen [ˋhɛlən] *s* Hélène *f*

helicopter [ˋhɛlɪ‚kɑptər] *s* hélicoptère *m*

hel′icopter land′ing *s* hélistation *f*

heliport [ˋhɛlɪ‚pɔrt] *s* héliport *m*

helium [ˋhilɪəm] *s* hélium *m*

helix [ˋhilɪks] *s* (*pl* **helixes** or **helices** [ˋhɛlɪ‚siz]) hélice *f*; (anat) hélix *m*

he'll *contr* he will

hell [hɛl] *s* enfer *m*; **a hell of a lot of** tout un tas de; **come hell or high water** en dépit de tout, quoiqu'il arrive; **go to hell!** va te faire voir!, la barbe!; **to give s.o. hell** passer une engueulade à qn; **to raise hell** faire la foire

hell′bent′ *adj* (slang) hardi; **hellbent on** (slang) acharné en diable à

hell′cat′ *s* (*bad-tempered woman*) harpie *f*; (*witch*) sorcière *f*

Hellene [ˋhɛlin] *s* Hellène *mf*

Hellenic [hɛˋlɛnɪk], [hɛˋlinɪk] *adj* hellène

hell′fire′ *s* feu *m* de l'enfer

hellish [ˋhɛlɪʃ] *adj* infernal

hel•lo [hɛˋlo] *s* (*pl* -los) bonjour *m* ‖ *interj* bonjour!; (*on telephone*) allô!

helm [hɛlm] *s* gouvernail *m*

helmet [ˋhɛlmɪt] *s* casque *m*

helms′man *s* (*pl* -men) homme *m* de barre

help [hɛlp] *s* aide *f*, secours *m*; (*workers*) main-d'œuvre *f*; (*office workers*) employés *mpl*; (*domestic servants*) domestiques *mfpl*; **help wanted** (*public sign*) offres d'emploi, on embauche, recrutons; **there's no help for it** il n'y a pas de remède ‖ *tr* aider, secourir; **so help me God!** que Dieu me juge!; **to help down** aider à descendre; **to help oneself** se défendre; (*to food*) se servir; **to not be able to help** ne pouvoir s'empêcher de ‖ *intr* aider ‖ *interj* au secours!

helper [ˋhɛlpər] *s* aide *mf*, assistant *m*

helpful [ˋhɛlpfəl] *adj* utile; (*person*) serviable, secourable

helping [ˋhɛlpɪŋ] *s* (*of food*) portion *f*

helpless [ˋhɛlplɪs] *adj* (*weak*) faible; (*powerless*) impuissant; (*penniless*) sans ressource; (*confused*) désemparé; (*situation*) sans recours

help′mate *s* compagnon *m*, compagne *f*; (*husband or wife*) époux *m*, épouse *f*

helter-skelter [ˋhɛltərˋskɛltər] *adj* désordonné ‖ *s* débandade *f* ‖ *adv* pêle-mêle

hem [hɛm] *s* ourlet *m*, bord *m* ‖ *v* (*pret & pp* **hemmed**; *ger* **hemming**) *tr* ourler, border; **to hem in** entourer, cerner ‖ *intr* faire un ourlet; **to hem and haw** ânonner; (fig) tourner autour du pot ‖ *interj* hum!

hemisphere [ˋhɛmɪ‚sfɪr] *s* hémisphère *m*

hemistich [ˋhɛmɪ‚stɪk] *s* hémistiche *m*

hem′line′ *s* ourlet *m* de la jupe

hem′lock′ *s* (*Tsuga canadensis*) sapin *m* du Canada, pruche *f;* (*herb and poison*) ciguë *f*

hemoglobin [‚hɛmə′globɪn] *s* hémoglobine *f*

hemophilia [‚hɛmə′fɪlɪ•ə] *s* hémophilie *f*

hemophiliac [‚hɛmə′fɪlɪ•æk] *s* hémophile *mf*

hemorrhage [′hɛmərɪdʒ] *s* hémorragie *f*

hemorrhoids [′hɛmə‚rɔɪdz] *spl* hémorroïdes *fpl*

hemostat [′hɛmə‚stæt] *s* hémostatique *m*

hemp [hɛmp] *s* chanvre *m*

hem′stitch′ *s* ourlet *m* à jour ‖ *tr* ourler à jour ‖ *intr* faire un ourlet à jour

hen [hɛn] *s* poule *f*

hence [hɛns] *adv* d'ici; (*therefore*) d'où, donc

hence′forth′ *adv* désormais, dorénavant

hench•man [′hɛnt∫mən] *s* (*pl* **-men**) partisan *m,* acolyte *m,* complice *mf*

hen′coop′ *s* cage *f* à poules, épinette *f*

hen′house′ *s* poulailler *m*

henna [′hɛnə] *s* henné *m* ‖ *tr* teindre au henné

hen′peck′ *tr* mener par le bout du nez

hep [hɛp] *adj* (slang) à la page, dans le train; **to be hep to** (slang) être au courant de

hepatitis [‚hɛpə′taɪtɪs] *s* (pathol) hépatite *f*

her [hʌr] *adj poss* son **§88** ‖ *pron pers* elle **§85;** la **§87;** lui **§87**

herald [′hɛrəld] *s* héraut *m;* (fig) avant-coureur *m* ‖ *tr* annoncer; **to herald in** introduire

herald•ry [′hɛrəldri] *s* (*pl* **-ries**) héraldique *f,* blason *m*

herb [ʌrb], [hʌrb] *s* herbe *f;* (pharm) herbe médicinale or officinale; **herbs for seasoning** fines herbes

herbalist [′hʌrbəlɪst] *ou* [′ʌrbəlɪst] *s* herboriste *mf*

herbicide [′hʌrbɪ‚saɪd] *s* herbicide *m*

herb′ shop′ *s* herboristerie *f*

herculean [hʌr′kjulɪ•ən] *adj* herculéen

herd [hʌrd] *s* troupeau *m* ‖ *tr* rassembler en troupeau ‖ *intr*—**to herd together** s'attrouper

herds′man *s* (*pl* **-men**) pâtre *m;* (*of sheep*) berger *m;* (*of cattle*) bouvier *m*

here [hɪr] *adv* ici; **from here to there** d'ici là; **here and there** çà et là, par-ci par-là; **here below** ici-bas; **here is** or **here are** voici; **here lies** ci-gît; **that's neither here nor there** ça n'a rien à y voir ‖ *interj* tenez!; (*answering roll call*) présent!

hereabouts [′hɪrə‚baʊts] *adv* près d'ici

here•af′ter *s*—**the hereafter** l'autre monde ‖ *adv* désormais, à l'avenir; (*farther along*) ci-après

here•by′ *adv* par ce moyen, par ceci; (*in legal language*) par les présentes

hereditary [hɪ′rɛdɪ‚tɛri] *adj* héréditaire

heredi•ty [hɪ′rɛdɪti] *s* (*pl* **-ties**) hérédité *f*

here•in′ *adv* ici; (*on this point*) en ceci; (*in this writing*) ci-inclus

here•of′ *adv* de ceci, à ce sujet

here•on′ *adv* là-dessus

here's *contr* **here is**

here•sy [′hɛrəsi] *s* (*pl* **-sies**) hérésie *f*

heretic [′hɛrətɪk] *adj & s* hérétique *mf*

heretical [hɪ′rɛtɪkəl] *adj* hérétique

heretofore [‚hɪrtu′for] *adv* jusqu'ici

here•upon′ *adv* là-dessus

here•with′ *adv* ci-joint, avec ceci

heritage [′hɛrɪtɪdʒ] *s* héritage *m*

hermetic(al) [hʌr′mɛtɪk(əl)] *adj* hermétique

hermit [′hʌrmɪt] *s* ermite *m*

hermitage [′hʌrmɪtɪdʒ] *s* ermitage *m*

herni•a [′hʌrnɪ•ə] *s* (*pl* **-as** or **-ae** [‚i]) hernie *f*

he•ro [′hɪro] *s* (*pl* **-roes**) héros *m*

heroic [hɪ′ro•ɪk] *adj* héroïque ‖ **heroics** *spl* (*verse*) vers *m* héroïque; (*language*) grandiloquence *f*

heroin [′hɛro•ɪn] *s* héroïne *f*

her′oin ad′dict *s* héroïnomane *mf*

heroine [′hɛro•ɪn] *s* héroïne *f*

heroism [′hɛro‚ɪzəm] *s* héroïsme *m*

heron [′hɛrən] *s* héron *m*

herpes [′hʌr‚piz] *s* (pathol) herpès *m*

herring [′hɛrɪŋ] *s* hareng *m*

her′ring•bone′ *s* (*in fabrics*) point *m* de chausson; (*in hardwood floors*) parquet *m* à batons rompus; (*in design*) arête *f* de hareng

hers [hʌrz] *pron poss* le sien **§89**

her•self′ *pron pers* elle **§89;** soi **§85;** elle-même **§86;** se **§87**

he's *contr* **he is; he has**

hesitan•cy [′hɛzɪtənsi] *s* (*pl* **-cies**) hésitation *f*

hesitant [′hɛzɪtənt] *adj* hésitant

hesitate [′hɛzɪ‚tet] *intr* hésiter

hesitation [‚hɛzɪ′te∫ən] *s* hésitation *f*

heterodox [′hɛtərə‚dɑks] *adj* hétérodoxe

heterodyne [′hɛtərə‚daɪn] *adj* hétérodyne

heterogeneous [‚hɛtərə′dʒɪni•əs] *adj* hétérogène

hew [hju] *v* (*pret* **hewed;** *pp* **hewed** or **hewn**) *tr* tailler, couper; **to hew down** abattre ‖ *intr*—**to hew close to the line** (coll) agir dans les rèles, être très méticuleux

hex [hɛks] *s* porte-guigne *m* ‖ *tr* porter la guigne à

hey [he] *interj* hé!; attention!

hey′day′ *s* meilleure période *f,* fleur *f*

hi [haɪ] *interj* salut!

hia•tus [haɪ′etəs] *s* (*pl* **-tuses** or **-tus**) (*gap*) lacune *f;* (*in a text; in verse*) hiatus *m*

hibernate [′haɪbər‚net] *intr* hiberner

hibiscus [hɪ′bɪskəs] *s* hibiscus *m,* ketmie *f*

hiccough or **hiccup** [′hɪkəp] *s* hoquet *m* ‖ *intr* hoqueter

hick [hɪk] *adj* (pej) péquenaud ‖ *s* (pej) péquenaud *m,* plouc *m*

hicko•ry [′hɪkəri] *s* (*pl* **-ries**) hickory *m*

hidden [′hɪdən] *adj* caché, dérobée; (*mysterious*) occulte

hide [haɪd] *s* peau *f,* cuir *m* ‖ *v* (*pret* **hid** [hɪd]; *pp* **hid** or **hidden** [′hɪdən]) *tr* cacher; **to hide s.th. from** cacher q.ch. à ‖ *intr* se cacher; **to hide from** se cacher à

hide′-and-seek′ *s* cache-cache *m*

hide′bound′ *adj* à l'esprit étroit

hideous [′hɪdɪ•əs] *adj* hideux

hide′-out′ *s* (coll) repaire *m,* planque *f*

hiding [ˈhaɪdɪŋ] *s* dissimulation *f*; (*punishment*) (coll) raclée *f*, rossée *f*; **in hiding** caché

hid'ing place' *s* cachette *f*

hierar•chy [ˈhaɪ•ə‚rɑrki] *s* (*pl* **-chies**) hiérarchie *f*

hieroglyphic [‚haɪ•ərə'glɪfɪk] *adj* hiéroglyphique ‖ *s* hiéroglyphe *m*

hi-fi [ˈhaɪˈfaɪ] *adj* (coll) de haute fidélité ‖ *s* (coll) haute fidélité *f*, hi-fi *f invar*

hi'-fi' fan' *s* (coll) fanatique *mf* de la haute fidélité

hi'-fi' set' *s* appareil *m* de la haute fidélité

hi'-fi' ster'eo sound' *s* son *m* stéréophonique de haute fidélité

high [haɪ] *adj* haut; (*river, price, rate, temperature, opinion*) élevé; (*fever, wind*) fort; (*sea, wind*) gros; (*cheekbones*) saillant; (*sound*) aigu; (*on alcohol*) (coll) éméché, gris; (*on drugs*) (coll) drogué; (culin) avancé; **high and dry** à sec; **high and mighty** prétentieux; **to be high** (coll) avoir son pompon ‖ *s* (aut) prise *f* directe; **on high** en haut, dans le ciel ‖ *adv* haut; à un prix élevé; **high and low** partout; **to aim high** viser haut; **to come high** se vendre cher

high' al'tar *s* maître-autel *m*

high'ball' *s* whisky *m* à l'eau

high' blood' pres'sure *s* hypertension *f*

high'born' *adj* de haute naissance

high'boy' *s* chiffonnier *m* semainier

high'brow' *adj* & *s* (slang) intellectuel *m*

high' chair' *s* chaise *f* d'enfant

high' command' *s* haut commandement *m*

high' cost of liv'ing *s* cherté *f* de la vie

high'-end' *s* (comp) haute gamme *f*

high'er educa'tion [ˈhaɪ•ər] *s* enseignement *m* supérieur

high'er-up' *s* (coll) supérieur *m* hiérarchique

high'est bid'der [ˈhaɪ•ɪst] *s* dernier enchérisseur *m*

high' explo'sive *s* haut explosif *m*, explosif puissant

highfalutin [‚haɪfə'lutən] *adj* (coll) pompeux, ampoulé

high' fidel'ity *s* haute fidélité *f*

high' fre'quency *s* haute fréquence *f*

high' gear' *s* (aut) prise *f* directe

high'-grade' *adj* de qualité supérieure

high'-hand'ed *adj* autoritaire, arbitraire

high' hat' *s* chapeau *m* haut de forme

high'-hat' *adj* (coll) snob, poseur ‖ **high'-hat'** *v* (*pret* & *pp* **-hatted;** *ger* **-hatting**) *tr* (coll) traiter de haut en bas

high'-heeled' *adj* à talons hauts

high' horse' *s* raideur *f* hautaine; **to get up on one's high horse** monter sur ses grands chevaux

high'jack' *tr var* de **hijack**

high' jinks' [‚dʒɪŋks] *s* (slang) clownerie *f*, drôlerie *f*

high' jump' *s* saut *m* en hauteur

high'-key' *adj* (phot) lumineux

highland [ˈhaɪlənd] *s* pays *m* de montagne; **highlands** hautes terres *fpl*

high'-level lan'guage *s* (comp) langage *m* évolué

high' life' *s* grand monde *m*

high'light' *s* (*big moment*) clou *m*, instant *m* le plus marquant, point *m* culminant; (*of a career*) grand succès *m*; **highlights** (*in a picture*) clairs *mpl* ‖ *tr* mettre en vedette

highly [ˈhaɪli] *adv* hautement; (*very*) extrêmement, fort; haut, e.g., **highly colored** haut en couleur; **to think highly of** avoir une bonne opinion de

High' Mass' *s* grand-messe *f*

high'-mind'ed *adj* magnanime, noble

highness [ˈhaɪnɪs] *s* hauteur *f*; **Highness** Altesse *f*

high' noon' *s* plein midi *m*

high'-oc'tane *adj* à indice d'octane élevé

high'-pitched' *adj* aigu; (*roof*) à forte pente

high'-powered' *adj* de haute puissance

high'-pres'sure *adj* à haute pression; (fig) dynamique, persuasif ‖ *tr* (coll) gonfler à bloc

high'-pres'sure sales' person *s* vendeur *m* de choc, vendeuse *f* de choc

high'-priced' *adj* de prix élevé

high' priest' *s* grand prêtre *m*; (fig) pontife *m*

high'-rise' *s* immeuble *m* à beaucoup d'étages

high'-risk' *adj* à risques élevés

high' road' *s* grand-route *f*; (fig) bonne voie *f*

high' school' *s* école *f* secondaire publique; (*in France*) lycée *m*

high'-school stu'dent *s* lycéen *m*; collégien *m*

high' sea' *s* houle *f*, grosse mer *f*; **high seas** haute mer

high' soci'ety *s* la haute société, le beau monde

high'-sound'ing *adj* pompeux, prétentieux

high'-speed' *adj* à grande vitesse, en accéléré

high'-spir'ited *adj* fougueux, plein d'entrain

high' spir'its *spl* gaieté *f*, entrain *m*

high' stakes' *spl*—**to play for high stakes** jouer gros jeu

high-strung [ˈhaɪˈstrʌŋ] *adj* tendu, nerveux

high-tech [ˈhaɪˈtɛk] *adj* de la haute technologie, high-tech

high' technol'ogy *s* la haute technologie *f*, high-tech *f invar*

high'-test' gas'oline *s* supercarburant *m*

high' tide' *s* marée *f* haute, haute marée

high' time' *s* heure *f*, e.g., **it is high time for you to go** c'est certainement l'heure de votre départ; (slang) bombance *f*, bombe *f*

high'trea'son *s* haute trahison *f*

high' volt'age *s* haute tension *f*

high wa'ter *s* marée *f* haute, hautes eaux *fpl*

high'way' *s* route *f*, voie *f* publique

high'way commis'sion *s* administration *f* des ponts et chaussées

high'way'man *s* (*pl* **-men**) voleur *m* de grand chemin

high'way map' *s* carte *f* routière

hijack [ˈhaɪ‚dʒæk] *tr* (coll) arrêter et voler sur

la route; (coll) saisir de force; (*an airplane*) (coll) détourner

hijacker [`haɪˌdʒækər] *s* (coll) bandit *m*, bandit de grand chemin; (coll) pirate *m* de l'air, pirate aérien

hijacking [`haɪˌdʒækɪŋ] *s* (coll) piraterie *f* aérienne, détournement *m*

hike [haɪk] *s* excursion *f* à pied, voyage *m* pédestre; (*e.g., in rent*) hausse *f*‖ *tr* hausser, faire monter ‖ *intr* faire de longues promenades à pied

hiker [`haɪkər] *s* excursionniste *mf* à pied, touriste *mf* pédestre

hilarious [hɪ`lɛrɪ•əs], [haɪ`lɛrɪ•əs] *adj* hilare, gai; (*joke*) hilarant

hill [hɪl] *s* colline *f*, coteau *m*; (*incline*) côte *f*; (mil) cote *f*; **over hill and dale** par monts et par vaux ‖ *tr* (*a plant*) butter, chausser

hill′bil′ly *s* (*pl* **-lies**) montagnard *m* rustique

hillock [`hɪlək] *s* tertre *m*, butte *f*

hill′side′ *s* versant *m*, coteau *m*

hill•y [`hɪli] *adj* (*comp* **-ier**; *super* **-iest**) montueux, accidenté; (*steep*) en pente, à fortes pentes

hilt [hɪlt] *s* poignée *f*; **up to the hilt** jusqu'à la garde

him [hɪm] *pron pers* lui §85, §87; le §87

him•self′ *pron* lui §85; soi §85; lui-même §86; se §87

hind [haɪnd] *adj* postérieur, de derrière ‖ *s* biche *f*

hind′ end′ *s* (slang) train *m*

hinder [`hɪndər] *tr* empêcher

hind′ legs′ *spl* pattes *fpl* de derrière

hind′most′ *adj* dernier, ultime

hind′quar′ter *s* arrière-train *m*, train *m* de derrière; (*of horse*) arrière-main *m*

hindrance [`hɪndrəns] *s* empêchement *m*

hind′sight′ *s* (*of firearm*) hausse *f*; compréhension *f* tardive

Hindu [`hɪndu] *adj* hindou ‖ *s* Hindou *m*

hinge [hɪndʒ] *s* charnière *f*, gond *m*; (*of mollusk*) charnière; (bb) onglet *m* ‖ *intr*—**to hinge on** axer sur, dépendre de

hin•ny [`hɪni] *s* (*pl* **-nies**) bardot *m*

hint [hɪnt] *s* insinuation *f*; (*small quantity*) soupçon *m*; **to take the hint** comprendre à demi-mot, accepter le conseil ‖ *tr* insinuer ‖ *intr* procéder par insinuation; **to hint at** laisser entendre

hinterland [`hɪntɛrˌlænd] *s* arrière-pays *m*

hip [hɪp] *adj* (slang) à la page, dans le train; **to be hip to** (slang) être au courant de ‖ *s* hanche *f*; (*of roof*) arête *f*

hip′bone′ *s* os *m* coxal, os de la hanche

hip′boots′ *spl* cuissardes *fpl*

hipped *adj*—**to be hipped on** (coll) avoir la manie de

hippety-hop [`hɪpɪtɪ`hɑp] *adv* (coll) en sautillant

hip•po [`hɪpo] *s* (*pl* **-pos**) (coll) hippopotame *m*

hippopota•mus [ˌhɪpə`pɑtəməs] *s* (*pl* **-muses** or **-mi** [ˌmaɪ]) hippopotame *m*

hip′ roof′ *s* toit *m* en croupe

hire [haɪr] *s* (*salary*) gages *mpl*; (*renting*) louage *m*; **for hire** à louer; (*public sign*) libre; **in the hire of** aux gages de ‖ *tr* (*a person*) engager, embaucher; (*to rent*) louer, prendre en location ‖ *intr*—**to hire out** (*said of person*) se louer, entrer en service

hired′ man′ *s* (*pl* **men′**) *s* (coll) valet *m* de ferme, garçon *m* de ferme

hireling [`haɪrlɪŋ] *adj & s* mercenaire *m*

hiring [`haɪrɪŋ] *s* embauchage *m*

his [hɪz] *adj poss* son §88 ‖ *pron poss* le sien §89

Hispanic [hɪs`pænɪk] *adj* hispanique

hiss [hɪs] *s* sifflement *m* ‖ *tr & intr* siffler

hist [hɪst] *interj* psitt!, pst!

histology [hɪs`talədʒi] *s* histologie *f*

historian [hɪs`torɪ•ən] *s* historien *m*

historic(al) [hɪs`tɔrɪk(əl)] *adj* historique

histo•ry [`hɪstəri] *s* (*pl* **-ries**) histoire *f*

histrionic [ˌhɪstrɪ`ɑnɪk] *adj* théâtral ‖ **histrionics** *s* art *m* du théâtre; (fig) attitude *f* spectaculaire

hit [hɪt] *s* coup *m*; (*blow that hits its mark*) coup au but, coup heureux; (*sarcastic remark*) coup de patte, trait *m* satirique; (*on the hit parade*) tube *m*; (baseball) coup de batte; (theat) succès *m*, spectacle *m* très couru; (coll) réussite *f*; **to make a hit** (coll) faire sensation ‖ *v* (*pret & pp* **hit**; *ger* **hitting**) *tr* frapper; (*the mark*) atteindre; (*e.g., a car*) heurter, heurter contre; (*to move the emotions of*) toucher; **to hit it off** (coll) s'entendre, se trouver d'accord ‖ *intr* frapper; **to hit on** tomber sur, trouver; (slang) faire des avances amoureuse à

hit′-and-run′ driv′er *s* chauffard *m* qui abandonne la scène d'un accident, qui prend la fuite

hitch [hɪtʃ] *s* saccade *f*, secousse *f*; obstacle *m*, difficulté *f*; (*knot*) nœud *m*, e.g., **timber hitch** nœud de bois; **without a hitch** sans accroc ‖ *tr* accrocher; (naut) nouer; **to hitch up** (*e.g., a horse*) atteler

hitch′hike′ *intr* (coll) faire de l'auto-stop

hitch′hik′er *s* auto-stoppeur *m*

hitch′hik′ing *s* auto-stop *m*

hitch′ing post′ *s* poteau *m* d'attache

hither [`hɪðər] *adv* ici; **hither and thither** çà et là

hith′er•to′ *adv* jusqu'ici, jusqu'à présent

hit′-or-miss′ *adj* capricieux, éventuel

hit′ parade′ *s* (coll) chansons *fpl* populaires du moment, palmarès *m*

hit′ rec′ord *s* (coll) disque *m* à succès

HIV [`eɪtʃˌaɪ`vi] *s* (letterword) (**Human Immunodeficiency Virus**) VIH *or* V.I.H. *m* (Virus de l'Immunodéficience Humaine)

HIV pos′itive *adj* séropositif; **to be HIV positive** être porteur du virus du sida, être séropositif

hive [haɪv] *s* ruche *f*; **hives** (pathol) urticaire *f*

hoard [hord] *s* entassement *m*, trésor *m* ‖ *tr* accumuler secrètement, thésauriser ‖ *intr* accumuler, entasser, thésauriser

hoarding [ˈhordɪŋ] *s* accumulation *f* secrète, thésaurisation *f*

hoarfrost [ˈhor͵frɔst] *s* givre *m*, gelée *f* blanche

hoarse [hors] *adj* enroué, rauque

hoarseness [ˈhorsnɪs] *s* enrouement *m*

hoar·y [ˈhori] *adj* (*comp* **-ier;** *super* **-iest**) chenu, blanchi

hoax [hoks] *s* mystification *f*, canard *m* ‖ *tr* mystifier

hob [hɑb] *s* (*of fireplace*) plaque *f*; **to play hob** (coll) causer des ennuis; **to play hob with** (coll) bouleverser

hobble [ˈhɑbəl] *s* (*limp*) boitillement *m*; (*rope used to tie legs of animal*) entrave *f* ‖ *tr* faire boiter; (*e.g., a horse*) entraver ‖ *intr* boiter, clocher

hob·by [ˈhɑbi] *s* (*pl* **-bies**) distraction *f*, violon *m* d'Ingres; (orn) hobereau *m*; **to ride one's hobby** enfourcher son dada

hob′by·horse′ *s* cheval *m* de bois

hob′gob′lin *s* lutin *m*; (*bogy*) épouvantail *m*

hob′nail′ *s* caboche *f*

hob·nob [ˈhɑb͵nɑb] *v* (*pret & pp* **-nobbed;** *ger* **-nobbing**) *intr* trinquer ensemble; **to hobnob with** être à tu et à toi avec

ho·bo [ˈhobo] *s* (*pl* **-bos** or **-boes**) chemineau *m*, vagabond *m*

hock [hɑk] *s* (*of horse*) jarret *m*; (*wine*) vin *m* du Rhin; (*pawn*) (coll) gage *m*; **in hock** (coll) au clou; (*in prison*) (coll) au bloc ‖ *tr* couper le jarret à; (*to pawn*) (coll) mettre en gage, mettre au clou

hockey [ˈhɑki] *s* hockey *m*

hock′ey play′er *s* hockeyeur *m*

hock′shop′ *s* (slang) mont-de-piété *m*, clou *m*

hocus-pocus [ˈhokəsˈpokəs] *s* tour *m* de passe-passe; (*meaningless formula*) abracadabra *m*

hod [hɑd] *s* oiseau *m*, auge *f*

hod′ car′rier *s* aide-maçon *m*

hodgepodge [ˈhɑdʒ͵pɑdʒ] *s* salmigondis *m*, méli-mélo *m*

hoe [ho] *s* houe *f*, binette *f* ‖ *tr* houer, biner

hog [hɔg] *s* pourceau *m*, porc *m*; (*pig*) cochon ‖ *v* (*pret & pp* **hogged;** *ger* **hogging**) *tr* (slang) s'emparer de, saisir avidement

hog′back′ *s* dos *m* d'âne

hoggish [ˈhɔgɪʃ] *adj* glouton

hogs′head′ *s* barrique *f*

hog′wash′ *s* eaux *fpl* grasses; vinasse *f*; (fig) boniments *mpl* à la noix de coco

hoist [hɔɪst] *s* monte-charge *m*, grue *f*; (*shove*) poussée *f* vers le haut ‖ *tr* lever, guinder; (*a flag, sail, boat, etc.*) hisser

hoity-toity [ˈhɔɪtiˈtɔɪti] *adj* hautain; **to be hoity-toity** le prendre de haut

hokum [ˈhokəm] *s* (coll) boniments *mpl*, fumisterie *f*

hold [hold] *s* (*grasp*) prise *f*; (*handle*) poignée *f*, manche *m*; (*domination*) pouvoir *m*, autorité *f*; (electron) mise-en-garde *f*; (mus) point *m* d'orgue; (naut) cale *f*; **hold for arrival**

(*formula on envelope*) garder jusqu'à l'arrivée; **to be on hold** (telp) être en ligne, attendre; **to get hold of** (*s.th.*) trouver; (*s.o.*) contacter; **to take hold of** empoigner, saisir ‖ *v* (*pret & pp* **held** [hɛld]) *tr* tenir; (*one's breath; s.o.'s attention*) retenir; (*to contain*) contenir; (*a job; a title*) avoir, posséder; (*e.g., a university chair*) occuper; (*a fort*) défendre; (*a note*) (mus) tenir, prolonger; **to be held to be. . .** passer pour. . .; **to hold** (telp) rester en ligne, attendre; **to hold back** or in retenir; **to hold one's own** rivaliser, se défendre; **to hold out** tendre, offrir; **to hold over** continuer, remettre; **to hold s.o. to be. . .** tenir qn pour. . .; **to hold s.o. to his word** obliger qn à tenir sa promesse; **to hold up** (*to delay*) retarder; (*to keep from falling*) retenir, soutenir; (*to rob*) (coll) voler à main armée ‖ *intr* (*to hold good*) rester valable, rester en vigueur; **hold on!** (telp) restez en ligne!; **to hold back** se retenir, hésiter; **to hold forth** disserter; **to hold off** se tenir à distance; **to hold on** or out tenir bon; **to hold on to** s'accrocher à, se cramponner à; **to hold out for** insister pour

hold′ but′ton *s* bouton *m* de rester en ligne

holder [ˈholdər] *s* possesseur *m*; (*of stock*) porteur *m*; (*of stock; of a record*) détenteur *m*; (*of degree, fellowship, etc.*) impétrant *m*; (*for a cigarette*) porte-cigarettes *m*; (*of a post, a right, etc.*) titulaire *mf*; (*for holding, e.g., a hot dish*) poignée *f*

holding [ˈholdɪŋ] *s* possession *f*; **holdings** valeurs *fpl*; (*of an investor*) portefeuille *m*; (*of a landlord*) propriétés *fpl*

hold′ing bay′ *s* (aer) aire *f* d'attente

hold′ing com′pany *s* holding trust *m*, holding *m*, société *f* d'unigestion

hold′ing pat′tern *s* (aer) trajectoire *f* d'attente

hold′up′ *s* (*stop, delay*) arrêt *m*; (coll) attaque *f* à main armée, hold-up *m*; **what's the holdup?** (coll) qu'est-ce qu'on attend?

hole [hol] *s* trou *m*; **in the hole** (coll) dans l'embarras; **to burn a hole in s.o.'s pocket** (coll) brûler la poche à qn; **to get s.o. out of a hole** (coll) tirer qn d'un mauvais pas; **to pick holes in** (coll) trouver à redire à, démolir; **to wear holes in** (*e.g., a garment*) trouer ‖ *intr*—**to hole up** se terrer

holiday [ˈhɑlɪ͵de] *s* jour *m* de fête, jour férié; (*vacation*) vacances *fpl*

holiness [ˈholɪnɪs] *s* sainteté *f*; **His Holiness** Sa Sainteté

holla [ˈhɑlə], [həˈlɑ] *interj* holà!

Holland [ˈhɑlənd] *s* Hollande *f*; la Hollande

Hollander [ˈhɑləndər] *s* Hollandais *m*

hollow [ˈhɑlo] *adj & s* creux *m* ‖ *adv*—**to beat all hollow** (coll) battre à plate couture ‖ *tr* creuser

hol·ly [ˈhɑli] *s* (*pl* **-lies**) houx *m*

hol′ly·hock′ *s* primerose *f*, rose *f* trémière

Hol′ly wood′ *adj* hollywoodien ‖ *s* Hollywood *m* (*centre de l'industrie cinématographique*)

holm′ oak′ [hom] *s* yeuse *f*

holocaust [ˈhɑləˌkɔst] *s* (*sacrifice*) holocauste *m;* (*disaster*) sinistre *m*
hologram [ˈholəɡræm] *s* hologramme *m*
holography [hoˈlɑɡrəfi] *s* holographie *f*
holster [ˈholstər] *s* étui *m;* (*on saddle*) fonte *f*
ho•ly [ˈholi] *adj* (*comp* **-lier;** *super* **-liest**) saint; (*e.g., water*) bénit
Ho′ly Ghost′ *s* Saint-Esprit *m*
ho′ly or′ders *spl* ordres *mpl* sacrés
Ho′ly Scrip′ture *s* l'Écriture *f* Sainte
Ho′ly See′ *s* Saint-Siège *m*
Ho′ly Sep′ulcher *s* Saint Sépulcre *m*
Ho′ly Spir′it *s* Saint-Esprit *m*
ho′ly wa′ter *s* eau *f* bénite
Ho′ly Writ′ *s* l'Écriture *f* Sainte
homage [ˈhɑmɪdʒ] *s* hommage *m*
home [hom] *adj* (*family*) domestique, de famille; (econ, pol) national, du pays ‖ *s* foyer *m,* chez-soi *m,* domicile *m;* (*house*) maison *f;* (*of the arts; native land*) patrie *f;* (*for the sick, poor, etc.*) asile *m,* foyer, hospice *m;* **at home** à la maison; (*at ease*) à l'aise; **make yourself at home** faites comme chez vous ‖ *adv* à la maison; **to see s.o. home** raccompagner qn jusqu'à chez lui; **to strike home** frapper juste, toucher au vif
home′ address′ *s* adresse *f* personnelle; (*on a form*) domicile *m* (permanent)
home′-baked′ *adj* fait à la maison
home′bod′y *s* (*pl* **-ies**) casanier *m,* pantouflard *m*
homebred [ˈhomˌbrɛd] *adj* élevé à la maison; du pays, indigène
home′-brew′ *s* boisson *f* faite à la maison
home′-care nurs′ing *s* soins *mpl* à domicile
home′com′ing *s* retour *m* au foyer; (*at university, church, etc.*) journée *f* or semaine *f* des anciens
home′ comput′er *s* micro-ordinateur *m,* ordinateur *m* domestique
home′ coun′try *s* pays *m* natal
home′ deliv′ery *s* livraison *f* à domicile
home′ econom′ics *s* économie *f* domestique; (*instruction*) enseignement *m* ménager
home′ front′ *s* théâtre *m* d'opérations à l'intérieur du pays
home′ ground′ *s* domaine *m,* terrain *m*
home′-grown′ *adj* (*e.g., vegetables*) du jardin
home′land′ *s* patrie *f,* pays *m* natal
homeless [ˈhomlɪs] *adj* sans foyer
home′ life′ *s* vie *f* familiale
home′like′ *adj* familial, comme chez soi
home′-lov′ing *adj* casanier
home•ly [ˈhomli] *adj* (*comp* **-lier;** *super* **-liest**) (*not good-looking*) laid, vilain; (*not elegant*) sans façons
home′made′ *adj* fait à la maison, de ménage
home′mak′er *s* maîtresse *f* de maison, ménagère *f*
home′ of′fice *s* siège *m* social
homeopathy [ˌhomɪˈɑpəθi] *s* homéopathie *f*
home′own′er *s* propriétaire *mf*
home′ plate′ *s* (baseball) marbre *m*
home′ port′ *s* port *m* d'attache
home′ rule′ *s* autonomie *f,* gouvernement *m* autonome
home′ sick′ *adj* nostalgique; **to be homesick** avoir le mal du pays
home′ sick′ness *s* mal *m* du pays, nostalgie *f*
homespun [ˈhomˌspʌn] *adj* filé à la maison; (fig) simple, sans apprêt
home′stead *s* bien *m* de famille, ferme *f*
home′stretch′ *s* fin *f* de course, dernière étape *f*
home′ team′ *s* locaux *mpl,* équipe *f* qui reçoit
home′town′ *s* ville *f* natale
homeward [ˈhomwərd] *adj* de retour ‖ *adv* vers la maison; vers son pays
home′work′ *s* travail *m* à la maison; devoirs *mpl*
homey [ˈhomi] *adj* (*comp* **homier;** *super* **homiest**) (coll) familial, intime
homicidal [ˌhɑmɪˈsaɪdəl] *adj* homicide
homicide [ˈhɑmɪˌsaɪd] *s* (*act*) homicide *m;* (*person*) homicide *mf*
homi•ly [ˈhɑmɪli] *s* (*pl* **-lies**) homélie *f*
hom′ing head′ *s* (*of missile*) tête *f* chercheuse
hom′ing pi′geon *s* pigeon *m* voyageur
hominy [ˈhɑmɪni] *s* semoule *f* de maïs
homo [ˈhomo] *s* (slang, pej) (*homosexual*) tapette *f,* tante *f*
homogeneous [ˌhoməˈdʒinɪ•əs], [ˌhɑməˈdʒinɪ•əs] *adj* homogène
homogenize [hɑˈmɑdʒəˌnaɪz] *tr* homogénéiser
homonym [ˈhɑmənɪm] *s* homonyme *m*
homonymous [həˈmɑnɪməs] *adj* homonyme
homosexual [ˌhoməˈsɛkʃʊ•əl] *adj* homosexuel ‖ *s* homosexuel *m;* (rare) homosexuelle *f*
homosexuality [ˌhoməˌsɛkʃʊˈælɪti] *s* homosexualité *f*
honcho [ˈhɑntʃo] *s* (coll) grand caïd *m*
hone [hon] *s* pierre *f* à aiguiser ‖ *tr* aiguiser, affiler
honest [ˈɑnɪst] *adj* honnête; (*money*) honnêtement acquis
honesty [ˈɑnɪsti] *s* honnêteté *f;* (bot) monnaie *f* du pape
hon•ey [ˈhʌni] *s* miel *m* ‖ *v* (*pret & pp* **-eyed** or **-ied**) *tr* emmieller
hon′ey•bee′ *s* abeille *f* à miel
hon′ey•comb′ *s* rayon *m,* gâteau *m* de cire; (*anything like a honeycomb*) nid *m* d'abeilles ‖ *tr* cribler
hon′ey dew′ mel′on *s* melon *m* d'hiver *or* d'Antibes
honeyed *adj* emmiellé
hon′ey•moon′ *s* lune *f* de miel; voyage *m* de noces ‖ *intr* passer la lune de miel
hon′ey•suck′le *s* chèvrefeuille *m*
honk [hɔŋk] *s* (aut) klaxon *m* ‖ *tr* (*the horn*) sonner ‖ *intr* klaxonner
honkytonk [ˈhɔŋkiˌtɔŋk] *s* (slang) boui-boui *m*
honor [ˈɑnər] *s* honneur *m;* (*award*) distinction *f;* **honors** honneurs ‖ *tr* honorer; **in honor of** en l'honneur de
honorable [ˈɑnərəbəl] *adj* honorable

hon'orable dis'charge *s* (mil) démobilisation *f* honorable

honorari•um [ˌɑnəˈrɛrɪ•əm] *s* (*pl* **-ums** or **-a** [ə]) *s* honoraires *mpl*

honorary [ˈɑnəˌrɛri] *adj* honoraire

honorific [ˌɑnəˈrɪfɪk] *adj* honorifique ‖ *s* formule *f* de politesse

hood [hʊd] *s* capuchon *m*, chaperon *m*; (*of chimney*) hotte *f*; (*academic hood*) capuce *m*; (aut) capot *m*; (slang) gangster *m*, loubard *m* ‖ *tr* capoter

hoodlum [ˈhʊdləm] *s* (coll) chenapan *m*

hoodoo [ˈhʊdu] *s* (*bad luck*) guigne *f*; (*rites*) vaudou *m* ‖ *tr* porter la guigne à

hood'wink' *tr* tromper, abuser, anarquer

hooey [ˈhu•i] *s* (slang) blague *f*

hoof [hʊf] *s* sabot *m*; **on the hoof** sur pied ‖ *tr*—**to hoof it** (coll) aller à pied

hoof' and mouth' disease' *s* (vet) fièvre *f* aphteuse

hoof'beat' *s* pas *m* de cheval

hook [hʊk] *s* crochet *m*; (*for fishing*) hameçon *m*; (*to join two things*) croc *m*; (*boxing*) crochet *m*; **by hook or by crook** (coll) de bric ou de broc, coûte que coûte; **hook line and sinker** (coll) tout à fait, avec tout le bataclan; **to get one's hooks on to** (coll) mettre le grappin sur; **to take off the hook** décrocher ‖ *tr* accrocher; (*e.g., a dress*) agrafer; (*e.g., a boat*) crocher, gaffer; (slang) amorcer, attraper; **to hook up** (*e.g., a loudspeaking system*) monter ‖ *intr* s'accrocher

hookah [ˈhʊkə] *s* narguilé *m*

hook' and eye' *s* agrafe *f* et porte *f*

hook' and lad'der *s* camion *m* équipé d'une échelle d'incendie

hooked' rug' *s* tapis *m* à points noués

hook' shot' *s* (sports) bras *m* roulé

hook'up' *s* (*diagram*) (rad, telv) montage *m*; (*network*) (rad, telv) chaîne *f*

hook'worm' *s* ankylostome *m*

hooky [ˈhʊki] *s*—**to play hooky** (coll) faire l'école buissonnière

hooligan [ˈhʊlɪgən] *s* voyou *m*

hooliganism [ˈhʊlɪgənˌɪzəm] *s* voyouterie *f*

hoop [hʊp] *s* cerceau *m*; (*of cask*) cercle *m* ‖ *tr* cercler, entourer

hoop' skirt' *s* crinoline *f*

hoot [hʊt] *s* huée *f*; (*of owl*) ululement *m*; **I don't care a hoot** (slang) je m'en bats l'œil, je m'en fiche ‖ *tr* huer ‖ *intr* huer; (*said of owl*) ululer; **to hoot at** huer

hoot' owl' *s* chat-huant *m*, hulotte *f*

hop [hɑp] *s* saut *m*; (*dance*) (coll) sauterie *f*, boum *f*; (coll) vol *m* en avion, étape *f*; **hops** (bot) houblon *m* ‖ *v* (*pret & pp* **hopped**; *ger* **hopping**) *tr* sauter, franchir; (*e.g., a taxi*) (coll) prendre ‖ *intr* sauter, sautiller; **to hop on one foot** sauter à cloche-pied; **to hop over** sauter

hope [hop] *s* (*feeling of hope*) espérance *f*; (*instance of hope*) espoir *m*; (*person or thing one puts one's hope in*) espérance, espoir ‖ *tr & intr* espérer; **to hope for** espérer; **to hope to** + *inf* espérer + *inf*

hope' chest' *s* trousseau *m*

hopeful [ˈhopfəl] *adj* (*feeling hope*) plein d'espoir; (*giving hope*) prometteur

hopeless [ˈhoplɪs] *adj* sans espoir

hopper [ˈhɑpər] *s* (*funnel-shaped container*) trémie *f*; (*of blast furnace*) gueulard *m*

hop'per car' *s* wagon-trémie *m*

hop'scotch' *s* marelle *f*

horde [hɔrd] *s* horde *f*

horehound [ˈhɔrˌhaʊnd] *s* (bot) marrube *m*

horizon [həˈraɪzən] *s* horizon *m*

horizontal [ˌhɔrɪˈzɑntəl] *adj* horizontal ‖ *s* horizontale *f*

hor'izon'tal hold' *s* (telv) commande *f* de stabilité horizontale, molette *f* horizontale

hormone [ˈhɔrmon] *s* hormone *f*

horn [hɔrn] *s* (*bony projection on head of certain animals*) corne *f*; (*of anvil*) bigorne *f*; (*of auto*) klaxon *m*; (*of snail; of insect*) antenne *f*; (mus) cor *m*; (*French horn*) (mus) cor d'harmonie; **horns** (*of deer*) bois *m*; **to blow one's own horn** (coll) se vanter, exalter son propre mérite; **to draw in one's horns** (fig) rentrer les cornes; **to toot the horn** corner ‖ *intr*—**to horn in** (slang) intervenir sans façon

horn'beam' *s* (bot) charme *m*

horned *adj* cornu

horned' owl' *s* duc *m*

hornet [ˈhɔrnɪt] *s* frelon *m*; **to stir up a hornet's nest** mettre le feu aux poudres

hor'net's nest' *s* guêpier *m*

horn' of plen'ty *s* corne *f* d'abondance

horn'pipe' *s* chalumeau *m*; (*dance*) matelote *f*

horn'rimmed glas'ses *spl* lunettes *fpl* à monture en corne

horn•y [ˈhɔrni] *adj* (*comp* **-ier;** *super* **-iest**) (*like horn*) corné; (*hands*) calleux; (*sexually aroused*) (slang) en rut, excité

horoscope [ˈhɔrəˌskop] *s* horoscope *m*; **to cast s.o.'s horoscope** tirer l'horoscope de qn

horrible [ˈhɔrɪbəl] *adj* horrible; (coll) horrible, détestable

horrid [ˈhɔrɪd] *adj* affreux; (coll) affreux, très désagréable

horri•fy [ˈhɔrɪˌfaɪ] *v* (*pret & pp* **-fied**) *tr* horrifier

horror [ˈhɔrər] *s* horreur *f*; **to have a horror of** avoir horreur de

hors d'oeuvre [ɔrˈdʌrvz] *s* (*pl* **hors d'oeuvres** [ɔrˈdʌrvz]) hors-d'œuvre *m invar*

horse [hɔrs] *s* cheval *m*; (*of carpenter*) chevalet *m*; **hold your horses!** (coll) arrêtez un moment!; **to back the wrong horse** (coll) miser sur le mauvais cheval; **to be a horse of another color** (coll) être une autre paire de manches; **to eat like a horse** (coll) manger comme un ogre; **to ride a horse** monter à cheval ‖ *intr*—**to horse around** (slang) muser, se baguenauder

horse'back' *s*—**on horseback** à cheval ‖ *adv*—**to ride horseback** monter à cheval

horse′back rid′ing s équitation f, exercise m à cheval

horse′ blan′ket s couverture f de cheval

horse′ break′er s dompteur m de chevaux

horse′car′ s tramway m à chevaux

horse′ chest′nut s (tree) marronnier m d'Inde; (nut) marron m d'Inde

horse′cloth′ s housse f

horse′ coll′ar s collier m de cheval

horse′ deal′er s marchand m de chevaux

horse′ doc′tor s (coll) vétérinaire m

horse′ fly′ s (pl **flies**) taon m

horse′hair′ s crin m

horse′hide′ s peau f or cuir m de cheval

horse′laugh′ s gros rire m bruyant

horse′less car′riage [ˈhɔrslɪs] s voiture f sans chevaux

horse′man s (pl **-men**) cavalier m; (at race track) turfiste m

horsemanship [ˈhɔrsmən,ʃɪp] s équitation f

horse′ meat′ s viande f de cheval

horse′ op′era s (coll) western m

horse′ pis′tol s pistolet m d'arçon

horse′play′ s jeu m de mains, clownerie f

horse′pow′er s (746 watts) cheval-vapeur m anglais

horse′ race′ s course f de chevaux

horse′rad′ish s raifort m

horse′ sense′ s (coll) gros bon sens m

horse′shoe′ s fer m à cheval

horse′shoe′ing s ferrure f, ferrage m

horse′shoe mag′net s aimant m en fer à cheval

horse′ show′ s exposition f de chevaux, concours m hippique

horse′tail′ s queue f de cheval; (bot) prèle f

horse′ thief′ s voleur m de chevaux

horse′ trad′er s maquignon m

horse′ trad′ing s maquignonnage m

horse′whip′ s cravache f ‖ v (pret & pp **-whipped**; ger **-whipping**) tr cravacher

horse′wom′an s (pl **-wom′en**) s cavalière f, amazone f

hors•y [ˈhɔrsi] adj (comp **-ier**; super **-iest**) chevalin; (coll) hippomane; (awkward in appearance) (coll) maladroit

horticultural [ˌhɔrtɪˈkʌltʃərəl] adj horticole

horticulture [ˈhɔrtɪ,kʌltʃər] s horticulture f

hose [hoz] s (flexible tube) tuyau m ‖ s (pl **hose**) (stocking) bas m; (sock) chaussette f

hosier [ˈhoʒər] s bonnetier m

hosiery [ˈhoʒəri] s la bonneterie; (stockings) les bas mpl

hospice [ˈhɑspɪs] s hospice m

hospitable [ˈhɑspɪtəbəl] adj hospitalier

hospital [ˈhɑspɪtəl] s hôpital m, clinique f, maison f de santé

hospitali•ty [ˌhɑspɪˈtælɪti] s (pl **-ties**) hospitalité f

hospitalize [ˈhɑspɪtə,laɪz] tr hospitaliser

hos′pital plane′ s avion m sanitaire

hos′pital ship′ s navire-hôpital m

hos′pital train′ s train m sanitaire

hos′pital ward′ s pavillon m

host [host] s hôte m; (who entertains dinner guests) amphitryon m; (multitude) foule f, légion f; (army) armée f; **Host** (eccl) hostie f

hostage [ˈhɑstɪdʒ] s otage m

hostel [ˈhɑstəl] s hôtellerie f; (youth hostel) auberge f de la jeunesse

hostel•ry [ˈhɑstəlri] s (pl **-ries**) hôtellerie f

hostess [ˈhostɪs] s hôtesse f; (taxi dancer) entraîneuse f

hostile [ˈhɑstɪl] adj hostile

hostili•ty [hɑsˈtɪlɪti] s (pl **-ties**) hostilité f

hostler [ˈhɑslər], [ˈɑslər] s palefrenier m, valet m d'écurie

hot [hɑt] adj (comp **hotter**; super **hottest**) chaud; (spicy) piquant; (fight, pursuit, etc.) acharné; (in rut) en chaleur; (radioactive) (coll) fortement radioactif; **hot off** (e.g., the press) (coll) sortant tout droit de; **to be hot** (said of person) avoir chaud; (said of weather) faire chaud; **to get hot under the collar** (coll) s'emporter; **to make it hot for** (coll) rendre la vie intenable à, harceler

hot′ air′ s (coll) hâblerie f, discours mpl vides, baratin m

hot′-air′ fur′nace s calorifère m à air chaud

hot′ and cold′ run′ning wa′ter s eau f courante chaude et froide

hot′ bed′ s (hort) couche f, couche de fumier; (e.g., of vice) foyer m; (e.g., of intrigue) officine f

hot′-blood′ed adj au sang fougueux

hot′box′ s (rr) coussinet m échauffé

hot′-but′ton is′sue s sujet m brûlant

hot′ cake′ s crêpe f; **to sell like hot cakes** (coll) se vendre comme des petits pains

hot′ dog′ s saucisse f de Francfort, saucisse chaude, hot-dog m

hotel [hoˈtɛl] adj hôtelier ‖ s hôtel m

hotel′keep′er s hôtelier m

hotel′ room′ s chambre f d'hôtel

hot′foot′ adv (coll) à toute vitesse ‖ tr—**to hotfoot it after** (coll) s'élancer à la pour-suite de

hot′head′ed adj exalté, fougueux

hot′house′ s serre f chaude

hot′ line′ s (pol) téléphone m rouge

hot′ mon′ey s (slang) capitaux mpl fébriles

hot′ pad′ s (for plates at table) garde-nappe m, dessous-de-plat m

hot′ pep′per s piment m rouge

hot′ plate′ s réchaud m

hot′ pota′to s (fig) sujet m brûlant

hot′ rod′ s (slang) bolide m

hot′ rod′der [ˌrɑdər] s (slang) bolide m, casse-cou m

hot′ springs′ spl sources fpl thermales

hot′-temp′ered adj coléreux, irascible

hot′ wa′ter s (coll) mauvaise passe f; **to be in hot water** (coll) être dans le pétrin

hot′-wa′ter boil′er s chaudière f à eau chaude

hot′-wa′ter bot′tle s bouillotte f

hot′-wa′ter heat′er s calorifère m à eau

hot-water heating *s* (*with instantaneous delivery of hot water*) chauffe-eau *m*

hot'-wa'ter heat'ing *s* chauffage *m* par eau chaude

hot'-wa'ter tank' *s* réservoir *m* d'eau chaude, bâche *f*

hound [haʊnd] *s* chien *m* de chasse, chien courant; **to follow the hounds** or **to ride to hounds** chasser à courre ‖ *tr* poursuivre avec ardeur, pourchasser

hound's'-tooth' *adj* pied-de-poule

hour [aʊr] *s* heure *f;* **by the hour** à l'heure; **hours of credit** (educ) unités *fpl* de valeur; **on the hour** à l'heure sonnante; **to keep late hours** se coucher tard

hour'glass' *s* sablier *m*, horloge *f* à sable

hour'-glass fig'ure *s* taille *f* de guêpe

hour' hand' *s* petite aiguille *f*, aiguille des heures

hourly ['aʊrli] *adj* à l'heure, horaire ‖ *adv* toutes les heures; (*hour by hour*) d'heure en heure

house [haʊs] *s* (*pl* **houses** ['haʊzɪz]) maison *f;* (*legislative body*) chambre *f;* (theat) salle *f,* e.g., **full house** salle comble; **to be on the house** (coll) être au frais du patron; **to bring down the house** (theat) faire crouler la salle sous les applaudissements; **to keep house for** tenir la maison de; **to put one's house in order** (fig) mettre de l'ordre dans ses affaires ‖ [haʊz] *tr* loger, abriter

house' arrest' *s*—**under house arrest** en résidence surveillée

house'boat' *s* péniche *f,* bateau-maison *m*

house'boy' *s* boy *m*

house'break'er *s* cambrioleur *m*

house'break'ing *s* effraction *f,* cambriolage *m*

housebroken ['haʊs,brokən] *adj* (*dog or cat*) dressé à la propreté

house' clean'ing *s* grand nettoyage *m* de la maison

house'coat' *s* peignoir *m*

house' cur'rent *s* courant *m* de secteur, secteur *m*

house'fly' *s* (*pl* **-flies**) mouche *f* domestique

houseful ['haʊs,fʊl] *s* pleine maison *f*

house' fur'nishings *spl* ménage *m*

house'hold' *adj* domestique, du ménage ‖ *s* ménage *m,* maisonnée *f*

house'hold'er *s* chef *m* de famille, maître *m* de maison

house' hunt'ing *s* chasse *f* aux appartements

house'keep'er *s* ménagère *f;* (*employee*) femme *f* de charge; (*for a bachelor*) gouvernante *f*

house'keep'ing *s* le ménage, l'économie *f* domestique; **to set up housekeeping** se mettre en ménage

house'maid' *s* bonne *f*

house'mates' *spl* partenaires *mfpl* qui habite la même maison

house'moth'er *s* maîtresse *f* d'internat

house' of cards' *s* château *m* de cartes

House' of Com'mons *s* Chambre *f* des communes

house' of ill' repute' *s* maison *f* mal famée, maison borgne

House' of Represen'tatives *s* Chambre *f* des Représentants

house' paint'er *s* peintre *m* en bâtiments

house' physi'cian *s* (*in hospital*) interne *m;* (*e.g., in hotel*) médecin *m*

house'top' *s* toit *m;* **to shout from the housetops** (coll) crier sur les toits

house' trail'er *s* caravane *f*

house'warm'ing *s*—**to have a housewarming** pendre la crémaillère

house'wife' *s* (*pl* **-wives'**) maîtresse *f* de maison, ménagère *f*

house'work' *s* travaux *mpl* ménagers; **to do the housework** faire le ménage

housing ['haʊzɪŋ] *s* logement *m,* habitation *f;* (*horsecloth*) housse *f;* (mach) enchâssure *f,* carter *m*

hous'ing devel'oper *s* promoteur *m* immobilier

hous'ing devel'opment *s* grand ensemble *m,* habitations *fpl* neuves, ensemble immobilier, lotissement *m,* complexe *m* résidentiel

hous'ing pro'ject *s* (*apartments*) projet *m* immobilier, cité *f*

hous'ing short'age *s* crise *f* du logement

hovel ['hʌvəl] *s* bicoque *f,* masure *f;* (*shed for cattle, tools, etc.*) appentis *m,* cabane *f*

hover ['hʌvər] *intr* planer, voltiger; (*to move to and fro near a person*) papillonner; (*to hang around threateningly*) rôder; (*said of smile on lips*) errer; hésiter

Hovercraft ['hʌvər,kræft] *s* (trademark) aéroglisseur *m*

how [haʊ] *s* comment *m;* **the how, the when, and the wherefore** (coll) tous les détails ‖ *adv* comment; **how** + *adj* quel + *adj,* e.g., **how beautiful a morning!** quelle belle matinée!; comme + c'est + *adj,* e.g., **how beautiful it is!** comme c'est beau!; que + c'est + *adj,* e.g., **how beautiful it is!** que c'est beau!; **how are you?** comment allez-vous?, ça va?' **how early** quand, à quelle heure; **how else** de quelle autre manière; **how far** jusqu'où; à quelle distance, e.g., **how far is it?** à quelle distance est-ce?; **how long** (*in time*) jusqu'à quand, combien de temps; **how long is the stick?** quelle est la longueur du bâton?; **how many** combien; **how much** combien; (*at what price*) combien; **how often** combien de fois; **how old are you?** quel âge avez-vous?; **how soon** quand, à quelle heure; **how to order** mode *m* de commande; **to know how to** savoir

how-do-you-do ['haʊdəjə'du] *s*—**that's a fine how-do-you-do!** (coll) en voilà une affaire!

how•ev'er *adv* cependant, pourtant, toutefois; **however little it may be** si peu que ce soit; **however much** or **many it may be** autant que ce soit; **however pretty she may be** quelque jolie qu'elle soit; **however that may be**

quoi qu'il en soit ‖ *conj* comme, e.g., **do it however you want** faites-le comme vous voudrez

howitzer [ˈhaʊ•ɪtsər] *s* obusier *m*

howl [haʊl] *s* hurlement *m* ‖ *tr* hurler; **to howl down** faire taire en poussant des huées ‖ *intr* hurler; (*said of wind*) mugir

howler [ˈhaʊlər] *s* hurleur *m;* (coll) grosse gaffe *f,* bourde *f,* bévue *f*

hoyden [ˈhɔɪdən] *s* petite coquine *f*

H.P. or **hp** *abbr* (**horsepower**) CV

hub [hʌb] *s* moyeu *m;* (fig) centre *m*

hubbub [ˈhʌbəb] *s* vacarme *m,* tumulte *m*

hub′cap′ *s* enjoliveur *m,* chapeau *m* de roue

huckster [ˈhʌkstər] *s* (*peddler*) camelot *m;* (*adman*) publicitaire *mf*

huddle [ˈhʌdəl] *s* (coll) conférence *f* secrète; **to go into a huddle** (coll) entrer en conclave ‖ *intr* s'entasser, se presser

hue [hju] *s* teinte *f,* nuance *f*

hue′ and cry′ *s* clameur *f* de haro; **with hue and cry** à cor et à cri

huff [hʌf] *s* accès *m* de colère; **in a huff** vexé, offensé

hug [hʌg] *s* étreinte *f* ‖ *v* (*pret & pp* **hugged;** *ger* **hugging**) *tr* étreindre; (*e.g., the coast*) serrer; (*e.g., the wall*) raser ‖ *intr* s'étreindre

huge [hjudʒ] *adj* énorme, immense

huh [hʌ] *interj* hein!, hé!

hulk [hʌlk] *s* (*body of an old ship*) carcasse *f;* (*old ship used as warehouse, prison, etc.*) ponton *m;* (*heavy, unwieldy person*) mastodonte *m*

hulking [ˈhʌlkɪŋ] *adj* massif, pesant, gros

hull [hʌl] *s* (*of certain vegetables*) cosse *f;* (*of nuts*) écale *f;* (*of ship or hydroplane*) coque *f* ‖ *tr* (*e.g., peas*) écosser; (*e.g., almonds*) écaler

hullabaloo [ˈhʌləbəˌlu] *s* (coll) boucan *m,* brouhaha *m*

hum [hʌm] *s* (*e.g., of bee*) bourdonnement *m;* (*e.g., of motor*) vrombissement *m;* (*of singer*) fredonnement *m* ‖ *v* (*pret & pp* **hummed;** *ger* **humming**) *tr* (*a melody*) fredonner, chantonner ‖ *intr* (*said of bee*) bourdonner; (*said of machine*) vrombir; (*said of singer*) fredonner, chantonner; (*to be active*) (coll) aller rondement ‖ *interj* hum!

human [ˈhjumən] *adj* humain

hu′man be′ing *s* être *m* humain

humane [hjuˈmen] *adj* humain, compatissant

hu′man immun′odefi′ciency vi′rus (HIV) *s* virus *m* de l'immunodéficience humaine (VIH)

humanist [ˈhjumənɪst] *adj & s* humaniste *m*

humanitarian [hjuˌmænɪˈtɛrɪ•ən] *adj & s* humanitaire *mf*

humani•ty [hjuˈmænɪti] *s* (*pl* **-ties**) humanité *f;* **humanities** (*Greek and Latin classics*) humanités classiques; (*belles-lettres*) humanités modernes

hu′man•kind′ *s* genre *m* humain

humble [ˈhʌmbəl], [ˈʌmbəl] *adj* humble ‖ *tr* humilier; **to humble oneself** s'humilier

hum′ble pie′ *s*—**to eat humble pie** faire amende honorable, s'humilier

hum′bug′ *s* blague *f;* (*person*) imposteur *m* ‖ *v* (*pret & pp* **-bugged;** *ger* **-bugging**) *tr* mystifier

hum′drum′ *adj* monotone, banal

humer•us [ˈhjumərəs] *s* (*pl* **-i** [ˌaɪ]) humérus *m*

humid [ˈhjumɪd] *adj* humide, moite

humidifier [hjuˈmɪdɪˌfaɪ•ər] *s* humidificateur *m*

humidi•fy [hjuˈmɪdɪˌfaɪ] *v* (*pret & pp* **-fied**) *tr* humidifier

humidity [hjuˈmɪdɪti] *s* humidité *f*

humiliate [hjuˈmɪlɪˌet] *tr* humilier

humiliating [hjuˈmɪlɪˌetɪŋ] *adj* humiliant

humili•ty [hjuˈmɪlɪti] *s* (*pl* **-ties**) humilité *f*

hum′ming•bird′ *s* oiseau-mouche *m,* colibri *m*

humor [ˈhjumər], [ˈjumər] *s* (*comic quality*) humor *m;* (*frame of mind; fluid*) humeur *f;* **out of humor** maussade, grognon; **to be in the humor to** être d'humeur à ‖ *tr* ménager, satisfaire; (*s.o.'s fancies*) se plier à, accéder à

humorist [ˈhjumərɪst], [ˈjumərɪst] *s* humoriste *mf,* comique *mf*

humorous [ˈhjumərəs], [ˈjumərəs] *adj* humoristique; (*writer*) humoriste

hump [hʌmp] *s* bosse *f*

hump′back′ *s* bossu *m;* (*whale*) mégaptère *m*

humus [ˈhjuməs] *s* humus *m*

hunch [hʌntʃ] *s* (*hump*) bosse *f;* (*premonition*) (coll) pressentiment *m* ‖ *tr* arrondir, voûter ‖ *intr* s'accroupir

hunch′back′ *s* bossu *m*

hundred [ˈhʌndrəd] *adj* cent ‖ *s* cent *m,* centaine *f;* **about a hundred** une centaine; **a hundred** or **one hundred** cent; une centaine; **by the hundreds** par centaines

hun′dred•fold′ *adj & s* centuple *m;* **to increase a hundredfold** centupler ‖ *adv* au centuple

hundredth [ˈhʌndrədθ] *adj, pron, & s* centième *m*

hun′dred•weight′ *s* quintal *m*

Hungarian [hʌŋˈgɛrɪ•ən] *adj* hongrois ‖ *s* (*language*) hongrois *m;* (*person*) Hongrois *m*

Hungary [ˈhʌŋgəri] *s* Hongrie *f;* la Hongrie

hunger [ˈhʌŋgər] *s* faim *f* ‖ *intr* avoir faim; **to hunger for** être affamé de

hun′ger march′ *s* marche *f* de la faim

hun′ger strike′ *s* grève *f* de la faim

hun•gry [ˈhʌŋgri] *adj* (*comp* **-grier;** *super* **-griest**) affamé; **to be hungry** avoir faim

hunk [hʌŋk] *s* gros morceau *m*

hunt [hʌnt] *s* (*act of hunting*) chasse *f;* (*hunting party*) équipage *m* de chasse; **on the hunt for** à la recherche de; **to use the hunt-and-peck system** taper à tâtons ‖ *tr* chasser; (*to seek, look for*) chercher; **to hunt down** donner la chasse à, traquer; **to hunt out** faire la chasse à ‖ *intr* chasser; (*with dogs*) chasser à courre; **to go hunting** aller à la chasse; **to hunt for** chercher; **to take hunting** emmener à la chasse

hunter [ˈhʌntər] *s* chasseur *m*

hunting [ˈhʌntɪŋ] *adj* de chasse ‖ *s* chasse *f*

hunt′ing dog′ s chien m de chasse
hunt′ing ground′ s terrain m de chasse, chasse f
hunt′ing horn′ s cor m de chasse
hunt′ing jack′et s paletot m de chasse
hunt′ing knife′ s couteau m de chasse
hunt′ing li′cense s permis m de chasse
hunt′ing lodge′ s pavillon m de chasse
hunt′ing per′mit s permis m de chasse
hunt′ing sea′son s saison f de la chasse
huntress [ˈhʌntrɪs] s chasseuse f
hunts′ man s (pl **-men**) chasseur m
hurdle [ˈhʌrdəl] s (hedge over which horses jump) haie f; (wooden frame over which runners jump) barrière f; (fig) obstacle m; **hurdles** course f d'obstacles ‖ tr sauter
hur′dle race′ s course f d'obstacles; (turf) course de haies
hurdy-gur•dy [ˈhʌrdiˈɡʌrdi] s (pl **-dies**) orgue m de Barbarie
hurl [hʌrl] s lancée f ‖ tr lancer; **to hurl back** repousser, refouler
hurrah [hʌˈrɑ] or **hurray** [hʊˈre] s hourra m ‖ interj hourra!; **hurrah for…!** vive…!
hurricane [ˈhʌrɪˌken] s ouragan m, hurricane m
hurried [ˈhʌrid] adj pressé, précipité; (hasty) hâtif, fait à la hâte
hur•ry [ˈhʌri] s (pl **-ries**) hâte f; **to be in a hurry** être pressé ‖ v (pret & pp **-ried**) tr hâter, presser ‖ intr se hâter, se presser; **to hurry after** courir après; **to hurry away** s'en aller bien vite; **to hurry back** revenir vite; **to hurry over** venir vite; **to hurry up** se dépêcher
hurt [hʌrt] adj blessé ‖ s blessure f; (pain) douleur f ‖ v (pret & pp **hurt**) tr faire mal à ‖ intr faire mal, e.g., **does that hurt?** ça fait mal?; avoir mal, e.g., **my head hurts** j'ai mal à la tête
hurtful [ˈhʌrtfəl] adj nuisible
hurtle [ˈhʌrtəl] intr se précipiter
husband [ˈhʌzbənd] s mari m, époux m ‖ tr ménager, économiser
hus′band•man s (pl **-men**) cultivateur m
husbandry [ˈhʌzbəndri] s agriculture f; (raising of livestock) élevage m
hush [hʌʃ] s silence m, calme m ‖ tr faire taire; **to hush up** (e.g., a scandal) étouffer ‖ intr se taire ‖ interj chut!
hushaby [ˈhʌʃəˌbaɪ] interj fais dodo!
hush′-hush′ adj très secret
hush′ mon′ey s prix m du silence
husk [hʌsk] s (of certain vegetables) cosse f, gousse f; (of nuts) écale f; (of corn) enveloppe f; (of oats) balle f; (of onion) pelure f ‖ tr (grain) vanner; (vegetables) éplucher; (peas) écosser; (nuts) écaler
husk′ing bee′ s réunion f pour l'épluchage du maïs
husk•y [ˈhʌski] adj (comp **-ier**; super **-iest**) (burly) costaud; (hoarse) enroué ‖ s (pl **-ies**) (dog) chien m esquimau
hus•sy [ˈhʌsi] s (pl **-sies**) (coll) coquine f, mâtine f; (pej) garce f, traînée f

hustle [ˈhʌsəl] s (coll) bousculade f, énergie f, allant m ‖ tr pousser, bousculer ‖ intr se dépêcher, se presser; (to work hard) (coll) se démener, s'activer
hustler [ˈhʌslər] s (go-getter) homme m d'action; (swindler) (slang) filou m; (streetwalker) (slang) traînée f, grue f
hut [hʌt] s hutte f, cabane f; (mil) baraque f
hutch [hʌtʃ] s (for rabbits) clapier m; (used by baker) huche f, pétrin m
hyacinth [ˈhaɪəsɪnθ] s (stone) hyacinthe f; (flower) jacinthe f
hybrid [ˈhaɪbrɪd] adj & s hybride m
hy•dra [ˈhaɪdrə] s (pl **-dras** or **-drae** [dri]) hydre f
hydrant [ˈhaɪdrənt] s prise f d'eau; (faucet) robinet m; (fire hydrant) bouche f d'incendie
hydrate [ˈhaɪdret] s hydrate m ‖ tr hydrater ‖ intr s'hydrater
hydraulic [haɪˈdrɔlɪk] adj hydraulique ‖ **hydraulics** s hydraulique f
hydrau′lic lift′ s vérin m hydraulique
hydrau′lic ram′ s bélier m hydraulique
hydrau′lic suspen′sion s suspension f hydraulique
hydrocarbon [ˌhaɪdrəˈkɑrbən] s hydrocarbure m
hy′drochlo′ric ac′id [ˌhaɪdrəˈklɔrɪk] s acide m chlorhydrique
hydroelectric [ˌhaɪdroˈɪˈlɛktrɪk] adj hydro-électrique
hydrofoil [ˈhaɪdrəˌfɔɪl] s hydrofoil m, hydroptère m
hydrogen [ˈhaɪdrədʒən] s hydrogène m
hy′drogen bomb′ s bombe f à hydrogène
hy′drogen perox′ide s eau f oxygénée
hy′drogen sul′fide s hydrogène m sulfuré
hydrometer [haɪˈdrɑmɪtər] s aréomètre m, hydromètre m
hydrophobia [ˌhaɪdrəˈfobɪ•ə] s hydrophobie f
hydroplane [ˈhaɪdrəˌplen] s hydravion m
hydroxide [haɪˈdrɑksaɪd] s hydroxyde m
hyena [haɪˈinə] s hyène f
hygiene [ˈhaɪdʒin] s hygiène f
hygienic [ˌhaɪdʒɪˈɛnɪk] adj hygiénique
hymn [hɪm] s hymne m; (eccl) hymne f, cantique m
hymnal [ˈhɪmnəl] s livre m d'hymnes
hymen [ˈhaɪmən] s hymen m
hyper [ˈhaɪpər] adj hyperactif
hyperacidity [ˌhaɪpərəˈsɪdɪti] s hyperacidité f
hy′per•ac′tive adj & s hyperactif m
hyperactivity [ˌhaɪpəræˈktɪvəti] s suractivité f
hyperbola [haɪˈpʌrbələ] s hyperbole f
hyperbole [haɪˈpʌrbəli] s hyperbole f
hy′per•link′ s (comp) hyperconnexion f
hypersensitive [ˌhaɪpərˈsɛnsɪtɪv] adj hypersensible, hypersensitif
hypertension [ˌhaɪpərˈtɛnʃən] s hypertension f
hy′per•text′ s (comp) hypertexte m
hy′per•ven′tila′tion s hyperventilation f
hyphen [ˈhaɪfən] s trait m d'union

hyphenate [ˈhaɪfəˌnet] *tr* joindre avec un trait d'union
hypno•sis [hɪpˈnosɪs] *s* (*pl* **-ses** [siz]) hypnose *f*
hypnotic [hɪpˈnɑtɪk] *adj & s* hypnotique *m*
hypnotism [ˈhɪpnəˌtɪzəm] *s* hypnotisme *m*
hypnotist [ˈhɪpnətɪst] *s* hypnotiseur *m*
hypnotize [ˈhɪpnəˌtaɪz] *tr* hypnotiser
hypochondriac [ˌhaɪpəˈkɑndrɪˌæk] *adj & s* hypocondriaque *mf*
hypocri•sy [hɪˈpɑkrəsɪ] *s* (*pl* **-sies**) hypocrisie *f*
hypocrite [ˈhɪpəkrɪt] *s* hypocrite *mf*
hypocritical [ˌhɪpəˈkrɪtɪkəl] *adj* hypocrite

hypodermic [ˌhaɪpəˈdʌrmɪk] *adj* hypodermique
hyposulfite [ˌhaɪpəˈsʌlfaɪt] *s* hyposulfite *m*
hypotenuse [haɪˈpɑtɪˌn(j)us] *s* hypoténuse *f*
hypothe•sis [haɪˈpɑθɪsɪs] (*pl* **-ses** [ˌsiz]) hypothèse *f*
hypothetic(al) [ˌhaɪpəˈθɛtɪk(əl)] *adj* hypothétique
hysteria [hɪsˈtɪrɪ•ə] *s* agitation *f*, frénésie *f*; (pathol) hystérie *f*
hysteric [hɪsˈtɛrɪk] *adj* hystérique ‖ **hysterics** *spl* crise *f* de nerfs, crise de larmes, fou rire *m*
hysterical [hɪsˈtɛrɪkəl] *adj* hystérique

I

I, i [aɪ] *s* IXe lettre de l'alphabet
I *pron* je §87; moi §85
iambic [aɪˈæmbɪk] *adj* ïambique
Iberian [aɪˈbɪrɪ•ən] *adj* ibérien, ibérique ‖ *s* Ibérien *m*
ibex [ˈaɪbɛks] *s* (*pl* **ibexes** or **ibices** [ˈɪbɪˌsiz]) bouquetin *m*
ice [aɪs] *s* glace *f*; **to break the ice** (fig) rompre la glace; **to cut no ice** (coll) ne rien casser, ne pas prendre; **to skate on thin ice** (coll) s'engager sur un terrain dangereux ‖ *tr* glacer; (*e.g., champagne*) frapper; (*e.g., melon*) rafraîchir ‖ *intr* geler; **to ice up** (*said of windshield, airplane wings, etc.*) se givrer
ice′ age′ *s* époque *f* glaciaire
ice′ bag′ *s* sac *m* à glace
ice′ bank′ *s* banquise *f*
iceberg [ˈaɪsˌbʌrg] *s* banquise *f*, iceberg *m*; (*person*) (coll) glaçon *m*
ice′ boat′ *s* (*icebreaker*) brise-glace *m*; (*for sport*) bateau *m* à patins
icebound [ˈaɪsˌbaʊnd] *adj* pris dans les glaces
ice′ box′ *s* glacière *f*
ice′ break′er *s* brise-glace *m*
ice′ cap′ *s* calotte *f* glaciaire
ice′-cream′ *s* glace *f*
ice′-cream′ cone′ *s* cornet *m* de glace, glace *f* en cornet
ice′-cream′ freez′er *s* sorbetière *f*
ice′ crush′er *s* broyeur *m* de glace
ice′ cube′ *s* glaçon *m*
ice′-cube′ tray′ *s* bac *m* à glaçons
iced′ tea′ *s* thé *m* glacé
ice′ floe′ *s* banquise *f*
ice′ hock′ey *s* hockey *m* sur glace
ice′ jam′ *s* embâcle *m*
Iceland [ˈaɪslənd] *s* Islande *f*; l'Islande
Icelander [ˈaɪsˌlændər] *s* Islandais *m*
Icelandic [aɪsˈlændɪk] *adj & s* islandais *m*
ice′ man′ *s* (*pl* **-men′**) glacier *m*
ice′ pack′ *s* (*pack ice*) embâcle *m*; (med) vessie *f* de glace

ice′ pail′ *s* seau *m* à glace
ice′ pick′ *s* poinçon *m* à glace; (*of mountain climber*) piolet *m*
ice′ resur′facer *s* lisseuse *f*
ice′ skate′ *s* patin *m* à glace ‖ *intr* patiner (sur glace), faire du patin à glace
ice′ skat′er *s* patineur *m*, patineuse *f*
ice′ skat′ing *s* patinage *m* à glace
ice′ tray′ *s* bac *m* à glaçons
ice′ wa′ter *s* eau *f* glacée *f*
ichthyology [ˌɪkθɪˈɑlədʒi] *s* ichtyologie *f*
icicle [ˈaɪsɪkəl] *s* glaçon *m*, chandelle *f* de glace
icing [ˈaɪsɪŋ] *s* (*on cake*) glaçage *m*; (aer) givrage *m*
icon [ˈaɪkɑn] *s* icône *f*
iconoclast [aɪˈkɑnəˌklæst] *s* iconoclaste *mf*
iconoclastic [aɪˌkɑnəˈklæstɪk] *adj* iconoclaste
Iconoscope [aɪˈkɑnəˌskop] *s* (trademark) iconoscope *m*
icy [ˈaɪsi] *adj* (*comp* **icier**; *super* **iciest**) glacé; (*slippery*) glissant; (fig) froid, glacial
I.D. *abbr* **identification card, identity card**
I'd *contr* **I would**
idea [aɪˈdi•ə] *s* idée *f*; **the very idea!** par exemple!
ideal [aɪˈdi•əl] *adj & s* idéal *m*
idealist [aɪˈdi•əlɪst] *adj & s* idéaliste *mf*
idealistic [aɪˌdɪ•əlˈɪstɪk] *adj* idéaliste
idealize [aɪˈdi•əˌlaɪz] *tr* idéaliser
identic(al) [aɪˈdɛntɪk(əl)] *adj* identique
identification [aɪˌdɛntɪfɪˈkeʃen] *s* identification *f*
identifica′tion card′ *s* carte *f* d'identité
identifica′tion tag′ *s* plaque *f* d'identité
identi•fy [aɪˈdɛntɪˌfaɪ] *v* (*pret & pp* **-fied**) *tr* identifier
identi•ty [aɪˈdɛntɪti] *s* (*pl* **-ties**) identité *f*
iden′tity card′ *s* carte *f* d'identité
iden′tity tag′ *s* plaque *f* d'identité
ideolo•gy [ˌaɪdɪˈɑlədʒi] *s* (*pl* **-gies**) idéologie *f*
ides [aɪdz] *spl* ides *fpl*
idio•cy [ˈɪdɪ•əsi] *s* (*pl* **-cies**) idiotie *f*

idiolect [ˈɪdɪ•ə,lɛkt] *s* idiolecte *m*

idiom [ˈɪdɪ•əm] *s* (*expression that is contrary to the usual patterns of the language*) idiotisme *m;* (*the linguistic communication used in a country or community*) idiome *m*, langue *f;* (*individual linguistic style of a person or of a group*) langage *m*, idiolecte *m*

idiomatic [,ɪdɪ•əˈmætɪk] *adj* idiomatique

idiosyncra•sy [,ɪdɪ•əˈsɪnkrəsi] *s* (*pl* **-sies**) idiosyncrasie *f*

idiot [ˈɪdɪ•ət] *s* idiot *m*

idiotic [,ɪdɪˈɑtɪk] *adj* idiot

idle [ˈaɪdəl] *adj* oisif, désœuvré; (*futile*) oiseux; **to run idle** marcher au ralenti ‖ *tr*—**to idle away** (*time*) passer à ne rien faire ‖ *intr* fainéanter; (*mach*) tourner au ralenti

idleness [ˈaɪdəlnɪs] *s* oisiveté *f*

idler [ˈaɪdlər] *s* oisif *m*

idling [ˈaɪdlɪŋ] *s* (*of motor*) ralenti *m*

idol [ˈaɪdəl] *s* idole *f*

idola•try [aɪˈdɑlətri] *s* (*pl* **-tries**) idolâtrie *f*

idolize [ˈaɪdə,laɪz] *tr* idolâtrer

idyll [ˈaɪdəl] *s* idylle *f*

idyllic [aɪˈdɪlɪk] *adj* idyllique

i.e. *abbr* (Lat **id est** that is) c.-à-d., à savoir

if [ɪf] *s*—**ifs and buts** des si et des mais ‖ *conj* si; **even if** quand même; **if it is true that** si tant est que; **if not** sinon; **if so** dans ce cas, s'il en est ainsi

ignis fatuus [ˈɪgnɪsˈfætʃu•əs] *s* (*pl* **ignes fatui** [ˈɪgnizˈfætʃu,aɪ]) feu *m* follet

ignite [ɪgˈnaɪt] *tr* allumer ‖ *intr* prendre feu

ignition [ɪgˈnɪʃən] *s* ignition *f;* (*aut*) allumage *m;* **to switch on the ignition** mettre le contact

igni′tion coil′ *s* (aut) bobine *f* d'allumage

igni′tion key′ *s* clef *m* de contact, clef d'allumage

igni′tion switch′ *s* (aut) contact *m*

ignoble [ɪgˈnobəl] *adj* ignoble

ignominious [,ɪgnəˈmɪnɪ•əs] *adj* ignominieux

ignoramus [,ɪgnəˈreməs] *s* ignorant *m*

ignorance [ˈɪgnərəns] *s* ignorance *f*

ignorant [ˈɪgnərənt] *adj* ignorant; **to be ignorant of** ignorer

ignore [ɪgˈnor] *tr* ne pas tenir compte de, ne pas faire attention à; (*a suggestion*) passer outre à; (*to snub*) faire semblant de ne pas voir, ignorer à dessein

iguana [ɪˈgwɑnə] *s* iguane *m*

ilk [ɪlk] *s* espèce *f;* **of that ilk** de cet acabit

I'll *contr* **I will**

ill [ɪl] *adj* (*comp* **worse** [wʌrs]; *super* **worst** [wʌrst]) malade, souffrant ‖ *adv* mal; **to take ill** prendre en mauvaise part; (*to get sick*) tomber malade

ill′-advised′ *adj* (*person*) malavisé; (*action*) peu judicieux

ill′ at ease′ *adj* mal à l'aise, gêné

ill-bred [ˈɪlˈbrɛd] *adj* mal élevé

ill′-consid′ered *adj* peu réfléchi, hâtif

ill′-disposed′ *adj* mal disposé, malintentionné

illegal [ɪˈligəl] *adj* illégal

illegible [ɪˈlɛdʒɪbəl] *adj* illisible

illegitimate [,ɪlɪˈdʒɪtɪmɪt] *adj* illégitime

ill′-famed′ *adj* mal famé

ill′-fat′ed *adj* malheureux, infortuné

ill-gotten [ˈɪlˈgɑtən] *adj* mal acquis

ill′ health′ *s* mauvaise santé *f*

ill′-hu′mored *adj* de mauvaise humeur, maussade

illicit [ɪˈlɪsɪt] *adj* illicite

illitera•cy [ɪˈlɪtərəsi] *s* (*pl* **-cies**) ignorance *f;* analphabétisme *m*

illiterate [ɪˈlɪtərɪt] *adj* (*uneducated*) ignorant, illettré; (*unable to read or write*) analphabète ‖ *s* analphabète *mf*

ill′-man′nered *adj* malappris, mal élevé

ill′-na′tured *adj* désagréable, méchant

illness [ˈɪlnɪs] *s* maladie *f*

illogical [ɪˈlɑdʒɪkəl] *adj* illogique

ill-spent [ˈɪlˈspɛnt] *adj* gaspillé

ill′-starred′ *adj* néfaste, de mauvais augure

ill′-tem′pered *adj* désagréable, de mauvais caractère

ill′-timed′ *adj* intempestif, mal à propos

ill′-treat′ *tr* maltraiter, rudoyer

illuminate [ɪˈlumɪ,net] *tr* illuminer; (*a manuscript*) enluminer

illu′minating gas′ *s* gaz *m* d'éclairage

illumination [ɪˈlumɪˈneʃən] *s* illumination *f;* (*in manuscript*) enluminure *f*

illusion [ɪˈluʒən] *s* illusion *f*

illusive [ɪˈlusɪv] *adj* illusoire, trompeur

illusory [ɪˈlusəri] *adj* illusoire

illustrate [ˈɪləs,tret] *tr* illustrer

illustration *s* [,ɪləsˈtreʃən] *s* illustration *f;* (*explanation*) explication *f*, éclaircissement *m*

illustrative [ɪˈlʌstrətɪv] *adj* explicatif, éclairant

illustrator [ˈɪləs,tretər] *s* illustrateur *m*, dessinateur *m*

illustrious [ɪˈlʌstrɪ•əs] *adj* illustre

ill′ will′ *s* rancune *f*

I'm *contr* **I am**

image [ˈɪmɪdʒ] *s* image *f*

im′age map′ *s* (comp) carte *f* mère

image•ry [ˈɪmɪdʒri] *s* (*pl* **-ries**) images *fpl*

imaginary [ɪˈmædʒɪ,nɛri] *adj* imaginaire

imagination [ɪ,mædʒɪˈneʃən] *s* imagination *f*

imagine [ɪˈmædʒɪn] *tr* imaginer, s'imaginer ‖ *intr* imaginer; **imagine!** figurez-vous!

imbecile [ˈɪmbɪsɪl] *adj & s* imbécile *mf*

imbecili•ty [,ɪmbɪˈsɪlɪti] *s* (*pl* **-ties**) imbécillité *f*

imbibe [ɪmˈbaɪb] *tr* absorber ‖ *intr* boire, lever le coude

imbue [ɪmˈbju] *tr* imprégner, pénétrer; **imbued with** imbu de

imitate [ˈɪmɪ,tet] *tr* imiter

imitation [,ɪmɪˈteʃən] *adj* d'imitation ‖ *s* imitation *f*

imitator [ˈɪmɪ,tetər] *s* imitateur *m*

immaculate [ɪˈmækjəlɪt] *adj* immaculé

Immac′ulate Concep′tion *s* (rel) Immaculée Conception *f*

immaterial [,ɪməˈtɪrɪ•əl] *adj* immatériel;

(*pointless*) sans conséquence; **it's immaterial to me** cela m'est égal

immature [ˌɪmə'tjʊr] *adj* pas mûr, peu mûr; pas adulte

immeasurable [ɪ'mɛʒərəbəl] *adj* immensurable

immediacy [ɪ'midɪ•əsi] *s* caractère *m* immédiat, imminence *f*

immediate [ɪ'midɪ•ɪt] *adj* immédiat

immediately [ɪ'midɪ•ɪtli] *adv* immédiatement

immemorial [ˌɪmɪ'morɪ•əl] *adj* immémorial

immense [ɪ'mɛns] *adj* immense

immerse [ɪ'mʌrs] *tr* immerger, plonger

immersion [ɪ'mʌrʒən] *s* immersion *f*

immigrant ['ɪmɪgrənt] *adj* & *s* immigrant *m*

immigrate ['ɪmɪˌgret] *intr* immigrer

immigration [ˌɪmɪ'greʃən] *s* immigration *f*

imminent ['ɪmɪnənt] *adj* imminent, très prochain

immobile [ɪ'mobɪl] *adj* immobile

immobilize [ɪ'mobɪˌlaɪz] *tr* immobiliser

immoderate [ɪ'madərɪt] *adj* immodéré

immodest [ɪ'madɪst] *adj* impudique

immoral [ɪ'morəl] *adj* immoral

immortal [ɪ'mortəl] *adj* & *s* immortel *m*

immortalize [ɪ'mortəˌlaɪz] *tr* immortaliser

immune [ɪ'mjun] *adj* dispensé, exempt; (med) immunisé

immune′ sys′tem *s* système *m* immunitaire

immunize ['ɪmjəˌnaɪz] *tr* immuniser

immunodeficiency ['ɪmjənodɪ'fɪʃənsi] *s* immunodéficience *f*

imp [ɪmp] *s* suppôt *m* du diable; (*child*) diablotin *m*, polisson *m*

impact ['ɪmpækt] *s* impact *m*

impair [ɪm'pɛr] *tr* endommager, affaiblir; (*health, digestion*) délabrer

impan•el [ɪm'pænəl] *v* (*pret* & *pp* **-eled** or **-elled**; *ger* **-eling** or **-elling**) *tr* appeler à faire partie de; (*a jury*) dresser la liste de

impart [ɪm'part] *tr* imprimer, communiquer; (*to make known*) communiquer

impartial [ɪm'parʃəl] *adj* impartial

impassable [ɪm'pæsəbəl] *adj* (*road*) impraticable; (*mountain*) infranchissable

impassible [ɪm'pæsɪbəl] *adj* impassible

impassioned [ɪm'pæʃənd] *adj* passionné

impassive [ɪm'pæsɪv] *adj* insensible; (*look, face*) impassible, composé

impatience [ɪm'peʃəns] *s* impatience *f*

impatient [ɪm'peʃənt] *adj* impatient

impeach [ɪm'pitʃ] *tr* accuser; (*s.o.'s honor, veracity*) attaquer; (pol) entamer la procédure d'impeachment contre

impeachment [ɪm'pitʃmənt] *s* accusation *f*; (*of honor, veracity*) attaque *f*; (pol) procédure *f* d'impeachment, mise *f* en accusation devant le Sénat, destitution *f*

impeccable [ɪm'pɛkəbəl] *adj* impeccable

impecunious [ˌɪmpɪ'kjunɪ•əs] *adj* besogneux, impécunieux

impede [ɪm'pid] *tr* entraver, empêcher

impediment [ɪm'pɛdɪmənt] *s* obstacle *m*, empêchement *m*

im•pel [ɪm'pɛl] *v* (*pret* & *pp* **-pelled;** *ger* **-pelling**) *tr* pousser, forcer

impending [ɪm'pɛndɪŋ] *adj* imminent

impenetrable [ɪm'pɛnətrəbəl] *adj* impénétrable

impenitent [ɪm'pɛnɪtənt] *adj* impénitent *m*

imperative [ɪ'pɛrɪtɪv] *adj* & *s* impératif *m*

imperceptible [ˌɪmpər'sɛptɪbəl] *adj* imperceptible

imperfect [ɪm'pʌrfɪkt] *adj* & *s* imparfait *m*

imperfection [ˌɪmpər'fɛkʃən] *s* imperfection *f*

imperforate [ɪm'pʌrfərɛt] *adj* (phila) nondentelé

imperial [ɪm'pɪrɪ•əl] *adj* impérial

imperialist [ɪm'pɪrɪ•əlɪst] *adj* & *s* impérialiste *mf*

imper•il [ɪm'pɛrɪl] *v* (*pret* & *pp* **-iled** or **-illed;** *ger* **-iling** or **illing**) *tr* mettre en péril, exposer au danger

imperious [ɪm'pɪrɪ•əs] *adj* impérieux

imperishable [ɪm'pɛrɪʃəbəl] *adj* impérissable

impersonal [ɪm'pʌrsənəl] *adj* impersonnel

impersonate [ɪm'pʌrsəˌnet] *tr* contrefaire, singer; jouer le rôle de

impertinent [ɪm'pʌrtɪnənt] *adj* impertinent

impetuous [ɪm'pɛtʃʊ•əs] *adj* impétueux

impetus ['ɪmpɪtəs] *s* impulsion *f*; (mech) force *f* impulsive; (fig) élan *m*

impie•ty [ɪm'paɪ•əti] *s* (*pl* **-ties**) impiété *f*

impinge [ɪm'pɪndʒ] *intr*—**to impinge on** or **upon** empiéter sur; (*to violate*) enfreindre

impious ['ɪmpɪ•əs] *adj* impie

impish ['ɪmpɪʃ] *adj* espiègle

implacable [ɪm'plekəbəl] *adj* implacable

implant [ɪm'plænt] *tr* implanter

implement ['ɪmplɪmənt] *s* outil *m*, ustensile *m* ‖ *tr* mettre en œuvre, réaliser; (*to provide with implements*) outiller

implicate ['ɪmplɪˌket] *tr* impliquer

implicit [ɪm'plɪsɪt] *adj* implicite

implied [ɪm'plaɪd] *adj* implicite, sousentendu

implore [ɪm'plor] *tr* implorer, supplier, solliciter

im•ply [ɪm'plaɪ] *v* (*pret* & *pp* **-plied**) *tr* impliquer

impolite [ˌɪmpə'laɪt] *adj* impoli

import ['ɪmport] *s* importance *f*; (*meaning*) sens *m*, signification *f*; (*extent*) portée *f*; (com) article *m* d'importation; **imports** importations *fpl* ‖ *tr* importer; (*to mean*) signifier, vouloir dire

importance [ɪm'portəns] *s* importance *f*

important [ɪm'portənt] *adj* important

importer [ɪm'portər] *s* importateur *m*

importune [ˌɪmpor't(j)un] *tr* importuner, harceler

impose [ɪm'poz] *tr* imposer ‖ *intr*—**to impose on** or **upon** en imposer à, abuser de

imposing [ɪm'pozɪŋ] *adj* imposant

imposition [ˌɪmpə'zɪʃən] *s* (*laying on of a burden or obligation*) imposition *f*; (*rudeness, taking unfair advantage*) abus *m*

impossible [ɪmˈpɑsɪbəl] *adj* impossible

impostor [ɪmˈpɑstər] *s* imposteur *m*

imposture [ɪmˈpɑstjər] *s* imposture *f*

impotence [ˈɪmpətəns] *s* impuissance *f*

impotent [ˈɪmpətənt] *adj* impuissant

impound [ɪmˈpaʊnd] *tr* confisquer, saisir; (*a dog, an auto, etc.*) mettre en fourrière

impoverish [ɪmˈpɑvərɪʃ] *tr* appauvrir

impracticable [ɪmˈpræktɪkəbəl] *adj* impraticable, inexécutable

impractical [ɪmˈpræktɪkəl] *adj* peu pratique; (*plan*) impraticable

impregnable [ɪmˈprɛgnəbəl] *adj* imprenable, inexpugnable

impregnate [ɪmˈprɛgnet] *tr* imprégner; (*to make pregnant*) féconder

impresari•o [ˌɪmprɪˈsɑrɪˌo] *s* (*pl* **-os**) imprésario *m*

impress [ɪmˈprɛs] *tr* (*to have an effect on the mind or emotions of*) impressionner; (*to mark by using pressure*) imprimer; (*on the memory*) graver; (mil) enrôler de force; **to impress s.o. with** pénétrer qn de

impression [ɪmˈprɛʃən] *s* impression *f*

impressive [ɪmˈprɛsɪv] *adj* impressionnant

imprint [ˈɪmprɪnt] *s* empreinte *f*; (typ) rubrique *f*, griffe *f* ‖ [ɪmˈprɪnt] *tr* imprimer

imprison [ɪmˈprɪzən] *tr* emprisonner

imprisonment [ɪmˈprɪzənmənt] *s* emprisonnement *m*

improbable [ɪmˈprɑbəbəl] *adj* improbable

impromptu [ɪmˈprɑmpt(j)u] *adj & adv* impromptu ‖ *s* (mus) impromptu *m*

impromp′tu speech′ *s* improvisation *f*, discours *m* improvisé

improper [ɪmˈprɑpər] *adj* (*not the right*) impropre; (*contrary to good taste or decency*) inconvenant, incorrect

improve [ɪmˈpruv] *tr* améliorer, perfectionner ‖ *intr* s'améliorer, se perfectionner

improvement [ɪmˈpruvmənt] *s* amélioration *f*, perfectionnement *m*; (*of a building site*) viabilité *f*

improvident [ɪmˈprɑvɪdənt] *adj* imprévoyant

improvise [ˈɪmprəˌvaɪz] *tr & intr* improviser

imprudent [ɪmˈprudənt] *adj* imprudent

impudent [ˈɪmpjədənt] *adj* impudent, effronté

impugn [ɪmˈpjun] *tr* contester, mettre en doute

impulse [ˈɪmpʌls] *s* impulsion *f*

impulsive [ɪmˈpʌlsɪv] *adj* impulsif

impunity [ɪmˈpjunɪti] *s* impunité *f*

impure [ɪmˈpjʊr] *adj* impur

impuri•ty [ɪmˈpjʊrɪti] *s* (*pl* **-ties**) impureté *f*

impute [ɪmˈpjut] *tr* imputer

in [ɪn] *adv* en dedans, à l'intérieur; (*at home*) à la maison, chez soi; (pol) au pouvoir; **all in** (*tired*) (coll) éreinté; **in here** ici, par ici; **in there** là-dedans, lá ‖ *prep* dans; en; (*inside*) en dedans de, à l'intérieur de; (*in ratios*) sur, e.g., **one in a hundred** un sur cent; **in that** du fait que; **in one's life** de sa vie ‖ *s* (coll) entrée *f*, e.g., **to have an in with** avoir ses entrées chez

inability [ˌɪnəˈbɪlɪti] *s* incapacité *f*, impuissance *f*

inaccessible [ˌɪnækˈsɛsɪbəl] *adj* inaccessible, inabordable

inaccura•cy [ɪnˈækjərəsi] *s* (*pl* **-cies**) inexactitude *f*, infidélité *f*

inaccurate [ɪnˈækjərɪt] *adj* inexact, infidèle

inaction [ɪnˈækʃən] *s* inaction *f*

inactive [ɪnˈæktɪv] *adj* inactif

inactivity [ˌɪnækˈtɪvɪti] *s* inactivité *f*

inadequate [ɪnˈædɪkwɪt] *adj* insuffisant

inadvertent [ˌɪnədˈvʌrtənt] *adj* distrait, étourdi; commis par inadvertance

inadvisable [ˌɪnədˈvaɪzəbəl] *adj* imprudent, peu sage

inane [ɪnˈen] *adj* inepte, absurde

inanimate [ɪnˈænɪmɪt] *adj* inanimé

inappropriate [ˌɪnəˈproprɪ•ɪt] *adj* inapproprié; (*word*) impropre

inarticulate [ˌɪnɑrˈtɪkjəlɪt] *adj* inarticulé; (*person*) muet, incapable de s'exprimer

inartistic [ˌɪnɑrˈtɪstɪk] *adj* peu artistique; (*person*) peu artiste

inasmuch as [ˌɪnəzˈmʌtʃ ˌæz] *conj* attendu que, vu que

inattentive [ˌɪnəˈtɛntɪv] *adj* inattentif

inaudible [ɪnˈɔdɪbəl] *adj* inaudible

inaugural [ɪnˈɔgjərəl] *adj* inaugural ‖ *s* discours *m* d'inauguration

inaugurate [ɪnˈɔgjəˌret] *tr* inaugurer

inauguration [ɪnˌɔgjəˈreʃən] *s* inauguration *f*; (*investiture*) installation *f*

inborn [ˈɪnˌbɔrn] *adj* inné, infus

in′breed′ing *s* croisement *m* consanguin

Inc. *abbr* (**Incorporated**) S.A. (société anonyme)

incandescent [ˌɪnkənˈdɛsənt] *adj* incandescent

incapable [ɪnˈkepəbəl] *adj* incapable

incapacitate [ˌɪnkəˈpæsɪˌtet] *tr* rendre incapable

incarcerate [ɪnˈkɑrsəˌret] *tr* incarcérer

incarnate [ɪnˈkɑrnɪt] *adj* incarné ‖ *tr* incarner

incarnation [ˌɪnkɑrˈneʃən] *s* incarnation *f*

incendiar•y [ɪnˈsɛndɪˌɛri] *adj* incendiaire ‖ *s* (*pl* **-ies**) incendiaire *mf*

incense [ˈɪnsɛns] *s* encens *m* ‖ *tr* (*to burn incense before*) encenser ‖ [ɪnˈsɛns] *tr* exaspérer, irriter

in′cense burn′er *s* brûle-parfum *m*

incentive [ɪnˈsɛntɪv] *adj & s* stimulant *m*

inception [ɪnˈsɛpʃən] *s* début *m*

incessant [ɪnˈsɛsənt] *adj* incessant

incest [ˈɪnsɛst] *s* inceste *m*

incestuous [ɪnˈsɛstʃuˑəs] *adj* incestueux

inch [ɪntʃ] *s* pouce *m*; **by inches** peu à peu, petit à petit; **not to give way an inch** ne pas reculer d'une semelle; **within an inch of** à deux doigts de ‖ *intr*—**to inch along** se déplacer imperceptiblement; **to inch forward** avancer peu à peu

incidence [ˈɪnsɪdəns] *s* incidence *f*; (*range of occurrence*) portée *f*

incident [ˈɪnsɪdənt] *adj & s* incident *m*

incidental [ˌɪnsɪˈdɛntəl] *adj* accidentel, fortuit;

(*expenses*) accessoire ‖ **incidentals** *spl* faux frais *mpl*

incidentally [,ɪnsɪ'dɛntəli] *adv* incidemment, à propos

incinerate [ɪn'sɪnə,ret] *tr* incinérer

incipient [ɪn'sɪpɪ•ənt] *adj* naissant

incision [ɪn'sɪʒən] *s* incision *f*

incisive [ɪn'saɪsɪv] *adj* incisif

incisor [ɪn'saɪzər] *s* incisive *f*

incite [ɪn'saɪt] *tr* inciter

inclement [ɪn'klɛmənt] *adj* inclément

inclination [,ɪnklɪ'neʃən] *s* inclination *f;* (*slope*) inclinaison *f*

incline ['ɪnklaɪn] *s* inclinaison *f,* pente *f* ‖ [ɪn'klaɪn] *tr* incliner ‖ *intr* s'incliner

include [ɪn'klud] *tr* comprendre, comporter; (*to contain*) renfermer; (*e.g., in a letter*) inclure

including [ɪn'kludɪŋ] *prep* y compris; **up to and including page ten** jusqu'à la page dix incluse

inclusive [ɪn'klusɪv] *adj* global; (*including everything*) tout compris; **from Wednesday to Saturday inclusive** de mercredi à samedi inclus; **inclusive of . . .** qui comprend . . . ‖ *adv* inclusivement

incogni•to [ɪn'kagnɪ,to] *adj & adv* incognito ‖ *s* (*pl* **-tos**) incognito *m*

incoherent [,ɪnko'hɪrənt] *adj* incohérent

incombustible [,ɪnkəm'bʌstɪbəl] *adj* incombustible

income ['ɪnkʌm] *s* revenu *m,* revenus; (*annual income*) rentes *fpl,* rentrée *f*

in'come tax' *s* impôt *m* sur le revenu

in'come-tax' blank' *s* feuille *f* d'impôt

in'come-tax return' *s* déclaration *f* de revenus

in' com'ing *adj* entrant, rentrant; (*tide*) montant ‖ *s* arrivée *f*

incomparable [ɪn'kampərəbəl] *adj* incomparable

incompatible [,ɪnkəm'pætɪbəl] *adj* incompatible

incompetent [ɪn'kampɪtənt] *adj & s* incompétent *m,* incapable *mf*

incomplete [,ɪnkəm'plit] *adj* incomplet

incomprehensible [,ɪnkamprɪ'hɛnsɪbəl] *adj* incompréhensible

inconceivable [,ɪnkən'sivəbəl] *adj* inconcevable

inconclusive [,ɪnkən'klusɪv] *adj* peu concluant, non concluant

incongruous [ɪn'kaŋgru•əs] *adj* incongru, impropre; disparate

inconsequential [ɪn,kansɪ'kwɛnʃəl] *adj* sans importance

inconsiderate [,ɪnkən'sɪdərɪt] *adj* inconsidéré

inconsisten•cy [,ɪnkən'sɪstənsi] *s* (*pl* **-cies**) (*lack of coherence; instability*) inconsistance *f;* (*lack of logical connection or uniformity*) inconséquence *f*

inconsistent [,ɪnkən'sɪstənt] *adj* (*lacking coherence of parts; unstable*) inconsistant; (*not agreeing with itself or oneself*) inconséquent

inconspicuous [,ɪnkən'spɪkju•əs] *adj* peu apparent; peu impressionnant

inconstant [ɪn'kanstənt] *adj* inconstant

incontinent [ɪn'kantɪnənt] *adj* incontinent

incontrovertible [,ɪnkantrə'vʌtɪbəl] *adj* incontestable

inconvenience [,ɪnkən'vinɪ•əns] *s* incommodité *f* ‖ *tr* incommoder, gêner

inconvenient [,ɪnkən'vinɪ•ənt] *adj* incommode, gênant; (*time*) inopportun

incorporate [ɪn'kɔrpə,ret] *tr* incorporer; (com) constituer en société anonyme ‖ *intr* s'incorporer; (com) se constituer en société anonyme

incorporation [ɪn,kɔrpə're ʃən] *s* incorporation *f;* (*of company*) constitution *f* en société anonyme; (*of town*) érection *f* en municipalité

incorrect [,ɪnkə'rɛkt] *adj* incorrect

increase ['ɪnkris] *s* augmentation *f;* **on the increase** en voie d'accroissement ‖ [ɪn'kris] *tr & intr* augmenter

increasingly [ɪn'krisɪŋli] *adv* de plus en plus

incredible [ɪn'krɛdɪbəl] *adj* incroyable

incredulous [ɪn'krɛdʒələs] *adj* incrédule

increment ['ɪnkrɪmənt] *s* augmentation *f;* (comp, econ, math, pol) incrément *m* ‖ *tr* (comp) incrémenter

incriminate [ɪn'krɪmɪ,net] *tr* incriminer

incrust [ɪn'krʌst] *tr* incruster

incubate ['ɪnkjə,bet] *tr* incuber, couver ‖ *intr* couver

incubator ['ɪnkjə,betər] *s* incubateur *m*

inculcate [ɪn'kʌlket] *tr* inculquer

incumben•cy [ɪn'kʌmbənsi] *s* (*pl* **-cies**) charge *f;* période *f* d'exercice

incumbent [ɪn'kʌmbənt] *adj*—**to be incumbent on** incomber à ‖ *s* titulaire *mf;* (pol) sortant *m*

incunabula [,ɪnkjʊ'næbjələ] *spl* origines *fpl;* (*books*) incunables *mpl*

in•cur [ɪn'kʌr] *v* (*pret & pp* **-curred;** *ger* **-curring**) *tr* encourir, s'attirer; (*a debt*) contracter

incurable [ɪn'kjʊrəbəl] *adj & s* incurable *mf,* inguérissable *mf*

incursion [ɪn'kʌrʒən] *s* incursion *f*

indebted [ɪn'dɛtɪd] *adj* endetté; **indebted to s.o. for** redevable à qn de

indebtedness [ɪn'dɛtɪdnɪs] *s* dette *f,* dettes *fpl*

indecen•cy [ɪn'disənsi] *s* (*pl* **-cies**) indécence *f,* impudeur *f,* incorrection *f*

indecent [ɪn'disənt] *adj* indécent, impudique, incorrect

inde'cent expo'sure *s* attentat *m* à la pudeur

indecisive [,ɪndɪ'saɪsɪv] *adj* indécis

indeclinable [,ɪndɪ'klaɪnəbəl] *adj* (gram) indéclinable

indeed [ɪn'did] *adv* en effet, vraiment, en vérité; (as an intensifier) effectivement, extrêmement, infiniment; **is it indeed!** vraiment?, c'est vrai?; **yes indeed!** bien sûr!, certainement!

indefatigable [,ɪndɪ'fætɪgəbəl] *adj* infatigable

indefensible [,ɪndɪ'fɛnsɪbəl] *adj* indéfendable

indefinable [,ɪndɪ'faɪnəbəl] *adj* indéfinissable

indefinite [ɪnˈdɛfɪnɪt] *adj* indéfini
indelible [ɪnˈdɛlɪbəl] *adj* indélébile
indelicate [ɪnˈdɛlɪkɪt] *adj* indélicat
indemnification [ɪnˌdɛmnɪfɪˈkeʃən] *s* indemnisation *f*
indemni•fy [ɪnˈdɛmnɪˌfaɪ] *v* (*pret & pp* **-fied**) *tr* indemniser
indemni•ty [ɪnˈdɛmnɪti] *s* (*pl* **-ties**) indemnité *f*
indent [ɪnˈdɛnt] *tr* denteler; (*to make a dent in*) laisser une empreinte sur; (*a sheet of metal*) bosseler; (*to recess*) renfoncer; (*typ*) mettre en alinéa, rentrer ‖ *intr* (*typ*) faire un alinéa
indentation [ˌɪndɛnˈteʃən] *s* (*notched edge*) dentelure *f*, découpure *f*; (*act*) découpage *m*; (*hollow mark*) empreinte *f*; (*in metal*) bosse *f*; (*recess*) renfoncement *m*; (*typ*) alinéa *m*
indented *adj* (*typ*) en alinéa
indenture [ɪnˈdɛntʃər] *s* contrat *m* d'apprentissage ‖ *tr* mettre en apprentissage
independence [ˌɪndɪˈpɛndəns] *s* indépendance *f*
independen•cy [ˌɪndɪˈpɛndənsi] *s* (*pl* **-cies**) indépendance *f*; nation *f* indépendante
independent [ˌɪndɪˈpɛndənt] *adj & s* indépendant *m*
indescribable [ˌɪndɪˈskraɪbəbəl] *adj* indescriptible, indicible
indestructible [ˌɪndɪˈstrʌktɪbəl] *adj* indestructible
index [ˈɪndɛks] *s* (*pl* **indexes** or **indices** [ˈɪndɪˌsiz]) index *m*; (*of prices*) indice *m*; (*typ*) main *f*; **Index** Index ‖ *tr* répertorier; (*a book*) faire un index á
in'dex card' *s* fiche *f*
in'dex fin'ger *s* index *m*
in'dex tab' *s* onglet *m*
India [ˈɪndɪ•ə] *s* Inde *f*; l'Inde
In'dia ink' *s* encre *f* de Chine
Indian [ˈɪndɪ•ən] *adj* indien ‖ *s* Indien *m*
In'dian club' *s* mil *m*, massue *f*
In'dian corn' *s* maïs *m*
In'dian file' *s* file *f* indienne ‖ *adv* en file indienne, à la queue leu leu
In'dian O'cean *s* mer *f* des Indes, océan *m* Indien
In'dian sum'mer *s* l'été *m* de la Saint-Martin
In'dia rub'ber *s* caoutchouc *m*, gomme *f*
indicate [ˈɪndɪˌket] *tr* indiquer
indication [ˈɪndɪˈkeʃən] *s* indication *f*
indicative [ɪnˈdɪkətɪv] *adj & s* indicatif *m*
indicator [ˈɪndɪˌketər] *s* indicateur *m*
indict [ɪnˈdaɪt] *tr* (*law*) inculper
indictment [ɪnˈdaɪtmənt] *s* inculpation *f*, mise *f* en accusation
indifferent [ɪnˈdɪfərənt] *adj* indifférent; (*poor*) médiocre
indigenous [ɪnˈdɪdʒɪnəs] *adj* indigène
indigent [ˈɪndɪdʒənt] *adj* indigent
indigestible [ˌɪndɪˈdʒɛstɪbəl] *adj* indigeste
indigestion [ˌɪndɪˈdʒɛstʃən] *s* indigestion *f*
indignant [ɪnˈdɪgnənt] *adj* indigné
indignation [ˌɪndɪgˈneʃən] *s* indignation *f*
indigni•ty [ɪnˈdɪgnɪti] *s* (*pl* **-ties**) indignité *f*

indi•go [ˈɪndɪˌgo] *adj* indigo ‖ *s* (*pl* **-gos** or **-goes**) indigo *m*
indirect [ˌɪndɪˈrɛkt] *adj* indirect
in'direct dis'course *s* discours *m* indirect, style *m* indirect
indiscreet [ˌɪndɪsˈkrit] *adj* indiscret
indispensable [ˌɪndɪsˈpɛnsəbəl] *adj* indispensable
indispose [ˌɪndɪsˈpoz] *tr* indisposer
indisposed *adj* indisposé; (*disinclined*) peu enclin, peu disposé
indisputable [ˌɪndɪˈspjutəbəl] *adj* incontestable, indiscutable
indissoluble [ˌɪndɪˈsaljəbəl] *adj* indissoluble
indistinct [ˌɪndɪˈstɪŋkt] *adj* indistinct
individual [ˌɪndɪˈvɪdʒʊ•əl] *adj* individuel ‖ *s* individu *m*
individuali•ty [ˌɪndɪˌvɪdʒʊˈæliti] *s* (*pl* **-ties**) individualité *f*
indivisible [ˌɪndɪˈvɪzɪbəl] *adj* indivisible
Indochina [ˈɪndoˈtʃaɪnə] *s* Indochine *f*; l'Indochine
Indo-Chi•nese [ˈɪndotˈʃaɪˈniz] *adj* indochinois ‖ *s* (*pl* **-nese**) Indochinois *m*, Indochinoise *f*
indoctrinate [ɪnˈdɑktrɪˌnet] *tr* endoctriner, catéchiser
Indo-European [ˈɪndoˌjurəˈpi•ən] *adj* indo-européen ‖ *s* (*language*) indo-européen *m*; (*person*) Indo-Européen *m*
indolent [ˈɪndələnt] *adj* indolent
Indonesia [ˌɪndoˈniʒə] *s* Indonésie *f*; l'Indonésie
Indonesian [ˌɪndoˈniʒən] *adj* indonésien ‖ *s* (*language*) indonésien *m*; (*person*) Indonésien *m*
indoor [ˈɪnˌdor] *adj* d'intérieur; (*home-loving*) casanier; (*tennis*) couvert; (*swimming pool*) fermé
indoors [ˈɪnˈdorz] *adv* á l'intérieur
indubitable [ɪnˈd(j)ubɪtəbəl] *adj* indubitable
induce [ɪnˈd(j)us] *tr* induire; (*to bring about*) provoquer; **to induce s.o.** porter qn á
induced *adj* provoqué; (*elec*) induit
inducement [ɪnˈd(j)usmənt] *s* encouragement *m*, mobile *m*, invite *f*
induct [ɪnˈdʌkt] *tr* installer; (*mil*) incorporer
inductee [ˌɪnˈdʌkti] *s* appelé *m*
induction [ɪnˈdʌkʃən] *s* installation *f*; (*elec*, *logic*) induction *f*; (*mil*) incorporation *f*
induc'tion coil' *s* bobine *f* d'induction
indulge [ɪnˈdʌldʒ] *tr* favoriser; (*s.o.'s desires*) donner libre cours à; (*a child*) tout passer à ‖ *intr* (*coll*) boire; (*coll*) fumer; **to indulge in** se livrer á
indulgence [ɪnˈdʌldʒəns] *s* indulgence *f*; **indulgence in** jouissance de
indulgent [ɪnˈdʌldʒənt] *adj* indulgent
industrial [ɪnˈdʌstrɪ•əl] *adj* industriel
industrialist [ɪnˈdʌstrɪ•əlɪst] *s* industriel *m*
industrialize [ɪnˈdʌstrɪ•əˌlaɪz] *tr* industrialiser
industrious [ɪnˈdʌstrɪ•əs] *adj* industrieux, appliqué, assidu

indus•try [ˈɪndəstri] *s* (*pl* **-tries**) industrie *f;* (*zeal*) assiduité *f*

inebriation [ɪnˌibriˈeʃən] *s* ébriété *f*

inedible [ɪnˈɛdɪbəl] *adj* incomestible

ineffable [ɪnˈɛfəbəl] *adj* ineffable

ineffective [ˌɪnɪˈfɛktɪv] *adj* inefficace; (*person*) incapable

ineffectual [ˌɪnɪˈfɛktʃu•əl] *adj* inefficace

inefficiency [ˌɪnəˈfɪʃənsi] *s* (*action, machine*) inefficacité *f;* (*person*) incapacité *f,* incompétence *f*

inefficient [ˌɪnɪˈfɪʃənt] *adj* (*action, machine*) inefficace; (*person*) incapable, incompétent

ineligible [ɪnˈɛlɪdʒɪbəl] *adj* inéligible

inept [ɪnˈɛpt] *adj* inepte

inequali•ty [ˌɪnɪˈkwɑlɪti] *s* (*pl* **-ties**) inégalité *f*

inequi•ty [ɪnˈɛkwɪti] *s* (*pl* **-ties**) injustice *f*

inertia [ɪnˈʌrʃə] *s* inertie *f*

inescapable [ˌɪnɛsˈkepəbəl] *adj* inéluctable

inevitable [ɪnˈɛvɪtəbəl] *adj* inévitable

inexact [ˌɪnɛgˈzækt] *adj* inexact

inexcusable [ˌɪnɛksˈkjuzəbəl] *adj* inexcusable

inexhaustible [ˌɪnɛgˈzɔstɪbəl] *adj* inexhaustible, inépuisable

inexorable [ɪnˈɛksərəbəl] *adj* inexorable

inexpedient [ˌɪnɛkˈspidɪ•ənt] *adj* inopportun, peu expédient

inexpensive [ˌɪnɛkˈspɛnsɪv] *adj* pas cher, bon marché

inexperience [ˌɪnɛkˈspɪrɪ•əns] *s* inexpérience *f*

inexperienced *adj* inexpérimenté

inexplicable [ɪnˈɛksplɪkəbəl] *adj* inexplicable

inexpressible [ˌɪnɛkˈsprɛsɪbəl] *adj* inexprimable, indicible

I.N.F. [ˈaɪˈɛnˈɛf] *spl* (letterword) (**intermediate-range nuclear forces**) F.N.I. *fpl* (forces nucléaires intermédiaires)

infallible [ɪnˈfælɪbəl] *adj* infaillible

infamous [ˈɪnfəməs] *adj* infâme

infa•my [ˈɪnfəmi] *s* (*pl* **-mies**) infamie *f*

infan•cy [ˈɪnfənsi] *s* (*pl* **-cies**) première enfance *f;* (fig) enfance

infant [ˈɪnfənt] *adj* infantile; (*in the earliest stage*) (fig) débutant ‖ *s* nourrisson *m,* bébé *m;* enfant *mf* en bas âge

infantile [ˈɪnfənˌtaɪl], [ˈɪnfəntɪl] *adj* infantile; (*childish*) enfantin

in′fantile paral′ysis *s* paralysie *f* infantile

infan•try [ˈɪnfəntri] *s* (*pl* **-tries**) infanterie *f*

in′fantry•man *s* (*pl* **-men**) militaire *m* de l'infanterie, fantassin *m*

in′fant seat′ *s* (aut) siège sit-up *m,* baby sit-up *m*

infarct [ɪnˈfɑrkt] *s* infarctus *m*

infatuated [ɪnˈfætʃu‚etɪd] *adj* entiché, épris; **infatuated with oneself** infatué; **to be infatuated** s'engouer

infect [ɪnˈfɛkt] *tr* infecter

infection [ɪnˈfɛkʃən] *s* infection *f*

infectious [ɪnˈfɛkʃəs] *adj* infectieux; (*laughter*) communicatif, contagieux

in•fer [ɪnˈfʌr] *v* (*pret & pp* **-ferred**; *ger* **-ferring**) *tr* inférer

inferior [ɪnˈfɪrɪ•ər] *adj & s* inférieur *m*

inferiority [ɪnˌfɪrɪˈɑrɪti] *s* infériorité *f*

inferior′ity com′plex *s* complexe *m* d'infériorité

infernal [ɪnˈfʌrnəl] *adj* infernal

infest [ɪnˈfɛst] *tr* infester

infidel [ˈɪnfɪdəl] *adj & s* infidèle *mf*

infideli•ty [ˌɪnfɪˈdɛlɪti] *s* (*pl* **-ties**) infidélité *f*

in′field′ *s* (baseball) petit champ *m,* avant-champ *m,* champ intérieur

infiltrate [ˈɪnfɪlˌtret] *tr* s'infiltrer dans, pénétrer; (*with conspirators*) noyauter ‖ *intr* s'infiltrer

infinite [ˈɪnfɪnɪt] *adj & s* infini *m*

infinitely [ˈɪnfɪnɪtli] *adv* infiniment

infinitive [ɪnˈfɪnɪtɪv] *adj & s* infinitif *m*

infini•ty [ɪnˈfɪnɪti] *s* (*pl* **-ties**) infinité *f;* (math) infini *m*

infirm [ɪnˈfʌrm] *adj* infirme, maladif

infirma•ry [ɪnˈfʌrməri] *s* (*pl* **-ries**) infirmerie *f*

infirmi•ty [ɪnˈfʌrmɪti] *s* (*pl* **-ties**) infirmité *f*

in′fix *s* infixe *m*

inflame [ɪnˈflem] *tr* enflammer ‖ *intr* s'enflammer

inflammable [ɪnˈflæməbəl] *adj* inflammable

inflammation [ˌɪnfləˈmeʃən] *s* inflammation *f*

inflammatory [ɪnˈflæməˌtori] *adj* incendiaire, provocateur; (pathol) inflammatoire

inflate [ɪnˈflet] *tr* gonfler ‖ *intr* se gonfler

inflation [ɪnˈfleʃən] *s* gonflement *m;* (com) inflation *f*

inflationary [ɪnˈfleʃənˌɛri] *adj* inflationniste

inflect [ɪnˈflɛkt] *tr* infléchir; (*e.g., a noun*) décliner; (*a verb*) conjuguer; (*the voice*) moduler

inflection [ɪnˈflɛkʃən] *s* inflexion *f*

inflexible [ɪnˈflɛksɪbəl] *adj* inflexible

inflict [ɪnˈflɪkt] *tr* infliger

influence [ˈɪnflu•əns] *s* influence *f* ‖ *tr* influencer, influer sur

in′fluence ped′dling *s* trafic *m* d'influence

influential [ˌɪnfluˈɛnʃəl] *adj* influent

influenza [ˌɪnfluˈɛnzə] *s* influenza *f*

in′flux′ *s* afflux *m*

inform [ɪnˈfɔrm] *tr* informer, renseigner; **keep me informed** tenez-moi au courant ‖ *intr*—**to inform on** informer contre, dénoncer

informal [ɪnˈfɔrməl] *adj* sans cérémonie; (*person; manners*) familier; (*unofficial*) officieux

infor′mal dance′ *s* sauterie *f*

informant [ɪnˈfɔrmənt] *s* informateur *m;* (*in, e.g., language study*) source *f* d'informations

information [ˌɪnfərˈmeʃən] *s* information *f,* renseignements *mpl;* (telp) service *m* des renseignements téléphoniques; **piece of information** information, renseignement

informational [ˌɪnfərˈmeʃənəl] *adj* instructif, documentaire; (comp) informatique

informa′tion bu′reau *s* bureau *m* de renseignements

informa′tion desk′ *s* comptoir *m* informations

informa′tion high′way *s* (comp) autoroute *f* de l'information, autoroute électronique, inforoute *f*

informa′tion proc′essing *s* (comp) traitement *m* des données, traitement de l'information

in′forma′tion sci′ence *s* (comp) informatique *f*

in′forma′tion the′ory *s* (comp) théorie de l'information

informative [ɪn′fɔrmətɪv] *adj* instructif, édifiant

informed′ sour′ces *spl* sources *fpl* bien informées

informer [ɪn′fɔrmər] *s* délateur *m*, dénonciateur *m*; (*police spy*) indicateur *m*, mouchard *m*

infraction [ɪn′fræk∫ən] *s* infraction *f*

infrared [,ɪnfrə′rɛd] *adj & s* infrarouge *m*

infrastructure [′ɪnfrə,strʌkt∫ər] *s* infrastructure *f*

infrequent [ɪn′frikwənt] *adj* peu fréquent, rare

infringe [ɪn′frɪndʒ] *tr* enfreindre; (*a patent*) contrefaire ‖ *intr*—**to infringe on** empiéter sur, enfreindre

infringement [ɪn′frɪndʒmənt] *s* infraction *f*; (*on patent rights*) contrefaçon *f*

infuriate [ɪn′fjʊrɪ,et] *tr* rendre furieux

infuse [ɪn′fjuz] *tr* infuser

infusion [ɪn′fjuʒən] *s* infusion *f*

ingenious [ɪn′dʒinjəs] *adj* ingénieux

ingenui•ty [,ɪndʒɪˈn(j)uˈɪti] *s* (*pl* **-ties**) ingéniosité *f*

ingenuous [ɪn′dʒɛnjuˈəs] *adj* ingénu, naïf

ingenuousness [ɪn′dʒɛnjuˈəsnɪs] *s* ingénuité *f*, naïveté *f*

ingest [ɪn′dʒɛst] *tr* ingérer

ingot [′ɪŋɡət] *s* lingot *m*

in•grained′ *adj* imprégné; (*habit*) invétéré; (*prejudice*) enraciné

ingrate [′ɪnɡret] *adj & s* ingrat *m*

ingratiate [ɪn′gre∫i,et] *tr*—**to ingratiate oneself (with)** se faire bien voir (de)

ingratiating [ɪn′gre∫i,etɪŋ] *adj* insinuant, persuasif

ingratitude [ɪn′grætɪ,t(j)ud] *adj* ingratitude *f*

ingredient [ɪn′gridiˈənt] *s* ingrédient *m*

in′growing nail′ *s* ongle *m* incarné

ingulf [ɪn′gʌlf] *tr* engouffrer

inhabit [ɪn′hæbɪt] *tr* habiter

inhabitant [ɪn′hæbɪtənt] *s* habitant *m*

inhale [ɪn′hel] *tr* inhaler, aspirer; (*smoke*) avaler ‖ *intr* (*while smoking*) avaler

inherent [ɪn′hɪrənt] *adj* inhérent

inherit [ɪn′hɛrɪt] *tr* (*e.g., money*) hériter; (*e.g., money to become the heir or successor of*) hériter de; **to inherit s.th. from s.o.** hériter q.ch. de qn

inheritance [ɪn′hɛrɪtəns] *s* héritage *m*

inher′itance tax′ *s* droits *mpl* de succession

inheritor [ɪn′hɛrɪtər] *s* héritier *m*

inhibit [ɪn′hɪbɪt] *tr* inhiber

inhibition [,ɪnɪ′bɪ∫ən] *s* inhibition *f*

inhospitable [ɪn′hɑspɪtəbəl] *adj* inhospitalier

in′-house′ *adj & adv* dans les bureaux de la société commerciale

inhuman [ɪn′hjumən] *adj* inhumain

inhumane [,ɪnhju′men] *adj* inhumain, insensible

inhumani•ty [,ɪnhju′mænɪti] *s* (*pl* **-ties**) inhumanité *f*

inimical [ɪ′nɪmɪkəl] *adj* inamical

iniqui•ty [ɪ′nɪkwɪti] *s* (*pl* **-ties**) iniquité *f*; (*wickedness*) méchanceté *f*

ini•tial [ɪ′nɪ∫əl] *adj* initial ‖ *s* initiale *f;* **initials** parafe *m*, initiales ‖ *v* (*pret* **-tialed** or **-tialled; ger -tialing** or **-tialing**) *tr* signer de ses initiales, parapher

initiate [ɪ′nɪ∫i,et] *s* initié *m* ‖ *tr* initier; (*a project*) commencer

initiation [ɪ,nɪ∫i′e∫ən] *s* initiation *f*

initiative [ɪ′nɪ∫iˈətɪv] *s* initiative *f*

inject [ɪn′dʒɛkt] *tr* injecter; (*a remark or suggestion*) introduire

injection [ɪn′dʒɛk∫ən] *s* injection *f;* (med) injection *f*, piqûre *f*

injudicious [,ɪndʒu′dɪ∫əs] *adj* peu judicieux

injunction [ɪn′dʒʌŋk∫ən] *s* injonction *f;* (law) mise *f* en demeure

injure [′ɪndʒər] *tr* (*to harm*) nuire à; (*to wound*) blesser; (*to offend*) faire tort à, léser

injurious [ɪn′dʒʊrɪˈəs] *adj* nuisible, préjudiciable; (*offensive*) blessant, injurieux

inju•ry [′ɪndʒəri] *s* (*pl* **-ries**) blessure *f*, lésion *f;* (*harm*) tort *m;* injure *f*, offense *f*

injustice [ɪn′dʒʌstɪs] *s* injustice *f*

ink [ɪŋk] *s* encre *f* ‖ *tr* encrer

ink′ blot′ *s* pâté *m*, macule *f*

ink′-jet print′er *s* (comp) imprimante *f* à jet d'encre

inkling [′ɪŋklɪŋ] *s* soupçon *m*, pressentiment *m*

ink′ pad′ *s* tampon *m* encreur

ink′stand′ *s* encrier *m*

ink′well′ *s* encrier *m* de bureau

ink•y [′ɪŋki] *adj* (comp **-ier;** super **-iest**) noir foncé; taché d'encre

inlaid [′ɪn,led], [,ɪn′led] *adj* incrusté

inland [′ɪnlənd] *adj & s* intérieur *m* ‖ *adv* à l'intérieur, vers l'intérieur

in′-law′ *s* (coll) parent *m* par alliance, pièce *f* rapportée; **the in-laws** (coll) la belle-famille, les beaux-parents *mpl*

in•lay [′ɪn,le] *s* incrustation *f* ‖ [′ɪn,le] *v* (*pret & pp* **-laid**) *tr* incruster

in′let *s* bras *m* de mer, crique *f;* (*e.g., of air*) arrivée *f*

in′mate *s* habitant *m;* (*of an institution*) pensionnaire *mf*

inn [ɪn] *s* auberge *f*

innate [ɪ′net] *adj* inné, infus

inner [′ɪnər] *adj* intérieur; (*e.g., ear*) interne; intime, secret

in′ner ci′ty *ou* **in′ner core′** *s* zones *fpl* urbaines en déclin

in′ner ear′ *s* oreille *f* interne

in′ner•spring mat′tress *s* sommier *m* à ressorts internes

in′ner tube′ *s* chambre *f* à air

inning [′ɪnɪŋ] *s* (*turn*) tour *m;* (baseball) manche *f*

inn'keep'er *s* aubergiste *mf*

innocence [ˈɪnəsəns] *s* innocence *f*

innocent [ˈɪnəsənt] *adj* & *s* innocent *m*

innocuous [ɪˈnɑkjuˑəs] *adj* inoffensif

innovate [ˈɪnəˌvet] *tr* & *intr* innover

innovation [ˌɪnəˈveʃən] *s* innovation *f*

innuen·do [ˌɪnjuˈɛndo] *s* (*pl* **-does**) allusion *f*, sous-entendu *m*

innumerable [ɪˈn(j)umərəbəl] *adj* innombrable

inoculate [ɪnˈɑkjəˌlet] *tr* inoculer

inoculation [ɪnˌɑkjəˈleʃən] *s* inoculation *f*

inoffensive [ˌɪnəˈfɛnsɪv] *adj* inoffensif

inoperative [ɪnˈɑpərətɪv] *adj* inopérant

inopportune [ɪnˌɑpərˈt(j)un] *adj* inopportun, mal choisi

inordinate [ɪnˈɔrdɪnɪt] *adj* désordonné, déréglé; (*unrestrained*) démesuré

inorganic [ˌɪnɔrˈgænɪk] *adj* inorganique

in'put' *s* (comp) information *f* fournie, données *fpl;* (elec) prise *f,* entrée *f,* énergie *f;* (mach) consommation *f*

inquest [ˈɪnkwɛst] *s* enquête *f*

inquire [ɪnˈkwaɪr] *tr* s'informer de, e.g., **to inquire the price of** s'informer du prix de ‖ *intr* s'enquérir; **to inquire about** s'enquérir de, se renseigner sur; **to inquire into** faire des recherches sur

inquir·y [ˈɪnkwɪri] *s* (*pl* **-ies**) investigation *f,* enquête *f;* (*question*) demande *f;* **to make inquiries** s'informer

inquisition [ˌɪnkwɪˈzɪʃən] *s* inquisition *f*

inquisitive [ɪnˈkwɪzɪtɪv] *adj* curieux, questionneur

in'road' *s* incursion *f,* empiètement *m*

ins' and outs' *spl* tours et détours *mpl*

insane [ɪnˈsen] *adj* dément, fou; (*unreasonable*) insensé, insane

insane' asy'lum *s* (obs) asile *m* d'aliénés

insani·ty [ɪnˈsænɪti] *s* (*pl* **-ties**) démence *f,* aliénation *f*

insatiable [ɪnˈseʃəbəl] *adj* insatiable

inscribe [ɪnˈskraɪb] *tr* inscrire; (*a book*) dédier

inscription [ɪnˈskrɪpʃən] *s* inscription *f;* (*of a book*) dédicace *f;* (*on a medal*) exergue *m,* inscription

inscrutable [ɪnˈskrutəbəl] *adj* impénétrable, fermé

insect [ˈɪnsɛkt] *s* insecte *m*

insecticide [ɪnˈsɛktɪˌsaɪd] *adj* & *s* insecticide *m*

insecure [ˌɪnsɪˈkjʊr] *adj* peu sûr; (*nervous*) inquiet

insensitive [ɪnˈsɛnsɪtɪv] *adj* insensible

inseparable [ɪnˈsɛpərəbəl] *adj* inséparable

insert [ˈɪnsʌrt] *s* (sewing) incrustation *f;* (typ) hors-texte *m,* encart *m* ‖ [ɪnˈsʌrt] *tr* insérer, introduire; (typ) encarter

insertion [ɪnˈsʌrʃən] *s* insertion *f;* (sewing) incrustation *f*

in·set [ˈɪnˌsɛt] *s* (*map, picture, etc.*) médaillon *m,* cartouche *m;* (sewing) incrustation *f;* (typ) hors-texte *m,* encart *m* ‖ [ɪnˈsɛt], [ˈɪnˌsɛt] *v* (*pret* & *pp* **-set;** *ger* **-setting**) *tr* insérer; (*a page or pages*) encarter

in'shore' *adj* côtier ‖ *adv* près de la côte

in'side' *adj* d'intérieur, interne; (*information*) secret, à la source ‖ *s* intérieur *m,* dedans *m;* **insides** (coll) entrailles *fpl* ‖ *adv* à l'intérieur; **inside and out** au-dedans et au-dehors; **inside of** à l'intérieur de; **inside out** à l'envers; **to turn inside out** (*e.g., a coat*) retourner ‖ *prep* à l'intérieur de, dans

in'side informa'tion *s* tuyau *m,* tuyaux *mpl*

insider [ˌɪnˈsaɪdər] *s* initié *m*

in'sider trad'ing *s* abus *m* de l'information privilégiée

in'side track' *s*—**to have the inside track** prendre à la corde; (fig) avoir un avantage

insidious [ɪnˈsɪdiˑəs] *adj* insidieux

in'sight' *s* pénétration *f;* (psychol) défoulement *m*

insigni·a [ɪnˈsɪɡniˑə] *s* (*pl* **-a** or **-as**) insigne *m*

insignificant [ˌɪnsɪɡˈnɪfɪkənt] *adj* insignifiant

insincere [ˌɪnsɪnˈsɪr] *adj* insincère, peu sincère

insinuate [ɪnˈsɪnjuˌet] *tr* insinuer

insipid [ɪnˈsɪpɪd] *adj* insipide

insist [ɪnˈsɪst] *intr* insister; **to insist on** insister sur; **to insist on** + *ger* insister pour + *inf*

insofar as [ˌɪnsoˈfarəz] *conj* pour autant que, dans la mesure où

insolence [ˈɪnsələns] *s* insolence *f*

insolent [ˈɪnsələnt] *adj* insolent

insoluble [ɪnˈsaljəbəl] *adj* insoluble

insolven·cy [ɪnˈsalvənsi] *s* (*pl* **-cies**) insolvabilité *f*

insolvent [ɪnˈsalvənt] *adj* insolvable

insomnia [ɪnˈsamniˑə] *s* insomnie *f*

insomuch [ˌɪnsoˈmʌtʃ] *adv*—**insomuch as** vu que; **insomuch that** à tel point que

inspect [ɪnˈspɛkt] *tr* inspecter

inspection [ɪnˈspɛkʃən] *s* inspection *f*

inspector [ɪnˈspɛktər] *s* inspecteur *m*

inspiration [ˌɪnspɪˈreʃən] *s* inspiration *f*

inspire [ɪnˈspaɪr] *tr* inspirer

inspiring [ɪnˈspaɪrɪŋ] *adj* inspirant

install [ɪnˈstɔl] *tr* installer

installer [ɪnˈstɔlər] *s* installateur *m,* installatrice *f;* (comp) installateur *m*

installment [ɪnˈstɔlmənt] *s* installation *f;* (*delivery*) livraison *f;* (*serial story*) feuilleton *m;* (*partial payment*) acompte *m,* versement *m;* **in installments** par acomptes, par tranches

install'ment buy'ing *s* achat *m* à tempérament

install'ment plan' *s* vente *f* à tempérament or à crédit; **on the installment plan** avec facilités de paiement

instance [ˈɪnstəns] *s* cas *m,* exemple *m;* **for instance** par exemple

instant [ˈɪnstənt] *adj* imminent, immédiat; **on the fifth instant** le cinq courant ‖ *s* instant *m,* moment *m*

instantaneous [ˌɪnstənˈteniˑəs] *adj* instantané

in'stant cof'fee *s* café *m* en poudre, café instantané

instantly [ˈɪnstəntli] *adv* à l'instant

instead [ɪnˈstɛd] *adv* plutôt, au contraire; à ma (votre, sa, etc.) place; **instead of** au lieu de

in'step' *s* cou-de-pied *m*
instigate [ˈɪnstɪˌget] *tr* inciter
instigation [ˌɪnstɪˈgeʃən] *s* instigation *f*
instill [ɪnˈstɪl] *tr* instiller
instinct [ˈɪnstɪŋkt] *s* instinct *m*
instinctive [ɪnˈstɪŋktɪv] *adj* instinctif
institute [ˈɪnstɪˌt(j)ut] *s* institut *m* ‖ *tr* instituer
institution [ˌɪnstɪˈt(j)uʃən] *s* institution *f*
instruct [ɪnˈstrʌkt] *tr* instruire
instruction [ɪnˈstrʌkʃən] *s* instruction *f*; (comp) instructions
instruc'tional soft'ware [ɪnˈstrʌkʃənəl] *s* (comp) didacticiel *m*
instruc'tion man'ual *s* livret *m* d'instruction
instruc'tions for use' *spl* mode *m* d'emploi
instructive [ɪnˈstrʌktɪv] *adj* instructif
instructor [ɪnˈstrʌktər] *s* instructeur *m*
instrument [ˈɪnstrəmənt] *s* instrument *m* ‖ [ˈɪnstrəˌmɛnt] *tr* instrumenter
instrumental [ˌɪnstrəˈmɛntəl] *adj* instrumental; **to be instrumental in** contribuer à
instrumentalist [ˌɪnstrəˈmɛntəlɪst] *s* instrumentiste *mf*
instrumentali•ty [ˌɪnstrəmənˈtælɪti] *s* (*pl* -ties) intermédiaire *m*, intervention *f*
in'strument board' *s* tableau *m* de bord
in'strument fly'ing *s* radio-navigation *f*, vol *m* aux instruments
in'strument land'ing *s* atterrissage *m* aux instruments, aide *f* à la navigation
in'strument pan'el *s* tableau *m* de bord
insubordinate [ˌɪnsəˈbɔrdɪnɪt] *adj* insubordonné
insufferable [ɪnˈsʌfərəbəl] *adj* insupportable, intolérable, imbuvable
insufficient [ˌɪnsəˈfɪʃənt] *adj* insuffisant
insuffi'cient ev'idence *s* insuffisance *f* de preuves
insular [ˈɪnsələr], [ˈɪnsjʊlər] *adj* insulaire
insulate [ˈɪnsəˌlet] *tr* insoler
in'sulating tape' *s* ruban *m* isolant, chatterton *m*
insulation [ˌɪnsəˈleʃən] *s* isolation *f*
insulator [ˈɪnsəˌletər] *s* isolant *m*
insulin [ˈɪnsəlɪn] *s* insuline *f*
insult [ˈɪnsʌlt] *s* insulte *f* ‖ [ɪnˈsʌlt] *tr* insulter
insulting [ɪnˈsʌltɪŋ] *adj* insultant, injurieux
insurable [ɪnˈʃʊrəbəl] *adj* assurable
insurance [ɪnˈʃʊrəns] *s* assurance *f*
insur'ance pol'icy *s* police *f* d'assurance
insure [ɪnˈʃʊr] *tr* assurer
insurer [ɪnˈʃʊrər] *s* assureur *m*
insurgent [ɪnˈsʌrdʒənt] *adj & s* insurgé *m*
insurmountable [ˌɪnsərˈmaʊntəbəl] *adj* insurmontable
insurrection [ˌɪnsəˈrɛkʃən] *s* insurrection *f*
intact [ɪnˈtækt] *adj* intact
intaglio [ɪnˈtælyo] *s* taille-douce *f*
in'take' *s* (*place*) entrée *f*; (*act or amount*) prise *f*; (mach) admission *f*
in'take man'ifold *s* tubulure *f* d'admission, collecteur *m* d'admission
in'take valve' *s* soupape *f* d'admission

intangible [ɪnˈtændʒɪbəl] *adj* intangible
intan'gible as'sets *spl* actif *m* incorporel
integer [ˈɪntɪdʒər] *s* nombre *m* entier
integral [ˈɪntɪgrəl] *adj* intégral (*part*) intégrant; **integral with** solidaire de ‖ *s* intégrale *f*
integrate [ˈɪntɪˌgret] *tr* intégrer; (*to desegregate*) éliminer la ségrégation raciale de
integration [ˌɪntɪˈgreʃən] *s* intégration *f*
integrity [ɪnˈtɛgrɪti] *s* intégrité *f*
intellect [ˈɪntəˌlɛkt] *s* intellect *m*; (*person*) intelligence *f*
intellectual [ˌɪntəˈlɛktʃuˌəl] *adj & s* intellectuel *m*
intelligence [ɪnˈtɛlɪdʒəns] *s* intelligence *f*
intel'ligence bu'reau *s* deuxième bureau *m*, service *m* de renseignements
intel'ligence quo'tient *s* quotient *m* intellectuel
intel'ligence test' *s* test *m* d'habileté mentale, test de capacité intellectuelle
intelligent [ɪnˈtɛlɪdʒənt] *adj* intelligent
intelligentsia [ɪnˌtɛlɪˈdʒɛntsi•ə] *s* intelligentsia *f*
intelligible [ɪnˈtɛlɪdʒɪbəl] *adj* intelligible
intemperate [ɪnˈtɛmpərɪt] *adj* intempérant
intend [ɪnˈtɛnd] *tr* destiner; signifier; vouloir dire; **to intend to** avoir l'intention de, penser; **to intend to become** se destiner à
intended *adj & s* (coll) futur *m*
intense [ɪnˈtɛns] *adj* intense
intensi•fy [ɪnˈtɛnsɪˌfaɪ] *v* (*pret & pp* -fied) *tr* intensifier ‖ *intr* s'intensifier
intensi•ty [ɪnˈtɛnsɪti] *s* (*pl* -ties) intensité *f*
intensive [ɪnˈtɛnsɪv] *adj* intensif
intent [ɪnˈtɛnt] *adj* attentif; (*look, gaze*) fixe, intense; **intent on** résolu à ‖ *s* intention *f*; **to all intents and purposes** en fait, pratiquement
intention [ɪnˈtɛnʃən] *s* intention *f*
intentional [ɪnˈtɛnʃənəl] *adj* intentionnel, délibéré
intentionally [ɪnˈtɛnʃənəli] *adv* exprès, à dessein
in•ter [ɪnˈtʌr] *v* (*pret & pp* -terred; *ger* -terring) *tr* enterrer
interact [ˌɪntərˈækt] *intr* agir réciproquement
interaction [ˌɪntərˈækʃən] *s* interaction *f*
in'ter•ac'tive *adj* interactif, conversationnel
inter•breed [ˌɪntərˈbrid] *v* (*pret & pp* -bred) *tr* croiser ‖ *intr* se croiser
intercalate [ɪnˈtʌrkəˌlet] *tr* intercaler
intercede [ˌɪntərˈsid] *intr* intercéder
intercept [ˌɪntərˈsɛpt] *tr* intercepter
interceptor [ˌɪntərˈsɛptər] *s* intercepteur *m*
interchange [ˈɪntərˌtʃɛndʒ] *s* échange *m*, permutation *f*; (*transfer point*) correspondance *f*; (*on highway*) échangeur *m* ‖ [ˌɪntərˈtʃɛndʒ] *tr* échanger, permuter ‖ *intr* permuter
in'ter•ci'ty *adj* interurbain
intercollegiate [ˌɪntərkəˈlidʒɪ•ɪt] *adj* interuniversitaire, entre universités
intercom [ˈɪntərˌkɑm] *s* (coll) interphone *m*, intervox *m*
intercourse [ˈɪntərˌkors] *s* relations *fpl*, rapports *mpl*; (*copulation*) copulation *f*, coït *m*

intercross [ˌɪntərˈkrɔs], [ˌɪntərˈkrɑs] *tr* entrecroiser ‖ *intr* s'entrecroiser

interdict [ˈɪntərˌdɪkt] *s* interdit *m* ‖ [ˌɪntərˈdɪkt] *tr* interdire; **to interdict s.o. from** + *ger* interdire à qn de + *inf*

interdisciplinary [ˌɪntərˈdɪsəplənɛri] *adj* interdisciplinaire

interest [ˈɪntərɪst] *s* intérêt *m* ‖ [ˈɪntəˌrɛst] *tr* intéresser

interested *adj* intéressé; **to be interested in** s'intéresser à *or* dans

interesting [ˈɪntrɪstɪŋ] *adj* intéressant

in'terest rate' *s* taux *m* d'intérêt

interface [ˈɪntərˌfes] *s* interface *f;* (comp) interface *f* ‖ *intr* (comp) se connecter

interfere [ˌɪntərˈfɪr] *intr* (*to meddle*) s'ingérer, s'immiscer; (phys) interférer; **to interfere with** intervenir dans, se mêler de; (*e.g., one's plans*) entraver, contrecarrer; **to interfere with each other** interférer (entre eux)

interference [ˌɪntərˈfɪrəns] *s* ingérence *f,* immixtion *f;* (phys) interférence *f;* (*static*) (rad) parasites *mpl;* (*jamming*) (rad) brouillage *m;* **interference with** immixtion dans

interim [ˈɪntərɪm] *adj* provisoire, par intérim ‖ *s* intérim *m*

interior [ɪnˈtɪri•ər] *adj & s* intérieur *m*

inte'rior dec'orator *s* décorateur *m* d'intérieurs

interject [ˌɪntərˈdʒɛkt] *tr* interposer; (*questions*) lancer

interjection [ˌɪntərˈdʒɛkʃən] *s* intervention *f;* (gram) interjection *f*

interlard [ˌɪntərˈlɑrd] *tr* entrelarder

in'terli'brary loan' *s* le prêt interbibliothèque, le service des prêts entre bibliothèques

interline [ˌɪntərˈlaɪn] *tr* interligner

interlining [ˈɪntərˌlaɪnɪŋ] *s* doublure *f* intermédiaire

interlock [ˌɪntərˈlɑk] *tr* emboîter, engager ‖ *intr* s'emboîter, s'engager

interloper [ˌɪntərˈlopər] *s* intrus *m*

interlude [ˈɪntərˌlud] *s* (mov, mus, telv) interlude *m;* (theat, fig) intermède *m*

intermediar•y [ˌɪntərˈmidiˌɛri] *adj* intermédiaire ‖ *s* (*pl* **-ies**) intermédiaire *mf,* interprète *mf*

intermediate [ˌɪntərˈmidi•ɪt] *adj* intermédiaire

interme'diate-range' mis'sile *s* missile *m* à portée intermédiaire

interment [ɪnˈtɑrmənt] *s* enterrement *m,* sépulture *f*

interminable [ɪnˈtɑrmɪnəbəl] *adj* interminable

intermingle [ˌɪntərˈmɪŋɡəl] *tr* entremêler ‖ *intr* s'entremêler

intermission [ˌɪntərˈmɪʃən] *s* relâche *m,* pause *f;* (theat) entracte *m*

intermittent [ˌɪntərˈmɪtənt] *adj* intermittent

intermix [ˌɪntərˈmɪks] *tr* entremêler ‖ *intr* s'entremêler

intern [ˈɪntɑrn] *s* interne *mf* ‖ [ɪnˈtɑrn] *tr* interner

internal [ɪnˈtɑrnəl] *adj* interne

inter'nal-combus'tion en'gine *s* moteur *m* à explosion

inter'nal rev'enue *s* recettes *fpl* fiscales

international [ˌɪntərˈnæʃənəl] *adj* international; (*exposition*) universel

in'terna'tional date' line' *s* ligne *f* de changement de date

interna'tional phonet'ic al'phabet (IPA) *s* alphabet *m* phonétique international (API)

in'terna'tional time' zone' *s* fuseau *m* horaire international

internecine [ˌɪntərˈnisɪn] *adj* domestique, intestin; (*war*) sanguinaire, d'extermination

internee [ˌɪntɑrˈni] *s* interné *m*

internet [ˈɪntɑrnɛt] *adj* (comp) internautique ‖ **Internet** *s* (comp) Internet *m or* internet *m,* Internet *or* l'Internet; **to surf the Internet** surfer sur Internet

In'ternet us'er *s* internaute *mf*

internment [ɪnˈtɑrnmənt] *s* internement *m*

in'tern•ship' *s* internat *m*

interpellate [ˌɪntərˈpɛlet] *tr* interpeller

interplanetary [ˌɪntərˈplænəˌtɛri] *adj* interplanétaire

interplan'etary trav'el *s* voyages *mpl* interplanétaires

interplay [ˈɪntərˌple] *s* interaction *f*

interpolate [ɪnˈtɑrpəˌlet] *tr* interpoler

interpose [ˌɪntərˈpoz] *tr* interposer

interpret [ɪnˈtɑrprɪt] *tr* interpréter

interpretation [ɪnˌtɑrprɪˈteʃən] *s* interprétation *f*

interpreter [ɪnˈtɑrprɪtər] *s* interprète *mf*

interracial [ˌɪntərˈreʃəl] *adj* interracial

interrogate [ɪnˈtɛrəˌget] *tr* interroger

interrogation [ɪnˌtɛrəˈgeʃən] *s* interrogation *f*

interroga'tion mark' *s* point *m* d'interrogation

interrupt [ˌɪntəˈrʌpt] *tr* interrompre

interruption [ˌɪntəˈrʌpʃən] *s* interruption *f*

intersect [ˌɪntərˈsɛkt] *tr* entrecouper ‖ *intr* s'entrecouper

intersection [ˌɪntərˈsɛkʃən] *s* intersection *f*

intersperse [ˌɪntərˈspɑrs] *tr* entremêler

interstellar [ˌɪntərˈstɛlər] *adj* interstellaire

interstice [ɪnˈtɑrstɪs] *s* interstice *m*

intertwine [ˌɪntərˈtwaɪn] *tr* entrelacer ‖ *intr* s'entrelacer

interval [ˈɪntərvəl] *s* intervalle *m*

intervene [ˌɪntərˈvin] *intr* intervenir

intervening [ˌɪntərˈvinɪŋ] *adj* (*period*) intermédiaire; (*party*) intervenant

intervention [ˌɪntərˈvɛnʃən] *s* intervention *f*

interview [ˈɪntərˌvju] *s* entrevue *f;* (journ) interview *f* ‖ *tr* avoir une entrevue avec; (journ) interviewer

inter•weave [ˌɪntərˈwiv] *v* (*pret* **-wove** *ou* **-weaved**) *pp* **-wove, woven** *ou* **weaved**) *tr* entrelacer; (*to intermingle*) entremêler

intestate [ɪnˈtɛstet] *adj & s* intestat *m*

intestine [ɪnˈtɛstɪn] *adj & s* intestin *m*

intima•cy [ˈɪntɪməsi] *s* (*pl* **-cies**) intimité *f;* rapports *mpl* sexuels

intimate [ˈɪntɪmɪt] *adj & s* intime *mf* ‖ [ˈɪntɪˌmet] *tr* donner à entendre

intimation [ˌɪntɪˈmeʃən] *s* suggestion *f*, insinuation *f*

intimidate [ɪnˈtɪmɪˌdet] *tr* intimider

into [ˈɪntʊ] *prep* dans, en

intolerant [ɪnˈtɑlərənt] *adj* intolérant

intonation [ˌɪntoˈneʃən] *s* intonation *f*

intone [ɪnˈton] *tr* (*to begin to sing*) entonner; (*to sing or recite in a monotone*) psalmodier ‖ *intr* psalmodier

intoxicant [ɪnˈtɑksɪkənt] *s* boisson *f* alcoolique

intoxicate [ɪnˈtɑksɪˌket] *tr* enivrer; (*to poison*) intoxiquer

intoxication [ɪnˌtɑksɪˈkeʃən] *s* ivresse *f*; (*poisoning*) intoxication *f*; (fig) enivrement *m*

intractable [ɪnˈtræktəbəl] *adj* intraitable

Intranet [ˈɪntrəˌnɛt] *s* (comp) Intranet *m*, intranet *m*

intransigent [ɪnˈtrænsɪdʒənt] *adj* intransigeant

intransitive [ɪnˈtrænsɪtɪv] *adj* intransitif

intravenous [ˌɪntrəˈvinəs] *adj* intraveineux

intraveˈnous drip *s* goutte-à-goutte *m invar*

intrepid [ɪnˈtrɛpɪd] *adj* intrépide

intricate [ˈɪntrɪkɪt] *adj* compliqué

intrigue [ɪnˈtrig] *s* intrigue *f* ‖ *tr & intr* intriguer

intrinsic(al) [ɪnˈtrɪnsɪk(əl)] *adj* intrinsèque

introduce [ˌɪntrəˈd(j)us] *tr* introduire; (*to make acquainted*) présenter

introduction [ˌɪntrəˈdʌkʃən] *s* introduction *f*; (*the beginning part*) entrée en matière, exorde *m* (*of one person to another or others*) présentation *f*

introductory [ˌɪntrəˈdʌktəri] *adj* préliminaire; (*text*) liminaire; (*speech, letter, etc.*) de présentation

introducˈtory ofˈfer *s* offre *f* de présentation, prix *m* de lancement

introspective [ˌɪntrəˈspɛktɪv] *adj* introspectif; (*person*) méditatif

introvert [ˈɪntrəˌvʌrt] *adj & s* introverti *m*

intrude [ɪnˈtrud] *intr* s'ingérer, s'immiscer; **to intrude on s.o.** déranger qn

intruder [ɪnˈtrudər] *s* intrus *m*

intrusion [ɪnˈtruʒən] *s* intrusion; (*upon privacy*) immixtions *fpl*, ingérences *fpl*

intrusive [ɪnˈtrusɪv] *adj* importun

intuition [ˌɪnt(j)uˈɪʃən] *s* intuition *f*

inundate [ˈɪnənˌdet] *tr* inonder

inundation [ˌɪnənˈdeʃən] *s* inondation *f*

inure [ɪnˈjʊr] *tr* aguerrir, endurcir ‖ *intr* entrer en vigueur; **to inure to** rejaillir sur

invade [ɪnˈved] *tr* envahir

invader [ɪnˈvedər] *s* envahisseur *m*

invalid [ɪnˈvælɪd] *adj* invalide, nul ‖ [ˈɪnvəlɪd] *adj & s* malade *mf*, invalide *mf*

invalidate [ɪnˈvælɪˌdet] *tr* invalider

invalidity [ˌɪnvəˈlɪdɪti] *s* invalidité *f*, nullité *f*

invaluable [ɪnˈvæljuˑəbəl] *adj* inappréciable, inestimable

invariable [ɪnˈvɛrɪˑəbəl] *adj* invariable

invasion [ɪnˈveʒən] *s* invasion *f*

invective [ɪnˈvɛktɪv] *s* invective *f*

inveigh [ɪnˈve] *intr*—**to inveigh against** invectiver contre

inveigle [ɪnˈvegəl] *tr* séduire, enjôler; **to inveigle s.o. into** + *ger* entraîner qn à + *inf*

invent [ɪnˈvɛnt] *tr* inventer

invention [ɪnˈvɛnʃən] *s* invention *f*

inventive [ɪnˈvɛntɪv] *adj* inventif

inventiveness [ɪnˈvɛntɪvnɪs] *s* esprit *m* inventif

inventor [ɪnˈvɛntər] *s* inventeur *m*

invenˑtory [ˈɪnvənˌtori] *s* (*pl* **-ries**) inventaire *m*; **beginning inventory** (com) stock *m* d'ouverture; **ending inventory** (com) stock de fermeture ‖ *v* (*pret & pp* **-ried**) *tr* inventorier

inverse [ɪnˈvʌrs] *adj & s* inverse *m*

inversion [ɪnˈvʌrʒən] *s* interversion *f*, inversion *f*

invert [ˈɪnvʌrt] *adj & s* inverti *m* ‖ [ɪnˈvʌrt] *tr* inverser; (*an image*) invertir

invertebrate [ɪnˈvʌrtɪˌbret] *adj & s* invertébré *m*

invest [ɪnˈvɛst] *tr* investir; (*money*) investir, placer; **to invest with** investir de ‖ *intr* investir *or* placer de l'argent

investigate [ɪnˈvɛstɪˌget] *tr* examiner, rechercher

investigation [ɪnˌvɛstɪˈgeʃən] *s* investigation *f*

investigator [ɪnˈvɛstɪˌgetər] *s* investigateur *m*, chercheur *m*

investment [ɪnˈvɛstmənt] *s* investissement *m*, placement *m*, mise *f* de fonds; (*with an office or dignity*) investiture *f*; (siege) investissement

investˈment trust *s* fonds *m* de placement fermé

investor [ɪnˈvɛstər] *s* actionnaire *mf*, investisseur *m*, investisseuse *f*, capitaliste *mf*

inveterate [ɪnˈvɛtərɪt] *adj* invétéré

invidious [ɪnˈvɪdɪˑəs] *adj* odieux

invigorate [ɪnˈvɪgəˌret] *tr* vivifier, fortifier

invigorating [ɪnˈvɪgəˌretɪŋ] *adj* vivifiant, fortifiant

invincible [ɪnˈvɪnsɪbəl] *adj* invincible

invisible [ɪnˈvɪzɪbəl] *adj* invisible

invisˈible inkˈ *s* encre *f* sympathique

invitation [ˌɪnvɪˈteʃən] *s* invitation *f*

invite [ɪnˈvaɪt] *tr* inviter

inviting [ɪnˈvaɪtɪŋ] *adj* invitant

invoice [ˈɪnvɔɪs] *s* facture *f*; **as per invoice** suivant facture ‖ *tr* facturer

invoke [ɪnˈvok] *tr* invoquer

involuntary [ɪnˈvɑlənˌtɛri] *adj* involontaire

involve [ɪnˈvɑlv] *tr* impliquer, entraîner, engager

invulnerable [ɪnˈvʌlnərəbəl] *adj* invulnérable

inward [ˈɪnwərd] *adj* intérieur ‖ *adv* intérieurement, en dedans

iodide [ˈaɪˑəˌdaɪd] *s* iodure *m*

iodine [ˈaɪˑəˌdin] *s* (chem) iode *m* ‖ [ˈaɪˑəˌdaɪn] *s* (pharm) teinture *f* d'iode

ion [ˈaɪˑən], [ˈaɪˑɑn] *s* ion *m*

ionize [[ˈaɪˑəˌnaɪz] *tr* ioniser

ionosphere [aɪˈɑnəˌsfɪr] *s* ionosphère *f*

I.O.U. [ˈaɪˌoʊˈju] s (letterword) (**I owe you**) reconnaissance f de dette

IPA [ˈaɪˈpiˈe] s (letterword) (**International Phonetic Alphabet**) API m (alphabet phonétique international)

I.Q. [ˈaɪˈkju] s (letterword) (**intelligence quotient**) quotient m intellectuel

IRA abbr **Irish Republican Army; Individual Retirement Account**

Iran [ɪˈrɑn], [aɪˈræn] s l'Iran m

Iranian [aɪˈreɪnɪən] adj iranien ‖ s (language) farsi m; (person) Iranien m

Iraq [ɪˈrɑk] s l'Irak m

Ira•qi [ɪˈrɑki] adj irakien ‖ s (pl **-qis**) Irakien m

irate [ˈaɪret], [aɪˈret] adj irrité

ire [aɪr] s courroux m, colère f

Ireland [ˈaɪrlənd] s Irlande f; l'Irlande

iris [ˈaɪrɪs] s iris m

Irish [ˈaɪrɪʃ] adj irlandais ‖ s (language) irlandais m, **the Irish** les Irlandais

I′rish•man s (pl **-men**) Irlandais m

I′rish stew′ s ragoût m irlandais

I′rish•wom′an s (pl **-wom′en**) Irlandaise f

irk [ʌrk] tr ennuyer, fâcher

irksome [ˈʌrksəm] adj ennuyeux

iron [ˈaɪ•ərn] s fer m; (for pressing clothes) fer à repasser; **irons** (fetters) fers; **to have too many irons in the fire** courir deux lièvres à la fois; **to strike while the iron is hot** battre le fer tant qu'il est chaud ‖ tr (clothes) repasser; **to iron out** (a difficulty) aplanir

i′ron and steel′ in′dustry s sidérurgie f

i′ron-bound′ adj cerclé de fer; (unyielding) inflexible; (rock-bound) plein de récifs

ironclad [ˈaɪ•ərnˌklæd] adj blindé, ferré, cuirassé; (e.g., contract) infrangible

i′ron cur′tain s rideau m de fer

i′ron diges′tion s estomac m d'autruche

i′ron gate′ s grille f d'entrée

i′ron horse′ s coursier m de fer

ironic(al) [aɪˈrɑnɪk(əl)] adj ironique

ironing [ˈaɪˌərnɪŋ] s repassage m

i′roning board′ s planche f à repasser

i′ron lung′ s poumon m d'acier

i′ron ore′ s minerai m de fer

i′ron-tipped′ adj ferré

i′ron•ware′ s quincaillerie f, ferblanterie f

i′ron will′ s volonté f inflexible

i′ron•work′ s ferrure f, ferronnerie f

i′ron•work′er s ferronnier m

iro•ny [ˈaɪrəni] s (pl **-nies**) ironie f

irradiate [ɪˈrediˌet] tr & intr irradier

irrational [ɪˈræʃənəl] adj irrationnel

irredeemable [ˌɪrɪˈdiməbəl] adj irrémédiable; (bonds) non remboursable

irrefutable [ˌɪrɪˈfjutəbəl] irréfutable

irregular [ɪˈrɛɡjələr] adj & s irrégulier m

irrelevant [ɪˈrɛləvənt] adj non pertinent, hors de propos

irreligious [ˌɪrɪˈlɪdʒəs] adj irréligieux

irremediable [ˌɪrɪˈmidɪ•əbəl] adj irrémédiable

irreparable [ɪˈrɛpərəbəl] adj irréparable

irreplaceable [ˌɪrɪˈplesəbəl] adj irremplaçable

irrepressible [ˌɪrɪˈprɛsɪbəl] adj irrépressible, irrésistible

irreproachable [ˌɪrɪˈprotʃəbəl] adj irréprochable

irresistible [ˌɪrɪˈzɪstɪbəl] adj irrésistible

irrespective [ˌɪrɪˈspɛktɪv] adj—**irrespective of** indépendant de

irresponsible [ˌɪrɪˈspɑnsɪbəl] adj irresponsable

irretrievable [ˌɪrɪˈtrivəbəl] adj irréparable; (lost) irrécupérable

irreverent [ɪˈrɛvərənt] adj irrévérencieux

irreversible [ˈɪrəˈvʌrsəbəl] adj irréversible

irrevocable [ɪˈrɛvəkəbəl] adj irrévocable

irrigate [ˈɪrɪˌget] tr irriguer

irrigation [ˌɪrɪˈgeʃən] s irrigation f

irritant [ˈɪrɪtənt] adj & s irritant m

irritate [ˈɪrɪˌtet] tr irriter

irritation [ˌɪrɪˈteʃən] s irritation f

irruption [ɪˈrʌpʃən] s irruption f

IRS [ˈaɪˈarˈɛs] s (letterword) (**Internal Revenue Service**) recette f (service de la recette des finances)

Isaiah [aɪˈzeˈə] s Isaïe m

isinglass [ˈaɪzɪŋˌglæs] s gélatine f, colle f de poisson; (mineral) mica m

Islam [ˈɪsləm], [ɪsˈlɑm] s l'Islam m

Islamic [ɪsˈlɑmɪk] adj islamique

Islam′ic fun′damen′talism s fondamentalisme m islamique

island [ˈaɪlənd] adj insulaire ‖ s île f

islander [ˈaɪləndər] s insulaire mf

isle [aɪl] s îlot m; (poetic) île f

isolate [ˈaɪsəˌlet] tr isoler

isolation [ˌaɪsəˈleʃən] s isolement m

isolationist [ˌaɪsəˈleʃənɪst] adj & s isolationniste mf

isometric [ˌaɪsəˈmɛtrɪk] adj isométrique ‖ **isometrics** spl exercices mpl isométriques

isosceles [aɪˈsɑsəˌliz] adj isocèle

isotope [ˈaɪsəˌtop] s isotope m

Israel [ˈɪzrɪ•əl] s Israël m; **in Israel** en Israël; **of Israel** d'Israël, e.g., **the state of Israel** l'état d'Israël; **to Israel** (to give to) à Israël; (to go to) en Israël

Israe•li [ɪzˈreli] adj israélien ‖ s (pl **-lis** [liz]) Israélien m

Israelite [ˈɪzrɪ•əˌlaɪt] adj israélite ‖ s Israélite mf

issuance [ˈɪʃu•əns] s émission f

issue [ˈɪʃu] s (way out) sortie f, issue f; (outcome) issue; (of a magazine) numéro m; (offspring) descendance f; (of banknotes, stamps, etc.) émission f; (under discussion) point m à discuter; (pathol) écoulement m; **at issue** en jeu, en litige; **to take issue with** être en désaccord avec; **without issue** sans enfants ‖ tr (a book, a magazine) publier; (banknotes, stamps, etc.) émettre; (a summons) lancer; (an order) donner; (a proclamation) faire; (a verdict) rendre ‖ intr sortir, déboucher

isthmus [ˈɪsməs] s isthme m

it [ɪt] pron pers ce §82B, §85; lui §85; il §87; le §87; y §87; en §87

Italian [ɪˈtæljən] *adj* italien ‖ *s* (*language*) italien *m;* (*person*) Italien *m*

italic [ɪˈtælɪk] *adj* (typ) italique; **Italic** italique ‖ **italics** *spl* caractères *mpl* penchés, italique *m;* **italics mine** c'est moi qui souligne

italicize [ɪˈtælɪˌsaɪz] *tr* mettre en italique

Italy [ˈɪtəli] *s* Italie *f;* l'Italie

itch [ɪtʃ] *s* démangeaison *f;* (pathol) gale *f* ‖ *tr* démanger à ‖ *intr* (*said of part of body*) démanger; (*said of person*) avoir une démangeaison; **to itch to** (fig) avoir une démangeaison de

itch•y [ˈɪtʃi] *adj* (*comp* -ier; *super* -iest) piquant; (pathol) galeux

item [ˈaɪtəm] *s* article *m;* (*in a list*) point *m;* (*piece of news*) nouvelle *f*

itemize [ˈaɪtəˌmaɪz] *tr* spécifier, énumérer

itinerant [aɪˈtɪnərənt] *adj & s* itinérant *m*

itinerar•y [aɪˈtɪnəˌrɛri] *adj* itinéraire ‖ *s* (*pl* -ies) itinéraire *m*

it'll *contr* it will

its [ɪts] *adj poss* son **§88** ‖ *pron poss* le sien **§89**

it's *contr* it is; it has

it's = **it is** c'est; il est, elle est

it'self' *pron pers* soi **§85;** lui-même **§86;** se **§87**

IV [ˈaɪˈvi] *s* (letterword) (**intravenous**) injection *f* intraveineuse

I've *contr* I have

ivied [ˈaɪvid] *adj* couvert de lierre

ivo•ry [ˈaɪvəri] *adj* d'ivoire, en ivoire ‖ *s* (*pl* -ries) ivoire *m;* **to tickle the ivories** (slang) taquiner l'ivoire

i'vory tow'er *s* (fig) tour *f* d'ivoire

I.V. stand [ˌaɪˈviˈstænd] *s* (med) goutte-à-goutte *m invar*

ivy [ˈaɪvi] *s* (*pl* ivies) lierre *m*

J

J, j [dʒe] *s* Xᵉ lettre de l'alphabet

jab [dʒæb] *s* (*with a sharp point; with a penknife; with the elbow*) coup m; (*with a needle*) piqûre *f;* (*with the fist*) coup sec ‖ *v* (*pret & pp* jabbed; *ger* jabbing) *tr* donner un coup de coude à; piquer; donner un coup sec à; (*a knife*) enfoncer

jabber [ˈdʒæbər] *tr & intr* jaboter

jack [dʒæk] *s* (aut) cric *m*, vérin *m;* (cards) valet *m;* (elec) jack *m*, prise *f;* (coll) fric *m;* **Jack** Jeannot *m* ‖ *tr*—**to jack up** soulever au cric; (*prices*) faire monter

jackal [ˈdʒækəl] *s* chacal *m*

jack'ass' *s* baudet *m*

jack'daw' *s* choucas *m*

jacket [ˈdʒækɪt] *s* (*of a woman; of a book*) jaquette *f;* (*of a man's suit*) veston *m;* (*metal casing*) chemise *f*

Jack' Frost' *s* le Bonhomme Hiver

jack'-in-the-box' *s* diable *m* à ressort, boîte *f* à surprise

jack'knife' *s* (*pl* -knives) couteau *m* de poche, couteau pliant; (*fancy dive*) saut *m* de carpe

jack'-of-all'-trades' *s* bricoleur *m*

jack-o'-lantern [ˈdʒækə ˌlæntərn] *s* potiron *m* lumineux

jack'pot' *s* gros lot *m*, poule *f;* **to hit the jackpot** décrocher la timbale

jack' rab'bit *s* lièvre *m* des prairies

Jacob [ˈdʒekəb] *s* Jacques *m*

jade [dʒed] *s* (*stone; color*) jade *m;* (*horse*) haridelle *f;* (*woman*) coquine *f,* friponne *f*

jaded *adj* éreinté, excédé; blasé

jag [dʒæg] *s* dentelure *f;* **to have a jag on** (slang) être paf

jagged [ˈdʒægɪd] *adj* dentelé

jaguar [ˈdʒægwɑr] *s* jaguar *m*

jail [dʒel] *s* prison *f* ‖ *tr* emprisonner

jail'bird' *s* cheval *m* de retour

jailer [ˈdʒelər] *s* geôlier *m*

jalop•y [dʒəˈlɑpi] *s* (*pl* -ies) bagnole *f,* tacot *m,* guimbarde *f,* clou *m*

jam [dʒæm] *s* confiture *f;* **to be in a jam** (coll) être dans le pétrin ‖ *v* (*pret & pp* jammed; *ger* jamming) *tr* coincer ‖ *intr* se coincer

Jamaican [dʒəˈmekən] *adj* jamaïquain, jamaïcain ‖ *mf* Jamaïquain *m,* Jamaïquaine *f,* Jamaïcain *m,* Jamaïcaine *f*

jamboree [ˌdʒæmbəˈri] *s* (*of boy scouts*) jamboree *m;* (slang) bombance *f*

James [dʒemz] *s* Jacques *m*

jamming [ˈdʒæmɪŋ] *s* (rad) brouillage *m*

Jane [dʒen] *s* Jeanne *f*

Jane' Doe' *s* (*unidentified female body*) inconnue *f*

jangle [ˈdʒæŋgəl] *s* cliquetis *m* ‖ *tr* faire cliqueter; (*nerves*) mettre en boule ‖ *intr* cliqueter

janitor [ˈdʒænɪtər] *s* concierge *m*

janitress [ˈdʒænɪtrɪs] *s* concierge *f*

January [ˈdʒænjuˌɛri] *s* janvier *m*

ja•pan [dʒəˈpæn] *s* laque *m* du Japon; **Japan** le Japon ‖ *v* (*pret & pp* -panned; *ger* -panning) *tr* laquer

Japa•nese [ˌdʒæpəˈniz] *adj* japonais ‖ *s* (*language*) japonais *m* ‖ *s* (*pl* -nese) (*person*) Japonais *m*

Jap'anese bee'tle *s* cétoine *f*

Jap'anese lan'tern *s* lanterne *f* vénitienne

jar [dʒɑr] *s* (*container*) pot *m,* bocal *m;* (*jolt*) secousse *f* ‖ *v* (*pret & pp* jarred; *ger* jarring) *tr* ébranler, secouer ‖ *intr* trembler, vibrer; (*to be out of harmony*) ne pas s'accorder, jurer; **to jar on the nerves** taper sur les nerfs

jargon [ˈdʒɑrgən] *s* jargon *m*

jasmine [ˈdʒæsmɪn] *s* jasmin *m*

jasper [ˈdʒæspər] *s* jaspe *m*

jaundice [ˈdʒɔndɪs] *s* jaunisse *f*, ictère *m*

jaundiced *adj* ictérique; (fig) amer

jaunt [dʒɔnt] *s* excursion *f*

jaun•ty [ˈdʒɔnti] *adj* (*comp* **-tier;** *super* **-tiest**) vif, dégagé; (*smart*) chic

javelin [ˈdʒævlɪn] *s* javelot *m*

jaw [dʒɔ] *s* mâchoire *f*; (*of animal*) gueule *f*; **jaws** (*e.g., of death*) griffes *fpl* ‖ *tr* (slang) engueuler ‖ *intr* (*to gossip*) (slang) bavarder

jaw′bone′ *s* mâchoire *f*, maxillaire *m*

jay [dʒe] *s* geai *m*

jay′walk′ *intr* traverser la rue en dehors des clous

jaw′walk′er *s* piéton *m* distrait

jazz [dʒæz] *s* jazz *m* ‖ *tr*—**to jazz up** (coll) animer, égayer

jazz′ band′ *s* orchestre *m* de jazz

jazz′ sing′er *s* chanteur *m* de rythme

jealous [ˈdʒɛləs] *adj* jaloux

jealous•y [ˈdʒɛləsi] *s* (*pl* **-ies**) jalousie *f*

jean [dʒin] *s* treillis *m*; **Jean** Jeanne *f*; **jeans** pantalon *m* de treillis

jeep [dʒip] *s* jeep *f*

jeer [dʒɪr] *s* raillerie *f* ‖ *intr* railler; **to jeer at** se moquer de

Jehovah [dʒɪˈhovə] *s* Jéhovah *m*

jell [dʒɛl] *s* gelée *f* ‖ *intr* se convertir en gelée; (*to take hold*) prendre forme, se préciser

jel•ly [ˈdʒɛli] *s* (*pl* **-lies**) gelée *f* ‖ *v* (*pret & pp* **-lied**) *tr* convertir en gelée ‖ *intr* se convertir en gelée

jel′ly•fish′ *s* méduse *f*; (*person*) chiffe *f*

jel′ly roll′ *s* gâteau *m* roulé

jeopardize [ˈdʒɛpər,daɪz] *tr* mettre en danger, compromettre

jeopardy [ˈdʒɛpərdi] *s* danger *m*

jerk [dʒʌrk] *s* saccade *f*, secousse *f*; (slang) mufle *m* ‖ *tr* tirer brusquement, secouer ‖ *intr* se mouvoir brusquement

jerk′water town′ *s* trou *m*, petite ville *f* de province

jerk•y [ˈdʒʌrki] *adj* (*comp* **-ier;** *super* **-iest**) saccadé

Jerome [dʒɔˈrom] *s* Jérôme *m*

jersey [ˈdʒʌrzi] *s* jersey *m*

Jerusalem [dʒɪˈrusələm] *s* Jérusalem *f*

jest [dʒɛst] *s* plaisanterie *f*; **in jest** en plaisantant ‖ *intr* plaisanter

jester [ˈdʒɛstər] plaisantin *m*; (*medieval clown*) bouffon *m*

Jesuit [ˈdʒɛʒu•ɪt] *adj* jésuite, jésuitique ‖ *s* Jésuite *m*

Jesus [ˈdʒizəs] *s* Jésus *m*

Je′sus Christ′ *s* Jésus-Christ *m*

jet [dʒɛt] *s* (*color; mineral*) jais *m*; (*of water, gas, etc.*) jet *m*; avion *m* à réaction ‖ *v* (*pret & pp* **jetted;** *ger* **jetting**) *intr* gicler, jaillir; voyager en jet

jet′-black′ *adj* noir de jais

jet′ en′gine *s* moteur *m* à réaction

jet′ fight′er *s* chasseur *m* à réaction

jet′ fu′el *s* carburéacteur *m*, kérosène *m* aviation

jet′ lag′ *s* troubles *mpl* dûs au décalage horaire

jet′ lin′er *s* avion *m* de ligne à réaction

jet′ plane′ *s* avion *m* à réaction

jet′ propul′sion *s* propulsion *f* par réaction

jetsam [ˈdʒɛtsəm] *s* marchandise *f* jetée à la mer

jet′ set′ *s* monde *m* des playboys

jet′ stream′ *s* (meteo) courant-jet *m*

jettison [ˈdʒɛtɪsən] *s* jet *m* à la mer ‖ *tr* jeter à la mer; (fig) mettre au rebut, rejeter

jet•ty [ˈdʒɛti] *s* (*pl* **-ties**) (*wharf*) appontement *m*; (*breakwater*) jetée *f*

Jew [dʒu] *s* Juif *m*; (rel) juif *m*

jewel [ˈdʒu•əl] *s* joyau *m*, bijou *m*; (*of a watch*) rubis *m*; (*of a clock*) pierre *f*; (*person*) bijou *m*

jew′el case′ *s* écrin *m*

jeweler or **jeweller** [ˈdʒu•ələr] *s* horloger-bijoutier *m*, bijoutier *m*

jewelry [ˈdʒu•əlri] *s* joaillerie *f*

jew′elry store′ *s* bijouterie *f*; (*for watches*) horlogerie *f*

Jewess [ˈdʒu•ɪs] *s* Juive *f*; (rel) juive *f*

Jewish [ˈdʒj•ɪʃ] *adj* juif, judaïque

jews′-harp or **jew′s-harp** [ˈdʒuz,hɑrp] *s* guimbarde *f*

jib [dʒɪb] *s* (mach) flèche *f*; (naut) foc *m*

jibe [dʒaɪb] *s* moquerie *f* ‖ *intr* railler; (*to agree*) concorder; (naut) passer d'un bord à l'autre du mât; **to jibe at** se moquer de, railler; **jibe with** (*to be in accord with*) coller à

jif•fy [ˈdʒɪfi] *s* (*pl* **-fies**)—**in a jiffy** (coll) en un clin d'œil

jig [dʒɪg] *s* (*dance*) gigue *f*; **the jig is up** (slang) il n'y a pas mèche, tout est dans le lac

jigger [ˈdʒɪgər] *s* mesure *f* qui contient une once et demie; (*for fishing*) leurre *m*; (*tackle*) palan *m*; (*flea*) puce *f*; (*for separating ore*) crible *m*; (naut) tapecul *m*; (*gadget*) (coll) machin *m*

jiggle [ˈdʒɪgəl] *s* petite secousse *f* ‖ *tr* agiter, secouer ‖ *intr* se trémousser

jig′saw′ *tr* chantourner, scie à découper, scie sauteuse

jig′ saw′ *s* scie *f* à chantourner

jig′saw puz′zle *s* casse-tête *m* chinois, puzzle *m*

jihad [dʒiˈhɑd] *s* (*holy war*) guerre *f* sainte; (*sacred war*) guerre sacré (de l'Islam); (*crusade*) croisade *f*

jilt [dʒɪlt] *tr* lâcher, repousser

Jim [dʒɪm] *s* (*dimunitif de* **James**) Jacquot *m*

Jim Crow *s* (pej) (*policy*) politique *f* raciste; (*Negro*) nègre *m* (pej)

jim•my [ˈdʒɪmi] *s* (*pl* **-mies**) pince-monseigneur *f*; (*sobriquet de* **James**) Jacquot *m* ‖ *v* (*pret & pp* **-mied**) *tr* forcer à l'aide d'une pince-monseigneur

jingle [ˈdʒɪngəl] *s* (*small bell*) grelot *m*; (*sound*) grelottement *m*, tintement *m*, cliquetis *m*; (*poem*) rimes *fpl* enfantines; (*catchy verse*) petit couplet, slogan *m* à rimes; **advertising jingle** couplet *m* publicitaire, refrain *m* publicitaire, réclame *f* chantée, sonal *m* ‖ *tr* faire grelotter ‖ *intr* grelotter

jin•go [ˈdʒɪŋgo] *adj* chauvin ‖ *s* (*pl* **-goes**) chauvin *m;* **by jingo!** (coll) sapristi!

jingoism [ˈdʒɪŋgoˌɪzəm] *s* chauvinisme *m*

jinx [dʒɪŋks] *s* guigne *f* ‖ *tr* (coll) porter la guigne à

jitters [ˈdʒɪtərz] *spl* (coll) frousse *f,* trouille *f;* **to give the jitters to** (coll) flanquer la trouille à

jittery [ˈdʒɪtəri] *adj* froussard

Joan' of Arc' *s* Jeanne *f* d'Arc

job [dʒɑb] *s* (*piece of work*) travail *m;* (*chore*) besogne *f,* tâche *f;* (*employment*) emploi *m;* (*work done by contract*) travail à forfait; (slang) vol *m;* **bad job** (fig) mauvaise affaire *f;* **by the job** à la pièce; **on the job** faisant un stage; (slang) attentif; **soft job** (coll) filon *m,* fromage *m;* **to be out of a job** être en chômage; **to lie down on the job** (slang) tirer au flanc

job' ac'tion *s* grève *f* du zèle

jobber [ˈdʒɑbər] *s* grossiste *m;* (*piece-worker*) ouvrier *m* à la tâche; (*dishonest official*) agioteur *m*

job' descrip'tion *s* définition *f* de fonction

job' hold'er *s* employé *m;* (*in the government*) fonctionnaire *m*

job' lot' *s* solde *m* de marchandises

job' print'ing *s* bilboquet *m,* travaux *mpl* de ville

job' secur'ity *s* sécurité *f* de l'emploi

job' va'cancy *s* poste *m* à pourvoir

job' work' *s* (printing) bilboqet *m,* travaux *mpl* de ville

jock [dʒɑk] *s* (coll) athlète *mf*

jockey [ˈdʒɑki] *s* jockey *m* ‖ *tr* (coll) manœuvrer

jockstrap [ˈdʒɑkˌstræp] *s* suspensoir *m,* slip *m* de soutien

jocose [dʒoˈkos] *adj* jovial, joyeux

jocular [ˈdʒɑkjələr] *adj* facétieux

jog [dʒɑg] *s* saccade *f* ‖ *v* (*pret & pp* **jogged;** *ger* **jogging**) *tr* secouer; (*the memory*) rafraîchir ‖ *intr*—**to jog along** aller au petit trot

jogger [ˈdʒɑgər] *s* joggeur *m,* joggeuse *f*

jogging [ˈdʒɑgɪŋ] *s* jogging *m*

John [dʒɑn] *s* Jean *m;* **john** (slang) toilettes *fpl;* (*prostitute's customer*) (slang) micheton *m*

John' Bull' *s* l'Anglais *m* typique

John' Doe' *s* M. Dupont, M. Durand; (*unidentified male body*) inconnu *m*

Johnny [ˈdʒɑni] *s* (coll) Jeannot *m*

John'ny•cake' *s* galette *f* de farine de maïs

John'ny-come'-late'ly *s* (coll) nouveau venu *m*

join [dʒɔɪn] *tr* joindre; (*to meet*) rejoindre; (*a club, a church*) se joindre à, entrer dans; (*a political party*) s'affilier à; (*the army*) s'engager dans; **to join s.o. in** + *ger* se joindre à qn pour + *inf* ‖ *intr* se joindre

joiner [ˈdʒɔɪnər] *s* menuisier *m;* (coll) clubiste *mf*

joint [dʒɔɪnt] *adj* commun, conjugué, joint, réuni ‖ *s* (*articulation*) joint *m;* (culin) rôti *m;*

(*place*) (slang) boîte *f;* (*notorious drinking place*) (slang) bistrot *m* mal famé; (*gambling den*) (slang) tripot *m;* (*reefer*) (slang) joint; **out of joint** disloqué; (fig) de travers

joint' account' *s* compte *m* indivis

joint' commit'tee *s* commission *f* mixte

joint' estate' *s* (*of husband and wife*) communauté *f*

joint' own'er *s* copropriétaire *mf*

joint'-stock' com'pany *s* société *f* par actions

joist [dʒɔɪst] *s* solive *f,* poutre *f*

joke [dʒok] *s* plaisanterie *f;* **to play a joke on** faire une attrape à ‖ *intr* plaisanter

joker [ˈdʒokər] *s* farceur *m,* blagueur *m;* (cards) joker *m,* fou *m;* (coll) clause *f* ambiguë

jol•ly [ˈdʒɑli] *adj* (*comp* **-lier;** *super* **-liest**) joyeux, enjoué ‖ *adv* (coll) rudement

Jol'ly Rog'er [ˈrɑdʒər] *s* pavillon *m* noir

jolt [dʒolt] *s* cahot *m,* secousse *f* ‖ *tr* cahoter, secouer ‖ *intr* cahoter

Jonah [ˈdʒonə] *s* Jonas *m*

jonquil [ˈdʒɑŋkwɪl] *s* jonquille *f*

Jordan [ˈdʒɔrdən] *s* (*country*) Jordanie *f;* la Jordanie; (*river*) Jourdain *m*

Jordanian [dʒɛrˈdeni•ən] *adj & s* Jordanien *m,* Jordanienne *f*

josh [dʒɑʃ] *tr & intr* (coll) blaguer

jostle [ˈdʒɑsəl] *tr* bousculer ‖ *intr* se bousculer

jot [dʒɑt] *s*—**not a jot** pas un iota ‖ *v* (*pret & pp* **jotted;** *ger* **jotting**) *tr*—**to jot down** prendre note de

journal [ˈdʒʌrnəl] *s* journal *m;* (*magazine*) revue *f;* (mach) tourillon *m;* (naut) journal de bord

jour'nal box' *s* boîte *f* d'essieu

journalese [ˌdʒʌrnəˈliz] *s* (pej) jargon *m* journalistique

journalism [ˈdʒʌrnəˌlɪzəm] *s* journalisme *m*

journalist [ˈdʒʌrnəlɪst] *s* journaliste *mf*

journalistic [ˌdʒʌrnəˈlɪstɪk] *adj* journalistique

journey [ˈdʒʌrni] *s* voyage *m;* trajet *m,* parcours *m* ‖ *intr* voyager

jour'ney•man *s* (*pl* **-men**) compagnon *m*

joust [dʒaʊst] *s* joute *f* ‖ *intr* jouter

Jove [dʒov] *s* Jupiter *m;* **by Jove!** parbleu!

jovial [ˈdʒovi•əl] *adj* jovial

jowl [dʒaʊl] *s* bajoue *f*

joy [dʒɔɪ] *s* joie *f*

joyful [ˈdʒɔɪfəl] *adj* joyeux

joyless [ˈdʒɔɪlɪs] *adj* sans joie

joyous [ˈdʒɔɪ•əs] *adj* joyeux

joy' ride' *s* (coll) balade *f* en auto

joy' stick' *s* manche *m* à balai

Jr. *abbr* (**junior**) fils, e.g., **Mr. Martin, Jr.** M. Martin fils

jubilant [ˈdʒubɪlənt] *adj* jubilant

jubilee [ˈdʒubɪˌli] *s* jubilé *m*

Judaism [ˈdʒude,ɪzəm] *s* judaïsme *m*

judge [dʒʌdʒ] *s* juge *m* ‖ *tr & intr* juger; **judging by** à en juger par

judge' ad'vocate *s* commissaire *m* du gouvernement

judgment [ˈdʒʌdʒmənt] *s* jugement *m*

judg′ment day′ s jour m du jugement dernier
judicial [dʒuˈdɪʃəl] adj judiciaire; (legal) juridique
judiciar•y [dʒuˈdɪʃiˌɛri] adj judiciaire ‖ s (pl -ies) pouvoir m judiciaire; (judges) judicature f
judicious [dʒuˈdɪʃəs] s judicieux
jug [dʒʌg] s (of earthenware) cruche f; (of metal) broc m; (jail) (slang) bloc m, taule f
juggle [ˈdʒʌgəl] tr jongler avec; **to juggle away** escamoter ‖ intr jongler
juggler [ˈdʒʌglər] s jongleur m; imposteur m, mystificateur m
juggling [ˈdʒʌglɪŋ] s jonglerie f; (trickery) passe-passe m
Jugoslavia [ˈjugoˈslɑvɪ•ə] s Yougoslavie f; la Yougoslavie
jugular [ˈdʒʌgjələr] adj & s jugulaire f
juice [dʒus] s jus m; (coll) courant m électrique
juice′ bar′ s juterie f
juic•y [ˈdʒusi] adj (comp -ier; super -iest) juteux; (fig) savoureux
jukebox [ˈdʒukˌbɑks] s pick-up m électrique à sous, distributeur m de musique
July [dʒuˈlaɪ] s juillet m
jumble [ˈdʒʌmbəl] s fouillis m, enchevêtrement m ‖ tr brouiller
jumbo [ˈdʒʌmbo] adj (coll) géant
jum′bo jet′ s avion-géant m, gros-porteur m
jump [dʒʌmp] s saut m, bond m; (nervous start) sursaut m; (sports) saut m; (sports) obstacle m ‖ tr sauter; **to jump ship** tirer une bordée; **to jump the gun** démarrer trop tôt; **to jump the track** dérailler ‖ intr sauter, bondir; **to jump at the chance** sauter sur l'occasion
jump′ ball′ s (sports) entre-deux m, chandelle f d'arbitre
jumper [ˈdʒʌmpər] s sauteur m, sauteuse f; (dress) robe-chasuble f
jump′er ca′ble s câble m de démarrage
jump′ing bean′ s petit pois m sauteur
jump′ing jack′ s pantin m
jump′ rope′ s corde f à sauter
jump′ seat′ s strapontin m
jump′ start′ s (aut) démarrage au moyen des câbles (deux câbles épissés mettent en contact les accumulateurs de deux autos)
jump′ -start′ tr (aut) démarrer au moyen des câbles; (fig) (an economy, enthusiasm, patriotism, donations) stimuler
jump′ suit′ s (aer) combinaison f de saut
jump•y [ˈdʒʌmpi] adj (comp -ier; super -iest) nerveux
junction [ˈdʒʌŋkʃən] s jonction f; (of railroads, roads) embranchement m
juncture [ˈdʒʌŋktʃər] s jointure f; (occasion)

conjoncture f; **at this juncture** en cette occasion
June [dʒun] s juin m
June′ bug′ s hanneton m
jungle [ˈdʒʌŋgəl] s jungle f
jun′gle war′fare s guerre f de la brousse
junior [ˈdʒunjər] adj cadet; **Bobby Watson, Junior** le jeune Bobby Watson; **Martin, Junior** Martin fils ‖ s cadet m; (educ) étudiant m de troisième année
jun′ior of′ficer s officier m subalterne
juniper [ˈdʒunɪpər] s genévrier m
ju′niper ber′ry s genièvre m
junk [dʒʌŋk] s (old metal) ferraille f; (worthless objects) bric-à-brac m; (cheap merchandise) camelote f, pacotille f; (coll) gnognote f; (naut) jonque f ‖ tr mettre au rebut
junk′ deal′er s fripier m; marchand m de ferraille
junket [ˈdʒʌŋkɪt] s excursion f; voyage m officiel aux frais de la princesse
junk′ food′ s camelote f alimentaire, mauvaise bouffe f
junkie [ˈdʒʌŋki] s (slang) camé m, drogué m
junk′man′ s (pl -men′) ferrailleur m; chiffonnier m
junk′ shop′ s boutique f de bric-à-brac et friperie; bric-à-brac m
junk′yard′ s cimetière m de ferraille
jurisdiction [ˌdʒurɪsˈdɪkʃən] s juridiction f; **within the jurisdiction of** du ressort de
jurist [ˈdʒurɪst] s légiste m
juror [ˈdʒurər] s juré m
ju•ry [ˈdʒuri] s (pl -ries) jury m
just [dʒʌst] adj juste ‖ adv seulement; justement; **just as** à l'instant où; (in the same way that) de même que; **just as it is** tel quel; **just out** vient de paraître; **to have just** venir de
justice [ˈdʒʌstɪs] s justice f; (judge) juge m
jus′tice of the peace′ s juge m de paix
justi•fy [ˈdʒʌstɪˌfaɪ] v (pret & pp -fied) tr justifier
justly [ˈdʒʌstli] adv justement
jut [dʒʌt] v (pret & pp **jutted;** ger **jutting**) intr—**to jut out** faire saillie
jute [dʒut] s jute m
juvenile [ˈdʒuveˌnaɪl] adj juvénile, adolescent; (e.g., books) pour la jeunesse ‖ s adolescent m
ju′venile court′ s tribunal m tutélaire de mineurs
ju′venile delin′quency s délinquance f juvénile
ju′venile delin′quent s délinquant m juvénile; **juvenile delinquents** jeunes délinquants mpl
juxtapose [ˌdʒʌkstəˈpoz] tr juxtaposer

K

K, k [ke] *s* XI*ᵉ* lettre de l'alphabet
kale [kel] *s* chou *m* frisé
kaleidoscope [kə'laɪdəˌskop] *s* kaléidoscope *m*
kamikaze [ˌkɑmə'kɑzi] *s* kamikaze *m*
kangaroo [ˌkæŋgə'ru] *s* kangourou *m*
kan'garoo court' *s* tribunal *m* bidon
kaput [kə'pʊt] *adj* (slang) fichu, foutu, dans le lac
karate [kə'rɑti] *s* karaté *m*
Kashmir ['kæʃmɪr] *s* le Cachemire
kash'mir shawl' *s* châle *m* de cachemire
katydid ['ketɪdɪd] *s* sauterelle d'Amérique
kayak ['kaɪæk] *s* kayak *m*
keel [kil] *s* quille *f* ‖ *intr*—**to keel over** (naut) chavirer; (coll) tomber dans les pommes
keen [kin] *adj* (*having a sharp edge*) aiguisé, affilé; (*sharp, cutting*) mordant, pénétrant; (*sharp-witted*) perçant, perspicace; (*eager, much interested*) enthousiaste, vif; (slang) formidable; **keen on** engoué de, passionné de
keep [kip] *s* (*of medieval castle*) donjon *m;* **for keeps** (*for good*) (coll) pour de bon; (*forever*) (coll) à tout jamais; **to earn one's keep** (coll) gagner sa nourriture, gagner sa vie; **to play for keeps** (coll) jouer le tout pour le tout ‖ *v* (*pret & pp* **kept** [kɛpt] *tr* garder, conserver; (*one's word or promise; accounts, a diary*) tenir; (*animals*) élever; (*a garden*) cultiver; (*a hotel, a school, etc.*) diriger; (*an appointment*) ne pas manquer à; (*a holiday*) observer; (*a person*) avoir à sa charge, entretenir; **keep it up!** ne flanchez pas!, continuez!; **keep off the flowers** (*public sign*) respecter les fleurs; **keep out of the bushes** (*public sign*) il est interdit de pénétrer dans le bosquet; **to keep away** éloigner; **to keep back** retenir; **to keep down** baisser; (*prices*) maintenir bas; (*a revolt*) réprimer; (*a student after school*) garder en retenue; (*dust, fire, etc.*) entretenir; **to keep off** éloigner; **to keep out** tenir éloigné, empêcher d'entrer; **to keep quiet** faire taire; **to keep running** laisser marcher; **to keep score** marquer les points; **to keep servants** avoir des domestiques; **to keep s.o. busy** occuper qn; **to keep s.o. clean (cool, warm, etc.)** tenir qn propre (au frais, au chaud, etc.); **to keep s.o. or s.th. from** + *ger* empêcher qn or q.ch. de + *inf;* **to keep s.o. informed about** mettre or tenir qn au courant de; **to keep s.o. waiting** faire attendre qn; **to keep up** maintenir; (*e.g., all night*) faire veiller ‖ *intr* rester, se tenir; (*in good shape*) demeurer, se conserver; (*e.g., from rotting*) se garder; **keep out** (public sign) entrée interdite; **that can keep** (coll) ça peut attendre; **to keep** + *ger* continuer à + *inf;* **to keep away** s'éloigner, se tenir à l'écart; **to keep from** + *ger* s'abstenir de + *inf;* **to keep in with** rester en bons termes avec; **to keep on** + *ger* continuer à + *inf;* **to keep out** rester dehors; **to keep out of** ne pas se mêler de; **to keep quiet**

rester tranquille, se taire; **to keep to** (*e.g., the right*) garder (*e.g., la droite*); **to keep up** tenir bon, tenir ferme; **to keep up with** aller de pair avec
keeper ['kipər] *s* gardien *m,* garde *m;* (*of a game preserve*) garde forestier; (*of a horseshoe magnet*) armature *f*
keeping ['kipɪŋ] *s* garde *f,* surveillance *f;* (*of a holiday*) observance *f;* **in keeping with** en accord avec; **in safe keeping** sous bonne garde; **out of keeping with** en désaccord avec
keep'sake' *s* souvenir *m,* gage *m* d'amitié
keg [kɛg] *s* tonnelet *m;* (*of herring*) caque *f*
ken [kɛn] *s*—**beyond the ken of** hors de la portée de
kennel ['kɛnəl] *s* chenil *m*
kep·i ['kɛpi] *s* (*pl* **-is**) képi *m*
kept [kɛpt] *s* (*pl* **wom'en**) femme *f* entretenue
kerchief ['kʌrtʃif] *s* fichu *m*
kernel ['kʌrnəl] *s* (*inner part of a nut or fruit stone*) amande *f;* (*of wheat or corn*) grain *m;* (fig) noyau *m,* cœur *m*
kerosene ['kɛrəˌsin] *s* kérosène *m,* pétrole *m* lampant
ker'osene lamp' *s* lampe *f* à pétrole
kerplunk [ˌkʌr'plʊŋk] *interj* patatras!
ketchup ['kɛtʃəp] *s* ketchup *m*
kettle ['kɛtəl] *s* chaudron *m,* marmite *f;* (*teakettle*) bouilloire *m;* **that's not my kettle of fish** (coll) ça n'est pas mes oignons
ket'tle·drum' *s* timbale *f*
key [ki] *adj* clef, clé ‖ *s* clef *f,* clé *f;* (*of piano, typewriter, etc.*) touche *f;* (*wedge or cotter used to lock parts together*) cheville *f,* clavette *f;* (*reef or low island*) caye *f;* (*answer book*) livre *m* du maître; (*tone of voice*) ton *m;* (*to a map*) légende *f;* (bot) samare *f;* (mus) tonalité *f;* (telg) manipulateur *m;* **key to the city** droit *m* de cité; **off key** faux; **on key** juste ‖ *tr* claveter, coincer; **to be keyed up** être surexcité, être tendu
key'board' *s* clavier *m*
key'board'er *s* claviste *mf;* (comp) opérateur *m* (*or* opératrice *f*) (de) console
key'hole' *s* trou *m* de la serrure; (*of clock*) trou de clef
key'man' *s* (*pl* **-men'**) pivot *m,* homme *m* indispensable
key' mon'ey *s* pas *m* de porte
key'note' *s* (mus) tonique *f;* (fig) dominante *f*
key'note speech' *s* discours *m* d'ouverture
key'pad *s* (comp) bloc *m* de touches, clavier *m*
key'punch' *s* (mach) perforatrice *f*
key'punch op'erator *s* perforeur *m*
key' ring' *s* porte-clefs *m*
key' sig'nature *s* (mus) armature *f* de la clé
key'stone' *s* clef *f* de voûte
key' word' *s* mot-clé *m*
kha·ki ['kɑki], ['kæki] *adj* kaki ‖ *s* (*pl* **-kis**) kaki *m*

khan [kɑn] *s* khan *m*

kibitz [ˈkɪbɪts] *intr* (coll) faire la mouche du coche

kibitzer [ˈkɪbɪtsər] *s* (coll) casse-pieds *mf*, curieux *m*

kick [kɪk] *s* coup *m* de pied; (*e.g., of a horse*) ruade *f*; (*of a gun*) recul *m*; (*complaint*) (slang) plainte *f*; (*thrill*) (slang) effet *m*, frisson *m*; **to get a kick out of** (slang) s'en payer une tranche de ‖ *tr* donner un coup de pied à; (*a ball*) botter; **to kick off** mettre en train, démarrer; **to kick out** (coll) chasser à coups de pied; **to kick s.o. in the pants** (coll) botter le derrière à qn; **to kick the bucket** (coll) casser sa pipe, passer l'arme à gauche; **to kick up a row** (slang) déclencher un chahut ‖ *intr* donner un coup de pied; (*said of gun*) reculer; (*said of horse*) ruer; (sports) botter; **to kick against** regimber contre; **to kick off** (football) donner le coup d'envoi; (*an event or project*) démarrer

kick′back′ *s* contrecoup *m*; (slang) ristourne *f*

kick′box′er *s* boxeur *m* qui pratique la savate *or* la boxe française

kick′box′ing *s* la savate, la boxe française

kicker [ˈkɪkər] *s* (sports) botteur *m*

kick′off′ *s* (football) coup *m* d'envoi; (fig) démarrage *m*

kid [kɪd] *s* chevreau *m*; (*child*) (coll) gosse *mf*; mioche *mf*; poulot *m* ‖ *v* (*pret & pp* **kidded;** *ger* **kidding**) *tr & intr* (slang) blaguer; **to kid oneself** (slang) se faire des illusions

kidder [ˈkɪdər] *s* (slang) blagueur *m*, plaisantin *m*

kidding [ˈkɪdɪŋ] *s* (slang) blague *f*; **no kidding!** (slang) sans blague!; **you're kidding!** (slang) tu galèges!

kid′ gloves′ *spl* gants *mpl* de chevreau; **to handle with kid gloves** traiter avec douceur, ménager

kid′nap *v* (*pret & pp* **-napped** or **-napped;** *ger* **-napping** or **-napping**) *tr* kidnapper, enlever

kidnaper or **kidnapper** [ˈkɪdnæpər] *s* kidnappeur *m*

kidnaping or **kidnapping** [ˈkɪdnæpɪŋ] *s* kidnappage *m*, enlèvement *m*

kidney [ˈkɪdni] *s* rein *m*; (culin) rognon *m*

kid′ney bean′ *s* haricot *m* de Soissons

kid′ney-shaped′ *adj* réniforme

kid′ney stone′ *s* calcul *m* rénal

kid′ney trans′plant *s* greffe *f* du rein

kill [kɪl] *s* mise *f* à mort; (*bag of game*) gibier *m* tué ‖ *tr* tuer; (*an animal*) abattre; (*a bill, amendment, etc.*) mettre son veto à, faire échouer

killer [ˈkɪlər] *s* assassin *m*

kill′er whale′ *s* épaulard *m*, orque *f*

killing [ˈkɪlɪŋ] *adj* meurtrier; (*exhausting; ridiculous*) crevant ‖ *s* tuerie *f*; **to make a killing** (coll) réussir un beau coup

kill′-joy′ *s* rabat-joie *m*, trouble-fête *mf*

kiln [kɪl], [kɪln] *s* four *m*

kil-o [ˈkilo] *s* (*pl* **-os**) kilo *m*, kilogramme *m*; kilomètre *m*

kilocycle [ˈkɪlə,saɪkəl] *s* kilocycle *m*

kilogram [ˈkɪlə,græm] *s* kilogramme *m*

kilometer [ˈkɪlə,mitər] *s* kilomètre *m*

kilowatt [ˈkɪlə,wɑt] *s* kilowatt *m*

kilowatt-hour [ˈkɪlə,wɑtˈaʊr] *s* (*pl* **-hours**) kilowatt-heure *m*

kilt [kɪlt] *s* kilt *m*

kilter [ˈkɪltər] *s*—**to be out of kilter** (coll) être détraqué

kimo-no [kɪˈmono] *s* (*pl* **-nos**) kimono *m*

kin [kɪn] *s* (*family relationship*) parenté *f*; (*relatives*) les parents *mpl*; **of kiln** apparenté; **the next of kin** le plus proche parent, les plus proches parents

kind [kaɪnd] *adj* bon, bienveillant; **kind to** bon pour; **to be so kind as to** être assez aimable pour ‖ *s* espèce *f*, genre *m*, sorte *f*, classe *f*; **all kinds of** (coll) quantité de; **in kind** en nature; **kind of** (coll) plutôt, en quelque sorte; **of a kind** semblable, de même nature; **to pay in kind** payer en nature

kindergarten [ˈkɪndər,gɑrtən] *s* jardin *m* d'enfants

kindergartner [ˈkɪndər,gɑrtnər] *s* élève *mf* de jardin d'enfants; (*teacher*) jardinière *f*

kind′-heart′ed *adj* bon, bienveillant

kindle [ˈkɪndəl] *tr* allumer ‖ *intr* s'allumer

kindling [ˈkɪndlɪŋ] *s* allumage *m*; (*wood*) bois *m* d'allumage

kin′dling wood′ *s* bois *m* d'allumage

kind•ly [ˈkaɪndli] *adj* (*comp* **-lier;** *super* **-liest**) (*kind-hearted*) bon, bienveillant; (*e.g., climate*) doux; (*e.g., terrain*) favorable ‖ *adv* avec bonté, avec bienveillance; **to take kindly** prendre en bonne part; **to take kindly to** prendre en amitié

kindness [ˈkaɪndnɪs] *s* bonté *f*, obligeance *f*

kindred [ˈkɪndrɪd] *adj* apparenté, de même nature ‖ *s* parenté *f*, famille *f*; parenté, ressemblance *f*

Kinescope [ˈkɪnɪ,skop] *s* (trademark) kinescope *m*

kinetic [kɪˈnɛtɪk] *adj* cinétique ‖ **kinetics** *s* cinétique *f*

kinet′ic en′ergy *s* énergie *f* cinétique

king [kɪŋ] *s* roi *m*; (cards, chess, & fig) roi; (checkers) pion *m* doublé, dame *f* ‖ *tr* (checkers) damer

king′bolt′ *s* cheville *f* maîtresse

kingdom [ˈkɪŋdəm] *s* royaume *m*; (*one of three divisions of nature*) règne *m*

king′fish′er *s* martin-pêcheur *m*

king•ly [ˈkɪŋli] *adj* (*comp* **-lier;** *super* **-liest**) royal, de roi, digne d'un roi ‖ *adv* en roi, de roi, comme un roi

king′pin′ *s* cheville *f* ouvrière; (bowling) quille *f* du milieu; (coll) ponte *m*, pontife *f*

king′ post′ *s* poinçon *m*

kingship [ˈkɪŋ,ʃɪp] *s* royauté *f*

king′-size′ *adj* grand format, géant

king′s′ ran′som *s* rançon *f* de roi

kink [kɪŋk] *s* (*twist, e.g., in a rope*) nœud *m;* (*in a wire*) faux pli *m;* (*in hair*) frisette *f,* bouclette *f;* (*soreness in neck*) torticolis *m;* (*flaw, difficulty*) point *m* faible; (*mental twist*) lubie *f;* (naut) coque *f* ‖ *tr* nouer, entortiller ‖ *intr* se nouer, s'entortiller

kink·y [ˈkɪŋki] *adj* (*comp* **-ier;** *super* **-iest**) crépu, bouclé

kinsfolk [ˈkɪnzˌfok] *spl* parents *mpl*

kin'ship *s* parenté *f*

kins·man [ˈkɪnzmən] *s* (*pl* **-men**) parent *m*

kins·woman [ˈkɪnzˌwʊmən] *s* (*pl* **-wom'en**) parente *f*

kipper [ˈkɪpər] *s* kipper *m* ‖ *tr* saurer

kiss [kɪs] *s* baiser *m;* **to blow a kiss** donner un baiser en l'air ‖ *tr* embrasser, donner un baiser à ‖ *intr* s'embrasser

kit [kɪt] *s* nécessaire *m;* (*tub*) tonnelet *m;* (*to put together*) prêt-à-monter *m;* (*of traveler*) trousse *f* de voyage; (mil) équipement *m,* sac *m;* **the whole kit and caboodle** (coll) tout le saint-frusquin

kitchen [ˈkɪtʃən] *s* cuisine *f*

kitch'en cup'board *s* vaisselier *m*

kitchenette [ˌkɪtʃəˈnɛt] *s* petite cuisine *f,* cuisinette *f*

kitch'en gar'den *s* jardin *m* potager

kitch'en·maid *s* fille *f* de cuisine

kitch'en police' *s* (mil) corvée *f* de cuisine

kitch'en range' *s* cuisinière *f*

kitch'en sink' *s* évier *m;* **everything but the kitchen sink** tout sauf les murs

kitch'en·ware' *s* ustensiles *mpl* de cuisine

kite [kaɪt] *s* cerf-volant *m;* (orn) milan *m;* **to fly a kite** lancer ou enlever un cerf-volant

kith' and kin' [kɪθ] *spl* amis et parents *mpl,* cousinage *m*

kitsch [kɪtʃ] *adj & s* kitsch *m invar,* kitch *m invar*

kitten [ˈkɪtən] *s* chaton *m,* petit chat *m*

kittenish [ˈkɪtənɪʃ] *adj* enjoué, folâtre; (*woman*) coquette, chatte

kit·ty [ˈkɪti] *s* (*pl* **-ties**) minet *m,* minou *m;* (*in card games*) cagnotte *f,* poule *f;* **Kitty, kitty, kitty!** minet, minet, minet!

kiwi [ˈkiwi] *s* kiwi *m*

kleptomaniac [ˌklɛptəˈmeni,æk] *adj & s* kleptomane *mf*

klutz [klʌts] *s* (coll) gros lourdaud *m,* gros ballot *m*

knack [næk] *s* adresse *f,* chic *m*

knapsack [ˈnæpˌsæk] *s* sac *m* à dos, havresac *m*

knave [nev] *s* fripon *m;* (cards) valet *m*

knaver·y [ˈnevəri] *s* (*pl* **-ies**) friponnerie *f*

knead [nid] *tr* pétrir; (*to massage*) masser

knee [ni] *s* genou *m;* **to bring s.o. to his knees** mettre qn à genoux; **to go down on one's knees** se mettre à genoux

knee' breech'es *spl* culotte *f* courte

knee'cap' *s* rotule *f;* (*protective covering*) genouillère *f*

knee'-deep' *adj* jusqu'aux genoux

knee'-high' *adj* à la hauteur du genou

knee'hole' *s* trou *m,* évidement *m* pour l'entrée des genoux

knee' jerk' *s* réflexe *m* rotulien

kneel [nil] *v* (*pret & pp* **knelt** [nɛlt] or **kneeled**) *intr* s'agenouiller, se mettre à genoux

knee'pad' *s* genouillère *f*

knee'pan' *s* rotule *f*

knee' swell' *s* (*of organ*) genouillère *f*

knell [nɛl] *s* glas *m;* **to toll the knell of** sonner le glas de ‖ *intr* sonner le glas

knickers [ˈnɪkərz] *spl* pantalons *mpl* de golf, knickerbockers *mpl*

knickknack [ˈnɪkˌnæk] *s* colifichet *m*

knife [naɪf] *s* (*pl* **knives** [naɪvz]) couteau *m;* (*of paper cutter or other instrument*) couperet *m,* lame *f;* **to go under the knife** (coll) monter ou passer sur le billard ‖ *tr* poignarder

knife' sharp'ener *s* fusil *m,* affiloir *m*

knife' switch' *s* (elect) interrupteur *m* à couteau

knight [naɪt] *s* chevalier *m;* (chess) cavalier *m* ‖ *tr* créer ou faire chevalier

knight-errant [ˈnaɪtˈɛrənt] *s* (*pl* **knights-errant**) chevalier *m* errant

knighthood [ˈnaɪthʊd] *s* chevalerie *f*

knightly [ˈnaɪtli] *adj* chevaleresque

knit [nɪt] *v* (*pret & pp* **knitted** or **knit;** *ger* **knitting**) *tr* tricoter; (*one's brows*) froncer; **to knit together** lier, unir ‖ *intr* tricoter; (*said of bones*) se souder

knit' goods' *spl* tricot *m,* bonneterie *f*

knitting [ˈnɪtɪŋ] *s* (*action*) tricotage *m;* (*product*) tricot *m*

knit'ting machine' *s* tricoteuse *f*

knit'ting nee'dle *s* aiguille *f* à tricoter

knit'wear' *s* tricot *m*

knob [nɑb] *s* (*lump*) bosse *f;* (*of a door, drawer, etc.*) bouton *m,* poignée *f;* (*of a radio*) bouton *m*

knock [nɑk] *s* coup *m,* heurt *m;* (*of an internal-combustion engine*) cognement *m;* (slang) éreintement *m,* dénigrement *m* ‖ *tr* frapper; (*repeatedly*) cogner à, contre, ou sur; (slang) éreinter, dénigrer; **to knock about** bousculer; **to knock against** heurter contre; **to knock down** (*with a blow, punch, etc.*) renverser; (*to the highest bidder*) adjuger; **to knock in** enfoncer; **to knock off** faire tomber; **to knock out** faire sortir en cognant; (boxing) mettre knock-out; (*to fatigue*) (coll) claquer, fatiguer; **to knock up** (slang) engrosser ‖ *intr* frapper; (*said of internal-combustion engine*) cogner; **to knock about** vagabonder, se balader; **to knock against** se heurter contre; **to knock at** or **on** (*e.g., a door*) heurter à, frapper à; **to knock off** (*to stop working*) (coll) débrayer

knock' down' *adj* (*dismountable*) démontable ‖ *s* (*blow*) coup *m* d'assommoir; (*discount*) escompte *m*

knocked' out' *adj* éreinté, sonné; (boxing) knock-out

knocker [ˈnɑkər] *s* (*on a door*) heurtoir *m,* marteau *m;* (*critic*) (coll) éreinteur *m*

knock-kneed [ˈnɑk͵nid] *adj* cagneux
knock'out' *s* (boxing) knock-out *m;* (*person*) (coll) type *m* renversant; (*thing*) (coll) chose *f* sensationnelle
knock'out drops' *spl* (slang) narcotique *m*
knoll [nol] *s* mamelon *m*, tertre *m*
knot [nɑt] *s* nœud *m;* (*e.g. of people*) groupe *m;* (naut) nœud *m*, mille *m* marin à l'heure; (*loosely*) (naut) mille marin; **to tie a knot** faire un nœud; **to tie the knot** (coll) prononcer le conjungo ‖ *v* (*pret & pp* **knotted;** *ger* **knotting**) *tr* nouer; **to knot one's brow** froncer le sourcil ‖ *intr* se nouer
knot'hole' *f* trou *m* de nœud
knot•ty [ˈnɑti] *adj* (*comp* **-tier;** *super* **-tiest**) noueux; (*e.g., question*) épineux
know [no] *s*—**to be in the know** (coll) être au courant, être à la page, être au parfum ‖ *v* (*pret* **knew** [n(j)u];* *pp* **known**) *tr & intr* (*by reasoning or learning*) savoir; (*by the senses or by perception; through acquaintance or recognition*) connaître; **as far as I know** autant que je sache; **to know about** être informé de, savoir; **to know best** être le meilleur juge; **to know how to** + *inf* savoir + *inf;* **to let s.o. know about** faire part à qn de; **you ought to know better** vous devriez avoir honte; **you ought to know better than to. . .** vous devriez vous bien garder de. . .; **you wouldn't know s.o. from. . .** on prendrait qn pour. . .
knowable [ˈno•əbəl] *adj* connaissable
know'-how' *s* technique *f*, savoir-faire *m*
knowing [ˈno•ɪŋ] *adj* avisé; (*look, smile*) entendu
knowingly [ˈno•ɪŋli] *adv* sciemment, en connaissance de cause; (*on purpose*) exprès
know'-it-all' *adj* (coll) omniscient ‖ *s* (coll) Monsieur Je-sais-tout *m*
knowledge [ˈnɑlɪdʒ] *s* (*faculty*) science *f*, connaissances *fpl*, savoir *m;* (*awareness, familiarity*) connaissance *f;* **not to my knowl-** edge pas que je sache; **to have a thorough knowledge of** posséder une connaissance approfondie de; **to my knowledge, to the best of my knowledge** à ma connaissance, autant que je sache; **without my knowledge** à mon insu
knowledgeable [ˈnɑlɪdʒəbəl] *adj* (coll) intelligent, bien informé
know'-noth'ing *s* ignorant *m*
knuckle [ˈnʌkəl] *s* jointure *f or* articulation *f* du doigt; (*of a quadruped*) jarret *m;* (mach) joint *m* en charnière; **knuckle of ham** jambonneau *m;* **to rap s.o. over the knuckles** donner sur les doigts or ongles à qn ‖ *intr*—**to knuckle down** se soumettre; (*to work hard*) s'y mettre sérieusement
knuck'le ball' *s* (baseball) jointure *f* tire-bouchon *m*
knurl [nʌrl] *s* molette *f* ‖ *tr* moleter
k.o. [ˈkeˈo] (letterword) (**knockout**) *s* k.o. *m* ‖ *tr* mettre k.o.
kook [kuk] *s* (slang) drôle *mf* d'oiseau, drôle de numéro, type *m*
Koran [koˈrɑn], [koˈræn] *s* Coran *m*
Koranic [koˈrænɪk] *adj* coranique
Korea [koˈri•ə] *s* Corée *f;* la Corée
Korean [koˈri•ən] *adj* coréen ‖ *s* (*language*) coréen; (*person*) Coréen *m*
kosher [ˈkoʃər] *adj* casher, kasher, kascher; (coll) convenable; **it's kosher** c'est kascher
kowtow [ˈkaʊˈtaʊ] *intr* se prosterner à la chinoise; **to kowtow to** faire des courbettes à *or* devant
K.P. [ˈkeˈpi] *s* (letterword) (**kitchen police**) (mil) corvée *f* de cuisine; **to be on K.P. duty** (mil) être de soupe
Kremlin [ˈkrɛmlɪn] *s*—**the Kremlin** le Kremlin
kudos [ˈk(j)udɑs] *s* (coll) gloire *f*, éloges *mpl*, flatteries *fpl*
Kuwait [kuˈwet] *s* Koweït *m*
Kuwaiti [kuˈweti] *adj* koweïtien ‖ *s* Koweïtien *m*, Koweïtienne *f*

L

L, l [ɛl] *s* XIIe lettre de l'alphabet
la•bel [ˈlebəl] *s* étiquette *f;* (*brand*) marque *f;* (*in a dictionary*) rubrique *f*, référence *f* ‖ *v* (*pret & pp* **-beled** *or* **-belled;** *ger* **-beling** *or* **-belling**) *tr* étiqueter
labeling [ˈlebəlɪŋ] *s* étiquetage *m;* **labeling and sealing** habillage *m*
labial [ˈlebi•əl] *adj* labial ‖ *s* labiale *f*
labor [ˈlebər] *adj* ouvrier ‖ *s* travail *m;* (*toil*) labeur *m*, peine *f;* (*job, task*) tâche *f*, besogne *f;* (*manual work involved in an undertaking; the wages for such work*) main-d'œuvre *f;* (*wage-earning worker as contrasted with capital and management*) le salariat, le tra- vail; (*childbirth*) couches *fpl*, travail; **to be in labor** être en couches ‖ *tr* (*a point, subject, etc.*) insister sur; (*one's style*) travailler, élaborer ‖ *intr* travailler; (*to toil*) travailler dur, peiner; (*to exert oneself*) s'efforcer; (*said of ship*) fatiguer, bourlinguer; **to labor under** être victime de; **to labor up** (*a hill, slope, etc.*) gravir; **to labor uphill** peiner en côte; **to labor with child** être en travail d'enfant
la'bor and man'agement *spl* la classe ouvrière et le patronat
laborato•ry [ˈlæbərə͵tori] *s* (*pl* **-ries**) laboratoire *m*

lab′oratory class′ s classe f de travaux pratiques

La′bor Day′ s Jour m du Travail

labored [′lebərd] adj travaillé, trop élaboré; (e.g., breathing) pénible

laborer [′lebərər] s travailleur m, ouvrier m; (unskilled worker) journalier m, manœuvre m

laborious [lə′borı•əs] adj laborieux

la′bor move′ment s mouvement m syndicaliste

la′bor un′ion s syndicat m, syndicat ouvrier

Labourite [′lebə,raıt] adj & s (Brit) travailliste mf

La′bour Par′ty [′lebər] adj (Brit) travailliste ‖ s parti m travailliste

Labrador [′læbrə,dɔr] s le Labrador

laburnum [lə′bʌrnəm] s cytise m

labyrinth [′læbırınθ] s labyrinthe m

lace [les] s dentelle f; (string to tie shoe, corset, etc.) lacet m, cordon m; (braid) broderies fpl ‖ tr garnir or border de dentelles; (shoes, corset, etc.) lacer; (to braid) entrelacer; (coll) flanquer une rossée à rosser

lace′ trim′ming s passementerie f

lace′work′ s dentelles fpl, passementerie f

lachrymose [′lækrı,mos] adj larmoyant

lacing [′lesıŋ] s lacet m, cordon m; (trimming) galon m, passement m; (coll) rossée f

lack [læk] s manque m, défaut m; (lack of necessities) pénurie f; for lack of faute de ‖ tr manquer de, être dépourvu de ‖ intr (to be lacking) manquer, faire défaut

lackadaisical [,lækə′dezıkəl] adj languissant, apathique

lackey [′læki] s laquais m

lacking [′lækıŋ] prep dépourvu de, dénué de

lack′lus′ter adj terne, fade

laconic [lə′kɑnık] adj laconique

lacquer [′lækər] s laque m & f ‖ tr laquer

lac′quer ware′ s laques mpl, objets mpl d'art en laque

lacrosse [lə′krɔs] s crosse f, jeu m de crosse; **to play lacrosse** jouer à la crosse

lacu•na [lə′kjunə] s (pl -nas or -nae [ni]) lacune f

lac•y [′lesi] adj (comp -ier; super -iest) de dentelle; (fig) fin, léger

lad [læd] s garçon m, gars m

ladder [′lædər] s échelle f; (stepping stone) (fig) marchepied m, échelon m; (stepladder) marchepied, escabeau m; (run in stocking) (Brit) démaillage m; (stairway) (naut) escalier m

lad′der truck′ s fourgon-pompe m à échelle

la′dies′ room′ s toilettes fpl pour dames, lavabos mpl pour dames

ladle [′ledəl] s louche f ‖ tr servir à la louche

la•dy [′ledi] s (pl -dies) dame f; **ladies** (public sign) dames; **ladies and gentlemen!** (formula used in addressing an audience) mesdames, mesdemoiselles, messieurs!; messieurs dames! (coll)

la′dy•bird′ or **la′dy•bug′** s cocinelle f, bête f à bon Dieu

la′dy•fin′ger s biscuit m à la cuiller

la′dy-in-wait′ing s (pl **ladies-in-waiting**) demoiselle f d'honneur

la′dy-kil′ler s bourreau m des cœurs, tombeur m de femmes

la′dy•like′ adj de bon ton, de dame

la′dy•love′ s bien-aimée f, dulcinée f

la′dy of the house′ s maîtresse f de maison

la′dy's maid′ s camériste f

la′dy's man′ s homme m à succès

lag [læg] s retard m ‖ v (pret & pp **lagged**; ger **lagging**) intr traîner; **to lag behind** rester en arrière

la′ger beer′ [′lɑgər] s bière f de fermentation basse, lager m

laggard [′lægərd] adj tardif ‖ s traînard m

lagoon [lə′gun] s lagune f

laid′ pa′per [led] s papier m vergé

laid′ up′ adj mis en réserve; (naut) mis en rade; (coll) alité, au lit

lair [lɛr] s tanière f; (fig) repaire m

laity [′le•ıti] s profanes mfpl; (eccl) laïques mfpl

lake [lek] adj lacustre ‖ s lac m

lamb [læm] s agneau m

lambaste [læm′best] tr (to thrash) (coll) flanquer une rossée à; (to reprimand harshly) (coll) passer un savon à

lamb′ chop′ s côtelette f d'agneau

lambkin [′læmkın] s agnelet m

lamb′skin′ s peau f d'agneau; (dressed with its wool) mouton m, agnelin m

lame [lem] adj boiteux; (sore) endolori; (e.g., excuse) faible, piètre ‖ tr estropier, rendre boiteux

lament [lə′mɛnt] s lamentation f; (dirge) complainte f ‖ tr déplorer ‖ intr lamenter, se lamenter

lamentable [′læmntəbəl] adj lamentable

lamentation [,læmən′te/ən] s lamentation f

laminate [′læmı,net] tr laminer

lamp [læmp] s lampe f

lamp′black′ s noir m de fumée

lamp′ chim′ney s verre m de lampe

lamp′light′ s lumière f de lampe

lamp′light′er s allumeur m de réverbères

lampoon [læm′pun] s libelle m, pasquinade f ‖ tr faire des libelles contre

lamp′post′ s réverbère m, poteau m de réverbère

lamprey [′læmpri] s lamproie f

lamp′shade′ s abat-jour m

lamp′wick′ s mèche f de lampe

lance [læns] s lance f; (surg) lancette f, bistouri m ‖ tr percer d'un coup de lance; (surg) donner un coup de lancette or bistouri à

lancet [′lænsıt] s (surg) lancette f, bistouri m

land [lænd] adj terrestre, de terre ‖ s terre f; **land of milk and honey** pays de cocagne; **to make land** toucher terre; **to see how the land lies** sonder or tâter le terrain ‖ tr débarquer, mettre à terre; (an airplane) atterrir; (a fish) amener à terre; (e.g., a job) (coll) décrocher; (a blow) (coll) flanquer ‖ intr débarquer, des-

cendre à terre; (*said of airplane*) atterrir; **to
land on one's feet** retomber sur ses pieds; **to
land on the moon** alunir; **to land on the
water** amerrir

land′ breeze′ *s* brise *f* de terre

landed *adj* (*owning land*) terrien; (*real-estate*)
immobilier

land′ed prop′erty *s* propriété *f* foncière

land′fall′ *s* (*sighting land*) abordage *m*; (*landing of ship or plane*) atterrissage *m*; (*landslide*) glissement *m* de terrain

land′fill′ *s* dépotoir *m*, terre *f* remplie d'ordures

landing [′lændɪŋ] *s* (*of plane*) atterrissage *m*;
(*of ship*) mise *f* à terre, débarquement *m*;
(*place where passengers and goods are landed*) débarcadère *m*; (*of stairway*) palier *m*;
(*on the moon*) alunissage *m*

land′ing bea′con *s* (aer) radiophare *m* d'atterrissage

land′ing craft′ *s* (nav) péniche *f* de débarquement

land′ing field′ *s* (aer) terrain *m* d'atterrissage

land′ing force′ *s* (nav) détachement *m* de débarquement

land′ing gear′ *s* (aer) train *m* d'atterrissage

land′ing par′ty *s* (nav) détachement *m* de débarquement

land′ing stage′ *s* débarcadère *m*

land′ing strip′ *s* (aer) piste *f* d'atterrissage, aire
f d'atterrissage

land′la′dy *s* (*pl* **-dies**) (*e.g., of an apartment*)
logeuse *f*, propriétaire *f*; (*of a lodging house*)
patronne *f*; (*of an inn*) aubergiste *f*

land′locked′ *adj* entouré de terre

land′lord′ *s* (*e.g., of an apartment*) logeur *m*,
propriétaire *m*; (*of a lodging house*) patron
m; (*of an inn*) aubergiste *m*

landlubber [′lænd,lʌbər] *s* marin *m* d'eau
douce

land′mark′ *s* point *m* de repère, borne *f*; (*important event*) étape *f* importante; (naut) amer
m

land′ of′fice *s* bureau *m* du cadastre

land′own′er *s* propriétaire *m* foncier

landscape [′lænd,skep] *s* paysage *m* ‖ *tr* aménager en jardins

land′scape ar′chitect *s* architecte *m* paysagiste

land′scape gar′dener *s* jardinier *m* paysagiste

land′scape paint′er *s* paysagiste *m f*

landscapist [′lænd,skepɪst] *s* paysagiste *m f*

land′slide′ *s* glissement *m* de terrain, éboulement *m*; (*in an election*) raz *m* de marée, majorité *f* écrasante

landward [′lændwərd] *adv* du côté de la terre,
vers la terre

land′ wind′ [wɪnd] *s* vent *m* de terre

lane [len] *s* (*narrow street or passage*) ruelle *f*;
(*in the country*) sentier *m*; (*of an automobile
highway*) voie *f*; (*line of cars*) file *f*; (*of an
air or ocean route*) route *f* de navigation

langsyne [′læŋ′saɪn] *s* (Scotch) le temps jadis
‖ *adv* (Scotch) au temps jadis

language [′læŋgwɪdʒ] *s* (*the linguistic commu-*

nication used in a country or community) langue *f*, idiome *m*; (*way of speaking or writing,
style; figurative or poetic expression; communication of meaning said to be employed by
flowers, birds, art, etc.*) langage *m*; (*of a special group of people*) jargon *m*

lan′guage lab′oratory *s* laboratoire *m* de langues

languid [′læŋgwɪd] *adj* languissant

languish [′læŋgwɪʃ] *intr* languir

languor [′læŋgər] *s* langueur *f*

languorous [′læŋgərəs] *adj* langoureux

lank [læŋk] *adj* efflanqué; maigre; (*hair*) plat,
e.g., **lank hair** cheveux plats

lank•y [′læŋki] *adj* (*comp* **-ier;** *super* **-iest**)
grand et maigre

lanolin [′lænəlɪn] *s* lanoline *f*

lantern [′læntərn] *s* lanterne *f*

lan′tern slide′ *s* diapositive *f*

lanyard [′lænjərd] *s* (*around the neck*) cordon
m; (naut) tire-feu *m*; (naut) ride *f*

lap [læp] *s* (*of human body or clothing*) genoux
mpl, giron *m*; (*of garment*) genoux, pan *m*;
(*with the tongue*) coup *m* de langue; (*of the
waves*) clapotis *m*; (*in a race*) (sports) tour
m; **last lap** dernière étape *f* ‖ *v* (*pret & pp*
lapped; *ger* **lapping**) *tr* (*with the tongue*)
laper; **to lap up** laper; (coll) gober ‖ *intr* laper;
(*said of waves*) clapoter; **to lap over** déborder

lap′ dog′ *s* bichon *m*, chien *m* de manchon

lapel [lə′pɛl] *s* revers *m*

Lap′land′ *s* Laponie *f*; la Laponie

Laplander [′læp,lændər] *s* Lapon *m*

Lapp [læp] *s* (*language*) lapon *m*; (*person*)
Lapon *m*

lap′ robe′ *s* couverture *f* de voyage

lapse [læps] *s* intervalle *m*; (*slipping into guilt
or error*) faute *f* légère, écart *m*; (*fall, decline*)
disparition *f*, oubli *m*, déchéance *f*; (*e.g., of
an insurance policy*) expiration *f*, échéance *f*;
(*of memory*) trou *m*, absence *f*; **a lapse of time**
un laps de temps ‖ *intr* (*to elapse*) s'écouler,
passer; (*to err*) manquer à ses devoirs; (*to
decline*) déchoir; (*said, e.g., of a right*) périmer, tomber en désuétude; (*said, e.g., of a
legacy*) devenir caduc; (*said, e.g., of an insurance policy*) cesser d'être en vigueur

lap′top′ *s* (comp) portatif *m*

lap′top comput′er *s* ordinateur *m* portatif

lap′wing′ *s* (orn) vanneau *m* huppé

larce•ny [′lɑrsəni] *s* (*pl* **-nies**) larcin *m*, vol *m*

larch [lɑrtʃ] *s* (bot) mélèze *m*

lard [lɑrd] *s* saindoux *m* ‖ *tr* larder

larder [′lɑrdər] *s* garde-manger *m*

large [lɑrdʒ] *adj* grand; **at large** en liberté

large′ intes′tine *s* gros intestin *m*

largely [′lɑrdʒli] *adv* principalement

largeness [′lɑrdʒnɪs] *s* grandeur *f*

large′-scale′ *adj* sur une large échelle, de
grande envergure

lariat [′lærɪ•ət] *s* (*for catching animals*) lasso
m; (*for tying grazing animals*) longe *f*

lark [lɑrk] *s* alouette *f;* (*prank*) espièglerie *f;* **to go on a lark** (coll) faire la bombe
lark′spur′ *s* (*rocket larkspur*) pied-d'alouette *m;* (*field larkspur*) consoude *f* royale
lar•va [ˈlɑrvə] *s* (*pl* **-vae** [vi]) larve *f*
laryngeal [ˌlærɪnˈdʒi•əl] *adj* laryngé, laryngien
laryngitis [ˌlærɪnˈdʒaɪtɪs] *s* laryngite *f*
laryngoscope [ləˈrɪŋgəˌskop] *s* laryngoscope *m*
larynx [ˈlærɪŋks] *s* (*pl* **larynxes** or **larynges** [ləˈrɪndʒiz]) larynx *m*
lascivious [ləˈsɪvɪ•əs] *adj* lascif
lasciviousness [ləˈsɪvɪ•əsnɪs] *s* lasciveté *f*
laser [ˈlezər] *s* (acronym) (**light amplification by stimulated emission of radiation**) laser *m*
la′ser beam′ *s* rayon *m* laser
la′ser print′er *s* (comp) imprimante *f* à laser
lash [læʃ] *s* (*cord on end of whip*) mèche *f;* coup *m;* (*splatter of rain on window*) fouettement *m;* (*eyelash*) cil *m* ‖ *tr* fouetter, cingler; (*to bind, tie*) lier; (naut) amarrer ‖ *intr* fouetter; **to lash out at** cingler
lashing [ˈlæʃɪŋ] *s* fouettée *f;* (*rope*) amarre *f;* (naut) amarrage *m*
lass [læs] *s* jeune fille *f,* jeunesse *f;* bonne amie *f*
lassitude [ˈlæsɪˌt(j)ud] *s* lassitude *f*
las•so [ˈlæso] *s* (*pl* **-sos** or **-soes**) lasso *m*
last [læst] *adj* (*in a series*) dernier (before noun), e.g., **the last week of the war** la dernière semaine de la guerre; (*just elapsed*) dernier (after noun), e.g., **last week** la semaine dernière; **before last** avant-dernier, e.g., **the time before last** l'avant-dernière fois; **the last two** les deux derniers ‖ *s* dernier *m;* (*the end*) fin *f,* bout *m;* (*for holding shoe*) forme *f;* **at last** enfin, à la fin; **at long last** à la fin des fins; **the last of the month** la fin du mois; **to the last** jusqu'à la fin, jusqu'au bout ‖ *intr* durer; (*to hold out*) tenir
last′ eve′ning *adv* hier soir
lasting [ˈlæstɪŋ] *adj* durable
lastly [ˈlæstli] *adv* pour finir, en dernier lieu, enfin
last′-minute news′ *s* nouvelles *fpl* de dernière heure
last′ name′ *s* nom *m,* nom de famille
last′ night′ *adv* hier soir; cette nuit
last′ quar′ter *s* dernier quartier *m*
last′ sleep′ *s* sommeil *m* de la mort
last′ straw′ *s*—**that's the last straw!** c'est le comble!
Last′ Sup′per *s* (eccl) Cène *f*
last will′ and tes′tament *s* testament *m,* acte *m* de dernière volonté
last′ word′ *s* dernier mot *m;* (*latest style*) (coll) dernier cri *m*
latch [lætʃ] loquet *m* ‖ *tr* fermer au loquet
latch′key′ *s* clef *f* de porte d'entrée
latch′string′ *s* cordon *m* de loquet
late [let] *adj* (*happening after the usual time*) tardif; (*person; train, bus, etc.*) en retard; (*e.g., art*) de la dernière époque; (*events*) dernier, récent; (*news*) de la dernière heure; (*incumbent of an office*) ancien; (*deceased*) défunt, feu; **at a late hour in** (*the night, the day*) bien avant dans, à une heure avancée de; **in the late seventeenth century (eighteenth century, etc.)** vers la fin du dix-septième siècle (dix-huitième siècle, etc.); **it is late** il est tard; **of late** dernièrement, récemment, depuis peu; **to be late** être en retard; **to be late in** + *ger* tarder à + *inf* ‖ *adv* tard, tardivement; (*after the appointed time*) en retard; **better late than never** mieux vaut tard que jamais; **late in** (*the afternoon, the season, the week, the month*) vers la fin de; **late in life** sur le tard; **very late in** (*the night, the day*) bien avant dans, à une heure avancée de
late-comer [ˈletˌkʌmər] *s* (*newcomer*) nouveau venu *m;* (*one who arrives late*) retardataire *mf*
lateen′ sail′ [læˈtin] *s* voile *f* latine
lateen′ yard′ *s* antenne *f*
lately [ˈletli] *adv* dernièrement, récemment, depuis peu
latency [ˈletənsi] *s* latence *f*
latent [ˈletənt] *adj* latent
later [ˈletər] *adj comp* plus tard, plus tardif; (*event*) subséquent, plus récent; (*kings, luminaries, etc.*) derniers en date; **later than** postérieur à ‖ *adv comp* plus tard; **later on** plus tard, par la suite; **see you later** (coll) à tout à l'heure
lateral [ˈlætərəl] *adj* latéral
lath [læθ] *s* latte *f* ‖ *tr* latter
lathe [leð] *s* (mach) tour *m;* **to turn on a lathe** façonner au tour
lather [ˈlæðər] *s* (*of soap*) mousee *f;* (*of horse*) écume *f* ‖ *tr* savonner ‖ *intr* (*said of soap*) mousser; (*said of horse*) être couvert d'écume
lathing [ˈlæθɪŋ] *s* lattage *m*
Latin [ˈlætən] *adj* latin ‖ *s* (*language*) latin *m;* (*person*) Latin *m*
Lat′in Amer′ica *s* l'Amérique *f* latine
Lat′in-Amer′ican *adj* latino-américain ‖ *s* Latino-américain *m*
latitude [ˈlætɪˌt(j)ud] *s* latitude *f*
latrine [ləˈtrin] *s* latrines *fpl*
latter [ˈlætər] *adj* dernier; **the latter part of** (*e.g., a century*) la fin de ‖ *pron*—**the latter** celui-ci **§84;** le dernier
lattice [ˈlætɪs] *adj* treillissé ‖ *s* treillis *m* ‖ *tr* treillisser
lat′tice gird′er *s* poutre *f* à croisillons
lat′tice•work′ *s* treillis *m,* grillage *m*
laud [lɔd] *tr* louer
laudable [ˈlɔdəbəl] *adj* louable
laudanum [ˈlɔdənəm] *s* laudanum *m*
laudatory [ˈlɔdəˌtori] *adj* laudatif, élogieux
laugh [læf] *s* rire *m* ‖ *tr*—**to laugh away** chasser en riant; **to laugh off** tourner en plaisanterie ‖ *intr* rire; **to laugh at** rire de, se moquer de
laughable [ˈlæfəbəl] *adj* risible
laughing [ˈlæfɪŋ] *adj* riant, rieur; **it's no**

laughing matter il n'y a pas de quoi rire ‖ *s* rire *m*

laugh′ing gas′ *s* gaz *m* hilarant

laugh′ing•stock′ *s* risée *f*, fable *f*

laughter [ˈlæftər] *s* rire *m*

launch [lɔntʃ] *s* (*open motorboat*) canot *m* automobile, vedette *f*; (naut) chaloupe *f* ‖ *tr* lancer; (*an attack*) déclencher ‖ *intr*—**to launch into, to launch out on** se lancer dans

launcher [ˈlɔn/ər] *s* (rok) lanceur *m*

launching [ˈlɔntʃɪŋ] *s* lancement *m*

launch′ing pad′ *s* rampe *f* de lancement, aire *f* de lancement

launder [ˈlɔndər] *tr* faire la lessive, blanchir; (*money*) blanchir

launderer [ˈlɔndərər] *s* blanchisseur *m*, buandier *m*

laundering [ˈlɔndərɪŋ] *s* blanchissage *m;* (*of money*) blanchiment *m*

laundress [ˈlɔndrɪs] *s* blanchisseuse *f;* buandière *f*

Laundromat [ˈlɔndrə‚mæt] *s* (trademark) laverie *f* automatique, laverie libre-service, lavromat *m*

laun•dry [ˈlɔndri] *s* (*pl* **-dries**) linge *m* à blanchir, lessive *f;* (*room*) buanderie *f;* (*business*) blanchisserie *f;* (*with individual machines*) laverie *f* (*blanchisserie équipée de machines à laver individuelles*)

laun′dry•man *s* (*pl* **-men**) blanchisseur *m*, buandier *m*

laun′dry room′ *s* buanderie *f*

laun′dry•wom′an *s* (*pl* **-wom′en**) blanchisseuse *f*, buandière *f*

laureate [ˈlɔrɪ•ɪt] *adj & s* lauréat *m*

lau•rel [ˈlɔrəl] *s* laurier *m;* **to rest on one's laurels** s'endormir sur ses lauriers ‖ *v* (*pret & pp* **-reled** or **-relled;** *ger* **-reling** or **-relling**) *tr* couronner de lauriers

lava [ˈlɑvə] *s* lave *f*

lavaliere [‚lævə′lɪr] *s* pendentif *m*

lavato•ry [ˈlævə‚tori] *s* (*pl* **-ries**) (*room equipped for washing hands and face; bowl with running water*) lavabo *m;* (*toilet*) lavabos

lavender [ˈlævəndər] *s* lavande *f*

lav′ender wa′ter *s* eau *f* de lavande

lavish [ˈlævɪʃ] *adj* prodigue; (*reception, dinner, etc.*) somptueux, magnifique ‖ *tr* prodiguer

law [lɔ] *s* (*of man, of nature, of science*) loi *f;* (*branch of knowledge concerned with law; body of laws; study of law, profession of law*) droit *m;* **to go to law** recourir à la justice; **go to law with s.o.** citer qn en justice; **to lay down the law** faire la loi; **to practice law** exercer le droit; **to read law** étudier le droit, faire son droit

law′-abid′ing *adj* soumis aux lois, respectueux des lois

law′ and or′der *s* ordre *m* public; **to maintain law and order** maintenir or faire régner l'ordre

law′break′er *s* transgresseur *m* de la loi

law′ court′ *s* cour *f* de justice, tribunal *m*

lawful [ˈlɔfəl] *adj* légal, légitime

lawless [ˈlɔlɪs] *adj* sans loi; (*unbridled*) sans frein, déréglé

law′mak′er *s* législateur *m*

lawn [lɔn] *s* pelouse *f*, gazon *m;* (*fabric*) batiste *f*, linon *m*

lawn′ mow′er *s* tondeuse *f* de gazon

lawn′ trim′mer *s* (*nylon cord*) tondeuse *f* à fouet, coupe-herbe *m*

law′ of′fice *s* étude *f* (d'avocat)

law′ of na′tions *s* loi *f* des nations

law′ of the jun′gle *s* loi *f* de la jungle

law′ stu′dent *s* étudiant *m* en droit

law′suit′ *s* procès *m*

lawyer [ˈlɔjər] *s* avocat *m*

lax [læks] *adj* (*in morals, discipline, etc.*) relâché, négligent; (*loose, not tense*) lâche; (*vague*) vague, flou

laxative [ˈlæksətɪv] *adj & s* laxatif *m*

lay [le] *adj* (*not belonging to clergy*) laïc or laïque; (*not having special training*) profane ‖ *s* situation *f;* (*poem*) lai *m* ‖ *v* (*pret & pp* **laid** [led]) *tr* poser, mettre; (*a trap*) tendre; (*eggs*) pondre; (*e.g., bricks*) ranger; (*a foundation*) jeter, établir; (*a cable*) poser; (*a mine*) (naut) mouiller; **to be laid in Rome (in France, etc.)** (*said, e.g., of scene*) se passer à Rome (en France, etc.); **to lay aside, away,** or **by** mettre de côté; **to lay down** (*one's life*) sacrifier; (*one's weapons*) déposer; (*conditions*) imposer; **to lay down the law to s.o.** (coll) rappeler qn à l'ordre; **to lay in** (*supplies*) faire provision de; **to lay into s.o.** (coll) sauter dessus qn; **to lay it on thick** (coll) y aller fort; **to lay low** (*to overwhelm*) abattre, terrasser; **to lay off** (*an employee*) congédier; (*to mark the boundaries of*) tracer; (*to stop bothering*) (coll) laisser tranquille; **to lay on** (*paint*) appliquer; (*hands; taxes*) imposer; **to lay open** mettre à nu; **to lay out** arranger; (*to display*) étaler; (*to outline*) tracer; (*money*) débourser; (*a corpse*) faire la toilette de; (*a garden*) aménager; **to lay up** (*to stock up on*) amasser; (*to injure*) aliter; (*a boat*) mettre en rade ‖ *intr* (*said of hen*) pondre; **to lay about** frapper de tous côtés; **to lay for** être à l'affût de, guetter; **to lay into** (slang) rosser, battre; **to lay off** (coll) cesser; **to lay off smoking** (coll) renoncer au tabac; **to lay over** faire escale; **to lay to** (naut) se mettre à la cape

lay′ broth′er *s* frère *m* lai, frère convers

layer [ˈle•ər] *s* couche *f;* (hen) pondeuse *f* ‖ *tr* (hort) marcotter

lay′er cake′ *s* gâteau *m* sandwich

layette [leˈɛt] *s* layette *f*

lay′ fig′ure *s* mannequin *m*

laying [ˈle•ɪŋ] *s* (*of carpet*) pose *f;* (*of foundation*) assise *f;* (*of eggs*) ponte *f*

lay′man *s* (*pl* **-men**) (*person who is not a clergyman*) laïc *m* or laïque *mf;* (*person who has no special training*) profane *mf*

lay′off′ *s* (*discharge*) renvoi *m;* (*unemployment*) chômage *m*

lay′ of the land′ s configuration f du terrain; (fig) aspect m de l'affaire

lay′out′ s plan m, dessin m, tracé m; (of tools) montage m; (organization) disposition f; (banquet) (coll) festin m

lay′o′ver s arrêt m en cours de route

lay′ sis′ter s sœur f laie, sœur converse

laziness [ˈlezɪnɪs] s paresse f

la•zy [ˈlezi] adj (comp **-zier;** super **-ziest**) paresseux

la′zy•bones′ s (coll) flemmard m, fainéant m

la′zy Su′san s plateau m tournant

lb. abbr (**pound**) livre f

lea [li] s (meadow) pâturage m, prairie f

lead [lɛd] adj en plomb, de plomb ‖ [lɛd] s plomb m; (of lead pencil) mine f (de plombagine); (for sounding depth) (naut) sonde f; (typ) interligne f ‖ [lɛd] v (pret & pp **leaded;** ger **leading**) tr plomber; (typ) interligner ‖ [lid] s (foremost place) avance f; (guidance) direction f, conduite f; (leash) laisse f; (of a newspaper article) article m de fond; (leading role) premier rôle m; (leading man) jeune premier m; (elec) câble m de canalisation, conducteur m; (elec, mach) avance; (min) filon m; **to follow s.o.'s lead** suivre l'exemple de qn; **to have the lead** (cards) avoir la main; **to return the lead** (cards) rejouer la couleur; **to take the lead** prendre le pas ‖ [lid] v (pret & pp **led** [lɛd] tr conduire, mener; (to command) commander, diriger; (to be foremost in) être à la tête de; (e.g., an orchestra) diriger; (a good or bad life) mener; (a certain card) attaquer de; (a certain card suit) attaquer; (elec, mach) canaliser; **to lead away** or **off** emmener; **to lead off** (to start) commencer; **to lead on** encourager; **to lead s.o. to believe** mener qn à croire ‖ intr aller devant, tenir la tête; (cards) avoir la main; **to lead to** conduire à, mener à; (another street, a certain result, etc.) aboutir à; **to lead up to** (a great work) préluder à (un grand ouvrage); (a subject) amener (un sujet)

leaden [ˈlɛdən] adj (of lead; like lead) de plomb, en plomb; (heavy as lead) pesant; (sluggish) alangui; (complexion) plombé

leader [ˈlidər] s chef m, guide mf; (ringleader) tête f; chef d'orchestre; (in a dance; among animals) meneur m; (in a newspaper) article m de fond; (of a reel of tape or film) amorce f; (bargain) article réclame; (vein of ore) filon m

leadership [ˈlidər,ʃip] s direction f; don m de commandement

leading [ˈlidɪŋ] adj principal, premier

lead′ing edge′ s (aer) bord m d'attaque

lead′ing la′dy s vedette f, étoile f, jeune première f

lead′ing man′ s (pl **men′**) jeune premier m

lead′ing ques′tion s question f tendancieuse

lead′-in wire′ [ˈlidˈɪn] s (rad, telv) fil m d'amenée

lead′ pen′cil [lɛd] s crayon m (à mine de graphite)

lead′ poi′soning [lɛd] s saturnisme m

leaf [lif] s (pl **leaves** [livz]) feuille f; (inserted leaf of table) rallonge f; (hinged leaf of door or table top) battant m; **to shake like a leaf** trembler comme une feuille; **to turn over a new leaf** tourner la page, faire peau neuve ‖ intr—**to leaf through** feuilleter

leafless [ˈliflɪs] adj sans feuilles, dénudé

leaflet [ˈliflɪt] s dépliant m, papillon m, feuillet m; (bot) foliole f

leaf′stalk′ s (bot) pétiole m

leaf•y [ˈlifi] adj (comp **-ier;** super **-iest**) feuillu, touffu

league [lig] s (unit of distance) lieue f; (association, alliance) ligue f ‖ tr liguer ‖ intr se liguer

League′ of Na′tions s Société f des Nations

leak [lik] s fuite f; (in a ship) voie f d'eau; (of electricity, heat, etc.) perte f, fuite; (of news, secrets, money, etc.) fuite; **to spring a leak** avoir une fuite; (naut) faire une voie d'eau ‖ tr faire couler; (gas, steam; secrets, news) laisser échapper ‖ intr fuire, s'écouler; (naut) faire eau; **to leak away** se perdre; **to leak out** (said of news, secrets, etc.) transpirer, s'ébruiter

leakage [ˈlikɪdʒ] s fuite f; (elec) perte f

leak•y [ˈliki] adj (comp **-ier;** super **-iest**) percé, troué; qui a des fuites; (shoes) qui prennent l'eau; (coll) indiscret

lean [lin] adj maigre; (gasoline mixture) pauvre ‖ s (leaning) inclinaison f; (of meat) maigre m ‖ v (pret & pp **leaned** or **leant** [lɛnt] tr incliner; **to lean s.th. against s.th.** appuyer q.ch. contre q.ch. ‖ intr s'incliner, pencher; **to lean against** s'appuyer contre; **to lean forward** s'incliner or se pencher en avant; **to lean out of** (e.g., a window) se pencher par; **to lean over** se pencher; (e.g., s.o.'s shoulder) se pencher sur; **to lean toward** (fig) incliner à or vers, pencher pour or vers

leaning [ˈlinɪŋ] adj penché ‖ s inclinaison f; (fig) inclination f, penchant m

lean′-to′ s (pl **-tos**) appentis m

lean′ years′ spl années fpl maigres

leap [lip] s saut m, bond m; **by leaps and bounds** par sauts et par bonds; **leap in the dark** saut m à l'aveuglette ‖ v (pret & pp **leaped** or **leapt** [lɛpt]) tr sauter, franchir ‖ intr sauter, bondir; **to leap across** or **over** sauter; **to leap up** sursauter; (said, e.g., of flame) jaillir

leap′ day′ s jour m intercalaire

leap′frog′ s saute-mouton m

leap′ year′ s année f bissextile

learn [lʌrn] v (pret & pp **learned** [lʌrnt] or **learnt** [lʌrnt] tr apprendre ‖ intr apprendre; **to learn to** apprendre à

learned [ˈlʌrnɪd] adj savant, érudit

learn′ed jour′nal s revue f d'une société savante

learn′ed profes′sion s profession f libérale

learn′ed soci′ety *s* société *f* savante
learn′ed word′ *s* mot *m* savant
learner [ˈlʌrnər] *s* élève *mf;* *(beginner)* débutant *m,* apprenti *m*
learn′er′s per′mit *s* (aut) permis *m* de conduire (*d′un élève chauffeur*)
learning [ˈlʌrnɪŋ] *s* (*act and time devoted*) étude *f;* (*scholarship*) savoir *m,* érudition *f,* science *f*
lease [lis] *s* bail *m;* **to give a new lease on life** donner un regain de vie ‖ *tr* (*in the role of landlord*) donner or louer à bail; (*in the role of tenant*) prendre à bail
lease′hold′ *adj* tenu à bail ‖ *s* tenure *f* à bail
leash [liʃ] *s* laisse *f;* **on the leash** en laisse, à l'attache; **to strain at the leash** (fig) ruer dans les brancards ‖ *tr* tenir en laisse
leasing [ˈlisɪŋ] *s* crédit-bail *m*
least [list] *adj* super (le) moindre §91 ‖ *s* (le) moins *m;* **at least** du moins; **at the very least** tout au moins; **it's the least of my worries** c'est le cadet de mes soucis; **not in the least** pas le moins du monde, nullement; **to say the least** pour ne pas dire plus ‖ *adv* super (le) moins §91
least′ com′mon denom′inator (L.C.D.) *s* plus petit commun multiple *m* (P.P.C.M.)
leather [ˈlɛðər] *s* cuir *m*
leath′er•back tur′tle *s* luth *m*
leath′er-bound′ *adj* relié cuir
leath′er•neck′ *s* (slang) fusilier *m* marin
leathery [ˈlɛðəri] *adj* (*e.g.,* steak) (coll) coriace
leave [liv] *s* permission *f;* (mil) permission de détente; **by your leave** ne vous en déplaise; **on leave** en congé; (mil) en permission; **to give leave to s.o.** to permettre or accorder à qn de; **to take leave (of)** prendre congé (de), faire ses adieux (à) ‖ *v* (*pret & pp* **left** [lɛft] *tr* (*to let stay; to stop, give up; to disregard*) laisser; (*to go away from*) partir de, quitter; (*to bequeath*) léguer, laisser; (*a wife*) quitter, abandonner; **to be left** rester, e.g., **the letter was left unanswered** la lettre est restée sans réponse; e.g., **there are three dollars left** il reste trois dollars; **to be left for s.o.** to être à qn de; **to be left over** rester; **to leave about** (*without putting away*) laisser traîner; **to leave alone** laisser tranquille; **to leave it up to** s'en remettre à, s'en rapporter à; **to leave no stone unturned** faire flèche de tout bois, mettre tout en œuvre; **to leave off** (*a piece of clothing*) ne pas mettre; (*a passenger*) déposer; **to leave off** + *ger* cesser de + *inf,* renoncer à + *inf;* **to leave out** omettre ‖ *intr* partir, s'en aller; **where did we leave off?** où en sommes-nous restés?
leaven [ˈlɛvən] *s* levain *m* ‖ *tr* faire lever; (fig) transformer, modifier
leavening [ˈlɛvənɪŋ] *adj* transformateur ‖ *s* levain *m*
leave′ of ab′sence *s* congé *m*
leave′-tak′ing *s* congé *m,* adieux *mpl*
leavings [ˈlivɪŋz] *spl* restes *mpl,* reliefs *mpl*

Leba•nese [ˌlɛbəˈniz] *adj* libanais ‖ *s* (*pl* **-nese**) Libanais *m*
Lebanon [ˈlɛbənən] *s* le Liban
lecher [ˈlɛtʃər] *s* débauché *m,* libertin *m* ‖ *intr* vivre dans la débauche
lecherous [ˈlɛtʃərəs] *adj* lubrique, lascif
lechery [ˈlɛtʃəri] *s* lubricité *f,* lasciveté *f*
lectern [ˈlɛktərn] *s* lutrin *m*
lecture [ˈlɛktʃər] *s* conférence *f;* (*tedious reprimand*) sermon *m* ‖ *tr* faire une conférence à; (*to rebuke*) sermonner ‖ *intr* faire une conférence or des conférences
lecturer [ˈlɛktʃərər] *s* conférencier *m*
ledge [lɛdʒ] *s* saillie *f,* corniche *f;* (*projection in a wall*) corniche *f*
ledger [ˈlɛdʒər] *s* (*slab*) pierre *f* tombale; (com) grand livre *m*
ledg′er line′ *s* (mus) ligne *f* supplémentaire
lee [li] *s* (*shelter*) (naut) abri *m;* (*quarter toward which wind blows*) côté *m* sous le vent; **lees** lie *f*
leech [litʃ] *s* sangsue *f;* **to stick like a leech to s.o.** s'accrocher à qn
leek [lik] *s* poireau *m*
leer [lɪr] *s* regard *m* lubrique, œillade *f* ‖ *intr* lancer or jeter une œillade; **to leer at** lorgner
leer•y [ˈlɪri] *adj* (*comp* **-ier;** *super* **-iest**) (coll) soupçonneux, méfiant
leeward [ˈliwərd], [ˈluˈərd] *adj & adv* sous le vent ‖ *s* côté *m* sous le vent; **to pass to leeward of** passer sous le vent de
Lee′ward Is′lands [ˈliwərd] *spl* îles *fpl* Sous-le-Vent
lee′way′ *s* (aer, naut) dérive *f;* (*of time, money*) (coll) marge *f;* (*for action*) (coll) champ *m,* liberté *f*
left [lɛft] *adj* gauche; (*left over*) de surplus ‖ *s* (*left hand*) gauche *f;* (boxing) gauche *m;* **on the left, to the left** à gauche; **the Left** (pol) la gauche; **to make a left** tourner à gauche ‖ *adv* à gauche
left′ field′ *s* (baseball) gauche *f* du grand champ
left′-hand′ drive′ *s* (aut) conduite *f* à gauche
left′-hand′ed *adj* gaucher; (*clumsy*) gauche; (*counterclockwise*) à gauche, en sens inverse des aiguilles d'une montre; (*e.g.,* compliment) douteux, ambigu
leftish [ˈlɛftɪʃ] *adj* gauchisant
leftism [ˈlɛftɪzəm] *s* gauchisme *m*
leftist [ˈlɛftɪst] *adj & s* gauchiste *mf*
left′o′ver *adj* de surplus, restant ‖ **leftovers** *spl* restes *mpl*
left′-wing′ *adj* gauchiste, gauchisant
left-winger [ˈlɛftˈwɪŋər] *s* (coll) gauchiste *mf*
left•y [ˈlɛfti] *adj* (coll) gaucher ‖ *s* (*pl* **-ies**) (coll) gaucher *m*
leg [lɛg] *s* jambe *f;* (*of boot or stocking*) tige *f;* (*of fowl; of frogs*) cuisse *f;* (*of journey*) étape *f;* **to be on one's last legs** n'avoir plus de jambes; **to pull the leg of** (coll) se payer la tête de, faire marcher
lega•cy [ˈlɛgəsi] *s* (*pl* **-cies**) legs *m*
legal [ˈligəl] *adj* légal; (*practice*) juridique

le′gal flaw′ *s* vice *m* de forme
le′gal hol′iday *s* jour *m* férié
legali·ty [lɪˈgælɪti] *s* (*pl* **-ties**) légalité *f*
legalization [ˌligələˈzeʃən] *s* légalisation *f*
legalize [ˈligəˌlaɪz] *tr* légaliser
le′gal ten′der *s* cours *m* légal, monnaie *f* libératoire
legate [ˈlɛgɪt] *s* ambassadeur *m*, envoyé *m*; (eccl) légat *m*
legatee [ˌlɛgəˈti] *s* légataire *mf*
legation [lɪˈgeʃən] *s* légation *f*
legend [ˈlɛdʒənd] *s* légende *f*
legendary [ˈlɛdʒənˌdɛri] *adj* légendaire
legerdemain [ˌlɛdʒərdɪˈmen] *s* escamotage *m*, passe-passe *m*
leggings [ˈlɛgɪŋz] *spl* jambières *fpl*, guêtres *fpl*, leggings *fpl*
leg·gy [ˈlɛgi] *adj* (*comp* **-gier;** *super* **-giest**) (*awkward*) dégingandé; (*attractive*) aux longues jambes élégantes
leg′horn′ *s* (*hat*) chapeau *m* de paille d'Italie; (*chicken*) leghorn *f*; **Leghorn** Livourne *f*
legibility [ˌlɛdʒɪˈbɪlɪti] *s* lisibilité *f*
legible [ˈlɛdʒɪbəl] *adj* lisible
legion [ˈlidʒən] *s* légion *f*
le′gionnaire′s′ disease′ [ˈlidʒəˌnɛrz] *s* (pathol) maladie *f* du légionnaire
legislate [ˈlɛdʒɪsˌlet] *tr* imposer à force de loi ‖ *intr* faire des lois, légiférer
legislation [ˌlɛdʒɪsˈleʃən] *s* législation *f*
legislative [ˈlɛdʒɪsˌletɪv] *adj* législatif
legislator [ˈlɛdʒɪsˌletər] *s* législateur *m*
legislature [ˈlɛdʒɪsˌletʃər] *s* assemblée *f* législative, législature *f*
legitimacy [lɪˈdʒɪtɪməsi] *s* légitimité *f*
legitimate [lɪˈdʒɪtɪmɪt] *adj* légitime ‖ [lɪˈdʒɪtɪˌmet] *tr* légitimer
legit′imate dra′ma *s* théâtre *m* régulier
legitimize [lɪˈdʒɪtɪˌmaɪz] *tr* légitimer
leg′ of lamb′ *s* gigot *m* d'agneau
leg′ of mut′ton *s* gigot *m*
leg′-of-mut′ton sleeve′ *s* manche *f* gigot
legume [ˈlɛgjum], [lɪˈgjum] *s* (*pod*) légume *m*; (bot) légumineuse *f*
leg′warm′er *s* jambière *f*
leg′ work′ *s* assemblage *m* d'information
leisure [ˈliʒər], [ˈlɛʒər] *s* loisir *m*; **at leisure** à loisir; **in leisure moments** à temps perdu; **leisure activities** loisirs *mpl*
lei′sure class′ *s* désœuvrés *mpl*, rentiers *mpl*
lei′sure hours′ *spl* heures *fpl* de loisir
leisurely [ˈliʒərli] *adj* tranquille, posé ‖ *adv* posément, sans hâte
lemon [ˈlɛmən] *s* citron *m*; (*e.g., worthless car*) (coll) clou *m*
lemonade [ˌlɛməˈned] *s* citronnade *f*
lem′on squeez′er *s* presse-citron *m*
lem′on tree′ *s* citronnier *m*
lem′on verbe′na [vərˈbinə] *s* verveine *f* citronnelle
lend [lɛnd] *v* (*pret & pp* **lent** [lɛnt]) *tr* prêter
lender [ˈlɛndər] *s* prêteur *m*
lend′ing li′brary *s* bibliothèque *f* de prêt

length [lɛŋθ] *s* longueur *f*; (*e.g., of string*) bout *m*, morceau *m*; (*of time*) durée *f*; **at length** longuement, en détail; (*finally*) enfin, à la fin; **in length** de longueur; **to go to any length** to ne reculer devant rien pour; **to keep at arm's length** tenir à distance
lengthen [ˈlɛŋθən] *tr* allonger, rallonger ‖ *intr* s'allonger
length′wise′ *adj* longitudinal ‖ *adv* en longueur, dans le sens de la longueur
length·y [ˈlɛŋθi] *adj* (*comp* **-ier;** *super* **-iest**) prolongé, assez long
leniency [ˈliniˌənsi] *s* douceur *f*, clémence *f*
lenient [ˈliniˌənt] *adj* doux, clément
lens [lɛnz] *s* lentille *f*; (anat) cristallin *m*
Lent [lɛnt] *s* le Carême
Lenten [ˈlɛntən] *adj* de carême
lentil [ˈlɛntəl] *s* lentille *f*
Leo [ˈliˌo] *s* (astr, astrol) le Lion
leopard [ˈlɛpərd] *s* léopard *m*
leotard [ˈliˌəˌtɑrd] *s* maillot *m* de gym; maillot de danseur, combinaison *f* de danse; (*tights*) maillot, collant *m*
leper [ˈlɛpər] *s* lépreux *m*
lep′er house′ *s* léproserie *f*
leprosy [ˈlɛprəsi] *s* lèpre *f*
leprous [ˈlɛprəs] *adj* lépreux
lesbian [ˈlɛzbiˌən] *adj* lesbien ‖ *s* (*female homosexual*) lesbienne
lesbianism [ˈlɛzbiˌəˌnɪzəm] *s* lesbianisme *m*
lese majesty [ˈlizˈmædʒɪsti] *s* crime *m* de lèse-majesté
lesion [ˈliʒən] *s* lésion *f*
less [lɛs] *adj comp* moindre §91 ‖ *s* moins *m* ‖ *adv comp* moins §91; **less and less** de moins en moins; **less than** moins que; (followed by numeral) moins de; **the less . . . the less** (or **the more**) moins . . . moins (or plus)
lessee [lɛsˈi] *s* preneur *m*; (*e.g., of house*) locataire *mf*; (*e.g., of gasoline station*) concessionnaire *mf*
lessen [ˈlɛsən] *tr* diminuer, amoindrir ‖ *intr* se diminuer, s'amoindrir
lesser [ˈlɛsər] *adj comp* moindre §91; **the lesser of two evils** le moindre de deux maux
lesson [ˈlɛsən] *s* leçon *f*
lessor [ˈlɛsər] *s* bailleur *m*
lest [lɛst] *conj* de peur que, de crainte que
let [lɛt] *v* (*pret & pp* **let;** *ger* **letting**) *tr* laisser; (*to rent*) louer; **let** + *inf* que + *subj*, e.g., **let him come in** qu'il entre; **let alone** sans parler de, sans compter; **let well enough alone** le mieux est souvent l'ennemi du bien; **let us eat, work, etc.** mangeons, travaillons, etc.; **to be let off with** en être quitte pour; **to let** à louer, e.g., **house to let** maison à louer; **to let alone, to let be** laisser tranquille; **to let by** laisser passer; **to let down** baisser, descendre; (*one's hair*) dénouer, défaire; (*e.g., a garment*) allonger; (*to leave in the lurch*) laisser en panne, faire faux bond à; **to let fly** décocher; **to let go** laisser partir; **to let have** laisser, e.g., **he let Robert have it for three**

dollars il l'a laissé à Robert pour trois dollars; **to let in** laisser entrer; **to let in the clutch** (aut) embrayer; **to let into** admettre dans; **to let loose** lâcher; **to let off** laisser partir; (*e.g., steam from a boiler*) laisser échapper, lâcher; (*e.g., a culprit*) pardonner à; **to let oneself go** se laisser aller; **to let on that** (coll) faire croire que; **to let out** faire or laisser sortir; (*e.g., a dress*) élargir; (*a cry; a secret; a prisoner*) laisser échapper; (*to reveal*) révéler, divulguer; **to let out on bail** relâcher sous caution; **to let out the clutch** débrayer; **to let slip** laisser tomber; **to let s.o.** + *inf* permettre à qn de + *inf*; laisser qn + *inf*, e.g., **he let Mary go to the theater** il a laissé Marie aller au théâtre; **to let s.o. in on** (*a secret*) (coll) confier à qn; (*e.g., a racing tip*) (coll) tuyauter qn sur; **to let s.o. know s.th.** faire savoir q.ch. à qn, mettre qn au courant de q.ch.; **to let s.o. off with** faire grâce à qn de; **to let stand** laisser, e.g., **he let the errors stand** il a laissé les fautes; **to let s.th. go for** (*a low price*) laisser q.ch. pour; **to let through** laisser passer; **to let up** laisser monter || *intr* (*said of house, apartment, etc.*) se louer; **to let down** (coll) ralentir; **to let go of** lâcher prise de; **to let out** (*said of class, school, etc.*) finir, se terminer; **to let up** (coll) ralentir, diminuer; (*on discipline; on a person*) devenir moins sévère

let′down′ s diminution f; (*disappointment*) déception f
lethal [′liθəl] adj mortel; (*weapon*) meurtrier
lethargic [lɪ′θɑrdʒɪk] adj léthargique
lethar•gy [′lɛθərdʒi] s (*pl* **-gies**) léthargie f
letter [′lɛtər] s lettre f; **letters** (*literature*) lettres; **to the letter** à la lettre, au pied de la lettre || *tr* marquer avec des lettres
let′ter box′ s boîte f aux lettres
let′ter car′rier s facteur m
let′ter drop′ s passe-lettres m, fente f (dans la porte pour le courrier)
lettered adj (*person*) lettré
let′ter file′ s classeur m de lettres
let′ter•head′ s en-tête m
lettering [′lɛtərɪŋ] s (*action*) lettrage m; (*title*) inscription f
let′ter of cred′it s lettre f de crédit
let′ter o′pener s coupe-papier m
let′ter pa′per s papier m à lettres
let′ter•per′fect adj correct; sûr
let′ter press′ s presse f à copier
let′ter•press′ s impression f typographique; (*in distinction to illustrations*) texte m
let′ter scales′ spl pèse-lettre m
let′ter•word′ s sigle m
lettuce [′lɛtɪs] s laitue f
let′up′ s accalmie f, pause f; **without letup** sans relâche
leucorrhea [,lukə′ri•ə] s leucorrhée f
leukemia [lu′kimɪ•ə] s leucémie f
Levant [lɪ′vænt] s Levant m

Levantine [′lɛvən,tin], [lɪ′væntin] adj levantin || s Levantin m
levee [′lɛvi] s (*embankment*) levée f, digue f; réception f royale
lev•el [′lɛvəl] adj de niveau; (*flat*) égal, uni; (*spoonful*) arasé; **level with** de niveau avec, à fleur de || s niveau m; **on a level with** au niveau de; **to be on the level** (coll) être de bonne foi; **to find one's level** trouver son niveau || v (*pret & pp* **-eled** or **-elled**; *ger* **-eling** or **-elling**) tr niveler; (*to smooth, flatten out*) aplanir, araser; (*to bring down*) raser; (*a gun*) braquer; (*accusations, sarcasm*) lancer, diriger; **to level out** égaliser; **to level up** (aer) redresser || *intr* (aer) redresser; **to level with** (coll) parler franchement à
lev′el•head′ed adj équilibré, pondéré
lev′eling rod′ s (surv) jalon-mire m, jalon m d'arpentage
lever [′livər] s levier m || *tr* soulever or ouvrir au moyen d'un levier
leverage [′lɛvərɪdʒ] s puissance f or force f de levier; (fig) influence f, avantage m
lev′eraged buy′out s (com, econ) désintéressement m avec le financement en dehors du actif
leviathan [lɪ′vaɪ•əθən] s léviathan m
levitation [,lɛvɪ′te∫ən] s lévitation f
levi•ty [′lɛvɪti] s (*pl* **-ties**) légèreté f
lev•y [′lɛvi] s (*pl* **-ies**) levée f || v (*pret & pp* **-ied**) tr lever; (*a fine*) imposer
lewd [lud] adj luxurieux, lubrique
lewdness [′ludnɪs] s luxure f, lubricité f
lexical [′lɛksɪkəl] adj lexical
lexicographer [,lɛksɪ′kɑgrəfər] s lexicographe mf
lexicographic(al) [,lɛksɪkə′græfɪk(əl)] adj lexicographique
lexicography [,lɛksɪ′kɑgrəfi] s lexicographie f
lexicology [,lɛksɪ′kɑlədʒi] s lexicologie f
lexicon [′lɛksɪkən] s lexique m
liabili•ty [,laɪ•ə′bɪlɪti] s (*pl* **-ties**) responsabilité f; (*e.g., to disease*) prédisposition f; **liabilities** obligations fpl, dettes fpl
liabil′ity insur′ance s assurance f tous risques
liable [′laɪ•əbəl] adj sujet; **liable for** (*a debt, fine, etc.*) passible de, responsable de; **we (you, etc.) are liable to** + *inf* (coll) il se peut que nous (vous, etc.) + *pres subj*; (coll) il est probable que nous (vous, etc.) + *pres ind*
liaison [li′ezən] s liaison f
liar [′laɪ•ər] s menteur m
libation [laɪ′be∫ən] s libation f
li•bel [′laɪbəl] s diffamation f, calomnie f; (*in writing*) écrit m diffamatoire || v (*pret & pp* **-beled** or **-belled**; *ger* **-beling** or **-belling**) tr diffamer, calomnier
libelous [′laɪbələs] adj diffamatoire, calomnieux
liberal [′lɪbərəl] adj libéral; (*share, supply, etc.*) libéral, généreux, copieux; (*ideas*) large || s libéral m
liberali•ty [,lɪbə′rælɪti] s (*pl* **-ties**) libéralité f; (*breadth of mind*) largeur f de vues

lib′eral•mind′ed adj tolérant
liberate [ˈlɪbə‚ret] tr libérer
liberation [‚lɪbəˈreʃən] s libération f
liberator [ˈlɪbə‚retər] s libérateur m
libertine [ˈlɪbərˌtin] adj & s libertin m
liber•ty [ˈlɪbərti] s (pl **-ties**) liberté f; (mil) permission f exceptionnelle; **at liberty** en liberté; **at liberty to** libre de; **to take the liberty to** se permettre de, prendre la liberté de
libidinous [lɪˈbɪdɪnəs] adj libidineux
libido [lɪˈbido], [lɪˈbaɪdo] s libido f
Libra [ˈlɪbrə] s (astr, astrol) la Balance
librarian [laɪˈbrɛrɪˌən] s bibliothécaire mf
librar•y [ˈlaɪ‚brɛri] s (pl **-ies**) bibliothèque f
li′brary card′ s carte f de lecteur, carte de bibliothèque
li•brary num′ber s cote f
li′brary sci′ence s bibliothéconomie f
libret•to [lɪˈbrɛto] s (pl **-tos**) livret m, libretto m
license [ˈlaɪsəns] s permis m, licence f; (to drive) permis de conduire ‖ tr accorder un permis à, autoriser
li′cense num′ber s numéro m d'immatriculation; (aut) numéro minéralogique
li′cense plate′ or **tag′** s plaque f d'immatriculation, plaque minéralogique
licentious [laɪˈsɛnʃəs] adj licencieux
lichen [ˈlaɪkən] s lichen m
lick [lɪk] s (with the tongue) coup m de langue; (salt lick) terrain m salifère; (blow) (coll) coup m; **at full lick** (coll) à plein gaz; **to give a lick and a promise to** (coll) nettoyer à la six-quatre-deux; (coll) faire un brin de toilette à ‖ tr lécher; (e.g., the fingers) se lécher; (to beat, thrash) (coll) enfoncer les côtes à, rosser; (to beat, surpass, e.g., in a sporting event) (coll) battre, enfoncer; (e.g., a problem) (coll) venir à bout de; **to lick into shape** (coll) dégrossir; **to lick up** lécher
licking [ˈlɪkɪŋ] s léchage m; (drubbing) (coll) raclée f
licorice [ˈlɪkərɪs] s réglisse f
lid [lɪd] s (on a dish, kettle, etc.) couvercle m; (eyelid) paupière f; (hat) (slang) couvrechef m
lie [laɪ] s mensonge m; **to give the lie to** donner le démenti à ‖ v (pret & pp **lied**; ger **lying**) tr—**to lie one's way out** se tirer d'affaire par des mensonges ‖ intr mentir ‖ v (pret **lay**; pp **lain** [lɛn]; ger **lying**) intr être couché; (to be located) se trouver; (e.g., in the grave) gésir, e.g., **here lies** ci-gît; **to lie down** se coucher
lie′ detec′tor s détecteur m de mensonges, polygraphe m
lien [lin] s privilège m, droit m de rétention
lieu [lu] s—**in lieu of** au lieu de
lieutenant [luˈtɛnənt] s lieutenant m; (nav) lieutenant m de vaisseau
lieuten′ant colo′nel s lieutenant-colonel m
lieuten′ant comman′der s (nav) capitaine m de corvette

lieuten′ant gov′ernor s (U.S.A.) vice-gouverneur m; (Brit) lieutenant-gouverneur m
lieuten′ant jun′ior grade′ s (nav) enseigne m de première classe
life [laɪf] s (pl **lives** [laɪvz]) vie f; (of light bulb, lease, insurance policy) durée f; **bigger than life** plus grand que nature; **for dear life** de toutes ses forces; **for life** à vie, pour la vie, à perpétuité; **for the life of me!** (coll) de ma vie!; **lives lost** morts mpl; **long life** longévité f; **never in my life!, not on your life!** jamais de la vie!; **run for your life!** sauve qui peut!; **such is life!** c'est la vie!; **taken from life** pris sur le vif; **to come to life** revenir à la vie; **to depart this life** quitter ce monde; **to risk life and limb** risquer sa peau
life′ annu′ity s rente f viagère
life′ belt′ s ceinture f de sauvetage
life′ blood′ s sang m; (fig) vie f
life′ boat′ s chaloupe f de sauvetage; (for shore-based rescue services) canot m de sauvetage
life′ buoy′ s bouée f de sauvetage
life′ expect′ancy s espérance f de vie
life′ float′ s radeau m de sauvetage
life′ guard′ s (mil) garde f du corps
life′guard′ s sauveteur m, maître nageur m
life′ impris′onment s emprisonnement m à vie, détention f perpétuelle
life′ insur′ance s assurance f sur la vie, assurance-vie f
life′ jack′et s gilet m de sauvetage
lifeless [ˈlaɪflɪs] adj sans vie, inanimé; (colors) embu, terne
life′like′ adj vivant, ressemblant
life′ line′ s ligne f or corde f de sauvetage, planche f de salut
life′long′ adj de toute la vie, perpétuel
life′ mem′ber s membre m à vie, membre perpétuel
life′ of lei′sure s vie f de château
life′ of Ri′ley [ˈraɪli] s (slang) joyeuse vie f, vie oisive
life′ of the par′ty s (coll) boute-en-train m
life′ preserv′er [prɪˈzʌrvər] s appareil m de sauvetage
lifer [ˈlaɪfər] s (slang) condamné m à perpétuité m
life′ raft′ s radeau m de sauvetage
lifesaver [ˈlaɪf‚sevər] s sauveteur m; (fig) planche f de salut
life′sav′ing s sauvetage m
life′ sci′ences spl sciences fpl biologiques
life′ sen′tence s condamnation f à perpétuité
life′-size′ adj de grandeur nature
life′ span′ s durée f de vie, espérance f de vie
life′style′ s style m de vie
life′time′ adj à vie ‖ s vie f, toute une vie; **in his lifetime** de son vivant
life′work′ s travail m de toute une vie
lift [lɪft] s haussement m, levée f; (aer) poussée f, portance f; (Brit) ascenseur m; (of dumbbell or weight) (sports) arraché m; **to give a lift to** (by offering a ride) conduire d'un coup de voiture, faire monter dans la voiture; (to aid)

donner un coup de main à; (*to raise the morale of*) remonter le moral de, ranimer ‖ *tr* lever, soulever; (*heart, mind, etc.*) élever, ranimer; (*a sail*) soulager; (*an embargo*) lever; (*e.g., passages from a book*) démarquer, plagier; (*to rob*) (slang) dérober; **to lift up** (*the hands*) lever; (*the head*) relever; (*the voice*) élever ‖ *intr* se lever, se soulever; (*said of clouds, fog, etc.*) se lever, se dissiper

lift' bridge' *s* pont *m* levant, pont-levis *m*

lift'off' *s* (rok) montée verticale, chandelle *f*

lift' truck' *s* chariot *m* élévateur

ligament ['lɪgəmənt] *s* ligament *m*

ligature ['lɪgət/ər] *s* ligature *f*

light [laɪt] *adj* léger; (*having illumination*) élairé; (*color, complexion, hair*) clair; (*beer*) blond; (*wine*) léger; **to make light of** faire peu de cas de ‖ *s* lumière *f;* (*to control traffic*) feu *m;* (*window or other opening in a wall*) jour *m;* (*example, shining figure*) lumière; (*headlight of automobile*) phare *m;* du feu, e.g., **do you have a light?** (*e.g., to light a cigarette*) avez-vous du feu?; **according to one's lights** selon ses lumières, dans la mesure de son intelligence; **against the light** à contre-jour; **in a false light** sous un faux jour; **in a new light** sous un jour nouveau; **in the same light** sous le même aspect; **it is light** (**out**) il fait jour; **lights** (*navigation lights; parking lights*) feux *mpl;* (*of sheep, calf, etc.*) mou *m;* **lights out** (mil) l'extinction *f* des feux; **to bring to light** mettre au jour; **to come to light** se révéler; **to shed** or **throw light on** éclairer; **to strike a light** allumer ‖ *adv* à vide; **to run light** (*said of engine*) aller haut le pied ‖ *v* (*pret & pp* **lighted** or **lit** [lɪt]) *tr* (*to furnish with illumination*) éclairer, illuminer; (*to set afire, ignite*) allumer; **to light the way for** éclairer; **to light up** illuminer ‖ *intr* s'éclairer, s'illuminer; allumer; (*to perch*) se poser; **to light from** or **off** (*an auto, carriage, etc.*) descendre de; **to light into** (*to attack; to berate*) (slang) tomber sur; **to light out** (*to skedaddle*) (slang) décamper; **to light up** s'éclairer, s'illuminer; **to light upon** (*by happenstance*) tomber sur, trouver par hasard

light' bulb' *s* ampoule *f* électrique, lampe *f* électrique

light' complex'ion *s* teint *m* clair

lighten ['laɪtən] *tr* (*to make lighter in weight*) alléger, soulager; (*to provide more light*) éclairer, illuminer; (*to give a lighter or brighter hue to*) éclaircir; (*grief, punishment, etc.*) adoucir ‖ *intr* (*to become less dark or sorrowful*) s'éclairer; (*to give off flashes of lightning*) faire des éclairs; (*to become less weighty*) s'alléger

lighter ['laɪtər] *s* (*to light cigarette*) briquet *m;* (*flat-bottomed barge*) chaland *m*, péniche *f*

light'-fin'gered *adj* à doigts agiles

light'-foot'ed *adj* au pied léger

light'-head'ed *adj* étourdi

light'-heart'ed *adj* joyeux, allègre, au cœur léger

light'house' *s* phare *m*

lighting ['laɪtɪŋ] *s* allumage *m*, éclairage *m*

light'ing en'gineer *s* éclairagiste *mf*

light'ing fix'tures *spl* appareils *mpl* d'éclairage

light' me'ter *s* posemètre *m*

lightness ['laɪtnɪs] *s* (*in weight*) légèreté *f;* (*in illumination; of complexion*) clarté *f*

light'ning ['laɪtnɪŋ] *s* (*electric discharge*) foudre *f;* (*light produced by this discharge*) éclairs *mpl* ‖ *v* (*ger* **-ning**) *intr* faire des éclairs

light'ning arrest'er [ə,rɛstər] *f* parafoudre *m*

light'ning bug' *s* luciole *f*

light'ning rod' *s* paratonnerre *m*

light' op'era *s* opérette *f*

light' pen' *s* (comp) photostyle *m*

light' read'ing *s* livres *mpl* d'agrément; lecture *f* légère or amusante

light'ship' *s* bateau-feu *m*

light-struck ['laɪt,strʌk] *adj* (phot) voilé

light' wave' *s* onde *f* lumineuse

light'weight' *adj* léger ‖ *s* (sports) poids *m* léger

light'weight coat' *s* surtout *m* de demisaison

light'-year' *s* année-lumière *f*

likable ['laɪkəbəl] *adj* sympathique, agréable

like [laɪk] *adj* (*alike*) pareils, semblables; pareil à, semblable à; (*typical of*) caractéristique de; (*poles of a magnet*) (elec) de même nom; **like father like son** tel père tel fils; **that is like him** il n'en fait pas d'autres ‖ *s* pareil *m*, semblable *m;* **likes** (*desires*) goût *m*, inclinations *fpl;* **the likes of him** son pareil ‖ *adv*—**like as not** le cas échéant, éventuellement; probablement; **like enough** probablement; **like mad** comme un fou ‖ *prep* comme; **like that** de la sorte ‖ *conj* (coll) de la même manière que, comme ‖ *tr* aimer, aimer bien, trouver bon; plaire à, e.g., **I like milk** le lait me plaît; se plaire, e.g., **I like it in the country** je me plais à la campagne ‖ *intr* vouloir; **as you like** comme vous voudrez; **if you like** si vous voulez

likelihood ['laɪklɪ,hʊd] *s* probabilité *f*, vraisemblance *f*

like•ly ['laɪkli] *adj* (*comp* **-lier;** *super* **-liest**) probable, vraisemblable; **to be likely to** + *inf* être probable que + *ind*, e.g., **Mary is likely to come to see us tomorrow** il est probable que Marie viendra nous voir demain ‖ *adv* probablement, vraisemblablement

like'-mind'ed *adj* du même avis

liken ['laɪkən] *tr* comparer, assimiler

likeness ['laɪknɪs] *s* (*picture or image*) portrait *m;* (*similarity*) ressemblance *f*

like'wise' *adv* également, de même; **to do likewise** en faire autant

liking ['laɪkɪŋ] *s* sympathie *f*, penchant *m;* **to one's liking** à souhait; **to take a liking to** (*a thing*) accueillir avec sympathie; (*a person*) montrer de la sympathie à, se prendre d'amitié pour

lilac ['laɪlək] *adj & s* lilas *m*

Lilliputian [ˌlɪlɪˈpjuʃən] *adj* & *s* lilliputien *m*
lilt [lɪlt] *s* cadence *f*
lil•y [ˈlɪlɪ] *s* (*pl* **-ies**) lis *m*, lis blanc; (*royal arms of France*) fleur *f* de lis; **to gild the lily** renchérir sur la perfection
lil′y of the val′ley *s* muguet *m*
lil′y pad′ *s* feuille *f* de nénuphar
lil′y-white′ *adj* blanc comme le lis, lilial
Li′ma bean′ [ˈlaɪmə] *s* (*Phaseolus limensis*) haricot *m* de Lima
limb [lɪm] *s* (*arm or leg*) membre *m*; (*of a tree*) branche *f*; (*of a cross; of the sea*) bras *m*; (astr, bot) limbe *m*; **to be out on a limb** (coll) être sur la corde raide
limber [ˈlɪmbər] *adj* souple, flexible ‖ *intr*—**to limber up** se dégourdir
lim•bo [ˈlɪmbo] *s* (*pl* **-bos**) limbes *mpl*
lime [laɪm] *s* (*calcium oxide*) chaux *f*; (*linden tree*) tilleul *m*; (*Citrus aurantifolia*) citron *m*; **sweet lime** (*Citrus limetta*) lime *f*
lime′kiln′ *s* four *m* à chaux
lime′light′ *s*—**to be in the limelight** être sous les feux de la rampe
limerick [ˈlɪmərɪk] *s* poème *m* humoristique en cinq vers
lime′stone′ *adj* calcaire ‖ *s* calcaire *m*, pierre *f* à chaux
limit [ˈlɪmɪt] *s* limite *f*, borne *f*; **to be the limit** (*to be exasperating*) (coll) être le comble; (*to be bizarre*) (coll) être impayable; **to go the limit** aller jusqu'au bout ‖ *tr* limiter, borner
limitation [ˌlɪmɪˈteʃən] *s* limitation *f*
lim′ited-ac′cess high′way *s* autoroute *f*
lim′ited edi′tion *s* édition *f* à tirage limité
lim′ited mon′archy *s* monarchie *f* constitutionnelle
limitless [ˈlɪmɪtlɪs] *adj* sans bornes, illimité
limousine [ˌlɪməˈzin] *s* (aut) limousine *f*
limp [lɪmp] *adj* mou, flasque, souple ‖ *s* boiterie *f* ‖ *intr* boiter
limpid [ˈlɪmpɪd] *adj* limpide
linchpin [ˈlɪntʃˌpɪn] *s* cheville *f* d'essieu, esse *f*
linden [ˈlɪndən] *s* tilleul *m*
line [laɪn] *s* ligne *f*; (*of poetry*) vers *m*; (*rope, string*) cordage *m*, corde *f*; (*wrinkle*) ride *f*; (*dash*) trait *m*; (*bar*) barre *f*; (*lineage*) lignée *f*; (*trade*) métier *m*; (*of merchandise*) article *m*; (*of traffic*) file *f*; (mil) rang *m*; (*of the spectrum*) (phys) raie *f*; **along the same line** suivant le même plan; dans cet ordre d'idées, de la même opinion; de la même façon; **fault line** ligne de faille; **hold the line!** (telp) ne quittez pas!; **in line** aligné, en rang; **in line with** conforme à, d'accord avec; **off line** (comp) autonome; **on line** (comp) en ligne; **on the line** (telp) au bout du fil; **out of line** désaligné; en désaccord; **straight line** ligne droite; **the line is busy** (telp) la ligne est occupée; **to bring into line with** mettre d'accord avec; **to drop s.o. a line** envoyer un mot à qn; **to fall into line** se mettre en ligne, s'aligner; **to hand s.o. a line** (slang) faire du baratin à qn, bourrer le crâne de qn; **to have**

a line on (coll) se tuyauter sur; **to learn one's lines** apprendre son texte or rôle; **to read between the lines** lire entre les lignes; **to stand** or **wait in line** faire la queue; **to toe the line** se mettre au pas ‖ *tr* aligner; (*a face*) rider; (*a suit, coat, etc.*) doubler; (*brakes*) fourrer; **to be lined with** (*e.g., trees*) être bordé de ‖ *intr*—**to line up** s'aligner, se mettre en ligne; faire la queue
lineage [ˈlɪnɪˌɪdʒ] *s* lignée *f*, race *f*, lignage *m*
lineal [ˈlɪnɪəl] *adj* linéal; (*succession*) en ligne directe
lineaments [ˈlɪnɪəmənts] *spl* linéaments *mpl*
linear [ˈlɪnɪər] *adj* linéaire
lined′ pa′per *s* papier *m* rayé
line′man *s* (*pl* **-men**) (elec) poseur *m* de lignes; (rr) garde-ligne *m*
linen [ˈlɪnən] *adj* de lin ‖ *s* (*fabric*) toile *f* de lin; (*yarn*) fil *m* de lin; (*sheets, tablecloths, underclothes, etc.*) linge *m*, lingerie *f*; **don't wash your dirty linen in public** il faut laver son linge sale en famille; il ne faut pas laver en public un linge sanglant; **pure linen** pur fil
lin′en clos′et *s* lingerie *f*
line′ of attack′ *s* (mil) plan *m* d'attaque
line′ of fire′ *s* (mil) ligne *f* de tir
line′ of least′ resis′tance *s* solution *f* de facilité
line′ of sight′ *s* ligne *f* de mire, ligne de visée
liner [ˈlaɪnər] *s* (naut) paquebot *m*
line′-up′ *s* (*row*) file *f*, mise *f* en rang; (*arrangement*) disposition *f*; (*of suspects*) séance *f* d'identification d'un suspect; (pol) front *m*; (sports) composition *f* de l'équipe
linger [ˈlɪŋgər] *intr* s'attarder; (*said of hope, doubt, etc.*) persister; **to linger on** traîner; **to linger over** s'attarder sur
lingerie [ˌlænʒəˈri] *s* lingerie *f* fine pour dames, lingerie de dame
lingering [ˈlɪŋgərɪŋ] *adj* prolongé, lent
lingual [ˈlɪŋgwəl] *adj* lingual ‖ *s* (*consonant*) linguale *f*
linguist [ˈlɪŋgwɪst] *s* (*person skilled in several languages*) polyglotte *mf*; (*specialist in linguistics*) linguiste *mf*
linguistic [lɪŋˈgwɪstɪk] *adj* linguistique ‖ **linguistics** *s* linguistique *f*
liniment [ˈlɪnɪmənt] *s* liniment *m*
lining [ˈlaɪnɪŋ] *s* (*of a coat*) doublure *f*; (*of a hat*) coiffe *f*; (*of auto brake*) garniture *f*; (*of furnace, wall, etc.*) revêtement *m*
link [lɪŋk] *s* maillon *m*, chaînon *m*; (fig) lien *m*; **links** terrain *m* de golf ‖ *tr* enchaîner; lier ‖ *intr*—**to link in, on,** or **up** se lier
linkage [ˈlɪŋkɪdʒ] *s* lien *m*, relation *f*; (aerosp) accouplement *m*; (comp) liaison *f*; (gen) linkage *m*
link′up′ *s* lien *m*, rapport *m*; (aerosp) arrimage *m*, jonction *f*; (rad, telv) liaison *f*
linnet [ˈlɪnɪt] *s* (orn) linotte *f*
linoleum [lɪˈnolɪəm] *s* linoléum *m*
Linotype [ˈlaɪnəˌtaɪp] (trademark) *s* linotype *f* ‖ *tr* & *intr* composer à la lino

lin′otype op′erator *s* linotypiste *mf*
lin′otype slug′ *s* ligne-bloc *m*
linseed [ˈlɪn,sid] *s* linette *f*, graine *f* de lin
lin′seed oil′ *s* huile *f* de lin
lint [lɪnt] *s* (*minute shreds*) petites parcelles *fpl* de fil; (*fluff*) peluches *fpl*; (*used to dress wounds*) charpie *f*; tissu *m* ouaté
lintel [ˈlɪntəl] *s* linteau *m*
lion [ˈlaɪ•ən] *s* lion *m*; (fig) lion; **to put one's head in the lion's mouth** se fourrer dans la gueule du loup ou du lion
lioness [ˈlaɪ•ənɪs] *s* lionne *f*
li′on-heart′ed *adj* au cœur de lion
lionize [ˈlaɪ•ə,naɪz] *tr* faire une célébrité de, traiter en vedette
li′ons′ den′ *s* (Bib) fosse *f* aux lions
li′on's share′ *s* part *f* du lion
lip [lɪp] *s* lèvre *f*; (*edge*) bord *m*; (slang) impertinence *f*; **to hang on the lips of** être suspendu aux lèvres de; **to smack one's lips** se lécher les babines
lip′read′ *v* (*pret & pp* **-read** [ˌrɛd]) *tr & intr* lire sur les lèvres
lip′ read′ing *s* lecture *f* sur les lèvres
lip′ serv′ice *s* dévotion *f* des lèvres
lip′stick′ *s* bâton *m* de rouge à lèvres
lique•fy [ˈlɪkwɪ,faɪ] *v* (*pret & pp* **-fied**) *tr* liquéfier
liqueur [lɪˈkʌr] *s* liqueur *f*
liquid [ˈlɪkwɪd] *adj* liquide ‖ *s* liquide *m*; (*consonant*) liquide *f*
liq′uid as′sets *spl* valeurs *fpl* disponibles
liquidate [ˈlɪkwɪ,det] *tr & intr* liquider
liquidity [lɪˈkwɪdɪti] *s* liquidité *f*
li′quid mea′sure *s* mesure *f* de capacité pour les liquides
liquor [ˈlɪkər] *s* boisson *f* alcoolique, spiritueux *m*; (culin) jus *m*, bouillon *m*
Lisbon [ˈlɪzbən] *s* Lisbonne *f*
lisle [laɪl] *s* fil *m* d'Ecosse, fil retors de coton
lisp [lɪsp] *s* zézayement *m*, blésement *m* ‖ *intr* zézayer, bléser
lissome [ˈlɪsəm] *adj* souple, flexible; (*nimble*) agile, leste
list [lɪst] *s* liste *f*; (*selvage*) lisière *f*; (naut) bande *f*, inclinaison *f*; **to enter the lists** entrer en lice; **to have a list** (naut) donner de la bande ‖ *tr* cataloguer, enregistrer; (comp) lister ‖ *intr* (naut) donner de la bande
listen [ˈlɪsən] *intr* écouter; **to listen in** rester à l'écoute; **to listen to** écouter; **to listen to reason** entendre raison
listener [ˈlɪsənər] *s* auditeur *m*; (educ) auditeur libre
listening [ˈlɪsənɪŋ] *s* écoute *f*
lis′tening post′ *s* poste *m* d'écoute
listing [ˈlɪstɪŋ] *s* énumération *f*, compte *m*; (comp) listage *m*
listless [ˈlɪstlɪs] *adj* apathique, inattentif
list′ price′ *s* prix *m* courant, cote *f*
lita•ny [ˈlɪtəni] *s* (*pl* **-nies**) litanie *f*
liter [ˈlitər] *s* litre *m*
literacy [ˈlɪtərəsi] *s* fait *m* de savoir lire et écrire

literal [ˈlɪtərəl] *adj* littéral; (*person*) prosaïque
literally [ˈlɪtərəli] *adv* littéralement, mot à mot, au sens propre; (*without interpretation*) au pied de la lettre, à la lettre; (*really*) réellement; (*absolutely*) (coll) littéralement
literary [ˈlɪtə,rɛri] *adj* littéraire
literate [ˈlɪtərɪt] *adj* qui sait lire et écrire; (*well-read*) lettré ‖ *s* personne *f* qui sait lire et écrire; lettré *m*, érudit *m*
literati [ˌlɪtəˈrɑti] *spl* littérateurs *mpl*
literature [ˈlɪtərətʃər] *s* littérature *f*; (com) documentation *f*
lithe [laɪð] *adj* souple, flexible
lithia [ˈlɪθɪ•ə] *s* (chem) lithine *f*
lithium [ˈlɪθɪ•əm] *s* (chem) lithium *m*
lithograph [ˈlɪθə,græf] *s* lithographie *f* ‖ *tr* lithographier
lithographer [lɪˈθɑgrəfər] *s* lithographe *mf*
lithography [lɪˈθɑgrəfi] *s* lithographie *f*
litigant [ˈlɪtɪgənt] *adj* plaidant ‖ *s* plaideur *m*
litigate [ˈlɪtɪ,get] *tr* mettre en litige ‖ *intr* plaider
litigation [ˌlɪtɪˈgeʃən] *s* litige *m*
lit′mus pa′per [ˈlɪtməs] *s* papier *m* de tournesol
lit′mus test′ *s* (chem) preuve *f* d'acidité; (fig) preuve déterminante ou décisive
litter [ˈlɪtər] *s* (*disorder*) fouillis *m*; (*things strewn about*) jonchee *f*; (*scattered rubbish*) ordures *fpl*; (*young brought forth at one birth*) portée *f*; (*bedding for animals*) litière *f*; (*vehicle carried by men or animals*) palanquin *m*; (*stretcher*) civière *f* ‖ *tr* joncher ‖ *intr* (*to bring forth young*) mettre bas
lit′ter•bug′ *s* souillon *m*, malpropre *m*, personne *f* qui dépose des ordures et des papiers dans la rue
littering [ˈlɪtərɪŋ] *s*—**no littering** (*public sign*) défense de déposer des ordures
little [ˈlɪtəl] *adj* petit; (*in amount*) peu de, e.g., **little money** peu d'argent; **a little** un peu de, e.g., **a little money** un peu d'argent ‖ *s* peu *m*; **a little** un peu; **to make little of, to think little of** faire peu de cas de; **wait a little** attendez un petit moment, attendez quelques instants ‖ *adv* peu §91; ne ... guère §90, e.g., **she little thinks that** elle ne se doute guère que; **little by little** peu à peu, petit à petit
Lit′tle Bear′ *s* Petite Ourse *f*
Lit′tle Dip′per *s* Petit Chariot *m*
lit′tle fin′ger *s* petit doigt *m*, auriculaire *m*; **to twist around one's little finger** mener par le bout du nez
lit′tle•neck′ *s* coque *f* de Vénus
littleness [ˈlɪtəlnɪs] *s* petitesse *f*
lit′tle owl′ *s* (*Athene noctua*) chouette *f* chevêche, chevêche *f*
lit′tle peo′ple *spl* (*fairies*) fées *fpl*; (*common people*) menu peuple *m*
Lit′tle Red Rid′ing-hood′ *s* le Petit Chaperon rouge
lit′tle slam′ *s* (bridge) petit chelem *m*
liturgic(al) [lɪˈtʌrdʒɪk(əl)] *adj* liturgique
litur•gy [ˈlɪtərdʒi] *s* (*pl* **-gies**) liturgie *f*

livable [ˈlɪvəbəl] *adj* (*house*) habitable; (*life, person*) supportable

live [laɪv] *adj* vivant, vif; (*coals; flame*) ardent; (*microphone*) actif; (elec) sous tension; (telv) en direct ‖ [lɪv] *tr* vivre; **to live down** faire oublier ‖ *intr* vivre; (*in a certain locality*) demeurer, habiter; **live and learn** qui vivra verra; **to live high** mener grand train; **to live in** (*e.g., a city*) habiter; **to live on** continuer à vivre; (*e.g., meat*) vivre de; (*a benefactor*) vivre aux crochets de; (*one's capital*) manger; **to live up to** (*e.g., one's reputation*) faire honneur à

live′ am′muni′tion *s* munitions *fpl* de combat

live′ coal′ [laɪv] *s* charbon *m* ardent

live-in [ˈlɪvɪn] *adj* & *s* résident *m*

live′-in part′ners *spl* partenaires *mfpl* qui habitent sous le même toit

livelihood [ˈlaɪvlɪ,hʊd] *s* vie *f;* **to earn one's livelihood** gagner sa vie

livelong [ˈlɪv,lɔŋ] *adj*—**all the livelong day** toute la sainte journée

live•ly [ˈlaɪvli] *adj* (*comp* **-lier;** *super* **-liest**) animé, vivant, plein d'entrain; (*merry*) enjoué, gai; (*active, keen*) vif; (*resilient*) élastique

liven [ˈlaɪvən] *tr* animer ‖ *intr* s'animer

liver [ˈlɪvər] *s* vivant *m;* (*e.g., in cities*) habitant *m;* (anat) foie *m*

liver•y [ˈlɪvəri] *s* (*pl* **-ies**) livrée *f*

liv′ery•man *s* (*pl* **-men**) loueur *m* de chevaux

liv′ery sta′ble *s* écurie *f* de louage

live′ show′ [laɪv] *s* (telv) prise *f* de vues en direct

live′stock′ *s* bétail *m*, bestiaux *mpl*, cheptel *m*

live′ tel′evision broad′cast *s* prise *f* de vues en direct

live′ wire′ *s* fil *m* sous tension; (slang) type *m* dynamique, boute-en-train *m invar*

livid [ˈlɪvɪd] *adj* livide

living [ˈlɪvɪŋ] *adj* vivant, en vie ‖ *s* vie *f;* **to earn** or **to make a living** gagner sa vie

liv′ing quar′ters *spl* appartements *mpl*, habitations *fpl*

liv′ing room′ *s* salle *f* de séjour, salon *m;* (*in a studio apartment*) living *m*

liv′ing space′ *s* espace *m* vital

liv′ing wage′ *s* salaire *m* suffisant pour vivre, salaire de base

lizard [ˈlɪzərd] *s* lézard *m*

load [lod] *s* charge *f;* **loads (of)** (coll) énormément (de); **to get a load of** (slang) observer, écouter; **to have a load on** (slang) avoir son compte ‖ *tr* charger ‖ *intr* charger; se charger

loaded *adj* chargé; (*very drunk*) (slang) soûl; (*very rich*) (slang) huppé

load′ed dice′ *spl* dés *mpl* pipés

load′stone′ *s* pierre *f* d'aimant; (fig) aimant *m*

loaf [lof] *s* (*pl* **loaves** [lovz]) pain *m* ‖ *intr* flâner

loafer [ˈlofər] *s* (*shoe*) flâneur *m;* (*person*) flemmard *m*, tire-au-flanc *m*

loam [lom] *s* terre *f* franche, glaise *f;* (*mixture used in making molds*) potée *f*

loamy [ˈlomi] *adj* franc, glaiseux

loan [lon] *s* prêt *m*, emprunt *m* ‖ *tr* prêter

loan′ of′fice *s* entreprise *f* de prêt, caisse *f* de prévoyance

loan′ shark′ *s* usurier *m*

loan′ word′ *s* mot *m* d'emprunt

loath [loθ] *adj*—**loath to** peu enclin à

loathe [loð] *tr* détester

loathing [ˈloðɪŋ] *s* dégoût *m*

loathsome [ˈloðsəm] *adj* dégoûtant

lob [lɑb] *s* (tennis) lob *m* ‖ *v* (*pret & pp* **lobbed; ger lobbing**) *tr* frapper en hauteur, lober

lob•by [ˈlɑbi] *s* (*pl* **-bies**) vestibule *m;* (*e.g., in a theater*) foyer *m;* (*pressure group*) groupe *m* de pression, lobby *m* ‖ *v* (*pret & pp* **-bied**) *intr* faire les couloirs

lobbying [ˈlɑbɪ•ɪŋ] *s* intrigues *fpl* de couloir

lobbyist [ˈlɑbɪ•ɪst] *s* intrigant *m* de couloir

lobe [lob] *s* lobe *m*

lobster [ˈlɑbstər] *s* (*spiny lobster*) langouste *f;* (*Homarus*) homard *m*

lob′ster pot′ *s* casier *m* à homards

local [ˈlokəl] *adj* local ‖ *s* (*of labor union*) succursale *f;* (journ) informations *fpl* régionales; (rr) train *m* omnibus

lo′cal call′ *s* (telp) communication *f* urbaine

locale [loˈkæl] *s* lieu *m*, milieu *m;* scène *f*

locali•ty [loˈkælɪti] *s* (*pl* **-ties**) localité *f*

localize [ˈlokə,laɪz] *tr* localiser

lo′cal supply′ cir′cuit *s* secteur *m*

locate [ˈloket] *tr* (*to discover the location of*) localiser; (*to place, to settle*) placer, installer; (*to ascribe a particular location to*) situer; **to be located** se trouver ‖ *intr* se fixer, s'établir

location [loˈkeʃən] *s* (*place, position*) situation *f*, emplacement *m;* (*act of placing*) établissement *m;* (*act of finding*) localisation *f*, détermination *f;* (*of a railroad line*) tracé *m;* **on location** (mov) en extérieur

loca′tion shot′ *s* (mov) extérieur *m*

lock [lɑk] *s* serrure *f;* (*of a canal*) écluse *f;* (*of hair*) mèche *f*, boucle *f;* (*of a firearm*) platine *f;* (wrestling) clef *f;* **lock, stock, and barrel** tout le bataclan, tout le fourbi; **under lock and key** sous clé ‖ *tr* fermer à clef; (*to key*) caler, bloquer; (*a boat*) écluser, sasser; (*a switch*) (rr) verrouiller; **to be locked in each other's arms** être enlacés; **to lock in** enfermer à clef; **to lock out** fermer la porte à or sur; (*workers*) fermer les ateliers contre; **to lock up** fermer à clef, mettre sous clé; (*e.g., a prisoner*) boucler, enfermer; (*a form*) (typ) serrer ‖ *intr* (*said of door*) fermer à clef; (*said of brake, wheel, etc.*) se bloquer; **to lock into** s'engrener dans

locker [ˈlɑkər] *s* armoire *f*, coffre *m* de sûreté; (*in a station or airport*) casier *m;* (*for keeping clothes*) vestiaire *m*, placard *m* individuel; (*locker room*) vestiaire

lock′er room′ *s* vestiaire *m*, vestiaire à placards individuels

locket [ˈlɑkɪt] *s* médaillon *m*

lock′jaw′ *s* trisme *m*

lock′ nut′ s contre-écrou m

lock′ out′ s lock-out m

lock′smith′ s serrurier m

lock′ step′ s —**to march in lock step** emboîter le pas

lock′ stitch′ s point m indécousable

lock′ten′der s éclusier m

lock′up′ s (prison) (coll) bloc m, violon m

lock′ wash′er s rondelle à ressort

locomotive [ˌlokə′motɪv] s locomotive f

lo•cus [′lokəs] s (pl **-ci**) [saɪ]) lieu m; (math) lieu géométrique

locust [′lokəst] s (Pachytylus) (ent) criquet m migrateur, locuste f; (Cicada) (ent) cigale f; (bot) faux acacia m

lode [lod] s filon m, veine f

lode′star′ s (astr) étoile f polaire; (fig) pôle m d'attraction

lodge [lɑdʒ] s (of gatekeeper; of animal; of Mason) loge f; (residence, e.g., for hunting) pavillon m; (hotel) relais m, hostellerie f ‖ tr loger; **to lodge a complaint with** porter plainte auprès de ‖ intr loger; (said of arrow, bullet) se loger

lodger [′lɑdʒər] s locataire mf, pensionnaire mf

lodging [′lɑdʒɪŋ] s logement m; (of a complaint) déposition f

loft [lɔft] s (attic) grenier m, soupente f; (hayloft) fenil m; (in theater or church) tribune f; (in store or office building) atelier m

loft•y [′lɔfti] adj (comp **-ier;** super **-iest**) (towering; sublime) élevé, exalté; (haughty) hautain

log [lɔg] s (of wood) bûche f, rondin m; (record book) registre m de travail; (aer) livre m de vol; (record book) (naut) journal m de bord; (chip log) (naut) loch m; (rad) carnet m d'écoute; **to sleep like a log** dormir comme une souche ‖ v (pret & pp **logged;** ger **logging**) tr (wood) tronçonner; (an event) porter au journal; (a certain distance) (naut) filer ‖ intr (to cut wood) couper des rondins

logarithm [′lɔgəˌrɪðəm] s logarithme m

log′book′ s (aer) livre m de vol; (naut) journal m de bord, livre de loch

log′ cab′in s cabane f en rondins

log′ chip′ s (naut) flotteur m de loch

log′ driv′er s flotteur m

log′ driv′ing s flottage m

logger [′lɔgər] s bûcheron m; (loader) (mach) grue f de chargement; (mach) tracteur m

log′ger•head′ s tête f de bois; **at loggerheads** en bisbille, aux prises

logic [′lɑdʒɪk] s logique f

logical [′lɑdʒɪkəl] adj logique

log′ic board′ s (comp) plaque f logique

logician [lo′dʒɪ.ʃən] s logicien m

logistic(al) [lo′dʒɪstɪk(əl)] adj logistique

logistics [lo′dʒɪstɪks] s logistique f

log′ jam′ s embâcle m de bûches; (fig) bouchon m, embouteillage m

log′ line′ s (naut) ligne f de loch

logo [′logo] s logo m, logotype m (obs)

log′roll′ intr faire trafic de faveurs politiques

log′wood′ s bois m de campêche; (tree) campêche m

loin [lɔɪn] s (of beef) aloyau m; (of veal) longe f; (of pork) échine f; **to gird up one's loins** se ceindre les reins

loin′cloth′ s pagne m

loiter [′lɔɪtər] tr—**to loiter away** perdre en flânant ‖ intr flâner

loiterer [′lɔɪtərər] s flâneur m

loll [lɑll] intr se prélasser, s'allonger, s'affaler

lollipop [′lɑli,pɑp] s sucette f

Lom′bardy pop′lar [′lɑmbərdi] s peuplier m noir

London [′lʌndən] adj londonien ‖ s Londres m

Londoner [′lʌndənər] s Londonien m

lone [lon] adj (alone) solitaire, seul; (sole, single) unique

loneliness [′lonlɪnɪs] s solitude f

lone•ly [′lonli] adj (comp **-lier;** super **-liest**) solitaire, isolé

lonesome [′lonsəm] adj solitaire, seul

lone′ wolf′ s (fig) solitaire mf, ours m

long [lɔŋ] (comp **longer** [′lɔŋgr]; super **longest** [′lɔŋgɪst]) adj long; de long, de longueur, e.g., **two meters long** deux mètres de long or de longueur ‖ adv longtemps; **as long as** aussi longtemps que; (provided that) tant que; **before long** sous peu; **how long?** combien de temps?, depuis combien de temps?, depuis quand?; **long ago** il y a longtemps; **long before** longtemps avant; **longer** plus long; **long since** depuis longtemps; **no longer** ne . . . plus longtemps; ne . . . plus, e.g., **I could no longer see him** je ne pouvais plus le voir; **so long!** (coll) à bientôt!; **so long as** tant que; **to be long in** tarder à ‖ intr—**to long for** soupirer pour or après

long′boat′ s chaloupe f

long′ dis′tance s (telp) l'interurbain m; **to call s.o. long distance** appeler qn par l'interurbain

long′-dis′tance call′ s (telp) appel m interurbain

long′-dis′tance flight′ s (aer) vol m au long cours, raid m aérien

long′-drawn′-out′ adj prolongé; (story) délayé

longevity [lɑn′dʒɛvɪti] s longévité f

long′ face′ s (coll) triste figure f

long′hair′ adj & s intellectuel m; fanatique mf de la musique classique

long′-haired′ adj à cheveux longs

long′hand′ s écriture f ordinaire; **in long-hand** à la main

longing [′lɔŋɪŋ] adj ardent ‖ s désir m ardent

longitude [′lɑndʒɪ,t(j)ud] s longitude f

long′ jump′ s saut m en longueur

long-lived [′lɔŋ′laɪvd], [′lɔŋ′lɪvd] adj à longue vie; persistant

long′-play′ing rec′ord s disque m de longue durée

long′ prim′er [′prɪmər] s (typ) philosophie f

long′-range′ adj à longue portée; (e.g., plan) à long terme

long′-range plane′ s long-courrier m
long′shore′man s (pl **-men**) arrimeur m, débardeur m
long′ shot′ s (turf) outsider m
long′-stand′ing adj de longue date
long′-suf′fering adj patient, endurant
long′ suit′ s (cards) couleur f longue, longue f; (fig) fort m
long′-term′ adj à longue échéance
long′-wind′ed [ˈwɪndɪd] adj interminable; (person) intarissable
look [lʊk] s (appearance) aspect m; (glance) regard m; **looks** apparence f, mine f; **to take a look at** jeter un coup d'œil sur or à ∥ tr regarder; (e.g., one's age) paraître; **to look daggers at** lancer un regard furieux à; **to look the part** avoir le physique de l'emploi; **to look up** (e.g., in a dictionary) chercher, rechercher; (to visit) aller voir, venir voir ∥ intr regarder; (to seek) chercher; **it looks like rain** le temps est à la pluie; **look here!** dites donc!; **look out!** gare!, attention!; **to look after** s'occuper de; (e.g., an invalid) soigner; **to look at** regarder; **to look away** détourner les yeux; **to look back** regarder en arrière; **to look down on** mépriser; **to look for** chercher; (to expect) s'attendre à; **to look forward to** s'attendre à, attendre avec impatience, se réjouir d'avance; **to look ill** avoir mauvaise mine; **to look in on** passer voir; **to look into** examiner, vérifier; **to look like** (s.o. or s.th.) ressembler à; (to give promise of) avoir l'air de; **to look out** faire attention; (e.g., the window) regarder par; **to look out on** donner sur; **to look through** (a window) regarder par; (a telescope) regarder dans; (a book) feuilleter; **to look toward** regarder du côté de; **to look up** lever les yeux; **to look up to** respecter; **to look well** avoir bonne mine
looker-on [ˌlʊkərˈɑn] s (pl **lookers-on**) spectateur m, assistant m
look′ing glass′ s miroir m
look′out′ s (observation) guet m, surveillance f; (person) guetteur m; (place) poste m d'observation; (person or place) (naut) vigie f; **that's his lookout** (coll) ça, c'est son affaire; **to be on the lookout for** être à l'affût de
loom [lum] s métier m ∥ intr (to appear) apparaître indistinctement; (to threaten) menacer, paraître imminent; **to loom up** surgir, s'élever
loon [lun] s lourdaud m, sot m; (orn) plongeon m
loon•y [ˈluni] adj (comp **-ier;** super **-iest**) (slang) toqué ∥ s (pl **-ies**) (slang) toqué m
loop [lup] s boucle f; (for fastening a button) bride f; (circular route) boulevard m périphérique; (in skating) croisé m; **to loop the loop** (aer) boucler la boucle ∥ tr & intr boucler
loop′hole′ s meurtrière f; (fig) échappatoire f
loop′-the-loop′ s looping m
loose [lus] adj lâche; (stone, tooth) branlant; (screw) desserré; (pulley, wheel) fou; (rope) mou, détendu; (coat, dress) vague, ample;

(earth, soil) meuble, friable; (bowels) relâché; (style) décousu; (translation) libre, peu exact; (life, morals) relâché, dissolu; (woman) facile; (unpackaged) en vrac; (unbound, e.g., pages) détaché; **to become loose** se détacher; **to break loose** (from captivity) s'évader; (fig) se déchaîner; **to let loose** lâcher, lâcher la bride à ∥ s—**to be on the loose** (to debauch) (coll) courir la prétantaine; (to be out of work) (coll) être sans occupation ∥ tr lâcher; (to untie) détacher
loose′ end′ s (fig) affaire f pendante; **at loose ends** désœuvré, indécis
loose′-leaf note′book s cahier m à feuilles mobiles
loosen [ˈlusən] tr lâcher, relâcher; (a screw) desserrer ∥ intr se relâcher
looseness [ˈlusnɪs] s relâchement m; (of garment) ampleur f; (play of screw) jeu m, desserrage m
loose′strife′ s (common yellow type) chassebosse f, grande lysimaque f; (spiked-purple type) salicaire f
loose′-tongued′ adj—**to be loose-tongued** avoir la langue déliée
loot [lut] s butin m, pillage m ∥ tr piller, saccager
lop [lɑp] v (pret & pp **lopped;** ger **lopping**) tr—**to lop off** abattre, trancher; (a tree, a branch) élaguer ∥ intr pendre
lope [lop] s galop m lent ∥ intr—**to lope along** aller doucement
lop′sid′ed adj déjeté, bancal
loquacious [loˈkweʃəs] adj loquace
lord [lɔrd] s seigneur m; (hum & poetic) époux m; (Brit) lord m ∥ tr—**to lord it over** dominer despotiquement, traiter avec arrogance
lord•ly [ˈlɔrdli] adj (comp **-lier;** super **-liest**) de grand seigneur, majestueux; (arrogant) hautain, altier
Lord's′ Day′ s jour m du Seigneur
lordship [ˈlɔrdʃɪp] s seigneurie f
Lord's′ Prayer′ s oraison f dominicale
Lord's Sup′per s communion f, cène f; Cène f
lore [lor] s savoir m, science f; tradition f populaire
lorgnette [lɔrnˈjɛt] s (eyeglasses) face-à-main m; (opera glasses) lorgnette f
lor•ry [ˈlɔri] s (pl **-ries**) lorry m, wagonnet m; (truck) (Brit) camion m; (wagon) (Brit) fardier m
lose [luz] v (pret & pp **lost** [lɔst]) tr perdre; (a patient who dies) ne pas réussir à sauver; (several minutes, as a timepiece does) retarder de; **to lose oneself in** s'absorber dans; **to lose one's way** s'égarer ∥ intr perdre; (said of timepiece) retarder
loser [ˈluzər] s perdant m
losing [ˈluzɪŋ] adj perdant ∥ **losings** spl pertes fpl
loss [lɔs] s perte f; **to be at a loss** ne savoir que faire; **to be at a loss to** avoir de la peine à, être bien embarrassé pour; **to sell at a loss** vendre à perte

loss' of face' s perte f de prestige

lost [lɔst] adj perdu; **lost in thought** perdu or absorbé dans ses pensées; **lost to** perdu pour

lost'-and-found' depart'ment s bureau m des objets trouvés

lost' sheep' s brebis f perdue, brebis égarée

lot [lɑt] s lot m; (*for building*) lotissement m, lot; (*fate*) sort m, lot; **a bad lot** (coll) un mauvais sujet, de la mauvaise graine; **a lot of** or **lots of** (coll) un tas de; **a queer lot** (coll) un drôle de numéro; **in a lot** en bloc; **to cast** or **to throw in one's lot with** tenter la fortune avec; **to draw** or **to cast lots** tirer au sort; **such a lot of** tellement de; **what a lot of. . .!** que de. . .!

lotion ['loʃən] s lotion f

lotter•y ['lɑtəri] s (*pl* **-ies**) loterie f

lotto ['lɑto] s loto m

lotus ['lotəs] s lotus m

loud [lɑud] adj (*volume*) haut, fort; (*noisy*) bruyant; (*voice*) fort; (*showy*) voyant ‖ *adv* fort; (*noisily*) bruyamment; **out loud** à haute voix

loud' mouth' s gueulard m

loud-mouthed ['lɑud,mɑuθt] adj au verbe haut, gueulard

loud'speak'er s haut-parleur m

Louisiana [lu,izɪ'ænə] s Louisiane f; la Louisiane

lounge [lɑundʒ] s divan m, sofa m; (*room*) petit salon m, salle f de repos; (*in a hotel*) hall m ‖ *intr* flâner; (*e.g., in a chair*) se vautrer

lounge' liz'ard s (slang) gigolo m

louse [lɑus] s (*pl* **lice** [lɑis]) pou m; (slang) salaud m ‖ *tr*—**to louse up** (slang) bâcler

lous•y ['lɑuzi] adj (*comp* **-ier;** *super* **-iest**) pouilleux; (*mean; ugly*) (coll) moche; (*bungling*) (coll) maladroit, gauche; **lousy with** (slang) chargé de

lout [lɑut] s lourdaud m, balourd m

louver ['luvər] s abat-vent m; (aut) auvent m

lovable ['lʌvəbəl] adj aimable, sympathique

love [lʌv] s amour m; (*ending a letter*) affectueusement, bons baisers, je t'embrasse; passion f, e.g., **the theater was her great love** le théâtre était sa grande passion; (tennis) zéro m; **in love with** amoureux de; **love at first sight** le coup de foudre; **love to all!** vives amitiés à tous!; **not for love or money** pour rien au monde, à aucun prix; **to make love to** faire la cour à; **with much love!** avec mes affectueuses pensées! ‖ *tr & intr* aimer

love' affair' s affaire f de cœur

love'birds' spl (orn) perruches fpl inséparables; (*persons*) (fig) tourtereaux mpl

love' child' s enfant mf de l'amour

love' feast' s (eccl) agape f

love' game' s (tennis) jeu m blanc

love' knot' s lacs m d'amour

loveless ['lʌvlɪs] adj sans amour; (*feeling no love*) insensible à l'amour

love' let'ter s billet m doux

lovelorn ['lʌv,lɔrn] adj délaissé d'amour; éperdu d'amour

love•ly ['lʌvli] adj (*comp* **-lier;** *super* **-liest**) beau; (*adorable*) charmant, gracieux; (*enjoyable*) (coll) agréable, aimable

love' match' s mariage m d'amour

love' nest' s nid m d'amoureux

love' po'tion s philtre m d'amour

lover ['lʌvər] s amoureux m, amant m; (*of hunting, sports, music, etc.*) amateur m, fanatique mf

love' seat' s causeuse f

love'sick' adj féru d'amour

love'sick'ness s mal m d'amour

love' song' s romance f, chanson f d'amour

love' sto'ry s histoire f d'amour

loving ['lʌvɪŋ] adj aimant, affectueux; affectionné, e.g., **your loving daughter** votre fille affectionnée

lov'ing cup' s coupe f de l'amitié; trophée m

lov'ing-kind'ness s bonté f d'âme

low [lo] adj bas; (*speed; price*) bas; (*speed; price; number; light*) faible; (*opinion*) défavorable; (*dress*) décolleté; (*sound, note*) bas, grave; (*fever*) lent; (*bow*) profond; **to lay low** étendre, terrasser; **to lie low** se tenir coi ‖ s bas m; (*moo of cow*) meuglement m; (aut) première vitesse f; (meteo) dépression f ‖ *adv* bas; **to speak low** parler à voix basse ‖ *intr* (*said of cow*) meugler

low'born' adj de basse naissance

low'boy' s commode f basse

low'brow' adj (coll) peu intellectuel ‖ s (coll) ignorant m

low'-cost' hous'ing s habitations fpl à loyer modéré or à bon marché

Low' Coun'tries spl Pays-Bas mpl

low'-down' adj (coll) bas, vil ‖ **low'-down'** s (slang) faits mpl véritables; **to give s.o. the low-down on** (slang) tuyauter qn sur

lower ['lo•ər] adj inférieur, bas ‖ *tr & intr* baisser ‖ ['lɑu•ər] *intr* se renfrogner, regarder de travers

low'er berth' s couchette f inférieure

low'er case' s (typ) bas m de casse

low'er mid'dle class' s petite bourgeoisie f

lowermost ['lo•ər,most] adj (le) plus bas

low'-fre'quency adj à basse fréquence

low' gear' s première vitesse f

low'-in'come hous'ing s habitations fpl à bon marché (HBM)

low'-key' adj modéré

lowland ['lolənd] s plaine f basse; **Lowlands** (*in Scotland*) Basse-Écosse f

low'-lev'el lan'guage s (comp) langage m de bas niveau

low•ly ['loli] adj (*comp* **-lier;** *super* **-liest**) humble, modeste; (*in growth or position*) bas, infime

Low' Mass' s messe basse f, petite messe

low'-mind'ed adj d'esprit vulgaire

low' neck' s décolleté m

low'-necked' adj décolleté

low'-pitched' *adj* (*sound*) grave; (*roof*) à faible inclinaison
low'-pres'sure *adj* à basse pression
low'-priced' *adj* à bas prix
low' shoe' *s* soulier *m* bas
low'-speed' *adj* à petite vitesse
low'-spir'ited *adj* abattu
low' spir'its *spl* abattement *m*, accablement *m*
low' tide' *s* marée *f* basse
low' vis'ibil'ity *s* (aer) mauvaise visibilité *f*
low'-warp' *adj* (tex) de basse lice
low' wa'ter *s* (*of river*) étiage *m*; (*of sea*) niveau *m* des basses eaux; marée *f* basse
loyal [ˈlɔɪ•əl] *adj* loyal
loyalist [ˈlɔɪ•əlɪst] *s* loyaliste *mf*
loyal•ty [ˈlɔɪ•əlti] *s* (*pl* **-ties**) loyauté *f*
lozenge [ˈlɑzɪndʒ] *s* (*candy cough drop*) pastille *f*; (geom) losange *m*
LP [ˈɛlˈpi] *s* (letterword) (trademark) (**long-playing**) disque *m* de longue durée
lubricant [ˈlubrɪkənt] *adj* & *s* lubrifiant *m*
lubricate [ˈlubrɪˌket] *tr* lubrifier
lubricous [ˈlubrɪkəs] *adj* (*slippery*) glissant; (*lewd*) lubrique; inconstant
lucerne [luˈsʌrn] *s* luzerne *f*
lucid [ˈlusɪd] *adj* lucide
luck [lʌk] *s* (*good or bad*) chance *f*; (*good*) chance, bonne chance; **to be down on one's luck, to be out of luck** avoir de la malchance, être dans la déveine; **to be in luck** avoir de la chance, avoir de la veine; **to bring luck** porter bonheur; **to try one's luck** tenter la fortune, tenter l'aventure; **worse luck!** tant pis!, pas de chance!
luckily [ˈlʌkɪli] *adv* heureusement, par bonheur
luckless [ˈlʌklɪs] *adj* malheureux, malchanceux
luck•y [ˈʌki] *adj* (*comp* **-ier;** *super* **-iest**) heureux, fortuné; (*supposed to bring luck*) porte-bonheur; **how lucky!** quelle chance!; **lucky dog!** le veinard!, la veinarde!; **to be lucky** avoir de la chance, être verni, avoir du pot
luck'y charm' *s* porte-bonheur *m*
luck'y dog' *s* (coll) veinard *m*
luck'y find' (coll) trouvaille *f*
luck'y hit' *s* (coll) coup *m* de bonheur, coup de chance
lucrative [ˈlukrətɪv] *adj* lucratif
ludicrous [ˈludɪkrəs] *adj* ridicule, risible
lug [lʌg] *s* oreille *f*; (*pull, tug*) saccade *f* ‖ *v* (*pret & pp* **lugged;** *ger* **lugging**) *tr* traîner, tirer; (*to bring up irrelevantly*) (coll) ressortir, amener de force
luggage [ˈlʌgɪdʒ] *s* bagages *mpl*
lug'gage car'rier *s* porte-bagages *m*
lugubrious [luˈg(j)ubri•əs] *adj* lugubre
lukewarm [ˈlukˈwɔrm] *adj* tiède
lull [lʌl] *s* accalmie *f* ‖ *tr* bercer, endormir, calmer
lulla•by [ˈlʌləˌbaɪ] *s* (*pl* **-bies**) berceuse *f*
lumbago [lʌmˈbego] *s* lumbago *m*
lumber [ˈlʌmbər] *s* bois *m* de charpente, bois de construction ‖ *intr* se traîner lourdement
lum'ber•jack' *s* bûcheron *m*

lum'ber jack'et *s* canadienne *f*
lum'ber•man *s* (*pl* **-men**) (*dealer*) exploitant *m* forestier, propriétaire *m* forestier; (*man who cuts down lumber*) bûcheron *m*
lum'ber raft' *s* train *m* de flottage
lum'ber room' *s* fourre-tout *m*, débarras *m*
lum'ber•yard' *s* chantier *m* de bois, dépôt *m* de bois de charpente
luminar•y [ˈlumɪˌnɛri] *s* (*pl* **-ies**) corps *m* lumineux; (astr) luminaire *m*; (*person*) (fig) lumière *f*
luminescent [ˌlumɪˈnɛsənt] *adj* luminescent
luminous [ˈlumɪnəs] *adj* lumineux
lummox [ˈlʌməks] *s* (coll) lourdaud *m*
lump [lʌmp] *s* masse *f*; (*of earth*) motte *f*; (*of sugar*) morceau *m*; (*of salt, flour, porridge, etc.*) grumeau *m*; (*swelling*) bosse *f*; (*of ice, stone, etc.*) bloc *m*; **in the lump** en bloc; **to get a lump in one's throat** avoir un serrement de gorge ‖ *tr* réunir; **to lump together** prendre en bloc, englober ‖ *intr*—**to lump along** marcher d'un pas lourd
lumpish [ˈlʌmpɪʃ] *adj* balourd
lump' sug'ar *s* sucre *m* en morceaux
lump' sum' *s* somme *f* globale
lump•y [ˈlʌmpi] *adj* (*comp* **-ier;** *super* **-iest**) grumeleux; (*covered with lumps*) couvert de bosses; (*sea*) clapoteux
luna•cy [ˈlunəsi] *s* (*pl* **-cies**) folie *f*
lu'nar land'er [ˈlunər] *s* alunisseur *m*
lu'nar land'ing *s* alunissage *m*
lu'nar mod'ule *s* (rok) module *m* lunaire
lunatic [ˈlunətɪk] *adj* & *s* fou *m*
lu'natic asy'lum *s* maison *f* de fous
lu'natic fringe' *s* minorité *f* fanatique, frange *f* des dingues
lunch [lʌntʃ] *s* (*midday meal*) déjeuner *m*; (*light meal*) collation *f*, petit repas *m* ‖ *intr* déjeuner; (*to snack*) casser la croûte, manger sur le pouce
lunch' bas'ket *s* panier *m* à provisions
lunch' cloth' *s* nappe *f* à thé
lunch' coun'ter *s* snack *m*, buffet *m*
luncheon [ˈlʌntʃən] *s* déjeuner *m*
luncheonette [ˌlʌntʃəˈnɛt] *s* brasserie *f*, café-restaurant *m*
lunch'room' *s* brasserie *f*, café-restaurant *m*
lunch' time' *s* heure *f* du déjeuner
lung [lʌŋ] *s* poumon *m*
lung' can'cer *s* cancer *m* du poumon
lunge [lʌndʒ] *s* mouvement *m* en avant; (*with a sword*) botte *f* ‖ *intr* se précipiter en avant; (*with a sword*) se fendre; **to lunge at** porter une botte à
lurch [lʌrtʃ] *s* embardée *f*; (*of person*) secousse *f*; **to leave in the lurch** laisser en plan ‖ *intr* faire une embardée; (*said of person*) vaciller
lure [lʊr] *s* (*decoy*) leurre *m*, amorce *f*; (fig) attrait *m* ‖ *tr* leurrer; **to lure away** détourner
lurid [ˈlʊrɪd] *adj* sensationnel; (*gruesome*) terrible, macabre; (*fiery*) rougeoyant; (*livid*) blafard
lurk [lʌrk] *intr* se cacher; (*to prowl*) rôder

luscious [ˈlʌʃəs] *adj* délicieux, succulent; luxueux, somptueux

lush [lʌʃ] *adj* plein de sève; (*abundant*) luxuriant; opulent, luxueux

lust [lʌst] *f* désir *m* ardent; (*greed*) convoitise *f*, soif *f*; (*strong sexual appetite*) luxure *f*

luster [ˈlʌstər] *s* lustre *m*

lus'ter•ware' *s* poterie *f* lustrée, poterie à reflets métalliques

lustful [ˈlʌstfəl] *adj* luxurieux, lascif, lubrique

lustrous [ˈlʌstrəs] *adj* lustré, chatoyant

lust•y [ˈlʌsti] *adj* (*comp* **-ier**; *super* **-iest**) robuste, vigoureux

lute [lut] *s* (mus) luth *m*; (*substance used to close or seal a joint*) (chem) lut *m*

Lutheran [ˈluθərən] *adj* luthérien ‖ *s* Luthérien *m*

Luxemburg [ˈlʌksəm,bʌrg] *s* le Luxembourg

luxuriant [lʌgˈʒurɪ•ənt] *adj* luxuriant; (*overornamented*) surchargé

luxurious [lʌgˈʒurɪ•əs] *adj* luxueux, somptueux

luxu•ry [ˈlʌgʒəri] *s* (*pl* **-ries**) luxe *m*

lux'ury i'tem *s* produit *m* de luxe

lux'ury tax' *s* taxe *f* de luxe

lyceum [laɪˈsi•əm] *s* lycée *m*

lye [laɪ] *s* lessive *f*

lying [ˈlaɪ•ɪŋ] *adj* menteur ‖ *s* le mensonge

ly'ing-in' hos'pital *s* maternité *f*, clinique *f* d'accouchement

lymph [lɪmf] *s* lymphe *f*

lymphatic [lɪmˈfætɪk] *adj* lymphatique

lynch [lɪntʃ] *tr* lyncher

lynching [ˈlɪntʃɪŋ] *s* lynchage *m*

lynx [lɪŋks] *s* lynx *m*

Lyons [ˈlaɪ•ənz] *s* Lyon *m*

lyre [laɪr] *s* (mus) lyre *f*

lyric [ˈlɪrɪk] *adj* lyrique ‖ *s* poème *m* lyrique; **lyrics** (*of song*) paroles *fpl*; (theat) chansons *fpl* du livret

lyrical [ˈlɪrɪkəl] *adj* lyrique

lyricism [ˈlɪrɪ,sɪzəm] *s* lyrisme *m*

lyricist [ˈlɪrɪsɪst] *s* poète *m* lyrique; (*writer of words for songs*) parolier *m*

M

M, m [ɛm] XIIIᵉ lettre de l'alphabet

ma [mɑ] *s* (coll) maman *f*

ma'am [mæm], [mɑm] *s* (coll) madame *f*

mac *ou* **Mac** [mæk] *s* (*form of address*) (coll) mon ami *m*

macadam [məˈkædəm] *s* macadam *m*

macadamize [məˈkædə,maɪz] *tr* macadamiser

macaroon [,mækəˈrun] *s* macaron *m*

macaw [məˈkɔ] *s* (orn) ara *m*

mace [mes] *s* masse *f*

mace'bear'er *s* massier *m*

Machiavellian [ˈmæki•əˈvɛli•ən] *adj* machiavélique

machination [,mækɪˈneʃən] *s* machination *f*

machine [məˈʃin] *s* machine *f*; (*of a political party*) noyau *m* directeur, leviers *mpl* de commande ‖ *tr* usiner, façonner

machine' gun' *s* mitrailleuse *f*

ma•chine'-gun' *v* (*pret & pp* **-gunned**; *ger* **-gunning**) *tr* mitrailler

ma•chine'-made' *adj* fait à la machine

machiner•y [məˈʃinəri] *s* (*pl* **-ies**) machinerie *f*, machines *fpl*; (*of a watch; of government*) mécanisme *m*; (*in literature*) merveilleux *m*

machine' screw' *s* vis *f* à métaux; vis à tôle

machine' shop' *s* atelier *m* d'usinage

machine' tool' *s* machine-outil *f*

machine' transla'tion *s* traduction *f* automatique

machinist [məˈʃinɪst] *s* mécanicien *m*

mackerel [ˈmækərəl] *s* maquereau *m*

mack'erel sky' *s* ciel *m* pommelé *or* moutonné

mad [mæd] *adj* (*comp* **madder**; *super* **maddest**) fou; (*dog*) enragé; (coll) fâché, irrité; **as mad as a hatter** fou à lier; **like mad** (coll) comme un fou, éperdument; **to be mad about** (coll) être fou or passionné de; **to drive mad** rendre fou

madam [ˈmædəm] *s* madame *f*; (*of a brothel*) (slang) tenancière *f*

mad'cap' *adj & s* écervelé *m*, étourdi *m*

mad' cow' disease' *s* (vet) encéphalopathie *f* spongiforme; maladie *f* de la vache folle

madden [ˈmædən] *tr* rendre fou ‖ *intr* devenir fou

made-to-order [ˈmedtəˈɔrdər] *adj* fait sur demande; (*clothing*) fait sur mesure

made'-up' *adj* inventé; (*artificial*) postiche; (*face*) maquillé

mad'house' *s* maison *f* de fous

mad'man' *s* (*pl* **-men'**) fou *m*

madness [ˈmædnɪs] *s* folie *f*; (*of dog*) rage *f*

Madonna [məˈdɑnə] *s* madone *f*; (eccl) Madone

maelstrom [ˈmelstrəm] *s* maelstrom *m*, tourbillon *m*

Mafia or **Maffia** [ˈmɑfi•ə] *s* mafia *f*, maffia *f*

magazine [ˈmægə,zin], [,mægəˈzin] *s* (*periodical*) revue *f*, magazine *m*; (*warehouse; for cartridges of gun or camera; for munitions or powder*) magasin *m*; (naut) soute *f*

mag'azine' rack' *s* casier *m* à revues

Magdalen [ˈmægdələn] *s* Madeleine *f*

Maggie [ˈmægi] *s* (coll) Margot *f*

maggot [ˈmægət] *s* asticot *m*

Magi [ˈmedʒaɪ] *spl* mages *mpl*

magic [ˈmædʒɪk] *adj* magique ‖ *s* magie *f;* **as
if by magic** comme par enchantement
magician [məˈdʒɪʃən] *s* magicien *m*
mag′ic mark′er pen′ *s* crayon-feutre *m*
magisterial [ˌmædʒɪsˈtɪrɪ•əl] *adj* magistral
magistrate [ˈmædʒɪs,tret] *s* magistrat *m*
Magna Charta [ˈmægnəˈkɑrtə] *s* la Grande
Charte *f*
magnanimous [mægˈnænɪməs] *adj* magnanime
magnate [ˈmægnet] *s* magnat *m*
magnesium [mægˈniʃi•əm] *s* magnésium *m*
magnet [ˈmægnɪt] *s* aimant *m*
magnetic [mægˈnɛtɪk] *adj* magnétique; (fig) attrayant, séduisant
magnet′ic de′viation *s* déviation *m* magnétique
magnet′ic tape′ *s* bande *f* magnétique
magnetism [ˈmægnɪ,tizəm] *s* magétisme *m*
magnetize [ˈmægnɪ,taɪz] *tr* aimanter
magne•to [mægˈnito] *s* (*pl* **-tos**) magnéto *f*
magnificent [mægˈnɪfɪsənt] *adj* magnifique
magni•fy [ˈmægnɪ,faɪ] *v* (*pret & pp* **-fied**) *tr*
grossir; (opt) grossir
mag′nifying glass′ *s* loupe *f*
magnitude [ˈmægnɪ,t(j)ud] *s* grandeur *f;* (astr)
magnitude *f*
magpie [ˈmæg,paɪ] *s* (orn, fig) pie *f*
mahlstick [ˈmɑl,stɪk] *s* appui-main *m*
mahoga•ny [məˈhɑgəni] *s* (*pl* **-nies**) acajou *m*
mahout [məˈhaut] *s* cornac *m*
maid [med] *s* (*servant*) bonne *f;* (*young woman*)
jeune fille *f,* demoiselle *f*
maiden [ˈmedən] *s* jeune fille *f,* demoiselle *f*
maid′en•hair′ *s* (bot) capillaire *m*
maid′en•head′ *s* hymen *m*
maid′en•hood′ *s* virginité *f*
maid′en la′dy *s* demoiselle *f,* célibataire *f*
maidenly [ˈmedənli] *adj* virginal, de jeune fille
maid′en name′ *s* nom *m* de jeune fille
maid′en voy′age *s* premier voyage *m*
maid′-in-wait′ing *s* (*pl* **maids-in-waiting**)
fille *f* d'honneur, dame *f* d'honneur
maid′ of hon′or *s* demoiselle *f* d'honneur
maid′serv′ant *s* fille *f* de service, servante *f*
mail [mel] *adj* postal ‖ *s* courrier *m;* (*system*)
poste *f;* (*armor*) mailles *fpl,* cotte *f* de mailles;
by return mail par retour du courrier; **mails**
poste ‖ *tr* mettre à la poste, envoyer par la
poste
mail′bag′ *s* sac *m* postal
mail′boat′ *s* paquebot *m,* bateau-poste *m*
mail′box′ *s* boîte *f* aux lettres
mail′ car′ *s* fourgon *m* postal, bureau *m* ambulant, wagon-poste *m*
mail′ car′rier *s* facteur *m,* préposé *m*
mail′ clerk′ *s* postier *m;* (mil, nav) vaguemestre
m; (rr) convoyeur *m* des postes
mailing [ˈmelɪŋ] *s* envoi *m;* (*preparation*)
adressage *m*
mail′ing list′ *s* liste *f* d'adresses, (*of subscribers*) liste d'abonnés
mail′ing per′mit *s* (label on envelopes) dispensé du timbrage

mail′man′ *s* (*pl* **-men′**) facteur *m*
mail′ or′der *s* commande *f* par la poste
mail′-order house′ *s* établissement *m* de vente
par correspondance or de vente sur catalogue;
comptoir *m* postal (Canad)
mail′-order sell′ing *s* vente *f* par correspondance
mail′plane′ *s* avion *m* postal
mail′ train′ *s* train-poste *m*
maim [mem] *tr* mutiler, estropier
main [men] *adj* principal ‖ *s* (*sewer*) égout *m*
collecteur, canalisation *f* or conduite *f* principale; **in the main** en général, pour la plupart
main′ clause′ *s* proposition *f* principale
main′ course′ *s* (culin) plat *m* principal, pièce
f de résistance
main′ deck′ *s* pont *m* principal
main′ en′trance *s* entrée *f* principale
main′ floor′ *s* rez-de-chaussée *m*
mainland [ˈmen,lænd], [ˈmenlənd] *s* terre *f*
ferme, continent *m*
main′ line′ *s* (rr) grande ligne *f*
mainly [ˈmenli] *adv* principalement
mainmast [ˈmenmɑst] *s* grand mât *m*
mainsail [ˈmensəl] *s* grand-voile *f*
main′spring′ *s* (*of watch*) ressort *m* moteur,
grand ressort; (fig) mobile *m* essentiel, principe *m*
main′stay′ *s* (naut) étai *m* de grand mât; (fig)
point *m* d'appui
main′stream′ *adj* établi, dominant ‖ *s* voie *f*
principale, courant *m* dominant, ligne *f* centrale
main′ street′ *s* rue *f* principale
maintain [menˈten] *tr* maintenir; (*e.g., a family*)
entretenir, faire subsister
maintenance [ˈmentɪnəns] *s* entretien *m,* maintien *m;* (*department entrusted with upkeep*)
services *mpl* d'entretien, maintenance *f*
maître d'hôtel [ˌmetərdoˈtɛl] *s* maître *m* d'hôtel
maize [mez] *s* maïs *m*
majestic [məˈdʒɛstɪk] *adj* majestueux
majes•ty [ˈmædʒɪsti] *s* (*pl* **-ties**) majesté *f*
major [ˈmedʒər] *adj* majeur ‖ *s* (*person of full
legal age*) majeur *m;* (educ) spécialisation *f;*
(mil) commandant *m* ‖ *intr* (educ) se spécialiser
Majorca [məˈdʒɔrkə] *s* Majorque *f;* île *f* de Majorque
Majorcan [məˈdʒɔrkən] *adj* majorquin ‖ *s* Majorquin *m*
ma′jor gen′eral *s* général *m* de division
majori•ty [məˈdʒɑrɪti], [məˈdʒɔrɪti] *adj* majoritaire ‖ *s* (*pl* **-ties**) majorité *f;* (mil) grade *m*
de commandant; **the majority of** la plupart
de
major′ity vote′ *s* scrutin *m* majoritaire
make [mek] *s* (*brand name*) marque *f;* (*production*) fabrication *f;* **on the make** (coll) prêt à
tout pour faire fortune ‖ *v* (*pret & pp* **made**
[med]) *tr* faire; rendre, e.g., **to make sick**
rendre malade; (*money*) gagner; (*the cards*)
battre; (*a train*) attraper; **to make into** trans-

former en; **to make known** faire savoir; **to make out** déchiffrer, distinguer; (*a bill, receipt, check*) écrire; (*a list*) dresser; **to make s.o.** + *inf* faire + *inf* + qn, e.g., **I will make my uncle talk** je ferai parler mon oncle ‖ *intr* être, e.g., **to make sure** être sûr; **to make believe** feindre; **to make good** réussir; **to make off** filer, décamper

make'-believe' *adj* simulé ‖ *s* faux-semblant *m*, feinte *f*

maker [ˈmekər] *s* fabricant *m*

make'shift' *adj* de fortune, de circonstance ‖ *s* expédient *m*; (*person*) bouche-trou *m*

make'-up' *s* arrangement *m*, composition *f*; (*cosmetic*) maquillage *m*; (typ) mise *f* en pages, imposition *f*

make'-up man' *s* (theat) maquilleur *m*; (typ) metteur *m* en pages, imposeur *m*

make'weight' *s* complément *m* de poids

making [ˈmekɪŋ] *s* fabrication *f*; (*of a dress; of a cooked dish*) confection *f*; **makings** éléments *mpl* constitutifs; (*money*) recettes *fpl*; **to have the makings of** avoir l'étoffe de

maladjusted [ˌmæləˈdʒʌstɪd] *adj* inadapté

maladjustment [ˌmæləˈdʒʌstmənt] *s* inadaptation *f*

mala•dy [ˈmælədi] *s* (*pl* **-dies**) maladie *f*

malaise [mæˈlez] *s* malaise *m*

malaria [məˈlɛrɪ•ə] *s* malaria *f*, paludisme *m*

Malay [ˈmele], [məˈle] *adj* malais ‖ *s* (*language*) malais *m*; (*person*) Malais *m*

Malaya [məˈle•ə] *s* Mallaisie *f*; la Malaisie

malcontent [ˈmælkənˌtɛnt] *adj* & *s* mécontent *m*

male [mel] *adj* & *s* mâle *m*

male' chau'vinism *s* machisme *m*

male' chau'vinist *s* machiste *m*, phallocrate *m*

male' chau'vinist pig's *s* cochon *m* de phallocrate

malediction [ˌmælɪˈdɪkʃən] *s* malédiction *f*

malefactor [ˈmælɪˌfæktər] *s* malfaiteur *m*

male' nurse' *s* infirmier *m*

malevolent [məˈlɛvələnt] *adj* malveillant

malfeasance [ˌmælˈfizəns] *s* prévarication *f*, trafic *m*

malfunction [ˌmælˈfʌŋkʃən] *s* mauvaise fonction *f* ‖ *intr* mal fonctionner

malice [ˈmælɪs] *s* méchanceté *f*, malice *f*

malicious [məˈlɪʃəs] *adj* méchant

malign [məˈlaɪn] *adj* pernicieux; malveillant ‖ *tr* calomnier

malignan•cy [məˈlɪgnənsi] *s* (*pl* **-cies**) malignité *f*

malignant [məˈlɪgnənt] *adj* méchant, malin, malfaisant; (med) malin, maligne

malinger [məˈlɪŋgər] *intr* faire le malade

malingerer [məˈlɪŋgərər] *s* simulateur *m*

mall [mɔl], [mæl] *s* (*tree-lined walk*) mail *m*, allée *f*; (*shopping mall*) galerie *f* marchande

mallard [ˈmælərd] *s* (orn) col-vert *m*

malleable [ˈmælɪ•əbəl] *adj* malléable

mallet [ˈmælɪt] *s* maillet *m*

mallow [ˈmælo] *s* (bot) mauve *f*

malnutrition [ˌmæln(j)uˈtrɪʃən] *s* sousalimentation *f*, malnutrition *f*

malodorous [mælˈodərəs] *adj* malodorant

malpractice [mælˈpræktɪs] *s* incurie *f*, méfait *m*; (med) incurie professionnelle, négligence *f*, faute *f* professionnelle

malt [mɔlt] *s* malt *m*

maltreat [mælˈtrit] *tr* maltraiter

mamma [ˈmɑmə], [məˈmɑ] *s* maman *f*

mammal [ˈmæməl] *s* mammifère *m*

mammalian [mæˈmelɪ•ən] *adj* & *s* mammifère *m*

mammogram [ˈmæməgræm] *ou* **mammograph** [ˈmæməgræf] *s* mammographie *f*

mammoth [ˈmæməθ] *adj* énorme, colossal ‖ *s* mammouth *m*

man [mæn] *s* (*pl* **men** [mɛn]) *s* homme *m*; (*servant*) domestique *m*; (*worker*) ouvrier *m*, employé *m*; (checkers) pion *m*; (chess) pièce *f*; **a man** on, e.g., **what can a man do?** qu'est-ce qu'on peut faire?; **every man for himself!** sauve qui peut!; **man alive!** (coll) tiens!; fichtre!; **man and wife** mari et femme; **men at work** (public sign) travaux en cours ‖ *v* (*pret & pp* **manned;** *ger* **manning**) *tr* (*a ship*) équiper; (*a fort*) garnir; (*a cannon, the pumps, etc.*) armer; (*a battery*) servir

man' about town' *s* boulevardier *m*, coureur *m* de cabarets

manacle [ˈmænəkəl] *s* manilla *f*; **manacles** menottes *fpl* ‖ *tr* mettre les menottes à

manage [ˈmænɪdʒ] *tr* gérer, diriger; (*to handle*) manier ‖ *intr* se débrouiller; **how did you manage to ...?** comment avez-vous fait pour ...?; **to manage to** s'arranger pour

manageable [ˈmænɪdʒəbəl] *adj* maniable

management [ˈmænɪdʒmənt] *s* direction *f*, gérance *f*; (*group who manage*) direction, administration *f*; (*in contrast to labor*) patronat *m*; **under new management** (public sign) changement de propriétaire

manager [ˈmænədʒər] *s* directeur *m*, gérant *m*; (*e.g., of a department*) chef *m*; (*impresario*) manager *m*; (baseball) gérant *m*, instructeur-chef *m*

managerial [ˌmænəˈdʒɪrɪ•əl] *adj* patronal

man'aging ed'itor *s* rédacteur *m* gérant

Manchuria [mænˈtʊrɪə] *s* Mandchourie *f*; la Mandchourie

man'darin or'ange [ˈmændərɪn] *s* mandarine *f*

mandate [ˈmændet] *s* mandat *m* ‖ *tr* placer sous le mandat de

mandatory [ˈmændə,tori] *adj* obligatoire

mandolin [ˈmændəlɪn] *s* mandoline *f*

mandrake [ˈmændrek] *s* mandragore *f*

mane [men] *s* crinière *f*

maneuver [məˈnuvər] *s* manœuvre *m* ‖ *tr* & *intr* manœuvrer

manful [ˈmænfəl] *adj* viril, hardi

manganese [ˈmæŋgə,nis] *s* manganèse *m*

mange [mendʒ] *s* gale *f*

manger [ˈmendʒər] *s* mangeoire *f*, crèche *f*

mangle [ˈmæŋgəl] s calandre f ‖ tr lacérer, mutiler; (to press) calandrer

man•gy [ˈmendʒi] adj (comp **-gier;** super **-giest**) galeux; (dirty, squalid) miteux

man'han'dle tr malmener

man'hole' s trou m d'homme, regard m

manhood [ˈmænhʊd] s virilité f; humanité f

man'hunt' s chasse f à l'homme; chasse au mari

mania [ˈmenɪ•ə] s manie f

maniac [ˈmenɪˌæk] adj & s maniaque mf

maniacal [məˈnaɪ•əkəl] adj maniaque

manic-depressive [ˈmænɪkdɪˈprɛsɪv] adj maniaco-dépressif

manicure [mænɪˌkjʊr] s soins mpl esthétiques des mains et des ongles; (person) manucure mf ‖ tr manucurer

manicurist [ˈmænɪˌkjʊrɪst] s manucure mf

manifest [ˈmænɪˌfɛst] adj manifeste ‖ s (naut) manifeste m ‖ tr & intr manifester

manifestation [ˌmænɪfɛsˈteʃən] s manifestation f

manifes•to [ˌmænɪˈfɛsto] s (pl **-toes**) manifeste m

manifold [ˈmænɪˌfold] adj multiple, nombreux ‖ s (aut) tuyauterie f, collecteur m

manikin [ˈmænɪkɪn] s mannequin m; (dwarf) nabot m

man' in the moon' s homme m dans la lune

man' in the street' s homme m de la rue

manipulate [məˈnɪpjəˌlet] tr manipuler

man'kind' s le genre humain, l'humanité f ‖ **man'kind'** s le sexe fort, les hommes mpl

manliness [ˈmænlɪnɪs] s virilité f

man•ly [ˈmænli] adj (comp **-lier;** super **-liest**) viril, masculin

man'-made' adj (fibers) synthétique; (lake) artificiel

manna [ˈmænə] s manne f

manned' space'craft s vaisseau m spatial habité

mannequin [ˈmænɪkɪn] s mannequin m

manner [ˈmænər] s manière f; **by all manner of means** certainement; **by no manner of means** en aucune manière; **in a manner of speaking** pour ainsi dire; **in the manner of** à la, e.g., **in the manner of the French, in the French manner** à la manière française, à la française; **manners** manières; **manners of the time** mœurs fpl de l'époque; **to the manner born** créé et mis au monde pour ça

mannerism [ˈmænəˌrɪzm] s maniérisme m

mannish [ˈmænɪʃ] adj hommasse

man' of let'ters s homme m de lettres, bel esprit m

man' of parts' s homme m de talent

man' of straw' s homme m de paille

man' of the world' s homme m du monde

man-of-war [ˌmænəvˈwɔr] s (pl **men-of-war**) navire m de guerre

manor [ˈmænər] s seigneurie f

man'or house' s château m, manoir m

man' o'verboard' interj un homme, à la mer!

man'pow'er s main-d'œuvre f; (mil) effectifs mpl

manse [mæns] s maison f du pasteur

man'serv'ant s (pl **-men'serv'ants**) valet m

mansion [ˈmænʃən] s hôtel m particulier; château m, manoir m

man'slaugh'ter s (law) homicide m involontaire

mantel [ˈmæntəl] s manteau m de cheminée

man'tel•piece' s manteau m de cheminée; dessus m de cheminée

mantilla [mænˈtɪlə] s mantille f

mantle [ˈmæntəl] s manteau m, mante f; (of gaslight) manchon m ‖ tr envelopper d'une mante; couvrir, revêtir; (to hide) voiler ‖ intr (said of face) rougir

manual [ˈmænjʊ•əl] adj manuel ‖ s (book) manuel m; (of arms) (mil) maniement m; (mus) clavier m d'orgue

man'ual dexter'ity s habileté f manuelle

man'ual train'ing s apprentissage m manuel

manufacture [ˌmænjəˈfæktʃər] s fabrication f; (thing manufactured) produit m fabriqué ‖ tr fabriquer

manufacturer [ˌmænjəˈfæktʃərˌʃr] s fabricant m

manure [məˈn(j)ʊr] s fumier m ‖ tr fumer

manuscript [ˈmænjəˌskrɪpt] adj & s manuscrit m

many [ˈmɛni] adj beaucoup de; **a good many** bien des, maintes; **how many** combien de; **many another** bien d'autres; **many more** beaucoup d'autres; **so many** tant de; **too many** trop de; **twice as many** deux fois autant de ‖ pron beaucoup; **as many as** autant de; jusqu'à, e.g., **as many as twenty** jusqu'à vingt; **how many** combien; **many a** maint; **many another** bien d'autres; **many more** beaucoup d'autres; **so many** tant; **too many** trop; **twice as many** deux fois autant

man'y-sid'ed adj polygonal; (having many interests or capabilities) complexe

map [mæp] s carte f; (of a city) plan m ‖ v (pret & pp **mapped;** ger **mapping**) tr faire la carte de; **to map out** tracer le plan de; **to put on the map** (coll) faire connaître, mettre en vedette

maple [ˈmepəl] s érable m

ma'ple sug'ar s sucre m d'érable

mar [mɑr] v (pret & pp **marred;** ger **marring**) tr défigurer, gâcher

marathon [ˈmærəˌθɑn] s marathon m

maraud [məˈrɔd] tr piller ‖ intr marauder

marauder [məˈrɔdər] s maraudeur m

marauding [məˈrɔdɪŋ] adj maraudeur ‖ s maraude f

marble [ˈmɑrbəl] s marbre m; (little ball of glass) bille f; **marbles** (game) jeu m de billes; **to lose one's marbles** (coll) perdre la boule ‖ tr marbrer; (the edge of a book) jasper

march [mɑrtʃ] s marche f; **March** mars m; **to steal a march on** prendre de l'avance sur ‖ tr faire marcher ‖ intr marcher

marchioness [`mɑrʃənɪs] s marquise f
mare [mɛr] s (*female horse*) jument m; (*female donkey*) ânesse f
Margaret [`mɑrgərɪt] s Marguerite f
margarine [`mɑrdʒərɪn] s margarine f
margin [`mɑrdʒɪn] s marge f; (*border*) bord m; (com) acompte m
mar'gin account' s (com) compte m de couverture
marginal [`mɑrdʒɪnəl] adj marginal
marginalization [ˌmɑrdʒɪnələˈzeʃən] s marginalisation f
marginalize [ˌmɑrdʒɪnəˈlaɪz] tr marginaliser
mar'gin release' s déclenche-marge f, touche f marge libre, touche passe-marge
mar'gin set'ter s pose-marge f
mar'gin stop' s margeur m
marigold [`mærɪˌgold] s (*Calendula*) souci m; (*Tagetes*) illet m d'Inde
marihuana or **marijuana** [ˌmɑrɪˈhwɑnə] s marihuana f or marijuana f
marinate [`mærɪˌnet] tr mariner
marine [məˈrin] adj marin, maritime ‖ s flotte f; (nav) fusilier m marin; **tell it to the marines!** (coll) à d'autres!
Marine' Corps' s infanterie f de marine
mariner [`mærɪnər] s marin m
marionette [ˌmærɪ•əˈnɛt] s marionette f
marital [`mærɪtəl] adj matrimonial
mar'ital sta'tus s état m civil
maritime [`mærɪˌtaɪm] adj maritime
marjoram [`mɑrdʒərəm] s marjolaine f; origan m
mark [mɑrk] s marque f, signe m; (*of punctuation*) point m; (*in an examination*) note f; (*spot, stain*) tache f, marque; (*monetary unit*) mark m; (*starting point in a race*) ligne f de départ; **as a mark of** en témoignage de; **Mark** Marc m; **on your mark!** à vos marques!; **to hit the mark** mettre dans le mille, atteindre le but; **to leave one's mark** laisser son empreinte; **to make one's mark** se faire un nom, marquer; **to miss the mark** manquer le but; **to toe the mark** se conformer au mot d'ordre ‖ tr marquer; (*a student; an exam*) donner une note à; (*e.g., one's approval*) témoigner; **to mark down** noter; (com) démarquer; **to mark off** distinguer; **to mark up** (com) majorer
mark'down' s rabais m
marker [`mɑrkər] s marqueur m; (*of boundary*) borne f; (*landmark*) repère m
market [`mɑrkɪt] s marché m; **to bear the market** jouer à la baisse; **to bull the market** jouer à la hausse; **to play the market** jouer à la bourse; **to put on the market** lancer, vendre, or mettre sur le marché ‖ tr commercialiser
marketable [`mɑrkɪtəbəl] adj vendable
mar'ket bas'ket s panier m à provisions
marketing [`mɑrkɪtɪŋ] s marketing m; (*of a product*) commercialisation f, exploitation f
mar'ket•place' s place f du marché

mar'ket price' s cours m du marché, prix m courant
marking [`mɑrkɪŋ] s marquage m; (*numbering*) chiffrage m; (educ) correction f de copies; (zool) marques fpl, taches fpl
mark'ing gauge' s trusquin m
marks•man [`mɑrksmən] s (pl **-men**) tireur m
marks'man•ship' s habileté f au tir, adresse f au tir
mark'up' s (*profit*) marge f bénéficiaire; (*price increase*) majoration f de prix
marl [mɑrl] s marne f ‖ tr marner
marmalade [`mɑrməˌled] s marmelade f
maroon [məˈrun] adj & s (*color*) lie f de vin, rouge m violacé, bordeaux ‖ tr abandonner, isoler
marquee [mɑrˈki] s marquise f
marquis [`mɑrkwɪs] s marquis m
marquise [mɑrˈkiz] s marquise
marriage [`mærɪdʒ] s marriage m
marriageable [`mærɪdʒəbəl] adj mariable
mar'riage certif'icate s acte m de mariage
mar'riage por'tion s dot f
mar'riage rate' s taux m de nuptialité
mar'ried life' [`mærɪd] s vie f conjugale
marrow [`mæro] s moelle f
mar•ry [`mæri] v (pret & pp **-ried**) tr (*to join in wedlock*) marier; (*to take in marriage*) se marier avec; **to get married to** se marier avec; **to marry off** marier ‖ intr se marier
Mars [mɑrz] s Mars m
Marseilles [mɑrˈselz] s Marseille f
marsh [mɑrʃ] s marais m, marécage m
mar•shal [`mɑrʃəl] s maître m des cérémonies; (*policeman*) shérif m; (mil) maréchal m ‖ v (pret & pp **-shaled** or **-shalled**; ger **-shaling** or **-shalling**) tr conduire; (*one's reasons, arguments, etc.*) ranger, rassembler
marsh' mal'low s (bot) guimauve f
marsh'mal'low s (*sweetened paste*) pâte f de guimauve; (*candy*) bonbon m à la guimauve
marsh•y [`mɑrʃi] adj (comp **-ier**; super **-iest**) marécageux
mart [mɑrt] s marché m, foire f
marten [`mɑrtən] s (*pine marten*) martre f; (*beech marten*) fouine f
Martha [`mɑrθə] s Marthe f
martial [`mɑrʃəl] adj martial
mar'tial law' s loi f martiale
Martian [`mɑrʃən] adj & s martien m, martienne f
martin [`mɑrtɪn] s (orn) martinet m
martinet [ˌmɑrtɪ`nɛt] s pètesec m
martyr [`mɑrtər] s martyr m ‖ tr martyriser
martyrdom [`mɑrtərdəm] s martyre m
mar•vel [`mɑrvəl] s merveille f ‖ v (pret & pp **-veled** or **-velled**; ger **-veling** or **-velling**) intr s'émerveiller; **to marvel at** s'émerveiller de
marvelous [`mɑrvələs] adj merveilleux
Marxist [`mɑrksɪst] adj & s marxiste mf
Maryland [`mɛrələnd] s le Maryland
marzipan [`mɑrzɪˌpæn] s massepain m
mascara [mæsˈkærə] s rimmel m

mascot [`mæskɑt] *s* mascotte *f*

masculine [`mæskjələn] *adj* & *s* masculin *m*

mash [mæʃ] *s* (*crushed mass*) bouillie *f;* (*to form wort*) fardeau *m* ‖ *tr* écraser; (*malt, in brewing*) brasser

mashed' pota'toes *spl* purée *f* de pommes de terre

masher [`mæʃər] *s* (*device*) broyeur *m;* (*slang*) tombeur *m*

mask [mæsk] *s* masque *m;* (*around the eyes*) loup *m;* (*phot*) cache *m* ‖ *tr* masquer; (*phot*) poser un cache à ‖ *intr* se masquer

masked' ball' *s* bal *m* masqué

mask'ing tape' *s* ruban *m* cache

masochist [`mæsəkɪst] *s* masochiste *mf*

masochistic [,mæsə`kɪstɪk] *adj* masochiste, maso (coll)

mason [`mesən] *s* maçon *m;* **Mason** Maçon

mason·ry [`mesənri] *s* (*pl* -**ries**) maçonnerie *f;* **Masonry** Maçonnerie

masquerade [,mæskə`red] *s* mascarade *f* ‖ *intr* se déguiser; **to masquerade as** se faire passer pour

mas'querade' ball' *s* bal *m* masqué

mass [mæs] *s* masse *f;* (*eccl*) messe *f* ‖ *tr* masser ‖ *intr* se masser

massacre [`mæsəkər] *s* massacre *m* ‖ *tr* massacrer

massage [mə`sɑʒ] *s* massage *m* ‖ *tr* masser

mass' arrest' *s* rafle *f*

masseur [mə`sʌr] *s* masseur *m*

masseuse [mə`suz] *s* masseuse *f*

massive [`mæsɪv] *adj* massif

mass' me'dia [`midɪ·ə] *spl* communication *f* de masse, media *mpl;* journalistes *mfpl;* presse *f,* radio *f,* télé *f*

mass' meet'ing *s* meeting *m* monstre, rassemblement *m*

mass' produc'tion *s* fabrication *f* en série

mast [mæst] *s* mât *m;* (*food for swine*) gland *m,* faîne *f;* **before the mast** comme simple matelot

mastecto·my [ma`stɛktəmi] *s* (*pl* -**mies**) mammectomie *or* mastectomie *f*

master [`mæstər] *s* maître *m;* (*employer*) chef *m,* patron *m;* (*male head of household*) maître de maison; (*title of respect*) Monsieur *m;* (naut) commandant *m* ‖ *tr* maîtriser; (*a subject*) connaître à fond, posséder

mas'ter bed'room *s* chambre *f* du maître

mas'ter build'er *s* entrepreneur *m* de bâtiments

masterful [`mæstərfəl] *adj* magistral, expert; impérieux, en maître

mas'ter key' *s* passe-partout *m*

masterly [`mæstərli] *adj* magistral, de maître ‖ *adv* magistralement

mas'ter mechan'ic *s* maître *m* mécanicien

mas'ter·mind' *s* organisateur *m,* cerveau *m* ‖ *tr* organiser, diriger

mas'ter of cer'emonies *s* maître *m* des cérémonies; (*in a night club, on television, etc.*) animateur *m*

mas'ter·piece' *s* chef-d'œuvre *m*

mas'ter stroke' *s* coup *m* de maître

mas'ter tape' *s* bande *f* génératrice, bande mère, bande souche

mas'ter·work' *s* chef-d'œuvre *m*

master·y [`mæstəri] *s* (*pl* -**ies**) maîtrise *f*

mast'head' *s* (*of a newspaper*) en-tête *m;* (naut) tête *f* de mât

masticate [`mæstɪ,ket] *tr* mastiquer

mastiff [`mæstɪf] *s* mâtin *m*

masturbate [`mæstər,bet] *tr* masturber ‖ *intr* se masturber

masturbation [,mæstər`beʃən] *s* masturbation *f*

mat [mæt] *s* (*for floor*) natte *f;* (*for a cup, vase, etc.*) dessous *m* de plat; (*before a door*) paillasson *m* ‖ *v* (*pret* & *pp* **matted;** *ger* **matting**) *tr* (*to cover with matting*) couvrir de mattes; (*hair*) emmêler; (*with blood*) coller ‖ *intr* s'emmêler

match [mætʃ] *s* (*producing fire*) allumette *f;* (*wick*) mèche *f;* (*counterpart*) égal *m,* pair *m;* (*suitable partner in marriage*) parti *m;* (*suitably associated pair*) assortiment *m;* (*game, contest*) match *m,* partie *f;* **to be a match for** être de la force de, être à la hauteur de; **to meet one's match** trouver son pareil ‖ *tr* égaler; (*objects*) faire pendant à, assortir ‖ *intr* s'assortir

match'box' *s* boîte *f* d'allumettes, porteallumettes *m*

matchless [`mætʃlɪs] *adj* incomparable, sans pareil

match'mak'er *s* marieur *m*

match' point' *s* (tennis) balle *f* de set, balle de match

mate [met] *s* (*husband*) conjoint *m;* (*wife*) conjointe *f;* (*to a female*) mâle *m;* (*to a male*) femelle *f;* (*fellow worker*) camarade *mf;* (*one of a pair*) l'autre gant *m,* l'autre soulier *m,* l'autre chaussette *f* (*etc.*); (*checkmate*) mat *m;* (naut) officier *m* en second, second maître *m* ‖ *tr* marier; (zool) accoupler ‖ *intr* se marier; s'accoupler

material [mə`tɪrɪ·əl] *adj* matériel; important ‖ *s* matériel *m;* (*what a thing is made of*) matière *f;* (*cloth, fabric*) étoffe *f;* (archit) matériau *m;* **materials** matériaux *mpl*

materialist [mə`tɪrɪ·əlɪst] *s* matérialiste *mf*

materialistic [mə`tɪrɪ·ə`lɪstɪk] *adj* matérialiste, matériel

materialize [mə`tɪrɪə,laɪz] *intr* se matérialiser; (*to be realized*) se réaliser

matériel [mə,tɪrɪ`ɛl] *s* matériel *m*

maternal [mə`tʌrnəl] *adj* maternel

maternity [mə`tʌrnɪti] *s* maternité *f*

mater'nity dress' *s* robe *f* de grossesse

mater'nity hos'pital *s* maternité *f*

mater'nity leave' *s* congé de maternité

mater'nity room' *s* salle *f* d'accouchement

mater'nity ward' *s* salle *f* des accouchées

math [mæθ] *s* (coll) math *fpl*

mathematical [,mæθɪ`mætɪkəl] *adj* mathématique

mathematician [ˌmæθɪməˈtɪʃən] s mathématicien m

mathematics [ˌmæθɪˈmætɪks] s mathématiques fpl

matinée [ˌmætɪˈne] s matinée f

mat′ing sea′son s saison f des amours

matins [ˈmætɪnz] spl matines fpl

matriarch [ˈmetrɪˌɑrk] s matrone f

matriar·chy [ˈmetrɪˌɑrki] s (pl **-chies**) matriarcat m

matricide [ˈmætrɪˌsaɪd] s (person) matricide mf; (action) matricide m

matriculate [məˈtrɪkjəˌlet] tr immatriculer ‖ intr s'inscrire à l'université, prendre ses inscriptions

matriculation [məˌtrɪkjəˈleʃən] s inscription f; immatriculation f

matrimonial [ˌmætrɪˈmonɪ·əl] adj matrimonial

matrimo·ny [ˈmætrɪˌmoni] s (pl **-nies**) marriage m, vie f conjugale

ma·trix [ˈmetrɪks] s (pl **-trices** [trɪˌsiz] or **-trixes**) matrice f

matron [ˈmetrən] s (woman no longer young, and of good standing) matrone f; intendante f, surveillante f

matronly [ˈmetrənli] adj de matrone, digne, respectable

ma′tron of hon′or s dame f d'honneur

matter [ˈmætər] s matière f; (pathol) pus m; **a matter of** affaire de, une question de; **for that matter** à vrai dire; **no matter** n'importe, pas d'importance; **no matter when** n'importe quand; **no matter where** n'importe où; **no matter who** n'importe qui; **what is the matter?** qu'y a-t-il?; **what is the matter with you?** qu'avez-vous? ‖ intr importer; **it doesn't matter** cela ne fait rien

mat′ter of course′ s chose f qui va de soi

mat′ter of fact′ s—**as a matter of fact** en réalité, effectivement, de fait

matter-of-fact [ˈmætərəvˌfækt] adj prosaïque, terre à terre

mattock [ˈmætək] s pioche f

mattress [ˈmætrɪs] s matelas m

mat′tress cov′er s alaise f or alèse f

mature [məˈtʃʊr], [məˈtʊr] adj mür; (due) échu ‖ tr faire mûrir ‖ intr mûrir; (to become due) échoir

maturity [məˈtʃʊrɪti], [məˈtʊrɪti] s maturité f; (com) échéance f

maudlin [ˈmɔdlɪn] adj larmoyant

maul [mɔl] tr malmener; (to split) fendre au coin

maulstick [ˈmɔlˌstɪk] s appui-main m

Maun′dy Thurs′day [mɔndi] s jeudi m saint

mausole·um [ˌmɔsəˈli·əm] s (pl **-ums** or **-a** [ə]) mausolée m

maw [mɔ] s (of birds) jabot m; (of fish) poche f d'air

mawkish [ˈmɔkɪʃ] adj à l'eau de rose; (sickening) écœurant

maxim [ˈmæksɪm] s maxime f

maximum [ˈmæksɪməm] adj & s maximum m

May [me] s mai m ‖ (l.c.) v (pret & cond **might** [maɪt]) aux—**it may be** il ne peut; **may I?** vous permettez?; **may I** + inf puis-je + inf, est-ce que je peux + inf; **may I (may we, etc.)** + inf peut-on + inf; **may you be happy!** puissiez-vous être heureux!

maybe [ˈmebi] adv peut-être

May′ Day′ s le premier mai m

Mayday [ˈmeˌde] interj (ships, airplanes) au secours!

mayhem [ˈmehɛm] s mutilation f

mayonnaise [ˌme·əˈnez] s mayonnaise f

mayor [ˈme·ər], [mɛr] s maire m

May′pole′ s mai m

May′ queen′ s reine f du premier mai

maze [mez] s labyrinthe m, dédale m

me [mi] pron moi §85, §87; me §87

meadow [ˈmɛdo] s prairie f, pré m

mead′ow·land′ s herbage m, prairie f

meager [ˈmigər] adj maigre

meal [mil] s (dinner, lunch, etc.) repas m; (grain) farine f; **to miss a meal** serrer la ceinture d'un cran

meal′ tick′et s ticket-repas m; (job) gagne-pain m

meal′time′ s heure f du repas

meal·y [ˈmili] adj (comp **-ier**; super **-iest**) farineux

mean [min] adj (intermediate) moyen; (low in station or rank) bas, humble; (shabby) vil, misérable; (stingy) mesquin; (small-minded) bas, vilain, méprisable; (vicious) sauvage, mal intentionné; **no mean** fameux, excellent ‖ s milieu m, moyen terme m; (math) moyenne f; **by all means** de toute façon, je vous en prie; **by means of** au moyen de; **by no means** en aucune façon; **means** ressources fpl, fortune f; (agency) moyen m; **means to an end** moyens d'arriver à ses fins; **not by any means!** jamais de la vie! ‖ v (pret & pp **meant** [mɛnt]) tr vouloir dire, signifier; (to intend) entendre; (to entail) entraîner; **to mean s.th. for s.o.** destiner q.ch à qn; **to mean to** avoir l'intention de, compter ‖ intr—**to mean well** avoir de bonnes intentions

meander [mɪˈændər] s méandre m ‖ intr faire des méandres

meaning [ˈminɪŋ] s signification f, sens m; intention f

meaningful [ˈminɪŋfəl] adj significatif

meaningless [ˈminɪŋlɪs] adj sans signification, dénué de sens

meanness [ˈminnɪs] s bassesse f, vilenie f; (stinginess) mesquinerie f

mean′time′ s—**in the meantime** dans l'intervalle, sur ces entrefaites ‖ adv entretemps, en attendant

mean′while′ s & adv var of **meantime**

measles [ˈmizəlz] s rougeole f; (German measles) rubéole f

mea·sly [ˈmizli] adj (comp **-slier**; super **-sliest**) rougeoleux; (slang) piètre, insignifiant

measurable [ˈmɛʒərəbəl] adj mesurable

measure ['mɛʒər] *s* mesure *f;* (*step, procedure*) mesure, démarche *f;* (*legislative bill*) projet *m* de loi; (*mus, poetic*) mesure; **in a large measure** en grande partie; **in a measure** dans une certaine mesure; **to take measures to** prendre des mesures pour; **to take s.o.'s measure** (fig) prendre la mesure de qn ‖ *tr* mesurer; **to measure out** mesurer, distribuer ‖ *intr* mesurer

measurement ['mɛʒərmənt] *s* mesure *f;* **to take s.o.'s measurements** prendre les mesures de qn

meas'uring cup' *s* verre *m* gradué

meat [mit] *s* viande *f;* (*food in general*) nourriture *f;* (*gist*) moelle *f,* substance *f*

meat'ball' *s* boulette *f* de viande

meat'hook' *s* croc *m,* allonge *f*

meat' loaf' *s* pain *m* de viande

meat' mar'ket *s* boucherie *f*

meat' pie' *s* tourte *f* à la viande, pâté *m* en croûte

meat·y ['miti] *adj* (*comp* **-ier;** *super* **-iest**) charnu; (fig) plein de substance, étoffé

Mecca ['mɛkə] *s* La Mecque

mechanic [mə'kænɪk] *s* mécanicien *m;* **mechanics** mécanique *f*

mechanical [mə'kænɪkəl] *adj* mécanique; (fig) mécanique, machinal

mechan'ical draw'ing *s* dessin *m* industriel

mechan'ical engineer' *s* ingénieur *m* mécanicien

mechan'ical toy' *s* jouet *m* mécanique

mechanics [mɪ'kænɪks] *s* mécanique *f*

mechanism ['mɛkə,nɪzəm] *s* mécanisme *m*

mechanize ['mɛkə,naɪz] *tr* mécaniser

medal ['mɛdəl] *s* médaille *f*

medallion [mɪ'dæljən] *s* médaillon *m*

meddle ['mɛdəl] *intr* s'ingérer; **to meddle in** or **with** se mêler de, s'immiscer dans

meddler ['mɛdlər] *s* intrigant *m,* touche-à-tout *m*

meddlesome ['mɛdəlsəm] *adj* intrigant

media ['midɪ•ə] *s* (journ, rad, telv) journalistes *mfpl;* presse *f,* radio *f,* télé *f;* **the media** les media *mpl*

median ['midɪ•ən] *adj* médian ‖ *s* médiane *f*

me'dian strip' *s* bande *f* médiane

mediate ['midɪ,et] *tr* procurer par médiation, négocier ‖ *intr* s'entremettre, s'interposer

mediation [,midɪ'eʃən] *s* médiation *f*

mediator ['midɪ,etər] *s* médiateur *m*

medical ['mɛdɪkəl] *adj* médical

med'ical exam'ina'tion *s* examen *m* mêdical

med'ical rec'ords *spl* dossier *m* mêdical

med'ical stu'dent *s* étudiant *m* en médicine

medicinal [mə'dɪsɪnəl] *adj* médicinal

medicine ['mɛdɪsɪn] *s* (*science and art*) médecine *f;* (pharm) médicament *m*

med'icine cab'inet *s* armoire *f* à pharmacie, armoire *f* de toilette

med'icine kit' *s* pharmacie *f* portative

med'icine man' *s* (*pl* **men'**) sorcier *m* indien; (*mountebank*) charlatan *m*

medi·co ['mɛdɪ,ko] *s* (*pl* **-cos**) (slang) carabin *m,* morticole *m*

medieval [,midɪ'ivəl], [,mɛdɪ'ivəl] *adj* médiéval, moyenâgeux; (pej) périmé, funeste

medievalist [,mɛdɪ'ivəlɪst] *s* médiéviste *mf*

mediocre [,midɪ'okər] *adj* médiocre

mediocri·ty [,midɪ'ɑkrɪti] *s* (*pl* **-ties**) médiocrité *f*

meditate ['mɛdɪ,tet] *tr* & *intr* méditer

meditation [,mɛdɪ'teʃən] *s* méditation *f*

Mediterranean [,mɛdɪtə'renɪ•ən] *adj* méditerranéen ‖ *s* Méditerranée *f*

medi·um ['midɪ•əm] *adj* moyen; (culin) à point ‖ *s* (*pl* **-ums** or **-a** [ə]) milieu *m;* (*means*) moyen *m;* (*in spiritualism*) médium *m;* (journ) organe *m;* **through the medium of** par l'intermédiaire de

me'dium of exchange' *s* agent *m* monétaire

me'dium-range' *adj* à portée moyenne

me'dium-sized' *adj* de grandeur moyenne

medlar ['mɛdlər] *s* (*fruit*) nèfle *f;* (*tree*) néflier *m*

medley ['mɛdli] *s* mélange *m;* (mus) potpourri *m*

medul·la [mɪ'dʌlə] *s* (*pl* **-lae** [li]) moelle *f*

Medusa [mə'duzə] *s* Méduse *f*

meek [mik] *adj* doux, humble

meekness ['miknɪs] *s* douceur *f,* humilité *f*

meerschaum ['mɪrʃəm] *s* écume *f* de mer; pipe *f* d'écume de mer

meet [mit] *adj*—**it is meet that** il convient que ‖ *s* (sports) meeting *m* ‖ *v* (*pret* & *pp* **met** [mɛt]) *tr* rencontrer; (*to make the acquaintance of*) faire la connaissance de; (*to go to meet*) aller au-devant de; (*a car in the street; a person on the sidewalk*) croiser; (*by appointment*) retrouver, rejoindre; (*difficulties; expenses*) faire face à; (*one's debts*) honorer; (*one's death*) trouver; (*a need*) satisfaire à; (*an objection*) réfuter; (*the ear*) frapper; **meet my wife (my friend, etc.)** je vous présente ma femme (mon ami, etc.) ‖ *intr* se rencontrer; (*for an appointment*) se retrouver, se rejoindre; (*to assemble*) se réunir; (*to join, touch*) joindre, se toucher; (*said of rivers*) confluer; (*said of roads; said of cars, persons, etc.*) se croiser; **till we meet again** au revoir; **to meet with** se rencontrer avec, rencontrer; (*difficulties, an affront, etc.*) subir

meeting ['mitɪŋ] *s* rencontre *f;* (*session*) séance *f;* (*assemblage*) réunion *f,* assemblée *f;* (*of an association*) congrès *m;* (*of two rivers*) confluent *m;* (*of two cars; of two roads*) croisement *m;* (pol) meeting *m*

meet'ing of the minds' *s* bonne entente *f*

meet'ing place' *s* rendez-vous *m*

megacycle ['mɛgə,saɪkəl] *s* mégacycle *m*

megaphone ['mɛgə,fon] *s* mégaphone *m,* portevoix *m*

megohm ['mɛg,om] *s* mégohm *m*

melancholia [,mɛlən'kolɪ•ə] *s* mélancolie *f*

melanchol·y ['mɛlən,kɑli] *adj* mélancholique ‖ *s* (*pl* **-ies**) mélancolie *f*

melee [ˈmele] *s* mêlée *f*

mellow [ˈmɛlo] *adj* moelleux; enjoué, débonnaire; (*ripe*) mûr ‖ *tr* rendre moelleux, mûrir

melodic [mɪˈlɑdɪk] *adj* mélodique

melodious [ˌmɪˈlodɪ•əs] *adj* mélodieux

melodramatic [ˌmɛlədrəˈmætɪk] *adj* mélodramatique

melo•dy [ˈmɛlədi] *s* (*pl* **-dies**) mélodie *f*

melon [ˈmɛlən] *s* melon *m*

melt [mɛlt] *tr & intr* fondre; **to melt into** (*e.g., tears*) fondre en

melt'ing pot' *s* creuset *m*

member [ˈmɛmbər] *s* membre *m*

mem'ber•ship' *s* membres *mpl*; (*in a club, etc.*) association *f*; (*belonging*) appartenance *f*

mem'bership blank' *s* bulletin *m* d'adhésion

membrane [ˈmɛmbren] *s* membrane *f*

memen•to [mɪˈmɛnto] *s* (*pl* **-tos** or **-toes**) mémento *m*

mem•o [ˈmɛmo] *s* (*pl* **-os**) (coll) note *f*, rappel *m*

mem'o book' *s* calepin *m*, mémento *m*

memoir [ˈmɛmwɑr] *s* biographie *f*; **memoirs** mémoires *mpl*

mem'o pad' *s* bloc-notes *m*, bloc *m*

memoran•dum [ˌmɛməˈrændəm] *s* (*pl* **-dums** or **-da** [də]) memorandum *m*; note *f*, rappel *m*

memorial [mɪˈmorɪ•əl] *adj* commémoratif ‖ *s* mémorial *m*; pétition *f*, mémoire *m*

memo'rial arch' *s* arc *m* de triomphe

Memo'rial Day' *s* la journée du Souvenir

memorialize [mɪˈmorɪ•ə‚laɪz] *tr* commémorer

memorize [ˈmɛmə‚raɪz] *tr* apprendre par cœur

memo•ry [ˈmɛməri] *s* (*pl* **-ries**) mémoire *f*; **from memory** de mémoire; **in memory of** en souvenir de, à la mémoire de

menace [ˈmɛnɪs] *s* menace *f* ‖ *tr & intr* menacer

menagerie [məˈnæʒəri] *s* ménagerie *f*

mend [mɛnd] *s* raccommodage *m*, reprise *f* ‖ *tr* réparer; (*to patch*) raccommoder; (*stockings*) repriser; (*to reform*) améliorer ‖ *intr* s'améliorer, s'amender

mendacious [mɛnˈdeʃəs] *adj* mensonger

mendicant [ˈmɛndɪkənt] *adj & s* mendiant *m*

mending [ˈmɛndɪŋ] *s* raccommodage *m*; (*of stockings*) reprisage *m*

menfolk [ˈmɛn‚fok] *spl* hommes *mpl*

menial [ˈminɪ•əl] *adj* servile ‖ *s* domestique *mf*

menses [ˈmɛnsiz] *spl* menstrues *fpl*

men's' fur'nishings *spl* confection *f* pour hommes

men's' room' *s* toilettes *fpl* pour hommes, lavabos *mpl* pour messieurs

menstrual [ˈmɛnstrʊ•əl] *adj* menstruel

menstruate [ˈmɛnstrʊ‚et] *intr* avoir ses règles

menstruation [ˌmɛnstrʊ ˈeʃən] *s* menstruation *f*

mental [ˈmɛntəl] *adj* mental

men'tal arith'metic *s* calcul *m* mental

men'tal case' *s* cas *m* mental

men'tal cru'elty *s* cruauté *f* mentale

men'tal defec'tive *s* débile *mf*

men'tal hy'giene *s* hygiène *f* mentale

men'tal ill'ness *s* maladie *f* mentale

mentali•ty [mɛnˈtælɪti] *s* (*pl* **-ties**) mentalité *f*

men'tal reserva'tion *s* arrière-pensée *f*, restriction *f* mentale

men'tal telep'athy *s* télépathie *f*

men'tal test' *s* test *m* psychologique

mention [ˈmɛnʃən] *s* mention *f* ‖ *tr* mentionner; **don't mention it** il n'y a pas de quoi, je vous en prie

menu [ˈmɛnju] *s* menu *m*, carte *f*

men'u bar' *s* (comp) barre *f* de menu

meow [mɪˈaʊ] *s* miaou *m* ‖ *intr* miauler

Mephistophelian [ˌmɛfɪstəˈfilɪ•ən] *adj* méphistophélique

mercantile [ˈmʌrkən‚taɪl] *adj* commercial, commerçant

mercenar•y [ˈmʌrsə‚nɛri] *adj* mercenaire ‖ *s* (*pl* **-ies**) mercenaire *mf*

merchandise [ˈmʌrtʃən‚daɪz] *s* marchandise *f*

merchandizing [ˈmʌrtʃən‚daɪzɪŋ] marchandisage *m*

merchant [ˈmʌrtʃənt] *adj & s* marchand *m*

mer'chant•man *s* (*pl* **-men**) navire *m* marchand

mer'chant marine' *s* marine *f* marchande

mer'chant ves'sel *s* navire *m* marchand

merciful [ˈmʌrsɪfəl] *adj* miséricordieux

merciless [ˈmʌrsɪlɪs] *adj* impitoyable

mercurial [mɛrˈkjʊrɪ•əl] *adj* inconstant, versatile; (*lively*) vif

mercu•ry [ˈmʌrkjəri] *s* (*pl* **-ries**) mercure *m*

mer•cy [ˈmʌrsi] *s* (*pl* **-cies**) miséricorde *f*, pitié *f*; **at the mercy of** à la merci de

mere [mɪr] *adj* simple, pur; seul, e.g., **at the mere thought of it** à la seule pensée de cela; rien que, e.g., **to shudder at the mere thought of it** frissoner rien que d'y penser

meretricious [ˌmɛrɪˈtrɪʃəs] *adj* factice, postiche; de courtisane

merge [mʌrdʒ] *tr* fusionner ‖ *intr* fusionner; (*said of two roads*) converger; **to merge into** se fondre dans

merger [ˈmʌrdʒər] *s* fusion *f*

meridian [məˈrɪdɪ•ən] *adj & s* méridien *m*

meringue [məˈræŋ] *s* meringue *f*

merit [ˈmɛrɪt] *s* mérite *m* ‖ *tr* mériter

meritorious [ˌmɛrəˈtorɪ•əs] *adj* méritoire; (*person*) méritant

merlin [ˈmʌrlɪn] *s* (orn) émerillon *m*

mermaid [ˈmʌr‚med] *s* sirène *f*

merriment [ˈmɛrɪmənt] *s* gaieté *f*, réjouissance *f*

mer•ry [ˈmɛri] *adj* (*comp* **-rier**; *super* **-riest**) gai, joyeux; **to make merry** se divertir

Mer'ry Christ'mas *s* Joyeux Noël *m*

mer'ry-go-round' *s* chevaux *mpl* de bois, manège *m* forain

mer'ry•mak'er *s* noceur *m*, fêtard *m*

mesh [mɛʃ] *s* (*network*) réseau *m*; (*each open space of net*) maille *f*; (*net*) filet *m*; (*engagement of gears*) engrenage *m*; **meshes** rets *m*, filets *mpl* ‖ *tr* (mach) engrener ‖ *intr* s'engrener

mesmerize [ˈmɛsmə‚raɪz] *tr* magnétiser

mess [mɛs] s (*disorder*) gâchis m; (*refuse*) saleté f; (*meal*) (mil) ordinaire m; (*for officers*) (mil) mess m; **to get into a mess** se mettre dans le pétrin; **to make a mess of** gâcher ‖ tr—**to mess up** (*to botch*) gâcher; (*to dirty*) salir ‖ intr—**to mess around** (*to putter*) (coll) bricoler; (*to waste time*) (coll) lambiner

message [ˈmɛsɪdʒ] s message m

mes′sage board′ s (comp) planche f de messages

messenger [ˈmɛsəndʒər] s messager m; (*one who goes on errands*) commissionnaire m

mess′ hall′ s cantine f; (*for officers*) mess m

Messiah [məˈsaɪə] s Messie m

mess′ kit′ s gamelle f

mess′ mate′ s camarade mf de table; (nav) camarade de plat

mess′ of pot′tage [ˈpɑtɪdʒ] s (Bib) plat m de lentilles

Messrs. [ˈmɛsərz] pl of **Mr.**

mess•y [ˈmɛsi] adj (*comp* -**ier**; *super* -**iest**) en désordre; (*dirty*) sale, poisseux

metal [ˈmɛtəl] s métal m

metallic [mɪˈtælɪk] adj métallique

metallurgy [ˈmɛtəˌlʌrdʒi] s métallurgie f

met′al pol′ish s brilliant m à métaux

met′al•work′ s serrurerie f, travail m des métaux

metamorpho•sis [ˌmɛtəˈmɔrfəsɪs] s (*pl* -**ses** [ˌsiz]) métamorphose f

metaphony [məˈtæfəni] s métaphonie f, inflexion f

metaphor [ˈmɛtəˌfɔr] s métaphore f

metaphorical [ˌmɛtəˈfɔrɪkəl] adj métaphorique

metathe•sis [mɪˈtæθɪsɪs] s (*pl* -**ses** [ˌsiz]) métathèse f

mete [mit] tr—**to mete out** distribuer

meteor [ˈmitɪˌər] s étoile f filante, météore m; (*atmospheric phenomenon*) météore m; (fig) météore m

meteoric [ˌmitɪˈɔrɪk] adj météorique; (fig) fulgurant

meteorite [ˈmitɪˌəˌraɪt] s météorite m & f

meteorology [ˌmitɪˈəˈrɑlədʒi] s météorologie f

me′teor show′er s averse f météorique

meter [ˈmitər] s (*unit of measurement; verse*) mètre m; (*instrument for measuring gas, electricity, water*) compteur m; (mus) mesure f

me′ter maid′ s contractuelle f, aubergine f

me′ter read′er s releveur m de compteurs

methane [ˈmɛθen] s méthane m

method [ˈmɛθəd] s méthode f

methodic(al) [mɪˈθɑdɪk(əl)] adj & s méthodique

Methodist [ˈmɛθədɪst] adj & s méthodiste mf

Methuselah [mɪˈθuzələ] s Mathusalem m

meticulous [mɪˈtɪkjələs] adj méticuleux

metric(al) [ˈmɛtrɪk(əl)] adj métrique

metrics [ˈmɛtrɪks] s métrique f

metronome [ˈmɛtrəˌnom] s métronome m

metropolis [mɪˈtrɑpəlɪs] s métropole f

metropolitan [ˌmɛtrəˈpɑlɪtən] adj & s métropolitain m

mettle [ˈmɛtəl] s ardeur f, fougue f; **to be on one's mettle** se piquer au jeu

mettlesome [ˈmɛtəlsəm] adj ardent, vif, fougueux

mew [mju] s miaulement m ‖ intr miauler

Mexican [ˈmɛksɪkən] adj mexicain ‖ s Mexicain m

Mexico [ˈmɛksɪˌko] s le Mexique

Mex′ico Cit′y s Mexico

mezzanine [ˈmɛzəˌnin] s entresol m; (theat) mezzanine m & f, corbeille f

mica [ˈmaɪkə] s mica m

microbe [ˈmaɪkrob] s microbe m

microbiologist [ˌmaɪkrəbaɪˈɑlədʒɪst] s microbiologiste mf

microbiology [ˌmaɪkrəbaɪˈɑlədʒi] s microbiologie f

microchip [ˈmaɪkrotʃɪp] s microchip m

microcomputer [ˈmaɪkrəkəmˌpjutər] s microordinateur m

microeconomics [ˌmaɪkroˌɛkəˈnɑmɪks] s microéconomie f

microfilm [ˈmaɪkrəˌfɪlm] s microfilm m ‖ tr microfilmer

microgroove [ˈmaɪkrəˌgruv] adj & s microsillon m

mi′crogroove rec′ord s disque m à microsillons

microphone [ˈmaɪkrəˌfon] s microphone m

microprocesser [ˈmaɪkrəˈprɑsəsər] s microprocesseur m

microscope [ˈmaɪkrəˌskop] s microscope m

microscopic [ˌmaɪkrəˈskɑpɪk] adj microscopique

microsurgery [ˈmaɪkroˈsʌrdʒəri] s microchirurgie f

microwave [ˈmaɪkrəˌwev] s micro-onde f; (*oven*) micro-ondes m invar

mi′cro•wave′ ov′en s micro-ondes m invar

mid [mɪd] adj—**in mid course** à mi-chemin

mid′day′ s midi m

middle [ˈmɪdəl] adj moyen, du milieu ‖ s milieu m; **in the middle of** au milieu de

mid′dle age′ s âge m moyen; **Middle Ages** moyen-âge m

middle-aged [ˈmɪdəlˌedʒd] adj d'un âge moyen

mid′dle class′ s classe f moyenne, bourgeoisie f

mid′dle-class′ adj bourgeois

Mid′dle East′ s Moyen-Orient m

Mid′dle Eng′lish s moyen anglais m

mid′dle fin′ger s majeur m, doigt m du milieu

mid′dle•man′ s (*pl* -**men′**) intermédiaire mf

mid′dle•weight′ s (boxing) poids m moyen

middling [ˈmɪdlɪŋ] adj moyen, assez bien, passable ‖ adv (coll) assez bien, passablement

mid•dy [ˈmɪdi] s (*pl* -**dies**) (coll) aspirant m

mid′dy blouse′ s marinière f

midget [ˈmɪdʒɪt] s nain m, nabot m

midland [ˈmɪdlənd] adj de l'intérieur ‖ s centre m du pays

mid′night′ adj de minuit; **to burn the mid-**

night oil pâlir sur les livres, se crever les livres ‖ *s* minuit *m*

midriff [ˈmɪdrɪf] *s* diaphragme *m*

mid′ship′man *s* (*pl* **-men**) aspirant *m*

midst [mɪdst] *s* centre *m;* **in our (your, etc.) midst** parmi nous (vous, etc.); **in the midst of** au milieu de

mid′stream′ *s*—**in midstream** au milieu du courant

mid′sum′mer *s* milieu *m* de l'été

mid′way′ *adj & adv* à mi-chemin ‖ **mid′way′** *s* fête *f* foraine

mid′week′ *s* milieu *m* de la semaine

mid′wife′ *s* (*pl* **-wives′**) sage-femme *f*

mid′win′ter *s* milieu *m* de l'hiver

mid′year′ *s* mi-année *f*

mien [min] *s* mine *f,* aspect *m*

miff [mɪf] *s* (coll) fâcherie *f* ‖ *tr* (coll) fâcher

might [maɪt] *s* puissance *f,* force *f;* **with might and main, with all one's might** de toute sa force ‖ *aux* used to form the potential mood, e.g., **she might not be able to come** il se pourrait qu'elle ne puisse pas venir

mightily [ˈmaɪtɪli] *adv* puissamment; (coll) énormément

mightn't *contr* **might not**

might·y [ˈmaɪti] *adj* (*comp* **-ier;** *super* **-iest**) puissant; (*of great size*) grand, vaste ‖ *adv* (coll) rudement, diablement

mignonette [ˌmɪnjəˈnɛt] *s* réséda *m*

migraine [ˈmaɪgren] *s* migraine *f*

migrant [ˈmaɪgrənt] *adj & s* (*animal*) migrateur *m;* (*person*) nomade *mf;* **migrant worker** travailleur *m,* migrant *m;* (*seasonal*) travailleur saisonnier

migrate [ˈmaɪgret] *intr* émigrer

migratory [ˈmaɪgrəˌtori] *adj* migratoire

milch [mɪltʃ] *adj* laitier

mild [maɪld] *adj* doux

mildew [ˈmɪlˌd(j)u] *s* moisissure *f;* (*on vine*) mildiou *m,* blanc *m*

mildness [ˈmaɪldnɪs] *s* douceur *f*

mile [maɪl] *s* mille *m*

mileage [ˈmaɪlɪdʒ] *s* distance *f* en milles; (*charge*) tarif *m* au mille

mile′post′ *s* borne *f* milliaire

mile′stone′ *s* borne *f* milliaire; (fig) jalon *m*

militancy [ˈmɪlɪtənsi] *s* esprit *m* militant

militant [ˈmɪlɪtənt] *adj & s* militant *m*

militarism [ˈmɪlɪtəˌrɪzəm] *s* militarisme *m*

militarize [ˈmɪlɪtəˌraɪz] *tr* militariser

military [ˈmɪlɪˌtɛri] *adj & s* militaire *m*

mil′itary acad′emy *s* académie *f* militaire

mil′itary police′man *s* (*pl* **-men**) agent *m* de la police militaire

militate [ˈmɪlɪˌtet] *intr* militer

militia [mɪˈlɪʃə] *s* milice *f*

mili′tia·man *s* (*pl* **-men**) milicien *m*

milk [mɪlk] *adj* laitier ‖ *s* lait *m* ‖ *tr* traire; abuser de, exploiter; **to milk s.th. from s.o.** soutirer q.ch. à

milk′ can′ *s* pot *m* à lait, berthe *f*

milk′ car′ton *s* boîte *f* de lait, berlingot *m*

milk′ choc′olate *s* chocolat *m* au lait

milk′ di′et *s* régime *m* lacté

milk′maid′ *s* laitière *f*

milk′man′ *s* (*pl* **-men**) laitier *m,* crémier *m*

milk′ pail′ *s* seau *m* à lait

milk′ shake′ *s* milk-shake *m*

milk′sop′ *s* poule *f* mouillée

milk′ tooth′ *s* dent *f* de lait

milk′weed′ *s* laiteron *m*

milk·y [ˈmɪlki] *adj* (*comp* **-ier;** *super* **-iest**) laiteux

Milk′y Way′ *s* Voie *f* Lactée

mill [mɪl] *s* moulin *m;* (*factory*) fabrique *f,* usine *f;* millième *m* de dollar; **to put through the mill** (coll) faire passer au laminoir ‖ *tr* moudre, broyer; (*a coin*) créneler; (*gears*) fraiser; (*steel*) laminer; (*ore*) bocarder; (*chocolate*) faire mousser ‖ *intr*—**to mill around** circuler

millennial [mɪˈlɛnɪ·əl] *adj* millénaire

millenni·um [mɪˈlɛnɪ·əm] *s* (*pl* **-ums** or **-a** [ə]) millénaire *m*

miller [ˈmɪlər] *s* meunier *m*

millet [ˈmɪlɪt] *s* millet *m*

milligram [ˈmɪlɪˌgræm] *s* milligramme *m*

millimeter [ˈmɪlɪˌmitər] *s* millimètre *m*

milliner [ˈmɪlɪnər] *s* modiste *f*

mil′linery shop′ [ˈmɪlɪˌnɛri] *s* boutique *f* de modiste

milling [ˈmɪlɪŋ] *s* (*of grain*) mouture *f*

mill′ing machine′ *s* fraiseuse *f*

million [ˈmɪljən] *adj* million de ‖ *s* million *m*

millionaire [ˌmɪljənˈɛr] *s* millionnaire *mf*

millionth [ˈmɪljənθ] *adj & pron* millionième (*masc, fem*) ‖ *s* millionième *m*

mill′pond′ *s* retenue *f,* réservoir *m*

mill′race′ *s* bief *m*

mill′stone′ *s* meule *f;* (fig) boulet *m*

mill′ wheel′ *s* roue *f* de moulin

mill′work′ *s* ouvrage *m* de menuiserie

mime [maɪm] *s* mime *mf* ‖ *tr & intr* mimer

mimeograph [ˈmɪmɪ·əˌgræf] *s* ronéo *f* ‖ *tr* ronéocopier, ronéotyper

mim·ic [ˈmɪmɪk] *s* mime *mf,* imitateur *m* ‖ *v* (*pret & pp* **-icked;** *ger* **-icking**) *tr* mimer, imiter

mimic·ry [ˈmɪmɪkri] *s* (*pl* **-ries**) mimique *f,* imitation *f*

minaret [ˌmɪnəˈrɛt] *s* minaret *m*

mince [mɪns] *tr* (*meat*) hacher menu ‖ *intr* minauder

mince′ meat′ *s* hachis *m* de viande et de fruits aromatisés; **to make mincemeat of** (coll) mettre en marmelade

mind [maɪnd] *s* esprit *m;* **to be of one mind** être d'accord; **to change one's mind** changer d'avis; **to have a mind to** avoir envie de; **to have in mind** avoir en vue; **to lose one's mind** perdre la raison; **to make up one's mind to** prendre le parti de; **to slip one's mind** échapper à qn; **to speak one's mind** donner son avis ‖ *tr* (*to take care of*) garder; (*to obey*) obéir à; (*to be troubled by*) s'inquiéter de; (*e.g., one's manners*) faire attention à;

(*e.g., a dangerous step*) prendre garde à; **mind your own business!** occupez-vous de vous affaires! ‖ *intr*—**do you mind?** cela ne vous ennuie pas?, cela ne vous gêne pas?; **if you don't mind** si cela ne vous fait rien, si cela vous est égal; **never mind!** n'importe!

mind'-bend'ing *s* renversant

mind'-blow'ing *s* hallucinant

mindful [ˈmaɪndfəl] *adj* attentif; **mindful of** attentif à, soigneux de

mind' read'er *s* liseur *m* de la pensée

mind' read'ing *s* lecture *f* de la pensée

mine [maɪn] *s* mine *f* ‖ *pron poss* le mien §89; à moi §85 A, 10 ‖ *tr* (*coal, minerals, etc.*) extraire; (*to undermine; to lay mines in*) miner

mine'field' *s* champ *m* de mines

mine'lay'er *s* poseur *m* de mines

miner [ˈmaɪnər] *s* mineur *m*

mineral [ˈmɪnərəl] *adj & s* minéral *m*

mineralogy [ˌmɪnəˈralədʒi] *s* minéralogie *f*

min'eral wool' *s* laine *f* minérale, laine de scories

mine'sweep'er *s* dragueur *m* de mines

mingle [ˈmɪŋgəl] *tr* mêler, mélanger ‖ *intr* se mêler, se mélanger

miniature [ˈmɪnɪ•ətˌʃər] *s* miniature *f;* **in miniature** en abrégé

min'iature golf' *s* golf *m* miniature, minigolf *m*

miniaturization [ˌmɪnɪ•ətˌʃərɪˈzeʃən] *s* miniaturisation *f*

miniaturize [ˈmɪnɪ•ətˌʃəˌraɪz] *tr* miniaturiser

minicomputer [ˈmɪnɪkəmˌpjutər] *s* micro-ordinateur *m*

minimal [ˈmɪnɪməl] *adj* minimum

minimize [ˈmɪnəˌmaɪz] *tr* minimiser

minimum [ˈmɪnɪməm] *adj* minimum; (*temperature*) minimal ‖ *s* minimum *m*

min'imum wage' *s* salaire *m* minimum, minimum *m* vital, SMIC *m*

min'imum-wage' earn'er *s* smicard *m*

mining [ˈmaɪnɪŋ] *adj* minier ‖ *s* exploitation *f* des mines; (nav) pose *f* de mines

minion [ˈmɪnjən] *s* favori *m;* (*henchman*) séide *m*

miniskirt [ˈmɪnɪˌskʌrt] *s* minijupe *f*

minister [ˈmɪnɪstər] *s* ministre *m;* (eccl) pasteur *m* ‖ *intr*—**to minister to** (*the needs of*) subvenir à; (*a person*) soigner; (*a parish*) desservir

ministerial [ˌmɪnɪsˈtɪrɪ•əl] *adj* ministériel

minis•try [ˈmɪnɪstri] *s* (*pl* **-tries**) ministère *m;* (eccl) clergé *m;* (eccl) pastorat *m*

mink [mɪŋk] *s* vision *m*

minnow [ˈmɪno] *s* vairon *m*

minor [ˈmaɪnər] *adj & s* mineur *m,* mineure *f;* (mus) mineur *m*

Minorca [mɪˈnɔrkə] *s* Minorque *f;* île *f* de Minorque

minori•ty [mɪˈnɔriti] *adj* minoritaire ‖ *s* (*pl* **-ties**) minorité *f*

minstrel [ˈmɪnstrəl] *s* (*in a minstrel show*) interprète *m* de chants nères; (hist) ménestrel *m*

mint [mɪnt] *s* hôtel *m* des Monnaies, Monnaie *f;* (bot) menthe *f;* (fig) mine *f* ‖ *tr* frapper, monnayer; (fig) forger

minuet [ˌmɪnjuˈɛt] *s* menuet *m*

minus [ˈmaɪnəs] *adj* négatif ‖ *s* moins *m* ‖ *prep* moins; (coll) sans, dépourvu de

minute [maɪˈn(j)ut] *adj* (*tiny*) minime; (*meticulous*) minutieux ‖ [ˈmɪnɪt] *s* minute *f;* **minutes** compte *m* rendu, procès-verbal *m* de séance; (*often omitted in expressions of time*), e.g., **ten after two, ten minutes after two** deux heures dix; **up to the minute** de la dernière heure; à la dernière mode; au courant

min'ute hand' [ˈmɪnɪt] *s* grande aiguille *f*

min'ute rice' *s* riz *m* précuit

min'ute steak' *s* entrecôte *f* minute

minutiae [mɪˈn(j)uʃi,i] *spl* minuties *fpl*

minx [mɪŋks] *s* effrontée *f*

miracle [ˈmɪrəkəl] *s* miracle *m*

mir'acle play' *s* miracle *m*

miraculous [mɪˈrækjələs] *adj* miraculeux

mirage [mɪˈrɑʒ] *s* mirage *m*

mire [maɪr] *s* fange *f*

mirror [ˈmɪrər] *s* miroir *m,* glace *f* ‖ *tr* refléter

mirth [mʌrθ] *s* joie *f,* gaieté *f*

mir•y [ˈmaɪri] *adj* (*comp* **-ier;** *super* **-iest**) fangeux

misadventure [ˌmɪsədˈvɛntʃər] *s* mésaventure *f*

misanthrope [ˈmɪsənˌθrop] *s* misanthrope *mf*

misapprehension [ˌmɪsæprɪˈhɛnʃən] *s* fausse idée *f,* malentendu *m*

misappropriation [ˌmɪsəˌproprɪˈeʃən] *s* détournement *m* de fonds

misbehave [ˌmɪsbɪˈhev] *intr* se conduire mal

misbehavior [ˌmɪsbɪˈhevɪ•ər] *s* mauvaise conduite *f*

miscalculation [ˌmɪskælkjəˈleʃən] *s* mécompte *m*

miscarriage [mɪsˈkærɪdʒ] *s* fausse couche *f;* (*e.g., of letter*) perte *f;* (*of justice*) déni *m,* mal-jugé *m;* (fig) avortement *m,* insuccès *m*

miscar•ry [mɪsˈkæri] *v* (*pret & pp* **-ried**) *intr* faire une fausse couche; (*said, e.g., of letter*) s'égarer; (fig) avorter, échouer

miscellaneous [ˌmɪsəˈlenɪ•əs] *adj* divers, mélangé

miscella•ny [ˈmɪsəˌleni] *s* (*pl* **-nies**) miscellanées *fpl*

mischief [ˈmɪstʃɪf] *s* (*harm*) tort *m;* (*disposition to annoy*) méchanceté *f;* (*prankishness*) espièglerie *f*

mis'chief-mak'er *s* brandon *m* de discorde

mischievous [ˈmɪstʃɪvəs] *adj* (*harmful*) nuisible; (*mean*) méchant; (*prankish*) espiègle, coquin

misconception [ˌmɪskənˈsɛpʃən] *s* conception *f* erronée

misconduct [mɪsˈkɑndʌkt] *s* inconduite *f;* (*e.g., of a business*) mauvaise administration *f* ‖ [ˌmɪskənˈdʌkt] *tr* mal administrer; **to misconduct oneself** se conduire mal

misconstrue [ˌmɪskən'stru], [mɪs'kanstru] *tr* mal interpréter

miscount [mɪs'kaunt] *s* erreur *f* de calcul ‖ *tr* & *intr* mal compter

miscue [mɪs'kju] *s* fausse queue *f*; (*blunder*) bévue *f* ‖ *intr* faire fausse queue; (theat) se tromper de réplique

mis•deal [ˈmɪsˌdil] *s* maldonne *f*, mauvaise donne *f* ‖ [mɪs'dil] *v* (*pret* & *pp* **-dealt**) *tr* mal distribuer ‖ *intr* faire maldonne

misdeed [ˈmɪsˌdid] *s* méfait *m*

misdemeanor [ˌmɪsdɪ'minər] *s* mauvaise conduite *f*; (law) délit *m* correctionnel

misdirect [ˌmɪsdɪ'rɛkt] *tr* mal diriger

misdoing [mɪs'du•ɪŋ] *s* méfait *m*

miser [ˈmaɪzər] *s* avare *mf*

miserable [ˈmɪzərəbəl] *adj* misérable

miserly [ˈmaɪzərli] *adj* avare

miser•y [ˈmɪzəri] *s* (*pl* **-ies**) misère *f*, détresse *f*

misfeasance [mɪs'fizəns] *s* (law) abus *m* de pouvoir

misfire [mɪs'faɪr] *s* raté *m* ‖ *intr* rater

mis•fit [ˈmɪsˌfɪt] *s* (*clothing*) vêtement *m* manqué; (*thing*) laissé-pour-compte *m*; (*person*) (fig) inadapté *m*

misfortune [mɪs'fɔrt∫ən] *s* infortune *f*, malheur *m*; **misfortunes** misères *fpl*

misgiving [mɪs'gɪvɪŋ] *s* pressentiment *m*, appréhension *f*, soupçon *m*

misgovern [mɪs'gʌvərn] *tr* mal gouverner

misguidance [mɪs'gaɪdəns] *s* mauvais conseils *mpl*

misguided [mɪs'gaɪdɪd] *adj* mal placé, hors de propos; (*e.g., youth*) dévoyé

mishap [ˈmɪshæp] *s* contretemps *m*, mésaventure *f*

mishmash [ˈmɪ∫ˌmæ∫] *s* méli-mélo *m*

misinform [ˌmɪsɪn'fɔrm] *tr* mal renseigner

misinterpret [ˌmɪsɪn'tʌrprɪt] *tr* mal interpréter

misjudge [mɪs'dʒʌdʒ] *tr* & *intr* mal juger

mis•lay [mɪs'le] *v* (*pret* & *pp* **-laid**) *tr* égarer, perdre

mis•lead [mɪs'lid] *v* (*pret* & *pp* **-led**) *tr* égarer; corrompre; tromper

misleading [mɪs'lidɪŋ] *adj* trompeur

mismanagement [mɪs'mænɪdʒmənt] *s* mauvaise administration *f*

misnomer [mɪs'nomər] *s* faux nom *m*

misplace [mɪs'ples] *tr* mal placer; (*to mislay*) (coll) égarer, perdre

misprint [ˈmɪsˌprɪnt] *s* erreur *f* typographique, coquille *f* ‖ [mɪs'prɪnt] *tr* imprimer incorrectement

mispronounce [ˌmɪsprə'nauns] *tr* mal prononcer

mispronunciation [ˌmɪsprəˌnʌnsɪ'e∫ən] *s* faute *f* de prononciation; **a mispronunciation of . . .** une prononciation incorrecte de. . .

misquote [mɪs'kwot] *tr* citer à faux, citer inexactement

misrepresent [ˌmɪsrɛprɪ'zɛnt] *tr* représenter sous un faux jour; (*e.g., facts*) dénaturer, travestir

miss [mɪs] *s* coup *m* manqué; **a miss!** à côté!; **Miss** Mademoiselle *f*, Mlle; (*winner of beauty contest*) Miss *f* ‖ *tr* manquer; (*the mark, an opportunity, a train*) rater; (*to feel the absence of*) regretter; (*not to run into*) ne pas voir, ne pas rencontrer; (*e.g., one's way*) se tromper de; **he misses you very much** vous lui manquez beaucoup ‖ *intr* manquer

missal [ˈmɪsəl] *s* missel *m*

misshapen [mɪs'∫epən] *adj* difforme, contrefait

missile [ˈmɪsɪl] *s* projectile *m*; (*guided missile*) missile *m*

mis'sile gap' *s* déséquilibre *m* (de missiles)

mis'sile launch'er *s* lance-fusées *m*

missing [ˈmɪsɪŋ] *adj* manquant, absent; perdu; **missing in action** (mil) porté disparu; **to be missing** manquer, e.g., **three are missing** il en manque trois

miss'ing link' *s* maillon *m* qui manque à la chaine; (gen) chaînon *m* manquant

miss'ing per'sons *spl* disparus *mpl*

mission [ˈmɪ∫ən] *s* mission *f*

missionar•y [ˈmɪ∫ənˌɛri] *adj* missionaire ‖ *s* (*pl* **-ies**) missionnaire *m*

missis [ˈmɪsɪz] *s*—**the missis** (coll) votre femme *f*

missive [ˈmɪsɪv] *adj* & *s* missive *f*

mis•spell [mɪs'spɛl] *v* (*pret* & *pp* **-spelled** or **-spelt**) *tr* & *intr* écrire incorrectement

misspelling [mɪs'spɛlɪŋ] *s* faute *f* d'orthographe

misspent [mɪs'spɛnt] *adj* gaspillé; dissipé

misstatement [mɪs'stetmənt] *s* rapport *m* inexact, erreur *f* de fait

misstep [mɪs'stɛp] *s* faux pas *m*

miss•y [ˈmɪsi] *s* (*pl* **-ies**) (coll) mademoiselle *f*

mist [mɪst] *s* brume *f*, buée *f*; (*fine spray*) vapeur *f*; (*of tears*) voile *m*

mis•take [mɪs'tek] *s* faute *f*; **by mistake** par erreur, par méprise; **to make a mistake** se tromper ‖ *v* (*pret* **-took;** *pp* **-taken**) *tr* (*to misunderstand*) mal comprendre; (*to be wrong about*) se tromper de; **to mistake s.o. for s.o. else** prendre qn pour qn d'autre

mistaken [mɪs'tekən] *adj* erroné, faux; (*person*) dans l'erreur

mistak'en iden'tity *s* erreur *f* d'identité, erreur sur la personne

mistakenly [mɪs'tekənli] *adv* par erreur

mister [ˈmɪstər] *s*—**the mister** (coll) votre mari *m* ‖ *interj* (slang & pej) Jules!, mon petit bonhomme!

mistletoe [ˈmɪsəlˌto] *s* gui *m*

mistreat [mɪs'trit] *tr* maltraiter

mistreatment [mɪs'tritmənt] *s* mauvais traitement *m*

mistress [ˈmɪstrɪs] *s* maîtresse *f*

mistrial [mɪs'traɪ•əl] *s* (law) procès *m* entaché de nullité

mistrust [mɪs'trʌst] *s* méfiance *f* ‖ *tr* se méfier de ‖ *intr* se méfier

mistrustful [mɪs'trʌstfəl] *adj* méfiant

mist•y [ˈmɪsti] *adj* (*comp* **-ier;** *super* **-iest**) brumeux; vague, indistinct

misunder‑stand [ˌmɪsʌndərˈstænd] v (pret & pp **-stood**) tr mal comprendre

misunderstanding [ˌmɪsʌndərˈstændɪŋ] s malentendu m

misuse [mɪsˈjus] s mauvais usage m, abus m; (of words) emploi m abusif ‖ [mɪsˈjuz] tr faire mauvais usage de, abuser de; (a person) maltraiter

misword [mɪsˈwʌrd] tr mal rédiger, mal exprimer

mite [maɪt] s (small contribution) obole f; (small amount) brin m, bagatelle f; (ent) mite f

miter [ˈmaɪtər] s (carpentry) onglet m; (eccl) mitre f ‖ tr tailler à onglet

mi′ter box′ s boîte f à onglets

mitigate [ˈmɪtɪˌget] tr adoucir, atténuer

mitt [mɪt] s (fingerless glove) mitaine f; (mitten) moufle f; (baseball) gant m de prise; (hand) (slang) main f

mitten [ˈmɪtən] s moufle f

mix [mɪks] tr mélanger, mêler; (cement; a cake) malaxer; (the cards; the salad) touiller; **to mix up** (to confuse) confondre ‖ intr se mélanger, se mêler; **to mix with** s'associer à or avec

mixed adj mélangé; (races; style; colors) mêlé; (feelings; marriage; school; doubles) mixte; (candy) assorti; (salad, vegetables, etc.) panaché; (number) fractionnaire; **to be all mixed up** (facts, account) être embrouillé; (person) être déboussolé, pédaler dans le choucroute

mixed′ drink′ s boisson f mélangée

mixer [ˈmɪksər] s (device) mélangeur m; (for, e.g., concrete) malaxeur m; **to be a good mixer** (coll) avoir le don de plaire

mix′ing fau′cet s robinet m mélangeur

mixture [ˈmɪkstʃər] s mélange m

mix′-up′ s embrouillage m

mizzen [ˈmɪzən] s artimon m

moan [mon] s gémissement m ‖ intr gémir

moat [mot] s fossé m

mob [mɑb] s (mass of common people) foule f, masse f; (crush of people) cohue f grouillante; (crowd bent on violence) foule en colère; (criminal gang) bande f, gang m; (pej) populace f ‖ v (pret & pp **mobbed**; ger **mobbing**) tr s'attrouper autour de; (to attack) fondre sur, assaillir

mobile [ˈmobɪl], [ˈmobɪl] adj & s mobile m

mo′bile home′ s résidence f mobile, mobil-home m

mo′bile tel′ephone s téléphone m mobile, téléphone cellulaire, radiotéléphone m

mobility [moˈbɪlɪti] s mobilité f

mobilization [ˌmobɪlɪˈzeʃən] s mobilisation f

mobilize [ˈmobɪˌlaɪz] tr & intr mobiliser

mob′ rule′ s loi f de la populace

mobster [ˈmɑbstər] s (slang) gangster m

moccasin [ˈmɑkəsɪn] s mocassin m

Mo′cha cof′fee [ˈmokə] s moka m

mock [mɑk] adj simulé, contrefait ‖ s moquerie f ‖ tr se moquer de, moquer; (to imitate) contrefaire, singer; (to deceive) tromper ‖ intr se moquer; **to mock at** se moquer de; **to mock up** construire une maquette de

mock′ elec′tion s élection f blanche

mocker‑y [ˈmɑkəri] s (pl **-ies**) moquerie f; (subject of derision) objet m de risée; (poor imitation) parodie f; (e.g., of justice) simulacre m

mockingbird [ˈmɑkɪŋˌbʌrd] s moqueur m, oiseau m moqueur

mock′ or′ange s seringa m

mock′ tur′tle soup′ s potage m à la tête de veau

mock′-up′ s maquette f

mode [mod] s (kind) mode m; (fashion) mode f; (gram, mus) mode m

mod‑el [ˈmɑdəl] adj modèle ‖ s modèle m; (artist's model) poseur m, poseuse f; (for dressmaker or artist; at a fashion show) mannequin m; (of a statue) maquette f ‖ v (pret & pp **-eled** or **-elled**; ger **-eling** or **-elling**) tr modeler ‖ intr dessiner des modèles; servir de modèle, poser

mod′el air′plane s aéromodèle m

mod′el-air′plane build′er s aéromodéliste mf

mod′el-air′plane build′ing s aéromodélisme m

mod′el home′ s (sample home) maison f exposition, pavillon m témoin, villa f modèle

modeling [ˈmɑdlɪŋ] s profession f de modèle; (making models) modélisme m; (comp, econ) modélisation f; (fa) modelé m

modem [ˈmoˌdɛm] s (comp) modem m (modulator demodulator) modem m (modulateur démodulateur)

moderate [ˈmɑdərɪt] adj modéré ‖ [ˈmɑdəˌret] tr modérer; (a meeting) présider ‖ intr se modérer; présider

moderator [ˈmɑdəˌretər] s (over an assembly) président m; (mediator; substance used for slowing down neutrons) modérateur m

modern [ˈmɑdərn] adj moderne

modernize [ˈmɑdərˌnaɪz] tr moderniser

mod′ern lan′guages spl langues fpl vivantes

modest [ˈmɑdɪst] adj modeste

modes‑ty [ˈmɑdɪsti] s (pl **-ties**) modestie f

modicum [ˈmɑdɪkəm] s petite quantité f

modifier [ˈmɑdɪˌfaɪ·ər] s (gram) modificateur m

modi‑fy [ˈmɑdɪˌfaɪ] v (pret & pp **-fied**) tr modifier

modish [ˈmodɪʃ] adj à la mode, élégant

modulate [ˈmɑdʒəˌlet] tr & intr moduler

modulation [ˌmɑdʒəˈleʃən] s modulation f

mohair [ˈmoˌhɛr] s mohair m

moist [mɔɪst] adj humide; (e.g., skin) moite

moisten [ˈmɔɪsən] tr humecter ‖ intr s'humecter

moisture [ˈmɔɪstʃər] s humidité f

molar [ˈmolər] adj & s molaire f

molasses [məˈlæsɪz] s mélasse f

mold [mold] s moule m; (fungus) moisi m, moisissure f; (agr) humus m, terreau m; (fig) trempe f ‖ tr mouler; (to make moldy) moisir ‖ intr moisir, se moisir

molder [ˈmoldər] s mouleur m ‖ intr tomber en poussière

molding [ˈmoldɪŋ] s moulage m; (cornice, shaped strip of wood, etc.) moulure f

mold·y [ˈmoldi] adj (comp **-ier**; super **-iest**) moisi

mole [mol] s (breakwater) môle m; (inner harbor) bassin m; (spot on skin) grain m de beauté; (small mammal) taupe f

molec′ular phys′ics [məˈlɛkjələr] s physique f moléculaire

molecule [ˈmalɪˌkjul] s molécule f

mole′hill′ s taupinière f

mole′skin′ s (fur) taupe f; (fabric) moleskine f

molest [məˈlɛst] tr déranger, inquiéter; molester, rudoyer

moll [mal] s (slang) femme f du Milieu

molli·fy [ˈmalɪˌfaɪ] v (pret & pp **-fied**) tr apaiser, adoucir

mollusk [ˈmaləsk] s mollusque m

mollycoddle [ˈmalɪˌkadəl] s poule f mouillée ‖ tr dorloter

molt [molt] s mue f ‖ intr muer

molten [ˈmoltən] adj fondu

molybdenum [məˈlɪbdɪnəm] s molybdène m

mom [mam] f (coll) maman f

moment [ˈmomənt] s moment m; **at any moment** d'un moment à l'autre; **at that moment** à ce moment-là; **at this moment** en ce moment; **in a moment** dans un instant; **of great moment** d'une grande importance; **one moment please!** (telp) ne quittez pas!

momentary [ˈmomənˌtɛri] adj momentané

momentous [moˈmɛntəs] adj important, d'importance

momen·tum [moˈmɛntəm] s (pl **-tums** or **-ta** [tə]) élan m; (mech) force f d'impulsion, quantité f de mouvement

mom-mom [ˈmammam] f (child's language) grand-maman f, mémé f

monarch [ˈmanərk] s monarque m

monarchic(al) [məˈnarkɪk(əl)] adj monarchique

monar·chy [ˈmanərki] s (pl **-chies**) monarchie f

monaster·y [ˈmanɛsˌtɛri] s (pl **-ies**) monastère m

monastic [məˈnæstɪk] adj monastique

monasticism [məˈnæstɪˌsɪzəm] s monachisme m

Monday [ˈmʌndi] s lundi m

monetary [ˈmanɪˌtɛri] adj (pertaining to coinage) monétaire; (pertaining to money) pécuniaire

money [ˈmʌni] s argent m; (legal tender of a country) monnaie f; **to get one's money's worth** en avoir pour son argent; **to make money** gagner de l'argent

mon′ey·bag′ s sacoche f; **moneybags** (wealth) (coll) sac m; (wealthy person) (coll) richard m

mon′ey belt′ s ceinture f porte-monnaie

moneychanger [ˈmʌniˌtʃendʒər] s changeur m, cambiste m

moneyed [ˈmʌnid] adj possédant

mon′ey laun′dering s blanchiment m d'argent sale

mon′ey·lend′er s bailleur m de fonds

mon′ey·mak′er s amasseur m d'argent; (fig) source f de gain

mon′ey or′der s mandat m postal

Mongol [ˈmaŋgəl] adj mongol ‖ s (language) mongol m; (person) Mongol m

mon·goose [ˈmaŋgus] s (pl **-gooses**) mangouste f

mongrel [ˈmʌŋgrəl] adj & s métis m

monitor [ˈmanɪtər] s contrôleur m; (at school) pion m, moniteur m; (comp) moniteur m ‖ tr contrôler; (rad) écouter

monk [mʌŋk] s moine m

monkey [ˈmʌŋki] s singe m; (female) guenon f; **to make a monkey of** tourner en ridicule ‖ intr—**to monkey around** tripoter; **to monkey around with** tripoter; **to monkey with** (to tamper with) tripatouiller

mon′key·shine′ s (slang) singerie f

mon′key wrench′ s clé f anglaise

monks′hood s (bot) napel m

monocle [ˈmanəkəl] s monocle m

monogamy [məˈnagəmi] s monogamie f

monogram [ˈmanəˌgræm] s monogramme m

monograph [ˈmanəˌgræf] s monographie f

monolingual [ˌmanəˈlɪŋgwəl] adj monolingue

monolithic [ˌmanəˈlɪθɪk] adj monolithique

monologue [ˈmanəˌlɔg] s monologue m

monomania [ˌmanəˈmenɪ·ə] s monomanie f

monomial [məˈnomɪ·əl] s monôme m

monoplane [ˈmanəˌplen] s monoplan m

monopolize [məˈnapəˌlaɪz] tr monopoliser

monopo·ly [məˈnapəli] s (pl **-lies**) monopole m

monorail [ˈmanəˌrel] s monorail m

monosyllable [ˈmanəˌsɪləbəl] s monosyllabe m

monotheist [ˈmanəˌθi·ɪst] adj & s monothéiste mf

monotonous [məˈnatənəs] adj monotone

monotony [məˈnatəni] s monotonie f

monotype [ˈmanəˌtaɪp] s monotype m; (machine to set type) monotype f

monoxide [məˈnaksaɪd] s oxyde m, e.g., **carbon monoxide** oxyde m de carbone

monsignor [manˈsinjər] s (pl **monsignors** or **monsignori**) [ˌmansiˈnjori] (eccl) monseigneur m

monsoon [manˈsun] s mousson f

monster [ˈmanstər] adj & s monstre m

monstrance [ˈmanstrəns] s ostensoir m

monstrous [ˈmanstrəs] adj monstrueux

month [mʌnθ] s mois m

month·ly [ˈmʌnθli] adj mensuel ‖ s (pl **-lies**) revue f mensuelle; **monthlies** (coll) règles fpl ‖ adv mensuellement

monument [ˈmanjəmənt] s monument m

moo [mu] s meuglement m ‖ intr meugler ‖ interj meuh! meuh!

mood [mud] s humeur f, disposition f; (gram)

mode *m;* **moods** accès *mpl* de mauvaise humeur

mood•y [ˈmudi] *adj* (*comp* **-ier;** *super* **-iest**) d'humeur changeante; (*melancholy*) maussade

moon [mun] *s* lune *f* ‖ *intr*—**to moon about** musarder; (*to daydream about*) rêver à

moon′beam′ *s* rayon *m* de lune

moon′light′ *s* clair *m* de lune ‖ *intr* cumuler

moon′light′ing *s* travail *m* noir

moon′lighting job′ *s* accessoire *m*, deuxième emploi *m*

moonscape [ˈmunskep] *s* paysage *m* lunaire

moon′shine′ *s* clair *m* de lune; (*idle talk*) baliverne *f;* (coll) alcool *m* de contrebande

moon′ shot′ *s* tir *m* à la lune

moor [mʊr] *s* lande *f*, bruyère *f;* **Moor** Maure *m* ‖ *tr* amarrer ‖ *intr* s'amarrer

Moorish [ˈmʊrɪʃ] *adj* mauresque

moose [mus] *s* (*pl* **moose**) élan *m* du Canada, orignal *m;* (*European elk*) élan *m*

moot [mut] *adj* discutable

moot′ point′ question *f* discutable

mop [map] *s* balai *m* à franges; (*of hair*) tignasse *f* ‖ *v* (*pret & pp* **mopped;** *ger* **mopping**) *tr* nettoyer avec un balai à franges; (*e.g., one's brow*) s'essuyer; **to mop up** (mil) nettoyer

mope [mop] *intr* avoir le cafard

moped [ˈmopɛd] *s* cyclomoteur *m*, mobylette *f* (trademark)

moral [ˈmɔrəl] *adj* moral ‖ *s* (*of a fable*) morale *f;* **morals** mœurs *fpl*

morale [məˈræl] *s* moral *m*

morali•ty [məˈrælɪti] *s* (*pl* **-ties**) moralité *f*

morass [məˈræs] *s* marais *m*

moratori•um [ˌmɔrəˈtoriˑəm] *s* (*pl* **-ums** or **-a** [ə]) moratoire *m*, moratorium *m*

morbid [ˈmɔrbɪd] *adj* morbide

mordacious [mɔrˈdeʃəs] *adj* mordant

mordant [ˈmɔrdənt] *adj & s* mordant *m*

more [mor] *adj comp* plus de §91; plus nombreux; de plus, e.g., **one minute more** une minute de plus; **more than** plus que; (followed by numeral) plus de ‖ *s* plus *m;* **all the more so** d'autant plus; **what is more** plus est; **what more do you need?** que vous faut-il de plus? ‖ *pron indef* plus, davantage ‖ *adv comp* plus §91; davantage; **more and more** de plus en plus; **more or less** plus ou moins; **more than** plus que, davantage que; (followed by numeral) plus de; **neither more nor less** ni plus ni moins; **never more** jamais plus, plus jamais; **no more** ne . . . plus §90; **once more** une fois de plus; **the more . . . the more** (or **the less**) plus . . . plus (or moins)

more•o′ver *adv* de plus, du reste

Moresque [moˈrɛsk] *adj* mauresque

morgue [mɔrg] *s* institut *m* médico-légal, morgue *f;* (journ) archives *fpl*

Mormon [ˈmɔrmən] *adj & s* mormon *m*

morning [ˈmɔrnɪŋ] *adj* matinal, du matin ‖ *s* matin *m;* (*time between sunrise and noon*) matinée *f*, matin; **in the morning** le matin;

the morning after le lendemain matin; (coll) le lendemain de bombe

morn′ing coat′ *s* jaquette *f*

morn′ing-glo′ry *s* (*pl* **-ries**) belle-de-jour *f*

morn′ing sick′ness *s* des nausées *fpl*

morn′ing star′ *s* étoile *f* du matin

Moroccan [məˈrakən] *adj* marocain ‖ *s* Marocain *m*

morocco [məˈrako] *s* (*leather*) maroquin *m;* **Morocco** le Maroc

moron [ˈmoran] *s* arriéré *m;* (coll) minus *mf*, minus habens *mf*

morose [məˈros] *adj* morose

morphine [ˈmɔrfin] *s* morphine *f*

morphology [mɔrˈfalədʒi] *s* morphologie *f*

morrow [ˈmoro] *s*—**on the morrow (of)** le lendemain (de)

Morse′ code′ [mɔrs] *s* alphabet *m* morse

morsel [ˈmɔrsəl] *s* morceau *m*

mortal [ˈmɔrtəl] *adj & s* mortel *m*

mortality [mɔrˈtælɪti] *s* mortalité *f*

mortar [ˈmɔrtər] *s* mortier *m*

mor′tar-board′ *s* bonnet *m* carré; (*of mason*) taloche *f*

mortgage [ˈmɔrgɪdʒ] *s* hypothèque *f* ‖ *tr* hypothéquer

mortgagee [ˌmɔrgɪˈdʒi] *s* créancier *m* hypothécaire

mortgagor [ˈmɔrgɪdʒər] *s* débiteur *m* hypothécaire

mortician [mɔrˈtɪʃən] *s* entrepreneur *m* de pompes funèbres

morti•fy [ˈmɔrtɪˌfaɪ] *v* (*pret & pp* **-fied**) *tr* mortifier

mortise [ˈmɔrtɪs] *s* mortaise *f* ‖ *tr* mortaiser

mortuar•y [ˈmɔrtʃuˌɛri] *adj* mortuaire ‖ *s* (*pl* **-ies**) morgue *f;* chapelle *f* mortuaire

mosaic [moˈzeˑɪk] *adj & s* mosaïque *f*

Moscow [ˈmaskau] *s* Moscou *m*

Moses [ˈmoziz] *s* Moïse *m*

Mos•lem [ˈmazləm] *adj & s* var of **Muslim**

mosque [mask] *s* mosquée *f*

mosqui•to [məsˈkito] *s* (*pl* **-toes** or **-tos**) moustique *m*

mosqui′to control′ *s* démoustication *f*

mosqui′to net′ *s* moustiquaire *f*

moss [mɔs] *s* mousse *f*

moss•y [ˈmɔsi] *adj* (*comp* **-ier;** *super* **-iest**) moussu

most [most] *adj super* (le) plus de §91, (la) plupart de; **for the most part** pour la plupart ‖ *s* (le) plus, (la) plupart; **at the most** au plus, tout au plus; **most of** la plupart de; **to make the most of** tirer le meilleur parti possible de ‖ *pron indef* la plupart ‖ *adv super* (le) plus §91, e.g., **what I like (the) most** ce que j'aime le plus; **the** (or **his, etc.**) **most** + *adj* le (or son, etc.) plus + *adj* ‖ *adv* très, bien, fort, des plus

mostly [ˈmostli] *adv* pour la plupart, principalement

motel [moˈtɛl] *s* motel *m*

moth [mɔθ] *s* teigne *f*, papillon *m* nocturne; (*clothes moth*) mite *f*

moth′ball′ s boule f antimite, boule de naphtaline

moth′-ball′ fleet′ s (nav) flotte f en réserve

moth-eaten [′mɔθ,itən] adj mité

mother [′mʌðər] s mère f ‖ tr servir de mère à; (to coddle) dorloter

moth′er coun′try s mère patrie f

Moth′er Goos′e's Nurs′ery Rhymes′ spl les Contes de ma mère l'oie

moth′er•hood s maternité f

mothering [′mʌðərɪŋ] s maternage m

moth′er•land s patrie f

moth′er-in-law s (pl **mothers-in-law**) belle-mère f

motherless [′mʌðərlɪs] adj orphelin de mère

motherly [′mʌðərli] adj maternel

mother-of-pearl [′mʌðərəv′pʌrl] adj de nacre, en nacre ‖ s nacre f

Moth′er's Day′ s la Fête des mères

moth′er supe′rior s mère f supérieure

moth′er tongue′ s langue f maternelle

moth′er wit′ s bon sens m, esprit m

moth′ hole′ s trou m de mite

moth′proof′ adj antimite ‖ tr rendre antimite

moth•y [′mɔθi] adj (comp **-ier**; super **-iest**) mité, plein de mites

motif [mo′tif] s motif m

motion [′moʃən] s mouvement m; (gesture) geste m; (in a deliberating assembly) motion f, proposition f ‖ intr—**to motion to** faire signe à

motionless [′moʃənlɪs] adj immobile

mo′tion pic′ture s film m; **motion pictures** cinéma m

mo′tion-pic′ture adj cinématographique

mo′tion-pic′ture the′ater s cinéma m

motivate [′motɪ,vet] tr animer, inciter, pousser; (to provide with a motive) motiver

motive [′motɪv] adj moteur ‖ s mobile m, motif m

mo′tive pow′er s force f motrice

motley [′matli] adj bigarré; (mixed) mélangé

motor [′motər] adj & s moteur m ‖ intr aller en voiture

mo′tor•bike′ s vélomoteur m

mo′tor•boat′ s canot m automobile

mo′tor•bus′ s autocar m

motorcade [′motər,ked] s défilé m de voitures

mo′tor•car′ s automobile f

mo′tor•cy′cle s moto f

motorist [′motərɪst] s automobiliste mf

motorize [′motə,raɪz] tr motoriser

mo′tor launch′ s chaloupe f à moteur

mo′tor•man s (pl **-men**) conducteur m, wattman m

mo′tor pool′ s parc m automobile

mo′tor scoot′er s scooter m

mo′tor ship′ s navire m à moteurs

mo′tor truck′ s camion m automobile

mo′tor ve′hicle s véhicule m automobile

mottle [′matəl] tr marbrer, tacheter

mot•to [′mato] s (pl **-toes** or **-tos**) devise f

mound [maʊnd] s monticule m

mount [maʊnt] s montage m; (hill, mountain) mont m; (horse for riding) monture f ‖ tr & intr monter

mountain [′maʊntən] s montagne f

moun′tain climb′ing s alpinisme m

mountaineer [,maʊntə′nɪr] s montagnard m; (climber) alpiniste mf

mountainous [′maʊntənəs] adj montagneux

moun′tain range′ s chaîne f de montagnes

mountebank [′maʊntɪ,bæŋk] s saltimbanque mf

mounting [′maʊntɪŋ] s montage m

mourn [morn] tr & intr pleurer

mourner [′mornər] s affligé m; (woman hired as mourner) pleureuse f; pénitent m; **mourners** (funeral procession) cortège m funèbre, deuil m

mourn′er's bench′ s banc m des pénitents

mournful [′mornfəl] adj lugubre

mourning [′mornɪŋ] s deuil m

mourn′ing band′ s crêpe m

mouse [maʊs] s (pl **mice** [maɪs]) souris f

mouse′hole′ s trou m de souris

mouser [′maʊzər] s souricier m

mouse′trap′ s souricière f

moustache [məs′tæʃ] s moustache f

mouth [maʊθ] s (pl **mouths** [maʊðz]) bouche f; (of gun; of, e.g., wolf) gueule f; (of river) embouchure f; **by mouth** par voie buccale; **to make s.o.'s mouth water** faire venir l'eau à la bouche à qn

mouthful [′maʊθ,fʊl] s bouchée f

mouth′ or′gan s harmonica m

mouth′piece′ s embouchure f; (person) porte-parole m

mouth′-to-mouth′ resus′cita′tion s méthode f insufflatoire bouche à bouche

mouth′wash′ s rince-bouche m, eau f dentifrice

movable [′muvəbəl] adj mobile

move [muv] s mouvement m; (from one house to another) déménagement m; (player's turn) tour m; (in chess and checkers) coup m; (maneuver) démarche f; **knight's move** marche f du cavalier; **on the move** en mouvement ‖ tr remuer; (to excite the feelings of) émouvoir; **to move that** (parl) proposer que; **to move up** (a date) avancer ‖ intr remuer; (to stir) se remuer; (said of traffic, crowd, etc.) circuler; (e.g., to another city) déménager; **don't move!** ne bougez pas!; **to move away** or **off** s'éloigner; **to move back** reculer; **to move in** emménager

movement [′muvmənt] s mouvement m

movie [′muvi] s (coll) film m; **movies** (coll) cinéma m

mov′ie cam′era s caméra f

movie-goer [′muvi,go•ər] s (coll) amateur m de cinéma

mov′ie house′ s (coll) cinéma m, salle f de spectacles

moving [′muvɪŋ] adj mouvant, en marche; (touching) émouvant; (force) moteur ‖ s mouvement *m;* (*from one house to another*) déménagement *m*

mov′ing pic′ture *s* film *m;* **moving pictures** cinéma *m*

mov′ing-pic′ture the′ater *s* cinéma *m*

mov′ing side′walk *s* trottoir *m* roulant

mov′ing spir′it *s* âme *f*

mov′ing stair′way *s* escalier *m* mécanique, escalier roulant

mov′ing van′ *s* voiture *f* de déménagement, camion *m* de déménagement

mow [mo] *v* (*pret* **mowed;** *pp* **mowed** or **mown**) *tr* faucher; (*a lawn*) tondre; **to mow down** faucher

mower [ˈmoˑər] *s* faucheur *m;* (mach) faucheuse *f;* (*for lawns*) (mach) tondeuse *f*

m.p.h. [ˈɛmˈpiˈetʃ] *spl* (letterword) (**miles per hour**—*six-tenths of a mile equaling approximately one kilometer*) km/h

Mr. [ˈmɪstər] *s* Monsieur *m,* M.

Mrs. [ˈmɪsɪz] *s* Madame *f,* Mme

much [mʌtʃ] *adj* beaucoup de, e.g., **much time** beaucoup de temps; bien de + *art,* e.g., **much trouble** bien du mal ‖ *pron indef* beaucoup; **too much** trop ‖ *adv* beaucoup, bien §91; **however much** pour autant que; **how much** combien; **much less** encore moins; **too much** trop; **very much** beaucoup

mucilage [ˈmjusɪlɪdʒ] *s* colle *f* de bureau; (*gummy secretion in plants*) mucilage *m*

muck [mʌk] *s* fange *f*

muck′rake′ *intr* (coll) dévoiler des scandales

mucous [ˈmjukəs] *adj* muqueux

mu′cous lin′ing *s* (anat) muqueuse *f*

mucus [ˈmjukəs] *s* mucus *m,* mucosité *f*

mud [mʌd] *s* boue *f;* **to sling mud at** couvrir de boue

muddle [ˈmʌdəl] *s* confusion *f,* fouillis *m* ‖ *tr* embrouiller ‖ *intr*—**to muddle through** se débrouiller

mud′dle•head′ *s* brouillon *m*

mud•dy [ˈmʌdi] *adj* (*comp* **-dier;** *super* **-diest**) boueux; (*clothes*) crotté ‖ *v* (*pret & pp* **-died**) *tr* salir; (*clothes*) crotter; (*a liquid*) troubler; (fig) embrouiller

mud′guard′ *s* garde-boue *m*

mud′hole′ *s* bourbier *m*

mudslinger [ˈmʌdˌslɪŋər] *s* (fig) calomniateur *m*

muezzin [mjuˈɛzɪn] *s* (rel) muezzin *m*

muff [mʌf] *s* manchon *m;* (*failure*) coup *m* raté ‖ *tr* rater, louper

muffin [ˈmʌfɪn] *s* petit pain *m* rond, muffin *m*

muffle [ˈmʌfəl] *tr* (*a sound*) assourdir; (*the face*) emmitoufler

muffler [ˈmʌflər] *s* (*scarf*) cache-nez *m;* (aut) pot *m* d'échappement, silencieux *m*

mufti [ˈmʌfti] *s* vêtement *m* civil; **in mufti** en civil, en pékin, en bourgeois

mug [mʌg] *s* timbale *f,* gobelet *m;* (*tankard*) chope *f;* (slang) gueule *f,* museau *m* ‖ *v* (*pret & pp* **mugged;** *ger* **mugging**) *tr* (*e.g., a suspect*) (slang) photographier; (*a victim*) (slang) saisir à la gorge ‖ *intr* (slang) faire des grimaces

mugger [ˈmʌgər] *s* agresseur *m*

mug•gy [ˈmʌgi] *adj* (*comp* **-gier;** *super* **-giest**) lourd, étouffant

Muhammad [muˈhæməd] *s* Mahomet *m,* Muhammad *m*

mulat•to [məˈlæto] *s* (*pl* **-toes**) mulâtre *m*

mulber•ry [ˈmʌlˌbɛri] *s* (*pl* **-ries**) mûre *f;* (*tree*) mûrier *m*

mulct [mʌlkt] *tr* (*a person*) priver, dépouiller; (*money*) carotter, extorquer

mule [mjul] *s* (*female mule; slipper*) mule *f;* (*male mule*) mulet *m*

muleteer [ˌmjuləˈtɪr] *s* muletier *m*

mulish [ˈmjulɪʃ] *adj* têtu, entêté

mull [mʌl] *tr* chauffer avec des épices; (*to muddle*) embrouiller ‖ *intr*—**to mull over** réfléchir sur, remâcher

mullion [ˈmʌljən] *s* meneau *m*

multigraph [ˈmʌltɪˌgræf] *s* (trademark) ronéo *f* ‖ *tr* ronéotyper, polycopier

multilateral [ˌmʌltɪˈlætərəl] *adj* multilatéral

multinational [ˌmʌltɪˈnæʃənəl] *adj* multinational ‖ **multinationals** *spl* (*corporations*) mégagroupes *mpl* mondiaux, multinationales *fpl*

mul′tina′tional corpora′tion *s* société *f* multinationale

multiple [ˈmʌltɪpəl] *adj & s* multiple *m*

mul′tiple sclero′sis *s* (pathol) sclérose *f* en plaques

multiplex [ˈmʌltɪˌplɛks] *adj* multiplex ‖ *s* (mov) multiplexe *m,* complexe *m* multisalle

multiplici•ty [ˌmʌltɪˈplɪsɪti] *s* (*pl* **-ties**) multiplicité *f*

multi•ply [ˈmʌltɪˌplaɪ] *v* (*pret & pp* **-plied**) *tr* multiplier ‖ *intr* se multiplier

multiprocessing [ˌmʌltɪˈprasɛsɪŋ] *s* (comp) multitraitement *m*

multiprocessor [ˌmʌltɪˈprasɛsər] *s* (comp) multiprocesseur *m*

multitasked [ˈmʌltɪˈtæskt] *adj* (comp) multitâche, multiprogrammé

multitasking [ˈmʌltɪˈtæskɪŋ] *s* (comp) multiprogrammation *f*

multitude [ˈmʌltɪˌt(j)ud] *s* multitude *f*

mum [mʌm] *adj* silencieux; **mum's the word!** motus!, bouche cousue!; **to keep mum about** ne souffler mot de

mumble [ˈmʌmbəl] *tr & intr* marmotter

mumbo jumbo [ˈmʌmboˈdʒʌmbo] *s* (pej) jargon *m,* baragouin *m,* charabia *m*

mummer•y [ˈmʌməri] *s* (*pl* **-ies**) momerie *f*

mum•my [ˈmʌmi] *s* (*pl* **-mies**) momie *f;* (slang) maman *f*

mumps [mʌmps] *s* oreillons *mpl*

munch [mʌntʃ] *tr* mâchonner

mundane [ˈmʌnden] *adj* mondain

municipal [mjuˈnɪsɪpəl] *adj* municipal

municipali•ty [mjuˌnɪsɪˈpælɪti] *s* (*pl* **-ties**) municipalité *f*

munificent [mjuˈnɪfɪsənt] *adj* munificent

munition [mjuˈnɪʃən] *s* munition *f* ‖ *tr* approvisionner de munitions

muni′tions dump′ *s* dépôt *m* de munitions

mural [ˈmjʊrəl] *adj* mural ‖ *s* peinture *f* murale

murder [ˈmʌrdər] *s* assassinat *m*, meurtre *m* ‖ *tr* assassiner; (*a language, proper names, etc.*) (coll) estropier, écorcher

murderer [ˈmʌrdərər] *s* meurtrier *m*, assassin *m*

murderess [ˈmʌrdərɪs] *s* meurtrière *f*

murderous [ˈmʌrdərəs] *adj* meurtrier

murk·y [ˈmʌrki] *adj* (*comp* **-ier;** *super* **-iest**) ténébreux, nébuleux

murmur [ˈmʌrmər] *s* murmure *m* ‖ *tr* & *intr* murmurer

Mur′phy bed′ *s* (trademark) lit *m* escamotable

muscle [ˈmʌsəl] *s* muscle *m*

muscular [ˈmʌskjələr] *adj* musclé, musculeux; (*system, tissue, etc.*) musculaire

muse [mjuz] *s* muse *f;* **the Muses** les Muses ‖ *intr* méditer; **to muse on** méditer

museum [mjuˈziˑəm] *s* musée *m*

muse′um piece′ *s* pièce *f* de musée

mush [mʌʃ] *s* bouillie *f;* (coll) sentimentalité *f* de guimauve

mush′room′ *s* champignon *m* ‖ *intr* pousser comme un champignon

mush′room cloud′ *s* champignon *m* atomique

mush·y [ˈmʌʃi] *adj* (*comp* **-ier;** *super* **-iest**) mou; (*ground*) détrempé; (coll) à la guimauve, sentimental

music [ˈmjuzɪk] *s* musique *f;* **to face the music** (coll) affronter les opposants; **to set to music** mettre en musique

musical [ˈmjuzɪkəl] *adj* musical

mus′ical chairs′ *s* (game) jeu *m* de chaises musicales; **to play at musical chairs** (fig) changer tout le temps de place

mu′sical com′edy *s* comédie *f* musicale

musicale [ˌmjuzɪˈkæl] *s* soirée *f* musicale; matinée *f* musicale

mu′sic box′ *s* boîte *f* à musique

mu′sic cab′inet *s* casier *m* à musique

mu′sic hall′ *s* salle *f* de musique; (Brit) music-hall *m*

musician [mjuˈzɪʃən] *s* musicien *m*

mu′sic lov′er *s* mélomane *mf*

musicology [ˌmjuzɪˈkalədʒi] *s* musicologie *f*

mu′sic rack′ or **mu′sic stand′** *s* pupitre *m* à musique

musk [mʌsk] *s* musc *m*

musk′ deer′ *s* porte-musc *m*

musketeer [ˌmʌskɪˈtɪr] *s* mousquetaire *m*

musk′mel′on *s* melon *m;* cantaloup *m*

musk′rat′ *s* rat *m* musqué, ondatra *m*

Mus·lim [ˈmʌzlɪm] *ou* [ˈmʌslɪm] *adj* & *s* (*pl* **-lims** *ou* **-lim**) musulman *m*, musulmane *f*

Mus′lim cal′endar *s* calendrier *m* musulman

muslin [ˈmʌzlɪn] *s* mousseline *f*

muss [mʌs] *tr* (*the hair*) ébouriffer; (*the clothing*) froisser

muss·y [ˈmʌsi] *adj* (*comp* **-ier;** *super* **-iest**) en désordre, froissé

must [mʌst] *s* moût *m;* nécessité *f* absolue ‖ *aux* used to express 1) necessity, e.g., **he must go away** il doit s'en aller; 2) conjecture, e.g., **he**

must be ill il doit être malade; **he must have been ill** il a dû être malade

mustache [məsˈtæʃ] *s* moustache *f*

mustard [ˈmʌstərd] *s* moutarde *f*

mus′tard gas′ *s* ypérite *f*, gaz *m* de combat suffocant et vésicant

mus′tard plas′ter *s* sinapisme *m*

muster [ˈmʌstər] *s* rassemblement *m;* (mil) revue *f;* **to pass muster** être porté à l'appel; (fig) être acceptable ‖ *tr* rassembler; **to muster in** enrôler; **to muster out** démobiliser; **to muster up courage** prendre son courage à deux mains

mus′ter roll′ *s* feuille *f* d'appel

mustn′t *contr* must not

mus·ty [ˈmʌsti] *adj* (*comp* **-tier;** *super* **-tiest**) (*moldy*) moist; (*stale*) renfermé; (*antiquated*) désuet

mutation [mjuˈteʃən] *s* mutation *f*

mute [mjut] *adj* muet ‖ *s* muet *m;* (mus) sourdine *f* ‖ *tr* amortir; (mus) mettre une sourdine à

mutilate [ˈmjutɪˌlet] *tr* mutiler

mutineer [ˌmjutɪˈnɪr] *s* mutin *m*

mutinous [ˈmjutɪnəs] *adj* mutiné

muti·ny [ˈmjutɪni] *s* (*pl* **-nies**) mutinerie *f* ‖ *v* (*pret* & *pp* **-nied**) *intr* se mutiner

mutt [mʌt] *s* (*dog*) (slang) cabot *m*, clebs *m;* (*person*) (slang) nigaud *m*

mutter [ˈmʌtər] *tr* & *intr* marmonner

mutton [ˈmʌtən] *s* mouton *m*

mut′ton-chop′ *s* côtelette *f* de mouton; **mutton-chops** favoris *mpl* en côtelette

mutual [ˈmjutʃʊˑəl] *adj* mutuel

mu′tual aid′ *s* entraide *f*

mu′tual fund′ *s* société *f* d'investissement à capital variable

mu′tual insur′ance com′pany *s* mutuelle *f*

muzzle [ˈmʌzəl] *s* (*projecting part of head of animal*) museau *m;* (*device to keep animal from biting*) muselière *f;* (*of firearm*) gueule *f* ‖ *tr* museler

my [maɪ] *adj poss* mon §88

myriad [ˈmɪriˑəd] *adj* innombrable ‖ *s* myriade *f*

myrrh [mɪr] *s* myrrhe *f*

myrtle [ˈmʌrtəl] *s* myrte *m;* (*periwinkle*) pervenche *f*

my·self′ *pron pers* moi §85; moi-même §86; me §87

mysterious [mɪsˈtɪriˑəs] *adj* mystérieux

myster·y [ˈmɪstəri] *s* (*pl* **-ies**) mystère *m*

mystic [ˈmɪstɪk] *adj* & *s* mystique *mf*

mystical [ˈmɪstɪkəl] *adj* mystique

mysticism [ˈmɪstɪˌsɪzəm] *s* mysticisme *m*

mystification [ˌmɪstɪfɪˈkeʃən] *s* mystification *f*

mysti·fy [ˈmɪstɪˌfaɪ] *v* (*pret* & *pp* **-fied**) *tr* mystifier

myth [mɪθ] *s* mythe *m*

mythical [ˈmɪθɪkəl] *adj* mythique

mythological [ˌmɪθəˈladʒɪkəl] *adj* mythologique

mytholo·gy [mɪˈθalədʒi] *s* (*pl* **-gies**) mythologie *f*

N

N, n [ɛn] *s* XIVᵉ lettre de l'alphabet

n. *abbr* **name, neuter, nominative, noon, north, northern, noun, number**

N. *abbr* **Nationalist, Navy, Noon, Norse, North, Northern, November**

NA *abbr* not applicable; not available

N.A. *abbr* **North America;** not applicable

NAACP *abbr* **National Association for the Advancement of Colored People**

nab [næb] *v* (*pret & pp* **nabbed;** *ger* **nabbing**) *tr* (slang) happer; (*to arrest*) (slang) pincer, harponner

NAFTA [ˈnæftə] *s* (acronym) (**North American Free Trade Agreement**) ALENA *m* (accord de libre-échange nord-américain)

nag [næg] *s* bidet *m* ‖ *v* (*pret & pp* **nagged;** *ger* **nagging**) *tr & intr* gronder constamment; **to nag at** gronder constamment

nail [nel] *s* (*of finger*) ongle *m;* (*to be hammered*) clou *m;* **to bite one's nails** se ronger les ongles; **to hit the nail on the head** mettre le doigt dessus, frapper juste ‖ *tr* clouer; (*a lie*) mettre à découvert; (coll) saisir, attraper

nail' brush' *s* brosse *f* à ongles

nail' clip'pers *spl* coupe-ongles *m*

nail' file' *s* lime *f* à ongles

nail' pol'ish *s* vernis *m* à ongles

nail' scis'sors *s & spl* ciseaux *mpl* à ongles

nail' set' *s* chasse-clou *m*

naïve [nɑˈiv] *adj* naïf

naked [ˈnekɪd] *adj* nu; **to be naked** être au poil; **to strip naked** se mettre tout nu; mettre tout nu; **with the naked eye** à l'œil nu

namby-pamby [ˈnæmbɪˈpæmbi] *adj* minaudier

name [nem] *s* nom *m;* (*reputation*) renom *m;* **by name** de nom; **by the name of** sous le nom de; **to call names** traiter de tous les noms; **what is your name?** comment vous appelez-vous? ‖ *tr* nommer; (*a price*) fixer, indiquer

name' brand' *s* image *f* de marque

name' day' *s* fête *f*

nameless [ˈnemlɪs] *adj* sans nom, anonyme; (*horrid*) odieux

namely [ˈnemli] *adv* à savoir, nommément

name' sake' *s* homonyme *m*

name' tag' *s* insigne *m* d'identité, barrette *f*

nan·ny [ˈnæni] *s* (*pl* **-nies**) nounou *f*

nan' ny goat' *s* (coll) chèvre *f,* bique *f*

nanotechnology [ˈnænɔtɛkˌnɔlɔdʒi] *s* nanotechnologie *f*

nap [næp] *s* (*short sleep*) somme *m,* sieste *f;* (*of cloth*) poil *m,* duvet *m;* **to take a nap** faire un petit somme ‖ *v* (*pret & pp* **napped;** *ger* **napping**) *intr* faire un somme; manquer de vigilance; **to catch napping** prendre au dépourvu

napalm [ˈnepɑm] *s* (mil) naplam *m*

nape [nep] *s* nuque *f*

naphtha [ˈnæfθə] *s* naphte *m*

napkin [ˈnæpkɪn] *s* serviette *f*

nap' kin ring' *s* rond *m* de serviette

napoleon [nəˈpolyən] *s* (culin) mille-feuille *m*

Napoleonic [nəˌpolɪˈɑnɪk] *adj* napoléonien

narcissus [nɑrˈsɪsəs] *s* narcisse *m;* **Narcissus** Narcisse

narcotic [nɑrˈkɑtɪk] *adj & s* narcotique *m*

narrate [næˈret] *tr* narrer, raconter

narration [næˈreʃən] *s* narration *f*

narrative [ˈnærətɪv] *adj* narratif ‖ *s* narration *f,* récit *m*

narrator [næˈretər] *s* narrateur *m*

narrow [ˈnæro] *adj* étroit; (*e.g., margin of votes*) faible ‖ **narrows** *spl* détroit *m,* goulet *m* ‖ *tr* rétrécir ‖ *intr* se rétrécir

nar' row escape' *s*—**it was a narrow escape** il était moins une; **to have a narrow escape** l'échapper belle

nar' row gauge' *s* voie *f* étroite

nar' row-mind'ed *adj* à l'esprit étroit, intolérant

nasal [ˈnezəl] *adj* nasal; (*sound, voice*) nasillard ‖ *s* (phonet) nasale *f*

nasalize [ˈnezəˌlaɪz] *tr & intr* nasaliser

nasturtium [nəˈstʌrʃəm] *s* capucine *f*

nas·ty [ˈnæsti] *adj* (*comp* **-tier;** *super* **-tiest**) mauvais, sale, dégoûtant; féroce, farouche; désagréable

nation [ˈneʃən] *s* nation *f*

national [ˈnæʃənəl] *adj* national ‖ *s* national *m,* ressortissant *m*

na' tional an'them *s* hymne *m* national

nationalism [ˈnæʃənəˌlɪzəm] *s* nationalisme *m*

nationali·ty [ˌnæʃənˈælɪti] *s* (*pl* **-ties**) nationalité *f*

nationalize [ˈnæʃənəˌlaɪz] *tr* nationaliser, étatiser, fonctionnariser

na' tion·wide' *adj* de toute la nation

native [ˈnetɪv] *adj* natif; (*land, language*) natal; **native of** originaire de ‖ *s* natif *m;* (*original inhabitant*) naturel *m,* indigène *mf,* autochtone *mf*

na' tive land' *s* pays *m* natal

nativi·ty [nəˈtɪvɪti] *s* (*pl* **-ties**) naissance *f;* (astrol) nativité *f;* **Nativity** Nativité *f*

NATO [ˈneto] *s* (acronym) (**North Atlantic Treaty Organization**) l'O.T.A.N. *f,* l'OTAN *f* (Organisation du traité de l'Atlantique Nord)

nat·ty [ˈnæti] *adj* (*comp* **-tier;** *super* **-tiest**) coquet, élégant, soigné

natural [ˈnætʃərəl] *adj* naturel ‖ *s* (mus) bécarre *m;* (mus) touche *f* blanche; **a natural** (coll) juste ce qu'il faut

naturalism [ˈnætʃərəˌlɪzəm] *s* naturalisme *m*

naturalist [ˈnætʃərəlɪst] *s* naturaliste *mf*

naturalization [ˌnætʃərəlɪˈzeʃən] *s* naturalisation *f*

naturaliza' tion pa'pers *spl* déclaration *f* de naturalisation

naturalize [ˈnætʃərəˌlaɪz] *tr* naturaliser

nature [ˈnetʃər] *s* nature *f;* (*disposition*) naturel *m*

naught [nɔt] *s* zéro *m;* rien *m;* **to come to naught** n'aboutir à rien

naugh•ty [`nɔti] *adj* (*comp* **-tier;** *super* **-tiest**) méchant, vilain; (*story*) risqué

nausea [`nɔʃɪ•ə], [`nɔsɪ•ə] *s* nausée *f*

nauseate [`nɔʃɪ,et], [`nɔsɪ,et] *tr* donner la nausée à ‖ *intr* avoir des nausées

nauseating [`nɔʃɪ,etɪŋ], [`nɔsɪ,etɪŋ] *adj* nauséabond

nauseous [`nɔʃɪ•əs], [`nɔsɪ•əs] *adj* nauséeux

nautical [`nɔtɪkəl] *adj* nautique; naval, marin

naval [`nevəl] *adj* naval

na′val acad′emy *s* école *f* navale

na′val of′ficer *s* officier *m* de marine

na′val sta′tion *s* station *f* navale

nave [nev] *s* (*of a church*) nef *f,* vaisseau *m;* (*of a wheel*) moyeu *m*

navel [`nevəl] *s* nombril *m*

na′vel or′ange *s* orange *f* navel

navigable [`nævɪgəbəl] *adj* (*river*) navigable; (*aircraft*) dirigeable; (*ship*) bon marcheur

navigate [`nævɪ,get] *tr* gouverner, conduire; (*the sea*) naviguer sur ‖ *intr* naviguer

navigation [,nævɪ`geʃən] *s* navigation *f*

navigator [`nævɪ,getər] *s* navigateur *m*

na•vy [`nevi] *adj* bleu marine ‖ *s* (*pl* **-vies**) marine *f* militaire, marine de guerre; (*color*) bleu *m* marine

na′vy bean′ *s* haricot *m* blanc

na′vy blue′ *s* bleu *m* marine

na′vy yard′ *s* chantier *m* naval

nay [ne] *adv* non; voire, même ‖ *s* non *m;* (*parl*) vote *m* négatif

Nazarene [,næzə`rin] *adj* nazaréen ‖ *s* (*person*) Nazaréen *m*

Nazi [`nɑtsi] *adj* & *s* nazi *m*

n.d. *abbr* (**no date**) s.d.

N.E. *abbr* **New Era** (*used to replace A.D.*)

Ne′apol′itan ice′ cream′ [,ni•ə`pɑlɪtən] *s* glace *f* panachée

neap′ tide′ [nip] *s* morte-eau *f*

near [nɪr] *adj* proche, prochain; **near at hand** tout près; **near side** (*of horse*) côté *m* de montoir ‖ *adv* près, de près; (*nearly*) presque; **to come near** s'approcher ‖ *prep* près de ‖ *tr* s'approcher de

near′by′ *adj* proche ‖ *adv* tout près

Near′ East′ *s*—**the Near East** le Proche Orient

nearly [`nɪrli] *adv* presque, de près; faillir, manquer de, e.g., **I nearly fell** j'ai failli tomber

near′ miss′ *s* (*near collision*) (aer) collision *f* manquée, quasi-collision *f*

near′-sight′ed *adj* myope

near′-sight′edness *s* myopie *f*

neat [nit] *adj* soigné, rangé; concis; (*clever*) adroit; (*liquor*) nature; (slang) chouette

neat′s′-foot oil′ *s* huile *f* de pied de bœuf

nebu•la [`nɛbjələ] *s* (*pl* **-lae** [,li] or **-las**) nébuleuse *f*

nebulous [`nɛbjələs] *adj* nébuleux

necessarily [,nɛsɪ`sɛrɪli] *adv* nécessairement, forcément

necessary [`nɛsɪ,sɛri] *adj* nécessaire; **if necessary** si besoin est

necessitate [nɪ`sɛsɪ,tet] *tr* nécessiter, exiger

necessi•ty [nɪ`sɛsɪti] *s* (*pl* **-ties**) nécessité *f*

neck [nɛk] *s* cou *m;* (*of bottle*) col *m,* goulot *m;* (*of land*) cap *m;* (*of tooth*) collet *m;* collet; (*of violin*) manche *m,* (*strait*) étroit *m;* **neck and neck** manche à manche; **to break one's neck** (coll) se rompre le cou; **to stick one's neck out** prêter le flanc; **to win by a neck** gagner par une encolure ‖ *intr* (slang) se bécoter

neck′ and neck′ *adj* & *adv* à égalité

neck′band′ *s* tour *m* de cou

neckerchief [`nɛkərtʃɪf] *s* foulard *m*

necking [`nɛkɪŋ] *s* (slang) pelotage *m,* bécotage *m*

necklace [`nɛklɪs] *s* collier *m*

neck′piece′ *s* col *m* de fourrure

neck′tie′ *s* cravate *f*

neck′tie pin′ *s* épingle *f* de cravate

necrolo•gy [nɛ`krɑlədʒi] *s* (*pl* **-gies**) nécrologie *f*

nectar [`nɛktər] *s* nectar *m*

nectarine [,nɛktə`rin] *s* brugnon *m*

nee [ne] *adj* (*used before maiden name*) née

need [nid] *s* besoin *m;* (*want, poverty*) besoin, indigence *f,* nécessité *f;* **if need be** au besoin, s'il le faut ‖ *tr* avoir besoin de, falloir, e.g., **he needs money** il a besoin d'argent, il lui faut de l'argent; demander, e.g., **the motor needs oil** le moteur demande de l'huile ‖ *aux* devoir

needful [`nidfəl] *adj* nécessaire

needle [`nidəl] *s* aiguille *f;* **to look for a needle in a haystack** chercher une aiguille dans une botte de foin ‖ *tr* (*to prod*) aiguillonner; (coll) taquiner; (*a drink*) (coll) corser

needless [`nidlɪs] *adj* inutile

nee′dle•work′ *s* ouvrage *m* à l'aiguille

need•y [`nidi] *adj* (*comp* **-ier;** *super* **-iest**) nécessiteux ‖ *s*—**the needy** less nécessiteux

ne′er-do-well [`nɛrdu,wɛl] *adj* propre à rien ‖ *s* vaurien *m*

nefarious [nɪ`fɛrɪ•əs] *adj* scélérat

negate [nɪ`get] *tr* invalider; nier

negation [nɪ`geʃən] *s* négation *f*

negative [`nɛgətɪv] *adj* négatif ‖ *s* (*opinion*) négative *f;* (*gram*) négation *f* (phot) négatif *m*

neglect [nɪ`glɛkt] *s* négligence *f* ‖ *tr* négliger; **to neglect to** négliger de

négligée or **negligee** [,nɛglɪ`ʒe] *s* négligé *m,* robe *f* de chambre

negligence [`nɛglɪdʒəns] *s* négligence *f*

negligent [`nɛglɪdʒənt] *adj* négligent

negligible [`nɛglɪdʒɪbəl] *adj* négligeable

negotiable [nɪ`goʃɪ•əbəl] *adj* négociable

negotiate [nɪ`goʃɪ•et] *tr* & *intr* négocier

negotiation [nɪ,goʃɪ`eʃən] *s* négociation *f*

negotiator [nɪ,goʃɪ,etər] *s* négociateur *m*

Ne•gro [`nigro] *adj* (usually offensive) noir,

nègre ‖ *s* (*pl* **-groes**) (usually offensive) Noir *m*, Noire *f*

neigh [ne] *s* hennissement *m* ‖ *intr* hennir

neighbor [ˈnebər] *adj* voisin ‖ *s* voisin *m*; (fig) prochain *m* ‖ *tr* avoisiner ‖ *intr* être voisin

neigh′bor·hood′ *s* voisinage *m;* **in the neighborhood of** aux environs de; (*approximately, about*) (coll) environ

neighborliness [ˈnebərlɪnɪs] *s* bon voisinage *m*

neighborly [ˈnebərli] *adj* bon voisin

neither [ˈniðər], [ˈnaɪðər] *adj indef* ni, e.g., **neither one of us** ni l'un ni l'autre ‖ *pron indef* ni, e.g., **neither** ni l'un ni l'autre ‖ *conj* ni; ni . . . non plus, e.g., **neither do I** ni moi non plus; **neither . . . nor** ni . . . ni

neme·sis [ˈnɛmɪsɪs] *s* (*pl* **-ses** [ˌsɪz]) juste châtiment *m;* **Nemesis** Némésis *f*

neologism [niˈɑləˌdʒɪzəm] *s* néologisme *m*

neon [ˈniˌɑn] *s* néon *m*

ne′on lamp′ *s* lampe *f* au néon

ne′on sign′ *s* réclame *f* lumineuse

neophyte [ˈniˌəˌfaɪt] *s* néophyte *mf*

nephew [ˈnɛfju], [ˈnɛvju] *s* neveu *m*

neptunium [nɛpˈt(j)uniˌəm] *s* neptunium *m*

Nero [ˈnɪro] *s* Néron *m*

nerve [nʌrv] *adj* nerveux ‖ *s* nerf *m;* (*self-confidence*) assurance *f,* courage *m;* **to get on s.o.'s nerves** porter sur les nerfs à qn; **to have a lot of nerve** (*to have a lot of cheek*) avoir du toupet; **to have nerves of steel** avoir du nerf; **to lose one's nerve** avoir le trac

nerve′ cen′ter *s* (anat) centre *m* nerveux; (fig) centre *m* opérations, nœud *m* vital

nerve′ end′ing *s* terminaison *f* nerveuse

nerve′ gas′ *s* gaz *m* asphyxiant

nerve′-rack′ing [ˈrækɪŋ] *adj* énervant, agaçant

nervous [ˈnʌrvəs] *adj* nerveux; **to get nervous** s'énerver

ner′vous break′down *s* épuisement *m* nerveux, dépression *f* nerveuse

nerv·y [ˈnʌrvi] *adj* (*comp* **-ier;** *super* **-iest**) nerveux, musclé; (coll) audacieux, culotté; (slang) dévergondé

nest [nɛst] *s* nid *m;* (*set of things fitting together*) jeu *m* ‖ *intr* se nicher

nest′ egg′ *s* nichet *m;* (fig) boursicot *m,* bas *m* de laine

nestle [ˈnɛsəl] *intr* se blottir, se nicher

nest′ of ta′bles *s* table *f* gigogne

net [nɛt] *adj* net ‖ *s* filet *m;* (*for fishing; for catching birds*) nappe *f;* (tex) tulle *m* ‖ *v* (*pret & pp* **netted;** *ger* **netting**) *tr* (*a profit*) réaliser

Netherlander [ˈnɛðərˌlændər] *s* Néerlandais *m*

Netherlands [ˈnɛðərləndz] *s*—**The Netherlands** les Pays-Bas *mpl*

net′ in′come *s* revenu *m* net

net′ prof′it *s* bénéfice *m* net

nettle [ˈnɛtəl] *s* ortie *f* ‖ *tr* piquer au vif

net′ weight′ *s* poids *m* net

net′work′ *s* réseau *m;* (rad, telv) chaîne *f,* réseau; (comp) réseau d'ordinateurs ‖ *tr* entrer en relations avec; (comp) joindre dans un ré-

seau ‖ *intr* échanger des informations; avoir des relations

net′work′ing *s* échange *m* d'informations; travail *m* en réseau; recherche *f* de connaissances et de relations; (comp) création *f* d'un réseau d'ordinateurs

neuralgia [n(j)uˈrældʒə] *s* névralgie *f*

neuron [ˈn(j)uran] *s* neurone *m*

neuro·sis [n(j)uˈrosɪs] *s* (*pl* **-ses** [siz]) névrose *f*

neurotic [n(j)uˈratɪk] *adj & s* névrosé *m*

neuter [ˈn(j)utər] *adj & s* neutre *m*

neutral [ˈn(j)utrəl] *adj* neutre ‖ *s* neutre *m;* (*gear*) point *m* mort

neutrality [n(j)uˈtrælɪti] *s* neutralité *f*

neutralize [ˈn(j)utrəˌlaɪz] *tr* neutraliser

neutron [ˈn(j)utran] *s* neutron *m*

neu′tron bomb′ *s* bombe *f* à neutrons

never [ˈnɛvər] *adv* jamais §90B; ne . . . jamais §90, e.g., **he never talks** il ne parle jamais

nev′er·more′ *adv* ne . . . plus jamais ‖ *interj* jamais plus!, plus jamais!

nev′er·the·less′ *adv* néanmoins

new [n(j)u] *adj* (*unused*) neuf; (*other, additional, different*) nouveau (before noun); (*recent*) nouveau (after noun); (*inexperienced*) novice; (*wine*) jeune; **what's new?** quoi de nouveau?, quoi de neuf?

new′born′ *adj* nouveau-né

new′born′ child′ *s* nouveau-né *m*

New′cas′tle *s*—**to carry coals to Newcastle** porter de l'eau à la rivière

newcomer [ˈn(j)uˌkʌmər] *s* nouveau venu *m*

New′ Cov′enant *s* (Bib) nouvelle alliance *f*

newel [ˈn(j)uˌəl] *s* (*of winding stairs*) noyau *m;* (*post at end of stair rail*) pilastre *m*

New′ Eng′land *s* Nouvelle-Angleterre *f;* la Nouvelle-Angleterre

newfangled [ˈn(j)uˌfæŋgəld] *adj* à la dernière mode, du dernier cri

Newfoundland [ˈn(j)ufəndˌlænd] *s* TerreNeuve *f;* **in** or **to Newfoundland** à TerreNeuve ‖ [n(j)uˈfaʊndlənd] *s* (*dog*) terreneuve *m*

newly [ˈn(j)uli] *adv* nouvellement

new′ly·wed′ *s* nouveau marié *m*

new′ moon′ *s* nouvelle lune *f*

newness [ˈn(j)unɪs] *s* nouveauté *f*

New′ Or′leans [ˈɔrliˌənz] *s* la Nouvelle-Orléans

news [n(j)uz] *s* nouvelles *fpl;* **a news item** un fait-divers; **a piece of news** une nouvelle

news′ a′gency *s* agence *f* d'information, agence de presse; (com) agence à journaux

news′beat′ *s* exclusivité *f*

news′boy′ *s* vendeur *m* de journaux

news′ bul′letin *s* bulletin *m* d'actualités

news′ cam′era·man *s* reporter *m* d'images

news′cast′ *s* journal *m* parlé; journal télévisé

news′cast′er *s* reporter *m* de la radio

news′ con′ference *s* conférence *f* de presse

news′ cov′erage *s* reportage *m*

news′deal′er *s* marchand *m* de journaux

news′ ed′itor s rédacteur m des actualités, rédacteur de la chronique du jour

news′let′ter s (*of a company, organization, etc.*) bulletin m (de . . .) (*de la compagnie, etc.*)

news′man′ s (*pl* **-men′**) journaliste m; (*dealer*) marchand m de journaux

New′ South′ Wales′ s la Nouvelle-Galles du Sud

news′pa′per adj journalistique ‖ s journal m

news′paper clip′ping s coupure f de presse

news′paper•man′ s (*pl* **-men′**) journaliste m; (*dealer*) marchand m de journaux

news′paper rack′ s casier m à journaux

news′paper route′ s tournée f de distribution de journaux

news′paper se′rial s feuilleton m

news′print′ s papier m journal

news′reel′ s actualités fpl (filmées)

news′room′ s salle f de rédaction

news′stand′ s kiosque m

news′week′ly s (*pl* **-lies**) hebdomadaire m

news′wor′thy adj d'actualité

New′ Tes′tament s Nouveau Testament m

New′ World′, The s Le Nouveau Monde m

New′ Year′s′ Day′ s le jour de l'an, le nouvel an

New′ Year′s′ Eve′ s la Saint-Sylvestre

New′ Year′s′ greet′ings spl souhaits mpl de nouvel An

New′ Year′s′ resolu′tion s résolution f de nouvel An

New′ York′ [jɔrk] adj newyorkais ‖ s New York m

New′ York′er [ˈjɔrkər] s newyorkais m

next [nɛkst] adj (*in time*) prochain, suivant; (*in place*) voisin; (*first in the period which follows*) prochain (before noun), e.g., **the next time** la prochaine fois; (*following the present time*) prochain (after noun), e.g., **next week** la semaine prochaine; **next to** à côté de ‖ adv après, ensuite; la prochaine fois; **who comes next?** à qui le tour? ‖ interj au premier de ces messieurs!, au suivant!

next′-door′ adj d'à côté, voisin ‖ **next′-door′** adv à côté; **next-door to** à côté de; à côté de chez

next′ of kin′ s (*pl* **next of kin**) proche parent m

Niag′ara Falls′ [naɪˈægərə] s les chutes fpl du Niagara

nib [nɪb] s pointe f; (*of pen*) bec m

nibble [ˈnɪbəl] s grignotement m; (*on fish line*) touche f; (fig) morceau m ‖ tr & intr grignoter

nice [naɪs] adj agréable, gentil, aimable; (*distinction*) subtil, fin; (*weather*) beau; **nice and . . .** (coll) très; **not nice** (coll) vilain

nicely [ˈnaɪsli] adv bien; avec délicatesse

nice•ty [ˈnaɪsəti] s (*pl* **-ties**) précision f; (*subtlety*) finesse f

niche [nɪtʃ] s niche f; (*job, position*) place f, poste m

nick [nɪk] s (*e.g., on china*) brèche f; **in the**

nick of time à point nommé, à pic ‖ tr ébrécher; (*for money, favors*) (slang) cramponner

nickel [ˈnɪkəl] s (*metal*) nickel m; (*coin*) pièce f de cinq sous ‖ tr nickeler

nick′el plate′ s nickelure f

nick′el-plate′ tr nickeler

nicknack [ˈnɪkˌnæk] s colifichet m

nick′name′ s sobriquet m, surnom m ‖ tr donner un sobriquet à, surnommer

nicotine [ˈnɪkəˌtin] s nicotine f

niece [nis] s nièce f

nif•ty [ˈnɪfti] adj (*comp* **-tier**; *super* **-tiest**) (slang) coquet, pimpant

niggard [ˈnɪgərd] adj & s avare mf

night [naɪt] s nuit f; (*evening*) soir m; **last night** (*night that has just passed*) cette nuit; (*last evening*) hier soir; **night before last** avant-hier soir

night′cap′ s bonnet m de nuit, casque m à mèche; (*drink*) posset m

night′ club′ s boîte f de nuit

night′ driv′ing s conduite f pendant la nuit

night′fall′ s tombée f de la nuit

night′gown′ s chemise f de nuit

night′hawk′ s noctambule mf; (orn) engoulevent m

nightingale [ˈnaɪtənˌgel] s rossignol m

night′latch′ s serrure f à ressort

night′ light′ s veilleuse f

night′long′ adj de toute la nuit ‖ adv pendant toute la nuit

nightly [ˈnaɪtli] adj nocturne; de chaque nuit ‖ adv nocturnement; chaque nuit

night′mare′ s cauchemar m

nightmarish [ˈnaɪtˌmɛrɪʃ] adj (coll) cauchemardesque, cauchemardeux

night′ owl′ s (coll) noctambule mf

night′ school′ s cours mpl du soir

night′shade′ s morelle f

night′ shift′ s équipe f de nuit

night′ ta′ble s table f de chevet

night′ watch′man s (*pl* **-men**) veilleur m de nuit

nihilism [ˈnaɪ•ɪˌlɪzəm] s nihilisme m

nil [nɪl] s rien m

Nile [naɪl] s Nil m

nimble [ˈnɪmbəl] adj agile, leste; (*mind*) délié

nim•bus [ˈnɪmbəs] s (*pl* **-buses** or **-bi** [baɪ]) nimbe m, auréole f; (meteo) nimbus m

nincompoop [ˈnɪnkəmˌpup] s nigaud m

nine [naɪn] adj & pron neuf ‖ s neuf m; **nine o'clock** neuf heures

nine′/elev′en (9/11 *ou* 9-11 *ou* Sept. 11) s neuf/onze m (*destruction du World Trade Center par une attaque terroriste*)

nine′pins′ s quilles fpl

nineteen [ˈnaɪnˈtin] adj, pron, & s dix-neuf m

nineteenth [ˈnaɪnˈtinθ] adj & pron dix-neuvième (*masc, fem*); **the Nineteenth** dix-neuf, e.g., **John the Nineteenth** Jean dix-neuf ‖ s dix-neuvième m; **the nineteenth** (*in dates*) le dix-neuf

ninetieth [`nainti•iθ] *adj & pron* quatre-vingt-dixième (*masc, fem*) ‖ *s* quatre-vingt-dixième *m*

nine•ty [`nainti] *adj & pron* quatre-vingt-dix ‖ *s* (*pl* **-ties**) quatre-vingt-dix *m*

nine'ty-first' *adj & pron* quatre-vingt-onzième (*masc, fem*) ‖ *s* quatre-vingt-onzième *m*

nine'ty-one' *adj, pron, & s* quatre-vingt-onze *m*

ninth [nainθ] *adj & pron* neuvième (*masc, fem*); **the Ninth** neuf, e.g., **John the Ninth** Jean neuf ‖ *s* neuvième *m;* **the ninth** (*in dates*) le neuf

nip [nip] *s* pincement *m,* petite morsure *f;* (*of cold weather*) morsure; (*of liquor*) goutte *f* ‖ *v* (*pret & pp* **nipped;** *ger* **nipping**) *tr* pincer, donner une petite morsure à; **to nip in the bud** tuer dans l'œuf ‖ *intr* (coll) biberonner, picoler

nipple [`nipəl] *s* mamelon *m;* (*of nursing bottle*) tétine *f;* (mach) raccord *m*

nip•py [`nipi] *adj* (*comp* **-pier;** *super* **-piest**) piquant; (*cold*) vif; (Brit) leste, rapide

nirvana [nir`vɑnə] *s* le nirvâna

nit [nit] *s* pou *m;* (*egg*) lente *f*

nit'pick' *intr* chercher la petite bête

niter [`naitər] *s* nitrate *m* de potasse; nitrate de soude

nitrate [`naitret] *s* azotate *m,* nitrate *m;* (*fertilizer*) engrais *m* nitraté ‖ *tr* nitrater

nitric [`naitrik] *adj* azotique, nitrique

nitrogen [`naitrədʒən] *s* azote *m*

nitroglycerin [,naitrə`glisərin] *s* nitroglycérine *f*

nitrous [`naitrəs] *adj* azoteux

ni'trous ox'ide *s* oxyde *m* azoteux, protoxyde *m* d'azote

nit'wit' *s* (coll) imbécile *mf*

no [no] *adj indef* aucun, nul, pas de §90B; **no admission, no admittance** entrée *f* interdite; **no answer** pas de réponse; **no comment!** rien à dire!; **no entry** entrée *f* interdite, défense *f* d'entrer; **no go** or **no soap** (coll) pas mèche *f;* **no kidding** (coll) blague *f* à part; **no littering** défense *f* de déposer des ordures; **no loitering** vagabondage *m* interdit; **no parking** stationnement *m* interdit; **no place** nulle part; **no place else** nulle part ailleurs; **no shooting** chasse *f* réservée; **no smoking** défense de fumer; **no thoroughfare** circulation *f* interdite, passage *m* interdit; **no use** inutile; **with no** sans ‖ *s* non *m* ‖ *adv* non; **no good** vil; **no longer** ne ... plus §90, e.g., **he no longer works here** il travaille plus ici; **no more** ne ... plus §90, e.g., **he has no more** il n'en a plus; **no more** ... (or *comp* in **-er**) **than** ne ... pas plus ... que, e.g., **she is no happier than he** elle n'est pas plus heureuse que lui

No'ah's Ark' [`no•əz] *s* l'arche *f* de Noé

nobili•ty [no`biliti] *s* (*pl* **-ties**) noblesse *f*

noble [`nobəl] *adj & s* noble *mf*

no'ble•man *s* (*pl* **-men**) noble *m*

nobleness [`nobəlnis] *s* noblesse *f*

nobod•y [`no,bɑdi] *s* (*pl* **-ies**) nullité *f* ‖ *pron indef* personne; ne ... personne §90, e.g., **I see nobody there** je n'y vois personne; personne ne, nul ne §90, e.g., **nobody knows it** personne ne le sait, nul ne le sait

nocturnal [nɑk`tʌrnəl] *adj* nocturne

nocturne [`nɑktʌrn] *s* nocturne *m*

nod [nɑd] *s* signe *m* de tête; (*greeting*) inclination *f* de tête ‖ *v* (*pret & pp* **nodded;** *ger* **nodding**) *tr* (*the head*) incliner; **to nod assent** faire un signe d'assentiment ‖ *intr* (*with sleep*) dodeliner de la tête; (*to greet*) incliner la tête

node [nod] *s* nœud *m*

no'-fault' *adj* (*divorce, insurance*) libre de culpabilité

no'-good' *adj* (coll) propre à rien

no'-how' *adv* (coll) aucunement, en aucune façon

noise [nɔiz] *s* bruit *m* ‖ *tr* (*a rumor*) ébruiter

noiseless [`nɔizlis] *adj* silencieux

nois•y [`nɔizi] *adj* (*comp* **-ier;** *super* **-iest**) bruyant

no' kid'ding? *s* (coll) sérieusement?, blague *f* à part?

nomad [`nomæd] *adj & s* nomade *mf*

no' man's' land' *s* région *f* désolée; (mil) zone *f* neutre

nominal [`nɑminəl] *adj* nominal

nominate [`nɑmi,net] *tr* désigner; (*to appoint*) nommer

nomination [,nɑmi`ne∫ən] *s* désignation *f,* investiture *f*

nominative [`nɑminətiv] *adj & s* nominatif *m*

nominee [,nɑmi`ni] *s* désigné *m,* candidat *m*

non'-agres'sion pact' *s* pacte *m* de non-agression

non'-aligned' na'tions *spl* pays *mpl* non-alignés; le Tiers-Monde *m*

nonbelligerent [,nɑnbə`lidʒərənt] *adj & s* non-belligérant *m*

nonbreakable [nɑn`brekəbəl] *adj* incassable

nonchalant [`nɑn∫ələnt] *adj* nonchalant

noncom [`nɑn,kɑm] *s* (coll) sous-off *m*

noncombatant [nɑn`kɑmbətənt] *adj & s* non-combattant *m*

noncommissioned [,nɑnkə`mi∫ənd] *adj* non-breveté

non'commis'sioned of'ficer *s* sous-officier *m*

noncommittal [,nɑnkə`mitəl] *adj* évasif, réticent

nonconductor [,nɑnkən`dʌktər] *s* non-conducteur *m,* mauvais conducteur *m*

nonconformist [,nɑnkən`fɔrmist] *adj & s* non-conformiste *mf*

nondenominational [,nɑndi,nɑmi`ne∫ənəl] *adj* indépendant, qui ne fait partie d'aucune secte religieuse; (*school*) laïque

nondescript [`nɑndi,skript] *adj* indéfinissable, inclassable

nondiscriminating [,nɑndis`krimi,netiŋ] *adj* (*employment, etc.*) égalitaire

none [nʌn] *pron indef* aucun §90B; (*nobody*) personne, nul §90B; ne ... aucun, ne ... nul

§90; n'en . . . pas, e.g., **I have none** je n'en ai pas; (*as a response on the blank of an official form*) néant ‖ *adv*—**to be none the wiser** ne pas en être plus sage

nonenti·ty [nɑnˋɛntɪtɪ] *s* (*pl* **-ties**) nullité *f*

none'such' *s* nonpareil *m;* (*apple*) nonpareille *f;* (bot) lupuline *f,* minette *f*

nonfiction [nɑnˋfɪkʃən] *s* littérature *f* autre que le roman

nonfulfillment [ˌnɑnfʊlˋfɪlmənt] *s* inaccomplissement *m*

nonintervention [ˌnɑnɪntərˋvɛnʃən] *s* nonintervention *f,* non-ingérence *f*

nonmetal [ˋnɑnˌmɛtəl] *s* métalloïde *m*

no'-no' *s* (coll) quelque chose défendu

no'-non'sense *adj* pratique, sensé

nonpartisan [nɑnˋpɑrtɪzən] *adj* neutre, indépendant

nonpayment [nɑnˋpemənt] *s* non-paiement *m*

non·plus [nɑnˋplʌs] *s* perplexité *f* ‖ *v* (*pret & pp* **-plused** or **-plussed;** *ger* **-plusing** or **-plussing**) *tr* déconcerter, dérouter

nonprof'it or'ganization *s* organisation *f* sans but lucratif

nonresident [nɑnˋrɛzɪdənt] *adj & s* non-résident *m*

nonresidential [nɑnˌrɛzɪˋdɛnʃəl] *adj* commercial

nonreturnable [ˌnɑnrɪˋtʌrnəbəl] *adj* (*bottle*) perdu

nonscientific [nɑnˌsaɪ•ənˋtɪfɪk] *adj* antiscientifique

nonsectarian [ˌnɑnsəkˋtɛrɪ•ən] *adj* nonsectaire; qui ne fait partie d'aucune secte religieuse; (*education*) laïque

nonsense [ˋnɑnsɛns] *s* bêtise *f,* non-sens *m*

nonskid [ˋnɑnˋskɪd] *adj* antidérapant

nonstop [ˋnɑnˋstɑp] *adj & adv* sans arrêt, continu; (*without landing*) sans escale

nonsupport [ˌnɑnsəˋport] *s* faute *f* d'entretien familial

nonviolence [nɑnˋvaɪ•ələns] *s* nonviolence *f*

noodle [ˋnudəl] *s* nouille *f;* (*fool*) (slang) niais *m;* (*head*) (slang) tronche *f*

noo'dle soup' *s* potage *m* à vermicelle

nook [nʊk] *s* coin *m,* recoin *m*

noon [nun] *s* midi *m*

no' one' or **no'-one'** *pron indef* personne **§90B;** ne . . . personne **§90,** e.g., **I see no one there** je n'y vois personne; personne ne, nul ne **§90B,** e.g., **no one knows it** personne ne le sait, nul ne le sait; **no one else** personne d'autre

noon'time' *s* midi *m*

noose [nus] *s* nœud *m* coulant; (*for hanging*) corde *f,* hart *f*

nor [nɔr] *conj* ni

Nordic [ˋnɔrdɪk] *adj & s* nordique *n*

norm [nɔrm] *s* norme *f*

normal [ˋnɔrməl] *adj* normal

Norman [ˋnɔrmən] *adj* normand ‖ *s* (*dialect*) normand *m;* (*person*) Normand *m*

Normandy [ˋnɔrməndi] *s* Normandie *f;* la Normandie

Norse [nɔrs] *adj & s* norrois *m*

Norse'man *s* (*pl* **-men**) Norrois *m*

north [nɔrθ] *adj & s* nord *m* ‖ *adv* au nord, vers le nord

North' Af'rican *adj* nord-africain ‖ *s* Nord-Africain *m*

North' Amer'ica *s* l'Amérique du Nord

North' Amer'ican *adj* nord-américain, d'Amérique du Nord ‖ *s* Nord-Américain *m,* Nord-Américaine *f*

north'east' *adj & s* nord-est *m*

north'east'er *s* vent *m* du nord-est

northern [ˋnɔrðərn] *adj* septentrional, du nord

North' Kore'a *s* Corée *f* du Nord; la Corée du Nord

North' Kore'an *adj* nord-coréen ‖ *s* (*person*) Nord-Coréen *m*

North' Pole' *s* pôle *m* Nord

northward [ˋnɔrθwərd] *adv* vers le nord

north'west' *adj & s* nord-ouest *m*

north' wind' *s* bise *f*

Norway [ˋnɔrwe] *s* Norvège *f;* la Norvège

Norwegian [nɔrˋwidʒən] *adj* norvégien ‖ *s* (*language*) norvégien *m;* (*person*) Norvégien *m*

nose [noz] *s* nez *m;* (*of certain animals*) museau *m;* **to blow one's nose** se moucher; **to have a nose for** avoir le flair de; **to keep one's nose to the grindstone** travailler sans relâche, buriner; **to lead by the nose** mener par le bout du nez; **to look down one's nose at** faire un nez à; **to talk through one's nose** parler du nez; **to thumb one's nose at** faire un pied de nez à; **to turn up one's nose at** faire la nique à; **under the nose of** à la barbe de ‖ *tr* flairer, sentir; **to nose out** flairer, dépister ‖ *intr*—**to nose about** fouiner; **to nose over** capoter

nose'bag' *s* musette *f*

nose'bleed' *s* saignement *m* de nez

nose' cone' *s* ogive *f*

nose' dive' *s* piqué *m*

nose'-dive' *intr* descendre en piqué

nose' drops' *spl* instillations *fpl* nasales

nose'gay' *s* bouquet *m*

nose' glass'es *spl* pince-nez *m,* binocle *m*

no'-show' *s* (aer) passager *m* manquant

no'-smok'ing *adj* (*section; room*) pour les non-fumeurs ‖ *s* défense *f* de fumer

nostalgia [nɑˋstældʒə] *s* nostalgie *f*

nostalgic [nɑˋstældʒɪk] *adj* nostalgique

nostril [ˋnɑstrɪl] *s* narine *f;* (*of horse, cow, etc.*) naseau *m*

nostrum [ˋnɑstrəm] *s* (*quack and his medicine*) orviétan *m;* panacée *f*

nos·y [ˋnozi] *adj* (*comp* **-ier;** *super* **-iest**) fureteur, indiscret

not [nɑt] *adv* ne **§87, §90C;** ne . . . pas **§90,** e.g., **he is not here** il n'est pas ici; non, non pas; **not at all** pas du tout; **not much** peu de chose; **not one** pas un; **not that** non pas que; **not yet** pas encore; **to think not** croire que non

notable [`notəbəl] *adj* & *s* notable *m*

notarize [`notə‚raɪz] *tr* authentiquer

notarized *adj* authentique

nota‧ry [`notəri] *s* (*pl* **-ries**) notaire *m*

notation [no`teʃən] *s* notation *f*

notch [nɑtʃ] *s* coche *f*, entaille *f*; (*of a belt*) cran *m*; (*of a wheel*) dent *f*; (*gap in a mountain*) brèche *f* ‖ *tr* encocher, entailler

note [not] *s* note *f*; (*short letter*) billet *m*; **notes** commentaires *mpl*; (*of a speech*) feuillets *mpl*; **note to the reader** avis *m* au lecteur; **to hit a wrong note** faire un canard ‖ *tr* noter; **to note down** prendre note de

note′book′ *s* cahier *m*; (*bill book, memo pad, etc.*) carnet *m*, calepin *m*

note′book cov′er *s* protège-cahier *m*

noted [`notɪd] *adj* éminent, distingué, connu

note′ pad′ *s* bloc-notes *m*

note′wor′thy *s* notable, remarquable

nothing [`nʌθɪŋ] *s* rien *m*; **nothing of importance** rien à signaler; **to count for nothing** compter pour du beurre ‖ *pron indef* rien §90B; ne . . . rien §90, e.g., **I have nothing** je n'ai rien; **nothing at all** rien du tout; **nothing doing!** (slang) pas mèche! ‖ *adv*—**nothing less than** rien moins que

nothingness [`nʌθɪŋnɪs] *s* néant *m*

notice [`notɪs] *s* (*warning; advertisement*) avis *m*; (*in a newspaper*) annonce *f*; (*observation*) attention *f*; (*of dismissal*) congé *m*; **at short notice** à bref délai; **to take notice of** faire attention à; **until further notice** jusqu'à nouvel ordre ‖ *tr* s'apercevoir de, remarquer

noticeable [`notɪsəbəl] *adj* apparent, perceptible

notification [‚notɪfɪ`keʃən] *s* notification *f*, avertissement *m*

noti‧fy [`notɪ‚faɪ] *v* (*pret* & *pp* **-fied**) *tr* aviser, avertir

notion [`noʃən] *s* notion *f*; intention *f*; **notions** mercerie *f*; **to have a notion to** avoir dans l'idée, avoir envie de

notorie‧ty [‚notə`raɪɪti] *s* (*pl* **-ties**) renom *m* déshonorant, triste notoriété *f*

notorious [no`toriəs] *adj* insigne, mal famé; (*person*) d'une triste notoriété

no′-trump′ *adj* & *s* sans-atout *m*

notwithstanding [‚nɑtwɪθ`stændɪŋ] *adv* nonobstant, néanmoins ‖ *prep* malgré ‖ *conj* quoique

nought [nɔt] *s* var of **naught**

noun [naʊn] *s* nom *m*

nourish [`nʌrɪʃ] *tr* nourrir

nourishment [`nʌrɪʃmənt] *s* nourriture *f*, alimentation *f*

Nova Scotia [`novə`skoʃə] *s* Nouvelle-Écosse *f*; la Nouvelle-Écosse

novel [`nɑvəl] *adj* nouveau; original, bizarre ‖ *s* roman *m*

novelette [‚nɑvəl`ɛt] *s* nouvelle *f*, bluette *f*

novelist [`nɑvəlɪst] *s* romancier *m*

novel‧ty [`nɑvəlti] *s* (*pl* **-ties**) nouveauté *f*; **novelties** bibelots, *mpl*, souvenirs *mpl*

November [no`vɛmbər] *s* novembre *m*

novice [`nɑvɪs] *s* novice *mf*

novitiate [no`vɪʃiɪt] *s* noviciat *m*

novocaine [`novə‚ken] *s* novocaïne *f*

NOW *abbr* **National Organization for Women**

now [naʊ] *adv* maintenant; **just now** tout à l'heure, naguère; **now and again** de temps en temps ‖ *interj* allez-y!

nowadays [`naʊ‧ə‚dez] *adv* de nos jours

no′ way′ or **no′ ways′** *adv* en aucune façon

no′where′ *adv* nulle part; ne . . . nulle part; **nowhere else** nulle autre part, nulle part ailleurs

noxious [`nɑkʃəs] *adj* nocif

nozzle [`nɑzəl] *s* (*of hose*) ajutage *m*; (*of fire hose*) lance *f*; (*of sprinkling can*) pomme *f*; (*of candlestick*) douille *f*; (*of pitcher; of gas burner*) bec *m*; (*of carburetor*) buse *f*; (*of vacuum cleaner*) suceur *m*; (*nose*) (slang) museau *m*

nth [ɛnθ] *adj* énième, nième; **for the nth time** pour la énième fois; **the nth power** la énième puissance

nuance [nju`ɑns], [`nju‧ɑns] *s* nuance *f*

nub [nʌb] *s* protubérance *f*; (*piece*) petit morceau *m*; (slang) nœud *m*

Nubia [`nubjə] *s* Nubie *f*

Nubian [`nubjən] *adj* & *s* nubien *m*, nubienne *f*

nuclear [`n(j)uklɪ‧ər] *adj* nucléaire

nu′clear ac′cident *s* accident *m* nucléaire

nu′clear en′ergy *s* énergie *f* nucléaire

nu′clear fis′sion *s* fission *f* nucléaire

nu′clear fu′sion *s* fusion *f* nucléaire

nu′clear phys′ics *s* physique *f* nucléaire

nu′clear pow′er′ *s* énergie *f* nucléaire

nu′clear pow′er plant′ *s* centrale *f* nucléaire

nu′clear reac′tor *s* réacteur *m* nucléire

nu′clear re′search lab′oratory *m* laboratoire *m* nucléaire

nu′clear test′ *s* test *m* nucléaire, essai *m* nucléaire

nu′clear test′ ban′ *s* interdiction *f* des essais nucléaires

nucleolus [n(j)u`kli‧ələs] *s* nucléole *m*

nucleon [`n(j)ukli‧ɑn] *s* nucléon *m*

nucle‧us [`n(j)ukli‧əs] *s* (*pl* **-i** [‚aɪ] or **-uses**) noyau *m*

nude [n(j)ud] *adj* nu ‖ *s* nu *m*; **in the nude** nu, sans vêtements

nudge [nʌdʒ] *s* coup *m* de coude ‖ *tr* pousser du coude

nudist [`n(j)udɪst] *adj* & *s* nudiste *mf*

nudity [`n(j)udɪti] *s* nudité *f*

nugget [`nʌgɪt] *s* pépite *f*

nuisance [`n(j)usəns] *s* ennui *m*; (*person*) peste *f*

nuke [njuk] *ou* [nuk] *s* (coll) arme *f* nucléaire; (*power plant*) centrale *f* nucléaire ‖ *tr* (coll) bombarder avec des armes nucléaires

null [nʌl] *adj indef* nul

null′ and void′ *adj* nul et non avenu

nulli‧fy [`nʌlɪ‚faɪ] *v* (*pret* & *pp* **-fied**) *tr* annuler

numb [nʌm] *adj* engourdi; **to grow numb** s'engourdir ‖ *tr* engourdir

number [ˈnʌmbər] *s* (*quantity*) nombre *m;* (*figure, numeral, digit*) chiffre *m;* (*house, page, registration, telephone, magazine*) numéro *m;* (*circus or vaudeville act*) numéro; (*car, manufactured goods, clothes*) modèle *m;* **even** (**odd, whole, cardinal, ordinal**) **number** nombre pair (impair, entier, cardinal, ordinal); **round number** chiffre rond; **wrong number** faux numéro ‖ *tr* numéroter; nombrer; (*to amount to*) s'élever à, compter; **to number among** compter parmi

numbering [ˈnʌmbərɪŋ] *s* numérotage *m,* numérotation

numberless [ˈnʌmbərlɪs] *adj* innombrable

numbness [ˈnʌmnɪs] *s* engourdissement *m*

numeracy [ˈnjumərəsi] *s* fait *m* de savoir les mathématiques

numeral [ˈn(j)umərəl] *adj* numéral ‖ *s* numéro *m,* chiffre *m;* **Arabic numeral** chiffre arabe; **Roman numeral** chiffre romain

numeration [ˌn(j)uməˈreʃən] *s* numération *f,* numérotage *m,* numérotation f

numerical [n(j)uˈmɛrɪkəl] *adj* numérique

numerous [ˈn(j)umərəs] *adj* nombreux

numismatic [ˌn(j)umɪzˈmætɪk] *adj* numismatique ‖ **numismatics** *s* numismatique *f*

numskull [ˈnʌmˌskʌl] *s* (coll) sot *m*

nun [nʌn] *s* religieuse *f,* nonne *f*

nunci•o [ˈnʌnʃɪˌo] *s* (*pl* **-os**) nonce *m*

nuptial [ˈnʌpʃəl] *adj* nuptial ‖ **nuptials** *spl* noces *fpl*

nurse [nʌrs] *s* (*female nurse*) infirmière *f;* (*male nurse*) infirmier *m;* (*wet nurse*) nourrice *f;* (*practical nurse*) garde-malade *mf;* (*children's nurse*) bonne *f* d'enfant, nurse *f* ‖ *tr* soigner; (*hopes; plants; a baby*) nourrir

nurse′maid′ *s* bonne *f* d'enfant

nurser•y [ˈnʌrsəri] *s* (*pl* **-ies**) chambre *f* des enfants; (*for day care*) crèche *f,* pouponnière *f;* (*hort*) pépinière *f*

nurs′ery•man *s* (*pl* **-men**) pépiniériste *m*

nurs′ery school′ *s* maternelle *f,* école *f* maternelle

nurs′e's aid′ *s* aide-soignante *f*

nursing [ˈnʌrsɪŋ] *s* (*care of invalids*) soins *mpl* infirmière; (*profession*) métier *m or* profession *f* d'infirmière; (*suckling*) allaitement *m;* (*mothering*) maternage *m*

nurs′ing bot′tle *s* biberon *m*

nurs′ing home′ *s* maison *f* de repos, maison de santé

nursling [ˈnʌrslɪŋ] *s* nourrisson *m*

nurture [ˈnʌrtʃər] *s* (*training*) éducation *f;* (*food*) nourriture *f* ‖ *tr* élever; (*to nurse*) nourrir

nut [nʌt] *s* noix *f,* e.g., **Brazil nut** noix du Brésil; (*of walnut tree*) noix; (*of filbert*) noisette *f;* (*to screw on a bolt*) écrou *m;* (slang) extravagant *m;* **to be nuts about** (slang) être follement épris de

nut′crack′er *s* casse-noisettes *m,* cassenoix *m;* (orn) casse-noix

nut′hatch′ *s* sittelle *f*

nut′meat′ *s* graine *f* de fruit sec, graine de noix

nutmeg [ˈnʌtˌmɛg] *s* (*seed or spice*) noix *f* muscade, muscade *f;* (*tree*) muscadier *m*

nutriment [ˈn(j)utrɪmənt] *s* nourriture *f*

nutrition [n(j)uˈtrɪʃən] *s* nutrition *f*

nutritious [n(j)uˈtrɪʃəs] *adj* nutritif

nuts [nʌts] *adj* (coll) dingue, cinglé, toqué; **to be nuts about** être emballé par ‖ *interj* la barbe!, je m'en fiche!

nut′shell′ *s* coquille *f* de noix; **in a nutshell** en un mot

nut•ty [ˈnʌti] *adj* (*comp* **-tier;** *super* **-tiest**) à goût de noisette, à goût de noix; (slang) cinglé, dingue

nuzzle [ˈnʌzəl] *tr* fouiller du groin ‖ *intr* fouiller du groin; s'envelopper chaudement; **to nuzzle up to** se pelotonner contre

nylon [ˈnaɪlɑn] *s* nylon *m;* **nylons** bas *mpl* de nylon, bas nylon

nymph [nɪmf] *s* nymphe *f*

O

O, o [o] *s* XVᵉ lettre de l'alphabet

oaf [of] *s* lourdaud *m,* rustre *m*

oak [ok] *s* chêne *m*

oaken [ˈokən] *adj* de chêne, en chêne

oakum [ˈokəm] *s* étoupe *f*

oar [or], [ɔr] *s* rame *f,* aviron *m*

oar′lock′ *s* tolet *m*

oars′man′ *s* (*pl* **-men′**) rameur *m*

oa•sis [oˈesɪs] *s* (*pl* **-ses** [siz]) oasis *f*

oat [ot] *s* avoine *f;* **oats** (*edible grain*) avoine; **to feel one's oats** être imbu de sa personne; **to sow one's wild oats** (coll) jeter sa gourme

oath [oθ] *s* (*pl* **oaths** [oðz]) serment *m;* (*swearword*) juron *m;* **to administer an oath to** (law) faire prêter serment à; **to take an oath** prêter serment

oat′meal′ *s* farine *f* d'avoine; (*breakfast food*) flocons *mpl* d'avoine

obbligato [ˌɑblɪˈgɑto] *s* accompagnement *m* à volonté

obdurate [ˈɑbdjərɪt] *adj* obstiné, endurci

obedience [oˈbidɪəns] *s* obéissance *f*

obedient [oˈbidɪ•ənt] *adj* obéissant

obeisance [oˈbesəns] *s* hommage *m;* (*greeting*) révérance *f*

obelisk [ˈɑbəlɪsk] *s* obélisque *m*

obese [o'bis] *adj* obèse
obesity [o'bisɪti] *s* obésité *f*
obey [ə'be] *tr* obéir à; **to be obeyed** être obéi ‖ *intr* obéir
obfuscate ['abfəs,ket] *tr* offusquer
obituar·y [o'bɪtʃu,ɛri] *adj* nécrologique ‖ *s* (*pl* **-ies**) nécrologie *f*
object ['abdʒɪkt] *s* objet *m* ‖ [ab'dʒɛkt] *tr* objecter, rétorquer ‖ *intr* faire des objections; **to object to** s'opposer à, avoir des objections contre
objection [ab'dʒɛk/ən] *s* objection *f*
objectionable [ab'dʒɛk/ənəbəl] *adj* répréhensible; répugnant, désagréable
objective [ab'dʒɛktɪv] *adj & s* objectif *m*
obligate ['ablɪ,get] *tr* obliger
obligation [,ablɪ'ge/ən] *s* obligation *f*
obligatory [ə'blɪgə,tori] *adj* obligatoire
oblige [ə'blaɪdʒ] *tr* obliger; **much obliged** bien obligé, très reconnaissant; **to be obliged to** être obligé de
obliging [ə'blaɪdʒɪŋ] *adj* accommodant, obligeant
oblique [ə'blik] *adj* oblique
obliterate [ə'blɪtə,ret] *tr* effacer, oblitérer
oblivion [ə'blɪvɪ·ən] *s* oubli *m*
oblivious [ə'blɪvɪ·əs] *adj* oublieux
oblong ['ablɔŋ] *adj* oblong
obnoxious [ab'nak/əs] *adj* odieux, désagréable
oboe ['obo] *s* hautbois *m*
oboist ['obo·ɪst] *s* hautboïste *mf*
obscene [ab'sin] *adj* obscène
obsceni·ty [ab'sɛnɪti] *s* (*pl* **-ties**) obscénité *f*
obscure [əb'skjʊr] *adj* obscur; (*vowel*) relâché, neutre
obscuri·ty [əb'skjʊrɪti] *s* (*pl* **-ties**) obscurité *f*
obsequies ['absɪkwiz] *spl* obsèques *fpl*
obsequious [əb'sikwɪ·əs] *adj* obséquieux
observance [əb'zʌrvəns] *s* observance *f*
observant [əb'zʌrvənt] *adj* observateur
observation [,abzər've/ən] *s* observation *f*
observato·ry [əb'zʌrvə,tori] *s* (*pl* **-ries**) observatoire *m*
observe [əb'zʌrv] *tr* observer; (*silence*) garder; (*a holiday*) célébrer; dire, remarquer
observer [əb'zʌrvər] *s* observateur *m*
obsess [əb'sɛs] *tr* obséder
obsession [əb'sɛ/ən] *s* obsession *f*
obsolescent [,absə'lɛsənt] *adj* vieillissant
obsolete ['absəlit] *adj* désuet, vieilli; (gram) obsolète
obstacle ['abstəkəl] *s* obstacle *m*
ob'stacle course' *s* champ *m* d'obstacles, piste *f* d'obstacles
obstetrical [ab'stɛtrɪkəl] *adj* obstétrique
obstetrics [ab'stɛtrɪks] *spl* obstétrique *f*
obstina·cy ['abstɪnəsi] *s* (*pl* **-cies**) obstination *f*, entêtement *m*
obstinate ['abstɪnɪt] *adj* obstiné
obstreperous [əb'strɛpərəs] *adj* turbulent
obstruct [əb'strʌkt] *tr* obstruer; (*movements*) empêcher, entraver
obstruction [əb'strʌk/ən] *s* obstruction *f*; (*on*

railroad tracks) obstacle *m*; (*to movement*) empêchement *m*, entrave *f*
obtain [əb'ten] *tr* obtenir, se procurer ‖ *intr* prévaloir
obtrusive [əb'trusɪv] *adj* importun, intrus
obtuse [əb't(j)us] *adj* obtus
obviate ['abvɪ,et] *tr* obvier à
obvious ['abvɪ·əs] *adj* évident; **that's obvious** ça s'impose
occasion [ə'keʒən] *s* occasion *f*; **on occasion** en de différentes occasions ‖ *tr* occasionner
occasional [ə'keʒənəl] *adj* fortuit, occasionnel; (*verses*) de circonstance; (*showers*) épars; (*chair*) volant
occasionally [ə'keʒənəli] *adv* de temps en temps, occasionnellement
occident ['aksɪdənt] *s* occident *m*
occidental [,aksə'dɛntəl] *adj & s* occidental *m*
occlusion [ə'kluʒən] *s* occlusion *f*
occlusive [ə'klusɪv] *adj* occlusif ‖ *s* occlusive *f*
occult [ə'kʌlt], ['akʌlt] *adj* occulte
occupancy ['akjəpənsi] *s* occupation *f*, habitation *f*
occupant ['akjəpənt] *s* occupant *m*
occupation [,akjə'pe/ən] *s* occupation *f*
occupational [,akjə'pe/ənəl] *adj* professionnel; de métier
oc'cupa'tional ther'apy *s* thérapie *f* rééducative, réadaptation *f* fonctionnelle
occu·py ['akjə,paɪ] *v* (*pret & pp* **-pied**) *tr* occuper; **to be occupied with** s'occuper de
oc·cur [ə'kʌr] *v* (*pret & pp* **-curred;** *ger* **-curring**) *intr* arriver, avoir lieu; (*to be found; to come to mind*) se présenter; **it occurs to me that** il me vient à l'esprit que
occurrence [ə'kʌrəns] *s* événement *m*; cas *m*, exemple *m*; **everyday occurrence** fait *m* journalier
ocean ['o/ən] *s* océan *m*
oceanic [,o/i'ænɪk] *adj* océanique
o'cean lin'er *s* paquebot *m* transocéanique
ocher ['okər] *s* ocre *f*
o'clock [ə'klak] *adv*—**it is one o'clock** il est une heure; **it is two o'clock** il est deux heures
octane ['akten] *s* octane *m*
oc'tane num'ber *s* indice *m* d'octane
octave ['aktɪv], ['aktev] *s* octave *f*
October [ak'tobər] *s* octobre *m*
octo·pus ['aktəpəs] *s* (*pl* **-puses** or **-pi** [,paɪ]) pieuvre *f*, poulpe *m*
octoroon ['aktə'run] *s* octavon *m*
ocular ['akjələr] *adj & s* oculaire *m*
oculist ['akjəlɪst] *s* oculiste *mf*
odd [ad] *adj* (*number*) impair; (*that doesn't match*) dépareillé, déparié; (*queer*) bizarre, étrange; (*occasional*) divers; quelque, e.g., **three hundred odd horses** quelque trois cents chevaux; et quelques ‖ **odds** *spl* chances *fpl;* (*disparity*) inégalité *f;* (*on a horse*) cote *f;* **at odds** en désaccord, en bisbille; **by all odds** sans aucun doute; **to be at odds with** être mal avec; **to give odds to** donner de l'avance à; **to set at odds** brouiller

odd′ball′ *s* (coll) excentrique *mf;* (*dissident*) opposant *m*

odd′ duck′ *s* (coll) excentrique *mf*

oddi•ty [`adɪti] *s* (*pl* **-ties**) bizarrerie *f*

odd′ jobs′ *spl* bricolage *m*, petits travaux *mpl*

odd′ man′ out′ *s*—**to be odd man out** être en trop

odds′ and ends′ *spl* petits bouts *mpl*, bribes *fpl;* (*trinkets*) bibelots *mpl;* (*food*) restes *mpl*

ode [od] *s* ode *f*

odious [`odɪ•əs] *adj* odieux

odor [`odər] *s* odeur *f;* **to be in bad odor** être mal vu

odorless [`odərlɪs] *adj* inodore

Odyssey [`adɪsi] *s* Odyssée *f*

Œdipus [`ɛdɪpəs], [`idəpəs] *s* Œdipe *m*

of [ʌv], [ʌv], [əv] *prep* de; à, e.g., **to think of** penser à; e.g., **to ask s.th. of s.o.** demander q.ch. à qn; en, e.g., **a doctor of medicine** un docteur en médecine; moins, e.g., **a quarter of two** deux heures moins le quart; entre, e.g., **he of all people** lui entre tous; d'entre, e.g., **five of them** cinq d'entre eux; par, e.g., **of necessity** par nécessité; (*made of*) en, de, e.g., **made of wood** en bois, de bois; (not translated), e.g., **the fifth of March** le cinq mars; e.g., **we often see her of a morning** nous la voyons souvent le matin

off [ɔf], [ɑf] *adj* mauvais, e.g., **off day** (*bad day*) mauvaise journée; libre, e.g., **off day** journée libre; de congé, e.g., **off day** jour de congé; (*account, sum*) inexact; (*meat*) avancé; (*electric current*) coupé; (*light*) éteint; (*radio; faucet*) fermé; (*street*) secondaire, transversal; (*distant*) éloigné, écarté ‖ *adv* loin; à . . . de distance, e.g., **three kilometers off** à trois kilomètres de distance; parti, e.g., **they're off!** les voilà partis!; bas, e.g., **hats off!** chapeaux bas!; (naut) au large; (theat) à la cantonade ‖ *prep* de; (*at a distance from*) éloigné de, écarté de; (naut) au large de, à hauteur de; **from off** de dessous; **off line** (comp) autonome

offal [`ɔfəl] *s* (*of butchered meat*) abats *mpl;* (*refuse*) ordures *fpl*

off′ and on′ *adv* de temps en temps, par intervalles

off′beat′ *adj* (slang) insolite, rare

off′ chance′ *s* chance *f* improbable

off′-col′or *adj* décoloré; (*e.g., story*) grivois, vert

offend [ə`fɛnd] *tr* offenser; **to be offended** s'offenser ‖ *intr*—**to offend against** enfreindre

offender [ə`fɛndər] *s* offenseur *m;* (*criminal*) délinquant *m*, coupable *mf*

offense [ə`fɛns] *s* offense *f;* (law) délit *m;* **to take offense (at)** s'offenser (de)

offensive [ə`fɛnsɪv] *adj* offensant, blessant; (mil) offensif ‖ *s* offensive *f*

offer [`ɔfər] *s* offre *f* ‖ *tr* offrir; (*excuses; best wishes*) présenter; (*prayers*) adresser ‖ *intr*—**to offer to** faire l'offre de; faire mine

de, e.g., **he offered to fight** il a fait mine de se battre

offering [`ɔfərɪŋ] *s* offre *f;* (eccl) offrande *f*

off′hand′ *adj* improvisé; brusque ‖ *adv* au pied levé; brusquement

office [`ɔfɪs] *s* (*function*) charge *f*, fonction *f*, office *m;* (*in business, school, government*) bureau *m;* (*national agency*) office *m;* (*of lawyer*) étude *f;* (*of doctor*) cabinet *m;* **elective office** poste *m* électif; **good offices** bons offices; **to run for office** se présenter aux élections

of′fice boy′ *s* coursier *m*, commissionaire *m* de bureau

of′fice desk′ *s* bureau *m* ministre

of′fice•hold′er *s* fonctionnaire *mf*

of′fice hours′ *spl* heures *fpl* de bureau; (*of doctor, counselor, etc.*) heures de consultation

officer [`ɔfɪsər] *s* (*of a company*) administrateur *m*, dirigeant *m;* (*of army, an order, a society, etc.*) officier *m;* (*police officer*) agent *m* de police, officier de police; **officer of the day** (mil) officier de service

of′ficer can′didate *s* élève-officier *m*

of′fice seek′er *s* solliciteur *m*

of′fice supplies′ *spl* fournitures *fpl* de bureau, articles *mpl* de bureau

of′fice-supply′ store′ *s* papeterie *f*

of′fice work′ *s* travail *m* de bureau

official [ə`fɪʃəl] *adj* officiel; (*e.g., stationery*) réglementaire ‖ *s* fonctionnaire *mf*, officiel *m;* **officials** cadres *mpl;* (*executives*) dirigeants *mpl*

offi′cial board′ *s* comité *m* directeur

offi′cial chan′nels *spl* filière *f* administrative

officialese [ə‚fɪʃə`liz] *s* jargon *m* administratif

officiate [ə`fɪʃɪ‚et] *intr* (eccl) officier; **to officiate as** exercer les fonctions de

officious [ə`fɪʃəs] *adj* trop empressé; **to be officious** faire l'officieux

offing [`ɔfɪŋ] *s*—**in the offing** au large; (fig) en perspective

off′key′ *adj & adv* faux; **to sing off-key** chanter faux

off′-lim′its *adj* défendu; (public sign) défense d'entrer, entrée interdite; (mil) interdit aux troupes

off′line′ *adj* (*printer; storage*) (comp) automatique

off′-peak heat′er *s* thermosiphon *m* à accumulation

off′peak hours′ *spl* heures *fpl* creuses

off′print′ *s* tiré *m* à part

off′-seas′on *s adj* hors-saison ‖ *s* mortesaison *f;* **in the off season** à la mortesaison

off′set′ *s* compensation *f;* (typ) offset *m* ‖ **off′set′** *v* (*pret & pp* **-set;** *ger* **-setting**) *tr* compenser

off′shoot′ *s* rejeton *m*

off′shore′ *adj* éloigné de la côte, du côté de la terre; (*wind*) de terre ‖ *adv* au large, vers la haute mer

off′side′ *adv* (sports) hors jeu

off′spring′ *s* descendance *f;* (*descendant*) rejeton *m,* enfant *mf;* (*result*) conséquence *f*

off′stage′ *adj* dans les coulisses ‖ *adv* à la cantonade

off′-the-cuff′ *adj* (coll) impromptu

off′-the-rec′ord *adj* confidentiel

off′-white′ *adj* blanc cassé

often [′ɔfən], [′ɑfən] *adv* souvent; **how often?** combien de fois?; tous les combien?; **not often** rarement; **once too often** une fois de trop

ogive [′odʒaɪv], [o′dʒaɪv] *s* ogive *f*

ogle [′ogəl] *tr* lancer une œillade à; (*to stare at*) dévisager

ogre [′ogər] *s* ogre *m*

ohm [om] *s* ohm *m*

oil [ɔɪl] *s* huile *f;* (*painting*) huile, peinture *f* à l'huile; **holy oil** huile sainte, saintes huiles; **to pour oil on troubled waters** calmer la tempête, verser de l'huile sur les plaies de qn; **to smell of midnight oil** sentir l'huile; **to strike oil** atteindre une nappe pétrolifère; (fig) trouver le filon ‖ *tr* huiler; (*to bribe*) graisser la patte à ‖ *intr* (naut) faire le plein de mazout

oil′-and-vin′egar cru′et *s* huilier *m*

oil′ burn′er *s* réchaud *m* à pétrole

oil′can′ *s* bidon *m* d'huile, burette *f* d'huile

oil′cloth′ *s* toile *f* cirée

oil′com′pany *s* société *f* pétrolière

oil′cup′ *s* (mach) godet *m* graisseur

oil′ drum′ *s* bidon *m* d'huile

oil′ field′ *s* gisement *m* pétrolifère

oil′ gauge′ *s* jauge *f* de niveau d'huile

oil′ lamp′ *s* lampe *f* à huile, lampe à pétrole

oil′man′ *s* (*pl* **-men′**) (*retailer*) huilier *m;* (*operator*) pétrolier *m*

oil′ pipe′line *s* oléoduc *m*

oil′ pump′ *s* pompe *f* à huile

oil′ rig′ *s* derrick *m,* tour *f* de forage; (*in water*) plate-forme *f* pétrolière

oil′ short′age *s* pénurie *f* de pétrole

oil′ stove′ *s* poêle *m* à mazout, fourneau *m* à pétrole

oil′ tank′er *s* pétrolier *m,* tanker *m*

oil′ well′ *s* puits *m* à pétrole

oil·y [′ɔɪli] *adj* (*comp* **-ier;** *super* **-iest**) huileux, oléagineux; (fig) onctueux

ointment [′ɔɪntmənt] *s* onguent *m,* pommade *f*

O.K. [′o′ke] (letterword) *adj* (coll) très bien, parfait ‖ *s* (coll) approbation *f* ‖ *adv* (coll) très bien ‖ *v* (*pret & pp* **O.K.'d;** *ger* **O.K.'ing**) *tr* (coll) approuver ‖ *interj* **O.K.!** ça colle!, d'accord!

okra [′okrə] *s* gombo *m,* ketmie *f* comestible

old [old] *adj* vieux; (*of former times*) ancien; (*wine*) vieux; **any old** n'importe, e.g., **any old time** n'importe quand; quelconque, e.g., **any old book** un livre quelconque; **at . . . years old** à l'âge de . . . ans; **how old is . . . ?** quel âge a . . . ?; **of old** d'autrefois, de jadis; **to be . . . years old** avoir . . . ans

old′ age′ *s* vieillesse *f,* âge *m* avancé

old′-clothes′man′ *s* (*pl* **-men′**) fripier *m*

old′ coun′try *s* mère patrie *f*

Old′ Cov′enant *s* (Bib) ancienne alliance *f*

old′-fash′ioned *adj* démodé, suranné, vieux jeu; (*literary style*) vieillot

old′ fo′gey or **old′ fo′gy** [′fogi] *s* (*pl* **-gies**) vieux bonhomme *m,* grime *m*

Old′ French′ *s* ancien français, *m*

Old′ Glo′ry *s* le drapeau des Etats-Unis

old′ hag′ *s* vieille fée *f*

old′ hand′ *s* vieux routier *m*

old′ lad′y *s* vieille dame *f;* (coll) grandmère *f*

old′ maid′ *s* vieille fille *f*

old′ mas′ter *s* grand maître *m;* œuvre *f* d'un grand maître

old′ moon′ *s* lune *f* à son décours

old′ peo′ple's home′ *s* hospice *m* de vieillards

old′ salt′ *s* loup *m* de mer

old′ school′ *s* vieille école *f,* vieille roche *f*

oldster [′oldstər] *s* vieillard *m,* vieux *m*

Old′ Tes′tament *s* Ancien Testament *m*

old′-time′ *adj* du temps jadis, d'autrefois

old′-tim′er *s* (coll) vieux *m* de la vieille, vieux routier *m*

old′ wives′′ tale′ *s* conte *m* de bonne femme

Old Wom′an who lived′ in a shoe′ *s* mère *f* Gigogne

Old′ World′ *s* vieux monde *m*

old′-world′ *adj* de l'ancien monde; du vieux monde

oleander [,olɪ′ændər] *s* laurier-rose *m*

olfactory [ɑl′fæktori] *adj* olfactif

oligar·chy [′ɑlɪ,gɑrki] *s* (*pl* **-chies**) oligarchie *f*

olive [′ɑlɪv] *adj* olive; (*complexion*) olivâtre ‖ *s* olive *f;* (*tree*) olivier *m*

ol′ive branch′ *s* rameau *m* d'olivier

ol′ive grove′ *s* olivaie *f*

ol′ive oil′ *s* huile *f* d'olive

Oliver [′ɑlɪvər] *s* Olivier *m*

ol′ive tree′ *s* olivier *m*

olympiad [o′lɪmpɪ,æd] *s* olympiade *f*

Olympian [o′lɪmpɪ·ən] *adj* olympien

Olympic [o′lɪmpɪk] *adj* olympique ‖ **Olympics** *spl* jeux *mpl* olympiques

ombudsman [′ɑmbʌdz,mæn] *s* intercesseur *m,* médiateur *m*

omelet [′ɑmlɪt] *s* omelette *f*

omen [′omən] *s* augure *m,* présage *m*

ominous [′ɑmɪnəs] *adj* de mauvais augure

omission [o′mɪʃən] *s* omission *f*

omit [o′mɪt] *v* (*pret & pp* **omitted;** *ger* **omitting**) *tr* omettre

omnibus [′ɑmnɪbəs] *adj & s* omnibus *m*

omnipotent [ɑm′nɪpətənt] *adj* omnipotent

omniscient [ɑm′nɪʃənt] *adj* omniscient

omnivorous [ɑm′nɪvərəs] *adj* omnivore

on [ɑn], [ɔn] *adj* (*light, radio*) allumé; (*faucet*) ouvert; (*machine, motor*) en marche; (*electrical appliance*) branché; (*brake*) serré; (*steak, chops, etc.*) dans la poêle; (*game, program, etc.*) commencé ‖ *adv*—**and so on** et ainsi de suite; **come on!** (coll) allons donc!; **farther on** plus loin; **from this day on** à dater de ce jour; **later on** plus tard; **move on!** circulez!;

to be on (theat) être en scène; **to be on to s.o.** (coll) voir clair dans le jeu de qn; **to have on** être vêtu de, porter; **to . . . on** continuer à + *inf*, e.g., **to sing on** continuer à chanter; **well on** avancé, e.g., **well on in years** d'un âge avancé ‖ *prep* sur; (*at the time of*) lors de; à, e.g., **on foot** à pied; e.g., **on my arrival** à mon arrivée; e.g., **on page three** à la page trois; e.g., **on the first floor** au rez-de-chaussée; e.g., **on the right** à droite; en, e.g., **on a journey** en voyage; e.g., **on arriving** en arrivant; e.g., **on fire** en feu; e.g., **on sale** en vente; e.g., **on the** or **an average** en moyenne; e.g., **on the top of** en dessus de; dans, e.g., **on a farm** dans une ferme; e.g., **on the jury** dans le jury; e.g., **on the street** dans la rue; e.g., **on the train** dans le train; par, e.g., **he came on the train** il est venu par le train; e.g., **on a fine day** par un beau jour; de, e.g., **on good authority** de source certaine, de bonne part; e.g., **on the north** du côté du nord; e.g., **on the one hand . . . on the other hand** d'une part . . . d'autre part; e.g., **on this side** de ce côté-ci; e.g., **to have pity on** avoir pitié de; e.g., **to live on bread and water** vivre de pain et d'eau; sous, e.g., **on a charge of** sous l'inculpation de; e.g., **on pain of death** sous peine de mort; (not translated), e.g., **on Tuesday** mardi; e.g., **on Tuesdays** le mardi, tous les mardis; e.g., **on July fourteenth** le quatorze juillet; contre, e.g., **an attack on** une attaque contre; **it's on me** (*it's my turn to pay*) (coll) c'est ma tournée; **it's on the house** (coll) c'est la tournée du patron; **on examination** après examen; **on it y, e.g., there is the shelf; put the book on it** voilà l'étagère; mettez-y le livre; **on line** (comp) en ligne; **on or about** (*a certain date*) aux environs de; **on or after** (*a certain date*) à partir de; **on tap** en perce, à la pression; **on the spot** (*immediately*) sur-le-champ; (*there*) sur place; (slang) en danger imminent; **to be on the committee** faire partie du comité; **to march on a city** marcher sur une ville

on' and on' *adv* continuellement, sans fin
on'-board comput'er *s* ordinateur *m* à bord
once [wʌns] *s*—**this once** pour cette fois-ci ‖ *adv* une fois; (*formerly*) autrefois; **all at once** (*all together*) tous à la fois; (*suddenly*) tout à coup; **at once** tout de suite, sur-le-champ; (*at the same time*) à la fois, en même temps; **for once** pour une fois; **once and for all** une bonne fois, une fois pour toutes; **once in a while** de temps en temps; **once more** encore une fois; **once or twice** une ou deux fois; **once upon a time there was** il était une fois ‖ *conj* une fois que, dès que
once'-o'ver *s* (slang) examen *m* rapide; travail *m* hâtif; **to give the once-over to** (slang) jeter un coup d'œil à
one [wʌn] *adj & pron* un §77; un certain, e.g., **one Dupont** un certain Dupont; un seul, e.g., **with one voice** d'une seule voix; unique, e.g.,

one price prix unique; (not translated when preceded by an adjective), e.g., **the red pencil and the blue one** le crayon rouge et le bleu; **not one** pas un; **one and all** tous; **one and only** unique, e.g., **the one and only closet in the house** l'armoire unique de la maison; seul et unique, e.g., **my one and only umbrella** mon seul et unique parapluie; **one another** l'un l'autre; les uns les autres; **one by one** à un; **one on one** en tête-à-tête, discussion *f* en têtê-à-têtê; **that one** celui-là; **the one that** celui que, çelui qui; **this one** celui-ci; **to become one** s'unir, se marier ‖ *s un m;* **one o'clock** une heure ‖ *pron indef* or §87, **one cannot go there alone** on ne peut pas y aller seul; **one's** son, e.g., **one's son** son fils
one'-horse *adj* à un cheval; (coll) provincial, insignifiant
one'-horse town' *s* (coll) trou *m*
one'-man band' *s* homme-orchestre *m*
one'-man show' *s* spectacle *m* solo
onerous [ˈɑnərəs] *adj* onéreux
one·self' *pron* soi §85; soi-même §86; se §87, e.g., **to cut oneself** se couper; **to be oneself** se conduire sans affectation
one'-sid'ed *adj* à un côté, à une face; (*e.g., decision*) unilatéral; (*unfair*) partial, injuste
one'-track' *adj* à une voie; (coll) routinier
one'-way friend'ship *s* amitié *f* non partagé
one'-way street' *s* rue *f* à sens unique
one'-way tick'et *s* billet *m* d'aller, billet simple
onion [ˈʌnjən] *s* oignon *m;* **to know one's onions** (coll) connaître son affaire
on'ion·skin' *s* papier *m* pelure
on'line' *adj & adv* à Internet, à l'Internet, en ligne sur Internet; **to go online** se connecter à Internet
on'look'er *s* assistant *m,* spectateur *m*
only [ˈonli] *adj* seul, unique; (*child*) unique ‖ *adv* seulement; ne . . . que, e.g., **I have only two** je n'en ai que deux; réservé, e.g., **staff only** (public sign) réservé au personnel ‖ *conj* mais, si ce n'était que
on'ly child' *s* enfant *mf* unique
on'rush' *s* ruée *f*
on'set' *s* attaque *f;* **at the onset** de prime abord, au premier abord
onslaught [ˈɑn,slɔt] *s* assaut *m*
on'stage' *adj* en scène
on'-the-job' *adj* (*training*) en stage; (coll) alerte
onus [ˈonəs] *s* charge *f,* fardeau *m*
onward [ˈɑnwərd] or **onwards** [ˈɑnwərdz] *adv* en avant
onyx [ˈɑnɪks] *s* onyx *m*
ooze [uz] *s* suintement *m;* (*mud*) vase *f,* limon *m* ‖ *tr* filtrer ‖ *intr* suinter, filtrer; **to ooze out** s'écouler
opal [ˈopəl] *s* opale *f*
opaque [oˈpek] *adj* opaque; (*style*) obscur
OPEC [ˈopɛk] *s* (acronym) (**organization of petroleum-exporting countries**) OPEP (organisation des pays exportateurs de pétrole)

open [ˈopən] *adj* ouvert; (*personality*) franc, sincère; (*job, position*) vacant; (*hour*) libre; (*automobile*) découvert; (*market; trial*) public; (*question*) pendant, indécis; (*wound*) béant; (*to attack, to criticism, etc.*) exposé; (sports) international; **to break** or **crack open** éventrer; **to throw open the door** ouvrir la porte toute grande ‖ *s* ouverture *f;* (*in the woods*) clairière *f;* **in the open** au grand air, à ciel ouvert; (*in the open country*) en rase campagne; (*in the open sea*) en pleine mer; (*without being hidden*) découvert; (*openly*) ouvertement ‖ *tr* ouvrir; (*a canal lock*) lâcher; **to open fire** déclencher le feu ‖ *intr* ouvrir, s'ouvrir; (*said, e.g., of a play*) commencer, débuter; **to open into** aboutir à, déboucher sur; **to open on** donner sur; **to open up** s'épanouir, s'ouvrir

o'pen-air' *adj* en plein air, au grand air

o'pen ar'chitec'ture *s* (comp) architecture *f* ouverte

o'pen-eyed' *adj* les yeux écarquillés

o'pen-hand'ed *adj* libéral, la main ouverte

o'pen-heart'ed *adj* ouvert, franc

o'pen-heart' sur'gery *s* chirurgie *f* à cœur ouvert

o'pen house' *s* journée *f* d'accueil; **to keep open house** tenir table ouverte

opening [ˈopənɪŋ] *s* ouverture *f;* (*in the woods*) clairière *f*, percée *f;* (*vacancy*) vacance *f*, poste *m* vacant; (*chance to say something*) occasion *f* favorable

o'pening night' *s* première *f*

o'pening num'ber *s* ouverture *f*

o'pening price' *s* cours *m* de début

o'pen-mind'ed *adj* à l'esprit ouvert, sans parti pris

o'pen se'cret *s* secret *m* de Polichinelle

o'pen shop' *s* atelier *m* ouvert aux nonsyndiqués

o'pen tick'et *s* coupon *m* date libre

o'pen·work' *s* ouvrage *m* à jour, ajours *mpl*

opera [ˈapərə] *s* opéra *m*

op'era glass'es *spl* jumelles *fpl* de spectacle

op'era hat' *s* claque *m*, gibus *m*

op'era house' *s* opéra *m*

operate [ˈapəˌret] *tr* actionner, faire marcher; exploiter ‖ *intr* fonctionner; s'opérer; (surg) opérer; **to operate on** (surg) opérer

operatic [ˌapəˈrætɪk] *adj* d'opéra

opera'ting expen'ses *spl* (*overhead*) frais *mpl* généraux, frais d'exploitation

op'erating room' *s* salle *f* d'opération

opera'ting sys'tem *s* (comp) système *m* d'exploitation

op'erating ta'ble *s* table *f* d'opération, billard *m*

operation [ˌapəˈreʃən] *s* opération *f;* (*of a business, of a machine, etc.*) fonctionnement *m;* (med) intervention *f* chirurgicale, opération; **to have an operation (for)** se faire opérer (de); passer sur le billard (coll)

operative [ˈapərətɪv] *adj* opératif; (surg) opéra

toire ‖ *s* (*workman*) ouvrier *m;* (*spy*) agent *m*, espion *m*

operator [ˈapəˌretər] *s* opérateur *m;* (*e.g., of a mine*) propriétaire *m* exploitant; (*of an automobile*) conducteur *m;* (telp) téléphoniste *mf*, standardiste *mf;* (slang) chevalier *m* d'industrie, aigrefin *m;* **operator on duty** opérateur de permanence

operetta [ˌapəˈrɛtə] *s* opérette *f*

opiate [ˈopɪˌet] *adj* opiacé ‖ *s* médicament *m* opiacé; (coll) narcotique *m*

opinion [əˈpɪnjən] *s* opinion *f;* **in my opinion** à mon avis

opinionated [əˈpɪnjəˌnetɪd] *adj* fier de ses opinions, dogmatique

opin'ion poll' *s* sondage *m* d'opinion

opium [ˈopɪ•əm] *s* opium *m*

o'pium den' *s* fumerie *f*

o'pium pop'py *s* œillette *f*

opossum [əˈpasəm] *s* opossum *m*, sarique *f*

opponent [əˈponənt] *s* adversaire *mf*, opposant *m*

opportune [ˌapərˈt(j)un] *adj* opportun, convenable

opportunist [ˌapərˈt(j)unɪst] *s* opportuniste *mf*

opportuni·ty [ˌapərˈt(j)unɪti] *s* (*pl* **-ties**) (*appropriate time*) occasion *f;* (*favorable condition or good chance for advancement*) change *f;* **at your first** (or **earliest**) **opportunity** à votre première occasion

oppose [əˈpoz] *tr* s'opposer à

opposite [ˈapəsɪt] *adj* opposé, contraire; d'en face, e.g., **the house opposite** la maison d'en face ‖ *s* opposé *m*, inverse *m*, contraire *m* ‖ *adv* en face, vis-à-vis ‖ *prep* en face de, à l'opposite de

op'posite num'ber *s* (fig) homologue *mf*

opposition [ˌapəˈzɪ/ən] *s* opposition *f*

oppress [əˈprɛs] *tr* opprimer; (*to weigh heavily upon*) oppresser

oppression [əˈprɛ/ən] *s* oppression *f*

oppressive [əˈprɛsɪv] *adj* oppressif; (*stifling*) étouffant, accablant

oppressor [əˈprɛsər] *s* oppresseur *m*

opprobrious [əˈprobrɪ•əs] *adj* infamant, injurieux, honteux

opprobrium [əˈprobrɪ•əm] *s* opprobre *m*

optic [ˈaptɪk] *adj* optique ‖ **optics** *s* optique *f*

optical [ˈaptɪkəl] *adj* optique

op'tical illu'sion *s* illusion *f* d'optique

op'tical scan'ner *s* lecture *f* optique

optician [apˈtɪ/ən] *s* opticien *m*

optimism [ˈaptɪˌmɪzəm] *s* optimisme *m*

optimist [ˈaptɪmɪst] *s* optimiste *mf*

optimistic [ˌaptɪˈmɪstɪk] *adj* optimiste

optimize [ˈaptɪˌmaɪz] *tr* optimiser

option [ˈap/ən] *s* option *f*

optional [ˈap/ənəl] *adj* facultatif

optometrist [apˈtamɪtrɪst] *s* opticien *m;* optométriste *mf* (Canad)

opulent [ˈapjələnt] *adj* opulent

or [ɔr] *conj* ou

oracle [ˈɔrəkəl] *s* oracle *m*

oracular [oˈrækjələr] *adj* d'oracle; dogmatique, sentencieux; (*ambiguous*) équivoque

oral [ˈorəl] *adj* oral

orange [ˈorɪndʒ] *adj* orangé, orange ‖ *s* (*color*) orangé *m*, orange *m*; (*fruit*) orange *f*

orangeade [ˌorɪndʒˈed] *s* orangeade *f*

or'ange blos'som *s* fleur *f* d'oranger

or'ange grove' *s* orangeraie *f*

or'ange juice' *s* jus *m* d'orange

or'ange peel' *s* écorce *f* d'orange

or'ange squeez'er *s* presse-fruits *m*

or'ange tree' *s* oranger *m*

orangutan [əˈræŋəˌtæŋ] *s* orang-outan *m*

oration [oˈreʃən] *s* discours *m*

orator [ˈorətər] *s* orateur *m*

oratorical [ˌorəˈtorɪkəl] *adj* oratoire

oratori•o [ˌorəˈtorɪˌo] *s* (*pl* **-os**) oratorio *m*

orato•ry [ˈorəˌtori] *s* (*pl* **-ries**) art *m* oratoire; (*eccl*) oratoire *m*

orb [orb] *s* orbe *m*

orbit [ˈorbɪt] *s* orbite *f;* **in orbit** sur orbite ‖ *tr* (*e.g., the sun*) tourner autour de; (*e.g., a rocket*) mettre en orbite, satelliser ‖ *intr* se mettre en orbite

or'bital space' sta'tion *s* station *f* orbitale, station spatiale

orchard [ˈortʃərd] *s* verger *m*

orchestra [ˈorkɪstrə] *s* orchestre *m;* (*pit for musicians*) fosse *f* d'orchestre; (*for spectators*) fauteuils *mpl* d'orchestre

orchestrate [ˈorkɪˌstret] *tr* orchestrer

orchid [ˈorkɪd] *s* orchidée *f*

ordain [orˈden] *tr* destiner; (*eccl*) ordonner; **to be ordained** (*eccl*) recevoir les ordres

ordeal [orˈdi•əl] *s* épreuve *f;* (*hist*) ordalie *f*

order [ˈordər] *s* ordre *m;* (*of words*) ordonnance *f;* (*for merchandise, a meal, etc.*) commande *f;* (*military formation*) ordre; (*law*) arrêt *m,* arrêté *m;* **in order** en ordre; **in order of appearance** (*theat*) dans l'ordre d'entrée en scène; **in order that** pour que, afin que; **in order to** + *inf* pour + *inf,* afin de + *inf;* **on order** en commande, commandé; **order!** à l'ordre!; **orders** (*eccl*) les ordres; (*mil*) la consigne; **pay to the order of** (*com*) payez à l'ordre de; **to get s.th. out of order** détraquer q.ch.; **to put in order** mettre en règle ‖ *tr* ordonner; (*com*) commander; **to order around** faire aller et venir; **to order s.o. to** + *inf* ordonner à qn de + *inf*

or'der blank' *s* bon *m* de commande, bulletin *m* de commande

or'der form' *s* formulaire *m* de commande

order•ly [ˈordərli] *adj* ordonné; (*life*) réglé; **to be orderly** avoir de l'ordre ‖ *s* (*pl* **-lies**) (*med*) ambulancier *m,* infirmier *m;* (*mil*) planton *m*

ordinal [ˈordɪnəl] *adj & s* ordinal *m*

ordinance [ˈordɪnəns] *s* ordonnance *f*

ordinary [ˈordɪnˌɛri] *adj* ordinaire; **out of the ordinary** exceptionnel

ordination [ˌordɪnˈeʃən] *s* ordination *f*

ordnance [ˈordnəns] *s* artillerie *f;* (*branch of an army*) service *m* du matériel

ore [or] *s* minerai *m*

oregano [əˈrɛɡəˌno] *s* origan *m*

organ [ˈorɡən] *s* (anat, journ) organe *m;* (mus) orgue *m*

organdy [ˈorɡəndi] *s* organdi *m*

or'gan grind'er *s* joueur *m* d'orgue

organic [orˈɡænɪk] *adj* organique; (*food, agriculture*) biologique

organism [ˈorɡəˌnɪzəm] *s* organisme *m*

organist [ˈorɡənɪst] *s* organiste *mf*

organization [ˌorɡənɪˈzeʃən] *s* organisation *f*

organize [ˈorɡəˌnaɪz] *tr* organiser

organizer [ˈorɡəˌnaɪzər] *s* organisateur *m*

or'gan loft' *s* tribune *f* d'orgue

orgasm [ˈorɡæzəm] *s* orgasme *m*

or•gy [ˈordʒi] *s* (*pl* **-gies**) orgie *f*

orient [ˈori•ənt] *s* orient *m;* **Orient** Orient ‖ [ˈori,ɛnt] *tr* orienter

oriental [ˌoriˈɛntəl] *adj* oriental ‖ (*cap*) *s* Oriental *m*

orien'tal rug' *s* tapis *m* d'orient

orientate [ˈori•ɛn,tet] *tr* orienter

orientation [ˌori•ɛnˈteʃən] *s* orientation *f*

orifice [ˈorɪfɪs] *s* orifice *m*

origin [ˈorədʒɪn] *s* origine *f*

original [əˈrɪdʒɪnəl] *adj* (*new, not copied; inventive*) original; (*earliest*) originel, primitif; (*first*) originaire, premier ‖ *s* original *m*

originality [əˌrɪdʒɪˈnælɪti] *s* originalité *f*

originate [əˈrɪdʒəˌnet] *tr* faire naître, créer ‖ *intr* prendre naissance; **to originate from** provenir de

oriole [ˈori,ol] *s* loriot *m*

ormolu [ˈormə,lu] *s* bronze *m* doré; (*powdered gold for gilding*) or *m* moulu; (*alloy of zinc and copper*) similor *m*

ornament [ˈornəmənt] *s* ornement *m* ‖ [ˈornə,mɛnt] *tr* ornementer, orner

ornamental [ˌornəˈmɛntəl] *adj* ornemental

ornate [orˈnet], [ˈornet] *adj* orné, fleuri

ornery [ˈornəri] *adj* (coll) acariâtre, intraitable

ornithology [ˌornɪˈθalədʒi] *s* ornithologie *f*

orphan [ˈorfən] *adj & s* orphelin *m*

orphanage [ˈorfənɪdʒ] *s* (*asylum*) orphelinat *m;* (*orphanhood*) orphelinage *m*

Orpheus [ˈorfi•əs] *s* Orphée *m*

orthodontics [ˌorθəˈdantɪks] *s* orthodontie *f*

orthodox [ˈorθə,daks] *adj* orthodoxe

orthogra•phy [orˈθaɡrəfi] *s* (*pl* **-phies**) orthographe *f*

orthopedics [ˌorθəˈpidɪks] *s* orthopédie *f*

oscillate [ˈasɪ,let] *intr* osciller

osier [ˈoʒər] *s* osier *m*

osmosis [azˈmosɪs] *s* osmose *f*

osprey [ˈaspri] *s* aigle *m* pêcheur

ossi•fy [ˈasɪ,faɪ] *v* (*pret & pp* **-fied**) *tr* ossifier ‖ *intr* s'ossifier

ostensible [asˈtɛnsɪbəl] *adj* prétendu, apparent, soi-disant

ostentatious [ˌastɛnˈteʃəs] *adj* ostentatoire, fastueux

osteopathy [ˌastiˈapəθi] *s* ostéopathie *f*

ostracism [ˈastrə,sɪzəm] *s* ostracisme *m*

ostracize [ˈɑstrəˌsaɪz] *tr* frapper d'ostracisme

ostrich [ˈɑstrɪtʃ] *s* autruche *f*

other [ˈʌðər] *adj* autre; **every other day** tous les deux jours; **every other one** un sur deux ‖ *pron indef* autre ‖ *adv*—**other than** autrement que

otherwise [ˈʌðərˌwaɪz] *adv* autrement, à part cela ‖ *conj* sinon, e.g., **come at once, otherwise it will be too late** venez tout de suite, sinon il sera trop tard; sans cela, e.g., **thanks, otherwise I'd have forgotten** merci, sans cela j'aurais oublié

oth′er•world′ly *adj* détaché des contingences de ce monde

otter [ˈɑtər] *s* loutre *f*

Ottoman [ˈɑtəmən] *adj* ottoman ‖ (*l.c.*) *s* (*corded fabric*) ottoman *m;* (*divan*) ottomane *f;* (*footstool*) pouf *m;* **Ottoman** (*person*) Ottoman *m*

ouch [aʊtʃ] *interj* aïe!

ought [ɔt] *s* zéro *m;* **for ought I know** pour autant que je sache ‖ *aux* used to express obligation, e.g., **he ought to go away** il devrait s'en aller; e.g., **he ought to have gone away** il aurait dû s'en aller

ounce [aʊns] *s* once *f*

our [aʊr] *adj poss* notre §88

ours [aʊrz] *pron poss* le nôtre §89

our•selves′ *pron pers* nous-mêmes §86; nous §85, §87

oust [aʊst] *tr* évincer, chasser

out [aʊt] *adj* extérieur; absent; (*fire*) éteint; (*secret*) divulgué; (*tide*) bas; (*flower*) épanoui; (*rope*) filé; (*lease*) expiré; (*gear*) débrayé; (*unconscious person*) évanoui; (*boxer*) knockouté; (*book, magazine, etc.*) paru, publié; (*out of print, out of stock*) épuisé; (*a ball*) (sports) hors jeu; (*a player*) (sports) éliminé ‖ *s* (*pretext*) échappatoire *f;* (baseball) retrait *m;* **to be on the outs with** être brouillé avec ‖ *adv* dehors, au dehors; (*outdoors*) en plein air; **out and out** complètement; **out for** en quête de; **out for lunch** parti déjeuner; **out of** (*cash*) démuni de; (*a glass, cup, etc.*) dans; (*a bottle*) à; (*the window; curiosity, friendship, respect, etc.*) par; (*range, sight*) hors de; de, e.g., **to cry out of joy** pleurer de joie; e.g., **made out of** fait de; sur, e.g., **nine times out of ten** neuf fois sur dix; **out of gas** en panne sèche; **out of play** hors jeu; **out of sight, out of mind** loin des yeux, loin du cœur; **out with it!** allez, dites-le!; **to be out** (*to be absent*) être sorti; faire, e.g., **the sun is out** il fait du soleil; **to be out of bounds** (sports) être hors jeu ‖ *prep* par ‖ *interj* hors d'ici!, ouste!

out′ and away′ *adv* de beaucoup, de loin

out′-and-out′ *adj* vrai; (*fanatic*) intransigeant; (*liar*) achevé

out′-and-out′er *s* (coll) intransigeant *m*

out′bid′ *v* (*pret* -**bid**; *pp* -**bid** or -**bidden**; *ger* -**bidding**) *tr* enchérir sur; (fig) renchérir sur ‖ *intr* surenchérir

out′board mo′tor *s* moteur *m* hors-bord, motogodille *f*

out′break′ *s* déchaînement *m;* (*of hives; of anger; etc.*) éruption *f;* (*of epidemic*) manifestation *f;* (*insurrection*) révolte *f*

out′build′ing *s* annexe *f,* dépendance *f*

out′burst′ *s* explosion *f;* (*of anger*) accès *m;* (*of laughter; etc.*) éclat *m;* (*e.g., of generosity*) élan *m*

out′cast′ *adj & s* banni *m,* proscrit *m*

out′caste′ *adj* hors caste ‖ *s* hors-caste *mf*

out′come′ *s* résultat *m,* dénouement *m*

out′cry′ *s* (*pl* -**cries**) clameur *f;* (*of indignation*) levée *f* de boucliers, tollé *m*

out•dat′ed *adj* démodé, suranné

out′dis′tance *tr* dépasser; (sports) distancer

out′do′ *v* (*pret* -**did**; *pp* -**done**) *tr* surpasser, l'emporter sur; **to outdo oneself** se surpasser

out′door′ *adj* au grand air; (sports) de plein air

out′door grill′ *s* rôtisserie *f* en plein air

out′doors′ *s* rase campagne *f,* plein air *m* ‖ *adv* au grand air, en plein air; en plein air; (*outside of the house*) hors de la maison; (*at night*) à la belle étoile

out′door swim′ming pool′ *s* piscine *f* à ciel ouvert

outer [ˈaʊtər] *adj* extérieur, externe

out′er ear′ *s* oreille *f* externe

out′er space′ *s* cosmos *m,* espace *m* cosmique

out′field′ *s* (baseball) grand champ *m,* arrière-champ *m,* champ extérieur

out′fit′ *s* équipement *m,* attirail *m;* (*caseful of implements*) trousse *f,* nécessaire *m;* (*ensemble*) costume et accessoires *mpl;* (*of a bride*) trousseau *m;* (*team*) équipe *f;* (*group of soldiers*) unité *f;* (com) compagnie *f* ‖ *v* (*pret & pp* -**fitted**; *ger* -**fitting**) *tr* équiper

out′go′ing *adj* en partance, partant; (*office-holder*) sortant; (*friendly*) communicatif, sympathique

out′grow′ *v* (*pret* -**grew**; *pp* -**grown**) *tr* devenir plus grand que; (e.g., *childhood clothes, activities, etc.*) devenir trop grand pour; abandonner, se défaire de

out′growth′ *s* excroissance *f;* (fig) résultat *m,* conséquence *f*

out′house′ *s* (*privy*) cabane *f* rustique où logent des cabinets extérieurs

outing [ˈaʊtɪŋ] *s* excursion *f,* sortie *f*

outlandish [aʊtˈlændɪʃ] *adj* bizarre, baroque

out′last′ *tr* durer plus longtemps que; survivre (with *dat*)

out′law′ *s* hors-la-loi *m,* proscrit *m* ‖ *tr* mettre hors la loi, proscrire

out′lay′ *s* débours *mpl,* dépenses *fpl* ‖ **out′lay′** *v* (*pret & pp* -**laid**) *tr* débourser, dépenser

out′let′ *s* (*for water, etc.*) sortie *f,* issue *f;* (*escape valve*) déversoir *m;* (*for, e.g., pent-up emotions*) exutoire *m;* (*market for goods*) débouché *m;* (*discount house*) magasin entrepôt *m,* minimarge *f;* (elec) prise *f* de courant, prise électrique; **no outlet** (public sign) rue sans issue

out′line′ *s* (*profile*) contour *m;* (*sketch*) esquisse *f; (summary)* aperçu *m; (of a work in preparation)* plan *m; (main points)* grandes lignes *fpl* ‖ *tr* esquisser; *(a work in preparation)* ébaucher

out′live′ *tr* survivre (with *dat*)

out′lived′ *adj* caduc, désuet

out′look′ *s* perspective *f,* point *m* de vue

out′ly′ing *adj* éloigné, écarté, isolé

outmoded [ˌaʊtˈmodɪd] *adj* démodé

out′num′ber *tr* surpasser en nombre

out′ of bounds′ *adj* hors jeu

out′-of-date′ *adj* démodé, suranné; *(document)* périmé

out′-of-door′ *adj* au grand air

out′-of-doors′ *adj* au grand air ‖ *s* rase campagne *f,* plein air *m* ‖ *adv* au grand air, hors de la maison

out′ of or′der *adj* en panne, en dérangement; **to be out of order** *(to be out of sequence)* ne pas être dans l'ordre

out′ of print′ *adj* épuisé

out′ of step′ *s*—**to be out of step** ne pas être au pas; **to be out of step with** marcher à contre-pas de; **to get out of step** perdre le pas

out′ of tune′ *adj* désaccordé ‖ *adv* faux, e.g., **to sing out of tune** chanter faux

out′ of work′ *adj* en chômage

out′ pa′tient *s* malade *mf* de consultation externe

out′patient clin′ic *s* consultation *f* externe

out′post′ *s* avant-poste *m,* antenne *f*

out′put′ *s* rendement *m,* débit *m; (of a mine; of a worker)* production *f*

out′rage *s* outrage *m; (wanton violence)* atrocité *f,* attentat *m* honteux ‖ *tr* faire outrage à, outrager; *(a woman)* violer

outrageous [aʊtˈredʒəs] *adj* outrageux; *(intolerable)* insupportable

out′rank′ *tr* dépasser en grade, dépasser en rang

out′rid′er *s* explorateur *m;* cow-boy *m; (mounted attendant)* piqueur *m*

outrigger [ˈaʊtˌrɪgər] *s (outboard framework)* balancier *m; (oar support)* porte-en-dehors *m*

out′right′ *adj* pur, absolu; *(e.g., manner)* franc, direct ‖ **out′right′** *adv* complètement; *(frankly)* franchement; *(at once)* sur le coup

out′set′ *s* début *m,* commencement *m*

out′side′ *adj* du dehors, d'extérieur ‖ **out′side′** *s* dehors *m,* extérieur *m;* surface *f;* **at the outside** tout au plus, au maximum ‖ **out′side′** *adv* dehors, à l'extérieur; *(outdoors)* en plein air; **outside of** en dehors de, à l'extérieur de; *(except for)* sauf ‖ **out′side′** or **out′side′** *prep* en dehors de, à l'extérieur de

outsider [ˌaʊtˈsaɪdər] *s* étranger *m; (intruder)* intrus *m; (uninitiated)* profane *mf; (dark horse)* outsider *m*

out′size′ *adj* hors série

out′skirts′ *spl* approches *fpl,* périphérie *f*

out′spo′ken *adj* franc; **to be outspoken** avoir son franc-parler

out′stand′ing *adj* saillant; *(eminent)* hors pair, hors ligne; *(debts)* à recouvrer, impayé

outward [ˈaʊtwərd] *adj* extérieur; *(apparent)* superficiel; *(direction)* en dehors ‖ *adv* au dehors, vers le dehors

out′weigh′ *tr* peser plus que; *(in value)* l'emporter en valeur sur

out′wit′ *v (pret & pp* **-witted;** *ger* **-witting)** *tr* duper, déjouer; *(a pursuer)* dépister

oval [ˈovəl] *adj & s* ovale *m*

ova·ry [ˈovəri] *s (pl* **-ries)** ovaire *m*

ovation [oˈveʃən] *s* ovation *f*

oven [ˈʌvən] *s* four *m; (fig)* fournaise *f*

over [ˈovər] *adj* fini, passé; *(additional)* en plus; *(excessive)* en excès; plus, e.g., **eight and over** huit et plus ‖ *adv* au-dessus, dessus; *(on the other side)* de l'autre côté; *(again)* de nouveau; *(on the reverse side of sheet of paper)* au verso; *(finished)* passé, achevé; **all over** *(everywhere)* partout; *(finished)* fini; *(completely)* jusqu'au bout des ongles; **I'll be right over** (coll) j'arrive tout de suite; **over!** *(turn the page!)* voir au verso!, tournez!; (rad) à vous!; **over again** de nouveau, encore une fois; **over against** en face de; *(compared to)* auprès de; **over and above** en plus de; **over and out!** (rad) terminé!; **over and over** à coups répétés, à plusieurs reprises; **over here** ici, de ce côté; **over there** là-bas; **to be over** *(an illness)* s'être remis de; **to hand over** remettre ‖ *prep* au-dessus de; *(on top of)* sur, par-dessus; *(with motion)* pardessus, e.g., **to jump over a fence** sauter par-dessus une barrière; *(a period of time)* pendant, au cours de; *(near)* près de; *(a certain number or amount)* plus de, audessus de; *(concerning)* à propos de, au sujet de; *(on the other side of)* au delà de, de l'autre côté de; à, e.g., **over the telephone** au téléphone; *(while doing s.th.)* tout en prenant, e.g., **over a cup of coffee** tout en prenant une tasse de café; **all over** répandu sur; **over and above** en sus de, en plus de; **to fall over** *(e.g., a cliff)* tomber du haut de; **to reign over** régner sur ‖ *interj (CB language)* terminé!

o′ver·all′ *adj* hors tout, complet; général, total ‖ **overalls** *spl* combinaison *f* d'homme, cotte *f,* salopette *f*

o′ver·awe′ *tr* impressionner, intimider

o′ver·bear′ing *adj* impérieux, tranchant, autoritaire

o′ver·board′ *adv* par-dessus bord; **man overboard!** un homme à la mer!; **to throw overboard** jeter par-dessus le bord; (fig) abandonner

o′ver·book′ing *s* surréservation *f*

o′ver·cast′ *adj* obscurci, nuageux ‖ *s* ciel *m* couvert ‖ *v (pret & pp* **-cast)** *tr* obscurcir, couvrir

o′ver·charge′ *s* prix *m* excessif, majoration *f* excessive; (elec) surcharge *f* ‖ **o′ver·charge′** *tr (a customer)* rançonner; (elec) surcharger; **to overcharge s.o. for s.th.** faire payer trop cher q.ch. à qn ‖ *intr* demander un prix excessif

o′ver·coat′ *s* pardessus *m*

o'ver•come' v (pret -came; pp -come) tr vaincre; (difficulties) surmonter

o'ver•con'fidence s témérité f, confiance f exagérée

o'ver•con'fident adj téméraire, excessivement confiant

o'ver•cooked' adj trop cuit

o'ver•crowd' tr bonder; (a town, region, etc.) surpeupler

o'ver•do' v (pret -did; pp -done) tr exagérer; overdone (culin) trop cuit || intr se surmener

o'ver•dose' s dose f excessive, surdosage m

o'ver•draft' s découvert m, solde m débiteur

o'ver•draw' v (pret -drew; pp -drawn) tr tirer à découvert || intr excéder son crédit

o'ver•drive' s (aut) surmultiplication f

o'ver•due' adj en retard; (com) échu, arriéré

o'ver•eat' v (pret -ate; pp -eaten) tr & intr trop manger

o'ver•exer'tion s surmenage m

o'ver ex'ploita'tion s (of resources) exploitation f abusive

o'ver•expose' tr surexposer

o'ver•expo'sure s surexposition f

o'ver•flow' s débordement m; (pipe) tropplein m || o'ver•flow' tr & intr déborder

o'ver•fly' v (pret -flew; pp -flown) tr survoler

o'ver•grown' adj démesuré; (e.g., child) trop grand pour son âge; overgrown with (e.g., weeds) envahi par, recouvert de

o'ver•hang' v (pret & pp -hung) tr surplomber, faire saillie au-dessus de; (to threaten) menacer || intr (to jut out) faire saillie

o'ver•haul' s remise f en état || o'ver•haul' tr remettre en état; (to catch up to) rattraper

o'ver•head' adj élevé; aérien, surélevé || s (overpass) pont-route m; (com) frais mpl généraux || o'ver•head' adv au-dessus de la tête, en haut

o'ver•head projec'tor s rétroprojecteur m

o'ver•head valve' s soupape f en tête

o'ver•hear' v (pret & pp -heard) tr entendre par hasard; (a conversation) surprendre

o'ver•heat' tr surchauffer

overjoyed [,ovər'dʒɔɪd] adj ravi, transporté de joie

o'ver kill' s surextermination f; (fig) excès m || intr excéder le nécessaire

overland ['ovər,lænd] adj & adv par terre, par voie de terre

o'ver•lap' v (pret & pp -lapped; ger -lapping) tr enchevaucher, imbriquer || intr chevaucher

o'ver•lap'ping s recouvrement m, chevauchement m, imbrication f; (of functions, offices, etc.) double emploi m

o'ver•load' s surcharge f; (comp) surcharge; sudden overload (elec) coup m de collier || o'ver•load' tr surcharger

o'ver•look' tr (to survey) donner sur, avoir vue sur; (to ignore) fermer les yeux sur, passer sous silence; (to neglect) oublier, négliger

o'ver•lord' s suzerain m || o'ver•lord' tr dominer, tyranniser

overly ['ovərli] adv (coll) trop, à l'excès

o'ver•med'icate intr (med) surmédicaliser

o'ver•night' adv toute la nuit; du jour au lendemain; to stay overnight passer la nuit

o'ver•night' bag' s sac m de nuit

o'ver•pass' s passage m supérieur, pontroute m, saut-de-mouton m

o'ver•pay'ment s surpaye f, rétribution f excessive

o'ver•pop'ula'tion s surpeuplement m, surpopulation f

o'ver•pow'er tr maîtriser; overpowered with grief accablé de douleur

o'ver•pow'ering adj accablant, irrésistible

o'ver•produc'tion s surproduction f

o'ver•rate' tr surestimer

o'ver•reach' tr dépasser

o'ver•ripe' adj blet, trop mûr

o'ver•rule' tr décider contre; (to set aside) annuler, casser

o'ver•run' v (pret -ran; pp -run; ger -running) tr envahir; (to flood) inonder; (limits, boundaries, etc.) dépasser || intr déborder

o'ver•sea' or o'ver•seas' adj d'outre-mer || o'ver•sea' or o'ver•seas' adv outre-mer

o'ver•see' v (pret -saw; pp -seen) tr surveiller

o'ver•se'er s surveillant m, inspecteur m

o'ver•sexed' adj hypersexué

o'ver•shad'ow tr ombrager; (fig) éclipser

o'ver•shoes' spl caoutchoucs mpl

o'ver•shoot' v (pret & pp -shot) tr aller au delà de, dépasser

o'ver•sight' s inadvertance f, étourderie f

o'ver•sleep' v (pret & pp -slept) intr dormir trop longtemps

o'ver•step' v (pret & pp -stepped; ger -stepping) tr dépasser, outrepasser

o'ver•stock' tr surapprovisionner

o'ver•stuffed' adj rembourré

o'ver•sup•ply' s (pl -plies) excédent m, abondance f || o'ver•sup•ply' v (pret & pp -plied) tr approvisionner avec excès

overt ['ovərt], [o'vʌrt] adj ouvert, manifeste; (intentional) prémédité

o'ver•take' v (pret -took; pp -taken) tr rattraper; (a runner) dépasser; (an automobile) doubler; (to surprise) surprendre

o'ver•tax' tr surtaxer; (to tire) surmener, excéder

o'ver•the-coun'ter adj vendu directement à l'acheteur

o'ver•throw' s renversement m || o'ver•throw' v (pret -threw; pp -thrown) tr renverser

o'ver•time' adj & adv en heures supplémentaires || s heures fpl supplémentaires

o'ver•time pe'riod s prolongation f

o'ver•tone' s (mus) harmonique m; (fig) signification f, sous-entendue m

o'ver•trump' tr surcouper

overture ['ovərtʃər] s ouverture f

o'ver•turn' tr renverser, chavirer || intr chavirer; (aer, aut) capoter

overweening [,ovər'winɪŋ] adj arrogant, outrecuidant

o′ver•weight′ *adj* au-dessus du poids normal; (*fat*) obèse ‖ *s* excédent *m* de poids

overwhelm [,ovər′hwɛlm] *tr* accabler, écraser; (*with favors, gifts, etc.*) combler

o′ver•work′ *s* surmenage *m*, excès *m* de travail ‖ **o′ver•work′** *tr* surmener, surcharger; abuser de, trop employer ‖ *intr* se surmener

Ovid [′avɪd] *s* Ovide *m*

ow [aʊ] *interj* aïe!

owe [o] *tr* devoir ‖ *intr* avoir des dettes; **to owe for** avoir à payer, devoir

owing [′o•ɪŋ] *adj* dû, redû; **owing to** à cause de, en raison de

owl [aʊl] *s* (*Asio*) hibou *m;* (*Strix*) chouette *f,* hulotte *f;* (*Tyto alba*) effraie *f*

own [on] *adj* propre, e.g., **my own brother** mon propre frère ‖ *s*—**all its own** spécial, authentique, e.g., **an aroma all its own** un parfum spécial, un parfum authentique; **my own (your own, etc.)** le mien (le vôtre, etc.) §89; **of my own (of their own, etc.)** bien à moi (bien à eux, etc.); **on one's own** à son propre compte, de son propre chef; **to come into one's own** entrer en possession de son bien; (*to win out*) obtenir de succès; (*to receive due praise*) recevoir les honneurs qu'on mérite; **to hold one's own** se maintenir, se défendre ‖ *tr* posséder; être propriétaire de; (*to acknowledge*) reconnaître ‖ *intr*—**to own to** convenir de, reconnaître; **to own up** (coll)

faire des aveux; **to own up to** (coll) faire l'aveu de, avouer

owner [′onər] *s* propriétaire *mf,* possesseur *m*

ownership [′onər,ʃɪp] *s* propriété *f,* possession *f*

own′er's li′cense *s* carte *f* grise

ox [aks] *s* (*pl* **oxen** [′aksən]) bœuf *m*

ox′cart′ *s* char *m* à bœufs

oxfords [′aksfərdz] *spl* richelieus *mpl*

oxide [′aksaɪd] *s* oxyde *m*

oxidize [′aksɪ,daɪz] *tr* oxyder ‖ *intr* s'oxyder

oxygen [′aksɪdʒən] *s* oxygène *m*

oxygenate [′aksɪdʒə,net] *tr* oxygéner

ox′ygen tent′ *s* tente *f* à oxygène

oxytone [′aksɪ,ton] *adj & s* oxyton *m*

oyster [′ɔɪstər] *adj* huîtrier ‖ *s* huître *f*

oys′ter bed′ *s* huîtrière *f,* banc *m* d'huîtres

oys′ter cock′tail *s* huîtres *fpl* écaillées aux condiments

oys′ter farm′ *s* parc *m* à huîtres, clayère *f*

oys′ter fork′ *s* fourchette *f* à huîtres

oys′ter knife′ *s* couteau *m* à huîtres

oys′ter•man *s* (*pl* **-men**) écailler *m*

oys′ter o′pener *s* (*person*) écailler *m;* (*implement*) ouvre-huîtres *m*

oys′ter plant′ *s* salsifis *m*

oys′ter shell′ *s* coquille *f* d'huître

oys′ter stew′ *s* soupe *f* à huîtres

ozone [′ozon] *s* ozone *m;* (coll) air *m* frais

o′zone hole′ *s* trou *m* d'ozone

o′zone lay′er *s* couche *f* d'ozone

ozonosphere [o′zonə,sfɪr] *s* ozonosphère *f*

P

P, p [pi] *s* XVIᵉ lettre de l'alphabet

pace [pes] *s* pas *m;* **to keep pace with** marcher de pair avec; **to put through one's paces** mettre à l'épreuve; **to set the pace** mener le train ‖ *tr* arpenter; **to pace off** mesurer au pas ‖ *intr* aller au pas; (equit) ambler

pace′mak′er *s* meneur *m* de train; (med) stimulateur *m* (cardiaque)

pacific [pə′sɪfɪk] *adj* pacifique ‖ **Pacific** *adj & s* Pacifique *m*

pacifier [′pæsɪ,faɪər] *s* pacificateur *m;* (*teething ring*) sucette *f*

pacifism [′pæsɪ,fɪzəm] *s* pacifisme *m*

pacifist [′pæsɪfɪst] *adj & s* pacifiste *mf*

paci•fy [′pæsɪ,faɪ] *v* (*pret & pp* **-fied**) *tr* pacifier

pack [pæk] *s* (*of peddler*) ballot *m;* (*of soldier*) paquetage *m,* sac *m;* (*of beast of burden*) bât *m;* (*of hounds*) meute *f;* (*of evildoers; of wolves*) bande *f;* (*of lies*) tissue *m;* (*of playing cards*) jeu *m;* (*of cigarettes*) paquet *m;* (*of floating ice*) banquise *f;* (*of troubles*) foule *f;* (*of fools*) tas *m;* (med) enveloppement *m* ‖ *tr* emballer, empaqueter; mettre en boîte; (*e.g., earth*) tasser; (*to stuff*) bourrer; **to send pack-**

ing (coll) envoyer promener ‖ *intr* faire ses bagages

package [′pækɪdʒ] *s* paquet *m* ‖ *tr* empaqueter

pack′age deal′ *s* accord *m* global, achat *m* forfaitaire

pack′age plan′ *s* voyage *m* à forfait

pack′age tour′ *s* voyage *m* organisé

pack′aging *s* conditionnement *m*

pack′aging and prepara′tion *s* habillage *m*

pack′ an′imal *s* bête *f* de somme

packet [′pækɪt] *s* paquet *m;* (naut) paquebot *m;* (pharm) sachet *m*

pack′ horse′ *s* cheval *m* de bât

pack′ing box′ or **case′** *s* caisse *f* d'emballage

pack′ing house′ *s* conserverie *f*

pack′sad′dle *s* bât *m*

pack′thread′ *s* ficelle *f*

pack′train′ *s* convoi *m* de bêtes de somme

pact [pækt] *s* pacte *m*

pad [pæd] *s* (*to prevent friction or damage*) bourrelet *m;* (*of writing paper*) bloc *m;* (*for inking*) tampon *m;* (*of an aquatic plant*) feuille *f;* (*for launching a rocket*) rampe *f;* (*sound of footsteps*) pas *m;* (*one's home*) (slang) piaule *f*, turne *f*, baraque *f*; (*a room*) (slang) carrée *f* (coll) ‖ *v* (*pret & pp* **padded;** *ger* **padding**) *tr* rembourrer; (*to expand unnecessarily*) délayer ‖ *intr* aller à pied

pad′ded cell′ *s* cellule *f* matelassée, cabanon *m*

paddle [′pædəl] *s* (*of a canoe*) pagaie *f*; (*for table tennis*) raquette *f*; (*of a wheel*) aube *f*; (*for beating*) palette *f* ‖ *tr* pagayer; (*to spank*) fesser ‖ *intr* pagayer; (*to splash*) barboter

pad′dle wheel′ *s* roue *f* à aubes

paddock [′pædək] *s* enclos *m*; (*at race track*) paddock *m*

pad′dy wag′on [′pædi] *s* (slang) panier *m* à salade

pad′lock′ *s* cadenas *m* ‖ *tr* cadenasser

pagan [′pagən] *adj & s* païen *m*

paganism [′pegə‚nızəm] *s* paganisme *m*

page [pedʒ] *s* (*of a book*) page *f*; (*boy attendant*) page *m*; (*in a hotel or club*) chasseur *m* ‖ *tr* (*a book*) paginer; appeler, demander, e.g., **you are being paged** on vous demande

pageant [′pædʒənt] *s* parade *f* à grand spectacle

pageant•ry [′pædʒəntri] *s* (*pl* **-ries**) grand apparat *m*; vaines pompes *fpl*

page′ proof′ *s* épreuve *f* de pages, seconde épreuve; (journ) morasse *f*

page′ set′up *s* (comp, type) composition *f* programmée

paginate [′pædʒı‚net] *tr* paginer

paging [′pedʒıŋ] *s* mise *f* en pages

paid′ in full′ [ped] *adj* (*formula stamped on bill*) pour acquit

paid′ vaca′tion *s* congé *m* payé

pail [pel] *s* seau *m*

pain [pen] *s* douleur *f*; **on pain of** sous peine de; **pain in the neck** (fig) casse-pieds *m*; **to take pains** se donner de la peine ‖ *tr* faire mal à; **it pains me to** il me coûte de ‖ *intr* faire mal

painful [′penfəl] *adj* douloureux, pénible

pain′kil′ler *s* (coll) calmant *m*

painless [′penlıs] *adj* sans douleur

pains′tak′ing *adj* soigneux; (*work*) soigné

paint [pent] *s* peinture *f*; **wet paint** peinture fraîche; (*public sign*) attention à la peinture! ‖ *tr & intr* peindre

paint′box′ *s* boîte *f* de couleurs

paint′brush′ *s* pinceau *m*

paint′ buck′et *s* camion *m*

painter [′pentər] *s* peintre *mf*

painting [′pentıŋ] *s* peinture *f*

paint′ remov′er *s* décapant *m*

pair [pɛr] *s* paire *f*; (*of people*) couple *m* ‖ *tr* accoupler ‖ *intr* s'accoupler

pair′ of scis′sors *s* ciseaux *mpl*

pair′ of trou′sers *s* pantalon *m*

pajam′a par′ty [pə′dʒamə] *s* soirée-hébergement *f*

pajamas *spl* pyjama *m*, pyjamas

Pakistan [′pakı′stan] *s* le Pakistan

Pakista•ni [‚pakı′stani] *adj* pakistanais ‖ *s* (*pl* **-nis**) Pakistanais *m*

pal [pæl] *s* copain *m* ‖ *v* (*pret & pp* **palled;** *ger* **palling**) *intr* (coll) être de bons copains; **to pal with** être copain de

palace [′pælıs] *s* palais *m*

palatable [′pælətəbəl] *adj* savoureux; (*acceptable*) agréable

palatal [′pælətəl] *adj* palatal ‖ *s* palatale *f*

palate [′pælıt] *s* palais *m*

pale [pel] *adj* pâle ‖ *s* (*stake*) pieu *m*; **beyond the pale** au-delà de la limite permise ‖ *intr* pâlir

pale′face′ *s* visage *m* pâle

palette [′pælıt] *s* palette *f*

palfrey [′pɔlfri] *s* palefroi *m*

palisade [‚pælı′sed] *s* palissade *f*; (*line of cliffs*) falaise *f*

pall [pɔl] *s* (*over a casket*) poêle *m*, drap *m* mortuaire; (*coffin*) cercueil *m*, poêle; (*to cover chalice*) pale *f*; (*vestment*) pallium *m* ‖ *intr* devenir fade; **to pall on** rassasier

pall′bear′er *s* porteur *m* d'un cordon du poêle; **to be a pallbearer** tenir les cordons du poêle

pallet [′pælıt] *s* grabat *m*

palliate [′pælı‚et] *tr* pallier

pallid [′pælıd] *adj* pâle, blême

pallor [′pælər] *s* pâleur *f*

palm [pam] *s* (*of the hand*) paume *f*; (*measure*) palme *m*; (*leaf*) palme *f*; (*tree*) palmier *m*; **to carry off the palm** remporter la palme; **to grease the palm of** (slang) graisser la patte à ‖ *tr* (*a card*) escamoter; **to palm off s.th. on s.o.** refiler q.ch. à qn

palmet•to [pæl′mɛto] *s* (*pl* **-tos** or **-toes**) palmier *m* nain

palmist [′pamıst] *s* chiromancien *m*

palmistry [′pamıstri] *s* chiromancie *f*

palm′ leaf′ *s* palme *f*

palm′ oil′ *s* huile *f* de palme

Palm′ Sun′day *s* le dimanche des Rameaux

palm′ tree′ *s* palmier *m*

palpable [′pælpəbəl] *adj* palpable

palpitate [′pælpı‚tet] *intr* palpiter

pal•sy [′pɔlzi] *s* (*pl* **-sies**) paralysie *f* ‖ *v* (*pret & pp* **-sied**) *tr* paralyser

pal•try [′pɔltri] *adj* (*comp* **-trier;** *super* **-triest**) misérable

pamper [′pæmpər] *tr* choyer, gâter

pamphlet [′pæmflıt] *s* brochure *f*

pan [pæn] *s* (*for cooking*) casserole *f*; (*basin; scale of a balance*) bassin *m*; (slang) binette *f*; **Pan** Pan *m* ‖ *v* (*pret & pp* **panned;** *ger* **panning**) *tr* (*gold*) laver à la batée; (coll) débiner, éreinter ‖ *intr* laver à la batée; (mov) panoramiquer; **to pan out well** (coll) réussir

panacea [‚pænə′si•ə] *s* panacée *f*

Panama [′pænə‚ma] *s* le Panama

Pan′ama Canal′ *s* canal *m* de Panama

Pan′ama Canal′ Zone′ *s* zone *f* canal du Panama

Pan′ama hat′ *s* panama *m*

Pan-American [‚pænə′mɛrıkən] *adj* panaméricain

pan'cake' s crêpe f ‖ intr (aer) descendre à plat, se plaquer

pan'cake land'ing s atterrissage m plaque, sur le ventre, or à plat

panchromatic [,pænkro`mætɪk] adj panchromatique

pancreas [`pænkrɪ•əs] s pancréas m

panda [`pændə] s panda m

pander [`pændər] s entremetteur m ‖ intr servir d'entremetteur; **to pander to** se prêter à; encourager

pane [pen] s carreau m, vitre f

pan•el [`pænəl] s panneau m; (on wall) lambris m; (door, wall) panneau m; (ceiling) caisson m; (discussion group) groupe m de discussion; (law) liste f, tableau m ‖ v (pret & pp **-eled** or **-elled**; ger **-eling** or **-elling**) tr (a room) garnir de boiseries; (a wall) lambrisser

pan'el discus'sion s colloque m

panelist [`pænəlɪst] s membre m d'un groupe de discussion

pang [pæŋ] s élancement m, angoisse f

pan'han'dle s queue f de la poêle; (geog) projection f d'un territoire dans un autre ‖ intr (slang) mendigoter

pan'han'dler s (slang) mendigot m

pan•ic [`pænɪk] adj & s panique f ‖ v (pret & pp **-icked**; ger **-icking**) tr semer la panique dans ‖ intr être pris de panique

pan'ic-strick'en adj pris de panique

pano•ply [`pænəplɪ] s (pl **-plies**) panoplie f

panorama [,pænə`ramə] s panorama m

pan•sy [`pænzɪ] s (pl **-sies**) pensée f; (slang) tapette f

pant [pænt] s halètement m; **pants** pantalon m; **to wear the pants** (coll) porter la culotte ‖ intr haleter, panteler

pantheism [`pænθɪ,ɪzəm] s panthéisme m

pantheon [`pænθɪ,ɑn] s panthéon m

panther [`pænθər] s panthère f

panties [`pæntɪz] spl culotte f, slip m de femme

pantomime [`pæntə,maɪm] s pantomime f

pan•try [`pæntrɪ] s (pl **-tries**) office m & f, dépense f

pant'y hose' [`pæntɪ] s collant m

pant'y lin'er s protège-slip m

pap [pæp] s bouillie f

papa [`papə], [pə`pa] s papa m

papa•cy [`pepəsɪ] s (pl **-cies**) papauté f

paper [`pepər] s papier m; (newspaper) journal m; (of needles) carte f ‖ tr tapisser

pa'per•back s livre m broché; (easily carried) livre de poche

pa'per•boy s vendeur m de journaux

pa'per clip' s attache f, trombone m

pa'per cone' s cornet m de papier

pa'per cup' s verre m en carton, gobelet m de papier

pa'per cut'ter s (knife) coupe-papier m; (office equipment) massicot m

pa'per hand'kerchief s mouchoir m à jeter, mouchoir en papier

pa'per•hang'er s tapissier m

pa'per knife' s coupe-papier m

pa'per mill' s papeterie f

pa'per mon'ey s papier-monnaie m

pa'per nap'kin s serviette f en papier

pa'per plate' s assiette f en carton, assiette de papier

pa'per tape' s bande f de papier

pa'per tow'el s serviette f de toilette en papier

pa'per tow'eling s essuie-mains m invar en papier

pa'per•weight' s presse-papiers m

pa'per work' s travail m de bureau

papier-mâché [,pepərmə`ʃe] s papier-pierre m, papier m mâché

paprika [pæ`prikə] s paprika m

Pap' smear' ou **Pap' test'** s (med) examen m cytologique des seins, frottis m sanguin Papanicolau

papy•rus [pə`paɪrəs] s (pl **ri** [raɪ]) papyrus m

par [pɑr] s pair m; (golf) normale f du parcours, par m; **at par** au pair; **to be on a par with** aller de pair avec

parable [`pærəbəl] s parabole f

parabola [pə`ræbələ] s parabole f

parachute [`pærə,ʃut] s parachute m ‖ tr & intr parachuter

par'achute jump' s saut m en parachute

parachutist [`pærə,ʃutɪst] s parachutiste mf

parade [pə`red] s défilé m; (ostentation) parade f; (mil) parade ‖ tr faire parade de ‖ intr défiler; parader

paradise [`pærə,daɪs] s paradis m

paradox [`pærə,dɑks] s paradoxe m

paradoxical [,pærə`dɑksɪkəl] adj paradoxal

paraffin [`pærəfɪn] s paraffine f ‖ tr paraffiner

paragon [`pærə,gɑn] s parangon m

paragraph [`pærə,græf] s paragraphe m

Paraguay [`pærə,gwaɪ] s le Paraguay

Paraguayan [,pærə`gwaɪ•ən] adj paraguayen ‖ s Paraguayen m

parakeet [`pærə,kit] s perruche f

paral•lel [`pærə,lɛl] adj parallèle ‖ s (line) parallèle f; (latitude; declination; comparison) parallèle m; **parallels** (typ) barres fpl; **without parallel** sans pareil ‖ v (pret & pp **-leled** or **-lelled**; ger **-leling** or **-lelling**) tr mettre en parallèle; entrer en parallèle avec, égaler

par'allel bars' spl barres fpl parallèles

paraly•sis [pə`rælɪsɪs] s (pl **-ses** [,siz]) paralysie f

paralytic [,pærə`lɪtɪk] adj & s paralytique mf

paralyze [`pærə,laɪz] tr paralyser

paramount [`pærə,maunt] adj suprême, capital

paranoiac [,pærə`nɔɪ•æk] adj & s paranoïaque mf

parapet [`pærə,pɛt] s parapet m

paraphernalia [,pærəfər`nelɪ•ə] spl effets mpl personnels; attirail m

paraphrase [`pærə,frez] s remaniement m ‖ tr remanier

paraplegic [,pærə`plidʒɪk] adj & s paraplégique mf

parasite [`pærə,saɪt] s parasite m

parasitic(al) [ˌpærə'sɪtɪk(əl)] *adj* parasite

parasol ['pærə,sɔl] *s* parasol *m*, ombrelle *f*

paratrooper ['pærə,trupər] *s* parachutiste *m*

parboil ['par,bɔɪl] *tr* faire cuire légèrement; (*vegetables*) blanchir

par·cel ['parsəl] *s* colis *m*, paquet *m* ‖ *v* (*pret & pp* -celed or -celled; *ger* -celing or -celling) *tr* morceler; **to parcel out** répartir

par'cel post' *s* colis *mpl* postaux

parch [partʃ] *tr* dessécher; (*beans, grain, etc.*) griller

parchment ['partʃmənt] *s* parchemin *m*

pardon ['pardən] *s* pardon *m;* (*remission of penalty by the state*) grâce *f;* **I beg your pardon** je vous demande pardon ‖ *tr* pardonner; pardonner à; (*a criminal*) grâcier; **to pardon s.o. for s.th.** pardonner q.ch. à qn

pardonable ['pardənəbəl] *adj* pardonnable

pare [pɛr] *tr* (*potatoes, fruit, etc.*) éplucher; (*the nails*) rogner; (*costs*) réduire

parent ['pɛrənt] *s* père *m or* mère *f;* origine *f*, base *f;* **parents** parents *mpl*, père et mère

parentage ['pɛrəntɪdʒ] *s* paternité *f or* maternité *f;* naissance *f*, origine *f*

par'ent com'pany *s* maison *f* mère, société *f* mère

parenthe·sis [pə'rɛnθɪsɪs] *s* (*pl* -ses [ˌsiz]) parenthèse *f;* **in parentheses** entre parenthèses

parenthood ['pɛrənt,hʊd] *s* paternité *f or* maternité *f*

pariah [pə'raɪ·ə], ['parɪ·ə] *s* paria *m*

par'ing knife' *s* couteau *m* à éplucher

Paris ['pærɪs] *s* Paris *m*

parish ['pærɪʃ] *adj* paroissien ‖ *s* paroisse *f*

parishioner [pə'rɪʃənər] *s* paroissien *m*

Parisian [pə'riʒən] *adj & s* parisien *m*

parity ['pærɪti] *s* parité *f*

park [park] *s* parc *m* ‖ *tr* garer, parquer ‖ *intr* stationner

parked *adj* en stationnement

parking ['parkɪŋ] *s* parcage *m;* (*e.g., in a city street*) stationnement *m;* **no parking** (*public sign*) stationnement interdit

park'ing ar'ea *s* aire *f* de stationnement

park'ing lights' *spl* (aut) feux *mpl* de stationnement, feux de position

park'ing lot' *s* parking *m*, parc *m* à autos

park'ing me'ter *s* parcomètre *m*, compteur *m* de stationnement

park'ing spot' *s* stalle *f*

park'ing tick'et *s* contravention *f*, papillon *m*

park'way' *s* route *f* panoramique; (*turnpike*) autoroute *f*

parley ['parli] *s* pourparlers *mpl* ‖ *intr* parlementer

parliament ['parlɪmənt] *s* parlement *m*

parliamentarian [ˌparlɪmɛn'tɛrɪ·ən] *s* expert *m* en usages parlementaires

parlor ['parlər] *s* salon *m;* (*in an institution*) parloir *m*

par'lor car' *s* (rr) wagon-salon *m*

par'lor game' *s* jeu *m* de société

Parnassus [par'næsəs] *s* le Parnasse

parochial [pə'rokɪ·əl] *adj* paroissial; (*attitude*) provincial

paro'chial school' *s* école *f* confessionnelle, école libre

paro·dy ['pærədi] *s* (*pl* -dies) parodie *f* ‖ *v* (*pret & pp* -died) *tr* parodier

parole [pə'rol] *s* parole *f* d'honneur; liberté *f* sur parole ‖ *tr* libérer sur parole

par·quet [par'ke], [par'kɛt] *s* parquet *m;* (theat) premiers rangs *mpl* du parterre ‖ *v* (*pret & pp* -queted ['ked], ['kɛtɪd]; *ger* -queting ['ke·ɪŋ], ['kɛtɪŋ]) *tr* parqueter

parricide ['pærɪ,saɪd] *s* (*act*) parricide *m;* (*person*) parricide *mf*

parrot ['pærət] *s* perroquet *m* ‖ *tr* répéter or imiter comme un perroquet

par·ry ['pæri] *s* (*pl* -ries) parade *f* ‖ *v* (*pret & pp* -ried) *tr* parer; (*a question*) éluder

parse [pars] *tr* faire l'analyse grammaticale de

parsimonious [ˌparsɪ'monɪ·əs] *adj* parcimonieux, regardant

parsley ['parsli] *s* persil *m*

parsnip ['parsnɪp] *s* panais *m*

parson ['parsən] *s* curé *m;* pasteur *m* protestant

parsonage ['parsənɪdʒ] *s* presbytère *m*

part [part] *s* (*section, division*) partie *f;* (*share*) part *f;* (*of a machine*) organe *m*, pièce *f;* (*of the hair*) raie *f;* (theat) rôle *m;* **for my part** pour ma part; **for the most part** pour la plupart; **in part** en partie; **in these parts** dans ces parages; **on the part of** de la part de; **parts** (*personal qualities*) talent *m;* (anat) parties (génitales); (geog) région(s) *f* (*pl*); **to be or form part of** faire partie de; **to be part and parcel of** faire partie intégrante de; **to do one's part** faire son devoir; **to live a part** (theat) entrer dans la peau d'un personnage; **to look the part** avoir le physique de l'emploi; **to take part in** prendre part à; **to take the part of** prendre parti pour; jouer le rôle de ‖ *adv* partiellement, en partie; **part . . . part** moitié . . . moitié ‖ *tr* séparer; **to part the hair** se faire une raie ‖ *intr* se séparer; (*said, e.g., of road*) diverger; (*to break*) rompre; **to part with** se défaire de; se dessaisir de

par·take [par'tek] *v* (*pret* -took; *pp* -taken) *intr*—to partake in participer à; **to partake of** (*e.g., a meal*) prendre; (*e.g., joy*) participer de

parthenogenesis [ˌparθəno'dʒɛnəsəs] *s* parthénogenèse *f*

Parthenon ['parθɪ,nan] *s* Parthénon *m*

partial ['parʃəl] *adj* partiel; (*prejudiced*) partial

participant [par'tɪsɪpənt] *adj & s* participant *m*

participate [par'tɪsɪ,pet] *intr* participer

participation [par,tɪsɪ'peʃən] *s* participation *f*

participle ['partɪ,sɪpəl] *s* participe *m*

particle ['partɪkəl] *s* particule *f;* **a particle of truth** un grain de vérité; **not a particle of evidence** pas l'ombre d'une preuve

par'ticle phys'ics *s* physique de la particule

particular [pər'tɪkjələr] *adj* particulier; difficile, exigeant; méticuleux; **a particular ...** un certain ... ‖ *s* détail *m*

particularize [pər`tɪkjələ,raɪz] *tr & intr* individualiser, particulariser

parting [`pɑrtɪŋ] *s* séparation *f*

partisan [`pɑrtɪzən] *adj & s* partisan *m*

partition [pɑr`tɪʃən] *s* (*dividing*) partage *m*, division *f*; (*of land*) morcellement *m*; (*wall*) paroi *f*, cloison *f* ‖ *tr* partager; **to partition off** séparer par des cloisons

partner [`pɑrtnər] *s* partenaire *mf*; (*husband*) conjoint *m*; (*wife*) conjointe *f*; (*in a dance*) cavalier *m*; (*in business*) associé *m*

part′ner•ship′ *s* association *f*; (com) société *f*

part′ of speech′ *s* partie *f* du discours

part′ own′er *s* copropriétaire *mf*

partridge [`pɑrtrɪdʒ] *s* perdrix *m*

part′-time′ *adj & adv* à mi-temps

par•ty [`pɑrti] *adj* de gala ‖ *s* (*pl* **-ties**) fête *f*, soirée *f*; (*social gathering; dance*) boum *f* (coll); (*diversion of a group of persons; individual named in contract or lawsuit*) partie *f*; (*with whom one is conversing*) interlocuteur *m*; (mil) détachement *m*, peloton *m*; (pol) parti *m*; (telp) correspondant *m*; (coll) individu *m*; **to be a party to** être complice de

party-goer [`pɑrti,go•ər] *s* invité *m*; (*nightlifer*) noceur *m*

par′ty hack′ *s* politicien *m* à la petite semaine

par′ty line′ *s* (*between two properties*) limite *f*; (telp) ligne *f* à postes groupés ‖ **par′ty line′** *s* ligne du parti; (*of communist party*) directives *fpl* du parti

par′ty pol′itics *s* politique *f* de parti

par′ty wall′ *s* mur *m* mitoyen

pass [pæs] *s* (*navigable channel; movement of hands of magician; in sports*) passe *f*; (*straits*) pas *m*; (*in mountains*) col *m*, passage *m*; (*document*) laissez-passer *m*; difficulté *f*; (mil) permission *f*; (rr) permis *m* de circulation; (theat) billet *m* de faveur ‖ *tr* passer; (*an exam*) réussir à; (*e.g., a student*) recevoir; (*a law*) adopter, voter; (*a red light*) brûler; (*to get ahead of*) dépasser; (*a car going in the same direction*) doubler; (*s.o. or s.th. coming toward one*) croiser; (*a certain place*) passer devant; **to pass around** faire circuler; **to pass oneself off as** se faire passer pour; **to pass out** distribuer; **to pass over** passer sous silence; (*to hand over*) transmettre; **to pass s.th. off on s.o.** repasser ou refiler q.ch. à qn ‖ *intr* passer; (educ) être reçu; **to bring to pass** réaliser; **to come to pass** se passer; **to pass as** or **for** passer pour; **to pass away** disparaître; (*to die out*) s'éteindre; (*to die*) mourir; **to pass by** passer devant; **to pass out** sortir; (slang) s'évanouir; **to pass over** passer sur; (*an obstacle*) franchir; (*said of storm*) s'éloigner; (*to pass through*) traverser; **to pass over to** (*e.g., the enemy*) passer à

passable [`pæsəbəl] *adj* passable; (*road, river, etc.*) franchissable

passage [`pæsɪdʒ] *s* passage *m*; (*of time*) cours *m*; (*of a law*) adoption *f*

pass′book′ *s* carnet *m* de banque

passenger [`pæsəndʒər] *adj* (*e.g., train*) de voyageurs; (*e.g., pigeon*) de passage ‖ *s* voyageur *m*, passager *m*

passer-by [`pæsər`baɪ] *s* (*pl* **passers-by**) passant *m*

passing [`pæsɪŋ] *adj* passager ‖ *s* passage *m* (*act of passing*) dépassement *m*; (*death*) trépas *m*; (*of time*) écoulement *m*; (*of a law*) adoption *f*; (*in an examination*) la moyenne; une mention passable; **in passing** (*in parenthesis*) du passage

passion [`pæʃən] *s* passion *f*

passionate [`pæʃənɪt] *adj* passionné

passive [`pæsɪv] *adj & s* passif *m*

pass′key′ *s* passe-partout *m*

pass′-out′ check′ *s* contremarque *f*

Pass′o′ver *s* Pâque *f*

pass′port′ *s* passeport *m*

pass′word′ *s* mot *m* de passe

past [pæst] *adj* passé, dernier; (*e.g., president*) ancien ‖ *s* passé *m* ‖ *prep* au-delà de, passé, plus de; hors de, e.g., **past all understanding** hors de toute compréhension; **it's twenty past five** il est cinq heures vingt; **its past three o'clock** il est trois heures passées

pasta [`pɑstə] *s* (culin) pâtes *fpl*, pâtes alimentaires

paste [pest] *s* (*glue*) colle *f* de pâte; (*jewelry*) strass *m*; (culin) pâte *f* ‖ *tr* coller

paste′board′ *s* carton *m*

pastel [pæs`tɛl] *adj & s* pastel *m*

pasteurize [`pæstə,raɪz] *tr* pasteuriser

pastime [`pæs,taɪm] *s* passe-temps *m*

past′ mas′ter *s* expert *m* en la matière, passé maître

pastor [`pæstər] *s* pasteur *m*

pastoral [`pæstərəl] *adj* pastoral ‖ *s* pastorale *f*

pastorate [`pæstərɪt] *s* pastorat *m*

pas•try [`pestri] *s* (*pl* **-tries**) pâtisserie *f*

pas′try cook′ *s* pâtissier *m*

pas′try shop′ *s* pâtisserie *f*

pasture [`pæstʃər] *s* pâturage *m*, pâture *f* ‖ *tr* faire paître ‖ *intr* paître

past•y [`pesti] *adj* (*comp* **-ier**; *super* **-iest**) pâteux; (*face*) terreux

pat [pæt] *adj* à propos; (*e.g., excuse*) tout prêt ‖ *s* (*light stroke*) petite tape *f*; (*on an animal*) caresse *f*; (*of butter*) coquille *f* ‖ *v* (*pret & pp* **patted**; *ger* **patting**) *tr* tapoter; caresser; **to pat on the back** encourager, complimenter

patch [pætʃ] *s* (*e.g., of cloth*) pièce *f*, raccommodage *m*; (*of land*) parcelle *f*; (*of ice*) plaque *f*; (*of inner tube*) rustine *f*; (*e.g., of color*) tache *f*; (*beauty spot*) mouche *f* ‖ *tr* rapiécer; **to patch up** rapetasser; (*e.g., a quarrel*) arranger, raccommoder

patent [`petənt] *adj* patent ‖ [`pætənt] *adj* breveté ‖ *s* brevet *m* d'invention; **patent applied for** une demande de brevet a été déposée ‖ *tr* breveter

pat′ent leath′er [ˈpætənt] s cuir m verni

pat′ent med′icine s specialité f pharmaceutique

pat′ent rights′ spl propriété f industrielle

paternal [pəˈtʌrnəl] adj paternel

paternity [pəˈtʌrnɪti] s paternité f

path [pæθ] s (way) sentier m; (in garden) allée f; (of bullet, heavenly body, etc.) trajectoire f; (for, e.g., riding horses) piste f; (course) route f; **to beat a path** frayer un chemin

pathetic [pəˈθɛtɪk] adj pathétique

path′find′er s pionnier m

pathology [pəˈθɑlədʒi] s pathologie f

pathol′ogy lab′oratory s laboratoire m d'analyses

pathos [ˈpeθɑs] s pathétique m

path′way′ s sentier m; (fig) voie f

patience [ˈpeʃəns] s patience f

patient [ˈpeʃənt] adj patient ‖ s malade mf; (undergoing surgery) patient m

pati•o [ˈpɑtɪˌo] s (pl -os) patio m

patriarch [ˈpetrɪˌɑrk] s patriarche m

patrician [pəˈtrɪʃən] adj & s patricien m

patricide [ˈpætrɪˌsaɪd] s (act) parricide m; (person) parricide mf

Patrick [ˈpætrɪk] s Patrice m, Patrick m

patrimo•ny [ˈpætrɪˌmoni] s (pl -nies) patrimoine m

patriot [ˈpetrɪ•ət] s patriote mf

patriotic [ˌpetrɪˈɑtɪk] adj patriotique, patriote

patriotism [ˈpetrɪ•əˌtɪzəm] s patriotisme m

pa•trol [pəˈtrol] s patrouille f ‖ v (pret & pp -trolled; ger -trolling) tr faire la patrouille dans ‖ intr patrouiller

patrol′ car′ s voiture f de ronde

patrol′man s (pl -men) s agent m de police

patrol′ wag′on s voiture f cellulaire

patron [ˈpetrən] adj patron ‖ s protecteur m; (com) client m

patronage [ˈpetrənɪdʒ] s patronage m, clientèle f; (pol) politique f du place-sous

patronize [ˈpetrəˌnaɪz] tr patronner, protéger; traiter avec condescendance; (com) acheter chez

patronizing [ˈpetrəˌnaɪzɪŋ] adj condescendant

pa′tron saint′ s patron m

patsy [ˈpætsi] s (scapegoat) tête f de Turc; (easy mark) naïf m ‖ **Patsy** surnom de Patrice

patter [ˈpætər] s (sounds) petit bruit m; (of rain) fouettement m; (of magician, peddler, etc.) boniment m ‖ intr (said of rain) fouetter; (said of little feet) trottiner

pattern [ˈpætərn] s (design) dessin m, motif m; (salient characteristics) profil m; (model) modèle m, exemple m; (sewing) patron m; **behavior pattern** type m de comportemente ‖ tr (to decorate) orner de motifs; **to pattern s.th. on** modeler q.ch. sur

pat′tern book′ s album m d'échantillons; (sewing) album de modes

pat•ty [ˈpæti] s (pl -ties) petit pâté m

paucity [ˈpɔsɪti] s rareté f; manque m, disette f

paunch [pɔntʃ] s panse f

paunch•y [ˈpɔntʃi] adj (comp -ier; super -iest) ventru

pauper [ˈpɔpər] s indigent m

pau′per's grave′ s fosse f commune

pause [pɔz] s pause f; (mus) point m d'orgue; **to give pause to** faire hésiter ‖ intr faire une pause; hésiter

pave [pev] tr paver

pavement [ˈpevmənt] s pavé m; (surface) chaussée f

pavilion [pəˈvɪljən] s pavillon m

paw [pɔ] s patte f; (coll) main f ‖ tr donner un coup de patte à ‖ intr (said of horse) piaffer

pawl [pɔl] s cliquet m d'arrêt

pawn [pɔn] s (in chess) pion m; (security, pledge) gage m; (tool of another person) jouet m ‖ tr mettre en gage; **to pawn s.th. off on s.o.** (coll) refiler q.ch. à qn

pawn′bro′ker s prêteur m sur gages

pawn′shop′ s mont-de-piété m, crédit m municipal

pawn′ tick′et s reconnaissance f du mont-de-piété

pay [pe] s paye f; (mil) solde f ‖ v (pret & pp **paid** [ped]) tr payer; (mil) solder; (a compliment; a visit; attention) faire; **to pay back** payer de retour; **to pay down** payer comptant; **to pay off** (a debt) acquitter; (a mortgage) purger; (a creditor) rembourser; **to pay s.o. for s.th.** payer qn de q.ch., payer q.ch. à qn ‖ intr payer, rapporter; **to pay for** payer; **to pay off** (coll) avoir du succès; **to pay up** se libérer que un paiement

payable [ˈpe•əbəl] adj payable

pay′ boost′ s augmentation f

pay′check′ s paye f

pay′day′ s jour m de paye

pay′dirt′ s alluvion f exploitable; (coll) source f d'argent

payee [peˈi] s bénéficiaire mf

pay′ en′velope s sachet m de paye; paye f

payer [ˈpe•ər] s payeur m

pay′load′ s charge f payante, charge utile; (aer) poids m utile

pay′mas′ter s payeur m

payment [ˈpemənt] m paiement m; (installment, deposit, etc.) versement m; **payment in full** règlement m complet

pay′ off′ s (outcome) dénouement m; (bribe) pot-de-vin m; (com) règlement m complet, désintéressement m

pay′ phone′ s taxiphone m

pay′roll′ s bulletin m de paye; (for officers) état m de solde; (for enlisted men) feuille f de prêt

pay′ sta′tion s téléphone m public

pay′ tel′evision s télévision f payante

PC [ˈpiˈsi] s (letterword) (**personal computer**) PC (ordinateur personnel)

pea [pi] s pois m; **green peas** petits pois

peace [pis] s paix f

peaceable [ˈpisəbəl] adj pacifique

peaceful [ˈpisfəl] adj paisible, pacifique

peace′mak′er s pacificateur m

peace′ of mind′ *s* tranquillité *f* d'esprit
peace′ pipe′ *s* calumet *m* de paix
peach [pitʃ] *s* pêche *f;* (slang) bijou *m*
peach′ tree′ *s* pêcher *m*
peach•y [ˈpitʃi] *adj* (*comp* **-ier;** *super* **-iest**) (slang) chouette
pea′coat′ *s* (naut) caban *m*
pea′cock′ *s* paon *m*
pea′hen′ *s* paonne *f*
peak [pik] *s* cime *f,* sommet *m;* (*mountain; mountain top*) pic *m;* (*of beard*) pointe *f;* (*of a cap*) visière *f;* (elec) pointe
peak′ hour′ *s* heure *f* de pointe
peak′ load′ *s* (elec) charge *f* de point
peak′ vol′tage *s* tension *f* de crête
peal [pil] *s* retentissement *m;* (*of bells*) carillon *m* ‖ *intr* carillonner
peal′ of laugh′ter *s* éclat *m* de rire
peal′ of thun′der *s* coup *m* de tonnerre
pea′nut′ *s* cacahuète *f;* (bot) arachide *f*
pea′nut but′ter *s* beurre *m* de cacahuètes *or* d'arachide
pear [pɛr] *s* poire *f*
pearl [pʌrl] *s* perle *f*
pearl′ oys′ter *s* huître *f* perlière
pear′ tree′ *s* poirier *m*
peasant [ˈpɛzənt] *adj* & *s* paysan *m*
pea′shoot′er *s* sarbacane *f*
pea′ soup′ *s* (culin, fig) purée *f* de pois
peat [pit] *s* tourbe *f*
pebble [ˈpɛbəl] *s* caillou *m;* (*on seashore*) galet *m*
pebbled *adj* (*leather*) grenu
peck [pɛk] *s* (*pecking*) coup *m* de bec; (*eight quarts*) picotin *m;* (*kiss*) (coll) baiser *m* d'oiseau, bécot *m;* (coll) tas *m* ‖ *tr* becqueter ‖ *intr* picorer; **to peck at** picorer; (*food*) pignocher
peculation [ˌpɛkjəˈləʃən] *s* péculat *m,* détournement *m* de fonds
peculiar [pɪˈkjuljər] *adj* particulier; (*strange*) bizarre
pedagogue [ˈpɛdəˌgag] *s* pédagogue *mf*
pedagogy [ˈpɛdəˌgadʒi] *s* pédagogie *f*
ped•al [ˈpɛdəl] *s* pédale *f* ‖ *v* (*pret* & *pp* **-aled** or **-alled;** *ger* **-aling** or **-alling**) *tr* actionner les pédales de ‖ *intr* pédaler
pe′dal push′ers *spl* pantalon *m* corsaire
pedant [ˈpɛdənt] *s* pédant *m*
pedantic [pɪˈdæntɪk] *adj* pédant
pedant•ry [ˈpɛdəntri] *s* (*pl* **-ries**) pédanterie *f*
peddle [ˈpɛdəl] *tr* & *intr* colporter
peddler [ˈpɛdlər] *s* colporteur *m*
pederast [ˈpɛdəˌræst] *s* pédéraste *m*
pedestal [ˈpɛdɪstəl] *s* piédestal *m*
pedestrian [pɪˈdɛstri•ən] *adj* (*style*) prosaïque ‖ *s* piéton *m; **pedestrian right of way** (*public sign*) priorité piétons
pedes′trian mall′ *s* rue *f* piétonne
pediatrics [ˌpidiˈætrɪks] *s* pédiatrie *f*
pedicure [ˈpɛdɪˌkjʊr] *s* soins *mpl* des pieds
pedigree [ˈpɛdɪˌgri] *s* généalogie *f;* (*table*) arbre *m* généalogique; (*of animal*) pedigree *m*
pediment [ˈpɛdɪmənt] *s* fronton *m*

peek [pik] *s* coup *m* d'œil furtif ‖ *intr*—**to peek at** regarder furtivement
peel [pil] *s* pelure *f;* (*of lemon*) zeste *m* ‖ *tr* peler; **to peel off** enlever ‖ *intr* se peler; (*said of paint*) s'écailler
peeler [ˈpilər] *s* éplucheur *m;* (*electric*) éplucheuse *f*
peel′ing knife′ *s* éplucheur *m*
peep [pip] *s* regard *m* furtif; (*of, e.g., chickens*) piaulement *m* ‖ *intr* piauler; **to peep at** regarder furtivement
peep′hole′ *s* judas *m*
peer [pɪr] *s* pair *m* ‖ *intr* regarder avec attention; **to peer at** or **into** scruter
peerless [ˈpɪrlɪs] *adj* sans pareil
peeve [piv] *s* (coll) embêtement *m* ‖ *tr* (coll) irriter, embêter, fâcher
peevish [ˈpivɪʃ] *adj* maussade
peg [pɛg] *s* (*of wood*) cheville *f;* (*of metal*) fiche *f;* (*for coat and hat*) patère *f;* (*for tent*) piquet *m;* **to take down a peg** (coll) rabattre le caquet de ‖ *v* (*pret* & *pp* **pegged;** *ger* **pegging**) *tr* cheviller; (*e.g., prices*) indexer, fixer; (*points*) marquer ‖ *intr* piocher; **to peg away at** travailler ferme à
Pegasus [ˈpɛgəsəs] *s* Pégase *m*
peg′ leg′ *s* jambe *f* de bois
peg′ top′ *s* toupie *f;* **peg tops** pantalon *m* fuseau
Pekin•ese [ˌpikiˈniz] *adj* pékinois ‖ *s* (*pl* **-ese**) Pékinois *m*
Peking [ˈpiˈkɪŋ] *s* Pékin *m*
pelf [pɛlf] *s* (pej) lucre *m*
pelican [ˈpɛlɪkən] *s* pélican *m*
pellet [ˈpɛlɪt] *s* (*of paper or bread*) boulette *f;* (*bullet*) grain *m* de plomb; (pharm) pilule *f*
pell-mell [ˈpɛlˈmɛl] *adj* confus ‖ *adv* pêle-mêle
pelt [pɛlt] *s* (*hide*) peau *m;* (*whack*) coup *m* violent; (*of stones, insults, etc.*) grêle *f* ‖ *tr* cribler; (*e.g., stones*) lancer ‖ *intr* tomber à verse
pen [pɛn] *s* (*for writing*) plume *f;* (*fountain pen*) stylo *m;* (*corral*) enclos *m;* (fig) plume; (*prison*) (slang) bloc *m* ‖ *v* (*pret* & *pp* **penned;** *ger* **penning**) *tr* écrire ‖ *v* (*pret* & *pp* **penned** or **pent** [pɛnt]; *ger* **penning**) *tr* parquer
penalize [ˈpinəˌlaɪz] *tr* (*an action*) sanctionner; (*a person*) punir; (sports) pénaliser
penal•ty [ˈpɛnəlti] *s* (*pl* **-ties**) peine *f;* (*for late payment; in a game*) pénalité *f;* **under penalty of** sous peine de
penance [ˈpɛnəns] *s* pénitence *f*
penchant [ˈpɛnʃənt] *s* penchant *m*
pen•cil [ˈpɛnsəl] *s* crayon *m;* (*of light*) faisceau *m* ‖ *v* (*pret* & *pp* **-ciled** or **-cilled;** *ger* **-ciling** or **-cilling**) *tr* crayonner
pen′ cil sharp′ener *s* taille-crayon *m*
pendent [ˈpɛndɛnt] *adj* pendant ‖ *s* pendant *m,* pendentif *m;* (*of chandelier*) pendeloque *f*
pending [ˈpɛndɪŋ] *adj* pendant ‖ *prep* en attendant
pendulum [ˈpɛndʒələm] *s* pendule *m*
pen′dulum bob′ *s* lentille *f*
penetrate [ˈpɛnɪˌtret] *tr* & *intr* pénétrer

penguin [ˈpɛŋgwɪn] *s* manchot *m*
pen'hold'er *s* porte-plume *m;* (*rack*) pose-plumes *m*
penicillin [ˌpɛnɪˈsɪlɪn] *s* pénicilline *f*
peninsula [pəˈnɪnsələ] *s* presqu'île *f;* (*large peninsula like Spain or Italy*) péninsule *f*
peninsular [pəˈnɪnsələr] *adj* péninsulaire
penis [ˈpinɪs] *s* pénis *m*
penitence [ˈpɛnɪtəns] *s* pénitence *f*
penitent [ˈpɛnɪtənt] *adj & s* pénitent *m*
penitentiary [ˌpɛnəˈtɛnʃəri] *s* pénitencier *m*
pen'knife' *s* (*pl* **-knives**) canif *m*
penmanship [ˈpɛnmənˌʃɪp] *s* calligraphie *f;* (*person's handwriting*) écriture *f*
pen' name' *s* pseudonyme *m*
pennant [ˈpɛnənt] *s* flamme *f;* (sports) bande-role *f* du championnat
penniless [ˈpɛnɪlɪs] *adj* sans le sou
pen•ny [ˈpɛni] *s* (*pl* **-nies**) (U.S.A.) centime *m;* **not a penny** pas un sou ‖ *s* (*pl* **pence** [pɛns]) (Brit) penny *m*
pen'ny-pinch'ing *adj* regardant
pen'ny•weight' *s* poids *m* de 24 grains
pen' pal' *s* (coll) correspondant *m*
pen'point' *s* bec *m* de plume
pension [ˈpɛnʃən] *s* pension *f* ‖ *tr* pensionner
pensioner [ˈpɛnʃənər] *s* pensionné *m*
pensive [ˈpɛnsɪv] *adj* pensif
Pentagon, the [ˈpɛntəˌgɑn] *s* le Pentagone
Pentecost [ˈpɛntɪˌkɔst] *s* la Pentecôte
penthouse [ˈpɛntˌhaʊs] *s* toit *m* en auvent, appentis *m;* appartement *m* sur toit, maison *f* à terrasse
pent-up [ˈpɛntˌʌp] *adj* renfermé, refoulé
penult [ˈpinʌlt] *s* pénultième *f*
penum•bra [pɪˈnʌmbrə] *s* (*pl* **-brae** [bri] or **-bras**) pénombre *f*
penurious [pɪˈnʊrɪ•əs] *adj* (*stingy*) mesquin, parcimonieux; (*poor*) pauvre
penury [ˈpɛnjəri] *s* indigence *f,* misère *f*
pen'wip'er *s* essuie-plume *m*
peo•ny [ˈpi•əni] *s* (*pl* **-nies**) pivoine *f*
people [ˈpipəl] *spl* gens *mpl,* personnes *fpl;* **many people** beaucoup de monde; **my people** ma famille, mes parents; **people say** on dit ‖ *s* (*pl* **peoples**) peuple *m,* nation *f* ‖ *tr* peupler
pep [pɛp] *s* (coll) allant *m* ‖ *v* (*pret & pp* **pepped;** *ger* **pepping**) *tr*—**to pep up** (coll) animer
pepper [ˈpɛpər] *s* (*spice*) poivre *m;* (*fruit*) grain *m* de poivre; (*plant*) poivrier *m;* (*plant or fruit of the hot or red pepper*) piment *m* rouge; (*plant or fruit of the sweet or green pepper*) piment doux, poivron *m* vert ‖ *tr* poivrer; (*e.g., with bullets*) cribler
pep'per•box' *s* poivrière
pep'per mill' *s* moulin *m* à poivre
pep'per•mint' *s* menthe *f* poivrée; (*lozenge*) pastille *f* de menthe
per [pʌr] *prep* par; **as per** suivant
perambulator [pərˈæmbjəˌletər] *s* voiture *f* d'enfant
per capita [pərˈkæpɪtə] par tête, par personne

perceive [pərˈsiv] *tr* (*by the senses*) apercevoir; (*by understanding*) percevoir
per cent or **percent** [pərˈsɛnt] pour cent
percentage [pərˈsɛntɪdʒ] *s* pourcentage *m;* **to get a percentage** (slang) avoir part au gâteau
perceptible [pərˈsɛptəbəl] *adj* perceptible, sensible, appréciable
perception [pərˈsɛpʃən] *s* perception *f;* compréhension *f,* pénétration *f*
perch [pʌrtʃ] *s* (*vantage point*) perchoir *m;* (ichth) perche *f* ‖ *tr* percher ‖ *intr* percher, se percher
percolate [ˈpʌrkəˌlet] *tr & intr* filtrer
percolator [ˈpʌrkəˌletər] *s* cafetière *f* à filtre
percussion [pərˈkʌʃən] *s* percussion *f*
percus'sion cap' *s* capsule *f* fulminante
per diem [pərˈdai•əm] par jour
perdition [pərˈdɪʃən] *s* perdition *f*
peremptory [pəˈrɛmptəri] *adj* péremptoire
perennial [pəˈrɛnɪ•əl] *adj* perpétuel; (bot) vivace ‖ *s* plante *f* vivace
perfect [ˈpʌrfɪkt] *adj & s* parfait *m* ‖ [pərˈfɛkt] *tr* perfectionner
perfidious [pərˈfɪdɪ•əs] *adj* perfide
perfi•dy [ˈpʌrfɪdi] *s* (*pl* **-dies**) perfidie *f*
perforate [ˈpʌrfəˌret] *tr* perforer; (phila) denteler
per'forated line' *s* pointillé *m*
perforation [ˌpʌrfəˈreʃən] *s* perforation *f;* (*of postage stamp*) dentelure *f*
perforce [pərˈfors] *adv* forcément
perform [pərˈfɔrm] *tr* exécuter; (surg) faire; (theat) représenter ‖ *intr* jouer; (*said of machine*) fonctionner
performance [pərˈfɔrməns] *s* (*accomplishing*) exécution *f;* (*production*) rendement *m;* (*of a machine*) fonctionnement *m* (*of actor, singer, dancer*) interprétation *f;* (sports) performance *f;* (theat) représentation *f;* **in the performance of his duties** dans l'exercice de ses fonctions
performer [pərˈfɔrmər] *s* artiste *mf,* interprète *mf*
perform'ing arts' *spl* arts *mpl* du spectacle
perfume [ˈpʌrfjum] *s* parfum *m* ‖ [pərˈfjum] *tr* parfumer
perfunctory [pərˈfʌŋktəri] *adj* superficiel; négligent
perhaps [pərˈhæps] *adv* peut-être; **perhaps not** peut-être que non
per hour' à l'heure
peril [ˈpɛrəl] *s* péril *m*
perilous [ˈpɛrɪləs] *adj* périlleux
period [ˈpɪrɪ•əd] *s* période *f;* (*in school*) heure *f* de cours; (gram) point *m;* (sports) division *f*
pe'riod cos'tume *s* costume *m* d'époque
pe'riod fur'niture *s* meubles *m* d'époque
periodic [ˌpɪrɪˈɑdɪk] *adj* périodique
periodical [ˌpɪrɪˈɑdɪkəl] *adj* périodique ‖ *s* publication *f* périodique
period'ical room' *s* (*in a library*) salle *f* des imprimés

peripheral [pə`rıfərəl] *adj* périphérique

peripher•y [pə`rıfəri] *s* (*pl* **-ies**) périphérie *f*

periscope [`pɛrɪ,skop] *s* périscope *m;* (*of a tank*) épiscope *m*

perish [`pɛrɪʃ] *intr* périr

perishable [`pɛrɪ/əbəl] *adj* périssable

perjure [`pʌrdʒər] *tr*—**to perjure oneself** se parjurer

perju•ry [`pʌrdʒəri] *s* (*pl* **-ries**) parjure *m*

perk [pʌrk] *s* bénéfice *m* extra, avantage *m* ‖ *tr*—**to perk up** (*the head*) redresser; (*the ears*) dresser; (*the appetite*) ravigoter ‖ *intr* (*coffee*) filtrer; **to perk up** se ranimer

perks [pʌrks] *abbr* **perquisites**

permafrost [`pərmə,frɔst] *s* pergélisol *m*

permanence [`pʌrmənəns] *s* permanence *f*

permanent [`pʌrmənənt] *adj* permanent ‖ *s* permanente *f*

per'manent address' *s* domicile *m* fixe

per'manent ten'ure *s* inamovibilité *f*

per'manent wave' *s* ondulation *f* permanente

permeate [`pʌrmɪ,et] *tr* & *intr* pénétrer

permissible [pər`mɪsɪbəl] *adj* permis

permission [pər`mɪ/ən] *s* permission *f*

permissive [pər`mɪsɪv] *adj* tolérant; (*morals, law*) laxiste; (*society*) de tolérance; (pej) trop tolérant

permissiveness [pər`mɪsɪvnɪs] *s* tolérance *f;* (pej) excès *m* de tolérance, mollesse *f,* laxisme *m*

per•mit [`pʌrmɪt] *s* permis *m;* (com) passavant *m* ‖ [pər`mɪt] *v* (*pret* & *pp* **-mitted;** *ger* **-mitting**) *tr* permettre; **to permit s.o. to** permettre à qn de

permute [pər`mjut] *tr* permuter

pernicious [pər`nɪ/əs] *adj* pernicieux

pernickety [pər`nɪkɪti] *adj* (coll) pointilleux

perox'ide blonde' [pər`aksaɪd] *s* blonde *f* décolorée

perp [pʌrp] *abbr* **perpetrator**

perpendicular [,pʌrpən`dɪkjələr] *adj* & *s* perpendiculaire *f*

perpetrate [`pʌrpɪ,tret] *tr* perpétrer

perpetual [pər`pɛt/ʊ•əl] *adj* perpétuel

perpetuate [pər`pɛt/ʊ,et] *tr* perpétuer

perplex [pər`plɛks] *tr* rendre perplexe

perplexed [pər`plɛkst] *adj* perplexe

perplexi•ty [pər`plɛksɪti] *s* (*pl* **-ties**) perplexité *f*

perp' walk' *s defilé dirigé par la police pour faire voir les accusés*

perquisite [`pʌrkwɪzɪt] *s* à-côté *m,* gratification *f*

per se [pʌr`se] *adv* par soi-même, de soi-même, essentiellement

persecute [`pʌrsɪ,kjut] *tr* persécuter

persecution [,pʌrsɪ`kju/ən] *s* persécution *f*

persecu'tion com'plex *s* manie *f* de la persécution

persevere [,pʌrsɪ`vɪr] *intr* persévérer

Persian [`pʌrʒən] *adj* persan ‖ *s* (*language*) persan *m;* (*person*) Persan *m*

Per'sian blind' *s* persienne *f*

Per'sian Gulf' *s* Golfe *m* Persique

Per'sian rug' *s* tapis *m* de Perse

persimmon [pər`sɪmən] *s* plaquemine *f;* (*tree*) plaqueminier *m*

persist [pər`sɪst] *intr* persister; **to persist in** persister dans + *ger,* persister à + *inf*

persistent [pər`sɪstənt] *adj* persistant

person [`pʌrsən] *s* personne *f;* **no person** personne; **per person** par personne, chacun

personage [`pʌrsənɪdʒ] *s* personnage *m*

personal [`pʌrsənəl] *adj* personnel ‖ *s* (journ) note *f* dans la chronique mondaine; **personals** (journ) de particulier à particulier

per'sonal comput'er *s* (comp) ordinateur *m* personnel *or* individual

personali•ty [,pʌrsə`nælɪti] *s* (*pl* **-ties**) personnalité *f*

personal'ity cult' *s* culte *m* de la personnalité

personal prop'erty *s* biens *mpl* mobiliers

personi•fy [pər`sɑnɪ,faɪ] *v* (*pret* & *pp* **-fied**) *tr* personnifier

personnel [,pʌrsə`nɛl] *s* personnel *m*

per'son-to-per'son tel'ephone call' *s* communication *f* avec préavis

perspective [pər`spɛktɪv] *s* perspective *f*

perspicacious [,pʌrspɪ`ke/əs] *adj* perspicace

perspiration [,pʌrspɪ`re/ən] *s* transpiration *f*

perspire [pər`spaɪr] *intr* transpirer

persuade [pər`swed] *tr* persuader; **to persuade s.o. of s.th.** persuader q.ch. à qn, persuader qn de q.ch.; **to persuade s.o. to** persuader à qn de

persuasion [pər`sweʒən] *s* persuasion *f;* (*faith*) (coll) croyance *f*

pert [pʌrt] *adj* effronté; (*sprightly*) animé

pertain [pər`ten] *intr*—**to pertain to** avoir rapport à

Peru [pə`ru] *s* le Pérou

peruse [pə`ruz] *tr* lire; lire attentivement

Peruvian [pə`ruvɪ•ən] *adj* péruvien ‖ *s* Péruvien *m*

pervade [pər`ved] *tr* pénétrer, s'infiltrer dans

perverse [pər`vʌrs] *adj* pervers; obstiné; capricieux

perversion [pər`vʌrʒən] *s* perversion *f*

perversi•ty [pər`vʌrsɪti] *s* (*pl* **-ties**) perversité *f;* obstination *f*

pervert [`pʌrvərt] *s* pervers *m,* perverti *m* ‖ [pər`vʌrt] *tr* pervertir

pes•ky [`pɛski] *adj* (*comp* **-kier;** *super* **-kiest**) (coll) importun

pessimism [`pɛsɪ,mɪzəm] *s* pessimisme *m*

pessimist [`pɛsɪmɪst] *s* pessimiste *mf*

pessimistic [,pɛsɪ`mɪstɪk] *adj* pessimiste

pest [pɛst] *s* insecte *m* nuisible; (*pestilence*) peste *f;* (*annoying person*) raseur *m*

pester [`pɛstər] *tr* casser la tête à, importuner

pest'house' *s* lazaret *m*

pesticide [`pɛstɪ,saɪd] *s* pesticide *m*

pestiferous [pɛs'tɪfərəs] *adj* pestiféré; (coll) ennuyeux

pestilence ['pɛstɪləns] *s* pestilence *f*

pestle ['pɛsəl] *s* pilon *m*

pet [pɛt] *s* animal *m* favori, animal familial; (*child*) enfant *m* gâté; (*anger*) accès *m* de mauvaise humeur; **teacher's pet** chouchou *m* (*or* chouchoute *f*) du professeur ‖ *v* (*pret & pp* **petted;** *ger* **petting**) *tr* choyer; (*e.g., an animal's fur*) caresser ‖ *intr* (slang) se bécoter

petal ['pɛtəl] *s* pétale *m*

pet' cock' *s* robinet *m* de purge

Peter ['pitər] *s* Pierre *m;* **to rob Peter to pay Paul** découvrir saint Pierre pour habiller saint Paul ‖ (*l.c.*) *intr*—**to peter out** (coll) s'épuiser, s'en aller en fumée

petition [pɪ'tɪʃən] *s* pétition *f* ‖ *tr* adresser or présenter une pétition à

pet' name' *s* mot *m* doux, nom *m* d'amitié

Petrarch ['pitrɑrk] *s* Pétrarque *m*

petri•fy ['pɛtrɪ,faɪ] *v* (*pret & pp* **-fied**) *tr* pétrifier ‖ *intr* se pétrifier

petrochemical [,pɛtro'kɛmɪkəl] *adj* pétrochimique

petrol ['pɛtrəl] *s* (Brit) essence *f*

petroleum [pɪ'trolɪ•əm] *s* pétrole *m*

pet' shop' *s* boutique *f* aux petites bêtes; (*for birds*) oisellerie *f*

petticoat ['pɛtɪ,kot] *s* jupon *m*

pet•ty ['pɛti] *adj* (*comp* **-tier;** *super* **-tiest**) insignifiant, petit; (*narrow*) mesquin; intolérant

pet' ty cash' *s* petite caisse *f*

pet' ty expen'ses *s* menus frais *mpl*

pet' ty lar'ceny *s* vol *m* simple

pet' ty of'ficer *s* (naut) officier *m* marinier

petulant ['pɛtjələnt] *adj* irritable, boudeur

pew [pju] *s* banc *m* d'église

pewter ['pjutər] *s* étain *m*

Pfc. ['pi'ɛf'si] *s* (letterword) (**private first class**) soldat *m* de première

phalanx ['felæŋks] *s* phalange *f*

phallic ['fælɪk] *adj* phallique

phallus ['fæləs] *s* phallus *m,* pénis *m*

phantasm ['fæntæzəm] *s* fantasme *m*

phantom ['fæntəm] *s* fantôme *m*

Pharaoh ['fɛro] *s* Pharaon *m*

pharisee ['færɪ,si] *s* pharisien *m;* **Pharisee** Pharisien *m*

pharmaceutical [,fɑrmə'sutɪkəl] *adj* pharmaceutique

pharmacist ['fɑrməsɪst] *s* pharmacien *m*

pharma•cy ['fɑrməsi] *s* (*pl* **-cies**) pharmacie *f*

pharynx ['færɪŋks] *s* pharynx *m*

phase [fez] *s* phase *f;* **out of phase** (*said of motor*) décalé ‖ *tr* mettre en phase; développer en phases successives; (coll) inquiéter; **to phase out** faire disparaître peu à peu

phat [fæt] *adj* (slang) beau, attrayant, bon

pheasant ['fɛzənt] *s* faisan *m*

phenobarbital [,fino'bɑrbɪ,tæl] *s* phénobarbital *m*

phenomenal [fɪ'nɑmɪ,nəl] *adj* phénoménal

phenome•non [fɪ'nɑmɪ,nɑn] *s* (*pl* **-na** [nə]) phénomène *m*

phial ['faɪəl] *s* fiole *f*

philanderer [fɪ'lændərər] *s* coureur *m,* galant *m*

philanthropist [fɪ'lænθrəpɪst] *s* philanthrope *mf*

philanthrop•y [fɪ'lænθrəpi] *s* (*pl* **-pies**) philanthropie *f*

philatelist [fɪ'lætəlɪst] *s* philatéliste *mf*

philately [fɪ'lætəli] *s* philatélie *f*

Philippine ['fɪlɪ,pin] *adj* philippin ‖ **Philippines** *spl* Philippines *fpl*

Philistine ['fɪlɪ,stin] *adj & s* philistin *m*

philologist [fɪ'lɑlədʒɪst] *s* philologue *mf*

philology [fɪ'lɑlədʒi] *s* philologie *f*

philosopher [fɪ'lɑsəfər] *s* philosophe *mf*

philosophic(al) [,fɪlə'sɑfɪk(əl)] *adj* philosophique

philoso•phy [fɪ'lɑsəfi] *s* (*pl* **-phies**) philosophie *f*

philter ['fɪltər] *s* philtre *m*

phlebitis [flɪ'baɪtɪs] *s* phlébite *f*

phlegm [flɛm] *s* flegme *m;* **to cough up phlegm** cracher des glaires, tousser gras

phlegmatic(al) [flɛg'mætɪk(əl)] *adj* flegmatique

phobia ['fobɪ•ə] *s* phobie *f*

Phoebe ['fibi] *s* Phébé *f*

Phoenicia [fɪ'niʃə] *s* Phénicie *f;* **la Phénicie**

Phoenician [fɪ'niʃən] *adj* phénicien ‖ *s* Phénicien *m*

phoenix ['finɪks] *s* phénix *m*

phone [fon] *s* (coll) téléphone *m* ‖ *tr & intr* (coll) téléphoner

phone' book' *s* annuaire *m* (du téléphone)

phone' booth' *s* cabine *f* téléphonique

phone' call' *s* coup *m* de téléphone, coup de fil

phone' card' *s* carte *f* de téléphone

phoneme ['fonim] *s* phonème *m*

phonetic [fo'nɛtɪk] *adj* phonétique ‖ **phonetics** *s* phonétique *f*

phone-in' show' *s* (rad, telv) tribune *f* téléphonique

phonics ['fɑnɪks] *s* (educ) instruction *f* phonique

phonograph ['fonə,græf] *s* phonographe *m*

phonology [fə'nɑlədʒi] *s* phonologie *f*

pho•ny ['foni] *adj* (*comp* **-nier;** *super* **-niest**) faux, truqué ‖ *s* (*pl* **-nies**) charlatan *m*

pho'ny war' *s* drôle *f* de guerre

phosphate ['fɑsfet] *s* phosphate *m*

phosphorescent [,fɑsfə'rɛsənt] *adj* phosphorescent

phospho•rus ['fɑsfərəs] *s* (*pl* **-ri** [,raɪ]) phosphore *m*

pho•to [foto] *s* (*pl* **-tos**) (coll) photo *f*

pho'to•cop'ier *s* photocopieur *m*

pho'to•cop'y *s* photocopie *f*

pho'to•elec'tric cell' *s* cellule *f* photoélectrique

pho'to•engrav'ing *s* photogravure *f*

pho'to fin'ish *s* photo-finish *f*

photogenic [,foto'dʒɛnɪk] *adj* photogénique

pho′to•graph′ s photographie f ‖ tr photographier ‖ intr—**to photograph well** être photogénique

photographer [fə'tɑgrəfər] s photographe mf

pho′to•graph′ li′brary s photothèque f

photography [fə'tɑgrəfi] s photographie f

Photostat ['fotə,stæt] s (trademark) photostat m ‖ tr & intr photocopier

phrase [frez] s locution f, expression f; (mus) phrase f ‖ tr exprimer, rédiger; (mus) phraser

phrenology [frɪ'nɑlədʒi] s phrénologie f

phys•ic ['fɪzɪk] s médicament m; (laxative) purgatif m ‖ v (pret & pp **-icked;** ger **-icking**) tr purger

physical ['fɪzɪkəl] adj physique

phys′ical de′fect s vice m de conformation

phys′ical ed′uca′tion s education f physique et sportive

phys′ical fit′ness s état m physique; (physical culture) gymnastique f

phys′ical hand′icap s handicap m physique

phys′ical ther′apy s thérapie f physique

physician [fɪ'zɪʃən] s médecin m

physicist ['fɪzɪsɪst] s physicien m

physics ['fɪzɪks] s physique f

physiogno•my [,fɪzɪ'ɑgnəmi] s (pl **-mies**) physionomie f

physiological [,fɪzɪə'lɑdʒɪkəl] adj physiologique

physiology [,fɪzɪ'ɑlədʒi] s physiologie f

physique [fɪ'zik] s physique m

pi [paɪ] s (math) pi m; (typ) pâté m ‖ v (pret & pp **pied;** ger **piing**) tr (typ) mettre en pâte

pianist ['pi•ənɪst] s pianiste mf

pian•o [pɪ'æno] s (pl **-os**) piano m

pian′o stool′ s tabouret m de piano

pian′o tun′er s accordeur m (de piano)

pian′o wire′ s corde f à piano

picayune [,pɪkə'jun] adj mesquin

picco•lo ['pɪkəlo] s (pl **-los**) piccolo m

pick [pɪk] s (tool) pic m, pioche f; (choice) choix m; (choicest) élite f, fleur f ‖ tr choisir; (flowers) cueillir; (fibers) effiler; (one's teeth, nose, etc.) se curer; (a scab) gratter; (a fowl) plumer; (a bone) ronger; (a lock) crocheter; (the ground) piocher; (e.g., guitar strings) toucher; (a quarrel; flaws) chercher; **to pick off** enlever; (to shoot) descendre; **to pick out** trier; **to pick pockets** voler à la tire; **to pick to pieces** (coll) éplucher; **to pick up** ramasser; (one's strength) reprendre; (speed) accroître; (a passenger; the phone) prendre; (a man overboard) recueillir; (an anchor; a stitch; a fallen child) relever; (information; a language) apprendre; (the scent) retrouver; (rad) capter ‖ intr (said of birds) picorer; **to pick at** (to scold) gronder; **to pick to eat one's food** manger du bout des dents; **to pick on** choisir; (coll) gronder; **to pick up** (coll) se rétablir

pick′ax′ s pioche f

picket ['pɪkɪt] s (stake, pale) pieu m; (of strikers; of soldiers) piquet m ‖ tr entourer de piquets de grève ‖ intr faire le piquet

pick′et fence′ s palis m

pick′et line′ s piquet m de grève

pickle ['pɪkəl] s (gherkin) cornichon m; (brine) marinade f, saumure f; (coll) gâchis m ‖ tr conserver dans du vinaigre

pick′lock′ s crochet m; (person) crocheteur m

pick′-me-up′ s (coll) remontant m

pick′pock′et s voleur m à la tire

pick′up′ s (passenger) passager m; (of a motor) reprise f; (truck; phonograph cartridge) pick-up m; (restorative) remontant m; (casual lover) partenaire mf de rencontre

pick′up arm′ s bras m de pick-up

pick′up truck′ s camionnette f; pick-up m invar

pic•nic ['pɪknɪk] s pique-nique m ‖ v (pret & pp **-nicked;** ger **-nicking**) intr pique-niquer

pictorial [pɪk'tɔrɪ•əl] adj & s illustré m

picture ['pɪktʃər] s tableau m, image f; (photograph) photographie f; (painting) peinture f; (engraving) gravure f; (mov) film m; (screen) (mov, telv) écran m; **a picture is worth a thousand words** une image vaut mieux que dix mille mots; **the very picture of** le portrait de, l'image de; **to receive the picture** (telv) capter l'image ‖ tr dépeindre, représenter; **to picture to oneself** s'imaginer

pic′ture gal′lery s musée m de peinture

pic′ture post′ card′ s carte f postale illustrée

pic′ture search′ s (electron) exploration f visuelle

pic′ture show′ s exhibition f de peinture; (mov) cinéma m

pic′ture sig′nal s signal m vidéo

picturesque [,pɪktʃə'rɛsk] adj pittoresque

pic′ture tube′ s tube m de l'image

pic′ture win′dow s fenêtre f panoramique

piddling ['pɪdlɪŋ] adj insignifiant

pidgin ['pɪdʒɪn] s (ling) pidgin m, sabir m, petit nègre m

Pid′gin Eng′lish s pidgin m, pidgin-english m

pie [paɪ] s pâté m; (dessert) tarte f; (bird) pie f

piece [pis] s (of music; of bread) morceau m; (cannon, coin, chessman, pastry, clothing) pièce f; (of land) parcelle f; (e.g., of glass) éclat m; **a piece of advice** un conseil; **a piece of furniture** un meuble; **to break into pieces** mettre en pièces, mettre en morceaux; **to give s.o. a piece of one's mind** (coll) dire son fait à qn; **to go to pieces** se désagréger; (to be hysterical) avoir ses nerfs; **to pick to pieces** (coll) éplucher ‖ tr rapiécer; **to piece together** rassembler, coordonner

piece′meal′ adv pièce à pièce

piece′work′ s travail m à la tâche

piece′work′er s ouvrier m à la tâche

pied [paɪd] adj bigarré, panaché; (typ) tombé en pâte

pier [pɪr] s (with amusements) jetée f; (breakwater) brise-lames m; (of a bridge) pile f; (of *a harbor*) jetée *f;* (*wall between two openings*) (archit) trumeau *m*

pierce [pɪrs] *tr & intr* percer

piercing [ˈpɪrsɪŋ] *adj* perçant; (*sharp*) aigu

pier′ glass′ *s* grand miroir *m*

pie•ty [ˈpaɪ•əti] *s* (*pl* **-ties**) piété *f*

piffle [ˈpɪfəl] *s* (coll) futilités *fpl*, sottises *fpl*

pig [pɪg] *s* cochon *m*, porc *m*

pigeon [ˈpɪdʒən] *s* pigeon *m*

pi′geon•hole′ *s* boulin *m;* (*in desk*) case *f* ‖ *tr* caser; mettre au rancart

pi′geon house′ *s* pigeonnier *m*

piggish [ˈpɪgɪʃ] *adj* goinfre

piggyback [ˈpɪgiˌbæk] *adv* sur le dos, sur les epaules; (rr) en auto-couchette

pig′gy bank′ [ˈpɪgi] *s* tirelire *f*, grenouille *f*

pig′-head′ed *adj* cabochard, têtu

pig′ i′ron *s* gueuse *f*

piglet [ˈpɪglɪt] *s* cochonnet *m*

pigment [ˈpɪgmənt] *s* pigment *m*

pig′pen′ *s* porcherie *f*

pig′skin′ *s* peau *f* de porc; (coll) ballon *m* du football

pig′sty′ *s* (*pl* **-sties**) porcherie *f*

pig′tail′ *s* queue *f*, natte *f;* (*of tobacco*) carotte *f*

pike [paɪk] *s* pique *f;* autoroute *f* à péage; (*fish*) brochet *m*

piker [ˈpaɪkər] *s* (slang) rat *m*

pile [paɪl] *s* (*heap*) tas *m;* (*stake*) pieu *m;* (*of rug*) poil *m;* (*of building*) masse *f;* (elec, phys) pile *f;* (coll) fortune *f;* **piles** (pathol) hémorroïdes *fpl* ‖ *tr* empiler ‖ *intr* s'empiler

pile′ dri′ver *s* batteur *m* de pieux; sonnette *f*

pile up′ *s* (aut) carambolage *m*

pilfer [ˈpɪlfər] *tr & intr* chaparder

pilgrim [ˈpɪlgrɪm] *s* pèlerin *m*

pilgrimage [ˈpɪlgrɪmɪdʒ] *s* pèlerinage *m*

pill [pɪl] *s* pilule *f;* (*something unpleasant*) pilule; (coll) casse-pieds *m;* **to sweeten the pill** dorer la pilule

pillage [ˈpɪlɪdʒ] *s* pillage *m* ‖ *tr & intr* piller

pillar [ˈpɪlər] *s* pilier *m*

pillo•ry [ˈpɪlər] *s* (*pl* **-ries**) pilori *m* ‖ *v* (*pret & pp* **-ried**) *tr* clouer au pilori

pillow [ˈpɪlo] *s* oreiller *m*

pil′low•case′ or **pil′low•slip′** *s* taie *f* d'oreiller

pilot [ˈpaɪlət] *s* pilote *m;* (*of gas range*) veilleuse *f* ‖ *tr* piloter

pi′lot en′gine *s* locomotive-pilote *f*

pi′lot light′ *s* veilleuse *f*

pimp [pɪmp] *s* entremetteur *m*

pimple [ˈpɪmpəl] *s* bouton *m*

pim•ply [ˈpɪmpli] *adj* (*comp* **-plier;** *super* **-pliest**) boutonneux

pin [pɪn] *s* épingle *f;* (*of wearing apparel*) agrafe *f;* (*bowling*) quille *f;* (mach) clavette *f*, cheville *f*, goupille *f;* **to be on pins and needles** être sur les chardons ardents ‖ *v* (*pret & pp* **pinned;** *ger* **pinning**) *tr* épingler; (mach) cheviller, goupiller; **to pin down** fixer, clouer

pinafore [ˈpɪnəˌfor] *s* tablier *m* d'enfant

pin′ball′ *s* billard *m* américain

pin′ball machine′ *s* flipper *m*

pincers [ˈpɪnsərz] *s & spl* pinces *fpl*

pinch [pɪntʃ] *s* (*pinching*) pincement *m;* (*of salt*) pincée *f;* (*of tobacco*) prise *f;* (*of hunger*) morsure *f;* (*trying time*) moment *m* critique; (slang) arrestation *f;* **in a pinch** au besoin ‖ *tr* pincer; (*to press tightly on*) serrer; (*e.g., one's finger in a door*) se prendre; (*to arrest*) (slang) pincer; (*to steal*) (slang) chiper ‖ *intr* (*said, e.g., of shoe*) gêner; (*to save*) lésiner

pinchers [ˈpɪntʃərz] *s & spl* pinces *fpl*

pin′cush′ion *s* pelote *f* d'épingles

pine [paɪn] *s* pin *m* ‖ *intr* languire; **to pine for** soupirer après

pine′ap′ple *s* ananas *m*

pine′ cone′ *s* pomme *f* de pin

pine′ nee′dle *s* aiguille *f* de pin

ping [pɪŋ] *s* sifflement *m;* (*in a motor*) cognement *m* ‖ *intr* siffler; cogner

Ping-Pong [ˈpɪŋˌpɔŋ] *s* (trademark) ping-pong *m*, tennis *m* de table

Ping′-Pong play′er *s* pongiste *mf*

pin′head′ *s* tête *f* d'épingle; (pej) crétin *m*

pink [pɪŋk] *adj* rose ‖ *s* rose *m;* (bot) œillet *m;* **to be in the pink** se porter à merveille

pin′ mon′ey *s* argent *m* de poche

pinnacle [ˈpɪnəkəl] *s* pinacle *m*

pin′point′ *adj* exact ‖ *s* (fig) point *m* critique ‖ *tr* situer avec précision

pin′prick′ *s* piqûre *f* d'épingle

pin′-striped′ *adj* rayé

pint [paɪnt] *s* chopine *f*

pin′up girl′ *s* pin up *f*

pin′wheel′ *s* (*fireworks*) soleil *m;* (*child's toy*) moulinet *m*

pioneer [ˌpaɪ•əˈnɪr] *s* pionnier *m* ‖ *tr* défricher ‖ *intr* faire œuvre de pionnier

pious [ˈpaɪ•əs] *adj* pieux, dévot

pip [pɪp] *s* (*in fruit*) pépin *m;* (*on cards, dice, etc.*) point *m;* (rad) top *m;* (vet) pépie *f*

pipe [paɪp] *s* tuyau *m*, tube *m*, conduit *m;* (*to smoke tobacco*) pipe *f;* (*of an organ*) tuyau; (mus) chalumeau *m* ‖ *tr* canaliser ‖ *intr* jouer du chalumeau; **pipe down!** (slang) boucle-la!

pipe′ clean′er *s* cure-pipe *m*

pipe′ dream′ *s* rêve *m*, projet *m* illusoire

pipe′ line′ *s* pipe-line *m;* (*of information*) tuyau *m*

pipe′ or′gan *s* grandes orgues *fpl*

piper [ˈpaɪpər] *s* joueur *m* de chalumeau; (*bagpiper*) cornemuseur *m;* **to pay the piper** payer les violons

pipe′ wrench′ *s* clef *f* à tubes

piping [ˈpaɪpɪŋ] *s* tuyauterie *f;* (sewing) passepoil *m*

pippin [ˈpɪpɪn] *s* (*apple*) reinette *f;* (*highly admired person or thing*) bijou *m*

piquancy [ˈpikənsi] *s* piquant *m*

piquant [ˈpikənt] *adj* piquant

pique [pik] *s* pique *f* ‖ *tr* piquer; **to pique oneself on** se piquer de

pira•cy [ˈpaɪrəsi] *s* (*pl* **-cies**) piraterie *f*

Piraeus [paɪˈriˑəs] *s* Le Pirée

pirate [ˈpaɪrɪt] *s* pirate *m* ‖ *tr* piller ‖ *intr* pirater

pirouette [ˌpɪruˈet] *s* pirouette *f* ‖ *intr* pirouetter

Pisces [ˈpaɪsiz] *s* (astr, astrol) les Poissons *mpl*

piss [pɪs] *s* (vulg) pisse *f* ‖ *tr & intr* (vulg) pisser

pistol [ˈpɪstəl] *s* pistolet *m*

piston [ˈpɪstən] *s* piston *m*

pis'ton ring' *s* segment *m* de piston

pis'ton rod' *s* tige *f* de piston

pis'ton stroke' *s* course *f* de piston

pit [pɪt] *s* fosse *f,* trou *m;* (*in the skin*) marque *f;* (*of certain fruit*) noyau *m;* (*for cockfights, etc.*) arène *f;* (*of the stomach*) creux *m;* (min) puits *m;* (theat) fauteuils *mpl* d'orchestre derrière les musiciens ‖ *v* (*pret & pp* **pitted;** *ger* **pitting**) *tr* trouer; (*the face*) grêler; (*fruit*) dénoyauter; **to pit oneself against** se mesurer contre

pitch [pɪtʃ] *s* (*black sticky substance*) poix *f;* (*throw*) lancement *m,* jet *m;* (*of a boat*) tangage *m;* (*of a roof*) degré *m* de pente; (*of, e.g., a screw*) pas *m;* (*of a tone, of the voice, etc.*) hauteur *f;* (coll) boniment *m,* tamtam *m;* **to such a pitch that** à tel point que ‖ *tr* lancer, jeter; (*hay*) fourcher; (*a tent*) dresser; enduire de poix; (mus) donner le ton de ‖ *intr* (*said of boat*) tanguer; **to pitch in** (coll) se mettre à la besogne; (coll) commencer à manger; **to pitch into** s'attaquer à

pitch' ac'cent *s* accent *m* de hauteur

pitcher [ˈpɪtʃər] *s* broc *m,* cruche *f;* (baseball) lanceur *m*

pitch'fork' *s* fourche *f;* **to rain pitchforks** pleuvoir à torrents

pitch'man' *s* (*high-pressure salesman*) vendeur *m* de choc; (*street vendor*) marchand *m* ambulant; (rad, telv) représentant *m* du produit vendu

pitch' pipe' *s* diapason *m* de bouche

pitch'wom'an *s* (*high-pressure saleswoman*) vendeuse *f* de choc; (*street vendor*) marchande *f* ambulante; (rad, telv) représentante *f* du produit vendu

pit'fall' *s* trappe *f;* (fig) écueil *m,* pierre *f* d'écueil

pith [pɪθ] *s* moelle *f;* (fig) suc *m*

pith•y [ˈpɪθi] *adj* (*comp* **-ier;** *super* **-iest**) moelleux; (fig) plein de suc

pitiful [ˈpɪtɪfəl] *adj* pitoyable

pitiless [ˈpɪtɪlɪs] *adj* impitoyable

pit•y [ˈpɪti] *s* (*pl* **-ies**) pitié *f;* **for pity's sake!** par pitié!; **what a pity!** quel domage! ‖ *v* (*pret & pp* **-ied**) *tr* avoir pitié de, plaindre

pivot [ˈpɪvət] *s* pivot *m* ‖ *tr* faire pivoter ‖ *intr* pivoter

placard [ˈplækɑrd] *s* placard *m,* affiche *f* ‖ *tr* placarder

placate [ˈpleket] *tr* apaiser

place [ples] *s* (*location*) endroit *m,* lieu *m;* (*job*) poste *m,* emploi *m;* (*seat*) place *f;* (*rank*) rang *m;* **everything in its place** chaque chose à sa place; **in no place** nulle part; **in place of** au lieu de; **in your place** à votre place; **out of**

place déplacé; **to change places** changer de place; **to keep one's place** (fig) tenir ses distances; **to take place** avoir lieu ‖ *tr* mettre, placer; (*to find a job for; to invest*) placer; (*to recall*) remettre, se rappeler; (*to set down*) poser ‖ *intr* (turf) finir placé

place•bo [pləˈsibo] *s* (*pl* **-bos** or **-boes**) remède *m* factice

place' card' *s* marque-place *f,* carton *m* marque-place

place' mat' *s* garde-nappe *m*

placement [ˈplesmənt] *s* placement *m;* (*location*) emplacement *m*

place'ment exam' *s* examen *m* probatoire

place'-name' *s* nom *m* de lieu, toponyme *m*

placid [ˈplæsɪd] *adj* placide

plagiarism [ˈpledʒəˌrɪzəm] *s* plagiat *m*

plagiarist [ˈpledʒərɪst] *s* plagiaire *mf*

plagiarize [ˈpledʒəˌraɪz] *tr* plagier

plague [pleg] *s* peste *f;* (*great public calamity*) fléau *m* ‖ *tr* tourmenter

plaid [plæd] *s* plaid *m*

plain [plen] *adj* (*manifest*) clair, évident; (*unambiguous*) clair, franc; (*talk*) sans équivoque; (*dress, style, diet, food*) simple; (*sheer, utter*) pur, tout pur; (*color*) uni; (*ugly*) sans attraits ‖ *s* plaine *f*

plain' clothes' *spl*—**in plain clothes** en civil, en bourgeois

plain'clothes'man *s* (*pl* **-men'**) agent *m* en civil

plain' cook'ing *s* cuisine *f* bourgeoise

plain' om'elet *s* omelette *f* nature

plain' speech' *s* franc-parler *m*

plaintiff [ˈplentɪf] *s* (law) demandeur *m,* plaignant *m*

plaintive [ˈplentɪv] *adj* plaintif

plan [plæn] *s* plan *m,* project *m;* (*drawing, diagram*) plan, dessein *m* ‖ *v* (*pret & pp* **planned;** *ger* **planning**) *tr* projecter; **to plan to** se proposer de ‖ *intr* faire des projets

plane [plen] *adj* plan, plat ‖ *s* (aer) avion *m;* (bot) platane *m;* (carpentry) rabot *m;* (geom) plan *m* ‖ *tr* raboter

plane' sick'ness *s* mal *m* de l'air

planet [ˈplænɪt] *s* planète *f*

plane' tree' *s* platane *m*

plan'ing mill' *s* atelier *m* de rabotage

plank [plæŋk] *s* planche *f;* (pol) article *m* d'une plate-forme électorale

planning [ˈplænɪŋ] *s* planification *f,* planning *m*

plant [plænt] *s* (*factory*) usine *f;* (*building and equipment*) installation *f;* (bot) plante *f* ‖ *tr* planter

plantation [plænˈteʃən] *s* plantation *f*

planter [ˈplæntər] *s* planteur *m*

plant' louse' *s* puceron *m*

plasma [ˈplæzmə] *s* plasma *m*

plaster [ˈplæstər] *s* plâtre *m;* (*poultice*) emplâtre *m* ‖ *tr* plâtrer; (*a bill, poster*) coller; (slang) griser

plas'ter•board' *s* placoplâtre *m*

plas'ter cast' *s* plâtre *m*

plas′ter of Par′is *s* plâtre *m* à mouler

plastic [ˋplæstɪk] *adj* & *s* plastique *m*

plas′tic bomb′ *s* plastic *m*, bombe *f* de plastique

plas′tic explo′sive *s* explosif *m* plastique, plastique *m*, plastic *m*

plas′tic sur′gery *s* chirurgie plastique

plate [plet] *s* (*dish*) assiette *f;* (*platter*) plateau *m;* (*sheet of metal*) tôle *f*, plaque *f;* vaisselle *f* d'or ou d'argent; (anat, elec, phot, rad, zool) plaque; (typ) planche *f;* (baseball) marbre *m* ‖ *tr* plaquer; (elec) galvaniser; (typ) clicher

plateau [plæˋto] *s* plateau *m*, massif *m*

plate′ glass′ *s* verre *m* cylindré

platen [ˋplætən] *s* rouleau *m*

platform [ˋplætˏfɔrm] *s* plate-forme *f;* (*for arrivals and departures*) quai *m;* (*of a speaker*) estrade *f;* (*political program*) plate-forme

plat′form car′ *s* (rr) plate-forme *f*

platinum [ˋplætɪnəm] *s* platine *m*

plat′inum blonde′ *s* blonde *f* platinée

platitude [ˋplætɪˏt(j)ud] *s* platitude *f*

Plato [ˋpleto] *s* Platon *m*

platoon [pləˋtun] *s* section *f*

platter [ˋplætər] *s* plat *m;* (slang) disque *m*

plausible [ˋplɔzɪbəl] *adj* plausible

play [ple] *s* jeu *m;* (*drama*) pièce *f;* (mach) jeu; **to give full play to** donner libre cours à ‖ *tr* jouer; (*e.g., the fool*) faire; (*cards; e.g., football*) jouer à; (*an instrument*) jouer de; **to play back** (*a tape*) faire repasser; **to play down** diminuer; **to play hooky** faire l'école buissonnière; **to play off** (sports) rejouer; **to play up** accentuer ‖ *intr* jouer; **to play out** s'épuiser; **to play safe** prendre des précautions; **to play sick** faire semblant d'être malade; **to play up to** passer de la pommade à

play′back′ *s* (*device*) lecteur *m;* (*reproduction*) lecture *f*, réécoute *f*, surjeu *m;* (*act*) présonorisation *f*

play′back head′ *s* tête *f* de lecture

play′bill′ *s* programme *m;* (*poster*) affiche *f*

player [ˋpleˏər] *s* joueur *m;* (mus) musicien *m*, joueur, exécutant *m;* (theat) acteur *m*, interprète *mf*

play′er pian′o *s* piano *m* mécanique

playful [ˋplefəl] *adj* enjoué, badin

playgoer [ˋpleˏgoˏər] *s* amateur *m* de théâtre

play′ground′ *s* terrain *m* de jeu

play′house′ *s* théâtre *m;* (*dollhouse*) maison *f* de poupée

play′ing card′ *s* carte *f* à jouer

play′ing field′ *s* terrain *m* de sports

play′mate′ *s* compagnon *m* de jeu

play′-off′ *s* finale *f*, match *m* d'appui

play′ on words′ *s* jeu *m* de mots

play′pen′ *s* parc *m* d'enfants

play′room′ *s* salle *f* de jeux

play′thing′ *s* jouet *m*

play′time′ *s* récréation *f*

playwright [ˋpleˏraɪt] *s* auteur *m* dramatique, dramaturge *mf*

play′writ′ing *s* dramaturgie *f*

plea [pli] *s* requête *f*, appel *m;* prétexte *m;* (law) défense *f*

plead [plid] *v* (*pret* & *pp* **pleaded** or **pled** [plɛd]) *tr* & *intr* plaider; **to plead not guilty** plaider non coupable

pleasant [ˋplɛzənt] *adj* agréable

pleasant•ry [ˋplɛzəntri] *s* (*pl* **-ries**) plaisanterie *f*

please [pliz] *tr* plaire à; **it pleases him to** il lui plaît de; **please** + *inf* veuillez + *inf;* **to be pleased with** être content *or* satisfait de ‖ *intr* plaire; **as you please** comme vous voulez; **if you please** s'il vous plaît

pleasing [ˋplizɪŋ] *adj* agréable

pleasure [ˋplɛʒər] *s* plaisir *m;* **at the pleasure of** au gré de; **what is your pleasure?** qu'y a-t-il pour votre service?, que puis-je faire pour vous?

pleas′ure car′ *s* voiture *f* de tourisme

pleas′ure trip′ *s* voyage *m* d'agrément

pleat [plit] *s* pli *m* ‖ *tr* plisser

plebe [plib] *s* élève *m* de première année

plebeian [plɪˋbi•ən] *adj* & *s* plébéien *m*

plebiscite [ˋplɛbɪˏsaɪt] *s* plébiscite *m*

pledge [plɛdʒ] *s* (*security*) gage *m;* (*promise*) engagement *m* d'honneur, promesse *f* ‖ *tr* mettre en gage; (*one's word*) engager

plentiful [ˋplɛntɪfəl] *adj* abondant

plenty [ˋplɛnti] *s* abondance *f;* **I have plenty** j'en ai plein; **plenty of** beaucoup de ‖ *adv* (coll) largement

pleurisy [ˋplʊrɪsi] *s* pleurésie *f*

pliable [ˋplaɪ•əbəl] *adj* (*substance*) pliable, flexible; (*character*) docile, souple, malléable

pliers [ˋplaɪ•ərz] *s* & *spl* pinces *fpl*, tenailles *fpl*

plight [plaɪt] *s* embarras *m;* (*promise*) engagement *m* ‖ *tr* engager; **to plight one's troth** promettre fidélité

PLO [ˋpiˋɛlˋo] *s* (letterword) (**Palestine Liberation Organization**) O.L.P. (Organisation de la libération de la Palestine)

plod [plɑd] *v* (*pret* & *pp* **plodded;** *ger* **plodding**) *tr* parcourir lourdement et péniblement ‖ *intr* cheminer; travailler laborieusement

plot [plɑt] *s* (*conspiracy*) complot *m;* (*of a play or novel*) intrigue *f;* (*of ground*) lopin *m*, parcelle *f;* (*map*) tracé *m*, plan *m;* (*of vegetables*) caré *m* ‖ *v* (*pret* & *pp* **plotted;** *ger* **plotting**) *tr* comploter, tramer; (*a tract of land*) faire le plan de; (*a point*) relever; (*lines*) tracer ‖ *intr* comploter; **to plot to** + *inf* comploter de + *inf*

plough [plaʊ] *s, tr,* & *intr* var of **plow**

plover [ˋplʌvər], [ˋplovər] *s* pluvier *m*

plow [plaʊ] *s* charrue *f;* (*for snow*) chasseneige *m* ‖ *tr* labourer; (*the sea; the forehead*) sillonner; (*snow*) déblayer; **to plow back** (com) affecter aux investissements ‖ *intr* labourer; **to plow through** avancer péniblement dans

plow′man *s* (*pl* **-men**) laboureur *m*

plow′share′ *s* soc *m* de charrue

pluck [plʌk] *s* courage *m*, cran *m;* (*tug*) petit coup *m* ‖ *tr* arracher; (*flowers*) cueillir; (*a* *fowl*) plumer; (*one's eyebrows*) épiler; (*e.g., the strings of a guitar*) pincer; **to pluck off** or **out** arracher; **to pluck up the courage to** trouver le courage de ‖ *intr*—**to pluck at** arracher d'un coup sec; **to pluck up** reprendre courage

pluck•y [ˈplʌki] *adj* (*comp* **-ier;** *super* **-iest**) courageux, crâne

plug [plʌg] *s* (*stopper*) tampon *m*, bouchon *m;* (*of sink, bathtub, etc.*) bonde *f;* (*of tobacco*) chique *f;* (aut) bougie *f;* (*on wall*) (elec) prise *f;* (*prongs*) (elec) fiche *f*, prise; (*old horse*) (coll) rosse *f;* (*hat*) (slang) haut-de-forme *m;* (slang) annonce *f* publicitaire ‖ *v* (*pret & pp* **plugged;** *ger* **plugging**) *tr* boucher; (*a melon*) entamer; **to plug in** (elec) brancher ‖ *intr*—**to plug away** (coll) persévérer

plum [plʌm] *s* prune *f;* (*tree*) prunier *m;* (slang) fromage *m*

plumage [ˈplumɪdʒ] *s* plumage *m*

plumb [plʌm] *adj* d'aplomb; (coll) pur ‖ *s* plomb *m;* **out of plumb** hors d'aplomb ‖ *adv* d'aplomb; (coll) en plein; (coll) complètement ‖ *tr* sonder

plumb′ bob′ *s* plomb *m*

plumber [ˈplʌmər] *s* plombier *m*

plumbing [ˈplʌmɪŋ] *s* plomberie *f*

plumb′ line′ *s* fil *m* à plomb

plume [plum] *s* (*cluster of feathers*) plumes *fpl;* (*small plume on hat*) plumet *m;* (*of a hat, of smoke, etc.*) panache *m* ‖ *tr* orner de plumes; (*feathers*) lisser; **to plume oneself on** se piquer de

plummet [ˈplʌmɪt] *s* plomb *m* ‖ *intr* tomber d'aplomb, se précipiter

plump [plʌmp] *adj* grassouillet, potelé, dodu ‖ *s* (coll) chute *f* lourde; (coll) bruit *m* sourd ‖ *adv* en plein; brusquement ‖ *tr* jeter brusquement; **to plump oneself down** s'affaler ‖ *intr* tomber lourdement

plum′ toma′to *s* olivette *f*

plunder [ˈplʌndər] *s* pillage *m;* (*booty*) butin *m* ‖ *tr* piller

plunge [plʌndʒ] *s* (*dive*) plongeon *m;* (*steep fall*) chute *f;* (*pitching movement*) tangage *m* ‖ *tr* plonger ‖ *intr* plonger; se précipiter; (fig) se plonger; (naut) tanguer; (slang) risquer de grosses sommes

plunger [ˈplʌndʒər] *s* (*for blocked drain*) ventouse *f*, débouchoir *m;* (*gambler*) (slang) risque-tout *m*

plunk [plʌŋk] *adv* d'un coup sec; (*squarely*) carrément ‖ *tr* jeter bruyamment ‖ *intr* tomber raide

plural [ˈplurəl] *adj & s* pluriel *m*

plus [plʌs] *adj* positif ‖ *s* (*sign*) plus *m;* quantité *f* positive ‖ *prep* plus

plush [plʌʃ] *adj* en peluche; (coll) rupin ‖ *s* peluche *f*

plush•y [ˈplʌʃi] *adj* (*comp* **-ier;** *super* **-iest**) pelucheux; (coll) rupin

plus′ sign′ *s* signe *m* plus

Plutarch [ˈplutɑrk] *s* Plutarque *m*

Pluto [ˈpluto] *s* Pluton *m*

plutonium [pluˈtoniˑəm] *s* plutonium *m*

ply [plaɪ] *s* (*pl* **plies**) (*e.g., of a cloth*) pli *m;* (*of rope, wool, etc.*) brin *m* ‖ *v* (*pret & pp* **plied**) *tr* manier; (*a trade*) exercer; **to ply s.o. with** presser qn de ‖ *intr* faire la navette

ply′wood′ *s* bois *m* de placage, contreplaqué *m*

P.M. [ˈpiˈɛm] *adv* (letterword) (**post meridiem**) de l'après-midi, du soir

pneumatic [n(j)uˈmætɪk] *adj* pneumatique

pneumat′ic drill′ *s* foreuse *f* à air comprimé, marteau-piqueur *m*

pneumonia [n(j)uˈmoniˑə] *s* pneumonie *f*

P.O. [ˈpiˈo] *s* (letterword) (**post office**) poste *f*

poach [potʃ] *tr* (*eggs*) pocher ‖ *intr* (hunting) braconner

poached′ egg′ *s* œuf *m* poché

poacher [ˈpotʃər] *s* braconnier *m*

pock [pɑk] *s* pustule *f*

pocket [ˈpɑkɪt] *s* poche *f;* (billiards) blouse *f;* (aer) trou *m* d'air ‖ *tr* empocher; (*a billiard ball*) blouser; (*insults*) avaler

pock′et•book′ *s* portefeuille *m;* (*small book*) livre *m* de poche

pock′et cal′culator *s* calculatrice *f* de poche, calculette *f*

pock′et comput′er *s* ordinateur *m* de poche

pock′et hand′kerchief *s* mouchoir *m* de poche

pock′et•knife′ *s* (*pl* **-knives**) couteau *m* de poche, canif *m*

pock′et mon′ey *s* argent *m* de poche

pock′mark′ *s* marque *f* de la petite vérole

pock′marked′ *adj* grêlé

pod [pɑd] *s* cosse *f*, gousse *f*

podiatrist [pəˈdaɪˑətrəst] *s* podologue *mf*, pédicure *mf*

podiatry [pəˈdaɪˑətri] *s* podologie *f*, soins *mpl* des pieds

poem [ˈpoˑɪm] *s* poème *m*

poet [ˈpoˑɪt] *s* poète *m*, poétesse *f*

poetess [ˈpoˑɪtɪs] *s* poétesse *f*

poetic [poˈɛtɪk] *adj* poétique ‖ **poetics** *s* poétique *f*

poetry [ˈpoˑɪtri] *s* poésie *f*

pogrom [ˈpogrəm] *s* pogrom *m*

poignancy [ˈpɔɪnənsi] *s* piquant *m*

poignant [ˈpɔɪnənt] *adj* poignant

point [pɔɪnt] *s* (*spot, dot, score, etc.*) point *m;* (*tip*) pointe *f;* (*of pen*) bec *m;* (*of conscience*) cas *m;* (*of a star*) rayon *m;* (*of a joke*) piquant *m;* (*of, e.g., grammar*) question *f;* (geog, naut) pointe; (typ) point; **beside the point, off the point** hors de propos; **on the point of** sur le point de; (*death*) à l'article de; **on this point** à cet égard, à ce propos; **point of a compass** aire *f* de vent; **point of order** rappel *m* au règlement; **point of view** point de vue; **points** (aut) vis *f* platinées; **to carry one's point** avoir gain de cause; **to come to the point** venir au fait; **to have one's good points** avoir ses qualités; **to make a point of** se faire un devoir de ‖ *tr* (*a gun, telescope, etc.*) braquer, pointer; (*a finger*) tendre; (*the way*) indiquer;

(*a wall*) jointoyer; (*to sharpen*) tailler en point; **to point out** signaler, faire remarquer ‖ *intr* pointer; (*said of hunting dog*) tomber en arrêt; **to point at** montrer du doigt

point′-blank′ *adj & adv* (*fired straight at the mark*) à bout portant; (*straight forward*) à brûle-pourpoint

pointed *adj* pointu; (*remark*) mordant

pointer [ˈpɔɪntər] *s* (*stick*) baguette *f*; (*of a dial*) aiguille *f*; (*dog*) chien *m* d'arrêt, pointeur *m*; (comp) (*white arrow on the screen following the mouvements of the mouse*) pointeur *m*

pointing [ˈpɔɪntɪŋ] *s* (archit) jointoiement *m*; (comp) (*white arrow*) pointeur *m*

point′ of view′ *s* point *m* de vue

poise [pɔɪz] *s* équilibre *m*; (*assurance*) aplomb *m* ‖ *tr* tenir en équilibre ‖ *intr* être en équilibre; (*in the air*) planer

poison [ˈpɔɪzən] *s* poison *m* ‖ *tr* empoisonner

poi′son gas′ *s* gaz *m* asphyxiant, gaz de combat

poi′son i′vy *s* sumac *m* vénéneux

poisonous [ˈpɔɪzənəs] *adj* toxique; (*plant*) vénéneux; (*snake*) venimeux

poi′son-pen′ let′ter *s* lettre *f* anonyme venimeuse

poke [pok] *s* poussée *f*; (*with elbow*) coup *m* de coude; (coll) traînard *m* ‖ *tr* pousser; (*the fire*) tisonner; **to poke fun at** se moquer de; **to poke one's nose into** (coll) fourrer son nez dans; **to poke s.th. into** fourrer q.ch. dans ‖ *intr* aller sans se presser; **to poke about** fureter

poker [ˈpokər] *s* tisonnier *m*; (cards) poker *m*

pok′er face′ *s* visage *m* impassible

pok•y [ˈpoki] *adj* (*comp* **-ier**; *super* **-iest**) (coll) lambin, lent

Poland [ˈpolənd] *s* Pologne *f*; la Pologne

polar [ˈpolər] *adj* polaire

po′lar bear′ *s* ours *m* blanc

po′lar ice′ cap′ *s* calotte *f* glaciaire polaire

polarize [ˈpolə,raɪz] *tr* polariser

pole [pol] *s* (*long rod or staff*) perche *f*; (*of flag*) hampe *f*; (*upright support*) poteau *m*; (astr, biol, elec, geog, math) pôle *m*; **Pole** (*person*) Polonais *m* ‖ *tr* pousser à la perche

pole′cat′ *s* putois *m*

pole′star′ *s* étoile *f* polaire

pole′ vault′ *s* saut *m* à la perche

police [pəˈlis] *s* police *f* ‖ *tr* maintenir l'ordre dans

police′ brutal′ity *s* brutalité *f* policière

police′ car′ *s* voiture *f* de police

police′ commis′sioner *s* préfet *m* de police

police′ force′ *s* police *f*,

police′man *s* (*pl* **-men**) agent *m* de police

police′ pre′cinct *s* commissariat *m* de police

police′ rec′ord *s* casier *m* judiciaire

police′ state′ *s* régime *m* policier

police′ sta′tion *s* poste *m* de police, commissariat *m*

police′wom′an *s* (*pl* **-wom′en**) femme *f* agent

poli•cy [ˈpɑlɪsi] *s* (*pl* **-cies**) politique *f*; (ins) police *f*

pol′icy hold′er *s* (ins) assuré *m*, assurée *f*

polio [ˈpoliˌo] *s* (coll) polio *f*

polish [ˈpɑlɪʃ] *s* (*shine*) poli *m*; (*for household uses*) cire *f*; (*for shoes*) cirage *m*; (fig) politesse *f*, vernis *m* ‖ *tr* polir; (*shoes, floor, etc.*) cirer; (*one's nails*) vernir; **to polish off** (coll) expédier; (*e.g., a meal*) (slang) engloutir ‖ **Polish** [ˈpolɪʃ] *adj & s* polonais *m*

polite [pəˈlaɪt] *adj* poli

politeness [pəˈlaɪtnɪs] *s* politesse *f*

politic [ˈpɑlɪtɪk] *adj* (*prudent*) diplomatique, politique; (*shrewd*) rusé

political [pəˈlɪtɪkəl] *adj* politique

polit′ical correct′ness *s* opinions *fpl* politiquement correctes

polit′ically correct′ *adj* politiquement correct

politician [,pɑlɪˈtɪʃən] *s* politicien *m*

politico [pəˈlɪtɪko] *s* politicien *m* marron, politicien (pej)

politics [ˈpɑlɪtɪks] *s & spl* politique *f*

poll [pol] *s* (*list of voters*) liste *f* électorale; (*vote*) scrutin *m*; (*head*) tête *f*; (*opinion survey*) sondage *m* d'opinion; **to go to the polls** aller aux urnes; **to take a poll** faire une enquête par sondage ‖ *tr* (*e.g., a delegation*) dépouiller le scrutin de; (*a certain number of votes*) recevoir

pollen [ˈpɑlən] *s* pollen *m*

pollinate [ˈpɑlɪ,net] *tr* féconder (avec du pollen)

poll′ing booth′ [ˈpolɪŋ] *s* isoloir *m*

polliwog [ˈpɑlɪ,wɑg] *s* têtard *m*

pol′liwog initia′tion *s* baptême *m* de la ligne

pollster [ˈpolstər] *s* sondeur *m*, enquêteur *m*

poll′ tax′ *s* taxe *f* par tête

pollute [pəˈlut] *tr* polluer

polluting [pəˈlutɪŋ] *adj* polluant

pollution [pəˈluʃən] *s* pollution *f*

polo [ˈpolo] *s* polo *m*

polonium [pəˈlonɪˌəm] *s* polonium *m*

polo shirt′ *s* chemise *f* polo

polygamist [pəˈlɪgəmɪst] *s* polygame *mf*

polygamous [pəˈlɪgəməs] *adj* polygame

polyglot [ˈpɑlɪ,glat] *adj & s* polyglotte *mf*

polygon [ˈpɑlɪ,gan] *s* polygone *m*

polynomial [,pɑlɪˈnomɪˌəl] *s* polynôme *m*

polyp [ˈpɑlɪp] *s* polype *m*

polytheist [ˈpɑlɪ,θiˌɪst] *s* polythéiste *mf*

polytheistic [,pɑlɪˈθiˌɪstɪk] *adj* polythéiste

polyvalent [pɑliˈvelənt] *adj* polyvalent

pomade [pəˈmed] *s* pommade *f*

pomegranate [ˈpɑm,grænɪt] *s* (*shrub*) grenadier *m*; (*fruit*) grenade *f*

pom•mel [ˈpʌməl] *s* pommeau *m* ‖ *v* (*pret & pp* **-meled** *or* **-melled**; *ger* **-meling** *or* **-melling**) *tr* rosser

pomp [pamp] *s* pompe *f*

pompous [ˈpampəs] *adj* pompeux

pon•cho [ˈpantʃo] *s* (*pl* **-chos**) poncho *m*

pond [pand] *s* étang *m*, mare *f*

ponder [ˈpandər] *tr* peser ‖ *intr* méditer; **to ponder over** réfléchir sur

ponderous [ˈpandərəs] *adj* pesant

poniard [ˈpanjərd] *s* poignard *m* ‖ *tr* poignarder

pontiff [`pɑntɪf] s pontife m
pontifical [pɑn`tɪfɪkəl] adj (e.g., air) de pontife
pontoon [pɑn`tun] s ponton m
po‧ny [`poni] s (pl **-nies**) poney m; (for drinking liquor) petit verre m; (coll) aide-mémoire m illicite
po′ny‧tail′ s queue-de-cheval f
poodle [`pudəl] s caniche m
pool [pul] s (small puddle) mare f; (for swimming) piscine f; (game) billard m; (in certain games) poule f; (of workers) équipe f; (combine) pool m; (com) fonds m commun ‖ tr mettre en commun
pool′room′ s salle f de billard
pool′ ta′ble s table f de billard
poop [pup] s poupe f; (deck) dunette f ‖ tr (slang) casser la tête à
pooped adj (slang) vanné, à plat, flagada
poor [pur] adj pauvre; (mediocre) piètre; (unfortunate) pauvre (before noun); (without money) pauvre (after noun)
poor′ box′ s tronc m des pauvres
poor′house′ s asile m des indigents
poorly [`purli] adj souffrant ‖ adv mal
pop [pɑp] s bruit m sec; (soda) boisson f gazeuse; (coll) papa m ‖ v (pret & pp **popped;** ger **popping**) tr (corn) faire éclater ‖ intr (said, e.g., of balloon) crever; (said of cork) sauter
pop′corn′ s maïs m éclaté, maïs explosé; grains mpl de maïs soufflés, pop-corn m
pope [pop] s pape m
pop′eyed′ adj aux yeux saillants
pop′gun′ s canonnière f
poplar [`pɑplər] s peuplier m
pop-pop [`pɑppɑp] s (child's language) grand-papa m, pépé m
pop‧py [`pɑpi] s (pl **-pies**) pavot m; (corn poppy) coquelicot m
pop′py‧cock′ s (coll) fadaises fpl
populace [`pɑpjələs] s peuple m, populace f
popular [`pɑpjələr] adj populaire
popularize [`pɑpjələ‚raɪz] tr populariser, vulgariser
populate [`pɑpjə‚let] tr peupler
population [‚pɑpjə`leʃən] s population f
populous [`pɑpjələs] adj populeux
pop′-up win′dow [`pɑpʌp] s (comp) fenêtre f dépliante
porcelain [`pɔrslɪn] s porcelaine f
porch [pɔrtʃ] s (portico) porche m; (enclosed) véranda f
porcupine [`pɔrkjə‚paɪn] s porc-épic m
pore [por] s pore m ‖ intr—**to pore over** examiner avec attention, s'absorber dans
pork [pɔrk] s porc m
pork′ and beans′ spl fèves fpl au lard
pork′chop′ s côtelette f de porc
porn [pɔrn] s (coll) porno m & f
pornographic [‚pɔrnə`græfɪk] adj pornographique
pornography [pɔr`nɑgrəfi] s pornographie f
porous [`porəs] adj poreux

porphy‧ry [`pɔrfɪri] s (pl **-ries**) porphyre m
porpoise [`pɔrpəs] s marsouin m
porridge [`pɔrɪdʒ] s bouillie f, porridge m
port [pɔrt] s port m; (opening in ship's side) hublot m, sabord m; (left side of ship or airplane) bâbord m; (wine) porto m; (mach) orifice m
portable [`pɔrtəbəl] adj portatif
port′able stand′ s (for a television set) socle m roulant
port′able type′writer s machine f à écrire portative
portage [`pɔrtɪdʒ] s transport m; portage m
portal [`pɔrtəl] s portail m
portcullis [pɔrt`kʌlɪs] s herse f
portend [pɔr`tɛnd] tr présager
portent [`pɔrtɛnt] s présage m
portentous [pɔr`tɛntəs] adj extraordinaire; de mauvais augure
porter [`pɔrtər] s (doorkeeper) portier m, concierge m; (in hotels and trains) porteur m
portfoli‧o [pɔrt`folɪ‚o] s (pl **-os**) portefeuille m
port′hole′ s hublot m
porti‧co [`pɔrtɪ‚ko] s (pl **-coes** or **-cos**) portique m
portion [`pɔrʃən] s portion f; (dowry) dot f ‖ tr—**to portion out** partager, répartir
port‧ly [`pɔrtli] adj (comp **-lier;** super **-liest**) corpulent
port′ of call′ s port m d'escale
portrait [`pɔrtret] s portrait m; **to sit for one's portrait** se faire faire son portrait
portray [pɔr`tre] tr faire le portrait de; dépeindre, décrire; (theat) jouer le rôle de
portrayal [pɔr`tre‧əl] s représentation f; description f
Portugal [`pɔrt/əgəl] s le Portugal
Portu‧guese [`pɔrt/ə‚giz] adj portugais ‖ s (language) portugais m ‖ s (pl **-guese**) (person) Portugais m
port′ wine′ s porto m
pose [poz] s pose f ‖ tr & intr poser; **to pose as** se poser comme
posh [pɑʃ] adj (slang) chic, élégant
position [pə`zɪʃən] s position f; (job) poste m; **in position** en place; **in your position** à votre place
positive [`pɑzɪtɪv] adj & s positif m
possess [pə`zɛs] tr posséder
possession [pə`zɛʃən] s possession f; **to take possession of** s'emparer de
possible [`pɑsɪbəl] adj possible
possibly [`pɑsəblɪ] adv peut-être
possum [`pɑsəm] s opossum m; **to play possum** (coll) faire le mort
post [post] s (upright) poteau m; (job, position) poste m; (post office) poste f; (mil) poste m ‖ tr (a notice, placard, etc.) afficher, placarder; (a letter) poster, mettre à la poste; (a sentinel) poster; (with news) tenir au courant; **post no bills** (public sign) défense d'afficher
postage [`postɪdʒ] s port m, affranchissement m

post′age due′ *s* port *m* dû, affranchissement *m* insuffisant

post′age me′ter *s* affranchisseuse *f* à compteur

post′age stamp′ *s* timbre-poste *m*

postal [ˈpostəl] *adj* postal

post′al card′ *s* carte *f* postale

post′al clerk′ *s* postier *m*

post′al mon′ey or′der *s* mandat-poste *m*

post′al per′mit *s* franchise *f* postale, dispensé *m* du timbrage

post′al sav′ings bank′ *s* caisse *f* d'épargne postale

post′ card′ *s* carte *f* postale

post′date′ *s* postdate *f* ‖ **post′date′** *tr* postdater

poster [ˈpostər] *s* affiche *f*

pos′ter board′ *s* carton *m* pour les affiches

posterity [pɑsˈtɛrɪti] *s* postérité *f*

postern [ˈpostərn] *s* poterne *f*

post′haste′ *adv* en toute hâte

posthumous [ˈpɑstʃʊməs] *adj* posthume

post′man *s* (*pl* **-men**) facteur *m*, préposé *m*

post′mark′ *s* cachet *m* d'oblitération, timbre *m* ‖ *tr* timbrer

post′mas′ter *s* receveur *m* des postes, administrateur *m* du bureau de postes

post′master gen′eral *s* ministre *m* des Postes et Télécommunications

post-mortem [ˌpostˈmɔrtəm] *adj* après décès; (fig) après le fait ‖ *s* autopsie *f*; discussion *f* après le fait

post′ of′fice *s* bureau *m* de poste

post′-office box′ *s* case *f* postale, boîte *f* postale

post′paid′ *adv* port payé, franc de port, franco de port

postpone [postˈpon] *tr* remettre, différer; (*a meeting*) ajourner

postponement [postˈponmənt] *s* remise *f*, ajournement *m*

postscript [ˈpostˌskrɪpt] *s* post-scriptum *m*

posture [ˈpɑstʃər] *s* posture *f* ‖ *intr* prendre une posture

post′war′ *adj* d'après-guerre

po·sy [ˈpozi] *s* (*pl* **-sies**) fleur *f*; bouquet *m*

pot [pɑt] *s* pot *m*; (*in gambling*) mise *f*; (culin) marmite *f*, pot; (*marijuana*) (slang) kif *m*, marie-jeanne *f*; **to go to pot** (slang) s'en aller à vau-l'eau

potash [ˈpɑtˌæʃ] *s* potasse *f*

potassium [pəˈtæsɪəm] *s* potassium *m*

pota·to [pəˈteto] *s* (*pl* **-toes**) pomme *f* de terre; (*sweet potato*) patate *f*

pota′to chips′ *spl* pommes *fpl* chips; croustelle *f* (Canad)

pota′to peel′er *s* éplucheur *m*

potbellied [ˈpɑtˌbɛlid] *adj* ventru

poten·cy [ˈpotənsi] *s* (*pl* **-cies**) puissance *f*; virilité *f*

potent [ˈpotənt] *adj* puissant, fort; (*effective*) efficace

potentate [ˈpotənˌtet] *s* potentat *m*

potential [pəˈtɛnʃəl] *adj* & *s* potentiel *m*

pot′hang′er *s* crémaillère *f*

pot′herb′ *s* herbe *f* potagère

pot′hold′er *s* poignée *f*

pot′hole′ *s* nid-de-poule *m*

pot′hook′ *s* croc *m*

potion [ˈpoʃən] *s* potion *f*

pot′luck′ *s*—**to take potluck** manger à la fortune du pot

pot′ shot′ *s* coup *m* tiré à courte distance

potter [ˈpɑtər] *s* potier *m* ‖ *intr*—**to potter around** s'occuper de bagatelles, bricoler

pot′ter's clay′ *s* terre *f* à potier

pot′ter's field′ *s* fosse *f* commune

pot′ter's wheel′ *s* roue *f* or tour *m* de potier

potter·y [ˈpɑtəri] *s* (*pl* **-ies**) poterie *f*

pouch [pautʃ] *s* poche *f*, petit sac *m*; (*of kangaroo*) poche *f* ventrale; (*for tobacco*) blague *f*

poultice [ˈpoltɪs] *s* cataplasme *m*

poultry [ˈpoltri] *s* volaille *f*

poul′try·man *s* (*pl* **-men**) éleveur *m* de volailles; (*dealer*) volailleur *m*

pounce [pauns] *intr*—**to pounce on** fondre sur, s'abattre sur

pound [paund] *s* (*weight*) livre *f*; (*for automobiles, stray animals, etc.*) fourrière *f* ‖ *tr* battre; (*to pulverize*) piler, broyer; (*to bombard*) pilonner; (*e.g., an animal*) mettre en fourrière; (*e.g., the sidewalk*) (fig) battre ‖ *intr* battre

pound′ cake′ *s* quatre-quarts *m invar*

pound′ ster′ling *s* livre *f* sterling

pour [por] *tr* verser; (*tea*) servir; **to pour off** décanter ‖ *intr* écouler; (*said of rain*) tomber à verse; **to pour out of** sortir à flots

pout [paut] *s* moue *f* ‖ *intr* faire la moue

poverty [ˈpɑvərti] *s* pauvreté *f*

POW [ˈpiˈoˈdʌblˌju] *s* (letterword) (**prisoner of war**) P.G.

powder [ˈpaudər] *s* poudre *f* ‖ *tr* réduire en poudre; (*to sprinkle with powder*) poudrer ‖ *intr* se poudrer

pow′dered cof′fee *s* café *m* soluble

pow′dered sug′ar *s* sucre *m* de confiseur, sucre en poudre, sucre glace

pow′der puff′ *s* houppe *f*

pow′der room′ *s* toilettes *fpl* pour dames; (*downstairs lavatory or toilet*) cabinet *m* de toilette

powdery [ˈpaudəri] *adj* (*like powder*) poudreux; (*sprinkled with powder*) poussiéreux; (*crumbly*) friable

power [ˈpauər] *s* (*authority; capacity*) pouvoir *m*; (*influential nation; energy, force, strength; of a machine, microscope, number*) puissance *f*; (*talent, capacity, etc.*) faculté *f*; **the powers that be** les autorités *fpl*; **to seize power** saisir le pouvoir ‖ *tr* actionner

pow′er brake′ *s* (aut) servo-frein *m*

pow′er dive′ *s* piqué *m* à plein gaz

pow′er-dive′ *intr* piquer à plein gaz

powerful [ˈpauˌərfəl] *adj* puissant

pow′er·house′ *s* usine *f* centrale; (coll) foyer *m* d'énergie

pow′er lawn′mower *s* tondeuse *f* à gazon à moteur

powerless [ˈpauˌərlɪs] *adj* impuissant

pow′er line′ s secteur m de distribution
power′ lunch′ s déjeuner m d'affaires (*rencontre stratégique avec des personnes haut placées*)
pow′er mow′er s tondeuse f à gazon à moteur; motofaucheuse f
pow′er of attorn′ey s procuration f, mandat m
pow′er pack′ s (rad) unité f d'alimentation
pow′er plant′ s (*powerhouse*) centrale f électrique; (aer, aut) groupe m motopropulseur
pow′er saw′ s tronçonneuse f
pow′er steer′ing s (aut) servo-direction f
power′ tool′ s outil m à moteur
practicable [′præktɪkəbəl] adj praticable
practical [′præktɪkəl] adj pratique
prac′tical joke′ s farce f, attrape f
prac′tical jok′er s fumiste m
practically [′præktɪkəli] adv pratiquement; (*more or less*) à peu près
prac′tical nurse′ s garde-malade mf
practice [′præktɪs] s (*habit, usage*) pratique f; (*of a profession*) exercice m; (*of a doctor*) clientèle f; (*exercise, training*) entraînement m; (*rehearsal*) répétition f; **in practice** en pratique, pratiquement; (*well-trained*) en forme; **out of practice** rouillé ‖ tr pratiquer; (*a profession*) exercer, pratiquer; (*e.g., the violin*) s'exercer à; **to practice what one preaches** prêcher d'exemple ‖ intr faire des exercices, s'exercer; (*said of doctor, lawyer, etc.*) exercer
practiced adj expert
practitioner [præk′tɪʃənər] s praticien m
Prague [prɑg] ou [preg] s Prague, Praha
prairie [′prɛri] s steppes fpl; **the prairie** les Prairies fpl
praise [prez] s louange f ‖ tr louer
praise′wor′thy adj louable, digne d'éloges
pram [præm] s voiture f d'enfant
prance [præns] intr caracoler, cabrioler
prank [præŋk] s espièglerie f
prate [pret] intr bavarder, papoter
prattle [′prætəl] s bavardage m, papotage m ‖ intr bavarder, papoter; (*said of children*) babiller
prawn [prɔn] s crevette f rose, bouquet m
pray [pre] tr & intr prier
prayer [prɛr] s prière f
prayer′ book′ s livre m de prières
pray′ing man′tis [′mæntɪs] s mante f religieuse
preach [pritʃ] tr & intr prêcher
preacher [′pritʃər] s prédicateur m
preamble [′pri,æmbəl] s préambule m
precarious [prɪ′kɛri•əs] adj précaire
precaution [prɪ′kɔʃən] s précaution f
precede [prɪ′sid] tr & intr précéder
precedent [′prɛsɪdənt] s précédent m
precept [′prisɛpt] s précepte m
precinct [′prisɪŋkt] s enceinte f; circonscription f électorale
precious [′prɛʃəs] adj précieux ‖ adv—**precious little** (coll) très peu

precipice [′prɛsɪpɪs] s précipice m
precipitate [prɪ′sɪpɪ,tet] adj & s précipité m ‖ tr précipiter ‖ intr se précipiter
precipitous [prɪ′sɪpɪtəs] adj escarpé; (*hurried*) précipité
precise [prɪ′saɪs] adj précis
precision [prɪ′sɪʒən] s précision f
preclude [prɪ′klud] tr empêcher
precocious [prɪ′koʃəs] adj précoce
preconceived [,prikən′sivd] adj préconçu
predatory [′prɛdə,tori] adj rapace; (zool) prédateur
predecessor [,prɛdɪ′sɛsər] s prédécesseur m, devancier m
predicament [prɪ′dɪkəmənt] s situation f difficile
predict [prɪ′dɪkt] tr prédire
prediction [prɪ′dɪkʃən] s prédiction f
predispose [,pridɪs′poz] tr prédisposer
predominant [prɪ′dɑmɪnənt] adj prédominant
preeminent [prɪ′ɛmɪnənt] adj prééminent
preempt [prɪ′ɛmpt] tr s'approprier
preen [prin] tr lisser; **to preen oneself** se bichonner; être fier, se piquer
prefabricated [pri′fæbrɪ,ketɪd] adj préfabriqué
preface [′prɛfɪs] s préface f ‖ tr préfacer
pre-fer [prɪ′fʌr] v (*pret & pp* -**ferred;** *ger* -**ferring**) tr préférer
preferable [′prɛfərəbəl] adj préférable
preference [′prɛfərəns] s préférence f
preferred′ stock′ s action f privilégiée, actions privilégiées
prefix [′prifɪks] s préfixe m ‖ tr préfixer
pregnan•cy [′prɛgnənsi] s (*pl* -**cies**) grossesse f
pregnant [′prɛgnənt] adj enceinte, grosse; (fig) gros
prehistoric [,prihɪs′tɔrɪk] adj préhistorique
prejudice [′prɛdʒədɪs] s préjugé m; (*detriment*) préjudice m ‖ tr prévenir, prédisposer; (*to harm*) porter préjudice à
prejudicial [,prɛdʒə′dɪʃəl] adj préjudiciable
prelate [′prɛlɪt] s prélat m
prelim [′prilɪm] s (educ) examen m préliminaire; (sports) épreuve f éliminatoire
preliminar•y [prɪ′lɪmɪ,nɛri] adj préliminaire ‖ s (*pl* -**ies**) préliminaire m
prelude [′prɛljud] s prélude m ‖ tr introduire; préluder à; (*a piece of music*) préluder par
premature [,primə′t(j)ʊr] adj prématuré; (*plant*) hâtif
premeditate [pri′mɛdɪ,tet] tr préméditer
premier [prɪ′mɪr] adj (*first of its kind*) premier, primordial ‖ s (pol) premier ministre m
première [prə′mjɛr], [prɪ′mɪr] s (theat) première f; (*actress*) vedette f
premise [′prɛmɪs] s prémisse f; **on the premises** sur les lieux; **premises** local m, locaux mpl
premium [′primi•əm] s prime f; **to be at a premium** faire prime
premonition [,primə′nɪʃən] s prémonition f
preoccupation [pri,ɑkjə′peʃən] s préoccupation f

preoccu•py [prɪˋakjə‚paɪ] *v* (*pret & pp* **-pied**) *tr* préoccuper

prepaid [priˋped] *adj* payé d'avance; (*letter*) affranchi

preparation [‚prɛpəˋreʃən] *s* préparation *f*; **preparations** (*for a trip; for war*) préparatifs *mpl*

preparatory [prɪˋpærə‚tori] *adj* préparatoire

prepare [prɪˋpɛr] *tr* préparer ‖ *intr* se préparer

preparedness [prɪˋpɛrdnɪs] *s* préparation *f*; armement *m* préventif

pre•pay [priˋpe] *v* (*pret & pp* **-paid**) *tr* payer d'avance

preponderant [prɪˋpɑndərənt] *adj* prépondérant

preposition [‚prɛpəˋzɪʃən] *s* préposition *f*

prepossessing [‚pripəˋzɛsɪŋ] *adj* avenant, agréable

preposterous [prɪˋpɑstərəs] *adj* absurde, extravagant

preppie [ˋprɛpi] *s* (slang) bon chic bon genre *m* (B.C.B.G.)

prep' school [prɛp] *s* école *f* préparatoire

prerecorded [‚prirɪˋkɔrdɪd] *adj* (rad, telv) différé, en différé

prerequisite [priˋrɛkwɪzɪt] *s* préalable *m*; (educ) cours *m* préalable

prerogative [prɪˋrɑgətɪv] *s* prérogative *f*

presage [ˋprɛsɪdʒ] *s* présage *m*; (*foreboding*) pressentiment *m* ‖ [prɪˋsedʒ] *tr* présager; pressentir

Presbyterian [‚prɛzbɪˋtɪrɪ•ən] *adj & s* presbytérien *m*

preschool [ˋpriskul] *adj* préscolaire

prescribe [prɪˋskraɪb] *tr* prescrire ‖ *intr* faire une ordonnance

prescription [prɪˋskrɪpʃən] *s* prescription *f*; (*pharm*) ordonnance *f*

prescrip'tion glass'es *spl* lunettes *fpl* prescrites

presence [ˋprɛzəns] *s* présence *f*

present [ˋprɛzənt] *adj* (*at this time*) actuel; (*at this place or time*) présent; **to be present at** assister à ‖ *s* cadeau *m*, présent *m*; (*present time or tense*) présent; **at present** à présent ‖ [prɪˋzɛnt] *tr* présenter

presentable [prɪˋzɛntəbəl] *adj* présentable, sortable

presentation [‚prɛzənˋteʃən] *s* présentation *f*

presenta'tion cop'y *s* exemplaire *m* offert à titre d'hommage

presentiment [prɪˋzɛntɪmənt] *s* pressentiment *m*

presently [ˋprɛzəntli] *adv* tout à l'heure; (*now*) à présent

preserve [prɪˋzʌrv] *s* confiture *f*; (*for game*) chasse *f* gardée ‖ *tr* préserver, conserver; (*to can*) conserver

pre-shrunk [priˋʃʌŋk] *adj* irrétrécissable

preside [prɪˋzaɪd] *intr* présider; **to preside over** présider

presiden•cy [ˋprɛzɪdənsi] *s* (*pl* **-cies**) présidence *f*

president [ˋprɛzɪdənt] *s* président *m*; (*of a university*) recteur *m*

pres'ident-elect' *s* président *m* désigné

presidential [‚prɛzɪˋdɛnʃəl] *adj* présidentiel

press [prɛs] *s* presse *f*; (e.g., *for wine*) pressoir *m*; (*pressure*) pression *f*; (*for clothes*) armoire *f*; (*in weight lifting*) développé *m*; **in press** (*said of clothes*) lisse et net; (*said of book being published*) sous presse; **to go to press** être mis sous presse ‖ *tr* presser; (e.g., *a button*) appuyer sur, presser; (*clothes*) donner un coup de fer à, repasser ‖ *intr* presser; **to press against** se serrer contre; **to press forward, to press on** presser le pas

press' a'gent *s* agent *m* de publicité, attaché(e) *mf* de presse

press' box' *s* tribune *f* des journalistes

press' card' *s* coupe-file *m* d'un journaliste

press' con'ference *s* conférence *f* de presse

press' gal'lery *s* tribune *f* de la presse

pressing [ˋprɛsɪŋ] *adj* pressé, pressant

press' pass' *s* placard *m* de presse

press' release' *s* communiqué *m* de presse

pressure [ˋprɛʃər] *s* pression *f*

pres'sure cook'er *s* autocuiseur *m*, cocotte *f* minute

pressurize [ˋprɛʃə‚raɪz] *tr* pressuriser

prestige [prɛsˋtiʒ] *s* prestige *m*

pre'stressed con'crete [ˋpri‚strɛst] *s* béton *m* précontraint

presumably [prɪˋz(j)uməbli] *adv* probablement

presume [prɪˋz(j)um] *tr* présumer; **to presume to** présumer ‖ *intr* présumer; **to presume on** or **upon** abuser de

presumption [prɪˋzʌmpʃən] *s* présomption *f*

presumptuous [prɪˋzʌmptʃu•əs] *adj* présomptueux

presuppose [‚prisəˋpoz] *tr* présupposer

pretend [prɪˋtɛnd] *tr* feindre; **to pretend to** + *inf* feindre de + *inf*; (*to claim*) prétendre, e.g., **I don't pretend to know everything** je ne pretends pas tout savoir; (*to imagine*) se dire, e.g., **I am going to pretend to be sitting at an outdoor café** je vais me dire que je m'assieds à une terrasse de café ‖ *intr* feindre; **let's pretend!** (*let's imagine that it's true*) imaginons-nous!; **to pretend to** (e.g., *the throne*) prétendre à

pretender [prɪˋtɛndər] *s* prétendant *m*; (*imposter*) simulateur *m*

pretense [prɪˋtɛns], [ˋpritɛns] *s* prétention *f*; feinte *f*; **under false pretenses** par des moyens frauduleux; **under pretense of** sous prétexte de

pretension [prɪˋtɛnʃən] *s* prétention *f*

pretentious [prɪˋtɛnʃəs] *adj* prétentieux

pretext [ˋpritɛkst] *s* prétexte *m*

pretonic [priˋtɑnɪk] *adj* prétonique

pret•ty [ˋprɪti] *adj* (*comp* **-tier**; *super* **-tiest**) joli; (coll) considérable ‖ *adv* assez; très

prevail [prɪˋvel] *intr* prévaloir, régner; **to prevail on** or **upon** persuader

prevailing [prɪˋvelɪŋ] *adj* (*opinion*) prédominant, courant; (*conditions*) actuel; (*wind*) dominant; (*fashion*) en vogue

prevalent [ˈprɛvələnt] *adj* commun, courant, regnant

prevaricate [prɪˈværɪˌket] *intr* mentir

prevent [prɪˈvɛnt] *tr* empêcher

prevention [prɪˈvɛnʃən] *s* empêchement *m;* (*e.g., of accidents*) prévention *f*

preventive [prɪˈvɛntɪv] *adj & s* préventif *m*

preview [ˈpriˌvju] *s* (*of something to come*) amorce *f;* (*private showing*) (mov) avant-première *f;* (*show of brief scenes for advertising*) film *m* annonce

previous [ˈpriviˑəs] *adj* précédent, antérieur; (*notice*) préalable; (coll) pressé ‖ *adv*—**previous to** antérieurement à

prewar [ˈpriˌwɔr] *adj* d'avant-guerre

prey [pre] *s* proie *f;* **to be a prey to** être en proie à ‖ *intr*—**to prey on** or **upon** faire sa proie de; (*e.g., a seacoast*) piller; (*e.g., the mind*) ronger, miner

price [praɪs] *s* prix *m* ‖ *tr* mettre un prix à, tarifer; s'informer du prix de

price′ control′ *s* contrôle *m* des prix

price′ cut′ting *s* rabais *m*, remise *f*

price′-earn′ings ra′tio *s* quotient *m* cours-bénéficie

price′ fix′ing *s* stabilisation *f* des prix

price′ freez′ing *s* blocage *m* des prix

priceless [ˈpraɪslɪs] *adj* sans prix, inestimable; (*very funny*) (coll) impayable, absurde

price′ list′ *s* liste *f* de prix, tarif *m*

price′ war′ *s* guerre *f* des prix

prick [prɪk] *s* piqûre *f;* (*spur; sting of conscience*) aiguillon *m* ‖ *tr* piquer; **to prick up** (*the ears*) dresser

prick·ly [ˈprɪkli] *adj* (*comp* **-lier;** *super* **-liest**) épineux

prick′ly heat′ *s* lichen *m* vésiculaire, miliaire *f*

prick′ly pear′ *s* figue *f* de Barbarie; (*plant*) figuier *m* de Barbarie

pride [praɪd] *s* (*self-respect*) orgueil *m;* (*satisfaction*) fierté *f;* (pej) arrogance *f*, orgueil; **to take pride in** être fier de ‖ *tr*—**to pride oneself on** or **upon** s'enorgueillir de

priest [prist] *s* prêtre *m*

priestess [ˈpristɪs] *s* prêtresse *f*

priesthood [ˈpristˑhʊd] *s* sacerdoce *m*

priest·ly [ˈpristli] *adj* (*comp* **-lier;** *super* **-liest**) sacerdotal

prig [prɪg] *s* poseur *m*, pédant *m*

prim [prɪm] *adj* (*comp* **primmer;** *super* **primmest**) compassé, guindé

prima·ry [ˈpraɪməri] *adj* primaire ‖ *s* (*pl* **-ries**) élection *f* primaire; (elec) primaire *m*

primate [ˈpraɪmet] *s* (eccl) primat *m;* (zool) primate *m*

prime [praɪm] *adj* (*first*) premier, principal; (*of the best quality*) de première qualité, (le) meilleur; (math) prime ‖ *s* fleur *f*, perfection *f;* commencement *m*, premiers jours *mpl;* **prime of life** fleur or force de l'âge ‖ *tr* amor-

cer; (*a surface to be painted*) appliquer une couche de fond à; (*to supply with information*) mettre au courant

prime′ min′ister *s* premier ministre *m*

primer [ˈprɪmər] *s* premier livre *m* de lecture, manuel *m* élémentaire ‖ [ˈpraɪmər] *s* (*for paint*) couche *f* de fond, impression, *f;* (mach) amorce *f*

prime′ rate′ *s* (com) taux *m* de base

primeval [praɪˈmivəl] *adj* primitif

primitive [ˈprɪmɪtɪv] *adj & s* primitif *m*

primordial [praɪˈmɔdɪˑəl] *adj* primordial

primp [prɪmp] *tr* bichonner, pomponner ‖ *intr* se bichonner, se pomponner

prim′rose′ *s* primevère *f*

prim′rose path′ *s* chemin *m* de velours

prince [prɪns] *s* prince *m*

Prince′ Charm′ing *s* le Prince Charmant

prince′ con′sort *s* prince *m* consort

prince·ly [ˈprɪnsli] *adj* (*comp* **-lier;** *super* **-liest**) princier

Prince′ of Wales′ *s* prince *m* de Galles

princess [ˈprɪnsɪs] *s* princesse *f*

principal [ˈprɪnsɪpəl] *adj & s* principal *m*

principali·ty [ˌprɪnsɪˈpælɪti] *s* (*pl* **-ties**) principauté *f*

principle [ˈprɪnsɪpəl] *s* principe *m*

print [prɪnt] *s* (*mark*) empreinte *f;* (*printed cloth*) imprimé *m;* (*design in printed cloth*) estampe *f;* (*lettering*) lettres *fpl* moulées; (*act of printing*) impression *f;* (phot) épreuve *f;* **out of print** épuisé; **small print** petits caractères *mpl* ‖ *tr* imprimer; écrire en lettres moulées; publier; (*an edition; a photographic negative*) tirer; **to print out** (comp) imprimer, restituer

print′ed cir′cuit *s* circuit *m* imprimé

print′ed mat′ter *s* imprimés *mpl*

printer [ˈprɪntər] *s* imprimeur *m;* (comp) imprimante *f*

prin′ter's dev′il *s* apprenti *m* imprimeur

prin′ter's er′ror *s* faute *f* d'impression, coquille *f*

prin′ter's ink′ *s* encre *f* d'imprimerie

prin′ter's mark′ *s* nom *m* de l'imprimeur

printing [ˈprɪntɪŋ] *s* imprimerie *f;* (*act*) impression *f;* (*by hand*) écriture *f* en caractères d'imprimerie; édition *f;* tirage *m;* (phot) tirage

print′ing frame′ *s* (phot) châssis-presse *m*

print′ing of′fice *s* imprimerie *f*

print′ing press′ *s* presse *f* typographique

print′out′ *s* (comp) tapuscrit *m*, listage *m*

prior [ˈpraɪˑər] *adj* antérieur ‖ *s* prieur *m* ‖ *adv* antérieurement; **prior to** avant; avant de

priori·ty [praɪˈɔrɪti] *s* (*pl* **-ties**) priorité *f*

prism [ˈprɪzəm] *s* prisme *m*

prison [ˈprɪzən] *s* prison *f* ‖ *tr* emprisonner

prisoner [ˈprɪznər] *s* prisonnier *m*

pris′on van′ *s* voiture *f* cellulaire

pris·sy [ˈprɪsi] *adj* (*comp* **-sier;** *super* **-siest**) (coll) bégueule

priva·cy [ˈpraɪvəsi] *s* (*pl* **-cies**) intimité *f;* secret *m*

private ['praɪvɪt] *adj* privé, particulier; confidentiel, secret; (*public sign*) défense d'entrer ‖ *s* simple soldat *m;* **in private** dans l'intimité, en particulier; **privates** parties *fpl*
pri′vate cit′izen *s* simple particulier *m,* simple citoyen *m*
pri′vate first′ class′ *s* soldat *m* de première
pri′vate hos′pital *s* clinique *f*
pri′vate school′ *s* école *f* privée, école libre
pri′vate sec′retary *s* secrétaire *m* particulier
pri′vate sid′ing *s* embranchement *m* particulier
privet ['prɪvɪt] *s* troène *m*
privilege ['prɪvɪlɪdʒ] *s* privilège *m*
priv•y ['prɪvi] *adj* privé; **privy to** averti de ‖ *s* (*pl* **-ies**) cabinets *mpl* au fond du jardin
prize [praɪz] *s* prix *m;* (*something captured*) prise *f* ‖ *tr* faire cas de, estimer
prize′ fight′ *s* match *m* de boxe
prize′ fight′er *s* boxeur *m* professionel
prize′ ring′ *s* ring *m*
prize′win′ner *s* lauréat *m;* **prizewinners** (*list*) palmarès *m*
pro [pro] *s* (*pl* **pros**) vote *m* affirmatif; (*professional*) (coll) pro *m;* **the pros and the cons** le pour et le contre ‖ *prep* en faveur de
probabili•ty [‚prɑbə'bɪlɪti] *s* (*pl* **-ties**) probabilité *f*
probable ['prɑbəbəl] *adj* probable
probably ['prɑbəbli] *adv* probablement
probate ['probet] *s* homologation *f* ‖ *tr* homologuer
probation [pro'beʃən] *s* liberté *f* surveillée; (*on a job*) stage *m*
probe [prob] *s* sondage *m;* (*instrument*) sonde *f;* (rok) échos *mpl;* (rok) engin *m* exploratoire ‖ *tr* sonder
problem ['prɑbləm] *s* problème *m*
probl′em child′ *s* enfant *mf* terrible
procedure [pro'sidʒər] *s* procédé *m*
proceed ['prosid] *s*—**proceeds** produit *m,* bénéfices *mpl* ‖ [pro'sid] *intr* avancer, continuer; continuer à parler; **to proceed from** procéder de; **to proceed to** se mettre à (*to go to*) se diriger à
proceeding [pro'sidɪŋ] *s* procédé *m;* **proceedings** actes *mpl*
process ['prɑsɛs] *s* (*technique*) procédé *m;* (*development*) processus *m;* **in the process of** en train de ‖ *tr* soumettre à un procédé, traiter; (comp) (*information*) traiter
pro′cessed cheese′ ['prɑsɛst] *s* fromage *m* fondu
processing ['prɑsɛsɪŋ] *s* (comp) traitement *m,* façonnage *m;* **processing by modem** (comp) télétraitement *m*
procession [pro'sɛʃən] *s* cortège *m,* défilé *m,* procession *f*
processor ['prɑ‚sɛsər] *s* (comp) mécanisme *m* pour traiter l'information
pro′cess serv′er *s* huissier *m* exploitant
pro′-choice′ move′ment *s* mouvement *m* du choix
proclaim [pro'klem] *tr* proclamer

proclitic [pro'klɪtɪk] *adj & s* proclitique *m*
procrastinate [pro'kræstɪ‚net] *tr* différer ‖ *intr* remettre les affaires à plus tard
proctor ['prɑktər] *s* surveillant *m*
procure [pro'kjʊr] *tr* obtenir, se procurer; (*a woman*) entraîner à la prostitution ‖ *intr* faire du proxénétisme
procurement [pro'kjʊrmənt] *s* obtention *f,* acquisition *f*
procurer [pro'kjʊrər] *s* proxénète *mf*
prod [prɑd] *s* poussée *f;* (*stick*) aiguillon *m* ‖ *v* (*pret & pp* **prodded;** *ger* **prodding**) *tr* aiguillonner
prodigal ['prɑdɪgəl] *adj & s* prodigue *mf*
prodigious [pro'dɪdʒəs] *adj* prodigieux
prodi•gy ['prɑdɪdʒi] *s* (*pl* **-gies**) prodige *m*
produce ['prɑd(j)us] *s* produit *m;* (*eatables*) denrées *fpl* ‖ [pro'd(j)us] *tr* produire; (*a play*) mettre en scène; (geom) prolonger
producer [pro'd(j)usər] *s* producteur *m*
product ['prɑdəkt] *s* produit *m*
production [pro'dʌkʃən] *s* production *f*
profane [pro'fen] *adj* profane; (*language*) impie, blasphématoire ‖ *s* profane *mf;* impie *mf* ‖ *tr* profaner
profani•ty [pro'fænɪti] *s* (*pl* **-ties**) blasphème *m*
profess [pro'fɛs] *tr* professer
profession [pro'fɛʃən] *s* profession *f*
professor [pro'fɛsər] *s* professeur *m*
proffer ['prɑfər] *s* offre *f* ‖ *tr* offrir, tendre
proficient [pro'fɪʃənt] *adj* compétent, expert
profile ['profaɪl] *s* profil *m;* courte biographie *f* ‖ *tr* profiler; **to be profiled against** se profiler sur
profit ['prɑfɪt] *s* bénéfice *m,* profit *m* ‖ *tr* profiter à ‖ *intr* profiter; **to profit from** profiter à, de, or en
profitable ['prɑfɪtəbəl] *adj* profitable
prof′it-and-loss′ account′ *s* compte *m* de profits et pertes
profiteer [‚prɑfɪ'tɪr] *s* profiteur *m* ‖ *intr* faire des bénéfices excessifs
prof′it mar′gin *s* marge *f* bénéficiaire
prof′it tak′ing *s* prise *f* de bénéfices
profligate ['prɑflɪgɪt] *adj & s* débauché *m*
pro′ for′ma in′voice [‚pro'fɔrmə] *s* facture *f* simulée
profound [pro'faʊnd] *adj* profond
pro-French′ *adj* francophile
profuse [prə'fjuz] *adj* abondant; (*extravagant*) prodigue
proge•ny ['prɑdʒəni] *s* (*pl* **-nies**) progéniture *f*
progno•sis [prɑg'nosɪs] *s* (*pl* **-ses** [siz]) pronostic *m*
prognosticate [prɑg'nɑstɪ‚ket] *tr* pronostiquer
pro•gram ['progræm] *s* programme *m* ‖ *v* (*pret & pp* **-gramed;** *ger* **-graming**) *tr* programmer
pro′gramed learn′ing *s* enseignement *m* séquentiel
programer ou **programmer** ['progræmər] *s* (comp) programmeur *m;* (mov, rad, telv) programmateur *m*

programing *ou* **programming** [ˈprogræmɪŋ] *s* programmation *f*

pro'gram pack'aging *s* (rad, telv) groupage *m* d'émissions

progress [ˈprogrɛs] *s* progrès *m;* cours *m,* e.g., **work in progress** travaux en cours; **to make progress** faire des progrès ‖ [prəˈgrɛs] *intr* progresser

progressive [prəˈgrɛsɪv] *adj* progressif; (pol) progressiste ‖ *s* (pol) progressiste *mf*

prohibit [proˈhɪbɪt] *tr* prohiber, interdire

prohibition [ˌproˑəˈbɪʃən] *s* prohibition *f*

project [ˈprɑdʒɛkt] *s* projet *m* ‖ [prəˈdʒɛkt] *tr* projeter ‖ *intr* (*to jut out*) saillir; (theat) passer la rampe

projectile [prəˈdʒɛktɪl] *s* projectile *m*

projection [prəˈdʒɛkʃən] *s* projection *f;* (*something jutting out*) saillie *f*

projec'tion booth' *s* (mov) cabine *f* de cinéma

projectionist [prəˈdʒɛkʃənɪst] *s* projectionniste *mf*

projector [prəˈdʒɛktər] *s* projecteur *m;* (mov, telv) sunlight *m invar*

proletarian [ˌproliˈtɛriˑən] *adj* prolétarien ‖ *s* prolétaire *m*

proletariat [ˌproliˈtɛriˑət] *s* prolétariat *m*

proliferate [prəˈlɪfəˌret] *intr* proliférer

prolific [prəˈlɪfɪk] *adj* prolifique

prolix [ˈprolɪks] *adj* prolixe

prologue [ˈprolog] *s* prologue *m*

prolong [proˈloŋ] *tr* prolonger

promenade [ˌprɑmɪˈned] *s* promenade *f;* bal *m* d'apparat; (theat) promenoir *m* ‖ *intr* se promener

prom'enade' deck' *s* (naut) pont-promenade *m*

prominent [ˈprɑmɪnənt] *adj* proéminent; (*well-known*) éminent

promiscuity [ˌprɑmɪsˈkjuˑəti] *s* promiscuité *f* sexuelle

promiscuous [prəˈmɪskjuˌas] *adj* (*in sexual matters*) de mœurs faciles, de mœurs légères, immoral; (*disorderly*) confus

promise [ˈprɑmɪs] *s* promesse *f* ‖ *tr & intr* promettre; **to promise s.o. to** promettre à qn de; **to promise s.th. to s.o.** promettre q.ch. à qn

prom'issory note' [ˈprɑmɪˌsori] *m* billet *m* à ordre

promonto•ry [ˈprɑmənˌtori] *s* (*pl* **-ries**) promontoire *m*

promote [prəˈmot] *tr* promouvoir

promoter [prəˈmotər] *s* promoteur *m*

promotion [prəˈmoʃən] *s* promotion *f*

prompt [prɑmpt] *adj* prompt; ponctuel ‖ *s* (comp) message *m* automatique pour l'opérateur informatique; (telp) message *m* automatique directeur ‖ *tr* inciter; (*an engine*) solliciter; (theat) souffler son rôle à

prompter [ˈprɑmptər] *s* (theat) souffleur *m*

promp'ter's box' *s* (theat) trou *m* du souffleur

promptness [ˈprɑmptnɪs] *s* promptitude *f*

promulgate [ˈprɑməlˌget] *tr* promulguer

prone [pron] *adj* à plat ventre, prostré; **prone to** enclin à

prong [proŋ], [prɑŋ] *s* dent *f*

pronoun [ˈpronaʊn] *s* pronom *m*

pronounce [prəˈnaʊns] *tr* prononcer

pronouncement [prəˈnaʊnsmənt] *s* déclaration *f*

pronunciation [prəˌnʌnsiˈeʃən] *s* prononciation *f*

proof [pruf] *adj*—**proof against** à l'épreuve de, résistant à ‖ *s* preuve *f;* (phot, typ) épreuve *f;* **to read proof** corriger les épreuves

proof'read'er *s* correcteur *m*

prop [prɑp] *s* appui *m;* (*to hold up a plant*) tuteur *m;* **props** (theat) accessoires *mpl* ‖ *v* (*pret & pp* **propped;** *ger* **propping**) *tr* appuyer; (hort) tuteurer

propaganda [ˌprɑpəˈgændə] *s* propagande *f*

propagate [ˈprɑpəˌget] *tr* propager

pro•pel [prəˈpɛl] *s* (*pret & pp* **-pelled;** *ger* **-pelling**) *tr* propulser

propellant [prəˈpɛlənt] *s* (rok) ergol *m*

propeller [prəˈpɛlər] *s* hélice *f*

propensi•ty [prəˈpɛnsɪti] *s* (*pl* **-ties**) propension *f*

proper [ˈprɑpər] *adj* (*fitting, correct*) convenable, correct; (*person*) comme il faut; (*name*) propre

proper•ty [ˈprɑpərti] *s* (*pl* **-ties**) propriété *f;* **properties** (theat) accessoires *mpl*

prop'erty own'er *s* propriétaire *mf*

prop'erty tax' *s* impôt *m* foncier

prophe•cy [ˈprɑfɪsi] *s* (*pl* **-cies**) prophétie *f*

prophe•sy [ˈprɑfɪˌsaɪ] *v* (*pret & pp* **-sied**) *tr* prophétiser

prophet [ˈprɑfɪt] *s* prophète *m*

prophetess [ˈprɑfɪtɪs] *s* prophétesse *f*

prophylactic [ˌprɑfɪˈlæktɪk] *adj* prophylactique ‖ *s* (*preventive*) prophylactique *m;* (*contraceptive*) préservatif *m,* capote *f* anglaise

propitiate [prəˈpɪʃiˌet] *tr* apaiser

propitious [prəˈpɪʃəs] *adj* propice

prop'jet' *s* turbopropulseur *m*

proportion [prəˈporʃən] *s* proportion *f;* **in proportion as** à mesure que; **in proportion to** en proportion de, en raison de; **out of proportion** hors de proportion ‖ *tr* proportionner

proportionate [prəˈporʃənt] *adj* proportionné

proposal [prəˈpozəl] *s* proposition *f;* demande *f* en mariage

propose [prəˈpoz] *tr* proposer ‖ *intr* faire sa déclaration; **to propose to** demander sa main à; (*to decide to*) se proposer de

proposition [ˈprɑpəˈzɪʃən] *s* proposition *f* ‖ *tr* faire des propositions malhonnêtes à

propound [prəˈpaʊnd] *tr* proposer

proprietor [prəˈpraɪˑətər] *s* propriétaire *mf*

proprietress [prəˈpraɪˑətrɪs] *s* propriétaire *f*

proprie•ty [prəˈpraɪˑəti] *s* (*pl* **-ties**) propriété *f;* (*of conduct*) bienséance *f;* **proprieties** convenances *fpl*

propulsion [prəˈpʌlʃən] *s* propulsion *f*

prorate [proˈret] *tr* partager au prorata

prosaic [proˈzeˑɪk] *adj* prosaïque
proscenium [proˈsinɪˑəm] *s* avant-scène *f*
proscribe [proˈskraɪb] *tr* proscrire
prose [proz] *adj* en prose ‖ *s* prose *f*
prosecute [ˈprɑsɪˌkjut] *tr* poursuivre
prosecutor [ˈprɑsɪˌkjutər] *s* (*lawyer*) procureur *m*; (*plaintiff*) plaignant *m*
proselyte [ˈprɑsɪˌlaɪt] *s* prosélyte *mf*
prose′ writ′er *s* prosateur *m*
prosody [ˈprɑsədi] *s* prosodie *f*
prospect [ˈprɑspɛkt] *s* (*outlook*) perspective *f*; (*future*) avenir *m*; (com) client *m* éventuel ‖ *tr & intr* prospecter; **to prospect for** (*e.g., gold*) chercher
prospector [ˈprɑspɛktər] *s* prospecteur *m*
prospectus [prəˈspɛktəs] *s* prospectus *m*
prosper [ˈprɑspər] *intr* prospérer
prosperity [prɑsˈpɛrɪti] *s* prospérité *f*
prosperous [ˈprɑspərəs] *adj* prospère
prostate (gland′) [ˈprɑstet] *s* prostate *f*
prostitute [ˈprɑstɪˌt(j)ut] *s* prostituée *f* ‖ *tr* prostituer
prostrate [ˈprɑstret] *adj* prosterné; (*exhausted*) prostré ‖ *tr* abattre; **to prostrate oneself** se prosterner
prostration [prɑsˈtreʃən] *s* prostration *f*; (*abasement*) prosternation *f*
protagonist [proˈtægənɪst] *s* protagoniste *m*
protect [prəˈtɛkt] *tr* protéger
protection [prəˈtɛkʃən] *s* protection *f*
protein [ˈprotiˑɪn] *s* protéine *f*
pro-tempore [proˈtɛmpəˌri] *adj* intérimaire, par intérim
protest [ˈprotɛst] *s* protestation *f* ‖ [proˈtɛst] *tr* protester de; protester ‖ *intr* protester
Protestant [ˈprɑtɪstənt] *adj & s* protestant *m*
protocol [ˈprotəˌkɑl] *s* protocole *m*
proton [ˈprotɑn] *s* proton *m*
protoplasm [ˈprotəˌplæzəm] *s* protoplasme *m*
prototype [ˈprotəˌtaɪp] *s* prototype *m*
protozoan [ˌprotəˈzoˑən] *s* protozoaire *m*
protract [proˈtrækt] *tr* prolonger
protrude [proˈtrud] *intr* saillir
protuberance [proˈt(j)ubərəns] *s* protubérance *f*
proud [praʊd] *adj* fier; (*vain*) orgueilleux
proud′ flesh′ *s* chair *f* fongueuse
prove [pruv] *v* (*pret* proved; *pp* proved *ou* proven [ˈpruvən]) *tr* prouver; (*to put to the test*) éprouver ‖ *intr* se montrer, se trouver; **to prove to be** se révéler, s'avérer
proverb [ˈprɑvərb] *s* proverbe *m*
provide [prəˈvaɪd] *tr* pourvoir, fournir; **to provide s.th. for s.o.** fournir q.ch. à qn ‖ *intr*—**to provide for** pourvoir à; (*e.g., future needs*) prévoir
provided *conj* pourvu que, à condition que
providence [ˈprɑvɪdəns] *s* providence *f*; (*prudence*) prévoyance *f*
providential [ˌprɑvɪˈdɛnʃəl] *adj* providentiel
providing [prəˈvaɪdɪŋ] *conj* pourvu que, à condition que

province [ˈprɑvɪns] *s* province *f*; (*sphere*) compétence *f*
prov′ing ground′ *s* terrain *m* d'essai
provision [prəˈvɪʒən] *s* (*supplying*) fourniture *f*; clause *f*; **provisions** provisions *fpl*
provi•so [prəˈvaɪzo] *s* (*pl* -sos *or* -soes) condition *f*, stipulation *f*
provocative [prəˈvɑkətɪv] *adj* provocant
provoke [prəˈvok] *tr* provoquer; fâcher, contrarier
provoking [prəˈvokɪŋ] *adj* contrariant
prow [praʊ] *s* proue *f*
prowess [ˈpraʊˑɪs] *s* prouesse *f*
prowl [praʊl] *intr* rôder
prowler [ˈpraʊlər] *s* rôdeur *m*
proximity [prɑkˈsɪmɪti] *s* proximité *f*
prox•y [ˈprɑksi] *s* (*pl* -ies) mandat *m*; (*agent*) mandataire *mf*; **by proxy** par procuration
prude [prud] *s* prude *mf*
prudence [ˈprudəns] *s* prudence *f*
prudent [ˈprudənt] *adj* prudent
pruder•y [ˈprudəri] *s* (*pl* -ies) pruderie *f*
prudish [ˈprudɪʃ] *adj* prude
prune [prun] *s* pruneau *m* ‖ *tr* élaguer
pruning [ˈprunɪŋ] *s* taille *f*, émondage *m*, cisaillement *m*
prun′ing shears′ *spl* cisailles *fpl*
Prussian [ˈprʌʃən] *adj* prussien ‖ *s* Prussien *m*
pry [praɪ] *v* (*pret & pp* pried) *tr*—**to pry open** forcer avec un levier; **to pry s.th. out of s.o.** extorquer, soutirer q.ch. à qn ‖ *intr* fureter; **to pry into** fourrer son nez dans
P.S. [ˈpiˈɛs] *s* (letterword) (**postscript**) P.-S.
psalm [sɑm] *s* psaume *m*
Psalter [ˈsɔltər] *s* psautier *m*
pseudo [ˈs(j)udo] *adj* faux, supposé, feint, factice
pseudonym [ˈs(j)udənɪm] *s* pseudonyme *m*
psyche [ˈsaɪki] *s* psyché *f*
psychedelic [ˌsaɪkɪˈdɛlɪk] *adj* psychédélique
psychiatrist [saɪˈkaɪˑətrɪst] *s* psychiatre *mf*
psychiatry [saɪˈkaɪˑətri] *s* psychiatrie *f*
psychic [ˈsaɪkɪk] *adj* psychique; médiumnique ‖ *s* médium *m*
psycho [ˈsaɪko] *adj & s* (slang) fou *m*, dingue *mf*, cinglé *m*, agité *m*
psychoanalysis [ˌsaɪkoˑəˈnælɪsɪs] *s* psychanalyse *f*
psychoanalyze [ˌsaɪkoˈænəˌlaɪz] *tr* psychanalyser
psychologic(al) [ˌsaɪkoˈlɑdʒɪk(əl)] *adj* psychologique
psychologist [saɪˈkɑlədʒɪst] *s* psychologue *mf*
psychology [saɪˈkɑlədʒi] *s* psychologie *f*
psychopath [ˈsaɪkəˌpæθ] *s* psychopathe *mf*
psycho•sis [saɪˈkosɪs] *s* (*pl* -ses [siz]) psychose *f*
psy′cho•ther′apy *s* psychothérapie *f*
psychotic [saɪˈkɑtɪk] *adj & s* psychotique *mf*
ptomaine [ˈtomen] *s* ptomaïne *f*
pub [pʌb] *s* (Brit) bistrot *m*, café *m*
puberty [ˈpjubərti] *s* puberté *f*
public [ˈpʌblɪk] *adj & s* public *m*

pub′lic-address′ sys′tem *s* sonorisation *f*

publication [ˌpʌblɪˈkeʃən] *s* publication *f*

pub′lic educa′tion *s* enseignement *m* public

publicity [pʌbˈlɪsɪti] *s* publicité *f*

public′ity stunt′ *s* canard *m* publicitaire

publicize [ˈpʌblɪˌsaɪz] *tr* publier

pub′lic li′brary *s* bibliothèque *f* municipale

pub′lic-opin′ion poll′ *s* sondage *m* de l'opinion, enquête *f* par sondage

pub′lic rela′tions *spl* relations *fpl* publiques

pub′lic-rela′tions ex′pert *s* publiciste *mf*, publicitaire *mf*

pub′lic school′ *s* (U.S.A.) école *f* primaire; (Brit) école privée

pub′lic serv′ant *s* fonctionnaire *mf*

pub′lic speak′ing *s* art *m* oratoire, éloquence *f*

pub′lic tel′ephone *s* téléphone *m* public

pub′lic toi′let *s* chalet *m* de nécessité

pub′lic transporta′tion *s* transport *m* en commun

pub′lic util′ity *s* entreprise *f* de service public; **public utilities** actions *fpl* émises par les entreprises de service public

publish [ˈpʌblɪʃ] *tr* publier

publisher [ˈpʌblɪʃər] *s* éditeur *m*

pub′lishing house′ *s* maison *f* d'édition

puck [pʌk] *s* palet *m*

pucker [ˈpʌkər] *s* fronce *m*, faux pli *m* || *tr* froncer || *intr* se froncer

pudding [ˈpʊdɪŋ] *s* entremets *m* sucré au lait, crème *f*

puddle [ˈpʌdəl] *s* flaque *f* || *tr* puddler

pudg•y [ˈpʌdʒi] *adj* (*comp* **-ier;** *super* **-iest**) bouffi, rondouillard

puerile [ˈpjuˌərɪl] *adj* puéril

puerili•ty [ˌpjuˈəˈrɪlɪti] *s* (*pl* **-ties**) puérilité *f*

Puerto Rican [ˈpwɛrtoˈrikən] *adj* portoricain || *s* Portoricain *m*

puff [pʌf] *s* (*of air*) souffle *m;* (*of smoke*) bouffée *f;* (*in clothing*) bouillon *m;* (*in sleeve*) bouffant *m;* (*for powder*) houppette *f;* (*swelling*) bouffissure *f;* (*praise*) battage *m;* (culin) moule *m* de pâte feuilletée fourré à la crème, à la confiture, etc. || *tr* lancer des bouffées de; **to puff oneself up** se rengorger; **to puff out** souffler; **to puff up** gonfler || *intr* souffler; (*to swell*) gonfler, se gonfler; **to puff at** or **on** (*a pipe*) tirer sur

puff′paste′ *s* pâte *f* feuilletée

pugilism [ˈpjudʒɪˌlɪzəm] *s* science *f* pugilistique, boxe *f*

pugilist [ˈpjudʒɪlɪst] *s* pugiliste *m*

pugnacious [pʌgˈneʃəs] *adj* pugnance

pug′-nosed′ *adj* camus

puke [pjuk] *s* (slang) dégobillage *m* || *tr & intr* (slang) dégobiller

pull [pʊl] *s* (*tug*) traction *f*, secousse *f*, coup *m;* (*handle of door*) poignée *f;* (*of the moon*) attraction *f;* (slang) piston *m*, appuis *mpl* || *tr* tirer; (*a muscle*) tordre; (*the trigger*) appuyer sur; (*a proof*) (typ) tirer; **to pull about** tirailler; **to pull away** arracher; **to pull down** bais-

ser; (*e.g., a house*) abattre; (*to degrade*) abaisser; **to pull in** rentrer; **to pull off** enlever; (fig) réussir; **to pull on** (*a garment*) mettre; **to pull oneself together** se ressaisir; **to pull out** sortir; (*a tooth*) arracher || *intr* tirer; bouger lentement, bouger avec effort; **to pull at** tirer sur; **to pull for** (slang) plaider en faveur de; **to pull in** rentrer; (*said of train*) entrer en gare; **to pull out** partir; (*said of train*) sortir de la gare; **to pull through** se tirer d'affaire; (*to get well*) se remettre

pull′ chain′ *s* chasse *f* d'eau

pull′-down′ men′u *s* (comp) menu *m* dépliant

pullet [ˈpʊlɪt] *s* poulette *f*

pulley [ˈpʊli] *s* poulie *f*

pulmonary [ˈpʌlməˌnɛri] *adj* pulmonaire

pulp [pʌlp] *s* pulpe *f;* (*to make paper*) pâte *f;* (*of tooth*) bulbe *m;* **to beat to a pulp** (coll) mettre en bouillie

pulp′ fic′tion *s* romans *mpl* à sensation; le roman de la concierge

pulpit [ˈpʊlpɪt] *s* chaire *f*

pulsate [ˈpʌlset] *intr* palpiter; vibrer

pulsation [pʌlˈseʃən] *s* pulsation *f*

pulse [pʌls] *s* pouls *m;* **to feel** or **take the pulse of** tâter le pouls à

pulverize [ˈpʌlvəˌraɪz] *tr* pulvériser

pu′mice stone′ [ˈpʌmɪs] *s* pierre *f* ponce

pum•mel [ˈpʌməl] *v* (*pret & pp* **-meled** or **-melled;** *ger* **-meling** or **-melling**) *tr* bourrer de coups

pump [pʌmp] *s* pompe *f;* (*slipperlike shoe*) escarpin *m* || *tr* pomper; (coll) tirer les vers du nez à; **to pump up** pomper; (*a tire*) gonfler || *intr* pomper

pump′han′dle *s* bras *m* de pompe

pumpkin [ˈpʌmpkɪn] *s* citrouille *f*, potiron *m*

pump-priming [ˈpʌmpˌpraɪmɪŋ] *s* amorçage *m* d'une pompe; (govt) renflouage *m* de l'économie, injection *f* dans l'économie

pun [pʌn] *s* calembour *m*, jeu *m* de mots || *v* (*pret & pp* **punned;** *ger* **punning**) *intr* faire des jeux de mots

punch [pʌntʃ] *s* (*blow*) coup *m* de poing; (*to pierce metal*) mandrin *m;* (*to drive a nail or bolt*) poinçon *m;* (*for tickets*) pince *f*, emporte-pièce *m;* (*drink; blow*) punch *m;* (mach) poinçonneuse *f;* (*energy*) (coll) allant *m*, punch; **to pull no punches** parler carrément || *tr* donner un coup de poing à; poinçonner

punch′ bowl′ *s* bol *m* à punch

punch′ card′ *s* carte *f* perforée

punch′ clock′ *s* horloge *f* de pointage

punch′-drunk′ *adj* abruti de coups; (coll) abruti, étourdi

punched′ tape′ *s* bande *f* enregistreuse perforée

punch′ing bag′ *s* punching-ball *m;* (fig) tête *f* de Turc, souffre-douleur *m invar*

punch′ line′ *s* point *m* final, phrase *f* clé

punctilious [pʌŋkˈtɪliˑəs] *adj* pointilleux, minutieux

punctual [ˈpʌŋktʃuˑəl] *adj* ponctuel

punctuate [`pʌŋkt∫ʊ,et] tr & intr ponctuer
punctuation [,pʌŋkt∫ʊˈe∫ən] s ponctuation f
punctua'tion mark' s signe m de ponctuation
puncture [`pʌŋkt∫ər] s (in skin, paper, leather) piqûre f; (of a tire) crevaison f; (med) ponction f ‖ tr perforer; (a tire) crever; (med) ponctionner
punc'ture-proof' adj increvable
pundit [`pʌndɪt] s pandit m; (savant) mandarin m; (pej) pontife m
pungent [`pʌndʒənt] adj piquant
punish [`pʌnɪ∫] tr & intr punir
punishment [`pʌnɪ∫mənt] s punition f; (for a crime) peine f; (severe handling) mauvais traitements mpl
punk [pʌŋk] adj (slang) moche, fichu; **to feel punk** (slang) être mal fichu ‖ s amadou m; mèche f d'amadou; (decayed wood) bois m pourri; (slang) voyou m, mauvais sujet m, loubard m
punster [`pʌnstər] s faiseur m de calembours
pu•ny [`pjuni] adj (comp -nier; super -niest) chétif, malingre
pup [pʌp] s chiot m
pupil [`pjupəl] s élève mf; (of the eye) pupille f, prunelle f
puppet [`pʌpɪt] s marionnette f; (person controlled by another) fantoche m, pantin m
pup'pet gov'ernment s gouvernement m fantoche
pup'pet show' ou **the'ater** s spectacle m de marionnettes, marionnettes fpl, guignol m; (hist) Grand Guignol m
pup-py [`pʌpi] s (pl -pies) petit chien m
pup'py love' s premières amours fpl
pup' tent' s tente-abri f
purchase [`pʌrt∫əs] s achat m; (leverage) point m d'appui, prise f ‖ tr acheter
pur'chasing pow'er s pouvoir m d'achat
pure [pjʊr] adj pur
purgative [`pʌrgətɪv] adj & s purgatif m
purgato•ry [`pʌrgə,tori] s (pl -ries) purgatoire m
purge [pʌrdʒ] s purge f ‖ tr purger
puri•fy [`pjʊrɪ,fai] v (pret & pp -fied) tr purifier
puritan [`pjʊrɪtən] adj & s puritain m; **Puritan** puritain
purity [`pjʊrɪti] s pureté f
purloin [pər`lɔɪn] tr & intr voler
purple [`pʌrpəl] adj pourpre ‖ s (violescent) pourpre m; (deep red, crimson) pourpre f; **born to the purple** né dans la pourpre
purport [`pʌrpɔrt] s sens m, teneur f; (intention) but m, objet m ‖ [pər`pɔrt] tr signifier, vouloir dire
purpose [`pʌrpəs] s intention f, dessein m; (goal) but m, objet m, fin f; **for all purposes** à tous usages; pratiquement; **for the purpose of, with the purpose of** dans le dessein de, dans le but de; **for this purpose** à cet effet; **for what purpose?** à quoi bon? à quelle fin?; **on purpose** exprès, à dessein, **to good purpose, to some purpose** utilement; **to no pur-**

pose vainement; **to serve the purpose** faire l'affaire
purposely [`pʌrpəsli] adv exprès, à dessein, de propos délibéré
purr [pʌr] s ronron m ‖ intr ronronner ‖ interj miam! miam!
purse [pʌrs] s bourse f, porte-monnaie m; (handbag) sac m à main ‖ tr (one's lips) pincer
purser [`pʌrsər] s commissaire m
purse' snatch'er [`snæt∫ər] s voleur m à la tire
purse' strings' spl cordons mpl de bourse
pursue [pər`s(j)u] tr poursuivre; (a profession) suivre
pursuit [pər`s(j)ut] s poursuite f; profession f
pursuit' plane' s chasseur m, avion m de chasse
purvey [pər`ve] tr fournir
pus [pʌs] s pus m
push [pʊ∫] s poussée f ‖ tr pousser; (a button) appuyer sur, presser; **to push around** (coll) rudoyer; **to push aside** écarter; **to push away** or **back** repousser; **to push in** enfoncer; **to push over** faire tomber; **to push through** amener à bonne fin; (a resolution, bill, etc.) faire adopter ‖ intr pousser; **to push forward** or **on** avancer; **to push off** se mettre en route; (naut) pousser au large
push' but'ton s bouton m électrique, poussoir m
push'-button tel'ephone s téléphone m à clavier
push'-but'ton war'fare s guerre f presse-bouton
push'cart' s voiture f à bras
pusher [`pʊ∫ər] s (slang) revendeur m de drogue, dealer m, vendeur m de mort, fourmi f
pushing [`pʊ∫ɪŋ] adj entreprenant; indiscret; agressif
pusillanimous [,pjusɪ`lænɪməs] adj pusillanime
puss [pʊs] s minet m; (slang) gueule f; **sly puss** (girl) (coll) futée f ‖ interj minet!
Puss' in Boots' s Chat m botté
puss' in the cor'ner s les quatre coins mpl
puss•y [`pʊsi] s (pl -ies) s minet m ‖ interj minet!
puss'y wil'low s saule m nord-américain aux chatons très soyeux
pustule [`pʌst∫ʊl] s pustule f
put [pʊt] v (pret & pp **put;** ger **putting**) tr mettre, placer; (to throw) lancer; (a question) poser; **to put across** passer; faire accepter; **to put aside** mettre de côté; **to put away** ranger; (to jail) mettre en prison; **to put back** remettre; retarder; **to put down** poser; (e.g., a name) noter; (a revolution) réprimer; (to lower) baisser; **to put off** renvoyer; (to mislead) dérouter; **to put on** (clothes) mettre; (a play) mettre en scène, monter; (a brake) serrer; (a light, radio, etc.) allumer; (to feign) feindre, simuler; **to put oneself out** se déranger; **to put on sale** mettre en vente; mettre en solde; **to put out** (the hand) étendre; (the fire, light, etc.) éteindre; (s.o.'s eyes) crever; (e.g., a book) publier; (to show to the door) mettre

dehors; (*to vex*) contrarier; **to put over** (coll) faire accepter; **to put s.o. through s.th.** faire subir q.ch. à qn; **to put through** passer; (*a resolution, bill, etc.*) faire adopter; **to put up** lever; (*a house*) construire, faire construire; (*one's collar, hair, etc.*) relever; (a picture) accrocher; (*a notice*) afficher; (*a tent*) dresser; (*an umbrella*) ouvrir; (*the price*) augmenter; (*money as an investment*) fournir; (*resistance*) offrir; (*an overnight guest*) loger; (*fruit, vegetables, etc.*) conserver; (coll) pousser, inciter ‖ *intr* se diriger; **to put on** feindre; **to put up** loger; **to put up with** tolérer, s'accommoder de

putative [ˈpjutətɪv] *adj* présumé, supposé; (law) putatif

put′down *s* brimade *f*

put′ op′tion *s* (econ) option *f* de vente

put′-out′ *adj* ennuyeux, fâcheux

putrid [ˈpjutrɪd] *adj* putride

putt [pʌt] *s* (golf) putt *m*, coup *m* roulé ‖ *tr* (*the ball*) frapper ‖ *intr* putter

putter [ˈpʌtər] *s* (*golf club*) putter *m* ‖ *intr*—**to putter around** s'occuper de bagatelles

putting [ˈpʌtɪŋ] *s* putting *m*

put′ting green′ *s* green *m*

put•ty [ˈpʌti] *s* (*pl* **-ties**) mastic *m* ‖ *v* (*pret & pp* **-tied**) *tr* mastiquer

put′ty knife′ *s* (*pl* **knives**) couteau *m* à mastiquer

put′-up′ *adj* (coll) machiné à l'avance, monté

put′-up job′ *s* (slang) coup *m* monté, micmac *m*

puzzle [ˈpʌzəl] *s* énigme *f* ‖ *tr* intriguer; **to puzzle out** déchiffrer ‖ *intr*—**to puzzle over** se creuser la tête pour comprendre

puzzler [ˈpʌzlər] *s* énigme *f*, colle *f*

puzzling [ˈpʌzlɪŋ] *adj* énigmatique

PW [ˈpiˈdʌbəl,ju] *s* (letterword) **(prisoner of war)** P.G.

pyg•my [ˈpɪgmi] *adj* pygméen ‖ *s* (*pl* **-mies**) pygmée *m*

pylon [ˈpaɪlɑn] *s* pylône *m*

pyramid [ˈpɪrəmɪd] *s* pyramide *f* ‖ *tr* augmenter graduellement ‖ *intr* pyramider

pyre [paɪr] *s* bûcher *m* funéraire

Pyrenees [ˈpɪrɪ,niz] *spl* Pyrénées *fpl*

pyrites [ˈpaɪraɪts] *s* pyrite *f*

pyrotechnical [,paɪrəˈtɛknɪkəl] *adj* pyrotechnique

pyrotechnics [,paɪrəˈtɛknɪks] *spl* pyrotechnie *f*

python [ˈpaɪθɑn] *s* python *m*

pythoness [ˈpaɪθənɪs] *s* pythonisse *f*

pyx [pɪks] *s* (eccl) ciboire *m*; (*for carrying Eucharist to sick*) (eccl) pyxide *f*; (*at a mint*) boîte *f* des monnaies

Q

Q,q [kju] *s* XVIIᵉ lettre de l'alphabet

quack [kwæk] *adj* frauduleux, de charlatan ‖ *s* charlatan *m* ‖ *intr* cancaner, faire couin-couin

quacker•y [ˈkwækəri] *s* (*pl* **-ies**) charlatanisme *m*

quadrangle [ˈkwɑd,ræŋgəl] *s* plan *m* quadrangulaire; cour *f* carrée

quadrant [ˈkwɑdrənt] *s* (*instrument*) quart *m* de cercle, secteur *m*; (math) quadrant *m*

quadroon [kwɑdˈrun] *s* quarteron *m*

quadruped [ˈkwɑdrə,pɛd] *adj & s* quadrupède *m*

quadruple [ˈkwɑdrupəl] *adj & s* quadruple *m* ‖ *tr & intr* quadrupler

quadruplets [ˈkwɑdru,plɛts] *spl* quadruplés *mpl*

quaff [kwɑf], [kwæf] *s* lampée *f* ‖ *tr & intr* boire à longs traits

quagmire [ˈkwæg,maɪr] *s* bourbier *m*, fondrière *f*

quail [kwel] *s* caille *f* ‖ *intr* fléchir

quaint [kwent] *adj* pittoresque, bizarre

quake [kwek] *s* tremblement *m*; (*earthquake*) tremblement de terre ‖ *intr* trembler

Quaker [ˈkwekər] *adj & s* quaker *m*

Quak′er meet′ing *s* réunion *f* de quakers; (coll) réunion où il y a très peu de conversation

qualification [,kwɑləfəˈkeʃən] *s* compétence *f*, aptitude *f*; (*requirement*) conditions *fpl* requises; (sports) (*testing to allow participation in a contest or activity*) qualification *f*; **qualifications** experience *f*, formation *f*; (*credentials*) diplômes *mpl*, titres *mpl*

qualified [ˈkwɑləfaɪd] *adj* compétent; (*with credentials*) diplômé; (*modified praise or support*) mitigé, conditionnel; (*a craftsman, athlete, or athletic team that has met the qualifications*) qualifié

quali•fy [ˈkwɑlɪ,faɪ] *v* (*pret & pp* **-fied**) *tr* qualifier; (*e.g., a statement*) apporter des réserves à, modifier; **to qualify oneself for** se préparer à, se rendre apte à ‖ *intr* se qualifier

quali•ty [ˈkwɑlɪti] *s* (*pl* **-ties**) qualité *f*; (*of a sound*) timbre *m*; **of good quality** de bonne facture; **quality of life** qualité de la vie

qualm [kwɑm] *s* scrupule *m*; (*remorse*) remords *m*; (*nausea*) soulèvement *m* de cœur

quanda•ry [ˈkwɑndəri] *s* (*pl* **-ries**) incertitude *f*, impasse *f*

quanti•ty [ˈkwɑntɪti] *s* (*pl* **-ties**) quantité *f*

quan•tum [ˈkwɑntəm] *adj* quantique ‖ *s* (*pl* **-ta** [tə]) quantum *m*

quan′tum the′ory *s* théorie *f* des quanta

quarantine [ˈkwɑrən,tin] *s* quarantaine *f* ‖ *tr* mettre en quarantaine

quar·rel [ˈkwɑrəl] s querelle f, dispute f; **to have no quarrel with** n'avoir rien à redire à; **to pick a quarrel with** chercher querelle à ‖ v (pret & pp **-reled** or **-relled**; ger **-reling** or **-relling**) intr se quereller, se disputer; **to quarrel over** contester sur, se disputer

quarrelsome [ˈkwɑrəlsəm] adj querelleur

quar·ry [ˈkwɑri] s (pl **-ries**) carrière f; (hunted animal) proie f ‖ v (pret & pp **-ried**) tr extraire ‖ intr exploiter une carrière

quart [kwɔrt] s quart m de gallon, pinte f

quarter [ˈkwɔrtər] s quart m; (American coin) vingt-cinq cents mpl; (of a year) trimestre m; (of town; of beef; of moon; of shield) quartier m; **a quarter after one** une heure et quart; **a quarter of an hour** un quart d'heure; **a quarter to one** une heure moins le quart; **at close quarters** corps à corps; **quarters** (mil) quartiers mpl, cantonnement m ‖ tr & intr (mil) loger, cantonner

quar'ter·deck' s gaillard m d'arrière

quar'ter-hour' s quart m d'heure; **every quarter-hour on the quarter-hour** tous les quarts d'heure au quart d'heure juste

quarter·ly [ˈkwɔrtərli] adj trimestriel ‖ s (pl **-lies**) publication f or revue f trimestrielle ‖ adv trimestriellement, par trimestre

quar'ter·mas'ter s (mil) quartier-maître m, intendant m militaire

Quar'ter·master Corps' s Intendance f, service m d l'Intendance

quar'ter note' s (mus) noire f

quar'ter rest' s (mus) soupir m

quar'ter tone' s (mus) quart m de ton

quartet [kwɔrˈtɛt] s quatuor m

quartz [kwɔrts] s quartz m

quartz' watch' s montre f à quartz

quasar [ˈkwesɑr] s (astr) quasar m

quash [kwɑʃ] tr étouffer; (to set aside) annuler, invalider

quatrain [ˈkwɑtren] s quatrain m

quaver [ˈkwevər] s tremblement m; (in the singing voice) trémolo m; (mus) croche f ‖ intr trembloter

quay [ki] s quai m, débarcadère m

Quebecois ou **Québecois** [ˌkebəˈkwɑ] adj & s québécois m, québécoise f

Quebec(k)er [kwɪˈbɛkər] s québécois m, québécoise f

queen [kwin] s reine f; (cards, chess) reine f

queen' bee' s reine f des abeilles

queen' dow'ager s reine f douairière

queen·ly [ˈkwinli] adj (comp **-lier**; super **-liest**) de reine, digne d'une reine

queen' moth'er s reine f mère

queen' post' s faux poinçon m

queer [kwɪr] adj (odd) bizarre, étrange, curieux, drôle; (suspicious) suspect, louche; (gay) (pej) de la pédale ‖ s excentrique mf; (gay) (pej) pédé m (pej), tante f (pej); (lesbian) (pej) gouine f (vulg) ‖ tr (coll) faire échouer, déranger

quell [kwɛl] tr étouffer, réprimer; (pain, sorrow, etc.) calmer

quench [kwɛntʃ] tr (the thirst) étancher; (a rebellion) étouffer; (a fire) éteindre

que·ry [ˈkwɪri] s (pl **-ries**) question f; doute m; (question mark) point m d'interrogation ‖ v (pret & pp **-ried**) tr questionner; mettre en doute; (to affix a question mark) marquer d'un point d'interrogation

quest [kwɛst] s quête f;, **in quest of** en quête de

question [ˈkwɛstʃən] s question f; (doubt) doute m; **beyond question** indiscutable, incontestable; **it is a question of** il s'agit de; **out of the question** impossible, impensable; **to ask s.o. a question** poser une question à qn; **to beg the question** faire une pétition de principe; **to call into question** mettre en question; **to move the previous question** (parl) demander la question préalable; **without question** sans aucun doute ‖ tr interroger, questionner; (to cast doubt upon) douter de, contester

questionable [ˈkwɛstʃənəbəl] adj discutable, douteux

ques'tion mark' s point m d'interrogation

questionnaire [ˌkwɛstʃənˈɛr] s questionnaire m

queue [kju] s queue f ‖ intr—**to queue up** faire la queue

quibble [ˈkwɪbəl] intr chicaner, ergoter

quibbling [ˈkwɪblɪŋ] s chicane f

quick [kwɪk] adj rapide, vif ‖ s—**the quick and the dead** les vivants et les morts; **to cut to the quick** piquer au vif

quicken [ˈkwɪkən] tr accélérer; (e.g., the imagination) animer ‖ intr s'accélérer; s'animer

quick'lime' s chaux f vive

quick' lunch' s casse-croûte m, repas m léger

quickly [ˈkwɪkli] adj vite, rapidement

quick'sand' s sable m mouvant

quick'sil'ver s vif-argent m, mercure m

quick'-tem'pered adj coléreux

quiet [ˈkwaɪət] adj (still) tranquille, silencieux; (person) modeste, discret; (market) (com) calme; **be quiet!** taisez-vous!; **to keep quiet** rester tranquille; (to not speak) se taire ‖ s tranquillité f; (rest) repos m; **on the quiet** en douce, à la dérobée ‖ tr calmer, tranquilliser; (a child) faire taire ‖ intr—**to quiet down** se calmer

quill [kwɪl] s plume f d'oie; (hollow part) tuyau m (de plume); (of hedgehog, porcupine) piquant m

quilt [kwɪlt] s courtepointe f ‖ tr piquer

quince [kwɪns] s coing m; (tree) cognassier m

quinine [ˈkwaɪnaɪn] s quinine f

quinsy [ˈkwɪnzi] s angine f

quintessence [kwɪnˈtɛsəns] s quintessence f

quintet [kwɪnˈtɛt] s quintette m

quintuplets [kwɪnˈtʌplɛts] spl quintuplés mpl

quip [kwɪp] s raillerie f, quolibet m ‖ v (pret & pp **quipped**; ger **quipping**) tr dire sur un ton railleur ‖ intr railler

quire [kwaɪr] s main f

quirk [kwʌrk] *s* excentricité *f;* (*subterfuge*) faux-fuyant *m;* **quirk of fate** caprice *m* du sort

quit [kwɪt] *adj* quitte; **to be quits** être quitte; **to call it quits** cesser, s'y renoncer; **we are quits** nous voilà quittes ‖ *v* (*pret & pp* **quit** or **quitted;** *ger* **quitting**) *tr* (*e.g., a city*) quitter; (*one's work, a pursuit, etc.*) cesser, **I quit!** j'abandonne!; **to quit** + *ger* s'arrêter de + *inf* ‖ *intr* partir; (coll) lâcher la partie

quite [kwaɪt] *adv* tout à fait; **quite a story** (coll) toute une histoire

quitter [ˈkwɪtər] *s* défaitiste *m,* lâcheur *m*

quiver [ˈkwɪvər] *s* tremblement *m;* (*to hold arrows*) carquois *m* ‖ *intr* trembler

quixotic [kwɪksˈɑtɪk] *adj* de don Quichotte; visionnaire, exalté

quiz [kwɪz] *s* (*pl* **quizzes**) interrogation *f,* colle *f* ‖ *v* (*pret & pp* **quizzed;** *ger* **quizzing**) *tr* examiner, interroger

quiz′ sec′tion *s* classe *f* d'exercices

quiz′ show′ *s* émission-questionnaire *f*

quizzical [ˈkwɪzɪkəl] *adj* curieux; (*laughable*) risible; (*mocking*) railleur

quoin [kɔɪn] *s* angle *m;* (*cornerstone*) pierre *f* d'angle; (*wedge*) coin *m,* cale *f* ‖ *tr* coincer, caler

quoit [kwɔɪt] *s* palet *m;* **to play quoits** jouer au palet

quondam [ˈkwɑndæm] *adj* ci-devant, d'autrefois

quorum [ˈkworəm] *s* quorum *m*

quota [ˈkwotə] *s* quote-part *f;* (*e.g., of immigration*) quota *m,* contingent *m*

quotation [kwoˈteʃən] *s* (*from a book*) citation *f;* (*of prices*) cours *m,* cote *f*

quota′tion marks *spl* guillemets *mpl;* **in quotation marks** entre guillemets

quote [kwot] *s* (*from a book*) citation *f;* (*of prices*) cours *m,* cote *f;* **in quotes** (coll) entre guillemets ‖ *tr* (*from a book*) citer; (*values*) coter ‖ *intr* tirer des citations; **to quote out of context** citer hors contexte ‖ *interj* je cite; (*in dictation*) ouvrez les guillemets

quote′ un′quote′ *interj* equivalent to the following: le mot est mal désigné *or* l'expression est mal désignée

quotient [ˈkwoʃənt] *s* quotient *m*

R

R, r [ɑr] *s* XVIIIᵉ lettre de l'alphabet

rabbet [ˈræbɪt] *s* feuillure *f* ‖ *tr* feuiller

rab•bi [ˈræbaɪ] *s* (*pl* **-bis** or **-bies**) rabbin *m*

rabbit [ˈræbɪt] *s* lapin *m*

rab′bit stew′ *s* lapin *m* en civet

rabble [ˈræbəl] *s* canaille *f*

rab′ble-rous′er *s* fomentateur *m,* agitateur *m*

rabies [ˈrebiz] *s* rage *f*

raccoon [ræˈkun] *s* raton *m* laveur

race [res] *s* (*ethnic background*) race *f;* (*contest*) course *f;* (*channel to lead water*) bief *m;* (*rapid current*) raz *m* ‖ *tr* lutter de vitesse avec; (*e.g., a horse*) faire courir; (*a motor*) emballer ‖ *intr* faire une course, courir; (*said of motor*) s'emballer

race′horse′ *s* cheval *m* de course

race′ ri′ot *s* émeute *f* raciale

race′ track′ *s* champ *m* de courses, hippodrome *m*

racial [ˈreʃəl] *adj* racial

rac′ing car′ *s* automobile *f* de course

rac′ing odds′ *spl* cote *f*

racism [ˈresɪzəm] *s* racisme *m*

racist [ˈresɪst] *s* raciste *mf*

rack [ræk] *s* (*shelf*) étagère *f;* (*to hang clothes*) portemanteau *m;* (*for baggage*) porte-bagages *m;* (*for guns; for fodder*) râtelier *m;* (*for torture*) chevalet *m;* (*bar made to gear with a pinion*) crémaillère *f;* **to go to rack and ruin** aller à vau-l'eau ‖ *tr* (*with hunger, remorse, etc.*) tenailler; (*one's brains*) se creuser

racket [ˈrækɪt] *s* (*noise*) vacarme *m;* (sports) raquette *f;* (slang) racket *m;* **to make a racket** faire du tapage

racketeer [ˌrækɪˈtɪr] *s* racketter *m* ‖ *intr* pratiquer l'escroquerie

rack′ rail′way *s* chemin *m* de fer à crémaillère

rac•y [ˈresi] *adj* (*comp* **-ier;** *super* **-iest**) plein de verve, vigoureux; parfumé (*off-color*) sale, grivois

radar [ˈredɑr] *s* (acronym) (**ra**dio **d**etecting **a**nd **r**anging) radar *m*

ra′dar sta′tion *s* poste *m* radar

ra′dial tire′ [ˈredɪ•əl] *s* pneu *m* radial, pneumatique *m* à carcasse radiale

radiant [ˈredɪ•ənt] *adj* radieux, rayonnant; (*astr, phys*) radiant

radiate [ˈredɪ,et] *tr* rayonner; (*e.g., happiness*) répandre ‖ *intr* rayonner

radiation [ˌredɪˈeʃən] *s* rayonnement *m,* radiation *f*

radia′tion sick′ness *s* mal *m* des rayons

radiator [ˈredɪ,etər] *s* radiateur *m*

ra′diator cap′ *s* bouchon *m* de radiateur

radical [ˈrædɪkəl] *adj & s* radical *m*

radi•o [ˈredɪ,o] *s* (*pl* **-os**) radio *f* ‖ *tr* radiodiffuser

ra′dio•ac′tive *adj* radioactif

ra′dio•ac′tive fall′out *s* retombées *fpl* radioactives

ra′dio•ac′tive waste′ *s* déchets *mpl* radioactifs

ra′dio am′ateur *s* sans-filiste *mf*

ra′dio announ′cer *s* speaker *m*

ra′dio•broad′cast′ing *s* radiodiffusion *f*

ra′dio control′ *s* (rok) radioguidage *m*

ra′dio•fre′quency *s* radiofréquence *f*

ra′dio•gram′ *s* radiogramme *m*

ra′dio ham′ *s* (coll) radioamateur *m*

ra′dio lis′tener *s* auditeur *m* de la radio

radiology [‚redɪ′ɑlədʒɪ] *s* radiologie *f*

ra′dio net′work *s* chaîne *f* de radiodiffusion

ra′dio news′cast *s* journal *m* parlé, radio-journal *m*

ra′dio•phone′ *s* radiotéléphone *m*

ra′dio receiv′er *s* récepteur *m* de radio

radioscopy [‚redɪ′askəpɪ] *s* radioscopie *f*

ra′dio set′ *s* poste *m* de radio

ra′dio sta′tion *s* poste *m* émetteur

ra′dio tax′i *s* radio-taxi *m*

ra′dio tel′ephone′ *s* radiotéléphone *m*

ra′dio•ther′apy *s* radiothérapie *f*

ra′dio tube′ *s* lampe *f* de radio

radish [′rædɪʃ] *s* radis *m*

radium [′redɪ•əm] *s* radium *m*

radi•us [′redɪ•əs] *s* (*pl* **-i** [‚aɪ] or **-uses**) rayon *m;* (anat) radius *m;* **within a radius of** dans un rayon de, à . . . à la ronde

raffish [′ræfɪʃ] *adj* bravache; (*flashy*) criard

raffle [′ræfəl] *s* tombola *f* ‖ *tr* mettre en tombola

raft [ræft] *s* (*floating on water*) radeau *m;* **a raft of** (*a lot of*) (coll) un tas de

rafter [′ræftər] *s* chevron *m*

rag [ræg] *s* chiffon *m;* **in rags** en haillons; **to chew the rag** (slang) tailler une bavette

ragamuffin [′rægə‚mʌfɪn] *s* gueux *m,* vanu-pieds *m;* (*urchin*) gamin *m*

rag′ doll′ *s* poupée *f* de chiffon

rage [redʒ] *s* rage *f;* **to be all the rage** faire fureur; **to fly into a rage** entrer en fureur ‖ *intr* faire rage

rag′ fair′ *s* marché *m* aux puces

ragged [′rægɪd] *adj* en haillons; (*edge*) hérissé

ragpicker [′ræg‚pɪkər] *s* chiffonnier *m*

rag′time′ *s* rythme *m* syncopé du jazz; musique *f* syncopée du jazz

rag′weed′ *s* ambrosie *f*

ragwort [′ræg‚wʌrt] *s* (*Senecio vulgaris*) séne-çon *m;* (*S. jacobaea*) jacobée *f*

raid [red] *s* incursion *f,* razzia *f;* (*by police*) descente *f;* (mil) raid *m* ‖ *tr* razzier; faire une descente dans

rail [rel] *s* rail *m;* (*railing*) balustrade *f;* (*of stairway*) rampe *f;* (*of, e.g., a bridge*) garde-fou *m;* (orn) râle *m;* **by rail** par chemin de fer ‖ *intr* invectiver; **to rail at** invectiver

rail′ fence′ *s* palissade *f* à claire-voie

rail′head′ *s* tête *f* de ligne

railing [′relɪŋ] *s* balustrade *f*

rail′road′ *adj* ferroviaire ‖ *s* chemin *m* de fer ‖ *tr* (*a bill*) faire voter en vitesse; (coll) empri-sonner à tort

rail′road cros′sing *s* passage *m* à niveau

railroader [′rel‚rodər] *s* cheminot *m*

rail′road sta′tion *s* gare *f*

rail′way′ *adj* ferroviaire ‖ *s* chemin *m* de fer

raiment [′remənt] *s* habillement *m*

rain [ren] *s* pluie *f;* **in the rain** sous la pluie ‖ *tr* faire pleuvoir ‖ *intr* pleuvoir; **it is raining cats and dogs** il pleut à seaux

rainbow [′ren‚bo] *s* arc-en-ciel *m*

rain′bow trout′ *s* truite *f* arc-en-ciel

rain′coat′ *s* imperméable *m*

rain′fall′ *s* chute *f* de pluie

rain′ for′est *s* selve *f,* selva *f,* forêt *m* vierge équatoriale, forêt amazonienne

rain′proof′ *adj* imperméable

rain′ wa′ter *s* eau *f* de pluie

rain•y [′renɪ] *adj* (*comp* **-ier;** *super* **-iest**) plu-vieux

raise [rez] *s* augmentation *f,* rallonge *f;* (*in poker*) relance *f* ‖ *tr* augmenter; (*plants, animals, children; one's voice; a number to a certain power*) élever; (*an army, a camp, a siege; anchor; game*) lever; (*an objection, questions, etc.*) soulever; (*doubts; a hope; a storm*) faire naître; (*a window*) relever; (*one's head, one's voice; prices; the land*) hausser; (*a flag*) arborer; (*the dead*) ressusciter; (*money*) se procurer; (*the ante*) relancer; **to raise up** soulever, dresser

raisin [′rezən] *s* raisin *m* sec, grain *m* de raisin sec

rake [rek] *s* râteau *m;* (*person*) débauché *m* ‖ *tr* ratisser; **to rake together** râteler

rake′-off′ *s* (coll) gratte *f*

rakish [′rekɪʃ] *adj* gaillard; dissolu

ral•ly [′rælɪ] *s* (*pl* **-lies**) ralliement *m;* (pol) réunion *f* politique; (*in a game*) reprise *f;* (*auto race*) rallye *m* ‖ *v* (*pret & pp* **-lied**) *tr* rallier ‖ *intr* se rallier; (*from illness*) se remettre; (sports) se reprendre; **to rally to the side of** se rallier à

ram [ræm] *s* bélier *m* ‖ *v* (*pret & pp* **rammed;** *ger* **ramming**) *tr* tamponner; **to ram down** or **in** enfoncer ‖ *intr* se tamponner; **to ram into** tamponner

RAM [′ɑr′e′em] *s* (letterword) (**random access memory**) RAM *f invar* (mémoire *f* vive)

Ramadan [′ræmədan] *s* (rel) Ramadan *m*

ramble [′ræmbəl] *s* flânerie *f* ‖ *intr* flâner, errer à l'aventure; (*to talk aimlessly*) divaguer

rami•fy [′ræmɪ‚faɪ] *v* (*pret & pp* **-fied**) *tr* rami-fier ‖ *intr* se ramifier

ramp [ræmp] *s* rampe *f,* bretelle *f*

rampage [′ræmpedʒ] *s* tempête *f;* **to go on a rampage** se déchaîner

rampart [′ræmpart] *s* rempart *m*

ram′rod′ *s* écouvillon *m*

ram′shack′le *adj* délabré

ranch [ræntʃ] *s* ranch *m,* rancho *m*

rancid [′rænsɪd] *adj* rance

rancor [′rænkər] *s* rancœur *f*

random [′rændəm] *adj* fortuit; **at random** au hasard

ran′dom ac′cess *s* (comp) accès *m* aléatoire, accès direct

ran′dom-ac′cess mem′ory (RAM) *s* (comp)

mémoire *f* vive, mémoire à accès sélectif, RAM *f invar*

range [rendʒ] *s* (*row*) rangée *f;* (*scope*) portée *f;* (*mountains*) chaîne *f;* (*stove*) cuisinière *f;* (*for rifle practice*) champ *m* de tir; (*of colors, musical notes, prices, speeds, etc.*) gamme *f;* (*or words*) répartition *f;* (*of voice*) tessiture *f;* (*of vision, of activity, etc.*) champ *m;* (*for pasture*) grand pâturage *m;* **within range of** à portée de ‖ *tr* ranger ‖ *intr* se ranger; **to range from** s'échelonner entre, varier entre; **to range over** parcourir

range′ find′er *s* télémètre *m*

rank [ræŋk] *adj* fétide, rance; (*injustice*) criant; (*vegetation*) luxuriant ‖ *s* rang *m* ‖ *tr* ranger ‖ *intr* occuper le premier rang; **to rank above** être supérieur à; **to rank with** aller de pair avec

rank′ and file′ *s* hommes *mpl* de troupe; commun *m* des mortels; (*of the party, union, etc.*) commun *m*

rankle [ˈræŋkəl] *tr* ulcérer; irriter ‖ *intr* s'ulcérer

ransack [ˈrænsæk] *tr* fouiller, fouiller dans; mettre à sac

ransom [ˈrænsəm] *s* rançon *f;* **to hold for ransom** mettre à rançon ‖ *tr* rançonner

rant [rænt] *intr* tempêter

rap [ræp] *s* (*blow*) tape *f;* (*noise*) petit coup *m* sec; (*slang*) éreintement *m;* **to not care a rap** (*slang*) s'en ficher; **to take the rap** (*slang*) se laisser châtier ‖ *v* (*pret & pp* **rapped;** *ger* **rapping**) *tr & intr* frapper d'un coup sec

rapacious [rəˈpeʃəs] *adj* rapace

rape [rep] *s* viol *m* ‖ *tr* violer

rapid [ˈræpɪd] *adj* rapide ‖ **rapids** *spl* rapides *mpl*

rap′id-fire′ *adj* à tir rapide

rapidity [rəˈpɪdəti] *s* rapidité *f*

rap′id tran′sit *s* reseau *m* ferroviaire urbain

rapier [ˈrepɪ•ər] *s* rapière *f*

rapt [ræpt] *adj* ravi; absorbé

rapture [ˈræptʃər] *s* ravissement *m*

rare [rer] *adj* rare; (*meat*) saignant; (*amusing*) (*coll*) impayable

rare′ bird′ *s* merle *m* blanc

rare′-book′ room′ *s* salle *f* de la réserve

rarely [ˈrerli] *adv* rarement

rascal [ˈræskəl] *s* coquin *m*

rash [ræʃ] *adj* téméraire ‖ *s* éruption *f*

rasp [ræsp] *s* crissement *m;* (*tool*) râpe *f* ‖ *tr* râper ‖ *intr* crisser

raspber•ry [ˈræz,beri] *s* (*pl* **-ries**) framboise *f*

rasp′berry bush′ *s* framboisier *m*

raster [ˈræstər] *s* (*telv*) lignes *fpl* successives pour former l'image grâce au balayage

rat [ræt] *s* rat *m;* (*false hair*) (*coll*) postiche *m;* (*deserter*) (*slang*) lâcheur *m;* (*informer*) (*slang*) mouchard *m;* (*scoundrel*) (*slang*) cochon *m;* **rats!** zut!; **to smell a rat** (*coll*) soupçonner anguille sous roche

ratchet [ˈrætʃit] *s* encliquetage *m*

rate [ret] *s* taux *m;* (*for freight, mail, a subscription*) tarif *m;* **at any rate** en tout cas; **at the**

rate of à raison de ‖ *tr* évaluer; mériter ‖ *intr* (*coll*) être favori

rate′ of exchange′ *s* cours *m*

rather [ˈræðər], [ˈrɑðər] *adv* plutôt; (*fairly*) assez; **rather than** plutôt que ‖ *interj* je vous crois!

rathskeller [ˈræts,kɛlər] *s* caveau *m*

rati•fy [ˈræti,faɪ] *v* (*pret & pp* **-fied**) *tr* ratifier

rating [ˈretiŋ] *s* classement *m,* cote *f*

ra•tio [ˈreʃo] *s* (*pl* **-tios**) raison *f,* rapport *m*

ration [ˈræʃən] *s* ration *f* ‖ *tr* rationner

rational [ˈræʃənəl] *adj* rationnel

ra′tion book′ *s* tickets *mpl* de rationnement

ra′tion card′ *s* carte *f* de ravitaillement

rat′ poi′son *s* mort *m* aux rats

rat′ race′ *s* foire *f* d'empoigne

rat′-tail file′ *s* queue-de-rat *f*

rattan [ræˈtæn] *s* rotin *m*

rattle [ˈrætəl] *s* (*number of short, sharp sounds*) bruit *m* de ferraille, cliquetis *m;* (*noisemaking device*) crécelle *f;* (*child's toy*) hochet *m;* (*in the throat*) râle *m* ‖ *tr* agiter; (*to confuse*) (*coll*) affoler; **to rattle off** débiter comme un moulin ‖ *intr* cliqueter; (*said of windows*) trembler

rat′tle•snake′ *s* serpent *m* à sonnettes

rat′trap′ *s* ratière *f*

raucous [ˈrɔkəs] *adj* rauque

ravage [ˈrævɪdʒ] *s* ravage *m;* **ravages** (*of time*) injure *f* ‖ *tr* ravager

rave [rev] *s* (*coll*) éloge *m* enthousiaste ‖ *intr* délirer; **to rave about** or **over** s'extasier devant or sur

raven [ˈrevən] *s* corbeau *m*

ravenous [ˈrævənəs] *adj* vorace

rave′ review′ *s* article *m* dithyrambique

ravine [rəˈvin] *s* ravin *m*

ravish [ˈrævɪʃ] *tr* ravir

ravishing [ˈrævɪʃiŋ] *adj* ravissant

raw [rɔ] *adj* (*uncooked*) cru; (*sugar, metal*) brut; (*silk*) grège; (*wound*) vif; (*wind*) aigre; (*weather*) humide et froid; novice, inexpérimenté

raw′boned′ *adj* décharné

raw′ deal′ *s* (*slang*) mauvais tour *m*

raw′hide′ *s* cuir *m* vert

raw′ mate′rial *s* matière *f* première, matières premières, matière brute

ray [re] *s* (*of light*) rayon *m;* (*fish*) raie *f*

rayon [ˈre•ɑn] *s* rayonne *f*

raze [rez] *tr* raser

razor [ˈrezər] *s* rasoir *m*

ra′zor blade′ *s* lame *f* de rasoir

ra′zor strop′ *s* cuir *m* à rasoir

razz [ræz] *tr* (*slang*) mettre en boîte

reach [ritʃ] *s* portée *f;* (*of a boxer*) allonge *f;* **out of reach (of)** hors d'atteinte (de), hors de portée (de); **within reach of** à portée de ‖ *tr* atteindre; arriver à; **to reach out** (*a hand*) tendre; (*an arm*) allonger ‖ *intr* s'étendre

react [rɪˈækt] *intr* réagir

reaction [rɪˈækʃən] *s* réaction *f*

reactionar•y [rɪˈækʃən͵ɛri] *adj* réactionnaire ‖ *s* (*pl* **-ies**) réactionnaire *mf*

reactivate [riˈæktə͵vet] *tr* réactiver

reactor [rɪˈæktər] *s* réacteur *m*

read [rid] *v* (*pret & pp* **read** [rɛd]) *tr* lire; **to read over** parcourir ‖ *intr* lire; (*said of passage, description, etc.*) se lire; (*said, e.g., of thermometer*) marquer; **to read on** continuer à lire; **to read up on** étudier

reader [ˈridər] *s* lecteur *m;* livre *m* de lecture

read'head' *s* (comp) lecteur *m* de disquette

readily [ˈrɛdɪli] *adv* (*willingly*) volontiers; (*easily*) facilement

reading [ˈridɪŋ] *s* lecture *f*

read'ing desk' *s* pupitre *m*

read'ing glass' *s* loupe *f;* **reading glasses** lunettes *fpl* pour lire

read'ing lamp' *s* lampe *f* de bureau

read'ing room' *s* salle *f* de lecture

readjust [͵riˈə·dʒʌst] *tr* réadapter; (*to correct*) rectifier; (*salaries*) rajuster

read'-on'ly mem'ory (ROM) *s* (comp) mémoire *f* morte, ROM *f invar*

read•y [ˈrɛdi] *adj* (*comp* **-ier;** *super* **-iest**) prêt; (*quick*) vif; (*money*) comptant ‖ *v* (*pret & pp* **-ied**) *tr* préparer ‖ *intr* se préparer

read'y cash' *s* argent *m* comptant

read'y-made' suit' *s* (*for men*) complet *m* de confection; (*for women*) costume *m* de confection

ready-to-eat [ˈrɛditəˈit] *adj* prêt à servir

ready-to-wear [ˈrɛditəˈwɛr] *adj* prêt à porter ‖ *s* prêt-à-porter *m*

reaffirm [͵riˈə·ˈfʌrm] *tr* réaffirmer

reagent [rɪˈedʒənt] *s* (chem) réactif *m*

real [ˈriˈəl] *adj* vrai, réel

re'al estate' *s* biens *mpl* immobiliers

re'al-estate' *adj* immobilier

re'al-estate a'gent *s* agent *m* immobilier, agent de location

realia [riˈæli•ə] *s* (educ) *des objets ou des activités de la vie réelle*

realism [ˈri•ə͵lɪzəm] *s* rélisme *m*

realist [ˈri•əlɪst] *s* réaliste *mf*

realistic [͵ri•əˈlɪstɪk] *adj* réaliste

reali•ty [riˈælɪti] *s* (*pl* **-ties**) réalité *f*

realize [ˈri•ə͵laɪz] *tr* se rendre compte de, s'apercevoir de; (*hopes, profits, etc.*) réaliser

really [ˈri•əli] *adv* vraiment réellement, en réalité

realm [rɛlm] *s* royaume *m;* (*field*) domaine *m*

re'al time' *s* (comp) temps *m* réel

Realtor [ˈri•əltər] *s* (*official member*) (U.S.A.) agent *m* immobilier, agent de location

ream [rim] *s* rame *f;* **reams** (coll) masses *fpl* ‖ *tr* aléser

reap [rip] *tr* moissonner; (*to gather*) recueillir

reaper [ˈripər] *s* moissonneur *m;* (mach) moissonneuse *f*

reappear [͵ri•əˈpɪr] *intr* réapparaître

reappearance [͵ri•əˈpɪrəns] *s* réapparition *f*

reapportionment [͵ri•əˈpɔrʃənmənt] *s* nouvelle répartition *f*

rear [rɪr] *adj* arrière, d'arrière, de derrière ‖ ‖ *s* derrière *m;* (*of a car, ship, etc.; of an army*) arrière *m;* (*of a row*) queue *f;* **to the rear!** (mil) demi-tour à droite! ‖ *tr* élever ‖ *intr* (*said of animal*) se cabrer

rear' ad'miral *s* contre-amiral *m*

rear'-axle assem'bly *s* (*pl* **-blies**) pont *m* arrière

rear' drive' *s* traction *f* arrière

rearmament [riˈɑrməmənt] *s* réarmement *m*

rearrange [͵ri•əˈrendʒ] *tr* arranger de nouveau

rear'-view mir'ror *s* rétroviseur *m*

rear' win'dow *s* (aut) lunette *f* arrière

reason [ˈrizən] *s* raison *f;* **by reason of** à cause de; **for good reason** pour cause; **to listen to reason** entendre raison; **to stand to reason** être de toute évidence ‖ *tr & intr* raisonner

reasonable [ˈrizənəbəl] *adj* raisonnable

reassessment [͵ri•əˈsɛsmənt] *s* réévaluation *f*

reassure [͵ri•əˈʃʊr] *tr* rassurer

reawaken [͵ri•əˈwekən] *tr* réveiller ‖ *intr* se réveiller

rebate [ˈribet] *s* (*discount*) rabais *m*, escompte *m*, ristourne *f;* (*money back*) remboursement *m*, ristourne *f* ‖ [rɪˈbet] *tr* faire un rabais sur

rebel [ˈrɛbəl] *adj & s* rebelle *mf* ‖ **re•bel** [rɪˈbɛl] *v* (*pret & pp* **-belled;** *ger* **-belling**) *intr* se rebeller

rebellion [rɪˈbɛljən] *s* rébellion *f*

rebellious [rɪˈbɛljəs] *adj* rebelle

re•bind [riˈbaɪnd] *v* (*pret & pp* **-bound**) *tr* (bb) relier à neuf

rebirth [rɪbʌrθ] *s* renaissance *f*

rebore [riˈbor] *tr* rectifier

rebound [ˈri͵baʊnd] *s* rebondissement *m* ‖ [ri·ˈbaʊnd] *intr* rebondir

rebroad•cast [riˈbrɔd͵kæst] *s* retransmission *f* ‖ *v* (*pret & pp* **-cast** or **-casted**) *tr* retransmettre

rebuff [rɪˈbʌf] *s* rebuffade *f* ‖ *tr* mal accueillir

re•build [riˈbɪld] *v* (*pret & pp* **-built**) *tr* reconstruire

rebuke [rɪˈbjuk] *s* réprimande *f* ‖ *tr* réprimander

re•but [rɪˈbʌt] *v* (*pret & pp* **-butted;** *ger* **-butting**) *tr* réfuter, repousser

rebuttal [rɪˈbʌtəl] *s* réfutation *f*

recall [ˈrikɔl] *s* rappel *m* ‖ [rɪˈkɔl] *tr* rappeler; se rappeler de

recant [rɪˈkænt] *tr* rétracter ‖ *intr* se rétracter

re•cap [ˈri͵kæp] *v* (*pret & pp* **-capped;** *ger* **-capping**) *tr* rechaper

recapitulation [͵rikə͵pɪtʃ/əˈleʃən] *s* récapitulation *f*

re•cast [ˈri͵kæst] *s* refonte *f* ‖ [riˈkæst] *v* (*pret & pp* **-cast**) *tr* (*metal; a play, novel, etc.*) refondre; (*the actors of a play*) redistribuer

recede [rɪˈsid] *intr* reculer; (*said of forehead, chin, etc.*) fuir; (*said of sea*) se retirer

receipt [rɪˈsit] *s* (*for goods*) récépissé *m;* (*for money*) récépissé, reçu *m;* (*recipe*) recette *f;* **receipts** recettes; **to acknowledge receipt of** accuser réception de ‖ *tr* acquitter

receive [rɪˈsiv] *tr* recevoir; (*stolen goods*) recéler; (*a station*) (rad) capter; **received payment** pour acquit ‖ *intr* recevoir

receiver [rɪˈsivər] *s* (*of letter*) destinataire *mf*; (*in bankruptcy*) syndic *m*, liquidateur *m*; (telp) récepteur *m*

receiv'ing set' *s* poste *m* récepteur

recent [ˈrisənt] *adj* récent

recently [ˈrisəntli] *adv* récemment

receptacle [rɪˈsɛptəkəl] *s* récipient *m*; (*in a coin phone*) sébile *f*; (elec) prise *f* femelle

reception [rɪˈsɛpʃən] *s* réception *f*; (*welcome*) accueil *m*

recep'tion desk' *s* réception *f*

receptionist [rɪˈsɛpʃənɪst] *s* préposé *m* à la réception

receptive [rɪˈsɛptɪv] *adj* réceptif

recess [ˈrisɛs] *s* (*of court, legislature, etc.*) ajournement *m*; (*at school*) récréation *f*; (*in a wall*) niche *f* ‖ [rɪˈsɛs] *tr* ajourner; (*s.th., e.g., in a wall*) encastrer ‖ *intr* s'adjourner

recession [rɪˈsɛʃən] *s* récession *f*

rechargeable [riˈtʃɑrdʒəbəl] *adj* rechargeable

recipe [ˈrɛsɪpi] *s* recette *f*

recipient [rɪˈsɪpɪ•ənt] *s* (*person*) bénéficiaire *mf*; (*of a degree, honor, etc.*) récipiendaire *m*; (*of blood*) receveur *m*; (*container*) récipient *m*

reciprocal [rɪˈsɪprəkəl] *adj* réciproque ‖ *s* (math) (*function*) inverse *m*

reciprocity [ˌrɛsɪˈprasɪti] *s* réciprocité *f*

recital [rɪˈsaɪtəl] *s* récit *m*; (*of music or poetry*) récital *m*

recite [rɪˈsaɪt] *tr* réciter; narrer

reckless [ˈrɛklɪs] *adj* téméraire, imprudent, insouciant

reckon [ˈrɛkən] *tr* calculer; considérer; (coll) supposer, imaginer ‖ *intr* calculer; **to reckon on** compter sur; **to reckon with** tenir compte de

reclaim [rɪˈklem] *tr* récupérer; (*e.g., waste land*) mettre en valeur; (*a person*) réformer

reclamation [ˌrɛkləˈmeʃən] *s* récupération *f*; (*e.g., of waste land*) mise *f* en valeur; (*of a person*) réforme *f*

recline [rɪˈklaɪn] *tr* appuyer, reposer ‖ *intr* s'appuyer, se reposer

reclin'ing seat' *s* siège *m* à dossier réglable

recluse [ˈrɛklus] *adj & s* reclus *m*

recognition [ˌrɛkəgˈnɪʃən] *s* reconnaissance *f*

recognize [ˈrɛkəgˌnaɪz] *tr* reconnaître; (parl) donner la parole à

recoil [rɪˈkɔɪl] *s* répugnance *f*; (*of, e.g., firearm*) recul *m* ‖ *intr* reculer

recollect [ˌrɛkəˈlɛkt] *tr* se rappeler

recollection [ˌrɛkəˈlɛkʃən] *s* souvenir *m*

recommend [ˌrɛkəˈmɛnd] *tr* recommander

recommendation [ˌrɛkəmɛnˈdaʃən] *s* recommandation *f*; (*written*) certificat *m*

recompense [ˈrɛkəmˌpɛns] *s* récompense *f* ‖ *tr* récompenser

reconcile [ˈrɛkənˌsaɪl] *tr* réconcilier; **to reconcile oneself to** se résigner à

reconnaissance [rɪˈkanɪsəns] *s* reconnaissance *f*

reconnoiter [ˌrɛkəˈnɔɪtər] *tr & intr* reconnaître

reconquer [riˈkaŋkər] *tr* reconquérir

reconquest [riˈkaŋkwɛst] *s* reconquête *f*

reconsider [ˌrikənˈsɪdər] *tr* reconsidérer

reconstruct [ˌrikənˈstrʌkt] *tr* reconstruire; (*a crime*) reconstituer

reconversion [ˌrikənˈvʌrʒən] *s* reconversion *f*

record [ˈrɛkərd] *s* enregistrement *m*, registre *m*; (*to play on the phonograph*) disque *m*; (mil) état *m* de service; (sports) record *m*; **off the record** en confidence; **records** archives *fpl*; **to break the record** battre le record; **to have a good record** être bien noté; (*at school*) avoir de bonnes notes ‖ [rɪˈkɔrd] *tr* enregistrer

rec'ord chang'er *s* tourne-disque *m* automatique

recorder [rɪˈkɔrdər] *s* (electron) appareil *m* enregistreur; (law) greffier *m*; (mus) flûte *f* à bec

rec'ord hold'er *s* recordman *m*

recording [rɪˈkɔrdɪŋ] *adj* enregistreur ‖ *s* enregistrement *m*

record'ing head' *s* tête *f* de graveur

record'ing tape' *s* ruban *m* magnétique

rec'ord li'brary *s* discothèque *m*

rec'ord play'er *s* électrophone *m*

recount [ˈriˌkaʊnt] *s* nouveau dépouillement *m* du scrutin ‖ [riˈkaʊnt] *tr* (*to count again*) recompter ‖ [rɪˈkaʊnt] *tr* (*to tell*) raconter

recoup [rɪˈkup] *tr* recouvrer; **to recoup s.o. for** dédommager qn de

recourse [rɪˈkors], [ˈrikors] *s* recours *m*; **to have recourse to** recourir à

recover [rɪkʌvər] *tr* (*to get back*) recouvrer; (*to cover again*) recouvrir ‖ *intr* (*to get well*) se rétablir

recov'er•y [rɪˈkʌvəri] *s* (*pl* **-ies**) récupération *f*, recouvrement *m*; (*e.g., of health*) rétablissement *m*

recov'ery room' *s* (med) salle *f* de reveil, salle de réanimation

recreant [ˈrɛkrɪ•ənt] *adj & s* lâche *mf*; traître *m*; apostat *m*

recreation [ˌrɛkrɪˈeʃən] *s* récréation *f*

rec'room' [rɛk] *s* salle *f* de détente

recruit [rɪˈkrut] *s* recrue *f* ‖ *tr* recruter; **to be recuited** se recruter

rectangle [ˈrɛkˌtæŋgəl] *s* rectangle *m*

rectifier [ˈrɛktəˌfaɪ•ər] *s* rectificateur *m*; (elec) redresseur *m*

recti•fy [ˈrɛktɪˌfaɪ] *v* (*pret & pp* **-fied**) *tr* rectifier; (elec) redresser

rec•tum [ˈrɛktəm] *s* (*pl* **-ta** [tə]) rectum *m*

recumbent [rɪˈkʌmbənt] *adj* couché

recuperate [rɪˈkjupəˌret] *tr & intr* récupérer

re•cur [rɪˈkʌr] *v* (*pret & pp* **-curred;** *ger* **-curring**) *intr* revenir, se reproduire; revenir à la mémoire de

recurrent [rɪˈkʌrənt] *adj* récurrent

recycle [riˈsaɪkəl] *tr* recycler

recycling [riˈsaɪklɪŋ] *s* recyclage *m*

red [rɛd] *adj* (*comp* **redder;** *super* **reddest**) rouge ‖ *s* (*color*) rouge *m;* **in the red** en déficit; **Red** (*communist*) rouge *mf;* (*nickname*) Rouquin *m;* **to glow** or **turn red** rougeoyer

red′bait′ *tr* taxer de communiste

red′bird′ *s* cardinal *m* d'Amérique, tangara *m*

red′ blood′ cell′ *s* globule *m* rouge

red blood′ cor′puscle *m* globule *m* rouge

red′-blood′ed *adj* vigoureux

red′breast′ *s* rouge-gorge *m*

red′cap′ porteur *m;* (Brit) soldat *m* de la police militaire

red′ cell′ *s* globule *m* rouge

Red′ Cross′ *s* Croix-Rouge *f*

redden [ˈrɛdən] *tr & intr* rougir

redeem [rɪˈdim] *tr* racheter; (*a pawned article*) dégager; (*a promise*) remplir; (*a debt*) s'acquitter de, acquitter

redeemer [rɪˈdimər] *s* rédempteur *m*

redemption [rɪˈdɛmpʃən] *s* rachat *m;* (rel) rédemption *f*

red′-haired′ *adj* roux

red′hand′ed *adj & adv* sur le fait, en flagrant délit

red′head′ *s* (*woman*) rousse *f*

red′ her′ring *s* hareng *m* saur; (fig) faux-fuyant *m*

red′-hot′ *adj* chauffé au rouge; ardent; (*news*) tout frais

rediscount [riˈdɪskaʊnt] *s* réescompte *m;* ‖ *tr* réescompter

rediscover [ˌridɪsˈkʌvər] *tr* redécouvrir

red′-let′ter day′ *s* jour *m* mémorable

red′ light′ *s* feu *m* rouge; **to go through a red light** brûler feu rouge

red′-light′ dis′trict *s* quartier *m* réservé

red′ man′ *s* (*pl* **men′**) Peau-Rouge *m*

re∙do [riˈdu] *v* (*pret* **-did;** *pp* **-done**) *tr* refaire

redolent [ˈrɛdələnt] *adj* parfumé; **redolent of** exhalant une senteur de; qui fait penser à

redouble [riˈdʌbəl] *s* (bridge) surcontre *m* ‖ *tr & intr* redoubler; (bridge) surcontrer

redoubt [rɪˈdaʊt] *s* redoute *f*

redound [rɪˈdaʊnd] *intr* contribuer; **to redound to** tourner à

red′ pep′per *s* piment *m* rouge

redress [ˈridrəs] *s* redressement *m* ‖ [rɪˈdrɛs] *tr* redresser

Red′ Rid′ing∙hood′ *s* Chaperon rouge *m*

Red′ Sea′ *s* Mer *f* Rouge

red′skin′ *s* (obs) Peau-Rouge *mf*

red′ tape′ *s* paperasserie *f,* chinoiseries *fpl* administratives

reduce [rɪˈd(j)us] *tr* réduire, diminuer ‖ *intr* maigrir

reduc′ing ex′ercises *spl* exercises *mpl* amaigrissants

reduction [rɪˈdʌkʃən] *s* réduction *f,* diminution *f;* **reduction in force** réduction *f* des effectifs

redundant [rɪˈdʌndənt] *adj* redondant

red′ wine′ *s* vin *m* rouge

red′ wing′ *s* (orn) mauvis *m*

red′wood′ *s* séquoia *m*

reed [rid] *s* (*of instrument*) anche *f;* (bot) roseau *m;* **reeds** (mus) instruments *mpl* à anche

reedit [riˈɛdɪt] *tr* rééditer

reef [rif] *s* récif *m;* (*of sail*) ris *m* ‖ *tr* (naut) prendre un ris dans

reefer [ˈrifər] *s* (slang) joint *m,* cigarette *f* de marijuana

reek [rik] *intr* fumer; **to reek of** or **with** empester, puer

reel [ril] *s* (*cylinder*) bobine *f;* (*of film*) rouleau *m,* bobine, bande *f;* (*of fishing rod*) moulinet *m;* (*sway*) balancement *m;* **off the reel** (coll) d'affilée ‖ *tr* bobiner; **to reel off** dévider; (coll) réciter d'un trait ‖ *intr* chanceler

reelection [ˌriɪˈlɛkʃən] *s* réélection *f*

reenlist [ˌriɛnˈlɪst] *tr* rengager ‖ *intr* rengager, se rengager

reenlistment [ˌriɛnˈlɪstmənt] *s* rengagement *m;* (*person*) rengagé *m*

reen∙try [riˈɛntri] *s* (*pl* **-tries**) rentrée *f;* (rok) retour *m* à la terre

reexamination [ˌriɛgˌzæmɪˈneʃən] *s* réexamen *m*

re∙fer [rɪˈfʌr] *v* (*pret & pp* **-ferred;** *ger* **-ferring**) *tr* renvoyer ‖ *intr*—**to refer to** se référer à

referee [ˌrɛfəˈri] *s* arbitre *m,* directeur *m* de jeu ‖ *tr & intr* arbitrer

reference [ˈrɛfərəns] *s* référence *f*

ref′erence room′ *s* bibliothèque *f* de consultation

referen∙dum [ˌrɛfəˈrɛndəm] *s* (*pl* **-da** [də]) référendum *m*

refill [ˈrifɪl] *s* recharge *f* ‖ [riˈfɪl] *tr* remplir à nouveau

refine [rɪˈfaɪn] *tr* raffiner

refinement [rɪˈfaɪnmənt] *s* raffinage *m;* (*e.g., of manners*) raffinement *m*

refiner∙y [rɪˈfaɪnəri] *s* (*pl* **-ies**) raffinerie *f*

reflect [rɪˈflɛkt] *tr* réfléchir, refléter ‖ *intr* (*to be reflected*) se refléter; (*to meditate*) réfléchir; **to reflect on** or **upon** réfléchir à or sur; (*to harm*) nuire à la réputation de

reflection [rɪˈflɛkʃən] *s* (*e.g., of light; thought*) réflexion *f;* (*reflected light; image*) reflet *m;* **to cast reflections on** faire des réflexions à

reflector [riˈflɛktər] *s* réflecteur *m*

reflex [ˈriflɛks] *adj & s* réflexe *m*

reflexive [rɪˈflɛksɪv] *adj & s* réflechi *m*

reforestation [ˌrifɔrɪsˈteʃən] *s* reboisement *m*

reform [rɪˈfɔrm] *s* réforme *f* ‖ *tr* réformer ‖ *intr* se réformer

reformation [ˌrɛfərˈmeʃən] *s* réformation *f;* **the Reformation** la Réforme

reformato∙ry [rɪˈfɔrməˌtori] *s* (*pl* **-ries**) maison *f* de correction

reformer [rɪˈfɔrmər] *s* réformateur *m*

reform′ school′ *s* maison *f* de correction

refraction [rɪˈfrækʃən] *s* réfraction *f*

refrain [rɪˈfren] *s* refrain *m* ‖ *intr* s'abstenir

refresh [rɪˈfrɛʃ] *tr* rafraîchir ‖ *intr* se rafraîchir

refreshing [rɪˈfrɛʃɪŋ] *adj* rafraîchissant

refreshment [rɪˈfrɛʃmənt] *s* rafraîchissement *m*

refresh′ment bar′ *s* buvette *f*

refrigerate [rɪˈfrɪdʒə,ret] *tr* réfrigérer

refrigerator [rɪˈfrɪdʒə,retər] *s* (*icebox*) glacière; réfrigérateur *m*, frigidaire *m*; (*condenser*) congélateur *m*

refrig′erator car′ *s* (rr) wagon *m* frigorifique

re•fuel [riˈfjul] *v* (*pret & pp* **-fueled** or **-fuelled;** *ger* **-fueling** or **-fuelling**) *tr* ravitailler en carburant ‖ *intr* se ravitailler en carburant

refuge [ˈrɛfjudʒ] *s* refuge *m;* **to take refuge (in)** se réfugier (dans)

refugee [,rɛfjuˈdʒi] *s* réfugié *m*

refund [ˈrifʌnd] *s* remboursement *m* ‖ [ˈrifʌnd] *tr* (*to pay back*) rembourser ‖ [riˈfʌnd] *tr* (*to fund again*) consolider

refurnish [riˈfʌrnɪʃ] *tr* remeubler

refusal [rɪˈfjuzəl] *s* refus *m*

refuse [ˈrɛfjus] *s* ordures *fpl*, détritus *mpl* ‖ [rɪˈfjuz] *tr & intr* refuser

refute [rɪˈfjut] *tr* réfuter

regain [rɪˈgen] *tr* regagner; (*consciousness*) reprendre

regal [ˈrigəl] *adj* royal

regale [rɪˈgel] *tr* régaler

regalia [rɪˈgelɪ•ə] *spl* atours *mpl*, ornements *mpl;* (*of an office*) insignes *mpl*

regard [rɪˈgard] *s* considération *f;* (*esteem*) respect *m;* (*look*) regard *m;* **in** or **with regard to** à l'égard de; **regards** sincères amitiés *fpl* ‖ *tr* considérer, estimer; **as regards** quant à

regarding [rɪˈgardɪŋ] *prep* au sujet de, touchant

regardless [rɪˈgardlɪs] *adj* inattentif ‖ *adv* (coll) coûte que coûte; **regardless of** sans tenir compte de

regatta [rɪˈgætə] *s* régates *fpl*

regen•cy [ˈridʒənsi] *s* (*pl* **-cies**) régence *f*

regenerate [rɪˈdʒɛnə,ret] *tr* régénérer ‖ *intr* se régénérer

regent [ˈridʒənt] *s* régent *m*

regicide [ˈrɛdʒɪ,saɪd] *s* (*act*) régicide *m;* (*person*) régicide *mf*

regime [reˈʒim] *s* régime *m*

regiment [ˈrɛdʒɪmənt] *s* régiment *m* ‖ [ˈrɛdʒɪ,mɛnt] *tr* enrégimenter, régenter

regimental [,rɛdʒɪˈmɛntəl] *adj* régimentaire ‖ **regimentals** *spl* tenue *f* militaire

region [ˈridʒən] *s* région *f*

register [ˈrɛdʒɪstər] *s* registre *m* ‖ *tr* enregistrer; (*a student; an automobile*) immatriculer; (*a letter*) recommander ‖ *intr* s'inscrire

reg′istered let′ter *s* lettre *f* recommandée

reg′istered mail′ *s* envoi *m* en recommandé

reg′istered nurse′ *s* infirmière *f* diplômée

registrar [ˈrɛdʒɪs,trar] *s* archiviste *mf*, secrétaire *mf*

registration [,rɛdʒɪsˈtreʃən] *s* enregistrement *m;* immatriculation *f*, inscription *f;* (*of mail*) recommandation *f*

registra′tion blank′ *s* fiche *f* d'inscription

registra′tion fee′ *s* frais *mpl* d'inscription, droit *m* d'inscription

registra′tion num′ber *s* (*of soldier or student*) numéro *m* matricule

re•gret [rɪˈgrɛt] *s* regret *m;* **regrets** excuses *fpl* ‖ *v* (*pret & pp* **-gretted;** *ger* **-gretting**) *tr* regretter

regrettable [rɪˈgrɛtəbəl] *adj* regrettable

regular [ˈrɛgjələr] *adj & s* régulier *m*

reg′ular fel′low *s* (coll) chic type *m*

regularity [,rɛgjəˈlærɪti] *s* régularité *f*

regularize [ˈrɛgjələ,raɪz] *tr* régulariser

regulate [ˈrɛgjə,let] *tr* régler; (*to control*) réglementer

regulation [,rɛgjəˈleʃən] *s* régulation *f;* (*rule*) règlement *m*

rehabilitate [,rihəˈbɪlɪ,tet] *tr* réadapter; (*in reputation, standing, etc.*) réhabiliter

rehearsal [rɪˈhʌrsəl] *s* répétition *f*

rehearse [rɪˈhʌrs] *tr & intr* répéter

reign [ren] *s* règne *m* ‖ *intr* régner

reimburse [,ri•ɪmˈbʌrs] *tr* rembourser

rein [ren] *s* rêne *f;* **to give free rein to** donner libre cours à ‖ *tr* contenir, freiner

reincarnation [,ri•ɪnkarˈneʃən] *s* réincarnation *f*

rein′deer′ *s* renne *m*

reinforce [,ri•ɪnˈfors] *tr* renforcer; (*concrete*) armer

reinforcement [,ri•ɪnˈforsmənt] *s* renforcement *m*

reinstate [,ri•ɪnˈstet] *tr* rétablir

reiterate [riˈɪtə,ret] *tr* réitérer

reject [ˈridʒɛkt] *s* pièce *f* or article *m* de rebut; **rejects** rebuts *mpl* ‖ [rɪˈdʒɛkt] *tr* rejeter

rejection [rɪˈdʒɛkʃən] *s* rejet *m*, refus *m*

rejoice [rɪˈdʒɔɪs] *intr* se réjouir

rejoin [rɪˈdʒɔɪn] *tr* rejoindre

rejoinder [rɪˈdʒɔɪndər] *s* réplique *f;* (law) réponse *f* à une réplique

rejuvenation [rɪ,dʒuviˈneʃən] *s* rajeunissement *m*

rekindle [riˈkɪndəl] *tr* rallumer

relapse [rɪˈlæps] *s* rechute *f* ‖ *intr* rechuter

relate [rɪˈlet] *tr* (*to narrate*) relater; (*e.g., two events*) établir un rapport entre; **to be related** être apparenté

relation [rɪˈleʃən] *s* (*relationship*) relation *f*, rapport *m;* (*telling*) récit *m*, relation; (*relative*) parent *m;* (*kinship*) parenté *f;* **in relation to** or **with** par rapport à; **relations** (*of a sexual nature*) rapports *mpl;* (*diplomatic*) relations *fpl*

relationship [rɪˈleʃən,ʃɪp] *s* (*connection*) rapport *m;* (*kinship*) parenté *f*

relative [ˈrɛlətɪv] *adj* relatif ‖ *s* parent *m*

relativity [,rɛləˈtɪvəti] *s* relativité *f*

relax [rɪˈlæks] *tr* détendre; **to be relaxed** être décontracté *or* détendu ‖ *intr* se détendre, décompresser

relaxation [,rilæksˈeʃən] *s* détente *f*, délassement *m*

relaxing [rɪˈlæksɪŋ] *adj* tranquillisant, apaisant; (*diverting*) délassant

relay [ˈrile] *s* relais *m* ‖ *v* (*pret & pp* **-layed**) *tr* relayer; (rad, telg, telp, telv) retransmettre ‖ [riˈle] *v* (*pret & pp* **-laid**) *tr* tendre de nouveau

re′lay race′ *s* course *f* de relais

re′lay sat′ellite *s* satellite *m* de relais

re′lay transmit′ter *s* (electron) réémetteur *m*

release [rɪ′lis] *s* (*from jail*) mise *f* en liberté, libération *f;* (*permission*) autorisation *f;* (*exemption*) dérogation *f;* (aer) lâchage *m;* (mach) déclenchement *m;* **release on bail** libération *f* sous caution; **release on parole** libération conditionnelle ‖ *tr* délivrer; (*from jail*) mettre en liberté; autoriser; (*a bomb*) lâcher

relegate [′rɛlɪˌget] *tr* reléguer

relent [rɪ′lɛnt] *intr* se laisser attendrir, s'adoucir

relentless [rɪ′lɛntlɪs] *adj* implacable

relevant [′rɛlɪvənt] *adj* pertinent

reliable [rɪ′laɪ•əbəl] *adj* digne de confiance, digne de foi, fiable

reliance [rɪ′laɪ•əns] *s* confiance *f*

relic [′rɛlɪk] *s* (rel) relique *f;* (fig) vestige *m*

relief [rɪ′lif] *s* (*from pain, anxiety*) soulagement *m;* (*projection of figures; elevation*) relief *m;* (*aid*) secours *m;* (*welfare program*) aide *f* sociale; (mil) relève *f;* **in relief** en relief

relief′ pitch′er *s* releveur *m,* lanceur *m* de relève

relieve [rɪ′liv] *tr* soulager; (*to aid*) secourir; (*to release from a post; to give variety to*) relever; (mil) relever

religion [rɪ′lɪdʒən] *s* religion *f*

religious [rɪ′lɪdʒəs] *adj* religieux

relinquish [rɪ′lɪŋkwɪʃ] *tr* abandonner

relish [′rɛlɪʃ] *s* (*enjoyment*) goût *m;* (*condiment*) assaisonnement *m;* **relish for** penchant pour ‖ *tr* goûter, apprécier

reluctance [rɪ′lʌktəns] *s* répugnance *f;* **with reluctance** à contrecœur

reluctant [rɪ′lʌktənt] *adj* hésitant, peu disposé

re•ly [rɪ′laɪ] *v* (*pret & pp* **-lied**) *intr*—**to rely on** compter sur, se fier à

REM [rɛm] *s* (acronym) (**rapid eye movement**) REM *m* (mouvements oculaires rapides)

remain [rɪ′men] *s*—**remains** restes *mpl;* œuvres *fpl* posthumes ‖ *intr* rester

remainder [rɪ′mendər] *s* reste *m;* **remainders** bouillons *mpl* ‖ *tr* solder

re•make [rɪ′mek] *v* (*pret & pp* **-made**) *tr* refaire

remark [rɪ′mɑrk] *s* remarque *f,* observation *f* ‖ *tr & intr* remarquer, observer; **to remark on** faire des remarques sur

remarkable [rɪ′mɑrkəbəl] *adj* remarquable

remar•ry [rɪ′mæri] *v* (*pret & pp* **-ried**) *tr* remarier; se remarier avec ‖ *intr* se remarier

reme•dy [′rɛmɪdi] *s* (*pl* **-dies**) remède *m* ‖ *v* (*pret & pp* **-died**) *tr* remédier à

remember [rɪ′mɛmbər] *tr* se souvenir de, se rappeler; **remember me to** rappelez-moi au bon souvenir de ‖ *intr* se souvenir, se rappeler

remembrance [rɪ′mɛmbrəns] *s* souvenir *m;* **in remembrance of** en souvenir de

remind [rɪ′maɪnd] *tr* rappeler

reminder [rɪ′maɪndər] *s* note *f* de rappel, mémento *m,* pense-bête *f*

reminisce [ˌrɛmɪ′nɪs] *intr* se livrer au souvenirs, raconter ses souvenirs

remiss [rɪ′mɪs] *adj* négligent

remission [rɪ′mɪʃən] *s* rémission *f*

re•mit [rɪ′mɪt] *v* (*pret & pp* **-mitted;** *ger* **-mitting**) *tr* remettre ‖ *intr* se calmer

remittance [rɪ′mɪtəns] *s* remise *f,* envoi *m*

remnant [′rɛmnənt] *s* (*remainder*) reste *m;* (*of cloth*) coupon *m;* (*at reduced price*) solde *m*

remod•el [rɪ′mɑdəl] *v* (*pret & pp* **-eled** or **-elled;** *ger* **-eling** or **-elling**) *tr* modeler de nouveau, remanier; (*a house*) transformer

remonstrance [rɪ′mɑnstrəns] *s* remontrance *f*

remonstrate [rɪ′mɑnstret] *intr* protester; **to remonstrate with** faire des remontrances à

remorse [rɪ′mɔrs] *s* remords *m*

remorseful [rɪ′mɔrsfəl] *adj* contrit, repentant, plein de remords

remote [rɪ′mot] *adj* loigné, retiré

remote′ control′ *s* commande *f* à distance, télécommande *f*

remote′-controlled′ *adj* téléguidé

remote′ serv′er *s* (comp) serveur *m* à distance

removable [rɪ′muvəbəl] *adj* amovible

removal [rɪ′muvəl] *s* enlèvement *m;* (*from house*) déménagement *m;* (*dismissal*) révocation *f*

remove [rɪ′muv] *tr* enlever, ôter; éloigner; (*furniture*) déménager; (*to dismiss*) révoquer ‖ *intr* se déplacer; déménager

remuneration [rɪˌmjunə′reʃən] *s* rémunération *f*

renaissance [ˌrɛnə′sɑns] *s* renaissance *f*

rend [rɛnd] *v* (*pret & pp* **-rent** [rɛnt]) *tr* déchirer; (*to split*) fendre; (*the air; the heart*) fendre

render [′rɛndər] *tr* rendre; (*a piece of music*) interpréter; (*lard*) fondre

rendez•vous [′rɑndəˌvu] *s* (*pl* **-vous** [ˌvuz]) rendez-vous *m* ‖ *v* (*pret & pp* **-voused** [ˌvud]; *ger* **-vousing** [ˌvuɪŋ]) *intr* se rencontrer

rendition [rɛn′dɪʃən] *s* (*translation*) traduction *f;* (mus) interprétation *f*

renegade [′rɛnɪˌged] *s* renégat *m*

renege [rɪ′nɪg] *s* renonce *f* ‖ *intr* renoncer; (coll) se dédire, ne pas tenir sa parole

renew [rɪ′n(j)u] *tr* renouveler ‖ *intr* se renouveler

renewable [rɪ′n(j)u•əbəl] *adj* renouvelable

renewal [rɪ′n(j)u•əl] *s* renouvellement *m;* (*of strength*) regain *m;* (*of a lease*) reconduction *f*

renounce [rɪ′naʊns] *s* renonce *f* ‖ *tr* renoncer à ‖ *intr* renoncer

renovate [′rɛnəˌvet] *tr* renouveler; (*a room, a house, etc.*) mettre à neuf, rénover, transformer

renown [rɪ′naʊn] *s* renom *m*

renowned [rɪ′naʊnd] *adj* renommé

rent [rɛnt] *adj* déchiré ‖ *s* loyer *m,* location *f;* (*tear, slit*) déchirure *f;* **for rent** à louer ‖ *tr* louer ‖ *intr* se louer

rental [′rɛntəl] *s* loyer *m,* location *f*

rent′al a′gen•cy *s* (*pl* **-cies**) agence *f* de location

rent′ed car′ *s* voiture *f* de louage, voiture de location; (*chauffeur-driven limousine*) voiture de grande remise

renter [′rɛntər] *s* locataire *mf*

renunciation [rɪ,nʌnsɪ′eʃən] *s* renonciation *f*

reopen [ri′opən] *tr* & *intr* rouvrir

reopening [ri′opənɪŋ] *s* réouverture *f*; (*of school*) rentrée *f*

reorganize [ri′ɔrgə,naɪz] *tr* réorganiser ‖ *intr* se réorganiser

repair [rɪ′pɛr] *s* réparation *f*; **in good repair** en bon état ‖ *tr* réparer ‖ *intr* se rendre

repair′man′ *s* (rad, telv) agent *m* de dépannage

repaper [ri′pepər] *tr* retapisser

reparation [,rɛpə′reʃən] *s* réparation *f*

repartee [,rɛpɑr′ti] *s* repartie *f*

repast [rɪ′pæst] *s* repas *m*

repatriate [ri′petrɪ,et] *tr* rapatrier

re•pay [rɪ′pe] *v* (*pret* & *pp* **-paid**) *tr* rembourser; récompenser

repayment [rɪ′pemənt] *s* remboursement *m*; récompense *f*

repeal [rɪ′pil] *s* révocation *f*, abrogation *f* ‖ *tr* révoquer, abroger

repeat [rɪ′pit] *s* répétition *f* ‖ *tr* & *intr* répéter

re•pel [rɪ′pɛl] *v* (*pret* & *pp* **-pelled;** *ger* **-pelling**) *tr* repousser; dégoûter

repent [rɪ′pɛnt] *tr* se repentir de ‖ *intr* se repentir

repentance [rɪ′pɛntəns] *s* repentir *m*

repentant [rɪ′pɛntənt] *adj* repentant

repercussion [,rɪpər′kʌʃən] *s* répercussion *f*, contrecoup *m*

reperto•ry [′rɛpər,tori] *s* (*pl* **-ries**) répertoire *m*

repetition [,rɛpɪ′tɪʃən] *s* répétition *f*

replace [rɪ′ples] *tr* (*to put back*) remettre en place; (*to take the place of*) remplacer

replaceable [rɪ′plesəbəl] *adj* remplaçable, amovible

replacement [rɪ′plesmənt] *s* (*putting back*) remise *f* en place, replacement *m*; (*substitution*) remplacement *m*; (*substitute part*) pièce *f* de rechange; (*person*) remplaçant *m*

replay [′riple] *s* match *m* rejoué; (telv) action *f* replay ‖ [ri′ple] *tr* rejouer

replenish [rɪ′plɛnɪʃ] *tr* réapprovisionner; remplir

replete [rɪ′plit] *adj* rempli, plein

replica [′rɛplɪkə] *s* reproduction *f*, réplique *f*

re•ply [rɪ′plaɪ] *s* (*pl* **-plies**) réponse *f*, réplique *f* ‖ *v* (*pret* & *pp* **-plied**) *tr* & *intr* répondre, répliquer

reply′ cou′pon *s* coupon-résponse *m*

report [rɪ′port] *s* (*account, statement*) rapport *m*; (*rumor*) bruit *m*; (*e.g., of firearm*) détonation *f* ‖ *tr* rapporter; dénoncer; **it is reported that** le bruit court que; **reported missing** porté manquant ‖ *intr* faire un rapport; (*to show up*) se présenter

report′ card′ *s* bulletin *m* scolaire

reportedly [rɪ′portɪdli] *adv* au dire de tout le monde

reporter [rɪ′portər] *s* reporter *m*

reporting [rɪ′portɪŋ] *s* reportage *m*

repose [rɪ′poz] *s* repos *m* ‖ *tr* reposer; (*confidence*) placer ‖ *intr* reposer

reprehend [,rɛprɪ′hɛnd] *tr* reprendre

represent [,rɛprɪ′zɛnt] *tr* représenter

representation [,rɛprɪzɛn′teʃən] *s* représentation *f*

representative [,rɛprɪ′zɛntətɪv] *adj* représentatif ‖ *s* représentant *m*

repress [rɪ′prɛs] *tr* réprimer; (psychoanal) refouler

repression [rɪ′prɛʃən] *s* répression *f*; (psychoanal) refoulement *m*

reprieve [rɪ′priv] *s* sursis *m* ‖ *tr* surseoir à l'exécution de

reprimand [′rɛprɪ,mænd] *s* réprimande *f* ‖ *tr* réprimander

reprint [′ri,prɪnt] *s* (*book*) réimpression *f*; (*offprint*) tiré *m* à part ‖ [ri′prɪnt] *tr* réimprimer

reprisal [rɪ′praɪzəl] *s* représailles *fpl*

reproach [rɪ′protʃ] *s* (*rebuke*) reproche *m*; (*discredit*) honte *f*, opprobre *m* ‖ *tr* reprocher; couvrir d'opprobre; **to reproach s.o. for s.th.** reprocher q.ch. à qn

reproduce [,riprə′d(j)us] *tr* reproduire ‖ *intr* se reproduire

reproduction [,riprə′dʌkʃən] *s* reproduction *f*

reproof [rɪ′pruf] *s* reproche *m*

reprove [rɪ′pruv] *tr* réprimander

reptile [′rɛtɪl] *s* reptile *m*

republic [rɪ′pʌblɪk] *s* république *f*

republican [rɪ′pʌblɪkən] *adj* & *s* républicain *m*

repudiate [rɪ′pjudɪ,et] *tr* répudier

repugnant [rɪ′pʌgnənt] *adj* répugnant

repulse [rɪ′pʌls] *s* refus *m*; (*setback*) échec *m* ‖ *tr* repousser

repulsive [rɪ′pʌlsɪv] *adj* répulsif

reputation [,rɛpjə′teʃən] *s* réputation *f*

repute [rɪ′pjut] *s* réputation *f*; **of ill repute** mal famé ‖ *tr*—**to be reputed to be** être réputé

reputedly [rɪ′pjutɪdli] *adv* suivant l'opinion commune

request [rɪ′kwɛst] *s* demande *f*; **on request** sur demande ‖ *tr* demander

Requiem [′rɛkwɪ,ɛm] *s* Requiem *m*

require [rɪ′kwaɪr] *tr* exiger

requirement [rɪ′kwaɪrmənt] *s* exigence *f*; besoin *m*

requisite [′rɛkwɪzɪt] *adj* requis ‖ *s* chose *f* nécessaire; condition *f* nécessaire

requisition [,rɛkwɪ′zɪʃən] *s* réquisition *f* ‖ *tr* réquisitionner

requital [rɪ′kwaɪtəl] *s* récompense *f*; (*retaliation*) revanche *f*

requite [rɪ′kwaɪt] *tr* récompenser; (*to avenge*) venger

re•read [ri′rid] *v* (*pret* & *pp* **-read** [′rɛd]) *tr* relire

rerun [′ri,rʌn] *s* reprise *f* ‖ [ri′rʌn] *tr* (*film, tape*) passer de nouveau; (*race*) courir de nouveau

resale [′ri,sel], [ri′sel] *s* revente *f*

rescind [rɪ′sɪnd] *tr* abroger

rescue ['rɛskju] *s* sauvetage *m;* **to the rescue** au secours, à la rescousse ‖ *tr* sauver, secourir

res'cue par'ty *s* équipe *f* de secours

research [rɪˈsʌrtʃ], [ˈrisʌrtʃ] *s* recherche *f* ‖ *intr* faire des recherches

re•sell [riˈsɛl] *v* (*pret & pp* **-sold**) *tr* revendre; (*to sell back*) recéder

resemblance [rɪˈzɛmbləns] *s* ressemblance *f*

resemble [rɪˈzɛmbəl] *tr* ressembler à; **to resemble one another** se ressembler

resent [rɪˈzɛnt] *tr* s'offenser de

resentful [rɪˈzɛntfəl] *adj* offensé

resentment [rɪˈzɛntmənt] *s* ressentiment *m*

reservation [ˌrɛzərˈveʃən] *s* (*booking*) location *f*, réservation *f;* (*Indian land*) réserve *f;* **without reservation** sans réserve

reserve [rɪˈzʌrv] *s* réserve *f* ‖ *tr* réserver

reserve' room' *s* (*in a library*) réserve *f*, salle *f* de services du prêt

reservist [rɪˈzʌrvɪst] *s* réserviste *m*

reservoir [ˈrɛzərˌvwar] *s* réservoir *m*

re•set [riˈsɛt] *v* (*pret & pp* **-set;** *ger* **-setting**) *tr* remettre; (*a gem*) remonter

re•ship [riˈʃɪp] *v* (*pret & pp* **-shipped;** *ger* **-shipping**) *tr* réexpédier; (*on a ship*) rembarquer ‖ *intr* se rembarquer

reshipment [riˈʃɪpmənt] *s* réexpédition *f;* (*on a ship*) rembarquement *m*

reside [rɪˈzaɪd] *intr* résider, demeurer

residence [ˈrɛzɪdəns] *s* résidence *f*, domicile *m*

residency [ˈrɛzɪdənsi] *s* (med) résidanat *m*

resident [ˈrɛzɪdənt] *adj & s* habitant *m*

residential [ˌrɛzɪˈdɛnʃəl] *adj* résidentiel

residue [ˈrɛzɪˌd(j)u] *s* résidu *m*

resign [rɪˈzaɪn] *tr* démissionner de, résigner; **to resign oneself to** se résigner à ‖ *intr* démissionner; se résigner; **to resign from** démissionner de

resignation [ˌrɛzɪgˈneʃən] *s* (*from a job, etc.*) démission *f;* (*submissive state*) résignation *f*

resin [ˈrɛzɪn] *s* résine *f*

resist [rɪˈzɪst] *tr* résister à; **to resist** + *ger* s'empêcher de + *inf* ‖ *intr* résister

resistance [rɪˈzɪstəns] *s* résistance *f*

resole [riˈsol] *tr* ressemeler

resolute [ˈrɛzəˌlut] *adj* résolu

resolution [ˌrɛzəˈluʃən] *s* résolution *f*

resolve [rɪˈzɔlv] *s* résolution *f* ‖ *tr* résoudre ‖ *intr* résoudre, se résoudre

resonance [ˈrɛzənəns] *s* résonance *f*

resort [rɪˈzɔrt] *s* station *f*, e.g., **health resort** station climatique; (*summer resort*) camp *m* de vacances; (*for help or support*) recours *m;* **as a last resort** en dernier ressort ‖ *intr*—**to resort to** recourir à, avoir recours à

resound [rɪˈzaund] *intr* résonner

resource [rɪˈsors], [ˈrisors] *s* ressource *f*

resourceful [rɪˈsorsfəl] *adj* débrouillard, de ressource

respect [rɪˈspɛkt] *s* respect *m;* **in many respects** à bien des égards; **in this respect** sous ce rapport; **to pay one's respects (to)** présenter ses respects (à); **with respect to** par rapport à ‖ *tr* respecter

respectable [rɪˈspɛktəbəl] *adj* respectable; considérable

respectful [rɪˈspɛktfəl] *adj* respectueux

respectfully [rɪˈspɛktfəli] *adv* respectueusement; **respectfully yours** (*complimentary close*) veuillez agréer l'assurance de mes sentiments très respectueux

respective [rɪˈspɛktɪv] *adj* respectif

res'piratory tract' [ˈrɛspɪrəˌtori] *s* appareil *m* respiratoire

respite [ˈrɛspɪt] *s* répit *m;* **without respite** sans relâche

resplendent [rɪˈsplɛndənt] *adj* resplendissant

respond [rɪˈspɑnd] *intr* répondre

response [rɪˈspɑns] *s* réponse *f*

responsibili•ty [rɪˌspɑnsɪˈbɪlɪti] *s* (*pl* **-ties**) responsabilité *f*

responsible [rɪˈspɑnsɪbəl] *adj* responsable; (*person*) digne de confiance; (*job, position*) de confiance; **responsible for** responsable de; **responsible to** responsable envers

responsive [rɪˈspɑnsɪv] *adj* sensible, réceptif; prompt à sympathiser

rest [rɛst] *s* (*repose*) repos *m;* (*lack of motion*) pause *f;* (*what remains*) reste *m;* (mus) silence *m;* **at rest** en repos; (*dead*) mort; **the rest** les autres; (*the remainder*) le restant; **the rest of us** nous autres; **to come to rest** s'immobiliser; **to lay to rest** enterrer ‖ *tr* reposer ‖ *intr* reposer, se reposer; **to rest on** reposer sur, s'appuyer sur

restaurant [ˈrɛstərənt] *s* restaurant *m*

rest' cure' *s* cure *f* de repos

restful [ˈrɛstfəl] *adj* reposant; (*calm*) tranquille, paisible

rest' home' *s* maison *f* de repos

rest'ing place' *s* lieu *m* de repos, gîte *m;* (*of the dead*) dernière demeure *f*

restitution [ˌrɛstɪˈt(j)uʃən] *s* restitution *f*

restive [ˈrɛstɪv] *adj* rétif

restless [ˈrɛstlɪs] *adj* agité, inquiet; sans repos

restock [riˈstɑk] *tr* réapprovisionner; (*with fish or game*) repeupler

restoration [ˌrɛstəˈreʃən] *s* restauration *f*

restore [rɪˈstor] *tr* restaurer; (*health*) rétablir; (*to give back*) restituer

restrain [rɪˈstren] *tr* retenir, contenir

restraint [rɪˈstrent] *s* restriction *f*, contrainte *f*

restrict [rɪˈstrɪkt] *tr* restreindre

restriction [rɪˈstrɪkʃən] *s* restriction *f*

rest' room' *s* cabinet *m* d'aisance

rest' stop' *s* (*on a superhighway*) restoroute *m* avec parking et un garage et des pompes à essence; (*on a highway*) petit parc *m* pourvu des toilettes

result [rɪˈzʌlt] *s* résultat *m;* **as a result of** par suite de ‖ *intr* résulter; **to result in** aboutir à

resume [rɪˈz(j)um] *tr & intr* reprendre

résumé [ˌrezʊˈme] *s* résumé *m*

resumption [rɪˈzʌmpʃən] *s* reprise *f*

resurface [ri`sʌrfɪs] *tr* refaire le revêtement de || *intr* (*said of submarine*) faire surface

resurrect [,rɛzə`rɛkt] *tr* & *intr* ressusciter

resurrection [,rɛzə`rɛkʃən] *s* résurrection *f*

resuscitate [ri`sʌsɪ,tet] *tr* & *intr* ressusciter

retail [`ritel] *adj* & *adv* au détail || *s* vente *f* au détail || *tr* vendre au détail, détailler || *intr* se vendre au détail

retailer [`ritelər] *s* détaillant *m*

retain [ri`ten] *tr* retenir; engager

retaliate [ri`tælɪ,et] *intr* prendre sa revanche, user de représailles

retaliation [ri,tælɪ`eʃən] *s* représailles *fpl*

retard [ri`tard] *s* retard *m* || *tr* retarder || [`ri tard] *s* (pej) retardé *m*, retardée *f*

retarded *adj* (pathol) retardé, arriéré; (pej) demeuré

retch [rɛtʃ] *tr* vomir || *intr* avoir un haut-le-cœur

retching [`rɛtʃiŋ] *s* haut-le-cœur *m*

reticence [`rɛtɪsəns] *s* réserve *f*

reticent [`rɛtɪsənt] *adj* réservé

retina [`rɛtɪnə] *s* rétine *f*

retinue [`rɛtɪ,n(j)u] *s* suite *f*, cortège *m*

retire [ri`taɪr] *tr* mettre à la retraite || *intr* se retirer

retired *adj* en retraite, retiré

retirement [ri`taɪrmənt] *s* retraite *f*

retire′ment pen′sion *s* retraite *f*, pension *f* de retraite

retire′ment pro′gram *s* programme *m* de prévoyance

retire′ment vil′lage *s* cité *f* retraite

retiring [ri`taɪriŋ] *adj* (shy) effacé; (*e.g., congressman*) sortant

retort [ri`tɔrt] *s* riposte *f*, réplique *f*; (chem) cornue *f* || *tr* & *intr* riposter

retouch [ri`tʌtʃ] *tr* retoucher

retrace [ri`tres] *tr* retracer; (one's steps) revenir sur

retract [ri`trækt] *tr* rétracter || *intr* se rétracter

retractable [ri`træktəbəl] *adj* (aer) escamotable

retraining [ri`treniŋ] *s* recyclage *m*

re•tread [`ri,trɛd] *s* pneu *m* rechapé || [ri`trɛd] *v* (pret & pp **-treaded**) *tr* rechaper || *v* (pret **-trod**; pp **-trod** or **-trodden**) *tr* repasser

retreat [ri`trit] *s* retraite *f;* **to beat a retreat** battre en retraite || *intr* se retirer

retrench [ri`trɛntʃ] *tr* restreindre || *intr* faire des économies

retribution [,rɛtri`bjuʃən] *s* rétribution *f*

retrieval [ri`trivəl] *s* récupération *f;* (comp) retrouve *f*

retrieve [ri`triv] *tr* retrouver, recouvrer; (a fortune, a reputation, etc.) rétablir; (game) rapporter || *intr* (said of hunting dog) rapporter

retriever [ri`trivər] *s* retriever *m*

retro [`rɛtro] *adj* (coll) (inspired by the fashions or styles of the past, particularly 1920 to 1960) rétro

retroactive [,rɛtro`æktɪv] *adj* rétroactif

retrogress [`rɛtrə,grɛs] *intr* rétrograder

retrorocket [`rɛtro,rakɪt] *s* rétrofusée *f*

retrospect [`rɛtrə,spɛkt] *s*—**to consider in retrospect** jeter un coup d'œil rétrospectif à

retrospective [,rɛtrə`spɛktɪv] *adj* rétrospectif

re•try [ri`traɪ] *v* (pret & pp **-tried**) *tr* essayer de nouveau; (law) juger à nouveau

return [ri`tʌrn] *adj* de retour; **by return mail** par retour du courrier || *s* retour *m;* (profit) bénéfice *m;* (yield) rendement *m;* (unwanted merchandise) rendu *m;* (of ball) renvoi *m;* (of income tax) déclaration *f;* (typewriter key) touche *f* de rappel de chariot, touche retour arrière; **in return** de retour; **in return for** en récompense de; **returns** (profits) recettes *fpl;* (of an election) résultats *mpl;* **many happy returns of the day!** bon anniversaire! || *tr* rendre; (to put back) remettre; (to bring back) rapporter; (e.g., a letter) retourner || *intr* (to go back) retourner; (to come back) revenir; (to get back home) rentrer; **return to sender** (on letter) retour à l'expéditeur; **to return empty-handed** revenir bredouille

return′able bot′tle *s* [ri`tʌrnəbəl] emballage *m* consigné

return′ address′ *s* adresse *f* de l'expéditeur

return′ bout′ *s* revanche *f*

return′ game′ *ou* **match′** *s* match *m* retour

return′ tick′et *s* aller et retour *m*

return′ trip′ *s* voyage *m* de retour

reunification [ri,junifɪ`keʃən] *s* réunification *f*

reunion [ri`junjən] *s* réunion *f*

reunite [,riju`naɪt] *tr* réunir || *intr* se réunir

reusable [ri`juzəbəl] *adj* réutilisable

rev [rɛv] *s* (coll) tour *m* || *v* (pret & pp **revved**; ger **revving**) *tr* (coll) accélérer; (to race) (coll) emballer || *intr* (coll) s'accélérer

revalue [ri`vælju] *tr* révaloriser

revamp [ri`væmp] *tr* refaire

reveal [ri`vil] *tr* révéler

reveille [`rɛvəli] *s* réveil *m*

rev•el [`rɛvəl] *s* fête *f;* **revels** ébats *mpl,* orgie *f* || *v* (pret & pp **-eled** or **-elled;** ger **-eling** or **-elling**) *intr* faire la fête, faire la bombe; **to revel in** se délecter à

revelation [,rɛvə`leʃən] *s* révélation *f;* **Revelation** (Bib) Apocalypse *f*

revel•ry [`rɛvəlri] *s* (pl **-ries**) réjouissances *fpl,* orgie *f*

revenge [ri`vɛndʒ] *s* vengeance *f;* **to take revenge on s.o. for s.th.** se venger de q.ch. sur qn || *tr* venger

revengeful [ri`vɛndʒfəl] *adj* vindicatif

revenue [`rɛvə,n(j)u] *s* revenu *m*

rev′enue cut′ter *s* garde-côte *m,* vedette *f*

rev′enue stamp′ *s* timbre *m* fiscal

reverberate [ri`vʌbə,ret] *intr* résonner, réverbérer

revere [ri`vir] *tr* révérer

reverence [`rɛvərəns] *s* révérence *f* || *tr* révérer

reverend [`rɛvərənd] *adj* & *s* révérend *m*

reverent [`rɛvərənt] *adj* révérenciel

reverie [`rɛvəri] *s* rêverie *f*

reversal [ri`vʌrsəl] *s* renversement *m*

reverse [ri`vʌrs] *adj* contraire || *s* (opposite)

contraire *m;* (*of medal; of fortune*) revers *m;* (*of page*) verso *m;* (aut) marche *f* arrière ‖ *tr* renverser; (*a sentence*) (law) révoquer ‖ *intr* renverser; (*said of motor*) faire machine arrière; (aut) faire marche arrière

reverse' lev'er *s* levier *m* de renvoi

reverse' side' *s* revers *m*, dos *m*

reversible [rɪ'vʌrsɪbəl] *adj* réversible

revert [rɪ'vʌrt] *intr* revenir, faire retour

review [rɪ'vju] *s* (*inspection*) revue *f;* (*of a book*) compte *m* rendu; (*of a lesson*) révision *f* ‖ *tr* revoir; (*a book*) faire la critique de; (*a lesson*) réviser, revoir; (*past events; troops*) passer en revue ‖ *intr* faire des révisions

revile [rɪ'vaɪl] *tr* injurier, outrager

revise [rɪ'vaɪz] *s* (typ) épreuve *f* de révision ‖ *tr* réviser, revoir

revised' edi'tion *s* édition *f* revue et corrigée

revision [rɪ'vɪʒən] *s* révision *f*

revisionist [rɪ'vɪʒənɪst] *adj & s* révisionniste *mf*

revival [rɪ'vaɪvəl] *s* retour *m* à la vie; (*of learning*) renaissance *f;* (rel) réveil *m;* (theat) reprise *f*

reviv'al meet'ings *spl* (rel) réveils *mpl*

revive [rɪ'vaɪv] *tr* ranimer; (*a victim*) ressusciter; (*a memory*) réveiller; (*a play*) reprendre; (*hopes*) faire renaître; ‖ *intr* reprendre; se ranimer

revoke [rɪ'vok] *tr* révoquer

revolt [rɪ'volt] *s* révolte *f* ‖ *tr* révolter ‖ *intr* se révolter

revolting [rɪ'voltɪŋ] *adj* dégoûtant, repoussant; rebelle, révolté

revolution [ˌrɛvə'luʃən] *s* révolution *f*

revolutionar•y [ˌrɛvə'luʃəˌnɛri] *adj* révolutionnaire ‖ *s* (*pl* **-ies**) révolutionnaire *mf*

revolve [rɪ'vɑlv] *tr* faire tourner; (*in one's mind*) retourner ‖ *intr* tourner

revolver [rɪ'vɑlvər] *s* revolver *m*

revolv'ing book'case *s* bibliothèque *f* tournante

revolv'ing door' *s* porte *f* à tambour, tambour *m* cylindrique

revolv'ing fund' *s* fonds *m* de roulement

revolv'ing stage' *s* scène *f* tournante

revue [rɪ'vju] *s* (theat) revue *f*

revulsion [rɪ'vʌlʃən] *s* aversion *f*, répugnance *f;* (*change of feeling*) revirement *m*

reward [rɪ'wɔrd] *s* récompense *f* ‖ *tr* récompenser

rewarding [rɪ'wɔrdɪŋ] *adj* rémunérateur; (*experience*) enrichissant

re•wind [ri'waɪnd] *v* (*pret & pp* **-wound**) *tr* (*film, tape, etc.*) renverser la marche de; (*a typewriter ribbon*) embobiner de nouveau; (*a clock*) remonter

rewire [ri'waɪr] *tr* (*a building*) refaire l'installation électrique dans

re•write [ri'raɪt] *v* (*pret* **-wrote;** *pp* **-written**) *tr* récrire

Rh *abbr* (**Rhesus factor**) Rh (facteur Rhésus)

rhapso•dy [ˈræpsədi] *s* (*pl* **-dies**) rhapsodie *f*

rheostat [ˈri•əˌstæt] *s* rhéostat *m*

Rhesus [ˈrisəs] *adj & s* (gen) Rhésus *m* ‖ (*l.c.*) *s* (zool) (*rhesus monkey*) rhésus *m*

Rhe'sus fac'tor *s* facteur *m* Rhésus

rhetoric [ˈrɛtərɪk] *s* rhétorique *f*

rhetorical [rɪ'tɑrɪkəl] *adj* rhétorique

rheumatic [ru'mætɪk] *adj* rhumatismal; (*person*) rhumatisant ‖ *s* rhumatisant *m*

rheumatism [ˈruməˌtɪzəm] *s* rhumatisme *m*

Rhine [raɪn] *s* Rhin *m*

Rhineland [ˈraɪnˌlænd] *s* Rhénanie *f*

rhine'stone' *s* faux diamant *m*

rhinoceros [raɪ'nɑsərəs] *s* rhinocéros *m*

rhubarb [ˈrubarb] *s* rhubarbe *f*

rhyme [raɪm] *s* rime *f;* **in rhyme** en vers ‖ *tr & intr* rimer

rhythm [ˈrɪðəm] *s* rythme *m*

rhythmic(al) [ˈrɪðmɪk(əl)] *adj* rythmique

rib [rɪb] *s* côte *f;* (*of umbrella*) baleine *f;* (*archit, biol, mach*) nervure *f* ‖ *v* (*pret & pp* **ribbed;** *ger* **ribbing**) *tr* garnir de nervures; (*slang*) taquiner

ribald [ˈrɪbəld] *adj* grivois

ribbon [ˈrɪbən] *s* ruban *m*

rice [raɪs] *s* riz *m*

rice' field' *s* rizière *f*

rice' pud'ding *s* riz *m* au lait

rich [rɪtʃ] *adj* riche; (*voice*) sonore; (*wine*) généreux; (*funny*) (coll) impayable; (coll) ridicule; **to get rich** s'enrichir; **to strike it rich** trouver le bon filon ‖ **riches** *spl* richesses *fpl*

rickets [ˈrɪkɪts] *s* rachitisme *m*

rickety [ˈrɪkɪti] *adj* (*object*) boiteux, délabré; (*person*) chancelant: (*suffering from rickets*) rachitique

rickshaw [ˈrɪkˌʃɔ] *s* pousse-pousse *m*

ricochet [ˈrɪkəˈʃe] *s* (*pl* **-chets** [-ʃez]) ricochet *m* ‖ *v* (*pret & pp* **-cheted** [-ʃed]; *ger* **-cheting** [-ʃe•ɪŋ]) *intr* ricocher

rid [rɪd] *v* (*pret & pp* **rid;** *ger* **ridding**) *tr* débarrasser; **to get rid of** se débarrasser de, débarquer

riddance [ˈrɪdəns] *s* débarras *m;* **good riddance!** bon débarras!

riddle [ˈrɪdəl] *s* devinette *f*, énigme *f* ‖ *tr*—**to riddle with** cribler de

ride [raɪd] *s* promenade *f;* **to take a ride** faire une promenade (en auto, à cheval, à motocyclette, etc.); **to take s.o. for a ride** (*to dupe s.o.*) (slang) faire marcher qn; (*to murder s.o.*) (slang) descendre qn ‖ *v* (*pret* **rode** [rod]; *pp* **ridden** [ˈrɪdən]) *tr* monter à; (coll) se moquer de; **ridden** dominé; **to ride out** (*e.g., a storm*) étaler ‖ *intr* monter à cheval (à bicyclette, etc.); **to let ride** (coll) laisser courir

rider [ˈraɪdər] *s* (*on horseback*) cavalier *m;* (*on a bicycle*) cycliste *mf;* (*in a vehicle*) voyageur *m;* (*to a document*) annexe *f*

ridge [rɪdʒ] *s* arête *f*, crête *f;* (*of a fabric*) grain *m*

ridge'pole' *s* faîtage *m*

ridicule [ˈrɪdɪˌkjul] *s* ridicule *m* ‖ tr ridiculiser

ridiculous [rɪ'dɪkjələs] *adj* ridicule

rid'ing acad'emy *s* école *f* d'équitation

rid′ing boot′ *s* botte *f* de cheval, botte à l'écuyère

rid′ing hab′it *s* habit *m* d'amazone

rid′ing mow′er *s* tondeuse *f* auto-portée

rife [raɪf] *adj* répandu; **rife with** abondant en

riffraff [ˈrɪf,ræf] *s* racaille *f*

rifle [ˈraɪfəl] *s* fusil *m; (spiral groove)* rayure *f* ‖ *tr* piller, mettre à sac; *(a gun barrel)* rayer

rift [rɪft] *s* fente *f*, crevasse *f; (disagreement)* désaccord *m*

rig [rɪg] *s* équipement *m; (carriage)* équipage *m;* (naut) gréement *m; (getup)* (coll) accoutrement *m* ‖ *v (pret & pp* **rigged;** *ger* **rigging)** *tr* équiper; *(to falsify)* truquer; (naut) gréer; **to rig out with** (coll) accoutrer de

rigging [ˈrɪgɪŋ] *s* gréement *m; (fraud)* truquage *m*

right [raɪt] *adj* droit; *(change, time, etc.)* exact; *(statement, answer, etc.)* correct; *(conclusion, word, etc.)* juste; *(name)* vrai; *(moment, house, road, etc.)* bon, e.g., **it's not the right road** ce n'est pas la bonne route; qu'il faut, e.g., **it's not the right village** (spot, boy, etc.) ce n'est pas le village (endroit, garçon, etc.) qu'il faut; **to be all right** aller très bien; **to be right** avoir raison ‖ *s (justice)* droit *m; (reason)* raison *f; (right hand)* droite *f; (fist or blow in boxing)* droit; **all rights reserved** tous droits réservés; **by right of** à titre de; **by rights** de plein droit; **by the right!** (mil) guide à droite!; **on the right** à droite; **right and wrong** le bien et le mal; **rights** droits; **to be in the right** avoir raison ‖ *adv* directement; correctement; complètement; bien, en bon état; *(to the right)* à droite; (coll) très, même, e.g., **right here** ici même; **all right!** d'accord!; **right and left** à droite et à gauche; **right away** tout de suite; **to put right** mettre bon ordre à, mettre en état ‖ *tr* faire droit à; *(to correct)* corriger; *(to set upright)* redresser ‖ *intr* se redresser ‖ *interj* parfait!

right′ about′ face′ *s* volte-face *f* ‖ *interj* (mil) demi-tour à droite!

righteous [ˈraɪtʃəs] *adj* juste; vertueux

right′ field′ *s* (baseball) champ *m* droit

rightful [ˈraɪtfəl] *adj* légitime

right′-hand drive′ *s* (aut) conduite *f* à droite

right-hander [ˈraɪtˈhændər] *s* droitier *m*

right′-hand man′ *s* bras *m* droit

rightist [ˈraɪtɪst] *adj & s* droitier *m*

rightly [ˈraɪtli] *adv* à bon droit, à juste titre; correctement, avec sagesse; **rightly or wrongly** à tort ou à raison

right′ of assem′bly *s* liberté *f* de réunion

right′ of asy′lum *s* droit *m* d'asile

right′ of way′ *s* droit *m* de passage; **to yield the right of way** céder le pas

rights′ of man′ *spl* droits *mpl* de l'homme

right′-to-life′ *adj* droit-à-la-vie

right′-to-lif′er *s* (coll) nataliste *mf*

right to work [ˈraɪttəˈwɜrk] *s* liberté *f* du travail des ouvriers non syndiqués

right′-wing′ *adj* de droite

right-winger [ˈraɪtˈwɪŋər] *s* (coll) droitier *m*

rigid [ˈrɪdʒɪd] *adj* rigide

rigmarole [ˈrɪgmə,rol] *s* galimatias *m*

rigor [ˈrɪgər] *s* rigueur *f;* (pathol) rigidité *f*

rigor mortis [ˈrɪgərˈmɔrtəs] *s* rigidité *f* cadavérique

rigorous [ˈrɪgərəs] *adj* rigoureux

rile [raɪl] *tr* (coll) exaspérer, agacer

rill [rɪl] *s* ruisselet *m*

rim [rɪm] *s* bord *m*, rebord *m; (of spectacles)* monture *f; (of wheel)* jante *f*

rind [raɪnd] *s* écorce *f; (of cheese)* croûte *f; (of bacon)* couenne *f*

ring [rɪŋ] *s* anneau *m; (for the finger)* bague *f*, anneau; *(for some sport or exhibition)* piste *f; (for boxing)* ring *m; (for bullfight)* arène *f; (of a group of people)* cercle *m; (of evildoers)* gang *m; (under the eyes)* cerne *m; (sound)* son *m; (of bell, clock, telephone, etc.)* sonnerie *f; (of a small bell; in the ears; of the glass of glassware)* tintement *m; (to summon a person)* coup *m* de sonnette; *(quality)* timbre *m;* (telp) coup de téléphone ‖ *v (pret & pp* **ringed)** *tr* cerner ‖ *intr* décrire des cercles ‖ *v (pret* **rang** [ræŋ]; *pp* **rung** [rʌŋ]) *tr* sonner; **to ring up** (telp) donner un coup de téléphone à ‖ *intr* sonner; *(said, e.g., of ears)* tinter; **to ring out** résonner

ring′bolt′ *s* piton *m*

ring′dove′ *s* (orn) ramier *m*

ring′ fin′ger *s* annulaire *m*

ringing [ˈrɪŋɪŋ] *adj* résonnant, retentissant ‖ *s* sonnerie *f; (in the ears)* tintement *m*

ring′lead′er *s* meneur *m*

ringlet [ˈrɪŋlɪt] *s* bouclette *f*

ring′mas′ter *s* maître *m* de manège, chef *m* de piste

ring′side′ *s* premier rang *m*

ring′snake′ *s (Tropidonotus natrix)* couleuvre *f* à collier

ring′worm′ *s* teigne *f*

rink [rɪŋk] *s* patinoire *f*

rinse [rɪns] *s* rinçage *m* ‖ *tr* rincer

riot [ˈraɪət] *s* émeute *f; (of colors)* orgie *f;* **to run riot** se déchaîner; *(said of plants or vines)* pulluler ‖ *intr* émeuter

rioter [ˈraɪətər] *s* émeutier *m*

ri′ot squad′ unité *f* antimanifestation

rip [rɪp] *s* déchirure *f* ‖ *v (pret & pp* **ripped;** *ger* **ripping)** *tr* déchirer; **to rip away** or **off** arracher; **to rip off** (slang) arnaquer; **to rip open** or **up** découdre; *(a letter, package, etc.)* ouvrir en le déchirant ‖ *intr* se déchirer

rip′ cord′ *s (of parachute)* cordelette *f* de déclenchement

ripe [raɪp] *adj* mûr; *(cheese)* fait; *(olive)* noir

ripen [ˈraɪpən] *tr & intr* mûrir

rip′off *s* (slang) arnaque *f*, vol *m* à main armée; (slang) *(conning)* mystification *f*

ripple [ˈrɪpəl] *s* ride *f; (sound)* murmure *m* ‖ *tr* rider ‖ *intr* se rider; murmurer

rise [raɪz] *s* hausse *f*, augmentation *f; (of ground; of the voice)* élévation *f; (of a* heavenly body; *of the curtain*) lever *m;* (*in one's employment, in one's fortunes*) ascension *f;* (*of water*) montée *f;* (*of a source of water*) naissance *f;* **to get a rise out of** (slang) se payer la tête de; **give rise to** donner naissance à ‖ *v* (*pret* **rose** [roz]; *pp* **risen** [ˈrɪzən]) *intr* s'élever, monter; (*to get out of bed; to stand up; to ascend in the heavens*) se lever; (*to revolt*) se soulever; (*said, e.g., of a danger*) se montrer; (*said of a fluid*) jaillir; (*in someone's esteem*) grandir; (*said of river*) prendre sa source; **to rise above** dépasser; (*unfortunate events, insults, etc.*) se montrer supérieur à; **to rise to** (*e.g., the occasion*) se montrer à la hauteur de

riser [ˈraɪzər] *s* (*of staircase*) contremarche *f;* (*of gas or water*) colonne montante; **to be a late riser** faire la grasse matinée; **to be an early riser** être matinal

risk [rɪsk] *s* risque *m* ‖ *tr* risquer

risk•y [ˈrɪski] *adj* (*comp* **-ier;** *super* **-iest**) dangereux, hasardeux, risqué

risqué [rɪsˈke] *adj* risqué, osé

rite [raɪt] *s* rite *m;* **last rites** derniers sacrements *mpl*

ritual [ˈrɪtʃʊ•ə] *adj & s* rituel *m*

ri•val [ˈraɪvəl] *adj & s* rival *m* ‖ *v* (*pret & pp* **-valed** or **-valled;** *ger* **-valing** or **-valling**) *tr* rivaliser avec

rival•ry [ˈraɪvəlri] *s* (*pl* **-ries**) rivalité *f*

river [ˈrɪvər] *adj* fluvial ‖ *s* fleuve *m;* (*tributary*) rivière *f;* (*stream*) cours *m* d'eau; **down the river** en aval; **up the river** en amont

riv′er bas′in *s* bassin *m* fluvial

riv′er•bed′ *s* lit *m* de rivière

riv′er•front′ *s* rive *f* d'un fleuve

riv′er•side′ *adj* riverain ‖ *s* rive *f*

rivet [ˈrɪvɪt] *s* rivet *m* ‖ *tr* river

riv′et gun′ *s* riveuse *f* pneumatique

rivulet [ˈrɪvjəlɪt] *s* ruisselet *m*

R.N. [ˈɑrˈɛn] *s* (letterword) (**registered nurse**) infirmière *f* diplômée

roach [rotʃ] *s* (ent) blatte *f,* cafard *m;* (ichth) gardon *m*

road [rod] *s* route *f,* chemin *m;* (naut) rade *f;* **road under construction** (*public sign*) travaux

road′bed′ *s* assiette *f;* (rr) infrastructure *f*

road′block′ *s* barrage *m*

road′ divid′er *s* séparateur *m*

road′ hog′ *s* écraseur *m,* chauffard *m*

road′house′ *s* guinguette *f* au bord de la route

road′ map′ *s* carte *f* routière

road′-salt′ing truck′ *s* saleuse *f*

road′ ser′vice *s* secours *m* routier

road′side′ *s* bord *m* de la route

road′ sign′ *s* poteau *m* indicateur

road′stead′ *s* rade *f*

road′way′ *s* chaussée *f*

roam [rom] *tr* parcourir; (*the seas*) sillonner ‖ *intr* errer, rôder

roar [ror] *s* (*of a lion*) rugissement *m;* (*of cannon, engine, etc.*) grondement *m;* (*of crowd*) hurlement *m;* (*of laughter*) éclat *m* ‖ *intr* rugir; gronder; hurler

roast [rost] *s* rôti *m;* (*of coffee*) torréfaction *f;* banquet *m* ‖ *tr* rôtir; (*coffee*) torréfier; (*chestnuts*) griller; (*to criticize severely*) éreinter ‖ *intr* se rôtir; se torréfier

roast′ beef′ *s* rosbif *m,* rôti *m* de bœuf

roaster [ˈrostər] *s* (*appliance*) rôtissoire *f;* (*for coffee*) brûloir *m;* (*fowl*) volaille *f* à rôtir

roast′ pork′ *s* porc *m* rôti

rob [rɑb] *v* (*pret & pp* **robbed;** *ger* **robbing**) *tr & intr* voler; **to rob s.o. of s.th.** voler q.ch. à qn

robber [ˈrɑbər] *s* voleur *m*

robber•y [ˈrɑbəri] *s* (*pl* **-ies**) vol *m*

robe [rob] *s* (*of a judge*) robe *f;* (*of a professor, judge, etc.*) toge *f;* (*dressing gown*) robe *f* de chambre; (*for lap in a carriage*) couverture *f* ‖ *tr* revêtir d'une robe ‖ *intr* revêtir sa robe

robin [ˈrɑbɪn] *s* (*Erithacus rubecula*) rougegorge *m;* (*Turdus migratorius*) grive *f* migratoire

robot [ˈrobɑt] *s* robot *m*

robotic [roˈbɑtɪk] *adj* robotique ‖ **robotics** *s* robotique *f*

robotize [ˈrobɑtaɪz] *tr* robotiser

robust [roˈbʌst] *adj* robuste

rock [rɑk] *s* roche *f;* (*eminence*) roc *m,* rocher *m;* (*sticking out of water*) rocher *m;* (*one that is thrown*) pierre *f;* (slang) diamant *m;* **on the rocks** (coll) fauché, à sec; (*said of liquor*) (coll) sur glace ‖ *tr* balancer; (*to rock to sleep*) bercer ‖ *intr* se balancer; se bercer

rock′-bot′tom *adj* (le) plus bas ‖ *s* (le) fin fond *m*

rock′ can′dy *s* candi *m*

rock′ crys′tal *s* cristal *m* de roche

rocker [ˈrɑkər] *s* bascule *f;* (*chair*) chaise *f* à bascule; **to go off one's rocker** (slang) perdre la boussole

rock′er arm′ *s* culbuteur *m*

rocket [ˈrɑkɪt] *s* fusée *f;* (arti, bot) roquette *f* ‖ *intr* monter en chandelle; (*said of prices*) monter en flèche

rock′et bomb′ *s* bombe *f* volante, fusée *f*

rock′et fu′el *s* kérosène *m* aviation

rock′et launch′er *s* lance-fuses *m;* (arti) lance-roquettes *m*

rock′et ship′ *s* fusée *f* interplanétaire, fusée interstellaire

rock′ gar′den *s* jardin *m* de rocaille

rock′ing chair′ *s* fauteuil *m* à bascule

rock′ing horse′ *s* cheval *m* à bascule

Rock′ of Gibral′tar [dʒɪˈbrɔltər] *s* rocher *m* de Gibraltar

rock′ salt′ *s* sel *m* gemme

rock′ sing′er *s* chanteur *m* de rock

rock′ wool′ *s* laine *f* minérale, laine *de* verre

rock•y [ˈrɑki] *adj* (*comp* **-ier;** *super* **-iest**) rocheux, rocailleux

Rock′y Moun′tains *spl* Montagnes *fpl* Rocheuses

rod [rɑd] *s* (*wooden stick*) baguette *f;* (*for pun-*

ishment) verge *f; (of the retina; elongated microorganism*) bâtonnet *m; (of authority*) main *f; (of curtain*) tringle *f; (for fishing*) canne *f;* (Bib) lignée *f,* race *f;* (mach) bielle *f;* (surv) jalon *m; (revolver*) (slang) pétard *m,* flingot *m,* flingue *m;* **rod and gun** la chasse et la pêche

rodent [ˈrodənt] *adj & s* rongeur *m*

roe [ro] *s (deer*) chevreuil *m; (of fish*) œufs *mpl*

roger [ˈradʒər] *interj* **O.K.!;** (rad) message reçu!

rogue [rog] *s adj (dishonest*) malhonnête; (*cruel*) méchant, sadique ‖ *s (scamp*) polisson *m; (crook*) gredin *m; (zool*) solitaire *m*

rogues'' gal'lery *s* fichier *m* de la police de portraits de criminels

roguish [ˈrogɪʃ] *adj* espiègle, polisson

roil [rɔɪl] *tr (to stir up*) remuer; (*to rile*) agacer, exaspérer ‖ *intr* (culin) bouillir à gros bouillons

roister [ˈrɔɪstər] *intr* faire du tapage

role or **rôle** [rol] *s* rôle *m*

roll [rol] *s (of paper, cloth, netting, wire, hair, etc.*) rouleau *m; (of thunder, drums, etc.*) roulement *m; (roll call*) appel *m; (list*) rôle *m; (of film*) rouleau *m; (of paper money*) liasse *f; (of dice*) coup *m; (of a boat*) roulis *m; (of fat*) bourrelet *m;* (culin) petit pain *m;* **to call the roll** faire l'appel ‖ *tr* rouler; (*to rob*) (slang) entôler; **to roll over** retourner; **to roll up** enrouler ‖ *intr* rouler; (*said of thunder*) gronder; (*to sway*) se balancer; (*to overturn*) faire panache; (*said of ship*) rouler; **to roll over** se retourner; **to roll up** se rouler

roll'back' *s* repoussement *m;* (com) baisse *f* de prix

roll' call' *s* appel *m; (vote*) appel nominal

roller [ˈrolər] *s* rouleau *m; (of a skate*) roulette *f; (wave*) lame *f* de houle

roll'er bear'ing *s* coussinet *m* à rouleaux

roll'er coast'er *s* montagnes *fpl* russes

roll'er skate' *s* patin *m* à roulettes

roll'er-skate' *intr* patiner sur des roulettes

roll'er-skating rink' *s* skating *m*

roll'er tow'el *s* essuie-mains *m* à rouleau, serviette *f* sans fin

roll'ing mill' *s* usine *f* de laminage; (*set of rollers*) laminoir *m*

roll'ing pin' *s* rouleau *m*

roll'ing stock' *s* (rr) matériel *m* roulant

roll'-top desk' *s* bureau *m* à cylindre

roly-poly [ˈroliˈpoli] *adj* rondelet

ROM [ˈɑrˈoˈɛm] *s* (letterword) **(read-only memory)** ROM *f invar* (mémoire *f* morte)

romaine [roˈmen] *s* romaine *f*

roman [ˈromən] *adj & s* (typ) romain *m;* **Roman** Romain *m*

Ro'man can'dle *s* chandelle *f* romaine

Ro'man Cath'olic *adj & s* catholique *mf*

Romance [ˈromæns], [roˈmæns] *adj* roman ‖ (*l.c.*) [roˈmæns], [ˈromæns] *s (chivalric narrative*) roman *m* de chevalerie; (*love story*) roman à l'eau de rose; (*made-up story*) conte *m* bleu; (*love affair*) idylle *f;* (mus) romance *f* ‖ (*l.c.*) [roˈmæns] *intr* exagérer, broder

Ro'mance lan'guages *spl* langues *fpl* romanes

Ro'man Em'pire *s* Empire *m* romain

Romanesque [ˌromənˈɛsk] *adj & s* roman *m*

Ro'man nose' *s* nez *m* aguilin

Ro'man nu'meral *s* chiffre *m* romain

romantic [roˈmæntɪk] *adj (genre; literature; scenery*) romantique; (*imagination*) romanesque

romanticism [roˈmæntɪˌsɪzəm] *s* romantisme *m*

romanticist [roˈmæntɪsɪst] *s* romantique *mf*

Rome [rom] *s* Rome *f*

romp [ramp] *intr* s'ébattre

rompers [ˈrampərz] *spl* barboteuse *f*

roof [ruf] *s* toit *m; (of the mouth*) palais *m;* **to raise the roof** (slang) faire un boucan de tous les diables

roofer [ˈrufər] *s* couvreur *m*

roof' gar'den *s* terrasse *f* avec jardin, pergola *f*

rook [rʊk] *s* (chess) tour *f;* (orn) freux *m,* corneille *f* ‖ *tr* (coll) rouler; **to rook s.o. out of s.th.** (coll) filouter q.ch. à qn

rookie [ˈrʊki] *s* (slang) bleu *m*

room [rum], [rʊm] *s* pièce *f; (especially bedroom*) chambre *f; (where people congregate*) salle *f; (space*) place *f;* **rooms** appartement *m;* **to make room for** faire place à ‖ *intr* vivre en garni; **to room with** partager une chambre avec

room' and board' *s* le vivre et le couvert, pension *f;* **for room and board** au pair

room' clerk' *s* employé *m* à la réception

roomer [ˈrumər] *s* locataire *mf*

roomette [ruˈmɛt] *s* chambrette *f* de sleeping

room'ing house' *s* maison *f* de rapport, immeuble *m* de rapport

room'mate' *s* camarade *mf* de chambre

room·y [ˈrumi] *adj (comp* **-ier;** *super* **-iest**) spacieux, ample; (*clothes*) large, ample

roost [rust] *s* perchoir *m;* (coll) logis *m,* demeure *f;* **to rule the roost** (coll) faire la loi ‖ *intr* se percher, percher

rooster [ˈrustər] *s* coq *m*

root [rut] *s* racine *f;* **to get to the root of** approfondir; **to take root** prendre racine ‖ *tr* fouiller; **to root out** déraciner ‖ *intr* s'enraciner; **to root around in** fouiller dans; **to root for** (coll) applaudir, encourager

rooter [ˈrutər] *s* (coll) fanatique *mf,* fana *mf*

rope [rop] *s* corde *f; (lasso*) corde à nœud coulant; **to jump rope** sauter à la corde; **to know the ropes** (slang) connaître les ficelles ‖ *tr* corder; (*cattle*) prendre au lasso; **to rope in** (slang) entraîner

rope' lad'der *s* échelle *f* de corde

rope' walk'er *s* funambule *mf,* danseur *m* de corde

rosa·ry [ˈrozəri] *s (pl* **-ries**) rosaire *m*

rose [roz] *adj* rose ‖ *s (color*) rose *m;* (bot) rose *f*

rose' bee'tle *s* cétoine *f* dorée

rose'bud' *s* bouton *m* de rose

rose'bush' *s* rosier *m*

rose'-col'ored *adj* rosé, couleur de rose; **to see**

everything through **rose-colored glasses** voir tout en rose

rose′ gar′den s roseraie f

rosemar•y [ˈroz,mɛri] s (pl **-ies**) romarin m

rose′ of Shar′on [ˈʃɛrən] s rose f de Saron

rosette [roˈzɛt] s rosette f; (archit, elec) rosace f

rose′ win′dow s rosace f, rose f

rose′wood′ s bois m de rose, palissandre m

rosin [ˈrazın] s colophane f

roster [ˈrɑstər] s liste f, appel m; (educ) heures fpl de classe; (mil) tableau m de service; (naut) ôle m

rostrum [ˈrɑstrəm] s tribune f

ros•y [ˈrozi] adj (comp **-ier**; super **-iest**) rosé; (complexion) vermeil; (fig) riant

rot [rɑt] s pourriture f; (slang) sottise f ‖ v (pret & pp **rotted**; ger **rotting**) tr & intr pourrir

ro′tary press′ [ˈrotəri] s rotative f

rotate [ˈrotet] tr & intr tourner; (agr) alterner

rotation [roˈteʃən] s rotation f; **in rotation** à tour de rôle

rote [rot] s routine f; **by rote** par cœur, machinalement

rot′ gut′ s (slang) tord-boyaux m

rotisserie [roˈtısəri] s rôtissoire f

rotogravure [ˌrotəgrəˈvjur] s rotogravure f

rototiller [ˈroto,tılər] s motoculteur m

rotten [ˈrɑtən] adj pourri

rotund [roˈtʌnd] adj rond, arrondi; (e.g., language) ampoulé

rotunda [roˈtʌndə] s rotonde f

rouge [ruʒ] s fard m, rouge m ‖ tr farder ‖ intr se farder, se mettre du rouge

rough [rʌf] adj (sound, voice, speech) rude; (uneven) inégal; (coarse) grossier; (unfinished) brut; (road) raboteux; (game) brutal; (sea) agité; (guess) approximatif ‖ tr—**to rough it** faire du camping, coucher sur la dure; **to rough up** malmener

roughage [ˈrʌfıdʒ] s fibres fpl alimentaires

rough′ cast′ s crépi m ‖ v (pret & pp **-cast**) tr crépir

rough′ cop′y s brouillon m

rough′ draft′ s ébauche f, avant-projet m, brouillon m

rough′ guess′ s approximation f

rough′house′ s boucan m, chahut m ‖ intr faire du boucan, chahuter

rough′ ide′a s aperçu m

roughly [ˈrʌfli] adv grossièrement; brutalement; approximativement

rough′neck′ s (coll) canaille f

roughshod [ˈrʌfˌʃɑd] adv—**to ride roughshod over** (an objection, observation, comment, etc.) passer outre à

rough′ sketch′ s croquis m, ébauche f

roulette [ruˈlɛt] s roulette f

round [raund] adj rond; (rounded) arrondi, rond; (e.g., shoulders) voûté; **three (four,** etc.) **feet round** trois (quatre, etc.) pieds de tour ‖ s rond m; (inspection) ronde f; (of golf; of drinks; of postman, doctor, etc.) tournée f;

(of applause) salve f; (of ammunition) cartouche f; (of veal) noix f; (in a game) manche f; (boxing) round m; **to go the rounds** faire le tour ‖ adv à la ronde; **round about** aux alentours; **the year round** pendant toute l'année; **to pass round** faire circuler, passer à la ronde ‖ prep autour de ‖ tr (to make round) arrondir; (e.g., a corner) tourner, prendre; (a cape) doubler; **to round off** or **out** arrondir; (to finish) achever; **to round up** rassembler; (suspects) cueillir ‖ intr s'arrondir

roundabout [ˈraundə,baut] adj indirect ‖ s détour m; (carrousel) (Brit) manège m; (traffic circle) (Brit) rond-point m

rounder [ˈraundər] s (coll) fêtard m

round′-headed screw′ s vis f à tête ronde

round′house′ s (rr) rotonde f

round′-shoul′dered adj voûté

round′ steak′ s gîte m à la noix

round′ ta′ble s table f ronde; **Round Table** Table ronde

round′-trip′ tick′et s billet m d'aller et retour

round′up′ s (of cattle) rassemblement m; (of suspects) rafle f

rouse [rauz] tr réveiller ‖ intr se réveiller

rout [raut] s déroute f ‖ tr mettre en déroute

route [rut] s route f; (of, e.g., bus) ligne f, parcours m ‖ tr acheminer

routine [ruˈtin] adj routinier, systématique ‖ s routine f

routine′ examina′tion s examen m de routine

rove [rov] intr errer, vagabonder

rover [ˈrovər] s vagabond m

row [rau] s (coll) altercation f, prise f de bec; **to raise a row** (coll) faire du boucan ‖ [ro] s rang m; (of, e.g., houses) rangée f; (boat ride) promenade f en barque; **in a row** à la file; (without interruption) de suite; **in rows** par rangs ‖ intr ramer

rowboat [ˈro,bot] s bateau m à rames, canot m

row•dy [ˈraudi] adj (comp **-dier**; super **-diest**) tapageur ‖ s (pl **-dies**) tapageur m

rower [ˈro•ər] s rameur m

rowing [ˈro•ıŋ] s nage f, canotage m, sport m de l'aviron

royal [ˈrɔı•əl] adj royal

royalist [ˈrɔı•əlıst] adj & s royaliste mf

royal•ty [ˈrɔı•əlti] s (pl **-ties**) royauté f; (remuneration) droit m d'auteur; redevance f, droit d'inventeur

r.p.m. [ˈɑrˈpiˈɛm] spl (letterword) (**revolutions per minute**) tr/mn, tours mpl à la minute

rub [rʌb] s frottement m; **there's the rub** (coll) voilà le hic ‖ v (pret & pp **rubbed**; ger **rubbing**) tr frotter; **to rub elbows with** coudoyer; **to rub out** effacer; (slang) descendre, liquider ‖ intr se frotter; (said, of moving parts) frotter; **to rub off** s'enlever, disparaître

rubber [ˈrʌbər] s caoutchouc m; (eraser) gomme f à effacer; (in bridge) robre m; (condom) préservatif m; **rubbers** (overshoes) caoutchoucs

rub′ber ball′ s balle f élastique

rub′ber band′ s élastique m

rub′ber bul′let s balle f de caoutchouc

rubberize [ˈrʌbəˌraɪz] tr caoutchouter

rub′ber·neck′ s (coll) badaud m ‖ intr (coll) badauder

rub′ber plant′ s figuier m élastique, caoutchoutier m; (tree) arbre m à caoutchouc, hévéa m

rub′ber stamp′ s tampon m; (coll) bénioui-oui m

rub′ber-stamp′ tr apposer le tampon sur; (with a person's signature) estampiller; (coll) approuver à tort et à travers

rub′bing al′cohol s alcool m pour les frictions

rubbish [ˈrʌbɪʃ] s détritus m, rebut m; (coll) imbécillités fpl

rubble [ˈrʌbəl] s (broken stone) décombres mpl; (used in masonry) moellons mpl

rub′down′ s friction f

rubric [ˈrubrɪk] s rubrique f

ru·by [ˈrubi] adj (lips) vermeil ‖ s (pl -bies) rubis m

rucksack [ˈrʌkˌsæk] s sac-à-dos m

rudder [ˈrʌdər] s gouvernail m

rud·dy [ˈrʌdi] adj (comp -dier; super -diest) rougeaud, coloré

rude [rud] adj (rough, rugged) rude; (discourteous) impoli, grossier

rudeness [ˈrudnɪs] s rudesse f; impolitesse f

rudiment [ˈrudɪmənt] s rudiment m

rue [ru] tr regretter amèrement

rueful [ˈrufəl] adj lamentable; triste

ruffian [ˈrʌfiən] s brute f

ruffle [ˈrʌfəl] s (in water) rides fpl; (of drum) roulement m; (sewing) jabot m plissé ‖ tr (to crease; to vex) froisser; (the water) rider; (its feathers) hérisser; (one's hair) ébouriffer

rug [rʌg] s tapis m, carpette f

rugged [ˈrʌgɪd] adj (manners, person, features) rude, sévère; (ground, landscape) accidenté; (coast) déchiqueté; (road, country, etc.) raboteux; (husky) robuste; (e.g., machine) résistant à toute épreuve

rug′ shampoo′er s shampouineur m, shampouineuse f

ruin [ˈruˑɪn] s ruine f; **to fall into ruins** se ruiner ‖ tr ruiner

rule [rul] s règle f; (regulation) règlement m; (custom) coutume f, habitude f; (authority) autorité f; (reign) règne m; (law) décision f; **as a rule** en général; **by rule of thumb** empiriquement, à vue de nez ‖ tr gouverner; (to lead) diriger, guider; (one's passions) contenir; (with lines) régler; (law) décider; **to rule out** écarter, éliminer ‖ intr gouverner; (to be the rule) prévaloir; **to rule over** régner sur

ruler [ˈrulər] s dirigeant m; souverain m; (for ruling lines and measuring) règle f

ruling [ˈrulɪŋ] adj actuel; (e.g., classes) dirigeant; (quality, trait, etc.) dominant ‖ s (of paper) réglage m; (law) décision f

rum [rʌm] s rhum m

Rumanian [ruˈmɛniˑən] adj roumain ‖ s (language) roumain m; (person) Roumain m

rumble [ˈrʌmbəl] s (of thunder) grondement m; (of a cart) roulement m; (of intestines) gargouillement m; (gang war) (slang) baroud m, rixe f entre gangs ‖ intr gronder, rouler

ruminate [ˈrumɪˌnet] tr & intr ruminer

rummage [ˈrʌmɪdʒ] intr fouiller

rum′mage sale′ s vente f d'objets usagés

rumor [ˈrumər] s rumeur f ‖ tr—**it is rumored that** le bruit court que

rump [rʌmp] s (of animal) croupe f; (of bird) croupion m; (cut of meat) culotte f; (buttocks) postérieur m

rumple [ˈrʌmpəl] s faux pli m ‖ tr (paper, cloth, etc.) froisser, chiffonner; (one's hair) ébouriffer

rump′ steak′ s romsteck m

rumpus [ˈrʌmpəs] s (coll) chahut m; (argument) (coll) prise f de bec; **to raise a rumpus** (coll) déclencher un chahut; faire une scène violente

rum′pus room′ s salle f de jeux

run [rʌn] s (act of running) course f; (e.g., of good or bad luck) suite f; (on a bank by depositors) descente f; (of salmon) remonte f; (of, e.g., a bus) parcours m; (in a stocking) échelle f, démaillage m, (baseball) point m; (cards) séquence f; (mus) roulade f; **in the long run** à la longue; **on the run** à la débandade, en fuite; **run of bad luck** série f noire; **the general run** la généralité; **to give free run** to donner libre carrière à; **to give s.o. a run for his money** en donner à qn pour son argent; **to have a long run** (theat) tenir longtemps l'affiche; **to have the run of** avoir libre accès à or dans; **to keep s.o. on the run** ne laisser aucun répit à qn; **to make a run in** (a stocking) démailler ‖ v (pret **ran** [ræn]; pp **run**; ger **running**) tr (the streets; a race; a risk) courir; (a motor, machine, etc.) faire marcher; (an organization, project, etc.) diriger; (a business, factory, etc.) exploiter; (a blockade) forcer; (a line) tracer; (turf) faire courir; **to run aground** échouer; **to run down** (to knock down) renverser; (to find) dépister; (game) mettre aux abois; (to disparage) (coll) dénigrer; **to run in** (a motor) roder; **to run off** (a liquid) faire écouler; (copies, pages, etc.) tirer; **to run through** (e.g., with a sword) transpercer; **to run up** (a flag) hisser; (a debt) (coll) laisser accumuler ‖ intr courir; (said, e.g., of water; said of fountain pen, nose, etc.) couler; (said of stockings) se démailler; (said of salmon) faire la montaison; (said of colors) s'étaler, se déteindre; (said of sore) suppurer; (said of rumor, news, etc.) circuler, courir; (for office) se présenter; (mach) fonctionner, marcher; (theat) rester à l'affiche, se jouer; **run along!** filez!; **to run across** (to meet by chance) rencontrer par hasard; **to run along** border, longer; (to go) s'en aller; **to run at** se jeter sur; **to run away** se sauver, s'enfuir; (said of horse) s'emballer, s'emporter; **to run away with** enlever; **to run down** (e.g., a hill) descendre en courant; (said of spring) se détendre; (said of watch) s'arrêter (faute d'être remonté); (said of storage battery) se décharger, s'épuiser; **to run for** (*an office*) poser sa candidature pour; **to run in the family** tenir de famille; **to run into** heurter; (*to meet*) (coll) rencontrer; **to run off** se sauver, s'enfuir; (*said of liquid*) s'écouler; **to run out** (*said of passport, lease, etc.*) expirer; **to run out of** être à court de; **to run over** (*said of a liquid*) déborder; (*an article, a text, etc.*) parcourir; (*s.th. in the road*) passer sur; (*e.g., a pedestrian*) écraser; **to run through** (*an article, text, etc.*) parcourir; (*a fortune*) gaspiller

run′ away′ *adj* fugitif; (*horse*) emballé ‖ *s* fugitif *m;* cheval *m* emballé

run′ down′ *s* compte rundu *m,* récit *m*

run′-down′ *adj* délabré; (*person; battery*) épuisé, à plat; (*clock spring*) détendu

rung [rʌŋ] *s* (*of ladder or chair*) barreau *m;* (*of wheel*) rayon *m*

runner [′rʌnər] *s* (*person*) coureur *m;* (*messenger*) courrier *m;* (*of ice skate or sleigh*) patin *m;* (*narrow rug*) rampe *f* d'escalier; (*strip of cloth for table top*) chemin *m* de table; (*in stockings*) démaillage *m;* (bot) coulant *m*

run′ner-up′ *s* (*pl* **runners-up**) bon second *m,* premier accessit *m*

running [′rʌnɪŋ] *adj* (*person; water; expenses*) courant; (*stream; knot; style*) coulant; (*sore*) suppurant; (*e.g., motor*) en marche ‖ *s* (*of man or animal*) course *f;* (*of water*) écoulement *m;* (*of machine*) fonctionnement *m,* marche *f;* (*of business*) direction *f*

run′ning board′ *s* marchepied *m*

run′ning com′mentar′y *s* (*pl* **-ies**) (rad, telv) reportage *m* en direct

run′ning head′ *s* titre *m* courant

run′ning mate′ *s* (pol) coéquipier *m,* colistier *m*

run′ning start′ *s* départ *m* lancé

run′off′ elec′tion *s* scrutin *m* de ballottage

run′-of-the-mill′ *adj* médiocre, banal, ordinaire

run′ proof′ *adj* indémaillable

runt [rʌnt] *s* avorton *m*

run′way′ *s* piste *f,* rampe *f*

rupture [′rʌptʃər] *s* rupture *f;* (pathol) hernie *f* ‖ *tr* rompre; (*a ligament, blood vessel, etc.*) se rompre ‖ *intr* se rompre

rural [′rʊrəl] *adj* rural

ru′ral free′ deliv′ery *s* distribution *f* gratuite par le facteur rural

ru′ral police′ man *s* garde *m* champêtre

ruse [ruz] *s* ruse *f*

rush [rʌʃ] *adj* urgent ‖ *s* (*rapid movement*) course *f* précipitée, ruée *f;* (*haste*) hâte *f,* précipitation *f;* (bot) jonc *m;* (*formula on envelope or letterhead*) urgent; **rushes** (mov) épreuves *fpl;* **to be in a rush to** être pressé de ‖ *tr* pousser vivement; (*e.g., to the hospital*) transporter d'urgence; (*a piece of work*) exécuter d'urgence; (*e.g., a girl*) (slang) insister auprès de; **to rush through** (*e.g., a law*) faire passer à la hâte ‖ *intr* se précipiter, se ruer; **to rush about** courir ça et là; **to rush headlong** foncer tête baissée; **to rush into** (*e.g., a room*) faire irruption dans; (*an affair*) se jeter dans; **to rush out** sortir précipitamment; **to rush through** (*one's lessons, prayers, etc.*) expédier; (*e.g., a town*) traverser à toute vitesse; (*a tourist attraction*) visiter au pas de course; (*a book*) lire à la hâte; **to rush to** s'empresser de; **to rush to one's face** (*said of blood*) monter au visage à qn; **to rush up to** accourir à *or* vers

rush′-bot′tomed chair′ *s* chaise *f* à fond de paille

rush′ hours′ *spl* heures *fpl* d'affluence *or* de pointe

rush′ or′der *s* commande *f* urgente

russet [′rʌsɪt] *adj* roussâtre, roux

Russia [′rʌʃə] *s* Russie *f;* la Russie

Russian [′rʌʃən] *adj* russe ‖ *s* (*language*) russe *m;* (*person*) Russe *mf*

rust [rʌst] *s* rouille *f* ‖ *tr* rouiller ‖ *intr* se rouiller

rustic [′rʌstɪk] *adj* rustique; simple, net; (pej) rustaud ‖ *s* paysan *m,* villageois *m*

rustle [′rʌsəl] *s* (*of leaves*) bruissement *m;* (*of a dress*) froufrou *m,* bruissement; (*of papers*) froissement *m* ‖ *tr* faire bruire; (*cattle*) (coll) voler ‖ *intr* bruire; (*said, e.g., of a dress*) froufrouter; **to rustle around** (coll) se démener

rustler [′rʌslər] *s* voleur *m* de bétail

rust′ proof′ *adj* inoxydable

rust·y [′rʌsti] *adj* (*comp* **-ier;** *super* **-iest**) rouillé

rut [rʌt] *s* ornière *f;* (zool) rut *m*

ruthless [′ruθlɪs] *adj* impitoyable

RV *abbr* **recreational vehicle**

rye [raɪ] *s* seigle *m;* whisky *m* de seigle

S

S, s [ɛs] *s* XIXᵉ lettre de l'alphabet

Sabbath [′sæbəθ] *s* (*Friday night to Saturday night*) sabbat *m;* (*Sunday*) dimanche *m;* (*Saturday*) samedi *m;* (*Friday*) vendredi *m*

sabbat′ical year′ [sə′bætɪkəl] *s* année *f* de congé

saber [′sebər] *s* sabre *m* ‖ *tr* sabrer

sable [′sebəl] *adj* noir ‖ *s* (*animal, fur*) zibeline *f;* noir *m;* **sables** vêtements *mpl* de deuil

sabotage [′sæbə,taʒ] *s* sabotage *m* ‖ *tr & intr* saboter

saccharin [′sækərɪn] *s* saccharine *f*

sachet [sæ′ʃe] *s* sachet *m* (à parfums)

sack [sæk] *s* sac *m;* (*wine*) xérès *m;* (*a base in* *baseball*) coussin *m* ‖ *tr* mettre en sac; (mil) saccager; (coll) saquer, congédier

sack'cloth' *s* grosse toile *f* d'emballage, serpillière *f;* (*worn for penitence*) cilice *m;* **in sackcloth and ashes** sous le sac et la cendre

sacrament ['sækrəmənt] *s* sacrement *m*

sacramental [,sækrə'mɛntəl] *adj* sacramentel

sacred ['sekrəd] *adj* sacré

sa'cred cow' *s* (fig) monstre *m* sacré

sacrifice ['sækrɪ,faɪs] *s* sacrifice *m;* **at a sacrifice** à perte ‖ *tr & intr* sacrifier

sacrilege ['sækrəlɪdʒ] *s* sacrilège *m*

sacrilegious [,sækrɪ'lɪdʒəs] *adj* sacrilège

sacristan ['sækrɪstən] *s* sacristain *m*

sad [sæd] *adj* (*comp* **sadder;** *super* **saddest**) triste

sadden ['sædən] *tr* attrister ‖ *intr* s'attrister

saddle ['sædəl] *s* selle *f* ‖ *tr* seller; **to saddle with** charger de, encombrer de

sad'dle•bag' *s* sacoche *f* (de selle)

saddlebow ['sædəl,bo] *s* arçon *m* de devant

saddler ['sædlər] *s* sellier *m*

sad'dle•tree' *s* arçon *m*

sadist ['sedɪst] *s* sadique *mf*

sadistic [sæ'dɪstɪk] *adj* sadique

sadness ['sædnɪs] *s* tristesse *f*

sad' sack' *s* (slang) bidasse *mf*

safe [sef] *adj* (*from danger*) sûr; (*unhurt*) sauf; (*margin*) certain; **safe and sound** sain et sauf; **safe from** à l'abri de ‖ *s* coffre-fort *m,* caisse *f*

safe'-con'duct *s* sauf-conduit *m*

safe'-depos'it box' *s* coffre *m* à la banque; coffret de sûreté (Canad)

safe'guard' *s* sauvegarde *f* ‖ *tr* sauvegarder

safe'keep'ing *s* bonne garde *f*

safe•ty ['sefti] *adj* de sûreté ‖ *s* (*pl* **-ties**) (*state of being safe*) sécurité *f,* sûreté *f;* (*avoidance of danger*) salut *m*

safe'ty belt' *s* ceinture *f* de sécurité

safe'ty depos'it box' *s* coffre *m* (d'un coffre-fort)

safe'ty fac'tor *s* (aer) coefficient *m* de sécurité

safe'ty match' *s* allumette *f* de sûreté

safe'ty pin' *s* épingle *f* de sûreté

saf'ty ra'zor *s* rasoir *m* de sûreté

safe'ty valve' *s* soupape *f* de sûreté

safe'ty zone' *s* zone *f* protégée pour piétons

saffron ['sæfrən] *adj* safrane ‖ *s* safran *m*

sag [sæg] *s* affaissement *m* ‖ *v* (*pret & pp* **sagged;** *ger* **sagging**) *intr* s'affaisser

sagacious [sə'geʃəs] *adj* sagace

sage [sedʒ] *adj* sage ‖ *s* sage *mf;* (*plant*) sauge *f*

sage'brush' *s* armoise *f*

Sagittarius [,sædʒɪ'tɛrɪ•əs] *s* (astr, astrol) le Sagittaire

sail [sel] *s* voile *f;* (*sails*) voilure *f;* (*of windmill*) aile *f;* **full sail** toutes voiles dehors; **to set sail** mettre les voiles; **to take a sail** faire une promenade à la voile; **to take in sail** baisser pavillon ‖ *tr* (*a ship*) gouverner, commander; (*to travel over*) naviguer sur ‖ *intr* naviguer;

to sail along the coast côtoyer; **to sail into** (coll) assaillir

sail'boat' *s* bateau *m* à voiles

sail'cloth' *s* toile *f* à voile

sailing ['selɪŋ] *s* navigation *f;* (*working of ship*) manœuvre *f;* (*of pleasure craft*) voile *f*

sail'ing ves'sel *s* voilier *m*

sail'mak'er *s* voilier *m*

sailor ['selər] *s* marin *m;* (*simple crewman*) matelot *m*

saint [sent] *adj & s* saint *m*

saint'hood *s* sainteté *f*

saintliness ['sentlɪnɪs] *s* sainteté *f*

Saint' Vi'tus's dance' ['vaɪtəsəz] *s* (pathol) danse *f* de Saint-Guy

sake [sek] *s*—**for the sake of** pour l'amour de, dans l'intérêt de; **for your sake** pour vous

salable ['seləbəl] *adj* vendable

salacious [sə'leʃəs] *adj* lubrique

salad ['sæləd] *s* salade *f*

sal'ad bar' *s* buffet *m* de salades, table *f* à salade

sal'ad bowl' *s* saladier *m*

sala•ry ['sæləri] *s* (*pl* **-ries**) salaire *m*

sal'ary freeze' *s* blocage *m* des salaires

sale [sel] *s* vente *f;* **for sale** en vente; **on sale** en solde, en réclame

sales' clerk' *s* vendeur *m*

sales' force' *s* ensemble *m* des représentants

sales'la'dy *s* (*pl* **-dies**) vendeuse *f,* demoiselle *f* de magasin

sales'man *s* (*pl* **-men**) vendeur *m,* commis *m*

sales' man'ager *s* directeur *m* commercial

sales'man•ship' *s* l'art *m* de vendre

sales' promo'tion *s* stimulation *f* de la vente

sales' rep'resen'tative *s* vendeur *m,* vendeuse *f*

sales'room' *s* salle *f* de vente

sales' talk' *s* raisonnements *mpl* destinés à convaincre le client

sales' tax' *s* taxe *f* à l'achat

saliva [sə'laɪvə] *s* salive *f*

salivate ['sælə,vet] *intr* saliver

sallow ['sælo] *adj* olivâtre

sal•ly ['sæli] *s* (*pl* **-lies**) saillie *f;* (mil) sortie *f* ‖ *v* (*pret & pp* **-lied**) *intr* faire une sortie

salmon ['sæmən] *adj & s* saumon *m*

salm'on trout' *s* truite *f* saumonée

saloon [sə'lun] *s* cabaret *m,* estaminet *m,* bistrot *m;* (naut) salon *m*

salt [sɔlt] *s* sel *m* ‖ *tr* saler; **to salt away** (coll) économiser, mettre de côté

salt'cel'lar *s* salière *f*

salt' lick' *s* terrain *m* salifère

salt'pe'ter *s* (*potassium nitrate*) salpêtre *m;* (*sodium nitrate*) nitrate *m* du Chili

salt' pork' *s* salé *m*

salt'sha'ker *s* salière *f*

salt•y ['sɔlti] *adj* (*comp* **-ier;** *super* **-iest**) salé

salute [sə'lut] *s* salut *m* ‖ *tr* saluer

salvage ['sælvɪdʒ] *s* sauvetage *m;* biens *mpl* sauvés ‖ *tr* sauver; récupérer

salvation [sæl've∫ən] *s* salut *m*

Salva'tion Ar'my *s* Armée *f* du Salut

salve [sæv] *s* onguent *m,* pommade *f;* (fig) baume *m* ‖ *tr* appliquer un onguent sur; (fig) apaiser

sal·vo [ˈsælvo] *s* (*pl* **-vos** or **-voes**) salve *f*

Samaritan [səˈmærɪtən] *adj* samaritain ‖ *s* Samaritain *m*

same [sem] *adj & pron indef* même (before noun); **at the same time** en même temps, au même moment, à la fois; **it's all the same to me** ça m'est égal; **just the same, all the same** malgré tout, quand même; **the same . . . as** le même . . . que

sameness [ˈsemnɪs] *s* monotonie *f*

sample [ˈsæmpəl] *s* échantillon *m* ‖ *tr* échantillonner; essayer

sam'ple cop'y *s* (*pl* **-ies**) numéro *m* spécimen, spécimen *m*

sam'ple home' *s* villa *f* modèle, maison *f* exposition, pavillon *m* témoin

samurai [ˈsæmə,raɪ] *s* samouraî *m*

sancti·fy [ˈsæŋktɪ,faɪ] *v* (*pret & pp* **-fied**) *tr* sanctifier

sanctimonious [,sæŋktɪˈmonɪ·əs] *adj* papelard, bigot

sanction [ˈsæŋkʃən] *s* sanction *f* ‖ *tr* sanctionner

sanctuar·y [ˈsæŋktʃU,ɛri] *s* (*pl* **-ies**) sanctuaire *m;* refuge *m,* asile *m*

sand [sænd] *s* sable *m* ‖ *tr* sablonner

sandal [ˈsændəl] *s* sandale *f*

san'dal·wood' *s* santal *m*

sand'bag' *s* sac *m* de sable ‖ *tr* protéger par moyen de sacs de sable; (*to bully*) (coll) intimider, assommer; (*to mislead*) (coll) tromper, égarer

sand'bank' *s* banc *m* de sable

sand'bar' *s* banc *m* de sable

sand'blast' *s* jet *m* de sable; (*apparatus*) sableuse *f* ‖ *tr* sabler

sand'box' *s* (rr) sablière *f*

sander [ˈsændər] *s* (mach) ponceuse *f*

sand'glass' *s* sablier *m*

sand'pa'per *s* papier *m* de verre ‖ *tr* polir au papier de verre

sand'pi'per *s* bécasseau *m*

sand'stone' *s* grès *m*

sand'storm' *s* tempête *f* de sable

sandwich [ˈsændwɪtʃ] *s* sandwich *m* ‖ *tr* intercaler

sand'wich man' *s* homme-affiche *m*

sand·y [ˈsændi] *adj* (*comp* **-ier;** *super* **-iest**) sablonneux; (*hair*) blond roux

sane [sen] *adj* sain, équilibré; (*principles*) raisonnable

sanitary [ˈsænɪ,tɛri] *adj* sanitaire

san'itary nap'kin *s* serviette *f* hygiénique

sanitation [,sænɪˈteʃən] *s* hygiène *f,* salubrité *f;* (*drainage*) assainissement *m*

sanity [ˈsænɪti] *s* santé *f* mentale; bon sens *m*

Santa Claus [ˈsæntə,klɔz] *s* le père Noël

sap [sæp] *s* sève *f;* (mil) sape *f;* (coll) poire *f,* nigaud *m* ‖ *v* (*pret & pp* **sapped; *ger* sapping**)

tr tirer la sève de; (*to weaken*) affaiblir; (mil) saper

sapling [ˈsæplɪŋ] *s* jeune arbre *m;* jeune homme *m*

sapphire [ˈsæfaɪr] *s* saphir *m*

Saracen [ˈsærəsən] *adj* sarrasin ‖ *s* Sarrasin *m*

sarcasm [ˈsɑrkæzəm] *s* sarcasme *m*

sarcastic [sɑrˈkæstɪk] *adj* sarcastique

sardine [sɑrˈdin] *s* sardine *f;* **packed in like sardines** serrés comme des harengs

Sardinia [sɑrˈdɪnɪ·ə] *s* Sardaigne; la Sardaigne

Sardinian [sɑrˈdɪnɪ·ən] *adj* sarde ‖ *s* (*language*) sarde *m;* (*person*) Sarde *mf*

SARS [sɑrz] *s* (acronym) (**severe acute respiratory syndrome**) SRAS *abbr* (syndrome *m* respiratoire aigu sévère) *or* pneumopathie *f* atypique

sarsaparilla [,sɑrsəpəˈrɪlə] *s* salsepareille *f*

sash [sæʃ] *s* ceninture *f;* (*of window*) châssis *m*

sash' win'dow *s* fenêtre *f* à guillotine

sas·sy [ˈsæsi] *adj* (*comp* **-sier;** *super* **-siest**) (coll) impudent, effronté

satchel [ˈsætʃəl] *s* sacoche *f;* (*of schoolboy*) carton *m*

sate [set] *tr* soûler

sateen [sæˈtin] *s* satinette *f*

satellite [ˈsætə,laɪt] *adj & s* satellite *m*

sat'ellite coun'try *s* pays *m* satellite

sat'ellite dish' *s* (telv) disque *m* de satellite

satiate [ˈseʃi,et] *adj* rassasié ‖ *tr* rassasier

satin [ˈsætɪn] *s* satin *m*

satire [ˈsætaɪr] *s* satire *f*

satiric(al) [səˈtɪrɪk(əl)] *adj* satirique

satirize [ˈsætɪ,raɪz] *tr* satiriser

satisfaction [,sætɪsˈfækʃən] *s* satisfaction *f*

satisfactory [,sætɪsˈfæktəri] *adj* satisfaisant

satis·fy [ˈsætɪs,faɪ] *v* (*pret & pp* **-fied**) *tr* satisfaire; (*a requirement, need, etc.*) satisfaire à ‖ *intr* satisfaire

saturate [ˈsætʃə,ret] *tr* saturer

satura'tion bom'ing [,sætʃəˈreʃən] *s* bombardement *m* en tapis, tactique *f* de saturation

Saturday [ˈsætərdi] *s* samedi *m*

Saturn [ˈsætərn] *s* Saturne *m*

sauce [sɔs] *s* sauce *f;* (coll) insolence *f,* toupet *m* ‖ *tr* assaisonner ‖ *tr* (coll) parler avec impudence à

sauce'pan' *s* casserole *f*

saucer [ˈsɔsər] *s* soucoupe *f*

sau·cy [ˈsɔsi] *adj* (*comp* **-cier;** *super* **-ciest**) impudent, effronté

Sau'di Ara'bia [ˈsaudi] *s* Arabie *f* Saoudite

Sau'di Ara'bian *ou* **Sau'di** *adj* saoudien, saoudite ‖ *s* Saoudien *m,* Saoudienne *f*

sauerkraut [ˈsaur,kraut] *s* choucroute *f*

saunter [ˈsɔntər] *s* flânerie *f* ‖ *intr* flâner

sausage [ˈsɔsɪdʒ] *s* saucisse *f,* saucisson *m*

sauté [soˈte] *tr* sauter, faire sauter

savage [ˈsævɪdʒ] *adj & s* sauvage *mf*

savant [ˈsævənt] *s* savant *m,* érudit *m*

save [sev] *prep* sauf, excepté ‖ *tr* sauver; (*money*) épargner; (*time*) gagner; (comp) protéger ‖ *intr* économiser

saving [ˈsevɪŋ] *adj* économe ‖ **savings** *spl* épargne *f,* économies *fpl*

sav′ings account′ *s* dépôt *m* d'épargne

sav′ings and loan′ associa′tion *s* caisse *f* d'épargne et de prêt

sav′ings bank′ *s* caisse *f* d'épargne

sav′ings book′ *s* livret *m* de caisse d'épargne

savior [ˈsevjər] *s* sauveur *m*

Saviour [ˈsevjər] *s* Sauveur *m*

savor [ˈsevər] *s* saveur *f* ‖ *tr* savourer ‖ *intr*—**to savor of** avoir un goût de

savor•y [ˈsevəri] *adj* (*comp* **-ier;** *super* **-iest**) (*taste*) savoureux; (*smell*) odorant ‖ *s* (*pl* **-ies**) (bot) sariette *f*

saw [sɔ] *s* scie *f;* (*proverb*) dicton *m* ‖ *tr* scier

saw′ dust′ *s* sciure *f* de bois

sawed′-off shot′gun *s* fusil *m* à canon scié

saw′horse′ *s* chevalet *m*

saw′mill′ *s* scierie *f*

Saxon [ˈsæksən] *adj* saxon *m;* (*person*) Saxon *m* ‖ *s* (*language*) saxon

saxophone [ˈsæksə,fon] *s* saxophone *m*

say [se] *s*—**to have one's say** avoir son mot à dire, avoir voix au chapitre ‖ *v* (*pret & pp* **said** [sɛd]) *tr* dire; **I should say not!** absolument pas!; **I should say so!** je crois bien!; **it is said** on dit; **no sooner said than done** sitôt dit, sitôt fait; **that is to say** c'est-à-dire; **to go without saying** aller sans dire; **what will the neighbors say?** qu'en dira-t-on?; **you don't say!** tu parles Charles!; **you said it!** (coll) et comment!, tu parles!

saying [ˈse•ɪŋ] *s* proverbe *m*

scab [skæb] *s* croûte *f;* (*strikebreaker*) jaune *m;* canaille *f*

scabbard [ˈskæbərd] *s* fourreau *m*

scab•by [ˈskæbi] *adj* (*comp* **-bier;** *super* **-biest**) croûteux; (coll) vil

scabrous [ˈskæbrəs] *adj* scabreux; (*uneven*) rugueux

scads [skædz] *spl* (slang) des tas *mpl*

scaffold [ˈskæfəld] *s* échafaud *m;* (*used in construction*) échafaudage *m*

scaffolding [ˈskæfəldɪŋ] *s* échafaudage *m*

scald [skɔld] *tr* échauder

scale [skel] *s* (*of thermometer, map, salaries, etc.*) échelle *f;* (*for weighing*) plateau *m;* (*incrustation*) tartre *m;* (bot, zool) écaille *f;* (mus) échelle; **on a large scale** sur une grande échelle; **scales** balance *f;* **to tip the scales** faire pencher la balance ‖ *tr* escalader; **to scale down** réduire l'échelle de

scallion [ˈskælɪ•ən] *s* échalote *f,* ciboule *f*

scallop [ˈskæləp] *s* (*seafood*) coquille *f* Saint-Jacques, peigne *m,* pétoncle *m;* (*thin slice of meat*) escalope *f;* (*on edge of cloth*) feston *m* ‖ *tr* (*the edges*) denteler, découper; (culin) gratiner et cuire au four et à la crème

scalp [skælp] *s* cuir *m* chevelu; (*trophy*) scalp *m* ‖ *tr* scalper; (*tickets*) (coll) faire le trafic de; (*to hoodwink*) (slang) abuser de

scalpel [ˈskælpəl] *s* scalpel *m*

scal•y [ˈskeli] *adj* (*comp* **-ier;** *super* **-iest**) écailleux

scamp [skæmp] *s* garnement *m*

scamper [ˈskæmpər] *intr* courir allégrement; **to scamper away** or **off** détaler

scan [skæn] *v* (*pret & pp* **scanned;** *ger* **scanning**) *tr* scruter; (*e.g., a page*) jeter un coup d'œil sur; (*verses*) scander; (astr, comp, telv, mil) explorer; (telv) balayer ‖ *intr* (med) se servir d'un scanographe

scandal [ˈskændəl] *s* scandale *m,* esclandre *m*

scandalize [ˈskændə,laɪz] *tr* scandaliser

scandalous [ˈskændələs] *adj* scandaleux

Scandinavian [,skændɪˈnevɪ•ən] *adj* scandinave ‖ *s* (*language*) scandinave *m;* (*person*) Scandinave *mf*

scanner [ˈskænər] *s* (comp) analyseur *m* du lexique; (med) scanographe *m,* scanner *m,* tomodensitomètre *m*

scanning [ˈskænɪŋ] *s* (telv) balayage *m*

scansion [ˈskæn,ʒən] *s* scansion *f*

scant [skænt] *adj* maigre; (*attire*) léger, sommaire ‖ *tr* réduire; lésiner sur

scant•y [ˈskænti] *adj* (*comp* **-ier;** *super* **-iest**) rare, maigre; léger

scapegoat [ˈskep,got] *s* bouc *m* émissaire, tête *f* de Turc

scar [skɑr] *s* cicatrice *f;* (*on face*) balafre *f* ‖ *v* (*pret & pp* **scarred;** *ger* **scarring**) *tr* balafrer

scarce [skɛrs] *adj* rare, peu abondant

scarcely [ˈskɛrsli] *adv* à peine, presque pas; ne ... guère §90; **scarcely ever** rarement

scarci•ty [ˈskɛrsiti] *s* (*pl* **-ties**) manque *m,* pénurie *f*

scare [skɛr] *s* panique *f,* effroi *m* ‖ *tr* épouvanter, effrayer; **to scare away** or **off** effaroucher; **to scare up** (coll) procurer ‖ *intr* s'effaroucher

scare′crow′ *s* épouvantail *m*

scarf [skɑrf] *s* (*pl* **scarfs** or **scarves** [skɑrvz]) foulard *m,* écharpe *f*

scarlet [ˈskɑrlɪt] *adj & s* écarlate *f*

scar′let fe′ver *s* scarlatine *f*

scar•y [ˈskɛri] *adj* (*comp* **-ier;** *super* **-iest**) (*easily frightened*) (coll) peureux, ombrageux; (*causing fright*) (coll) effrayant

scathing [ˈskeðɪŋ] *adj* cinglant

scatter [ˈskætər] *tr* éparpiller; (*a mob*) disperser ‖ *intr* se disperser

scat′ter•brained′ *adj* (coll) étourdi

scenari•o [sɪˈnɛrɪ,o] *s* (*pl* **-os**) scénario *m*

scenarist [sɪˈnɛrɪst] *s* scénariste *mf*

scene [sin] *s* scène *f;* (*landscape*) paysage *m;* **behind the scenes** dans les coulisses; **to make a scene** faire une scène

scener•y [ˈsinəri] *s* (*pl* **-ies**) paysage *m;* (theat) décor *m,* paysage

sceneshifter [ˈsin,fiftər] *s* (theat) machiniste *m*

scenic [ˈsinɪk] *adj* pittoresque; spectaculaire; (theat) scénique

sce′nic rail′way *s* chemin *m* de fer en miniature des parcs d'attraction

scent [sɛnt] *s* odeur *f;* parfum *m;* (*trail*) piste *f*

‖ *tr* parfumer; (*an odor*) renifler; (*game as a dog does; a trap*) flairer

scepter [ˈsɛptər] *s* sceptre *m*

sceptic [ˈskɛptɪk] *adj* & *s* sceptique *mf*

sceptical [ˈskɛptɪkəl] *adj* sceptique

scepticism [ˈskɛptɪˌsɪzəm] *s* scepticisme *m*

schedule [ˈskɛdjʊl] *s* (*of work*) plan *m*, programme *m*; (*of things to do*) emploi *m* du temps; (*of prices*) barème *m*; (rr) horaire *m*; **on schedule** selon l'horaire; selon les prévisions ‖ *tr* classer; inscrire au programme, à l'horaire, etc.; **scheduled to speak** prévu comme orateur

scheduled *adj* prévu, indiqué; (*train, bus, plane*) régulier

sched′uled air′line *s* compagnie *f* aérienne de transport régulier

sched′uled flight′ *s* vol *m* régulier

scheme [skim] *s* projet *m*; machination *f*, truc *m* ‖ *tr* projeter ‖ *intr* ruser

schemer [ˈskimər] *s* faiseur *m* de projets; intrigant *m*

schism [ˈsɪzəm] *s* schisme *m*, scisson *f*

schizophrenia [ˌskɪtsəˈfriniˑə] *s* schizophrénie *f*

scholar [ˈskɑlər] *s* (*pupil*) écolier *m*; (*learned person*) érudit *m*, savant *m*; (*holder of scholarship*) boursier *m*

scholarly [ˈskɑlərli] *adj* érudit, savant ‖ *adv* savamment

schol′ar•ship′ *s* érudition *f*; (*award*) bourse *f*

scholasticism [skəˈlæstɪˌsɪzəm] *s* scolastique *f*

school [skul] *adj* scolaire ‖ *s* école *f*; (*of a university*) faculté *f*; (*of fish*) banc *m* ‖ *tr* instruire, discipliner

school′ age′ *s* âge *m* scolaire

school′ board′ *s* conseil *m* de l'instruction publique

school′book′ *s* livre *m* de classe, livre scolaire

school′boy′ *s* écolier *m*

school′ bus′ *s* voiture *f* école

school′girl′ *s* écolière *f*

school′house′ *s* maison *f* d'école

schooling [ˈskulɪŋ] *s* instruction *f*, études *fpl*; (*teaching*) enseignement *m*

schoolmarm [ˈskulˌmɑrm] *s* maîtresse *f* d'école, institutrice *f*

school′mas′ter *s* maître *m* d'école, instituteur *m*

school′mate′ *s* camarade *mf* d'école, condisciple *m*

school′room′ *s* classe *f*, salle *f* de classe

school′teach′er *s* enseignant *m*, instituteur *m*

school′yard′ *s* cour *f* de récréation

school′ year′ *s* année *f* scolaire

school′ zone′ *s* (*public sign*) ralentir école

schooner [ˈskunər] *s* schooner *m*, goélette *f*

sciatica [saɪˈætɪkə] *s* (pathol) sciatique *f*

science [ˈsaɪˑəns] *s* science *f*

sci′ence fic′tion *s* science-fiction *f*

scientific [ˌsaɪˑənˈtɪfɪk] *adj* scientifique

scientist [ˈsaɪˑəntɪst] *s* homme *m* de science, savant *m*

sci-fi [ˈsaɪˈfaɪ] *s* (coll) SF *f* (*science-fiction*)

scimitar [ˈsɪmɪtər] *s* cimeterre *m*

scintillate [ˈsɪntɪˌlet] *intr* scintiller, étinceler

scion [ˈsaɪˑən] *s* héritier *m*; (hort) scion *m*

scissors [ˈsɪzərz] *s* & *spl* ciseaux *mpl*

scis′sors-grind′er *s* rémouleur *m*; (orn) engoulevent *m*

scoff [skɔf] *s* raillerie *f* ‖ *intr*—**to scoff at** se moquer de

scoff′law′ *s* violateur *m* méprisant

scold [skold] *s* harpie *f* ‖ *tr* & *intr* gronder

scolding [ˈskoldɪŋ] *s* gronderie *f*

scoop [skup] *s* (*for flour, sugar, etc.*) pelle *f* à main; (*for ice cream*) cuiller *f* à glace; (*kitchen utensil*) louche *f*; (*of dredge*) godet *m*; (*for coal*) seau *m*; (journ) nouvelle *f* à sensation, nouvelle en exclusivité, scoop *m*; (mach) benne *f* preneuse; (naut) écope *f* ‖ *tr* creuser; **to scoop out** excaver à la pelle; (*water*) écoper

scoot [skut] *intr* (coll) détaler

scooter [ˈskutər] *s* trottinette *f*, patinette *f*

scope [skop] *s* (*field*) domaine *m*, étendue *f*; (*reach*) portée *f*, envergure *f*; **to give free scope to** donner libre carrière à

scorch [skɔrtʃ] *tr* roussir; flétrir, dessécher

scorched′-earth′ pol′icy *s* politique *f* de la terre brûlée

scorching [ˈskɔrtʃɪŋ] *adj* brûlant; caustique, mordant

score [skor] *s* (*debt*) compte *m*; (*twenty*) vingtaine *f*; (*notch*) entaille *f*; (*on metal*) rayure *f*, éraflure *f*; (mus) partition *f*; (sports) score *m*, marque *f*; **on that score** à cet égard; **to keep score** compter les points; **to settle a score with s.o.** régler son compte à qn ‖ *tr* (*to notch*) entailler; (*to criticize*) blâmer; (*metal*) rayer, érafler; (*a success*) remporter; (*e.g., a goal*) marquer; (mus) orchestrer

score′board′ *s* tableau *m*

score′keep′er *s* marqueur *m*

scorn [skɔrn] *s* mépris *m*, dédain *m* ‖ *tr* mépriser, dédaigner ‖ *intr*—**to scorn to** dédaigner de

Scorpio [ˈskɔrpɪˌo] *s* (astr, astrol) le Scorpion

scorpion [ˈskɔrpɪˑən] *s* scorpion *m*

Scot [skɑt] *s* Écossais *m*

Scotch [skɑtʃ] *adj* écossais; (slang) avare, chiche *s* (*dialect*) écossais *m*; whiskey *m* écossais; **the Scotch** les Écossais ‖ (*l.c.*) *s* (*wedge*) cale *f*; (*notch*) entaille *f* ‖ *tr* caler; entailler; (*a rumor*) étouffer

Scotch′man *s* (*pl* -**men**) Écossais *m*

Scotch′ pine′ *s* pin *m* sylvestre

Scotch′ tape′ *s* (trademark) ruban *m* cellulosique, adhésif *m* scotch

Scotland [ˈskɑtlənd] *s* Écosse *f*; l'Écosse

Scottish [ˈskɑtɪʃ] *adj* écossais ‖ *s* (*dialect*) écossais *m*; **the Scottish** les Écossais

scoundrel [ˈskaʊndrəl] *s* coquin *m*, fripon *m*, canaille *f*

scour [skaʊr] *tr* récurer; (*e.g., the countryside*) parcourir

scourge [skʌrdʒ] *s* nerf *m* de bœuf, discipline *f*; (fig) fléau *m* ‖ *tr* fouetter, flageller

scour′ing sponge′ *s* tampon *m* abrasif

scout [skaʊt] *adj* scout ‖ *s* éclaireur *m; (boy scout)* scout *m,* éclaireur; **a good scout** (coll) un brave gars ‖ *tr* reconnaître; *(to scoff at)* repousser avec dédain ‖ *intr* aller en reconnaissance

scouting [ˈskaʊtɪŋ] *s* scoutisme *m*

scout′ing par′ty *s* (*pl* **-ties**) (mil) détachement *m* de reconnaissance

scout′mas′ter *s* chef *m* de troupe

scowl [skaʊl] *s* renfrognement *m* ‖ *intr* se renfrogner

scram [skræm] *v* (*pret & pp* **scrammed;** *ger* **scramming**) *intr* (coll) ficher le camp; **scram!** (coll) fiche-moi le camp!

scramble [ˈskræmbəl] *s* bousculade *f* ‖ *tr* brouiller ‖ *intr* se disputer; grimper à quatre pattes

scram′bled eggs′ *spl* œufs *mpl* brouillés

scrambling [ˈskræmblɪŋ] *s* (electron) embrouillage *m*

scrap [skræp] *s* (*metal*) ferraille *f; (little bit)* bout *m,* petit morceau *m; (fight)* (coll) chamaillerie *f* ‖ *v* (*pret & pp* **scrapped;** *ger* **scrapping**) *tr* mettre au rebut ‖ *intr* (coll) se chamailler

scrap′book′ *s* album *m* de découpures

scrape [skrep] *s* grincement *m; (coll)* mauvaise affaire *f* ‖ *tr* gratter, râcler

scrap′ heap′ *s* tas *m* de rebut

scrap′ i′ron *s* ferraille *f*

scrap′ pa′per *s* bloc-notes *m; (refuse)* papier *m* de rebut

scratch [skrætʃ] *s* égratignure *f;* **to start from scratch** partir de rien ‖ *tr* gratter, égratigner; *(to eliminate from an event)* déclarer forfait

scratch′ pad′ *s* bloc-notes *m,* brouillon *m*

scratch′ pa′per *s* bloc-notes *m*

scrawl [skrɔl] *s* griffonnage *m* ‖ *tr & intr* griffonner

scraw•ny [ˈskrɔni] *adj* (*comp* **-nier;** *super* **-niest**) décharné, mince

scream [skrim] *s* cri *m* perçant; (slang) personne *f* ridicule; (slang) chose *f* ridicule ‖ *tr & intr* pousser des cris, crier

screech [skritʃ] *s* cri *m* perçant ‖ *intr* jeter des cris perçants

screech′ owl′ *s* chat-huant *m; (barn owl)* effraie *f*

screen [skrin] *s* écran *m;* grillage *m* en fil de fer, treillis *m* métallique; *(for sifting)* crible *m* ‖ *tr* abriter; *(candidates)* trier; (mov) porter à l'écran

screen′ grid′ *s* (electron) grille *f* blindée

screening [ˈskrinɪŋ] *s* présélection *f;* (med) dépistage *m*

screen′play′ *s* scénario *m;* drame *m* filmé

screen′ test′ *s* bout *m* d'essai

screw [skru] *s* vis *f;* (naut) hélice *f;* **to have a screw loose** (coll) être toqué ‖ *tr* visser; **to screw off** dévisser; **to screw tight** visser à bloc; **to screw up** *(one's courage)* rassembler ‖ *intr* se visser

screw′ball′ *adj & s* (slang) extravagant *m,* loufoque *m*

screw′driv′er *s* tournevis *m*

screw′ eye′ *s* vis *f* à œil

screw′ press′ *s* cric *m* à vis

screw′ propel′ler *s* hélice *f*

screw′ top′ *s* couvercle *m* à pas de vis

screw•y [ˈskru•i] *adj* (*comp* **-ier;** *super* **-iest**) (slang) loufoque

scrib′al er′ror [ˈskraɪbəl] *s* faute *f* de copiste

scribble [ˈskrɪbəl] *s* griffonnage *m* ‖ *tr & intr* griffonner

scribe [skraɪb] *s* scribe *m*

scrimmage [ˈskrɪmɪdʒ] *s* mêlée *f*

scrimp [skrɪmp] *tr* lésiner sur ‖ *intr* lésiner

scrip [skrɪp] *s* monnaie *f* scriptural, script *m*

script [skrɪpt] *s* manuscrit *m,* original *m; (handwriting)* écriture *f;* (mov) scénario *m;* (typ) script *m;* (mov, telv) texte *m*

scriptural [ˈskrɪptʃərəl] *adj* biblique

scripture [ˈskrɪptʃər] *s* citation *f* tirée de l'Écriture; **Scripture** l'Écriture *f;* **the Scriptures** les Ecritures

script′writ′er *s* scénariste *mf*

scrofula [ˈskrɑfjələ] *s* scrofule *f*

scroll [skrol] *s* rouleau *m;* (archit) volute *f*

scroll′work′ *s* ornementation *f* en volute

scro•tum [ˈskrotəm] *s* (*pl* **-ta** [tə] or **-tums**) scrotum *m,* bourses *fpl*

scrub [skrʌb] *adj* rabougri ‖ *s* (*scrubbing*) nettoyage *m* à la brosse; *(underbrush)* broussailles *fpl;* (rok) vol *m* annulé; (sports) joueur *m* novice ‖ *v* (*pret & pp* **scrubbed;** *ger* **scrubbing**) *tr* frotter, nettoyer, récurer; *(to cancel)* (rok) annuler

scrub′bing brush′ *s* brosse *f* de chiendent

scrub′wom′an *s* (*pl* **-wom′en**) nettoyeuse *f*

scruff [skrʌf] *s* nuque *f*

scruple [ˈskrupəl] *s* scrupule *f*

scrupulous [ˈskrupjələs] *adj* scrupuleux

scrutinize [ˈskrutɪˌnaɪz] *tr* scruter

scruti•ny [ˈskrutɪni] *s* (*pl* **-nies**) examen *m* minutieux

scuba [ˈskubə] *s* scaphandre *m* autonome

scu′ba div′er *s* scaphandrier *m*

scuff [skʌf] *s* usure *f* ‖ *tr* érafler

scuffle [ˈskʌfəl] *s* bagarre *f* ‖ *intr* se bagarrer

scull [skʌl] *s* (*stern oar*) godille *f;* aviron *m* de couple ‖ *tr* godiller ‖ *intr* ramer en couple

sculler•y [ˈskʌləri] *s* (*pl* **-ies**) arrière-cuisine *f*

scul′lery maid′ *s* laveuse *f* de vaisselle

scullion [ˈskʌljən] *s* marmiton *m*

sculptor [ˈskʌlptər] *s* sculpteur *m*

sculptress [ˈskʌlptrɪs] *s* femme *f* sculpteur

sculpture [ˈskʌlptʃər] *s* sculpture *f* ‖ *tr & intr* sculpter

scum [skʌm] *s* écume *f; (of society)* canaille *f* ‖ *v* (*pret & pp* **scummed;** *ger* **scumming**) *tr & intr* écumer

scum•my [ˈskʌmi] *adj* (*comp* **-mier;** *super* **-miest**) écumeux; (fig) vil

scurrilous [ˈskʌrɪləs] *adj* injurieux, grossier, outrageant

scur•ry [ˈskʌri] *v* (*pret & pp* **-ried**) *intr*—**to scurry around** galoper; **to scurry away** or **off** déguerpir

scur·vy [ˈskʌrvi] *adj* (*comp* **-vier;** *super* **-viest**) méprisable, vil ‖ *s* scorbut *m*

scuttle [ˈskʌtəl] *s* (*bucket for coal*) seau *m* à charbon; (*trap door*) trappe *f;* (*run*) course *f* précipitée; (naut) écoutillon *m* ‖ *tr* saborder ‖ *intr* filer, déguerpir

scut·tle·butt' *s* (coll) on-dit *m*

scythe [saɪð] *s* faux *f*

sea [si] *s* mer *f;* **at sea** en mer; (fig) désorienté; **by the sea** au bord de la mer; **to put to sea** prendre le large

sea'board' *s* littoral *m*

sea' breeze' *s* brise *f* de mer

sea'coast' *s* côté *f*, littoral *m*

sea' dog' *s* (ichth) chien *m* de mer, roussette *f;* (*seal*) phoque *m* commun; **old sea dog** (naut) vieux loup *m* de mer

seafarer [ˈsi,fɛrər] *s* marin *m;* voyageur *m* par mer

sea'food' *s* fruits *mpl* de mer, marée *f*

seagoing [ˈsi,go·ɪŋ] *adj* de haute mer, au long cours

sea' gull' *s* mouette *f*, goéland *m*

seal [sil] *s* (*on a document*) sceau *m;* (zool) phoque *m* ‖ *tr* sceller; **in a sealed envelope** sous pli fermé

sea' legs' *spl* pied *m* marin

sea' lev'el *s* niveau *m* de la mer

seal'ing wax' *s* cire *f* à cacheter

sea' li'on *s* otarie *f*

seal'skin' *s* peau *f* de phoque

seam [sim] *s* couture *f;* (*of metal*) joint *m;* (geol) fissure *f;* (min) couche *f*

sea'man *s* (*pl* **-men**) marin *m*

sea' mile' *s* mille *m* marin

seamless [ˈsimlɪs] *adj* sans couture; (mach) sans soudure

seamstress [ˈsimstrɪs] *s* couturière *f*

seam·y [ˈsimi] *adj* (*comp* **-ier;** *super* **-iest**) plein de coutures; vil, vilain

séance [ˈse·ɑns] *s* séance *f* de spiritisme

sea'plane' *s* hydravion *m*

sea'port' *s* port *m* de mer

sea' pow'er *s* puissance *f* maritime

sear [sɪr] *adj* desséché ‖ *s* cicatrice *f* de brûlure ‖ *tr* dessécher; marquer au fer rouge

search [sʌrtʃ] *s* recherche *f;* **in search of** à la recherche de ‖ *tr* & *intr* fouiller; **to search for** chercher

searching [ˈsʌrtʃɪŋ] *adj* pénrant, scrutateur

search'light' *s* projecteur *m*

search' war'rant *s* mandat *m* de perquisition

seascape [ˈsi,skep] *s* panorama *m* marin; (*painting*) marine *f*

sea' shell' *s* coquille *f* de mer

sea'shore' *s* bord *m* de la mer

sea'sick' *adj*—**to be seasick** avoir le mal de mer

sea'sick'ness *s* mal *m* de mer

sea'side' *s* bord *m* de mer

sea'side' resort' *s* station *f* balnéaire

season [ˈsizən] *s* saison *f* ‖ *tr* assaisonner; (*troops*) aguerrir; (*wood*) sécher

seasonal [ˈsizənəl] *adj* saisonnier

seasoning [ˈsizənɪŋ] *s* assaisonnement *m*

sea'son's greet'ings *spl* meilleurs souhaits *mpl*, tous mes vœux *mpl*

sea'son tick'et *s* carte *f* d'abonnement

seat [sit] *s* siège *m;* (*place or right*) place *f;* (*in theater*) fauteuil *m;* (*on bus or train*) banquette *f;* (*on cycle*) selle *f;* (*of trousers*) fond *m;* **have a seat** asseyez-vous donc; **keep your seat** restez assis; **to have a good seat** (equit) avoir une bonne assiette ‖ *tr* asseoir; (*a number of persons*) contenir; **to be seated** (*to sit down*) s'asseoir; (*to be in sitting posture*) être assis

seat' belt' *s* ceinture *f* de sécurité

seat' cov'er *s* (aut) housse *f*

SEATO [ˈsito] *s* (acronym) (**Southeast Asia Treaty Organization**) l'OTASE *f* (Organisation du traité de l'Asie du Sud-Est)

sea' wall' *s* digue *f*

sea'way' *s* voie *f* maritime; (*of ship*) sillage *m;* (*rough sea*) mer *f* dure

sea'weed' *s* algue *f* marine; plante *f* marine

sea'wor'thy *adj* en état de naviguer

secede [sɪˈsid] *tr* tenir éloigné; (*to shut up*) faire sécession

secession [sɪˈsɛʃən] *s* sécession *f*

seclude [sɪˈklud] *tr* tenir éloigné; (*to shut up*) enfermer

secluded *adj* retiré, écarté

seclusion [sɪˈkluʒən] *s* retraite *f*

second [ˈsɛkənd] *adj* & *pron* deuxième (*masc, fem*), second; **the Second** deux, e.g., **John the Second** Jean deux; **to be second in command** commander en second; **to be second to none** ne le céder à personne ‖ *s* deuxième *m*, second *m;* (*in time; musical interval; of angle*) seconde *f;* (*in a duel*) témoin *m*, second *m;* (com) article *m* de deuxième qualité; **the second** (*in dates*) le deux ‖ *adv* en second lieu ‖ *tr* affirmer; (*to back up*) seconder

secondar·y [ˈsɛkən,dɛri] *adj* secondaire ‖ *s* (*pl* **-ies**) (elec) secondaire *m*

sec'ondary educa'tion *s* enseignement *m* secondaire

sec'ond best' *s* pis-aller *m*

sec'ond-best' *adj* (*everyday*) de tous les jours; **to come off second-best** être battu

sec'ond-class' *adj* de second ordre; (rr) de seconde classe

sec'ond cous'in *s* cousin *m or* cousine *f* issu(e) d'un(e) cousin(e) germain(e) du père *or* de la mère

sec'ond floor' *s* premier étage *m;* (*second floor above the ground floor = American third floor*) (Brit) deuxième étage

sec'ond hand' *s* (*of a timepiece*) trotteuse *f*

sec'ond·hand' *adj* d'occasion, de seconde main

sec'ond-hand book'dealer *s* bouquiniste *mf*

sec'ondhand book'shop *s* librairie *f* d'occasion

sec'ondhand smoke' *s* fumée *f* exhalée par les fumeurs

sec'ond lieuten'ant *s* sous-lieutenant *m*

sec′ond mate′ *s* (naut) second maître *m*
sec′ond-rate′ *adj* de second ordre
sec′ond sight′ *s* seconde vue *f*
sec′ond wind′ *s* second souffle *m;* **to get one's second wind** reprendre haleine
secre•cy [ˈsikrəsi] *s* (*pl* **-cies**) secret *m;* **in secrecy** en secret
secret [ˈsikrɪt] *adj* & *s* secret *m;* **in secret** en secret
secretar•y [ˈsɛkrɪ,tɛri] *s* (*pl* **-ies**) secrétaire *mf;* (*desk*) secrétaire *m*
se′cret bal′lot *s* scrutin *m* secret
secrete [sɪˈkrit] *tr* cacher; (physiol) sécréter
secretive [sɪˈkritɪv] *adj* cachottier
se′cret serv′ice *s* deuxième bureau *m*
sect [sɛkt] *s* secte *f*
sectarian [sɛkˈtɛrɪ•ən] *adj* sectaire; (*school*) confessionnel ‖ sectaire *mf*
section [ˈsɛkʃən] *s* section *f*
sectionalism [ˈsɛkʃənə,lɪzəm] *s* régionalisme *m*
sec′tion hand′ *s* cantonnier *m*
sector [ˈsɛktər] *s* secteur *m;* (*instrument*) compas *m* de proportion
secular [ˈsɛkjələr] *adj* (*worldly, of this world*) séculier; (*century-old*) séculaire ‖ *s* séculier *m*
secularism [ˈsɛkjələ,rɪzəm] *s* laïcisme *m,* mondanité *f*
secure [sɪˈkjʊr] *adj* sûr ‖ *tr* obtenir; (*to make fast*) fixer
securi•ty [sɪˈkjʊrɪti] *s* (*pl* **-ties**) sécurité *f;* (*pledge*) garantie *f;* (*person*) garant *m;* **securities** valeurs *fpl*
secu′rity risk′ *s* risque *m* d'un relâchement des mesures de sécurité; (*person*) *personne qui pourrait compromettre la sécurité d'une organisation ou la sûreté de l'État*
secu′rity sys′tem *s* (*in a home*) gardiennage *m* électronique
secu′rity-sys′tems com′pany *s* société *f* de gardiennage
sedan [sɪˈdæn] *s* (aut) conduite *f* intérieure
sedan′ chair′ *s* chaise *f* à porteurs
sedate [sɪˈdet] *adj* calme, discret
sedation [sɪˈdeʃən] *s* sédation *f*
sedative [ˈsɛdətɪv] *adj* & *s* sédatif *m*
sedentary [ˈsɛdən,tɛri] *adj* sédentaire
sedge [sɛdʒ] *s* (*Carex*) laîche *f*
sediment [ˈsɛdɪmənt] *s* sédiment *m*
sedition [sɪˈdɪʃən] *s* sédition *f*
seditious [sɪˈdɪʃəs] *adj* séditieux
seduce [sɪˈd(j)us] *tr* séduire
seducer [sɪˈd(j)usər] *s* séducteur *m*
seduction [sɪˈdʌkʃən] *s* séduction *f*
seductive [sɪˈdʌktɪv] *adj* séduisant
sedulous [ˈsɛdʒələs] *adj* assidu
see [si] *s* (eccl) siège *m* ‖ *v* (*pret* **saw** [sɔ]; *pp* **seen** [sin]) *tr* voir; **see other side** (*turn the page*) voir au dos; **to see s.o. play, to see s.o. playing** voir jouer qn, voir qn qui joue; **to see s.th. played** voir jouer q.ch. ‖ *intr* voir; **to see through s.o.** (fig) voir venir qn
seed [sid] *s* graine *f,* semence *f;* sperme *m;* (*in fruit*) pépin *m;* (fig) germe **to go to seed** monter en graine ‖ *intr* semer, ensemencer
seed′bed′ *s* semis *m*
seeder [ˈsidər] *s* (mach) semeuse *f*
seedling [ˈsidlɪŋ] *s* semis *m*
seed•y [ˈsidi] *adj* (*comp* **-ier;** *super* **-iest**) (coll) râpé, miteux
seeing [ˈsi•ɪŋ] *adj* voyant ‖ *s* vue *f* ‖ *conj* vu que
See′ing Eye′ dog′ *s* (trademark) chien *m* d'aveugle
seek [sik] *v* (*pret* & *pp* **sought** [sɔt]) *tr* chercher ‖ *intr* chercher; **to seek after** rechercher; **to seek to** chercher à
seem [sim] *intr* sembler
seemingly [ˈsimɪŋli] *adv* en apparence
seem•ly [ˈsimli] *adj* (*comp* **-lier;** *super* **-liest**) gracieux; (*correct*) bienséant
seep [sip] *intr* suinter
seer [sɪr] *s* prophète *m,* voyant *m*
see′saw′ *s* balançoire *f,* bascule *f;* (*motion*) va-et-vient *m* ‖ *intr* basculer, balancer
seethe [sið] *intr* bouillonner
segment [ˈsɛgmənt] *s* segment *m*
segregate [ˈsɛgrɪ,get] *tr* mettre à part, isoler
segregation [,sɛgrɪˈgeʃən] *s* ségrégation *f*
segregationist [,sɛgrɪˈgeʃənɪst] *s* ségrégationniste *mf*
seismic [ˈsaɪzmɪk] *adj* sismique
seismograph [ˈsaɪzmə,græf] *s* sismographe *m*
seismology [saɪzˈmɑlədʒi] *s* sismologie *f*
seize [siz] *tr* saisir
seizure [ˈsiʒər] *s* prise *f;* (law) saisie *f;* (pathol) attaque *f*
seldom [ˈsɛldəm] *adv* rarement
select [sɪˈlɛkt] *adj* choisi ‖ *tr* choisir, sélectionner
selection [sɪˈlɛkʃən] *s* sélection *f*
selective [sɪˈlɛktɪv] *adj* sélectif
self [sɛlf] *adj* de même ‖ *s* (*pl* **selves** [sɛlvz]) moi *m,* être *m;* **all by one's self** tout seul; **one's better self** notre meilleur côté ‖ *pron*—**payable to self** payable à moi-même
self′-addressed en′velope *s* enveloppe *f* adressée à l'envoyeur
self′-cen′tered *adj* égocentrique
self′-clean′ing ov′en *s* four *m* autonettoyant
self′-con′fidence *s* confiance *f* en soi
self′-con′fident *adj* sûr de soi
self′-con′scious *adj* gêné, embarrassé, emprunté
self′-contained′ *adj* content et peu communicatif; (mach) indépendant
self′-control′ *s* sang-froid *m,* maîtrise *f* de soi
self′-defense′ *s* autodéfense *f;* **in self-defense** en légitime défense
self′-deni′al *s* abnégation *f*
self′-deter′mina′tion *s* autodétermination *f*
self′-dis′cipline *s* discipline *f* personnelle
self′-ed′ucated *adj* autodidacte
self′-employed′ *adj* indépendant
self′-esteem′ *s* amour-propre *m*
self′-ev′ident *adj* évident aux yeux de tout le monde; **that's self-evident** ça s'impose

self'-explan'ator'y adj qui s'explique de soi-même

self'-gov'ernment s autonomie f; maîtrise f de soi

self'-impor'tant adj suffisant, présomptueux

self'-indul'gence s faiblesse f envers soi-même, intempérance f

self'-in'terest s intérêt m personnel

selfish [ˈsɛlfɪʃ] adj égoïste

selfishness [ˈsɛlfɪˌnɪs] s égoïsme m

selfless [ˈsɛlflɪs] adj désintéressé

self'-love' s égoïsme m

self'-made man' s (pl -men') fils m de ses œuvres

self'-por'trait s autoportrait m

self'-possessed' adj maître de soi

self'-pres'erva'tion s conservation f de soi-même

self'-reli'ant adj sûr de soi, assuré

self'-respect'ing adj correct, honorable

self'-right'eous adj pharisaïque

self'-sac'rifice' s abnégation f

self'same' adj identique

self'sat'isfied' adj content de soi

self'-seal'ing adj (envelope) autocollant, auto-adhésif; (container) à obturation automatique

self'-seek'ing adj égoïste, intéressé

self'-serv'ice s libre-service m

self'-serv'ice laun'dry s (pl -dries) laverie f libre-service, laverie automatique, lavromat m

self'-ser'vice res'taurant s restaurant m libre-service

self'-serv'ice sta'tion s (aut) station f libre-service

self'-start'er s démarreur m automatique

self'-styled' adj soi-disant

self'-taught' adj autodidacte

self'-tim'er s (phot) retardateur m

self'-willed' adj obstiné, entêté

self'-wind'ing adj à remontage automatique

sell [sɛl] v (pret & pp **sold** [sold]) tr vendre; **to sell back** réceder; **to sell out** solder; (to betray) vendre ‖ intr vendre; **to sell for** (e.g., ten dollars) se vendre à

seller [ˈsɛlər] s vendeur m

selling [ˈsɛlɪŋ] s vente f; **selling by mail** postalage m; **selling price** prix m de vente

sell'out' s (betrayal) trahison f, capitulation f; (person) traître m; (com) liquidation f totale; (mov, sports, theat) représentation f, séance f ou match m à guichets fermés

Selt'zer wa'ter [ˈsɛltsər] s eau f de Seltz

selvage [ˈsɛlvɪdʒ] s (of fabric) lisière f; (of lock) gâche f

semantic [sɪˈmæntɪk] adj sémantique ‖ **semantics** s sémantique f

semaphore [ˈsɛməˌfor] s sémaphore m

semblance [ˈsɛmbləns] s semblant m

semen [ˈsimɛn] s sperme m, semence f

semester [sɪˈmɛstər] adj semstriel ‖ s semestre m

semes'ter hour' s (educ) heure f semestrielle

semicircle [ˈsɛmɪˌsʌrkəl] s demi-cercle m

semicolon [ˈsɛmɪˌkolən] s point-virgule m

semiconductor [ˌsɛmɪkənˈdʌktər] s semiconducteur m

semiconscious [ˌsɛmɪˈkanʃəs] adj à demi conscient

semifinal [ˌsɛmɪˈfaɪnəl] adj avant-dernière ‖ s demi-finale f

semilearned [ˌsɛmɪˈlʌrnɪd] adj à moitié savant

seminar [ˈsɛmɪˌnar] s séminaire m

seminar•y [ˈsɛmɪˌnɛri] s (pl -ies) séminaire m

semiprecious [ˌsɛmɪˈprɛʃəs] adj fin, semi-précieux

Semite [ˈsɛmaɪt] s Sémite mf

Semitic [sɪˈmɪtɪk] adj (e.g., language) sémitique; (person) sémite

semitrailer [ˈsɛmɪˌtrelər] s semi-remorque f

senate [ˈsɛnɪt] s sénat m

senator [ˈsɛnətər] s sénateur m

send [sɛnd] v (pret & pp **sent** [sɛnt]) tr envoyer; (rad, telv) émettre; **to send back** renvoyer; **to send out** envoyer; **to send s.o. for s.th.** or **s.o.** envoyer qn chercher q.ch. or qn; **to send s.o. to** + inf envoyer qn + inf ‖ intr (rad, telv) émettre; **to send for** envoyer chercher

sender [ˈsɛndər] s expéditeur m; (telg) transmetteur m

send'-off' s manifestation f d'adieu

senile [ˈsinaɪl] adj sénile

senility [sɪˈnɪlɪti] s sénilité f

senior [ˈsinjər] adj aîné; (clerk, partner, etc.) principal; (rank) supérieur; père, e.g., **Maurice Laporte, Senior** Maurice Laporte père ‖ s aîné m, doyen m; (U.S. upperclassman) étudiant m de dernière année

sen'ior cit'izens spl les vieilles gens fpl

seniority [sinˈjɔrɪti] s ancienneté f, doyenneté f

sen'ior staff' s personnel m hors classe

sensation [sɛnˈseʃən] s sensation f

sensational [sɛnˈseʃənəl] adj sensationnel

sense [sɛns] s sens m; (wisdom) bon sens; (e.g., of pain) sensation f; **to make sense out of** arriver à comprendre ‖ tr percevoir, sentir

senseless [ˈsɛnslɪs] adj (lacking perception) insensible; (unconscious) sans connaissance; (unreasonable) insensé

sense' of guilt' s remords m

sense' of hu'mor s sens m de l'humour

sense' or'gans spl organes mpl des sens

sensibili•ty [ˌsɛnsɪˈbɪlɪti] s (pl -ties) sensibilité f; susceptibilité f

sensible [ˈsɛnsɪbəl] adj sensible; (endowed with good sense) sensé, raisonnable

sensitive [ˈsɛnsɪtɪv] adj sensible; (touchy) susceptible, sensitif

sensitize [ˈsɛnsɪˌtaɪz] tr sensibiliser

sensor [ˈsɛnˌsɔr] s (rok) capteur m

sensory [ˈsɛnsəri] adj sensoriel

sensual [ˈsɛnʃʊəl] adj sensuel

sensuous [ˈsɛnʃʊəs] adj sensuel

sentence [ˈsɛntəns] s (gram) phrase f; (law) sentence f ‖ tr condamner

sentiment [ˈsɛntɪmənt] s sentiment m

sentimental [ˌsɛntɪˈmɛntəl] *adj* sentimental

sentinel [ˈsɛntɪnəl] *s* sentinelle *f;* **to stand sentinel** être en sentinelle

sen•try [ˈsɛntri] *s* (*pl* **-tries**) sentinelle *f*

sen′try box′ *s* guérite *f*

separate [ˈsɛpərɪt] *adj* séparé ‖ [ˈsɛpəˌret] *tr* séparer ‖ *intr* se séparer

separation [ˌsɛpəˈreʃən] *s* séparation *f*

September [sɛpˈtɛmbər] *s* septembre *m*

Septem′ber elev′en *s* le onze septembre (fête solennelle à la mémoire de la mort d'innocentes victimes dans l'attaque terroriste contre le Centre du Commerce Mondial)

septic [ˈsɛptɪk] *adj* septique

sepulcher [ˈsɛpəlkər] *s* sépulcre *m*

sequel [ˈsikwəl] *s* conséquence *f;* (*something following*) suite *f*

sequence [ˈsikwəns] *s* succession *f*, ordre *m;* (cards, mov) séquence *f;* (*of tenses*) (gram) concordance *f*

sequester [sɪˈkwɛstər] *tr* séquestrer

sequin [ˈsikwɪn] *s* paillette *f*

ser•aph [ˈsɛrəf] *s* (*pl* **-aphs** or **-aphim** [əfɪm]) séraphin *m*

Serb [sʌrb] *adj* serbe ‖ *s* Serbe *mf* ‖ *s* (*language*) serbe *m*

Serbia [ˈsʌrbɪ•ə] *s* Serbie *f*

Serbian [ˈsʌrbɪ•ən] *adj* serbe ‖ *s* Serbe *mf* ‖ *s* (*language*) serbe *m*

Serbo-Croatian [ˌsʌrbokroˈeʃən] *s* (*language*) serbo-croate *m*

sere [sɪr] *adj* sec, desséché

serenade [ˌsɛrəˈned] *s* sérénade *f* ‖ *tr* donner une sérénade à ‖ *intr* donner des sérénades

serene [sɪˈrin] *adj* serein

serenity [sɪˈrɛnɪti] *s* sérénité *f*

serf [sʌrf] *s* serf *m*

serfdom [ˈsʌrfdəm] *s* servage *m*

serge [sʌrdʒ] *s* serge *f*

sergeant [ˈsɑrdʒənt] *s* sergent *m*

ser′geant-at-arms′ *s* (*pl* **sergeants-at-arms**) huissier *m*, sergent *m* d'armes

ser′geant ma′jor *s* (*pl* **sergeant majors**) sergent-major *m*

serial [ˈsɪrɪ•əl] *adj* de série ‖ *s* roman-feuilleton *m*

serially [ˈsɪrɪ•əli] *adv* en série; (*in installments*) en feuilleton

se′rial num′ber *s* numéro *m* d'ordre; (mil) numéro *m* matricule

se•ries [ˈsɪriz] *s* (*pl* **-ries**) série *f;* **in series** en série

serious [ˈsɪrɪ•əs] *adj* (*illness, injury, mistake, tone, attitude, smile, look*) grave, sérieux; (*damage*) important, considérable

seriousness [ˈsɪrɪ•əsnɪs] *s* sérieux *m*, gravité *f*

sermon [ˈsʌrmən] *s* sermon *m*

sermonize [ˈsʌrməˌnaɪz] *tr* & *intr* sermonner

seropositive [ˌsɪroˈpɑzətɪv] *adj* séropositif

serpent [ˈsʌrpənt] *s* serpent *m*

se•rum [ˈsɪrəm] *s* (*pl* **-rums** or **-ra** [rə]) sérum *m*

servant [ˈsʌrvənt] *s* domestique *mf;* (*civil ser-*

vant) fonctionnaire *mf;* (*housemaid*) bonne *f;* (*humble servant*) (fig) serviteur *m*

serv′ant girl′ *s* servante *f*

serv′ant prob′lem *s* crise *f* domestique

serve [sʌrv] *tr* servir; **to serve s.o. as** servir à qn de; **to serve time** purger une peine ‖ *intr* servir; **to serve as** (*to function as*) servir de; (*to be useful for*) servir à

server [ˈsʌrvər] *s* (*waiter or waitress*) serveur *m*, serveuse *f;* (*spoon, ladle or fork for serving*) couvert *m* à servir; (comp) serveur *m;* (tennis) serveur *m*, serveuse *f*

service [ˈsʌrvɪs] *s* service *m;* (eccl) office *m;* **the services** (mil) les forces *fpl* armées ‖ *tr* entretenir, réparer

serviceable [ˈsʌrvɪsəbəl] *adj* utile, pratique; résistant

ser′vice charge′ *s* service *m;* (*in banking*) commission *f*

serv′ice club′ *s* foyer *m* du soldat

serv′ice•man *s* (*pl* **-men′**) réparateur *m;* (mil) militaire *m*

serv′ice rec′ord *s* état *m* de service

serv′ice sta′tion *s* station-service *f*

ser′vice stop′ *s* (*on a superhighway*) restoroute *m* avec parking et un garage et des pompes à essence

serv′ice stripe′ *s* chevron *m*, galon *m*

servicing [ˈsʌrvɪsɪŋ] *s* entretien *m* courant

servile [ˈsʌrvɪl] *adj* servile

servitude [ˈsʌrvɪˌt(j)ud] *s* servitude *f*

sesame [ˈsɛsəmi] *s* sésame *m;* **open sesame!** sésame, ouvre-toi!

session [ˈsɛʃən] *s* session *f;* **to be in session** siéger

set [sɛt] *adj* (*rule*) établi; (*price*) fixe; (*time*) fixé; (*smile; locution*) figé ‖ *s* ensemble *m;* (*of dishes, linen, etc.*) service *m;* (*of dishes*) service *m;* (*of kitchen utensils*) batterie *f;* (*of pans; of weights; of tickets*) série *f;* (*of tools, chessmen, oars, etc.*) jeu *m;* (*of books*) collection *f;* (*of diamonds*) parure *f;* (*of tennis*) set *m;* (*of cement*) prise *f;* (*of a garment*) tournure *f;* (*group of persons*) coterie *f;* (mov) plateau *m;* (rad) poste *m;* (theat) mise *f* en scène; **set of false teeth** dentier *m;* **set of teeth** denture *f* ‖ *v* (*pret & pp* **set;** *ger* **setting**) *tr* mettre, placer, poser; (*a date, price, etc.*) fixer; (*a gem*) monter; (*a trap*) tendre; (*a timepiece*) mettre à l'heure, régler; (*the hair*) mettre en plis; (*a bone*) remettre; **to set aside** mettre de côté; annuler; **to set going** mettre en marche; **to set off** mettre en valeur; (*e.g., a rocket*) lancer, tirer ‖ *intr* se figer; (*said of sun, moon, etc.*) se coucher; (*said of hen*) couver; (*said of garment*) tomber; **to set about, to set out to** se mettre à; **to set upon** attaquer

set′back′ *s* revers *m*, échec *m*

set′screw′ *s* vis *f* de pression

settee [sɛˈti] *s* canapé *m;* (*for two*) canapé à deux places, causeuse *f*

setting [ˈsɛtɪŋ] *s* (*surroundings*) cadre *m;* (*of a* *gem*) monture *f;* (*of cement*) prise *f;* (*of sun*) coucher *m;* (*of a bone*) recollement *m;* (*of a watch*) réglage *m;* (*adjustment*) ajustage *m;* (theat) mise *f* en scène

set′ting-up′ ex′ercises *spl* gymnastique *f* rhythmique, gymnastique suédoise

settle [′sɛtəl] *tr* (*a region*) coloniser; (*a dispute, account, debt, etc.*) régler; (*a problem*) résoudre; (*doubts, fears, etc.*) calmer; (*to stop wobbling*) stabiliser ‖ *intr* se coloniser; se calmer; (*said of weather*) se mettre au beau; (*said of building*) se tasser; (*said of sediment, dust, etc.*) se déposer; (*said of liquid*) se clarifier; **to settle down** s'établir; (*to be less wild*) se ranger; **to settle down to** (*a task*) s'appliquer à; **to settle on** se décider pour

settlement [′sɛtəlmənt] *s* établissement *m,* colonie *f;* (*of an account, dispute, etc.*) règlement *m;* (*of a debt*) liquidation *f;* (*settlement house*) œuvre *f* sociale

settler [′sɛtlər] *s* colon *m*

set′up′ *s* port *m,* maintien *m;* (*of the parts of a machine*) installation *f;* (coll) organisation *f*

seven [′sɛvən] *adj & pron* sept ‖ *s* sept *m;* **seven o'clock** sept heures

seventeen [′sɛvən′tin] *adj, pron,* & *s* dix-sept *m*

seventeenth [′sɛvən′tinθ] *adj & pron* dix-septième (*masc, fem*); **the Seventeenth** dix-sept, e.g., **John the Seventeenth** Jean dix-sept ‖ *s* dix-septième *m;* **the seventeenth** (*in dates*) le dix-sept

seventh [′sɛvənθ] *adj & pron* septième (*masc, fem*); **the Seventh** sept, e.g., **John the Seventh** Jean sept ‖ *s* septième *m;* **the seventh** (*in dates*) le sept

seventieth [′sɛvənti•ɪθ] *adj & pron* soixante-dixième (*masc, fem*) ‖ *s* soixante-dixième *m*

seven‧ty [′sɛvənti] *adj & pron* soixante-dix ‖ *s* (*pl* **-ties**) soixante-dix *m*

sev′enty-first′ *adj & pron* soixante et onzième (*masc, fem*) ‖ *s* soixante et onzième *m*

sev′enty-one′ *adj, pron,* & *s* soixante et onze *m*

sever [′sɛvər] *tr* séparer; (*relations*) rompre ‖ *intr* se séparer

several [′sɛvərəl] *adj & pron indef* plusieurs

severance [′sɛvərəl] *s* séparation *f;* (*of relations*) rupture *f;* (*of communications*) interruption *f*

sev′erance pay′ *s* indemnité *f* pour cause de renvoi

severe [sɪ′vɪr] *adj* sévère; (*weather*) rigoureux; (*pain*) aigu; (*illness*) grave

sew [so] *v* (*pret* **sewed;** *pp* **sewed** or **sewn**) *tr & intr* coudre

sewage [′s(j)u•ɪdʒ] *s* eaux *fpl* d'égouts

sew′age dispos′al plant′ *s* installation *f* d'évacuation des vidanges

sewer [′s(j)u•ər] *s* égout *m* ‖ [′so•ər] *s* (*one who sews*) couseur *m*

sewerage [′s(j)u•ərɪdʒ] *s* (*removal*) vidange *f;*

(*system*) système *m* d'égouts; (*sewage*) eaux *fpl* d'égouts

sew′ing bas′ket *s* nécessaire *m* de couture

sew′ing machine′ *s* machine *f* à coudre

sew′ing ta′ble *s* chiffonnière *f*

sex [sɛks] *s* sexe *m;* (*sexualité*) sexe; **the fair sex** le beau sexe; **the sterner sex** le sexe fort; **to have sex with** (coll) avoir des rapports avec

sex′ appeal′ *s* sex-appeal *m*

sex′-change′ op′era′tion *s* intervention *f* de changement de sexe

sex′ ed′uca′tion *s* éducation *f* sexuelle

sexism [′sɛksɪzəm] *s* sexisme *m*

sexist [′sɛksɪst] *adj & s* sexiste *mf*

sextant [′sɛkstənt] *s* sextant *m*

sextet [sɛks′tɛt] *s* sextuor *m*

sexton [′sɛkstən] *s* sacristain *m*

sexual [′sɛkʃu•əl] *adj* sexuel

sex′ual abuse′ *s* abus *m* sexuel

sex′ual harass′ment *s* harcèlement *m* sexual

sex′ual in′ter•course′ *s* rapports *mpl* sexuels

sexuality [‚sɛksju′ælɪtɪ] *s* sexualité *f*

sex′ually transmit′ted disease′ (STD) *s* maladie *f* sexuellement transmissible (MST)

sex′ual or′ienta′tion *s* orientation *f* sexuelle

sex•y [′sɛksi] *adj* (*comp* **-ier;** *super* **-iest**) (slang) aguichant, grivois; (*story*) érotique; **to be sexy** avoir du chien

sh [ʃ] *interj* chut!

shab•by [′ʃæbi] *adj* (*comp* **-bier;** *super* **-biest**) râpé, usé; (*mean*) mesquin; (*house*) délabré

shack [ʃæk] *s* cabane *f,* case *f*

shackle [′ʃækəl] *s* boucle *f;* **shackles** entraves *fpl* ‖ *tr* entraver

shad [ʃæd] *s* alose *f*

shade [ʃed] *s* (*shadow*) ombre *f;* (*of lamp*) abat-jour *m;* (*of window*) store *m;* (*hue; slight difference*) nuance *f;* (*little bit*) soupçon *m* ‖ *tr* ombrager; (*to make gradual changes in*) nuancer

shadow [′ʃædo] *s* ombre *f* ‖ *tr* ombrager; (*to spy on*) filer, pister

shad′ow cab′inet cabinet *m* fantôme

shadowy [′ʃædo•i] *adj* ombreux, sombre; (fig) vague, obscur

shad•y [′ʃedi] *adj* (*comp* **-ier;** *super* **-iest**) ombreux, ombragé; (coll) louche

shaft [ʃæft] *s* (*of mine; of elevator*) puits *m;* (*of feather*) tige *f;* (*of arrow*) bois *m;* (*of column*) fût *m,* tige; (*of flag*) mât *m;* (*of wagon*) brancard *m,* limon *m;* (*of motor*) arbre *m;* (*of light*) rayon *m;* (*to make fun of s.o.*) trait *m*

shag•gy [′ʃægi] *adj* (*comp* **-gier;** *super* **-giest**) poilu, à longs poils

shag′gy dog′ sto′ry *s* (*pl* **-ries**) histoire *f* sans queue ni tête

shagreen [ʃə′grin] *s* peau *f* de chagrin

shake [ʃek] *s* secousse *f;* **the shakes** frissons *mpl;* tremblement *m* alcoolique ‖ *v* (*pret* **shook** [ʃʊk];* *pp* **shaken**) *tr* secouer; (*the head*) hocher, secouer; (*one's hand*) serrer; **to shake down** faire tomber; (*a thermometer*) secouer; (slang) escroquer; **to shake off** secouer; (*to get rid of*) se débarrasser de; **to shake up** (*a liquid*) agiter; (fig) ébranler ‖ *intr* trembler

shake′ down′ *adj* (*cruise*) préparatoire, préliminaire ‖ *s* (*search*) fouille *f;* (*extortion*) extorsion *f,* chantage *m*

shaker [′ʃekər] *s* (*for salt*) salière *f;* (*for cocktails*) shaker *m*

shake′up′ *s* bouleversement *m;* (*reorganization*) remaniement *m*

shak•y [′ʃeki] *adj* (*comp* **-ier;** *super* **-iest**) tremblant, chancelant; (*hand; writing*) tremblé; (*voice*) tremblotant

shale [ʃel] *s* schiste *m* (argileux)

shall [ʃæl] *v* (*cond* **should** [ʃʊd]) *aux* used to express 1) the future indicative, e.g., **I shall arrive** j'arriverai; 2) the future perfect indicative, e.g., **I shall have arrived** je serai arrivé; 3) the potential mood, e.g., **what shall he do?** que doit-il faire?

shallow [′ʃælo] *adj* peu profond; (*dish*) plat; (fig) creux, superficiel ‖ **shallows** *spl* hautfond *m*

sham [ʃæm] *adj* feint, simulé ‖ *s* feinte *f,* simulacre *m;* (*person*) imposteur *m* ‖ *v* (*pret* & *pp* **shammed;** *ger* **shamming**) *tr* & *intr* feindre, simuler

sham′ bat′tle *s* combat *m* simulé

shambles [′ʃæmbəlz] *spl* boucherie *f;* ravage *m,* ruine *f;* (*disorder*) pagaille *f*

shame [ʃem] *s* honte *f;* **shame on you!, for shame!** quelle honte!; **what a shame!** quel dommage! ‖ *tr* faire honte à

shame′faced′ *adj* penaud, honteux

shameful [′ʃemfəl] *adj* honteux

shameless [′ʃemlɪs] *adj* éhonté

shampoo [ʃæm′pu] *s* shampooing *m* ‖ *tr* (*the hair*) shampouiner; (*a person*) faire un shampooing à

shampooer [ʃæ̃puər] *s* shampouineur *m,* shampouineuse *f*

shamrock [′ʃæmrɑk] *s* trèfle *m* d'Irlande

Shanghai [′ʃæŋhaɪ] *s* Changhaï ‖ (*l.c.*) *tr* (coll) racoler

Shangri-la [‚ʃæŋgrɪ′lɑ] *s* le pays de Cocagne

shank [ʃæŋk] *s* jambe *f,* tibia *m;* (*of horse*) canon *m;* (*of anchor*) verge *f;* (culin) manche *m;* (*of a column*) fût *m*

shan't *contr* **shall not**

shan•ty [′ʃænti] *s* (*pl* **-ties**) masure *f,* bicoque *f*

shan′ty•town′ *s* bidonville *m*

shape [ʃep] *s* forme *f;* **in bad shape** (coll) mal en point; **in good shape** (*physically*) en bonne tenue; **out of shape** déformé; **to take shape** prendre tournure; ‖ *tr* former ‖ *intr* se former; **to shape up** prendre forme; avancer

shapeless [′ʃeplɪs] *adj* informe

shape•ly [′ʃepli] *adj* (*comp* **-lier;** *super* **-liest**) bien proportionné, bien fait, svelte

share [ʃɛr] *s* part *f;* (*of stock in a company*) action *f* ‖ *tr* partager ‖ *intr*—**to share in** prendre part à, participer à

share′ certif′icate *s* titre *m* d'actions, certificat *m* d'actions

sharecropper [′ʃɛr‚krɑpər] *s* métayer *m*

share′hold′er *s* actionnaire *mf*

shark [ʃɑrk] *s* requin *m;* (*swindler*) escroc *m;* (slang) as *m,* expert *m*

sharp [ʃɑrp] *adj* (*point; pain; intelligence; voice, sound*) aigu; (*wind, cold, pain, fight, criticism, edge, trot; person, mind*) vif; (*knife*) tranchant; (*point; needle, pin, nail; tongue*) acéré; (*slope*) raide; (*curve*) prononcé; (*turn*) brusque; (*photograph*) net; (*hearing*) fin; (*step, gait*) rapide; (*eyesight*) perçant; (*taste*) piquant; (*reprimand*) vert; (*keen*) éveillé; (*cunning*) rusé, fin; (mus) dièse; (*stylish*) (coll) chic; **sharp features** traits *mpl* accentués ‖ *adv* vivement; brusquement; précis, sonnant, tapant, e.g., **at four o'clock sharp** à quatre heures précises, sonnantes, or tapantes; **to stop short** s'arrêter net or pile ‖ *s* (mus) dièse *m* ‖ *tr* (mus) diéser

sharpen [′ʃɑrpən] *tr* aiguiser; (*a pencil*) tailler ‖ *intr* s'aiguiser

sharpener [′ʃɑrpənər] *s* aiguisoir *m*

sharper [′ʃɑrpər] *s* filou *m,* tricheur *m*

sharp′shoot′er *s* tireur *m* d'élite

shatter [′ʃætər] *tr* fracasser, briser ‖ *intr* se fracasser, se briser

shat′ter•proof′ *adj* de sécurité

shave [ʃev] *s*—**to get a shave** se faire raser, se faire faire la barbe; **to have a close shave** (coll) l'échapper belle ‖ *tr* (*hair, beard, etc.*) raser; (*a person*) faire la barbe à, raser; (*e.g., wood*) doler; (*e.g., expenses*) rogner ‖ *intr* se raser, se faire la barbe

shaving [′ʃevɪŋ] *s* rasage *m;* **shavings** rognures *fpl,* copeaux *mpl*

shav′ing brush′ *s* blaireau *m*

shav′ing cream′ *s* crème *f* à raser

shav′ing foam′ *s* mousse *f* à raser

shav′ing lo′tion *s* (*aftershave*) lotion *f* aprèsrasage

shav′ing soap′ *s* savon *m* à barbe, savonnade *f*

shawl [ʃɔl] *s* châle *m,* fichu *m*

she [ʃi] *s* femelle *f* ‖ *pron pers* elle §85, §87; ce §82B; **she who** celle qui §83

sheaf [ʃif] *s* (*pl* **sheaves** [ʃivz]) gerbe *f;* (*of papers*) liasse *f*

shear [ʃir] *s* lame *f* de ciseau; **shears** ciseaux *mpl;* (*to cut metal*) cisaille *f* ‖ *v* (*pret* **sheared;** *pp* **sheared** or **shorn** [ʃorn]) *tr* (*sheep*) tondre; (*velvet*) ciseler; (*metal*) cisailler; **to shear off** couper

sheath [ʃiθ] *s* (*pl* **sheaths** [ʃiðz]) gaine *f,* fourreau *m*

sheathe [ʃið] *tr* envelopper; (*a sword*) rengainer

she'd *contr* **she would**

shed [ʃɛd] *s* (*warehouse; engine shed; barn*) hangar *m;* (*for, e.g., tools*) remise *f;* (*rough shelter*) hutte *f,* cabane *f;* (*for cattle*) étable *f;* (*line from which water flows in two directions*) ligne *f* de faîte ‖ *v* (*pret* & *pp* **shed;** *ger*

shedding) *tr* répandre, verser; (*e.g., leaves*) perdre; (*e.g., light; skin*) jeter

sheen [ʃin] *s* lustre *m*, brilliant *m*

sheep [ʃip] *s* (*pl* **sheep**) mouton *m*; (*ewe*) brebis *f*

sheep'dog' *s* chien *m* de berger

sheep'fold' *s* bergerie *f*

sheepish [ˈʃipɪʃ] *adj* penaud, honteux

sheep'skin' *s* (*undressed*) peau *f* de mouton; (*dressed*) basane *f*; (*diploma*) (coll) peau d'âne

sheep'skin jack'et *s* canadienne *f*

sheer [ʃɪr] *adj* (*stocking*) extra-fin; (*steep*) à pic; (*impossibility; necessity; waste of time*) absolu; (*utter*) pur; (fig) vif, e.g., **by sheer force** de vive force ‖ *intr* faire une embardée

sheet [ʃit] *s* (*e.g., for the bed*) drap *m*; (*of paper*) feuille *f*; (*of metal*) tôle *f*, lame *f*; (*of water*) nappe *f*; (*of ice*) couche *f*; (naut) écoute *f*; **white as a sheet** blanc comme un linge

sheet' light'ning *s* fulguration *f*, éclairs *mpl* en nappe

sheet' met'al *s* tôle *f*

sheet' mu'sic *s* morceaux *mpl* de musique

sheik [ʃik] *s* cheik *m*; (coll) tombeur *m* de femmes

shelf [ʃɛlf] *s* (*pl* **shelves** [ʃɛlvz]) tablette *f*, planche *f*; (*of cupboard; of library*) rayon *m*; (geog) plateau *m*; **on the shelf** (*inactive*) (coll) au rancart, laissé à l'écart; **shelves** rayonnages *mpl*

she'll *contr* **she will**

shell [ʃɛl] *s* (*of egg, nut, oyster, snail, etc.*) coque *f*, coquille *f*; (*of nut*) écale *f*, coque; (*of pea*) cosse *f*; (*of oyster, clam, etc.*) écaille *f*; (*of tortoise, lobster, crab*) carapace *f*; (*of building, ship, etc.*) carcasse *f*; (*cartridge*) cartouche *f*; (*projectile*) obus *m*; (*long, narrow racing boat*) yole *f*, outrigger *m* ‖ *tr* écaler, écosser; (mil) bombarder, pilonner; **to shell out** (coll) débourser ‖ *intr*—**to shell out** (coll) casquer

shel•lac [ʃəˈlæk] *s* laque *f*, gomme *f* laque ‖ *v* (*pret & pp* **-lacked;** *ger* **-lacking**) *tr* laquer; (slang) tabasser

shell'fish' *s* fruits *mpl* de mer, coquillages *mpl*

shell' hole' *s* entonnoir *m*, trou *m* d'obus

shell' shock' *s* commotion *f* cérébrale

shelter [ˈʃɛltər] *s* abri *m* ‖ *tr* abriter

shelve [ʃɛlv] *tr* (*a place*) ranger; (*merchandise*) entreposer; (*a project, a question, etc., by putting it aside*) enterrer, classer; (*to provide with shelves*) garnir de tablettes, rayons, or planches

shelving [ˈʃɛlvɪŋ] *s* rayonnage *m*, étagères *fpl*

shepherd [ˈʃɛpərd] *s* berger *m*; (fig) pasteur *m* ‖ *tr* veiller sur, guider

shep'herd dog' *s* berger *m*, chien *m* de berger

shepherdess [ˈʃɛpərdɪs] *s* bergère *f*

sherbet [ˈʃɑrbət] *s* sorbet *m*

sheriff [ˈʃɛrɪf] *s* shérif *m*

sher•ry [ˈʃɛri] *s* (*pl* **-ries**) xérès *m*

she's *contr* **she is; she has**

shield [ʃild] *s* bouclier *m*; (elec) blindage *m*; (heral, hist) écu *m*, écusson *m* ‖ *tr* protéger; (elec) blinder

shift [ʃift] *s* (*change*) changement *m*; (*in wind, temperature, etc.*) saute *f*; (*group of workmen*) équipe *f* de relais; (fig) expédient *m* ‖ *tr* changer; (*the blame, the guilt, etc.*) rejeter; **to shift gears** changer de vitesse ‖ *intr* changer; changer de place; changer de direction; **to shift for oneself** se débrouiller tout seul

shift' key' *s* touche *f* majuscules

shiftless [ˈʃiftlɪs] *adj* mollasse, peu débrouillard

shift'-lock' key' *s* fixe-majuscules *m*

shift•y [ˈʃifti] *adj* (*comp* **-ier;** *super* **-iest**) roublard; (*look*) chafouin; (*eye*) fuyant

Shiite [ˈʃiˌaɪt] *adj & s* chiite *mf*

shimmer [ˈʃimər] *s* chatoiement *m*, miroitement *m* ‖ *intr* chatoyer, miroiter

shin [ʃin] *s* tibia *m*; (culin) jarret *m* ‖ *v* (*pret & pp* **shinned;** *ger* **shinning**) *intr*—**to shin up** grimper

shin'bone' *s* tibia *m*

shine [ʃaɪn] *s* (*shining*) éclat *m*, brillant *m*; (*of cloth, clothing, etc.*) luisant *m*; (*on shoes*) coup *m* de cirage; **to take a shine to** (slang) s'enticher de ‖ *v* (*pret & pp* **shined**) *tr* faire briller, faire reluire; (*shoes*) cirer ‖ *v* (*pret & pp* **shone** [ʃon]) *intr* briller, reluire

shiner [ˈʃaɪnər] *s* (slang) œil *m* poché

shingle [ˈʃiŋgəl] *s* bardeau *m*; (*of doctor, lawyer, etc.*) (coll) enseigne *f*; **shingles** (pathol) zona *m*

shining [ˈʃaɪnɪŋ] *adj* brillant, luisant

shin•y [ˈʃaɪni] *adj* (*comp* **-ier;** *super* **-iest**) brillant, reluisant; (*from much wear*) lustré

ship [ʃip] *s* navire *m*; (*steamer, liner*) paquebot *m*; (aer) appareil *m*; (nav) bâtiment *m* ‖ *v* (*pret & pp* **shipped;** *ger* **shipping**) *tr* expédier; (*a cargo; water*) embarquer; (*oars*) armer, rentrer ‖ *intr* s'embarquer

ship'board' *s* bord *m*; **on shipboard** à bord

ship'build'er *s* constructeur *m* de navires

ship'build'ing *s* construction *f* navale

ship'mate' *s* compagnon *m* de bord

shipment [ˈʃipmənt] *s* expédition *f*; (*goods shipped*) chargement *m*

ship'own'er *s* armateur *m*

shipper [ˈʃipər] *s* expéditeur *m*

shipping [ˈʃipɪŋ] *s* embarquement *m*, expédition *f*; (naut) transport *m* maritime

ship'ping clerk' *s* expéditionnaire *mf*

ship'ping mem'o *s* connaissement *m*

ship'ping room' *s* salle *f* d'expédition

ship'shape' *adj & adv* en bon ordre

ship's' pa'pers *spl* papiers *mpl* de bord

ships' time' *s* heure *f* locale du navire

ship'-to-shore' ra'di•o [ˈʃiptəˌʃor] *s* (*pl* **-os**) liaison *f* radio maritime

ship'wreck' *s* naufrage *m* ‖ *tr* faire naufrager ‖ *intr* faire naufrage

ship'yard' *s* chantier *m* de construction navale or maritime

shirk [ʃʌrk] *tr* manquer à, esquiver ‖ *intr* négliger son devoir

shirred' eggs' [ʃʌrd] *spl* œufs *mpl* pochés à la crème

shirt [ʃʌrt] *s* chemise *f*; **keep your shirt on!** (slang) ne vous emballez pas!; **to lose one's shirt** perdre jusqu'à son dernier sou

shirt'band' *s* encolure *f*

shirt' front' *s* plastron *m* de chemise

shirt' sleeve' *s* manche *f* de chemise; **in shirt sleeves** en bras de chemise

shirt'tails' *spl* pans *mpl* de chemise

shirt'waist' *s* chemisier *m*

shiver [ˈʃivər] *s* frisson *m* ‖ *intr* frissonner

shoal [ʃol] *s* banc *m*, bas-fond *m*

shock [ʃɑk] *s* (*bump, clash*) choc *m*, heurt *m*; (*upset, misfortune; earthquake tremor*) secousse *f*; (*of grain*) gerbe *f*, moyette *f*; (*of hair*) tignasse *f*; (elec) commotion *f*, choc; **to die of shock** mourir de saisissement ‖ *tr* choquer; (elec) commotionner, choquer

shock' absorb'er [æb,sɔrbər] *s* amortisseur *m*

shocking [ˈʃɑkɪŋ] *adj* choquant, scandaleux

shock' troops' *spl* troupes *fpl* de choc

shod•dy [ˈʃɑdi] *adj* (*comp* -dier; *super* -diest) inférieur, de pacotille

shoe [ʃu] *s* soulier *m*; **to be in the shoes of** être dans la peau de; **to put one's shoes on** se chausser; **to take one's shoes off** se déchausser ‖ *v* (*pret & pp* shod [ʃɑd]) *tr* chausser; (*a horse*) ferrer

shoe'black' *s* cireur *m* de bottes

shoe'horn' *s* chausse-pied *m*

shoe'lace' *s* lacet *m*, cordon *m* de soulier

shoe'mak'er *s* cordonnier *m*

shoe' pol'ish *s* cirage *m* de chaussures

shoe'shine' *s* cirage *m*

shoe' store' *s* magasin *m* de chaussures

shoe'string' *s* lacet *m*, cordon *m* de soulier; **on a shoestring** avec de minces capitaux

shoe'tree' *s* embauchoir *m*, forme *f*

shoo [ʃu] *tr* chasser ‖ *interj* ch!, filez!

shoot [ʃut] *s* (*sprout, twig*) rejeton *m*, pousse *f*; (*for grain, sand, etc.*) goulotte *f*; (*contest*) concours *m* de tir; (*hunting party*) partie *f* de chasse ‖ *v* (*pret & pp* shot [ʃɑt]) *tr* tirer; (*a person*) tuer d'un coup de fusil; (*to execute with a discharge of rifles*) fusiller; (*with a camera*) photographier; (*a scene; a motion picture*) tourner, roder; (*the sun*) prendre la hauteur de; (*dice*) jeter; **to shoot down** abattre; **to shoot up** (slang) cribler de balles ‖ *intr* tirer; s'élancer, se précipiter; (*said of pain*) lanciner; (*said of star*) filer; **to shoot at** faire feu sur; (*to strive for*) viser; **to shoot up** (*said of plant*) pousser; (*said of flame*) jaillir; (*said of prices*) augmenter; (*intravenously*) (slang) se shooter

shooting [ˈʃutɪŋ] *s* tir *m*; (phot) prise *f* de vues

shoot'ing gal'ler•y *s* (*pl* -ies) stand *m* de tir, tir *m*

shoot'ing match' *s* concours *m* de tir

shoot'ing script' *s* découpage *m*

shoot'ing star' *s* étoile *f* filante

shop [ʃɑp] *s* (*store*) boutique *f*; (*workshop*) atelier *m*; **to talk shop** parler boutique, parler affaires ‖ *v* (*pret & pp* shopped; *ger* shopping) *intr* faire des emplettes, faire des courses; magasiner (Canad); **to go shopping** faire des emplettes, faire des courses, faire des achats; **to shop around** être à l'affût de bonnes occasions; **to shop for** chercher à acheter

shop'girl' *s* vendeuse *f*

shop'keep'er *s* boutiquier *m*

shoplifter [ˈʃɑp,lɪftər] *s* voleur *m* à l'étalage

shop'lift'ing *s* vol *m* à l'étalage

shopper [ˈʃɑpər] *s* acheteur *m*

shopping [ˈʃɑpɪŋ] *s* achat *m*; (*purchases*) achats *mpl*, emplettes *fpl*

shop'ping bag' *s* sac *m* à provisions, cabas *m*

shop'ping cen'ter *s* centre *m* commercial

shop'ping dis'trict *s* quartier *m* commerçant

shop'ping mall' *s* galerie *f* marchande

shop' stew'ard *s* délégué *m* d'atelier

shop'win'dow *s* vitrine *f*, devanture *f*

shop'worn' *adj* défraîchi

shore [ʃor] *s* rivage *m*, rive *f*, bord *m*; (*sandy beach*) plage *f*; **shores** (poetic) pays *m* ‖ *tr*—**to shore up** étayer

shore' din'ner *s* dîner *m* de marée

shore' leave' *s* (nav) descente *f* à terre

shore'line' *s* ligne *f* de côte

shore' patrol' *s* patrouille *f* de garde-côte; (*police*) (nav) police *f* militaire de la marine

short [ʃɔrt] *adj* court; (*person*) petit; (*temper*) brusque; (phonet) bref; **in short** en somme; **short of breath** poussif; **to be short for** (coll) être le diminutif de; **to be short of** être à court de ‖ *s* (elec) court-circuit *m*; (mov) court-métrage *m*; **shorts** culotte *f* courte, culotte de sport ‖ *adv* court, de court; **to run short of** être à court de, manquer de; **to sell short** (com) vendre à découvert; **to stop short** s'arrêter net ‖ *tr* (elec) court-circuiter ‖ *intr* (elec) se mettre en court-circuit

shortage [ˈʃɔrtɪdʒ] *s* manque *m*, pénurie *f*; crise *f*, e.g., **housing shortage** crise du logement; (com) déficit *m*; **shortages** manquants *mpl*

short'cake' *s* gâteau *m* recouvert de fruits frais

short'-change' *tr* ne pas rendre assez de monnaie à; (*to cheat*) (coll) rouler

short' cir'cuit *s* court-circuit *m*

short'-cir'cuit *tr* court-circuiter

short'com'ing *s* défaut *m*

short'cut' *s* raccourci *m*

shorten [ˈʃɔrtən] *tr* raccourcir ‖ *intr* se raccourcir

shortening [ˈʃɔrtənɪŋ] *s* raccourcissement *m*; (culin) saindoux *m*

short'hand' *adj* sténographique ‖ *s* sténographie *f*; **to take down in shorthand** sténographier

short'hand notes' *spl* sténogramme *m*

short'hand typ'ist *s* sténodactylo *mf*

short-lived [ˈʃɔrtˈlaɪvd], [ˈʃɔrtˈlɪvd] *adj* de courte durée, bref

shortly [ˈʃɔrtli] *adv* tantôt, sous peu; brièvement; (*curtly*) sèchement; **shortly after** peu après

short'-range' *adj* à courte portée

short'-range plane' *s* court-courrier *m*

short' sale' *s* vente *f* à découvert

short'-sight'ed *adj* myope; **to be short-sighted** (fig) avoir la vue courte

short' sto'ry *s* nouvelle *f,* conte *m*

short'-tem'pered *adj* vif, emporté

short'-term' *adj* à court terme

short' wave' *adj* aux petites ondes, aux ondes courtes ‖ *s* petite onde *f,* onde courte

short' weight' *s* poids *m* insuffisant

shot [ʃɑt] *adj* (*silk*) changeant; (*e.g., chances*) (coll) réduit à zéro; (*drunk*) (slang) paf ‖ *s* coup *m* de feu, décharge *f;* (*marksman*) tireur *m;* (*pellets*) petits plombs *mpl;* (*of a rocket into space*) lancement *m,* tir *m;* (*in certain games*) shoot *m;* (*snapshot*) instantané *m;* (mov) plan *m;* (*hypodermic injection*) (coll) piqûre *f;* (*drink of liquor*) (slang) verre *m* d'alcool; **a long shot** un gros risque, une chance sur mille; **to fire a shot at** tirer sur; **to start like a shot** partir comme un trait

shot'gun' *s* fusil *m* de chasse

shot'-put' *s* (sports) lancement *m* du poids

should [ʃʊd] *aux* used to express 1) the present conditional, e.g., **if I waited for him, I should miss the train** si je l'attendais, je manquerais le train; 2) the past conditional, e.g., **if I had waited for him, I should have missed the train** si je l'avais attendu, j'aurais manqué le train; 3) the potential mood, e.g., **he should go at once** il devrait aller aussitôt; e.g., **he should have gone at once** il aurait dû aller aussitôt; 4) a softened affirmation, e.g., **I should like a drink** je prendrais bien quelque chose à boire; e.g., **I should have thought that you would have known better** j'aurais cru que vous auriez été plus avisé

shoulder [ˈʃoldər] *s* épaule *f;* (*of a road*) accotement *m;* **across the shoulder** en bandoulière, en écharpe; **shoulders** (*of a garment*) carrure *f;* **to cry on someone's shoulder** pleurer dans le gilet de qn ‖ *tr* (*a gun*) mettre sur l'épaule; **to shoulder aside** pousser de l'épaule

shoul'der blade' *s* omoplate *f*

shoul'der strap' *s* (*of underwear*) épaulette *f;* (mil) bandoulière *f*

shouldn't *contr* **should not**

shout [ʃaʊt] *s* cri *m* ‖ *tr* crier; **to shout down** huer ‖ *intr* crier

shove [ʃʌv] *s* poussée *f,* bourrade *f* ‖ *tr* pousser, bousculer ‖ *intr* pousser; **to shove off** pousser au large; (slang) filer, décamper

shov•el [ˈʃʌvəl] *s* pelle *f* ‖ *v* (*pret & pp* **-eled** or **-elled;** *ger* **-eling** or **-elling**) *tr* pelleter; (*e.g., snow*) balayer

show [ʃo] *s* (*of hatred or affection*) démonstration *f;* (*semblance*) apparence *f;* (*exhibition*) exposition *f;* (*display*) étalage *m,* parade *f;* (*of hands*) levée *f;* (*each performance*) séance *f;* (mov) film *m;* (theat) spectacle *m;* **by show of hands** à main levée; **to make a show of** faire parade de ‖ *v* (*pret* **showed;** *pp* **shown** [ʃon] or **showed**) *tr* montrer; (*one's passport*) présenter; (*a film*) projeter; (*e.g., to the door*) conduire; **to show off** faire étalage de; (*attract attention*) frimer; **to show up** (coll) démasquer ‖ *intr* se montrer; **to show through** transparaître; **to show up** (*against a background*) ressortir; (coll) faire son apparition

show' bill' *s* affiche *f*

show'boat' *s* bateau-théâtre *m*

show' busi'ness *s* l'industrie *f* du spectacle

show'case' *s* vitrine *f*

show'down' *s* cartes *fpl* sur table, moment *m* critique; **to come to a showdown** en venir au fait; **to force a showdown** mettre au pied du mur

shower [ˈʃaʊ•ər] *s* averse *f,* ondée *f;* (*of blows, bullets, kisses, etc.*) pluie *f;* (*bath*) douche *f* ‖ *tr* faire pleuvoir; **to shower with** combler de ‖ *intr* pleuvoir à verse

show' girl' *s* girl *f*

show'man *s* (*pl* **-men**) impresario *m;* **he's a great showman** c'est un as pour la mise en scène

show'-off' *s* (coll) m'as-tu-vu *m*

show'piece' *s* pièce *f* maîtresse

show'place' *s* lieu *m* célèbre

show'room' *s* salon *m* d'exposition

show' win'dow *s* vitrine *f*

show•y [ˈʃo•i] *adj* (*comp* **-ier;** *super* **-iest**) fastueux; (*gaudy*) voyant

shrapnel [ˈʃræpnəl] *s* shrapnel *m,* obus *m* à mitraille; éclat *m* d'obus

shred [ʃrɛd] *s* morceau *m,* lambeau *m;* **not a shred of** pas l'ombre de; **to tear to shreds** mettre en lambeaux ‖ *v* (*pret & pp* **shredded** or **shred;** *ger* **shredding**) *tr* mettre en lambeaux, déchiqueter

shrew [ʃru] *s* (*nagging woman*) mégère *f;* (zool) musaraigne *f*

shrewd [ʃrud] *adj* sagace, fin

shriek [ʃrik] *s* cri *m* perçant ‖ *intr* pousser un cri perçant

shrike [ʃraɪk] *s* pie-grièche *f*

shrill [ʃrɪl] *adj* aigu, perçant

shrimp [ʃrɪmp] *s* crevette *f;* (*insignificant person*) gringalet *m*

shrine [ʃraɪn] *s* tombeau *m* de saint; (*reliquary*) châsse *f;* (*holy place*) lieu *m* saint, sanctuaire *m*

shrink [ʃrɪŋk] *v* (*pret* **shrank** [ʃræŋk] or **shrunk** [ʃrʌŋk];* *pp* **shrunk** or **shrunken**) *tr* rétrécir ‖ *intr* se rétrécir; **to shrink away** or **back from** reculer devant

shrinkage [ˈʃrɪŋkɪdʒ] *s* rétrécissement *m*

shriv•el [ˈʃrɪvəl] *v* (*pret & pp* **-eled** or **-elled;** *ger* **-eling** or **-elling**) *tr* ratatiner, recroqueviller ‖ *intr* se ratatiner, se recroqueviller

shroud [ʃraʊd] *s* linceul *m;* (*veil*) voile *m;*

shrouds (naut) haubans *mpl* ‖ *tr* ensevelir; voiler

Shrove′ Tues′day [ˌʃrov] *s* mardi *m* gras

shrub [ʃrʌb] *s* arbuste *m*

shrubber•y [ˈʃrʌbəri] *s* (*pl* **-ies**) bosquet *m*

shrug [ʃrʌg] *s* haussement *m* d'épaules ‖ *v* (*pret & pp* **shrugged;** *ger* **shrugging**) *tr* (*one's shoulders*) hausser; **to shrug off** minimiser; ne tenir aucun compte de ‖ *intr* hausser les épaules

shudder [ˈʃʌdər] *s* frisson *m*, frémissement *m* ‖ *intr* frissonner, frémir

shuffle [ˈʃʌfəl] *s* (*of cards*) battement *m*, mélange *m;* (*of feet*) frottement *m;* (*change of place*) déplacement *m* ‖ *tr* (*cards*) battre; (*the feet*) traîner; (*to mix up*) mêler, brouiller ‖ *intr* battre les cartes; traîner les pieds

shuf′fle•board *s* jeu *m* de palets

shun [ʃʌn] *v* (*pret & pp* **shunned;** *ger* **shunning**) *tr* éviter, fuir

shunt [ʃʌnt] *tr* garer, manœuvrer; (elec) shunter, dériver

shut [ʃʌt] *adj* fermé ‖ *v* (*pret & pp* **shut;** *ger* **shutting**) *tr* fermer; **to shut in** enfermer; **to shut off** couper; **to shut out** (baseball) blanchir; **to shut up** enfermer; (coll) faire taire, clouer le bec à ‖ *intr* se fermer; **shut up!** (slang) tais-toi!, ferme-la!

shut′down′ *s* fermeture *f*

shut′out′ *s* (baseball) blanchissage *m*

shutter [ˈʃʌtər] *s* volet *m*, contrevent *m;* (*over store window*) rideau *m;* (phot) obturateur *m*

shuttle [ˈʃʌtəl] *s* navette *f* ‖ *intr* faire la navette

shut′tle train′ *s* navette *f*

shy [ʃaɪ] *adj* (*comp* **shyer** or **shier;** *super* **shyest** or **shiest**) timide, sauvage; (*said of horse*) ombrageux; **I am shy a dollar** il me faut un dollar; **to be shy of** se méfier de ‖ *v* (*pret & pp* **shied**) *intr* (*said of horse*) faire un écart; **to shy away from** éviter

shyster [ˈʃaɪstər] *s* (coll) avocat *m* marron

Sia•mese [ˌsaɪə̍miz] *adj* siamois ‖ *s* (*pl* **-mese**) Siamois *m*

Si′amese twins′ *spl* frères *mpl* siamois

Siberian [saɪˈbɪriən] *adj* sibérien ‖ *s* Sibérien *m*

sibling [ˈsɪblɪŋ] *s* parent *m* frère-sœur

sibyl [ˈsɪbɪl] *s* sibylle *f*

sic [sik] *adv* sic ‖ [sɪk] *v* (*pret & pp* **sicked;** *ger* **sicking**) *tr*—**sic 'em!** (coll) pille!; **to sic on** lancer après

Sicilian [sɪˈsiljən] *adj* sicilien ‖ *s* Sicilien *m*

Sicily [ˈsɪsɪli] *s* Sicile *f;* la Sicile

sick [sɪk] *adj* malade; **to be sick and tired of** (coll) en avoir plein le dos de, en avoir marre de; **to be sick at** or **to one's stomach** avoir mal au cœur, avoir des nausées; **to take sick** tomber malade

sick′bed′ *s* lit *m* de malade

sicken [ˈsɪkən] *tr* rendre malade ‖ *intr* tomber malade; (*to be disgusted*) être écœuré

sickening [ˈsɪkənɪŋ] *adj* écœurant, dégoûtant

sick′ head′ache *s* migraine *f* avec nausées

sickle [ˈsɪkəl] *s* faucille *f*

sick′ leave′ *s* congé *m* de maladie

sick′le cell′ ane′mia *s* (pathol) drépanocytose *f*

sick•ly [ˈsɪkli] *adj* (*comp* **-lier;** *super* **-liest**) maladif, débile

sickness [ˈsɪknɪs] *s* maladie *f;* nausée *f*

side [saɪd] *adj* latéral, de côté ‖ *s* côté *m;* (*of phonograph*) face *f;* (*of team, government, etc.*) camp *m,* parti *m,* côté; **this side up** (*on package*) haut ‖ *intr*—**to side with** prendre le parti de

side′ arm deliv′ery *s* (baseball) lancer *m* latéral

side′ arms′ *spl* armes *fpl* de ceinturon

side′board′ *s* buffet *m*, desserte *f*

side′burns′ *spl* favoris *mpl*

side′ dish′ *s* plat *m* d'accompagnement

side′ door′ *s* porte *f* latérale, porte *f* de service

side′ effect′ *s* effet *m* secondaire

side′ en′trance *s* entrée *f* latérale

side′ glance′ *s* regard *m* de côté

side′ is′sue *s* question *f* d'intérêt secondaire

side′line *s* occupation *f* secondaire; **on the sidelines** sans y prendre part

sidereal [saɪˈdɪriəl] *adj* sidéral

side′ road′ *s* chemin *m* de traverse

side′sad′dle *adv* en amazone

side′ show′ *s* spectacle *m* forain; (fig) événement *m* secondaire

side′slip′ *s* glissade *f* sur l'aile

side′split′ting *adj* désopilant

side′ step′ *s* écart *m*

side′-step′ *v* (*pret & pp* **-stepped;** *ger* **-stepping**) *tr* éviter ‖ *intr* faire un pas de côté

side′stroke′ *s* nage *f* sur le côté

side′ ta′ble *s* console *f*

side′track′ *s* voie *f* de garage ‖ *tr* écarter, dévier; (rr) aiguiller sur une voie de garage

side′ view′ *s* vue *f* de profil

side′walk′ *s* trottoir *m*

side′walk café′ *s* terrasse *f* de café

side′walk sale′ *s* vente *f* à l'éventaire

sideward [ˈsaɪdwərd] *adj* latéral ‖ *adv* latéralement, de côté

side′ways′ *adj* latéral ‖ *adv* latéralement, de côté

side′ whisk′ers *spl* favoris *mpl*

side′wise′ *adj* latéral ‖ *adv* latéralement, de côté

siding [ˈsaɪdɪŋ] *s* (*on a house*) bardage *m;* (rr) voie *f* d'évitement, voie *f* de garage

sidle [ˈsaɪdəl] *intr* avancer de biais; **to sidle up to** se couler auprès de

siege [sidʒ] *s* siège *m;* **to lay siege to** mettre le siège devant

siesta [siˈɛstə] *s* sieste *f;* **to take a siesta** faire la sieste

sieve [sɪv] *s* crible *m*, tamis *m* ‖ *tr* passer au crible, passer au tamis

sift [sɪft] *tr* passer au crible, passer au tamis; (*flour*) tamiser; (fig) examiner soigneusement

sigh [saɪ] *s* soupir *m* ‖ *intr* soupirer

sight [saɪt] *s* vue *f;* (*of firearm*) mire *f;* (*of telescope, camera, etc.*) viseur *m;* chose *f* digne d'être vue; **a sight of** (coll) énormément de; **at sight** à vue; à livre ouvert; **by sight de**, **in sight of** à la vue de; **sad sight** spectacle *m* navrant; **sights** curiosités *fpl;* **to catch sight of** apercevoir; **what a sight you are!** comme vous voilà fait! ‖ *tr & intr* viser

sight′ draft′ *s* (com) effet *m* à vue

sight′ less *adj* aveugle

sight′-read′ *v* (*pret & pp* **read** [ˌrɛd]) *tr & intr* lire à livre ouvert; (mus) déchiffrer

sight′ read′er *m* déchiffreur *m*

sight′see′ing *s* tourisme *m;* **to go sightseeing** visiter les curiosités

sightseer [ˈsaɪtˌsiˑər] *s* touriste *mf,* excursionniste *mf*

sign [saɪn] *s* signe *m;* (*on a store*) enseigne *f* ‖ *tr* signer; **to sign up** engager, embaucher ‖ *intr* signer; **to sign off** (rad) terminer l'émission; **to sign up for** (coll) s'inscrire à

sig•nal [ˈsɪɡnəl] *adj* signalé, insigne ‖ *s* signal *m* ‖ *v* (*pret & pp* **-naled** or **-nalled;** *ger* **-naling** or **-nalling**) *tr* faire signe à, signaler ‖ *intr* faire des signaux

sig′nal tow′er *s* tour *f* de signalisation

signature [ˈsɪɡnətʃər] *s* signature *f;* (bb) cahier *m* (d'imprimerie); (mus) armature *f;* (rad) indicatif *m*

sign′board′ *s* panneau *m* d'affichage

signer [ˈsaɪnər] *s* signataire *mf*

sig′net ring′ [ˈsɪɡnɪt] *s* chevalière *f*

significance [sɪɡˈnɪfɪkəns] *s* importance *f;* (*meaning*) signification *f*

significant [sɪɡˈnɪfəkənt] *adj* important; significatif

signi•fy [ˈsɪɡnɪˌfaɪ] *v* (*pret & pp* **-fied**) *tr* signifier

sign′ lan′guage *s* langage *m* gestuel, langage par signes; **to talk in sign language** parler par signes

Sign′ of the Cross′ *s* (eccl) signe *m* de la Croix

sign′post′ *s* poteau *m* indicateur

Sikh [sik] *adj & s* Sikh *mf*

silence [ˈsaɪləns] *s* silence *m* ‖ *tr* faire taire, réduire au silence

silencer [ˈsaɪlənsər] *s* (*of a gun*) silencieux *m*

silent [ˈsaɪlənt] *adj* silencieux

si′lent major′ity *s* majorité *f* silencieuse

si′lent mov′ie *s* film *m* muet

silhouette [ˌsɪluˈɛt] *s* silhouette *f* ‖ *tr* silhouetter

silicon [ˈsɪlɪkən] *s* silicium *m*

sil′icon chip′ *s* plaquette *f* de silicium

silicone [ˈsɪlɪˌkon] *s* silicone *f*

silk [sɪlk] *s* soie *f*

silk′-cotton tree′ *s* fromager *m*

silken [ˈsɪlkən] *adj* soyeux

silk′ hat′ *s* haut-de-forme *m*

silk′-stock′ing *adj* aristocratique ‖ *s* aristocrate *mf*

silk′worm′ *s* ver *m* à soie

silk•y [ˈsɪlki] *adj* (*comp* **-ier;** *super* **-iest**) soyeux

sill [sɪl] *s* (*of window*) rebord *m;* (*of door*) seuil *m;* (*of walls*) sablière *f*

sil•ly [ˈsɪli] *adj* (*comp* **-lier;** *super* **-liest**) sot, niais

si•lo [ˈsaɪlo] *s* (*pl* **-los**) silo *m* ‖ *tr* ensiler

silt [sɪlt] *s* vase *f*

silver [ˈsɪlvər] *s* argent *m* ‖ *tr* argenter; (*a mirror*) étamer

sil′ver-fish′ *s* (ent) poisson *m* d'argent

sil′ver foil′ *s* feuille *f* d'argent

sil′ver lin′ing *s* beau côté *m,* côté brillant

sil′ver plate′ *s* argenterie *f*

sil′ver screen′ *s* écran *m*

sil′ver•smith′ *s* orfèvre *m*

sil′ver spoon′ *s*—**born with a silver spoon in one's mouth** né coiffé

sil′ver-tongued′ *adj* à la langue dorée, éloquent

sil′ver•ware′ *s* argenterie *f*

similar [ˈsɪmɪlər] *adj* semblable

similari•ty [ˌsɪmɪˈlærɪti] *s* (*pl* **-ties**) ressemblance *f,* similitude *f*

simile [ˈsɪmɪli] *s* comparaison *f*

simmer [ˈsɪmər] *tr* mijoter ‖ *intr* mijoter; **to simmer down** s'apaiser

Simon [ˈsaɪmən] *s* Simon *m;* **Simon says . . .** (game) Caporal a dit . . .

simper [ˈsɪmpər] *s* sourire *m* niais ‖ *intr* sourire bêtement

simple [ˈsɪmpəl] *adj & s* simple *m*

sim′ple-mind′ed *adj* simple, naïf; niais

sim′ple sub′stance *s* (chem) corps *m* simple

simpleton [ˈsɪmpəltən] *s* niais *m*

simpli•fy [ˈsɪmplɪˌfaɪ] *v* (*pret & pp* **-fied**) *tr* simplifier

simulate [ˈsɪmjəˌlet] *tr* simuler

simulator [ˈsɪmjəˌletər] *s* (comp) simulateur *m*

simultaneous [ˌsaɪməlˈtenɪˑəs] *adj* simultané

si′multa′neous transla′tion *s* traduction *f* en simultanée

sin [sɪn] *s* péché *m* ‖ *v* (*pret & pp* **sinned;** *ger* **sinning**) *intr* pécher

since [sɪns] *adv & prep* depuis ‖ *conj* depuis que; (*inasmuch as*) puisque

sincere [sɪnˈsɪr] *adj* sincère

Sincere′ly yours′ [sɪnˈsɪrli] *adv* bien à vous, cordialement à vous; (formal) Je vous prie d'agréer, (*Monsieur, Madame, etc.*), l'expression de mes sentiments les meilleurs (or: de ma profonde considération); (*man to woman*) Je vous prie d'agréer, Madame, mes très respectueux hommages

sincerity [sɪnˈsɛrɪti] *s* sincérité *f*

sine [saɪn] *s* (trig) sinus *m*

sinecure [ˈsaɪnɪˌkjʊr] *s* sinécure *f*

sinew [ˈsɪnju] *s* tendon *m;* (fig) nerf *m,* force *f*

sinful [ˈsɪnfəl] *adj* (*person*) pécheur; (*act, intention*) coupable

sing [sɪŋ] *v* (*pret* **sang** [sæŋ] or **sung** [sʌŋ]; *pp* **sung**) *tr & intr* chanter

singe [sɪndʒ] *v* (*ger* **singeing**) *tr* roussir; (*poultry*) flamber

singer [ˈsɪŋər] *s* chanteur *m*

single [ˈsɪŋɡəl] *adj* seul, unique; (*unmarried*) célibataire; (*e.g., room in a hotel*) à un lit;

(*bed*) à une place; (*e.g., devotion*) simple, honnête ‖ *tr*—**to single out** distinguer, choisir

sin′gle bless′edness [ˈblɛsɪdnɪs] *s* le bonheur *m* du célibat

sin′gle•breast′ed *adj* droit

sin′gle-en′try *adj* (bk) en partie simple

sin′gle-en′try book′keeping *s* comptabilité *f* simple

sin′gle file′ *s*—**in single file** en file indienne, à la file

sin′gle-hand′ed *adj* sans aide, tout seul

sin′gle life′ *s* vie *f* de célibataire

sin′gle par′ent *s* mère *f* seule (*qui élève ses enfants sans partenaire*); père *m* seul (*qui élève ses enfants sans partenaire*)

sin′gle par′ent fam′ily *s* famille *f* monoparentale

sin′gle room′ *s* chambre *f* à un lit

sin′gle-spaced′ *s* à simple interligne

sin′gle-track′ *adj* (rr) à voie unique; (coll) d'une portée limitée

sing′song′ *adj* monotone ‖ *s* mélopée *f*

singular [ˈsɪŋgjələr] *adj* & *s* singulier *m*

sinister [ˈsɪnɪstər] *adj* sinistre

sink [sɪŋk] *s* (*in kitchen or laundry*) évier *m*; (*in bathroom*) lavabo *m*; (*drain*) égout *m* ‖ *v* (*pret* **sank** [sæŋk] *or* **sunk** [sʌŋk]; *pp* **sunk**) *tr* enfoncer; (*a ship*) couler, faire sombrer; (*a well*) creuser; (*money*) immobiliser ‖ *intr* s'enfoncer, s'affaisser; (*under the water*) couler, sombrer; (*said of heart*) se serrer; (*said of health, prices, sun, etc.*) baisser; **to sink into** plonger dans; (*an armchair*) s'effondrer dans

sink′ing fund′ *s* caisse *f* d'amortissement

sink′hole′ *s* (fig) cloaque *m* de vice

sinless [ˈsɪnlɪs] *adj* sans péché

sinner [ˈsɪnər] *s* pécheur *m*

sintering [ˈsɪntərɪŋ] *s* (metallurgy) frittage *m*

sinuous [ˈsɪnjʊ•əs] *adj* sinueux

sinus [ˈsaɪnəs] *s* sinus *m*

sip [sɪp] *s* petite gorgée *f*, petit coup *m* ‖ *v* (*pret* & *pp* **sipped;** *ger* **sipping**) *tr* boire à petit coups, siroter

siphon [ˈsaɪfən] *s* siphon *m* ‖ *tr* siphonner

si′phon bot′tle *s* siphon *m*

sir [sʌr] *s* monsieur *m*; (*British title*) Sir *m*; **Dear Sir** Monsieur

sire [saɪr] *s* sire *m*; (*of a quadruped*) père *m* ‖ *tr* engendrer

siren [ˈsaɪrən] *s* sirène *f*

sirloin [ˈsʌrlɔɪn] *s* aloyau *m*

sirup [ˈsɪrəp], [ˈsʌrəp] *s* sirop *m*

sis [sɪs] *s* (coll) soeur *f*

sis•sy [ˈsɪsi] *s* (*pl* **-sies**) efféminé *m*; fillette *f*; (*cowardly fellow*) poule *f* mouillée

sister [ˈsɪstər] *adj* (fig) jumeau ‖ *s* sœur *f*

sis′ter-in-law′ *s* (*pl* **sisters-in-law**) belle-sœur *f*

sit [sɪt] *v* (*pret* & *pp* **sat** [sæt]; *ger* **sitting**) *intr* s'asseoir; être assis; (*said of hen on eggs*) couver; (*for a portrait*) poser; (*said of legislature, court, etc.*) siéger; **to sit down** s'asseoir;

to sit still ne pas bouger; **to sit up** se redresser; se tenir droit; **to sit up and beg** (*said of dog*) faire le beau

sitcom [ˈsɪt,kɑm] *s* (rad, telv) sitcom *m* & *f* (*comédie de situation*)

sit′-down strike′ *s* grève *f* sur le tas

site [saɪt] *s* site *m*

sit′-in′ *s* occupation *f* sauvage

sitting [ˈsɪtɪŋ] *s* séance *f*

sit′ting duck′ *s* (coll) cible *f* facile

sit′ting room′ *s* salon *m*

situate [ˈsɪtʃʊ,et] *tr* situer

situation [,sɪtʃʊ e/ən] *s* situation *f;* poste *m,* emploi *m*

sit′ua′tion com′edy (sitcom) *s* comédie *f* de situation (*sitcom*)

sit′up′ *s* (*exercise*) redressement *m* assis

sitz′ bath′ [sɪts] *s* bain *m* de siège

six [sɪks] *adj* & *pron* six ‖ *s* six *m;* **at sixes and sevens** de travers, en désaccord; **six o'clock** six heures

sixteen [ˈsɪks′tin] *adj, pron,* & *s* seize *m*

sixteenth [ˈsɪks′tinθ] *adj* & *pron* seizième (*masc, fem*); **the Sixteenth** seize, e.g., **John the Sixteenth** Jean seize ‖ *s* seizième *m;* **the sixteenth** (*in dates*) le seize

sixth [sɪksθ] *adj* & *pron* sixième (*masc, fem*); **the Sixth** six, e.g., **John the Sixth** Jean six ‖ *s* sixième *m;* **the sixth** (*in dates*) le six

sixtieth [ˈsɪkstɪ•θ] *adj* & *pron* soixantième (*masc, fem*) ‖ *s* soixantième *m*

six•ty [ˈsɪksti] *adj* & *pron* soixante; **about sixty** une soixantaine de ‖ *s* (*pl* **-ties**) soixante *m;* (*age of*) soixantaine *f*

sizable [ˈsaɪzəbəl] *adj* assez grand, considérable

size [saɪz] *s* grandeur *f,* dimensions *fpl;* (*of a person or garment*) taille *f;* (*of a shoe, glove, or hat*) pointure *f;* (*of a shirt collar*) encolure *f;* (*of a book or box*) format *m;* (*to fill a porous surface*) apprêt *m;* **what size hat do you wear?** du combien coiffez-vous?; **what size shoes do you wear?** du combien chaussez-vous? ‖ *tr* classer; (*wood to be painted*) coller; **to size up** juger

sizzle [ˈsɪzəl] *s* grésillement *m* ‖ *intr* grésiller

skate [sket] *s* patin *m;* (ichth) raie *f;* **good skate** (slang) brave homme *m* ‖ *intr* patiner; **to go skating** faire du patin

skate′board′ *s* planche *f* à roulettes, skateboard *m,* skate *m*

skat′ing rink′ *s* patinoire *f*

skein [sken] *s* écheveau *m*

skeleton [ˈskɛlɪtən] *s* squelette *m;* **skeleton in the closet** squelette *m* dans un placard

skel′eton key′ *s* fausse clé *f,* passe-partout *m*

skeptic [ˈskɛptɪk] *adj* & *s* sceptique *mf*

skeptical [ˈskɛptɪkəl] *adj* sceptique

skepticism [ˈskɛptɪ,sɪzəm] *s* scepticisme *m*

sketch [skɛtʃ] *s* esquisse *f;* (*pen or pencil drawing*) croquis *m,* esquisse, (lit) aperçu *m;* (theat) sketch *m* ‖ *tr* esquisser ‖ *intr* croquer

sketch′book′ *s* album *m* de croquis

skew [skju] *adj* & *s* biais *m* ‖ *intr* biaiser

skewer [ˈskju•ər] *s* brochette *f* ‖ *tr* embrocher

ski [ski] *s* ski *m* ‖ *intr* skier; **to go skiing** faire du ski

ski' boots' *spl* chaussures *fpl* de ski

skid [skɪd] *s* (*sidewise*) dérapage *m;* (*forward*) patinage *m;* (*of wheel*) sabot *m,* patin *m* ‖ *v* (*pret & pp* **skidded**; *ger* **skidding**) *tr* enrayer, bloquer ‖ *intr* (*sidewise*) déraper; (*forward*) patiner

skid' chain' *s* chaîne *f* antidérapante

skid'ding *s* dérapage *m*

skid' row' [ro] *s* quartier *m* mal famé, quartier de clochards

skier [ˈski•ər] *s* skieur *m*

skiff [skɪf] *s* skiff *m,* esquif *m*

skiing [ˈski•ɪŋ] *s* ski *m*

ski'ing gog'gles *spl* lunettes *fpl* (protectrices) de ski

ski' jack'et *s* anorak *m*

ski' jump' *s* (*place to jump*) tremplin *m;* (*act of jumping*) saut *m* en skis

ski' lift' *s* remonte-pente *m,* téléski *m*

skill [skɪl] *s* habilité *f,* adresse *f;* (*job*) métier *m*

skilled *adj* habile, adroit

skillet [ˈskɪlɪt] *s* casserole *f;* (*frying pan*) poêle *f*

skillful [ˈskɪlfəl] *adj* habile, expert

skim [skɪm] *v* (*pret & pp* **skimmed**; *ger* **skimming**) *tr* (*milk*) écrémer; (*molten metal*) écumer; (*to graze*) raser ‖ *intr*—**to skim over** passer légèrement sur

ski' mask' *s* passe-montagne *m*

skimmer [ˈskɪmər] *s* écumoire *f;* (*straw hat*) canotier *m*

skim' milk' *s* lait *m* écrémé

skimp [skɪmp] *tr* bâcler ‖ *intr* lésiner; **to skimp on** lésiner sur

skimp•y [ˈskɪmpi] *adj* (*comp* **-ier;** *super* **-iest**) maigre; (*garment*) étriqué; avare, mesquin

skin [skɪn] *s* peau *f;* **by the skin of one's teeth** de justesse, par un cheveu; **soaked to the skin** trempé jusqu'aux os; **to strip to the skin** se mettre à poil ‖ *v* (*pret & pp* **skinned**; *ger* **skinning**) *tr* écorcher, dépouiller; (*e.g., an elbow*) s'écorcher; **to skin alive** (*coll*) écorcher vif

skin'-deep' *adj* superficiel; (*beauty*) à fleur de peau

skin' div'er *s* plongeur *m* autonome

skin'flint' *s* grippe-sou *m*

skin' game' *s* (*slang*) escroquerie *f*

skin' graft'ing *s* greffe *f* cutanée, autoplastie *f*

skin•ny [ˈskɪni] *adj* (*comp* **-nier;** *super* **-niest**) maigre, décharné

skin' test' *s* (*med*) cuti-réaction *f*

skin'tight' *adj* collant, ajusté

skip [skɪp] *s* saut *m* ‖ *v* (*pret & pp* **skipped**; *ger* **skipping**) *tr* sauter; **skip it!** ça suffit!, laisse tomber!; **to skip rope** sauter à la corde ‖ *intr* sauter; **to skip out** or **off** filer

skip' bomb'ing *s* (*aer*) bombardement *m* par ricochet

ski' pole' *s* bâton *m* de skis

skipper [ˈskɪpər] *s* patron *m* ‖ *tr* commander, conduire

skirmish [ˈskʌrmɪʃ] *s* escarmouche *f* ‖ *intr* escarmoucher

skirt [skʌrt] *s* jupe *f;* (*woman*) (*slang*) jupe ‖ *tr* côtoyer, longer; éviter

ski' run' *s* descente *f* en skis

ski' stick' *s* bâton *m* de skis

skit [skɪt] *s* sketch *m*

skittish [ˈskɪtɪʃ] *adj* capricieux; timide; (*e.g., horse*) ombrageux

ski' wax' *s* fart *m*

skulduggery [skʌlˈdʌgəri] *s* (*coll*) fourberie *f,* ruse *f,* cuisine *f*

skull [skʌl] *s* crâne *m*

skull' and cross'bones *s* tibias *mpl* croisés et tête *f* de mort

skull'cap' *s* calotte *f*

skunk [skʌŋk] *s* mouffette *f;* (*person*) (*coll*) salaud *m*

sky [skaɪ] *s* (*pl* **skies**) ciel *m;* **to praise to the skies** porter aux nues

sky'div'er *s* parachutiste *mf*

sky'div'ing *s* parachutisme *m,* saut *m* en chute libre

Sky'lab' *s* laboratoire *m* du ciel

sky'lark' *s* (*Alauda arvensis*) alouette *f,* alouette des champs ‖ *intr* (*coll*) batifoler

sky'light' *s* lucarne *f*

sky'line' *s* ligne *m* d'horizon; (*of city*) profil *m*

sky'rock'et *s* fusée *f* volante ‖ *intr* monter en flèche

sky'scrap'er *s* gratte-ciel *m*

sky'writ'ing *s* écriture *f* aérienne (*publicité tracée dans le ciel*)

slab [slæb] *s* (*of stone*) dalle *f;* (*slice*) tranche *f*

slack [slæk] *adj* (*loose*) lâche, mou; (*careless*) négligent ‖ *s* mou *m;* (*slowdown*) ralentissement *m;* **slacks** pantalon *m;* **to take up the slack** (*coll*) prendre le relais ‖ *tr* relâcher; (*lime*) éteindre; **to slack off** larguer ‖ *intr*—**to slack off** or **up** se relâcher

slacken [ˈslækən] *tr* relâcher; (*to slow down*) ralentir ‖ *intr* se relâcher; se ralentir

slacker [ˈslækər] *s* flemmard *m;* (*mil*) tire-au-flanc *m,* embusqué *m*

slack' hours' *spl* heures *fpl* creuses

slag [slæg] *s* scorie *f*

slake [slek] *tr* apaiser, étancher; (*lime*) éteindre

slalom [ˈslɑləm] *s* slalom *m*

slam [slæm] *s* claquement *m;* (*cards*) chelem *m;* (*coll*) critique *f* sévère ‖ *v* (*pret & pp* **slammed**; *ger* **slamming**) *tr* claquer; (*coll*) éreinter; **to slam down on** flanquer sur ‖ *intr* claquer

slam' dunk' *s* (*basketball*) panier marqué en lançant le ballon avec force d'en haut

slammer [ˈslæmər] *s* (*slang*) prison *f*

slander [ˈslændər] *s* calomnie *f* ‖ *tr* calomnier

slanderous [ˈslændərəs] *adj* calomnieux

slang [slæŋ] *s* argot *m;* (*e.g., of the underworld*) langue *f* verte

slant [slænt] *s* pente *f;* (*bias*) point *m* de vue ‖ *tr* mettre en pente, incliner; donner un biais spécial à ‖ *intr* être en pente, s'incliner

slap [slæp] *s* tape *f,* claque *f;* (*in the face*) soufflet *m,* gifle *f* ‖ *v* (*pret & pp* **slapped;** *ger* **slapping**) *tr* taper, gifler

slap′dash′ *adj*—**in a slapdash manner** à la vacomme-je-te-pousse ‖ *adv* à la six-quatre-deux

slap′stick′ *adj* bouffon ‖ *s* bouffonnerie *f*

slash [slæʃ] *s* entaille *f* ‖ *tr* taillader; (*e.g., prices*) réduire beaucoup

slat [slæt] *s* latte *f*

slate [slet] *s* ardoise *f;* (*of candidates*) liste *f* ‖ *tr* couvrir d'ardoises; inscrire sur la liste, désigner

slate′ pen′cil *s* crayon *m* d'ardoise

slate′ roof′ *s* toit *m* d'ardoises

slattern [′slætərn] *s* (*slovenly woman*) marie-salope *f;* (*slut*) voyoute *f,* gueuse *f*

slaughter [′slɔtər] *s* boucherie *f* ‖ *tr* abattre; massacrer

slaught′er•house′ *s* abattoir *m*

Slav [slɑv], [slæv] *adj* slave ‖ *s* (*language*) slave *m;* (*person*) Slave *mf*

slave [slev] *adj & s* esclave *mf* ‖ *intr* besogner, trimer

slave′ driv′er *s* (hist, fig) négrier *m*

slave′ la′bor *s* exploitation *f* des esclaves; (fig) travail *m* de forçat

slavery [′slevəri] *s* esclavage *m;* (*institution of keeping slaves*) esclavagisme *m*

slave′ ship′ *s* négrier *m*

slave′ trade′ *s* traite *f* des noirs

slave′ trad′er *s* négrier *m*

Slavic [′slævɪk] *adj & s* slave *m*

slavish [′slevɪʃ] *adj* servile

slaw [slɔ] *s* salade *f* de chou

slay [sle] *v* (*pret* **slew** [slu]; *pp* **slain** [slen]) *tr* tuer, massacrer

slayer [′sle•ər] *s* meurtrier *m*

sled [slɛd] *s* luge *f* ‖ *v* (*pret & pp* **sledded;** *ger* **sledding**) *intr* faire de la luge, luger

sled′ dog′ *s* chien *m* de traîneau

sledge′ ham′mer [slɛdʒ] *s* massette *f,* masse *f*

sleek [slik] *adj* lisse, luisant ‖ *tr* lisser

sleep [slip] *s* sommeil *m;* **to go to sleep** s'endormir; **to put to sleep** endormir ‖ *v* (*pret & pp* **slept** [slɛpt]) *tr*—**to sleep it over, to sleep on it** prendre conseil de son oreiller; **to sleep off** (*a hangover headache, etc.*) faire passer en dormant ‖ *intr* dormir; (*e.g., with a woman*) coucher; **to sleep late** faire la grasse matinée; **to sleep like a log** dormir comme un loir

sleeper [′slipər] *s* dormeur *m;* (*girder*) poutre *f* horizontale; (*tie*) (rr) traverse *f*

sleep′ing bag′ *s* sac *m* de couchage

Sleep′ing Beau′ty *s* La Belle au bois dormant

sleep′ing car′ *s* wagon-lit *m*

sleep′ing pill′ *s* somnifère *m*

sleep′ing sick′ness *s* maladie *f* du sommeil

sleepless [′sliplɪs] *adj* sans sommeil

sleep′less night′ *s* nuit *f* blanche

sleep′walk′er *s* somnambule *mf*

sleep•y [′slipi] *adj* (*comp* **-ier;** *super* **-iest**) endormi, somnolent; **to be sleepy** avoir sommeil

sleep′y•head′ *s* endormi *m,* grand dormeur *m*

sleet [slit] *s* grésil *m;* (*frozen coating on ground*) verglas *m* ‖ *intr* grésiller

sleet•y [′sliti] *adj* (*comp* **-tier;** *super* **-tiest**) de grésil; (*iced-over*) verglacé

sleeve [sliv] *s* manche *f;* (mach) manchon *m,* douille *f;* **to laugh in** or **up one's sleeve** rire sous cape

sleigh [sle] *s* traîneau *m* ‖ *intr* aller en traîneau

sleigh′ bell′ *s* grelot *m*

sleigh′ ride′ *s* promenade *f* en traîneau

sleight′ of hand′ [slaɪt] *s* prestidigitation *f,* tours *mpl* de passe-passe

slender [′slɛndər] *adj* svelte, mince, élancé; (*resources*) maigre

sleuth [sluθ] *s* limier *m,* détective *m*

slew [slu] *s* (coll) tas *m,* floppée *f*

slice [slaɪs] *s* tranche *f* ‖ *tr* trancher

slick [slɪk] *adj* lisse; (*appearance*) élégant; (coll) rusé ‖ *s* tache *f,* e.g., **oil slick** tache d'huile ‖ *tr* lisser; **to slick up** (coll) mettre en ordre

slicker [′slɪkər] *s* ciré *m,* imper *m;* (coll) enjôleur *m*

slide [slaɪd] *s* (*sliding*) glissade *f,* glissement *m;* (*sliding place*) glissoire *m;* (*of microscope*) plaque *f;* (*of trombone*) coulisse *f;* (*on a slide rule*) curseur *m;* (*piece that slides*) glissière *f;* (phot) diapositive *f,* diapo *f* ‖ *v* (*pret & pp* **slid** [slɪd]) *tr* glisser ‖ *intr* glisser; **to let slide** ne faire aucun cas de, laisser aller

slide′ fas′tener *s* fermeture *f* éclair

slide′ projec′tor *s* projecteur *m* de diapositives

slide′ rule′ *s* règle *f* à calcul

slide′ valve′ *s* soupape *f* à tiroir

slid′ing con′tact *s* curseur *m*

slid′ing door′ *s* porte *f* à coulisse

slid′ing scale′ *s* échelle *f* mobile

slight [slaɪt] *adj* (*small*) léger; (*slender*) mince; (*insignificant*) faible; (*e.g., effort*) faible ‖ *s* affront *m* ‖ *tr* faire peu de cas de, dédaigner; (*a person*) méconnaître

slim [slɪm] *adj* (*comp* **slimmer;** *super* **slimmest**) mince, svelte; (*chance, excuse*) mauvais; (*resources*) maigre

slime [slaɪm] *s* limon *m,* vase *f;* (*of snakes, fish, etc.*) bave *f*

slim•y [′slaɪmi] *adj* (*comp* **-ier;** *super* **-iest**) limoneux, vaseux

sling [slɪŋ] *s* (*to shoot stones*) fronde *f;* (*to hold up a broken arm*) écharpe *f;* (*shoulder strap*) bretelle *f,* bandoulière *f* ‖ *v* (*pret & pp* **slung** [slʌŋ]) *tr* lancer; passer en bandoulière

sling′shot′ *s* fronde *f*

slink [slɪŋk] *v* (*pret & pp* **slunk** [slʌŋk]) *intr*—**to slink away** s'esquiver

slip [slɪp] *s* (*slide*) dérapage *m,* glissade *f,* glissement *m;* (*small sheet*) bout *m* de papier; (*for* *indexing, filing, etc.*) fiche *f;* (*cutting from plant*) bouture *f;* (*piece of underclothing*) combinaison *f;* (*blunder*) faux pas *m,* bévue *f;* (naut) cale *f;* **to give the slip to** échapper à ‖ *v* (*pret & pp* **slipped;** *ger* **slipping**) *tr* glisser; **to slip off** (*a garment*) enlever, ôter; **to slip on** (*a garment, shoes, etc.*) enfiler; **to slip one's mind** sortir de l'esprit, échapper à qn ‖ *intr* glisser; (*to blunder*) faire un faux pas; **to let slip** laisser échapper; **to slip away** or **off** s'échapper, se dérober; **to slip by** s'échapper; (*said of time*) s'écouler; **to slip up** se tromper

slip′cov′er *s* housse *f*

slip′ of the pen′ *s* lapsus *m*

slip′ of the tongue′ *s* lapsus *m*

slipped′ disc′ *s* hernie *f* discale

slipper [ˈslɪpər] *s* pantoufle *f*

slippery [ˈslɪpəri] *adj* glissant; (*deceitful*) rusé

slip′pery slope′ *s* (fig) terrain *m* glissant, pente *f* savonneuse

slip′shod′ *adj* bâclé, négligent

slip′-up′ *s* (coll) erreur *f,* bévue *f*

slit [slɪt] *s* fente *f,* fissure *f* ‖ *v* (*pret & pp* **slit;** *ger* **slitting**) *tr* fendre; (*e.g., pages*) couper; **to slit the throat of** égorger

sliver [ˈslɪvər] *s* écharde *f,* éclat *m*

slob [slɑb] *s* (slang) rustaud *m*

slobber [ˈslɑbər] *s* bave *f;* (fig) sentimentalité *f* ‖ *intr* baver

sloe [slo] *s* (*shrub*) prunellier *m;* (*fruit*) prunelle *f*

slogan [ˈslogən] *s* mot *m* d'ordre, devise *f;* (com) slogan *m*

sloop [slup] *s* sloop *m*

slop [slɑp] *s* lavure *f,* rinçure *f* ‖ *v* (*pret & pp* **slopped;** *ger* **slopping**) *tr* répandre ‖ *intr* se répandre; **to slop over** déborder

slope [slop] *s* pente *f;* (*of a roof*) inclinaison *f;* (*of a region, mountain, etc.*) versant *m* ‖ *tr* pencher, incliner ‖ *intr* se pencher, s'incliner

slop•py [ˈslɑpi] *adj* (*comp* **-pier;** *super* **-piest**) mouillé; (*dress*) négligé, mal ajusté; (*work*) bâclé

slot [slɑt] *s* entaille *f,* rainure *f;* (*e.g., in a coin telephone*) fente *f*

sloth [sloθ] *s* paresse *f;* (zool) paresseux *m*

slot′ machine′ *s* (*for gambling*) appareil *m* à sous; (*for vending*) distributeur *m* automatique

slouch [slaʊtʃ] *s* démarche *f* lourde; (*person*) lourdaud *m* ‖ *intr* ne pas se tenir droit; (*e.g., in a chair*) se vautrer; **to slouch along** traîner le pas

slouch′ hat′ *s* chapeau *m* mou

slough [slaʊ] *s* bourbier *m* ‖ [slʌf] *s* (*of snake*) dépouille *f;* (pathol) escarre *f* ‖ *tr*—**to slough off** se débarrasser de, dépouiller ‖ *intr* muer, se dépouiller

Slovak [ˈslovæk] *adj* slovaque ‖ *s* (*language*) slovaque *m;* (*person*) Slovaque *mf*

Slovakia [sloˈvɑkɪ•ə] *s* la Slovaquie *f*

sloven•ly [ˈslʌvənli] *adj* (*comp* **-lier;** *super* **-liest**) négligé, malpropre

slow [slo] *adj* lent; (*sluggish*) traînard; (*clock, watch*) en retard; (*in understanding*) lourdaud ‖ *adv* lentement ‖ *tr & intr* ralentir; **SLOW** (*public sign*) ralentir; **to slow down** ralentir

slow′down′ *s* ralentissement *m,* ralenti *m*

slow′down′ strike′ *s* grève *f* perlée

slow′ mo′tion *s* ralenti *m;* **in slow motion** au ralenti, en ralenti

slowness [ˈslonɪs] *s* lenteur *f*

slow′poke′ *s* (coll) lambin *m,* traînard *m*

slug [slʌg] *s* (*used as coin*) jeton *m;* (*of linotype*) ligne-bloc *f;* (zool) limace *f;* (*blow*) (coll) bon coup *m;* (*drink*) (coll) gorgée *f* ‖ *v* (*pret & pp* **slugged;** *ger* **slugging**) *tr* (coll) flanquer un coup à

sluggard [ˈslʌgərd] *s* paresseux *m*

sluggish [ˈslʌgɪʃ] *adj* traînard

sluice [slus] *s* canal *m;* (*floodgate*) écluse *f;* (*dam; flume*) bief *m*

sluice′ gate′ *s* vanne *f*

slum [slʌm] *s* bas quartiers *mpl* ‖ *v* (*pret & pp* **slummed;** *ger* **slumming**) *intr*—**to go slumming** aller visiter les taudis

slumber [ˈslʌmbər] *s* sommeil *m,* assoupissement *m* ‖ *intr* sommeiller

slum′ber par′ty *s* soirée-hébergement *f*

slum′ dwell′ing *s* taudis *m*

slump [slʌmp] *s* affaissement *m;* (com) crise *f,* baisse *f* ‖ *intr* s'affaisser; (*said of prices, stocks, etc.*) dégringoler, s'effondrer

slur [slʌr] *s* (*in pronunciation*) mauvaise articulation *f;* (*insult*) affront *m;* (mus) liaison *f;* **to cast a slur on** porter atteinte à ‖ *v* (*pret & pp* **slurred;** *ger* **slurring**) *tr* (*a sound, a syllable*) mal articuler; (*a person*) déprécier; (mus) lier; **to slur over** glisser sur

slush [slʌʃ] *s* névasse *f,* fange *f,* boue *f* liquide; (*gush*) sensiblerie *f*

slush′ drink′ *s* barbotine *f*

slush′ fund′ *s* fonds *mpl* servant à des pots-de-vin

slut [slʌt] *s* chienne *f;* (*slovenly woman*) marie-salope *f*

sly [slaɪ] *adj* (*comp* **slyer** or **slier;** *super* **slyest** or **sliest**) rusé, sournois; (*mischievous*) espiègle, futé; **on the sly** furtivement, en cachette

smack [smæk] *s* (*sound*) claquement *m;* (*with the hand*) gifle *f,* claque *f;* (*trace, touch*) soupçon *m;* (*kiss*) (coll) gros baiser *m* ‖ *adv* en plein ‖ *tr* claquer ‖ *intr*—**to smack of** sentir; avoir un goût de

small [smɔl] *adj* petit §91; (*income*) modique; (*short in stature*) court; (*petty*) mesquin; (typ) minuscule

small′ arms′ *spl* armes *fpl* portatives

small′ beer′ *s* petite bière *f;* (slang) petite bière

small′ busi′ness *s* petite industrie *f*

small′ cap′ital *s* (typ) petite capitale *f*

small′ change′ *s* petite monnaie *f,* menue monnaie

small′ fry′ *s* menu fretin *m*

small′ intes′tine *s* intestin *m* grêle

small′-mind′ed *adj* mesquin, étriqué, étroit

small′ of the back′ *s* chute *f* des reins, bas *m* du dos

smallpox [ˈsmɔlˌpɑks] *s* variole *f*

small′ print′ *s* petits caractères *mpl*

small′ talk′ *s* ragots *mpl*, papotage *m*

small′-time′ *adj* de troisième ordre, insignifiant, petit

small′-town′ *adj* provincial

smart [smɑrt] *adj* intelligent, éveillé; (*pace*) vif; (*person, clothes*) élégant, chic; (*pain*) cuisant; (*saucy*) impertinent ‖ *s* douleur *f* cuisante ‖ *intr* brûler, cuire; (*said of person with hurt feelings*) être cinglé

smart′ al′eck [ˌælɪk] *s* (coll) fat *m*, présomptueux *m*

smart′ bomb′ *s* (coll) bombe *f* intelligente

smart′ card′ *s* (com) carte *f* intelligente

smart′ mon′ey *s* (fig) investissement *m* astucieux; investisseurs *mpl* bien informés

smart′ set′ *s* monde *m* élégant, gens *mpl* chic

smash [smæʃ] *s* fracassement *m*, fracas *m*; (coll) succès *m* ‖ *tr* fracasser ‖ *intr* se fracasser; **to smash into** emboutir, écraser

smash′ hit′ *s* (coll) succès *m*, succès fou; (coll) pièce *f* à succès

smash′-up′ *s* collision *f*; débâcle *f*, culbute *f*

smattering [ˈsmætərɪŋ] *s* légère connaissance *f*, teinture *f*

smear [smɪr] *s* tache *f*; (*vilification*) calomnie *f*; (med) frottis *m* ‖ *tr* tacher; calomnier; (*to coat*) enduire

smear′ campaign′ *s* campagne *f* de calomnies

smell [smɛl] *s* odeur *f*; (*aroma*) parfum *m*, senteur *f*; (*sense*) odorat *m* ‖ *v* (*pret & pp* **smelled** or **smelt** [smɛlt]) *tr & intr* sentir; **to smell of** sentir

smell′ing salts′ *spl* sels *mpl* volatils

smell•y [ˈsmɛli] *adj* (*comp* **-ier;** *super* **-iest**) malodorant, puant

smelt [smɛlt] *s* (*fish*) éperlan *m* ‖ *tr & intr* fondre

smile [smaɪl] *s* sourire *m* ‖ *intr* sourire; **to smile at** sourire à

smirk [smʌrk] *s* minauderie *f* ‖ *intr* minauder

smite [smaɪt] *v* (*pret* **smote** [smot]; *pp* **smitten** [ˈsmɪtən] or **smit** [smɪt]) *tr* frapper; **to smite down** abattre

smith [smɪθ] *s* forgeron *m*

smith•y [ˈsmɪθi] *s* (*pl* **-ies**) forge *f*

smitten [ˈsmɪtən] *adj* frappé, affligé; (coll) épris, amoureux

smock [smɑk] *s* blouse *f*; (*of artists*) sarrau *m*; (*buttoned in back*) tablier *m*

smock′ frock′ *s* sarrau *m*

smog [smɑg] *s* (coll) brouillard *m* fumeux, fumillard *m*

smoke [smok] *s* fumée *f*; (coll) cigarette *f*; **to go up in smoke** s'en aller en fumée ‖ *tr & intr* fumer

smoke′ detec′tor *s* détecteur *m* de fumées

smoked′ glass′es *spl* verres *mpl* fumés

smoke′ evac′uator *s* extracteur *m* de fumées

smoke′-filled room′ *s* tabagie *f*

smoke′less pow′der [ˈsmoklɪs] *s* poudre *f* sans fumée

smoker [ˈsmokər] *s* fumeur *m*; (*room*) fumoir *m*; (*meeting*) réunion *f* de fumeurs; (rr) compartiment *m* pour fumeurs

smoke′ rings′ *spl* ronds *mpl* de fumée

smoke′ screen′ *s* rideau *m* de fumée

smoke′ sig′nal *s* signal *m* de fumée

smoke′stack′ *s* cheminée *f*

smoking [ˈsmokɪŋ] *s* le fumer *m*; **no smoking** (*public sign*) défense de fumer

smok′ing car′ *s* voiture *f* de fumeurs

smok′ing gun′ *s* (coll) incident qui prouve la culpabilité

smok′ing jack′et *s* veston *m* d'intérieur

smok′ing room′ *s* fumoir *m*

smok•y [ˈsmoki] *adj* (*comp* **-ier;** *super* **-iest**) fumeux, enfumé

smolder [ˈsmoldər] *s* (*dense smoke*) fumée *f* épaisse; (*smoldering fire*) feu *m* qui couve ‖ *intr* brûler sans flamme; (*said of fire, anger, rebellion, etc.*) couver

smooch [smutʃ] *intr* (coll) se bécoter

smooching [ˈsmutʃɪŋ] *s* bécotage *m*

smooth [smuð] *adj* uni, lisse; (*gentle, mellow*) doux, moelleux; (*operation*) doux, régulier; (*style*) facile ‖ *tr* unir, lisser; **to smooth away** (*e.g., obstacles*) aplanir, enlever; **to smooth down** (*to calm*) apaiser, calmer; **to smooth out** défroisser

smooth′-faced′ *adj* imberbe

smooth-shaven [ˈsmuðˈʃevən] *adj* rasé de près

smooth•y *ou* **smooth•ie** [ˈsmuði] *s* (*pl* **-ies**) (coll) chattemite *f*, flagorneur *m*

smother [ˈsmʌðər] *tr* suffoquer, étouffer; (culin) recouvrir

smudge [smʌdʒ] *s* tache *f*; (*smoke*) fumée *f* épaisse ‖ *tr* tacher; (agr) fumiger

smudge′ pot′ *s* fumigène *m*

smug [smʌg] *adj* (*comp* **smugger;** *super* **smuggest**) fat, suffisant

smuggle [ˈsmʌgəl] *tr* introduire en contrebande, faire la contrebande de ‖ *intr* faire la contrebande

smuggler [ˈsmʌglər] *s* contrebandier *m*

smuggling [ˈsmʌglɪŋ] *s* contrebande *f*

smut [smʌt] *s* tache *f* de suie; (*obscenity*) ordure *f*; (agr) nielle *f*

smut•ty [ˈsmʌti] *adj* (*comp* **-tier;** *super* **-tiest**) taché de suie, noirci; (*obscene*) ordurier; (agr) niellé

snack [snæk] *s* casse-croûte *m*; amuse-bouche *m*, amuse-gueule *m* **to have a snack** casser la croûte

snack′ bar′ *s* snack-bar *m*, snack *m*

snag [snæg] *s* (*of tree; of tooth*) chicot *m*; **to hit a snag** se heurter à un obstacle, tomber sur un bec ‖ *v* (*pret & pp* **snagged;** *ger* **snagging**) *tr* (*a stocking*) faire un accroc à

snail [snel] *s* escargot *m*; **at a snail's pace** à pas de tortue, comme un escargot

snail′mail′ *s* (hum) courrier *m* envoyé par la poste

snake [snek] *s* serpent *m* ‖ *intr* serpenter

snake′ in the grass′ *s* serpent *m* caché sous les fleurs; ami *m* perfide, traître *m*, individu *m* louche

snap [snæp] *s* (*breaking*) cassure *f;* (*crackling sound*) bruit *m* sec; (*of the fingers*) chiquenaude *f;* (*bite*) coup *m* de dents; (*cookie*) biscuit *m* croquant; (*catch or fastener*) bouton-pression *m,* fermoir *m;* (phot) instantané *m;* (slang) jeu *m* d'enfant, coup facile; **cold snap** coup *m* de froid; **it's a snap!** (slang) c'est du tout cuit! ‖ *v* (*pret & pp* **snapped;** *ger* **snapping**) *tr* casser net; **to snap up** happer, saisir ‖ *intr* casser net; faire un bruit sec; (*from fatigue*) s'effondrer; **to snap at** donner un coup de dents à; (*to speak sharply to*) rembarrer; (*an opportunity*) saisir; **to snap out of it** (slang) se secouer; **to snap shut** se fermer avec un bruit sec

snap′ course′ *s* (slang) cours *m* tout mâché

snap′drag′on *s* (bot) gueule-de-loup *f*

snap′ fas′tener *s* bouton-pression *m*

snap′ judg′ment *s* décision *f* prise sans réflexion

snap•py [ˈsnæpi] *adj* (*comp* **-pier;** *super* **-piest**) mordant, acariâtre; (*quick, sudden*) vif; **make it snappy!** (slang) grouillez-vous!

snap′shot′ *s* instantané *m*

snare [snɛr] *s* collet *m;* (*trap*) piège *m;* (*of a drum*) timbre *m,* corde *f* de timbre ‖ *tr* prendre au collet, prendre au piège

snare′ drum′ *s* caisse *f* claire

snarl [snɑrl] *s* (*sound*) grognement *m;* (*intertwining*) enchevêtrement *m* ‖ *tr* dire en grognant; enchevêtrer ‖ *intr* grogner; s'enchevêtrer

snatch [snætʃ] *s* (*action*) geste *m* vif (pour saisir), arrachement *m;* (*theft*) vol *m* (à l'arraché); (*bit, scrap*) bribe *f,* fragment *m;* (*in weight lifting*) arraché *m* ‖ *tr* saisir brusquement, arracher; **to snatch from** arracher à; **to snatch up** ramasser vivement ‖ *intr*—**to snatch at** saisir au vol

sneak [snik] *adj* furtif ‖ *s* chipeur *m,* mauvais type *m* ‖ *tr* (*e.g., a drink*) prendre à la dérobée; glisser furtivement; (coll) chiper ‖ *intr* se glisser furtivement; **to sneak into** se faufiler dans; **to sneak out** s'esquiver

sneaker [ˈsnikər] *s* espadrille *f*

sneak′ thief′ *s* chipeur *m,* voleur *m* à la tire

sneak•y [ˈsniki] *adj* (*comp* **-ier;** *super* **-iest**) furtif, sournois

sneer [snɪr] *s* ricanement *m* ‖ *intr* ricaner; **to sneer at** se moquer de

sneeze [sniz] *s* éternuement *m* ‖ *intr* éternuer; **it's not to be sneezed at** (coll) il ne faut pas cracher dessus

snicker [ˈsnɪkər] *s* rire *m* bête; (*sneer*) rire narquois; (*in response to smut*) petit rire grivois ‖ *intr* rire bêtement; **to snicker at** se moquer de

sniff [snɪf] *s* reniflement *m;* (*odor*) parfum *m;* (*e.g., of air*) bouffée *f* ‖ *tr* renifler; (*e.g., fresh air*) humer; (*e.g., a scandal*) flairer; **to sniff up** renifler ‖ *intr* renifler; **to sniff at** flairer; (*to disdain*) cracher sur

sniffle [ˈsnɪfəl] *s* reniflement *m;* **to have the sniffles** être enchifrené ‖ *intr* renifler

snip [snɪp] *s* (*e.g., of cloth*) petit bout *m;* (*cut*) coup *m* de ciseaux; (coll) personne *f* insignifiante ‖ *v* (*pret & pp* **snipped;** *ger* **snipping**) *tr* couper; **to snip off** enlever, détacher

snipe [snaɪp] *s* (orn) bécassine *f* ‖ *intr*—**to snipe at** canarder

sniper [ˈsnaɪpər] *s* tireur *m* embusqué, tireur isolé

snippet [ˈsnɪpɪt] *s* petit bout *m,* bribe *f;* personne *f* insignifiante

snip•py [ˈsnɪpi] *adj* (*comp* **-pier;** *super* **-piest**) hautain, brusque

snitch [snɪtʃ] *tr* (coll) chaparder ‖ *intr* (coll) moucharder; **to snitch on** (coll) moucharder

sniv•el [ˈsnɪvəl] *s* pleurnicherie *f;* (*mucus*) morve *f* ‖ *v* (*pret & pp* **-eled** or **-elled;** *ger* **-eling** or **-elling**) *intr* pleurnicher; (*to have a runny nose*) être morveux

snob [snɑb] *s* snob *m*

snobbery [ˈsnɑbəri] *s* snobisme *m*

snobbish [ˈsnɑbɪʃ] *adj* snob

snoop [snup] *s* (coll) curieux *m* ‖ *intr* (coll) fouiner, fureter

snoop•y [ˈsnupi] *adj* (*comp* **-ier;** *super* **-iest**) (coll) curieux

snoot [snut] *s* (slang) nez *m*

snoot•y [ˈsnuti] *adj* (*comp* **-ier;** *super* **-iest**) (slang) snob, hautain

snooze [snuz] *s* (coll) petit somme *m* ‖ *intr* (coll) sommeiller

snore [snor] *s* ronflement *m* ‖ *intr* ronfler

snort [snɔrt] *s* ébrouement *m;* (*of person, horse, etc.*) reniflement *m* ‖ *tr* dire en reniflant, grogner ‖ *intr* s'ébrouer, renifler bruyamment

snot [snɑt] *s* (slang) morve *f*

snot•ty [ˈsnɑti] *adj* (*comp* **-tier;** *super* **-tiest**) (coll) morveux; (slang) snob, hautain

snout [snaʊt] *s* museau *m;* (*of pig*) groin *m;* (*of bull*) mufle *m;* (*something shaped like the snout of an animal*) bec *m,* tuyère *f*

snow [sno] *s* neige *f* ‖ *intr* neiger; **it is snowing** il neige; **to shovel snow** balayer la neige

snow′ball′ *s* boule *f* de neige ‖ *tr* lancer des boules de neige à ‖ *intr* faire boule de neige

snow′bank′ *s* talus *m* de neige, banc *m* de neige

snow′ blind′ness *s* cécité *f* des neiges

snow′ blow′er *s* chasse-neige *m*

snow′bound′ *adj* bloqué par la neige

snow′-capped′ *adj* couronné de neige

snow′-clad′ *adj* enneigé

snow′drift′ *s* congère *f*

snow'fall' *s* chute *f* de neige; (*amount*) enneigement *m*

snow' fence' *s* palissade *f* pour délimiter la neige

snow'flake' *s* flocon *m* de neige

snow' flur'ry *s* (*pl* -**ries**) bouffée *f* de neige

snow' job' *s* (slang) conte *m* (*récit mensonger*), tromperie *f*

snow' line' *ou* **lim'it** *s* limite *f* des neiges permanentes

snow'mak'ing *s* enneigement *m* artificiel

snow'man' *s* (*pl* -**men'**) bonhomme *m* de neige

snowmobile [ˈsnoməˌbil] *s* motoneige *f*

snow'plow' *s* chasse-neige *m*

snow' remov'al *s* déneigement *m*

snow'shoe' *s* raquette *f*

snow'slide' *s* avalanche *f*

snow'storm' *s* tempête *f* de neige

snow' tire' *s* pneu *m* à neige

snow'white' *adj* blanc comme la neige ‖ **Snow-white** *s* Blanche-Neige *f*

snow•y [ˈsnoˑi] *adj* (*comp* -**ier**; *super* -**iest**) neigeux

snow'y owl' *s* chouette *f* blanche

snub [snʌb] *s* affront *m*, rebuffade *f* ‖ *v* (*pret & pp* **snubbed**; *ger* **snubbing**) *tr* traiter avec froideur, rabrouer

snub•by [ˈsnʌbi] *adj* (*comp* -**bier**; *super* -**biest**) trapu; (*nose*) camus

snub'-nosed' *adj* camard

snuff [snʌf] *s* tabac *m* à priser; (*of a candlewick*) mouchure *f*; **to be up to snuff** (*to be shrewd*) (slang) être dessalé; (*to be up to par*) (slang) être dégourdi ‖ *tr* priser; (*a candle*) moucher; **to snuff out** éteindre

snuff'box' *s* tabatière *f*

snuffers [ˈsnʌfərz] *spl* mouchettes *fpl*

snug [snʌg] *adj* (*comp* **snugger**; *super* **snuggest**) confortable; (*garment*) bien ajusté; (*bed*) douillet; (*sheltered*) abrité; (*hidden*) caché; **snug and warm** bien au chaud; **snug as a bug in a rug** comme un poisson dans l'eau

snuggle [ˈsnʌgəl] *tr* serrer dans ses bras ‖ *intr* se pelotonner; **to snuggle up to** se serrer tout près de

so [so] *adv* si, tellement; ainsi; donc, par conséquent, aussi; **or so** plus ou moins; **so as to** afin de, pour; **so far** jusqu'ici; **so long!** (coll) à bientôt!; **so many** tant; tant de; **so much** tant; tant de; **so that** pour que, afin que; de sorte que; **so to speak** pour ainsi dire; **so what?** (slang) et alors?; **to hope so** espérer bien; **to think so** croire que oui ‖ *conj* (coll) de sorte que

soak [sok] *s* trempage *m*; (slang) sac *m* à vin, soûlard *m* ‖ *tr* tremper; (*to swindle*) (slang) estamper; **to soak to the skin** tremper jusqu'aux os ‖ *intr* tremper

so'-and-so' *s* (*pl* -**sos**) (pej) triste individu *m*, mauvais sujet *m*; **Mr. So-and-so** Monsieur Untel

soap [sop] *s* savon *m* ‖ *tr* savonner

soap'box' *s* caisse *f* à savon; (fig) plateforme *f*

soap'box or'ator *s* orateur *m* de carrefour

soap' bub'ble *s* bulle *f* de savon

soap' dish' *s* plateau *m* à savon

soap' fac'to•ry *s* (*pl* -**ries**) savonnerie *f*

soap' flakes' *spl* savon *m* en paillettes

soap' op'era *s* mélo *m*

soap' pow'der *s* savon *m* en poudre

soap'stone' *s* pierre *f* de savon; craie *f* de tailleur

soap'suds' *spl* mousse *f* de savon, eau *f* de savon

soap•y [ˈsopi] *adj* (*comp* -**ier**; *super* -**iest**) savonneux

soar [sor] *intr* planer dans les airs; prendre l'essor, monter subitement

sob [sab] *s* sanglot *m* ‖ *v* (*pret & pp* **sobbed**; *ger* **sobbing**) *intr* sangloter

sober [ˈsobər] *adj* sobre; (*expression*) grave; (*truth*) simple; (*not drunk*) pas ivre; (*no longer drunk*) dégrisé ‖ *tr* calmer; **to sober up** dégriser ‖ *intr*—**to sober up** se dégriser

sobriety [soˈbraɪˑəti] *s* sobriété *f*

sob' sis'ter *s* (slang) journaliste *f* larmoyante

sob' sto'ry *s* (*pl* -**ries**) histoire *f* larmoyante, histoire d'un pathétique facile, histoire à vous fendre le cœur

so'-called' *adj* dit; soi-disant, prétendu; ainsi nommé

soccer [ˈsakər] *s* football *m*

sociable [ˈsoʃəbəl] *adj* sociable

social [ˈsoʃəl] *adj* social ‖ *s* réunion *f* sans cérémonie

so'cial climb'er *s* parvenu *m*, arriviste *mf*

so'cial events' *spl* mondanités *fpl*

socialism [ˈsoʃəˌlɪzəm] *s* socialisme *m*

socialist [ˈsoʃəlɪst] *s* socialiste *mf*

socialite [ˈsoʃəˌlaɪt] *s* (coll) membre *m* de la haute société

so'cial reg'ister *s* annuaire *m* de la haute société

so'cial secu'rity *s* sécurité *f* sociale, assistance *f* familiale

so'cial serv'ice *s* assistance *f* sociale, aide *f* sociale, aide familiale

so'cial stra'ta [ˌstrætə] *spl* couches *fpl* sociales

so'cial work'er *s* assistant *m* social, travailleuse *f* familiale

socie•ty [səˈsaɪˑəti] *s* (*pl* -**ties**) société *f*

soci'ety col'umn *s* carnet *m* mondain

soci'ety ed'itor *s* chroniqueur *m* mondain

sociology [ˌsosɪˈalədʒi] *s* sociologie *f*

sock [sak] *s* chaussette *f*; (slang) coup *m* de poing ‖ *tr* (slang) donner un coup de poing à

socket [ˈsakɪt] *s* (*of bone*) cavité *f*, glène *f*; (*of candlestick*) tube *m*; (*of caster*) sabot *m*; (*of eye*) orbite *f*; (*of tooth*) alvéole *m*; (elec) douille *f*

sock'et joint' *s* joint *m* à rotule

sock'et wrench' *s* clé *f* à tube

Socrates [ˈsakrətiz] *s* Socrate *m*

Socratic [soˈkrætɪk] *adj* socratique

sod [sad] *s* gazon *m*; motte *f* de gazon ‖ *v* (*pret & pp* **sodded**; *ger* **sodding**) *tr* gazonner

soda [ˈsodə] *s* (*soda water*) soda *m;* (chem) soude *f*

so′da crack′er *s* biscuit *m* soda

so′da wa′ter *s* soda *m*

sodium [ˈsodɪ•əm] *s* sodium *m*

sodomy [ˈsadəmi] *s* sodomie *f*

sofa [ˈsofə] *s* canapé *m*, sofa *m*

so′fa bed′ *s* lit-canapé *m*

soft [sɔft] *adj* (*yielding*) mou; (*mild*) doux; (*weak in character*) faible; **to go soft** (coll) perdre la boule

soft′-boiled egg′ *s* œuf *m* à la coque

soft′ coal′ *s* houille *f* grasse

soft′ drink′ *s* boisson *f* non-alcoolisée

soften [ˈsɔfən] *tr* amollir; (*e.g., noise*) atténuer; (*one's voice*) adoucir; (*one's moral fiber*) affaiblir; **to soften up** amollir ‖ *intr* s'amollir; s'adoucir; s'affaiblir

soft′-head′ed *adj* faible d'esprit, cinglé

soft′-heart′ed *adj* au coeur tendre, compatissant

soft′ land′ing *s* (rok) arrivée *f* en douceur

soft′ ped′al *s* (mus) pédale *f* sourde

soft′-ped′al *v* (*pret & pp* -aled *or* -alled; *ger* -aling *or* -alling) *tr* (coll) atténuer, modérer

soft′ shoul′der *s* (aut) accotement *m* nonstabilisé

soft′ soap′ *s* savon *m* mou, savon noir; (coll) pommade *f*

soft′-soap′ *tr* (coll) passer de la pommade à

soft′ware *s* (comp) logiciel *m*, programmerie *f*

soft′ware engineer′ing *s* genie *m* logiciel

sog•gy [ˈsagi] *adj* (*comp* -gier; *super* -giest) saturé, détrempé

soil [sɔɪl] *s* sol *m*, terroir *m* ‖ *tr* salir, souiller ‖ *intr* se salir

soil′ pipe′ *s* tuyau *m* de descente

sojourn [ˈsodʒʌrn] *s* séjour *m* ‖ *intr* séjourner

solace [ˈsalɪs] *s* consolation *f* ‖ *tr* consoler

solar [ˈsolər] *adj* solaire

so′lar bat′tery *s* photopile *f*

so′lar cell *s* cellule *f* solaire, photopile *f*

so′lar heat′er *s* insolateur *m*

so′lar radia′tion *s* rayonnement *m* solaire

sold [sold] *adj*—**sold out** (*no more room*) complet; (*no more merchandise*) épuisé; **to be sold on** (coll) raffoler de ‖ *interj* (*to the highest bidder*) adjugé!

solder [ˈsadər] *s* soudure *f* ‖ *tr* souder

sol′dering i′ron *s* fer *m* à souder

soldier [ˈsoldʒər] *s* soldat *m*

sole [sol] *adj* seul, unique ‖ *s* (*of shoe*) semelle *f;* (*of foot*) plante *f;* (*fish*) sole *f* ‖ *tr* ressemeler

solemn [ˈsaləm] *adj* sérieux, grave; (*ceremony*) solennel

solemnize [ˈsalɛm,naɪz] *tr* solenniser

solenoid [ˈsolə,nɔɪd] *s* solénoïde *m*

solicit [səˈlɪsɪt] *tr* solliciter ‖ *intr* quêter; (*with immoral intentions*) racoler

solicitation [sə,lɪsəˈteʃən] *s* sollicitation *f*

solicitor [səˈlɪsɪtər] *s* (*for contributions*) solliciteur *m;* (*for trade*) agent *m*, représentant *m;*

(com) démarcheur *m;* (law) procureur *m;* (Brit) avoué *m*

solicitous [səˈlɪsɪtəs] *adj* soucieux

solid [ˈsalɪd] *adj* solide, consistant; (*clouds*) dense; (*gold*) massif; (*opinion*) unanime; (*color*) uni; (*hour, day, week*) entier; (*e.g., three days*) d'affilée ‖ *s* solide *m*

solidarity [,salɪˈdarɪtɪ] *s* solidarité *f;* **to declare solidarity with** se solidariser avec, se déclarer solidaire de; **to show solidarity** être solidaires

sol′id geom′etry *s* géométrie *f* dans l'espace

solidity [səˈlɪdɪti] *s* solidité *f*, consistance *f*

sol′id-state′ *adj* (electron) en état solide

sol′id-state′ phys′ics *s* physique *f* de l'état solide

solilo•quy [səˈlɪləkwi] *s* (*pl* -quies) soliloque *m*

solitaire [ˈsalɪ,tɛr] *s* solitaire *m;* (cards) patience *f*, réussite *f;* **to play solitaire** faire une réussite

solitar•y [ˈsalɪ,tɛri] *adj* solitaire ‖ *s* (*pl* -ies) solitaire *m*

sol′itary confine′ment *s* régime *m* cellulaire

solitude [ˈsalɪ,t(j)ud] *s* solitude *f*

so•lo [ˈsolo] *adj* solo ‖ *s* (*pl* -los) solo *m*

soloist [ˈsolo•ɪst] *s* soliste *mf*

so′ long′ *interj* (coll) à bientôt!, tchao! *or* ciao!, prochainement!, on se reverra!

solstice [ˈsalstɪs] *s* solstice *m*

soluble [ˈsaljəbəl] *adj* soluble

solution [səˈluʃən] *s* solution *f*

solvable [ˈsalvəbəl] *adj* soluble

solve [salv] *tr* résoudre

solvency [ˈsalvənsi] *s* solvabilité *f*

solvent [ˈsalvənt] *adj* (*substance*) solubilisant; (*person or business*) solvable ‖ *s* (*of a substance*) solvant *m*

somber [ˈsambər] *adj* sombre

some [sʌm] *adj indef* quelque, du; **some way or other** d'une manière ou d'une autre ‖ *pron indef* certains, quelques-uns §81; en §87 ‖ *adv* un peu, passablement, assez; environ; quelque, e.g., **some two hundred soldiers** quelque deux cents soldats

some′bod′y *pron indef* quelqu'un §81; **somebody else** quelqu'un d'autre ‖ *s* (*pl* -ies) (coll) quelqu'un *m*

some′day′ *adv* un jour

some′how′ *adv* dans un sens, je ne sais comment; **somehow or other** d'une manière ou d'une autre, vaille que vaille

some′one′ *pron indef* quelqu'un §81; **someone else** quelqu'un d'autre

somersault [ˈsʌmər,sɔlt] *s* culbute *f;* (sports) saut *m* périlleux

some′thing′ *s* (coll) quelque chose *m* ‖ *pron indef* quelque chose (*masc*) ‖ *adv* quelque peu, un peu

some′time′ *adj* ancien, ci-devant ‖ *adv* un jour; un de ces jours

some′times′ *adv* quelquefois, de temps en temps, des fois; **sometimes . . . sometimes** tantôt . . . tantôt

some′way′ *adv* d'une manière ou d'une autre

some′what′ *adv* un peu, assez

some′where′ *adv* quelque part; **somewhere else** ailleurs, autre part

somnambulist [sɑmˈnæmbjəlɪst] *s* somnambule *mf*

somnolent [ˈsɑmnələnt] *adj* somnolent

son [sʌn] *s* fils *m*

sonata [səˈnɑtə] *s* sonate *f*

song [sɔŋ] *s* chanson *f;* (*of praise*) hymne *m;* **to buy for a song** (coll) acheter pour une bouchée de pain

song′bird′ *s* oiseau *m* chanteur

song′ book′ *s* recueil *m* de chansons

Song′ of Songs′ *s* (Bib) Cantique *m* des Cantiques

song′thrush′ *s* grive *f* musicienne

song′writ′er *s* chansonnier *m*

sonic [ˈsɑnɪk] *adj* sonique

son′ic boom′ *s* double bang *m*

son′-in-law′ *s* (*pl* **sons-in-law**) gendre *m*, beau fils *m*

sonnet [ˈsɑnɪt] *s* sonnet *m*

son•ny [ˈsʌni] *s* (*pl* **-nies**) fiston *m*

soon [sun] *adv* bientôt; (*early*) tôt; **as soon as** aussitôt que, dès que, sitôt que; **as soon as possible** le plus tôt possible; **how soon** quand; **no sooner said than done** sitôt dit sitôt fait; **soon after** tôt après; **sooner** plus tôt; (*rather*) (coll) plutôt; **sooner or later** tôt ou tard; **so soon** si tôt; **too soon** trop tôt

soot [sʊt] *s* suie *f* ‖ *tr*—**to soot up** encrasser de suie ‖ *intr* s'encrasser

soothe [suð] *tr* calmer, apaiser; flatter

soothsayer [ˈsuθˌseɪər] *s* devin *m*

soot•y [ˈsʊti] *adj* (*comp* **-ier;** *super* **-iest**) (*color; flame*) fuligineux; couvert de suie

sop [sɑp] *s* morceaux *m* trempé; (fig) os *m* à ronger, cadeau *m* ‖ *v* (*pret & pp* **sopped;** *ger* **sopping**) *tr* tremper, faire tremper; **to sop up** absorber

sophisticated [səˈfɪstɪˌketɪd] *adj* mondain, sceptique; complexe; (comp) sophistiqué

sophistication [səˌfɪstɪˈkeʃən] *s* mondanité *f*

sophomore [ˈsɑfəˌmor] *s* étudiant *m* de deuxième année

sophomoric [ˌsɑfəˈmɔrɪk] *adj* naïf, suffisant, présomptueux

sopping [ˈsɑpɪŋ] *adj* détrempé, trempé ‖ *adv*—**sopping wet** trempé comme une soupe

sopran•o [səˈpræno] *adj* de soprano ‖ *s* (*pl* **-os**) soprano *f;* (*boy*) soprano *m*

sorcerer [ˈsɔrsərər] *s* sorcier *m*

sorceress [ˈsɔrsərɪs] *s* sorcière *f*

sorcer•y [ˈsɔrsəri] *s* (*pl* **-ies**) sorcellerie *f*

sordid [ˈsɔrdɪd] *adj* sordide

sore [sor] *adj* douloureux, enflammé; (coll) fâché ‖ *s* plaie *f*, ulcère *m*

sore′head′ *s* (coll) rouspéteur *m*, grincheux *m*

sorely [ˈsorli] *adv* gravement, grièvement; cruellement

soreness [ˈsornɪs] *s* douleur *f*, sensibilité *f*

sore′ throat′ *s*—**to have a sore throat** avoir mal à la gorge

sorori•ty [səˈrɔrɪti] *s* (*pl* **-ties**) club *m* d'étudiantes universitaires

sorrow [ˈsɔro] *s* chagrin *m*, peine *f*, affliction *f*, tristesse *f* ‖ *intr* s'affliger, avoir du chagrin; être en deuil; **to sorrow for** s'affliger de

sorrowful [ˈsɔrəfəl] *adj* (*person*) affligé, attristé; (*news*) affligeant

sor•ry [ˈsɔri] *adj* (*comp* **-rier;** *super* **-riest**) désolé, navré, fâché; (*appearance*) piteux, misérable; (*situation*) triste; **to be** or **feel sorry for** regretter; **to be** or **feel sorry for** regretter (*q.ch.*); plaindre (*qn*); **to be sorry to** + *inf* regretter de + *inf* ‖ *interj* pardon!

sort [sɔrt] *s* sorte *f*, espèce *f*, genre *m;* **a sort of** une espèce de; **to be out of sorts** être de mauvaise humeur, ne pas être dans son assiette ‖ *tr* classer; **to sort out** trier

so′-so′ *adj* (coll) assez bon, passable, supportable ‖ *adv* assez bien, comme ci comme ça

sot [sɑt] *s* ivrogne *mf*

soul [sol] *s* âme *f;* **not a soul** (coll) pas un chat; **upon my soul!** par ma foi!

soul′ food′ *s* (culin) plats *mpl* traditionnels dans le Sud des Etats-Unis

soul′mate′ *s* âme *f* sœur

sound [saʊnd] *adj* (*body, fruit, tree*) sain; (*structure, floor, bridge*) solide, en bon état; (*healthy, robust*) en bonne santé, bien portant; (*sleep*) profond ‖ *s* son *m;* (*probe*) sonde *f;* (geog) goulet *m*, détroit *m*, bras *m* de mer ‖ *adv* (*asleep*) profondément ‖ *tr* sonner; (*to take a sounding of*) sonder; **to sound out** sonder; **to sound the horn** klaxonner, corner ‖ *intr* sonner; sonder; **to sound off** parler haut; **to sound strange** sembler bizarre

sound′ bar′rier *s* mur *m* du son

sound′ effects′ *spl* (mov, rad, telv, theat) bruitage *m*

sound′ film′ *s* film *m* sonore

sound′ hole′ *s* (*of a violin*) ouïe *f*

sounding [ˈsaʊndɪŋ] *s* (*signal*) son *m;* (*act*) sondage *m;* (*measurements*) sondages *mpl*

sound′ing board′ *s* (*behind rostrum*) abat-voix *m invar;* (mus) table *f* d'harmonie

soundly [ˈsaʊndli] *adv* sainement; profondément; (*hard*) bien

sound′ post′ *s* (*of a violin*) âme *f*

sound′proof′ *adj* insonorisé, insonore ‖ *tr* insonoriser

sound′proof(ed) room′ *s* chambre *f* sourde

sound′proof′ing *s* insonorisation *f*

sound′track′ *s* piste *f* sonore, sonorisation *f*

sound′ wave′ *s* onde *f* sonore

soup [sup] *s* potage *m*, bouillon *m;* (*with vegetables*) soupe *f;* **in the soup** (coll) dans le pétrin or la mélasse

soup′ kitch′en *s* soupe *f* populaire

soup′ spoon′ *s* cuiller *f* à soupe

soup′ tureen′ *s* soupière *f*

sour [saʊr] *adj* aigre; (*grapes*) vert; (*apples*) sur; (*milk*) tourné ‖ *tr* rendre aigre ‖ *intr* tourner, s'aigrir

source [sors] *s* source *f*

source′ lan′guage *s* langue *f* source, langue de départ

source′ mate′rial *s* sources *fpl* originales

sour′ cher′ry *s* (*pl* -ries) griotte *f;* (*tree*) griottier *m*

sour′ cream′ *s* crème *f* fraîche

sour′ grapes′ *interj* ils sont trop verts!

sour′ puss′ *s* (slang) grincheux *m*

south [sauθ] *adj & s* sud *m;* **the South** (*of France, Italy, etc.*) le Midi; (*of U.S.A.*) le Sud ‖ *adv* au sud, vers le sud

South′ Af′rica *s* la République sud-africaine

South′ Amer′ica *s* Amérique *f* du Sud; l'Amérique du Sud

South′ Amer′ican *adj* sud-américain ‖ *s* (*person*) Sud-Américain *m*

south′east′ *adj & s* sud-est *m*

southern [′sʌðərn] *adj* du sud, méridional

South′ern Cross′ *s* Croix-du-Sud *f*

southerner [′sʌðərnər] *s* Méridional *m;* (U.S.A.) sudiste *mf*

South′ Kore′a *s* Corée *f* du Sud; la Corée du Sud

South′ Kore′an *adj* sud-coréen ‖ *s* (*person*) Sud-Coréen *m*

south′paw′ *adj & s* (coll) gaucher *m*

South′ Pole′ *s* pôle *m* Sud

southward [′sauθwərd] *adv* vers le sud

south′west′ *adj & s* sud-ouest *m*

souvenir [,suvə′nɪr] *s* souvenir *m*

souv′enir sheet′ *s* (phila) bloc *m* commémoratif

sovereign [′savrɪn] *adj* souverain ‖ *s* (*king; coin*) souverain *m;* (*queen*) souveraine *f*

sovereign·ty [′savrɪnti], *s* (*pl* -ties) souveraineté *f*

soviet [′sovɪ,ɛt] *adj* soviétique ‖ *s* soviet *m;* **Soviet** (*person*) Soviétique *mf*

So′viet Rus′sia *s* la Russie *f* soviétique

So′viet Un′ion *s* Union *f* soviétique

sow [sau] *s* truie *f* ‖ [so] *v* (*pret* **sowed;** *pp* **sown** or **sowed**) *tr* (*seed; a field*) semer; (*a field*) ensemencer

soybean [′sɔɪ,bin] *s* soya *m*, soja *m*

spa [spa] *s* ville *f* d'eau, station *f* thermale, bains *mpl*

space [spes] *s* espace *m;* (*in typing*) frappe *f;* (typ) espace *f* ‖ *tr* espacer

space′ age′ *s* âge *m* de l'exploration spatiale

space′ bar′ *s* barre *f* d'espacement

space′ cap′sule *s* capsule *f* spatiale

space′ cen′ter *s* centre *m* spatial

space′craft′ *s* astronef *m*

space′ flight′ *s* voyage *m* spatial, vol *m* spatial

space′ heat′er *s* chaufferette *f*

space′ hel′met *s* casque *m* de cosmonaute

space′man′ or **space′man** *s* (*pl* -**men′** or -**men**) homme *m* de l'espace, astronaute *m*, cosmonaute *m*

space′ probe′ *s* sonde *m* spatiale, coup *m* de sonde dans l'espace; (*rocket*) fusée *f* sonde

spacer [′spesər] *s* (*of typewriter*) barre *f* d'espacement

space′ race′ *s* course *f* spatiale

space′ship′ *s* vaisseau *m* spatial, astronef *m*

space′ shut′tle *s* navette *f* spatiale

space′ sta′tion *s* station *f* orbitale

space′ suit′ *s* (rok) scaphandre *m* des cosmonautes, scaphandre spatial, combinaison *f* spatiale

space′-time′ *s* espace-temps *m*

space′ ve′hicle *s* spationef *m*

space′ walk′ *s* promenade *f* dans l'espace ‖ **space′walk′** *intr* se promener dans l'espace

spacious [′speʃəs] *adj* spacieux

spade [sped] *s* bêche *f;* (cards) pique *m;* **to call a spade a spade** (coll) appeler un chat un chat

spade′work′ *s* gros travail *m*, défrichage *m*

spaghetti [spə′gɛti] *s* spaghetti *mpl*

Spain [spen] *s* Espagne *f;* l'Espagne

Spam [spæm] *s* (trademark) viande *f* froide en conserve; **spam** (comp) (slang) messages *mpl* commerciaux non sollicités envoyés par e-mail

span [spæn] *s* portée *f;* (*of time*) durée *f;* (*of hand*) empan *m;* (*of wing*) envergure *f;* (*of bridge*) travée *f* ‖ *v* (*pret & pp* **spanned;** *ger* **spanning**) *tr* couvrir, traverser

spangle [′spæŋgəl] *s* paillette *f* ‖ *tr* orner de paillettes

Spanglish [′spæŋglɪʃ] *s* espagnol-anglais *m* invar

Spaniard [′spænjərd] *s* Espagnol *m*

spaniel [′spænjəl] *s* épagneul *m*

Spanish [′spænɪʃ] *adj* espagnol ‖ *s* (*language*) espagnol *m;* **the Spanish** (*persons*) les Espagnols *mpl*

Span′ish-Amer′ican *adj* hispano-américain ‖ *s* Hispano-Américain *m*

Span′ish broom′ *s* genêt *m* d'Espagne

Span′ish fly′ *s* cantharide *f*

Span′ish Main′ *s* Terre *f* ferme; mer *f* des Antilles

Span′ish moss′ *s* tillandsie *f*

Span′ish-speak′ing *adj* hispanophone, d'expression espagnole; (*country*) de langue espagnole

spank [spæŋk] *tr* fesser

spanking [′spæŋkɪŋ] *adj* (Brit) de premier ordre; **at a spanking pace** à toute vitesse ‖ *s* fessée *f*

spar [spar] *s* (mineral) spath *m;* (naut) espar *m* ‖ *v* (*pret & pp* **sparred;** *ger* **sparring**) *intr* s'entraîner à la boxe; se battre

spare [spɛr] *adj* (*thin*) maigre; (*available*) disponible; (*interchangeable*) de rechange; (*left over*) en surnombre ‖ *tr* (*to save*) épargner, économiser; (*one's efforts*) ménager; (*a person*) faire grâce à, traiter avec indulgence; (*time, money, etc.*) disposer de; (*something*) se passer de

spare′ clothes′ *spl* vêtements *mpl* de rechange

spare′ parts′ *spl* pièces *fpl* détachées, pièces de rechange

spare′ rib′ *s* côte *f* découverte de porc, plat *m* de côtes

spare′ room′ *s* chambre *f* d'ami

spare′ time′ *s* moments *mpl* de loisir, heures *fpl* perdues

spare′ tire′ *s* pneu *m* de rechange

spare′ wheel′ *s* roue *f* de secours

sparing [ˈspɛrɪŋ] *adj* économe, frugal

spark [spɑrk] *s* étincelle *f*

spark′ coil′ *s* bobine *f* d'allumage

spark′ gap′ *s* (*of induction coil*) éclateur *m;* (*of spark plug*) entrefer *m*

sparkle [ˈspɑrkəl] *s* étincellement *m*, éclat *m* ‖ *intr* étinceler

sparkling [ˈspɑrklɪŋ] *adj* étincelant; (*wine*) mousseux; (*soft drink*) gazeux

spark′ plug′ *s* bougie *f*

spar′ring part′ner *s* adversaire *mf* dans un match de boxe; boxeur *m* avec qui on s'entraîne

sparrow [ˈspæro] *s* moineau *m*

spar′row hawk′ *s* épervier *m*

sparse [spɑrs] *adj* clairsemé, rare; peu nombreux

Spartan [ˈspɑrtən] *adj* spartiate ‖ *s* Spartiate *mf*

spasm [ˈspæzəm] *s* spasme *m*

spasmodic [spæzˈmɑdɪk] *adj* intermittent, irrégulier; (pathol) spasmodique

spastic [ˈspæstɪk] *adj* spasmodique

spat [spæt] *s* (coll) dispute *f*, prise *f* de bec; **spats** demi-guêtres *fpl* ‖ *v* (*pret & pp* **spatted;** *ger* **spatting**) *intr* se disputer

spatial [ˈspeʃəl] *adj* spatial, de l'espace

spatter [ˈspætər] *s* éclaboussure *f* ‖ *tr* éclabousser

spatula [ˈspætʃələ] *s* spatule *f*

spawn [spɔn] *s* frai *m* ‖ *tr* engendrer ‖ *intr* frayer

spay [spe] *tr* châtrer

speak [spik] *v* (*pret* **spoke** [spok]; *pp* **spoken**) *tr* (*a word, one's mind, the truth*) dire; (*a language*) parler ‖ *intr* parler; **so to speak** pour ainsi dire; **speaking!** à l'appareil!; **to speak out** or **up** parler plus haut, élever la voix; (fig) parler franc

speak′-eas′y *s* (*pl* **-ies**) bar *m* clandestin

speaker [ˈspikər] *s* parleur *m;* (*person addressing a group*) conférencier *m;* (*presiding officer*) speaker *m*, président *m;* (rad) haut-parleur *m*

speaking [ˈspikɪŋ] *adj* parlant; **to be on speaking terms with s.o.** adresser la parole à qn ‖ *s* art *m* de parler

spear [spɪr] *s* lance *f* ‖ *tr* percer d'un coup de lance

spear′head′ *s* fer *m* de lance; (mil) pointe *f*, avancée *f* ‖ *tr* (*e.g., a campaign*) diriger

spear′mint′ *s* menthe *f* verte

special [ˈspɛʃəl] *adj* spécial, particulier ‖ *s* train *m* spécial

spe′cial-deliv′ery let′ter *s* lettre *f* exprès

spe′cial ed′ucation *s* éducation *f* spéciale, éducation pour des étudiants handicapés

specialist [ˈspɛʃəlɪst] *s* spécialiste *mf*

speciali•ty [ˌspɛʃiˈælɪti] *s* (*pl* **-ties**) spécialité *f*

specialize [ˈspɛʃəˌlaɪz] *tr* spécialiser ‖ *intr* se spécialiser

special•ty [ˈspɛʃəlti] *s* (*pl* **-ties**) spécialité *f;* **cassoulet is a specialty of Toulouse** le cassoulet est une spécialité toulousaine

specie [ˈspisi] *s*—**in specie** en espèces, en numéraire

spe•cies [ˈspisiz] *s* (*pl* **-cies**) espèce *f*

specific [spɪˈsɪfɪk] *adj* & *s* spécifique *m*

specif′ic grav′ity *s* poids *m* spécifique

speci•fy [ˈspɛsɪˌfaɪ] *v* (*pret & pp* **-fied**) *tr* spécifier

specimen [ˈspɛsɪmən] *s* spécimen *m;* (coll) drôle *m* de type

specious [ˈspiʃəs] *adj* spécieux

speck [spɛk] *s* (*on fruit, face, etc.*) tache *f;* (*in the distance*) point *m;* (*small quantity*) brin *m*, grain *m*, atome *m* ‖ *tr* tacheter

speckle [ˈspɛkəl] *s* petite tache *f* ‖ *tr* tacheter, moucheter

spectacle [ˈspɛktəkəl] *s* spectacle *m;* **spectacles** lunettes *fpl*

spec′tacle case′ *s* étui *m* à lunettes

spectator [ˈspɛktetər] *s* spectateur *m*

specter [ˈspɛktər] *s* spectre *m*

spec•trum [ˈspɛktrəm] *s* (*pl* **-tra** [trə] or **-trums**) spectre *m*

speculate [ˈspɛkjəˌlet] *intr* spéculer

speculator [ˈspɛkjəˌletər] *s* spéculateur *m*, boursicotier *m*

speech [spitʃ] *s* (*faculty*) parole *f;* (*language*) langage *m;* (*of a people or region*) parler *m;* (*manner of speaking*) façon *f* de parler; (*enunciation*) articulation *f*, élocution *f;* (*formal address*) discours *m;* (theat) tirade *f;* **to make a speech** prononcer un discours

speech′ clin′ic *s* centre *m* de rééducation de la parole

speech′ correc′tion *s* rééducation *f* de la parole

speech′ de′fect *s* défaut *m* d'élocution

speechless [ˈspitʃlɪs] *adj* sans parole, muet; (fig) sidéré, stupéfié

speech′ ther′apy *s* phoniatrie *f*

speed [spid] *s* vitesse *f;* **at full speed** à toute vitesse ‖ *v* (*pret & pp* **speeded** or **sped** [spɛd]) *tr* dépêcher, hâter ‖ *intr* se dépêcher; **to speed up** aller plus vite

speed′ bump′ *s* dos *m* d'âne

speeding [ˈspidɪŋ] *s* excès *m* de vitesse

speed′ king′ *s* as *m* du volant

speed′ lim′it *s* vitesse *f* maximum

speedometer [spiˈdɑmɪtər] *s* indicateur *m* de vitesse

speed′ rec′ord *s* record *m* de vitesse

speed′ trap′ *s* (aut) piège *m* de police pour contrôle de vitesse

speed′-up′ *s* accélération *f*

speed′way′ *s* (*racetrack*) piste *f* d'autos; (*highway*) autoroute *f*

speed•y [ˈspidi] *adj* (*comp* **-ier;** *super* **-iest**) rapide, vite, prompt

speed′ zone′ *s* zone *f* de vitesse surveillée

spell [spɛl] *s* (*magic power*) sortilège *m*, charme *m;* (*brief period*) intervalle *m;* (*turn*) tour *m;* (*magic words*) formule *f* magique; (*attack*) accès *m* ‖ *v* (*pret & pp* **spelled** or **spelt** [spɛlt]) *tr* (*orally*) épeler; (*in writing*) orthographier, écrire; **to spell out** (coll) expliquer en détail ‖ *v* (*pret & pp* **spelled**) *tr* (*to relieve*) remplacer, relever, relayer

spell′bind′er *s* orateur *m* fascinant, orateur entraînant

spell′bound′ *adj* fasciné

spell′ check′er *s* (comp) vérificateur *m* orthographique

spelling [′spɛlɪŋ] *s* orthographe *f*

spell′ing bee′ *s* concours *m* d'orthographe

spelunker [spɪ′lʌŋkər] *s* spéléo *m*

spend [spɛnd] *v* (*pret & pp* **spent** [spɛnt]) *tr* dépenser; (*a period of time*) passer

spender [′spɛndər] *s* dépensier *m*

spend′ing mon′ey *s* argent *m* de poche pour les menues dépenses

spend′thrift′ *s* prodigue *mf*, grand dépensier *m*

sperm [spʌrm] *s* sperme *m*

sperm′ bank′ *s* banque *f* de sperme

sperm′ whale′ *s* cachalot *m*

spew [spju] *tr & intr* vomir

sphere [sfɪr] *s* sphère *f*; corps *m* céleste

spherical [′sfɛrɪkəl] *adj* sphérique

sphinx [sfɪŋks] *s* (*pl* **sphinxes** or **sphinges** [′sfɪndʒiz]) sphinx *m*

spice [spaɪs] *s* épice *f*; (fig) sel *m*, piquant *m* ‖ *tr* épicer

spick-and-span [′spɪkənd′spæn] *adj* (*room*) brillant comme un sou neuf; (*person*) tiré à quatre épingles

spic•y [′spaɪsi] *adj* (*comp* **-ier;** *super* **-iest**) épicé, aromatique; (*e.g., gravy*) relevé; (*conversation, story, etc.*) épicé, salé, piquant, grivois

spider [′spaɪdər] *s* araignée *f*

spi′der•web′ *s* toile *f* d'araignée

spiff•y [′spɪfi] *adj* (*comp* **-ier;** *super* **-iest**) (slang) épatant, élégant

spigot [′spɪgət] *s* robinet *m*

spike [spaɪk] *s* pointe *f*; (*nail*) clou *m* à large tête; (bot) épi *m*; (rr) crampon *m* ‖ *tr* clouer; ruiner, supprimer; (*a drink*) (coll) corser à l'alcool ‖ *intr* (bot) former des épis

spill [spɪl] *s* chute *f*, culbute *f* ‖ *v* (*pret & pp* **spilled** or **spilt** [spɪlt]) *tr* renverser; (*a liquid*) répandre; (*a rider*) désarçonner; (*passengers*) verser ‖ *intr* se répandre, s'écouler

spill′way′ *s* déversoir *m*

spin [spɪn] *s* (*turning motion*) tournoiement *m*, rotation *f*; (*on a ball*) effet *m*; (aer) vrille *f*; (pol) opérations *fpl* publicitaires dans le domaine des relations publiques; (pol) point *m* de vue spécial; **to go for a spin** (coll) se balader en voiture; **to go into a spin** (aer) descendre en vrille ‖ *v* (*pret & pp* **spun** [spʌn]; *ger* **spinning**) *tr* filer; faire tournoyer; (pol) faire un expertise publicitaire de; (pol) présenter un point de vue de ‖ *intr* filer; tournoyer

spinach [′spɪnɪtʃ] *s* épinard *m*; (*leaves used as food*) des épinards

spinal [′spaɪnəl] *adj* spinal

spi′nal col′umn *s* colonne *f* vertébrale

spi′nal cord′ *s* moelle *f* épinière

spindle [′spɪndəl] *s* fuseau *m*

spin′ doc′tor *s* (pol) (coll) expert *m* dans le domaine des relations publiques

spin′-dri′er *s* essoreuse *f*

spin′-dry′ *v* (*pret & pp* **-dried**) *tr* essorer

spine [spaɪn] *s* (*in body*) épine *f* dorsale, échine *f*; (*quill, fin*) épine; (*ridge*) arête *f*; (*of book*) dos *m*; (fig) courage *m*

spine′-chill′ing *adj* à vous glacer le sang

spineless [′spaɪnlɪs] *adj* sans épines; (*weak*) mou; **to be spineless** (fig) avoir l'échine souple

spinet [′spɪnɪt] *s* épinette *f*

spinner [′spɪnər] *s* fileur *m*; machine *f* à filer

spinning [′spɪnɪŋ] *adj* tournoyant ‖ *s* (*act*) filage *m*; (*art*) filature *f*

spin′ning wheel′ *s* rouet *m*

spin′-off′ *s* avantage *m* inattendu; (com) sous-produit *m*, application *f* secondaire; **to be a spin-off from** (telv) être tiré de, être issu de

spinster [′spɪnstər] *s* (usually offensive) célibataire *f*, vieille fille *f*

spiraea [spaɪ′riə] *s* spirée *f*

spi•ral [′spaɪrəl] *adj* spiral, en spirale ‖ *s* spirale *f* ‖ *v* (*pret & pp* **-raled** *ou* **-ralled;** *ger* **-raling** *ou* **-ralling**) *intr* tourner en spirale; (aer) vriller

spi′ral stair′ case *s* escalier *m* en colimaçon

spire [spaɪr] *s* aiguille *f*; (*of clock tower*) flèche *f*

spirit [′spɪrɪt] *s* esprit *m*; (*enthusiasm*) feu *m*; (*temper, genius*) génie *m*; (*host*) esprit, revenant *m*; **high spirits** joie *f*, abandon *m*; **spirits** (*alcoholic liquor*) esprit *m*, spiritueux *m*; **to raise the spirits of** remonter le courage de ‖ *tr*—**to spirit away** enlever, faire disparaître mystérieusement

spirited *adj* animé, vigoureux

spiritless [′spɪrɪtlɪs] *adj* sans force, abattu, déprimé

spir′it lev′el *s* niveau *m* à bulle

spiritual [′spɪrɪtʃu•əl] *adj* spirituel ‖ *s* chant *m* religieux populaire

spiritualism [′spɪrɪtʃu•ə₁lɪzəm] *s* spiritisme *m*

spiritualist [′spɪrɪtʃu•əlɪst] *s* spirite *mf*; (philos) spiritualiste *mf*

spir′ituous bev′erages [′spɪrɪtʃu•əs] *spl* boissons *fpl* spiritueuses

spit [spɪt] *s* salive *f*; (culin) broche *f* ‖ *v* (*pret & pp* **spat** [spæt] or **spit;** *ger* **spitting**) *tr & intr* cracher

spit′ball *s* petite balle *f* de papier mouillé; (baseball) balle *f* mouillée de salive

spit′ curl′ *s* rouflaquette *f*

spite [spaɪt] *s* dépit *m*, rancune *f*; **in spite of** en dépit de, malgré ‖ *tr* dépiter, contrarier

spiteful [′spaɪtfəl] *adj* rancunier

spit′fire′ *s* mégère *f*

spit′ting im′age *s* (coll) portrait *m* craché

spittoon [spɪ′tun] *s* crachoir *m*

splash [splæʃ] *s* éclaboussure *f*; (*of waves*) clapotis *m;* **to make a splash** (coll) faire sensation ‖ *tr & intr* éclabousser ‖ *interj* flic flac!

splash′down′ *s* (rok) amerrissage *m*

spleen [splin] *s* (anat) rate *f;* (fig) maussaderie *f,* mauvaise humeur *f;* **to vent one's spleen on** décharger sa bile sur

splendid [ˈsplɛndɪd] *adj* splendide; (coll) admirable, superbe

splendor [ˈsplɛndər] *s* splendeur *f*

splice [splaɪs] *s* (*in rope*) épissure *f;* (*in wood*) enture *f* ‖ *tr* (*rope*) épisser; (*wood*) enter; (*film*) réparer, coller; (slang) marier

splint [splɪnt] *s* éclisse *f* ‖ *tr* éclisser

splinter [ˈsplɪntər] *s* éclat *m,* éclisse *f;* (*lodged under the skin*) écharde *f* ‖ *tr* briser en éclats ‖ *intr* voler en éclats

splin′ter group′ *s* minorité *f* dissidente, groupe *m* fragmentaire

split [splɪt] *adj* fendu; (*pea*) cassé; (*skirt*) déchiré ‖ *s* fente *f,* fissure *f;* (*quarrel*) rupture *f;* (*one's share*) part *f;* (*bottle*) quart *m,* demi *m;* (gymnastics) grand écart *m* ‖ *v* (*pret & pp* **split;** *ger* **splitting**) *tr* fendre; (*money; work; ticket*) partager; (*in two*) couper; (*a hide*) dédoubler; **to split hairs** couper les cheveux en quatre; **to split one's sides laughing** se tenir les côtes de rire; **to split the difference** couper la poire en deux ‖ *intr* se fendre; **to split away (from)** se séparer (de)

split′ fee′ *s* (*between doctors*) dichotomie *f*

split′-lev′el *adj* à deux niveaux

split′ personal′ity *s* personnalité *f* dedoublée

split′-sec′ond *s* fraction *f* de seconde

split′ skirt′ *s* jupe-culotte *f*

split′ tick′et *s* (pol) panachage *m*

splitting [ˈsplɪtɪŋ] *adj* violent; (*headache*) atroce ‖ *s* fendage *m;* (*of the atom*) désintégration *f;* (*of the personality*) dédoublement *m*

splotch [splɑtʃ] *s* tache *f* ‖ *tr* tacher, barbouiller

splurge [splʌrdʒ] *s* (coll) épate *f* ‖ *intr* (coll) se payer une fête; (*to show off*) (coll) faire de l'épate

splutter [ˈsplʌtər] *s* crachement *m* ‖ *tr*—**to splutter out** bredouiller ‖ *intr* crachoter; (*said of candle, grease, etc.*) grésiller

spoil [spɔɪl] *s* (*object of plunder*) prise *f,* proie *f;* **spoils** (*booty*) butin *m,* dépouilles *fpl;* (*emoluments, especially of public office*) assiette *f* au beurre, part *f* du gâteau ‖ *v* (*pret & pp* **spoiled** or **spoilt** [spɔɪlt]) *tr* gâter, abîmer ‖ *intr* se gâter, s'abîmer; **to be spoiling for** (coll) brûler du désir de

spoilage [ˈspɔɪlɪdʒ] *s* déchet *m*

spoiled *adj* gâté

spoil′sport′ *s* rabat-joie *m*

spoils′ sys′tem *s* système *m* des postes aux petits copains

spoke [spok] *s* rai *m,* rayon *m;* (*of a ladder*) échelon *m;* (*of an umbrella*) baleine *f*

spokes′man *s* (*pl* **-men**) porte-parole *m,* interprète *mf*

sponge [spʌndʒ] *s* éponge *f* ‖ *tr* éponger; (*a*

meal) (coll) écornifler ‖ *intr* (coll) écornifler; **to sponge on** (coll) vivre aux crochets de

sponge′ cake′ *s* gâteau *m* de Savoie, gâteau mousseline, génoise *f*

sponger [ˈspʌndʒər] *s* écornifleur *m,* pique-assiette *mf*

sponge′ rub′ber *s* caoutchouc *m* mousse

spon·gy [ˈspʌndʒi] *adj* (*comp* **-gier;** *super* **-giest**) spongieux

sponsor [ˈspɑnsər] *s* patron *m;* sponsor *m,* parraineur *m;* (*godfather*) parrain *m;* (*godmother*) marraine *f;* (law) garant *m;* (rad, telv) commanditaire *m* ‖ *tr* patronner, parrainer; (law) se porter garant de; (rad, telv) commanditer

spon′sor·ship′ *s* patronnage *m*

spontaneous [spɑnˈtenɪ•əs] *adj* spontané

spoof [spuf] *s* (slang) mystification *f;* (slang) parodie *f* ‖ *tr* (slang) mystifier; (slang) blaguer ‖ *intr* (slang) blaguer

spook [spuk] *s* (coll) revenant *m,* spectre *m*

spool [spul] *s* bobine *f*

spoon [spun] *s* cuiller *f;* **to be born with a silver spoon in one's mouth** (coll) être né coiffé ‖ *tr* prendre dans une cuiller; **to spoon off** enlever avec la cuiller ‖ *intr* (coll) se faire des mamours

spooner [ˈspunər] *s* (coll) peloteur *m*

spoonerism [ˈspunə·rɪzəm] *s* contrepèterrie *f*

spoon′-feed′ *v* (*pret & pp* **-fed**) *tr* nourrir à la cuiller; (*an industry*) subventionner; (coll) mâcher la besogne à

spoonful [ˈspunˌfʊl] *s* cuillerée *f*

spoon·y [ˈspuni] *adj* (*comp* **-ier;** *super* **-iest**) (coll) peloteur

sporadic(al) [spəˈrædɪk(əl)] *adj* sporadique

spore [spor] *s* spore *f*

sport [sport] *adj* sportif, de sport ‖ *s* sport *m;* amusement *m,* jeu *m;* (biol) mutation *f;* (coll) chic type *m;* **a good sport** un bon copain; (*a good loser*) un beau joueur; **in sport** par plaisanterie; **to make sport of** tourner en ridicule ‖ *tr* faire parade de, arborer ‖ *intr* s'amuser, jouer

sport′ clothes′ *spl* vêtements *mpl* de sport

sport′ing goods′ *spl* articles *mpl* de sport

sports′cast′er *s* radioreporteur *m* sportif

sports′ ed′itor *s* rédacteur *m* sportif

sports′ fan′ *s* fanatique *mf,* enragé *m* des sports

sports′man *s* (*pl* **-men**) sportif *m*

sports′man·like′ *adj* sportif

sports′man·ship′ *s* sportivité *f*

sports′wear′ *s* vêtements *mpl* sport

sports′writ′er *s* reporter *m* sportif

sport·y [ˈsporti] *adj* (*comp* **-ier;** *super* **-iest**) (coll) sportif; (*smart in dress*) (coll) chic; (*flashy*) (coll) criard, voyant; (coll) dissolu, libertin

spot [spɑt] *s* (*stain*) tache *f;* (*place*) endroit *m,* lieu *m;* **on the spot** sur place, à pied d'œuvre; (slang) dans le pétrin; **spots** (*before eyes*) mouches *fpl* ‖ *v* (*pret & pp* **spotted;** *ger* **spot-**

ting) *tr* tacher; (coll) repérer, détecter ‖ *intr* se tacher

spot′ cash′ *s* argent *m* comptant

spot′ check′ *s* échantillonnage *m*

spot′-check′ *tr* échantillonner

spotless [ˈspɑtlɪs] *adj* sans tache

spot′light′ *s* spot *m;* (aut) projecteur *m* auxiliaire orientable; **to hold the spotlight** (fig) être en vedette ‖ *tr* diriger les projecteurs sur; (fig) mettre en vedette

spot′ remov′er [rɪˌmuvər] *s* détachant *m*

spot′ weld′ing *s* soudage *m* par points

spouse [spaʊz], [spaʊs], *s* (*man*) époux *m,* conjoint *m;* (*woman*) épouse *f,* conjointe *f*

spout [spaʊt] *s* (*discharge pipe or tube*) tuyau *m* de décharge; (*e.g., of teapot*) bec *m;* (*of sprinkling can*) col *m,* queue *f;* (*of water*) jet *m* ‖ *tr* faire jaillir; (*e.g., insults*) (coll) déclamer ‖ *intr* jaillir; **to spout off** (coll) déclamer

sprain [spren] *s* foulure *f,* entorse *f* ‖ *tr* fouler, se fouler

sprawl [sprɔl] *intr* s'étaler, se carrer

spray [spre] *s* (*of ocean*) embruns *mpl;* (*branch*) rameau *m;* (*for insects*) liquide *m* insecticide; (*for weeds*) produit *m* herbicide; (*for spraying insects or weeds*) pulvérisateur *m;* (*for spraying perfume*) vaporisateur *m,* atomiseur *m;* (med) pulvérisation *f* ‖ *tr* pulvériser; (*with a vaporizer*) vaporiser; (hort) désinfecter par pulvérisation d'insecticide; **to spray paint on** peindre au pistolet ‖ *intr*—**to spray out** gicler

sprayer [ˈspreˌər] *s* vaporisateur *m,* pulvérisateur *m*

spray′ gun′ *s* pulvérisateur *m;* (*for paint*) pistolet *m;* (hort) seringue *f*

spread [sprɛd] *adj* étendu, écarté, ouvert ‖ *s* (*extent, expanse*) étendue *f,* rayonnement *m;* (*of disease, fire*) propagation *f,* progression *f;* (*of wings*) envergure *f;* (*on bed*) dessus-de-lit *m,* couvre-lit *m;* (*on sandwich*) pâte *f;* (*buffet lunch*) collation *f* ‖ *v* (*pret & pp* **spread**) *tr* étendre, étaler; (*news*) répandre; (*disease*) propager; (*the wings*) déployer; (*a piece of bread*) tartiner ‖ *intr* s'étendre, s'étaler; se répandre, rayonner

spread′sheet′ *s* (comp) programme *m* de compatibilité; (*sheet*) page *f* de calcul

spree [spri] *s* bombance *f,* orgie *f;* **to go on a spree** (coll) faire la bombe

sprig [sprɪg] *s* brin *m,* brindille *f*

spright•ly [ˈspraɪtli] *adj* (*comp* **-lier;** *super* **-liest**) vif, enjoué

spring [sprɪŋ] *adj* printanier ‖ *s* (*of water*) source *f;* (*season*) printemps *m;* (*jump*) saut *m,* bond *m;* (*elastic device*) ressort *m;* (*quality*) élasticité *f* ‖ *v* (*pret* **sprang** [spræŋ] or **sprung** [sprʌŋ]; *pp* **sprung**) *tr* (*the frame of a car*) faire déjeter; (*a lock*) faire jouer; (*a leak*) contracter; (*a question*) proposer à l'improviste; (*a prisoner*) (coll) faire sortir de prison ‖ *intr* sauter, bondir; (*said of oil, water, etc.*) jaillir; **to spring up** se lever; naître

spring′-and-fall′ *adj* (*coat*) de demi-saison

spring′board′ *s* tremplin *m*

spring′ fe′ver *s* (hum) malaise *m* des premières chaleurs, flemme *f*

spring′like′ *adj* printanier

spring′time′ *s* printemps *m*

sprinkle [ˈsprɪŋkəl] *s* pluie *f* fine; (culin) pincée *f* ‖ *tr* (*with water*) asperger, arroser; (*with powder*) saupoudrer; (*to strew*) parsemer ‖ *intr* tomber en pluie fine

sprinkler [ˈsprɪŋklər] *s* arrosoir *m*

sprinkling [ˈsprɪŋklɪŋ] *s* aspersion *f,* arrosage *m;* (*with holy water*) aspersion; (*with powder*) saupoudrage *m;* (*of knowledge*) bribes *fpl,* notions *fpl;* (*of persons*) petit nombre *m*

sprin′kling can′ *s* arrosoir *m*

sprint [sprɪnt] *s* course *f* de vitesse, sprint *m* ‖ *intr* faire une course de vitesse, courir à toute vitesse

sprite [spraɪt] *s* lutin *m*

sprocket [ˈsprɑkɪt] *s* dent *f* de pignon; (*wheel*) pignon *m* de chaîne

sprock′et wheel′ *s* pignon *m* de chaîne

sprout [spraʊt] *s* pousse *f,* rejecton *m;* (*of seed*) germe *m* ‖ *intr* (*said of plant*) pousser, pointer; (*said of seed*) germer

spruce [sprus] *adj* pimpant, tiré à quatre épingles ‖ *s* sapin *m;* (*Norway spruce*) épicéa *m* commun ‖ *intr*—**to spruce up** se faire beau, se pomponner

spry [spraɪ] *adj* (*comp* **spryer** or **sprier;** *super* **spryest** or **spriest**) vif, alerte

spud [spʌd] *s* (*chisel*) bédane *f;* (agr) arracheracines *m;* (coll) pomme *f* de terre, patate *f*

spun′ glass′ [spʌn] *s* coton *m* de verre

spunk [spʌŋk] *s* (coll) cran *m,* courage *m*

spur [spʌr] *s* éperon *m;* (*of rooster*) ergot *m;* (*stimulant*) aiguillon *m,* stimulant *m;* (rr) embranchement *m;* **on the spur of the moment** sous l'impulsion du moment ‖ *v* (*pret & pp* **spurred;** *ger* **spurring**) *tr* éperonner; **to spur on** aiguillonner, stimuler

spurious [ˈspjʊriˌəs] *adj* faux; (*sentiments*) simulé, feint; (*document*) apocryphe

spurn [spʌrn] *tr* repousser avec mépris, faire fi de

spurt [spʌrt] *s* jaillissement *m,* giclée *f,* jet *m;* (*of enthusiasm*) élan *m;* effort *m* soudain ‖ *intr* jaillir; **to spurt out** gicler

sputnik [ˈspʊtnɪk] *s* spoutnik *m*

sputter [ˈspʌtər] *s* (*manner of speaking*) bredouillement *m;* (*of candle*) grésillement *m;* (*of fire*) crachement *m* ‖ *tr* (*words*) débiter en lançant des postillons ‖ *intr* postillonner; (*said of candle*) grésiller; (*said of fire*) cracher, pétiller

spu•tum [ˈspjutəm] *s* (*pl* **-ta** [tə]) crachat *m*

spy [spaɪ] *s* (*pl* **spies**) espion *m* ‖ *v* (*pret & pp* **spied**) *tr* (*to catch sight of*) entrevoir; **to spy out** découvrir par ruse ‖ *intr* espionner; **to spy on** épier, guetter

spy′glass′ *s* longue-vue *f*

spying [ˈspaɪˌɪŋ] *s* espionnage *m*

spy′ plane′ *s* avion *m* fugitif

spy′ ring′ *s* réseau *m* d'espionnage

spy′ sat′ellite *s* satellite *m* d'espionnage

squabble [ˈskwɑbəl] *s* chamaillerie *f* ‖ *intr* se chamailler

squad [skwɑd] *s* escouade *f*, peloton *m*; (*of detectives*) brigade *f*

squadron [ˈskwɑdrən] *s* (aer) escadrille *f*; (mil) escadron *m*; (nav) escadre *f*

squalid [ˈskwɑlɪd] *adj* sordide

squall [skwɑl] *s* (*of rain*) bourrasque *f*, rafale *f*; (*cry*) braillement *m*; (coll) grabuge *m* ‖ *intr* souffler en bourrasque; brailler

squalor [ˈskwɑlər] *s* saleté *f*; misère *f*

squander [ˈskwɑndər] *tr* gaspiller

square [skwɛr] *adj* carré; (*honest*) loyal, franc; (*real*) véritable; (*conventional*) (slang) formaliste; **nine** (**ten**, etc.) **inches square** de neuf (dix, etc.) pouces en carré; **nine** (**ten**, etc.) **square inches** neuf (dix, etc.) pouces carrés; **to get square with** (coll) régler ses comptes avec; **we'll call it square** (coll) nous sommes quittes ‖ *s* carré *m*; (*of checkerboard or chessboard*) case *f*; (*city block*) pâté *m* de maisons; (*open area in town or city*) place *f*; (*of carpenter*) équerre *f*; **to be on the square** (coll) jouer franc jeu; **to go back to square one** se retrouver à la case départ, repartir à zéro ‖ *adv* carrément ‖ *tr* carrer; (*a number*) élever au carré; (*wood, marble, etc.*) équarrir; (*a debt*) régler; (bk) balancer ‖ *intr*—**to square off** (coll) se mettre en posture de combat; **to square with** (*to tally with*) s'accorder avec; régler ses comptes avec

square′ dance′ *s* quadrille *m* américain

square′ deal′ *s* (coll) procédé *m* loyal

square′ meal′ *s* repas *m* copieux

square′ root′ *s* racine *f* carrée

squash [skwɑʃ] *s* écrasement *m*; (bot) courge *f*; (sports) squash *m* ‖ *tr* écraser ‖ *intr* s'écraser

squash•y [ˈskwɑʃi] *adj* (*comp* **-ier**; *super* **-iest**) mou et humide; (*fruit*) à pulpe molle

squat [skwɑt] *adj* (*heavyset*) tassé, trapu, ramassé ‖ *s* position *f* accroupie ‖ *v* (*pret & pp* **squatted**; *ger* **squatting**) *intr* s'accroupir; (*to settle*) s'installer sans titre légal

squatter [ˈskwɑtər] *s* squatter *m*

squatting [ˈskwɑtɪŋ] *adj* (*person*) accroupi; (*animal*) tapi, ramassé

squaw [skwɔ] *s* (pej) femme *f* peau-rouge

squawk [skwɔk] *s* cri *m* rauque; (slang) protestation *f*, piaillerie *f* ‖ *intr* pousser un cri rauque; (slang) protester, piailler

squeak [skwik] *s* grincement *m*; (*of living being*) couic *m*, petit cri *m* ‖ *intr* grincer; pousser des petits cris, couiner

squeal [skwil] *s* cri *m* aigu ‖ *intr* piailler; (slang) manger le morceau; **to squeal on** (slang) moucharder

squealer [ˈskwilər] *s* (coll) cafard *m*

squeamish [ˈskwimɪʃ] *adj* trop scrupuleux; prude; sujet aux nausées

squeeze [skwiz] *s* pression *f*; (coll) extorsion *f*;

it's a tight squeeze (coll) ça tient tout juste ‖ *tr* serrer; (*fruit*) presser; **to squeeze from** (coll) extorquer à; **to squeeze into** faire entrer de force dans ‖ *intr* se blottir; **to squeeze through** se frayer un passage à travers

squeezer [ˈskwizər] *s* presse *f*, presse-fruits *m*

squelch [skwɛltʃ] *s* (coll) remarque *f* écrasante ‖ *tr* écraser, réprimer

squid [skwɪd] *s* calmar *m*

squill [skwɪl] *s* (bot) scille *f*; (zool) squille *f*

squint [skwɪnt] *s* coup *m* d'œil furtif; (pathol) strabisme *m* ‖ *tr* fermer à moitié ‖ *intr* loucher; **to squint at** regarder furtivement

squint′-eyed′ *adj* bigle, strabique; malveillant

squire [skwaɪr] *s* (*knight's attendant*) écuyer *m*; (*lady's escort*) cavalier *m* servant; (*property owner*) propriétaire *m* terrien; (law) juge *m* de paix ‖ *tr* escorter

squirm [skwʌrm] *s* tortillement *m* ‖ *intr* se tortiller; **to squirm out of** se tirer de

squirrel [ˈskwʌrəl] *s* écureuil *m*

squirt [skwʌrt] *s* giclée *f*, jet *m*; (*syringe*) seringue *f*; (coll) morveux *m* ‖ *tr* faire gicler ‖ *intr* gicler, jaillir

stab [stæb] *s* coup *m* de poignard, de couteau; (*wound*) estafilade *f*; (coll) coup d'essai; **to make a stab at** (coll) s'essayer à ‖ *v* (*pret & pp* **stabbed**; *ger* **stabbing**) *tr* poignarder

stabilize [ˈstebəl‚aɪz] *tr* stabiliser

stab′ in the back′ *s* coup *m* de Jarnac, coup de traître

stable [ˈstebəl] *adj* stable ‖ *s* (*for cows*) étable *f*; (*for horses*) écurie *f*

stack [stæk] *s* (*of wood, books, papers*) tas *m*, pile *f*; (*of hay, straw, etc.*) meule *f*; (*of sheaves*) gerbier *m*; (*e.g., of rifles*) faisceau *m*; (*of ship or locomotive*) cheminée *f*; (*of fireplace*) souche *f*; (*airplanes in a holding pattern*) file *f* d'attente, pile *f* d'attente, manège *m* d'avions; **stacks** (*in library*) rayons *mpl* ‖ *tr* entasser, empiler; mettre en meule, en gerbier, ou en faisceau; (*a deck of cards*) truquer, donner un coup de pouce à; (aer) faire attendre (sur niveaux différents); **to be stacked** (aer) s'échelonner; **to stack arms** former les faisceaux

stadi•um [ˈstedɪ•əm] *s* (*pl* **-ums** or **-a** [ə]) stade *m*

staff [stæf] *s* (*rod, pole*) bâton *m*; (*of pilgrim*) bourdon *m*; (*of flag*) hampe *f*; (*of newspaper*) rédaction *f*; (*employees*) personnel *m*; (*servants*) domestiques *mfpl*; (*support*) soutien *m*; (mil) état-major *m*; (mus) portée *f* ‖ *tr* fournir, pourvoir de personnel; nommer le personnel pour

staff′ head′quarters *spl* (mil) état-major *m*

staff′ meet′ing *s* réunion *f* de service

staff′ of′ficer *s* officier *m* d'état-major

stag [stæg] *adj* exclusivement masculin; **to go stag** aller sans compagne ‖ *s* homme *m*; (*male deer*) cerf *m*

stage [stedʒ] *s* (*point in time, section, process*) stade *m*, étape *f*, phase *f*; (*of rocket*) étage *m*;

(*stagecoach*) diligence *f;* (*scene*) champ *m* d'action, scène *f;* (*staging*) échafaudage *m;* (*platform*) estrade *f;* (*of microscope*) platine *f;* (theat) scène; **by easy stages** par petites étapes; **by successive stages** par échelons; **to go on the stage** monter sur les planches ‖ *tr* (*a play, demonstration, riot, etc.*) monter; (*a play*) mettre en scène

stage′coach′ *s* diligence *f,* coche *m*

stage′craft′ *s* technique *f* de la scène

stage′ door′ *s* entrée *f* des artistes

stage′-door John′ny *s* (*pl* **-nies**) coureur *m* de girls

stage′ effect′ *s* effet *m* scénique

stage′ fright′ *s* trac *m*

stage′hand′ *s* machiniste *m*

stage′ left′ *s* côté *m* jardin

stage′ man′ager *s* régisseur *m*

stage′ name′ *s* nom *m* de théâtre

stage′ prop′erties *spl* accessoires *mpl*

stage′ right′ *s* côté *m* cour

stage′-struck′ [strʌk] *adj* entiché de théâtre

stage′ whis′per *s* aparté *m*

stagger [′stægər] *tr* faire chanceler, faire tituber; (*to upset*) atterrer, bouleverser; (*to surprise*) étonner; (*to arrange*) disposer en chicane, en zigzag; (*hours of work, train schedules, etc.*) échelonner ‖ *intr* chanceler, tituber

staggering [′stægərɪŋ] *adj* (*swaying*) chancelant; (*amazing*) étonnant, faramineux, hallucinant

staging [′stedʒɪŋ] *s* échafaudage *m;* (theat) mise *f* en scène

stagnant [′stægnənt] *adj* stagnant

stag′ par′ty *s* (*pl* **-ties**) (coll) réunion *f* entre hommes, réunion d'hommes seuls

staid [sted] *adj* posé, sérieux

stain [sten] *s* tache *f,* souillure *f* ‖ *tr* tacher, souiller; (*to tint*) teindre ‖ *intr* se tacher

stained′ glass′ *s* vitre *f* de couleur

stained′-glass win′dow *s* vitrail *m*

stain′less steel′ [′stenlɪs] *s* acier *m* inoxydable

stain′ remov′er *s* détachant *m*

stair [stɛr] *s* escalier *m;* (*step of a series*) marche *f,* degré *m;* **stairs** escalier *m*

stair′case′ or **stair′way′** *s* escalier *m*

stair′well′ *s* cage *f* d'escalier

stake [stek] *s* (*hammered in the ground*) pieu *m,* poteau *m;* (*of tent*) piquet *m;* (*marker*) jalon *m;* (*for burning condemned persons*) bûcher *m;* (*in a game of chance*) mise *f,* enjeu *m;* **at stake** en jeu; **to pull up stakes** (coll) déménager ‖ *tr* (*a road*) bornoyer; (*plants*) échalasser, ramer; (*money*) risquer; (*to back financially*) (slang) fournir aux besoins de; **to stake all** mettre tout en jeu; **to stake off** or **out** jalonner, piqueter

stake′ out′ *s* (coll) opération *f* de surveillance dans un lieu déterminé

stale [stel] *adj* (*bread*) rassis; (*wine or beer*) éventé; (*air*) confiné; (*joke*) vieux; (*check*) proscrit; (*subject*) rabattu; (*news*) défloré, dé-

fraîchi; **to smell stale** (*said of room*) sentir le renfermé

stale′mate′ *s* (chess) pat *m;* (fig) impasse *f;* **in stalemate** pat ‖ *tr* (chess) faire pat; (fig) paralyser

stalk [stɔk] *s* tige *f;* (*of flower or leaf*) queue *f* ‖ *tr* traquer, suivre à la piste ‖ *intr* marcher fièrement, marcher à grandes enjambées

stall [stɔl] *s* (*for a market*) stalle *f;* (*at a market*) étal *m,* échoppe *f;* (aer) décrochage *m;* (sports) anti-jeu *m;* (slang) prétexte *m* ‖ *tr* mettre dans une stalle; (*a car*) caler; (*an airplane*) mettre en perte de vitesse; **to stall off** (coll) différer sous prétexte ‖ *intr* (*said of motor*) se bloquer; **to stall for time** (slang) temporiser

stallion [′stæljən] *s* étalon *m*

stalwart [′stɔlwərt] *adj* robuste; vaillant ‖ *s* partisan *m* loyal

stamen [′stemən] *s* étamine *f*

stamina [′stæmɪnə] *s* vigueur *f,* résistance *f*

stammer [′stæmər] *s* bégaiement *m,* balbutiement *m* ‖ *tr & intr* bégayer, balbutier

stammerer [′stæmərər] *s* bègue *mf*

stamp [stæmp] *s* (*mark, impression*) empreinte *f;* (*for postage*) timbre *m;* (*for stamping*) poinçon *m* ‖ *tr* (*mail*) affranchir; (*money, leather; a medal*) frapper, estamper; (*a document*) timbrer; (*a passport*) viser; **to stamp one's feet** trépigner; **to stamp one's foot** frapper du pied; **to stamp out** (*e.g., a rebellion*) écraser, étouffer

stampede [stæm′pid] *s* (*of animals or people*) débandade *f;* (*rush*) ruée *f;* (*of people*) sauve-qui-peut *m* ‖ *tr* provoquer la ruée de ‖ *intr* se débander

stamped′ self′-addressed′ en′velope *s* enveloppe *f* timbrée par l'expéditeur

stamp′ing grounds′ *spl*—**to be on one's stamping grounds** (slang) être sur son terrain, être dans son domaine

stamp′ pad′ *s* tampon *m* encreur

stamp′-vend′ing machine′ *s* distributeur *m* automatique de timbres-poste

stance [stæns] *s* attitude *f,* posture *f*

stanch [stɑntʃ] *adj* ferme, solide; vrai, loyal; (*watertight*) étanche ‖ *tr* étancher

stand [stænd] *s* (*place, attitude*) position *f;* (*opposition*) résistance *f;* (*of a merchant*) étal *m,* éventaire *m;* (*of a speaker*) tribune *f,* estrade *f;* (*of a horse*) aplombs *mpl;* (*piece of furniture*) guéridon *m,* console *f;* (*to hold music, papers*) pupitre *m;* **stands** tribune *f,* stand *m* ‖ *v* (*pret & pp* **stood** [stʊd]) *tr* mettre, placer, poser; (*the cold*) supporter; (*a shock; an attack*) soutenir; (*a round of drinks*) (coll) payer; **to stand off** repousser; **to stand up** (*to keep waiting*) (coll) poser un lapin à ‖ *intr* se lever, se mettre debout; se tenir debout, être debout; en être, e.g., **how does it stand?** où en est-il?; **stand by!** en attente!; **to stand aloof** or **aside** se tenir à l'écart; **to stand by** se tenir prêt; (*e.g., a friend*) rester fidèle à; **to stand fast** tenir bon; **to stand for** (*to mean*) signifier; (*to affirm*) soutenir; (*to allow*) tolérer; **to stand in for** doubler, remplacer; **to stand in line** faire la queue; **to stand out** sortir, saillir; **to stand up** se lever, se mettre debout; se tenir debout, être debout; **to stand up against** or **to** tenir tête à; **to stand up for** prendre fait et cause pour

standard [ˈstændərd] *adj* (*product, part, unit*) standard, de série, normal; (*current*) courant; (*author, book, work*) classique; (*edition*) définitif; (*keyboard of typewriter*) universel; (*coinage*) au titre ‖ *s* norme *f*, mesure *f*, règle *f*, pratique *f*; (*of quantity, weight, value*) standard *m*; (*banner*) étendard *m*; (*of lamp*) support *m*; (*of wires*) pylône *m*; (*of coinage*) titre *m*; (*for a monetary system*) étalon *m*; (fig) degré *m*, niveau *m*; **standards** critères *mpl*; **up to standard** suivant la norme

stand′ard‑bear′er *s* porte-drapeau *m*
stand′ard gauge′ *s* voie *f* normale
standardize [ˈstændərˌdaɪz] *tr* standardiser
stand′ard of liv′ing *s* niveau *m* de vie
stand′ard time′ *s* heure *f* légale
standee [stænˈdi] *s* voyageur *m* debout; (theat) spectateur *m* debout
stand′‑in′ *s* (mov, theat) doublure *f*, remplaçant *m*; (coll) appuis *mpl*, piston *m*
standing [ˈstændɪŋ] *adj* (*upright*) debout; (*statue*) en pied; (*water*) stagnant; (*army, committee*) permanent; (*price; rule; rope*) fixe; (*custom*) établi, courant; (*jump*) à pieds joints ‖ *s* standing *m*, position *f*, importance *f*; **in good standing** estimé, accrédité; **of long standing** de longue date
stand′ing ar′my *s* armée *f* permanente
stand′ing room′ *s* places *fpl* debout
stand′ing vote′ *s* vote *m* par assis et levé
stand′off′ *s* impasse *f*
stand‑offish [ˌstændˈɔfɪʃ] *adj* réservé, distant, froid
stand′out′ *s* chose *f* saillante; personne *f* remarquable
stand′pat′ *adj & s* (coll) immobiliste *mf*
stand′pat′ter *s* (coll) immobiliste *mf*
stand′point′ *s* point *m* de vue; **from the standpoint of** sous le rapport de
stand′still′ *s* arrêt *m*, immobilisation *f*; **at a standstill** au point mort; **to come to a standstill** s'arrêter court
stand′‑up come′dian *s* monologuiste *mf* comique
stanza [ˈstænzə] *s* strophe *f*
staple [ˈstepəl] *adj* principal ‖ *s* (*product*) produit *m* principal; (*for holding papers together*) agrafe *f*; (bb) broche *f*; **staples** denrées *fpl* principales ‖ *tr* agrafer; (*books*) brocher
stapler [ˈsteplər] *s* agrafeuse *f*; (bb) brocheuse *f*
star [stɑr] *s* astre *m*; (*heavenly body except sun and moon; figure that represents a star*) étoile *f*; (*of stage or screen*) vedette *f* ‖ *v* (*pret & pp* **starred;** *ger* **starring**) *tr* étoiler, consteller; (mov, rad, telv, theat) mettre en vedette; (typ)

marquer d'un astérisque ‖ *intr* apparaître comme vedette
starboard [ˈstɑrˌbord] *adj* de tribord ‖ *s* tribord *m* ‖ *adv* à tribord
star′ board′er *s* (coll) pensionnaire *mf* de prédilection
starch [stɑrtʃ] *s* amidon *m*; (*for fabrics*) empois *m*; (*formality*) raideur *f*; (bot, culin) fécule *f*; (coll) force *f*, vigueur *f* ‖ *tr* empeser
starch‑y [ˈstɑrtʃi] *adj* (*comp* **-ier;** *super* **-iest**) empesé; (*foods*) féculent; (*manner*) raide, guindé
stare [ster] *s* regard *m* fixe ‖ *tr*—**to stare s.o. in the face** dévisager qn; (*to be obvious to s.o.*) sauter aux yeux de qn ‖ *intr* regarder fixement; **to stare at** regarder fixement, dévisager
star′fish′ *s* étoile *f* de mer
star′gaze′ *intr* regarder les étoiles; rêvasser, être dans la lune
stark [stɑrk] *adj* pur; rigide; désert, solitaire ‖ *adv* entièrement
stark′‑na′ked *adj* tout nu
star′light′ *s* lumière *f* des étoiles
starling [ˈstɑrlɪŋ] *s* étourneau *m*
star‑ry [ˈstɑri] *adj* (*comp* **-rier;** *super* **-riest**) étoilé
Stars′ and Stripes′ *spl* or **Star′-Spangled Ban′ner** *s* bannière *f* étoilée
start [stɑrt] *s* (*beginning*) commencement *m*, début *m*; (*sudden start*) sursaut *m*, haut-le-corps *m* ‖ *tr* commencer; (*a car, a motor, etc.*) mettre en marche, démarrer; (*a conversation*) entamer; (*a hare*) lever; (*a deer*) lancer; **to start** + *ger* se mettre à + *inf* ‖ *intr* commencer, débuter; démarrer; (*to be startled*) sursauter; **starting from** or **with** à partir de; **to start after** sortir à la recherche de; **to start out** se mettre en route
starter [ˈstɑrtər] *s* initiateur *m*; (aut) démarreur *m*; (sports) starter *m*
start′ing pit′cher *s* lanceur *m* partant
start′ing point′ *s* point *m* de départ
startle [ˈstɑrtəl] *tr* faire tressaillir ‖ *intr* tressaillir
startling [ˈstɑrtlɪŋ] *adj* effrayant; (*event*) sensationnel; (*resemblance*) saisissant
start′up′ *adj* initial ‖ *s* (comp) démarrage *m*
starvation [stɑrˈveʃən] *s* inanition *f*, famine *f*
starva′tion di′et *s* diète *f* absolue
starva′tion wag′es *spl* salaire *m* de famine
starve [stɑrv] *tr* affamer; faire mourir de faim; **to starve out** réduire par la faim ‖ *intr* être affamé; être dans la misère; mourir de faim; (coll) mourir de faim
starving [ˈstɑrvɪŋ] *adj* affamé; **I'm starving** je meurs de faim
state [stet] *s* état *m*; (*pomp*) apparat *m*; **to lie in state** être exposé solennellement ‖ *tr* affirmer, déclarer; (*an hour or date*) régler, fixer; (*a problem*) poser
stateless [ˈstetlɪs] *adj* apatride

state·ly [ˈstetli] *adj* (*comp* **-lier;** *super* **-liest**) majestueux, imposant

statement [ˈstetmənt] *s* énoncé *m,* exposé *m;* (*account, report*) compte rendu *m,* rapport *m;* (*of an account*) (com) relevé *m;* (comp) instruction *f*

state′ of mind′ *s* état *m* d'esprit, état d'âme

state′ of the art′ *s* état *m* or dernier cri *m* de la technique, état présent

state′room′ *s* (naut) cabine *f;* (rr) compartiment *m*

state′side *adj* (coll) aux Etats-Unis, dans les États-Unis

states′man *s* (*pl* **-men**) homme *m* d'État

states′man·like *adj* diplomatique

states′ rights′ *spl* droits *mpl* propres à chaque État des États-Unis

static [ˈstætɪk] *adj* statique; (rad) parasite ‖ *s* (rad) parasites *mpl*

station [ˈsteʃən] *s* station *f;* (*for police; for selling gasoline; for broadcasting*) poste *m;* (*of bus, subway, rail line, taxi; for observation*) station; (rr) gare *f* ‖ *tr* poster, placer

sta′tion a′gent *s* chef *m* de gare

stationary [ˈsteʃənˌɛri] *adj* stationnaire

sta′tion break′ *s* (rad) pause *f*

stationer [ˈsteʃənər] *s* papetier *m*

stationery [ˈsteʃənˌɛri] *s* papeterie *f,* fournitures *fpl* de bureau

sta′tionery store′ *s* papeterie *f*

sta′tion house′ *s* commissariat *m* de police

sta′tion identifica′tion *s* (rad) indicatif *m*

sta′tion·mas′ter *s* chef *m* de gare

Sta′tions of the Cross′ *s* (rel) stations *fpl* de la Croix

sta′tion wag′on *s* familiale *f,* break *m*

statistical [stəˈtɪstɪkəl] *adj* statistique

statistician [ˌstætɪsˈtɪʃən] *s* statisticien *m*

statistics [stəˈtɪstɪks] *s* (*science*) statistique *f* ‖ *spl* (*data*) statistique, statistiques

statue [ˈstætʃʊ] *s* statue *f*

Stat′ue of Lib′erty *s* Liberté *f* éclairant le monde, Statue *f* de la Liberté

statuesque [ˌstætʃʊˈɛsk] *adj* sculptural

stature [ˈstætʃər] *s* stature *f,* taille *f;* caractère *m,* stature

status [ˈstetəs] *s* condition *f;* rang *m,* standing *m;* **the status of** le statut de

sta′tus quo′ [kwo] *s* statu quo *m*

sta′tus seek′er *s* obsédé *m* du standing

sta′tus sym′bol *s* symbole *m* du rang social

statute [ˈstætʃʊt] *s* statut *m*

stat′ute of limita′tions *s* loi *f* concernant la prescription

statutory [ˈstætʃʊˌtori] *adj* statutaire

staunch [stɔntʃ] *adj* & *tr* var of **stanch**

stave [stev] *s* (*of barrel*) douve *f;* (*of ladder*) échelon *m;* (*mus*) portée *f* ‖ *v* (*pret* & *pp* **staved** or **stove** [stov]) *tr*—**to stave in** défoncer, crever; **to stave off** détourner, éloigner

stay [ste] *s* (*visit*) séjour *m;* (*prop*) étai *m;* (*of a corset*) baleine *f;* (*of execution*) sursis *m;* (fig) soutien *m* ‖ *tr* arrêter ‖ *intr* rester; séjour-

ner; (*at a hotel*) descendre; **to stay put** ne pas bouger; **to stay up** veiller

stay′-at-home′ *adj* & *s* casanier *m*

STD [ˈɛsˈtiˈdi] *s* (letterword) (**sexually transmitted disease**) MST (maladie sexuellement transmissible)

stead [stɛd] *s*—**in s.o.'s stead** à la place de qn; **to stand s.o. in good stead** être fort utile à qn

stead′fast′ *adj* ferme; constant

stead·y [ˈstɛdi] *adj* (*comp* **-ier;** *super* **-iest**) ferme, solide; régulier; (*market*) soutenu ‖ *v* (*pret* & *pp* **-ied**) *tr* raffermir ‖ *intr* se raffermir

steak [stek] *s* (*slice*) tranche *f;* bifteck *m*

steal [stil] *s* (coll) vol *m;* (*bargain*) (coll) occasion *f* ‖ *v* (*pret* **stole** [stol]; *pp* **stolen**) *tr* voler; **to steal s.th. from s.o.** voler q.ch. à qn ‖ *intr* voler; **to steal away** se dérober; **to steal into** se glisser dans; **to steal upon** s'approcher en tapinois de

stealth [stɛlθ] *s*—**by stealth** en tapinois, à la dérobée

steam [stim] *s* vapeur *f;* (*e.g., on a window*) buée *f;* **full steam ahead!** en avant à toute vapeur!; **to get up steam** faire monter la pression; **to let off steam** lâcher la vapeur; (fig) s'épancher ‖ *tr* passer à la vapeur; (culin) cuire à la vapeur; **to steam up** (*e.g., a window*) embuer ‖ *intr* dégager de la vapeur, fumer; s'évaporer; **to steam ahead** avancer à la vapeur; (fig) faire des progrès rapides; **to steam up** s'embuer

steam′boat′ *s* vapeur *m*

steam′ chest′ *s* boîte *f* à vapeur

steam′ en′gine *s* machine *f* à vapeur

steamer [ˈstimər] *s* vapeur *m*

steam′ heat′ *s* chauffage *m* à la vapeur

steam′ roll′er *s* rouleau *m* compresseur; (fig) force *f* irrésistible

steam′ship′ *s* vapeur *m*

steam′ shov′el *s* pelle *f* à vapeur

steam′ ta′ble *s* table *f* à compartiments chauffés à la vapeur

steed [stid] *s* coursier *m*

steel [stil] *adj* (*industry*) sidérurgique ‖ *s* acier *m;* (*for striking fire from flint*) briquet *m;* (*for sharpening knives*) fusil *m* ‖ *tr* aciérer; **to steel oneself against** se cuirasser contre

steel′ wool′ *s* laine *f* d'acier, paille *f* de fer, jex *m*

steel′works′ *spl* aciérie *f*

steelyard [ˈstilˌjɑrd] *s* romaine *f*

steep [stip] *adj* raide, abrupt; (*cliff*) escarpé; (*price*) (coll) exorbitant ‖ *tr* tremper; (*e.g., tea*) infuser; **steeped in** saturé de; (*ignorance*) pétri de; (*the classics*) nourri de

steeple [ˈstipəl] *s* clocher *m;* (*spire*) flèche *f*

stee′ple·chase′ *s* course *f* d'obstacles

stee′plejack′ *s* réparateur *m* de hautes cheminées et de clochers

steer [stɪr] *s* bouvillon *m* ‖ *tr* diriger, conduire; (naut) gouverner ‖ *intr* se diriger; (naut) se gouverner; **to steer clear of** (coll) éviter

steerage [ˈstɪrɪdʒ] *s* entrepont *m*

steer′age pas′senger *s* passager *m* d'entrepont

steer′ing col′umn *s* (aut) colonne *f* de direction

steer′ing commit′tee *s* comité *m* d'organisation

steer′ing wheel′ *s* volant *m;* (naut) roue *f* de gouvernail

stellar [ˈstɛlər] *adj* stellaire; (*rôle*) de vedette

stem [stɛm] *s* (*of plant; of key*) tige *f;* (*of column; of tree*) fût *m,* tige; (*of fruit*) queue *f;* (*of pipe; of feather*) tuyau *m;* (*of goblet*) pied *m;* (*of watch*) remontoir *m;* (*of word*) radical *m,* thème *m;* (naut) étrave *f;* **from stem to stern** de l'étrave à l'étambot, d'un bout à l'autre ‖ *v* (*pret & pp* **stemmed;** *ger* **stemming**) *tr* (*e.g., grapes*) égrapper; (*e.g., the flow of blood*) étancher; (*the tide*) lutter contre, refouler; (*to check*) arrêter, endiguer ‖ *intr*—**to stem from** provenir de

stem′ cell′ *s* (gen) cellule *f* souche, cellule mère

stem′-wind′er *s* montre *f* à remontoir

stench [stɛntʃ] *s* puanteur *f*

sten•cil [ˈstɛnsəl] *s* (*of metal, cardboard*) pochoir *m;* (*of paper*) poncif *m;* (*work produced by it*) travail *m* au pochoir; (*for reproducing typewriting*) stencil *m* ‖ *v* (*pret & pp*-ciled *ou* -cilled; *ger*-ciling *ou* -cilling) *tr* passer au pochoir; tirer au stencil

stenographer [stəˈnɑgrəfər] *s* sténo *f,* sténographe *mf*

stenography [stəˈnɑgrəfi] *s* sténographie *f*

step [stɛp] *s* pas *m;* (*of staircase*) marche *f,* degré *m;* (*footprint*) trace *f;* (*of carriage*) marchepied *m;* (*of ladder*) échelon *m;* (*procedure*) démarche *f;* **in step with** au pas avec; **step by step** pas à pas; **to march in step** marcher en cadence; **watch your step!** prenez garde de tomber!; (fig) évitez tout faux pas! ‖ *v* (*pret & pp* **stepped;** *ger* **stepping**) *tr* échelonner; **to step off** mesurer au pas ‖ *intr* faire un pas; marcher; (coll) aller en toute hâte; **to step aside** s'écarter; **to step back** reculer; **step in** entrer; **to step on it** (coll) mettre tous les gaz; **to step on the starter** appuyer sur le démarreur

step′broth′er *s* demi-frère *m*

step′child′ *s* (*pl* -child′ren) beau-fils *m;* belle-fille *f*

step′daugh′ter *s* belle-fille *f*

step′fa′ther *s* beau-père *m*

step′lad′der *s* échelle *f* double, marche-pied *m,* escabeau *m*

step′moth′er *s* belle-mère *f*

steppe [stɛp] *s* steppe *f*

step′ping stone′ *s* pierre *f* de passage; (fig) marchepied *m*

step′sis′ter *s* demi-sœur *f*

step′son′ *s* beau-fils *m*

stere•o [ˈstɛri,o] *adj* (coll) stéréo, stéréophonique; (coll) stéréoscopique ‖ *s* (*pl* -os) (coll) disque *m* stéréo; (coll) émission *f* en stéréophonique; (coll) photographie *f* stéréoscopique

stereotyped [ˈstɛri•ə,taipt] *adj* stéréotypé

sterile [ˈstɛrɪl] *adj* stérile

sterilize [ˈstɛrɪ,laɪz] *tr* stériliser

sterling [ˈstʌrlɪŋ] *adj* de bon aloi ‖ *s* livres *fpl* sterling; (*sterling silver*) argent *m* fin, argent de bon aloi

stern [stʌrn] *adj* sévère, austère; (*look*) rébarbatif ‖ *s* poupe *f*

stethoscope [ˈstɛθə,skop] *s* stéthoscope *m*

stevedore [ˈstivə,dor] *s* arrimeur *m*

stew [st(j)u] *s* ragoût *m* ‖ *tr* mettre en ragoût ‖ *intr* (coll) être dans tous ses états

steward [ˈst(j)u•ərd] *s* (*on estate, etc.*) régisseur *m,* intendant *m;* (*in a restaurant*) maître *m* d'hôtel; (aer) flight attendant; (naut) steward *m*

stewardess [ˈst(j)u•ərdɪs] *s* (aer) hôtesse *f* de l'air; (naut) stewardesse *f*

stewed′ fruit′ *s* compote *f*

stewed′ toma′toes *spl* purée *f* de tomates

stick [stɪk] *s* bâtonnet *m,* bâton *m;* (*rod*) verge *f;* (*wand; drumstick*) baguette *f;* (*of chewing gum; of dynamite*) bâton; (*firewood*) bois *m* sec; (*walking stick*) canne *f;* (naut) mât *m;* (typ) composteur *m* ‖ *v* (*pret & pp* **stuck** [stʌk]) *tr* piquer, enfoncer; (*to fasten in position*) clouer, ficher, planter; (*to glue*) coller; (*a pig*) saigner; (coll) confondre; **stick 'em up!** (slang) haut les mains!; **to be stuck** être pris; (*e.g., in the mud*) s'enliser; (*to be unable to continue*) (coll) être en panne; **to stick it out** (coll) tenir jusqu'au bout; **to stick out** (*one's tongue*) tirer; (*one's head*) passer; (*one's chest*) bomber; **to stick up** (*in order to rob*) (slang) voler à main armée ‖ *intr* se piquer, s'enfoncer; se ficher, se planter; (*to be jammed*) être pris, se coincer; (*to adhere*) coller; (*to remain*) continuer, rester; **to stick out** saillir, dépasser; (*to be evident*) sauter aux yeux; **to stick up for** (coll) prendre la défense de

sticker [ˈstɪkər] *s* (*label*) étiquette *f* gommée; (*difficult question*) (coll) colle *f*

stickler [ˈstɪklər] *s*—**to be a stickler for** insister sur, être pointilleux sur, être rigoriste en matière de

stick′pin′ *s* épingle *f* de cravate

stick′-up′ *s* (slang) attaque *f* à main armée, hold-up *m*

stick•y [ˈstɪki] *adj* (*comp* -ier; *super* -iest) gluant, collant; (*hands*) poisseux; (*weather*) étouffant; (*question*) épineux; (*unaccommodating*) tatillon

stiff [stɪf] *adj* raide; difficile, ardu; (*joint*) ankylosé; (*brush; batter*) dur; (*style, manner*) guindé, empesé; (*drink*) fort; (*price*) (coll) salé, exagéré; **to be scared stiff** (slang) les avoir à zéro ‖ *s* (*corpse*) (slang) macchabée *m*

stiff′ col′lar *s* col *m* empesé

stiffen [ˈstɪfən] *tr* raidir, tendre; (culin) épaissir ‖ *intr* se raidir

stiff′ neck′ *s* torticolis *m*

stiff′-necked′ *adj* obstiné, entêté

stiff′ shirt′ *s* chemise *f* empesée, chemise à plastron

stifle [ˈstaɪfəl] *tr & intr* étouffer

stig·ma [ˈstɪgmə] *s* (*pl* -mas or -mata [mətə]) stigmate *m*

stigmatize [ˈstɪgmə,taɪz] *tr* stigmatiser

stilet·to [stɪˈlɛto] *s* (*pl* -tos) stylet *m*

still [stɪl] *adj* (*peaceful, quiet*) tranquille, calme, silencieux; (*motionless*) immobile; (*water*) dormant; (*wine*) non mousseux ‖ *s* (*for distilling*) alambic *m;* (phot) image *f;* (mov) photogramme *m;* (poetic) silence *m* ‖ *adv* (*yet*) encore, toujours ‖ *conj* cependant, pourtant ‖ *tr* calmer, apaiser; (*to silence*) faire taire ‖ *intr* se calmer, s'apaiser; se taire

still′birth′ *s* mort *f* à la naissance

still′born′ *adj* mort-né

still′ life′ *s* (*pl* still lifes or still lives) nature *f* morte

stilt [stɪlt] *s* échasse *f;* (*in the water*) pilotis *m*

stilted *adj* guindé; (archit) surhaussé

stimulant [ˈstɪmjələnt] *adj & s* stimulant *m*

stimulate [ˈstɪmjə,let] *tr* stimuler

stimu·lus [ˈstɪmjələs] *s* (*pl* -li [,laɪ]) stimulant *m*, aiguillon *m;* (physiol) stimulus *m*

sting [stɪŋ] *s* piqûre *f;* (*stinging organ*) aiguillon *m*, dard *m* ‖ *v* (*pret & pp* stung [stʌŋ]) *tr & intr* piquer

stin·gy [ˈstɪndʒi] *adj* (*comp* -gier; *super* -giest) avare, pingre

stink [stɪŋk] *s* puanteur *f* ‖ *v* (*pret* stank [stæŋk]; *pp* stunk [stʌŋk]) *tr*—**to stink up** empester, empuantir ‖ *intr* puer, empester, **to stink of** puer, empester

stinker [ˈstɪŋkər] *s* (slang) peau *f* de vache, chameau *m*

stint [stɪnt] *s* tâche *f*, besogne *f;* **without stint** sans réserve, sans limite ‖ *tr* limiter, réduire; **to stint oneself** se priver ‖ *intr* lésiner, être chiche

stipend [ˈstaɪpənd] *s* traitement *m*, honoraires *mpl*

stipulate [ˈstɪpjə,let] *tr* stipuler

stir [stʌr] *s* remuement *m*, agitation *f;* (*prison*) (slang) bloc *m;* **to create a stir** faire sensation ‖ *v* (*pret & pp* stirred; *ger* stirring) *tr* remuer, agiter; **to stir up** (*trouble*) fomenter ‖ *intr* remuer, s'agiter, bouger

stirring [ˈstʌrɪŋ] *adj* entraînant

stirrup [ˈstʌrəp], [ˈstɪrəp] *s* étrier *m*

stitch [stɪtʃ] *s* (*in sewing*) point *m;* (*in knitting*) maille *f;* (surg) point de suture; **not a stitch of** (coll) pas un brin de; **stitch in the side** point de côté; **to be in stitches** (coll) se tenir les côtes ‖ *tr* coudre; (bb) brocher; (surg) suturer ‖ *intr* coudre

stock [stɑk] *s* (*supply*) réserve *f*, provision *f*, stock *m;* (*assortment*) assortiment *m;* capital *m*, fonds *m;* (*shares*) valeurs *fpl*, actions *fpl;* (*of meat*) bouillon *m;* (*of a tree*) tronc *m;* (*of an anvil*) billot *m;* (*of a rifle*) crosse *f;* (*of a tree; of a family*) souche *f;* (*livestock*) bétail

m, bestiaux *mpl;* (*handle*) poignée *f;* (*for dies*) tourne-à-gauche *m;* (hort) ente *f;* **in stock** en magasin; **on the stocks** (fig) sur le métier; **out of stock** épuisé; **stocks** (*for punishment*) pilori *m;* (naut) chantier *m;* **to take stock** (com) faire l'inventaire; (fig) faire le point; **to take stock in** (coll) faire grand cas de; **to take stock of** faire l'inventaire de ‖ *tr* approvisionner; garder en magasin; (*a forest or lake*) peupler; (*a farm*) monter en bétail; (*a pool*) empoissonner

stockade [stɑˈked] *s* palanque *f*, palissade *f* ‖ *tr* palissader

stock′breed′er *s* éleveur *m* de bestiaux

stock′breed′ing *s* élevage *m*

stock′bro′ker *s* agent *m* de change, courtier *m* de bourse

stock′ car′ *s* (aut) voiture *f* de série; (rr) wagon *m* à bestiaux

stock′-car race′ *s* course *f* de bolides

stock′ certif′icate *s* certificat *m* d'actions

stock′ com′pany *s* (com) société *f* anonyme; (theat) troupe *f* à demeure

stock′ div′idend *s* action *f* gratuite

stock′ exchange′ *s* bourse *f*

stock′hold′er *s* actionnaire *mf*

stock′hold′er of rec′ord *s* actionnaire *mf* dont les actions figurent sur une liste dans le registre de la société

stocking [ˈstɑkɪŋ] *s* bas *m*

stock′ mar′ket *s* bourse *f*, marché *m* des valeurs; **to play the stock market** jouer à la bourse

stock′pile′ *s* stocks *mpl* de réserve ‖ *tr & intr* stocker

stock′ rais′ing *s* élevage *m*

stock′room′ *s* magasin *m*

stock·y [ˈstɑki] *adj* (*comp* -ier; *super* -iest) trapu, costaud

stock′yard′ *s* parc *m* à bétail

stoic [ˈsto·ɪk] *adj & s* stoïque; **Stoic** stoïcien *m*

stoke [stok] *tr* (*a fire*) attiser; (*a furnace*) alimenter, charger

stoker [ˈstokər] *s* chauffeur *m;* (mach) stoker *m*

stolid [ˈstɑlɪd] *adj* flegmatique, impassible, lourd

stomach [ˈstʌmək] *s* estomac *m* ‖ *tr* digérer; (coll) digérer, avaler

stom′ach ache′ *s* mal *m* d'estomac

stom′ach pump′ *s* pompe *f* stomacale

stone [ston] *s* pierre *f;* (*of fruit*) noyau *m;* (pathol) calcul *m;* (typ) marbre *m* ‖ *tr* lapider; (*fruit*) dénoyauter

stone′-broke′ *adj* (coll) complètement fauché, raide

stone′-deaf′ *adj* sourd comme un pot

stone′ma′son *s* maçon *m*

stone′ quar′ry *s* (*pl* -ries) carrière *f*

stone′s′ throw′ *s*—**within a stone's throw** à un jet de pierre

stone′wall′ *intr* donner des réponses évasives

ston·y [ˈstoni] *adj* (*comp* -ier; *super* -iest) pierreux; (fig) dur, endurci

stooge [studʒ] *s* (theat) compère *m;* (slang) homme *f* de paille, acolyte *m*

stool [stul] *s* tabouret *m*, escabeau *m;* (*bowel movement*) selles *fpl*

stool′ pi′geon *s* appeau *m;* (slang) mouchard *m*, mouton *m*

stoop [stup] *s* courbure *f*, inclinaison *f;* (*porch*) véranda *f* ‖ *intr* se pencher; se tenir voûté; (*to debase oneself*) s'abaisser

stoop′-shoul′dered *adj* voûté

stop [stɑp] *s* arrêt *m;* (*in telegrams*) stop *m;* (*full stop*) point *m;* (*of a guitar*) touche *f;* (mus) jeu *m* d'orgue; (*public sign*) stop; **to pull out all the stops** (coll) mettre le paquet; **to put a stop to** mettre fin à ‖ *v* (*pret & pp* **stopped;** *ger* **stopping**) *tr* arrêter; (*a check*) faire opposition à; **to stop up** boucher ‖ *intr* s'arrêter, arrêter; **to stop +** *ger*, cesser de + *inf*, s'arrêter de + *inf;* **to stop off** descendre en passant; **to stop off at** s'arrêter un moment à; **to stop over** (aer, naut) faire escale

stop′ ac′tion *s* (electron) arrêt *m* sur image

stop′cock′ *s* robinet *m* d'arrêt

stop′gap′ *adj* provisoire ‖ *s* bouche-trou *m*

stop′light′ *s* signal *m* lumineux; (aut) feu *m* stop, stop *m*

stop′o′ver *s* arrêt *m* en cours de route, étape *f*

stoppage [ˈstɑpɪdʒ] *s* arrêt *m;* (*of payments*) suspension *f;* (*of wages*) retenue *f;* obstruction *f;* (pathol) occlusion *f*

stopper [ˈstɑpər] *s* bouchon *m*, tampon *m*

stop′ping for unload′ing *s* manutention *f*

stop′ sign′ *s* signal *m* d'arrêt

stop′ thief′ *interj* au voleur!

stop′watch′ *s* chronomètre *m* à déclic, compte-secondes *m*

storage [ˈstorɪdʒ] *s* emmagasinage *m*, entreposage *m;* **to put in storage** entreposer

stor′age bat′ter•y *s* (*pl* **-ies**) (elec) accumulateur *m*, accu *m*

store [stor] *s* (*where goods are sold*) magasin *m;* (*shop*) boutique *f;* (*supply*) provision *f*, réserve *f*, stock *m;* (*of learning, information*) fonds *m;* (*warehouse*) (Brit) entrepôt *m;* **stores** (*materials*) matériel *m;* (*provisions*) vivres *mpl;* **to set great store by** faire grand cas de ‖ *tr* emmagasiner; (*to warehouse*) entreposer; (*to supply or stock*) approvisionner; **to store away** or **up** accumuler

store′front church′ *s* église *f* dans une vieille boutique à côté de la rue

store′house′ *s* magasin *m*, entrepôt *m;* (*of information*) mine *f*

store′keep′er *s* boutiquier *m*

store′room′ *s* dépense *f*, office *f;* (*for furniture*) garde-meuble *m;* (naut) soute *f*

store′ win′dow *s* vitrine *f*

stork [stɔrk] *s* cigogne *f*

storm [stɔrm] *s* orage *m;* (mil) assaut *m;* (fig) tempête *f;* **to take by storm** prendre d'assaut ‖ *tr* livrer l'assaut à ‖ *intr* faire de l'orage; (fig) tempêter

storm′ cloud′ *s* nuage *m* orageux; (fig) nuage noir

storm′ door′ *s* contre-porte *f*

storm′ pet′rel [ˈpɛtrəl] *s* oiseau *m* des tempêtes

storm′ sash′ *s* contre-fenêtre *f*

storm′ sew′er *s* évacuateur *m* pluvial

storm′ troops′ *spl* troupes *fpl* d'assaut

storm′ win′dow *s* contre-fenêtre *f*, double fenêtre *f*

storm•y [ˈstɔrmi] *adj* (*comp* **-ier;** *super* **-iest**) orageux

sto•ry [ˈstori] *s* (*pl* **-ries**) (*narration*) histoire *f;* (*tale*) conte *m;* (*plot*) intrigue *f;* (*floor*) étage *m;* (coll) mensonge *m*, histoire

sto′ry-tel′ler *s* conteur *m;* (*fibber*) menteur *m*

stout [staut] *adj* (*fat*) corpulent, gros; (*courageous*) vaillant; (*determined*) ferme, résolu; (*strong*) fort ‖ *s* stout *m*

stout′-heart′ed *adj* au cœur vaillant

stove [stov] *s* (*for heating a house or room*) poêle *m;* (*for cooking*) fourneau *m* de cuisine, cuisinière *f*

stove′pipe′ *s* tuyau *m* de poêle; (*hat*) (coll) huit-reflets *m*, tuyau de poêle

stow [sto] *tr* mettre en place, ranger; (naut) arrimer; **to stow with** remplir de ‖ *intr*—**to stow away** s'embarquer clandestinement

stowage [ˈsto•ɪdʒ] *s* arrimage *m;* (*costs*) frais *mpl* d'arrimage

stow′away′ *s* passager *m* clandestin

straddle [ˈstrædəl] *tr* enfourcher, chevaucher ‖ *intr* se mettre à califourchon; (coll) répondre en normand

strafe [strɑf], [stref] *s* (slang) bombardement *m*, marmitage *m* ‖ *tr* (slang) bombarder, marmiter

straggle [ˈstrægəl] *intr* traîner; (*to be scattered*) s'éparpiller; **to straggle along** marcher sans ordre

straggler [ˈstræglər] *s* traînard *m*

straight [stret] *adj* (*not curved*) droit; (*shortest route*) direct; (*honest*) loyal, honnête; (*in order*) correct, en ordre; (*chair*) à dossier droit; (*hair*) raide; (*whiskey*) sec; (*candid*) franc; (*hanging straight*) d'aplomb; (*part in a play*) sérieux; (*not homosexual*) qui n'est pas homosexuel; (*not a drug addict*) qui ne se drogue pas; (*not a criminal*) qui n'est pas véreux; **to set s.o. straight** faire la leçon à qn ‖ *s* (poker) séquence *f* ‖ *adv* droit; directement; loyalement, honnêtement; (*without interruption*) de suite; **straight ahead** tout droit; **straight out** franchement, sans detours; **straight through** de part en part; d'un bout à l'autre; **to go straight** (coll) vivre honnêtement

straighten [ˈstretən] *tr* redresser; mettre en ordre ‖ *intr* se redresser

straight′ face′ *s*—**to keep a straight face** montrer un front sérieux

straight′for′ward *adj* franc, direct; loyal

straight′ off′ *adv* sur-le-champ, d'emblée

straight′ ra′zor *s* rasoir *m* à main

straight′way′ *adv* sur-le-champ, d'emblée

strain [stren] *s* tension *f*, effort *m*, pression *f*; (*of a muscle*) foulure *f*; (*descendants*) lignée *f*; (*ancestry; type of virus*) souche *f*; (*trait*) héritage *m*, tendance *f*; (*vein*) ton *m*, sens *m*; (*bit*) trace *f*; (coll) grand effort *m*; **mental strain** surmenage *m* intellectuel; **strains** (*of, e.g., the Marseillaise*) accents *mpl*; **sweet strains** doux accords *mpl* ‖ *tr* forcer; (*e.g., a wrist*) se fouler; (*e.g., one's eyes*) se fatiguer; (*e.g., part of a machine*) déformer; (*e.g., a liquid*) filtrer, tamiser; **to strain oneself** se surmener ‖ *intr* s'efforcer; filtrer, tamiser; (*to trickle*) suinter; (*said of beam, ship, motor, etc.*) fatiguer; **to strain at** (*a leash, rope, etc.*) tirer sur; (*to balk at*) reculer devant

strained *adj* (*smile*) forcé; (*friendship*) tendu; (*nervous*) crispé

strainer [ˋstrenər] *s* passoire *f*, filtre *m*

strait [stret] *s* détroit *m*; **straits** détroit; **to be in dire straits** être dans la plus grande gêne

strait′ jack′et *s* camisole de force

strait′-laced′ *adj* prude, collet monté, puritain

Straits′ of Do′ver *spl* Pas *m* de Calais

strand [strænd] *s* (*beach*) plage *f*, grève *f*; (*of rope or cable*) toron *m*; (*of thread*) brin *m*; (*of pearls*) collier *m*; (*of hair*) cheveu *m* ‖ *tr* toronner; (*to undo strands of*) décorder; (*a ship*) échouer

stranded *adj* abandonné; (*lost*) égaré; (*ship*) échoué; (*rope or cable*) à torons; **to leave s.o. stranded** laisser qn en plan

strange [strendʒ] *adj* étrange; (*unfamiliar*) inconnu, étranger; (*unaccustomed*) inhabituel

stranger [ˋstrendʒər] *s* étranger *m*; visiteur *m*

strangle [ˋstræŋɡəl] *tr* étrangler, étouffer ‖ *intr* s'étrangler

strap [stræp] *s* (*of leather, rubber, etc.*) courroie *f*; (*of cloth, metal, leather, etc.*) bande *f*; (*to sharpen a razor*) cuir *m* à rasoir; (*of, e.g., a harness*) sangle *f* ‖ *v* (*pret & pp* **strapped;** *ger* **strapping**) *tr* attacher avec une courroie, sangler; (*a razor*) repasser sur le cuir

strap′hang′er *s* (coll) voyageur *m* debout

strapping [ˋstræpɪŋ] *adj* bien découplé, robuste; (coll) énorme, gros

stratagem [ˋstrætədʒəm] *s* stratagème *m*

strategic(al) [strəˋtidʒɪk(əl)] *adj* stratégique

strategist [ˋstrætɪdʒɪst] *s* stratège *m*

strate•gy [ˋstrætɪdʒɪ] *s* (*pl* **-gies**) stratégie *f*

strati•fy [ˋstrætɪ͵faɪ] *v* (*pret & pp* **-fied**) *tr* stratifier ‖ *intr* se stratifier

stratosphere [ˋstrætə͵sfɪr] *s* stratosphère *f*

stra•tum [ˋstrætəm] *s* (*pl* **-ta** [tə] or **-tums**) couche *f*; (*e.g., of society*) classe *f*, couche

straw [strɔ] *s* paille *f*; (*for drinking*) chalumeau *m*, paille; **it's the last straw!** c'est le bouquet!, il ne manquait plus que cela!, c'est la fin des haricots!

straw′ber′ry *s* (*pl* **-ries**) fraise *f*; (*plant*) fraisier *m*

straw′hat′ *s* chapeau *m* de paille; (*skimmer*) canotier *m*

straw′ man′ *s* (*pl* **-men′**) (*figurehead*) homme *m* de paille, sanglier *m* de carton; (*scarecrow*) épouvantail *m*; (*red herring*) canard *m*, diversion *f*

straw′ mat′tress *s* paillasse *f*

straw′ vote′ *s* vote *m* d'essai

stray [stre] *adj* égaré; (*bullet*) perdu; (*scattered*) épars ‖ *s* animal *m* égaré ‖ *intr* s'égarer

streak [strik] *s* raie *f*, rayure *f*, bande *f*; (*of light*) trait *m*, filet *m*; (*of lightning*) éclair *m*; (*layer*) veine *f*; (*bit*) trace *f*; **like a streak** comme un éclair; **streak of luck** filon *m* ‖ *tr* rayer, strier, zébrer ‖ *intr* faire des raies; passer comme un éclair

stream [strim] *s* (*brook*) ruisseau *m*; (*steady flow of current*) courant *m*; (*of people, abuse, light, etc.*) flot *m*; (*of, e.g., automobiles*) défilé *m* ‖ *intr* couler; (*said of blood*) ruisseler; (*said of light*) jaillir; (*said of flag*) flotter; **to stream out** sortir à flots

streamer [ˋstrimər] *s* banderole *f*

stream′lined′ *adj* aérodynamique, caréné; (fig) abrégé, concis

stream′lin′er *s* train *m* caréné de luxe

street [strit] *s* rue *f*; (*surface of the street*) chaussée *f*

street′ ball′ *s* sport *m* de rue (*basket de rue, football de rue*)

street′car′ *s* tramway *m*

street′ clean′er *s* balayeur *m*; (mach) balayeuse *f*

street′ clothes′ *spl* vêtements *mpl* de ville

street′ floor′ *s* rez-de-chaussée *m*

street′light′ *s* réverbère *m*

street′ sprink′ler *s* arroseuse *f*

street′ u′rinal *s* vespasienne *f*, édicule *m*, urinoir *m*

street′walk′er *s* racoleuse *f*, fille *f* des rues

street′wise′ *adj* démerdard

strength [strɛŋθ] *s* force *f*, puissance *f*; (*of a fabric*) solidité *f*; (*of spirituous liquors*) degré *m*, titre *m*; (com) tendance *f* à la hausse; (mil) effectif(s) *m*(*pl*); **on the strength of** sur la foi de

strengthen [ˋstrɛŋθən] *tr* fortifier, renforcer ‖ *intr* se fortifier, se renforcer

strenuous [ˋstrɛnju•əs] *adj* actif, énergique; (*work*) ardu; (*effort*) acharné; (*objection*) vigoureux

strep′ throat′ [strɛp] *s* streptococcie *f* de la gorge

streptococcus [͵strɛptəˋkɑkəs] *s* streptocoque *m*

streptomycin [͵strɛptəˋmaɪsən] *s* (pharm) streptomycine *f*

stress [strɛs] *s* tension *f*, force *f*; (mach) stress *m*, tension; (phonet) accent *m* d'intensité; **to lay stress on** insister sur ‖ *tr* (*e.g., a beam*) charger; (*a syllable*) accentuer; (*a point*) insister sur, appuyer sur

stress′ ac′cent *s* accent *m* d'intensité

stretch [strɛtʃ] *s* (*act, gesture*) étirement *m*; (*span*) envergure *f*; (*of the arm; of the meaning*) extension *f*; (*of the imagination*) effort *m;* (*distance in time or space*) intervalle *m,* période *f;* (*section of road*) section *f;* (*section of country, water, etc.*) étendue *f;* **at a stretch** d'un trait; **in one stretch** d'une seule traite; **to do a stretch** (slang) faire de la taule ‖ *tr* tendre; (*the sense of a word*) forcer; (*a sauce*) allonger; **to stretch oneself** s'étirer; **to stretch out** allonger, étendre; (*the hand*) tendre ‖ *intr* s'étirer; (*said of shoes, gloves, etc.*) s'élargir; **to stretch out** s'allonger, s'étendre

stretcher [ˈstrɛtʃər] *s* (*for gloves, trousers, etc.*) tendeur *m;* (*for a painting*) châssis *m;* (*to carry sick or wounded*) civière *f,* brancard *m*

stretch′er·bear′er *s* brancardier *m*

strew [stru] *v* (*pret* **strewed;** *pp* **strewed** or **strewn**) *tr* semer, éparpiller; (*e.g., with flowers*) joncher, parsemer

stricken [ˈstrɪkən] *adj* frappé; (*e.g., with grief*) affligé; (*crossed out*) rayé; **stricken with** atteint de

strict [strɪkt] *adj* strict; (*exacting*) sévère

stricture [ˈstrɪktʃər] *s* critique *f* sévère; (*pathol*) rétrécissement *m*

stride [straɪd] *s* enjambée *f;* **to hit one's stride** attraper la cadence; **to make great** (or **rapid**) **strides** avancer à grands pas; **to take in one's stride** faire sans le moindre effort ‖ *v* (*pret* **strode** [strod]; *pp* **stridden** [ˈstrɪdən]) *tr* parcourir à grandes enjambées; (*to straddle*) enfourcher ‖ *intr*—**to stride across** or **over** enjamber; **to stride along** marcher à grandes enjambées

strident [ˈstraɪdənt] *adj* strident

strife [straɪf] *s* lutte *f*

strike [straɪk] *s* (*blow*) coup *m;* (*stopping of work*) grève *f;* (*discovery of ore, oil, etc.*) rencontre *f;* (*baseball*) coup du batteur, prise *f;* **to go on strike** se mettre en grève ‖ *v* (*pret & pp* **struck** [strʌk]) *tr* frapper; (*coins*) frapper; (*a match*) frotter; (*a bargain*) conclure; (*camp*) lever; (*the sails; the colors*) amener; (*the hour*) sonner; (*root; a pose*) prendre; **how does he strike you?** quelle impression vous fait-il?; **to strike it rich** trouver le filon; **to strike out** (baseball) retirer sur trois prises; **to strike out** or **off** rayer; **to strike up** (*a song, piece of music, etc.*) attaquer, entonner; (*an acquaintance, conversation, etc.*) lier ‖ *intr* frapper; (*said of clock*) sonner; (*said of workers*) faire la grève; (*mil*) donner l'assaut; **to strike out** se mettre en route; (*baseball*) se retirer sur trois prises

strike′break′er *s* briseur *m* de grève, jaune *m*

strike′ pay′ *s* salaire *m* de gréviste

striker [ˈstraɪkər] *s* frappeur *m;* (*on door*) marteau *m;* (*worker on strike*) gréviste *mf*

striking [ˈstraɪkɪŋ] *adj* frappant, saisissant; (*workers*) en grève

strik′ing pow′er *s* force *f* de frappe

string [strɪŋ] *s* ficelle *f;* (*of onions or garlic; of islands; of pearls; of abuse*) chapelet *m;* (*of words, insults*) enfilade *f,* kyrielle *f;* (*e.g., of cars*) file *f;* (*of beans*) fil *m;* (*for shoes*) lacet *m;* (mus) corde *f;* **strings** instruments *mpl* à cordes; **to pull strings** (fig) tirer les ficelles; **with no strings attached** (coll) sans restriction ‖ *v* (*pret & pp* **strung** [strʌŋ]) *tr* mettre une ficelle à, garnir de cordes; (*e.g., a violin*) mettre les cordes à; (*a bow*) bander; (*a tennis racket*) corder; (*beads, sentences, etc.*) enfiler; (*a cord, a thread, a wire, etc.*) tendre; (*to tune*) moner; **to string along** (slang) lanterner, faire marcher; **to string up** (coll) pendre ‖ *intr*—**to string along with** (slang) collaborer avec, suivre

string′ bean′ *s* haricot *m* vert

stringed′ in′strument *s* instrument *m* à cordes

stringent [ˈstrɪndʒənt] *adj* rigoureux; (*tight*) tendu; (*convincing*) convaincant

string′ quartet′ *s* quatuor *m* à cordes

string·y [ˈstrɪŋi] *adj* (*comp* **-ier;** *super* **-iest**) fibreux, filandreux

strip [strɪp] *s* (*of paper, cloth, land, stamps*) bande *f;* (*of metal*) lame *f,* ruban *m* ‖ *v* (*pret & pp* **stripped;** *ger* **stripping**) *tr* dépouiller; (*to strip bare*) mettre à nu; (*the bed*) défaire; (*a screw*) arracher le filet de, faire foirer; (*tobacco*) écoter; **to strip down** (*e.g., a motor*) démonter; **to strip off** enlever; (*e.g., bark*) écorcer ‖ *intr* se déshabiller

strip′ cen′ter *s* centre *m* commercial

stripe [straɪp] *s* raie *f,* bande *f;* (*on cloth*) rayure *f;* (*flesh wound*) marque *f;* (mil, nav) chevron *m,* galon *m;* **of any stripe** de tous poils; **to win one's stripes** gagner ses galons ‖ *tr* rayer

strip′ min′ing *s* exploitation *f* minière à ciel ouvert

stripper [ˈstrɪpər] *s* (*male stripper*) strip-teaseur *m;* (*female stripper*) strip-teaseuse *f;* (*paint remover*) décapant *m*

strip′ search′ *tr* faire déshabiller et fouiller

strip′tease′ *s* strip-tease *m,* déshabillage *m* suggestif

stripteaser [ˈstrɪpˌtizər] *s* effeuilleuse *f,* strip-teaseuse *f*

strive [straɪv] *v* (*pret* **strove** [strov]; *pp* **striven** [ˈstrɪvən]) *intr* s'efforcer; **to strive after** rechercher; **to strive against** lutter contre; **to strive to** s'efforcer à, s'évertuer à

strobe (light) [strob] *s* stroboscope *m,* appareil *m* stroboscopique

stroke [strok] *s* coup *m;* (*of pen; of wit*) trait *m;* (*of arms in swimming*) brassée *f;* (*caress with hand*) caresse *f* de la main; (*of a piston*) course *f;* (*of lightning*) foudre *f;* (pathol) attaque *f* d'apoplexie; **at the stroke of** sonnant, e.g., **at the stroke of five** à cinq heures sonnantes; **to not do a stroke of work** ne pas en ficher une ramée ‖ *tr* caresser de la main

stroll [strol] *s* promenade *f;* **to take a stroll** aller faire un tour ‖ *intr* se promener

stroller [ˈstrolər] *s* promeneur *m;* (*for babies*) poussette *f*

strong [strɔŋ] *adj* (*comp* **stronger** [ˈstrɔŋgər]; *super* **strongest** [ˈstrɔŋgɪst]) fort; (*stock mar-*

ket) ferme; (*musical beat* marqué; (*spicy*) piquant; (*rancid*) rance

strong′-arm′ man′ *s* gorille *m* (coll)

strong′box′ *s* coffre-fort *m*

strong′ drink′ *s* boissons *fpl* spiritueuses

strong′hold′ *s* place *f* forte

strong′ man′ *s* (*pl* **-men′**) (*e.g., in a circus*) hercule *m* forain; (*leader, good planner*) animateur *m;* (*dictator*) chef *m* autoritaire

strong′-mind′ed *adj* résolu, décidé; (*woman*) hommasse

strontium [ˈstrɑnʃɪ•əm] *s* strontium *m*

strop [strɑp] *s* cuir *m* à rasoir ‖ *v* (*pret & pp* **stropped;** *ger* **stropping**) *tr* repasser sur le cuir

strophe [ˈstrofɪ] *s* strophe *f*

structure [ˈstrʌktʃər] *s* structure *f;* (*building*) édifice *m*

struggle [ˈstrʌgəl] *s* lutte *f‖ intr* lutter; **to struggle along** avancer péniblement

strug′gle for exist′ence *s* lutte *f* pour la vie

strum [strʌm] *v* (*pret & pp* **strummed;** *ger* **strumming**) *tr* (*an instrument*) gratter de; (*a tune*) tapoter ‖ *intr* jouailler; **to strum on** plaquer des arpèges sur

strumpet [ˈstrʌmpɪt] *s* putain *f*

strut [strʌt] *s* (*brace, prop*) étai *m,* support *m,* entretoise *f;* démarche *f* orgueilleuse ‖ *v* (*pret & pp* **strutted;** *ger* **strutting**) *intr* se pavaner

strychnine [ˈstrɪknaɪn] *s* strychnine *f*

stub [stʌb] *s* (*fragment*) tronçon *m;* (*of a tree*) souche *f;* (*of a pencil, of a cigar, cigarette*) bout *m;* (*of a check*) talon *m,* souche ‖ *v* (*pret & pp* **stubbed;** *ger* **stubbing**) *tr*—**to stub one's toe** se cogner le bout du pied

stubble [ˈstʌbəl] *s* éteule *f,* chaume *m;* (*of beard*) poil *m* court et raide

stubborn [ˈstʌbərn] *adj* obstiné; (*headstrong*) têtu; (*resolute*) acharné; (*fever*) rebelle; (*soil*) ingrat

stuc•co [ˈstʌko] *s* (*pl* **-coes** or **-cos**) stuc *m* ‖ *tr* stuquer

stuck [stʌk] *adj* coincé, pris; (*glued*) collé; (*unable to continue*) en panne; **stuck on** (coll) entiché de

stuck′-up′ *adj* (coll) hautain, prétentieux

stud [stʌd] *s* (*nail, knob*) clou *m* à grosse tête; (*ornament*) clou doré; (*on shirt*) bouton *m;* (*studhorse*) étalon *m;* (*horse farm*) haras *m;* (*bolt*) goujon *m;* (archit) montant *m* ‖ *v* (*pret & pp* **studded;** *ger* **studding**) *tr* clouter; **studded with** jonché de, parsemé de

stud′ bolt′ *s* goujon *m*

stud′ded tire′ *s* pneu *m* à clou

student [ˈst(j)udənt] *adj* estudiantin ‖ *s* étudiant *m;* (*researcher*) chercheur *m*

stu′dent bod′y *s* étudiants *mpl*

stu′dent cen′ter *s* foyer *m* d'étudiants, centre *m* social des étudiants

stu′dent nurse′ *s* élève *f* infirmière

stu′dent teach′er *s* stagiaire *mf*

stud′ farm′ *s* haras *m*

stud′horse′ *s* étalon *m*

studied [ˈstʌdid] *adj* prémédité; recherché

studi•o [ˈst(j)udɪˌo] *s* (*pl* **-os**) studio *m,* atelier *m*

studious [ˈst(j)udɪ•əs] *adj* studieux, appliqué

stud•y [ˈstʌdi] *s* (*pl* **-ies**) étude *f;* rêverie *f;* cabinet *m* ‖ *v* (*pret & pp* **-ied**) *tr & intr* étudier

stuff [stʌf] *s* chose *f,* truc *m;* (*miscellaneous objects*) choses *fpl,* fatras *m;* (*possessions*) affaires *fpl;* **to know one's stuff** (coll) s'y connaître ‖ *tr* bourrer; (*with food*) gaver; (*furniture*) rembourrer; (*an animal*) empailler; (culin) farcir; **to stuff up** boucher ‖ *intr* se gaver

stuffed [stʌft] *adj* (e.g., *toy*) en peluche

stuffed′ shirt′ *s* collet *m* monté

stuffing [ˈstʌfɪŋ] *s* rembourrage *m;* (culin) farce

stuff•y [ˈstʌfi] *adj* (*comp* **-ier;** *super* **-iest**) (*room*) mal ventilé; (*tedious*) ennuyeux; (*pompous*) collet monté; **to smell stuffy** sentir le renfermé

stumble [ˈstʌmbəl] *intr* trébucher; (*in speaking*) hésiter

stum′bling block′ *s* pierre *f* d'achoppement

stump [stʌmp] *s* (*of tree*) souche *f;* (*e.g., of arm*) moignon *m;* (*of tooth*) chicot *m* ‖ *tr* (*a design*) estomper; (coll) embarrasser, coller; (*a state, district, region*) (coll) faire une tournée électorale en, dans, or à ‖ *intr* clopiner

stump′ speak′er *s* orateur *m* de carrefour

stump′ speech′ *s* harangue *f* électorale improvisée

stun [stʌn] *v* (*pret & pp* **stunned;** *ger* **stunning**) *tr* étourdir

stunning [ˈstʌnɪŋ] *adj* (coll) étourdissant, épatant

stunt [stʌnt] *s* (*underdeveloped creature*) avorton *m;* (*feat*) tour *m* de force, acrobatie *f;* (*trick*) truc *m;* **to do a stunt** (mov) faire une cascade ‖ *tr* atrophier ‖ *intr* (coll) faire des acrobaties

stunted *adj* rabougri

stunt′ fly′ing *s* vol *m* de virtuosité, acrobatie *f* aérienne

stunt′ man′ *s* (*pl* **men′**) cascadeur *m,* doublure *f*

stupe•fy [ˈst(j)upɪˌfaɪ] *v* (*pret & pp* **-fied**) *tr* stupéfier

stupendous [st(j)uˈpɛndəs] *adj* prodigieux, formidable

stupid [ˈst(j)upɪd] *adj* stupide

stupor [ˈst(j)upər] *s* stupeur *f*

stur•dy [ˈstʌrdi] *adj* (*comp* **-dier;** *super* **-diest**) robuste, vigoureux; (*resolute*) ferme, hardi

sturgeon [ˈstʌrdʒən] *s* esturgeon *m*

stutter [ˈstʌtər] *s* bégaiement *m* ‖ *tr & intr* bégayer

sty [staɪ] *s* (*pl* **sties**) porcherie *f;* (pathol) orgelet *m*

style [staɪl] *s* style *m;* (*fashion*) mode *f;* (*elegance*) ton *m,* chic *m;* **to live in great style** mener grand train ‖ *tr* appeler, dénommer; **to style oneself** s'intituler

stylish [ˈstaɪlɪ] *adj* à la mode, élégant, chic

sty•mie [ˈstaɪmi] *v* (*pret & pp* **-mied;** *ger* **-mieing**) *tr* contrecarrer

styp′tic pen′cil [ˈstɪptɪk] *s* crayon *m* styptique

suave [swɑv] *adj* suave; (*person*) affable; (*manners*) doucereux

sub *abbr* **submarine**

subconscious [səbˈkɑnʃəs] *adj & s* subconscient *m*

sub′contrac′tor *s* sous-traitant *m*

sub′divide′ or **sub′divide′** *tr* subdiviser; (*land for future sale*) lotir ‖ *intr* se subdiviser

sub′divi′sion *s* subdivision; (*land to be developed and sold*) lotissement *m;* (*plot*) parcelle *f,* lot *m*

subdue [səbˈd(j)u] *tr* subjuguer, vaincre, asservir; (*color, light, sound*) adoucir, amortir; (*passions, feelings*) dompter

sub′head′ *s* sous-titre *m*

subject [ˈsʌbdʒɪkt] *adj* sujet, assujetti, soumis ‖ *s* sujet *m;* (*e.g., in school*) matière *f* ‖ [səbˈdʒɛkt] *tr* assujettir, soumettre

sub′ject′ in′dex *s* index de matières

subjection [səbˈdʒɛk/ən] *s* sujétion *f,* soumission *f*

subjective [səbˈdʒɛktɪv] *adj* subjectif

sub′ject mat′ter *s* matière *f*

subjugate [ˈsʌbdʒə,get] *tr* subjuguer

subjunctive [səbˈdʒʌŋktɪv] *adj & s* subjonctif *m*

sub′lease′ *s* sous-location *f* ‖ **sub′lease′** *tr* sous-louer

sub•let [səbˈlɛt], [ˈsʌb,lɛt] *v* (*pret & pp* **-let;** *ger* **-letting**) *tr* sous-louer

sub′machine′ gun′ *s* mitraillette *f*

sub′marine′ *adj* sous-marin *m* ‖ *s* sous-marin *m;* (*culin*) sandwich *m* d'assiette anglaise et de fromage

sub′marine chas′er *s* chasseur *m* de sous-marins

submerge [səbˈmʌrdʒ] *tr* submerger ‖ *intr* (*said of submarine*) plonger .

submersion [səbˈmʌrʒən] *s* submersion *f*

submission [səbˈmɪʃən] *s* soumission *f;* (*delivery*) présentation *f*

submissive [səbˈmɪsɪv] *adj* soumis

sub•mit [səbˈmɪt] *v* (*pret & pp* **-mitted;** *ger* **-mitting**) *tr* soumettre ‖ *intr* se soumettre

subordinate [səbˈɔrdɪnɪt] *adj & s* subordonné *m* ‖ [səbˈɔrdɪ,net] *tr* subordonner

subpoena [səˈpinə] *s* assignation *f,* citation *f* ‖ *tr* citer

subscribe [səbˈskraɪb] *tr* souscrire ‖ *intr*—**to subscribe to** (*an opinion; a charity; a loan; a publication*) souscrire à; (*a newspaper, a magazine*) s'abonner à

subscriber [səbˈskraɪbər] *s* abonné *m*

subscription [səbˈskrɪpʃən] *s* souscription *f;* (*to newspaper or magazine*) abonnement *m;* (*to club*) cotisation *f;* **to take out a subscription for s.o.** abonner qn; **to take out a subscription to** s'abonner à

subsequent [ˈsʌbsɪkwənt] *adj* subséquent, suivant

subservient [səbˈsʌrvɪ•ənt] *adj* asservi, subordonné

subside [səbˈsaɪd] *intr* (*said of water, ground, etc.*) s'abaisser; (*said of storm, excitement, etc.*) s'apaiser

subsidiar•y [səbˈsɪdɪ,ɛri] *adj* subsidiaire ‖ *s* (*pl* **-ies**) filiale *f*

subsidize [ˈsʌbsɪ,daɪz] *tr* subventionner; suborner

subsi•dy [ˈsʌbsɪdi] *s* (*pl* **-dies**) subside *m,* subvention *f*

subsist [səbˈsɪst] *intr* subsister

subsistence [səbˈsɪstəns] *s* (*supplies*) subsistance *f;* existence *f*

sub′soil′ *s* sous-sol *m*

subsonic [,sʌbˈsɑnɪk] *adj* subsonique

substance [ˈsʌbstəns] *s* substance *f*

sub•stand′ard *adj* inférieur au niveau normal

substantial [səbˈstænʃəl] *adj* substantiel; (*wealthy*) aisé, cossu

substantiate [səbˈstænʃi,et] *tr* établir, vérifier

substantive [ˈsʌbstəntɪv] *adj & s* substantif *m*

sub′sta′tion *s* (*of post office*) bureau *m* auxiliaire; (*elec*) sous-station *f*

substitute [ˈsʌbstɪ,t(j)ut] *s* (*person*) remplaçant *m,* suppléant *m,* substitut *m;* (*e.g., for coffee*) succédané *m* ‖ *tr* remplacer, e.g., **they substituted copper for silver** ils ont remplacé l'argent par le cuivre; substituer, e.g., **a hind was substituted for Iphigenia** une biche fut substituée à Iphigénie ‖ *intr* servir de remplaçant; **to substitute for** remplacer, suppléer, e.g., **she substituted for the math teacher** elle a suppléé le professeur de maths

sub′sti′tute teach′er *s* suppléant *m,* suppléante *f,* professeur *m* suppléant

substitution [,sʌbstɪˈt(j)uʃən] *s* substitution *f*

sub′stra′tum *s* (*pl* **-ta** [tə] or **-tums**) substrat *m*

subterfuge [ˈsʌbtər,fjudʒ] *s* subterfuge *m,* faux-fuyant *m*

subterranean [,sʌbtəˈreni•ən] *adj* souterrain

sub′ti′tle *s* sous-titre *m*

subtle [ˈsʌtəl] *adj* subtil

subtle•ty [ˈsʌtəlti] *s* (*pl* **-ties**) subtilité *f*

subtract [səbˈtrækt] *tr* soustraire

subtraction [səbˈtrækʃən] *s* soustraction *f*

suburb [ˈsʌbʌrb] *s* ville *f* de la banlieue; **the suburbs** la banlieue, la périphérie *f*

suburban [səˈbʌrbən] *adj* suburbain, périphérique

sub′ur′ban devel′opment *s* lotissements *mpl* dans la périphérie; expansion *f* périphérique

suburbanite [səˈbʌrbə,naɪt] *s* banlieusard *m*

subvention [səbˈvɛnʃən] *s* subvention *f* ‖ *tr* subventionner

subversive [səbˈvʌrsɪv] *adj* subversif ‖ *s* factieux *m*

subvert [səbˈvʌrt] *tr* corrompre; renverser

sub′way′ *s* métro *m;* (*tunnel for pedestrians*) souterrain *m*

sub′way car′ *s* voiture *f* de métro
sub′way sta′tion *s* station *f* de métro
succeed [sək′sid] *tr* succéder à; **to succeed one another** se succéder ‖ *intr* réussir; **to succeed in** + *ger* réussir à + *inf;* **to succeed to** (*the throne; a fortune*) succéder à
success [sək′sɛs] *s* succès *m,* réussite *f;* **to be a howling success** (theat) faire un malheur; **to be a success** avoir du succès
successful [sək′sɛsfəl] *adj* réussi; heureux, prospère
succession [sək′sɛʃən] *s* succession *f;* **in succession** de suite
successive [sək′sɛsɪv] *adj* successif
succor [′sʌkər] *s* secours *m* ‖ *tr* secourir
succotash [′sʌkə,tæʃ] *s* plat *m* de fèves et de maïs
succumb [sə′kʌm] *intr* succomber
such [sʌtʃ] *adj & pron indef* tel, pareil, semblable; **such a** un tel; **such and such** tel et tel; **such as** tel que
suck [sʌk] *s*—**to give suck to** allaiter ‖ *tr* sucer; (*a nipple*) téter; **to suck in** aspirer; (*to absorb*) sucer ‖ *intr* sucer; téter
sucker [′sʌkər] *s* suceur *m;* (*sucking organ*) suçoir *m,* ventouse *f;* (bot) drageon *m;* (ichth) rémora *m;* (*gullible person*) (coll) gogo *m;* (*lollipop*) (coll) sucette *f*
suckle [′sʌkəl] *tr* allaiter
suck′ling pig′ *s* cochon *m* de lait
suction [′sʌkʃən] *s* succion *f*
suc′tion cup′ *s* ventouse *f*
suc′tion pump′ *s* pompe *f* aspirante
sudden [′sʌdən] *adj* brusque, soudain; **all of a sudden** tout à coup
sud′den death′ *s* mort *f* subite; (sports) verdict *m* instantané
sud′den in′fant death′ syn′drome *s* mort *f* subite du nourrisson, mort inexpliquée du nourrisson
suddenly [′sʌdənli] *adv* tout à coup
suds [sʌdz] *spl* eau *f* savonneuse; mousse *f* de savon
sue [s(j)u] *tr* poursuivre en justice ‖ *intr* intenter un procès
suede [swed] *s* suède *m;* (*for shoes*) daim *m*
suet [′s(j)uˑɪt] *s* graisse *f* de rognon
suffer [′sʌfər] *tr* souffrir; (*to allow*) permettre; (*a defeat*) essuyer, subir ‖ *intr* souffrir
sufferance [′sʌfərəns] *s* tolérance *f*
suffering [′sʌfərɪŋ] *adj* souffrant ‖ *s* souffrance *f*
suffice [sə′faɪs] *tr* suffire à ‖ *intr* suffire; **it suffices to** + *inf* il suffit de + *inf*
sufficient [sə′fɪʃənt] *adj* suffisant
suffix [′sʌfɪks] *s* suffixe *m*
suffocate [′sʌfə,ket] *tr & intr* suffoquer, étouffer
suffrage [′sʌfrɪdʒ] *s* suffrage *m*
suffragist [′sʌfrədʒɪst] *s* partisan *m* du droit de vote des femmes
suffuse [sə′fjuz] *tr* baigner, saturer
sugar [′ʃʊgər] *s* sucre *m* ‖ *tr* sucrer; (*a cake*)

saupoudrer de sucre; (*a pill*) recouvrir de sucre ‖ *intr* former du sucre
sug′ar beet′ *s* betterave *f* sucrière, betterave à sucre
sug′ar bowl′ *s* sucrier *m*
sug′ar cane′ *s* canne *f* à sucre
sug′ar-coat′ *tr* dragéifier; (fig) dorer
sug′ar dad′dy *s* (*pl* **-dies**) papa *m* gâteau
sug′ar ma′ple *s* érable *m* à sucre
sug′ar pea′ *s* mange-tout *m*
sug′ar tongs′ *spl* pince *f* à sucre
sugary [′ʃʊgəri] *adj* sucré; (fig) doucereux
suggest [səg′dʒɛst] *tr* suggérer
suggestion [səg′dʒɛstʃən] *s* suggestion *f;* nuance *f,* pointe *f,* soupçon *m*
suggestive [səg′dʒɛstɪv] *adj* suggestif
suicidal [,s(j)uˑɪ′saɪdəl] *adj* suicidaire
suicide [′s(j)uˑɪ,saɪd] *s* (*act*) suicide *m;* (*person*) suicidé *m;* **to commit suicide** se suicider
su′icide bomb′er *s* (*carrying explosives*) plastiqueur *m or* plastiqueuse *f* suicidant(e); (aer) pilote *mf* terroriste suicidant(e)
su′icide bomb′ing *s* (*on the ground*) attentat *m* suicidant au plastic; (aer) pilotage *m* terroriste suicide
su′icide squad′ *s* (football) équipe *f* suicide
suit [s(j)ut] *s* (*men's*) complet *m,* costume *m;* (*women's*) costume tailleur, tailleur *m;* (*lawsuit*) procès *m;* (*plea*) requête *f;* (cards) couleur *f;* **to follow suit** jouer la couleur; (fig) en faire autant ‖ *tr* adapter; convenir à, e.g., **does that suit him?** cela lui convient?; aller à, seoir à, e.g., **the dress suits her well** la robe lui va bien, la robe lui sied bien ‖ *intr* convenir, aller
suitable [′s(j)utəbəl] *adj* convenable, à propos; compétent
suit′case′ *s* valise *f*
suite [swit] *s* suite *f* ‖ [s(j)ut] *s* (*of furniture*) ameublement *m,* mobilier *m*
suiting [′s(j)utɪŋ] *s* étoffe *f* pour complets
suit′ of clothes′ *s* complet-veston *m*
suitor [′s(j)utər] *s* prétendant *m,* soupirant *m*
sul′fa drugs′ [′sʌlfə] *spl* sulfamides *mpl*
sulfide [′sʌlfaɪd] *s* sulfure *m*
sulfur [′sʌlfər] *adj* soufré ‖ *s* soufre *m* ‖ *tr* soufrer
sulfuric [sʌl′fjurɪk] *adj* sulfurique
sul′fur mine′ *s* soufrière *f*
sulk [sʌlk] *s* bouderie *f* ‖ *intr* bouder
sulk•y [′sʌlki] *adj* (*comp* **-ier;** *super* **-iest**) boudeur, maussade
sullen [′sʌlən] *adj* maussade, rébarbatif
sul•ly [′sʌli] *v* (*pret & pp* **-lied**) *tr* souiller
sulphate [′sʌlfet] *s* sulfate *m*
sulphur [′sʌlfər] *adj, s & tr* var of **sulfur**
sultan [′sʌltən] *s* sultan *m*
sul•try [′sʌltri] *adj* (*comp* **-trier;** *super* **-triest**) étouffant, suffocant
sum [sʌm] *s* somme *f;* tout *m,* total *m;* **in sum** somme toute ‖ *v* (*pret & pp* **summed;** *ger* **summing**) *tr*—**to sum up** résumer
sumac *ou* **sumach** [′sumæk] *s* sumac *m*

summarize [`sʌmə,raɪz] *tr* résumer
summa·ry [`sʌməri] *adj* sommaire || *s* (*pl* **-ries**) sommaire *m*
summer [`sʌmər] *adj* estival || *s* été *m* || *intr* passer l'été
sum'mer resort' *s* station *f* estivale
summersault *var* de **somersault**
sum'mer school' *s* cours *m* d'été, cours de vacances
summery [`sʌməri] *adj* estival, d'été
summit [`sʌmɪt] *s* sommet *m*
sum'mit con'ference *s* conférence *f* au sommet
summon [`sʌmən] *tr* appeler, convoquer; (law) sommer, citer, assigner
summons [`sʌmənz] *s* appel *m;* (law) mandat *m* d'amener, citation *f,* assignation *f,* exploit *m*
sump' pump' [sʌmp] *s* vide-cave *m*
sumptuous [`sʌmptʃʊ•əs] *adj* somptueux
sun [sʌn] *s* soleil *m* || *v* (*pret & pp* **sunned;** *ger* **sunning**) *tr* exposer au soleil || *intr* prendre le soleil
sun' bath' *s* bain *m* de soleil
sun'beam' *s* rayon *m* de soleil
sun'bon'net *s* capeline *f*
sun'burn' *s* coup *m* de soleil || *v* (*pret & pp* **-burned** or **-burnt**) *tr* hâler, basaner || *intr* se basaner
sun'burned' *adj* brûlé par le soleil
sundae [`sʌndi] *s* coupe *f* de glace garnie de fruits, sundae *m*
Sunday [`sʌndi] *adj* dominical || *s* dimanche *m*
Sun'day best' *s* (coll) habits *mpl* du dimanche
Sun'day driv'er *s* chauffeur *m* du dimanche
Sun'day school' *s* école *f* du dimanche
sunder [`sʌndər] *tr* séparer, rompre
sun'di'al *s* cadran *m* solaire, gnomon *m,* horloge *f* solaire
sun'down' *s* coucher *m* du soleil
sundries [`sʌndriz] *spl* articles *mpl* divers
sundry [`sʌndri] *adj* divers
sun'fish' *s* poisson-lune *m*
sun'flow'er *s* soleil *m,* tournesol *m*
sun'glass'es *spl* lunettes *fpl* de soleil, verres *mpl* fumés
sunken [`sʌŋkən] *adj* creux, enfoncé; (*rock*) noyé; (*ship*) sous-marin
sun' lamp' *s* lampe *f* à rayons ultraviolets
sun'light' *s* lumière *f* du soleil
Sunni [`suni] *adj & s* sunnite
sun·ny [`sʌni] *adj* (*comp* **-nier;** *super* **-niest**) ensoleillé; (*happy*) enjoué; **it is sunny** il fait du soleil
sun'ny side' *s* côté *m* exposé au soleil; (fig) bon côté
sun' par'lor *s* véranda *f*
sun' porch' *s* véranda *f*
sun'rise' *s* lever *m* du soleil
sun' roof' *s* (aut) toit *m* ouvrant
sun'set' *s* coucher *m* du soleil
sun'shade' *s* (*over door*) banne *f;* parasol *m;* abat-jour *m,* visière *f*
sun'shine' *s* clarté *f* du soleil, soleil *m;* (fig)

gaieté *f* rayonnante; **in the sunshine** en plein soleil
sun'spot' *s* tache *f* solaire
sun'stroke' *s* insolation *f*
sun' tan' *s* hâle *m*
sun'-tan oil' *s* huile *f* solaire
sun'up' *s* lever *m* du soleil
sun' vi'sor *s* abat-jour *m*
sup [sʌp] *v* (*pret & pp* **supped;** *ger* **supping**) *intr* souper
super [`supər] *adj* (slang) superbe, formidable || *s* (theat) figurant *m;* (slang) concierge *mf*
su'per·abun'dant *adj* surabondant
superannuated [,supər`ænjʊ,etɪd] *adj* (*person*) retraité; (*thing*) suranné
superb [sʊ`pʌrb] *adj* superbe
su'per·car'go *s* (*pl* **-goes** or **-gos**) subrécargue *m*
su'per·charge' *s* surcompression *f* || *tr* surcomprimer
supercilious [,supər`sɪli•əs] *adj* sourcilleux, hautain, arrogant
superficial [,supər`fɪʃəl] *adj* superficiel
superfluous [sʊ`pʌrflu•əs] *adj* superflu
su'per·high'way' *s* autoroute *f*
su'per·hu'man *adj* surhumain
su'per·impose' *tr* superposer
su'per·intend' *tr* surveiller; diriger
superintendent [,supərɪn`tɛndənt] *s* directeur *m,* directeur en chef; (*of a building*) concierge *mf*
superior [sə`pɪri•ər] *adj & s* supérieur *m*
superiority [sə,pɪri`arɪti] *s* supériorité *f*
superlative [sə`pʌrlətɪv] *adj & s* superlatif *m*
su'per·man' *s* (*pl* **-men'**) surhomme *m*
su'per·mar'ket *s* supermarché *m*
su'per·nat'ural *adj & s* surnaturel *m*
supersede [,supər`sid] *tr* remplacer
su'per·sen'sitive *adj* hypersensible
su'per·son'ic *adj* supersonique
superstition [,supər`stɪʃən] *s* superstition *f*
superstitious [,supər`stɪʃəs] *adj* superstitieux
su'per·tank'er *s* pétrolier *m* géant, tanker *m* géant
supervene [,supər`vin] *intr* survenir
supervise [`supər,vaɪz] *tr* surveiller; diriger
su'per·vi'sion *s* surveillance *f;* direction *f*
su'per·vi'sor *s* surveillant *m,* inspecteur *m;* directeur *m*
supper [`sʌpər] *s* souper *m*
sup'per·time' *s* heure *f* du souper
supplant [sə`plænt] *tr* supplanter
supple [`sʌpəl] *adj* souple, flexible
supplement [`sʌplɪmənt] *s* supplément *m* || *tr* ajouter à
supplementary [,sʌplə`mɛntəri] *adj* supplémentaire
suppliant [`sʌpli•ənt] *adj & s* suppliant *m*
supplicant [`sʌplɪkənt] *s* suppliant *m*
supplicate [`sʌplɪ,ket] *tr* supplier
supplier [sə`plaɪ•ər] *s* fournisseur *m,* pourvoyeur *m*
sup·ply [sə`plaɪ] *s* (*pl* **-plies**) (*action*) fourniture

f, provision *f,* approvisionnement *m; (store)* provision *f,* réserve *f,* stock *m;* **supplies** fournitures, approvisionnements; *(of food)* vivres *mpl* ‖ *v (pret & pp* **-plied**) *tr* fournir; *(a person, a city, a fort)* pourvoir, munir; *(a need)* répondre à; *(what is lacking)* suppléer; (mil) approvisionner

supply′ and demand′ *spl* l'offre *f* et la demande

supply′-side econom′ics *s* économie *f* de l'offre

support [sə`port] *s* soutien *m,* appui *m; (living expenses)* ressources *fpl,* de quoi vivre *m; (pillar)* support *m* ‖ *tr* soutenir, appuyer; *(e.g., a wife)* entretenir, soutenir; *(to hold up; to corroborate; to tolerate)* supporter; **to support oneself** gagner sa vie

supporter [sə`portər] *s* partisan *m,* supporter *m; (for part of body)* suspensoir *m,* slip *m* de soutien

suppose [sə`poz] *tr* supposer; **I suppose** so probablement; **suppose that . . .** à supposer que . . .; **suppose we take a walk?** si nous faisions une promenade?; **to be supposed to** + *inf* devoir + *inf; (to be considered to be)* être censé + *inf*

supposedly [sə`pozıdli] *adv* censément

supposition [,sʌpə`zı̣ʃən] *s* supposition *f*

supposito•ry [sə`pazı,tori] *s (pl* **-ries**) suppositoire *m*

suppress [sə`prɛs] *tr* supprimer; *(rebellion; anger)* réprimer, contenir; *(a yawn)* étouffer, empêcher

suppression [sə`prɛʃən] *s* suppression *f; (of a rebellion)* subjugation *f,* répression *f; (of a yawn)* empêchement *m*

suppurate [`sʌpjə,ret] *intr* suppurer

supremacy [sə`prɛməsi] *s* suprématie *f*

supreme [sə`prim], [sʊ`prim] *adj* suprême

Supreme Court, la *s* (U.S.A.) la Cour suprême

supreme′ court′ of appeals′ *s* cour *f* de cassation

surcharge [`sʌr,tʃardʒ] *s* surcharge *f* ‖ *tr* surcharger

sure [ʃʊr] *adj* sûr, certain; *(e.g., hand)* ferme; **for sure** à coup sûr, pour sûr; **to be sure to** + *inf* ne pas manquer de + *inf;* **to make sure** s'assurer ‖ *adv* (coll) certainement; **sure enough** (coll) effectivement, assurément ‖ *interj* (slang) mais oui!, bien sûr!, entendu!

sure′-foot′ed *adj* au pied sûr

surely [`ʃʊrli] *adv* sûrement, certainement; sans doute; *(frankly)* vraiment, tout de même

sure′ thing′ *interj* d'accord!, bien sûr! ‖ *s* (coll) pari *m* gagnant

sure•ty [`ʃʊrti] *s (pl* **-ties**) sûreté *f*

surf [sʌrf] *s* barre *f,* ressac *m,* brisants *mpl* ‖ *tr* surfer

surface [`sʌrfıs] *adj* superficiel ‖ *s* surface *f;* (area) superficie *f;* **on the surface** à la surface, en apparence; **to float under the surface** nager entre deux eaux ‖ *tr* polir la surface

de; *(a road)* recouvrir, revêtir ‖ *intr (said of submarine)* faire surface

sur′face mail′ *s* courrier *m* par voie ordinaire

surf′ and turf′ *s* (culin) pré *m* et marée

surf′board′ *s* planche *f* pour le surf, surfboard *m*

surfeit [`sʌrfıt] *s* satiété *f* ‖ *tr* rassasier ‖ *intr* se rassasier

surf′rid′ing *s* surfing *m,* planking *m*

surge [sʌrdʒ] *s* houle *f;* (elec) surtension *f* ‖ *intr* être houleux; se répandre; **to surge up** s'enfler, s'élever

surgeon [`sʌrdʒən] *s* chirurgien *m*

surger•y [`sʌrdʒəri] *s (pl* **-ies**) chirurgie *f;* salle *f* d'opération

surgical [`sʌrdʒıkəl] *adj* chirurgical

sur′gical gloves′ *spl* gants *npl* chirurgicaux

sur•ly [`sʌrli] *adj (comp* **-lier;** *super* **-liest**) hargneux, maussade, bourru

surmise [sər`maız] *s* conjecture *f* ‖ *tr & intr* conjecturer

surmount [sər`maʊnt] *tr* surmonter

surname [`sʌr,nem] *s* nom *m* de famille; surnom *m* ‖ *tr* donner un nom de famille à; surnommer

surpass [sər`pæs], [sər`pas] *tr* surpasser

surplice [`sʌrplıs] *s* surplis *m*

surplus [`sʌrplʌs] *adj* excédent, excédentaire, en excédent ‖ *s* surplus *m,* excédent *m*

sur′plus bag′gage *s* excédent *m* de bagages

surprise [sər`praız] *adj* à l'improviste, brusqué, inopiné ‖ *s* surprise *f;* **to take by surprise** prendre à l'improviste, prendre au dépourvu ‖ *tr* surprendre; **to be surprised at** être surpris de

surprise′ attack′ *s* attaque *f* brusquée

surprise′ pack′age *s* surprise *f,* pochette *f* surprise

surprise′ par′ty *s (pl* **-ties**) réunion *f* à l'improviste

surprising [sər`praızıŋ] *adj* surprenant

surrealism [sə`ri•ə,lızəm] *s* surréalisme *m*

surrender [sə`rɛndər] *s* reddition *f,* soumission *f; (e.g., of prisoners, goods)* remise *f; (e.g., of rights, property)* cession *f* ‖ *tr* rendre, céder ‖ *intr* se rendre

surren′der val′ue *s* valeur *f* de rachat

surreptitious [,sʌrɛp`tı̣ʃəs] *adj* subreptice

surrogate [`sʌrə,get] *s* substitut *m*

sur′rogate moth′er *s* femme *f* porteuse

surround [sə`raʊnd] *tr* entourer

surrounding [sə`raʊndıŋ] *adj* entourant, environnant ‖ **surroundings** *spl* environs *mpl,* alentours *mpl;* entourage *m,* milieu *m*

surtax [`sʌr,tæks] *s* surtaxe *f* ‖ *tr* surtaxer

surveillance [sər`vel(j)əns] *s* surveillance *f*

survey [`sʌrve] *s (for verification)* contrôle *m; (for evaluation)* appréciation *f,* évaluation *f; (report)* expertise *f,* aperçu *m; (of a whole)* vue *f* d'ensemble, tour *m* d'horizon; *(measured plan or drawing)* levé *m,* plan *m;* (surv) lever *m* or levé des plans; **to make a survey** *(to map out)* lever un plan; *(to poll)* effectuer un contrôle par sondage ‖ [sʌr`ve], [`sʌrve] *tr* contrôler; apprécier, évaluer, faire l'expertise de; (*as a whole*) jeter un coup d'œil sur; (*to poll*) sonder; (*e.g., a farm*) arpenter, faire l'arpentage de; (*e.g., a city*) faire le levé de

sur′vey course′ s cours *m* général

surveying [sʌr′ve•ɪŋ] s arpentage *m*, géodésie *f*, levé *m* des plans

surveyor [sər′ve•ər] s arpenteur *m*

survival [sər′vaɪvəl] s survivance *f*; (*after death*) survie *f*; **survival of the fittest** loi *f* sélective du plus fort, survie *f* du plus apte

surviv′al kit′ s équipement *m* de survie

survive [sər′vaɪv] *tr* survivre à ‖ *intr* survivre

surviving [sər′vaɪvɪŋ] *adj* survivant

survivor [sər′vaɪvər] s survivant *m*

survivorship [sər′vaɪvər‚ʃɪp] s (law) survie *f*

susceptible [sə′sɛptɪbəl] *adj* (*capable*) susceptible; (*liable, subject*) sensible; (*to love*) facilement amoureux

suspect [′sʌspɛkt], [səs′pɛkt] *adj* & s suspect *m* ‖ [səs′pɛkt] *tr* soupçonner ‖ *intr* s'en douter

suspend [səs′pɛnd] *tr* suspendre

suspenders [səs′pɛndərz] *spl* bretelles *fpl*

suspense [səs′pɛns] s suspens *m*

suspension [səs′pɛnʃən] s suspension *f*; **suspension of driver's license** retrait *m* de permis

suspen′sion bridge′ s pont *m* suspendu

suspicion [səs′pɪʃən] s soupçon *m*

suspicious [səs′pɪʃəs] *adj* (*inclined to suspect*) soupçonneux; (*subject to suspicion*) suspect

sustain [səs′ten] *tr* soutenir; (*a loss, injury, etc.*) éprouver

sustenance [′sʌstɪnəns] s subsistance *f*; (*food*) nourriture *f*

sustain′ing mem′ber [səs′tenɪŋ] s membre *m* bienfaiteur

suture [′sut/ər] s suture *f* ‖ *tr* suturer

SUV [′ɛs′ju′vi] s (letterword) (**Sport Utility Vehicle**) véhicule *m* suburbain utilitaire

swab [swɑb] s écouvillon *m*; (naut) faubert *m*; (surg) tampon *m* ‖ *v* (*pret & pp* **swabbed;** *ger* **swabbing**) *tr* écouvillonner

swaddle [′swɑdəl] *tr* emmailloter

swad′dling clothes′ *spl* maillot *m*

swagger [′swægər] s fanfaronnade *f* ‖ *intr* faire des fanfaronnades

swain [swen] s garçon *m*; jeune berger *m*; soupirant *m*

swallow [′swɑlo] s gorgée *f*; (orn) hirondelle *f* ‖ *tr* & *intr* avaler

swal′low-tailed coat′ s frac *m*

swamp [swɑmp] s marécage *m* ‖ *tr* submerger, inonder

swamp•y [′swɑmpi] *adj* (*comp* -ier; *super* -iest) marécageux

swan [swɑn] s cygne *m*

swan′ dive′ s saut *m* de l'ange

swank [swæŋk] *adj* (slang) élégant, chic

swan′ knight′ s chevalier *m* au cygne

swan's′-down′ s cygne *m*, duvet *m* de cygne

swan′ song′ s chant *m* du cygne

swap [swɑp] s (coll) troc *m* ‖ *v* (*pret & pp* **swapped;** *ger* **swapping**) *tr* & *intr* troquer

swarm [swɔrm] s essaim *m* ‖ *intr* essaimer; (fig) fourmiller

swarth•y [′swɔrði] *adj* (*comp* -ier; *super* -iest) basané, brun, noiraud

swashbuckler [′swɑʃ‚bʌklər] s rodomont *m*, bretteur *m*

swat [swɑt] s (coll) coup *m* violent ‖ *v* (*pret & pp* **swatted;** *ger* **swatting**) *tr* (coll) frapper; (*a fly*) (coll) écraser

sway [swe] s balancement *m*; (*domination*) empire *m* ‖ *tr* balancer ‖ *intr* se balancer; (*to hesitate*) balancer

swear [swɛr] *v* (*pret* **swore** [swor]; *pp* **sworn** [sworn]) *tr* jurer; **to swear in** faire prêter serment à; **to swear off** jurer de renoncer à ‖ *intr* jurer; **to swear at** injurier; **to swear by** (*e.g., a remedy*) préconiser; **to swear to** déclarer sous serment; jurer de + *inf*

swear′ words′ *spl* gros mots *mpl*

sweat [swɛt] s sueur *f* ‖ *v* (*pret & pp* **sweat** or **sweated**) *tr* (*e.g., blood*) suer; (slang) faire suer; **to sweat it out** (slang) en baver jusqu'à la fin ‖ *intr* suer

sweat′band′ s bandeau *m*

sweater [′swɛtər] s chandail *m*, sweater *m*

sweat′shirt′ s sweat-shirt *m*, sweat *m*

sweat′suit′ s survêtement *m*, jogging *m*, survêt *m*

sweat•y [′swɛti] *adj* (*comp* -ier; *super* -iest) suant

Swede [swid] s Suédois *m*

Sweden [′swidən] s Suède *f*; la Suède

Swedish [′swidɪʃ] *adj* & s suédois *m*

sweep [swip] s (*sweeping*) balayage *m*; (*range*) champ *m*, étendue *f*; (*movement of the arm*) grand geste *m*; (*curve*) courbe *f*; (*of wind*) souffle *m*; (*of well*) chadouf *m*; **at one sweep** d'un seul coup; **to make a clean sweep of** faire table rase de; (*to win all of*) rafler ‖ *v* (*pret & pp* **swept** [swɛpt]) *tr* balayer; (*the chimney*) ramoner; (*for mines*) draguer ‖ *intr* balayer; s'étendre

sweeper [′swipər] s balayeur *m*; (mach) balai *m* mécanique

sweeping [′swipɪŋ] *adj* (*movement*) vigoureux; (*statement*) catégorique ‖ s balayage *m*; **sweepings** balayures *fpl*

sweep′-sec′ond s trotteuse *f* centrale

sweep′stakes′ s or *spl* loterie *f*; (turf) sweepstake *m*

sweet [swit] *adj* doux; (*sugared*) sucré; (*perfume, music, etc.*) suave; (*sound*) mélodieux; (*milk*) frais; (*person*) charmant, gentil; (*dear*) cher; **to be sweet on** (coll) avoir un béguin pour; **to smell sweet** sentir bon ‖ **sweets** *spl* sucreries *fpl*

sweet′-and-sour′ *adj* aigre-doux

sweet′bread′ s ris *m* de veau

sweet′bri′er s églantier *m*

sweeten [′switən] *tr* sucrer; purifier; (fig) adoucir ‖ *intr* s'adoucir

sweetener [ˈswitənər] *s* édulcorant *m;* (*bribe*) pot-de-vin *m*

sweet′heart′ *s* (*male*) bon ami *m*, chéri *m;* (*female*) petite amie *f*, chérie *f;* **sweethearts** amoureux *mpl*

sweet′heart con′tract *s* contrat *m* syndical clandestin

sweetie [ˈswiti] *s* ami(e) *m(f)*, bien-aimé(é) *m(f);* (*as form of address*) mon chéri, ma chérie, mon chou, ma choute, mon ange

sweet′ mar′joram *s* marjolaine *f*

sweet′meats′ *spl* sucreries *fpl*

sweet′ pea′ *s* gesse *f* odorante, pois *m* de senteur

sweet′ pep′per *s* piment *m* doux, poivron *m*

sweet′ pota′to *s* patate *f* douce

sweet′-scent′ed *adj* parfumé

sweet′ talk′ *s* (coll) baratin *m*

sweet′-talk′ *tr* (coll) baratiner

sweet′-toothed′ *adj* friand de sucreries

sweet′ wil′liam *s* œillet *m* de poète

swell [swɛl] *adj* (coll) élégant; (slang) épatant ‖ *s* (*swelling*) gonflement *m;* (*of sea*) houle *f;* (mus) crescendo *m;* (pathol) enflure *f;* (*dandy*) (coll) rupin *m* ‖ *v* (*pret* **swelled;** *pp* **swelled** or **swollen** [ˈswolən]) *tr* gonfler, enfler ‖ *intr* se gonfler, s'enfler; (*said of sea*) se soulever; (fig) augmenter

swell′head′ *adj* suffisant, vaniteux

swelter [ˈswɛltər] *intr* étouffer de chaleur

swept′back wing′ *s* aile *f* en flèche

swerve [swʌrv] *s* écart *m*, déviation *f;* (aut) embardée *f* ‖ *tr* faire dévier ‖ *intr* écarter, dévier; (aut) faire une embardée

swift [swɪft] *adj* rapide ‖ *adv* vite ‖ *s* (orn) martinet *m*

swig [swɪg] *s* (coll) lampée *f*, trait *m* ‖ *v* (*pret & pp* **swigged;** *ger* **swigging**) *tr & intr* lamper

swill [swɪl] *s* eaux *fpl* grasses, ordures *fpl;* (*drink*) lampée *f* ‖ *tr & intr* lamper

swim [swɪm] *s* nage *f;* **to be in the swim** (coll) être dans le train ‖ *v* (*pret* **swam** [swæm]; *pp* **swum** [swʌm]; *ger* **swimming**) *tr* nager ‖ *intr* nager; (*said of head*) tourner; **to swim across** traverser à la nage; **to swim under water** nager entre deux eaux

swimmer [ˈswɪmər] *s* nageur *m*

swimming [ˈswɪmɪŋ] *s* natation *f*, nage *f*

swim′ming pool′ *s* piscine *f*

swim′ming suit′ *s* maillot *m* de bain

swim′ming trunks′ *spl* slip *m* de bain

swindle [ˈswɪndəl] *s* escroquerie *f* ‖ *tr* escroquer

swindler [ˈswɪndlər] *s* escroc *m*, filou *m*, charlatan

swine [swaɪn] *s* (*pl* **swine**) cochon *m*, pourceau *m*, porc *m*

swing [swɪŋ] *s* balancement *m*, oscillation *f;* (*device used for recreation*) escarpolette *f;* (*trip*) tournée *f;* (boxing, mus) swing *m;* **in full swing** en pleine marche ‖ *v* (*pret & pp* **swung** [swʌŋ]) *tr* balancer, faire osciller; (*the arms*) agiter; (*a sword*) brandir; (*e.g., an election*) mener à bien ‖ *intr* se balancer; (*said of pendulum*) osciller; (*said of door*) pivoter;

(*said of bell*) branler; **to swing open** s'ouvrir tout d'un coup

swing′ing door′ *s* porte *f* va-et-vient

swing′ing strike′ *s* (baseball) prise *f* sur élan

swing′ shift′ *s* roulement *m* entre deux postes de travail

swinish [ˈswaɪnɪʃ] *adj* cochon

swipe [swaɪp] *s* (*blow*) coup *m* à toute volée; (*punch*) (coll) coup *m* de poing; (*cutting remark*) remarque *f* cinglante ‖ *tr* frapper à toute volée; (*to steal*) (coll) chiper; (com) passer (*une carte de crédit*) à la rainure d'un mécanisme électronique

swirl [swʌrl] *s* remous *m*, tourbillon *m* ‖ *tr* faire tourbillonner ‖ *intr* tourbillonner

swish [swɪʃ] *s* (*e.g., of a whip*) sifflement *m;* (*of a dress*) froufrou *m;* (*e.g., of water*) susurrement *m* ‖ *tr* (*a whip*) faire siffler; (*its tail*) battre ‖ *intr* siffler; froufrouter; susurrer

Swiss [swɪs] *adj* suisse ‖ *s* Suisse *m;* **the Swiss** les Suisses *mpl*

Swiss′ chard′ [tʃɑrd] *s* bette *f*, poirée *f*

Swiss′ cheese′ *s* emmenthal *m*, gruyère *m*

Swiss′ Guard′ *s* suisse *m*

switch [swɪtʃ] *s* (*stick*) badine *f;* (*exchange*) échange *m;* (*hairpiece*) postiche *m;* (elec) interrupteur *m;* (rr) aiguille *f* ‖ *tr* cingler; (*places*) échanger; (rr) aiguiller; **to switch off** couper; (*a light*) éteindre; **to switch on** mettre en circuit; (*a light*) allumer ‖ *intr* changer de place

switch′back′ *s* chemin *m* en lacet

switch′blade knife′ *s* couteau *m* à cran d'arrêt

switch′board′ *s* tableau *m* de distribution; standard *m* téléphonique

switch′board op′erator *s* standardiste *mf*

switch′ing en′gine *s* locomotive *f* de manœuvre

switch′man *s* (*pl* **-men**) aiguilleur *m*

switch′ tow′er *s* poste *m* d'aiguillage

switch′yard′ *s* gare *f* de triage

Switzerland [ˈswɪtsərlənd] *s* Suisse *f;* la Suisse

swiv•el [ˈswɪvəl] *s* pivot *m;* (*link*) émerillon *m* ‖ *v* (*pret & pp* **-eled** or **-elled;** *ger* **-eling** or **-elling**) *tr* faire pivoter ‖ *intr* pivoter

swiv′el chair′ *s* fauteuil *m* tournant, chaise *f* pivotante

swiz′zle stick′ *s* agitateur *m*

swoon [swun] *s* évanouissement *m* ‖ *intr* s'évanouir

swoop [swup] *s* attaque *f* brusque; **at one fell swoop** d'un seul coup ‖ *intr* foncer, fondre; **to swoop down on** s'abattre sur

sword [sord] *s* épée *f;* **to cross swords with** croiser le fer avec; **to put to the sword** passer au fil de l'épée

sword′ belt′ *s* ceinturon *m*

sword′fish′ *s* espadon *m*

swords′man *s* (*pl* **-men**) épéiste *m*

sword′ swal′lower [ˈswɑlo•ər] *s* avaleur *m* de sabres

sword′ thrust′ *s* coup *m* de pointe, coup d'épée

sworn [sworn] *adj* (*enemy*) juré; **sworn in** assermenté

sycophant [ˈsɪkəfənt] *s* flagorneur *m*

syllable [ˈsɪləbəl] *s* syllabe *f*

sylla·bus [ˈsɪləbəs] *s* (*pl* **-bi** [ˌbaɪ] or **-buses**) programme *m*

syllogism [ˈsɪləˌdʒɪzəm] *s* syllogisme *m*

sylph [sɪlf] *s* sylphe *m*

sylvan [ˈsɪlvən] *adj* sylvestre

symbol [ˈsɪmbəl] *s* symbole *m*

symbolic(al) [ˈsɪmˈbɑlɪk(əl)] *adj* symbolique

symbolism [ˈsɪmbəˌlɪzm] *s* symbolisme *m*

symbolize [ˈsɪmbəˌlaɪz] *tr* symboliser

symmetric(al) [sɪˈmɛtrɪk(əl)] *adj* symétrique

symme·try [ˈsɪmɪtri] *s* (*pl* **-tries**) symétrie *f*

sympathetic [ˌsɪmpəˈθɛtɪk] *adj* (*kind*) compatissant; (*favoring*) bien disposé; (anat, physiol) sympathique

sympathize [ˈsɪmpəˌθaɪz] *intr*—**to sympathize with** compatir à; comprendre

sympa·thy [ˈsɪmpəθi] *s* (*pl* **-thies**) (*pity*) compassion *f*; (*fellow feeling*) solidarité *f*; sympathie *f*, e.g., **expressions of sympathy** témoignages de sympathie; **to be in sympathy with** être en sympathie avec; **to extend one's sympathy to** offrir ses condoléances à

sym'pathy strike' *s* grève *f* de solidarité

sympho·ny [ˈsɪmfəni] *s* (*pl* **-nies**) symphonie *f*

symposi·um [sɪmˈpozɪˈəm] *s* (*pl* **-a** [ə]) colloque *m*, symposium *m*

symptom [ˈsɪmptəm] *s* symptôme *m*

synagogue [ˈsɪnəˌgɔg] *s* synagogue *f*

sync *ou* **synch** [sɪŋk] *s* synchronisation *f*; **to be in sync with** être synchronisé avec

synchronize [ˈsɪŋkrəˌnaɪz] *tr* synchroniser

synchronous [ˈsɪŋkrənəs] *adj* synchrone

syncopated [ˈsɪŋkəˌpetəd] *adj* syncopé

syncopation [ˌsɪŋkəˈpeʃən] *s* syncope *f*

syncope [ˈsɪŋkəˌpi] *s* syncope *f*

syndicate [ˈsɪndɪkɪt] *s* (journ) syndicat *m* (de distribution) ‖ [ˈsɪndɪˌket] *tr* syndiquer ‖ *intr* se syndiquer

syndrome [ˈsɪndrom] *s* syndrome *m*

synonym [ˈsɪnənɪm] *s* synonyme *m*

synonymous [sɪˈnɑnɪməs] *adj* synonyme

synop·sis [sɪˈnɑpsɪs] *s* (*pl* **-ses** [siz]) abrégé *m*, résumé *m*; (mov) synopsis *m* & *f*

syntax [ˈsɪntæks] *s* syntaxe *f*

synthe·sis [ˈsɪnθɪsɪs] *s* (*pl* **-ses** [ˌsiz]) synthèse *f*

synthesize [ˈsɪnθɪˌsaɪz] *tr* synthétiser

synthetic(al) [sɪnˈθɛtɪk(əl)] *adj* synthétique

synthet'ic leath'er *s* cuir *m* synthétique

syphilis [ˈsɪfɪlɪs] *s* syphilis *f*

Syria [ˈsɪrɪ·ə] *s* Syrie *f*; la Syrie

Syrian [ˈsɪrɪˈən] *adj* syrien ‖ *s* (*language*) syrien *m*; (*person*) Syrien *m*

syringe [ˈsɪrɪndʒ] *s* seringue *f* ‖ *tr* seringuer

syrup [ˈsɪrəp], [ˈsʌrəp] *s* sirop *m*

system [ˈsɪstəm] *s* système *m*; (*of lines, wires, pipes, roads*) réseau *m*

systematic(al) [ˌsɪstəˈmætɪk(əl)] *adj* systématique

systematize [ˈsɪstəməˌtaɪz] *tr* systématiser

systole [ˈsɪstəli] *s* systole *f*

T

T, t [ti] *s* XXᵉ lettre de l'alphabet

tab [tæb] *s* patte *f*; (*label*) étiquette *f*; (*dinner check*) (coll) note *f*; **to keep tab on** (coll) garder à l'œil; **to pick up the tab** (coll) payer l'addition

tab·by [ˈtæbi] *s* (*pl* **-bies**) chat *m* moucheté; (*female cat*) chatte *f*; (*old maid*) vieille fille *f*; (*spiteful female*) vieille chipie *f*

tabernacle [ˈtæbərˌnækəl] *s* tabernacle *m*

table [ˈtebəl] *s* table *f*; (*tableland*) plateau *m*; (*list, chart*) tableau *m*, table; **to clear the table** ôter le couvert; **to set the table** mettre le couvert ‖ *tr* ajourner la discussion de

tab·leau [ˈtæblo] *s* (*pl* **-leaus** or **leaux** [loz]) tableau *m* vivant

ta'ble·cloth' *s* nappe *f*

table d'hôte [ˈtabəlˈdot] *s* repas *m* à prix fixe

ta'ble·land' *s* plateau *m*

ta'ble lin'en *s* nappage *m*, linge *m* de table

ta'ble man'ners *spl*—**to have good table manners** bien se tenir à table

tab'le·mate' *s* commensal *m*

ta'ble nap'kin *s* serviette *f* de table

ta'ble of con'tents *s* table *f* des matières

ta'ble salt' *s* sel *m* fin, sel de table

ta'ble soc'cer *m* (*played with figurines moved on mobile rods*) baby-foot *m*

ta'ble·spoon' *s* cuiller *f* à soupe

tablespoonful [ˈtebəlˌspun,fʊl] *s* cuillerée *f* à soupe or à bouche

tablet [ˈtæblɪt] *s* (*writing pad*) bloc-notes *m*, bloc *m*; (*lozenge*) pastille *f*, comprimé *m*; plaque *f* commémorative

ta'ble talk' *s* propos *mpl* de table

ta'ble ten'nis *s* ping-pong *m*, tennis *m* de table

ta'ble-ten'nis play'er *s* pongiste *mf*

ta'ble·top' *s* dessus *m* de table

ta'ble·ware' *s* ustensiles *mpl* de table

ta'ble wine' *s* vin *m* ordinaire

tabloid [ˈtæblɔɪd] *adj* (*press, article, etc.*) à sensation ‖ *s* journal *m* de petit format à l'affût du sensationnel, tableautier *m*

taboo [təˈbu] *adj* & *s* tabou *m* ‖ *tr* déclarer tabou

tabular [ˈtæbjələr] *adj* tabulaire

tabulate [ˈtæbjəˌlet] *tr* disposer en forme de table or en tableaux, dresser un tableau de, aligner en colonnes

tabulator [ˈtæbjə‚letər] *s* tabulateur *m*

tab′ulator set′ting *s* arrêt *m* de tabulateur

tacit [ˈtæsɪt] *adj* tacite

taciturn [ˈtæsɪtərn] *adj* taciturne

tack [tæk] *s* (*nail*) semence *f;* (*plan*) voie *f,* tactique *f;* (*of sail*) amure *f;* (naut) bordée *f;* (sewing) point *m* de bâti ‖ *tr* clouer; (sewing) bâtir ‖ *intr* louvoyer

tackle [ˈtækəl] *s* (*for lifting*) treuil *m;* (football) plaquage *m;* (naut) palan *m* ‖ *tr* empoigner, saisir; (*a problem, job, etc.*) chercher à résoudre, attaquer; (football) plaquer

tack•y [ˈtæki] *adj* (*comp* **-ier;** *super* **-iest**) collant; (coll) râpé, minable

tact [tækt] *s* tact *m*

tactful [ˈtæktfəl] *adj* plein de tact; **to be tactful** avoir du tact

tactical [ˈtæktɪkəl] *adj* tactique

tactician [tækˈtɪʃən] *s* tacticien *m*

tactics [ˈtæktɪks] *spl* tactique *f*

tactless [ˈtæktlɪs] *adj* sans tact

tadpole [ˈtæd‚pol] *s* têtard *m*

taffeta [ˈtæfɪtə] *s* taffetas *m*

taffy [ˈtæfi] *s* pâte *f* à berlingots; (coll) flagornerie *f*

tag [tæg] *s* (*label*) étiquette *f;* (*of shoelace*) ferret *m;* (*game*) chat *m* perché ‖ *v* (*pret & pp* **tagged;** *ger* **tagging**) *tr* étiqueter; (*in the game of tag*) attraper ‖ *intr* (coll) suivre de près; **to tag along behind s.o.** (coll) traîner derrière qn

tag′ day′ *s* jour *m* de collecte publique

tag′ end′ *s* queue *f;* (*remnant*) coupon *m*

Tagus [ˈtegəs] *s* Tage *m*

tail [tel] *s* queue *f;* (*of shirt*) pan *m;* **tails** (*of a coin*) pile *f;* (*formal dress*) (coll) frac *m,* queue-de-morue *f;* **to turn tail** tourner les talons ‖ *tr* (coll) suivre de tout près ‖ *intr*—**to tail after** marcher sur les talons de; **to tail off** s'éteindre, disparaître

tail′ assem′bly *s* (*pl* **-blies**) (aer) empennage *m*

tail′ end′ *s* queue *f,* fin *f*

tail′ gate′ *tr & intr* (aut) talonner

tail′ gat′ing *s* (aut) talonnage *m;* (sports) pique-nique *m* à l'occasion d'un match

tail′ light′ *s* feu *m* arrière

tailor [ˈtelər] *s* tailleur *m* ‖ *tr* (*a suit*) faire ‖ *intr* être tailleur

tailoring [ˈtelərɪŋ] *s* métier *m* de tailleur

tai′lor-made suit′ *s* (*men's*) costume *m* sur mesure, complet *m* sur mesure; (*women's*) costume tailleur, tailleur *m*

tai′lor's chalk′ *s* craie *f* de tailleur

tai′lor shop′ *s* boutique *f* de tailleur

tail′piece′ *s* queue *f;* (*of stringed instrument*) cordier *m*

tail′race′ *s* canal *m* du fuite

tail′spin′ *s* chute *f* en vrille

tail′wind′ *s* (aer) vent *m* arrière; (naut) vent en poupe

taint [tent] *s* tache *f* ‖ *tr* tacher; (*food*) gâter

Taiwan [taɪˈwɑn] *s* Taïwan *f*

take [tek] *s* prise *f;* (mov) prise *f* de vues; (slang) recette *f* ‖ *v* (*pret* **took** [tʊk]; *pp* **taken**) *tr* prendre; (*a walk; a trip*) faire; (*a course; advice*) suivre; (*an examination*) passer; (*a person on a trip*) emmener; (*the occasion*) profiter de; (*a photograph*) prendre; (*a newspaper*) être abonné à; (*a purchase*) garder; (*a certain amount of time*) falloir, e.g., **it takes an hour to walk there** il faut une heure pour y aller à pied; (*to lead*) conduire, mener; (*to tolerate, stand*) supporter; (*a seat*) prendre, occuper, e.g., **this seat is taken** cette place est prise *or* occupée; **do you take that to be important?** tenez-vous cela pour important?; **I take it that** je suppose que; **take it easy!** (coll) allez-y doucement!; **to be taken ill** tomber malade; **to take amiss** prendre mal; **to take away** enlever; emmener; (*to subtract*) soustraire, retrancher; **to take down** descendre; (*a building*) démolir; (*in writing*) noter; **to take in** (*a roomer*) recevoir; (*laundry*) prendre à faire à la maison; (*the harvest*) rentrer; (*a seam*) reprendre; (*to include*) embrasser; (*to deceive*) (coll) duper; **to take off** ôter, enlever; (*from the price*) rabattre; (*to imitate*) (coll) singer; **to take on** (*passengers*) prendre; (*a responsibility*) prendre sur soi; (*workers*) embaucher, prendre; **to take out** sortir; (*a bullet from a wound; a passage from a text; an element from a compound*) extraire; (*public sign*) à emporter; **to take over** (*to escort across*) transporter; (*to assume responsibility for*) reprendre, prendre à sa charge; **to take place** avoir lieu; **to take s.th. from s.o.** enlever, ôter, *or* prendre q.ch. à qn; **to take up** (*to carry up*) monter; (*to remove*) enlever; (*a dress*) raccourcir; (*an idea, method, etc.*) adopter; (*a profession*) embrasser, prendre; (*a question, a study, etc.*) aborder ‖ *intr* prendre; **to not take to** (*a person*) prendre en grippe; **to take after** ressembler à; (*to chase*) poursuivre; **to take off** s'en aller; (aer) décoller; **to take over** (pol) prendre le pouvoir; **to take over from s.o.** prendre la relève (*or* le relais) de qn; **to take to** (*flight; the woods*) prendre; (*a bad habit*) se livrer à; (*a person*) se prendre d'amitié avec; (*to like*) s'adonner à; **to take to** + *ger* se mettre à + *inf;* **to take up with s.o.** (coll) se lier avec qn

take′-home pay′ *s* salaire *m* net

take′-off′ *s* (aer) décollage *m;* (coll) caricature *f*

take′o′ver *s* (*of a corporation*) rachat *m*

take′over bid′ *s* offre *f* publique d'achat (O.P.A.)

tal′cum pow′der [ˈtælkəm] *s* poudre *f* de talc

tale [tel] *s* conte *m;* mensonge *m;* (*gossip*) racontar *m,* histoire *f*

tale′bear′er *s* rapporteur *m*

talent [ˈtælənt] *s* (*ability*) talent *m;* (*persons*) gens *mpl* de talent

talented [ˈtæləntɪd] *adj* doué, talentueux

tal′ent scout′ *s* dénicheur *m* de vedettes

tal′ent show′ *s* crochet *m* radiophonique, radio-crochet *m*

talk [tɔk] *s* paroles *fpl;* (*gossip*) racontars *mpl,* dires *mpl;* (*lecture*) conférence *f,* causerie *f;* **to cause talk** défrayer la chronique; **to have a talk with** s'entretenir avec ‖ *tr* parler; **to talk over** discuter; **to talk up** vanter ‖ *intr* parler; (*to chatter, gossip, etc.*) bavarder, jaser; **to talk back** répliquer; **to talk on** continuer à parler

talkative [′tɔkətɪv] *adj* bavard

talker [′tɔkər] *s* parleur *m;* **a great talker** (coll) un causeur, un hâbleur

talkie [′tɔki] *s* (coll) film *m* parlant

talk′ing doll′ [′tɔkɪŋ] *s* poupée *f* parlante

talk′ show′ *s* (rad, telv) causerie *f* (radiodiffusée *or* télévisée), tête-à-tête *m invar or* entretien *m* (radiodiffusé *or* télévisé)

tall [tɔl] *adj* haut, élevé; (*person*) grand; (coll) exagéré

tallow [′tælo] *s* suif *m*

tall′ tale′ *s* récit *m* mensonger, conte *m* (pej)

tal·ly [′tæli] *s* (*pl* **-lies**) compte *m,* pointage *m* ‖ *v* (*pret & pp* **-lied**) *tr* pointer, contrôler ‖ *intr* s'accorder

tallyho [′tæli,ho] *interj* taïaut!

tal′ly sheet′ *s* feuille *f* de pointage, bordereau *m*

talon [′tælən] *s* serre *f*

tamarack [′tæmə,ræk] *s* mélèze *m* d'Amérique

tambourine [,tæmbə′rin] *s* tambour *m* de basque

tame [tem] *adj* apprivoisé; (*e.g., lion*) dompté; (*e.g., style*) fade, terne ‖ *tr* apprivoiser; (*e.g., a lion*) dompter

tamp [tæmp] *tr* bourrer; (*e.g., a hole in the ground*) damer

tamper [′tæmpər] *intr*—**to tamper with** se mêler de; (*a lock*) fausser; (*a document*) falsifier; (*a witness*) suborner

tampon [′tæmpɑn] *s* (surg) tampon *m* ‖ *tr* (surg) tamponner

tan [tæn] *adj* jaune; (*e.g., skin*) bronzé, hâlé ‖ *v* (*pret & pp* **tanned;** *ger* **tanning**) *tr* tanner; (*e.g., the skin*) bronzer, hâler ‖ *intr* se hâler

tandem [′tændəm] *adj & adv* en tandem, en flèche ‖ *s* tandem *m*

tang [tæŋ] *s* goût *m* vif, saveur *f;* (*ringing sound*) tintement *m*

tangent [′tændʒənt] *adj* tangent ‖ *s* tangente *f;* **to fly off at** *or* **on a tangent** changer brusquement de sujet

tangerine [,tændʒə′rin] *s* mandarine *f*

tangible [′tændʒɪbəl] *adj* tangible

tan′gible as′sets *spl* actifs *mpl* corporels

Tangier [tæn′dʒɪr] *s* Tanger *m*

tangle [′tæŋgəl] *s* enchevêtrement *m* ‖ *tr* enchevêtrer ‖ *intr* s'enchevêtrer

tank [tæŋk] *s* réservoir *m;* (mil) char *m*

tank′ car′ *s* (rr) wagon-citerne *m*

tanker [′tæŋkər] *s* (*ship*) bateau-citerne *m,* pétrolier *m;* (*truck*) camion-citerne *m;* (*plane*) ravitailleur *m*

tank′ farm′ing *s* culture *f* hydroponique

tank′ top′ *ou* **tank** *s* (*shirt ou blouse*) débardeur *m,* maillot *m* tank (*d'épaules nues ou avec bretelles*)

tank′ truck′ *s* camion-citerne *m*

tanner [′tænər] *s* tanneur *m*

tanner·y [′tænəri] *s* (*pl* **-ies**) tannerie *f*

tantalize [′tæntə,laɪz] *tr* tenter, allécher

tantamount [′tæntə,maʊnt] *adj* équivalent

tantrum [′tæntrəm] *s* accès *m* de colère; **in a tantrum** en rogne

tap [tæp] *s* (*light blow*) petit coup *m;* (*faucet*) robinet *m;* (elec) prise *f;* (mach) taraud *m;* **on tap** au tonneau, en perce; (*available*) (coll) disponible; **taps** (mil) l'extinction *f* des feux ‖ *v* (*pret & pp* **tapped;** *ger* **tapping**) *tr* taper; (*a cask*) mettre en perce; (*a tree*) entailler; (*a telephone*) passer à la table d'écoute; (*a nut*) tarauder; (*resources, talent, etc.*) drainer; (elec) brancher sur ‖ *intr* taper

tap′ dance′ *s* danse *f* à claquettes

tap′-dance′ *intr* danser les claquettes, faire les claquettes

tap′ dan′cer *s* danseur *m* à claquettes

tape [tep] *s* ruban *m* ‖ *tr* (*an electric wire*) guiper; (*land*) mesurer au cordeau; (*to tape-record*) enregistrer sur ruban

tape′ deck′ *s* platine *f* de magnétophone

tape′ meas′ure *s* mètre-ruban *m,* centimètre *m*

taper [′tepər] *s* (*for lighting candles*) allumette-bougie *f;* (eccl) cierge *m* ‖ *tr* effiler ‖ *intr* s'effiler

tape′-record′ *tr* enregistrer sur ruban magnétique *or* au magnétophone

tape′ record′er *s* magnétophone *m*

tapes·try [′tæpɪstri] *s* (*pl* **-tries**) tapisserie *f* ‖ *v* (*pret & pp* **-tried**) *tr* tapisser

tape′worm′ *s* ver *m* solitaire

tappet [′tæpɪt] *s* (mach) taquet *m*

tap′room′ *s* débit *m* de boissons, buvette *f*

tap′ wa′ter *s* eau *f* du robinet

tap′ wrench′ *s* taraudeuse *f*

tar [tɑr] *s* goudron *m;* (coll) marin *m* ‖ *v* (*pret & pp* **tarred;** *ger* **tarring**) *tr* goudronner; **to tar and feather** enduire de goudron et de plumes

tar·dy [′tɑrdi] *adj* (*comp* **-dier;** *super* **-diest**) lent; retardataire, en retard

tare [tɛr] *s* (*weight*) tare *f;* (Bib) ivraie *f* ‖ *tr* tarer

target [′tɑrgɪt] *s* cible *f,* point *m* de mire; (*goal*) but *m;* (mil) objectif *m;* (*butt*) (fig) cible

tar′get ar′ea *s* zone *f* de tir

tar′get lan′guage *s* langue *f* cible, langue d'arrivée

tar′get prac′tice *s* tir *m* à la cible

tariff [′tærɪf] *s* (*duties*) droits *mpl* de douane; (*rates in general*) tarif *m*

tarnish [′tɑrnɪʃ] *s* ternissure *f* ‖ *tr* ternir ‖ *intr* se ternir

tar′ pa′per *s* papier *m* goudronné

tarpaulin [tɑr′pɔlɪn] *s* bâche *f,* prélart *m*

tarragon [′tærəgən] *s* estragon *m*

tar·ry [′tɑri] *adj* (*comp* **-rier;** *super* **-riest**) gou-

dronneux ‖ [ˈtæri] v (pret & pp **-ried**) intr
tarder; (to stay) rester, demeurer
tart [tɑrt] adj (taste) aigrelet; (reply) mordant
‖ s tarte f; (slang) grue f, poule f
tartar [ˈtɑrtər] adj (sauce) tartare; **Tartar** tartare ‖ s (on teeth) tartre m; **Tartar** Tartare mf
task [tæsk] s tâche f; **to bring** or **take to task**
prendre à partie
task′ force′ s (mil) groupement m stratégique
mixte
task′ mas′ter s chef m de corvée; (fig) tyran m
tassel [ˈtæsəl] s gland m; (on corn) barbe f; (on
nightcap) mèche f; (bot) aigrette f
taste [test] s goût m, saveur f; (sense of what is
fitting) goût, bon goût ‖ tr goûter; (to sample)
goûter à; (to try out) goûter de ‖ intr goûter;
to taste like avoir le goût de; **to taste of** avoir
un goût de
taste′ bud′ s papille f gustative
tasteless [ˈtestlɪs] adj sans saveur, fade; (in bad
taste) de mauvais goût
tast•y [ˈtesti] adj (comp **-ier;** super **-iest**) (coll)
savoureux; (coll) de bon goût
tatter [ˈtætər] s lambeau m ‖ tr mettre en lambeaux
tatterdemalion [ˌtætərdɪˈmeljən] s loqueteux m
tattered adj en lambeaux, en loques
tattle [ˈtætəl] s bavardage m; (gossip) cancan
m ‖ intr bavarder; cancaner
tat′ tle•tale′ adj révélateur ‖ s rapporteur m, cancanier m
tattoo [tæˈtu] s tatouage m; (mil) retraite f ‖ tr
tatouer
taunt [tɔnt] s sarcasme m ‖ tr bafouer
Taurus [ˈtɔrəs] s (astr, astrol) le Taureau
taut [tɔt] adj tendu
tavern [ˈtævərn] s café m, bar m, bistrot m; (inn)
taverne f
taw•dry [ˈtɔdri] adj (comp **-drier;** super
-driest) criard, voyant
taw•ny [ˈtɔni] adj (comp **-nier;** super **-niest**)
fauve; (skin) basané
tax [tæks] s impôt m; (on goods, services) taxe
f; **to reduce the tax on** dégrever ‖ tr imposer;
(e.g., one's patience) mettre à l'épreuve; **to
tax s.o. with** (e.g., laziness) taxer qn de
taxable [ˈtæksəbəl] adj imposable
tax′able in′come s revenu m imposable
taxation [tækˈseʃən] s imposition f; charges fpl
fiscales, impôts mpl
tax′ base′ s base f fiscale, assiette f fiscale
tax′ ba′sis m assiette f fiscale, base f fiscale
tax′ brack′et s niveau m d'imposition, tranche
f
tax′ collec′tor s percepteur m
tax′ cut′ s dégrèvement m d'impôt
tax′ deduc′tion s dégrèvement m
tax′ eva′sion s fraude f fiscale
tax′-exempt′ adj net d'impôt, exempt d'impôts
tax′-exemp′tion s exemption f d'impôts
tax′ ha′ven s refuge m fiscal, pays m étranger
qui offre des avantages fiscaux
tax•i [ˈtæksi] s (pl **-is**) taxi m ‖ v (pret & pp

-ied; ger **-iing** or **-ying**) tr (aer) rouler au sol
‖ intr aller en taxi; (aer) rouler au sol ‖ interj
hep taxi!
tax′i•cab′ s taxi m
tax′i danc′er s taxi-girl f
taxidermy [ˈtæksɪˌdʌrmi] s taxidermie f
tax′i driv′er s chauffeur m de taxi
tax′i•plane′ s avion-taxi m
tax′i stand′ s station f de taxis
tax′i•way′ s (aer) chemin m de roulement
tax′ loss′ s perte f de réclamation
tax′ pay′er s contribuable mf
tax′ rate′ s taux m de l'impôt
tax′ relief′ s dégrèvement m
tax′ return′ s déclaration f de revenus, déclaration d'impôts; (blank) feuille f de déclaration
de revenus
tax′ shel′ter s abri m fiscal
tea [ti] s thé m; (medicinal infusion) tisane f
tea′ bag′ s sachet m de thé
tea′ ball′ s boule f à thé
tea′cart′ s table f roulante
teach [titʃ] v (pret & pp **-taught** [tɔt]) tr enseigner; **to teach s.o. s.th.** enseigner q.ch à
qn; **to teach s.o. to** + inf enseigner à qn à
+ inf ‖ intr enseigner
teacher [ˈtitʃər] s instituteur m, enseignant m;
(such as adversity) (fig) maître m
teach′er's pet′ s élève m gâté
teaching [ˈtitʃɪŋ] s enseignement m
teach′ing aids′ spl matériel m auxiliaire d'enseignement
teach′ing staff′ s corps m enseignant
tea′cup′ s tasse f à thé
tea′ dance′ s thé m dansant
teak [tik] s teck m
tea′ket′tle s bouilloire f
team [tim] s (of horses, oxen, etc.) attelage m;
(sports) équipe f ‖ tr atteler ‖ intr—**to team
up with** faire équipe avec
team′mate′ s équipier m
teamster [ˈtimstər] s (of horses) charretier m;
(of a truck) camionneur m
team′work′ s travail m en équipe; (spirit) esprit
m d'équipe
tea′pot′ s théière f
tear [tɪr] s larme f; **to burst into tears** fondre
en larmes ‖ [tɛr] s déchirure f ‖ [tɛr] v (pret
tore [tor]; pp **torn** [torn] tr déchirer; **to tear
away, down, off** or **out** arracher; **to tear up**
(e.g., a letter) déchirer ‖ intr se déchirer; **to
tear along** filer précipitamment, aller à fond
de train
tear′ bomb′ [tɪr] s bombe f lacrymogène
tear′ duct′ [tɪr] s conduit m lacrymal
tearful [ˈtɪrfəl] adj larmoyant, éploré
tear′ gas′ [tɪr] s gaz m lacrymogène
tear•jerker [ˈtɪrˌdʒʌrkər] s (slang) comédie f
larmoyante
tea′room′ s salon m de thé
tease [tiz] mf taquin m, taquine f ‖ tr taquiner
tea′spoon′ s cuiller f à café
teaspoonful [ˈtiˌspun,fʊl] s cuillerée f à café

teat 688 temptation

teat [tit] *s* tétine *f*
tea′time′ *s* l'heure *f* du thé
technical [ˈtɛknɪkəl] *adj* technique
technicali•ty [ˌtɛknɪˈkælɪti] *s* (*pl* **-ties**) technicité *f*; (*fine point*) subtilité *f*
technician [tɛkˈnɪ/ən] *s* technicien *m*
technics [ˈtɛknɪks] *ssg* technique *f*
technique [tɛkˈnik] *s* technique *f*
technology [tɛkˈnɑlədʒi] *s* technologie *f*; **new technologies** technologies avancées; **up-to-date technology** technologie à pointe
ted′dy bear′ [ˈtɛdi] *s* ours *m* en peluche
tedious [ˈtidɪ•əs] *adj* ennuyeux, fatigant
teem [tim] *intr* fourmiller; **to teem with** abander en, fourmiller de
teeming [ˈtimɪŋ] *adj* fourmillant; (*rain*) torrentiel
teen•ager [ˈtin,edʒər] *s* adolescent *m* de 13 à 19 ans
teens [tinz] *spl* numéros anglais qui se terminent en **-teen** (de 13 à 19); adolescence *f* de 13 à 19 ans; **to be in one's teens** être adolescent
tee•ny [ˈtini] *adj* (*comp* **-nier**; *super* **-niest**) (*coll*) minuscule, tout petit
teeter [ˈtitər] *s* branlement *m*; balançoire *f* ‖ *intr* se balancer, chanceler
teethe [tið] *intr* faire ses dents
teething [ˈtiðɪŋ] *s* dentition *f*
teeth′ing ring′ *s* sucette *f*
teetotaler [tiˈtotələr] *s* antialcoolique *mf* (*qui s'abstient totalement de boissons alcooliques*)
tele•cast [ˈtɛlɪ,kæst] *s* émission *f* télévisée ‖ *v* (*pret & pp* **-cast** or **-casted**) *tr & intr* téléviser
telecommunications [ˈtɛləkə,mjunəˈke/ənz] *s* télécommunications *fpl*
telegram [ˈtɛlɪ,græm] *s* télégramme *m*
telegraph [ˈtɛlɪ,græf] *s* télégraphe *m* ‖ *tr & intr* télégraphier
telegrapher [tɪˈlɛgrəfər] *s* télégraphiste *mf*
tel′egraph pole′ *s* poteau *m* télégraphique
telemarketing [ˌtɛləˈmɑrkətɪŋ] *s* télémarketing *m*, télémercatique *f* (*utilisation des moyens de télécommunication au service du marketing*)
telemeter [tɪˈlɛmɪtər] *s* télémètre *m*
telemetry [trˈlɛmɪtri] *s* télémétrie *f*
telepathy [tiˈlɛpəθi] *s* télépathie *f*
telephone [ˈtɛlɪˈfon] *s* téléphone *m* ‖ *tr & intr* téléphoner
tel′ephone booth′ *s* cabine *f* téléphonique
tel′ephone call′ *s* appel *m* téléphonique, coup *m* de fil;
tel′ephone direc′tory *s* annuaire *m* du téléphone
tel′ephone exchange′ *s* central *m* téléphonique
tel′ephone num′ber *s* numéro *m* d'appel
tel′ephone op′erator *s* standardiste *mf*, téléphoniste *mf*
tel′ephone receiv′er *s* récepteur *m* de téléphone
tel′ephone ta′ble *s* table *f* du téléphone
tel′ephoto lens′ [ˈtɛlɪ,foto] *s* téléobjectif *m*
teleprinter [ˈtɛlɪ,prɪntər] *s* téléimprimeur *m*

teleprocessing [ˈtɛlə,prɑsɛsɪŋ] *s* télétraitement *m*
Teleprompter [ˈtɛlə,prɑmptər] *s* (trademark) télésouffleur *m*
telescope [ˈtɛlɪ,skop] *s* télescope *m* ‖ *tr* télescoper ‖ *intr* se télescoper
telescopic [ˌtɛlɪ,skɑpɪk] *adj* télescopique
teletext [ˈtɛlə,tɛkst] *s* télétexte *m*, vidéographie diffusée
Teletype [ˈtɛlɪ,taɪp] *s* (trademark) télétype *m*
tel′etype′ writ′er *s* téléscripteur *m*
televangelism [ˈtɛlɪˈvændʒəlɪzəm] *s* télévangélisme *m*
televangelist [ˈtɛlɪˈvændʒəlɪst] *s* télévangéliste *m*
teleview [ˈtɛlɪ,vju] *tr & intr* voir à la télévision
televiewer [ˈtɛlɪ,vju•ər] *s* téléspectateur *m*
televise [ˈtɛlɪ,vaɪz] *tr* téléviser
television [ˈtɛlɪ,vɪʒən] *adj* télévisuel ‖ *s* télévision *f*
tel′evision aud′ience *s* téléspectateurs *mpl*
tel′evision screen′ *s* écran *m* de télévision, petit écran
tel′evision set′ *s* téléviseur *m*
tel′evision view′er *s* téléspectateur *m*, téléspectatrice *f*
telex [ˈtɛlɛks] *s* télex *m* ‖ *tr* envoyer par télex
tell [tɛl] *v* (*prep, & pp* **told** [told]) *tr* dire; (*a story*) raconter; (*to count*) compter; (*to recognize as distinct*) distinguer; **tell me another!** (coll) à d'autres!; **to tell off** compter; (coll) dire son fait à; **to tell s.o. to** + *inf* dire à qn de + *inf* ‖ *intr* produire un effet; **do tell!** (coll) vraiment!; **to tell on** influer sur; (coll) dénoncer; **who can tell?** qui sait?
teller [ˈtɛlər] *s* narrateur *m*; (*of a bank*) caissier *m*; (*of votes*) scrutateur *m*
temper [ˈtɛmpər] *s* humeur *f*, caractère *m*; (*of steel, glass, etc.*) trempe *f*; **to keep one's temper** retenir sa colère; **to lose one's temper** se mettre en colère ‖ *tr* tremper ‖ *intr* se tremper
temperament [ˈtɛmpərəmənt] *s* tempérament *m*
temperamental [ˌtɛmpərəˈmɛntəl] *adj* constitutionnel; capricieux, instable
temperance [ˈtɛmpərəns] *s* tempérance *f*
temperate [ˈtɛmpərɪt] *adj* tempéré; (*in food or drink*) tempérant
temperature [ˈtɛmpərət/ər] *s* température *f*
tempest [ˈtɛmpɪst] *s* tempête *f*; **tempest in a teapot** tempête dans un verre d'eau
tempestuous [tɛmˈpɛst/ʊ•əs] *adj* tempétueux
template [ˈtɛmplet] *s* patron *m*, gabarit *m*, calibre *m*
temple [ˈtɛmpəl] *s* temple *m*; (*side of forehead*) tempe *f*; (*of spectacles*) branche *f*
tem•po [ˈtɛmpo] *s* (*pl* **-pos** or **-pi** [pi]) tempo *m*
temporal [ˈtɛmpərəl] *adj* temporel; (anat) temporal
temporary [ˈtɛmpə,rɛri] *adj* temporaire
temporize [ˈtɛmpə,raɪz] *intr* temporiser
tempt [tɛmpt] *tr* tenter
temptation [tɛmpˈte/ən] *s* tentation *f*

tempter [ˈtɛmptər] *s* tentateur *m*

tempting [ˈtɛmptɪŋ] *adj* tentant

ten [tɛn] *adj & pron* dix; **about ten** une dizaine de ‖ *s* dix *m;* **ten o'clock** dix heures

tenable [ˈtɛnəbəl] *adj* soutenable

tenacious [tɪˈneʃəs] *adj* tenace

tenacity [tɪˈnæsɪti] *s* ténacité *f*

tenant [ˈtɛnənt] *s* locataire *mf*

ten'ant farm'er *s* métayer *m*

Ten' Command'ments, the [ˌkəˈmændmənts] *spl* les dix commandements *mpl*

tend [tɛnd] *tr* soigner; (*sheep*) garder; (*a machine*) surveiller ‖ *intr*—**to tend to** (*to be disposed to*) tendre à; (*to attend to*) vaquer à; **to tend towards** tendre vers *or* à

tenden•cy [ˈtɛndənsi] *s* (*pl* **-cies**) tendance *f*

tender [ˈtɛndər] *adj* tendre ‖ *s* offre *f;* (aer, naut) ravitailleur *m;* (rr) tender *m* ‖ *tr* offrir

ten'der-heart'ed *adj* au cœur tendre

ten'der-loin *s* filet *m*

tenderness [ˈtɛndərnɪs] *s* tendresse *f;* (*of, e.g., the skin*) sensibilité *f;* (*of, e.g., meat*) tendreté *f*

tendon [ˈtɛndən] *s* tendon *m*

tendril [ˈtɛndrɪl] *s* vrille *f*

tenement [ˈtɛnɪmənt] *s* maison *f* d'habitation; (*slum tenement house*) taudis *m*

ten'ement house' *s* maison *f* de rapport; (*in the slums*) taudis *m*

tenet [ˈtɛnɪt] *s* doctrine *f,* principe *m*

tennis [ˈtɛnɪs] *s* tennis *m*

ten'nis ball' *s* balle *f* de tennis

ten'nis court' *s* court *m* de tennis

tenor [ˈtɛnər] *s* teneur *f,* cours *m;* (mus) ténor *m*

ten'or clef' *s* clef *f* d'ut

tense [tɛns] *adj* tendu ‖ *s* (gram) temps *m*

tension [ˈtɛnʃən] *s* tension *f*

tent [tɛnt] *s* tente *f*

tentacle [ˈtɛntəkəl] *s* tentacule *m*

tentative [ˈtɛntətɪv] *adj* provisoire; (*hesitant*) timide

tenth [tɛnθ] *adj & pron* dixième (*masc, fem*); **the Tenth** dix, e.g., **John the Tenth** Jean dix ‖ *s* dixième *m;* **the tenth** (*in dates*) le dix

tent' pole' *s* montant *m* de tente

tenuous [ˈtɛnju•əs] *adj* ténu

tenure [ˈtɛnjər] *s* (*possession*) tenure *f;* (*of an office*) occupation *f;* (*protection from dismissal*) inamovibilité *f*

tepid [ˈtɛpɪd] *adj* tiède

term [tʌrm] *s* terme *m;* (*of imprisonment*) temps *m;* (*of office*) mandat *m;* (*of the school year*) semestre *m;* **terms** conditions *fpl;* **to be on good terms with** avoir de bons rapports avec ‖ *tr* appeler, qualifier

termagant [ˈtʌrməgənt] *s* mégère *f*

terminal [ˈtʌrmɪnəl] *adj* terminal ‖ *s* (comp) terminal *m;* (elec) borne *f;* (rr) terminus *m*

terminate [ˈtʌrmɪˌnet] *tr* terminer ‖ *intr* se terminer

termination [ˌtʌrmɪˈneʃən] *s* conclusion *f;* (*ex-*

tremity) bout *m;* (*of word*) désinence *f;* (*of a treaty*) extinction *f*

terminus [ˈtʌrmɪnəs] *s* bout *m,* extrémité *f;* (*boundary*) borne *f;* (rr) terminus *m*

termite [ˈtʌrmaɪt] *s* termite *m*

term' pa'per *s* dissertation *f*

terrace [ˈtɛrəs] *s* terrasse *f* ‖ *tr* disposer en terrasse

terra firma [ˈtɛrəˈfʌrmə] *s* terre *f* ferme

terrain [tɛˈren] *s* terrain *m*

terrestrial [təˈrɛstri•əl] *adj* terrestre

terrible [ˈtɛrɪbəl] *adj* terrible; (*extremely bad*) atroce

terrific [təˈrɪfɪk] *adj* terrible, terrifiant; (coll) formidable, dynamite

terri•fy [ˈtɛrɪˌfaɪ] *v* (*pret & pp* **-fied**) *tr* terrifier

territo•ry [ˈtɛrɪˌtori] *s* (*pl* **-ries**) territoire *m*

terror [ˈtɛrər] *s* terreur *f*

terrorize [ˈtɛrəˌraɪz] *tr* terroriser

ter'ry cloth' [ˈtɛri] *s* tissu-éponge *m*

terse [tʌrs] *adj* concis, succinct

tertiary [ˈtʌrʃəri] *adj* tertiaire

test [tɛst] *s* (*physical, mental, moral*) épreuve *f;* (*exam*) examen *m;* (*trial*) essai *m;* (*e.g., of intelligence*) test *m* ‖ *tr* éprouver, mettre à l'épreuve; examiner, tester

testament [ˈtɛstəmənt] *s* testament *m*

test' ban' *s* interdiction *f* des essais nucléaires

test' flight' *s* vol *m* d'essai

testicle [ˈtɛstɪkəl] *s* testicule *m*

testi•fy [ˈtɛstɪˌfaɪ] *v* (*pret & pp* **-fied**) *tr* déclarer ‖ *intr* déposer; **to testify to** témoigner de

testimonial [ˌtɛstɪˈmoni•əl] *s* attestation *m*

testimo•ny [ˈtɛstɪˌmoni] *s* (*pl* **-nies**) témoignage *m*

test'ing ground' *s* terrain *m* d'essai

test' pat'tern *s* (telv) mire *f*

test' pi'lot *s* pilote *m* d'essai

testosterone [tɛˈstɑstəˌron] *s* testostérone *f*

test' tube' *s* éprouvette *f*

test'-tube ba'by *s* bébé *m* éprouvette

test•ty [ˈtɛsti] *adj* (*comp* **-tier;** *super* **-tiest**) susceptible

tetanus [ˈtɛtənəs] *s* tétanos *m*

tether [ˈtɛðər] *s* attache *f;* **at the end of one's tether** à bout de ressources ‖ *tr* mettre à l'attache

tetter [ˈtɛtər] *s* (pathol) dartre *f*

text [tɛkst] *s* texte *m*

text'book' *s* manuel *m* scolaire, livre *m* de classe

text' flow' *s* (comp) flux *m* de textes

textile [ˈtɛkstaɪl] *adj & s* textile *m*

textual [ˈtɛkstʃu•əl] *adj* textuel

texture [ˈtɛkstʃər] *s* texture *f;* (*woven fabric*) tissu *m*

Thai [ˈtɑ•i] [taɪ] *adj* thaï, thaïlandais ‖ *s* (*language*) thaï *m;* (*person*) Thaïlandais *m;* **the Thai** les Thaïlandais

Thailand [ˈtaɪlənd] *s* Thaïlande *f;* la Thaïlande

Thames [tɛmz] *s* Tamise *f*

than [ðæn] *conj* que; (*before a numeral*) de, e.g., **more than three** plus de trois

thank [θæŋk] *adj* (*e.g.*, *offering*) de reconnaissance ‖ **thanks** *spl* remerciements *mpl;* **thanks to** grâce à ‖ **thanks** *interj* merci!; **no thanks!** merci! ‖ **thank** *tr* remercier; **thank you** je vous remercie; **thank you for** merci de *or* pour; **thank you for** + *ger* merci de + *inf;* **to thank s.o. for** remercier qn de *or* pour; **to thank s.o. for** + *ger* remercier qn de + *inf*

thankful [ˈθæŋkfəl] *adj* reconnaissant

thankless [ˈθæŋklɪs] *adj* ingrat

Thanksgiv′ing Day′ *s* le Jour d'action de grâces

that [ðæt] *adj dem* (*pl* **those**) ce §82; **that one** celui-là §84 ‖ *pron dem* (*pl* **those**) celui §83; celui-là §84 ‖ *pron rel* qui; que ‖ *pron neut* cela, ça; **that is** c'est-à-dire; **that's all** voilà tout; **that will do** cela suffit ‖ *adv* tellement, si, aussi; **that far** si loin, aussi loin; **that much, that many** tant ‖ *conj* que; (*in order that*) pour que, afin que; **in that** en ce que

thatch [θætʃ] *s* chaume *m* ‖ *tr* couvrir de chaume

thatched′ cot′tage *s* chaumière *f*

thaw [θɔ] *s* dégel *m* ‖ *tr & intr* dégeler

the [ðə], [ðɪ], [ði] *art def* le §77 ‖ *adv* d'autant plus, *e.g.*, **she will be the happier for it** elle en sera d'autant plus heureuse; **the more . . . the more** plus . . . plus

theater [ˈθiˑətər] *s* théâtre *m*

the′ater club′ *s* association *f* des spectateurs

the′ater-go′er *s* habitué *m* du théâtre

the′ater page′ *s* chronique *f* théâtrale

theatrical [θiˈætrɪkəl] *adj* théâtral

thee [ði] *pron pers* (archaic, poetic, Bib) toi §85; te §87

theft [θɛft] *s* vol *m*

their [ðɛr] *adj poss* leur §88

theirs [ðɛrz] *pron poss* le leur §89

them [ðɛm] *pron pers* eux §85; les §87; leur §87; **of them** en §87; **to them** leur §87; y §87

theme [θim] *s* thème *m;* (*essay*) composition *f;* (mus) thème

theme′ song′ *s* leitmotiv *m;* (rad) indicatif *m*

them-selves′ *pron pers* soi §85; eux-mêmes §86; se §87; eux §85

then [ðɛn] *adv* alors; (*next*) ensuite, puis; (*therefore*) donc; **by then** d'ici là; **from then on, since then** depuis lors, dès lors; **then and there** séance tenante; **till then** jusque-là; **what then?** et après? ‖ *adj* d'alors

thence [ðɛns] *adv* de là; (*from that fact*) pour cette raison

thence′forth′ *adv* dès lors

theocra-cy [θiˈɑkrəsɪ] *s* (*pl* **-cies**) théocratie *f*

theolo-gy [θiˈɑlədʒɪ] *s* (*pl* **-gies**) théologie *f*

theorem [ˈθiˑərəm] *s* théorème *m*

theoretical [ˌθiˑəˈrɛtɪkəl] *adj* théorique

theorize [ˈθiˑəˌraɪz] *intr* faire de la théorie

theo-ry [ˈθiˑərɪ] *s* (*pl* **-ries**) théorie *f*

therapeutic [ˌθɛrəˈpjutɪk] *adj* thérapeutique ‖ **therapeutics** *spl* thérapeutique *f*

thera-py [ˈθɛrəpɪ] *s* (*pl* **-pies**) thérapie *f*

there [ðɛr] *adv* là; y §87; **down there, over there** là-bas; **from there** de là; en §87; **in there** là-dedans; **on there** là-dessus; **there is** *or* **there are** il y a; (*pointing out*) voilà; **under there** là-dessous; **up there** là-haut

there′abouts′ *adv* aux environs, près de là; (*approximately*) à peu près

there′af′ter *adv* par la suite

there′by′ *adv* par là; de cette manière

there'd *contr* **there would**

therefore [ˈðɛrˌfor] *adv* par conséquent, donc

there′in′ *adv* dedans, là-dedans

there'll *contr* **there will**

there′of′ *adv* de cela; en §87

there's *contr* **there is**

there′upon′ *adv* là-dessus §85A; sur ce

there′with′ *adv* avec cela

thermal [ˈθʌrməl] *adj* (*waters*) thermal; (*capacity*) thermique

ther′mal cone′ *s* bouclier *m* thermique

thermocouple [ˈθʌrmoˌkʌpəl] *s* thermocouple *m*

thermodynamic [ˌθʌrmodaɪˈnæmɪk] *adj* thermodynamique ‖ **thermodynamics** *spl* thermodynamique *f*

thermometer [θərˈmɑmɪtər] *s* thermomètre *m*

thermonuclear [ˌθʌrmoˈn(j)uklɪˑər] *adj* thermonucléaire

Thermopylae [θərˈmɑpɪˌli] *s* les Thermopyles *fpl*

ther′mos bot′tle [ˈθʌrməs] *s* thermos *m & f,* bouteille *f* thermos

thermostat [ˈθʌrməˌstæt] *s* thermostat *m*

thesau-rus [θɪˈsɔrəs] *s* (*pl* **-ruses** [rəsəs] *or* **-ri** [raɪ] trésor *m;* (*dictionary*) dictionaire *m* analogique; (*treasury*) trésor *m;* (comp) thesaurus *m*

these [ðiz] *adj dem pl* **ces** §82 ‖ *pron dem pl* ceux §83; ceux-ci §84

the-sis [ˈθisɪs] *s* (*pl* **-ses** [siz]) thèse *f*

they [θe] *pron pers* ils §87; eux §85; on §87, *e.g.*, **they say** on dit; ce §82B

they'd *contr* **they would; they had**

they'd've [ˈðedəv] *contr* **they would have**

they'll *contr* **they will**

they're *contr* **they are**

they've *contr* **they have**

thick [θɪk] *adj* épais; (*pipe, rod, etc.*) gros; (*forest, eyebrows, etc.*) touffu; (*grass, grain, etc.*) dru; (*voice*) pâteux; (*gravy*) court; (coll) stupide, obtus; (coll) intime ‖ *s* (*of thumb, leg, etc.*) gras *m;* **the thick of** (*e.g., a crowd*) le milieu de; (*e.g., a battle*) le fort de; **through thick and thin** contre vents et marées

thicken [ˈθɪkən] *tr* épaissir ‖ *intr* s'épaissir; (*said, e.g., of plot*) se corser

thicket [ˈθɪkɪt] *s* fourré *m,* maquis *m*

thick′-head′ed *adj* à la tête dure

thick′-lipped′ *adj* lippu

thickness [ˈθɪknəs] *s* épaisseur *f*

thick′-set′ *adj* trapu

thief [θif] *s* (*pl* **thieves** [θivz]) voleur *m*

thieve [θiv] *intr* voler

thiever·y [ˈθivəri] *s* (*pl* **-ies**) volerie *f*
thigh [θaɪ] *s* cuisse *f*
thigh′bone′ *s* fémur *m*
thimble [ˈθɪmbəl] *s* dé *m*
thin [θɪn] *adj* (*comp* **thinner;** *super* **thinnest**) mince; (*person*) élancé, maigre; (*hair*) rare; (*soup*) clair; (*gravy*) long; (*voice*) grêle; (*excuse*) faible ‖ *v* (*pret & pp* **thinned;** *ger* **thinning**) *tr* amincir; (*colors*) délayer; **to thin out** éclaircir ‖ *intr* s'amincir; **to thin out** s'éclaircir
thine [ðaɪn] *adj poss* (archaic, poetic, Bib) ton **§88** ‖ *pron poss* (archaic, poetic, Bib) le tien **§89**
thing [θɪŋ] *s* chose *f;* **for another thing** d'autre part; **for one thing** en premier lieu; **of all things!** par exemple!; **to be the thing** être le dernier cri; **to see things** avoir des hallucinations
thingamajig [ˈθɪŋəmə,dʒɪg] *s* (coll) truc *m*, machin *m*, bidule *f*
think [θɪŋk] *v* (*pret & pp* **thought** [θɔt]) *tr* penser; (*to deem, consider*) estimer; **to think of** (*to have as an opinion of*) penser de, e.g., **what do you think of your uncle?** que pensez-vous de votre oncle? ‖ *intr* penser, songer; **to think fast** avoir l'esprit alerte; **to think of** (*to direct one's thoughts toward*) penser à, songer à, e.g., **do you ever think of your uncle?** pensez-vous jamais à votre oncle?; **to think of it** or **them** y penser, y songer; **to think so** croire que oui
thinker [ˈθɪŋkər] *s* penseur *m*
think′tank′ *s* (govt) cabinet *m* de stratèges, comité de conseillers
third [θʌrd] *adj & pron* troisième (*masc, fem*); **the Third** trois, e.g., **John the Third** Jean trois ‖ *s* troisième *m;* (*in fractions*) tiers *m;* **the third** (*in dates*) le trois
third′ degree′ *s* (coll) passage *m* à tabac, cuisinage *m*
third′ fin′ger *s* annulaire *m*
third′ rail′ *s* (rr) rail *m* de contact; rail conducteur
third′-rate′ *adj* de troisième ordre
Third′ World′ *s* Tiers Monde *m*
thirst [θʌrst] *s* soif *f* ‖ *intr* avoir soif; **to thirst for** avoir soif de
thirst′-quench′ing *adj* désaltérant
thirst·y [ˈθʌrsti] *adj* (*comp* **-ier;** *super* **-iest**) altéré, assoiffé; **to be thirsty** avoir soif
thirteen [ˈθʌrˈtin] *adj, pron, & s* treize *m*
thirteenth [ˈθʌrˈtinθ] *adj & pron* treizième (*masc, fem*); **the Thirteenth** treize, e.g., **John the Thirteenth** Jean treize ‖ *s* treizième *m;* **the thirteenth** (*in dates*) le treize
thirtieth [ˈθʌrtɪ·ɪθ] *adj & pron* trentième (*masc, fem*) ‖ *s* trentième *m;* **the thirtieth** (*in dates*) trente
thir·ty [ˈθʌrti] *adj & pron* trente; **about thirty** une trentaine de ‖ *s* (*pl* **-ties**) trente *m;* **the thirties** les années *fpl* trente
this [ðɪs] *adj dem* (*pl* **these**) ce **§82;** **this one**

celui-ci **§84** ‖ *pron dem* (*pl* **these**) celui **§83;** celui-ci **§84** ‖ *pron neut* ceci ‖ *adv* tellement, si, aussi; **this far** si loin, aussi loin; **this much, this many** tant
thistle [ˈθɪsəl] *s* chardon *m*
thither [ˈθɪðər] *adv* là, de ce côté là
thong [θɔŋ] *s* courroie *f*
tho·rax [ˈθoræks] *s* (*pl* **-raxes** or **-races** [rə,siz]) thorax *m*
thorn [θɔrn] *s* épine *f*
thorn·y [ˈθɔrni] *adj* (*comp* **-ier;** *super* **-iest**) épineux
thorough [ˈθʌro] *adj* approfondi, complet; consciencieux, minutieux
thor′ough·bred′ *adj* de race, racé; (*horse*) pur sang ‖ *s* personne *f* racée; (*horse*) pur-sang *m*
thor′ough·fare′ *s* voie *f* de communication; **no thoroughfare** (*public sign*) rue barrée
thor′ough·go′ing *adj* parfait; consciencieux
thoroughly [ˈθʌroli] *adv* à fond
those [ðoz] *adj dem pl* ces **§82** ‖ *pron dem pl* ceux **§83;** ceux-là **§84**
thou [ðaʊ] *pron pers* (archaic, poetic, Bib) tu **§87** ‖ *tr & intr* tutoyer
though [ðo] *adv* cependant ‖ *conj* (*although*) bien que, quoique; (*even if*) même si; **as though** comme si
thought [θɔt] *s* pensée *f;* **on second thought** réflexion faite
thought′ control′ *s* asservissement *m* des consciences
thoughtful [ˈθɔtfəl] *adj* pensif; (*considerate*) prévenant, attentif; (*serious*) profond
thoughtless [ˈθɔtlɪs] *adj* étourdi, négligent; inconsidéré
thought′ transfer′ence *s* transmission *f* de pensée
thousand [ˈθaʊzənd] *adj & pron* mille; mil, e.g., **the year one thousand nineteen hundred and eighty-one** l'an mil neuf cent quatre-vingt-un ‖ *s* mille *m;* **a thousand** un millier de, mille
thousandth [ˈθaʊzəndθ] *adj & pron* millième (*masc, fem*) ‖ *s* millième *m*
thrash [θræʃ] *tr* rosser; (agr) battre; **to thrash out** débattre ‖ *intr* s'agiter; (agr) battre le blé
thread [θrɛd] *s* fil *m;* (bot) filament *m;* (mach) filet *m;* **threads** (slang) vêtements *mpl;* **to hang by a thread** ne tenir qu'à un fil; **to lose the thread of** perdre le fil de ‖ *tr* enfiler; (mach) fileter
thread′bare′ *adj* élimé, râpé; (*tire*) usé jusqu'à la corde
threat [θrɛt] *s* menace *f*
threaten [ˈθrɛtən] *tr & intr* menacer
threatening [ˈθrɛtənɪŋ] *adj* menaçant
three [θri] *adj & pron* trois ‖ *s* trois *m;* **three o'clock** trois heures; **three of a kind** (cards) un fredon
three′-cor′nered *adj* triangulaire
three′-cor′nered-hat′ *s* tricorne *m*
three′-ply′ *adj* à trois épaisseurs; (*e.g., wool*) à trois fils

three′ R's′ [ɑrz] *spl* la lecture, l'écriture et l'arithmétique, premières notions *fpl*

three′-ring′-cir′cus *s* cirque *m* à trois pistes; (fig) tapage *m*, désordre *m*, chaos *m*

three′score′ *adj* soixante

three′-quar′ters *pron* trois quarts *mpl*

three-sided [ˈθriˈsaɪdəd] *adj* à trois côtés, à trois faces

threno•dy [ˈθrɛnədi] *s* (*pl* **-dies**) thrène *m*

thresh [θrɛʃ] *tr* (agr) battre; **to thresh out** (*a problem*) débattre ‖ *intr* s'agiter; (agr) battre le blé

thresh′ing floor′ *s* aire *f*

thresh′ing machine′ *s* batteuse *f*

threshold [ˈθrɛʃold] *s* seuil *m;* **to cross the threshold** franchir le seuil

thrice [θraɪs] *adv* trois fois

thrift [θrɪft] *s* économie *f*, épargne *f*

thrift•y [ˈθrɪfti] *adj* (*comp* **-ier;** *super* **-iest**) économe, ménager, frugal; prospère

thrill [θrɪl] *s* frisson *m* ‖ *tr* faire frémir ‖ *intr* frémir

thriller [ˈθrɪlər] *s* roman *m*, film *m*, or pièce *f* à sensation; (*novel*) roman de série noire

thrilling [ˈθrɪlɪŋ] *adj* émouvant, passionnant

thrive [θraɪv] *v* (*pret* **thrived** or **throve** [θrov]; *pp* **thrived** or **thriven** [ˈθrɪvən]) *intr* prospérer; (*said of child, plant, etc.*) croître, se développer

throat [θrot] *s* gorge *f;* **to clear one's throat** s'éclaircir le gosier; **to have a sore throat** avoir mal à la gorge

throb [θrɑb] *s* palpitation *f*, battement *m;* (*of motor*) vrombissement *m* ‖ *v* (*pret & pp* **throbbed;** *ger* **throbbing**) *intr* palpiter, battre fort; (*said of motor*) vrombir

throes [θroz] *spl* (*of childbirth*) douleurs *fpl;* (*of death*) affres *fpl;* **in the throes of** luttant avec

thrombosis [θrɑmˈbosəs] *s* thrombose *f*

throne [θron] *s* trône *m*

throng [θrɛŋ] *s* foule *f*, affluence *f* ‖ *intr* affluer

throttle [ˈθrɑtəl] *s* (*of steam engine*) régulateur *m;* (aut) étrangleur *m* ‖ *tr* régler; étrangler

through [θru] *adj* direct; (*finished*) fini; (*traffic*) prioritaire ‖ *adv* à travers; complètement ‖ *prep* au travers de, par; grâce à, par le canal de

through•out′ *adv* d'un bout à l'autre ‖ *prep* d'un bout à l'autre de; (*during*) pendant tout; **throughout the world** de par le monde

through′ street′ *s* rue *f* à circulation prioritaire

through′way′ *s* autoroute *f*

throw [θro] *s* jet *m*, lancement *m;* (*scarf*) châle *m* ‖ *v* (*pret* **threw** [θru]; *pp* **thrown**) *tr* jeter, lancer; (*a glance; the dice*) jeter; (*e.g., a baseball*) lancer; (*e.g., a shadow*) projeter; (*blame; responsibility*) rejeter; (*a rider*) désarçonner; (*a game, career, etc.*) perdre à dessein; **to throw away** jeter; **to throw back** renvoyer; **to throw in** ajouter; **to throw out** expulser, chasser; (*e.g., an odor*) répandre; (*one's chest*) bomber; **to throw over** aban-

donner; **to throw up** jeter en l'air; vomir; (*one's hands*) lever; (*e.g., one's claims*) renoncer à ‖ *intr* jeter, lancer; jeter des dés; **to throw up** vomir

throw′back′ *s* recul *m;* (*setback*) échec *m;* (*reversion*) retour *m* atavique

thrum [θrʌm] *v* (*pret & pp* **thrummed;** *ger* **thrumming**) *intr* pianoter

thrush [θrʌʃ] *s* grive *f*

thrust [θrʌst] *s* poussée *f;* (*with a weapon*) coup *m* de pointe; (*with a sword*) coup d'estoc; (*jibe*) trait *m;* (rok) poussée *f;* **thrust and parry** la botte et la parade ‖ *v* (*pret & pp* **thrust**) *tr* pousser; (*e.g., a dagger*) enfoncer; **to thrust oneself on** s'imposer à

thud [θʌd] *s* bruit *m* sourd ‖ *v* (*pret & pp* **thudded;** *ger* **thudding**) *tr & intr* frapper avec un son mat

thug [θʌg] *s* bandit *m*, assassin *m*

thumb [θʌm] *s* pouce *m;* **all thumbs** (coll) maladroit; **to twiddle one's thumbs** se tourner les pouces; **under the thumb of** sous la coupe de ‖ *tr* tripoter; (*a book*) feuilleter; **to thumb a ride** faire de l'autostop; **to thumb one's nose at** (coll) faire un pied de nez à

thumb′ in′dex *s* onglet *m*, encoche *f*

thumb′print′ *s* marque *f* de pouce

thumb′screw′ *s* papillon *m*, vis *f* à ailettes

thumb′tack′ *s* punaise *f* ‖ *tr* punaiser

thump [θʌmp] *s* coup *m* violent ‖ *tr* cogner ‖ *intr* tomber avec un bruit sourd; (*said, e.g., of marching feet*) sonner lourdement; (*said of heart*) battre fort

thumping [ˈθʌmpɪŋ] *adj* (coll) énorme

thunder [ˈθʌndər] *s* tonnerre *m* ‖ *tr* fulminer ‖ *intr* tonner; **to thunder at** tonner contre, tempêter contre

thun′der•bolt′ *s* foudre *f;* (*disaster*) coup *m* de foudre

thun′der•clap′ *s* coup *m* de tonnerre

thunderous [ˈθʌndərəs] *adj* orageux; (*voice; applause*) tonnant

thun′der•show′er *s* pluie *f* d'orage

thun′der•storm′ *s* orage *m*

thunderstruck [ˈθʌndərˌstrʌk] *adj* foudroyé, pantois

Thursday [ˈθʌrzdi] *s* jeudi *m*

thus [ðʌs] *adv* ainsi; (*therefore*) donc; **thus far** jusqu'ici

thwack [θwæk] *s* coup *m* ‖ *tr* flanquer un coup à

thwart [θwɔrt] *adj* transversal ‖ *adv* en travers ‖ *tr* déjouer, frustrer

thy [ðaɪ] *adj poss* (archaic, poetic, Bib) ton §88

thyme [taɪm] *s* thym *m*

thyroid [ˈθaɪrɔɪd] *s* thyroïde *f;* (pharm) extrait *m* thyroïde

thyself [ðaɪˈsɛlf] *pron* (archaic, poetic, Bib) toi-même §86; te §87

tiara [taɪˈɑrə], [taɪˈɛrə] *s* tiare *f;* (*woman's headdress*) diadème *m*

tic [tɪk] *s* (pathol) tic *m*

tick [tɪk] *s* (*ticking*) tic-tac *m;* (*e.g., of pillow*) taie *f;* (*e.g., of mattress*) housse *f* de coutil; (ent) tique *f;* **on tick** à crédit ‖ *tr*—**to tick off** (*to check off*) pointer ‖ *intr* tictaquer; (*said of heart*) battre

ticker [ˈtɪkər] *s* téléimprimeur *m;* (*watch*) (slang) toquante *f;* (*heart*) (slang) cœur *m*

tick′er tape′ *s* bande *f* de téléimprimeur

ticket [ˈtɪkɪt] *s* billet *m;* (*of bus, subway, etc.*) ticket *m;* (*of baggage, checkroom*) bulletin *m;* (*of cloakroom*) numéro *m;* (*for boat trip*) passage *m;* (*of a political party*) liste *f* électorale; (*for violation*) (coll) papillon *m* de procès-verbal, contravention *f;* **that's the ticket** (coll) c'est bien ça, à la bonne heure; **tickets, please!** vos places, s'il vous plaît!

tick′et a′gent *s* guichetier *m*

tick′et collec′tor *s* contrôleur *m*

ticketing [ˈtɪkɪtɪŋ] *s* billetterie *f*

tick′et of′fice *s* guichet *m;* (theat) bureau *m* de location

tick′et scalp′er [ˌskælpər] *s* trafiquant *m* de billets de théâtre

tick′et win′dow *s* guichet *m*

ticking [ˈtɪkɪŋ] *s* (*of a clock*) tic-tac *m;* (tex) coutil *m*

tickle [ˈtɪkəl] *s* chatouillement *m* ‖ *tr* chatouiller; (*to amuse*) amuser; (*to please*) plaire à ‖ *intr* chatouiller

ticklish [ˈtɪklɪʃ] *adj* chatouilleux; (*touchy*) susceptible; (*subject, question*) épineux, délicat

tick′-tack-toe′ *s* morpion *m*

ticktock [ˈtɪk,tɑk] *s* tic-tac *m* ‖ *intr* faire tic-tac

tid′al ba′sin *s* bassin *m* à flot

tid′al wave′ [ˈtaɪdəl] *s* raz *m* de marée; (*e.g., of popular indignation*) vague *f*

tidbit [ˈtɪd,bɪt] *s* bon morceau *m*

tiddlywinks [ˈtɪdli,wɪŋks] *s* jeu *m* de puce

tide [taɪd] *s* marée *f;* **against the tide** à contre-marée; **to go with the tide** suivre le courant ‖ *tr*—**to tide over** dépanner, remettre à flot; (*a difficulty*) venir à bout de

tide′land′ *s* terres *fpl* inondées aux grandes marées

tide′wa′ter *s* eaux *fpl* de marée; bord *m* de la mer

tide′water pow′er plant′ *s* usine *f* marémotrice

tidings [ˈtaɪdɪŋz] *spl* nouvelles *fpl*

ti•dy [ˈtaɪdi] *adj* (*comp* **-dier;** *super* **-diest**) propre, net, bien tenu; (*considerable*) (coll) joli, fameux ‖ *s* (*pl* **-dies**) voile *m* de fauteuil ‖ *v* (*pret & pp* **-died**) *tr* mettre en ordre, nettoyer ‖ *intr*—**to tidy up** faire un brin de toilette

tie [taɪ] *s* (*connection*) lien *m,* attache *f;* (*knot*) nœud *m;* (*necktie*) cravate *f;* (*in games*) match *m* nul; (mus) liaison *f;* (rr) traverse *f* ‖ *v* (*pret & pp* **tied;** *ger* **tying**) *tr* lier; (*a knot, a necktie, etc.*) nouer; (*shoelaces; a knot; one's apron*) attacher; (*an artery*) ligaturer; (*a competitor*) être à égalité avec; (mus) lier; **tied up** (*busy*) occupé; **to tie down** assujettir; **to tie up** attacher; (*a package*) ficeler; (*a person*) ligoter; (*a wound*) bander; (*funds*) immobiliser; (*traffic, a telephone line*) embouteiller ‖ *intr* (sports) faire match nul, égaliser

tie′back′ *s* embrasse *f*

tie′ game′ *s* match *m* nul

tie′pin′ *s* épingle *f* de cravate

tier [tɪr] *s* étage *m;* (*of stadium*) gradin *m*

tiger [ˈtaɪgər] *s* tigre *m*

ti′ger lil′y *s* lis *m* tigré

tight [taɪt] *adj* serré, juste; (*e.g., rope*) tendu; (*clothes*) ajusté; (*container*) étanche; (*game*) serré; (*money*) rare; (*miserly*) (coll) chiche; (*drunk*) (coll) rond noir ‖ **tights** *spl* collant *m,* maillot *m,* maillot de danseur ‖ *adv* fermement, bien; **to hold tight** tenir serré; se tenir, se cramponner; **to sit tight** (coll) tenir bon

tighten [ˈtaɪtən] *tr* (*a knot, a bolt*) serrer, resserrer; (*e.g., a rope*) tendre ‖ *intr* se serrer; se tendre

tight-fisted [ˈtaɪtˈfɪstɪd] *adj* dur à la détente, serré

tight′-fit′ting *adj* collant, ajusté

tight′rope′ *s* corde *f* raide

tight′rope walk′er *s* funambule *mf*

tight′ squeeze′ *s* (coll) situation *f* difficile, embarras *m*

tight′wad′ *s* (coll) grippe-sou *m*

tigress [ˈtaɪgrɪs] *s* tigresse *f*

tile [taɪl] *s* (*for roof*) tuile *f;* (*for floor*) carreau *m* ‖ *tr* (*e.g., a house*) couvrir de tuiles; (*a floor*) carreler

tile′ roof′ *s* toit *m* de tuiles

till [tɪl] *s* tiroir-caisse *m* ‖ *prep* jusqu'à ‖ *conj* jusqu'à ce que ‖ *tr* labourer

tilt [tɪlt] *s* (*slant*) pente *f,* inclinaison *f;* (*contest*) joute *f;* **full tilt** à fond de train ‖ *tr* pencher, incliner; **to tilt back** renverser en arrière; **to tilt up** redresser ‖ *intr* se pencher, s'incliner; (*with lance*) jouter; (naut) donner de la bande; **to tilt at** attaquer, critiquer; **to tilt back** se renverser en arrière

timber [ˈtɪmbər] *s* bois *m* de construction; (*trees*) bois de haute futaie; (*rafter*) poutre *f*

tim′ber·land′ *s* bois *m* pour exploitation forestière

tim′ber line′ *s* limite *f* de la végétation forestière, ligne *f* des arbres

timbre [ˈtɪmbər] *s* (phonet, phys) timbre *m*

time [taɪm] *s* temps *m;* heure *f,* e.g., **what time is it?** quelle heure est-il?; fois, e.g., **five times** cinq fois; e.g., **five times two is ten** cinq fois deux font dix; (*period of payment*) délai *m;* (phot) temps d'exposition; **at that time** à ce moment-là; à cette époque; **at the present time** à l'heure actuelle; **at the same time** en même temps; **at times** parfois; **behind the times** en retard sur son époque; **between times** entre-temps; **full time** plein temps; **in due time** en temps et lieu; **in no time** en moins de rien; **in the time of** au temps de; **on time** à l'heure, à temps; **several times** à plusieurs reprises; **time and time again** maintes fois; **to beat time** (mus) battre la mesure; **to do time** (coll) faire son temps; **to have a**

good time s'amuser bien, se divertir; **to lose time** (*said of timepiece*) retarder; **to mark time** marquer le pas; **to play for time** (coll) chercher à gagner du temps ‖ *tr* mesurer la durée de; (sports) chronométrer

time′ bomb′ *s* bombe *f* à retardement

time′ cap′sule *s* capsule *f* du temps

time′ card′ *s* registre *m* de présence

time′ clock′ *s* horloge *f* enregistreuse

time′ expo′sure *s* (phot) pose *f*

time′ fuse′ *s* fusée *f* fusante

time′-hon′ored *adj* consacré par l'usage

time′keep′er *s* pointeur *m*, chronométreur *m;* (*clock*) pendule *f;* (*watch*) montre *f*

timeless [′taɪmlɪs] *adj* sans fin, éternel

time′ lim′it *s* limite *f* de temps, délai *m;* **without a time limit** sans une limitation de temps

time·ly [′taɪmli] *adj* (*comp* **-lier;** *super* **-liest**) opportun, à propos

time′-out′ *s* (sports) temps *m* mort

time′piece′ *s* (*clock*) pendule *f;* (*watch*) montre *f*

timer [′taɪmər] *s* (*person*) chronométreur *m;* (*of an electrical appliance*) minuterie *f*, compte-minutes *m invar;* (*on a stove*) minuteur *m*

time′-release medica′tion *s* médicament *m* à action prolongée, médication *f* retard

times [taɪmz] *prep* multiplié par, par

time′-shar′ing *adj* (comp) en temps partagé

time′ shar′ing *s* (comp) temps *m* partagé, partage *m* du temps

time′ sheet′ *s* feuille *f* de présence

time′ sig′nal *s* signal *m* horaire

time′ slot′ *s* créneau *m* temporel

time′ ta′ble *s* horaire *m;* (rr) indicateur *m*

time′ warp′ *s* saut *m* dans le temps, déformation *f* dans l'espace-temps; **stuck in a time warp** détenu dans le temps

time′work′ *s* travail *m* à l'heure

time′worn′ *adj* usé par le temps; (*venerable*) séculaire

time′ zone′ *s* fuseau *m* horaire

timid [′tɪmɪd] *adj* timide

timing [′taɪmɪŋ] *s* (*recording of time*) chronométrage *m;* (*selecting the right time*) choix *m* du moment propice; (*of an electrical appliance*) minuterie *f;* (aut, mach) réglage *m;* (sports) chronométrage; (theat) tempo *m*, minutage *m*

tim′ing gears′ *spl* engrenage *m* de distribution

timorous [′tɪmərəs] *adj* timoré, peureux

tin [tɪn] *s* (*element*) étain *m;* (*tin plate*) fer-blanc *m;* (*cup, box, etc.*) boîte *f* ‖ *v* (*pret & pp* **tinned;** *ger* **tinning**) *tr* étamer; (*to can*) (Brit) mettre en boîte

tin′ can′ *s* boîte *f* en fer-blanc, boîte de conserve

tincture [′tɪŋktʃər] *s* teinture *f*

tin′ cup′ *s* timbale *f*

tinder [′tɪndər] *s* amadou *m*

tin′der·box′ *s* briquet *m* à amadou; (fig) foyer *m* de l'effervescence

tin′ foil′ *s* feuille *f* d'étain, papier *m* d'argent

ting-a-ling [′tɪŋə,lɪŋ] *s* drelin *m*

tinge [tɪndʒ] *s* teinte *f*, nuance *f* ‖ *v* (*ger* **tingeing** or **tinging**) *tr* teinter, nuancer

tingle [′tɪŋgəl] *s* picotement *m*, fourmillement *m* ‖ *intr* picoter, fourmiller; (*e.g., with enthusiasm*) tressaillir

tin′ hat′ *s* (coll) casque *m* en acier

tinker [′tɪŋkər] *s* chaudronnier *m* ambulant; (*bungler*) bousilleur *m* ‖ *intr* bricoler; **to tinker with** tripatouiller

tinkle [′tɪŋkəl] *s* tintement *m* ‖ *tr* faire tinter ‖ *intr* tinter

tin′ plate′ *s* fer-blanc *m*

tin′-plate′ *tr* étamer

tin′ roof′ *s* toit *m* de fer-blanc

tinsel [′tɪnsəl] *s* clinquant *m;* (*for a Christmas tree*) paillettes *fpl*, guirlandes *fpl* clinquantes

tin′smith′ *s* ferblantier *m*

tin′ sol′dier *s* soldat *m* de plomb

tint [tɪnt] *s* teinte *f* ‖ *tr* teinter

tin′type′ *s* ferrotypie *f*

tin′ware′ *s* ferblanterie *f*

ti·ny [′taɪni] *adj* (*comp* **-nier;** *super* **-niest**) minuscule

tip [tɪp] *s* (*end*) bout *m*, pointe *f;* (*slant*) inclinaison *f;* (*fee to a waiter*) pourboire *m;* (*secret information*) (slang) tuyau *m* ‖ *v* (*pret & pp* **tipped;** *ger* **tipping**) *tr* incliner; (*the scales*) faire pencher; (*a waiter*) donner un pourboire à, donner la pièce à; **to tip off** (slang) tuyauter; **to tip over** renverser ‖ *intr* se renverser; donner un pourboire

tip′cart′ *s* tombereau *m*

tip′-in′ *s* (bb) hors-texte *m*

tip′-off′ *s* (coll) tuyau *m*

tipped′-in′ *adj* (bb) hors texte

tipple [′tɪpəl] *intr* biberonner

tip′staff′ *s* verge *f* d'huissier; huissier *m* à verge

tip·sy [′tɪpsi] *adj* (*comp* **-sier;** *super* **-siest**) gris, grisé

tip′toe′ *s* pointe *f* des pieds ‖ *v* (*pret & pp* **-toed;** *ger* **toeing**) *intr* marcher sur la pointe des pieds

tirade [′taɪred] *s* diatribe *f*

tire [taɪr] *s* pneu *m* ‖ *tr* fatiguer ‖ *intr* se fatiguer

tire′ chain′ *s* chaîne *f* antidérapante

tired [taɪrd] *adj* fatigué, las

tire′ gauge′ *s* manomètre *m*

tire′ i′ron *s* démonte-pneu *m*

tireless [′taɪrlɪs] *adj* infatigable

tire′ pres′sure *s* pression *f* des pneus

tire′ pump′ *s* gonfleur *m* pour pneus

tiresome [′taɪrsəm] *adj* fatigant, ennuyeux

tissue [′tɪsju] *s* (*thin paper*) papier *m* de soie; (*toilet tissue*) papier hygiénique; (*paper handkerchief*) mouchoir *m* en papier; (tex) tissu *m*, étoffe *f;* (*web, mesh*) (fig) tissu, enchevêtrement *m*

tis′sue pa′per *s* papier *m* de soie

tit [tɪt] *s* téton *m;* (orn) mésange *f;* **tit for tat** à bon chat bon rat

titanic [taɪ′tænɪk] *adj* titanesque; (chem) titanique

titanium [taɪ′teni•əm] *s* titane *m*

tithe [taɪð] *s* dixième *m;* (rel) dîme *f* ‖ *tr* soumettre à la dîme; payer la dîme sur

Titian [ˈtɪʃən] *s* le Titien *m*

Ti′tian red′ *s* blond *m* vénitien

title [ˈtaɪtəl] *s* titre *m;* (*of an automobile*) carte *f* grise ‖ *tr* intituler

ti′tle deed′ *s* titre *m* de propriété

ti′tle•hold′er *s* tenant *m* du titre

ti′tle page′ *s* page *f* de titre

ti′tle role′ *s* rôle *m* principal

tit′mouse′ *s* (*pl* -mice) (orn) mésange *f*

titter [ˈtɪtər] *s* rire *m* étouffé ‖ *intr* rire en catimini

titular [ˈtɪtʃələr] *adj* titulaire

to [tu], [tʊ], [tə] *adv*—**to and fro** de long en large ‖ *prep* à; (*towards*) vers; (*in order to*) afin de, pour; envers, pour, e.g., **good to her** bon envers elle, bon pour elle; jusqu'à, e.g., **to this day** jusqu'à ce jour; e.g., **to count to a hundred** compter jusqu'à cent; moins, e.g., **a quarter to eight** huit heures moins le quart; contre, e.g., **seven to one** sept contre un; dans, e.g., **to a certain extent** dans une certaine mesure; en, e.g., **from door to door** de porte en porte; e.g., **I am going to France** je vais en France; de, e.g., **to try to** + *inf* essayer de + *inf;* **to him** lui §87

toad [tod] *s* crapaud *m*

toad′stool′ *s* agaric *m;* champignon *m* vénéneux

to-and-fro [ˈtuˑəndˈfro] *adj* de va-et-vient

toast [tost] *s* pain *m* grillé; (*with a drink*) toast *m* ‖ *tr* griller; porter un toast à, boire à la santé de

toaster [ˈtostər] *s* grille-pain *m*

toast′er ov′en *s* grille-pain-four *m*

toast′mas′ter *s* préposé *m* aux toasts

tobac•co [təˈbæko] *s* (*pl* -cos) tabac *m*

tobac′co pouch′ *s* blague *f*

toboggan [təˈbɑgən] *s* toboggan *m*

tocsin [ˈtɑksɪn] *s* tocsin *m;* (*bell*) cloche *f* qui sonne le tocsin

today [tʊˈde] *s & adv* aujourd'hui *m*

toddle [ˈtɑdəl] *s* allure *f* chancelante ‖ *intr* marcher à petits pas chancelants

toddler [ˈtɑdlər] *s* tout-petit *m*

tod•dy [ˈtɑdi] *s* (*pl* -dies) grog *m*

to-do [təˈdu] *s* (*pl* -dos) embarras *mpl,* chichis *mpl,* façons *fpl*

toe [to] *s* doigt *m* du pied, orteil *m;* (*of shoe, of stocking*) bout *m* ‖ *v* (*pret & pp* **toed;** *ger* **toeing**) *tr*—**to toe the line** or **the mark** s'aligner, se mettre au pas

toe′nail′ *s* ongle *m* du pied

tofu [ˈtofu] *s* tofu *m,* pâte *f* de suc de soja

tog [tɑg] *v* (*pret & pp* **togged;** *ger* **togging**) *tr*—**to tog out** or **up** attifer, fringuer ‖ **togs** *spl* fringues *fpl*

together [tʊˈgɛðər] *adv* ensemble; (*at the same time*) en même temps, à la fois

tog′gle switch′ [ˈtɑgəl] *s* (elec) interrupteur *m* à culbuteur *or* à bascule

toil [tɔɪl] *s* travail *m* dur; **toils** filet *m,* piège *m* ‖ *intr* travailler dur

toilet [ˈtɔɪlɪt] *s* toilette *f;* (*rest room*) cabinet *m* de toilette, W.-C. *m,* la toilette *f* (Belgique); **toilets** toilettes *fpl,* cabinets *mpl* d'aisances; **to go to the toilet** aller aux toilettes, faire ses besoins

toi′let seat′ *s* siège *m* des cabinets, abattant *m*

toi′let ar′ticles *spl* objets *mpl* de toilette

toi′let bowl′ *s* cuvette *f*

toi′let pa′per *s* papier *m* hygiénique

toi′let seat′ *s* siège *m* des toilettes, abattant *m*

toi′let set′ *s* nécessaire *m* de toilette

toi′let soap′ *s* savonnette *f*

toi′let wa′ter *s* eaux *fpl* de toilette

token [ˈtokən] *adj* symbolique ‖ *s* (*symbol*) signe *m,* marque *f;* (*keepsake*) souvenir *m;* (*used as money*) jeton *m;* **by the same token** de plus; **in token of** en témoignage de

tolerance [ˈtɑlərəns] *s* tolérance *f*

tolerate [ˈtɑlə͵ret] *tr* tolérer

toll [tol] *s* (*of bells*) glas *m;* (*payment*) droit *m* de passage, péage *m;* (*number of victims*) mortalité *f;* (telp) tarif *m* ‖ *tr* tinter; (*to ring the knell for*) sonner le glas de ‖ *intr* sonner le glas

toll′ booth′ *s* cabine *f* de péage

toll′ bridge′ *s* pont *m* à péage

toll′ call′ *s* appel *m* interurbain

toll′gate′ *s* barrière *f* à péage

toll′ road′ *s* autoroute *f* à péage

toma•to [təˈmeto], [təˈmato] *s* (*pl* -toes) tomate *f*

toma′to paste *s* extrait *m* de tomate

tomb [tum] *s* tombeau *m*

tomboy [ˈtɑm͵bɔɪ] *s* garçon *m* manqué

tomb′stone′ *s* pierre *f* tombale

tomcat [ˈtɑm͵kæt] *s* matou *m*

tome [tom] *s* tome *m*

tomorrow [tʊˈmɔro] *adj, s, & adv* demain *m;* **tomorrow morning** demain matin; **until tomorrow** à demain

tom-tom [ˈtɑm͵tɑm] *s* tam-tam *m*

ton [tʌn] *s* tonne *f*

tone [ton] *s* ton *m* ‖ *tr* accorder; **to tone down** atténuer; **to tone up** renforcer; (*e.g., the muscles*) tonifier ‖ *intr*—**to tone down** se modérer

tone′ po′em *s* poème *m* symphonique

tone′ pulse′ *s* (telp) tonalité-pulsation *f*

tone′ tel′ephone *s* téléphone *m* à clavier

tongs [tɔŋz] *spl* pincettes *fpl;* (*e.g., for sugar*) pince *f;* (*of blacksmith*) tenailles *fpl*

tongue [tʌŋ] *s* (*language; part of body*) langue *f;* (*of wagon*) timon *m;* (*of buckle*) ardillon *m;* (*of shoe*) languette *f;* (*neck or narrow strip of land*) langue de terre; **to hold one's tongue** se mordre la langue

tongue′ lash′ing *s* savon *m,* engueulade *f*

tongue-tied [ˈtʌŋ͵taɪd] *adj* bouche cousue

tongue′ twist′er *s* phrase *f* à décrocher la mâchoire, casse-langue *m invar*

tonic [ˈtɑnɪk] *adj & s* tonique *m*

tonight [tʊˈnaɪt] *adj & s* ce soir

tonnage [ˈtʌnɪdʒ] *s* tonnage *m*

tonsil [ˈtɑnsəl] *s* amygdale *f*

tonsillitis [ˌtɑnsɪˈlaɪtɪs] *s* amygdalite *f*

ton‧y [ˈtoni] *adj* (*comp* **-ier;** *super* **-iest**) (slang) élégant, chic

too [tu] *adv* (*also*) aussi; (*more than enough*) trop; (*moreover*) d'ailleurs; **I did too!** mais si!; **too bad!** c'est dommage!; **too many, too much** trop, trop de

tool [tul] *s* outil ‖ *tr* (*a piece of metal*) usiner; (*leather*) repousser; (bb) dorer ‖ *intr*—**to tool along** rouler; **to tool up** s'outiller

tool′ bar′ *s* (comp) barre *f* d'outils

tool′ box′ *s* trousse *f* à outils

tool′ mak′er *s* taillandier *m*

toot [tut] *s* (*sound of tooting*) son *m* du cor; (*of auto*) coup *m* de klaxon; (*of locomotive*) coup de sifflet ‖ *tr* sonner ‖ *intr* corner; (aut) klaxonner

tooth [tuθ] *s* (*pl* **teeth** [tiθ]) dent *f;* **to grit, grind,** or **gnash the teeth** grincer des dents, crisser des dents

tooth′ ache′ *s* mal *m* de dents

tooth′ brush′ *s* brosse *f* à dents

toothless [ˈtuθlɪs] *adj* édenté

tooth′ paste′ *s* pâte *f* dentifrice

tooth′ pick′ *s* cure-dent *m*

tooth′ pow′der *s* poudre *f* dentifrice

top [tɑp] *adj* premier, de tête ‖ *s* sommet *m,* cime *f,* faîte *m;* (*of a barrel, table, etc.*) dessus *m;* (*of a page*) haut *m;* (*of a box*) couvercle *m;* (*of a carriage or auto*) capote *f;* (toy) toupie *f;* (naut) hune *f;* **at the top of** en haut de; (*e.g., one's class*) à la tête de; **at the top of one's voice** à tue-tête; **from top to bottom** de haut en bas, de fond en comble; **on top of** sur; (*in addition to*) en plus de; **tops** (*e.g., of carrots*) fanes *fpl;* **to sleep like a top** dormir comme un sabot ‖ *v* (*pret & pp* **topped;** *ger* **topping**) *tr* couronner, surmonter; (*to surpass*) dépasser; (*a tree, plant, etc.*) écimer

topaz [ˈtopæz] *s* topaze *f*

top′ bill′ing *s* tête *f* d'affiche

top′ coat′ *s* surtout *m* de demi-saison

toper [ˈtopər] *s* soiffard *m*

top′ hat′ *s* haut-de-forme *m*

top′-heav′y *adj* trop lourd du haut

topic [ˈtɑpɪk] *s* sujet *m*

top′ knot′ *s* chignon *m*

top′less swim′ suit *s* monokini *m*

top′-lev′el *adj* de haut niveau, haut

top′ mast′ *s* mât *m* de hune

top′ most′ *adj* (le) plus haut

top′ notch′ *adj* (coll) d'élite

top′-of-the-line′ *adj* haut de gamme

topography [təˈpɑgrəfi] *s* (*pl* **-phies**) topographie *f*

topple [ˈtɑpəl] *tr & intr* culbuter

top′ prior′ity *s* priorité *f* absolue, priorité numéro un

top′-rank′ing *adj* de haut niveau, important

topsail [ˈtɑpsəl], [ˈtɑp‚sel] *s* (naut) hunier *m*

top′-se′cret *adj* ultra-secret

top′soil′ *s* couche *f* arable

topsy-turvy [ˈtɑpsɪˈtʌrvi] *adj & adv* sens dessus dessous

torch [tɔrtʃ] *s* torche *f,* flambeau *m;* (Brit) lampe *f* torche; **to carry the torch for** (slang) avoir un amour sans retour pour

torch′ bear′er *s* porte-flambeau *m;* (fig) défenseur *m*

torch′ light′ *s* lueur *f* des flambeaux

torch′ light proces′sion *s* défilé *m* aux flambeaux

torch′ song′ *s* chanson *f* de l'amour non partagé

torment [ˈtɔrmɛnt] *s* tourment *m* ‖ [tɔrˈmɛnt] *tr* tourmenter

torna‧do [tɔrˈnedo] *s* (*pl* **-does** or **-dos**) tornade *f*

torpe‧do [tɔrˈpido] *s* (*pl* **-does**) torpille *f* ‖ *tr* torpiller

torpe′do-boat destroy′er *s* contre-torpilleur *m*

torpid [ˈtɔrpɪd] *adj* engourdi

torque [tɔrk] *s* effort *m* de torsion, couple *m* de torsion

torrent [ˈtɔrənt] *s* torrent *m*

torrid [ˈtɔrɪd] *adj* torride

tor‧so [ˈtɔrso] *s* (*pl* **-sos**) torse *m*

tort [tɔrt] *s* (law) acte *m* dommageable sauf rupture de contrat ou abus de confiance

tortoise [ˈtɔrtəs] *s* tortue *f*

tor′toise shell′ *s* écaille *f*

torture [ˈtɔrʃər] *s* torture *f* ‖ *tr* torturer

toss [tɔs] *s* (*throw*) lancement *m;* (*of the head*) mouvement *m* dédaigneux ‖ *tr* lancer; (*one's head*) relever dédaigneusement; (*a rider*) démonter; (*a coin*) jouer à pile et face avec; **to toss about** agiter, ballotter; **to toss off** (*e.g., work*) expédier; (*in one gulp*) lamper; **to toss up** jeter en l'air ‖ *intr* s'agiter; **to toss and turn** se tourner et retourner

toss′ up′ *s* (*flip of a coin*) (coll) coup *m* de pile ou face; (*fifty-fifty chance*) (coll) chances *fpl* égales

tot [tɑt] *s* bambin *m,* tout petit *m* ‖ *v* (*pret & pp* **totted;** *ger* **totting**) *tr*—**to tot up** additionner

to‧tal [ˈtotəl] *adj & s* total *m;* **as a total** au total ‖ *v* (*pret & pp* **-taled** or **-talled;** *ger* **-taling** or **-talling**) *tr* additionner, totaliser; (*to amount to*) s'élever à

totalitarian [to‚tælɪˈtɛrɪ•ən] *adj & mf* totalitaire

totem [ˈtotəm] *s* totem *m*

totter [ˈtɑtər] *intr* chanceler

touch [tʌtʃ] *s* (*act*) attouchement *m;* (*e.g., of color; with a brush*) touche *f;* (*sense; of pianist*) toucher *m;* (*of typist*) frappe *f;* (*little bit*) pointe *f,* brin *m;* **in touch** en communication; **to get in touch with** prendre contact avec ‖ *tr* toucher; (*for a loan*) (slang) taper; **to touch off** déclencher; **to touch up** retoucher ‖ *intr* se toucher; **to touch on** toucher à

touched *adj* touché; (*crazy*) timbré

touching [ˈtʌtʃɪŋ] *adj* touchant, émouvant ‖ *prep* touchant, concernant

touch′ type′writing *ou* **touch′ typ′ing** *s* dactylographie *f* au toucher

touch•y [ˈtʌtʃi] *adj* (*comp* **-ier;** *super* **-iest**) susceptible, irritable

tough [tʌf] *adj* dur, coriace; (*tenacious*) résistant; (*task*) difficile ‖ *s* voyou *m*

toughen [ˈtʌfən] *tr* endurcir ‖ *intr* s'endurcir

tough' luck' *s* déveine *f*

toupee [tuˈpe] *s* postiche *m*

tour [tʊr] *s* tour *m;* (*e.g., of inspection*) tournée *f;* **on tour** en tournée ‖ *tr* faire le tour de; (*e.g., a country*) voyager en; (theat) faire une tournée de, en, or dans ‖ *intr* voyager

tour'ing car' *s* voiture *f* de tourisme

tourist [ˈtʊrɪst] *adj* & *s* touriste *mf*

tour'ist indus'try *s* tourisme *m*

tour'ist resort' *s* complexe *m* touristique

tournament [ˈtʊrnəmənt], [ˈtʌrnəmənt] *s* tournoi *m*

tourney [ˈtʊrni] *s* tournoi *m* ‖ *intr* tournoyer

tourniquet [ˈtʊrnɪˌkɛt] *s* (surg) garrot *m*, tourniquet *m*

tousle [ˈtaʊzəl] *tr* (*to dishevel*) ébouriffer; (*to handle roughly*) tirailler, maltraiter

tow [to] *s* (*towing*) remorque *f;* (*e.g., of hemp*) filasse *f;* **to take in tow** prendre en remorque; (fig) se charger de ‖ *tr* remorquer

towage [ˈto•ɪdʒ] *s* remorquage *m;* (*fee*) droits *mpl* de remorquage

toward(s) [tord(z)], [təˈwɔrd(z)] *prep* vers; (*in regard to*) envers

tow'boat' *s* remorqueur *m*

tow•el [ˈtaʊ•əl] *s* serviette *f*, essuie-main *m* ‖ *v* (*pret* & *pp* **-eled** or **-elled;** *ger* **-eling** or **elling**) *tr* essuyer avec une serviette

tow'el rack' *s* porte-serviettes *m*

tower [ˈtaʊ•ər] *s* tour *f* ‖ *intr* s'élever

towering [ˈtaʊ•ərɪŋ] *adj* élevé, géant; (*e.g., ambition*) sans bornes

tow'er•man *s* (*pl* **-men**) (aer, rr) aiguilleur *m*

tow'ing serv'ice [ˈto•ɪŋ] *s* service *m* de dépannage

tow'line' *s* câble *m* de remorque

town [taʊn] *s* ville *f;* **in town** en ville

town' clerk' *s* secrétaire *m* de mairie

town' coun'cil *s* conseil *m* municipal

town' cri'er *s* crieur *m* public

town' hall' *s* hôtel *m* de ville

town' plan'ning *s* urbanisme *m*

towns'folk' *spl* citadins *mpl*

town'ship *s* commune *f;* (U.S.A.) circonscription *f* administrative de six milles carrée

towns'man [ˈtaʊnzmən] *s* (*pl* **-men**) citadin *m*

towns'peo'ple *spl* citadins *mpl*

town' talk' *s* sujet *m* du jour

tow'path' *s* chemin *m* de halage

tow'rope' *s* corde *f* de remorque

tow' truck' *s* dépanneuse *f*, voiture *f* de dépannage, camion *m* de remorquage

toxic [ˈtɑksɪk] *adj* & *s* toxique *m*

tox'ic shock' syn'drome *s* syndrome *m* de choc toxique

toy [tɔɪ] *adj* (*small*) petit; (*child's*) d'enfant ‖ *s* jouet *m;* (*trifle*) bagatelle *f* ‖ *intr* jouer, s'amuser; **to toy with** (*a person*) badiner avec; (*an idea*) caresser

toy' dog' *s* chien *m* de manchon

toy' sol'dier *s* soldat *m* de plomb

trace [tres] *s* trace *f;* (*of harness*) trait *m* ‖ *tr* tracer; (*the whereabouts of s.o. or s.th.*) pister; (*e.g., an influence*) retrouver les traces de; (*a design seen through thin paper*) calquer; **to trace back** remonter jusqu'à l'origine de

trace' el'ement *s* oligo-élément *m*

tracer [ˈtresər] *s* traceur *m*

trac'er bul'let *s* balle *f* traçante

trache•a [ˈtrekɪ•ə] *s* (*pl* **-ae** [ˌi]) trachée *f*

tracing [ˈtresɪŋ] *s* tracé *m*

trac'ing tape' *s* cordeau *m*

track [træk] *s* (*of foot or vehicle*) trace *f;* (*of an animal; in a stadium*) piste *f;* (*of a boat*) sillage *m;* (*of a railroad*) voie *f;* (*of an airplane, of a hurricane*) trajet *m;* (*of a tractor*) chenille *f;* (*course followed*) chemin *m* tracé; (sports) la course et le saut de barrières; (sports) athlétisme *m;* **off the beaten track** hors des sentiers battus; **on the right track** sur la bonne voie; **to be on the wrong track** faire fausse route; **to have an inside track** tenir la corde; **to keep track of** ne pas perdre de vue; **to make tracks** (coll) filer ‖ *tr* traquer; laisser des traces de pas dans; **to track down** dépister

tracking [ˈtrækɪŋ] *s* pistage *m;* (*of spaceship*) repérage *m;* (aer) poursuite *f*

track'ing sta'tion *s* poste *m* de repérage

track'less trol'ley *s* trolleybus *m*

track' meet' *s* concours *m* de courses et de sauts, épreuve *f* d'athlétisme

track' rec'ord *s* antécédents *mpl*

track' walk'er *s* garde-voie *m*

tract [trækt] *s* (*of land*) étendue *f;* (*leaflet*) tract *m;* (anat) voie *f*

traction [ˈtrækʃən] *s* traction *f*

trac'tion com'pany *s* entreprise *f* de transports urbains

tractor [ˈtræktər] *s* tracteur *m*

trade [tred] *s* (*business*) commerce *m*, négoce *m;* (*customers*) clientèle *f;* (*calling, job*) métier *m;* (*exchange*) échange *m;* (*in slaves*) traite *f;* **to take in trade** reprendre en compte ‖ *tr* échanger; **to trade in** (*e.g., a used car*) donner en reprise ‖ *intr* commercer; **to trade in** faire le commerce de; **to trade on** exploiter

trade'-in' *s* reprise *f*

trade'mark' *s* marque *f* déposée

trade' name' *s* raison *f* sociale

trader [ˈtredər] *s* commerçant *m*

trade' school' *s* école *f* des arts et métiers

trade' show' *s* exposition *f* interprofessionnelle

trades'man *s* (*pl* **-men**) commerçant *m;* (*shopkeeper*) boutiquier *m;* (Brit) artisan *m*

trades' un'ion or **trade' un'ion** *s* syndicat *m* ouvrier

trade' war' *s* guerre *f* commerciale

trade' winds' *spl* vents *mpl* alizés

trad'ing post' [ˈtredɪŋ] *s* factorerie *f*

trad′ing stamp′ *s* timbre-prime *m*

tradition [trə′dɪ∫ən] *s* tradition *f*

traditional [trə′dɪ∫ənəl] *adj* traditionnel

traf•fic [′træfɪk] *s* (*commerce*) négoce *m*; (*in the street*) circulation *f*; (*illegal*) trafic *m*; (*in, e.g., slaves*) traite *f*; (naut, rr) trafic ‖ *v* (*pret & pp* **-ficked;** *ger* **-ficking**) *intr* trafiquer

traf′fic ac′cident *s* accident *m* de circulation

traf′fic cir′cle *s* rond-point *m*

traf′fic cop′ *s* agent *m* de la circulation

traf′fic court′ *s* tribunal *m* de simple police (pour les contraventions au code de la route)

traf′fic jam′ *s* embouteillage *m*

traf′fic light′ *s* feu *m* de circulation

traf′fic sign′ *s* panneau *m* de signalisation, poteau *m* indicateur

traf′fic sig′nal *s* signal *m* routier

traf′fic tick′et *s* contravention *f*

traf′fic vi′olator *s* contrevenant *m*

tragedian [trə′dʒɪdɪ•ən] *s* tragédien *m*

trage•dy [′trædʒɪdi] *s* (*pl* **-dies**) tragédie *f*

tragic [′trædʒɪk] *adj* tragique

trail [trel] *s* trace *f*, piste *f*; (*e.g., of smoke*) traînée *f* ‖ *tr* traîner; (*to look for*) pister ‖ *intr* traîner; (*said of a plant*) grimper; **to trail off** se perdre

trail′blaz′er *m* pionnier *m*

trailer [′trelər] *s* remorque *f*; (*for vacationing*) remorque de plaisance, caravane *f*; (mov) film-annonce *m*

trail′er court′ *s* camp *m* pour caravanes

trail′er home′ *s* caravane *f*

train [tren] *s* (*of railway cars*) train *m*; (*of dress*) traîne *f*; (*of thought*) enchaînement *m*; (*streak*) traînée *f* ‖ *tr* entraîner, former; (*plants*) palisser; (*a gun; a telescope*) pointer ‖ *intr* s'entraîner

train′ crash′ *s* accident *m* ferroviaire

train′ crew′ *s* (rr) personnel de route

trained′ an′imals *spl* animaux *mpl* savants

trained′ nurse′ *s* infirmière *f* diplômée

trainee [tre′ni] *s* stagiaire *mf*, apprenti *m*

trainer [′trenər] *s* (*of animals*) dresseur *m*; (sports) entraîneur *m*

training [′trenɪŋ] *s* entraînement *m*, formation *f*, instruction *f*; (*of animals*) dressage *m*

train′ing school′ *s* école *f* technique; (*reformatory*) maison *f* de correction

train′ing ship′ *s* navire-école *m*

trait [tret] *s* trait *m*

traitor [′tretər] *s* traître *m*

traitress [′tretrɪs] *s* traîtresse *f*

trajecto•ry [trə′dʒɛktəri] *s* (*pl* **-ries**) trajectoire *f*

tramp [træmp] *s* (*hobo*) vagabond *m*; (*sound of steps*) bruit *m* de pas lourds ‖ *tr* parcourir à pied; (*the street*) battre ‖ *intr* vagabonder; marcher lourdement; **to tramp on** marcher sur

trample [′træmpəl] *tr* fouler, piétiner ‖ *intr*—**to trample on** or **upon** fouler, piétiner

trampoline [′træmpə,lin] *s* tremplin *m* de gymnase

tramp′ steam′er *s* tramp *m*

trance [træns] *s* transe *f*; **in a trance** en transe

tranquil [′træŋkwɪ] *adj* tranquille

tranquilize [′træŋkwɪ,laɪz] *tr* tranquilliser

tranquilizer [′træŋkwɪ,laɪzər] *s* tranquillisant *m*

tranquillity [træn′kwɪlɪti] *s* tranquillité *f*

transact [træn′zækt] *tr* traiter, négocier ‖ *intr* faire des affaires

transaction [træn′zæk∫ən] *s* transaction *f*; (*of business*) conduite *f*; **transactions** (*of a society*) actes *mpl*

transatlantic [,trænsət′læntɪk] *adj & s* transatlantique *m*

transcend [træn′sɛnd] *tr* transcender ‖ *intr* se transcender

transcribe [træn′skraɪb] *tr* transcrire

transcript [′trænskrɪpt] *s* copie *f*; (*of a meeting*) procès-verbal *m*; (educ) livret *m* scolaire

transcription [træn′skrɪp∫ən] *s* transcription *f*

transept [′trænsɛpt] *s* transept *m*

trans•fer [′trænsfər] *s* (*e.g., of stock, property, etc.*) transfert *m*; (*from one place to the other*) translation *f*; (*from one job to the other*) mutation *f*; (*of a design*) décalque *m*; (*for bus or subway*) billet *m* de correspondance; (public sign) correspondance ‖ [træns′fʌr], [′trænsfər] *v* (*pret & pp* **-ferred;** *ger* **-ferring**) *tr* transférer; transporter; (*e.g., a civil servant*) déplacer; (*a design*) décalquer ‖ *intr* se déplacer; changer de train (de l'autobus, etc.)

transfix [træns′fɪks] *tr* transpercer

transform [træns′fɔrm] *tr* transformer ‖ *intr* se transformer

transformer [træns′fɔrmər] *s* transformateur *m*

transfusion [træns′fjuʒən] *s* transfusion *f*

transgress [træns′grɛs] *tr & intr* transgresser

transgression [træns′grɛ∫ən] *s* transgression *f*

transient [′træn∫ənt] *adj* transitoire, passager; (*e.g., guest*) de passage ‖ *s* hôte *mf* de passage

transistor [træn′sɪstər] *s* transistor *m*

transistorize [træn′zɪstə,raɪz] *tr* transistoriser

transistorized *adj* transistorisé, à transistors

transis′tor ra′dio *s* transistor *m*

transit [′trænsɪt] *s* transit *m*

transition [træn′zɪ∫ən] *s* transition *f*

transitional [træn′zɪ∫ənəl] *adj* transitoire, de transition

transitive [′trænsɪtɪv] *adj* transitif ‖ *s* verbe *m* transitif

transitory [′trænsɪ,tori] *adj* transitoire

translate [′trænslet] *tr* traduire

translation [træns′le∫ən] *s* traduction *f*; (*transfer*) translation *f*

translator [træns′letər] *s* traducteur *m*

transliterate [træns′lɪtə,ret] *tr* translitérer

translucent [træns′lusənt] *adj* translucide, diaphane

transmission [træns′mɪ∫ən] *s* transmission *f*; (*gear change*) changement *m* de vitesse; (*housing for gears*) boîte *f* de vitesses

transmis′sion-gear′ box′ *s* boîte *f* de vitesses

trans•mit [træns′mɪt] *v* (*pret & pp* **-mitted;**

ger -mitting) *tr* & *intr* transmettre; (rad) émettre

transmitter [træns'mɪtər] *s* (telg, telp) transmetteur *m;* (rad) émetteur *m*

transmit'ting sta'tion *s* poste *m* émetteur

transmute [træns'mjut] *tr* transmuer

transom ['trænsəm] *s* (*crosspiece*) linteau *m;* (*window over door*) imposte *f*, vasistas *m;* (*of ship*) barre *f* d'arcasse

transparen•cy [træns'pɛrənsi] *s* (*pl* -cies) transparence *f;* (phot) diapositive *f*

transparent [træns'pɛrənt] *adj* transparent

transpire [træns'paɪr] *intr* se passer; (*to leak out*) transpirer

transplant ['træns,plænt] *s* (*organ or tissue*) greffon *m;* (*operation*) greffe *f* ‖ [træns'plænt] *tr* transplanter; (*e.g., a heart*) greffer

transport ['trænsport] *s* transport *m* ‖ [træns'port] *tr* transporter

transportation [,trænspor'teʃən] *s* transport *m;* billet *m* de train, de bateau, or d'avion; (*deportation*) transportation *f*

transport'er bridge' [træns'portər] *s* transbordeur *m*

trans'port work'er *s* employé *m* des entreprises de transport

transpose [træns'poz] *tr* transposer

trans•ship [træns'ʃɪp] *v* (*pret* & *pp* -shipped; *ger* -shipping) *tr* transborder

transshipment [træns'ʃɪpmənt] *s* transbordement *m*

transvestism [træns'vɛstɪzəm] *s* travestisme *m*

transvestite [træns'vɛstaɪt] *s* travesti *m*, travestie *f*

trap [træp] *s* piège *m;* (*pitfall*) trappe *f;* (*double-curved pipe*) siphon *m;* **traps** (mus) batterie *f* de jazz ‖ *v* (*pret* & *pp* **trapped;** *ger* **trapping**) *tr* prendre au piège, attraper

trap' door' *s* trappe *f*

trapeze [trə'piz] *s* trapèze *m*

trapezoid ['træpɪ,zɔɪd] *s* trapèze *m*

trapper ['træpər] *s* trappeur *m*

trappings ['træpɪŋz] *spl* (*adornments*) atours *mpl;* (*of horse's harness*) harnachement *m*

trap'shoot'ing *s* tir *m* au pigeon, ball-trap *m*

trash [træʃ] *s* déchets *mpl*, rebuts *mpl;* (*junk*) camelote *f;* (*nonsense*) ineptie *f;* (*worthless people*) racaille *f*

trash' bag' *s* sac *m* poubelle

trash' can' *s* poubelle *f*

trauma ['traumə] *s* traumatisme *m;* (psychol) trauma *m*, traumatisme *m*

traumatic [trau'mætɪk] *adj* traumatique

travail [trə'vel] *s* labeur *m;* douleur *f* de l'enfantement

trav•el ['trævəl] *s* voyages *mpl;* (mach) course *f* ‖ *v* (*pret* & *pp* -eled or -elled; *ger* -eling or -elling) *tr* parcourir ‖ *intr* voyager; (mach) se déplacer

trav'el a'gent *s* agent *m* touristique

trav'el a'gency *s* agence *f* de voyages

trav'el bur'eau *s* agence *f* de voyages

traveler ['trævələr] *s* voyageur *m*

trav'eler's check' *s* chèque *m* de voyage

trav'eling bag' *s* sac *m* de voyage

trav'eling expen'ses *spl* frais *mpl* de voyage

trav'eling sales'man *s* (*pl* -men) commis *m* voyageur

traverse [trə'vʌrs] *tr* parcourir, traverser

traves•ty ['trævɪsti] *s* (*pl* -ties) *s* travestissement *m* ‖ *v* (*pret* & *pp* -tied) *tr* travestir

trawl [trɔl] *s* chalut *m* ‖ *tr* traîner ‖ *intr* pêcher au chalut

trawler ['trɔlər] *s* chalutier *m*

tray [tre] *s* plateau *m;* (*of refrigerator*) bac *f;* (chem, phot) cuvette *f*

treacherous ['trɛtʃərəs] *adj* traître

treacher•y ['trɛtʃəri] *s* (*pl* -ies) trahison *f*

tread [trɛd] *s* (*step; sound of steps*) pas *m;* (*gait*) allure *f;* (*of stairs*) giron *m;* (*of tire*) chape *f;* (*of shoe*) semelle *f;* (*of egg*) cicatricule *f* ‖ *v* (*pret* **trod** [trad]; *pp* **trodden** ['tradən] or **trod**) *tr* marcher sur, piétiner ‖ *intr* marcher

treadle ['trɛdəl] *s* pédale *f*

tread'less *adj* (*tire*) à chape usée

tread'mill' *s* trépigneuse *f;* (*futile drudgery*) besogne *f* ingrate

treason ['trizən] *s* trahison *f*

treasonable ['trizənəbəl] *adj* traître

treasure ['trɛʒər] *s* trésor *m* ‖ *tr* garder soigneusement; (*to prize*) tenir beaucoup à

trea'sure hunt' *s* chasse *f* au trésor

treasurer ['trɛʒərər] *s* trésorier *m*

treasur•y ['trɛʒəri] *s* (*pl* -ies) trésorerie *f;* trésor *m*

treat [trit] *s* régal *m*, plaisir *m* ‖ *tr* traiter; régaler; (*to a drink*) payer à boire à; **to treat everyone to a round of drinks** offrir la tournée générale ‖ *intr* traiter

treatise ['tritɪs] *s* traité *m*

treatment ['tritmənt] *s* traitement *m*

trea•ty ['triti] *s* (*pl* -ties) traité *m*

treble ['trɛbəl] *adj* (*threefold*) triple; (mus) de soprano ‖ *s* soprano *mf;* (*voice*) soprano *m* ‖ *tr* & *intr* tripler

tre'ble clef' [klɛf] *s* clef *f* de sol

tree [tri] *s* arbre *m*

tree' farm' *s* taillis *m*

treeless ['trilɪs] *adj* sans arbres

tree'top' *s* cime *f* d'un arbre

trellis ['trɛlɪs] *s* treillis *m*, treillage *m;* (*summerhouse*) tonnelle *f* ‖ *tr* treillager

tremble ['trɛmbəl] *s* tremblement *m* ‖ *intr* trembler

tremendous [trɪ'mɛndəs] *adj* terrible; (coll) formidable

tremolo ['trɛmə,lo] *s* trémolo *m*

tremor ['trɛmər] *s* tremblement *m*

trench [trɛntʃ] *s* tranché *f*

trenchant ['trɛntʃənt] *adj* tranchant

trench' mor'tar *s* lance-bombes *m*

trend [trɛnd] *s* tendance *f*, cours *m*

trendy ['trɛndi] *adj* dernier cri, dans le vent, à la dernière mode

trespass ['trɛspəs] *s* (*illegal entry*) entrée *f* sans permission; (rel) offense f ‖ intr entrer sans permission; **no trespassing** (public sign) défense d'entrer; **to trespass against** offenser; **to trespass on** empiéter sur; (s.o.'s patience) abuser de

trespasser [ˈtrɛspəsər] s intrus m

tress [trɛs] s tresse f; **tresses** chevelure f

trestle [ˈtrɛsəl] s tréteau m; (bridge) pont m en treillis

trial [ˈtraɪ•əl] s essai m; (difficulty) épreuve f; (law) procès m; **on trial** à titre d'essai; (law) en jugement; **to bring to trial** faire passer en jugement

tri′al and er′ror s—**by trial and error** par tâtonnements

tri′al balloon′ s ballon m d'essai

tri′al by jur′y s jugement m par jury

tri′al ju′ry s jury m de jugement

tri′al or′der s commande f d'essai

tri′al run′ s course f d'essai

triangle [ˈtraɪˌæŋgəl] s triangle m

tribe [traɪb] s tribu f

tribunal [trɪˈbjunəl] s tribunal m

tribune [ˈtrɪbjun] s tribune f

tributar•y [ˈtrɪbjəˌtɛri] adj tributaire ‖ s (pl -ies) tributaire m

tribute [ˈtrɪbjut] s (homage; payment) tribut m; **to pay tribute to** (e.g., merit) rendre hommage à

trice [traɪs] s—**in a trice** en un clin d'œil

trichinosis [ˌtrɪkəˈnosɪs] s (pathol) trichinose f

trick [trɪk] s (prank, joke) tour m, farce f, blague f; (artifice) ruse f; (cards in one round) levée f; (habit) manie f; (girl) (coll) belle f; **to be up to one's old tricks again** faire encore des siennes; **to play a dirty trick on** faire un vilain tour à, faire un tour de cochon à; **tricks of the trade** trucs mpl du métier ‖ tr duper

tricker•y [ˈtrɪkəri] s (pl -ies) tromperie f

trickle [ˈtrɪkəl] s filet m ‖ intr dégoutter

trickster [ˈtrɪkstər] s fourbe mf

trick•y [ˈtrɪki] adj (comp -ier; super -iest) rusé; (difficult) compliqué, délicat

tricolor [ˈtraɪˌkʌlər] adj & s tricolore m

tricorn [ˈtraɪkɔrn] s tricorne m

tried [traɪd] adj loyal, éprouvé

trifle [ˈtraɪfəl] s bagatelle f; (article of little value) bricole f; **trifles** futilités fpl ‖ tr—**to trifle away** gaspiller ‖ intr badiner

trifling [ˈtraɪflɪŋ] adj frivole; insignifiant

trifocals [traɪˈfokəlz] spl lunettes fpl à trois foyers

trigger [ˈtrɪgər] s (of gun) détente f; (of any device) déclencheur m; **to pull the trigger** appuyer sur la détente ‖ tr déclencher

trig′ger-hap′py adj—**to be trigger-happy** (coll) avoir la gâchette facile

trigonometry [ˌtrɪgəˈnɑmɪtri] s trigonométrie f

trill [trɪl] s trille m ‖ tr & intr triller

trillion [ˈtrɪljən] s (U.S.A.) billion m; (Brit) trillion m

trilo•gy [ˈtrɪlɔdʒi] s (pl -gies) trilogie f

trim [trɪm] adj (comp **trimmer**; super **trim-**

mest) ordonné, coquet ‖ s (condition) état m; (adornment) ornement m; (of sails) orientation f; (around doors and windows) moulures fpl; **in good trim** (sports) en bonne forme ‖ v (pret & pp **trimmed**; ger **trimming**) tr enguirlander; (a Christmas tree) orner; (hat, dress, etc.) garnir; (the hair) rafraîchir; (a candle or lamp) moucher; (trees, plants) tailler; (the edges of a book) rogner; (the sails) orienter; (coll) battre

trimming [ˈtrɪmɪŋ] s (of clothes, hat, etc.) garniture f; (of hedges) taille f; (of sails) orientation f; **to get a trimming** (coll) essuyer une défaite

trini•ty [ˈtrɪnɪti] s (pl -ties) trinité f; **Trinity** Trinité

trinket [ˈtrɪŋkɪt] s colifichet m; (trifle) babiole f

tri•o [ˈtri•o] s (pl -os) trio m

trip [trɪp] s (journey) voyage m; (distance covered) trajet m, parcours m; (stumble; blunder) faux pas m; (act of causing a person to stumble) croc-en-jambe m; (on drugs) (slang) trip m, défonce f ‖ v (pret & pp **tripped**; ger **tripping**) tr faire trébucher; **to trip up** donner un croc-en-jambe à; prendre en défaut ‖ intr trébucher

tripartite [traɪˈpɑrtaɪt] adj tripartite

tripe [traɪp] s tripe f; (slang) fatras m

trip′ham′mer s marteau m à bascule

triple [ˈtrɪpəl] adj & s triple m ‖ tr & intr tripler

triplet [ˈtrɪplɪt] s (offspring) triplet m; (stanza) tercet m; (mus) triolet m; **triplets** (offspring) triplés mpl

triplicate [ˈtrɪplɪkɪt] adj triple ‖ s triplicata m; **in triplicate** en trois exemplaires

tripod [ˈtraɪpɑd] s trépied m

triptych [ˈtrɪptɪk] s triptyque m

trite [traɪt] adj banal, rebattu

triumph [ˈtraɪ•əmf] s triomphe m ‖ intr triompher; **to triumph over** triompher de

trium′phal arch′ [traɪˈʌmfəl] s arc m de triomphe

triumphant [traɪˈʌmfənt] adj triomphant

trivia [ˈtrɪvi•ə] spl vétilles fpl

trivial [ˈtrɪvi•əl] adj trivial, insignifiant

triviali•ty [ˌtrɪviˈælɪti] s (pl -ties) trivialité f, insignifiance f

Trojan [ˈtrodʒən] adj troyen ‖ s Troyen m

Tro′jan Horse′ s cheval m de Troie

Tro′jan war′ s guerre f de Troie

troll [trol] tr & intr pêcher à la cuiller

trolley [ˈtrɑli] s trolley m; (streetcar) tramway m

trol′ley car′ s tramway m

trol′ley pole′ s perche f

trolling [ˈtrolɪŋ] s pêche f à la cuiller

trollop [ˈtrɑləp] s souillon f; (prostitute) traînée f

trombone [ˈtrɑmbon] s trombone m

troop [trup] s troupe f; **troops** (mil) troupes fpl ‖ tr (the colors) présenter ‖ intr s'attrouper

troop′ car′rier s (aer) avion m de transport militaire; (aut) transport *m* de troupes; (nav) transport *m*

trooper [ˈtrupər] *s* membre *m* de la police montée; (*state trooper*) agent *m* de police; (mil) soldat *m* de cavalerie; **to swear like a trooper** jurer comme un charretier

tro•phy [ˈtrofi] *s* (*pl* **-phies**) trophée *m;* (sports) coupe *f*

tropic [ˈtrɑpɪk] *adj* & *s* tropique *m; tropics* tropiques, zone *f* tropicale

tropical [ˈtrɑpɪkəl] *adj* tropical

troposphere [ˈtrɑpə‚sfɪr] *s* troposphère *f*

trot [trɑt] *s* trot *m* ‖ *v* (*pret* & *pp* **trotted**; *ger* **trotting**) *tr* faire trotter; **to trot out** (slang) exhiber ‖ *intr* trotter

troth [troθ] *s* foi *f;* **in troth** en vérité; **to plight one's troth** promettre fidélité; donner sa promesse de mariage

trouble [ˈtrʌbəl] *s* (*unpleasantness*) ennuis *mpl,* dérangement *m;* (*problem*) difficulté *f,* problème *m;* (*bother, effort*) mal *m,* peine *f;* (*social unrest*) troubles *mpl;* **that's not worth the trouble** cela ne vaut pas la peine; **that's the trouble** voilà le hic; **the trouble is that . . .** la difficulté c'est que . . . ; **to be in trouble** avoir des ennuis; (*said of a woman*) (coll) faire Pâques avant les Rameaux; **to be looking for trouble** chercher querelle; **to get into trouble** se créer des ennuis, s'attirer une mauvaise affaire; **to take the trouble to** se donner la peine de; **with very little trouble** à peu de frais ‖ *tr* (*to disturb*) déranger; (*to grieve*) affliger; **to be troubled about** se tourmenter au sujet de; **to trouble oneself** s'inquiéter ‖ *intr* se déranger; **to trouble to** se donner la peine de

trou′ble-free′ *adj* sans ennuis, sans problèmes

trou′ble light′ *s* lampe *f* de secours

trou′ble•mak′er *s* fomentateur *m,* perturbateur *m*

troubleshooter [ˈtrʌbəl‚ʃutər] *s* dépanneur *m;* (*in disputes*) arbitre *m*

trou′ble•shoot′ing *s* dépannage *m;* (*of disputes*) composition *f,* arbitrage *m*

troublesome [ˈtrʌbəlsəm] *adj* ennuyeux

trou′ble spot′ *s* foyer *m* de conflit

trough [trɔf] *s* (*e.g., to knead bread*) pétrin *m;* (*for water for animals*) abreuvoir *m;* (*for feeding animals*) auge *f;* (*under the eaves*) chéneau *m;* (*between two waves*) creux *m*

troupe [trup] *s* troupe *f*

trouper [ˈtrupər] *s* membre *m* de la troupe; vieil acteur *m;* vieux routier *m*

trousers [ˈtrauzərz] *spl* pantalon *m*

trous•seau [truˈso], [ˈtruso] *s* (*pl* **-seaux** or **-seaus**) trousseau *m*

trout [traut] *s* truite *f*

trowel [ˈtrauˑəl] *s* truelle *f;* (*for gardening*) déplantoir *m*

Troy [trɔɪ] *s* Troie *f*

truant [ˈtruˑənt] *s*—**to play truant** faire l'école buissonnière

truce [trus] *s* trêve *f*

truck [trʌk] *s* camion *m,* poids *m* lourd; (*for baggage*) diable *m;* (*vegetables*) produits *mpl* maraîchers; **to have no truck with** (coll) refuser d'avoir affaire à ‖ *tr* camionner

truck′ driv′er *s* camionneur *m*

truck′ farm′ing *s* culture *f* maraîchère

truck′ gar′den *s* jardin *m* maraîcher

trucking [ˈtrʌkɪŋ] *s* camionnage *m*

truculent [ˈtrʌkjələnt] *adj* truculent

trudge [trʌdʒ] *intr* cheminer

true [tru] *adj* vrai; loyal; (*exact*) juste; (*copy*) conforme; **to come true** se réaliser ‖ *tr* rectifier, dégauchir

true′ cop′y *s* (*pl* **-ies**) copie *f* conforme

true′-heart′ed *adj* au cœur sincère

true′love *s* bien-aimé *m*

truffle [ˈtrʌfəl] *s* truffe *f*

truism [ˈtruˑɪzm] *s* truisme *m*

truly [ˈtruli] *adv* vraiment; sincèrement; **yours truly** (complimentary close) veuillez agréer, Monsieur (Madame, etc.), l'assurance de mes sentiments distingués

trump [trʌmp] *s* atout *m;* brave garçon *m,* brave fille *f;* **no trump** sans atout ‖ *tr* couper; **to trump up** inventer ‖ *intr* couper

trumpet [ˈtrʌmpɪt] *s* trompette *f* ‖ *tr* & *intr* trompeter

trumpeter [ˈtrʌmpətər] *s* trompette *m*

truncheon [ˈtrʌntʃən] *s* matraque *f,* casse-tête *m;* (*of policeman*) bâton *m*

trunk [trʌŋk] *s* (*chest for clothes*) malle *f;* (*of elephant*) trompe *f;* (anat, bot) tronc *m;* (aut) coffre *m;* **trunks** slip *m*

trunk′ light′ *s* (aut) lumière *f* du coffre

truss [trʌs] *s* (*framework*) armature *f;* (med) bandage *m* herniaire ‖ *tr* armer; (culin) trousser

trust [trʌst] *s* confiance *f;* (*hope*) espoir *m;* (*duty*) charge *f;* (*safekeeping*) dépôt *m;* (com) trust *m,* cartel *m* ‖ *tr* se fier à; (*to entrust*) confier; (com) faire crédit à ‖ *intr* espérer; **to trust in** avoir confiance en

trust′ com′pany *s* crédit *m,* société *f* de banque

trustee [trʌsˈti] *s* administrateur *m;* (*of a university*) régent *m;* (*of an estate*) fidéi-commissaire *m*

trusteeship [trʌsˈtiˑʃɪp] *s* tutelle *f*

trustful [ˈtrʌstfəl] *adj* confiant

trust′ fund′ *s* fonds *m* en fidéicommis

trust′wor′thy *adj* digne de confiance

trust•y [ˈtrʌsti] *adj* (*comp* **-ier;** *super* **-iest**) sûr, loyal ‖ *s* (*pl* **-ies**) forçat *m* bien noté

truth [truθ] *s* vérité *f;* **in truth** en vérité

truthful [ˈtruθfəl] *adj* véridique

try [traɪ] *s* (*pl* **tries**) essai *m* ‖ *v* (*pret* & *pp* **tried**) *tr* mettre à l'épreuve; (law) juger; **to try on** or **out** essayer ‖ *intr* essayer; **to try to** essayer de

trying [ˈtraɪˑɪŋ] *adj* pénible

try′out′ *s* essai *m;* (theat) essai d'un rôle; (theat) représentation *f* d'une pièce avant la première

tryst [trɪst], [traɪst] *s* rendez-vous *m*

T′-shirt′ *s* gilet *m* de peau avec manches

tub [tʌb] s cuvier m, baquet m; (clumsy boat) (coll) rafiot m

tube [t(j)ub] s tube m; (aut) chambre f à air; (subway) (Brit) métro m

tube′less tire′ s pneu m sans chambre à air

tuber [′t(j)ubər] s tubercule m

tubercle [′t(j)ubərkəl] s tubercule m

tuberculosis [t(j)u‚bʌrkjə′losɪs] s tuberculose f

tuck [tʌk] s pli m, rempli m ‖ tr plisser, remplier; **to tuck away** reléguer; **to tuck in** rentrer; **to tuck in bed** border; **to tuck up** retrousser

tucker [′tʌkər] tr—**to tucker out** (coll) fatiguer

Tuesday [′t(j)uzdi] s mardi m

tuft [tʌft] s touffe f ‖ tr garnir de touffes ‖ intr former une touffe

tug [tʌg] s tiraillement m, effort m; (boat) remorqueur m ‖ v (pret & pp **tugged;** ger **tugging**) tr tirer fort; (a boat) remorquer ‖ intr tirer fort

tug′boat′ s remorqueur m

tug′ of war′ s lutte f à la corde (de traction)

tuition [t(j)u′ɪʃən] s enseignement m; (fees) frais mpl de scolarité

tulip [′t(j)ulɪp] s tulipe f

tumble [′tʌmbəl] s chute f; (sports) culbute f ‖ tr culbuter ‖ intr tomber, culbuter; (sports) faire des culbutes; (to catch on) (slang) comprendre; **to tumble down** dégringoler

tum′ble‑down′ adj croulant, délabré

tumbler [′tʌmblər] s gobelet m, verre m; acrobate m; (self‑righting toy) poussah m, ramponneau m

tummy [′tʌmi] s (coll) bide f

tumor [′t(j)umər] s tumeur f

tumult [′t(j)umʌlt] s tumulte m

tun [tʌn] s tonne f

tuna [′tunə] s thon m

tune [t(j)un] s air m; (manner of acting or speaking) ton m; **in tune** (mus) accordé; (rad) en syntonie; **out of tune** (mus) désaccordé; **to change one's tune** (coll) changer de disque ‖ tr accorder; (a radio or television set) régler; **to tune in** (rad) syntoniser; **to tune up** régler

tungsten [′tʌŋstən] s tungstène m

tunic [′t(j)unɪk] s tunique f

tuning [′t(j)unɪŋ] s réglage m; (rad) syntonisation f

tun′ing coil′ s bobine f de syntonisation

tun′ing fork′ s diapason m

tun‑nel [′tʌnəl] s tunnel m; (min) galerie f ‖ v (pret & pp **‑neled** or **nelled;** ger **‑neling** or **‑nelling**) tr percer un tunnel dans or sous

tun′nel vi′sion s (opt) rétrécissement m du champ visuel; (fig) étroitesse f de vues

turban [′tʌrbən] s turban m

turbid [′tʌrbɪd] adj trouble

turbine [′tʌrbɪn] s turbine f

turbojet [′tʌrbo‚dʒɛt] s turboréacteur m; avion m à turboréacteur

turboprop [′tʌrbo‚prɑp] s turbopropulseur m; avion m à turbopropulseur

turbosupercharger [′tʌrbo′supər′t∫ɑrdʒər] s turbocompresseur m de suralimentation

turbulent [′tʌrbjələnt] adj turbulent

tureen [t(j)u′rin] s soupière f

turf [tʌrf] s gazon m; (sod) motte f de gazon; (peat) tourbe f; **the turf** le turf

turf′man s (pl **‑men**) turfiste mf

Turk [tʌrk] s Turc m

turkey [′tʌrki] s dindon m; (culin) dinde f; (flop) (slang) four m; **Turkey** Turquie f; la Turquie

Turkish [′tʌrkɪʃ] adj & s turc m

Turk′ish delight′ s loukoum m

Turk′ish tow′el s serviette f éponge

turmoil [′tʌrmɔɪl] s agitation f

turn [tʌrn] s tour m; (change of direction) virage m; (bend) tournant m; (of events; of an expression) tournure f; (in a wire) spire f; (coll) coup m, choc m; **at every turn** à tout propos; **by turns** tour à tour; **in turn** à tour de rôle; **to a turn** (culin) à point; **to do a good turn** rendre un service; **to take turns** alterner; **to wait one's turn** prendre son tour; **whose turn is it?** à qui le tour? ‖ tr tourner; **to turn about** or **around** retourner; **to turn aside** or **away** détourner; **to turn back** renvoyer; (an attack) repousser; (a clock) retarder; **to turn down** (a collar) rabattre; (e.g., the gas) baisser; (an offer) refuser; **to turn from** détourner de; **to turn in** replier; (a wrongdoer) dénoncer; **to turn into** changer en; **to turn off** (the water, the gas, etc.) fermer; (the light, the radio, etc.) éteindre; (a road) quitter; **to turn on** (the water, the gas, etc.) ouvrir; (the light, the radio, etc.) allumer; **to turn out** mettre dehors; (to manufacture) produire; (e.g., the light) éteindre; **to turn over and over** tourner et retourner; **to turn up** (a collar) relever; (one's sleeves) retrousser; (to unearth) déterrer ‖ intr tourner, se tourner; (said of milk) tourner; (to toss and turn) se retourner; (to be dizzy) tourner, e.g., **his head is turning** la tête lui tourne; **to turn about** or **around** se retourner, se tourner; **to turn aside** or **away** se détourner; **to turn back** rebrousser chemin; **to turn down** se rabattre; **to turn in** (coll) aller se coucher; **to turn into** tourner à or en; **to turn on** se jeter sur; (to depend on) dépendre de; **to turn out to be** se trouver être; **to turn out well** tourner bien; **to turn over** se retourner; (said of auto) capoter; **to turn up** (to increase) se relever; (to appear) se présenter, arriver

turn′ around′ s volte‑face f; (comp) traitement m

turn′ around time′ s (comp) temps m d'accès

turn′coat′ s transfuge m

turn′down′ adj rabattu ‖ s refus m

turn′ing point′ s moment m décisif

turnip [′tʌrnɪp] s navet m; (big watch) (slang) bassinoire f; (slang) tête f de bois

turn′key′ s geôlier m

turn′ of life′ s retour m d'âge

turn′ of mind′ s inclination f naturelle

turn′out′ s (*gathering*) assistance f; (*output*) rendement m; (*equipment*) attelage m

turn′o′ver s renversement m; (com) chiffre m d'affaires

turn′pike′ s autoroute f à péage

turn′pike res′taurants spl ponts mpl restaurants

turn′spit′ s tournebroche m

turnstile [′tʌrn,staɪl] s tourniquet m

turn′stone′ s (orn) tourne-pierre m

turn′ta′ble s (*of phonograph*) plateau m porte-disque; (rr) plaque f tournante

turpentine [′tʌrpən,taɪn] s térébenthine f

turpitude [′tʌrpɪ,t(j)ud] s turpitude f

turquoise [′tʌrkɔɪz] s turquoise f

turret [′tʌrɪt] s tourelle f

turreted adj en poivrière

turtle [′tʌrtəl] s tortue f

tur′tle•dove′ s tourterelle f

tur′tle•neck′ s col m roulé

tur′tle•neck sweat′er s sweater m or chandail m à col roulé

Tuscan [′tʌskən] adj & s toscan m

Tuscany [′tʌskəni] s Toscane f; la Toscane

tusk [tʌsk] s défense f

tussle [′tʌsəl] s bagarre f ‖ intr se bagarrer

tutor [′t(j)utər] s précepteur m, répétiteur m ‖ tr donner des leçons particulières à ‖ intr donner des leçons particulières

tuxe•do [tʌk′sido] s (*pl* **-dos**) smoking m

TV [′ti′vi] s (letterword) (**television**) tévé f, télé f

T′V′ din′ner s plateau-repas m congelé

twaddle [′twadəl] s fadaises fpl ‖ intr dire des fadaises

twang [twæŋ] s (*of musical instrument*) son m vibrant; (*of voice*) ton m nasillard ‖ tr faire résonner; dire en nasillant ‖ intr nasiller

twang•y [′twæŋi] adj (*comp* **-ier**; *super* **-iest**) (*nasal*) nasillard; (*resonant*) vibrant

'twas [twɑz], [twəz] abbr (poet) **it was**

tweed [twid] s tweed m

tweet [twit] s pépiement m ‖ intr pépier

tweeter [′twitər] s (rad) tweeter m

tweezers [′twizərz] spl brucelles fpl; pince f à épiler

twelfth [twɛlfθ] adj & pron douzième (*masc, fem*); **the Twelfth** douze, e.g., **John the Twelfth** Jean douze ‖ s douzième m; **the twelfth** (*in dates*) le douze

twelve [twɛlv] adj & pron douze; **about twelve** une douzaine de ‖ s douze m; **twelve o'clock** (*noon*) midi m; (*midnight*) minuit m

twentieth [′twɛntɪ•θ] adj & pron vingtième (*masc, fem*); **the Twentieth** vingt, e.g., **John the Twentieth** Jean vingt ‖ s vingt m; **the twentieth** (*in dates*) le vingt

twen•ty [′twɛnti] adj & pron vingt; **about twenty** une vingtaine de ‖ s (*pl* **-ties**) vingt m; **the twenties** les années fpl vingt

twen′ty-first′ adj & pron vingt et unième (*masc, fem*); **the Twenty-first** vingt et un, e.g., **John the Twenty-first** Jean vingt et un

‖ s vingt et unième m; **the twenty-first** (*in dates*) le vingt et un

twen′ty-one′ adj & pron vingt et un ‖ s vingt et un m; (cards) vingt-et-un

twen′ty-sec′ond adj & pron vingt-deuxième (*masc, fem*); **the Twenty-second** vingt-deux, e.g., **John the Twenty-second** Jean vingt-deux ‖ s vingt-deuxième m; **the twenty-second** (*in dates*) le vingt-deux

twen′ty-two′ adj, pron, & s vingt-deux m

twice [twaɪs] adv deux fois; **twice over** à deux reprises

twice′-told′ adj dit deux fois; bien connu

twiddle [′twɪdəl] tr tourner, jouer avec; (*e.g., one's moustache*) tortiller

twig [twɪg] s brindille f

twilight [′twaɪ,laɪt] adj crépusculaire ‖ s crépuscule m

twill [twɪl] s croisé m ‖ tr croiser

twin [twɪn] adj & s jumeau m ‖ v (*pret & pp* **twinned**; *ger* **twinning**) tr jumeler

twin′ beds′ spl lits mpl jumeaux

twin′ broth′er s jumeau m

twine [twaɪn] s ficelle f ‖ tr enrouler ‖ intr s'enrouler

twinge [twɪndʒ] s élancement m ‖ intr élancer

twin′jet′ plane′ s biréacteur m

twinkle [′twɪŋkəl] s scintillement m; (*of the eye*) clignotement m ‖ intr scintiller; clignoter

twin′-screw′ adj à hélices jumelles

twin′ sis′ter s jumelle f

twin′ tow′ers spl tours fpl jumelles

twirl [twʌrl] s tournoiement m ‖ tr faire tournoyer; (*e.g., a cane*) faire des moulinets avec ‖ intr tournoyer

twist [twɪst] s (*action*) torsion f; (*strand*) cordon m; (*of the wrist, of rope, etc.*) tour m; (*of the road, river, etc.*) coude m; (*of tobacco*) rouleau m; (*of the ankle*) entorse f; (*of mind or disposition*) prédisposition f ‖ tr tordre, tortiller ‖ intr se tordre, se tortiller; **to twist and turn** (*said, e.g., of road*) serpenter; (*said of sleeper*) se tourner et se retourner

twister [′twɪstər] s (coll) tornade f

twit [twɪt] v (*pret & pp* **twitted**; *ger* **twitting**) tr taquiner

twitch [twɪtʃ] s crispation f ‖ intr se crisper

twitter [′twɪtər] s gazouillement m ‖ intr gazouiller

two [tu] adj & pron deux ‖ s deux m; **to put two and two together** raisonner juste; **two o'clock** deux heures

two′-cy′cle adj (mach) à deux temps

two′-cyl′inder adj (mach) à deux cylindres

two′-edged′ adj à deux tranchants, à double tranchant

two′-faced′ adj hypocrite

two′-fist′ed adj fort, robuste, batailleur

two′ hun′dred adj, pron, & s deux cents m

twosome [′tusəm] s paire f; jeu m à deux joueurs

two′-time′ tr (slang) tromper

two′-way street′ s rue f à double sens

tycoon [taɪ′kun] s (coll) magnat m

type [taɪp] *s* type *m* ‖ *tr* typer; (*to typewrite*) taper; (*a sample of blood*) chercher le groupe sanguin sur ‖ *intr* taper

type′face′ *s* œil *m*

type′script′ *s* manuscrit *m* dactylographié

typesetter [ˈtaɪpˌsɛtər] *s* compositeur *m*, typographe *mf;* machine *f* à composer

type′write′ *v* (*pret* -**wrote;** *pp* -**written**) *tr* & *intr* taper à la machine

type′writ′er *s* machine *f* à écrire

type′writer rib′bon *s* ruban *m* encreur

type′writ′ing *s* dactylographie *f*

ty′phoid fe′ver [ˈtaɪfɔɪd] *s* fièvre *f* typhoïde

typhoon [taɪˈfun] *s* typhon *m*

typical [ˈtɪpɪkəl] *adj* typique

typi•fy [ˈtɪpɪˌfaɪ] *v* (*pret* & *pp* -**fied**) *tr* symboliser; être le type de

typ′ing er′ror *s* faute *f* de frappe

typist [ˈtaɪpɪst] *s* dactylo *f*

typographic(al) [ˌtaɪpəˈgræfɪk(əl)] *adj* typographique

typograph′ical er′ror *s* erreur *f* typographique

typography [taɪˈpɑgrəfi] *s* typographie *f*

tyrannic(al) [tɪˈrænɪk(əl)] *adj* tyrannique

tyran•ny [ˈtɪrəni] *s* (*pl* -**nies**) tyrannie *f*

tyrant [ˈtaɪrənt] *s* tyran *m*

ty•ro [ˈtaɪro] *s* (*pl* -**ros**) novice *mf*

U

U, u [ju] *s* XXIᵉ lettre de l'alphabet

ubiquitous [juˈbɪkwɪtəs] *adj* ubiquiste, omniprésent

udder [ˈʌdər] *s* pis *m*

UFO [ˈjuˈɛfˈo] *s* (letterword) (**unidentified flying object**) O.V.N.I. (objet volant nonidentifié)

UFOlogy [juˈfɑlədʒi] *s* étude *f* des ovnis

ugliness [ˈʌglɪnɪs] *s* laideur *f*

ug•ly [ˈʌgli] *adj* (*comp* -**lier;** *super* -**liest**) laid; (*disagreeable; mean*) vilain

Ukraine [ˈjukren], [juˈkren] *s* Ukraine *f;* l'Ukraine

Ukrainian [juˈkrenɪ•ən] *adj* ukrainien ‖ *s* (*language*) ukrainien *m;* (*person*) Ukrainien *m*

ulcer [ˈʌlsər] *s* ulcère *m*

ulcerate [ˈʌlsəˌret] *tr* ulcérer ‖ *intr* s'ulcérer

ulterior [ʌlˈtɪrɪ•ər] *adj* ultérieur; secret, inavoué

ultimate [ˈʌltɪmɪt] *adj* ultime, final, définitif

ultima•tum [ˌʌltɪˈmetəm] *s* (*pl* -**tums** or -**ta** [tə]) ultimatum *m*

ultrahigh [ˌʌltrəˈhaɪ] *adj* (electron) de fréquence très élevée

ultrashort [ˌʌltrəˈʃɔrt] *adj* (electron) ultracourt

ultrasound [ˈʌltrəˌsaʊnd] *s* (electron) ultrason *m*

ultraviolet [ˌʌltrəˈvaɪ•əlɪt] *adj* & *s* ultraviolet *m*

ul′travi′olet light′ *s* lumière *f* ultraviolette

umbil′ical cord′ [ʌmˈbɪlɪkəl] *s* cordon *m* ombilical

umbrage [ˈʌmbrɪdʒ] *s*—**to take umbrage at** prendre ombrage de

umbrella [ʌmˈbrɛlə] *s* parapluie *m;* (mil) ombrelle *f* de protection

umbrel′la stand′ *s* porte-parapluies *m*

umlaut [ˈumlaut] *s* métaphonie *f,* inflexion *f* vocalique; (*mark*) tréma ‖ *tr* changer le timbre de; écrire avec un tréma

umpire [ˈʌmpaɪr] *s* arbitre *m,* juge *m* arbitre; (baseball) officiel *m,* arbitre *m* ‖ *tr* & *intr* arbitrer

umpteen [ˈʌmpˈtin] *adj* beaucoup de

umpteenth [ˈʌmptinθ] *adj* énième

UN [ˈjuˈɛn] (letterword) (**United Nations**) ONU *f* (Organisation des Nations Unies)

unable [ʌnˈebəl] *adj* incapable; **to be unable to** être incapable de

unabridged [ˌʌnəˈbrɪdʒd] *adj* intégral

unaccented [ˌʌnækˈsɛntɪd] *adj* inaccentué

unacceptable [ˌʌnəkˈsɛptəbəl] *adj* inacceptable, irrecevable

unaccountable [ˌʌnəˈkaʊntəbəl] *adj* inexplicable; irresponsable

unaccounted-for [ˌʌnəˈkaʊntɪdˌfɔr] *adj* inexpliqué, pas retrouvé

unaccustomed [ˌʌnəˈkʌstəmd] *adj* inaccoutumé

unafraid [ˌʌnəˈfred] *adj* sans peur

unaligned [ˌʌnəˈlaɪnd] *adj* non-engagé

un′-Amer′ican *adj* antiaméricain, peu *or* pas américain

unanimity [ˌjunəˈnɪmɪti] *s* unanimité *f*

unanimous [juˈnænɪməs] *adj* unanime

unanswerable [ʌnˈænsərəbəl] *adj* incontestable, sans réplique; (*argument*) irréfutable

unappreciative [ˌʌnəˈpriʃɪˌetɪv] *adj* ingrat, peu reconnaissant

unapproachable [ˌʌnəˈprotʃəbəl] *adj* inabordable; (fig) incomparable

unarmed [ʌnˈarmd] *adj* sans armes

unascertainable [ʌnˌæsərˈtenəbəl] *adj* non vérifiable

unasked [ʌnˈæskt] *adj* non invité; **to do s.th. unasked** faire q.ch. spontanément

unassembled [ˌʌnəˈsɛmbəld] *adj* démonté

unassuming [ˌʌnəˈs(j)umɪŋ] *adj* modeste, sans prétentions

unattached [ˌʌnəˈtætʃt] *adj* indépendant; (*loose*) détaché; (*not engaged to be married*) seul; (mil, nav) en disponibilité

unattainable [ˌʌnəˈtenəbəl] *adj* inaccessible

unattractive [ˌʌnəˈtræktɪv] *adj* peu attrayant, peu séduisant

unavailable [ˌʌnəˈveləbəl] *adj* non disponible

unavailing [ˌʌnəˈvelɪŋ] *adj* inutile

unavoidable [ˌʌnəˈvɔɪdəbəl] *adj* inévitable

unaware [ˌʌnəˈwɛr] *adj* ignorant; **to be unaware of** ignorer ‖ *adv* à l'improviste; à mon (son, etc.) insu

unawares [ˌʌnəˈwɛrz] *adv* (*unexpectedly*) à l'improviste; (*unknowingly*) à mon (son, etc.) insu

unbalanced [ʌnˈbælənst] *adj* non équilibré; (*mind*) déséquilibré; (*bank account*) non soldé

unbandage [ʌnˈbændɪdʒ] *tr* débander

un•bar [ʌnˈbɑr] *v* (*pret & pp* **-barred;** *ger* **-barring**) *tr* débarrer

unbearable [ʌnˈbɛrəbəl] *adj* insupportable, imbuvable

unbeatable [ʌnˈbitəbəl] *adj* imbattable

unbecoming [ˌʌnbɪˈkʌmɪŋ] *adj* déplacé, inconvenant; (*dress*) peu seyant

unbelievable [ˌʌnbɪˈlivəbəl] *adj* incroyable

unbeliever [ˌʌnbɪˈlivər] *s* incroyant *m*

unbending [ʌnˈbɛndɪŋ] *adj* inflexible

unbiased [ʌnˈbaɪ•əst] *adj* impartial

un•bind [ʌnˈbaɪnd] *v* (*pret & pp* **-bound**) *tr* délier

unbleached [ʌnˈblitʃt] *adj* écru

unbolt [ʌnˈbolt] *tr* (*a gun; a door*) déverrouiller; (*a machine*) déboulonner

unborn [ʌnˈbɔrn] *adj* à naître, futur

unbosom [ʌnˈbuzəm] *tr* découvrir; **to unbosom oneself** ouvrir son cœur

unbound [ʌnˈbaʊnd] *adj* non relié

unbreakable [ʌnˈbrekəbəl] *adj* incassable; (*e.g., glasses*) impact résistant

unbroken [ʌnˈbrokən] *adj* intact; ininterrompu; (*spirit*) indompté; (*horse*) non rompu

unbuckle [ʌnˈbʌkəl] *tr* déboucler

unburden [ʌnˈbʌrdən] *tr* alléger; **to unburden oneself of** se soulager de

unburied [ʌnˈbɛrid] *adj* non enseveli

unbutton [ʌnˈbʌtən] *tr* déboutonner

uncalled-for [ʌnˈkɔld.fɔr] *adj* déplacé; (*e.g., insult*) gratuit

uncanny [ʌnˈkæni] *adj* inquiétant, mystérieux; rare, remarquable

uncared-for [ʌnˈkɛrd.fɔr] *adj* négligé; peu soignée

unceasing [ʌnˈsisɪŋ] *adj* incessant

unceremonious [ˌʌnsɛrɪˈmoni•əs] *adj* sans façon

uncertain [ʌnˈsʌrtən] *adj* incertain

uncertain•ty [ʌnˈsʌrtənti] *s* (*pl* **-ties**) incertitude *f*

unchain [ʌnˈtʃen] *tr* désenchaîner

unchangeable [ʌnˈtʃendʒəbəl] *adj* immuable

uncharted [ʌnˈtʃɑrtɪd] *adj* inexploré

unchecked [ʌnˈtʃɛkt] *adj* sans frein, non contenu; non vérifié

uncivilized [ʌnˈsɪvɪ.laɪzd] *adj* incivilisé

unclad [ʌnˈklæd] *adj* déshabillé

unclaimed [ʌnˈklemd] *adj* non réclamé; (*mail*) au rebut

unclasp [ʌnˈklæsp] *tr* dégrafer; (*one's hands*) desserrer

unclassified [ʌnˈklæsɪ.faɪd] *adj* non classé; (*documents, information, etc.*) pas secret

uncle [ˈʌŋkəl] *s* oncle *m*

unclean [ʌnˈklin] *adj* sale, immonde

Un'cle Sam' *s* Oncle *m* Sam, l'oncle *m* Sam

Un'cle Tom' *s* (pej) l'oncle Tom (*bon nègre*)

un•clog [ʌnˈklɑg] *v* (*pret & pp* **-clogged;** *ger* **-clogging**) *tr* dégager, désobstruer

unclouded [ʌnˈklaʊdɪd] *adj* clair, dégagé

uncollectible [ˌʌnkəˈlɛktɪbəl] *adj* irrécouvrable

uncomfortable [ʌnˈkʌmfərtəbəl] *adj* (*causing discomfort*) inconfortable; (*feeling discomfort*) mal à l'aise

uncommitted [ˌʌnkəˈmɪtɪd] *adj* non-engagé

uncommon [ʌnˈkɑmən] *adj* peu commun

uncompromising [ʌnˈkɑmprə.maɪzɪŋ] *adj* intransigeant

unconcerned [ˌʌnkənˈsʌrnd] *adj* indifférent

unconditional [ˌʌnkənˈdɪʃənəl] *adj* inconditionnel

uncongenial [ˌʌnkənˈdʒini•əl] *adj* peu sympathique; incompatible; désagréable

unconquerable [ʌnˈkɑŋkərəbəl] *adj* invincible

unconquered [ʌnˈkɑŋkərd] *adj* invaincu, indompté

unconscious [ʌnˈkɑnʃəs] *adj* inconscient; (*temporarily deprived of consciousness*) sans connaissance ‖ *s*—**the unconscious** l'inconscient *m*

unconsciousness [ʌnˈkɑnʃəsnɪs] *s* inconscience *f*; perte *f* de connaissance, évanouissement *m*

unconstitutional [ˌʌnkɑnstɪˈt(j)uʃənəl] *adj* inconstitutionnel

uncontrollable [ˌʌnkənˈtroləbəl] *adj* ingouvernable; (*e.g., desires*) irrésistible; (*e.g., laughter*) inextinguible

unconventional [ˌʌnkənˈvɛnʃənəl] *adj* original, peu conventionnel; (*person*) non-conformiste

uncork [ʌnˈkɔrk] *tr* déboucher

uncouple [ʌnˈkʌpəl] *tr* désaccoupler

uncouth [ʌnˈkuθ] *adj* gauche, sauvage; (*language*) grossier

uncover [ʌnˈkʌvər] *tr* découvrir

unction [ˈʌŋkʃən] *s* onction *f*

unctuous [ˈʌŋktʃu•əs] *adj* onctueux

uncultivated [ʌnˈkʌltɪ.vetɪd] *adj* inculte

uncultured [ʌnˈkʌltʃərd] *adj* inculte, sans culture

uncut [ʌnˈkʌt] *adj* non coupé; (*stone, diamond*) brut; (*crops*) sur pied; (*book*) non rogné

undamaged [ʌnˈdæmɪdʒd] *adj* indemne

undaunted [ʌnˈdɔntɪd] *adj* pas découragé; sans peur

undecided [ˌʌndɪˈsaɪdɪd] *adj* indécis

undefeated [ˌʌndɪˈfitɪd] *adj* invaincu

undefended [ˌʌndɪˈfɛndɪd] *adj* sans défense

undefiled [ˌʌndɪˈfaɪld] *adj* sans tache

undeniable [ˌʌndɪˈnaɪ•əbəl] *adj* indéniable

under [ˈʌndər] *adj* (*lower*) inférieur; (*underneath*) de dessous ‖ *adv* dessous; **to go under**

sombrer; **to keep under** tenir dans la soumission ‖ *prep* sous, au-dessous de, dessous; moins de, e.g., **under forty** moins de quarante ans; dans, e.g., **under the circumstances** dans les circonstances; en, e.g., **under treatment** en traitement; e.g., **under repair** en voie de réparation; à, e.g., **under the microscope** au microscope; e.g., **under examination** à l'examen; e.g., **under the terms of** aux termes de; e.g., **under the word** (*in dictionary*) au mot; **to serve under** servir sous les ordres de

un'der•age' *adj* mineur

un'der•arm pad' *s* dessous-de-bras *m*

un'der•bid' *v* (*pret & pp* -**bid**; *ger* -**bidding**) *tr* offrir moins que

un'der•brush' *s* broussailles *fpl*

un'der•car'riage *s* (aer) train *m* d'atterrissage; (aut) dessous *m*

un'der•clothes' *spl* sous-vêtements *mpl*

un'der•consump'tion *s* sous-consommation *f*

un'der•cov'er *adj* secret

un'der•cur'rent *s* courant *m* de fond; (fig) vague *f* de fond

un'der•devel'oped *adj* (pol) sous-développé

un'der•devel'oped coun'try *s* pays *m* en développement, pays moins avancé

un'der•dog' *s* opprimé *m*; (sports) parti *m* non favori, outsider *m*

underdone ['ʌndər,dʌn] *adj* pas assez cuit

un'der•es'timate *tr* sous-estimer

un'der•gar'ment *s* sous-vêtement *m*

un'der•go' *v* (*pret* -**went**; *pp* -**gone**) *tr* subir, éprouver, souffrir

un'der•grad'uate *adj & s* non diplômé *m*

un'der•ground' *adj* souterrain; (fig) clandestin ‖ *s* (*subway*) métro *m*; (pol) résistance *f*, maquis *m* ‖ *adv* sous terre; **to go underground** (fig) entrer dans la clandestinité, prendre le maquis

un'der•growth' *s* sous-bois *m*; (*underbrush*) broussailles *fpl*

un'der•hand'ed *adj* sournois, dissimulé

un'der•line' *or* un'der•line' *tr* souligner

underling ['ʌndərlɪŋ] *s* sous-ordre *m*, sous-fifre *m*

un'der•mine' *tr* miner, saper

underneath [,ʌndər'niθ] *adj* de dessous; (*lower*) inférieur ‖ *s* dessous *m* ‖ *adv* dessous, en dessous ‖ *prep* sous, audessous de

un'der•nour'ished *adj* sous-alimenté

un'der•nour'ishment *s* sous-alimentation *f*

underpaid [,ʌndər'ped] *adj* mal rétribué

un'der•pass' *s* passage *m* souterrain

un'der•pin' *v* (*pret & pp* -**pinned**; *ger* -**pinning**) *tr* étayer

un'der•priv'ileged *adj* déshérité, défavorisé, déshérité; (econ) économiquement faible

un'der•rate' *tr* sous-estimer

un'der•score' *tr* souligner

un'der•sea' *adj* sous-marin ‖ un'der•sea' *adv* sous la surface de la mer

un'der•sec'retar'y *s* (*pl* -**ies**) sous-ecrétaire *m*

un'der•sell' *v* (*pret & pp* -**sold**) *tr* vendre à meilleur marché que; (*for less than the actual value*) solder

un'der•shirt' *s* gilet *m*, maillot *m* de corps, tricot *m* de corps, tricot de peau

un'der•signed' *adj* soussigné

un'der•skirt' *s* jupon *m*

un'der•stand' *v* (*pret & pp* -**stood**) *tr & intr* comprendre, entendre

understandable [,ʌndər'stændəbəl] *adj* compréhensible; **that's understandable** cela se comprend

un'der•stand'ing *adj* compréhensif ‖ *s* compréhension *f*; (*intellectual faculty, mind*) entendement *m*; (*agreement*) accord *m*, entente *f*; **on the understanding that** à condition que; **to come to an understanding** arriver à un accord

un'der•stud'y *s* (*pl* -**ies**) doublure *f* ‖ *v* (*pret & pp* -**ied**) *tr* (*an actor*) doubler

un'der•take' *v* (*pret* -**took**; *pp* -**taken**) *tr* entreprendre; (*to agree to perform*) s'engager à faire; **to undertake to** s'engager à

undertaker ['ʌndər,tekər] *s* (*mortician*) entrepreneur *m* de pompes funèbres

undertaking [,ʌndər'tekɪŋ] *s* entreprise *f*; (*commitment*) engagement *m* ‖ ['ʌndər,tekɪŋ] *s* service *m* des pompes funèbres

un'der•tone' *s* ton *m* atténué; (*background sound*) fond *m* obscur; **in an undertone** à voix basse

un'der•tow' *s* (*countercurrent below surface*) courant *m* de fond; (*on beach*) ressac *m*

un'der•wear' *s* sous-vêtements *mpl*

un'der•world' *s* (*criminal world*) bas-fonds *mpl*, pègre *f*; (*pagan world of the dead*) enfers *mpl*

un'der•write' *or* un'der•write' *v* (*pret* -**wrote**; *pp* -**written**) *tr* souscrire; (ins) assurer

un'der•writ'er *s* souscripteur *m*; (ins) assureur *m*

undeserved [,ʌndɪ'zʌrvd] *adj* immérité

undesirable [,ʌndɪ'zaɪrəbəl] *adj* peu désirable; (*e.g., alien*) indésirable ‖ *s* indésirable *mf*

undetachable [,ʌndɪ'tæt∫əbəl] *adj* inséparable

undeveloped [,ʌndɪ'veləpt] *adj* (*land*) inexploité; (*country*) sous-développé

undigested [,ʌndɪ'dʒestɪd] *adj* indigeste

undignified [ʌn'dɪgnɪ,faɪd] *adj* sans dignité, peu digne

undiscernible [,ʌndɪ'zʌrnɪbəl], [,ʌndi'sʌrnəbəl] *adj* imperceptible

undisputed [,ʌndɪs'pjutɪd] *adj* incontesté

undo [ʌn'du] *v* (*pret* -**did**; *pp* -**done**) *tr* défaire; (fig) ruiner

undoing [ʌn'du•ɪŋ] *s* perte *f*, ruine *f*

undone [ʌn'dʌn] *adj* défait; (*omitted*) inaccompli; **to come undone** se défaire; **to leave nothing undone** ne rien négliger

undoubtedly [ʌn'dautɪdli] *adv* sans aucun doute, incontestablement

undramatic [,ʌndrə'mætɪk] *adj* peu dramatique

undress [ʌn'drɛs] *s* déshabillé *m*; (*scanty dress*)

petite tenue *f* || *tr* déshabiller || *intr* se déshabiller

undressing [ʌn'drɛsɪŋ] *s* déshabillage *m*, déculottage *m*

undrinkable [ʌn'drɪŋkəbəl] *adj* imbuvable

undue [ʌn'd(j)u] *adj* indu

undulate ['ʌndjə,let] *intr* onduler

unduly [ʌn'd(j)uli] *adv* indûment

undying [ʌn'daɪ•ɪŋ] *adj* impérissable

un′earned in′come ['ʌnʌrnd] *s* rente *f*, revenu *m* d'un bien

un′earned in′crement *s* plus-value *f*

unearth [ʌn'ʌrθ] *tr* déterrer

unearthly [ʌn'ʌrθli] *adj* surnaturel, spectral; bizarre; (*hour*) indu

uneasy [ʌn'izi] *adj* inquiet; contraint, gêné

uneatable [ʌn'itəbəl] *adj* immangeable

uneconomic(al) [,ʌnikə'namɪk(əl)] *adj* peu économique; (*person*) peu économe

uneducated [ʌn'ɛdjə,ketɪd] *adj* ignorant, sans instruction

unemployed [,ʌnɛm'plɔɪd] *adj* en chômage, sans travail || *spl* chômeurs *mpl*, sans-travail *mfpl*

unemployment [,ʌnɛm'plɔɪmənt] *s* chômage *m*

un′employ′ment insur′ance *s* assurance-chômage *f*, allocation *f* de chômage

unending [ʌn'ɛndɪŋ] *adj* interminable

unequal [ʌn'ikwəl] *adj* inégal; **to be unequal to** (*a task*) ne pas être à la hauteur de

unequaled or **unequalled** [ʌn'ikwəld] *adj* sans égal, sans pareil

unerring [ʌn'ʌrɪŋ] *adj* infaillible

UNESCO [ju'nɛsko] *s* (acronym) (**United Nations Educational, Scientific, and Cultural Organization**) l'Unesco *f*

unessential [,ʌnɛ'sɛnʃəl] *adj* non essentiel

uneven [ʌn'ivən] *adj* inégal; (*number*) impair

uneventful [,ʌnɪ'vɛntfəl] *adj* sans incident, peu mouvementé

unexceptionable [,ʌnɛk'sɛpʃənəbəl] *adj* irréprochable

unexpected [,ʌnɛk'spɛktɪd] *adj* inattendu, imprévu

unexplained [,nɛk'splɛnd] *adj* inexpliqué

unexplored [,ʌnɛk'splɔrd] *adj* inexploré

unexposed [,ʌnɛk'spozd] *adj* (phot) vierge

unfading [ʌn'fedɪŋ] *adj* immarcescible

unfailing [ʌn'felɪŋ] *adj* infaillible; (*inexhaustible*) intarissable

unfair [ʌn'fɛr] *adj* injuste, déloyal

unfaithful [ʌn'feθfəl] *adj* infidèle

unfamiliar [,ʌnfə'mɪljər] *adj* étranger, peu familier

unfasten [ʌn'fæsən] *tr* défaire, détacher

unfathomable [ʌn'fæðəməbəl] *adj* insondable

unfavorable [ʌn'fevərəbəl] *adj* défavorable

unfeeling [ʌn'filɪŋ] *adj* insensible

unfilled [ʌn'fɪld] *adj* vide; (*post*) vacant

unfinished [ʌn'fɪnɪʃt] *adj* inachevé

unfit [ʌn'fɪt] *adj* impropre, inapte

unfitted *adj* inapte, inhabile

unfold [ʌn'fold] *tr* déplier || *intr* se déplier

unforeseeable [,ʌnfor'si•əbəl] *adj* imprévisible

unforeseen [,ʌnfor'sin] *adj* imprévu

unforgettable [,ʌnfər'gɛtəbəl] *adj* inoubliable

unforgivable [,ʌnfər'gɪvəbəl] *adj* impardonnable

unfortunate [ʌn'fɔrtjənɪt] *adj* & *s* malheureux *m*

un•freeze [ʌn'friz] *v* (*pret* **-froze**; *pp* **-frozen**) *tr* dégeler

unfriend•ly [ʌn'frɛndli] *adj* (*comp* **-lier**; *super* **-liest**) inamical

unfruitful [ʌn'frutfəl] *adj* infructueux

unfulfilled [,ʌnfəl'fɪld] *adj* inaccompli

unfurl [ʌn'fʌrl] *tr* déployer

unfurnished [ʌn'fʌrnɪʃt] *adj* non meublé

ungain•ly [ʌn'genli] *adj* gauche, disgracieux

ungentlemanly [ʌn'dʒɛntəlmənli] *adj* mal élevé, impoli

ungird [ʌn'gʌrd] *tr* déceindre

ungodly [ʌn'gadli] *adj* impie; (*dreadful*) (coll) atroce

ungracious [ʌn'greʃəs] *adj* malgracieux

ungrammatical [,ʌngrə'mætɪkəl] *adj* peu grammatical

ungrateful [ʌn'gretfəl] *adj* ingrat

ungrudgingly [ʌn'grʌdʒɪŋli] *adj* de bon cœur, libéralement

unguarded [ʌn'gardɪd] *adj* sans défense; (*moment*) d'inattention; (*card*) sec

unguent ['ʌŋgwənt] *s* onguent *m*

unhandy [ʌn'hændi] *adj* maladroit; (*e.g., tool*) incommode, pas maniable

unhap•py [ʌn'hæpi] *adj* (*comp* **-pier**; *super* **-piest**) malheureux, triste; (*unlucky*) malheureux, malencontreux; (*fateful*) funeste

unharmed [ʌn'harmd] *adj* indemne

unharness [ʌn'harnɪs] *tr* dételer

unheal•thy [ʌn'hɛlθi] *adj* (*comp* **-thier**; *super* **-thiest**) malsain; (*person*) maladif

unheard-of [ʌn'hʌrd,ʌv] *adj* inouï

unhinge [ʌn'hɪndʒ] *tr* (fig) détraquer

unhitch [ʌn'hɪtʃ] *tr* décrocher; (*e.g., a horse*) dételer

unho•ly [ʌn'holi] *adj* (*comp* **-lier**; *super* **-liest**) profane; (coll) affreux

unhook [ʌn'hʊk] *tr* décrocher; (*e.g., a dress*) dégrafer

unhoped-for [ʌn'hopt,fɔr] *adj* inespéré

unhorse [ʌn'hɔrs] *tr* désarçonner

unhurt [ʌn'hʌrt] *adj* indemne

unicorn ['juni,kɔrn] *s* unicorne *m*

un′iden′tified fly′ing ob′ject [,ʌnaɪ'dɛntə,faɪd] *s* objet *m* volant non-identifié (O.V.N.I.)

unification [,junɪfɪ'keʃən] *s* unification *f*

uniform ['juni,fɔrm] *adj* & *s* uniforme *m* || *tr* uniformiser; vêtir d'un uniforme

uniformi•ty [,juni'fɔrmɪti] *s* (*pl* **-ties**) uniformité *f*

uni•fy ['juni,faɪ] *v* (*pret* & *pp* **-fied**) unifier

unilateral [,juni'lætərəl] *adj* unilatéral

unimpeachable [,ʌnɪm'pitʃəbəl] *adj* irrécusable

unimportant [ˌʌnɪm'pɔrtənt] *adj* peu important, sans importance

uninhabited [ˌʌnɪn'hæbɪtɪd] *adj* inhabité

uninspired [ˌʌnɪn'spaɪrd] *adj* sans inspiration, sans vigueur

unintelligent [ˌʌnɪn'tɛlɪdʒənt] *adj* inintelligent

unintelligible [ˌʌnɪn'tɛlɪdʒɪbəl] *adj* inintelligible

uninterested [ʌn'ɪntrɪstɪd], [ʌn'ɪntə,rɛstɪd] *adj* indifférent

uninteresting [ʌn'ɪntrɪstɪŋ], [ʌn'ɪntə,rɛstɪŋ] *adj* peu intéressant

uninterrupted [ˌʌnɪntə'rʌptɪd] *adj* ininterrompu

union ['junjən] *adj* (*leader, scale, card, etc.*) syndical ‖ *s* union *f;* (*of workmen*) syndicat *m*

unionize ['junjə,naɪz] *tr* syndiquer ‖ *intr* se syndiquer

un'ion shop' *s* atelier *m* syndical

un'ion suit' *s* sous-vêtement *m* d'une seule pièce

unique [ju'nik] *adj* unique

unisex ['juni,sɛks] *adj* unisex, unisexué

unison ['junɪsən] *s* unisson *m;* **in unison (with)** à l'unisson (de)

unit ['junɪt] *adj* unitaire ‖ *s* unité *f;* (elec, mach) groupe *m*

unite [ju'naɪt] *tr* unir ‖ *intr* s'unir

united [ju'naɪtɪd] *adj* uni

Unit'ed King'dom *s* Royaume-Uni *m*

Unit'ed Na'tions *spl* Nations *fpl* Unies

Unit'ed States' *adj* des États-Unis, américain ‖ *s*—**the United States** les États-Unis *mpl;* **the United States of America** les États-Unis d'Amérique

Unit'ed States' of Brazil' **the** les États-Unis de Brésil

uni•ty ['junɪti] *s* (*pl* **-ties**) unité *f*

universal [ˌjuni'vʌrsəl] *adj* & *s* universel *m*

u'niversal joint' *s* joint *m* articulé, cardan *m*

Un'iver'sal Prod'uct Code' (**UPC**) *s* code *m* universel de produit (*le code à barres plus une numération*)

universe ['juni,vʌrs] *s* univers *m*

universi•ty [ˌjuni'vʌrsɪti] *adj* universitaire ‖ *s* (*pl* **-ties**) université *f*

unjust [ʌn'dʒʌst] *adj* injuste

unjustified [ʌn'dʒʌstɪ,faɪd] *adj* injustifié

unkempt [ʌn'kɛmpt] *adj* dépeigné; matenu, négligé

unkind [ʌn'kaɪnd] *adj* désobligeant; (*pitiless*) impitoyable, dur

unknowable [ʌn'noəbəl] *adj* inconnaissable

unknowingly [ʌn'noɪŋli] *adv* inconsciemment

unknown [ʌn'non] *adj* inconnu; (*not yet revealed*) inédit; **unknown to** à l'insu de ‖ *s* inconnu *m;* (*math*) inconnue *f*

un'known quan'tity *s* (math, fig) inconnue *f*

Un'known Sol'dier *s* Soldat *m* inconnu

unlace [ʌn'les] *tr* délacer

unlatch [ʌn'lætʃ] *tr* lever le loquet de

unlawful [ʌn'lɔfəl] *adj* illégal, illicite

unleash [ʌn'liʃ] *tr* lâcher

unleavened [ʌn'lɛvənd] *adj* azyme

unless [ʌn'lɛs] *prep* sauf ‖ *conj* à moins que

unlettered [ʌn'lɛtərd] *adj* illettré

unlike [ʌn'laɪk] *adj* (*not alike*) dissemblables; différent de; (*not typical of*) pas caractéristique de; (*poles of a magnet*) (elec) de noms contraires ‖ *prep* (*contrary to*) à la différence de

unlikely [ʌn'laɪkli] *adj* peu probable

unlimited [ʌn'lɪmɪtɪd] *adj* illimité

unlined [ʌn'laɪnd] *adj* (*coat*) non fourré; (*paper*) non rayé; (*face*) sans rides

unlist'ed tel'ephone num'ber [ʌn'lɪstɪd] *s* numéro *m* qui figure en la liste des abonnés dans la liste rouge

unlist'ed tel'ephone subscrib'ers *spl* liste *f* rouge

unload [ʌn'lod] *tr* décharger; (*a gun*) désarmer; (coll) se décharger de ‖ *intr* décharger

unloading [ʌn'lodɪŋ] *s* déchargement *m;* (*stopping for unloading*) manutention *f*

unlock [ʌn'lɑk] *tr* ouvrir; (*a bolted door*) déverrouiller; (*the jaws*) desserrer

unloose [ʌn'lus] *tr* lâcher; (*to undo*) délier; (*a mighty force*) déchaîner

unloved [ʌn'lʌvd] *adj* peu aimé, haï

unlovely [ʌn'lʌvli] *adj* disgracieux

unluck•y [ʌn'lʌki] *adj* (*comp* **-ier;** *super* **-iest**) malchanceux, malheureux

un•make [ʌn'mek] *v* (*pret & pp* **-made**) *tr* défaire

unmanageable [ʌn'mænɪdʒəbəl] *adj* difficile à manier, ingouvernable

unmanly [ʌn'mænli] *adj* indigne d'un homme, poltron; efféminé

unmannerly [ʌn'mænərli] *adj* impoli, mal élevé

unmarketable [ʌn'mɑrkɪtəbəl] *adj* invendable

unmarriageable [ʌn'mærɪdʒəbəl] *adj* non mariable

unmarried [ʌn'mærid] *adj* célibataire

unmask [ʌn'mæsk] *tr* démasquer ‖ *intr* se démasquer

unmatched [ʌn'mætʃt] *adj* sans égal, incomparable; (*unpaired*) désassorti, dépareillé

unmerciful [ʌn'mʌrsɪfəl] *adj* impitoyable

unmesh [ʌn'mɛʃ] *tr* (mach) désengrener ‖ *intr* (mach) se désengrener

unmindful [ʌn'maɪndfəl] *adj* oublieux

unmistakable [ˌʌnmɪs'tekəbəl] *adj* évident, facilement reconnaissable

unmitigated [ʌn'mɪtɪ,getɪd] *adj* parfait, fieffé

unmixed [ʌn'mɪkst] *adj* sans mélange

unmoor [ʌn'mʊr] *tr* désamarrer

unmovable [ʌn'muvəbəl] *adj* inamovible

unmoved [ʌn'muvd] *adj* impassible

unmuzzle [ʌn'mʌzəl] *tr* démuseler

unnatural [ʌn'nætʃərəl] *adj* anormal, dénaturé; maniéré; artificiel

unnecessary [ʌn'nɛsə,sɛri] *adj* inutile

unnerve [ʌn'nʌrv] *tr* démonter, décontenancer, bouleverser

unnoticeable [ʌnˈnotisəbəl] *adj* imperceptible

unnoticed [ʌnˈnotɪst] *adj* inaperçu

unobserved [ˌʌnəbˈzʌrvd] *adj* inobservé, inaperçu

unobtainable [ˌʌnəbˈtenəbəl] *adj* introuvable

unobtrusive [ˌʌnəbˈtrusɪv] *adj* discret, effacé

unoccupied [ʌnˈakjəˌpaɪd] *adj* libre, inoccupé

unofficial [ˌʌnəˈfɪʃəl] *adj* officieux, non officiel

unopened [ʌnˈopənd] *adj* fermé; (*letter*) non décacheté

unopposed [ˌʌnəˈpozd] *adj* sans opposition; (*candidate*) unique

unorthodox [ʌnˈɔrθəˌdaks] *adj* peu orthodox

unpack [ʌnˈpæk] *tr* déballer

unpaid [ʌnˈped] *adj* impayé

unpalatable [ʌnˈpælətəbəl] *adj* fade, insipide

unparalleled [ʌnˈpærəˌlɛld] *adj* sans précédent, sans pareil

unpardonable [ʌnˈpardənəbəl] *adj* impardonnable

unpatriotic [ˌʌnpetrɪˈatɪk] *adj* antipatriotique

unperceived [ˌʌnpərˈsivd] *adj* inaperçu

unperturbable [ˌʌnpərˈtʌbəbəl] *adj* imperturbable

unpleasant [ʌnˈplɛzənt] *adj* désagréable, déplaisant

unpopular [ʌnˈpapjələr] *adj* impopulaire

unpopularity [ʌnˌpapjəˈlærɪti] *s* impopularité *f*

unprecedented [ʌnˈprɛsɪˌdɛntɪd] *adj* sans précédent, inédit

unprejudiced [ʌnˈprɛdʒədɪst] *adj* sans préjugés, impartial

unpremeditated [ˌʌnprɪˈmɛdɪˌtetɪd] *adj* non prémédité

unprepared [ˌʌnprɪˈpɛrd] *adj* sans préparation; (*e.g., speech*) improvisé

unprepossessing [ˌʌnpripəˈzɛsɪŋ] *adj* peu engageant

unpresentable [ˌʌnprɪˈzɛntəbəl] *adj* peu présentable

unpretentious [ˌʌnprɪˈtɛnʃəs] *adj* sans prétentions, modeste

unprincipled [ʌnˈprɪnsɪpəld] *adj* sans principes, sans scrupules

unproductive [ˌʌnprəˈdʌktɪv] *adj* improductif

unprofitable [ʌnˈprafɪtəbəl] *adj* peu profitable, inutile

unpronounceable [ˌʌnprəˈnaʊnsəbəl] *adj* imprononçable

unpropitious [ˌʌnprəˈpɪʃəs] *adj* défavorable

unpublished [ʌnˈpʌnɪʃt] *adj* inédit

unpunished [ʌnˈpʌnɪʃt] *adj* impuni

unqualified [ʌnˈkwaləˌfaɪd] *adj* incompétent; parfait, fieffé

unquenchable [ʌnˈkwɛntʃəbəl] *adj* inextinguible

unquestionable [ʌnˈkwɛstʃənəbəl] *adj* indiscutable

unquote [ˈʌnˌkwot] *adv* fermez les guillemets

unrav·el [ʌnˈrævəl] *v* (*pret & pp* -eled or -elled; *ger* -eling or -elling) *tr* effiler; (fig) débrouiller ‖ *intr* s'effiler; (fig) se débrouiller

unreachable [ʌnˈritʃəbəl] *adj* inaccessible

unreal [ʌnˈriəl] *adj* irréel

unreali·ty [ˌʌnrɪˈælɪti] *s* (*pl* -ties) irréalité *f*

unreasonable [ʌnˈrizənəbəl] *adj* déraisonnable

unrecognizable [ʌnˈrɛkəgˌnaɪzəbəl] *adj* méconnaissable

unreel [ʌnˈril] *tr* dérouler ‖ *intr* se dérouler

unrelenting [ˌʌnrɪˈlɛntɪŋ] *adj* implacable

unreliable [ˌʌnrɪˈlaɪəbəl] *adj* peu fidéle, instable, sujet à caution

unremitting [ˌʌnrɪˈmɪtɪŋ] *adj* incessant, infatigable

unrented [ʌnˈrɛntɪd] *adj* libre, sans locataires

unrepentant [ˌʌnrɪˈpɛntənt] *adj* impénitent

un'requit'ed love' [ˌʌnrɪˈkwaɪtɪd] *s* amour *m* non partagé

unresponsive [ˌʌnrɪˈspansɪv] *adj* peu sensible, froid, détaché

unrest [ʌnˈrɛst] *s* agitation *f,* trouble *m;* inquiétude *f*

un·rig [ʌnˈrɪg] *v* (*pret & pp* -rigged; *ger* -rigging) *tr* (naut) dégréer

unrighteous [ʌnˈraɪtʃəs] *adj* inique, injuste

unripe [ʌnˈraɪp] *adj* vert, pas mûr; précoce

unrivaled or **unrivalled** [ʌnˈraɪvəld] *adj* sans rival

unroll [ʌnˈrol] *tr* dérouler ‖ *intr* se dérouler

unromantic [ˌʌnroˈmæntɪk] *adj* peu romanesque, terre à terre

unruffled [ʌnˈrʌfəld] *adj* calme, serein

unruly [ʌnˈruli] *adj* indiscipliné, ingouvernable

unsaddle [ʌnˈsædəl] *tr* (*a horse*) desseller; (*a horseman*) désarçonner

unsafe [ʌnˈsef] *adj* dangereux

unsaid [ʌnˈsɛd] *adj*—**to leave unsaid** passer sous silence

unsalable [ʌnˈseləbəl] *adj* invendable

unsanitary [ʌnˈsænɪˌtɛri] *adj* peu hygiénique

unsatisfactory [ʌnˌsætɪsˈfæktəri] *adj* peu satisfaisant

unsatisfied [ʌnˈsætɪsˌfaɪd] *adj* insatisfait, inassouvi

unsavory [ʌnˈsevəri] *adj* désagréable; (fig) équivoque, louche

unscathed [ʌnˈskeðd] *adj* indemne

unscientific [ˌʌnsaɪənˈtɪfɪk] *adj* antiscientifique

unscrew [ʌnˈskru] *tr* dévisser

unscrupulous [ʌnˈskrupjələs] *adj* sans scrupules

unseal [ʌnˈsil] *tr* desceller

unsealed *adj* (*mail*) non clos

unseasonable [ʌnˈsizənəbəl] *adj* hors de saison; (*untimely*) inopportun

unseemly [ʌnˈsimli] *adj* inconvenant

unseen [ʌnˈsin] *adj* invisible

unselfish [ʌnˈsɛlfɪʃ] *adj* désintéressé

unsettled [ʌnˈsɛtəld] *adj* instable; (*region*) non colonisé; (*question*) en suspens; (*weather*) variable; (*bills*) non réglé; **to be unsettled** (*to be uneasy*) avoir du vague à l'âme

unshackle [ʌnˈʃækəl] *tr* désentraver

unshaken [ʌnˈʃekən] *adj* inébranlé

unshapely [ʌnˈʃepli] *adj* difforme, informe

unshaven [ʌnˈʃevən] *adj* non rasé
unsheathe [ʌnˈʃið] *tr* dégainer
unshod [ʌnˈʃɑd] *adj* déchaussé; (*horse*) déferré
unshrinkable [ʌnˈʃrɪŋkəbəl] *adj* irrétrécissable
unsightly [ʌnˈsaɪtli] *adj* laid, hideux
unsinkable [ʌnˈsɪŋkəbəl] *adj* insubmersible
unskilled [ʌnˈskɪld] *adj* inexpérimenté; de manœuvre
un′skilled la′borer *s* manœuvre *m*
unskillful [ʌnˈskɪlfəl] *adj* maladroit
unsnarl [ʌnˈsnɑrl] *tr* débrouiller
unsociable [ʌnˈsoʃəbəl] *adj* insociable
unsold [ʌnˈsold] *adj* invendu
unsolder [ʌnˈsɑdər] *tr* dessouder
unsophisticated [ˌʌnsəˈfɪstɪˌketɪd] *adj* ingénu, naïf, simple
unsound [ʌnˈsaʊnd] *adj* peu solide; (*false*) faux; (*decayed*) gâté; (*mind*) dérangé; (*sleep*) léger
unspeakable [ʌnˈspikəbəl] *adj* indicible; (*disgusting*) sans nom
unsportsmanlike [ʌnˈsportsmənˌlaɪk] *adj* antisportif
unstable [ʌnˈstebəl] *adj* instable
unsteady [ʌnˈstɛdi] *adj* chancelant, tremblant, vacillant
unstinted [ʌnˈstɪntɪd] *adj* abondant, sans bornes
unstitch [ʌnˈstɪtʃ] *tr* découdre
un•stop [ʌnˈstɑp] *v* (*pret & pp* **-stopped;** *ger* **-stopping**) *tr* déboucher
unstressed [ʌnˈstrɛst] *adj* inaccentué
unstrung [ʌnˈstrʌŋ] *adj* détraqué; (*necklace*) défilé; (*mus*) sans cordes
unsuccessful [ˌʌnsəkˈsɛsfəl] *adj* non réussi; **to be unsuccessful** ne pas réussir
unsuitable [ʌnˈs(j)utəbəl] *adj* impropre; (*time*) inopportun; **unsuitable for** peu fait pour, inapte à
unsuspected [ˌʌnsəsˈpɛktɪd] *adj* insoupçonné
unswerving [ʌnˈswʌrvɪŋ] *adj* ferme, inébranlable
unsympathetic [ˌʌnsɪmpəˈθɛtɪk] *adj* peu compatissant
unsystematic(al) [ˌʌnsɪstəˈmætɪk(əl)] *adj* non systématique, sans méthode
untactful [ʌnˈtæktfəl] *adj* indiscret, indélicat
untamed [ʌnˈtemd] *adj* indompté
untangle [ʌnˈtæŋgəl] *tr* démêler, débrouiller
untenable [ʌnˈtɛnəbəl] *adj* insoutenable
unthankful [ʌnˈθæŋkfəl] *adj* ingrat
unthinkable [ʌnˈθɪŋkəbəl] *adj* impensable
unthinking [ʌnˈθɪŋkɪŋ] *adj* irréfléchi
untidy [ʌnˈtaɪdi] *adj* désordonné, débraillé
un•tie [ʌnˈtaɪ] *v* (*pret & pp* **-tied;** *ger* **-tying**) *tr* délier, dénouer
until [ʌnˈtɪl] *prep* jusqu'à ‖ *conj* jusqu'à ce que, en attendant que
untimely [ʌnˈtaɪmli] *adj* inopportun; (*premature*) prématuré; (*excessive*) intempestif
untiring [ʌnˈtaɪrɪŋ] *adj* infatigable
untold [ʌnˈtold] *adj* incalculable; (*suffering*) inouï; (*joy*) indicible; (*tale*) non raconté

untouchable [ʌnˈtʌtʃəbəl] *adj & s* intouchable *mf*
untouched [ʌnˈtʌtʃt] *adj* intact; indifférent; non mentionné
untoward [ʌnˈtord] *adj* malencontreux
untrained [ʌnˈtrend] *adj* inexpérimenté; (*animal*) non dressé
untrammeled or **untrammelled** [ʌnˈtræməld] *adj* sans entraves
untried [ʌnˈtraɪd] *adj* inéprouvé
untroubled [ʌnˈtrʌbəld] *adj* calme, insoucieux
untrue [ʌnˈtru] *adj* faux; infidèle
untrustworthy [ʌnˈtrʌstˌwʌrði] *adj* indigne de confiance
untruth [ʌnˈtruθ] *s* mensonge *m*
untruthful [ʌnˈtruθfəl] *adj* mensonger
untwist [ʌnˈtwɪst] *tr* détordre ‖ *intr* se détordre
unused [ʌnˈjuzd] *adj* inutilisé, inemployé; **unused to** peu accoutumé à, inaccoutumé à
unusual [ʌnˈjuʒu•əl] *adj* insolite, inusité, inhabituel
unutterable [ʌnˈʌtərəbəl] *adj* indicible, inexprimable
unvanquished [ʌnˈvæŋkwɪʃt] *adj* invaincu
unvarnished [ʌnˈvɑrnɪʃt] *adj* non verni; (fig) sans fard, simple
unveil [ʌnˈvel] *tr* dévoiler; (*e.g., a statue*) inaugurer ‖ *intr* se dévoiler
unveiling [ʌnˈvelɪŋ] *s* dévoilement *m*
unventilated [ʌnˈvɛntɪˌletɪd] *adj* sans aération
unvoice [ʌnˈvɔɪs] *tr* dévoiser, assourdir
unwanted [ʌnˈwɑntɪd] *adj* non voulu
unwarranted [ʌnˈwɑrəntɪd] *adj* injustifié; sans garantie
unwary [ʌnˈwɛri] *adj* imprudent
unwavering [ʌnˈwevərɪŋ] *adj* constant, ferme, résolu
unwelcome [ʌnˈwɛlkəm] *adj* (*e.g., visitor*) importun; (*e.g., news*) fâcheux
unwell [ʌnˈwɛl] *adj* indisposé, souffrant; (*menstruating*) indisposée
unwholesome [ʌnˈholsəm] *adj* malsain, insalubre
unwieldy [ʌnˈwildi] *adj* peu maniable
unwilling [ʌnˈwɪlɪŋ] *adj* peu disposé
unwillingly [ʌnˈwɪlɪŋli] *adv* à contrecœur
un•wind [ʌnˈwaɪnd] *v* (*pret & pp* **-wound**) *tr* dérouler ‖ *intr* se dérouler
unwise [ʌnˈwaɪz] *adj* peu judicieux, malavisé
unwished-for [ʌnˈwɪʃtˌfor] *adj* non souhaité
unwittingly [ʌnˈwɪtɪŋli] *adv* inconsciemment, sans le savoir
unwonted [ʌnˈwʌntɪd] *adj* inaccoutumé, peu commun
unworldly [ʌnˈwʌrldli] *adj* peu mondain; simple, naïf
unworthy [ʌnˈwʌrði] *adj* indigne
un•wrap [ʌnˈræp] *v* (*pret & pp* **-wrapped;** *ger* **-wrapping**) *tr* dépaqueter, désenvelopper
unwrinkled [ʌnˈrɪŋkəld] *adj* uni, lisse, sans rides
unwritten [ʌnˈrɪtən] *adj* non écrit; oral; (*blank*) vierge, blanc

unwrit′ten law′ s droit m coutumier
unyielding [ʌn'jildɪŋ] adj ferme, solide; inébranlable
unyoke [ʌn'jok] tr dételer
up [ʌp] adj montant, ascendant; (raised) levé; (standing) debout; (time) expiré; (blinds) relevé; **up in arms** soulevé, indigné ∥ adv haut, en haut; **to be up against** se heurter à; **to be up against it** avoir la déveine; **to be up to** être capable de, être à la hauteur de; être à, e.g., **to be up to you (me, etc.)** être à vous (moi, etc.); **up and down** de haut en bas; (back and forth) de long en large; **up there** là-haut; **up to** jusqu'à; (at the level of) au niveau de, à la hauteur de; **up to and including** jusques et y compris; **what's up?** qu'est-ce qui se passe?; for expressions like **to go up** monter and **to get up** se lever, see the verb ∥ prep en haut de, vers le haut de; (a stream) en montant ∥ v (pret & pp **-upped;** ger **upping**) tr (coll) faire monter; (prices, wages) (coll) élever ∥ interj debout!
up-and-coming ['ʌpən'kʌmɪŋ] adj (coll) entreprenant
up-and-doing ['ʌpən'du•ɪŋ] adj (coll) entreprenant, alerte, énergique
up-and-up ['ʌpən'ʌp] s—**to be on the up-and-up** (coll) être en bonne voie; (coll) être honnête
up-braid′ tr réprimander, reprendre
upbringing ['ʌp,brɪŋɪŋ] s éducation f
UPC abbr **Universal Product Code**
up′coun′try adv (coll) à l'intérieur du pays ∥ s (coll) intérieur m du pays
up-date′ tr mettre à jour
upheaval [ʌp'hivəl] s soulèvement m
up′hill′ adj montant; difficile, pénible ∥ **up′hill′** adv en montant
up•hold′ v (pret & pp **-held**) tr soutenir, maintenir
upholster [ʌp'holstər] tr tapisser
upholsterer [ʌp'holstərər] s tapissier m
upholster•y [ʌp'holstəri] s (pl **-ies**) tapisserie f
up′keep′ s entretien m; (expenses) frais mpl d'entretien
upland ['ʌp,lænd] adj élevé ∥ s région f montagneuse; **uplands** hautes terres fpl
up′lift′ s élévation f; (moral improvement) édification f ∥ **up•lift′** tr soulever, élever
up′link′ s (aerosp) transmission f de données depuis la terre jusqu'au satellite
upon [ə'pɑn] prep sur; à, e.g., **upon my arrival** à mon arrivée; **upon** + ger en + ger, e.g., **upon arriving** en arrivant
upper ['ʌpər] adj supérieur; haut; (first) premier ∥ s (of shoe) empeigne f
up′per berth′ s couchette f du haut, couchette supérieure
up′per-case′ adj (typ) du haut de casse
up′per clas′ses spl hautes classes fpl
up′per hand′ s dessus m, haute main f
up′per mid′dle class′ s haute bourgeoisie f

up′per•most adj (le) plus haut, (le) plus élevé; (le) premier ∥ adv en dessus
Up′per Room′ s (eccl) cénacle m
uppish ['ʌpɪʃ] adj (coll) suffisant, arrogant
up•raise′ tr lever
up′right′ adj & adv droit ∥ s montant m
up′right pia′no s piano m droit
uprising ['ʌp,raɪzɪŋ] s soulèvement m, insurrection f
up′roar′ s tumulte m, vacarme m
uproarious [ʌp'rorɪ•əs] adj tumultueux; (funny) comique, impayable
up•root′ tr déraciner
ups′ and downs′ spl vicissitudes fpl
up′scale adj de première qualité
up•set′ or **up′set′** adj (overturned) renversé; (disturbed) bouleversé; (stomach) dérangé ∥ **up′set′** s (overturn) renversement m; (of emotions) bouleversement m ∥ **up•set′** v (pret & pp **-set;** ger **-setting**) tr renverser; bouleverser ∥ intr se renverser
up′set price′ s prix m de départ
upsetting [ʌp'sɛtɪŋ] adj bouleversant, inquiétant
up′shot′ s résultat m; point m essentiel
up′side down′ adv sens dessus dessous; **to turn upside down** renverser; se renverser; (said of carriage) verser
up′stage′ adj & adv au second plan, à l'arrière-plan; **to go upstage** remonter ∥ s arrière-plan m ∥ **up′stage′** tr (coll) prendre un air dédaigneux envers
up′stairs′ adj d'en haut ∥ s l'étage m supérieur ∥ adv en haut; **to go upstairs** monter, monter en haut
up•stand′ing adj droit; (vigorous) gaillard; (sincere) honnête, probe
up′start′ adj & s parvenu m
up′stream′ adj d'amont ∥ adv en amont
up′stroke′ s (in writing) délié m; (mach) course f ascendante
up′surge′ s poussée f
up′swing′ s mouvement m de montée; (com) amélioration f
up′tight′ adj (coll) inquiet, soucieux
up-to-date ['ʌptə'det] adj à la page; (e.g., account books) mis à jour
up-to-the-minute ['ʌptəðə'mɪnɪt] adj de la dernière heure
up′trend′ s tendance f à la hausse
up′turn′ s hausse f, amélioration f
up•turned′ adj (e.g., eyes) levé; (part of clothing) relevé; (nose) retroussé
upward ['ʌpwərd] adj ascendant ∥ adv vers le haut; **upward of** plus de
up′ward mobil′ity s mobilité f sociale ascendante
Ural ['jurəl] adj Ouralien ∥ s Oural m; **Urals** Oural
uranium [ju'reni•əm] s uranium m
Uranus [ju'renəs] s Uranus m
urban ['ʌrbən] adj urbain
urbane [ʌr'ben] adj urbain, courtois

ur′ban plan′ning *s* urbanisme *m*

ur′ban guer′rilla *s* guérillero *m* urbain

urbanite [ˈʌrbə‚naɪt] *s* citadin *m*, habitant *m* d'une ville

urbanity [ʌrˈbænɪti] *s* urbanité *f*

urbanize [ˈʌrbə‚naɪz] *tr* urbaniser

ur′ban renew′al *s* renouveau *m* urbain

urchin [ˈʌrtʃin] *s* gamin *m*, galopin *m*

ure•thra [juˈriθrə] *s* (*pl* **-thras** or **-thrae** [θri]) urètre *m*

urge [ʌrdʒ] *s* impulsion *f* ‖ *tr & intr* presser

urgen•cy [ˈʌrdʒənsi] *s* (*pl* **-cies**) urgence *f;* insistance *f*, sollicitation *f*

urgent [ˈʌrdʒənt] *adj* urgent, pressant; (*insistent*) pressant, importun

urinal [ˈjurinəl] *s* (*small building or convenience for men*) urinoir *m*, vespasienne *f;* (*for bed*) urinal *m*

urinary [ˈjuri‚nɛri] *adj* urinaire

urinate [ˈjuri‚net] *tr & intr* uriner; pisser (coll)

urine [ˈjurin] *s* urine *f*

urn [ʌrn] *s* urne *f;* (*for tea, coffee, etc.*) fontaine *f*

urology [juˈralədʒi] *s* urologie *f*

us [ʌs] *pron pers* nous §85, §87

U.S.A. [ˈjuˈɛsˈe] *s* (letterword) (**United States of America**) E.-U.A. *mpl* or U.S.A. *mpl*

usable [ˈjuzəbəl] *adj* utilisable

usage [ˈjuzɪdʒ] *s* usage *m*

use [jus] *s* emploi *m*, usage *m;* (*usefulness*) utilité *f;* **in use** occupé; **of what use is it?** à quoi cela sert-il?; **not in use** libre; **out of use** hors de service; **to be of no use** ne servir à rien; **to have no use for s.o.** tenir qn en mauvaise estime; **to make use of** se servir de; **what's the use?** à quoi bon? ‖ [juz] *tr* employer, se servir de, user de; **to use up** épuiser, user ‖ *intr*—**I used to visit my friend every evening** je visitais mon ami tous les soirs

used [juzd] *adj* usagé, usé; d'occasion, e.g., **used car** voiture *f* d'occasion; **to be used** (*to be put into use*) être usité, être employé; **to be used as** servir de; **to be used to** (*to be*

useful for) servir à; **used to** [ˈjustu] accoutumé à; **used up** épuisé

useful [ˈjusfəl] *adj* utile

usefulness [ˈjusfəlnɪs] *s* utilité *f*

useless [ˈjuslɪs] *adj* inutile

user [ˈjuzər] *s* usager *m;* (*of a machine, of a computer, of gas, etc.*) utilisateur *m*

usher [ˈʌ/ər] *s* placeur *m;* ouvreuse *f;* (*doorkeeper*) huissier *m* ‖ *tr*—**to usher in** inaugurer; (*a person*) introduire

U.S.S.R. [ˈjuˈɛsˈɛsˈar] *s* (letterword) (**Union of Soviet Socialist Republics**) U.R.S.S. *f*

usual [ˈjuʒuˈəl] *adj* usuel; **as usual** comme d'habitude

usually [ˈjuʒuˈəli] *adv* usuellement, d'habitude, d'ordinaire, par d'habitude

usurp [juˈzʌrp] *tr* usurper

usu•ry [ˈjuʒəri] *s* (*pl* **-ries**) usure *f*

utensil [juˈtɛnsɪl] *s* ustensile *m*

uter•us [ˈjutərəs] *s* (*pl* **-i** [‚aɪ]) utérus *m*

utilitarian [‚jutɪlɪˈtɛriˈən] *adj* utilitaire

utili•ty [juˈtɪlɪti] *s* (*pl* **-ties**) utilité *f;* service *m* public; **utilities** services en commun (*gaz, transports, etc.*)

util′ity room′ *s* lingerie *f;* pièce *f* pour la machine à laver, la chaudière ou d'autres appareils

utilize [ˈjutɪ‚laɪz] *tr* utiliser

utmost [ˈʌt‚most] *adj* extrême; (*larger*) plus grand; (*further away*) plus éloigné ‖ *s*—**the utmost** l'extrême *m*, le comble *m;* **to do one's utmost** faire tout son possible; **to the utmost** jusqu'au dernier point

utopia [juˈtopiˈə] *s* utopie *f*

utopian [juˈtopiˈən] *adj* utopique ‖ *s* utopiste *mf*

utter [ˈʌtər] *adj* complet, total, absolu ‖ *tr* proférer, émettre; (*a cry*) pousser

utterance [ˈʌtərəns] *s* expression *f*, émission *f;* (gram) énoncé *m;* **to give utterance to** exprimer

utterly [ˈʌtərli] *adj* complètement, tout à fait, totalement

U-turn [ˈju‚tʌrn] *s* demi-volte *f*

V

V, v [vi] *s* XXIIᵉ lettre de l'alphabet

vacan•cy [ˈvekənsi] *s* (*pl* **-cies**) (*emptiness; gap, opening*) vide *m;* (*unfilled position or job*) vacance *f;* (*in a building*) appartement *m* disponible; (*in a hotel*) chambre *f* de libre; **no vacancy** (public sign) complet

vacant [ˈvekənt] *adj* (*empty*) vide; (*having no occupant; untenanted*) vacant, libre, disponible; (*expression, look*) distrait, vague

va′cant lot′ *s* terrain *m* vague

vacate [ˈveket] *tr* quitter, évacuer ‖ *intr* (*to move out*) déménager

vacation [veˈke/ən] *s* vacances *fpl;* **on vacation**

en vacances ‖ *intr* prendre ses vacances, passer les vacances

vacationist [veˈke/ənɪst] *s* vacancier *m*

vaca′tion with pay′ *s* congé *m* payé

vaccinate [ˈvæksɪ‚net] *tr* vacciner

vaccination [‚væksɪˈne/ən] *s* vaccination *f*

vaccine [ˈvækˈsin] *s* vaccin *m*

vacillate [ˈvæsɪ‚let] *intr* vaciller

vacui•ty [væˈkjuˈiti] *s* (*pl* **-ties**) vacuité *f*

vacu•um [ˈvækjuˈəm] *s* (*pl* **-ums** or **-a** [ə]) vacuum *m*, vide *m* ‖ *tr* passer à l'aspirateur, dépoussiérer

vac′uum clean′er *s* aspirateur *m*

vac'uum-packed' adj emballé sous vide
vac'uum pump' s pompe f à vide
vac'uum tube' s tube m à vide
vagabond ['væɡə,bɑnd] adj & s vagabond m
vagar•y [və'ɡɛri] s (pl -ies) caprice m
vagina [və'dʒaɪnə] s vagin m
vagran•cy ['veɡrənsi] s (pl -cies) vagabondage m
vague [veɡ] adj vague
vain [ven] adj vain; **in vain** en vain
vainglorious [ven'ɡlori•əs] adj vaniteux
valance ['væləns] s cantonnière f, lambrequin m
vale [vel] s vallon m
valedicto•ry [,væli'dɪktəri] s (pl -ries) discours m d'adieu
valence ['veləns] s (chem) valence f
valentine ['vælən,taɪn] s (sweetheart) valentin m; (card) carte f de la Saint-Valentin
Val'entine Day' s la Saint-Valentin
vale' of tears' s vallée f de larmes
valet ['vælɪt], ['væle] s valet m
valiant ['væljənt] adj vaillant
valid ['vælɪd] adj valable, valide
validate ['væli,det] tr valider; (sports) homologuer
validation [,væli'deʃən] s validation f; (sports) homologation f
validi•ty [və'lɪdɪti] s (pl -ties) validité f
valise [və'lis] s mallette f
valley ['væli] s vallée f, vallon m; (of roof) cornière f
valor ['vælər] s valeur f, vaillance f
valorous ['vælərəs] adj valeureux
valuable ['vælju•əbəl], ['væljəbəl] adj précieux, de valeur ‖ **valuables** spl objets mpl de valeur
value ['vælju] s valeur f; (bargain) affaire f, occasion f; **to set a value on** estimer, évaluer ‖ tr (to think highly of) priser, estimer; (to set a price for) estimer, évaluer; **if you value your life** si vous tenez à la vie
val'ue-added tax' s taxe f à la valeur ajoutée, T.V.A.
valueless ['væljulɪs] adj sans valeur
valve [vælv] s soupape f; (of mollusk; of fruit; of tire) valve f; (of heart) valvule f; (mus) clé f
valve' cap' s chapeau m, bouchon m
valve' gears' spl (of gas engine) engrenages mpl de distribution; (of steam engine) mécanisme m de distribution
valve'-in-head' en'gine s moteur m à soupapes en tête, moteur à culbuteurs
valve' seat' s siège m de soupape
valve' spring' s ressort m de soupape
valve' stem' s tige f de soupape
vamp [væmp] s (of shoe) empeigne f; (patchwork) rapiéçage m; (woman who preys on man) (coll) femme f fatale, vamp f ‖ tr (a shoe) mettre une empeigne à; (to piece together) rapiécer; (a susceptible man) (coll)

vamper; (an accompaniment) (coll) improviser
vampire ['væmpaɪr] s vampire m; femme f fatale, vamp f
van [væn] s camion m, voiture f de déménagement; (mil, fig) avant-garde f; (railway car) (Brit) fourgon m
vandal ['vændəl] adj & s vandale m ‖ (cap) adj vandale ‖ (cap) s Vandale mf
vandalism ['vændə,lɪzəm] s vandalisme m
vane [ven] s (weathervane) girouette f; (of windmill) aile f; (of propeller or turbine) ailette f; (of feather) lame f; (of a wheel) aube f
vanguard ['væn,ɡɑrd] s (mil, fig) avant-garde f; **in the vanguard** à l'avant-garde
vanilla [və'nɪlə] s vanille f
vanish ['vænɪʃ] intr s'évanouir, disparaître
van'ishing cream' s crème f de jour
vani•ty ['vænɪti] s (pl -ties) vanité f; (dressing table) table f de toilette, coiffeuse f; (vanity case) poudrier m
van'ity case' s poudrier m, nécessaire m de toilette
van'ity strip' s (bank of lights in the dressing room) bande f de coiffeuse
vanquish ['væŋkwɪʃ] tr vaincre
van'tage point' ['væntɪdʒ] s position f avantageuse
vapid ['væpɪd] adj insipide
vapor ['vepər] s vapeur f
vaporize ['vepə,raɪz] tr vaporiser ‖ intr se vaporiser
va'por lock' s bouchon m de vapeur
va'por trail' s (aer) sillage m de fumée
variable ['vɛri•əbl] adj & s variable f
variance ['vɛri•əns] s différence f, variation f; **at variance with** en désaccord avec
variant ['vɛri•ənt] adj variant ‖ s variante f
variation [,vɛri'eʃən] s variation f
varicose ['væri,kos] adj variqueux
var'icose veins' spl (pathol) varice f
varied ['vɛrid] adj varié
variegated ['vɛri•ə,ɡetɪd] adj varié; (spotted) bigarré, bariolé
varie•ty [və'raɪ•əti] s (pl -ties) variété f
vari'ety show' s spectacle m de variétés
vari'ety store' s magasin m à prix unique
various ['vɛri•əs] adj divers, différent; (several) plusieurs; (variegated) bigarré
varnish ['vɑrnɪʃ] s vernis m ‖ tr vernir; (e.g., the truth) farder, embellir
varsi•ty ['vɑrsiti] adj (sports) universitaire ‖ s (pl -ties) (sports) équipe f universitaire principale
var•y ['vɛri] v (pret & pp -ied) tr & intr varier
vase [ves], [vez] s vase m
Vaseline ['væsə,lin] s (trademark) vaseline f
vassal ['væsəl] adj & s vassal m
vast [væst] adj vaste
vastness ['væstnɪs] s vaste étendue f, immensité f
vat [væt] s cuve f, bac m

VAT [væt] *s* (acronym) (**value-added tax**) TVA (taxe *f* à la valeur ajoutée)

Vatican ['vætɪkən] *adj* vaticane ‖ *s* Vatican *m*

vaudeville ['vodvɪl] *s* spectacle *m* de variétés, music-hall *m; (light theatrical piece interspersed with songs)* vaudeville *m*

vault [vɔlt] *s (underground chamber)* souterrain *m; (of a bank)* chambre *f* forte; *(burial chamber)* caveau *m; (leap)* saut *m;* (anat, archit) voûte *f* ‖ *tr & intr* sauter

vaunt [vɔnt], [vɑnt] *s* vantardise *f* ‖ *tr* vanter ‖ *intr* se vanter

VCR ['vi'si'ɑr] *s* (letterword) (**videocassette recorder**) magnétoscope *m* à cassettes

VD ['vi'di] *s* (letterword) (**venereal disease**) maladie *f* vénérienne

veal [vil] *s* veau *m*

veal' chop' *s* côtelette *f* de veau

veal' cut'let *s* escalope *f* de veau

veer [vɪr] *s* virage *m* ‖ *tr* faire virer ‖ *intr* virer

vegan ['vigən], ['vegən], ['vɛʒən] *s* végétarien *m* qui ne mange pas les produits laitiers

vegetable ['vɛdʒɪtəbəl] *adj* végétal ‖ *s (plant)* végétal *m; (edible part of plant)* légume *m*

veg'etable gar'den *s* potager *m*

veg'etable soup' *s* potage *m* aux légumes

vegetarian [,vɛdʒɪ'tɛrɪ•ən] *adj & s* végétarien *m*

vegetate ['vɛdʒɪ,tet] *intr* végéter

vehemence ['vi•ɪməns] *s* véhémence *f*

vehement ['vi•ɪmənt] *adj* véhément

vehicle ['vi•ɪkəl] *s* véhicule *m*

veil [vel] *s* voile *m; (fig)* voile *m;* **to take the veil** prendre le voile ‖ *tr* voiler ‖ *intr* se voiler

vein [ven] *s* veine *f* ‖ *tr* veiner

velar ['vilər] *adj & s* vélaire *f*

vellum ['vɛləm] *s* vélin *m;* papier *m* vélin

veloci•ty [vɪ'lɑsɪti] *s (pl* **-ties**) vitesse *f*

velvet ['vɛlvɪt] *s* velours *m*

velveteen [,vɛlvɪ'tin] *s* velvet *m*

velvety ['vɛlvɪti] *adj* velouté

vend [vɛnd] *tr* vendre, colporter

vend'ing machine' *s* distributeur *m* automatique

vendor ['vɛndər] *s* vendeur *m*

veneer [və'nɪr] *s* placage *m;* (fig) vernis *m* ‖ *tr* plaquer

venerable ['vɛnərəbəl] *adj* vénérable

venerate ['vɛnə,ret] *tr* vénérer

venereal ['vɛ'nɪrɪ•əl] *adj* vénérien

Venetian [vɪ'ni∫ən] *adj* vénitien ‖ *s* Vénitien *m*

Vene'tian blind' *s* jalousie *f,* store *m* vénitien

vengeance ['vɛndʒəns] *s* vengeance *f;* **with a vengeance** furieusement, à outrance; *(to the utmost limit)* tant que ça peut

vengeful ['vɛndʒfəl] *adj* vengeur

Venice ['vɛnɪs] *s* Venise *f*

venison ['vɛnɪsən] *s* venaison *f*

venom ['vɛnəm] *s* venin *m*

venomous ['vɛnəməs] *adj* venimeux

vent [vɛnt] *s* orifice *m; (for air)* ventouse *f;* **to give vent to** donner libre cours à ‖ *tr* décharger

ventilate ['vɛntɪ,let] *tr* ventiler

ventilation [,vɛntɪ'le∫ən] *s* aération *f,* ventilation *f*

ventila'tion shaft' *s* conduit *m* d'aération, bouche *f* d'aération

ventilator ['vɛntɪ,letər] *s* ventilateur *m*

ventricle ['vɛntrɪkəl] *s* ventricule *m*

ventriloquism [vɛn'trɪlə,kwɪzəm] *s* ventriloquie *f*

ventriloquist [vɛn'trɪləkwɪst] *s* ventriloque *mf*

venture ['vɛnt∫ər] *s* entreprise *f* risquée; **at a venture** à l'aventure ‖ *tr* aventurer ‖ *intr* s'aventurer; **to venture on** hasarder

ven'ture cap'ital *s* capital-risque *msg*

venturesome ['vɛnt∫ərsəm] *adj* aventureux

venturous ['vɛnt∫ərəs] *adj* aventureux

vent' win'dow *s* (aut) déflecteur *m*

venue ['vɛnju] *s* lieu *m* de rendez-vous; endroit *m,* site *m;* occasion *f,* moyen *m;* (law) lieu *m* du jugement *or* procès, juridiction *f;* **change of venue** (law) renvoi *m*

Venus ['vinəs] *s* Vénus *f*

veracious [vɪ're∫əs] *adj* véridique

veraci•ty [vɪ'ræsɪti] *s (pl* **-ties**) véracité *f*

veranda or **verandah** [və'rændə] *s* véranda *f*

verb [vʌrb] *adj* verbal ‖ *s* verbe *m*

verbalize ['vʌrbə,laɪz] *tr* exprimer par des mots; (gram) changer en verbe ‖ *intr* être verbeux

verbatim [vər'betɪm] *adj* textuel ‖ *adv* textuellement

verbiage ['vʌrbi•ɪdʒ] *s* verbiage *m*

verbose [vər'bos] *adj* verbeux

verdant ['vʌrdənt] *adj* vert; naïf, candide

verdict ['vʌrdɪkt] *s* verdict *m*

verdigris ['vʌrdɪ,gris] *s* vert-de-gris *m*

verdure ['vʌrdʒər] *s* verdure *f*

verge [vʌrdʒ] *s* bord *m,* limite *f;* **on the verge of** sur le point de ‖ *intr*—**to verge on** or **upon** toucher à; *(bad faith; the age of forty; etc.)* friser

verification [,vɛrɪfɪ'ke∫ən] *s* vérification *f*

veri•fy ['vɛrɪ,faɪ] *v (pret & pp* **-fied**) *tr* vérifier

verily ['vɛrɪli] *adv* en vérité

veritable ['vɛrɪtəbəl] *adj* véritable

vermilion [vər'mɪljən] *adj & s* vermillon *m*

vermin ['vʌrmɪn] *s (objectionable person)* vermine *f* ‖ *spl (objectionable animals or persons)* vermine

vermouth [vər'muθ], ['vʌrmuθ] *s* vermout *m*

vernacular [vər'nækjələr] *adj* vernaculaire ‖ *s* langue *f* vernaculaire; *(everyday language)* langage *m* vulgaire; *(language peculiar to a class or profession)* jargon *m*

versatile ['vʌrsətɪl] *adj* aux talents variés; *(e.g., mind)* universel, souple

verse [vʌrs] *s* vers *mpl; (stanza)* strophe *f;* (Bib) verset *m*

versed [vʌrst] *adj*—**versed in** versé dans; spécialiste de

versification [,vʌrsɪfɪ'ke∫ən] *s* versification *f*

versi•fy ['vʌrsɪ,faɪ] *v (pret & pp* **-fied**) *tr & intr* versifier

version ['vʌrʒən] *s* version *f*

ver•so [ˈvʌrso] *s* (*pl* **-sos**) (*e.g.*, *of a coin*) revers *m;* (typ) verso *m*

versus [ˈvʌrsəs] *prep* contre

verte•bra [ˈvʌrtɪbrə] *s* (*pl* **-brae** [ˌbri] or **-bras**) vertèbre *f*

vertebrate [ˈvʌrtɪˌbret] *adj & s* vertébré *m*

ver•tex [ˈvʌrtɛks] *s* (*pl* **-texes** or **-tices** [tɪˌsiz]) sommet *m*

vertical [ˈvʌrtɪkəl] *adj* vertical ‖ *s* verticale *f*

ver'tical hold' *s* (telv) commande *f* de stabilité verticale

ver'tical rud'der *s* gouvernail *m* de direction

ver'tical take'-off *s* décollage *m* vertical

verti•go [ˈvʌrtɪˌgo] *s* (*pl* **-gos** or **-goes**) vertige *m*

very [ˈvɛri] *adj* véritable; même, e.g., **at this very moment** à cet instant même ‖ *adv* très, e.g., **I am very hungry** j'ai très faim; bien, e.g., **you are very nice** vous êtes bien gentil; tout, e.g., **the very first** le tout premier; e.g., **my very best** tout mon possible; **for my very own** pour moi tout seul; **very much** beaucoup

vesicle [ˈvɛsɪkəl] *s* vésicule *f*

vespers [ˈvɛspərz] *spl* vêpres *fpl*

vessel [ˈvɛsəl] *s* bâtiment *m*, navire *m;* (*container*) vase *m;* (anat, bot, zool) vaisseau *m*

vest [vɛst] *s* gilet *m;* **to play it close to the vest** (coll) jouer serré ‖ *tr* revêtir; **to vest with** investir de, revêtir de

vest'ed in'terests *spl* classes *fpl* dirigeantes

vestibule [ˈvɛstɪˌbjul] *s* vestibule *m*

ves'tibule car' *s* (rr) wagon *m* à soufflets

vestige [ˈvɛstɪdʒ] *s* vestige *m*

vestment [ˈvɛstmənt] *s* vêtement *m* sacerdotal

vest'-pock'et *adj* de poche, de petit format

ves•try [ˈvɛstri] *s* (*pl* **-tries**) sacristie *f;* (*committee*) conseil *m* paroissial

ves'try•man *s* (*pl* **-men**) marguillier *m*

Vesuvius [vɪˈs(j)uviˌəs] *s* le Vésuve

vet [vɛt] *s* (coll) vétérinaire *mf;* (coll) véteran *m* ‖ *tr* examiner de près, examiner soigneusement; (*a manuscript*) corriger, revoir

vetch [vɛtʃ] *s* vesce *f;* (*Lathyrus sativus*) gesse *f*

veteran [ˈvɛtərən] *s* vétéran *m*

veterinarian [ˌvɛtərɪˈnɛriˌən] *s* vétérinaire *mf*

veterinar•y [ˈvɛtərɪˌnɛri] *adj* vétérinaire ‖ *s* (*pl* **-ies**) vétérinaire *mf*

ve•to [ˈvito] *s* (*pl* **-toes**) veto *m* ‖ *tr* mettre son veto à

vex [vɛks] *tr* vexer, contrarier

vexation [vɛkˈseʃən] *s* vexation *f*

via [ˈvaɪə] *prep* via

viaduct [ˈvaɪəˌdʌkt] *s* viaduc *m*

vial [ˈvaɪəl] *s* fiole *f*

viand [ˈvaɪənd] *s* mets *m*

vibrate [ˈvaɪbret] *intr* vibrer

vibration [vaɪˈbreʃən] *s* vibration *f*

vicar [ˈvɪkər] *s* vicaire *m;* (*in Church of England*) curé *m*

vicarage [ˈvɪkərɪdʒ] *s* presbytère *m;* (*duties of vicar*) cure *f*

vicarious [vaɪˈkɛriˌəs] *adj* substitut; (*punish-*

ment) souffert pour autrui; (*power, authority*) délégué; (*enjoyment*) partagé

vice [vaɪs] *s* vice *m;* (*device*) étau *m*

vice'-ad'miral *s* vice-amiral *m*

vice'-pres'ident *s* vice-président *m*

viceroy [ˈvaɪsrɔɪ] *s* vice-roi *m*

vice' squad' *s* brigade *f* des mœurs

vice versa [ˈvaɪsə ˈvʌrsə] *adv* vice versa

vicini•ty [vɪˈsɪnɪti] *s* (*pl* **-ties**) voisinage *m;* environs *mpl*, e.g., **New York and vicinity** New York et ses environs

vicious [ˈvɪʃəs] *adj* vicieux; (*mean*) méchant; (*ferocious*) féroce

vicissitude [vɪˈsɪsɪˌt(j)ud] *s* vicissitude *f*

victim [ˈvɪktɪm] *s* victime *f;* (*e.g., of a collision, fire*) accidenté *m*

victimize [ˈvɪktɪˌmaɪz] *tr* prendre pour victime; (*to swindle*) duper

victor [ˈvɪktər] *s* vainqueur *m*

victorious [vɪkˈtoriˌəs] *adj* victorieux

victo•ry [ˈvɪktəri] *s* (*pl* **-ries**) victoire *f*

victuals [ˈvɪtəlz] *spl* victuailles *fpl*

video [ˈvɪdiˌo] *s* (*pl* **videos**) vidéo; **on video** en vidéo ‖ *tr* (3d pers pres **videoes;** *pret & pp* **videoed;** *ger* **videoing**) enregistrer en vidéo, magnétoscoper

vid'eo arcade' *s* jeu *m* d'arcade

vid'eo cam'era *s* caméra *f* vidéo, caméscope *m*

vid'eo•cassette' *s* vidéocassette *f*

vid'eo•cassette' record'er *s* magnétoscope *m* à cassettes

vid'eo•cassette' record'ing *s* enregistrement *m* sur bande

vid'eo clip' *s* vidéo-clip *m*

vid'eo club' *s* vidéoclub *m*

vid'eo•con'ference *s* visioconférence *f*

vid'eo•disk' *ou* **vid'eo•disc'** *s* vidéodisque *m*

vid'eo display' u'nit *s* (comp) moniteur *m*

vid'eo film' *s* (mov, telv) film *m* vidéo

vid'eo game' *s* jeu *m* vidéo

vid'eo li'brary *s* vidéothèque *f*

vid'eo•phone' *s* vidéotex *m* (*assuré par un réseau téléphonique*)

vid'eo pi'racy *s* piraterie *f* vidéo

vid'eo projec'tor *s* projecteur *m* vidéo

vid'eo record'er *s* vidéogramme *m*, magnétoscope *m*

vid'eo record'ing *s* vidéogramme *m*, magnétoscope *m*

vid'eo sig'nal *s* vidéofrequence *f*

vid'eo•tape' *s* bande *f* magnétique (vidéo); (*recording*) vidéo *m* ‖ *tr* enregistrer en vidéo, magnétoscoper

vid'eo•tape' record'er *s* vidéogramme *m*, magnétoscope *m*

vid'eo•tape' record'ing *s* vidéogramme *m*, magnétoscope *m*

vid'eo•tap'ing *s* enregistrement *m* vidéo

videotex [ˈvɪdiˌoˌtɛks] *ou* **videotext** [ˈvɪdiˌoˌtɛkst] *s* vidéotex *m*, vidéographie *f* interactive

vie [vaɪ] *v* (*pret & pp* **vied;** *ger* **vying**) *intr* rivaliser, lutter

Vienna [vɪˈɛnə] *s* Vienne *f*
Vien•nese [ˌviˑəˈniz] *adj* viennois ‖ *s* (*pl* **-nese**) Viennois *m*
Vietnam [ˌvɪˑɛtˈnɑm] *s* le Vietnam
Vietnam•ese [vɪˌɛtnəˈmiz] *adj* vietnamien ‖ *s* (*pl* **-ese**) Vietnamien *m*
view [vju] *s* vue *f;* **in my view** à mon avis, selon mon opinion; **in view** en vue; **in view of** étant donné, vu; **on view** exposé; **with a view to** en vue de ‖ *tr* voir, regarder; considérer, examiner
viewer [ˈvjuˑər] *s* spectateur *m;* (*for film, slides, etc.*) visionneuse *f;* (telv) télé-spectateur *m*
view′find′er *s* viseur *m*
view′point′ *s* point *m* de vue
vigil [ˈvɪdʒɪl] *s* veille *f;* (eccl) vigile *f;* **to keep a vigil** veiller
vigilance [ˈvɪdʒɪləns] *s* vigilance *f*
vigilant [ˈvɪdʒɪlənt] *adj* vigilant
vignette [vɪnˈjɛt] *s* vignette *f*
vigor [ˈvɪgər] *s* vigueur *f*
vigorous [ˈvɪgərəs] *adj* vigoureux
vile [vaɪl] *adj* vil; (*smell*) infect; (*weather*) sale; (*disgusting*) détestable
vili•fy [ˈvɪlɪˌfaɪ] *v* (*pret & pp* **-fied**) *tr* diffamer, dénigrer
villa [ˈvɪlə] *s* villa *f*
village [ˈvɪlɪdʒ] *s* village *m*
villager [ˈvɪlɪdʒər] *s* villageois *m*
villain [ˈvɪlən] *s* scélérat *m;* (*of a play*) traître *m*
villainous [ˈvɪlənəs] *adj* vil, infame
villain•y [ˈvɪləni] *s* (*pl* **-ies**) vilenie *f,* infamie *f*
vim [vɪm] *s* énergie *f,* vigueur *f*
vinaigrette′ sauce′ [ˌvɪnəˈgrɛt] *s* vinaigrette *f*
vindicate [ˈvɪndɪˌket] *tr* justifier, défendre
vindictive [vɪnˈdɪktɪv] *adj* vindicatif
vine [vaɪn] *s* plante *f* grimpante; (*grape plant*) vigne *f*
vinegar [ˈvɪnɪgər] *s* vinaigre *m*
vinegary [ˈvɪnɪgəri] *adj* aigre, acide; (*ill-tempered*) acariâtre
vine′ stock′ *s* cep *m*
vineyard [ˈvɪnjərd] *s* vignoble *m,* vigne *f*
vintage [ˈvɪntɪdʒ] *s* vendange *f;* (*year*) année *f,* cru *m;* (coll) classe *f,* catégorie *f*
vin′tage wine′ *s* bon cru *m*
vin′tage year′ *s* grande année *f*
vintner [ˈvɪntnər] *s* négociant *m* en vins; (*person who makes wine*) vigneron *m*
vinyl [ˈvaɪnɪl] *s* vinyle *m*
viola [vaɪˈolə], [vɪˈolə] *s* alto *m*
violate [ˈvaɪˑəˌlet] *tr* violer
violation [ˌvaɪˑəˈleʃən] *s* violation *f*
violator [ˈvaɪˑəˌletər] *s* violateur *m*
violence [ˈvaɪˑələns] *s* violence *f*
violent [ˈvaɪˑələnt] *adj* violent
violet [ˈvaɪˑəlɪt] *adj* violet ‖ *s* (*color*) violet *m;* (bot) violette *f*
violin [ˌvaɪˑəˈlɪn] *s* violon *m*
violinist [ˌvaɪˑəˈlɪnɪst] *s* violoniste *mf*
violoncel•lo [ˌvaɪˑələnˈtʃɛlo] *s* (*pl* **-los**) violoncelle *m*

VIP [ˈviˈaɪˈpi] *s* (letterword) (**Very Important Person**) VIP *or* V.I.P. (personnalité de marque)
viper [ˈvaɪpər] *s* vipère *f*
vira•go [vɪˈrego] *s* (*pl* **-goes** or **-gos**) mégère *f*
virgin [ˈvʌrdʒɪn] *adj* vierge ‖ *s* vierge *f;* (*male virgin*) puceau *m*
vir′gin birth′ *s* parthénogenèse *f;* **Virgin Birth** (rel) conception *f* virginale de Jésus
Virgin′ia creep′er [vərˈdʒɪnɪˑə] *s* vigne *f* vierge
virginity [vərˈdʒɪnɪti] *s* virginité *f*
Virgo [ˈvʌrgo] *s* (astr, astrol) la Vierge
virility [vɪˈrɪlɪti] *s* virilité *f*
virology [vaɪˈralədʒi] *s* virologie *f*
virtual [ˈvʌrtʃuˑəl] *adj* véritable, effectif; (mech, opt, phys) virtuel
virtue [ˈvʌrtʃu] *s* vertu *f;* mérite *m,* avantage *m*
virtuosi•ty [ˌvʌrtʃuˈasɪti] *s* (*pl* **-ties**) virtuosité *f*
virtuo•so [ˌvʌrtʃuˈoso] *s* (*pl* **-sos** or **-si** [si]) virtuose *mf*
virtuous [ˈvʌrtʃuˑəs] *adj* vertueux
virulence [ˈvɪrjələns] *s* virulence *f*
virulent [ˈvɪrjələnt] *adj* virulent
virus [ˈvaɪrəs] *s* virus *m*
visa [ˈvizə] *s* visa *m* ‖ *tr* viser
visage [ˈvɪzɪdʒ] *s* visage *m*
vis-à-vis [ˌvizəˈvi] *adj* face à face ‖ *s & adv* vis-à-vis *m* ‖ *prep* vis-à-vis de
viscera [ˈvɪsərə] *spl* viscères *mpl*
viscount [ˈvaɪkaʊnt] *s* vicomte *m*
viscountess [ˈvaɪkaʊntɪs] *s* vicomtesse *f*
viscous [ˈvɪskəs] *adj* visqueux
vise [vaɪs] *s* étau *m*
visible [ˈvɪzɪbəl] *adj* visible
vision [ˈvɪʒən] *s* vision *f*
visionar•y [ˈvɪʒəˌnɛri] *adj* visionnaire ‖ *s* (*pl* **-ies**) visionnaire *mf*
visit [ˈvɪzɪt] *s* visite *f* ‖ *tr* visiter; (*e.g., a person*) rendre visite à ‖ *intr* faire des visites
visitation [ˌvɪzɪˈteʃən] *s* visite *f;* justice *f* du ciel; clémence *f* du ciel; (*e.g., in a séance*) apparition *f;* **Visitation** (eccl) Visitation *f*
vis′iting card′ *s* carte *f* de visite
vis′iting hours′ *spl* heures *fpl* de visite
vis′iting nurse′ *s* infirmière *f* visiteuse
vis′iting profes′sor *s* visiting *m*
vis′iting team′, the *s* les visiteurs *mpl*
visitor [ˈvɪzɪtər] *s* visiteur *m*
visor [ˈvaɪzər] *s* visière *f*
vista [ˈvɪstə] *s* perspective *f*
visual [ˈvɪʒuˑəl] *adj* visuel
vi′sual display′ u′nit *s* (comp) moniteur *m*
visualize [ˈvɪʒuˑəˌlaɪz] *tr* (*in one's mind*) se faire une image mentale de, se représenter; (*to make visible*) visualiser
vital [ˈvaɪtəl] *adj* vital ‖ **vitals** *spl* organes *mpl* vitaux
vitality [vaɪˈtælɪti] *s* vitalité *f*
vitalize [ˈvaɪtəˌlaɪz] *tr* vitaliser
vitamin [ˈvaɪtəmɪn] *s* vitamine *f*
vitiate [ˈvɪʃiˌet] *tr* vicier

vitreous ['vɪtrɪ•əs] *adj* vitreux
vitriolic [,vɪtrɪ'alɪk] *adj* (chem) vitriolique; (fig) trempé dans du vitriol
vituperate [vaɪ't(j)upə,ret] *tr* vitupérer
viva ['vivə] *s* vivat *m* ‖ *interj* vive!, vivent!
vivacious [vaɪ've∫əs] *adj* vif, animé
vivaci•ty [vaɪ'væsɪti] *s* (*pl* -ties) vivacité *f*
viva voce ['vaɪvə'vosi] *adv* de vive voix
vivid ['vɪvɪd] *adj* vif; (*description*) vivant; (*recollection*) vivace
vivi•fy ['vɪvɪ,faɪ] *v* (*pret & pp* -fied) *tr* vivifier
vivisection [,vɪvɪ'sɛk∫ən] *s* vivisection *f*
vixen ['vɪksən] *s* mégère *f*; (zool) renarde *f*
viz. *abbr* (Lat: **videlicet** namely, to wit) c.-à-d., à savoir
vizier [vɪ'zɪr], ['vɪzjər] *s* vizir *m*
vocabular•y [vo'kæbjə,lɛri] *s* (*pl* -ies) vocabulaire *m*
vocal ['vokəl] *adj* vocal; (*inclined to express oneself freely*) communicatif, démonstratif
vo'cal cords' *spl* cordes *fpl* vocales
vocalist ['vokəlɪst] *s* chanteur *m*
vocalize ['vokə,laɪz] *tr* vocaliser ‖ *intr* vocaliser; (phonet) se vocaliser
vocation [vo'ke∫ən] *s* vocation *f*; profession *f*, métier *m*
voca'tional guid'ance [vo'ke∫ənəl] *s* orientation *f* professionnelle
voca'tional school' *s* école *f* professionnelle
vocative ['vakətɪv] *s* vocatif *m*
vociferate [vo'sɪfə,ret] *intr* vociférer
vociferous [vo'sɪfərəs] *adj* vociférant, criard
vogue [vog] *s* vogue *f*; **in vogue** en vogue
voice [vɔɪs] *s* voix *f*; **in a loud voice** à voix haute; **in a low voice** à voix basse; **with one voice** unanimement ‖ *tr* exprimer; (*a consonant*) voiser, sonoriser ‖ *intr* se voiser
voiced *adj* (phonet) voisé, sonore
voiceless ['vɔɪslɪs] *adj* sans voix, aphone; (*consonant*) dévoisée, sourde
void [vɔɪd] *adj* vide; (law) nul; **void of** dénué de ‖ *s* vide *m* ‖ *tr* vider; (*the bowels*) évacuer; (law) rendre nul ‖ *intr* évacuer, excréter
voile [vɔɪl] *s* voile *m*
volatile ['valətɪl] *adj* (*solvent*) volatil; (*disposition*) volage; (*temper*) vif
volatilize ['valətə,laɪz] *tr* volatiliser ‖ *intr* se volatiliser
volcanic [val'kænɪk] *adj* volcanique
volca•no [val'keno] *s* (*pl* -noes or -nos) volcan *m*
volition [və'lɪ∫ən] *s* volition *f*, volonté *f*; **of one's own volition** de son propre gré
volley ['vali] *s* volée *f* ‖ *tr* lancer à la volée; (sports) reprendre de volée ‖ *intr* lancer une volée
vol'ley•ball' *s* volley-ball *m*
volplane ['val,plen] *s* vol *m* plané ‖ *intr* descendre en vol plané

volt [volt] *s* volt *m*
voltage ['voltɪdʒ] *s* voltage *m*, tension *f*; **high voltage** haute tension *f*
volt'age drop' *s* perte *f* de charge
volte-face [vɔlt'fas] *s* volte-face *f*
volt'me'ter *s* voltmètre *m*
voluble ['valjəbəl] *adj* volubile
volume ['valjəm] *s* volume *m*; **to speak volumes** en dire long
vol'ume num'ber *s* tomaison *f*
voluminous [və'luminəs] *adj* volumineux
voluntar•y ['valən,tɛri] *adj* volontaire ‖ *s* (*pl* -ies) (mus) morceau *m* d'orgue improvisé
volunteer [,valən'tɪr] *adj & s* volontaire *mf* ‖ *tr* offrir volontairement ‖ *intr* (mil) s'engager; **to volunteer to** + *inf* s'offrir à + *inf*
voluptuar•y [və'lʌpt∫u,ɛri] *adj* voluptuaire ‖ *s* (*pl* -ies) voluptueux *m*
voluptuous [və'lʌpt∫u•əs] *adj* voluptueux
vomit ['vamɪt] *s* vomissure *f* ‖ *tr & intr* vomir
voodoo ['vudu] *adj & s* vaudou *m*
voracious [və're∫əs] *adj* vorace
voraci•ty [və'ræsɪti] *s* (*pl* -ties) voracité *f*
vor•tex ['vɔrtɛks] *s* (*pl* -texes or -tices [tɪ,siz]) vortex *m*, tourbillon *m*
vota•ry ['votəri] *s* (*pl* -ries) fidèle *mf*
vote [vot] *s* vote *m*; **by popular vote** au suffrage universel; **to put to the vote** mettre aux voix; **to tally the votes** dépouiller le scrutin; **vote by show of hands** vote à main levée ‖ *tr* voter; **to vote down** repousser; **to vote in** élire ‖ *intr* voter; **to vote for** voter; **to vote on** passer au vote
voter ['votər] *s* votant *m*, électeur *m*
vot'ing booth' *s* isoloir *m*
vot'ing machine' *s* machine *f* électorale
votive ['votɪv] *adj* votif
vouch [vaut∫] *tr* affirmer, garantir ‖ *intr*—**to vouch for** répondre de
voucher ['vaut∫ər] *s* garant *m*; (*certificate*) récépissé *m*, pièce *f* comptable, bon *m* de change
vouch•safe' *tr* octroyer ‖ *intr*—**to vouch-safe to** + *inf* daigner + *inf*
vow [vau] *s* vœu *m*; **to take vows** entrer en religion ‖ *tr* (*e.g., revenge*) jurer ‖ *intr* faire un vœu; **to vow to** faire vœu de
vowel ['vau•əl] *s* voyelle *f*
voyage ['vɔɪ•ɪdʒ] *s* (*by air or sea*) traversée *f*; (*any journey*) voyage *m* ‖ *tr* traverser ‖ *intr* voyager
voyager ['vɔɪ•ɪdʒər] *s* voyageur *m*
vs. *abbr* (**versus**) contre
vulcanize ['vʌlkə,naɪz] *tr* vulcaniser
vulgar ['vʌlgər] *adj* grossier; (*popular, common; vernacular*) vulgaire
vulgari•ty [vʌl'gærɪti] *s* (*pl* -ties) grossièreté *f*, vulgarité *f*
Vul'gar Lat'in *s* latin *m* vulgaire
vulnerable ['vʌlnərəbəl] *adj* vulnérable
vulture ['vʌlt∫ər] *s* vautour *m*

W

W, w [ˈdʌbəlˌju] *s* XXIIIᵉ lettre de l'alphabet

wad [wɑd] *s* (*of cotton*) tampon *m;* (*of papers*) liasse *f;* (*in a gun*) bourre *f* ‖ *v* (*pret & pp* **wadded;** *ger* **wadding**) *tr* bourrer

waddle [ˈwɑdəl] *s* dandinement *m* ‖ *intr* se dandiner

wade [wed] *tr* traverser à gué ‖ *intr* marcher dans l'eau, patauger; **to wade into** (coll) s'attaquer à; **to wade through** (coll) avancer péniblement dans

wad′ing bird′ *s* (orn) échassier *m*

wad′ing pool′ *s* pataugeoire *f*

wafer [ˈwefər] *s* (*thin, crisp cake*) gaufrette *f;* (*pill*) cachet *m;* (*for sealing letters*) pain *m* à cacheter; (eccl) hostie *f*

waffle [ˈwɑfəl] *s* gaufre *f* ‖ *tr* (sports) faillir laisser tomber (*une balle*) ‖ *intr* vaciller, user d'équivoques; parler pour ne rien dire

waf′fle i′ron *s* gaufrier *m*, moule *m* à gaufre

waft [wæt], [wɑft] *tr* porter; (*a kiss*) envoyer ‖ *intr* flotter

wag [wæg] *s* (*of head*) hochement *m;* (*of tail*) frétillement *m;* (*jester*) farceur *m* ‖ *v* (*pret & pp* **wagged;** *ger* **wagging**) *tr* (*the head*) hocher; (*the tail*) remuer ‖ *intr* frétiller

wage [wedʒ] *s* salaire *m;* **wages** gages *mpl*, salaire *m;* (fig) salaire, récompense *f* ‖ *tr*—**to wage war** faire la guerre

wage′ earn′er [ˌʌrnər] *s* salarié *m*

wage′-price′ freeze′ *s* blocage *m* des prix et des salaires

wager [ˈwedʒər] *s* pari *m;* **to lay a wager** faire un pari ‖ *tr & intr* parier

wage′ work′er *s* salarié *m*

waggish [ˈwægɪʃ] *adj* plaisant, facétieux

wagon [wægən] *s* charrette *f;* (*Conestoga wagon; plaything*) chariot *m;* (mil) fourgon *m;* **to be on the wagon** (slang) s'abstenir de boissons alcooliques

wag′tail′ *s* hochequeue *m*, bergeronnette *f*

waif [wef] *s* (*founding*) enfant *m* trouvé; animal *m* égaré *or* abandonné; (*stray child*) voyou *m*

wail [wel] *s* lamentation *f*, plainte *f* ‖ *intr* se lamenter, gémir

wain·scot [ˈwenskət] *s* lambris *m* ‖ *v* (*pret & pp* **-scoted** *ou* **-scotted;** *ger* **-scoting** *ou* **-scotting**) *tr* lambrisser

waist [west] *s* (*of human body; corresponding part of garment*) taille *f*, ceinture *f;* (*garment*) corsage *m*, blouse *f*

waist′band′ *s* ceinture *f*

waist′cloth′ *s* pagne *m*

waistcoat [ˈwest,kot] *s* gilet *m*

waist′-deep′ *adj* jusqu'à la ceinture

waist′line′ *s* taille *f*, ceinture *f;* **to keep** or **watch one's waistline** garder or soigner sa ligne

wait [wet] *s* attente *f;* **to lie in wait for** guetter ‖ *tr*—**to wait one's turn** attendre son tour ‖ *intr* attendre; **to wait for** attendre; **to wait on** (*customers; dinner guests*) servir

wait′-and-see′ pol′icy *s* attentisme *m*

waiter [ˈwetər] *s* garçon *m;* (*tray*) plateau *m*

wait′ing list′ *s* liste *f* d'attente

wait′ing room′ *s* salle *f* d'attente; (*of a doctor*) antichambre *f*

waitress [ˈwetrɪs] *s* serveuse *f;* **waitress!** mademoiselle!

waive [wev] *tr* renoncer à; (*to defer*) différer

waiver [ˈwevər] *s* renonciation *f*, abandon *m*

wake [wek] *s* (*watch by the body of a dead person*) veillée *f* mortuaire; (*of a boat or other moving object*) silage *m;* **in the wake of** dans le sillage de, à la suite de ‖ *v* (*pret* **waked** or **woke** [wok]; *pp* **waked**) *tr* réveiller ‖ *intr*—**to wake to** se rendre compte de; **to wake up** se réveiller

wakeful [ˈwekfəl] *adj* éveillé

wakefulness [ˈwekfəlnɪs] *s* veille *f*

waken [ˈwekən] *tr* éveiller, réveiller ‖ *intr* s'éveiller, se réveiller

wale [wel] *s* zébrure *f* ‖ *tr* zébrer

Wales [welz] *s* le pays de Galles

walk [wɔk] *s* (*act*) promenade *f;* (*distance*) marche *f;* (*way of walking, bearing*) démarche *f;* (*of a garden*) allée *f;* (*calling*) métier *m;* **to fall into a walk** (*said of horse*) se mettre au pas; **to go for a walk** faire une promenade ‖ *tr* promener; (*a horse*) promener au pas ‖ *intr* aller à pied, marcher; (*to stroll*) se promener; **to walk away** s'en aller à pied; **to walk off with** (*a prize*) gagner; (*a stolen object*) décamper avec; **to walk out** sortir, partir subitement; (*to go on strike*) se mettre en grève; **to walk out on** abandonner; quitter en colère

walk′away′ *s* (coll) victoire *f* facile

walker [ˈwɔkər] *s* marcheur *m*, promeneur *m;* (*pedestrian*) piéton *m;* (*go-cart*) chariot *m* d'enfant; (*used by an infirm person*) déambulateur *m*

walkie-talkie [ˈwɔkiˈtɔki] *s* (rad) talkie-walkie *m*, émetteur-récepteur *m* portatif, parle-en-marche *m*

walk′ing pa′pers *spl*—**to give s.o. his walking papers** (coll) congédier qn

walk′ing shoes′ *spl* souliers *mpl* de marche

walk′ing stick′ *s* canne *f*

Walk′man′ (trademark) *s* (electron) baladeur *m*, somnambule *m*

walk′-on′ *s* (*actor*) figurant *m*, comparse *mf;* (*role*) figuration *f*

walk′out′ (coll) grève *f* improvisée

walk′o′ver *s* (coll) victoire *f* dans un fauteuil

walk′-up′ *s* appartement *m* sans ascenseur

wall [wɔl] *s* mur *m;* (*between rooms; of a pipe, boiler, etc.*) paroi *f;* (*of a fortification*) muraille *f;* **to go to the wall** succomber; perdre la partie ‖ *tr* entourer de murs; **to wall up** murer

wall′board′ *s* panneau *m* or carreau *m* de revêtement

wall′ clock′ *s* pendule *f* murale

wallet [ˈwɑlɪt] *s* portefeuille *m*

wall'flow'er s (bot) ravenelle f, giroflée f; **to be a wallflower** (coll) faire tapisserie

wall' lamp' s applique f

wall' map' s carte f murale

Walloon [wɑ'lun] adj wallon ‖ s (dialect) wallon m; (person) Wallon m

wallop ['wɑləp] s (coll) coup m, gnon m; **with a wallop** (fig) à grand fracas ‖ tr (coll) tanner le cuir à, rosser; (a ball) (coll) frapper raide; (to defeat) (coll) battre

wallow ['wɑlo] s souille f‖ intr se vautrer; (e.g., in wealth) nager

wall'pa'per s papier m peint ‖ tr tapisser

wall'-to-wall' car'peting s tapis m mur à mur, moquette f

walnut ['wɔlnət] s noix f; (tree and wood) noyer m

walrus ['wɔlrəs], [wɑlrəs] s morse m

Walter ['wɔltər] s Gautier m

waltz [wɔlts] s valse f ‖ tr & intr valser

wan [wɑn] adj (comp **wanner;** super **wannest**) pâle blême; (weak) faible

wand [wɑnd] s baguette f; (emblem of authority) bâton m, verge f

wander ['wɑndər] tr vagabonder sur, parcourir ‖ intr errer, vaguer; (said of one's mind) vagabonder

wanderer ['wɑndərər] s vagabond m

wan'der·lust' s manie f des voyages, bougeotte f

wane [wen] s déclin m; (of moon) décours m ‖ intr décliner; (said of moon) décroître

wangle ['wæŋgəl] tr (to obtain by scheming) (coll) resquiller; (accounts) (coll) cuisiner; (e.g., a leave of absence) (coll) carotter; **to wangle one's way out of** (coll) se débrouiller de ‖ intr (coll) pratiquer le système D

wannabe abbr want to be

want [wɔnt] s (need; misery) besoin m; (lack) manque m; **for want of** faute de, à défaut de; **to be in want** être dans la gêne ‖ tr vouloir; (to need) avoir besoin de; **to want s.o. to** + inf vouloir que qn + subj; **to want to** + inf avoir envie de + inf, vouloir + inf ‖ intr être dans le besoin; **to be wanting** manquer

want' ads' spl petites annonces fpl

wanton ['wɑntən] adj déréglé; (e.g., cruelty) gratuit; (e.g., child) espiègle; (e.g., woman) impudique

war [wɔr] s guerre f; **to go to war** se mettre en guerre; (as a soldier) aller à la guerre; **to wage war** faire la guerre ‖ v (pret & pp **warred;** ger **warring**) intr faire la guerre; **to war on** faire la guerre contre

warble ['wɔrbəl] s gazouillement m ‖ intr gazouiller

warbler ['wɔrblər] s (orn) fauvette f

war' cloud' s menace f de guerre

war' correspon'dent s correspondant m de guerre

war' crime' s crime m de guerre

war' cry' s (pl **cries**) cri m de guerre

ward [wɔrd] s (person, usually a minor under protection of another)** pupille mf; (guardianship) tutelle f; (of a city) circonscription f électorale, quartier m; (of a hospital) salle f; (of a lock) gardes fpl ‖ tr—**to ward off** parer

war' dance' s danse f guerrière

warden ['wɔrdən] s gardien m; (of a jail) directeur m; (of a church) marguillier m; (gamekeeper) garde-chasse m

ward' heel'er s politicailleur m servile

ward'robe' s garde-robe f

ward'robe trunk' s malle-armoire f

ward' room' s (nav) carré m des officiers

ware [wɛr] s faïence f; **wares** articles mpl de vente, marchandises fpl

ware'house' s entrepôt m

ware'house'man s (pl **-men**) garde-magasin m, magasinier m

war'fare' s guerre f

war'head' s charge f creuse

war'-horse' s cheval m de bataille; (coll) vétéran m

warily ['wɛrɪli] adv prudemment

war'like' adj guerrier

war' loan' s emprunt m de guerre

war' lord' s seigneur m de la guerre

warm [wɔrm] adj chaud; (welcome, thanks, friend, etc.) chaleureux; (heart) généreux; **it is warm** (said of weather) il fait chaud; **to be warm** (said of person) avoir chaud; **to keep s.th. warm** tenir q.ch. au chaud; **you're getting warm!** (you've almost found it!) vous brûlez! ‖ tr chauffer, faire chauffer; **to warm up** réchauffer ‖ intr se réchauffer; **to warm up** se réchauffer, chauffer, se chauffer; (said of speaker, discussion, etc.) s'animer s'échauffer

warm'-blood'ed adj passionné, ardent; (animals) à sang chaud

war' memor'ial s monument m aux morts de la guerre

warmer ['wɔrmər] s (culin) réchaud m

warm'-heart'ed adj au cœur généreux

warm'ing pan' s bassinoire f

warmonger ['wɔr,mʌŋgər] s belliciste mf

war' moth'er s marraine f de guerre

warmth [wɔrmθ] s chaleur f

warm'-up' s exercises mpl d'assouplissement; mise f en condition

warn [wɔrn] tr prévenir; **to warn s.o. to** avertir qn de

warning ['wɔrnɪŋ] s avertissement m; **without warning** par surprise

warn'ing shot' s coup m de semonce

war' of attri'tion s guerre f d'usure

war' of nerves' s guerre f des nerfs

warp [wɔrp] s (of a fabric) chaîne f; (of a board) gauchissement m; (naut) touée f ‖ tr gauchir; (the mind, judgment, etc.) fausser; (naut) touer ‖ intr se gauchir; (naut) se touer

war'path' s—**to be on the warpath** être sur le sentier de la guerre; (to be out of sorts) (coll) être d'une humeur de dogue

war'plane' s avion m de guerre

warp′ speed′ s (*in science fiction*) vitesse f de lumière

warrant [ˈwɔrənt] s (*guarantee*) garantie f; (*attestation*) certificat m; (*right*) justification f; (*for arrest*) mandat m d'arrêt ‖ tr garantir; certifier; justifier

war′rant of′ficer s (mil) sous-officier m breveté; (nav) premier maître m

warran•ty [ˈwɔrənti] s (*pl* **-ties**) garantie f; autorisation f

war′ ranty ser′vice s service m après vente

warren [ˈwɔrən] s garenne f

warrior [ˈwɔrjər] s guerrier m

Warsaw [ˈwɔrsɔ] s Varsovie f

war′ship′ s navire m de guerre

wart [wɔrt] s verrue f

war′time′ s temps m de guerre

war′-torn′ adj dévasté par la guerre

war•y [ˈwɛri] adj (*comp* **-ier**; *super* **-iest**) prudent, avisé

wash [wɔʃ] s (*washing*) lavage m; (*clothes washed or to be washed*) lessive f; (*dirty water*) lavure f; (*place where the surf breaks; broken water behind a moving ship*) remous m; (aer) souffle m ‖ tr laver; (*one's hands, face, etc.*) se laver; (*dishes, laundry, etc.*) faire; (*e.g., a seacoast*) baigner; **all washed up** (coll) tombé dans le lac, fichu; **to wash away** enlever; (*e.g., a bank*) affouiller, ronger ‖ intr se laver; (*to do the laundry*) faire la lessive

washable [ˈwɔʃəbəl] adj lavable

wash′-and-wear′ adj de repassage superflu de séchage rapide

wash′ba′sin s (*basin*) cuvette f; (*fixture*) lavabo m

wash′bas′ket s corbeille f à linge

wash′board′ s planche f à laver

wash′bowl′ s (*basin*) cuvette f; (*fixture*) lavabo m

wash′cloth′ s gant m de toilette

wash′day′ s jour m de lessive

washed′-out′ adj délavé, déteint; (coll) flapi, vanné, à plat, vaseux

washed′-up′ adj (coll) hors de combat, ruiné

washer [ˈwɔʃər] s (*person*) laveur m; (*machine*) laveuse f, lessiveuse f; (*ring of metal*) rondelle f; (*ring of rubber*) rondelle de robinet

wash′er•wom′an s (*pl* **-wom′en**) blanchisseuse f

wash′ goods′ spl tissus mpl grand teint

washing [ˈwɔʃiŋ] s lavage m; (*act of washing clothes*) blanchissage m; (*clothes washed or to be washed*) lessive f; **washings** lavures fpl

wash′ing machine′ s machine f à laver, laveuse f automatique

wash′ing so′da s cristaux mpl de soude

wash′out′ s affouillement m; (*person*) (coll) raté m; **to be a washout** (coll) faire fiasco, faire four

wasn't contr **was not**

wash′rag′ s gant m de toilette, torchon m

wash′room′ s cabinet m de toilette, lavabo m

wash′ sale′ s (com) lavage m des titres

wash′stand′ s lavabo m

wash′tub′ s baquet m, cuvier m

wash′ wa′ter s lavure f

wasp [wasp] s guêpe f

WASP [wasp] s (acronym) (**White, Anglo-Saxon, Protestant**) WASP adj invar & mf invar (de race blanche, d'origine anglo-saxonne, de religion protestante)

wasp′ waist′ s taille f de guêpe

waste [west] adj (*land*) inculte; (*material*) de rebut ‖ s (*loss*) gaspillage m; (*garbage*) déchets mpl; (*wild region*) région f inculte; (*of time*) perte f; (*for wiping machinery*) chiffons mpl de nettoyage, effiloche f de coton; **to lay waste** dévaster; **wastes** déchets; excrément m ‖ tr gaspiller, perdre ‖ intr—**to waste away** dépérir, maigrir

waste′bas′ket s corbeille f à papier

wasteful [ˈwestfəl] adj gaspilleur

waste′pa′per s papier m de rebut; (*public sign*) papers

waste′ pipe′ s tuyau m d'écoulement, vidange f

waste′ prod′ucts spl déchets mpl

wastrel [ˈwestrəl] s gaspilleur m, prodigue mf

watch [watʃ] s (*for telling time*) montre f; (*lookout*) garde f, guet m; (naut) quart m; **to be on the watch for** guetter; **to be on watch** (naut) être de quart; **to keep watch over** surveiller ‖ tr (*to look at*) observer, regarder; (*to oversee*) surveiller ‖ intr être aux aguets; (*to keep awake*) veiller; **to watch for** guetter; **to watch out** faire attention; **to watch out for** faire attention à; **to watch over** surveiller; **watch out!** attention! gare!

watch′case′ s boîtier m de montre

watch′ chain′ s chaîne f de montre

watch′ charm′ s breloque f

watch′ crys′tal s verre m de montre

watch′dog′ s chien m de garde; gardien m vigilant

watch′dog′ commit′tee s comité m de surveillance

watchful [ˈwatʃfəl] adj vigilant

watchfulness [ˈwatʃfəlnɪs] s vigilance f

watch′mak′er s horloger m

watch′man s (*pl* **-men**) gardien m

watch′ night′ s réveillon m du jour de l'an

watch′ pock′et s gousset m

watch′ strap′ s bracelet m d'une montre

watch′tow′er s tour f de guet

watch′word′ s (*password*) mot m d'ordre, mot de passe; (*slogan*) devise f

water [ˈwɔtər] s eau f; **of the first water** de premier ordre; (*diamond*) de première eau; **to back water** (naut) culer; reculer; **to be in hot water** (coll) être dans le pétrin; **to fish in troubled waters** pêcher en eau trouble; **to hold water** (coll) tenir debout, être bien fondé; **to make water** (*to urinate*) uriner; (naut) faire eau; **to pour** or **throw cold water**

on (fig) jeter une douche froide sur, refroidir; **to swim under water** nager entre deux eaux; **to tread water** nager debout ‖ *tr (e.g., plants)* arroser; *(horses, cattle, etc.)* abreuver; *(wine)* couper; **to water down** atténuer ‖ *intr (said of horses, cattle, etc.)* s'abreuver; *(said of locomotive, ship, etc.)* faire de l'eau; *(said of eyes)* se mouiller, larmoyer

wa′ter bed′ *s* matelas *m* à eau

wa′ter blis′ter *s* ampoule *f*

wa′ter bot′tle *s* carafe *f* à eau

wa′ter buf′fa•lo *s (pl* **-loes** or **-los)** buffle *m*

wa′ter car′rier *s* porteur *m* d'eau

wa′ter clock′ *s* horloge *f* à eau, horloge d'eau

wa′ter clos′et *s* water-closet *m*, waters *mpl*

wa′ter•col′or *s* aquarelle *f*

wa′ter-cooled′ *adj* à refroidissement d'eau

wa′ter•course′ *s* cours *m* d'eau; *(of a stream)* lit *m*

wa′ter•cress′ *s* cresson *m* de fontaine

wa′ter cure′ *s* cure *f* des eaux

wa′ter•fall′ *s* chute *f* d'eau

wa′ter•front′ *s* terrain *m* sur la rive

wa′ter gap′ *s* percée *f*, trouée *f*, gorge *f*

wa′ter ham′mer *s (in pipe)* coup *m* de bélier

wa′ter heat′er *s* chauffe-eau *m*, chauffe-bain *m*

wa′ter ice′ *s* boisson *f* à demi glacée

wa′tering can′ *s* arrosoir *m*

wa′tering place′ *s (for cattle)* abreuvoir *m*; *(for tourists)* ville *f* d'eau

wa′tering pot′ *s* arrosoir *m*

wa′tering trough′ *s* abreuvoir *m*

wa′ter jack′et *s* chemise *f* d'eau

wa′ter lil′y *s* nénuphar *m*

wa′ter line′ *s* ligne *f* de flottaison; niveau *m* d'eau

wa′ter•logged′ *adj* détrempé

wa′ter main′ *s* conduite *f* principale

wa′ter•mark′ *s (in paper)* filigrane *m;* (naut) laisse *f*

wa′ter•mel′on *s* pastèque *f*, melon *m* d'eau

wa′ter me′ter *s* compteur *m* à eau

wa′ter pick′ *s* (dentistry) jet *m* dentaire

wa′ter pipe′ *s* conduite *f* d'eau

wa′ter po′lo *s* water-polo *m*

wa′ter pow′er *s* force *f* hydraulique, houille *f* blanche

wa′ter•proof′ *adj & s* imperméable *m*

wa′ter•proof′ing *s* imperméabilisation *f*

wa′ter rights′ *spl* droits *mpl* de captation d'eau, droits d'irrigation

wa′ter•shed′ *s* ligne *f* de partage des eaux, ligne de faîte

wa′ter ski′er *s* skieur *m* nautique

wa′ter ski′ing *s* ski *m* nautique

wa′ter sof′tener *s* assouplisseur *m*

wa′ter span′iel *s* (zool) barbet *m*

wa′ter•spout′ *s* descente *f* d'eau, gouttière *f;* *(funnel of wet air)* trombe *f*

wa′ter-supply sys′tem *s* service *m* des eaux; réseau *m* de conduites d'eau

wa′ter ta′ble *s* (geol) nappe *f* phréatique

wa′ter•tight′ *adj* étanche; *(argument)* inattaquable; (law) sans clause échappatoire

wa′ter tow′er *s* château *m* d'eau

wa′ter va′por *s* vapeur *m* d'eau

wa′ter wag′on *s—***to be on the water wagon** (coll) s'abstenir de boissons alcooliques

wa′ter•way′ *s* voie *f* navigable

wa′ter wheel′ *s* roue *f* hydraulique; roue à aubes or à palettes; roue-turbine *f*

wa′ter wings′ *spl* flotteur *m* de natation

wa′ter•works′ *s (system)* canalisations *fpl* d'eau; *(pumping station)* usine *f* de distribution des eaux

watery ['wɔtəri] *adj* aqueux; *(eyes)* larmoyant; *(food)* insipide, fade

watt [wɑt] *s* watt *m*

wattage ['wɑtɪdʒ] *s* puissance *f* en watts

watt′-hour′ *s (pl* **watt-hours)** watt-heure *m*

wattle [wɑtəl] *s (of bird)* caroncule *f;* *(of fish)* barbillon *m*

watt′me′ter *s* wattmètre *m*

wave [wev] *s* onde *f*, vague *f;* *(in hair)* ondulation *f;* geste *m* de la main; *(of heat or cold; of people; of the future)* vague *f;* (phys) onde ‖ *tr (a handkerchief)* agiter; *(the hair)* onduler; *(a hat, newspaper, cane)* brandir; **to wave aside** écarter d'un geste; **to wave good-bye** faire un signe d'adieu; **to wave one's hand** faire un geste de la main ‖ *intr* s'agiter; *(said of a flag)* ondoyer; **to wave to** faire signe à

wave′band′ *s* bande *f* de fréquences

wave′length′ *s* longueur *f* d'onde

wave′ mo′tion *s* mouvement *m* ondulatoire

waver ['wevər] *intr* vaciller

wav•y ['wevi] *adj (comp* **-ier;** *super* **-iest)** onduleux, ondoyant; *(hair; road surface)* ondulé; *(line)* tremblé, onduleux

wax [wæks] *s* cire *f* ‖ *tr* cirer ‖ *intr—***to wax and wane** croître et décroître; **to wax indignant** s'indigner

wax′ bean′ *s* haricot *m* beurre

wax′ pa′per *s* papier *m* paraffiné

wax′ ta′per *s* allumette-bougie *f*

wax′wing′ *s* (orn) jaseur *m*

wax′works′ *s* musée *m* de cire

way [we] *s* voie *f;* *(road)* chemin *m;* *(direction)* côté *m*, sens *m;* *(manner)* façon *f*, manière *f;* *(means)* moyen *m;* *(habit, custom)* manière, habitude *f*, usage *m;* **across the way** en face; **all the way** jusqu'au bout; **by the way** à propos; **by way of** par; comme; **either way** d'une manière ou de l'autre; **get out of the way!** ôtez-vous de là!; **in a way** en un certain sens; **in every way** à tous les égards; **in my (his, etc.) own way** à ma (sa, etc.) façon or manière; **in no way** en aucune façon; **in some ways** par certains côtés; **in such a way that** de sorte que; **in that way** de la sorte; **in this way** de cette façon; **on the way** chemin faisant; **on the way to** en route pour; **out of the way** écarté **that way** par là; **the wrong way** le mauvais sens, la mauvaise route; *(the wrong manner)* la mauvaise façon; *(when brushing hair)* à contre-poil; **this way** par ici; **to be in the way** être encombrant; **to feel one's way** avancer à tâtons; **to get out of the way** s'écarter; **to get** (*s.th. or s.o.*) **out of the way** se débarrasser de (*q.ch. or qn*); **to give way** céder; **to go one's own way** faire bande à part; **to go one's way** passer son chemin; **to go out of one's way** faire un détour; (fig) se déranger; **to have one's way** avoir le dernier mot, l'emporter; **to keep out of s.o.'s way** se tenir à l'écart de qn; **to know one's way around** connaître son affaire, être à la coule; **to lead the way** montrer le chemin; **to make one's way** se frayer un chemin; **to make way for** faire place à; **to mend one's ways** s'amender; **to see one's way to** trouver moyen de; **to stand in the way of** barrer le chemin à; **under way** en marche, en cours; **way down** descente *f;* **way in** entrée *f;* **way out** sortie *f;* **ways** (*for launching a ship*) couette *f,* anguilles *fpl;* **way through** passage *m;* **way up** montée *f;* **which way?** par où?

way′bill′ *s* feuille *f* de route, lettre *f* de voiture
wayfarer [ˈwe,fɛrər] *s* voyageur *m,* vagabond *m*
way′lay′ *v* (*pret & pp* **-laid**) *tr* embusquer; (*to buttonhole*) arrêter au passage
way′ of life′ *s* manière *f* de vivre, genre *m* de vie, train *m* de vie
way′side′ *s* bord *m* de la route; **to fall by the wayside** rester en chemin
wayward [ˈwewərd] *adj* capricieux; rebelle
we [wi] *pron pers* nous §85, §87; nous autres, e.g., **we Americans** nous autres américains
weak [wik] *adj* faible
weaken [ˈwikən] *tr* affaiblir ‖ *intr* faiblir, s'affaiblir
weakling [ˈwiklɪŋ] *s* chétif *m,* malingre *mf;* (*in character*) mou *m*
weak′-mind′ed *adj* irrésolu, d'esprit faible; (*feeble-minded*) débile
weakness [ˈwiknɪs] *s* faiblesse *f*
weal [wil] *s* papule *f;* (archaic) bien *m*
wealth [wɛlθ] *s* richesse *f*
wealth•y [ˈwɛlθi] *adj* (*comp* **-ier;** *super* **-iest**) riche, opulent
wean [win] *tr* sevrer; **to wean away from** détacher de
weapon [ˈwɛpən] *s* arme *f*
weaponize [ˈwɛpənaɪz] *tr* transformer en une arme
weaponry [ˈwɛpənri] *s* armement *m*
wear [wɛr] *s* (*use*) usage *m;* (*wasting away from use*) usure *f;* (*clothing*) vêtements *mpl,* articles *mpl* d'habillement; **for evening wear** pour le soir; **for everyday wear** pour tous les jours ‖ *v* (*pret* **wore** [wor]; *pp* **worn** [worn]) *tr* porter; (*to put on*) mettre; **to wear down** or **out** user; (*e.g., one's patience*) épuiser ‖ *intr* s'user; **to wear off** s'effacer; **to wear on** s'écouler, s'avancer; **to wear out** s'user; **to wear well** durer
wearable [ˈwɛrəbəl] *adj* mettable
wear′ and tear′ [tɛr] *s* usure *f*
weariness [ˈwɪrɪnɪs] *s* lassitude *f,* fatigue *f;* (*boredom*) ennui *m*

wear′ing appar′el [ˈwɛrɪŋ] *s* vêtements *mpl,* habits *mpl*
wearisome [ˈwɪrɪsəm] *adj* lassant, ennuyeux
wea•ry [ˈwɪri] *adj* (*comp* **-rier;** *super* **-riest**) las ‖ *v* (*pret & pp* **-ried**) *tr* lasser ‖ *intr* se lasser
weasel [ˈwizəl] *s* (zool) belette *f;* (slang) mouchard *m*
wea′sel words′ *spl* mots *mpl* ambigus
weather [ˈwɛðər] *s* temps *m;* **to be under the weather** (coll) se sentir patraque; (*from drinking*) (coll) avoir mal aux cheveux; **what's the weather like?** quel temps fait-il? ‖ *tr* altérer; (*e.g., difficulties*) survivre à, étaler ‖ *intr* s'altérer
weath′er balloon′ *s* ballon *m* atmosphérique
weath′er-beat′en *adj* usé par les intempéries
weath′er bu′reau *s* bureau *m* météorologique, météo *f*
weath′er•cock′ *s* girouette *f;* (fig) girouette, caméléon *m*
weath′er fore′cast *s* bulletin *m* météorologique
weath′er fore′caster *s* météorologue *mf,* météorologiste *mf*
weath′er fore′casting *s* prévision *f* du temps
weath′er report′ *s* bulletin *m* de la météo
weath′er sta′tion *s* station *f* météorologique
weath′er strip′ping *s* bourrelet *m*
weath′er vane′ *s* girouette *f*
weave [wiv] *s* armure *f* ‖ *v* (*pret* **wove** [wov] or **weaved;** *pp* **wove** or **woven** [ˈwovən]) *tr* tisser; **to weave one's way through** se faufiler à travers, se faufiler entre ‖ *intr* tisser; serpenter, zigzaguer
weaver [ˈwivər] *s* tisserand *m*
Web [wɛb] *s* (comp) Web *m,* web *m,* WWW, La Toile
web [wɛb] *s* (*piece of cloth*) tissu *m;* (*roll of newsprint*) rouleau *m;* (*of spider*) toile *f;* (*between toes of birds and other animals*) palmure *f;* (*of an iron rail*) âme *f;* (fig) trame *f*
web′-foot′ed *adj* palmé, palmipède
Web′ page′ *s* page *f* Web
Web′ site′ *s* (comp) Site *m* Web, site *m*
we'd *contr* we would
wed [wɛd] *v* (*pret & pp* **wed** or **wedded;** *ger* **wedding**) *tr* (*to join in wedlock*) marier; (*to take in marriage*) épouser ‖ *intr* épouser, se marier
wedding [ˈwɛdɪŋ] *adj* nuptial ‖ *s* mariage *m,* noces *fpl*
wed′ding ban′quet *s* repas *m* de noce
wed′ding cake′ *s* gâteau *m* de mariage
wed′ding cer′emo•ny *s* (*pl* **-nies**) cérémonie *f* nuptiale
wed′ding day′ *s* jour *m* des noces; (*anniversary*) anniversaire *m* du mariage
wed′ding dress′ *s* robe *f* nuptiale, robe de noce, robe de mariée
wed′ding march′ *s* marche *f* nuptiale
wed′ding night′ *s* nuit *f* de noces
wed′ding pres′ent *s* cadeau *m* de mariage; **wedding presents** corbeille *f* de mariage
wed′ding ring′ *s* anneau *m* nuptial, alliance *f*
wedge [wɛdʒ] *s* coin *m* ‖ *tr* coincer

wedlock [ˈwɛdlɑk] *s* mariage *m*
Wednesday [ˈwɛnzdi] *s* mercredi *m*
wee [wi] *adj* tout petit
weed [wid] *s* mauvaise herbe *f;* **the weed** (coll) le tabac; **weeds** vêtements *mpl* de deuil ‖ *tr &* *intr* désherber, sarcler; **to weed out** éliminer, extirper
weed′ing hoe′ *s* sarcloir *m*
weed′ kill′er *s* herbicide *m*
weed′ whack′er [ˌhwækər] *s* taille-herbe *m*
week [wik] *s* semaine *f;* **a week from today** d'aujourd'hui en huit; **week in week out** d'un bout de la semaine à l'autre
week′day′ *s* jour *m* de semaine, jour ouvrable
week′ days′ *adv* en semaine
week′ end′ *s* fin *f* de semaine, week-end *m* ‖ *intr* passer le week-end
week‧ly [ˈwikli] *adj* hebdomadaire ‖ *s* (*pl* **-lies**) hebdomadaire *m* ‖ *adv* tous les huit jours
weep [wip] *v* (*pret & pp* **wept** [wɛpt]) *tr* pleurer ‖ *intr* pleurer; (*to drip*) suinter; **to weep for** pleurer; (*joy*) pleurer de
weep′ing wil′low *s* saule *m* pleureur
weep‧y [ˈwipi] *adj* (*comp* **-ier;** *super* **-iest**) (coll) pleurnicheur
weevil [ˈwivəl] *s* charançon *m*
weft [wɛft] *s* (*yarns running across warp*) trame *f;* (*fabric*) tissu *m*
weigh [we] *tr* peser; (*anchor*) lever; **to weigh down** faire pencher; **to weigh in one's hand** soupeser ‖ *intr* peser; **to weigh heavily with** avoir du poids auprès de; **to weigh in** (sports) se faire peser
weight [wet] *s* poids *m;* **to gain weight** prendre du poids; **to lift weights** faire des haltères; **to lose weight** perdre du poids; **to throw one's weight around** (coll) s'imposer ‖ *tr* charger; (*statistically*) pondérer; **to weight down** alourdir
weightless [ˈwetlɪs] *adj* sans pesanteur
weightlessness [ˈwetlɪsnɪs] *s* apesanteur *f*, impesanteur *f*
weight′ lift′er [ˌlɪftər] *s* (sports) haltérophile *m*
weight′ lift′ing *s* poids et haltères *mpl*
weight‧y [ˈweti] *adj* (*comp* **-ier;** *super* **-iest**) pesant, lourd; (*troublesome*) grave; important, puissant
weir [wɪr] *s* (*dam*) barrage *m;* (*trap*) filet *m* à poissons
weird [wɪrd] *adj* surnaturel; étrange
welcome [ˈwɛlkəm] *adj* bienvenu; (*change, news, etc.*) agréable; **to be welcome to** + *inf* être libre de + *inf;* **you are welcome!** (*i.e., gladly received*) soyez le bienvenu!; (*in response to thanks*) de rien!, je vous en prie!, il n'y a pas de quoi!; **you are welcome to it** c'est à votre disposition; (ironically) je ne vous envie pas ‖ *s* bienvenue *f*, bon accueil *m* ‖ *tr* souhaiter la bienvenue à, faire bon accueil à, accueillir; **to welcome coldly** faire mauvais accueil à, accueillir froidement
welcoming [ˈwɛlkəmɪŋ] *adj* (*friendly*) accueillant; (*party, speeches*) d'accueil

weld [wɛld] *s* soudure *f* autogène; (bot) gaude *f*, réséda *m* ‖ *tr* souder à l'autogène
welder [ˈwɛldər] *s* soudeur *m;* (mach) soudeuse *f*
welding [ˈwɛldɪŋ] *s* soudure *f* autogène
weld′ing gun′ *s* pistolet *m* à souder
welfare [ˈwɛlˌfɛr] *s* bien-être *m;* (*for under-privileged*) aide *f* sociale
wel′fare state′ *s* état-providence *m*
wel′fare work′ *s* assistance *f* sociale
we'll *contr* **we will**
well [wɛl] *adj* bien (*enjoying good health*) bien, bien portant; **all's well** tout est bien; **it would be just as well to** il serait bon de; **to be well** aller bien ‖ *s* (*drilled hole*) puits *m;* (*natural source of water*) source *f*, fontaine *f;* (*of stairway*) cage *f* ‖ *adv* bien; **as well** aussi; **as well as** aussi bien que; **well and good!** à la bonne heure! ‖ *intr*—**to well up** jaillir ‖ *interj* alors!, tiens!
well′-bal′anced *adj* bien équilibré
well′-behaved′ *adj* de bonne conduite; (*child*) sage
well′-be′ing *s* bien-être *m*
well′born′ *adj* bien né
well-bred [ˈwɛlˈbrɛd] *adj* bien élevé
well′built′ *adj* (*building*) bien construit, solide; (*person*) bien bâti, solide, costaud
well′-disposed′ *adj* bien dispose
well-done [ˈwɛlˈdʌn] *adj* bien fait; (culin) bien cuit
well′-dressed′ *adj* bien vêtu
well′-ed′ucated *adj* cultivé, instruit
well′-fixed′ *adj* (coll) bien renté, riche
well′-formed′ *adj* bien conformé
well′-found′ed *adj* bien fondé, consistant
well′-groomed′ *adj* paré, soigné
well′-heeled′ *adj* (coll) huppé, riche
well′-informed′ *adj* bien informé
well′-inten′tioned *adj* bien intentionné
well-kept [ˈwɛlˈkɛpt] *adj* bien tenu; (*secret*) bien gardé
well-known [ˈwɛlˈnon] *adj* bien connu, notoire
well′-matched′ *adj* bien assortis
well′-mean′ing *adj* bien intentionné
well′-nigh′ *adv* presque
well′-off′ *adj* fortuné, prospère
well′-preserved′ *adj* bien conservé
well-read [ˈwɛlˈrɛd] *adj* instruit, cultivé
well-spent [ˈwɛlˈspɛnt] *adj* bien employé
well′-spo′ken *adj* (*courteous*) poli, courtois; (*words*) bien choisi, bien trouvé
well′spring′ *s* source *f*, source intarissable
well′ sweep′ *s* chadouf *m*
well′-thought′-of′ *adj* de bonne réputation
well′-timed′ *adj* opportun
well-to-do [ˈwɛltəˈdu] *adj* aisé, cossu
well′-tried′ *s* éprouvé
well-wisher [ˈwɛlˈwɪˌʃər] *s* partisan *m*, ami *m* fidèle
well′-worn′ *adj* usé; (*subject*) rebattu
Welsh [wɛlʃ] *adj* gallois ‖ *s* (*language*) gallois *m;* **the Welsh** les Gallois *mpl* ‖ (*l.c.*) *intr*

(slang) manquer à sa parole, manquer à ses obligations; **to welsh on s.o.** (slang) manquer à qn

Welsh′man s (pl **-men**) Gallois m

Welsh′ rab′bit or **rare′bit** [′reɛrbɪt] s fondue f au fromage et à la bière sur canapé

welt [wɛlt] s zébrure f; (border) bordure f; (of shoe) trépointe f

welter [′wɛltər] s confusion f, fouillis m ‖ intr se vautrer

wel′ter•weight′ s (boxing) poids m mimoyen, poids welter, mi-moyen m

wen [wɛn] s kyste m sébacé, loupe f

wench [wɛntʃ] s jeune fille f, jeune femme f

wend [wɛnd] tr—**to wend one's way (to)** diriger ses pas (vers)

we're contr **we are**

weren't contr **were not**

west [wɛst] adj & s ouest m ‖ adv à l'ouest, vers l'ouest

western [′wɛstərn] adj occidental, de l'ouest ‖ s (mov) western m

westerner [′wɛstərnər] s habitant m de l'ouest, Occidental m

West′ In′dies [′ɪndiz] spl Indes fpl occidentales, Antilles fpl

westward [′wɛstwərd] adv vers l'ouest

wet [wɛt] adj (comp **wetter**; super **wettest**) mouillé; (damp) humide; (rainy) pluvieux; (paint) frais, (coll) antiprohibitionniste; **all wet** (slang) fichu, erroné ‖ s antiprohibitionniste mf ‖ v (pret & p **wet** or **wetted**; ger **wetting**) tr mouiller ‖ intr se mouiller

wet′back′ s (pej) immigré m or immigrée hispanique (ouvrier agricole mexicain)

wet′ bat′ter•y s (pl **-ies**) pile f à liquide

wet′ blan′ket s trouble-fête mf, rabat-joie m

wet′ dream′ s pollution f nocturne

wet′ nurse′ s nourrice f

wet′ paint′ s peinture f fraîche; (public sign) attention à la peinture

wet′ suit′ s combinaison f de plongée

we've contr **we have**

whack [hwæk] s (coll) coup m, gnon m; (try) (coll) tentative f; **to have a whack at** (coll) s'attaquer à ‖ tr (coll) cogner ‖ interj vlan!

whale [hwel] s baleine f; (sperm whale) cachalot m; **to have a whale of a time** (coll) s'amuser follement ‖ tr (coll) rosser

whale′bone′ s baleine f, fanon m de baleine

whaler [′hwelər] s baleinier m

wham [wæm] interj vlan!

wharf [hwɔrf] s (pl **wharves** [hwɔrvz] or **wharfs**) quai m, débarcadère m

what [hwɑt] adj interr quel §80, e.g., **what time is it?** quelle heure est-il?; e.g., **what is his occupation?** quel est son métier? ‖ adj rel ce qui, e.g., **I'll give you what water I have left** je vous donnerai ce qui me reste d'eau; ce que, e.g., **I know what drink you want** je sais ce que vous voulez comme boisson ‖ pron interr qu'est-ce qui, e.g., **what happened?** qu'est-ce qui s'est passé?; que, e.g., **what are**

you doing? que faites-vous?; qu'est-ce que, e.g., **what are you doing?** qu'est-ce que vous faites?; comment, e.g., **what is he like?** comment est-il?; combien, e.g., **what is two and two?** combien font deux et deux?; **so what!** tant pis!; **what** (did you say)? comment?; **what else?** quoi d'autre?, quoi encore; **what for?** pourquoi donc?; **what if** si, e.g., **what if I were to die?** si je venais à mourir?; **what if I did?, what of it?, so what?** qu'importe?; **what is it?** qu'est-ce que c'est?, qu'est-ce qu'il y a?; **what now?** alors?; **what's that?** qu'est-ce que c'est que cela?; **what then?** et après? ‖ pron rel ce qui, ce que; ce dont §79, e.g., **I have what you need** j'ai ce dont vous avez besoin; ce à quoi, e.g., **I know what you are thinking of** je sais ce à quoi vous pensez; (sometimes untranslated), e.g, **he asked them what time it was** il leur a demandé l'heure; **to know what's what** (coll) s'y connaître, être au courant ‖ interj comment!; **what a** que de, e.g., **what a lot of people!** que de monde!; quel §80, e.g., **what a pity!** quel dommage!

what•ev′er adj quel que §80; moindre or quelconque, e.g., **is there any hope whatever?** y a-t-il le moindre espoir?, y a-t-il un espoir quelconque? ‖ pron tout ce qui; tout ce que, e.g., **tell him whatever you like** dites-lui tout ce que vous voudrez; quoi que, e.g., **whatever you do** quoi que vous fassiez; **whatever comes** à tout hasard

what′not′ s étagère f

what's′-his-name′ s (coll) Monsieur un tel

wheal [wil] s papule f

wheat [hwit] s blé m

weedle [′hwidəl] tr enjôler

wheel [hwil] s roue f; **at the wheel** au volant ‖ tr (to turn) faire pivoter; (a wheelbarrow, table, etc.) rouler ‖ intr pivoter; (said, e.g., of birds in the sky) tournoyer; **to wheel about** or **around** faire demi-tour

wheelbarrow [′hwil,bæro] s brouette f

wheel′base′ s (aut) empattement m

wheel′chair′ s fauteuil m roulant pour malade, voiture f d'infirme, chaise f roulante

wheel′ horse′ s (horse) timonier m; (person) bûcheur m

wheelwright [′hwil,raɪt] s charron m

wheeze [hwiz] s respiration f sifflante; (pathol) cornage m ‖ intr respirer avec peine, souffler

wheezing [′hwizɪŋ] s sifflement m

whelp [hwɛlp] s petit m ‖ tr & intr mettre bas

when [hwɛn] adv quand ‖ conj quand, lorsque; (on which, in which) où; (whereas) alors que

whence [hwɛns] adv & conj d'où

when•ev′er conj chaque fois que, quand

where [hwɛr] adv & conj où; **from where** d'où

whereabouts [′hwɛrə,baʊts] s—**the whereabouts of** l'endroit où se trouve ‖ adv & conj où donc

whereas [hwɛr′æz] conj tandis que, attendu que ‖ s considérant m

where•by′ conj par lequel

wherefore ['hwɛrfor] *s & adv* pourquoi *m* ‖ *conj* à cause de quoi

where•from' *adv* d'où

where•in' *adv* d'où; en quoi ‖ *conj* où

where•of' *adv* de quoi ‖ *conj* dont §79

where•up•on' *adv* sur quoi, sur ce

wherever [hwɛr'ɛvər] *conj* partout où; où que, n'importe où

wherewithal ['hwɛrwɪð,ɔl] *s* ressources *fpl*, moyens *mpl*

whet [hwɛt] *v* (*pret & pp* **whetted**; *ger* **whetting**) *tr* aiguiser

whether ['wɛðər] *conj* si; que, e.g., **it is doubtful whether you can finish** il est douteux que vous puissiez finir; e.g., **whether he is rich or poor** qu'il soit riche ou qu'il soit pauvre; **whether or no** de toute façon; **whether or not** qu'il en soit ainsi ou non

whet'stone' *s* pierre *f* à aiguiser

whew [hwju] *interj* ouf!

whey [hwe] *s* petit lait *m*

which [hwɪtʃ] *adj interr* quel §80, e.g., **which university do you prefer?** quelle université préférez-vous?; **which one?** lequel? ‖ *adj rel* le . . . que, e.g., **choose which road you prefer** choisissez le chemin que vous préférez ‖ *pron interr* lequel §78; **which is which?** lequel des deux est-ce?; **which of them?** lequel d'entre eux? ‖ *pron rel* qui; que; dont §79

which•ev'er *adj rel* n'importe quel ‖ *pron rel* n'importe lequel

whiff [hwɪf] *s* bouffé *f*; **to get a whiff of** flairer

while [hwaɪl] *s* temps *m*, moment *m*; **a long while** longtemps; **a (little) while ago** tout à l'heure; **in a little while** sous peu, tout à l'heure ‖ *conj* pendant que; (*as long as*) tant que; (*although*) quoique ‖ *tr*—**to while away** tuer, faire passer

whim [hwɪm] *s* caprice *m*, lubie *f*

whimper ['hwɪmpər] *s* pleurnicherie *f* ‖ *tr* dire en pleurnichant ‖ *intr* pleurnicher

whimsical ['hwɪmzɪkəl] *adj* capricieux, lunatique

whine [hwaɪn] *s* geignement *m*; (*of siren*) hurlement *m* ‖ *intr* geindre; (*said of siren*) hurler

whin•ny ['hwɪni] *s* (*pl* **-nies**) hennissement *m* ‖ *v* (*pret & pp* **-nied**) *intr* hennir

whip [hwɪp] *s* fouet *m* ‖ *v* (*pret & pp* **whipped** or **whipt**; *ger* **whipping**) *tr* fouetter; (*to defeat*) battre; (*the end of a rope*) surlier; **to whip out** (*e.g., a gun*) sortir brusquement; **to whip up** (*e.g., a supper*) (coll) préparer à l'improviste; (*e.g., enthusiasm*) (coll) stimuler

whip'cord' *s* corde *f* à fouet

whip' hand' *s* main *f* du fouet; (*upper hand*) avantage *m*, dessus *m*

whip'lash' *s* mèche *f* de fouet; (aut) coup *m* de lapin

whip'lash' in'jury *s* lésion *f* traumatique

whipped' cream' *s* crème *f* fouettée, chantilly *m*

whipper-snapper ['hwɪpər,snæpər] *s* freluquet *m*, paltoquet *m*

whipping ['hwɪpɪŋ] *s* (*punishment*) correction *f*; (*of rope*) surliure *f*; **to give s.o. a whipping** fouetter qn

whip'ping boy' *s* tête *f* de Turc

whip'ping post' *s* poteau *m* des condamnés au fouet

whippoorwill [,hwɪpər'wɪl] *s* (*Caprimulgus vociferus*) engoulevent *m* américain

whir [hwʌr] *s* ronflement *m* ‖ *v* (*pret & pp* **whirred**; *ger* **whirring**) *intr* ronfler

whirl [hwʌrl] *s* tourbillon *m*; (*of events, parties, etc.*) succession *f* ininterrompue ‖ *tr* faire tourbillonner ‖ *intr* tourbillonner; **his head whirls** la tête lui tourne

whirligig ['hwʌrlɪ,gɪg] *s* tourniquet *m*; (ent) gyrin *m*, tourniquet

whirl'pool' *s* tourbillon *m*, remous *m*

whirl'wind' *s* tourbillon *m*

whirlybird ['hwʌrli,bʌrd] *s* (coll) hélicoptère *m*

whisk [hwɪsk] *s* (*rapid, sweeping stroke*) coup *m* léger; (*broom*) époussette *f*; (culin) fouet *m* ‖ *tr* balayer; (culin) fouetter; **to whisk out of sight** escamoter ‖ *intr* aller comme un trait

whisk' broom' *s* époussette *f*

whiskers ['hwɪskərz] *spl* barbe *f*, poils *mpl* de barbe; (*on side of face*) favoris *mpl*; (*of cat*) moustaches *fpl*

whiskey ['hwɪski] *s* whisky *m*

whisper ['hwɪspər] *s* chuchotement *m* ‖ *tr* chuchoter, dire à l'oreille ‖ *intr* chuchoter

whispering ['hwɪspərɪŋ] *s* chuchotement *m*

whist [hwɪst] *s* whist *m*

whistle ['hwɪsəl] *s* (*sound*) sifflement *m*; (*device*) sifflet *m*; **to wet one's whistle** (coll) s'humecter le gosier ‖ *tr* siffler, soffloter ‖ *intr* siffler; **to whistle for** siffler; attendre en vain, se voir obligé de se passer de

whis'tle stop' *s* arrêt *m* facultatif

whit [hwɪt] *s*—**not a whit** pas un brin; **to not care a whit** s'en moquer

white [hwaɪt] *adj* blanc ‖ *s* blanc *m*; blanc d'œuf; **whites** (pathol) pertes *fpl* blanches

white' blood' cell' *s* globule *m* blanc

white' caps' *spl* moutons *mpl*

white' coal' *s* houille *f* blanche

white' cof'fee *s* câfé *m* crème

white' -col'lar *adj* de bureau

white' -col'lar crimes' *spl* crimes *mpl* des employés de bureau

white' -col'lar work'er *s* employé ou employée de bureau

white' cor'puscle *s* globule *m* blanc

white' feath'er *s*—**to show the white feather** lâcher pied, flancher, caner

white'fish' *s* poisson *m* blanc, merlan *m*

white' goods' *spl* vêtements *mpl* blancs; tissus *mpl* de coton, cotonnade *f*; (*applicances*) appareils *mpl* électroménagers

white' -haired' *adj* aux cheveux blancs, chenu; (coll) favori

white' -hot' *adj* chauffé à blanc

White' House' *s*—**the White House** la Maison Blanche

white' lead' [lɛd] s céruse f, blanc m de céruse

white' lie' s mensonge m pieux

white' meat' s blanc m

whiten [ˈhwaɪtən] tr & intr blanchir

whiteness [ˈhwaɪtnɪs] s blancheur f

white' slav'ery s traite f des blanches

white' tie' s cravate f blanche; tenue f de soirée

white' wall' tire' s pneu m à flanc blanc

white'wash' s blanc m de chaux, badigeon m; (cover-up) couverture f‖ tr blanchir à la chaux; (e.g., a guilty person, a scandal) blanchir

whither [ˈhwɪðər] adv & conj où, là où

whitish [ˈhwaɪtɪʃ] adj blanchâtre

whitlow [ˈhwɪtlo] s panaris m

Whitsuntide [ˈhwɪtsən,taɪd] s saison f de la Pentecôte

whittle [ˈhwɪtəl] tr tailler au couteau; **to whittle away** or **down** amenuiser

whiz or **whizz** [hwɪz] s sifflement m; (slang) prodige m ‖ v (pret & pp **whizzed;** ger **whizzing**) intr—**to whiz by** passer en sifflant, passer comme le vent

who [hu] pron interr qui; quel §80; **who else?** qui d'autre?; qui encore?; **who is there?** (mil) qui vive? ‖ pron rel qui; celui qui §83

whoa [hwo] interj holà!, doucement!

who'd contr **who would**

whodunit [huˈdʌnɪt] s roman m noir

who•ev'er pron rel quiconque; celui qui §83; qui que, e.g., **whoever you are** qui que vous soyez

whole [hol] adj entier ‖ s tout m, totalité f, ensemble m; **on the whole** somme toute, à tout prendre

whole'heart'ed adj sincère, de bon cœur

whole' milk' s lait m entier

whole' note' s (mus) ronde f

whole' rest' s (mus) pause f

whole'sale' adj & adv en gros; (e.g., slaughter) en masse ‖ s gros m, vente f en gros ‖ tr & intr vendre en gros

whole'sale price' s prix m de gros

wholesaler [ˈhol,selər] s commerçant m en gros, grossiste mf

whole'sale trade' s commerce m de gros

wholesome [ˈholsəm] adj sain

whole'-wheat' bread' s pain m complet

who'll contr **who will**

wholly [ˈholi] adv entièrement

whom [hum] pron interr qui ‖ pron rel que; lequel §78; celui que §83; **of whom** dont, de qui §79

whom•ev'er pron rel celui que §83; tous ceux que; (with a preposition) quiconque

whoop [hup], [hwup] s huée f; (cough) quinte f ‖ tr—**to whoop it up** (slang) pousser des cris ‖ intr huer

whoop'ing cough' [ˈhupɪŋ] s coqueluche f

whopper [ˈhwɑpər] s (coll) chose f énorme; (lie) (coll) gros mensonge m

whopping [ˈhwɑpɪŋ] adj (coll) énorme

whore [hor] s putain f ‖ intr—**to whore around** courir la gueuse

whore'house' s maison f de débauche, maison publique, maison borgne, boxon m

who's contr **who is; who was**

whose [huz] pron interr à qui, e.g., **whose pen is that?** à qui est ce stylo? ‖ pron rel dont, de qui §79; duquel §78

why [hwaɪ] s (pl **whys** [hwaɪz]) pourquoi m; **the why and the wherefore** le pourquoi et le comment ‖ adv pourquoi; **why not?** pourquoi pas? ‖ interj tiens!; **why, certainly!** mais bien sûr!; **why, yes!** mais oui!

wick [wɪk] s mèche f

wicked [ˈwɪkɪd] adj méchant, mauvais

wicker [ˈwɪkər] s en osier ‖ s osier m

wicket [ˈwɪkɪt] s guichet m; (croquet) arceau m

wide [waɪd] adj large; (range) vaste, étendu; (spread, angle, etc.) grand; large de, e.g., **eight feet wide** large de huit pieds ‖ adv loin, partout; **open wide!** ouvrez bien!

wide'-an'gle adj grand-angulaire

wide'-an'gle lens' s (phot) grand-angle m, grand-angulaire m

wide'-awake' adj bien éveillé

widen [ˈwaɪdən] tr élargir ‖ intr s'élargir

wide'-o'pen adj grand ouvert

wide'-rang'ing adj de grande envergure

wide'screen' s (mov) écran m large

wide'spread' adj (arms, wings) étendu; répandu, universel

widow [ˈwɪdo] s veuve f ‖ tr—**to be widowed** devenir veuf

widower [ˈwɪdo•ər] s veuf m

widowhood [ˈwɪdo,hud] s veuvage m

wid'ow's mite' s obole f

wid'ow's weeds' spl deuil m de veuve

width [wɪdθ] s largeur f; (of cloth) lé m

wield [wild] tr (sword, pen) manier; (power) exercer

wife [waɪf] s (pl **wives** [waɪvz]) femme f, épouse f

wig [wɪg] s perruque f

wiggle [ˈwɪgəl] s tortillement m ‖ tr agiter ‖ intr tortiller, se tortiller

wig'wag' s télégraphie f optique ‖ v (pret & pp **-wagged;** ger **-wagging**) tr transmettre à bras avec fanions ‖ intr signaler à bras avec fanions

wigwam [ˈwɪgwɑm] s wigwam m

wild [waɪld] adj sauvage; (untamed) sauvage, fauve; (frantic, mad) frénétique; (hair; dance; dream) échevelé; (passion; torrent; night) tumultueux; (idea, plan) insensé, extravagant; (life) déréglé; (blows, bullet, shot) perdu; **wild about** or **for** fou de ‖ **wilds** spl régions fpl sauvages ‖ adv—**to run wild** dépasser toutes les bornes; (said of plants) pousser librement

wild' boar' s sanglier m

wild' card' s inconnu m, impondérable m

wild' cat' s chat m sauvage; lynx m, (well) sondage m d'exploration

wild'cat strike' s grève f sauvage, grève spontanée

wild' cher'ry s (pl **-ries**) merise f; (tree) merisier m

wilderness [ˈwɪldərnɪs] s désert m

wil′derness camp′ing s camping m sauvage

wild′fire′ s feu m grégeois; feu m follet; éclairs mpl en nappe; **like wildfire** comme une traînée de poudre

wild′ flow′er s fleur f des champs

wild′ goose′ s oie f sauvage

wild′-goose′ chase′ s—**to go on a wild-goose chase** faire buisson creux

wild′life′ s animaux mpl sauvages

wild′ oats′ spl—**to sow one's wild oats** jeter sa gourme

wild′ pitch′ s mauvais lancer m

wile [waɪl] s ruse f ‖ tr—**to while away** tuer, faire passer

will [wɪl] s volonté f; (law) testament m; **against one's will** à contre-cœur; **at will** à volonté; **to put s.o. in one's will** porter qn sur son testament; **with a will** de bon cœur ‖ tr vouloir; (to bequeath) léguer ‖ intr vouloir; **do as you will** faites comme vous voudrez ‖ (pret & cond **would** [wʊd]) aux used to express 1) the future indicative, e.g., **he will arrive early** il arrivera de bonne heure; 2) the future perfect indicative, e.g., **he will have arrived before I leave** il sera arrivé avant que je parte; 3) the present indicative denoting habit or custom, e.g., **after breakfast he will go out for a walk every morning** après le petit déjeuner il fait une promenade tous les matins

willful [ˈwɪlfəl] adj volontaire; (stubborn) obstiné

willfulness [ˈwɪlfəlnɪs] s entêtement m

William [ˈwɪljəm] s Guillaume m

willing [ˈwɪlɪŋ] adj disposé, prêt; **to be willing to** vouloir bien; **willing or unwilling** bon gré mal gré

willingly [ˈwɪlɪŋli] adv volontiers

willingness [ˈwɪlɪŋnɪs] s bonne volonté f, consentement m

will-o'-the-wisp [ˈwɪləðəˈwɪsp] s feu m follet; (fig) chimère f

willow [ˈwɪlo] s saule m

willowy [ˈwɪlo•i] adj souple, agile; svelte, élancé; couvert de saules

will′ pow′er s force f de volonté

willy-nilly [ˈwɪliˈnɪli] adv bon gré mal gré

wilt [wɪlt] tr flétrir ‖ intr se flétrir

wil•y [ˈwaɪli] adj (comp **-ier;** super **-iest**) rusé, astucieux

wimp [wɪmp] s poule f mouillée

wimple [ˈwɪmpəl] s guimpe f

win [wɪn] s (coll) victoire f; (baseball) gain m ‖ v (pret & pp **won** [wʌn]; ger **winning**) tr gagner; (a victory, a prize) remporter; **to win back** regagner; **to win over** gagner, convaincre ‖ intr gagner; convaincre; **to win out** (coll) réussir

wince [wɪns] s—**without a wince** sans sourciller ‖ intr tressaillir

winch [wɪntʃ] s treuil m; (handle, crank) manivelle f

wind [wɪnd] s vent m; (breath) haleine f, souffle m; **to break wind** lâcher un vent, faire un pet;

to get wind of avoir vent de; **to sail close to the wind** courir au plus près; **to sail into the wind** aller au lof, venir au lof ‖ tr faire perdre le souffle à ‖ intr flairer le gibier ‖ [waɪnd] v (pret & pp **wound** [waʊnd]) tr enrouler; (a timepiece) remonter; (yarn, thread, etc.) pelotonner; **to wind up** enrouler; remonter; (to finish) (coll) terminer, régler ‖ intr serpenter

windbag [ˈwɪndˌbæg] s (of bagpipe) outre f; (coll) moulin m à paroles

wind′break′ s abrivent m

wind′break′er s (jacket) blouson m

wind′-chill fac′tor s déperdition f de chaleur due au vent

wind′ cone′ s (aer) manche f à air

winded [ˈwɪndɪd] adj essoufflé

wind′fall s (fig) aubaine f

wind′ing road′ [ˈwaɪndɪŋ] s route f en lacet

wind′ing sheet′ s linceul m

wind′ing stairs′ spl escalier m en colimaçon

wind′ in′strument [wɪnd] s (mus) instrument m à vent

windlass [ˈwɪndləs] s treuil m

wind′mill′ s moulin m à vent; (on a modern farm) aéromoteur m; **to tilt at windmills** se battre contre des moulins à vent

window [ˈwɪndo] s fenêtre f; (of ticket office) guichet m; (of store) vitrine f; (of opportunity) ouverture f, occasion f; (aut) glace f; (comp) fenêtre f

win′dow box′ s jardinière f à plantes

win′dow dress′er s étalagiste mf

win′dow dress′ing s art m de l'étalage; (coll) façade f

win′dow en′velope s enveloppe f à fenêtre

win′dow frame′ s châssis m, dormant m

win′dow•pane′ s vitre f, carreau m

win′dow screen′ s grillage m, écran m en fil de fer

win′dow shade′ s store m

win′dow-shop′ v (pret & pp **-shopped;** ger **-shopping**) intr faire du lèche-vitrines, lécher les vitrines

win′dow shut′ter s volet m

win′dow sill′ s rebord m de fenêtre

wind′pipe′ s trachée-artère f

wind′ shear′ s cisaillement m du vent

wind′shield′ s pare-brise m

wind′shield wash′er s lave-glace m

wind′shield wip′er s essuie-glace m

wind′sock′ s manche f à air

wind′storm′ s tempête f de vent

wind′ surf′ing s planche f à voile

wind′ tun′nel s tunnel m aérodynamique

windup [ˈwaɪndˌʌp] s conclusion f, fin f; (baseball) élan m ‖ intr prendre son élan

windward [ˈwɪndwərd] adj & adv au vent ‖ s côté m du vent; **to turn to windward** louvoyer

wind•y [ˈwɪndi] adj (comp **-ier;** super **-iest**) venteux; (verbose) verbeux; **it is windy** il fait du vent

wine [waɪn] *s* vin *m* ‖ *tr*—**to wine and dine s.o.** fêter qn

wine′ cel′lar *s* cave *f*

wine′ glass′ *s* verre *m* à vin

winegrower [ˈwaɪnˌgro•ər] *s* viticulteur *m*, vigneron *m*

winegrowing [ˈwaɪnˌgro•ɪŋ] *s* viticulture *f*

wine′ list′ *s* carte *f* des vins

wine′ press′ *s* pressoir *m*

winer•y [ˈwaɪnəri] *s* (*pl* **-ies**) pressoir *m*

wine′skin′ *s* outre *f* à vin

wine′ stew′ard *s* sommelier *m*; (*of prince, king*) bouteiller *m*

winetaster [ˈwaɪnˌtestər] *s* (*person*) dégustateur *m*; (*pipette*) taste-vin *m*

wing [wɪŋ] *s* aile *f*; (*e.g., of hospital*) pavillon *m*; (pol) parti *m*, faction *f*; **in the wings** (theat) dans la coulisse; **on the wing** au vol; **to take wing** prendre son essor ‖ *tr* (*to wound*) blesser; **to wing one's way** voler

wing′ chair′ *s* fauteuil *m* à oreilles

wing′ col′lar *s* col *m* rabattu

wing′ load′ *s* (aer) charge *f* alaire

wing′ nut′ *s* écrou *m* ailé, vis *f* à ailettes

wing′spread′ *s* envergure *f*

wink [wɪŋk] *s* clin *m* d'œil; **to not sleep a wink** ne pas fermer l'œil; **to take forty winks** (coll) piquer un roupillon ‖ *tr* cligner ‖ *intr* cligner des yeux; **to wink at** cligner de l'œil à; (*e.g., an abuse*) fermer les yeux sur

winner [ˈwɪnər] *s* gagnant *m*, vainqueur *m*

winning [ˈwɪnɪŋ] *adj* gagnant; (*attractive*) séduisant ‖ **winnings** *spl* gains *mpl*

winnow [ˈwɪno] *tr* vanner, sasser; (*e.g., the evidence*) passer au crible

winsome [ˈwɪnsəm] *adj* séduisant, engageant

winter [ˈwɪntər] *s* hiver *m* ‖ *intr* passer l'hiver; (*said of animals, troops, etc.*) hiverner

win′ter•green *s* (*oil*) wintergreen *m*; (bot) gaulthérie *f*

winterize [ˈwɪntəraɪz] *tr* hivériser

win•try [ˈwɪntri] *adj* (*comp* **-trier**; *super* **-triest**) hivernal, froid

wipe [waɪp] *tr* essuyer; **to wipe away** essuyer; **to wipe off** or **out** effacer; (*to annihilate*) anéantir; **to wipe up** nettoyer

wiper [ˈwaɪpər] *s* torchon *m*; (elec) contact *m* glissant; (mach) came *f*

wire [waɪr] *s* fil *m*; télégramme *m*; **hold the wire!** (telp) restez à l'écoute!; **on the wire** (telp) au bout du fil; **reply by wire** réponse *f* télégraphique; **to get in under the wire** arriver juste à temps; terminer juste à temps; **to pull wires** (coll) tirer les ficelles ‖ *tr* attacher avec du fil de fer; (*a message*) télégraphier; (*a house*) canaliser ‖ *intr* télégraphier

wire′ cut′ter *s* coupe-fil *m*

wire′ draw′ *v* (*pret* **-drew**; *pp* **-drawn**) *tr* tréfiler

wire′ entan′glement *s* réseau *m* de barbelés

wire′ gauge′ *s* calibre *m* or jauge *f* pour fils métalliques

wire′-haired′ *adj* à poil dur

wireless [ˈwaɪrlɪs] *adj* sans fil

wire′ nail′ *s* clou *m* de Paris

Wire′pho′to *s* (*pl* **-tos**) (trademark) (*device*) bélinographe *m*; (*photo*) bélinogramme *m*

wire′ pull′ing *s* (coll) influences *fpl* secrètes, piston *m*

wire′ record′er *s* magnétophone *m* à fil d'acier

wire′ tap′ *s* (*device*) table *f* d'écoute ‖ *v* (*pret & pp* **-tapped**; *ger* **-tapping**) *tr* passer à la table d'écoute

wiring [ˈwaɪrɪŋ] *s* (*e.g., of house*) canalisation *f*; (*e.g., of radio*) montage *m*

wir•y [ˈwaɪri] *adj* (*comp* **-ier**; *super* **-iest**) nerveux; (*hair*) raide

wisdom [ˈwɪzdəm] *s* sagesse *f*

wis′dom tooth′ *s* dent *f* de sagesse

wise [waɪz] *adj* sage; (*step, decision*) judicieux, prudent; **to be wise to** (slang) voir clair dans le jeu de, percer le jeu de; **to get wise** (coll) se mettre au courant ‖ *s*—**in no wise** en aucune manière ‖ *tr*—**to wise up** (slang) avertir, désabuser

wiseacre [ˈwaɪzˌekər] *s* fat *m*, fierot *m*

wise′crack′ *s* (coll) blague *f*, plaisanterie *f* ‖ *intr* (coll) blaguer, plaisanter

wise′ guy′ *s* (slang) type *m* goguenard, fier-à-bras *m*

wish [wɪʃ] *s* souhait *m*, désir *m*; **best wishes** meilleurs vœux *mpl*; (formula used to close a letter) amitiés; **last wishes** dernières volontés *fpl*; **our best wishes** (*formula in letter writing*) nos meilleurs sentiments; **to make a wish** faire un vœu ‖ *tr* souhaiter, désirer; **to wish s.o. s.th.** souhaiter q.ch. à qn; **to wish s.o. to** + *inf* souhaiter que qn + *subj*; **to wish to** + *inf* vouloir + *inf*

wish′bone′ *s* fourchette *f*

wishful [ˈwɪʃfəl] *adj* désireux

wish′ful think′ing *s* optimisme *m* à outrance; **to indulge in wishful thinking** se forger des chimères

wish′ing well′ *s* puits *m* aux souhaits

wistful [ˈwɪstfəl] *adj* pensif, rêveur

wit [wɪt] *s* esprit *m*; (*person*) homme *m* d'esprit; **to be at one's wits' end** ne plus savoir que faire; **to keep one's wits about one** conserver toute sa présence d'esprit; **to live by one's wits** vivre d'expédients

witch [wɪtʃ] *s* sorcière *f*

witch′ craft′ *s* sorcellerie *f*

witch′ doc′tor *s* sorcier *m* guérisseur

witch′ es′ Sab′bath *s* sabbat *m*

witch′ ha′zel *s* teinture *f* d'hamamélis; (bot) hamamélis *m*

witch′ hunt′ *s* chasse *f* aux sorcières

with [wɪð], [wɪθ] *prep* avec; (*at the home of; in the case of*) chez; (*in spite of*) malgré; à, e.g., **the girl with the blue eyes** la jeune fille aux yeux bleus; e.g., **coffee with milk** café au lait; e.g., **with open arms** à bras ouverts; e.g., **with these words ...** à ces mots ... ; de, e.g., **with a loud voice** d'une voix forte; e.g., **with all his strength** de toutes ses forces;

e.g., **to be satisfied with** être satisfait de; e.g., **to fill with** remplir de
with·draw′ v (pret **-drew;** pp **-drawn**) tr retirer; (money) toucher ‖ intr se retirer
withdrawal [wɪð′drɔ·əl] s retrait m
withdraw′al symp′tom s symptôme m de l'état de manque
wither [′wɪðər] tr faner ‖ intr se faner
with·hold′ v (pret & pp **-held**) tr (money, taxes, etc.) retenir; (permission) refuser; (the truth) cacher
with·hold′ing tax′ s impôt m retenu à la source
with·in′ adv à l'intérieur; là-dedans §85A ‖ prep à l'intérieur de; (in less than) en moins de; (within the limits of) dans; (in the bosom of) au sein de; (not exceeding a margin of error of) à … près, e.g., **I can tell you what time it is within five minutes** je peux vous dire l'heure à cinq minutes près; à portée de, e.g., **within reach** à portée de la main
with·out′ adv au-dehors, dehors ‖ prep au dehors de; (lacking, not with) sans; **to do without** se passer de; **without** + ger sans + inf, e.g., **he left without seeing me** il est parti sans me voir; sans que + subj, e.g., **he left without anyone seeing him** il est parti sans que personne ne le voie
with·stand′ v (pret & pp **-stood**) tr résister à
witness [′wɪtnɪs] s témoin m; **in witness whereof** en foi de quoi; **to bear witness** rendre témoignage ‖ tr (to be present at) être témoin de, assister à; (to attest) témoigner; (e.g., a contract) signer
wit′ness stand′ s barre f des témoins
witticism [′wɪtɪ,sɪzəm] s trait m d'esprit
wittingly [′wɪtɪŋli] adv sciemment
wit·ty [′wɪti] adj (comp **-tier;** super **-tiest**) spirituel
wizard [′wɪzərd] s sorcier m
wizardry [′wɪzərdri] s sorcellerie f
wizened [′wɪzənd] adj desséché
woad [wod] s guède f
wobble [′wɑbəl] intr chanceler; (said of table) branler; (said of voice) chevroter; vaciller
wob·bly [′wɑbli] adj (comp **-blier;** super **-bliest**) vacillant
woe [wo] s malheur m, affliction f; **woe is me!** pauvre de moi!; **woes** misères fpl
woebegone [′wobɪ,gɔn] adj navré, abattu, désolé
woeful [′wofəl] adj triste, désolé; très mauvais
wolf [wʊlf] s (pl **wolves** [wʊlvz]) loup m; galant m, tombeur m de femmes; **to cry wolf** crier au loup; **to keep the wolf from the door** se mettre à l'abri du besoin, joindre les deux bouts; **wolf eel** (ichth) loup m de mer ‖ tr & intr engloutir
wolf′ cub′ s louveteau m
wolf′hound′ s chien-loup m
wolf′ pack′ s bande f de loups
wolfram [′wʊlfrəm] s (element) tungstène m; (mineral) wolfram m
wolf's′-bane′ or **wolfs′bane′** s tue-loup m, aconit m, napel m

woman [′wʊmən] s (pl **women** [′wɪmɪn]) femme f
wom′an doc′tor s femme f médecin, doctoresse f
womanhood [′wʊmən,hʊd] s le sexe féminin; les femmes fpl
womanish [′wʊmənɪʃ] adj féminin; (effeminate) efféminé
wom′an·kind′ s le sexe féminin
wom′an la′borer s femme f manœuvre
woman·ly [′wʊmənli] adj (comp **-lier;** super **-liest**) féminin, femme
wom′an preach′er s femme f pasteur
womb [wum] s utérus m, matrice f; (fig) sein m
wom′en's libera′tion move′ment m mouvement m de la libération de la femme (M.L.F.)
wonder [′wʌndər] s merveille f; (feeling of surprise) émerveillement m; (something strange) miracle m; **for a wonder** chose étonnante; **no wonder that …** rien d'étonnant que …; **to work wonders** faire des merveilles ‖ tr—**to wonder that** s'étonner que; **to wonder why, if, whether** se demander pourquoi, si ‖ intr—**to wonder at** s'émerveiller de, s'étonner de
won′der drug′ s remède m miracle, médicament m miracle, drogue-miracle f
wonderful [′wʌndərfəl] adj merveilleux, étonnant
won′der·land′ s pays m des merveilles
wonderment [′wʌndərmənt] s étonnement m
won't contr **will not**
wont [wɔnt] adj—**to be wont to** avoir l'habitude de ‖ s—**his wont** son habitude
wonted adj habituel, accoutumé
woo [wu] tr courtiser
wood [wʊd] s bois m; (for wine) fût m; **out of the woods** (coll) hors de danger, hors d'affaire; **to take to the woods** se sauver dans la nature; **woods** bois m or mpl
woodbine [′wʊd,baɪn] s (honeysuckle) chèvrefeuille m; (Virginia creeper) vigne f vierge
wood′ carv′ing s sculpture f sur bois
wood′chuck′ s marmotte f d'Amérique
wood′cock′ s bécasse f
wood′cut′ s (typ) gravure f sur bois
wood′cut′ter s bûcheron m
wooded [′wʊdɪd] adj boisé
wooden [′wʊdən] adj en bois; (style, manners) guindé, raide
wood′ engrav′ing s (typ) gravure f sur bois
wood′en-head′ed adj (coll) stupide, obtus
wood′en leg′ s jambe f en bois
wood′en shoe′ s sabot m
wood′ grouse′ s grand tétras m, grand coq m de bruyère
woodland [′wʊdlənd] adj sylvestre ‖ s pays m boisé
wood′land scene′ s (painting) paysage m boisé
wood′man s (pl **-men**) bûcheron m
woodpecker [′wʊd,pɛkər] s pic m; (green woodpecker) pivert m, pic-vert m
wood′ pig′eon s (orn) ramier m

wood′pile′ *s* tas *m* de bois
wood′ pulp′ *s* pâte *f* à papier
wood′ screw′ *s* vis *f* à bois
wood′shed′ *s* bûcher *m*
woods′man *s* (*pl* -**men**) bûcheron *m;* (*trapper*) trappeur *m,* chasseur *m*
wood′ tick′ *s* vrillette *f*
wood′winds′ *spl* (mus) bois *mpl*
wood′work′ *s* (*working in wood*) menuiserie *f;* (*things made of wood*) boiseries *fpl*
wood′work′er *s* menuisier *m*
wood′worm′ *s* (ent) artison *m*
wood•y [ˈwʊdi] *adj* (*comp* -**ier;** *super* -**iest**) boisé; (*like wood*) ligneux
wooer [ˈwuˑər] *s* prétendant *m*
woof [wuf] *s* trame *f;* (*fabric*) tissu *m*
woofer [ˈwʊfər] *s* (rad) boomer *m,* woofer *m*
wool [wʊl] *s* laine *f*
woolen [ˈwʊlən] *adj* de laine ‖ *s* tissu *m* de laine; **woolens** lainage *m*
wool′gath′ering *s* rêvasserie *f*
woolgrower [ˈwʊl,groˑər] *s* éleveur *m* des bêtes à laine
wool•ly [ˈwʊli] *adj* (*comp* -**lier;** *super* -**liest**) laineux
word [wʌrd] *s* mot *m;* (*promise, assurance*) parole *f;* **in other words** autrement dit; **in your own words** en vous propres termes; **my word!** ça alors!; **not a word!** motus!; **the Word** (eccl) le Verbe; **to break one's word** manquer à sa parole; **to have words with** échanger des propos désagréables avec; **to make s.o. eat his words** faire ravaler ses paroles à qn; **to put in a word** placer un mot; **to take s.o. at his word** prendre qn au mot, croire qn sur parole; **upon my word!** ma foi!; **without a word** sans mot dire; **words** (*e.g., of song*) paroles ‖ *tr* formuler, rédiger
word′ forma′tion *s* formation *f* de texte(s)
wording [ˈwʌrdɪŋ] *s* langage *m*
word′ or′der *s* ordre *m* des mots
word′ pro′cessing *s* traitement *m* des mots
word′ pro′cessor *s* (comp, electron) microprocesseur *m*
word′-stock′ *s* vocabulaire *m*
word•y [ˈwʌrdi] *adj* (*comp* -**ier;** *super* -**iest**) verbeux
work [wʌrk] *s* travail *m;* (*production, book*) Œuvre *f,* ouvrage *m;* **at work** en œuvre; (*not at home*) au travail, au bureau, à l'usine; **out of work** sans travail, en chômage; **to shoot the works** (slang) mettre le paquet, jouer le tout pour le tout; **works** Œuvres; mécanisme *m;* (*of clock*) mouvement *m* ‖ *tr* faire travailler; (*to operate*) faire fonctionner, faire marcher; (*wood, iron*) travailler; (*mine*) exploiter; **to work out** élaborer, résoudre; **to work up** préparer; stimuler ‖ *intr* travailler; (*said of motor, machine, etc.*) fonctionner, marcher; (*said of remedy*) faire de l'effet; (*said of wine, beer*) fermenter; **how will things work out!** à quoi tout cela aboutira-t-il?; **to work hard** travailler dur; **to work**

loose se desserrer; **to work out** (sports) s'entraîner; **to work too hard** se surmener
workable [ˈwʌrkəbəl] *adj* (*feasible*) réalisable; (*that can be worked*) ouvrable
workaholic [ˌwʌrkəˈhɔlɪk] *s* bourreau *m* de travail, drogué *m* du travail, travaillomane *mf*
work′bas′ket *s* corbeille *f* à ouvrage
work′bench′ *s* établi *m*
work′book′ *s* manuel *m;* (*notebook*) carnet *m;* (*for student*) cahier *m* de devoirs
work′box′ *s* boîte *f* à ouvrage; (*for needlework*) coffret *m* de travail
work′day′ *adj* de tous les jours; prosaïque, ordinaire ‖ *s* jour *m* ouvrable; (*part of day devoted to work*) journée *f*
worked′-up′ *adj* préparé, ouvré; (*excited*) agité, emballé
worker [ˈwʌrkər] *s* travailleur *m,* ouvrier *m,* employé *m*
work′er ant′ *s* ouvrière *f*
work′er bee′ *s* abeille *f* ouvrière
work′ flow′ *s* déroulement *m* des opérations
work′ force′ *s* main-d'œuvre *f;* personnel *m*
work′horse′ *s* cheval *m* de charge; (*tireless worker*) vrai cheval *m* de labour
work′house′ *s* maison *f* de correction; (Brit) asile *m* des pauvres
work′ing class′ *s* classe *f* ouvrière
work′ing day′ *s* jour *m* ouvrable; (*daily hours for work*) journée *f*
work′ing hours′ *spl* heures *fpl* de travail
work′ing•man′ *s* (*pl* -**men′**) travailleur *m*
work′ing•wom′an *s* (*pl* -**wom′en**) ouvrière *f*
work′man *s* (*pl* -**men**) ouvrier *m*
workmanship [ˈwʌrkmən,ʃɪp] *s* habileté *f* professionnelle, facture *f;* (*work executed*) travail *m*
work′ of art′ *s* œuvre *f* d'art
work′ or′der *s* bon *m* de travail
work′out′ *s* essai *m,* épreuve *f;* (*physical exercise*) séance *f* d'entraînement
work′room′ *s* atelier *m;* (*for study*) cabinet *m* de travail, cabinet d'études
work′shop′ *s* atelier *m*
work′ stop′page *s* arrêt *m* du travail
work′-to-rule′ strike′ *s* grève *f* du zèle
world [wʌrld] *adj* mondial ‖ *s* monde *m;* **a world of** énormément de; **for all the world** à tous les égards, exactement; **not for all the world** pour rien au monde; **since the world began** depuis que le monde est monde; **the other world** l'autre monde; **to bring into the world** mettre au monde; **to go around the world** faire le tour du monde; **to see the world** voir du pays; **to think the world of** estimer énormément, avoir une très haute opinion de
world′ affairs′ *spl* affaires *fpl* internationales
world′-fa′mous *adj* de renommée mondiale
world′ his′tory *s* histoire *f* universelle
world•ly [ˈwʌrldli] *adj* (*comp* -**lier;** *super* -**liest**) mondain

world′ly-wise′ *adj*—**to be worldly-wise** savoir ce que c'est que la vie

world′ map′ *s* mappemonde *f*

World′ Se′ries *s* championnat *m* mondial

world's′ fair′ *s* exposition *f* universelle

World′ Trade′ Cen′ter *s* World Trade Center *m* (*Centre du Commerce Mondial*)

world′ war′ *s* guerre *f* mondiale

world′wide′ *adj* mondial, universel

World′-Wide′ Web′ *s* (comp) La Toile *f* (mondiale)

worm [wʌrm] *s* ver *m* ‖ *tr* enlever les vers de; (*a secret, money, etc.*) soutirer; **to worm it out of him** lui tirer les vers du nez ‖ *intr* se faufiler

worm-eaten [ˈwʌrmˌitən] *adj* vermoulu

worm′ gear′ *s* engrenage *m* à vis sans fin

worm′wood′ *s* (*Artemisia*) armoise *f*; (*Artemisia absinthium*) armoise absinthe; (*something grievous*) (fig) absinthe *f*

worm•y [ˈwʌrmi] *adj* (*comp* **-ier;** *super* **-iest**) véreux

worn [worn] *adj* usé, fatigué

worn′-out′ *adj* épuisé, usé; éreinté

worrisome [ˈwʌrisəm] *adj* inquiétant; inquiet, anxieux

wor•ry [ˈwʌri] *s* (*pl* **-ries**) souci *m*, inquiétude *f*; (*cause of anxiety*) ennui *m*, tracas *m* ‖ *v* (*pret & pp* **-ried**) *tr* inquiéter; (*to harass, pester*) ennuyer, tracasser; **to be worried** s'inquiéter ‖ *intr* s'inquiéter; **don't worry!** ne vous en faites pas!

worse [wʌrs] *adj comp* pire, plus mauvais §91; **and to make matters worse** et par surcroît de malheur; **so much the worse** tant pis; **to make** or **get worse** empirer; **what's worse** qui pis est; **worse and worse** de pis en pis ‖ *adv comp* pis, plus mal §91

worsen [ˈwʌrsən] *tr & intr* empirer

wor•ship [ˈwʌrʃip] *s* culte *m*, adoration *f* ‖ *v* (*pret & pp* **-shiped** or **-shipped;** *ger* **-shiping** or **-shipping**) *tr* adorer ‖ *intr* prier; (*to go to church*) aller au culte

worshiper or **worshipper** [ˈwʌrʃipər] *s* adorateur *m*, fidèle *mf*

worst [wʌrst] *adj super* pire §91; pis ‖ *s* (le) pire, (le) pis; **to be hurt the worst** être le plus gravement atteint (blessé, etc.); **to get the worst of it** avoir le dessous ‖ *adv super* pis §91

worsted [ˈwʊstid] *adj* de laine peignée ‖ *s* peigné *m*, tissu *m* de laine peignée

wort [wʌrt] *s* (*of beer*) moût *m*

worth [wʌrθ] *adj* digne de; valant, e.g., **book worth three dollars** livre valant trois dollars; **to be worth** valoir; avoir une fortune de; **to be worth** + *ger* valoir la peine de + *inf*; **to be worth while** valoir la peine ‖ *s* valeur *f*; **a dollar's worth of** pour un dollar de

worthless [ˈwʌrθlɪs] *adj* sans valeur; (*person*) bon à rien, indigne

worth′while′ *adj* utile, de valeur

wor•thy [ˈwʌrði] *adj* (*comp* **-thier;** *super* **-thiest**) digne ‖ *s* (*pl* **-thies**) notable *mf*; (hum, ironical) personnage *m*

would [wʊd] *aux* used to express 1) the past future, e.g., **he said he would come** il a dit qu'il viendrait; 2) the present conditional, e.g., **he would come if he could** il viendrait s'il pouvait; 3) the past conditional, e.g., **he would have come if he had been able (to)** il serait venu s'il avait pu; 4) the potential mood, e.g., **would that I knew it!** plût à Dieu que je le sache!, je voudrais le savoir!; 5) the past indicative denoting habit or custom in the past, e.g., **he would visit us every day** il nous visitait tous les jours

would′-be′ *adj* prétendu

wouldn't *contr* would not

would've *contr* would have

wound [wʊnd] *s* blessure *f* ‖ *tr* blesser

wounded [ˈwʊndɪd] *adj* blessé ‖ *s*—**the wounded** les blessés *mpl*

wow [waʊ] *s* (*e.g., of phonograph record*) distorsion *f*; (slang) succès *m* formidable ‖ *tr* (slang) enthousiasmer ‖ *interj* (slang) formidable!

wrack [ræk] *s* vestige *m*; (*ruin*) naufrage *m*; (bot) varech *m*

wraith [reθ] *s* apparition *f*

wrangle [ˈræŋgəl] *s* querelle *f* ‖ *intr* se quereller

wrap [ræp] *s* couverture *f*; (*coat*) manteau *m* ‖ *v* (*pret & pp* **wrapped;** *ger* **wrapping**) *tr* envelopper, emballer

wrap′around skirt′ *s* jupe *f* portefeuille

wrap′around wind′shield *s* pare-brise *m* panoramique

wrapper [ˈræpər] *s* saut-de-lit *m*; (*of newspaper or magazine*) bande *f*; (*of tobacco*) robe *f*

wrap′ping pa′per *s* papier *m* d'emballage

wrath [ræθ] *s* colère *f*

wrathful [ˈræθfəl] *adj* courroucé, en colère

wreak [rik] *tr* assouvir

wreath [riθ] *s* (*pl* **wreaths** [riðz]) couronne *f*; (*of smoke*) volute *f*, panache *m*

wreathe [rið] *tr* enguirlander; (*e.g., flowers*) entrelacer ‖ *intr* (*said of smoke*) s'élever en volutes

wreck [rɛk] *s* (*shipwreck*) naufrage *m*; (*debris at sea or elsewhere*) épave *f*; (*of train*) déraillement *m*; (*of airplane*) écrasement *m*; (*of auto*) accident *m*; (*of one's hopes*) naufrage; **to be a wreck** être une ruine ‖ *tr* (*a ship, one's hopes*) faire échouer; (*a train*) faire dérailler; (*one's health*) ruiner

wreckage [ˈrɛkɪdʒ] *s* débris *mpl*, décombres *mpl*, ruines *fpl*

wrecker [ˈrɛkər] *s* (*tow truck*) dépanneuse *f*; (*person*) dépanneur *m*

wreck′ing car′ *s* voiture *f* de dépannage

wreck′ing crane′ *s* grue *f* de dépannage

wren [rɛn] *s* (orn) troglodyte *m*; (*kinglet*) (orn) roitelet *m*

wrench [rɛntʃ] *s* (*tool*) clef *f*; (*pull*) secousse *f*; (*twist of a joint*) foulure *f* ‖ *tr* (*e.g., one's ankle*) se fouler; (*to twist*) tordre

wrest [rɛst] *tr* arracher violemment
wrestle [ˈrɛsəl] *s* lutte *f* ‖ *intr* lutter
wrestling [ˈrɛslɪŋ] *s* (sports) lutte *f,* catch *m*
wres′tling match′ *s* rencontre *f* de catch
wretch [rɛtʃ] *s* misérable *mf*
wretched [ˈrɛtʃɪd] *adj* misérable
wriggle [ˈrɪgəl] *s* tortillement *m* ‖ *tr* tortiller ‖ *intr* se tortiller; **to wriggle out of** esquiver adroitement
wrig·gly [ˈrɪgli] *adj* (*comp* **-glier;** *super* **-gliest**) frétillant; évasif
wring [rɪŋ] *v* (*pret & pp* **wrung** [rʌŋ]) *tr* tordre; (*one's hands*) se tordre; (*s.o.'s hand*) serrer fortement; **to wring out** (*clothes*) essorer; (*money, a secret, etc.*) arracher
wringer [ˈrɪŋər] *s* essoreuse *f*
wrinkle [ˈrɪŋkəl] *s* (*in skin*) ride *f;* (*in clothes*) pli *m,* faux pli; (*clever idea or trick*) (coll) truc *m* ‖ *tr* plisser ‖ *intr* se plisser
wrin·kly [ˈrɪŋkli] *adj* (*comp* **-klier;** *super* **-kliest**) ridé, chiffonné
wrist [rɪst] *s* poignet *m*
wrist′band′ *s* poignet *m*
wrist′ watch′ *s* montre-bracelet *f*
writ [rɪt] *s* (eccl) écriture *f;* (law) acte *m* judiciaire
write [raɪt] *v* (*pret* **wrote** [rot]; *pp* **written** [ˈrɪtən]) *tr* écrire; **to write down** consigner par écrit; baisser le prix de; **to write in** insérer; **to write off** (*a debt*) passer aux profits et pertes; **to write up** rédiger un compte rendu de; (*to ballyhoo*) faire l'éloge de ‖ *intr* écrire; **to write back** répondre par écrit
write′-off *s* (com) révocation *f* d'une dette
writer [ˈraɪtər] *s* écrivain *m*
writ′er's cramp′ *s* crampe *f* des écrivains
write′-up′ *s* compte *m* rendu; (*ballyhoo*) battage *m;* (com) surestimation *f*
writhe [raɪð] *intr* se tordre
writing [ˈraɪtɪŋ] *s* l'écriture *f;* (*something written*) écrit *m,* œuvre *f;* (*profession*) métier *m*

d'écrivain; **at this writing** au moment où j'écris; **to put in writing** mettre par écrit
writ′ing desk′ *s* bureau *m,* écritoire *f;* (*in schoolroom*) pupitre *m*
writ′ing pa′per *s* papier *m* à lettres
writ′ten ac′cent *s* accent *m* orthographique
wrong [rɔŋ] *adj* (*unjust*) injuste; (*incorrect*) erroné; (*road, address, side, place, etc.*) mauvais; ne pas . . . qu'il faut, e.g., **I arrived at the wrong city** je ne suis pas arrivé à la ville qu'il fallait; (*word*) impropre; qui ne marche pas, e.g., **something is wrong with the motor** il y a quelque chose qui ne marche pas dans le moteur; **to be wrong** (*i.e., in error*) avoir tort; (*i.e., to blame*) être le coupable ‖ *s* mal *m;* injustice *f;* **to be in the wrong** être dans son tort, avoir tort; **to do wrong** faire du mal, faire du tort ‖ *adv* mal; **to go wrong** faire fausse route; (*said, e.g., of a plan*) ne pas marcher; (*said of one falling into evil ways*) se dévoyer; **to guess wrong** se tromper ‖ *tr* faire du tort à, être injuste envers
wrongdoer [ˈrɔŋˌduˑər] *s* malfaiteur *m*
wrong′do′ing *s* mal *m,* tort *m;* (*misdeeds*) méfaits *mpl*
wrong′ num′ber *s* (telp) mauvais numéro *m;* **you have the wrong number** vous vous trompez de numéro
wrong′ side′ *s* (*e.g., of material*) revers *m,* envers *m;* (*of the street*) mauvais côté *m;* **to drive on the wrong side** circuler à contrevoie; **to get out of bed on the wrong side** se lever du pied gauche; **wrong side out** à l'envers; **wrong side up** sens dessus dessous
wrought′ i′ron [rɔt] *s* fer *m* forgé
wrought′-up′ *adj* excité, agité
wry [raɪ] *adj* (*comp* **wrier;** *super* **wriest**) tordu, de travers; forcé, ironique
wry′neck′ *s* (orn) torcol *m;* (pathol) torticolis *m*
www. *abbr* (**World-Wide Web**) WWW, www (Web)

X

X, x [ɛks] *s* XXIVᵉ lettre de l'alphabet
Xavier [ˈzevɪ-ər] *s* Xavier *m*
xenon [ˈzinɑn], [ˈzɛnɑn] *s* xénon *m*
xenophobe [ˈzɛnəˌfob] *s* xénophobe *mf*
xenophobia [ˌzɛnəˈfobɪˑə] *s* xénophobie *f*
xerography [ziˈrɑgrəfi] *s* xérographie *f*
xerox [ˈzɪrɑks], [ˈzirɑks] *tr* faire une xérocopie de, photocopier ‖ *intr* faire des xérocopies
xeroxing [ˈzɪrɑksɪŋ] *s* xérographie *f*
Xerox [ˈzɪrɑks], [ˈzirɑks] *s* (trademark) xérocopie *f;* **to make a Xerox of** faire une xérocopie
Xer′ox cop′y *s* (trademark) xérocopie *f*
Xer′ox machine′ *s* (trademark) photocopieur *m*

Xerxes [ˈzʌrksiz] *s* Xerxès *m*
Xmas [ˈkrɪsməs] *adj* de Noël ‖ *s* Noël *m*
X-rated [ˈɛksˌretɪd] *adj* (*film, etc.*) pornographique; seulement pour les adultes
X′ ray′ *ou* **x′-ray′** *s* (*photograph*) radiographie *f;* **to have an X ray** passer à la radio; **X rays** rayons *mpl* X
X′-ray′ *ou* **x′-ray′** *adj* radiographique ‖ **X′-ray′** *ou* **x′-ray′** *tr* radiographier
X′-ray treat′ment *s* radiothérapie *f*
xylem [ˈzaɪlɛm] *s* xylème *m*
xylograph [ˈzaɪləˌgræf] *s* xylographie *f*
xylophone [ˈzaɪləˌfon] *s* xylophone *m*

Y

Y, y [waɪ] *s* XXVᵉ lettre de l'alphabet
yacht [jɑt] *s* yacht *m*
yacht′club′ *s* yacht-club *m*
yah [jɑ] *interj* (*in disgust*) pouah!; (*in derision*) oh là là!
yam [jæm] *s* igname *f;* (*sweet potato*) patate *f* douce
yank [jæŋk] *s* (coll) secousse *f* ‖ *tr* (coll) tirer d'un coup sec
Yankee [ˈjæŋki] *adj & s* yankee *mf*
yap [jæp] *s* jappement *m;* (slang) criaillerie *f* ‖ *v* (*pret & pp* **yapped;** *ger* **yapping**) *intr* japper; (slang) criailler; (slang) dégoiser
yard [jɑrd] *s* cour *f;* (*for lumber, for repairs, etc.*) chantier *m;* (*measure*) yard *m;* (naut) vergue *f;* (rr) gare *f* de triage
yard′arm′ *s* (naut) bout *m* de vergue
yard′mas′ter *s* (rr) chef *m* de dépôt
yard′ sale′ *s* braderie *f,* vente *f* bric-à-brac
yard′stick′ *s* yard *m* en bois (en métal, etc.); (fig) unité *f* de comparaison
yarn [jɑrn] *s* fil *m,* filé *m;* (coll) histoire *f*
yarrow [ˈjæro] *s* mille-feuille *f*
yaw [jɔ] *s* (naut) embardée *f;* **yaws** (pathol) pian *m* ‖ *intr* faire des embardées
yawl [jɔl] *s* yole *f*
yawn [jɔn] *s* bâillement *m* ‖ *intr* bâiller; être béant
ye (old spelling of **the** [ðə]) *art* le, e.g., **ye olde shoppe** la vieille boutique ‖ [ji] *pron pl* (obs) vous (*pl*)
yea [je] *s* oui *m;* vote *m* affirmatif ‖ *adv* oui, voire
yeah [je] *adv* (coll) oui; **oh yeah?** (coll) de quoi?; **oh yeah!** (coll) ouais!
yean [jin] *intr* (*said of ewe*) agneler; (*said of goat*) chevreter
year [jɪr] *s* an *m,* année *f;* (*of issue; vintage*) millésime *m;* **six-year-old, seven-year-old,** etc. de six ans, de sept ans, etc.; **to be ... years old** avoir ... ans; **year in year out** bon an mal an
year′book′ *s* annuaire *m*
yearling [ˈjɪrlɪŋ] *s* animal *m* d'un an; (*horse*) yearling *m*
yearly [ˈjɪrli] *adj* annuel ‖ *adv* annuellement
yearn [jʌrn] *intr*—**to yearn for** soupirer après; **to yearn to** brûler de
yearning [ˈjʌrnɪŋ] *s* désir *m* ardent
yeast [jist] *s* levure *f*
yell [jɛl] *s* hurlement *m;* (*school yell*) cri *m* de ralliement ‖ *tr & intr* hurler
yellow [ˈjɛlo] *adj* jaune; (*cowardly*) (coll) froussard; (*e.g., press*) à sensation; **to turn yellow** jaunir; (coll) avoir la frousse ‖ *s* jaune *m* ‖ *tr & intr* jaunir
yel′low fe′ver *s* fièvre *f* jaune
yel′low•ham′mer *s* (orn) bruant *m* jaune
yellowish [ˈjɛlo•ɪʃ] *adj* jaunâtre
yel′low•jack′et *s* (ent) frelon *m*
yel′low streak′ *s* (coll) trait *m* de lâcheté

yelp [jɛlp] *s* glapissement *m,* jappement *m* ‖ *intr* glapir, japper
yen [jɛn] *s*—**to have a yen to** or **for** (coll) avoir envie de
yeo•man [ˈjomən] *s* (*pl* **-men**) yeoman *m;* (*clerical worker*) (nav) commis *m* aux écritures
yeo′man of the guard′ *s* (Brit) hallebardier *m* de la garde du corps
yeo′man's serv′ice *s* effort *m* précieux
yes [jɛs] *s* oui *m* ‖ *adv* oui; (to contradict a negative statement or question) si or pardon, e.g., **"You didn't know." "Yes, I did!"** "Vous ne le saviez pas." "Si!" ‖ *v* (*pret & pp* **yessed;** *ger* **yessing**) *tr* dire oui à ‖ *intr* dire oui
yes′ man′ *s* (*pl* **men′**) (coll) M. Toujours; **to be a yes man** opiner du bonnet; **yes men** (coll) béni-oui-oui *mpl*
yesterday [ˈjɛstər,de] *adj, s, & adv* hier *m;* **yesterday morning** hier matin
yet [jɛt] *adv* encore; déjà, e.g., **has he arrived yet?** est-il déjà arrivé?; **as yet** jusqu'à présent; **not yet** pas encore ‖ *conj* cependant
yew′tree′ [ju] *s* if *m*
Yiddish [ˈjɪdɪʃ] *adj & s* yiddish *m invar,* yidich *m*
yield [jild] *s* rendement *m;* (*crop*) produit *m;* (*income produced*) rapport *m,* revenu *m* ‖ *tr* rendre, produire; (*a profit; a crop*) rapporter; (*to surrender*) céder ‖ *intr* (*to produce*) produire, rapporter; (*to give way*) céder, se rendre; (*public sign*) priorité (à droite; à gauche)
yippie [ˈjɪpi] *interj* *hourra! *interj & m*
yo•del [ˈjodəl] *s* tyrolienne *f* ‖ *v* (*pret & pp* **-deled** or **-delled;** *ger* **-deling** or **-delling**) *tr & intr* jodler
yoga [ˈjogə] *s* yoga *m*
yogi [ˈjogi] *s* yogi *m*
yogurt [ˈjogʊrt] *s* yaourt *m,* yogourt *m,* yoghourt *m*
yoke [jok] *s* (*pair of draft animals*) paire *f;* (*device to join a pair of draft animals*) joug *m;* (*of a shirt*) empiècement *m;* (elec) culasse *f;* (fig) joug; **to throw off the yoke** secouer le joug ‖ *tr* accoupler
yokel [ˈjokəl] *s* rustaud *m,* manant *m*
yolk [jok] *s* jaune *m* d'œuf
yonder [ˈjɑndər] *adj* ce ... -là là-bas, e.g., **that tree yonder** cet arbre-là là-bas ‖ *adv* là-bas
yore [jor] *s*—**of yore** d'antan
you [ju] *pron pers* vous, toi §85; vous, tu §87; vous, te §87 ‖ *pron indef* (coll) on §87, e.g., **you go in this way** on entre par ici
you'd *contr* **you had; you would**
you'll *contr* **you will**
young [jʌŋ] *adj* (*comp* **younger** [ˈjʌŋgər]; *super* **youngest** [ˈjʌŋgɪst]) jeune ‖ **the young** les jeunes; (*of animal*) les petits *mpl;* **to be with young** (*said of animal*) être pleine; **young and old** les grands et les petits
young′ la′dy *s* (*pl* **-dies**) jeune fille *f;* (*mar-*

ried) jeune femme *f;* **young ladies** jeunes personnes *fpl*

young′ man′ *s* (*pl* **men′**) jeune homme *m;* **young men** jeunes gens *mpl*

young′ peo′ple *spl* jeunes gens *mpl*

youngster [ˈjʌŋstər] *s* gosse *mf*

your [jʊr] *adj poss* votre, ton §88

you're *contr* **you are**

yours [jʊrz] *pron poss* le vôtre, le tien §89; **a friend of yours** un de vos amis; **cordially yours** (complimentary close) amitiés; **yours truly** or **sincerely yours** (complimentary close) veuillez agréer, Monsieur, l'expression de mes sentiments distingués

your·self [jʊrˈsɛlf] *pron pers* (*pl* **-selves** [ˈsɛlvz]) vous-même, toi-même §86; vous, te §87; vous, toi §85

youth [juθ] *s* (*pl* **youths** [juθs], [juðz]) jeunesse *f;* (*person*) jeune homme *m;* **youths** jeunes *mpl*

youthful [ˈjuθfəl] *adj* jeune, juvénile

youth′ hos′tel *s* auberge *f* de jeunesse

you've *contr* **you have**

yowl [jaʊl] *s* hurlement *m* ‖ *intr* hurler

Yugoslav [ˈjugoˈslɑv] *adj* yougoslave ‖ *s* Yougoslave *mf*

Yugoslavia [ˈjugoˈslɑvɪə] *s* Yougoslavie *f;* la Yougoslavie

Yule′ log′ [jul] *s* bûche *f* de Noël

Yule′ tide′ *s* les fêtes *fpl* de Noël

yummy [ˈjʌmi] *adj* délicieux

yum yum [ˈjʌm ˈjʌm] *interj* miam! miam!

yup·pi *ou* **yup·py** [ˈjʌpi] *s* (*pl* **-pies**) yuppie *mf*

Z

Z, z [zi] or [zɛd] (Brit) *s* XXVIᵉ lettre de l'alphabet

za·ny [ˈzeni] *adj* (*comp* **-nier;** *super* **-niest**) bouffon, toqué ‖ *s* (*pl* **-nies**) bouffon *m*

zap [zæp] *v* (*pret & pp* **zapped;** *ger* **zapping**) *tr* (coll) détruire, frapper; (com) eliminer, effacer; (telv) (*commercials*) éviter, omettre ‖ *intr* (coll) se sauver, passer comme un éclair ‖ *interj* pan!, boum!

zeal [zil] *s* zèle *m*

zealot [ˈzɛlət] *s* zélateur *m,* adepte *mf*

zealotry [ˈzɛlətri] *s* fanatisme *m*

zealous [ˈzɛləs] *adj* zélé

zebra [ˈzibrə] *s* zèbre *m*

zenith [ˈziniθ] *s* zénith *m*

zephyr [ˈzɛfər] *s* zéphyr *m*

zeppelin [ˈzɛpəlin] *s* zeppelin *m*

ze·ro [ˈziro] *s* (*pl* **-ros** or **-roes**) zéro *m* ‖ *intr* —**to zero in** (mil) régler la ligne de mire; **to zero in on** (coll) pointer sur

ze′ro grav′ity *s* apesanteur *f*

ze′ro growth′ *s* croissance *f* zéro

ze′ro hour′ *s* heure *f* H

ze′ro op′tion *s* option *f* nulle

zest [zɛst] *s* enthousiasme *m;* (*agreeable and piquant flavor*) saveur *f,* piquant *m*

Zeus [zus] *s* Zeus *m*

zig·zag [ˈzigˌzæg] *adj & adv* en zigzag ‖ *s* zigzag *m* ‖ *v* (*pret & pp* **-zagged;** *ger* **-zagging**) *intr* zigzaguer

zinc [zɪŋk] *s* zinc *m*

Zionism [ˈzaɪˌəˌnɪzəm] *s* sionisme *m*

zip [zɪp] *s* (coll) sifflement *m;* (coll) énergie *f* ‖ *v* (*pret & pp* **zipped;** *ger* **zipping**) *tr* fermer à fermeture éclair ‖ *intr* siffler; **to zip by** (coll) passer comme un éclair

Zip′ code′ *s* indicatif *m* postal

zipper [ˈzɪpər] *s* fermeture *f* éclair, fermeture à glissière

zircon [ˈzʌrkɑn] *s* zircon *m*

zirconium [zərˈkoniˌəm] *s* zirconium *m*

zither [ˈzɪðər] *s* cithare *f*

zodiac [ˈzodɪˌæk] *s* zodiaque *m*

zone [zon] *s* zone *f*

zoning [ˈzonɪŋ] *s* zonage *m,* zoning *m*

zon′ing code′ *s* plan *m* d'occupation des sols (P.O.S.)

zon′ing or′dinance *s* réglementation *f* urbaine

zon′ing per′mit *s* certificat *m* d'urbanisation

zoo [zu] *s* zoo *m*

zoologic(al) [ˌzoˈəˈlɑdʒɪk(əl)] *adj* zoologique

zoology [zoˈɑlədʒi] *s* zoologie *f*

zoom [zum] *s* vrombissement *m;* (aer) montée *f* en chandelle ‖ *intr* vrombir; **to zoom up** monter en chandelle

zoom′ lens′ *s* zoom *m*

zoot′ suit′ [zut] *s* costume *m* zazou

Zu·lu [ˈzulu] *adj* zoulou ‖ *s* (*pl* **-lus**) Zoulou *m*

zygote [ˈzaɪgot] *s* zygote *m*

FRENCH REGULAR VERBS

The letters (a) to (f) before the names of the tenses in this table correspond to the letters (a) to (f) that designate the tenses in the section on French irregular verbs. The forms printed in boldface correspond to the key forms described there.

TENSE	FIRST CONJUGATION	SECOND CONJUGATION	THIRD CONJUGATION
inf	**DONNER**	**FINIR**	**VENDRE**
ger	donnant	finissant	vendant
pp	donné	fini	vendu
(a) *impv*	donne	finis	vends
	donnons	finissons	vendons
	donnez	finissez	vendez
(b) *pres ind*	**donne**	**finis**	**vends**
	donnes	finis	vends
	donne	finit	vend
	donnons	**finissons**	**vendons**
	donnez	finissez	vendez
	donnent	**finissent**	**vendent**
(c) *pres subj*	donne	finisse	vende
	donnes	finisses	vendes
	donne	finisse	vende
	donnions	finissions	vendions
	donniez	finissiez	vendiez
	donnent	finissent	vendent
(d) *imperf ind*	donnais	finissais	vendais
	donnais	finissais	vendais
	donnait	finissait	vendait
	donnions	finissions	vendions
	donniez	finissiez	vendiez
	donnaient	finissaient	vendaient
(e) *fut ind*	**donnerai**	**finirai**	**vendrai**
	donneras	finiras	vendras
	donnera	finira	vendra
	donnerons	finirons	vendrons
	donnerez	finirez	vendrez
	donneront	finiront	vendront
pres cond	donnerais	finirais	vendrais
	donnerais	finirais	vendrais
	donnerait	finirait	vendrait
	donnerions	finirions	vendrions
	donneriez	finiriez	vendriez
	donneraient	finiraient	vendraient
(f) *pret ind*	**donnai**	**finis**	**vendis**
	donnas	finis	vendis
	donna	finit	vendit
	donnâmes	finîmes	vendîmes
	donnâtes	finîtes	vendîtes
	donnèrent	finirent	vendirent
imperf subj	donnasse	finisse	vendisse
	donnasses	finisses	vendisses
	donnât	finît	vendît
	donnassions	finissions	vendissions
	donnassiez	finissiez	vendissiez
	donnassent	finissent	vendissent

FRENCH IRREGULAR VERBS

In addition to the infinitive, gerund, and past participle, all simple tenses are shown in these tables if they contain one irregular form or more, except the conditional (which can always be derived from the stem of the future indicative) and the imperfect subjunctive (which can always be derived from the preterit indicative). Those forms are considered irregular that deviate morphologically and/or orthographically in root, stem, or ending from the paradigms of regular verbs. The infinitive is printed in boldface capital letters. And the following forms are printed in boldface: (1) key forms (that is, irregular forms from which other irregular forms can be derived, but not the derived forms), e.g., **buvons,** (2) individual irregular forms that occupy the place of key forms but cannot function as key forms because other irregular forms cannot be derived from them, e.g., **sommes,** and (3) individual irregular forms that cannot be derived from key forms, e.g., **dites.** The names of the key forms and the forms derived from each of them are listed below.

The numbers are those that accompany the respective verbs and verbs of identical patterns where they are listed in their alphabetical places in this Dictionary. The letters (a) to (f) identify the tenses as follows:

(a) imperative
(b) present indicative
(c) present subjunctive
(d) imperfect indicative
(e) future indicative
(f) preterit indicative

KEY FORM	DERIVED FORMS
1st sg pres ind	*2d & 3d sg pres ind & 2d sg impv**
1st pl pres ind	*2d pl pres ind, 1st & 2d pl pres subj,* whole *imperf ind, 1st & 2d pl impv, &* *ger*
3d pl pres ind	whole *sg & 3d pl pres subj*
1st sg fut ind	rest of *fut ind &* whole *conditional*
1st sg pret ind	rest of *pret ind &* whole *imperf subj*
1st sg pres subj of **faire, pouvoir,** & **savoir**	rest of *pres subj*
1st sg pres subj of **aller, valoir,** & **vouloir**	*2d & 3d sg & 3d pl pres subj*

§1　**ABRÉGER**—abrégeant—abrégé Combination of §10 and §38
(a) abrège, abrégeons, abrégez
(b) **abrège,** abrèges, abrège, **abrégeons,** abrégez, **abrègent**
(c) abrège, abrèges, abrège, abrégions, abrégiez, abrègent
(d) abrégeais, abrégeais, abrégeait, abrégions, abrégiez, abrégeaient
(f) **abrégeai,** abrégeas, abrégea, abrégeâmes, abrégeâtes, abrégèrent

§2　**ACHETER**—achetant—acheté
(a) achète, achetons, achetez
(b) **achète,** achètes, achète, achetons, achetez, **achètent**
(c) achète, achètes, achète, achetions, achetiez, achètent
(e) **achèterai,** achèteras, achètera, achèterons, achèterez, achèteront

§3　**ACQUÉRIR**—acquérant—**acquis**
(a) acquiers, acquérons, acquérez
(b) **acquiers,** acquiers, acquiert, **acquérons,** acquérez, **acquièrent**
(c) acquière, acquières, acquière, acquérions, acquériez, acquièrent
(d) acquérais, acquérais, acquérait, acquérions, acquériez, acquéraient
(e) **acquerrai,** acquerras, acquerra, acquerrons, acquerrez, acquerront
(f) **acquis,** acquis, acquit, acquîmes, acquîtes, acquirent

§4　**ALLER**—allant—allé

* Some irregular verbs of the third conjugation that end in **s,** not preceded by **d,** in the *1st sg pres ind,* end in **s** also in the *2d sg pres ind* and the *2d sg impv,* and in **t** in the *3d sg pres ind,* e.g., **crains, crains, craint** and **bois, bois, boit.** And three verbs, namely, **pouvoir, valoir,** and **vouloir,** which end in **x** in the *1st sg pres ind,* end in **x** also in the *2d sg pres ind* and the *2d sg impv,* and in **t** in the *3d sg pres ind,* e.g., **veux, veux, veut.**

        (a) **va,** allons, allez
        (b) **vais** [ve], **vas, va,** allons, allez, **vont**
        (c) **aille** [aj], ailles, aille, allions, alliez, aillent
        (e) **irai,** iras, ira, irons, irez, iront

§5A   **ASSEOIR**—asseyant—**assis**
        (a) assieds, asseyons, asseyez
        (b) **assieds,** assieds, assied, **asseyons,** asseyez, **asseyent**
        (c) asseye, asseyes, asseye, asseyions, asseyiez, asseyent
        (d) asseyais, asseyais, asseyait, asseyions, asseyiez, asseyaient
        (e) **assiérai,** assiéras, assiéra, assiérons, assiérez, assiéront
        (f) **assis,** assis, assit, assîmes, assîtes, assirent

§5B   **ASSEOIR**—assoyant—**assis**
        (a) assois, assoyons, assoyez
        (b) **assois,** assois, assoit, **assoyons,** assoyez, **assoient**
        (c) assoie, assoies, assoie, assoyions, assoyiez, assoient
        (d) assoyais, assoyais, assoyait, assoyions, assoyiez, assoyaient
        (e) **assoirai,** assoiras, assoira, assoirons, assoirez, assoiront
        (f) **assis,** assis, assit, assîmes, assîtes, assirent

§6   **AVOIR**—**ayant**—**eu** [y]
        (a) **aie** [e], **ayons, ayez**
        (b) **ai** [e], **as, a, avons,** avez, **ont**
        (c) **aie, aies, ait, ayons, ayez, aient**
        (d) avais, avais, avait, avions, aviez, avaient
        (e) **aurai,** auras, aura, aurons, aurez, auront
        (f) **eus** [y], eus, eut, eûmes, eûtes, eurent

§7   **BATTRE**—battant—battu
        (a) bats, battons, battez
        (b) **bats,** bats, bat, battons, battez, battent

§8   **BOIRE**—buvant—**bu**
        (a) bois, buvons, buvez
        (b) bois, bois, boit, **buvons,** buvez, **boivent**
        (c) boive, boives, boive, buvions, buviez, boivent
        (d) buvais, buvais, buvait, buvions, buviez, buvaient
        (f) **bus,** bus, but, bûmes, bûtes, burent

§9   **BOUILLIR**—bouillant—bouilli
        (a) bous, bouillons, bouillez
        (b) **bous,** bous, bout, **bouillons,** bouillez, **bouillent**
        (c) bouille, bouilles, bouille, bouillions, bouilliez, bouillent
        (d) bouillais, bouillais, bouillait, bouillions, bouilliez, bouillaient

§10   **CÉDER**—cédant—cédé
        (a) cède, cédons, cédez
        (b) **cède,** cèdes, cède, cédons, cédez, **cèdent**
        (c) cède, cèdes, cède, cédions, cédiez, cèdent

§11   **CONCLURE**—concluant—**conclu**
        (f) **conclus,** conclus, conclut, conclûmes, conclûtes, conclurent

§12   **CONNAÎTRE**—connaissant—**connu**
        (a) connais, connaissons, connaissez
        (b) **connais,** connais, connaît, **connaissons,** connaissez, **connaissent**
        (c) connaisse, connaisses, connaisse, connaissions, connaissiez, connaissent
        (d) connaissais, connaissais, connaissait, connaissions, connaissiez, connais-
            saient
        (f) **connus,** connus, connut, connûmes, connûtes, connurent

§13   **COUDRE**—cousant—**cousu**
        (a) couds, cousons, cousez
        (b) couds, couds, coud, **cousons,** cousez, **cousent**
        (c) couse, couses, couse, cousions, cousiez, cousent
        (d) cousais, cousais, cousait, cousions, cousiez, cousaient
        (f) **cousis,** cousis, cousit, cousîmes, cousîtes, cousirent

§14   **COURIR**—courant—**couru**
(a) cours, courons, courez
(b) **cours,** cours, court, **courons,** courez, **courent**
(c) coure, coures, coure, courions, couriez, courent
(d) courais, courais, courait, courions, couriez, couraient
(e) **courrai,** courras, courra, courrons, courrez, courront
(f) **courus,** courus, courut, courûmes, courûtes, coururent

§15   **CRAINDRE**—craignant—**craint**
(a) crains, craignons, craignez
(b) **crains,** crains, craint, **craignons,** craignez, **craignent**
(c) craigne, craignes, craigne, craignions, craigniez, craignent
(d) craignais, craignais, craignait, craignions, craigniez, craignaient
(f) **craignis,** craignis, craignit, craignîmes, craignîtes, craignirent

§16   **CROIRE**—croyant—**cru**
(a) crois, croyons, croyez
(b) crois, crois, croit, **croyons,** croyez, croient
(c) croie, croies, croie, croyions, croyiez, croient
(d) croyais, croyais, croyait, croyions, croyiez, croyaient
(f) **crus,** crus, crut, crûmes, crûtes, crurent

§17   **CROÎTRE**—croissant—**crû, crue**
(a) croîs, croissons, croissez
(b) **croîs,** croîs, croît, **croissons,** croissez, **croissent**
(c) croisse, croisses, croisse, croissions, croissiez, croissent
(d) croissais, croissais, croissait, croissions, croissiez, croissaient
(f) **crûs,** crûs, crût, crûmes, crûtes, crûrent

§18   **CUEILLIR**—cueillant—**cueilli**
(a) cueille, cueillons, cueillez
(b) **cueille,** cueilles, cueille, **cueillons,** cueillez, **cueillent**
(c) cueille, cueilles, cueille, cueillions, cueilliez, cueillent
(d) cueillais, cueillais, cueillait, cueillions, cueilliez, cueillaient
(e) **cueillerai,** cueilleras, cueillera, cueillerons, cueillerez, cueilleront

§19   **CUIRE**—cuisant—**cuit**
(a) cuis, cuisons, cuisez
(b) cuis, cuis, cuit, **cuisons,** cuisez, **cuisent**
(c) cuise, cuises, cuise, cuisions, cuisiez, cuisent
(d) cuisais, cuisais, cuisait, cuisions, cuisiez, cuisaient
(f) **cuisis,** cuisis, cuisit, cuisîmes, cuisîtes, cuisirent

§20   **DÉPECER**—dépeçant—dépecé Combination of §2 and §51
(a) dépèce, dépeçons, dépecez
(b) **dépèce,** dépèces, dépèce, **dépeçons,** dépecez, **dépècent**
(c) dépèce, dépèces, dépèce, dépecions, dépeciez, dépècent
(d) dépeçais, dépeçais, dépeçait, dépecions, dépeciez, dépeçaient
(e) **dépècerai,** dépèceras, dépècera, dépècerons, dépècerez, dépèceront
(f) **dépeçai,** dépeças, dépeça, dépeçâmes, dépeçâtes, dépecèrent

§21   **DEVOIR**—devant—**dû, due**
(a) missing
(b) **dois,** dois, doit, **devons,** devez, **doivent**
(c) doive, doives, doive, devions, deviez, doivent
(d) devais, devais, devait, devions, deviez, devaient
(e) **devrai,** devras, devra, devrons, devrez, devront
(f) **dus,** dus, dut, dûmes, dûtes, durent

§22   **DIRE**—disant—**dit**
(a) dis, disons, **dites**
(b) dis, dis, dit, **disons, dites, disent**
(c) dise, dises, dise, disions, disiez, disent
(d) disais, disais, disait, disions, disiez, disaient
(f) **dis,** dis, dit, dîmes, dîtes, dirent

§23   **DORMIR**—dormant—dormi *invar*
(a) dors, dormons, dormez

(b) **dors,** dors, dort, **dormons,** dormez, **dorment**
(c) dorme, dormes, dorme, dormions, dormiez, dorment
(d) dormais, dormais, dormait, dormions, dormiez, dormaient

§24 **ÉCLORE**—éclosant—**éclos**
(a) éclos
(b) éclos, éclos, **éclôt, éclosent**
(c) éclose, écloses, éclose, **éclosions, éclosiez,** éclosent
(d) missing
(f) missing

§25 **ÉCRIRE**—écrivant—**écrit**
(a) écris, écrivons, écrivez
(b) écris, écris, écrit, **écrivons,** écrivez, **écrivent**
(c) écrive, écrives, écrive, écrivions, écriviez, écrivent
(d) écrivais, écrivais, écrivait, écrivions, écriviez, écrivaient
(f) **écrivis,** écrivis, écrivit, écrivîmes, écrivîtes, écrivirent

§26 **ENVOYER**—envoyant—envoyé
(a) envoie, envoyons, envoyez
(b) **envoie,** envoies, envoie, envoyons, envoyez, **envoient**
(c) envoie, envoies, envoie, envoyions, envoyiez, envoient
(e) **enverrai,** enverras, enverra, enverrons, enverrez, enverront

§27 **ESSUYER**—essuyant—essuyé
(a) essuie, essuyons, essuyez
(b) **essuie,** essuies, essuie, essuyons, essuyez, **essuient**
(c) essuie, essuies, essuie, essuyions, essuyiez, essuient
(e) **essuierai,** essuieras, essuiera, essuierons, essuierez, essuieront

§28 **ÊTRE**—étant—été *invar*
(a) **sois, soyons, soyez**
(b) **suis, es, est, sommes, êtes, sont**
(c) **sois, sois, soit, soyons, soyez, soient**
(d) étais, étais, était, étions, étiez, étaient
(e) **serai,** seras, sera, serons, serez, seront
(f) **fus,** fus, fut, fûmes, fûtes, furent

§29 **FAIRE**—faisant—**fait**
(a) fais, faisons, **faites**
(b) fais, fais, fait, **faisons, faites, font**
(c) **fasse,** fasses, fasse, fassions, fassiez, fassent
(d) faisais, faisais, faisait, faisions, faisiez, faisaient
(e) **ferai,** feras, fera, ferons, ferez, feront
(f) **fis,** fis, fit, fîmes, fîtes, firent

§30 **FALLOIR**—missing—**fallu** *invar*
(a) missing
(b) **faut**
(c) **faille**
(d) **fallait**
(e) **faudra**
(f) **fallut**

§31 **FUIR**—fuyant—fui
(a) fuis, fuyons, fuyez
(b) fuis, fuis, fuit, **fuyons,** fuyez, **fuient**
(c) fuie, fuies, fuie, fuyions, fuyiez, fuient
(d) fuyais, fuyais, fuyait, fuyions, fuyiez, fuyaient

§32 **GRASSEYER**—grasseyant—grasseyé
(regular, unlike other verbs with stem ending in **y**)

§33 **HAÏR**—haïssant—**haï**
(a) hais [ɛ], haïssons, haïssez
(b) **hais** [ɛ], hais, hait, **haïssons,** haïssez, **haïssent**
(c) haïsse, haïsses, haïsse, haïssions, haïssiez, haïssent
(d) haïssais, haïssais, haïssait, haïssions, haïssiez, haïssaient
(f) haïs, haïs, haït, **haïmes, haïtes,** haïrent

739

§34 **JETER**—jetant—jeté
(a) jette, jetons, jetez
(b) **jette,** jettes, jette, jetons, jetez, **jettent**
(c) jette, jettes, jette, jetions, jetiez, jettent
(e) **jetterai,** jetteras, jettera, jetterons, jetterez, jetteront

§35 **JOINDRE**—joignant—**joint**
(a) joins, joignons, joignez
(b) **joins,** joins, joint, **joignons,** joignez, **joignent**
(c) joigne, joignes, joigne, joignions, joigniez, joignent
(d) joignais, joignais, joignait, joignions, joigniez, joignaient
(f) **joignis,** joignis, joignit, joignîmes, joignîtes, joignirent

§36 **LIRE**—lisant—**lu**
(a) lis, lisons, lisez
(b) lis, lis, lit, **lisons,** lisez, **lisent**
(c) lise, lises, lise, lisions, lisiez, lisent
(d) lisais, lisais, lisait, lisions, lisiez, lisaient
(f) **lus,** lus, lut, lûmes, lûtes, lurent

§37 **LUIRE**—luisant—**lui**
(a) luis, luisons, luisez
(b) luis, luis, luit, **luisons,** luisez, **luisent**
(c) luise, luises, luise, luisions, luisiez, luisent
(d) luisais, luisais, luisait, luisions, luisiez, luisaient
(f) archaic

§38 **MANGER**—mangeant—mangé
(a) mange, mangeons, mangez
(b) mange, manges, mange, **mangeons,** mangez, mangent
(d) mangeais, mangeais, mangeait, mangions, mangiez, mangeaient
(f) **mangeai,** mangeas, mangea, mangeâmes, mangeâtes, mangèrent

§39 **MAUDIRE**—maudissant—**maudit**
(a) maudis, maudissons, maudissez
(b) maudis, maudis, maudit, **maudissons,** maudissez, **maudissent**
(c) maudisse, maudisses, maudisse, maudissions, maudissiez, maudissent
(d) maudissais, maudissais, maudissait, maudissions, maudissiez, maudissaient
(f) **maudis,** maudis, maudit, maudîmes, maudîtes, maudirent

§40 **MÉDIRE**—médisant—**médit**
(a) médis, médisons, médisez
(b) médis, médis, médit, **médisons,** médisez, **médisent**
(c) médise, médises, médise, médisions, médisiez, médisent
(d) médisais, médisais, médisait, médisions, médisiez, médisaient
(f) **médis,** médis, médit, médîmes, médîtes, médirent

§41 **MENTIR**—mentant—menti
(a) mens, mentons, mentez
(b) **mens,** mens, ment, **mentons,** mentez, **mentent**
(c) mente, mentes, mente, mentions, mentiez, mentent
(d) mentais, mentais, mentait, mentions, mentiez, mentaient

§42 **METTRE**—mettant—**mis**
(a) mets, mettons, mettez
(b) **mets,** mets, met, mettons, mettez, mettent
(f) **mis,** mis, mit, mîmes, mîtes, mirent

§43 **MOUDRE**—moulant—**moulu**
(a) mouds, moulons, moulez
(b) mouds, mouds, moud, **moulons,** moulez, **moulent**
(c) moule, moules, moule, moulions, mouliez, moulent
(d) moulais, moulais, moulait, moulions, mouliez, moulaient
(f) **moulus,** moulus, moulut, moulûmes, moulûtes, moulurent

§44 **MOURIR**—mourant—**mort**
(a) meurs, mourons, mourez

(b) **meurs,** meurs, meurt, **mourons,** mourez, **meurent**
(c) meure, meures, meure, mourions, mouriez, meurent
(d) mourais, mourais, mourait, mourions, mouriez, mouraient
(e) **mourrai,** mourras, mourra, mourrons, mourrez, mourront
(f) **mourus,** mourus, mourut, mourûmes, mourûtes, moururent

§45 **MOUVOIR**—mouvant—**mû, mue, mus, mues**
(a) meus, mouvons, mouvez
(b) **meus,** meus, meut, **mouvons,** mouvez, **meuvent**
(c) meuve, meuves, meuve, mouvions, mouviez, meuvent
(d) mouvais, mouvais, mouvait, mouvions, mouviez, mouvaient
(e) **mouvrai,** mouvras, mouvra, mouvrons, mouvrez, mouvront
(f) **mus,** mus, mut, mûmes, mûtes, murent

§46 **NAÎTRE**—naissant—**né**
(a) nais, naissons, naissez
(b) **nais,** nais, naît, **naissons,** naissez, **naissent**
(c) naisse, naisses, naisse, naissions, naissiez, naissent
(d) naissais, naissais, naissait, naissions, naissiez, naissaient
(f) **naquis,** naquis, naquit, naquîmes, naquîtes, naquirent

§47 **NETTOYER**—nettoyant—nettoyé
(a) nettoie, nettoyons, nettoyez
(b) **nettoie,** nettoies, nettoie, nettoyons, nettoyez, **nettoient**
(c) nettoie, nettoies, nettoie, nettoyions, nettoyiez, nettoient
(e) **nettoierai,** nettoieras, nettoiera, nettoierons, nettoierez, nettoieront

§48 **PAÎTRE**—paissant—**pu** *invar*
(a) pais, paissez
(b) **pais,** pais, paît, **paissons,** paissez, **paissent**
(c) paisse, paisses, paisse, paissions, paissiez, paissent
(d) paissais, paissais, paissait, paissions, paissiez, paissaient
(f) missing

§49 **PAYER**—payant—payé
(a) paie or paye, payons, payez
(b) **paie,** paies, paie, payons, payez, **paient** or paye, payes, paye, payons, payez, payent
(c) paie, paies, paie, payions, payiez, paient or paye, payes, paye, payions, payiez, payent
(e) **paierai,** paieras, paiera, paierons, paierez, paieront or payerai, payeras, payera, payerons, payerez, payeront

§50 **PEINDRE**—peignant—**peint**
(a) peins, peignons, peignez
(b) **peins,** peins, peint, **peignons,** peignez, **peignent**
(c) peigne, peignes, peigne, peignions, peigniez, peignent
(d) peignais, peignais, peignait, peignions, peigniez, peignaient
(f) **peignis,** peignis, peignit, peignîmes, peignîtes, peignirent

§51 **PLACER**—plaçant—placé
(a) place, plaçons, placez
(b) place, places, place, **plaçons,** placez, placent
(d) plaçais, plaçais, plaçait, placions, placiez, plaçaient
(f) **plaçai,** plaças, plaça, plaçâmes, plaçâtes, placèrent

§52 **PLAIRE**—plaisant—**plu** *invar*
(a) plais, plaisons, plaisez
(b) plais, plais, **plaît, plaisons,** plaisez, **plaisent**
(c) plaise, plaises, plaise, plaisions, plaisiez, plaisent
(d) plaisais, plaisais, plaisait, plaisions, plaisiez, plaisaient
(f) **plus,** plus, plut, plûmes, plûtes, plurent

§53 **PLEUVOIR**—pleuvant—**plu** *invar*
(a) **pleus, pleuvons, pleuvez** (fig & rare)
(b) **pleut, pleuvent**
(c) pleuve, pleuvent
(d) **pleuvait, pleuvaient**

(e) **pleuvra, pleuvront**
(f) **plut, plurent**

§54 **POURVOIR**—pourvoyant—**pourvu**
(a) pourvois, pourvoyons, pourvoyez
(b) **pourvois,** pourvois, pourvoit, **pourvoyons,** pourvoyez, **pourvoient**
(c) pourvoie, pourvoies, pourvoie, pourvoyions, pourvoyiez, pourvoient
(d) pourvoyais, pourvoyais, pourvoyait, pourvoyions, pourvoyiez, pourvoyaient
(f) **pourvus,** pourvus, pourvut, pourvûmes, pourvûtes, pourvurent

§55 **POUVOIR**—pouvant—**pu** *invar*
(a) missing
(b) **peux** or **puis,** peux, peut, **pouvons,** pouvez, **peuvent**
(c) **puisse,** puisses, puisse, puissions, puissiez, puissent
(d) pouvais, pouvais, pouvait, pouvions, pouviez, pouvaient
(e) **pourrai,** pourras, pourra, pourrons, pourrez, pourront
(f) **pus,** pus, put, pûmes, pûtes, purent

§56 **PRENDRE**—prenant—**pris**
(a) prends, prenons, prenez
(b) prends, prends, prend, **prenons,** prenez, **prennent**
(c) prenne, prennes, prenne, prenions, preniez, prennent
(d) prenais, prenais, prenait, prenions, preniez, prenaient
(f) **pris,** pris, prit, prîmes, prîtes, prirent

§57 **PRÉVOIR**—prévoyant—**prévu**
(a) prévois, prévoyons, prévoyez
(b) **prévois,** prévois, prévoit, **prévoyons,** prévoyez, **prévoient**
(c) prévoie, prévoies, prévoie, prévoyions, prévoyiez, prévoient
(d) prévoyais, prévoyais, prévoyait, prévoyions, prévoyiez, prévoyaient
(f) **prévis,** prévis, prévit, prévîmes, prévîtes, prévirent

§58 **RAPIÉCER**—rapiéçant—rapiécé Combination of §10 and §51
(a) rapièce, rapiéçons, rapiécez
(b) **rapièce,** rapièces, rapièce, **rapiéçons,** rapiécez, **rapiècent**
(c) rapièce, rapièces, rapièce, rapiécions, rapiéciez, rapiècent
(d) rapiéçais, rapiéçais, rapiéçait, rapiécions, rapiéciez, rapiéçaient
(f) **rapiéçai,** rapiéças, rapiéça, rapiéçâmes, rapiéçâtes, rapiécèrent

§59 **RECEVOIR**—recevant—**reçu**
(a) reçois, recevons, recevez
(b) **reçois,** reçois, reçoit, **recevons,** recevez, **reçoivent**
(c) reçoive, reçoives, reçoive, recevions, receviez, reçoivent
(d) recevais, recevais, recevait, recevions, receviez, recevaient
(e) **recevrai,** recevras, recevra, recevrons, recevrez, recevront
(f) **reçus,** reçus, reçut, reçûmes, reçûtes, reçurent

§60 **RÉSOUDRE**—résolvant—**résolu; résout** *invar*
(a) résous, résolvons, résolvez
(b) **résous,** résous, résout, **résolvons,** résolvez, **résolvent**
(c) résolve, résolves, résolve, résolvions, résolviez, résolvent
(d) résolvais, résolvais, résolvait, résolvions, résolviez, résolvaient
(f) **résolus,** résolus, résolut, résolûmes, résolûtes, résolurent

§61 **RIRE**—riant—**ri** *invar*
(b) **ris,** ris, rit, rions, riez, rient
(f) **ris,** ris, rit, rîmes, rîtes, rirent

§62 **SAVOIR**—sachant—**su**
(a) **sache, sachons, sachez**
(b) **sais,** sais, sait, **savons,** savez, **savent**
(c) **sache,** saches, sache, sachions, sachiez, sachent
(d) savais, savais, savait, savions, saviez, savaient
(e) **saurai,** sauras, saura, saurons, saurez, sauront
(f) **sus,** sus, sut, sûmes, sûtes, surent

§63 **SERVIR**—servant—servi
(a) sers, servons, servez
(b) **sers,** sers, sert, **servons,** servez, **servent**

(c) serve, serves, serve, servions, serviez, servent
(d) servais, servais, servait, servions, serviez, servaient

§64 **SORTIR**—sortant—sorti
(a) sors, sortons, sortez
(b) **sors,** sors, sort, **sortons,** sortez, **sortent**
(c) sorte, sortes, sorte, sortions, sortiez, sortent
(d) sortais, sortais, sortait, sortions, sortiez, sortaient

§65 **SOUFFRIR**—souffrant—**souffert**
(a) souffre, souffrons, souffrez
(b) **souffre,** souffres, souffre, **souffrons,** souffrez, **souffrent**
(c) souffre, souffres, souffre, souffrions, souffriez, souffrent
(d) souffrais, souffrais, souffrait, souffrions, souffriez, souffraient

§66 **SUFFIRE**—suffisant—**suffi**
(a) suffis, suffisons, suffisez
(b) suffis, suffis, suffit, **suffisons,** suffisez, **suffisent**
(c) suffise, suffises, suffise, suffisions, suffisiez, suffisent
(d) suffisais, suffisais, suffisait, suffisions, suffisiez, suffisaient
(f) **suffis,** suffis, suffit, suffîmes, suffîtes, suffirent

§67 **SUIVRE**—suivant—**suivi**
(a) suis, suivons, suivez
(b) **suis,** suis, suit, suivons, suivez, suivent

§68 **TRAIRE**—trayant—**trait**
(a) trais, trayons, trayez
(b) trais, trais, trait, **trayons,** trayez, traient
(c) traie, traies, traie, trayions, trayiez, traient
(d) trayais, trayais, trayait, trayions, trayiez, trayaient
(f) missing

§69 **TRESSAILLIR**—tressaillant—tressailli
(a) tressaille, tressaillons, tressaillez
(b) **tressaille,** tressailles, tressaille, **tressaillons,** tressaillez, **tressaillent**
(c) tressaille, tressailles, tressaille, tressaillions, tressailliez, tressaillent
(d) tressaillais, tressaillais, tressaillait, tressaillions, tressailliez, tressaillaient
(e) **tressaillirai,** tressailliras, tressaillira, tressaillirons, tressaillirez, tressail-
liront, or **tressaillerai,** tressailleras, tressaillera, tressaillerons, tres-
saillerez, tressailleront

§70 **VAINCRE**—vainquant—vaincu
(a) vaincs [vɛ̃], vainquons, vainquez
(b) vaincs, vaincs, vainc, **vainquons,** vainquez, **vainquent**
(c) vainque, vainques, vainque, vainquions, vainquiez, vainquent
(d) vainquais, vainquais, vainquait, vainquions, vainquiez, vainquaient
(f) **vainquis,** vainquis, vainquit, vainquîmes, vainquîtes, vainquirent

§71 **VALOIR**—valant—**valu**
(a) vaux, valons, valez
(b) **vaux,** vaux, vaut, **valons,** valez, **valent**
(c) **vaille** [vaj], vailles, vaille, valions, valiez, vaillent
(d) valais, valais, valait, valions, valiez, valaient
(e) **vaudrai,** vaudras, vaudra, vaudrons, vaudrez, vaudront
(f) **valus,** valus, valut, valûmes, valûtes, valurent

§72 **VENIR**—venant—**venu**
(a) viens, venons, venez
(b) **viens,** viens, vient, **venons,** venez, **viennent**
(c) vienne, viennes, vienne, venions, veniez, viennent
(d) venais, venais, venait, venions, veniez, venaient
(e) **viendrai,** viendras, viendra, viendrons, viendrez, viendront
(f) **vins,** vins, vint, vînmes [vɛ̃m], vîntes [vɛ̃t], vinrent [vɛ̃r]

§73 **VÊTIR**—vêtant—**vêtu**
(a) vêts, vêtons, vêtez
(b) **vêts,** vêts, vêt, **vêtons,** vêtez, **vêtent**
(c) vête, vêtes, vête, vêtions, vêtiez, vêtent
(d) vêtais, vêtais, vêtait, vêtions, vêtiez, vêtaient

§74 **VIVRE**—vivant—**vécu**
 (a) vis, vivons, vivez
 (b) **vis,** vis, vit, vivons, vivez, vivent
 (f) **vécus,** vécus, vécut, vécûmes, vécûtes, vécurent

§75 **VOIR**—voyant—**vu**
 (a) vois, voyons, voyez
 (b) **vois,** vois, voit, **voyons,** voyez, **voient**
 (c) voie, voies, voie, voyions, voyiez, voient
 (d) voyais, voyais, voyait, voyions, voyiez, voyaient
 (e) **verrai,** verras, verra, verrons, verrez, verront
 (f) **vis,** vis, vit, vîmes, vîtes, virent

§76 **VOULOIR**—voulant—**voulu**
 (a) veux, voulons, voulez
 (b) **veux,** veux, veut, **voulons,** voulez, **veulent**
 (c) **veuille,** veuilles, veuille, voulions, vouliez, veuillent
 (d) voulais, voulais, voulait, voulions, vouliez, voulaient
 (e) **voudrai,** voudras, voudra, voudrons, voudrez, voudront
 (f) **voulus,** voulus, voulut, voulûmes, voulûtes, voulurent

FRENCH GRAMMATICAL REFERENCES

This section contains grammatical information that is cross-referenced by paragraph numbers in the body of the Dictionary (continuing the references numbered §1 to §76 of the section on French irregular verbs).

§77 le *art def* the. The following table shows the forms of the definite article, the combination of **le** with **à** and **de**, and the combinations of **les** with **à, de,** and **en.**

	masc	*fem*
sg	le; l' before a vowel or mute **h**	la; l' before a vowel or mute **h**
pl	les	les
with **à** *sg*	au; à l' before a vowel or mute **h**	à la; à l' before a vowel or mute **h**
with **à** *pl*	aux	aux
with **de** *sg*	du; de l' before a vowel or mute **h**	de la; de l' before a vowel or mute **h**
with **de** *pl*	des	des
with **en** *pl*	ès, e.g., **maître ès arts**	ès, e.g., **docteur ès lettres**

un *art indef* a, an. The following table shows the forms of the indefinite article.

	masc	*fem*
sg	un	une

The indefinite article does not have a plural form in modern French. Vestiges of earlier plural forms are seen in **quelques-uns** and **quelques-unes** (see §81). The plural is also shown when **un** is a pronoun, e.g., **les uns et les autres** the ones and the others; **ni les unes ni les autres** neither the ones nor the others. Instead of an indefinite plural article, modern French uses the contraction **de + les = des** to express the partitive idea of "some":
   Je voudrais des carottes parce que je n'ai qu'une carotte.
   I would like some carrots because I have only one carrot.

Mass nouns and uncountables. The preposition **de** plus the definite article (**du, de la, de l', des**) is used to indicate the partitive idea with a mass noun, e.g., **de l'eau** "(some) water." English and French nouns sometimes differ in regard to uncountable features. For example, the English speaker cannot say "I have a furniture" but must say "I have a piece of furniture." The French speaker, on the other hand, can say *J'ai un meuble.* Differences of this type are often noted in the body of this Dictionary.

§78 lequel *pron rel* who, whom; which • *pron interr* which, which one. The following table shows all the forms of the word **lequel** and their combinations with the prepositions **à** and **de.**

	masc	*fem*
sg	lequel	laquelle
pl	lesquels	lesquelles
with **à** *sg*	auquel	à laquelle
with **à** *pl*	auxquels	auxquelles
with **de** *sg*	duquel	de laquelle
with **de** *pl*	desquels	desquelles

The forms combined with **de** and used as relative pronouns sometimes mean "whose," e.g., **l'étudiant avec la sœur duquel j'ai dansé** the student with whose sister I danced.

§79 dont *rel pron* of whom; of which; from which; with which; on which; at which; which; whose. The relative pronoun **dont** may be: (a) the complement of the subject of the dependent verb, e.g., **cette malheureuse dont la jambe droite était brisée** that wretched woman whose right leg was broken; (b) the complement of the object of the dependent verb, e.g., **sa grande chambre dont on avait fermé les volets** his large bedroom the shutters of which they had closed; (c) the complement of the verb itself, e.g., **les termes dont il se servait** the expressions (that) he used.

If the antecedent is one of point of origin, **d'où** is used, e.g., **la porte d'où il est sorti** the door from which he went out, unless the point of origin is one of ancestry or extraction having to do with a person, e.g., **la famille distinguée dont il sortait** the distinguished family from which he came.

The relative pronoun **dont** cannot be the complement of a noun that is the object of a preposition but must be replaced by a form of **lequel** combined with **de** (see §78), or by **de qui**, e.g., **l'étudiante avec le frère de laquelle** (or **de qui**) **j'ai dansé** the student with whose brother I danced.

§80 quel *adj* what; what sort of; which; what a, e.g., **quelle belle ville!** what a beautiful city!; **n'importe quel** any ‖ *adj interr* what, e.g., **quel est le but de la vie?** what is the purpose of life?; who, e.g., **quel est cet homme?** who is that man? ‖ *adj indef*—**quel que** whoever, e.g., **quel que soit l'homme** whoever the man may be; whatever, e.g., **quelles que soient les difficultés** whatever difficulties there may be; whichever, e.g., **quel que soit le pied sur lequel il s'appuie** whichever foot he leans on. The following table shows all the forms of the word **quel**.

	masc	*fem*
sg	quel	quelle
pl	quels	quelles

§81 quelqu'un *pron indef* someone, somebody; anyone, anybody; **quelques-uns** some; any, a few. The following table shows all the forms of the word **quelqu'un**.

	masc	*fem*
sg	quelqu'un	quelqu'une
pl	quelques-uns	quelques-unes

§82A ce *adj dem* this; that; **ces** these; those. The following table shows all the forms of this word.

	masc	*fem*
sg	ce; cet before a vowel or mute **h**	cette
pl	ces	ces

This word has two meanings as exemplified by the following example:

cet homme this man; that man

However, the particles **-ci** and **-là** are attached to the noun modified by the forms of **ce** to distinguish what is near the person speaking (i.e., the first person) from what is near the person spoken to (i.e., the second person) or what is remote from both (i.e., the third person), for example:

cet homme-ci this man (*not that man*)
cet homme-là that man (*not this man*)
cet homme-là that man (*yonder*)

§82B ce *pron dem*
it, e.g., **c'est un bon livre** it is a good book;
he, e.g., **c'est un bon professeur** he is a good professor;
she, e.g., **c'est une belle femme** she is a beautiful woman;
they, e.g., **ce sont des élèves** they are students

§83 celui *pron dem* this one; that one. The following table shows all the forms of the demonstrative pronoun with their translations into English.

	masc	*fem*
sg	celui this one; that one; he	celle this one; that one; she
pl	ceux these; those	celles these; those

This word in all its forms is generally used with a following **de** or the relative pronouns **que** and **qui**:

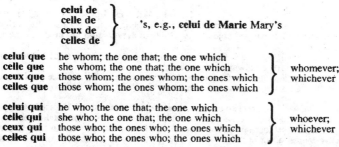

celui de ⎫	
celle de ⎬ 's, e.g., **celui de Marie** Mary's	
ceux de ⎬	
celles de ⎭	

celui que	he whom; the one that; the one which	⎫
celle que	she whom; the one that; the one which	⎬ whomever;
ceux que	those whom; the ones whom; the ones which	⎬ whichever
celles que	those whom; the ones whom; the ones which	⎭

celui qui	he who; the one that; the one which	⎫
celle qui	she who; the one that; the one which	⎬ whoever;
ceux qui	those who; the ones who; the ones which	⎬ whichever
celles qui	those who; the ones who; the ones which	⎭

§84 celui-ci *pron dem* this one; he; the latter. The particles **-ci** and **-là** are attached to the forms of **celui** to distinguish what is near the person speaking (i.e., the first person) from what is near the person spoken to (i.e., the second person) or remote from both (i.e., the third person). The following table shows all the forms of this word with particles attached and with their translations into English.

	masc	*fem*
sg	**celui-ci** this one	**celle-ci** this one
	celui-là that one	**celle-là** that one
pl	**ceux-ci** these	**celles-ci** these
	ceux-là those	**celles-là** those

The forms of **celui-ci** also mean the latter; and the forms of **celui-là**, the former, e.g., **Henri était roi et Catherine était reine. Celle-ci était espagnole et celui-là anglais.** Henry was a king, and Catherine was a queen. The former was English and the latter Spanish. (The English word order requires the inversion.)

§85 Disjunctive personal and reflexive pronouns. The following table shows all the forms of the disjunctive personal and reflexive pronouns with their translations into English.

moi	me; myself; I	**nous**	we, us; ourselves
toi	you, thee; yourself	**vous**	you; yourselves
lui	he, him, it; himself	**eux**	they, them *masc;* themselves *masc*
elle	she, her, it; herself	**elles**	they, them *fem;* themselves *fem*
soi	oneself; himself, herself, itself	**soi**	themselves

A. The disjunctive personal pronouns are used:
   (1) as the object of a preposition, e.g., **Jean a été invité chez elle** John was invited to her house; e.g., **il est très content de lui** he is very satisfied with himself. Disjunctive pronouns especially as objects of prepositions rarely stand for things. Prepositional phrases that would include them are generally expressed by **y** (see §87), e.g., **je m'y suis avancé** I walked up to it, as contrasted with **je me suis avancé vers lui** I walked up to him; or are expressed by one of the adverbs **là-dessus, là-dessous, là-dedans,** etc., e.g., **voilà mon nom; écrivez le vôtre là-dessous** there is my name; write yours under it, as contrasted with **il n'a pas d'argent sur lui** he has no money with him.
   (2) after the preposition **à** in phrases that are used to clarify or to stress the meaning of a conjunctive personal pronoun, e.g., **il lui a parlé, à elle** he spoke to her (or, he spoke to *her*).
   (3) after the preposition **à** in phrases that are used to clarify the meaning of a preceding possessive adjective, e.g., **son chapeau à elle** her hat.
   (4) as predicate pronouns after the verb **être**, especially after **c'est** and **ce sont:**

c'est moi	it is I, it is me	**c'est nous**	it is we, it is us
c'est toi	it is you, it is thee	**c'est vous**	it is you
c'est lui	it is he, it is him	**ce sont eux**	it is they, it is them *masc*
c'est elle	it is she, it is her	**ce sont elles**	it is they, it is them *fem*

(5) after **que** (than, as) in comparisons, e.g., **nous y allons plus souvent qu'eux** we go there more often than they; e.g., **nous y allons aussi souvent que vous** we go there as often as you.

(6) when the verb is not expressed, e.g., **qui a fait cela? Lui** who did that? He did.

(7) to stress the subject or object of the sentence, e.g., **lui, il a raison** he is right.

(8) in compound subjects and objects, e.g., **lui et moi, nous sommes médecins** he and I are doctors.

(9) when an adverb separates the subject pronoun from the verb, e.g., **lui toujours arrive en retard** he always arrives late.

(10) after **être** + **à** to contrast ownership, e.g., **ce stylo est à lui mais ce papier est à elle** this pen is his, but this paper is hers.

B. The disjunctive indefinite reflexive pronoun **soi** corresponds to **on** and is used mainly as the object of a preposition, i.e., according to **A**, 1 above, e.g., **on doit parler rarement de soi** one should seldom talk about oneself. But it may also be used in the predicate after the verb **être**, according to **A**, 4 above, e.g., **on a plus confiance quand c'est soi qui conduit** one has more confidence when it is oneself who drives.

§86 Intensive personal pronouns. The following table shows all the forms of these pronouns. They are made by combining the disjunctive personal pronouns with the forms of **même**.

moi-même	myself; I myself	**nous-mêmes**	ourselves; we ourselves
toi-même	yourself, thyself; you yourself	**vous-même**	yourself; you yourself
		vous-mêmes	yourselves; you yourselves
lui-même	himself; he himself; itself		
elle-même	herself; she herself; itself	**eux-mêmes**	themselves; they themselves
soi-même	oneself; itself	**elles-mêmes**	themselves; they themselves

§87 SEE PAGES xxiv–xxv.

§88 Possessive adjectives. The following table shows all the forms of possessive adjectives with their translations into English.

masc sg	*fem sg*	*masc & fem pl*	
mon	**ma***	**mes**	my
ton	**ta***	**tes**	your, thy, thine
son	**sa***	**ses**	his, her, its
notre	**notre**	**nos**	our
votre	**votre**	**vos**	your
leur	**leur**	**leurs**	their

* The forms **mon**, **ton**, and **son** are used instead of **ma**, **ta**, and **sa** respectively before feminine nouns and adjectives beginning with a vowel or mute **h**, e.g., **Marie a fait un cadeau à son aïeule** Mary gave a present to her grandmother; **elle y est venue avec son aimable tante** she came with her nice aunt.

The possessive adjectives:
(1) agree in gender and number with the thing possessed rather than with the possessor, e.g., **Marie lit son livre** Mary is reading her book.

(2) must be repeated before each noun in a series, e.g., **Marie apporte son stylo et son crayon** Mary is bringing her pen and pencil.

§89 Possessive pronouns. The following table shows all the forms of possessive pronouns with their translations into English.

	sg	*pl*	

masc	le mien	les miens	mine
fem	la mienne	les miennes	
	sg	*pl*	

| masc | le tien | les tiens | yours, thine |
| fem | la tienne | les tiennes | |

| masc | le sien | les siens | his, hers, its |
| fem | la sienne | les siennes | |

| masc | le nôtre | les nôtres | ours |
| fem | la nôtre | | |

| masc | le vôtre | les vôtres | yours |
| fem | la vôtre | | |

| masc | le leur | les leurs | theirs |
| fem | la leur | | |

The possessive pronouns:
(1) agree in gender and number with the thing possessed rather than with the possessor, e.g., **donnez votre livre à Marie, elle a perdu le sien** give your book to Mary; she has lost hers.
(2) are preceded by a definite article, e.g., **tu dois obéir à son ordre et au mien** you must obey his order and mine.
(3) are sometimes used without antecedent: (a) **le mien** mine, my own (*i.e., property*); **le sien** his, his own (*i.e., property*); hers, her own (*i.e., property*); etc.; (b) **les miens** my folks, my family; my friends; my men; **les siens** his folks, his family; his friends; his men; her folks, etc.; (c) **faire des siennes** (coll) to be up to one's (his, etc.) old tricks.

§90 The adverb **ne**. This is a conjunctive particle, i.e., it always precedes a verb and, like conjunctive pronouns, is unstressed. Because of its weakness, it is generally accompanied by another word, which follows the verb (or auxiliary) in most cases, is stressed, and gives force or added meaning to the negation, e.g., **il n'est pas ici** he is not here.

A. The following table shows **ne** with the various words with which it is associated. (For more detail, see each expression under the second word in the body of the Dictionary, e.g., s.v. **aucun**; s.v. **aucunement**.)

ne . . . aucun	no, none; no one, nobody	ne . . . ni . . . ni	neither . . . nor
		ne . . . nul	no, none
ne . . . aucunement	by no means	ne . . . nullement	not at all
ne . . . brin (archaic)	not a bit, not a single	ne . . . pas	not, no
		ne . . . pas que	not only
ne . . . davantage	no more	ne . . . pas un	not one
ne . . . goutte (archaic)	not a drop, nothing	ne . . . personne	no one, nobody
		ne . . . plus	no more, no longer
ne . . . guère	hardly, scarcely; hardly ever	ne . . . plus jamais	never any more
		ne . . . plus que	now only
ne . . . jamais	never	ne . . . point	not, no, not at all
ne . . . mie (archaic)	not a crumb, not	ne . . . que	only, but
ne . . . mot (archaic)	not a word, nothing	ne . . . rien	nothing

B. The position of **ne** in the sentence is that of column 2 of §87. The position of **pas** and all the other like words, with the exception of **aucun, ni . . . ni, nul, personne,** and **que** is that of column 9. The position of **aucun, nul, personne,** and **que** is that of column 11. And the position of the first **ni** of **ni . . . ni** is that of column 11 unless the past participle is one of the correlatives, in which case its position is that of column 9.

   Aucun, nul, pas un, personne, and **rien** may be used as subjects of the verb; they then precede **ne** and the verb, e.g., **personne n'est ici** no one is here. And **aucun, nul,** and **pas un** may be used as adjectives in the same position, e.g., **nul péril ne l'arrête** no danger stops him.

   Usually when an infinitive is in the negative, **pas** immediately follows **ne**, e.g., **il m'a dit de ne pas y aller** he told me not to go there; **il regrette de ne pas me l'avoir dit** he regrets not having told me it.

749

§87 Conjunctive personal and reflexive pronouns.

person	1 subject	2 negative	3 direct & indirect object	4 direct object	5 indirect object
1	je (j')—I		me (m')—me, to me; myself, to myself		
2	tu—you, thou		te (t')—you, to you; thee, to thee; thyself, to thyself		
3	il—he; it elle—she; it on—one, they	ne (n')—not §90B	se (s')—himself, herself, itself, oneself; to himself, to herself, to itself, to oneself	le (l')—him; it la (l')—her; it	lui—to him; to her
4	nous—we		nous—us, to us; ourselves, to ourselves		
5	vous—you		vous—you, to you; yourself, yourselves, to yourselves		
6	ils—they elles—they		se (s')—themselves; to themselves	les—them	leur—to them

This table shows all the forms of the conjunctive personal and reflexive pronouns with their translations into English and their positions (reading horizontally, not vertically) with respect to each other and with respect to the verb; and in negative declarative sentences, with respect to **ne** and **pas** and **personne.** All of the elements in this table except the verb and **pas** and **personne** (and the other negative words listed in §90) are unstressed.

In affirmative and negative interrogative sentences, the subject pronouns in column 1 are placed after the verb or auxiliary in column 8 and attached to it with a hyphen. A **t,** preceded and followed by hyphens, is intercalated between third-singular forms ending in a vowel and the subject pronoun. The interrogative forms of the first singular present indicative whose final sound is a nasal vowel or a consonant are not used, while those whose final sound is an oral vowel are, e.g., **où vais-je?** where am I going?; e.g., **que dirai-je?** what shall I say? And the ending **-e** of the first singular present indicative of verbs of the first conjugation is changed to **-é**, e.g., **donné-je?** do I give?, but these forms are not in current use in prose. All the forms not used are replaced by **est-ce que** in affirmative interrogative

sentences and by **n'est-ce pas que** in negative interrogative sentences. And **est-ce que** and **n'est-ce pas que** may be thus used in any person of any tense of the indicative. The ending **-e** of the first singular imperfect subjunctive of some verbs is likewise changed to **-é** in conditional clauses without **si** in literary usage, e.g., **dussé-je** if I should.

In affirmative imperative sentences, the subject pronouns are not expressed and the pronouns in columns 3, 4, 5, 6, and 7 are placed after the verb and attached to it and to each other with hyphens except where elision occurs, and the pronouns in column 4 precede those in column 3. And unless followed by **en** or **y, me** is replaced by **moi** and **te** is replaced by **toi;** and **moi** and **toi** are stressed.

In negative imperative sentences, the subject pronouns are not expressed either and columns 2, 3, 4, 5, 6, 7, 8, and 9 have the same order as in negative declarative sentences.

A pronoun of column 5 cannot **be** used with a pronoun of column 3 but is replaced by a disjunctive pronoun preceded by the preposition **à.**

person	6	7	8	9 negative	10	11 negative
1						
2						
3						
	y—there, to it; to them	en—some; of it; of them	VERB or AUXILIARY	pas—not §90B	past participle	personne—no one §90B
4						
5						
6						

C. The adverb **ne** is often used without **pas** or a similar word with the verbs **bouger, cesser, oser, pouvoir,** and **savoir,** e.g., **je ne saurais vous le dire** I can't tell you. And it is not

translated (1) with a compound tense after **il y a . . . que, voilà . . . que,** and **depuis que,** e.g., **il y a trois jours que je ne l'ai vu** it is three days since I saw him or (2) with the verb of a clause introduced by (a) **à moins que, avant que, empêcher . . . que,** and **éviter . . . que,** e.g., **à moins que je ne sois retenu** unless I am detained; (b) **si** meaning unless, e.g., **si je ne me trompe** unless I am mistaken; (c) a comparative + **que,** e.g., **vous étiez plus occupé qu'il ne l'était** you were busier than he was; (d) a verb or expression of fear such as **avoir peur que, craindre que, redouter que,** e.g., **je crains qu'il ne soit malade** I am afraid that he is sick; (e) a negative verb or expression of doubt, denial, despair such as **ne pas désespérer que, ne pas disconvenir que, ne pas douter que, ne pas nier que,** e.g., **je ne doute pas qu'il ne vienne** I do not doubt that he will come.

§91 *adj & adv comp & super* The comparative of superiority of adjectives and adverbs is formed by placing **plus** before the positive, e.g., **heureux** happy, **plus heureux** happier. The superlative of superiority of adjectives and adverbs is the same as the comparative, e.g., **heureux** happy, **plus heureux** happier and happiest. It is to be observed that the superlative is generally used in both French and English with the definite article or the possessive pronoun, e.g., **le plus heureux** the happiest, **son plus heureux** his happiest.

Some adjectives and adverbs have irregular comparatives and superlatives:

ADJECTIVES		ADVERBS	
positive	*comp and super*	*positive*	*comp and super*
bon good	**meilleur** better; best	**beaucoup** much	**plus** more; most
mauvais bad	**pire** worse; worst	**bien** well	**mieux** better; best
petit small	**moindre** lesser, less; least	**mal** badly	**pis** worse; worst
		peu little	**moins** less; least

The formation of adverbs. The feminine form of an adjective + the suffix *ment* constitutes an adverb.

masculine form	*feminine form*	*+ ment*
affectueux	**affectueuse**	**affectueusement**
brusque	**brusque**	**brusquement**
certain	**certaine**	**certainement**

Some adverbs are irregular in form, such as **absolument** (*fem adj* **absolue**), **assidûment** (*fem adj* **assidue**), **constamment** (*fem adj* **constante**), **énormément** (*fem adj* **énorme**), and many others. When an adverb has an irregular form, it may be found in the body of this Dictionary. When an adverb has a regular form, it is found in the body of this Dictionary when it has a meaning different from that of the adjective.

§92 Adjectives followed by **à** before a complementary infinitive. Many common adjectives are followed by an infinitive governed by **à:**

C'est facile à faire. It is easy to do.

When **il est** is used instead of **c'est,** then **de** is used before the infinitive:

Il est facile de faire le travail. It is easy to do the work.

In the above example, the infinitive has an object, and in such a case **il est** is generally used.

Other adjectives in this category are **accoutumé, bon, dernier, difficile, disposé, facile, habitué, léger, lent, lourd, mauvais, premier, prêt, propre, résolu, seul, utile.**

§93 Adjectives followed by **de** before a complementary infinitive. Many common adjectives are followed by an infinitive governed by **de:**

Ils sont fatigués de travailler. They are tired of working.
Je suis heureux de faire votre connaissance. I am happy to meet you.
Robert est absolument sûr de réussir. Robert is absolutely sure to succeed.

Other adjectives in this category are **capable, certain, chargé, content, coupable, curieux, digne, fatigué, heureux, libre, ravi, sûr, tenu.**

§94 Numerals. There are idiomatic characteristics of both French and English numerals. The entries for **trois** and **three** may be used as models for the other numerals:

trois [trwɑ] *adj & pron* three; the Third, e.g., **Jean trois** John the Third; **trois heures** three o'clock ‖ *m* three; third (*in dates*)

troisième [trwɑzjɛm] *adj, pron (masc, fem),* & *m* third

three [θri] *adj & pron* trois ‖ *s* trois *m;* **three o'clock** trois heures; **three of a kind** (cards) un frédon

third [θʌrd] *adj & pron* troisième (*masc, fem*); **the Third** trois, e.g., **John the Third** Jean trois ‖ *s* troisième *m;* (*in fractions*) tiers *m;* **the third** (*in dates*) le trois

§95 Verbs not followed by a preposition before an infinitive. Some verbs take no preposition before a dependent infinitive, as the verb **vouloir** in the following example.

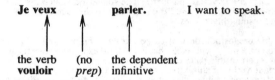

| **Je veux** | | **parler.** | I want to speak. |

the verb **vouloir**   (no *prep*)   the dependent infinitive

Here are five more examples:

Nous allons voir le film. We are going to see the film.
Henri doit respecter sa mère. Henry should respect his mother.
Elle ne sait pas jouer au tennis. She does not know how to play tennis.
Il faut manger. It is necessary to eat.
Ils pensent venir bientôt. They intend to come soon.

The most common of the verbs in this category are **accourir, affirmer, aimer, aimer mieux, aller, apercevoir, assurer, avoir beau, avouer, compter, confesser, courir, croire, daigner, déclarer, déposer, descendre, désirer, devoir, écouter, entendre, envoyer, espérer, être censé, faillir, faire, falloir, se figurer, s'imaginer, juger, jurer** (or **+ de**), **laisser, mener, mettre, monter, oser, ouïr, paraître, penser, pouvoir, préférer, prétendre, se rappeler, reconnaître, regarder, rentrer, retourner, revenir, savoir, sembler, sentir, souhaiter, soutenir, supposer, témoigner, valoir mieux, venir, voir, voler, vouloir.**

§96 Verbs followed by the preposition **à** before an infinitive. Some verbs take **à** before a dependent infinitive as do **chercher** and **commencer** in these examples:

Vous cherchez à comprendre? You are trying to understand?
Marie commence à parler. Mary is beginning to speak.

There are almost two hundred verbs in this category. Note that some of these verbs are sometimes used with **de** by native speakers. (One of these verbs is **commencer.**)

§97 Verbs followed by the preposition **de** before an infinitive. Here are three examples:

Robert décide de parler. (compare §100) Robert decides to speak.
Jean essaie de parler. John is trying to speak.
Hélène refuse de parler. Helen refuses to speak.

There are hundreds of verbs in this category.

Some verbs in this category are more likely to be followed by a past infinitive, e.g., **avoir fait,** than by a present infinitive, e.g., **faire.** Examples:

Jean attend de l'avoir fait. Jean expects to have it done.
Jean regrette de ne pas m'avoir téléphoné. Jean regrets not to have telephoned me.
Jean trouve bon d'y avoir assisté. Jean thinks it right to have taken part in it.

Other verbs of this kind are **douter, enrager, gémir, mourir, nier, rire, rougir, souffrir, sourire, trembler.**

§98 When the object of the verb is also the logical subject of the dependent infinitive—pattern à . . . de. Examples:

Le professeur a demandé à Marie de se taire. The professor asked Marie to stop talking.
Marie a dit au professeur de lire les examens. Mary told the professor to read the tests.
Le directeur conseille à Marie de chercher un autre emploi. The director is advising Mary to look for another job.

In this pattern the preposition **à** is used before the person or acting agent and the preposition **de** is used before the infinitive that follows the verb.

The most important verbs of this type or pattern are **accorder, commander, conseiller, crier, défendre, demander, dire, écrire, expliquer, imposer, inspirer, interdire, jurer, offrir, ordonner, parler, persuader, prescrire, promettre, proposer, recommander, refuser, répondre, reprocher, suggérer.**

§99 When the object of the verb is also the logical subject of the dependent infinitive—pattern (no *prep*) . . . de. Examples:

Le directeur prie Georges de choisir un métier. The director is begging George to choose a trade.
Le soldat a empêché le voleur de sortir. The soldier prevented the thief from leaving.
Le père ne doit pas dissuader son fils de finir ses études. The father should not dissuade his son from finishing his studies.

In this pattern the preposition **de** is used before the infinitive and no preposition is used before the person or acting agent. Note that in the third example above the use of **devoir** (*ne doit pas*) is not a part of this pattern but refers to the pattern in §95.

Some important verbs of this kind or pattern are **arrêter, avertir, aviser, charger, convaincre, décourager, défier, dégoûter, détourner, dispenser, dissuader, empêcher, exempter, menacer, persuader, prier, supplier.**

Some verbs of this kind are more likely to be followed by a past infinitive, e.g., **avoir fait,** than by a present infinitive, e.g., **faire.** Examples:

Jean accuse Paul de l'avoir fait. John accuses Paul of having done it.
Robert félicite Henri d'y avoir réussi. Robert congratulates Henry on having succeeded.

Other verbs in this latter category are **admirer, blâmer, consoler, excuser, gronder, louer, punir, remercier, réprimander.**

§100 When the object of the verb is also the logical subject of the dependent infinitive—pattern (no *prep*) . . . à. Examples:

Henri aide sa sœur à travailler. Henry is helping his sister work.
Madame Durand invitera ses amis à chanter. Mrs. Durand will invite her friends to sing.
Son père a décidé mon ami à chercher un emploi. His father persuaded my friend to look for a job.

In this pattern the preposition **à** is used before the infinitive and no preposition is used before the person or acting agent. Note that in the third example above, **décider** does not take **de** as it does in §97 because now it is set in a different pattern.

The most important verbs of this type or pattern are **accoutumer, aider, autoriser, condamner, décider, destiner, disposer, dresser, employer, engager, entraîner, exciter, exhorter, forcer, habituer, inciter, inviter, obliger, porter, pousser, préparer, réduire.**

§101 When the object of the verb is also the logical subject of the dependent infinitive—pattern à . . . à. Examples:

Marie enseigne à ses étudiants à prononcer correctement les voyelles. Mary is teaching her students to pronounce the vowels correctly.
Robert apprendra à son frère à écouter les instructions! (coll) Robert will teach his brother to listen to the directions!

In this pattern the preposition **à** is used both before the person or acting agent and before the infinitive.

There are only two verbs in this pattern, **enseigner** and **apprendre,** and they appear in the examples above.

§102 Plurals of nouns and adjectives. The general rule for plurals is to add an **s: la reine /
les reines; joli / jolis**
The principal exception to the general rule is that nouns and adjectives ending in **-s, -x,**
and **-z** remain unchanged in the plural: (*nouns*) **le bras / les bras; la voix / les voix; le nez
/ les nez;** (*adjectives*) singular: **frais, doux;** plural: **frais, doux**
Instead of referencing irregular plurals to the grammatical tables, this Dictionary gives
that information in the body of the Dictionary. Nouns with two plural forms, foreign nouns,
and compound nouns are also explained in the respective entry in the body of the Dictionary.
However, a short summary of some irregularities follows here:

(1) Nouns in **-au** and **-eu** add an **-x** to form the plural: **château / châteaux; jeu / jeux.** But
note these exceptions: **landau / landaus; pneu / pneus**
(2) Adjectives in **-eau** and **-eu** add an **-x** to form the plural: **beau / beaux; hébreu /
hébreux.** But note these exceptions: **bleu / bleus; feu / feus**
(3) Nouns and adjectives in **-al** change the **-al** to **-au** and add an **-x** to form the plural: **cheval
/
chevaux; égal / égaux.** But note these exceptions: **fatals, finals, avals, bals, cals,
carnavals, chacals, régals**
(4) Seven nouns ending in **-ou** do not take the **-s** of the general rule but add **-x** to form the
plural; their plurals are **bijoux, cailloux, choux, genoux, hiboux, joujoux, poux.**
(5) The following are the plurals of seven nouns ending in **-ail:**
baux, coraux, soupiraux, travaux, vantaux, ventaux, vitraux. But note, e.g.: **détail
/ détails; éventail / éventails**

FRENCH PRONUNCIATION

The following phonetic symbols represent all sounds of the French language.

VOWELS

SYMBOL	SOUND	EXAMPLE
[a]	A little more open than the **a** in English **hat**.	**patte** [pat]
[ɑ]	Like **a** in English **father**.	**pâte** [pɑt] **phase** [fɑz]
[ɛ]	Like **e** in English **met**. Native French pronunciation of this vowel in an open syllable is often somewhere between [ɛ] the **e** in **met** and [e] the **a** in **fate**.	**sec** [sɛk] **fer** [fɛr] **fête** [fɛt] **aile** [ɛl] **parallèle** [paralɛl]
[e]	Like **a** in English **fate**, but without the glide the English sound sometimes has.	**été** [ete] **fée** [fe] **et** [e] **créer** [kree]
[ə]	Like **a** in English **comma** or like **o** in English **pardon**.	**le** [lə] **petit** [pəti]
[i]	Like **i** in English **machine** or like **e** in English **she**.	**si** [si]
[ɔ]	A little more open and rounded than **aw** in English **law**.	**donne** [dɔn] **dormir** [dɔrmir]
[o]	Like **o** in English **note** but without the glide the English sound sometimes has.	**mot** [mo] **eau** [o] **faute** [fot]
[u]	Like **u** in English **rude**.	**sou** [su] **four** [fur]
[y]	The lips are rounded for [u] and held without moving while the sound [i] is pronounced.	**su** [sy] **sûr** [syr]
[ø]	The lips are rounded for [o] and held without moving while the sound [e] is pronounced	**peu** [pø] **eux** [ø] **feutre** [føtr]
[œ]	The lips are rounded for [ɔ] and held without moving while the sound [ɛ] is pronounced.	**peur** [pœr] **seul** [sœl]

NASAL VOWELS

To produce the nasal vowels, sound is emitted through both nose and mouth by means of a lowering of the velum. The orthographic **m** or **n** has no consonantal value.

SYMBOL	SOUND	EXAMPLE
[ã]	Like **a** in English **father** and nasalized.	**en** [ã] **tant** [tã] **temps** [tã] **paon** [pã]
[ɔ̃]	More close than **aw** in English **law** and nasalized.	**on** [ɔ̃] **pont** [pɔ̃] **comte** [kɔ̃t]
[ɛ̃]	Like **e** in English **met** and nasalized.	**pin** [pɛ̃] **pain** [pɛ̃] **faim** [fɛ̃] **teint** [tɛ̃]
[œ̃]	Like [œ] of French **bœuf** and nasalized. There has been a tendency in this century to assimilate the nasal sound [œ̃] to the nasal sound [ɛ̃], making **brun** [brœ̃] and **brin** [brɛ̃] sound much the same.	**un** [œ̃] **parfum** [parfœ̃]

DIPHTHONGS

The sounds [j], [ɥ], and [w] are used to form French diphthongs. In addition, [aɪ] and [aʊ] occur in some words of foreign origin.

SYMBOL	SOUND	EXAMPLE
[j]	Like **y** in English **year** or like **y** in English **toy**.	**hier** [jɛr] **ail** [aj]

SYMBOL	SOUND	EXAMPLE
[ɥ]	Like the letter **u** [y] pronounced with consonantal value preceding a vowel.	**lui** [lɥi] **situation** [sitɥɑsjɔ̃] **nuage** [nɥaʒ] **écuelle** [ekɥɛl]
[w]	Like **w** in English **water**.	**oie** [wa] **jouer** [ʒwe] **jouir** [ʒwir]
[aɪ]	Like **i** in English **fine**.	**sunlight** [sœnlaɪt]
[aʊ]	Like **ou** in English **house**.	**clubhouse** [klybaʊs]

CONSONANTS

The speaker of French characteristically keeps the tip of the tongue down behind the lower teeth and arches the back of the tongue at the same time. Thus, sounds such as [t], [d], [n], [s], [z] and [r] must in French be articulated with the tongue tip and blade in the proximity of the back surface of the teeth.

SYMBOL	SOUND	EXAMPLE
[b]	Like **b** in English **baby**.	**basse** [bɑs]
[d]	Like **d** in English **dead**.	**doux** [du]
[f]	Like **f** in English **face**.	**fou** [fu]
[g]	Like **g** in English **go**.	**gare** [gar]
[k]	Like **k** in English **kill**, but without the aspiration that normally accompanies **k** in English.	**cas** [kɑ] **kiosque** [kjɔsk]
[l]	Like **l** in English **like** or in English **slip**—pronounced toward the front of the mouth. Not like **l** in **old**.	**lit** [li] **houle** [ul]
[m]	Like **m** in English **more**.	**masse** [mas]
[n]	Like **n** in English **nest**.	**nous** [nu]
[ɲ]	Like **ny** in English **canyon** or like **ni** in English **onion**.	**signe** [siɲ] **agneau** [aɲo]
[ŋ]	Like **ng** in English **parking**.	**parking** [parkiŋ]
[p]	Like **p** in English **pen**, but without the aspiration that normally accompanies **p** in English.	**passe** [pɑs]
[r]	Sometimes the uvular **r** but for some decades now usually a friction **r** with the point of articulation between the rounded back of the tongue and the hard palate. It resembles the Spanish aspirate in **jota**, the German aspirate in **ach**, and the **g** in modern Greek **gamma** more than it resembles American retroflex **r**. The tip of the tongue must point down near the back of the lower teeth and must not move during the utterance of the French [r].	**rire** [rir] **caractère** [karaktɛr] **roi** [rwa] **roue** [ru]
[s]	Like **s** in English **send**.	**sot** [so] **leçon** [ləsɔ̃] **place** [plas] **lassitude** [lɑsityd] **attention** [atɑ̃sjɔ̃]
[ʃ]	Like **sh** in English **shall** or **ch** in English **machine**.	**cheval** [ʃval] **mèche** [mɛʃ]
[t]	Like **t** in English **ten**, but without the aspiration that normally accompanies **t** in English.	**toux** [tu] **thé** [te]
[v]	Like **v** in English **vest**.	**verre** [vɛr]
[z]	Like **z** in English **zeal**.	**zèle** [zɛl] **oser** [oze]

SYMBOL	SOUND	EXAMPLE
[ʒ]	Like **s** in English **pleasure**.	**joue** [ʒu] **rouge** [ruʒ] **mangeur** [mɑ̃ʒœr]

Note that truly French sounds are made by speaking in the front of the mouth, with vigorous movements of the lips (unlike English, which is spoken in the back, and with lazy lips).

LAW OF POSITION

In the modern French standard cultured pronunciation in France, the choice of the vowels [e] and [ɛ] (written variously as **e** + *cons,* **è, é, ai** + *cons,* **ais, ait, ei**) and the choice of the vowels [o] and [ɔ] (written variously as **o, ô, au, aux, eau, eaux**) follow what can be called the "law of position" (*la loi de position*). This is a rule of thumb that can be stated briefly as follows: Closed vowels are used in accented open syllables, and open vowels are used in closed syllables. The closed variants are [e] (**a** as in **fate**) and [o] (**o** as in **note**). An open syllable is one that does not end in a consonant sound. Examples: **est** [e], **allait** [ale], **été** [ete], **mot** [mo], **piano** [pjano], **ruisseau** [rɥiso]. In the examples just cited, the vowel is not followed by a consonant sound, and the closed variant is used. On the other hand, the open variants are [ɛ] (**e** as in **met**) and [ɔ] (**aw** as in **law**). A closed syllable is one that ends in a consonant sound. Examples: **père** [pɛr], **terre** [tɛr], **laisse** [lɛs], **donne** [dɔn], **encore** [ɑ̃kɔr]. In the examples just cited, the vowel is followed by a consonant sound, and the open variant is used. However, with the spellings **au** or **ô**, the closed variant is used even when followed by a pronounced consonant: **faute** [fot], **fausse** [fos], **hôte** [ot].

In this Dictionary the law of position is not used to explain pronunciation. For example, **très** [trɛ] is not presented with the pronunciation [tre] even though the latter pronunciation is frequently used today. Since the use of the law of position varies from speaker to speaker and from region to region, and the use of the law of position is inconsistent even in the same speaker (who might pronounce **est** as [e] but **paix** as [pɛ]), the notation of pronunciation in this Dictionary is traditional and conservative.

FRENCH STRESS

Stress is not shown on French words in this Dictionary because stress is not a fixed characteristic of the pronunciation of French words. It depends on the position of the word in the sentence and it falls on the last syllable of the word that terminates a rhythmic or sense grouping unless the vowel of that syllable is a mute **e** [ə], in which case it falls on the immediately preceding syllable.

VOWEL LENGTH

Vowel length is not shown in the phonetic transcription of French words in this Dictionary because it, like stress, is not a fixed characteristic of the pronunciation of French words.

Furthermore, vowel length in French is not phonemic: Whether the vowel is long or short does not make a difference in the meaning of the word. To take the word **maître** as an illustration, some reference sources use a colon [ː] to indicate that the length of the preceding vowel has been increased: [mɛːtr] / [mɛtr]. The meaning of the word has not been changed by the lengthening of the vowel, and so the change is stylistic, not phonemic. Only phonemes are afforded the user in the pronunciation in the body of this Dictionary, and therefore the length is not shown by a colon [ː].

A third reason for not indicating length of vowel is pedagogical: The student's task should not be complicated by the idea that the number of vowels has doubled. Instead, the student should realize that the length of vowels in French depends upon the environment of the vowel—where it finds itself in the rhythmic grouping or which vowel and/or consonant sounds surround it. There are regular rules for vowel length. The student may follow these simple rules:

The following vowel sounds in the positions indicated are long when stressed: (1) all when followed by [r], [z], [v], [ʒ], or [vr]; (2) all spelled with a circumflex accent and followed by a consonant sound; and (3) [ɑ̃], [ɔ̃], [ɛ̃], [œ̃], [ɑ], [o], and [ø] followed by a consonant sound. When these conditions are not fulfilled, all vowel sounds are normal in length (or sometimes they may be short in length, even when stressed, if followed by [k], [p], [t], [kt], [rk], [rp], or [rt]).

ELISION AND LIAISON

Elision in French is the omission of the **a** in **la** and the **e** in words such as **le, de, que, se, me, te,** etc. Examples: **je + ai = j'ai, de + autres = d'autres.** Liaison is the pronunciation of a final written and usually silent consonant of a word as the first sound of the following word. Examples: **vous êtes, grand homme.** The **s** of **vous** is pronounced as a **z** and is the first sound of the following word as if that word were "zêtes." The **d** of **grand** becomes a **t,** and the following word might be represented by "tomme." Elision and liaison are usually made when the following word begins with a vowel or a mute **h.** Examples: **vous avez, beaux hommes.** Elision and liaison are made with some words beginning with **y,** such as: **yèbe, yeuse, yeux, Yonne,** and **York.**

However, there are words that begin with a vowel or an **h** with which elision and liaison are not made. Most of these words begin with **h,** called aspirate **h,** although it has not been pronounced for centuries. In this Dictionary these words are indicated by an asterisk placed before the opening bracket of the phonetic symbols, e.g., **hameau** *[amo], **onze** *[ɔ̃z], **a** *[a], **s** *[ɛs].

Liaison is not always obligatory but depends upon level of speech. More liaison is used in formal speech than in informal speech. The standard cultured pronunciation of **ont attendu** takes the **t** of **ont** in liaison and sets it as the first sound of the word **attendu.** The informal pronunciation omits this liaison. There are some words that never make liaison, such as **et.** There are some combinations that always make liaison no matter what the level of speech, such as the pronouns and their following verbs, e.g., **nous avons, elles ont.**

LINKING

Linking (*enchaînement*) is the general term that refers to the final consonant of a word pronounced as the first sound of the following word. Thus, **autre ami** has three syllables: (1) **au,** (2) **tra,** (3) **mi.** This practice follows from the basic tendency of French pronunciation to end a syllable wherever possible with a vowel: consonant + vowel, consonant + vowel, etc. Note in these examples that the linked consonant need not be the last letter in the spelling of its word (**autre, quatre,** etc.). Examples:

Elle a quatre anges pour Anne. She has four angels for Ann.

Pronunciation division:

E	*lla*	*qua*	*tranges*	*pou*	*rAnne.*
V	CV	CV	CV	CV	CVC

Paul a mal au dents. Paul has a toothache.

Pronunciation division:

Pau	*la*	*ma*	*lau*	*dents.*
CV	CV	CV	CV	CV

Sometimes, of course, as in the case of a double consonant (**gouver*n*ement**) or a final position (**Anne,** above), the consonant must end the syllable.

Note that linking differs from liaison (see explanation above) in that liaison is a specialized type of linking that concerns a spelled but silent letter that would not otherwise be pronounced.

LA PRONONCIATION DE L'ANGLAIS

Les signes suivants représentent à peu près tous les sons de la langue anglaise.

VOYELLES

SIGNE	SON	EXEMPLE
[æ]	Plus fermé que **a** dans **patte**.	**hat** [hæt]
[ɑ]	Comme **a** dans **pâte**.	**father** [fɑðər] **proper** [prɑpər]
[ɛ]	Comme **e** dans **sec**.	**met** [mɛt]
[e]	Comme **e** dans **récit**. Surtout en position finale, [e] se prononce comme s'il était suivi de [ɪ].	**fate** [fet] **they** [ðe]
[ə]	C'est **e** muet, par ex., **e** dans **gouvernement**.	**heaven** [hɛvən] **pardon** [pɑrdən]
[i]	Comme **i** dans **mine**.	**she** [ʃi] **machine** [məʃin]
[ɪ]	Moins fermé que **i** dans **mirage**.	**it** [fɪt] **beer** [bɪr]
[o]	Comme **au** dans **haut**. Surtout en position finale, [o] se prononce comme s'il était suivi de [ʊ].	**nose** [noz] **road** [rod] **row** [ro]
[ɔ]	Un peu plus fermé que **a** dans **donne**.	**bought** [bɔt] **law** [lɔ]
[ʌ]	Plus ou moins comme **eu** dans **peur**.	**cup** [kʌp] **come** [kʌm] **mother** [mʌðər]
[ʊ]	Moins fermé que **ou** dans **doublage**.	**pull** [pʊl] **book** [bʊk] **wolf** [wʊlf]
[u]	Comme **ou** dans **doublage**.	**move** [muv] **tomb** [tum]

DIPHTONGUES

SIGNE	SON	EXEMPLE
[aɪ]	Plus ou moins comme **ai** dans **ail**.	**night** [naɪt] **eye** [aɪ]
[aʊ]	Plus ou moins comme **aou** dans **caoutchouc**.	**found** [faʊnd] **cow** [kaʊ]
[ɔɪ]	Comme **oy** dans **boy**.	**voice** [vɔɪs] **oil** [ɔɪl]

CONSONNES

SIGNE	SON	EXEMPLE
[b]	Comme b dans bébé.	bed [bɛd] robber [rɑbər]
[d]	Comme d dans don.	dead [dɛd] add [æd]
[dʒ]	Comme dj dans djinn.	gem [dʒɛm] jail [dʒel]
[ð]	Comme la consonne castillane d intervocalique de moda.	this [ðis] father ['fɑðər]
[f]	Comme f dans fin.	face [fes] phone [fon]
[g]	Comme g dans gallois.	go [go] get [gɛt]
[h]	Comme la consonne allemande h de Haus ou comme la consonne espagnole j de jota mais moins aspiré.	hot [hɑt] alcohol ['ælkə,hɔl]
[j]	Comme i dans hier ou comme y dans yod.	yes [jɛs] unit ['junɪt]
[k]	Comme k dans kiosque ou comme e dans cote, mais accompagné d'une aspiration.	cat [kæt] chord [kɔrd] kill [kɪl]
[l]	Comme l ou ll dans pulluler.	late [let] allow [ə'laʊ]
[m]	Comme m dans mère.	more [mor] command [kə'mænd]
[n]	Comme n dans note.	nest [nest] manner ['mænər]
[ŋ]	Comme ng dans parking.	king [kiŋ] conquer ['kɑŋkər]
[p]	Comme p dans père, mais accompagné d'une aspiration.	pen [pɛn] cap [kæp]
[r]	Le r rétroflexe, une semi-voyelle dont l'articulation se produit par la pointe de la langue élevée vers la voûte du palais.	run [rʌn] far [fɑr] art [ɑrt] carry ['kæri]
[s]	Comme ss dans classe.	send [sɛnd] cellar ['sɛlər]
[ʃ]	Comme ch dans chose.	shall [ʃæl]
[t]	Comme t dans table, mais accompagné d'une aspiration.	ten [tɛn] dropped [drɑpt]
[tʃ]	Comme tch dans caoutchouc.	child [tʃaɪld]
[θ]	Comme la consonne castillane c de cinco.	think [θɪŋk]
[v]	Comme v dans veuve.	vest [vɛst] of [ʌv]
[w]	Comme w dans watt; comme le [w] produit en prononçant le mot bois.	work [wʌrk] tweed [twid] queen [kwin]
[z]	Comme s dans rose ou comme z dans zèbre.	zeal [zil] his [hɪz]
[ʒ]	Comme j dans jardin.	azure ['eʒər] measure ['mɛʒər]

American Measurements and the Metric System*

	AMERICAN UNIT	METRIC EQUIVA-LENT	METRIC UNIT	AMERICAN EQUIVA-LENT
Length	one mile (mi.)	1.6 kilometers	un kilomètre (km)	.6 mile
	one yard (yd.)	.9 meter	un mètre (m)	39.34 inches
	one foot (ft.)	30 centimeters	un centimètre (cm)	or 3.28 feet
				.39 inch
	one inch (in.)	25.4 millime-ters	un millimètre (mm)	.039 inch
Surface	one acre (a.)	.4 hectare	un hectare (ha)	2.5 acres
	one square mile (sq. mi.)	259 hectares	un kilomètre carré (km²)	.39 square mile
Volume	one cubic foot (cu. ft.)	.028 cubic meter	un mètre cube (m³)	35.314 cubic feet
Capacity	one liquid quart (qt.)	.95 liter	un litre (l)	1.057 quarts or .26 gal-lon
	one gallon (gal.)	3.8 liters		
Weight	one pound (lb.)	.45 kilogram	un kilogram (kg) (un kilo)	2.2 pounds
	one ounce (oz.)	28.35 grams	100 grammes	3.5 ounces
	one ton (2,000 pounds)	907.2 kilo-grams	un gramme (g)	15.432 grains

* International System of Units—Le système international d'unités (SI).

Approximate Comparison of Fahrenheit and Centigrade (Celsius) Temperatures

FAHRENHEIT		CENTIGRADE	
Boiling point ▶	212	100 ◀	Point d'ébullition
	140	60	
	104	40	
	100	38	
Normal body temperature ▶ (physiol)	98.6	37 ◀	Température normale (physiol)
	97	36	
	88	31	
	77	25	
	68	20	
	59	15	
	50	10	
	41	5	
Freezing point ▶	32	0 ◀	Point de congélation
	23	−5	
	14	−10	
	5	−15	
	0	−18	
	−13	−25	
	−22	−30	
	−40	−40	

For exact conversion, use the following:

(a) To convert Fahrenheit into centigrade, subtract 32, multiply by 5, and divide by 9.

(b) To convert centigrade into Fahrenheit, multiply by 9, divide by 5, and add 32.

Tire Pressure

Pounds per square inch *Livres par pouce carré*	Kilograms per square centimeter *Kilogrammes par centimètre carré*	Pounds per square inch *Livres par pouce carré*	Kilograms per square centimeter *Kilogrammes par centimètre carré*
16	1,12	30	2,10
18	1,26	32	2,24
20	1,40	36	2,52
22	1,54	40	2,80
24	1,68	50	3,50
26	1,82	60	4,20
28	1,96	70	4,90

Sizes of Clothing in the United States and France

LADIES—*DAMES*

Size of coats, dresses—*Taille de manteaux, de robes*

American	8	10	12	14	16	18	20
French	38	40	42	44	46	48	50

Size of blouses, sweaters, and slips—*Taille de chemisiers (corsages), de chandails et de combinaisons*

American	32	34	36	38	40	42
French	38	40	42	44	46	48

Size of shoes, slippers—*Pointure de chaussures, de pantoufles*

American	4	5	6	7	8	9
French	36	37	38	39	40	41

MEN—*MESSIEURS*

Size of topcoats, suits—*Taille de pardessus, de costumes*

American	30	32	34	36	38	40	42	44	46
French	40	42	44	46	48	50	52	54	56

Size (neck size) of shirts—*Taille (encolure) de chemises*

American	14	14½	15	15½	16	16½
French	37	38	39	40	41	42

Size of shoes, slippers—*Pointure de chaussures, de pantoufles*

American	8	8½	9	9½	10	10½	11
French	41	42	43	44	45	46	47

Size of hats—*Pointure (tours de la tête en centimètres) de chapeaux*

American	6⅝	6¾	6⅞	7	7⅛	7¼	7⅜	7½	7⅝
French	53	54	55	56	57	58	59	60	61

LABELS AND ABBREVIATIONS
RUBRIQUES ET ABRÉVIATIONS

abbr abbreviation—abréviation
(acronym) word formed from the initial letters or syllables of a series of words—mot formé de la suite des lettres initiales ou des syllabes initiales d'une série de mots
adj adjective—adjectif
adv adverb—adverbe
(aer) aeronautics—aéronautique
(aerosp) aerospace—aérospatiale
(agr) agriculture—agriculture
(alg) algebra—algèbre
(anat) anatomy—anatomie
(archaic) archaïque
(archeol) archeology—archéologie
(archit) architecture—architecture
(arith) arithmetic—arithmétique
art article—article
(arti) artillery—artillerie
(astr) astronomy—astronomie
(astrol) astrology—astrologie
(aut) automobile—automobile
aux auxiliary verb—verbe auxiliaire
(bact) bacteriology—bactériologie
(baseball) base-ball
(bb) bookbinding—reliure
(Bib) Biblical—biblique
(billiards) billard
(biochem) biochemistry—biochimie
(biol) biology—biologie
(bk) bookkeeping—comptabilité
(bot) botany—botanique
(bowling) jeu de quilles, jeu de boules
(boxing) boxe
(Brit) British—britannique
(Canad) Canadian—canadien
(*cap*) capital—majuscule
(cards) cartes
(carpentry) charpenterie
(checkers) jeu de dames
(chem) chemistry—chimie
(chess) échecs
(coll) colloquial—familier
(com) commercial—commercial
comp comparative—comparatif
(comp) computers—ordinateurs
(complimentary close) formule de politesse
cond conditional—conditionnel
conj conjunction—conjonction; conjunctive—atone
contr contraction—contraction
(culin) cooking—cuisine
(dated) vieilli
def definite—défini

dem demonstrative—démonstratif
(dentistry) art dentaire
(dial) dialectal—dialectal
(dipl) diplomacy—diplomatie
disj disjunctive—tonique
(eccl) ecclesiastical—ecclésiastique
(ecol) ecology—écologie
(econ) economics—économique
(educ) education—éducation, pédagogie
e.g. par ex.
(elec) electricity—électricité
(electron) electronics—électronique
(embryol) embryology—embryologie
(eng) engineering—ingénierie, genie
(ent) entomology—entomologie
(equit) horseback riding—équitation
(escr) fencing—escrime
f feminine noun—nom féminin
(fa) fine arts—beaux-arts
fem feminine—féminin
(feudal) feudalism—féodalité
(fig) figurative—figuré
(fishing) pêche
fpl feminine noun plural—nom féminin pluriel
fut future—futur
(game) jeu
(gen) genetics—génétique
(geog) geography—géographie
(geol) geology—géologie
(geom) geometry—géométrie
ger gerund—gérondif
(govt) government—gouvernement
(gram) grammar—grammaire
(gymnastics) gymnastique
(heral) heraldry—héraldique, blason
(hist) history—histoire
(hort) horticulture—horticulture
(hum) humorous—humoristique
(hunting) chasse
(ichth) ichthyology—ichtyologie
i.e. c.-à-d.
imperf imperfect—imparfait
impers impersonal verb—verbe impersonnel
impv imperative—impératif
ind indicative—indicatif
indef indefinite—indéfini
inf infinitive—infinitif
(ins) insurance—assurance
interj interjection—interjection
interr interrogative—interrogatif
intr intransitive—intransitif
invar invariable—invariable

765

(ironical) ironique
(jewelry) bijouterie
(journ) journalism—journalisme
(Lat) Latin—latin
(law) droit
(*l.c.*) lower case—bas de casse
(letterword) word in the form of an abbreviation that is pronounced by sounding the names of its letters in succession and that functions as a part of speech—mot en forme d'abréviation qu'on prononce en faisant sonner le nom de chaque lettre consécutivement et qui fonctionne comme partie du discours
(ling) linguistics—linguistique
(lit) literary—littéraire
(logic) logique
m masculine noun—nom masculin
(mach) machinery—machinerie
(mas) masonry—maçonnerie
masc masculine—masculin
(Masonry) franc-maçonnerie
(math) mathematics—mathématiques
(mech) mechanics—mécanique
(med) medicine—médecine
(metallurgy) métallurgie
(meteo) meteorology—météorologie
mf masculine or feminine noun according to sex—nom masculin ou nom féminin selon le sexe
[for *m* & *f* see abbreviation following (mythol)]
(mil) military—militaire
(min) mining—travail des mines
(mineral) mineralogy—minéralogie
(mountaineering) alpinisme
(mov) moving pictures—cinéma
mpl masculine noun plural—nom masculin pluriel
(mus) music—musique
(mythol) mythology—mythologie
m & f masculine and feminine noun without regard to sex—nom masculin et féminin sans distinction de sexe
(naut) nautical—nautique
(nav) naval—naval
neut neuter—neutre
(nucl) nuclear physics—physique nucléaire
(obs) obsolete—vieilli, vieux
(obstet) obstetrics—obstétrique
(offensive) offensant, blessant
(opt) optics—optique
(orn) ornithology—ornithologie
(painting) peinture
(parl) parliamentary procedure—usages parlementaires
(pathol) pathology—pathologie
(pej) pejorative—péjoratif
perf perfect—parfait
pers personal—personnel; person—personne
(pharm) pharmacy—pharmacie
(phila) philately—philatélie
(philos) philosophy—philosophie
(phonet) phonetics—phonétique
(phot) photography—photographie
(phys) physics—physique

(physiol) physiology—physiologie
pl plural—pluriel
(poetic) poetical—poétique
(pol) politics—politique
poss possessive—possessif
pp past participle—participe passé
prep preposition—préposition
pres present—présent
pret preterit—prétérit, passé simple
pron pronoun—pronom
(pros) prosody—métrique, prosodie
(psychoanal) psychoanalytic—psychanalytique
(psychol) psychology—psychologie
(psychopathol) psychopathology—psychopathologie
(*public sign*) affiche, écriteau
q.ch. or *q.ch.* quelque chose—something
qn or *qn* quelqu'un—someone
(rad) radio—radio
(rare) rare
ref reflexive verb—verbe pronominal, réfléchi ou réciproque
reflex reflexive—réfléchi
rel relative—relatif
(rel) religion—religion
(rhet) rhetoric—rhétorique
(rok) rocketry—fusées
(rowing) canotage
(rr) railroad—chemin de fer
s substantive—substantif
(sculp) sculpture—sculpture
(seismol) seismology—sismologie
(sewing) couture
sg singular—singulier
(slang) populaire, argotique
s.o. or *s.o.* someone—quelqu'un
spl substantive plural—substantif pluriel
(sports) sports
s.th. or *s.th.* something—quelque chose
subj subjunctive—subjonctif
super superlative—superlatif
(surg) surgery—chirurgie
(surv) surveying—topographie
(swimming) nage
(taur) bullfighting—tauromachie
(telg) telegraphy—télégraphie
(telp) telephony—téléphonie
(telv) television—télévision
(tennis) tennis
(tex) textile—textile
(theat) theater—théâtre
(theol) theology—théologie
tr transitive verb—verbe transitif
(trademark) marque déposée
(turf) horse racing—courses de chevaux
(typ) printing—imprimerie
(U.S.A.) U.S.A., É.-U.A.
v verb—verbe
var variant—variante
(vet) veterinary medicine—médecine vétérinaire
(vulg) vulgar—grossier
(weight lifting) haltérophilie
(wrestling) lutte, catch
(zool) zoology—zoologie

ROGER J. STEINER is Emeritus Professor of Linguistics, University of Delaware. He is the author of numerous articles on lexicography and language.

AMSCO SCHOOL PUBLICATIONS, INC.